Handbook of

Education Policy Research

Educational policy continues to be of major concern. Policy debates about economic growth and national competitiveness, for example, commonly focus on the importance of human capital and a highly educated workforce. Defining the theoretical boundaries and methodological approaches of education policy research are the two primary themes of this comprehensive, AERA-sponsored Handbook.

Organized into seven sections, the Handbook focuses on (1) disciplinary foundations of educational policy, (2) methodological perspectives, (3) the policy process, (4) resources, management, and organization, (5) teaching and learning policy, (6) actors and institutions, and (7) education access and differentiation.

Drawing from multiple disciplines, the Handbook's over one hundred authors address three central questions: What policy issues and questions have oriented current policy research? What research strategies and methods have proven most fruitful? And what issues, questions, and methods will drive future policy research? Topics such as early childhood education, school choice, access to higher education, teacher accountability, and testing and measurement cut across the 62 chapters and 14 commentaries in the volume. The politics surrounding these and other issues are objectively analyzed by authors and commentators.

Each of the seven sections concludes with two commentaries by leading scholars in the field. The first considers the current state of *policy design*, and the second addresses the current state of *policy research*.

This book is appropriate for scholars and graduate students working in the field of education policy and for the growing number of academic, government, and think-tank researchers engaged in policy research.

HANDBOOK OF EDUCATION POLICY RESEARCH

Edited by

Gary Sykes

Barbara Schneider

David N. Plank

with

Timothy G. Ford

American
Educational
Research
Association

Routledge
Taylor & Francis Group

NEW YORK AND LONDON

The American Educational Research Association (AERA) publishes books and journals based on the highest standards of professional review to ensure their quality, accuracy, and objectivity. Findings and conclusions in publications are those of the authors and do not reflect the position or policies of the Association, its Council, or its officers.

© 2009 American Educational Research Association

First published 2009
by Routledge
270 Madison Ave, New York, NY 10016

Simultaneously published in the UK
by Routledge
2 Park Square, Milton Park, Abingdon, Oxon OX14 4RN

Routledge is an imprint of the Taylor & Francis Group, an informa business

Typeset in Times by EvS Communication Networx, Inc.
Printed and bound in the United States of America on acid-free paper by Sheridan Books, Inc.

Library of Congress Cataloging in Publication Data
Handbook of education policy research / edited by Gary Sykes, Barbara Schneider, David N. Plank with Timothy G. Ford.
p. cm.
Includes bibliographical references and indexes.
1. Education and state—Research—Handbooks, manuals, etc. I. Sykes, Gary. II. Schneider, Barbara. III. Plank, David Nathan. IV. Ford, Timothy G.
LC71.H363 2009
379—dc22
2008040170

ISBN 10: 0-415-98991-4 (hbk)
ISBN 10: 0-415-98992-2 (pbk)
ISBN 10: 0-203-88096-X (ebk)

ISBN 13: 978-0-415-98991-6 (hbk)
ISBN 13: 978-0-415-98992-3 (pbk)
ISBN 13: 978-0-203-88096-8 (ebk)

This book is dedicated to:

William L. Boyd

(1935–2008)

Writing about composing *Rhapsody in Blue* George Gershwin said, "I tried to express our manner of living, the tempo of our modern life with its speed and chaos and vitality." His words capture the spirit, insight, and dedication of William L. Boyd, a leading researcher of educational policy for over 30 years, who also was an accomplished musician. He served as the first vice president of the American Educational Research Association's Division of Educational Policy and Politics after the division was established in 1996. We speak for our field in mourning the loss of a great contributor and friend.

Contents

Section III. Politics and the Policy Process
Section Editor: Jane Clark Lindle

Section IV. Policy Implications of Educational Resources, Management, and Organization
Section Editor: Linda Skrla

Section V. Teaching and Learning Policy
Section Editor: Gary Sykes

Section VI: Actors and Institutions in the Policy Process
Section Editor: Carolyn Herrington

Section VII. Educational Access and Differentiation
Section Editor: Barbara Schneider

Foreword

It is significant that the *Handbook of Education Policy Research*, the first book published in the AERA Handbook Series in Education Research, is being released at this defining moment in our nation's history. This is a time when individuals are confronting concerns about economic and social survival and the nation is facing urgent challenges to its position as a leader in the global economy and in world affairs. Education has become the focal point for many of these concerns, and politicians at the local as well as the national level have made education a visible and robust campaign issue. Competing ideas and insights about how to respond to problems confronting our schools are packaged in education policy proposals that are continuously debated and often debunked. Within this atmosphere, it can be difficult to identify the kind of ideas, innovations, and programs that can be used to improve our educational system.

The editors of the *Handbook of Education Policy Research* have collected in a single volume a wealth of information including statistics, analyses, and studies that highlight the role that research can play in helping school administrators, governmental leaders, higher-education policy makers, and others to better understand the nature of the problems they are confronting and make informed and thoughtful decisions as they seek to address them. The handbook is an essential resource for the research community and those seeking to comprehend and make gains in education policy research. In addition to decision makers who are confronting and working to resolve serious challenges in our education system, graduate students in policy programs, as well as doctoral candidates in related fields, will find the discussions on research methods and techniques, which are interspersed throughout the volume, invaluable as they engage in education policy research.

The 62 chapters and 14 commentaries in this handbook include a mix of established and new voices in education policy research. The mix of voices results in chapters that balance critical approaches with chapters that focus on solutions. The chapters fall into seven sections. Each section addresses important dimensions of education policy ranging from its historical and social science foundations to social stratification and other issues that are implicated in educational access and differentiation. The chapter authors discuss a wide range of topics, including long-standing policy interests such as education access, language learning, accountability, charter schools, school vouchers, assessment, and, more broadly, No Child Left Behind, as well as topics that highlight important new and emerging interdisciplinary and global policy perspectives in education policy research. In some cases, complex topics such as the value of educational investments and production are discussed by several chapter authors who examine different elements of the topic. This enables readers to deepen their understanding of the policy issue as well as the impact of its implementation. The commentaries at the end of each section add value to the research discussed in the section by pointing to areas where such research is or should be particularly useful and by identifying unmet policy needs.

The Handbook Series was designed and implemented by the AERA Books Editorial Board. At the time the proposal for the *Handbook of Education Policy Research* was approved, the Board was composed of founding Board members Carl A. Grant, Patrick B. Forsyth, Felice J. Levine, Gary J. Natriello, Ana Maria Villegas, Carol Camp Yeakey, and myself. Carl A. Grant, in his capacity as chair of the Publication Committee, has since transitioned off the Board. Robert J. Sternberg, the current chair of the Publication Committee, now serves on the Books Editorial Board along with Board member Robert E. Floden.

The AERA Handbook Series in Education Research is part of an overall AERA books publication program that aims to "publish works that advance knowledge, expand access to significant research and research analyses and syntheses, and promote knowledge utilization." The series specifically seeks to publish volumes of excellence that are conceptually and substantively distinct. The volumes in the series "offer state-of-the-art knowledge and the foundation to advance research to scholars and students in education research and related social science fields." When the Books Editorial Board issued its call for proposals for handbooks in education research, the editors of the *Handbook of Education Policy Research* were among the first to respond. Their proposal was accepted after a substantive review and revision process directed by the Books Editorial Board.

The following criteria outlined in guidelines for preparing handbook proposals were used to review the proposal for the *Handbook of Education Policy Research*. First and foremost, the Board examined the proposed handbook in terms of whether it would provide an opportunity for readers to take stock of and advance their thinking about current and future directions of education policy research. Second, the Board focused on the extent to which the proposed handbook would draw on the strongest research—including from within and outside the United States. Third, the Board was interested in the ability of the editors of the proposed handbook to bring together a team of authors who could assess the knowledge base of education policy research and do so with respect to the diverse populations served by contemporary educational systems. Finally, the Board reviewed the proposed content of the handbook to get a sense of the book's scope and the extent to which it would include a "critical analysis of the strengths and limitations of extant studies as well as address the essential tools and elements for research progress."

At the end of the review process, the Board enthusiastically approved and moved the *Handbook of Education Policy Research* into development. Support was given to the editors during the manuscript development process, and when the manuscript was complete, it was reviewed

and approved for publication by the Board. We are very pleased to make this comprehensive and well-conceptualized handbook available to readers interested in education policy. It advances both theory and practice in the field of education policy, and, if seriously engaged by policy makers, the *Handbook of Education Policy Research* will help them better understand, identify, and implement policies that can improve our nation's education systems and help strengthen the quality of education policy research.

On behalf of the AERA Books Editorial Board, I want to thank editors Gary Sykes, Barbara Schneider, and David Plank for their substantial investment in this research handbook and for producing a timely volume of significance. Special thanks are also due to Tim Ford, who assisted the lead editors in bringing this handbook to fruition. Finally I wish to thank the many authors, commentators, and reviewers for their important contributions.

Cherry A. McGee Banks
Chair, AERA Books Editorial Board
University of Washington Bothell

Acknowledgments

A volume of this magnitude could not have come to fruition without major resource commitments from a whole host of individuals. First, we need to thank the 99 authors who allowed us to endlessly bother them with revisions and agree to have their work blind reviewed by two outside reviewers. Second, a special thanks to the 107 reviewers who helped the authors identify the holes, inconsistencies, and maintain objectivity that in such a large volume, is in many ways a feat unto itself. We are especially grateful to several reviewers, Kathryn Anderson-Leavitt, David Baker, Susan Bodilly, Jere Brophy, Dorinda Carter, Margaret Eisenhart, Chandra Muller, Donald Peurach, John Tyler, and Ronald Zimmer, who gave us immediate, extensive, and in many cases, multiple reviews that were extraordinarily helpful not only to the authors but to us as we tried to provide a balance on issues of content, method, and theoretical perspectives. Third, we also owe our deep appreciation to the fourteen commentators who within a tight and short schedule provided clear and insightful syntheses of the material in each section, highlighting additional ideas, policies, and research that all play a significant role in the formulation of educational policy. Fourth, we would like to thank section editors Carolyn Herrington, Jane Clark Lindle, and Linda Skrla for their initial work in selecting authors for chapters and providing initial feedback to authors regarding the scope and organization of their chapters.

Behind the scenes of any manuscript are the real workers who make a book possible. Leigh Ann Halas, who helped with editing and seemingly endless rounds of reference checking, we thank you for all of your hard work. Nathan Jones, Venessa Keesler, and Adam Maier, all graduate students at Michigan State University, played a critical role not only serving as co-authors on chapters but assisting in the organization and preparation of the volume. But the person who really deserves our immense gratitude is Timothy Ford, a graduate student in educational policy at Michigan State University, who beyond any other individual made this volume possible. He was the command central, the chief editor, and overall task-master without whose assistance this volume would still be sheets of unorganized papers on three messy desks.

At AERA, we also would like to thank Felice Levine for her encouragement and support and continued prodding to make sure this volume is an authentic series of chapters that underscore the importance and value of educational policy research. A special thanks to Todd Reitzel, Director of Publications at AERA, who kept us to our deadlines, and secured copyright and all other legal documentation required for publication. Additionally, we would like to acknowledge the hard work of the AERA Books Editorial Board, established in 2005 to oversee selection of editors for the AERA/LEA Research Handbook Series and ensure high quality standards for the series volumes, of which this Handbook is a part. We extend our gratitude to this board, made up of chair Cherry McGee Banks and members Robert Floden, Patrick Forsyth, Felice Levine, Gary Natriello, Robert Sternberg, and Carol Camp Yeakey, for taking the time to review the manuscript to be sure it met the standards of scholarship AERA is continually striving to improve and achieve.

To our publisher Lane Akers, we thank you for assisting a rather unruly set of editors on keeping deadlines and making sure there would be books for the 2009 AERA annual meeting. To Carole Ames, Dean of the College of Education at Michigan State University, thank you for the resources from the John A. Hannah chair to make this process progress more smoothly than it might have otherwise.

But in the end, the three of us have to take responsibility for what we all hoped and envisioned is a timely and useful compilation of high quality scholarship on educational policy research. Thank you all.

Gary Sykes
Barbara Schneider
David N. Plank

Introduction

GARY SYKES, BARBARA SCHNEIDER, AND TIMOTHY G. FORD
MICHIGAN STATE UNIVERSITY

Over the past several decades, political leaders and governments around the world have come to assign an increasingly central role to education. Public initiatives to revitalize cities, encourage physical fitness and healthy lifestyles, and promote democratic and civic participation likewise rely heavily on the education system for the accomplishment of their goals. Policy discussions about economic growth and national competitiveness, for example, commonly focus on the importance of "human capital" and a highly-educated workforce. Policy debates about the sources of poverty and inequality quickly turn to the need to expand and improve the educational opportunities for all children, especially those facing initial and sustaining economic and social disadvantages.

"Education" is no longer just about what happens in classrooms and schools, but increasingly about rules and regulations promulgated in state capitals and the federal government designed to improve student academic performance and social development as well as the management and operation of the schools they attend. As "policy" has assumed an increasingly pivotal role in the educational system, a growing number of scholars have turned their attention to the process through which rules and regulations are adopted, and the consequences they have on teaching and learning. Education policy research has in turn expanded its reach and its relationship to these developments.

Today, policy research traverses the full spectrum of issues in education, from governance and finance to curriculum, pedagogy, and assessment, and across all levels of the educational system, from the federal government to the classroom. Virtually all aspects of the educational enterprise are now the objects of "policy," and appropriate subjects for policy research. New methodological tools also have been developed and are being deployed on many policy issues, while conceptual approaches with origins in multiple disciplines frame policy questions. Defining the boundaries of the field and identifying a parsimonious set of organizing principles to bring order to the vast diversity of topics is a

central challenge, but the importance of education policy research today merits the effort.

This handbook joins a set of companion volumes, all of which have contributed to recent efforts at synthesizing the field of educational policy. These include the *Handbook of Research in Education Finance and Policy* (Ladd & Fiske, 2008), *The State of Education Policy Research* (Fuhrman, Cohen, & Mosher, 2007), and the *International Handbook of Educational Policy* (Bascia, Cumming, Datnow, Leithwood, & Livingstone, 2005), among others. This volume offers a broad survey of topics on educational policy ranging from global to local perspectives (although the bulk of the chapters center on the United States given the extent of research found there); diverse and competing theoretical disciplinary frameworks and the multiple methodologies that underpin them; and the development and implementation of educational policy in other countries.

The volume is organized into seven sections, some more tightly bounded by theme than others. These include: the disciplinary foundations of education policy research (Section I); methodological issues in education policy research (Section II); a wide-ranging set of chapters on politics and the policy process (Section III); policy implications of resources, management, and organization (Section IV); teaching and learning policy (Section V); actors and institutions in the policy process (Section VI); and issues of access and differentiation in education and policy systems (Section VII). The remainder of this introduction provides an abstract of each chapter and overviews of the parts under which they are organized.

One important contribution to this volume is the chapters by commentators that follow each of the seven sections. These commentaries are written by a range of scholars who represent not only those who have had experience on the ground as practicing school leaders, but also as directors of major federal research and development offices. Additionally, some of the commentators work on reporting educational policy initiatives for the broader public, while others are chronicling the impact of state policies on classroom practices and teacher qualifications and credentialing processes. Some serve as leaders in bi-partisan academies that provide assessments, challenges, and future directions for specific policy initiatives. All of these commentators have established records of high-quality scholarship in investigating the impact of educational policy on students, their teachers, families and the communities in which they live. Together, they critique, emphasize, and recommend where the field of educational policy needs to focus if it is to be useful to the educational enterprise.

Section I: Social Science Disciplines and Education Policy Research

Education policy research can trace its roots in part to the social science disciplines. Section I addresses how knowledge from history, economics, political science, sociology, anthropology, and public policy (considered here as a distinct field of study) has formed a foundation for policy research in education. In the opening chapter, Vinovskis reviews the ebb and flow of the role of history in informing policy debates over the past decades, concentrating on federal education policy in particular. The chapter underscores the value that historical studies can have in identifying the risks and unintended consequences of former policies that future policies may well avoid. Vinovskis encourages historians to reclaim their discipline, and shore up on approaches and methods being eclipsed by other social scientists for describing and interpreting the contributions of history in education policy research.

Next, two economists explore the burgeoning field of economics of education which is having a major influence on many federal, state, and local education policies. Carnoy begins by explaining how the field of economics has influenced debates on school improvement along several dimensions. Economists argue that education has economic value on both an individual and societal level by increasing productivity, hence wages, and economic growth. Carnoy emphasizes however, that the evidence for this argument has been difficult to achieve and the results controversial. He underscores how education may influence economic productivity not simply through the addition of skills to the workforce but also through the pace and progress of technological innovation and change. Economists have also contributed methodologically to measuring the impact of school inputs on student outcomes. Carnoy provides a series of examples of how economists have used sophisticated statistical techniques to develop models (controlling for selection bias) that estimate causal effects using large-scale observational data.

Hanushek examines more specifically the issue of economic returns to education both in the United States and other countries. Like Carnoy, he argues that the U. S. may be reaching the limits of the economic benefits of *more* schooling such that greater attention is now warranted to the *quality* of schooling and to what students are learning in school. While simple measures of school quality have been elusive, economic research has demonstrated the importance of teacher quality (despite its uncertain relationship to teacher qualifications of various types). He concludes that school quality may help explain the puzzle of why low school-completion rates exist when the individual returns to education are high. These chapters should be read in conjunction with that of Plecki and Castañeda, which explores the question, does money matter.

Turning to political science, McDonnell draws on this disciplinary framework to explore the interaction of three conceptual "building blocks"—interests, ideas, and institutions. She examines how each has been incorporated into theories to explain cycles of policy stability and change. In moving beyond short-term snapshots of single policies, political scientists have looked to the interplay between interests and ideas, the institutions that insulate existing policies from change, and policy entrepreneurs who act strategically to advance new agendas.

More recently, political scientists have used the same concepts to consider how policies can alter patterns of citizen participation and distributional consequences. She concludes her chapter with a rationale for why political science can be a useful framework for informing education policy research.

The contributions of sociology to education policy are examined by Lauen and Tyson. They highlight processes of social stratification in society; the social organization of schooling; the effects of families, schools, and neighborhoods on student cognitive and social development; and the importance of modeling social context as a multi-level phenomenon. The chapter discusses how sociological studies have made major contributions to policy discourse and practice, with the Coleman Report standing as one of the most influential in debates over equality of opportunity in education. They argue for using qualitative sociological methods, in the tradition of the Chicago School, for exploring questions such as, what's happening? and why or how is it happening? that can help interpret and understand results from experimental and quasi experimental studies and evaluations.

Dixon, Borman, and Cotner introduce the reader to an anthropological approach to education. While they indicate that ethnographic studies "on the ground" are a useful accompaniment to experimental studies, they also note that the concept of "culture" as a distinct and bounded sphere has become blurred in the post-modern, global world prompting anthropologists to rethink this fundamental concept in their discipline. Drawing on a variety of studies, they show how anthropological work has helped to understand how policies are affecting children's lives, particularly No Child Left Behind and new instructional and curricular designs. The chapter concludes by noting that this discipline tends to adopt a critical perspective on policy, especially with regard to issues of equity and social justice for marginalized students, and to advocate for activist and participatory research that aims to uncover power relations and the lived experiences of "the other," as representing the full social spectrum of humanity suspended in webs of meaning (to use Geertz's phrase).

In the final chapter of Section I, Weimer distinguishes three domains that play complementary but different roles in the relationship between research and policy. *Disciplinary research,* that other authors in this section have described, employs methods, models, and concepts in the social sciences that inform our understanding of phenomena that may—or may not—be subject to policy intervention. *Policy research* aims to produce sound assessments of some policy problem or impact. Finally, the main topic of his chapter, *policy analysis* examines the impact of policy alternatives in relation to a policy problem. This analysis, he proposes, treats trade-offs entailed in policy alternatives around such issues as costs, problem identification, response to variability and uncertainty, and discovery of "Type III" errors, described as finding the correct response to the wrong question. Weimer succinctly brings this section to a close by describing general approaches to policy analysis that occur closer to actual and specific policies which have, in turn, been influenced by ideas, concepts, and findings from the social sciences. The methods of analysis he advocates then serve as a bridge to Section II.

Section II: Conducting Policy Research, Methodological Perspectives

Section II of the handbook turns to issues associated with the conduct of policy research and of its relationship to policymaking. Orland begins with a discussion of the prospects that "scientifically base research," randomized clinical trials (RCTs) in particular, may exert greater influence on policy making. While he advocates for research of this kind, his chapter also points out some of the main difficulties in linking research to policymaking. Some of these issues reside in the nature of the policy process (timing, politics, preferences), others in the nature of research (preferences for new discoveries vs. replication), and still others in the relationship between research and policy (e.g., funding, communication issues). In any event, he characterizes the relationship as filled with disjunctions, concluding that the current emphasis on scientifically based research in federal R & D policy in education is a promising and worthwhile development, but one whose ultimate success in fostering stronger research/policy linkages is far from assured. He urges caution in overstating the likely positive impacts of such reforms in addressing current pressing policy needs, as well as a greater near-term emphasis on R & D policies supporting research translation and tailored knowledge use.

Borman continues and deepens Orland's arguments by supplying a careful discussion of the issues associated with conducting randomized field trials in education. His chapter systematically considers the range of challenges to the conduct of RCTs, then proposes methods for dealing with them. Ethical issues, such as the withholding of treatments from students, are addressed along with others. Ultimately, he

argues, if education is to follow medicine in developing an "evidence based field," then the methods used to supply both internal and external validity for educational "treatments" of various kinds will require a similar level and kind of rigor that has come to characterize the field of medical research. The "gold standard" in this perspective is the experiment, as appropriately combined with methods that include an appropriate qualitative accompaniment.

Kaplan advocates a somewhat different approach in contrasting what he terms the "structural" and "experimental" traditions for dealing with problems of causality. While experimental designs have the advantage of testing well-specified counterfactuals, there exists a non-experimental, observational approach to causality that has taken shape in the field of econometrics, known variously as path analysis or structural equation modeling (SEM). His chapter provides an introduction to this alternative to experiments, cautioning that both approaches to causal inference rest on some "heroic assumptions." Following a careful exposition of the philosophical literature on causality originating in the work of the British Enlightenment empiricist David Hume, he makes the case for the value and practice of SEM as an underutilized method for drawing causal inferences in educational policy research. His essential point, though, is that policy analysts require a thorough conceptual understanding of theories of causality (and of their intellectual history) in order to make wise use of both experimental and non-experimental approaches. With this argument he rejects the claim that experiments alone constitute the "gold standard" for policy research.

Next, Pigott takes up a different but equally important issue in policy research, the conduct and uses of research syntheses or meta-analyses to inform education policymaking (see also Smith and Smith, chapter 30). Often policy makers seek an accurate and up-to-date summation of knowledge on a particular issue as one basis for policy development, and they turn to analysts with requests for such syntheses. She first proposes how research syntheses can contribute to policy development, what quality standards should be applied to meta-analyses, and how such work might be made more valuable to the policy process. While research syntheses can map fields of study and explore the boundaries of inference (around such matters as types of study method, varying contexts, and differences by participant), she argues in favor of expanding the kinds of questions addressed in meta-analyses together with procedures for producing more timely reviews that enter cycles of policy development and research.

Desimone further expands conceptions of how policy research might influence policy development through a consideration of the uses of mixed methods that move beyond formal means for ensuring causal inference or summarizing effects across studies. She argues that selection of methods depends on the questions asked. Whereas experimental and quasi-experimental methods seek confirmation around well-specified questions, other methods pursue aims that seek to generate hypotheses rather than test them. She also argues that the selection of methods should not be inherently ideological (for example as aligned with supporting vs. challenging the status quo in policy). In the second half of her chapter, she reprises a framework (see Green, Caracelli, & Graham, 1989) for the productive mix of methods based on five purposes: triangulation (different methods around same question); complementarity (different methods for different components of a study); development (using methods sequentially to refine knowledge); initiation (different methods to uncover contradictory or non convergent knowledge); and expansion (multiple methods to expand the scope or breadth of a study). She concludes with three "best practices" recommendations—using an integrative framework, applying an iterative approach, and grounding mixed methods in theory.

In the next chapter, Herman and Baker take up a particularly important topic at the intersection of research and policy—the nature of assessment policy. Assessments depend on standards of rigor established in the psychometric field, yet they also originate from policy decisions, in turn informing policy and political processes. Hence, assessment policy involves a complex mix of the technical and the political (see also Lindle). The complexity of assessment policy resides in part in the multiple purposes for assessments (which the chapter reviews) together with the multiple criteria for evaluating assessment policy (another topic in the chapter). After reviewing the research evidence on the effects of assessment, the authors demonstrate that most state assessment systems fail to meet quality criteria. Future U.S. developments, they argue, would do well to emulate assessment models already implemented in countries such as England and New Zealand. Incremental approaches toward such models appear the best bet for future assessment policy in the United States, dependent upon the necessary political will.

The final chapter in Section II takes up a wide range of issues for conducting policy and program evaluation research. While a conventional view might regard program evaluation as a simple matter—design and execute a study of a program—McDonald frames evaluation research in the context of scaling up programs and practices found to be effective. Scale-up as a contemporary policy concern points to evaluation research as an extended, multi-stage process in the "discovery to implementation" cycle: first, proof of concept, then establishing efficacy, demonstrating effectiveness, scaling up and testing again; and finally, post-marketing research. The chapter explores issues at each stage in this process while arguing that such a complete cycle is required if education policy is to benefit from evaluation research.

Section III: Politics and the Policy Process

A wide range of issues related to the theme of politics and the policy process constitute the third section of the Handbook. The first four chapters pose theoretical alternatives for interpreting education policies including those implemented on behalf of racially and ethnically diverse students, families, and the communities in which they live, and the discourse by which these initiatives are symbolized and framed in policy documents. The next two chapters look at the political institutions of the law and of collective bargaining as influences on the policy process, followed by four chapters on public involvement in educational politics and policy, and the tensions involved in the process of policy implementation. The final chapters explore the challenges to the political process in education offered by public choice theory, and what its prospects may be for influencing educational policy.

Torres and Van Heertum discuss how the philosophical and historical roots of critical theory have been applied to education policy. Included in their discussion are a series of constructs and ideas that define this field and key researchers who have contributed to it. Critiquing both critical theory and positivism, they argue that education research should be committed to tying together theory and practice, communicating positionality, emphasizing results over methods, and linking them to relevant policies. Finally, using teacher unions and NCLB as examples, they demonstrate the value of critical theory in questioning the bases of these frameworks and the importance of striving for moral and ethical imperatives to guide policy research and formulation.

Mickelson paints a sociological and historical portrait of the racial and ethnic diversity among American students. She uses the common (and contested) racial and ethnic categories Asians, Blacks, Latinos/as, Native Americans and Alaskan Natives, Whites, Bi- and Multiracial, and Immigrant youth as she examines various school processes. She discusses a range of theories that help to explain the racially correlated nature of educational outcomes. Many of these theories focus on the structured inequality in educational opportunities that intersect with socioeconomic, political, and cultural differences among families, communities, and social networks. While acknowledging there has been some narrowing in achievement gaps among groups (see also Farkas), she concludes by noting how resilient these gaps are, and how, "the institutional basis of racial stratification in education remains the single most urgent challenge facing educational policy makers, students, and their parents."

Stovall documents how critical race theory (CRT) and critical race feminism (CRF) supply alternative but complementary models for interpreting both the intent and character of policies associated with the plight of urban schools. In societies where overt and subtle forms of discrimination by race, gender, and other social characteristics are endemic, education is called on to perform emancipatory or liberatory functions, and to tackle both the manifest and latent causes of educational inequalities. To illustrate such an analysis, the chapter considers the case of housing reform in Chicago and its relation to education. Reforms in the name of improved housing served a variety of corporate and class interests while dispossessing poor and working class people of color in schools and their respective neighborhoods. The case illustrates the importance of taking a wide angle view of reforms from critical perspectives linked to race, gender, and class.

Rosen presents us with yet another theoretical perspective, symbolic action, as an analytic tool for understanding educational policy, its origins and expressions. Within this framework, she argues that policy serves two functions: the *expressive*, to communicate articles of faith; and the *constitutive*, to construct policy realities. Pursuing the expressive function, she then illustrates how policy and policymaking serve as myths, rituals, and spectacles. Pursuing the constitutive function, she shows how public problems are defined, how the rhetoric of policy exerts influence, and how "frames" shape policy development. Along with the first three chapters, Rosen's exposition has value in challenging official policy discourses and in noticing policy's cultural underpinnings in relation to instrumental purposes and consequences. She wants not to dismiss instrumental perspectives but rather to include symbolic perspectives in the appraisal of policy and policy making.

Two specific kinds of policy—the law and collective bargaining—are analyzed by Mead and Koppich and Callahan, respectively. Mead begins by distinguishing law from policy, noting that while law tends to answer the questions, may we? and must we? policy seeks to answer the question, should we? Law creates boundary conditions while policies attempt to determine what is to be done. Legal scholarship has challenged many of the premises and bases for policy frameworks and decisions. To illustrate the relationship between law and policy, she presents four examples that contrast legal with legislative decisions at federal and state levels. These cases help illustrate the interplay between law and policy, where constitutional principles set boundaries; legislation captures relatively changeable values of time and locale; and litigation interprets legislation and seeks to uphold constitutional precedent. As she describes, future critical arenas for such contestation will be the reauthorization of NCLB and the aftermath of the Supreme Court decision disallowing voluntary integration programs that use race as one consideration for student assignment.

Koppich and Callahan review the hotly disputed and understudied issue of collective bargaining agreements, which regulate aspects of schooling and teaching and shape the educational environment. Two perspectives on collective bargaining frame the debate, one that is critical (see chapter by West), the other cautiously positive. The authors review the history of collective bargaining in education, and then describe contemporary efforts to introduce professional unionism and reform bargaining as an alternative to traditional, industrial bargaining, highlighting vanguard experiments in some districts. Their main point is that policy research has not kept up with these developments. Thus, the saliency of reform bargaining and its potential effects on student outcomes remains largely unknown. Clearly, more studies are needed to guide the future of collective bargaining in education.

Jacobsen, in the next chapter, argues that poll formulation can be understood as a form of discourse that captures public voice regarding satisfaction (or dissatisfaction) with public education. When the public's voicing of dissatisfaction is ignored, increased exit from the public system is a rational alternative. Jacobsen reviews how opinion polling about the goals and purposes of American education has evolved over the years, underscoring that polling surveys are highly sensitive to the questions asked, the formats they are presented in, and other factors. She notes that by using key concepts and words, polls suggest that the public wants public schools to pursue a relatively broad range of goals. The public places some emphasis on core academic outcomes, but also expects public education to develop students' skills in other goals such as citizenship, critical thinking, and work ethic. To gain greater specificity with regard to the desires of the public, an important and under-studied field in politics and education, contemporary work on polling has asked respondents to indicate relative weights or trade-offs among major goals. Future work, she advocates, must provide finer breakdowns by state and subpopulations together with attention to new policies and political actors.

Political discourse on assessments, specifically performance standards and accountability policy, is the focus of the next chapter by Lindle. Her political discourse analysis of *Education Week* and *Lexis Nexis* reveals that political and professional elites are quoted most frequently, with only 10% of attention going to assessment experts/educational researchers. Although heard less frequently, experts fulfill an important role by supplying two kinds of checks on elite opinions: They challenge and critique elite views and help explain the complexities of assessment policy to the public. Given the politicized role that experts' opinions have, she questions their future role in an environment that is likely to continue to be assessment and accountability driven.

The next pair of chapters turns from the politics of public discourse to the mobilization and implementation of policy to address public concerns. Honig's chapter on policy implementation argues that the basic evaluation question, What works? should be replaced by the question, What works for whom, where, when, and why? She frames implementation as a highly contingent and locally situated process involving the interaction of policy, people, and places. She next uses these three categories to supply an historical review of implementation research, advocating for better use of theory to guide future work. As illustration, she selects three promising theories and demonstrates how each helps to illuminate policy implementation issues. Her choices—complexity theory, organizational learning theory, and critical race theory (see chapters by Stovall and by Torres and Van Heertum)—demonstrate the wide range of lenses that might be employed usefully to study implementation.

Datnow and Park closely examine three large-scale reforms and the theories and rationale behind their implementation. They offer three major perspectives to understanding policy implementation—technical/rational conceptions, mutual adaptation, and sensemaking/co-construction—and how they are embodied in Comprehensive School Reform, NCLB, and data-driven decision making at the district level. Several assumptions about the change of direction, the policy process, spheres of influence, and the role of context and values are compared and contrasted from these three perspectives. The authors suggest that, when assessing the effectiveness of large-scale education reforms, policy makers and researchers need to be more analytically sophisticated and theoretically multifaceted when constructing complex reform efforts that can be sustainable (see also McDonald's chapter 9 for discussion of large-scale reforms and their sustainability).

To conclude this section, chapters by West and by Smith and Smith each provide overviews of the relationship between research and policy. West offers a brief introduction to public choice theory as a lens for understanding the productivity puzzle: Why have the costs of education risen while educational outcomes have remained flat (see Hanushek, Carnoy, Plecki and Castañeda, and Hess on this point)? Many theorists in this tradition rely on "principal-agent" models to understand behavior in public bureaucracies, and while such models have been challenged for underestimating altruism and mission-oriented behavior, they provide a basic framework for understanding the powerful role of self-interested behavior—individually and collectively—in public service organizations. West suggests that low productivity attributed in part to the weaknesses of market forces in the education sector, unionization of employees, and incentives for excessive bureaucratization within public education. He notes that such diagnoses have helped spur calls for the increased use of self-interested incentives through test-based accountability and school choice to improve student outcomes (see also chapters by Vergari, Witte, Hess, and Belfield and Levin). However, he recognizes the difficulties of allowing for a systematic evaluation of such initiatives.

In their chapter, Smith and Smith address questions concerning how research might better inform policy and program development. In a wide-ranging treatment, their chapter mines past efforts to link research and policy via examination of a set of topics that includes the pros and cons of large foundation support; the conditions under which research has influenced policies; why many reforms have failed; what we know about more successful efforts; dimensions for policies that are more likely to succeed; the importance of theory in policy-oriented research; and recommendations for policy researchers and policymakers. Viewed in contrast to the chapters that concentrate on the politics of the policy process, this synthesis makes a persuasive argument for how research might play a more powerful and consequential role in the policy process.

Section IV: Policy Implications of Educational Resources, Management, and Organization

Section IV examines some of the extensive policy levers that are used in designing and implementing major changes in educational systems. Many of these reforms are associated with different types of educational resources and with alterations in the organizational and managerial landscape of schools, districts, and state systems. While some policies have been incremental and targeted, others have had large-scale, transformative goals. The first chapters in this section discuss proposed and enacted reforms in resource allocations, with later chapters taking up system changes in organization and management.

The chapter by Spillane, Gomez, and Mesler could be considered a companion to the chapters by Honig and Datnow and Park, but here the emphasis is on organizations and organizational change as a context for understanding outcomes of policy implementation. In the authors' reframing of the role of organizations, they consider the public or idealized characterization of resources—defined as its ostensive property—and what people do with resources in particular places and times—as its performative property—and how both of these enable and constrain practice and policy implementation. Their analysis considers four different resources that exhibit these two properties: human capital, social capital, organizational routines, and technology. These resources are situated within contexts or "fields of interaction." The theoretical framework described here provides several suggestions for future work including the study of work practice within and between organizations; attention to the broader institutional system within which practice is nested; and moving beyond the study of natural variations in organizations. The authors recommend that the design and implementation of planned change be conducted using a wide range of research approaches including randomized trials and/or experiments.

In their chapter, Ahn and Brewer describe a particular structural aspect of school organization that has attracted considerable attention from policy makers: class and school size. In part one of the chapter, they review the arguments and theories that have been put forward supporting the benefits of small classes and schools. In part two, they examine the evidence on each reform. While some evidence, based mostly on the Tennessee STAR experiment, reveals causal effects for small classes on student achievement, there is very little evidence based on well-designed experiments or quasi-experiments to support the claimed benefits of small schools. Ahn and Brewer also address issues concerning the policy tradeoffs related to class size reduction (e.g., more building space, hiring of more qualified teachers), and question the cost effectiveness of class and school reductions relative to other reforms. In sum, while this policy intervention in school organization appears attractive to many analysts and advocates, the research base for such reforms remains thin.

Issues of equity and adequacy of financial resources are the focus of the chapter by Baker and Green. Beginning with the historical roots of the language used in school finance cases, the authors argue why conventional definitions for framing school finance solutions lead to oversimplified, inadequate programs that fail to meet student needs, especially those in low income households. Questioning the role of state finance legislative and legal actions, using examples from three states, they raise concerns with when, whether, and how state courts should be involved in defining educational adequacy and the difficulty of legislatures to meet the financial obligations imposed by court actions. Resource disparities continue to be the norm in state school finance with states struggling to strike a balance between equity and adequacy; judicial and legislative roles; and politics versus empirical evidence as the basis for school finance reform.

Plecki and Castañeda complement Baker and Green by exploring what is known about the value of educational investments. In common with the chapters by Carnoy, Hanushek, and West, they also look at the educational production function literature, reiterating (as Hess also indicates) that while expenditures have been rising, student educational outcomes have not improved. Their chapter notes the measurement and methodological challenges in some of the economic models, primarily educational production functions, that have contributed to controversies in determining whether money matters, and if so in relation to what particular kinds of investments. Six investments appear to be candidates for policy pay-off, although each has pros and cons. They include improving teacher quality, lowering pupil-teacher ratios (see the chapter by Ahn and Brewer), expanding early-childhood programs (see the chapter by Schweinhart and Fulcher-Dawson), improving high school, decentralizing spending authority, and providing incentives to improve performance. The chapter closes with thoughts on future studies, including a more cautious note on the use of various models, including randomized trials, for estimating the value of educational investments.

While fiscal resources serve as one source of and target for policy, organizational and management features of educational systems also have been implicated as the next set of chapters indicates. Reconstituting public schools, introducing charter schools, voucher plans, other elements of market-based approaches all seek either retail improvements in low performing schools or wholesale transformations in school systems. The next five chapters explore these policy options. First, Malen and King Rice examine theory and evidence on school reconstitution, defined as the "blanket replacement of personnel in schools." This policy prescription bears attention today as one potential remedy under the NCLB sanctions, and the evidence to date is not promising. Theory specifies positive effects via some combination of sanctions and capacity-building, but the critical issues concern whether the new capacity is well aligned with what low performing schools need, and how contextual factors affect the coherence of the intervention. Evidence from studies of reconstitution policies in Chicago, San Francisco, Baltimore, Portland, and other locales has turned up only a few favorable outcomes. Instead, such a policy more often increases stress, demoralization, and instability, actually weakens staff quality, and focuses schools on short-term fixes rather than long term improvements.

Better designed policies and studies might improve this track record, but the authors urge caution in future recourse to this policy remedy.

Vergari provides an update on the many research questions provoked by the rise of charter schools in the United States and of their counterparts elsewhere around the world. Her chapter examines the growth of charter schools in the U.S. and their impact on a wide range of issues including equity, the exercise of parental choice, student mobility and attrition, educational innovation, local school finance and accountability. Fifteen years into the experiment with charter schools in the U.S., she argues that many questions remain unanswered and require greater attention by policy researchers, even as the pace of charter school growth has leveled off.

The concluding three chapters in this section consider the prospects of market-based reforms in education, especially as those stimulated by school choice policies associated with voucher plans, tuition tax credits, and the like. Witte's chapter takes stock of voucher plans in a cross-national, comparative context, assessing the evidence pertaining to effects it has on segregation by class and race, student achievement, and quality of other non-voucher schools. Reviewing arguments pro and con for vouchers, he identifies five design features of voucher plans and then describes how these features operate in nine countries around the world, including the United States. To take but one contrast, the Netherlands has the oldest system of educational choice (dating from 1917) that features public subsidies for Protestant and Catholic schools alike. Due to small class differences, there has been substantial equality across schooling options, but the recent influx of Muslim immigrants may be altering this accommodation. Chile, in contrast, launched its national voucher plan in 1980, but their system features very large between school differences associated with social stratification. Witte ultimately argues that voucher systems alone are unlikely to work wholesale changes on educational systems even as the idea retains power and influence.

Hess provides a provocative and straightforward argument concerning the potential power of a competitive marketplace of schools for transforming education. He parses arguments for school choice differently than Witte by distinguishing competitive effects for improving existing schools (termed "public sector response") from effects associated with new entrants into the education market (termed "displacement"). While competition is already a feature in certain segments of education (e.g., higher education and supplemental services under NCLB), he notes that the bulk of K–12 education in the United States has been insulated from substantial competition by an array of forces that blunt, distort, and weaken its potential productive effects (see also West's chapter for concurring arguments). Moreover, competition's rough edges, its tendency toward what Austrian economist Joseph Schumpeter called "creative destruction," have caused even ardent reformers to pull back from the full implications of competition. There may, he suggests, not be a coalition powerful enough to overcome the political opposition to market reforms other than those that operate on the margins. But he argues in favor of the raw potential for this transformative change.

Belfield and Levin supply a broader context in which to consider both Witte's and Hess' analysis of public school choice policies. Building on Levin's prior work, they note that any form of school choice will require trade-offs among four values—freedom to choose; productive efficiency, equity, and social cohesion. In any choice plan, more of one value is likely to mean less of some other value. For example, if families are allowed full freedom to choose schools for their children, this might improve productive efficiency but at the expense of the state's interest in equity and social cohesion. Their chapter then provides a review of empirical studies around each of these values. They conclude from the evidence that competition and choice are likely to greatly improve freedom to choose; to exert small improvements in student achievement but certainly not revolutionary change; to increase inequalities unless choices are restricted, e.g., to the poor; and it is not clear what effects these might have on social cohesion. Taken together, these analyses seem to indicate that choice policies involve a set of clear preferences around core values, none of which may be dismissed; that they produce relatively modest effects on many important outcomes; that they may be one means of improving equity (under plans targeted to the poor); and that a fully competitive market system is unlikely to replace—or even strongly supplement—government provision of K–12 schools in the United States.

Section V: Teaching and Learning Policy

The chapters in Section V move the focus of policy research and intervention closer to the core of education and to the immediate influences on teachers and teaching, on learners and learning. The chapters examine critical policy questions related to curriculum, the education of special student populations, teacher preparation and the labor market, instructional designs as policy reform, interactions between students and teachers in classrooms, factors underlying the persistent achievement gaps among student groups, and the challenges and promises associated with the new teaching and learning technologies.

In the first chapter, Schmidt and Maier review the literature on "opportunity to learn" (OTL), a critically important policy variable, that they argue has been narrowly defined as students' exposure to curriculum content. The authors provide OTL's rich history in educational research, and how it has been conceptualized and operationalized in three large-scale and influential studies of education: The Third International Mathematics and Science Study (TIMSS); the Study of Instructional Improvement (SII); and the instructional measurement studies flowing out of the Institute for Research on Teaching (IRT). The chapter then describes strategies for measuring OTL, which serves both as an outcome in some studies and as a mediating vari-

able in other studies, and the similarities and differences in results from these studies (see Rowan et al.'s chapter for further exposition on SII). Evidence from the U.S. indicates great variability in math OTL within schools as well as between schools. The authors suggest that this is partially the consequence of a slow-moving and poorly sequenced curriculum weak in academic rigor and content coverage out of step with many other countries. The authors' critical point, though, is that OTL is a central variable in education policy research and development that must be considered in studies that examine effects of other variables (e.g., teacher quality) on achievement, that, if not considered, will bias estimates of the effect of instruction and content coverage on mathematics, science, and other subjects.

Schoenfeld and Pearson describe the history of tensions and controversies that have swirled around the teaching of reading and mathematics. Both school subjects have been party to theoretical and empirical disputes, changes in practices, and political interventions strongly driven by ideological positions that can be traced to beliefs about the goals of education. The chapter reviews many similarities and some of the differences in the narrative account of some of the most acrimonious scientific and political debates that engulfed curricular approaches, instructional techniques, and assessment strategies for measuring student performance in reading and mathematics. The authors' views of the events surrounding these controversies should be read alongside Orland's account and that of Smith and Smith to round out an understanding of how scientific and political forces have interacted over the years and the consequences they have had on educational research and practice.

If the curriculum constitutes one important factor for understanding the relationships among teaching and learning, policy, politics, and research, then students constitute another. The next chapter considers particular populations of students—English Language Learners. Gándara and Gómez review the contentious and troubled history of language policy in the U.S., noting how politicized this issue has been and how seldom research has been used to adjudicate the controversies. One way of underscoring the importance of language policy is to note that the U.S linguistic minority population has grown dramatically; it currently constitutes 20% of all school-age children. They note how language policy differs among nations, based on their ideology, ranging from monolingual (e.g., France, the U.S.) to multilingual (e.g., India, South Africa). Then, they examine the key policy issues and questions at stake, and the research methods used to study such questions. They conclude by suggesting that a richer research agenda for language studies could be achieved by viewing it through a lens that sees language as a personal and societal resource that could be used for improving the preparation of teachers.

Teachers serve as the focus of the next two chapters. First, Béteille and Loeb summarize what is known about the nature of teacher labor markets. The chapter describes the teacher workforce which is large (over 8% of working college graduates) and diverse. It then summarizes the research linking teacher characteristics to student outcomes. While most studies reveal only weak associations between most measured characteristics of teachers, such as whether or not they have an advanced degree, and student outcomes, they consistently find that new teachers are less effective than more experienced teachers. Yet, new teachers are over represented in schools with students most at risk. This difference in teacher characteristics is systematic of the broader pattern that teachers are unequally distributed across schools and districts. Inner city schools and those serving minority students have lower proportions of experienced teachers and teachers with higher qualifications, and they have higher teacher attrition rates. The chapter then reviews factors that attract and retain teachers in particular locales, including wages, job characteristics, location, entrance requirements, and local hiring practices. The chapter concludes with a review of policy options developed at state and local levels that hold some promise in addressing staffing problems in poor minority schools and districts.

Darling-Hammond, Wei, and Johnson next examine issues associated with teacher preparation, selection, and learning opportunities. The chapter focuses on what qualifications and training matter most for producing effective teachers. The topics they cover include teacher preparation, certification, licensure, mentoring and induction, and professional support. They also review policies and their effects for reducing restrictions to entry, opening up alternative routes, terminating ineffective teachers. Some of these policies are generally under the umbrella of market mechanisms to address problems of supply, demand, and quality (see Hess for exposition of this view). While an accumulating body of evidence provides empirical support for many aspects of teacher preparation, many questions remain to be answered. They suggest more studies that can help inform policies particularly related to mentoring, teacher retention and classroom practices that can be associated with learning results.

The next two chapters narrow the focus of teaching and learning in schools to classrooms. First, Rowan and colleagues report results from a large, quasi-experimental study conducted between 1999 and 2004 that examined the implementation of three prominent whole-school reforms—the Accelerated Schools Project (ASP); America's Choice (AC); and Success for All (SFA). Beginning in the 1990s, one significant approach to school reform was predicated on the idea that external agents might develop designs for new schools that then might be implemented in many schools with external assistance supplied by the designers. The Study of Instructional Improvement (SII) followed the course of three of these designs in multiple schools around the country. This chapter supplies a summary of results from this study, concentrating on features of the designs themselves; effects on instructional practice; and effects on student achievement. The study finds (1) that the designs were different one from another, and, not surprisingly, achievement results vary by model; (2) that instructional interventions require fine-grained information and careful measurement strategies; (3) that it is important to specify the "logic model" or theory of action when studying complex interventions (see also Smith and Smith on this point); and (4) that the designs are fragile in practice such that attention to implementation is critical. Of particular note, is that student mobility in schools with high proportions of poor and minority students proved to be a crucial factor in undermining the effectiveness of otherwise successful designs and implementation strategies.

Pianta and Hamre second the importance of concentrating on and carefully measuring instruction as an aspect of policy development. Operating out of a tradition of research on classroom behavior, the authors argue that attention to instruction is critical because of the emphasis on performance in NCLB; the renewed attention to school readiness (see also Farkas, and Schweinhart and Fulcher-Dawson); and increasing emphasis on teacher quality, which calls for direct measures of teachers' performance and student-teacher interactions. They present a framework for studying classrooms that introduces three dimensions—the emotional, organizational, and instructional—each carefully theorized. Studies reveal that considerable time in many classrooms is not devoted to instruction; that variability in instruction among classrooms is high and inequitable; and that consistency of high-quality instruction varies from year to year. An intervention program based on their framework reveals modest but positive relationship to student outcomes, leading them to conclude with recommendations for research and education policy. Together with Darling-Hammond, Wei, and Johnson, they argue for direct measures of teaching performance as an important complement to conventional teacher licensure policies.

Inequalities in learning that both Rowan and colleagues, and Pianta and Hamre uncover are documented in detail in the Farkas chapter. The term "achievement gap" has now entered the educational lexicon, but its particular characteristics are important to note. Farkas carefully examines the evidence for the racial achievement gap over the life course, beginning with differences at the outset of formal schooling. An important finding whose etiology is not well understood, is that the achievement gap between Blacks and Whites widens as children move through the grade levels, resulting in significant differences in cognitive achievement, school completion rates, post-secondary attendance, and employment outcomes. Still, between 1980 and 2002, gaps have narrowed somewhat, although Farkas notes that the problem is akin to catching a moving train: African American and Hispanic students must increase more rapidly than Whites in order to "catch up" with rising White achievement. However, when parent education is held constant, achievement gaps have narrowed substantially, indicating that family structure and parental education are strongly implicated in student achievement. Quality instruction in the early grades and parent education may all be parts of a successful strategy to narrow the gaps, but so too must be larger efforts to ameliorate the effects of family and neighborhood poverty. Farkas concludes by advocating for better and more universal pre-school education to promote greater equality "at the starting gate," since early deficits continue to play a role as determinants of future achievement.

If equity is one watchword in education policy, then another is "innovation" with technology often touted as the wave of the future. In their chapter Zhao and Lei examine the history of technology in the schools and find that enthusiasm typically has outrun results. In its latest incarnation, the new information technologies appear to offer promise for a great leap forward, yet to date evidence on effectiveness is mixed, costs of maintaining and replacing computers are high, and unintended consequences have emerged around such problems as addiction to computer games; online bullying and harassment; access to sexually explicit and/or violent material; plagiarism and others. At the same time, the authors note the great symbolic value or appeal of technology as opposed to its actual impact and the problems with vague goals and poor implementation (often featuring blame visited on teachers). For several reasons they argue that the productivity gains from technology in the world of business are not likely to appear in education, but note as well that technology use outside of schools is likely to have major impact on schooling in a variety of ways. They suggest that we need to reconsider the role of technology in education, particularly in relation to human teachers. They conclude with recommendations for policy and research on this beguiling but challenging topic that is coming to have global influence through and in the new virtual world.

Next, Plank and Keesler discuss one tendency that has emerged among many nation-states that has been characterized as the "shrinking state." The term refers to pressures to reduce state involvement in and funding of education in the face of rising expenditures coupled with political dissatisfaction with the inability of educational systems to improve the literacy and numeracy of many of its students (see also West's exposition of public choice theory). After reviewing the history of and rationale for educational expansion over the last century, the authors note some of the counter-pressures today to reduce the state's role in educational systems that provide schooling options from early childhood through adult education. Along with Mundy and Ghali (see Section VI), they document the growing influence of trans-national organizations, then consider how public dissatisfaction with education may lead to state failure, which, in turn, may provoke policies that replace public provisions of education with market arrangements, shifting costs to a variety of private providers especially around pre-school and higher education. Families, local school districts, and neighborhood communities are all bearing the costs of unsuccessful schooling systems and many groups are calling for administrative decentralization that challenges the state's role (see the chapter by Fuller). This dissatisfaction with public systems is reinforced by religious and ethnic groups who are demanding various forms of private education through school choice policies partially subsidized by the state. Whether these developments presage a new trend is open to question, as some counter-movements have developed in the face of problems with "failed states" around the globe.

Section VI: Actors and Institutions in the Policy Process

It is widely recognized that power and influence are distributed across all levels of educational systems. This has meant that the policy process consists of a complex configuration of institutions and actors that frequently interact—sometimes in conflict and at other times reinforcing the actions of each other. Section VI presents a broad array of organizations and actors to answer the classic political question: Who governs? The chapters depict a wide range of pluralistic and elitist views for understanding and predicting policy stability and change.

"Globalization" has become the lexicon of many of today's policy analysts, fueled in part by massive economic and technological developments throughout the world. Mundy and Ghali examine the rise of international and trans-national organizations from post-World War II to the present. Beginning with the formation of the United Nations and UNESCO, they argue that these organizations failed to exert much influence in the immediate post-war period, stalemated in part by the Cold War. International interests took on a greater role in the 1960s with the Organization for Economic Cooperation and Development (OECD), and went on to gather momentum with subsequent organizations such as the World Bank, UNICEF, and the International Monetary Fund (IMF). These "second cycle" organizations were able to muster more attention and influence because of their investments in strategies directed at increasing human capital. In the 1970s and 1980s, globalization became the watchword as developments began to "deterritorialize" policy together with efforts to "shrink the state" (see Plank and Kessler's chapter) by privatizing education. By the 1990s, another round of organizations arose (e.g., the European Union, the World Trade Organization, various regional cooperatives), including international nongovernmental organizations (INGOs), with concerns such as "education for all," equity, and poverty. Some of these initiatives took on an instrumentalist approach advocating cross-nation-state testing such as the Program for International Student Assessment (PISA)—to identify which countries were able to raise and improve the educational productivity of their students (see also Baker's chapter). Turning from history to theory, the authors then review macro sociological theories of world systems, concluding with the promise of International Relations for demonstrating how international institutions can matter in formulating educational policy.

The next chapter also uses a political science perspective to examine the expansion of federal and state education policy in the U.S. Cohen-Vogel and McLendon organize their chapter on the federal role in education around recent theories in political science to explain policy influence, stability, and change (see also McDonnell). Some theorists have stressed the intractability of the American political system, whereas a second group has underscored the openness and adaptability of the system, while the third has produced an integrated or synthetic account of policy development that encompass both policy stability and change. The authors maintain that synthetic theories help to illuminate aspects of federal education policy while raising new questions for study. They advocate longitudinal research that takes a wide angle perspective, while noting new databases that can assist with inquiries of this type.

McDermott next reviews empirical studies of state education policy in the United States and some of the methodological issues associated with them. She describes the growing influence of states beginning with school finance (see also Baker and Green's chapter), then, examines the waves of reform in the 1980s to the present,, with a special emphasis on state studies that analyze the effects of state assessment and accountability systems on student performance and low performing schools. She discusses how policy ideas at the state level are appropriated at the federal level (e.g., NCLB), and at other times, influence flows from the federal to the state level (e.g., IDEA). States then mediate various kinds of influence that arise from the federal level or local level of the educational system. McDermott concludes with suggestions for future research for studying the state's role in education policy.

School districts in the United States, originating as agents of local control, are somewhat unique relative to the world pattern of centralized, ministerial systems. Today, school districts are often required to exert influence over instruction, a trend that Sykes, O'Day, and Ford analyze in their chapter. After setting the stage by reviewing arguments for the importance of districts as both policy initiators and enactors, the chapter describes the contemporary challenges facing districts; includes a brief history of this distinctive institution; a précis of the research on districts; and then an agenda for future policy studies. The chapter's main point focuses on the importance of conceiving districts as learning organizations in conjunction with their role in operating and monitoring systems of accountability.

One of the organizations directly involved in educational policy making, are those organizations that represent teachers. Bascia describes how these organizations that include teacher unions on one hand, and various subject matter professional organizations on the other have altered the wages and working conditions of teachers. She notes that the standard policy paradigm, which attends to formal governmental processes, tends to overlook the informal ways that teacher organizations affect classroom practice. Organized teachers occupy an anomalous and contested position in education due to jurisdictional disputes with administrators, constraints of labor laws, and cross purposes represented by their organizations. Still, teacher organizations offer opportunities for teacher leadership through which they can exercise informal influence on education policies. Bascia suggests that research on teacher organizations can help to discern how policy ideas are formed and

the networks through which policies are disseminated and institutionalized over time.

Mintrom's chapter examines the role of local, democratic institutions in education, orienting his approach around Gutmann's (1987) theory of democratic education. Local school boards, superintendents, and interest groups serve as agents of local democracy in pursuit of goals traditionally associated with citizenship and participation in civic life. At the same time, criticisms of these institutions have arisen, particularly in large urban districts where school bureaucracies often appear to insulate educators from families and local communities. The future of these institutions face four dilemmas including: the tensions among democratic controls and the promotion of learning for all, local versus national priorities, efforts to hold accountable the private and personal work of teachers, and the imperative to improve schools while holding them accountable. Three strategies of reform have emerged including: incremental adjustments to current institutions; large-scale institutional reforms; and alternative forms of institutions. Mintrom closes by advocating more theory-driven, empirical studies of the relationship between institutional designs and the behaviors of institutional actors with a focus on improving local democracy in education.

Lugg and Rorrer's chapter details the rise of home-schooling in the United States, where estimates place the number of home-schooled children at over one million (2.2% of all students), with dramatic increases over the past 20 years. State policy related to home-schooling runs the gamut from permissive to relatively regulated on a variety of dimensions including teacher qualifications, instructional time, testing requirements, and others. A strong interest group with historical roots in liberalist Protestantism has been a vigorous proponent of home-schooling. In particular, Protestant Right legal organizations have drawn on selective Supreme Court decisions involving religion and education in bolstering their arguments in support of home-schooling. However, at present, there are no Supreme Court decisions on home-schooling. Furthermore, while state courts have established parental rights to educate children at home, questions remain unsettled around whether the rights of children are adequately safeguarded, and whether the public interest is well-served with increasing numbers of families withdrawing from institutions of public schooling. The authors conclude by raising concerns about what we do not know about home-schooling especially given the diversity of regulatory and implementation policies across the states, and whether such policies are serving the best interests of children.

The final two chapters in this section focus specifically on students. In her chapter, Mitra reviews the concept of student voice. Employing a developmental perspective, she conceptualizes how students can partner with adults to support their agency, sense of belonging, and competence. While the threat exists for partnerships to result in co-optive and inauthentic relationships, most of the research from the United Kingdom, Australia, Canada, and the United States provide positive exemplars. Mitra examines three forms of student voice—as data sources around reform efforts; as collaborators in communities of learning; and as co-leaders of change efforts—and concludes with a discussion of conditions that facilitate student voice in the policy and educative process.

The next student chapter by Hehir presents a contrasting view of the ways in which students, in this instance, students with special needs have sometimes been unfairly treated in the educational process. He argues that over its 30-year history the Individuals with Disabilities Education Act (IDEA) for the most part, has promoted significant improvements in the education of children with special needs around such outcomes as dropping out, attending postsecondary education, and gaining employment. He underscores that while these results have been positive, they vary by social class so that special needs students from lower income families who attend large urban districts are less likely to achieve such positive outcomes. This disparity in services has largely been attributed to the inequitable distribution of resources. In poor urban districts serving concentrations of poor families, the lack of specially trained personnel and other instructional materials has meant that special needs students are isolated in resource rooms even though such practices violate least restrictive environment provisions of the law. When parents and other advocates use the law to force changes, the results appear to be positive, leading Hehir to advocate the law and policies as effective tools in promoting improved education for special needs students.

Section VII: Educational Access and Differentiation

The final section of the handbook looks across the educational enterprise from early childhood to higher education to examine how education systems provide access and opportunity to some populations of students and not others. Key social categories such as class, race, and gender are implicated as well as social, institutional, and political processes. While the chapters tend to reveal interesting differences from a national perspective, several of the authors (e.g., Jones and Schneider and Baker) suggest that such patterns of differentiation regarding access and opportunity exist throughout the world.

Decentralizing control and resources down to parents or local educators offers one policy strategy for equalizing access to a more colorful spectrum of schools. Fuller asks what has been learned empirically over the past generation, as faith in the de-centering of power and dollars has grown among reformers on the political Right and Left. He reviews evidence and methodological advances in studying charter schools, vouchers, small schools, and early education. Fuller also traces the ideals and intellectual currents that have energized decentralized reforms, going back to the 1950s, including theories of rational choice, institutional pluralism, communitarian localism, and culturally situated notions of learning. The chapter argues that policy researchers have focused largely on the summative ques-

tion, does the reform work, rather than examining the social mechanisms or economic incentives that explain success or failure. Certain forms of decentralization, including high-quality charter schools and preschools, have shown notable effect sizes, while other forms have shown disappointing results to date.

A convincing body of research now demonstrates the importance of early childhood education. Learning trajectories are powerfully determined by developments in the pre-school years, giving rise to calls for better early childhood education. Schweinhart and Fulcher-Dawson review the evidence on early childhood education, including studies of programs that have demonstrated the long-term cost-effectiveness of quality education, returning anywhere from $4 to $16 for every dollar spent on such efforts. However, access to such programs is very uneven across states and localities. While federal (e.g., Headstart, Evenstart) and state programs now are available in all 50 states (only 38 have their own pre-kindergarten programs, however), two facts stand out: few programs meet all of the quality benchmarks established for such programs; and together they account for modest effects at best (presumably related to their uneven quality). International studies also support the value of early childhood programs, but here too, program quality has been shown to be uneven. Based on their review of evidence, they recommend expansion of public programs that include such features as qualified teachers; a validated child development curriculum; a strong parent involvement component; and a strong, competent educational leader.

Jones and Schneider review several major studies that have examined how schools and other institutions stratify educational opportunities for students, focusing specifically on studies in which the scope and rigor of the work appears to be linked to major educational policies over the last 50 years. They begin by examining the early contributions of sociologists to the study of social stratification, focusing on the ways in which family background characteristics interact with experiences that impact students' educational attainment. The authors then explore the mechanisms of stratification that emerge between schools (e.g., racial segregation) and within schools (e.g., tracking, ability grouping), and document how neighborhoods have unique effects on educational experiences and outcomes. They conclude with a discussion of strategies that policy makers have taken to raise the educational expectations of young people from disadvantaged backgrounds, as well as directions for future reforms. They advocate the steady accumulation of policies that together might promote greater social and educational mobility.

Another differentiating phenomenon that has emerged worldwide but with particular emphasis in Asian countries is "shadow education," defined as a complementary educational (or supplementary tutorial) program—often privately funded—that operates independently of the formal system. Lee, Park, and Lee describe the emergence and effects of shadow education which has attracted considerable policy attention in countries like Korea, Japan, China (Hong

Kong), and others. They describe how the dramatic rise in private tutoring is associated with credentialism and high-stakes entrance examinations that determine admittance into prestigious universities that have highly selective limited enrollments. Explanations for this development can thus be explained at institutional, organizational, and individual levels. Policy concerns include the effects of shadow education on student achievement and performance; inequalities in access to private tutoring; and the potential for undercutting or corrupting public school systems as shadow education gains in power and influence. Evidence on these matters has been mixed and so too have government policies that range from turning a blind eye, to prohibitions, to recognition and regulation, or active encouragement. Given the growing importance of this development, they advocate for studies that allow for stronger causal inferences about the demand and effects of shadow education.

If issues of access begin in early childhood, they also are crucial at the transition from secondary to post-secondary education. Recognition of this has prompted considerable policy attention to so-called "K–16 transitions" and access to higher education. Williams, in her chapter, reviews the issues, research, and policy on K–12 transitions around five themes: readiness for college; improving access to higher education, assisting students with transitions to college, college completion, and partnerships that link K–12 to higher education. Across these topics research shows marked disparities by race, gender, and class (as Jones and Schneider also demonstrate) attributable to a range of factors that include information about and access to financing; social and academic integration of students from diverse backgrounds; counseling and placement services; and others. Two distinct problems emerge from this work: adequacy of preparation for postsecondary education, and inequities in access to higher education. Williams describes the many policy initiatives underway to address these problems, while calls for more urgent and systematic attention to them.

Stephan and Rosenbaum provide a complementary perspective on these issues. First, they note that while disparities exist (as Williams emphasizes), the pattern over the past 30 years has been increasing enrollments among minority groups in various forms of postsecondary education. Then, they present a conceptual framework for the analysis of evidence and policies on pathways to and through higher education for different groups of students. Two factors appear to encourage and sustain the transition process—*permeability* (defined as ease of movement into and within higher education); and *transparency* (ease of understanding pathways from enrollment to completion). Their chapter documents how the U.S. system has changed from low permeability but high transparency (also known as "known limits") to high permeability but low transparency (also known as "uninformed choice"). They examine how this development has played out with respect to three policies—high school counseling, community college open admission and financial aid policies. Overall, they show

that the United States has an elaborate, complex system of choices and options for higher education that extends opportunity on one hand, while on the other, making navigation of the system difficult, particularly for low income families who possess limited social and cultural capital. Conceding that this perspective places heavy emphasis on the role of information, they conclude by noting topics this framework suggests for further study and policies that might improve the transparency of pathways to higher education.

Hearn and Lacy then examine how policies and politics have affected the organization of higher education systems. The authors show how state and federal governments have influenced core organizational features of colleges and universities, despite our country's decentralized and market-driven approach to higher education. They document that the policy context of higher education has changed in several important ways, including: the rapid evolution in financing systems; increased enrollments and college aspirations among a wider, more diverse student clientele; a policy shift from equity and access issues toward emphasis on a market orientation and matters of educational quality; and the turn toward greater accountability in higher education. Three themes dominate the research literature in this area: federal and state roles in research and graduate education; state governance and policy issues; and legal issues involving such matters as affirmative action, open meeting laws, and privacy. The chapter's concluding section recommends an expansion of the research agenda around methods, topics, and theoretical approaches.

The volume's final chapter focuses again on the global theme of world education culture as a context for understanding issues of access and differentiation. Baker charts the cross-national development of education that reveals convergence on a common pattern from small, decentralized formal educational systems to mass state systems of education. The author discusses one line of influential theory that regards this world-wide phenomenon not as a product, e.g., of economic development but of cultural attitudes and beliefs in personal achievement and collective progress. In this account, transnational influences have played a powerful role in the development of a distinctive model of formal education (see also Mundy and Ghali). Discourse on the "common culture" of worldwide education has focused on four elements: equal opportunity and social justice, development of education for the common good, dominance of academic intelligence, and meritocratic achievement and credentialism. Taken together, these four ideas form a global "cultural faith" that helps explain specific instances of policy development and reform, as Baker illustrates with the cases of diploma expansion and efforts to reform U.S. science and mathematics education. Today, the availability of international comparative data on education systems and outcomes abets the trend toward a global orientation around images of competition at all levels. "Thinking globally, acting locally" takes on new meanings for researchers and policy makers alike as the many chapters of this handbook now attest.

References

Bascia, N., Cumming, A., Datnow, A., Leithwood, K., & Livingstone, D. (Eds.). (2005). *International handbook of education policy.* Dordrecht, the Netherlands: Kluwer.

Fuhrman, S. H., Cohen, D. K., & Mosher, F. (Eds.). (2007). *The state of education policy research.* Mahwah, NJ: Erlbaum.

Green, J. C., Caracelli, V. J., & Graham, W. F. (1989). Toward a conceptual framework for mixed-method evaluation designs. *Educational Evaluation and Policy Analysis, 11*(x), 255–274.

Gutmann, A. (1987). *Democratic education.* Princeton, NJ: Princeton University Press.

Ladd, H., & Fiske, E. (Eds.). (2008). *Handbook on research in education finance and policy.* Mahwah, NJ: Erlbaum.

Section I

Social Science Disciplines and Education Policy Research

Section Editors: Barbara Schneider and David N. Plank

1

Historians and Educational Policy Research in the United States

Maris A. Vinovskis
University of Michigan

In colonial and 19th-century America, policy makers frequently turned to history for guidance and inspiration. During the first half of the 20th century, historians continued working with policy makers—especially during World War I and II. Gradually historians reduced their involvement in trying to directly influence policy makers. Today historians are returning to their earlier interest in policy research. More scholars are providing historical perspectives on current education policies such as early childhood learning and No Child Left Behind. Yet federal education research agencies and many private foundations are reluctant to fund education policy studies that are historically oriented. Moreover, some scholars involved in policy studies are not well-prepared to undertake certain types of historical analyses.

History and Policymaking

Colonial American leaders frequently turned to the classics for historical models of ideal individual and national behavior (Gay, 1966). American revolutionaries and the founding fathers worried about potential conspiracies against their new republic. They studied Greek and Roman history to understand how tyrants subverted liberty and destroyed republics in the past (Bailyn, 1967; Cohen, 1980). Pre-Civil War readers flocked to well-written, inspiring historical accounts by popular authors such as George Bancroft and Francis Parkman. Many antebellum policy makers also read and enjoyed historical literature, but it provided more moral instruction rather than specific policy guidance (Callcott, 1970; Roorbach, 1937).

In the late 19th century, popular amateur historians were gradually supplemented by professional historians who wrote for a smaller, more scholarly audience. These scholars saw themselves as scientific historians and created the American Historical Association (AHA) in 1884. By the early 20th century, disciplines such as political science, economics, and sociology left the AHA to create their own professional associations. Compared to other scholars, professional historians were less likely to address policy issues or participate in social reform movements (Furner, 1975; Novick, 1988; Vinovskis, 1999).

Professional historians and government officials continued to recognize the importance of using historical models for informing policy makers. The U.S. Bureau of Education, for example, turned to historian Herbert B. Adams to oversee the commissioning of higher education state histories. Charles Francis Adams even called for a special July AHA session, before each presidential election, so that historians could offer candidates and voters guidance on major issues (Vinovskis, 1999).

During the first half of the 20th century, historians stressed the practical benefits of their discipline and sometimes personally participated in policymaking. Historians as well as other scholars were involved in policy-related work during World War I and II. Some government officials also utilized historical analyses in areas such as judicial decision making. But many decision makers and agencies, including the U.S. Bureau of Education, gradually paid less attention to historical studies. Instead, policy makers increasingly turned to the other social sciences for guidance and assistance (Featherman & Vinovskis, 2001).

After the 1950s most historians concentrated on investigating the past for itself, rather than directly trying to inform current policymaking. Concerns about the perceived excesses of the so-called progressive historians in making policy recommendations during the 1930s and 1940s led many historians to focus more narrowly on their own scholarly investigations. When Professor Richard Bauer (1948) reviewed the value of history for students, he cautioned that "it is neither the business of the historian to read lessons into history nor to predict the future course of events. ...His main function is to portray the past as sincerely, objectively, and truthfully as possible, without consciously injecting his own biases and prejudices" (p. 156).

During the past 50 years, historians once again have gradually become more involved in policy-related matters (Vinovskis, 1999; Zelizer, 2005). The decades of the 1960s and 1970s were particularly important as the Vietnam War and the Great Society programs stimulated debates about the roles of academics in policymaking. A few prominent historians, such as Arthur Schlesinger, Jr., participated in politics and policymaking. Schlesinger served in the John F. Kennedy White House and wrote popular contemporary accounts of that administration (Schlesinger, 1971). Since the mid-1960s, however, only a few prominent academic historians have been involved in federal or state-level policymaking. Yet historians continued to trail their colleagues in the other social sciences in working with the federal government.

The Vietnam War divided the nation and provoked heated debates on college campuses. As policy makers and others debated the war, there were frequent references to the foreign policies of the 1930s as well as to those of the more recent Korean War. Many of these discussions involved a rather limited understanding of earlier foreign policies, partly because most contemporary decision makers did not seek advice from professional historians (May, 1973; Pipes, 1990). There were a few policy makers, however, who possessed a more thorough understanding of the past and relied upon it in their foreign policy analyses. For example, political scientist Henry Kissinger, a controversial but distinguished international affairs expert, played a key role on Vietnam and other foreign policy issues in both the Richard M. Nixon and Gerald R. Ford administrations (Dickson, 1978).

Whereas policy makers often turned to the past in foreign affairs, when the Great Society programs were created, less attention was paid to earlier domestic policy initiatives. The John F. Kennedy, Lyndon B. Johnson, and Richard M. Nixon administrations increasingly relied upon social scientists and policy analysts to create, implement, and evaluate their domestic programs, but historians rarely, if ever, were consulted. Instead, policy makers turned to policy analysts trained or familiar with the increasingly sophisticated quantitative methods of analysis (Featherman & Vinovskis, 2001).

While there were some historians pursuing policy issues, they were not seen as important contributors, as Hugh Graham (1993), a senior policy historian, explains:

> In the modern marketplace for policy advice, historians compete at a disadvantage for the attention of decision-makers, whose habit it is to turn to their experienced line staff, to lawyers and "hard" social scientists, or to policy analysts trained in systems analysis and operations research. Such policy advisers are trained in problem solving; they compare the costs and benefits of alternative solutions, predict outcomes, and recommend courses of action. Historians, on the other hand, are cautionary and seem more comfortable with negative advice. Historians are quickest to see what's wrong with politically tempting analogies ...We refuse to predict. Given the generally weak instrumental

case that policy historians have made for the importance of their advice to decision-makers, and given as well the severe economic pressures of recent years on public payrolls and private taxpayers, it is not surprising that political leaders, agency officials, and corporate decision-makers have sought policy advice from lawyers and social scientists rather than historians. (p. 15)

At the same time, some scholars became more active in the analysis of policy history. They established the *Journal of Policy History* in 1989 and published essays and books that addressed past and contemporary policy issues. Richard Neustadt and Ernest May (1986) published an important guide for policy makers interested in history, *Thinking in Time: The Uses of History for Decision-makers*. Moreover, the number of historians writing about policy-related topics has greatly expanded in the past 10 to 15 years. Pennsylvania State University Press, for example, is publishing a series of collected policy history essays on topics such as abortion and birth control (Critchlow, 1996), civil rights (Graham, 1994), drug control policy (Walker, 1992), health care (Marcus & Cravens, 1997), refugees (Loescher, 1992), social policy (Critchlow & Hawley, 1988), and urban policy (Melosi, 1993).

As questions were raised about the relevance of history for policy makers and the public in the 1980s, some historians continued to be optimistic about the future of the discipline (Kammen, 1980). Other historians, such as Theodore Hamerow (1987), however, feared that the perceived value of history was steadily declining. AHA President William Leuchtenburg (1992), one of the few prominent historians personally involved with policymaking, offered a complex, but cautious view of historians engaged in contemporary policymaking:

> One can agree that history has value wholly apart from any utilitarian end it serves without accepting the conclusion that historians must refrain from public involvement, and one can acknowledge that historians have an obligation to their community without dismissing the sage admonitions that the skeptics raise. (p. 17)

Leuchtenburg also reminded historians involved in policy analysis of the

> … need constantly to remind ourselves that we are not omniscient, and that we must never, no matter how worthy the cause, compromise our commitment to, in John Higham's words, 'the simple axiom that history is basically an effort to tell the truth about the past.' (p. 17)

Today, there is a gradual, but still somewhat limited, revival of interest among professional historians in policymaking (Gillon, 1997; Graham, 1993; Zelizer, 2000, 2005). Policy-oriented scholars in the other social sciences are returning to their early 20th-century interest in the past as part of the recent historic turn in most of their disciplines (McDonald, 1996; Monkkonen, 1994). As a result, more policy-related research now includes at least a brief historical perspective than two or three decades ago.

Historians and Educational Policy Research

There was considerable historical education research, though not necessarily of stellar quality, produced in the first half of the 20th century (Lagemann, 2000; Reese, 2007, chap. 2). Historians sometimes provided assistance for federal agencies such as the U.S. Bureau of Education (later renamed the U.S. Office of Education). Yet that education agency gradually abandoned its support of historical policy studies. During World War II, while other federal agencies increased their research and even hired a few more historians, the U.S. Office of Education actually reduced its overall research activities and did not solicit more help from historians (Vinovskis, 1999; Warren, 1974).

At the same time, historians in the late 19th- and early 20th-centuries helped to design and implement K-12 history teaching reforms. By the 1920s and 1930s, most academic historians and the AHA increasingly focused more upon their own professional research and teaching and quietly abandoned their earlier involvement in elementary and secondary school teaching issues. Instead, social studies teachers and administrators sought a larger role in deciding how history and related subjects were taught in the K-12 grades (Halvorsen, 2006; Novick, 1988; Saxe, 1991).

A few post-World War II education scholars continued writing historical textbooks on U.S. education development; these volumes were mainly intended for school of education students rather than policy makers. Some historians, such as Arthur Bestor (1953) and Richard Hofstadter (1963), raised serious policy questions about the K-12 curriculum, including the teaching of history. In the mid-1960s, however, the field of education history was revitalized from two different directions (Gaither, 2003). On the one hand, scholars such as Bernard Bailyn (1960) and Lawrence Cremin (1965) questioned the often laudatory, in-house education histories written by school of education professors; instead, they called for more critical and scholarly studies as well as a broader conception of the nature and role of education in America's past.

At the same time, another new group of education historians, often characterized as "revisionists," also questioned the earlier one-sided, positive accounts of the triumph of public schools. The revisionists, however, stressed the failings of urban public schools today. Their research focused on the 19th- and early 20th-century education reformers and the public schools they created. The revisionists found that reformers designed schools to produce the disciplined, more compliant labor force needed for industrial growth—often at the expense of the overall well-being and intellectual development of working-class children (Bowles & Gintis, 1976; Katz, 1968). However, critics of the revisionists' scholarship, such as Diane Ravitch (1978), challenged their research and interpretations of the past. Ravitch objected to the revisionists' unbalanced account of American education, their one-sided and negative portrayal of the motivations of reformers such as Horace Mann, and their dismissal of any relationship between education and social mobility in the past. The revisionists defended their analyses and

questioned why the National Academy of Education had commissioned her to critique their work (Feinberg, Kantor, Katz, & Violas, 1980).

In 1968, Michael Katz published one of the first and most influential revisionist monographs, *The Irony of School Reform: Educational Innovation in Mid-nineteenth Century Massachusetts*. The debates over this seminal book, especially the study of the abolition of the Beverly Public High School in 1860, nicely illustrate some of the continuing differences among educational historians on the proper role of scholars and policymaking today. While *Irony of Early School Reform* focused on mid-19th century Massachusetts controversies, Katz compared them to the views of James Bryant Conant and others in the mid-1960s. Katz concluded that reforms in both eras were:

> … spearheaded by the socially and intellectually prominent concerned for the preservation of domestic tranquility and an ordered, cohesive society. In both cases this group has been joined and supported by middle-class parents anxious about the status of their children and, somewhat tardily, for the most part, by the organized schoolmen, who understandably enough have usually evaluated reform theory in terms of its impact upon their own precarious status. (pp. 214–215)

Katz further explained that:

> … very largely both movements of urban reform have been impositions; communal leaders have mounted an ideological and noisy campaign to sell education to an often skeptical, sometimes hostile, and usually uncomprehending working class. The reformers have been determined to foist their innovations upon the community, if necessary by force. (p. 214)

Almost two decades later, Vinovskis (1985) reanalyzed in more depth and using more sophisticated statistical techniques the abolition of the Beverly Public High School. Vinovskis agreed with some of Katz's findings, but rejected Katz's overall portrayal of the creation, abolition, and then quick re-establishment of that institution. In the conclusion of his book, Vinovskis more generally cautioned that:

> … the recent debate among some educational historians over the ideological motivations of groups of scholars or the political implications of their efforts is likely to be counterproductive in the long run unless it leads to a more scholarly and objective reexamination of the work in this area. (pp. 119–120)

When Katz (1987) reviewed Vinovskis' study of the abolition of the Beverly Public High School, he continued to defend his work. He also responded to Vinovskis' plea for a "scholarly and objective" reexamination of important issues. Katz argued that:

> politics cannot be divorced from scholarship, and numbers are no more neutral than words. Vinovskis is as partisan as the rest of us. I mean this as no criticism. Rather, I only wish he would make his assumptions and commitments

more explicit and drop the fiction of neutrality. For history, after all, is about questions that matter. (p. 247)

The editors of the journal containing both Michael Katz's and Edward Steven's extended reviews also gave Vinovskis an opportunity to respond. In that response, Vinovskis (1987) provided a somewhat different view of the role of historians in working with education policy issues and decision makers than Katz implied:

> While I find much to admire in Katz's enthusiasm and work in policy analysis, I am not sure that we share the same approach in our scholarship. Certainly I strongly agree with him that as historians we can and should be deeply involved in formulating and implementing policy. I reject the notion that scholars must distance themselves from the policy-making arena—as many of us were advised in graduate school. I also agree with Katz that history can and does inform policy making—though the connection is usually much more distant and tenuous than some of us would like. Yet as a professional historian, I see it as my responsibility to try to be as "scholarly and objective" as possible even though we are all inevitably influenced to some degree by our prior experiences and commitments. Using a social science approach does not guarantee objectivity, but it encourages us to be more explicit about our assumptions and methodology so that our colleagues, such as Katz and Stevens, can correct us if we stray too far from the evidence. (p. 257)

In his later mid-1990s historical work on education and poverty in America, Katz (1995) elaborated his views on policy-making by pointing to the limitations faced by historians in trying to predict the future on the basis of the past:

> I offer no concrete solutions. Historians and other social scientists who offer interpretative accounts of social issues always face a "last chapter" problem. Readers expect them to extract clear lessons from history, offer unambiguous recommendations, and foresee the future. My standard response—my role is to analyze and explain the problem; I have no special expertise in devising solutions—although honest, rarely satisfies. When historians tack on a set of conclusions, more often than not they appear, banal, not very different from what others have suggested, marginally related to the analysis that precedes them and far less subtle. The reason, of course, is that no set of recommendations flows directly from any historical analysis. Understanding the origins and dimensions of a social issue can lead in very different policy directions. (p. 7)

Over time some of the divisions and most of the rancorous debate between the revisionists and their opponents faded. Substantive differences of opinion on education development in the past, however, remain and are still contested today—but the focus is now even more on what the research shows, rather than the ideological orientations of the participants. Some scholars still regret the tone and nature of the earlier disagreements between the revisionists and their critics; others have come to acknowledge and appreciate the energy and excitement that the earlier debates

brought to the otherwise rather dormant field of educational history after World War II (Moran & Vinovskis, 2007).

Since the mid-1960s, historically-oriented education policy studies have increased. In part this reflects the expansion of federal education programs started during the Johnson administration; as these initiatives were reauthorized and expanded over the next four decades, policy analysts sometimes reviewed the historical origins of those programs as well as discussed their subsequent developments (Nelson, 2007). Federal assistance for pre-school education through Project Head Start, for example, was part of activities of the Office of Economic Opportunity (OEO) under the 1964 Economic Opportunity legislation. Most of the initial studies of Head Start and early childhood education focused on the current programs or were memoirs of the participants (Greenberg, 1969; Zigler & Valentine, 1979). In the early 1990s, however, psychologist Edward Zigler, a prominent Head Start proponent, co-authored a history of the program (Zigler & Muenchow, 1992).

Historians had not studied much American early childhood education or Head Start during the 1960s or 1970s. A few monographs addressed early childhood education by investigating the development of American kindergartens (Shapiro, 1983), and historians discovered the short-lived, but widespread, infant school movement in the early 19th-century (Kaestle & Vinovskis, 1980; May & Vinovskis, 1977). Barbara Beatty (1995) published a comprehensive history of preschool education in 1995; a decade later a reinterpretation of the origins and development of Head Start in the Kennedy and Johnson administrations was produced (Vinovskis, 2005).

Initial studies of the Elementary and Secondary Education Act (ESEA) of 1965 were written by political scientists and policy analysts. Most of the focus was on contemporary events, but there was some attention to earlier efforts to enact federal education programs (Bailey & Mosher, 1968; Eidenberg & Morey, 1969; Meranto, 1967). Historian Julie Jeffrey (1978), a decade later, published a useful overview of ESEA's origins and early implementation.

ESEA continued as the major federal compensatory education program over the next 40 years and was revised substantially under the No Child Left Behind Act signed in January 2002. Political scientists and education policy analysts periodically wrote about ESEA, often with a brief historical preface (Jennings, 1998; McLaughlin, 1974; Thomas, 1975). During the past five years, scholars from a variety of disciplines, including historians, have written broader ESEA histories (Cross, 2004; Davies, 2007; Kosar, 2005; McGuinn, 2006; Manna, 2006; Vinovskis, in press). Thus, over time, in part because of the increasing importance of federal programs such as Head Start and ESEA, policy analysts are reconsidering these and other education programs from a more historical perspective.

Education historians periodically complain that government officials ignore their contributions. During the first Bush administration, however, education historians had a unique opportunity to share their ideas about school reforms with a more policy-oriented audience. Diane Ravitch, Assistant Secretary of the Office of Educational Research and Improvement (OERI), commissioned 14 individual essays from historically-minded analysts (mostly education historians) about current education reforms. Joined by her fellow education historian Maris Vinovskis (and at the time OERI's Research Adviser), they co-edited the volume, *Learning from the Past: What History Teaches Us About School Reform* (Ravitch & Vinovskis, 1995).

In the introduction to the book, Ravitch and Vinovskis (1995) noted that, "the authors of these essays, reflecting quite different intellectual and disciplinary orientations, provide a useful historical context for the current education reforms. They caution us about the tendency of education advocates to exaggerate the benefits of school reforms and to minimize the difficulty of implementing them" (p. xiv). In some ways similar to Katz's statement about the value of history for policy makers, Ravitch and Vinovskis state that, "although studies of past educational reforms do not necessarily provide immediate and specific suggestions for improving our present system of schooling, they do contribute to a better understanding and appreciation of the complex and diverse nature of educational development and change today" (p. xiv). Individual essays from *Learning from the Past* were read by some policy makers and federal employees—in part because relevant portions of the book were distributed to quite a few individuals in Washington, DC, at that time. The book continues to be used modestly in some college courses—including graduate seminars in schools of education and public policy schools.

Almost a decade later, Carl Kaestle, with funding from the Annenberg Foundation as well as the Spencer Foundation at Brown University, created a post-doctoral program for scholars providing historical perspectives on education reforms. The program participants assembled their historical policy analyses in a useful collection of essays entitled, *To Educate a Nation: Federal and National Strategies of School Reform* (Kaestle & Lodewick, 2007). In their introduction to the volume, Carl Kaestle and Alyssa Lodewick acknowledge that historical studies usually do not produce a single answer to policy dilemmas today. But they hope "… that the case studies, political analyses, and insights of *To educate a nation* will help readers draw their own conclusions about how the education polity has evolved over time and how education policy makers can best foster equity, quality, and diversity in our nation's schools in the future" (p. 11).

There is neither time nor space to discuss in detail the many contributions of historians in other areas of education that may be of interest to policy makers. A few recent examples, however, will illustrate the possibilities. In the area of higher education, for example, one might consult the writings of Linda Eisenmann (2006), Roger Geiger (2004), Morton Keller and Phyllis Keller (2001), Miriam Levin (2005), George Marsden (1994), and Julie Reuben (1996). On college admissions, the studies of Elizabeth Duffy and Idana Goldberg (1998) or Arthur Levine and Jana Nidiffer (1996) are available. In the area of education and affirmative

action, books by Terry Anderson (2004), Patricia Gurin, Jeffrey Lehman, and Earl Lewis (2004), Hugh Graham (2002), and Ira Katznelson (2005) may be useful.

Historians have also produced valuable studies of elementary and secondary schools. Studies of the curriculum and books are available in David Angus and Jeffrey Mirel (1999), Herbert Kliebard (1999), Joseph Moreau (2003), John Rudolph (2002), and Jonathan Zimmerman (2002). Joel Perlmann and Robert Margo (2001), Kate Rousmaniere (1997), and Wayne Urban (2000) analyzed teachers. Studies of urban public schools have been provided by Jesse Hoffnung-Garskof (2008), Stephen Lassonde (2005), Jeffrey Mirel (1999), Adam Nelson (2005), and John Rury (2005). Historians who have investigated school segregation are Jack Dougherty (2004), Ellen Lagemann and Lamar Miller (1996), Matthew Lassiter and Andrew Lewis (1998), and James Patterson (2001). Elementary and secondary school reforms and research have been investigated by David Cohen and Heather Hill (2001), Kenneth Gold (2002), Patricia Graham (1992, 2005), John Rury (2004), Ellen Lagemann (2000), Diane Ravitch (1995, 2000), William Reese (2005), Harold Silver and Pamela Silver (1991), David Tyack (2004), David Tyack and Larry Cuban (1995), and Maris Vinovskis (2001).

Challenges of Doing Policy-Related Historical Research

As scholars analyze education policies historically, they employ a wide variety of strategies. Some analysts, for example, provide broad overviews of education policies over long time-periods. Of course, this raises questions about how one selects which education issues are to be studied as well as which aspects of the historical context need to be included.

Other studies investigate federal involvement in schooling. This is particularly true of those dealing with the past 50 years as the federal government is playing a larger role in state and local education policies and practices. Naturally, the particular education policies examined, as well as the time periods covered, are important considerations. Moreover, how policy issues are addressed depends upon which branches of the federal government are considered. Does the analysis focus on the executive branch by analyzing White House education policies or those of federal agencies such as the U.S. Department of Education? Are congressional education policies and politics analyzed? What about the role of the federal judicial system in adjudicating and implementing education policies?

Similar questions can be asked about studies of state and local education. Does the analysis focus on state boards of education, school districts, or the local schools? What education issues are studied and what other related institutions and participants are included in these investigations? Given the considerable diversity among state, district, and local schools in the United States, what are the implications of choosing any particular sample of sites as case studies?

Rather than studying education policies at the federal, state, or local school levels, one might focus on the classroom level by studying teachers, the curriculum, the textbooks or equipment used, the students, or their parents. In addition, analysts might pursue any of these classroom-level issues more broadly. For example, one might study the careers of teachers in general, rather than just investigating their classroom activities.

This brief and incomplete discussion of what types of past education policies might be studied reminds us of the many research options facing analysts. Perhaps historians might consider adopting a broader life-course framework for conceptualizing and analyzing their projects (Vinovskis, 1999, pp. 203–237). Otherwise historians may undertake policy studies without adequate attention to what they are investigating, how it relates to other institutions and key participants, what is being implicitly omitted from their analysis, and how the overall research design might affect their findings.

As a consequence of the diversity of topics and possible approaches to the study of past education policies, scholars need to consider using many different types of sources. Published documents, especially from government and agency sources, are a major component of many projects. Newspapers, magazines and newsletters often are consulted. For more contemporary documents, as well as some from the more distant past, many of these materials now are available through the Internet.

Unpublished documents often provide important additional information. Some unpublished reports are available through various Web sites or the ERIC (Education Resources Information Center) system. Scholars sometimes utilize the relatively well-preserved archival collections at the presidential libraries scattered throughout the nation. Yet analysts sometimes forget that presidential libraries usually only collect certain types of White House information (Smith & Stern, 2006). As a result, they may neglect to consult related agency records, such as those from the U.S. Department of Education, housed at the National Archives at College Park, Maryland.

Congressional documents and unpublished committee proceedings are available through the National Archives in Washington, DC. Unfortunately, many congressional committees have not always deposited all of their materials with the National Archives, and individual Senators and Representatives frequently take their personal and public papers with them. Some of these individual congressional papers, however, have been deposited elsewhere and can be located through the Library of Congress THOMAS Web site.

The U.S. Department of Education continues to maintain its own education archive. This archive provides a useful supplement to the documents available at the National Archives. Unfortunately, the agency discarded some of its primary documents as well as much of its published materials when the archives were transferred in the mid-1990s to smaller quarters in the basement of the main U.S. Department of Education building.

Some important unpublished education documents from policy makers such as former Health Education and Welfare Secretary Wilbur Cohen or former OERI Assistant Secretary Chester "Checker" Finn at other archives, such as the Wisconsin Historical Society or the Hoover Institution, may still be available. And key documents, such as the successive drafts of the America 2000 Excellence in Education proposal, for example, may be available from former Washington, DC, participants who worked on those initiatives.

The availability of state and local school records varies considerably by locality. Many of these documents are considered public information and should be available, but some institutions are reluctant to provide access to them—partly due to the hassle of locating and making them available. Educational organizations, such as the National Education Association, sometimes maintain their own archives and are willing to share their documents with researchers (Urban, 2000).

Another source frequently used by historians is oral histories. Some of these oral histories were recorded in the past and are now available to researchers at archives such as the presidential libraries. In addition, many analysts often undertake their own formal or informal interviews with policy makers as they write their histories of past education policies; often such oral histories are not recorded or transcribed so that they are not available for use by other researchers. A general problem with using oral histories, especially those not done by experts in this methodology, is the lack of appreciation of the problems involved in relying upon oral histories for accurate and reliable accounts of the past (Perks & Thomson, 2006; Ritchie, 2003). For example, not only do policy makers have trouble remembering details about policy issues many years later, but they also may exaggerate their own role as they may forget, or were not even fully aware at that time, the contributions of others.

The use of quantitative data in policy analyses has grown considerably during the past half century (Featherman & Vinovskis, 2001). Social scientists involved in policy analyses increasingly have turned to quantitative measures and assessments; quantitative program evaluations have become commonplace in program evaluations such as assessments of Head Start and Title I of the Elementary and Secondary Education Act (ESEA) of 1965. As a result, education policy historians often need the ability to read and re-interpret these earlier social science studies.

While the use and sophistication of statistical analysis of education policies has improved over time, the training of historians in understanding and using quantitative techniques has diminished (Archdeacon, 1994; Feinstein & Thomas, 2002; Hudson, 2000). Many social science historians in the 1960s and 1970s acquired the skills necessary to use quantitative data, but subsequent cohorts of historians have moved away from social science history toward more qualitative-oriented cultural and anthropological studies. The current generation of historians is less interested or capable of dealing with social science history than their predecessors (Iggers, 1997). As a result, scholars trained in other social sciences such as political science, economics, or sociology, or graduating from schools of education, are often better prepared for analyzing quantitative education data than historians.

Another challenge for historians studying education policies is their lack of involvement in the policy process itself (Schlesinger, 1971). Though some historians before 1945 were involved in the policymaking process, since the mid-1960s few have worked in the federal government (Vinovskis, 1999). Consequently, historians often lack an understanding of how Washington operates. Interestingly, a few education historians have participated more in federal education policies than historians from many other areas of historical analysis. Patricia Graham, Diane Ravitch, and Maris Vinovskis, for instance, have worked in the National Institute of Education (NIE) or the Office of Educational Research and Improvement (OERI) in recent decades.

Most funding agencies and reviewers have not been very receptive to historical education policy proposals. While periodically some historical education policy studies have been funded by federal agencies, they are few and far between. The National Endowment for the Humanities (NEH), for example, does not preclude funding of historical policy studies, but some historians on their review panels have questioned the appropriateness or value of historical policy studies. While the U.S. Department of Education has occasionally commissioned historical studies of agencies such as the National Assessment Governing Board or the National Education Goals Panel, OERI or the Institute of Education Sciences (IES) rarely have shown interest in funding historical education policy analyses. One notable exception was OERI's commissioning of essays on historical perspectives on current education reforms during the early 1990s (Ravitch & Vinovskis, 1995).

Private, non-profit foundations have been more open to funding historical policy studies. The most important funding source has been the Spencer Foundation, which has provided funds for pre-doctoral and post-doctoral fellowships for historical policy studies as well as general funding for policy-oriented education history projects. But other foundations have also occasionally funded historical education policy studies. For example, the Bradley Foundation, the Andrew W. Mellon Foundation, the Annenberg Foundation, the Olin M. Foundation, the Russell Sage Foundation, the Smith Richardson Foundation, and the William and Flora Hewlett Foundation have supported historically-oriented education policy studies at various points.

Policy-Related Research on Teaching American History

As we explore how historians address policy-related issues today, perhaps we might also consider what particular aspects of the past, if any, attract the attention of policy makers. Many analysts have compiled lists of the benefits of historical understandings for individuals as well as society

as a whole—such as producing educated citizens, promoting patriotism, and understanding history as an academic discipline (Reese, 2007, chap. 1; Vaughn, 1985). Leaders such as presidents George H. W. Bush, William J. Clinton, and Harry S. Truman, as well as the general public, often enjoyed reading inspiring biographies or well-written popular histories rather than perusing academic monographs. These biographies and popular histories usually were written by publicly-acclaimed historians such as Stephen Ambrose (1996) and David McCullough (2001), who often were looked down upon by their academic colleagues (Jackson, 2002; Rosenzweig & Thelen, 1998).

Most political leaders see history's primary role as promoting patriotism and providing citizenship training for students. Citing disappointing scores on national American history tests, educators and policy makers in the 1980s and 1990s called for more rigorous national and state history standards, improved history curricula, and more challenging student assessments (Nash, Crabtree, & Dunn, 1997; Vinovskis, 2006). After President George H. W. Bush and the nation's governors met at the historic Charlottesville Education Summit in September 1989, they agreed upon six national education goals. Among them was Goal Three, which stated that "by the year 2000, American students will leave grades four, eight and twelve having demonstrated competency in challenging subject matter including English, mathematics, science, history, and geography; and every school in America will ensure that all students learn to use their minds well, so they may be prepared for responsible citizenship, further learning, and productive employment in our modern economy" (White House, 1990, p. 3).

As part of their unsuccessful attempt to enact the America 2000 program, the George H. W. Bush administration designated history as one of the five core subjects; the National Endowment for the Humanities as well as the U.S. Department of Education funded the development of voluntary national history standards by a consortium of major history and social studies organizations. Similarly, President Clinton reiterated his earlier promise that all students would be competent in history by the year 2000, and in 1994 the Clinton administration included history as one of the core subjects in its Goals 2000 program (McGuinn, 2006; Vinovskis, 2006).

During these deliberations, historians and their organizations worked closely with policy makers in both the Bush and Clinton administrations as well as with congressional members. The release of the 1994 draft of the national history standards was praised by most professional historians and many elementary and secondary school teachers. Many conservatives such as former NEH Chair Lynn Cheney, however, were outraged because they felt that the national history standards were politically biased and unpatriotic. After considerable public debate, the U.S. Senate condemned the history standards by a vote of 99 to 1 and President Clinton denounced them as well (Nash et al., 1997).

During the mid-1990s, discussion of the National

Education Goals diminished—especially once it became evident that none of the goals would be reached by the year 2000. Renewed efforts were then made to improve math, reading, and science education in the elementary grades, but serious attention to other core subjects such as history and geography was quietly abandoned by the federal government.

Following the election of George W. Bush, Congress passed the administration's No Child Left Behind Act of 2001, which specifies that by the school year 2013–14, all students in Grades 3–8 had to demonstrate proficiency in math and reading. Subjects such as history and geography, however, were left to the discretion of the states (McGuinn, 2006). Continued inadequate student performance on history tests led Senator Robert Byrd (D-WV) in 2001 to appropriate $50 million for the Teaching American History (TAH) program. In the 7-year period from FY2001 to FY2007, almost three-quarters of a billion dollars have been spent to improve the teaching of traditional American history. These annual expenditures are the most the federal government has ever directly invested in the teaching of K-12 American history (Vinovskis, 2006).

The TAH program called for partnerships between elementary and secondary school history teachers with institutions such as colleges and universities, museums, and other non-profit organizations. The programs were intended to raise student history achievement scores by improving teachers' American history knowledge and employing research-proven teaching strategies and programs. In addition, the TAH activities were expected to result "in systematic information about the effectiveness of the program to strengthen American history instruction and improve student achievement" (U.S. Department of Education, 2006). Yet the quality of the TAH assessments to date have been neither very scientific nor rigorous (Humphrey, Chang-Ross, Donnelly, Hersh, & Skolnik, 2005).

Thus, although historians had only limited involvement in policy-related activities in recent decades, they actively participated in the drafting of the voluntary national history standards as well as the design and implementation of the TAH program. The controversy over the history standards, however, did not endear historians to many policy makers; the lack of knowledge and experience among most professional historians and K-12 teachers about designing, implementing, and analyzing history assessments has hampered their contributions to the TAH program.

Conclusion

Though historians are now producing more policy-oriented studies, most of them have been written for other scholars rather than policy makers. Gradually, policy historians are gaining more respect and acceptance from the history profession, but much work remains to be done to attract the attention of policy makers (Zelizer, 2005). In the area of history of education policy, however, historians and other scholars currently are doing a much better job of providing policy makers with studies that address present as well as past concerns. This process is helped by the fact that many historians and other historically-minded scholars are now trying to offer advice and assistance to current policy makers. Thus, the interactions between historically-oriented policy analysts and education policy decision makers are likely to be expanded substantially in the years to come.

References

Ambrose, S. (1996). *Undaunted courage: Meriwether Lewis, Thomas Jefferson, and the opening of the American West.* New York: Simon and Shuster.

Anderson, T. H. (2004). *The pursuit of fairness: A history of affirmative action.* New York: Oxford University Press.

Angus, D. L., & Mirel, J. E. (1999). *The failed promise of the American high school, 1890–1995.* New York: Teachers College Press.

Archdeacon, T. J. (1994). *Correlation and regression analysis: A historian's guide.* Madison: University of Wisconsin Press.

Bailey, S., & Mosher, E. (1968). *ESEA: The Office of Education administers a law.* Syracuse, NY: Syracuse University Press.

Bailyn, B. (1960). *Education in the forming of American society: Needs and opportunities for study.* New York: Vintage Books.

Bailyn, B. (1967). *The ideological origins of the American Revolution.* Cambridge, MA: Harvard University Press.

Bauer, R. H. (1948). The study of history. *Social Studies, 39,* 150–158.

Beatty, B. (1995). *Preschool education in America: The culture of young children from the colonial era to the present.* New Haven, CT: Yale University Press.

Bestor, A. E. (1953). *Educational wastelands: The retreat from learning in our public schools.* Urbana: University of Illinois Press.

Bowles, S., & Gintis, H. (1976). *Schooling in capitalist America: Educational reform and the contradictions of economic life.* New York: Basic Books.

Callcott, G. H. (1970). *History in the United States, 1800–1860: Its practice and purpose.* Baltimore: Johns Hopkins University Press.

Cohen, D. K., & Hill, H. C. (2001). *Learning policy: When state education reform works.* New Haven, CT: Yale University Press.

Cohen, L. H. (1980). *The revolutionary histories: Contemporary narratives of the American Revolution.* Ithaca, NY: Cornell University Press.

Cremin, L. A. (1965). *The wonderful world of Ellwood Patterson Cubberly: An essay on the historiography of American education.* New York: Teachers College Press.

Critchlow, D. T. (Ed.). (1996). *The politics of abortion and birth control in historical perspective.* University Park: Pennsylvania State University Press.

Critchlow, D. T., & Hawley, E. W. (Eds.). (1988). *Federal social policy: The historical dimension.* University Park: Pennsylvania State University Press.

Cross, C. (2004). *Political education: National policy comes of age.* New York: Teachers College Press.

Davies, G. (2007). *See government grow: Education politics from Johnson to Reagan.* Lawrence: University Press of Kansas.

Dickson, P. W. (1978). *Kissinger and the meaning of history.* New York: Cambridge University Press.

Dougherty, J. (2004). *More than one struggle: The evolution of black school reform in Milwaukee.* Chapel Hill: University of North Carolina Press.

Duffy, E. A., & Goldberg, I. (1998). *Crafting a class: College admissions and financial aid, 1955–1994.* Princeton, NJ: Princeton University Press.

Eidenberg, E., & Morey, R. (1969). *An act of Congress: The legislative process and the making of education policy.* New York: W. W. Norton.

Eisenmann, L. (2006). *Higher education for women in postwar America, 1945–1965.* Baltimore: Johns Hopkins University Press.

Featherman, D. L., & Vinovskis, M. A. (2001). Growth and use of social and behavioral science in the federal government since World War II.

In D. L. Featherman & M. A. Vinovskis (Eds.), *Social science and policy-making: A Search for relevance in the twentieth century* (pp. 40–82). Ann Arbor: University of Michigan Press.

Feinberg, W., Kantor, H., Katz, M., & Violas, P. (1980). *Revisionists respond to Ravitch.* Washington, DC: National Academy of Education.

Feinstein, C. H., & Thomas, M. (2002). *Making history count: A primer in quantitative methods for historians.* New York: Cambridge University Press.

Furner, M. O. (1975). *Advocacy and objectivity: A crisis in the professionalization of American social science, 1865–1905.* Lexington: University Press of Kentucky.

Gaither, M. (2003). *American educational history revisited: A critique of progress.* New York: Teachers College Press.

Gay, P. (1966). *A loss of mastery: Puritan historians in colonial America.* Berkeley: University of California Press.

Geiger, R. L. (2004). *Knowledge and money: Research universities and the paradox of the marketplace.* Stanford, CA: Stanford University Press.

Gillon, S. M. (1997). The future of political history. *Journal of Policy History, 9,* 240–255.

Gold, K. M. (2002). *School's in: The history of summer education in American public schools.* New York: Peter Lang.

Graham, H. D. (1993). The stunted career of policy history: A critique and an agenda. *Public Historian, 15*(2), 15–37.

Graham, H. D. (Ed.). (1994). *Civil rights in the United States.* University Park: Pennsylvania State University Press.

Graham, H. D. (2002). *Collision course: The strange convergence of affirmative action and immigration policy in America.* New York: Oxford University Press.

Graham, P. A. (1992). *SOS: Sustain our schools.* New York: Hill and Wang.

Graham, P. A. (2005). *Schooling America: How the public schools meet the nation's changing needs.* New York: Oxford University Press.

Greenberg, P. (1969). *The devil has slippery shoes: A biased biography of the Child Development Group of Mississippi (CDGM)—A story of maximum feasible poor parent participation.* New York: MacMillan.

Gurin, P., Lehman, J. S., & Lewis, E. (Eds.). (2004). *Defending diversity: Affirmative action at the University of Michigan.* Ann Arbor: University of Michigan Press.

Halvorsen, A. (2006). *The origins and rise of elementary social studies education, 1884 to 1941.* Unpublished doctoral dissertation, University of Michigan, Ann Arbor.

Hamerow, T. S. (1987). *Reflections on history and historians.* Madison: University of Wisconsin Press.

Hoffnung-Garskof, J. (2008). *A tale of two cities: Santo Domingo and New York after 1950.* Princeton, NJ: Princeton University Press.

Hofstadter, R. (1963). *Anti-intellectualism in American life.* New York: Alfred A. Knopf.

Hudson, P. (2000). *History by numbers: An introduction to quantitative approaches.* New York: Oxford University Press.

Humphrey, D. C., Chang-Ross, C., Donnelly, M. B., Hersh, L., & Skolnik, H. (2005). *Evaluation of the Teaching American History Program.* Washington, DC: U.S. Department of Education.

Iggers, G. G. (1997). *Historiography in the twentieth century: From scientific objectivity to the postmodern challenge.* Hanover, NH: Wesleyan University Press.

Jackson, K. T. (2002). The power of history: The weakness of the profession. *Journal of American History, 88,* 1299–1314.

Jeffrey, J. R. (1978). *Education for children of the poor: A study of the origins and implementation of the Elementary and Secondary Education Act of 1965.* Columbus: Ohio State University Press.

Jennings, J. F. (1998). *Why national standards and tests? Politics and the quest for better schools.* Thousand Oaks, CA: Sage.

Kaestle, C. F., & Lodewick, A. E. (Eds.). (2007). *To educate a nation: Federal and national strategies of school reform.* Lawrence: University Press of Kansas.

Kaestle, C. F., & Vinovskis, M. A. (1980). *Education and social change in nineteenth-century Massachusetts.* New York: Cambridge University Press.

Kammen, M. (Ed.). (1980). *The past before us: Contemporary historical writing in the United States.* Ithaca, NY: Cornell University Press.

Katz, M. B. (1968). *The irony of early school reform: Educational innovation in mid-nineteenth century Massachusetts.* Cambridge, MA: Harvard University Press.

Katz, M. B. (1987). Forum: The origins of public high schools. *History of Education Quarterly, 27,* 241–247.

Katz, M. B. (1995). *Improving poor people: The welfare state, the "underclass," and urban schools as history.* Princeton, NJ: Princeton University Press.

Katznelson, I. (2005). *When affirmative action was white: An untold history of racial inequality in twentieth-century America.* New York: W. W. Norton.

Keller, M., & Keller, P. (2001). *Making Harvard modern: The rise of America's university.* New York: Oxford University Press.

Kliebard, H. M. (1999). *Schooled to work: Vocationalism and the American curriculum, 1876–1946.* New York: Teachers College Press.

Kosar, K. R. (2005). *Failing grades: The federal politics of education standards.* Boulder, CO: Lynne Rienner.

Lagemann, E. C. (2000). *An elusive science: The troubling history of education research.* Chicago: University of Chicago Press.

Lagemann, E. C., & Miller, L. P. (Eds.). (1996). *Brown v. Board of Education: The challenge of today's schools.* New York: Teachers College Press.

Lassiter, M. D., & Lewis, A. B. (Eds.). (1998). *The moderates' dilemma: Massive resistance to school desegregation in Virginia.* Charlottesville: University Press of Virginia.

Lassonde, S. (2005). *Learning to forget: Schooling and family life in New Haven's working class, 1870–1940.* New Haven, CT: Yale University Press.

Leuchtenburg, W. E. (1992). The historian and the public realm. *American Historical Review, 97,* 1–18.

Levin, M. R. (2005). *Defining women's scientific enterprise: Mount Holyoke faculty and the rise of American science.* Hanover, NH: University Press of New England

Levine, A., & Nidiffer, J. (1996). *Beating the odds: How the poor get to college.* San Francisco: Jossey-Bass.

Loescher, G. (Ed.). (1992). *Refugees and the asylum dilemma in the west.* University Park: Pennsylvania State University Press.

Manna, P. (2006). *School's in: Federalism and the national education agenda.* Washington, DC: Georgetown University Press.

Marcus, A. I., & Cravens, H. (Eds.). (1997). *Health care policy in contemporary America.* University Park: Pennsylvania State University Press.

Marsden, G.M. (1994). *The soul of the American university: From Protestant establishment to established nonbelief.* New York: Oxford University Press.

May, D., & Vinovskis, M. A. (1977). A ray of millennial light: Early education and social reform in the infant school movement in Massachusetts, 1826–1840. In T. K. Hareven (Ed.), *Family and kin in American urban communities, 1800–1940* (pp. 62–99). New York: Watts.

May, E. R. (1973). *"Lessons" of the past: The use and misuse of history in American foreign policy.* New York: Oxford University Press.

McCullough, D. (2001). *John Adams.* New York: Simon and Shuster.

McDonald, T. J. (Ed.). (1996). *The historic turn in the human sciences.* Ann Arbor: University of Michigan Press.

McGuinn, P. J. (2006). *No Child Left Behind and the transformation of federal education policy, 1965–2005.* Lawrence: University Press of Kansas.

McLaughlin, M. (1974). *Evaluation and reform: The Elementary and Secondary Education Act of 1965, Title I.* Santa Monica: RAND.

Melosi, M. V. (Ed.). (1993). *Urban public policy: Historical modes and methods.* University Park: Pennsylvania State University Press.

Meranto, P. (1967). *The politics of federal aid to education in 1965: A study in political innovation.* Syracuse, NY: Syracuse University Press.

Mirel, J. (1999). *The rise and fall of an urban school system: Detroit, 1907–81* (2nd ed.). Ann Arbor: University of Michigan Press.

Monkkonen, E. H. (Ed.). (1994). *Engaging the past: The uses of history across the social sciences.* Durham, NC: Duke University Press.

Moran, G. F., & Vinovskis, M. A. (2007). Literacy, common schools, and high schools in colonial and antebellum America. In J. L. Rury & W. J. Reese (Eds.), *Rethinking the history of American education* (pp. 17–46). New York: Palgrave.

Moreau, J. (2003). *Schoolbook nation: Conflicts over American history textbooks from the Civil War to the present.* Ann Arbor: University of Michigan Press.

Nash, G. B., Crabtree, C., & Dunn, R. E. (1997). *History on trial: Culture wars and the teaching of the past.* New York: Alfred A. Knopf.

Nelson, A. R. (2005). *The elusive ideal: Equal educational opportunity and the federal role in Boston's public schools, 1950–1985.* Chicago: University of Chicago Press.

Nelson, A. R. (2007). The federal role in American education: A historiographical essay. In J. L. Rury & W. J. Reese (Eds.), *Rethinking the history of American education* (pp. 261–280). New York: Palgrave.

Neustadt, R. E., & May, E. R. (1986). *Thinking in time: The uses of history for decision makers.* New York: Free Press.

Novick, P. (1988). *The noble dream: The "objectivity question" and the American historical profession.* New York: Cambridge University Press.

Patterson, J. T. (2001). *Brown v. Board of Education: A civil rights milestone and its troubled legacy.* New York: Oxford University Press.

Perlmann, J., & Margo, R. A. (2001). *Women's work? American schoolteachers, 1650–1920.* Chicago: Chicago University Press.

Perks, R., & Thomson, A. (Eds.). (2006). *Oral history reader* (2nd ed.). London: Routledge.

Pipes, R. (1990). *How Washington makes Soviet policy: Observations of a visitor.* Stanford, CA: Hoover Institution Press.

Ravitch, D. (1978). *The revisionists revised: A critique of the radical attack on the schools.* New York: Basic Books.

Ravitch, D. (1995). *National standards in American education: A citizen's guide.* Washington, DC: Brookings Institution Press.

Ravitch, D. (2000). *Left back: A century of failed school reforms.* New York: Simon and Schuster.

Ravitch, D., & Vinovskis, M. A. (Eds.). (1995). *Learning from the past: What history teaches us about school reform.* Baltimore: Johns Hopkins University Press.

Reese, W. J. (2005). *America's public schools: From the common school to "No Child Left Behind."* Baltimore: Johns Hopkins University Press.

Reese, W. J. (2007). *History, education, and the schools.* New York: Palgrave.

Reuben, J. A. (1996). *The making of the modern university: Intellectual transformation and the marginalization of morality.* Chicago: University of Chicago Press.

Ritchie, D. A. (2003). *Doing oral history: A practical guide.* New York: Oxford University Press.

Roorbach, A. O. (1937). *The development of the social studies in American secondary education before 1861.* Philadelphia: University of Pennsylvania Press.

Rosenzweig, R., & Thelen, D. (1998). *The presence of the past: Popular uses of history in American life.* New York: Columbia University Press.

Rousmaniere, K. (1997). *City teachers: Teaching and school reform in historical perspective.* New York: Teachers College Press.

Rudolph, J. L. (2002). *Scientists in the classroom: The cold war reconstruction of American science education.* New York: Palgrave.

Rury, J. (2004). *Education and social change: Themes in the history of American schooling* (2nd ed.). Mahwah, NJ: Erlbaum.

Rury, J. (Ed.). (2005). *Urban education in the United States: A historical reader.* New York: Palgrave.

Saxe, D. W. (1991). *Social studies in schools: A history of the early years.* Albany: State University of New York Press.

Schlesinger, A., Jr. (1971). The historian as participant. *Daedalus, 100,* 339–358.

Shapiro, M. S. (1983). *Child's garden: The kindergarten movement from Froebel to Dewey.* University Park: Pennsylvania State University Press.

Silver, H., & Silver, P. (1991). *An educational war on poverty: American and British policy-making, 1960–1980.* Cambridge, UK: Cambridge University Press.

Smith, N. K., & Stern, G. M. (2006). A historical review of access to records in presidential libraries. *Public Historian, 28*(3), 79–116.

Thomas, N. (1975). *Education in national politics.* New York: David McKay.

Tyack, D. (2004). *Seeking common ground: Public schools in a diverse society.* Cambridge, MA: Harvard University Press.

Tyack, D., & Cuban, L. (1995). *Tinkering toward utopia: A century of public school reform.* Cambridge, MA: Harvard University Press.

Urban, W. J. (2000). *Gender, race, and the National Education Association: Professionalism and its limitations.* New York: Routledge Falmer.

U.S. Department of Education, Teaching American History Program, Frequently asked questions. Retrieved March 20, 2006, from http://www.ed.gov/print/programs/teaching history

Vaughn, S. (Ed.). (1985). *The vital past: Writings on the uses of history.* Athens: University of Georgia Press.

Vinovskis, M. A. (1985). *The origins of public high schools: A reexamination of the Beverly high school controversy.* Madison: University of Wisconsin Press.

Vinovskis, M. A. (1987). Forum: The origins of public high schools. *History of Education Quarterly, 27,* 250–258.

Vinovskis, M. A. (1999). *History and educational policymaking.* New Haven, CT: Yale University Press.

Vinovskis, M. A. (2001). *Revitalizing federal education research and development: Improving the R&D centers, regional educational laboratories, and the "new" OERI.* Ann Arbor: University of Michigan Press.

Vinovskis, M. A. (2005). *The birth of Head Start: Preschool education policies in the Kennedy and Johnson administrations.* Chicago: University of Chicago Press.

Vinovskis, M. A. (2006). History assessments and elementary and secondary education. In B. Bain & R. Orrill (Eds.), *History education.* Manuscript submitted for publication.

Vinovskis, M. A. (in press). *From a Nation at Risk to No Child Left Behind: National education goals and the creation of federal education policy.* New York: Teachers College Press.

Walker, W. O., III. (Ed.). (1992). *Drug control policy: Essays in historical and comparative perspective.* University Park: Pennsylvania State University Press.

Warren, D. R. (1974). *To enforce education: A history of the founding years of the United States Office of Education.* Detroit, MI: Wayne State University Press.

White House. (1990, February 26). National goals for education. Washington, DC: Office of the Press Secretary.

Zelizer, J. E. (2000). Clio's lost tribe: Public policy history since 1978. *Journal of Policy History, 12,* 369–394.

Zelizer, J. E. (2005). Introduction: New directions in policy history. *Journal of Policy History, 17,* 1–11.

Zigler, E., & Muenchow, S. (1992). *Head Start: The inside story of America's most successful educational experiment.* New York: Basic Books.

Zigler, E., & Valentine, J. (Eds.). (1979). *Project Head Start: A legacy of the war on poverty.* New York: Free Press.

Zimmerman, J. (2002). *Whose America?: Culture wars in the public schools.* Cambridge, MA: Harvard University Press.

2

Policy Research in Education

The Economic View

MARTIN CARNOY
Stanford University

Economists have had a profound impact on education policy research. By showing that education has an important economic dimension, they have inserted education policy near the center of the debate on economic development and material well-being. They have also greatly influenced the debate on school improvement in two important ways. First, by developing economic notions of educational production, in which schools, districts, and states are economic decision units, allocating resources to produce educational outputs, and where incentives and resource allocation decisions affect the productivity of teachers and student learning, economists have been able to model a number of school improvement issues and test them empirically. Second, economists have been at the forefront of applying new and increasingly sophisticated statistical techniques to estimate quantitatively the effects of various educational policies.

One of the most important contributions of economics to educational policy analysis is the focus on costs and returns. As a society we may want all children to go to college, or we may want the achievement gaps between different groups to close, but accomplishing these goals requires sacrifice, and economics can help us to think about how great those sacrifices may have to be and whether the gain to society is worth the cost. Economics can also help us decide how to achieve goals most "efficiently" (in terms of costs) by debating which educational strategies provide the biggest effect for the sacrifice required.

The Economic Dimension of Education

Economists became interested in educational policy because, after two centuries of evolving modern economic theory, they concluded that education has economic value. In the late 1950s and early 1960s, when economists were first thinking systematically about the economics of education, Theodore Schultz, a professor of economics at the University of Chicago, who later received the Nobel Prize, wrote:

The economic value of education rests on the proposition that people enhance their capabilities as producers and as consumers by investing in themselves and that schooling is the largest investment in human capital. This proposition implies that most of the economic capabilities of people are not given at birth or at the time when children enter upon their schooling. These acquired capabilities are anything but trivial. They are of a magnitude to alter radically the usual measures of the amount of savings and of capital formation that is taking place. They also alter the structure of wages and salaries and the amount of earnings from work relative to the amount of income from property. (Schultz, 1963, pp. 10–11)

The development of human capital theory by Schultz (1963), Gary Becker (1964), and Jacob Mincer (1958, 1962) focused on individual behavior; that is, they envisaged that human capital formation is carried out by individuals, acting in their own interests, making decisions about their education and training. This "methodological individualism," as Blaug (1976) called it, is useful for understanding the demand for education and the choices that individuals make regarding education and jobs. However, in a world where government supplies most education and training, the more relevant issue is whether human capital investment has economic value to the society.

Determining this broader economic value of education is not simple. We know that individuals with more schooling earn, on average, more income and have higher status jobs. However, it is not clear whether they earn higher income because schooling taught them skills that are more highly valued by employers, or whether school merely certifies that smarter, harder-working, more disciplined individuals—who would be more productive whether they took more schooling or not—are more likely to finish higher levels of schooling. Schooling may play mainly a social legitimation function in an ostensibly meritocratic society. That is, more schooling may just provide a "signal" to employers that those who finish more schooling are the smarter, harder working, and more highly disciplined individuals—the qualities for which employers are willing to pay higher wages (Spence, 1973; Bedard, 2001). Or schooling may act as a "screen" that selects more productive individuals from those who would be less productive (Arrow, 1973; Stiglitz, 1975).

Economists have generally come to the conclusion over the past four decades that the skills learned with more years of schooling do have economic value in terms of increasing productivity and economic growth. Yet, empirical evidence for this proposition has not been easy to come by. Early on, in the 1970s, analysts such as Mark Blaug suggested that empirical research in human capital theory had *not* been successful in proving that skills learned in school had economic value in and of themselves (Blaug, 1976). Griliches (1977) thought that there was a good case for skills contributing to earnings, arguing that measurement error in the education variable offset any ability bias in the relation between higher wages and more schooling. That is, the nominal amount of schooling that an individual takes varies greatly in quality and content, creating a major source of error that biases downward estimates of the relation between education and earnings.

Later research using data on twins (Ashenfelter & Krueger, 1994) and longitudinal data from the 1970s and 1980s that included information on academic credits taken in college (Kane & Rouse, 1995) supported the Griliches' position. So did Card's (1993) seminal work showing that college proximity to where a person lives is a significant positive predictor of men's educational attainment. Correcting for this potential "selection bias" increases the economic returns to college attendance, the opposite of what would be the case if there were only an ability effect. These studies suggest that individuals with more time in school (credit hours) earn higher wages because they spent more time in school and/or took more courses, independent of their native ability and socialization (the twins study), pre-college test scores, or proximity to a college (for a summary of the research, see Card, 1999).

Economists estimate the payoff to more education relative to the cost of that education just like they would estimate the payoff to any investment. They calculate what the amount invested in education yields in higher earnings over the lifetime of those with more education. The private rate of return is the payoff to the individual in higher earnings associated with additional schooling compared to the income foregone and direct private costs of that schooling. The social rate of return measures the payoff to society—higher productivity (earnings) plus "externalities" the economic payoffs that accrue to society as a whole, rather than to the individual—compared to the total costs of the schooling, which include private costs and public spending. The rates of return to the investment in education are generally positive in almost every country. In Europe, social rates of return (not including externalities) are about 7%–8%, but in many developing countries, they can be much higher. In Chile, for example, the social rate of return to the investment in education is more than 12%–14% per year of schooling. A positive rate of return to education suggests that investing in education contributes to economic growth. The higher the rate of return, the more likely that investment in education contributes to growth.

One of the continuing discussions among economists is whether the payoff to certain levels of education is higher than to others, and whether the payoff to certain fields of study is higher than to others. This would have important implications for policy if it could be argued that governments invest resources in education based on estimated economic payoffs to education. There is little evidence that this is the case. Most countries such as the United States invest historically in education from the bottom up—first expanding primary, then secondary, then post-secondary higher education—although there are exceptions, such as Brazil, where until recently, public investment in university education exceeded that in secondary education. These patterns of expansion by governments, whether they are national governments or state governments, do not seem to be related to the economic payoffs to education in any systematic way.

Some early analyses of the economic payoff (additional income earned by those with higher levels of schooling relative to the cost of that schooling) across countries argued that primary education had a higher economic value relative to private (income foregone and direct family expenditures) plus public (government spending) cost of primary schooling than did higher levels of schooling (Psacharopoulos, 1993). That implied that governments would be more likely to foster national economic growth by investing more in lower levels of schooling (which most countries start out by doing anyway). Whether or not this was the actual pattern of rates of return in the 1970s, recent evidence suggests that the economic value of post-secondary education relative to costs is now higher in more developed countries than to other levels of schooling (Carnoy, 1995a; Task Force on Higher Education, 2000). This implies that the better investment strategy as countries become more developed is to shift government spending to expanding access to universities (which is what most countries do anyway). Of course, public investment strategy should be driven by more than just returns measured by higher wages. Increased levels of pre-school, primary school, and secondary education could result in lower crime rates (Lochner & Moretti, 2001), improved civic behavior (Milligan, Moretti, & Oreopoulos, 2004), and healthier children borne to more educated mothers (Carnoy, 1993), all of which would benefit the society at large. Increased investment in higher education could also lead to more rapid overall technological progress—again, this could yield society-wide benefits.

Because of such "externalities," economists reasoned that the economic value of investment in schooling might be better measured by its contribution to economic growth rather than the relation of individual earnings gains relative to costs as measured by rates of return (Krueger & Lindahl, 2001). Such a *macroeconomic approach* to the relation between education and economic growth emphasizes the correlation between the stock of human capital and the increase in economic output per capita. This may just indicate that as individuals earn more income, they purchase more schooling for their children, just like they would buy a refrigerator or a family automobile. In that case, schooling would be primarily a durable *consumption* good whose benefits are realized over time, not an *investment* good like a machine or a computer system. However, many economists have argued that, *on average*, countries that have sustained high levels of economic growth are also those who have invested steadily in raising the education of their labor force (e.g., Barro, 1990; Barro & Lee, 1994).

With the shift to an information economy, globalization, and flexible organizations of production, economists have taken these arguments about human capital in the production process a step farther. Theories of development now argue that developing nations have a better chance of catching up with the more advanced economies when they have a stock of labor that has the skills to develop new technologies themselves or to adopt and use foreign technology.

The claim that educated workers adjust more effectively to rapid change in opportunities and technology implies that in today's swiftly changing and more competitive markets, the payoff to education should rise (Schultz, 1975; Welch, 1970). The growth of science-based industries, such as chemicals, biotechnology, telecommunications, and information systems, also means that economic development depends increasingly on highly educated and scientifically trained labor. Yet, more than simply increasing the demand for scientifically-trained labor, economists argue that the new types of production reward innovation and learning-by-doing on a broader scale, even among non-scientifically-oriented workers. In this kind of model, more education in the labor force increases output in two ways: (a) education adds skills to labor, increasing the capacity of labor to produce more output; and (b) education increases the worker's capacity to innovate (learn new ways of using existing technology and creating new technology) in ways that increase his or her own productivity and the productivity of other workers.

The first of these emphasizes the human capital aspect of education (education improves the quality of labor as a factor of production and permits technological development); the second places human capital at the core of the economic process and assumes that the externalities generated by human capital are the source of self-sustaining economic growth process—human capital not only produces higher productivity for more educated workers, but for most other labor, as well.

This second model sees innovation and learning-by-doing as *endogenous* to the production process itself. It assumes that productivity increases are a self-generating process inside firms and economies (Lucas, 1988; Romer, 1990). Such learning-by-doing and innovation as part of the work process are facilitated in firms and societies that foster greater participation and decision making by work-

ers, since those are the firms and societies in which more educated workers will have the greatest opportunities to express their creative capacity.

The model of endogenous innovation and learning-by-doing has major implications for the economic value of education. The value of higher educated labor, particular highly skilled scientific and management labor—those who are able to create the most valuable innovation—increases relative to other levels and kinds of educated labor. More importantly, the economic value of education is generated by a much more complex set of relations between the potential of human capacity to produce more economic output and its realization through organizations of work that are both geared to realize that capacity and to innovate using their human capacity. Thus, the value of education is not just a function of the jobs that workers with more education can get in the labor market. Instead, information, ideology, political power, property rights, citizenship rights in the workplace, and the willingness of organizations to innovate all condition the economic value of education.

At a theoretical level, then, there seems to be a consensus that education increases economic productivity, innovation, and other economic and social factors that contribute positively to economic growth. However, empirical estimates of the education-economic growth relationship have showed mixed results. Focusing just on research done in the 1990s, some of the cross-country analyses suggested that the countries that had initially higher levels of education attained a more sustained level of economic growth (e.g., Barro & Lee, 1994), but others found little or no relation (see discussion, below). Barro (1990) was the first to show that for a given level of wealth, the economic growth rate was positively related to the initial human capital level of a country, whereas for a given level of human capital, the growth rate was negatively related to the initial level of gross domestic product (GDP) per capita. Macroeconomic convergence, therefore, appears to be strongly conditioned by the initial level of education.

Economists also showed that the correlation between education and economic growth is weaker when the education variable is measured as the investment in education (and not the stock of education in the labor force) or when the econometric tests include measures of educational change over time (panel data; Islam, 1995). These analyses tended to show that there is no significant relationship between investment in education and economic growth. Using the same model as Barro (1990), Barro and Lee (1994) showed that the increase in the number of those who attended secondary school in 1965–85 had a positive effect on growth. But estimates by others did not confirm this result. Using an aggregated production function, Benhabib and Spiegel (1994) and Pritchett (1996) also measured the impact of human capital investment on the economic growth rate. They used various measurements of human capital, including the number of years of education as calculated by Kyriacou (1991) or, as in Barro and Lee (1994), the literacy rate and the secondary enrollment rate. Whatever the education variable chosen, the associated coefficients appear either to be insignificant, or to have a negative sign. In short, the initial level of education may be a strong correlate of later economic development (the countries which had a higher level of education in 1960 experienced stronger growth rates). But it is much more uncertain that the rate of investment in education is followed (after a lag) by an increase in the economic growth rate. This apparent contradiction has not been resolved in the education-economic growth literature.

Most recently, the discussion about education's contribution to economic growth has included the role of education quality, as measured by student performance on international tests, in influencing economic output. Hanushek and Kimko (2000) used data from international student achievement tests through 1991 for their measure of educational quality and found that this measure was significantly and positively related to economic growth in 1960–1990 that is much greater than the association between the quantity of education and growth. Hanushek and Wössmann (2007) used test data for a larger group of countries and found that a one standard deviation higher in test score is associated with a 2% higher average annual growth rate over the period 1960–2000. Once this measure of educational quality was included in the growth regressions, school attainment (years of schooling in the labor force) seemed to have little or no role in economic growth. The importance of educational quality in growth remained important even when they included variables that proxy economic institutions, such as the openness of the economy and the strength of property rights. Further, they estimated that the effect of quality on growth is greater in low-income countries. For example, Hanushek and Wössmann's (2007) estimate of the effect of a one standard deviation increase in test score (100 points on the PISA test) means that if the United States could raise its students' average math score to the level of average students in Korea (one-half a standard deviation), it potentially could increase the U.S. growth rate by 1% annually (see Hanushek, this volume).[1]

Notably, estimates of the probable effect of quality on growth do not discuss the costs of increasing educational quality, even though the costs of improving labor force quality through increasing how much students learn in each year of school may be substantial. For example, what would it cost to get the math scores of U.S. 15-year-olds up to those of Korean students? As we suggest in the following section, economic research over the past 40 years has not provided many answers as to how to improve student performance through educational policy interventions, and especially how much it would cost to improve student performance substantially.[2]

School Production Functions and Educational Policy

The first attempt to model and estimate how school inputs, such as teacher characteristics, produce an educational good such as test scores, school attainment, or student engagement was by James Coleman, a sociologist (Coleman et al., 1966). However, economists soon engaged school production as a policy problem and gave it their own cast. The fundamental analytic tool economists used in this line of work is the education production function. At the most basic level, these functions are intended to show how much educational output can be produced from a certain set of inputs, with educational "technology" (curriculum, organization of the classroom and school) usually assumed to be a given, not in control of the education production unit. The concept is rooted in the theory of the firm, where schools are typically assumed to be the production unit, school supplies and physical plant are the capital inputs of the school, and teachers and students are the labor inputs (where labor is differentiated by its human capital). In essence, the estimated contribution of each input to school output constitutes the marginal productivity of an additional unit of the input. When this estimated marginal productivity of a particular input—say years of teacher experience—was compared to its marginal cost, economists could compare this effectiveness-cost ratio to a similar ratio for other inputs (e.g., Levin, Glass, & Meister, 1987). The rational firm (school) could (in theory) increase its output most efficiently by increasing the highest payoff inputs at the expense of those with lower payoffs.

By the late 1960s, stimulated by Coleman's study, there was a growing industry of production function estimates. These controlled for individual student socioeconomic background and focused mainly on the relationship between student achievement and teacher characteristics, class size, and other school variables. In theory, economists' findings regarding each of these questions were intended to inform the education policymaking process as to which policies should be implemented by governments and school administrators. If, for example, the results were to reveal that test scores in mathematics were higher when teachers have advanced training in mathematics, and that the effectiveness-cost ratio of advanced training in mathematics for student outcomes was higher than to other inputs, one could argue for the implementation of an education policy requiring more math teachers to have a college degree in mathematics.

Nevertheless, in practice economists had difficulty finding significant effects of school variables on student performance. One reason was that they were using very broad "human capital" proxies for teachers' potential productivity, such as years of education and experience teaching. Another reason was that other school inputs (as well as teacher quality) were highly correlated with the academic capital students brought with them to school. A major review in the mid-1980s of educational production function research suggested, for example, that neither class size (the number of students in a class with a teacher) nor the amount spent per student was significantly related to student achievement (Hanushek, 1986). Even today, strong arguments are being made, based on 30 years of empirical studies, that student social class is the dominant determinant of school success (Rothstein, 2004).

In addition, other difficulties existed with economists' conception of production as it applied to schools. For one, economists did not derive their models of education production from any theory of learning; that is, they did not specify the process of production itself in modeling the relationship between inputs and outputs (Levin, 1980). Second, economists generally assumed that the main output of schools was student academic performance as measured by subject matter tests. Tests scores were favored partly because they were the most readily available measure of school outcomes. Yet, schools produce other outcomes, and the importance of these outcomes varies across schools and districts (or even classrooms). For example, in addition to academic performance, schools try to socialize children into certain types of behavior (Dreeben, 1968). Such non-cognitive outcomes may be more important than cognitive outcomes in explaining wage differences in the labor force (Bowles, Gintis, & Osborne, 2001; Carneiro, Heckman, & Masterov, 2005). Assigning all inputs to the production of only one output mis-specifies the nature of production in a multi-product firm. Some inputs can be estimated to have high marginal effects on student academic performance but low marginal effects on, say, student socialization (although the two outputs are likely to be complementary).

Furthermore, student achievement as measured at one moment in a student's academic career reflects an accumulation of classroom and school effects, so as a measure of output related to this year's classroom and school inputs it could produce highly biased estimates of those inputs' effects. An early theoretical analysis of these problems showed that estimates from panel data resolved many of the issues associated with such cumulated effects (Boardman & Murnane, 1979). A more recent contribution to estimating the determinants of cognitive achievement suggests that, ultimately, to understand the production of achievement, economists need to unravel earlier from later effects and accept the limitations of experiments that measure the effect of a single intervention on academic outcomes (Todd & Wolpin, 2003).

Economists face another problem in these production function estimates: they usually assume that the "firm" producing learning is the school. Yet, some resource allocation decisions are made at the classroom level, others at the school level, others at the district level, and others at the state level. For example, curriculum decisions, which have considerable influence on how time is allocated in the education system, are made at the state or even national level, although textbook decisions could be made partially at the classroom or school level. Class size is usually another decision made outside the school, and this, in turn determines how many teachers have to be hired. Teacher hiring decisions may be made at the school level or district level, depending on the district, but time allocation decisions within a subject matter and the degree of teacher effort are made at the classroom level (Levin, 1980). Furthermore, the educational process could be viewed as joint production between the family and the school (Carnoy, 1995b).

With the advent in the 1970s of longitudinal studies that measured the same students' achievement in two different grades, analysts could begin to deal with one of these problems; namely, how much a student learned in a particular classroom or school in a defined period of time. This provided a more accurate measure of productivity in terms of student achievement. The main focus of these studies was on the relative effectiveness of private Catholic high schools compared to public high schools (Coleman & Hoffer, 1987), but it contained a larger discussion of what schooling factors might be contributing to variation in student performance (Alexander & Pallas, 1987; Bryk, Lee, & Holland, 1993).

Economists influenced these new policy debates in three important ways. Milton Friedman (1955) provided the underlying theoretical justification for the greater efficiency of market-type competition between private and public schools. His arguments were derived from neo-classical economic theories of consumer choice and from the notion that public schooling was a public monopoly. Friedman argued that providing school choice through publicly financed vouchers would raise consumer (parent) satisfaction, hence economic welfare. Further, since monopolies are able to price products above competitive market equilibrium, competition among schools would result in both public and (publicly subsidized) private schools delivering education at lower cost per student than when only neighborhood public schools provided free education. Although many non-economists also analyzed the relative effectiveness of private schools compared to public (e.g., Chubb & Moe, 1990; Witte, Sterr, & Thorn, 1995; Greene, Peterson, & Du, 1996; Howell, Peterson, Wolf, & Campbell, 2006), economists were deeply involved in the relative effectiveness debate, which also included charter schools (Rouse, 1998a, 1998b; McEwan & Carnoy, 2000; Hoxby, 2003; Carnoy, Jacobsen, Mishel, & Rothstein, 2005; Bifulco & Ladd, 2006; Hanushek, Kain, Rivkin, & Branch, 2007). They also added the dimension of the effectiveness of private schooling relative to the amount spent per student and attempted to estimate the effects of competition on public school performance (Hoxby, 1994; Belfield & Levin, 2002; Hsieh & Urquiola, 2006; Hoxby, 2003; Rothstein, 2007; Carnoy, Adamson, Chudgar, Luschei, & Witte, 2007).

Significantly, despite early claims that privately run alternatives to public education would be more effective than public schools, and that competition among schools would increase student performance across the board, empirical studies have shown overall that this is not the case. In the case of vouchers, perhaps the most interesting results were those of a voucher experiment in New York City. The results of the experiment seemed to suggest that after 3 years Black (but not Hispanic) voucher recipients had significant academic gains relative to those who stayed in public schools (Howell, Peterson, Wolf, & Campbell, 2006). However, a reanalysis of the data found that even the gains for Black students were statistically insignificant (for a review, see Witte, this volume).

In the case of charter schools (discussed further in the methodology section, below), there is also considerable controversy over whether charter students show greater test score gains than public school students, but *on average*, the claim that freeing (charter) schools from the heavy hand of public bureaucracy produces significant academic gains seems to be unfounded. Nevertheless, some economists have argued—using computational theoretical models—that certain types of vouchers would be more likely to produce positive effects than others (Epple & Romano, 1998). Neither does competition seem to lower the costs of educating students, although many charter and private schools are able to provide education at lower cost per student than public schools, mainly by hiring younger teachers and taking fewer students with special needs (McEwan & Carnoy, 2000, on the Chilean voucher plan).

The second important influence economists had on the discussion of how much inputs raised student achievement was to introduce an emphasis on the *cost of those inputs*—that is cost-effectiveness and cost-benefit analysis of educational improvement (Levin & McEwan, 2000). For example, the Tennessee class size experiment, which randomly assigned students and teachers to normal size and small classes, suggested a significant positive class size effect on student achievement and attainment (Finn & Achilles, 1999). Economic analysis estimated that despite the high costs of class size reduction, the long-term economic benefits for students who had been placed in the smaller classes in Tennessee was also relatively high (Krueger & Whitmore, 2001).

A second example is the cost-benefit studies of early childhood interventions for low-income children on later adult outcomes (Lynch, 2007). Although these studies showed that pre-school interventions had little effect on student achievement in primary schooling, the interventions resulted in higher school attainment, which in turn reduced welfare costs and incarceration rates, and produced high social benefits relative to the costs of the programs. A third example is studies of learning improvement interventions in schools. One such study was Levin et al.'s (1987) comparison of a number of interventions—computer software to teach mathematics, peer tutoring, reducing class size, and lengthening the school day—relative to the costs of those interventions. They found much larger effects on achievement of computer-based math training (an expensive intervention) than peer tutoring (an inexpensive intervention), but on a cost-effectiveness basis, a better result for peer tutoring. They found both of these interventions more cost effective than reducing class size and lengthening the school day (but this was before data were available on class size effects from the Tennessee experiment). They argued that from a cost-efficiency standpoint, putting resources in peer tutoring made more sense than in computer-based learning, even though the effect size of the latter intervention was larger.

Economists' focus on the costs of educational production has produced another controversial debate in educational policy: Does spending more per student result in better student outcomes? The broad outlines of the argument against any spending effect is that the educational cost per pupil rose more than 35% in the United States in real terms (adjusted for inflation) between 1980 and the mid-1990s, but that average test scores did not rise significantly in the same period (Hanushek, 1994). Another version of this argument is that average international test scores in a variety of developed countries hardly changed in 1970–1994, but real spending per pupil rose substantially (Pritchett, 2003). Thus, economists have been largely responsible for a widely held belief in some education policy circles that more spending per pupil does not result in better student performance, but rather is absorbed almost entirely in higher teacher salaries that are not linked to teacher productivity.

Yet, there have been strong counter-arguments. One is that using the consumer price index (CPI) to estimate the inflation-corrected increase in education costs is a misleading adjustment because the components of the CPI are not the main products purchased by school systems. Rather, nominal spending on education over time should be deflated by an index of higher educated labor costs, especially the salaries of higher educated women. Using such an index instead of the CPI to deflate education spending per pupil suggests that real costs in education increased little in the 1980s and 1990s (Rothstein & Miles, 1995). Further, much of the increases that did occur came in special education spending and transportation costs, elements that have little to do with instructing the vast majority of students. Thus, in the United States, it is likely that most state education systems increased spending on teachers about enough to keep pace with the increasing salaries of professional women in the rest of the labor market. Some states increased spending more than average in the 1980s and early 1990s (e.g., Texas), and some states, much less (e.g., California). On the other side of the equation, U.S. mathematics test scores of fourth- and eighth-grade students increased substantially in the 1990s (NCES, 2005), suggesting that teacher productivity as measured by math outcomes rose even as the relative salaries of teachers compared to other professionals was constant.

The third and most recent contribution economists have made to our understanding of school improvement policy debate is to provide compelling evidence that teacher "quality" is essential to improving student performance (Rivkin, Hanushek, & Kain, 2005; Clotfelter, Ladd, & Vigdor, 2007). This evidence has emerged from state data that track individual students' performance over time and from classroom to classroom as they progress through the school system. These data have allowed researchers to estimate the test score gains that students make from grade to grade and to associate those gains with particular teachers. Data are also available on students' social characteristics and teachers' social and educational characteristics, as well as work experience. The results suggest that some teachers do consistently better across student cohorts than other teachers, although there is disagreement whether teacher education and work experience is important in explaining these differences in performance (Rivkin, Hanushek, and Kain's, 2005 results suggest that they do not; Clotfelter, Ladd, and Vigdor, 2007, suggest that they do).

These results and those of experiments that reward teachers for outcomes (Lavy, 2002, 2005; Figlio & Kenny, 2006) have led to an important debate among economists about improving student performance through performance-based teacher pay systems. Since this volume contains a chapter that deals specifically with teacher labor markets (see Béteille & Loeb), we will not go into much detail on this issue, nor on the important contributions which economists have made to teacher labor markets more generally. However, it is worth noting some of the elements of economists' thinking about teacher pay systems (see Béteille & Loeb, this volume).

If, as one argument goes, it is difficult to identify the characteristics of teachers that increase student performance, but we do know that students do consistently better with some teachers than others, economists suggest that the best way to recruit such high performing teachers is to offer higher salaries to those starting teachers who are able to show, over, say, a 3-year initiation period, their ability to produce high student performance. Eventually, as older teachers retire, this would gradually raise the overall quality of teachers in the labor force and greatly raise teacher salaries. A second approach would be to pay proven high performing teachers in the system more (merit pay) in the hope that lower performing teachers would be induced to greater effort in order to increase their wages. Although earlier studies were pessimistic (Murnane & Cohen, 1986) recent limited experimental research (Lavy, 2002, 2005) suggests that merit pay may produce a positive effect on student performance.

If it is possible to identify characteristics of teachers that are associated with higher student performance, economists contend that teacher pay could be set to attract individuals with those characteristics into teaching, or, alternatively, that the costs of entering teaching could be decreased for such individuals, for example by eliminating requirements for teacher certification. One teacher characteristic that has been alleged to produce higher student performance is greater subject content knowledge (e.g., Shulman, 1987). Programs such as Teach for America (TFA) adopt this assumption as its underlying rationale for recruiting individuals from more elite universities into teaching. TFA teachers are paid the same salaries as other starting teachers. The recruitment incentive is a short training period instead of the 1-year program teacher certification requirement. On the other hand, Chile raised its teacher salaries sharply in the 1990s in part to attract more highly qualified high school students into university teacher preparation programs. The average entrance exam scores of Chile's university students in education faculties did rise substantially in the 2000s (Organization for Economic Cooperation and Development [OECD], 2003).

Such teacher improvement schemes might attract a better talent pool and many of them would result in higher teacher pay. If these increases in teacher pay were tied to student performance in some way, student performance would also increase. However, if teacher pay is not directly related to student performance, the evidence suggests that school/district recruitment, selection, evaluation, and tenure decisions might continue to be based on institutional practices that do not capitalize much on the better talent pool (Ballou & Podgursky, 1997). The bottom line is that economists are far from answering the question of how much teacher pay would have to increase in order to produce substantial increases in student performance. Little is known about the current distribution of the capacity to teach well among university graduates, or about how teacher education programs would respond to teacher pay schemes that emphasize student performance results by producing new sets of teacher skills, assuming that those skill sets were identifiable.

Economists and Methodology in Educational Policy Analysis

Economists have had a major influence on educational policy analysis by developing and applying statistical methods that correct for selection bias in the analysis of large scale data sets. These methods attempt to approximate the causal inference associated with randomized assignment.

Selection bias in educational policy analysis is usually quite obvious. The performance of suburban schools catering to upper middle class students having all the advantages of highly educated, high income families cannot be compared directly to the performance of inner city schools. James Heckman (1979) calls this "observable selection bias," and it can be corrected by adjusting outcomes for relevant observables that are correlated with the outcome variable and the independent (treatment) variable of interest. But some selection bias is more subtle. On the one hand, charter schools may attract students that have similar family characteristics as public school students, but are having academic difficulties in public schools. Families may enroll their children in a charter school specifically because they are already not doing as well as their classmates. On the other hand, charter schools may have much more flexibility than regular public schools to pick their students, so may be able to deny admission to potentially troublesome students. Charter schools may also appeal to the most motivated parents, eager to provide opportunities to their children that they feel are lacking in regular private schools. These are usually "unobservables," or omitted variables. They are correlated with the educational intervention in question and therefore bias estimates of that effect of the intervention on outcomes.

Economists use several methods to deal with selection bias as represented by omitted variables. The four we review here are fixed effects, instrumental variables, regression discontinuities, which are a form of an instrumental variable, and propensity scores (or propensity matching; Schneider, Carnoy, Kilpatrick, Schmidt, & Shavelson, 2007).

Student and School Fixed Effects A key problem in estimating the impact of educational treatment variables on student performance in longitudinal data sets containing multiple observations of students and schools over time is that unobserved characteristics of students or schools are correlated with both treatment and outcome variables. Controlling for these unobserved characteristics would help reduce the bias in the estimate of the treatment effect. When student outcomes are measured over time, analysts can control for student and school characteristics that are invariant over time and correlated with the dependent variable by including a series of dummy (0/1) variables for each student or school. This series of dummy variables can capture, say, the fact that during the time period we are studying certain schools achieve at a higher level or lower level for reasons that we cannot observe but may be correlated with our treatment variable. Correcting for such fixed effects should provide a less biased estimate of the effect on achievement of the treatment (say, class size).

For example, Rouse (1998a, 1998b) compared student performance in Milwaukee private voucher schools compared to students in public school in the period 1991–1994 (4 years). She used student fixed effects to control for time invariant observable *and* unobservable student characteristics. In a recent extension of earlier research mentioned above, Rivkin, Hanushek, and Kain (2005) test whether teachers have a significant impact on student achievement, and what it is about teachers that may account for that difference. They used 5 years of longitudinal data on students in grades 4 through 8 in one large urban district in which they were able to get data identifying each student with his or her teacher, grade by grade. In order to correct for possible selection bias from students and teachers choosing schools, Rivkin and colleagues used school fixed effects to restrict all achievement variation among students and teachers to within schools variance.

Bifulco and Ladd (2006) analyzed a statewide sample of North Carolina students that included the third-grade cohorts for 5 years, 1996–2000, following them to the eighth grade or to the 2001–2002 school year, whichever came first. Besides end-of-grade reading and math test scores, the data include the students' grade, gender, race or ethnicity, parents' education, whether the school was a charter or regular public school, and a school identifier. This allowed Bifulco and Ladd to tell which type of school individual students were attending in any given year. They could compare student gains in charter and in regular public schools—about 65% of students in the sample who spent some time in a charter school between 1996 and 2000 also spent at least 1 year in a public school during that period. To help correct for selection bias, they use repeated observations on individual students to control for individual fixed effects. The study found that across all students, grades, and years, students in charter schools scored significantly lower on both the reading test (0.16 standard deviations) and math test (0.26 standard deviations). They also found gains to be significantly lower in charter schools on both

tests. The negative effect of being in a charter school was larger when the student fixed effects model was used. For the large number of students who changed from a public school to a charter or vice-versa in a given year, Bifulco and Ladd estimated gains controlling for the fact that the change itself may have had a negative effect.

Hanushek, Kain, Rivkin, and Branch's (2007) work on charter schools in Texas had a similar data set and served as a model methodology for Bifulco and Ladd. Hanushek et al. (2007) also used student fixed effects to control for observed and unobserved time invariant pupil characteristics, hence correcing for possible selection bias for students who received the treatment (attending charter school). But the fact that a large group in the sample attended both charter and regular public schools in the time period observed provided an even stronger control than fixed effects for selection bias.

Instrumental Variables Another popular method economists use to correct for variables is to include an "instrumental variable" unobservable to include the analysis (Heckman, 1979; Angrist & Krueger, 2001). An instrumental variable must have the properties that it is correlated with the independent variable of interest but not with the dependent variable conditional on the other independent variables. The instrumental variables method allows us to estimate the coefficient of interest consistently and free from asymptotic bias from omitted variables, without actually having data on the omitted variables or even knowing what they are (Angrist & Krueger, 2001, p. 73).

For example, Angrist and Krueger (1991) used birth date (quarter of birth) and compulsory school laws (students cannot leave school before their 16th or 18th birthday, depending on the state) to estimate the effect of staying in school longer (those whose birthdays occur earlier stay in school longer) on earnings. Birth date is a good instrument because it determines who starts school in a given year or a year later, but is not a priori related to an individual's ability, family resources, or other omitted variables that might influence earnings. Nevertheless, there are critiques of Angrist and Krueger's instrumental variable, notably that conception/birth quarter may itself depend on wage seasonality (Bound, Jaeger, & Baker, 1995).

In comparing school achievement and attainment for those attending Catholic private and public schools, a number of economists (Hoxby, 1994; Evans & Schwab, 1995; Neal, 1997) have used the instrumental variable of whether the student identifies himself or herself as Catholic. Catholic is not as "good" an instrument as birth date. But once observables such as a student's family background are controlled for, delimiting the comparison to students who identify themselves as Catholic, particularly in school districts where both public and parochial schools are available, may reduce selection bias. The key is whether we believe that those Catholic students from similar socioeconomic status (SES) families who attend Catholic and public schools do so more or less randomly, not because of ability, motivational, or other differences correlated with, in this case, school achievement or attainment. Below, in reviews of studies using regression discontinuity analysis, we show other examples of instrumental variables—in these cases, the discontinuity provides the instrument, just as, in a sense, birth date in the Angrist and Krueger birth date analysis is a discontinuity.

Regression Discontinuity A third method that can be used to simulate random assignment is regression discontinuity, which in turn is related to an instrumental variables approach. A regression discontinuity occurs when a group is subject to a treatment because they fell either above or below a certain cutoff score that put them into or out of the treatment group. The model example for regression discontinuity (Campbell, 1969) is the effect of National Merit Scholarships on later incomes The fact that those just above the cutoff and those just below the cutoff are likely to be similar on a set of unobserved variables that predict the score on the test determining National Merit Scholarship awards suggest that the effect of the treatment on a dependent variable (in this case, future incomes) could be estimated by comparing this restricted group—those just above the cutoff (received the treatment) and those just below the cutoff (did not receive the treatment). Campbell argued that:

> If the assignment mechanism used to award scholarships is discontinuous, e.g., there is a threshold value of past achievement that determines whether an award is made, then one can control for any smooth function of past achievement and still estimate the effect of the award at the point of discontinuity. This is done by matching discontinuities or nonlinearities in the relationship between outcomes and past achievement to discontinuities or nonlinearities in the relationship between awards and past achievement. (as cited in Angrist & Lavy, 1999, p. 548)

Economists using the regression discontinuity approach assume, in effect, that individuals in this restricted group would approximate a random assignment to the treatment and control groups (at this particular cutoff point). That implies that the estimate of the regression coefficient at the cutoff point yields an unbiased estimate of the treatment. When there are multiple discontinuities, this provides an even better estimate of the treatment effect. Multiple discontinuities provide estimates across a broader range of the initial independent variable (in the merit scholarship case, at different levels of test scores; discussion of the Campbell model can be found in greater detail in Schneider et al., 2007, pp. 52–53).

A typical policy problem that has been addressed by this method is the effect on academic achievement of attending summer school and of grade retention. Both remediations kick in on the basis of test scores and a cutoff above which the student is promoted and below which they are required to attend summer school or repeat a grade. Jacob and Lefgren (2004) use Chicago Public School data to estimate achievement 1 year after third and sixth graders were either

(a) promoted to the next grade based on June math and reading tests, (b) sent to summer school and given another set of tests in August, or (c) retained in third or sixth grade based on the August test results. The method they use to estimate the effect of the treatment variable (either summer school or grade retention) is equivalent to an instrumental variable approach in which they control for a linear trend of reading ability (they limit their sample to those students that passed the math portion of the test but failed the reading portion) and instrument for treatment using a dummy that takes on a value of 1 for students who exceed the cutoff. Briefly summarized, they find that summer school and retention have a significant positive effect on achievement 1 year and 2 years later for third graders but not for sixth graders. The effects were largest for Black students and female students.

A second study that uses regression discontinuity addresses the issue of class size in Israel. Angrist and Lavy (1999) use an administrative rule in the Israeli educational system to analyze the effect of class size on achievement. The rule (called Maimonides Rule) limits the class size to 40 and requires schools with enrollment in a grade with 41, 81, 121, and so forth students to create an additional classroom. As a result, when enrollment exceeds 40, 80, 120, and so forth, class size drops sharply on the other side of the discontinuity. Since small schools in Israel are mainly rural and are characterized by low achievement scores, and larger enrollment school are generally more highly regarded, attracting a higher social class student body, enrollment is positively correlated with enrollment. Angrist and Lavy estimate the relation of student achievement averaged at the classroom level to class size to an instrumental variable that captures the class size discontinuity, controlling for school enrollment and SES. They also estimate the regression restricted to the range of enrollment plus or minus 5 around each discontinuity (40, 80, 120, etc.). They find strong evidence of a significant negative relation between reading and math scores and predicted class size for fifth graders, but the effect of class size for fourth-grade reading scores are smaller and for fourth-grade math scores are not significantly different from zero. The main problem with the instrument in this case is that schools may be able to manipulate the assignment variable, namely school enrollments, allowing them to choose a precise class size, introducing selection bias. This is part of a more general problem with regression discontinuity designs: individuals or schools may "game" values of the assignment variable (Imbens & Lemieux, 2007).

Implications of the Results for Causal Inference Economists have long used large data sets to address the impact of various educational policies on student performance—policies such as reducing class size, grade retention, and summer school; having students attend Catholic schools, or charter schools rather than traditional public schools, and hiring teachers with particular characteristics. Beginning in the 1980s, economists began using statistical methodologies to address the selection bias that is inherent in the non-random assignment typical of these data.[3]

In addition, almost all the studies were able to deal with the effects on different groups. Rivkin et al. (2005) estimated differential effects of Black teachers on Black students, for example. Morgan (2001) estimated the effect of attending Catholic school by social class, Jacob and Lefgren (2004) estimate the effect of summer school and promotion by grade, ethnicity, gender , and social class, and Angrist and Lavy (1999) discuss the differential impact of the class size on different types of schools (smaller schools and schools with fewer disadvantaged pupils).

Furthermore, some of these studies reinforce other studies of the same treatment that used other methodologies but come to similar conclusions. For example, the Morgan analysis of the effect of attending Catholic secondary schools summarizes two decades of discussion and concludes that the effect of the treatment is positive and significant, but is driven by the larger impact on those groups in Catholic schools least likely to attend them. This is a similar conclusion to Bryk et al.'s (1993) study a decade earlier. Angrist and Lavy's (1999) analysis of the effect of class size, while applied to the Israeli case, supports earlier results from the Tennessee class size experiment.

Because these analyses generate estimated relationships that policy makers can infer are "causal," and because educational policy decisions usually involve resources (costs), means that—for better or worse—they have considerable influence in policy circles. At the same time, there is considerable disagreement among economists on many of these prominent issues, particularly in how important many touted interventions are for improving student performance and economic outcomes.

Directions for Further Policy Research

Much of the work that economists are doing in educational policy research recently is to examine the effect of interventions using either experimental design or sophisticated statistical analysis on longitudinal data that corrects for selection bias. This is valuable research, because it puts educational policy on much more secure empirical ground than it has been in the past. Much more work needs to be done, in order to assess what works to improve student performance (both achievement and attainment).

A second area that is on the verge of producing valuable insights into the production process in education is research on teacher labor markets. This chapter has only touched on this subject because it is covered elsewhere in this volume, but economic research will have a lot to say about how to improve the quality of teaching through incentives, wage policy, and workplace management, and how effective such policies might be in improving student performance for different types of students.

Third, as economists are concerned with costs, much more research is needed on the costs of increasing human capital through improving the quality of education (student achievement in each year of schooling) that students take compared to increasing the quantity of schooling (number of years of schooling) they attain. As in the case of teacher incentives, the push for higher quality—although seemingly not very controversial—requires a great deal more empirical work in order to understand the full policy implications of upgrading educational systems.

Notes

1. Although the focus of Hanushek and Wössman's analysis is on the relation between school quality and student achievement, student achievement level is the result of many factors outside school, such as family and community emphasis on academic persistence and discipline—factors that contribute both to doing well on tests and to workplace productivity.

2. Outside-of-school factors in some societies could also be associated with higher yields to investment in schooling, so trying to raise test scores through school interventions in societies where these factors are less pervasive may be more costly. The other side of the coin is that total educational costs per student in societies that score high on tests may be greatly underestimated by public spending per pupil on education. For example, recent estimates show that families in Korea spend about 2.3% of gross domestic product on private tutoring in 2003, one-half of public spending on education (Korean Education Development Institute [KEDI], 2003). Many other countries are also characterized by high private costs borne by families—costs not counted in the usual accounting for spending on schooling (Tsang, 2002; Kim, 2007).

3. These are not the only methods available for correcting selection bias. For example, one method not commonly found in economic analysis and used by others is propensity scores. Most regression analyses in non-randomized observational studies are carried out for the full range of a particular sample, without regard for the probability that individuals have of being in the treatment or control groups. A propensity score is a technique developed by Rosenbaum and Rubin (1983) to represent the predicted probability that individuals with certain characteristics would be assigned to a treatment group when assignment is non-random. The advantage of a propensity score is that it aggregates a number of characteristics that individually would be difficult to match among those in the treatment and non-treatment groups. Take the example of student performance in private compared to public schools. Students from disadvantaged families are much less likely to attend a private school than a public school. At the other end of the spectrum, students from well-off families, particularly minority high-income families, have a relatively high probability of attending a private school. To approach a random assignment trial, we should compare observations from our non-randomized survey of individuals that have a similar probability of being in the treatment or control group—that is, a group with similar propensities, based on an aggregate of characteristics, of being in the treatment group or the control group Students with similar propensities to be in the treatment group (whether they are in the treatment group or not) can be matched on the basis of their scores. The difference in their achievement scores would be closer to the difference we could expect in a random assignment of students to the two groups, since it is much more likely that their omitted characteristics are similar (see Schneider et al., 2007, for further discussion of this point). Propensity scores address an important issue endemic to all empirical research, namely the specificity of estimates to certain groups (e.g., Hong & Raudenbush, 2005; Morgan, 2001).

References

Alexander, K. L., & Pallas, A. M. (1987). School sector and cognitive performance: When is a little a little? In E. H. Haertel, T. James, & H.

M. Levin (Eds.), *Comparing public and private schools. Vol. 2: School achievement* (pp. 89–111). New York: Falmer Press.

Angrist, J. D., & Krueger, A. B. (1991). Does compulsory school attendance affect schooling and earnings? *Quarterly Journal of Economics, 106,* 979–1014.

Angrist, J. D., & Krueger, A. B. (2001). Instrumental variables and the search for identification: From supply and demand to natural experiments. *Journal of Economic Perspectives, 15,* 69–85.

Angrist, J. D., & Lavy, V. (1999). Using Maimonides' rule to estimate the effects of class size on academic achievement. *Quarterly Journal of Economics, 114),* 533–576.

Arrow, K. (1973). Higher education as a filter. *Journal of Public Economics, 2,* 193–216.

Ashenfelter, O., & Krueger, A. B. (1994). Estimates of the economic return to schooling from a new sample of twins. *American Economic Review, 84,* 1157–1173.

Ballou, D., & Podgursky, M. (1997). *Teacher pay and teacher quality.* Kalamazoo, MI: W. E. Upjohn Institute for Employment Research.

Barro, R. J. (1990). Government spending in a simple model of endogenous growth. *Journal of Political Economy, 98,* S103–S125

Barro, R. J., & Lee, J. W. (1994, June). Sources of economic growth. *Carnegie Rochester Conference Series on Public Policy, 40,* 1–46.

Becker, G. (1964). *Human capital.* Chicago: University of Chicago Press.

Bedard, K. (2001). Human capital versus signaling models: University access and high school dropouts. *Journal of Political Economy, 109,* 749–775.

Benhabib, J., & Spiegel, M. (1994). The role of human capital in economic development: Evidence for aggregate cross country data. *Journal of Monetary Economics, 34,* 143–173.

Belfield, C., & Levin, H. M. (2002). The effects of competition on educational outcomes: A review of U.S. evidence. *Review of Educational Research, 72,* 279–341.

Bifulco, R., & Ladd, H. F. (2006). The impacts of charter schools on student achievement: Evidence from North Carolina. *Education Finance and Policy, 1,* 50–90.

Blaug, M. (1976). The empirical status of human capital theory: A slightly jaundiced survey. *Journal of Economic Literature, 14,* 827–855.

Boardman, A., & Murnane, R. (1979). Using panel data to improve estimates of the determinants of educational achievement. *Sociology of Education, 52,* 113–121.

Bowles S., Gintis, H., & Osborne, M. (2001). The determinants of earnings: A behavioral approach. *Journal of Economic Literature, 39,* 1137–1176.

Bryk, A. S., Lee, V. E., & Holland, P. B. (1993). *Catholic schools and the common good.* Cambridge, MA: Harvard University Press.

Campbell, D. T. (1969). Reforms as experiments. *American Psychologist, 24,* 409–429.

Card, D. (1993). *Using geographic variations in college proximity to estimate the returns to schooling* (Working Paper No. 4483). Cambridge, MA: National Bureau of Economic Research.

Card, D. (1999). The causal effects of education on earnings. In O. Ashenfelter & D. Card (Eds.), *Handbook of labor economics: Vol. 3* (pp. 1801–1863). Amsterdam, Holland: Elsevier Science.

Carneiro, P., Heckman, J., & Masterov, D. (2005). *Labor market discrimination and racial differences in premarket factors* (Discussion Paper 1453). Bonn, Germany: Institute for the Study of Labor (IZA).

Carnoy, M. (1993). *The case for basic education.* New York: UNICEF.

Carnoy, M. (1995a). Rates of return to education. In M. Carnoy (Ed.), *The international encyclopedia of the economics of education* (pp. 364–369). Oxford, UK: Pergamon.

Carnoy, M. (1995b). Joint production of education. In M. Carnoy (Ed.), *The international encyclopedia of the economics of education* (pp. 297–303). Oxford, UK: Pergamon.

Carnoy, M., Jacobsen, R., Mishel, L., & Rothstein, R. (2005). *The charter school dust-up.* New York: Teachers College Press and the Economic Policy Institute.

Carnoy, M., Adamson, F., Chudgar, A., Luschei, T. F., & Witte, J. F.

(2007). *Vouchers and public school performance: A case study in the Milwaukee parental choice program.* Washington, DC: Economic Policy Institute.

Chubb, J., & Moe, T. (1990). *Politics, markets, and America's schools.* Washington, DC: The Brookings Institution.

Clotfelter, C., Ladd, H., & Vigdor, J. (2007). *How and why do teacher credentials matter for student achievement?* (Working Paper 12828). Cambridge, MA: National Bureau of Economic Research.

Coleman, J. S., Campbell, E. Q., Hobson, C. J., McPartland, F., Mood, A. M., Weinfeld, F. D., et al. (1966). *Equality of educational opportunity.* Washington, DC: Government Printing Office.

Coleman, J., & Hoffer, T. (1987). *Public and private high schools: The impact of communitie*s. New York: Basic Books.

Dreeben, R. (1968). *On what is learned in school.* Reading, MA: Addison-Wesley.

Epple, D., & Romano, R. (1998). Competition between public and private school, vouchers, and peer-group effects. *American Economic Review, 88,* 33–62.

Evans, W. N., & Schwab, R. M. (1995). Finishing high school and starting college: Do Catholic schools make a difference? *Quarterly Journal of Economics, 110,* 941–974.

Figlio, D., & Kenny, L. (2006). *Individual teacher incentives and student performance* (Working Paper 12627). Cambridge, MA: National Bureau of Economic Research.

Finn, J. D., & Achilles, C. M. (1999). Tennessee's class size study: Findings, implications, and misconceptions. *Educational Evaluation and Policy Analysis. 21,* 97–109.

Friedman, M. (1955). The role of government in education. In R. A. Solo (Ed.), *Economics and the Public Interest* (pp. 123–144). New Brunswick, NJ: Rutgers University Press.

Greene, J. P., Peterson, P. E., & Du, J. (1996, August 30). *The effectiveness of school choice in Milwaukee: A secondary analysis of data from the program's evaluation.* Paper presented before the Panel on the Political Analysis of Urban School Systems, American Political Science Association, San Francisco.

Griliches, Z. (1977). Estimating the returns of schooling: Some econometric problems. *Econometrica, 45*(1), 1–22.

Hanushek, E. A. (1986). The economics of schooling: Production and efficiency in public schools. *Journal of Economic Literature, 24,* 1141–1177.

Hanushek, E. A. (1994). *Making schools work: Improving performance and controlling costs.* Washington, DC: Brookings Institution.

Hanushek, E. A., & Kimko, D. D. (2000). Schooling, labor force quality, and the growth of nations. *American Economic Review, 90*(5), 1184–1208.

Hanushek, E. A., Kain, J. F., Rivkin, S. G., & Branch, G. F. (2007). Charter school quality and parental decision making with school choice. *Journal of Public Economics, 91,* 823–848.

Hanushek, E. A., & Wössmann. L. (2007). *The role of school improvement in economic development* (Working Paper 12832). Cambridge, MA: National Bureau of Economic Research.

Heckman, J. J. (1979). Sample selection bias as a specification error. *Econometrica, 47*(1), 153–161.

Hong, G. & Raudenbush, S. (2005). Effects of kindergarten retention policy on children's cognitive growth in reading and mathematics. *Educational Evaluation and Policy Analysis, 27,* 205–224.

Hoxby, C. M. (1994). *Do private schools provide competition for public schools?* (Working Paper No. W4978). Cambridge, MA: National Bureau of Economic Research, .

Hoxby, C. M. (2003). School choice and school competition: Evidence from the United States [Electronic version]. *Swedish Economic Policy Review, 10,* 11–67.

Howell, W., Peterson, P., Wolf, P., & Campbell, D. (2006). *The education gap: Vouchers and urban schools.* Washington, DC: The Brookings Institution.

Hsieh, C-T., & Urquiola, M. (2006). The effects of generalized school choice on achievement and stratification: Evidence from Chile's school voucher program. *Journal of Public Economics, 90,* 1477–1503.

Imbens, G., & Lemieux, T. (2007). *Regression discontinuity designs: A guide to practice* (Working Paper No. 13039). Cambridge, MA: National Bureau of Economic Research.

Islam, N. (1995). Growth empirics: A panel data approach. *Quarterly Journal of Economics, 110*, 1127–1170.

Jacob, B., & Lefgren, L. (2004). Remedial education and student achievement: A regression discontinuity analysis. *Review of Economics and Statistics, 86,* 226–244.

Kane, T. J., & Rouse, C. E. (1995). Labor-market returns to two- and four-year college. *The American Economic Review, 85*, 600–614.

Kim, J-H. (2007). *The determinants of demand for private tutoring in South Korea.* Retrieved December 12, 2007, from the National Center for the Study of School Privatization in Education Web site: http://www.ncspe.org/publications_files/OP143.pdf

Korean Education Development Institute (KEDI). (2003). *Monitoring private tutoring and analyzing the cost of private tutoring* (CR2003-19). Seoul: Author.

Krueger, A. B., & Lindahl, M. (2001). Education for growth: Why and for whom? *Journal of Economic Literature, 39*, 1101–1136.

Krueger, A. B., & Whitmore, D. (2001). The effect of attending a small class in the early grades on college-test taking and middle school test results: Evidence from Project Star. *The Economic Journal, 111*(468), 1–28.

Kyriacou, G. (1991). *Level and growth effects of human capital* (Working Paper 91–26). New York: C.V. Starr Center.

Lavy, V. (2002). Evaluating the effect of teachers' group performance incentives on pupil achievement. *Journal of Political Economy, 110*, 1286–1317.

Lavy, V. (2005, June). *Performance pay and teachers' effort, productivity and grading ethics.* Jerusalem: Hebrew University.

Levin, H. M. (1980). Educational production theory and teacher inputs. In C. Bidwell & D. Windham (Eds.), *The analysis of educational productivity, Vol. 2: Issues in macro analysis* (pp. 203–231). Cambridge, MA: Ballinger.

Levin, H. M., Glass, G. V., & Meister, G. L. (1987). Cost-effectiveness of computer-assisted instruction. *Evaluation Review, 11*, 50–72.

Levin, H. M., & McEwan, P. (2000). *Cost-effectiveness analysis: Methods and applications* (2nd ed.). Thousand Oaks, CA: Sage.

Lochner. L., & Moretti, E. (2001). *The effect of education on crime: Evidence from prison inmates, arrests, and self-reports* (Working Paper No. 8605). Cambridge, MA: National Bureau of Economic Research.

Lucas, R. (1988). On the mechanics of economic development. *Journal of Monetary Economics, 22*, 3–42.

Lynch, R.G. (2007). *Enriching children, enriching the nation.* Washington, DC: Economic Policy Institute.

McEwan, P., & Carnoy, M. (2000). The effectiveness and efficiency of private schools in Chile's voucher system. *Educational Evaluation and Policy Analysis, 22*(3), 213–239.

Mincer, J. (1958). Investment in human capital and personal income distribution. *Journal of Political Economy, 66*, 281–302.

Mincer, J. (1962). On-the-job training: Costs, returns, and some implications. *Journal of Political Economy, 70*(5, Suppl. 2), 50–79.

Milligan, K., Moretti, E., & Oreopoulos, P. (2004). Does education improve citizenship? Evidence from the United States and the United Kingdom. *Journal of Public Economics, 88*, 1667–1695.

Morgan, S. L. (2001). Counterfactuals, causal effect heterogeneity, and the Catholic school effect on learning. *Sociology of Education, 74*, 341–374.

Murnane, R., & Cohen, D. (1986, February). Merit pay and the evaluation problem: Why most merit pay plans fail and a few survive. *Harvard Educational Review, 56*, 1–17.

National Center for Educational Statistics, National Assessment of Educational Progress. (2005). *NAEP 2004 Trends in academic progress: Three decades of student performance in reading and mathematics.* Washington, DC: National Center Educational Statistics.

Neal, D. (1997). The effect of Catholic secondary schooling on educational attainment. *Journal of Labor Economics, 15*, 98–123.

Organization.for Economic Cooperation and Development (OECD). (2003). *Reviews of national policies for education: Chile.* Paris: Author.

Pritchett, L. (1996). *Where has all the education gone?* (Policy Research Working Paper No. 1581). Washington, DC: World Bank.

Pritchett, L. (2003, August 26). Calidad y costos de la educacion: Cinco posibles piezas de un gran romecabezas. Santiago, Chile: Educarchile. Retrieved December 12, 2007, from http://www.educarchile.cl/Portal.Base/Web/VerContenido.aspx?GUID=123.456.789.000&ID=76902

Psacharopoulos, G. (1993). *Returns to investment in education : A global update* (Policy Research Working Paper No. 1067). Washington, DC: World Bank.

Rivkin, S. G., Hanushek, E. A., & Kain, J. F. (2005). Teachers, schools, and academic achievement. *Econometrica, 72*, 417–458.

Romer, P. (1990). Endogenous technological change. *Journal of Political Economy, 98*(5), S71–S102.

Rosenbaum, P. R., & Rubin, D. B. (1983). The central role of the propensity score in observational studies for causal effects. *Biometrika, 70*, 41–55.

Rothstein, R. (2004). Class and schools: *Using social, economic, and educational reform to close the Black/White achievement gap.* Washington, DC: Economic Policy Institute.

Rothstein, J. (2007). Does competition among public schools benefit students and taxpayers? Comment. *American Economic Review, 97*, 2026–2037.

Rothstein, R., & Miles, K. H. (1995). *Where's all the money gone? Changes in the level and composition of education spending.* Washington, DC: Economic Policy Institute.

Rouse, C. (1998a). Private school vouchers and student achievement: An evaluation of the Milwaukee Choice Program. *Quarterly Journal of Economics, 113*, 553–602.

Rouse, C. (1998b). Schools and student achievement: More evidence from the Milwaukee Parental Choice Program. *Federal Reserve Bank of New York Economic Policy Review, 4*, 61–76.

Schneider, B., Carnoy, M., Kilpatrick, J., Schmidt, W. H., & Shavelson, R. J., (2007). *Estimating causal effects: Using experimental and observational designs.* Washington DC: American Educational Research Association.

Schultz, T. W. (1963). *The economic value of education.* New York: Columbia University Press.

Schultz, T.W. (1975). The value of the ability to deal with disequilibria. *Journal of Economic Literature, 13*, 827–846.

Shulman, L. (1987). Knowledge and teaching: Foundations of the new reform. *Harvard Educational Review, 57*, 1–22.

Spence, A. M. (1973). Job market signaling. *Quarterly Journal of Economics, 87*(3), 355–374.

Stiglitz, J. (1975). The theory of 'screening', education, and the distribution of income. *American Economic Review, 65*, 283–300.

Task Force on Higher Education and Society. (2000, February). *Higher education in developing countries: Peril and promise.* Washington, DC: World Bank.

Todd, P., & Wolpin, K. (2003). On the specification and estimation of the production function for cognitive achievement. *Economic Journal, 113*(485), F3-F33.

Tsang, M. (2002). Comparing the costs of public and private schools in developing countries. In H. M. Levin & P. McEwan (Eds.), *Cost-effectiveness and educational policy: American Education Finance Association 2002 Yearbook* (pp. 111–136). Larchmont, NY: Eye on Education.

Welch, F. (1970). Education in production. *Journal of Political Economy 78*, 35–59.

Witte, J. F., Sterr, T. D., & Thorn, C. A. (1995). *Fifth year report: Milwaukee Parental Choice Program.* Madison, WI: Department of Political Science and the Robert M. La Follette Center for Public Affairs, University of Wisconsin.

3

The Economic Value of Education and Cognitive Skills

ERIC A. HANUSHEK
Hoover Institution of Stanford University

Education is one of the top priority policy areas of governments around the world. It is often viewed as an essential element in global economic competition. It is further taken as a force for improving the economic standing of disadvantaged populations within borders and, in the case of foreign aid, across borders. At the same time, some question whether this common model is true, as many economic outcomes appear impervious to increased schooling. This chapter reviews the evidence on the economic impact of education with a special emphasis on cognitive skills.

In terms of student performance, most developed countries are acutely aware of how their students do in comparison to students elsewhere in the world. The now frequent scores on PISA and TIMSS provide direct feedback on the performance of students.[1] But, as comparative test scores have become more plentiful, two key questions arise. First, do scores on these tests make any difference? Second, how can they be changed by governmental policies? This chapter emphasizes the first but addresses both of these questions.

Economists are now accustomed to looking at issues of skill development from the vantage point of human capital theory. The simplest notion is that individuals make investments in skills that have later payoffs in outcomes that matter. And, in this, it is commonly presumed that formal schooling is one of several important contributors to the skills of an individual and to human capital. It is not the only factor. Parents, individual abilities, and friends undoubtedly contribute. Schools nevertheless have a special place because they are most directly affected by public policies.

The human capital and investment perspective immediately makes it evident that the real issues are ones of long-run outcomes. Future incomes of individuals are related to their past investments. It is neither their income while in school nor their income in their first job. Instead, it is their income over the course of their working life. These later outcomes are the focus of this chapter.

The distribution of income in the economy similarly involves both the mixture of people in the economy and the pattern of their incomes over their lifetime. Specifically, most measures of how income and well-being vary in the population do not take into account the fact that some of the low-income people have low incomes only because they are just beginning a career. Their lifetime income is likely to be much larger as they age, gain experience, and move up in their firms and career. What is important is that any noticeable effects of the current quality of schooling on the distribution of skills and income will only be realized years in the future, when those currently in school become a significant part of the labor force. In other words, most workers in the economy were educated years and even decades in the past—and they are the ones that have the most impact on current levels of productivity and growth, if for no reason other than that they represent the larger share of active workers.

Much of the early and continuing development of empirical work on human capital concentrates on the role of school attainment, that is, the quantity of schooling. The revolution in the United States during the 20th century was universal schooling. This has spread around the world, encompassing both developed and developing countries. Quantity of schooling is easily measured, and data on years attained, both over time and across individuals, are readily available. But quantity of schooling proves to be a poor measure of the skills of individuals both within and across countries.

Today, policy concerns in most corners of the world revolve much more around issues of school quality than issues of quantity. This brings us back to PISA and TIMSS. Do standardized tests such as these identify qualities that have economic benefits? The next sections assess what we know about the payoff to cognitive skills for individuals and for nations. In short, there are very large payoffs to such skills. Individuals with more measured cognitive skills systematically do better than those with less, and nations with a more skilled population grow faster than those with a less skilled population. Again, however, because cognitive skills reflect a variety of factors, the level of cognitive skills may or may not reflect varying school quality.

School Attainment

A look at the history of the 20th century suggests that schooling has generally been a good investment, buoyed by steady increases in the demand for skilled workers.[2] Individuals have dramatically increased their own investments in education, presumably in response to these potential rewards. In the United States, at the beginning of the 20th century, only 6% of the adult population had finished high school. After World War I, high school graduation rates began to increase rapidly. But changes in education work their way slowly through the overall population. By 1940, only half of Americans aged 25 or older had completed more than eight years of school, that is, had any high school education at all. Not until 1967 did the median attainment for an adult aged 25 or over exceed high school.[3] Since 1967, however, the increase in the number of years of schooling completed by Americans has begun to level off. The young adult population, aged 25 to 29, has had stable completion rates for almost two decades. At the turn of the 21st century, over 80% of Americans over age 25 had completed high school or more.[4]

The changes in other nations have been even more dramatic. Table 3.1 shows the percentages of different age groups completing upper secondary schools for a sample of the Organization for Economic Cooperation and Development (OECD) and other countries.[5] By examining the oldest age cohort (column 5), and comparing them with each successive one, the trend of increased educational attainment can be observed. The different age groups effectively trace the normal schooling in different decades in the past, so that the changes with age show the rate of increase in schooling. While the United States has been stable since the 1960s, most of the other countries have undergone massive increases in high school completion—mirroring the historical developments in the U.S. before and immediately after World War II (Goldin, 1998).

By 2003, however, the secondary completion rates in the United States were below the average of the developed countries in the OECD. As Figure 3.1 shows, the United States actually trails many developed and developing countries in terms of expected school completion.

The benefits of education to individuals also appear clear. The average incomes of workers with a high school education remain significantly above those of the less educated, and the average income of workers with a college education now dwarf those of the high-school educated. In the United States, the rapidly increasing earnings of college-educated workers during the past two decades currently provides them with a premium of more than 70% higher earnings than a high school graduate with similar job experience.[6]

For individuals, the rate of return on investments in

TABLE 3.1

Percentage of Population Attaining Upper Secondary Education or More, by Country and Age: 1999

	Ages 25–64	Ages 25–34	Ages 35–44	Ages 45–54	Ages 55–64
OECD countries					
Australia	57	65	59	55	44
Austria[a]	74	83	78	69	59
Belgium	57	73	61	50	36
Canada	79	87	83	78	62
Czech Republic	86	93	89	85	75
Denmark	80	87	80	79	70
Finland	72	86	82	67	46
France[a]	62	76	65	57	42
Germany	81	85	85	81	73
Greece	50	71	58	42	24
Hungary	67	80	76	70	36
Iceland	56	64	59	53	40
Ireland[a]	51	67	56	41	31
Italy	42	55	50	37	21
Japan	81	93	92	79	60
Korea	66	93	72	47	28
Luxembourg	56	61	57	52	41
Mexico	20	25	22	16	9
New Zealand	74	79	77	71	60
Norway[a]	85	94	89	79	68
Poland[a]	54	62	59	53	37
Portugal	21	30	21	15	11
Spain	35	55	41	25	13
Sweden	77	87	81	74	61
Switzerland	82	89	84	79	72
Turkey	22	26	23	18	12
United Kingdom[a]	62	66	63	60	53
United States	87	88	88	88	81
OECD mean	**62**	**72**	**66**	**58**	**45**
World Education Indicators participants					
Brazil[a]	24	29	27	21	12
Chile[a]	43	55	45	35	24
Indonesia	22	33	21	15	9
Jordan	51	55	55	43	25
Malaysia[a]	35	50	35	20	10
Peru[a]	46	58	48	35	24
Philippines	44	55	45	34	24
Sri Lanka[a]	36	46	36	31	21
Thailand[a]	16	23	17	9	6
Tunisia	8	11	9	6	3
Uruguay[a]	32	39	34	28	20
Zimbabwe	29	51	19	11	7

Note: [a]Year of reference is 1998. Source: Organisation for Economic Co-operation and Development (2001).

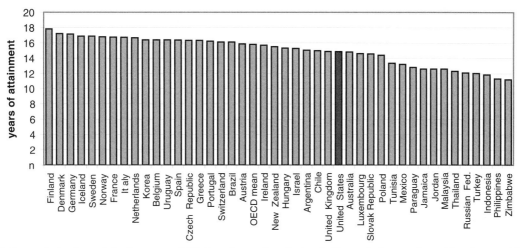

Figure 3.1 Expected school completion by country, 2003. *Data Source:* Organisation for Economic Co-operation and Development (2005).

higher education has been sufficient to offset the costs.[7] An individual can expect significant financial benefit from extended schooling, even after appropriately considering costs.[8] Individuals also gain non-financial benefits from education. For example, there is evidence that more educated people make better choices concerning health, so they tend to live longer and to have healthier lives. There is also evidence that the children of more educated parents get more out of school. They attend longer and learn more. Such benefits of schooling simply reinforce those from the labor market.[9] The common interpretation of the overall returns is that high technology economies produce large demands for skilled workers, workers who can adapt to new technologies and manage complicated production processes effectively.[10]

Society as a whole also benefits from education. National income rises directly with earnings from workers with more and better skills. The more educated are more prone to be civically involved, to vote in local and national elections, and to be better informed and a more responsible electorate.[11] Increases in the level of education are associated with reductions in crime (e.g., Lochner & Moretti, 2001).

Recent economic studies argue that education may provide economic benefits to society greater than the sum of its benefits to individuals—by providing a rich environment for innovation and scientific discovery—education can accelerate the growth rate of the economy (see, e.g., the analyses of growth by Lucas, 1988; Romer, 1990; Barro, 1991; Jorgenson & Fraumeni, 1992; Barro & Sala-i-Martin, 2004). The economics literature has focused on different ways to model the relationship between schooling and growth, but the basic idea is that human capital will directly affect the improvements in productivity and national income. Indeed, in the analysis of differences in economic growth across countries, measures of the amount of schooling—either enrollment rates or attainment—are one of the most common measures of international differences.[12]

Recent studies suggest that education is important both as an investment in human capital and in facilitating re-

search and development and the diffusion of technologies (see Benhabib & Spiegel, 2005). Extending this, Vandenbussche, Aghion, and Meghir (2006) suggest that innovation is more important than imitation for countries close to the technological frontier. As a consequence, the composition of human capital between basic and higher education may be important, with initial levels of education being more important for imitation and higher education being more important for innovation. They provide evidence from a panel of OECD countries in line with this argument, but the small number of countries makes this analysis difficult and leaves some ambiguity.

Education appears also to have helped to achieve both greater social equality and greater equity in the distribution of economic resources. Schooling was a centerpiece of the U.S. War on Poverty in the 1960s, and the benefits of improved schooling are demonstrated in comparisons of the earnings of different social and ethnic groups. Earnings by Blacks and Whites have converged noticeably since World War II, and much of this convergence is attributable to improved educational opportunities for African Americans (see Smith & Welch, 1989; Jaynes & Williams, 1989). However, that convergence slowed down noticeably in the 1980s with skill differences being cited as a prime determinant (Juhn, Murphy, & Pierce, 1993; Neal, 2006).

While there are many well-documented associations between amount of schooling—either individually or in the aggregate—and desirable economic outcomes, significant questions remain about the magnitude and interpretation of these relationships. First, the association may misstate the causal impact of changes in schooling for individuals and the aggregate. Two studies focus on how school attainment affects growth. Bils and Klenow (2000) suggest that the causal effect of higher economic growth to additional education may be at least as important as the effect of education on economic growth across countries.[13] Pritchett (2001, 2006) notes the fragility of the evidence linking changes in education to economic growth and suggests that the institutional framework of the economy may be a primary concern.[14] Second, the measurement issues, as highlighted in the next section, are significant.[15] These topics have received surprisingly limited attention and are a fertile area for future work. In many contexts, they are key to both analytical and policy concerns.

Consideration of Cognitive Skills

Most policy and analytical attention has now switched to quality dimensions of schooling. In the United States, with the slowing of individual income growth[16] and of income convergence by race,[17] improving the quality of schooling, or how much is learned for each year, has been seen as the natural policy focus. Similar concerns, albeit generally with a lag, have diffused to other developed and developing countries.

The economic effects of differences in the cognitive skills of graduates of elementary and secondary schools are now becoming clearer, particularly with regard to the performance of the aggregate economy. It is natural to focus on the knowledge base and analytical skills that are the focal point of schools. Moreover, to add concreteness to this discussion, much of it relies on information provided by standardized tests of academic achievement, ability, and general cognitive skills.

Policy concerns revolve much more around issues of achievement and cognitive skills than issues of quantity of schooling or attainment. The U.S. completion rates for high school and college have been roughly constant for a quarter of a century (see Heckman & LaFontaine, 2007). Meanwhile, the standards movement in schools has focused on what students know as they progress through schools. This trend is substantially reinforced by federal accountability legislation (the No Child Left Behind Act of 2001), which emphasizes student proficiency in basic subjects as measured by standardized achievement tests.[18]

Much of the discussion of school quality—in part related to new efforts to provide better accountability—has identified cognitive skills as the important dimension. And, while there is ongoing debate about the testing and measurement of these skills, most parents and policy makers alike accept the notion that cognitive skills are a key dimension of schooling outcomes. The question here is whether these measured skills—students' performance on standardized tests—are systematically and causally related to individuals' performance in the labor market and the economy's ability to grow. Until recently, little comprehensive data have been available to show any relationship between differences in cognitive skills and any related economic outcomes. Such data are now becoming available.

But, again, a word of caution about interpretation is important. Cognitive skills and measured test scores are not synonymous with school quality. Just as much of the discussion surrounding accountability relates to the preparation of students entering the schools and the influence of nonschool factors on assessments, cognitive skills must be recognized as broader than just school quality. Higher quality schools undoubtedly contribute to higher cognitive skills, but so do other things such as families, peers, neighborhoods, and health status. From a policy perspective, improving school quality may be the most viable way to improve cognitive skills, but it is neither the only way nor the only contributor to observed differences in skills across individuals and across countries.

Impacts of Cognitive Skills on Individual Incomes— Developed Countries   There is now considerable evidence that cognitive skills measured by test scores are directly related to individual earnings, productivity, and economic growth. A variety of researchers document that the earnings advantages to higher achievement on standardized tests are quite substantial.[19] While these analyses emphasize different aspects of individual earnings, they typically find that measured achievement has a clear impact on earnings after allowing for differences in the quantity of schooling, the experiences of workers, and other factors that might also influence earnings. They also span different time periods so that they give some support to the long term nature of skills in the U.S. economy. In simplest terms, skills measured by tests similar to those currently used in accountability systems are closely related to individual productivity and earnings.

Three recently published studies provide direct and quite consistent estimates of the impact of test performance on earnings (Mulligan, 1999; Murnane, Willett, Duhaldeborde, & Tyler, 2000; Lazear, 2003). These studies employ different nationally representative data sets that follow students after they leave schooling and enter the labor force. When scores are standardized, they suggest that one standard deviation increase in mathematics performance at the end of high schools translates into 12% higher annual earnings.[20] By way of summary, median earnings in 2001, while differing some by age, were about $30,000, implying that a one standard deviation increase in performance would boost these by $3,600 for each year of work life. The full value to individual earnings and productivity is simply the annual premium for skills integrated over the working life.

A limited number of additional studies are available for developed countries outside of the United States. McIntosh and Vignoles (2001) study wages in the United Kingdom and find strong returns to both numeracy and literacy.[21] Finnie and Meng (2002) and Green and Riddell (2003) investigate returns to cognitive skills in Canada. Both suggest that literacy has a significant return, but Finnie and Meng (2002) find an insignificant return to numeracy. This latter finding stands at odds with most other analyses that have emphasized numeracy or math skills.

There are reasons to believe that these estimates provide a lower bound on the impact of higher achievement. First, these estimates are obtained fairly early in the work career (mid-20s to early 30s), and another analysis suggests that the impact of test performance becomes larger with experience.[22] Second, these analyses concentrate on labor market experiences from the mid-1980s and into the mid-1990s, but these might not be entirely representative of the current situation because other evidence suggests that the value of skills and of schooling has grown throughout and past that period.

These problems are partially avoided by Hanushek and Zhang (2008), who analyze the situation in a set of countries. Their analysis relies on data from the International Adult Literacy Survey (IALS), which collected consistent data on basic skills of literacy and numeracy for a representative sample of the population aged 15–65 for a sample of countries between 1994 and 1998. Hanushek and Zhang (2008) estimate returns to school attainment and to literacy scores for the 13 countries where continuous measures of individual earnings are available.[23] As in the prior analyses, both school attainment and cognitive skills are seen to enter into the determination of individual incomes. With the exception of Poland, literacy scores have a consistent positive impact on earnings, lending more support to the significance of cognitive skills as a consistent measure of human capital.[24] All of the estimated returns to cognitive skills may be too low if the demands for skilled workers continues to evolve as in the past few decades. Future general improvements in productivity might lead to larger returns to skill if the recent trends of higher rewards to more skilled workers continue.[25]

Another part of the return to higher skills comes through continuation in school. There is substantial U.S. evidence that students who do better in school, either through grades or scores on standardized achievement tests, tend to go farther in school.[26] Murnane, Willett, Duhaldeborde, and Tyler (2000) separate the direct returns to measured skill from the indirect returns of more schooling and suggest that perhaps one-third to one-half of the full return to higher achievement comes from further schooling. Note also that the effect of quality improvements (measured by increases in cognitive skills of students) on school attainment incorporates concerns about dropout rates. Specifically, higher student achievement keeps students in school longer, which leads to, among other things, higher graduation rates at all levels of schooling.

This work has not, however, investigated how achievement affects the ultimate outcomes of higher education. For example, if over time lower-achieving students tend increasingly to attend college, colleges may be forced to offer more remedial courses, and the variation of what students know and can do at the end of college may expand commensurately. This possibility, suggested in *A Nation at Risk*, has not been fully investigated but may fit into considerations of the widening of the distribution of income within schooling categories.[27]

The impact of test performance on individual earnings provides a simple summary of the primary economic rewards to an individual. This estimate combines the impacts on hourly wages and on employment/hours worked. It does not include any differences in fringe benefits or nonmonetary aspects of jobs, nor does it make any allowance for aggregate changes in the labor market that might occur over time. These estimates also do not directly provide information about the source of any skill differences. As the education production function literature suggests, a variety of factors influence achievement, including family background, peers, school factors, and individual ability (Hanushek, 1979, 1986). This analysis suggests that skill improvements, regardless of their source, have strong economic effects.[28]

Impacts of Cognitive Skills on Individual Incomes— Developing Countries Questions remain about whether the clear impacts of quality in the United States and developed countries generalize to other countries, particularly developing countries. The literature on returns to cognitive skills in developing countries is restricted to a relatively limited number of countries: Ghana, Kenya, Morocco, Pakistan, South Africa, and Tanzania. Moreover, a number of studies actually employ the same basic data—albeit with different analytical approaches, but come up with somewhat different results.

Table 3.2 provides a simple summary to the quantitative estimates available for developing countries. The summary of the evidence permits a tentative conclusion that the returns to quality may be even larger in developing countries than in developed countries. This, of course, would be consistent with the range of estimates for returns to quantity of schooling (e.g., Psacharopoulos, 1994), which are frequently interpreted as indicating diminishing marginal returns to schooling.

There are some reasons for caution in interpreting the precise magnitude of estimates. First, the estimates appear to be quite sensitive to the estimation methodology itself. Both within individual studies and across studies using the same basic data, the results are quite sensitive to the techniques employed in uncovering the fundamental parameter for cognitive skills.[29] Second, the evidence on variations within developing countries is not entirely clear. For example, Jolliffe (1998) finds little impact of skills on farm income, while Behrman, Ross, and Sabot (2008) suggest an equivalence across sectors at least on theoretical grounds.

Nevertheless, the overall summary is that the available estimates of the impact of cognitive skills on outcomes suggest strong economic returns within developing countries. The substantial magnitude of the typical estimates indicates that quality concerns are very real for developing countries and that this aspect of schools simply cannot be ignored.

Impacts of Cognitive Skills on Economic Growth The relationship between measured labor force quality and economic growth is perhaps even more important than the impact of human capital and cognitive skills on individual productivity and incomes. Economic growth determines how much improvement will occur in the overall standard of living. Moreover, the education of each individual has the possibility of making others better off (in addition to the individual benefits just discussed). Specifically, a more skilled society may lead to higher rates of invention; may

TABLE 3.2
Summary of Estimated Returns to a Standard Deviation Increase in Cognitive Skills

Country	Study	Estimated effect[a]	Notes
Ghana	Glewwe (1996)	0.21**–0.3** (government) 0.14-0.17 (private)	Alternative estimation approaches yield some differences; math effects shown generally more important than reading effects, and all hold even with Raven's test for ability.
Ghana	Jolliffe (1998)	0.05–0.07*	Household income related to average math score with relatively small variation by estimation approach; effect from off-farm income with on-farm income unrelated to skills.
Ghana	Vijverberg (1999)	?	Income estimates for math and reading with nonfarm self-employment; highly variable estimates (including both positive and negative effects) but effects not generally statistically significant.
Kenya	Boissiere, Knight, and Sabot (1985); Knight and Sabot (1990)	0.19**–0.22**	Total sample estimates: small variation by primary and secondary school leavers.
Morocco	Angrist and Lavy (1997)	?	Cannot convert to standardized scores because use indexes of performance; French writing skills appear most important for earnings, but results depend on estimation approach.
Pakistan	Alderman, Behrman, Ross, and Sabot (1996)	0.12–0.28*	Variation by alternative approaches and by controls for ability and health; larger and more significant without ability and health controls.
Pakistan	Behrman, Ross, and Sabot (2008)	?	Estimates of structural model with combined scores for cognitive skill; index significant at .01 level (but cannot translate directly into estimated effect size).
South Africa	Moll (1998)	0.34**–0.48**	Depending on estimation method, varying impact of computation; comprehension (not shown) generally insignificant.
Tanzania	Boissiere, Knight, and Sabot (1985); Knight and Sabot (1990)	0.07–0.13*	Total sample estimates: smaller for primary than secondary school leavers.

*significant at .05 level; **significant at .01 level.
Note: [a]Estimates indicate proportional increase in wages from a one standard deviation increase in measured test scores.

make everyone more productive through the ability of firms to introduce new and better production methods; and may lead to more rapid introduction of new technologies. These externalities provide extra reason for being concerned about cognitive skills and the quality of schooling.

The potential effect of differences in growth rates on economic well-being is easy to see. Figure 3.2 begins with the value of gross domestic product (GDP) per capita for a medium income country in the year 2000 and shows its value in 2050 under different growth rates.[30] If it grows at 1% each year, this measure (in U.S. dollars) would increase from $5,000 to $8,000—or increasing by almost two-thirds over the period. If it were to grow at 2% per year, it would

reach $13,500 in 2050. For the United States, the numbers are also dramatic. The level of gross domestic product (GDP) per capita in 2000 was roughly $30,000 per person. Other things equal, a 1% higher growth rate would increase this to $50,000 over 50 years. Small differences in growth rates have huge implications for the income and wealth of society.

The current economic position of the United States, for example, is largely the result of its strong and steady growth over the 20th century. As previously suggested, economists have developed a variety of models and ideas to explain differences in growth rates across countries—invariably featuring the importance of human capital.[31]

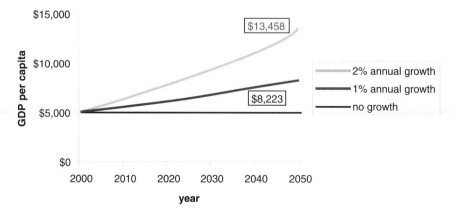

Figure 3.2 Effect of economic growth on GDP per capita (medium income country). *Source:* Author's calculations.

The empirical work supporting growth analyses has, as mentioned, largely emphasized school attainment differences across countries. Again, this is natural because, while compiling comparable data on many things for different countries is difficult, assessing quantity of schooling is more straightforward. The typical study finds that quantity of schooling is highly related to economic growth rates. But, quantity of schooling is a very crude measure of the knowledge and cognitive skills of people—particularly in an international context. A year of schooling in Egypt is not the same as a year of schooling in France. Additionally, formal schooling is just one element of cognitive skills; other factors may also impact cognitive skills.

Hanushek and Kimko (2000) go beyond simple quantity of schooling and delve into the role of cognitive skills in growth.[32] They incorporate the information about international differences in mathematics and science knowledge that has been developed through testing over the past four decades. They find a remarkable impact of differences in school quality on economic growth.

The international comparisons of quality come from piecing together results of a series of tests administered over the past four decades. In 1963 and 1964, the International Association for the Evaluation of Educational Achievement (IEA) administered the first of a series of mathematics tests to a voluntary group of countries. These initial tests suffered from a number of problems, but they did prove the feasibility of such testing and set in motion a process to expand and improve on the undertaking.[33]

Subsequent testing, sponsored by the IEA and the OECD, has included both math and science and has expanded on the group of countries that have been tested. In each, the general model has been to develop a common assessment instrument for different age groups of students and to work at obtaining a representative group of students taking the tests. An easy summary of the participating countries and their test performance is found in Figure 3.3. This figure records performance aggregated across the age groups and subject area of the various tests and scaled to a common test mean of 500.[34]

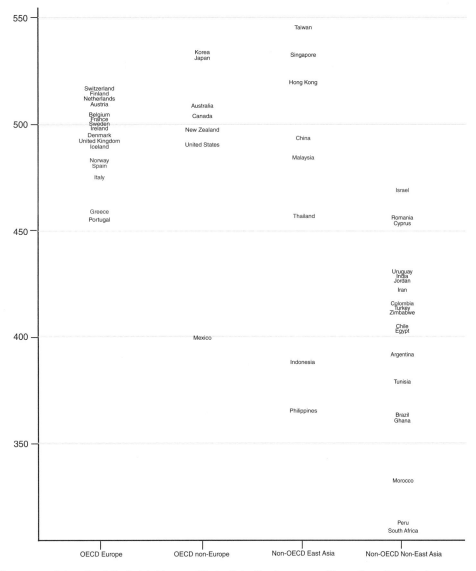

Figure 3.3 Performance on International Student Achievement Tests. *Note:* Simple average of the mathematics and science scores over all available international tests, using the re-scaled data by Hanushek and Wössmann (in preparation) that puts performance at different international tests on a common scale.

The United States and the United Kingdom are the only countries to participate in all 13 of the past testing opportunities, but participation in one or more of the tests has expanded quite broadly as can be seen by the figure. This figure, and the subsequent analysis of the data, aggregate scores across any testing experience. There is some movement across time of country performance on the tests, but for the one country that can be checked—the United States—the pattern on the international tests is consistent with other data. The National Assessment of Educational Progress (NAEP) in the United States is designed to follow performance of U.S. students for different subjects and ages. The movement of scores on NAEP follows the same rough pattern as U.S. scores on the individual international tests.[35]

The Hanushek and Kimko (2000) analysis of economic growth is very straightforward. They combine all of the available earlier test scores into a single composite measure of quality and consider statistical models that explain differences in growth rates across nations during the period 1960 to 1990. The basic statistical models, which include the initial level of income, the quantity of schooling, and population growth rates, explain three-fourths of the variation in economic growth across countries.

The quality of the labor force as measured by math and science scores is extremely important. One standard deviation difference on test performance is related to 1% difference in annual growth rates of gross domestic product (GDP) per capita.[36]

This effect of cognitive skills, while possibly sounding small, is actually very large and significant. Because the added growth compounds, it leads to powerful effects on national income and on societal well-being. One needs only to return to the calculations presented in Figure 3.2 to understand the impact of such skill-based improvements in economic growth.

This analysis of cognitive skills and growth has been confirmed and extended by a variety of authors. Another early contribution, by Lee and Lee (1995), found an effect size similar to Hanushek and Kimko (2000) using data from the 1970–71 First International Science Study on the participating 17 countries; also leaving quantitative measures of education with no significant effect on growth. Using a more encompassing set of international tests, Barro (2001) also finds that, while both the quantity of schooling and test scores matter for economic growth, measured cognitive skills are much more important. Employing the measure of cognitive skills developed by Hanushek and Kimko (2000) in a development accounting framework, Woessmann (2002, 2003) finds that the share of cross-country variation in levels of economic development attributable to international differences in human capital rises dramatically when cognitive skills are taken into account. Building on Gundlach, Rudman, and Woessmann (2002), this work analyzes output per worker in 132 countries in 1990. The variation that can be attributed to international differences in human capital rises from 21% to 45% once the international achievement measures are taken into account, and to over 60% in samples with reasonable data quality.

Extensions of the measure of Hanushek and Kimko (2000) and its imputation in Woessmann (2003) are also used in the cross-country growth regressions by Bosworth and Collins (2003) and in the cross-country industry-level analysis by Ciccone and Papaioannou (2005). Both also find that measured cognitive skills strongly dominate any effect of educational quantity on growth.[37] Coulombe, Tremblay, and Marchand (2004) and Coulombe and Tremblay (2006) use test-score data from the International Adult Literacy Survey in a panel of 14 OECD countries, confirming the result that the test-score measure outperforms quantitative measures of education.

Jamison, Jamison, and Hanushek (2007) further extend the Hanushek and Kimko (2000) framework. They replicate and strengthen the previous results by using test data from a larger number of countries, controlling for a larger number of potentially confounding variables, and extending the time period of the analysis. Using the panel structure of their growth data, they suggest that cognitive skills seem to improve income levels mainly though speeding up technological progress, rather than shifting the level of the production function or increasing the impact of an additional year of schooling.

Finally, the newest estimates of the impact of cognitive skills on economic growth are found in Hanushek and Woessmann (2008). They expand the number of countries with tests from 31 to 50. They also add the decade of the 1990s, which is important because of the potential impacts of economic disruptions during that period. Interestingly, the results from this extension are very similar to those from the earlier period. In both qualitative and quantitative terms, the impacts of cognitive skills over the longer period of time point to the same strong influences on differences in growth. Moreover, the results are very similar in developed and developing countries—all countries seem to benefit from having a well-educated population.

While Hanushek and Woessmann (2008) confirmed that the results would apply to developing countries, they did find that the size of the impact of cognitive skills depends on whether a nation's economy is open to outside trade and other external influences. For greatest positive economic impact, the more open the economy, the more important it is that a country's students are acquiring high levels of cognitive skills. This analysis confirms the arguments by Pritchett (2006) that the institutional framework is very important in determining the impact of schooling and cognitive skills.

Importance of Cognitive Skills The frequent focus of governmental programs has been increasing school attainment and expanding on the years of schooling of the population. The previous discussion, however, highlights the central importance of cognitive skills. While years of schooling attainment are important, that holds only if the student outcomes in terms of skill are maintained. The

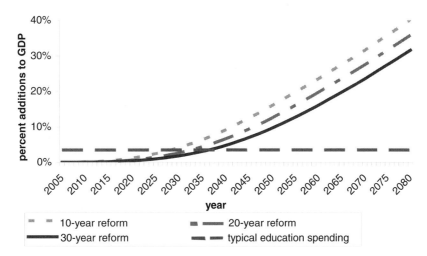

Figure 3.4 Improved GDP with moderately strong knowledge improvement. *Source:* Author's calculations.

impact of improved cognitive skills can be calculated from the considerations of how quality affects growth rates for economies. Consider the effects of beginning a successful school improvement program in 2005. Of course, school reform takes time. And, even if successful, it takes some time before the school graduates work their way into the labor force and thus some time before the impact will be felt.

Figure 3.4 illustrates the impact that reform could be expected to have over time if it is successful at achieving moderately strong knowledge improvement (corresponding to a 0.5 standard deviation increase in test score achievement, or cognitive skills).[38] The curves sketch out the path of GDP improvement that would occur with a reform plan that reaches its improvement goal within 10, 20, or 30 years.[39] An increase in performance of this magnitude (one-half of a standard deviation) roughly corresponds to the goals set out by the U.S. governors in 1989—that is, making the United States first in the world in math and science by 2000. (Note that this pledge of the governors also corresponded to a very fast reform, making it similar to the 10 years portion of Figure 3.4.) Of course, the United States did not meet these ambitious goals, but the figure gives some indication of what meeting those goals might have meant for the country.[40] An increase of this magnitude also corresponds to bringing a number of developing countries—for example, Mexico or Brazil—halfway to the average scores in Europe.

The impact of improvements in cognitive scores is vividly shown. Consider just the slow improvement of schools over a 30-year period. In 2040, the GDP would be almost 4% higher than projected without the schooling reforms. Of course, faster reforms would yield even greater gains in GDP. This magnitude of gain would cover total school spending in most countries of the world. In other words, the projected gains in GDP holding other things constant would be greater than our current expenditure on schooling.

Causality One common concern in analyses such as these is that schooling or cognitive skills might not be the actual cause of growth but, in fact, may just reflect other attributes

of the economy that are beneficial to growth.[41] For example, as seen in Figure 3.3, the East Asian countries consistently score very highly on the international tests, and they also had extraordinarily high growth over the 1960–2000 period. It may be that other aspects of these East Asian economies have driven their growth and that the statistical analysis of labor force quality simply is picking out these countries. But in fact, even if the East Asian countries are excluded from the analysis, a strong—albeit slightly smaller—relationship is still observed with test performance (see Hanushek & Kimko, 2000; Hanushek & Woessmann, 2008). This test of sensitivity of the results seems to reflect a basic importance of school quality, a factor that contributes also to the observed growth of East Asian countries.

Another concern might be that other factors that affect growth, such as efficient market organizations, are also associated with efficient and productive schools—so that, again, the test measures are really a proxy for other attributes of the country. In order to investigate this, we concentrate on immigrants to the United States who received their education in their home countries. Hanushek and Kimko (2000) find that immigrants who were schooled in countries that have higher scores on the international math and science examinations earn more in the United States. This analysis makes allowance for any differences in school attainment, labor market experience, or being native English-language speakers. In other words, skill differences as measured by the international tests are clearly rewarded in the United States labor market, reinforcing the validity of the tests as a measure of individual skills and productivity.

Finally, the observed relationships could simply reflect reverse causality, that is, that countries that are growing rapidly have the resources necessary to improve their schools and that better student performance is the result of growth, not the cause of growth. As a simple test of this, Hanushek and Kimko (2000) investigated whether the international math and science test scores were systematically related to the resources devoted to the schools in the years prior to the tests. They were not. If anything, they found relatively better performance in those countries spending less on their schools. This finding is reinforced by Hanushek and Woessmann (2006), Hanushek (1995, 2003a), and Woessmann (2005, 2007).

In sum, the relationship between math and science skills on the one hand and productivity and growth on the other comes through clearly when investigated in a systematic manner across countries. This finding underscores the importance of policies that can increase cognitive skills.

Why Has U.S. Growth been so Strong?

Figure 3.3 on international test score differences introduces an important issue of interpretation. Namely, that the United States has not been truly competitive on an international level in terms of tests. It has scored below the median of countries taking the various tests. Moreover, this figure—which combines scores across different age groups—disguises the fact that performance on tests of U.S. students is much stronger at young ages but falls off dramatically at the end of high school (Hanushek, 2003b).

Earlier, we introduced the discussion of the importance of growth by recounting America's successful economic growth during the 20th century. Yet, looking at Figure 3.3, we see that the United States has been, at best, mediocre in mathematics and science ability. Regardless of the set of countries taking the test, the United States has performed in the middle of the pack or below. Some people find this anomalous: How could math and science ability be important in light of the strong U.S. growth over a long period of time?[42]

The answer is that quality of the labor force and the level of cognitive skills are just one component of the economy that enters into the determination of growth. A variety of factors clearly contribute, and these factors work to overcome any deficits in quality. These other factors may also be necessary for growth. In other words, simply providing more or higher-quality schooling may yield little in the way of economic growth in the absence of other elements, such as the appropriate market, legal, and governmental institutions to support a functioning modern economy.[43] Past experiences investing in less developed countries that lack these institutional features demonstrate that schooling is not itself an entirely sufficient engine of growth.

Indeed, some have questioned the precise role of schooling in growth. Easterly (2001), for example, notes that education without other facilitating factors such as functioning institutions for markets and legal systems, may not have much impact. He argues that World Bank investments in schooling for less-developed countries that do not ensure that the other attributes of modern economies are in place have been quite unproductive.

It is useful to describe some of the other contributing factors to U.S. growth. This is done in part to understand more fully the character of economic growth, but more importantly to highlight some important related issues that are central to thinking about human capital policies.

Economic Structure Almost certainly the most important factor sustaining the growth of the U.S. economy is the openness and fluidity of its markets. The United States maintains generally freer labor and product markets than most countries in the world. The government generally has less regulation on firms (both in terms of labor regulations and in terms of overall production), and trade unions are less extensive than those in many other countries. Even broader, the United States has less intrusion of government in the operation of the economy—not only less regulation but also lower tax rates and minimal government production through nationalized industries. These factors encourage investment, permit the rapid development of new products and activities by firms, and allow U.S. workers to adjust to new opportunities. While identifying the precise importance of these factors is difficult, a variety of analyses suggest that such market differences could be very important explanations for differences in growth rates.[44]

Substitution of Quantity for Quality Over the 20th century, the expansion of the education system in the United States outpaced that around the world. The United States pushed to open secondary schools to all citizens (Goldin, 1998; Goldin & Katz, 2008). With this came also a move to expand higher education with the development of land grant universities, the G.I. bill, and direct grants and loans to students. In comparison with other nations of the world, the U.S. labor force has been better educated, even after allowing for the lesser achievement of its graduates. In other words, more schooling with less learning each year has yielded more human capital than found in other nations that have less schooling but learn more in each of those years.

This historical approach, however, has reached its limits for the United States. Other developed and developing nations have rapidly expanded their schooling systems, and many now surpass the United States (see Figure 3.1 and Table 3.1). The past advantage of the United States in amount of school completed has gone away as other nations have discovered the importance of schooling. Thus, going into the future, the United States appears unlikely to continue dominating others in human capital unless it can improve on the cognitive skills dimension.

Note, however, that this story about U.S. school quality does not generalize well to developing countries—countries that are often not close in any quality dimension. Indeed, as discussed below and as argued in Hanushek (1995) and Hanushek and Woessmann (2006), it appears to be a considerable mistake for developing countries to expand quantity or access to schools while ignoring quality, or what is being learned. Indeed there is an argument that improving quality would actually make it easier to expand access by reducing repetition and other counterproductive aspects of schools (see Harbison & Hanushek, 1992; Hanushek, Lavy, & Hitomi, 2008).

Quality of U.S. Colleges The analysis of growth rates across countries emphasizes quality of the elementary and secondary schools of the United States. It did not include any measures of the quality of U.S. colleges. By most evaluations, U.S. colleges and universities rank at the very top in the world. Few broad measurements of quality of colleges across countries exist.[45] However, there is indirect evidence. Foreign students by all accounts are not tempted to emigrate to the United States to attend elementary and secondary schools—except perhaps if they see this as a way of gaining entry into the country. They do emigrate in large numbers to attend U.S. colleges and universities. They even tend to pay full, unsubsidized tuitions at U.S. colleges, something that few American citizens do.

A number of the models of economic growth in fact emphasize the importance of scientists and engineers as a key ingredient to growth (e.g., Romer, 1990). By these views, the technically trained college students who contribute to invention and to development of new products provide a special element to the growth equation. Here, again, the United States appears to have the best programs. If this view is correct, U.S. higher education may continue to provide a noticeable advantage over other countries. But the raw material for U.S. colleges is the graduates of our elementary and secondary schools. As has been frequently noted, the lack of preparation of our students leads to extensive remedial education at the postsecondary level, detracting from the ability of colleges and universities to be most effective. Moreover, pre-college preparation is likely an important factor driving the increased proportions of foreign-born students graduating from the science and engineering programs of U.S. colleges and universities (Committee on Science, 2005).

Improving Cognitive Skills

The value of improving school quality and cognitive skills has been intuitively grasped by policy makers around the world. Unfortunately, school reforms or other policies have often not achieved their objectives. Much of school policy is traditionally thought of as an exercise in selecting and ensuring that the optimal set of resources, however defined, is available. Matched with this policy perspective has been a line of research considering the relationship between resource use and student performance. If the effectiveness of different resources or combinations of resources were known, it would be straightforward to define an optimal set of resources. Moreover, we could often decide about policies that would move us toward such an optimal set of resources. Unfortunately, this eludes us.

Schools in the United States have been the focus of extensive research. Both aggregate data about performance of schools over time and more detailed school and classroom data point to a simple conclusion: There is a lack of any consistent or systematic effect of resources on student achievement. While controversial, partly because of the conflict with existing school policies, the evidence is very extensive (Hanushek, 2003a).[46] Existing statistical analyses in less developed countries have shown a similar

inconsistency of estimated resource effects as that found in the United States (Hanushek, 1995; Glewwe & Kremer, 2006). The evidence on resources is remarkably consistent across countries, both developed and developing. Had there been distinctly different results for some subsets of countries, issues of what kinds of generalizations were possible would naturally arise. Such conflicts do not appear particularly important.

In sum, a wide range of analyses indicate that overall resource policies have not led to discernible improvements in student performance. It is important to understand what is and is not implied by this conclusion. First, it does not mean that money and resources *never* matter. There clearly are situations where small classes or added resources have an impact. It is just that no good description of when and where these situations occur is available, so that broad resource policies such as those legislated from central governments may hit some good uses but also hit bad uses that generally lead to offsetting outcomes. Second, this statement does not mean that money and resources *cannot* matter. Instead, as described below, altered sets of incentives could dramatically improve the use of resources.

Many countries have, of course, attempted to improve their schools. While some have succeeded, many have not. One explanation for past failure is simply that insufficient attention has been paid to teacher quality (see Beteille & Loeb, this volume). By many accounts, the quality of teachers is the key element to improving student performance. The research evidence also suggests that many of the policies that have been pursued around the world have not been very productive. Specifically, the chosen policies of individual countries may have led to changes in measured aspects of teachers such as degrees or teacher qualifications, but they have not tended to improve the quality of teachers—at least when quality is identified by student performance.[47]

Rivkin, Hanushek, and Kain (2005) describe estimates of differences in teacher quality on an output basis.[48] Specifically, the concern is identifying good and bad teachers on the basis of their performance in obtaining gains in student achievement.[49] An important element of that work is distinguishing the effects of teachers from the selection of schools by teachers and students and the matching of teachers and students in the classroom. In particular, highly motivated parents search out schools that they think are good, and they attempt to place their children in classrooms where they think the teacher is particularly able. Teachers follow a similar selection process (Hanushek, Kain, & Rivkin, 2004a, 2004b; Boyd, Lankford, Loeb, & Wyckoff, 2005). Thus, from an analytical viewpoint, it is difficult to sort out the quality of the teacher from the quality of the students that she has in her classroom. In their analysis of teacher performance, Rivkin et al. (2005) go to great lengths to avoid contamination from any such selection and matching of students and teachers.

Estimates of the differences in annual achievement growth between an average and a good teacher are large.

Within one academic year, a good teacher can move a typical student up at least four percentiles in the overall distribution (equal to a change of 0.12 standard deviations of student achievement). From this, it is clear that having a series of good teachers can dramatically affect the achievement of any student. In fact, a series of good teachers can erase the deficits associated with poor preparation for school.

The difficulty, as pointed out in the preceding discussion, is that hiring good teachers is not easily done. Teaching ability is not closely related to training or experience. Moreover, common salary systems do not target particularly high quality teachers. From a policy viewpoint the primary objective should be improving the overall quality of the teaching force. If one were simply to redistribute existing teachers, the overall policy goals would not be achieved. Moreover, the historical reforms in many countries of the world have failed to improve teacher quality by significant amounts that are reflected in student outcomes.

Conclusions

For most of the 20th century, the international debate over the economic consequences of schooling concentrated on the amount of school attained or, simply, the quantity of schooling of the population. Policy deliberations focused on school completion rates, on the proportion of the population attending postsecondary schooling, and the like. Analyses of the benefits of schooling were most concerned with the effects of quantity of schooling—whether benefits are seen in terms of individual incomes or social benefits like the improved voting participation of citizens.

These discussions have now moved to consider more quality dimensions of schooling and of individual skills. This policy attention to student achievement is most easily seen through attention to test-based accountability. The recent economic analysis into impacts of human capital has underscored the correctness of this policy focus. Cognitive skills, as measured by commonly available achievement scores, have a clear and powerful impact on individual earnings and on aggregate outcomes through altering national growth rates.

In making decisions about schools, countries always face limited budgets. If there are the commonly accepted two objectives of expanding access and of improving quality, these objectives will conflict because they must compete for the same budget. Thus, by this standard policy makers are faced with a particularly unpleasant dilemma: choose between broad availability of schools and good schools.

An alternative view, while apparently different, is actually quite closely related. Analyses of labor market implications and the rate of return to schooling in developing countries suggest strongly that schooling is a very good investment. A year of schooling typically shows a 25%–30% real rate of return. Such a return often looks noticeably better than other investment alternatives. At the same time, school completion rates in low-income countries are very low. These two facts do not go together. If it is such a high rate of return activity, why are people not taking advantage of those high returns?

Work on the role of cognitive skills has something to say about both elements of education policy, since the historic concentration on school attainment ignores variations in cognitive skills and in the value-added of schools. First, the simple trade-off story about access and school quality is very misleading, if not wrong in important ways. In fact, in many circumstances, there may not really be the trade-off suggested, but quality may support added attainment. Second, the unifying idea is that school quality may be an important explanation for the "strange" investment behavior that does not take advantage of the available high returns, because those not taking advantage of the high returns may in fact have low skills.

School quality is directly related to decisions about attending schools and to promotion through schools. High quality schools raise student achievement and speed students through primary (and perhaps secondary) schools, thus conserving on costs. Additionally, students respond to school quality in deciding whether or not to drop out of school. They tend to stay in high quality schools and drop out of low quality schools.[50]

Both of these mechanisms indicate a direct relationship between the quantity of schooling attained and the quality of that schooling. Thus, studies of the rate of return to schooling which only consider quantity of schooling produce a misleading estimate of the potential gains. Estimation of the rate of return to schooling that does not account for quality differences will systematically overstate the productivity gains that are associated with additional years of schooling, because the estimates will include quality differences that are correlated with quantity.

Notes

1. The Programme for International Student Assessment (PISA) has been conducted in 2000, 2003, and 2006; retrieved January 12, 2008, from http://www.oecd.org/pages/0,2966,en_32252351_32235731_1_1_1_1_1,00.html. TIMSS is the Trends in International Mathematics and Science Study (formerly the Third International Mathematics and Science Study) and is a continuation of international testing begun in the 1960s; retrieved January 12, 2008, http://timss.bc.edu/

2. A history of changing demands for skills along with changes in schooling can be found in Goldin and Katz (2008).

3. See U.S. Bureau of the Census (1975, 2000) and Goldin (1998).

4. The data have themselves been questioned. Different sources provide very different views about graduation rates overall and by subgroup. Heckman and LaFontaine (2007) show how the various estimates of graduation rates can be reconciled by allowing, among other things, for changes in the attainment of GEDs.

5. A comprehensive comparison of schooling across nations can be found in Barro and Lee (2001).

6. More detail on the patterns of earnings can be found in Murphy and Welch (1989, 1992), Kosters (1991), Pierce and Welch (1996), and Deere (2001). McMahon (1991) reports slightly lower private rates of return for high school completion than for college completion, although they remain substantial. These calculations all rely on just salary differentials, and greater equality in the provision of fringe benefits may act to compress the differences for total compensation.

However, no analysis of schooling returns in terms of total compensation is available.

7. Costs and benefits generally occur at different times with costs occurring early in life and benefits accruing later. Thus, in order to compare them, it is necessary to discount all costs and benefits back to a common time. For this reason, the simple sum of costs or of future earnings does not give an accurate picture of the economic value of different investments.

8. While most economists think of schooling as involving the production of human capital in individuals, the screening or signaling perspective is a clear alternative (e.g., Spence, 1973; Wolpin, 1977; Weiss, 1995). The screening model in the extreme suggests that individuals begin schooling with differing abilities and that schooling merely allows employers to identify those with more ability. From the individual's viewpoint, it does not matter what the source of earnings enhancement is, be it production by schools or screening. The individual will be equally induced to make schooling investments based on the comparison of returns and costs. The two may, however, yield quite different incentives to governments to invest, because signaling may lead to different social and private returns to schooling. As a general matter, these models are not identified with just labor market outcome data. A variety of specialized tests under different maintained assumptions about individual motivations and firm behavior has been conducted but has not provided clear support for screening. These tests include looking for "sheepskin effects," particularly high returns to completing given institutional levels, as in Layard and Psacharopoulos (1974). Some support of screening does come from analysis of incentives to complete high school when there are fewer college graduates Bedard (2001). Tyler, Murnane, and Willett (2000) also interpret the earnings outcomes of GED receipt as reflecting signaling. See Riley (2001) for a review of general theoretical and empirical work. The key difficulty with these tests, however, remains that they focus on labor market outcomes, where the private returns to schooling are generally expected to exist independent of the underlying causal mechanism. The analysis below concentrates importantly on outcomes that relate directly to the schooling process (the point where the two models are hypothesized to differ significantly).

9. See, for example, Michael (1982); Haveman and Wolfe (1984); Wolfe and Zuvekas (1995); and Leibowitz (1974). Many factors are unclear, however, because of questions of causality; see, for example, Farrell and Fuchs (1982).

10. Formal models with this character are developed in Nelson and Phelps (1966) and Welch (1970) and summarized in the ideas of dealing with disequilibrium in Schultz (1975).

11. The pattern of U.S. voting over time can be found in Stanley and Niemi (2000). An analysis of the partial effects of educational attainment (which are positive in the face of overall declines in voter turnout over time) is presented in Teixeira (1992).

12. The exact form of the growth relationship is open to dispute. Much of the empirical analysis relates growth to the aggregate level of education in the economy. These so-called endogenous growth models imply that the overall level of schooling in society affects the earnings ability and productivity of the individual, creating an externality where individuals both gain from the investment and affect the earnings of others. In the terminology of economists, this would be called an "externality," because the actions of one person have direct impacts on others. Here, when one person becomes more educated, the value of everybody else's schooling increases. Estimation by Acemoglu and Angrist (2000), however, questions the presence of such an externality, at least at the U.S. state level.

13. See also the perspectives in Mankiw, Romer, and Weil (1992) and Benhabib and Spiegel (1994). At the individual level, see Card (1999).

14. Much of these arguments relates more directly to school attainment, as opposed to cognitive skills that is the subject of the subsequent discussion; see Hanushek and Woessmann (2006).

15. A third topic is whether schooling creates an externality that raises the value of schooling for others. In general externalities have been notoriously elusive and difficult to estimate convincingly, and education proves to be no exception.

16. See, for example, Levy and Murnane (1992) and Welch (1999) for reviews and interpretation of distributional patterns. An updated evaluation is found in Deere and Vesovic (2006).

17. Discussion of distributional issues including earnings differences by race can be found in Smith and Welch (1989); O'Neill (1990); Card and Krueger (1992); Levy and Murnane (1992); Bound and Freeman (1992); Boozer, Krueger, and Wolkon (1992); Juhn, Murphy, and Pierce (1993); Hauser (1993); Kane (1994); Grogger (1996); Welch (1999); and Deere (2001). Reviews of general trends plus Black-White changes can be found in Deere and Vesovic (2006) and Neal (2006).

18. For a discussion and analysis of accountability systems, see Hanushek and Raymond (2005) and Figlio and Ladd (2007).

19. These results are derived from different specific approaches, but the basic underlying analysis involves estimating a standard "Mincer" earnings function and adding a measure of individual cognitive skills. This approach relates the logarithm of earnings to years of schooling, experience, and other factors that might yield individual earnings differences. The clearest analyses are found in the following references (which are analyzed in Hanushek, 2002). See Bishop (1989, 1991); O'Neill (1990); Grogger and Eide (1993); Blackburn and Neumark (1993, 1995); Murnane, Willett, and Levy (1995); Neal and Johnson (1996); Mulligan (1999); Murnane, Willett, Duhaldeborde, and Tyler (2000); Altonji and Pierret (2001); Murnane, Willett, Braatz, and Duhaldeborde (2001); Lazear (2003); and Rose (2006).

20. Murnane, Willett, Duhaldeborde, and Tyler (2000) provide evidence from the High School and Beyond and the National Longitudinal Survey of the High School Class of 1972. Their estimates suggest some variation with males obtaining a 15% increase and females a 10% increase per standard deviation of test performance. Lazear (2003), relying on a somewhat younger sample from NELS:88, provides a single estimate of 12%. These estimates are also very close to those in Mulligan (1999), who finds 11% for the normalized AFQT score in the NLSY data. By way of comparison, estimates of the value of an additional year of school attainment are typically 7%–10%, suggesting that the economic value of an additional year of schooling is equivalent to 0.6 to 0.8 standard deviations of test scores. For policy purposes, the right comparison would reflect the costs of the alternatives. While these comparisons are not currently feasible, we return to this discussion below.

21. Because they look at discrete levels of skills, it is difficult to compare the quantitative magnitudes directly to the U.S. work.

22. Altonji and Pierret (2001) find that the impact of achievement grows with experience, because the employer has a chance to observe the performance of workers.

23. An element of the analysis in Hanushek and Zhang (2008) is adjusting the years of schooling obtained in different time periods to be equivalent in quality terms. This procedure involves equating the marginal impact of a year of schooling on literacy scores across time (after allowing for other influences on literacy scores). All references to school attainment here refer to their quality-adjusted school attainment.

24. Analysis by Altonji and Pierret (2001) can reconcile the difference in quantitative magnitudes of the impact of cognitive skills on U.S. earnings. Hanushek and Zhang (2008) find that the impact of literacy scores rises from that for the youngest workers. These findings are consistent with Altonji and Pierret, who argue that the impact of cognitive skills will become greater as employers have more time to observe individual skills.

25. These estimates of labor market returns typically compare workers of different ages at one point in time to obtain an estimate of how earnings will change for any individual. If, however, productivity improvements occur in the economy, these will tend to raise the earnings of individuals over time. In the past few decades, these increases have favored the more educated and skilled, thus increasing the return to skill. If these trends continue, the impact of

improvements in student skills are likely to rise over the work life instead of being constant as portrayed here. On the other hand, such skill-biased change has not always been the case, and technology could push returns in the opposite direction. See the longer historical look of Goldin and Katz (2008).

26. See, for example, Dugan (1976) and Manski and Wise (1983). Rivkin (1995) finds that variations in test scores capture a considerable proportion of the systematic variation in high school completion and in college continuation, so that test score differences can fully explain Black-White differences in schooling. Bishop (1991) and Hanushek, Rivkin, and Taylor (1996), in considering the factors that influence school attainment, find that individual achievement scores are highly correlated with continued school attendance. Neal and Johnson (1996) in part use the impact of achievement differences of Blacks and Whites on school attainment to explain racial differences in incomes. Behrman, Kletzer, McPherson, and Schapiro (1998) find strong achievement effects on both continuation into college and quality of college; moreover, the effects are larger when proper account is taken of the various determinants of achievement. Hanushek and Pace (1995) find that college completion is significantly related to higher test scores at the end of high school.

27. This logic is most clear for the college graduates. For high school graduates, the movement into the college category could leave the high school group more homogeneous and could work in the opposite direction. Empirical evidence on income inequality within schooling groups suggests that inequality has increased over time for both college and high school groups, but the increase for college is larger (Murnane, Willett, & Levy, 1995). This analysis also suggests that increased demand for skills is one of the elements in this growing inequality.

28. Note that this does take into account recent work that has introduced the possibility that noncognitive skills also enter into economic outcomes. Because evidence suggests that cognitive and noncognitive skills are correlated and are both affected by school factors, our evidence is interpreted as the effects of cognitive skills including their correlated components with noncognitive skills. See Bowles, Gintis, and Osborne (2001); Heckman, Stixrud, and Urzua (2006); and Cunha, Heckman, Lochner, and Masterov (2006). Hanushek and Woessmann (2008) integrate noncognitive skills into the interpretation of general models such as above and show how this affects the interpretation of the parameter on school attainment and other estimates.

29. The sensitivity to estimation approach is not always the case (see, e.g., Jolliffe, 1998). A critique and interpretation of the alternative approaches within a number of these studies can be found in Glewwe (2002).

30. These calculations indicate how changing the growth, holding other things equal, affects incomes. Specifically, if other processes also influence growth, these calculations show the *added* effect from an increase in growth rates.

31. Barro and Sala-i-Martin (2004) review recent analyses and the range of factors that are included.

32. Barro and Lee (2001) provide an analysis of qualitative differences that also includes literacy.

33. The problems included issues of developing an equivalent test across countries with different school structure, curricula, and language; issues of selectivity of the tested populations; and issues of selectivity of the nations that participated. The first tests did not document or even address these issues in any depth.

34. For a description of past testing, see Hanushek and Woessmann (2006).

35. See Hanushek and Woessmann (2006) for a description of how tests are equated across time.

36. The details of this work can be found in Hanushek and Kimko (2000) and Hanushek and Woessmann (2008). Importantly, adding other factors potentially related to growth, including aspects of international trade, private and public investment, and political instability, leaves the effects of labor force quality unchanged.

37. Bosworth and Collins (2003) cannot distinguish the effect of cognitive skills from the effect of quality of government institutions. The analysis of Hanushek and Woessman (2008) shows, however, that they can be separated when we use our new measure of cognitive skills that also extends the country sample by several additional data points on international tests scores.

38. These calculations are calibrated to scores on international mathematics and science exams. The "moderately strong" improvement implies an increase in scores by 0.5 standard deviations across the international comparisons. This is equivalent of bringing a country at the 31st percentile of performance up to the median for the world.

39. For the calibration, policies are assumed to begin in 2005—so that a 20-year reform would be complete in 2025. The actual reform policy is presumed to operate linearly such that, for example, a 20-year reform that ultimately yielded one-half standard deviation higher achievement would see the performance of graduates increasing by 0.025 standard deviations each year over the period. It is assumed that the impact on the economy is proportional to the average achievement levels of prime age workers. Finally, for this exercise we project the growth impact according to the basic achievement model that also includes the independent impact of economic institutions.

40. A direct discussion of these goals and the implications is found in Hanushek, Jamison, Jamison, and Woessmann (2008).

41. This issue, in terms of school attainment, was forcefully raised by Bils and Klenow (2000).

42. In fact, Gerald Bracey (2002) and other commentators have used evidence about U.S. economic performance as rebuttal of the argument that there is any real need to improve the schools. For example, Bracey argues that people calling for reform are simply wrong: "None of these fine gentlemen provided any data on the relationship between the economy's health and the performance of schools. Our long economic boom suggests there isn't one—or that our schools are better than the critics claim."

43. See the analysis in Hanushek and Woessmann (2008).

44. See, for example, Krueger (1974), World Bank (1993), and Parente and Prescott (1994, 1999).

45. In the 2007 academic rankings of the world's research universities by the Institute of Higher Education, Shanghai Jiao Tong University, the United States had 17 of the top 20 universities and 54 of the top 99 (see http://ed.sjtu.edu.cn/rank/2007/ARWU2007TOP500list.htm, accessed January 12, 2008). In a 2007 professional ranking by the Ecole des mines de Paris based on graduates who were CEOs at Global Fortune 500 countries, U.S. institutions had 10 of the top 22 places and 24 of the top 59 places (see http://www.ensmp.fr/Actualites/PR/EMP-ranking.html, accessed January 12, 2008). These remain, however, narrow measures of the quality of the overall higher education sector.

46. For more on the historical debates about resources, see Hedges, Laine, and Greenwald (1994) and Hanushek (1994). The discussion of specialized topics such as class size reduction can be found in Krueger (1999), Hanushek (1999), and Mishel and Rothstein (2002); for more on teacher salaries, see Loeb and Page (2000).

47. For a review of existing U.S. literature, see Hanushek and Rivkin (2004, 2006). Those papers describe various attempts to estimate the impact of teacher quality on student achievement. Similar studies are currently much less available in other countries.

48. A number of other analyses similarly pursue this approach. See Hanushek, Kain, O'Brien, and Rivkin (2005), and Hanushek and Rivkin (2006).

49. For other analyses of this sort, see among others Hanushek (1971, 1992), Murnane (1975), Armor et al. (1976), Murnane and Phillips (1981), Aaronson, Barrow, and Sander (2007), Rockoff (2004), Boyd, Grossman, Lankford, Loeb, and Wyckoff (2006), and Kane, Rockoff, and Staiger (2006).

50. In Egyptian schools, Hanushek, Lavy, and Hitomi (2008) find that students tend to dropout much more frequently from low value-added schools as compared to high value-added schools. Similarly, in U.S. charter schools student exit rates are significantly higher for

low value-added schools as compared to high value-added schools (Hanushek, Kain, Rivkin, & Branch, 2007).

References

Aaronson, D., Barrow, L., & Sander, W. (2007). Teachers and student achievement in the Chicago public high schools. *Journal of Labor Economics, 25*, 95–135.

Acemoglu, D., & Angrist, J. D. (2000). How large are the social returns to education? Evidence from compulsory schooling laws. In B. S. Bernanke & K. Rogoff (Eds.), *NBER Macroeconomics Annuals, 2000* (pp. 9–59). Cambridge, MA: MIT Press.

Alderman, H., Behrman, J. R., Ross, D. R., & Sabot, R. (1996). The returns to endogenous human capital in Pakistan's rural wage labour market. *Oxford Bulletin of Economics and Statistics, 58*, 29–55.

Altonji, J. G., & Pierret, C. R. (2001). Employer learning and statistical discrimination. *Quarterly Journal of Economics, 116*, 313–350.

Angrist, J. D., & Lavy, V. (1997). The effect of a change in language of instruction on the returns to schooling in Morocco. *Journal of Labor Economics, 15*(S1), S48–S76.

Armor, D. J., Conry-Oseguera, P., Cox, M., King, N., McDonnell, L., Pascal, A., et al. (1976). *Analysis of the school preferred reading program in selected Los Angeles minority schools*. Santa Monica, CA: RAND Corp.

Barro, R. J. (1991). Economic growth in a cross section of countries. *Quarterly Journal of Economics, 106*, 407–443.

Barro, R. J. (2001). Human capital and growth. *American Economic Review, 91*, 12–17.

Barro, R. J., & Lee, J-W. (2001). International data on educational attainment: Updates and implications. *Oxford Economic Papers, 53*, 541–563.

Barro, R. J., & Sala-i-Martin, X. (2004). *Economic growth* (2nd ed.). Cambridge, MA: MIT Press.

Bedard, K. (2001). Human capital versus signaling models: University access and high school dropouts. *Journal of Political Economy, 109*, 749–775.

Behrman, J. R., Kletzer, L. G., McPherson, M. S., & Schapiro, M. O. (1998). The microeconomics of college choice, careers, and wages: Measuring the impact of higher education. *Annals of the American Academy of Political and Social Science, 559*, 12–23.

Behrman, J. R., Ross, D., & Sabot, R. (2008). Improving the quality versus increasing the quantity of schooling: Estimates of rates of return from rural Pakistan. *Journal of Development Economics, 85*, 94–104.

Benhabib, J., & Spiegel, M. M. (1994). The role of human capital in economic development: Evidence from aggregate cross-country data. *Journal of Monetary Economics, 34*, 143–174.

Benhabib, J., & Spiegel, M. M. (2005). Human capital and technology diffusion. In P. Aghion & S. N. Durlauf (Eds.), *Handbook of economic growth* (pp. 935–966). Amsterdam: North Holland.

Bils, M., & Klenow, P. J. (2000). Does schooling cause growth? *American Economic Review, 90*, 1160–1183.

Bishop, J. H. (1989). Is the test score decline responsible for the productivity growth decline? *American Economic Review, 79*, 178–197.

Bishop, J. H. (1991). Achievement, test scores, and relative wages. In M. H. Kosters (Ed.), *Workers and their wages* (pp. 146–186). Washington, DC: The AEI Press.

Blackburn, M. L., & Neumark, D. (1993). Omitted-ability bias and the increase in the return to schooling. *Journal of Labor Economics, 11*, 521–544.

Blackburn, M. L., & Neumark, D. (1995). Are OLS estimates of the return to schooling biased downward? Another look. *Review of Economics and Statistics, 77*, 217–230.

Boissiere, M. X., Knight, J. B., & Sabot, R. H. (1985). Earnings, schooling, ability, and cognitive skills. *American Economic Review, 75*, 1016–1030.

Boozer, M. A., Krueger, A. B., & Wolkon, S. (1992). Race and school quality since *Brown v. Board of Education*. In M. N. Baily & C. Winston (Eds.), *Brooking papers on economic activity: Microeconomics* (pp. 269–338). Washington, DC: Brookings Institution.

Bosworth, B. P., & Collins, S. M. (2003). The empirics of growth: An update. *Brookings papers on economic activity, 2003, No. 2* (pp. 113–206). Washington, DC: Brookings Institution.

Bound, J., & Freeman, R. B. (1992). What went wrong? The erosion of relative earnings and employment among young black men in the 1980s. *Quarterly Journal of Economics, 107*, 201–232.

Bowles, S., Gintis, H., & Osborne, M. (2001). The determinants of earnings: A behavioral approach. *Journal of Economic Literature, 39*, 1137–1176.

Boyd, D., Grossman, P., Lankford, H., Loeb, S., & Wyckoff, J. (2006). How changes in entry requirements alter the teacher workforce and affect student achievement. *Education Finance and Policy, 1*, 176–216.

Boyd, D., Lankford, H., Loeb, S., & Wyckoff, J. (2005). The draw of home: How teachers' preferences for proximity disadvantage urban schools. *Journal of Policy Analysis and Management, 24*, 113–132.

Bracey, G. W. (2002, May 5). Why do we scapegoat the schools? *Washington Post*, p. B01.

Card, D. (1999). Causal effect of education on earnings. In O. Ashenfelter & D. Card (Eds.), *Handbook of labor economics* (pp. 1801–1863). Amsterdam: North-Holland.

Card, D., & Krueger, A. B. (1992). School quality and Black-White relative earnings: A direct assessment. *Quarterly Journal of Economics, 107*, 151–200.

Ciccone, A., & Papaioannou, E. (2005). *Human capital, the structure of production, and growth* (CEPR Discussion Paper No. 5354). Barcelona, Spain: Universitat Pompeu Fabra.

Committee on Science, Engineering, and Public Policy. (2005). *Rising above the gathering storm: Energizing and employing America for a brighter economic future*. Washington, DC: National Academies Press.

Coulombe, S., & Tremblay, J-F. (2006). Literacy and growth. *Topics in Macroeconomics, 6*, 1404.

Coulombe, S., Tremblay, J-F., Marchand, S. (2004). *Literacy scores, human capital and growth across fourteen OECD countries*. Ottawa: Statistics Canada.

Cunha, F., Heckman, J. J., Lochner, L., & Masterov, D. V. (2006). Interpreting the evidence on life cycle skill formation. In E. A. Hanushek & F. Welch (Eds.), *Handbook of the Economics of Education, Vol. 1* (pp. 697–812). Amsterdam: Elsevier.

Deere, D. (2001). Trends in wage inequality in the United States. In F. Welch (Ed.), *The causes and consequences of increasing inequality* (pp. 9–35). Chicago: University of Chicago Press.

Deere, D. & Vesovic, J. (2006). Educational wage premiums and the U.S. income distribution: A survey. In E. A. Hanushek & F. Welch (Eds.), *Handbook of the economics of education, Vol. 1* (pp. 55–306). Amsterdam: North Holland.

Dugan, D. J. (1976). Scholastic achievement: Its determinants and effects in the education industry. In J. T. Froomkin, D. T. Jamison, & R. Radner (Eds.), *Education as an industry* (pp. 53–83). Cambridge, MA: Ballinger.

Easterly, W. (2001). *The elusive quest for growth: An economists' adventures and misadventures in the tropics*. Cambridge, MA: MIT Press.

Farrell, P., & Fuchs, V. R. (1982). Schooling and health: The cigarette connection. *Journal of Health Economics, 1*, 217–230.

Figlio, D. N., & Ladd, H. F. (2007). School accountability and student achievement. In H. F. Ladd & E. B. Fiske (Eds.), *Handbook of research in education finance and policy* (pp. 166–182). Mahwah, NJ: Erlbaum.

Finnie, R., & Meng, R. (2002). Minorities, cognitive skills, and incomes of Canadians. *Canadian Public Policy, 28*, 257–273.

Glewwe, P. (1996). The relevance of standard estimates of rates of return to schooling for educational policy: A critical assessment. *Journal of Development Economics, 51*, 267–290.

Glewwe, P. (2002). Schools and skills in developing countries: Education policies and socioeconomic outcomes. *Journal of Economic Literature, 40*, 436–482.

Glewwe, P., & Kremer, M. (2006). Schools, teachers, and educational outcomes in developing countries. In E. A. Hanushek & F. Welch (Eds.), *Handbook of the economics of education, Vol. 2* (pp. 943–1017). Amsterdam: North Holland.

Goldin, C. (1998). America's graduation from high school: The evolution and spread of secondary schooling in the twentieth century. *Journal of Economic History, 58*, 345–374.

Goldin, C., & Katz, L. F. (2008). *The race between education and technology: The evolution of U.S. educational wage differentials, 1890 to 2005*. Cambridge, MA: Harvard University Press.

Green, D. A., & Riddell, W. C. (2003). Literacy and earnings: An investigation of the interaction of cognitive and unobserved skills in earnings generation. *Labour Economics, 10*, 165–184.

Grogger, J. T. (1996). Does school quality explain the recent black/white wage trend? *Journal of Labor Economics, 14*, 231–253.

Grogger, J. T., & Eide, E. (1993). Changes in college skills and the rise in the college wage premium. *Journal of Human Resources, 30*, 280–310.

Gundlach, E., Rudman, D., & Woessmann, L. (2002). Second thoughts on development accounting. *Applied Economics, 34*, 1359–1369.

Hanushek, E. A. (1971). Teacher characteristics and gains in student achievement: Estimation using micro data. *American Economic Review, 60*, 280–288.

Hanushek, E. A. (1979). Conceptual and empirical issues in the estimation of educational production functions. *Journal of Human Resources, 14*, 351–388.

Hanushek, E. A. (1986). The economics of schooling: Production and efficiency in public schools. *Journal of Economic Literature, 24*, 1141–1177.

Hanushek, E. A. (1992). The trade-off between child quantity and quality. *Journal of Political Economy, 100*, 84–117.

Hanushek, E. A. (1994). Money might matter somewhere: A response to Hedges, Laine, and Greenwald. *Educational Researcher, 23*, 5–8.

Hanushek, E. A. (1995). Interpreting recent research on schooling in developing countries. *World Bank Research Observer, 10*, 227–246.

Hanushek, E. A. (1999). The evidence on class size. In S. E. Mayer & P. E. Peterson (Eds.), *Earning and learning: How schools matter* (pp. 131–168). Washington, DC: Brookings Institution.

Hanushek, E. A. (2002). Publicly provided education. In A. J. Auerbach & M. Feldstein (Eds.), *Handbook of public economics* (pp. 2045–2141). Amsterdam: Elsevier.

Hanushek, E. A. (2003a). The failure of input-based schooling policies. *Economic Journal, 113*, F64–F98.

Hanushek, E. A. (2003b). The importance of school quality. In P. E. Peterson & J. E. Chubb (Eds.), *Our schools and our future: Are we still at risk?* (pp. 141–173). Stanford, CA: Hoover Institution Press.

Hanushek, E. A., Jamison, D. T., Jamison, E. A., & Woessmann, L. (2008). Education and economic growth: It's not just going to school but learning that matters. *Education Next, 8*(2), 62–70.

Hanushek, E. A., Kain, D. F., O'Brien, J. F., & Rivkin, S. G. (2005, February). *The market for teacher quality* (Working Paper No. 11154). Cambridge, MA: National Bureau of Economic Research.

Hanushek, E. A., Kain, J. F., & Rivkin, S. G. (2004a). The revolving door. *Education Next, 4*(1), 77–82.

Hanushek, E. A., Kain, J. F., & Rivkin, S. G. (2004b). Why public schools lose teachers. *Journal of Human Resources, 39*, 326–354.

Hanushek, E. A., Kain, J. F., Rivkin, S. G., & Branch, G. F. (2007). Charter school quality and parental decision making with school choice. *Journal of Public Economics, 91*, 823–848.

Hanushek, E. A., & Kimko, D. D. (2000). Schooling, labor force quality, and the growth of nations. *American Economic Review, 90*, 1184–1208.

Hanushek, E. A., Lavy, V., & Hitomi, K. (2008). Do students care about school quality? Determinants of dropout behavior in developing countries. *Journal of Human Capital, 1*, 69–105.

Hanushek, E. A., & Pace, R. R. (1995). Who chooses to teach (and why)? *Economics of Education Review, 14*, 101–117.

Hanushek, E. A., & Raymond, M. E. (2005). Does school accountability lead to improved student performance? *Journal of Policy Analysis and Management, 24*, 297–327.

Hanushek, E. A., & Rivkin, S. G. (2004). How to improve the supply of high quality teachers. In D. Ravitch (Ed.), *Brookings Papers on Education Policy, 2004* (pp. 7–25). Washington, DC: Brookings Institution.

Hanushek, E. A., & Rivkin, S. G. (2006). Teacher quality. In E. A. Hanushek & F. Welch (Eds.), *Handbook of the economics of education, Vol. 2* (pp. 1051–1078). Amsterdam: North Holland.

Hanushek, E. A., Rivkin, S. G., & Taylor, L. L. (1996). Aggregation and the estimated effects of school resources. *Review of Economics and Statistics, 78*, 611–627.

Hanushek, E. A., & Woessmann, L. (2006, October). The role of school improvement in economic development (NBER Working Paper No. 12832). Cambridge, MA: National Bureau of Economic Research.

Hanushek, E. A., & Woessmann, L. (2008). The role of cognitive skills in economic development. *Journal of Economic Literature, 46*, 607–668.

Hanushek, E. A., Woessmann, L. (in preparation). *The human capital of nations*.

Hanushek, E. A., & Zhang, L. (2008, March). *Quality consistent estimates of international returns to skill* [mimeo]. Stanford, CA: Stanford University, Hoover Institution.

Harbison, R. W., & Hanushek, E. A. (1992). *Educational performance of the poor: Lessons from rural northeast Brazil*. New York: Oxford University Press.

Hauser, R. M. (1993). The decline in college entry among African Americans: Findings in search of explanations. In P. M. Sniderman, P. E. Tetlock, & E. G. Carmines (Eds.), *Prejudice, politics, and the American dilemma* (pp. 271–306). Stanford, CA: Stanford University Press.

Haveman, R. H., & Wolfe, B. L. (1984). Schooling and economic well-being: The role of nonmarket effects. *Journal of Human Resources, 19*, 377–407.

Heckman, J. J., & LaFontaine, P. A. (2007, December). *The American high school graduation rate: Trends and levels* (NBER Working Paper No. 13670). Cambridge, MA: National Bureau of Economic Research.

Heckman, J. J., Stixrud, J., & Urzua, S. (2006). The effects of cognitive and noncognitive abilities on labor market outcomes and social behavior. *Journal of Labor Economics, 24*, 411–482.

Hedges, L. V., Laine, R. D., & Greenwald, R. (1994). Does money matter? A meta-analysis of studies of the effects of differential school inputs on student outcomes. *Educational Researcher, 23*(3), 5–14.

Jamison, E. A., Jamison, D. T., & Hanushek, E. A. (2007). The effects of education quality on income growth and mortality decline. *Economics of Education Review, 26*, 772–789.

Jaynes, G. D., & Williams, R. M., Jr. (Eds.). (1989). *A common destiny: Blacks and American society*. Washington, DC: National Academy Press.

Jolliffe, D. (1998). Skills, schooling, and household income in Ghana. *World Bank Economic Review, 12*, 81–104.

Jorgenson, D. W., & Fraumeni, B. M. (1992). Investment in education and U.S. economic growth. *Scandinavian Journal of Economics, 94*(Suppl.), S51–S70.

Juhn, C., Murphy, K. M., & Pierce, B. (1993). Wage inequality and the rise in returns to skill. *Journal of Political Economy, 101*, 410–442.

Kane, T. J. (1994). College entry by Blacks since 1970: The role of college costs, family background, and the returns to education. *Journal of Political Economy, 102*, 878–911.

Kane, T. J., Rockoff, J. E., & Staiger, D. O. (2006, April). What does certification tell us about teacher effectiveness? Evidence from New York City (NBER Working Paper No. 12155). Cambridge, MA: National Bureau of Economic Research.

Knight, J. B., & Sabot, R. H. (1990). *Education, productivity, and inequality: The East African Natural Experiment*. New York: Oxford University Press.

Kosters, M. H. (1991). Wages and demographics. In M. H. Kosters (Ed.), *Workers and their wages* (pp. 1–32). Washington, DC: The AEI Press.

Krueger, A. B. (1999). Experimental estimates of education production functions. *Quarterly Journal of Economics, 114*, 497–532.

Krueger, A. O. (1974). The political economy of the rent seeking society. *American Economic Review, 64*, 291–303.

Layard, R., & Psacharopoulos, G. (1974). The screening hypothesis and the returns to education. *Journal of Political Economy, 82*, 985–998.

Lazear, E. P. (2003). Teacher incentives. *Swedish Economic Policy Review, 10*, 179–214.

Lee, D. W., & Lee, T. H. (1995). Human capital and economic growth: Tests based on the international evaluation of educational achievement. *Economics Letters, 47*, 219–225.

Leibowitz, A. (1974). Home investments in children. *Journal of Political Economy, 82,* S111–S131.

Levy, F., & Murnane, R. J. (1992). U.S. earnings levels and earnings inequality: A review of recent trends and proposed explanations. *Journal of Economic Literature, 30*, 1333–1381.

Lochner, L., & Moretti, E. (2001, November). *The effect of education on crime: Evidence from prison inmates, arrests, and self-reports* (NBER Working Paper No. 8605). Cambridge, MA: National Bureau of Economic Research.

Loeb, S., & Page, M. E. (2000). Examining the link between teacher wages and student outcomes: The importance of alternative labor market opportunities and non-pecuniary variation. *Review of Economics and Statistics, 82*, 393–408.

Lucas, R. E. (1988). On the mechanics of economic development. *Journal of Monetary Economics, 22*, 3–42.

Mankiw, N. G., Romer., D., & Weil, D. (1992). A contribution to the empirics of economic growth. *Quarterly Journal of Economics, 107*, 407–437.

Manski, C. F., & Wise, D. A. (1983). *College choice in America.* Cambridge, MA: Harvard University Press.

McIntosh, S., & Vignoles, A. (2001). Measuring and assessing the impact of basic skills on labor market outcomes. *Oxford Economic Papers, 53*, 453–481.

McMahon, W. W. (1991). Relative returns to human and physical capital in the U.S. and efficient investment strategies. *Economics of Education Review, 10*, 283–296.

Michael, R. T. (1982). Measuring non-monetary benefits of education: A survey. In W. W. McMahon & T. G. Geske (Eds.), *Financing education: Overcoming inefficiency and inequity* (pp. 119–149). Urbana: University of Illinois Press.

Mishel, L., & Rothstein, R. (Eds.). (2002). *The class size debate.* Washington, DC: Economic Policy Institute.

Moll, P. G. (1998). Primary schooling, cognitive skills, and wage in South Africa. *Economica, 65*(258), 263–284.

Mulligan, C. B. (1999). Galton versus the human capital approach to inheritance. *Journal of Political Economy, 107*, S184–S224.

Murnane, R. J. (1975). *The impact of school resources on the learning of inner city children.* Cambridge, MA: Ballinger.

Murnane, R. J., & Phillips, B. (1981). What do effective teachers of inner-city children have in common? *Social Science Research, 10*, 83–100.

Murnane, R. J., Willett, J. B., Braatz, M. J., & Duhaldeborde, Y. (2001). Do different dimensions of male high school students' skills predict labor market success a decade later? Evidence from the NLSY. *Economics of Education Review, 20*, 311–320.

Murnane, R. J., Willett, J. B., Duhaldeborde, Y., & Tyler, J. H. (2000). How important are the cognitive skills of teenagers in predicting subsequent earnings? *Journal of Policy Analysis and Management, 19,* 547–568.

Murnane, R. J., Willett, J. B., & Levy, F. (1995). The growing importance of cognitive skills in wage determination. *Review of Economics and Statistics, 77*, 251–266.

Murphy, K. M., & Welch, F. (1989). Wage premiums for college graduates: Recent growth and possible explanations. *Educational Researcher, 18*(4), 17–26.

Murphy, K. M., & Welch, F. (1992). The structure of wages. *Quarterly Journal of Economics, 107*, 285–326.

Neal, D. (2006). Why has Black-White skill convergence stopped? In E. A. Hanushek & F. Welch (Eds.), *Handbook of the economics of education, Vol. 1* (pp. 511–576). Amsterdam: North Holland.

Neal, D. A., & Johnson, W. R. (1996). The role of pre-market factors in Black-White differences. *Journal of Political Economy, 104*, 869–895.

Nelson, R. R., & Phelps, E. (1966). Investment in humans, technological diffusion and economic growth. *American Economic Review, 56*, 69–75.

O'Neill, J. (1990). The role of human capital in earnings differences between Black and White men. *Journal of Economic Perspectives, 4*(4), 25–46.

Organisation for Economic Co-operation and Development (OECD). (2001). *Education at a glance: OECD Indicators 2001.* Paris: Author.

Organisation for Economic Co-operation and Development (OECD). (2005). *Education at a glance: OECD Indicators 2005.* Paris: Author.

Parente, S. L., & Prescott, E. C. (1994). Barriers to technology adoption and development. *Journal of Political Economy, 102*, 298–321.

Parente, S. L., & Prescott, E. C. (1999). Monopoly rights: A barrier to riches. *American Economic Review, 89*, 1216–1233.

Pierce, B., & Welch, F. (1996). Changes in the structure of wages. In E. A. Hanushek & D. W. Jorgenson (Eds.), *Improving America's schools: The role of incentives* (pp. 53–73). Washington, DC: National Academy Press.

Pritchett, L. (2001). Where has all the education gone? *World Bank Economic Review, 15*, 367–391.

Pritchett, L. (2006). Does learning to add up add up? The returns to schooling in aggregate data. In E. A. Hanushek & F. Welch (Eds.), *Handbook of the Economics of Education, Vol. 1* (pp. 635–695). Amsterdam: North Holland.

Psacharopoulos, G. (1994). Returns to investment in education: A global update. *World Development, 22*, 1325–1344.

Riley, J. G. (2001). Silver signals: Twenty-five years of screening and signaling. *Journal of Economic Literature, 39*, 432–478.

Rivkin, S. G. (1995). Black/White differences in schooling and employment. *Journal of Human Resources, 30*, 826–852.

Rivkin, S. G., Hanushek, E. A., & Kain, J. F. (2005). Teachers, schools, and academic achievement. *Econometrica, 73*, 417–458.

Rockoff, J. E. (2004). The impact of individual teachers on student achievement: Evidence from panel data. *American Economic Review, 94*, 247–252.

Romer, P. (1990). Endogenous technological change. *Journal of Political Economy, 98*, S71–S102.

Rose, H. (2006). Do gains in test scores explain labor market outcomes? *Economics of Education Review, 25*, 430–446.

Schultz, T. W. (1975). The value of the ability to deal with disequilibria. *Journal of Economic Literature, 13*, 827–846.

Smith, J. P., & Welch, F. (1989). Black economic progress after Myrdal. *Journal of Economic Literature, 27*, 519–564.

Spence, A. M. (1973). Job market signalling. *Quarterly Journal of Economics, 87*, 355–374.

Stanley, H. W., & Niemi, R. G. (2000). *Vital statistics on American politics.* Washington, DC: CQ Press.

Teixeira, R. A. (1992). *The disappearing American voter.* Washington, DC: Brookings Institution.

Tyler, J. H., Murnane, R. J., & Willett, J. B. (2000). Estimating the labor market signaling value of the GED. *Quarterly Journal of Economics, 115*, 431–468.

U.S. Bureau of the Census. (1975). *Historical statistics of the United States, colonial times to 1970, bicentennial edition* (Parts 1-2). Washington, DC: U.S. Government Printing Office.

U. S. Bureau of the Census. (2000). *Statistical abstract of the United States: 2000.* Washington, DC: U.S. Government Printing Office.

Vandenbussche, J., Aghion, P., & Meghir, C. (2006). Growth, distance to frontier and composition of human capital. *Journal of Economic Growth, 11*, 97–127.

Vijverberg, W. P. M. (1999). The impact of schooling and cognitive skills on income from non-farm self-employment. In P. Glewwe (Ed.), *The economics of school quality investments in developing countries: An empirical study of Ghana* (pp. 206–252). New York: St. Martin's Press.

Weiss, A. (1995). Human capital vs. signalling explanations of wages. *Journal of Economic Perspectives, 9*(4), 133–154.

Welch, F. (1970). Education in production. *Journal of Political Economy, 78*, 35–59.

Welch, F. (1999). In defense of inequality. *American Economic Review, 89*(2), 1–17.

Wolfe, B. L., & Zuvekas, S. (1995, May). Nonmarket outcomes of schooling (Discussion Paper No. 1065-95). Madison: University of Wisconsin, Institute for Research on Poverty.

Wolpin, K. I. (1977). Education and screening. *American Economic Review, 67*, 949–958.

World Bank. (1993). *The East Asian miracle: Economic growth and public policy*. New York: Oxford University Press.

Woessmann, L. (2002). *Schooling and the quality of human capital*. Berlin, Germany: Springer.

Woessmann, L. (2003). Specifying human capital. *Journal of Economic Surveys, 17*, 239–270.

Woessmann, L. (2005). Educational production in Europe. *Economic Policy, 20*, 446–504.

Woessmann, L. (2007). International evidence on expenditure and class size: A review. In *Brookings Papers on Education Policy 2006–2007* (pp. 245–272). Washington, DC: Brookings Institution.

4

A Political Science Perspective on Education Policy Analysis

Lorraine M. McDonnell
University of California, Santa Barbara

Political science is not a discipline whose theories and methods will likely contribute to a better understanding of how specific policies can be designed to increase student learning. Rather, its empirically-based theories can help specify the conditions under which policies are likely to change or remain stable, explain how politics shapes education policy, and in turn, how those policies influence political participation and future policy design. Its normative theories provide the rationale for why politics has a legitimate role in public education, and more importantly, for why education should be a valued collective good in a democratic society.

Political scientists came to what is now called policy analysis later than economists whose theoretical approaches initially defined the field. Many political scientists conducting policy research adopted the dominant rational choice paradigm from economics. That paradigm is grounded in normative assumptions about the appropriate rationales for policy action (e.g., market failure, public goods provision), how policy actors behave in pursuing their self or group interest, and the criteria for evaluating policy options (e.g., efficiency, distributional outcomes; Weimer & Vining, 2005). The dominance of rational choice models in economics, policy analysis, and political science over the past 30 years placed the concept of interest front and center in policy research.

However, some researchers found this approach unsatisfying, arguing that it underestimated the role of institutions in shaping and constraining choices and that it did not give adequate consideration to how interests are formed or how they are framed to gain advantage in various political arenas. Over time, critiques of "the rationality project" (Stone, 2002) prompted a growing consensus that whatever the preferred political science approach, the three common building blocks needed to understand policy development, stability, and change are ideas, interests, and institutions (Heclo, 1994, p. 375). Although political scientists use similar types of data and analytical techniques, their theo-

retical approaches to policy research tend to accord greater weight (than does traditional policy analysis) to explanations that augment interest-based ones with institutional and ideational factors.

Within the general framework of ideas, interests, and institutions, two questions are currently at the forefront of policy studies by political scientists. The first has intrigued researchers for more than 20 years, with the explanatory power of its answers growing through cumulative theory-building and testing. That question is: Under what conditions are policy regimes likely to remain stable, and under what conditions are they altered in fundamental ways? This focus originated in attempts to explain how particular issues get on decision-makers' agendas. It later expanded to consider the broader puzzle of why, in a system where most policymaking is incremental, large and profound changes sometimes occur—even to the point of reversing well-established policies.

The second question is: How do policies, once enacted, influence political attitudes and actions? In traditional policy research, political factors are typically the independent variables explaining policy enactment and implementation outcomes. More recently, some political scientists have reversed the causal nexus to examine how policies, once enacted, influence public attitudes and actions, thus creating a form of policy feedback.

This chapter first provides an overview of institutions, ideas, and interests as explanatory factors. The second and third sections examine the conceptual approaches political scientists have used to understand change and stability and policy feedback. Because the methods that political scientists use are common to all the social sciences, the emphasis in this review is on conceptual frameworks rather than research methods. In each section, several education policy studies based on the approach under discussion are reviewed. These studies not only illustrate the application of political science theory, but they are also indicative of political scientists' growing interest in education policy research over the past decade. The theoretical frameworks and empirical studies discussed in this chapter are all drawn from scholarship in and about the United States. Because one of the lessons analysts have drawn from earlier policy studies is the importance of historical, cultural, and political contexts, findings from the specific studies cited here are only illustrative with limited generalizability beyond the United States. However, the basic conceptual building blocks of institutions, interests, and ideas are broadly applicable to cross-national research, and variants of the theories discussed are used in comparative research. The chapter concludes with a brief discussion of the likely intellectual and practical pay-offs from grounding more education policy research in political science theories and concepts.

Major Determinants of Policy

Even as political scientists have recognized the need to understand the interplay among institutions, interests, and ideas, individual policy studies have tended to emphasize one of these factors more than the other two in explaining why particular policies are enacted, what policy makers intend for them to accomplish, and the extent to which they are implemented and actually produce their expected effects. The choice of which factor to emphasize is frequently based on judgments about the conceptual lens likely to produce the greatest explanatory payoff, given the type of policy or political phenomenon being studied. For example, in education policy research, implementation studies have typically been grounded in an institutional perspective, while research on the politics of enactment have focused on interests and studies of curricular value conflicts often concentrate on ideational factors. Consequently, in this section, each of the three factors is discussed separately. Nevertheless, even when one factor is emphasized, its explanatory power is typically derived from the interaction between it and other factors.

Institutions Over the past 20 years, a body of theoretical literature has developed arguing that institutions matter because they define the framework in which policymaking occurs, thus shaping its outcomes, and because different institutional arrangements advantage some societal interests and policy alternatives at the expense of others (March & Olsen, 1989, 1995; Kelman, 1987).[1] These effects occur through the structure of rules and norms, which determines who may participate in the policymaking process, who is granted formal authority to choose among proposals, and what procedures must be followed before those with formal authority can make a decision. In education policy, institutional arrangements are particularly critical to explaining policy outcomes because political power is exercised and policy decisions made in multiple venues or arenas. As Mazzoni (1991) notes, these arenas are never neutral in their allocation of access and power: "They legitimate a set of participants, establish the institutional

and social context—including the governing rules of the game—mediate the potency of resources and strategies, and encourage some means (and discourage other means) of reaching agreements" (p. 116).

Rules governing school board elections are examples of institutional arrangements that have historically been central to education policy. After focusing little attention on local decision-making arenas for nearly two decades, political scientists are once again examining them. These studies are still limited in number and tentative in their conclusions. Nevertheless, they suggest promising research directions, and reinforce the need for timely and nationally-representative data on local institutions.[2]

One question that has been explored recently is the relationship between electoral arrangements and representation on school boards. In her study of Black and Hispanic representation on school boards in four metropolitan areas, Marschall (2005) found that rules governing whether school board elections are at-large or by ward affect Black representation, with district elections having a significant positive effect on the number of Blacks elected, but having no significant effect on Hispanic school board representation. In their study of Texas districts, Meier and Juenke (2005) found that electoral structures matter to the ethnic composition of boards, to teachers hired, and to educational outcomes—even after controlling for whether Hispanics constitute a minority or majority of the local population. Using national census data, Berkman and Pultzer (2005) found that between 1987 and 1992, Black representation on school boards improved across the country, but increased most significantly in those districts that changed their voting rules from either at-large or ward-based to the other type of system. Because of the limitations of their data, the authors could only surmise that change, regardless of its substance, was significant because pressure from affected interests—whether through court order, settlement, or threat of litigation—reinforced the effect of the new electoral rules.

These disparate findings highlight both the significance of research on representation and the need for additional studies. Developing a more nuanced understanding of the relationship between electoral arrangements and the presence of minorities on local boards speaks to issues at the core of politics and policy—the role institutional rules play in shaping how citizens' preferences are reflected in decision-making bodies and the links between who makes policy decisions (descriptive representation) and the content and effects of those decisions (substantive representation).

Other recent research on local education governance has focused on mayoral control of the schools (Wong & Shen, 2005; Henig & Rich, 2004; Kirst, 2003). These studies have generally concluded that it is too early to tell whether changing institutional structures to give urban mayors greater control over school systems will improve educational outcomes. But like the relationship between electoral rules and school board representation, this reform is premised on the assumption that institutional arrangements, including who holds authority over resource allocation, the rules by which those resources are allocated, and how elected officials are held accountable, influence district and school performance. The ambiguous relationship between governance changes and improved instructional practices and outcomes points to the contingent nature of governing institutions. Although their effect on student learning is necessarily indirect, they have the potential to shape those factors that directly influence classroom practice, such as teacher quality and resource levels. However, their impact depends on the specific structures and rules embodied in each local institution, and these can vary considerably across communities.

Not only do governance structures vary locally, but they are embedded in a highly fragmented system of state and federal institutions. Education policy analysts have long noted that the most distinctive institutional characteristic of U.S. public education is its fragmentation. Not only do multiple levels of government share authority over public education and responsibility for its funding, but power is also fragmented among institutions within each level. It is intuitively clear that this institutional fragmentation helps explain the significant variation in educational services and quality across states and localities. Recently, however, analysts have examined the causal processes by which institutions shape policy outcomes to gain a more systematic understanding of that relationship, and its long-term effects on the system's ability to produce and sustain coherent and effective policy.

As one example, Reed (2001), in analyzing the politics of school finance litigation, addresses the question of why the egalitarian assumptions underlying decisions in school finance lawsuits are often diminished when state legislatures fashion remedies in response to judicial mandates. He identifies the institutional configuration "by which resources are delivered to children according to a regime of property taxes, home values, and local control of revenues" (p. 128) as the source of an explanation. Based on his analysis of public opinion data from four states, Reed concludes that even though there has been a trend away from local control, its persistence as a defining characteristic of the U.S. educational system shapes public attitudes toward educational opportunity, particularly opposition to school finance reform viewed as a threat to localism.

In emphasizing the institutional design of public education, Reed details how the local governance of municipalities and school districts and local control of property tax receipts "… implicitly structures our beliefs about the proper way to organize education, and indirectly, they inform a good deal of our democratic politics surrounding education" (p. 132). His analysis indicates that the link between the primacy of local control and public attitudes influences state legislative behavior. Legislatures are political arenas that have traditionally reinforced geographically-based inequalities by preserving local control over a significant proportion of school funding. However, in their school finance rulings, state supreme courts threaten to disrupt this equilibrium by

requiring redistributive remedies. It is this constellation of rules, norms, and structures that explains why the legislative crafting of school finance remedies is often so prolonged, and why the primacy of local control over local resources persists even as state courts have moved to change distributional rules and make them more equitable.

Reed's analysis illustrates how institutional designs can buttress some interests and thwart others, and it provides a critical example of the effects of fragmented policymaking across institutional arenas. That fragmentation has resulted in less coherent policy, but it has also increased access to the policy process giving interests multiple entry points and the ability to "shop" for the venue likely to give them the greatest advantage. Education policy analysts have examined the strategic use of multiple venues, particularly how groups choose between legislative and judicial routes in pursuing their interests (e.g., Reed, 2001; Melnick, 1995). However, less attention has been paid to how institutional norms with regard to participation and decision making vary across arenas, and the effect of those differences on policy outcomes. This strand of research, informed by institutional approaches, would be especially important now that the scope of centralized authority, with its emphasis on decision making through bargaining, has grown simultaneously with expanded school-site governance where deliberative norms and consensual decision making are more likely.

Not all fragmentation occurs among institutions with formal authority over education governance and resources. Public education, at the national, state, and particularly the local level, is embedded in overlapping webs of formal and informal relationships. In the past, education policy research tended to focus on the formal institutions of governance and to consider education as a stand-alone enterprise. More recent studies, however, have conceived of education as a subsystem located in a wider set of political and social relationships, and have focused equal attention on formal and informal institutions. The extent to which those institutional relationships are either strong or fragmented is often a determinant of policy outcomes. One set of examples comes from recent research on the politics of urban school reform (Clarke, Hero, Sidney, Fraga, & Erlichson, 2006; Shipps, 2006; Stone, Henig, Jones, & Pierannunzi, 2001; Henig, Hula, Orr, & Pedescleaux, 1999; Orr, 1999; Portz, Stein, & Jones, 1999; Stone, 1998; Rich, 1996). Although several of these are case studies of a single city and others look comparatively across multiple cities, they share two characteristics: (a) they take an institutional perspective and (b) they seek explanations for why cities vary in their ability to initiate and sustain reform efforts.

Most are grounded in Clarence Stone's concept of urban regime as the informal arrangements that surround and complement the formal workings of governmental authority. In comparing across 11 cities, Stone and his colleagues (2001) found that superintendents at best can promote educational interests in a community, but they typically do not act as change agents in big-city school systems. Similarly, boards of education are not major actors in school reform, usually focusing on constituency service and narrow issues rather than broad systemic reform. Consequently, civic mobilization or the degree to which various sectors of the community join together in support of school reform and related efforts to improve educational opportunities and performance is a key factor in explaining variation in reform outcomes. In cities with the highest levels of mobilization, community-wide coalitions and support structures—civic capacity in Stone and his fellow researchers' parlance—were formed by a variety of actors, including the business community, city officials, community organizations, and foundations.

Although researchers have been able to identify some patterns associated with levels of mobilization, the relatively small number of cities that have been studied has made it difficult to explain anomalies in expected relationships (e.g., between demographic composition and mobilization). Nevertheless, these studies suggest potentially fruitful avenues for future research. For example, business involvement appears to be crucial to building strong civic capacity but such involvement is not guaranteed, and there seems to be a trade-off between business participation and alternative forms of civic mobilization that occur through interventions external to the city such as judicial desegregation orders (Stone et al., 2001). At the same time, even if business leaders become involved, they cannot be major facilitators of civic mobilization unless they can interact with a wide array of other actors and skillfully build coalitions. Just as business leaders may see mobilization in their economic interest, elected politicians may also have incentives and resources to mobilize broad coalitions capable of taking action to improve the schools. However, one consistent finding across all these studies is that civic mobilization is insufficient to sustain reform efforts unless it can be institutionalized in ongoing partnerships and organizations (Shipps, 2006; Stone et al., 2001; Portz et al., 1999).

Two other conclusions from these studies suggest, on the one hand, the power of institutional relationships in constraining attempts at change and on the other, the limitations of governing institutions in altering student outcomes. The first is that civic mobilization cannot be understood independently of a city's ethnic and racial politics, but that politics occurs within the constraints of existing institutional relationships. For example, in their studies of school reform in Black-majority cities governed by Black leaders, Henig and his co-authors (1999) document the role of race not just in complicating access to private resources typically held by White elites, but also in defining the role of the school system as part of a broader employment regime—thus explaining the opposition of teacher unions, Black ministers, and community activists to school reform efforts if they seem to threaten jobs. Orr (1999) found in Baltimore that while social capital within the Black community was strong, it hindered African American leaders' ability to gain corporate and suburban cooperation necessary for school reform because that social capital had been built on intra-group solidarity and opposition to White control of the city. In their study of four multiethnic cities, Clarke and her colleagues (2006) found that although students of color, their parents, and advocates presented new ideas for overcoming the institutional constraints that limited educational opportunities, these ideas led at most to marginal institutional transformations and were not easily sustained.

In contrast to the power of institutions in hindering change, a second conclusion points to their limitations in accomplishing instrumental goals. Civic mobilization and high civic capacity do not directly translate into improved educational performance. This limitation is especially evident in Shipps' (2006) analysis of the role of the business community in Chicago school reform. She characterizes the situation as a "recurring dynamic of strong influence and poor results" (p. 170), and attributes it to the business community's attachment to a bureaucratic model of top-down coordination and control along with deep distrust of educators on whom they must rely to execute the core process of teaching and learning. Although the reasons for the disjuncture between governing institutions and educational outcomes may vary across localities, the Chicago example illustrates the more general point that central institutions set the context for teaching and learning and constrain the choices educators can make, but a myriad of other institutional relationships, inside and outside schools, shape the causal process linking policy choices and their outcomes.

More could be said about education policy research grounded in an institutional perspective, but the studies discussed here illustrate three significant points about this approach. First, after years of researchers focusing on federal and state policy to the neglect of the local level, these studies point to the centrality of local political institutions in facilitating or hindering change in education policy and practice. Their suggestive, but not conclusive, findings indicate that more comparative research of both urban and non-urban jurisdictions—using common theoretical frameworks and data collection strategies—is needed. Second, these studies highlight the need to look beyond school systems to understand current policies and the potential for change. A more expansive view of institutions also requires that researchers consider the informal norms, behaviors, and relationships that become institutionalized patterns in addition to examining formal institutions. Studies such as Reed's (2001) also point to the importance of understanding how institutions shape individual attitudes and how those attitudes can, in turn, influence policy decisions. Finally, although the studies reviewed in this section identify institutions as a primary factor in explaining policy outcomes, they also point to the critical interaction of institutional factors with interests such as those of teacher unions, ethnic groups, and business, and with ideas such as the notion of local control over local resources. Even if researchers approach a question through an institutional lens, identifying and understanding the nature of these interactions is likely to be where the greatest payoff is.

Interests Within political science, differing conceptions of interests and the groups that represent them have long been central to most analyses of political processes and outcomes. In the post-war period, American political science was dominated by what has been called the pluralist or group approach to politics that assumed "a nation's political system could best be understood by looking at how groups focused and interacted with each other and with the government" (Baumgartner & Leech, 1998, p. 44). Although the group approach contributed to the development of analytical concepts still in current use, such as issue networks and policy subsystems, it fell into disfavor as empirical research began to show that political inequalities and high barriers to entry constrained who participated in the political process. Not only did these findings challenge the idea that interest groups provided a valid or seemingly comprehensive lens through which to view politics, but critics also questioned whether the group approach had moved from a theoretical framework to guide empirical studies to a normative theory of how politics should be constituted.

Recent research has continued to focus on interests as they are manifested through formal organizations and social movements, but has concentrated on how groups overcome collective action problems, the range of incentives for individual and group mobilization, and the use of lobbying and grassroots action strategies. As this literature has evolved, greater attention has been paid to measuring group influence more precisely, particularly their informal role in setting governmental policy agendas, and to understanding how organizational strategies vary depending on the type of group, policy issue, and arena. (For in-depth reviews of interest group research in political science, see Mawhinney, 2001; Baumgartner & Leech, 1998.)

A focus on interests has also long been a part of descriptive analyses of the politics of education. The major textbook in the field (Wirt & Kirst, 2005) devotes considerable attention to a wide range of interest groups at the local, state, and federal levels—portraying them as transfer agents that formulate and convey to political officials the demands of particular interests.

Somewhat surprisingly, given this recognition of the centrality of interests, research knowledge about them in education is limited. With the notable exception of teacher unions, much of what we know about education interest groups comes not from studying the groups as the unit of analysis, but rather as a byproduct of research on specific policy issues and local communities. Although not numerous, studies specifically focused on teacher unions and their dual roles as collective bargaining agents and political interest groups have analyzed the nature of their influence as it grew over the 1970s and then began to wane as new actors entered the education policy arena (e.g., Berkman & Plutzer, 2005; Moe, 2005; Boyd, Plank, & Sykes, 2000). In contrast, much of what we know about the role of business groups in education has come as a byproduct either of studies of single policies such as No Child Left Behind (NCLB; Manna, 2006; McGuinn, 2006) and Reading First (Miskel & Song, 2004), or of research on specific governmental levels and their educational institutions (e.g., Stone

et al., 2001; Henig et al., 1999; Longoria, 1998). While research knowledge about business groups has emerged incidentally from studies with other foci, it is considerably more comprehensive and systematic than for a number of other interests that have become increasingly significant in education policy. These include textbook and test publishers (particularly after the passage of NCLB), private sector providers such as those offering tutoring or school management services, foundations, community-based organizations, and various non-profits.[3]

Because of this dearth of studies with organized groups as the unit of analysis, our knowledge of education interests is spotty and unconnected to the research base on interest groups in political science. So, for example, the broader interest group literature is quite informative about what scholars call "demand aggregation"—how groups mobilize, how group leaders relate to their membership, and how they recruit members or otherwise maintain themselves (Cigler, 1994). However, we lack systematic information on these topics for most groups active in the education arena. We even lack another type of more descriptive information available from large-scale surveys of interest groups in other policy domains—namely, a systematic overview of the various tactics that groups use in their attempts to influence policy.

However, a potential advantage of heightened scholarly attention to the politics of education policy is that researchers will recognize the advantages of conducting such studies. A recent one illustrates the payoff from using interest groups as the unit of analysis and grounding that analysis in a conceptual framework derived from political science. Itkonen (2007) examined the interest groups testifying before Congress in all federal special education legislation since 1975 as well as those filing amicus briefs before the Supreme Court. Her analysis is grounded in the theoretical literature on policy framing and in research that distinguishes groups whose members are motivated by personal pain or loss from conventional interest groups.

In the case of special education, the pain/loss groups represent parents of students with disabilities. These groups tend to frame their advocacy differently than the organizations representing education professionals, and they use different tactics. Itkonen (2007) found that family disability groups typically premise their political action on the argument that special education is a civil rights entitlement protected by the federal government, and they tell a hopeful story of the positive outcomes that will result if students with disabilities are served. In contrast, professional groups, particularly school administrator organizations, view special education as a set of procedural rules governing a grant-in-aid program. They advocate for greater state or local control, equitable funds distribution, and against expansions to the statutes (e.g., through new eligibility categories), and they typically tell stories of decline, emphasizing the negative consequences of federal legislation (e.g., that special education mandates undermine the ability of state and local governments to provide high-quality education for all students). By focusing on the range of interests operating within one area of education policy, Itkonen provides an example of how such studies can help explain policy outcomes across multiple institutional venues, and also inform the larger issue of the conditions under which professional and parental interests diverge.

Although the focus of most studies of political interests is on their role in policy enactment, interest-based perspectives are also used to explain the persistence of policies over time. These explanations typically link interests with institutional factors by focusing on how organizational rules and structures protect the policy preferences of particular interests from opponents attempting to alter or replace those policies. An example is Moe's (1990) theory of the politics of structural choice. His initial premise is that in a democracy all interests must cope with political uncertainty: they will not always be in the political majority, and when other interests come to dominate, opponents may significantly change or reverse their policies. One way for current majorities to lock-in their legislative victories and to protect them from future tampering is through the structures by which policies are implemented and administered. Consequently, the dominant coalition attempts to ensure that those structures embody a set of rules governing institutional behavior—decision-making criteria, allocational rules, personnel evaluation standards—that insulates the agency from legislative oversight and alteration of its policies (e.g., by placing a greater emphasis on professionalism than is technically justified because professionals resist political interference). However, to the extent that a dominant coalition must engage in political compromise with its opponents, the resulting administrative structure may also include elements that will make them vulnerable when majorities change.

The politics of structural choice links institutional and interest-based explanations, and it points to the role of political considerations in overriding effectiveness and efficiency concerns. Chubb and Moe (1990) argue that the politics of structural choice has resulted in a highly bureaucratized educational system that is overly responsive to organized interests such as teacher unions at the expense of parents. Their recommended voucher solution reflects a strong normative stance, and has sparked years of scholarly and political debate. Nevertheless, researchers attempting to understand the growing bureaucratization of education and the structures that become institutionalized around specific policies such as student testing are likely to find Moe's theory valid and useful even if they disagree with his solution.

Ideas For some scholars who find interest-based explanations of policy outcomes invalid or incomplete, the concept of ideas represents an alternative that assumes there is a public interest which transcends self-interest (Mansbridge, 1990; Reich, 1988; Kelman, 1987). Other researchers have defined ideas more broadly as beliefs about preferred policy goals and the strategies for achieving those goals whether they stem from public- or self-interested motivations (Kingdon, 1993). In essence, then, policy ideas refer to specific policy alternatives (e.g., test-based accountability, school finance reform) as well as to the organized principles, values, and causal beliefs in which policy proposals are embedded (e.g., democratic representation, distributional equity; Béland, 2005a, p. 2). Because they typically embody a set of desired ends and the strategy or theory about how best to produce those results, ideas capture both normative and instrumental dimensions of policy.

Policy preferences are typically motivated by self or group interest, whether it is politicians' desires to be re-elected or interest groups' efforts to enhance their members' material advantages. Nevertheless, political scientists have come to recognize that ideas are often necessary to persuade others to accept even the most self-interested policy options. Even when a policy outcome is best explained by the actions of groups seeking to advance their material interests, they often must build support for their position through arguments based on the merits of the case (Majone, 1989; Kingdon, 1993). That process typically involves framing their alternative in ways that will increase elite and popular support prior to enactment and then during implementation.[4] In essence, frames are normative and cognitive ideas undergirding policy debates that political elites strategically craft and can use to legitimize their policy preferences (Campbell, 2002).

Research also suggests that comprehensive and far-reaching policies are more likely than narrow, specialized ones to be motivated by ideology and by concepts that transcend self-interest (Kelman, 1987). In fact, ideas and interests can be so intertwined that it becomes difficult to measure their independent effects (Kingdon, 1993). Education is among the domestic policy domains where the distinction between interests and ideas are often the most blurred. Although much of the politics of education revolves around material interests such as the allocation of financial resources, debates over which values should be reflected in the curriculum have also been enduring and central to its politics. Some analysts, using an ideational perspective to understand value conflicts in education, have examined the competing goals of education as a basis for understanding major policy disputes.

In a recent example, Hochschild and Scovronick (2003) provide a useful conceptual framework for understanding the bases of contention in policies ranging from school finance reform to bilingual and special education. They argue that from its inception, American public education has been defined by two broad goals with a third added more recently. The first is to promote individual attainment, articulated in the ideology of the American dream promising that all U.S. residents will have a reasonable chance to achieve success as they define it. The second is the collective purpose of promoting democracy through the teaching of democratic values and practices, and the provision of equal opportunity for all children. A third goal that has become prominent over the past two decades is the expectation that schools should meet the distinctive needs of particular racial, ethnic, religious, and gender groups.

By examining a variety of policy debates through the lens of each of these goals, we can begin to understand why the politics surrounding some education policies have been so virulent and difficult to resolve. Although Hochschild and Scovronick (2003) assume that all three goals are valid, the legitimacy of the third one continues to be questioned in debates over policies ranging from affirmative action to special education. Even when a goal's legitimacy is not in question, its advocates must compete for scarce resources and for time in the school curriculum, with one goal typically preeminent at a given time. The result is continual jockeying among proponents of those goals not currently in ascendancy to upset the status quo and to gain a higher place on the public agenda for the values they espouse. Consequently, "the combination of multiple goals, competing interests, and a fragmented governance structure has often made policies incoherent and decisions unstable" (Hochschild & Scovronick, 2003, p. 18).

Hochschild and Scovronick's framework is useful for understanding ideational policy disputes at a general level and for explaining why several major themes have endured in defining the sides in these debates. Taking a narrower but more in-depth approach and drawing on a variety of theoretical frameworks, other researchers have examined specific policies that have become flash-points in the cultural politics of education. For example, using a policy instruments framework and focusing on hortatory instruments that rely on information and values rather than material inducements to advance their goals, McDonnell (2004) examined the conflicts that arose in the 1990s over the curricular values embodied in some state assessments. She concluded that even when tangible incentives were attached to test results, curricular and professional values played a major part in motivating educators' actions. However, values that were strong enough to motivate educators were also powerful enough to mobilize small, but strategically influential, groups of cultural conservatives in opposition to the assessments.

In another example, Binder (2002) compared two very different curricular values—Afrocentrism and creationism— through seven cases grounded in a well-specified theoretical framework that draws on institutional perspectives and social movements research. Binder found that despite having very different constituencies, there were notable similarities between Afrocentrists and creationists. Both made comparable arguments about oppression by the majority culture and about their children's welfare, and educators were skeptical about the factual claims of both groups. She also found that Afrocentrists and creationists often directed their arguments for change at insiders within the school establishment, and not just at outsiders such as mobilizable members of the public. She concludes, "once we have taken note of the fact that insiders are sometimes the targets of challenger frames and even occasionally, they, themselves, become challenge advocates, then we have to recognize that the old line separating

'insiders' from 'outsiders' in challenge events is suspect" (p. 217). The finding that challengers' frames or arguments sometimes connected with insiders' frames helps explain why Afrocentrists were more successful, even if only at a symbolic level,[5] and it suggests an important enhancement of classical social movement theory. The status of creationists, some of whom were elected to school boards, also allowed Binder to make an important distinction between political and institutional power. As school board members, creationists had formal political authority over educators. However, because they did not share their professional socialization and were not involved in routine education decision making, they lacked the legitimacy that would have converted their political authority into institutional power over district policy and practice.

Once again, we return to the intersection of ideas, interests, and institutions. Creationism represents an idea whose adherents attempted to integrate it into the curriculum. Those attempts occurred within the institutional framework of school district bureaucracies whose rules and norms advantage insiders. Binder's analysis reminds us that challengers to the educational status quo must disrupt existing patterns of interest among policy makers and organized groups. However, even when they are successful at the enactment stage, they must also permeate well-established bureaucratic interests during implementation if they are to convert whatever political influence they can garner into sustained institutional influence.

Summary: Institutional, Interest-Based, and Ideational Approaches This review of research grounded in conceptions of institutions, interests, and ideas is necessarily selective. However, in presenting a diverse array of studies that draw on different theoretical approaches and research methods and that focus on different aspects of the education policy system, the hope is to demonstrate the potential payoff of using these concepts to guide future empirical analyses. Referring to institutions, interests, and ideas as building blocks is appropriate for several reasons, and suggests how their use as analytical concepts needs to be approached.

First, they should be viewed as hollow blocks that represent general parameters, but how they are filled depends on how the concept is defined and measured in an individual study. These three concepts do not provide a uniform recipe or theoretical template; they only point the researcher to a generic class of variables and set of assumptions that must be tailored to specific phenomena and research questions. Related to the need to tailor these concepts is a caution that has often been a critique of these approaches. Without precise specifications, they can easily fall prey to the problem of explaining everything and thus explaining nothing. Although these concepts may have come into vogue as a reaction to the artifactual constraints of the formal models derived from rational choice assumptions, they still require grounding in clear conceptualizations and well-defined causal assumptions if they are to produce valid research.

Second, these concepts are truly building blocks in the

sense that while one may serve as a keystone variable in a given study, a single block is unlikely to support a valid and comprehensive explanation. How these blocks are arranged will again depend on the phenomenon under study and the analytical strategy. One set of questions for which they are especially relevant are those dealing with the conditions for policy stability and change discussed in the next section.

Policy Stability and Change

Historical Institutionalism The focus on behavioral and later rational choice approaches in the post-war period threatened to make U.S. political science an ahistorical discipline. However, at about the same time that institutional perspectives once again gained currency, greater attention began to be paid in studies of American political development and comparative politics research to the role of historical events and institutions in shaping subsequent politics and policy. One question addressed in this line of historical institutional research is what factors explain the stability of policy regimes over time? Historical institutionalists have used the concept of path dependence to explain how and why social policies can become entrenched and difficult to alter. In its simplest form, path dependence refers to the process by which policy choices create institutional arrangements that make reversal or change costly.[6] Large consequences may result from relatively small or contingent events, but once particular courses of action are introduced, they may be virtually impossible to reverse (Pierson, 2000, p. 251). Those who examine policy stability and change from a path dependent perspective also stress the importance of timing and sequence, and they distinguish formative moments in policy development from periods that reinforce the status quo.[7]

Few education policy studies have been structured around an explicitly historical institutional framework and notions of path dependence. However, some analysts have used this approach to explain aspects of their findings. For example, Shipps (2006) notes, in explaining the persistence of corporate influence in the Chicago schools, that "vocational purposes, efficiency criteria, and management orientations embedded in the structure of the system have created a form of path dependence ... Once the initiating era passed, such self-reinforcing patterns of preference and access were no longer as dependent on logical argument, or organizational learning, or the strength of rational evidence" (p. 174). In contrast, McGuinn (2006) argues in his analysis of the history of federal education policy after 1965 that, contrary to studies of other federal policies such as social security that find they become path dependent with only incremental changes, the emergence of NCLB suggests that education is different with "the ends and means of national school policy hav[ing] changed dramatically since 1965" (p. 209).[8] However, even these partial tests of the explanatory power of historical institutionalism in education policy research are the exceptions, distinguishing it from other policy domains such as healthcare, pensions, and im-

migration where major studies have been grounded in this framework (e.g., Hacker, 2002; Tichenor, 2002; Gordon, 2003; Béland, 2005b).

Historical institutionalists acknowledge that change can occur, but assume that it is typically bounded until something erodes or overwhelms mechanisms that generate continuity (Pierson, 2004). However, this approach, while acknowledging that policy paths can be disrupted and diverted, lacks a detailed theory of change. Consequently, to understand policy change, we need to turn to other theorists.

Agenda-Setting and Policy Change Two models have withstood numerous empirical tests in a variety of policy domains, and they now dominate the political science and policy analysis research literature. The first, proposed by John Kingdon (1995) and based on research he conducted in the late 1970s, explains the process by which a proposal reaches the governmental agenda and is considered by policy makers, though not necessarily enacted into law. Kingdon hypothesized that policy emerges from the coupling of three independent process streams—problems, policy proposals, and politics. "They are largely independent of one another, and each develops according to its own dynamics and rules. But at some critical junctures the three streams are joined, and the greatest policy changes grow out of that coupling of problems, policy proposals, and politics ... a problem is recognized, a solution is developed and available to the policy community, a political change makes it the right time for policy change, and potential constraints are not severe" (p. 19, 165). Policy entrepreneurs are often critical to the process of bringing the three streams together—in effect, opening a policy window. They are willing to invest their resources in calling attention to problems and mobilizing support for pet proposals in the hope of obtaining future policies they favor.

Kingdon's model is designed to explain the agenda-setting process for most social policies whether they involve major changes or only incremental ones.[9] In contrast, the second model focuses on policy enactment as well as on agenda-setting, and it seeks to explain cycles of policy stability and change. In their research, now being replicated in other studies, Baumgartner and Jones (1993, 2002) set out to explain a persistent condition in U.S. public policy: the fact that most policymaking is incremental, but dramatic and deep changes in policy do occur. Borrowing from the natural sciences, Baumgartner and Jones call this condition punctuated equilibrium—long periods of stability interrupted by major alterations to the system (for an extended discussion of this topic, see also Cohen-Vogel & McLendon, this volume). This stability is maintained through the creation of policy monopolies that are structural arrangements supported by powerful policy ideas. These ideas or policy images are generally connected to core political values, combine empirical information and emotive appeals, can be easily understood, and are communicated directly and simply through image and rhetoric.

However, policy monopolies and the interests they represent can be disrupted, resulting in major policy changes. A primary reason such changes occur is that those opposed to the policy monopoly or excluded from it constitute slack resources policy entrepreneurs can mobilize. They do so through a redefinition of the dominant policy image using ideas that challenge it and capture the imagination of the media, policy makers, and the public. They provide new understandings of policy problems and new ways of conceptualizing solutions. These ideas can fuel powerful changes as they are communicated through a variety of rhetorical mechanisms, including stories about decline or negative consequences resulting from the current policy monopoly and stories of hope about what can be accomplished with a new framing of the policy problem and solution (Stone, 2002, p. 138).

Yet new ideas "are not controlled or created by any single group or individual, but are the result of multiple interactions among groups seeking to propose new understandings of issues, political leaders seeking new issues on which to make their name, agencies seeking to expand their jurisdictions, and voters reacting to the whole spectacle" (Baumgartner & Jones, 1993, p. 237). Although the fragmentation of the U.S. policy system often makes coherent policy difficult, its multiple arenas give policy entrepreneurs alternative points of entry as they move among institutions at the same and different governmental levels. Even when new ideas lead to policy changes, however, the old policy monopoly often continues until the institutional structures and norms through which new policies are implemented are also transformed.

The Kingdon and the Baumgartner and Jones models have significantly advanced scholarly understanding of agenda-setting and policy change. However, more work needs to be done. First, because most studies based on these models have focused on the national level in the United States and abroad, additional research is needed examining policy change and stability across levels in federalist systems and within sub-national governments. A second weakness is that although the two strands are quite complementary, historical institutional studies and those using a policy dynamics framework have developed independently with little attempt to link them systematically. Finally, these theories are primarily intended to be ex post—explaining cycles of stability and change after they occur—rather than predictive of future shifts. Yet these shortcomings only highlight the potential payoff from additional research focused on one of the most critical parts of the policy puzzle: the conditions under which a policy is likely to continue with only incremental changes as compared with those that lead to fundamental alterations in a dominant policy image.

Illustrative Studies of Education Policy Change Two education policy studies illustrate possible directions for refining the existing models. In a recent analysis of the origins of NCLB, Manna (2006) supplements Baumgartner and Jones' theory, focusing on policy change in a federalist system. In his analysis, Manna develops the concept of *borrowing strength* that "occurs when policy entrepreneurs at one level of government attempt to push their agendas by leveraging the justification and capabilities that other governments elsewhere in the federal system possess" (p. 5). Manna argues that the passage of NCLB was possible because state governments had earlier enacted reforms organized around standards and assessments. Policy entrepreneurs promoting NCLB could mobilize around the *license* or arguments states had already made to justify the involvement of higher levels of government in classroom processes and outcomes, and around the *capacity* or resources and administrative structures that state reforms had created. Manna notes that although federal officials were able to borrow strength from the states in the case of NCLB, the process can also work in the other direction. For example, state officials may take advantage of the license provided by a president using the bully pulpit to advance reform arguments as a point of leverage in promoting their own policy agenda (p. 15).

A number of Manna's major conclusions—including his finding that, beginning in the 1990s, the federal government's involvement began to touch the core functions of schools and that its expanded license to act was directly related to the widening role of state governments in education during the 1980s—have also been documented by other analysts (e.g., McDonnell, 2005). Similarly, Manna notes that in their analysis of state-local relationships, Fuhrman and Elmore (1990) countered the claim that influence in the federalist system is zero-sum, with one governmental level's increase in influence coming at the expense of another. Rather, they found that entrepreneurial local school districts can use state policies as leverage to promote their own priorities through much the same process as Manna's notion of borrowing strength. His analysis of federal agenda-setting with its caution that neither a solely top-down nor bottom-up perspective is sufficient also complements the forward- and backward-mapping strategies derived from decades of implementation research on the relationship between inadequate federal capacity and state and local policy.

So Manna's contribution is not one of significant new insights about the evolution of the federal role in education. Rather, it provides a conceptual framework linking the education case to the broader research literature on agenda-setting and federalism. As a result, his account is more systematic and coherent than earlier ones. Manna outlines a set of predictions about the circumstances under which policy entrepreneurs are likely to borrow strength from other governmental levels, and about the conditions under which states will seek to extract concessions from federal officials (e.g., when state policy makers think their federal counterparts have overestimated state license or capacity). In assessing how federalism has shaped the nation's education policy agenda over the past 40 years, Manna uses a political development approach, identifying the constraints and opportunities that past policies have created for future choices, and taking into account both incremental and more rapid change.

The second study analyzes the role of policy entrepreneurs in promoting school choice, and it provides a deeper, more nuanced picture of these critical agents than is typically available from studies that examine them as one factor in a particular case of policy change. In promoting policy innovations, policy entrepreneurs typically tap into issue networks that allow them to communicate their ideas to those with shared interests and to be linked by formal and informal contacts (Kingdon, 1995; Wirt & Kirst, 2005). A good example of this process is the role of policy entrepreneurs and issue networks in the diffusion of ideas about school choice. Drawing on a survey of state education policy experts, Mintrom (1997) found that policy entrepreneurs were identified as advocates of school choice in 26 states. Then, using event history analysis models of the diffusion of school choice ideas across the U.S., Mintrom and Vergari (1998) found that greater involvement in policy networks significantly increased the likelihood that policy entrepreneurs achieved their legislative goals.

However, the explanatory variables for getting the school choice issue on a state's legislative agenda differed from those explaining whether or not a choice policy was subsequently enacted. The researchers found that in getting the choice issue on the agenda, policy entrepreneurs used both interstate or external policy networks and internal, in-state networks consisting of individuals with ties to members of the local policymaking community. The external networks served as sources for generating new ideas, while the internal networks provided relevant contacts and a source of information about how best to present proposals for innovation to garner serious attention. However, once the issue was on the agenda, the factors that predicted legislative approval were different. At the approval stage, not only was the presence of an internal network significant, but approval was more likely if the teacher union did not strongly oppose the policy and student test scores had declined, signaling a need for policy change.

This example illustrates the critical role of policy entrepreneurs and issue networks in spreading new ideas and in altering established policy monopolies. But it also shows how ideas and interests intersect. In this case, the strength of union opposition had no effect on the likelihood of legislative consideration of school choice, but such opposition did reduce chances for legislative approval. In essence, the influence of a critical group whose interests could be threatened by school choice was not a significant factor in determining whether this new idea was seriously considered, but the group's position did make a difference to whether it was transformed into policy.

Our understanding of the dynamics of policy stability and change is incomplete, and additional work is needed. Yet despite significant gaps in the theoretical and empirical research literature, a focus on long-term policy development is likely to result in more sophisticated and valid policy analyses. As Pierson (2005) notes, it moves the field from a "snapshot" view of individual policy decisions to a perspective that "pays attention to processes that play out over considerable periods of time" (p. 34). Such an emphasis is especially important in education policy because it is characterized by remarkable stability in some core elements such as instructional delivery systems, while at the same time, punctuated by significant shifts in underlying policy theories and institutional arrangements.

Policy Feedback

More than 70 years ago, Schattschneider (1935) argued that "new policies create a new politics" (p. 288). However, it has only been within the last 15 years that Schattschneider's assertion has been incorporated into a framework for studying the political effects of policy. This approach, called policy feedback, has two analytical purposes. The first is to reverse the causal arrow of most research on the politics of public policy in which political variables are used to explain policy outcomes. Instead, policy feedback studies examine how policies, once enacted, create political interests that mobilize and shape future policies (Pierson, 1993). The second purpose is to connect research on mass political behavior with more institutionally-focused policy studies (Mettler & Soss, 2004). In essence, the second purpose is a subset of the first in that not all policies directly influence mass political attitudes and actions, but most, in advantaging some interests and disadvantaging others, lead to some form of mobilization. Although the research literature is not always clear about policies' differing potential for mobilization, we can think of policy feedback occurring at just the elite level or at both the elite and mass levels. For example, policies giving tax advantages to specific industries are likely to mobilize support coalitions limited to groups representing those industries, while Social Security has mobilized a broad swath of senior citizens (Campbell, 2003).

The assumed causal process that underlies policy feedback, however, is similar at the elite and mass levels, and is related to the institutional regimes that policies create. In allocating resources or in regulating their use, policies create incentives for targets to organize to preserve and expand their benefits or to minimize their costs. These efforts occur within a set of rules and structures that the policy establishes and that can become institutionalized. Not all policies result in enduring regimes. But if it persists, a policy's allocational rules and administrative structures will lead, over time, to patterns of interest group formation and for some policies, to distributions of public opinion.

The nature of policy feedback, then, depends on the incentive structures created, but it also depends on the types of access to the governmental system the policy provides and to the signals it sends about the political standing of its targets. This latter dimension is what Pierson (1993) classifies as interpretative effects: how policies serve as sources of information and meaning with implications for citizens' political learning. It is this aspect of policy feedback that scholars see as the link to mass attitudes and behavior. In outlining a future research agenda, Mettler and Soss (2004) suggest a number of ways that policies signal targets about their political status: by influencing how individuals understand their rights and responsibilities as members of a political community, by conveying messages about group characteristics directly to members of a target group and to broader public audiences, by playing a role in building and distributing civic skills among the public, by defining policy problems and their solutions in particular ways, by encouraging or discouraging demand making, and by creating arenas for citizen demands.

Empirical Studies of Policy Feedback Two examples related to education illustrate several ways that policies can shape political behavior. First, the Individuals with Disabilities Education Act (IDEA) and subsequent judicial rulings have given parents of special education students a major role in deciding which educational services are most appropriate for their children, and have led to the effective mobilization of parent groups (Itkonen, 2007). Yet one could imagine a different policy design for IDEA in which professional educators and school districts were more clearly preeminent in the decision-making process with less equal standing for parents. Such a design would have sent a strong message about assumed parental deference to professional expertise and would have given them weaker legal standing from which to mobilize. Mettler and Soss (2004) suggest a second example that illustrates a significant gap in the link between knowledge about individual political behavior and policy effects. One of the most robust conclusions from political behavior research is that education enhances political knowledge and skills, levels of interest, and engagement in civic affairs. Because education is unevenly distributed, the result is considerable political inequality. Yet political behavior studies rarely consider government policy as a significant factor in explaining observed outcomes, and "policy studies that focus on social and economic outcomes say almost nothing about how education policies affect the political process" (p. 56).

Over the past decade, several studies have examined the nature of policy feedback as it relates to mass political attitudes and participation. They have been characterized by creative analyses of multiple data sources, and significant insight into the links between policy and individual behavior. However, these studies have represented easy tests of the concept because the policy designs are ones that send strong messages about how the larger polity views program targets—for example, the universalism and social insurance framing of Social Security (Campbell, 2003), the reward for sacrifices on behalf of country embodied in the Servicemen's Readjustment Act of 1944 (G.I. Bill; Mettler, 2005), and the means-testing and tight regulations associated with the Temporary Assistance to Needy Families program (Soss, 1999). Although the interpretative effects of these policies are major factors in shaping targets' political attitudes and their conceptions of themselves as political actors, they are also buttressed by the level and type of material resources

the policies allocate and by the institutional arrangements through which government agencies interact with program recipients.

Thus far, only one study in education has used an explicit policy feedback approach. Abernathy (2005) examines the effects of school choice on political participation in resource-rich and resource-poor communities. Drawing on a variety of survey and observational data, he finds that choice options do seem to encourage greater parental participation, but that the effects of this increased participation are largely felt within the choice school and not in the broader community.

Consistent with an earlier study of public school choice (Schneider, Teske, & Marschall, 2000), Abernathy finds that parents who left the Milwaukee public school system for either a public choice or private school option are more involved in their school community, and that once their children entered the choice school, they became even more active. From a survey of Minnesota principals, he finds that charter school principals and those with charter schools operating in their districts are more customer-focused than those with no nearby charter schools. Charter school principals are also more likely to offer parents an opportunity to participate in meaningful areas of policy related to school-level governance and budgetary decisions. In examining school budget referenda in New Jersey, Abernathy finds that charter school districts are associated with higher voter turnout, but lower budget approval rates than in non-charter districts. He argues that this latter finding is consistent with a "process of withdrawal from the collective enterprise into the cocoon of the charter school" (p. 105).

Abernathy acknowledges that the patterns emerging from his disparate analyses are only suggestive and warrant additional research. However, they do indicate a significant relationship between policy design and participatory patterns that, if found to be valid in other studies, has serious implications for districts designing choice programs. The major one is that researchers and policy designers need to distinguish between the building- and community-level effects of various choice policies. The policy feedback effects may be positive for individual choice schools, but may be quite negative for the broader community if the most active parents exit traditional public schools and then focus their efforts only within the choice school. These effects are likely to be most serious in resource-poor communities where even if non-choice principals attempt to be responsive and competitive, the withdrawal of active parents may leave them with insufficient human and social capital.

School choice is an obvious test of the theory of policy feedback because one of its goals is to alter the relationship between schools and the parents and students they serve. But more studies are needed that focus on education policies as well as on ones in other domains. For example, within education, what elements of the Elementary and Secondary Education Act's (ESEA) design have led to a different politics around it than around IDEA? What effects have those differences had on program services? To what extent do state categorical programs lead to different types of claims and allocational decisions than general aid? These and similar questions will require creative research designs that draw on survey, budgetary, and historical data. However, the potential benefits from such research can be considerable. If policy feedback can be shown to be a robust concept, it can play both retrospective and prospective functions in policy analysis. Retrospectively, it can expand conventional policy evaluation research by considering outcomes beyond immediate instrumental effects of a particular policy to its broader impact on democratic citizenship. Prospectively, it can provide policy makers with more complete information about the likely effects of the options presented them. In addition to predictions about likely costs, distributional, and educational effects, a policy feedback approach would also provide information about the potential effects of different administrative structures a policy could establish—such as, who will have standing to make claims, how are program targets likely to be treated under different organizational arrangements, and how accessible and transparent will information about program operations and outcomes be under different structures?

Conclusions

Given political science's emphasis on theory-building and its focus on factors distant from the classroom, it seems fair to ask what payoffs are likely from grounding more education policy research in political science theory and concepts. This question seems especially relevant at a time when student achievement, as measured on standardized tests, has become the dominant standard for policy success and the major dependent variable to be explained. There are three possible answers, each related to the different audiences for policy research. The first involves those within the academic community. Grounding education policy research in political science frameworks, or those of other disciplines such as economics, sociology, social psychology, or anthropology, will make the theories that guide it less derivative and better integrate the field into the broader social sciences. Linking education research more directly into the disciplinary social sciences is likely to benefit its standing within academia and to attract a broader range of scholars to the field. However, just as education stands to gain from stronger ties to the disciplines, so the disciplines can benefit from studying education policy. Seeking to understand policies that affect the lives of children may not have the same cachet as studying war, peace, or presidents, but there is no question that the politics of education policy represents a microcosm of the U.S. political system, and provides an excellent opportunity for testing disciplinary theories. Education is an especially productive policy domain for refining theory because its fragmented institutions allow for more extensive tests than are typical with the national focus of much political science research. The values that define the politics of education, such as competing definitions of equity, the place of religion, and the role of markets, as

well as the range of interests that advance them, also make it fertile ground for developing a better understanding of the contours of American politics.

A second answer relates to the analyses that researchers can provide the policy community. Studies applying concepts such as policy regime, path dependency, punctuated equilibrium, and civic capacity have shown us that snapshot views of single policies over a relatively short period and a focus on policy only within the narrow confines of school systems have provided incomplete information to policy makers. Certainly, officials often have shortened time frames dictated by electoral cycles, and education's isolation from other civic institutions and social policies contributes to this narrow perspective. Nevertheless, those seeking either to change policy directions or to improve the status quo will be better equipped if they are informed by analyses that situate education policy in broader institutional contexts, that pay attention to informal norms and behaviors as well as to formal institutions, and that understand the causal processes that constrain change or provide opportunities and critical junctures for new policies to emerge.

The final answer speaks to the public about the role of education in a democratic society. Despite efforts over the past century to place public schooling above politics, it remains a profoundly political institution. A central part of its mission since the founding of the Republic has been to prepare students for democratic citizenship; it is the arena in which we decide how one of society's most precious resources will be distributed and what values will be reflected in the curriculum, and it is an institution that has directly touched the lives of most citizens. For much of the late 20th century, politics was viewed as little more than one of the independent variables explaining education policy outcomes—in effect, a production function for delivering policies rather than a process important in its own right, with particular normative and practical outcomes. One of the benefits of recent studies that have drawn on political science concepts has been to remind us of education's role as a political institution. While understanding the academic functions of schooling will—and should—remain preeminent, the capacity of education policy and politics to encourage or hinder democratic aspirations should also continue as a worthy object of scholarship.

Notes

1. Even researchers who start with very different models of politics and assumptions about the role of institutions agree that they are important to explaining outcomes. For example, Moe (2000) presents a model in which political institutions largely reflect the interests of dominant groups, while March and Olsen (2000) assume that those same institutions embody rules and norms encouraging the development of shared identities that extend beyond self-interest. Nevertheless, both sets of authors see institutions as critical for understanding education policy and for changing its outcomes.

2. The last national census of governments that included information about local school boards was conducted by the U.S. Census Bureau in 1992 (Berkman & Pultzer, 2005). As a result, most studies of local boards are based on comparative case studies, often a sample

of urban districts or districts within a single state or region (e.g., see the studies presented in Howell, 2005).

3. In his review of two major political science journals, Orr (2004) finds that over a 118-year period, only 12 of the 6,800 articles published focused on education. Somewhat ironically, however, the first education-related article published in the *Political Science Quarterly* (Jenks, 1891) analyzed the book agents' lobby, portraying them as a powerful interest group whose political activities in state capitals shaped decisions about which textbooks students would use.

4. Ideas are used after policy enactment as rationalizations that provide a broader conceptual framework for what would otherwise be discrete and disjointed decisions. These idea-based arguments help: develop popular understandings of a policy by linking it to other policies and normative beliefs; anticipate and answer criticism; facilitate communication among those implementing it and similar policies; and identify new implications of the policy (Majone, 1996).

5. Binder concludes that Afrocentrists were more successful in getting their values embodied in curriculum because they appeared to be offering a solution to problems of urban school failure, and school administrators were sympathetic to their arguments that African history and culture had been excluded from the curriculum. In contrast, the creationists were attempting to change the curriculum in suburban schools that appeared to be effective in educating their students; they were trying to change the higher status science curriculum as opposed to history; and their opponents had the added lever of the courts because creationism raised separation of church and state issues.

6. Historical institutionalists have borrowed the concept of *increasing returns* from economists as a more precise way to examine the extent of path dependence and the possibilities for institutional change. Increasing returns processes pinpoint how the costs of switching from one alternative to another will, in certain social contexts, increase significantly over time. The reasons are varied, but include large set-up or fixed costs, learning effects that lead to the continued use of familiar institutional arrangements and processes, and coordination effects with the benefits to one individual or jurisdiction increasing as others adopt similar policies and procedures (Pierson, 2000).

7. Most studies grounded in an historical institutional perspective have focused on the determinants of policy stability, and have paid less attention to developing theories of change. However, a few political scientists have begun to formulate theories of change from this perspective. For example, Lieberman (2002) hypothesized that change arises out of friction among mismatched institutional and ideational patterns. His illustrative case is U.S. race policy in the 1960s and 1970s when the friction between the strong ideological underpinnings of antidiscrimination policy were at odds with the weak institutional capacity to enforce it. That situation led from a convergence on color-blindness to an embrace of race-conscious remedies for discrimination as incentives were created to move enforcement away from a sole concentration in Washington to multiple institutional venues throughout the country, including local collective bargaining agreements and employee lawsuits.

8. In contrast, other analyses of NCLB (McDonnell, 2005) have concluded that although NCLB expanded the scope of federal regulation, this newest version reflects an evolution of the federal role rather than a radical redefinition or major departure from its developmental path. Along with other analysts (e.g., Manna, 2006), she also finds that NCLB's design was only possible because of profound changes in the state role over the past 20 years.

9. At least one policy analyst has argued that a variant of Kingdon's framework is also a useful way to conceptualize the conditions necessary for policy termination. Of particular relevance is the fact that Kingdon's framework focuses on two devices that maintain organizational stability: (a) the existing structure of an institution and (b) the definition of a policy problem. Consequently, it provides clues about how policy makers can counteract factors that work against termination (Geva-May, 2004).

References

Abernathy, S. F. (2005). *School choice of the future of American democracy.* Ann Arbor: University of Michigan Press.

Baumgartner, F. R., & Jones, B. D. (1993). *Agendas and instability in American politics.* Chicago: University of Chicago Press.

Baumgartner, F. R., & Jones, B. D. (Eds.). (2002). *Policy dynamics.* Chicago: University of Chicago Press.

Baumgartner, F. R., & Leech, B. L. (1998). *Basic interests: The importance of groups in politics and political science.* Princeton, NJ: Princeton University Press.

Béland, D. (2005a). Ideas and social policy: An institutionalist perspective. *Social Policy and Administration, 39,* 1–18.

Béland, D. (2005b). *Social Security: History and politics from the New Deal to the privatization debate.* Lawrence: University Press of Kansas.

Berkman, M. B., & Pultzer, E. (2005). *Ten thousand democracies: Politics and public opinion in America's school districts.* Washington, DC: Georgetown University Press.

Binder, A. J. (2002). *Contentious curricula: Afrocentism and creationism in American public schools.* Princeton, NJ: Princeton University Press.

Boyd, W. L., Plank, D. N., & Sykes, G. (2000). Teachers unions in hard times. In T. Loveless (Ed.), *Conflicting missions? Teachers unions and education reform* (pp. 174–210). Washington, DC: Brookings Institution Press.

Campbell, A. L. (2003). *How policies make citizens: Senior political activism and the American welfare state.* Princeton, NJ: Princeton University Press.

Campbell, J. L. (2002). Ideas, politics, and public policy. *Annual Review of Sociology, 28,* 21–38.

Chubb, J. E., & Moe, T. M. (1990). *Politics, markets, and America's schools.* Washington, DC: Brookings Institution.

Cigler, A. J. (1994). Research gaps in the study of interest group representation. In W. Crotty, M. A. Schwartz, & J. C. Green (Eds.), *Representing interests and interest groups* (pp. 29–36). Lanham, MD: University Press of America.

Clarke, S. E., Hero, R. E., Sidney, M. S., Fraga, L. R., & Erlichson, B. A. (2006). *Multiethnic moments: The politics of urban education reform.* Philadelphia: Temple University Press.

Fuhrman, S. H., & Elmore, R. F. (1990). Understanding local control in the wake of state education reform. *Educational Evaluation and Policy Analysis, 12,* 82–96.

Geva-May, I. (2004). Riding the wave of opportunity: Termination in public policy. *Journal of Public Administration Research and Theory, 14,* 309–333.

Gordon, G. (2003). *Dead on arrival: The politics of health care in twentieth-century America.* Princeton, NJ: Princeton University Press.

Hacker, J. S. (2002). *The divided welfare state: The battle over public and private social benefits in the United States.* New York: Cambridge University Press.

Heclo, H. (1994). Ideas, interests, and institutions. In L. C. Dodd & C. Jillson (Eds.), *The dynamics of American politics: Approaches and interpretations* (pp. 366–392). Boulder, CO: Westview Press.

Henig, J., Hula, R., Orr, M., & Pedescleaux, D. (1999). *The color of school reform: Race, politics, and the challenge of urban education.* Princeton, NJ: Princeton University Press.

Henig, J. R., & Rich, W. C. (Eds.). (2004). *Mayors in the middle: Politics, race, and mayoral control of urban schools.* Princeton, NJ: Princeton University Press.

Hochschild, J., & Scovronick, N. (2003). *The American dream and the public schools.* New York: Oxford University Press.

Howell, W. G. (Ed.). (2005). *Besieged: School boards and the future of education politics.* Washington, DC: Brookings Institution.

Itkonen, T. (2007). Politics of passion: Collective action from pain and loss. *American Journal of Education, 113,* 577–604.

Jenks, J. W. (1891). School-book legislation. *Political Science Quarterly, 6,* 90–125.

Kelman, S. (1987). *Making public policy: A hopeful view of American government*. New York: Basic Books.

Kingdon, J. W. (1993). Politicians, self-interest, and ideas. In G. E. Marcus & R. L. Hanson (Eds.), *Reconsidering the democratic public* (pp. 73–89). University Park: Pennsylvania State University Press.

Kingdon, J. W. (1995). *Agendas, alternatives, and public policies* (2nd ed.). New York: HarperCollins.

Kirst, M. W. (2003). Mayoral influence, new regimes, and public school governance. *Yearbook of the National Society for the Study of Education, 102*(10), 196–218.

Lieberman, R. C. (2002). Ideas, institutions, and political order: Explaining political change. *American Political Science Review, 96*, 697–712.

Longoria, T., Jr. (1998). School politics in Houston: The impact of business involvement. In C. Stone (Ed.), *Changing urban education* (pp. 184–198). Lawrence: University Press of Kansas.

Majone, G. (1989). *Evidence, argument and persuasion in the policy process.* New Haven, CT: Yale University Press.

Majone, G. (1996). Public policy and administration: Ideas, interests, and institutions. In R. E. Goodin & H. Klingemann (Eds.), *A new handbook of political science* (pp. 610–627). New York: Oxford University Press.

Manna, P. (2006). *School's in: Federalism and the national education agenda*. Washington, DC: Georgetown University Press.

Mansbridge, J. J. (Ed.). (1990). *Beyond self-interest*. Chicago: University of Chicago Press.

March, J. G., & Olsen, J. P. (1989). *Rediscovering institutions: The organizational basis of politics*. New York: Free Press.

March, J. G., & Olsen, J. P. (1995). *Democratic governance*. New York: Free Press.

March, J. G., & Olsen, J. P. (2000). Democracy and schooling: An institutional perspective. In L. M. McDonnell, P. M. Timpane, & R. Benjamin (Eds.), *Rediscovering the democratic purposes of education* (pp. 148–173). Lawrence: University Press of Kansas.

Marschall, M. J. (2005). Minority incorporation and local school boards. In W. G. Howell (Ed.), *Besieged: School boards and the future of education politics* (pp. 173–198). Washington, DC: Brookings Institution.

Mawhinney, H. B. (2001). Theoretical approaches to understanding interest groups. *Educational Policy, 15*, 187–214.

Mazzoni, T. L. (1991). Analyzing state school policymaking: An arena model. *Educational Evaluation and Policy Analysis, 13*, 115–138.

McDonnell, L. M. (2004). *Politics, persuasion, and educational testing*. Cambridge, MA: Harvard University Press.

McDonnell, L. M. (2005). No Child Left Behind and the federal role in education: Evolution or revolution? *Peabody Journal of Education, 80*(2), 19–38.

McGuinn, P. J. (2006). *No Child Left Behind and the transformation of federal education policy, 1965–2005*. Lawrence: University Press of Kansas.

Meier, K. J., & Juenke, E. G. (2005). Electoral structure and the quality of representation on school boards. In W. G. Howell (Ed.), *Besieged: School boards and the future of education politics* (pp. 199–227). Washington, DC: Brookings Institution.

Melnick, R. S. (1995). Separation of powers and the strategy of rights: The expansion of special education. In M. K. Landy & M. Levin (Eds.), *The new politics of public policy* (pp. 23–46). Baltimore: Johns Hopkins University Press

Mettler, S. (2005). *Soldiers to citizens: The G.I. Bill and the making of the greatest generation*. New York: Oxford University Press.

Mettler, S., & Soss, J. (2004). The consequences of public policy for democratic citizenship: Bridging policy studies and mass politics. *Perspectives on Politics, 2*, 55–73.

Mintrom, M. (1997). Policy entrepreneurs and the diffusion of innovation. *American Journal of Political Science, 41*, 738–770.

Mintrom, M., & Vergari, S. (1998). Policy networks and innovation diffusion: The case of state education reforms. *The Journal of Politics, 60*, 126–148.

Miskel, C., & Song, M. (2004). Passing Reading First: Prominence and processes in an elite policy network. *Educational Evaluation and Policy Analysis, 26*, 89–109.

Moe, T. M. (1990). Political institutions: The neglected side of the story. *Journal of Law, Economics, and Organization, 6*(Special Issue), 213–254.

Moe, T. M. (2000). The two democratic purposes of public education. In L. M. McDonnell, P. M. Timpane, & R. Benjamin (Eds.), *Rediscovering the democratic purposes of education* (pp. 127–147). Lawrence: University Press of Kansas.

Moe, T. M. (2005). Teacher unions and school board elections. In W. G. Howell (Ed.), *Besieged: School boards and the future of education politics* (pp. 254–287). Washington, DC: Brookings Institution.

Orr, M. (1999). *Black social capital: The politics of school reform in Baltimore, 1986–1998*. Lawrence: University Press of Kansas.

Orr, M. (2004). Political Science and Education Research: An exploratory look at two political science journals. *Educational Researcher, 33*(5), 11–16.

Pierson, P. (1993). When effect becomes cause: Policy feedback and political change. *World Politics, 45*, 595–628.

Pierson, P. (2000). Increasing returns, path dependence, and the study of politics. *American Political Science Review, 94*, 251–267.

Pierson, P. (2004). *Politics in time: History, institutions, and social analysis*. Princeton, NJ: Princeton University Press.

Pierson, P. (2005). The study of policy development. *Journal of Policy History, 17*, 34–51.

Portz, J., Stein, L., & Jones, R. R. (1999). *City schools and city politics: Institutions and leadership in Pittsburgh, Boston, and St. Louis*. Lawrence: University Press of Kansas.

Reed, D. S. (2001). *On equal terms: The constitutional politics of educational opportunity*. Princeton, NJ: Princeton University Press.

Reich, R. B. (Ed.). (1988). *The power of public ideas*. Cambridge, MA: Ballinger.

Rich, W. C. (1996). *Black mayors and school politics: The failure of reform in Detroit, Gary, and Newark*. New York: Garland.

Schattschneider, E. E. (1935). *Politics, pressures, and the tariff*. New York: Prentice-Hall.

Schneider, M., Teske, P., & Marschall, M. (2000). *Choosing schools: Consumer choice and the quality of American schools*. Princeton, NJ: Princeton University Press.

Shipps, D. (2006). *School reform, corporate style: Chicago 1880–2000*. Lawrence: University Press of Kansas.

Soss, J. (1999). Lessons of welfare: Policy design, political learning, and political action. *American Political Science Review, 93*, 363–380.

Stone, C. N. (Ed.). (1998). *Changing urban education*. Lawrence: University Press of Kansas.

Stone, C. N., Henig, J. R., Jones, B. D., & Pierannunzi, C. (2001). *Building civic capacity: The politics of reforming urban schools*. Lawrence: University Press of Kansas.

Stone, D. (2002). *Policy paradox: The art of political decision making* (Rev. ed.). New York: W. W. Norton.

Tichenor, D. J. (2002). *Dividing lines: The politics of immigration control in America*. Princeton, NJ: Princeton University Press.

Weimer, D. L., & Vining, A. R. (2005). *Policy analysis: Concepts and practice* (4th ed.). Upper Saddle River, NJ: Pearson/Prentice Hall.

Wirt, F. M., & Kirst, M. W. (2005). *The political dynamics of American education* (3rd ed.). Richmond, CA: McCutchon Publishing.

Wong, K. K., & Shen, F. X. (2005). When mayors lead urban schools: Assessing the effects of mayoral takeover. In W. G. Howell (Ed.), *Besieged: School boards and the future of education politics* (pp. 81–101). Washington, DC: Brookings Institution.

5

Perspectives from the Disciplines

Sociological Contributions to Education Policy Research and Debates

Douglas Lee Lauen and Karolyn Tyson
University of North Carolina at Chapel Hill

Introduction

Émile Durkheim and Max Weber laid the foundation for a sociological approach to the study of education, but the sub-discipline of the sociology of education did not emerge until the late 1950s and early 1960s in the U.S. and the U.K. (Dreeben, 1994; Karabel & Halsey, 1977). The dominant social science perspectives on education at the time included psychology, which examined cognition and the learning process; economics, which through human capital theory attempted to account for individual and societal investments in education; and structural functionalism, a sociological theory which attempted to describe the major social systems, including education, and their interrelationships.

Since the time of the emergence of the sociology of education as a sub-discipline, sociological research has shed light on the contribution of educational achievement and attainment to occupational attainment, equality of educational opportunity, the role of schooling in reproducing the existing social order, the social organization of schools, tracking and other within-school processes, and approaches to examining the effects of schools as institutions. While these topics are varied, sociological research on education often shares one implicit goal: to contribute to knowledge that may be used to understand and in some cases improve society, education, and schools.

Advancing theory about schools has advanced popular conceptions of schools, so we begin this essay with some of the major theoretical and empirical contributions of the sociology of education. Following a summary of how sociological theory and research has contributed to the way we think about education and schools, we will outline some of the successes, failures, and challenges inherent in making sociological contributions to educational policy. This chapter will focus on the contributions of the sociological study of education to public policy about K-12 education, though it must be noted that assessing the impact of sociological theory and research on education policy, or indeed theory

and research from *any* of the social sciences, is probably impossible to pin down precisely.

We conclude this chapter with reflections on the differences between academic and policy research, the audiences for social science research, and the major modes of empirical inquiry, including a discussion of qualitative research and the recent turn towards causal analysis, and draw implications about how mode of inquiry affects the policy relevance of research.

Major Theoretical and Empirical Contributions to Education Research

Since the mid-1950s, sociology has developed a rich tradition of theoretical work on education and schools. This broad base of knowledge covers questions big and small and addresses macro- and micro-level processes, ranging from analyses of education as an institution and its purpose and effects on society, to analyses of classroom practices and policies and the influence of schooling on individuals.

The public's understanding of the limits and possibilities of schooling is informed to a large degree by knowledge gained from sociological analyses of education, both theoretical and empirical. Sociological theory outlines the general purposes of education as an institution, the effects of schooling on individuals, and how schools facilitate particular societal goals, such as preparing young people for their adult roles. These theories, in turn, contribute to empirical studies of education and schools. Sociologists conduct research to assess how well schools are meeting society's varied needs, the factors that explain the allocation of individuals to positions in society, and how factors such as funding, leadership, curriculum, pedagogy, school practices and policies, and teacher, student, and parent attitudes and behaviors impact educational outcomes. Indeed, sociology plays an important, although largely anonymous, role in education policy, because as Stevenson (2000) notes, much of the "standard empirical work of sociologists of education

[has] become the background knowledge of policymakers" (p. 548). In the sections that follow we highlight some of the theoretical and empirical findings of sociological research on education that have made a significant contribution to our knowledge of the effects of schools.

Functionalist Theory At the core of the sociological study of education are questions about social change and the relationship between schools and society. When the sub-discipline was emerging in the 1950s, structural functionalism was the dominant theoretical approach to understanding how society and its various institutions, including schools, work. Early sociologists like Émile Durkheim, Pitirim Sorokin, and Talcott Parson were interested in schools not just in and of themselves, but in relation to the wider society, to their connection and value to other institutions, and the overall functioning of the social system. The functionalist perspective posits a view of society as a system of interrelated institutions, each fulfilling particular roles but working in concert to maintain the stability of the system. The school's primary roles in the social system are to socialize young people in the national culture and prepare them for social life, and to determine and develop their particular talents and abilities so that they are prepared to fulfill the adult roles for which they are best suited. Functionalists contend that the school's allocation of individuals to positions in society is based on the principle of meritocracy and therefore provides a mechanism for social mobility because it reduces the effects of ascribed characteristics such as gender, race, and social class. By the 1960s, however, the view of school as a neutral institution charged with socializing youth and allocating them to their appropriate place in the occupational structure according to ability and motivation began to fall out of favor as approaches with a less cohesive view of society became more popular.

Conflict Theory Advancing a decidedly Marxist perspective and building as well on the work of Max Weber, conflict theory views education as a tool of domination that aids in the maintenance of the existing stratification order. Conflict theorists argue that as elite-driven institutions, schools inculcate in young people attitudes and values that foster respect for the dominant culture. Thus social stability is maintained through coercion, and not, as functionalists posit, as a result of a consensus of values and interests. The conflict perspective holds that socialization and allocation function for the benefit of the elite rather than the society as a whole, because students are allocated according to race, class, and gender. This set of arrangements creates a source of constant tension among competing status groups in schools, as the less advantaged challenge the elite in an attempt to gain a greater share of the society's relatively scarce resources.

The conflict perspective continued to develop through the 1970s with a number of other significant theoretical contributions from sociologists and other social scientists (e.g., Bowles & Gintis, 1976). Sociologists such as Basil Bernstein (1975) and Pierre Bourdieu and Jean Claude Passeron (1977) offered theories that elaborated on the process by which the class structure is reproduced through schooling, with a focus on language and cultural codes. Bourdieu's (1977) concept of cultural capital, used to explain the intergenerational transmission of privilege and disadvantage, is now widely used among scholars conducting education research. At the same time, however, other scholars were critical of reproduction theories, arguing that they placed too much emphasis on structure and too little on human agency, leaving individuals powerless to resist the forces of institutions (MacLeod, 1995). Scholars such as Paul Willis (1977) called for greater attention to the lived experience of youth in schools and to their capacity to respond in a variety of ways to systems of domination.

The concept of credentialism, used by Randall Collins (1979) to explain the rise in the level of education required in the labor market, has also become a common term in the discourse of education researchers. Collins rejected the functionalist position that the change in educational requirements reflects the increasing complexity of jobs and argued instead that it is a strategy of the elite to maintain and justify their high-status positions. Collins proposed that as the percentage of the population possessing the minimum educational requirement (e.g., a high school diploma) becomes universal, occupational groups raise the educational requirement. This action provides a means to ration high-status positions and allows employers to select applicants whose credentials signal particular cultural characteristics.

These more critical approaches to understanding education presented new ways to understand social change, stability, and inequality. They also presented new questions for study. Thus, sociological research on education shifted from a focus on the forms, structure, and function of schools to questions about the effects of the determinants of inequality (social class, race, and gender). For example, research framing the educational problems of poor, working-class, and minority students in terms of the groups' cultural shortcomings gave way to studies examining the impact of background characteristics on students' educational and occupational outcomes. Status attainment research burgeoned during this period.

Status Attainment Research Status attainment research focuses on social mobility by attempting to identify the contribution of family background, parental education, and achievement on educational, occupational, and economic aspiration and attainment. Beginning in the 1950s with rural Wisconsin males and then expanded to other populations, studies in this tradition have proliferated during the past 50 years (Blau & Duncan, 1967; Duncan & Hodge, 1963; Featherman & Hauser, 1976; Sewell, Haller, & Portes, 1969; Sewell, Haller, & Strauss, 1957; Sewell & Hauser, 1980; Sewell, Hauser, Springer, & Hauser, 2001), and represent the dominant paradigm in the sociology of education and the study of stratification (Dreeben, 1994). Consistent findings of status attainment research are that (a) educational attainment explains a large portion of variance in occupational attainment, (b) school or neighborhood characteristics have virtually no effect on educational aspirations after controlling for individual characteristics, and (c) schools have no effects on educational aspirations because most variance in educational aspirations is *within* and not *between* schools (Sewell & Hauser, 1980).

Arguably, the most prominent and influential piece of education research in the 1960s was a report commissioned by the federal government in 1966 called the Equality of Educational Opportunity study (EEOS; Coleman et al., 1966) conducted by a team of researchers led by Columbia-trained sociologist James Coleman. Ten years after the Supreme Court outlawed segregated schools in the landmark *Brown vs. Board of Education* decision, the United States Department of Health, Education, and Welfare hired Coleman and his colleagues to study how minority students were faring in American schools compared to Whites. The report concluded that family background and other non-school factors have a greater impact on student achievement than school factors such as resources and curriculum, a conclusion which raised doubts about federal policies designed to improve life outcomes through school reform.

The Coleman report (1966) was significant because its findings ran counter to conventional wisdom, and because it reconceptualized equality of educational opportunity to include equality of results by including analysis of both inputs (the resources to which students had access) and outputs (the academic achievement of students). The report signaled a major shift in focus in debates on educational inequality and accountability. Although this focus on outputs is now standard practice throughout the United States (as evidenced in federal policy such as No Child Left Behind, NCLB, for example), it was the Coleman report that ushered in this momentous shift toward examining inequality in outcomes, particularly student test scores (Heckman & Neal, 1996).

Building on Coleman's findings by reanalyzing the EEOS data and conducting secondary analysis on many other (mostly cross-sectional) surveys, Christopher Jencks and colleagues (1972) argued that government attempts to reduce inequality through education were misguided because economic success is due to luck and on-the-job competence (which is largely due to personality, not test scores). Jencks argued that the War on Poverty was based on the assumption of equal opportunity—that everyone enters the competition for status and income with equal chances of winning—and that school reform should equalize cognitive skill and bargaining power in the marketplace. Jencks found, however, that (a) helping children escape poverty would be ineffective because poverty was not primarily hereditary or intergenerational, (b) raising cognitive skills would not reduce poverty because there was just as much economic inequality among those with high test scores as in the general population, and (c) education reform could not compensate for inadequate parenting because there was no evidence that either school resources or segregation had an appreciable effect on test scores or educational attainment. Jencks et al. (1972) concluded by arguing that public policy that proceeds by "ingenious manipulations of marginal institutions like the schools" will lead to only glacial progress on reducing inequality. Instead he argued for income redistribution and "what other countries usually call socialism" (p. 265).

Studies in the status attainment tradition raised questions about the effectiveness of education as a means for social mobility. These studies, however, have been critiqued for conceptualizing schools as "black boxes" in an economic production function in which inputs (student and parent characteristics) lead to outputs (life outcomes). This approach has been criticized for methodological individualism (Lynch, 2000) that discounts the role that social structural features such as school and neighborhood contexts can play in status attainment. It has also failed to distinguish between "school" (an institution) and "schooling" (a social process; Bidwell & Kasarda, 1980).

The Social Organization of Schooling The status attainment model conceptualized school as a homogenous entity theorized to have common effects across students.[1] This model limited the policy relevance of this type of education research because it failed to identify and examine levers to drive school improvement. It was assumed that schools did not differentiate the treatment of students based on student background, prior achievement, or learning style. Scholars who spent time in schools, however, understood that teachers and administrators made adaptations in practice based on student background, behavior, and local circumstances (Metz, 1978; Swidler, 1979; Cookson & Persell, 1985). Bidwell and Kasarda (1980) argued that the status attainment model mistakenly attributed variation in school organization to individual students. They argued that teachers and administrators set formal and informal policies that influenced student access to resources for learning. For example, teachers make decisions about pedagogy and ability grouping that condition student access to educational opportunity.

As scholars began examining the formal and informal organization of schools, a puzzle began to emerge. Schools did not seem to be organized like other enterprises, such as businesses. In one of the earliest theoretical treatments of the school as a formal organization, Bidwell (1965) hypothesized that while schools attempted to apply universalistic principles to students (e.g., equal access to rigorous math instruction), this task was made difficult by the diversity of their clientele. The implications of this tension and the difficulty of simultaneously coping with turbulence in the external environment (i.e., changes in law, policy, culture) for the formal organization of schools were twofold: (a) internal differentiation to adjust instruction to student background, and (b) structural looseness, which provides teachers the autonomy to adapt instruction to individual student needs (Bidwell, 1965). This concept of structural looseness was independently developed by Weick (1976), who argued that schools were "loosely coupled systems" due to the uncertainty about the goals of schooling, the technology to bring about improved student learning, and the influence of changes in the external environment. He noted that schools tended not to be organized around authority of office or close attention to the technical core (i.e., teaching and learning), but rather were loosely coupled to cope with conflicting interests both inside and outside the school walls. As noted by Dreeben (1994), the conceptualization of schools as loosely coupled both opened up the possibility of systematic analysis of the internal workings of schools and also provided an explanation for the paradoxical lack of school effects found in empirical research. Meyer, Scott, and Deal (1983), for example, argued that schools are organized not to coordinate their technical activities, but rather to adhere to rules institutionalized by external actors (parent groups, unions, business groups, district, state, and federal officials).

Status attainment research and neoinstitutional theory about schools as organizations raised doubts about the effects of schools as institutions that promote student learning. Later work with more sophisticated methods advanced our understandings of the effects of schools on outcomes and the effects of within-school processes on students.

School and Teacher Effects School effects research seeks to understand the effects of educational context on life chances while taking into account the characteristics of the individuals themselves. Dreeben (2000) defines structural effects as "net of the effect of an individual characteristic believed to shape a pattern of conduct, a group property based on the aggregation of that characteristic influences that conduct" (p. 108). For example, one may consider the effect of socio-economic status (SES) on test scores at two levels: individual SES and average SES of a school. Assuming proper specification of a multi-level analysis framework, if one finds that net of the effect of individual SES, average SES has an association with an individual's test score, one could call this a structural effect of SES on achievement. In the case of racial school segregation, we might want to examine whether Black students who attend racially homogenous schools have lower achievement, attainment, and aspirations, holding constant important student-level variables that also predict achievement, attainment, and aspirations. While there are many varieties of structural or contextual analysis—some that rely on social psychology, some that rely on social networks, for example—the analytic task is to attempt to explain individual behavior and/ or life outcomes by membership in some group, whether it be a workplace, a neighborhood, a gang, or a school. This harkens back to Durkheim (1897/1951), who sought to explain differing rates of suicide by membership in different social groupings such as family circumstances and religious faith.

In contradiction to early school effects research, where one goes to school can also affect the likelihood one stays

in school and graduates, an important precondition of attending college and increasing one's probability of a middle-class lifestyle and a lifetime of positive wage differentials. Toles, Schulz, and Rice (1986) noted that there is wide between-school variation in dropout rates even once student differences are controlled. Bryk and Thum (1989) found that high levels of differentiation within high schools and weak normative environments were associated with the probability of dropping out. Rumberger and Thomas (2000) found that while much of the between-school variation in dropout rates can be attributed to student characteristics, about half was due to factors under the control of policy makers such as student-teacher ratios, teacher quality, school control, school size, and average daily attendance. Lee and Bryk (1988) found that curriculum, school size, and positive student-teacher relationships affected school dropout rates.

Though the Coleman report (1966) called into question the impact of schools on student achievement, more recent work has highlighted the important role teachers play in raising student achievement. To the extent that teachers are the main resource schools provide to students, it may seem to be merely an academic matter whether it is schools rather than teachers that influence student achievement. The fact that there is more variance in student achievement within schools than between them (Sewell & Hauser, 1980; Nye, Konstantopoulos, & Hedges, 2004) has important policy implications, however. Specifically, this suggests that policies aimed at altering the sorting process of students among schools (i.e., school choice, desegregation) may be less effective than policies aimed at raising teacher quality or altering the distribution of teachers across classrooms. Given that econometric studies find substantial cumulative effects of being assigned a high quality teacher over a number of years (Aaronson, Barrow, & Sander, 2007; Rivkin, Hanushek, & Kain, 2005; Rockoff, 2004), the match of high quality teachers with disadvantaged students has important implications for equality of educational opportunity and closing test score gaps.

Perhaps the most important factor affecting student achievement, other than teachers, is the curriculum to which students are exposed. Sociological interest in the curriculum has centered on what is taught, in both the informal (e.g., Dreeben, 1968; Swidler, 1976) and formal curriculum (e.g., Cookson & Persell, 1985), and to whom (Rosenbaum, 1976; Oakes, 1985; Spade, Columba, & Vanfossen, 1997). Most schools use some form of curriculum differentiation, either tracking or ability grouping, to separate students for instruction based on measured ability. However, studies of these practices consistently show a correlation between student assignment and social class and race and ethnicity: working-class and minority students are more likely to be placed in lower-ability groups and tracks, and middle-class and White students are more likely to be assigned to higher-ability groups and tracks (Rist, 1970; Barr & Dreben, 1983; Gamoran & Mare, 1989; Hallinan, 1996; Lucas, 1999). The evidence to explain this pattern is less consistent (Dougherty, 1996). Some studies find that the variation is explained by group differences in prior achievement and other factors such as aspirations, motivation, or significant others' expectations, but other studies find a significant direct effect of social class even after controlling for these factors.

Nevertheless, the evidence is clear that even if there is no discrimination in track and ability group assignment, students in the lower groups do not benefit from these practices as much as students in the higher groups do. Research on the effects of curriculum differentiation on student achievement shows that compared to their peers in the higher groups, students in the lower groups do not learn as much because they are exposed to less challenging curricular materials and are given less rigorous assignments (Barr & Dreeben, 1983; McPartland & Schneider, 1996; Hallinan & Kubitschek, 1999; Lucas, 1999), tend to have less experienced teachers (Oakes, 1985), and to be in classrooms that experience more disruptions (Eder, 1981). Thus, rather than catching up to their higher-status peers, working-class and minority students assigned to low-track classes tend to fall further behind. The preponderance of evidence on tracking and ability grouping, then, suggests that these practices mostly reinforce rather than reduce inequality. Consequently, calls for schools to detrack have been increasing in recent years (Wells & Oakes, 1998; Burris & Welner, 2005).

In summary, sociologists have changed conceptions about the role of education in social mobility, developed and tested hypotheses about the equality of educational opportunity, opened up the black box of schooling to uncover hidden within-school processes such as ability grouping and tracking, and have advanced the theory and measurement of school, sector, and teacher effects.

Social Processes Findings from studies using qualitative research methods have also made important contributions to our understanding of schooling processes. Although qualitative research may have a less direct impact on education policy, for reasons we discuss below, the findings from these studies are no doubt part of the taken-for-granted and background knowledge of policy makers and other researchers. Qualitative studies have been particularly effective in highlighting the subtle everyday practices that often go unnoticed in the classroom but which have significant consequences for the educational outcomes we care most about, including students' social and cognitive development. As Hugh Mehan (1992) has written, "It often takes intimate contact with people and a close analysis of their words and deeds to capture subtleties, contradictions, and nuances of everyday life" (p. 1).

Sociologists of education have been especially engaged in studies examining race, social class, and gender socialization processes. These studies reveal a variety of ways that schools fall short of the goal of leveling the effects of background characteristics and instead reinforce social inequality through the curriculum, textbooks, and school policies and practices. Sociologists have used ethnographic research methods to describe the context of schooling in rich, vivid detail and show how race, class, and gender structure students' daily lives at school. The findings show the various ways that students' identities are constructed and reinforced through the schooling process (e.g., Bettie, 2003), as well as how some youth resist the identities and the norms that schools attempt to impose on them (Stinchcombe, 1965; Willis, 1977; MacLeod, 1995). Paul Willis's (1977) study shed light on the nature of resistance to school norms among working-class, disaffected youth in England and brought us to an improved understanding of both the school's and the student's role in reproducing the class structure. Indeed, sociologists have helped us to understand how profoundly social class shapes the culture and structure of schools and how the middle-class culture of schools often alienates and disadvantages working-class children and their families (Lareau & Horvat, 1999; Lareau, 2000).

Other sociological studies show the deeply rooted nature of gendered patterns of interaction in the classroom. These studies find that children enter the classrooms as gendered beings and that schools reinforce gendered social relations and identities in the messages conveyed by teachers and peers about the appropriate role for girls and boys (Grant, 1983, 1984; Eder & Parker, 1987; Thorne, 1993). For example, researchers find that teachers reward and punish the behavior of girls and boys differentially according to particular gender norms. These studies have helped us to understand how some schooling processes may be linked to children's future family and career aspirations, choices, and attainment, and enduring patterns of gender inequality.

Numerous ethnographic studies have also helped us to understand the ways in which race and ethnicity affect students' schooling experiences, peer relationships, and achievement outcomes, and how students from diverse racial and ethnic backgrounds make sense of and respond to schooling (Lee, 1996; Valenzuela, 1999; Ferguson, 2000; Perry, 2002; Lewis, 2003; Carter, 2005). For example, various studies have helped us to understand how some of the negative behavior, attitudes, and outcomes of minority students are linked to school structures. These studies show the complexity of the students' behaviors and explain that minority students, like working-class students, are often resisting the ways in which the school's treatment of them denies them their full humanity and dignity by viewing them solely in terms of their race and/or class and gender. Ann Ferguson's (2000) study examining the beliefs and practices that produce a racialized system of discipline in an elementary school describes how teachers' negative beliefs about Black males leads to the heavy policing and disciplining of this group in ways that mark Black boys as dangerous and in need of fixing, and push them further and further from the mainstream.

Sociologists have also devoted considerable attention to understanding the effects of peers in school, and their findings reveal the powerful effect that youth have on one another, particularly during adolescence (Coleman, 1961; MacLeod, 1995). The literature on peer effects provides greater understanding of how peer relationships and interactions affect school engagement and achievement, attitudes toward school, and involvement in illicit activities, as well as how the goals of schools are misaligned with the goals of adolescents. This work has contributed to changes in the way many schools structure academic activities to encourage and improve student learning, motivation, and academic achievement (Coleman, 1996; Heckman & Neal, 1996).

Understanding the day-to-day experiences and interactions of individuals in schools is a central objective in research in the sociology of education. The extensive body of literature on social processes has substantially informed our knowledge of the development of student attitudes and identity, how teacher practices affect student behavior and achievement, and how peers influence on one another. Indeed, qualitative research in the sociological tradition has been especially instrumental in calling attention to "possible hidden or latent consequences" of schooling as well as "how conditions outside the consciousness of individuals can affect their actions" (Schlechty & Noblit, 1982, p. 291).

Sociology and Education Policy Debates The power of sociological conceptions of schools, whether from quantitative research of large scale datasets or nuanced studies of the social relations of a single school, has influenced public policy through several avenues. Today sociologists and other social scientists are often called upon to provide expert testimony before Congress and the courts on a variety of education-related issues, and their research is used by policy makers to provide a public rationale for policies as well as to design policies (Stevenson, 2000). Sociologists in particular play an increasingly active role in policy debates because the public and governmental concerns with equality of opportunity and equity in access are in line with what have been and continue to be primary areas of research interests to sociologists (Schlechty & Noblit, 1982). Thus, litigators and policy makers are likely to turn to sociologists and sociological research to understand educational phenomenon and address the pressing educational problems of the day (Hallinan, 2000). Sociologists also take an active approach to education policy by filing amicus briefs in court cases on which sociological research has something to say. Although it is not clear just how much influence amicus briefs have on court decisions, they have become an increasingly important way for sociologists and other social scientists to have access to the judicial decision-making process and input on important educational issues of the day (Kearney & Merrill, 2000).[2]

The contribution of sociologists and sociological research to education-related litigation, while not new, has not always been as prominent or visible as it is today, particularly compared to other social science fields, especially psychology. The *Brown vs. Board of Education* (1954) case relied most heavily on psychological research: psychologists accounted for seven of the nine social scientists providing expert testimony (only one sociologist was involved). And it is the testimony of psychologists, particularly Kenneth Clark and Mamie Clark, which is best remembered for its influence on the Court's ruling on the psychologically damaging effects of segregation on children's developing personalities. A decade later, sociological research gained national visibility in education policy circles with the EEO study. Since that time, sociologists have remained actively involved in policy-relevant education research and are regularly called upon to provide research findings to government agencies as well as expert testimony in education-related cases, especially on some of the more challenging questions of equality of educational opportunity and issues of equity.

Through the power of their ideas, high quality research, congressional testimony, and expert testimony in court cases, sociologists have played an important role in shaping policy debates about education. We turn next to the challenges and opportunities sociologists face when attempting to conduct research relevant to policy debates. These include becoming aware of the important differences between academic and policy research, understanding the differences in the audiences for academic and policy research, and how mode of inquiry affects the policy relevance of sociological research.

Challenges and Opportunities

Academic vs. Policy Research When considering the contribution of sociology to education policy research, it is important to keep in mind the differences between academic research in sociology—indeed in any academic discipline—and policy research. To be clear, most sociologists pursue academic rather than policy research (Bulmer, 1996). However, understanding the differences between these two enterprises will help elucidate what kind of sociological research is more likely to influence education policy. Weimer and Vining (2005) outline the differences between academic and policy research. These differences are shown in Table 5.1. Policy research employs the methods of social science disciplines to examine "relationships between variables that reflect social problems and other variables that can be manipulated by public policy" (Weimer & Vining, 2005, p. 25). Academic research, on the other hand, is about constructing and testing broad theories for understanding society. In policy research there are three types of variables: outcomes, policy variables, and control variables. Policy variables measure something policy makers can alter, such as class size, rather than something they cannot, like gender. Control variables are included in the analysis to better understand the effect of the policy variable on the outcome. This is particularly important when the analysis is conducted with non-experimental (i.e., regression analysis) rather than experimental (i.e., random assignment) methods.

For example, if policy research is aimed at determining the impact of class size reduction on student achievement gain using regression analysis, the policy variable is class size and the outcome is the year-to-year student gain in academic achievement as measured by test score. If teacher

TABLE 5.1
Differences Between Academic and Policy Research

Paradigm	Major Objective	"Client"	Common Style	Time Constraints	General Weaknesses
Academic Social Science Research	Construct theories for understanding society	"Truth," as defined by the disciplines, other scholars	Rigorous methods for constructing and testing theories; usually retrospective	Rarely external time constraints	Often irrelevant to information needs of decision makers
Policy Research	Predict impacts of changes in variables that can be altered by public policy	Actors in the policy arena; the related disciplines	Application of formal methodology to policy-relevant questions; prediction of consequences	Sometimes deadline pressure; perhaps mitigated by issue recurrence	Difficulty in translating findings into government action

Note: Adapted from Weimer and Vining, 2005, Table 2.1. © 2005 by Pearson Education, Inc. Reprinted by permission.

skill is associated with class size and student test score gain, however, we must somehow include teacher skill in our analysis. Assume that high skill teachers are better at raising student test scores and we do not account for teacher skill in the analysis. In this case, if high skill teachers are assigned to smaller classes, then the estimate of class size on student test score gain would *overstate* the true effect. In other words, we would assume that smaller class size had a positive effect on student test score gain when in fact at least part of this effect is due to the fact that highly skilled teachers are more likely to teach smaller classes. On the other hand, if high skill teachers are assigned to *larger* classes, then the estimate of class size would *understate* the true effect. Therefore, it makes sense to statistically control for teacher skill in a regression equation estimating the effect of class size reduction on student test score gain. In fact, the importance of controlling for relevant control variables applies to both academic and policy research; the difference is in what kind of research questions are of most relevance to policy makers.

The types of variables that are of most interest to policy makers are within the political and cultural domain of policymaking control. While the "effect" of gender on test score gain may be of interest to policy makers, policy makers can do little to change students' gender. The same may be said of racial or ethnic background. While the Black-White test score gap is of great interest to policy makers, simply noting the presence of a gap does not inform policy makers about what to do about the problem. To better inform policy about the test score gap requires analysis of policies and practices that may reduce this gap, such as teacher treatment of students, school desegregation, tracking, "double-dose" instruction of basic subjects like reading and math, tutoring programs, and summer school.[3] Moreover, social practices within the domain of the family, for example, may be considered beyond the reach of policy makers. Child discipline practices, such as parental spanking, may be related to student incidence of disciplinary infractions in elementary school, but because parental spanking is considered an acceptable practice in most U.S. states, policy makers may be reluctant to intervene.[4]

Therefore, while academic sociologists might be interested in gender, race, and class, policy makers are more interested in the effectiveness of educational policies that "work" for all students regardless of background. The preferences of the audiences for the findings of education research can shape not only research questions, but methodology and interpretation of findings as well.

Social Science Research Audience and Use Like other social science research, most sociological research on education is published in scholarly journals and other outlets targeting an academic audience. Sociologists are generally more interested in speaking to other sociologists and social scientists than to educational practitioners and policy makers. Indeed, Pamela Walters (2007) argues that much of the current scholarship in the sociology of education is oriented to advancing sociological theory rather than to improving education. This is no doubt related to the ever-present concern within sociology with maintaining the discipline's legitimacy as a scientific enterprise. Yet because the audience for academic research is other academic researchers, the common style of social scientific academic research is elegance of formal theory, rigorous methods for testing these theories, and retrospective analysis of empirical evidence.

Policy research, on the other hand, is targeted to two audiences: actors in the policy arena, and other academics with an interest in the type of policy research being conducted. Research problems in policy research tend to come from practical considerations of social or policy problems rather than theoretical debates in the discipline, and the results are tailored to what Coleman (1972) called the "world of action," which is characterized by time constraints and the necessity of making decisions under uncertainty. In a perfect world, researchers could produce flawless information with great dispatch. In reality, and especially in the policy world, the best we can hope for is imperfect information in a timely fashion. This fact led Coleman to propose redundancy as a safety mechanism: multiple studies, each using different data sources addressing the same question, allowing policy makers to "triangulate" each of the admittedly imperfect studies to aid decision making.

The ultimate purpose of policy research is to serve the public good. Defining the public good, however, is complex and subject to multiple interpretations and value conflicts.

For example, in the case of policy research funded by a governmental entity, the researcher's and the client's perception of the public good may, in fact, conflict. Neutral problem definition and interpretation of research findings is quite difficult to carry out in practice and, in fact, much policy research reflects the interests of the client and is advocacy-oriented. This tendency conflicts with academic norms to retain objectivity, at least with respect to the analysis and interpretation of results. For this reason, policy research is not as highly valued in the academy as is academic research. Moreover, translation of research findings into policies that can be implemented often requires attention to practical considerations of little interest to other academics but of great interest to policy makers. On the other hand, if research is too technical or not policy-relevant enough, it is not of much use to policy makers. Therefore, scholars wishing to conduct policy research must traverse the narrow bounds of ideological and pragmatic considerations when deciding how much time to devote to academic and policy research, respectively.

Sociologists have long wrestled with questions about the uses of sociological knowledge and the role social scientists should play in public policy. C. Wright Mills (2000) believed that the social scientist, particularly the sociologist, has a social responsibility to reveal to the public the connections between the problems they encounter in their individual lives and larger structural forces. The social scientist also has the obligation to make those in positions of power, that is, those who have a hand in creating institutional and structural conditions, aware of how their decisions and actions are affecting the lives others. Mills did not believe that social scientists could "save the world," but he saw nothing wrong with their attempting to do so; thus he posed the question, "If there *are* any ways out of the crises of our period by means of intellect, is it not up to the social scientist to state them?" (p. 193).

Like Mills, many sociologists believe that sociology can make unique contributions to public policy with the tools of empirical data and social theory. James Coleman has written extensively on the role of sociology in social policy. For him, conducting research that has the potential to contribute to policy issues and "make a difference" was among the most important motivations for undertaking a project. He has described social policy research as "the systematic search for information that can aid social policy" (Coleman, 1976, p. 304), and he believed strongly that social science research findings should form the basis of policy debates.

Social science findings, whether about the contribution of educational resources, tracking, the effects of desegregation, or teacher treatment, are subject to interpretation and debate. As Bulmer (1996) reports in his analysis of Coleman's contribution to social policy, people interpreted the EEOS findings to suit their own interests, and this led to differing conclusions about the implications of the results. For some, the results suggested the need to intervene in family and community rather than to change schools; for others, the results indicated that the way to improve Black children's academic performance was to integrate schools; and for others the results suggested the need for Black community control of neighborhood schools. Such disagreement among social scientists is a major obstacle to the vision of the improvement of social policy research that many hold and it calls into question the extent to which social scientists should be involved in making policy recommendations, which some view as over-advocacy (Bulmer, 1996). Many scholars believe that academics are uniquely positioned to provide objective input in the policy arena, but as Bulmer points out, academics also have "value standpoints" and "interests at stake" which may affect their policy recommendations (p. 112).

Modes of Empirical Research and Policy Implications

Qualitative Research Ethnography is the preferred method of many education researchers (Rist, 1980; Eisenhart, 2001). Schooling is a social enterprise, consisting of a complex set of social arrangements and interactions, which qualitative methods like ethnography are well-suited to illuminate. When done well, both with respect to design and analysis, qualitative studies, as described earlier in this chapter, present rich and vivid portraits of life in school and reveal perspectives and experiences of school actors that previously had not been widely known or well understood. For example, according to Schlechty and Noblit (1982), in the 1960s sociologically oriented qualitative research was instrumental in helping evaluators to understand why federally funded school innovations did not produce the expected outcomes. The authors contend that sociologists brought attention to the importance of the "cultural, social, political, and organizational contexts in and around schools" for how programs are understood and implemented at the local level (Schlechty & Noblit, 1982, p. 289). Indeed, qualitative studies reveal much in their detail about school context, cultures, and social systems, and about how individuals make sense of their lives within these institutions, and they have greatly enhanced our knowledge and understanding of various schooling processes, including school (Mehan, 1979) and classroom organization (Rist, 1970), student conformity and resistance (McFarland, 2001), and parental involvement (Lareau, 2000).

While qualitative research can enrich our understanding of the complexity of how social processes unfold, research of this kind has its limitations for informing policy. Among the most serious is the lack of generalizability beyond the communities and individuals studied. Although team ethnographies with numerous researchers and multiple sites are becoming more common, ethnographic studies are typically relatively small in scale, focusing in depth on one or two schools and a limited number of informants, usually no more than 20 or 30.[5] As Coleman (1994) has argued, the increase in government funding for social science research in the late 1950s contributed to a "decisive shift" from studies combining qualitative and survey methods, in the tradition of the classic community studies of sociologists such as Robert Lynd's Middletown, to pure survey methods: "Governments are less interested in analysis of social system functioning than in descriptive statistics for well-defined populations, such as the population for which they have some responsibility. Thus they will favor research which gathers data on a representative sample, from which inferences about the population can be rigorously drawn" (p. 30). Hence, for all their richness, critics contend that many qualitative studies are not useful for informing policy, because while they reveal a great deal about one or two schools or a small group of individuals, they tell us very little about larger trends and the degree to which the findings can be generalized to other schools, regions of the country, or groups. Furthermore, qualitative studies do not easily lend themselves to replication, a hallmark of the scientific model of research. In fact, many qualitative studies are impossible to replicate, and thus limit opportunities for the research community to test the reliability and validity of their findings.

Qualitative research is also widely criticized because of the poor quality of data collection and/or analysis of some studies (Rist, 1980), but this criticism is not uniformly applicable. There are many examples of well-designed qualitative research studies that use rigorous and systematic techniques of data collection and analysis. Indeed, notwithstanding the criticisms about generalizability and causation, qualitative research once held a rather prominent place in the discipline of sociology, built on work by sociologists such as Robert Lynd, W. Lloyd Warner, W. E. B. DuBois, Robert E. Park, William Foote Whyte, and Sinclair Drake. In fact, qualitative research was once the dominant research method in the discipline of sociology.

The criticisms of qualitative research are neither new nor unique to sociology or educational research. Nevertheless, they are not trivial issues, and they are of particular consequence for education policy research because of the significance Americans accord to education and its relationship to other important quality of life outcomes. Thus, research used to inform education policy must be high quality, and the evidence must be solid because, as Karl Alexander (1997) has argued, eventually we all suffer "if misguided thinking about the schools leads to misguided policy" (p. 18). To achieve sound education policy, we must have sound evidence to support policy recommendations. This is a point with which everyone can agree. It underscores the need for more publications dedicated to addressing the concerns and criticisms about qualitative methods in education policy research and offering proven prescriptions for overcoming them. In this way, the potential contributions of qualitative methods to policy are not lost. A number of publications like this already exist (Eisenhart, 2001; Levinson, Cade, Padawer, & Elvir, 2002; Stritikus & Wiese, 2006), but sociologists have been less involved than anthropologists have in this endeavor.

Quantitative Research and Causal Inference The field of education policy research has expanded and matured

since the publication of the Coleman report, but the lessons learned from that study continue to influence the field. The report provided a model for education policy research, demonstrating, as Heckman and Neal (1996) assert, "the value of large-scale data sets and empirical social science research for evaluating social programs" (p. 84). Although findings from such studies often are vigorously contested, as they were even with the Coleman report, nationally representative survey data are still considered to be among the most valid, rigorous, and reliable sources of evidence for education policy research, second perhaps only to experiments.

Since the publication of *A Nation at Risk* (U. S. National Commission on Excellence in Education, 1983), American education policy has been dominated by standards-based reform and accountability. These policies involve setting standards for what students should know and be able to do, designing assessments linked to these standards, testing students on a regular basis, and establishing sanctions and rewards for schools, principals, teachers, and, at times, students based on high-stakes test results. Though there is some evidence that school-based accountability programs may increase achievement (Figlio & Ladd, 2008; Carnoy & Loeb, 2002; Hanushek & Raymond, 2005; Jacob, 2005), there is also some concern that accountability based on high-stakes tests may narrow and fragment the curriculum, promote rote, teacher-directed instruction, and encourage schools to teach test-preparation skills rather than academic content, tendencies that may be stronger in schools with high minority and low income populations (Orfield & Kornhaber, 2001; Valenzuela, 2005; Nichols & Berliner, 2007).

The emphasis placed on accountability has increased the desire among policy makers and funding agencies for methods that provide stronger causal inference. The strongest causal inference comes from a randomized research design, which involves randomly assigning subjects to treatment conditions, as is commonly done in drug trial studies. Such a design, if carried out correctly, ensures that subjects are alike in all respects with the exception of the treatment.[6] For example, suppose we want to test the causal effect of teacher experience on student test score gains, defined as the test score gain difference between students who had a teacher with less than three years of experience and students who had a teacher with more than 20 years of experience. Randomly assigning students to treatment (novice vs. experienced teachers), eliminates the problem of selection bias (that students in the treatment and control conditions would differ on "pre-treatment" covariates). Eliminating selection bias is one of the most important conditions of establishing a causal inference. Others include temporal precedence, which in this case could be addressed by ensuring that the outcome (test score gain) is measured subsequent to teacher assignment; causal manipulability, discussed previously; and eliminating alternative explanations. Due to the cost and difficulty of implementing random design trials, and the political and ethical barriers of withholding treatment to a subgroup of students, such designs have been relatively rare in social scientific studies of educational programs. In some cases, it is possible to use observational data analysis techniques that approximate random design to reduce selection bias. These techniques, which include fixed effects models, regression discontinuity, propensity score matching, and instrumental variables estimation are becoming increasingly prominent, especially in policy analysis and the economics of education.

The recent turn toward causal analysis for policy research is made clear in the 2003 reauthorization of the Elementary and Secondary Education Act, NCLB. This act encourages research studies based on scientifically based evidence, and the U.S. Department of Education has signaled its preference for random assignment and quasi-experimental designs in grant competition announcements.[7] These designs have also been a point of emphasis for education research funding at the National Science Foundation, the National Institute of Child Health and Human Development, and are becoming institutionalized through the What Works Clearinghouse (funded by the newly formed Institute of Education Sciences) and disseminated through the Interagency Education Research Initiative, a program designed to bring promising interventions to scale.[8]

Conclusion

The institutionalization of causal analysis through federal funding priorities has shifted the balance toward understanding systematic effects. It is important to keep in mind, however, that an understanding of systematic effects is only one question that drives scientific research. There are at least two others: (a) what is happening? and (b) why or how is it happening? (National Research Council, 2002).

Due to the breadth of the discipline of sociology, sociologists are perhaps uniquely situated to address all three realms of scientific research on education. Sociologists, along with psychologists and economists, are designing randomized field trials and using quasi-experimental techniques to estimate the causal effects of educational interventions. Accounting for the presence or absence of causal effects, however, requires understanding "the implementation problem," that is, what is happening and why or how it comes about. Such an understanding requires systematic analysis of how the "cultural, social, political, and organizational contexts in and around schools directly shape the meaning of given programs and the actions that take place within programs" (Schlechty & Noblit, 1982, p. 289). This type of analysis involves developing a qualitative understanding of such things as how process emerges over time, how actors create meaning in the face of complexity, and how norms of cooperation and competition shape the pursuit of collective goals. These nuances will not emerge from a regression equation, causal or not, but are also critical to our understanding of the educational process and the effects causes are theorized to bring about.

Therefore, sociologists can contribute to education

research designed to test causal effects of "what works," describe in great depth what is happening in schools, and test hypotheses about why and how. This unique perspective bodes well for the continuing relevance of sociological inquiry on education despite the many differences between academic and applied research. One of the strengths of sociology is the interplay between qualitative and quantitative research methods, the ability of each to inform the other. Good sociologists understand and appreciate both types of research and they understand the importance of selecting the appropriate methods for the research questions.

Notes

1. This section draws heavily from Dreeben (1994).
2. According to legal scholar Rachel Moran (2008), it is very rare for amicus briefs to be cited in court decisions.
3. In the case of reducing the Black-White test score gap, it may be most effective to target effective educational services and programs specifically at low-achieving Black students rather than providing for all students, Black or White. Targeted policies, however, may lack the necessary political support that more universalistic policies can garner.
4. Corporal punishment in schools is banned in about half of U.S. states. Corporal punishment in the home is explicitly allowed in some legislation and it is banned by statute in only one state, Minnesota.
5. Here we are referring to in-depth qualitative interviews as opposed to survey interviews.
6. There is the possibility that due to sampling error there may be some observable differences between treatment and control groups. The likelihood of detecting a statistically significant difference between treatment and control on an observable characteristic would shrink toward zero as sample size increases.
7. See, for example, the January 25, 2005, Federal register, p. 3586, as cited in Schneider and Keesler (2007).
8. See Schneider, Carnoy, Kilpatrick, Schmidt, and Shavelson (2007) for a discussion of how causal analysis is becoming institutionalized through federal funding initiatives and useful summaries of education research studies that use experimental and quasi-experimental methods.

References

Aaronson, D., Barrow, L., & Sander, W. (2007). Teachers and student achievement in the Chicago Public High Schools. *Journal of Labor Economics, 25,* 95–135.

Alexander, K. (1997). Public schools and the public good. *Social Forces, 76,* 1–30.

Barr, R., & Dreeben, R. (1983). *How schools work.* Chicago: University of Chicago Press.

Bernstein, B. (1975). *Class, codes, and control.* London: Routledge and Kegan Paul.

Bettie, J. (2003). *Women without class: Girls, race, and identity.* Berkeley: University of California Press.

Bidwell, C. E. (1965). The school as a formal organization. In J. G. March (Ed.), *Handbook of organizations* (pp. 972–1022). Chicago: Rand McNally.

Bidwell, C. E., & Kasarda, J. D. (1980). Conceptualizing and measuring the effects of school and schooling. *American Journal of Education, 88,* 401–430.

Blau, P. M., & Duncan, O. D. (1967). *The American occupational structure.* New York: Wiley.

Bourdieu, P. (1977). Cultural reproduction and social reproduction. In J. Karabel & A. H. Halsey (Eds.), *Power and ideology in education* (pp. 487–511). New York: Oxford University Press.

Bourdieu, P., & Passeron, J. C. (1977). *Reproduction in education, society, and culture* (R. Nice, Trans.). London: Sage. (Original work published 1970)

Bowles, S., & Gintis, H. (1976). *Schooling in capitalist America*. New York: Basic Books.

Brown v. Board of Education, 347 U.S. 483 (1954).

Bryk, A. S., & Thum, Y. M. (1989). The effects of high school organization on dropping out: An exploratory investigation. *American Educational Research Journal, 26*, 353–383.

Bulmer, M. (1996). The sociological contribution to social policy research. In J. Clark (Ed.), *James S. Coleman* (pp. 103–118). London: Falmer Press.

Burris, C., & Welner, K. (2005). Closing the achievement gap by detracking. *Phi Delta Kappan, 86*, 594–598.

Carnoy, M., & Loeb, S. (2002). Does external accountability affect student outcomes? A cross-state analysis. *Educational Evaluation and Policy Analysis, 24*, 305–331.

Carter, P. (2005). *Keepin' it real: School success beyond Black and White*. New York: Oxford University Press.

Coleman, J. S. (1961). *The adolescent society: The social life of the teenager and its impact on education*. New York: Free Press of Glencoe.

Coleman, J. S. (1972). *Policy research in the social sciences*. Morristown, NJ: General Learning Press.

Coleman, J. S. (1976). Policy decisions, social science information, and education. *Sociology of Education, 49*, 304–312.

Coleman, J. S. (1994). A vision for sociology. *Society, 32*, 29–34.

Coleman, J. S. (1996). Reflections on schools and adolescents. In J. Clark, (Ed.), *James S.Coleman* (pp. 17–22). London: Falmer Press.

Coleman, J., Campbell, E. Q., Hobson, C. J., McPartland, J., Mood, A. M., Weinfeld, F. D., et al. (1966). *Equality of educational opportunity*. Washington, DC: U.S. Government Printing Office.

Collins, R. (1979). *The credential society*: *An historical sociology of education and stratification*. New York: Academic Press.

Cookson, P., & Persell, C. H. (1985). *Preparing for power: America's elite boarding schools*. New York: Basic Books.

Dougherty, K. (1996). Opportunity-to-learn standards: A sociological critique. *Sociology of Education, 69*(Extra Issue), 40–65.

Dreeben, R. (1968). *On what is learned in school*. Reading, MA: Addison-Wesley.

Dreeben, R. (1994). The sociology of education: Its development in the United States. In A. Pallas (Ed.), *Research in sociology of education and socialization, Vol. 10* (pp. 7–52). Greenwich, CT: JAI Press

Dreeben, R. (2000). Structural effects in education: A history of an idea. In M. Hallinan (Ed.*), Handbook of the sociology of education* (pp. 107–136). New York: Kluwer Academic/Plenum Publishers.

Duncan, O. D., & Hodge, R. W. (1963). Education and occupational mobility: A regression analysis. *American Journal of Sociology, 68*, 629–644.

Durkheim, É. (1951). *Suicide: A study in sociology* (J. A. Spalding & G. Simpson, Trans.). Glencoe, IL: Free Press. (Original work published 1897)

Eder, D. (1981). Ability grouping as a self-fulfilling prophecy: A micro-analysis of teacher-student interaction. *Sociology of Education, 54*, 151–162.

Eder, D., & Parker, S. (1987). The cultural production and reproduction of gender: The effect of extracurricular activities on peer-group culture. *Sociology of Education, 60*, 200–213.

Eisenhart, M. (2001). Educational ethnography past, present, and future: Ideas to think with. *Educational Researcher, 30*(8), 16–27.

Featherman, D. L., & Hauser, R. M. (1976). Changes in the socioeconomic stratification of the races, 1962–1973. *American Journal of Sociology, 82*, 621–651.

Ferguson, A. A. (2000). *Bad boys: Public schools and the making of Black masculinity*. Ann Arbor: University of Michigan Press.

Figlio, D. N., & Ladd, H. F. (2008). School accountability and student achievement. In H. F. Ladd & E. B. Fiske (Eds.), *Handbook of research in education finance and policy* (pp. 166–182). New York: Routledge.

Gamoran, A., & Mare, R. (1989). Secondary school tracking and educational inequality: Compensation, reinforcement or neutrality? *American Journal of Sociology, 94*, 1146–1183.

Grant, L. (1983). Gender roles and status in school children's peer interactions. *Western Sociological Review, 14*(1), 58–76.

Grant, L. (1984). Black females' "place" in desegregated classrooms. *Sociology of Education, 57*, 98–111.

Hallinan, M. (1996). Track mobility in secondary school. *Social Forces, 74*, 983–1002.

Hallinan, M. (2000). Introduction: Sociology of education at the threshold of the twenty-first century. In M. Hallinan (Ed.), *Handbook of the sociology of education* (pp. 1–12). New York: Kluwer Academic/ Plenum Publishers.

Hallinan, M., & Kubitschek, W. (1999). Curriculum differentiation and high school achievement. *Social Psychology of Education, 3*, 41–62.

Hanushek, E., & Raymond, M. (2005). Does accountability lead to improved student performance? *Journal of Policy Analysis and Management, 24*, 297–327.

Heckman, J., & Neal, D. (1996). Coleman's contribution to education: Theory, research styles, and empirical research. In J. Clark (Ed.), *James S. Coleman* (pp. 81–102). London: Falmer Press.

Jacob, B. (2005). Accountability, incentives and behavior: The impact of high-stakes testing in Chicago Public Schools. *Journal of Public Economics, 89*, 761–796.

Jencks, C., Smith, M., Acland, H., Bane, M. J., Cohen, D., Gintis, H. et al. (1972). *Inequality: A reassessment of the effect of family and schooling in America*. New York: Basic Books.

Karabel, J., & Halsey, A. H. (1977). Educational research: A review and an interpretation. In J. Karabel & A. H. Halsey (Eds.), *Power and ideology in education* (pp. 1–86). New York: Oxford University Press.

Kearney, J., & Merrill, T. (2000). The influence of amicus curiae briefs on the Supreme Court. *University of Pennsylvania Law Review, 148*, 743–855.

Lareau, A. (2000). *Home advantage: Social class and parental intervention in elementary education*. Berkeley: University of California Press.

Lareau, A., & Horvat, E. (1999). Moments of social inclusion and exclusion: Race, class, and cultural capital in family-school relationships. *Sociology of Education, 72*, 37–53.

Lee, S. (1996). *Unraveling the "model minority" stereotype: Listening to Asian American youth*. New York: Teachers College Press.

Lee, V. E., & Bryk, A. S. (1988). Curriculum tracking as mediating the social distribution of high school achievement. *Sociology of Education, 61*, 78–94.

Levinson, B. A., Cade, S. L., Padawer, A., & Elvir, A. P. (Eds.). (2002). *Ethnography and education policy across the Americas*. Westport, CT: Praeger.

Lewis, A. (2003). *Race in the schoolyard: Negotiating the color line in classrooms and communities*. New Brunswick, NJ: Rutgers University Press.

Lucas, S. (1999). *Tracking inequality: stratification and mobility in American high schools*. New York: Teachers College Press.

Lynch, K. (2000). Research and theory on equality and education. In M. T. Hallinan (Ed.), *Handbook of the sociology of education* (pp. 85–106). New York: Kluwer Academic/Plenum Publishers.

MacLeod, J. (1995). *"Ain't no makin' it:" Aspirations and attainment in a low-income neighborhood*. Boulder, CO: Westview Press.

McFarland, D. (2001). Student resistance: How the formal and informal organization of classrooms facilitate everyday forms of student defiance. *The American Journal of Sociology, 107*, 612–678.

McPartland, J., & Schneider, B. (1996). Opportunities to learn and student diversity: Prospects and pitfalls of a common core curriculum. *Sociology of Education, 69*(Extra Issue), 66–81.

Mehan, H. (1979). *Learning lessons: Social organization in the classroom*. Cambridge, MA: Harvard University Press.

Mehan, H. (1992). Understanding inequality in schools: The contribution of interpretive studies. *Sociology of Education, 65*, 1–20.

Metz, M. H. (1978). *Classrooms and corridors: The crisis of authority in desegregated secondary schools*. Berkeley: University of California Press.

Meyer, J. W., Scott, W. R., & Deal, T. E. (1983). Institutional and technical sources of organizational structure: Explaining the structure of educational organizations. In J. W. Meyer & W. R. Scott (Eds.), *Organizational environments: Ritual and rationality* (pp. 45–67). Beverly Hills, CA: Sage.

Mills, C. W. (2000). *The sociological imagination* (2nd ed). New York: Oxford University Press.

Moran, R. (2008, May). [Keynote address]. Paradoxes of race, law and inequality in the United States conference, California, Irvine, CA.

National Research Council. (2002). *Scientific research in education*. Washington, DC: National Academy Press.

Nichols, S. L., Berliner, D. (2007). *Collateral damage: How high-stakes testing corrupts America's schools*. Cambridge, MA: Harvard University Press.

Nye, B., Konstantopoulos, S., & Hedges, L. (2004). How large are teacher effects? *Educational Evaluation and Policy Analysis, 26*, 237–257.

Oakes, J. (1985). *Keeping track: How schools structure inequality*. New Haven, CT: Yale University Press.

Orfield, G., & Kornhaber, M. L. (Eds.). (2001). *Raising standards or raising barriers? Inequality and high-stakes testing in public education*. New York: Century Foundation Press.

Perry, P. (2002). *Shades of White: White kids and racial identities in high school*. Durham, NC: Duke University Press.

Rist, R. C. (1970). Student social class and teacher expectations: The self-fulfilling prophecy in ghetto education. *Harvard Educational Review. 40*, 411–450.

Rist, R. C. (1980). Blitzkrieg ethnography: On the transformation of a method into a movement. *Educational Researcher, 9*(2), 8–10.

Rivkin, S. G., Hanushek, E. A., & Kain, J. F. (2005). Teachers, schools, and academic achievement. *Econometrica, 73*, 417–458.

Rockoff, J. E. (2004). The impact of individual teachers on student achievement: Evidence from panel data. *American Economic Review, 94*, 247–252.

Rosenbaum, J. E. (1976). *Making inequality*: *The hidden curriculum of high school tracking*. New York: Wiley.

Rumberger, R. W., & Thomas, S. L. (2000). The distribution of dropout and turnover rates among urban and suburban high schools. *Sociology of Education, 73*, 39–67.

Schlechty, P., & Noblit, G. (1982). Some uses of sociological theory in educational evaluation. In A. C. Kerckhoff & R. G. Corwin (Eds.), *Research in sociology of education and socialization, Vol. 3* (pp. 283–306). Greenwich, CT: JAI Press

Schneider, B., Carnoy, M., Kilpatrick, J., Schmidt, W., & Shavelson, R. (2007). *Estimating causal effects: Using experimental and observational designs*. New York: American Educational Research Association.

Schneider, B., & Keesler, V. (2007). School Reform 2007: Transforming education into a scientific enterprise. *Annual Review of Sociology, 33*, 197–217.

Sewell, W. H., Haller, A. O., & Portes, A. (1969). The educational and early occupational attainment process. *American Sociological Review, 34*, 82–92.

Sewell, W. H., Haller, A. O. & Strauss, M. A. (1957). Social status and educational and occupational aspiration. *American Sociological Review, 22*, 67–73.

Sewell, W. H., & Hauser, R. M. (1980). The Wisconsin Longitudinal Study of social and psychological factors in aspirations and achievements. In A. C. Kerckhoff (Ed.), *Research in sociology of education and socialization, Vol. 1* (pp. 59–99). Greenwich, CT: JAI Press.

Sewell, W. H., Hauser, R. M., Springer, K. W., & Hauser, T. S. (Eds.). (2001). *As we age: A review of the Wisconsin Longitudinal Study, 1957–2001*. Madison: University of Wisconsin, Department of Sociology.

Spade, J., Columba, L., & Vanfossen, B. (1997). Tracking in mathematics and science: Courses and course selection procedures. *Sociology of Education, 70*, 108–127.

Stevenson, D. L. (2000). The fit and misfit of sociological research and educational policy. In M. Hallinan, (Ed.), *Handbook of the sociology of education* (pp. 547–563). New York: Kluwer Academic/Plenum Publishers.

Stinchcombe, A. (1965). *Rebellion in a high school*. Chicago: Quadrangle Books.

Stritikus, T., & Wiese, A-M. (2006). Reassessing the role of ethnographic methods in education policy research: Implementing bilingual education policy at local levels. *Teachers College Record, 108*, 1106–1131.

Swidler, A. (1976). What free schools teach. *Social Problems, 24*, 214–227.

Swidler, A. (1979). *Organization without authority: Dilemmas of social control in free schools*. Cambridge, MA: Harvard University Press.

Thorne, B. (1993). *Gender play: Girls and boys in school*. New Brunswick, NJ: Rutgers University Press.

Toles, R., Schulz, E. M., & Rice, W. K., Jr. (1986). A study of variation in dropout rates attributable to effects of high schools. *Metropolitan Education, 2*, 30–38.

U.S. National Commission on Excellence in Education. (1983). *A nation at risk: The imperative for educational reform*. Washington, DC: U.S. Government Printing Office.

Valenzuela, A. (1999). Subtractive schooling: U.S.-Mexican youth and the politics of caring. Albany: State University of New York Press.

Valenzuela, A. (Ed.). (2005). *Leaving children behind: How "Texas style" accountability fails Latino youth*. Albany: State University of New York Press.

Walters, P. (2007). Betwixt and between discipline and profession: A history of sociology of education. In C. Calhoun (Ed.), *Sociology in America* (pp. 639–665). Chicago: University of Chicago Press.

Wells, A. S., & Oakes, J. (1998). Tracking, detracking, and the politics of educational reform: A sociological perspective. In C. A. Torres & T. R. Mitchell (Eds.), *Sociology of education: Emerging perspectives* (pp. 155–180). Albany: State University of New York Press.

Weick, K. (1976). Educational organizations as loosely coupled systems. *Administrative Science Quarterly, 21*, 1–19.

Weimer, D., & Vining, A. (2005). *Policy analysis: Concepts and practice* (4th ed.). Upper Saddle River, NJ: Pearson Prentice Hall.

Willis, P. (1977). *Learning to labor: How working class kids get working class jobs*. New York: Columbia University Press.

6

Current Approaches to Research in Anthropology and Education

MARESSA L. DIXON, KATHRYN M. BORMAN, AND BRIDGET A. COTNER[1]
University of South Florida

History of Anthropology of Education

For anthropologists of education, the beginnings of the field are readily identified. They are closely linked with the efforts of George and Louise Spindler at Stanford University who first defined the field. Their own academic histories included considerable work over 50 years in what George Spindler (2000) identifies as their "four careers": psychological anthropology, anthropology and education, teaching, and editing. The key event that ushered the new field of anthropology and education into play was a conference held at Stanford in the 1950s that included many of those associated with the field from its earliest beginnings. Attending the conference were activists and philosophers, as well as academic anthropologists, including Theodore Brameld, Cora Du Bois, Jules Henry, Dorothy Lee, and Solon Kimball. These individuals made contributions during the 1950s and 60s to the emerging field of education and anthropology by introducing courses of study at both the elementary and the secondary levels, including the study of Eskimo and Iroquois culture (Ellison, 1960). In addition, these pioneers saw the potential for anthropology and education to inform educational theory and practice, especially with respect to the "improvement of understanding of school and society as socio-cultural phenomena" (Hoebel, 1955, p. 301). Establishing academic programs focused on anthropology and education also occurred during this period at Stanford's College of Education by the Spindlers, but even earlier at Harvard and New York University—as early as the 1940s according to Hoebel (1955). Additional early programs came into being at Teachers College, Columbia University, Washington University, and The University of Chicago.

The proceedings of the Stanford conference were later published as a book entitled *Anthropology and Education* edited by Spindler (1955); in it he argued that a major contribution to be made to the general field of educational research and theory was anthropology's methodological toolkit, particularly ethnographic approaches, including participant observation, interviewing, and a long-term commitment to understanding the ethnographic context of communities in which schools were embedded. The focus of initial ethnographic work was the school, although some adventurous researchers included in the collection of chapters also investigated the playground and the classroom. According to a review of the volume that appeared in the *Annals of the American Academy,* topics useful for "the analysis of the educative process" using ethnographic techniques and strategies included "the school in the context of the community, conflicts between cultural ideals and educational action, problems relating to intercultural understanding, contrasts between pre-pubertal and post-pubertal education, communication theory in learning situations, and the relationships between anthropological and educational theory" (Wronski, 1956, p. 174).

The single criticism Wronski (1956) offers of this otherwise "excellent compilation" is the failure to give attention to the links between the newly emerging field of anthropology and education and that part of sociology "closely linked to cultural and social anthropology" (p. 174), a charge that is still relevant 50 years later. In fact, in this chapter we will argue that it is time for anthropologists of education to abandon the role of the lone ethnographer, the sole and ultimate instrument of research in the ethnographic tradition, for a more collaborative and interactive role on a team of social and behavioral scientists.

Anthropology and Education Policy

In their recent edited volume *Policy as Practice,* Sutton and Levinson (2001) highlight ethnographic studies of education policy and implementation that span local, national, and global contexts. Key components of anthropological research concerning education policy are the sociohistorical connections among policy makers at several levels.

Policy formation, in the anthropological sense, does not reside solely within the realm of powerful political elites who mandate institutional changes that other stakeholders blindly follow. Rather, policy is a process of negotiation and meaning-making, a process that requires individuals and groups to define and redefine educational outcomes that are valued and to identify those individuals who can gain access to educational resources (Sutton & Levinson, 2001). Anthropologists of education use single cases, multisite comparisons, and mixed-methods designs to study the multiple ways that institutional actors at different levels understand, mold, and change education policy to meet the needs of particular policy-related issues. Anthropologists analyze education policy with a context-conscious (i.e., ethnographic) perspective in order to better understand the mechanisms through which individuals and groups shape or are prohibited from shaping education policy in their own image.

The Utility of Ethnography as the Signature Method in Educational Anthropology

Anthropology of education has emerged as a field useful in informing methodological approaches in educational research. Even in an era that emphasizes the importance of the so-called "gold standard" or Randomized Controlled Trial (RCT) in educational research, currently requirements for studies supported by the Institute of Education Sciences still emphasize the importance of capturing the on-the-ground effects of the intervention being implemented. Utilizing ethnography as both a set of methodological tools and as a perspective for viewing policy analysis, anthropologists of education investigate the wider cultural context involving groups of people incorporating, resisting, reconstituting, and changing education policy to accomplish goals specific (though not necessarily exclusive) to their daily lived reality. Participant observation, interviewing, archival data analysis, oral histories, statistical analysis, and other data collection methods are the instruments used by anthropologists to examine education policy. These instruments serve the larger purpose of understanding education policy as "a complex social practice" (Sutton & Levinson, 2001, p. 1), a process through which groups of human actors make decisions about the education available in their community (p. 3). Ethnography, however, is meant to also go beyond the *what* of policy formation and implementation to examine the *how* and *why*. Anthropologists of education examine the ways people experience and perceive education policy, the patterns of social interaction used by individuals to translate education policy into education practice, and the intended and unintended outcomes of education policy for various stakeholders. Finally, anthropologists of education "study up" and "study through" (Nader, 1974) to understand the mechanisms that individuals and groups employ to wield power and to develop and/or influence education policy.

Among those in the field of anthropology and education who have been most persistent and most passionate in underscoring the importance of educational ethnography

informing research is Margaret Eisenhart (1999, 2001, 2006). In her recent work she argues that ethnographic work is problematic in several ways. First, "culture" itself is no longer readily associated with either a given community or group, much less with lives in schools, either "prepubertal or postpubertal," to invoke Wronski. In a postmodern world it is virtually impossible to capture "culture" because of the ebb and flow of children through many worlds at once: the media, schools, families, sports activities, and other pursuits. Therefore, Eisenhart (2001) argues, we can "no longer conceive of social groups of people with a culture that is clearly bounded and determined, internally coherent and uniformly meaningful" (p. 17). This is of grave concern to ethnographers and to ethnography as a scientific method because it puts the very subject of ethnographic research— culture—in jeopardy. According to Judith Preissle (1999), "Educational ethnography is the study of the culture of human teaching and learning as they occur in people's ordinary daily activities" (p. 650). In understanding culture as a constantly negotiated process of meaning-making— rather than a neatly packaged set of actions and ideals— anthropologists of education attempt to unpack the complex social, political, and historical relationships that undergird educational policy outcomes.

Eisenhart (2001) considers additional dilemmas confronting the contemporary ethnographer. She points to the importance historically in carrying out ethnographies of education to pursue changes "designed to improve minority children's success in school" (p. 20), as an example. She identifies the problem of giving voice to a plethora of voices that might, in fact, be in conflict in such a scenario. She finally resolves the "muddles" that she has identified with an "untidy" methodological approach—ethnography—by offering several solutions, ways she herself has chosen to represent the "products" of her ethnographic work with middle-school girls learning science (pp. 20–24). First, the tools of communication, including the Internet, may be usefully explored and used to inform an understanding of relationships, communication, and the like. She seems to reluctantly conclude that ethnographers *might* be able to insert themselves into educational research only perhaps by working as members of an interdisciplinary research effort, somewhat wistfully noting that "we will have to participate [as ethnographers] along with others, with one perspective or voice among many [voices]" (p. 24).

Judith Preissle (1999) is resigned but much more sanguine about the prospects of ethnography and ethnographic research than Eisenhart. In her essay "An Educational Ethnographer Comes of Age," Preissle boldly asserts that, while it is the case that who does ethnographic research, how it is done, and what the topic of that approach is might certainly have changed, ethnography has not so much been "conventionalized" as it has been "systemized." In other words, with the publication of an extraordinary number of research methods books—she counts over 300 in her own personal library—over the 30 years surveyed by Preissle, there is now greater method to ethnography's madness. So, who, according to Preissle is the new ethnographer? She argues that the role of professional ethnographer (Agar, 1980) may be obsolete. Instead, thanks to a variety of critics whose work has changed our thinking forever, namely, feminist scholars, postmodernists, and participatory and post-colonial scholars, we can no longer view professional researchers as wholly legitimate. Rather, the researcher as outsider's comprehension and motives are now suspect, and the ethnographic perspective is often viewed by critics as unethical and naïve. It may be, she concludes, that we will *all* be field workers. Indeed, some have argued just that (Ellis & Bochner, 1996). By virtue of the rise of research methods including auto-ethnography, where the researcher monitors him or herself and employs the first person in setting forth the research perspective and findings, the landscape of ethnographic methods has been irrevocably changed.

So, what role and what territory can we envision for the new ethnographer of education in the tradition of anthropology and education? We take on this topic toward the end of the chapter and argue that the trends in postcolonial, feminist, and other approaches have opened windows and doors that now allow more researchers under the broad tent of ethnographic research methods, a very useful thing in our view. Therefore, this chapter is meant to highlight recent (i.e., in the last 10–15 years) policy-related research that is grounded in a holistic perspective, one that foregrounds human agency and the various mechanisms employed by groups of people in different local sites to negotiate education policies. Such research investigates the process of policy development and implementation as people engage with educational policy in their daily lives. In examining policy as a cultural process itself, *all* anthropologists of education inevitably consider issues of policy. Rather than attempt to account for all anthropological investigations of education and schooling, the specific studies we include in this chapter were selected to represent some themes that have recently captured the attention of anthropologists of education who either explicitly consider policy as a topic of research or offer recommendations for future policy development and analysis. By foregrounding some themes over others, we are not suggesting that the work of anthropological researchers not included in this review are less important or less influential in understanding education policy. Rather, the studies selected provide an analysis of one of the four topical areas of central interest to contemporary working anthropologists of education, namely No Child Left Behind (NCLB; 2002) and accountability, cross-cultural and international studies, culturally relevant curriculum, and critical research.

In the next section, we turn to the role of anthropological research in explicating the most salient national policy issue of today: NCLB. With the passage in 2001 of the No Child Left Behind legislation, the role of ethnographic research in showing the mundane particulars that provided the detail needed to show the impact of the policy at the school and classroom levels became important to those who

were careful to document the range of both anticipated and unanticipated outcomes of the policy.

NCLB and Educational Accountability

The No Child Left Behind Act of 2001 ushered in sweeping reforms in U.S. public K-12 education, requiring students and teachers to meet accountability standards through extensive standardized testing. These reforms base school and district funding, student academic advancement, and often teacher salary bonuses on those test results. Since 2001, anthropologists of education have researched the effects of these sweeping, high-stakes changes on students and their families, teachers, classrooms, schools, and districts, including the historical and cultural contexts that allowed for and continue to abet these policy reforms. Even before Congress authorized NCLB, anthropologists conducted school-based ethnographic research that asked whether or not increasing emphasis on standardized testing benefited low performing students in states that would become models for "accountability" reforms nationwide (e.g., Valenzuela, 1999). Educational disparities based on ethnic/racial status, socioeconomic status, English language proficiency, and disability—and the potential for "accountability" reforms to ameliorate these educational inequities—remain pertinent issues that anthropologists of education routinely explore and address.

Broadly stated, anthropologists of education are increasingly orienting their research toward the effects of NCLB accountability requirements on particular groups and/or educational processes. Anthropologists of education pursue two major trajectories of research on NCLB-like accountability policies: (a) the cultural contexts shaping accountability policies, and (b) the effects of these policies after implementation. Anthropologists of education have long studied the impact of policy on ethnically and/or economically marginalized groups. With NCLB's definition of "accountability" explicitly focusing on disaggregating achievement outcomes by race/ethnicity, socioeconomic status, gender, English language proficiency, and disability indicators, the development and implementation of this policy is of particular concern to anthropologists of education.

Direct research concerning NCLB and related policies documents the sociocultural contexts within which political and business elites develop, implement, and nurture accountability reforms through time. This body of research analyzes sociocultural processes that set the stage for accountability policies at the city, state, and national levels, often connecting NCLB to earlier local and state policies. Sites for these studies include such disparate locations as Chicago (Lipman & Haines, 2007), Texas (Salinas & Reidel, 2007), and North Carolina (Bartlett, Frederick, Gulbrandsen, & Murillo, 2002). These researchers investigate the ways such mandates develop and achieve salience through specific discourses and actions adopted by school boards, politicians, businesspeople, and politically influential parents. In Texas, for example, "the efficiency and excellence values of the state's economic elite became a definitive feature of Texas's educational system" (Salinas & Reidel, 2007, p. 46) throughout more than two decades of legislative recommendations made by officially appointed educational committees, an influential non-profit organization, and personal communications between legislators and representatives of these entities (McNeil, 2000; Salinas & Reidel, 2007). Researchers working in the tradition of ethnographic approaches to conducting educational research in anthropology include both sociologists of education and anthropologists. With these methodological tools, researchers document developments in educational policy by analyzing relevant documents, participating in local education events, interviewing stakeholders, and observing in classrooms and other sites where education policy is implemented.

The anthropological study of accountability policies relies heavily upon archival document analysis, observation and participant-observation, and in-depth interviewing of key individuals. Such studies necessitate sociocultural and historical perspectives, linking specific policy outcomes (e.g., school choice options, high stakes testing) to larger discourses and practices going back 25 years and more. This research aims to demystify our educational system's progression toward more standardization by highlighting the cultural basis for politicized, market-driven discourses of educational quality. Ethnographic research reveals the ways the actors who helped shape accountability policies translated ideologies of efficiency, competition, and standardization into educational policies and curriculum (Bartlett et al., 2002; Salinas & Reidel, 2007). What results is, ultimately, an unapologetically critical analysis of the effects of neoliberal ideology on educational policy (Bartlett et al., 2002).

The majority of research on NCLB in anthropology concerns the impacts of accountability policies on students, teachers, classrooms, and schools (Sloan, 2007). That is, the anthropology of education is concerned with the affects of educational policies on the culture of education in local sites and the impact of different cultural processes on the implementation of those policies. Anthropologists producing these types of studies realize that the complexity of NCLB reforms and their impact on education at the local level must be understood by conducting research in, "the very places where such policies ultimately play themselves out: classrooms" (Sloan, 2007, p. 38).

One of the most salient concerns to anthropologists researching education is the impact of NCLB accountability mandates on learning and teaching. These researchers investigate "accountability" as an overarching category that includes such multiple policy outcomes as the proliferation of schools of choice, English-only mandates, and high stakes standardized testing. The question underlying these studies of accountability measures is whether or not the implementation of NCLB policies is truly accomplishing what it is purported to accomplish: "to close the achievement gap with accountability, flexibility, and choice" (107th

Congress, 2002, p. 1439). In other words, anthropologists investigating the impact of accountability policies are most often also ultimately investigating issues of educational equity for linguistically, ethnically, and economically diverse and differently-abled students.

From studies of one teacher (e.g., Valli & Chambliss, 2007), to studies of one school site (e.g., Valenzuela, 1999), to multiple site studies (e.g., Hubbard & Datnow, 2005), anthropologists of education produce descriptive analyses of multi-layered sociocultural processes surrounding the implementation of one or a few specific policies. For example, Hubbard and Datnow's (2005) 2-year study of single-sex academies revealed that positive teacher-student interactions and liberal funding—combined with the single-sex environment—contributed to the success of low-income and minority students in these schools.

Another example of an anthropological analysis of NCLB policy mandates—this time, high-stakes testing—comes from Fine, Jaffe-Walter, Pedraza, Futch, and Stoudt's (2007) multi-site study of the impact of standardized exit exams on the education English Language Learners receive. From class-action lawsuits in California to the International High Schools in New York, these researchers explore sites and instances of resistance to high-stakes testing and the potential for that resistance to usher in a new approach to educational equity. Studies of resistance to policy mandates stand to provide important gains in new knowledge in the anthropology of education because they highlight the sociocultural components of sites of educational activism. As Sutton and Levinson (2001) argue, resistance is one form of policy appropriation and "through this kind of appropriation, new kinds of local normative policies may take shape" (pp. 4–5). In the case of Fine et al. (2007) in particular, it is both the focus on observable alternatives to the status quo as well as the employment of multiple research methods (e.g., surveying, interviewing, student-generated maps) that will increase our understanding of the multiple ways local actors experience, interpret, and act in response to educational policies, forming alternative policies in the process. Long-term ethnographies of sites of resistance could offer diverse communities diverse solutions to educational problems that cannot be addressed by increasing accountability measures alone.

Cross-Cultural and International Education

With the publication of *Coming of Age in Samoa*, Margaret Mead (1928/1961) argued the value of cross-cultural comparison. Cross-cultural comparative data have been used to inform educational policies in many countries around the world—in particular, the United States. Historically, the United States has been influenced by Japan and Germany's education policies (LeTendre, Baker, Akiba, Goesling, & Wiseman, 2001). However, the United States and Western ideals have recently played an influential role in global trends in educational policy. According to Anderson-Levitt (2003), "World culture theorists see an increase in common educational principles, policies, and even practices among countries with varying national identities" (p. 2). Next, a brief overview of the U.S. educational system and trends in education are presented and are followed by methodological issues for cross-cultural and international anthropological research in education.

From its inception, the United States has fostered one of the most decentralized systems of schooling in the world (Cogan, 2004). According to Cogan (2004), this is due in large part to the lack of presence taken, until recent years, by a federal role in education policy: "because there is no federal provision for education in the *U.S. Constitution*" (p. 575). With the absence of a federal presence for education, individual states in the union are given authority to provide this important societal function. States maintained their authority over education throughout the first half of the 20th century. This autonomy began to fade in the second half of the 20th century with the beginning of space exploration, marked by the launching of Sputnik by the former Soviet Union in April 1957. Aware that space exploration was critical to national security, the U.S. Congress passed the National Defense Education Act (1959) in 1958. This statute was the first legislated by the federal government to assume authority in creating a national educational policy, as it was believed that better academic preparation for high school graduates was needed to remain competitive with our Cold War rivals. Subsequent statutes, including the current No Child Left Behind Act, have enabled the U.S. federal government to play a much more prominent role in education without relevant, specific mandates of constitutional authority.

Current trends in U.S. education policy feature the reliance on both standards-based instruction and high levels of accountability. Although NCLB is the principal engine for this approach, high-stakes accountability policies have taken center stage in other countries' educational policies. Curriculum and assessment policies in Australia have evolved through time in sync with philosophical changes in approaches to public schooling. For example, during the 1960s and 1970s practices were focused on the individual child. These practices in turn were followed by a "back-to basics" movement in the U.S. during the mid- to late 1970s. Beginning in the 1970s, and continuing today, there has been a push by the Commonwealth for national control of curriculum and increased monitoring and accountability of student and school performance in Australia. In contrast, States and Territories in Australia have contested the need for a national curriculum; however, according to Halse (2004), "[Policy in Australia] has conceded that increased public testing and accountability seemed unavoidable given the local political climate and global trends" (p. 529). Additionally, while the Commonwealth supports policies similar to NCLB, the States and Territories have cited NCLB as "an undesirable model of educational practice that led to short-term interventions for underachieving students at the expense of broader structural changes for long-term effective school improvement" (p. 529).

LeTendre et al. (2001) have examined the cultural appropriateness of international data to inform educational practice. The debate centers on the feasibility of transferring educational practices from one culture to another. In their work, LeTendre et al. (2001) describe two types of cultural perspectives: national cultures and global cultural dynamics. National cultures are homogenous within nations. An example of how a national culture influences teaching and learning can be found in the work of Stigler and Hiebert (1999) who argue that teaching is a cultural activity. That is, teachers across the United States follow a "script" for teaching that is driven by cultural norms and expectations. Similarly, the Trends in International Mathematics and Science Study (TIMSS) found that educational practice in teaching mathematics and science in the U.S. is "a mile wide and inch deep" compared, for example, to teaching in Japan where coverage of a smaller number of concepts is institutionalized in Japanese pedagogy. Cultural differences in teaching by country are very important to consider when attempting to adapt an educational policy or practice.

Global cultural dynamics, or "world culture," according to LeTendre et al. (2001), evolved from Western ideas and provides an overarching theory where educational change comes from both local idiosyncratic histories as well as broad global trends. Similar educational processes are repeated around the world to varying degrees, creating what LeTendre et al. and others (Anderson-Levitt, 2003) refer to as "international isomorphism in schooling." An example of this is in a school year with the schedule of holidays and the curriculum being organized about "the rationalized model of schooling, which now pervades the world system" (LeTendre et al., 2001, p. 5). Both national and global cultural perspectives have implications for cross-cultural comparisons.

Using cultural factors to explain phenomena in education has been a focus of anthropological and sociological research. Van Zanten (1997) pointed out, "as cultural deprivation theories were replaced by cultural difference theories in the 1970s, an entire new area of research gained recognition in the academic field" (p. 351). Van Zanten looked at the main differences in education of immigrant and minority groups in the United States and France by focusing on cultural factors that help construct national ideologies (a set of values and beliefs that frame political thinking and action) and interact with the global society.

Legitimizing knowledge of participants is a methodological issue that scholarship in education, anthropology, and sociology has significantly contributed to through research with historically marginalized communities in the United States and in the world (Subedi, 2007). For educational anthropologists, representing "the other" as accurately as possible is of critical importance (Ansell, 2001). Ansell (2001) presents the perspective that "the researcher cannot perform a neutral role, but inevitably participates in the (re) production of power relations in the field" (p. 103). This perspective highlights the impossibility of avoiding subordination and exploitation of the researched. However, it is the role of the anthropologist to strive for legitimatization and representation of the people participating in our research.

Culturally Relevant Curriculum

"Culturally relevant," "culturally based," or "culturally responsive" curriculum refers to the conscious and sustained effort to develop curriculum and pedagogy that is built upon and enhances the cultural worlds students occupy. Studies of culturally relevant curriculum are grounded in the idea that students bring knowledge and perspective, molded by the culture(s) in which they are raised, to every educational setting. In fact, a central premise of educational anthropology is that *all* education is culturally based, and learning takes place both inside and outside the school walls. Researchers of culturally based curriculum development argue for a more sustained and conscious effort at ensuring educational equity by opening spaces where all students' cultures are valued and incorporated explicitly into the formal curriculum. The challenge that remains is translating this sentiment into practice; the research discussed in this section represents three specific situations contributing to an understanding and valuing of students' out-of-school lives leading to school-based practices that improved the quality of the education they received.

Advocates for culturally relevant curriculum development range from educators (Ladson-Billings, 2000), to anthropologists (Brenner, 1998; Lipka et al., 2005), to African-centered scholars (Hilliard, 1995; Murrell, 2002), and also span many decades (Deyhle & McCarty, 2007). In the current era of accountability policies, educational anthropologists are linking the language of culturally based curriculum and instruction to the language of standards and accountability. Three major goals for research on culturally relevant curriculum are examined here: using research to support calls for more culturally based curriculum development, investigating outcomes for students and teachers engaged in a culturally based curriculum program, and studying the process of culturally based curriculum development.

Loutzenheiser (2002) interviewed young women in an alternative education program who have been doubly and triply marginalized based on ethnicity, economic status, sexuality, academics, or a combination of multiple identities. The author demonstrates how these young women have rejected either/or typologies that label them "at-risk," and thus failures. Loutzenheiser's (2002) "practice- and policy-oriented analysis" (p. 443) highlights the ways, "events, actions, and decisions made at the school, classroom, and teacher levels can, to a greater or lesser degree, also alter students' feelings of connection to school and to the teachers themselves" (p. 449). It is within the setting of an alternative school that students were supported as whole, complex people rather than as stereotypes or caricatures; this policy of emotionally honest "caring" supported student growth socially, emotionally, as well as academically (see also Valenzuela, 1999, for an extended discussion of "caring,"

school culture, and academic outcomes). What is needed, Loutzenheiser concludes, is more time structured into teachers' routine that allows them to develop a curriculum that responds to students' cultural, academic, and personal needs (pp. 461–462).

For the alternative school involved in the Loutzenheiser study, "culturally relevant" was broadly conceived and included sensitivity to familial issues, learning styles, gender, sexuality—what Loutzenheiser (2002, calls, "the complicatedness of students' lives" (p. 461). Most importantly, the author uses non-standardized open-ended interview techniques to "illuminate differences, similarities, and contradictions within and between the young women's experiences" (p. 445). This study highlights an overarching goal for many anthropologists doing education policy research: the desire to demonstrate that the success of policies directed toward any group depends a great deal on researchers' and policy makers' willingness to understand the experiences and perspectives of the people themselves.

While Loutzenheiser calls for a school-based policy to percolate into mainstream educational settings, it is more often the case that anthropologists of education examine school-based responses to larger policy initiatives. In the last decade policy makers have focused their attention more and more on promoting measures that ensure the attainment of basic skills, particularly mathematical and reading skills. In fact, it can be argued that this reform movement has been underway for over 30 years, with NCLB being the latest iteration of efforts at school reform. What anthropologists of education have and continue to argue is that these movements require an understanding that diverse students learn in diverse ways, and everyday learning is the foundation supporting school-based learning (Lipka et al., 2005, p. 369). Still, as Lipka et al. (2005) suggest, the empirical studies that support claims for culturally based learning are scarce. Lipka et al.'s ethnographic work in predominantly Yup'ik Indian schools in Alaska combines two strivings: one for more empirical knowledge concerning the affects of culturally based curricula and another for more effective methods of mathematical instruction for students living in ethnic communities.

Lipka has worked for more than a decade to develop, cooperatively with Yup'ik elders, teachers, schools, and communities, "Math in a Cultural Context" (MCC), a curricular and pedagogical supplement to the normal math curriculum Yup'ik elementary school students' experience. Lipka et al. (2005) investigate the ways two novice teachers implement MCC, connecting the culturally based program to higher student conceptual understanding and achievement in math. Classroom observations and interviews with these two teachers lead the authors to conclude that, as a result of immersion in the program, "each [teacher] created a strong sense of community among the various stakeholders" (p. 381), fostering a classroom culture of support, trust, and cooperative learning that falls in line with the underlying intent of the MCC curriculum.

Though this particular study is firmly situated in the

ethnographic tradition, the overarching project combines qualitative and quantitative methods, employs a quasi-experimental design, and analyzes student gains on tests administered before and after exposure to the curriculum (that is, for the treatment group; Lipka et al., 2005). In utilizing a plethora of methods—both culturally based and positivist in nature—this research team consciously mobilized, "the language of power" (Sleeter, 2004, p. 135) to argue that culturally based curriculum development is possible, and this curriculum is more effective for American Indian/Alaskan Native students than existing reforms.

Like the work of Lipka's research team, much of the culturally relevant curriculum development programs in U.S. schools that have been evaluated by anthropologists occur in indigenous American Indian or Hawaiian communities. Researchers with the Kamehameha Early Education Program (KEEP) have worked to develop culturally appropriate curricula and teacher training programs for Native Hawaiian students since 1970 (Brenner, 1998). As a researcher associated with KEEP, Brenner uses mathematical testing in both standard and Hawaiian Creole English (HCE) and observations of family shopping to ascertain the amount of mathematical knowledge two samples of students (urban and rural) brought to school before starting kindergarten. She finds that, "the strategic use of HCE and more everyday-like activities in the classroom might promote understanding of task demands ... and facilitate children's utilization of their existing knowledge base" (Brenner, 1998, p. 230).

Brenner then uses this knowledge of Native Hawaiian cultural acquisition of mathematical skills as a basis for instructional experiments at the kindergarten and second-grade levels. In the kindergarten class, the regular teacher incorporated more HCE into instruction, used more hands-on activities, sequenced the text topics to build upon student knowledge, and allowed student autonomy (a common occurrence in Native Hawaiian households) at a math-based game center. By the end of the first year of implementation for the kindergarteners, standardized test scores were statistically significantly higher and students completed more of the text than the control class. The second-graders took turns occupying different "staff" positions in a school store, thereby using mathematical skills in realistic situations. The students' money knowledge, their skills using calculators, and their standardized test scores improved as a result of participating in an ongoing activity that had purpose and relevance in their own day-to-day lives (Brenner, 1998).

Brenner (1998) blends, "a combination of anthropological and cognitive science research strategies" (p. 219)—a quasi-experimental pre-test/posttest design, ethnographic observation, interviewing, and experimental instruction. This approach is especially promising for policy development because it clearly links the desired outcome of current reform policies—higher standardized test scores—to curricula and pedagogy specifically developed around cultural knowledge and informal education. The development of culturally relevant math curricula, as Lipka et al. and Brenner demonstrate, is a promising method of

promoting educational equity for students whose cultures are often erroneously considered a barrier, rather than a springboard, to achievement. Although these studies occurred in relatively distinctive ethnic communities, they put into practice a concept of culturally informed pedagogy that is foundational to the anthropology of education and can be applied to school sites around the world. That is, these researchers investigated the daily activities and experiences of students in the communities that served as homes to these schools, translated those experiences into pedagogy at the classroom level, and then tested whether or not students exposed to this curriculum outperformed students not exposed to the curriculum. What we learn from this type of research is that incorporating outside-of-school learning into the formal school curriculum can positively impact student achievement.

Contemporary anthropologists of education are approaching culturally relevant curriculum development in ways that build upon and expand previous studies. What remains constant in the anthropological tradition of culturally relevant education is the recognition that education occurs both inside and outside the classroom, and the more these two arenas of life are connected, the better chance *all* students have of achieving well academically. Anthropologists of education have studied sites where educators, students, and communities have reclaimed formal schooling to reflect culturally informed understandings of the world, infusing those understandings into the formal curricular structure and advocating for that infusion.

New Directions: Critical Research, in Theory and Practice

Ethnographic research has the ability to uncover complex sociocultural processes influencing educational outcomes for students. As anthropologists of education look toward the future, it is in the areas of theory and methodology that their work has the most promise to expand our knowledge of the relationships between culture and education. When it comes to policy research and analysis, the anthropology of education is in a unique position to connect local, community-based processes to national and global educational movements. Building upon a long-standing tradition of activist-oriented research, anthropologists of education are approaching policy research more and more with a critical lens. Critical research perspectives allow anthropologists to examine questions of educational equity within local and national policy contexts simultaneously, investigating educational justice and injustice as it affects communities.

Critical approaches call upon the researcher to consider her or his practice—methodology, analysis, interpretation—as itself a promotion of educational equity. Critical anthropologists of education interrogate their own researcher roles as elements of an inequitable education system, developing more sensitive and culturally appropriate approaches to data collection and analysis in marginalized communities (Lynn & Parker, 2006), and redirecting that insight toward developing more equitable policies. In this way, local knowledge is not only recorded and analyzed, but incorporated as an element in further knowledge production.

Participatory Action Research (PAR) goes a step further by engaging communities as producers of knowledge rather than subjects of study. As we explored in the section focusing on NCLB, a new direction in critical policy research is to investigate the ways local communities resist, impact, and change the policy setting for their community's schools. PAR is a combination of critical theory, critical methodology and critical action. PAR practitioners facilitate research endeavors involving practices that allow youth and/or adult community members to define, investigate, and analyze research questions that are fundamental to their everyday experiences within schools and communities, then use that research to develop plans of action meant to disrupt existing systems of inequality. Though anthropologists of education have engaged in PAR and other participatory and/or activist-oriented education research for decades, more and more scholars from different disciplines are acknowledging the potential for this type of research to shed new light on the impact of education policies on local communities and the impact local communities can make on education policies.

Agbo (2001) defines Participatory Action Research done with a Mohawk Indian community in New York State as a method for developing a culturally relevant curriculum for students. As Agbo indicates, the project involved much more than curriculum development; it was, "an intrinsically multi-layered process of knowledge creation and sharing" (p. 39). This project engaged a group of teachers, community members, a SUNY Potsdam faculty member, and an American Indian graduate student in researching and defining culturally-relevant educational standards and developing a curriculum based on those standards. As a PAR project, this research called upon participants to critically examine the current policy context that defined "standards" for their students and change those standards in ways that better served their students' needs. Anthropologists of education are engaging in PAR projects in communities around the nation (see also Cammarota, 2008; Hurtig, 2008), increasingly conducting research that is itself a promotion of educational equity. The March 2008 edition of *Anthropology and Education Quarterly,* devoted to activist-oriented research, reflects this growing movement toward connecting educational policy to action research aimed at changing policy.

Critical researchers often call for greater interdisciplinary understanding and expanded methodological tools as avenues for investigating educational policies in practice. Stambach and David (2005) examine, "histories of educational reforms and mothers' narrative accounts" (p. 1634) to analyze the often overlooked gendered rhetoric embedded in school choice policies. The authors suggest that, not only are these and other policies imbued with dichotomous, normative gender ideologies, but exposing these ideologies "show[s] how gender, race, and class intertwine, not simply

add on to one another. This interconnection is as much a factor in considering the formulation of policy as it is in considering how consumerist and class-oriented ideals are crafted into policy" (p. 1652). School choice initiatives, then, are as much products of cultural conceptions of education as they are of cultural conceptions of gender. As Stambach and David illustrate, a more sensitive critical and interdisciplinary lens refracts light onto the interaction of gender, education, and culture in the realm of policies currently impacting the lives of millions of families.

Critical ethnographers also analyze the potential for developing educational policies that acknowledge and encourage educators to negotiate issues of gender, class, race, and educational equity in the classroom. Chapman (2007) explores the multicultural education (MCE) movement catalyzed by *Brown vs. the Board of Education* (1954) by situating one high school class within multiple contexts laden with sociocultural discourses of race and education. Chapman analyzes the methods a multicultural group of students use to navigate racially sensitive topics that arise in class exercises, protecting themselves from the racial volatility of overlapping classroom-school-community contexts. Approaching the research using Critical Race Theory in education, Chapman concludes that defensive student reactions to issues of race were an understandable response to the negative racial undertones that permeated in- and out-of-school settings, and that led in turn to missed opportunities for true multicultural learning in this classroom. She suggests that multicultural education initiatives should be embraced by entire schools, making classrooms safe spaces for cross-cultural learning and understanding instead of another stage for reenacting community-wide racial friction.

Although these studies cannot encompass the entirety of critical approaches to the anthropology of education, it is clear that a salient feature of this type of research is the culture-policy-culture cycle. In other words, critical anthropologists trace the ancestry of educational policies to deep-seated cultural assumptions, and then trace the legacies of these policies to the cultural mechanisms diverse groups of people have developed to negotiate them. The ultimate goal is not to simply understand policy, but to critically examine policies in order to mobilize positive change.

Conclusion

The studies we have reviewed in this chapter highlight the importance of anthropological approaches to understanding policy formation and implementation as a complex sociocultural process that involves stakeholders at all levels. A *perennial* challenge to anthropologists of education is the capacity to carve out a space within educational research as a whole that foregrounds the importance of understanding social processes that influence the ways individuals and groups affect and are affected by education policy mandates at different levels.

Because of anthropologists' particular concern with culture, a variable also of interest to psychologists and sociologists, one avenue for creating opportunities for collaborative research involves studies that have questions of culture central to the enterprise. While there are many studies that take up questions related to the quality and effects of culture on participants in, say, the schooling process in grades pre-K-12, few have involved collaborative teams including anthropologists of education. Hampering the formation of collaborative teams is the reluctance to abandon roles of independence in conducting ethnographic studies that have been a hallmark of research in the field. There is little question that anthropologists of education have long been wrapped in the cloak of the lone researcher, bolstered by images of perhaps the most well-known early anthropologist of education, Margaret Mead, armed only with her own intrepid will, conducting research among adolescent young women in Samoa. It will be predictably difficult to engage in more collaborative policy-related research with colleagues from other disciplines, but we believe it will signal the coming of age of the field in important ways. For one thing, it will indicate that anthropology of education is now secure enough as a field to risk having its boundaries challenged. Lessons can be learned from other sub-disciplines of anthropology, especially those sub-disciplines that comprise contemporary applied anthropology. Medical anthropologists, increasingly engaging in collaborative research with others in related fields, constitute an extremely useful example that could be fruitfully explored by anthropologists of education who wish to take up the complex burden of undertaking policy-related research.

Note

1. The authors would like to acknowledge the help and support of Barbara Schneider and the editors of this handbook along with the two anonymous reviewers, whose helpful comments improved the chapter. Of course, the authors take full responsibility for any errors or omissions that may remain.

References

Agar, M. (1980). *The professional stranger: An informal introduction to ethnography.* New York: Academic Press.

Agbo, S. A. (2001). Enhancing success in American Indian students: Participatory research at Akwesasne as part of the development of a culturally relevant curriculum. *Journal of American Indian Education, 40*(1), 31–56.

Anderson-Levitt, K. M. (Ed.). (2003). *Local meanings, global schooling: Anthropology and world culture theory.* New York: Palgrave Macmillan.

Ansell, N. (2001). Producing knowledge about "Third world women:" The politics of fieldwork in a Zimbabwean secondary school. *Ethics, Place and Environment, 4*(2), 101–116.

Bartlett, L., Frederick, M., Gulbrandsen, T., & Murillo, E. (2002). The marketization of education: Public schools for private ends. *Anthropology and Education Quarterly, 33*, 5–29.

Brenner, M. E. (1998). Adding cognition to the formula for culturally relevant instruction in mathematics. *Anthropology and Education Quarterly, 29*, 214–244.

Brown v. Board of Education, 347 U.S. 483 (1954).

Cammarota, J. (2008). The cultural organizing of youth ethnographers:

Formalizing a praxis-based pedagogy. *Anthropology and Education Quarterly, 39*, 45–58.

Chapman, T. K. (2007). The power of contexts: Teaching and learning in recently desegregated schools. *Anthropology and Education Quarterly, 38*, 297–315.

Cogan, J. J. (2004). Schooling for the future in United States of America: Educational policy at the crossroads. *International Journal of Educational Research, 41*, 574–583.

Deyhle, D., & McCarty, T. L. (2007). Beatrice Medicine and the anthropology of education: Legacy and vision for critical race/critical language research and praxis. *Anthropology and Education Quarterly, 38*, 209–220.

Eisenhart, M. (1999). Reflections on educational intervention in light of postmodernism. *Anthropology and Education Quarterly, 30*, 462–465.

Eisenhart, M. (2001). Educational ethnography past, present, and future: Ideas to think with. *Educational Researcher, 30*(8), 16–27.

Eisenhart, M. (2006). Qualitative science in experimental time. *International Journal of Qualitative Studies in Education, 19*, 697–707.

Ellis, C., & Bochner, A. P. (Eds.). (1996). *Composing ethnography: Alternative forms of qualitative writing.* Walnut Creek, CA: Altamira Press.

Ellison, J. L. (1960). Anthropology brings human nature into the classroom. *Social Education, 24*, 313–316.

Fine, M., Jaffe-Walter, R., Pedraza, P., Futch, V., & Stoudt, B. (2007). Swimming: On oxygen, resistance, and possibility for immigrant youth under siege. *Anthropology and Education Quarterly, 38*, 76–96.

Halse, C. (2004). Striving for balance: Australian perspectives on the future of schooling. *International Journal of Educational Research, 41*, 523–533.

Hilliard, A. G. (1995). *The maroon within us: Selected essays on African American community socialization.* Baltimore: Black Classic Press.

Hoebel, E. A. (1955). Anthropology in education. In W. Thomas (Ed.), *Yearbook of Anthropology* (pp. 391–395). New York: Wenner-Gren Foundation for Anthropological Research.

Hubbard, L., & Datnow, A. (2005). Do single-sex schools improve the education of low-income and minority students? An investigation of California's public single-gender academies. *Anthropology and Education Quarterly, 36*, 115–131.

Hurtig, J. (2008, March). Community writing, participatory research, and an anthropological sensibility. *Anthropology and Education Quarterly, 39*, 92–106.

Ladson-Billings, G. (2000). Culturally relevant pedagogy in African-centered schools: Possibilities for progressive educational reform. In D. S. Pollard & C. S. Ajirotutu (Eds.), *African-centered schooling in theory and practice* (pp. 187–198). Westport, CT: Bergin and Garvey.

LeTendre, G. K., Baker, D. P., Akiba, M., Goesling, B., & Wiseman, A. (2001). Teachers' work: Institutional isomorphism and cultural variation in the US, Germany, and Japan. *Educational Researcher, 30*(6), 3–15.

Lipka, J., Hogan, M. P., Webster, J. P., Yanez, E., Adams, B., Clark, S.,et al. (2005). Math in a cultural context: Two case studies of a successful culturally based math project. *Anthropology and Education Quarterly, 36*, 367–385.

Lipman, P., & Haines, N. (2007). From accountability to privatization and African American exclusion: Chicago's "Renaissance 2010." *Educational Policy, 21*, 471–502.

Loutzenheiser, L. W. (2002). Being seen and heard: Listening to young women in alternative schools. *Anthropology and Education Quarterly, 33*, 441–464.

Lynn, M., & Parker, L. (2006). Critical race studies in education: Examining a decade of research on U.S. schools. *The Urban Review, 38*(4), 257–290.

McNeil, L. M. (2000). *Contradictions of school reform: Educational costs of standardized testing.* New York: Routledge.

Mead, M. (1961). Coming to age in Samoa: A psychological study of primitive youth for Western civilization. New York: Marrow. (Original published 1928)

Murrell, P. C., Jr. (2002). *African-centered pedagogy: Developing schools of achievement for African American children.* Albany: State University of New York Press.

Nader, L. (1974). Up the anthropologist: Perspectives gained by studying up. In D. Hymes (Ed.), *Reinventing anthropology* (pp. 284–311). New York: Vintage Books.

National Defense Education Act of 1958, Pub. L. No. 85-864, 72 Stat. 1581-1591 (1959).

No Child Left Behind Act of 2001, Pub L. No. 107-110, 115 Stat, 1425 (2002).

Preissle, J. (1999). An educational ethnographer comes of age. *Journal of Contemporary Ethnography, 28,* 650–659.

Salinas, C. S., & Reidel, M. (2007). The cultural politics of the Texas Educational Reform Agenda: Examining who gets what, when, and how. *Anthropology and Education Quarterly, 38,* 42–56.

Sleeter, C. E. (2004). Context-conscious portraits and context-blind policy. *Anthropology and Education Quarterly, 35,* 132–136.

Sloan, K. (2007). High-stakes accountability, minority youth, and ethnography: Assessing the multiple effects. *Anthropology and Education Quarterly, 38,* 24–41.

Spindler, G. D. (Ed.). (1955). *Education and anthropology.* Stanford, CA: Stanford University Press.

Spindler, G. D. (2000). The four careers of George and Louise Spindler: 1948–2000. *Annual Review of Anthropology, 29,* xv–xxxviii.

Stambach, A., & David, M. (2005). Feminist theory and educational policy: How gender has been "involved" in family school choice debates. *Signs: Journal of Women in Culture and Society, 30,* 1633–1658.

Stigler, J. W., & Hiebert, J. (1999). *The teaching gap: Best ideas from the world's teachers for improving education in the classroom.* New York: The Free Press.

Subedi, B. (2007). Recognizing respondents' ways of being and knowing: Lessons un/learned in researching Asian immigrant and Asian-American teachers. *International Journal of Qualitative Studies in Education, 20,* 51–71.

Sutton, M., & Levinson, B. (Eds.). (2001). *Policy as practice: Toward a comparative sociocultural analysis of educational policy.* Norwood, NJ: Ablex.

Valenzuela, A. (1999). *Subtractive schooling: U.S.-Mexican youth and the politics of caring.* Albany: State University of New York Press.

Valli, L., & Chambliss, M. (2007). Creating classroom cultures: One teacher, two lessons, and a high-stakes test. *Anthropology and Education Quarterly, 38,* 57–75.

van Zanten, A. (1997). Schooling immigrants in France in the 1990s: Success or failure of the Republican model of integration? *Anthropology and Education Quarterly, 28,* 351–374.

Wronski, S. P. (1956). Education and anthropology. *The Annals of the American Academy of Political and Social Science, 304,* 173–174.

7

Making Education Research More Policy-Analytic

David L. Weimer
University of Wisconsin–Madison

Introduction

Many researchers seek answers to questions relevant to the design, implementation, assessment, and administration of education policy in the United States. A veritable army of researchers, including not only those trained specifically as educational researchers but also economists, psychologists, sociologists, political scientists, and lawyers working in universities, think tanks, advocacy groups, and government, do research that has potential relevance to improving education. They generally produce *policy research*. Although they often do so with the express purpose of informing education policy, they rarely engage in *policy analysis* to assess systematically the alternative policy choices that could be made to address any particular problem or to exploit any identified opportunity. I argue in this chapter that by adopting a more policy-analytic perspective, those producing research relevant to education policy would potentially increase the usefulness of their research and the prudence of their policy claims.

In the following discussion, I draw out distinctions between policy research and policy analysis in some detail. As a starting point, and at the risk of oversimplification, I see policy research as generally emphasizing the methodologically valid assessment of some important policy problem or impact, and policy analysis emphasizing the assessment of the valued impacts of concrete policy alternatives. Thus, being more policy-analytic means specifying detailed alternatives and predicting the full range of their impacts.

It may be helpful to begin by distinguishing between good disciplinary and good policy research. Disciplinary research in the social sciences informs our understanding of human behavior in the various spheres of life—the personal, social, economic, and political. To the extent it helps us understand better how the world works, it is potentially relevant to making good public policy. However, good disciplinary research need not have any immediate relevance to specific policy issues, sometimes because the causal

relationships it identifies cannot be affected by policies reasonably within the purview of government.

In contrast, the defining characteristic of policy research is its direct relevance to some aspect of public policy. Sometimes policy research involves assessing the extent or nature of a condition that may be worthy of public attention. For example, is the racial gap in educational performance growing or shrinking? Is it the same for girls and boys? Does it vary by subject? What consequences does it have for individuals or society more broadly? Other times policy research involves assessing the impact of variables that can be manipulated through public policy—a more or less verified hypothesis of the sort: If government adopts policy X, then consequence Y will result. For example, policy research answers questions such as: Does reduction in class size substantially increase student achievement? Are reductions more valuable in some grades than others? Do gains made in one grade persist in subsequent grades?

Policy analysis systematically assesses the alternative ways that government can address problems of public concern. Canonical policy analysis defines the problem being addressed, identifies the social values, or goals, relevant to the problem, constructs concrete policy alternatives, projects the impacts of the alternative policies in terms of the identified goals, and makes a recommendation based on an explicit assessment of the tradeoffs among goals offered by the alternatives (Bardach, 2005; MacRae & Whittington, 1997; Weimer & Vining, 2005). As professional practice, it typically aims to inform decisions by specific policy makers.

Policy research clearly informs policy analysis, especially about the magnitude and nature of problems and the likely impacts of particular policy alternatives. Policy research also often contributes to the demand for policy analysis by raising the visibility of undesirable conditions or by indicating the possible efficacy of particular policy interventions to address such conditions. The concepts and demands of policy analysis have less influence on the conduct of policy research. This is unfortunate, because anticipating the potential use of research findings in subsequent policy analyses may enable researchers to make their findings more useful. Ignoring policy analysis is also unfortunate, in that adopting its more comprehensive view of social values could potentially help temper some of the advocacy, and hence controversy, that seems to be so common in educational research.

Differences between Policy Research and Policy Analysis

Policy research as it is commonly practiced differs in several important ways from canonical policy analysis. These differences, summarized in Table 7.1, suggest ways policy research can be made more useful to policy choice. They also help explain why academic incentives push policy research away from policy analysis.

Both policy research and policy analysis seek to contribute to a better society. Policy research typically does so by focusing on a particular value, or goal (such as increasing student achievement) that is important and affected by some policy whose impacts can be assessed through systematic study. Often the value itself is implicit, perhaps because greater impact is inherently desirable. In contrast, policy analysis seeks to consider the full range of social values. If for no other reason than the inevitable limits to social and governmental resources, the set of values considered almost always includes minimizing the use of these scarce resources that could be used to produce other things valued by society. Identifying the relevant values to consider is itself a value judgment, so a good policy analysis makes an explicit argument as to why a particular set of values should be employed.

Policy research typically focuses on a single policy, perhaps because an application of the policy has generated data to assess its impacts. Indeed, policy research often follows the "evaluation model," which seeks to assess the impacts actually produced by some intervention. Good policy research clearly documents the essential elements of the policy (to make clear the "treatment" producing the impacts), but rarely in sufficient detail to allow for its immediate implementation in some other context. It thus generally offers assessment relevant to a generic, rather than specific, application of the policy alternative. Policy analysis, driven more by a desire to solve a problem than assess a particular policy, typically considers several policies as alternative courses of action. In order to make predictions of impacts, including demands on resources, and provide a clear starting point for implementation, policy analysts specify alternatives very concretely.

Policy researchers want to influence policy choice. However, researchers, particularly those in academia, typically aim their work primarily at other researchers who can be expected to be familiar with sophisticated research design and statistical methods. Rather than attempting to inform a particular decision-maker, they aim to change thinking within what John Kingdon (1995) calls the "policy stream," or Paul Sabatier and Hank Jenkins-Smith (1993) call the "advocacy coalition system." Although ongoing policy debates influence the subject and rapidity of policy research, and sometimes the availability of research funding, the speed with which good policy research can be produced and disseminated depends very much on the methodology being employed and the reviewing processes of the journals where it is to be published. If high standards that garner the respect of the community of researchers are to be met, then the motto must be "no study before its time." In contrast, policy analysts tailor their work to specific individual or institutional clients who seek advice about a perceived problem or proposed courses of action. Advice may have no value to these clients after circumstances such as legislative, budgetary, or administrative cycles have forced them to make decisions, therefore policy analysts often do not have the luxury of waiting for better data or more sophisticated studies. Of course, as many issues recur, forward-looking policy analysts encourage investments in longer term research projects that have potential for filling important gaps in knowledge.

The contributions of policy researchers often reflect the strong influences of disciplinary training and scholarly incentives. For better or worse, status in the academy tends to favor those who contribute to disciplinary progress as well as social improvement. Publishing research in a disciplinary journal generally contributes more to career advancement than publishing in a topic-area journal. Consequently, career incentives encourage use of the dominant methodology within the discipline whether or not it fully encompasses the problem being addressed. In contrast, good policy analysis is eclectic in its methods, drawing both evidence and methods from any sources that can shed light on the nature of problems or help predict the consequences of alternative policies for addressing them.

Policy research usually offers recommendations, though often only implicitly. A common approach is to conduct some sort of evaluation of a single policy already in place, such as a program or project in a school, school district, or state. Usually, based on whether or not the policy ap-

TABLE 7.1
Comparison of Policy Research with Policy Analysis

Approach Characteristics	Policy Research (common practice)	Policy Analysis (canonical)
Values	Selective; Implicit	Comprehensive; Explicit
Alternatives	Single; Generic	Multiple; Concrete
Primary Client	Research community	Decision maker
Time Frame	Driven by methodology	Driven by decision
Intellectual Resources	Disciplinary	Eclectic
Recommendation	Single impact; General	Tradeoffs; Very specific
Dissemination	Broad	Narrow

pears to produce an important impact, the research implies that the policy is either desirable (and therefore worthy of continuation, expansion, or replication) or undesirable (and therefore appropriately shrunk, radically reformed, or terminated). Rarely do policy researchers consider the full range of values relevant to making such a judgment. Additionally, they tend to report results as relevant to the policy in its generic form rather than in terms of a concrete policy proposal. In contrast, good policy analysis considers tradeoffs among the full set of relevant values in making a very specific recommendation that indicates exactly what steps a decision maker would have to take to adopt and implement it.

Policy research, especially when relevant to important issues, often disseminates widely. The general statements about problems or policies it makes gives it an audience within the community of researchers interested in the substantive area; they may also spill into the popular media, though in very abbreviated and sometimes distorting formats. Further, as noted above, it may also receive disciplinary attention if it explicitly contributes to theory or methods recognized within the discipline. In contrast, the demands of informing a particular decision force policy analysis to be narrow in focus. Although many researchers, analysts, and other decision-makers would benefit from access to good analyses despite their specificity to a particular context, there are few publishing venues for making them broadly available. By reducing the cost of dissemination, the Internet may expand availability. For example, the work of Aos, Lieb, Mayfield, Miller, and Pennucci (2004) at the Washington State Institute for Public Policy comparing the net benefits of various policies relevant to youth are available on the organization's webpage (www.wsipp.wa.gov), even though it is not published in a journal. However, moving good policy analyses to publishable form is often difficult, especially as an exemplary policy analysis need not necessarily involve any of the methodological innovations so valued by scholarly journals. As the marginal professional value of publication for practicing analysts is much lower than for academic or think-tank researchers, and because collective authorship of policy analyses within organizations often dilutes the incentive for any one analyst to take the lead in bearing the usually after-work costs of publication, analysts rarely make their work available in refereed journals.

Possible Gains from Being More Policy-Analytic

The long term prospects for improving education depend on a continuing flow of good policy research that informs, however indirectly, policy choice. It would be a great loss if this flow slowed because large numbers of researchers diverted their efforts to producing policy analyses—any short term gains would likely come at the expense of long term progress in understanding how to make education more effective. Nevertheless, more policy-analytic thinking might help researchers ask more policy-relevant questions and make more prudent recommendations that recognize the relevance of multiple, and often conflicting, values to policy choice.

The differences between policy research and policy analysis point to ways that the former can gain from the latter—that is, ways that policy research can become more policy-analytic. At the risk of perhaps conveying too strong an admonition to be more policy-analytic, the following discussion is hortatory. It should be viewed as offering different ways of thinking about how to make policy research more useful rather than as a call for substantially changing its conduct. In some cases, it simply calls policy researchers back to good practices that run counter to disciplinary incentives.

Let Problems as well as Alternatives Drive Research The most typical approach of policy research, which I label the evaluation model, assesses policies already in place for which available data permit inferences about one or more important impacts. Our multitude of school districts and variety of state laws offer many opportunities for applying the evaluation model to innovative policies, though opportunities may be lost if innovators do not collect data in anticipation of eventual evaluation. Truly novel policy ideas cannot be assessed within this model because they have yet to produce data that can be used to assess impacts.

By looking only under the proverbial lamppost, that is, by looking only where data permit confident impact assessment, researchers miss opportunities for potentially making large contributions to the improvement of education. The research community, including foundations, referees, and editors, should be more aware of this limitation and encourage more research that does not closely fit the evaluation model. For example, what does theory tell us about possible ways to deal with some problem? Have similar problems been faced in the past? Can similar approaches in other policy areas be found to offer indications of likely impacts? Can a practical experiment or demonstration be designed to provide data for assessing promising approaches in the future? Judging the quality of research employing more eclectic and often more qualitative approaches is harder than determining if the standards and conventions of the evaluation model have been followed. Nevertheless, looking forward to potential, if uncertain, solutions to problems offers a broadening of perspective beyond the more certain retrospective assessments of what has actually been tried.

A problem orientation may help counter the natural tendency of education researchers to restrict their attention to policies that can be implemented through schools. Since 1960, real per pupil expenditures have risen substantially in the United States, yet average student performance has not (Hanushek, 1997). One explanation recognizes that education is jointly produced by schooling and families. If some families fail to provide supportive environments, then schools face a more difficult task. A problem orientation leads one to ask how these families could be made better contributors to education. Could these families be helped more effectively through school-based or social welfare programs? At the margin, would additional public expenditures be more effective in improving the performance of students from poor family environments if they were directed at the families, rather than at the students? If so, how could these services be most effectively delivered?

Looking broadly at problems may also identify opportunities. For example, education researchers know the many undesirable consequences of failure to complete high school, including increased risk of criminal behavior. Contact with the criminal justice system also provides an opportunity for coercive intervention not otherwise available. Judges may help offenders' future life prospects by requiring completion of schooling, perhaps through general education degrees, as a condition of diversion or probation. Can policies that encourage judges to consider this approach be crafted? Would they be desirable? Looking solely within the boundaries of school policy may miss opportunities for answering such questions.

Acknowledge Multiple Goals The evaluation model of policy research tends to focus attention on one or a small number of policy impacts with unambiguous desirability. Other things equal, we all want students to be knowledgeable, well behaved both in and out of school, prepared to participate in the economy, and good citizens. In comparing policies, however, other things are rarely equal. Policies aimed at producing the same educational impact typically differ in ways of relevance to a variety of other social values that we wish to promote, such as economy in the use of scarce resources, democratic participation, and personal autonomy. Acknowledging the relevance of these multiple goals encourages researchers to give attention to more policy impacts. It may also promote a more constructive engagement among advocates for conflicting policies, where it is the other, less explicitly addressed, social values that seem to be predispose researchers to particular policies.

Relevant social values include not only those things that all see as desirable. Things valued by segments of society generally deserve consideration in policy making. The values people hold deserve respect for their own sake. Their values and interests also demand attention to help anticipate and further political feasibility. In education policy, these stakeholder values include those held by students, parents, taxpayers, and teachers.

Some of the most heated debates among education researchers tend to focus on one or a few policy impacts without engagement of all the relevant values. Consider, for example, the fights in the literature over the impacts of school choice on the performance of students who exercise it as well as on the traditional public schools these students leave. Most of the studies focus on student achievement as measured by standardized test scores, though some consider the satisfaction levels of parents and participating teachers. Student achievement is certainly important, though standardized tests do not assess it perfectly. Minimizing budgetary cost certainly has relevance to taxpayers; all else

equal, including student achievement, the less expensive policy is desirable because it permits other expenditures that produce things of value. Thus, even if voucher or charter schools produced the same level of achievement as traditional schools, they would be preferred if they were less expensive. Of course, choice policies have a number of impacts that affect other relevant values as well. On the positive side, they give parents the opportunity to play a more meaningful role in the schooling of their children. They may change parents' residential choices in ways that benefit the diversity and vibrancy of neighborhoods, perhaps with fiscal spillovers to city governments. They may create incentives for public schools to improve or at least be more responsive to parents. They may also provide more desirable working conditions for the teachers who staff them. On the negative side, choice policies may drain resources from public schools that have little flexibility in the short run for responding, resulting in lower achievement levels and reduced organizational capacity. They may leave public schools with higher concentrations of children with less motivated parents. They may thus reduce the quality of the working environment for public school teachers, which in turn may encourage departures by the most effective teachers. They also may bring along with them regulations that constrain the previously existing private schools in undesirable ways.

A good policy analysis of a choice program would consider all of these possible effects, not just student achievement on standardized tests. Predicting the magnitude, or in some cases even the sign, of these sorts of effects, would likely only be possible if they have been addressed by policy researchers. Thus, policy researchers can make their work more valuable by assessing as many of the impacts of choice programs as they can. Acknowledging the multiple values at stake helps researchers anticipate the relevant impacts.

Inform Tradeoffs The consideration of multiple goals almost always leads to tradeoffs, as one alternative rarely dominates another in all respects. Good policy analysis directly confronts these tradeoffs. Policy researchers should as well.

Consider, for example, proposals to reduce class size. The most useful research would not just infer the gains in student performance that result from a reduction in class size from, say, 25 to 15 students. Rather, because class size reductions are very expensive, it would be more informative if it produced a schedule of gains by size of reduction, which in turn would allow analysts to produce a schedule of gains per dollar of additional expenditure. Such a schedule would make clear tradeoffs between two things of value to society—gains in student achievement and tax dollars that could be spent on many things of value. Even if such a schedule cannot be confidently produced because of uncertainties about effects on achievement, cost estimates of the sort produced by Brewer, Krop, Gill, and Reichardt (1999) make a valuable contribution to the class size debate from a policy perspective. More generally, policy researchers can potentially contribute to analysis by paying more attention to costs. For example, the finding of Stiefel, Berne, Iatarola, and Fruchter (2000) that the size of high schools does not substantially affect budgetary costs per 4-year pupil tells analysts that the size of high schools can be assessed in terms of their other impacts.

When it is reasonable to limit attention to one quantified impact and the costs required to produce it, policy researchers may make their work more policy informative by pushing it toward cost-effectiveness, which compares the incremental cost of a policy with its incremental impact on some important outcome. That is, they can attempt to assess social costs exclusive of the non-monetized impact broadly so that a cost-effectiveness ratio can be estimated. Levin (2001) argues that there is a dearth of actual cost-effectiveness analyses, as opposed to the use of cost-effectiveness jargon, in the education policy literature. Adding good cost-effectiveness studies to this literature would increase its potential influence on policy choice.

... But Look for Ways to Monetize
Illuminating tradeoffs challenges analysts when the number of relevant goals is large. Measuring impacts relevant to various goals using a common metric promotes simplification by allowing impacts to be algebraically combined. Cost-benefit analysis provides a protocol for measuring all impacts relevant to efficiency in the common metric of present value dollars. The net benefits accruing in aggregate can be broken out in useful ways, such as those accruing to a client, such as a student, and those that spill over to the rest of society in terms of taxes and externalities—see Karoly, Kilburn, and Cannon (2005) for an example of the application of this approach to the valuation of early childhood interventions.

Examples of good cost-benefit analyses of education policies are few. Those that are available often do not fully take account of social benefits, say by limiting attention to gains in market earnings of participants (Krueger, 2004; Levin, 2006; Aos, Miller, & Mayfield, 2007), which probably underestimate the social benefits of schooling by a half (Wolfe & Haveman, 2001). However, recent applications to early childhood programs such as Perry Preschool (Belfield, Nores, Barnett, & Schweinhart, 2006), Abecedian (Barnett & Masse, 2007), and Child Parent Centers (Temple & Reynolds, 2007) suggest there is a growing number of education researchers with the capabilities and inclination to apply cost-benefit analysis to provide overall assessments of potentially desirable policy interventions.

Researchers can make their work more useful by anticipating the demand for information from analysts who wish to assess efficiency through cost-benefit analysis. They may also contribute by helping to estimate better commonly used "shadow prices" that allow researchers to monetize impacts. For example, cost-benefit analysts may be relatively comfortable valuing high school completion in terms of increased future earnings (Tyler, Murnane, & Willet, 2000), reduced criminal behavior, and delayed fertility (Haveman & Wolfe, 1984; Wolfe & Haveman, 2001).

Programs that increase achievement in lower grades can be translated into this framework only if researchers estimate the magnitude of the link between achievement gains and the probability of high school completion.

Describe Policies in Detail
The evaluation model of policy research considers an existing policy such as a pilot or ongoing program. Interest usually focuses on some specific feature of the program that differs from common practice. Researchers wish to attribute the inferred impacts to that feature. However, such programs often operate in complex social environments that may be relevant to the impacts that the feature produces. The best research designs for ensuring internal validity seek ways of controlling for these confounding environmental factors through experiments employing randomization of subjects into treatment and control groups. Not only cost, but also administrative barriers and ethical concerns, may preclude such experiments when they are otherwise technically feasible, as with innovations at the student or classroom level. Experiments may not be technically feasible for innovations at the school, district, or state levels. When true experiments cannot be done, creative researchers look for quasi-experimental designs to support inferences, such as comparing outcomes before and after the innovation or across units with and without the innovation. In all cases, but especially for studies based on quasi-experimental designs, the full value of such research for informing decisions about replication will not be realized without a detailed description of what was actually evaluated.

Good policy analysis requires detailed specification of policy alternatives for two reasons. First, one can only predict the consequences of a very concrete proposal. A generic policy such as reducing class size could have almost any effect, depending on the circumstances of its implementation. Only with details, such as the number of students in the reduced-size classes, their grade levels, and the socioeconomic status of their families, can one begin to make predictions, with or without the support of policy research. Second, one can only identify the resources needed to implement a very concrete proposal—reductions of class size to 15 students will be much more costly than reductions to 20 students and the overall extent of the reductions may have implications for the availability of skilled teachers and appropriate classroom spaces. Policy research that specifies the details of what has been evaluated helps policy analysts design alternatives, predict their consequences, and anticipate resources needed for their implementation.

Producing detailed descriptions should be easier for policy researchers who can look at what has been done than for policy analysts who must design alternatives that might be. However, several factors work against policy researchers providing their audiences with detailed descriptions of what they have evaluated. First, discovering what has actually been done is labor intensive, and therefore costly. Official descriptions of innovations often do not reflect adaptations made during implementation to deal with unanticipated difficulties or opportunities. Finding out what actually happened during implementation often requires interviews with those on the ground. Confirming what is happening often requires direct observation. Second, the data relevant to impacts and their analysis often become the focus for researchers and referees, deflecting attention away from program description. Third, editors, seeking to economize on scarce journal pages, trained earlier generations of researchers to cut description to a minimum to allow more space for the presentation of methods and results. Although the first factor lies largely beyond the control of the research community, the technology of the Internet should enable editors to reduce the effect of the other two factors. Editors can, and should, require researchers to post extensive descriptions of evaluated programs on journal-sponsored web pages. In the meantime, researchers can do their own postings, though without the benefits of permanent availability and easy comparability that would result from archiving by journals.

Recognize Variability Policy researchers naturally want their work to garner attention and be influential. This desire, perhaps reinforced by an ideologically motivated policy preference, may tempt researchers to make overly bold and unqualified claims. Lost within very general claims may be useful information about situations in which policies that appear effective overall are likely to be ineffective, or situations in which policies that appear ineffective overall are likely to be effective. Although bold and unequivocal claims often grab public and political attention, more nuanced assessments may lead to better policies in the long run.

An example from criminology illustrates this danger. In 1974, Robert Martinson published a review of criminal rehabilitation programs in *The Public Interest* that made the bold claim that there was no systematic evidence that any approach was generally effective in reducing recidivism. This claim contributed to a policy shift during the 1980s away from the rehabilitative model and toward the deterrence and "just desserts" models of criminal punishment. Researchers eventually challenged the general claim, identifying particular types of rehabilitative programs that worked for specific populations, such as juveniles and substance abusers (e.g., Gendreau & Ross, 1987). Had the inherent variability in effectiveness across program types and target populations been conveyed rather than the general claim, it is quite possible that the policies governing juvenile justice and the punishment of drug offenders would have followed very different paths over the last 30 years.

The casual reader of the education policy literature, which would include many policy makers, might encounter sweeping, and contradictory, claims about policies such as vouchers, class size, and phonics versus whole language reading instruction. Although careful review may reveal appropriate caveats, media coverage tends to focus on bold claims—see, for example, Schemo (2004) on charter schools—and researchers themselves sometimes seem to be engaged in winning heated debates rather than making

the best possible assessments. Carefully identifying the situations in which various policies are likely to be effective or ineffective makes debate more productive and supports more sophisticated policy choice.

Acknowledge Uncertainty Good inferential policy research conveys not only the point estimates of model parameters but also their precision. Simple models often produce standard errors of estimates as a byproduct. With the advance of computing resources, researchers have become more skillful in using sophisticated methods, such as bootstrapping, for estimating standard errors in more complicated models. These methods insure that Type I errors, rejecting the null hypothesis for some alternative hypothesis when in fact the null is true, are correctly assessed *assuming* that the researcher has applied the correct model. (Type II error is failing to reject the null hypothesis in favor of the alternative when, in fact, the latter is true.) Failure to use the correct model can be thought of as what is commonly referred to as Type III error—finding a correct answer to the wrong question (Kimball, 1957). Assessing the risk of Type III error is an important part of acknowledging uncertainty.

Policy analysts, especially without access to original data, must generally rely on the judgment of researchers (and for published work, referees and editors) that appropriate models were employed in estimating the reported findings. Researchers can reassure analysts that the risk of Type III error has been minimized by reporting the extent to which substantive results differed when plausible alternative models were estimated. They can also be explicit about the assumptions inherent in a model and the likelihood that these assumptions are met. For example, hierarchical models are commonly employed in education research, because they take account of the nesting of students within classrooms and classrooms within schools. Yet, these models require researchers to make the strong assumption that the random components of higher level coefficients are independent, an assumption that may not be warranted. Addressing such concerns in the research report enables policy analysts to more confidently draw on findings.

... But Provide Estimates Policy researchers may be conditioned by their experiences with publishing in scholarly journals to disregard statistically insignificant findings. Editors are loath to allocate scarce space to null-findings, and both editors and referees may be skeptical about null-findings because of the difficulty of assessing the power of tests to reject the null in favor of substantively meaningful effects. This conditioning may lead unthinking, or unethical, researchers to torture their data until it speaks the desired conventional significance (Weimer, 1986). These processes—editorial bias against null-findings and researcher responses to this bias—may result in a literature that paints a distorted picture of policy effectiveness.

The under-representation of null-findings means that policy analysts may incorrectly believe that some alternative has not been evaluated rather than it has been found to be not effective. Researchers with null findings do a service by finding some venue, even if only self-publication on the Internet, to make their research accessible to policy analysts.

Researchers should also recognize that policy analysts may have a different interpretation of null-findings. Unlike researchers, who follow standard conventions of hypothesis testing that require the null to be very unlikely in view of the observed data before it is rejected in favor of an alternative of some non-zero effect, policy analysts must make a prediction. Although they would most like to base their predictions on statistically and substantively significant effects, they would rather have a very imprecise but substantively relevant effect as the basis for prediction than no empirical basis at all. In the regression context, for example, a positive coefficient such that there is a 20% probability of observing a value as large or larger when in fact the true effect is zero would nevertheless be useful to a policy analyst forced to make a prediction even if it would not earn a star in a regression table in a journal. A good policy analyst would convey the uncertainty in the prediction resulting from the large standard error of the coefficient—perhaps using Monte Carlo techniques to assess the implications of the uncertainty on derivative estimates, such as net benefits. In any event, policy researchers should realize that their work may have utility for policy analysis even if it does not yield the conventionally statistically significant results that earn it a place in a major journal.

Write to Your Audience(s) Successful policy researchers internalize the prevailing norms for presentation within their intellectual communities. If these norms are indeed widely shared, then they facilitate economy in presentation. However, these presentational norms may also serve as barriers to understanding for those not in the community. For example, researchers who seek to measure the value-added provided by various school interventions will likely be familiar with the difference-in-differences estimators or the distinction between intent-to-treat and as-treated experimental assessments—even quite sophisticated state-level policy makers may not. Researchers can increase the potential influence of their work by presenting it in ways that make it accessible to those not familiar with the prevailing norms within the research community.

Many students of policy analysis see clear writing that communicates effectively with the intended audience as an essential feature of effective analysis—not just as a means of packaging a final product, but also as integral to the analytical process itself (see Mintrom, 2003; Musso, Biller, & Myrtle, 2000; Weimer & Vining, 2005). The key idea is to communicate with the intended audience. For policy researchers seeking to reach policy makers, this generally requires that the version of the research presented to the research community be translated into clear, jargon-free language that can be readily understood by an intelligent reader untrained in the research methods employed.

As decision makers are typically busy people, the trans-lated work should begin with an executive summary that places the recommendation in the last sentence of the first paragraph and then rehearses the reasoning that supports it. The report itself should tell the story of the research clearly and concisely, referring as appropriate to the more technical report written for colleagues. Researchers can facilitate dissemination by posting their general-audience reports on their Web pages along with their working papers. Sending links to the reports by e-mail to potentially interested parties is a low-cost way of promoting dissemination.

Conclusion

Well-executed policy research contributes to good public policy both by expanding our general knowledge about problems and policies and by informing specific policy choices. By virtue of their training and the intellectual communities within which they work, policy researchers tend to focus on expanding general knowledge through the application of recognized research methods drawn from the scholarly disciplines. In this chapter, I have argued that policy researchers may be able to increase the utility of their work by anticipating its potential use in policy analysis. Such anticipation need not interfere with the production of high quality research, though it may divert some resources to a more careful description and more varied assessments than might otherwise be done, or at least reported. Although these diversions could go too far, my occasional visits to the education policy literature make me comfortable urging researchers to be more policy-analytic in their work at the margin.

References

Aos, S., Lieb, R., Mayfield, J., Miller, M., & Pennucci, A. (2004). *Benefits and costs of prevention and early intervention programs for youth.* Olympia: Washington State Institute for Public Policy.

Aos, S., Miller, M., & Mayfield, J. (2007). *Benefits and costs of k-12 educational policies: Evidence-based effects of class size reductions and full-day kindergarten* (Document No. 07-03-2201). Olympia: Washington State Institute for Public Policy.

Bardach, E. (2005). *A practical guide for policy analysis: The eightfold path to more effective problem solving* (2nd ed.). Washington, DC: CQ Press.

Barnett, W. S., & Masse, L. N. (2007). Comparative benefit-cost analysis of the Abecedarian Program and its policy implications. *Economics of Education Review, 26,* 113–125.

Belfield, C. R., Nores, M., Barnett, S., & Schweinhart, L. (2006). The High/Scope Perry preschool program: Cost-benefit analysis using data from the age-40 follow up. *Journal of Human Resources, 41,* 162–190.

Brewer, D. J., Krop, C., Gill, B. P., & Reichardt, R. (1999). Estimating the costs of national class size reductions under different policy alternatives. *Educational Evaluation and Policy Analysis, 21,* 179–192.

Gendreau, P., & Ross, R. R. (1987). Revivification of rehabilitation: Evidence from the 1980s. *Justice Quarterly, 4,* 349–408.

Hanushek, E. A. (1997). Assessing the effects of school resources on student performance: An update. *Educational Evaluation and Policy Analysis, 19,* 141–164.

Haveman, R. H., & Wolfe, B. L. (1984). Schooling and economic well-being: The role of nonmarket effects. *Journal of Human Resources, 19,* 377–407.

Karoly, L. A., Kilburn, M. R., & Cannon, J. S. (2005). *Early childhood interventions: Proven results, future promise.* Santa Monica, CA: RAND Corporation.

Kimball, A. W. (1957). Errors of the third kind in statistical consulting. *Journal of the American Statistical Association, 52,* 133–142.

Kingdon, J. W. (1995). *Agendas, alternatives, and public policies* (2nd ed). New York: HarperCollins College Publishers.

Krueger, A. (2004). Inequality: Too much of a good thing? In J. Heckman & A. Krueger (Eds.), *Inequality in America: What role for human capital policies?* (pp. 1–76). Cambridge, MA: MIT Press.

Levin, H. M. (2001). Waiting for Godot: Cost-effectiveness analysis in education. *New Directions for Evaluation, 90,* 55–68.

Levin, H. M. (2006, June). *The public returns to public educational investments in African-American males.* Paper presented at the international conference Economics of Education: Major Contributions and Future Directions, Dijon, France.

MacRae, D., Jr., & Whittington, D. (1997). *Expert advice for policy choice: Analysis and discourse.* Washington, DC: Georgetown University Press.

Martinson, R. (1974). What works? Questions and answers about prison reform. *The Public Interest, 35,* 22–38.

Mintrom, M. (2003). *People skills for policy analysts.* Washington, DC: Georgetown University Press.

Musso, J., Biller, R., & Myrtle, R. (2000). Tradecraft: Professional writing as problem solving. *Journal of Policy Analysis and Management, 19,* 635–646.

Sabatier, P. A., & Jenkins-Smith, H. (Eds.). (1993). *Policy change and learning: An advocacy coalition framework.* Boulder, CO: Westview Press.

Schemo, D. J. (2004, August 17). Nation's charter schools lag behind, U.S. test scores reveal. *New York Times,* p. A1.

Stiefel, L., Berne, R. Iatarola, P., & Fruchter, N. (2000). High school size: Effects on budgets and performance in New York City. *Educational Evaluation and Policy Analysis, 22,* 27–39.

Temple, J. A., & Reynolds, A. J. (2007). Benefits and costs of investments in preschool education: Evidence from the child-parent centers and related programs. *Economics of Education Review, 26,* 126–144.

Tyler, J. H., Murnane, R. J., & Willet, J. B. (2000). Estimating the labor market signaling value of the GED. *Quarterly Journal of Economics, 115,* 431–468.

Weimer, D. L. (1986). Collective delusion in the social sciences. *Policy Studies Review, 5,* 705–708.

Weimer, D. L., & Vining, A. R. (2005). *Policy analysis: Concepts and practice* (4th ed.). Upper Saddle River, NJ: Pearson Prentice Hall.

Wolfe, B., & Haveman, R. (2001). Accounting for the social and non-market benefits of education. In J. F. Helliwell (Ed.), *The contribution of human and social capital to sustained economic growth and well being* (pp. 221–250). Vancouver, BC: University of British Columbia Press.

8

COMMENTARY
Disciplined Education Policy Research

Michael J. Feuer
National Research Council[1]

God's connection to the people of Israel "is analogous to a person who tethered two ships together with anchor chains and iron moorings, put them out to sea, and built a palace on them. The palace endures so long as the ships are tethered to one another; were the ships to float apart, the palace could not endure …"
—Simeon ben Yohai, circa 135 C.E.
(cited in Heschel, 2006, p. 109)

It is a truism that good interdisciplinary research requires strong disciplines: to build durable bridges across silos, we need sturdy silos. It is perhaps less obvious, though, how to handle an inherent paradox: disciplinary allegiances are both necessary for—and a barrier against—effective interdisciplinarity. Most scholars working in their own fields do not have time and resources to know much about, no less integrate, the work of colleagues in other fields. Moreover, as disciplines grow more rigorous, their private linguistic code—jargon—grows more opaque. Ultimately, the collective good of interdisciplinary research is constrained by the rational choice of scholars who burrow in and focus on ever more isolated areas of expertise.

And the plot thickens in the world of policy research. Often the complexity of a policy domain—such as "education," shorthand for myriad overlapping issues involving teaching, learning, and the organization of schooling—is a main reason policy makers and the general public are loath to rely on any single perspective or body of research as the basis for decisions. This is especially true when decisions can have significant consequences, when deeply-held historical traditions and cultural values are at stake, or when basic social and political goals are contested (in education we frequently encounter all of those conditions). At the same time, though, it is precisely in such situations that policy makers are most likely to turn to scholarship for clarity, or at least guidance, based on coherent, logical, dispassionate, and defensible interpretations of evidence. Whether they seek "cover" for preconceived positions or are more genuinely willing to base their judgments on research, they yearn for straightforward answers to complex questions. But these are difficult to produce, and the result is more paradox: policy domains characterized by the greatest complexity demand interdisciplinary attention, but the complexity of interdisciplinary evidence is a barrier to its understanding and application.

Lest we despair, though, from yet another "tragedy" of individual choice and social outcomes (e.g., Schelling, 1978; Feuer, 2008) it pays to remember that the awareness of potential collective benefit often leads to institutional or social arrangements that mitigate, albeit imperfectly, the undesired effects of purely self-interested behavior. Human resilience and the creative ingenuity of people who sense the social benefits of concerted action enable and encourage collective responses.

There are at least three existing mechanisms that have evolved in order to promote integrative research and buck the natural forces that would otherwise keep scholars apart. One is the professional association, such as AERA, which thrives on the ingathering of scholars with diverse intellectual traditions and which, occasionally, makes explicit efforts at interdisciplinarity. (The conference theme for the 2009 annual meeting is a powerful example. See http://aera.net/ for details.) Of course, it is not surprising that some critics of AERA see only the negative side of inclusion and bemoan what they perceive as an erosion of quality; but apparently the overwhelming sentiment of the membership is to favor diversity, even at the risk of potential compromise to scholarly standards. Over 15,000 participants attended the 2008 annual meeting.[2]

A second institutional remedy to the paradox of interdisciplinarity is the one most commonly associated with the National Research Council of the National Academy of Sciences. The staple product of this organization is the consensus report written by a carefully-conceived interdisciplinary committee and reviewed by an equally interdisciplinary group of peers. Not a natural act for most academics, this type of collaboration invites experts in various fields to accept a form of collective self-coercion, partially suspend disciplinary allegiances, agree to disagree civilly about data and evidence, and aspire to a set of findings and recommendations that are more interesting than would be attained from a mundane collation of individual studies and interpretations. When it works well, the process results in the best available interdisciplinary consensus on a complex issue, offered in hopes of fulfilling the Academy's mandate to "advise the nation." The Academy releases about 200 such reports each year. Here, too, critics wonder if strong evidentiary standards enforced by specific research communities are diluted for the sake of consensus, but the general sense is that small chips in the disciplinary armor are justified by the collective benefits of scientific consensus, the accumulation of knowledge, and the cultivation of hybrid research disciplines.[3]

A third example of corrective action to the collective action problem is this Handbook. It is admittedly weighty and perhaps a bit unwieldy, but is clearly intended to create opportunities for education researchers to look out the windows of their silos and at least contemplate the advantages of building new bridges. Whether education is or ever will be considered a bona fide discipline of its own is an interesting question, but in the meantime we are fortunate to be involved in a field of research that benefits from—and contributes to—many existing disciplines. As the chapters in this section demonstrate, education *policy* has long been a special interest of scholars working from diverse perspectives and intellectual traditions. Can bridges be built?

It would be naïve and presumptuous to attempt a grand synthesis of even the seven fascinating chapters in just this one section of the Handbook. As a start, though, I recommend that readers take the time to read each chapter—*and then go back and read them each again, only this time with at least two or three critical questions in mind that arise from the first reading.* I do not mean to inflict on readers a combinatoric nightmare—life is too short to attempt a complete mapping of all the possible connections even for this subset of the anthology—but my sense is that most readers will find even a partial effort at integration to be worthwhile.

For example, consider Hanushek's broad-ranging chapter on the economics of education, which provides a clear and concise summary of many complex issues, including the relationship between cognitive skills and individual and national economic capacity, the effects of schooling and family characteristics on student achievement, the evolving nature of work and its implications for skill formation in and out of school, and the prospects for continued U.S. productivity and international competitiveness in the light of substantial catching-up by many European and Asian nations. In itself, the Hanushek chapter is worth studying by anyone wanting a good snapshot of the value of economic analysis in education policy research. Surely all his findings and interpretations are not unanimously held in either the economics or education research communities, but the chapter is as good a first approximation of the key issues as one can find.

Now consider Hanushek again in the light of the chapters by Vinovskis and by Lauen and Tyson. Although Vinovskis is mostly concerned with the on-again off-again role of historians in the formation and implementation of education policy, he points to the longstanding historical debate over the purposes of schooling, the equitable distribution of resources, and the role of schooling in preparing young people for productive lives in the American democracy. His detailed recounting of a well-known dispute between so-called "revisionists" (e.g., Katz, 1968) and their critics (e.g., Ravitch, 1978), on the question of what the common school reformers of the 19th century had in mind, should spur education policy buffs as well as academic researchers to plumb the historical literature more deeply.

Meanwhile, though, Vinovskis stimulates us to revisit some of Hanushek's necessarily abridged conclusions. For example, Hanushek argues that policy discussions today have "moved to consider more *quality* dimensions of schooling and of individual skills," in a break from earlier 20th century focus on *quantity* of schooling attained. But a more nuanced historical analysis would suggest that issues of quantity, quality, and standards have always been part of the big policy discourse, at least since the reform movements of the 19th century (e.g., Kaestle, 1983), which suggests that current arguments have deeper historical and cultural roots than conventional economic analysis might imply.

Looking from the other direction, it pays to reread Vinovskis after digesting the important trend data summarized by Hanushek, for example, with regard to international comparisons. Among the important questions that might emerge from such juxtaposition is one that is routinely lost in the fog of public debate over the condition of U.S. schools compared to those in other countries. We hear plenty about how European and Asian competitors are catching up (e.g., Phillips, 2008), but there is scant attention paid to whether convergence among nations as measured by educational indicators such as participation, completion, and attainment is correlated with (or is somehow causally linked with) convergence in social and economic indicators such as productivity growth. (Neither Hanushek nor Carnoy discuss "convergence" although it is a well-known concept in economics; see, e.g., Baumol, Batey Blackman, & Wolff, 1989). Historical and economic research together could shed new light on this and related questions.

Similarly, if one is mainly concerned with effects of schooling on individual and aggregate outcomes of interest—earnings, productivity, competitiveness—both Hanushek and Carnoy certainly provide adequate summaries of relevant research. We learn, for example, that "economists have generally come to the conclusion … that the skills learned with more years of schooling do have economic value in terms of increasing productivity and economic growth …" (Carnoy), although "significant questions remain about the magnitude and interpretation of these relationships ..." (Hanushek). But the story grows even more interesting—and complex—if one reads the economists in conjunction with Lauen and Tyson, who provide a restatement of selected findings from what was surely the most influential empirical study of schooling and education of the 20th century, led by the distinguished sociologist James Coleman (Coleman et al., 1966).

As Lauen and Tyson note, the effects of schooling on achievement differed for minority and White students, and the overall impacts of formal education were significantly conditioned by other factors. "The [Coleman] study found ... that the effect of home remained strong across grade levels, leading the authors to infer that schools matter ... not through the mechanisms the school system controls but because of peer effects and other factors outside the school system's control." Clearly, overlaying economic "production function" studies with the conceptual frame of sociology offers benefits to both lines of research.

Moving to other insights from sociology, we are drawn to issues such as the role of teachers in raising student achievement, a topic that has (again) risen to the top of the education policy and political agendas. Lauen and Tyson note that "to the extent that teachers are the main resource schools provide to students, it may seem to be merely an academic matter whether it is schools rather than teachers that influence achievement. *The fact that there is more variance in student achievement within schools than between them* ... suggests that policies aimed at altering the sorting process of students among schools (i.e., school choice, desegregation) may be less effective than policies aimed at raising teacher quality or altering the distribution of teachers across classrooms." Note that the phrase I have italicized, about within-group vs. between-group variance, is a key finding from sociological research (e.g., Hauser, Sewell, & Alwin, 1976). My point here is not to take a stand on the validity of these findings as much as to argue for more efforts aimed at bridging the models and methods of economists and sociologists who are clearly interested in similar problems.

The chapter by Dixon, Borman, and Cotner begins with a clarion call to anthropologists of education "to abandon the role of the lone ethnographer, the sole and ultimate instrument of research in the ethnographic tradition, for a more collaborative and interactive role on a team of social and behavioral scientists." This is a noble recommendation, and the magnitude of the challenge it poses would seem insurmountable if not for the accessibility to the work of at least some of those prospective members of the "team" afforded in this section of the Handbook.

It is daunting, for example, to consider the chasm that separates researchers whose main concern is with differences across "cultures" from those whose baseline assumption is that generalizability (or replicability) is a reasonable criterion in policy research and who hope to find some basis for inferring that policy or program effects will be at least approximately reproduced beyond the specific popula-

tions in which they are first introduced. (For discussion of replicability as a principle of scientific inquiry, see, e.g., National Research Council, 2002; for a more general history of scientific education research see Lagemann, 2000.) This is not to say that economists and sociologists don't care about culture, but rather to note that it carries different weight than for ethnographers. We learn from Dixon, Borman, and Cotner that anthropologists of education are interested in "the cultural contexts in which accountability policies form," but we see little or no reference to that particular construct in the other disciplines represented here (I distinguish between looking at differential effects of policies across racial and ethnic classifications and categorizing individuals or groups according to definitions of "culture"). Economists rarely ask, and political scientists and historians only slightly more frequently ask, how different organizational arrangements favor or discourage the formation of various policy strategies (but see my discussion of McDonnell, whose chapter in this section of the Handbook does include an important discussion of the effects of institutions on policy); in any case, one rarely sees much interest among these social scientists in the ethnographers' concern with "the ways the actors who helped shape 'accountability' policies translated ideologies of efficiency, competition, and standardization into educational policies and curriculum...." The motif typical in economics, and to some extent in sociology, emphasizes the validity of predictions about outcomes without worrying quite so much about the ideological or cultural origins of educators, policy makers, or the researchers themselves.

Other subtle differences can be gleaned from a rereading of Dixon, Borman, and Cotner in conjunction with the other chapters. For example, it is worth revisiting Carnoy's characterization of one of the main contributions of economic thinking to education policy research: "Economics can ... help us decide how to achieve goals most 'efficiently' (in terms of costs) by debating which educational strategies provide the biggest effect for the sacrifice required." In the tradition of neoclassical, positive economics, this approach skates over the more intricate delicacies of culture and ideology, avoids the messiness of the "black box," and aims for valid predictions based on parsimonious assumptions. Ethnography, on the other hand, is typically more concerned with description than with prediction and causal inference, a difference manifest by the nature of data, the unit of analysis, and the strength and generalizability of inferential claims that ethnographic research supports. As Dixon, Borman, and Cotner note, "from studies of one teacher ... to studies of one school site ... to multiple site studies ... anthropologists of education produce descriptive analyses of multi-layered sociocultural processes surrounding the implementation of one or a few specific policies."

Having mentioned descriptive research and hinted at the role of institutions in theories of education policy, I segue now to the chapter by McDonnell, which provides an extremely useful summary of major strands in political science generally and their connections to education policy research specifically. The chapter begins with the perhaps overly modest observation that theories from political science do not easily contribute to better understanding of how specific policies might improve student learning, but rather helps "specify the conditions under which policies are likely to change or remain stable, explain how politics shapes education policy, and in turn how those policies influence political participation and future policy design." Granted, the chief concern of political science is with institutions, interests, and ideas, and the orientation is largely descriptive; but I would argue valid *explanation* of complex historical or contemporary phenomena is an important—perhaps essential—element in the *prediction* of outcomes associated with alternative policies, and prediction is surely a desirable component of policy formation. (On the philosophy of explanation and prediction, see, e.g., Blaug, 1980.)

Consider the significance of institutional arrangements. McDonnell argues that they shape and explain policy outcomes through the imposition of rules and norms that determine "who may participate in the policy making process, who is granted formal authority to choose among proposals, and what procedures must be followed before those with formal authority can make a decision." A good example is the role of school boards, and more specifically, the way that elections to school boards influence (or at least explain) policy outcomes. (Whether institutions influence policy or policy influences institutions is another problem tackled by political scientists, as McDonnell carefully notes.)

Similarly, McDonnell draws attention to models of local educational governance, such as mayoral control of schools, to argue that such reforms are "premised on the assumption that institutional arrangements, including who holds authority over resource allocation, the rules by which those resources are allocated, and how elected officials are held accountable and influence district and school performance." These observations, powerful in their own right, are enriched when considered alongside micro-level ethnographies that permit more detailed case-by-case dissection of the origins and architecture of organizational arrangements; or against more macro-level sociological and economic research that assumes institutional arrangements and focuses then on the implications of decisions taken within them.

If we integrate political concepts such as institutions and interests with historical trends in the design and conduct of school systems, as emphasized by Vinovskis and others, the research agenda becomes more complicated, but its results are likely to be even more useful, at least for certain kinds of broad policy debates. *Why* do localities choose mayoral control? *How* do such choices square with long-held values and traditions in educational history? *What* are the likely consequences of shifts in institutional arrangements, given prior experience? A core question—what explains the emergence and sustainability of various modes of organizing economic and social transactions?—is not typically a concern of political science (although McDonnell addresses it), and would be worth considering through a cross-disciplinary

lens that includes psychology and cognitive science, which are not sufficiently represented in this section of the Handbook (see, e.g., Williamson, 1975; Feuer, 2006).

McDonnell's note that "the causal processes by which institutions shape policy outcomes" is a topic of increasing interest among political scientists of education suggests a fruitful line of research, especially if it is open to integration with other disciplinary perspectives. Clearly, if one cares about such matters as how individuals decide to translate ideas and values into institutions, political science research would be well-served by connecting with the more intensely cultural orientation of anthropology. In any event, McDonnell's bottom line, that there are likely to be important payoffs "from grounding education policy research in political science theory and concepts," seems imminently sensible.

The proposition that disciplinary—and interdisciplinary—studies might bring payoffs to policy-relevant education research begs a more basic question: what exactly *is* policy-relevant research? A good place to begin this conversation is with the chapter by David Weimer, who defines policy research as "generally emphasizing the methodologically valid assessment of some important policy problem or policy impact …" Weimer is perhaps the most concerned, among the authors represented here, with the distinction between disciplinary and policy research: the former "informs our understanding of human behavior in the various spheres of life—the personal, social, economic, and political … [but] need not have any immediate relevance to specific policy issues.…" Good applied research, therefore, hinges on good basic research, but how to design institutions and incentives to foster the needed cross-fertilization is, obviously, a continuing challenge.

Weimer's central argument is that policy research is self-consciously oriented toward the analysis of policy alternatives, and that the design of valid and reliable policies rests on multiple and intersecting disciplinary foundations. Thus, for example, he notes that "the contributions of policy researchers often reflect the strong influences of disciplinary training and scholarly incentives," an idea that resonates strongly with my concern for overcoming paradoxes of interdisciplinarity. Weimer offers a number of suggestions for how policy research can be improved, for example, more explicit attention to the nature of error and the presence of uncertainty, acceptance of variability as a limiting factor on otherwise extravagant claims about the effects of policy choices, and the description of policies in as exact detail as possible.

Alert readers will note how each of these suggestions links to one or more of the disciplines represented in this section. To cite one perhaps obvious example, describing the equivalent of wiring diagrams for proposed policy initiatives seems like a task for which case-study methods perfected in ethnography and anthropology are germane. Similarly, Weimer's plea for more conscious attention to uncertainties associated with policy prescriptions and predictions raises fundamental questions about the organization and management of policy analysis and policymaking, for which political science, economics, and history all have potentially valuable contributions. As for the suggestion that researchers curb their enthusiasm for grandiose claims, he is, of course correct, though an argument can be made for the role of rhetoric in motivating public attention and marshaling public funds for policy research (see, e.g., Feuer, 2006).

Which brings me back to the promise and peril of interdisciplinary policy studies. As expected, my own reading of these chapters has reinforced my hope for continued value in integrative research. It has also reinforced my conviction that the most important goal for policy research is not necessarily to reach optimal or definitive answers to complex questions, but rather to establish what might be called "comfort zones" for policy makers. Faced with dauntingly complex questions for which even the best research—within and across conventional disciplinary terrains—provides incomplete results, policy makers are well-served by evidence that at least points them in the right direction, even if it doesn't give them foolproof solutions.

Granted, there is a natural desire for answers that settle complex and controversial policy debates once and for all; but when research doesn't settle problems, researchers and policy makers need to settle for reasonable answers. Rigorous interdisciplinary scholarship of the sort included in this Handbook can advance knowledge, challenge conventional wisdom, help eliminate policy strategies that rest on thin or dubious evidence, and enable policy makers to concentrate on courses of action that are most likely—if not guaranteed—to achieve articulated goals. To hold out for research that "clinches" rather than "vouches for" certain policy choices (Cartwright, 2007), or to insist on "optimal" rather than reasonably good solutions (Feuer, 2006), is to risk raising the evidentiary bar just high enough to discourage—if not disqualify—any action whatsoever. The problems of education require dedicated attention by scholars of many disciplines and traditions, and are just too urgent to be deferred until interdisciplinary research is permanently cleansed of its inevitable uncertainties and imperfections.

Notes

1. The opinions expressed in this chapter are the author's and do not necessarily reflect the views and positions of the National Research Council, the National Academy of Sciences, or its constituent boards and committees.
2. In its struggle to sustain high standards while striving for diversity and inclusion, the AERA is a microcosm of American education. See Cremin (1990) for an eloquent argument about the historical tension between standards and participation in U.S. schooling.
3. The author's bias is noted.

References

Baumol, W., Batey Blackman, S. A., & Wolff, E. N. (1989). *Productivity and American leadership: The long view.* Cambridge, MA: The MIT Press.

Blaug, M. (1980). *The methodology of economics.* Cambridge, UK: Cambridge University Press.

Cartwright, N. (2007). *Hunting causes and using them: Approaches in philosophy and economics.* Cambridge, UK: Cambridge University Press.

Coleman, J., Campbell, E. Q., Hobson, C. J., McPartland, J., Mood, A. J., Weinfeld, F. D., et al. (1966). *Equality of educational opportunity.* Washington, DC: United States Government Printing Office.

Cremin, L. (1990). *Popular education and its discontents.* New York: Harper and Row.

Feuer, M. J. (2006). *Moderating the debate: Rationality and the promise of American education.* Cambridge, MA: Harvard Education Press.

Feuer, M. J. (2008). Future directions for educational accountability: Notes for a political economy of measurement. In K. Ryan & L. Shepard (Eds.), *The future of test-based educational accountability* (pp. 293–306). New York: Routledge.

Hauser, R. M., Sewell, W. H., & Alwin, D. F. (1976). High school effects on achievement. In W. H. Jewell & D. L. Featherman (Eds.), *Schooling and achievement in American society* (pp. 309–341). New York: Academic Press.

Heschel, A. J. (2006). *Heavenly Torah—as refracted through the generations.* Edited and translated from the Hebrew with commentary by Gordon Tucker and Leonard Levin, New York: Continuum International.

Kaestle, C. (1983). *Pillars of the republic.* New York: HarperCollins.

Katz, M. B. (1968). *The irony of early school reform: Educational innovation in mid-nineteenth century Massachusetts.* Cambridge, MA: Harvard University Press

Lagemann, E. C. (2000). *An elusive science: The troubling history of education research.* Chicago: University of Chicago Press.

National Research Council. (2002). *Scientific research in education.* Washington, DC: National Academy Press.

Phillips, G. (2008). *Chance favors the prepared mind: Mathematics and science indicators for comparing states and nations.* Washington, DC: American Institutes for Research.

Ravitch, D. (1978). *The revisionists revised: A critique of the radical attack on the schools.* New York: Basic Books.

Schelling, T. (1978). *Micromotives and macrobehavior.* New York: Norton.

Williamson, O. E. (1975). *Markets and hierarchies.* New York: Free Press.

9

COMMENTARY
The Disciplinary Foundations
of Education Policy Research

Adam Gamoran[1]
University of Wisconsin–Madison

In what ways do the social science disciplines provide a foundation for education policy research? In what areas do they fall short? Reflecting on a century or so of discipline-based research on education, is it reasonable to anticipate that scholars working in the disciplinary traditions will, to use Weimer's terms, supply the sort of policy *research* that will permit productive policy *analysis*? The aim of this chapter is to take stock of the disciplinary contributions outlined in the preceding chapters and to identify new avenues by which disciplinary research can fruitfully contribute to educational policy analysis and, ultimately, policy decisions. This assessment also points towards ways that practitioners and policy makers can find value in social science research on education.

As several of the authors in this introductory section of the Handbook have noted or implied, contributing to policy research is far from the only agenda of disciplinary scholarship (see, e.g., Lauen & Tyson). On the contrary, the usual goals of social scientists are to establish theories and test hypotheses that derive from disciplinary knowledge, not necessarily to inform policy debates. Yet as Coleman (1976) has argued, research on education is inherently policy relevant, so that studies of education have the potential to contribute to decisions about improving education, even if educational improvements were not central to their mission. Consequently, it is reasonable to ask whether and how the social sciences have supported and can support policy research in education.

Weimer's distinction between policy research and policy analysis offers a useful starting point for examining themes that are common to the preceding chapters. Policy research, he explains, answers questions about existing programs or practices in education, whereas policy analysis provides comparisons among possible alternatives, in terms of both impact and cost, allowing the policy maker to make an informed choice. The disciplines are not typically charged with policy analysis in this sense, but they may offer con-tributions to policy research, which is essential grist for the analyst's mill.

To preview my conclusions, I find that, on the one hand, the disciplines contribute by advancing theories that guide research and point towards causal mechanisms, and by developing research techniques that serve as tools for policy research. On the other hand, despite significant accomplishments, wide gaps remain in policy-relevant knowledge, and disciplinary boundaries tend to limit the contributions of social science research to policy analysis. For the practitioner and the policy maker, existing research findings offer ideas and insights that they can weigh in light of their own contexts, capabilities, and resources, even if existing findings do not provide unambiguous guidance for specific decisions.

Four Themes: Theoretical and Methodological Contributions, Gaps in Findings and Collaboration

Taken as a whole, the chapters on the foundations of policy research in education yield four common themes. First, the social sciences offer theoretical perspectives and concepts that help frame policy research. Second, the tools of policy research are those of the methods of social science. Third, while half a century or more of research has yielded useful knowledge, the amount of knowledge gained is modest compared to the wide gaps that remain. Fourth, despite overlapping interests among the disciplines, most studies remain bounded within their disciplinary borders, a limitation that constrains the policy value of discipline-based research.

Theoretical Frameworks and Concepts from the Social Sciences Applied to Education Perhaps the most prominent contribution of the social sciences to education policy research is the provision of theories and concepts that guide research. These ideas lead to hypotheses about the

effects of education programs and practices and about the mechanisms through which programs have their desired (or undesired) effects.

Each of the discipline-based chapters in this section identifies a number of theories that are used in research. In economics, for instance, Carnoy summarizes the theoretical basis for encouraging market competition in education. These claims have not only supported policies that promote choice in education, but also have motivated a large and growing body of research on topics such as vouchers, competition, private schools, magnet schools, and charter schools. Moreover, economic theory identifies the mechanisms through which more choice is expected to improve educational outcomes: the competition of the marketplace creates incentives for schools to become more productive, and in the cases of private schools and charter schools, fewer bureaucratic constraints may result in more efficient operations. As Carnoy notes, empirical studies of choice and competition have not consistently upheld the theoretical positions, so more theoretical work is needed to understand the complexities of the empirical findings. In this sense, education research offers a useful testing ground for social science theories. To be useful to policy analysts, however, theories need to be refined and more empirical work undertaken in light of findings that are inconsistent with the theories.

Another theoretical concept that helps guide research is the notion of policy feedback from political science (McDonnell). Researchers in this line of thought point out that not only does the political process shape policy decisions, but that policies that are enacted create new political interests that may influence subsequent policies. Research on federal and local policies has proceeded from this standpoint, and helps us understand the give and take between politics and policies. As McDonnell argues, new studies may contribute to policy research that allows analysts to make better recommendations about the implementation of standards-based reforms that are at the heart of current federal education policy.

As a third example, sociologists have developed the theoretical concept of loose coupling to describe the organizational context of schools (Lauen & Tyson). According to this notion, decisions and activities occurring in one part of the school system do not necessarily resonate elsewhere. Loose coupling has proven useful to policy-relevant research in several ways. First, it helps explain why external mandates often fail to make an impact inside the classroom. Second, it points towards elements within schools that may be more closely linked to the production of achievement. If one wishes to influence teaching and learning, for example, one may reach the classroom through the allocation of resources that guide and constrain teachers' work, and by promoting teacher learning (Gamoran, Secada, & Marrett, 2000). Empirical studies have built on that insight and are partly responsible for the current emphasis on professional development as the key to enhancing teaching and learning.

Social Science Methods Applied to Research on Education A second theme that runs through all the chapters is that social sciences have provided the tools through which policy research is conducted. In his chapter on history and education policy research, Vinovskis acknowledges that historians have been less engaged with education policy than other social scientists. Yet the tools of the historian are nevertheless essential for policy research. To make policy recommendations, analysts need information about the prospects for implementation of a program under consideration, and historical comparisons offer useful guidance. In addition, other researchers in other disciplines such as sociology and political science often use the tools of the historian to understand patterns in past efforts to bring about change. These studies typically aim to reach more general conclusions than those of the historian, who is ordinarily concerned with the unique features of the case at hand.

Like history, each of the other social science disciplines offers methodological tools for the policy researcher's toolkit. (This includes psychology, which is not covered in this section of the volume but whose methods are evident in the "Methodological Perspectives" section.) Carnoy reviews methodological approaches from economics that are common in education policy research. The economist's production function—the measured relation between an "output" and a list of "inputs"—is as much a theoretical notion as it is a methodological technique. Production functions have often been estimated with ordinary regression analysis, but more sophisticated econometric techniques are designed to address what is perhaps the biggest challenge to quantitative studies of education: selectivity bias, the problem that what appears to be the effect of an educational program may actually reflect other differences between those who offer the program and those who do not, or between those who are enrolled in the program and those who are not enrolled. Among these econometric approaches are fixed effects models, instrumental variables, and regression discontinuity, each of which seeks estimates of program effects that are not contaminated by selectivity. In addition, a method that is increasingly popular among economists is the randomized controlled trial, which avoids selection bias through random assignment of participants to intervention and comparison groups (besides the chapters in this section by Carnoy and Hanushek, see also the chapters by Geoffrey Borman and by David Kaplan in the "Methodological Perspectives" section).

Sociologists have also contributed work on quantitative methods (Lauen & Tyson), particularly in the application of structural equation modeling, hierarchical linear modeling, and other approaches aimed at disentangling program effects from measurement error in education research. Other sociologists, however, rely on qualitative methods from the anthropological tradition (Lauen & Tyson). As the chapter by Dixon, Borman, and Cotner makes clear, the anthropology of education consists of the application of ethnographic methods to the content area of education. Ethnographic techniques can deepen understanding of how policies play out in the lives of those affected and, like historical work, can shed light on the prospects for implementation as well as possible unintended consequences. For example, current ethnographic work on responses to federal education policy highlight resistance to policy mandates as well as the negative side of standardization in education systems (see Dixon, Borman, & Cotner for details). McDonnell does not identify a unique methodological contribution from political scientists, but she shows how scholars from that discipline use historical, ethnographic, and quantitative tools to provide a distinctive perspective on education policy, focusing particularly on stability and change in policy regimes, and on the relation between policies and political attitudes and actions.

While theoretical and methodological contributions are essential, their value to policy research is limited by the extent to which they have been used to generate useful empirical findings. We next turn to that issue.

Discipline-Based Answers to Policy Questions The disciplines of history, economics, political science, sociology, and anthropology have yielded modest gains towards answering questions that confront education policy makers and practitioners on a daily basis. This observation reflects the complexities of educational policy and practice and the extensive range and depth of problems that must be addressed.

Research on teacher effects on student achievement offers a prominent example. Each of the disciplines has something to say on the topic and, in the fields of economics (Hanushek; Carnoy) and sociology (Lauen & Tyson) (not to mention psychology, which is not addressed here), researchers have attempted to provide quantitative estimates of teacher effects. In this line of work, researchers have convincingly demonstrated that student achievement differs from teacher to teacher, and that part of this variation is causal: from a student's perspective, it matters which teacher he or she encounters (Carnoy; Lauen & Tyson). This is a significant accomplishment that is policy relevant: It encourages decision makers to invest in the quality of their teachers as a key means to improving student achievement (Carnoy). The form that this investment should take, however, is less clear. Financial incentives for boosting achievement? Professional development? Better pre-service preparation? Each of these strategies, and others, is being attempted at present and is the subject of ongoing research. At present, however, researchers have been more successful at establishing that teachers matter and less successful at showing what characteristics or practices make some teachers more effective at raising test scores than others. This can only frustrate the policy maker who needs to know what investment will maximize outcomes (however defined). Other examples of this situation include, from economics, the finding that increasing school "quality" as reflected in higher test scores enhances productivity, but how to improve school quality is uncertain (Carnoy; Hanushek); from sociology, that Catholic schools produce higher achievement

than public schools, particularly for the students who are least likely to attend Catholic schools, but whether there are features of Catholic schools that might be adopted by public schools to produce similar effects is undemonstrated (Lauen & Tyson); and from political science, that institutional interests shape policy change as much or more than rational calculations, but that it is difficult to anticipate how those interests may play out in a given context (McDonnell; for parallel findings from anthropology about cultural contexts, see Dixon, Borman, & Cotner). These examples reflect policy-relevant findings, but also show that there is much more to be learned.

In some cases, researchers have provided clear evidence of the payoffs that can be expected from more specific investments. In these cases, however, the utility of the research findings has been limited by insufficient knowledge about costs, implementation, and outcomes other than cognitive skills. For example, class size reduction is one policy for which strong evidence exists of boosting test scores (Carnoy; Lauen & Tyson). Moreover, the costs of class size reduction have been calculated and compared to other policy options (Carnoy). Yet the costs have sometimes been ignored by policy makers, as in the case of Florida, a state which is unable to fund its state-wide mandate, or calculated with incomplete information, as in the case of California, which funded class size reduction but lacked sufficient teachers and classroom space to accommodate the increased number of smaller classes (Milesi & Gamoran, 2006). Moreover, the mechanisms through which smaller classes raise test scores are not well understood, so even this relatively strong finding is tempered by uncertainty (Ehrenberg, Brewer, Gamoran, & Willms, 2001). Problems with implementation and ambiguous mechanisms may account for the difficulty of generalizing the class size finding on a national scale (Milesi & Gamoran, 2006).

Tutoring one-on-one or in small groups is another policy for which strong evidence of effectiveness exists: students who receive tutoring exhibit cognitive gains (Carnoy). Presumably on the basis of this finding, tutoring was included in the federal No Child Left Behind (NCLB) law as a means to help low achievers catch up and bring low-performing schools up to state standards. Yet the research on tutoring has had little to offer on implementation, and unfortunately, tutoring under NCLB has been implemented so weakly, inconsistently, and with so little monitoring and accountability (ironically, since the law that requires it is all about accountability), that it has not had its desired effect (Burch, Steinberg, & Donovan, 2007; Farkas & Durham, 2007). These findings resonate well with McDonnell's argument that institutions, interests, and ideas shape policies and policy implementation, and with Dixon, Borman, and Cotner's point that policy impacts need to be understood in their sociocultural contexts, but they also highlight the difficulty of translating even the clearest empirical findings into effective policy decisions.

Despite the demonstrated importance of cognitive skills (Hanushek), economists as well as social scientists from other disciplines recognize that test scores are not the only valued outcome of schooling (Carnoy; Lauen & Tyson; Dixon, Borman, & Cotner). Although most policy-relevant evidence is in the realm of cognitive performance, research on other outcomes is growing. For example, the What Works Clearinghouse, an effort by the U.S. Department of Education to provide evidence for practitioners of effective educational programs and practices, reports mainly program effects on test scores, but in the areas of dropout prevention and character education, non-cognitive outcomes are also addressed.[2] This development is important because, as Dixon, Borman, and Cotner explain, policies that boost test scores may have unintended consequences in other arenas.

The Need for Interdisciplinary Social Science Research on Education

The fourth theme that emerges from the chapters is that while the disciplines exhibit substantial overlap in their main interests, discipline-based researchers tend to work separately from one another, and this limits the applicability of their findings. Examples of overlaps abound: Political science and history share a common focus on institutions; economics and sociology are both centrally concerned with levels and distributions of valued goods, such as schooling and earnings; another line of work in sociology shares with anthropology a mutual interest in culture; and so on. Yet when it comes to assessing the impact of programs and practices in education—that is, when it comes to conducting policy research—researchers usually labor within their disciplinary confines (Dixon, Borman, & Cotner). Moreover, policies that are examined from the perspective of one disciplinary tradition may not be addressed in another. As a result, our policy knowledge is incomplete.

To weigh evidence and reach a recommendation, policy analysts need information of at least the following sorts:

- estimates from a production function, which specifies the impact of introducing a program or practice into the existing system (economics, sociology);
- a cost-benefit analysis, including the full costs of implementation (economics);
- an interpretive understanding of the meaning and significance of the new program or practice to participants, including possible unintended consequences (anthropology, history, sociology); and
- an understanding of the political context of the potential reform (political science, history).

This combination of knowledge does not exist for any single policy, often because the production function estimates are not available, as noted above. Even when plausible estimates of impact are available, however, the rest of the package is typically lacking. Tutoring under NCLB again furnishes an instructive example. Tutoring is a case for which both impact estimates and cost-benefit analyses are available (Carnoy). Yet little or no research is available on

the subjective meaning of assignment to tutoring programs (Dixon, Borman, & Cotner do not report work in this area), even though a study along these lines could be very helpful in understanding one of the major shortcomings of NCLB tutoring: Eligible students do not enroll, and when they do enroll they exhibit poor attendance (Farkas & Durham, 2007). Similarly, research on the politics of implementing extensive tutoring programs in a way that ensures quality control either has not occurred or has not been connected to current policy efforts (McDonnell; Vinovskis). Had such links been drawn, policy makers might have been able to anticipate the weak and inconsistent implementation of NCLB tutoring and to include provisions in the law that would boost its prospects for success.

Other potential policies have substantial findings about their cultural significance or political ramifications, but lack evidence of impact. For example, culturally relevant pedagogy has particular resonance for members of under-represented minority groups (Dixon, Borman, & Cotner), but how curriculum and instructional reforms that reflect this insight might affect cognitive and non-cognitive outcomes has not been assessed. As a result, the policy analyst lacks a common metric on which to weigh this reform compared to other possibilities. Were economists or sociologists to respond to this need with a production function design (and with consideration of non-cognitive as well as cognitive outcomes), the policy analyst would be more fully informed. Along similar lines, valuable historical findings about school reform (Vinovskis) would be complemented by measures of impact.

In sum, both the gaps in our knowledge about impact and the dearth of interdisciplinary findings means that social science research has far to go towards providing the sort of policy research that is needed by policy analysts. At the same time, research from the disciplines can aid policy research and policy analysis by constructing theoretical frameworks and concepts, testing hypothesis, and continuing to develop analytic tools that are essential for policy research and analysis.

Making the Most of Social Science Contributions

In light of the limitations of empirical research from the social sciences, what can policy analysts and practitioners find that is useful at the present time? Notwithstanding the efforts of the What Works Clearinghouse, decision makers will not find a neat array of policy options with cost and impact estimates alongside implementation concerns lined up for rational decisions. Still, practitioners and analysts can find much that is useful in social science contributions, if they consider available research in light of their own particular contexts.

My own experience with research on ability grouping allows me to illustrate how decision makers can make use of research findings despite modest evidence. Research on ability grouping and achievement suggests that students in honors or advanced groups tend to benefit from their privileged placements, whereas students in low or remedial groups tend to fall further and further behind (e.g., Gamoran, Nystrand, Berends, & LePore, 1995). To the best of my ability to judge, this increasing inequality represents more than just selectivity bias (i.e., high achieving students are assigned to high groups and low-achieving students to low groups). Part of this increasing inequality is attributable to instructional differences between groups. Because some students benefit while others are disadvantaged, the policy implications are ambiguous.

Qualitative work by other scholars further shows that ability grouping stratifies opportunities and is bound up with differences in how young people view themselves and their futures (e.g., Oakes, 2005). Still other authors, however, show that eliminating ability grouping is not simple and may not benefit the achievement of all students (e.g., Loveless, 1999). With respect to both impact and implementation, then, some evidence is available, but mainly it shows that the issue is complex and there is no clear solution. How can the practitioner and decision maker respond?

Often, I am asked for a simple "thumbs up or thumbs down" on ability grouping. Unfortunately, the evidence does not afford a simple response. Instead, I believe the responsibility of the researcher is to show what ability grouping tends to produce and why. Researchers can indicate who tends to benefit and who tends to lose out under both ability grouping and mixed-ability grouping, and can speak to the challenges of moving from one system to another. This answer is not the full array of policy research in Weimer's terms—estimates of impact are debated, there are no indicators of cost, and no truly comparable measures of alternatives—but it is policy relevant. With this information, the practitioner is positioned to consider his or her own context. What is the achievement distribution of my school? How is it linked to demographic characteristics of the student body? How are teachers assigned to classes? Are teachers well equipped to instruct students at widely varying levels of performance? What new resources might be needed to support change, in light of past research? The practitioner's decision will thus be informed, even if we cannot make a confident prediction of the results of the decision.

This sort of deliberation falls well short of policy analysis in Weimer's terms, but it is likely to afford better decisions than simply going on instinct or following the latest fashion. Decisions about pressing topics, from accountability to mathematics instruction to English language learning to many others, will be more likely to bring about desired results and to avoid unintended consequences if they are undertaken in light of evidence from systematic studies, even if that evidence is limited. At the same time, the social sciences can support more informed policy decisions by striving for rigor (regardless of the methodological paradigm), by collaborating across disciplines, and by developing new theories and concepts that respond to empirical findings and that point towards the mechanisms that underlie policy effects.

Notes

1. The author is grateful for helpful comments from Anat Gofen.
2. See www.whatworks.ed.gov.

References

Burch, P., Steinberg, M., & Donovan, J. (2007). Accountability and supplemental education services: Market assumptions and emerging policy issues. *Educational Evaluation and Policy Analysis, 29*(2), 115–133.

Coleman, J. S. (1976). Policy decisions, social science information, and education. *Sociology of Education, 49*, 304–312.

Ehrenberg, R. G., Brewer, D. J., Gamoran, A., & Willms, J. D. (2001). Class size and student achievement. *Psychological Science in the Public Interest, 2*(1).

Farkas, G., & Durham, R. (2007). The role of tutoring in standards-based reform. In A. Gamoran (Ed.), *Standards-based reform and the poverty gap: Lessons for No Child Left Behind* (pp. 203–230). Washington, DC: Brookings Institution.

Gamoran, A., Nystrand, M., Berends, M., & LePore, P. E. (1995). An organizational analysis of the effects of ability grouping. *American Educational Research Journal, 32*, 687–713.

Gamoran, A., Secada, W. G., & Marrett, C. B. (2000). The organizational context of teaching and learning: Changing theoretical perspectives. In M. T. Hallinan (Ed.), *Handbook of the sociology of education* (pp. 37–63). New York: Kluwer Academic/Plenum Publishers.

Loveless, T. (1999). *The tracking wars: State reform meets school policy.* Washington, DC: Brookings Institution.

Milesi, C., & Gamoran, A. (2006). Effects of class size and instruction on kindergarten achievement. *Educational Evaluation and Policy Analysis, 28*, 287–313.

Oakes, J. (2005). *Keeping track: How schools structure inequality* (2nd ed.). New Haven, CT: Yale University Press.

Section II

Conducting Policy Research

Methodological Perspectives

SECTION EDITORS: BARBARA SCHNEIDER AND DAVID N. PLANK

10

Separate Orbits

The Distinctive Worlds of Educational Research and Policymaking

Martin Orland
WestEd

Introduction

In the world of education policy making, research findings often do not seem to matter much. Whether the issue is early childhood education, grade retention, student testing regimes, the professional development of teachers, or any one of the dozens of other areas where choices are regularly made about how to structure and deliver educational services, although research may frequently be cited (Kirst, 2000; Center on Education Policy, 2007), it is much more likely to serve as a bit player than a main attraction in shaping actual decisions (Corcoran, 2003). Why are the fruits from research so often ignored in education policymaking, or a marginal influence at best? Why aren't research findings seen more often by education leaders as helpful in exercising their responsibilities? Why, even when seriously considered, is research so often misapplied in developing and executing education policies? What are reasonable objectives for the role that research and sustained scholarly attention should play in shaping the decisions and actions of policy makers and educators? How far is educational research from attaining these objectives and what, if anything, might serve to foster such attainment?

Questions like these are particularly important in this No Child Left Behind era. Accountability demands from the law are causing policy makers to more aggressively seek "answers" to perennial and seemingly intractable system performance problems, including low student achievement levels in core content areas, large achievement gaps among student subgroups, and unacceptably high dropout rates. It is also an era where the nature of the educational research enterprise has achieved unusual visibility and prominence in policy circles. For the first time, specific models for the appropriate conduct of educational research are being aggressively promoted at the federal level (see, e.g., U.S. Department of Education, 2002; No Child Left Behind Act of 2001 [NCLB]; Education Sciences Reform Act of 2002

[ESRA]). The models appear under the generic banner of scientifically-based research (SBR). In some manifestations, they actively promote a research hierarchy in which the conduct of experimental studies employing randomized control designs are viewed as a "gold standard" for judging the effectiveness of educational policies, programs, and practices. The express goal for such unprecedented federal involvement is to ensure that policy makers and educators receive trustworthy research evidence about "what works" in education. In this context, understanding the factors that can help explain the longstanding relationships (or lack of such) between the worlds of educational research and policymaking, and whether and how current aggressive federal efforts to promote SBR and experimental studies are likely to alter them in significantly ways, seems especially timely.

The main purpose of the following analysis is to explore whether and under what circumstances this current concerted federal level emphasis on scientifically-based research and randomized control trials is likely to bring the orbits of educational research and policy into greater alignment. I do so by first outlining some basic assumptions and expectations about the role of research in enhancing public decision making, and the criteria that education policy makers employ—at least implicitly—in judging whether existing research is likely to provide such enhancements. Next I look at the distinct cultures and incentive structures as explanations for the frequent disconnects between research-based knowledge and policy actions. This includes well-documented explanations inherent to the tensions between academic research and public policy in any applied area, as well as those that appear particularly relevant to education. Lastly, I leverage the preceding analyses to explore significant recent changes in federal law and policy with regard to educational research, the implicit theory behind these changes, and the likelihood that these might eventually foster greater integration and synergy between the educational research and policy communities. I argue that current federal efforts represent self-conscious attempts to bring the worlds of educational research and policymaking into greater alignment, that they offer unique potential for doing so, but also that the movement is a fragile one and some early tendencies pose significant risks to the likelihood of long-term success.

Before proceeding, it is important to note that the primary focus of this chapter is on the relationship between research and educational *policy* as opposed to *practice*. The former refers to laws, regulations, requirements, and operating procedures that govern the general manner in which educational services are provided, while the latter concerns the specific behaviors of teachers and others who directly interact with students. Obviously, research can directly affect the behavior of educational practitioners through their application of research-based knowledge in schools and classrooms. Similarly, nearly all significant education policies have implications for practice, and many, such as those regarding curricula, professional development, or assessment, are often expressly designed to change existing practice. Nevertheless, questions concerning the role of research in directly influencing practitioner behaviors, the exceedingly complex relationship between educational policy and school level practice, and the current and possible future role of research in affecting this relationship are largely beyond the scope of this paper. Where I do touch on questions of practice, it is as a mediating factor helping to explain the potential, limitations, and challenges for educational research to inform policy in ways likely to improve the ultimate quality and effectiveness of educational service provision.

Public Policymaking and the Role of Research

As most policy makers would certainly attest, public policymaking in this country is a complex process involving multiple nodes of policymaking—or policy networks—shaping policy development, enactment, and implementation on different issues (Helco, 1978; Kirst, Meister, & Rowley, 1984). For example, in U.S. foreign policy, separate networks shape policies on such issues as human rights, bioterrorism, arms control, and world hunger. Within any one of these areas, different groups of legislative, executive, and judicial level bodies, government officials, and external "influentials" are involved on an ongoing basis in enacting legislation, administering programs, and setting the proper boundaries for government action. Indeed, even within any one issue area such as human rights, there will typically be separate policy networks around different sub-issues such as the treatment of terrorist suspects (which, for example, at the executive level will have heavy Defense Department and CIA involvement), or the application of trade sanctions (significant executive level involvement by the State and Commerce Department).

The existence of distinctive policy networks is not unique to high stakes national level policymaking. They exist at the state and local levels as well, where decisions on all manner of public affairs from public works, to economic development, to social service provision and education, are all shaped by distinct combinations of elected leaders, bureaucrats, judicial officials, legislators, and outside interests. Within any policy network, the ultimate preferences and actions of the relevant policy makers will be influenced by a number of factors. They can be grouped into three basic sets: (a) external influences, (b) organizational culture and operating procedures, and (c) personal values and dispositions.

External Influences The perceived needs and expectations of constituents represent one key influence on policy makers, since those who lose touch with constituent preferences risk alienating themselves from those responsible (either directly or indirectly) for their holding power. Not surprisingly, perceptions of constituent preference are most influential with policy makers on issues that are considered important or *salient* by the general public (Weaver, 1991).

A second type of externally-based influence comes from opinion leaders (i.e., outsiders who are well respected for their expertise and influence in a particular policy domain or more generally) and special interest groups (Burstein & Linton, 2002; Dye, 2004). The less salient an issue is to the general public, the greater the role that this types of influence can be expected to play, since policy makers and their institutions will be more responsive to those for whom they know an issue "counts," than to those who are indifferent.

A third external influence comes from political party affiliation. To the extent political party leaders stake out policy positions on different issues, both elected officials and those working for them can be expected to be influenced by the perspective of the leadership (Cooper & Herring, 2003; Snyder & Groseclose, 2000; Cox & McCubbins, 2005). At least at the national level, party influence has generally increased in recent years, as they have become more ideological, and party leadership more effective in enforcing discipline in the ranks (Owens, 1997; Cooper & Young, 2002).

Organizational Culture and Operating Procedures The organizational cultures and operating procedures of the institutions involved in policy making also help shape the preferences and actions of policymakers representing that institution (Wilson, 1989; Downs, 1994). All policymaking bodies, but especially large well-established ones with rich and longstanding histories, have distinct norms, values, traditions, methods for arriving at decisions, and institutional goals. Policies that are generally well-aligned with the organizational culture, as well as those that are seen as likely to enhance the authority and influence of the organization, are more likely to be advocated by public officials acting on behalf of the institution than policies lacking in such attributes.

Personal Values and Dispositions Last, but not least, the fundamental attitudes, values, and dispositions emanating from policy makers' own backgrounds influence their preferences and actions (Anderson, 1979). Officials with public policy responsibilities are not merely reactive automatons who are tossed hither and yon by the complex interplay of outside forces. Rather, how they interact with these influences and determine their own preferences and actions will be shaped by their family and cultural heritage, education, personal experiences, and so forth.

Educational Policy Networks and the Role of Research

The influence factors described are generally applicable to issues confronting policy development and implementation in education. Education policy networks are particularly complex because of the significant amount of shared responsibilities for education service provision encompassing different government levels (i.e., federal, state, and local), non-governmental entities (e.g., private colleges and universities), and each of the three government branches—legislative, executive, and judiciary.

Education analysts could easily identify dozens of separate decision networks and sub-networks, each housing sets of relevant policy actors on such issues as assisting the educationally disadvantaged, higher education, teacher education, curriculum and instructional programs, and education finance (to name but a few). For example, in the single area of assisting the educationally disadvantaged, distinct and only partially overlapping groups of actors shape policies and programs regarding civil rights enforcement, funding levels and allocation formulas, and developing and enforcing requirements under different provisions of No Child Left Behind on such questions as student testing, teacher quality, curriculum choices, and accountability. Comparable policymaking groups exist at the state level around each of these sub-issues. For some—such as funding of state aid to disadvantaged schools and students—the state policy networks will tend to act relatively independently of their federal counterparts. However, for others—such as those related to NCLB—one can expect the relevant state and federal networks to work together closely in both policy development and execution.[1]

How might educational research influence such policy preferences and actions? As in other areas, in gauging the contribution of research to policy one should be careful not to look for simple "straight line" relationships in which the results from one or more research investigations can easily be mapped to specific policies. The policy process has too many actors and complex incentive structures, and the problems too bound by site-specific contextual factors to expect this kind of linear impact (Kirst, 2000). Further, we know that policy makers are invariably constrained by limited or bounded rationality with respect to their policy choices (Lindblom, 1959; Lindblom & Cohen, 1979; Feuer, 2006). They tend to search for solutions that are easily apparent, build on previous efforts, and considered adequate rather than optimal (or that "satisfice" to use Lindblom's term). As such, the results from research will only, at best, be one of many factors shaping educational policy. Even

the most compelling and relevant research findings may fail to penetrate the policymaking process and, where research influences are manifest, their contributions are likely to be both indirect and incremental.

Carol Weiss (1977), in her groundbreaking examination of knowledge diffusion for policymaking, introduced the concept of an "enlightenment" function of social research in which research-based knowledge affects policy gradually by shaping how decision makers understand and frame a problem and decide on potential solutions. She argues persuasively that this is a realistic and reasonable standard for viewing the influence of research on policy, and that by this standard the impact of research can at times be profound. Corcoran (2003) makes a similar point in arguing for an important but limited role for research-based knowledge in influencing decisions about local instructional improvement strategies in education.

As relevant policy makers in any policy network consider specific laws, regulations, and administrative actions, the influence of educational research on what they propose and do will be shaped by the three types of factors previously identified (i.e., external influences such as from public attitudes and interest groups, the culture and operating procedures of their organization, and their own personal values and dispositions). One could cite examples where the fruits from research may well have impacted policymaking through influencing public attitudes. The issue of global warming certainly seems to be one current case in point (Zogby International, 2006). However, it is more likely in education as well in most other areas that research impacts on policy will more frequently be felt by affecting the positions of opinion leaders, interest groups, or political leaders, altering the legitimacy by which different objectives, priorities, or methods are perceived by relevant policymaking institutions, and directly acting on the fundamental attitudes and beliefs of the policy makers themselves.

Creating Useable Knowledge for Educational Decision Making

Whatever the specific conduits for the influence of research in any policy network, there are numerous examples in sectors outside of education (e.g., macroeconomic policy, public health policy, environmental policy) where research contributions to policy are clearly substantial, affecting which issues get on the policy agenda, what new policies and programs look like, and how existing ones are implemented. The critical question is under what circumstances knowledge from educational research is likely to enlighten the policymaking process among the relevant actors in a policy network, and produce useable knowledge that will enhance sound decision making.

For an educational research activity to serve this function successfully, there are three broad criteria that need to be met. Failure to meet any one of the criteria will result in a flawed connection between research-based knowledge and its appropriate application in educational policy. I label these criteria rigor, relevance, and usefulness, and argue that education poses some special challenges in meeting each; some of which are a function of the fundamental nature and difficulties for research inherent to the educational enterprise, and some of which relate to the current infrastructure for the conduct and application of educational research.

Rigor Policy makers have come to uniquely value and trust scientific ways of knowing and to give findings from research perceived as sufficiently rigorous and scientific special standing in policy deliberations and determinations (Branscomb, 2004). At the national level, this is reflected in a number of ways including the obligatory expert testimony at congressional hearings, the heavy reliance on scientific and technical advisors to guide policymaking throughout government, and significant annual appropriations for scientific research and development, including two large agencies whose principal mission is advancing scientific knowledge generation: the National Institutes of Health and the National Science Foundation. It is manifest on issues as disparate as global warming, the U.S. trade imbalance, welfare reform, and the accuracy of electronic voting machines.

This is not, of course, to argue that the different experts and researchers advising policy makers on questions of this type all agree on the scientific evidence coming from their work (indeed that would be atypical), or that either they or the policy makers they are informing agree on its policy implications.[2] Nor is it to say that even where consensus exists, the scientific evidence will necessarily trump other considerations in policy determinations. It is to say, rather, that—consistent with the concept of research as enlightening the policy process—the framing of the policy questions and options for consideration, the arguments for and against the different options, and the resulting policies and their justifications, all pay significant heed to the research findings when they are considered rigorous and scientifically based. Because the knowledge claims are considered "evidence-based" and emanating from "scientific authority," they are "uniquely warranted" and readily distinguished from claims made in other ways (Jenkins, 1983; Black, 2001; Branscomb, 2004).

Throughout its some 100-year history, educational research has not enjoyed a reputation for scientific rigor within either academic or policy circles (Kaestle, 1993; Sroufe, 1997; Lagemann, 2000; National Research Council, 2002). Such criticisms find support in a number of synthetic research reviews conducted over the past decade that have employed explicit quality research standards for research study inclusion. The 2000 report of the National Reading Panel (National Institute of Child Health and Human Development, 2000), for example, found that fewer than half of the studies reviewed from refereed journals on the topic of effective approaches for teaching beginning reading met minimum quality criteria. Similarly, in 2001, a comprehensive review of studies on teacher preparation research found that only 57 of 300 studies published in

refereed journals met minimum quality standards (Wilson, Floden, & Ferrini-Mundy, 2001). And most recently, an updated review by the American Institutes for Research of studies of comprehensive school reform research (Comprehensive School Reform Quality Center, 2006) found that only 95 of 800 of the studies examined met its minimum quality criteria.[3]

At least partly because of its overall weak reputation for scientific rigor, findings from educational research investigations are rarely perceived by policy makers as having unique warrants on knowledge claims that distinguish it from other information sources. This condition, of course, hampers the influence of research on the education policy process. Perversely, it is the ubiquity of problematic educational research which limits the impacts of the smaller number of methodologically strong studies by weakening the currency of educational research in general.

That said, it is important to keep in mind that the role for which we should reasonably expect more scientifically rigorous research studies to affect what occurs in education is likely to vary by the type(s) of policy under consideration. In describing evidence-based policy in health, Black (2001) makes useful distinctions between practice policies (i.e., what practitioners should do), service policies (what services government should provide and for who), and governance policies (how the system of services and practices should be organized and managed). He argues that evidence-based policy making holds up best for influencing practice policy and least well for governance policy. Hess (2005) makes a similar point in education, arguing that the recent emphasis on scientifically-based research and randomized control studies in education is quite appropriate for guiding questions of appropriate educational practices in the schools, but not for broad policies relating to school organization and governance which, by their nature, must rely on other knowledge sources (including common sense) as a principal basis for policymaking.

Relevance/Usefulness Educational research must also examine questions and concerns that are *relevant* to decision makers and communicated in ways that policy makers are able to apply it. It is important, as Donald Stokes (1997) and others argue (National Research Council, 2003), that there be an adequate supply of research that is inspired by, and responsive to, considerations of its usefulness. This does *not* mean that policy makers should only invest in applied, as opposed to basic, research. Indeed, in Stokes' now well-known quadrant model of scientific research (p. 73), he pays special attention to Pasteur's Quadrant of use-inspired basic research that is simultaneously applicable to both real world decisions and uses *and* basic knowledge generation and understandings.

However, one cannot assume that the knowledge generated by the education research community will necessarily and naturally come to address issues and concerns that are of high import to policy makers. Indeed, there is good reason to believe that much of it will not. In education, as in other areas of public policy, what interests academic researchers does not typically intersect with the high priority questions of educational policy (National Research Council, 2003). Even where researchers do address topic areas of high policy interest, the questions, policy options, and recommendations from their work will often not be well-aligned with the typically bounded and incremental policy alternatives considered by decision makers (Lindblom, 1959; Lindblom & Cohen, 1979; Feuer, 2006).

Similarly, one should not assume that the *usefulness* of findings from research investigations—even when directly relevant to significant policy needs—are either self-evident, or will naturally find their way into the policy process. For this to occur, the findings and what they imply for policy must be communicated in ways that decision makers understand and ultimately find useful in exercising their responsibilities. Research on knowledge utilization indicates that the successful application of research-based insights into policies is associated with the development of long-term relationships between researchers and decision makers (Weiss, 1991; Hood, 2002). However, education currently lacks mechanisms to foster these types of ongoing relationships (National Research Council, 2003).

Critical Disjunctures Between the Worlds of Education Policy and Research

It has often been noted (Hood, 2002; National Academy of Education, 1999; National Research Council, 1999, 2003) that the fundamental reason behind the lack of adequate connections between education research and policy is their distinctive and misaligned cultures. Yet, many of the elements and factors cited in distinguishing these cultures are not unique to education, and other policy areas such as health, transportation, and agriculture are viewed as having enjoyed greater success in integrating research with policy and ultimately practice (National Research Council, 2003). In this section, I will highlight both generic factors that comprise the "cultural misalignment" between the worlds of research and policy and those that seem particularly pronounced in education.

General Factors   One can identify five general factors in which the cultures and reward structures operate completely differently in the worlds of research versus policy:

- Original contribution versus replication/refinement
- Understanding versus fixing problems
- Communications conventions
- Interdisciplinarity/collaboration
- Time horizons

These factors inhibit greater articulation between the separate cultures in all public policy areas, not just education.

Original Contribution vs. Replication/Refinement   As reflected in the emphasis on numbers of publications in

peer-reviewed academic journals, research that is most highly valued and likely to be rewarded in the academe is that which demonstrates an *original contribution* to the field, as opposed to *replicating* or *refining* the work of others (Brunn, 1988; Burkhardt & Schoenfeld, 2003). In contrast, in order to be most applicable for policymaking, it is the ability to replicate findings multiple times in different contexts, and in understanding the specific refinements that should be taken into account in order to successfully apply the research to specific conditions and circumstances; that is crucial for the work to be considered both trustworthy and useful. This disjuncture limits the supply of potentially relevant and useful research available to inform policy in all applied fields,[4] and, in education, has been one factor in limiting the ability of scientifically based research insights to accumulate (National Research Council, 2002) in ways that benefit the conduct of educational policy and practice.

Understanding vs. Fixing Problems   Even when academic research focuses on particular policy problems, the emphasis is more often on creating a better conceptual understanding of the broad issue rather than on how to ameliorate or improve the specific condition under study (Burkhardt & Schoenfeld, 2003; Vermuelen, 2005). In other words, Pasteur's Quadrant (Stokes, 1997) is often neglected in the academe. Generating adequate theoretical and conceptual understandings of a policy problem is a necessary condition for taking appropriate knowledge-based actions. But it is not a sufficient one. Without concomitant attention by researchers to the question of remedies, their work is not likely to be perceived as relevant or useful to meeting the needs of decision makers. Perhaps even worse, when policy makers extrapolate research aimed at generating understanding into what appear to be logical applications, the policy prescriptions may well prove inadequate and deficient. Problematic applications of research on class size reduction (Bohrnstedt & Stecher, 2002) and the literature on school size (National Evaluation of High School Transformation, 2005) are two recent examples in education.

Communications Conventions   Researchers, even those who investigate questions with high potential relevance to public policy, are typically trained and rewarded for communicating with their peers, not the policy professionals who are also potential audiences for their efforts. Academic journals are intended for use primarily by academic scholars, not research consumers. The same holds for academic conferences. The emphasis in the academe on research method explication, developing well-justified theoretical constructs, and preparing complex narratives with tightly woven and carefully nuanced arguments are endemic to high-quality research scholarship. However, because the communications conventions are specific to the academe, these same attributes inhibit adequate communication of potentially relevant and useful research to those outside it. The result again is either ignorance by policy makers of research that is potentially applicable to their needs, or its misapplication because of a failure to appreciate its nuances and complexities.

Interdisciplinarity/Collaboration   Most academic research is conducted within a single traditional academic discipline or sub-discipline, with the investigator working alone or with one or two colleagues. This structure is functional for the continued development and growth of academic fields and sub-fields, as well as for rewarding individual researcher productivity. However, it is not well-aligned with the nature of most policy problems which require knowledge expertise from multiple disciplines and therefore disciplinary collaborations involving many researchers and research traditions. This condition again limits the supply of potentially policy-relevant research being generated (National Research Council, 2004). In education, one implication is that much of the research of this type that does take place occurs not within traditional academic settings, but rather through government contracts to for-profit and non-profit research organizations specializing in applied research.

Time Horizon   Policy makers operate in an environment with relatively short-term and time-sensitive information needs. Further, it is frequently difficult to predict the nature of such needs well in advance, because they are influenced by dynamic and shifting conditions that change the relative priority for different knowledge at particular times. By contrast, the incentives driving most academic research and knowledge production is for longer term study that is relatively fixed in content, and driven by calendars of peer review and academic productivity requirements for individual career advancement. Concern about meeting the time horizons of policy makers is rarely considered. As a result, it is not unusual for potentially relevant research to be unavailable in time to inform policy determinations. Similarly, in those instances where such research is brought to bear, its availability at an opportune moment is much more likely to have been a function of serendipity than design.

Special Factors in Education   The above five factors present substantial challenges for applying relevant insights from research to public policy and service delivery in any policy area. However, the challenge in the area of education is compounded because of the presence of three interrelated additional factors:

- The public/political nature of the education enterprise
- The conditional nature of salient explanations for nearly all educational phenomena
- The size and nature of the federal knowledge investment in education

The Public/Political Nature of the Education Enterprise   Since its inception as a publicly funded and government-managed activity in the early 19th century, educational policy in this country has been an area of

heavily contested political terrain (Lagemann, 1996). This reflects the often profound differences between citizens over their societal visions and the values that should therefore be promoted through the public education system. Such differences continue unabated today, and are debated continuously and passionately at the local, state, and national levels. What generally distinguishes education in this regard from other public service areas is that the public debates and decisions tend to cover *all* aspects of education; not just its broad system goals and policies (e.g., determining the proper balance between academic, vocational, and social objectives, or between maximizing individual potential vs. ensuring equality of opportunity), but also defining very specific service delivery mechanisms to be employed for goal attainment. These include the proper instructional and curriculum content (e.g., evolution, sex education, English vs. native language instruction, a phonics vs. whole language approach to reading), who should be allowed to provide services, and how many and what types of resources and services should be made available to which students. Such decisions are not considered to be the purview of distant and unaccountable technocrats judging the "scientific evidence but rather legitimate and expected areas for debate and decision through democratic processes (National Research Council, 2002). In other words, the general culture around educational decision making revolves much more around the public allocation of individual and societal values than discoveries of objective fact or truth (Brighouse, 2006).

Given this context, it should not be surprising that the contributions of independent, objective, and scientifically rigorous research have encountered significant difficulties as a major resource to improve educational policymaking, since the very essence of scientifically-based knowledge generation is to disentangle questions of fact from value. To the extent it is relied on at all, educational research is much more likely to be paid attention to by educational policy leaders when it buttresses arguments about particular policy directions or prescriptions *already* being advocated, thus furthering a particular political/policy position.[5] It is research as ammunition, not knowledge discovery.

This condition, in turn, has led to two consequences for the educational research enterprise. First, until recently as far as policy makers were concerned, high-quality and rigorous academic research in education was largely off the hook as far as being expected to contribute significantly to solving educational problems. It was by-and-large not a big issue to them that the worlds of academic research in education and policymaking were operating in separate orbits.

Second, because it is relatively easy to create research ammunition, there has been a proliferation of research studies supported by groups with unabashed political agendas making policy-relevant claims in line with political/policy positions. These works are unfiltered by any commonly accepted standards or quality control mechanisms (even peer review in most cases), and they tend to be the only research that education policy makers are exposed to, further devaluing the reputation of educational research as a uniquely warranted source of credible knowledge.

The Multiplicity of Objectives and Contexts Confronting Educational Policy Makers and Practitioners   The skepticism with which policy makers view educational research as a potential source of useable knowledge is not completely a function of its inherently value-laden nature. It is also because the nature of education does not lend itself easily to the technology of scientifically rigorous research investments.

Tangible payoffs to research in education are often compared unfavorably with returns to investments in the field of medicine (Coalition for Evidence-Based Policy, 2002). However, one clear distinction between medicine and education is that in most cases the goals of the medical practitioner are reasonably clear and straightforward: to cure the patient's illness. To be sure, there are judgments that medical professionals must make made regarding alternative ways to accomplish this objective, and not infrequent considerations of other (usually subsidiary) treatment goals such as minimizing potential side effects so that the patient's enjoys a reasonable quality of life. Still, it is reasonable to conclude that in most instances the medical practitioner has a limited set of clear goals in mind when treating a patient.

By contrast, even in this age of increasing test-based accountability and focus on academic content knowledge, teachers are still expected to meet a variety of implicit and explicit objectives in successfully exercising their responsibilities. These include the familiar expectations for fostering adequate levels of student knowledge and skills in the curricula areas they are responsible for, but also other goals such as motivating their students and giving them the skills to be lifelong learners, ensuring that each student achieves to their potential, promoting socially desirable values and behaviors, and pleasing both their supervisor (i.e., the principal) and their customers (i.e., parents of their students). Because these multiple objectives need to be continually balanced, and because they often conflict with one another, they complicate the ability of educational research to provide relevant and useful guidance either to classroom teachers directly, or policy makers setting the conditions for instructional service delivery.

Even if the performance goals for teachers and schools were simpler and clearer, decisions about what intervention(s) are most likely to achieve the desired outcome(s) still invariably depend on site-specific conditions. For example, let us imagine that a school's *only* goal is to ensure that all students reached a designated level of reading proficiency. The principal would still need to weigh a number of factors in deciding on an appropriate program regimen including; (a) the current reading level of the students, (b) the current reading program(s) in the school, (c) the variability of student reading proficiency within and across classrooms, (d) whether teachers in the school have the knowledge and skills needed to implement the intervention(s), (e) the amount of professional development needed, and (f) the extent of coordination and cooperation needed between different teachers and between teachers and parents. Again, all this assumes that the goals themselves that the principal is responsible for are singular and clear (i.e., increased reading proficiency), rather than the considerably more complex environment that actually exists where objectives tend to be vague, multiple, unstable, and often conflicting.

One can identify nearly any educational problem area and quickly come up with a lengthy list of conditional questions that will (or should) be actively considered before making a decision about whether and how to adopt a particular policy or program. The appropriate question that therefore needs to be addressed if educational research is to be perceived as relevant and useful is rarely, if ever, just, what works? It is, rather, what works for whom and under what conditions?[6] While educational research has occasionally been able to provide insights about general prevalence patterns or main effects of policies and programs, they have not, in general, developed a scientifically grounded and trustworthy knowledge base that can inform the vast multiplicity of distinct real world decision-making contexts. And it is this knowledge limitation that has largely prevented the ability of educational interventions that frequently appear effective (based on sound research) in limited and controlled settings from being successfully scaled-up so that such impacts result in large-scale system-wide educational improvements.

This circumstance is *not* meant to suggest that education is unique in its need for knowledge that takes into account locally-specific conditions. Medical practitioners too, for example, need to know such things as the age and medical history of their patient, other medical conditions they present, and other medications that they are taking before deciding on a treatment regimen. Nor does it imply that such knowledge about relevant contextual and conditional factors is theoretically unattainable through programs of scientifically rigorous research investigations and systematic knowledge building. It is only to say that given the inherently social and co-dependent nature of educational service delivery, the number of variables for educational policy makers to consider in deciding on approaches or interventions likely to work in achieving particular outcomes is much larger than it is in medicine. It has taken generations of systematic medical research and a research infrastructure conducive to knowledge building and knowledge sharing over those generations to allow medical practitioners to make informed decisions about what factors to consider, and how to weigh these factors, in deciding on appropriate medical interventions. Given the highly conditional nature of effective education service provision, it will require *at least* comparable commitments of time, resources, highly disciplined and sustained inquiry, and investments in information sharing and knowledge infrastructures, for the fruits of educational research investigations to begin to yield significant amounts of readily discernible and useful insights in education. This brings us to the last critical disjuncture that has contributed to the "separate orbits" of educational research and policy.

The Size and Nature of the Federal Knowledge Investment in Education   Since the original passage of ESEA in 1965, through the creation and reauthorizations of the National Institute of Education (NIE) and Office of Educational Research and Improvement (OERI), and most recently, the creation in 2002 of the Institute of Education Sciences (IES), there has been a decidedly cyclical pattern to federal policy supporting educational research. The pattern begins when, usually to some considerable rhetorical fanfare, the federal government declares a new era of federal support for educational research by creating a new or substantially revamped educational research entity.[7] This entity then spends several years attempting to organize its efforts and manage a new program (always a complex undertaking in Washington, DC) amidst a continuously shifting set of priorities and expectations on the part of both government and critical interest group constituents.[8] After a few years, the federal government looks at its educational research investment, finds it has not delivered what was hoped or expected, and then again vows to fix educational research by stipulating a new structure complete with rationales about why the new enterprise will succeed where the old one failed. The pattern then more or less repeats itself.

This consistent failure of educational research to live up to policy maker expectations resembles Cuban's (1990) now classic analysis of the cyclical nature of educational reform more generally. In this case, the pattern can be attributed to a number of factors, but at its core, it reflects the fundamental disconnect between what policy makers expect from educational research (when they consider it at all), and what is needed to deliver on these expectations. As just noted, the multiple and often conflicting objectives for our educational system as well as the complex and conditional nature of educational problems makes the challenge in providing scientifically rigorous, relevant, and useful educational research extremely difficult. What is required is systematic, sustained, and adequate levels of investment in high-quality research and its applications over a number of years before significant returns can be expected. However, precisely because educational research is not seen by the vast majority of educational policy makers and practitioners as being relevant to meeting their needs, there is at present only limited demand to provide more than very modest levels of financial support. In fiscal year (FY) 2005, federal government expenditures on basic and applied research in the U.S. Department of Education was estimated at $186 million compared with about $28 billion in the Department of Health and Human Services, $2 billion in the Department of Agriculture, and $461 million in the Department of Transportation (Office of Science and Technology Policy, n.d.). With FY 2005 total federal K-12 education spending estimated at about $44 billion (Office of Management and Budget, n.d., p. 108), and total K-12 spending by all levels of government at $536 billion (U.S. Department of Education, 2005, p. 1), the $186 million spent on basic and applied research in education at the Department of Education represents less than one half of 1% of all federal K-12 education spending, and less than one twentieth of 1% of estimated spending by all levels of government.[9]

What is more, befitting an enterprise for which they have only limited respect and trust, Congress has not been shy in stipulating how even such limited funds be spent. So, for example, the 1994 reauthorization of the Office of Educational Research and Improvement in the U.S. Department of Education (Title IX, Part C of the Goals 2000: Educate America Act of 1994) required that research funds be divided among distinct areas of study including early childhood, student achievement, curriculum, and assessment, postsecondary education and lifelong learning, at-risk students, and education finance, policy, and management. The law even required that within each area, 25% of the funding be reserved for research initiated by individual researchers in the field (Goals 2000, § 931). And they further earmarked significant funds for "a national system of dissemination, development and educational improvement," including 10 regional educational laboratories and an educational resources information clearinghouse (Goals 2000, § 941). Such legislatively mandated fragmentation from an already small funding base of course further limits the leadership potential of those administering the educational research program (at that time, the Office of Educational Research and Improvement) from making the kinds of resource prioritizations and continuous, coherent, and adequately supported investments needed for significantly advancing the state of useable knowledge in the field.

It can be argued that the current authorization for educational research as reflected in ESRA represents more than just the latest incarnation of the failure cycle. It is rather a self-conscious effort to learn from past experiences and profoundly alter policy maker perceptions of educational research through promoting a different paradigm that is explicitly grounded in a scientifically based approach to educational scholarship, and which is deliberately modeled after federally supported research investments in medical research. It is to this latest round of research reform initiatives attempting to get the orbits of educational research and policymaking to cross more frequently that I now turn.

The Current Landscape

Scientifically based research is the watchword for the most recent cycle of federally-driven educational R & D reform. It incorporates an unprecedented federal-level involvement in research method, in effect removing determinations of what constitutes legitimate educational research from the traditional purview of the research professionals in the field to definitions and specifications contained in legislative statute.

Policy makers focus on SBR began taking shape in the 1990s, stimulated to a large extent by an increasing awareness of advances in knowledge about effective practices in teaching young children to read. These advances were documented in two major federally supported and highly respected research syntheses reports: *Preventing Reading Difficulties in Young Children* (National Research Council, 1998) and *Teaching Children to Read* (National Institute of Child Health and Human Development, 2000). They were also heavily promoted by a federal administrator whose agency had sponsored a good portion of this work and who was a strong advocate of both enhancing the scientific rigor of educational research, and distinguishing research findings and conclusions from high-quality scientifically-based studies from other research, employing what he considered to be weaker methods and designs (see, e.g., Congressional testimony from Reid Lyon [Statement on Education Research], 1999). Significantly, Dr. Lyon did not work for the U.S. Department of Education's research unit (the Office of Educational Research and Improvement), but rather for the National Institute of Child Health and Human Development (NICHD) in the National Institutes of Health. And the educational research designs and programs that NICHD supported more closely resembled investigations of medical interventions than typical educational research studies and programs. Like medical investigations of efficacy and effectiveness, these efforts relied heavily on randomized control trials (RCTs) as the "gold standard" for documenting a causal linkage between an educational intervention and its impacts.

It is a short path from federal policy makers becoming persuaded that advances in knowledge about early reading instruction is directly attributable to more scientifically rigorous research designs, to their believing that a more explicit focus on scientifically based research and randomized control studies in education had strong potential to improve the quality of educational policies and practices more generally (Eisenhart & Towne, 2003). Thus, beginning with the Reading Excellence Act in 1999, and continuing through the No Child Left Behind Act (2001) and the Education Sciences Reform Act (2002), federal education legislation has explicitly endorsed scientifically based research as the basis for knowing about the effectiveness of educational intervention or programs. They have also defined in statute the key characteristics of such research as a basis to instruct federal program grantees on the criteria to use in selecting particular program models and interventions, as well as in recasting the orientation, structure, and focus of federally supported research within the U.S. Department of Education.

By one count, the No Child Left Behind Act of 2001 contained 111 separate references to the use of scientifically based research (SBR) as a basis for guiding local program offerings (Feuer, Towne, & Shavelson, 2002). The legislation defines SBR as "… research that involves the application of rigorous, systematic, and objective procedures to obtain reliable and valid knowledge relevant to education activities and programs" (No Child Left Behind Act of 2001, § 9101). Evidence suggests that these provisions have had

discernible though limited impacts on the behaviors of local NCLB grantees in seeking more rigorous research as a basis for their program design determinations (Center on Education Policy, 2007; Corcoran, 2003).

In 2002, the Congress authorized a new research unit for the U.S. Department of Education, the Institute of Education Sciences (IES). The functions specified for this new entity have consistently emphasized the conduct, support, dissemination, development, and strengthening of national capacity in the area of "scientifically valid research" (Education Sciences Reform Act of 2002, § 112). The ESRA legislation defined "scientifically-based research standards" as those that:

(i) apply rigorous, systematic, and objective methodology to obtain reliable and valid knowledge relevant to education activities and programs; and
(ii) present findings and make claims that are appropriate to and supported by the methods that have been employed. (Education Sciences Reform Act of 2002, § 102)

In its short history, the IES has been extremely attentive in all of its operations to questions of the quality and rigor of research designs as reflected in how it structures and manages research grant competitions, federal program evaluations, and dissemination to the field on "what works" in education. Their efforts have consistently emphasized the more frequent use, wherever feasible, of randomized control designs in order to make causal inferences about the effectiveness of specific educational interventions (see, e.g., Whitehurst, 2003). Because of the pivotal institutional and financial role played by the research office of the U.S. Department of Education, IES' priorities and orientation have already played a significant role in shaping educational research; focusing unprecedented levels of attention to questions of education research design, method, and quality, supporting a number of large-scale randomized control studies of both federal programs and other educational interventions, and influencing the behaviors of other organizations toward directions compatible with the IES emphasis. Witness, for example, the standards for reporting on research methods recently adopted by the American Educational Research Association (2006), and the creation of a major new independent research organization—The Society for Research on Educational Effectiveness—whose mission is to promote scientifically rigorous and methodologically sound research to questions of educational effectiveness (Society for Research on Educational Effectiveness Advisory Board, 2005), as just two illustrations of IES' impacts on the educational research community.

Toward More Overlapping Orbits: Likely Impacts of Current SBR Reforms

Is the current concerted federal government emphasis on scientifically based research and randomized control studies in education likely to improve the relationship between educational research and policy? Will it lead to the production of more "useable knowledge" that will play a significant role in enhancing educational quality and effectiveness? These, of course, are critical questions that emerge from the current round of federally-driven educational research reforms. To understand this likelihood, it is necessary first to recognize that these efforts do *not* only represent epistemological beliefs about educational research. They also reflect strategic political and administrative judgments about how best to use real but limited federal institutional and financial resources to leverage current systems engaged in producing and consuming educational research. There is a theory of change implicit in the current federal emphasis on SBR whose ultimate goal is to succeed where previous efforts have failed in improving the credibility and usefulness of educational research for policy and practice and, by doing so, sustaining and eventually increasing levels of federal educational research investments. The theory has two cornerstones: the preeminence of scientific rigor and methodological adequacy as criteria for designing and judging the value of educational research investigations, and the preeminence of randomized control trials as the scientific research method most worthy of current support and investment.

Scientific Rigor and Methodological Adequacy
One feature of the current SBR strategy that readily distinguishes it from past approaches is its incessant focus on questions of scientific rigor and methodological adequacy. As noted earlier, these concerns are paramount in driving new federally supported educational research studies, in federal dissemination of research findings, and in deciding which research should count when federal grantees design their service offerings under programs such as Reading First. Nowhere has this shift been more dramatic than in federal efforts at disseminating educational research findings to research, policy, and practitioner audiences. Traditionally, the federal government's role was to serve as a megaphone for educational research—that is, it amplified to communities of research, policy, and practice the findings and potential applicability of research insights. Now, however, the federal role is much more a scientific filter whose policies and actions distinguish high-quality scientifically-based research from other efforts. This change is manifest in a number of current operations at the Institute of Education Sciences including the What Works Clearinghouse, which identifies specific programs and practices with evidence of effectiveness from scientifically-based studies, and the much more constrained and scientifically-driven missions of the Educational Resources Information Clearinghouse (ERIC) and the regional educational laboratories network.

Separating out and privileging the relatively small portion of educational research that can be trusted because it is considered scientifically sound from other research, allows the federal government to accomplish two strategic objectives. First, it is expropriating into the education sphere the high levels of confidence and trust that policy

makers and service providers generally have for results from scientifically-based inquiries and research more generally, but which has heretofore been largely lacking in education (National Research Council, 2003). Second, it is sending a clear signal both to the educational research community and consumers of such research to pay much greater attention to issues of scientific rigor and research design quality. Accomplishing these objectives, in turn, can change over time the very culture in which educational research is both conducted and consumed in this country to a culture in which evidence from scientifically sound research plays a much more prominent role in shaping educational policies and practices (U.S. Department of Education, 2002).

Randomized Control Trials
A second feature of the current strategy is to support randomized control trials (RCTs) as a principal vehicle for securing relevant and useful scientifically based advances from educational research. Here, federal officials and other well-placed national advocates of more randomized studies in education frequently make direct and non-flattering comparisons between the inexorable progress that has been made in treating disease as a result of the accumulated knowledge derived from scientifically based medical research, with the decided lack of progress made in solving educational problems where randomized design studies have been infrequent (Coalition for Evidence Based Policy, 2002; U.S. Department of Education, 2002). The implicit message to the policy and practice communities is that more randomized studies in education will eventually yield comparable useful knowledge advances.

While the terms *scientifically based research* and *randomized control trials* are often conflated, it is important to point out that the legislation establishing the Institute of Education Sciences (the Education Sciences Reform Act) contains a relatively broad definition of scientifically based research that does not prescribe a preferred research method, nor require that only certain types of studies (e.g., those that test hypotheses) be conducted (Eisenhart & Towne, 2003).[10] The unprecedented current focus on RCTs in the IES portfolio reflects, by-and-large, federal policy judgments about how to structure agency knowledge resource investments, and not a pronouncement that RCTs are the only legitimate form of scientific inquiry in education. Indeed, a significant portion of IES activities include support for work other than RCTs (e.g., the entire program of the National Center for Education Statistics), and policies in such areas as reviewing grant proposals (U.S. Department of Education, 2006a) and publishing manuscripts (U.S Department of Education, 2006b) are consistent with a research agency adhering to furthering principles of scientific inquiry generally, rather than any single methodology or approach.

What makes the current emphasis on RCTs so interesting is *not* that it is viewed as uniquely scientific, but rather that it represents a deliberate policy strategy for more closely linking the fruits of educational research with the needs of decision-maker audiences. That view is based on the belief that, above all, educational decision makers are looking to the research community for clear guidance on very particular questions—What curriculum should be used with second grade students in my school who are falling behind in reading? What dropout preventions programs are most likely to be effective in reducing the incidence of dropping out in my school district? If I want to increase student achievement in my state, am I better off implementing policies that will lower class size, or ones that will create more charter schools and school choice? Because these questions are about causal relationships (i.e., what effect am I likely to get if I implement a particular program, policy, or practice), they are considered to be best addressed scientifically through research incorporating RCT designs (National Research Council, 2002). The implicit theory appears to be that, by using much larger proportions of limited federal research resources to address questions of "what works" through support of RCTs, the federal government will be providing educational decision makers with new and eagerly sought information that will allow them to make more scientifically grounded choices about particular policies or programs. This, in turn, will bring the orbits of educational research and policy/practice into closer alignment, change the culture of educational policymaking to one that more actively considers findings and evidence from educational research, and encourage policy makers over time to support larger federal educational research investments, both for RCTs and other purposes.

Major Threats to the SBR Reform Strategy and how to Address Them I would argue that both because of its direct focus on enhancing the public credibility of educational research and in producing results directly intended to serve the needs of policy and practice, the strategic logic anchoring the current federal emphases on scientific rigor and increased use of RCTs is reasonable. Of all the reforms around federal education research investments over the past 35 years, this one has the greatest chance to have a sustainable and positive impact on not only the quality of educational research, but also its relationship to policy. However, I would also argue that some tendencies seen in current efforts fail to account for important challenges in the current educational research and policy environment. If not modified, they pose substantial risks for the ultimate success of the strategy.

One danger is in harboring unrealistic expectations about the magnitude of impacts to expect from SBR in education, and when to expect them. While SBR can reasonably be expected to improve educational quality, it should not be seen as the key to "curing" our nation's educational ills. In this respect, simple comparisons to medical advances are seriously misguided (Coalition for Evidence-Based Policy, 2002) and likely to be counterproductive. The problems that educators are now expected to address—such as getting all students to become proficient in reading and mathematics and closing the achievement gap between student subgroups—are enormous. Both empirical evidence on educational program effects,[11] and what is reasonable to as-

sume about the limits of school (at least given their existing basic structures and funding levels) to overcome preexisting social and economic inequities (Rothstein, Jacobsen, & Wilder, 2006), strongly suggest that expectations should be tempered, especially in the short-term, for dramatic educational improvements as a result of knowledge gains from scientifically based research.

Further, there are a number of reasons to believe that even modest though useful knowledge advances from SBR will come slowly and incrementally. They include the previously mentioned difficulties in separating—for both education policy makers and researchers—questions of value and ideology from questions of evidence, and the conditional circumstances that are so often critical factors in distinguishing the appropriateness and likely impacts of particular educational policies or programs. Making the challenge even more daunting is the current shortage, in virtually every policy-relevant area of inquiry, of an adequate existing supply of high-quality scientifically-based research that has accumulated and been refined over time and which can serve as a jumping off point for subsequent knowledge building investments.[12] There is also a shortage of researchers who have the skills to conduct methodologically rigorous educational research studies (National Research Council, 2005). Nor have educators, by-and-large, been trained to be knowledgeable consumers of educational research, or has the culture surrounding educational policy and practice encouraged decision makers to look to research as a principal basis for policy and program choices.[13]

All of this suggests that advocates of SBR in education need to be not only modest in their expectations, but also vigilant in their support for continued investments, and patient in their time horizons for when such investments can be expected to reap clear dividends. There is a need for long-term and stable funding that will allow for the growth of a scientifically-based knowledge infrastructure in educational research. Over time, these investments can be increasingly expected to provide educational decision makers with informative evidence-based guidance. However, vigilance and patience may be in short supply given the real world pressures from federal mandates like NCLB to continuously improve student achievement, and the more general aversion by policy makers to invest in the promise of the future versus spending on the expressed needs of the present. For this reason, it is advisable for the federal education research portfolio to be in balance; keeping one eye on present needs in the field, while still maintaining a long-term strategic vision coupled with the requisite needed investments in the future. This has implications for the current federal emphasis on studies incorporating RCT designs.

In her recent essay on the warranting of causal claims in scientific research, philosopher of science Nancy Cartwright (2007) makes the important distinction between research methods that *clinch* conclusions but are narrow in their applications, versus those that merely *vouch* for conclusions, but are broader in their range of applications. She lists RCTs in the former category, and the appeal of RCTs in education clearly lies in their ability to clinch conclusions. However, any single RCT is likely to have only a narrow range of real-world applications and therefore can be expected to provide only limited guidance to educational policy makers.[14] It is only through the accumulated knowledge built over time from multiple well-designed and implemented RCTs combined with insights from other forms of knowledge generation (both scientific and nonscientific) that we can expect to gain broadly applicable and policy-relevant research insights.

This, in fact, is largely the story of the advances made in the teaching and learning of early reading (National Research Council, 2002, pp. 38–41), which has benefited from over 30 years of relatively systematic knowledge accretion through randomized studies and other research methods. As noted earlier, early reading has been the existence proof most responsible for animating the current level of interest in SBR. But even here, the knowledge advances are relatively narrow. So, for example, while we can now confidently assert and inform policy makers and educators about the major components of effective early reading instruction that must be attended to, we still know relatively little about how to impart in teachers the necessary knowledge and skills so that they may effectively provide such instruction. Nor does our knowledge of effective early reading teaching and learning transfer well to address questions of what works in adolescent literacy.

All this is to say that there should be an important place in the current federal education research portfolio for the conduct and dissemination of high-quality scientifically based research that does not necessarily clinch causal conclusions. A failure to do so is likely to lead to a selection of research investigations and communications that are both too narrow (at least in the short-term) and not timely enough to be considered relevant and useful by educational decision makers. That in turn may well lead to the diminution of support for needed long-term SBR investments.

Well-designed and scientifically rigorous descriptive and correlational studies, formal meta-analyses and evidence-based research syntheses, as well as qualitative investigations of significant educational programs and phenomena, can be enormously informative to educational decision makers, and perceived as helping them with their immediate knowledge needs. One promising avenue in this regard may be to enhance support for, and the dissemination of, research that applies multivariate analytic models to extant data sets such as those maintained by the National Center for Educational Statistics (Schneider, Carnoy, Kilpatrick, Schmidt, & Shavelson, 2007). Another would be to re-conceptualize the current What Works Clearinghouse so that its synthetic reviews and meta-analyses capture additional potentially informative extant research investigations. Expanded investments in these areas are fully consistent with the role of scientifically-based research in vouching for policy-relevant causal claims. A third strategy is to conduct more well-designed case studies and/or surveys examining

the implementation of major educational policy reforms such as charter schools, class-size reduction, or new teacher compensation systems. Findings from investments of this type can sensitize policy makers to issues and challenges that they are unaware of and which need to be addressed if their policy expectations are to be realized.

The federal government can also become much more active in providing high-quality "research translation" support through both user-friendly synthetic reviews of relevant research and technical assistance services. Such support, particularly if it fosters continuous and long-term relationships between policy makers and research experts, could help policy makers understand the strengths and limitations of the current knowledge base with respect to important questions at hand (therefore sensitizing them to critical distinctions in research quality), and assist them in relating the best evidence currently available to their own local context.[15] While there is always the risk that these efforts may lead education decision makers to overstate the causal inferences that can be responsibly asserted, this risk can be minimized through effective communications, management, and quality-control strategies. For the long term strategic interests of SBR in education, it is, I would argue, a risk worth taking given the benefits that would be perceived by research consumers currently yearning for useable knowledge to enhance their decision making.[16]

Summary and Conclusions

My principal purposes in this chapter have been two-fold. First, I wanted to identify those factors most responsible for inhibiting greater recognition and use of educational research by educational policy makers. Second, I wished to explore whether and under what circumstances the current concerted federal level emphasis on scientifically based research and randomized control trials is likely to bring the orbits of educational research and policy into greater alignment.

Like other areas of public policymaking, findings from educational research should be viewed as but one of many factors expected to influence educational decision making. Further, the nature of such influence will often be indirect and incremental (i.e., "enlightening") rather than directly causal. Three basic conditions need to be met if educational research is to play a larger role in influencing policy; it should be perceived by educational decision makers as scientifically rigorous, address issues considered relevant to their needs, and communicate findings, conclusions, and recommendations effectively to non-research audiences of educational policy makers.

Several factors make the attainment of these conditions challenging. These include the emphasis in academic research on original contributions to the field as opposed to replicating or refining the work of others, on understanding rather than fixing problems, on communicating with peers (i.e., other academic researchers) rather than non-specialist audiences, on single disciplinary perspectives, and on time horizons for research production that are not well-aligned with policy information needs. In addition to these difficulties, which tend to be endemic to real-world applications of social science research generally, there are also special factors in education that make alignment even more difficult. These include the highly public, political, and value-laden nature of educational decision making, the fact that the technology for providing a scientifically rigorous basis to guide educational policy is not easily adapted to the breadth and diversity of conditions characterizing actual decision-maker contexts, and the limited and largely failed history of past federal research investments in educational research.

The unprecedented current federal emphasis on conducting scientifically-based research in education (SBR) in general, and randomized control trials (RCTs) in particular, is a strategic response to many of these difficulties. It represents an attempt to at least partially displace the culture of educational decision making from one where considerations of politics and values predominate to one where scientifically-based knowledge insights receive greater acknowledgement and weight. It also appears intended to shift the supply of educational research so that it focuses more directly on questions that policy makers most want guidance on—questions on what works.

The current SBR and RCT foci represent both a reasonable and overdue strategy for addressing many of the barriers that have, in the past, stifled greater alignment between the worlds of educational research and policymaking. Whether it will ultimately prove any more successful than past federal research reform efforts may well depend on minimizing tendencies that some have associated with these still nascent efforts; including *overstating* the likely positive impacts of SBR reforms in addressing current pressing needs, *overvaluing* knowledge advances from randomized controlled trials versus other scientifically-based research approaches that, while less definitive, are likely to have a broader range of policy-relevant applications, and *undervaluing* the importance of direct and ongoing decision-maker services and supports aimed at research translation and tailored knowledge use.

In a curious sense, the knowledge use challenges facing leaders of the SBR agenda in education writ large are analogous to those facing education researchers investigating a significant policy issue or problem. For even the highest quality research to influence policy and ultimately system effectiveness requires that its design and application reflect the actual environments where the findings are likely to be employed. Such findings should, for example, be available and adequately communicated during policy adoption cycles, relevant to actual policy maker choice-sets given tendencies such as "satisficing" and biases favoring incremental change, and accurate in their assumptions about any assumed relationships between recommended policies and school/classroom level practices. The same holds true more generally for the prospects of the scientifically based research reform movement to influence more effective policy making and better services and outcomes for students.

While there is little doubt that SBR reforms will result in more research meeting the highest standards of scientific rigor, research reformers should be at least equally attentive to the context for the application of research-based knowledge in real-world policy environments if their efforts are to result in more synchronous orbits of educational knowledge production and appropriate decision maker actions.

Notes

1. For an illustration of how such networks have emerged and influenced state-level reading policies see Song and Miskel (2005).

2. Nor does this mean that the characterization of such evidence as "scientific" and therefore valid is necessarily accurate. For example, Allington (2000) claims that the evidence has been distorted to support particular policies regarding the teaching of reading, while Hanushek (1998) makes a similar contention regarding research on class-size reduction.

3. It should be noted that the research quality standards used do not appear to be unreasonably restrictive or harsh. The Wilson et al. review, for example (2001, pp. 2–4) accepted studies employing a variety of research methodologies including experimental, quasi-experimental, multiple regression, longitudinal studies of change, and qualitative case studies as long as they met generally accepted quality standards within the appropriate research tradition.

4. For critiques in the fields of business and public management research, see Davenport and Markus (1999), and Vermuelen (2005).

5. See, for example, the use of research from the Tennessee class size reduction experiment as argument by interest groups for reduced class-size (Achilles, 1997; American Federation of Teachers, 2003). Or, on the other side of the ideological divide, see how findings from the evaluation of the Teach For America program have been used by those opposed to current barriers to entry into the teaching profession (Holland, 2004; Walsh, 2004). For a more general discussion of research as ideological ammunition, see Petrilli (2006).

6. McRobbie, Finn, and Harman (1998), to cite but one example, attempt to take this approach in examining the lessons learned from the myriad studies on class-size reduction. Their effort is instructive not only for the nature of the conditional questions asked, but also for the relative paucity of high-quality evidence apparent in the research review (despite this being such a heavily studied area of federal education policy) to inform these questions in ways that will likely be perceived as both trustworthy and valuable to educational policy makers.

7. For an early critique of educational research and development that was influential in creating the National Institute of Education, see Chase (1971).

8. For a rich discussion on the difficulties confronting the National Institute of Education, see Sproull, Weiner, and Wolf (1978).

9. For a strikingly similar argument made over 15 years ago see Guthrie (1990).

10. This conflation is no doubt partially attributable to the No Child Left Behind Act legislation in which the definition of scientifically based research mentions only experimental or quasi-experimental designs as methods for evaluating research (pp. 126–127). The fact that SBR in NCLB is used exclusively in the context of grantees evaluating research on the effectiveness of educational programs and program components in order to shape their own design choices probably explains this inappropriately narrow definition.

11. For example, the average 1-year effect size in the Tennessee class size experiment was only .1 (Nye, Hedges, & Konstantopoulos, 2001).

12. This has become a common refrain of high-quality research syntheses addressing very different areas. See, for example, *Adding it Up* (National Research Council, 2001, p. 26), and Wilson et al. (2001, p. 6). One can argue that the assumption that high-quality scientifically

based research exists when it may well have trivialized most grantee responses to SBR requirements in NCLB, and thus is unlikely to promote greater educator responsiveness to evidence as a significant basis for decision making.

13. As a recent prominent example of the difficulties in the federal government attempting to introduce scientifically based research considerations as the basis for curricular decisions, one need only look at recent controversies surrounding the implementation of the Reading First program (U.S. Department of Education, 2006d).

14. It is true that small-scale RCTs provide less general guidance than larger ones covering diverse conditions, target populations, etc. However, given the heavily conditional nature of factors associated with the success or failure of nearly all educational interventions, even single large-scale experiments tend to be limited in their applications to future policy. In fact, the failure to appreciate questions of condition and context may well lead to inappropriate policy inferences such as occurred in California's use of the findings from the Tennessee class-size experiment (Bohrnstedt & Stecher, 2002). See also Ioannidis (2005) and Raudenbush (2005) for discussions of appropriate cautions and constraints in commissioning many large-scale RCTs.

15. This had been one ostensible function of the network of regional education laboratories that has been federally supported since the 1960s. However, probably in response to criticism that the program has paid inadequate attention to questions of scientific rigor and responsiveness to the policy needs of their service areas (Vinovskis, 2001), the most recent national laboratories contract deemphasizes their technical assistance role while placing heavy emphasis on conducting descriptive surveys and new randomized control studies.

16. There is some evidence that the Institute of Education Sciences is becoming more aware of this need and is attempting to be responsive. See, for example, pages 10 and 11 of the Statement of Work originally issued on December 19, 2006, for the What Works Clearinghouse (U.S. Department of Education, 2006c).

References

Achilles, C. M. (1997, October). Exploring class-size research issues. *The School Administrator*. Retrieved February 27, 2007, from http://www.aasa.org/publications/content.cfm?ItemNumber=4511

Allington, R. (2000). Broad claims from slender findings. *Reading Rockets*. Retrieved February 13, 2007, from http://www.readingrockets.org/article/366

American Educational Research Association. (2006). Standards for reporting on empirical social science research in AERA publications. *Educational Researcher, 35*(6), 33–40.

American Federation of Teachers. (2003, November). *Benefits of small class size* (Issue Brief). Retrieved February 24, 2007, from http://www.aft.org/topics/classsize/downloads/ClassSizeBrief.pdf

Anderson, J. E. (1979). *Public policy-making* (2nd ed.). New York: Holt, Rinehart, and Winston.

Black, N. (2001). Evidence based policy: Proceed with care. *British Medical Journal, 323*(7307), 275–279.

Bohrnstedt, G. W., & Stecher, B. M. (Eds.). (2002). *What have we learned about class-size reduction in California?* (CSR Research Consortium Capstone Report). Palo Alto, CA: American Institutes for Research.

Branscomb, L. M. (2004). Science, politics, and U.S. democracy. *Issues in Science and Technology, 21*(1), 53–59.

Brighouse, H. (2006, September 27). Is 'evidence' enough? Why values and context matter in education policymaking. *Education Week*. Retrieved February 24, 2007, from http://www.edweek.org/ew/articles/2006/09/27/05brighouse.h26.html?levelId=1000&print=1

Brunn, S.D. (1988). The manuscript review process and advice to prospective authors. *Professional Geographer, 40*, 8–14.

Burkhardt, H., & Schoenfeld, A. H. (2003). Improving educational research: Toward a more useful, more influential, and better-funded enterprise. *Educational Researcher, 32*(9), 3–14.

Burstein, P., & Linton, A. (2002). The impact of political parties, interest groups, and social movement organizations on public policy: Some recent evidence and theoretical concerns. *Social Forces, 81*, 381–408.

Cartwright, N. (2007). Causes: Warranting them and using them. In *Hunting causes and using them: Approaches in philosophy and economics* (chap. 3). New York: Cambridge University Press.

Center on Education Policy. (2007, January). *No Child Left Behind at five: A review of changes to state accountability plans*. Washington, DC: Author.

Chase, F. (1971). Educational research and development in the sixties. *Curriculum Theory Network, No. 7* (Monograph Supplement: Elements of Curriculum Development), 142–163.

Coalition for Evidence-Based Policy. (2002). *Bringing evidence-driven progress to education: A recommended strategy for the U.S. Department of Education*. Washington, DC: Author.

Comprehensive School Reform Quality Center. (2006). *CSRQ Center report on elementary school comprehensive school reform models*. Washington, DC: American Institutes for Research.

Cooper, J., & Herring, M. (2003, April). *Proximity voting versus party effects: A revised theory of the importance of party in Congressional decision making*. Paper presented at the annual meeting of the Midwest Political Science Association, Chicago.

Cooper, J., & Young, G. (2002). Party and preference in Congressional decision making: Roll call voting in the House of Representatives, 1889–1999. In D. W. Brady & M. D. McCubbins (Eds.), *Party, process, and political change in Congress: New perspectives on the history of Congress* (pp. 64–106). Stanford, CA: Stanford University Press.

Corcoran, T. (2003). The use of research evidence in instructional improvement. (CPRE Policy Brief, RB-40). Philadelphia: University of Pennsylvania, Graduate School of Education.

Cox, G. W., & McCubbins, M. D. (2005). *Setting the agenda: Responsible party government in the U.S. House of Representatives*. New York: Cambridge University Press.

Cuban, L. (1990). Reforming again, again, and again. *Educational Researcher, 19*(1), 3–13.

Davenport, T. H., & Markus, M. L. (1999). Rigor vs. relevance revisited: Response to Benbaset and Zmud. *MIS Quarterly, 23*, 19–23.

Downs, A. (1994). *Inside bureaucracy* (Reissue ed.). Prospect Heights, IL: Waveland Press.

Dye, T. R. (2004). *Understanding public policy* (11th ed.). Upper Saddle River, NJ: Prentice Hall.

Education Sciences Reform Act of 2002, Pub. L. No. 107-279.

Eisenhart, M., & Towne, L. (2003). Contestation and change in national policy on "scientifically based" education research. *Educational Researcher, 32*(7), 31–38.

Feuer, M. J. (2006). *Moderating the debate: Rationality and the promise of American education*, Cambridge, MA: Harvard Education Press.

Feuer, M. J., Towne, L., & Shavelson, R. J. (2002). Scientific culture and educational research. *Educational Researcher, 31*(8), 4–14.

Goals 2000: Educate America Act of 1994, Pub. L. No. 103-227.

Guthrie, J. W. (1990). Education R&D's lament (and what to do about it). *Educational Researcher, 19*(2), 26–34.

Hanushek, E. A. (1998). *The evidence on class size* (Occasional Paper 98-1). Rochester, NY: University of Rochester, W. Allen Wallis Institute of Political Economy.

Helco, H. (1978). Issue networks in the executive establishment. In A. King (Ed.), *The new American political system* (pp. 87–124). Washington, DC: American Enterprise Institute.

Hess, F. M. (2005, May). Science and nonscience: The limits of scientific research. *AEI On the Issues*. Retrieved February 24, 2007, from http://www.aei.org/publications/pubID.22461/pub_detail.asp

Holland, R. (2004, October 1). Teach for America shows its mettle. *School Reform News*. Retrieved February 27, 2007, from http://www.heartland.org/PrinterFriendly.cfm?theType=artId&theID=15696

Hood, P. (2002). Perspectives on knowledge utilization in education. San Francisco: WestEd.

Ioannidis, J. P. A. (2005). Why most published research findings are false [Electronic version]. *PLoS Medicine, 2*(8), 696–704.

Jenkins, J. C. (1983). Resource mobilization theory and the study of social movements. *Annual Review of Sociology, 9*, 527–553.

Kaestle, C. F. (1993). The awful reputation of educational research. *Educational Researcher, 22*(1), 23–31.

Kirst, M. W. (2000). Bridging education research and education policymaking. *Oxford Review of Education, 26*, 379–391.

Kirst, M., Meister, G., & Rowley, S. (1984). Policy issue networks: Their influence on state policymaking. *Policy Studies Journal, 13*, 247–264.

Lagemann, E. C. (1996). Contested terrain: A history of education research in the United States, 1890–1990. *Educational Researcher, 26*(9), 5–17.

Lagemann, E. C. (2000). *An elusive science: The troubling history of education research*. Chicago: University of Chicago Press.

Lindblom, C. E. (1959). The science of "muddling through." *Public Administration Review, 19*, 79–88.

Lindblom, C. E., & Cohen, D. K. (1979). *Usable knowledge: Social science and social problem solving*. New Haven, CT: Yale University Press.

McRobbie, J., Finn, J. D., & Harman, P. (1998, August). *Class size reduction: Lessons learned from experience* (WestEd Policy Brief No. 23). Retrieved February 24, 2007, from http://www.wested.org/policy/pubs/full_text/pb_ft_csr23.htm

National Academy of Education. (1999, March). *Recommendations regarding research priorities: An advisory report to the National Educational Research Policy and Priorities Board*. New York: Author.

National Evaluation of High School Transformation. (2005). *Getting to results: Student outcomes in new and redesigned high schools*. Washington, DC: American Institutes for Research/SRI International. Retrieved March 1, 2007, from http://www.gatesfoundation.org/nr/downloads/Ed/researchevaluation/OutcomesYr3.pdf

National Institute of Child Health and Human Development. (2000). *Report of the National Reading Panel, Teaching children to read: An evidence-based assessment of the scientific research literature on reading and its implications for reading instruction* (NIH Publication No. 00-4769). Washington, DC: U.S. Government Printing Office.

National Research Council. (1998). *Preventing reading difficulties in young children*. Committee on the Prevention of Reading Difficulties in Young Children. C. E. Snow, M. S. Burns, & P. Griffin (Eds.). Washington, DC: National Academy Press.

National Research Council. (1999). *Evaluating federal research programs: Research and the Government Performance and Results Act*. Committee on Science, Engineering, and Public Policy. Washington, DC: National Academy Press.

National Research Council. (2001). *Adding it up: Helping children learn mathematics*. Mathematics Learning Study Committee. J. Kilpatrick, J. Swafford, & F. Findell (Eds.). Washington, DC: National Academy Press.

National Research Council. (2002). *Scientific research in education*. Committee on Scientific Principles for Education Research. R. J. Shavelson & L. Towne (Eds.). Washington, DC: National Academy Press.

National Research Council. (2003). *Strategic education research partnership*. Committee on a Strategic Education Research Partnership. M. S. Donovan, A. K. Wigdor, & C. E. Snow (Eds.). Washington, DC: National Academy Press.

National Research Council. (2004). *Facilitating interdisciplinary research*. Committee on Science, Engineering, and Public Policy. Washington, DC: National Academies Press.

National Research Council. (2005). *Advancing scientific research in education*. Committee on Research in Education. L. Towne, L. L. Wise, & T. M. Winters (Eds.). Washington, DC: National Academies Press.

No Child Left Behind Act of 2001, Pub. L. No. 107-110.

Nye, B., Hedges, L. V., & Konstantopoulos, S. (2001). Are the effects of small classes cumulative? Evidence from a Tennessee experiment. *Journal of Educational Research, 94*, 336–345.

Office of Management and Budget. (n.d.). *Budget of the federal government, fiscal year 2006* (pp. 97–108). Retrieved February 28, 2007, from http://www.whitehouse.gov/omb/budget/fy2006/pdf/budget/education.pdf

Office of Science and Technology Policy. (n.d.). *Federal research and development spending (FY 2006)*. Retrieved February 28, 2007, from http://www.ostp.gov/html/budget/2006/Tables/FederalR&DSpendingTable.pdf

Owens, J. E. (1997). The return of party government in the U.S. House of Representatives: Central leadership – committee relations in the 104th Congress. *British Journal of Political Science, 27*, 247–272.

Petrilli, M. J. (2006, August 24). Unprincipled. *Education Gadfly, 6*(32). Retrieved February 27, 2007, from http://www.edexcellence.net/institute/gadfly/issue.cfm?id=254&edition=#25

Raudenbush, S. W. (2005). Learning from attempts to improve schooling: The contribution of methodological diversity. *Educational Researcher, 34*(5), 25–31.

Reading Excellence Act. Pub. L. No. 105-277, 112 Stat. 2681.

Rothstein, R., Jacobsen, R., & Wilder, T. (2006, November). 'Proficiency for all' — an oxymoron. Paper prepared for the symposium "Examining America's Commitment to Closing Achievement Gaps: NCLB and Its Alternatives," New York.

Schneider, B., Carnoy, M., Kilpatrick, J., Schmidt, W., & Shavelson, R. (2007). *Estimating causal effects using experimental and observational designs*. Washington, DC: American Educational Research Association.

Snyder, J. M., Jr., & Groseclose, T. (2000). Estimating party influence in Congressional roll-call voting. *American Journal of Political Science, 44*, 193–211.

Society for Research on Educational Effectiveness Advisory Board. (2005). *Mission statement*. Retrieved January 15, 2008, from http://www.educationaleffectiveness.org/pages/pressrelease/mission.shtml

Song, M., & Miskel, C. G. (2005). Who are the influentials? A cross-state social network analysis of the reading policy domain. *Educational Administration Quarterly, 41*, 7–48.

Sproull, L., Weiner, S., & Wolf, D. (1978). *Organizing an anarchy: Belief, bureaucracy, and politics in the National Institute of Education*. Chicago: University of Chicago Press.

Sroufe, G. E. (1997). Improving the "awful reputation" of education research. *Educational Researcher, 26*(7), 26–28.

Statement on education research: Is what we don't know hurting our children?: Hearings before the Subcommittee on Basic Research, of the House Science Committee, 106th Cong. (1999) (written testimony of G. Reid Lyon). Retrieved February 28, 2007, from http://www.hhs.gov/asl/testify/t991026b.html

Stokes, D. E. (1997). *Pasteur's quadrant: Basic science and technological innovation*. Washington, DC: Brookings Institution.

U.S. Department of Education. (2002). *Strategic plan 2002–2007*. Washington, DC: Author.

U.S. Department of Education. (2005). *10 facts about K-12 education funding*. Washington, DC: Author. Retrieved March 1, 2007, from http://www.ed.gov/about/overview/fed/10facts/10facts.pdf

U.S. Department of Education. (2006a). *Procedures for peer review of grant applications*. Washington, DC: Author. Retrieved February 28, 2007, from http://ies.ed.gov/director/pdf/SRO_grant_peerreview.pdf

U.S. Department of Education. (2006b). *Procedures for peer review of reports*. Washington, DC: Author. Retrieved February 28, 2007, from http://ies.ed.gov/director/pdf/SRO_reports_peerreview.pdf

U.S. Department of Education. (2006c). *Statement of work: The What Works Clearinghouse*. Washington, DC: Author. Retrieved May 12, 2008, from https://www.fbo.gov/utils/view?id=84fa9e9e919f8c619fe12ce5d4d1c8a5

U.S. Department of Education. (2006d). *The reading first program's grant application process: Final inspection report*. Washington DC: Author. Retrieved December 28, 2007, from http://www.ed.gov/about/offices/list/oig/aireports/i13f0017.pdf

Vermuelen, F. (2005). On rigor and relevance. Fostering dialectic progress in management research. *Academy of Management Journal, 48*, 978–982.

Vinovskis, M. A. (2001). *Revitalizing federal education research and development: Improving the R&D centers, regional educational laboratories, and the "new" OERI*. Ann Arbor: The University of Michigan Press.

Walsh, K. (2004, June 14). Study finds Teach for America teachers as good in reading and better in math. *Teacher Quality Bulletin, 5*(13). Retrieved February 27, 2007, from http://www.nctq.org/nctq/jsp/view_bulletin.jsp?title=Archives&search_page=volumes.jsp&issueTypeId=0&regionId=0&bulletinId=185&x=6&y=22

Weaver, D. (1991). Issue salience and public opinion: Are there consequences of agenda-setting? *International Journal of Public Opinion, 3*, 53–68.

Weiss, C. H. (1977). Research for policy's sake: The enlightenment function of social research. *Policy Analysis, 3*, 531–545.

Weiss, C. H. (1991). The many meanings of research utilization. In D. S. Anderson & B. J. Biddle (Eds.), *Knowledge for policy: Improving education through research* (pp. 173–182). London: Falmer Press.

Whitehurst, G. J. (2003, April). *The Institute of Education Sciences: New wine, new bottles.* Presentation at the annual meeting of the American Educational Research Association, Chicago. Retrieved March 1, 2007, from http://ies.ed.gov/director/speeches2003/04_22/2003_04_22.asp

Wilson, J. Q. (1989). *Bureaucracy: What government agencies do and why they do it.* New York: Basic Books.

Wilson, S. M., Floden, R. E., & Ferrini-Mundy, J. (2001). Teacher preparation research: Current knowledge, gaps, and recommendations (CTP Research Report). University of Washington, Center for the Study of Teaching and Policy.

Zogby International. (2006). *Zogby International/National Wildlife Federation survey.* New York: Author. Retrieved February 24, 2007, from http://www.zogby.com/wildlife/NWFfinalreport8-17-06.htm

11

The Use of Randomized Trials to Inform Education Policy

GEOFFREY D. BORMAN
University of Wisconsin–Madison

Beginning in 1965, with the authorization of the Elementary and Secondary Education Act (ESEA), the United States government mandated large-scale annual evaluations of the effectiveness of Title I of the ESEA (most recently reauthorized as the No Child Left Behind Act of 2002) and enacted major educational research and development (R&D) initiatives through Title IV of the ESEA. These efforts, and others, generated some initial optimism among researchers and policy makers that education could be a field informed by research and fueled by the development of new educational processes and programs that were derived from science rather than speculation and tradition. However, as Slavin (1997) noted, these federally funded educational R&D efforts produced few well-validated programs or practices that entered widespread use. Many reasons for this disappointing outcome have been proffered. Most observers suggest that the educational R&D infrastructure has never been adequately funded, the national research agenda is fragmented, and that the field is highly politicized (Guthrie, 1990; Vinovskis, 1999). These are serious handicaps. Most fundamentally and most disturbingly, though, the field of educational research has been widely perceived as methodologically and scientifically inferior to the "hard sciences" and the other so-called "soft sciences" in the social and behavioral disciplines. As a result of these shortcomings, the research that has been funded rarely builds the critical mass to move an important field forward, has been open to varying partisan perspectives, and has left educational practice to be dictated by faddishness and craft knowledge rather than by scientific principles.

The latest wave of national attention to educational R&D provides several notable indications that policy makers are intent on addressing these shortcomings. First, in 1998, Congress began making a $150 million funding source, the Comprehensive School Reform Demonstration (CSRD) program, available only to those schools that proposed to implement "proven" educational practices and programs

with solid evidence of effectiveness. Congressmen David Obey and John Porter, who crafted the CSRD legislation, defined "proven" practices and programs as those that have been rigorously evaluated using experimental-control comparisons on standards-based measures. By 2001, funding for this unprecedented program had reached over $300 million annually (Borman, Hewes, Overman, & Brown, 2003).

Second, concerned about the widespread dissemination of flawed, untested educational initiatives that can be detrimental to children, the U.S. Congressional Committee on Education and the Work Force developed a bill, the Scientifically Based Education Research, Evaluation, and Statistics and Information Act of 2000, that called for more rigor in educational research and tried to specify what this meant. The bill did not pass, but as Boruch and Mosteller (2002) noted, it provided a clear sign of congressional interest in making more explicit the standards of evidence that are appropriate for both quantitative and qualitative research. Also, though not formally enacted as law, clearer definitions of high-quality scientific research have emerged from national organizations, including the National Research Council's publication, *Scientifically Based Research* (Shavelson & Towne, 2002).

Third, in January of 2002, the reauthorization of the ESEA of 1965 and the federal government's single largest investment in America's elementary and secondary schools, the No Child Left Behind Act (NCLB), required practices based on high-quality research for everything from the technical assistance provided to schools to the choice of anti-drug-abuse programs. Within the No Child Left Behind Act, phrases like "scientifically based research" appear more than 100 times (Olson & Viadero, 2002). Like CSRD, this legislation also places a premium on randomized experiments for developing and assessing new and innovative practices, as the following excerpt suggests: "The Secretary shall evaluate the demonstration projects supported under this title, using rigorous methodological designs and techniques, including control groups and random assignment, to the extent feasible, to produce reliable evidence of effectiveness" (No Child Left Behind Act of 2001, 115 Stat 1425, 1597). This legislation, urging the use of scientifically based educational methods and procedures, is meant to revolutionize not only the cornerstone of the ESEA, Title I schoolwide and targeted assistance programs for the disadvantaged, but also the Reading First and Early Reading First programs, the Even Start family literacy programs, services for limited English proficient students, and other federal initiatives.

Finally, established by the Education Sciences Reform Act of 2002 and under the leadership of Grover (Russ) Whitehurst, the Institute of Education Sciences—the research arm of the U.S. Department of Education—has led a prominent nationwide push to promote the use of randomized experiments for evidence-based decision making (Whitehurst, 2002). Since 2002, new grant competitions designed by IES have focused on the development of practical solutions to improve U.S. public schools and have emphasized application of high-quality methods of causal inference including, when possible, randomized designs. Also, in 2006, IES continued the federal commitment to educational R&D by funding 10 regional educational laboratories committed to providing policy makers and practitioners with expert advice, training, and technical assistance on how to interpret the latest findings from scientifically valid research pertaining to the requirements of NCLB (Bowler & Thomas, 2006). In instances where scientific evidence is not readily available and schools need appraisals of alternative strategies to improve learning, IES charged the laboratories to devote approximately one-third of their operating budgets to carrying out rigorous randomized trials to evaluate potentially promising practices and programs.

Recognizing a need to build the capacity within the educational research community to perform randomized trials, in 2004 IES also funded 18 universities to establish Pre- and Postdoctoral Interdisciplinary Research Training Programs in the Education Sciences (Pre- and Postdoctoral Interdisciplinary Research Training in the Education Sciences Home Page, n.d.). These programs receive support from IES to produce a cadre of education researchers capable of and willing to conduct a new generation of methodologically rigorous and educationally relevant scientific research that will provide solutions to pressing problems and challenges facing American education. Fellows completing these training programs receive financial support and access to specialized resources and experts in the field of study and become part of an emerging national network of students and faculty contributing to the field of education sciences by conducting rigorous evaluation studies, developing new products and approaches that are grounded in a science of learning, and designing valid tests and measures.

These recent developments, among others, have begun to produce important changes in the national educational R&D infrastructure. It was not long ago that many other fields, including medicine, agriculture, and technology, were at similar turning points. These fields, among others, have benefited humanity through remarkable advances over the 20th century. Over the last 50 years in medicine, for instance, clinical advances tested through randomized clinical trials have virtually eliminated diseases such as polio, measles, mumps, and rubella and hundreds of thousands of Americans have been saved from other life-threatening conditions, such as coronary heart disease and stroke. Indeed, it is difficult to overstate the magnitude of the effect that randomized trials have had on the lives of Americans. Education now appears to be on the same brink of rapid development and innovation.

The question remains: Will educational R&D respond to calls for more rigorous research and will researchers help the field take advantage of this unusual opportunity? Is the scientific model of R&D one that can be applied to questions in education? Can experimentation lead to the widespread dissemination of educational programs and practices that are truly research proven? In this chapter, I provide a brief overview of the logic of experiments, present several tensions that have inhibited the widespread application of experiments to questions in education, and discuss several ways that researchers may apply experiments to the special circumstances surrounding educational policy.

To help develop and improve programs and practices in U.S. schools and classrooms, research methods must separate fact from advocacy, provide the most believable results, and inform with great confidence the question, "what works?" The field of educational research is highly variegated. As Labaree (1998) noted, this can be both a blessing and a curse. It is a blessing in that the various methodologies and perspectives create a rich, vibrant, and democratic discourse about what really matters in education and what should be done to improve it. It is a curse because all too often this diversity in educational research is perceived as confusion and contradiction and, as a result, little consensus seems to emerge about what needs improvement and how we should go about doing it. As Cook and Payne (2002) noted, many features of educational research are today healthy, particularly as concerns historical scholarship, the use of surveys to describe students, classrooms, schools, and districts, the use of individual measures to assess students' academic performance, and the use of longitudinal methods to measure change in student outcomes. The use of qualitative methods also has benefited the field of education in describing and analyzing the interactions and processes that occur within schools and classrooms. For the reasons outlined below, I also believe that the best answers to questions like "what works" or "what makes a difference" come from one type of study: the experiment. It is also quite clear that this sort of evidence in education is extremely limited.

The Logic of Experiments

What is an experiment and what makes it such a potentially powerful design for causal inference? The most familiar examples of experiments are those that take place in controlled laboratory settings or those that occur in the area of health, where each person or group is randomly assigned to receive either a new drug or medical treatment or a placebo or no treatment. The central element that distinguishes a true experiment from all other methods of research is the random assignment of alternate treatments to the individuals or groups involved in the study. Another important, though not unique, component of the randomized experiment is that it involves conscious manipulation of the environment. Typically, the new intervention is assigned at random to one set of individuals or groups, the treatment group, and is withheld from another set of individuals or groups, the no-treatment or control group. In other cases, though, the researcher may not have a true no-treatment control group and may decide, instead, to assign randomly individuals or groups to different types of interventions, or to conditions providing varying intensities or versions of a single intervention model. In these cases, we may discern the relative effects of interventions rather than their absolute effects.

The process of randomization also needs not to be confined to the laboratory. Randomized field trials in education, for instance, may take place in the natural surroundings of classrooms and schools. Field trials introduce a variety of complexities—most notably assuring that the treatment group actually received the treatment as it was intended and that the control group did not receive the treatment—but they generally provide results that will help researchers and policy makers best understand the effects one can expect from an intervention once it is implemented beyond the laboratory in the "real world" of schools and classrooms.

One can understand the logic and statistical theory of randomized experiments by applying Rubin's causal model (Holland, 1986; Rubin, 1974). Rubin's causal model considers each participant in an experiment to have two theoretical outcomes: the outcome, Y_T, she would have attained if assigned to the treatment group, and the outcome Y_C, she would have attained if assigned to the control condition. The causal effect of the treatment for a participant is simply the difference between her two theoretical outcomes, $Y_T - Y_C$. The problem, though, is that this person-specific effect generally remains hypothetical, in that it is not usually observable because participants are assigned to the treatment or control condition but not to both. As a result, we must estimate the average person-specific causal effect of treatment based on the outcomes for the two distinct groups of participants who were assigned to the treatment and control groups. Specifically, if μ_T is the population mean outcome when all participants are assigned to the treatment and μ_C is the population mean outcome when all participants are assigned to the control group, the population causal effect is $\delta = \mu_T - \mu_C$. If we have a randomized experiment in which the sample mean outcomes, $\bar{y}_T$ and $\bar{y}_C$, are from, respectively, participants randomly assigned to the treatment and control group, taking the difference between these sample means, $\bar{y}_T - \bar{y}_C$, provides an unbiased estimate of δ. In other words, the randomized experiment produces

an outcome for the control group that accurately represents what the treatment group's outcome would have been in the absence of the intervention—the counterfactual. Therefore, any observed differences between the two groups' outcomes can be understood as the causal effect of the intervention.

The reason that we can be sure that the intervention caused the differences in the outcome is that the assignment of participants to the treatment and control conditions is independent of all other variables that may have confounded this casual interpretation. That is, if we begin with a sample of individuals, classrooms, or schools that is representative of a known population, using random assignment allows us to draw two samples, a treatment and control group, that are representative of the original population and that are comparable to one another. In assigning people or units to the two groups at random, in expectation we will form two groups that are, on average, equivalent with respect to things that we can measure, such as baseline achievement levels, motivation, and socioeconomic status, and other things that we may not have measured or even considered. It is not inevitable that the two groups will be comparable, but if the random assignment is done properly and if the samples are large enough, it will result in two groups that will be essentially the same, except that one group receives the intervention and the other does not. From such a sample, we are in a unique position to generate an unbiased estimate of the causal effect of a treatment.

Ruling Out Selection Bias and Confounds

The principal reason to conduct a randomized study is to help rule out selection bias and confounds such that we can isolate the effect of one independent variable—for example, whether or not a student was assigned to receive an educational intervention—on the dependent variables, including test scores, graduation rates, and academic engagement. Other designs do not rule out competing explanations, or rival hypotheses, regarding the outcomes observed for the treatment group to the extent that true experiments do. As a result, an increasing body of evidence has emerged suggesting that such comparison-group studies in social policy (e.g., employment, training, welfare-to-work, education) generally produce inaccurate estimates of an intervention's effects, because of unobservable differences between the intervention and comparison groups that differentially affect their outcomes (Glazerman, Levy, & Myers, 2002). It is also the case that when one compares directly randomized experiments and non-experiments that were designed to answer the same research questions, the non-experiments provide more highly variable estimates of the treatment effects (Bloom, 2005; Lipsey & Wilson, 1993). This result can be explained by the fact that experimental estimates of treatment effects have but one source of random error—the error attributable to sampling a finite number of individuals or units—its standard error reflects a single component. On the other hand, non-experimental estimates have two sources of error: the same sampling error to which the experiment is subject and non-experimental mismatch error. Reflecting both components, the standard error of the non-experimental estimator is necessarily larger that that of its corresponding experimental estimator if the non-experimental comparison group and the experimental control group are the same size (Bloom, 2005). In this way, non-experiments are less efficient than true experiments.

Researchers conducting non-experiments apply a range of statistical procedures in attempts to control selection bias and confounds. Some methods have shown promise, including those that generate probabilistic models of the selection process of groups or individuals into the program and that use the predicted probability that one will enter the treatment group as a covariate in the analysis (Rosenbaum & Rubin, 1983). These methods, though, clearly lack the intuitive and transparent qualities of randomized experiments. As Burtless (2002) noted, this simplicity and rigor makes the results convincing to other scholars and understandable to policy makers and practitioners. A carefully conducted experiment allows the researcher to describe the results in very straightforward and convincing language, for instance: "a new reading program boosted the test scores of the students in the treatment group by X% over the control group." This simplicity is usually not possible in non-experimental studies in which complex statistical procedures are used—in general to rule out selection bias and make equivalent groups that are not—to generate findings that are subject to a bewildering number of qualifications.

The Application of Experiments to Education Policy Research

In other fields within the social sciences, including economics and criminology, there has been a considerable increase in the number of randomized experiments over the last 50 years (Boruch, de Moya, & Snyder, 2002). Since the 1948 watershed in medicine, the randomized controlled trial of streptomycin for treating polio, there has been an increase in the number of large trials involving 100 or more participants (McDonald, Westby, Clarke, Lefebvre, & The Cochrane Centre's Working Group on 50 Years of Randomized Trials, 2002). As most other fields have placed increasing emphasis on randomized experiments, education has lagged behind. Nave, Meich, and Mosteller (1999) showed that less than 1% of dissertations in education or of the studies archived in ERIC Abstracts involved randomized experiments. Boruch and his colleagues (2002) found that just one of 84 program evaluations and studies planned by the Department of Education for fiscal year 2000 involved a randomized field trial.

In discussing many of the major issues in education today, Cook (2001) pointed to the lack of experimental evidence available to evaluate the effects of virtually every policy. This general lack of evidence is apparent when one considers three educational policy areas most recently and most strongly tied to higher standards of evidence: Title I of the No Child Left Behind Act, the CSRD program, and the

federally sponsored What Works Clearinghouse (WWC). Despite an annual expenditure of approximately $13 billion in 2006 and its 42-year history, Title I itself has never been subjected to randomized trials (Borman & D'Agostino, 1996). Although the recent CSRD legislation suggested that schools should adopt only those comprehensive school reform (CSR) models with solid evidence of effectiveness, a comprehensive meta-analysis of 232 studies of the achievement outcomes associated with 29 of the most widely implemented models found only 7 completed studies, or about 3%, of all studies on the achievement effects associated with CSR had generated evidence from randomized experiments (Borman, Hewes, Overman, & Brown, 2003). Finally, the WWC, which collects, screens, and identifies studies of the effectiveness of various programs, products, practices, and policies that could be implemented in schools using federal funds, has not identified overwhelming experimental evidence either. In assessing the research base to support programs, products, practices, and policies from across various topic areas including beginning reading, character education, dropout prevention, early childhood education, elementary school math, English language learners, and middle school math curricula, the WWC found strong evidence of positive effects from randomized trials for only 18 of the 88 interventions reviewed (What Works Clearinghouse Home Page, 2008).

Recently, several authors have provided compelling explanations for the rarity of randomized trials in education. Cook and Payne (2002) contended that many influential theorists of educational evaluation have explicitly rejected randomized experiments. The elitist scientific model suggested by experimentation is not in accord with the ontology, epistemology, or methodology that educational researchers prefer, they do not believe that randomization is practical, and they do not consider it to be compatible with their preferred metaphor of schools as complex social organizations that should be improved using the tools of management consulting more than science. As a result, most experiments in education have been done by scholars with appointments in public health, psychology, economics, and the policy sciences. Cook and Payne stated that for more experiments to take place, R&D in schools will require different intellectual assumptions from those now prevalent among evaluation specialists in schools of education.

Burtless (2002) identified several other obstacles to random assignment in education. First, relative to states and localities, the federal government plays a minor role in funding elementary and secondary education and in establishing policy. Thus, even with growing federal support for randomized trials, Burtless argued that there may be limited political support to champion randomization as a major research tool. Second, many people have ethical troubles with random assignment in education because it involves denying potentially beneficial treatments to teachers or students, who are all regarded as "deserving." Third, random assignment often requires that teachers and administrators provide researchers with some authority over curriculum, student placements, or pedagogical technique. Yet, most educators resist surrendering authority to people they do not consider professionally competent to judge their work. Finally, educators, parents, and students are far from politically weak. If there are suspicions concerning the ethics or general merits of random assignment, they have many formal and informal channels through which to register their opposition.

Clearly, these and other considerations make randomization difficult in educational settings. In reviewing the problems cited by Cook and Payne (2002), Burtless (2002), and by others, three general themes emerge. First, if randomization is to be more widely accepted and implemented in education, the ethical and political dilemma of withholding services must be addressed. Second, randomized field trials must be adapted to fit the messy and complex world of schools and classrooms. Third, continued development of a strong centralized, federal role is needed to foster and sustain experimentation and improvement of educational practices. In the following sections, I discuss these three themes and offer practical suggestions of how they may be addressed. Based on lessons learned in the field of medicine and based on my own experiences conducting randomized experiments, I believe that these problems are not insurmountable and, indeed, may be addressed directly and constructively by educational researchers.

The Ethical and Political Dilemma of Withholding Services

Experiments are not always desirable or useful. It should be clear by now that they help answer cause-effect questions: Is the program, practice, or intervention effective, does it make a difference, what is the effect, and for whom does the service work best? If the researcher is not interested in answering a causal question, there is, obviously, no need for a randomized experiment. What other criteria are important to consider in justifying the need for randomized trials and in justifying withholding services from students and teachers who might benefit from the intervention? First, the effectiveness of the intervention, or the relative effectiveness of two or more competing services, must be in some doubt. Second, if there are limited opportunities to participate in the intervention, random assignment can be a fair and equitable way to allocate the scarce resources. If the researcher and stakeholders do not know which intervention is preferable, or if there are not adequate resources to serve everyone who might benefit from a program, a randomized experiment is a logical and ethical alternative to consider.

Silverman and Chalmers (2001) reminded us that the idea of casting or drawing lots to help deal with uncertainty and assure fairness has been accepted for millennia. From events that were akin to experiments in the Bible, to military draft lotteries dating back to the 17th century, to the decision of who should win the investments of the millions of people who bought lottery tickets, societies through the ages have depended on processes similar to the modern methods of random assignment. Silverman and Chalmers further argued that these methods have helped physicians in making life and death decisions and have helped transform medicine from a practice dominated by the opinions of authorities to one based on rules of evidence. Indeed, as the observations of Sir Richard Doll (1998), a noted British epidemiologist, made clear, opinion and uncertainty had a strong history in medicine:

> When I qualified in medicine in 1937, new treatments were almost always introduced on the grounds that in the hands of professor A … the results in a small series of patients … had been superior to those recorded by professor B … The treatment of peptic ulcer was, perhaps, more susceptible to claims of benefit than most other chronic diseases; so that in 1948, when I began to investigate it, I was soon able to prepare a list of treatments beginning with each letter of the alphabet. Standard treatments, for their part, tended to be passed from one textbook to another without ever being adequately evaluated. (p. 1217)

Today, physicians may not always know the best treatment or medication for a particular condition, but the widespread use of clinical trials in medicine has underscored the point that it is unethical not to find out. The medical advances made and lives that have been saved through randomized trials reveal the true ethical character of basing decisions on evidence.

The similarities within education are striking. Historically, the primary technology of education, teaching, has been fraught with what Lortie (1975) called "endemic uncertainties." The work of teachers is not usually driven by scientific knowledge of the efficacy of their practices, but, instead, tends to be reinforced by "psychic rewards" that teachers feel when they reach their students. As a result, key instructional decisions within the classroom are driven and perpetuated by highly subjective criteria that often have no foundation in evidence on what works. These subjective decisions are often reinforced by the highly variable and politicized nature of educational policymaking that occurs beyond the classroom, as Slavin and Fashola (1998) described it:

> Change in educational practice more resembles change in fashion; hemlines go up and down according to popular tastes, not evidence. We do give lip service to research in education. Yet practices from use of phonics in beginning reading to use of ability grouping in secondary schools go in and out of fashion, often in direct contradiction to well-established evidence, but more often in the absence of adequately rigorous and compelling research. (p. 6)

Akin to the importance of a physician's bedside manner, which is generally not the subject of scientific inquiry nor dictated by evidence, not every educational practice could or should be formed based on research, and the schooling of children, indeed, benefits from the humanity of a caring teacher. Education is not an exact science, but it is too important to allow so much of it to be determined by unfounded technologies and general opinions, whether of politicians, teachers, researchers or anyone else. Researching and developing the best quality educational interventions to promote the healthy cognitive development of children is as important as promoting the best medical procedures to improve children's general health.

The conditions under which a researcher may conduct a randomized experiment that responds to legitimate and important ethical concerns are somewhat limited. For some practitioners and researchers, the idea of withholding potentially beneficial interventions, even under these limited circumstances, is simply not one that is comprehensible. For instance, when interventions, such as compensatory education programs, are assigned based on need and it is known that the program responds particularly well to that need, the most reasonable and ethical solution may be assignment to the most needy children rather than assignment by lottery. This position, of course, presumes that the intervention has proven to be beneficial when, as both practitioners and researchers, we share a history of uncertainty about the efficacy of a range of educational programs and practices. Even in medicine, only half of the new treatments subjected to randomized experiments actually show benefits beyond the standard treatments patients would have received (Gilbert, McPeek, & Mosteller, 1977). Concern should also be shown for the ethics of mandating unproven educational policies or implementing programs with unknown potentials. Without the benefit of evaluation through randomized trials, many widely implemented educational practices have simply wasted the time of teachers and students, and others, including compensatory education pullout programs and the use of tracking, have been regarded by some researchers as counterproductive and potentially harmful.

Sometimes even more prominent than ethical considerations are the political problems associated with random assignment. As Gueron (2002) noted, it is far more difficult, and may even be illegal or unethical, to use a lottery to deny services that would have been received in the absence of research. On the other hand, randomization is far more politically viable when it offers new and enriched resources or services that would not have existed if it had not been for the research. These points are illustrated by contrasting the experiences with random assignment in two recent studies. Only after very intensive national outreach efforts spanning two years and the offer of substantial incentives to both treatment and control schools did we obtain a sufficient sample of 41 schools to agree to be randomized for the recently completed trial involving the Success for All program (Borman et al., 2007). Rather than strictly ethical concerns for students, administrators far more often suggested that they faced political pressures to raise test scores. Leaving their schools' accountability up to, essentially, the flip of a coin was unpalatable to principals. They had to do something to improve their schools and, likely, to retain their jobs. These concerns weighed even more heavily on the minds of principals than the potential ethical considerations involved with random assignment.

In contrast, when a supplemental summer school program was offered to 10 high poverty schools in Baltimore, with the condition that a randomized process be used to allocate the limited number of seats in the program and to test its effects, principals were generally willing and eager participants (Borman & Dowling, 2006). At the time, Baltimore had no city-sponsored summer school programs and schools had few, if any, options for offering their students other summer learning opportunities. The chance to offer a promising program, even to a limited number of their students, allowed the schools to extend their services through participation in the experiment. Using rules of random assignment, every child and parent who applied to participate had the same fair chance of winning one of the limited number of spots available in the free pilot program. Some parents were disappointed that their child was not selected, but all were assured that no favoritism or preferential treatment was shown. The intuitive and democratic nature of this selection process appealed to nearly every parent who raised concerns about the matter.

In addition to the important idea that experiments can often overcome political obstacles by simply offering a fair process for distributing scarce resources that would not have existed in the absence of the trial, several other methodological and practical ideas can help overcome political opposition. First, researchers need not necessarily employ a balanced 50%–50% allocation of sample members to treatment and control groups. If there are resources available to serve 70% of the applicants interested in a new program, for instance, there are few methodological or practical reasons to deny services to individuals in order to achieve a balanced allocation to the alternate experimental groups. Generally overlooked is the fact that a design's precision erodes slowly as sample allocation departs from balance. Under conditions when the homoscedasticity assumption is reasonable, researchers can construct samples with allocations to treatment ranging from 20% to 80% with little impact on the precision of the design (Bloom, 2005). Such flexibility can be quite important when implementing randomized designs in the face of some political opposition.

Second, it is sometimes desirable to utilize pre-randomization blocking to guarantee equitable distribution of new treatments across groups. For instance, if several school districts were interested in implementing a new school reform program in some of their struggling schools, a strict random assignment design with no blocking could produce imbalances in the assignment of schools to treatment across districts. By chance, some districts may have a large number of schools assigned to treatment while others have only a few. By blocking by district before randomization and by conducting the random assignment of schools within each of the districts using the same selection probability, the researcher can guarantee an equitable distribution of the treatment across the districts and can also achieve a more representative sample across the districts having enhanced face validity.

Finally, another benefit of the experimental design that has an important bearing on overcoming political opposition to random assignment resides in the evidence it can produce for the stakeholders. For instance, in the previously mentioned trial of summer school in Baltimore, our arguments that the experiment could help produce high-quality evidence that could convince school officials and policy makers to expand the availability of summer programming in the future were met with great enthusiasm from principals and parents alike. On the other hand, if the trial suggested that the summer program was not particularly effective, this evidence could provide valuable formative information that could help students benefit more from subsequent implementations of the program. In this sense, the delayed treatment afforded the control group after the study can sometimes be the preferred treatment relative to the unstudied pilot innovation offered during the experimental phase.

Experimenting in the Complex Environments of Schools and Classrooms

Scholars have observed that schooling occurs within a complex and multilevel system (Barr, Dreeben, & Wiratchai, 1983). Federal policies affect how states operate their school systems, states mandate district-level requirements, districts influence school-level policies, school-level leadership affects classrooms, and classrooms and subgroups (e.g., reading groups of "robins," "blue birds," and "sparrows") within them affect the content, pace, duration, and quality of instruction. How can such a complicated and multivariate setting be studied through the relatively simple causal connections suggested by experimental designs?

In addition, Cook and Payne (2002) argued that the prevailing theories of change in education are not consistent with the scientific model of experimentation and improvement. These authors contended that the prominent beliefs in education are based on assumptions from management consulting, which suggests that educational organizations are so complex and distinctive that any one change attempt will lead to quite variable responses, depending on a school's history, organization, personnel, and politics. As a consequence, Cook and Payne suggested that educational change ideas typically come from the creative blending of many different kinds of knowledge—deep historical and ethnographic insight into the district or school under study, craft knowledge about what is likely to improve this particular school or district, and the application of existing general theories of organizational change. Seen from this perspective, the causal knowledge provided by randomized experiments will obscure each school's unique qualities, will oversimplify the nature and explanation of change, and will fail to create knowledge that educators can use to improve their schools.

Typical "black box" experiments may have some of these drawbacks. The Tennessee class size study has received considerable deserved attention for providing high-quality experimental evidence on the effects of class-size reductions in the early elementary grades (Mosteller, Light, &

Sachs, 1996). The study, though, provided considerably less information regarding the actual mechanisms through which the reductions in class size promoted improved student outcomes. Fortunately, a reduction in class size is a relatively straightforward and replicable policy. However, one can imagine a number of ways in which the reduced class sizes helped raise student achievement, for example through improved behavioral management, through more one-on-one help offered to students by the teachers, or by promoting teachers' use of more complex instructional strategies. Indeed, it is possible that alternative, and potentially less costly interventions than reductions in class size, such as a high-quality professional development program on behavioral management, could promote similar effects to those found for the STAR experiment. Randomized trials that take the typical black-box approach to studying program effects often miss the important nuances of the intervention's effects and may fail to create reliable knowledge that will help improve schools.

Recent thought on evaluation and educational change, though, presents the researcher with a variety of methods for dealing with these complexities and uncertainties. First, in many circumstances mixed-method designs can combine the strengths of qualitative research with randomized experiments and uncover the actual school and classroom processes and practices that underlie causal effects. This combination of findings is likely to provide practitioners and policy makers better information about how to improve practice. Second, researchers in search of causal effects can define and implement experimental interventions that represent discrete and clear proximal causes of student outcomes. For instance, Cohen, Raudenbush, and Ball (2002) suggested that instructional practices, rather than general school resources, should be viewed as the proximal causes of learning. In this scheme, the causal effects of instruction would provide a clear foundation for educational improvement. Ways of supporting specific instructional techniques within schools and districts of varying contexts might then be designed and evaluated. Third, randomized experiments that are composed of relatively large and heterogeneous samples of schools and districts allow researchers to test causal effects over a range of contexts. These studies can address empirically the extent to which treatment effects generalize across diverse settings and can generate casual conclusions that are sensitive to context. The clear tradeoff with an experiment is that some schools will receive the innovation now and others assigned to the control condition will receive the program later, if it proves to be worthwhile and effective. Approaches such as these are necessary to facilitate replication of practices that improve student learning and that help educators understand how to adapt the model of improvement to their specific circumstances.

Recent approaches to advancing educational change, most notably through the movement toward school-based adoption of externally developed educational interventions, also have strong implications for these perceptions of schools as highly distinctive and complex institutions that are resistant to research-based models of change. The Success for All program, for instance, which is a relatively uniform and consistent intervention implemented across high-poverty schools throughout the United States, has been scaled up to thousands of schools serving over 1 million children (Slavin & Madden, 2001). This development, and the increasing use of a variety of other externally developed educational interventions, shows that research-based models of educational improvement can be successfully replicated across many schools and children from varying contexts. There are adaptations that are sensitive to context—for instance there is a Spanish version of the Success for All program, *Exito Para Todos*, designed for English language learners—but the general models of school improvement also include well-founded and widely applicable instructional and organizational components that are likely to work under a variety of situations.

The complexities of school systems also may result in less-than-ideal program implementations or imperfect compliance with participants' treatment assignments. Again, these issues point to the importance of collecting data that will help differentiate between the treatment that participants received as a result of random assignment and the treatment that they received in reality. The implications of this distinction may also be meaningfully understood by applying two classes of analytical methods to the resulting data. First, an intention-to-treat (ITT) analysis requires that individuals be analyzed in the groups they were randomized into, regardless of whether they complied with the treatment they were given or received the full dose of the program implementation. This type of analysis tends to generate a more conservative, and generally more realistic, estimate of the treatment effect than an analysis of only those individuals who complied with their original treatment assignment or those who received the full dose of the program implementation. If one were to analyze only compliant individuals, the control and experimental groups defined by compliance would no longer be formed on the basis of randomization and are, thus, subject to bias. Also, the groups defined by compliance may not accurately represent the practical impact of the treatment, as similar noncompliance is likely to occur in implementations of the program beyond the experiment in replications. In this way, the effect that is estimated through an ITT analysis is often likely to provide policy makers an indication of the program effect that can be expected in typical school settings in which students and schools often do not fully comply with program assignments.

To complement the ITT analysis, other methods may be applied to understand the impact of receiving the full treatment. In a randomized experiment with full treatment compliance, analyzing this result is simply a matter of comparing the treatment and control groups' outcome measures as in an ITT analysis. In many studies, though, assignment to treatment and control conditions is random but treatment compliance is not perfect. There may be a range of attendance rates among students assigned to the treatment group

or there may be a range of program implementation levels among schools. For instance, Borman and Dowling (2006) found a range of attendance rates among students assigned to a voluntary summer school program, from those who were "no shows" to those with perfect attendance. In such cases, a simple comparison between treatment and control outcomes is an investigation of the effect of intention to treat rather than the effect of the full treatment.

Drawing on Rubin's causal model, a Complier Average Causal Effect (CACE) analysis may distinguish classes of individuals or schools who actively participated in a program versus those who did not. For those schools or students randomized into the program group, their treatment compliance is observed, but for schools or students in the control group membership in the compliant or non-compliant group is missing. Thus, for controls, treatment compliance may be viewed as a latent categorical variable. The application of a latent variable mixture model provides one method to identify among the control students those who would have complied with the treatment, had they been assigned to treatment, and then to compare the outcomes of these would-be compliers with the outcomes for the actual treatment compliers (Little & Yau, 1998; Muthén, 2001). These concepts and methods, which originated with Bloom's (1984) no-show adjustment and also include the instrumental variables approach proposed by Angrist, Imbens, and Rubin (1996), provide the means for adjusting the experimental ITT estimate to calculate an estimate of the effect of the treatment on the treated. Though this estimate is nonexperimental, it often provides important supplementary information that helps stakeholders understand the potential effects of the treatment when it is implemented as intended.

A Federal Role in Fostering Experimentation

Largely fueled by the leadership provided by IES, there has been a strong federal commitment over the past five years to a guiding premise that the key to progress in education is scientific research and evaluation together with systematically collected data on education performance. Indeed, these efforts have, in many ways, been inspired by what evidence-based health care has done for the health profession. With the early success of the polio vaccine randomized trials, one might think that the medical profession saw a rapid acceptance and expansion of experiments. This was not the case. It was not until such studies were demanded by federal policy makers as a requirement for the licensing of new drugs that the randomized controlled trial became widely accepted and used in medicine (Doll, 1998). The 1962 Kefauver-Harris Amendments to the Food, Drug, and Cosmetic Act, as implemented by the Food and Drug Administration (FDA), required that the effectiveness of any new drug be demonstrated in randomized controlled trials before the FDA would approve it for marketing. This legislation, along with significant federal funding for randomized trials through the National Institutes of Health (NIH), was the primary reason for the proliferation of randomized controlled trials in medicine (Chassin, 1998). Chassin noted that between 1966 and 1995, the number of clinical research articles based on randomized trials increased from approximately 100 to 10,000 annually.

In education, nationally disseminated interventions, such as the Comer School Development Program and Success for All whole-school reform models, the I CAN Learn pre-algebra and algebra computerized intervention, and the Open Court Reading and Everyday Mathematics curricula, are being invented and scaled up across the country. The implementation of these interventions, especially within high-poverty schools, is largely supported by various federal funding sources, including Title I and Reading First. Yet, only a few of such programs have convincing experimental or non-experimental evidence of their effects on student outcomes. If the federal government were to restrict funding to only those educational interventions that have been rigorously evaluated—similar to the FDA's standards for pre-marketing drug approval—there would be few interventions from which schools could choose.

To develop an evidence-based field, the efforts and funds of the federal government can be productively applied toward continued development and dissemination of clear standards of evidence, through the WWC and other organizations, and by continuing investments in formative and summative evaluations of a variety of educational interventions. Scholars in fields other than education, such as medicine and public health, agree that randomized experiments provide the "gold standard" for evidence on the effects of new treatments (Jorland, Opinel, & Weisz, 2005). This type of information is also vital for understanding the casual effects of educational interventions. It is not, however, the only information that is needed to develop and evaluate new educational innovations. Like the series of studies required in the FDA's pre-marketing drug approval process, a similar set of studies should guide the research, development, and ultimate dissemination of educational programs. First, qualitative, descriptive, and survey research is needed to understand the current parameters of educational problems. The data sets produced by the National Center for Education Statistics, such as the National Assessment of Educational Progress (NAEP), address many important issues, including historical achievement trends for the United States and for various student subgroups. These data sets also provide correlational data to help us understand, for instance, potential barriers to implementing standards-based reform in Title I schools and how implementation may be associated with other general contextual and organizational factors of school systems. Second, specific models of how Title I, or other federal programs, can support standards-based reform could be observed as small qualitative case studies or relatively small quantitative studies, which would help reveal the general promise of the approaches, troubles with implementation, sustainability of the efforts, and unexpected side effects of the reforms.

Third, after identifying a smaller number of promising and replicable models of standards-based reform initia-

tives, effects on students, and others, could be evaluated through the use of randomized designs or well-designed non-experimental studies. The programs that showed convincing effects through a variety of methods, including randomized trials, could then be disseminated and funded through Title I or other federal resources to interested school systems. Follow-up studies would assess the long-term consequences of the reforms on student outcomes and would investigate whether unforeseen complications arose in the implementation of the interventions. Government policy regarding pharmaceutical drugs and many medical procedures requires the accumulation of a similar series of experimental and non-experimental evidence before those drugs or procedures are allowed on the market. Applying this process to education would, in the same way, promote the development, dissemination, and funding of school-based treatments that work.

Donald Campbell (1969) related a famous vision for educational and social reform through experimentation:

> The United States and other modern nations should be ready for an experimental approach to social reform, an approach in which we try out new programs designed to cure specific social problems, in which we learn whether or not these programs are effective, and in which we retain, imitate, modify, or discard them on the basis of apparent effectiveness on the multiple imperfect criteria available. (p. 409)

We may, indeed, be on the brink of the "experimenting society" Campbell had envisioned, in which we may take advantage of unbiased assessments of the effects of social and educational interventions to better the country. As Cook and Payne (2002) suggested, though, educational researchers and practitioners may not be easily convinced of the merits of randomized designs. In certain situations randomized experiments will not be ethical to implement, and, if conceived as a "black box," they may not provide the information needed to truly understand the process of change and the implications of it. Randomized experiments are not replacements for the variety of other methods in educational research. However, policy makers and practitioners should demand the best evidence on the effects of educational interventions. As researchers in nearly every other discipline, and especially in medicine, already acknowledge, the experiment is the best method for establishing the causal effects of innovations.

References

Angrist, J. D., Imbens, G. W., & Rubin, D. B. (1996). Identification of causal effects using instrumental variables. *Journal of the American Statistical Association, 91*, 444–455.

Barr, R., Dreeben, R., & Wiratchai, N. (1983). *How schools work.* Chicago: University of Chicago Press.

Bloom, H. S. (1984). Accounting for no shows in experimental evaluation designs. *Evaluation Review, 8*, 225–246.

Bloom, H. S. (Ed.). (2005). *Learning more from social experiments: Evolving analytic approaches.* New York: Russell Sage Foundation.

Borman, G. D., & D'Agostino, J. V. (1996). Title I and student achievement:

A meta-analysis of federal evaluation results. *Educational Evaluation and Policy Analysis, 18,* 309–326.

Borman, G. D., & Dowling, N. M. (2006). The longitudinal achievement effects of multi-year summer school: Evidence from the Teach Baltimore randomized field trial. *Educational Evaluation and Policy Analysis, 28,* 25–48.

Borman, G. D., Hewes, G., Overman, L. T., & Brown, S. (2003). Comprehensive school reform and achievement: A meta-analysis. *Review of Educational Research, 73,* 125–230.

Borman, G. D., Slavin, R. E., Cheung, A., Chamberlain, A., Madden, N., & Chambers, B. (2007). Final reading outcomes of the national randomized field trial of Success for All. *American Educational Research Journal, 44,* 701–731.

Boruch, R., de Moya, D., & Snyder, B. (2002). The importance of randomized field trials in education and related areas. In F. Mosteller & R. Boruch (Eds.), *Evidence matters: Randomized trials in education research* (pp. 50–79). Washington, DC: Brookings Institution.

Boruch, R., & Mosteller, F. (2002). Overview and new directions. In F. Mosteller & R. Boruch (Eds.), *Evidence matters: Randomized trials in education research* (pp. 1–14). Washington, DC: Brookings Institution.

Bowler, M., & Thomas, D. (2006). *Regional educational laboratories awarded* (press release). Retrieved June 2, 2008, from http://www.ed.gov/news/pressreleases/2006/03/03282006.html

Burtless, G. (2002). Randomized field trials for policy evaluation: Why not in education? In F. Mosteller & R. Boruch (Eds.), *Evidence matters: Randomized trials in education research* (pp. 179–197). Washington, DC: Brookings Institution.

Campbell, D. T. (1969). Reforms as experiments. *American Psychologist, 24,* 409–429.

Chassin, M. R. (1998). Is health care ready for six sigma quality? *The Milbank Quarterly, 76,* 565–591.

Cohen, D. K., Raudenbush, S. W., & Ball, D. L. (2002). Resources, instruction, and research. In F. Mosteller & R. Boruch (Eds.), *Evidence matters: Randomized trials in education research* (pp. 80–119). Washington, DC: Brookings Institution.

Cook, T. D. (2001). Sciencephobia: Why education researchers reject randomized experiments. *Education Next, 1*(3), 63–68.

Cook, T. D., & Payne, M. R. (2002). Objecting to the objections to using random assignment in educational research. In F. Mosteller & R. Boruch (Eds.), *Evidence matters: Randomized trials in education research* (pp. 150–178). Washington, DC: Brookings Institution.

Doll, R. (1998). Controlled trials: The 1948 watershed. *British Medical Journal, 317,* 1217–1220.

Gilbert, J., McPeek, B., & Mosteller, F. (1977). Statistics and ethics in surgery and anesthesia. *Science, 198,* 684–689.

Glazerman, S., Levy, D. M., & Myers, D. (2002). *Nonexperimental replications of social experiments: A systematic review.* Princeton, NJ: Mathematica Policy Research, Inc.

Gueron, J. (2002). The politics of random assignment: Implementing studies and affecting policy. In F. Mosteller & R. Boruch (Eds.), *Evidence matters: Randomized trials in education research* (pp. 15–49). Washington, DC: Brookings Institution.

Guthrie, J. W. (1990). Education R&D's lament (and what to do about it). *Educational Researcher, 19*(2), 26–34.

Holland, P. (1986). Statistics and causal inference. *Journal of the American Statistical Association, 91,* 444–472.

Jorland, G., Opinel, A., & Weisz, G. (Eds.). (2005). Body counts: Medical quantification in historical and sociological perspectives. Montreal: Mc-Gill-Queen's University Press.

Labaree, D. F. (1998). Educational researchers: Living with a lesser form of knowledge. *Educational Researcher, 27*(8), 4–12.

Lipsey, M. W., & Wilson, D. B. (1993). The efficacy of psychological, educational, and behavioral treatment: Confirmation from meta-analysis. *American Psychologist, 48,* 1181–1209.

Little, R. J., & Yau, L. H. Y. (1998). Statistical techniques for analyzing data from prevention trials: Treatment of no-shows using Rubin's causal model. *Psychological Methods, 3,* 147–159.

Lortie, D.C. (1975). *Schoolteacher: A sociological study.* Chicago: University of Chicago Press.

McDonald, S., Westby, M., Clarke, M., Lefebvre, C., & The Cochrane Centre's Working Group on 50 Years of Randomized Trials (2002). Number and size of randomized trials reported in general health care journals from 1948 to 1997. *International Journal of Epidemiology, 31,* 125–127.

Mosteller, F., Light, R. J., & Sachs, J. A. (1996). Sustained inquiry in education: Lessons from skill grouping and class size. *Harvard Educational Review, 66,* 797–842.

Muthén, B. O. (2001). Second-generation structural equation modeling with a combination of categorical and continuous latent variables: New opportunities for latent class/latent growth modeling. In A. Sayer & L. Collins (Eds.), *New methods for the analysis of change* (pp. 291–322). Washington, DC: American Psychological Association.

Nave, B., Meich, E., & Mosteller, F. (1999). *A rare design: The role of field trials in evaluating school practices.* Paper presented at The American Academy of Arts and Sciences, Cambridge, MA.

No Child Left Behind Act of 2001, Pub L. No. 107-110, 115 Stat, 1425 (2002).

Olson, L., & Viadero, D. (2002). Law mandates scientific base for research. *Education Week, 21*(20), 1, 14–15.

Pre- and Postdoctoral Interdisciplinary Research Training in the Education Sciences Home Page. (n.d.). Retrieved June 2, 2008, from http://pirt.wceruw.org/

Rosenbaum, P., & Rubin, D. B. (1983). The central role of the propensity score in observational studies for causal effects. *Biometrika, 70,* 41–55.

Rubin, D. (1974). Estimating causal effects of treatments in randomized and nonrandomized studies. *Journal of Educational Psychology, 66,* 688–701.

Shavelson, R. J., & Towne, L. (Eds.). (2002). *Scientifically based research.* Washington, DC: National Academy Press. Retrieved April 24, 2008, from http://www.nap.edu/books/0309082919/html/R1.html

Silverman, W. A., & Chalmers, I. (2001). Casting and drawing lots: A time honoured way of dealing with uncertainty and ensuring fairness. *British Medical Journal, 323,* 1467–1468.

Slavin, R. E. (1997). Design competitions: A proposal for a new federal role in educational research and development. *Educational Researcher, 26*(1), 22–28.

Slavin, R. E., & Fashola, O. S. (1998). *Show me the evidence! Proven and promising programs for America's schools.* Thousand Oaks, CA: Corwin Press.

Slavin, R., & Madden, N. (2001). *One million children: Success for All.* Thousand Oaks, CA: Corwin Press.

Vinovskis, M. A. (1999). *History and educational policymaking.* New Haven, CT: Yale University Press.

What Works Clearinghouse Home Page. (2008). Retrieved June 2, 2008, from http://ies.ed.gov/ncee/wwc/

Whitehurst, G. (2002, April). *Charting a new course for the U.S. Office of Educational Research and Improvement.* Paper presented at the annual meeting of the American Educational Research Association, New Orleans, LA.

12

Causal Inference in Non-Experimental Educational Policy Research

David Kaplan[1]

University of Wisconsin–Madison

Introduction

With the passage of the No Child Left Behind Act (NCLB; 2002), attention has focused on the need for evidence-based educational research, particularly educational policies and interventions that rest on what NCLB refers to as "scientifically based research." In practice, this focus on scientifically based educational research has translated into a preference for research studies based on the principles of randomized experimental designs. Specifically, Part A, Section 9101 of the No Child Left Behind Act, under the definition "Scientifically Based Research" states:

> The term 'scientifically based research' (A) means research that involves the application of rigorous, systematic, and objective procedures to obtain reliable and valid knowledge relevant to education activities and programs; and (B) includes research that … (iv) is evaluated using experimental or quasi-experimental designs in which individuals, entities, programs, or activities are assigned to different conditions and with appropriate controls to evaluate the effects of the condition of interest, with a preference for random-assignment experiments, or other designs to the extent that those designs contain within-condition or across-condition controls …

Before proceeding, it may be useful to provide definitions of randomized experimental designs, quasi-experimental designs, and observational/non-experimental studies. Following Shadish, Cook, and Campbell (2002), a *randomized experiment* is "an experiment in which units are assigned to receive the treatment or alternative condition by a random process such as the toss of a coin or a table of random numbers" (p. 12). When a randomized experiment is properly conducted, the groups formed by random assignment are probabilistically equivalent to each other. A *quasi-experiment* is "an experiment in which units are not assigned to conditions randomly" (Shadish et al., 2002, p. 12). In quasi-experimental studies, units self-select into

treatment. Such self-selection can result in pre-treatment differences that may confound any causal conclusions drawn regarding the efficacy of the treatment. Careful use of various statistical controls can provide a degree of pre-treatment equivalence that can increase confidence in causal conclusions. Finally, a *correlational* study is "usually synonymous with non-experimental or observational study: a study that simply observes the size and direction of a relationship among variables" (Shadish et al., 2002, p. 12).

The underlying theory of randomization and the statistical equivalency it can provide is, arguably, the ostensible reason for its stated preference in NCLB. Indeed, this preference for experimental designs stated in NCLB has led to it being referred to as the "gold standard" for educational research. As an example, the standards of the U.S. Department of Education's Institute of Educational Sciences-sponsored "What Works Clearinghouse" brooks no room for non-experimental studies as meeting the standard. Quoting from the standards document:

> Studies that provide strong evidence for an intervention's effectiveness are characterized as *Meet Evidence Standards*. Studies that offer weaker evidence *Meet Evidence Standards with Reservations*. Studies that provide insufficient evidence … [*Do*] *Not Meet Evidence Screens*. In order to meet evidence standards (either with or without reservations), a study has to be a randomized controlled trial or a quasi-experiment with one of the following three designs: quasi-experiment with equating, regression discontinuity designs, or single-case designs. (U.S. Department of Education, 2008, p. 1)

Although randomized experimental and quasi-experimental designs can, under ideal conditions, provide a sound basis for evaluating causal claims, it does not preclude the possibility that reliable causal inferences can be drawn from non-experimental/observational settings where random assignment of units to treatments perhaps may not be practical or ethical. The choice of randomized experimental, quasi-experimental, or observational studies is dependent on a number of factors, the most important of which is that the choice be based on the research question being asked.

As will be described below, randomized experimental designs have the advantage of testing well-defined counterfactual claims. Moreover, when properly implemented, the randomized experiment controls for biases resulting from the self-selection of units to treatments. Under certain conditions, quasi-experiments can also provide control over self-selection. These strengths notwithstanding, randomized experimental designs and quasi-experimental designs are often employed to address efficacy questions that fit the model of a clinical drug trial and rest on fairly heroic assumptions—not the least of which is the need to rely on asymptotics to guarantee true statistical equivalency and that no systematic biases creep into the implementation of the treatment after randomization occur. A general critique of experimental designs can be found in Worrall (2002, 2004). Perhaps more importantly, however, certain kinds of educational policy questions might simply not be well-suited to experimental designs—particularly questions that involve testing the impact of numerous and complex counterfactual propositions while accounting for ongoing dynamics.

In contrast to the experimental design approach, there exists a non-experimental/observational approach to causal inference that is grounded in structural econometrics via the method of simultaneous equation modeling. The *structural* approach, as it will be referred to in this chapter, has had a long history in educational, psychological, and sociological research under the names *path analysis* and *structural equation modeling*. In this chapter I provide an overview of the structural approach for addressing problems in educational policy situated in non-experimental settings. It should be noted, though, that as with randomized experimental designs, the structural approach also rests on heroic assumptions. In particular, causal information encoded in over-identifying restrictions is often hard to justify, and, in practice, structural models often do not fit observed data. Nevertheless, I argue that a structural approach to non-experimental educational policy research can yield more than "… simply … the size and direction of a relationship among variables" (Shadish et al., 2002). However, for the structural approach to be employed successfully in the domain of educational policy research, a deeper synthesis of modern work on causal inference is required.

At the outset it must be noted that the topic of causation and causal inference is enormous, and space limitations preclude a comprehensive literature review and synthesis. Therefore, the literature examined in this chapter is highly selective and does not represent all of the extant scholarship on the problem. Rather, the focus of this chapter is on how a structural approach to educational policy analysis can yield reliable causal inferences when supported by a deeper philosophical understanding of causation. With this caveat in mind, the chapter will begin with a brief overview of David Hume's notions of causation, as it is Hume's writings

that permeate much of the relevant theoretical and practical work that followed. The chapter then examines the standard critique of Hume. Although there are serious critiques of Hume's position, his writings set the groundwork for the experimental design tradition as embodied in the work of J. S. Mill, D. Campbell and J. Stanley, and more recently, in Donald Rubin and Paul Holland's model of causal inference. The experimental tradition is then elucidated. The chapter then reviews somewhat more modern conceptions of causation, particularly the work of Mackie (1980) and Woodward (2003). I focus mainly on Mackie because, as I will argue, his work on counterfactuals serves to bridge the divide between the experimental tradition and the structural tradition. The chapter then proceeds to a discussion of causal inference from the structural econometric tradition embodied in the early work of Haavelmo (1943), and more recently in positions put forth by Hoover (1990, 2001) and Heckman (2000, 2005). Focus in this section will be on the idea of strengthening causal inferences in the context of observational studies; that is, examining the causes of effects so as to provide more accurate predictions derived from policy counterfactuals. Next, I will advance an argument that the structural approach is well-suited to a science and practice of educational policy analysis in non-experimental settings. I will adopt the manipulationist view of causal analysis (Woodward, 2003) embedded in the structural approach, but also bring in Mackie's earlier ideas on counterfactual propositions. The chapter closes with a general conclusion outlining some of the important work that is missing from this review.

Early Historical Foundation

Providing a review of the historical foundations of the problem of causation is a difficult task. One can start by examining work dating far back in recorded history—at least as far back as the ancient Greeks, and specifically Aristotle. However, for the purposes of a chapter that attempts to review the problem of causal inference as it relates to education policy analysis, it is convenient to start relatively more recently with the work of David Hume. The rationale for beginning with Hume is twofold. First, as discussed by Hoover (2001), Hume's work on problems of causation stemmed from problems of economic policy analysis, and therefore may be relevant to educational policy analysis. Indeed, Hume made very important contributions to the theory of money as it was understood in the 18th century. Second, much subsequent work on problems of causal inference can trace their origins to Hume's essential insights.

Hume's Philosophy of Causation Hume's position on causation is contained in two of his seminal books, *A Treatise of Human Nature* (1739/2000, Book 1, Part 3) and *An Enquiry Concerning Human Understanding* (1748/1999, §§4-8). In line with the philosophy of empiricism of his time, Hume viewed all human perception as arising from sense impressions. Intellectual ideas were no different, and were also considered by Hume to be based ultimately in sense impressions, but perhaps of a more ephemeral sort. Thus, for Hume the question arises as to what constitutes the sense impressions that give rise to the perception of a necessary connection between events.

For Hume, the outward sense impression that leads to the perception of necessary connection is one of the constant conjunction of events. Using the famous metaphor of billiard balls colliding with one another, Hume argued that three elements are required to give rise to an inward idea of cause and effect. The first requirement is spatial contiguity, with one ball moving after it is touched by another. The second requirement is that the cause precedes the effect. The third requirement is necessary connection in the sense that the cause must reliably give rise to the effect.

In Hume's analysis, the first two requirements reside in the outward sense experience, while the last requirement, the inner idea of necessary connection, arises in the mind. For Hume, the idea of a necessary connection arising from the empirical experiences of contiguity and constant conjunction gives rise to the inner idea of necessary connection.

It appears that Hume is drawing the negative conclusion that we can have no outward knowledge of necessary connection or, for that matter, the forces of nature at all. This view is consistent with Hume's classic critique of induction, which he articulates in *A Treatise of Human Nature*: "There can be no *demonstrative* arguments to prove that those instances, of which we have had no experience, resemble those, *of which we have had experience*" (1739/2000, Book 1, Part 3, §5, p. 62). For example, when an individual first experiences a billiard ball colliding with another and causing the second ball to move, that individual cannot logically form a general rule about future events. However, upon witnessing numerous instances of the same conjoined events, that individual will feel compelled to claim that they are necessarily connected, with one billiard ball moving—referred to as the cause and the other the moving upon being struck—referred to as the effect. Thus, necessary connection comes from the experience of numerous similar instances of conjunction. Hume argued though that this inductive fallacy is not mitigated by experiencing numerous like events any more than the experience of a single event. The only difference is that the experience of numerous instances of the event (unlike the single instance) leads the individual to feel that they are connected, and that now forecasting the future events is justified. This feeling of necessary connection is a habit or "custom" of the mind (Hume, 1739/2000).

At first glance, it appears that Hume was espousing an anti-realist position. However, as pointed out by Hoover (2001), Hume was a realist in the sense that he believed that there were indeed actual forces of nature independent of our senses that cause events to take place. But, Hume denied that necessary connection is independent of our senses. Returning to the metaphor of the billiard ball, Hume accepted that there were natural forces at work that caused a billiard ball to move upon being struck by another bil-

liard ball—Hume simply believed we could not know what those forces were. "We are never able, in a single instance, to discover any power or necessary connexion; any quality, which binds the effect to the cause, and renders the one an infallible consequence of the other" (Hume, 1748/1999, §6, Part 1, p. 136).

Despite this rather negative conclusion, Hume argued that there was virtually nothing more important than the understanding of cause and effect: "By means of it alone we attain any assurance concerning objects, which are removed from the present testimony of our memory and senses" (1748/1999, §29, p. 145). He further stated, "The only immediate utility of all sciences, is to teach us, how to control and regulate future events by their causes" (1748/1999, §29, p. 145). Given Hume's view that a causal connection arises in the mind as a function of observing the constant conjunction of events, he arrived at his definition of causation: "We may define a cause to be *an object, followed by another, and where all the objects, similar to the first, are followed by objects similar to second*. Or in other words *where, if the first object had not been, the second never had existed*" (1748/1999, §29, p. 146).

What is particularly noteworthy about this definition is the second part. What appeared to Hume as a synonymous rephrasing of his definition of causation is, in fact, two different ways of considering cause. The latter part, which is of major concern in this chapter, concerns the role of the counterfactual conditional proposition in a theory of causation. The role of the counterfactual conditional proposition figures predominantly in later theories of causation and will be a major focus of this chapter.

Critiques of Hume Hume's analysis of the problem of causation has been criticized on numerous grounds and was nicely summarized by Mackie (1980). For Mackie, perhaps the most serious problem relates to the condition of constant conjunction. Specifically, the argument that necessary connection arises in the mind after experiencing the constant conjunction of events, implies that constant conjunction is, indeed, constant—in other words, that the conjunction of events will always take place. But, by Hume's own critique of induction, this assumption is not tenable.

On the same point, Mackie (1980) noted that not all experience of constant conjunction can sensibly give rise to the idea of necessary connection. For example, Mackie asked, "… are there not causal sequences which nevertheless are not regular?" (p. 4). Mackie then answered his own question by giving an example of a coin toss. A coin toss is an indeterministic process, whereby each time I toss the coin, either it will land heads or land tails. Thus, on the one hand, tossing a coin is not a regular process, but on the other hand, surely my tossing the coin caused it to land heads. Mackie even questioned the necessity of assuming temporal precedence. He asked if there were not causes that could occur simultaneously with events. This latter concern is particularly crucial in the context of economic modeling as statistical models for supply and demand assume simultaneous causation (however, see Fisher, 1970, for a discussion of some of the temporal assumptions associated with simultaneous equation modeling).

More recently, Pearl (2000) pointed to three problems with Hume's definition of causation. First, regularity, or correlation, is simply not sufficient for causation—namely, counterfactual sentences—is comparable to regular succession. That is, regular succession is based on observation and counterfactuals are mental exercises (p. 238). Third, Hume's addition of counterfactuals came 9 years after his original definition that argued only for regularity. As noted earlier, a counterfactual condition for causation is not synonymous with the notion of regularity as stated in the first part of Hume's second definition nor his earlier regularity definition. On the basis of these problems, Mackie (1980) concluded that Hume's definition of causation was "imprecise and carelessly formulated" (p. 6).

The Experimental Tradition

Much more can be said regarding the problems with Hume's analysis of causation. For now, however, it is important to examine Hume's role in setting the stage for the problem of drawing causal inferences in experimental designs. In this section, I discuss three important contributions to the underlying theory of experimental designs and the conditions that give such designs their efficacy. The first contribution is that of John Stuart Mill who, following Hume, set down many of the conditions of experimental designs. Indeed, Mackie (1980) notes that Mill's work was a vast improvement on Hume insofar as Mill recognized the existence of what Mackie much later referred to as factors that could operate as conditions for causation. The second contribution is that of Campbell and Stanley, whose work on elucidating the threats to causal conclusions drawn from experimental designs, and how randomization can be used to address those threats, is considered the classic treatment on the subject. I also briefly examine extensions of Campbell and Stanley, including the work of Cook and Campbell. The third contribution is that of Rubin (1974) and Holland (1986), who provided the statistical underpinnings which give experimental designs their legitimacy in testing causal claims. The Rubin-Holland framework has focused the statistics and econometrics community on the counterfactual theory of causal inference.

John Stuart Mill In discussing the origins of the experimental tradition, it is safe to start with the ideas of Mill (1851). It should be noted, though, that many of Mill's ideas stemmed from some of Hume's basic thoughts about causation. Specifically, we find instances of Hume's contributions in Mill's different methods of experimental inquiry as espoused in *A System of Logic*. Nevertheless, Mill's ideas are fundamental to more modern treatments of experimental logic and design.

The goal for Mill (1851) was to isolate from the circumstances (that precede or follow a phenomenon) those which are linked to the phenomenon by some constant law (III.viii.1). That is, the approach taken by Mill is to test if a presumed causal connection exists by experiment—by observing the relevant phenomena under a variety of experimental situations. To take an example from education policy analysis, suppose we wish to know whether the reduction of class size causes improvement in achievement. How can this be proved? For Mill, causal inference rested on three factors. First, the cause must precede the effect; second, the cause and effect must be related, and third, other explanations for the cause-effect relationship must be ruled out. Mill's major contributions to experimental design concerned his work on the third factor for causal inference. Mill suggested three methods for dealing with this third factor. The first is the *Method of Agreement*, which states that the effect will be present when the cause is present. The second is the *Method of Difference*, which states that the effect will be absent when the cause is absent. The third is the *Method of Concomitant Variation*, which states that assuming the method of agreement and the method of difference are satisfied, and inference of causation is stronger when alternative reasons for the covariation between the cause and effect are eliminated.

Campbell and Stanley Perhaps the most important instantiation of Mill's codification of experimental logic, and the one that has had the most profound influence in experimental studies in the social and behavioral sciences, is the work of Campbell and Stanley (1966). In their small but seminal monograph *Experimental and Quasi-experimental Designs for Research*, Campbell and Stanley (1966) lay out the logic of experimental and quasi-experimental designs. They provide the major sources of confounding in these types of designs and describe their strengths and weaknesses with regard to internal versus external validity.

For Campbell and Stanley (1966), internal validity "is the basic minimum without which any experiment is uninterpretable" (p. 5). In contrast to internal validity, the external validity of an experiment concerns the capability of the findings to generalize outside the experimental arrangement. These two types of validity often clash. Experimental designs that are strong in both internal and external validity are desirable; however, the fact remains that designs that are strong with respect to internal validity are often implemented at the cost of strong external validity. Indeed, Campbell and Stanley (1966) suggest that "while *internal validity* is the *sine qua non*, and while the question of *external validity*, like the question of inductive inference, is never completely answerable, the selection of designs strong in both types of validity is obviously our ideal" (p. 5).

A number of factors can serve as threats to the internal validity and hence causal conclusions that can be drawn from an experimental design. To take an example, consider the so-called "one-group pretest-posttest design." Here, measures are taken prior to the implementation of an intervention, say to boost reading comprehension, after which the same measures are taken again. Campbell and

Stanley (1966) provide this bad example of an experiment in order to elucidate the types of confounds that threaten causal claims regarding the effect of an intervention. For example, the confound of history suggests that exogenous factors taking place between the first and second observation periods could be the explanation for the shift in mean reading comprehension rather than the intervention. A second threat to the internal validity of the experiment is maturation, where endogenous changes to the individual might induce a shift in the measures over time, having nothing to do with the treatment intervention. These two threats, and many others, provide a sense of the types of criticisms that can be leveled against certain types of experimental arrangements.

To mitigate these threats, Campbell and Stanley suggest adding a group that does not receive the intervention—the so-called *control group*. The addition of the control group along with the treatment group affords a very powerful defense against the threats to internal validity. One process by which the addition of a control group eliminates threats to the internal validity of an experiment is the concept of *random assignment*. Random assignment, in this context, simply means that each individual in the defined sample has an equal probability of being in the treatment group or the control group. The introduction of a control group along with random assignment eliminates most threats to internal validity as discussed in Campbell and Stanley (1966).[2] Thus, for example, in the case of maturation, we would expect that individuals in the treatment group receiving the reading comprehension intervention are as likely to experience the same endogenous changes as those in the control group. It is the power of random assignment that, arguably, lends experimental designs their strength. However, it is important to point out that random assignment removes threats to internal validity in infinitely large samples. In finite samples, problematic outcomes of random assignment to treatment and control can still occur, and these problems become more likely with small samples.

But what if random assignment is not feasible, or perhaps not ethical? In the nomenclature of Campbell and Stanley (1966), designs that resemble true experiments in their arrangement but do not enjoy the benefits of random assignment are considered *quasi-experimental designs*. The ability to draw causal conclusions in the context of quasi-experimental designs is directly related to the degree of pre-treatment equivalence of the treatment and control groups. Numerous design and analysis methods have been employed to attempt pretreatment equivalence. These include propensity score matching, covariate analysis, and others (see, e.g., Rosenbaum & Rubin, 1983; Rosenbaum, 1995). In the end, if pre-treatment equivalence can be attained, then most (but not all) of the threats to internal validity are addressed.

Cook and Campbell The primary focus of Campbell and Stanley's monograph (1966) was to outline the conditions under which experimental arrangements were more or less robust to threats to internal validity. In later and equally important work, Cook and Campbell (1979) extended the Campbell and Stanley framework to consider quasi-experimental designs that are applicable to field settings where random assignment might not be feasible. They begin their book by stating that, "… this book is to outline the experimental approach to causal research …" and, "… since this book is largely about drawing causal inferences in field research, we obviously need to define cause" (p. 1).

What follows in the first chapter of Cook and Campbell is an excellent overview of positions on the problem of causation, ending in what they refer to as an evolutionary critical-realist perspective. The evolutionary critical realist perspective of Cook and Campbell arises first out of the activity theory of causation proposed by Collingwood (1940) among others, and might now be referred to as the *manipulationist* view proposed by Woodward (2003). The idea is that what constitutes a cause is something that can be manipulated to bring about an effect. The evolutionary perspective refers to the notion that the human species (and perhaps other species) have a strong psychological predisposition to infer causal relations, and that this predisposition is the result of biological evolution and the survival value conferred on species having such a predisposition. Their critical-realist perspective suggests that they view causes as actually operating in the real world, but that our knowledge of these causes is conjectural and open to critical discussion. The critical nature of their work is in line with the critical-rationalist perspective of Karl Popper (1959, 1963) and his students.

The Rubin-Holland Model A very important set of papers that have provided the statistical underpinnings for causal inference in experimental studies is the work of Rubin (1974) and Holland (1986); here referred to as the Rubin-Holland Model. Their papers provide a framework for how statistical models that test causal claims are different from those that test associational claims, and that statistical theory has a great deal to add to the discussion of causal inference. Moreover, their work has led both the statistics and econometrics community to a deeper appreciation of the counterfactual theory of causation and has served as an impetus for extensions of the counterfactual theory of causation to the estimation of treatment effects (see, e.g., Morgan & Winship, 2007).

In the more recent of the two papers, Holland (1986) makes clear that his interest is in "*measuring the effects of causes* because this seems to be a place where statistics, which is concerned with measurement, has contributions to make" (p. 945). Holland is clear, however, that experiments are not the only setting where causal claims can be tested, but he does believe they are the simplest.

In outlining the Rubin-Holland model, it is noted that their terminology of cause is not confined to cases of randomized experiments. The notion of cause (or, interchangeably, treatment) in the Rubin-Holland model is relative to some other cause. Specifically, in considering the phrases

"*X causes Y*," the ideas is that *X* causes *Y* relative to another cause—including the possibility of "*not* X." Holland (1986) states that "For causal inference, it is critical that each unit must be potentially exposable to any one of its causes" (p. 946). Note how the Rubin-Holland model equates exposability to the notion of a counterfactual proposition. Using a reading intervention example, we can envision a reading comprehension intervention as causing an increase in a student's reading ability, because we can also envision exposing the same student to no intervention (or perhaps another intervention). That is, we can set up a sensible counterfactual conditional statement of the sort: What if the student was not exposed to the reading comprehension intervention? Rubin and Holland thus link exposability to counterfactual propositions.

To formalize these ideas, Holland starts by defining a selection variable *S* that assigns a unit *u* (e.g., a student) who is a member of population *U* to either a treatment, *t*, or a control, *c*. In randomized experiments, *S* is created by the experimenter, but in observational (i.e., uncontrolled) experiments, such assignments often occur naturally. In the Rubin-Holland model, the critical characteristic is that the value $S(u)$ for each individual could potentially be different.

The role of the outcome variable *Y* in the Rubin-Holland model is also crucial to their framework. First, for the variable *Y* to measure the effect of the cause, *Y* must be measured post-exposure—that is, after exposure to the treatment. Then, the value of the post-exposure outcome variable must be a result of either the cause *t* or the cause *c* defined on a particular student. Therefore, the Rubin-Holland model conceives of the same student providing an outcome variable after being exposed to the treatment, $Y_t(u)$ or after being exposed to the control $Y_c(u)$. The causal effect defined within the Rubin-Holland framework is then the difference between Y_t and Y_c for student *u*. That is:

$$Y_t - Y_c \qquad (1)$$

This is the fundamental idea of the Rubin-Holland model—namely, that causal inference is defined on individual units. However, as Holland (1986) points out, this fundamental notion has a serious problem—namely, that it is impossible to observe the value of Y_t and Y_c on the same unit, and therefore impossible to observe the effect of *t* on *u*. Holland refers to this as the *Fundamental Problem of Causal Inference*.

Holland's approach to this fundamental problem is to draw a distinction between a scientific solution to the problem and a statistical solution. For Holland, the scientific solution requires that certain assumptions be made regarding temporal stability, causal transience, and unit homogeneity. Temporal stability refers to the assumption that the application of the control condition to a unit does not depend on when it occurred. Causal transience refers to the assumption that the response to the treatment is not affected by exposure of the units to the control condition— that the effect of the control condition is transient. Finally,

unit homogeneity refers to the assumption that the response to a treatment applied to one unit is equal to the response to the treatment for another unit—that is $Y_t(u_1) = Y_t(u_2)$. As Holland notes, however, these assumptions are generally not testable but are not uncommon in supporting causal claims in laboratory science.

The statistical solution to the Fundamental Problem offered by Holland (1986) is to make use of the population of individuals *U*. In this case, the *average causal effect*, *T* of *t* can be defined (relative to the control group) as the expected value of the difference between Y_t and Y_c over the units in the population—namely:

$$E(Y_t - Y_c) = T, \qquad (2)$$

Where T is the average causal effect, simplified as:

$$T = E(Y_t) - E(Y_c). \qquad (3)$$

According to Holland (1986), "The important point is that the statistical solution replaces the impossible-to-observe causal effect of *t* on a specific unit with the possible-to-estimate average causal effect of *t* over a population of units" (p. 947).

Much more can be said about the Rubin-Holland model, but what must be discussed is Holland's notion of what constitutes a cause, as his views are central to the arguments made in this chapter:

> Put as bluntly and as contentiously as possible … I take the position that causes are only those things that could, in principle, be treatments in experiments. The qualification, "in principle" is important because practical, ethical, and other considerations might make some experiments infeasible, that is, limit us to contemplatingd *hypothetical experiments.* (1986, p. 954)

Holland (1986) goes on to say that what constitutes a cause is the same in both experimental and observational studies, except that in experimental studies, the investigator has a greater degree of control over the outcome than in the case of observational studies. From this, Holland points out that certain variables simply cannot be causes. For example, an attribute of an individual, such as gender or race cannot be a cause since the notion of *potential exposability* of the unit to all levels of the treatment is not possible without also changing the individual. We cannot conceive of a situation in which we wish to know what an achievement score would be if a female child were male, because potential exposability is simply not possible. In the context of attributes, all that can be derived are associations, and although associations are important and suggestive of variables that might moderate causal variables, they cannot be causes in the sense of the Rubin-Holland framework.

In the final analysis, four points are crucial to an understanding of the Rubin-Holland framework. First, the goal should be to seek out the effects of causes, and not necessarily the causes of effects. For Holland, seeking out the causes of effects is valuable, but because our knowledge of causes is provisional, it is more valuable for a theory of causation to examine effects of causes. Second, effects of causes are always relative to other causes—particularly, the control. For Holland, and Campbell and Stanley before him, experiments that do not have a control condition are not experiments. Third, not everything can be a cause, and specifically, attributes cannot be causes. The law of causality simply states, according to Holland, that everything has a cause, but not everything can be a cause. Finally, for Rubin (1974) and Holland (1986), there can be "*no causation without manipulation*" (Holland, 1986, p. 959).

Counterfactual Propositions and a Manipulability Theory of Causation

Before discussing the structural approach for causal inference, more detailed attention must be paid to philosophical ideas regarding counterfactual propositions that connect to both the experimental tradition and the structural tradition. In the interest of space, I will focus on the work of Mackie (1980), as it is his work on counterfactual propositions that helps to bridge the gap between the two traditions of causal inference. For an additional detailed study of counterfactuals from the philosophical tradition, see Lewis (1973). An excellent review of counterfactuals within social science research can be found in Morgan and Winship (2007).

Mackie and the INUS Condition   Earlier in this chapter mention was made of Mackie's criticism of Hume's ideas about causality. In this section, I briefly outline Mackie's important contribution to our understanding of causation, as developed in his seminal work *The Cement of the Universe: A Study of Causation* (1980). I concentrate on two specific aspects of Mackie's work on causation because his ideas appear in later econometric treatments of causal inference, and which I believe lay a strong logical groundwork for how to consider causal inference in educational policy analysis. The first aspect of Mackie's work addresses a regularity theory of causation and the second aspect concerns a conditional analysis of causation. It should be understood that Mackie's overall contributions are much deeper than I have the space to present.

Mackie (1980) situates the issue of causation in the context of a modified form of a counterfactual conditional statement. Recall that a counterfactual conditional statement is of the form, *if X causes Y, then this means that X occurred and Y occurred, and Y would not have occurred if X had not*. This strict counterfactual statement is problematic for the following reason: We can conceive of Y occurring if X had not. The example used by Mackie is that of striking a match. It is possible that a flame can appear without the act of striking the match, if, say, the match was lit by another source, for example, another lit match. Thus, Mackie suggests that a counterfactual conditional must be augmented by considering the *circumstances* in which the causal event took place. In the case of the match, the circumstances under which striking the match produces the flame include no other potential cause of the match lighting. Thus, under

the circumstances, the flame would not have occurred if the match had not been struck. Similarly, in our example of improved reading comprehension, we can conceive of improved reading comprehension without the intervention. Thus, if we are to attribute improved reading comprehension to our intervention, we must define the conditions under which the intervention took place.

Mackie then discusses the distinction between *conditions* and *causes*. Another example used by Mackie is one of an individual lighting a cigarette inside a flat of apartments, causing an explosion due to a gas leak. The temptation is to say that the explosion was caused by lighting the cigarette. In this regard, the gas leak is a standing condition, and therefore not the cause of the explosion. However, as it is the case that lighting a cigarette in an apartment is not terribly unusual, but a gas leak is, we might be inclined to say that the gas leak was the cause of the explosion and not the lighting of the cigarette.

Mackie suggests that the problem of distinguishing between conditions and causes is addressed by considering that causes take place in a context, or what Mackie refers to as a *causal field*. In addressing the question of what caused the explosion, Mackie (1980) argues that the question should be rephrased as:

> What made the difference between those times, or those cases, within a certain range, in which no such explosion occurred, and this case in which an explosion did occur? Both cause and effect are seen as differences within a field; anything that is part of the assumed (but commonly understated) description of the field itself will, then, be automatically ruled out as a candidate for the role of cause. (p. 35)

Mackie goes on to say:

> What is said to be caused, then, is not just an event, but an event-in-a-certain-field, and some 'conditions' can be set aside as not causing this-event-in-this-field simply because they are part of the chosen field, though if a different field were chosen, in other words if a different causal question were being asked, one of those conditions might well be said to cause this-event-in-that-field. (p. 35)

In the context of a causal field, there can be a host of factors that qualify as causes of an event. Following Mackie (1980), let A, B, C..., etc, be a list of factors that lead to some effect whenever some conjunction of the factors occurs. A conjunction of events may be *ABC*, or *DEF*, or *JKL*, etcetera. This allows for the possibility that *ABC* might be a cause or *DEF* might be a cause, and so on. So, all (*ABC* or *DEF* or *JKL*) are followed by the effect. For simplicity, assume the collection of factors is finite, that is, only *ABC*, *DEF*, and *JKL*. Now, this set of factors (*ABC* or *DEF* or *JKL*) is a condition that is both necessary and sufficient for the effect to occur. Each specific conjunction, such as *ABC*, is sufficient but not necessary for the effect. In fact, following Mackie, *ABC* is a "minimal sufficient" condition insofar as none of its constituent parts are redundant. That is, *AB* is not sufficient for the effect, and *A* itself is neither a necessary nor sufficient condition for the effect. However, Mackie states that the single factor, in this case, *A*, is related to the effect in an important fashion—namely, "it is an *insufficient* but *non-redundant* part of an *unnecessary* but *sufficient* condition: it will be convenient to call this ... an *inus* condition" (p. 62).

It may be useful to examine Mackie's ideas in the context of our reading comprehension example. Mackie's concept of inus conditions alerts us to the importance of carefully specifying the causal field in which causal claims regarding the intervention are made, and to attempt to isolate those factors that serve as *inus* conditions for causal inferences.[3] Specifically, in the context of examining policies or interventions centered on improving reading proficiency in young children, Mackie would have us first specify the causal field or context under which the development of reading proficiency takes place. We could envision a large number of factors that could qualify as causes of reading proficiency. In Mackie's analysis, the important step would be to isolate the set of conjunctions, any one of which might be necessary and sufficient for improved reading proficiency. A specific conjunction might be phonemic awareness, parental support and involvement, teacher training. This set is the minimal sufficient condition for reading proficiency in that none of the constituent parts are redundant. Any two of these three factors is not sufficient for reading proficiency, and one alone—say focusing on parental reading activities, is neither necessary nor sufficient. However, parental reading activities is an inus condition for reading proficiency. That is, the emphasis on reading activities is insufficient as it stands, but it is also a non-redundant part of a set of unnecessary but (minimally) sufficient conditions.

Mackie's analysis, therefore, provides a framework for unpacking the role of inus conditions for reading proficiency. I will argue later in this chapter that Mackie's notion of the inus condition, supported by structural econometric methodologies, provides a basis for sound causal inferences in non-experimental educational policy settings.

Woodward and the Manipulability Theory of Causation

Mackie's notions of causal fields and the inus condition are essential in providing a deeper background for a counterfactual theory of causation. However, Mackie does not provide specific advice with regard to developing notions of causal explanation. Recently, a manipulability theory of causation was put forth by Woodward (2003) in an attempt to provide a foundation for causal explanation. Briefly, Woodward first considers the difference between descriptive knowledge versus explanatory knowledge. While not demeaning the usefulness of description for purposes of classification and prediction, Woodward is clear that his focus is on causal explanation. For Woodward (2003), a causal explanation is an explanation that provides information for purposes of manipulation and control:

> My idea is that one ought to be able to associate with any successful explanation a hypothetical or counterfactual experiment that shows us that and how manipulation of the factors mentioned in the explanation ... would be a way of manipulating or altering the phenomenon explained ... Put in still another way, and explanation ought to be such that it can be used to answer what I call the what-if-things-had-been-different question ... (p. 11)

It is certainly the case that the experimental approach allows one to ask the *what-if things-had-been-different question*. This is the centerpiece of the Rubin-Holland framework because it bases this question at the level of the individual. However, the *what-if-things-had-been-different question* is not restricted to experimental settings.

An important aspect of Woodward's theory involves clarifying the problem of *intervention* and *invariance*. Intervention, in Woodward's theory, relates to the notion of an ideal experimental manipulation of a variable, *X*, with the goal of determining if this ideal manipulation changes *Y*, and that no change in *Y* would have occurred without the change in *X*. According to Woodward, a necessary and sufficient condition for the description of a causal relationship is that it be invariant under some appropriate set of interventions. If a purported causal relationship is not *invariant* under a set of interventions, it is not, in fact, a causal relationship—and indeed might only describe a correlation. Take the example given by Woodward of an observed change in barometer reading and the occurrence of a storm. We might say that changing the barometer caused the storm to occur. Clearly, however, almost any set of interventions on the barometer would not yield a storm—and therefore, in Woodward's terminology, the correlation between the barometer's change and the storm's occurrence is a *non-invariant generalization*.

At the forefront of Woodward's manipulability account of causal explanation is the idea of a hypothetical experiment. However, Woodward makes clear that experiments are not the only way that we can learn about causal relationships. Under certain assumptions, we can learn about causal relationships from a combination of observation and experiment:

> A plausible manipulability theory will not deny that reliable causal inference on the basis of nonexperimental evidence is possible, but rather, suggests a specific way of thinking about such inferences: we should think of them as an attempt to determine (on the basis of other kinds of evidence) what the results of a suitably designed hypothetical experiment or manipulation would be without actually carrying out this experiment. (p. 35)

I argue that Mackie's theory of causal fields and the inus condition provides a philosophical foundation for Woodward's manipulability theory of causal explanation. Specifically, articulating the causal field and identifying an inus condition for causality are not enough. We need an account of how identifying an inus condition for causation provides a possible explanation for some observed effect. Woodward's detailed account of manipulation and intervention, along with the crucial notion of invariance, provides, in my view, precisely the philosophical grounding needed to advance a non-experimental/observational approach to causal inference in educational policy analysis. However, what is required is a methodology for testing causal explanations with non-experimental data. In my view, this methodology arises from the structural econometric tradition.

The Structural (Econometric) Tradition

In this section, I outline the structural econometric approach as it relates to causal inference and in contrast to the experimental paradigm discussed earlier. I will focus attention on the methodology of simultaneous equation modeling as opposed to other standard statistical methodologies used in econometrics—such as time series analysis. Although issues of causality appear in the time series literature, the simultaneous equations approach provides a richer framework for a discussion of causal inference and is also a methodology whose extensions have been applied in educational policy analysis under the names *path analysis* and *structural equation modeling* (see, e.g., Kaplan, 2009).

This section begins with a very brief history of simultaneous equation modeling. It is recognized that this approach to economic models is not without criticism and the form of the criticism is briefly discussed. Regardless, I examine the issue of causal inference within this perspective and focus heavily on the work of Hoover (1990, 2001) and Heckman (2000, 2005).

Brief History of Simultaneous Equation Modeling Mathematical models of economic phenomena have a long history dating back at least to the 17th century (see Spanos, 1986, for a review). However, the development of simultaneous equation modeling must be credited to the work of Haavelmo (1943). Haavelmo was interested in modeling the interdependence among economic variables utilizing the form for systems of simultaneous equations.

The simultaneous equations model was a major innovation in econometric modeling. The development and refinement of the simultaneous equations model was the agenda of the Cowles Commission for Research in Economics, a conglomerate of statisticians and econometricians that met at the University of Chicago in 1945 and subsequently moved to Yale (see Berndt, 1991). This group wedded the newly developed simultaneous equations model with the method of maximum likelihood estimation and associated hypothesis testing methodologies (see Hood & Koopmans, 1953; Koopmans, 1950). For the next 25 years, the thrust of econometric research was devoted to the refinement of the simultaneous equations approach. Particularly notable during this period was the work of Fisher (1976) on model identification.

Utilizing notation familiar in the social sciences, the general form of the simultaneous equation model can be written as

$$y = \alpha + By + \Gamma x + \zeta, \qquad (4)$$

Where y is a vector of observed endogenous variables, x is vector of observed exogenous variables, α is vector of structural intercepts, B is a coefficient matrix that relates endogenous variables to each other, Γ is a coefficient matrix that relates endogenous variables to exogenous variables, and ζ is a vector of disturbance terms.

Of relevance to policy analysis are the elements in B and Γ representing the structural relationships among the variables. In standard practice, *over-identifying restrictions* are placed in specific elements of B and Γ. Typically, these elements are fixed to zero representing the hypothesized absence of a relationship. In terms of causal inference, the elements in Γ give the effect of changes in a set of variables x on the respective endogenous variables y. The total effect of a change in a causal variable x on an outcome y, taking into account the full set of direct and mediating relationships is obtained by arranging Equation (4) so that the outcomes are on the left side of the equation and the causal variables are on the right side. Specifically, under standard assumptions, Equation (4) can be written in "reduced-form" as

$$y = (1 - B)^{-1}\alpha + (1 - B)^{-1}\Gamma x + (1 - B)^{-1}\zeta,$$
$$= \Pi_0 + \Pi_1 x + \zeta^*. \qquad (5)$$

where Π_0 is the vector of reduced form intercepts, Π_1 is the vector of reduced form slopes that give the total effect of a change in x on the outcomes y as specified by the model, and ζ^* is the vector of reduced form disturbances. Details regarding identification, estimation, testing, and improvement of the simultaneous equation model in Equation (4), along with extensions to latent variables, longitudinal, multilevel data, and mixture models can be found in Kaplan (2009).

It is important to note that while the simultaneous equations framework enjoyed a long history of development and application, it was not without its detractors. As Heckman (2000) pointed out, by the mid-1960s, the dominant view was that the program of the Cowles Commission was an "intellectual success but an empirical failure" (p. 48). Critics asserted that a serious problem with large macroeconomic simultaneous equations models was that they could not compete with the relatively theory-free methods of the Box-Jenkins time series model or its multivariate extension—the so-called vector auto-regressive model—when it came to accurate predictions (e.g., Cooper, 1972). The underlying problem was related to the classic distinction between theory-based but relatively static models versus the dynamic time series approach. Its widespread popularity was argued to be due to the fact that time series models are more closely aligned with the data, and therefore, much better at prediction and forecasting than the more theoretical methods arising out of the structural approach to econometrics (Heckman, 2000). The counterargument to the time series approach has been that it is not well-suited for the evaluation of economic policy or testing policy relevant counterfactual claims.

Hoover and the Logic of Causal Inference in Econometrics A crucial analysis that incorporated much of Mackie's ideas of causation within the structural econometric framework can be found in the work of Hoover (1990, 2001). Hoover argues, among other things, that causal inference is a logical problem, and not a problem whose solution is to be found within a statistical model, per se. Moreover, Hoover argues that discussions of causal inference in econometrics are essential and that we should not eschew these discussions because it may appear to some as bordering on realm of metaphysics. Rather, as with medicine but perhaps without the same consequences, the success or failure of economic policy might very well hinge on a logical understanding of causation. A central thesis of this chapter is that such a logical understanding of causation is equally essential to rigorous educational policy analysis.

An important aspect of Hoover's work that is of relevance to our consideration of causal inference in educational policy is his focus on Mackie's inus condition. Hoover sees the inus condition as particularly attractive to economists because it focuses attention on some aspect of the causal problem without having to be concerned directly with knowing every minimally sufficient subset of the full cause of the outcome of interest. I argue later in this chapter that Hoover's analysis of Mackie's ideas serves as a starting point for a rigorous analysis of causal inference in observational settings.

Returning to the reading proficiency example to illustrate the point, recall that the inus condition focuses on a disjunction of minimally sufficient subsets of antecedent conditions for reading proficiency. Following Hoover's notation, this comprehensive set, denoted as A, is the *full cause* of reading proficiency, which, as argued above, may not be possible to fully enumerate. However, we may be able to enumerate a minimally sufficient subset A_i representing the *complete cause* of reading proficiency. From the complete cause A_i, an element a_i is then designated as a cause of reading proficiency if it is an insufficient but necessary member of an unnecessary but (minimally) sufficient set of antecedents of reading proficiency. Therefore, in considering any particular substantive problem in educational policy, it may be possible to divide the universe of possible antecedents into those that are relevant to the effect of interest, A, and those that are irrelevant, *non-A*. Among the relevant antecedents are those that we can divide into their disjuncts A_i, and then further restrict our attention to conjuncts that satisfy the definition of an inus condition.

But what of the remaining relevant causes of reading proficiency? According to Mackie, these remaining causes are relegated to the *causal field*. Hoover acknowledges the notion of the causal field and views it as containing the standing conditions of the problem that are known not to change, or perhaps to be extremely stable for the purposes at hand. In Hoover's words, they represent the "boundary conditions" of the problem. The causal field, however, is much more than simply the standing conditions of a particular problem. Indeed, from the standpoint of classical linear regression, those variables that are relegated to the causal field are part of what is typically referred to as the *disturbance term* represented by the vector ζ in Equation (4). Introducing random error into the discussion allows Mackie's notions to be possibly relevant to indeterministic problems, such as those usually encountered in educational policy analysis. However, according to Hoover, this is only possible if the random error terms are components of Mackie's notion of a causal field.

Hoover argues that the notion of a causal field has to be expanded for Mackie's ideas to be relevant to indeterministic problems. In the first instance, certain parameters of a causal process such as those referenced by the matrices $\mathbf{B}$ and $\mathbf{\Gamma}$ in Equation (4) may not, in fact, be constant. If parameters of a causal question were truly constant, then they can be relegated to the causal field. Parameters that are mostly stable over time can also be relegated to the causal field, but should they in fact change, the consequences for the problem at hand may be profound. In Hoover's analysis, these parameters are part of the boundary conditions of the problem. Hoover argues that most interventions are defined within certain, presumably constant, boundary conditions. In addition to parameters, there are also variables that are not of immediate concern and are thus part of the causal field. Random errors, in Hoover's analysis contain the variables omitted from the problem and are therefore "impounded" in the causal field.

> The causal field is a background of standing conditions and, within the boundaries of validity claimed for the causal relation, must be invariant to exercises of controlling the consequent by means of the particular causal relation (INUS condition) of interest. (Hoover, 2001, p. 222)

Hoover points out that for the inus condition to be a sophisticated approach to the problem of causal inference, the antecedents must truly be antecedent. Often this is argued by appealing to temporal priority, but this is sometimes unsatisfactory. Hoover gives the example of laying one's head on a pillow and the resulting indentation in the pillow as an example of the problem of simultaneity and temporal priority. For all practical purposes, the indentation occurs simultaneously with laying one's head on the pillow.[4] Mackie, however, sees the issue somewhat more simply—namely, the antecedent must be directly controllable. This notion of direct controllability, which is also an important feature of Woodward's (2003) theory and of the Rubin-Holland model, leads to the problem of *invariance*.

Invariance is essential to causal claims, and particularly counterfactual propositions. As noted earlier when discussing Woodward's (2003) manipulability theory, invariance under interventions distinguishes causal explanations from accidental associations. Hoover, as well as Cartwright (1989), have both argued that for an antecedent to be a cause, it must have the capacity to change a consequent, and that capacity must be somewhat stable over time. The stability of a relationship in response to control of the antecedent is the problem of invariance which, for Hoover, also constitutes a possible strategy for determining causal order. Specifically, consider a model in which changes in reading achievement are caused only by changes in parental involvement in reading practices—which, say, we can control. We could just as easily "reverse" the regression and use reading achievement as a cause of parental involvement. Which causal order is correct? Using historical information from large representative longitudinal or trend data, we may be able to locate periods of time in which no major interventions took place that would have changed reading achievement or parental reading practices. Then either causal order would yield stable regression coefficients. However, during periods of time in which there have been interventions that were targeted toward reading achievement and interventions targeted toward parental reading practices, then examining the relative stability of the coefficients to the different regressions would provide information regarding causal order. A discussion of the reverse regression problem in the context of exogeneity and invariance can be found in Kaplan (2004).

Although this is a somewhat contrived example, it is offered to make two important points about the structural approach to causal inference in non-experimental educational policy research. First, as discussed by Cartwright (1989), invariance is an essential foundation for counterfactual propositions. Using Cartwright's notation, the antecedent of a counterfactual proposition, say C, must have a stable causal relationship to the consequent, say E, when C comes under direct control. To quote Cartwright, "If Cs do ever succeed in causing Es (by virtue of being Cs), it must be because they have the capacity to do so. That capacity is something they can be expected to carry with them from situation to situation" (p. 145). Second, the structural approach provides a way to examine causal ordering, and this alone can provide important insights into the functioning of complex systems such as education. Gaining an understanding of causal ordering and invariance is crucial for ascertaining the behavior of policies and interventions—particularly when those policies or interventions are being taken to scale.

Heckman's Scientific Model of Causality

Recently, Heckman (2000, 2005) provided an important contribution to the problem of causal inference from a structural econometric perspective. Heckman's perspective centers on two essential points. First, Heckman views causality as the property of a model of hypothetical statements, and that a fully developed model should represent a set of precisely formulated counterfactual propositions. According to Heckman (2005), the problem with modeling the effects of causes, which is the mainstay of the experimental paradigm, is that such a perspective does not speak to how the processes by which causal inferences are being drawn have been generated.

> The ambiguity and controversy surrounding discussion of causal models are consequences of analysts wanting something for nothing: a definition of causality without a clearly articulated model of the phenomenon being described (i.e., a model of counterfactuals). (p. 2)

For Heckman, models such as that in Equation (4) are descriptions of hypothetical worlds and interest should be in how these hypothetical worlds change as a function of manipulating the causal **x**-variables that determine the **y**-outcomes. Thus for Heckman, science is about constructing these causal models, and that the growth of human knowledge is based on constructing counterfactuals and developing supportive theories.

Heckman's second point is that causal inference within statistics conflates three tasks that he argues need to be clearly separated: (a) definitions of counterfactuals, (b) identification of causal models from population distributions, and (c) identification of causal models from actual data. Heckman views the definition of counterfactuals as located in the realm of a scientific theory. The problem of the identification of causal models from population distributions falls into the purview of the mathematical analysis of identification (see Fisher, 1976). Finally, identification of causal models from actual data is a problem for estimation and sampling theory.

Heckman (2005) then compares his view with the approach to causal inference favored in epidemiology and clinical drug trials, and now educational research—namely, the randomized experimental design approach described earlier. In Heckman's view, there are two essential problems with the experimental design approach. The first problem relates to the issue of selection bias—specifically, the experimental approach does not model the mechanism by which counterfactuals are selected or how hypothetical interventions might be realized. This problem is seen when units making the intervention choices are not the same as the units receiving the intervention—as in the case of parents ultimately making choices for their children, although the latter are those actually receiving the intervention. The structural approach guided by theory can provide information that would allow the construction and testing of various selection mechanisms. The capability of structural models to provide insights into the selection process is potentially of great importance in education in the context of taking an intervention to scale.

The second problem is that the experimental approach does not specify the sources of randomness embedded in the error terms. Modeling these unobservable sources of random variation is, according to Heckman, essential in choosing the correct estimation method. Heckman goes on to suggest that the "treatment" in randomized designs is a conglomerate of factors that are not related to a theory of what actually produced the effect. Finally, and perhaps of most relevance to educational policy analysis, the experimental approach cannot be used for out-of-sample forecasting to new populations. In the context of educational policy analysis, the experimental approach does not yield insights into the behavior of the treatment when scaled up. The structural approach, on the other hand:

> Like the goal of all science, is to model phenomena at a deeper level, to understand the causes producing the effects

so that we can use empirical versions of the models to forecast the effects of interventions never previously experienced, to calculate a variety of policy counterfactuals, and to use scientific theory to guide the choices of estimators and the interpretation of the evidence. These activities require development of a more elaborate theory than is envisioned in the current literature on causal inference in epidemiology and statistics. (Heckman, 2005, p. 6)

With respect to non-experimental educational policy analysis, the structural approach allows historically experienced policies to be examined in light of new policies not yet experienced. Of course, in the context of non-experimental educational policy analysis, this depends on support for research and development into better strategies for large-scale data collection.

A third and quite serious issue is that the experimental approach cannot address the problem of *general equilibrium*, a problem that is intimately tied to the *generalizability* of a causal inference. To place the issue of general equilibrium in the context of non-experimental educational policy, consider the problem of class size reduction. A well-controlled experimental approach to class size reduction would provide an unbiased estimate of the population average causal effect of a specified class size change on the achievement outcome of interest. Other variables that would be affected by class size reduction and are correlated with achievement (e.g., teacher quality) are not explicitly considered in the experimental framework, and indeed, are averaged out due to random assignment (or some other rigorous form of pre-treatment equating). Thus, the experimental design approach to studying class size reduction is identical to a *partial equilibrium* analysis of the problem.

Upon reflection however, it is clear that the potential real life influence of class size reduction on other aspects of the educational system becomes extremely serious if the class size reduction policy is fully implemented. For example, if a policy to reduce class size was, in fact, implemented (e.g., all middle school math classes would be reduced to no more than 15 children in a classroom) the real effect on teacher hiring, teacher quality, teacher salaries, buildings, and a host of other important variables, could all be effected. The adjustments that would take place in these other variables in response to a class size reduction policy represent the general equilibrium effects. Again, the experimental (partial equilibrium) approach simply does not address these generalizability issues, whereas the structural approach can provide an explicit rigorous framework for modeling these effects and to test how various changes in causal variables of interest might manifest themselves in terms of the general equilibrium effects.

Toward an Approach to Causal Inference Suitable for Non-Experimental Educational Policy Analysis

In this section, I argue that the structural approach advocated by Heckman (2005), particularly when supplemented by Hoover's synthesis of Mackie's inus conditions, contains the

methodology for formulating a number of precisely stated counterfactuals within a well-specified, albeit hypothetical, model. The structural approach allows testing of varying counterfactual propositions that can reflect the complex reality of educational systems. Such modeling efforts can provide important substantive feedback regarding how policies or interventions might work to effect outcomes under different counterfactual scenarios, including issues of treatment and/or outcome selection. In a related manner, the flexibility of the structural approach allows for the study and anticipation of general equilibrium effects under a variety of realistic scenarios that could be faced when an intervention or policy goes to scale. The structural approach to non-experimental educational policy analysis is also well suited to examine the potential for how policies and interventions might operate out-of-sample. Finally, the structural approach can provide a framework for theory development in educational policy analysis.

The advantages of the structural approach to causal inferences notwithstanding, much more work needs to be done to fully integrate this approach into educational policy research. This is particularly true given the way in which path analysis and structural equation modeling have traditionally been applied in education, sociology, and psychology. A critique of the standard approach to path analysis and structural equation modeling as applied in education, psychology, and sociology is given in Kaplan (2009). The essence of the critique is that conventional applications of structural equation modeling have not gone much beyond the presentation of goodness-of-fit measures. Although goodness-of-fit is important, as it provides information regarding how well a hypothesized model matches the data generating process, additional information can be gained from other forms model evaluation, such as testing model predictions "out-of-sample."

An alternative framework developed by Spanos and referred to as the *probabilistic reduction approach*, was advocated by Kaplan (2009) as a means of improving on the conventional approach to structural equation modeling. Among other things, the probabilistic reduction approach makes explicit the differences among data generating mechanisms, theoretical models, and statistical models. Kaplan (2009) argued that the probabilistic reduction approach applied within a manipulationist philosophical perspective could enhance the use of structural equation modeling for causal inferences in non-experimental settings.

Also, much greater effort needs to be focused on precisely articulating the identifying assumptions as they pertain to conceptual or theoretical frameworks. Specifically, a conceptual framework and the theoretical equations that are suggested by the framework do not necessarily imply that causal parameters can be uniquely identified from the data. In some cases, identifying restrictions must be imposed, and these restrictions require justification within the theoretical framework. Furthermore, in the context of cross-sectional data, it is essential that assumptions associated with the estimation of "contemporaneous" equations be carefully argued. For example, in a cross-sectional study, there is the implicit assumption that only the exogenous variables at the current time point are relevant to explaining the outcome, or that exogenous variables are unchanging and they capture the entire history of the inputs, and the exogenous variables are unrelated to any unobserved set of variables (Todd & Wolpin, 2003).

The issues raised above point to the need for bold theoretical development in educational policy analysis and aggressive support for research and development in high quality data sources that can be brought to bear on testing theoretical claims. Regarding high quality data sources, a recent monograph by Schneider, Carnoy, Kilpatrick, Schmidt, and Shavelson (2007) dealt explicitly with this issue by comparing and contrasting the experimental approach with approaches to causal inference gleaned from observational and non-experimental approach designs in education, particularly through the careful analysis of large scale, nationally representative databases. The Schneider et al. (2007) monograph is to be commended for its emphasis on supporting the development of large-scale educational databases to be used to test causal claims in education. However, the monograph did not provide an updated view of the philosophical or methodological developments relevant to a deeper understanding of how causal inferences can be warranted using large-scale databases.

I maintain along with Schneider et al. (2007) that well-designed, large-scale educational databases, such as the Early Childhood Longitudinal Study (National Center for Educational Statistics, 2001) or the Program for International Student Assessment (Organization for Economic Cooperation and Development, 2004) are the types of observational studies that should be continually supported, developed, and utilized to test causal propositions. To do so, however, requires a bridging of counterfactual theories in the experimental literature and the structural literature.

In the final analysis, neither the experimental nor structural approach to causal inference can legitimately lay claim to being a "gold standard" for methodological rigor. Both approaches have many well-known strengths and weaknesses. As such, claiming that one methodology is the gold standard while others are, by implication, of lesser methodological rigor is unfair, inaccurate, and unproductive in advancing educational policy research. A more productive stance would be to recognize overlapping areas of agreement across all approaches and to exploit those areas of agreement in order to improve the full array of evidence-based methodologies for causal inference in educational policy research. In terms of basic principles, both approaches (a) rightly reject the nihilistic post-modern relativism that seems to have infected education research of late, (b) urge rigorous standards of empirical data collection and measurement, and (c) subscribe to some variant of the counterfactual theory of causation.

It is this last area of agreement where I believe there exists considerable overlap between the Rubin-Holland approach and the econometric approach advocated by Heckman, Hoover, and others. Perhaps the main area of agreement is the notion of exposability to potential treatment conditions and the general notion of manipulability articulated by Woodward (2003) as the basis for inferring causation. However, given their shared agreement in the importance of manipulability, potential exposability, and counterfactuals, it is surprising that neither Holland nor Heckman mention Mackie's (1980) philosophical analysis of counterfactual propositions and inus conditions, nor does Heckman refer to Hoover's (1990, 2001) work on causal analysis in econometrics. One purpose of the present paper was to link the structural approach to the experimental approach via Mackie's ideas of counterfactuals, causal fields, and inus conditions framed with Woodward's (2003) manipulability theory of causal explanation.

It is also the case that the experimental approach and structural approach can be combined in fruitful ways (see, e.g., Shadish, Cook, & Campbell, 2002, chap. 12). Indeed, recent research has shown that experimental studies can be used to validate predictions developed from complex structural models. In a recent paper, Todd and Wolpin (2006) examined the effect of a school subsidy program in Mexico that was implemented as a randomized social experiment. In addition, they specified a complex dynamic structural model that captured parental decisions about fertility and child schooling. The model was capable of reproducing the treatment effect quite closely. However, whereas the results of the social experiment stopped at the treatment effect, the structural model allowed specification and testing of other ex ante policy scenarios that produced information regarding general equilibrium effects. In the context of educational policy, we can imagine a similar exercise in a study of, say, class size and student achievement. Specifically, we can envision attempting to estimate a model of class size, examine its prediction under conditions similar to an actual class size experiment in order to use the experimental results to validate the model, but then use the model to examine a variety of realistic policy alternatives. Clearly, a great deal of forethought would be required to anticipate the type of data needed to conduct such a study.

Conclusion

As noted in the introduction, a considerable amount of research on the problem of causal inference has been omitted from this chapter. There is simply not enough space to cover all of the work on this problem, and I have likely omitted writings that are relevant to both a defense and criticism of my central arguments. Suffice to say that there are other essential ideas that deserve further exploration within the context of advancing methodologies for causal inference in educational policy research. For example, within the counterfactual theory of causal inference, a considerable amount of work has been conducted on different causal estimands—such as estimates of *local average treatment effects* and *complier average causal effects*. For an excellent summary of these issues, see Morgan and Winship

(2007). I did not review the work on probabilistic causality, originally considered by Suppes (1970), and expanded by Eells (1991). My review also did not cover the important work of Pearl (2000) or the work of Spirtes, Glymour, and Scheines (2000). Nor have I discussed Hausman's (1998) work on causal asymmetry. The work of these scholars, and many others, must be thoroughly studied and critiqued as we further attempt to build a rigorous science of causal inference for education policy research.

Space limitations notwithstanding, the goal of this chapter was to review certain central ideas of causality and to argue for an approach to causal inference in non-experimental educational policy analysis that rests on modern philosophical and methodological work arising from structural econometrics. The arguments raised in this chapter speak to the need to support basic and applied research on methodologies for non-experimental and observational studies and to vigorously support research and development into the design and analysis of large-scale databases as a means of testing invariance assumptions and hypothetical counterfactual experiments. In summary, although it is clear that much more philosophical and methodological work remains, it is hoped that this chapter will stimulate a broader discussion on the development of a rigorous empirical science and practice of educational policy analysis.

Notes

1. Support for this research was made possible by a Vilas Associate Award from the University of Wisconsin-Madison. I am grateful to Jane Cooley, Adam Gamoran, Daniel Hausman, Salvador Navarro, and Barbara Schneider for valuable comments and criticisms on an earlier draft of this chapter. The opinions expressed herein are mine alone.
2. Perhaps the only threat that remains is bias due to non-random attrition from the study.
3. Pearl (2000) notes that in legal circles, the convoluted meaning of the acronym *inus* has been replace by the easier acronym NESS, which stands for necessary element of a sufficient set.
4. This example was originally put forth by Kant in the context of an iron ball depressing a cushion. In any case, we are ignoring causal processes at the quantum level.

References

Berndt, E. R. (1991). *The practice of econometrics: Classic and contemporary.* New York: Addison-Wesley.

Campbell, D. T., & Stanley, J. C. (1966). *Experimental and quasi-experimental designs for research.* Boston: Houghton Mifflin.

Cartwright, N. (1989). *Nature's capacities and their measurement.* Oxford, UK: Oxford University Press.

Collingwood, R. G. (1940). *An essay on metaphysics.* Oxford, UK: Clarendon Press.

Cook, T. D., & Campbell, D. T. (1979). *Quasi-experimentation: Design and analysis issues for field settings.* Boston: Houghton Mifflin.

Cooper, R. L. (1972). The predictive performance of quarterly econometric models of the United States. In B. G. Hickman (Ed.), *Econometric models of cyclical behavior* (pp. 813–974). New York: Columbia University Press.

Eells, E. (1991). *Probabilistic causality.* Cambridge, UK: Cambridge University Press.

Fisher, F. M. (1970). A correspondence principle for simultaneous equation models. *Econometrica, 38*(4), 73–92.

Fisher, F. M. (1976). *The identification problem in econometrics.* Huntington, NY: Robert Kreiger.

Haavelmo, T. (1943). The statistical implications of a system of simultaneous equations. *Econometrica, 11,* 1–12.

Hausman, D. M. (1998). *Causal asymmetries.* Cambridge, UK: Cambridge University Press.

Heckman, J. J. (2000). Causal parameters and policy analysis in economics: A twentieth century retrospective. *The Quarterly Journal of Economics, 115,* 45–97.

Heckman, J. J. (2005). The scientific model of causality. *Sociological Methodology, 35,* 1–97.

Holland, P. W. (1986). Statistics and causal inference. *Journal of the American Statistical Association, 81,* 945–960.

Hood, W. C., & Koopmans, T. C. (Eds.). (1953). Studies in econometric methods. *Cowles Commission Monograph, Vol. 14.* New York: Wiley.

Hoover, K. D. (1990). The logic of causal inference: Econometrics and the conditional analysis of causality. *Economics and Philosophy, 6,* 207–234.

Hoover, K. D. (2001). *Causality in macroeconomics.* Cambridge, UK: Cambridge University Press.

Hume, D. (1999). *An enquiry concerning human understanding.* (T. L. Beauchamp, Ed.). Oxford, UK: Oxford University Press. (Original work published 1748)

Hume, D. (2000). *A treatise of human nature.* (D. F. Norton & M. J. Norton, Eds.). Oxford, UK: Oxford University Press. (Original work published 1739)

Kaplan, D. (2004). On exogeneity. In D. Kaplan (Ed.), *The Sage handbook of quantitative methodology for the social sciences* (pp. 407–421). Newbury Park, CA: Sage.

Kaplan, D. (2009). *Structural equation modeling: Foundations and extensions* (2nd ed.). Newbury Park, CA: Sage.

Koopmans, T. C. (Ed.). (1950). Statistical inference in dynamic economic models. *Cowles Commission Monograph, Vol. 10.* New York: Wiley.

Lewis, D. (1973). *Counterfactuals.* Malden, MA: Blackwell.

Mackie, J. L. (1980). *The cement of the universe: A study of causation.* Oxford, UK: Clarendon.

Mill, J. S. (1851). *A system of logic: Vol. I* (3rd ed.). London: John W. Parker.

Morgan, S. L., & Winship, C. (2007). Counterfactuals and causal inference: Methods and principles for social research. Cambridge, UK: Cambridge University Press.

National Center for Education Statistics (NCES). (2001). Early childhood longitudinal study: Kindergarten class of 1998–99. Kindergarten fifth grade public-use data files user's manual (Tech. Rep. Nos. 2001-029). Washington, DC: U.S. Government Printing Office.

The No Child Left Behind Act of 2001. Pub. L. No. 107-110, 115 Stat. 1425 (2002).

Organization for Economic Cooperation and Development (OECD). (2004). *The PISA 2003 assessment framework: Mathematics, reading, science, and problem solving knowledge and skills.* Paris: Author.

Pearl, J. (2000). *Causality: Models, reasoning, and inference.* New York: Cambridge University Press.

Popper, K. (1959). *The logic of scientific discovery.* New York: Basic Books.

Popper, K. (1963). *Conjectures and refutations: The growth of scientific knowledge.* New York: Routledge.

Rosenbaum, P. R. (1995). *Observational studies.* New York: Springer-Verlag.

Rosenbaum, P. R., & Rubin, D. B. (1983). The central role of the propensity score in observational studies for causal effects. *Biometrika, 70,* 41–55.

Rubin, D. B. (1974). Estimating causal effects of treatments in randomized and nonrandomized studies. *Journal of Educational Psychology, 66,* 688–701.

Schneider, B., Carnoy, M., Kilpatrick, J., Schmidt, W. H., & Shavelson,

R. J. (2007). *Estimating causal effects: Using experimental and observational designs*. Washington, DC: American Educational Research Association.

Shadish, W. R., Cook, T. D., & Campbell, D. T. (2002). *Experimental and quasi-experimental designs for generalized causal inference*. New York: Houghton Mifflin.

Spanos, A. (1986). *Statistical foundations of econometric modeling*. Cambridge, UK: Cambridge University Press.

Spirtes, P., Glymour, C., & Scheines, R. (2000). *Causation, prediction, and search* (2nd ed.). Cambridge, MA: MIT Press.

Suppes, P. (1970). A probabilistic theory of causality. *Acta Philosophica Fennica, 24*, 5–130.

Todd, P. E., & Wolpin, K. I. (2003). On the specification and estimation of the production function for cognitive achievement. *Economic Journal, 113*, F3–F33.

Todd, P. E., & Wolpin, K. I. (2006). Using a social experiment to validate a dynamic behavioral model of child schooling and fertility: Assessing the impact of a school subsidy program in Mexico. *American Economic Review, 96*, 1384-1417.

United States Department of Education, Institute for Educational Sciences (2008). *What Works Clearing House Standards*. Retrieved April 11, 2008, from http://www.ed.gov/about/offices/list/ies/ncee/wwc.html

Woodward, J. (2003). *Making things happen: A theory of causal explanation*. Oxford, UK: Oxford University Press.

Worrall, J. (2002). What evidence in evidence-based medicine? *Philosophy of Science, 69*, S316–S330.

Worrall, J. (2004). *Why there's no cause to randomize* (Tech. Rep.). London: Centre for Philosophy of Natural and Social Science.

13

Research Synthesis and Education Policy

THERESE D. PIGOTT
Loyola University Chicago

Introduction

The current educational policy environment focuses on scientific evidence as the basis for decisions in our schools and other education institutions. While this emphasis on research ensures stronger warrants for important education policy decisions, the problem lies not only in determining what constitutes scientific evidence but in actually sifting through the large amount of research that exists. How do we develop an understanding of a research base that includes hundreds of diverse studies?

Comprehensive research synthesis and the statistical tools of meta-analysis provide a set of systematic methods for organizing and mapping the knowledge that exists in a literature. Cooper (1998) defines the aims of a comprehensive or systematic review as seeking "to summarize past research by drawing overall conclusions from many separate investigations that address related or identical processes" (p. 3). The techniques of meta-analysis allow the statistical modeling of variation among study results as a function of the methods used in a study. Together the methods of comprehensive research synthesis and meta-analysis provide a transparent and systematic assessment of the literature that can directly aid in the goal of using research evidence as the basis for sound educational policy.

Background on Research Synthesis and Meta-Analysis

Literature reviews in education and the social sciences take many different forms. As Cooper (1998) describes, some literature reviews introduce and provide a rationale for a new primary study. Other literature reviews are theoretical in nature, describing and analyzing the theories operating in a given literature. For Kennedy (2007), these conceptual reviews add new insights and frameworks to thinking about a given research area. Conceptual reviews do not necessarily attempt a synthesis of all literature, but instead provide

new ways to think about the literature. In this chapter, I define comprehensive research syntheses as reviews that describe the current state of empirical evidence in a field. They depend completely on the nature of the research that exists in the literature and thus are bound by the methods used by primary researchers in a field. While research syntheses use past research, they can also provide guidelines for future research by identifying areas where more research is warranted.

Comprehensive research syntheses also employ statistical techniques collectively referred to as meta-analysis. Like all statistical methods, meta-analysis provides a set of tools to help organize and examine a large amount of data, in this case, studies. The reviewer usually extracts a measure of the study's effect—the difference between two treatment groups, or the correlation between two measures, for example—and uses meta-analysis to examine the variation across studies in this measure of a study's effect. Reviewers often test models of how different study methods relate to variations in effect size magnitude. A number of statistical modeling strategies exist for meta-analysis as represented by the work of Cooper and Hedges (1994), Hunter and Schmidt (2004), and Rosenthal (1991). While these techniques differ in assumptions and procedures, they all focus on examining the distribution of effect sizes and the relationships between effect size magnitude and variation in study design and samples.

Comprehensive research reviews and meta-analysis can contribute to policy in three ways: (a) by mapping the existing research base on an issue, (b) by expanding the external validity of single studies through the use of multiple studies, and (c) by providing multiple views of the causal explanations explored in a given research area. Not all comprehensive reviews, however, hold to standards that warrant their use in policy decisions. A reviewer makes many decisions when conducting a review that directly influences the quality of that review and the ability of that review to provide usable knowledge for policy decisions.

In addition, the methods for comprehensive reviews and meta-analysis limit our ability to assess the evidence available in a given literature.

This chapter outlines the potential role that systematic research reviews and meta-analysis can play in the development of educational policy. The chapter will focus on three questions about the relationship between research synthesis and educational policy:

1. How can comprehensive research reviews contribute to policy decisions?
2. What reasonable quality standards should we hold for a comprehensive synthesis that can contribute to policy debate?
3. What are current areas of research in research synthesis that could strengthen its contribution to education policy?

In addition, the chapter will illustrate the potential and the limitations of the role of research synthesis in policy using the National Reading Panel's (NRP; 2000) review of strategies for reading instruction. The NRP's review provides an interesting example given its genesis as a U.S. Congress-mandated report intended to influence directly federal reading policy, and given the controversy it engendered among various stakeholders throughout the educational system.

Contributions of Research Synthesis to Policy

In 1997, Congress asked the National Institute of Child Health and Human Development (NICHD) to convene a panel of experts to assess the research on teaching children to read. This panel of reading research experts, the NRP, was charged with assessing "the status of research-based knowledge, including the effectiveness of various approaches to teaching children to read" (National Reading Panel, 2000). When the deadline for a report to Congress was due in 1998, the panel asked for an extension given that they had identified 100,000 studies on reading published since 1966. The sheer size of the task before this volunteer panel led to the use of techniques for comprehensive research synthesis to organize and interpret this large body of literature. The NRP's meta-analysis illustrates the potentials and limitations of research synthesis to map the field, to generalize to other research and practice contexts, and to provide causal explanations for a phenomenon.

Mapping the Field   In many areas of educational research, the number of studies conducted reach into the thousands, or as in the case of the National Reading Panel, in the hundreds of thousands. No single researcher or policy maker can hope to read and understand this literature in the time allotted for making important decisions. As Feuer (2006) points out, the complexity of the tasks involved in educational decision making can be likened to the famous traveling salesperson problem; by the time we rationally

choose the optimal route for visiting a number of cities, the salesperson will have already visited these cities and moved on to other tasks. Thus, by the time we have read and summarized thousands of studies, the policy community will have moved to a new arena. We need a time-bounded but rational method for understanding the complex literature. Research synthesis and the techniques of meta-analysis provide tools for mapping and organizing a set of studies. As in any statistical modeling strategy, the summary of the literature is necessarily a simplification of the data at hand. But if this simplification contributes to a bounded rational decision about an educational policy, then we have moved beyond the use of single favored studies and anecdote as warrants for particular courses of action as Kingdon (2003) has demonstrated.

The mapping of the literature occurs through systematic and transparent rules about what studies should be included and excluded in a synthesis. The National Reading Panel report (2000) includes appendices outlining the types of studies on instructional strategies for reading that remained in the review. One set of criticisms (Pressley, Duke, & Boling, 2004) of the NRP review centered on the nature of the studies included in the review. Among Pressley et al.'s arguments is that the NRP focused more effort on a narrowly defined set of reading instruction strategies, including those that were more easily studied using experimental and quasi-experimental techniques. Pressley et al. conclude that this decision limits the usefulness of the NRP results for policymaking and ignores observational and interpretive research. Thus, the map provided by the NRP may outline only the instructional strategy research that uses experimental designs, missing other types of reading strategies that may be important but cannot or have not yet been studied using experimental methods. Since, as Pressley et al. point out, the Reading First initiative relied heavily on the NRP report's findings, the partial NRP map may not provide the range and extent of evidence that could be brought to bear on reading instruction.

Beyond the External Validity of Single Studies   Research in the social sciences rarely follows a replication model. Interventions are developed and tested under numerous conditions, contexts, and participants. Research synthesis capitalizes on this diversity by allowing systematic investigation of the relationship between variation in study design and study results. More formally, Shadish, Cook, and Campbell (2002) provide the rationale for generalized causal explanation from research synthesis and more specifically, meta-analysis. Three of Shadish et al.'s principles for causal inference apply directly to the external validity of meta-analysis. These principles are surface similarity, ruling out irrelevancies, and making discriminations.

Surface Similarity   Scientists who are attempting generalizations to a target from a single study use the principle of surface similarity to strengthen their argument. When a primary study utilizes constructs, procedures, and operations known as similar to the target context, the warrant is stronger for the generalization. Research synthesis capitalizes on surface similarity through the range of studies included in the review. It is more likely in a review that the constructs and operations relevant to a research area are represented in one or more of the studies included in the review. In the NRP meta-analysis, a wide range of literacy assessments were used to measure children's phonemic awareness, comprehension, fluency, and other literacy skills. Not every assessment or subtest of these assessments is relevant for every target skill, but across the set of studies included in each meta-analysis were assessments considered a more direct test of the target skill. More specifically, in the Ehri, Nunes, Stahl, and Willows (2001) review, a number of measures of reading ability were used including pseudo-word reading, reading fluency, reading comprehension, and spelling. With a range of reading skills measured, the meta-analysis can go beyond any of the individual studies in examining the possible outcomes of phonics instruction.

Ruling Out Irrelevancies   Scientists also attempt to rule out irrelevancies when making inferences to a target. Given a large causal field with several plausible explanations for an event, ruling out those elements that do not contribute to the issue helps to refine the theory explaining the event. Techniques of meta-analysis allow the formal test of elements of a given event that are relevant to the theoretical causal chain. Models of effect size examine the relationships between potential moderators of events and effect size magnitude. Thus, reviewers can identify relevant and irrelevant factors in a given causal explanation. One motivation for the formation of the NRP was to summarize what reading interventions work, for what sets of children, under what sets of conditions. For example, Ehri et al. (2001) present results from a series of single moderator analyses examining variation in effect size for phonemic awareness programs. For example, studies with kindergarten and first-grade children found larger effects for the phonemic awareness programs than studies with children in second grade or older. In addition, there was a larger effect on children's decoding than on other literacy skills measured in the studies. Other factors such as the type of assignment to treatment groups in the study, and whether the treatment was implemented in small groups or in a whole class were not statistically related to effect size magnitude.

Causal Explanation   While comprehensive research reviews potentially reach beyond the external validity of any single study, the ultimate goal of much of educational research is to make causal inferences. Causal description, as Shadish et al. (2002) write, is best accomplished through experimentation, where a researcher can observe the consequences attributable to varying a treatment. Causal explanation, on the other hand, clarifies the potential mechanisms and conditions where the causal relationship holds. Research reviews and meta-analysis cannot provide causal description given that the range of methods, contexts, and participants are not randomly assigned or determined by the reviewer. However, causal explanation is suited to comprehensive reviews not only due to the potential for mapping and setting the boundaries for the external validity of results of a literature but also for the ability of meta-analysis models to examine causal mediating processes not systematically examined in every study. These methods, however, require more information than is typically provided in studies, and more expertise in meta-analysis than is available to many reviewing teams. The NRP meta-analyses (2000) used simple models that examined single moderators at a time. For example, the Ehri et al. (2001) review on phonemic instruction examined the effect of grade level, type of phonemic awareness program, socioeconomic status of the students, prior ability level of students, type of assessment, and many other potential moderators. One difficulty with making generalizations from these one-variable models is that the critical elements of the relationship between study moderators and effect sizes are not explored—there is potential that relevant moderators are confounded with other moderators. A reviewer can attempt to disentangle these micro-mediating processes by examining multivariate models either through regression models or more sophisticated instrumental variable methods. Ehri et al.'s (2001) review of phonics programs states that there were not sufficient numbers of studies to explore more complex models. In the NRP report, the timeline imposed on the review may have also precluded the involvement of consultants who could assist in fitting these models. Using more complex techniques in a research review could potentially clarify important mediating processes in reading instruction.

The current education policy environment has highlighted the importance of scientific evidence when making decisions about instructional practices at all levels of schooling. Comprehensive research synthesis and the statistical modeling strategies of meta-analysis contribute methods for mapping systematically the literature in a given area. In addition, if the literature is sufficiently developed, a comprehensive research synthesis and meta-analysis provides modeling techniques both to examine the boundaries of the external validity of the literature as a whole and to test particular causal explanations for the results found.

Quality Standards for Research Synthesis

The contributions of a comprehensive research review are necessarily limited by the quality of the methods and conduct of the review. As Kennedy (2007) points out, every stage of a comprehensive review requires decisions that affect the kinds of inferences and generalizations possible from the review. The sections below examine each stage of a comprehensive research review, highlighting the consequences of making particular types of choices at each stage. The National Reading Panel (2000) report illustrates many of these choices and the impact on the generalizations possible from this review.

The National Reading Panel submitted their report in

2000 after conducting a series of eight research reviews in the areas of phonics, phonemic awareness, fluency, vocabulary instruction, text comprehension, comprehension strategies, teacher education, and technology and reading instruction. Of the eight areas, the meta-analysis on phonics instruction generated the most criticism. The details of this meta-analysis were also published in the *Review of Educational Research* by Ehri et al. (2001). As Shanahan (2005) states, there has been a steady stream of criticism of the findings of the report that extend "over a longer period than the panel worked on the original eight studies that make up the report" (p. 452). The criticisms were wide-ranging, and continue to generate debate in the literature as seen in a recent special issue of the *Elementary School Journal* (Allington, 2006; Camilli, Wolfe, & Smith, 2006; Hammill & Swanson, 2006). Some of these criticisms relate to the decisions made in each stage of a review as outlined below.

Problem Formulation A research review as well as a primary study should have a well-articulated research question. The question guiding the National Reading Panel report was one provided by the U.S. Congress—to assess the status of research-based knowledge on early reading instruction. For the phonics instruction review, the NRP focused on the following questions: "Does phonics instruction improve reading achievement? If so, how is this instruction best provided?" (National Reading Panel, 2000). This question implies a broad examination of the literature, looking not only at the magnitude of the effect of phonics instruction on reading achievement but also on the moderators that may influence that effect size.

Kennedy's (2007) reflections about comprehensive research synthesis lead her to temper her enthusiasm for meta-analysis, concluding that comprehensive reviews cannot provide the kinds of important insights that may change the course of a field of research. One answer to Kennedy's conclusions relates to the nature of the question guiding the review. In the case of Kennedy's review of teacher quality and quality of teaching, the research question was a comprehensive and broad one—focusing on how teacher qualifications relate to the quality of teaching. Organizing and mapping out this literature may be a more important contribution than arriving at elegant models of effect size moderators. Smaller samples of studies included in this comprehensive project, studies that focus on just alternatively certified teachers, for example, may allow inferences that could address directly some of the area's most pressing questions. Thus, the nature of the research question guiding the review, whether broad or narrow, does dictate the types of inferences possible. It may be a large contribution to understand where the most effort has been expended in a given research area to the detriment of other equally important questions, a result that comes from a systematic mapping of the literature. The NRP meta-analysis has been criticized for not using more comprehensive search and inclusion criteria for identifying relevant studies (Pressley et al., 2004), and

thus may not have provided as comprehensive an outline of the literature than was theoretically possible.

Data Collection Also critical to the quality of both research reviews and primary studies is data collection. When comprehensive research reviews aim to characterize the full domain of the literature on a given topic, then the search procedures should be comprehensive and thorough. Early in the development of meta-analysis, researchers debated the merit of including unpublished studies, citing the generally poorer quality of research that does not survive the peer-review process (Slavin, 1986). However, other researchers have established the bias that does exist in the published literature toward larger and statistically significant effects (Mahoney, 1977; Sterne et al., 2002). Kennedy (2007) also shows that in the teacher qualification review, journal articles were of higher quality than book chapters, but of lower quality than dissertations and reports from independent research organizations.

The NRP decided to include only published results, opening up the possibility that the review overestimates the effect of phonics instruction. Ehri et al. (2001) use Rosenthal's (1992) fail-safe computation to conclude that over 800 other effect size comparisons in unpublished sources are needed to change the findings of the review. While it is unlikely that this number of studies exist somewhere in unpublished form, the fail-safe computation does not provide the most sensitive test of the potential for publication bias. More contemporary methods to address the effect of publication bias are outlined in Rothstein, Sutton, and Borenstein (2005). These methods examine the distribution of the effect sizes to produce more sensitive tests of possible bias such as the funnel plot first introduced by Light and Pillemer (1984), or the trim-and-fill method (Duval & Tweedie, 2000). Thus, we cannot discount the possibility that the panel's estimate of the effect of systematic phonics on reading achievement overestimates the true effect.

The current debate about studies to include in meta-analysis now centers on the type and quality of evidence required for making decisions about policy. A recent issue of *Educational Researcher* includes an essay by Slavin (2008) that argues for a hierarchy of study designs when judging the effectiveness of a program. Slavin characterizes the differences between a number of organized efforts such as the What Works Clearinghouse (2007) and the Best Evidence Encyclopedia (Center for Data-Driven Reform in Education, 2008) as a difference in the nature of the evidence considered strong enough to judge program effectiveness. These differences mainly consist of the types of studies included for the review with the randomized clinical trial at the top of the hierarchy followed by other well-controlled quasi-experiments. In one response to Slavin, Dynarski (2008) argues that all evidence on a given program should be reviewed, leaving the decision about whether the evidence supports a particular policy to those stakeholders who can assess how well the evidence fits their particular context. This debate can be framed as a discussion about whether reviewers or users of evidence are in the best position to evaluate the generalizability and validity of evidence from a review. If we are going to rely on a stakeholder to evaluate this evidence, the review itself must be usable and understandable—a question of the presentation of results. This issue will be explored in a later section.

The NRP made the decision to examine studies of phonics instruction that use experimental and well-controlled quasi-experimental research designs, a decision derived directly from the research question posed that focused on identifying effective methods for reading instruction. Many of the critics of the NRP report found the inclusion criteria for studies in the phonics review as too limiting. One set of criticisms focused on the inclusion of only experimental studies (Cunningham, 2001; Pressley et al., 2004). These criticisms make the point that limiting the review to experimental studies then limits the questions that can be addressed in the review. In fact, the National Reading Panel did limit their ability to produce reviews of particular areas of reading research because of the lack of experimental and quasi-experimental studies in these areas. Studies of the efficacy of systematic phonics instruction naturally employ experimental and quasi-experimental methods. In the decision to focus only on experimental studies, the Panel limits its ability to generalize results of the meta-analysis (a) to areas where experimental studies are more easily and regularly conducted, (b) to instructional contexts (including settings and implementation variables) that are similar to those used in the experimental studies, and most importantly, (c) to questions that can be addressed in experiments and quasi-experiments. Questions of how a program works, for example, cannot be addressed using experiments.

In some ways, these criticisms put an unfair burden on the research review. The NRP's charge from Congress was to examine evidence about program efficacy, and not to produce a review that could focus on questions of either statistical relationships or on questions about how or why a given program would work. These questions are critical to policy decisions, but are not ones that can be addressed by current methods for comprehensive research reviews and meta-analysis. A second criticism in Pressley et al. (2004) legitimately points out the retrospective nature of the studies included in a review. Cutting edge work pushing the boundaries of the research in a given area may not find its way to a comprehensive review and will likely not influence the results. Comprehensive research reviews may be limited in their ability to move the field in a new direction because of their retrospective nature, as Kennedy (2007) points out.

Data Evaluation In this stage of a research review, a researcher examines each included study, extracting a measure of the study's effect size, and codes aspects of the study's procedures, samples, and methods. Researchers developing codes for a set of studies need to have a thorough understanding of the studies included in the review as well as a breadth of knowledge of the literature in a given area. The difficult task in most research syntheses is the definition of the critical constructs in the review.

Another area of criticism of the report on phonics concerned the definitions of systematic phonics instruction. Allington (2006) writes that only 9 of the 38 studies on systematic phonics instruction examined reading text as a student outcome; the other studies measured reading isolated words. It is unlikely that any given definition of systematic phonics instruction for the purposes of a meta-analysis will satisfy all interested parties. What is reasonable to expect from a meta-analysis is transparency in the definition and consistency in applying that definition to the studies included in the review. Allington argues that the many interpretations of the NRP report including its executive summary were inconsistent in their definitions and in their reports of findings. The definition of key constructs does place boundaries on the types of inferences possible. With a large enough literature, a reviewer could examine how the results of primary studies vary with the operational definition of a construct. The report did examine differences in the magnitude of the effect size by the types of phonics programs finding no differences between synthetic phonics programs and other approaches, but as detailed below, these modeling strategies had some shortcomings.

Data Analysis and Interpretation When the studies in a comprehensive research review use quantitative measures, then the statistical techniques termed meta-analysis are usually employed. As described in earlier sections, these techniques include methods for describing the effect sizes extracted from the study, analyzing the variation among studies and examining models that account for the inevitable variation in studies' effect size.

At least one set of researchers raised issues about the analysis presented in the report (Camilli, Vargas, & Yurecko, 2003; Camilli et al., 2006). Their criticisms could reasonably be interpreted as providing a less optimistic estimate of the effects of phonics instruction. More important, however, to the results of the National Reading Panel is the comprehensiveness of the analysis presented in both the report (2000) and the subsequent publication by Ehri et al. (2001). Ehri et al. describe the statistical tests used as assessing

> … whether mean weighted effect sizes (d) were significantly greater than zero, whether mean effect sizes were derived from a homogeneous set (Q statistic), and whether pairs of mean effect sizes differed significantly for different levels of a moderator variable…. The analysis did not include tests of interactions between moderator variables because the numbers of comparisons were insufficient in many cases. (p. 403)

The analysis presented in the research review is equivalent to examining a series of t-tests, comparing two effect size means from two different study groups. For example, the studies with kindergarten and first graders were compared to studies with second through sixth graders. Unfortunately, these series of paired comparisons provide a restricted picture of the literature. We cannot tell from this analysis how the different characteristics of the studies relate to one another. For example, are most of the studies with kindergarten and first-grade children using particular outcome measures (such as decoding pseudowords) and using synthetic phonics programs? In general, the analyses presented in the phonics meta-analysis do not go far enough in providing a detailed model and description of the literature using the full range of meta-analysis tools available at the time of the report. Thus, it is difficult to arrive at reading policies that could be directly implemented given the lack of knowledge about how the context variables relate to each other and to effect size magnitude.

Public Presentation Educational research cannot influence policymaking if the results of that research cannot be understood by policy makers. The usability of the findings for policy decisions is a direct function of the presentation of the results. Allington (2006) and Camilli et al. (2006) both point to subsequent reporting of the results of the original NRP report and of the results of Camilli et al. (2003) as misrepresentations of the findings. Basing policies on inaccurate understandings of the complex findings could lead to faulty policy decisions. The presentation of results must balance the need for usability with an accurate and perhaps complex picture of the findings.

What should be standards guiding the reporting of comprehensive reviews that contribute to policy? The standards that guide the reporting of results in academic journals are not necessarily those guiding accessible user reports. This issue relates to the larger problem of translating results into practice that plagues all of our research efforts in education. The Evidence for Policy and Practice Information and Co-ordinating Centre (EPPI-Centre) at the Institute of Education, University of London, produces systematic reviews that involve users throughout the review process (EPPI-Centre, 2006). The reports produced by the research teams involve both technical researchers and potential consumers of the information. The Nordic Campbell Centre at the Danish National Centre for Social Research also focuses on the usability of research reviews. Their library includes review summaries written for a general audience and approved by the original systematic review authors (Nordic Campbell Centre, 2008). These efforts have the potential of providing accurate information to policy makers that can influence decisions.

Summary of Characteristics of Thorough Comprehensive Research Reviews What are reasonable quality standards for a comprehensive research synthesis using meta-analysis? The most important standard for a research review is transparency in the decisions made in each stage of the review. Though others may disagree with the decisions made by a reviewer, a thorough discussion of the rationale for the choices made in a review provides the boundaries for the inferences possible in the review. For reviews that

aim at assessing the current state of the literature for policy makers, the most thorough and current methods of analysis should be employed to understand the nature of the evidence available. The thoroughness of the analysis directly impacts how well we understand the nature of the evidence available in a given literature. Naturally, decisions made in the NRP report limit the types of inferences possible, and also suffer from the possibility that the estimates reflect publication bias. More importantly, however, the analysis itself does not serve to illuminate the important patterns and relationships among studies. These relationships could be examined using techniques analogous to one-way ANOVA or regression in the review. The information we would derive from the review would reflect the complexity of the evidence in the literature, and provide detail about how contextual variables relate to each other and to the efficacy of phonics instruction. But, as Feuer (2006) argues, this information, however imperfect, can be used in a bounded rational way to arrive at policy recommendations. The next section discusses areas of research in comprehensive synthesis that may increase the ability of findings to translate to policymaking.

Strengthening the Contribution of Research Syntheses

Research syntheses can contribute to policy by providing a comprehensive map of the literature in a given research area, and by exploring the boundaries of the inferences that can be made in a given literature, that is, by systematically examining how the effects of a program vary by types of study methods, contexts, and participant characteristics. There are a number of areas, however, where continued research on methods for research synthesis could expand and strengthen the contribution of reviews to policy.

Expanding the Questions Addressed in Research Synthesis Techniques for meta-analysis tend to dominate many comprehensive research reviews, focusing the review on studies that use quantitative measures of either differences between experimental groups or of relationships between important constructs. The focus on quantitative studies leaves out the range of studies concerned with how and why a program may work. How can we incorporate the contextual and detailed information contained in interpretive and qualitative studies of a program's implementation and results? For example, Thomas et al. (2004) illustrate how they integrated qualitative studies into their review on promoting healthy eating among children. They produce three separate syntheses, one for the quantitative studies, one for the qualitative and one that combines the two. They illustrate a summary matrix that maps out the kinds of evidence available for the set of recommendations found in the qualitative studies.

Chatterji (2008) argues for a broader inclusion of studies in a review that focuses on environmental, systemic, and implementation factors. Chatterji draws on the work of Pawson, Greenhalgh, Harvey, and Walshe (2005) on realist reviews—reviews based on the principles of theory-based evaluation.

Instead of a singular focus on a program's outcomes, Chatterji and Pawson et al. argue for review methods that explore underlying program theory and its implementation in diverse settings. Thus, inclusion rules in realist reviews encompass in-depth, qualitative studies of implementation and program processes. The Campbell Collaboration's (2001) guidelines for review protocols also requires potential reviewers to indicate how qualitative evidence will be synthesized in the review. Finding ways to incorporate and integrate evidence of various forms is an important challenge for the field of comprehensive research reviews.

Presenting Results in Usable Ways As discussed earlier, the contribution of research syntheses to policy depends on how those results are communicated to relevant policy makers and stakeholders. The EPPI-Centre (2006) and the Nordic Campbell Centre (2008) have both produced models of review summaries that are intended for users. Petticrew and Roberts (2003) also provide a method for characterizing the evidence in a particular field that illuminates not only the nature of the evidence for a given research question but also shows the areas where more research is warranted.

While the Ehri et al. (2001) review provided details about the analysis, the findings are not directly applicable either to practice or to policy decisions. One reason for the difficulty in translating the results centers on the nature of the analysis. A series of single predictor variable analyses does not allow the review to highlight what aspects of the context or of the program are most relevant to the magnitude of the effect of the program. Knowing that phonics instruction relates to larger effect sizes in earlier grades and to larger effect sizes on decoding skills than other measured skills does not necessarily lead to the inference that phonics instruction does not make a difference in later grades. It might be that all of the studies on phonics instruction's effect on decoding skills also used only kindergarten children. Ways to map systematically how the contextual and program variations are distributed across the studies in the review would also help policy makers to understand where we have good evidence about a program's effectiveness and where we need to invest resources to develop a deeper understanding of a program. In addition, models such as those of the EPPI-Centre and the Nordic Campbell Centre that foster collaboration between the review authors and potential users may both produce more usable reviews and avoid the translation problems cited by Allington (2006) and Camilli et al. (2006).

Methodological Advances for Meta-Analysis that Match Primary Studies Primary studies published in academic journals are increasingly using complex statistical modeling procedures such as structural equation modeling or multi-level models. In evaluation studies, these models are used to understand how contextual and program variables are related to variation in a program's effectiveness. Statistical methods in meta-analysis have not kept pace with advances in the modeling strategies of primary studies. For example,

the literature on education production functions uses models that relate school expenditures to student achievement while controlling for a number of factors at the school and student level. Each of these studies uses differing sets of control variables as well as variables measured at different levels (student versus school versus district). How to arrive at an estimate of the effect of school expenditures on student achievement requires techniques for synthesizing regression results, a technique that we are just beginning to explore (Wu & Pigott, 2008). We need to expand our ability to synthesize results beyond bivariate effect sizes such as correlation coefficients and standardized mean differences.

Timeliness of Reviews Comprehensive research reviews can take several years to complete. As seen in the experience of the NRP, reviews cannot be produced quickly, especially in areas where the literature is mature and diverse. Thus, reviews have a limited ability to address timely policy decisions. However, in the medical sciences at least, the Cochrane Collaboration (2008) and the EPPI-Centre (2006) provide models for more responsive reviews. The Cochrane Collaboration supports both new systematic reviews in areas of medicine and updates of existing reviews. Keeping a review current, and adjusting findings to new research allows medical professionals to have updated knowledge about the effects of a treatment regimen, or the progress of a disease. The EPPI-Centre's model is one of responsiveness to policy makers. As issues arise in the policy arena, the EPPI-Centre organizes and supports teams of researchers to produce reviews that have immediate policy relevance.

The Campbell Collaboration focuses on supporting and updating reviews in the areas of crime and justice, education and social welfare. As the library of reviews continues to expand in Campbell, these reviews could provide a more timely resource for policy makers in education to consult for the latest mapping of knowledge on a given topic. The Campbell Collaboration has some years to go before it develops a library as extensive as its sister organization, the Cochrane Collaboration. However, this volunteer and international group may eventually produce resources that educational policy makers and stakeholders can use directly in their decisions.

Discussion

In a series of lectures, Feuer (2006) argues for more rational and reasonable expectations of how educational research influences practice. One of Feuer's recommendations for educational researchers is:

> to specify clearly the limits of the analysis relating to specific policy choices that are otherwise left as an exercise to the listener....[I]t would involve articulating as precisely as possible the intended and unintended causal inferences imbedded in the work; the different standards of evidence that would need to obtain if the results were to translate into policy or programs; cautions about unintended effects of alternate interpretations of the data; and how the discovery of

new patterns and reinforcement or refutation of known patterns strengthens the base for testable hypotheses. (p. 93)

This set of recommendations applies to the use of comprehensive research syntheses in policy debates. Systematic reviews should report on the boundaries of the inferences and generalizations possible from a review, providing a map of types of evidence available in the literature, and where more resources are needed to provide a fuller understanding of an area. If the review is concerned with program efficacy, this map should include a discussion of the causal inferential landscape—the links in the causal description chain that are illuminated by the various studies in a given literature. For example, the NRP review on phonics instruction illustrates that we have relatively more information about the efficacy of phonics programs for kindergarten and first-grade children than we have for older students. We also need to understand how strong the evidence is based on the nature of the designs used in the literature and on how the design of the study relates to variation in effect sizes.

To create an understandable and usable map of the literature will require more attention to the presentation of research synthesis results and how these results relate to the underlying theory of the program or phenomenon. Some efforts in this arena have focused on the participation of stakeholders and potential users in all stages of the research review. Other efforts should concentrate on the presentation of results, perhaps using graphical techniques to illuminate the parts of the causal field that have received focus in the research. The results of a research synthesis reflect the complexity of the research in the field, and thus, research reviewers need to represent their results and the types of inferences possible as accurately as possible.

Research syntheses of high quality can contribute to policymaking if they are comprehensive in both scope and analysis. One limitation of their use in policy, however, is the timeliness of producing results. The Campbell Collaboration represents one volunteer effort to support syntheses in education, social welfare, and criminal justice. One goal of the Campbell Collaboration involves the updating of these syntheses so that these maps of the evidence in the literature can influence time-sensitive policy decisions. This system is already in place in Great Britain, for example, through the work of the EPPI-Centre.

The current policy window has brought a focus on the nature of the evidence supporting educational decisions. Comprehensive research reviews and meta-analysis can provide systematic methods for examining the evidence in a given policy area so that important decisions about educating our children are based more on research than on anecdote.

References

Allington, R. L. (2006). Reading lessons and federal policy making: An overview and introduction to the special issue. *Elementary School Journal, 107*, 3–15.

Camilli, G., Vargas, S., & Yurecko, M. (2003). Teaching children to read: The fragile link between science and federal education policy. *Education Policy Analysis Archives, 11*(15). Retrieved November 12, 2008, from http://epaa.asu.edu/epaa/v11n15/

Camilli, G., Wolfe, P. M., & Smith, M. L. (2006). Meta-analysis and reading policy: Perspectives on teaching children to read. *Elementary School Journal, 107*, 27–36.

Campbell Collaboration. (2001). *Guidelines for the preparation of review protocols.* Retrieved April 30, 2008, from http://www.campbellcollaboration.org/library/C2_Protocols_guidelines.pdf

Center for Data-Driven Reform in Education. (2008). *Best Evidence Encyclopedia.* Retrieved April 20, 2008, from http://www.bestevidence.org

Chatterji, M. (2008). Synthesizing evidence from impact evaluations in education to inform action. *Educational Researcher, 37*(1), 23–26.

The Cochrane Collaboration. (2008). *The Cochrane Collaboration: The reliable source of evidence in health care.* Retrieved April 30, 2008, from http://www.cochrane.org/

Cooper, H. (1998). *Synthesizing research: A guide for literature reviews* (3rd ed.). Thousand Oaks, CA: Sage.

Cooper, H., & Hedges, L. V. (Eds.). (1994). *The handbook of research synthesis.* New York: Russell Sage Foundation.

Cunningham, J. W. (2001). Review: Essay book reviews: The National Reading Panel Report. *Reading Research Quarterly, 36*, 326–335.

Duval, S., & Tweedie, R. (2000). Trim and fill: A simple funnel-plot-based method of testing and adjusting for publication bias in meta-analysis. *Biometrics, 56*, 455–463.

Dynarski, M. (2008). Bringing answers to educators: Guiding principles for research syntheses. *Educational Researcher, 37*(1), 27–29.

Ehri, L. C., Nunes, S. R., Stahl, S. A., & Willows, D. M. (2001). Systematic phonics instruction helps students learn to read: Evidence from the National Reading Panel's Meta-analysis. *Review of Educational Research, 71*, 393–447.

EPPI-Centre. (2006). *User driven evidence: Informed policy and practice.* Retrieved April 28, 2008 from http://eppi.ioe.ac.uk/cms/Default.aspx?tabid=65

Feuer, M. J. (2006). *Moderating the debate: Rationality and the promise of American education.* Cambridge, MA: Harvard Education Press.

Hammill, D. D., & Swanson, H. L. (2006). The National Reading Panel's meta-analysis of phonics instruction: Another point of view. *Elementary School Journal, 107*, 17–26.

Hunter, J. E., & Schmidt, F. L. (2004). *Methods of meta-analysis: Correcting error and bias in research findings* (2nd ed.). Thousand Oaks, CA: Sage.

Kennedy, M. M. (2007). Defining a literature. *Educational Researcher, 36*(3), 139–147.

Kingdon, J. W. (2003). *Agendas, alternatives and public policies* (2nd ed.). Upper Saddle River, NJ: Longman.

Light, R. J., & Pillemer, D. B. (1984). *Summing up: The science of reviewing research.* Cambridge, MA: Harvard University Press.

Mahoney, M. J. (1977). Publication prejudices: An experimental study of confirmatory bias in the peer review system. *Cognitive Therapy and Research, 1*, 161–175.

National Reading Panel. (2000). *Report of the National Reading Panel: Teaching children to read. An evidence-based assessment of the scientific research literature on reading and its implications for reading instruction: Report of the subgroups.* Bethesda, MD: National Institutes of Health, National Institute of Child Health and Human Development.

Nordic Campbell Centre. (2008). *Nordic Campbell Centre Library.* Retrieved April 28, 2008, from http://www.sfi.dk/sw28636.asp

Pawson, R., Greenhalgh, T., Harvey, G., & Walshe, K. (2005). Realist review: A new method of systematic review designed for complex policy interventions. *Journal of Health Services Research and Policy, 10*(Suppl. 1), 21–34.

Petticrew, M., & Roberts, H. (2003). Evidence, hierarchies, and typologies: Horses for courses. *Journal of Epidemiology and Community Health, 57*, 527–529.

Pressley, M., Duke, N. K., & Boling, E. C. (2004). The educational science and scientifically based instruction we need: Lessons from reading research and policymaking. *Harvard Educational Review, 74*, 30–61.

Rosenthal, R. (1991). *Meta-analytic procedures for social research* (Rev. ed.). Thousand Oaks, CA: Sage.

Rosenthal, R. (1992). Effect size estimation, significance testing, and the file-drawer problem. *Journal of Parapsychology, 56*, 57–58.

Rothstein, H. R., Sutton, A. J., & Borenstein, M. (Eds.). (2005). *Publication bias in meta-analysis: Prevention, assessment and adjustments.* West Sussex, England: Wiley.

Shadish, W. R., Cook, T. D., & Campbell, D. T. (2002). *Experimental and quasi-experimental designs for generalized causal inference.* Boston: Houghton Mifflin.

Shanahan, T. (2005). A special section on reading research: But does it really matter? *Phi Delta Kappan, 86*, 452–461.

Slavin, R. E. (1986). Best-evidence synthesis: An alternative to meta-analytic and traditional reviews. *Educational Researcher, 15*(9), 5–11.

Slavin, R. E. (2008). Perspectives on evidence-based research in education—what works? Issues in synthesizing educational program evaluations. *Educational Researcher, 37*(1), 5–14.

Sterne, J. A. C., Juni, P., Schulz, K. F., Altman, D. G., Bartlett, C., & Egger, M. (2002). Statistical methods for assessing the influence of study characteristics on treatment effects in 'meta-epidemiological' research. *Statistics in Medicine, 21*, 1513–1524.

Thomas, J., Harden, A., Oakley, A., Oliver, S., Sutcliffe, K., Rees, R., et al. (2004). Integrating qualitative research with trials in systematic reviews. *British Medical Journal, 328*, 1010–1012.

What Works Clearinghouse. (2007). Welcome to WWC: A central and trusted source of scientific evidence for what works in education. Retrieved May 15, 2008, from http://www.w-w-c.org/

Wu, M.-J., & Pigott, T. D. (2008, March). *Synthesizing regression results.* Paper presented at the Annual meeting of the American Educational Research Association, New York.

14

Complementary Methods for Policy Research

Laura M. Desimone
University of Pennsylvania

Debates about the relative merits of different research methodologies have persisted for decades in education research. The appropriateness, benefits, tradeoffs, and challenges of combining paradigmatic, design, data collection, and analytic approaches in conducting education research have been the subject of journal articles (e.g., Ercikan & Roth, 2006; Raudenbush, 2005), book chapters (e.g., Shulman, 1997), even entire books (e.g., Bernard, 1999; Creswell & Clark, 2006). Building on such previous work, I discuss here complementary methods as they apply specifically to education program and policy research.

What is Policy Research?

The first step in a discussion of methodological complementarities in education program and policy research is to define what qualifies as education policy research. Policy research has multiple dimensions, tiers, and levels of specificity (Kraft & Furlong, 2004; Munger, 2000). At one extreme, policy is a funding stream with global targets. Title I fits this definition of policy—the government gives Title I money to districts and schools to achieve broad goals such as decreasing the achievement gap between high and low poverty students. A more explicit policy might delineate specific targets for success and accompany them with sanctions and incentives, as do the accountability provisions of the No Child Left Behind Act (NCLB).

At the other end of the policy continuum are programs, where policy not only has established global targets, but specifies a particular intervention that states, districts, or schools are to use to meet the targets. Examples are comprehensive school reform programs required by many districts to meet their overarching policy of improved student achievement; and reading programs funded by the federal government's Reading First initiative. The distinctions between programs and policy are the subject of much discussion, and subsequently the lines between program evaluation and policy research are not clear (Cronbach et al.,

1980; Weiss, 1998). In this chapter, the conception of education policy includes both broad policy directives as well as programmatic initiatives designed to respond to those broad policy directives. I use the terms program and policy research and education policy research interchangeably.

Policy can be conceived and implemented at multiple levels. Often a policy conceived at one level is implemented at another. The education system has many levels at which policy might be developed and implemented, including national policy (e.g., Title VII), state policy (e.g., certification requirements for teachers, content standards and assessment regimes), district policy (e.g., required professional development hours), school policy (e.g., in-school mentoring/coaching), and classroom policy (e.g., behavior modification programs). Education policy can operate at more than one of these levels simultaneously. For example, a textbook or curriculum adoption can occur at the district, school, or classroom level.

Activities that fall under the guise of policy research can include the study of policy formation, implementation, effects, and cost-benefit analyses (Munger, 2000; Patton & Sawicki, 1993; Weimer & Vining, 1998). In the context of education, these same distinctions apply. Education policy research might study the formation of state policy in higher education (McLendon, Hearn, & Deaton, 2006), the diffusion and variation in a school or district's implementation of a reform (Massell, 2001; McLaughlin, 1976), the facilitators and barriers to a program's implementation (Desimone, Payne, Federovicious, Henrich, & Finn-Stevenson, 2004), the effects of broad education policy initiatives such as systemic reform (Clune et al., 1997; Supovitz & Taylor, 2005), state policies (e.g., Firestone, Goertz, & Natriello, 1997), and federal funding streams (Birman & Porter, 2002), the effects of specific programmatic reforms such as an after-school program designed to meet the requirements of district or state policy (James-Burdumy et al., 2005), or the effects of a particular curriculum reform such as Success for All (Borman et al., 2005).

A distinction is sometimes made between policy research and policy-relevant research (Majchrzak, 1984). Policy research looks directly at the formation, implementation, effects, and tradeoffs of programs and policies. Policy-relevant research does not directly assess a particular program or policy, but instead provides data and information with the potential of informing or shaping policy. In one sense, policy-relevant research in education might be any information that contributes to a better understanding of how states, districts, schools, and classrooms work. By this definition, much, if not all, of education research might be considered "policy-relevant." In this chapter I focus on policy research that is explicitly targeting the study of the implementation and/or effects of a particular education program or policy.

Chapters in this section of the Handbook focus on alternative methodologies for studying education policy, such as clinical trials, meta-analysis, and sophisticated techniques to perform rigorous quasi-experiments. The purpose of the current chapter is to discuss how these and other alternative methodologies might be combined to improve our ability to answer important education policy questions. This chapter first briefly describes the myriad of methodologies available to education policy research, and then discusses the relationship that methods have with research questions and with ideology. The following sections explain several ways of combining methods and how complementary methods can increase the quality of policy research. Then, suggestions are made for best practice in using complementary methods, and the relative strengths of quantitative and qualitative research as they apply to education policy questions are presented. The final section highlights current issues and challenges in integrating methods to provide better insights into how and why certain education policies succeed or fail.

Alternative Methods for Conducting Education Policy Research

The diverse array of techniques we have at our disposal to study education policy forms a "methodological mosaic" (Shulman, 1997, p. 14). Advancing from the design experiments, place-based experiments, quasi-experiments, and correlational methods that dominated social science in the early 19th century, we now have in our arsenal of methods ethnographic techniques (Merriam, 1988), discourse analysis (Wooffitt, 2005), think aloud and other forms of protocol analysis (Desimone & LeFloch, 2004), and case study approaches that usually include a combination of in-depth interviewing, document analysis, and observation. Each type of research methodology must in some way deal with questions of precision and generalizability, though standards and criteria for these differ across modes of inquiry (Shulman, 1997). With each of these methodologies, alternative approaches are possible. For example, within the framework of correlational and quasi-experimental studies, we have developed powerful and sophisticated techniques

from which researchers must choose—for example, for analyzing nested hierarchical systems, imputing missing data, accounting for selection bias, and generating the correct standard errors (e.g., fixed or random effects; e.g., Allison, 2001; Burnham & Anderson, 2002; Little & Rubin, 2002; Raudenbush & Bryk, 2002).

Research methods are most commonly dichotomized into qualitative and quantitative modes of inquiry. Such broad categories, however, mask substantive differences in approaches to inquiry. One might imagine a continuum with exploratory or naturalistic inquiry on one end of the continuum, and manipulation and hypothesis testing on the other end. Another way of looking at this progression is the continuum of investigative techniques from low levels of inference (more exploratory, descriptive inquiry) to high levels of inference (hypothesis-confirming studies; Ercikan & Roth, 2006).

Considering this continuum or progression, it is clear that qualitative or quantitative designs, data collection, or analysis methods might be used at either end (Lynch, 1983; Tashakkori & Teddlie, 1998). Thus it is important to distinguish at least three dimensions of methods—type of inquiry (e.g., manipulation vs. naturalistic inquiry), type of data to collect, and methods to collect that data (Lynch, 1983). For example, classroom observations or interviews (methods of data collection) might be used to create narratives, or coded to provide quantitative data (type of data). Typically, however, quantitative methods such as quasi-experiments and experiments are used in a confirmatory way—to test formal hypotheses—while case studies, ethnographies, and other field based observational studies generally are used for in-depth exploration or naturalistic inquiry (LeTendre, 2002).

Linking Methods to Questions

Given the myriad of choices about design, type of data and data collection, how should researchers decide which are the best methods to use in pursuing education policy questions? The answer, true of all types of research and fundamental to this discussion of integrating methods for policy research, is that research questions should drive methods. Our choice of methodologies should be in direct response to the type of policy question we are asking. At a basic level, questions about policy or program effectiveness are best answered with experiments and quasi-experiments. When properly executed, these designs give us the most confidence in causal conclusions, because they have stronger internal validity (i.e., they account for confounding factors and alternative explanations for effects). In contrast, questions focused on how and why a program or policy works nearly always necessitate in-depth data generated from qualitative approaches like case studies. Understanding the complexities and interactions and contextual influences of policy implementation and effects requires rich data that surveys and assessments cannot capture.

Shulman (1997) provides an example that explicates the

appropriateness of different methodologies for different questions. In examining reading programs, an investigator might ask one of several questions:

1. What predicts good reading?
2. What is the best method for teaching reading?
3. How does reading achievement differ across groups?
4. How is reading instruction implemented?

Each type of question corresponds to a different set of methods. Identifying factors that predict reading achievement necessitates a correlational study; choosing the best method for teaching reading requires a series of impact studies with an experimental or quasi-experimental design; examining differences across groups requires a comparative descriptive analysis with quantitative assessment data, and characterizing how teachers instruct reading requires an implementation study, which may use both quantitative and qualitative measures of instruction. Further, each of these four questions contributes to policy in a different way—the first question informs the development of good reading programs (this would fall under the policy-relevant category discussed above), the second identifies programs to adopt, the third targets individuals for the program or policy, and the fourth informs policy implementation.

Once our policy question is defined, we must make decisions about appropriate data and analytic techniques. For example, if we want to know how a particular program or policy changed a teacher's instruction, we need data with at least two time points (Singer & Willett, 2003). If we want to better understand children's achievement growth trajectories, we need at least 3 time points of data (Bryk & Raudenbush, 1987; Rogosa, Brandt, & Zimowski, 1982). Thus, while in a general sense our choice of methods should reflect the particular policy questions we are asking, even without our broad choice of methods there are a multitude of decisions about proper data collection and analytic techniques.

The challenge of choosing the appropriate methodology is compounded when multiple methodologies are employed to answer related policy questions. Paradigms differ in the manner in which they formulate their questions, how they define the content of their domains and organize that content conceptually, and the principles of discovery and verification that constitute the ground rules for creating and testing knowledge in their fields (Shulman, 1997). These differences underlie the basic tensions between multiple methods and different disciplines. Other work has taken on these debates directly (e.g., Brewer & Hunter, 2005). Here we start from the perspective that important policy questions need to be studied from multiple perspectives using multiple paradigms. This in turn implies that policy studies need to be asking multi-dimensional questions.

Do Methods Equal Ideology?

One of the key challenges in asking multi-dimensional questions in policy studies is that often the questions we ask, and thus the modes of inquiry we choose, are associated, rightly or wrongly, with our political or epistemological beliefs. A widely accepted idea in policy and politics is that defining the problem or question serves an agenda-setting role (Kingdon, 1984). The questions we ask say something about the kinds of problems we think are important.

While few would argue that politics and policy are inextricably intertwined, to what extent do the methods that education policy researchers choose equate with their supposed political and epistemological ideologies? Modes of research are often thought to reflect the researcher's political or ideological dispositions. Shulman (1997) argues that choosing methods is not primarily a technical endeavor, but that it is associated with underlying theoretical, political, or social purposes. For example, qualitative investigations focused on answering questions about how current policies differentially affect minority or high-poverty students (e.g., McNeil, 2000) are frequently thought to be challenging the status quo, while "empiricists" who seek to answer straightforward questions about how current policies or programs are working (e.g., Borman & Hewes, 2003), may be interpreted to support the status quo.

There is no evidence that these interpretations are accurate, however. A reading of education policy research in the past several decades supports the notion that methodologies themselves do not necessarily favor particular political ideologies. While methodology and ideology are often correlated (e.g., critical theory analysis with particular beliefs about race and class in our society), such an association is not inevitable or required. In answering questions about policy formation, implementation, and effectiveness, our choice of methods is not inherently ideological. It is in how we administer those methods, what areas we emphasize and ignore, and how we interpret our results where ideology plays the most substantive role. State-of-the-art policy inquiry should acknowledge the particular stance dictated by its set of research questions, and should strive whenever possible to integrate alternative frameworks into designing studies—for example, by pairing straightforward "what works" questions with inquiry into unintended consequences and differential effects across racial/ethnic and income groups.

However, the very issue of how closely tied ideology is to methods calls into question the sensibility and value of mixing paradigms and methods. At one extreme is the thought that mixing methods where there are different paradigms is not meaningful, sensible, or useful (Guba & Lincoln, 1988). The other extreme believes that paradigms are logically interdependent and that methods can be mixed and matched to achieve the combination most appropriate for a given inquiry problem (Reichardt & Cook, 1979; Miles & Huberman, 1984). The middle ground supports the notion that different methodologies can retain their distinct paradigms and simultaneously enhance inquiry into a research problem by exploring convergences in stories generated by the alternative paradigms (Kidder & Fine, 1987). It is this middle ground where policy research can most benefit from calling on different paradigms and methodologies.

Complementary Methods: To What End?

Having argued that paradigms and methods are separate from ideology, and can be used productively in combination, this leads to the question of why we would want to use different methods to study a policy or program. What purposes are served by combining paradigms and methods? Consistent with calls for mixed methodology for education research in general (see Johnson & Onwuegbuzie, 2004), this section describes a framework for combining methods to provide insights into policy implementation and effects that would otherwise be unattainable from only one paradigm or method.

Greene, Caracelli, and Graham (1989) offer a sensible schema to distinguish the main purposes of using different methodologies in education research. Though they apply the scheme to education in a general sense, the framework is directly applicable to policy research. They identify five purposes for mixed method studies: (a) triangulation, (b) complementarity, (c) development, (d) initiation, and (e) expansion. Below, I briefly discuss each of these and how they apply to education policy research.

Triangulation Triangulation refers to the use of different research methods to answer the same question. The goal is to establish "convergence, corroboration and correspondence of results across different method types" (Greene et al., 1989, p. 257). In other words, triangulation provides similar but alternative measures of the same phenomena (LeTendre, 2002). By using methods whose biases counteract each other, the validity of research results are strengthened (Greene et al., 1989). The use of triangulation is based on the premise that every method has particular biases and limitations, so that the use of only one method to answer a policy question will inevitably yield biased and limited results.

Triangulation is enhanced when each method used has a similar weight and influence on the research design, data collection, and analysis, and when each component is implemented independently and simultaneously. Triangulation is rarely employed in education policy research, in part due to limited resources and pressures for quick results, which often precludes the collection and analysis of multiple measures of the same inputs and outcomes.

Complementarity A more common way of mixing methods is for complementary purposes. This is when different methods are used for different components of a study (Cook, 1985) or to measure separate levels of a phenomena (Mark & Shotland, 1987). In a "complementarity" mixed-method study, qualitative and quantitative methods are used to measure overlapping but different facets of a phenomenon.

Results from one method type are intended to enhance, enrich, elaborate, illustrate, or clarify results from the other. Complementarity can increase the depth and confidence in interpretation of whatever policy is under study. The most common mixed methodology in policy research and program evaluation is embedding case studies in a larger quantitative study, where the quantitative study answers questions about who the policy is affecting, and its outcomes, and the case studies offer insights to explain effects, give examples, and illustrate how effects and implementation might differ across class, race, or gender lines (e.g., Berger, Desimone, Herman, Garet, & Margolin, 2002; Garet, Porter, Desimone, Birman, & Yoon, 2001; Weiss, Banilower, Crawford, & Overstreet, 2003). Case studies might also be used to explain how and why a policy or program has particular effects (e.g., Aladjem et al., 2002).

Development A third way to use different methods in the same study is to use methods sequentially in the development of the study (Greene et al., 1989). Here the intent is to use the results of one method to help develop or inform the other method. A recommended use here is employing case studies or cognitive interviews to develop surveys or observation protocols (Desimone & LeFloch, 2004; LeTendre, 2002). Qualitative inquiry such as focus groups or interviews can also be used to refine a study's conceptual model. Other examples are where an initial descriptive survey might be administered to identify state, districts, schools, or classrooms as candidates for a study; or where results of questionnaires are used to indicate areas that justify follow-up with qualitative methods.

Development can also be conducted *across* policy studies. For example, in research on teacher pay for performance, qualitative work has indicated that unintended negative outcomes are possible, such as teacher competition, cheating, and teaching to the test (Cullen & Reback, 2002; Hatry, Greiner, & Ashford, 1994); this work has in turn informed subsequent policy studies which explicitly include measures of these unintended effects (Jacob & Levitt, 2003; Springer, 2006). Similarly, early case study data has shown that communication with the community and parents is critical to student participation in school choice programs. Such data was used in the development of part of a national policy study targeting the evaluation of school choice options. In response to the earlier qualitative results, researchers included on the national survey specific questions about the level and type of school-parent-community communication about the availability of school choice options (RAND, AIR, & NORC, 2005).

Initiation The fourth purpose of mixed methods in Greene et al.'s (1989) framework is to use different methods to inquire into the same questions, to increase the chances of identifying paradox or contradiction (Rossman & Wilson, 1985). In "initiation" studies, the researcher intentionally seeks areas of non-convergence to initiate interpretations and conclusions, suggest areas for further analysis or recast research questions or the problem itself. Here mixing paradigms is encouraged, consistent with Cook's (1985) call for multiple theoretical and value frameworks in applied social inquiry. Initiation designs are meant to be provocative through the recasting of questions or results from one method type with questions or results from the contrasting method type.

An example from education policy research might use initiation to investigate the effects of high-stakes testing on students, teachers, and principals. A hypothesis-testing paradigm might quantitatively measure rewards and sanctions associated with high-stakes testing, and subsequent student achievement scores on standardized tests, to test whether the incentive systems of NCLB are affecting student learning. A more inquiry-oriented paradigm might use teacher and student interviews and classroom observation and lesson plan analyses to examine how teaching, content coverage, and student attitude/motivation have changed as a result of NCLB mandates. Both methods are designed to answer the global questions of effects, but using them together creates the potential to identify non-convergence with implications for redefining interpretations, research questions, or the initial problem. For example, such an "initiation" design might uncover undesirable teaching practices, perverse incentives to perform, and questions about appropriate ways of measuring student achievement. These findings in turn could affect the conceptualization of the original policy question.

Expansion The last purpose of mixed methodology that Greene et al. (1989) describe is the use of multiple methods to expand the scope, breadth, or range of a study. In expansion uses, the methods are often kept separate, since they are answering different policy questions. Pure expansion studies do not realize the benefits of mixing methods in answering the same question, which results in increased confidence in inferences, as in complementary designs (Greene et al., 1989). The advantage lies primarily in enabling the study to answer more questions, though similar concepts, complementary and expansion methods differ in at least one major way. In complementary designs, mixed methods are used to examine different levels or aspects of a question. For example, survey data might be used to demonstrate the existence of associations and interview data might describe those associations and how they work. In expansion studies, mixed methods are used to examine separate questions. In the example above, survey data might be used to show a correlation, while interview data might be used to shed light on how those associations came to be—a different question than what the relationships are.

A common use of expansion in program and policy research is for quantitative paradigms and methods to be used for assessing program and policy outcomes, while qualitative paradigms and methods are used to describe implementation and unintended consequences (Rossi, Lipsey, & Freeman, 2004; Weiss, 1998). Thus a policy study might measure implementation through case study data, and outcomes through survey and assessment data, which is a typical way to expand a program evaluation or policy study.

Mixing Mixed Methods Of course, each of these strategies for using multiple methods can be used in combination, and at different points in the study—for design, data collection, analysis, and interpretation. Greene et al. (1989) developed a framework that lists a continuum from full integration in both analyses and interpretation, to separate analyses but some integration during interpretation, to no integration. This framework can be extended to consider the degree of integration in development, design, and data collection. Decisions about which component(s) of the study merit the integration of methods should be guided by the overarching policy questions at the heart of the study, and the purpose(s) of the combination methods, as just described.

Elevating the Quality of Policy Research Using Complementary Methods: Or Why Policy Research Needs Complementary Methods

Most education research can benefit from the use of complementary methods, as reflected in the argument that "the best research programs will reflect intelligent deployment of a diversity of research methods applied to their appropriate research questions" (Shulman, 1997, p. 25). Policy research in particular often demands it, for a myriad of reasons. Education policy plays out amidst the dynamic complexity of everyday life in school districts, schools and classrooms. The complexity of on-the-ground policy calls into question the usefulness of single dimensional studies as traditionally conducted (Lather & Moss, 2005).

Capturing the interactions, real-time changes, and multiple perspectives of policy actors at various levels requires multiple methods. Previous policy work has shown beyond a doubt that context matters (e.g., Berends, 2000; Bryk & Driscoll, 1988; Clune, 1998; Cohen & Hill, 2001; McLaughlin, 1976). The pressure for policy research to produce generalizable, valid answers to how a particular policy or program is working, combined with the need to understand implementation challenges and how context might influence implementation, perceptions, and outcomes necessitates the use of multiple methodologies.

In addition, use of complementary methods has gained wide support as a way to increase the accuracy of the interpretation of results. This is especially important when policies or programs are being evaluated for decisions about continuation. For example, leaders of national policy studies focus attention on the importance of including "narrative methodologies in order to provide potential for rich interpretations for … statistical data, and in this way providing decision makers [with] more comprehensive information" (Plomp, 1990, p. 9).

Further, consistent with an "expansion" purpose, using different methods enables researchers to answer different policy questions (Tashakkori & Teddlie, 1998), often necessary to obtain a complete picture of the policy's effects. Policy inquiry might rely on quantitative data to provide information about the proliferation of charter schools, qualifications of teachers who teach in them, and trends in student achievement over time, either in the context of an experiment or quasi-experiment. In contrast, qualitative methods can ask questions about how teachers come to teach in charter schools, how their goals and motivations shape their teaching practices, and how the contextual issues and uncertainty around the development of a new charter school influences teaching and learning (Berends, Watral, Teasley, & Nicotera, 2006; Goldring & Cravens, 2006). Together quantitative and qualitative inquiry provide a more complete answer to policy questions about the formation, execution, and effects of charter schools than would be possible with only one methodology.

Similarly, combining methods, such as embedding case studies in experimental designs, results in greater explanatory power. Such a combination enables us to learn about the determinants and consequences of implementation quality and about the viability of the substantive theory undergirding program design (Cook, 2002). A simple experiment without implementation or case study data would likely leave too many question unanswered about how and why the program succeeded or failed.

Using complementary methods can also improve cross-cultural policy studies. Combining qualitative and quantitative methodologies can "maximize understanding of educational processes cross-nationally" (LeTendre, 2002, p. 204). Incorporating cultural analyses into cross-national studies of schooling enable the effects of beliefs, values, ideological conflicts or habitual practices to be incorporated into the analysis. For example, the TIMSS-Repeat (TIMSS-R) and Civic Education studies combine video and surveys and by doing so make advances in integrating qualitative and quantitative methods in cross-national studies of academic achievement. The video-survey combination enables a holistic analysis that incorporates a more dynamic model of culture than would otherwise be available with just one methodology. For an illustration of this, take the statistical analyses of survey data showing a correlation between large class size and the use of more procedural (e.g., lecture) instruction in the U.S., but not in the high-achieving countries of Singapore and Japan (Desimone, Smith, Baker, & Ueno, 2005). These data might be used to shape policy and mandate smaller class size to enable more inquiry-oriented types of instruction. However, analysis of classroom lessons on video reveal how Singapore and Japanese teachers are able to use inquiry-oriented methods with larger classes, providing an existence proof that conceptual teaching can be conducted with large classes, and thus a point of departure for shaping U.S. policy designed to foster such teaching (Stigler & Stevenson, 1991).

Still another purpose of using complementary methods is that it might increase the use of the results in policy-making. In public policy textbooks, the rational decision-making framework describes a process where the problem is defined, alternatives are laid out along with decision criteria, information is collected along the dimensions of the criteria and then an analysis is conducted to come to a decision. As any student of policy knows, policy decisions do not follow this organized, linear path. Empirical work on how social science data are used in policy decisions show that such straightforward and direct uses are rare (Weiss & Bucuvalas, 1977; Weiss, 1988). Instead, policy decisions are based on the interaction of a number of factors, given more or less weight depending on the circumstances, including research information blended with current perceptions, beliefs and theories, political tensions, existence proofs, etc. (Cook, 2002; Cohen & Garet, 1991; Kingdon, 1984). Research use is much more complex than simply making an evidence-based rational choice (Cook, 2002; Weiss, 1998). Given this reality, the more different types of data and multi-dimensional answers to policy questions we can provide using multiple methods, the more chance we have that education policy research will have an influence on policy decisions.

Best Practice in Using Complementary Methods

Working from the tenet that policy research can be more informative when using multiple methods, what are the principles of best practice in using complementary methods? While the benefits of using a multiplicity of methods for social inquiry were recognized centuries ago by great philosophers such as Aristotle (1941), the proper use and application in current education policy research is less clear. Previous work points to at least three recommendations for the use of complementary methods in policy research; using an integrative framework, applying an iterative approach, and grounding the study in theory.

Use of an Integrative Framework One recommendation is to have an inclusive framework for policy studies, which includes questions answered by multiple techniques. Too often in mixed methods studies each methodology operates in isolation, and thus does not yield benefits to analysis and interpretation. An integrated framework allows the results of the different research components to be used in ways that increase the overall analytic strength of a study (LeTendre, 2002). Here a plan for how each method will be integrated with the other is made explicit in the study design. Such detailed analysis plans (e.g., American Institutes for Research, 2000) provide a guiding framework for subsequent data collection, analysis and interpretation.

Application of an Iterative Approach A second suggestion for strengthening policy research through complementary methods is by iterative use of multiple methods. This is most consistent with the development and initiation methods, where each method informs the other. The idea behind interactive sequential methodology is not to measure the same phenomenon at the same time, but to use the findings of one methodology to inform the issues to be addressed in the subsequent study. Qualitative data are employed to ensure that the quantitative study is current, and quantitative data in turn are used to reformulate issues for the qualitative study (Moran, 1987). For example, in the IEA Civic Education study, experts moved back and forth between two sets of data and used findings from the qualitative to alter the collection of quantitative data (LeTendre, 2002). This iterative integration allowed the strength of qualitative studies—to generate high quality hypotheses grounded in empirical reality—to be incorporated into the overall research process. This allowed key questions that arose in the early stages of research to drive the development of focus and instrument creation in subsequent stages (LeTendre, 2002). Such an approach increases the likelihood of "maximiz[ing] the analytic capacity of individual components" of a study (LeTendre, 2002, p. 217).

Grounding the Study in Theory   A third component to best practice in using complementary methods is grounding the study in theory. Having a core set of characteristics that we know are related to effective policy implementation, and measuring them every time we study education policy initiatives, would help move the field forward. We know that there are competing policy initiatives that affect the coherence of the policy environment; we know that policies have different levels of specificity that affect respondent behavior; we know that policies have different levels of backing and buy-in that affect implementation; and we know policies have different rewards and sanctions, both implicit and explicit, associated with their use (Desimone, 2002; Porter, Floden, Freeman, Schmidt, & Schwille, 1988). Why not include these and other key components in our studies of education policies? This does not prevent each study from having its own unique characteristics, or require each study to be constrained to measure only the features in a core framework. Using a shared conceptual framework as a basis for developing measures of the policy and school environment would contribute to our building a consistent set of data over time on critical aspects of policy formation, implementation, and effects. A shared conceptual framework could also steer us toward using an appropriate timeline. Cook (2002) criticizes the reliance on theory to make causal conclusions from non-experimental data, in part because theories rarely espouse an appropriate timeline for the expectation of results. If education policy were to adopt a core framework it could serve as a guide for the appropriate timing of program and policy effects.

Relative Strengths of Different Methods for Policy Research

As indicated earlier in the chapter, there are a multitude of methods from which to choose, and different points in the study (development, design, data collection, analysis, interpretation) to apply them. But the major distinction most commonly made among methods is between those representing qualitative and quantitative modes of inquiry. I use this rough dichotomy to frame a discussion of what each overarching paradigm and methodology brings to the study of education policy, to make even more clear how complementary methods are vital to high-quality policy studies.

Use of Qualitative Methods for Policy Research   Qualitative research that follows a naturalistic paradigm tends not to use an a priori theoretical or analytic perspective to understand the phenomena under study (Riehl, 2001). This allows discovery of unintended consequences, as well as relationships and links that might not have been originally hypothesized by the policy designers or implementers. Such a perspective can be invaluable in understanding policy implementation challenges and explaining outcomes. For example, a qualitative inquiry into a school's practice of holding a vote on whether to adopt a particular comprehensive school reform model revealed that teachers often felt pressure from their principal and fellow teachers to vote a particular way, so a vote in favor of a particular program did not necessarily reflect teachers' support for the program. This lack of real support was manifested later in weak implementation (Datnow, 2000). A quantitative study design that measured only whether there was a vote and its results, and linked that to quality of implementation, might have erroneously concluded that faculty support (as proxied by a unanimous faculty vote) was unrelated to implementation. Clearly, the politics and pressure of the voting procedure and other measures of support and buy-in is something districts and schools need to consider in their adoption and implementation of policies and programs. This is an explicit example of how qualitative approaches "can be a powerful tool for debugging policy" (Sadler, 1985, p. 144).

Qualitative inquiry also is especially useful for answering questions about how policies operate in different classroom and school contexts (Asay & Hennon, 1999; Ercikan & Roth, 2006). Since we know that policies may be differentially effective across contexts, insights into contextual interactions and effects are critical to shaping policies and programs to bring to scale, particularly in identifying adaptations and flexibility that needs to be built into the policy to reflect alternative local contexts (McLaughlin, 1976, 1987).

Another strength of exploratory, in-depth approaches to data collection is their ability to capture dynamic, interactive, subjective phenomena, which often undergird the success or failure of policies and programs. Current education program and policy reforms such as school choice, coaching/mentoring, professional development interventions, and curriculum changes are all subject to the complex dynamics of relationships between district administrators, principals, teachers and students, information sharing, and school culture and norms. Qualitative inquiry is ideally situated to describe and analyze these phenomena to inform our understanding of how such dynamics facilitate or constrain policy implementation and effectiveness.

Certain important policy questions are answerable only with qualitative inquiry. For example, what are the policy's unintended consequences? What constraints operate within organizations to inhibit how policy is implemented? How does a new policy interact/coordinate with school and district policies already in place, and how do principals and teachers respond to any lack of coherence in the policy system (Sadler, 1985)? Another question that qualitative inquiry is uniquely able to answer is: What variations in implementation have occurred, and how did they come about? Program and policy directives have to be interpreted and implemented; street-level bureaucrats often shape the policy in ways unintended by the original designers (Sadler, 1985; Weatherly & Lipsky, 1977). These interpretations directly influence the effects of the policy, and are best studied with open-ended approaches unfettered by preconceived hypotheses.

Additionally, qualitative inquiry is useful for unpacking constructs in a way that makes them more tangible targets for policy. For example, assigning novice teachers mentors is a popular reform designed to increase teacher retention. Qualitative studies of these programs showed that many were unsuccessful, and revealed that the most productive relationships occurred when mentors and their mentees shared the same subject expertise, and worked at the same school (Feiman-Nemser & Parker, 1990; Feiman-Nemser, 1996). These ideas have formed the basis for the movement toward school-based content mentors (Fideler & Haselkorn, 1999; Ingersoll & Kralik, 2004).

On a more global level, Sadler (1985) argues that qualitative research is especially appropriate to analytic inquiry into policy, given that "general enlightenment [results] in specific policy payoffs" (p. 144). The idea here is that through inquiry uninhibited by a priori theoretical boundaries, we are able to discover ideas and relationships that we had not previously conceived, many of which have implications for how we might design, implement, and measure effects of policy. Of course, qualitative inquiry can be designed within a conceptual framework that integrates previous work, while simultaneously being open-ended. Further, qualitative inquiry can help prevent mistakes or erroneous assumptions in interpretation about how practitioners interpret the policy system (LeTendre, 2002). For example, a quantitative study that attempts to link rewards and sanctions of NCLB to teacher behavior would likely miss what a more-qualitative open-ended approach found— that even in this time of high-stakes testing, the rewards and sanctions still most salient to teachers are their students' learning, not the outside policy system that threatens their school (Desimone & LeFloch, 2004). Thus, qualitative insights can help improve accurate causal modeling of the social system (LeTendre, 2002).

Use of Experiments and Other Quantitative Methods for Policy Research At the opposite end of the continuum from naturalistic inquiry using qualitative methods is policy experimentation or rigorous quasi-experimentation. In experimentation, a particular policy or program is put into place with participants randomly assigned to the intervention or a control group, and results are measured to judge the effects on participants. Quasi-experimental designs seek similar causal conclusions without the benefit of random assignment. Common quasi-experimental designs are regression discontinuity designs, which draw treatment and comparison groups from around a particular cut-off point;[1] and matched comparison designs where districts, schools, or classrooms not participating in the policy intervention are matched to intervention participants based on key demographic or achievement variables likely to be associated with program effects. There are a myriad of quasi-experimental designs, which vary in the strength of their validity in attributing effects to a particular policy or program (see Rossi et al., 2004).

As Borman points out in chapter 11 of this volume, the power of the experiment is its unique capacity to attribute cause (but see Kaplan, this volume, for an extensive treatment of causality). The argument here, dating back decades, is that it is only through the systematic study of planned modifications that we can distinguish causal relationships between events or characteristics from mere chance co-occurrences (Cronbach, 1957). Borman's chapter talks in depth about the strengths and limits of randomized designs—here, I would like to focus on the strengths that experiments and other quantitative analyses bring to program and policy studies.

One of the fundamental questions we ask about a program or a policy is, does it work? Experiments and rigorous quasi-experiments are uniquely equipped to answer that question. Their internal validity is high; in other words, the likelihood of the effect being caused by something besides the intervention is very low. Testing causal claims is a fundamental goal of program and policy studies.[2]

In addition, quantitative designs, such as time series analysis and trend analysis, are useful for charting change over time (Singer & Willett, 2003). Often in the policy arena we want to know how interventions affect student or teacher growth trajectories—are effects strong in the first year and then fade? Do they persist for several years? Quantitative studies of preschool have tracked data for several decades to show long-term life outcomes for participants (e.g., Schweinhart, Barnes, Weikart, Barnett, & Epstein, 1993). Techniques such as growth curve modeling and cross-classified modeling (Ding, Davison, & Peterson, 2005; Singer & Willett, 2003; Raudenbush & Bryk, 2002), and value-added analyses (Braun, 2005; Raudenbush, 2004; Sanders & Rivers, 1996; Kupermintz, 2003) are able to quantitatively account for some of the complex changes that schools, teachers, and students experience (e.g., children changing teachers, differing achievement growth rates).

Another essential policy need that requires quantitative inquiry is for representative descriptive data that is generalizable to a particular population. Studies of certain education policy issues require representative data from samples drawn so that all members of the population of interest have a known probability of being drawn; this in turn enables national, state, or local estimates to be drawn with a specific level of precision. Researchers and policy makers usually rely on such survey data to provide representative descriptions of the policy environment and outcomes, especially for state and national policy (e.g., Porter, Garet, Desimone, Suk Yoon, & Birman, 2000; LeFloch, et al., 2007).

Quantitative data also play a primary role in the development and evaluation of education policy. Research designed to inform state and national policy questions—Is a particular policy or program working? How is it being implemented? What are its effects? What factors are associated with positive outcomes?—often rely on standardized student assessments and large-scale survey data. Survey data are used by scholars, practitioners, and policy makers for many purposes, including to inform policy development and improvement, to evaluate the effectiveness of reform (e.g., Carpenter, Fennema, Peterson, Chiang, & Loef, 1989; Cobb et al., 1991; Council of Chief State School Officers [CCSSO], Wisconsin Center for Education Research [WCER], & Eleven-State Collaborative [ECS], 2000; Knapp & Associates, 1995; Simon & Schifter, 1993; U.S. Department of Education, 1998), to examine the prevalence of effective practices (Garet et al., 2001), to make international comparisons (Schmidt et al., 2001), and to compare conditions of teaching and teachers across districts and states (Ingersoll, 2001). Survey data are also commonly used to measure implementation in large-scale studies of state and local efforts such as comprehensive school reform (e.g., Ross et al., 1997), and in the context of experimental design, where they can be employed to measure the quality of the implementation of an intervention (e.g., Cook et al., 1999; Foorman, Francis, Fletcher, & Schatschneider, 1998). Survey research also plays an important role in education policy debates about what works and how big effects are (Rowan, Correnti, & Miller, 2002).

Current Issues and Challenges in Using Complementary Methods for Policy Research

Given the host of ways quantitative and qualitative methods can be integrated, and the unique strengths of both types of methods, the real challenges lie not in deciding whether to use mixed methods for policy research, but determining the appropriate combination of strategies to maximize explanatory power. Since research questions should drive methods, the choice of complementary methods depends on the parameters of the policy question. Do we just want to know if a particular program worked? Do we want to learn how or why it worked? Do we want to know about unintended consequences and how contextual influences facilitated or served as barriers to implementation and effects?

The answers to these questions depend on the policy or program. For example, randomized experiments are best when the causal question "is simple, sharply focused and easily justified" (Cook, 2002, p. 179). Results of single experiments typically show that one form of intervention affected achievement at a particular time in the particular sample of schools that volunteered for an experiment. When policy questions are multi-dimensional, they benefit from descriptive correlational studies and qualitative inquiry. Basically, the tradeoff is between getting a biased answer to a big explanatory question or an unbiased answer to a smaller causal descriptive question. Combining experimental or quasi-experimental designs with descriptive survey data and qualitative inquiry enjoys the benefits of strong internal validity from the experiment, good external validity with descriptive data, and in-depth insights from the qualitative inquiry.

Disagreement about the relative strengths, weaknesses, and value of alternative methodologies in the education research field continue (e.g., Ercikan & Roth, 2006; Mayer & Jackson, 2005; Soller, 2004) and will likely persist. As a result, one of the challenges for using complementary methods is the pressure to place one's work at a particular point on the continuum, either with advocates for the use of experiments, qualitative methods, or correlational/non-experimental methods. Best practice in policy research should push us toward an integration of these various points on the continuum, and a merging of these methods to yield more informative policy studies.

Policy research at once demands the confidence in causal conclusions that experiments or rigorous quasi-experiments generate, the understanding of situation and context provided by qualitative data, and generalizable descriptions garnered only from representative survey data. To the extent that we can incorporate these elements simultaneously into education policy studies, our knowledge and understanding of policy will be exponentially increased.

Still another challenge that pervades policy studies is the lack of consensus on how to measure high-profile outcomes like teacher quality, effective teaching, and student achievement. Some policy studies rely on standardized student assessments, while others advocate for alternative assessments such as portfolios or diagnostic assessments more closely linked to classroom curriculum than standardized tests. Such disagreements can be addressed by including multiple measures of critical constructs, both quantitative and qualitative, to increase the validity of the results.

Another current challenge is continuing to refine the analytic tools available to analyze quantitative data. Recent advances include the ability to analyze nested data and cross-classified models that account for students changing teachers (Raudenbush & Bryk, 2002), techniques for growth modeling with longitudinal data (Kaplan, 2002), value-added analyses (Braun, 2005) and propensity score analysis to account for selection bias (McCaffery, Ridgeway, & Morral, 2004). Current work continues to seek advances in these areas, as well as to develop even more sophisticated methodology for analyzing non-experimental data, to better account for selection bias and control for fixed and random effects (Raudenbush, 2006; Schneider, Carnoy, Kilpatrick, Schmidt, & Shavelson, 2007).

Still another challenge is reconciling the different results that alternative methodologies reap. When using multiple methods to measure the same aspect of the policy environment (triangulation), to provide different levels of insight into the same phenomena (complementarity), or to broaden the study (expansion), one of the key challenges is reconciling any conflicting results from the different methods (Greene et al., 1989). This reconciliation is often left unaddressed, and occurs both within and across studies.

Conclusions garnered from different methodologies often do not converge, but even conclusions from the same paradigm often do not converge.

This is evident from examining the research on several major policy issues whose conclusions conflict, such as the role of resources in educational effectiveness (Hanushek, 1989, 1994; Hedges, Lane, & Greenwald, 1994), the effects of high-stakes testing on teaching and learning (Amrein & Berliner, 2002; Braun, 2004; Carnoy & Loeb, 2002; McNeil, 2000; Porter & Chester, 2002), or the effects of certification (Darling-Hammond, Berry, & Thorenson, 2001; Goldhaber & Brewer, 2000; Smith, Desimone, & Ueno, 2005). Interpreting conflicting findings from both similar and disparate methodologies continues to be a challenge. In these situations it is critical to make explicit the biases and limitations of the methodologies used, and how those biases and limitations affect the results and their interpretation.

Still another challenge is finding the proper expertise to implement a complementary methods design. Few scholars have the expertise to implement multiple methodologies to a high standard. With our richly diverse collection of methods and techniques, it is nearly impossible for a single person or even those from a single discipline to develop expertise in several methodologies (Jaeger, 1997). The recommended practice is to develop collaborative policy research teams that integrate researchers with expertise in different modes of research (Ercikan & Roth, 2006). A shared sense of research methods holds a scholarly community together and permits it to operate communally and collaboratively (Shulman, 1997). Perhaps we might apply the communities of practice idea (McLaughlin & Talbert, 1993) to education policy researchers, by developing teams of researchers with expertise in different methods, all working together to answer a series of policy questions. Such a model is common in policy and evaluation work conducted by think tank and consulting firms (Aladjem et al., 2002; Weiss et al., 2003) and is becoming more common as researchers from various universities join forces to study high-profile policy issues (see the National Study of Charter Schools; Berends, Watral, Teasley, & Nicotera, 2006; Goldring & Cravens, 2006; the National Study of Pay for Performance; Springer, 2006).

Conclusions

Lee Shulman (1997) defined methods as "the organization and application of a coherent, well-reasoned and persuasive argument that can enlighten and shape the understandings of others" (p. 26). Education policy research can be greatly strengthened by the application of multiple methods to develop and execute more holistic and insightful policy studies.

Debates about the relative strengths and weaknesses of alternative methods have persisted for decades. Even great philosophers could not agree; John Stuart Mill advocated for scientific methods with increased precision and known error in the search to create "unanimous assent" for certain truths, whose absence was a "blot on the face of science;"

in contrast, philosopher Alfred North Whitehead observed that "Some of the major disasters of mankind have been produced by the narrowness of men with a good methodology … to set limits to speculation is treason to the future."[3]

Though these debates will likely continue, the education policy research community is in a position of strength, where we are able to designs studies with precision enough to be reasonably confident of effects, while simultaneously employing methods that allow for speculation, discovery, and unanticipated occurrences. We know the benefits and tradeoffs of different methods and have sophisticated tools and technologies to assist us in their application. Our challenge is to put multiple methods to good use in complementary ways, crafting the most rigorous and comprehensive studies that are able to provide informative answers to pressing education policy questions.

Notes

1. A regression discontinuity design works when program participation is decided based on a quantitative measure that has a specific cut-off point, such as a grade point average or score on an assessment. For example, in a study to determine the effectiveness of an honors program that required a 3.5 grade point average (GPA), a regression discontinuity design would form the control group from students who had a 3.3–3.49 grade point average and wanted to enlist in the honors program; the treatment group would be students with a 3.5–3.6 GPA. The reasoning is that students just above and below the cut-off point are statistically equivalent, and thus form a natural experimental and control group.

2. The external validity of experiments depends largely on the extent to which the process of choosing districts and schools to participate mirrors the real-life process the district or school would otherwise experience. For example, an experiment might require that districts mandate schools to participate when otherwise they would not choose that particular reform. On the other hand, often experiments use only principals who volunteer for the treatment because they think it will help their school. The extent to which either scenario strengthens external validity depends on how decisions are made in a particular district. If a district usually chooses and mandates particular school-level reform, then scenario one would have stronger external validity. If a district's practice was to allow school principal's to choose their own reforms, then the second scenario would have stronger external validity.

3. Quotes taken from Lee Shulman (1997, pp. 23–24) where he highlights these opposing philosophical arguments.

References

Aladjem, D., Shive, J., Fast, E. F., Herman, R., Borman, K., Katzenmeyer, W., et al. (2002). *A large-scale mixed-methods approach to studying comprehensive school reform*. Washington, DC: American Institutes for Research.

Allison, P. D. (2001). *Missing data*. Thousand Oaks, CA: Sage.

American Institutes for Research. (2000). *Study of Goals 2000 study and analysis plan*. Washington, DC: Author.

Amrein, A. L., & Berliner, D. C. (2002). High-stakes testing, uncertainty, and student learning. *Education Policy Analysis Archives, 10*(18). Retrieved March 7, 2008, from http://epaa.asu.edu/epaa/v10n18/

Aristotle. (1941). De anima [On the soul]. In R. P. McKeon (Ed.), *Basic works of Aristotle*. New York: Random House.

Asay, S., & Hennon, C. (1999). The challenge of conducting qualitative family research in international settings. *Family and Consumer Sciences Research Journal, 27*, 409–427.

Berends, M. (2000). Teacher-reported effects of New American Schools design: Exploring relationships to teacher background and school context. *Education Evaluation and Policy Analysis, 22*, 65–82.

Berends, M., Watral, C., Teasley, B., & Nicotera, A. (2006, September). *Charter school effects on achievement: Where we are and where we're going.* Paper presented at the National Center on School Choice conference, Nashville, TN.

Berger, A., Desimone, L., Herman, R., Garet, M., & Margolin, J. (2002). *Content of state standards and the alignment of state assessments with state standards.* Washington, DC: U.S. Department of Education.

Bernard, H. R. (1999). *Social research methods: Qualitative and quantitative approaches* (4th ed.). Thousand Oaks, CA: Sage.

Birman, B. F., & Porter, A. C. (2002). Evaluating the effectiveness of education funding streams. *Peabody Journal of Education, 77*(4), 59–85.

Borman, G. D., & Hewes, G. (2003). The long-term effects and cost-effectiveness of Success for All. *Educational Evaluation and Policy Analysis, 24*, 243–266.

Borman, G. D., Slavin, R. E., Cheung, A., Chamberlain, A. M., Madden, N. A., & Chambers, B. (2005). Success for All: First-year results from the national randomized field trial. *Educational Evaluation and Policy Analysis, 27*, 1–22.

Braun, H. (2004). Reconsidering the impact of high-stakes testing. *Education Policy Analysis Archives, 12*(1). Retrieved March 10, 2008, from http://epaa.asu.edu/epaa/v12n1/

Braun, H. (2005). *Using student progress to evaluate teachers: A primer on value-added models.* Princeton, NJ: Educational Testing Service.

Brewer, J., & Hunter, A. (2005). *Foundations of multimethod research: Synthesizing styles.* Thousand Oaks, CA: Sage.

Bryk, A. S., & Driscoll, M. E. (1988). *The high school as community: Contextual influences and consequences for students and teachers.* Madison, WI: National Center on Effective Secondary Schools. (ERIC Document Reproduction Service No. ED 302 539)

Bryk, A. S., & Raudenbush, S. W. (1987). Application of hierarchical linear models to assessing change. *Psychological Bulletin, 101,* 147–158.

Burnham, K., & Anderson, D. (2002). *Model selection and multi-model inference: A practical information-theoretic approach* (2nd ed.). New York: Springer-Verlag.

Carnoy, M., & Loeb, S. (2002). Does external accountability affect student outcomes? A cross-state analysis. *Educational Evaluation and Policy Analysis, 24*, 305–332.

Carpenter, T. P., Fennema, E., Peterson, P. L., Chiang, C., & Loef, M. (1989). Using knowledge of children's mathematics thinking in classroom teaching: An experimental study. *American Educational Research Journal, 26*, 499–531.

Clune, W. (1998). Toward a theory of systemic reform: The case of nine NSF statewide systemic initiatives (National Institute for Science Education Research Monograph No. 16). Madison, WI: NISE.

Clune, W., Miller, S., Raizen, S., Webb, N., Bowcock, D., Britton, E., et al. (Eds.). (1997). *Research on systemic reform. What have we learned? What do we need to know?* Madison: University of Wisconsin, National Institute for Science Education.

Cobb, P., Wood, T., Yackel, E., Nicholls, J., Grayson, W., Trigatti, B., et al. (1991). Assessment of a problem-centered second-grade mathematics project. *Journal for Research in Mathematics Education, 22*, 3–29.

Cohen, D., & Garet, M. (1991). Reforming educational policy with applied social research. In D. Anderson & B. Biddle (Eds.), *Knowledge for policy:Improving education through research* (pp. 123–140). London: Falmer Press.

Cohen, D. K., & Hill, H. C. (2001). *Learning policy: When state education reform works.* New Haven, CT: Yale University Press.

Cook, T. D. (1985). Postpositivist critical multiplism. In R. L. Shotland & M. M. Mark (Eds.), *Social science and social policy* (pp. 21–62). Beverly Hills, CA: Sage.

Cook, T. D. (2002). Randomized experiments in educational policy research: A critical examination of the reasons the educational evaluation community has offered for not doing them. *Educational Evaluation and Policy Analysis, 24*, 175–199.

Cook, T. D., Habib, F., Phillips, M., Settersten, R. A., Shagle, S. C., &

Degirmencioglu, S. M. (1999). Comer's school development program in Prince George's County, Maryland: A theory-based evaluation. *American Educational Research Journal, 36*, 543–597.

Council of Chief State School Officers (CCSSO), Wisconsin Center for Education Research (WCER), & Eleven-State Collaborative (ESC). (2000). *Using data on enacted curriculum in mathematics and science: Sample results from a study of classroom practices.* Washington, DC: Author.

Creswell, J. W., & Clark, V. P. (2006). *Designing and conducting mixed methods research.* Thousand Oaks, CA: Sage.

Cronbach, L. J. (1957). The two disciplines of scientific psychology. *American Psychologist, 12,* 671–684.

Cronbach, L., Ambron, S., Dornbusch, S., Hess, R., Hornik, R., Phillips, D., et al. (1980). Where evaluation stands today. In L. Cronbach & Associates (Eds.), *Toward reform of program evaluation: Aims, methods and institutional arrangements* (pp. 12–35). San Francisco: Jossey-Bass.

Cullen, J. B., & Reback, R. (2002). *Tinkering towards accolades: School gaming under a performance accountability system* (NBER Working Paper 12286). Ann Arbor: University of Michigan.

Darling-Hammond, L., Berry, B., & Thorenson, A. (2001). Does teacher certification matter? Evaluating the evidence. *Educational Evaluation and Policy Analysis, 23*, 57–77.

Datnow, A. (2000). Power and politics in the adoption of school reform models. *Educational Evaluation and Policy Analysis, 22*, 357–374.

Desimone, L. (2002). How can comprehensive school reform models be successfully implemented? *Review of Educational Research, 72*, 433–479.

Desimone, L., & LeFloch, K. (2004). Are we asking the right questions? Using cognitive interviews to improve surveys in education research. *Educational Evaluation and Policy Analysis, 26*, 1–22.

Desimone, L., Payne, B., Federovicious, N., Henrich, C., & Finn-Stevenson, M. (2004). Comprehensive school reform: An implementation study of preschool programs in elementary schools. *The Elementary School Journal, 104*, 369–389.

Desimone, L., Smith, T., Baker, D., & Ueno, K. (2005). The distribution of teaching quality in mathematics: Assessing barriers to the reform of United States mathematics instruction from an international perspective. *American Educational Research Journal, 42*, 501–535.

Ding, C., Davison, M., & Peterson, A. (2005). Multidimensional scaling analysis of growth and change. *Journal of Educational Measurement, 42,* 171–191.

Ercikan, K., & Roth, W. M. (2006). What good is polarizing research into qualitative and quantitative? *Educational Researcher, 35*(5), 14–23.

Feiman-Nemser, S. (1996). *Teacher mentoring: A critical review.* Washington, DC: ERIC Clearinghouse on Teaching and Teacher Education. (ERIC Digest No. ED397060)

Feiman-Nemser, S., & Parker, M. B. (1990). Making subject matter part of the conversation in learning to teach. *Journal of Teacher Education, 41*(3), 32–43.

Fideler, E., & Haselkorn, D. (1999). *Learning the ropes: Urban teacher induction programs and practices in the United States.* Belmont, MA: Recruiting New Teachers, Inc.

Firestone, W., Goertz, M. E., & Natriello, G. (1997). *From cashbox to classroom: The struggle for fiscal reform and educational change in New Jersey.* New York: Teachers College Press.

Foorman, B., Francis, D., Fletcher, J., & Schatschneider, C. (1998). The role of instruction in learning to read: Preventing reading failure in at-risk children. *Journal of Educational Psychology, 90*, 37–55.

Garet, M., Porter, A., Desimone, L., Birman, B., & Yoon, K. (2001). What makes professional development effective? Analysis of a national sample of teachers. *American Educational Research Journal, 38*, 915–945.

Goldhaber, D. D., & Brewer, D. J. (2000). Does teacher certification matter? High school teacher certification status and student achievement. *Educational Evaluation and Policy Analysis, 22*, 129–145.

Goldring, E., & Cravens, X. (2006, September). *Teachers' academic focus on learning in charter and non-charter schools.* Paper presented at the National Center on School Choice conference, Nashville, TN.

Greene, J. C., Caracelli, V. J., & Graham, W. F. (1989). Toward a conceptual framework for mixed-method evaluation designs. *Educational Evaluation and Policy Analysis, 11,* 255–274.

Guba, E. G., & Lincoln, Y. S. (1988). Do inquiry paradigms imply inquiry methodologies? In D. M. Fetterman (Ed.), *Qualitative approaches to evaluation in education: The silent scientific revolution* (pp. 89–115). London: Praeger.

Hanushek, E. (1989). Impact of differential expenditures on school performance. *Educational Researcher, 18*(4), 45–51.

Hanushek, E. (1994). Money might matter somewhere: A response to Hedges, Laine, and Greenwald. *Educational Researcher, 23*(4), 5–8.

Hatry, H., Greiner, J., & Ashford, B. (1994). *Issues and case studies in teacher incentive plans* (2nd ed.). Washington, DC: Urban Institute Press.

Hedges, L., Laine, R., & Greenwald, R. (1994). Does money matter? A meta-analysis of studies of the effects of differential school inputs on student outcomes. *Educational Researcher, 23*(3), 5–14.

Ingersoll, R. M. (2001). Teacher turnover and teacher shortages: An organizational analysis. *American Educational Research Journal, 38,* 499–534.

Ingersoll, R., & Kralik, J. M. (2004). *The impact of mentoring on teacher retention: What the research says.* Denver, CO: Education Commission of the States.

Jacob, B., & Levitt, S. (2003). Rotten apples: An investigation of the prevalence and predictors of teacher cheating. *Quarterly Journal of Economics, 118,* 843–877.

Jaeger, R. (1997). Survey research methods in education. In R. Jaeger (Ed.), *Complementary methods for research in education* (2nd ed., pp. 449–485). Washington, DC: American Educational Research Association.

James-Burdumy, S., Dynarski, M., Moore, M., Deke, J., Mansfield, W., Pistorino, C., et al. (2005). *When schools stay open late: The national evaluation of the 21st Century Community Learning Centers Program.* Washington, DC: U.S. Department of Education.

Johnson, R. B., & Onwuegbuzie, A. J. (2004). Mixed methods research: A research paradigm whose time has come. *Educational Researcher, 33*(7), 14–26.

Kaplan, D. (2002). Methodological advances in the analysis of individual growth with relevance to education policy. *Peabody Journal of Education, 77*(4), 189–215.

Kidder, L. H., & Fine, M. (1987). Qualitative and quantitative methods: When stories converge. In M. M. Mark & R. L. Shotland (Eds.), *Multiple methods in program evaluation: New directions for program evaluation No. 35* (pp. 57–75). San Francisco: Jossey-Bass.

Kingdon, J. (1984). *Agendas, alternatives, and public policies.* Boston: Little, Brown & Co.

Knapp, M. S., & Associates. (1995). Introduction. In M.S. Knapp & Associates (Eds.), *Teaching for meaning in high poverty classrooms* (pp. 1–10). New York: Teachers College Press.

Kraft, M., & Furlong, S. (2004). *Public policy: Politics, analysis, and alternatives.* Washington, DC: Congressional Quarterly Press.

Kupermintz, H. (2003). Teacher effects and teacher effectiveness: A validity investigation of the Tennessee value added assessment system. *Educational Evaluation and Policy Analysis, 25,* 287–298.

Lather, P., & Moss, P. A. (2005). Introduction: Implications of the scientific research in education report for qualitative inquiry. *Teachers College Record, 107,* 1–3.

LeFloch, K., Martinez, F., O'Day, J., Stecher, B., Taylor, J., & Cook, A. (2007). *State and Local Implementation of the No Child Left Behind Act, Vol. 3. Accountability under NCLB: Interim Report.* Washington, DC: U.S. Department of Education.

LeTendre, G. (2002). Advancements in conceptualizing and analyzing cultural effects in cross-national studies of educational achievement. In A. Porter & A. Gamoran (Eds.), *Methodological advances in cross-national surveys of educational achievement* (pp. 198–228). Washington, DC: National Academy Press.

Little, R., & Rubin, D. (2002). S*tatistical analysis with missing data* (2nd ed.). Hoboken, NJ: Wiley.

Lynch, K. B. (1983). Qualitative and quantitative evaluation: Two terms in search of a meaning. *Educational Evaluation and Policy Analysis, 5,* 461–464.

Majchrzak, A. (Ed.). (1984). *Methods for policy research.* Thousand Oaks, CA: Sage

Mark, M. M., & Shotland, R. L. (1987). Alternative models for the use of multiple methods. In M. M. Mark & R. L. Shotland (Eds.), *Multiple methods in program evaluation: New directions for program evaluation No. 35* (pp. 95–100). San Francisco: Jossey-Bass.

Massell, D. (2001). The theory and practice of using data to build capacity: State and local strategies and their effects. In S. Furhman (Ed.), *From the capitol to the classroom: Standards-based reform in the states. One hundredth yearbook of the National Society for the Study of Education, Part II* (pp. 148–169). Chicago: University of Chicago Press.

Mayer, R. E., & Jackson, J. (2005). The case for coherence in scientific explanations: Quantitative details can hurt qualitative understanding. *Journal of Experimental Psychology Applied, 11,* 13–18.

McCaffery, D., Ridgeway, G., & Morral, A. (2004). Propensity score estimation with boosted regression for evaluating causal effects in observational studies. *Psychological Methods, 9,* 403–425.

McLaughlin, M. (1976). Implementation as mutual adaptation: Change in classroom organization. *Teachers College Record, 77,* 339–351.

McLaughlin, M. (1987). Learning from experience: Lessons from policy implementation. *Educational Evaluation and Policy Analysis, 9,* 171–178.

McLaughlin, M. W., & Talbert, J. E. (1993). Introduction: New visions of teaching. In D. K. Cohen, M. W. McLaughlin, & J. E. Talbert (Eds.), *Teaching for understanding: Challenges for policy and practice* (pp. 1–10). San Francisco: Jossey-Bass.

McLendon, M. K., Hearn, J. C., & Deaton, R. (2006). Called to account: Analyzing the origins and spread of state performance-accountability policies for higher education. *Educational Evaluation and Policy Analysis, 28,* 1–24.

McNeil, L. (2000). *Contradictions of school reform: Educational costs of standardized testing.* New York: Routledge.

Merriam, S. (1988). *Case study research in education: A qualitative approach.* San Francisco: Jossey-Bass.

Miles, M. B., & Huberman, A. M. (1984). *Qualitative data analysis: A sourcebook of new methods.* Beverly Hills, CA: Sage.

Moran, T. K. (1987). Research and managerial strategies for integrating evaluation research into agency decision making. *Evaluation Review, 11,* 612–630.

Munger, M. C. (2000). *Analyzing policy: Choices, conflicts and practices.* New York: W.W. Norton.

Patton, C., & Sawicki, D. (1993). *Basic methods of policy analysis and planning* (2nd ed.). Englewood Cliffs, NJ: Prentice Hall.

Plomp, T. (1990, April). *IEA: Its role and plans for international comparative research in education.* Paper presented at the Annual Meeting of the American Educational Research Association, Boston.

Porter, A., & Chester, M. (2002). Building a high-quality assessment and accountability program: The Philadelphia example. In D. Ravitch (Ed.), *Brookings papers on education policy 2002* (pp. 285–337). Washington, DC: Brookings Institution.

Porter, A., Floden, R., Freeman, D., Schmidt, W., & Schwille, J. (1988). Content determinants in elementary school mathematics. In D. Grouws & T. Cooney (Eds.), *Perspectives on research on effective mathematics teaching* (pp. 96–113). Reston, VA: The National Council of Teachers of Mathematics.

Porter, A., Garet, M., Desimone, L., Suk Yoon, K., & Birman, B. (2000). *Does professional development change teaching practice? Results from a three-year study.* Washington, DC: U.S. Department of Education.

RAND, AIR, NORC. (2005). *NCLB accountability, 2002–2005 interim report of National Longitudinal Study of No Child Left Behind* (OMB #1875-0227).

Raudenbush, S. W. (2004). What are value-added models estimating and what does this imply for statistical practice? *Journal of Educational and Behavioral Statistics, 29,* 121–130.

Raudenbush, S. W. (2005). Learning from attempts to improve schooling:

The contribution of methodological diversity. *Educational Researcher, 34*(5), 25–31.

Raudenbush, S. (2006, December). *Fixed effects vs. random effects.* Paper presented at the first annual meeting of the Society for Research on Educational Effectiveness, Leesburg, VA.

Raudenbush, S. W., & Bryk, A. S. (2002). *Hierarchical linear models: Applications and data analsis methods* (2nd ed.). Thousand Oaks, CA: Sage.

Reichardt, C. S., & Cook, T. D. (1979). Beyond qualitative versus quantitative methods. In T. D. Cook & C. S. Reichardt (Eds.), *Qualitative and quantitative methods in evaluation research: Vol. 1* (pp. 7–32). Beverly Hills, CA: Sage.

Riehl, C. (2001). Bridges to the future: The contributions of qualitative research to the sociology of education. *Sociology of Education, 74,* 115–134.

Rogosa, D. R., Brandt, D., & Zimowski, M. (1982). A growth curve approach to the measurement of change. *Psychological Bulletin, 90,* 726–748.

Ross, S. M., Troutman, A., Horgan, D., Maxwell, S., Laitinen, R., & Lowther, D. (1997). The success of schools in implementing eight restructuring designs: A synthesis of first-year evaluation outcomes. *School Effectiveness and School Improvement, 8,* 95–124.

Rossi, P., Lipsey, M., & Freeman, H. (2004). An overview of program evaluation. In P. Rossi, H. Freeman, & M. Lipsey (Eds.), *Evaluation: A systematic approach* (7th ed., pp. 1–28). Beverly Hills, CA: Sage.

Rossman, G. B., & Wilson, B. L. (1985). Numbers and words: Combining quantitative and qualitative methods in a single large-scale evaluation study. *Education Review, 9,* 627–643.

Rowan, B., Correnti, R., & Miller, R. (2002). *What large-scale survey research tells us about teacher effects on student achievement: Insights from the Prospects study of elementary schools.* Philadelphia: University of Pennsylvania, Consortium for Policy Research in Education.

Sadler, D. R. (1985). Evaluation, policy analysis, and multiple case studies: Aspects of focus and sampling. *Educational Evaluation and Policy Analysis, 7,* 143–149.

Sanders, W., & Rivers, J. (1996, November). *Cumulative and residual effects of teachers on future student academic achievement.* Knoxville: University of Tennessee, Value-Added Research and Assessment Center.

Schmidt, W. H., McKnight, C. C., Houang, R. T., Wang, H. C., Wiley, D. E., Cogan, L. S., et al. (2001). *Why schools matter: A cross-national comparison of curriculum and learning.* San Francisco: Jossey-Bass.

Schneider, B., Carnoy, M., Kilpatrick, J., Schmidt, W. H., & Shavelson, R. J. (2007). *Estimating causal effects: Using experimental and observational designs.* Washington DC: American Educational Research Association.

Schweinhart, L., Barnes, H., Weikart, D., Barnett, S., & Epstein, A. (1993). Significant benefits: The High-Scope Perry Preschool Study through age 27 (*Monographs of the High/Scope Educational Research Foundation, No. 10*). Ypsilanti, MI: The High/Scope Press.

Shulman, L. (1997). Disciplines of inquiry in rducation: A new overview. In R. Jaeger (Ed.), *Complementary methods for research in education* (2nd ed., pp. 3–31). Washington, DC: American Educational Research Association.

Simon, M., & Schifter, D. (1993). Toward a constructivist perspective: The impact of a mathematics teacher inservice program on students. *Educational Studies in Mathematics, 25,* 331–340.

Singer, J. D., & Willett, J. B. (2003). *Applied longitudinal data analysis: Modeling change and event occurrence.* New York: Oxford University Press.

Smith, T., Desimone, L., & Ueno, K. (2005). "Highly qualified" to do what? The relationship between NCLB teacher quality mandates and the use of reform-oriented instruction in middle school math. *Educational Evaluation and Policy Analysis, 27,* 75–109.

Soller, A. (2004). Understanding knowledge-sharing breakdowns: A meeting of the quantitative and qualitative minds. *Journal of Computer Assisted Learning, 20,* 212–223.

Springer, M. (2006). *Pay for performance experiment.* Nashville, TN: Vanderbilt University.

Stigler, J., & Stevenson, H. (1991). How Asian teachers polish each lesson to perfection. *American Educator, 15*(1), 12–20.

Supovitz, J. A., & Taylor, B. S. (2005). Systemic education evaluation: Evaluating the impact of systemwide reform in education. *American Journal of Evaluation, 26,* 204–230.

Tashakkori, A., & Teddlie, C. (1998). *Mixed methodology: Combing qualitative and quantitative approaches.* Thousand Oaks, CA: Sage.

U.S. Department of Education. (1998, September). *Promising practices: New ways to improve teacher quality.* Retrieved March 25, 2006, from http://www.ed.gov/pubs/PromPractice

Weatherly, R., & Lipsky, M. (1977). Street level bureaucrats and institutional innovation: Implementing special education reform. *Harvard Educational Review, 47,* 171–197.

Weimer, D., & Vining, A. (1998). *Policy analysis: Concepts and practices* (3rd ed.). Englewood Cliffs, NJ: Prentice Hall.

Weiss, C. H. (1988). Evaluation for decisions: Is anybody there? Does anybody care? *Evaluation Practice, 9,* 5–20.

Weiss, C. (1998). *Evaluation: Methods for studying programs and policies* (2nd ed.). Upper Saddle River, NJ: Prentice Hall.

Weiss, C. H., & Bucuvalas, M. J. (1977). The challenge of social research to decision making. In C. H. Weiss (Ed.), *Using social research in public policy making* (pp. 213–234). Lexington, MA: Lexington.

Weiss, I. R., Banilower, E. R., Crawford, R. A., & Overstreet, C. M. (2003). *Local systemic change through teacher enhancement, year eight cross-site report.* Chapel Hill, NC: Horizon Research, Inc.

Wooffitt, R. (2005). *Conversation analysis and discourse analysis: A comparative and critical introduction.* Thousand Oaks, CA: Sage.

15

Assessment Policy

Making Sense of the Babel

JOAN L. HERMAN AND EVA L. BAKER
University of California, Los Angeles, CRESST

Consider the word Babel and what happens in its circumstance. Merriam-Webster's collegiate dictionary (1993) defines the word as:

1. a city in Shinar where the building of a tower is held in Genesis to have been halted by the confusion of tongues;
2. often not capitalized a: a confusion of sounds or voices b: a scene of noise or confusion.

According to the Bible story referenced in the first definition, a plan to build a tower to heaven goes awry when people cannot understand one another. A recent, award-winning movie of the same name illustrates a similar point: Catastrophe ensues when characters miscommunicate, and bad decisions result when people think they understand, but in fact misinterpret evidence because of their unique personal knowledge and experience, and then act on those misconceptions.

Assessment policy may present a similar case in point: It is the source of many, often conflicting meanings; where diverse stakeholders, speaking from different perspectives, forge expectations that appear clear but devolve into cacophony; then, widespread misunderstanding produces confusion as well as bad decisions. In this policy chapter, we attempt to impose some order on current understandings of assessment and suggest critical considerations in moving from the present babel to more unified, effective assessment systems. We start with definitions of the multitude of terms that convey various aspects of the "assessment" concept and the assessment and accountability systems that are forged from them. We then move to the policy motivation for such assessments, the policy purposes they are intended to serve. Concentrating on systems intended to promote accountability and improvement, we consider common wisdom about what constitutes quality in assessment and review research evidence on how well current systems are working. After laying out challenging tensions in current

policy and practice, we conclude with priorities for future research.

A Confusion of Meaning

As a prelude to our main arguments, consider the many terms that comprise the assessment argot. It can be a confusing babel of overlapping meaning, where the referents of one stakeholder may be considerably different from those of another, raising the strong probability of miscommunication and the possibility that presumed policy consensus is illusory. Without getting into the details of psychometrics (IRT scores, alphas, and the like) or highly technical jargon, consider just a few of the terms that are commonly used.

What Is "It" Called? Assessment, test, measure, instrument, examination, metric? Tests or assessments are instruments used to collect and provide information; they are composed of measures that can be numerically summarized. Summarized quantitatively, singly, or in simple or weighted combination, assessment results can be used to produce an indicator. A metric is an indicator divided by some other variable, such as time or cost. Although the term "test" often connotes more traditional kinds of measures (multiple-choice or short-answer items, easily hand-scored or machine-scored), and assessment a wider array of task and item types, we use the two terms interchangeably.

What Is Being Assessed? Is it learning, achievement, performance, proficiency, readiness, capability, ability? Status or change in status (progress), trends? Combined with "purpose," as we discuss below, the intent of a test and subsequent test development strategies will vary.

What Kind of Score Is Produced and How Are Scores Combined and Reported? Raw, scale, proficiency, percentile, percentage correct, percent at or above particular cut points? All scores start out as "raw" but are then transformed in various ways to produce indicators that are more interpretable and comparable. Score type matters—for example, in looking at progress from one year to the next, comparison of scale scores credits change at all points on the distribution, whereas changes in percent proficient functionally only give credit for students who move from below the proficiency cut point and miss progress achieved by lower performing students because they fail to reach the cut-point.

How Is the Test Conceptualized?

How Is the Test Conceptualized? Norm-referenced, criterion-referenced, standards-based? The distinctions have been blurred by both vendors and consumers. Today's standardized tests are yesterday's criterion-referenced, where test content is referenced to standards rather than objectives. Norm-referenced tests report scores relative to a nationally representative group of students—and provide a sense of how students or other schools rank relative to this norm. However, even though referenced to standards, today's standardized tests use item development and selection procedures very similar to those used for the norm-referenced tests of the past.

How Widely and Frequently Is It Given? Large scale, annual, interim (benchmark, interim, progress), curriculum embedded, classroom, teacher? As the name implies, large-scale assessments are administered widely and usually in a common, standard form over a jurisdiction (e.g., nation, state, district), whereas teacher and classroom assessments are typically largely unique to each teacher. Large-scale tests may sample a proportion of students (as in the National Assessment of Educational Progress, NAEP) or test every student in an educational authority. Large-scale assessments are typically administered annually; so-called interim, benchmark, or progress tests typically are administered periodically (e.g., quarterly) throughout the academic year. Curriculum-embedded assessments are those that often come with specific instructional materials and may be end-of-chapter examinations or integrated in educational software.

Who Mandates It; How Wide Is the Purview Under Which It Is Given? Federal, state, local educational agency, school, teacher? Each level has legitimate needs and concerns, but whether and how these are coordinated and mutually consistent has serious ramifications.

What Is the Unit(s) of Interest, the Organizational Level that Is Being Assessed? Individual students, classes/teachers, schools, local educational agencies, states, particular programs or interventions or institutions? A test that is administered to individual students can provide insight about those individuals or can be aggregated and summarized at higher levels (classroom/teacher, school, local educational agency, state) to provide insight on the educational performance at these levels, including the status of current performance and progress (i.e., trends or changes across testing periods). However, to be aggregated from one level to the next or compared from one year to the next, the measures must be comparable on conceptual and technical grounds.

What Happens as a Result? Stakes refer to the consequences of assessment results. Low or high stakes? Policy makers often attempt to support policy goals by attaching incentives or sanctions to particular results, presumably to motivate effort. For example, high school exit exams that are required for graduation attach serious, life-time consequences for students who fail to pass. Even results from nominally low-stakes examinations, if published, develop consequences.

The foregoing questions become critical considerations in the design and use of assessment to serve policy goals. In recent practice, such goals have concerned the creation of test-based accountability systems (largely state level) intended both to leverage and support the improvement of educational performance (that of educators, students, and the institutions in which they are constituted), and to promote evidence-based or assessment-based practice. In addition, by default, if not by direct intent, because such assessment results exist, they become "available" assessment data, which are commonly used to evaluate the effectiveness of policies and programs at the state, local, and even national levels. Assessment thus is used as an instrument of policy to directly and indirectly advance education and social goals and as a tool to determine the effectiveness of educational policies, practices, programs, and individuals as well as institutions.

The Purposes of Assessment

Articulating the specifics of how assessment can be orchestrated to serve these various policy goals is a matter of understanding an array of potential purposes of assessment. While historically these purposes have been conceptualized in terms of the general decision areas test data are intended to serve (e.g., see Table 15.1), more recent observations of the actual use and effects of testing have given rise to a more complex picture (Firestone, Schorr, & Monfils, 2004; Herman, 2008). Tests or assessments do result in technical evidence that can inform specific categories of decisions and policy functions (e.g., accountability, admissions/selection, placement, diagnosis, progress monitoring, certification, accreditation, and evaluation), but the attention to and use of the technical data also carry important social meanings and consequences. These consequences also make murky theoretical distinctions between formative and summative purposes (Scriven, 1967), between evaluation and assessment used for purposes of improvement as opposed to those used for making judgments of effectiveness.

Consider, for example, a state high school exit exam that students need to pass for a high school diploma, whose results are reported to the individual students who take the test and to their parents, and when aggregated at the school, district, and state levels, are publicly communicated through

TABLE 15.1
Purposes of Assessment

I. Accountability for individuals and institutions
   a. Monitor performance: status, progress
   b. Quality assurance: certification, accreditation
   c. Evaluation, grading
   d. Fair selection
II. Improvement
   a. Diagnosis of individuals, groups, programs
   b. Guidance for improvement
      i. Analysis of curriculum and instruction
      ii. Professional development priorities
      iii. Resource allocation
      iv. Identification of effective practices and people
        (and the reverse)
      v. Feedback for system participants, including students
        and parents
   c. Placement
III. Communication/motivation
   a. Distribute rewards and punishment
   b. Motivate effort
   c. Articulation of goals for educators and trainers
   d. Promote outcomes orientation
   e. Systematic planning and ongoing evaluation/continuous
      improvement
   f. Fuel competitive instincts
   g. Reassure public

newspapers and Web sites. The ostensible purpose of the test is to *certify* that students have the knowledge and skills that the state has determined are expected of high school graduates, ideally to assure that students have the proficiencies they need for success after high school, in college, and/or the workplace.

By mandating the test, policy makers among other things communicate that they are concerned about education and its improvement, that high school graduates need to be at least minimally prepared for their future, and that they are serious about accountability and using "hard" data to hold individuals and institutions responsible for performance. Because getting a high school diploma is important to students' futures, the existence of the test is expected *to motivate* students to learn, to prepare for the test, and to acquire the knowledge and skills that are assessed, as well as to motivate parents to pay attention and support their children's education. Moreover, because they care about their students (and their futures) and, even in the absence of tangible rewards and benefits, see public reports of their students' test performance as evidence of their own professional efficacy, educators are motivated to do what they can to assure that their students will succeed on the test. To do so, they may modify the content of their classes to be sure it is relevant to the test content and format, develop or purchase special materials to prepare students, use practice tests to assess student progress, and so forth. For students who do not pass the exit exam initially, educators may use the results to *place* students in special classes, provide extra tutoring options, and if the test provides subscale data on different aspects of performance, they may use the results to *diagnose* individual students' learning needs. Those same

results aggregated at the class or school level may be used to *analyze and respond to curriculum strengths and weaknesses*, to suggest specific content areas in which teachers may benefit from *professional development*, or to infer priorities for *budget allocations*. Actors at the district, regional, and state levels may be similarly analyzing and responding to the same data at different levels of aggregation, and identifying schools and districts that are doing particularly well or that are in most need of help, including deriving implications for immediate programs for current students as well as for the prior courses and schooling that were supposed to provide students with necessary prerequisite skills, and so forth. While this example is not meant to be exhaustive, it does serve to illustrate the confounding of test purposes, of distinctions between accountability/summative and improvement/formative functions, and of the technical, sociopolitical, and symbolic roles that assessment plays in current practice. A single test, ostensibly aimed at a single purpose, launches a whole network of interrelated motivations and cascading actions, only some of which directly involve the use of the test and its technical results.

As another example, take a state-mandated teacher competency assessment that teachers must pass to gain tenure in the system. By mandating such an assessment, state policy makers communicate their commitment to educational quality, their recognition of the importance of students having access to good teachers, and their responsibility for assuring the quality of the teaching force. As the assessment is developed, it makes concrete and communicates valued knowledge and competencies for beginning teachers. Just as high schools respond to the requirements of high school exit exams, so too can teacher preparation institutions be expected to adapt their curriculum and instructional pedagogy to the expectations of the teacher assessment and to use their students' results to strengthen their program's success in enabling students to pass. To the extent that sizable proportions are not passing, an institution may change its admission procedures, create special test preparation courses or tutoring opportunities, and/or try to pressure pre-preparation institutions to better prepare potential candidates. To the extent that the assessment delves deeply into meaningful aspects of teachers' content and pedagogical knowledge and requires demonstration of quality practice, preparing for the test may well help new teachers become more effective, and responding to the assessment requirements may strengthen and deepen existing preparation programs. In any event, unless it is a trivial assessment, the assessment is likely to have a homogenizing or standardizing effect on preparation programs and expectations for them.

Leaders and faculty in all such programs will want their students to do well on the assessment, not only because it is necessary for entry into the profession, but also because they will recognize that the assessment results will provide an indicator of their own effectiveness and influence future recruitment. Who would want to attend an institution that does not have a high success rate for their graduating teachers? This example illustrates both that assessment fuels the competition motives and the fact that researchers and the public use whatever data are available to evaluate their institutions.

Finally, take an example of a state accountability system such as that mandated by No Child Left Behind (NCLB, 2002), which is intended to hold organizations, schools, districts, states, and departments of education accountable for their students' learning to state standards and for reducing the gap between traditionally underachieving subgroups. NCLB requires states to articulate academic standards in English-language arts and mathematics[1] and to create and administer annual assessments aligned to them for students in Grades 2 through 8 and during at least one grade in high school, as of this writing. Cut scores define what is considered proficient for tests at each grade level, and states must establish annual measurable objectives (AMO) as targets in terms of the percentage of students who must be proficient each year, if the state is to be on track and attain universal proficiency in reading and math by the year 2014. Hardly any serious educator believes that the 2014 goal is reasonable, but it is set as an aspiration and a message about desired performance of "all" students. Schools and districts must meet their annual goals in both reading and math for both the school as a whole and for every numerically significant subgroup (e.g., English learners, African American students, Latino students, Title I students, and students with disabilities). Schools and districts that fail to meet these targets are deemed "in need of improvement," must engage in systematic needs assessment and improvement planning, and, over time, face successively more punitive sanctions, including reconstitution or takeover by the state or other approved entity. Thus, the assessments' attendant student proficiency classifications provide a de facto definition of effective or successful schools (schools that meet goals in terms the percentage of their students who are proficient are not "in need of improvement"). By requiring schools to meet the target for every numerical subgroup, the legislation is intended to hold schools accountable for and assure their attention to historically underserved groups. As the research summarized below shows, these assessment mandates indeed have spawned such attention and a burgeoning interest in ongoing assessment. However, as also discussed below, the choice of a conjunctive rather than a compensatory model for determining school success may adversely affect motivation, particularly for large schools serving diverse student populations. The conjunctive model means that schools must attain AMO in both reading and math for the school as a whole as well as for each numerically significant subgroup; for large urban high schools this may mean meeting 20 or more separate targets. Surpassing standards in one subject or grade does not compensate for underachieving in another and raises challenges of feasibility. The essentially arbitrary annual benchmarks for moving from current levels of performance to all students proficient by 2014 raise a second concern, as does the mere chance impact of failing to meet one of a large number of targets, relevant in particular to large, diverse schools.

Challenges notwithstanding, these examples are intended to illustrate the purposes that assessment currently plays in educational policy. No longer only "after-the-fact" events to evaluate how well individuals are doing or to make decisions about selection and placement, assessments nominally aligned with content and performance standards are intended to provide motivation, clear performance expectations, and evidence of accruing progress. The same set of test results, aggregated at different levels of analysis, may be used to evaluate individuals, programs, and/or institutions; to determine whether individuals or groups of students are making adequate progress; to provide the basis for grades, rewards, and sanctions; for purposes of accreditation and quality assurance; and to certify readiness for particular options.

Beyond accountability purposes, the same set of findings, again aggregated at different levels of analysis, are intended to be used to guide the improvement of performance. Depending on granularity of reporting, results may influence how an institution establishes priorities, diagnoses the learning needs of individuals and groups, evaluates the strengths and weaknesses of programs and institutions, and/or makes a myriad of decisions about curriculum, professional development, and resource allocations. The data also may be used to identify individuals, institutions, or programs that are performing extraordinarily well or poorly (an accountability/evaluation problem) in order to try to infer promising practices that can be used to help other individuals, institutions, or programs to improve their performance. Prime within the improvement domain is the value of feedback from assessment results to students and parents. In fact, research consistently shows the strong effects of feedback on student learning (Nyquist, 2003).

Moving to communication and motivation purposes, the examples above provide instances of how assessment results communicate goals, motivate attention and effort, promote outcomes and performance improvement orientation, activate competitive instincts, and encourage systematic analysis and planning. Test results, whether viewed by parents or the community at large, also have an enormous impact on perceptions of public education.

These multiple and related uses and effects of assessment make clear that a single assessment mandate may contribute to many functions, and that it makes sense to take account of these cascading and interacting effects in the formulation of assessment policy. The politics of assessment policy creation, in fact, may contribute to such proliferation of expected effects. As McDonnell (1994) has noted, policy makers may have varying or even conflicting expectations about what a particular assessment mandate is expected to accomplish, and given resource and other constraints, are apt to push for using the same assessment for multiple purposes. Motivated to make a mark within 2- or 4-year electoral cycles, policy makers are attracted to the cheap, quick fix that assessment seems to be—that is, rather than funding systemic reform itself, they fund an assessment to leverage the reform—and tend to mandate short timelines for bringing their initiatives to fruition (see also Linn, 1998).

At the same time, professional standards require that assessments be designed, developed, and validated with respect to each intended assessment use (American Educational Research Association, American Psychological Association, & National Council on Measurement in Education [AERA, APA, & NCME], 1999), potentially bringing political and technical concerns into conflict. From a technical standpoint, it is foolhardy to apply an assessment to purposes beyond its evidence base, even as such practice is common. From a political standpoint, assessments that do not have strong political support, regardless of their technical characteristics, are bound to fail. Thus, for example, there are important lessons to be learned from the performance assessments popular in state assessment programs from the 1990s (see, e.g., McDonnell, 1997). Intended to serve both accountability and improvement purposes, these assessments fell short on the technical quality and cost effectiveness required for accountability systems. In addition, in some states, where new assessments signaled a major change in the status quo of school curriculum and pedagogy, a lack of consensus on the desired changes produced public upheaval and short-lived assessment programs (McDonnell, 1997). In contrast, the National Center for Research on Evaluation, Standards, and Student Testing (CRESST) assessment models provide a common architecture for creating tiered assessment systems for large-scale accountability and classroom use, and validation evidence exists to support both uses (Baker, 1997, 2007b). Yet the implementation of such models would require a transformation of assessment technology, amongst other things, violating policy makers' apparent desires for quick and cheap fixes.

Criteria for Evaluating the Quality of Existing Assessments

Policy assessments thus require marriage of the political and the technical. How well is the marriage working? To answer that question, we first consider common professional wisdom about what constitutes quality assessment, as articulated by current professional standards, the *Standards for Educational and Psychological Testing* (AERA, APA, & NCME, 1999). Validity is the overarching term measurement experts use to express the fundamental quality of an assessment or an assessment system. Drawing on Messick's (1989) landmark reformulation, the *Standards* define validity as "the degree to which evidence and theory support the interpretations of test scores entailed by proposed uses of tests" (AERA, APA, & NCME, 1999, p. 9). Validity is thus a matter of accumulating and integrating evidence that demonstrates the extent to which inferences drawn from an assessment's results are justified for particular uses or purposes. Such evidence, according to the *Standards*, can and should be drawn from a number of sources: evidence based on test content, on response processes, on internal structure, on relations to other variables (convergent and divergent evidence), test-criterion relationships, validity generalization, and on evidence of consequences.

By this definition, particular assessments cannot be classified as either absolutely valid or absolutely invalid; rather validity is a matter of degree and is strongly dependent on the specific use(s) to which assessment results are applied. An assessment that is valid for one purpose (e.g., providing a general indicator of students' understanding of science) may be invalid for another (e.g., providing details of students' understandings of particular topics, or detecting misconceptions to guide subsequent instruction). Reliability and accuracy are necessary but not sufficient prerequisites for valid assessment: A test may be reliable and consistent in the estimates it provides without well-serving its intended purposes.

Validity Criteria CRESST built on this conception to articulate an expanded set of validity criteria for evaluating large-scale state and local assessments. The criteria focused attention on the consequences and character of such assessments as well as more traditional technical and practical issues (Linn, Baker, & Dunbar, 1991). The criteria evolved to include:[2]

- *Consequences.* To what extent do the assessments model and encourage good teaching practice? Are intended positive consequences achieved? What are the unintended negative consequences?
- *Content representativeness/alignment.*
  - *Content quality.* Is the assessment content consistent with the best current understanding of the subject matter? Do the items reflect the enduring themes and/or priority principles, concepts, and topics of the subject?
  - *Cognitive complexity.* Does the assessment reflect the intellectual demands evident in the standards? Does the assessment require students to use complex thinking and problem solving?
  - *Comprehensiveness.* To what extent does the assessment cover key elements of the standards and/or curriculum?
  - *Fairness.* Does the assessment enable students, regardless of race, ethnicity, gender, or economic status, to show what they know and can do? Are the items free from bias, including linguistic complexities that may confound students' abilities to display their understandings? Have students had the opportunity to learn what is being assessed?
  - *Instructional sensitivity.* Is the test sensitive to effective instructional opportunities? If students are well taught, does their performance on the assessment show it?
  - *Transfer and generalizability.* Will the results of an assessment transfer and generalize to new settings?
  - *Credibility.* Do students find the assessment tasks realistic and worthwhile? Do parents and the public find the assessment and its results credible?

- *Practicality and cost.* Is the information about students worth the cost and time to obtain it?

Reinforcing the Learning Base *Knowing What Students Know* (*KWSK*; National Research Council, 2001) renewed the call for assessments that could directly benefit the teaching and learning process. Combining recent research in learning with modern advances in measurement theory, *KWSK* laid a new foundation for educational assessment based in cognitive models operationalizing the content within a specific domain and how learning develops in that domain. In addition, other research has examined how assessment design may be optimized by using some elements of domain-independent cognition, for instance, drawn from expert-novice studies (Chi, Glaser, & Farr, 1988) or from studies of metacognition (Pintrich, 2000).

Cognizant of the reality of current accountability demands, *KWSK* also argued for the development of balanced assessment systems that could accommodate both large-scale and classroom learning needs. Three critical principles were identified: coherence, comprehensiveness, and continuity. A *coherent* assessment system is built on a well-structured conceptual base, which serves as the foundation for *both* the large-scale and classroom assessments. A *comprehensive* assessment system uses a range of measurement methods to assure adequate measurement of intended constructs and measures of different grain size to serve decision-making needs at different levels of the education system. Assessments at all levels need to be seen as part of a continuous stream of evidence that tracks the progress of both individual students and educational programs over time. Such a system requires consistency in the definition of the constructs over time, termed *continuity* by the NRC committee.

In summary, decades of theory and research on test validity establish a variety of indicators for judging the quality of individual assessments for specific purposes, with recent advances particularly emphasizing the importance of an assessment's cognitive underpinnings. Moreover, the growing use of assessment as a policy tool to promote accountability and improvement from the statehouse down to the classroom has encouraged a systems view of assessment, with strong recognition of the need for multiple measures, and a systems view of validity, with attention to assessment systems' coherence, comprehensiveness, and continuity.

The Consequences and Use of Assessment Systems

Ample research suggests that accountability systems can be powerful in communicating expectations and stimulating teachers and schools to modify their teaching and to work to attain established performance goals. For example, see studies of the consequences of state assessments in Arizona (Smith & Rottenberg, 1991), California (Gross & Goertz, 2005; Herman & Klein, 1997; McDonnell & Choisser, 1997), Florida (Gross & Goertz, 2005), Kentucky (Borko

& Elliott, 1998; Koretz, Barron, Mitchell, & Stecher, 1996; Stecher, Barron, Kaganoff, & Goodwin, 1998; Wolf & McIver, 1999), Maine (Firestone, Mayrowetz, & Fairman, 1998), Maryland (Firestone et al., 1998; Goldberg & Rosewell, 2000; Lane, Stone, Parke, Hansen, & Cerrillo, 2000), Michigan (Gross & Goertz, 2005), New Jersey (Firestone, Camilli, Yurecko, Monfils, & Mayrowetz, 2000; Firestone et al., 2004), North Carolina (Gross & Goertz, 2005; McDonnell & Choisser, 1997), New York (Gross & Goertz, 2005), Pennsylvania (Gross & Goertz, 2005), Vermont (Koretz, McCaffrey, Klein, Bell, & Stecher, 1993), and Washington (Borko & Stecher, 2001; Stecher, Barron, Chun, & Ross, 2000). These studies, using a variety of quantitative and qualitative methodologies, have shown consistent results:

Testing Signals Curriculum Priorities; State Tests Serve to Focus Instruction Teachers and principals pay attention to what is tested, analyze test results, and adapt their curriculum and teaching accordingly. Koretz (2005) noted the variety of forms in which educators may adapt: from increasing their allocations of time to what is assessed (do more of the same) to meaningful alignment of instruction (do something different in curriculum and instruction) to substantive and non-substantive coaching (coaching or test preparation on specific skills likely to be assessed) to inappropriate test preparation or cheating.

Teachers Model What Is Assessed Teachers tend to model the pedagogical approach reflected on high-visibility tests. When a state or district assessment is composed of multiple-choice tests, teachers tend to rely heavily on multiple-choice worksheets in their classroom instruction. However, when the assessments use open-ended items and/or extended writing and rubrics to judge the quality of student work, teachers prepare students for the test by incorporating these same types of activities in their classroom practice.

Schools Work Actively to Align their Students' Opportunity to Learn (OTL) with State Standards and Assessments Across grade and school levels, national studies show that schools, particularly those that have failed to meet their performance targets, are concentrating on aligning curriculum and instruction with state assessments—through revisions in their regular curriculum, the addition of new courses, test preparation, and remedial and extra-school tutoring (Center on Education Policy [CEP], 2006; Gross & Goertz, 2005; U.S. Department of Education, 2004).

Districts, Schools, and Teachers Are More Attuned to Using Assessment and Student Data National studies show that the vast majority of schools use student achievement data to target their instruction and to identify students who need special help (CEP, 2006; U. S. Department of Education, 2004). More and more districts also are mandating interim assessments, largely mimicking the expected content and format of their state tests, to provide quarterly or so feedback on how students are doing, and encouraging teachers to keep their eye on student progress on the knowledge and skills that will be tested (Herman, 2003). Moreover, many districts have become more prescriptive about how and what teachers are supposed to teach and have created pacing guides detailing what is to be covered, and at what time.

Growing Attention to Formative Assessment The focus on assessment results has moved down to the classroom. Black and Wiliam's (1998) review reintroduced the power of formative assessment, ongoing classroom assessment that is used to "form" and improve ongoing teaching and learning (see also Markle, 1967; Scriven, 1967). Studies show that educators value and use curriculum-embedded, classroom assessment more than annual state or periodic interim testing for reaching learning goals (Hamilton et al., 2007; Herman & Yamashiro, 2001). At the same time, however, taking an up-close look at practice in this area suggests the challenges of developing teachers' capacities to engage in valid, formative practice (Gearhart et al., 2006) and the gap between teachers' assessments and their actual use of results (Herman, Osmundson, Ayala, Schneider, & Timms, 2006).

While the above points demonstrate some important benefits of accountability assessment, other research shows unintended, negative consequences:

Schools Focus on the Test Rather than the Standards With sanctions and incentives riding on test performance, educators appear to give their primary attention to what is tested and how it is tested, rather than to the standards underlying the test. Teachers shift how much classroom instruction time is accorded to core curriculum subjects depending on whether or not a particular subject is tested at their grade levels (Koretz, Linn, Dunbar, & Shepard, 1991; Stecher & Barron, 1999; Stecher et al., 2000). However, what "teaching to the test" actually means depends on the beliefs and capacities of the educators who are responding (see Firestone et al., 2004). In response to the same test, some schools make meaningful and productive changes to teaching and learning, while others react more rotely with a "drill and kill" curriculum of test preparation.

What Is Not Tested Becomes Invisible As a corollary, focusing on the test rather than the standards also means that that which is not tested tends to get less attention or may be ignored all together. Both the broader domain of the tested disciplines and important subjects that are not tested may get short shrift. Many state tests tend to give relatively little attention to complex thinking and problem solving and tend to focus on lower levels of learning, and this has strong implications for what is likely to be taught. Moreover, when tests and standards are not well aligned, it seems clear that the test and not the standards will be the focus of attention.

At-Risk Students Face Impoverished Curriculum The higher stakes of the current NCLB policy (2002) seem to have intensified the curriculum narrowing that may occur when a test becomes the focus of instruction. Evidence suggests that schools are increasingly focusing on reading and mathematics, to the exclusion of science, social studies, and the arts, and at the secondary level, low-performing students are being pulled from academic courses to concentrate on literacy development (Greenleaf, Jiménez, & Roller, 2002; Gross & Goertz, 2005; Mintrop & Trujillo, 2005). Indeed one recent national study showed that 71% of school districts indicated that they have reduced instructional time in at least one other subject to make more time for reading and mathematics, and in some districts, struggling students receive double periods of reading and/or math, missing electives or other subjects (CEP, 2006). At the extreme, there are anecdotes as well about schools using "triage" strategies to focus on what they consider "pushables" and "slippables" (relative to reaching proficiency) and virtually ignoring students in greatest educational need or overriding issues of instructional quality (Booher-Jennings, 2006).

Unanticipated Effects In addition to consequences based on intended effects, state tests also have been demonstrated to have a range of unanticipated effects. For example, motivation theory suggests possible negative effects of large-scale accountability on teachers and students. Expectancy theory, for instance, posits that motivation is a function of valence, expectancy, and instrumentality, or how strongly one wants goals, the expectancy that one can achieve the goals, and the probability that performance will result in reward (Vroom, 1964). Expectancy theory would predict negative effects of establishing unrealistic accountability goals, such as those of NCLB (2002), that some schools and teachers have little chance of attaining. Data from North Carolina, for example, shows how accountability exacerbates the problem of attracting and retaining quality teachers in low performing schools (Clotfelter, Ladd, Vigdor, & Diaz, 2004).

Similarly, with regard to students, goal theory suggests that an overemphasis on testing and evaluation can reduce students' intrinsic motivation to learn and produce a performance orientation, where students work toward performance goals rather than toward learning and actually becoming and feeling competent (Stipek, 1998). A performance orientation can work against students' engagement and persistence in learning, metacognition, and self regulation (see also Shepard, 2005). While these characteristics bode poorly for students' future success, there also is continuing debate over the effects of high stakes tests and students' persistence in school. That is, evidence suggests that general high school exit exams are associated with higher dropout rates, while course-based exams seem to increase student achievement without the negative effects on school leaving, and thus students' future economic success (Bishop, 2005). The potential economic effects of testing, in fact, as real estate values extend as far as housing values (Brasington & Hauren, 2006).

State Test Scores Appear Inflated Test score inflation is still another unintended consequence of accountability and assessment. If teachers teach only to the test and not to the larger domain that the test is intended to represent, the test score results may represent just that—higher scores on a specific test and not genuine learning that generalizes to other settings. Research findings showing disparities between student performance on state accountability tests and performance on other achievement measures that are intended to measure similar areas of learning raise questions about the meaning of increasing test scores. For example, Dan Koretz and colleagues have found limited correspondence between gains on state tests and those on the National Assessment of Educational Progress (Koretz & Barron, 1998), and Linn's (2006) recent state-by-state analyses shows wide disparities for many states in the proportion of students classified as proficient based on their state test compared with the proportion so classified by the National Assessment of Educational Progress, the nation's independent report card.

Challenges to Validity of Current State Tests

The possibility that scores from state accountability tests are inflated bears directly on the validity of state tests and the extent to which they provide accurate information for intended decision-making purposes. As we indicated above, modern measurement theory regards validity as an accumulated set of data from various sources to support the argument that a particular assessment provides sound inferences to support a particular purpose and that validity must be established for each purpose an assessment is intended to serve. It is disappointing that current test development practice generally fails to meet this dictum. Rather than establishing validity for particular purposes, current practice continues to emphasize traditional psychometric indices of technical quality (reliability indices for scores and for scorers and raters, differential item functioning indices to detect possible bias, indices of comparability of scores from year to year) and largely superficial expert reviews and judgments of test items without regard to purpose. For example, while NCLB legislation mandates that state tests provide diagnostic as well as accountability information for schools and parents, states are not required to demonstrate the reliability of the diagnosis. We summarize below some crucial validity issues that have been inadequately addressed and/or largely ignored.

Alignment If state assessments are to communicate priorities for students' learning, and results are to be used to provide feedback that helps schools and the teachers and students within them to attain state standards, then it is essential that state standards and assessments be aligned.

Because there is vagueness and lack of specificity of standards in many states, available evidence suggests that the alignment of current tests remains problematic. Studies conducted in more than 10 states by Achieve (Rothman, Slattery, Vranek, & Resnick, 2002) and those led in a number of other states by Norman Webb (1999) suggest that existing tests do not fully cover intended standards and tend to emphasize lower levels of knowledge and skills to the detriment of complex thinking and problem solving. What is tested seems to be a function of the proclivities of particular item writers and items that survive psychometric field-testing (e.g., items that are at appropriate levels of item difficulty and that relate in empirically coherent ways to other items). Rather, we would argue that sets of items should be selected to provide a comprehensive and balanced view of how students are achieving relative to standards (Herman, Webb, & Zuniga, 2003).

At the same time, research shows the fragility of current methods used to evaluate alignment. A typical procedure involves the assembly of four to six content experts (expert teachers or content specialists in the area assessed, college faculty) who then review each item on the test to identify what standard and/or objective it addresses at what level of cognitive demand. Results across raters are then summarized mathematically to provide various indices characterizing the concurrence between the content and cognitive demands of the tests and those of standards, and judgments are made about the adequacy of the alignment based on established targets for each index (see Porter, Smithson, Blank, & Zeidner, 2007; Webb, 2007). Yet despite its careful attention to each assessment item and the well-rationalized and seemingly objective indices produced, the method has a number of soft spots. A first issue is the accuracy of expert judgment, that is, whether experts actually can know what an item measures by simply looking at it. In the old days of measurement theory, such methods, albeit absent the intricate procedures, were considered "face validity" and not regarded as serious evidence. In fact, there are research studies demonstrating a disjunction between what test items may look as if they are assessing and the response processes that students actually use to solve the items (see, e.g., Baxter, Glaser, & Raghavan, 1994). For this reason, the current measurement standards (AERA, APA, & NCME, 1999) call for validity evidence based directly on student response processes, such as the use of think-aloud protocols, to examine the concepts and processes that students actually apply in problem solution. Additional questions about the reliability of alignment ratings and the indices they produce are raised by evidence showing how widely judgments may vary depending on the specific calculations used to summarize the data and on the specific individuals that constitute the expert rating group (see Herman, Webb, & Zuniga, 2007; Webb, Herman, & Webb, 2007).

Fairness Test developers, as noted above, have standard content and empirical review procedures for detecting obvious bias in test items. Test items undergo multiple content reviews to detect and weed out stereotypes, item content that might be offensive to particular cultural groups, and items whose contexts are likely to be less familiar to some groups than to others. Differential item functioning and other statistical techniques are used routinely to tag items that behave differently for students of similar ability from different cultural groups—for example, an item that is difficult for high-ability, African American students, but easy for similarly high-ability students from other cultural groups. The intent is to discover and fix items that may exhibit construct-irrelevant variance (AERA, APA, & NCME, 1999, pp. 73–84; Messick, 1989), that is, features of an item or test that are unrelated to the construct or subject of the assessment but that nevertheless influence (impede or boost) students' ability to show what they know.

Language proficiency is a prime example of a construct-irrelevant factor that can impede English Learner (EL) students' ability to demonstrate their knowledge in academic subjects. If an assessment is in English, then EL students may have difficulty understanding the questions and/or the response called for, and these difficulties impede their performance. Test scores then are the result of an unknown combination of subject matter knowledge (the construct that presumably is the goal of the assessment) and language capability (the construct irrelevant factor). Research on test accommodations continues to address how the testing situation may be adapted appropriately for EL students to reduce the interference of language, for example, through provision of extra time, modification to reduce the language load of items, provision of glossaries, and so forth (see, e.g., Abedi, 2005; Francis, Rivera, Lesaux, Kieffer, & Rivera, 2006). Accommodations are being similarly explored for students with disabilities.

Yet, fairness in testing is more than the absence of obvious bias in test items. Culturally based differences in students' out-of-school experiences undoubtedly influence their background knowledge, motivation, and interests, which in turn influence students' ability to respond to particular test tasks and result in the impossibility of any test being fully "culture free." Although critics of testing have been particularly vocal about the bias of typical, standardized tests using predominantly multiple-choice items, the problems of potential cultural bias also are apparent in more performance-oriented assessments that ask students to probe deeply and to apply complex thinking and problem solving. For example, Edmund Gordon noted that what is authentic and motivating to one individual or group may not be to another, and for any assessment system needs to accommodate diversity and incorporate options that respond to it (Gordon, 1992). Similarly, from a psychometric perspective, the fact of measurement error and the fallibility of any and all tests argue that important decisions about individuals or institutions should never be made on the basis of a single test (AERA, APA, & NCME, 1999). The fact of individual and cultural differences as well as the reality of measurement error then would seem to argue for multiple measures of student performance. Yet the dictum is routinely ignored by states that base high school graduation on a single exit exam.

Multiple measures, as described in the Improving America's Schools Act (IASA, 1994) and policy analyses (National Council on Education Standards and Testing, 1992) leading up to its enactment, were intended to provide alternative means to demonstrate proficiency, rather than herding all students into the same chute. However, in the design of the policy guidelines, during rule negotiation, the term "multiple measures" was changed to mean "noncognitive measures." Oddly, these were not the usual contrast between cognitive and affective or preference measures, but signaled approval to use measures such as absences and dropouts or other archival information in the accountability system. The term "alternative" assessment now survives as description for assessments for students with special needs, either intellectually, or perhaps of non-English language backgrounds. In any case, the intention of choice and adaptation came to a screaming halt at the negotiation table, a change because of cost implications that was reified in practice.

Concern for fairness also has given rise to concern for equity in students' opportunity to learn (OTL): That is, if students are going to be held accountable for test performance, they must be given the opportunity to learn that which is assessed, a principle that has been well established in law (see, e.g., Pullin, 1994; *Williams v. State of California*, 2005). What constitutes adequate opportunity and how to measure it are open issues. At the same time it is interesting to note the negative consequences of an overemphasis on providing students opportunity to learn *only* what is tested. Strong accountability, as we noted above, has fostered curriculum narrowing, particularly for schools and classes serving large numbers of students who perform poorly. The result can be a dual curriculum: one concentrating on test preparation in reading and mathematics for students who are disproportionately poor and ethnically and culturally diverse, and the other providing more advantaged students an academically richer 21st century curriculum addressing knowledge and skills essential for future success.

Instructional Sensitivity The logic of accountability in standards-based reform rests on the assumption that what happens in schools—the quality of teaching and learning within them—is responsible for how well students perform on tests, and that if teaching and learning improve in schools, these improvements will be reflected in higher test scores. Scores on a test that is sensitive to instruction will detect improvements (or the reverse) if they occur, and thus it is reasonable to hold educators responsible for results. As central as this assumption is to the validity argument for accountability testing, however, the assumption is rarely tested (Baker & Linn, 2004).

Why might it be important to do so? Why can't instructional sensitivity be assumed if items on an assessment ostensibly are aligned with standards that schools are supposed to be teaching? First, current test development and scaling procedures continue to be based on normal distribution assumptions similar to those on which yesterday's intelligence testing was based, tests designed to detect presumed innate and immutable differences in student ability (and therefore immune to change). This underlying methodology thus gives rise to continuing questions about whether there may be a disjunction between items that are psychometrically effective in defining a scale of accomplishment and those that are most sensitive to instruction. In addition, consider the distance between the requirements laid out by the Commission on Instructionally Supportive Assessment (2001) and current practice, notably with regard to focusing on a limited number of high-priority learning goals, providing clear descriptions of what is to be tested, reporting results in instructionally useful ways, and assuring evidence of validity for intended purposes, including accountability, and instructional improvement.

Transfer and Meaning of Test Performance At the most basic level, accountability testing assumes that students' performance on the assessment has meaning beyond the specifics of how many items a student was able to answer correctly, that students' scores reflect important capability that *transfers* and is usable in other situations (see Baker, 2007b; Bassok, 1990; Bjork, deWinstanley, & Storm, 2007; Bjork & Richardson-Klavehn, 1989). Moreover, that capability, as articulated by state standards, presumably represents the knowledge and skills that students need for success—in school and ultimately for success in postsecondary education and/or the world of work. Strangely, these fundamental assumptions are rarely subjected to empirical testing. Scanty available evidence on score inflation (see above) raises questions about students' ability to transfer their performance on state tests to NAEP (Koretz et al., 1991), as does the need for remedial courses by increasing numbers of entering college students despite increases in proficiency as judged by state high school tests (CEP, 2003). Basic studies of test-criterion relationships and validity generation are needed.

Challenges in the transfer and meaning of results from standards-based tests can arise from three sources: (a) problems in the nature and content of the assessment, (b) problems with instruction, and (c) problems with the performance standards themselves (e.g., what score is considered sufficient to be considered proficient). For example, suppose a study showed only a weak relationship between proficiency as judged by a high school mathematics test and the need for remedial mathematics coursework at college entry. Among other things, the weak relationship could be the result of the weak alignment between the knowledge and skills tested (and presumably state high school standards) and those required for college entry. If the test content is not college synchronized with expectations (e.g., college entry requirements), passing the test (or not) tells little about whether a student needs college remediation. Teachers may have taught students the narrowest interpretation

of assessed content and skills, rather than linking them to broader contexts and applications and so test results do not generalize to college settings. Alternatively, the test content could be appropriate, but the performance standard—or passing score—may be set too low (or too high) to be a good determiner of college preparation.

Like alignment, although performance standards are a critical component of standards-based testing, the methodology for their establishment sits on shaky ground. Typical procedures essentially bring together a group of judges (educators, content specialists, parents, community members), each of whom is asked to inspect individual items and to make a judgment about whether a minimally proficient student should be able to answer them correctly, or for an open-ended item, whether the response reflects a minimally proficient student's response. Individual judgments are summarized for the group to arrive at an initial cut score. Subsequent rounds of judgment usually occur after group discussion and consideration of item difficulty data, with the final round of individual judgments used to establish the official cut score.

Even though it incorporates empirical data on item difficulty and mathematically summarizes results, the standard-setting process is essentially a judgmental process that is subject to the same criticisms mentioned above with regard to alignment methodology. What does proficiency really mean? Can judges infer how a "proficient" student would respond by just looking at an item? Would a different group of judges arrive at a different judgment? If "proficiency" is an obvious state and obvious to infer from test items, wouldn't one expect all states to have similar standards? The arbitrary nature of the process may be inferred from the differences in the percentage of students deemed proficient on their state test compared to the percentage who score at that level based on NAEP (Linn, 2006).

Measurement theory would suggest the need to conduct empirical studies to validate decisions about cut scores (see, e.g., AERA, APA, & NCME, 1999; Kane, 1994, 2001). For example, a criterion-related study might look at whether a given cut score predicted subsequent success (for instance, the relationship between a particular cut score on a promotion test and success in the next grade), and whether and how the cut score might need to be modified to optimize the prediction. Such studies are rarely conducted in practice for state assessments.

The Three C's As noted above, researchers in learning and assessment have articulated the need for a system of assessments that can serve both accountability and student learning and well recognize the multiple levels at which assessment might be initiated and used (e.g., state, district, classroom; Baker, 2003; Baker, Griffin, & Choi, 2008; NRC, 2001). With others, *KWSK* envisioned a system of multiple measures to address the depth and the breadth of expectations for student learning, to provide students with diverse opportunities to show their capability, and to provide ongoing, diagnostic information to inform teaching and learning (see, e.g., Baker, 2003; Baker, Linn, Herman, & Koretz, 2002; Herman, 2003).

Certainly today's landscape features a number of different kinds and sources of measures. Spurred by current accountability demands, the results of annual state testing are little and too late to guide instruction, to catch and catch up students who may be left behind, or to try to assure that annual accountability goals will be met. Research, furthermore, suggests that successful schools and districts (successful in raising test scores) often supplement state assessment results with other local data and institute periodic testing to get regular information during the school year about whether and how students are progressing (Baker, Griffin, & Choi, 2008; Borko & Elliott, 1998; Casserly, 2006). As a result, districts across the country have acted to institute quarterly or more frequent testing programs, variously called benchmark testing, progress monitoring, and interim tests, and spawning a burgeoning commercial interest in such tests.

At the same time, as noted above, there is growing interest in teachers' formative assessment practices. Teachers are encouraged to use assessment during the course of instruction to support their students' learning and progress toward proficiency, using their own and curriculum-embedded assessments, observations of student responses, and a growing array of commercial item banks and products.

Thus certainly multiple measures are emanating from different levels of the system obstensibly to support student learning, but one might ask how well such measures constitute the types of learning-based assessment system and criteria advocated by *KWSK*. Does the collection of state, benchmark, and classroom assessments available represent a *coherent* system of assessment that provides *comprehensive* and *continuous* data to fuel educationally better decision-making at various levels of the educational system? The answer unfortunately is no.

In terms of *coherence*, instead of building on a firm conceptual base, informed by a rich conception of the meaning of state standards and of how knowledge develops in a domain, the system largely concentrates on the idiosyncrasies of the state test. There typically is tight coupling between the periodic district benchmark tests and the specific content and format of the state assessment, with the former built to directly mirror and mimic the latter, and indeed the system seems driven largely by the economics of sticking with existing testing technology. While all would acclaim the importance of high-quality indicators of student learning and school performance, the time and cost of new development impedes progress. Other inhibitors include a small, concentrated group of vendors who wish to maximize profit, the constraints of tradition, the strong trust of and experience with the psychometric argument underlying current assessment strategies, and policy makers' and political activists' appetites for measuring all "standards" and rather than expending the political energy and capital on reaching consensus on a fewer number of standards to be measured well. Perhaps most salient is the constraint of the fiscal cycle that often restricts states and always the federal government to annual budget plans based on estimated revenues. Public debt seems acceptable for many areas, but traditionally not for education, which frequently suffers the ups and downs of budgetary shifts.

As a result, rather than being *comprehensive,* the picture of student learning is severely constrained by the multiple-choice formats that are dominant in current tests. Further, while teachers generally find the results of benchmark tests more helpful than annual state results, educators continue to value most their own classroom assessments (Hamilton, 2003; Stecher, 2002; Stecher & Hamilton, 2002), which are unlikely to be of high quality or based in a coherent, continuous sense of learning progression. Responses to accountability may have reduced the babel by encouraging attention to a single set of goals, but is a test the right goal? Rather than a symphony, the result is a weak chord.

Toward System Validity

It is true that the system is moving toward more coherence, *if* coherence based on an annual, predominantly multiple-choice test counts. But judged from the criterion of learning, assessment data do not speak clearly to teaching, and system validity is highly suspect. Existing large-scale accountability measures have been developed independent of models of cognition and of concerns for adverse effects on curriculum and instruction. The result is assessment systems about which there are many questions: Do existing measures represent meaningful and transferable learning? Do they support students' opportunities to learn important 21st century knowledge and skills? Are measures sensitive to good instruction? Do they leverage and collectively support the best of teaching and learning? Available evidence would suggest the need for some improvements.

In the search for serious systemic reform (Smith & O'Day, 1991) and the proffering of various remedies since, including the No Child Left Behind mandates (2002), calls for a national system of standards and assessments (National Council on Education Standards and Testing, 1992), the exploration of a Voluntary National Test (Heubert & Hauser, 1999), and calls for a national curriculum, we seem to have arrived thus far at an efficient "work-around" based on traditional, standardized testing technology and narrow tests. Standardization means uniform requirements for all, designed to assure fairness in a diverse educational system, yet at the same time standardization reduces the potential richness of such diversity and with it the richness of student learning.

We think it is time to try a new approach, a system that builds from the competencies and dispositions that students need for future success in the 21st century and the curriculum, teaching and learning that will help them to get there. Rather than insisting on strict standardization and its attendant superficial assessments, consider how accountability systems can directly enable students to develop and be assessed in 21st century competencies and engaged in meaningful contexts that both respond to the reality of individual difference and fuel students' interest and future aspirations. While history suggests the futility of trying to abolish current standardized tests in their entirety, we believe we should be exploring new models that reduce the narrow focus on traditional tests, build on the success cited earlier of course-based assessment strategies (cf. Bishop, 2005), and open up possibilities for comparable, but locally adapted course-based evidence of essential competencies.

One model worth exploring is a system of alternative, co-ordinated syllabuses, professional development, and student performance requirements for satisfying specified learning goals from which local schools and/or students can choose may be worth exploring. Such a system currently exists in England, where the Qualifications and Curriculum Authority (http://www.qca.org.uk/) supervises the development of assessments, cut scores, and curriculum. Schools or local authorities are able to select the integrated set of syllabus, professional development, materials, and assessment that will serve their needs. Through a moderation process, comparable scores are developed within subjects (e.g., algebra), and alignment is naturally built in, a function of the design of the instruction and assessments. A qualifications-oriented approach, where students demonstrate the specific acquisition of competency and have the opportunity to apply complex thinking and problem solving in specific areas of interest (e.g., vocational or academically oriented), offers another, related possibility that is in place in many other countries (e.g., New Zealand, http://www.nzqa.govt.nz/ncea/assessment/resources/visualart/index.html) and recommended in the United States (Achieve Inc., http://www.achieve.org/; Baker, 2007a).

What can be done to strengthen the system and to work toward necessary modifications in short order? First, as we have noted, consider an incremental approach that retains some standardized measures for their credibility and cost virtues and, second, work first in the area where the U.S. currently performs the worst, in its secondary schools. One might start with the current movement directed to creating high-quality, end-of-course examinations and assure that such examinations build in opportunities for 21st century skills. This effort alone would link goals, instruction, and assessment more operationally, and design in alignment. A corollary initiative would be to offer secondary students a much wider range of choice, including academic certifications that could count for exit examinations, such as Advanced Placement Examinations or the International Baccalaureate. In addition, schools could begin to offer additional options for students relevant to job skills, or to the construct of cognitive readiness (Fletcher & Morrison, 2008). Cognitive readiness involves skills that have general applicability problem solving, information search, and metacognition, but must be embedded in content domains for application. The term "readiness" is used less as a "beginner set of prerequisites" and more to suggest that the student is ready for the uncertain future that may demand a combination of learned skills and knowledge combined in

new ways to meet unforeseen circumstances. Here "readiness" means readiness for action. If such a system targeted to both academic learning and usable skills could be developed for all students, college bound or not, we might be able to make rapid progress without lumbering bureaucratic holdups. Instead of large-scale agreement on one syllabus, the use of a range of certifying options could be proposed and vetted. These might supplement those coming from schools and involve industry, universities, and the community. The requirement to succeed would not necessarily be only institutional (at the school), but because of student active choice, could be more strongly shared by the students themselves. Arbitrary seat time limits and sanctions would be mitigated, and an expanding menu of options, perhaps available through the Internet and sometimes as a public service could be available.

How could this shift be possible? What kind of political will would be necessary to adopt this or other departures from present practice? Unfortunately, political deliberations do not map at all to the speed of change in the society, or even to the speed needed to prepare U.S. students adequately. Wildavsky (1993) argued for incrementalism because bargains were easier to strike and tradeoffs could be made within sub-areas of activity. What if American politics cannot conduct its business fast enough to produce the changes it needs? Historically, the United States has managed to gather its resources and act expeditiously when its perceived national interest is threatened. That was the message 25 years ago in *A Nation At Risk* (National Commission on Excellence in Education, 1983), but perceived as a metaphor rather than a call to speedy action. It took more than 10 years before the enactment of a modified educational plan focusing on outcomes for all children, and 10 years more since the most recent modification, No Child Left Behind (2002) had been implemented. Twenty years is too long. It is about two generations of students.

So, there is an inherent conflict between the speed required to take serious decisions and make them real, and the traditional practices of politics, educational policymaking, and teaching. Like global warming used to seem an alarmist prediction that we now experience, so very well might our competition with new economic powers with greater agility and alacrity in policy implementation. Unless all major players in the United States recognize that our educational system needs more significant and much faster attention, the particular details of our accountability processes may fade from centrality as the bulk of our nation's students lose competitive advantage in jobs, science, technology, and economic product.

If the U.S. education system of assessments could change its priorities and less useful traditions, real shifts in the interaction of policy and performance could be seen. While continuing to maintain the importance of closing differential gaps among groups, accountability systems could respond to the diversity and special skills of many individuals, promote tasks and tests that produce students' ability to use knowledge in different settings (transfer), and to prepare all students to adapt to changing requirements. Our accountability system could align with our larger hopes and aspirations for our children and our country.

Notes

1. The legislation also requires states to create standards and annual assessments in science for at least one grade level during each of elementary, middle, and high school, but these assessments do not "count" in the calculations for meeting annual accountability targets.
2. Adapted from CRESST Criteria for Evaluating Assessment (National Center for Research on Evaluation, Standards, and Student Testing, Los Angeles, UCLA).

References

Abedi, J. (2005). Issues and consequences for English language learners. In J. L. Herman & E. Haertel (Eds.), *Uses and misuses of data in accountability testing. Yearbook of the National Society for the Study of Education* (pp. 175–198). Malden, MA: Blackwell.

American Educational Research Association, American Psychological Association, & National Council on Measurement in Education. (1999). *The standards for educational and psychological testing.* Washington, DC: American Educational Research Association.

Baker, E. L. (1997). Model-based performance assessment. *Theory into Practice, 36,* 247–254.

Baker, E. L. (2003). Multiple measures: Toward tiered systems. *Educational Measurement: Issues & Practice, 22*(2), 13–17.

Baker, E. L. (2007a). The end(s) of testing (2007 AERA Presidential Address). *Educational Researcher, 36*(6), 309–317.

Baker, E. L. (2007b). Model-based assessments to support learning and accountability: The evolution of CRESST's research on multiple-purpose measures. *Educational Assessment, 12,* 179–194.

Baker, E. L., Griffin, N. C., & Choi, K. (2008, April). *The achievement gap in California: Context, status, and approaches for improvement.* Paper prepared for the California Department of Education, P-16 Closing the Gap Research Council, Davis, CA. Retrieved April 18, 2008, from http://cap-ed.ucdavis.edu/sites/cap-ed.ucdavis.edu/files/BakerFINALPFD2_WEB.pdf

Baker, E. L., & Linn, R. L. (2004). Validity issues for accountability systems. In S. H. Fuhrman & R. F. Elmore (Eds.), *Redesigning accountability systems for education* (pp. 47–72). New York: Teachers College Press.

Baker, E. L., Linn, R. L., Herman, J. L., & Koretz, D. (2002, Winter). *Standards for educational accountability systems* (CRESST Policy Brief 5). Los Angeles: University of California, National Center for Research on Evaluation, Standards, and Student Testing.

Bassok, M. (1990). Transfer of domain-specific problem solving procedures. *Journal of Experimental Psychology: Learning, Memory, and Cognition, 16,* 522–533.

Baxter, G. P., Glaser, R., & Raghavan, K. (1994). *Analysis of cognitive demand in selected alternative science assessments* (CSE Tech. Rep. 382). Los Angeles: University of California, Center for Research on Evaluation, Standards, and Student Testing.

Bishop, J. (2005). High school exit examinations: When do learning effects generalize? In J. L. Herman & E. Haertel (Eds.), *Uses and misuses of data in accountability testing. Yearbook of the National Society for the Study of Education* (pp. 260–288). Malden, MA: Blackwell.

Bjork, E. L., deWinstanley, P. A., & Storm, B. C. (2007). Learning how to learn: Can experiencing the outcome of different encoding strategies enhance subsequent encoding? *Psychonomic Bulletin & Review, 14,* 207–211.

Bjork, R. A., & Richardson-Klavehn, A. (1989). On the puzzling relationship between environmental context and human memory. In C. Izawa (Ed.), *Current issues in cognitive processes: The Tulane Flowerree Symposium on Cognition* (pp. 313–344). Hillsdale, NJ: Erlbaum.

Black, P., & Wiliam, D. (1998). Assessment and classroom learning. *Assessment in Education: Principles, Policy and Practice, 5,* 7–73.

Booher-Jennings, J. (2006). Rationing education in an era of accountability. *Phi Delta Kappan, 87,* 756–761.

Borko, H., & Elliott, R. (1998, November). *Tensions between competing pedagogical and accountability commitments for exemplary teachers of mathematics in Kentucky* (CSE Tech. Rep. No. 495). Los Angeles: University of California, National Center for Research on Evaluation, Standards, and Student Testing (CRESST).

Borko, H., & Stecher, B. M. (2001, April). *Looking at reform through different methodological lenses: Survey and case studies of the Washington state education reform.* Paper presented at the annual meeting of the American Educational Research Association, Seattle, WA.

Brasington, D., & Hauren, D. (2006). Educational outcomes and house values: A test of the value-added approach. *Journal of Regional Science, 46,* 245–268.

Casserly, M. (2006). *Beating the odds: A city-by-city analysis of student performance and achievement gaps on state assessments: Results from the 2004–2005 school year.* Washington, DC: Council of the Great City Schools.

Center on Education Policy. (2003). *State high school exit exams: Put to the test.* Washington, DC: Author.

Center on Education Policy. (2006). *From the capital to the classroom: Year 4 of the No Child Left Behind Act.* Washington, DC: Author.

Chi, M. T. H., Glaser, R., & Farr, M. (Eds.). (1988). *The nature of expertise.* Hillsdale, NJ: Erlbaum.

Clotfelter, T., Ladd, H., Vigdor, J., & Diaz, R. (2004). Do school accountability systems make it more difficult for low performing schools to attract and retain high quality teachers? *Journal of Policy Analysis and Management 23,* 251–271.

Commission on Instructionally Supportive Assessment. (2001). *Building tests to support instruction and accountability.* Retrieved August 7, 2007, from http://www.nea.org/accountability/buildingtests.html

Firestone, W. A., Camilli, G., Yurecko, M., Monfils, L., & Mayrowetz, D. (2000). State standards, socio-fiscal context and opportunity to learn in New Jersey. *Education Policy Analysis Archives, 8*(35), 1068–2341.

Firestone, W. A., Mayrowetz, D., & Fairman, J. (1998). Performance-based assessment and instructional change: The effects of testing in Maine and Maryland. *Educational Evaluation and Policy Analysis, 20,* 95–113.

Firestone, W. A., Schorr, R. Y., & Monfils, L. F. (2004). *The ambiguity of teaching to the test: Standards, assessment, and educational reform.* Mahwah, NJ: Erlbaum.

Fletcher, J. D., & Morrison, J. E. (2008). Representing cognition in games and simulations. In E. L. Baker, J. Dickieson, W. Wulfeck, & H. F. O'Neil (Eds.), *Assessment of problem solving using simulations* (pp. 107–137). Mahwah, NJ: Erlbaum.

Francis, D. J., Rivera, M. O., Lesaux, N., Kieffer, M., & Rivera, H. (2006). *Practical guidelines for the education of English language learners: Research-based recommendations for instruction and academic interventions.* Portsmouth, NH: RMC Corporation.

Gearhart, M., Nagashima, S., Pfotenhauer, J., Clark, S., Schwab, S., Vendlinski, T. et al. (2006). Developing expertise with classroom assessment in K-12 science. *Educational Assessment, 11,* 237–263.

Goldberg, G. L., & Rosewell, B. S. (2000). From perception to practice: The impact of teachers' scoring experience on performance based instruction and classroom practice. *Educational Assessment, 6,* 257–290.

Gordon, E. W. (1992). *Implications of diversity in human characteristics for authentic assessment* (CSE Tech. Rep. No. 341). Los Angeles: University of California, National Center for Research on Evaluation, Standards, and Student Testing.

Greenleaf, C. L., Jiménez, R. T., & Roller, C. M. (2002). Reclaiming secondary reading interventions: From limited to rich conceptions, from narrow to broad conversations. *Reading Research Quarterly, 37,* 484–496.

Gross, B., & Goertz, M. E. (Eds.). (2005). *Holding high hopes: How high schools respond to state accountability policies* (CPRE Research

Report Series. RR-056). Philadelphia: The University of Pennsylvania, Consortium for Policy Research in Education.

Hamilton, L. S. (2003). Assessment as a policy tool. *Review of Research in Education, 27,* 25–68.

Hamilton, S., Stecher, B., Marsh, J. A., Sloan McCombs, J., Robyn, A., Russell, J., et al. (2007). *Standards-based accountability under No Child Left Behind: Experiences of teachers and administrators in three states.* Santa Monica, CA: RAND.

Herman, J. L. (2003). The effects of testing on instruction. In S. Fuhrman & R. Elmore (Eds.), *Redesigning accountability systems for education* (pp. 141–166). New York: Teachers College Press.

Herman, J. L. (2008). Accountability and assessment: Is public interest in K-12 education being served? In K. Ryan & L. A. Shepard (Eds.), *The future of test-based educational accountability* (pp 211–231). Mahwah, NJ: Erlbaum.

Herman, J. L., & Klein, D. C. D. (1997). *Assessing opportunity to learn: A California example* (CSE Rep. 453). Los Angeles: University of California, National Center for Research on Evaluation, Standards, and Student Testing.

Herman, J. L., Osmundson, E., Ayala, C., Schneider, S., & Timms, M. (2006). *The nature and impact of teachers' formative assessment practices* (CSE Tech. Rep. 703). Los Angeles: University of California, National Center for Research on Evaluation, Standards, and Student Testing.

Herman, J. L., Webb, N. M., & Zuniga, S. A. (2003). *Alignment and college admissions: The match of expectations, assessments, and educator perspectives* (CSE Tech. Rep. No. 593). Los Angeles: University of California, National Center for Research on Evaluation, Standards, and Student Testing.

Herman, J. L., Webb, N. M., & Zuniga, S. A. (2007). Measurement issues in the alignment of standards and assessments. *Applied Measurement in Education, 20,* 101–126.

Herman, J. L., & Yamashiro, K. (2001). *Exploring data use and school performance in urban public schools.* Los Angeles: University of California, National Center for Research on Evaluation, Standards, and Student Testing.

Heubert, J. P., & Hauser, R. M. (Eds.). (1999). *High Stakes: Testing for tracking, promotion, and graduation.* Washington, DC: National Academy Press.

Improving America's Schools Act of 1994, Pub. L. No. 103-382, 108 Stat. 3518 (1994).

Kane, M. T. (1994). Validating the performance standards associated with passing scores. *Review of Educational Research, 64,* 425–461.

Kane, M. T. (2001). So much remains the same: Conception and status of validation in setting standards. In G. J. Cizek (Ed.), *Setting performance standards: Concepts, methods and perspectives* (pp. 53–88). Mahwah, NJ: Erlbaum.

Koretz, D. (2005). Alignment, high stakes, and the inflation of test scores. In J. L. Herman & E. Haertel (Eds.), *Uses and misuses of data in accountability testing. Yearbook of the National Society for the Study of Education* (pp. 99–118). Malden, MA: Blackwell.

Koretz, D. & Barron, S. (1998). *The validity of gains in scores on the Kentucky Instructional Results Information System (KIRIS).* Santa Monica, CA: RAND.

Koretz, D., Barron, S., Mitchell, K. J., & Stecher, B. M. (1996). *Perceived effects of the Kentucky Instructional Results Information System (KIRIS).* Santa Monica, CA: RAND.

Koretz, D, Linn, R. L., Dunbar, S. B., & Shepard, L. A. (1991, April). *The effects of high-stakes testing on achievement: Preliminary findings about generalization across tests.* Paper presented at the annual meeting of the American Educational Research Association, Chicago.

Koretz, D., McCaffrey, D., Klein, S., Bell, R., & Stecher, B. (1993). *The reliability of scores from the 1992 Vermont portfolio assessment program* (CSE Tech. Rep. No. 355). Los Angeles: University of California, National Center for Research on Evaluation, Standards, and Student Testing (CRESST).

Lane, S., Stone, C. A., Parke, C. S., Hansen, M. A., & Cerrillo, T. L. (2000, April). *Consequential evidence for MSPAP from the teacher, principal, and student perspective.* Paper presented at the annual

meeting of the National Council of Measurement in Education, New Orleans, LA.

Linn, R. L. (1998). *Standards-based accountability: Ten suggestions* (CRESST Policy Brief). Los Angeles: University of California, Center for Research on Evaluation, Standards, and Student Testing.

Linn, R. L. (2006). *Educational accountability systems* (CSE Tech. Rep. 687). Los Angeles: University of California, National Center for Research on Evaluation, Standards, and Student Testing.

Linn, R. L., Baker, E. L., & Dunbar, S. B. (1991). Complex, performance-based assessment: Expectations and validation criteria. *Educational Researcher, 20*(8), 15–21. (ERIC Document Reproduction Service No. EJ 436999)

Markle, S. M. (1967). Empirical testing of programs. In P. C. Lange (Ed.), *Programmed instruction: The sixty-sixth yearbook of the National Society for the Study of Education, Part 2* (pp. 104–140). Chicago: National Society for the Study of Education, University of Chicago Press.

McDonnell, L. M. (1994). Assessment policy as persuasion and regulation. *American Journal of Education, 102,* 394–420.

McDonnell, L. M. (1997). The politics of state testing: Implementing new student assessments (CSE Tech. Rep. 424). Los Angeles: University of California, National Center for Research on Evaluation, Standards, and Student Testing.

McDonnell, L. M., & Choisser, C. (1997). *Testing and teaching: Local implementation of new state assessments* (CSE Tech. Rep. No. 442). Los Angeles: University of California, National Center for Research on Evaluation, Standards, and Student Testing.

Merriam-Webster, Inc. (1993). *Merriam-Webster's collegiate dictionary* (10th ed.). Springfield, MA: Author.

Messick, S. (1989). Validity. In R. L. Linn (Ed.), *Educational measurement* (3rd ed., pp. 13–103). New York: MacMillan.

Mintrop, H., & Trujillo, T. M. (2005). Corrective action in low performing schools: Lessons for NCLB implementation from first-generation accountability systems [Electronic version]. *Education Policy Analysis Archives, 13*(48).

National Commission on Excellence in Education. (1983). *A nation at risk: The imperative for educational reform. A report to the nation and the Secretary of Education.* Washington, DC: U.S. Government Printing Office.

National Council on Education Standards and Testing. (1992). *Raising standards for American education: A report to Congress, the Secretary of Education, the National Education Goals Panel, and the American people.* Washington, DC: U.S. Government Printing Office.

National Research Council. (2001). *Knowing what students know: The science and design of educational assessment.* Committee on the Foundations of Assessment. J. Pellegrino, N. Chudowsky, & R. Glaser (Eds.). Board on Testing and Assessment, Center for Education, Division of Behavioral and Social Sciences and Education. Washington, DC: National Academy Press.

No Child Left Behind Act of 2001, Pub. L. No. 107-110, § 115 Stat. 1425 (2002).

Nyquist, J. B. (2003, December). *The benefits of reconstructing feedback as a larger system of formative assessment: A meta-analysis.* Unpublished master's thesis, Vanderbilt University, Nashville, TN.

Pintrich, P. R. (2000). The role of goal orientation in self-regulated learning. In M. Boekaerts, P. R. Pintrich, & M. Zeidner (Eds.), *Handbook of self-regulation* (pp. 451–502). San Diego, CA: Academic Press.

Porter, A. C., Smithson, J., Blank, R., & Zeidner, T. (2007). Alignment as a teacher variable. *Applied Measurement in Education, 20,* 27–51.

Pullin, D. C. (1994). Learning to work: The impact of curriculum and assessment standards on educational opportunity. *Harvard Educational Review, 64,* 31–54.

Rothman, R., Slattery, J. B., Vranek, J. L., & Resnick, L. B. (2002). *Benchmarking and alignment of standards and testing* (CSE Rep. 566). Los Angeles: National Center for Research on Evaluation, Standards, and Student Testing.

Scriven, M. (1967). The methodology of evaluation. In R. W. Tyler, R. M. Gagné, & M. Scriven (Eds.), *Perspectives of curriculum evaluation. American Educational Research Association Monograph Series on Curriculum Evaluation, No. 1* (pp. 39–83). Chicago: Rand McNally.

Shepard, L. A. (2005). *Formative assessment: Caveat emptor*. Paper presented at the ETS Invitational Conference, New York City.

Smith, M., & O'Day, J. (1991). Systemic school reform. In S. Fuhrman & B. Malen (Eds.), *The politics of curriculum and testing* (pp. 233–267). Philadelphia: Falmer Press.

Smith, M. L., & Rottenberg, C. (1991). Unintended consequences of external testing in elementary schools. *Educational Measurement: Issues and Practice, 10*(4), 7–11.

Stecher, B. M. (2002). Consequences of large-scale, high-stakes testing on school and classroom practice. In L. S. Hamilton, B. M. Stecher, & S. P. Klein (Eds.), *Making sense of test-based accountability in education* (pp. 79–100). Santa Monica, CA: RAND.

Stecher, B. M., & Barron, S. (1999). *Quadrennial milepost accountability testing in Kentucky* (CSE Tech. Rep. No. 505). Los Angeles: University of California, National Center for Research on Evaluation, Standards, and Student Testing (CRESST).

Stecher, B. M., Barron, S. L., Chun, T., & Ross, K. (2000). *The effects of the Washington state education reform on schools and classrooms* (CSE Tech. Rep. No. 525). Los Angeles: University of California, National Center for Research on Evaluation, Standards, and Student Testing (CRESST).

Stecher, B. M., Barron, S. L., Kaganoff, T., & Goodwin, J. (1998). *The effects of standards-based assessment on classroom practices: Results of the 1996–97 RAND survey of Kentucky teachers of mathematics and writing* (CSE Tech. Rep. No. 482). Los Angeles: University of California, National Center for Research on Evaluation, Standards, and Student Testing (CRESST).

Stecher, B. M., & Hamilton, L. S. (2002). Putting theory to the test: Systems of "educational accountability" should be held accountable. *Rand Review, 26*(1), 16–23.

Stipek, D. (1998). *Motivation to learn: From theory to practice* (3rd ed.). Needham Heights, MA: Allyn and Bacon.

U.S. Department of Education. (2004). *Evaluation of Title I accountability systems and school improvement efforts (TASSIE): First-year findings*. Washington, DC: Author.

Vroom, V. H. (1964) *Work and motivation*. New York: Wiley.

Webb, N. L. (1999). *Alignment of science and mathematics standards and assessments in four states* (Research Monograph No. 18). Madison: University of Wisconsin, Wisconsin Center for Education Research.

Webb, N. L. (2007). Issues related to judging the alignment of curriculum standards and assessments. *Applied Measurement in Education, 20*, 7–25.

Webb, N. M., Herman, J. L., & Webb, N. L. (2007). Alignment of mathematics state-level standards and assessments: The role of reviewer agreement. *Educational Measurement: Issues and Practice, 26*(2), 17–29.

Wildavsky, A. (1993). *Speaking truth to power: The art and craft of policy analysis*. New Brunswick, NJ: Transaction Publishers.

Williams v. State of California, AB 831, § 15, EC 60119(a)(1)(A) (2005).

Wolf, S. A., & McIver, M. C. (1999). When process becomes policy: The paradox of Kentucky state reform for exemplary teachers of writing. *Phi Delta Kappan, 80*, 401–406.

16

Scale-Up as a Framework for Intervention, Program, and Policy Evaluation Research[1]

SARAH-KATHRYN MCDONALD
NORC at the University of Chicago

This chapter discusses the steps traditionally taken by educational researchers as they design, conduct, and implement evaluation studies, and relates these activities to recent efforts to provide evaluations that use evidence generated by scientifically based research models. The evolving focus on the standards of evidence has critical implications for policy makers and practitioners as they consider how to weigh, when to apply, and when to discount the results of educational evaluations at each stage of the evidence-generation process. Together, these considerations underscore the importance of designing evaluations to meet evidence quality standards with careful attention to who seeks (and who could benefit from) the results of the evaluation, in what time frame, for what purpose(s). They also suggest how evaluators can increase the prospects that the evidence they produce can be collated and communicated in ways that enhance policy and practice.

Defining the Evaluation Research Process

Evaluation is intuitively a four-step process. The first step is to establish the objective of the evaluation. Fundamentally, this entails determining the nature of the impact a specific intervention, program, policy, strategy, or course of action played in achieving a specified outcome. Consistent with this aim is documenting any unanticipated outcomes, and establishing who the intended audiences for the evaluation's findings are and how they can use them. The second step, following closely from the first, is to select the appropriate outcome measures and the optimal instrumentation and designs for ascribing impacts to the evaluand or evaluee (i.e., the intervention, policy, program, or organization under study; see Scriven, 1981; Stufflebeam & Shinkfield, 2007). The third step is to conduct the evaluation thus designed to generate evidence of outcomes and impact. The fourth step is to share the evidence. Key here is ensuring the results of the evaluation are clearly and effectively communicated to its intended audiences—a feedback loop that provides both

the study commissioner and the evaluator an opportunity to assess how well the initial objectives for the evaluation were ultimately achieved. The issues and challenges associated with how to implement studies with fidelity are well-documented elsewhere thus are not discussed here. Key questions and issues associated with the other three steps—establishing objectives, selecting measures and specifying designs, and sharing evidence—are outlined below.

Establishing the Objectives of the Evaluation

The fundamental goal of evaluation is to provide evidence of impact whereby the evaluator matches outcomes to objectives to determine whether or not the desired result was achieved. This achievement-of-objectives, gap-detection approach to evaluation research is closely associated with the work of education researcher Ralph Tyler (1950), who defined evaluation as "the process of determining to what extent the educational objectives are actually being realized" (p. 69). Yet the results of such a matching process on their own provide insufficient grounds for proclaiming the evaluand a "success." Mechanistic matching of actual to anticipated outcomes may yield evidence that is overly descriptive, inappropriately ascribing effects to interventions. Determining whether or not the evaluand led to the observed outcome requires something more of the evaluation. "How much more?" is a critical question, which the evaluator needs to establish unequivocally from the outset. Is it enough to demonstrate an association between the evaluand and the observed outcomes? Must a causal link be established? Is it necessary to rule out competing explanations for observed outcomes? What, if any, expectations need to be met regarding the generalizability of the findings?

Clarifying these objectives is essential in identifying the study design options, and selecting from the range of scientifically based research methods the one(s) most appropriate to the study objectives.[2] Yet it is not only the *standards of evidence* that the evaluator must take care to establish; careful attention must also be given to the *intended use(s) of the evidence*. The ability to speak confidently about the evidence of impact in summative terms (reporting in absolute terms whether or not the evaluand "worked") may require less information than formative applications of the findings. Formative applications typically seek not only evidence of impact, but also data that speak to whether the evaluand is the most efficient and effective way to achieve the desired outcome. In such cases, the evaluator needs to establish the dimensions on which alternative courses of action are to be valued and compared.

It is important, then, for investigators to ascertain, before they commit to conduct an evaluation, what are its objectives, who are its audiences, and what role the evaluator is expected (or will be allowed) to play in communicating the results. Many typologies categorizing evaluation research along these dimensions have been suggested, and can be helpful in conceptualizing the scope of an evaluation.[3] Similarly, it is desirable to be as specific as possible in identifying the evaluand's objectives. These objectives are the touchstone of the assessment effort; they identify the changes to be looked for, and may suggest the most appropriate measures to use or provide rubrics for determining whether the evaluand can be deemed a "success" at various "keep fishing or cut bait?" checkpoints in the evolution of potentially scalable interventions. In short, clear statements of (and agreement upon) the objectives of the evaluand and the evaluation effort itself are essential to success in the second key step in the evaluation research process: *designing a study which it is feasible to implement that satisfies the objective(s) of the evaluation.*

Specifying Measures and Designs Having specified what should be measured to what degree of specificity in order to establish whether the evaluand and its evaluation meet their objectives, the next step is to identify (or develop and validate) instruments capable of accurately and reliably detecting sufficiently finely grained changes in outcome(s) of interest. Scriven (1991) and Rossi, Lipsey, and Freeman (2004) are among those who distinguish two distinct roles for evaluators at this stage in the assessment process. The first, data-gathering, role involves specifying how "detailed and precise ... description[s] of program performance" must be (Rossi et al., 2004, p. 16). The second—a value/standards/criteria collection, clarification, and verification role—entails establishing data quality and design parameters. Is it, for example, enough to compare measures of the outcome of interest before and after the administration of the intervention, and to deem an intervention a success on the basis of a change in the anticipated direction? Or must other factors be taken into account, for example, to support causal inferences not just about the effect of the presumed cause of interest (the evaluand) but also other potential causes of observed (intended and unanticipated) consequences? Here the goals of the evaluation are critical for (a) the insights they provide into how *certain* conclusions need to be (regarding the magnitude, nature, rate of, and rea-

sons for change, including variations in outcomes across subjects), and (b) the deciding the study design best suited to provide the quality of evidence required to satisfy the evaluation's information requirements.

The "ideal" design(s) for particular information needs are well described in the literature,[4] and practical guidelines and checklists to facilitate the evaluation research design process abound.[5] Unfortunately adherence to scientific research principles is not always sufficient to ensure a successful evaluation, as demonstrated by a 2008 U.S. Department of Education decision to terminate a random assignment evaluation of the Upward Bound program.[6] The many challenges to implementing methodologically sound evaluations in real-world educational settings are well-rehearsed in the literature—as, increasingly, are strategies for overcoming them.[7] The latter continue, by and large, to consist of exhortations to develop close relationships with and achieve buy-in from district and school administrators and teachers (and to a lesser extent, parents). Unfortunately, there are no magic formulae for developing commitment to the goals of an evaluation research enterprise. Instead, such commitments are extensions of trust relationships that evolve over time, enriched by traditions of mutual respect for the objectives and products of the practitioners' and the researchers' professions. An important benefit of such relationships is the climate of acceptance for rigorous educational evaluations they foster. Another is the insights they provide into the information these stakeholders look to evaluators to provide, and the most efficient and effective means of communicating with them.

Sharing Evidence Evaluation is inherently summative, looking backward to "sum up" the impacts of an intervention. Whether or not this retrospective information has prospective (formative) uses depends largely on how well it is communicated to potential stakeholders—a task that may or may not fall to the evaluator. Evaluators are not always expected or prepared to be advocates for their findings; yet evaluators can have a pivotal role to play in working with communication specialists to ensure study findings are accessible to and usable by target audiences. The expectation that evidence will inform subsequent judgments and actions is so central that it has shaped the way in which several noted experts conceptualize[8] and define (see, e.g., Rossi et al., 2004) evaluation research. A major sub-specialization is concerned with the utilization of evaluation research findings (or perhaps more accurately, how to address the apparent dearth thereof; see, e.g., Patton, 1997; Shadish, 1998; Shulha & Cousins, 1997; Stufflebeam, 1968; Weiss, 1978, 1998). Yet merely disseminating study findings—or providing access by storing them in some central depository—may be insufficient to ensure even the most rigorous evidence will be used to good effect. A key consideration for the evaluator-as-communicator is how best to balance the information provided by specific instruments and designs with the information required (or desired) by various stakeholders—each of whom may have different interests and power at different stages in the innovation-to-implementation process.

Frequently framed as a "translational" task (implying the need to turn the jargon of the researcher into the language of the mayor, the congressman, or the elementary school teacher) or an accessibility issue (e.g., emphasizing the importance of synthesizing complex findings and providing executive reviews in multiple formats), the considerations go far beyond the mechanisms (terms, graphs, and media) used to communicate messages to the nature of the messages themselves. Like other products, the knowledge gleaned from evaluation research activities is typically best received when developed with the market in mind. This is not to imply that consumer-driven evaluation should tell people what they "want" to hear—rather, that it should communicate its findings, whatever they are, in ways that are relevant, timely, accessible, and actionable. Properly communicated, evaluation research findings should resonate even when they differ with the prevailing discourse and individuals' webs of knowledge and beliefs.

Returning to the first step in the evaluation research process, how and by whom it is intended the evaluation research findings will be used should be clarified in the objectives of the study. While neither guaranteeing the results will be used as envisaged, nor precluding the possibility they will find other uses (including by other audiences), incorporating explicit expectations vis-à-vis knowledge use in the statement of objectives provides valuable guidelines and additional criteria for assessing the success of the evaluation effort. It encourages the evaluator (and those commissioning the evaluation) to consider from the outset the information needs of each target audience, to distinguish the ideal from the possible from the likely uses of research findings, and to allocate resources to presenting and communicating findings in ways that facilitate both current usage and accumulation for the future. Critically, it highlights the importance of considering, appreciating, and balancing issues central to the philosophy of science (e.g., the effort required to draw causal inferences with confidence) with issues central to the study of decision-making (including the roles not only scientifically based research findings but also values and judgments ultimately play in even the most "rational" evidence-based decisions, plans, and strategies; see, e.g., Bazerman, 2005; Committee on Science, Engineering, and Public Policy, National Academy of Sciences, 1986; Simon, 1976). Put another way, it reminds us that approaching evaluation as a logic game designed to provide the most robust evidence may be a wonderful training exercise for philosophers and methodologists. It may, however, prove disappointing when the success of the evaluation effort is gauged not on the quality of the evidence it produces, but by the extent to which it affects subsequent decisions and courses of action. The challenge for the evaluator is to ensure the evidence that is shared meets the appropriate standards associated with its intended uses at each stage in the intervention, program, and policy development-to-implementation cycle.

Conceptualizing Intervention, Program, and Policy Evaluation Research in Stages Interventions, programs, and policies are developed and evidence regarding their impacts is generated and accumulated in stages. Innovations—rooted in theory or the result of creative insights—are explored in basic research. With sufficient data, faith, and/or resources, some innovative ideas are instantiated in prototypes, typically tested at small scales in idealized conditions before their impacts in "real world" conditions at scale are assessed. This prudent approach to investing resources in and taking the decision to expose individuals to social interventions, programs, and policies is intuitively appealing and has arguably characterized the evolution of educational reforms for decades. However it was not until the end of the last century that these principles and their implications for educational evaluation were addressed in federal educational policy.

In 1997 the President's Committee of Advisors on Science and Technology (PCAST) Panel on Educational Technology issued a *Report to the President on the use of technology to strengthen K-12 education in the United States*. Like other documents issued at the time, the PCAST report "emphasized the need for a strong research base for educational improvement" (National Science Foundation [NSF], 2004, p. 5); in addition, it recommended "a large-scale program of rigorous, systematic research on education in general and educational technology in particular" be initiated. Critically, it suggested this program of research be conceived in stages, from "basic research" to "early-stage research" to "rigorous, well-controlled, peer-reviewed, large-scale empirical studies designed to determine which educational approaches are in fact most effective in practice" (President's Committee of Advisors on Science and Technology, 1997, p. 7). The result was a unique federal education research program launched the same year the Reading Excellence Act set the scientifically based research (SBR) precedent: the Interagency Education Research Initiative (IERI).

IERI began as a collaborative venture of the National Science Foundation, the U.S. Department of Education's Office of Educational Research and Improvement, and the National Institute for Child Health in Human Development in the National Institutes of Health. Its primary objective was "to develop the knowledge and experimental methods that will allow for the implementation and evaluation of large-scale educational interventions, which will, in turn, inform educational policy and practice" (NSF, 1999a, p. 1).[9] While early solicitations in particular supported the development of promising interventions, IERI's interest in "developing sustainable and scalable interventions in education" (p. 4) was a hallmark of the program, and later cohorts of funded projects included more evaluations of exemplary interventions as they were being brought to scale.

In 2002 the NSF established a research and technical center to support funded projects and the program overall, among other things by undertaking a program of research designed to contribute to the development of the nascent

IERI-supported science of scale-up in education. Drawing on frameworks for conceptualizing and undertaking scale-up of innovations in other disciplines and fields of practice, the Data Research and Development Center advanced a conceptual model which emphasizes the critical importance of context in scale-up research, and the methods appropriate to providing evidence of interventions' impacts at distinct stages in a discovery-to-scale-up process that is designed to develop and extend the reach of exemplary interventions to larger numbers of students, teachers, schools, and districts (see, e.g., Hedges, 2007; Hedges & Hedberg, 2007; McDonald, Keesler, Kauffman, & Schneider, 2006; Schneider & McDonald, 2007a, 2007b). Analogous to the steps pharmaceutical firms take in testing potential treatments to determine whether—and if so, under what conditions—they should be approved for use in specific populations, this conceptual framework highlights the benefits and limitations of different designs and methods for assessing effects at five distinct different stages in the discovery-to-implementation cycle: (a) providing proof of concept, (b) establishing efficacy, (c) demonstrating effectiveness, (d) scaling-up and testing again, and (e) post-marketing research. It clarifies the guidance policy makers and practitioners can expect to obtain at each stage in the process. It underscores the importance—and the challenges—of forging multi-year, multi-party partnerships of teachers, district officials, researchers, parents, and students committed to learning what programs and policies work best, for whom, and under what conditions, to improve learning and attainment. It focuses attention on the resources required to support such collaborations. It also underscores the importance at each stage in the innovation-to-implementation cycle of: (a) establishing the precise objectives of the evaluation exercise, including how and by whom the findings will (and could, and should) be used; (b) designing studies that both satisfy the objective(s) of the evaluation and are feasible to implement; and (c) considering, from the outset and throughout the evaluation research process, to whom, when, and how new evidence should be communicated.

Stage 1: Provide Proof of Concept The first stage in a program of research designed to culminate in the dissemination and adoption of an innovation on a large scale is the identification or development of a promising intervention. In this context, "promising" refers to an intervention far enough along in the research and development cycle that it is possible (a) to articulate a theory of action (specifying the cause-and-effect relationship assumed to hold between the intervention and the outcome(s) of interest), and (b) to review evidence of its efficacy (i.e., its power or capacity to effect the outcome as—e.g., in the direction—intended). Analogous in some fields (e.g., chemistry; see Zlokarnik, 2002) to bench testing, in others (e.g., pharmacology; see Lipsky & Sharp, 2001) to pre-clinical and Phase 1 clinical trials, the evidence base must be sufficient to warrant testing using a greater number of (typically volunteer) subjects. The primary audiences for the results of Stage 1 evaluations are:

(a) the members of the research team, (b) frequently (although not always, e.g., if the work is deemed proprietary) the wider research community, and (c) those who fund (and are likely to fund future iterations of) the work.

The primary objective of Stage 1 research is to provide proof of concept, and to demonstrate an innovation is sufficiently promising to warrant either further refinement or to progress "as is" for more rigorous assessments of its efficacy. Not surprisingly, the standard of evidence deemed appropriate to support the latter is more stringent than that sought for the former. In either case, researchers typically point to supportive literature as a justification for further exploration of an intervention's impacts. So, for example, high school reformers might reference the research on aligned ambition, academic preparation, tracking, peer influences, and other social supports[10] to buttress a claim that a particular course sequencing, counseling, or other school-based initiative should be assessed to determine whether or not it assists secondary school students in making successful transitions to postsecondary education. Before the transition to efficacy trials, however, it is increasingly common practice to provide more proximal evidence, for example, from secondary analyses of individual student observational data or small-scale descriptive studies with primary data collection.[11]

As in the model provided by the U.S. Food and Drug Administration's drug development and approval process,[12] these initial explorations are frequently carried out by individuals and/or organizations with vested interests in their outcomes. Unlike the drug review process, there are no steps analogous to the Investigational New Drug Application (IND) stage to establish the evidence base required to justify initial testing on the ultimate population of interest[13]—in this case, students and/or their teachers. This places an even greater burden on theory, coupled with insights gained from the application of interventions further along the developmental process, to suggest that an innovation is likely to produce desirable outcomes for some while doing no harm to others on whom it must be tested to warrant further investigation. Thus both aspects of formative evaluation—a "preformative phase" in which one engages in planning, and the "usual formative phase, where you have actually got a preliminary version and you are part of the R&D operation" (Scriven, 1979, p. 69)—typically combine in this first stage of educational scale-up research.

An important consideration at this juncture is the distinction between programs or policies as interventions, and interventions embedded in distinct program and/or policy contexts. In evaluation terms, is the evaluand an intervention (e.g., a reading curriculum that provides daily instruction to students grouped by ability rather than age) or a more comprehensive program providing resources including one-to-one tutors, and staff and family support teams (e.g., Success for All) within which such a curriculum is enacted?

While partly a semantic issue (a wide range of initiatives, including complex, multi-faceted programs are described as "interventions" in the literature), clearly distinguishing the unit of analysis is important for both providers and consumers of Stage 1 evaluation research findings. The key to an intervention's success may be the programmatic context which supports and surrounds it—yet in practice stand-alone interventions may be more easily replicable than the larger (and more resource-intensive) programs in which they are most appropriately or productively provided to given audiences. An ostensible benefit of comprehensive school reform (CSR) programs is that they facilitate "portable reform" by providing whole-school "packaged" models for integrating "proven strategies and methods… used successfully multiple schools" (U.S. Department of Education, Office of Elementary and Secondary Education, 2004). Yet even the externally developed CSR models, which are most uniformly scaffolded and supported and most widely "replicated," are often adapted to fit local circumstances (see Borman, 2007).

In practice, such modification may be much more desirable than rigid adherence to a single standard one-size-fits-all intervention package. It is useful, then, to anticipate and consider the likely impacts of such adaptations from the outset. In pharmaceutical research, where such derogations can have severe adverse consequences, a primary purpose of Phase 1 clinical trials is to establish safe dosage parameters. A similarly advantageous parallel in educational research might be a Stage 1 plan to establish zones of adaptability around promising evaluands (e.g., to indicate how much variation is acceptable in each of a program's or policy's key characteristics before one is effectively evaluating a different evaluand). From a methodological perspective, this would have the benefit of suggesting a full range of fidelity of implementation indicators to employ in order to identify initiatives that are sufficiently robust to merit Stage 2 efficacy trials. From a communications perspective, it suggests the value in even the earliest discussions with practitioners and policy makers of promising interventions of distinguishing interventions from the programmatic and policy contexts within which they are embedded. Practitioners, through experience, are likely to already have anticipated the distinction, but may appreciate this sign of awareness from R&D and evaluation experts of the practicalities of implementing idealized interventions in field settings. Shaping the discourse with (and within) the policymaking community to appreciate the pervasive influence of context on educational innovations' outcomes may help to level expectations regarding the benefits that can be achieved by classroom- or school-based educational reform. It may also reduce the prospect of unpleasant surprises when innovations that seem highly promising in hot-house Stage 1 assessments produce minimal or no discernable effects in increasingly more naturalistic settings.

The heavily contextualized nature of individual students' classroom-based learning means multiple factors must be considered and controlled for in order to establish the efficacy of educational treatments in formal settings. The number of relevant factors is likely to increase when the evaluand is a de-contextualized intervention rather than a comprehensive program. Given the commitment of resources necessary to provide robust estimates of an evaluand's efficacy, the most responsible course of action may be to bring to Stage 2 only those innovations which seem highly likely to withstand subsequent variation in the field. Conceptualizing the demands of Stage 1 evaluations suggests the potential benefits of applying more stringent standards of evidence earlier in the innovation-to-implementation cycle. It also suggests the value of prolonging Stage 1 evaluations to: (a) more fully illuminate theories of action, (b) specify logic models, (c) determine whether "the proposed intervention [is] a reasonable operationalization of the theory," (d) develop measures that "tap the constructs that the intervention is intended to address," (e) enumerate the salient features of the evaluand, and (f) understand its practical importance (see U.S. Department of Education, Institute of Education Sciences, 2007, p. 54). Evaluation data that enable innovators to more clearly establish, from the earliest stage in the innovation cycle, what are, and are not, acceptable variations in educational program or policy characteristics can be invaluable in achieving the objectives of evidence-based education. More immediately, the ability to judge how well an innovation performs within these parameters is critical in deciding whether an intervention—on its own, or as embedded in a given programmatic or policy context—requires further Stage 1 R&D elaboration, or is ready for Stage 2 evaluation.

Stage 2: Establish Efficacy   The primary purpose of Stage 2 evaluations is to determine the efficacy of the evaluand. Efficacy studies are concerned with establishing the evaluand's *capacity* to effect the object as intended (whether it "*can* be successful when it is properly implemented under controlled conditions;" Marlowe, 2004, ¶ 4) as distinguished from the likelihood it will produce this same effect in actual practice (its effectiveness; see Marlowe, 2004; Howard, Moras, Brill, Martinovich, & Lutz, 1996). This means it is not only appropriate but necessary to specify and adhere to the ideal features and context of implementation. The primary audiences for the results of Stage 2 investigations are: the members of the research team, the wider research community (although the motivation to share findings with this community may stem as much from the publication requirements associated with career advancement in the academy as from a desire to see one's work replicated or adapted for testing in other educational settings), and those who fund (or are likely to fund future iterations of) the work. Other key stakeholders include the principals, teachers, school district and state administrators who need to be convinced to participate in future efficacy and effectiveness trials, and the practitioners and policy makers in a position to jeopardize such trials by enacting apparently efficacious programs prematurely.

Once again, there are important analogies—and distinctions—between efficacy trials in education and in medicine. Individual Stage 2 evaluations in education's innovation-to-implementation cycles, like Phase 2 clinical evaluations in pharmaceutical research, typically seek to enroll the smallest number of subjects required "to provide sufficient statistical power to determine efficacy" (Lipsky & Sharp, 2001, p. 365).[14] In each case, efficacy trials are intended to ensure Stage 3 effectiveness studies do not suffer from the "theory failure" (Suchman, 1969) which "occurs when a program is well implemented but does not have the impact hypothesized by the program theory" (Raudenbush, 2007, p. 25). In both cases efficacy evaluations are unlikely to proceed to larger-scale effectiveness trials without the benefits of triangulating information from multiple replications. However in education, Stage 2 studies typically collect a wide range of data that are neither suited nor intended to answer the "did it work?" question. Spurred in part by efficiency concerns (e.g., the marginal costs associated with collection additional data in a study already in the field), educational evaluations frequently collect data with the goal of elaborating theories of action and stimulating additional innovations and refinements to the evaluand. In the language of the evaluation researcher, Stage 2 education evaluations frequently record data to serve both summative and formative purposes. Similarly, while theory failure's corollary—"implementation failure" (Suchman, 1969)—is typically associated with Stage 3 scale-up studies, invaluable information on the parameters within which variation in the fidelity of implementation do not cause outright failure of the intervention are frequently captured in replications of Stage 2 studies. Nevertheless, the primary goal of Stage 2 trials in education, like Phase 2 trials in medical and pharmaceutical research, is to establish the capacity of the evaluand to produce the desired outcome(s)—a goal that drives the research design process.

From a methodological perspective, the ideal designs for establishing efficacy are experimental randomized controlled trials (RCTs).[15] Logically, it is only these designs that adequately address (control for) threats to internal validity (the ability to rule-out pretreatment characteristics of subjects as the causes of observed effects, thereby increasing the likelihood that the experimental treatment may be the cause of the effect).[16] Thus when they are "ethically, logistically, and financially feasible, randomized field trials are generally acknowledged to be the best design for making causal inferences about the effects of specific interventions (see, e.g., Cook, 2003; Holland, 1986; Raudenbush, 2005; Shadish, Cook, & Campbell, 2002)" (Hoogstra & McDonald, 2007, p. 229).

Many educational researchers—with cooperation from district superintendents, principals, teachers, students, and their parents—have succeeded in implementing RCTs to establish the impacts of educational interventions. Examples include experimental examinations of technological innovations for the Texas Primary Reading Inventory developed "to assist teachers in becoming expert in linking results to instruction" (Foorman, Santi, & Berger, 2007, p. 69); Tennessee's Student/Teacher Achievement Ratio (STAR) project (see Finn & Achilles, 1990; Finn, Fulton, Zaharias, & Nye, 1989); and teachers' "effectiveness in promoting

their students' academic achievement" (Nye, Konstantopoulos, & Hedges, 2004, p. 237). The deep integration of cutting-edge technology in the administration and assessment of increasingly large numbers of interventions holds the promise of additional opportunities to embed RCTs within interventions—-an opportunity already exploited by Project LISTEN's automated Reading Tutor (see Mostow & Beck, 2007).[17]

Evaluators have also been successful in employing RCTs to explore the impacts of programs and policies. Examples include Cook and his colleagues' assessments of James Comer's school development program in Chicago and Prince George's county (see Cook, Habib, et al., 1999; Cook, Hunt, & Murphy, 1999); and evaluations of the Even Start Family Literacy program (St. Pierre, Swartz, Murray, & Deck, 1996), the School Drop-out Demonstration Assistance Program (Dynarski, Gleason, Rangarajan, & Wood, 1998), and the Ypsilanti Preschool Demonstration Project (Schweinhart, Barnes, Weikart, 1993); see Boruch, DeMoya, and Snyder (2002).

These successes notwithstanding, the challenges of conducting RCTs in educational settings are widely noted. Sometimes they are overstated (masking opportunities, given sufficient resources and cooperation, to employ these more rigorous designs). Still, for a wide range of evaluands, RCTs are neither a viable nor even the optimal approach to demonstrating efficacy.[18] Logically, for example, we could be more confident that impacts associated with grade retention policies were in fact caused by these programs if children were randomly selected for promotion or retention—yet it is difficult to imagine students or their caregivers would be content to find their futures decided by such a lottery. Similarly, it seems reasonable to support continued testing of innovations for which initial evaluations provide ambiguous evidence of efficacy before reconciling them to the "promising, but ultimately unsuccessful" category. However, subsequent Stage 2 investigations might be better explored through other, less costly (on a variety of dimensions) designs that nevertheless provide strong evidence of evaluands' causal effects (see, e.g., Schneider, Carnoy, Kilpatrick, Schmidt, & Shavelson, 2007).[19] Appropriately applied, these methods allow us to estimate causal effects both when RCTs are inappropriate or infeasible, and using existing observational data. They hold great promise, then, to increase the efficiency of the education research enterprise, allowing us to re-purpose and leverage the informational content of large-scale national data sets.[20]

Stage 2 is the place in education's innovation-to-implementation cycle where the notion of the "value" of the evaluand begins to take shape. It is the first place at which evaluators are well-positioned to begin to take note of not only its expected but also its unanticipated consequences. It is also the stage after which consumers of the evaluation's findings need to begin to weigh evidence regarding the comparative merits of distinct evaluands. It is critically important at this early stage in the discovery-to-implementation cycle not to fall into the trap of assuming "no effects" findings preclude future exploration of interventions (Deutscher's "goal trap;" see Deutscher, 1977; Chen & Rossi, 1980). Chen and Rossi (1980) recommend evaluators employ a "multi-goal, theory-driven approach to evaluation" to assist them in identifying potentially positive impacts beyond the narrow set of originally intended intervention, program, or policy objectives. Narrower than the "goal free" evaluation Scriven (1972) describes, the system Chen and Rossi propose involves "defining a set of outcomes as potential effects of a program, some given by the official goals of the program and others derived from social science knowledge and theory concerning the subject matter in question" (1980, p. 108). Such an approach effectively embeds Stage 1 proof-of-concept perspectives within Stage 2 efficacy studies, an efficient, multi-purposed assessment exercise consistent with the iterative nature of the knowledge discovery to implementation cycle with its many feedback loops.

The logic of the staged evidence model implies any Stage 2 evaluation that demonstrates an evaluand's capacity to affect the desired outcome in ideal circumstances merits further examination of its effectiveness in real-world Stage 3 settings. In practice this transition is unlikely to occur, for a variety of reasons. Traditionally, financial support for educational research has been such that relatively small numbers of Stage 3 scale-up studies can be supported. Moreover, evaluators' demand for teachers, schools, and districts willing to participate in studies of intervention, program, and policy effectiveness seem to outstrip the supply—at least the supply of those eager to collaborate in such evaluations. Paradoxically, the current accountability climate may exacerbate this mismatch; schools and districts participating in effectiveness studies are not rewarded for their participation with diminished expectations regarding their ability to achieve adequate yearly progress (AYP) or other accountability standards. As a result they may be less willing to commit their staff and other resources to assist evaluators in testing new reform initiatives—more likely, when they are willing, to seek out the innovations which preliminary (i.e., efficacy) studies suggest are most likely to produce the best impacts most efficiently. In short, the evaluator looking to enroll subjects in Stage 3 trials may find the sell an easier one when it is possible to provide some sense of its relative worth. Similarly, the innovator seeking funding to sustain a program of evaluation research into Stage 3 may find the sell an easier one if a persuasive case can be made that, of all the innovations whose efficacy has been established, this one is particularly promising for a given set of reasons. Both sales jobs require insights into the relative merits of alternative "products"—the evaluands that compete for access to schools and funding. So, while not logically required of efficacy trials, access to evidence from others' Stage 2 trials—ideally, calibrated to standard outcome measures—would be invaluable in making the case for (or against) further evaluations, just as evidence from multiple Stage 2 trials of a single evaluand may increase confidence

and comfort in committing public resources to its ongoing implementation and evaluation in the field. Further buttressing the case in favor of continued exploration of an evaluand is information on the cost at which efficacy is obtained. Given the comparatively limited resources available for Stage 3 effectiveness studies in education, funders need to weigh carefully evidence on the benefits and costs of alternative approaches to achieving the same educational outcomes. Ideally, then, "efficacy at what cost" data should be a part of the package of information placed before funders asked to support Stage 3 studies.

Other important audiences for Stage 2 educational evaluations are practitioners and policy makers in a position to enact efficacious programs prematurely. While the current accountability climate may diminish decision makers' interest in supporting trials of as yet unproven interventions, it may also "push promising interventions into practice before researchers are given the time to complete rigorous assessments of their effectiveness in multiple contexts" (Hoogstra & McDonald, 2007, p. 232). There is no analogous temptation associated with evidence derived from Phase 2 drug trials, as treatments are not approved for use outside the evaluation process until that process is complete. No such restriction holds in the case of educational interventions, programs, and policies. Thus educational evaluators arguably have a moral (if a typically unfunded) mandate to document and make available clear statements of the limitations associated with Stage 2 efficacy trial findings— including information on unanticipated consequences, and the populations, contexts, and support structures within which the evaluand has—and has not—been tested. This includes, for example, describing the characteristics of the classrooms within which interventions have—and have not—been evaluated. The potential homogenizing impact of retention policies on ability levels within grade levels notwithstanding, the standard practice of allocating children to grade levels based upon their age leads to considerable heterogeneity in the physical, mental, and emotional development of children within grades and classrooms. It is therefore vital for reports of Stage 2 evaluations to disclose, along with the results of the efficacy investigation, the characteristics of the classroom or other educational environments within which the intervention, program, or policy was enacted.

Stage 3: Demonstrate Effectiveness Efficacy is clearly a necessary yet not a sufficient condition for an evaluand to be deemed effective (see Marlowe, 2004). Efficacy trials establish the evaluand's capacity to produce the desired outcome(s) in ideal circumstances, but common usage may vary from the ideal on numerous dimensions. Even the most rigorous evidence of an intervention's efficacy, then, is not enough to warrant its adoption on a large scale. Neither are repeated Stage 2 studies. The latter may increase, through successful replication, confidence in the likelihood an intervention will achieve desired effect(s) under specified conditions—but real confidence in an intervention develops only when its functionality in typical, real-world conditions has been demonstrated.

Providing this more realistic assessment of the prospects an intervention, program, or policy will (continue to) achieve its objectives outside the hothouse efficacy trial context is the goal of Stage 3 effectiveness investigations. Their defining objective is to establish whether an intervention "works" as typically used by the population(s) of interest. More formally, effectiveness trials seek to determine the likelihood that the same cause will continue to create the same effect in "authentic education delivery settings" (U.S. Department of Education, Institute of Education Sciences, 2007, p. 56). The primary audiences for the results of Stage 3 research are the likely purchasers (e.g., districts, state and federal agencies), users (e.g., teachers, principals), and gatekeepers (e.g., parents) controlling access to the intervention.[21]

This seems an appropriate point at which to remind ourselves that knowledge generation is an iterative process. Posing only "do we have evidence that the evaluand produces the desired changes in the outcome of interest when implemented in real-world conditions" questions in an effectiveness trial is a myopic approach with considerable opportunity costs. Failing to consider *why* something made—or failed to make—a difference limits opportunities to develop or refine interventions and/or the guidelines that need to be offered, and followed, to ensure their success. Focusing only on how well (or poorly) a program affects one subgroup can obscure its potential to be scaled-up to reach larger, potentially more diverse populations. Looking only at changes in projected outcomes may mask beneficial or negative unanticipated consequences, which again, may have different implications for different target audiences. For all these reasons, effectiveness trials typically employ a mix of methods designed to generate data that can be mined for multiple purposes—including to suggest refinements in theory and logic models that may suggest the development of new or enhanced innovations, and insights into implementation challenges that may inform Stage 4 scale-up evaluations. Disentangling the objectives of program and policy evaluation research at different stages in the discovery-implementation cycle can go a long way towards clarifying the evidence that speaks best to each individual objective (e.g., is sufficiently precise and reliable) and how confident one can be of decisions based upon that evidence; it should not be taken to imply, however, that the knowledge generation process is—or should be—a rigidly linear one.

Because classroom-based learning is so heavily contextualized, testing programs and policies with the same population (as described by individual-level characteristics) in multiple contexts is analogous in some respects to assessing the impact of the evaluand on multiple populations (e.g., groups of individuals for whom higher-level family, school, and community contexts are effectively fixed). The increased availability of school choice options may make it more feasible for members of one such "population" to

move to another, yet as decades of sociological and public policy research have demonstrated, many of the boundaries established by factors operating at level two and above in hierarchical models of factors influencing individual-level behavior remain relatively impermeable. Logically it may be both appropriate and beneficial, then, to conceptualize these as distinct populations, rather than as the same population operating (e.g., learning) in different contexts. Such a conceptualization is beneficial from an evaluation research perspective as it underscores the continued merit of designs with random assignment of subjects to treatment and control conditions. Put another way, it reminds us that programs, policies, and interventions that prove efficacious for one student or teacher population may not be equally efficacious for others—and if efficacy is not separately tested for each population at Stage 2, Stage 3 trials are likely to simultaneously pursue both efficacy and effectiveness issues.

This is another point of departure from the medical model of evidence generation. In Phase 3 drug approval trials, the extension of the evaluation seeks evidence on effectiveness and further data on safety and optimum dosage (see Lipsky & Sharp, 2001); in education's Stage 3 studies evaluators are often juggling (and thus need to disentangle) the impacts of differential support for and fidelity of implementation, from different organizational, climate, and leadership structures associated with different implementation contexts, from different family, social, and community contexts influencing individual-level student learning (see, e.g., Bidwell & Friedkin, 1988; Dreeben, 1994; Hallinan, 2000; Levinson, Cookson, & Sadovnik, 2001; McDonald et al., 2006; Schneider, 2003).

The design ramifications are considerable and are widely discussed in a burgeoning literature that seeks to refine and extend a core corpus of social science research methodology with extensions and analyses of implications in educational research settings (see, e.g., Cook, 2001a, 2001b, 2003; Myers & Dynarski, 2003; National Research Council, 2002, 2004, 2005; Raudenbush, 2007; Raudenbush & Willms, 1995; Shadish et al., 2002). In some cases the issues addressed in the latter are extensions of those raised by the former, for example, Raudenbush's (2007) consideration of "how evaluations should proceed when innovations are taken to scale"—specifically, "how studies might be designed to minimize bias, maximize precision, and facilitate causal generalization" (p. 24) given the interrelationships among evaluands, resources, instruction, and student learning. Others are even more particular to the educational context, such as the need to address, if one cannot eliminate, "bleeding" across treatment conditions (including possible impacts on the "control" condition).

Another design consideration raises once again the value (and the price) of the additional confidence one can place in causal inferences drawn from evaluations of effectiveness based on randomized field trials. On a variety of dimensions (including the continued need to establish efficacy for discrete populations described above), multi-site RCTs would seem to be the design of choice for establishing the root causes for observable variation in outcomes of interest. Yet, as in Stage 2, for a variety of reasons multi-site RCTs may not be the optimal design. In Raudenbush's (2007) discussion of the advantages and feasibility of designing randomized field trials of educational innovations to "establish compelling empirical evidence of the innovation's impact across a broad array of new settings" (p. 23), he suggests it is possible to implement large-scale randomized field trials at scale to "provide persuasive evidence of an intervention's effectiveness" (see Hoogstra & McDonald, 2007, p. 233). Raudenbush also cautions that "educational evaluation is characterized by specific features that offer unique, interesting, and difficult methodological challenges" (p. 39). Thus there may be times when it is wise to exercise "some restraint about the utility of randomized experiments," for example when there is reason to anticipate differential attrition in longitudinal experiments, as both "differential attrition and nonrandom missing data convert an initially randomized experiment into a nonrandomized experiment, or 'quasi experiment'" (Raudenbush, 2007, pp. 23, 33). While this advice is offered in the context of a discussion of the challenges of providing evidence of impact at scale (Stage 4), it has implications for the specification of designs to minimize bias at Stage 3 as well.

Another important consideration in effectiveness evaluations is whether the fidelity of implementation to guidelines for enacting interventions, programs, or policies achieved in efficacy studies can be maintained when evaluands are implemented in practice, which may be influenced by how closely implementation is observed by those perceived to have a stake in the evaluand's performance (e.g., researchers as evaluators). Citing evaluations of one of the most well-known and widely disseminated CSR models, Success for All, Borman (2007) relates replicability to implementation, noting that even when programs are "replicated with a good deal of consistency … effects depend on the quality of the implementation" (p. 59; see also Slavin & Madden, 2001). Determining the extent to which program and policy impacts vary with different degrees of fidelity of implementation (an issue long known to be critical in determining program success; see, e.g., Pressman & Wildavsky, 1984) is often an explicit goal of Stage 4 scale-up evaluations (see below). Prior to committing the considerable resources such a study would require, however, it is prudent to seek evidence of challenges teachers, schools, and districts encounter in enacting evaluands as intended in replications of effectiveness evaluations, and to develop the measures, instruments, and processes required to monitor the quality of implementation over time. The importance of tracking and unpacking the impact of fidelity of implementation upon programmatic outcomes at Stage 3 draws the administrative or managerial variables that traditionally have been the focus of performance audits (e.g., "organizational structure, plans, procedures, and monitoring"; see Davis, 1990, p. 37) more centrally into the realm of program evaluation.[22] It also underscores the benefits of incorporating sufficient observational methods in Stage 3 studies to

identify "superrealized" program development which, like Stage 2 efficacy studies, may result in optimal rather than realistic assessments of probable impacts of evaluands at scale (see Borman, 2007; Cronbach et al., 1980).

The above design considerations underscore the caution with which individual study findings should be approached and understandings of the central messages of multiple studies should be constructed. A key question is whether the results of Stage 3 effectiveness investigations should be disseminated on a case-by-case basis, or if dissemination should await the accumulation of a corpus of case data from which a preponderance of evidence might emerge. Here, as in Stage 2 studies, researchers' inability to control the spread of information about an intervention and its impacts can be problematic, and not only because of the contamination of carefully designed studies that can occur when features (or effects) of interventions bleed into controlled comparison conditions. Well-designed effectiveness studies typically require multi-year investigations to establish trends and the sustainability of impacts. In medicine, such studies typically last from 2 to 10 years (Lipsky & Sharp, 2001, p. 365), although in education it can prove difficult to obtain funding for such a prolonged period of effectiveness research.[23] Early results of effectiveness studies may differ substantially from those achieved at the end of a study period—yet the pressure political and accountability systems combine to place on educators to demonstrate results may make early adoption of initially promising programs or policies seem a reasonable course of action. It is not clear who should be held responsible for the inefficient use of resources and/or potentially detrimental impacts of early adoption of interventions, programs, and policies whose effectiveness has not yet been established. And while the logic of evidence-informed education suggests the best decisions would be those made on the basis of the best evidence—evidence of impacts when interventions are scaled-up "with the goal of producing similarly positive effects in larger, more diverse populations" (McDonald et al., 2006, p. 15)—it is also not clear that either local education or federal policymaking systems are prepared to wait for the results of the multi-year studies required to determine the impacts of evaluands at scale.

Stage 4: Scale-Up and Test Again The primary objective of research on evaluands as they are taken to scale is to provide compelling evidence of the impact of innovations already shown to be effective in one or more settings when they are enacted with larger numbers of individuals across a wide range of educational contexts (Schneider & McDonald, 2007b, p. xiii). Evaluating innovations at scale poses four distinct methodological challenges. The first, how to design and conduct studies that provide compelling evidence, is concerned with the methods for conducting research. Key issues, given the potential magnitude of the research enterprise, involve balancing the costs against the information content of a particular information study; examples include: the optimal allocation of resources in sample design between the number of Level 2 units and Level 1 elements within each unit to be studied (see, e.g., Raudenbush, 2007); the statistical power considerations which (should) influence sample design (see, e.g., Cuijpers, 2003; Dignam, 2007; Halpern, Karlawish, & Berlin, 2002; Konstantopoulos, 2004; Raudenbush & Liu, 2000); and the availability of the "definitive prior information" on the variance structure of academic achievement required to construct adequately powered designs[24] (Hedberg, Santana, & Hedges, 2004, p. 2; see also Hedges & Hedberg, 2007).

The second major challenges for scale-up research, how to implement a specific intervention with fidelity once it has been successfully tested in one or more local settings—and how to establish, if the quality of implementation is breached, its impacts on effectiveness—are concerned with issues of study design, measurement, and quality control. Foorman et al. (2007) include a candid discussion of the challenges encountered in scaling-up assessment-driven instruction and technological innovations for the Texas Primary Reading Inventory that may prove extremely helpful to those concerned to anticipate (and avoid) the potential impacts of "communication, timing, and research knowledge" (p. 82) issues upon the ability to implement experiments as designed. Such challenges underscore the importance of ensuring evaluations of innovations at scale, like Stage 2 efficacy and Stage 3 effectiveness trials, are designed to "obtain information useful for *post hoc* explanations of why the [evaluand] … does or does not improve student learning [or other proximal or distal outcomes of interest] relative to the counterfactual" (U.S. Department of Education, Institute of Education Sciences, 2007, p. 60). Here the primary comparison condition of interest is the evaluand as demonstrated to operate at smaller scales and in previous effectiveness evaluations. So, for example, the national evaluation of the Early Reading First (ERF) program[25] included as one of its three focal questions "To what extent are variations in ERF program quality and implementation associated with differences in the language and literacy skills of the children served?" (see Jackson et al., 2007, p. xiv). As in Stage 1 proof of concept studies, to answer such questions Stage 4 evaluations typically make provision for systematic assessment of factors that may mediate or moderate the impacts of the evaluand (e.g., using observational methods to document how the evaluand is functioning, and any derogation from implementation guidelines). In addition to identifying reasons for any observed discrepancies, these data can be invaluable in providing feedback to refine the evaluand and/or develop guidelines (akin to medical treatment dosage schedules) for adopting it to ensure it operates as intended in specific contexts with particular populations.

It may also be helpful, in Stage 4 evaluations, to consider the evaluand's effectiveness relative to another treatment at scale. Such comparisons once again require careful attention to issues of selection bias. Given historical levels of funding for educational research, it seems unlikely that even a fraction of the interventions, programs, and policies already demonstrated to be effective at smaller scales would be experimentally evaluated to determine if and why their impacts might vary when implemented with larger numbers in potentially diverse circumstances. However, depending upon the mechanism used to control assignment to the treatment condition, here, as in Stage 2 and Stage 3, evaluations selection bias may be minimized using techniques Schneider and her colleagues (2007) describe. Again, the ERF evaluation is a case in point. The selection criteria used to select ERF sites enabled evaluators to employ a regression discontinuity design, selecting for inclusion in a comparison group unfunded applicant sites with scores close to the score of the least highly rated funded site (see Jackson et al., 2007, p. xiv).

The third major challenge for scale-up research follows logically from the first two: How generalizable are observed treatment effects? As framed by Hedges (2007), "the key generalizability question is, if an intervention is found to produce effects of a certain magnitude in a particular intervention study carried out in a particular context, how applicable are those findings about treatment effects to other implementations carried out in other contexts?" or "given what we know about the effectiveness of this intervention, how dependable are those findings of intervention's effects when applied elsewhere?" (p. 55). Importantly, given the likely uses to which practitioners and policy makers aware of a set of findings would put them, this may mean distinguishing from average treatment effects at various levels of analysis (e.g., how dependably we expect treatment effects will be reproduced, on average, at the classroom, school, district, and/or state level; see Hedges, 2007, p. 55). Hedges presents a theory of generalization of treatment effects with important implications for research design that may prove helpful both for those commissioning and those conducting evaluation research at scale.

A fourth major challenge for scale-up research, closely related to the third, is concerned with the communication and accumulation of evidence from evaluations of innovations at scale. What methods are best for communicating scale-up research findings to affect policymaking and practice? Are those the same methods that work best to facilitate the accumulation of knowledge across (while maintaining key distinctions among) efficacy, effectiveness, and scale-up investigations? Scale-up investigations are typically multi-year (multi-million dollar) research studies; how—indeed can—early results from scale-up studies in the field be contained so that early adopting does not contaminate research designs, and to minimize the possibility of as-yet unidentified, potentially negative consequences? Alternatively, are there times when the goals of science (generating rigorous evidence of an evaluand's impacts at scale) should be sacrificed to avoid needless negative effects or to allow extremely promising programs and policies to reach wider audiences more quickly? Currently education has no institutions analogous to medicine's data monitoring committees to guide decisions regarding early stopping of clinical trials (see, e.g., Grant, 2004; Mueller, Montori,

Bassler, Koenig, & Guyatt, 2007). For a variety of reasons (discussed below) it is not clear that medical models for moving evidence into practice are the most appropriate for educators to follow. Yet the commitment of resources required to support scientific educational evaluations at scale is such that clear strategies should be developed to balance the scientific and social objectives of evaluations at scale—issues meriting careful consideration by both evaluators and those who commission their work.

Stage 5: Post-Marketing Research If, as the logic of evidence-informed education suggests ought to be the case, an evaluand demonstrated to work at scale is increasingly widely adopted, what more do we need to learn regarding its effectiveness in additional contexts, at larger scales? And what more can and should we seek to learn about the sustainability of impacts and the relevance of the evaluand once a market has been saturated and an innovation becomes the status quo? These are the challenges of a fifth stage of scale-up research which, given the many analogies to medical and new product development experiences with widespread implementation, it seems useful to describe as "post-marketing research."

Post-marketing research has an important role to play in extending understandings of how contextual variations affect educational outcomes—both those of interest from the outset, and unanticipated consequences. Such research is vital in accumulating scientific research evidence "that distinguishes responses to interventions implemented with varying degrees of fidelity in complex, dynamic, nested school contexts from other factors that influence achievement" (Schneider & McDonald, 2007b, p. 4). It has a key role to play in accumulating a preponderance of evidence on the sustainability of effects—information that can be critical to systematic reviews and meta-analyses distilling key common and dissenting findings from a range of experiences with an intervention or class of interventions over time. Post-marketing research can enrich understandings of how impacts vary when the evaluand is employed in slightly different populations, and to develop a keener appreciation of the cut-points above and below which adaptation versus adoption with specific fidelity of implementation boundaries are tolerable. The latter might point to circumstances in which an evaluand should not be implemented, not originally identified in effectiveness and scale-up research—yet absent a mechanism analogous to medicine's "adverse incidents" reporting structure, we again face questions regarding whose responsibility it is to couch such incidents in a larger body of evidence.

Evaluation Research and Evidence-Informed Education

The notion that rigorous, robust information on the effects of interventions, programs, and policies should affect educational policymaking and practice is logically persuasive and intuitively appealing. So, too, is the notion that im-

proving the quality of evidence may improve the quality of decisions based upon or informed by it, and the idea that the perceived quality of the evidence base affects both the likelihood individuals will seek evidence out and how they will weigh it. Yet the promise of evidence-informed education[26] has yet to be realized.

There are many reasons why this is the case—from difficulties linking and sharing longitudinal data systems, and concerns with the disclosure and re-disclosure of data permissible under the Family Educational Rights and Privacy Act, to the dearth of mechanisms and time required to systematically review findings and clarify their implications for practice. The latter challenges are not unique to education; efforts to increase the impact of evidence are increasingly seen in management and organizational behavior, psychology, and medicine (see, e.g., Pfeffer & Sutton, 2006a, 2006b, 2007; Rousseau, 2006). Many of medicine's efforts to increase the speed and extent to which work conducted at the bench translates into treatments offered at the bedside seem particularly promising for education. Examples include the use of confirmatory trials and consensus development initiatives (see Dignam, 2007) and translational research, which seeks to forge clearer links between basic science findings and pre-clinical research, and to develop medical care standards from multiple RCT findings. But before we turn too quickly to take a leaf from medicine's book, it is worth remembering some of the key differences between medical and educational evaluations at different stages in the innovation-to-implementation cycle.

In medicine, it is only at the end of the clinical trial process that applications for approval to make interventions available outside the tightly controlled trial process are submitted; and it is only after that approval is received that the intervention can be marketed. Thus it seems appropriate to describe the innovation-to-commercialization process characteristic of new drug development and approval processes as a "discovery-translate-disseminate" model of knowledge generation, accumulation, and utilization. Educational reformers and evaluators are not protected by a similar set of intervention approval requirements; they do not have the same control over knowledge about and the potential dissemination of their innovations throughout the evidence accumulation process. Instead, educational innovators run the risk that new (potentially incomplete) evidence will leak out, possibly bleeding into (thus contaminating) controlled comparison conditions.

It seems translation is an activity that education evaluators must be prepared (and resourced) to carry-out much earlier in the knowledge generation and accumulation process. Those commissioning as well as those conducting education evaluations may therefore need throughout that process to consider: (a) What are the communication goals of distributing results of effectiveness trials study by study? (b) Who is responsible for ensuring their achievement, and what sorts of cautions or contraindications should accompany statements of findings to guard against misuse? (c) NCLB stipulates scientifically based research shall guide decisions regarding the implementation of interventions, programs, and practices supported with federal funding. Should this influence the way evaluators communicate (and qualify) their findings? Are evaluators who warrant the impacts interventions have for particular sub-populations in particular conditions at risk if they fail to communicate clearly the conditions in which and populations on whom effectiveness has not been assessed? (d) What actions or decisions should target users be cautioned against making on the basis of single—or even small numbers of—studies? (e) If multiple study findings are to be integrated, by whom will this be done, and when? And if multiple study findings are less conclusive than one would like because of flaws or inconsistencies in the realization of effectiveness study designs, how will this be distinguished, by whom, from deficiencies in the intervention itself? (f) When should (and can) evaluators serve as the advocates for their research findings, and when should (and will) this role be taken on by intermediaries in the knowledge diffusion process? (g) What role(s) do (and should) we expect evaluators to play in facilitating appropriate accumulation of multi-, meta-, and single-study findings? How can we ensure they exercise these roles to the best of their ability? And how should (and will) they be rewarded for this additional expenditure of effort?

In the more than 40 years since Lyndon Johnson sat outside his childhood school in Stonewall, Texas, with his first school teacher beside him and signaled the start of a new era in educational evaluation by signing the Elementary and Secondary Education Act of 1965 (ESEA) into law, many advances in educational evaluation have been made. The teaching and conduct of educational evaluation (and its capacity to impact subsequent program and policy development) have been enhanced by the rise of social experimentation; the development and subsequent professionalization of evaluation as a field of study and application; the definition, promulgation, and adoption of new standards of evidence; and over four decades of practical experience assessing the efficacy and effectiveness of interventions, programs, and policies designed to improve student learning outcomes. The fundamental logic of evaluation research design has been enriched with new tools and techniques that provide (a) better (richer, more consistent thus comparable, repeated, disaggregated) outcome measures; (b) more methods of analysis for making causal inferences with observational data and for adjusting for observed and unobserved characteristics when making comparisons across groups using such data; (c) more information on the variance structure of academic achievement to ascertain optimal design parameters for multilevel studies of educational interventions; (d) greater potential to link and analyze linked data; (e) increased capacity to synthesize and more mechanisms for sharing the results of evaluation research; and (f) more support for training programs that build capacity to leverage and further develop these and other methodological advances.

At the same time, frameworks for conceptualizing evaluation's roles in program and policy development, implementation, assessment, refinement, continuation, and withdrawal have evolved. More stakeholders at all levels of the educational system see evaluation as a critical component of, rather than an after-the-fact supplement to, program and policy development and enactment. Practitioners and policy makers are more sensitive to the core precepts of program and policy evaluation research (e.g., the importance of clarifying program objectives and ensuring the comparability of available outcome measures and anticipated programmatic results). Randomized clinical trials—still the gold standard for establishing internal validity—are increasingly appreciated for providing an important, yet not always the optimal (financially, logistically, or ethically) method for making causal inferences about the impacts of educational interventions. Similarly, epistemological differences are understood to provide alternative mechanisms for triangulating data to develop richer understandings of phenomena—offering complementing rather than competing views of the world.

United in the goal of improving access to the benefits of a sound educational system, researchers, legislators, agency staff, teachers, principals, and district administrators continue to work collaboratively to generate, accumulate, disseminate, and make decisions informed by sound evidence of what did, and did not, work to improve students' learning outcomes. Such collaborations are at times strained, and tense relationships have been stretched further by national and international attention to the lackluster performance of America's youth on standardized tests of academic achievement, by the increasingly high stakes federal policies placed upon state and local efforts to fix what is still widely agreed to be an under- (if not a poorly) performing educational system, and by the increasingly inescapable political significance of education to elected officials. Identifying and rectifying the factors contributing to poor student performance are no longer matters reserved for teachers, principals, district administrators, and state education agencies—they have been redefined as the responsibilities of mayors, governors, legislators, and presidents. Following ESEA's lead, each decade has seen renewed federal efforts to stimulate the production and use of high quality evidence from intervention, program, and policy evaluation research in classrooms, districts, agency offices, and the halls of Congress.[27] Increasingly these efforts have employed guidelines for generating evidence as a lever for change. Yet evaluation research findings still appear less central to educational policy agendas and program adoption than policy makers' proclaimed commitment to evidence-based education suggests ought to be the case.

There is no reason to suspect educators or the administrators and legislators charged with regulating and enabling their efforts to support student learning will be any more successful drawing on evidence to inform their plans and actions than are medical practitioners, for-profit managers, or members of any other profession critiqued for the too-small role evidence—of any quality—seems to play in their decision-making processes. There is every reason to believe that they will remain frustrated in any attempts they may make to do so if better mechanisms are not developed for communicating the information that is relevant to particular audiences faced with specific types of decisions more efficiently and effectively. It would be a serious oversight in a discussion of educational evaluation not to consider the importance of designs and methods for disseminating evidence in the evaluators' methods arsenal. As efforts to improve the quality of the evidence base mature, these issues take on renewed importance.

If the ultimate test of the quality of evaluation research is not only the scientific rigor of the evidence it generates, but also the extent to which it influences educational policy and practice, we have much as a field—in collaboration with those we hope will find it valuable to use the results of our work—to do. In particular, it seems educational evaluators will need to give more careful consideration, at all stages in the evidence generation process, to how evidence from proof of concept, efficacy, effectiveness, scale-up, and post-marketing evaluations can, and should not, be used—including how it is best communicated, when, to whom, in order to shape agendas[28] and influence educational policies and practices. This suggests it may be time to rethink how educational evaluations are resourced. Of critical concern is the possibility that efforts to *provide* versus to *enhance others' ability to utilize* the "best" evidence may be dangerously out of sync. Technological and methodological advances make it possible to dramatically increase the depth and rigor of the evidence available to those who develop, propose, secure support for, implement, and argue against specific educational programs and policies. The challenge is to ensure we strike an appropriate balance between the resources allocated to generating this evidence and the resources committed to ensuring that evidence is available to influence the substance and the politics of the educational policymaking process. The jury is still out on the extent to which rigorous evidence will shape policy makers' and practitioners' decisions and actions.[29] Conducting and carefully communicating the results of evaluations designed to address the distinct objectives and standards of evidence required to warrant continued investment in the development and application of educational interventions, programs, and policies at each stage in the innovation-to-implementation scale-up process holds considerable promise to close these gaps.

Notes

1. This material is based upon work supported by the National Science Foundation under Grant No. 0129365. Any opinions, findings, and conclusions or recommendations expressed in this material are those of the author, and do not necessarily reflect the views of the National Science Foundation.

2. Early efforts to define scientifically based research methods in U.S. federal education policy include measures in the Omnibus Consolidated and Emergency Supplemental Appropriations Act of 1999 (Pub.L. 105-277) enacting the Reading Excellence Act (REA). Title II of the Elementary and Secondary Education Act was amended to require that applications for REA's competitive reading and literacy grants would ensure professional development and other practices were "based on scientifically based reading research" for example, "… the application of rigorous, systematic, and objective procedures to obtain valid knowledge relevant to reading development, reading instruction, and reading difficulties … that—(i) employs systematic, empirical methods that draw on observation or experiment; (ii) involves rigorous data analyses that are adequate to test the stated hypotheses and justify the general conclusions drawn; (iii) relies on measurements or observational methods that provide valid data across evaluators and observers and across multiple measurements and observations; and (iv) has been accepted by a peer-reviewed journal or approved by a panel of independent experts through a comparably rigorous, objective, and scientific review." The following year H.R. 4875 (proposing the Scientifically Based Education Research, Statistics, Evaluation, and Information Act of 2000) operationalized "scientifically valid research" (Scientifically Based Education Research, Statistics, Evaluation, and Information Act, 2000). Two years later, the National Research Council's (2002) Committee on Scientific Principles for Education Research articulated "six guiding principles [that] underlie all scientific inquiry, including education research" in *Scientific Research in Education*. Scientifically based research was defined again in the No Child Left Behind Act of 2001, at the time of writing, due to be reauthorized.

3. No single, comprehensive taxonomy of the objectives of evaluation research has as yet been assembled, although several researchers have endeavored to codify and/or critically review key approaches (see, e.g., Guba & Lincoln, 1981; House, 1980; Worthen & Sanders, 1973). Notable efforts include Nevo's (1983) 10-dimension framework for reviewing educational evaluation literature and Williams's (1989) "taxonomy of evaluation theory and practice" developed by administering questionnaires to 14 selected theorists (Abt, Alkin, Cook, Cronbach, Eisner, Freeman, House, Patton, Popham, Scriven, Stake, Stufflebeam, Weiss, and Wholey) who assessed how similar their approaches were to their counterparts' (p. 20). Stufflebeam and Shinkfield's (2007) description of evaluation as "a process for giving attestations on such matters as reliability, effectiveness, cost-effectiveness, efficiency, safety, ease of use, and probity" (p. 4) concurs with the importance attached to effectiveness and efficiency while suggesting several additional objectives. Boruch and Cordray (1980) identify more in their federally mandated review of evaluation practices and procedures (e.g., "who is served by the program? Who needs services? What are the services, how well are they delivered, and what do they cost? What are the effects of services on recipients? What are costs and benefits of alternatives?" (p. 21) as do Rossi, Lipsey, and Freeman (2004) in their seminal text (e.g., understanding "the need for a program, its design, operation and service delivery, or efficiency," p. 7). Additional objectives are suggested in a literature which compares and contrasts consumer-oriented approaches to program evaluation with goal-free evaluation, monitoring evaluation, context/input/process/product (CIPP) evaluation, heuristic evaluation, and formative and summative evaluation. Evaluations have also been characterized as formal or informal, comparative or non-comparative, proactive or retroactive, utilization-focused, responsive, integrative, illuminative, transactional, objectives-based, and conceived to confirm gap reductions over time (see, e.g., Draper, Brown, Henderson, & McAteer, 1996; Lam, 1992; Long, 1984; Nielsen, 1994; Parlett & Dearden, 1977; Patton, 1997; Rippey, 1973; Scriven, 1967, 1979; Stufflebeam, 1972, 1980; Stufflebeam & Shinkfield, 2007; Stake, 1975; Tyler, 1950).

4. See, e.g., Boruch, 2002; Campbell, 1969; Campbell & Stanley, 1963; Cronbach, 1982; Hempel, 1966; Lipsey & Cordray, 2000; Mosteller & Boruch, 2002; Myers & Dynarski, 2003; Rossi & Freeman, 1993; Shadish et al., 2002; Weiss, 1998.

5. See, e.g., the resources provided by The Evaluation Center at Western Michigan University (http://www.wmich.edu/evalctr/); the Online Evaluation Resource Library (OERL) designed to "collect and make available evaluation plans, instruments, and reports for NSF

projects that can be used as examples by Principal Investigators, project evaluators, and others outside the NSF community as they design proposals and projects" (see http://oerl.sri.com/); and the National Science Foundation's *The 2002 User-friendly Handbook for Project Evaluation* (see http://www.nsf.gov/pubs/2002/nsf02057/start.htm) and *User-friendly Handbook for Mixed Method Evaluations* (see http://www.nsf.gov/publications/pub_summ.jsp?ods_key=nsf97153).

6. Of particular concern were questions regarding the services to be provided to eligible students assigned to the control condition.

7. See, e.g., Cook, 2001a, 2001b, 2003; National Research Council, 2002, 2004, 2005.

8. Influenced by his experiences assisting Columbus (Ohio) Public Schools in evaluating their Title I projects, Stufflebeam (1980) suggested "that we ought to rethink evaluation and begin defining it as a process aimed at helping people make better decisions about their educational programs and projects," a rethinking that led to the development of the Context/Input/Process/Product (CIPP) evaluation model (see pp. 86–87).

9. In 1999 the first round of IERI awards was made, providing over $28 million to 14 projects based in 12 institutions in nine states (National Science Foundation, 1999b, p. 1); at the time of writing, IERI had awarded over $220 million to educational studies in 31 states (Brown, McDonald, & Schneider, 2007, p. 2). Ultimately, IERI supported over 100 studies of mathematics, science, and reading interventions with a common focus on the evidence required to warrant continued investments in interventions as they move forward from the "proof-of-concept" research and development stage of innovation to implementation at scale, in a continuous cycle of innovation and learning (see NSF, 2007). Additional information on the IERI program is available in announcements and requests for applications (see e.g., National Science Foundation, 1999a, 2000, 2001, 2002, 2004; U.S. Department of Education, Institute of Education Sciences, 2002, 2003a, 2003b, 2003c) and from the research and technical center, the Data Research and Development Center (http://drdc.uchicago.edu).

10. See, e.g., Schneider & Stevenson, 1999; Martinez & Klopott, 2005; Adelman, 1999; Cabrera & LaNasa, 2000; McDonough, 1997; Wimberly & Noeth, 2004.

11. For example, the sorts of studies the Institute of Education Sciences proposed to support in FY08 "Identification projects" (see U.S. Department of Education, Institute of Education Sciences, 2007).

12. For more information on the Food and Drug Administration's drug approval process, see U.S. Food and Drug Administration (FDA), 2002; and the FDA Center for Drug Evaluation and Research (CDER) online at http://www.fda.gov/cder/index.html.

13. In the drug review process, preclinical testing typically combines theoretical insights and advances in basic science with exploratory investigations in other living animals to establish the likely safety of the proposed treatment in human populations (see Lipsky & Sharp, 2001; U.S. FDA, 2002).

14. In the medical case, it is not only resource but also patient safety considerations which place powerful constraints on sample size. As a result, in the new drug development process "typically, phase 2 studies involve 100 to 300 patients who suffer from the condition the new drug is intended to treat" (Lipsky & Sharp, 2001, p. 365).

15. Campbell and Stanley consider three such designs in their 1963 treatise—the pretest-posttest control group design, the Solomon four-group design, and the posttest-only control group design—noting that the last two also address a key treat to external validity (the ability to generalize findings to other populations, settings, and treatment and measurement variables): the "reactive" or "interaction effect of testing" (see Campbell & Stanley, 1963, pp. 5, 8, 13–27).

16. Threats to internal validity include: history, maturation, testing, instrumentation, statistical regression, selection, experimental mortality, and selection-maturation interaction (see Campbell & Stanley, 1963, pp. 5, 13).

17. As described by Mostow and Beck, "automated experiments embedded in the Reading Tutor evaluate its own interventions in a way that combines the methodological rigor of controlled experiments, the ecological validity of school settings, and the statistical power of large samples" (Mostow & Beck, 2007, pp. 198–200).

18. Referencing the Joint Committee on Standards for Educational Evaluation's (2007) utility, feasibility, propriety, and accuracy standards for program evaluation, Patton (2004) argues that while RCTs are "especially appropriate" in particular circumstances, they are not the only, not always the best, and at times inappropriate (e.g., unethical) designs for "generating understandings of causality" (pp. 4–6, 12, 14). Patton notes RCTs are especially appropriate when the evaluand is "discrete, concrete … singular, well-specified;" "when implementation can be standardized … [and] controlled;" when "valid and reliable measures exist for the outcome to be tested;" and when "random assignment is possible … [and] ethical" (see p. 14).

19. Schneider and her colleagues (2007) provide an excellent review of four analytic methods that address the root causes of threats to internal validity, enabling evaluators to be extremely confident in causal inferences drawn from analyses of non-experimental data: fixed effects models, instrumental variables, propensity score matching, and regression discontinuity designs. *Fixed effects models* allow analysts to control for characteristics of students and their schools which do not vary over time, but which are correlated with the outcome of interest (see pp. 42–45; Bifulco & Ladd, 2006; Currie & Thomas, 1995; Winship & Morgan, 1999). *Instrumental variables* can be used to overcome omitted variable problems in estimating causal relationships (see Schneider et al., 2007, pp. 46–48; Angrist, Imbens, & Rubin, 1996; Angrist & Krueger, 1991; Heckman, 1979). *Propensity score matching* can increase confidence in causal inferences made outside an RCT context by correcting for bias from observed covariates (see Schneider et al., 2007, pp. 49–52; Rosenbaum & Rubin, 1983; Rubin, 1997; Hong & Raudenbush, 2005). *Regression discontinuity designs* assume the similarity of groups of individuals falling just below and above cut-points of interest (e.g., birthdates used to determine date of enrollment in school; achievement test scores required for promotion to the next grade) thus focus on only those individuals as a means of controlling for selection bias, approximating random assignment (see Schneider et al., 2007, pp. 52–54; Cook, 2008; Cook & Wong, in press; Thistlewaite & Campbell, 1960; Rubin, 1977; Jacob & Lefgren, 2004).

20. For example, the National Longitudinal Study of Adolescent Health (Add Health, see http://www.cpc.unc.edu/projects/addhealth); the Common Core of Data (CCD, see http://nces.ed.gov/ccd/); the Early Childhood Longitudinal Study (ECLS, see http://nceds.ed.gov/ecls); High School and Beyond (HS&B, see http://nces.ed.gov/surveys/hsb/); the National Assessment of Educational Progress (NAEP, see http://nces.ed.gov/nationsreportcard/); the National Education Longitudinal Study (NELS, see http://nces.ed.gov/surveys/nels88/); the National Longitudinal Survey (NLS, see http://www.bls.gov/nls), including the National Longitudinal Survey of Youth (NLSY); and the Schools and Staffing Survey (SASS, see http://nces.ed.gov/surveys/sass/).

21. Echoing the days before direct advertising of pharmaceutical products to prospective patients was allowed, students who directly or indirectly are intended to benefit from the evaluand are rarely considered an important (or even an appropriate) audience for information about its potential benefits, dosing guidelines, or contraindications.

22. See Davis (1990) for a comparison of program evaluations and performance audits, and the blurring of traditional differences between the two fields of practice.

23. As an example, in its 2008 requests for applications for education research grants, the Institute of Education Sciences indicated funds for such studies would typically be awarded for a maximum of 4 years; see U.S. Department of Education, Institute of Education Sciences, 2007, p. 61.

24. Such designs ensure an acceptable likelihood that differences in

outcomes attributable to the evaluand will be detected when they exist.

25. The early reading first program was established by NCLB "to enhance teacher practices, instructional content, and classroom environments in preschools and to help ensure that young children start school with the skills needed for academic success" (see Jackson et al., 2007, p. xii).

26. The term "evidence-informed education" recognizes the importance that factors such as professional judgment do and should play in decision making by practitioners and policy makers alike. This point was underscored by the first Secretary of the Institute of Education Sciences in addressing the Student Achievement and School Accountability Conference in 2002. There, he described evidence-based education as "the integration of professional wisdom with the best available empirical evidence in making decisions about how to deliver instruction" (Whitehurst, 2002).

27. Select federal initiatives that have shaped expectations regarding the goals and conduct of, and the evidence standards to be achieved by educational intervention, program, and policy evaluations include: (a) the *Education Amendments of 1974* which among other things authorized the President of the United States to "call and conduct a White House Conference on Education…in order to stimulate a national assessment of the conditions, needs, and goals of education" (U.S. Library of Congress, 1974); (b) the *Education Amendments of 1978* (1978; which required the Commissioner of Education to conduct a comprehensive study of evaluation policies and procedures, see Boruch & Cordray, 1980); (c) the *Educational Research, Development, Dissemination, and Improvement Act* (1994); (d) the *Department of Education Appropriations Act* (1998) which explicitly linked standards of evidence to formative program evaluation in the Comprehensive School Reform demonstration program; (e) the *Reading Excellence Act* (1999); which reinforced and extended the notion that formative program evaluation should be grounded in a particular type of evidence; (f) the *Omnibus Consolidated and Emergency Supplemental Appropriations Act of 1999* (1999; which further specified the standards of evidence evaluations would need to produce in order to warrant the adoption of specific educational practices); (g) H.R. 4875 (the Scientifically Based Education Research, Statistics, Evaluation, and Information Act of 2000 to reauthorize the U.S. Department of Education's Office of Educational Research and Improvement); (h) the decision by the U.S. Department of Education's National Educational Research Policy and Priorities Board to sponsor the National Research Council in convening the Committee on Scientific Principles for Education Research, resulting in the 2002 report *Scientific research in education* (see National Educational Research Policy and Priorities Board, 2001), (i) the *No Child Left Behind Act of 2001* (2002) with its numerous references to scientifically based research; (j) the announcement—one day after *Scientific Research in Education* was issued in prepublication form—by then Assistant Secretary Grover (Russ) Whitehurst of the U.S. Department of Education's intention to establish a "what works" clearinghouse, whose mission would include "establish[ing] a series of standards for evaluating claims with respect to educational intervention" (Society for Research in Child Development, 2001, p. 1); (k) the *Education Sciences Reform Act of 2002* (2002; establishing the Institute of Education Sciences, defining "scientifically valid education evaluation," and making conducting, supporting, and widely disseminating the results of such evaluations key functions of the new IES); and (l) the 2005 *Scientifically Based Evaluation Methods—Notice of Final Priority* that among other things codified a preference for random assignment of participants to intervention or control groups, as "[e]valuation methods using an experimental design are best for determining project effectiveness" (see 34 CFR 75.105.c; U.S. Department of Education, 2005).

28. With respect to the role of evidence in agenda-setting, see Smith and Patton on the "enlightenment" versus the instrumental uses of evaluation findings (Patton et al., 1977; Patton, 1997; Smith, 1993).

29. On November 8, 2006, the UK House of Commons Science and Technology Committee's report *Scientific Advice, Risk and Evidence Based Policy Making* was published, presenting results of an inquiry launched a year earlier into that government's "handling of scientific advice, risk and evidence in policy making" (UK House of Commons, 2006, p. 5). It observed, "in considering evidence based policy, we conclude that the Government should not overplay this mantra, but should acknowledge more openly the many drivers of policy making, as well as any gaps in the relevant research base" (p. 3). An analogous study, initiated in 2007 in the U.S. by the National Research Council's Division of Behavioral and Social Sciences and Education, "Evidence for Use: Improving the Quality and Utility of Social Science Research," had not issued a report at the time of writing (see National Research Council, Division of Behavioral and Social Sciences in Education, 2007).

References

Adelman, C. (1999). *Answers in the tool box: Academic intensity, attendance patterns, and bachelor's degree attainment.* Washington, DC: U.S. Department of Education.

Angrist, J. D., Imbens, G. W., & Rubin, D. B. (1996). Identification of causal effects using instrumental variables (with commentary). *Journal of the American Statistical Association, 91*, 444–472.

Angrist, J. D., & Krueger, A. B. (1991). Does compulsory school attendance affect schooling and earnings? *Quarterly Journal of Economics, 106*, 979–1014.

Bazerman, M. H. (2005). *Judgment in managerial decision making* (6th ed.). Hoboken, NJ: Wiley.

Bidwell, C. E., & Friedkin, N. E. (1988). The sociology of education. In N. J. Smelser (Ed.), *Handbook of sociology* (pp. 449–471). Newbury Park, CA: Sage.

Bifulco, R., & Ladd, H. F. (2006). The impacts of charter schools on student achievement: Evidence from North Carolina. *Education Finance and Policy, 1*, 50–90.

Borman, G. D. (2007). National efforts to bring reform to scale in high-poverty schools: Outcomes and implications. In B. Schneider & S-K. McDonald (Eds.), *Scale-up in education, Vol. 2: Issues in practice* (pp. 41–67). Lanham, MD: Rowman and Littlefield.

Boruch, R. F. (2002). The virtues of randomness. *Education Next, 2*(3), 37–41.

Boruch, R. F., & Cordray, D. S. (Eds.). (1980). *An appraisal of educational program evaluations: Federal, state, and local agencies.* Washington, DC: U.S. Department of Education.

Boruch, R., DeMoya, D., & Snyder, B. (2002). The importance of randomized field trials in education and related areas. In F. Mosteller & R. Boruch (Eds.), *Evidence matters: Randomized trials in education research* (pp. 50–79). Washington, DC: Brookings Institution.

Brown, K., McDonald, S-K., & Schneider, B. (2007). *Just the facts: Results from IERI scale-up research.* Retrieved June 26, 2007, from http://drdc.uchicago.edu/extra/just-the-facts.pdf

Cabrera, A. F., & LaNasa, S. M. (2000). *On the path to college: Three critical tasks facing America's disadvantaged.* University Park: The Pennsylvania State University, Center for the Study of Higher Education.

Campbell, D. T. (1969). Reforms as experiments. *American Psychologist, 24*, 409–429.

Campbell, D. T., & Stanley, J. C. (1963). *Experimental and quasi-experimental designs for research.* Chicago: Rand McNally.

Chen, H-T., & Rossi, P. H. (1980). The multi-goal, theory-driven approach to evaluation: A model linking basic and applied social science. *Social Forces, 59*, 106–122.

Committee on Science, Engineering, and Public Policy, National Academy of Sciences. (1986). Report of the Research Briefing Panel on decision making and problem solving. In *Research Briefings 1986 for the Office of Science and Technology Policy, the National Science Foundation, and selected federal departments and agencies* (pp. 17–36). Washington, DC: National Academy Press.

Cook, T. D. (2001a). *A critical appraisal of the case against using experiments to assess school (or community) effects.* Retrieved March 23, 2006, from http://media.hoover.org/documents/ednext20013unabridged_cook.pdf

Cook, T. D. (2001b). Sciencephobia: Why education researchers reject randomized experiments [Electronic version]. *Education Next, 1*(3), 62–68.

Cook, T. D. (2003). Why have educational evaluators chosen not to do randomized experiments? *Annals of American Academy of Political and Social Science, 589*, 114–149.

Cook, T. D. (2008) "Waiting for life to arrive:" A history of the regression-discontinuity design in psychology, statistics and economics. *Journal of Econometrics, 142*, 636–654.

Cook, T. D., Habib, F-N., Phillips, M., Settersten, R. A., Shagle, S. C., & Degirmencioglu, S. M. (1999). Comer's school development program in Prince George's County: A theory-based evaluation. *American Educational Research Journal, 36*, 543–597.

Cook, T. D., Hunt, H. D., & Murphy, R. F. (1999). *Comer's school development program in Chicago: A theory-based evaluation.* Chicago: Northwestern University Press.

Cook, T. D., & Wong, V. C. (in press). Empirical tests of the validity of the regression discontinuity design. *Annales d'Economie et de Statistique.* Retrieved May 25, 2007, from http://www.northwestern.edu/ipr/publications/papers/cook_empirical_tests.pdf

Cronbach, L. J. (1982). *Designing evaluations of educational and social programs.* San Francisco: Jossey-Bass.

Cronbach, L. J., Ambron, S. R., Dornbusch, S. M., Hess, R. D., Hornik, R. C., Phillips, D. C., et al. (1980). *Toward reform of program evaluation: Aims, methods, and institutional arrangements.* San Francisco: Jossey-Bass.

Cuijpers, P. (2003). Examining the effects of prevention programs on the incidence of new cases of mental disorders: The lack of statistical power. *The American Journal of Psychiatry, 160*, 1385–1391.

Currie, J., & Thomas, D. (1995). Does Head Start make a difference? *American Economic Review, 85*, 341–364.

Davis, D. F. (1990). Do you want a performance audit or a program evaluation? *Public Administration Review, 50*, 35–41.

Department of Education Appropriations Act, Pub. L. 105-78 (1998).

Deutscher, I. (1977). Toward avoiding the goal trap in evaluation research. In F. G. Caro (Ed.), *Reading in evaluation research* (2nd ed., pp. 221–238). New York: Russell Sage Foundation.

Dignam, J. J. (2007). From efficacy to effectiveness: Translating randomized controlled trial findings into treatment standards. In B. Schneider & S-K. McDonald (Eds.), *Scale-up in education, Vol. 1: Ideas in principle* (pp. 123–144). Lanham, MD: Rowman and Littlefield.

Draper, S. W., Brown, M. I., Henderson, F. P., & McAteer, E. (1996). Integrative evaluation: An emerging role for classroom studies of CAL. *Computers and Education, 26*, 17–32.

Dreeben, R. (1994). The sociology of education: Its development in the United States. In A. M. Pallas (Ed.), *Research in sociology of education and socialization, Vol. 10* (pp. 7–52). Greenwich, CT: JAI Press.

Dynarski, M., Gleason, P., Rangarajan, A., & Wood, R. (1998). *Impacts of dropout prevention programs: Final report.* Princeton, NJ: Mathematica Policy Research.

The Education Amendments of 1978, Pub. L. 95-561, 92 Stat. 2143 (1978).

Education Sciences Reform Act of 2002, Pub. L. 107-279 (2002).

Educational Research, Development, Dissemination, and Improvement Act, Pub. L. 103-227 (1994).

Finn, J. D., & Achilles, C. M. (1990). Answers and questions about class size: A statewide experiment. *American Educational Research Journal, 27*, 557–577.

Finn, J. D., Fulton, D., Zaharias, J., & Nye, B. A. (1989). Carry-over effects of small classes. *Peabody Journal of Education, 67*(1), 75–84.

Foorman, B. R., Santi, K. L., & Berger, L. (2007). Scaling assessment-driven instruction using the internet and handheld computers. In B. Schneider & S-K. McDonald (Eds.), *Scale-up in education, Vol. 2: Issues in practice* (pp. 69–90). Lanham, MD: Rowman and Littlefield.

Grant, A. (2004). Stopping clinical trials early: Data monitoring committees may have important role. *BMJ, 329*, 525–526.

Guba, E. G., & Lincoln, Y. S. (1981). *Effective evaluation: Improving the usefulness of evaluation results through responsive and naturalistic approaches.* San Francisco: Jossey-Bass.

Hallinan, M. T. (Ed.). (2000). *Handbook of the sociology of education.* New York: Kluwer Academic/Plenum.

Halpern, S. D., Karlawish, J. H. T., & Berlin, J. A. (2002). The continuing unethical conduct of underpowered clinical trials. *Journal of the American Medical Association, 288*, 358–362.

Heckman, J. J. (1979). Sample selection bias as a specification error. *Econometrica, 47*, 153–161.

Hedberg, E. C., Santana, R., & Hedges, L. V. (2004, April). *The variance structure of academic achievement in America.* Paper presented at the Annual Meeting of the American Educational Research Association, San Diego, California.

Hedges, L. V. (2007). Generalizability of treatment effects: Psychometrics and education. In B. Schneider & S-K. McDonald (Eds.), *Scale-up in education, Vol. 1: Ideas in principle* (pp. 55–78). Lanham, MD: Rowman and Littlefield.

Hedges, L. V., & Hedberg, E. C. (2007). Intraclass correlation values for planning group-randomized trials in education. *Educational Evaluation and Policy Analysis, 29*, 60–87.

Hempel, C. G. (1966). *Philosophy of natural science.* Englewood Cliffs, NJ: Prentice Hall.

Holland, P. (1986). Statistics and causal inference. *Journal of the American Statistical Association, 81*, 945–960.

Hong, G., & Raudenbush, S. W. (2005). Effects of kindergarten retention policy on children's cognitive growth in reading and mathematics. *Educational Evaluation and Policy Analysis, 27*, 205–224.

Hoogstra, L., & McDonald, S-K. (2007). Challenges, incentives, and obligations of conducting scale-up research. In B. Schneider & S-K. McDonald (Eds.), *Scale-up in education, Vol. 2: Issues in practice* (pp. 229–236). Lanham, MD: Rowman and Littlefield.

House, E. R. (1980). *Evaluating with validity.* Beverly Hills, CA: Sage.

Howard, K. I., Moras, K., Brill, P. L., Martinovich, Z., & Lutz, W. (1996). Evaluation of psychotherapy: Efficacy, effectiveness, and patient progress. *American Psychologist, 51*, 1059–1064.

Jackson, R., McCoy, A., Pistorino, C., Wilkinson, A., Burghardt, J., Clark, M., et al. (2007). *National evaluation of Early Reading First: Final report* (NCEE 2007-4007). Washington, DC: National Center for Educational Evaluation and Regional Assistance.

Jacob, B., & Lefgren, L. (2004). Remedial education and student achievement: A regression discontinuity analysis. *Review of Economics and Statistics, 86*, 226–244.

Joint Committee on Standards for Educational Evaluation. (2007). *The program evaluation standards: Summary of the standards.* Retrieved May 25, 2007, from http://www.wmich.edu/evalctr/jc/

Konstantopoulos, S. (2004, April). Planning sample sizes for multilevel studies of educational interventions. Paper presented at the Annual Meeting of the American Educational Research Association, San Diego, California.

Lam, T. C. M. (1992). Analysis of performance gaps in program evaluation: A review of the gap reduction design. *Evaluation Review, 16*, 618–633.

Levinson, D. L., Cookson, P. W., Jr., & Sadovnik, A. R. (Eds.). (2001). *Education and sociology: An encyclopedia.* New York: Routledge Falmer.

Lipsey, M. W., & Cordray, D. S. (2000). Evaluation methods for social intervention. *Annual Review of Psychology, 51*, 345–375.

Lipsky, M. S., & Sharp, L. K. (2001). From idea to market: The drug approval process [Electronic version]. *Journal of the American Board of Family Practice, 14*, 362–367.

Long, M. H. (1984). Process and product in ESL program evaluation. *TESOL Quarterly, 18*, 409–425.

Marlowe, D. B. (2004). Commentary: Drug court efficacy vs. effectiveness. *Join Together Online.* Retrieved March 29, 2007, from http://www.jointogether.org/news/yourturn/commentary/2004/drug-court-efficacy-vs.html

Martinez, M., & Klopott, S. (2005). *The link between high school reform and college access and success for low-income and minority youth* [Electronic version]. Washington, DC: American Youth Policy Forum and Pathways to College Network.

McDonald, S-K., Keesler, V., Kauffman, N., & Schneider, B. (2006). Scaling-up exemplary interventions. *Educational Researcher, 35*(3), 15–24.

McDonough, P. M. (1997). *Choosing colleges: How social class and schools structure opportunity*. Albany: State University of New York Press.

Mosteller, F., & Boruch, R. (Eds.). (2002). *Evidence matters: Randomized trials in education research*. Washington, DC: Brookings Institution.

Mostow, J., & Beck, J. (2007). When the rubber meets the road: Lessons from the in-school adventures of an automated reading tutor that listens. In B. Schneider & S-K. McDonald (Eds.), *Scale-up in education, Vol. 2: Issues in practice* (pp. 183–200). Lanham, MD: Rowman and Littlefield.

Mueller, P. S., Montori, V. M., Bassler, D., Koenig, B. A., & Guyatt, G. H. (2007). Ethnical issues in stopping randomized trials early because of apparent benefit. *Annals of Internal Medicine, 146*, 878–881.

Myers, D., & Dynarski, M. (2003). *Random assignment in program evaluation and intervention research: Questions and answers*. Washington, DC: National Center for Education Evaluation and Regional Assistance.

National Educational Research Policy and Priorities Board. (2001). *Minutes of quarterly meeting, November 30, 2001*. Retrieved May 30, 2007, from http://www.ed.gov/offices/OERI/NERPPB/minutes113001.html

National Research Council. (2002). *Scientific research in education*. R. J. Shavelson & L. Towne (Eds.). Washington, DC: National Academy Press.

National Research Council. (2004). *Implementing randomized field trials in education: Report of a workshop*. L. Towne & M. Hilton (Eds.). Washington, DC: The National Academies Press.

National Research Council. (2005). *Advancing scientific research in education*. L. Towne, L. L. Wise, & T. M. Winter (Eds.). Washington, DC: The National Academies Press.

National Research Council, Division of Behavioral and Social Sciences and Education. (2007). *Pilot project in brief: Structured abstracts in education research*. Retrieved July 2, 2007, from http://www7.nationalacademies.org/dbasse/Standards%20of%20Evidence%20Pilot%20Description.html

National Science Foundation (NSF). (1999a). *Interagency Education Research Initiative (IERI)* (Program Announcement NSF 99-84). Retrieved June 26, 2007, from http://www.nsf.gov/pubs/1999/nsf9984/nsf9984.htm

National Science Foundation (NSF). (1999b). Unique Interagency Education Research Initiative kicks off with first grants: Projects to build new learning, teaching strategies in core subjects (NSF Press Release 99-62). Retrieved June 27, 2007, from http://www.nsf.gov/od/lpa/news/press/99/pr9962.htm

National Science Foundation (NSF). (2000). *Interagency Education Research Initiative (IERI)* (Program Solicitation NSF 00-74). Retrieved June 26, 2007, from http://www.nsf.gov/pubs/2000/nsf0074/nsf0074.htm

National Science Foundation (NSF). (2001). *Interagency Education Research Initiative (IERI)* (Program Solicitation NSF 01-92). Retrieved June 26, 2007, from http://www.nsf.gov/pubs/2001/nsf0192/nsf0192.htm

National Science Foundation (NSF). (2002). *Interagency Education Research Initiative (IERI)* (Program Solicitation NSF 02-062). Retrieved June 26, 2007, from http://www.nsf.gov/pubs/2002/nsf02062/nsf02062.html

National Science Foundation (NSF). (2004). *Interagency Education Research Initiative (IERI)* (Program Solicitation NSF 04-553). Retrieved June 26, 2007, from http://www.nsf.gov/pubs/2004/nsf04553/nsf04553.htm

National Science Foundation (NSF). (2007). *Research and Evaluation on Education in Science and Engineering (REESE)* (Program Solicitation NSF 07-595). Retrieved April 28, 2008, from http://www.nsf.gov/pubs/2007/nsf07595/nsf07595.pdf

Nevo, D. (1983). The conceptualization of educational evaluation: An analytical review of the literature. *Review of Educational Research, 53*, 117–128.

Nielsen, J. (1994). Heuristic evaluation. In J. Nielsen, & R. L. Mack (Eds.), *Usability inspection methods* (pp. 25–62). New York: Wiley.

No Child Left Behind Act of 2001, Pub. L. 107-110, 115 Stat. 1425 (2002).

Nye, B., Konstantopoulos, S., & Hedges, L. V. (2004). How large are teacher effects? *Educational Evaluation and Policy Analysis, 26*, 237–257.

Omnibus Consolidated and Emergency Supplemental Appropriations Act of 1999, Pub. L. 105-277, 112 Stat. 2681 (1999).

Parlett, M., & Dearden, G. (1977). *Introduction to illuminative evaluation: Studies in higher education*. Cardiff-by-the-Sea, CA: Pacific Soundings Press.

Patton, M. Q. (1997). *Utilization-focused evaluation: The new century text* (3rd ed.). Thousand Oaks, CA: Sage.

Patton, M. Q. (2004). *The debate about randomized controls in evaluation: The gold standard question*. Retrieved March 23, 2007, from http://videocast.nih.gov/ppt/nci_patton091404.ppt#256

Patton, M. Q., Grimes, P. S., Guthrie, K. M., Brennan, N. J., French, B. D., & Blyth, D. A. (1977). In search of impact: An analysis of the utilization of federal health evaluation research. In C. Weiss (Ed.), *Using social research in public policy making.* (pp. 141–164). Lexington, MA: D.C. Heath.

Pfeffer, J., & Sutton, R. I. (2006a). Evidence-based management. *Harvard Business Review, 84*(1), 63–74.

Pfeffer, J., & Sutton, R. I. (2006b). *Hard facts, dangerous half-truths, and total nonsense: Profiting from evidence-based management*. Boston: Harvard Business School Press.

Pfeffer, J., & Sutton, R. I. (2007). Suppose we took evidence-based management seriously: Implications for reading and writing management. *The Academy of Management Learning and Education, 6*, 153–155.

President's Committee of Advisors on Science and Technology, Panel on Educational Technology. (1997). *Report to the President on the use of technology to strengthen K-12 education in the United States: Findings related to research and evaluation*. Washington, DC: Office of Science and Technology Policy.

Pressman, J. L., & Wildavsky, A. B. (1984). *Implementation: How great expectations in Washington are dashed in Oakland; Or, why it's amazing that federal programs work at all, this being a saga of the economic development administration as told by two sympathetic observers who seek to build morals on a foundation of ruined hopes* (3rd ed.). Berkeley: University of California Press.

Raudenbush, S. W. (2005). Learning from attempts to improve schooling: The contribution of methodological diversity. *Educational Researcher, 34*(5), 25–31.

Raudenbush, S. W. (2007). Designing field trials of educational innovations. In B. Schneider & S-K. McDonald (Eds.), *Scale-up in education, Vol. 2: Issues in practice* (pp. 23–40). Lanham, MD: Rowman and Littlefield.

Raudenbush, S. W., & Liu, X. (2000). Statistical power and optimal design for multi-site randomized trials. *Psychological Methods, 5*, 199–213.

Raudenbush, S. W., & Willms, J. D. (1995). The estimation of school effects. *Journal of Educational and Behavioral Statistics, 20*, 307–335.

Reading Excellence Act, H.R. 2614, 105th Cong. (1997).

Rippey, R. M. (1973). *Studies in transactional evaluation*. Berkeley, CA: McCutchan.

Rosenbaum, P. R., & Rubin, D. B. (1983). The central role of the propensity score in observational studies for causal effects. *Biometrika, 70*, 41–55.

Rossi, P. H., & Freeman, H. E. (1993). *Evaluation: A systematic approach* (5th ed.). Newbury Park, CA: Sage.

Rossi, P. H., Lipsey, M. W., & Freeman, H. E. (2004). *Evaluation: A systematic approach* (7th ed.). Thousand Oaks, CA: Sage.

Rousseau, D. M. (2006). Is there such a thing as "evidence based management?" *Academy of Management Review, 31,* 256–269.

Rubin, D. B. (1977). Assignment to treatment group on the basis of a covariate. *Journal of Educational Statistics, 2,* 1–26.

Rubin, D. B. (1997). Estimating causal effects from large data sets using propensity scores. *Annals of Internal Medicine, 127,* 757–763.

Schneider, B. (2003). Sociology of education: An overview of the field at the turn of the twenty-first century. In M. T. Hallinan, A. Gamoran, W. Kubitschek, & T. Loveless (Eds.), *Stability and change in American education: Structure, process, and outcomes* (pp. 193–226). Clinton Corners, NY: Eliot Werner.

Schneider, B., Carnoy, M., Kilpatrick, J., Schmidt, W. H., & Shavelson, R. J. (2007). *Estimating causal effects: Using experimental and observational designs.* Washington, DC: American Educational Research Association.

Schneider, B., & McDonald, S-K. (Eds.). (2007a). *Scale-up in education, Vol. 1: Ideas in principle.* Lanham, MD: Rowman and Littlefield.

Schneider, B., & McDonald, S-K. (Eds.). (2007b). *Scale-up in education, Vol. 2: Issues in practice.* Lanham, MD: Rowman and Littlefield.

Schneider, B., & Stevenson, D. (1999). *The ambitious generation: America's teenagers, motivated but directionless.* New Haven, CT: Yale University Press.

Schweinhart, L. J., Barnes, H. V., & Weikart, D. P. (1993). *Significant benefits: The High/Scope Perry Preschool Study through age 27.* Ypsilanti, MI: High/Scope Press.

Scientifically Based Education Research, Statistics, Evaluation, and Information Act of 2000. H.R. 4875, 106th Cong. (2000).

Scriven, M. (1967). The methodology of evaluation. In R. W. Tyler, R. M. Gagné, & M. Scriven (Eds.), *Perspectives of curriculum evaluation* (pp. 39–83). Chicago: Rand McNally.

Scriven, M. (1972). Pros and cons about goal-free evaluation. *Evaluation Comment, 3*(4), 1–4.

Scriven, M. (1979). Michael Scriven: Viewpoints on education evaluation. *Educational Evaluation and Policy Analysis, 1*(2), 66–72.

Scriven, M. (1981). *Evaluation thesaurus* (3rd ed.). Inverness, CA: Edgepress.

Scriven, M. (1991). The science of valuing. In W. R. Shadish, Jr., T. D. Cook, & L. C. Leviton (Eds.), *Foundations of program evaluation: Theories of practice* (pp. 73–118). Newbury Park, CA: Sage.

Shadish, W. R. (1998). Some evaluation questions. *Practical Assessment, Research and Evaluation, 6*(3). Retrieved February 26, 2007, from http://PAREonline.net/getvn.asp?v=6&n=3

Shadish, W. R., Cook, T. D., & Campbell, D. T. (2002). *Experimental and quasi-experimental designs for generalized causal inference.* Boston: Houghton Mifflin.

Shulha, L. M., & Cousins, J. B. (1997). Evaluation use: Theory, research and practice since 1986. *Evaluation Practice, 18,* 195–208.

Simon, H. (1976). *Administrative behavior* (3rd ed.). New York: The Free Press.

Slavin, R. E., & Madden, N. A. (2001). *One million children: Success for all.* Thousand Oaks, CA: Corwin.

Smith, N. L. (1993). Improving evaluation theory through the empirical study of evaluation practice. *American Journal of Evaluation, 14,* 237–242.

Society for Research in Child Development. (2001). *Washington update, November 2001: Science policy.* Retrieved May 30, 2007, from http://srcd.org/policywashupdate11-01.html

Stake, R. E. (1975). Program evaluation particularly responsive evaluation (Occasional Paper Series No. 5). Retrieved March 20, 2007, from http://www.wmich.edu/evalctr/pubs/ops/ops05.html

St. Pierre, R. G., Swartz, J. P., Murray, S., & Deck, D. (1996). *Improving family literacy: Findings from the National Even Start Evaluation.* Cambridge, MA: Abt Associates.

Stufflebeam, D. L. (1968). *Evaluation as enlightenment for decision-making.* Columbus: The Ohio State University, Evaluation Center.

Stufflebeam, D. L. (1972). The relevance of the CIPP evaluation model for educational accountability. *SRIS Quarterly, 5,* 3–6.

Stufflebeam, D. L. (1980). An EEPA interview with Daniel L. Stufflebeam. *Educational Evaluation and Policy Analysis, 2*(4), 85–90.

Stufflebeam, D. L., & Shinkfield, A. J. (2007). *Evaluation theory, models, and applications.* San Francisco: Jossey-Bass.

Suchman, E. A. (1969). Evaluating educational programs: A symposium. *The Urban Review, 3*(4), 15–17.

Thistlewaite, D. L., & Campbell, D. T. (1960). Regression-discontinuity analysis: An alternative to the ex-post facto experiment. *Journal of Educational Psychology, 51,* 309–317.

Tyler, R. W. (1950). *Basic principles of curriculum and instruction.* Chicago: University of Chicago Press.

UK House of Commons Science and Technology Committee. (2006). *Scientific advice, risk and evidence based policy making: Seventh report of Session 2005–06, Vol. 1* (HC 900-I). London: The Stationery Office, Limited.

U.S. Department of Education. (2005, January 25). Department of Education—Scientifically based evaluation methods, notice of final priority [Electronic version]. *Federal Register, 70*(15), 3586–3589.

U.S. Department of Education, Institute of Education Sciences. (2002). *Interagency Education Research Initiative (IERI), Request for applications number NCER-03-04.* Washington, DC: Author.

U.S. Department of Education, Institute of Education Sciences. (2003a). *Teacher quality research grants, request for applications NCER-04-02.* Washington, DC: Author.

U.S. Department of Education, Institute of Education Sciences. (2003b). *Mathematics and science education research grants, request for applications NCER-04-03.* Washington, DC: Author.

U.S. Department of Education, Institute of Education Sciences. (2003c). *Reading comprehension and reading scale-up research grants, request for applications number NCER-04-04.* Washington, DC: Author.

U.S. Department of Education, Institute of Education Sciences. (2007). *Education research grants, request for applications number IES-NCER-2008-01.* Washington, DC: Author.

U.S. Department of Education, Office of Elementary and Secondary Education. (2004). Comprehensive School Reform Program: About CSR. Retrieved January 3, 2007, from http://www.ed.gov/programs/compreform/2pager.html

U.S. Food and Drug Administration Office of Public Affairs. (2002). The FDA's drug review process: Ensuring drugs are safe and effective. *FDA Consumer Magazine,* Pub. No. FDA05-3242. Retrieved March 22, 2007, from http://www.fda.gov/fdac/features/2002/402_drug.html

U.S. Library of Congress. (1974). *Summary of Public Law 93-380.* Washington, DC: U.S. Library of Congress.

Weiss, C. H. (1978). Improving the linkage between social research and public policy. In L. E. Lynn, Jr. (Ed.), *Knowledge and policy: The uncertain connection* (pp. 23–81). Washington, DC: National Academy of Sciences.

Weiss, C. H. (1998). Improving the use of evaluations: Whose job is it anyway? *Advances in Educational Productivity, 7,* 263–276.

Whitehurst, G. J. (2002, October). *Evidence-based education.* Presentation to the Student Achievement and School Accountability Conference. Retrieved June 29, 2007, from http://www.ed.gov/nclb/methods/whatworks/eb/edlite-slide001.html

Williams, J. E. (1989). A numerically developed taxonomy of evaluation theory and practice. *Evaluation Review, 13,* 18–31.

Wimberly, G. L. & Noeth, R. J. (2004). *Schools involving parents in early postsecondary planning: ACT policy report.* Iowa City, IA: American College Testing.

Winship, C., & Morgan, S. L. (1999). The estimation of causal effects from observational data. *Annual Review of Sociology, 25,* 659–706.

Worthen, B. R., & Sanders, J. R. (1973). *Educational evaluation: Theory and practice.* Belmont, CA: Wadsworth.

Zlokarnik, M. (2002). *Scale-up in chemical engineering.* Weinheim, Germany: Wiley-VCH Verlag.

17

COMMENTARY
Conducting Policy Research

Methodological Perspectives

Spyros Konstantopoulos
Boston College

Education policy is innate in much empirical research in education. Lately, there has been an increasing federal and state activity in education policy with focus on gauging the effects of educational interventions on student achievement. Specifically, with the passage of the No Child Left Behind Act much emphasis has been put on accountability for school intervention outcomes, in particular academic achievement. Nowadays the most critical questions that concern education policy makers are what works and what are the effects of educational interventions? Hence, much of the current trend in education research has been driven by the need to evaluate school related interventions and their effects on student achievement. This critical evaluation component involves the use of multiple methods. Some of these methods are quantitative in nature such as modern statistical and econometric techniques, whilst other methods are qualitative in nature. Regardless of the methods used in any specific study the current education policy research requires a spectrum of methodological expertise and skills that have become sophisticated over time. Thus, the education policy researcher needs to continuously improve methodologically in order to evaluate the effects of educational interventions most efficiently/adequately. The chapters by Martin Orland, Geoffrey Borman, David Kaplan, Terri Pigott, Laura Desimone, Joan Herman and Eva Baker, and Sarah-Kay McDonald provide a comprehensive anthology of the methodological perspectives and issues involved in modern education policy research.

Indeed, all seven chapters are very informative and each one of them is worthy of more detailed discussion that can be provided in this brief commentary. Each chapter discusses thoroughly important methodological perspectives and challenges in education policy research.

The chapters discuss educational policy issues that range from the alignment of educational research and policymaking (Orland), the role of field experiments and casual inferences in education policy research (Borman), causal inferences in non-experimental education policy research,

the role of meta-analytic methods that combine evidence from multiple studies in education policy research (Pigott), the use of multiple methodologies in education policy research (Desimone), the role of assessment in education policy research (Herman and Baker), to the processes involved in evaluation research (McDonald). Although these chapters are diverse, collectively they carefully cover the methodological challenges the current education policy research faces and provide useful suggestions for the future. In addition, these chapters are interrelated and underscore the significance of employing multiple methods in order to provide a more complete picture of education policy research.

Separate Orbits: The Distinctive Worlds of Educational Research and Policymaking

The main objective of this chapter is to clarify the relationship between educational research and policymaking. First, Orland provides a nice discussion of the role of educational research policymaking and the circumstances under which findings from educational research are likely to influence policymaking. He defines three criteria that educational research needs to meet in order to affect education policy making: rigor, relevance, and usefulness. Rigor refers to the degree that educational research is rigorous and based on scientific methods. Relevance refers to the connection between the questions addressed in educational research and the topics of interest in educational policymaking. Finally usefulness suggests that findings from educational research needs to be communicated in appropriate ways that are understood by policy makers. This point is also highlighted in McDonald's chapter in which she argues that the results from educational research need to be clearly communicated to the target audience.

Second, Orland discusses the differences and tensions between educational research and policy. Third, he discusses how recent variations of Federal law and policy may affect the relationship between educational research and policy. Orland argues that the recent focus on scientifically based research and randomized control trials in education sanctioned by federal education laws may contribute to a closer alignment between educational research and policy. The main argument is that if much of educational research uses rigorous scientific methods, the findings produced from such work will more likely be used by education policy makers. In addition, the emphasis on scientific based work is suitable for asking questions of what works, which is closely related to education policymaking. Orland suggests that multiple methods can be used to inform education policymaking including meta-analytic methods, which are highlighted in Pigott's chapter as well, field experiments which are discussed by Borman, non-experimental methods discussed by Kaplan, and qualitative methods discussed by Desimone.

The Use of Randomized Trials to Inform Education Policy

This chapter discusses the logic and recent use of field experiments in education and ways that experimental designs can be used to inform education policy. Borman argues that experimental studies can provide definite answers about what works and strong evidence about the effects of educational interventions. Indeed when randomization is successful and threats to the validity of the experiment are minimized (or not taken into account), results from field experiments facilitate causal inferences. Borman does an excellent job discussing ways that address the ethical and political dilemma of withholding services in experiments, and ways that experimental studies can be adapted to fit school and classroom practices. He highlights the importance of using multiple methods when conducting experimental studies in education and discusses how qualitative methods as well as methods from biostatistics and econometrics can be used fruitfully in experimental studies. The chapter ends with a thoughtful discussion about how qualitative, descriptive, and survey research can be useful in educational policy.

Although randomized experiments are considered by many the gold standard and perhaps rightfully so, it is crucial that researchers monitor the randomization process carefully and ensure that randomization is successful. In addition, it is critical that possible validity threats are minimized, or taken into account in the statistical analysis phase.

Causal Inference in Non-Experimental Educational Policy Research

In this chapter Kaplan discusses a non-experimental approach to causal inference, the structural approach, and reminds us that there are other methods, besides randomized experiments or quasi-experimental designs, researchers could employ to draw causal inferences. This is an important chapter that provides a thorough discussion about the main

ideas of causation, reviews recent conceptions of causation in the econometric literature, and discusses causal analysis in non-experimental designs via the structural approach. The discussion about causal inferences and the potential caveats of experimental designs is very careful and articulate. Kaplan concludes by arguing that the experimental and structural approach can complement each other in policy research. I find Kaplan's chapter inspiring because it addresses critical issues about causality as well as issues about the generality of findings. Indeed using different methodologies appropriately and in a complementary way can help advance policy research.

Research Synthesis and Education Policy

This is a useful chapter that stresses the importance of combining evidence across studies in policy research. Indeed research synthesis and meta-analysis can be useful tools for providing estimates of the average effects and the range of effects of educational interventions that can inform policy research. Pigott provides a thorough discussion about ways that research synthesis and meta-analysis can inform education policy. The chapter also reviews carefully the potential pitfalls and strengths of research synthesis and meta-analysis in informing education policy. Pigott and Orland (in the first chapter) both argue that well conducted meta-analyses can produce useful estimates of the range of the effects of educational interventions, which can indicate what effects are plausible to take place. An important advantage of meta-analysis is the generality of findings that was also stressed by Kaplan and by McDonald. Note that the consistency of effects across various studies can be considered an index of the generality of findings or whether the effects scale up.

Complementary Methods for Policy Research

This is an important chapter that reviews complementary methods for education policy research. The main objective of the chapter is to present alternative methodologies of qualitative nature that can used in combination with more quantitatively oriented methods (such as field experiments, structural approaches, meta-analysis, etc.) to address adequately important policy issues. Desimone first clarifies the kind of information produced from quantitative and qualitative methods, argues that the methods used should be driven by policy questions of interest, and proposes that multiple perspectives need to be employed when studying policy issues. Then, she describes carefully the advantages of studies that employ mixed methods (a combination of quantitative and qualitative approaches) and makes a strong case for the need to mix methods. A good example in education policy is related to the effects of class size on student achievement. Although Project STAR (a large-scale randomized experiment) suggested convincing evidence about the positive effects of small classes, the questions about the mechanism of class size remained unanswered for the most part, because classroom practices were not documented. Both Desimone and Kaplan make an important point that it is crucial to understand the nature of the effect of an educational intervention. In other words, it is essential to answer the questions of what works and why? The why something works in this case is related to a more micro perspective (e.g., classroom practices) that can inform what works.

Assessment Policy: Making Sense of the Babel

This chapter discusses a significant aspect of education policy, namely assessment, which is closely related to what is being measured. The authors illustrate the current assessment system and propose ways of moving towards a more effective and unified system. Herman and Baker ask the question of whether there is or should be one "best" way of assessment or whether multiple ways of assessment are warranted. The authors make a convincing case about the need for multiple measures and a more comprehensive assessment system. They argue that multiple measures of student performance are necessary and that traditional measures of performance (e.g., standardized tests) can co-exist with measures that are well aligned with classroom practices and provide opportunities for complex thinking and problem solving. Herman and Baker conclude with an important statement that the assessment system needs to be clear about its objectives and closely connected to the objectives of the society. Indeed, any changes in the U.S. assessment system should go hand in hand with changes in U.S. education and society.

Scale-Up as a Framework for Intervention, Program, and Policy Evaluation Research

This chapter connects the evaluation research process followed by researchers with the recent emphasis on conducting research based on rigorous scientific methods. McDonald starts by reviewing three of the steps of the evaluation research process: the goal of the evaluation, the assessment and design phase of the evaluation, and the dissemination of the findings in appropriate ways. Then, she describes the distinct stages that take place in a discovery-to-scale-up process that begins with the degree of promise of an intervention, continues with evaluating the effects of the intervention (ideally in diverse settings) as well as scaling-up the effects in larger and diverse samples, and ends with post-marketing research that provides information about the sustainability and variability of effects across different contexts. The author concludes with an excellent discussion about evidence-informed education. McDonald makes an important point that it is equally important to generate rigorous scientific evidence and make evidence available to education policymaking via appropriate communication channels.

Conclusion

These are high-quality chapters that provide excellent discussions about important methodological perspectives in education policy. It is impressive that although each chapter focuses on one method, all authors discuss the usefulness of other methods and encourage the use of multiple methods in education policy research. In addition, all authors suggest adapting a multidisciplinary approach when conducting education policy research and underscore the benefits of using different methods to generate evidence that will inform education policy the most. Indeed, the modern education policy researcher needs to be aware of the various methods from different disciplines and hopefully use them appropriately to address questions of interest. In addition, researchers need to be aware of the advantages and limitations of different methods, since as Kaplan argues, methodologies are based on assumptions that are not always met. Finally, what we also gain from these chapters is the realization that policy research is interdisciplinary and that different methodologies in policy research can be complementary, as Desimone argues.

18

COMMENTARY
An Applied Perspective on Research, Method, and Policy

Christopher B. Swanson[1]
Editorial Projects in Education

Taking the Good with the Bad

To the best of my knowledge, I have never been burned in effigy. But I do have a sinking suspicion that some public officials out there may think a bonfire is not a half-bad idea. On occasion, my research on high school graduation rates has been denounced in rather public ways by elected officials, policy makers, and educational administrators disputing my methods or, more often, just the results of the research. My work has been called "false," "faulty," "flawed," "damaging," "intellectually dishonest," "totally erroneous," and "rubbish." And those words all come from one spokesperson for one major urban school system.

Disagreement comes along with the territory. Quite frankly, policy researchers should be more concerned when their work is greeted with silence because that might mean that no one is paying attention. On a lighter note, along with a healthy dose of criticism, recent studies on high school graduation have also received strong expressions of support in more-than-equal measure. Work by myself and other analysts has sparked renewed and sustained attention to the issue. I would further argue that this work has contributed in constructive ways to new public dialogues over the nation's graduation crisis in communities from coast to coast. That's why we, applied policy researchers, get into this line of work in the first place.

This is all to say that policy research can get a bit rough-and-tumble in the trenches, and that success comes hard-earned and with its share of scrapes and bruises. Research in academe, admittedly, does have its share of disputes over theory, method, substance, and values. But scholarly disagreements typically do not play out from the pressroom podium, in the pages of print dailies, over the airwaves, or on the evening news. However, the contentiousness that some-times accompanies applied policy research may bespeak its value. Would we expect to see such strong reactions if the research was not cutting close to the bone?

The other chapters in this section thoughtfully elaborate on a variety of methodological issues pertinent to research on educational policy. This commentary will be something of a departure, offering a decidedly applied practitioner's first-person perspective on policy research and method. But in doing so, I hope to speak to a number of issues addressed by other authors in this volume.

I will draw, in part, on experiences gained while work-ing on a particular issue—high school graduation rates. This work serves as a useful case study for several reasons. First, research by myself and others has enjoyed an unusual amount of attention among public policy circles and in the press. For the most part, the debates over graduation rates have also unfolded within a particular, well-defined (although often-criticized) legal and policy context, namely the federal No Child Left Behind Act. This body of work also exemplifies the type of research that often comes into play during the policy process. To boot, and as hard as it may be to believe, the seemingly arcane issue of statisti-cal methodology has emerged as a pivotal piece of public dialogue over graduation rates, prompting calls for high school reform more broadly.

What Influences Public Policy?

What sorts of factors influence policymaking? I cannot speak to this issue across all domains of public policy. But it just so happens that I conducted a study several years ago (Swanson & Barlage, 2006) investigating that very question in the realm of educational policy. The answer: anything and everything, in its own way.

This particular study—Influence: A Study of the Factors Shaping Educational Policy—was once described to me as "cute." That appellation was not intended to be entirely complimentary, as one might guess. While perhaps not strictly "scientific" in the now-common usage of the term, the study did nevertheless systematically survey a couple hundred leading educational policy experts to glean their views on the studies, information sources, people, and organizations that have shaped the field in recent years. So, the results do bear directly on the question at hand.

The expression "policy research" is used to mean any number of things. I am not particularly concerned with what Mr. Webster and his dictionary have to say. But in my mind, the term embraces research intended to define and quantify the nature and extent of social and educational problems, inform public policy formulation, monitor program implementation, evaluate and measure the effectiveness of interventions, and contribute to the promulgation of the rules, regulations, and practices that govern the application of policy mandates on the ground. While this covers quite a bit of ground, a broad understanding of policy research would appear to be merited, given the results of the Influence study.

The research that ranked as the most influential proved to be surprisingly diverse, including: large-scale government data collections like the National Assessment of Educational Progress (NAEP) and Trends in International Mathematics and Science (TIMSS), several volumes reporting proceedings from National Research Council and other blue-ribbon commissions, the Tennessee class-size experiment (Project STAR), the value-added methodology of William Sanders, and the work of several individual researchers and organizations on various topics. Those "influentials" also run the gamut methodologically, encompassing randomized control trial (RCT) experiments, quasi-experimental and correlational research, rigorous but descriptive statistical treatments, research synthesis, policy analysis, and everything in between. This collection of research spans any number of the dividing lines we commonly use to describe the research enterprise: basic versus applied; formative versus summative; quantitative versus qualitative versus analytical; scientific versus non-scientific. It is also interesting to note that while one entry on the influential short list qualifies as "gold standard" experimental research, the bulk of the top-ranked studies would probably not merit that label in the narrow sense in which it has come to be used recently.

Dividers can be useful devices, whether we are waiting at the supermarket checkout or attempting to conceptually organize a large and diverse body of research. A distinction I personally find helpful when it comes to policy research is one between "problems research" and "solutions research." The former deals with identifying and measuring deficiencies in educational practice and outcomes that, if sufficiently severe, would be viewed as cause for alarm and decisive action. The latter type of research concentrates on finding effective interventions to counteract recognized educational problems.

I lean toward that framing, in part, because it is inclusive. The problems-solutions distinction recognizes the value both of broad descriptive research intended to raise the profile of an educational problem on policy makers' agendas and also of methodologically-sophisticated experimental and non-experimental studies designed to inform precisely

defined questions of program effectiveness. This way of thinking also resonates strongly with the nature of public policy cycles. As discussed below, this may help to explain why certain types of research typically play a larger role at particular stages of that cycle.

Research and the Policy Cycle

In reflecting on the connection between research and policy, the words of Chicago-based social activist Saul Alinsky often come to mind. To paraphrase: To change the world, you must start with the world as it is, not as you would like it to be. The same sentiment also applies to matters of educational policy. In principle, policy research may seek to fundamentally change the manner in which public policymaking comes about. In general practice, however, the ambitions of policy research tend to be more circumscribed. So, for present purposes, we will assume that the nature, rhythms, and peculiarities of the policymaking process are themselves set in stone. In other words, my premise is that research aims to inform policy decisions but not to change the rules of the policymaking game in more fundamental ways.

That means, by extension, that policy decisions are inherently political insomuch as they arise from and are embedded in a politically oriented rather than purely rational, technocratic system of governance. Those decisions are also shaped by difficult-to-predict cycles of public attention and swayed by constituent pressure. Policy makers can be influenced directly by voters and indirectly by advocacy organizations, membership associations, and the like. A short time horizon often characterizes the policymaking process, as does the need to make decisions with whatever information is available or attainable within a given amount of time. Competing demands and priorities vie with one another for attention and resources, both within and across domains of social policy. Accordingly, policy decisions will be based on multiple criteria, only one of which is the value or quality of research-based evidence.

It may very well be the case that policy makers have every intention of basing decisions on the systematic use of solid research; and that may actually happen sometimes. But, as is well known, research may ultimately be employed opportunistically to support issue positions or policy decisions that have already been made largely on other grounds. This is the post hoc use of research to justify rather than ex ante use to inform policy. If the fundamental relevance of research can be called into doubt from the start, then the question of that research's quality (while of extraordinary importance to researchers) becomes at best a second-order consideration to policy makers.

Lest we become unduly pessimistic, I would quickly add that the preceding does not mean that research is incapable of influencing the policy process. But this does mean that researchers must often make a strong case that their work is salient to a live policy issue. We cannot take for granted that policy makers or others will do that work for us, nor can we fall into a build-it-and-they-will-come mindset. If researchers want their work to be relevant, they have to make it relevant by dint of design or dissemination. The "relevancing" of research requires an understanding of the ebbs and flows that characterize the typical policy cycle.

According to Swanson, at least, the public policy cycle consists of the following reasonably discernable stages: (a) discovery, (b) formulation, (c) authorization, (d) implementation, (e) regulation and guidance, (f) evaluation, and (g) reformulation and reauthorization. This is a process through which policy makers come to understand a problem, devise legal mechanisms to address that problem (e.g., legislation, executive order, administrative rule), formally enact that policy, put the respective mandates into effect with additional guidance for the implementing agents, evaluate the effectiveness of the policy's programmatic manifestations (this being, ideally, part of the original policy framework), and eventually amend, reauthorize, or discontinue the policy based on evidence generated by evaluation and other pertinent considerations.

The first three stages can be thought of as the front end of the policy cycle dealing with formulation and enactment. The next three stages constitute the back end of implementation and assessment, with the final step feeding back to the beginning of the process. There is no special science to these stages, which could well have been devised a bit differently. The important point here is that there are multiple opportunities for research to intersect with the policy cycle. Further, different types of research and different methodologies may be more likely to come into play at various points in that cycle, given the questions they best answer (problem vs. solution) and their own time horizons (quick-turnaround vs. long-term studies).

Timing is Everything

There is a classic chicken-and-egg dilemma at work here. How can new policy, which must be formed in a short amount of time, be adequately informed by top-notch research that may not even exist? The short answer is simple: It can't, in many cases.

Windows of opportunity to shape the policy process and policymaking decisions are usually narrow and unable to wait for new studies to be commissioned, conducted, and communicated. Research poised to make a difference from the onset of a new policy cycle generally exhibits one or more distinguishing features, which are not necessarily compatible with one another. Such well-positioned work is: already completed, well-known and respected, reasonably free of controversy, easily communicated to lay audiences, and/or strongly advocated by activists, researchers, or other stakeholder communities. The latter suggests that, in addition to the merits of the research itself, the underlying agendas, motivations, and interests of advocates are likely to affect the policy process in general and utilization of research in particular. This state of affairs is not exactly tailor-made for methodologically complex or otherwise

scientifically based research, which may help to explain why comparatively simple descriptive research and other problems-oriented studies tend to factor prominently into the early stages of the policy cycle.

Gold standard experimental research, by contrast, requires a significant fiscal investment, sometimes substantial political will, plenty of time to design and execute properly, and additional time for the results to be effectively disseminated. Experimental research is also ideally suited to offer definitive answers about narrowly framed questions, such as may be posed within a particular policy or programmatic framework. As a result, such methods probably fit best into the back end of a policy cycle. In most cases, expensive large-scale RCT research will be an intermediary product of a policy cycle rather than a major factor in initial policy formation. Similar timeliness considerations also pertain to systematic synthesis of existing research literature such as meta analysis (the utility of which, incidentally, depends heavily on the quality of the respective literature) and to any research that must navigate the less-than-swift channels of peer review.

We may be inclined to assume that if research does not inform the initial formulation of policy then the story ends there. Actually, that is only the beginning, and there are usually second and third acts still to come, in keeping with the cyclical nature of policymaking. Even when researchers miss the opportunity to shape policy on the front end, there may still be openings to inform the process on the back end, particularly though high-quality evaluation efforts. However, a caveat is in order. During the several years that elapse while an evaluation is being conducted, an influential constituency may grow up around the program in question. This is especially likely when the program involves significant funding or addresses issues of concern to a preexisting advocacy community. Such groups may hold significant political sway and advocate for continued funding in the absence of proof that a program is effective or, sometimes, in the face of evidence to the contrary. In other words, political considerations may surface in the back end of the policy cycle and compete against even definitive research-based evidence. And evidence, despite our best efforts, is rarely definitive.

An Unscientific Case Study (Part 1) My own work on high school graduation offers some useful insights about how research can fit into the dynamics of a policy cycle. I began this line of work in late 2002 as a think-tank researcher relatively new to the policy world. At that point, the final regulations for Title I of the No Child Left Behind Act had just been released and everyone, myself included, was trying to wrap their heads around the implications of the new rules for the practical implementation of the law. One piece of NCLB that happened to catch my eye was its requirement that high schools be held accountable for graduation rates as well as test scores. It turned out that this was a good time to start working on the topic. We were still early in the implementation process, with policy makers and educational officials trying to gain a better understanding of these provisions. And because most attention was focused on test scores, the graduation issue offered a relatively uncrowded playing field with plenty of opportunity for well-positioned research to make a difference.

As I would come to learn, those graduation rate provisions were written into NCLB for largely technical reasons related to the design of accountability schemes. Specifically, Congress was concerned that an accountability system based solely on test scores would create perverse incentives to push out low-performing high school students, thereby artificially inflating test scores at the expense of creating or exacerbating a real dropout problem. Graduation rate accountability was incorporated into NCLB as a check against the law's primary focus on assessment outcomes.

When drafting the legislation, policy makers were aware that decades of research had thoroughly documented the detrimental effects of leaving high school without a diploma. But there was little appreciation, at that point, that the nation's public schools might be facing a serious or widespread graduation crisis. That realization came about a bit later, as a result of subsequent research. As we will see below, that work has factored prominently into debates over the law's implementation and its eventual reauthorization.

From Public Awareness to Policy Action

On the "problems" side of the problem-solution continuum, a major role of educational policy research is to help the public and public officials understand the nature and dynamics of problems facing the nation's schools. This, in turn, can motivate the solutions phase of the cycle by making a compelling case for a policy intervention and by pointing to specific targets or strategies for programmatic remedies.

In the problems business, a critical factor to keep in mind is the distinction between the severity of a problem and the prevalence of a problem. For example, an undesired educational condition, phenomenon, or outcome may have dire consequences for individuals directly affected; but it may impact relative few individuals. This would result in a weak case for broad and dramatic policy intervention, one reason being that it leaves the door open to a not-in-my-backyard (NIMBY) mentality, expressed along the lines of "it sure is a shame that some of those children aren't graduating from high school, but my own kids are doing just fine, thank you very much." Conversely, an adverse outcome may be more widespread but may have only modest consequences for those affected. That situation, likewise, may not rise to the level of a "serious" problem needing an immediate policy fix, given other issues competing for policy-maker attention and public dollars.

We should also keep in mind a related consideration—the distinction between direct (individual) versus indirect (social) consequences. For instance, failing to finish high school carries serious, well-known, and highly visible implications for a dropout's life prospects along virtually

any dimension we would care to name, be that economic, social, further education, health, criminal justice involvement, public aid dependency, and so forth. However, each dropout also exacts a harder-to-see social cost on employers who desire more-skilled workers, the broader economy, victims of crime, and the public at large who are deprived of potential tax revenue and the other benefits of well-educated fellow citizens and neighbors. In the absence of accessible information and evidence, such indirect connections and social costs often go unappreciated in policy debates.

We can think of the practical importance and policy relevance of a given social problem as a function of both the per-capita severity of the outcome and the total number of individuals impacted. The ideal conditions for aggressive, decisive policy action are problems that: are experienced by a large number of individuals, exact a heavy toll on those affected, and impose significant and well-documented indirect or social costs. It also helps when problems affect diverse populations and geographically dispersed communities, because this can elevate an issue above parochial interest-group politics and counteract NIMBY thinking. It might seem like a relatively straightforward matter to identify a serious and widespread educational problem when it exists. But that is not necessarily so. Among the greatest challenges facing policy researchers can actually be convincingly documenting such problems and, just as importantly, communicating that evidence clearly to the public and policy makers.

Research and the Perfect Storm (Unscientific Case Study, Part 2) For decades, the most widely cited public statistics on high school graduation came from economic sources like the Current Population Survey and other census-related databases. To some extent this is still true. But here is the problem. For a variety of reasons I won't go into here, there is now growing consensus that those economic statistics considerably overestimate what we in the educational policy world would think of as the high school graduation rate. Those data gave the impression that overall high school completion rates were high (in the neighborhood of 85%) and that most major demographic groups were doing alright. That is not exactly a recipe for action.

Fast-forward to 2002. No Child Left Behind comes into effect and requires that public schools be held accountable for their graduation rates. Among other things, this new mandate sparks a renewed interest in the issue among researchers who bring educational data on actual public schools to bear to answer a seemingly simple question: What is the graduation rate? Specifically, analysts started using the U.S. Department of Education's Common Core of Data (CCD), an annual census of public schools and districts. Those researchers consistently found a much different state of affairs than the conventional wisdom from economic data and research suggested.

Using my own work as an example, this new research found: an overall graduation rate around 70%, graduation gaps as large as 25 to 30 percentage points across demographic groups, consistently lower rates for males, and very large disparities from state-to-state and at even-more-local levels. This is a *potentially* potent combination of factors. Graduation rates are much lower than previously thought. The problem seems to affect everyone—for example, the new research places graduation rates for white students lower than conventional economic statistics for African Americans. But there is also a crisis of devastating proportions for a significant segment of the population—minority males basically have a fifty-fifty chance of graduating with a diploma. Further, the graduation crisis extends across the nation's geographical regions and political jurisdictions.

I used the qualifier "potentially" above intentionally. Simply having a compelling finding is no guarantee that anyone will see it, understand it, agree with it, or act upon it. This new line of graduation research has not been without its share of controversy and disagreement, particularly over finer points of methodology. However, the conclusions of this work are now generally accepted and widely cited by key players in the education policy world, including the U.S. Secretary of Education. Of course, a critical factor driving research "pick up" among policy makers is exactly how that research is targeted, packaged, and communicated. We will turn to this issue shortly.

Research with Legs that Go on for Miles

Here is a question: What are the chances that policy makers will read this handbook? As they used to say when I was a kid in Mississippi, the answer is: Slim to none, and Slim just left town. Admittedly, that is not an entirely fair question since this volume was not produced with a policy-maker audience specifically in mind. On the other hand, there is much here that policy makers could conceivably use to inform the way they consume research and use research-based evidence to make decisions. So what's the problem? Good information is only part of the equation. To be actionable as well, that information must also be crafted and presented in a manner that is relevant and easily accessed by the desired audience.

Policy makers and particularly elected officials (as distinct, to some extent, from government administrators) are experts of the political, policy, and legislative realms, at least if they hope to be reelected. They may also happen to possess deep and abiding interests and perhaps technical expertise in particular domains of public policy. But while those officials may specialize to some extent on areas related committee assignments, they ultimate hold responsibilities over very broad swaths of policy. So, it is unrealistic to expect public officials to be content experts in every issue on which they cast a vote. While staff bring additional capacity, they, like their bosses, typically have crammed schedules, work under tight timelines, juggle multiple portfolios, and develop their expertise over a period of time.

So, if policy makers are truly an audience researchers would like to reach with their work, then we are faced

with the often-noted and nearly-as-often-lamented task of "translation." That entails converting technical research-speak into a form better suited to a non-specialist audience like policy makers. We often think of this as something that must be done over and above the "real" work of the research enterprise. But anyone aspiring to a career as a successful applied policy researcher should think about this not as a chore but as an important and essential responsibility. Otherwise, the frequently heard goal of informing the policy process amounts to little more than lip service.

In most cases, it is not that the substance of the research needs to be dumbed-down. Policy makers and others working in the field are smart folks. The real challenge is identifying the information relevant for a particular audience or stakeholder (given their interests and role in the policy process), excising extraneous technical details (while maintaining context essential for interpretability), and then presenting that information in a format and style that resonates and can be acted upon. More often than not, when researchers fail to make their point, the problem is not that policy makers do not "get it." Failure to communicate is, generally, a group effort.

Moving from A Problem to My Problem (Unscientific Case Study, Part 3) In the course of studying high school graduation, I have gained an appreciation for what tends to work, or sometimes not work, in communicating research findings. I suspect there are some more general lessons to be learned here.

For starters, and this may sound either obvious or stupid, policy research generally needs a solid policy connection to be relevant. Policy provides a framework and system of meaning in which research finds its relevance. For example, the terms "graduation rate" and "graduate" have specific definitions under the federal No Child Left Behind Act that do not necessarily correspond to conventional research practice, state and local policy, or common sense understandings of the public. It is also worth adding that NCLB is concerned exclusively with the performance of *public* schools, private education being essentially outside the law's purview. Researchers who do not appreciate such basic ground rules, either because they are unaware of them or think they know better, are flirting with irrelevancy in the policy realm. The research on graduation rates that has gained the most traction firmly roots itself in understandings of: the workings of the federal law, the critical implementation role played by the states, and the issues about which policy makers and the public most need guidance.

Brevity is the soul of wit. Successful communication in the policy world revolves first and foremost around short, focused, relevant treatments of an issue tailored for the intended audience. Press releases and executive summaries—which can be crafted in both thoughtful and informative ways—tend to get more play than extensive treatises and tomes, although the latter have a place too. Researchers love nuance. Policy makers have little use for it; and, in fact, it makes their jobs more difficult. It is certainly possible to communicate high-quality, substantial research. But it is also worth noting that some forms of research just travel better than others. Basic statistics, for example, are highly portable. They may be inherently interesting, can be easily picked up by the media and worked into news coverage, and (if well-constructed) require relatively little contextualization, qualification, and explanation to be interpretable to a generalist audience. Profound theoretical discourse and involved methodological considerations tend to have much more limited mass appeal and are difficult, if not impossible, to boil down into a sound bite. Like it or not, that gives research legs. A couple useful rules of thumb: no lengthy exposition, no unexplained technical jargon (no jargon at all, ideally), and absolutely no Greek. Although sound bites, catchphrases, and clichés may strike some as inane or low-brow forms of communication, they can help researchers to make their point clearly and succinctly. And a little Shakespeare never hurts.

We have all heard the expression that all politics is local. By extension, if policy (or at least the policy maker) has an inherently political character, then locally oriented data and analysis could provide a key leverage point for research in the policy process. This proposition proves particularly salient in educational policy, where so much authority rests at the state and local levels. I know a former governor and member of Congress, now a high-profile advocate for high school reform, who puts it this way. Legislators hear about educational problems from national reports all the time. But what gets their attention, and really makes a problem their own, is when they start hearing about it directly from constituents during trips home to their districts. That is what ultimately motivates many policy makers. And therein lies the power of localizing data and research.

Perhaps the most important decision I have made in my own work on graduation rates was one to report not only national and state statistics but to also publish graduation rates for every school district in the country, all 11,000 or so of them (2006). The public can access this information through a GIS-based Web site (maps.edweek.org) that lets users view graduation patterns visually (think, a picture is worth a thousand words) and download reports for their own school districts (putting actionable data into their hand). Access to such localized data makes research particularly relevant for policy makers and the general public alike and ultimately generates much of the coverage our work receives in the media. These data quite literally enable every daily paper and local television or radio station in the country to produce a graduation story for their own community. Admittedly, a local dissemination strategy is also a double-edged sword. Enhanced relevance goes hand-in-hand with the prospect of generating controversy and criticism on a whole new scale. Every school district superintendent or local official might decide to denounce the results of your research. Fortunately, my experience has been that most do not. In fact many find that the research, even if unflattering, can help them to better address the challenges their schools and students face.

Parting Shots—On Perfection

Perfection is a wonderful thing, if you can find it. And if you cannot, it can still be a lofty standard to which you might aspire. But perfection is not an especially practical or constructive notion when it comes to public policy or applied research.

At the risk of appearing incredibly unsophisticated, unscientific, or just plain-old trite, let me share a rule of thumb that has long guided researchers hoping to inform and improve public policy. Do not let the perfect be the enemy of the good. I would offer a slightly amended and updated version of my own—Do not let the perfect be the enemy of the better.

All of us working in the field of applied policy research are dealing in shades of imperfection. Policy and, dare I say, policy makers, are imperfect creatures. And so are research and researchers. After all, we are talking about social science here, not magic or divine intervention. I firmly believe the large majority of those engaged in the broader policy enterprise do so with the best of intentions. That is not to say, of course, that we are without vigorous and legitimate disagreements over the goals of public policy and the best means for achieving those ends. But expecting perfection of policy or research (or the intersection between the two) is a recipe for failure and disappointment. Or, at the very least, we risk turning ourselves inside-out and being overcome by inertia and cynicism attempting to attain an unattainable goal.

As far as policy is concerned, No Child Left Behind is a notable object lesson. No one should realistically expect a law as far-reaching and ambitious to be perfect. Remember, NCLB has as its stated purpose and guiding principle the goal of raising all students to academic proficiency and eliminating all achievement gaps between historically high- and low-performing groups. And the plan, no less, is to accomplish this in little more than a dozen years. The merits and demerits of the law could be, and have been, endlessly debated. But rather than demanding perfection, it is more productive to ask whether the law on the whole has helped to improve the situation of the nation's schools. If so, how could the law be tweaked and further strengthened? If not, can the law be fixed or is it time for the scrap yard?

A similar sensibility should be applied to the world of research. The connections between research and policy are complex, and no single study, however well-designed and executed, can be all thing to all people. Still, one crucial function of methodology is to help signal the quality of research and evidence. The educational research world could really use a better strategy for populating the critical in-between terrain of the knowledge landscape. This territory, where much applied policy research resides, falls somewhere between gold standards and the rigors of full-blown peer review at one extreme and the unmoderated marketplace of ideas at the other. Not that there is anything inherently wrong with a free market approach that over time adjudicates the merit of ideas and evidence. But the research community itself also has a responsibility to become a more active member of that larger community of knowledge and to bring its expertise more fully to bear in service of the larger good.

One final word of caution, or advice, if you will: Beware of perfection when it is used as the basis for criticism; because this is often just a ploy. In my experience, detractors who raise the specter of perfection can rarely live up to that loft of standard themselves. Indeed, I believe that to be an unrealistic standard for any of us. But more to the point, such critics may have no practical solution to offer at all, let alone constructive ideas any better than those under attack. The ultimate touchstone for applied policy research should be whether it holds relevance to key audiences and represents a meaningful advancement compared with the status quo. Policy research, like policymaking, is an incre-

mental business. And I, for one, will chose imperfection and incrementalism over inaction any day of the week.

Notes

1. I would like to extend all of the customary acknowledgements and disclaimers. *Influence*, the EPE Research Center's study of the factors shaping educational policy, was commissioned by the Thomas B. Fordham Foundation. Much of my work on graduation rates, including *Education Week*'s annual *Diplomas Count* report, has been made possible through generous support from the Bill & Melinda Gates Foundation. All views expressed in this commentary, insightful or otherwise, are my own and should not be attributed to Editorial Projects in Education or its funders.

Reference

Swanson, C. B., & Barlage, J. (2006). *Influence: A study of the factors shaping educational policy.* Bethesda, MD: Editorial Projects in Educations Research Center.

III

Politics and the Policy Process

SECTION EDITOR: JANE CLARK LINDLE

19

Education and Domination

Reforming Policy and Practice through Critical Theory

CARLOS ALBERTO TORRES AND RICHARD VAN HEERTUM
University of California, Los Angeles

Introduction

We stand at an important historical conjuncture, with great possibility confronted by great peril. Global poverty and growing economic inequality, environmental threats, health care crises, and challenges to democracy and freedom endanger our future while new social and political movements and technological, scientific, and medical advances offer opportunities to address global poverty, improve longevity, and enhance quality of life. Within education, neoliberal reforms have profoundly challenged holistic notions of education, replacing them with instrumental, corporate models based primarily on sorting and training. The question becomes how governments and industry will address these contradictory trends, working to balance the interests of the market and security with those of personal freedom and the common good.

In this chapter we explore the role critical theory (CT) can play in addressing these contradictory phenomena and offering potential policy and practice reforms in education. We start by offering a set of arguments defending the framework of critical theory as a timely and energetic legacy that may help teachers, practitioners, researchers, policy activists, parents, and students work to collectively address these issues and challenge the central tenets of neoliberal reforms and positivistic movements in educational research. Critical social theory can help advance a clearer and more compelling agenda for social research that incorporates ethical concerns and projects for social transformation into educational research and practice. It provides valuable research to policy makers and stakeholders in education and it provides a powerful inspiration for those practitioners working in classroom to practice a liberatory education that can empower students and provide the hope necessary for engagement in the political arena.

Critical Theory and Education

Definition(s)[1] In the 1920s and 30s, a group of German philosophers and intellectuals at the Institute for Social Research began to study culture and its critical importance in the rise of Nazism, witnessing first hand the ways radio, newspapers, and other media were used as powerful forces of persuasion. Building on an idea from a short Marx and Engels (1932/1998) essay in *The German Ideology*—"the ideas of the ruling class are in every epoch the ruling ideas: i.e., the class which is the ruling *material* force of society is at the same time its ruling *intellectual* force" (p. 302)—they began to systemically consider how the superstructure (culture) reproduced the economic base and power relations. The group, made up predominantly of Jews, escaped Germany right before the Holocaust and moved to America where, over time, they came to see our culture as extremely ideological as well, working to promote and maintain the capitalist system.

Over time this group, comprised of Horkheimer, Adorno, Benjamin, Fromm, Kirchheimer, Lowenthal, Neumann, Pollack, and Marcuse, combined traditional Marxist critique with psychoanalysis, Weberian sociology and theories of the administered society and Nietzschean critiques of science and knowledge claims to alter the focus and methodological approach of Marxism. The group centered their work on three related aspects of modernity and how capitalism had altered its mechanisms of domination and control. The first was to explore the ways in which the promises of enlightenment had turned on themselves and science and reason had become tools for domination, control, and the fascist attempt to destroy an entire race of people. This was coupled with a general critique of positivism and the ways in which objectivity and scientism had undermined the transgressive and emancipatory possibilities of science and reason. Third was an analysis of the changing nature of capitalism itself, focused on the rise and consolidation of instrumental rationality and the strength of the culture industry (media culture) and the administered society (the state and its tools of social, political, and economic control) to define and delimit human wants, needs, and dreams, and thus undermine more humanistic visions of the common good and good society. Critical theory in its original instantiation can thus be seen as an attempt to modify Marxist social theory to more accurately describe the contemporary society of their time (Kellner, 1989).

Leading members Adorno and Horkheimer (1947/2002) started their critique of contemporary society by exploring the failure of Enlightenment and reason to improve society and the human condition. In their seminal work *Dialectics of Enlightenment,* they argued that "In the most general sense of progressive thought the Enlightenment has always aimed at liberating men from fear and establishing their sovereignty. Yet the fully enlightened earth radiates disaster triumphant" (p. 1). They were thus among the first to recognize the dialectic nature of objectivity and offer a trenchant critique of positivism and its over-reliance on science, reason, and objectivity.

They argued that instrumental rationality had penetrated all aspects of quotidian life and that science had become a vehicle of social domination and control that actually denied the critical faculty of reason in deference to the empirically provable fact. In their view, science had fallen prey to the scientific method and analysis had become separated from the questions of ethics and ends, instead focusing solely on description, classification, and means. Positivism thus ushered in a paradigm that always stopped short of critique, and was forever stuck in describing the world as it was seen, heard, and felt.

Critical theory instead sought to use critique as a mechanism to delve below surface experience to the deeper psychological and ontological ways of being in the world. Marcuse, for one, starts with the determinate negation in Hegelian analysis, which lies in Marx's commitment to the "merciless criticism of everything existing" (as cited in Lenin, 1914, p. 10). Yet what is the role of determinate negation in this process? As Smith (1989) explains:

> The logic of "determinate negation" is the principle of development which exhibits the movement from one category or form of consciousness to another. It constitutes a method for moving from one stage to another that is not externally imposed ... the logic of determinate negation has both a critical and a constructive aspect. It is critical because it does not merely accept what a body of thought, a philosophical system, or even an entire culture says about itself, but is concerned to confront that thought, system, or culture with its own internal tensions, incoherencies, and anomalies. It is constructive because out of this negation or confrontation we are able to arrive at ever more complete, comprehensive, and coherent bodies of propositions and forms of life. (p. 188–189)

The notion of negative philosophy is intimately associated with the notion of negation in dialectics, and to the concept of determinate negation developed by Hegel and later transformed by Marx in *Capital* (1990/1867–1894). As Torres (1994) has argued, following Marcuse, Hegelian dialectics is the rational construction of reality through which the subject assimilates his vital experiences in an ongoing fashion until it finds itself in the positivity of the determinate negation. Hegel saw that the subject would not only appropriate things (basic property) but would attempt to appropriate other subjects as well (the struggle of the opposed consciousnesses). When the conflict of the two self-consciousnesses ensued (that of consciousness that had gone out of itself and was for itself), both fighting to appropriate the same good, it offered a road toward resolution. This road resulted in the *pact,* where one of the two consciousnesses submitted to the other to survive, creating an independent and dependent consciousness; or in classical terms, the Master (Lord) and the Slave (Servant).

Marcuse (1964) argues that the power of negative reason and thinking is being obliterated in the context of authoritarian industrial societies that constrict the ability to think outside the logic of dominant technological and instrumental rationality. History would thus be the road of the Mind, wholly self-conscious, which identifies with the totality of the historical process, whereas this historical process, in its logic, is nothing more than the manifestation of immanent life at the historical unfolding of the Mind.

It is in the reconstruction of Hegel's philosophy that Marx established the foundations for the elaboration of his dialectical-historical philosophy, and the basic concepts he employed to study the relationships between and among human beings and historically constituted structures. In so doing, Marx challenges the traditional epistemology in the subject-object relation, drawing from the Hegelian premise that material reality is a concrete totality constituted through social relations and antagonisms. Within this Hegelian-Marxist framework, which underpins the work of critical social theory, the concept of labor is posited as determining the development of consciousness because human beings transform (and appropriate the fruits of) nature through their labor. More current work in critical theory from Habermas, feminists, critical race theorists, and others has challenge this focus on work and labor, a topic we turn to at the end of the section. Marx then follows Hegel's suggestion that the opposition of consciousnesses is the result of the confrontation resulting from the desire of ego to appropriate things and even consciousness itself.[2]

In short, critical social theory appears as a negative philosophy not only because it challenges the tenets of the philosophy of positivism (a positive philosophy) but because theory helps to deconstruct the premises of common sense as contradictory and building hegemony, á la Gramsci (1971). Or as Horkheimer (1972/1937) puts it: "Among the vast majority of the ruled there is the unconscious fear that theoretical thinking might show their painfully won adaptation to reality to be perverse and unnecessary" (pp. 231–232).

Horkheimer (1972) was among the first to systematize the goals and methods of Critical Theory in its formative stage. He offered dialectical social theory as an alternative to the over-reliance on the scientific method (Kellner, 1989). Dialectical social theory is founded on empirical evidence but is underwritten by values and a normative political standpoint to attack injustice, suffering, and alienation. It assails the notion of "value free," or objective, research and calls for the centrality of critique—based on a symbiotic relationship between theory, morality, and politics. It is further underwritten by an ethical foundation based on minimizing the unhappiness of the poor and suffering and maximizing the happiness of all. This involves locating the socio-historical sources of suffering and injustice and working to overcome them. The project is thus based on reconstructing society on non-exploitative relations and placing humans at the center of history and social formation.

Jürgen Habermas (1973) furthered this line of reasoning by arguing that adherence to reason alone eliminated the ability to hope, to take a position, to desire, to strive for happiness, and to dignify all other aspects of human experience that did not fit into the scientifically observable fact. In Habermas' view, science had separated reason from desire and suffering, and had increasingly centered itself on production, technological "progress," and efficiency alone. As a result, anything associated with transcending reality was deemed nonsensical and outside the scope of scientific study. In the end, he felt, science had abandoned its role in aiding the progress of humanity. We will discuss this critique more in the section on objectivity and educational research.

Habermas' (1972) engagement with critical theory, of course, goes well beyond this insight. He is considered the preeminent critical theorist today, although many have critiqued his turn toward a more democratic socialist tradition in recent years. Habermas sees three functions for critical theory: (a) a critique of society, (b) developing agents of social transformation, and (c) self-reflective critique of critical theory itself. His theoretic contributions have been profound in this area and beyond the scope of this chapter, but one of his main contributions has been to question the focus on production and class in Marxism and Critical Theory, to move from a philosophy of consciousness to one of language and to foreground the centrality of communication. This turn is dedicated to preserving the importance of Marxism to critical social theory, staking a space between the skepticism of post-structuralism, continued attachment to production-centered, economistic Marxism and the absolutism of positivism, while recognizing their individual strengths and shortcomings. Ultimately, Habermas (1984) believes a normative foundation and rational base can be forged for a critical social theory that can be emancipatory in nature, critiquing society and establishing the grounds for increased democracy and freedom. This is based on his theory of communicative reason, which locates rationality in structures of linguistic communication rather than in subjectivity or absolute truth claims. A more just, humane

and egalitarian society can thus be formed through the realization of human potential for autonomy and freedom, particularly through discourse ethics (communicative competency) and deliberative democratic dialogue and processes.

A third aspect of the critical theory heritage relates to their engagement with culture and its increased importance in the consolidation of instrumental rationality and the administered society. Leading members Adorno and Horkheimer (1947/2002) thus developed a theory of the culture industry starting in fascist Germany and then in the Fordist era of American society, which worked to establish the centrality of production and create a system of values, interests, lifestyles and institutions that supported maintenance of the status quo. In Dialectic of Enlightenment, they systemized this critique, showing the critical importance of movies, television, radio, and magazines in how people perceived their world and created meaning. The culture industry thus came to serve a key role in social reproduction, with Adorno and Horkheimer giving the culture industry an almost totalizing power over a homogenized, pacified and massified public.

Marcuse (1964), another founding member of the Frankfurt School, went even further in arguing that the media and technology contained their own discourse that prevails over the ability to think negatively and question the validity of the system in which one resides. By erecting a "technological society" that integrates individuals into a world of thought and behavior that demands administrative submission, a meme of conformity or "one dimensionality" prevails. The central feature of this mode of thought is a repression of values, aspirations, and ideas that are not consistent with the prevailing operational attitudes and rationality. The ability to think negatively, or outside the strictures of the system, became all but impossible and one was forced to instead conform to a naturalized set of needs and wants in line with capitalist logic. Marshall McLuhan (1965), in his seminal book Understanding Media, came to a similar conclusion, placing media and technology at the center of reality, controlling individuals who simply adapted to their imperatives and rationality (after a period of negotiation with new technology); although he had a more sanguine view of the influence of television.

Marcuse (1966) also provides the most extensive—and we would argue compelling—incorporation of psychoanalysis in critical theory. He argued that contemporary society has established a system of repression more complex than that described by Freud. There was the necessary repression that accompanied agreeing to live in society with others (the performance or reality principle) and a surplus repression, which was the source of social domination. Forms that this surplus repression took included the monogamous, patriarchal family, the hierarchical division of labor and public control of an individual's private existence.

With the advent of surplus repression, individuals became encased within an overarching technological and instrumental rationality that seriously circumscribes thought, dreams, and even needs. The resulting organization of desire altered the very nature of the pleasure principle, orienting it toward the perpetuation of the system of domination and control. A phenomenon that emerged in response is *repressive desublimation*, where the promise of immediate gratification and small measures of freedom led people to embrace the system and work to sustain it. Simulation and simulacra become the mechanisms for social control as the commodified object replaces the unattainable deeper libidinal desires. The system thus creates an internal process of self-perpetuation where want and desire that can never be filled but ephemerally become the basis of a repression that is internalized. Since we cannot see outside the imposed rationality and sensibility, we are trapped in a system that never offers the happiness and satisfaction available outside it.

In this way, one can argue, we become estranged from our own deeper libidinal desires and a new form of alienation emerges, where we cannot find satisfaction in the system that we see as a natural extension of our psyche. Instead of looking for ways to transcend this reality, we instead seek only to consume more, to work harder, and to strive for more material satisfaction, assuming this as the route to happiness. But in the failure this effort continues to sustain, we become further and further alienated from ourselves and our desiring systems and become victims of a vicious circle of internal dissatisfaction and confusion that can easily result in cynicism and disengagement.

The problem for social transformation then becomes more than reaching critical consciousness through ideology critique. It must be accompanied by a new way to view the world and, as Kellner has argued, a more radical subjectivity that breaks the failed essentialism, idealism, and various prejudices of the past (Kellner, 2000). In this movement, the *great refusal* is one key component, finding ways to awaken a sense that more than freedom and satisfaction on the cheap are available and an alternative worldview and order of things is possible.[3] Desire and its embodiment in a more ecumenical Eros can then become a revolutionary force, rather than one of the main sources of oppression. This is a necessary but not easy precondition to any radical project for change not destined for ultimate failure.

The Frankfurt School thus offered a model of analysis that centered on ideological critique toward unearthing the deeper political and economic interests that underwrote cultural production and state activity. They utilized an approach that situated analysis within the larger context of social, political, and economic life, exploring the role of various social institutions and structures in the development of normative values, desires, and needs. The approach is transdisciplinary, incorporating sociology, political economy, history, political science, philosophy, and psychoanalysis. It explored social phenomena from a variety of optics seeking to deconstruct culture toward emancipating people from a capitalist society that continued to exploit, dominate, and alienate in the name of instrumentalized notions of progress.

Critical theorists are committed to penetrating objective appearance and exploring the underlying social relations the surface often conceals. They rejected rationality that subordinated human consciousness and action to the imperatives of universal law and instead highlighted the contradictions, alienation, and subjugation that existed below the cohesiveness and universality of functionalist traditions (Giroux, 1983). By looking at the relationship between political domination and culture, subjectivity, and consciousness, Frankfurt School theorists hoped to critique the social order as part of a radical project for change that offered a normative vision of what society should be like.

Since this formative work, critical theory has expanded its analytical breadth to engage with a more diverse set of oppressions that transcend class alone. These include exploring the interrelationship between class, gender, race, nationality, and other lines of difference that better describe the diverse forms of domination and control today. The focus among some scholars has moved away from class consciousness and revolution toward radical democracy or even more delimited political projects. Others have challenged the ideas of democracy themselves (Laclau, 1988, 1990; Benhabib, 2006). Many of the movements away from the original theorists have been driven by insights about difference, otherness, critiques of grand narratives and essentialism, and other insights from post-structuralism and postmodernism.

Certain strands of feminist theory have led many of these critiques. This work began, arguably, with Nancy Fraser (1985) who critiqued the original work of Habermas (1962/1989) on the public sphere and his rather truncated and limited notion of its White, male-propertied nature. Fraser highlighted racial and gender public spheres that Habermas neglected and offered a more general critique of the ways in which the public/private sphere analysis left women and their work outside the model. This critique would lay the foundation for the work of others, like Butler and Benhabib, who more forcefully challenged the commitments of critical theory and their reliance on outdated Enlightenment ideas of democracy, pluralism, otherness, and subjectivity; as well as their paternalism and masculinist tendencies (Benhabib, 2006; Butler & Mouffe, 1997; Butler & Scott, 1992). This move more generally informed critical race theory, queer studies, and other attempts to take the tools of critical theory and post-structuralism and synthesize them into a more appropriate model for dealing with difference and otherness.

Within education, critical theory first emerges in a serious, comprehensive way with the work of Paulo Freire (1970), the Brazilian educator who uses the tools of critical theory and liberation theology to critique the educational system of his time and offer a new liberatory pedagogy. In the United States, critical theory was first taken up by Michael Apple (1971, 2004) and then Henry Giroux (1983), who focused on its critique of science toward offering a critique of schooling, curriculum and pedagogy, and alternative pedagogical projects that fit within the spirit of Critical Theories commitment to social transformation, though both come to explore multiple forms of oppression and domination. Stanley Aronowitz (2000) was also instrumental in bringing CT to the academic and educational communities, as was Wexler, who was the first to use the psychoanalytic insights of CT in education. A host of other critical educational theorists have emerged in education since then including bell hooks, Peter McLaren, Antonia Darder, Carlos Torres, Richard Delgado, Derek Bell, and many others. We look at their work in more detail below, as well as the critiques that have been levied particularly by critical feminists like Ellsworth, Lather, and Weiler.

Principles   What is the meaning and nature of the concept of critical in critical social theory? Canadian critical theorist Raymond Morrow offers an insightful set of distinctions when he argues that:

> The term *critical* itself, in the context of "critical social theory" has a range of meanings not apparent in common sense where critique implies negative evaluations. This is, to be sure, one sense of critique in critical social theory, given its concern with unveiling ideological mystifications in social relations; but another even more fundamental connotation is methodological, given a concern with critique as involving establishing the presuppositions of approaches to the nature of reality, knowledge, and explanation; yet another dimension of critique is associated with the self-reflexivity of the investigator and the linguistic basis of representation. (Morrow & Brown, 1994, p. 7)

Following Morrow's contribution, we would like to argue that as a research program, critical social theory implies several dimensions. It is a *human science*, providing a humanistic, anti-positivist approach to social theory. It is also a *historical science of society*, providing a form of historical sociology. Finally it is a *sociocultural critique*, concerned with normative theory or a "theory about values and what ought to be. Critical imagination is required to avoid identifying where we live here and now as somehow cast, in stone by natural laws" (Morrow & Brown, 1994, p. 11). To be truly critical, it must also engage with the multiple forms of oppression and difference and transcend the traditional approach focused predominantly on production and class.

Douglas Kellner (1989) has forcefully argued that there is no unitary critical social theory. A definitive feature of this theoretical cluster and research program is its interdisciplinary nature, defying the logic of separate disciplines analyzing discrete objects of study: "critical social theory has refused to situate itself within an arbitrary or conventional division of labor. It thus traverses and undermines boundaries between competing disciplines, and stresses interconnections between philosophy, economics and policies, and culture and society" (p. 7). Another important insight from Kellner's analysis is the notion that critical social theory attempts a synthesis that, as a research program, can only be accomplished through collective groups of intellectuals aiming at social transformation: "The project requires a collective, supradisciplinary synthesis of philosophy, the science and politics, produced by groups of theorists and scientists from various disciplines working together to produce a critical social theory of the present age aimed at radical social-political transformation" (p. 7).

This notion of critical social theory has serious implications for the role of intellectuals in contemporary capitalist societies, for the role of social theory in the context of debates about modernism and postmodernism, and for the role that education can play in social transformation. For the critical social theory tradition, theory cannot be easily separated from practice. Hence a political sociology of education improves not only the understanding of social reality and the epistemological, logical, and analytical perspectives of theory and empirical research, but contributes to improving the practice of policy makers, policy brokers, and policy constituencies, and the cognitive and non-cognitive outcomes of the process of teaching and learning. A byproduct of this discussion is the role of intellectuals employing critical social theory as opposed to liberal, neoliberal, and neoconservative intellectuals employing mainstreams theories, and the centrality of praxis (or the synthesis of theory and practice) to their work.

Implications   Foucault (2000) once argued that "There exists an international citizenship that has its rights and its duties, and that obliges one to speak out against every abuse of power, whoever the author, whoever the victim" (p. 474). The answer to this challenge from the perspective of critical social theory is to be critics of the social order following the logic of determinate negation. Not a critic who is necessarily intransigent or intolerant in all cases, but one who is able to offer society perspectives on critical aspects that need to be considered in dealing with mechanisms of sociability, production, and political exchanges. Universities, as places inhabited by intellectuals and technocrats, have a role to play in developing critical modes of thinking for society. This implies a critique of the commodification of human relations, and in the context of universities themselves, a critique of the corporatization of academic institutions as currently outlined by the graduate employee unionization movement in the United States (Rhoads & Rhoades, 2005).

Critical social theory also assumes that a central role of intellectuals is to create a social imaginary, relating to Gramsci's hypotheses about organic and traditional intellectuals (Morrow & Torres, 2002a). The creation of social imaginary implies a moral responsibility and a political commitment. The moral responsibility is to imagine social scenarios where people can deliberate and construct mechanisms of participation which may expand the workings of democracy. The political commitment is to create an autonomous sphere of public debate, as suggested by Habermas, which is neither controlled by the market nor by the State (Torres, 2008).

Gramsci (1971) proposed a forceful hypothesis when he argues that everybody has the capacity to do intellectual work, but only a few recognize it and work in intellectual professions. Two key elements then emerge from Gramsci's suggestion. First, that intellectual work is not only a trade, profession, or set of techniques, but the capacity to realize refined analysis that leads to praxis and social transformation. Second, a critical intellectual is one who is able not only to teach but to learn from people. Or, to paraphrase Mao Tse Tung, a critical intellectual is one who is able to capture the collective imagination of the people in all its disorganized richness and insightfulness and to return this knowledge back to the people in a more systematic and organized fashion so the very same producers of the knowledge are able to appraise, reinterpret, and rethink their own knowledge and insights, conceptually and practically.

The production of knowledge in the human sciences is a process that involves a great deal of persuasion. Intellectuals are always attempting to persuade each other, to show that they have a better explanation and a more powerful, far-reaching, and/or comprehensive analysis than the previous or competing one. From a constructivist perspective, however, critical intellectuals are convinced that there is never a perfect or comprehensive interpretation or understanding nor a conclusive analysis that cannot be challenged or subjected to debate and criticism. Perhaps the best way to put it is the notion of Hegelian *Aufhebung*: Knowledge creation is always the negation of the previous negation, the criticism of previous knowledge which, in and of itself, is a criticism of previous knowledge (Torres, 2008).

Hence, assuming this notion of Aufhebung invites a sense of humility and introspection in intellectual work. Intellectuals always work with knowledge produced by other individuals and collectives and critical intellectuals recognize this fact and further see their work as always provisional and limited. They cannot be detached clinicians offering "objective" advice. So, while intellectual work is conventionally seen as eminently individual, or produced in small team of individuals who share similar analytical, theoretical, and methodological premises, for critical intellectuals it is collective work because it always draws from previous knowledge and the criticism of that previous knowledge. The notion of learning then becomes as important as the notion of teaching in knowledge construction.

Critical intellectuals assume an agonistic perspective in knowledge production, assuming that no intellectual work can provide a definitive answer to any domain or problematic of the human sciences. They cannot, however, for moral and political reasons, give up continuing the process of mutual persuasion, even if their intellectual product may be short-lived. Marcuse offers a compelling argument to justify the moral dimensions of the work of critical intellectuals speaking, perhaps for the last time, to his disciple Jürgen Habermas: "Look, I know wherein our most basic value judgment are rooted—in compassion, in our sense for the suffering of others" (Habermas, 1984, p. 77).

In political terms, critical intellectuals pay considerable attention to the process of intellectual work. In so doing, they remain key facilitators of intellectual exchanges in the production of collective symbolism and rituals. They remain important sources working to create spaces for public conversation, as Freire exemplified throughout his life. A few years ago, Torres asked Freire what he would like his legacy to be. He answered that when he died, he would like people to say of him: "Paulo Freire lived, loved, and wanted to know" (personal communication, June 15, 1991). In his poetic style, he provided a simple and yet powerful message about the role of critical intellectuals. For him, critical intellectuals should passionately embody and live their own ideas, building spaces of deliberation and tolerance in their quest for knowledge and empowerment. They should love what they do, and those with whom they interact. Love, then, becomes another central element of the political project of intellectuals in producing knowledge for empowerment and liberation.

Finally, it is their love for knowledge itself that makes them sensitive to the popular knowledge and common sense. Following Gramsci, critical intellectuals know that common sense always has a nucleus of "good sense." From this good sense, critical intellectuals can develop a criticism of conventional wisdom, knowledge, and practices. In educational policy and planning, this good sense can be a powerful starting point for a critique of instrumental rationalization. In this context critical intellectuals can use political sociology of education to understand educational policy formation.[4]

The lessons of critical social theory for education are clear, and need to be remembered: politics and education intersect continually, and a neutral, objective educational practice is thus impossible (Freire 1998a, 1998b). Power plays a major role in configuring schooling and social reproduction (Apple, 2004; Giroux, 1983; Bowles & Gintis, 1976). Social change cannot be simply articulated as social engineering from the calm environment of the research laboratory. It needs to be forged in negotiations, compromise, and struggle in the political arena through social movements and in the streets (Torres, 2002). It also needs to be conquered in the schools struggling against bureaucratic and authoritarian behavior, defying the growing corporatization of educational institutions (particularly in higher education), and striving to implement substantive rationality through communicative dialogue. Finally, it needs to be achieved in the cozy and joyful environment of our gatherings with family and friends. Dialogue and reason cannot take vacations if one pursues the dream of social justice education and peace.

The current process of globalization if it is not simply understood as globalization from above (neoliberalism) could contribute to a bottom-up, grassroots social movement to challenge the current principles neglecting human rights and freedom in capitalist societies, enhancing the chances for cosmopolitan democracies and radical educational reform. Critical social theory has a major role to play in achieving these goals.

Critical Theory Contributions to U.S. Education

Critical theory first emerges in education in a serious analytical way with the work of Paulo Freire (1970), with the publication of his book *Pedagogy of the Oppressed* in the early 1970s. In this and his other work, Freire attempted to critique traditional education and pedagogy, particularly what he called *banking education* and its adherence to a subject-object relationship between teacher and student. Freire instead advocated a problem-posing education that centered on dialogue and using student's specific cultural knowledge and experience to help move them toward critical consciousness and hope and empowerment for social change. His work inspired the critical pedagogy movement that followed in this country, led by Apple (1971) and Giroux (1983) among others, who used the tools of critical theory to offer a systematic critique of schooling and its role in reproducing class, race, and gender inequalities and maintaining and reinforcing capitalist logic and rationality.

Many critical social theorists thus see education as a key site for their work, given the role that schools, colleges, and universities play in social reproduction and preparing citizens for participation in the broader society (Giroux, 1983; Morrow & Torres, 2002b; Rhoads & Valadez, 2006; Tierney & Rhoads, 1993; Torres, 1998, 2008). For them, critical theory provides valuable tools to explore the relationship of knowledge, schooling, and the social order and the role schools play in spreading ideology, maintaining or challenging social inequality, and serving democracy. Critical theorists in this sense use inquiry as a means for challenging forms of oppression and marginality that limit full and equitable participation in public life. Thus, a key contribution of critical theory in education is the belief that research ought to serve an emancipatory goal. That is, paraphrasing Karl Marx, social scientists should not simply interpret the world, but use their inquiry as a vehicle for improving, reforming, or revolutionizing social life. Critical theory thus provides *theoretical* tools that are then used by theorists in advocating for educational reform, critical pedagogy, or other radical or progressive pedagogical practices that can advance democratic ideals and practices and address and challenge social inequalities.

This work has, as previously mentioned, expanded beyond its focus on social reproduction and ideology to explore the interrelationship between class, race, gender, sexuality, and other lines of demarcation. Critical Race Theory, for example, has used the tools of critical theory to deconstruct the ways schools undermine the opportunities and achievement of minority students. Recent works in this vein analyze a diverse array of factors working to undermine the success of minority students in schools, including traditional issues of inequities in funding, resources, and access to quality teachers, as well as overcrowded and crumbling schools (Bell, 1960; Delgado, 1999; Solórzano & Yosso, 2004; Valencia, 2002; Valenzuela, 1999). They also include analyses of the overrepresentation of minorities, particularly Chicanos, in special education and remedial classes, the re-segregation of schools along race lines, and the key issue of language and bilingual training. These trends fit with the general critique of critical pedagogues who argue for a more culturally-specific curriculum, local control of schools, and other mechanisms to ensure that curriculum and learning be relevant to the lives and experiences of students from diverse cultural and socioeconomic backgrounds.

Feminists have also sought to expand the work of critical theory to address their specific concerns. This critique emanates particularly from the work of Ellsworth, Lather, Luke and Gore, and Weiler. Their critique centers on the masculine and paternalistic tendencies of much critical pedagogy, the resulting "performative contradiction" in their work, and ways to foreground subjectivity and difference in critical pedagogy. They argue that difference is often subsumed within the consensus or solidarity-building dialogue that critical theorists and critical pedagogues advocate. Here Habermas' theory of communicative action comes under scrutiny as does the work of McLaren, Giroux, and Freire, using education as a mechanism in the struggle for critical consciousness and emancipatory collective action. They wonder at the "we" that is being created in these critical dialogues and whose voices and subjectivities are excluded in the call for solidarity and transformative political projects.

Weiler (1991) maintains many critical and potentially emancipatory elements of CT while attempting to use insights from feminist pedagogy in providing a space for excluded and formerly silenced groups to challenge dominant approaches to learning and knowledge systems and, at the level of theory, question modernist claims to universal truth and rationality. She calls for a reformulation of critical pedagogy that challenges too-rigid dichotomies like oppressor/oppressed, confronts its sexist attitudes, and combines sensitivity to difference and personal experience with a renewed commitment to universal emancipation. Luke and Gore (1992) follow this line of reasoning, arguing for daily pedagogical practices that empower students to demystify canonical knowledge and to show the ways in which relationship of domination oppress subjects along the lines of gender, race, class, and other forms of difference. Both seek to critique the paternalism of critical pedagogy and reformulate it within feminist critiques of humanist emancipatory projects and post modern discourses in general (Gur-Ze'ev, 2005).

A more profound critique emerges in the work of Ellsworth (1989), who seeks to negate all elements of essentialism, foundationalism, and any call for universalism and collectivism from critical pedagogy, arguing against the vestiges of enlightenment reason that continue to inhere today. Unlike Weiler, she largely rejects the notion of human subjects and critical consciousness and the ways in which structures and institutions limit and undermine humanistic aims. She instead follows Foucault in avoiding commitment to any project that is devoted to controlling justice and truth, instead exploring the possibility of a non-hierarchical feminist alternative to what she sees as the elitism and symbolic and real violence of the modernist rationalist emancipatory project.

Ellsworth centers her work on personal experience, individual subjectivities, and an imminent critique of any project with a positive utopianism or effort toward solidarity, as largely based on an illusory dialogue and as being potentially repressive by its very nature. In many ways, she thus follows Butler in emphasizing the omnipotence of social and cultural manipulation of consciousness, its constructiveness, and its ways of seeing and being in the world. As Gur-Ze'ev (2005) argues, however, this leaves little room for escaping, criticizing, or changing society—directly challenging Freire's call for hope and recognition of our power as subjects to act in the world and transform it. Gur-Ze'ev believes a middle ground must be forged that includes understanding the limits of dialogue and the real nature of power in the construction and limitations of the subject, to create a counter-education based on helping individuals to understand, critique, and decipher reality and its codes, and "critically reconstruct and demolished potential for human solidarity, cooperation, and the realization of their ideological essence, while acknowledging that at the current historical stage, these two missions contradict each other" (pp. 24–25). She is thus against the idea that it offers antidotes to the present circumstance, but does believe it can offer partial, local, and painful successes toward this ultimate goal.

In this sense, a more recent work by Nancy Fraser (1997, chap. 1) might be informative in drawing a middle ground between the two camps. Fraser argues that the politics of difference and coming-to-voice must come together with a broader critique of economic distribution and the material reality of oppression in contemporary society. We believe there are valuable insights in all of this work and that an effective critical social theory must engage with the multifarious forms of oppression and domination—including race, gender, class, sexuality, nationality, and the like. But we believe that critical theory should entail a struggle for a more just and democratic world that serves the needs of the many. Along with Apple (2001), we believe a strategy of *decentered unity* allows for a politics of difference and solidarity where the various factions of the left can work together toward specific group goals and the broader goals of social justice and democratization within and outside education. The social imaginary is in our minds a powerful tool toward that end, engaging with social transformation at the level of the society we envision as an alternative to the present order of things. This utopia would be provisional, local, and bottom–up, and can vary from community to community. But as Jameson (2004) has argued, it allows for two important elements essential to counter-hegemonic politics: a diagnosis of what is wrong with society and a provisional roadmap for change. We believe a critical theory and pedagogy based solely on difference and coming-to-voice ignores the broader and worthy project critical theory has been dedicated to since its inception.

Within the limited space of a chapter, we cannot discuss the multiple themes, analytical options, methodological strategies, or policy choices that emerge from the implementation of critical theory in U.S. education. Here, we have identified three key areas of concern: educational research and objectivity; teaching, teacher education, and teachers unions; and educational policy as it relates to high-stakes testing and No Child Left Behind. After exploring these three themes, we offer a brief rendition of the principal challenges of critical theory in educational research.

Critique of Objectivity and Neutrality in Research In this section, we explore the positivistic tendencies in educational research and its role in undermining efforts to explore larger structural and ethical issues or the particular concerns of the most oppressed groups. We argue, for example, against the recent work of Paul Tough (2006) and others attempting to place the blame for racial and class educational inequality on cultural differences or deficiencies; forgoing broader critiques of social institutions and power structures that promote and maintain inequality.[5] The positivist tradition encompasses a diverse array of theorists from Henri de Saint-Simon, Auguste Comte, the Vienna Circle, and early Ludwig Wittgenstein to Karl Popper. Their shared commitment is to parallel the social sciences with the natural sciences by co-opting the scientific method to study human behavior and interaction. They center this position on a binding faith in sensory data and the ability to quantify what is seen, heard, or felt. Any theory must be validated through the experience of facts, quantified in a rigorous process that eliminates subjective intervention. That which cannot be shown through observation or experimentation becomes de facto inferior, a mere exercise in speculative dreaming (Giroux, 1983).

Popper (1992)—as a strong advocate of this approach and critic of all forms of skepticism, conventionalism, and relativism—added the idea of *falsifiability*, where no theory is scientific if it cannot in principal be shown false by observation (leading him to claim theories like Marxism and psychoanalysis outside the realm of science). The theorists in this tradition then set out to separate science from questions of ethics and ends, and instead prided themselves on their ability to suspend judgment, bias, and politics in lieu of the type of increasingly complex statistical manipulation that purports to maximize reliability and validity. Within education, a subset of theorists and researchers has increasingly followed the central tenets of this project, working to gain legitimacy and respect in the broader research community and among policy makers.

As outlined in detail above, the Frankfurt School and other critical theorists are dedicated to penetrating empirical reality and exploring the ways in which manipulation, domination, and control undermine our ability to see the world as it really exists. They believed positivism had become a powerful mechanism in this manipulation, by separating science from ethical concerns and a normative project to improve society. Instead it became a force to recapitulate reality without any real project to change it, or serve the original goal of human emancipation from suffering and oppression. Their goal was to reaffirm the transformative and radical potential of science to reduce suffering and increase freedom, social equality, and happiness.

Within education, Freire (1998a) mirrors these thinkers in first locating, and then rejecting, the oxymoron of objective, apolitical knowledge. Freire recognized that teaching and research were by their very nature political acts that necessarily involve taking a position: "It seems fundamental to me to clarify in the beginning that a neutral, uncommitted, and apolitical educational practice does not exist" (p. 39). He believed that separating education from its underlying politics worked toward dehumanizing students and facilitating the interests of neoliberalism and its fatalistic exodus from hope. The positivism that was coming to dominate educational research in the 1980s and early 1990s was thus of great concern to Freire and his followers, particularly its reliance on a "value free" methodology. The obvious manipulative potential of statistics was secondary, in their view, to the more insidious nature of extricating ethical considerations.

In the introduction to Freire's (1998a) last book, *Pedagogy of Freedom*, Donaldo Macedo outlines his particular concern with the power of positivistic overemphasis to effectively cloak ideology: "behind a facile call for 'scientific rigor' and 'absolute objectivity'" (p. xi). He claims that attempts to adopt the methods of the "hard sciences" have led toward scientism, where intellectual work cultivated by specialists fragmented knowledge and extricated it from broader social critique. He further argues that many researchers had come to believe that facts were not human statements about the world but embodied the world itself. In the process, they were eliding the lessons of contemporary philosophy and social theory—that human beings are cultural animals who see the world and interpret it through socially constructed lenses. Then Macedo highlights the ways adherence to neutrality absolves researchers of responsibility for their work and its implications.

Many since Freire have continued and enriched this work. In *Theory and Resistance in Education*, Giroux (1983) outlined a new vision of educational reform focused on resistance and radical social transformation, basing much of his analysis within the critical theory tradition. Apple (2004), in his classic *Ideology and Curriculum*, modified Gramscian ideas to examine the profound ways in which official knowledge cloaks ideology and indoctrinates children into a worldview that serves the powerful. hooks (1994) highlighted the centrality of lived experience in knowledge, while challenging the essentialism that some critical theory and feminism invoked. And a host of others, from Stanley Aronowitz and Ira Shor to Cameron McCarthy and Antonia Darder, have augmented the discussion by incorporating deeper discussion of class, race, gender, the body, and difference as essential components of critical educational research.

Some empirical work in education has turned to anthropology and its use of interpretative research to address the problems of objectivity. Instead of looking at larger structural issues through a purely quantitative lens, some have turned to participatory research and direct observation (Anderson, 1989; Hargreaves, 1997; Carspection, 1995). One of the key benefits of critical ethnography is that anthropology had long ago recognized and corrected its adherence to a false methodological objectivity and thus offered educational researchers a more critical starting point where the centrality of the researcher's point-of-view in what is observed, what is recorded, how it is recorded, and how it is later adapted into a research report were well established. These educational researchers realize that data are always for some hypothesis and both include and exclude, and that underlying theories generally affect the method of data collection, data analysis, and reporting. They offer a powerful critique of positivism and focus on symbolic action and place human actors and their interpretive and negotiating capacity at the center of analysis (Anderson, 1989). Some, like Rhoads (2003), Hargreaves (1997), and Noguera (2001), have gone even further, using action or participatory action research and critical ethnography as ways to foreground political and ethical questions. In adopting a more critical, interpretive, and reflexive approach in this vein, this research has taken a huge step along the path away from objectivity and positivism and toward intervention. But a question that remains is the extent to which this research reframes larger ethical questions by offering information within a relatively narrow context hard to extrapolate to the larger whole. And when grounded theory is the starting point, a further question is whether research becomes trapped in an extreme form of positivism where data and experience alone dictate the nature of inquiry.

Horkheimer argued that positivism presents a view of knowledge and science that strips them of their critical potential (as cited in Giroux, 1983). Likewise, feminists have spent years critiquing the ways that objectivity maintains current power dynamics along the lines of gender, race, class, and sexuality. Harding put it succinctly when she noted the conventional view that, "politics can only obstruct and damage the production of scientific knowledge" (Harding, 2004, p. 1). Even forgoing the obvious biases and ideologies that underwrite all language, if researchers refuse to take positions by clinging to a discourse of neutrality, it seems fair to claim that they are essentially supporting the current order of things. If, as researchers, we neglect discussion of the political ramifications of our research, then what purpose does it serve? If we only look at the present and past in our studies, don't we miss reporting what could be? Objectivity in this broader view becomes but a shroud protecting us from the deeper theoretical and systemic issues at the heart of social injustice.

The problem that looms largest, perhaps, is thus that objective empirical work cannot really quantify a new or unique solution, but only reiterate a problem and the past efforts to eradicate it. It implicitly disavows utopia as "Utopian," and thus outside the sphere of the scientific method. Empirical researchers can quantify what was or is, but cannot quantify what can be, and any effort at the latter is a bête noire to the positivistic community that is to be condemned for falling outside the rigor of the scientific method and the requirement of falsifiability. So, while critical pedagogues and feminists in the United States and abroad continue offering normative alternatives to prevailing practices in schools and the larger society, they generally exist at the periphery, outside the acceptable continuum of science and official knowledge.

In critiquing positivism, Horkheimer again offered *dialectical social theory* as an alternative to the over-reliance on the scientific method (as cited in Kellner, 1989), starting with empirical evidence but underwritten by values and a normative political standpoint to attack injustice, suffering, and alienation. It challenges neutral research and calls for the centrality of critique based on bringing together theory, morality, and politics, to use research as a tool for social transformation. Freire follows this approach, advocating *critical hermeneutics* as a way out of the impasse of strict positivism and absolute relativity, employing phenomenological epistemology toward reaching a provisional and generalizable knowledge that can be used constructively in the struggle to define and redefine the world (Freire, 1970, 1998a, 1998b). This new knowledge is tied to everyday life, rather than universalizing principles, where dialogue and experimentation allow people to produce new knowledge based on *collective lived experience*. In the process, research assists subjects in becoming conscious of the social, cultural, and political world around them, as well as the power relations that underwrite those spheres. Haraway (2004) offers a similar research agenda, arguing that a power-charged social relation of conversation between active agents in history is the best way to overcome the extremes of social constructionist relativity and absolute empiricism. The knowledge created by this research then as a provisional and collective nature, tied to place and time, and to larger issues of culture, language, and social structures. It is social in nature and highlights the centrality of intersubjectivity and the social nature of all knowledge and reality.

Freire advocated this approach to bridge the line between an excessive reliance on an unattainable objectivity and the complete rejection of knowledge claims from the revisionist camp. He argued that we could reach a provisional, generalizable knowledge at a given moment that could be used constructively in the struggle to define the world:

> The process of conscientization makes use of two different forms of knowledge that produce distantiation. On the one hand, there is the possibility of bringing to the learning situation empirical knowledge with respect to how society works. This type of critical insight corresponds to the Enlightenment model of critical consciousness. The second type of distantiation is more characteristic of problem-posing education, which starts by discovering the theory hidden in the practices of human agents and social movements. (Morrow & Torres, 2002b, p. 46)

bell hooks (1994) offers us hints to the first step in this direction with her call for "Hearing each other's voices, individual thoughts, and sometimes associating these voices with personal experience [which] make us more acutely aware of each other. Sharing experiences and confessional narratives in the classroom helps establish communal commitment to learning" (p. 148). The entire research community could benefit greatly from this mediated position, between positivistic adherence to objectivity and an intractable subjectivity, moving away from general reliance on "neutral" empirical research and methodological rigor that simply reproduces evidence of intuitive problems without any real prescriptions for change, or from the opposite extreme reject theories that dissolve all attempts at analyzing problems from the start. Science can still serve the cause of radicalism, if it takes a radically different course than that offered today—as an active advocate and effective apologist for conservative ideology.[6]

Yet, while we have been arguing for the limitation of objectivity as a goal of inquiry, it is absurd to argue that researchers should abandon its spirit completely. Instead, research can move to a position where balance, fairness, and reflexivity replace value-free norms. Science can then return to the study of uncertainty rather than the attempt to overcome it, and thereby, re-engage the centrality of questioning official knowledge. Researchers would then be in a position to recognize their own biases and prejudices and, to the extent practicable, communicate those to the audience. They should be clear about their political objectives and offer a project for positive social transformation together with the now ubiquitous critique.

Educational research could also benefit greatly from acknowledging the dialectical nature of all reality and the subjectivity that confronts all empirical work. Rather than simply saying that factor x led to positive outcome y or negative outcome z, research could study the ambiguity of outcomes associated with different educational policies and practices, as well as the ambiguity of the goals themselves. Better test scores and grades could be measured against self-esteem, critical thinking skills, and motivation to learn. Students' performance could be measured against whether the teacher provides a nurturing and caring environment that fosters learning, imagination, and humanization. School performance could be measured against funding differentials, a real measure of teacher quality, civic educational goals, and the motivation of students to do well on the tests that increasingly decide their future.

At the same time, balance and fairness are goals that should continue to stand at the forefront of all research. Educational researchers can have a political end in mind, but must not allow this to cloud their judgment or make them blind to disconfirming evidence. Accomplishing this involves acknowledging the biases inherent in all research, the larger structural issues empirical work often cannot see, the diversity of opinions and perspectives ignored among the group actually observed, and the limitations of the findings. The work should acknowledge its political implications and attempt to limit essentializing narratives, while working toward replicable and generalizable findings grounded in the present, and comprehensiveness in its offering provisional utopian alternatives.

Empirical work should never be marginalized or dismissed as sometimes occurs among critical theorists. It should be remembered that Adorno and Horkheimer (1947/2002) undertook extensive empirical work in laying the groundwork for critical theory and many who have followed have done the same. Empirical work is critical to any project for social change, but this work must itself be critical in nature. This does not mean a return to positivistic "fetishizing" of statistical methods and neutrality. Instead it involves a new vision of educational research underwritten by a commitment to tying together theory and practice, communicating positionality, emphasizing results over methods, and linking research to material circumstances and relevant policy. More than anything it involves a movement from the cataloging of what is to the struggle to define what can be.

The Attack on Teachers, Teaching, and Unions Another area where critical theory can play a profound role is in teacher education, on-the-job training, and pedagogical practice. Freire (1998b) believed teaching necessarily entailed taking a position: "It seems fundamental to me to clarify in the beginning that a neutral, uncommitted, and apolitical educational practice does not exist" (p. 39). With Freire, we witness the emergence of a more radical educational project—dedicated to positive social transformation. In his grand opus *Pedagogy of the Oppressed* (1970), Freire inaugurated a movement that has spread across the globe in ways he could never have imagined. In Africa and the rest of the Americas, he has come to embody a popular form of revolt against the great imperialist and capitalist oppressors. Even in the United States, a coterie of theorists who have labeled themselves critical pedagogues have started a movement to reinvigorate education with transformative and emancipatory messages.

In *Pedagogy of the Oppressed* and his subsequent books, Freire (1970) attacks the traditional learning environment where authoritarian teachers implant knowledge into passive, subjugated students, aptly labeling this approach "banking education." Instead, Freire advocates "problem-posing education" where teachers and students dialogue in an attempt to address the "unfinishedness" of students and bring them to a sense of their own surrounding reality and their agency as subject in history:

> In order for the oppressed to be able to wage the struggle for their liberation, they must perceive the reality of oppression not as a closed world from which there is no exit, but as a limiting situation which they can transform. (p. 49)

Freire believes education can serve as a transformative institution that helps the oppressed first recognize their dehumanized state, move toward *critical consciousness*, and then use this newly discovered knowledge to transform it. Freire thus becomes the first philosopher of education to focus his attention on class and race and on

those citizens most aversely affected by capitalism and its underlying logic. Unlike Lenin and Trotsky, however, Freire sees education as the key vehicle moving the exploited to critical consciousness of their situation and the immutable contradiction of capital and labor. While he later tempered his adherence to the Marxist project of communist revolution, instead embracing radical democracy,[7] he continued to struggle throughout his career for a more humane society that eliminated the subjugation of the majority for the interests of the few:

> Concern for humanization leads at once to the recognition of dehumanization, not only as an ontological possibility but as an historical reality ... But while both humanization and dehumanization are real alternatives, only the first is the people's vocation. This vocation is constantly negated, yet it is affirmed by that very negation. It is thwarted by injustice, exploitation, oppression, and the violence of the oppressors; it is affirmed by the yearning of the oppressed for freedom and justice, and by their struggle to recover their lost humanity. (Freire, 1970, pp. 43–44)

For Freire, as for Dewey, Rousseau, and Wollstonecraft, the road to the good society is paved with the educational imperative. As the most radical of educational theorists, Freire envisioned the potential of education to transform our consciousness and, in the process, society. But he never believed this to be a foregone conclusion. All education could do was offer an environment most conducive to emancipation—it would still be up to individuals working collectively to change the world for the better.

In actualizing these insights in the classroom, Freire argues for great vigilance in recognizing that teaching is not exhausted by the transmission of knowledge—whether it be hegemonic or counter-hegemonic in nature. Teachers must respect the knowledge that students bring into the classroom, constantly question their own assumptions and techniques and work to embrace cultural and ideological differences toward opening rather than closing the student's mind. The progressive teacher must build on our collective "unfinishedness," showing students the profound power of social conditioning while respecting their autonomy and creative impulse to look at the world in ways different than progressives might find appropriate. This is fortified by the power of hope and joy to embolden students to become excited about education, knowledge, and political action. Progressive educators can then spread hope by embodying it themselves, ensuring that their practice is self-confident, competent, generous, committed, humble, dialogical, two-sided, caring, and able to effectively balance freedom and authority. This last aspect is among the most crucial, as Freire does not believe in a classroom absent of authority or in one based solely on informing students of the "truth," but instead one where freedom is tempered by responsibility, growth, and recognition of the interconnectivity of all life:

> If in fact the dream that inspires us is democratic and grounded in solidarity, it will not be by talking to others

from on high as if we were inventors of the truth that we will learn to speak with them. Only the person who listens patiently and critically is able to speak *with* the other, even if at times it should be necessary to speak *to* him or her. Even when, of necessity, she/he must speak against ideas and convictions of the other person, it is still possible to speak as if the other were a subject who is being invited to listen critically and not an object submerged by an avalanche of unfeeling, abstract words. (Freire, 1998a, pp. 110–111)

To ignite hope in students, Freire believed we must consider teaching as an act of love. Teachers must be passionate about their work and bring a love of their students and learning into the classroom every day. Antonia Darder (2002) in fact advocates a pedagogy of love as essential to combating the racism, sexism, and class inequality that continue to plague our schools and larger society.[8] She follows Freire in arguing that authentic dialogue, in fact, requires love of the world and its citizens. The love not only connects teachers to their students, but provides the strength, faith, and humility necessary to establish solidarity and collective struggle to transform the oppressive ideologies and practices of public education. Only through love and solidarity can teachers realize and transmit the spirit of liberatory education, founded on the fervent belief that hope represents an "ontological requirement for human beings" (Freire, 1997, p. 44).

Freire also offered a profound critique of neoliberalism and its exodus from hope (Freire, 1998a). At the heart of the paradigm is the notion that teachers, teaching, and teachers' unions are one of the greatest barriers to global prosperity. As Lois Weiner has pointed out, a World Bank (2003) draft report, *World Development Report 2004: Making Services Work for Poor People*, makes this claim explicit, arguing that "unions, especially teachers union, are one of the greatest threats to global prosperity" and that unions have "captured governments holding poor people hostage to demands for more pay" (as cited in Compton & Weiner, 2008, p. 68). The report suggest that teachers should be fired in large numbers if they strike or refuse reduced pay, and that governments should implement a policy of privatizing services, charging user fees (essentially parents pay to send their children to school), devolving control of schools to neighborhoods and greatly reducing public funding for schools at all levels. Many of these policies have been implemented across Latin America and beyond, often by making loans and aid contingent on these economic restructuring plans. In Argentina, Torres and Puiggros (1997) have argued that these policies have caused great harm to students from the poorer strata of society.

The move to attack teachers and teacher unions relates to the underlying logic of neoliberalism and its project of market liberation—essentially transforming schools to serve as the primary institution of sorting and training in the economy. This explains the overall neoliberal model of education, which really entails deskilling teachers, focusing instruction on tests and specific knowledge, using outside experts and funding to ensure business interests trump all

others in the school, and pushing outside the United States to weaken or abolish teachers unions (Apple, 2004; Kozol, 2005). In the United States, ex-Secretary of Education Rod Paige went as far as calling the National Education Association (NEA) a "terrorist organization" (King, 2004, ¶ 1).

At a deeper level, it can be argued that the neoliberal agenda attacks schools as ideological institutions that could challenge the discourses and rationality behind neoliberalism itself (Compton & Weiner, 2008). If this claim is true, it would explain the move to weaken the power of teachers and establish teacher-proof curriculum, to call for neutrality and apolitical classrooms all the way through to the university (á la David Horowitz's Academic Bill of Rights movement in the U.S.) and to standardize curriculum and use high-stakes testing to all but erase time for education outside its vocational and job training aspects (Berliner & Nichols, 2007). By undermining teacher autonomy and authority, neoliberal advocates ensure that education serves the needs of global competition and segmented labor needs in different countries and among different classes within a country. Luke and Luke (2000) describe two fundamental shifts in pedagogy resulting from the ongoing neoliberal educational reforms:

> To refocus on teachers and teaching, what is most interesting are not the most overt aspects of such reforms—the change in systems-level administration and school management to fit mercantile practices and new age metaphors—but rather the ways in which teaching has increasingly been appropriated both by curriculum and instructional commodities and the extent to which teachers have moved toward consumer-like behavior. (p. 1430)

This is accompanied by attempts to undermine the political power of unions in general and teachers in the classroom, by disavowing the relationship between politics and education and advocating objectivity and neutrality across the curriculum. Freire (1998b) once warned, "washing one's hands of the conflict between the powerful and the powerless means to side with the powerful, not to be neutral" (p. 102). Yet politics is always implicated in education, and education always serves political causes. Teaching means taking a position in the world, as Freire (1970, 1998a) repeatedly argued, and can serve the cause of democracy and social change only if it implicitly engages with political questions relevant to those oppressed, disenfranchised, or otherwise disadvantaged by the social and political order. Education defines the content and breadth of official knowledge, what perspectives frame that knowledge and whose voices are included and excluded in learning. In attempting to remain neutral and balanced, teachers effectively take the hegemonic position of maintaining the status quo, by failing to offer students alternative perspectives and knowledge claims that can broaden their understanding and offer critical tools to engage with the world and redefine it. This is particularly so when teachers do not listen carefully to their students, do not understand their private and public codes, and do not analyze with them their lifeworld narratives.

The extrication of politics from education thus serves to undermine efforts at social transformation, providing a cynical view of learning that undermines its more radical potential. bell hooks (1994), for example, argued for education as "the practice of freedom" and Freire and his followers for a liberatory education. Neoliberalism undermines education in this vein, replacing hope, freedom, and emancipation with a proscribed notion of education that closes, rather than opens, the mind.

The educational system in the United States and across much of the globe stands in jeopardy of doing just that by attempting to eradicate politics and real critical thinking from the classroom at all levels and by ensuring inequalities along the lines of gender, race, nationality, and class continue to persist and grow. Jonathon Kozol outlined in *Savage Inequality* (1991) and the more recent *The Shame of the Nation* (2005), that class and race still define the access and opportunity available to students—undermining a central promise of democracy and freedom (see also Anyon, 1980; Bowles & Gintis, 1976, 2002; Oakes, 1985). Outside the United States, these trends are only amplified in many cases. By disavowing the connection between education and politics, neoliberal advocates dismantle the role education can play in awakening students to their surroundings and allowing them to critically engage with that world. Rather, the new paradigm assumes ideas are dangerous and works to protect students from any knowledge that might challenge the current order of things.

Critical theory becomes useful in deconstructing the underlying politics of neoliberal reforms and breaks through the call for accountability and increased efficiency to analyze who benefits and who is hurt by these changes, and what power and institutional relationships are implemented in these actions. We conclude our educational policy analysis looking at No Child Left Behind and its largely neoliberal model of educational reform.

Critique: Identify Flaws and Contradictions in Policy Making If we ask the question of the possible connection between power, domination, and education, we must begin to question the predominant notion of instrumental rationality, pervasive in the federal and state governments and in academia. In this section, we analyze the No Child Left Behind Act (NCLB) and its underlying rationality within the critical theory tradition. We essentially follow the arguments from above, believing NCLB largely fits within the neoliberal attempt to redefine schooling as serving the needs of the market and thus dedicated primarily to training and sorting.

NCLB also attempts to move control over curriculum and instructional issues away from teachers, classrooms, schools, and local districts where it should be, and puts it in the hands of state and federal educational bureaucracies and politicians, representing the single biggest assault on local control of schools in the history of federal education policy (Ovando, 2004). At the same time, it includes provisions that try to push prayer, military recruiters, and homophobia into schools while pushing multiculturalism, teacher innovation, and creative curriculum out.[9]

While there have been many voices of dissent in school districts and state departments of education struggling to comply with the letter and the spirit of the law, we will argue that even the spirit of the law, based on the notion of accountability, should be carefully inspected and criticized. Technocrats and bureaucrats take for granted that accountability is one of those terms that cannot be challenged because accountability refers to the process of holding actors responsible for their actions. Nevertheless:

> Operationalizing such an open-ended concept is fraught with complications, starting with the politically and technically contested issue of assessing performance. Even if the measurement problem were solved, the factors explaining the process have received remarkably little research attention. For example, although political science has sought broad generalizations to explain wars, treaties, military coups, legislation, electoral behavior, and transitions to democracy, it has not produced empirically grounded conceptual frameworks that can explain how public accountability is constructed across diverse institutions. (Fox & Brown, 1998, p. 12)

Valencia, Valenzuela, Sloan, and Foley (2001) make a similar point, arguing that the push toward accountability has tended to hurt not help students of color. They argue for a more sensible system that measures inputs, processes, and outcomes—rather than just focusing on the last. This provides further information for policy makers in considering and combating educational inequalities and achievement gaps and for teachers and administrators to improve pedagogy, curriculum, and local school organization.

We believe No Child Left Behind largely follows the neoliberal educational reforms that have spread across the globe in the last 25 years. These include a push toward standardization, professionalism, testing/accountability regimes, and the decentralization and privatization of education (Macedo, Dendrinos, & Gounari, 2003). While NCLB clearly works against decentralization, George W. Bush and many other conservatives continue to push for privatization and school choice, and essentially achieve it to some degree with NCLB, in that it appears many schools will fail under the strict testing targets and thus free parents to choose alternative educational options.[10] NCLB also continues the trend of deskilling and disempowering teachers, by enforcing a de facto curriculum focused predominantly on passing tests—particularly for poor and workin-class schools where meeting mandated thresholds is more difficult (Torres, 2005). And it further instrumentalizes knowledge by taking it outside its broader context, making it a series of barely related facts and formulas and treating learning solely as a means to an end (for both teachers and students).

NCLB thus creates a condition in which the federal government diminished the educational autonomy of the states (Debray, 2003). It claims to raise standards while defining what those standards are and what quality of education is or ought to be—primarily a mechanism to ensure the economic competitiveness and prosperity of the larger society. It is also cloaked in the movement toward professionalism of education. This involves attempts to replace teacher autonomy with outside experts, often from the business community, who work to "improve" the efficiency and effectiveness of schools—often by implementing business models of success that ignore the nature of education as a public good (Apple, 2001). Professionalism is predicated on the belief that specialization is implicitly positive, even if it means neglecting the cultural, class, and racial/ethnic specificity of schools and students and the ability of teachers to creatively construct the classroom experience around the specific needs of their students. The result is more uniform curriculum and teaching methods that parse the ability to address the particularity of student populations. Berliner makes this very case using empirical research to argue against government policy of high stake testing because they do not work at improving teaching and learning and tend to corrupt and deskill the teaching profession (Berliner & Biddle, 1995; Berliner & Nichols, 2007).

bell hooks argued in *Teaching to Transgress* (1994) that "the classroom remains the most radical space of possibility in the academy ... undermined by teachers and students alike who seek to use it as a platform for opportunistic concerns rather than as a place to learn" (p. 12). Freire, Giroux, and a host of others have argued for a similar potential in K-12 and beyond, seeing schooling and education more generally as an opening for a revaluation of values. Neoliberal reforms undermine this dream, altering the nature of schooling to predominantly serve the role of training. Lost is the more holistic notion of education that involves the formation of good citizens that will contribute not only to the economy but the public good (Apple, 2001; Dewey, 1916; Giroux, 2003) Weakened is the notion that schools can create more tolerant and socially able adults that are well-adjusted and prepared to deal with their familial and social responsibilities. Largely disabled are efforts to cultivate the imagination, to critically engage with the world and see it in diverse ways and to teach students the rudiments of democratic participation and civic engagement. And disavowed are efforts for education to serve the project of social transformation.

The deskilling of teachers disables their ability to empower and inspire students from diverse backgrounds and to serve as progenitors of individual and social transformation (Berliner & Nichols, 2007). Teachers have been stripped of their relative autonomy in the classroom and forced to comply with standards, tests, and pedagogical methods that they often recognize as disadvantageous to their own students and the larger society. Schools are set up as competitive environments where individual achievement is paramount, losing touch with social development and the rudiments of active citizenry, which involves balancing individual wants with the common good. Also lost are arts, physical education, and other facets of education that fall outside the new mandates.

Teachers become mere service workers that deliver highly scripted and prefabricated content to their "consumers," or students. As Apple (1998, 2001) argues, school curricula under the auspices of efficiency, cost effectiveness, and accountability have become increasingly controlled, limiting the ability of teachers to engage students with relevant or interesting content. The uniformity ignores cultural difference and specificity in deference to uniformity and sculpting content to the tests that will largely determine future economic prospects. These tests, like the curriculum, are often normed to White, middle-class students, thus disadvantaging students of color and working-class students and ensuring that content rarely relates to their lived experiences.

This may be the most important change in curriculum and pedagogy associated with the neoliberal movement in education, with the higher level of prescription of teachers' activities in the classroom and an emphasis on monitoring performance undermining the very professionals once entrusted with the social, political, and economic development of the nation's children.[11] This often involves textbooks and curriculum that define the specter of acceptable "official knowledge," with elected officials, business leaders, parents, professors, and increasingly, publishers in the academic market defining what knowledge is appropriate and acceptable.[12] Adoption programs at the state level are awash in political battles that limit the types of knowledge available to students and publishers increasingly elide content that might make it hard to sell the books to broader audiences unwilling to accept progressive themes or ideas or even broach topics like racism, abortion, sex education, or most obviously, evolution without alternative theories. As a result, new curriculum like Open Court are developed, that constrain teachers' autonomy and essentially script large portions of the school day.

Many will probably argue that Realpolitiks calls for an understanding of systemic issues and the need of solving pressing institutional needs through practical or pragmatic solutions. While recognizing the importance of those practical needs, the logic underpinning the rationales for policy formation, or the legal constraints of policymaking and institutional negotiation, there is no reason to base all policy on economic rationality that ignores centuries of humanistic education, pedagogical research, or alternative models and critical perspectives. Or perhaps one simply may ask why a reform like NCLB ignores vast amounts of contemporary scientific research which shows the difficulties of implementing its measures, and the pitfalls and dangers of those measures if implemented (Berliner & Biddle, 1995; Berliner & Nichols, 2007).

The complexities of NCLB call for a more reflexive and critical understanding of contemporary schooling in the U.S. While criticizing social reproduction, critical educators have been struggling to promote equity and equality in schools, alongside achieving a quality education. To this end, critical educators believe that better research findings, more consistent policy, better school management, teacher training, curriculum and instruction theories, and textbooks make a difference. To critically examine the foundations, instruments, methods, and policy orientation of NCLB and its implementation makes a lot of pedagogical and political sense. Yet, there are other pressing questions of a greater order that we cannot ignore.

Even if NCLB were to succeed in its implementation and premises, what difference do better schools—as defined by NCLB—make for the betterment of our society if the overall orientation of the U.S. government is to achieve global hegemony through the use of brutal force (disguised through new military euphemisms like "smart bombs"), and acting as a world policeman in neo-imperialist fashion, exporting democracy through carpet bombing in Iraq? What difference do schools make in educating students if they will eventually become the new centurions of neoconservative foreign policy? What difference do schools make in the education of people of color, if they will become "green card Marines" in the imperial army or among the increasing corps of the unemployed? What difference do schools make in promoting social mobility if there are no jobs for the graduates after most of the best jobs have been outsourced out of the local markets and into a globalized market, benefiting the surplus value of globalized corporations (Burbules & Torres, 2000)? What difference do schools make in promoting multicultural traditions if, as many scholars have argued, there is only one dominant, hegemonic culture in capitalism, and that is the commodification of labor and knowledge and the culture of class (Jacoby, 1994; McCarthy, 1997; Torres, 1998)? What difference do schools make if, as some scholars have argued, they represent the broken promises of public education and the American dream of equal opportunity (Dimitriadis & Carlson, 2003)? What difference do schools make if—under the burden of heavy school districts and union bureaucracies, in rundown buildings, managed by self-serving politicians, stuffed by technocratic curriculum, demoralized administrators and teachers, and tested-to-death, disenfranchised students, with overworked and underpaid parents, and assailed by the world of business as another site for-profit taking—they have abandoned the key tenets of reason and utopia, betraying the principles of the Enlightenment?

What difference schools make is the question that educational research concerned with the interactions between education and domination should be continuously asking. To be able to ask good questions is a prerequisite to finding good answers.

Challenges of Critical Theory in Educational Research

Two main challenges undermine efforts to institute critical social theory in policy reform efforts and the research and practice of education. The first is a strong technocracy that is firmly established in K-12, universities, and funding institutions. This is coupled with the move toward professionalism in education, replacing teacher and professor autonomy with strong influence among outside consultants and administrators who believe in the business models of governance, management, and training. These changes are associated with the neoliberal goal of shrinking the state and subjecting the sources of knowledge to market competition and dictates. Privatization policies are crucial elements of the reforms oriented toward promoting open markets and reducing public expenditures on education.

It also serves as a powerful tool for depoliticizing the regulatory practices of the state in the public policy and depoliticizing teaching and learning in the classroom, as business interests elide more holistic notions of schooling. The implications of growing privatization and the push for market policies in the public realm thus have serious potential ramifications:

> In the context of the market forces, the state's interventionist role is likely to decline. This will have implications for all categories of people who, by virtue of their already weak position in spheres of knowledge, skills, access to goods and services and control over resources, need some protective legislations and provisions. Left to themselves in the open market, their situation is likely to get further deteriorated. (Kaur, 1999, p. 126)

Privatization policies are generally preferred even if the outcomes are unclear—as, for example, with vouchers. In August 2000, in the midst of the U.S. presidential debate, a Harvard professor and vouchers advocate, Paul E. Peterson, released a study of voucher programs in New York, Dayton, Ohio, and Washington, DC. His analysis, based on randomized field trails, appeared to demonstrate that vouchers significantly improved test scores of African American students. The work of Peterson and associates gained immediate national prominence in the presidential race, with then presidential candidates Bush supporting vouchers and Gore opposing them. Conservative editorial writers and columnists seized on the occasion to show how out of touch Gore was on pressing educational matters, arguing that the facts were clear and persuasive. Yet three weeks after those findings were first reported, Mathematica, a Princeton-based research firm and partner in the study, issued a sharp dissent, questioning the implications of the findings, considering them quite provisional—even as they noted it was probably already too late to impact public opinion (Winerip, 2003).

More recently, Alan Krueger, a Princeton University economist with access to the full database made available by Mathematica, reanalyzed the data showing that the results reported came from only one of the five grades studied in New York (Krueger & Zhu, 2004). This was also Mathematica's emphasis in questioning the findings released by Peterson. Moreover, by reanalyzing the way race was defined in the original analysis of the data—including the race of the father rather than only of the mother—Krueger was able to expand the total sample size of African Americans from 519 to 811. Considering this new sample, one could infer that vouchers appear to have made no difference for any group. Clearly, as Hank Levin indicated years ago, data is a political prisoner of governments, and we would add, of political ideologies as well (Levin, 2001).

The problem then lies in combating the ability of data and research manipulation to dominate the public debate on key issues and undermine broader concerns. Another example is a recent article in the *New York Times Magazine* on Kipp schools that follows much contemporary mainstream discourse in essentially placing the blame for achievement gaps between White and minority students on the students, their families, and their communities (Tough, 2006). This article and others, including, for example, the Thernstrom books (Glazer, 2003), base themselves on deficit theories that ignore larger structural issues and institutional barriers to learning for students of color (Valencia, 1997).

Apple (2001) has pointed out the ways in which a loose confederation of neoliberals, neoconservatives, authoritarian populists, and the professional and managerial new middle class have collectively worked to implement neoliberal and, in many cases, more conservative educational reforms that tend to reflect the trends we have discussed throughout this chapter, in a general sense attacking egalitarian norms and values and depoliticizing education. It also includes the concomitant trends toward disempowering and deskilling teachers and undermining the transformative potential of schooling envisioned by radical theorists like Plato, Rousseau, Dewey, and Freire.

A second related challenge in the current environment is how to break the stranglehold of positivism on practice and research in education. Positivism demands an objective, neutral research agenda that extricates ethical concerns and subjectivity from research and politics from the classroom. These notions have strong currency in America today among policy makers, practitioners, and parents. The belief that these goals are both normatively superior and possible are firmly ensconced in the popular consciousness and it will be a slow process to convince the public that politics and education are implicitly tied, particularly when most of the preeminent schools of education (e.g., Harvard, Stanford, Columbia) advocate positivistic empirical research as the only valid form of inquiry.

Overcoming this rationale involves engaging in the public sphere to alter the nature of the debate and reestablish the broader goals of education. Parents are obviously interested in their children's future, and the notion that education can serve the common good must be backed by the belief that the two goals are largely consonant. Once again, the contributions of Freire may resonate with unusual force here. Freire addresses a serious dilemma of democracy and the constitution of a democratic citizenship, arguing that domination, aggression, and violence are intrinsic part of human and social life. He thus argued that few human encounters are exempt from one form of oppression or another—by virtue of race, ethnicity, class, or gender—and that most people tend to be victims and/or perpetrators of oppression. For Freire, sexism, racism, and class exploitation were the most salient forms of domination, yet exploitation and domination exist along other grounds as well including religious beliefs, political affiliation, national origin and language, age, size, and physical and intellectual abilities to name just a few. The challenge then becomes finding ways to combat and transcend the barriers that keep groups apart and find mechanisms for coalition building, border crossing and solidarity in diversity.

Starting from a psychology of oppression, influenced by psychoanalytical theorists like Freud, Jung, Adler, Fanon, and Fromm, Freire developed his "pedagogy of the oppressed." With the spirit of the Enlightenment, he believed in education as a means to improve the human condition, confronting the effects of a psychology and sociology of oppression, contributing ultimately to what Freire considered the ontological vocation of the human race: humanization. This work could be instrumental in dialogue with other efforts to address prejudice and oppression in all its multivariate forms and work to bring people back together as a collective that can work in solidarity for social transformation.

Conclusion

Critical theory offers valuable tools in the policy arena, bringing together sound empirical research with ethical concerns and a project for social transformation. It allows for a challenge to the logic of neoliberal reforms, to the deskilling and disempowering of teachers and unions, to the shortcomings of No Child Left Behind and high-stakes testing, and offers avenues to a more critical educational research. We have argued that educational research cannot be easily separated from moral commitments, and that critical scholars cannot be mere witnesses to the truth, but must strive to actualize, and make sure that the "truth," as a social construction and as a set of ethical imperatives, can be implemented dialogically in classrooms and communities. We must also make sure that teaching and learning, which requires a fair amount of humbleness and wisdom from teachers, professors and researchers, will be done with careful consideration and respect for the notion of otherness and the need for constant border crossing of lines of difference. This political project can only be accomplished with the passion that the struggle for social transformation can spark.

To those who are burned out by the failures of the past, who find themselves skeptical of the possibility of change, who feel asphyxiated by bureaucratic structures or the cynical actions of the power elites, or who have adopted a commodious, though self-destructive, cynical perspective, we say go back to the sources of inspiration and hope. Many of these lie within the critical social theory tradition, actualized in research and practice in classrooms across the globe. There are many out there. Some are anonymous, practicing like butterflies in the quotidian world, but constantly renewing the beauty of educational landscapes. Some are well known and have served as source of inspiration for educational change for centuries. We would like to conclude this chapter with the voice of one of those sources who has been so influential in our own lives and struggles, Paulo Reglus Neves Freire. In the introduction to his highly acclaimed *Pedagogy of the Oppressed*, Freire (1970) states what we consider to be the central ethical and political ethos of critical theory; the one most able to inspire our dreams and tame our fears: "From these pages I hope it is clear my trust in the people, my faith in men and women, and my faith in the creation of a world in which it will be easier to love" (p. 19).

Notes

1. The reader who believes that philosophy has no role in education should skip this section. Those who believe, on the other hand, that we cannot develop a set of critical arguments without a solid epistemology, gnoseology, and even metaphysics, should read this segment with the appropriate devotion and critical gaze.

2. There is no question that there are as many interpretations of Marxist contributions to the analysis of power and domination as there are Marxist schools of thought. A systematic research article with an analytical and quite complete survey of Marxist schools in the last 100 years is Javier Amadeo, "Mapeando el Marxismo," CLACSO, virtual library, Buenos Aires, Argentina, 2007. Also see Atilio Boron, who in his inimitable style and erudition, has provided us in his inaugural teachings in the course on CLACSO, virtual teaching, 2007, with a fundamental piece of analysis on the origin and destiny of the Marxist discourse and theory in Latin America, "Clase inaugural: Por el necesario (y demorado) retorno al marxismo."

3. The great refusal, as embodied for example in art, offers ways to step outside the dominant discourse and rationality and engage alternative ways of seeing and being in the world. Marcuse saw art as having a strong counterhegemonic potential, because of its ability to escape the prison house of ideology and language.

4. See the arguments of one of the authors of this article in defense of a political sociology of education in Torres (1999).

5. See Tough (2006).

6. In this way we can reengage praxis, or the unity of theory and practice, toward research that seeks to find deeper structural phenomenon and power relations and offer movement toward critical consciousness and real avenues for change. At the same time, we should not use this as a call to reject all other research, or become strictly anti-positivist in the critical theory tradition. Instead, we should heed the advice of Morrow and Torres (2002a), who opine, "a critical theory of methodology, we would argue, is reflexively pluralist but not relativist because there are both situational (pragmatic) and universalizing criteria for assessing and evaluating research traditions and specific research practices" (p. 54).

7. In his final book, *Pedagogy of Freedom*, Freire (1998a) offered a trenchant critique of neoliberalism and its end of history proclamations (see Fukuyama, 1992, for the first popular articulation of the theory of liberal democracy and capitalism as the final stage of human evolution and the highest form of social organization).

8. Some might argue that a pedagogy of love fits too closely with attempts by the right to bring religion back into school. We believe Darder's work is clear in its incantation of love in a way that enriches the learning environment by embracing difference, nurturing children, and providing them with a safe place for learning and coming-to-voice. bell hooks has made similar claims.

9. See http://www.rethinkingschools.org/special_reports/bushplan/hoax.shtml

10. Some have also posited that NCLB is set up to fail and thus open the door to more popular support for vouchers and the dismantling of public education in a broader sense.

11. Teaching as a profession is different than the critique we made earlier of professionalism in schools, which relates to outside experts that undermine the ability of teachers to move beyond a merely technical trade to engage as professionals in educating students.

12. This has been discussed by Apple, in his books *Ideology and Curriculum* (2004), *Teachers and Text* (1986), and *Official Knowledge* (1993).

References

Adorno, T. W., & Horkheimer, M. (2002). *Dialectic of enlightenment* (J. Cumming, Trans.). New York: Continuum. (Original work published 1947)

Anderson, G. (1989). Critical ethnography in education: Origins, current status, and new directions. *Review of Educational Research, 59*, 249–270.

Anyon, J. (1980). Social class and the hidden curriculum of work. *Journal of Education, 162*(1), 67–92.

Apple, M. (1971). The hidden curriculum and the nature of conflict. *Interchange, 2*(4), 27–40.

Apple, M. (1986). *Teachers and text: A political economy of class and gender relations in education.* New York: Routledge.

Apple, M. (1993). *Official knowledge: Democratic education in a conservative age* (2nd ed.). New York: Routledge.

Apple, M. (1998). *Teaching and texts: A political economy of class and gender relations in education.* New York: Routledge.

Apple, M. (2001). *Educating the right way: Markets, standards, God, and inequality.* New York: Routledge Falmer.

Apple, M. (2004). *Ideology and curriculum* (3rd ed.). New York: RoutledgeFalmer.

Aronowitz, S. (2000). *The knowledge factory: Dismantling the corporate university and creating true higher learning.* Boston: Beacon Press.

Bell, D. (1960). *The end of ideology: On the exhaustion of political ideas in the fifties.* New York: Free Press.

Benhabib, S. (2006). *Another cosmopolitanism.* Oxford, UK: Oxford University Press.

Berliner, D. C., & Biddle, B. J. (1995). *The manufactured crisis: Myths, fraud and the attack on America's public schools.* Reading, MA: Addison-Wesley.

Berliner, D. C., & Nichols, S. L. (2007). *Collateral damage: How high stakes testing corrupts America's schools.* Cambridge, MA: Harvard Educational Press.

Bowles, S., & Gintis, H. (1976). *Schooling in capitalist America: Educational reform and the contradictions of economic life.* New York: Basic Books.

Bowles, S., & Gintis, H. (2002). Schooling in capitalist America revisited. *Sociology of Education, 75*, 1–18.

Burbules, N., & Torres, C. A. (Eds.). (2000). *Globalization and education: Critical perspectives.* New York: Routledge.

Butler, J., & Mouffe, C. (1997). The uses of equality. *Diacritics, 27*(1), 3–12.

Butler, J., & Scott, J. W. (Eds.). (1992). *Feminists theorize the political.* New York: Routledge.

Carspection, P. F. (1995). *Critical ethnography in educational research: A theoretical and practical guide.* New York: Routledge.

Compton, M., & Weiner, L. (2008). *The global assault on teaching, teachers, and their unions: Stories for resistance.* New York: Palgrave MacMillan.

Darder, A. (2002). *Reinventing Paulo Freire: A pedagogy of love.* Boulder, CO: Westview Press.

Debray, E. (2003). The federal role in schools accountability: Assessing recent history and the new law. *Voices in Urban Education, 1*, 56–62.

Delgado, R. (1999). *Critical race theory: The cutting edge* (2nd ed.). Philadelphia: Temple University Press.

Dewey, J. (1916). *Democracy and education: An introduction to the philosophy of education.* New York: Macmillan.

Dimitriadis, G., & Carlson, D. (Eds.). (2003). *Promises to keep: Cultural studies, democratic education, and public life.* New York: Routledge Falmer.

Ellsworth, E. (1989). Why doesn't this feel empowering? Working through the repressive myths of critical pedagogy. *Harvard Educational Review, 59*, 297–324.

Foucault, M. (2000). *Power: Essential works of Foucault, 1954–1984, Vol. 3.* New York: New Press.

Fox, J., & Brown, L. D. (Eds.). (1998). *The struggle for accountability: The World Bank, NGOs, and grassroots movements.* Cambridge, MA: MIT Press.

Fraser, N. (1985). What's critical about critical theory? The case of Habermas and gender. *New German Critique, 35*, 97–131.

Fraser, N. (1997). *Justice interruptus: Critical reflections on the "postsocialist" condition.* New York: Routledge.

Freire, P. (1970). *Pedagogy of the oppressed.* New York: Continuum.

Freire, P. (1997). *Pedagogy of the heart.* New York: Continuum.

Freire, P. (1998a). *Pedagogy of freedom.* Lanham, MD: Rowman and Littlefield.

Freire, P. (1998b). *Politics and education.* Los Angeles: UCLA Latin American Center Publications.

Fukuyama, F. (1992). *The end of history and the last man.* London: Penguin Books.

Giroux, H. (1983). *Theory and resistance: A pedagogy for the opposition.* South Hadley, MA: J. F. Bergin.

Giroux, H. (2003). *Public spaces, private lives: Democracy beyond 9/11.* Lanham, MD: Rowman and Littlefield.

Glazer, N. (2003, October 13–20). Will anything work? [Review of the book *No excuses: Closing the racial gap in learning*]. *The New Republic,* p. 383.

Gramsci, A. (1971). *Selections from the prison notebooks.* New York: International Publishers.

Gur-Ze'ev, I. (2005). Feminist critical pedagogy and critical theory today. *Journal of Thought, 40*(2), 55–72.

Habermas, J. (1989). *The structural transformation of the public sphere: An inquiry into a category of bourgeois society* (T. Burger, Trans.). Cambridge, MA: MIT Press. (Original work published 1962)

Habermas, J. (1972). *Knowledge and human interest.* Boston: Beacon Press.

Habermas, J. (1973). *Theory and practice* (J. Viertel, Trans.). Boston: Beacon Press.

Habermas, J. (1984). *The theory of communicative action, Vol. 1: Reason and the rationalization of society* (T. McCarthy, Trans.). Boston: Beacon.

Haraway, D. (2004). Situated knowledges: The science question in feminism and the privilege of partial perspective. In S. Harding (Ed.), *The feminist standpoint theory reader: Intellectual and political controversies* (pp. 81–102). New York: Routledge.

Harding, S. (Ed.) (2004). *The feminist standpoint theory reader: Intellectual and political controversies.* New York: Routledge.

Hargreaves, A. (Ed.). (1997). *Rethinking educational change with heart and mind.* Alexandria, VA: Association of Supervision and Curriculum Development.

Horkheimer, M. (1972). *Critical theory: Selected essays.* (M. J. O'Connell et al., Trans.). New York: Seabury Press.

hooks, b. (1994). *Teaching to transgress: Education as the practice of freedom.* New York: Routledge.

Jacoby, R, (1994) The myth of multiculturalism. *New Left Review, 208,* 121–126.

Jameson, F. (2004). The politics of utopia. *New Left Review, 25,* 35–54.

Kaur, M. (1999). Globalization and women: Some likely consequences. In R. M. Sethi (Ed.), *Globalization, culture and women's development* (pp. 250–274). New Delhi, India: Rawat Publications.

Kellner, D. (1989). *Critical theory, Marxism and modernity.* Baltimore: John Hopkins University Press.

Kellner, D. (2000). Marcuse and the quest for radical subjectivity. In M. Peters, C. Lankshear, & M. Olssen (Eds.), *Critical theory and the human condition: Founders and praxis* (pp. 1–24). New York: Peter Lang.

King, J. (2004, February 23). Paige calls NEA "terrorist organization." Retrieved May 21, 2008, from http://www.cnn.com/2004/EDUCATION/02/23/paige.terrorist.nea/

Kozol, J. (1991). *Savage inequality: Children in America's schools.* New York: Harper Collins.

Kozol, J. (2005). *The shame of the nation: The restoration of apartheid schooling in America.* New York: Three Rivers Press.

Krueger, A., & Zhu, P. (2004). Inefficiency, subsample selection bias, and nonrobustness: A response to Paul E. Peterson and Williwm G Howell. *American Behavioral Scientist, 47,* 718–728.

Laclau, E. (1988). Politics and the limits of modernity. In A. Ross (Ed.), *Universal abandon? The politics of postmodernism* (pp. 63–82). Minneapolis: University of Minnesota Press.

Laclau, E. (1990). *New reflections on the revolution of our time.* New York: Verso.

Lenin, V. (1914). *Karl Marx: A brief biographical sketch with an exposition on Marxism.* Retrieved May 23, 2008, from http://www.gannz.com/ebooks/lenin.pdf

Levin, H. M. (Ed.). (2001). *Privatizing education.* Boulder, CO: Westview Press.

Luke, A. (2004). Teaching after the market: From commodity to cosmopolitan. *Teachers College Record, 106,* 1422–1443.

Luke, A., & Luke, C. (2000). A situated perspective on cultural globalization. In N. C. Burbules & C. A. Torres (Eds.), *Globalization and education: Critical perspectives* (pp. 275–298). New York: Routledge.

Luke, C., & Gore, J. (1992). *Feminisms and critical pedagogy.* New York: Routledge.

Macedo, D., Dendrinos, B., & Gounari, P. (2003). *The hegemony of English.* Boulder, CO: Paradigm Publishers.

Marcuse, H. (1964). *One-dimensional man: Studies in the ideology of advanced industrial society.* Boston: Beacon Press.

Marcuse, H. (1966). *Eros and civilization: A philosophical inquiry into Freud.* Boston: Beacon Press.

Marx, K. (1990). *Capital* (B. Fowkes & D. Fernbach, Trans.; Vol. 1–3). New York: Penguin Books. (Original work published 1867–1894)

Marx, K., & Engels, F. (1998). *The German ideology.* Amherst, NY: Prometheus Books. (Original work published 1932)

McCarthy, C. (1997). *The uses of culture: Education and the limits of ethnic affiliation.* New York: Routledge.

McLuhan, M. (1965). *Understanding media: The extensions of man.* New York: McGraw-Hill.

Morrow, R., & Brown, D. (1994). *Critical theory and methodology.* Thousand Oaks, CA: Sage.

Morrow, R. & Torres, C. A. (2002a). Gramsci and popular education in Latin America: From revolution to democratic transition. In C. Borg, J. Buttigieg, & P. Mayo (Eds.), *Gramsci and education* (pp. 179–200). New York: Rowman and Littlefield,.

Morrow, R., & Torres, C. A. (2002b). *Reading Freire and Habermas: Critical pedagogy and transformative social change.* New York: Teachers College Press.

Noguera, P. (2001). Listen first: How student perspectives on violence can be used to create safer schools. In V. Polakow (Ed.), *The public assault on America's children: Poverty, violence, and juvenile injustice* (pp. 130–156). New York: Teachers College Press.

Oakes, J. (1985). *Keeping track: How schools structure inequality.* New Haven, CT: Yale University Press.

Ovando, C. (2004, February). *Teaching for social justice: A critique of the No Child Left Behind Act.* Paper presented at the California Association of Educators Conference, Los Angeles.

Popper, K. (1992). *Logic of scientific discovery* (Rev. ed.). London: Routledge.

Rhoads, R. (2003). Traversing the great divide: Writing the self into qualitative research and narrative. *Studies in Symbolic Interaction, 26,* 235–259.

Rhoads, R., & Rhoades, G. (2005). Graduate employee unionization as symbol of and challenge to the corporatization of U.S. research universities. *Journal of Higher Education, 76*(3), 243–275.

Rhoads, R., & Valadez, J. (2006). *Democracy, multiculturalism, and the community college: A critical perspective.* New York: Garland.

Smith, S. (1989). *Hegel's critique of liberalism: Rights in context.* Chicago: University of Chicago Press.

Solórzano, D., & Yosso, T. (2004). From racial stereotyping and deficit discourse toward a critical race theory of teacher education. In W. De La Torre, L. Rubalclava, & B. Cabello (Eds.), *Urban education in America: A critical perspective* (pp. 67–81). Dubuque, IA: Kendall/Hunt.

Tierney, G. W., & Rhoads, R. (1993). Postmodernism and critical theory in higher education: Implications for research and practice. In J. C.

Smart (Ed.), *Higher education: Handbook of theory and research* (pp. 308–343). New York: Agathon Press.

Torres, C. A. (1994). Education and the archeology of consciousness: Freire and Hegel. *Educational Theory, 44*, 429–445.

Torres, C. A. (1998). *Democracy, education and multiculturalism: Dilemmas of citizenship in a global world.* Lanham, MD: Rowman and Littlefield.

Torres, C. A. (1999). Critical social theory and political sociology of education: Arguments. In T. J. Popkewitz & L. Fendler (Eds.), *Critical theories in education: Changing terrains of knowledge and politics, Vol. 9* (pp. 87–116). New York: Routledge

Torres, C. A. (2002). Globalization, education and citizenship: Solidarity versus markets? *American Educational Research Journal, 39*(2), 363–378.

Torres, C. A. (2005). The NCLB: A brainchild of neoliberalism and American politics. *New Politics, 10*(2), 94–100.

Torres, C. A. (2009). *Globalizations and education: Collected essays on class, race, gender, and the State.* New York: Columbia University Press.

Torres, C. A., & Puiggros, A. (1997). *Latin American education: Comparative perspectives.* Boulder, CO: Westview Press.

Tough, P. (2006, November 26). What it takes to make a student. *The New York Times Magazine*, p. 44.

Valencia, R. (Ed.). (1997). *The evolution of deficit thinking: Educational thought and practice.* Washington, DC: The Falmer Press.

Valencia, R. (Ed.). (2002). *Chicano school failure and success: Past, present and future.* New York: RoutledgeFalmer.

Valencia, R., Valenzuela, A., Sloan, K., & Foley, D. (2001). Let's treat the cause, not the symptoms: Equity and accountability in Texas schools revisited. *Phi Delta Kappan, 83*, 318–326.

Valenzuela, A. (1999). *Subtractive schooling: U.S.-Mexican youth and politics of caring.* Albany: State University of New York Press.

Weiler, K. (1991). Freire and a feminist pedagogy of difference. *Harvard Educational Review, 61*, 449–474.

Winerip, M. (2003, May 7). What some much-noted data really showed about vouchers. *New York Times*, p. B12.

World Bank. (2003). *World development report 2004: Making services work for poor people.* Washington, DC: Author.

20

Race, Ethnicity, and Education

ROSLYN ARLIN MICKELSON
University of North Carolina at Charlotte

The United States has been an ethnically and racially diverse society since its inception. The mix of people brought together by European colonization of Native American lands, the African slave trade, the annexation of large parts of the Southwest, and centuries of voluntary immigration from all parts of the globe has resulted in a diverse society. Ethnicity and race also have always been markers of inequality in public life in the United States. This fact is especially true in education.

The racial and ethnic diversity of the U.S. student population presents both opportunities and challenges to public education. The richness and diversity of U.S. students' cultural and social backgrounds, the nation's extraordinary resources, and the high priority parents and communities place on education offer significant opportunities to public schools. Arguably, one of the biggest challenges public schools face is persistent racial stratification in educational outcomes. That racial disparities are woven into the fabric of public education is not surprising given the nation's historical legacy of providing racially segregated and unequal public education to its children.

Racially separate and unequal public education was not an accident; it was created by laws and policies enacted and enforced by state governments and local school systems. The nature of the education historically provided to U.S. children has been intimately tied to their race, ethnicity, social class, and their gender. From the establishment of the common school in the 19th century until the middle of the 20th century, racial inequality in educational opportunities was an explicit policy of the state (Mickelson, 2003; Walters, 2001). The epochal *Brown v. Board of Education* (1954) decision challenged the principle undergirding educational stratification, but in practice its legacy survives in many forms.

This chapter examines ethnicity, race, and education in the United States from an institutional perspective. It begins with an examination of the definitions and uses of the concepts of race and ethnicity. Following an overview of the educational history of the major American racial and ethnic groups, the chapter presents a number of indicators that reveal the contours of contemporary race and ethnicity stratification in education. The chapter then reviews a variety of social and behavior science models that seek to account for the disparities in outcomes. It concludes with observations about the policy issues this chapter has raised.

Defining Race and Ethnicity

Race Social scientists generally agree that commonly used racial categories are socially constructed in loose relation to perceived phenotypical differences among humans. The idea that race (and ethnicity) are socially constructed derives from critical race theory (Crenshaw, Gotanda, Peller, & Thomas, 1995; Delgado, 1995; Ladson-Billings, 1999; Omi & Winant, 1994; Tate, 1997). Official racial categories are socially, politically, and historically contingent. For example, the categories used in the 2000 census are: American Indian or Alaskan Native; Asian, Black, or African American; Hispanic or Latino/a; Native Hawaiian or other Pacific Islanders; and White (Snipp, 2003, p. 577). In 1997 a successful political campaign waged by many racial and ethnic minority citizens culminated in new response options that allowed census people, for the first time, to declare on their 2000 census form more than one category as their racial heritage. Permitting people to express a multiracial heritage legitimized a new racial category and broadened the official set of recognized racial groups in the United States (Snipp, 2003).

Ethnicity Ethnicity refers to ancestry and denotes a shared cultural, linguistic, and historical background. Key aspects of ethnicity are shared beliefs among those who identify with a given ethnic group that they descend from common ancestors and share a culture with co-ethnics (Waters, 1990). Like race, ethnicity is socially constructed rather than fixed. A group's history of contact with the United States, the conditions of its incorporation into U.S. society, its relationship to other ethnic groups, and contemporary politics influence the way an ethnic group constructs its identity vis-à-vis other ethnic groups. For example, how certain ethnic groups became White is an ongoing topic of scholarly debate (Allen, 1994). The Irish (Ignatiev, 1995) and Jews (Brodkin, 1998) have become White, but it is not clear whether Iranians are "White." Whether the 40,000 Lumbee of eastern North Carolina are a distinct Native American tribe (entitled to recognition and federal benefits) or members of other tribes remains an unsettled dispute among Lumbee and the federal government (Klug & Whitfield, 2003).

Simply categorizing students into a racial group fails to capture the complexity of their social locations, which are also shaped by their gender, social class, home language, ethnicity, and generation. Panethnic labels such as Asian or Latino/a mask important ethnic distinctions within these larger categories (Lopez & Espiritu, 1990; Rumbaut, 2006). Within each racial category are multiple ethnic groups, each with its own history and relationship to the larger U.S. society. Similarly, members of different racial groups can have a common ethnicity. Issues of measurement error due to response variability and classification error especially by third party observers (such as school officials) further complicate measurement of race/ethnicity (Snipp, 2003, p. 583).

Labels Racial and ethnic self-identity has two complementary aspects: how others identify a person's ethnicity/race and how the person constructs her or his own identity, in part as a reaction to others' behavior. Pollock (2004) describes the phenomenon of race-bending, wherein biracial students strategically identify themselves as one race or another, illustrating the highly fluid and socially constructed nature of their racial identities. A number of scholars report that that Black students construct their ethnic identities by registering and reacting to others' responses to them and then by interpreting and performing their identities (O'Connor, 2001; Sellers & Shelton, 2003; Smalls, White, Chavous, & Sellers, 2007). How students construct their racial identity may also depend on social structural features in the student's environment. Dutton, Singer, and Devlin (1998) and Perry (2002) found that the self-reported racial identity of students varies with their school's racial composition.

Despite the fluid boundaries and socially constructed nature of the concepts of race and ethnicity, this chapter will, nevertheless, utilize the five static labels of Asian, Black, Latino/a, Native American, and White even though they do not capture the concepts' nuances. The use of the labels is necessary in order to position people relative to others in the social and educational landscape that will be covered in this chapter. A second reason for the use of these problematic, static ahistorical labels is that data necessary to discuss race, ethnicity, and education are typically collected in these categories.

Racial and Ethnic Distribution of U.S. Students

The population of U.S. school children is becoming more diverse. The growth of peoples of color as a proportion of the U.S. population has been driven primarily by the recent influx of Latinos/as. Latinos/as were 6% of public school enrollments in 1972, but by 2005 they had grown to over 19% (Dillon, 2007). Previously, minority students were concentrated in the west, southwest, northeast, and the major cities of the midwest. Today, racial and ethnic minority students attend schools in most communities in every state, although the midwest has the fewest minority students of any region (Dillon, 2007).

As Table 20.1 indicates, peoples of color are one third of the U.S. population. The age distribution has important implications for education. Approximately 25% of the overall population is under the age of 18. Black, Latino/a, Native American, and multiracial children are more likely to fall within that age category than are Whites or Asians.

The racial distribution of the student population is somewhat different from the racial distribution in the overall proportion because of the varying proportion of children under 18 in each racial and ethnic group (see Table 20.1). Currently, 57.4% of U.S. school children in kindergarten through 12th grade are White; 19.3% are Latino/a; 16% are Black; 4.1% are Asian; and 3.2% are multiracial and other racial groups (U.S. Census Bureau, 2005).

The Social Context of Racial and Ethnic Educational Stratification

Asians As the name suggests, Asians include people whose ancestry traces back to the Asian continent, the Pacific Rim, the Indian subcontinent, and the Pacific Islands. In 1997 Hawaiian and Pacific Islander were added as ethnic options

TABLE 20.1
Percent of U.S. Population and Percent under 18 by Race/Ethnicity

	Asian	Black	Latino/a	Native American	White	Multiracial
Percent of Population[a]	4.3	12.8	14.0	1.0	67.0	< 2.0
Percent of Race/Ethnic Group under 18	23.0	29.9	33.9	29.9	21.6	45.4

Note: [a]Exceeds 100 percent because of rounding errors.
Source: U.S. Census Bureau, 2005.

to the 2000 census (Snipp, 2003). As of 2005, 14 million Americans identified themselves as Asian, Native Hawaiian, or other Pacific Islander (U.S. Census Bureau, 2005). Asian Americans immigrated to the west coastal states of California, Oregon, and Washington during the 19th and 20th centuries. They were relegated to low-paying jobs (such as building the transcontinental railroad, agricultural labor) and suffered legal, cultural, and social marginalization. The contemporary stereotype of Asians as "model minorities" stands in sharp contrast to the historically hostile treatment of Asian immigrants and citizens during the significant portions of the last two centuries (Takaki, 1993). Emblematic of that distrust and hostility was the 1942 Executive Order 9066 signed by President Franklin Roosevelt imprisoning west coast Japanese families in concentration camps through the end of World War II.

Asian student populations vary by ethnicity, social class, gender, generation, and immigration status, all factors with important implications for school outcomes. Compared to students from other ethnic and racial groups, Asian students from many ethnic backgrounds are highly likely to persist in school and have high levels of attainment. In fact, the remarkable educational accomplishments of many Southeast Asian refugee children prompted Caplan, Choy, and Whitmore (1991) to proclaim that, indeed, the U.S. educational system actually still works.

This "model minority" stereotype masks a more complex reality (Lee, 1996; Lew, 2007). Many Asian students struggle to achieve, and certain ethnic groups and recent immigrants have high dropout and school failure rates. Asian American students face many of the obstacles to school success that other minority students encounter. These may include ethnic hostility from other students and teachers, overcrowded classrooms, and limited English proficiency. The Supreme Court decision recognizing the right to linguistically appropriate education in *Lau v. Nichols* (1974) was brought on behalf of a Chinese American child. Many contemporary Asian immigrant children struggle in school, especially if they have limited English proficiency. Similarly, Native Hawaiian students often struggle in public schools that are not responsive to their culture and language (Kana'iaupuni, 2004). Specific norms among some Asian ethnic groups may pose barriers to academic success. Hmong teenage females may leave school in order to have children because of the centrality of fertility to women's status within the culture (Fadiman, 1998).

Blacks The Black population of the United States was about 38 million in 2005 (U.S. Census Bureau, 2005). Along with descendants of African slaves, the population includes several million Blacks born in the Caribbean, Africa, Latin America, and Western Europe. Educational performance among Blacks varies widely by ethnicity, immigration status, and generation. Historically, Black educational outcomes, such as test scores, have been markedly lower than those of Whites. Since the middle of the 20th century, Black educational achievement and attainment levels have improved on virtually all indicators. Nevertheless, their educational achievement and attainment continue to lag behind Whites and other ethnic and racial groups in the United States. On average, first and second generation foreign-born Blacks tend to perform better and attain more education than native-born Blacks. Black immigrants' academic advantage relative to the native population is similar to patterns seen among Asian and Latino/a immigrants.

At present, the majority of Blacks are urban residents, but growing numbers of middle-class (and increasingly working-class) families are moving to suburbs. Black suburbanization has had a marked effect on urban communities and the children who remain in urban schools. As the middle class moves to the suburbs, once-socioeconomically heterogeneous central city neighborhoods typically become isolated islands of concentrated poverty adjacent to the vibrant financial and commercial centers of major cities. Compared to suburban schools, schools in central cities are less likely to offer high-quality educational opportunities to their students. Central city schools typically are minority segregated, poorly resourced, and have high concentrations of children living in poverty. This constellation of characteristics creates challenges for educators working in these schools and families sending their children to them (Natriello, McDill, & Pallas, 1990; Rumberger & Palardy, 2005). At the same time, the suburbanization of middle-class Black students has not resulted in the anticipated substantial narrowing of race gaps, even among children of educated and prosperous Black parents (Ferguson, 2001; Ogbu, 2003).

Black students' underperformance is historically rooted in absent or unequal education. Most Blacks lived in the South from the 17th century until the early part of the 20th century. During the era of slavery, formal schooling for Blacks was illegal. Literate Blacks tended to live outside the south. The era of Reconstruction brought the opportunity for former slaves to go to school and large numbers of adults and children attend school along with poor and working-class Whites. Following the election of 1876 and the compromise that removed federal troops from the south, schools along with other public accommodations were re-segregated as Jim Crow laws that codified the breadth and depth of the racial oppression that continued well into the next century (Anderson, 1988; Kluger, 1975).

Black parents, educators, and communities responded to resource-starved schools and culturally inappropriate curricula in many ways since Reconstruction (Anderson, 1988; Watkins, 2001). Responses include community actions for self determination (King, 2005; Walker, 1996), homeschooling (Sampson, 2005), Afrocentric education (Lee, Lomotey, & Shujaa, 1991), and Muslim schools (Akom, 2008; Muhammed, 2005). These responses of the Black community share many themes with the struggles waged by other disadvantaged ethnic communities for culturally responsive schooling (Kana'iaupuni, 2004; Klug & Whitfield, 2003; McCarty, 2002; Valenzuela, 1999; Woodrum, 2004).

School segregation is intimately tied to the education

of Black Americans and to racially stratified education more broadly. The *Brown* decision ending de jure racial segregation in public schools also set the stage for the end to formal legal segregation in other domains of public life.[1] It was followed by a series of Supreme Court decisions that eliminated the formal legal foundation of segregated schools (Boger, 2002). Despite the Supreme Court's ruling in *Brown* outlawing state-sanctioned segregation, informal segregation was often encouraged or recreated through racially discriminatory public policies and private practices in housing, transportation, lending for home purchases, and a host of school district decisions.

During the more than 50 years since the *Brown* decision, some regions of the United States have been more successful in desegregating their schools than others. Southern schools remained segregated well into the 1960s and northern schools until the 1970s. Southern and border states eventually experienced the greatest degree of desegregation. In some southern school systems, the percentage of Blacks attending extremely segregated minority schools dropped from 78% in the late 1960s to 25% at its lowest in the mid-1980s (Orfield & Eaton, 1996). Other regions of the country where de facto segregation was the norm also desegregated to a large degree. Importantly, trends in the reduction in Black-White achievement gaps followed the reduction in levels of Black-White segregation (Grissmer, Flanagan, & Williamson, 1998).

By the mid-1980s, the national trend toward greater levels of desegregation stalled and slowly reversed (Clotfelter, 2004; Orfield & Eaton, 1996). By the first decade of the 21st century, levels of resegregation in U.S. public schools approached those of the 1960s (Logan, Oakley, & Stowell, 2008; Orfield & Frankenberg, 2008), although currently levels of segregation appear to be greater between districts than within school systems. In 2007, in twin cases involving voluntary desegregation in Seattle and Louisville (*Parents Involved in Community Schools* [PICS] *v. Seattle School District No. 1*, 2007; *Meredith v. Jefferson County Board of Education*, 2007), a majority of the Supreme Court affirmed the nation's compelling interest in creating an integrated society and avoiding racially isolated schools, but it struck down both plans' use of individual student race in their pupil assignment plans. However, it also held that the Seattle and Louisville race-conscious assignment plans were unconstitutional because they were not sufficiently narrowly tailored to satisfy a compelling state interest in the use of an individual student's race in assignment plans. At the same time, Justice Kennedy's controlling opinion suggested possible race neutral alternatives that a school district could use to promote diversity. These include strategic site selection of new schools, drawing attendance zones with general recognition of neighborhood demographics, allocating resources for special programs, recruiting students and faculty in a targeted fashion, and tracking enrollments, performance, and other statistics by race. Moreover, Kennedy's controlling opinion left the door open (even if only slightly) to the possibility that a school district could constitutionally use racial classifications to remedy de facto segregation if race is only one of several factors that a school board considers in making admissions decisions, although it cannot be the primary criterion for admission.

Latinos/as Although desegregation is commonly associated with the education of Black students, the larger issues raised by the struggle for integrated schools—diversity, opportunity, equity—are not confined to only one racial/ethnic group. In fact, a case involving Latino/a students that ended segregation in an Orange County, California school system set a legal precedent for the Supreme Court's decision declaring all de jure racial segregation unconstitutional in *Brown* in 1954 (Valencia, 2005). *Mendez v. Westminster School District* (1947) was the first case in which a federal court ruled that racial segregation of schooling was unconstitutional. The circumstances of the Mendez family's livelihood reflected a great deal about U.S. society at that time: the Mendez family came to the city of Westminster, California to rent farmland from the Munemitsu family, a Japanese American family sent to an internment camp during World War II (House Congressional Resolution 200, 2003).

The Latino population of the United States is the fastest growing of any group; one in eight Americans is a Latino/a. Latinos/as are relatively young and have high fertility rates. Students of Latino/a origin will enter school systems in the future in greater proportions than most other population (see Table 20.1). Some large city school systems, like the Los Angeles Unified School District, are already majority Latino/a. In 2005, over 41 million Americans of all races identified themselves as Latino/a (U.S. Census Bureau, 2005). The educational achievement of Latino students is, on average, lower than Whites and Asians, similar to Native Americans, and surpasses Blacks. As is true of other ethnic groups, many Latino/a immigrant students perform better than their native-born co-ethnics.

Latinos/as are an ethnically diverse population that includes persons whose ancestry traces to Mexico, Puerto Rico, Cuba, the islands of the Caribbean, as well as Central and South American countries (Garcia, 2001). Sixty-six percent of Latinos/as are of Mexican heritage, 14% are of Central or South American ethnicity, 9% are Puerto Rican, 4% are of Cuban descent, and 7% have other Latino ethnicities (U.S. Census Bureau, 2005). Generational issues, ethnicity, social class, English-language proficiency, and immigration status shape Latino/a educational achievement and attainment processes and outcomes (Matute-Bianchi, 1986, 2008). There is a growing, well-educated, fluent bilingual or monolingual English-speaking Latino/a middle class, whose children perform better in school than their low-income counterparts. But poverty and limited English proficiency characterizes the life of many Latino/a students, especially recent immigrants from Mexico who are likely to attend overcrowded and underfunded inner city schools (Valenzuela, 1999).

The majority of Latinos/as live in the western and southwestern states of California, Nevada, Colorado, Arizona, New Mexico, and Texas, much of which became part of the United States following Mexico's defeat in the Mexican-American War. The 1848 Treaty of Guadalupe Hidalgo guaranteed to former Mexican citizens the rights to their culture, including the use of the Spanish language. Nevertheless, the use of the Spanish language in schools was proscribed in many states in the southwest, Florida, and New York City through the 1960s. Since the 1970s various bilingual education models have been employed across the country with limited English-speaking children, most of who are Spanish-speaking. In recent years, several western and southwestern states (e.g., Arizona, California, and Colorado) have attempted to eliminate bilingual education programs (Garcia, 2005). These political efforts, especially the English-only movement, ignore the issue of what happens when the language of the school shuts out the language of the child's culture (Valenzuela, 1999).

The issues of English language fluency and bilingual education are particularly relevant to Latino educational issues because of the large limited English-proficient population among Latino students. Research indicates that students classified as fluent bilingual speakers surpass monolingual English speakers and limited bilingual speakers on various cognitive tests. Some scholars speculate that fluent bilingualism itself has a positive effect on speakers' cognitive skills, while others posit the likely association between cognitive skills and bilingualism occurs because of the relationship of higher socioeconomic status to both of them (Portes & Rumbaut, 2006).

The nature of the pedagogy, curricula, and social relations of classrooms in which Latinos/as are educated often subtracts, rather than affirms, embraces, and builds upon their community-based language and culture (Valenzuela, 1999). Such schools are formally and informally organized in ways that fracture students' ethnic identities and cultures and undermine their academic success, what Valenzuela (1999) describes as subtractive schooling. These processes, in essence, assimilate students by subtracting from their funds of knowledge (Moll & González, 2001) rather than by accommodating indigenous language and culture by adding the dominant ones to what students already have (Gibson, 1988). Other researchers have identified similar threats to learning for Native Americans (Deyhle, 2008), Native Hawaiians (Kana'iaupuni, 2004), African Americans (King, 2005), and Appalachian Whites (Woodrum, 2004).

Native Americans and Alaskan Natives Almost 4.5 million people identified themselves as Native Americans (American Indians and Alaskan Natives—Inuits and Aluets; U.S. Census Bureau, 2005). The Native American population has been growing during the past half century. Roughly 2 million people are non-Latino Native Americans, although over 7 million Americans identify themselves as having some Native American ancestry. Inuits and Aluets, who live primarily in Alaska, number about 100,000 individu-

als. If language is considered a marker of unique ethnicity, then there are over 200 ethnic groups among Native Americans.

Reservations are home to about one-fifth of the American Indian population. Over 530,000 Native Americans live on 557 reservations and trust lands across 33 states (U.S. Census Bureau, 2004). The majority of tribes suffer from a dearth of fertile land or other exploitable natural resources on the reservations and lack of capital. Reservation residents are relatively uneducated, unskilled, and poor compared to their co-ethnics living off the reservation, or to other racial and ethnic groups. Most reservations have high poverty and unemployment rates due to their relative isolation from the U.S. economic mainstream. Farming, tourism, and recently, casino gambling, are major sources of revenue for residents of reservations.

A small Native American middle class has emerged recently, although most Native Americans are likely to have low incomes, high unemployment, and low educational and occupational attainment whether they live on reservations or in urban areas. Migration to urban areas is difficult for rural people, especially those with low levels of education and occupational skills. Nevertheless, urban American Indians are relatively more prosperous than their counterparts on reservations.

Contemporary educational challenges for Native American students are similar to those of students from other economically marginalized and culturally oppressed racial and ethnic groups. These conditions are exacerbated by the relative isolation and small size of the American Indian population. Native American students have the highest dropout rates of any ethnic group and, while they have achieved gains in outcomes since the 1980s, key indicators show their achievement and attainment levels are lower than most other American racial and ethnic groups (Klug & Whitfield, 2003).

Beginning in 1940, the federal government created the first Bureau of Indian Affairs (BIA) boarding schools. Native American children placed in BIA schools were taught mainstream curricula. Native American languages and cultures were absent from BIA schools. Curricula were designed as a conscious attempt to strip Native American children of their own culture and assimilate them into dominant White one (Crow Dog, 1991). By the middle of the 20th century, opposition to this type of schooling led to the decline of BIA schools and transfer of most Native American children into local public schools where the new curricula included elements of their culture, language, and history. Some Native American communities' struggle for educational self-determination culminated in community-controlled indigenous schools such as the Navajo's Rough Rock Demonstration School (McCarty, 2002). Because there is no pan Native American culture, a culturally responsive education for American Indian children requires specific bicultural curricula and pedagogy that embody both the dominant and Native cultures (Deyhle, 2008; Klug & Whitfield, 2003; Seale & Slapin, 2005).

Whites Almost 200 million Americans identified themselves as Whites (U.S. Census Bureau, 2005). Although the majority of Whites claim one or more European ethnic groups as their heritage, about one-tenth of Whites identify their ethnic group as American. The 11 most common ethnic identities among Whites are German, Irish, English, Italian, French, Polish, Scottish, Scotch-Irish, Dutch, Norwegian, and Swedish. Lieberson and Waters (1986) report that by the third generation, there was a great deal of ethnic intermarriage and Whites began to identify themselves as having multiple European ancestries. Racial boundaries among European ethnics have always been fluid. For instance, Jews and Irish were not always considered Whites (Brodkin, 1998; Ignatiev, 1995).

Historically, public schools were created for Whites but access to public education in colonial times was highly stratified by social class and gender. Tyack and Hansot (1990) note that initially public schools were for boys only. Boys and girls were informally taught to read in their homes, but public schools were part of the male domain. By the early 1800, when America was a nation of small farmers and shopkeepers, most male and female students were not educated beyond the fifth grade. Before 1870, secondary schools offered classical liberal educations to a small number of middle class and elite males.

Trow (1961) identifies two key transformations of the American public education system. The first was its transformation into a mass system of secondary schools. The transformation of public schools after 1870 was a response to the demands of the industrial leaders for white collar workers with educations beyond elementary schools, the imperative to socialize and "Americanize" the millions of European immigrants into a blue collar workforce, and political struggles among the working class and business leaders for access to education among the working classes. The second transformation occurred after World War II when U.S. public education became a mass college preparatory system. Both transformations were driven by rapid increases in demand for workers with certain kinds of education and skill, and by popular demands for greater access to education. By the 20th century, these struggles bore fruit as White women and working-class students gained greater access to higher education.

In general, Whites enjoy relatively greater access to educational resources than other groups and their overall outcomes reflect these advantages. Whites' achievement levels exceed those of other racial and ethnic groups, with the exception of Asian students whose mathematics and science achievement surpasses that of Whites in the later grades. Patterns of achievement among Whites are influenced by students' social class and gender, but with few exceptions, ethnicity no longer influences Whites' educational outcomes as it did in the past. The congruence of mainstream middle-class White culture with the formal curriculum positions middle-class Whites to excel in school. Among Whites, females tend to outperform males in all social classes; in fact, at almost all levels of education middle-class White female students outperforming their working-class and male counterparts.

The schools attended by rural, poor, and working-class Whites have fewer human and material resources than middle-class suburban schools. For example, the educational performance of isolated rural Whites from Appalachia and the Ozarks is markedly lower than the outcomes of urban and suburban Whites. Woodrum (2004) attributes poor student performance among Appalachian students not only to inadequate schools, but also to cultural and economic dissonance between poor families and their public schools. Woodrum observes that much of Appalachia's economic and political history reads like that of an internal colony— isolated both physically and culturally from mainstream America. She reports isolated rural White parents express fears that the values taught in their public schools will diverge from those taught in their home. In this sense, these Appalachian parents share ambivalence toward public education sometimes found among Blacks (Boykin, 1986; Spencer, 1999), Asians (Lee, 1996; Lew, 2007), and Latinos/as (Matute-Bianchi, 1986, 2008).

Bi- and Multiracial Youth The addition of biracial and multiracial categories to the 2000 census did not radically alter the proportion of people who self-identified as Blacks or Whites. Less than 2% of Americans identify themselves as biracial and multiracial (U.S. Census Bureau, 2005), and those who did tend to be from Native Americans, Asians, Pacific Islanders, and Latinos populations (Snipp, 2003). In part because of the newness of the category and in part because of their proportionally small size, school systems typically do not separately report outcome data for their biracial and multiracial students. National sources do not provide sufficient systematic data to allow comparisons of biracial and multiracial students' outcomes with those with other race/ethnicities.

Individual researchers have explored the relationship between biracial identity and school outcomes. Using a national sample, Kao (1999) examined if school outcomes for biracial youth more closely resembled the achievement patterns of their minority or White counterparts. She found that subjective identification with one race or another plays a role in shaping academic performance for Black biracial but not for Asian biracial students. Herman (2009) investigated achievement patterns of 1,492 multiracial students from nine high schools in California and Wisconsin. She found that ethnic identity and experiences of racism were not strong factors in explaining achievement among multiracial *or* monoracial students. Instead, the school achievement of multiracial youth is most clearly related to the racial composition of the contexts in which they live, including peer group, family, neighborhood, and school. Herman (2009) found that achievement patterns among biracial youth are significantly different than those of monoracial Blacks and monoracial Asians, but not significantly different than monoracial Whites or Latinos.

Immigrants Growing numbers of students are immigrants or children of immigrants. How well immigrant students do in school depends on many of the same factors that shape other students' performance as well as a number of circumstances unique to immigrants (Suarez-Orozco & Suarez-Orozco, 2001). Immigrants' personal resources are essential factors that contribute to how successfully they and their children assimilate or whether they become marginalized in U.S. society. But, as Portes and Rumbaut (2006) observe, the social context in which the immigrant enters a country renders individualistic models of assimilation or acculturation insufficient. The different contexts of reception into the United States (generous economic aid from the federal government and networks of co-ethnics, or a hostile political climate) as well as the context of emigration (political refugees or family visa) means some immigrants are formally embraced while others are hounded by the host society. The cases of Cuban and Haitian immigrant students are illustrative: the U.S. government extends special educational privileges to most Cuban American children because of their status as political refugees from a communist state. Haitians, in contrast, are defined as economic refugees and thus do not enjoy these privileges (Schmidt, 2001; Van Hook, 2002). Cuban students also tend to have higher levels of achievement and attainment than Haitians.

English language fluency is closely linked to immigrant students' academic outcomes (Garcia, 2005; Portes & Rumbaut, 2006). According to the 2000 census, 18% of the population spoke a language other than English at home, up from 14% in 1990. Many immigrants speak their native tongue at home and English in public. Time erodes their bilingualism so that 84% of third generation youth are monolingual English speakers. Grandchildren of immigrants typically become linguistic outsiders to their own ancestral heritage (Portes & Rumbaut, 2006, p. 208).

Immigrants' class of origin is also a key factor in their subjective and objective well-being and their children's performance in school. Immigrant parents with high levels of education and technical skill provide their children with cultural, human, social, and financial resources to which the children of poorly educated, low-skilled, immigrant parents do not have access. For example, poorly educated low-income immigrant parents may hold pro-school values and high expectations for their children's educational attainment. But if their children attend poor quality public schools they are likely to be exposed to youth cultural norms and behaviors that are inimical to educational success and social mobility (Portes & Rumbaut, 2006).

Portes and Rumbaut (2006) investigated the educational aspirations and expectations of various immigrant students in Miami and San Diego. A comparison of their educational aspirations and expectations with those of native-born students consistently shows that irrespective of ethnic origins, all immigrants' dropout rates were lower and expectations for college and postgraduate education were higher than those of the general population. Kao and Tienda (1995) conclude that because most foreign-born youth are at a disadvantage due to their limited English language skills and because immigrant parents promote academic achievement, second generation immigrant youth (native-born offspring of immigrant parents) who are fluent in English are in the best position to achieve academically. Even so, second generation immigrant students report a wide gap between their aspirations and their expectations for educational attainment. By the third generation immigrants are far less committed to schooling than the second generation.

Educational Outcomes by Ethnicity and Race

The previous section's brief overview of the status of education among the major racial and ethnic groups described the historical forces and institutional contexts that generated and perpetuated racial and ethnic stratification in educational outcomes. This section presents data on selected indicators of educational attainment and achievement beginning with the National Assessment of Educational Progress (NAEP) scores for 4th, 8th, and 12th graders and concluding with postsecondary attainment by race and ethnicity.

National Assessment of Educational Progress NAEP measures how well students have learned the formal curriculum. NAEP assesses student academic performance in a variety of subjects in grades 4, 8, and 12. Table 20.2 presents NAEP results from 2005. Racial and ethnic gaps in reading, science, and mathematics that appear in fourth grade continue into high school. Overall, Asian and White students outperform Blacks, Latinos/as, and Native Americans at each grade level in reading, science, and mathematics.

Advanced Placement Advanced Placement (AP) courses offer the most rigorous coverage of the formal curriculum and are taken primarily by those who expect to go on to higher education. AP courses provide students with college-

TABLE 20.2

NAEP Reading and Mathematics Scale Score by Race/Ethnicity in Grades 4, 8, and 12, 2005

	Asian	Black	Latino	Native American	White
Reading					
Grade 4	229	200	203	204	229
Grade 8	271	243	246	249	271
Grade 12	287	267	272	279	293
Science					
Grade 4	158	129	133	138	162
Grade 8	156	124	129	n.a.	160
Grade 12	153	120	128	139	156
Mathematics					
Grade 4	251	220	226	226	246
Grade 8	295	255	262	264	289
Grade 12	163	127	133	134	157

Source: U.S. Department of Education 2006a, 2006b, 2007a, 2007b.

TABLE 20.3
Mean AP Scores in Selected Subjects by Race/Ethnicity, 2003

	Asian	Black	Latino	Native American	White	All
U.S. History	2.8	1.9	2.1	2.3	2.	2.7
English language/composition	3.1	2.2	2.4	2.6	3.1	3.0
Calculus (AB and BC)	3.2	2.2	2.4	2.5	3.2	3.1
Chemistry	2.9	1.7	1.9	1.9	2.8	2.7

Source: College Board, 2003.

level coursework. If they pass the AP exam with a high enough score, students may receive college course credit. In the past 10 years, the average AP cut score (above which a student receives college credit) has shifted upwards. Previously, most selective colleges accepted a score of 3, but recently the most selective colleges require scores of 4 or 5 to receive college credit (Lichten, 2007).

Access to AP course varies with the ethnic and socio-economic composition of schools. The high schools that middle-class White and Asian students typically attend offer greater access to AP courses than the high schools Black, Latino, and Native American students likely attend (Pachón, Federman, & Castillo, 2005). In response to demands for greater equity of access to AP courses, programs have expanded to more rural and inner city schools. The number of exams taken has tripled every decade since the 1980s (Lichten, 2007). The number of students of color taking AP courses more than doubled between 1997 and 2005 (Dillon, 2007).

Despite greater minority students' access to AP courses, there remain substantial racial and ethnic disparities in AP scores as Table 20.3 shows. Black, Latino, and American Indian students' pass rates are lower than Whites or Asians' rates. Some scholars have questioned the quality of expanded AP programs in schools that serve minority students. Lichten (2007) suggests that the expansion of access has not been sufficiently monitored for quality. Other observers point out that merely enrolling in AP courses, irrespective of exam results, benefits students because the courses expand students' intellectual horizons and social networks.

High School Graduation Rates Nearly two-thirds of students in public high school graduate from them, although racial and ethnic variations in dropout rates are a major source of stratified educational outcomes (Swanson, 2004). Urban school systems account for disproportionate numbers of dropouts (Swanson, 2008). In 2001, an estimated 74.5% of Whites, 76.8% of Asian Americans, 50.2% of Blacks, 53.2% of Latinos/as, and 51.1% of Native Americans graduated from high school (Swanson, 2004). Females graduated at higher rates across all ethnic groups: among Whites, 71.5 of males compared to 77% of females graduated from high school; among Asian Americans, 72.6 of males compared to 80% of females graduated; among Blacks, 56.2% of women compared to 42.8% of men graduated; among Latinos/as, 48% of males compared to 58.5% of females graduated, and among Native Americans, 47% of males compared to 51.4% of females graduated from high school. Graduation rates are increasing for all male ethnic groups, except Latinos/as for whom rates are holding steady (Freeman, 2004).

SAT College entrance exams such as the SAT are highly influential because of their role in college admissions, and the importance of higher education in the status attainment process. The majority of SAT-takers are females (54.6%) and overall scores reflect a large racial and ethnic gap in favor of Whites and Asians (College Board, 2006). Table 20.4 shows that, on average, White students' scores in critical reading and writing exceed those of all other ethnic groups. Asians score higher in mathematics than students in all other racial groups. Even though the population of students taking SAT tests is more selective than those taking NAEP tests, patterns in NAEP results by subject area and ethnic group are similar to those in SAT scores.

Postsecondary Enrollments In 2003, 41.6% of White, 32.3% of Black, and 23.5% of Latino 18 to 24 year olds were enrolled in a postsecondary degree-granting institution (U.S. Census Bureau, 2003). Social class background and gender are important predictors of college participation as well. Students from low-income families are less likely to attend college than their peers from more prosperous backgrounds. Forty years ago men were the majority of

TABLE 20.4
Mean Scores Selected SAT Indicators by Race/Ethnicity, 2006

	Asian	Black	Latino[a]	Native American	White
Critical Reading	510	434	454	487	527
Math	578	429	465	494	536
Writing	512	428	452	474	519

Note: [a]Excludes Puerto Ricans.
Source: College Board, 2006.

students at all levels of postsecondary education. Today, the reverse is largely true. There are striking ethnic variations in undergraduate enrollments by gender: 49% of White, 37% of Black, 34% of Latino, 30% of American Indian, and 54% of Asian undergraduate students are male (Freeman, 2004). Additionally, the type of postsecondary institution in which students are enrolled varies by their race, ethnicity, and social class background. Students from lower income, Black, Latino, and Native American backgrounds are more likely to be enrolled in two-year than in four-year institutions.

Postsecondary Attainment While enrollment is the first step to obtaining a higher education, persistence to graduation is the most important step. Racial and ethnic differences in persistence to degree exist at all levels of postsecondary education. Table 20.5 shows the percent of bachelor's, doctoral, and first-professional degrees awarded by racial/ethnic group in 2003. Relative to their population, Blacks, Latinos/as, and Native Americans earn disproportionately fewer postsecondary degrees. Whites and Asians earn a disproportionately greater share of bachelor's and first-professional degrees.

In general, females earn 59% of undergraduate degrees awarded. There are important within-group gender gaps that reveal key contours of racial stratification in higher education. For all racial/ethnic groups, within-group gender gaps favoring females are greatest at the associate's degree level and smallest at doctoral and first-professional degree levels. Among White bachelor's degree recipients, 57% are female; among Blacks 66% are female; among Latinos/as, 60% are females; among Asians, 54% are females (even though more Asian males enroll in higher education); and among Native American students, 61% are females (Freeman, 2004).

Master's, doctoral, and first-professional degree attainment patterns by ethnicity and gender follow undergraduate trends, with a few notable exceptions. In most racial groups more females than males received their doctorate in 2003. The one exception is Asians—males enjoy a small advantage over females in receipt of their doctorate. Among first-professional degree recipients who were White, 54% were males. But Black and Asian first-professional degree recipients are more likely to be females, and there are no first-professional degree gender differences among Latinos/as and Native Americans (U.S. Dept of Education, 2004).

Accounting for Ethnic and Racial Variations in Educational Outcomes

The previous section presented data demonstrating consistent patterns of racial and ethnic disparities in educational outcomes from elementary through postsecondary education. This section reviews explanations that have been advanced to account for racial and ethnic gaps. It begins with four theories of how macro-structural dynamics affect educational stratification. Next, the section considers how school characteristics and family background contribute to racial variations in outcomes. The section then considers a variety of theories that address the role of culture and cultural dynamics in school outcomes. It ends with a critique of biological determinist explanations for race and ethnic differences in educational outcomes.

Social Structure In light of the relationship between race and social class, it is necessary to consider the racial gap in educational outcome through the lens of social class. About one-third of the race gap in achievement is likely due to social class differences among students (Hedges & Nowell, 1998; Sirin, 2005). The relationship between social class and educational outcomes in the United States is far from unique. Shavit and Blossfeld (1993) examined 13 industrialized nations and found that the relative likelihood of graduating from secondary school and entering higher education for people from different social class backgrounds has remained essentially the same over the past several decades despite an enormous expansion of educational capacity in all 13 nations. In the Netherlands and Sweden, where overall social inequality declined, so have the effects of social background on educational attainment. The following four theories discuss how macro dynamics in the social structure can affect educational stratification.

Reproduction Theory Bowles and Gintis (1976) argued that schools in capitalist societies are designed to reproduce the class system by providing qualitatively and quantitatively different education to children according to their class of origin. Because the social relations of school (and the home) correspond to the social relations of production, schools foster capitalist structures of production and reproduce class inequities. Poor and working-class students, who are disproportionately Black, Latino'a, and Native Americans, receive an education that corresponds to their likely destination as member of the working class.

TABLE 20.5
Percent of Postsecondary Degrees Awarded by Race/Ethnicity, 2003

	Asian	Black	Latino	Native American	White	Internationals
Bachelor	7.5	9.1	6.6	0.7	73.7	2.4
Doctoral	5.2	5.5	3.4	0.3	60.0	25.6
First-professional	12.8	7.3	5.0	0.8	72.5	1.6

Source: U.S. Dept. of Education, 2004.

Middle-class and elite students—predominantly White—are prepared for management, ownership, and technical/analytic positions. Reproduction theory has been criticized for undertheorizing race and gender and for being overdeterministic, leaving no space for students' human agency in generating school outcomes.

Resistance Theory Resistance theorists (Giroux, 1983; MacLeod, 1987; Willis, 1977) incorporate human agency into accounts of how schools reproduce class inequality. They argue that youths respond to the perceived disjuncture between promises of mobility and social transformation through educational success and the stratified political economy in which class inequalities are daily realities. Adolescents' partial understanding of this disjuncture results in their conscious challenges to schooling. At the same time, when they resist acquiring educational credentials, students foreclose any possibilities of upward mobility through education. MacFarland (2000) argues that the formal and informal organization of classrooms may facilitate resistant behavior. While some theorists attend to issues of race and ethnicity—for example, Foley's (1990) examination of the reproduction of and resistance to capitalist culture among White and Latino high school students in Texas—most resistance theory scholarship concentrate on social class and pay insufficient attention to race and gender aspects of social and educational inequality.[2]

Maximally Maintained Inequality Raftery and Hout (1993) theorize that in a maximally maintained inequality (MMI) system, as soon as historically disadvantaged groups (like working-class youth, Blacks, Latinos/as, and Native Americans) attain the educational credentials previously held by the dominant groups, the credential requirements for the higher-status jobs necessary for status maintenance and mobility are ratcheted up. Dominant groups are better positioned to attain the new credentials. In this way, dominant social groups preserve their advantaged social locations, and class inequality in education does not decline despite expanded educational access. MMI is consistent with Collins' (1979) description of credentialism that fosters the credential inflation that, in turn, perpetuates the social class advantages of elites.

Effectively Maintained Inequality Lucas's (2001) theory of effectively maintained inequality (EMI) refines MMI. Advantages of social background effectively maintain educational privilege for children of the privileged in at least two ways: they influence who completes a given level of education if completion is not universal at that level, and they influence the kind of education people will receive within levels of education that are nearly universal (such as high school). Curricular tracking is a central mechanism through which EMI operates. As students make the transitions from elementary school through higher education, their location in the stratified curriculum at any given point has implications for their curricular trajectories during the remainder of their educational careers. Because working-class, Black, Latino, and Native American students are disproportionately found in lower tracks beginning in elementary school, their secondary and postsecondary educational trajectories tend to be distinct from those of middle-class Whites.

School Characteristics The organizational structures of the over 15,000 U.S. school systems are stratified on three key dimensions related to educational outcomes: resources, ability grouping and tracking, and school racial composition. There is a large literature that establishes how the organization of schools influences opportunities to learn specific subjects in high school, such as math and science (Lee, Smith, & Croninger, 1997). The organizational features of schools that optimize learning are rarely found in low-income racially isolated minority schools.

Resources Access to material and human resources varies by state, school districts within states, and by schools within school districts. Overall, low-income and disadvantaged minority students are less likely than middle-class, White, and Asian students to have access to material and human resources associated with greater opportunities to learn (Duncan & Brooks-Gunn, 1997; Lee & Burkam, 2002; Payne & Biddle, 1999). Given the system of public school financing, which depends largely on property taxes at the local level, and the racial segregation in public and private housing markets (Powell, Kearney, & Kay, 2001), it is not surprising to find race, ethnic, and social class differences in school resources and the opportunities to learn that they provide.

Debates as to whether money matters for school outcomes date back, at least, to the Coleman Report's finding that funding was not closely related to achievement (Coleman et al., 1966; Hanushek, 1996, 1997; Hedges, Laine, & Greenwald, 1994). However, new evidence suggests that money *does* matter, particularly for students from disadvantaged backgrounds and minority students, but may not matter for students from more highly advantaged backgrounds (Wenglinsky, 1997). Money buys not only buildings, books, instructional supplies, and smaller class size, but it also enables schools to hire high-quality, experienced, credentialed teachers instructing in their area of expertise (Darling-Hammond, 2000; Lankford, Loeb, & Wyckoff, 2002). This last point is crucial because teacher resources are the single most important element of the opportunities to learn a school offers.

Tracking Curricula differentiation—tracking in secondary school and ability grouping in elementary grades—is an almost universal organizational feature of the formal curriculum. Fine (1997) describes tracking as institutional choreography that funnels opportunities to some students but not to others. Numerous studies indicate that students in higher tracks—even less academically able youngsters—learn more in them because they are exposed to broader curricula, better teaching, and more academically oriented peers (Braddock & Dawkins, 1993; Cohen & Lotan, 1997; Gamoran & Mare, 1989; Hallinan, 2001; Oakes, 2005). The relative absence of disadvantaged minority students in higher tracks and their disproportionate enrollment in lower-level ones (Lucas, 1999; Oakes, 2005) is a contributing factor to the race gap in achievement.

Tracking and ability grouping begin very early in children's school careers (Alexander, Entwisle, & Lettgers, 1998; Oakes, 2005; Kornhaber, 1997) and have consequences that follow students throughout the course of their education (Lucas, 2001; Oakes, 2005). Black, Latino, and Native American students are more likely than White and Asian students to be identified for special education in elementary school. However, Hibel, Morgan, and Farkas (2006) found that once they controlled for test scores and learning environment, there is no evidence that ethnic minority students are over-placed into special education. The effects of ability grouping and tracking are cumulative: young students who possess similar social backgrounds and cognitive abilities but who learn in different tracks become more and more academically dissimilar each year they spend in school (Mickelson, 2001; Oakes, 2005). Research on heterogeneously grouped classrooms and detracked schools suggest widespread cognitive gains from more equitable approaches to organizing the delivery of the curriculum such as detracked schools and complex instruction in heterogeneous classrooms (Burris & Welner, 2005; Rubin, 2006; Cohen & Lotan, 1997).

Because the racially correlated tracking system contributes to educational stratification, it is important to understand how students are assigned to tracks. Several other factors shape placements in addition to students' prior achievement. Southworth and Mickelson (2007) found that school racial composition affected the likelihood of college track placement for comparably able students from different race-by-gender cohorts. Rhiel, Pallas, and Natriello (1999) show that arbitrary and idiosyncratic placement decisions are common. A large body of research (Baker & Stevenson, 1986; Kornhaber, 1997; Oakes, 2005; Useem, 1992; Wells & Serna, 1996; Welner, 2001; Yonazawa, 1997) documents how privileged parents use their superior financial resources, knowledge, and social networks to ensure that their children are placed in the top academic trajectories. That schools and school personnel respond favorably to parental exercises of their race and class privileges also contributes to the problem (Lareau & Horvat, 1999).

School Racial Composition The original social science rationale for school desegregation rested largely on claims that desegregation improves disadvantaged minority youths' access to the higher quality education more often provided to Whites. Early empirical evidence on desegregation's effects on minority youths' achievement was inconsistent (Armor, 1995; Cook, 1984; Wells & Crain, 1994), although there is little debate over the positive relationship between desegregation and minority students' status attainment (Braddock & McPartland, 1988). A recent meta-analysis by Pettigrew and Tropp (2006) reaffirmed earlier research showing that intergroup contact reduces prejudice and bias among both majority and minority students.

Recent empirical studies provide more conclusive findings on cognitive gains associated with attending diverse schools. New studies using local, state, and national level data show modest positive cognitive outcomes are associated with desegregated learning environments. Saatcioglu (2006) found that desegregated schools in Cleveland, Ohio, were much more successful in helping students to succeed because they were able to cope with non-school impediments that affected the typical student. Mickelson (2001, 2006) reported that both Black and White students achieved higher in desegregated schools in Charlotte, North Carolina. Borman and her colleagues (2005) demonstrated that school segregation in Florida negatively influenced mathematics achievement among minority students. Hanushek, Kain, and Rivkin (2008) reported that an increased percentage of Black classmates had a strong adverse effect on the achievement of Black students, but no significant adverse effect on White and Hispanic students.

Analyses of national-level data provide similar results. Borman and Dowling (2006) replicated the 1966 Coleman Report using the original data but they employed multilevel modeling (a technique not available 40 years ago) to analyze them. They report that going to a high-poverty school or a highly segregated Black school had a large negative effect on a student's achievement outcomes, above and beyond the effect of his or her individual poverty or minority status. In dramatic contrast to previous analyses of the Coleman data, these findings reveal that school context effects dwarf the effects of family background on achievement. Harris (2006) analyzed national test score data required by the federal No Child Left Behind Act (NCLB) to examine the effects of segregation in more than 22,000 schools across the country that enroll more than 18 million students. He found that Blacks and Hispanics learn more in integrated schools. Armor (2006), using NAEP data, found that after controlling for socioeconomic status, most of the negative relationship with segregated schools and achievement is eliminated for White but not for Black students. He reported that the size and significance of the relationships varied among states.

In short, the preponderance of new evidence points to a moderate positive relationship between racially diverse schools and higher achievement especially for racial/ethnic minority students (Brief of 553 Social Scientists, 2006) Ironically, just as social science evidence is showing more conclusively that achievement and intergroup relations benefit from diverse schools, public education is becoming increasingly racially isolated (Orfield & Lee, 2004; Orfield & Frankenberg, 2008).

Family Characteristics and Dynamics Parents from different ethnic and social class backgrounds possess different levels and types of resources critical for their children's education (Roscigno, 2000). Family background resources fall into two broad categories. The first is the characteristics of families, such as number of children, whether the parents are married, how many adults are in the household, wealth and income, and the adults' own educational attainment. All of these indicators correlate with race. The second category of resources concerns social dynamics of family-school relations, how parents socialize their children for schooling, how families use networks, and how parents participate in their children's education (Epstein, 2001). It is useful to consider family resources as human, financial, and social capital.[3]

Financial and Human Capital   Race is strongly correlated with variations in financial capital (Oliver & Shapiro, 2006). Families' financial capital influences children's nutrition, their health, residential stability, and access to books. In addition to the necessities of life, money purchases access to the best developmental preschools, tutors, computers, psychologists who test for giftedness, and homes with quiet bedrooms for doing homework.

Parents' human capital influences student outcomes as well. For example, the more education parents have, the better able they are to help with their children's homework. Race and class inequalities in children's school readiness are evident when they first walk through the kindergarten classroom door (Lee & Burkam, 2002). Social class and racial differences in child-rearing influence children's acquisition of cognitive skills, and noncognitive traits and behaviors that contribute to school outcomes (Farkas, 2003; Phillips, Brooks-Gunn, Duncan, Klebanov, & Crane, 1998).

Social Capital   In relation to education, social capital refers to parental access to networks and relationships that foster educational success. Such networks and relationships help parents learn what questions to ask, how to ask them, and to whom those questions should be addressed in schools. Those with social capital have networks of parents who share information on how to customize their children's educational careers, and share confidence and trust in school personnel (Baker & Stevenson, 1986; Bourdieu, 1977; de Graaf, 1986; Ma, 1999; Muller, 1998). Bryk, Lee, and Holland (1993) found that one reason for the success of Catholic schools was the participants' sense of community, trust, common mission, and shared responsibility for all children. In general, because of the ways in which public schools are organized, staffed, operate, and respond to parents, the social capital of educated middle-class White families facilitates their children's school success.

Cultural Forms

Cultural Capital   Bourdieu (1977) viewed cultural capital as a mechanism for transferring class advantage from one generation to another. Bourdieu argued because schools embody dominant cultural forms (expressed as the sanctioned dialect, demeanor, tastes, sensibilities, stock of elite knowledge manifest in the formal curricula), students who possess more of the valued cultural capital fare better than do their otherwise comparable peers who possess less of it. A great deal of empirical research demonstrates the positive relationships between possession of cultural capital and higher school outcomes (DiMaggio, 1982; Dumais, 2002; Farkas, 1996; Lareau, 2003).

Lareau and Horvat (1999) show that the value of cultural capital depends heavily on the particular social setting in which parents activate their cultural capital resources, and on the reciprocal, negotiated process by which social actors in schools respond to the activation and accord it legitimacy. The historical legacy of racial discrimination makes it more difficult for Black parents (and other peoples of color), independent of their social class, to activate their cultural capital on behalf of their children.

Cultural Deficit and Cultural Difference   Cultural deprivation theories (Lewis, 1966) proposed that racially stratified educational outcomes stemmed from cultural values and norms ill-suited for school success. Cultural deprivation or deficit theories, now largely discredited (Lee, 2005a, 2005b) informed the ideological underpinnings of the original compensatory education movement that arose in the 1960s. Without implying cultural superiority of mainstream culture, one version of cultural difference theory posits that racial variations in educational outcomes exist because cultural practices and values of certain racial and ethnic groups are more conducive to educational success (Bernstein, 1971; Bialystok & Hakuta, 1994; Delpit, 1996). However, the core educational values among peoples of color who are less successful in school, such as Blacks and Latinos/as, are essentially different from the values of groups who are more successful, like Asians and Whites (Blau, 2003). There is ample evidence that at some level, all racial and ethnic groups value learning, scholarship, and educational attainment.

Another version of cultural difference theory argues that racially stratified educational outcomes are linked to the failure of White-dominated educational institutions to incorporate non-dominant cultures into the formal curricula, pedagogical approaches, or structures (Hallinan, 2001; Kana'iaupuni, 2004; Klug & Whitfield, 2003; McCarty, 2002; Valenzuela, 1999; Woodrum, 2004). The multicultural education movement is, in some sense, a response to this critique of the formal curricula (Banks & McGee Banks, 2003).

Oppositional Cultural Framework   One of the more controversial approaches to understanding variations in minority achievement is Ogbu's (2004) cultural ecological model (CEM), a part of which is his theory of oppositional cultural frameworks. CEM posits that structural forces (e.g., discrimination and poor quality schools) and community forces (e.g., collective identity) shape minority school performance. Ogbu argues that cultural and language differences between disadvantaged peoples of color and Whites become markers of the former's collective identity as an oppressed people. Ogbu contends that many Black, Latino, and Native American students eschew behaviors that lead to educational achievement (speaking standard English, carrying books, doing homework, studying for tests) because engaging in them can be viewed as compromises of authenticity, ethnic identity, and group solidarity.

Ethnographic and survey research by other scholars both confirms and challenges the presence and influence of an oppositional cultural framework among Blacks (Ainsworth-Darnell & Downey, 1998; Carter, 2006; Cook & Ludwig, 1998; Farkas, Lleras, & Maczuga, 2002; Ferguson, 2001; Horvat & O'Connor, 2006; Spencer, 1999; Tyson, 2002; Tyson, Darity, & Castellino, 2005). Whether or not Black students—and other nonimmigrant minority youths—possess or reject oppositional cultural identities remains a subject of intense and ongoing debate.[4]

Abstract and Concrete Attitudes Mickelson (1990, 2001) demonstrated that students' attitudes toward education reflect, on the one hand, a cultural value embracing education and on the other hand, a material reality in which their families encounter a racially stratified opportunity structure. She argues that attitudes toward education and opportunity take two forms. The first is abstract attitudes, which are based on the dominant ideology that holds that education is the solution to most individual and social problems. All adolescents value education in the abstract, but these views do not necessarily predict differences in academic achievement because abstract attitudes do not vary in relation to achievement differences. Achievement is affected by students' perceptions of the opportunities that await them, which are reflected in their concrete attitudes. Concrete attitudes fluctuate according to the race, ethnicity, and social class forces that shape individuals' and groups' experiences in the U.S. opportunity structure. Mickelson, Okazaki, and Zheng (1995) demonstrated that Asian and Black students had more cynical concrete attitudes than Whites. By simultaneously examining both abstract and concrete attitudes toward education in relation to high school achievement, Mickelson and colleagues explained how widely held positive educational attitudes can exist across race and class lines, while at the same time there can be significant racial and class differences in actual school behavior and achievement.

Stereotype Threat Steele and Aronson (1998) examine how the stereotype of Black intellectual inferiority affects the academic performance of the most accomplished and most capable Black students. Steele and Aronson used experimental data to demonstrate that if academically able Black students were cued about race before engaging in an intellectual task, their performance was lower than students who did not receive such a cue. Given the salience of achievement to high performers and the pernicious cultural stereotype of Black intellectual inferiority, Steele and Aronson argue that stereotype threat inhibits academic performance because the most able Black students are reluctant

to engage fully in intellectual challenges lest they validate the stereotype through trying *and* failing. Their anxiety unconsciously leads them to disengage, and disengagement undermines performance. Steele and Aronson have demonstrated that the effects of stereotype threat operate similarly among other populations. Stereotype threat theory does not account for underperformance of Blacks who are not academically able.

Biological Determinism Periodically during the 20th century, theories that attribute racial gaps in educational outcomes to inherited, fixed racial differences in cognitive abilities circulate in the popular and scientific press (Herrnstein & Murray, 1994; Jensen, 1969, 2006; Rushton & Jensen, 2005; Terman, 1923). The precise extent to which these theories have influenced decisions about school racial composition, educational testing, curricula, tracking and ability grouping, pedagogy, the allocation of material and human resources, social norms, and the cultural climates of schools is impossible to assess. But it is apparent from a cursory review of American educational history from colonial times, through the Jim Crow era, to certain contemporary educational practices, that theories of inherited, fixed racial differences in cognitive abilities influenced public education in various ways.

Two conclusions about biological determinist theories are unambiguous. First, educational policies and practices grounded in such theories wreak havoc on the education of the low-income people of color labeled as cognitively deficient under their imprimatur. Second, biological determinist theories for racially stratified outcomes have no scientific merit. Molecular anthropologists (Marks, 2002a), cognitive psychologists (Gardner, 1993; Myerson, Frank, Rains, & Schnitzler, 1998), and sociologists (Fisher et al., 1996) have discredited biological determinist explanations for racial differences in academic performance. For example, decades before the human genome project established that there is greater within group genetic variation than between group variation, biological anthropologists demonstrated that the relationship between genetic diversity and racial and ethnic diversity is weak; and diversity in the former does not map easily onto the latter because genetic variation *within* socially constructed racial groups is greater than *between* two groups (Marks, 2002a). Moreover, genetic variations among humans do not predict patterns of behavioral diversity (Marks, 2002b).

Biological determinist attributions for racial gaps in educational outcomes are expressions of racism. Most racism in education rarely appears in such a blatant, pure form. Rather, racism is more subtly woven into the warp and weft of school cultures and organizations, their processes and contents. Consequently, racism as an explanatory category offers limited insight into persistent race and ethnic gaps in educational performance. Instead of discussing racism, qua racism, this chapter has framed the multiple intersections of race and education within a larger societal context of racial and ethnic stratification; that is, school success and failure can be understood as part of the larger racial conflict in America.

Conclusion

This chapter's focus on racially stratified school processes and outcomes should not obscure the important fact that U.S. schools successfully educate millions of students. Since 1954, access to education at every level has expanded for all children; NAEP scores show modest but steady improvements in many subjects; racially disaggregated SAT scores are rising for all racial and ethnic groups; more students—including more students of color and children of the working class—are taking AP courses; more students from all racial, ethnic, and social class backgrounds are going to college and graduating from them than in the past. For all its flaws, public education is the most accessible and democratic institution in the nation—far more accessible and democratic than the housing market, the healthcare system, the media, and most certainly the economy.

There has been progress in narrowing racial and ethnic gaps (Grissmer et al., 1998; Hedges & Nowell, 1999; U. S. Department of Education, 2006a, 2006b, 2007a). Nevertheless, there is striking variability in the opportunities to learn available in public education and that variability is strongly related to a student's race, ethnicity, and social class. From elementary through graduate school, all key measures of academic achievement and attainment are stratified by race and ethnicity. The patterns are consistent. White and Asian educational outcomes surpass those of Black, Latino, and Native Americans. To be sure, there are gender and social class differences in outcomes, and striking social class and gender gaps within race groups. However, social class and gender gaps in outcomes are dwarfed by the racial and ethnic disparities in achievement and attainment.

During the past five decades, a number of educational policies designed to eliminate the racial and ethnic gaps have been implemented with varying degrees of success. Some equity-oriented reforms like desegregation, compensatory education, bilingual education, and affirmative action have had modest success in closing some gaps for some students in some locales. Market-oriented reforms like school choice, privatization, and the standards and accountability movement have yet to produce systematic results that indicate these reforms will close the race gap.

Race and social class gaps in outcomes remain fairly resilient, and this chapter has described several reasons for this resilience. First, racial and ethnic inequalities in educational outcomes are derivative of the inequality in the economic, political, legal, and social institutional contexts in which families, students, and educators live, learn, and work. Many educational policies and practices still tend to compound rather than ameliorate the effects of neighborhood and family disadvantages. And second, the political and legal environment has changed and the federal government, especially the judiciary, is no longer dismantling the institutional bases of educational stratifi-cation. The Supreme Court's decision in the Seattle and Louisville voluntary desegregation cases is emblematic of the judiciary's retrenchment from its former role.

The structure of nested inequalities among states, districts, schools, and classrooms (Hochschild & Scovronick, 2003) has not disappeared in the 50 years since the U.S. began to dismantle the legal framework of Jim Crow education. The institutional basis of racial stratification in education remains the single most urgent challenge facing educational policy makers, educators, students, and their parents.

Notes

1. A number of Black parents, educators, and leaders today lament the loss of control, culture, and community that came with desegregation. Segregated Black schools, along with churches, were critical nerve centers for Black communities. The fact that many veteran educators lost their jobs as school systems desegregated was a blow to the Black community.
2. Foley distinguishes between Anglos and Mexicanos; for consistency of language, I refer to his subjects as Whites and Latinos.
3. Smith and Kulynych (2002) argue that the term *social capital* unnecessarily privileges capitalist culture and that the phrases social networks, or trust networks are better suited to convey the core relationships under consideration.
4. John Ogbu's (2008) posthumously published *Minority Status, Oppositional Culture, and Schooling* is the definitive presentation of his cultural ecological model and the various debates it generated. The volume's 24 chapters are organized as a dialogue between Ogbu and the larger scholarly community, including his many critics. See Foster (2004, 2008) for an incisive analysis and critique of Ogbu's contribution to many fields, including anthropology and sociology of education.

References

Ainsworth-Darnell, J. W., & Downey, D. B. (1998). Assessing the oppositional culture explanation for racial/ethnic differences in school performance. *American Sociological Review, 63*, 536–553.

Akom, A. A. (2008). Reexamining resistance as oppositional behavior: The Nation of Islam and the creation of a black achievement ideology (The remix). In J. U. Ogbu (Ed.), *Minority status, oppositional culture, and schooling* (pp. 190–221). New York: Routledge.

Alexander, K., Entwisle, D., & Lettgers, N. (1998, August). *On the multiple faces of first grade tracking.* Paper presented at the annual meeting of the American Sociological Association, San Francisco.

Allen, T. (1994). *The invention of the White race: Vol.1.* New York: Verso.

Anderson, J. D. (1988). *The education of Blacks in the South, 1860–1935.* Chapel Hill: University of North Carolina Press.

Armor, D. (1995). *Forced justice: School desegregation and the law.* New York: Oxford University Press.

Armor, D. (2006). Lessons learned from school desegregation. In P. Peterson (Ed.), *Generational change: Closing the test score gap* (pp. 115–142). Lanham, MD: Rowman and Littlefield.

Baker, D., & Stevenson, D. (1986). Mothers' strategies for children's school achievement: Managing the transition to high school. *Sociology of Education, 59,* 156–166.

Banks, J., & McGee Banks, C. A. (Eds.). (2003). *Handbook of research on multicultural education* (2nd ed.). San Francisco: Jossey-Bass.

Bernstein, B. (1971). *Class, codes, and control: Vol. 1.* London: Routledge & Kegan Paul.

Bialystok, A., & Hakuta, K. (1994). *In other words: The science and psychology of second-language acquisition.* New York: Basic Books.

Blau, J. (2003). *Race in the schools: Perpetuating White dominance?* Boulder, CO: Lynne Rienner.

Boger, J. (2002). *A quick look at the remedial responsibilities under the Federal Constitution For School Districts found to have practiced de jure, or intentional segregation of their public schools—And at judicial consideration of the relation between continuing school segregation and private housing choices in formerly segregated school districts.* Unpublished manuscript. Chapel Hill: University of North Carolina Law School.

Borman, G., & Dowling, M. (2006, April). *Schools and inequality: A multi-level analysis of Coleman's Equality of Educational Opportunity data.* Paper presented at the annual meeting of the American Educational Research Association, San Francisco.

Borman, K., Eitle, T. M., Michael, D., Eitle, D. J., Lee, R., Johnson, L., et al. (2005). Accountability in a postdesegregation era: The continuing significance of racial segregation in Florida's schools. *American Educational Research Journal, 41*, 605–631.

Bourdieu, P. (1977). *Outline of a theory of practice* (R. Nice, Trans.). London: Cambridge University Press. (Original work published 1972)

Bowles, S., & Gintis, H. (1976). *Schooling in capitalist America: Educational reform and the contradictions of economic life.* New York: Basic Books.

Boykin, A. W. (1986). The triple quandary and the schooling of Afro-American children. In U. Neisser (Ed.), *The school achievement of minority children: New perspectives* (pp. 57–92). Mahwah, NJ: Erlbaum.

Braddock, J., & Dawkins, M. (1993). Ability grouping, aspirations, and attainments. *Journal of Negro Education, 62*, 324–336.

Braddock, J., II, & McPartland, J. M. (1988). The social and academic consequences of school desegregation. *Equity and Choice, 4*(2), 50–73.

Brief of 553 Social Scientists as Amici Curiae in Support of Respondents in *Parents Involved in Community Schools v. Seattle School District One* and *Meredith v. Jefferson County Board of Education*. (2006).

Brodkin, K. (1998). *How Jews became White folks and what that says about race in America.* New Brunswick, NJ: Rutgers University Press.

Brown v. Board of Education, 347 U.S. 483 (1954).

Bryk, A., Lee, V., & Holland, P. (1993). *Catholic schools and the common good.* Cambridge, MA: Harvard University Press.

Burris, C., & Welner, K. (2005). Closing the achievement gap by detracking. *Phi Delta Kappan, 86*, 594–598.

Caplan, N., Choy, M., & Whitmore, J. (1991). *Children of the boat people: A study of educational success.* Ann Arbor: University of Michigan Press.

Carter, P. (2006). *Keepin' it real: School success beyond Black and White.* New York: Oxford University Press.

Clotfelter, C. T. (2004) *After Brown: The rise and retreat of school desegregation.* Princeton, NJ: Princeton University Press.

Cohen, E., & Lotan, R. (Eds.). (1997). *Working for equity in heterogeneous classrooms: Sociological theory in practice.* New York: Teachers College Press.

Coleman, J., Campbell, E. Q., Hobson, C., McPartland, J., Mood, A., Winfield, F., et al. (1966). *Equality of educational opportunity.* Washington, DC: U.S. Government Printing Office.

College Board. (2003). *School AP grade distributions by total and ethnic group.* Retrieved May 14, 2008, from http://www.collegeboard.com/prod_downloads/student/testing/ap/sumrpts/2003/xls/national_2003.xls

College Board. (2006). *College-bound seniors 2006: Total group profile.* Washington, DC: Author.

Collins, R. (1979). *The credential society: An historical sociology of education and stratification.* New York: Academic Press.

Cook, P. J., & Ludwig, J. (1998). The burden of "acting White:" Do Black adolescents disparage academic achievement? In C. Jencks & M. Phillips (Eds.), *The Black-White test score gap* (pp. 375–401). Washington, DC: Brookings Institution.

Cook, T. (Ed.). (1984). *School desegregation and Black achievement.* Washington, DC: U.S. Department of Education.

Crenshaw, K., Gotanda, N., Peller, G., & Thomas, K. (Eds.). (1995). *Critical race theory: The key writings that formed the movement.* New York: The New Press.

Crow Dog, M. (1991). *Lakota woman.* New York: Harper Perennial.

Darling-Hammond, L. (2000). Teacher quality and student achievement: A review of state policy evidence [Electronic version]. *Education Policy Analysis Archives, 8*(1), 1–50.

de Graaf, P. M. (1986). The impact of financial and cultural resources on educational attainment in the Netherlands. *Sociology of Education, 59*, 237–246.

Delpit, L. (1996). *Other people's children: Cultural conflict in the classroom.* New York: New Press.

Delgado, R. (Ed.). (1995). *Critical race theory: The cutting edge.* Philadelphia: Temple University Press.

Deyhle, D. (2008). Navajo youth and Anglo racism: Cultural integrity and resistance. In J. U. Ogbu (Ed.), *Minority status, oppositional culture, and schooling* (pp. 433–480). New York: Routledge.

Dillon, S. (2007, June 1). U.S. data show rapid minority growth in school rolls. *New York Times*, p. A27.

DiMaggio, P. (1982). Cultural capital and school success: The impact of status culture participation on grades of U.S. high school students. *American Sociological Review, 47*, 189–201.

Dumais, S. A. (2002). Cultural capital, gender, and school success: The role of habitus. *Sociology of Education, 75*, 44–68.

Duncan, G., & Brooks-Gunn, J. (Eds.). (1997). *Consequences of growing up poor.* New York: Russell Sage Foundation.

Dutton, S. E., Singer, J., & Devlin, A. S. (1998). Racial identity of children in integrated, predominantly White, and Black schools. *Journal of Social Psychology, 138*, 41–53.

Epstein, J. (2001). *School, family, and community partnerships: Preparing educators and improving schools.* Boulder, CO: Westview.

Fadiman, A. (1998). *The spirit catches you and you fall down: A Hmong child, her American doctors, and the collision of two cultures.* New York: Farrar, Strauss, & Giroux.

Farkas, G. (1996). *Human capital or social capital? Ethnicity and poverty groups in an urban school district.* New York: Aldine De Gruyter.

Farkas, G. (2003). Cognitive skills and noncognitive traits and behaviors in stratification processes. *Annual Review of Sociology, 29*, 541–562.

Farkas, G., Lleras, C., & Maczuga, S. (2002). Does oppositional culture exist in minority and poverty peer groups? *American Sociological Review, 67*, 148–155.

Ferguson, R. F. (2001). A diagnostic analysis of Black-White GPA disparities in Shaker Heights, Ohio. *Brookings Papers on Education Policy, 2001*, 403–408.

Fine, M. (1997). Witnessing whiteness. In M. Fine, L. Weis, L. C. Powell, & L. M. Wong (Eds.), *Off White: Readings on race, power, and society* (pp. 57–65). New York: Routledge.

Fisher, C., Hout, M., Janowski, M. S., Lucas, S., Swidler, A., & Voss, K. (1996). *Inequality by design: Cracking the Bell Curve myth.* Princeton, NJ: Princeton University Press.

Foley, D. E. (1990). *Learning capitalist culture deep in the heart of Tejas.* Philadelphia: University of Pennsylvania Press.

Foster, K. M. (2004). Coming to terms: A discussion of John Ogbu's cultural-ecological theory of minority academic achievement. *Intercultural Education, 15*, 369–384.

Foster, K. M. (2008). Forward-looking criticism: Critiques and enhancements for the next generation of the cultural-ecological model. In J. U. Ogbu (Ed.), *Minority status, oppositional culture, and schooling* (pp. 577–592). New York: Routledge.

Freeman, C. E. (2004). *Trends in educational equity of girls and women: 2004* (NCES 2005-016). Washington, DC: National Center for Educational Statistics.

Gamoran, A., & Mare, R. (1989). Secondary school tracking and educational inequity: Compensation, reinforcement, or neutrality. *American Journal of Sociology, 94*, 1146–1183.

Garcia, E. E. (2001). *Hispanic education in the United States: Raíces y alas.* Lanham, MD: Rowman and Littlefield.

Garcia, E. E. (2005). *Teaching and learning in two languages: Bilingualism and schooling in the United States.* New York: Teachers College Press.

Gardner, H. (1993). *Frames of mind: The theory of multiple intelligences* (Rev. ed.). New York: Basic Books.

Gibson, M. (1988). *Accommodation without assimilation: Sikh immigrants in American high schools.* Ithaca, NY: Cornell University Press.

Giroux, H. A. (1983). *Theory and resistance in education: A pedagogy for the opposition.* New York: Bergin and Garvey.

Grissmer, D. W., Flanagan, A., & Williamson, S. (1998). Why did the Black-White score gap narrow in the 1970s and 1980s? In C. Jencks & M. Phillips (Eds.), *The Black-White test score gap* (pp. 182–228). Washington, DC: Brookings Institution.

Hallinan, M. T. (2001). Sociological perspectives on Black-White inequalities in American schooling. *Sociology of Education, 34,* 50–70.

Hanushek, E. (1996). A more complete picture of school resource policies. *Review of Educational Research, 66,* 397–409.

Hanushek, E. (1997). Assessing the effects of school resources on student performance: An update. *Educational Evaluation and Policy Analysis, 19,* 141–164.

Hanushek, E., Kain, T., & Rivkin, S. (2006). *New evidence on Brown v. Board of Education.* Unpublished manuscript.

Harris, D. (2006, November 29). *Lost learning, forgotten promises: A national analysis of school segregation, student achievement, and "controlled choice" plans.* Washington, DC: Center for American Progress.

Hedges, L. V., Laine, R. D., & Greenwald, R. (1994). Does money matter? A meta-analysis of studies of the effects of differential inputs on student outcomes. *Educational Researcher, 23,* 5–14.

Hedges, L. V., & Nowell, A. (1998). Black-White test score convergence since 1965. In C. Jencks & M. Phillips (Eds.), *The Black-White test score gap* (pp. 149–181). Washington, DC: Brookings Institution.

Hedges, L. V., & Nowell, A. (1999). Changes in the Black-White gap in achievement test scores. *Sociology of Education, 72,* 111–135.

Herman, M. (2009). The Black-White-Other test score gap: Academic achievement among mixed race adolescents. *Sociology of Education, 82,* 30–44.

Herrnstein, R., & Murray, C. (1994). *The bell curve: Intelligence and class structure in American life.* New York: Free Press.

Hibel, J., Morgan, P., & Farkas, G. (2006, August 11). *Who is placed into special education?* Paper presented at the annual meeting of the American Sociological Association, Montreal, Quebec, Canada.

Hochschild, J., & Scovronick, N. (2003). *The American dream and the public schools.* New York: Oxford University Press.

Horvat, E., & O'Connor, C. (Eds.). (2006). *Beyond acting White: Reassessments and new directions in research on Black students and school success.* Lanham, MD: Rowman and Littlefield.

H.R. Con. Concurrent Resolution 200 (2003).

Ignatiev, N. (1995). *How the Irish became White.* New York: Routledge.

Jensen, A. (1969). How much can we boost IQ and scholastic achievement? *Harvard Educational Review, 39,* 1–123.

Jensen, A. R. (2006) *Clocking the mind: Mental chronometry and individual differences.* Oxford: Elsevier.

Kana'iaupuni, S. M. (2004). Ka'akālai kū kanaka: A call for strengths-based approaches from a Native Hawaiian perspective. *Educational Researcher, 34*(5), 32–38.

Kao, G. (1999). Racial identity and academic performance: An examination of biracial Asian and African American youth. *Journal of Asian American Studies, 2,* 223–249.

Kao, G., & Tienda, M. (1995). Optimism and achievement: The educational performance of immigrant youth. *Social Science Quarterly, 76,* 1–19.

King, J. E. (2005). A transformative vision of Black education for human freedom. In J. E. King (Ed.), *Black education: A transformative research and action agenda for the new century* (pp. 3–18). Mahwah, NJ: Erlbaum.

Klug, B. J., & Whitfield, P. T. (2003). *Widening the circle: Culturally relevant pedagogy for American Indian children.* New York: RoutledgeFalmer.

Kluger, R. (1975). *Simple justice: The history of Brown v. Board of Education and Black America's struggle for equality.* New York: Random House.

Kornhaber, M. (1997). *Seeking strengths: Equitable identification for gifted education and the theory of multiple intelligences.* Unpublished doctoral dissertation, Harvard University, Cambridge, MA.

Ladson-Billings, G. (1999). Just what is critical race theory, and what's it doing in a *nice* field like Education? In L. Parker, D. Deyhle, & S. Villenas (Eds.), *Race is…race isn't: Critical race theory and qualitative studies in education* (pp. 7–30). Boulder, CO: Westview Press.

Lankford, H., Loeb, S., & Wyckoff, J. (2002). Teacher sorting and the plight of urban schools: A descriptive analysis. *Educational Evaluation and Policy Analysis, 24,* 37–62.

Lareau, A. (2003). *Unequal childhoods: Class, race, and family life.* Berkeley: University of California Press.

Lareau, A., & Horvat, E. M. (1999). Moments of social inclusion and exclusion: Race, class, and cultural capital in family-school relationships. *Sociology of Education, 72,* 37–53.

Lau v. Nichols, 414 U.S. 563 (1974).

Lee, C. D. (2005a). Intervention research based on current views of cognition and learning. In J. E. King (Ed.), *Black education: A transformative research and action agenda for the new century* (pp. 73–114). Mahwah, NJ: Erlbaum.

Lee, C. D. (2005b). The state of knowledge about the education of African Americans. In J. E. King (Ed.), *Black education: A transformative research and action agenda for the new century* (pp. 45–72). Mahwah, NJ: Erlbaum.

Lee, C. D., Lomotey, K., & Shujaa, M. (1991). How shall we sing our sacred song in a strange land? The dilemma of double consciousness and the complexities of an African centered pedagogy. *Journal of Education, 172*(2), 45–61.

Lee, S. J. (1996). *Unraveling the "model minority" stereotype: Listening to Asian American youth.* New York: Teachers College Press.

Lee, V. E., & Burkam, D. (2002). *Inequality at the starting gate: Social background differences in achievement as children begin school.* Washington, DC: Economic Policy Institute.

Lee, V. E., Smith, J. B., & Croninger, R. G. (1997). How high school organization influences the equitable distribution of learning in mathematics and science. *Sociology of Education, 70,* 128–150.

Lew, J. (2007). A structural analysis of the success and failure of Asian Americans: A case study of Koreans in urban schools. *Teachers College Record, 109,* 369–390.

Lewis, O. (1966). The culture of poverty. *Scientific American, 215,* 19–25.

Lichten, W. (2007). Equity and excellence in the College Board Advanced Placement program. *Teachers College Record, 109,* 245–267.

Lieberson, S., & Waters, M. C. (1986). Ethnic groups in flux: The changing ethnic responses of American Whites. *The Annals of the American Academy of Political and Social Science, 487,* 79–91.

Logan, J., Oakley, D., & Stowell, J. (2008). School segregation in metropolitan regions, 1970–2000: The impact of policy choices on public education. *American Journal of Sociology, 113,* 1611–1644.

Lopez, D., & Espiritu, Y. (1990). Panethnicity in the United States: A theoretical framework. *Ethnic and Racial Studies, 13,* 198–224.

Lucas, S. R. (1999). *Tracking inequality: Stratification and mobility in American high schools.* New York: Teachers College Press.

Lucas, S. R. (2001). Effectively maintained inequality: Education transitions, track mobility, and social background effects. *American Journal of Sociology, 106,* 1642–1690.

Ma, X. (1999). Dropping out of advanced placement mathematics: The effects of parental involvement. *Teachers College Record, 101,* 60–81.

MacFarland, D. (2000). Student resistance: How the formal and informal organization of classrooms facilitate everyday forms of student defiance. *American Journal of Sociology, 107,* 612–678.

MacLeod, J. (1987). *Ain't no makin' it: Aspirations and attainment in a low-income neighborhood.* Boulder, CO: Westview Press.

Marks, J. (2002a). Anthropology and the bell curve. In H. Gusterson & C. Besteman (Eds.), *On deeper reflection: Why America's top pundits are wrong about the world* (pp. 206–227). Philadelphia: University of Pennsylvania Press.

Marks, J. (2002b). *What it means to be 98% chimpanzee: Apes, people, and their genes.* Berkeley: University of California Press.

Matute-Bianchi, M. E. (1986). Ethnic identities and patterns of school success and failure among Mexican-descent and Japanese-American students in a California high school: An ethnographic analysis. *American Journal of Education, 95,* 233–255.

Matute-Bianchi, M. E. (2008). Situational ethnicity and patterns of school performance among immigrant and nonimmigrant Mexican-descent students. In J. U. Ogbu (Ed.), *Minority status, oppositional culture, and schooling* (pp. 397–432). New York: Routledge.

McCarty, T. L. (2002). *A place to be Navajo. Rough Rock and the struggle for self-determination in indigenous schooling.* Mahwah, NJ: Erlbaum.

Mendez v. Westminster School District, 161 F.2d 774 (9th Cir. 1947).

Meredith v. Jefferson County Board of Education, 127 S. Ct. 2738 (2007).

Mickelson, R. A. (1990). The attitude-achievement paradox among Black adolescents. *Sociology of Education, 63,* 44–61.

Mickelson, R. A. (2001). Subverting *Swann:* First- and second- generation segregation in the Charlotte-Mecklenburg schools. *American Educational Research Journal, 38,* 215–252.

Mickelson, R. A. (2003). When are racial disparities in education the result of discrimination? A social science perspective. *Teachers College Record, 105,* 1052–1086.

Mickelson, R. A. (2006). Segregation and the SAT. *Ohio State Law Journal, 67,* 157–199.

Mickelson, R. A., Okazaki, S., & Zheng, D. (1995). Reading reality more carefully than books: A structural approach to race and class differences in adolescent educational performance. In P. Cookson, Jr. & B. Schneider (Eds.), *Transforming schools* (pp. 81–105). New York: Garland.

Moll, L., & González, N. (2001). Engaging life: A funds-of-knowledge approach to multicultural education. In J. Banks & C. A. McGee Banks (Eds.), *Handbook of research on multicultural education.* San Francisco: Jossey-Bass.

Muller, C. (1998). Gender differences in parental involvement and adolescents' math achievement. *Sociology of Education, 71,* 336–356.

Muhammad, Z. (2005). Faith and courage to educate our own: Reflections on Islamic schools in the African American community. In J. E. King (Ed.), *Black education: A transformative research and action agenda for the new century* (pp. 261–279). Mahwah, NJ: Erlbaum.

Myerson, J., Frank, M., Rains, F., & Schnitzler, M. (1998). Race and general cognitive ability: The myth of diminishing returns to education. *Psychological Science, 9,* 139–142.

Natriello, G., McDill, E., & Pallas, A. (1990). *Schooling disadvantaged children: Racing against catastrophe.* New York: Teachers College Press.

Oakes, J. (2005). *Keeping track: How schools structure inequality* (2nd ed.). New Haven, CT: Yale University Press.

O'Connor, C. (2001). Making sense of the complexity of social identity in relation to achievement: A sociological challenge in the new millennium. *Sociology of Education, 34,* 159–168.

Ogbu, J. U. (2003). *Black American students in an affluent suburb: A study of academic disengagement.* Mahwah, NJ: Erlbaum.

Ogbu, J. U. (2004). Collective identity and the burden of "acting White" in Black history, community, and education. *The Urban Review, 36,* 1–35.

Ogbu, J. U. (Ed.). (2008). *Minority status, oppositional culture, and schooling.* Mahwah, NJ: Erlbaum.

Oliver, M., & Shapiro, T. (2006). *Black wealth/White wealth: A new perspective on racial inequality* (2nd ed.). New York: Routledge.

Omi, M., & Winant, H. (1994). *Racial formation in the United States: From the 1960s to the 1980s* (2nd ed.). New York: Routledge.

Orfield, G., & Eaton, S. (1996). *Dismantling desegregation: The quiet reversal of Brown v. Board of Education.* Cambridge, MA: Harvard University Press.

Orfield, G., & Frankenberg, E. (2008). *The last have become first: Rural and small town America lead the way on desegregation.* The Civil Rights Project/Proyecto Derechos Civiles: University of California, Los Angeles.

Orfield, G., & Lee, C. (2004). *Brown at 50: King's dream or Plessy's nightmare.* Cambridge, MA: Harvard University: The Civil Rights Project.

Pachón, H., Federman, M., & Castillo, L. (2005). High school race and class composition and advanced placement course availability. In A. Wells & J. Petrovich (Eds.), *Putting equity back in school reform* (pp. 175–187). New York: Teachers College Press.

Parents Involved in Community Schools v. Seattle School District No. 1 127 S.Ct. 2738 (2007).

Payne, K. J., & Biddle, B. J. (1999). Poor school funding, child poverty, and mathematics achievement. *Educational Researcher, 28*(6), 4–13.

Perry, P. (2002). *Shades of White: White kids and racial identities in high school.* Durham, NC: Duke University Press.

Pettigrew, T., & Tropp, L. (2006). A meta-analytic test of intergroup contact theory. *Journal of Personality and Social Psychology, 90,* 751–783.

Phillips, M., Brooks-Gunn, J., Duncan, G., Klebanov, P., & Crane, J. (1998). Family background, parenting practices, and the Black-White test score gap. In C. Jencks & M. Phillips (Eds.), *The Black-White test score gap* (pp. 103–148). Washington, DC: Brookings Institution.

Pollock, M. (2004). *Colormute: Race talk dilemmas in an American school.* Princeton, NJ: Princeton University Press.

Portes, A., & Rumbaut, R. (2006). *Immigrant America: A portrait* (3rd ed.). Berkeley: University of California Press.

Powell, J. A., Kearney, G., & Kay, V. (Eds.). (2001). *In pursuit of a dream deferred: Linking housing and education policy.* New York: Peter Lang.

Raftery, A., & Hout, M. (1993). Maximally maintained inequality: Expansion, reform, and opportunity in Irish education, 1921–75. *Sociology of Education, 66,* 41–62.

Rhiel, C., Pallas, A., & Natriello, G. (1999). Rites and wrongs: Institutional explanations for the student course-scheduling process in urban high schools. *American Journal of Education, 107,* 116–154.

Roscigno, V. J. (2000). Family/school inequality and African American/ Hispanic achievement. *Social Problems, 47,* 266–290.

Rubin, B. C. (2006). Tracking and detracking: Debates, evidence, and best practices for a heterogeneous world. *Theory into Practice, 45,* 4–14.

Rumbaut, R. (2006). The making of a people. In M. Tienda & F. Mitchell (Eds.), *Hispanics and the future of America* (pp. 16–65). Washington, DC: The National Academies Press.

Rumberger, R. W., & Palardy, G. J. (2005). Does segregation still matter? The impact of student composition on academic achievement in high school. *Teachers College Record, 107,* 1999–2045.

Rushton, J. P., & Jensen, A. R. (2005). Thirty years of research on race differences in cognitive ability. *Psychology, Public Policy, and Law, 11*(2), 235–294.

Saatcioglu, A. (2006, August). *Non-school factors and the effectiveness of urban public schools.* Paper presented at the annual meeting of the American Sociological Association, Montreal, Quebec, Canada.

Sampson, Z. C. (2005, December 11). Home schools are becoming more popular among Blacks. *New York Times,* p. A34.

Schmidt, C. L. (2001). Educational achievement, language-minority students, and the new second generation. *Sociology of Education, 34,* 71–87.

Seale, D. & Slapin, B. (2005). *A broken flute: The native experience in books for children.* Walnut Creek, CA: AltaMira Press.

Sellers, R., & Shelton, J. N. (2003). The role of racial identity in perceived racial discrimination. *Journal of Personality and Social Psychology, 84,* 1079–1092.

Shavit, Y., & Blossfeld, H.-P. (Eds.). (1993). *Persistent inequality: Changing educational attainment in thirteen countries.* Boulder, CO: Westview.

Sirin, S. (2005). Socioeconomic status and academic achievement: A meta-analytic review of research. *Review of Educational Research, 75*(3), 417–453.

Smalls, C., White, R., Chavous, T., & Sellers, R. (2007). Racial ideological beliefs and racial discrimination experiences as predictors of academic engagement among African American adolescents. *Journal of Black Psychology, 33*(3), 299–330.

Smith, S. S., & Kulynych, J. (2002). It may be social, but why is it capital? The social construction of social capital and the politics of language. *Politics and Society, 30*, 149–186.

Snipp, C. M. (2003). Racial measurement in the American census: Past practices and implications for the future. *Annual Review of Sociology, 29*, 563–588.

Southworth, S., & Mickelson, R. A. (2007). The interactive effects of race, gender, and school composition on college track placement. *Social Forces, 86*, 497–524.

Spencer, M. B. (1999). Social and cultural influences on school adjustment: The application of an identity-focused cultural ecological perspective. *Educational Psychologist, 34*, 43–57.

Steele, C., & Aronson, J. (1998). Stereotype threat and the test performance of academically successful African Americans. In C. Jencks & M. Phillips (Eds.), *The Black-White test score gap* (pp. 401–430). Washington, DC: Brookings Institution.

Suarez-Orozco, C., & Suarez-Orozco, M. (2001). *Children of immigration.* Cambridge, MA: Harvard University Press.

Swanson, C. (2004). *Who graduates? Who doesn't? A statistical portrait of public high school graduates, class of 2001.* Washington, DC: The Urban Institute.

Swanson, C. (2008). Cities in crisis: A special analytic report on high school graduation. Bethesda, MD: Editorial Projects in Education Research Center.

Takaki, R. (1993). *A different mirror: A history of multicultural America.* Boston: Little, Brown.

Tate, W. (1997). Critical race theory and education: History, theory, and implications. *Review of Research in Education, 23*, 195–247.

Terman, L. (1923). *Intelligence tests and school reorganization.* New York: World Book Company.

Trow, M. (1961). The second transformation of American secondary education. *International Journal of Comparative Sociology, 2*, 144–165.

Tyack, D., & Hansot, E. (1990). *Learning together: A history of coeducation in American public schools.* New Haven, CT: Yale University Press.

Tyson, K. (2002). Weighing in: Elementary-age students and the debate on attitudes toward school among Black students. *Social Forces, 80*, 1157–1189.

Tyson, K., Darity, W. A., Jr., & Castellino, D. (2005). It's not "a Black thing:" Understanding the burden of acting White and other dilemmas of high achievement. *American Sociological Review, 70*, 582–605.

U.S. Census Bureau. (2004, September 30). *State and local characteristics.* Washington, DC: Author.

U.S. Census Bureau. (2005, July 1). *Population profile of the United States: Dynamic version.* Washington, DC: Author.

U.S. Census Bureau. (2003, October). *Enrollment of 18-24-year-olds in degree-granting institutions by sex and race/ethnicity.* Washington, DC: Author.

U.S. Department of Education. (2004). *Percent postsecondary degrees by race and ethnicity.* Washington, DC: National Center for Educational Statistics, Institute of Educational Science.

U.S. Department of Education. (2006a). *Reading 2005: Reading grades 4 and 8* (NCES 2006-451). Washington, DC: National Center for Educational Statistics, Institute of Educational Sciences.

U.S. Department of Education. (2006b). *Science 2005: Grades 4, 8, and 12* (NCES 2006-466). National Center for Educational Statistics, Institute of Educational Sciences.

U.S. Department of Education. (2007a). 12th Grade reading and mathematics 2005 (NCES 207-468). National Center for Educational Statistics, Institute of Educational Sciences.

U.S. Department of Education (2007b). America's high school graduates. Results from the 2005 NAEP High School Transcript Study. U.S. Department of Education. NCES2007-467.

Useem, E. (1992). Middle schools and math groups: Parents' involvement in children's placement. *Sociology of Education, 65*, 263–279.

Valencia, R. (2005). The Mexican American struggle for equal educational opportunity in *Mendez v. Westminster:* Helping to pave the way for *Brown v. Board of Education. Teachers College Record, 107*, 389–423.

Valenzuela, A. (1999). *Subtractive schooling: U.S.-Mexican youth and the politics of caring.* Albany: State University of New York Press.

Van Hook, J. (2002). Immigration and African American educational opportunity: The transformation of minority schools. *Sociology of Education, 75*, 169–189.

Walker, V. S. (1996). *Their highest potential: An African American school community in the segregated south.* Chapel Hill: University of North Carolina Press.

Walters, P. B. (2001). Educational access and the state: Historical continuities and discontinuities in racial inequality in American education. *Sociology of Education, 34*, 35–149.

Waters, M. (1990). *Ethnic options: Choosing identities in America.* Berkeley: University of California Press.

Watkins, W. (2001). *The White architects of Black education: Ideology and power in America 1865–1954.* New York: Teachers College Press.

Wenglinsky, H. (1997). How money matters: The effects of school district spending on academic achievement. *Sociology of Education, 70*, 221–237.

Wells, A. S., & Crain, R. L. (1994). Perpetuation theory and the long-term effects of school desegregation. *Review of Educational Research, 64*, 531–556.

Wells, A. S., & Serna, I. (1996). The politics of culture: Understanding the local political resistance to detracking in racially mixed schools. *Harvard Educational Review, 66*, 93–118.

Welner, K. G. (2001). *Legal rights, local wrongs: When community control collides with educational equity.* Albany: State University of New York Press.

Willis, P. (1977). *Learning to labor: How working class kids get working class jobs.* New York: Columbia University Press.

Woodrum, A. (2004). State-mandated testing and cultural resistance in Appalachian schools: Competing values and expectations. *Journal of Research in Rural Education, 19*(1), 1–10.

Yonazawa, S. (1997). *Making decisions about students' lives: An interactive study of secondary school students' academic program selection.* Unpublished doctoral dissertation, University of California, Los Angeles.

21

Race(ing), Class(ing), and Gender(ing) Our Work

Critical Race Theory, Critical Race Feminism, Epistemology, and New Directions in Educational Policy Research

DAVID O. STOVALL
University of Illinois at Chicago

The following chapter seeks to demonstrate how Critical Race Theory (CRT) and Critical Race Feminism (CRF) work in concert as epistemologies and methodological frameworks that contribute to a critical analysis of educational policy in the United States. In order to address the aforementioned theoretical constructs, this chapter is centered in addressing two questions:

- How can CRT and CRF, as both epistemological and methodological frameworks, address the conditions of those adversely affected by the enforcement of educational policy in urban school districts?
- How can CRT and CRF contribute to a critical analysis of educational policy in urban areas?

To engage this task the chapter begins with a discussion of epistemology and critical policy analysis in education. Second, the chapter provides a brief overview of CRT, CRF, and Critical Race Praxis in education. The third section provides an example of CRT and CRF analysis in an urban school district in the United States and its implications for current trends in urban educational policy. The chapter concludes with a discussion of the possibilities of CRT and CRF in forging new directions in educational policy research.

Epistemology and Critical Policy Analysis in Educational Policy Research

Webster's *New International Dictionary of the English Language* defines epistemology as "the theory or science of the method and grounds of knowledge, especially with reference to its limits and validity (Webster, 1940, p. 861). Using this definition, the work of William Schubert (1986) is useful in his discussion of epistemology as dealing with "the nature of knowledge and the knowing process" (p. 121). For those interested in educational policy research and praxis,

the nature of knowledge is informed by the work we do with students, communities, teachers, parents, community organizations, teachers, and administrators.

Schubert continues in his inquiry to ask a number of questions that remain relevant to educational policy research: *By what methods can knowledge be acquired and validated? To what extent is knowledge generalizable, and to what extent does it depend on particular circumstances* (p. 122)? In relation to action and reflection (praxis), Schubert's inquiries allow researchers to frame a research agenda aimed at the investigation of phenomena with regards to race, class, and gender. The "particular circumstances" under which phenomena occur is critical when posing questions in relationship to what knowledge informs our understanding. However, it should be noted that the aim of CRT and CRF research is not to demonstrate generalizability, but to provide a framework by which to perform educational policy research and analysis with regard to race, class, and gender. Reviewed later in the document in relationship to CRT and CRF, these epistemological foundations provide the necessary building blocks to provide alternative frameworks.

If we understand education as intensely political (intimately connected to systems of power and domination), the work of Paulo Freire (2003) challenges the critical research community to reflect on themselves, their responsibilities, and their role in posing alternative approaches to educational policy. By posing the problems that are experienced in urban communities, we are able to engage tangible solutions by reflecting on the work created to address said issues. This reflexive practice allows those who engage CRT and CRF to engage in praxis. Discussed in detail in later sections, a critical race praxis provides researchers the chance to explain, discuss, and challenge traditional paradigms around students of color that operate utilizing deficit models. For researchers who work in solidarity with groups that seek to address issues of historically underserved communities of color in schools and education writ large, a critical race praxis approach has the potential to be extremely beneficial.

Additionally, it allows us to ask a different set of questions in relationship to policy under the assumption that the work we suggest is in direct relation to a particular outcome that has the potential to adversely affect the lives of young people in schools. Mentioned as *critical* policy analysis in the work of Taylor, Rizvi, Lingard, and Henry (1997), the following questions are political as they are critical in that they challenge the status quo in educational policy:

- Why was this policy adopted?
- On whose terms? Why?
- On what grounds have these selections been justified? Why?
- In whose interests? Indeed, how have competing interests been negotiated. (Kenway, as cited in Taylor et al., 1997, p. 39)

Utilizing Kenway's framework, Taylor et al. offer a final question: What are the consequences? Embedded in this inquiry is a type of skepticism that allows researchers to challenge traditional airs of positivism around the implementation of policy. In the ensuing sections, CRT and CRF are explained and discussed as epistemology and method that encourages praxis while utilizing a critical framework aimed at addressing the aforementioned policy questions.

Critical Race Theory, Critical Race Feminism, and Critical Race Praxis in Education

CRT has evolved as a theoretical and methodological construct over the last 30 years. In response to the Critical Legal Studies (CLS) movement, CRT was the attempt by scholars of color to critique liberalism in legal scholarship. As the CLS scholars understood the legal system to be unjust, CRT scholars felt that it did not take into account all the necessary "evils" that contributed to an unjust society. Challenging their primary focus on class, CRT scholars felt it was just as important to include race as a necessary "evil." Their understanding was that "racism will not be understood or go away" because CLS proves that "legalisms are indeterminate and the law reflects the interests of the power structure." The operating premise was that social reality "is constructed by the creation and exchange of stories about individual situations" (Tate, 1997, p. 216). Narrative, in creating such an exchange, is the compound agent that embraces an interdisciplinary approach. To the CRT scholar, the theoretical construct expands the scope of CLS through the addition of a racial component by way of critique of the liberal tradition in legal scholarship. Where this account will primarily focus on its recent application to education over the last 12 years, its origins in legal scholarship are central to its development.

In addition to the outgrowths of CRT that challenged the Black-White binary on race (Lat Crit, Asian Crit, First Nations Crit, etc.) and heterosexuality (Queer Crit, etc.) Critical Race Feminism (CRF) emerged from a particular critique of CRT with regards to gender. Noted by Adrien Katherine Wing (1997), women of color in some instances felt excluded by their male peers in the CRT movement. Addressing the absence of gender in the construct, women of color in the legal CRT movement made a call for inclusion from a feminist perspective. The result was "race-ing" patriarchy and feminism. In terms of the tenets, many CRF scholars adhere to the idea that:

> while mainstream feminism asserts that society is patriarchal, it does not "race" patriarchy; it overlooks the fact that this domination affects women and men of color differently than White women. Fundamental to Critical Race Feminism is the idea that women of color are not simply White women plus some ineffable and secondary characteristic, such as skin tone, added on. (Wing, 1997, p. 3)

Crucial to the development of the paradigm, female legal scholars of color began to write in observation of said realities. Maintaining the critique, CRF scholars recognize "how various factors, such as race, gender, and class, interact within a system of white make patriarchy and racist oppression to make the experiences of women of color distinct from those both of men of color and White women" (Onwuachi-Willig, 2006, p. 733).

Such a process includes challenging the essentialist notion that all women of color are facing the same barriers. Instead, CRF pushes scholars and activists to recognize the diversity of women's experiences (Sedilla, as cited in Wing, 2000, p. 71). By including the intersections of class and race, CRF scholars can provide substantive analysis that can be utilized to holistically address the issues and concerns of women of color in education.

In educational policy analysis, CRT operates as an intersection of theoretical constructs through the incorporation of legal, social science, humanities, and educational scholarship. However, the most crucial link between the various disciplines lies in the inclusion of "real life experience" (i.e., narrative). Throughout the process, CRT analysis of K-12 policy acknowledges the:

1. White middle-class American (male) … as the standard against which all other groups are compared.
2. Instruments used to measure differences are universally applied across all groups.
3. Although we need to recognize sources of potential variance such as social class, gender, cultural orientation, and proficiency in English, these factors are viewed as extraneous and can later be ignored. (Tate, 1997, p. 265)

"Standards" in the traditional sense are rarely challenged as to their validity or rationale. Instead, they are often accepted as benign measures that demonstrate a particular skill set. Conversely, if we understand standards as racialized educational policy, CRT analysis challenges questions around the "achievement gap" and other comparisons that favor the test scores of White students as normative. Upon reading this rationale, many would argue that the test scores of Asian American students from particular ethnic groups would complicate this analysis. To this rationale I would offer the example of college admissions, specifically in the instance of the University of California, Berkeley in the mid-1980s. When the school made a decision to grant admission solely on test scores, the result was an incoming freshman class that was almost half Asian and Asian American. Upon viewing the results, the school switched to a policy that incorporated factors other than test scores for admissions (Chi-Ching Sun, 1997).

Understanding racism as endemic to American life, CRT becomes integral in the identification of the intricate relationships in the urban school setting. In order to address the current state of urban education, there must be new systemic and external efforts to address the needs and concerns of students, parents, and teachers. For many this statement may appear too broad. In terms of creating a space to utilize CRT to analyze school policy in urban areas, researchers must be careful not to create a site-specific model for educational change, but to declare the intersection of disciplines in CRT as necessary to the development of new approaches.

In order to develop said approaches, Solorzano and Yosso (2002) suggest the use of CRT in creating a series of tenets that advocate for a critical race method. Leading to a community-centered praxis, this methodology is a theoretically grounded approach that:

1. foregrounds race and racism in all aspects of the research process;
2. challenges the traditional research paradigms, texts, and theories used to explain the experiences of students of color;
3. offers a liberatory or transformative solution to racial, gender, and class subordination;
4. focuses on the racialized, gendered and classed experiences of students of color. Furthermore, it views the experiences as sources of strength; and
5. uses the interdisciplinary knowledge base of ethnic studies, women's studies, sociology, history, humanities, and the law to better understand the experiences of students of color. (Solorzano & Yosso, 2002, p. 24)

Eric Yamamoto (1997), in championing the method known as critical race praxis, has made the parallel attempt to create a constructive method of "bridging" theoretical concepts and justice practice. He challenges CRT scholars to expand its boundaries through the implementation of praxis. At its center lies the idea of "racial justice as anti-subordination practice" (p. 875). CRT, although sufficient to explain the relationships of people of color to White supremacy, does not provide proper analysis of intra-group racial politics. These dynamics can become important as racial/ethnic groups are pitted against each other in false competition through divide and conquer tactics for resources. Using a

recent district court decision on the admission of Chinese American students to a prestigious magnet school in San Francisco (*Ho v. San Francisco Unified School District*), Yamamoto argues for a critical race praxis enabling lawyers to address "color-on-color" racial conflict in addition to White racism (p. 877). As a delegation of Chinese Americans sued the school district for discrimination, support came from conservative factions arguing for the end of quotas in public schooling. The plaintiffs, arguing that their children were more deserving than Mexican and African American students due to high test performance, sought the end of a policy guaranteeing spaces for said groups.

The combination of color-on-color conflict and White supremacy prompts Yamamoto (1997) to suggest a *race practice* (p. 873). Fusing the possible contributions of academics and lawyers to the paradigm, Yamamoto suggests the work of Robert Williams, Jr. calling for professors "unconnected with actual anti-racist struggles" to "spend less time on abstract theorizing and more time on actual community law-based antisubordination practice" (p. 873). Race practice in the law consisted of establishing legal clinics, working in conjunction with community organizations, guiding student activists, establishing relationships with sympathetic politicians, and drafting possible ordinances/laws to address race-based inequity. In education, as a outgrowth of CRT and CRF, critical race praxis would include (but is not limited to) providing policy analysis for community organizations that focus on educational issues, team-teaching courses at a local K-12 school, developing popular education strategies with community organizations, working with parent groups in developing strategies for parental inclusion in school decision-making processes, publishing articles in community newspapers and journals, and engendering authentic relationships with school stakeholders by establishing research agendas *with* them in opposed to *on* them to address their issues and concerns with regards to education. In short, the focus is to stand in solidarity with communities in opposed to using them solely for research sites.

Such praxis is also characterized by "reflexive action." Through this process, anti-racist practice is infused with "aspects of critical inquiry and pragmatism" to recast "theory in light of practical experience" (Yamamoto, 1997, p. 874). In shifting thought into action, CRT shifts into academic activism in terms of incorporating methods of the academy to address practical issues. Challenging the classical "top-down" theoretical paradigm of educational research, critical race praxis encourages the concept of "engaged researchers" where theoretical assumptions are secondary to the experiential knowledge of the groups in question. Incorporating Yamamoto's process, CRT scholars, in critique of U.S. racial dynamics, should recognize and work to alleviate problems that generate such tensions. Justice, as an "experienced" phenomenon, involves grappling with the often "messy and conflictual racial realities" often absent from traditional research literature (Yamamoto, 1997, p. 875). In developing praxis, the idea is to create a method by which to discuss these realities while engaging in anti-racist practice.

Yamamoto (1997) suggests four starting points of "race praxis inquiry:" conceptual analysis, performative inquiry, material analysis, and reflexive action (p. 878). Included in the construct is the effect of White supremacy as an endemic reality on communities of color in struggles against each other for resources (i.e., the *Ho* case). Performative inquiry involves the action necessary to enact a critical race praxis. In the development of community-based initiatives, theoretical approaches are enhanced through experiential knowledge gained in the process. Based on his own experiences in the attempt to fuse activist and academic communities, Yamamoto observes possible tensions if theorists do not engage in praxis:

> One conclusion I draw from interactions with political lawyers and community activists is that theoretical insights about race and critical socio-legal analyses of particular controversies are unlikely to be meaningfully developed and translated for frontline anti-subordination practice unless theorists personally engage with the difficult, entangled, shifting realities of that practice. (p. 880)

In education, the process of addressing the material realities of the communities that we work with is in concert with reflexive action. By developing strategies to identify and challenge the systemic nature of racism, we are able to theorize, identify, and create action plans that are centered in the day-to-day lives of communities. Discussed at length in a subsequent section by way of a specific example of educational policy, a critical race praxis challenges members of the academic community to make tangible connections between communities and our research.

Continuing the argument of critical race praxis in K–12 education, Lynn (1999) offers a critical race pedagogy that enables teachers to respect and honor the cultures of their students. Where his work is situated primarily in the K–12 classroom, his insights provide important lessons that can inform policy research. By expanding the previous work of Woodson (2004), Lynn argues that urban public schools are not "created with the intent of being spiritually, emotionally, and intellectually emancipating (p. 607). Instead, they are promoted and utilized as systems of control and punishment (often under the language of "discipline") for the students who attend them.

Lynn utilizes the work of Ladson-Billings (1998) to highlight the process of culturally relevant teaching as a process that places an emphasis on culture while "facilitating the development of basic skills that will allow the students to successfully navigate the White world" (p. 608). For Lynn this approach in the K–12 classroom allows teachers to incorporate issues of "race, gender and class oppression" (p. 609). This is important in educational policy analysis if we return to the critical questions posed by Kenway with regard to what grounds policies have been selected and for what schools. From this space we are able to identify patterns that could possibly speak to what schools are provided

the necessary resources to allow students to make informed decisions about their lives. Lynn's conclusion that "one cannot *not* prioritize one facet of his or her identity over another because it creates a false dichotomy that negates the fact that we all live our daily lives as raced, classed, and gendered subjective entities" (p. 619). In the attempt to create critical race praxis, Lynn's account connects to the efforts of pedagogical approaches to research on race.

A CRT and CRT analysis of Renaissance 2010 and the Chicago Housing Authority's Plan for Transformation: Lessons from the Ground

Returning to the interdisciplinary method of CRT, it becomes important to rely on history in the discussion of educational policy in Chicago. Where this section will focus on Chicago Housing Authority's (CHA) Plan for Transformation and Renaissance 2010, the connection to education, housing, and business can be located some 37 years prior (1971) with the Chicago 21 Plan. As a plan created to rid the city of blight and to curb White flight, 21 wards were targeted as areas to expand development. As the mayor (Richard J. Daley—father of the current mayor, Richard M. Daley) could not implement the plan at the time, it has returned in the form of the Plan for Transformation and Renaissance 2010 under the leadership of his son. For the remainder of this section, the aforementioned plans should not be considered to be mutually exclusive policies. Instead, they should be understood as part of a collective strategy aimed at reshaping the economic, housing, and educational landscape of the city. In Chicago (and in many other urban centers in the United States), it is impossible to understand the effect of these policies absent of a race and gender analysis. Through CRT and CRF, Chicago provides a tangible example of how the implementation of urban educational policy can aversely affect low-income communities of color.

As a matter of record, it is impossible to understand current educational policy in Chicago without its intimate connections to housing policy and economic development. Where Renaissance 2010 operates as the educational arm of a larger urban redevelopment agenda (combined with the Chicago Housing Authority's Plan for Transformation), further analysis of the policy identifies a plan that has resulted in uneven development and extreme gentrification in communities that have been historically populated by people of color. Extensively studied in the works of Lipman (2003, 2004, 2006; Lipman & Haines, 2007; Greenlee, Hudspeth, Lipman, Smith, & Smith, 2008; Arrastia, 2007), a CRT and CRF analysis of current school policy in Chicago identifies serious implications for urban school districts both nationally and internationally. In order to fully grasp the policy's scope and intention, it is important to begin with the Chicago Housing Authority's Plan for Transformation.

Public housing is perhaps the most extreme example of an economically segregated and isolated community in the United States. The trend in many cities has been to demolish the "projects" (nickname for public housing) and redevelop them as lower density "mixed-income" communities. In Chicago, miles of high-rise buildings razed along the city's South Side—most built in the late 1950s and early 1960s—are now being replaced with low density, low and mid-rise buildings that will contain substantially fewer public housing units and significant numbers of market rate housing for middle-income families (Chicago Housing Authority, 2000). While the new market-rate housing is selling, it is still relatively early in the process to know if these new communities are sustainable.

The mixed-income strategy employed to redevelop public housing in Chicago is a product of this thinking. The Chicago Housing Authority (CHA) is implementing a $1.6 billion Plan for Transformation to redevelop areas once occupied by high-rise public housing as mixed-income communities. As housing stock in the redeveloped areas will be distributed in thirds amongst very low-income, moderate-income, and market rate homes, questions arise as dubious qualifications have been placed on the low-income group (Olivio, 2004). To receive any of the homes in the recent developments, public housing families have to go through a battery of screenings for health (specifically for substance abuse), employment (applicants must now work at least 30 hours per week unless they are not able or are in a training/educational program), and criminal activity (a person cannot rent an apartment if anyone in the household has a felony conviction).

In the Plan for Transformation, schools are framed as an important part of the plan, and that change in the housing will mean an increase in families of moderate and affluent incomes that requires strategic planning on the part of Chicago Public Schools (CPS). For example, *A New Business Plan for Chicago Public Schools*—a report prepared by a global management consulting firm for CPS, recommends that:

> Knowing exactly who your customers are and how best to meet their needs is an ongoing study for businesses. With the city envisioning its schools effectively becoming community centers, its "customers" are everyone in the community. And as new housing is built, the neighborhood demographics will undergo dramatic changes. Accounting for such flux in both the final product and the transition plan is essential. (Kearny, 2005, p. 49)

In Chicago, the expected or likely change in neighborhood demographics resulting from public housing redevelopment is not spelled out. Again where this should not be considered conspiratorial, it is important to note the racialized, coded language of the "dramatic changes" that will come with the new developments. Further deepening the code is the general rule that city officials and developers refer to income and not race when they talk about what the new "mixed" communities will look like. Nevertheless, race is critical in this analysis as 95% of Chicago public housing residents are African American. Additionally, of the 95% African American residents, 40% are senior citizens that live on a fixed income. If we incorporate a CRF analysis to the situation, many of the senior citizens living on fixed incomes are women (specifically grandmothers) who have the responsibility of childrearing in their particular families. With them rests the responsibilities for registering children for school, staying current with immunizations, and remaining abreast to any shifts in current educational policy that may affect their grandchildren. Instead of acknowledging these facts, public officials point to fact that the majority of units will not be public housing—usually no more than one-third of the total. In its current state, it appears that a similar effect is sought by restricting enrollment of lower-income and public housing residents, or "customers" as described above, at newly transformed neighborhood schools.

Masking these conditions, the race of new and old residents or customers creates intricate and broad-reaching intersections of race and class promulgated through education and housing policy. In broad terms, the poor are not the likely beneficiaries of these policies in Chicago or elsewhere. As Lipman (2003) describes, Chicago serves as the place to:

> Secure the claims on urban space of a new (mainly White), urban gentry of managers and professionals by reinforcing a corporate culture of efficiency and rationality while regulating and evicting these marginalized others. This process is legitimated by discourses of regeneration, progress and purification: the state assists real estate developers and elite civic leaders in cleaning up bad neighborhoods, revitalizing blighted areas and keeping gangbangers off the streets. (p. 333)

In other words, we find evidence that while the discourses of "transformation" and "renaissance" evoke such promise for the new gentry, a counter-story is omitted, or masked. In excavating the counter-story, CRT is utilized to help reveal the realities of such projects. The contrasting discourse of "dysfunctional" and "healthy" speak directly to an alleged pathology of the long-time residents who are being displaced. Such dichotomies become problematic in school and community development. In the case of schools, historic inequity is justified by lack of necessary curricular and infrastructure support. As a result, poorly performing schools are in need. The solution to shut down or transform a school is in response to the effects of historic inequity has little to do with the causes of it. By focusing on the conditions and not the source of inequity, changing curriculum, and then restricting access to newly redeveloped schools makes sense. A similar logic underpins public housing policy, where mixed-income developments become the logical solution to the problem of the "project." As noted in Lipman's account, Chicago secures its "transformation" at the expense of poor, working-class, communities of color:

> As public housing is torn down and its residents dispersed to make way for expensive new town homes and condominiums, racially coded accountability policies also justify

the segregation and or removal of African-American communities much as the vocabulary of the "urban frontier" justifies gentrification and displacement of working class residents and people of color in the wave of civilizing urban neighborhoods. (Smith, as cited in Lipman, 2003, p. 346)

Despite the provisions for low-income families in the new mixed-income communities, the aforementioned health, employment, and criminal compliances help to carefully sanitize the community marketed to newcomers. Schools, as the final frontier, provide the necessary push for buyers to take the final step in "coming home" to a "renaissance" of quality education. Still, the question remains: quality for whom?

CRT provides a framework to analyze the ever-shifting phenomenon of race, class, and gender in housing and education. As a result of the normalizing nature of racism in U.S. society, strategies vis-à-vis laws and rules aimed at treating Blacks and Whites "alike" only get at extreme cases of injustice. Further, little is done about business-as-usual forms of racism confronting people daily (Delgado & Stefancic, 2001). This includes overt acts such as racial profiling, but also policy and programs that privilege the White position. Consider, for example, efforts that aimed to promote racial integration by restricting the number of African Americans to literally be the minority in order to assuage fears of Whites that "too many" Blacks will make a neighborhood change. Not only does this reproduce a racist position, it also sustains a belief that there is such a thing as a tipping point that can be predicted and manipulated vis-à-vis policy and practice, which in mixed-income housing means making sure public housing is the minority (Smith, 2006).

To supplement the Plan for Transformation, the mayor, with CPS, in conjunction with the Civic Committee of The Commercial Club of Chicago (a conglomerate of the main business interests in Metropolitan Chicago) produced Renaissance 2010, an overarching policy proposing to close 70 existing underperforming schools and re-open them as 100 new schools under the rubric of charter, contract, or performance school. Beginning with the Civic Committee's report "Left Behind," the discourse of the "problems" of school are mildly coded to name numerous enemies. A section from the introduction reads as follows:

The problem lies in the system, which lacks competitive pressures pushing it to achieve desired results. It responds more to politics and pressures from the school unions that to community or parental demands for quality. Schools, principals and teachers are largely insulated from accountability or responsibility for results … The constraints of the city-wide teachers' union contract, including the tenure system and the difficulty of removing teachers for cause, make management of the system's human resources difficult. State achievement tests are not given in every grade every year, so it is impossible to see exactly where gains are made—or where students consistently fail to advance. Success is not rewarded; and failure is not—or infrequently—penalized. (Ahlquist et al., 2003, p. 3)

The rhetoric of the previous excerpt is loaded for several reasons. A CRT analysis would identify "politics" as merely pressures from teachers' unions, excluding the inability of CPS to disclose its policies around school closings in gentrifying neighborhoods and the sale of CPS-owned land to commercial and residential real estate developers. "Accountability" and "responsibility" are interpreted as test scores as the definitive marker for learning. The neoliberal rhetoric of "constraints," "management," and "gains" speak to a desired emphasis on the primacy of market economies and the centrality of individual self-interest in all spheres of economic and social life (Lipman & Haines, 2007, p. 480). CRT and CRF counter neoliberal rhetoric through analysis of the implementation of said policy. As Renaissance 2010 was rolled out in the summer of 2004, 20 of 22 schools in the Mid-South community in Chicago were scheduled for closing due to underperformance. Upon reviewing the data, Lipman, by collaborating with community members, discovered a vast contradiction in CPS rhetoric, discovering that 10 of the schools were not underperforming according to CPS standards. However, what they did discover was that building permits for residential construction and condominium conversion were peaking in the same area. Additionally, the Mid-South is close to the downtown central business district, has proximity to two major expressways, and has an ample number of recreational outlets in the form of lakefront public parks, bike paths, and a surge in new restaurants and cafes. As this information was dispersed throughout the community, residents were able to stage a series of actions that halted the initial rollout of the plan.

The Mid-South instance highlights another set of complications from a critical race praxis perspective in that intra-racial tensions are substantial, in that a significant portion of the gentrifying community are upper middle-class African American families. Where some would argue that this dynamic refutes CRT's claim to the endemic nature of racism/White supremacy, a closer analysis would state that racism should not be reduced to individual acts of bigotry. Instead, it should be understood as a complex system of oppressions where members of historically oppressed racial groups can be individually rewarded to enact and enforce the policies of the dominant society. In the case of Mid-South, the reward for new affluent African American residents and low-income residents that are allowed to remain would be access to new homes and new schools. The challenge to researchers who work in solidarity with communities would be to get both the middle-class and low-income residents of the city to work as a unified front in opposing the closing of schools. By engaging with both groups, there is a greater chance for both groups to recognize that these new homes and new schools may be a false premise in that both sets of residents may not have access to them in the final analysis.

Nevertheless, the mayor's office, with the support of developers and administrators from the central office, has continued with their sale of this policy throughout the city. As a result of converging policies, many educational initiatives operate in concert with redevelopment efforts to foster displacement among the city's working-class African American and Latino/a populations (Lipman, 2004). In Chicago, many schools in communities experiencing gentrification have changed rapidly and drastically. Schools once classified as neighborhood schools become magnet schools, language academies, math and science academies, or visual and performing arts centers. For the incoming resident, the "academy" title seems appealing, but it is part of a larger concept that provides "incentive for professional and middle-class families to live in the city" (Lipman, 2004, p. 56). Such curricular change needs to be examined more carefully and in the context of the shifts in community redevelopment initiatives. Key to the argument for building new public schools and redeveloping public housing was that current residents would benefit. However, it can also help to attract middle-income families who might otherwise move to the suburbs or are likely to once their children reach school age. Strategies to redevelop poorly performing inner city schools and the poor neighborhoods where they are usually located has real potential to do more harm than good for the families the policy is supposed to benefit. Examining how CHA's Plan for Transformation and CPS's Renaissance 2010 play out in a community reveals the subtle and overt implications of housing and education policy's impact on communities of color in urban space. For this reason Renaissance 2010 should not be considered an education plan. Instead, it is the educational arm of a business plan in the form of education policy. Through the lens of CRT, this becomes a matter of public policy, not conspiracy.

The most recent development of Renaissance 2010 has come in the form of closing 18 schools, all (except one) of which are in predominantly African American and Latino/a neighborhoods. Where many of these neighborhoods are in the final stages of gentrification or are being prepared for initial stages of development, community residents are forced to scramble to find schools for their children in the fall (Greenlee et al., 2008, p. 1). Mired in the rhetoric of "underutilized" and "underperforming," community residents provide an entirely different story than what CPS is offering. Many of these schools have demonstrated vast improvements in areas like attendance, teacher mobility rates, and test scores. Nevertheless, despite efforts from parents and community groups to request CPS policies on what constitutes underutilization or underperformance, Greenlee and colleagues highlight the contradictions in CPS rhetoric. For example, CPS considers any elementary school "overcrowded" if enrollment exceeds 80% of a schools design capacity (Greenlee et al., 2008, p. 7). In the current round of proposed closings, 6 of the 18 schools were under 80%. If a CRT lens is applied to this dynamic, we would have to look deeper into the history of each of the "under-populated" schools to see if families have been moving out of the area due to rising housing costs, eminent domain, condominium conversions, and new housing stock. Of the six previously mentioned schools, three

are in severely gentrifying neighborhoods, with a fourth being primed for new development. As this information is distributed to communities, residents are aware of the numerous connections their school has to macro-policy in education, housing, and economic development. Similar to the residents of Mid-South, if communities are armed with this information early on in the process, they are able to engage proactive strategies that can thwart the current wave of closings.

With the current turn in closings, CPS has developed a new term for schools, which receive students from a neighboring school that has been closed. Known as "receiver schools," some institutions with these classifications have doubled in size in the course of one year. However, it must be noted that the new population does not come with additional resources from central office. As a consequence, many of these schools are experiencing increased rates of student-on-student violence and expulsions. Where this document does not address the specific ramifications of the school-to-prison pipeline, a CRT and CRF analysis alerts researchers to the proximity of certain stidents to the criminal justice system. As schools are starved of resources, students, in turn, are criminalized as educational options become fewer.

The national and international implications loom large in that the Chicago model of reform has been duplicated in cities like New York, Los Angeles, and Houston. Officials from all three cities have come to Chicago to study mayoral control (of the school board) and solidifying business interests to foster development. Internationally Chicago has been deemed a "global city," being cited for its improvements in business, housing, and education. As a central hub for global finance, informational technological advancements, and management for systems of production, Chicago has fashioned itself as a viable competitor for investment from transnational global firms in business, industry, and entertainment. Currently, over 10 Fortune 500 companies have their international headquarters in Chicago. Coupled with a construction boom that has 50 new skyscrapers scheduled for construction in the downtown area, Chicago has created:

> A massive market for upscale residential and leisure spaces built out of, and over, the homes and factories and neighborhoods of formal industrial workforces. The new luxury living and recreational spaces become gated security zones, policed and controlled to ensure the "safety" of their new occupants and global tourists against the menacing "others," particularly disenfranchised youth of color who increasingly have place in the new economy and refashioned city. (Lipman, 2004, p. 8)

As education is linked to the economy through the suggestions of Bill Gates, the Business Roundtable, and the Civic Committee of the Commercial Club of Chicago, CRT analysis of educational policy provides a narrative that counters the positivistic language of "development" and "educational opportunity." Instead, the critical policy question around who has access to what knowledge becomes critical in the attempt to develop social movements that challenge "the discourse of inevitability" (p. 11).

Conclusion: Critical Policy Questions for a Research Agenda of Community Engagement

As students are placed in the lanes of college prep, low-wage service sector/military employment, or incarceration (the most proximal outcome if young people are unable to matriculate through the first two tracks), a CRT analysis of educational policy enables researchers to work in solidarity with communities adversely affected by policies that occur in similar fashion. If CHA and CPS had the interests of the community in mind, equitable education and housing policy would be configured differently. Where both entities currently hold public hearings to field the issues and concerns of the community, the current iteration has little connection to the direct implementation of policy. Instead, the city could have used the numerous reports on public housing and public education, taken a complete audit of the state of both systems, and guaranteed a one-to-one rebuilding plan for public housing, assuring current residents would have a place to live. Additionally, the new housing should have been coupled with education and job readiness programs for former CHA residents. With schools, CPS could have been transparent with its policies on school closings and developed a needs-based assessment of each school in the district. This would have ensured public documentation and access of the needs of schools as stated by a combination of community members, students, teachers, and administrators. But alas, I am only offering a utopian construct of equitable education policy.

Again, leaning on an interdisciplinary perspective, history demonstrates that centralized structures best respond to pressures initiated from people on the ground. If CRT and CRF theorists plan to join such a struggle, it must come in the form of working with communities to develop strategies to address their conditions. Similar to the efforts of Lipman in the Mid-South, scholars must humble themselves and offer their skill set to supplement the dearth of community knowledge that can be critical in informing our strategies. As an introductory step in this direction, the editors of the education magazine *Rethinking Schools* have suggested a set of critical questions communities can mobilize around if "new" schools are solicited to them.

- What role have teachers, parents, and community representatives played in developing the plans for creating new schools?
- What populations will the new schools serve? Will the students select the schools or will the schools select the students? What procedures are in place to ensure that new schools will not cream the best students, but will serve a representative cross-section of the population, including special education students and English language learners?

- What impact will the new schools have on existing schools in the district, including racial balance and the distribution of experienced teachers?
- Where will the new schools be housed? What facilities studies have been done? How are these plans being balanced with existing facilities needs in the district?
- Are the new schools intended to be system-wide models for improvement and reform? If so, how will their experience be shared, reviewed, and implemented in the district? (Au et al., 2005, p. 6)

Specific attention must be paid to race, class, and gender when looking at the answers to all these questions. By doing so, as evidenced by the example presented here, community members, community organizations, researchers, and policy analysts will be able to identify the broad and nuanced factors endemic of a racist system that contributes to the displacement of people who may not have access to material resources to remain in gentrifying communities.

For researchers, we must return to Yamamoto's suggestion of challenging CRT scholars to answer critical questions with regard to addressing the conditions of the lives of the people we do research with. The mere suggestion of engagement stands counter to traditional notions of "objective" research that seeks to spin a positive light on current trends in economic development, housing, and educational policy.

Essentially, one of the roles of CRT scholars is to understand the urgency of the situations faced by many communities of color with regard to urban schools. As significant populations of people of color classified as working-class and/or low-income make drastic geographic shifts within large urban areas and their outlying suburbs, it behooves those of us concerned with their situation to understand their situation not to be one of conspiracy, but of public policy. Through the epistemology and methods of CRT and CRF, we are able to connect the dots.

References

Ahlquist, G., Brodsky, W. J., Farrell, W. J., Lubin, D. G., Martin, R. E., McKenna, A. J., et al. (2003). *Left behind: Student achievement in Chicago Public Schools.* Chicago: Civic Committee of the Commercial Club of Chicago.

Arrastia, L. (2007). Capital's daisy chain: Exposing Chicago's corporate coalition. *Journal of Critical Education Policy Studies, 5*(1). Retrieved July 8, 2008, from http://www.jceps.com/index.php?pageID=article&articleID=86

Au, W., Burrant, T., Bigelow, B., Christensen, L., Karp, S., Miller, L., et al. (2005). The small schools express. *Rethinking Schools, 19*(4), 4–6.

Chi-Ching Sun, T. (1997). *The admissions dispute: Asian Americans versus the University of California at Berkeley.* New York: University Press of America.

Chicago Housing Authority (2000). *Change: A plan for transformation.* Chicago: Chicago Housing Authority.

Delgado, R., & Stefancic, J. (2001). *Critical race theory: An introduction.* New York: New York University Press.

Freire, P. (2003). *Education for critical consciousness.* New York: Continuum.

Greenlee, A., Hudspeth, N., Lipman, P., Smith, D. A., & Smith, J. (2008). *Data and Democracy Project: Investing in neighborhoods.* Chicago:

University of Illinois, Collaborative for Equity and Justice in Education and Natalie P. Vorhees Center for Neighborhood and Community Improvement.

Kearny, A. T. (2005). A new business plan for Chicago Public Schools. *Executive Agenda*, 47–51.

Ladson-Billings, G. (1998). Just what is critical race theory and what's it doing in a "nice" field like education. *International Journal of Qualitative Studies in Education, 11*(1), 7—24.

Lipman, P. (2003). Chicago school policy: Regulating Black and Latino youth in the global city. *Race, Ethnicity, and Education, 6,* 331–355.

Lipman, P. (2004). *High stakes education: Inequality, globalization, and urban school reform*. New York: Routledge Falmer.

Lipman, P. (2006). Chicago school reform: Advancing the global city agenda. In J. P. Koval, L. Bennett, M. I. J. Bennett, F. Demissie, R. Garner, & K. Kim (Eds.), *The new Chicago: A social and cultural analysis* (pp. 248–258). Philadelphia: Temple University Press.

Lipman, P., & Haines, N. (2007). From accountability to privatization and African-American exclusion: Chicago's "Renaissance 2010." *Education Policy, 2,* 471–502.

Lynn, M. (1999). Toward a critical race pedagogy: A research note. *Urban Education, 33*(5), 606–627.

Olivio, A. (2004, September 22). New CHA housing is tied to jobs: Adults must work 30 hours a week. *The Chicago Tribune*, p. A8.

Onwuachi-Willig, A. (2006). This bridge called our backs: An introduction to "the future of critical race feminism." *UC Davis Law Review, 39,* 733–742.

Schubert, W. (1986). *Curriculum: Perspective, paradigm and possibility*. New York: Macmillan.

Solorzano, D., & Yosso, T. (2002). Critical race methodology: Counter-storytelling as an analytical framework. *Qualitative Inquiry, 8,* 23–44.

Smith, J. L. (2006). Mixed-income communities: Designing out poverty or pushing out the poor? In L. Bennett, J. Smith, & P. Wright (Eds.), *Where are poor people to live: Transforming public housing communities* (pp. 259–281). London: M.E. Sharpe.

Tate, W. (1997). Critical race theory and education: History, theory and implications. *Review of Research in Education, 22,* 195–247.

Taylor, S., Rizvi, F., Lingard, B., & Henry, M. (1997). *Educational policy and the politics of change*. New York: Routledge.

Webster Group (1940). *Webster's New International Dictionary of the English Language*. New York: C&C Merriam Company.

Wing, A. K. (1997). (Ed.). *Critical race feminism: A reader*. New York: New York University Press.

Wing. A. K. (2000). (Ed.). *Global critical race feminism: An international reader*. New York: New York University Press.

Woodson, C. G. (2004). *The mis-education of the Negro*. Trenton, NJ: Africa World Press.

Yamamoto, E. (1997). Critical race praxis: Race theory and political lawyering practice in post-civil rights America. *Michigan Law Review, 95,* 821–900.

22

Rhetoric and Symbolic Action in the Policy Process[1]

Lisa Rosen
University of Chicago

This chapter reviews both empirical and theoretical work that illuminates the role of symbolic action in the policy process. I begin by considering why this approach to policy analysis (in education as well as in other policy domains) has been neglected or underutilized and what has been lost as a consequence. I then demonstrate that educational policy is an especially salient arena for symbolic action and that full understanding of the educational policy process therefore requires attention to its understudied symbolic dimensions. Next, I identify the major conceptual themes in the analysis of policy as a form of symbolic action, distinguishing its constitutive and expressive dimensions. The remaining discussion is devoted to elaborating these two dimensions of policy activity. My conclusion considers both the strengths and potential weaknesses of symbolic analysis for illuminating educational policy processes and the implications of this approach for the practice of policy analysis.

An Underutilized Approach

Policy research has historically been limited by conventional assumptions about the instrumental nature of policy activity: that is, by the received view of policy as the construction of instruments (e.g., regulations and programs) designed to address public needs. In this received view, which Deborah Stone (1997) labels "the rationality project," policy is understood primarily as a form of utilitarian (i.e., goal-seeking) behavior, in which there is a direct, logical connection between the instruments of policy and specific objectives. As a consequence of these assumptions, policy analyses typically focus on the purposes and functions of policies and the extent to which they produce the outcomes stated or intended by their creators. This emphasis has led policy analysts to adopt a "naïve rationalism" (Cohen & Rosenberg, 1977, p. 136) concerning the policy process, ignoring the non-rational, non-utilitarian dimensions of the policy process.[2]

Compounding this "obsession with instrumentalism" (Rowan, 1984, p. 76), policy research has also been characterized by a positivist orientation which regards the policy process "as a set of factual propositions, where those facts are treated as explicit and objective realities that can be discovered by direct observation and perception" (Yanow, 1993, p. 42). This orientation has caused many policy analysts to overlook those aspects of the policy process that cannot be understood through exclusive attention to explicit facts and "objective realities" and thus to ignore or downplay the role of implicit meanings, subjective perceptions, and tacit or taken-for-granted understandings within the policy process. In contrast, analyses of symbolic activity deal with the "gap between the overt superficial statement of action and its underlying meaning" and involve identifying what is unstated or implied by particular actions through situating their analysis within a broader consideration of the social, cultural, and political contexts in which they occur (Firth, 1973, p. 26). In other words, the study of symbolic action involves the contextualized interpretation of subjective meanings in addition to the identification of objective facts. Consequently, the analysis of symbolic action is not exclusively concerned with validity or proof in the traditional sense, but with "degrees of plausibility of inference" (Firth, 1973, p. 176). Thus, symbolic studies are more vulnerable to charges of interpretive bias or subjectivity, making them less authoritative as grounds for policy decisions, an issue I return to in the conclusion.

Likewise, policy research has also historically been biased toward quantitative studies.[3] This bias, bolstered by policy makers' often narrow conceptions of science (see Erickson & Gutierrez, 2002), is more pronounced than ever in the present educational policy environment, in which the federal government is aggressively promoting and sponsoring a view of research that deems large-scale, quantitative studies (especially randomized, controlled experiments) more "scientific" than other forms of scholarship. However, while quantitative techniques are clearly well-suited to measuring outcomes and ascertaining facts, the symbolic or cultural dimensions of policy are more difficult to study using methods such as surveys and experiments because these dimensions cannot be easily quantified. Rather, symbolic processes are more amenable to in-depth qualitative analysis using ethnographic or other interpretive methods.

Finally, the applied nature of much policy research, together with the sense of urgency that frequently surrounds policy problems, create an expectation that studies of policy will yield straightforward, unambiguous, and practical answers to these urgent problems. This further encourages policy researchers to emphasize the instrumental dimensions of policy processes and to build their studies around examining cause-effect relationships between particular problems and the policies addressed to solving them. As we shall see, symbolic analyses of policy rarely produce such simple and unambiguous answers. At the same time, they also suggest that the certainty and simplicity policy makers seek from research is largely an illusion. Yet, the analysis of policy as symbolic action need not necessarily be understood as a repudiation of instrumentally oriented approaches. Rather, a view of policy as symbolic action directs attention to an important, but understudied *dimension* of policy activity. As Firth (1973) argues: "Man does not live by symbols alone, but man orders and interprets his reality by his symbols, and even reconstructs it" (p. 20).

Understanding the Symbolic Dimensions of Policy: Education as a Particularly Salient Arena for Symbolic Action

Dissatisfied with prevailing approaches to analyzing policy, the scholars whose work this chapter highlights share a concern with understanding policy as a sociocultural process that involves not simply overt, explicit, and rational behavior, but also (a) tacit meanings, implicit understandings, and attempts to define, categorize, and interpret an intrinsically ambiguous reality; (b) contestation over those culturally constructed meanings among individuals and groups with different degrees of power to impose their interpretations on others; and (c) the display, enactment, and validation of particular cultural beliefs, values, and ideals.

At the same time, while directing attention to the latter, intangible dimensions of policy, symbolic analyses nevertheless remain concerned with the tangible and material consequences of particular policies (e.g., their effects on students, parents, administrators, teachers, and everyday citizens).[4] However, such analyses demonstrate that the tangible effects of policies are frequently *mediated by* intangible cultural or symbolic processes. In other words, policies do not necessarily directly shape action. Rather, how various actors interpret or make sense of policies partly determines their consequences. For example, individuals' prior beliefs, cultural understandings, and so forth influence not only the initial construction of policies, but also how policies get translated into practice or enacted in particular settings. At the same time, the body of work reviewed in this chapter also shows that policies influence actions by shaping or reinforcing particular ways of interpreting and conceptualizing educational situations or problems (e.g., particular ways of understanding student achievement or educational equality). In short, there is a dynamic, mutually shaping relationship between policy instruments and the interpretive, sense-making, or symbolic activities of social actors.

Analyses of policy as a form of symbolic action make a strong case that studies of policy that ignore or overlook its symbolic aspects miss much that is important about policy as a human endeavor.[5] This is true of policy in general, but may be particularly true of educational policy, for a number of reasons. First, Americans have historically imbued education with the almost miraculous power to alleviate a range of social problems, from the assimilation of immigrants to the redress of racial inequalities. This belief in the redeeming power of education is akin to a national faith (cf. Mead, 1943, pp. 638–639). Consequently, education policy is an especially intense focus for symbolic action, making schools and the policy activity surrounding them "a place in which great stories can be told and great dramas acted out" (Cohen & Rosenberg, 1977, pp. 134–135). For example, as we shall see, the prominent role that schooling plays within American cultural narratives of success and social mobility (especially for immigrants and ethnic minorities) makes educational policy a kind of national theater for the dramatization of these cultural stories (see Bigler, 1999, pp. 81–118). Specifically, educational policy serves as a medium for displaying, enacting, celebrating, and reinforcing a "sacred narrative" at the heart of conceptions of American national identity: that the United States is a meritocratic society in which each person has an equal opportunity to achieve the American dream through hard work and individual effort. Structural factors (such as race or class privilege—or conversely, disadvantage—and institutionalized practices that reproduce such inequality) have no place in this explanatory cultural model. It is this blindness to the latter factors (which social scientists have repeatedly demonstrated play a significant role in influencing both social mobility and educational outcomes) that has led sociologists to dub this model the American "achievement ideology" (see Mehan, 1994). This ideology legitimates existing social inequalities because it suggests that individuals who enjoy greater social or economic advantages have achieved these rewards on their own merits and are therefore deserving of their success. Those who have not succeeded in life are likewise to blame for their own failure. The fact that reality frequently falls short of this and other cherished cultural ideals does not make the beliefs associated with this ideology irrelevant or meaningless. On the contrary, from a symbolic perspective, the discrepancy between a society's abstract ideals and reality on the ground makes such stories, and the policies that reinforce them, all the more important as validations of key articles of cultural faith.

Second, the potency of children as political symbols further enhances the salience of educational policy as an arena for symbolic activity. As Senator John D. Rockefeller IV recently commented on the debate surrounding a proposed expansion to the State Children's Health Insurance Program, "There are very few symbols as powerful as kids."[6] This potency derives from the lofty, emotionally charged ideas children are often invoked to represent, including, among other things: innocence, hope, the future, human potential, and humanity's essential goodness (or evil, depending on one's perspective).[7]

Third, educational policy is also an especially potent arena for symbolic action because the "endemic uncertainties" of schooling (Lortie, 1975, p. 134) magnify the innate human drive to impose order, meaning, and certainty on experience. For example, the impact of schooling experiences on student outcomes is far from linear, uniform, or direct. Rather, student learning is variable and complex and the relationship between schooling and learning is mediated by a host of interacting factors, not all of which are fully understood and only some of which schools and policy makers can control: for example, teachers' professional knowledge and skill; individual differences in ability and learning styles among children; students' home environments and peer culture; and the broader social and cultural context of schooling (such as systemic inequalities based on race and economic class, prejudices arising from received understandings of ability, beliefs about the relative intelligence of different categories of students, the structure of economic opportunity, and students' perceptions of the value of education as a means of social mobility). The relationship between educational policy and practice is equally complex, uncertain, and indirect, as the literature on policy implementation attests (see Honig, this volume). Yet, educational policy activity implicitly denies and suppresses these overwhelming complexities and endemic uncertainties, operating *as if* the relationship between teaching and learning, and between policy and practice, was as straightforward as simply choosing the right textbook for a given subject, placing a "highly qualified teacher" in every classroom, or choosing "scientifically validated" curricula and assessments. Likewise, participants in educational policy processes generally act as if they are engaged in strictly instrumental behavior; indeed, for policy actors to acknowledge the irrational aspects of policy activity discussed in this chapter would be to confront directly the limits of their capacity to control and manage educational outcomes.

The dominant instrumentalist mode of policy analysis perpetuates this illusion, thereby shoring up faith in the rationality of the policy project and the possibility of achieving certainty regarding intrinsically uncertain questions. As such, the "obsession with instrumentalism" (Rowan, 1984, p. 76) that generally characterizes policy research is part and parcel of the same symbolic processes that such instrumentally oriented research ignores. That is, the underutilization of the symbolic approach within policy scholarship is a consequence not simply of the preference for certain scientific methods or the prevalence of "naïve

rationalist" assumptions about policy activity as discussed earlier, but also of the very non-rational impulses that mainstream policy analysts tend to deny or ignore: the drive for certainty and order in the face of a chaotic and uncertain world. This situation evinces Firth's (1973) argument that symbolization is a "mode of dealing with reality" that simplifies its complexities and disguises painful truths (pp. 90–91). The abundant uncertainties of the educational process make such coping mechanisms particularly necessary. (I return to the issue of mainstream policy analysis and its role in perpetuating particular views of reality toward the end of the chapter.)

Finally, the special significance of symbolic action for education policy also derives from the unique character of schools as arenas for public discussion and debate over competing cultural ideals (as evidenced by education policy's key role in the ongoing culture wars) and as institutions dedicated to the creation of a common culture and promotion of the common good. Indeed, because schools are widely regarded as agents of socialization as well as academic instruction, a range of social groups have historically sought to use schools as tools or platforms for promoting their particular ideologies and cultural worldviews. Thus, at stake in educational policy debates are not only the explicit issues at hand, but also a range of implicit concerns that particular policy issues stand in for or *represent*: for example, in the case of controversy over multicultural and bilingual education, fears and anxieties provoked by perceived threats to a particular conception of national identity and American culture (see Bigler, 1999).

Conceptual Themes

Three interrelated premises undergird the analysis of policy as a form of symbolic activity. The first is that all human perception is necessarily indirect or mediated. This premise—drawn primarily from phenomenological philosophy (especially the work of Alfred Schutz, 1932/1967)—holds that reality is too overwhelmingly complex and ambiguous for human beings to perceive directly. We cannot perceive everything that we encounter and so require a means of selective perception: a way to filter or process experience and thereby render it into a simpler and more manageable form. The second premise is that human beings possess an innate drive to create order, certainty, and meaning out of the chaos, complexity, and intrinsic ambiguity of experience. Culture, which provides a symbolic toolkit for making sense of experience, is the primary means by which we fulfill the latter needs. The third premise is that reality and its experience do not have inherent meaning. Rather, human beings *give* meaning and order to the natural and social world by means of cultural or symbolic constructs that help us define situations and thus make sense of or filter experience. These symbolic structures shape perception by directing attention toward particular aspects of experience (and away from others) and shape cognition and behavior by naming and classifying that experience, defining expectations about events, and suggesting ways of interpreting and reacting to those events. As a form of cultural activity, policy is part of this meaning-making process.

My discussion is organized in terms of two distinct, but interrelated dimensions of symbolic activity manifested in the policy arena: (a) the role of policy in communicating and reinforcing important articles of cultural faith (its *expressive* aspects); and (b) policy's role in the ongoing construction of social reality (its *constitutive* aspects). The distinction I make between these two dimensions is primarily one of emphasis: the former dimension highlights the ceremonial or ritualistic, while the latter foregrounds the persuasive or rhetorical aspects of policy processes.[8] At the same time, a crosscutting theme in the studies I consider is the role of conflict, competition, and the power to control meaning as central elements of symbolic activity. Symbolic analyses assume a fundamental interrelation between policy and politics. They are especially concerned with how particular policies may either reinforce or undermine dominant cultural beliefs and ideologies, either bolstering or challenging the existing social order by shaping educational actors' interpretations of reality and consequently their actions.[9]

Policy as a Form of Expressive Activity

A policy can be said to have expressive import when *the act of having passed the policy* is of equal or greater importance than its intended instrumental effects. All policies can be shown to have expressive aspects. However, these aspects are more visible in the case of initiatives that actually lack instrumental mechanisms for achieving their stated goals. For example, Smith, Miller-Kahn, Heinecke, and Jarvis (2004) note that following recent, high profile school shootings in the United States, several states passed laws mandating the posting of the Ten Commandments in schools, presumably with the objective of reducing school violence. Yet, these laws do not provide any substantive instruments that could logically be expected to achieve this objective (p. 9).

Such policies constitute public expressions and exaltations of particular values and principles, rather than instrumental means to achieving particular ends. For example, requiring the posting of the Ten Commandments in schools sends a more general or abstract symbolic message about the importance of Judeo-Christian values, the role of schools in imparting these traditional values, the commitment of policy makers to upholding them, and the religious basis of the nation more generally. This example illustrates that policies can be thought of as public performances designed to dramatize particular ideals and values, elicit or inspire particular emotions, and communicate particular symbolic messages. Indeed, as later discussion shows, this dramatization frequently involves many of the same elements as theatrical performances, including the use of imagery, stories, props, and staging. Consequently, many studies that analyze policy as a form of expressive activity draw an analogy between policy/politics and theater.

Instrumental Failure and Symbolic Success Moreover, while many educational policies may fail on strictly instrumental grounds, they may nevertheless be highly effective as symbolic acts. Abstinence-only sex education programs are an example of this phenomenon. The debates surrounding such programs—which are favored by religious and social conservatives in both the United States and Britain—also illustrate the role of policy in struggles over competing values within the ongoing culture wars (see Apple, 1989, 1996, 2001). Abstinence-only policies require schools to teach about sex within a "moral framework" that emphasizes abstinence until marriage and prohibits or discourages teaching about sexuality, sexual orientation, contraception, and safe sex. On the one hand, when measured against the instrumental goals of reducing risky sexual behavior and teen pregnancy, such policies are a clear failure. For example, researchers have consistently found that such programs not only do not achieve these goals, but may even work at cross-purposes to them because they deny students access to information on birth control and methods for protecting against sexually transmitted diseases.[10]

On the other hand, however, when viewed as a form of expressive activity, the failure of such policies to achieve the aforementioned goals is irrelevant. Indeed, to the proponents of such programs the display, enactment, and validation of a particular vision of social and moral order may be of equal or greater importance. For example, by portraying sex outside of marriage as both immoral and dangerous and prohibiting discussions of sexual practices that deviate from this traditional mold, abstinence-only sex education policies send the message that ours is a society that values heterosexual marriage as the ideal family form (in spite of the fact that increasingly fewer families actually conform to this mold). Indeed, advocates of abstinence-only programs view them as a critical counterweight to the permissiveness and moral relativism that they believe has infiltrated the culture since the 1960s (see Lewis & Knijn, 2002; Thomson, 1994). Thus, from the perspective of supporters, such policies constitute "a symbolic barrier to a culture's disintegration" (Firth, 1973, pp. 17–18), regardless of their instrumental effect on students' sexual behavior or attitudes.[11] At the same time, to direct attention to the symbolic dimensions of instrumentally ineffective policies such as abstinence-only sex education is not to deny that such policies have effects or consequences. On the contrary, in the case of abstinence-only sex education, such policies may have the very real consequences of actually increasing the likelihood of teenagers becoming pregnant or contracting sexually transmitted diseases, as suggested previously.

Policy and Status Politics As symbolic acts, policies also involve what Gusfield (1986)—following Richard Hofstadter and Seymour Lipset—calls "status politics": conflict arising "from status aspirations and discontents" in which the primary stakes are the allocation of respect and prestige via institutionalized signs of social status (pp. 17–18). For example, abstinence-only sex education policies confer social status on the worldviews of religious and cultural conservatives by making them part of the officially sanctioned curriculum. Indeed, symbolic analyses of social policy controversies ranging from debates over temperance (Gusfield, 1986), to abortion (Luker, 1984), to progressive education (Kliebard, 2004) demonstrate that such struggles are as much about the legitimacy and respect accorded to particular values, belief systems, and lifestyles as they are about the specific policy issues in question.

Status politics tend to emerge under conditions of social transformation or social upheaval, in which groups clinging to older or more traditional values seek to preserve their social status in the face of (real or perceived) threats to their way of life and the respect accorded to it. From this perspective, conservative, fundamentalist, and other reactionary social movements can be seen as part of the metaphorical "rear guard" of troops defending an embattled traditional worldview in a struggle against the forces of secularism, moral relativism, and modernity (Gusfield, 1986, p. 9). At issue in such struggles is the respect accorded to not only particular values, but also particular social roles and the identities of the individuals who adopt them, such as traditional gender roles in a culture that increasingly celebrates and valorizes gender equality (cf. Luker, 1984).[12]

Reinforcing Articles of Cultural Faith   As a form of expressive activity, policy also reinforces key articles of cultural faith: those taken-for-granted beliefs and ideas that we do not think to (or are reluctant to) question. Such beliefs and ideas impart a reassuring sense of order, meaning, and certainty to daily living. Bailey (2003) characterizes them as "sacred" because they are rarely examined and tend to be accepted on faith alone, regardless of disconfirming evidence. Following Ibsen, he describes such beliefs and ideas as "saving lies": the fictions on which daily living depends. Most relevant to the present discussion is the faith in the capacity to control educational outcomes. In the face of overwhelming complexity and the uncertainty it engenders, educational policy activity helps shore up and validate a "saving lie" at the heart of the policy enterprise: the belief in the ability to remedy persistent educational problems with technocratic solutions guided by expert knowledge. The need for such validation arises from the ambiguities and complexities of reality discussed previously, which require that culturally constructed beliefs and understandings about how the world works be periodically reinforced and shored up against the chaos, confusion, and anxiety that would otherwise result from confronting a world of conflicting facts, ambiguous alternatives, and the actual limits on our capacity to control educational processes. In the remainder of this section, I elaborate in closer detail three concepts—myth, ritual, and spectacle—that more fully illustrate the expressive aspects of policy, particularly its role in helping to create a reassuring sense of order, certainty, and control in relationship to the schooling process.

Policy as Myth   One way in which policy imparts this sense of reassurance is by providing explanations for complex and troubling social conditions together with plans to address or improve them. For example, when children or schools are not producing the outcomes we imagine they should, we seek or create interpretations to explain the cause of those failures and guide our efforts at addressing them. These explanations are embedded in policy solutions and often take the form of compelling narratives that allocate responsibility for these problems to particular evils and provide persuasive, relatively simple solutions for them. These reassuring accounts contain and reduce the inherent complexities of education, assigning simple, stable explanations and motives to unstable, ambiguous, and highly complex events and conditions.

Such accounts can be thought of as myths: stories that help individuals makes sense of social life. The conventional understanding of myth is a story that is not true or "made up." However, when used as an analytical construct for the examination of social processes, the truth or falsehood of a narrative is not the essential consideration. Rather, use of this concept draws attention to the fact that social conditions are *always* ambiguous and the evidence for any interpretation always incomplete. As Bailey (1994) notes:

> The heart of the matter is a tension between certainty and uncertainty. We pin things down intellectually—we escape chaos—by making intellectual models that identify patterns of events and, beyond the patterns, their causes. These models let us recognize what has happened, tell us what is the appropriate action, and even sometimes allow us to shape future events—at least to plan to do so. (p. 82)

Myths depend upon processes of selection and interpretation to assign meaning to intrinsically uncertain circumstances. These processes produce coherent "storylines" that reduce ambiguities and compensate for gaps in evidence by presenting interpretations that highlight some aspects of those conditions, while directing attention away from others. The central consideration in the analysis of narrative or myth-making as a social process is thus not the accuracy of a given account, but the extent to which it provides a satisfactory explanation for a situation that helps people make sense of their experience and orient their future action: that is, its commensurability with *perceived* reality (regardless of whether or not it also conforms to "the facts," which are frequently ambiguous anyway). Indeed, powerful myths actually shape the interpretation of evidence, such that facts that contradict them may be overlooked or ignored.

An example of this can be seen in the federal No Child Left Behind (NCLB) policy. This policy defines as core obstacles to educational improvement the inappropriate and excessive influence of ideology and the poor quality of educational research. As solutions, it promises to make educational research more rigorous and educational practice more evidence-based. Specifically, the policy establishes stringent standards for what counts as scientific research (with randomized controlled trials being held up as the "gold standard") and requires that federal funds be used only for educational programs proven by research that fits this definition. The discourse surrounding this policy asserts that scientific research is central not only to effective educational policymaking in general, but particularly to solving the persistent and troubling problem of disparities in achievement between White students and students of color (see Paige, 2002).

This example illustrates the processes of selection, interpretation, and simplification involved in the construction of policy myths. For example, as I argue in further detail in the second half of the chapter, the suggestion that unscientific practices are responsible for the achievement gap ignores other equally plausible causes of disparities in student achievement and therefore leaves a great deal unsaid. At the same time, this example also shows how policy myths, like most stories, rely upon the use of stock characters to cast particular individuals as heroes or enemies (see Smith et al., 2004, pp. 18–19). For instance, this particular story constructs "dogmatic ideologues" as the enemies of educational progress and policy makers as champions of rationality and truth. At the same time, the claim that ideology and fads are the main obstacles to educational progress provides a relatively simple explanation for complex educational conditions that also suggests a relatively simple solution: make education more "scientific." It is difficult to argue against this explanation because of the status of scientific knowledge as a cultural ideal—to be *against science* has no standing in the public arena—and because there is some truth to arguments about the poor quality of some educational research. Moreover, pinning the issue on science suggests reason for optimism: that is, for believing that these problems can be solved by purely technical means, avoiding the need to address more politically troubling issues. (For examples of studies that highlight the role of myth or narrative in educational policy processes, see Bigler, 1999, pp. 81–118; Rosen, 2001; Smith et al., 2004, pp. 20–22; also see Edelman, 1971, p. 83; 1985, pp. 191–192.)

Of course, NCLB is not simply a collection of stories with no real world consequences, nor does the view of policy as myth require this interpretation. For example, as a consequence of new rules established under NCLB, researchers wishing to receive federal funding or be listed in federally sponsored library sources must revise their research designs to fit the criteria laid out in the policy. This, in turn, has consequences for the kinds of studies conducted and the knowledge they produce. However, symbolic approaches direct attention to how policies achieve their effects not only through such concrete rules and regulations, but also through more abstract symbolic means, such as the creation of powerful and persuasive narratives. Such narratives help establish legitimacy for the rules and regulations that policies create. In other words, the symbolic dimensions of policies often serve to reinforce or legitimize their material aspects. For example, the story that the influence of ideology and the poor quality of educational research are primary obstacles to educational improvement helps justify new restrictions on federal funding for research and the educational programs schools may adopt.

Policy as Ritual   Policy may also be thought of as a form of ritual. Following Durkheim (1915), social theorists generally define ritual as stylized or formalized activity that helps sustain social order by conveying messages that: (a) reflect and reinforce sacred beliefs, (b) display and legitimate the social distinctions involved in the established social structure, and (c) produce feelings of social solidarity by providing occasions in which individuals come together and experience a sense of membership in a larger community (see Firth, 1973, pp. 130–135; see also Moore & Myerhoff, 1977).[13] As Firth notes: "What ritual performances do is to recall and present in symbolic form the underlying order that is supposed to guide the members of the community in their social activities" (1973, p. 167). This presentation (whether in ritual or myth) sometimes involves what critical social theorists call "mystification": "symbolic representation of the political order in a way that systematically differs from the actual power relations found in a society" (Kertzer, 1988, p. 48). Such mystification is particularly important for obscuring contradictions between a society's espoused ideals and reality (e.g., in societies with the espoused belief that all people are equal, but an actual social structure in which the few hold power over the many). "In capitalist countries," as Kertzer (1988) notes, this "commonly entails attributing an individual's power position to his or her individual virtues—for example, intelligence or hard work—rather than conceiving of inequality as created and perpetuated by the economic system itself" (p. 48). Educational policy, as we shall see, plays a role in such mystification.

The rituals of policy also provide reassurance that idealized beliefs about how government works are actually true. As Edelman (1985) notes:

> We tell ourselves that the people determine what government will do, and we point to elections, legislative actions, and "soundings" of the public as evidence. We believe that our machinery of government functions so that administrators carry out the will of the legislature, and therefore of the people, rather than making policy by themselves... Finally, we tell ourselves that government has the power and knowledge to produce the results the people want. (p. 192)

The reality, however, is considerably more complex and contradictory. For example, as suggested previously, policy makers frequently possess neither the knowledge nor the capacity to produce desired results for public schools. Yet, by continually passing laws, enacting statutes, issuing proclamations, commissioning reports, holding public hearings, soliciting public testimony, and so forth, policy makers nevertheless reassure the public that the instruments of government are working to address potent problems in service of the public good. Much of the formal activity surrounding policy processes can be understood as rituals proclaiming and reinforcing these beliefs. For example, the form of school board, town hall, and other public meetings devoted to education policy convey in dramatic form a reassuring message that government indeed functions according to this idealized view. This dramatic effect is achieved by use of many of the same elements as theatrical presentations, including the staging of events, props such as

American flags and presidential seals, and costumes such as formal dress.[14]

Ritual, like myth, also gives people a sense of control in the face of uncertainty, helping to drive out the sense of helplessness and despair that may be associated with events or processes (be it crop failure in traditional agrarian societies or school failure in contemporary urban settings) which seem to be governed by mysterious forces. From this perspective, the discourses and practices surrounding test-based accountability policies such as No Child Left Behind can be seen in a different light: as ritual proclamations of faith in the redeeming power of science (in the form of evidence-based practice), the possibility of progress on troubling educational issues, and the meritocratic basis of the social order (with standardized tests as measures of such merit). Cohen and Rosenberg (1977) make precisely this point in a historical analysis of the institutionalization of standardized testing in American schools. Specifically, they interpret testing as a ritual expression of Americans' faith in the role of science in the achievement of social progress:

> [T]ests captured three essential elements in ideas about modernization. First, the tests were scientific: as such they provided a seemingly authoritative measure of students' skills and abilities. Second, there was Merit: assigning students within schools on the basis of this authoritative knowledge would be fair— to each according to his or her ability and need. And finally, there was Progress: the combination of tests and ability groups would allow schools to connect their "product" to society's "economic needs." (pp. 128–129)

Commenting on the role of testing as an expression of the unwavering faith in science characteristic of American society in the first half of the 20th century, they draw an analogy between testing and the symbolism of religious practice:

> [The] prominent display of these [testing] rituals in schools, like the prominent display of sacred figures and texts in other holy places, gave evidence that the institution was securely connected to those deeper sacred forces on which everything in the modern West is founded—science, economic progress, and merit. Their display was a visible, tactile declaration of faith. (p. 133)

The emphasis on science and testing as the route to progress within the discourse surrounding No Child Left Behind can be seen as a similar declaration or act of faith.

Rowan (1984) offers a way of further understanding the uses of ritual in educational policy and practice and the role of science in this. In an analysis grounded in insights from anthropological research on revitalization movements in traditional societies, he suggests that applied social scientists function as modern shamans in relation to crises over school improvement. Specifically, he argues that science is a form of stylized knowledge, which, from the point of view of practitioners and policy makers, operates in a manner similar to magic in premodern societies. Rowan draws particular attention to what he calls "research rituals that

heal and revitalize sectors of education" (p. 79). Based on studies showing that magic or ritual becomes particularly important in the presence of "(a) high levels of technical uncertainty; (b) structural cleavages that create great stress among social groups; and (c) social disorganization that creates problematic mood states among participants," Rowan argues that "research shamanism" is likewise of greatest significance in areas of education where these conditions of uncertainty, social conflict, and distress are most evident (pp. 79–80).

As an example, Rowan (1984) points to the "effective schools" research (e.g., Edmonds, 1978), which has "held out hope that the pervasive ills of modern urban schooling can be cured" (p. 80). This body of research aimed to challenge the pessimism encouraged by a number of influential studies in the late 1960s and early 1970s (e.g., Coleman et al., 1966) which demonstrated that schools have limited effects on student outcomes when compared with students' family backgrounds, socioeconomic status, and so forth. The latter research created a powerful sense of discouragement and despair among researchers, practitioners, and the public, undermining collective belief in the capacity of schooling to make a positive difference in students' lives. The effective schools research sought to counter this despair by identifying schools that defied this pessimistic outlook so as to raise expectations for what schools could achieve and thus restore a sense of hope (p. 80).

When examined in relation to the predictive conditions of uncertainty, structural cleavage, and social distress Rowan (1984) identifies, policies such as No Child Left Behind can be seen in a similar light: not only as declarations of faith in the role of scientifically based testing to produce a meritocratic social order, but also as ritual efforts to (a) "heal and revitalize sectors of education," by encouraging an optimistic outlook toward the learning of very disadvantaged students (p. 79); (b) probe the mysteries of teaching and learning using specialized techniques endowed with almost magical power to reveal these mysteries (e.g., randomized controlled trials); and (c) provide a sense of reassurance concerning our capacity to control these mysterious processes. However, ritual acts, like myths, have tangible as well as intangible consequences. Indeed, in addition to the intangible consequences of healing, reassurance, inspiration, and so forth, suggested by Rowan's analysis, NCLB's expressions of faith in testing and science have also had profound material consequences on schools and the experience of teachers and students within them: for example, dramatically ratcheting up pressure to increase student achievement on standardized tests. This pressure, in turn, may have had effects such as increasing the incidence of students dropping out of school or being assigned to special education, with important consequences for their future life chances.

Policy as Spectacle   A more critical view of the role of ritual and myth in the policy process can be found in Edelman's concept of political spectacle (1971, 1985, 1988), a synthesis of ideas about symbolic action from social, psychological, and linguistic theory. Many elements of political spectacle theory (such as the expressive or non-instrumental dimensions of policy and politics, mystification of unequal power relations, illusions of rationality, and the analogy between policy/politics and theater) are common to other theories of symbolic action and have already been discussed. However, spectacle theory takes a darker and more psychologically oriented view of these processes.

Taking the theatrical analogy a degree further, spectacle theory conceptualizes politics and policymaking as a type of performance in which a largely passive and politically disenfranchised audience is entertained, aroused, confused, distracted, and lulled into submission by a dazzling array of political symbols controlled by an elite and powerful cadre of image-makers. In the first major study to apply these ideas comprehensively to educational policy, Smith et al. (2004) summarize the central claim of spectacle theory as follows: "that contemporary politics resemble theater, with directors, stages, casts of actors, narrative plots, and (most importantly) a curtain that separates the action onstage—what the audience has access to—from the backstage," where decisions are actually made and resources and values allocated (p. 11). This process ultimately results in concrete, tangible benefits for the few who are actors in this drama, but exclusively symbolic benefits (such as the stemming of anxieties that may be the product of political spectacle in the first place, validation of cherished myths, and the reinforcement of positive self conceptions) for the audience. A central tenant of this theory is that the few who control the policy process "backstage" shape the perceptions of the masses of people who do not have access to this privileged space.

Edelman (1985) insists that this process should not be seen as one of deliberate manipulation: "There is no implication here that leaders consciously mold political myths and rituals to serve their ends. Attempts at such manipulation usually become known for what they are and fail. What we find is social role taking, not deception" (pp. 19–20). The concept of "social role taking" describes a mutually constitutive relationship between governmental actions, on the one hand, and the self-conceptions, desires, and political cognitions of individual citizens, on the other. Through this relationship, policy and politics actually shape the identities or social roles of their spectators and the symbolic needs associated with these identities in turn shape politics and policy.[15] This suggests that individuals support particular policies because doing so provides them with gratifying reinforcement for their view of themselves as certain kinds of people (e.g., "compassionate conservatives," loyal citizens, or defenders of civil rights). The use of rhetorical techniques to associate policies with cherished cultural themes such as equality or patriotism facilitates this process of identification. For example, an anti-bilingual education initiative framed in the language of equality of educational opportunity (e.g., the argument that teaching children in their first language unfairly inhibits their chances for success in life) can gain support not only from conservatives

identified with its nationalistic or assimilationist impulses, but also from liberals who would be disinclined to support an explicitly racist or anti-immigrant policy (cf., Woolard, 1989). (I discuss the role of language in framing policy issues in greater detail in the second half of the chapter.)

However, Smith et al.'s (2004) interpretation of Edelman's theory comes closer to suggesting that political spectacle involves deliberate manipulation, rather than simply social role-taking. The way in which they characterize the NCLB policy illustrates this more sinister view:

> This law instituted harsh and far-reaching federal mandates on schools. It is ironic that an administration that professes (onstage) its belief in freedom above other values passed the most standardized and centralized program in the nation's history ... Whatever readers might think about systematic phonics as the sole official method of teaching kids how to read and whatever readers might think about the efficacy of high-stakes tests to make schools accountable and raise achievement, they ought to be clear about the elements of political spectacle in this program. First, know that this program allocates tangible benefits backstage and symbols onstage. Schools and students bear the costs. Second, policy makers appropriate the term 'scientific research' as the foundation and justification of its provisions. (p. xii)

As discussed previously, expressive analysis might traditionally suggest an interpretation of this policy as an element of contemporary revitalization rituals involving the use of inspirational myths and "research magic" aimed at restoring a sense of hope and possibility in the face of persistent educational problems. However, spectacle theory casts these rituals, myths, and magical acts in a darker light. Specifically, it views them as elaborate performances involving the use of smoke and mirrors (e.g., the rhetoric of science) to dazzle and confuse audience members into believing in the necessity of the policy's provisions and direct attention away from its consequences (e.g., the punishing effects of high-stakes testing on students and schools; the economic benefits to publishers of federally authorized textbooks, reading programs, and assessments and the costs borne by developers of alternative programs; and the benefits accrued to practitioners of particular research methods as well as the costs to researchers of other kinds).

The preceding example illustrates the differing conceptions of the role of symbols involved in the application of spectacle theory to educational policy (as interpreted by Smith et al., 2004) when compared with traditional expressive analysis. There are other differences as well. For instance, Smith et al. label policies that lack instrumental means for achieving their stated intentions "symbolic policies," while policies that contain such mechanisms are excluded from this category. In contrast, traditional symbolic analysis presumes that all policies have symbolic (i.e., constitutive and/or expressive) elements, even those that also contain concrete and practical mechanisms for achieving their goals. Such analysis regards symbolization as an intrinsic human activity and thus an inseparable element of the policy process. Smith et al. (2004) further suggest that the extent to which policy makers offer the public symbolic rather than instrumental policies is symptomatic of the strength of a society's democracy more generally (pp. 34–35). This analysis assumes that symbolic action primarily serves the interests of elites in maintaining their power. In contrast, while conventional expressive analysis recognizes the role of symbolic action in the maintenance of social inequality, it involves a more balanced view of the role of symbols, suggesting that the illusions of rationality, democracy, and control involved in policy processes may function as much to reassure policy makers themselves as to placate their audiences. At the same time, the analysis of policy as a form of expressive activity (whether through myth, ritual, or spectacle) only tells half of the story of policy's symbolic role. Indeed, many of the same policy activities discussed in this section can be seen as not only ceremonial or performative acts, but also as forms of rhetoric or persuasion that actually shape social reality. I turn to the latter aspects of policy in the second half of the chapter, below.

Policy as a Form of Constitutive Activity

The diversity of scholars who view policy as a form of constitutive action share in common a social constructionist perspective on reality in general (see Berger & Luckmann, 1966; Douglas, 1977) and on the policy process specifically (see Mehan, 1993, pp. 241–244; Fischer, 2003, pp. 53–55). This perspective holds that human actions shape or construct social reality through collective processes that produce, reinforce, or transform meanings that define the social world. As Mehan (1992) explains:

> Constitutive action defines the meaning of objects and events through elaborate enactments of cultural conventions, institutional practices, and constitutive rules. Constitutive rules, in turn, are those rules that create the very possibility of human activities and the rights and duties of the people associated with them. (p. 10)[16]

For instance, culturally constructed meanings provide categories for classifying objects and establish criteria for what counts as instances of particular categories, such as the concept of an educated or successful person, the characteristics of individuals who fit these categories, and criteria for what counts as education or success (cf. Levinson, Foley, & Holland, 1996; Valdes, 1996; Varenne & McDermott, 1999). These classification schema, in turn, shape the perception of individuals and situations and become the basis for subsequent social action. As Edelman (1977) observes in *Political Language*: "To place an object in one class of things rather than another establishes its central characteristics and creates assumptions about matters that are not seen" (p. 23). These meanings tend to become naturalized or taken for granted, encouraging the belief that the order we perceive in the world around us "is not of our own (cultural) making, but rather an order that belongs to the external world itself" (Kertzer, 1988, p. 85).

Educational policy is part and parcel of these constitutive social processes. For example, numerous studies have documented the role of state, district, or school-level policy in the social construction of categories of students that become normalized or taken for granted in school practice, frequently with the effect of reinforcing existing social inequalities based on race and class. For instance, constitutive analyses have illuminated how educational policies have helped to create "dropouts" (Fine, 1991), "bad boys" (Ferguson, 2000), "gifted" (Wells & Serna, 1996), "at risk" (Swadener & Lubeck, 1995), and "learning disabled" (Mehan, 1993) students, to name a few.[17] Such analyses illuminate the constitutive processes involved not only in the initial stages of conceptualizing and formulating policy, but also in how policies are interpreted, implemented, and enacted (e.g., how policies as written get remade in schools through the interpretive activities of individuals charged with enacting them).

An example of recent research that illuminates these constitutive processes—particularly the meaning-making activities of school-based actors tasked with enacting a policy initially formulated elsewhere—is Anagnostopoulos' (2006) "cultural sociological" examination of the enactment of merit promotion policies in two Chicago high schools. Her study analyzes "the meanings with which teachers and students invest the classification schema" that merit promotion policies offered "and the practices through which these meanings enter into and inform teachers' and students' interactions and the distribution of instructional resources" (p. 10). Her investigation reveals how this policy facilitated the creation of distinct social categories of "deserving" and "undeserving" students that: (a) limited the learning opportunities for students who were categorized as "undeserving" because they had been retained in grade; and (b) served as a resource for the creation of "moral boundaries" that constituted both mechanisms of social exclusion and bases for students' own processes of identity construction. Specifically, Anagnostopoulos demonstrates that merit promotion policies in these two urban schools enabled a form of "moral boundary work" that justified the failure of large numbers of poor and minority students by generating "moral distinctions" which made this failure seem both natural and deserved. Moreover, these distinctions also constructed identities for students that shaped their own self-conceptions, thus acting "as mechanisms for cultural reproduction that ultimately called upon the students to endorse, if not internalize, their own subordination" (p. 30). That is, these distinctions drew upon "an ideology of deservingness," to which students themselves adhered, that obscured recognition of the structural forces (such as racial and economic inequality and their impact on the systemic inadequacies of urban schools) that also contribute to student failure (p. 31). In this way, the policy also functioned as a form of symbolic mystification, reinforcing the American achievement ideology discussed previously.

The Role of Policy in Constructing Social Problems By

showing how policy reinforces and/or helps to construct belief systems, social categories, and other meanings that become part of taken-for-granted understandings of reality, constitutive or constructionist analyses call into question the common sense understanding of policy as a response to objective social conditions. Such analyses instead regard social or policy problems as the consequence of constitutive social activity. Loseke and Best (2003) explain: "In comparison to *objectivist* approaches that examine social problems as objective conditions in the environment, *constructionist* approaches explore how meaning is created by people who say things and do things to convince others that a problem is at hand and that something must be done" (p. 251). This is not to suggest that actors in the policy process necessarily or deliberately misrepresent reality or fabricate claims (although sometimes they do). However, it is to say that characterizations of policy problems (like all representations of reality) are unavoidably partial and selective, focusing attention on some conditions and away from others. As a consequence, particular conditions come to be defined as problematic and worthy of public attention and redress, while others conditions are overlooked, accepted, or denied. At the same time, particular interpretations of those conditions come to be publicly accepted or legitimized, while other interpretations are discredited or marginalized (Edelman, 1987; Gusfield, 1981, 1986; Rosen, 2001; Spector & Kitsuse, 2006).[18]

Both citizens and government officials participate in this process of problem construction. For example, individual citizens or groups of citizens strive to bring particular issues or conditions to the attention of government and to promote particular interpretations of those issues. At the same time, government officials do not simply respond to expressions of concern by citizens, but also may help define such problems through policy activity. For example, in an analysis that draws on concepts of both myth and constitutive social action, Rosen (2001) examines a series of local school board meetings in the midst of the "math wars" in California, showing how local policy makers tacitly colluded in helping to define or construct the problems their meetings were ostensibly meant to address. Specifically, the way in which they organized their meetings, allocated time for public testimony, and responded to citizens' concerns helped give credence to the claims advanced by a particular group of parents (who blamed the district's newly adopted "reform" mathematics curriculum for a recent decline in district test scores). This example illustrates the reciprocal dynamic that exists between government actions and citizen concern vis-à-vis the construction of policy problems (Spector & Kitsuse, 2006, p. 155).

The process of problem construction is also intrinsically political. This is not only because individuals hold different views of the same conditions and compete to have their own views prevail, but also because how a problem is defined shapes understandings of its causes, implicitly or explicitly *attributing responsibility* to particular individuals, institutions, or conditions (see Gusfield, 1981, pp.

6–16). As Edelman (1977, 1985, 1987, 1988) and others (see, e.g., Rosen, 2001; Smith et al., 2004) have suggested, relatively simple and straightforward constructions of policy problems tend to have greater currency in the public policy arena. This is particularly the case when these explanations resonate with powerful cultural beliefs and ideologies. The previously discussed research on merit promotion policies in Chicago illustrates this. For example, such policies, combined with the way in which both teachers and students interpreted them, defined the problem of student failure in largely individualistic terms. That is, how the policy initially constructed the problem of student achievement, teachers translated the policy into their own settings, and students made sense of this enactment all encouraged a conception of students who fail as deficient, ultimately suggesting that *responsibility for addressing this problem rested primarily with students themselves*. This mode of constructing the problem suggested a relatively straightforward solution that resonated with dominant cultural assumptions about achievement.

However, if the problem of student failure were defined in institutional, rather than individual terms, this would imply a very different allocation of responsibility. For example, such a redefinition might place greater responsibility on teachers to provide more meaningful, culturally relevant instruction; on administrators to critically examine and alter institutional practices of exclusion that stigmatize or marginalize particular groups of students; on citizens and policy makers to provide urban schools with more adequate resources; and on government to remedy the effects of systemic inequalities (such as persistent racism, residential segregation, and inequalities in access to quality public schooling) and address the constellation of social problems that plague urban neighborhoods and impact students' motivation, engagement, and readiness to learn. Yet, the latter modes of allocating responsibility suggest a more complex and politically controversial understanding of the problem of student failure.

An Intrinsically Rhetorical View of Language Constitutive analyses of policy also involve an intrinsically rhetorical conception of language: the view that words unavoidably exert a persuasive influence on the interpretation of situations (see Fish, 1995). Contrary to the received view of language as simply a means of reporting facts or neutrally describing events, this analytical stance regards language as a resource or tool for filtering, ordering, and otherwise making sense of experience. From this perspective, words do not simply create a transparent windowpane through which we view the world. Rather, language is a form of social action that shapes reality by giving meaning to the objects it names (Austin, 1962).[19] Edelman (1977) provides an illustration of the implications of this perspective on language for the examination of policy processes. He observes that the basic categories or labels that structure policy discourse and action—the division of policy activity into different "domains" such as education policy, labor policy, economic policy, trade policy, healthcare policy, and so forth—presuppose that the issues and problems in each "domain" are separable from and unrelated to those in other "domains." Yet, by "cueing" or encouraging a perception of them as distinct, these labels obscure and inhibit an understanding of the fact that the "various issues with which governments deal are highly interrelated in the contemporary world" (p. 40).

The received view of language as a "transparent verbal medium" for objectively portraying reality (Fish, 1995, p. 206) inhibits acknowledgment of the rhetorical functions of language within policy processes. This recognition is further obscured by the posture of objectivity, rationality, and neutrality typical of policy discourse. For example, the arid, technical, and bureaucratic language in which policies are written presents an image of rationality, impartiality, and detachment. Yet, language is never neutral, because any description of an individual, object, or situation always already involves a particular set of assumptions that shape its perception and impose a particular perspective on its interpretation. Consequently, the usual language in which policies are written and discussed promotes a false image of political neutrality. As Shapiro (1988) argues, the "language of public policy is ideological to the extent that it poses as non-valuational" (p. 26).

The Politics of Representation   As discussed previously, educational policy functions as an arena for asserting and promoting particular visions of social and moral order and particular social constructions of educational policy problems. These ideas are frequently contested and individuals compete to have their views or versions of reality prevail over those of their opponents. This process involves the "politics of representation" (Shapiro, 1988; Mehan, 1993; Rosen & Mehan, 2003): competition between differently situated actors for the power to define a situation for others. In contests over policy, individuals compete to attain social acceptance or legitimacy for their own way of defining or understanding a situation. The prize in such competitions is having one's own ideas authorized or made official by virtue of being enshrined in policy.

The analysis of the politics of representation starts from the recognition that not all forms of language have equal social status. For example, professional, technical, and scientific language, with its connotations of expertise and esoteric knowledge, tends to exert more influence in policy contexts than more informal language. That is, individuals and groups who use such language tend to be accorded greater credibility, legitimacy, and respect than opponents communicating in a lower status idiom and are thus more likely to be successful in policy debates (Epstein, 1996; Gusfield, 1981). For example, Mehan (1993) shows how the enactment at the school building level of policies related to the designation of students as "learning disabled" are shaped by the relative power of various vocabularies for representing student learning and development. In an analysis of a meeting in which school officials were deciding whether to designate a particular student as learning disabled, he shows how the formal, technical, abstract, and decontextualized vocabulary of the school psychologist won out over the more informal, concrete, and context-specific language of the child's parent, who questioned the appropriateness of a special education placement. In light of the complexity and ambiguity of the issues citizens and policy makers must confront when it comes to deciding and implementing policy, the reputation or perceived expertise of a speaker often serves as a proxy for deeper understanding and evaluation. Yet, more powerful groups tend to have greater access to and mastery of higher status languages, along with the credentials to legitimate their use, and thus have more resources at their disposal to impose their meanings on others in discussions of policy.

Framing   Fundamental to the politics of representation and the construction of social or policy problems is the process of framing policy issues. Frames (a term adapted from the work of Erving Goffman, 1974) are interpretive schema that allow people to categorize and understand reality by drawing on "the extant stock of meanings, beliefs, ideologies, practices, values, myths, narratives, and the like" in order to shape the interpretation of situations and issues and create a favorable impression of their own positions or arguments (Benford & Snow, 2000, p. 629; see also Mills, 1940).[20] Framing techniques are used to *diagnose* particular conditions as problematic, to offer a *prognosis* for improving or addressing those conditions, and to consolidate the *identities* of groups on various sides of an issue (e.g., to draw boundaries between individuals defined as either part of the problem or part of the solution; Snow & Benford, 1988).[21]

Claims-makers in the United States frequently draw upon the theme of equality to frame issues and buttress the claim that a particular situation is problematic and therefore demands redress via policy. This is clearly evident in both sides of the debate over affirmative action policies in education. For example, challenging the historical framing of affirmative action as a vehicle for achieving equality, the ballot initiative that succeeded in outlawing affirmative action in public institutions in California was named the Civil Rights Initiative and used the discourse of equality in its campaign to associate *opposition* to affirmative action with the egalitarian principles of the civil rights movement. In so doing, the initiative successfully contested the historical framing of affirmative action as a practice that promotes equality and "reframed" it as both discriminatory and ultimately harmful to minorities. The effectiveness of these framing activities derived from how they made these associations seem logical and commonsensical, such that they appeared as "natural causal relations" rather than as the effect of associations forged in rhetoric (Woolard, 1989, pp. 269–270).

This type of "counter-framing" or "frame contestation" (Benford & Snow, 2000, pp. 625–627) in relation to themes of equality is particularly apparent in educational policies aimed at addressing the so-called achievement gap. For example, challenging the historical association of *liberal* educational policies with egalitarian values, President Bush's framing of the No Child Left Behind Act as an assault on the "soft bigotry of low expectations"[22] draws on the theme of equality to diagnose the problem of minority student achievement as a problem of academic permissiveness, excuse-making, and prejudice in the form of lower standards for minority students as compared to Whites. This diagnosis implicitly suggests that traditional liberal interpretations of low minority student achievement as consequences of poverty and disadvantage are in fact discriminatory because they lead to lower expectations for these students.[23] This framing offers as a solution increasing academic standards and holding both students and schools accountable for working harder to meet them, simultaneously framing advocates of the policy as defenders of accountability, integrity, and equality, and its opponents as enemies of these same values.

This mode of framing the problem of minority student achievement, with its emphasis on student effort and school-level factors as keys to academic success, fits well with a series of more general ideological shifts that have accompanied the increasing strength of the "New Right" in American politics over the last two decades. Conservatives have particularly sought to undermine new understandings of equality introduced into American culture by the social movements of the 1960s. In place of an emergent definition of equality advocated by the latter movements, which emphasized structural or institutional factors (such as income inequality and institutionalized racial biases) and compensating for the effect of past group oppression, conservatives have substituted a notion of equality that emphasizes individual freedom from constraints on opportunity. In education, this manifests in a renewed emphasis on "excellence" that has shifted the language of educational achievement so that success and failure are framed once again in largely individualistic terms. In response, researchers, activists, and citizen groups have worked to reframe (see Lakoff, 2004) the problem of minority student achievement as one of cumulative historical injustice. For instance, drawing an analogy between educational outcomes and economic processes, Ladson-Billings (2006) proposes that instead of the "achievement gap," the problem of lagging achievement on the part of specific racial subgroups of students should instead be termed "the education debt." When viewed in the context of such political contestation, the federal agenda to close the "achievement gap" can be seen as part of a broader cultural struggle over competing understandings of equality and explanations of inequality (i.e., as part of the "culture wars"; Apple, 1989, p. 35; 1993, p. 19; Bigler, 1999, pp. 81–84, 114; Hunter, 1987; Mehan, 1993, 1994, p. 79; Omi & Winant, 1994; Rieder, 1985; Rosen & Mehan, 2003).

The preceding discussion illustrates that the framing processes involved in constructing and representing policy problems are generally implicit rather than explicit (e.g.,

evoking structures of interrelated beliefs and understandings without necessarily stating them directly). This implicit quality partly accounts for the effectiveness of such framing techniques; direct statements bring to mind their opposites, but indirect invocations of cultural understandings have no direct contraries and are thus more difficult to dispute. Moreover, individuals are frequently strongly invested in these structures of beliefs and understandings, particularly when they serve their social and economic interests. For example, references to closing the achievement gap by raising standards and increasing accountability for teachers and students metonymically evoke the larger structure of beliefs involved in the American achievement ideology: that educational success and failure are principally a consequence of individual effort and character and that holding students of color accountable to higher standards is the solution to these problems (see Edelman, 1977, p. 16). This manner of framing problems of academic achievement suggests an explanation for educational inequality that helps to preserve the existing order of things by implying that educational equality can be achieved without drastic changes to the existing social order. (For a discussion of the relevance of frame analysis for policy, see Rein & Schön, 1993; for examples of frame analysis applied to educational policy, see Binder, 2002; Coburn, 2006; Davies, 1999.)

The Relationship Between Policy and Research Researchers also participate in the process of framing policy issues and thus constructing policy problems. For example, Berliner (2006) and others (Slee & Weiner, 1998) have argued that the focus of educational reform researchers on school-level factors as explanations for academic achievement ignores or directs attention away from the role of economic, social, and political factors that exert an equal or greater influence on student learning and academic performance. They contend that research directed exclusively at school-level factors contributes to the social construction of student achievement as a problem of urban school effectiveness, rather than of poverty. Indeed, Berliner (2006) suggests that the failure of large employers such as Wal-Mart to provide health insurance and pay a living wage to their workers is just as culpable as the school-level factors on which researchers and policy makers traditionally focus because of the relationship that can be shown between family income, health care, and school performance (p. 987).

This brief example illustrates that researchers are far from objective in the pure, idealized sense assumed by the dominant cultural conception of scientific research. This hegemonic conception—what anthropologists would call a "folk model" of science (see Holland & Quinn, 1987)—assumes the capacity of research to mirror reality by generating knowledge that directly corresponds to an objective world. This model endorses the "ideal of mechanical objectivity, knowledge based completely on explicit rules ... [and] the application of sanctioned methods to presumably neutral facts" (Porter, 1995, p. 7). However, this folk conception of science—also endorsed in more sophisticated, academic form by many mainstream, positivist policy researchers (see Fischer, 2003, pp. 117–130)—has been strongly challenged by research in the social studies of science (e.g., see Haraway, 1988).[24] The latter research, partly drawing on constitutive theory, demonstrates that mechanical objectivity is an unattainable ideal because scientific research involves significant elements of judgment and interpretation and is especially shaped by the standards, values, and assumptions of particular academic disciplines and the professional communities that comprise them. For example, the conduct of research is fundamentally shaped by what a researcher has chosen to pay attention to and the theories and methods he or she draws upon to gather and interpret evidence. It may also be shaped by his or her political commitments, social position or identity (such as gender, race, or class), and sources of funding or sponsorship.

A "Post-Positivist" Conception of Research In place of the positivist conception of scientific research that dominates mainstream policy research and practice, constitutive theorists substitute a view of science as an epistemic toolkit for probing and representing reality. This perspective on science involves the recognition that choices of research methods and interpretations of data they generate are guided by theoretical frameworks that embed particular, discipline-based assumptions and propose particular models of the social world and how to understand it. Different models, moreover, draw attention to different kinds of phenomena and away from others. Thus, research methods should be understood as tools for mapping or modelling, not mirroring, the social and natural world. As such, while researchers themselves strive harder than others to produce valid and comprehensive accounts of policy problems and are held to higher standards in this regard, research is no different from other representations of reality. That is, like all cultural constructions, research arguments are necessarily partial and selective, consisting of abstractions or models that considerably simplify and smooth over the complexities, contradictions, and ambiguities of reality itself (cf. Bailey, 2003, pp. 2–10).[25]

The Role of Science in the Politics of Representation Nevertheless, because of the power of the folk model of science and the collective faith in science and technology discussed in the first half of the chapter, researchers enjoy a privileged status as arbiters of truth in the arena of public policy. Indeed, the current historical moment is one in which scientists are increasingly called upon to adjudicate political and policy disputes and provide answers to complex problems that are subject to multiple, competing interpretations. Particularly when such disputes involve strong ideological differences, as is virtually always the case in education, "science is the resource called on to promote consensus, and experts are brought in to 'settle' political and social controversies" (Epstein, 1996, p. 6). For this reason, science and scientific language play a particularly prominent role in the politics of representation surrounding education policy.

For example, much has been written about the federal government's current effort to "transform education into an evidence-based field,"[26] most vividly symbolized in the Education Sciences Reform Act of 2002. As discussed previously, this law and the policy efforts surrounding it decry the purported tendency within the field of education to "value ideology over evidence" (U.S. Department of Education, 2002, p. 10), promising to eliminate the influence of ideology over education through the use of sanctioned research methods, particularly randomized, controlled trials. Yet, by suggesting the possibility of attaining value-free knowledge through the use of sanctioned procedures, federal policy implicitly endorses the folk model of science discussed above. In so doing, this policy constructs and represents reality in a particular way, constituting hierarchical, value-laden social categories—such as "ideological" versus "scientific"—for distinguishing and labelling different types of research. And, much as labels for categorizing students provide a basis for justifying their differential treatment, the distinctions that federal policy creates for labelling different kinds of research likewise serve as the basis for legitimizing particular educational policy decisions (e.g., forbidding the use of federal funding for reading programs not based on research defined as "scientific"). (For a detailed constitutive analysis of how the definition of scientific research involved in federal educational policy functions to legitimate particular political agendas and policy decisions see Smith et al., 2004, pp. 151–189.)

As the brief preceding discussion of federal policy illustrates, when viewed as a form of constitutive social activity, "science" can be seen as not simply a way of investigating social and natural phenomena, but also a way of making and legitimizing claims about them, especially in situations of political conflict or policy debate. Constitutive analysis particularly foregrounds the role of science and technical/scientific language as tools for constructing, presenting, and asserting particular images of reality. Indeed, as the earlier discussion of "research shamanism" illustrated, symbolic analysis opposes the conventional distinctions or oppositions between science, rhetoric, and ritual (see Gusfield, 1981). As such, it posits science as not simply a rational means of creating and validating knowledge (i.e., a means to an end), but also as both an end in itself (i.e., an expressive or ritual activity that validates articles of faith) and a form of rhetoric or argument that can be used to justify or legitimate particular policy decisions.[27]

The latter legitimating power derives from the fact that scientific language "both enlist(s) and generate(s)" an interpretive context that assigns facticity to arguments framed in its terms (Gusfield, 1981, pp. 107–108), while concealing the processes of selection and interpretation by which such arguments are constructed. This interpretive frame is evoked by the language and imagery of objectivity, logic, precision, and technical expertise. This symbolism produces "the illusion of certainty, of being accurately in correspondence with an objective world" (Bailey, 1994, p. 83), and constructs a "cognitive and moral order which appears external and unyielding to human choice and design" (Gusfield, 1981, p. 18). In other words, the use of scientific and technical language is a form of constitutive activity that constructs an authoritative image of reality and is therefore a powerful tool in the politics of representation, the rhetorical force of which derives from its perceived correspondence with objective reality. For these reasons, many professional, political, and educational reform advocacy organizations employ researchers and/or ground their educational policy claims in evidence from research. However, such research tends to be carefully selected and represented so as to support particular policy agendas. For example, by summarizing research in ways that eliminate ambiguities, qualifications, and uncertainties, advocates of particular policy positions can present an image of objectivity and certainty in relation to their particular agendas.[28]

Moreover, as Mehan's (1993) work on the social construction of learning disabilities demonstrates, technical language also bolsters the authority of its users by removing the grounds for negotiating meaning from under a conversation because such language makes it more difficult for non-experts to challenge information presented (p. 258). As Lave (1993) argues with regard to the use of technical language in educational settings, "the effect of technical language (its technologism is not an accident) is to bracket and delegitimize the situated understanding of other participants, including parents and teachers" (p. 26; also see Fischer, 1993). For example, the use of scientific research and scientific language to legitimize particular policy decisions can serve to narrow the conversation about a policy's effects, discrediting alternative views and restricting such conversation to a small group of socially designated "experts."

The Tension between Science and Democracy   This phenomenon underscores the tension between the privileged status of science as arbiter of truth in policy discussions, on the one hand, and the goal of democratic decision making, on the other. As Fischer (2003) observes:

> Whereas democracy stands for open discussion on the part of all citizens, science has always been the domain of knowledge elites. Whereas democracy seeks to encourage a wide range of viewpoints and perspectives, science strives to limit the number of participants in pursuit of the one correct answer or assessment. (p. 205)

These comments point to a key difference between the view of science involved in mainstream (or what Fischer, 2003, refers to as "neopositivist/empiricist") policy research and that involved in the constitutive perspective summarized here. Specifically, the focus within mainstream policy research on obtaining "objective," certain explanations of educational phenomenon lends itself to a technocratic approach to policymaking. This is not only because it tends to restrict decision making to an elite group of designated

technical experts, but also because the search for definitive, "objective" truth denies or obscures the processes of framing, problem construction, and the politics of representation that I have argued are intrinsic to policy activity. In so doing, mainstream policy research contributes to the construction of "regimes of truth" (Foucault, 1980, pp. 131–133) that reify particular views of reality by cloaking them in the mantle of objectivity. As Fischer (2003) observes:

> Insofar as empiricist social science's emphasis on 'objective reality' diverts attention from the struggles grounded 'in other realities' that challenge existing arrangements, social science—wittingly or unwittingly—serves as much to provide ideological support for a configuration of power as it does to explain it. (p. 129)

In contrast, the constitutive view argued here suggests a "multiple perspectives" approach to policy scholarship (see Malen & Knapp, 1997). This approach recognizes the value not only of multiple forms of research, but also of broader participation in the policy process so as to include a range of citizens' perspectives, not just those of socially designated experts. This suggests that symbolic analysis should complement, rather than supplant, more instrumentally oriented studies. It further suggests a view of the policy analyst as a facilitator of broad-based reflection and ongoing discussion on the meaning and consequences of particular policy decisions, rather than a purveyor of "technical answers designed to bring political discussions to an end" (Fischer, 2003, p. 221). In the conclusion, I further elaborate the implications of the ideas discussed in this section for the practice of policy analysis and consider both the strengths and weaknesses of the symbolic approach to the study of policy processes.

Conclusion

The main contribution of the symbolic approach is its power to (a) unmask the illusions of rationality and objectivity at the heart of the policy enterprise (including policy research as it is traditionally practiced) and (b) demonstrate the role of policy in producing and reinforcing taken-for-granted meanings that define the social world, shaping thought and action in ways that have profound effects, both tangible and intangible. Moreover, by revealing what lies under the surface of claims about particular policy problems (i.e., their status as social constructions rather than neutral descriptions of objective conditions) symbolic analyses suggest the need to problematize received understandings of policy problems, as these are as likely to reflect cultural myths as actual conditions (Loseke & Best, 2003, pp. 252–253; also see Fischer & Forester, 1993, pp. 6–7).

This problematizing also involves rethinking the conventional way of evaluating a policy's impact: that is, expanding the conception of impact beyond tangible outcomes such as test scores or changes in teacher practice to include less tangible consequences in the realm of cultural beliefs, ideologies, and understandings, thereby revealing a dynamic relationship between the symbolic and material effects of policy. For example, my discussion has shown that both the expressive and constitutive aspects of policy help to create and reinforce social categories and understandings that have real consequences for students' lives. As Cohen and Rosenberg (1977) note:

> The institutions and culture of schools today are in many respects simply the cold and hardened organizational results of myths and rituals believed and celebrated several generations ago ... Being told and believed the stories took on institutional form, and then had all manner of effects—many weighing heavily on us for generations thereafter. (pp. 135–136)

Beliefs and understandings shape reality. When people act on these ideas, reality changes.

At the same time, however, the questioning of received understandings that symbolic analysis encourages is also its greatest weakness, in two respects. First, such analysis cannot provide the sense of certainty and control over educational outcomes that policy makers and the public have come to expect from research. In place of this reassuring sense of order and control, symbolic analysis posits a chaotic and conflictual world of multiple, competing realities in which certain, objective knowledge is unattainable. A sense of paralysis and disillusionment could easily follow. Second, symbolic analysis also holds the potential for promoting a view of individuals as cultural dupes of the policy process: passive victims of myths, rituals, and rhetorical processes that shape their perceptions of reality, while concealing their status as cultural constructions. I will try to address each of these potential weaknesses in the brief space that remains.

While symbolic analysis cannot provide the sense of certainty and control that many crave, it can provide a more reliable foundation for educational decision making: a deeper understanding of the assumptions underlying particular policy decisions, together with their consequences, that can inform an ongoing process of democratic deliberation. This type of understanding is particularly important given the intrinsically value-laden nature of educational policy questions. Education is intrinsically, unavoidably ideological (especially educational policy). As Bruner (1999) observes, education's "objectives—the cultivation of mind, the betterment of life, or whatever else—are in principle culturally contestable issues that inevitably become ideological or political issues not readily resolved by scientific research alone" (p. 401). At the same time, however, research can help to clarify what goals are worth striving for and the effects of pursuing particular culturally constructed objectives, thus contributing to "the task of discerning the consequences of such culturally constituted ends as a society prescribes for its education system" (p. 405). Evidence from research is crucial both to the advancement of general understanding and also to informing decision making in particular cases. However, it is equally crucial to resist succumbing to the tempta-

tions of expecting evidence from research to (a) provide a degree of certainty that it cannot; and (b) obviate the need for interpretation, judgment, and open discussion of the beliefs, values, and assumptions associated with different educational policies. Indeed, the intrinsic role of values and ideology in education ought to be openly acknowledged as a defense against the rhetorical (mis)use of the language of scientific objectivity and neutrality to legitimize particular policy decisions.

Symbolic analysis suggests that perhaps research can more productively contribute to the improvement of education not by pandering to a collective yearning for certainty packaged in the form of expert proclamations about "what works," but by instead providing data and analyses to inform thoughtful public conversation about the framing of policy problems. It further suggests that an important leverage point for policy actors, including researchers, lies precisely in questioning the *discourse* that helps to construct particular policy problems (cf. Lipman, 2004, pp. 171–173). As Kertzer (1988) notes: "Our symbol system ... is not a cage which locks us into a single view of the political world, but a mélange of symbolic understandings by which we struggle, through a continuous series of negotiations, to assign meaning to events" (pp. 174–175). This suggests that, rather than induce a sense of helplessness or victimization in the face of powerful cultural processes of meaning-making, symbolic analysis aids in identifying points of strategic intervention in these processes. Such "postempiricist policy analysis," as Fischer (2003) explains:

> is frame-critical policy analysis. Uncovering the multiple and conflicting frames involved in a given policy dispute, it inquires into the sources of conflicting frames by examining the histories, roles, institutional context, and interests of those who advance them. Such analysis explores the assumptions, ambiguities and inconsistencies underlying conflicting frames, along with the consequences to which their uses may lead. (p. 146)

More generally, the insights emerging from symbolic analysis suggest that, rather than providing technical solutions to problems pre-defined by policy makers, researchers should instead aim to foster broad-based discussion of how such problems are constructed or defined in the first place. To the extent that these efforts provoke or support discussion of the values, goals, and assumptions involved in such definitions and the consequences of acting on them, policy analysts can play a more constructive, educative role in policy processes.

Notes

1. I wish to thank Gary Sykes for his foresight in thinking to include a chapter on rhetoric and symbolic action in this volume and his generosity in believing I was the correct person to write it. This chapter was his idea and benefited greatly from his early feedback. I am grateful to Barbara Schneider for supporting the idea as well. I also wish to thank the reviewers of the manuscript, one of whom—Hugh Mehan—revealed his identity to me and one of whom

remains anonymous. Both provided extremely helpful comments that ultimately sharpened the manuscript. Finally, my thanks go out to Jim Scheurich and Bradley Levinson for their comments on the manuscript and encouragement of my work more generally.

2. The work of Murray Edelman (1971, 1977, 1985, 1987, 1988), which in many ways anticipated more recent theoretical developments within policy studies, constitutes a very important exception to the historical tendency within mainstream policy-oriented disciplines to ignore or neglect the non-rational dimensions of policy.

3. For discussions of the reasons for this bias in relation to the founding epistemological assumptions of policy research as a field, see Ball (1998), Fischer (2003), and O'Connor (2001).

4. In popular or journalistic discussions of policy and politics, the label "symbolic" is often used in a dismissive manner: for example, describing something as "merely a symbolic gesture" or "only" symbolic to suggest that symbolic objects or behaviors are somehow not real or have no consequences. Challenging this assumption, the body of work I discuss in this chapter endorses a view of symbols and symbolization as a mode of constructing and dealing with reality that has real, material consequences, rather than as a realm of human activity distinct from or opposed to reality (Firth, 1973, p. 90).

5. The ideas summarized in this chapter constitute an element of a larger body of scholarship addressed to the sociocultural analysis of policy. For a useful introduction to this work from the perspective of anthropology, see Shore and Wright (1997). For syntheses of this approach addressed to key ideas and schools of thought within political science, see Fischer and Forrester (1993) and Fischer (2003). For an introduction to interpretive policy analysis from public policy studies, see Yanow (1996, 2000). Finally, for an overview of interpretive and sociocultural approaches to the study of educational policy in particular, see Levinson and Sutton (2001); also see Ball (1994, pp. 14–27); Taylor, Rizvi, Lingard, and Henry (1997).

6. As quoted in *Newsweek*, July 30, 2007, p. 19.

7. This diversity of meanings underscores an important quality of symbols in general: their intrinsic ambiguity and multi-valence. Symbolic actions have "no single precise meaning," but rather stand for and bring together or "condense" an array of diverse meanings, such that these meanings are "not just simultaneously elicited but also interact with one another so that they become associated together" in the mind of their audience (Kertzer, 1988, p. 11). Moreover, different people might understand the same symbol in different ways. This ambiguity accounts for an important characteristic of symbols and symbolic action: their capacity to evoke strong feelings of identification among diverse actors and thus build feelings of solidarity among them in the absence of actual consensus.

8. However, much symbolic activity is simultaneously both ceremonial/ ritualistic and persuasive/rhetorical. For example, ceremonies and rituals can also be understood as a form of rhetoric or persuasion: a way of constructing compelling narratives or images of reality intended to shape the perception of situations (Kertzer, 1988, p. 101). Consequently, many symbolic studies deal with both dimensions simultaneously and the distinctions I make between them are primarily a heuristic for organizing my discussion.

9. In this respect, symbolic analyses map a similar terrain as critical policy research, which focuses on the relationship between policy and domination (see Torres & Van Heertum, this volume).

10. In contrast, programs promoting the use of condoms, in particular, significantly reduce students' risk of HIV infection. See "Abstinence-only fails to stop" (2007); "Ex-surgeon general says he was silenced" (2007); Santelli, Ott, Lyon, Rogers, Summers, and Schleifer (2006); "No-sex programs 'not working,'" (2007); Underhill, Montgomery, & Operario (2007).

11. Another example can be seen in widely popular policy initiatives aimed at ending "social promotion" in schools by requiring students to repeat a grade if they do not meet minimum academic standards. Empirical research has consistently called into doubt the efficacy of such initiatives. (For a summary of this research and the symbolic dimensions of grade retention policies more generally, see Labaree, 1997, pp. 53–74. Also see the series of reports on "ending social promotion" in the Chicago Public Schools conducted by the Consortium on Chicago School Research: http://ccsr.uchicago.edu/content/publications.php.) Nevertheless, such policies perform vital "cultural work" by dramatizing and reinforcing understandings of academic achievement associated with the American achievement ideology. For example, grade retention policies display a commitment to the values of hard work and individual effort, depict the consequences that befall those who fail to work hard, and symbolize intolerance for methods of social advancement that are not merit-based.

12. Gusfield (1986) notes: "In a society of diverse cultures and of rapid change, it is quite clear that systems of culture are as open to downward and upward mobility as are occupations or persons. Yesterday's moral virtue is today's ridiculed fanaticism" (p. 180). Educational policy, as Gusfield reminds, is consequently an arena for struggle over the relative legitimacy and status of competing value systems in a time of social change. It is these latent dynamics of symbolic domination and degradation that are responsible, Gusfield suggests, for the intense feelings and expressions of moral condemnation that policy debates over such issues as school prayer, abstinence-only sex education, and the teaching of creationism tend to inspire. Similarly, efforts since the late 1960s by ethnic, women's, disability, and gay/lesbian advocacy organizations to raise their social status by promoting curricula espousing diversity, multiculturalism, gender equality, and tolerance for diverse lifestyles can all be understood as "instances of attempts to enhance or defend a level of prestige under conflict" (Gusfield, 1986, p. 18; for a related analysis, see Kliebard, 2004, p. 289).

13. Of course, rituals can also be important tools for challenging the social and political status quo (see Kertzer, 1988). However, in keeping with Durkheim's emphasis on ritual as a vehicle for maintaining social stability, analyses of policy as a form of ritual typically focus on its role in validating the established social order.

14. The holding of hearings to accept public commentary on policy documents is another instance of such ritual activity. For example, as Smith et al. (2004) observe, state and local agencies frequently create committees to write educational standards, frameworks, etc. They then hold public hearings to take commentary on these documents. However, such hearings frequently perform expressive rather than instrumental functions, providing individuals the opportunity to participate in a ritual of democracy that bears little connection to actual decision making. For example, public commentary is typically limited to only a few minutes per speaker, there is generally very little substantive dialogue about any issues raised, few changes occur as a result of such meetings, and most of the actual decisions take place backstage, out of public view. Yet, "staging public meetings creates the impression that democracy has been served" (Smith et al., 2004, p. 24; cf., Rosen, 2001).

15. As Edelman (1971) explains:

> [P]olitical goals … are socially cued by others who are significant to a person, creating faith in a belief that is not susceptible to empirical disproof and at the same time creating a valued self-conception for those who believe in the goal as well as for those who reject it. The man who sees himself as a fighter in the war against the Communist conspiracy, as a bulwark of the movement for civil rights, or as one who recognizes that welfare measures promote sloth and moral softness has strong reason to cling to the political role that is gratifying. He will shape and select other perceptions to accord with the central, salient one, and will seek out, emphasize, and usually exaggerate social support for his belief. Government plays an especially salient function in the shaping of cognitions about political issues. On many of the most controversial ones the impact of governmental actions upon mass beliefs and perceptions is, in fact, the major, or the only, consequence of political activity (p. 174).

16. Mehan compares constitutive rules to the rules of football, which determine what counts as a touchdown, who can score one (only uniformed players), when (only during the game), and under what circumstances (only when their team has the ball). Similarly, in everyday life, constitutive rules, social norms, and cultural conventions govern the games of everything from courtship to gift giving, from workplace behavior to elevator riding, from greetings to grocery shopping, and from classroom instruction to job interviewing. These social rules, which exert a powerful influence on behavior, tend to be tacit and are often learned unconsciously through experience and observation, rather than being explicitly taught. Indeed, their taken-for-granted status is a major source of their power. (For examples of how constitutive theory has been applied in studies of education, see Datnow, Hubbard, & Mehan, 2002; Erickson & Shultz, 1982; Hall & McGinty, 1997; Mehan, 1993; McDermott, Gospodinoff, & Aron, 1978; Rosen, 2001; Rosen & Mehan, 2003.)

17. In this respect, constitutive analyses share common ground with Foucault's work on how particular "discourses" construct their subjects (see Foucault, 1980). For discussions of how Foucault's ideas have been applied to the analysis of policy, see Fischer (2003) and Shore and Wright (1997).

18. The process of problem construction frequently involves the evocation of a sense of crisis, which is then used to justify subsequent policy measures. This perception of crisis is partly achieved by the use of dramatic language to generate feelings of anxiety on the part of the public and induce acquiescence to deprivations in the name of addressing it (Edelman, 1971, 1988, p. 31). Many scholars have pointed to the 1983 educational reform report *A Nation at Risk*, which claimed that "a rising tide of mediocrity" in U.S. schools threatened the future prosperity of the nation, as a textbook example of this (see Hall, 1983; Smith et al., 2004, p. 14).

19. To illustrate with a simple example, ostensibly neutral descriptions of particular educational policy proposals or preferences do not merely describe, but also suggest ways of interpreting particular educational approaches. For instance, in California's heated debates over mathematics curriculum policy in the 1990s, organized proponents of changing how mathematics has historically been taught described new programs and policies by the label "mathematics reform," thereby associating such programs with improvement, modernity, innovation, and progress. In contrast, critics of such new programs described their preferred approach as "traditional mathematics," thus associating this approach with stability, academic rigor, classical or canonical knowledge, and practices that have stood the test of time. Such discourse strategies contribute to the social construction of educational policy problems, creating representations that shape the way educational conditions are interpreted and consequently the development of policies addressed to those conditions.

20. The literature on framing processes comes out of institutional sociology and has primarily focused on the activities of social movement organizations, rather than policy. The primary contribution of this literature is the provision of a specific set of concepts for understanding the characteristics, features, and social uses of framing techniques, as well as a theoretical framework for understanding framing processes and dynamics. (For a review of this literature, see Benford & Snow, 2000; for discussions of framing processes applied to the policy context, see Lakoff, 2004; Schön & Rein, 1994.)

21. An example can be seen in the "English for the Children" ballot initiative (sponsored by an organization calling itself One Nation/ One California) that successfully outlawed bilingual education in California and subsequently inspired a similar successful effort in Arizona. Drawing on cultural myths and ideologies concerning the centrality of assimilation to social mobility, the initiative campaign constructed its proponents as advocates of children's welfare and national unity, while implicitly suggesting that supporters of bilingual education were not only "against the children," but also divisive cultural separatists. Similarly, proponents of voucher programs for public education draw on capitalist values of freedom and economic competition to create a favorable impression of such programs. For

example, they characterize voucher initiatives as "school choice" programs, while representing critics of such programs as both opponents of parents' freedom to choose and defenders of a failed bureaucratic system and the entrenched special interests who benefit from it (such as teachers' unions). In recent years, they have also increasingly drawn on the theme of equality, arguing that parents of public school students should have the same right to choose their children's schools enjoyed by those who can afford the option of private education.

27. This is a phrase Bush has repeatedly used throughout his administration (e.g., see Noe, 2004).

23. Hirschman (1991) refers to this rhetorical strategy as the "perversity thesis" because it holds that a given course of action will, in fact, produce the opposite of its intended effects.

24. For a useful review of this literature, particularly in relation to the social construction of expertise, see Epstein (1996, pp. 14–26; see also Fischer, 2003, pp. 117–130).

25. To offer an analogy, just as a weather map highlights different aspects of a landscape than a topographic, population, or street map, so too do different kinds of research studies offer different kinds of accounts of the social and natural world, highlighting some aspects of a given terrain, while ignoring or minimizing others. Moreover, both kinds of landscapes, those of interest to researchers or cartographers, are complex, dynamic systems that are in constant flux. Yet, the kinds of renderings that both researchers and mapmakers construct, whether research studies or maps, cannot capture this dynamic complexity. Instead, they artificially freeze their objects, constructing static portraits that significantly simplify, and thus to some extent distort, the phenomena they seek to represent. For all of these reasons—as well as for reasons of practicality and coherence—both maps and research studies offer only simplified, partial, and selective accounts of their respective landscapes. Furthermore, a topographic map is not intrinsically more valid than a street map and both are necessary for a more complete understanding of the territory. The same holds for research studies. (For a detailed elaboration of this point, see Malen & Knapp, 1997, who advocate a multiple perspectives approach to educational policy research.) Indeed, the postempiricist conception of research (Fischer, 2003) involved in constructionist analyses holds that it is impossible to obtain a complete or fully objective view of reality, partly because of the impossibility of unmediated perception discussed previously, but also because of the intrinsic complexity of reality itself.

26. This is Goal 4 of the U.S. Department of Education Strategic Plan for 2002-2007, available at www.ed.gov/pubs/stratplan2002-07/index.html

27. It does not follow, however, from the conception of science as a form of rhetoric or ritual that research is merely symbolic (i.e., that it has no reference to reality). Rather, in keeping with the "post-positivist" conception of research discussed previously, the constitutive view argued here is that research studies are representations of the world that may more or less accurately represent reality and that can be evaluated using the agreed-upon criteria of particular disciplinary communities. In short, the view of science as a form of rhetoric or ritual is not mutually exclusive with the more conventional notion of science as a way of probing reality in order to generate reliable conclusions about the world. However, as discussed previously, it rejects the notion of mechanical objectivity as an unattainable and problematic ideal.

28. For discussion of these dynamics in relation to debate over educational policy in California's "math wars," see Wilson, 2003; Rosen, 2001.

References

Abstinence-only fails to stop early pregnancies, diseases. (2007, July 30) *USA Today*. Retrieved August 17, 2007, from http://blogs.usatoday.com/oped/2007/07/our-view-on-sex.html

Anagnostopoulos, D. (2006). "Real students" and "true demotes": Ending social promotion and the moral ordering of urban high schools. *American Educational Research Journal, 43,* 5–42.

Apple, M. W. (1989). The politics of common sense: Schooling, populism, and the new right. In H. A. Giroux & P. L. McLaren (Eds.), *Critical pedagogy, the state, and cultural struggle* (pp. 32–49). Albany: State University of New York Press.

Apple, M. W. (1993). *Official knowledge: Democratic education in a conservative age.* New York: Routledge.

Apple, M. W. (1996). *Cultural politics and education.* New York: Teachers College Press.

Apple, M. W. (2001). *Educating the "right" way: Markets, standards, God, and inequality.* New York: RoutledgeFalmer.

Austin, J. L. (1962). *How to do things with words.* Cambridge, MA: Harvard University Press.

Bailey, F. G. (1994). *The witch-hunt: Or, the triumph of morality.* Ithaca, NY: Cornell University Press.

Bailey, F. G. (2003). *The saving lie: Truth and method in the social sciences.* Philadelphia: University of Pennsylvania Press.

Ball, S. J. (1994). *Education reform: A critical and post-structural approach.* Buckingham, England: Open University Press.

Ball, S. J. (1998) Educational studies, policy entrepreneurship and social theory. In R. Slee, G. Weiner, & S. Tomlinson (Eds.), *School effectiveness for whom? Challenges to the school effectiveness and school improvement movements* (pp. 70–83). Bristol, PA: Falmer Press.

Benford, R. D., & Snow, D. A. (2000). Framing processes and social movements: An overview and assessment. *Annual Review of Sociology, 26,* 611–639.

Berger, P., & Luckmann, T. (1966). *The social construction of reality: A treatise in the sociology of knowledge.* London: Penguin Books.

Berliner, D. (2006). Our impoverished view of educational research. *Teachers College Record, 108,* 949–995.

Bigler, E. (1999). *American conversations: Puerto Ricans, white ethnics, and multicultural education.* Philadelphia: Temple University Press.

Binder, A. J. (2002). *Contentious curricula: Afrocentrism and creationism in American public schools.* Princeton, NJ: Princeton University Press.

Bruner, J. (1999). Postscript: Some reflections on education research. In E. C. Lagemann & L. S. Shulman (Eds.), *Issues in education research* (pp. 399–409). San Francisco: Jossey-Bass.

Coalition for Evidence-Based Policy. (2002). *Bringing evidence-driven progress to education: A recommended strategy for the U.S. Department of Education.* Washington, DC: Author.

Coburn, C. (2006). Framing the problem of reading instruction: Using frame analysis to uncover the microprocesses of policy implementation. *American Educational Research Journal, 43,* 343–349.

Cohen, D. K., & Rosenberg, B. H. (1977). Functions and fantasies: Understanding schools in capitalist America. *History of Education Quarterly, 17,* 113–137.

Coleman, J., Campbell, E., Hobson, C., McPartland, J., Mood, A., Weinfeld, F. D., et al. (1966). *Equality of educational opportunity.* Washington, DC: U.S. Government Printing Office.

Datnow A., Hubbard L., & Mehan, H. (2002) *Extending educational reform: From one school to many.* New York: RoutledgeFalmer.

Davies, S. (1999). From moral duty to cultural rights: A case study of political framing in education. *Sociology of Education, 72,* 1–21.

Douglas, M. (Ed.). (1977). *Rules and meanings: The anthropology of everyday knowledge.* New York: Penguin Books.

Durkheim, E. (1915). *The elementary forms of the religious life.* New York: Free Press.

Edelman, M. (1971). *Politics as symbolic action: Mass arousal and quiescence.* Chicago: Markham Publishing.

Edelman, M. (1977). *Political language: Words that succeed and policies that fail.* New York: Academic Press.

Edelman, M. (1985). *The symbolic uses of politics* (Rev. ed.). Urbana: University of Illinois Press.

Edelman, M. (1987). The construction of social problems as buttresses of inequalities. *University of Miami Law Review, 42,* 7–28.

Edelman, M. (1988). *Constructing the political spectacle.* Chicago: University of Chicago Press.

Edmonds, R. (1978). *A discussion of the literature and issues related to effective schooling.* St. Louis, MO: CEMREL.

Epstein, S. (1996). *Impure science: AIDS, activism, and the politics of knowledge.* Berkeley: University of California Press.

Erickson, F., & Gutierrez, K. (2002). Culture, rigor, and science in educational research. *Educational Researcher, 31*(8), 21–24.

Erickson, F., & Schultz, J. (1982). *The counselor as gatekeeper: Social interaction in interviews.* New York: Academic Press.

Ex-surgeon general says he was silenced. (2007, July 10). *USA Today.* Retrieved August 17, 2007, from www.usatoday.com/news/washington/2007-07-10-carmona-testimony_n.htm

Ferguson, A. A. (2000). *Bad boys: Public schools in the making of black masculinity.* Ann Arbor: University of Michigan Press.

Fine, M. (1991). *Framing dropouts: Notes on the politics of an urban public high school.* Albany: State University of New York Press.

Firth, R. (1973). *Symbols public and private.* Ithaca, NY: Cornell University Press.

Fischer, F. (1993). Policy discourse and the politics of Washington think tanks. In F. Fischer & J. Forester (Eds.), *The argumentative turn in policy analysis and planning* (pp. 21–42). Durham, NC: Duke University Press.

Fischer, F. (2003). *Reframing public policy: Discursive politics and deliberative practices.* New York: Oxford University Press.

Fischer, F., & Forester, J. (Eds.). (1993). *The argumentative turn in policy analysis and planning.* Durham, NC: Duke University Press.

Fish, S. (1995). Rhetoric. In F. Lentricchia & T. McLaughlin (Eds.), *Critical terms for literary study* (2nd ed., pp. 203–222). Chicago: University of Chicago Press.

Foucault, M. (1980). *Power/knowledge: Selected interviews and other writings 1972–77* (C. Gordon, Ed.). Brighton, UK: Harvester Press.

Goffman, E. (1974). *Frame analysis: An essay on the organization of experience.* Boston: Northeastern University Press.

Gusfield, J. R. (1981). *The culture of public problems: Drinking-driving and the symbolic order.* Chicago: University of Chicago Press.

Gusfield, J. R. (1986). *Symbolic crusade: Status politics and the American temperance movement* (2nd ed.). Chicago: University of Illinois Press.

Hall, P. M. (1983). A social construction of reality. *The Elementary School Journal, 84,* 142–148.

Hall, P. M., & McGinty, P. J. W. (1997). Policy as the transformation of intentions: Producing program from statute. *The Sociological Quarterly, 38,* 439–467.

Haraway, D. (1988). Situated knowledges: The science question in feminism and the privilege of the partial perspective. *Feminist Studies, 14,* 575–600.

Hirschman, A. (1991). *The rhetoric of reaction: Perversity, futility, jeopardy.* Cambridge, MA: Harvard University Press.

Holland, D., & Quinn, N. (Eds.). (1987). *Cultural models in language and thought.* Cambridge, England: Cambridge University Press.

Hunter, A. (1987). The role of liberal political culture in the construction of Middle America. *University of Miami Law Review, 42,* 93–126.

Kertzer, D. I. (1988). *Ritual, politics, and power.* New Haven, CT: Yale University Press.

Kliebard, H. M. (2004). *The struggle for the American curriculum, 1893–1958* (3rd ed.). New York: RoutledgeFalmer.

Labaree, D. F. (1997). *How to succeed in school without really learning: The credentials race in American education.* New Haven, CT: Yale University Press.

Ladson-Billings, G. (2006). From the achievement gap to the education debt: Understanding achievement in U.S. schools. *Educational Researcher, 35*(7), 3–12.

Lakoff, G. (2004). *Don't think of an elephant! Know your values and frame the debate: The essential guide for progressives.* White River Junction, VT: Chelsea Green.

Lave, J. (1993). The practice of learning. In S. Chaiklin & J. Lave (Eds.), *Understanding practice: Perspectives on activity and context* (pp. 3–32). Cambridge, England: Cambridge University Press.

Levinson, B. A. U., Foley, D. E., & Holland, D. C. (Eds.). (1996). *The cultural production of the educated person: Critical ethnographies of schooling and local practice.* Albany: State University of New York Press.

Levinson, B. A. U., & Sutton, M. (2001). Introduction: Policy as/in practice—a sociocultural approach to the study of educational policy. In B. A. U. Levinson & M. Sutton (Eds.), *Policy as practice: Toward a comparative sociocultural analysis of educational policy* (pp. 1–22). Westport, CT: Ablex.

Lewis, J., & Knijn, T. (2002). The politics of sex education policy in England and Wales and The Netherlands since the 1980s. *Journal of Social Policy, 31,* 669–694.

Lipman, P. (2004). *High stakes education: Inequality, globalization, and urban school reform.* New York: RoutledgeFalmer.

Lortie, D. (1975). *Schoolteacher: A sociological study.* Chicago: University of Chicago Press.

Loseke, D. R., & Best, J. (Eds.). (2003). *Social problems: Constructionist readings.* New York: Aldine de Gruyter.

Luker, K. (1984). *Abortion and the politics of motherhood.* Berkeley: University of California Press.

Malen, B., & Knapp, M. (1997). Rethinking the multiple perspectives approach to education policy analysis: Implications for policy-practice connections. *Education Policy, 12,* 419–445.

McDermott, R., Gospodinoff, K., & Aron, J. (1978). Criteria for an ethnographically adequate description of concerted activities and their contexts. *Semiotica, 24,* 245–275.

Mead, M. (1943). Our educational emphases in primitive perspective. *The American Journal of Sociology, 48,* 633–639.

Mehan, H. (1992). Understanding inequality in schools: The contribution of interpretive studies. *Sociology of Education, 65,* 1–20.

Mehan, H. (1993). Beneath the skin and between the ears: A case study in the politics of representation. In S. Chaiklin & J. Lave (Eds.), *Understanding practice: Perspectives on activity and context* (pp. 241–268). Cambridge, UK: Cambridge University Press.

Mehan, H. (1994). The role of discourse in learning, schooling, and reform. In B. McLeod (Ed.), *Language and learning: Educating linguistically diverse students* (pp. 71–96). Albany: State University of New York Press.

Mills, C. W. (1940). Situated actions and vocabularies of motive. *American Sociological Review, 5,* 904–913.

Moore, S. F., & Myerhoff, B. G. (Eds.). (1977). *Secular ritual.* Amsterdam: Van Gorcum.

No-sex programs "not working." (2007, August 2). *BBC News.* Retrieved August 3, 2007, from http://news.bbc.co.uk/2/hi/health/6927733.stm

Noe, C. (2004, January 9). Bush decries Democrats' "Soft bigotry of low expectations." *NewsMax.Com.* Retrieved May 8, 2008, from http://archive.newsmax.com/archives/articles/2004/1/9/110923.shtml

O'Connor, A. (2001). *Poverty knowledge: Social science, social policy, and the poor in twentieth-century U.S. history.* Princeton, NJ: Princeton University Press.

Omi, M., & Winant, H. (1994). *Racial formation in the United States: From the 1960s to the 1990s* (2nd ed.). New York: Routledge.

Paige, R. (2002, November 18). Speech presented at the Consolidation Conference, Washington, DC. Retrieved May 8, 2008, from http://www.ed.gov/news/speeches/2002/11/11182002.html

Porter, T. M. (1995). *Trust in numbers: The pursuit of objectivity in science and public life.* Princeton, NJ: Princeton University Press.

Rein, M., & Schön, D. (1993). Reframing policy discourse. In F. Fischer & J. Forester (Eds.), *The argumentative turn in policy analysis and planning* (pp. 145–166). Durham, NC: Duke University Press.

Rieder, J. (1985). *Canarsie: The Jews and Italians of Brooklyn against liberalism.* Cambridge, MA: Harvard University Press.

Rosen, L. (2001). Myth making and moral order in a debate on mathematics. In B. A. U. Levinson & M. Sutton (Eds.), *Policy as practice: Toward a comparative sociocultural analysis of educational policy* (pp. 295–316). Westport, CT: Ablex.

Rosen, L., & Mehan, H. (2003). Reconstructing equality on new political ground: The politics of representation in the charter school debate at UCSD. *American Educational Research Journal, 40,* 655–682.

Rowan, B. (1984). Shamanistic rituals in effective schools. *Issues in Education, 2*(1), 76–87.

Santelli, J., Ott, M. A., Lyon, M., Rogers, J., Summers, D., & Schleifer, R. (2006). Abstinence and abstinence-only education: A review of U.S. policies and programs. *Journal of Adolescent Health, 38,* 72–81.

Schön, D., & Rein, M. (1994). *Frame reflection: Toward the resolution of intractable controversies.* New York: Basic Books.

Schutz, A. (1967). *The phenomenology of the social world.* (G. Walsh & F. Lehnert, Trans.). Evanston, IL: Northwestern University Press. (Original work published 1932)

Shapiro, M. J. (1988). *The politics of representation: Writing practices in biography, photography, and policy analysis.* Madison: University of Wisconsin Press.

Shore, C., & Wright, S. (Eds.). (1997). *Anthropology of policy: Critical perspectives on governance and power.* London: Routledge.

Slee, R., & Weiner, G. (1998). Introduction: School effectiveness for whom? In R. Slee, G. Weiner, & S. Tomlinson (Eds.), *School effectiveness for whom? Challenges to the school effectiveness and school improvement movements* (pp. 1–10). Bristol, PA: Falmer Press.

Smith, M. L., Miller-Kahn, L., Heinecke, W., & Jarvis, P. F. (2004). *Political spectacle and the fate of American schools.* New York: RoutledgeFalmer.

Snow, D. A., & Benford, R. D. (1988). Ideology, frame resonance, and participant mobilization. *International Social Movement Research, 1,* 197–218.

Spector, M., & Kitsuse, J. I. (2006). *Constructing social problems* (Rev. ed.). New Brunswick, NJ: Transaction Publishers.

Stone, D. (1997). *Policy paradox: The art of political decision-making* (2nd ed.). New York: W. W. Norton.

Swadener, B. B., & Lubeck, S. (Eds.). (1995). *Children and families "at promise": Deconstructing the discourse of risk.* Albany: State University of New York Press.

Taylor, S., Rizvi, F., Lingard, B., & Henry, M. (1997). *Educational policy and the politics of change.* New York: Routledge.

Thomson, R. (1994). Moral rhetoric and public health pragmatism: The recent politics of sex education. *Feminist Review, 48,* 40–60.

Underhill, K., Montgomery, P., & Operario, D. (2007). Sexual abstinence only programmes to prevent HIV infection in high income countries: Systematic review [Electronic version]. *British Medical Journal, 335*(7613), 248.

U.S. Department of Education. (2002). *U. S. Department of Education strategic plan 2002–2007.* Jessup, MD: ED Pubs.

Valdes, G. (1996). *Con respeto: Bridging the distance between culturally diverse families and schools, an ethnographic portrait.* New York: Teachers College Press.

Varenne, H., & McDermott, R. (1999). *Successful failure: The school America builds.* Boulder, CO: Westview Press.

Wells, A. S., & Serna, I. (1996). The politics of culture: Understanding local political resistance to detracking in racially mixed schools. *Harvard Educational Review, 66,* 93–118.

Wilson, S. (2003). *California dreaming: Reforming mathematics education.* New Haven, CT: Yale University Press.

Woolard, K. (1989). Sentences in the language prison: The rhetorical structuring of an American language policy debate. *American Ethnologist, 16,* 268–278.

Yanow, D. (1993). The communication of policy meanings: Implementation as interpretation and text. *Policy Sciences, 26,* 41–61.

Yanow, D. (1996). *How does a policy mean? Interpreting policy and organizational actions.* Washington, DC: Georgetown University Press.

Yanow, D. (2000). *Conducting interpretive policy analysis.* Newbury Park, CA: Sage.

23

The Role of Law in Educational Policy Formation, Implementation, and Research

JULIE F. MEAD
University of Wisconsin–Madison

What is the relationship between educational law and educational policy? What role do courts play in relation to school policy? How has that role changed over time? What is legal research and how does it relate to school policy? Addressing these questions forms the focus of this chapter. The first section provides an overview of the link between law and policy and the influence of legal research on that role. Then the chapter briefly examines the influence of litigation and legislation on school policy and how it has evolved over time. Next, four illustrative examples of judicial and legislative intervention, at both the federal and state levels, are presented. The chapter concludes with a brief discussion of legal issues that appear to loom largest on the educational policy horizon.

The Relationship Between Law and Policy

School law is, of course, one form of school policy. Conversely, school policy may be considered a form of local law in some instances. The terms, however, are not synonymous, and the relationship between the concepts may be best understood as a simple maxim. Law bounds practice. Federal and state constitutions establish broad principles; federal and state legislatures both prescribe and proscribe action; state and local executive agencies promulgate rules to guide statutory implementation; courts check discretion by settling disputes, construing statutes, and interpreting constitutional principles. Accordingly, understanding school law is not about knowing answers. It is about knowing what questions to ask and what information to gather. Understanding school law involves the quest to discern what boundaries school policy makers, school authorities, and school teachers have when accomplishing the important work of schools.

The law, therefore, not only defines our limits, but has limitations itself. Distilled to its essence, knowing what the "law" says about a particular school policy or practice can only help educators consider two types of questions: "may we?" or "must we?" For example, in the last few years, the Supreme Court has been asked several "may we" questions in relation to schools:

- May we, as school officials, require students to submit to random urinalysis as a condition for playing sports or participating in extracurricular activities and still be consistent with the Fourth Amendment's prohibition against unreasonable searches and seizures? (*Vernonia School District 47J v. Acton,* 1995; *Board of Education of Independent School District No. 92 of Pottawatomie County v. Earls,* 2002)
- May we, as state lawmakers, create a voucher plan that allows public funds to pay for private religious education without violating the Establishment of Religion Clause of the First Amendment? (*Zelman v. Simmons-Harris,* 2002)
- May we, as teachers, have students grade each other's papers without violating the provisions of the Federal Educational Rights and Privacy Act? (*Owasso Independent School Dist. No. I-011 v. Falvo,* 2002)

Courts are also asked to address "must we" questions, such as:

- Must we, as school officials, have an Individualized Education Program in place before the school year begins in order to comply with the dictates of the Individuals with Disabilities Education Act? (Individuals with Disabilities Education Act, 20 U.S.C. §1414(d)(2)(2004); *E.P. v. San Ramon Valley Unified School Dist.,* 2007)
- Must we fund religious education if we fund other types of training through a college scholarship program in order to comply with the First Amendment's Free Exercise of Religion and Freedom of Speech Clauses? (*Locke v. Davey,* 2004)

- Must we provide access to classes for students who are being homeschooled? (*Swanson v. Guthrie Independent School District I-L*, 1998).
- Must we, as schoolteachers, supervise students at all times? (*Wallmuth v. Rapides Parish School Board*, 2002)

Ascertaining the answers to these legal questions helps school officials, teachers, and policy makers to discern the bounds of their discretion, while failure to understand the legal bounds of discretion for either making or implementing policy risks two types of errors. Actions that exceed those boundaries may be determined to be unlawful or unconstitutional and may confer legal liability on the actors, the school district, or the state. Just as troubling, policy makers and practitioners unaware of their legal discretion may unnecessarily constrain their activities under a mistaken belief that the "law" limits more than it actually does. Discerning the precise boundaries various forms of legal authority create may not always be clear, however, which is why disputes arise. In these cases, litigation is sparked and the judiciary is frequently called upon to define where those boundaries are.

Examining issues of policy formation and implementation from a legal perspective is necessarily limited, however, for legal advice cannot address the question, "should we?" "Should we?" is an issue of policy. Given the separation of powers enshrined in our constitution, lawyers and judges cannot tell us what we should do. Only educators and those that create or enact educational policy can answer that question, and only they can determine whether or not to exercise the discretion enjoyed given the boundaries of the law. For example:

- The Supreme Court has held that school officials may require students to submit to random urinalysis as a condition for playing sports or participating in extracurricular activities. But should we? And if we do, will it prove an effective tool against the problem of childhood substance abuse? What message will we send students if we use such practices and what message will we send if we do not? Those are questions of policy, not law.
- The Supreme Court has determined that states may create voucher programs that channel money to religious schools. But are such programs a good idea? Do they make effective use of limited educational funds? Those are questions of policy, not law.
- The Supreme Court has concluded that teachers may have students grade each other's papers. But is that good instructional practice? That is a question of policy, not law.

In other words, understanding school law helps to discern the bounds of discretion (authority) for school policymaking and practice, but cannot determine whether exercising that discretion in a certain manner is a good or bad idea wise or misguided policy, effective or ineffective practice. Those determinations are the province of school policy, and all of the political forces that influence its development.

Research on school law, then, is the study of the various sources of legal authority in order to determine both what is and what could be. Research on school law that focuses on the present attempts to understand the various sources of legal authority that apply to a given problem or set of facts. As shown in Table 23.1, legal authority may derive from each level and each branch of government.

In other words, legal research may seek to capture the current statutory boundaries and jurisprudential thinking on a topic in order to describe its implications, both for current practice and for future policy development.

What is more, legal scholarship also may address the future in another way. "One of the earliest insights of law and society scholarship is that there is very often a gap between law's aspirations and its actual social consequences"

TABLE 23.1
Sources of Legal Authority

		Level of Government		
		Federal	**State**	**Local School District**
Branch of Government		U.S. Constitution	State Constitution	(derived from state constitution)
	Legislative	Federal Statutes (U. S. Congress)	State Statutes State Legislature)	Board Policies (Local School Board)
	Executive	Federal Administrative Regulations and Rules (U.S. Dept. of Education)	State Administrative Regulations and Rules (State Educational Agencies [e.g., Dept. of Education, Dept. of Public Instruction])	Administrative Policies and Procedures (Superintendent and other Administrators)
	Judicial	Case Law (Federal District Courts, Federal Courts of Appeals, U.S. Supreme Court)	Case Law (all state courts)	Board Decisions from Hearings

Note: Table adapted from Underwood & Mead, 1995, p. 1

(Sarat, Constable, Engle, Hans, & Lawrence, 1998, p. 4). As such, legal scholarship may seek to construct a legal theory that might be used to move jurisprudential thinking in one direction or another. Likewise, legal research may adopt a "critical" vantage point in order to "attack … the legitimacy and power of established forms of legal authority" (Munger, 1998, p. 36). This approach is particularly common in constructions of identity and how "equality" is or is not achieved under the law and courts' interpretations of it. Legal research from this perspective may employ "critical race theory," "feminist legal theory," and "queer theory," to name a few (see, e.g., Delgado, 1995; Crenshaw, Gotanda, Peller, & Thomas, 1997; West, 1988). Such critical treatments of the law may also point out the entrenched nature of the status quo and the frequent inadequacy of litigation as a means to effect meaningful change and thus encourage the exploration of other political avenues to advance toward social justice. As such, there is a dynamic interplay between policy makers and political factions that try to persuade them, educators who implement the policy, the judiciary that settles disputes that arise between various educational stakeholders and researchers, from both legal and policy perspectives, who seek to shed light on the significant questions of the time.

Historical Overview

There is no question that, as a field, education law has grown over time. For example, a book written in 1913 to prepare one-room school teachers makes only one mention of the courts: "Corporal punishment as viewed by the courts" (Culter & Stone, 1913, pp. 149–150). Twenty years later, an early school law text concentrated its treatment of the legal aspects of education to the state's authority to establish, fund, and operate schools with only marginal attention to issues of teacher dismissal, religion, segregation, and student discipline (Edwards, 1933). In contrast, modern school law textbooks routinely cover topics such as religion, student expression, teacher expression, student discipline, contract law, liability, curricular control, segregation, English language learners, and special education (Alexander & Alexander, 2005; McCarthy, Cambron-McCabe, & Thomas, 2004). Present day texts attest to the marked increase in both legislative and judicial intervention at both the state and federal levels of government in the operation of the nation's public schools. And while early texts deal almost entirely with discussions of state law and local school board authority, current treatments of the law must, by necessity, discuss the influence of federal law on educational delivery.

Educating young children began, of course, as a local enterprise. As the nation grew, states assumed the responsibility for providing and even compelling education (Alexander & Alexander, 2005; Yudof, Kirp, Levin, & Moran, 2002). In fact, all 50 state constitutions establish a legislative responsibility for the creation of public schools (McCarthy et al., 2004). Each state legislature, then, has had the task of enacting laws that define public education

for its citizenry, provide funds for their operation, and designate or delegate authority for their oversight. As such, the tension between state and local control of public schools is largely defined by each state's legislative body and the statutes they create in response to the state constitutional mandate. State enactments may dictate how school districts will be organized, what programs public schools must offer, and require local districts to reform their practices to conform to state requirements. Local educational authorities (e.g., school boards) may only exercise that authority delegated to them. Moreover, state legislatures may alter that balance between state and local control whenever the political will to do so asserts itself. In fact, many view the last two decades as a period in which the states increased their control over educational delivery by divesting local school boards of much of the authority for school operation by adopting strict educational standards and various accountability mechanisms to enforce them (Koski, 2001; Howard, 1996).

At the federal level, judicial intervention largely preceded legislative activity. McCarthy et al. (2004) report:

> Traditionally, the federal judiciary did not address educational concerns; fewer than 300 cases involving education had been initiated in federal courts prior to 1954. However, starting with the landmark desegregation decision, *Brown v. Board of Education of Topeka* (1954), federal courts assumed a significant role in resolving educational controversies. By 1970, litigation was clearly viewed as an important tool to influence social policies, and more legal challenges to school practices were initiated in the 1970s than in the preceding seven decades combined. (p. 22, footnotes omitted)

As noted, the Supreme Court's landmark decision in *Brown v. the Board of Education* (1954) marked the beginning of a series of important constitutional decisions related to public education. Chief Justice Earl Warren's decision, which spoke for a unanimous court, not only declared that segregation was "inherently unequal," it recognized the important place education plays in the "liberty" guaranteed by the United States Constitution. The decision also linked the benefit gained by a single individual through education to the benefit that accrues to the collective when educational opportunity is available to all. Finally, the *Brown* decision put states on notice that while courts would and should defer to state and local authorities on many educational matters, judicial deference was not without limit and courts should not hesitate to scrutinize educational policy whenever evidence showed authorities had strayed from the values safeguarded by the principles enunciated in the Constitution.

Since *Brown*, the Supreme Court has articulated several constitutional boundaries to school's work that heretofore had been unrecognized. For example, the Court held that students retained rights to free speech under the First Amendment even while at school (*Tinker v. Des Moines Independent Community School District*, 1969) and continued to enjoy the Fourth Amendment's protection from unreasonable searches at the hands of school authorities (*New Jersey v. T.L.O.*, 1985). What is more, the Court declared that education is a property right protected by the 14th Amendment's Due Process Clause such that even short term suspensions from school require a modicum of due process (*Goss v. Lopez*, 1975) and that the 14th Amendment's Equal Protection Clause requires that all children, even those whose parents are undocumented aliens, must have access to benefits of public education whenever states provide it (*Plyler v. Doe*, 1982). Likewise, the Court held that teachers do not shed their constitutional rights to speak out on matters of public concern (*Pickering v. Board of Education*, 1968) and must be given adequate due process before being dismissed from public employment (*Board of Regents v. Roth*, 1972). And yet, the Court also concluded that education was not a federal fundamental right protected by the same constitutional principles (*San Antonio Independent School District v. Rodriguez*, 1973). These decisions, of course, represent just a sampling of the educational issues considered by the Supreme Court in the period following *Brown*.

After *Brown* and in response to states' failure to move with "all deliberate speed" (*Brown v. Board of Education*, 1955) toward the provision of educational opportunity for all students (Orfield, 1999), the United States Congress also increased its role in setting educational policy. While Congress has no direct authority to legislate education, the legislature has used its "power of the purse" (the spending clause of Article I of the Constitution) to "promote the general welfare" by enacting educational legislation.

Congress has used its spending authority in three distinct but related ways by adopting (a) general funding statutes, (b) incentive funding statutes, and (c) conditional funding statutes (Underwood & Mead, 1995). General funding statutes create pools of money that states can access in order to pursue goals established by Congress (e.g., the Charter School Expansion Act). Incentive funding states provide funds for specified purposes, but require that states bind themselves to a particular set of rules in order to get the funds (e.g., the Individuals with Disabilities Education Act). Funds made available in this way become the "carrot" Congress uses to get state compliance with its policy directives. Conditional funding statutes provide no money. Rather, they use withdrawal of federal funds as a penalty for state behavior, such as discrimination, that Congress has deemed inappropriate (e.g., Section 504 of the Rehabilitation Act of 1973). In this instance, the threat of removal of other federal money is the "stick" Congress uses to get state compliance. Table 23.2 lists a number of major federal statutes and their purposes.

If *Brown* was the defining moment of judicial intervention into public education, then the Elementary and Secondary Education Act (ESEA) of 1965 marks the turning point for federal legislative activism. The ESEA coupled with the Title VI of the Civil Rights Act of 1964 established powerful avenues by which the federal government could influence state and local educational policy. While the ESEA provided funds to encourage states to move in the policy directions established by Congress, Title VI threatened to remove all federal funds if states did not desegregate. This pairing of incentives and punishments also provided the

TABLE 23.2
Federal Statutes Affecting Public Education

Federal Statute	Type	Purpose
Carl Perkins Vocational Education Act (20 U.S.C. 2301)	general	provides funds for vocational education programs
No Child Left Behind Act of 2001 (20 U.S.C. 6301 et seq.)	General/ incentive	provides funds for programs for students disadvantaged by poverty and more
Individuals with Disabilities Education Act (20 U.S.C. 1400 et seq.)	incentive	provides funds for special education and related services
McKinney-Vento Homeless Education Assistance Improvements Act of 2001 (42 U.S.C. 11301)	incentive	provides funds for educational services for children who are homeless
Child Abuse Prevention and Treatment Act (42 U.S.C. 5101)	incentive	provides funds to state who enact legislation for the mandatory reporting of child abuse and neglect
Title IX of the Education Amendments (20 U.S.C. 1681)	conditional	prohibits discrimination on the basis of sex in educational institutions
Section 504 of the Rehabilitation Act (29 U.S.C. 794)	conditional	prohibits discrimination on the basis of disability
Title VI of the Civil Rights Act (42 U.S.C. 2000e-2)	conditional	prohibits discrimination in employment on the basis of race, color, religion, sex, or national origin
Family Educational Rights and Privacy Act (20 U.S.C. 1232g)	conditional	protects students' rights to privacy in school records, requires parental access to those records
Equal Access Act (20 U.S.C. 4071)	conditional	prohibits content-based discrimination in access to high school forums (e.g., student-led clubs)

Note: Adapted from Mead (2000).

Executive Branch potent means to monitor and influence state and local educational policy makers.

Undoubtedly, while federal legislative activity has become an increasing presence in school operation since 1965, the reauthorization of the ESEA as the No Child Left Behind Act of 2001 (NCLB) marks another step in federal educational policymaking and influence. NCLB's myriad provisions not only determine what educational activities enjoy federal financial support, but also dictate ways in which schools and states will be held accountable for their instructional efforts. The far-reaching impact of NCLB has implicated the federal government in teaching and learning enterprise to a greater extent than ever. NCLB provides a compelling example of how policy ideas become enacted into law, which in turn spurs the development of more policy at the state and local levels. For example, NCLB requires, as a condition of receiving funds under the act, that states adopt uniform statewide achievement standards, develop tests to track student performance, engage in annual testing, and report test results. NCLB also mandates that states penalize those schools and districts that fail to achieve "adequate yearly progress" toward a goal in 2014 of having 100% of their students demonstrating proficiency in reading, math, and science. Consequently, NCLB illustrates how much "law" in the form of federal legislation has come to impact educational delivery.

Illustrative Examples

As noted by the historical overview presented above, law in the form of both litigation and legislation has impacted school policymaking in meaningful and enduring ways. In this section, four illustrative examples of the interplay between law and policy are presented. First, as an example of the impact of litigation at the federal level, the jurisprudence that developed to permit the enactment of publicly funded school voucher programs is presented. Then, to exemplify federal legislative intervention, the 30-year evolution of the Individuals with Disabilities Education Act (IDEA) is traced. Third, an example of state judicial impact in the form of finance equity litigation is presented. Finally, the proliferation of charter schools is offered as an example of state legislative intervention.

Judicial Intervention–Voucher Programs Vouchers as means to use public funds to pay for education was first proffered by Milton Friedman in his classic book, *Capitalism and Freedom* (1962). Friedman argued that by allowing parents to select the school their child would attend, schools' competition for students would result in better educational outcomes. Strong schools would attract more students. Weak schools would fold because they could not compete. This radical idea suggested that the "public" in education should only reflect the funding source rather than those setting policy and directing instruction. Rather, parents should be allowed to select from all educational options, public or private, religious or non-religious, and

use a voucher provided by public tax dollars to pay for all or part of the educational costs. This free market approach, however, was met with substantial opposition, and at least part of that opposition argued that creating such programs would violate the United States Constitution insofar as religious schools were included in any plan (for an extended discussion of vouchers, see Witte, this volume).

Specifically, some opposed to vouchers argued that allowing public funds to pay for all or part of a child's religious education, even if selected by the parents, would violate the Establishment of Religion Clause of the First Amendment. A series of cases in the early 1970s seemed to solidify this thinking (*Lemon v. Kurtzman,* 1971; *Sloan v. Lemon,* 1973; *Levitt v. Committee for Public Education and Religious Liberty,* 1973; *Committee for Public Education and Religious Liberty v. Nyquist,* 1973). The last of these, *Committee for Public Education and Religious Liberty v. Nyquist,* required the Court to consider the constitutionality of a group of New York state programs that provided funds to non-public schools for maintenance and repair of facilities, "a tuition grant program and a tax benefit program" (*Committee for Public Education and Religious Liberty v. Nyquist,* 1973, p. 764). The court invalidated the programs finding that they had the "primary effect" of advancing religion.

While it might have appeared that *Nyquist* settled the matter, it did not, in fact. Subsequent cases asked the court to consider the constitutional viability of a variety of programs challenged as being impermissible direct aid to religious schools or organizations. Each of these decisions was then essentially mined to determine how the resulting jurisprudence might be used to craft a voucher program that would survive constitutional scrutiny.

While the Court heard a number of Establishment Clause cases after Nyquist, five decisions would ultimately lay the foundation for a legal theory that could support a public voucher program. First, the Court held that a Minnesota statute that allowed parents a tax deduction for educational expenses was constitutional, even though the provision predominantly benefited those whose children attended private religious schools (*Mueller v. Allen,* 1983). The Court reasoned that any "attenuated financial benefit, ultimately controlled by the private choices of individual parents, that eventually flows to parochial schools from the neutrally available tax benefit" (*Mueller,* 1983, p. 400) did not have the effect of advancing religion. Similarly, the Court held that providing funds for vocational assistance to a blind student studying at religious college did not violate the Establishment Clause because the student chose the educational institution he wished to attend and the program entailed no financial incentives for students to undertake sectarian education (*Witters v. Washington Department of Services for the Blind,* 1986). Drawing again on the constitutional import of the fact that private, not state, actors selected the school and that the funds in question were made available to a "broad class" of citizens without regard to religion, the Court next foreshadowed its ultimate approval of vouchers in *Zobrest v. Catalina Foothills School District* (1993). In *Zobrest*, the Court ruled that nothing in the constitution prohibited the expenditure of federal funds to support the provision of a sign language interpreter for a child enrolled in a private religious school. Likewise, the Court upheld the constitutionality of aid to parochial schools under the Elementary and Secondary Education Act first in *Agostini v. Felton* (1997) and then in *Mitchell v. Helms* (2000), and thus expanded on this thinking. As Justice Thomas, writing for the plurality in *Mitchell*, explained:

> If the religious, irreligious, and areligious are all alike eligible for governmental aid, no one would conclude that any indoctrination that any particular recipient conducts has been done at the behest of the government. For attribution of indoctrination is a relative question. If the government is offering assistance to recipients who provide, so to speak, a broad range of indoctrination, the government itself is not thought responsible for any particular indoctrination. To put the point differently, if the government, seeking to further some legitimate secular purpose, offers aid on the same terms, without regard to religion, to all who adequately further that purpose, then it is fair to say that any aid going to a religious recipient only has the effect of furthering that secular purpose. (pp. 809–810)

Two years after this pronouncement, the Court heard *Zelman v. Simmons-Harris* (2002), which considered the constitutionality of the voucher program created by the Ohio legislature and made available to children in the Cleveland City School District. In a contentious 5–4 decision, the Court upheld the program because it served a secular purpose and satisfied two essential characteristics as a program providing indirect benefit to religious organizations: (a) that the program did not define recipients based on religious criteria, and (b) that the recipients had "genuine and independent private choice" between religious and nonreligious alternatives (*Zelman*, 2002, p. 652). In so doing, the Court definitively responded that states had the discretion to create such programs, or in other words, that states "may" establish vouchers consistent with the federal constitution.

Perhaps not surprisingly, legal challenges mounted by both proponents and opponents of vouchers did not end with *Zelman*. At the federal level, proponents of vouchers next argued that not only *may* states create vouchers including religious options, they *must* do so in order to comply with the First Amendment's Free Exercise of Religion Clause (*Locke v. Davey*, 2004). The Supreme Court rejected this premise ruling that while the federal Constitution permitted voucher programs that included religious schools, it did not require them. Opponents shifted their litigation strategy to state courts and found some success there. For example, the Florida Supreme Court invalidated a state voucher program as violative of the legislature's duty under the state constitution to provide for a "uniform" system of public education (*Bush v. Holmes*, 2006; for a similar ruling interpreting the Colorado Constitution, see *Owens v. Congress of Parents,*

Teachers, and Students, 2004). Nonetheless, after the *Zelman* decision, arguments about vouchers have largely left various legal arenas and have played out in political venues where advocates of each position argue the wisdom, rather then the legality of voucher programs (Forman, 2007).

Federal Legislative Intervention—IDEA The evolution of the Individuals with Disabilities Education Act (IDEA) provides a compelling example of the how Congress and its ability to enact statutes to "promote the general welfare" impact educational policy. IDEA's development also illustrates how the interaction between the legislative and judicial branches shapes educational policy.

The IDEA was first enacted as the Education for All Handicapped Children Act (EAHCA) in 1975 and provided substantial federal funds to states to support the education of children with disabilities. The act followed 2 years after Congress voted to prohibit discrimination on the basis of disability by passing Section 504 of the Rehabilitation Act of 1973 (1973). EAHCA's enactment also followed courts' rulings in two highly publicized cases which considered constitutional challenges to the exclusion and inappropriate education of children with disabilities available in the nation's public schools of the time (*Mills v. Board of Education of the District of Columbia*, 1972; *Pennsylvania Association for Retarded Children [PARC] v. Commonwealth of Pennsylvania*, 1973). As the Senate report accompanying the bill explained:

> Over the past few years, parents of handicapped children have begun to recognize that their children are being denied services which are guaranteed under the Constitution. It should not, however, be necessary for parents throughout the country to continue utilizing the courts to assure themselves a remedy. (S. Rep. No. 94-168, 1975)

In fact, the provisions of the EAHCA were largely a codification of the consent decree that resulted from the 1972 decision in *Mills v. Board of Education* (Underwood & Mead, 1995). The EAHCA required states, as a condition of receiving the funds made available, to commit to ensuring that each child with a disability within its borders had available a "free appropriate public education." Moreover, the law detailed elaborate procedures to document those efforts and involve parents in all decision making and established mechanisms for parents to challenge school districts both administratively and judicially whenever they believed districts had failed to realize their obligations under the act.

Since that initial passage, the law has been amended four times, including re-naming the act the Individuals with Disabilities Education Act (IDEA) in 1990. The most recent reauthorization of the act occurred in 2004 under the title the Individuals with Disabilities Education Improvement Act (IDEIA). Though only 10 states mandated that schools educate children with disabilities in 1970 (Underwood & Mead, 1995), currently all 50 states accept IDEA funds and thus are bound by its provisions.

A comprehensive treatment of the IDEA, all its provisions, and the myriad judicial opinions shaping its interpretation and application is beyond the scope of this chapter. Instead, two examples of how the law was amended in response to judicial rulings demonstrate how litigation influences legislation and how both sources of law memorialize the policy choices of the time and therefore dictate the direction of educational policy development. One of the first of such examples is available by reviewing the Supreme Court's decision in *Smith v. Robinson* in 1984 and the passage 2 years later of the Handicapped Children's Protection Act (HCPA). In *Smith*, the Court denied parents' attempt to recover attorneys' fees expended while advocating for their child's right to an appropriate education. The Court, while sympathetic to the parents' argument, determined that such reimbursement was not possible because nothing in the act explicitly made such recovery possible. Congress was then spurred to correct this situation and did so with the HCPA which amended the law simply by adding a provision that now allows parents to recover attorney's fees if they are successful in demonstrating that school authorities denied their child an appropriate education (Individuals with Disabilities Education Act, 20 U.S.C. §1415 (e)(4)(2004)). The Senate report accompanying the bill explained this linkage:

> The situation which has resulted from the *Smith v. Robinson* decision was summarized by Justices Brennan, Marshall, and Stevens in their dissenting opinion: "Congress will now have to take the time to revisit the matter." Seeking to clarify the intent of Congress with respect to the educational rights of handicapped children guaranteed by the EHA, the Handicapped Children's Protection Act . . . was introduced. (S. Rep. No. 99-112, 1986)

Similarly, Congress added provisions related to discipline in 1997 (Individuals with Disabilities Education Act, 20 U.S.C. §1415(k)(2004)) in response to the Court's decision in *Honig v. Doe* (1988) that the law created no exception for children who engaged in dangerous behaviors (Mead, 1998).

Over the history of the act, Congress has also responded to calls from researchers to make various changes. For example, in 1997 Congress created a presumption of regular class placement and in so doing essentially codified a national policy of inclusion for children with disabilities (Mead, 1999). Most recently, the 2004 reauthorization of the act included a provision that prohibits states from requiring the use of so-called "discrepancy formulas" for determining whether a child is eligible under the act as a child with a "severe learning disability." Such formulas calculate the difference between intellectual potential as measured by an IQ test and actual performance on achievement measures. A learning disability is then operationally defined as a significant discrepancy between the two. Having heard testimony about the inaccuracy of such formulas and given the concerns about over-identification of children as learning disabled, Congress now prohibits states from mandating such formulas by including a provision which reads:

> a local educational agency shall not be required to take into consideration whether a child has a severe discrepancy between achievement and intellectual ability in oral expression, listening comprehension, written expression, basic reading skill, reading comprehension, mathematical calculation, or mathematical reasoning. (Individuals with Disabilities Education Act, 20 U.S.C. §1414(b)(6) (A)(2004))

Moreover, Congress has spurred considerable activity at the state and local level by also expressly permitting "a process that determines if the child responds to scientific, research-based intervention as a part of the evaluation procedures" (Individuals with Disabilities Education Act, 20 U.S.C. §1414(b)(6)(B)(2004)). Again, such legislative activity has the effect of establishing a national policy preference for a particular way of identifying and educating children with disabilities.

As each of the above examples illustrate, federal legislative activity establishes national policy, codifies its parameters, and responds to issues raised by the judiciary. Not all litigation or legislation affecting education occurs at the federal level—quite the contrary, in fact. In the same way that the federal judiciary must resolve educational disputes, so, too, do state courts in each jurisdiction.

State Judicial Intervention–School Finance Litigation

One example of where judicial intervention at the state level has significantly impacted educational policy in recent years is in school finance litigation. Prior to 1973, challenges to state school finance practices were often litigated in federal courts under theories that they violated poor children's rights to equal protection and/or due process under the 14th Amendment (Underwood & Verstegen, 1990). Since that time, however, litigation on school finance has occurred "almost exclusively" in state courts (Alexander & Alexander, 2005, p. 949). What caused the shift? In 1973, the United States Supreme Court ruled in *San Antonio v. Rodriguez* that education was not a fundamental right under the federal constitution. As such, state finance schemes needed only to justify their programs by explaining how they bore a rational relationship to a legitimate state interest—the lowest and most deferential judicial test employed by the Court. Though not completely foreclosing federal challenges (Underwood & Verstegan, 1990), *Rodriguez* made federal courts much less receptive venues for such challenges.

As such, litigation aimed at forcing legislatures to devise finance systems which resulted in more equitable allocations of resources shifted to state courts and arguments made under state constitutions. As Alexander and Alexander (2005) explain:

> School finance litigation under state constitutions usually emanates from two sources. First, the positive law in the body of state constitutions requires legislatures to establish and maintain a system of public schools. These "shalt" provisions in the framework of state constitutions place obligations on state legislatures to provide public school

systems that are "uniform," "adequate," "thorough," "efficient," "high quality," etc., depending on the wording of the state constitution. Second, the negative state constitutional provisions, the "shalt nots," prohibit state legislatures from denying individual rights of equal protection and due process of law. These provisions are the state counterparts to the liberties and freedoms provisions in the Bill of Rights and the Fourteenth Amendment of the U.S. Constitution. (p. 949)

Such lawsuits have met with varying success depending on the state and the precise wording of the state constitutional provisions in question. Zirkel and Kearns-Barber (2005) report that 41 states have considered one or more lawsuits challenging school finance systems between 1973 and 2005. Of these, litigants in 27 states won by having all or part of school finance programs declared unconstitutional.

Once a state court has declared a system of school finance unconstitutional, the general remedy ordered is for the legislature to revamp the system in order to address the inadequacies identified by the judiciary. As before, what then results is a cycle of legislation followed by litigation followed by more legislation and so on. Whether successful to date or not in a particular state, this type of litigation is likely to continue as long as disparities in funding exist in a state such that some districts appear to "have" and others to "have not" (Thro, 2005).

State Legislative Intervention—Charter Schools As mentioned earlier, state constitutions and state laws define what public education is for a given state. Accordingly, since public education is a creature of state law, state legislatures enjoy considerable discretion to define and redefine the nature of that public benefit. A recent example of state legislative action that has had the effect of redefining public education is the advent of charter schools. As Green and Mead (2004) explain:

> Appearing first in the 1990s, charter schools are public schools that are formed by a 'charter' between a designated chartering authority and those who wish to operate a school. State legislatures grant charter schools autonomy from many laws and regulations that apply to traditional public schools. In exchange for this autonomy, charter schools must achieve the educational goals that are established in the charter. Failure to do so may result in the closing of the school. (Green & Mead, 2004, p. 1)

Currently 40 states, the District of Columbia, and Puerto Rico have state laws that permit charter schools (United States Department of Education, 2007). Charter school statutes—and hence the definition of what constitutes a "charter school"—vary considerably from state to state (Green & Mead, 2004). For example, some states allow universities to charter schools, others do not; some states allow private schools to convert to charter schools, others do not; some states specify procedures for contract renewal, others do not; some provide blanket waivers from state rules, others do not. Regardless of the specific policy choices a

state has adopted pursuant to charter schools, it is undeniable that they have constructed a new type of public school that did not exist even two decades ago (Green & Mead, 2004). What is interesting to note is that the policy decisions about whether or not a state legislature should enact a charter school statute proceeded before, not after, research began being conducted about charter schools' effectiveness (Vergari, 2002; Fuller, 2000). Not surprisingly, altering the public school landscape to include charter schools invited legal challenge. Some of the earliest challenges alleged that permitting charter schools violated state constitutional provisions regarding public education (Green & Mead, 2004). While unsuccessful, the challenges illustrate the evolving concept of "public" education and constitutional mandates that bound such conceptions.

The spread of charter schools also illustrates another struggle that has faced state legislatures across the county. How can legislators set policies that promote educational excellence and to what degree should schools be controlled by state educational or local educational authorities (Fuller, 2000)? In addition, like voucher programs, charter schools necessarily consider how and to what degree parental choice should play a role in public education.

Looking Forward

As each of the examples above shows, legislation and litigation play an irrefutable role in educational policy. While legislation sets policy at the federal and state levels, litigation both construes the application of that policy and considers its congruence with constitutional principles. While it may seem self-evident, it is also worth remembering that in addition to setting boundaries, law expresses and codifies values. Constitutional provisions typically articulate a society's highest principles and accordingly change only through a lengthy process. Legislation and local policy capture the values of the time and locale. Finally, litigation both interprets those principles and provides a check when actions taken violate the foundational values contained in constitutional guarantees. Thus, all law including that applicable to education is constantly evolving. As Alexander and Alexander (2005) explain:

> The evolution of the law gives new shape to the public schools that emerge from the social forces that proscribe and portend the direction of the law. Contained therein is a discernible pattern of the ebb and flow of student and teacher rights and freedoms that ultimately define the nature and context of the public schools. (p. xxxviii)

At present, a number of legislative and judicial developments will likely affect the next steps in that evolution. While such issues are too numerous to review here, two issues appear to loom most prominently on the legal and policy horizon. At the national level, Congress is just beginning the process of reauthorizing NCLB. As congressional committees hear testimony, lobbyists proffer their arguments and legislative staff members attempt to summarize the input from constituents, education policy will take center stage on the national policy arena. We know what NCLB now requires. The question will be whether its provisions will remain, or what new requirements and inducements will be crafted to take their place—what values it will express. As such, a new cycle of regulatory activity, state level responses, and perhaps even possible litigation will inexorably follow and another chapter will be written in the use of law to balance the roles of federal, state, and local control of education.

Likewise, state and local educational policy makers are currently in the process of trying to discern the meaning and impact of the Supreme Court's latest pronouncements. The most significant of the decisions recently rendered is that of *Parents Involved in Community Schools v. Seattle Public District No. 1* (2007). Through that decision, a sharply divided Court determined that the voluntary integration programs that allocated student assignments using race as a consideration in both Seattle, Washington, and Louisville, Kentucky, violated the Equal Protection Clause of the 14th Amendment. While a majority of justices concurred on the holding, the Court was not able to reach a majority on the legal reasoning to support it. Four justices, Chief Justice Roberts and Justices Scalia, Thomas, and Alito, reasoned that race-conscious objectives in public schools could not be compelling unless pursued as a remedy to a judicial finding of improper de jure segregation. Justice Kennedy, while agreeing that the programs under scrutiny exceeded constitutional boundaries, concluded that some use of race to further integration could be constitutionally permissible. And yet, many school policy makers are passionately committed to integration as means of achieving values held dear—social justice and equality. Accordingly, state and local school officials across the county are engaged in processes to try to determine the features of that permissibility, attempting to discern from Kennedy's concurrence a possible road map to further efforts to establish and maintain racially integrated public schools. Just as surely, more litigation will be necessary to determine whether the policy responses adopted conform to the necessary constitutional principles.

This example also illustrates the influence of the Supreme Court and the collective character of a given group of nine justices. Clearly, the Warren Court that decided *Brown v. Board of Education* differed markedly in its approach to jurisprudence than the current Roberts Court that decided *Parents Involved*. In fact, Justice Stevens made the following observation in his dissent to *Parents Involved*: "It is my firm conviction that no Member of the Court that I joined in 1975 would have agreed with today's decision" (p. 2800). Much has been written about the conservative, moderate, or liberal leanings of the Supreme Court throughout time (see, e.g., Toobin, 2007). Suffice it to say here that the orientation of the Court has significant impact on numerous school law issues, including but not limited to parental rights, student rights, teacher rights, discrimination law, and federalism.

In both forward looking examples presented—NCLB's

pending reauthorization and the implications of the recent *Parents Involved* decision–it becomes clear how "law"– both legislation and litigation—create flux in the process of policy formation and implementation. Accordingly, in addition to policy research that considers the wisdom of various policy objectives and the effectiveness of the means available to realize them, legal research will likewise be undertaken to consider the contours and implications of the new boundaries set and how they relate to the values expressed by our constitutional foundation. For while "policy" may be distinguished from "law," the two concepts are inextricably bound together in the cycle of activity that determines what public education is and should be in these United States.

References

Agostini v. Felton, 521 U.S. 203, 117 S.Ct. 1997 (1997).

Alexander, K., & Alexander, M. D. (2005). *American public school law* (6th ed.). Belmont, CA: Wadsworth/Thomson Learning.

Board of Education of Independent School District No. 92 of Pottawatomie County v. Earls, 536 U.S. 822 (2002).

Board of Regents v. Roth, 408 U.S. 564, 92 S. Ct. 2701 (1972).

Brown v. Board of Education of Topeka, 347 U.S. 483, 74 S. Ct. 686 (1954).

Brown v. Board of Education of Topeka, 349 U.S. 294, 754 S. Ct. 753 (1955). (Brown II)

Bush v. Holmes, 919 So.2d 392 (Fla. 2006).

Committee for Public Education and Religious Liberty v. Nyquist, 413 U.S. 756, 93 S. Ct. 3062 (1973).

Crenshaw, K., Gotanda, N., Peller G., & Thomas, K. (Eds.). (1997). *Critical race theory: The key writings that formed the movement.* New York: New Press.

Culter, H. M., & Stone, J. M. (1913). *The rural school: Its methods and management.* Boston: Silver, Burdett & Company.

Delgado, R. (Ed.). (1995). *Critical race theory: The cutting edge.* Philadelphia: Temple University Press.

Edwards, N. (1933). *The courts and the public schools: The legal basis of school organization and administration.* Chicago: The University of Chicago Press.

E.P. v. San Ramon Valley Unified School Dist., 2007 U.S. Dist. LEXIS 47553 (N.D. Cal. 2007).

Forman, J. (2007). The rise and fall of school vouchers: A story of religion, race, and politics. *UCLA Law Review, 54*, 547–604.

Friedman, M. (1962). *Capitalism and freedom.* Chicago: University of Chicago Press.

Fuller, B. (Ed.). (2000). *Inside charter schools: The paradox of radical decentralization.* Cambridge, MA: Harvard University Press.

Goss v. Lopez, 419 U.S. 565, 95 S. Ct. 729 (1975).

Green, P. C., & Mead, J. F. (2004). *Charter schools and the law: Establishing new legal relationships.* Norwood, MA: Christopher-Gordon.

Honig v. Doe, 484 U.S. 305 (1988).

Howard, D. (1996). Rewarding and sanctioning school district performance by decreasing or increasing the level of state control. *Kansas Journal of Law and Public Policy, 5*(3), 187–198.

Individuals with Disabilities Education Act, 20 U.S.C. §1400 *et seq.*, 34 C.F.R. §300 *et seq.* (2004).

Koski, W. (2001). Educational opportunity and accountability in an era of standards-based school reform. *Stanford Law and Policy Review, 12*, 301-331.

Lemon v. Kurtzman, 403 U.S. 602, 91 S. Ct. 2105 (1971).

Levitt v. Committee for Public Education and Religious Liberty, 413 U.S. 472, 93 S. Ct. 2814 (1973).

Locke v. Davey, 540 U.S. 712, 124 S. Ct. 1307 (2004).

McCarthy, M. M., Cambron-McCabe, N. H., & Thomas, S. B. (2004).

Legal rights of teachers and students. Boston: Pearson Education/ Allyn & Bacon.

Mead, J. F. (1998). Expressions of Congressional intent: Examining the 1997 amendments to the IDEA. *West's Education Law Reporter, 127,* 511–531.

Mead, J. F. (1999). The reauthorization process of the IDEA: Expressions of equity. *The Journal for a Just and Caring Education, 5,* 476–492.

Mills v. Board of Education of the District of Columbia, 348 F.Supp. 866 (D.D.C. 1972).

Mitchell v. Helms, 530 U.S. 793, 120 S. Ct. 2530, 147 L.Ed.2d 660 (2000).

Mueller v. Allen, 463 U.S. 388, 103 S. Ct. 3062 (1983).

Munger, F. (1998). Mapping law and society. In A. Sarat, M. Constable, D. Engle, V. Hans, & S. Lawrence (Eds.), *Crossing boundaries: Traditions and Transformations in law and society research* (pp. 21–80). Evanston, IL: Northwestern University Press.

New Jersey v. T.L.O., 469 U.S. 325, 105 S.Ct. 733 (1985).

No Child Left Behind Act of 2001, 20 U.S.C. §6301 *et seq.* (2002).

Orfield, G. (1999). Conservative activists and the rush toward resegregation. In J. P. Heubert (Ed.), *Law and school reform: Six strategies for promoting educational equity* (pp. 39–87). New Haven, CT: Yale University Press.

Owens v. Congress of Parents, Teachers, and Students, 92 P.3d 933 (Colo. 2004).

Owasso Independent School Dist. No. I-011 v. Falvo, 534 U.S. 426, 122 S. Ct. 934 (2002).

Parents Involved In Community Schools v. Seattle School District No. 1, U.S., 127 S. Ct. 2738 (2007).

Pennsylvania Association for Retarded Children (PARC) v. Commonwealth of Pennsylvania, 343 F. Supp. 279 (E.D. Pa. 1972).

Pickering v. Board of Education, 391 U.S. 563, 88 S. Ct. 1731 (1968).

Plyler v. Doe, 457 U.S. 202, 102 S.Ct. 2382 (1982).

San Antonio Independent School District v. Rodriguez, 411 U.S. 1, 93 S. Ct. 1278 (1973).

Sarat, A., Constable, M., Engle, D., Hans, V., & Lawrence, S. (Eds.). (1998). *Crossing boundaries: Traditions and transformations in law and society research.* Evanston, IL: Northwestern University Press.

Section 504 of the Rehabilitation Act of 1973, 29 U.S.C. §794; 34 C.F.R. 104 *et seq.*

S. Rep. No. 94-168 (1975).

S. Rep. No. 99-112 (1986).

Sloan v. Lemon, 413 U.S. 825, 93 S. Ct. 2982 (1973).

Smith v. Robinson, 468 U.S. 992, 104 S. Ct. 3457 (1984).

Swanson v. Guthrie Independent School District I-L, 135 F.3d 694 (1998).

Thro, W. E. (2005). An essay: The school finance paradox: How the Constitutional values of decentralization and judicial restraint inhibit the achievement of quality education. *West's Education Law Reporter, 197,* 477–497.

Tinker v. Des Moines Independent Community School District, 393 U.S. 503 (1969).

Toobin, J. (2007). *The nine: Inside the secret world of the Supreme Court.* New York: Doubleday.

Underwood, J. K., & Mead, J. F. (1995). *Legal aspects of special education and pupil services.* Needham Heights, MA: Allyn & Bacon.

Underwood, J. K., & Verstegen, D. A. (1990). School finance challenges in federal courts: Changing equal protection analysis. In J. K. Underwood & D. A. Verstegen (Eds.), *The impacts of litigations and legislation on public school finance: Adequacy, equity, and excellence* (pp. 177–191). New York: Harper & Row.

United States Department of Education. (2007). *U.S. charter schools: State information.* Retrieved July 31, 2007, from http://www.uscharterschools.org/pub/uscs_docs/sp/index.htm

Vergari, S. (Ed.). (2002). *The charter school landscape.* Pittsburgh, PA: University of Pittsburgh Press.

Vernonia School District 47J v. Acton, 515 U.S. 646, 115 S. Ct. 2386 (1995).

Wallmuth v. Rapides Parish School Board, 813 So.2d 341 (La. 2002).

West, R. (1988). Jurisprudence and gender. *The University of Chicago Law Review, 55,* 1–72.

Witters v. Washington Department of Services for the Blind, 474 U.S. 481 (1986).

Yudof, M., Kirp, D., Levin, B., & Moran, R. (2002). *Education policy and the law* (4th ed.). Belmont, CA: West-Thomson Learning.

Zelman v. Simmons-Harris, 536 U.S. 639, 122 S. Ct. 2460 (2002).

Zirkel, P., & Kearns-Barber, J.A. (2005). A tabular overview of the school finance litigation. *West's Education Law Reporter, 197,* 21–28.

Zobrest v. Catalina Foothills School District, 509 U.S. 1, 113 S. Ct. 2462 (1993).

24

Teacher Collective Bargaining

What We Know and What We Need to Know

Julia E. Koppich
J. Koppich and Associates

Mary Alice Callahan
University of California, Berkeley

Collective bargaining in education is much like Mark Twain's aphorism about the weather. Everybody talks about it but no one does much about it—or, in this case, does much research about it. Teacher unions and collective bargaining are often the topic of heated political and policy debate and discussion, with vocal defenses of union actions on one side and equally vociferous protestations on the other.

Research and writing about unions and contract bargaining typically put forth one of two competing theories. One theory holds that unions are necessary to preserve and protect teachers' workplace rights, serve to advance the place of teachers as professionals, and further the cause of educational reform. Adherents to this school of thought believe that unions are, and should be, equal partners with school district management in ongoing efforts to improve student learning and should have a central place at the education decision-making table.[1]

A second and competing theory holds that unions are obstructionist organizations that wield their considerable power only to serve the self-interested (and no longer relevant) aims of their own members. Proponents of this theory assert that unions' interest in the fundamental work of schools, namely, improving student achievement, is fleeting, at best, as they focus their attention on stifling the needed educational reforms that would have a fighting chance if only the power of unions was curtailed.[2]

In the real world of schools and districts, both theories have merit and neither alone is entirely accurate. This is because the two theories represent opposite poles within the bargaining relationship and are more easily recognized than any middle ground. But what do we know from research about unions and collective bargaining? Why do some contracts incorporate education reform efforts while others are unabashedly tethered to the traditional, and traditionally defined, contract triumvirate of wages, hours, and terms and conditions of employment? What kinds of short- or long-term impacts do negotiated contracts have on the ex-penditure of public (school district) resources? How do the negotiated provisions of contracts impact the operation of school districts and the results they achieve? To what extent do contracts (or selected contact provisions) help or hinder districts' efforts to attract and retain high quality teachers? Are contracts linked to improving, or dampening, student achievement results?

The short answer to all of these questions about what we know about unions and collective bargaining is, "not nearly as much as we should." In other words, we do not know nearly as much as we should from available research to be able to extract adequate data and craft worthwhile education policy. Nor do we know nearly as much as we should from available research and data to use the results of collective bargaining to improve education decision making.

This conclusion may be somewhat surprising given that, while researchers and policy makers often disagree about many aspects of education, there seems to be fairly widespread consensus that teacher unions are powerful and the implications of their actions—whether those be participation in federal, state, and local election contests, or lobbying efforts on behalf of a wide range of education-related policies and initiatives, or through local collective bargaining—are significant.

A recent spate of policy reports and online postings, many of them highly critical of teacher unions and collective bargaining, have taken up this topic, or at least some portion of negotiated labor-management contracts. The Rhode Island-based Education Partnership (2005) published *Teacher Contracts: Restoring the Balance: Volume 1*, a critique of teacher contracts, including how they allocate resources and the issues on which they focus. Though centered on collective bargaining in Rhode Island, the Partnership received a significant amount of play for its work by sponsoring a conference in December 2006 that brought together many of the most prominent teacher union leaders from around the country with policy analysts and union critics for a wide-ranging conversation about the status and future of collective bargaining.

The New Teacher Project's widely cited *Unintended Consequences: The Case for Reforming the Staffing Rules in Urban Teachers Contracts* report takes to task collectively bargained teacher assignment practices, asserting that these agreements undermine districts' abilities to hire teachers in a timely manner and place them in assignments in which they are most needed (Levin, Mulhern, & Schunk, 2005).[3] The National Center on Teacher Quality in 2006 assembled and launched a much-publicized Web site designed to offer transparency about the content of teacher contracts. Titled *Teacher Rules, Roles, and Rights*, the Web-based tool allows an online search of contract provisions from the collectively bargained agreements in the 50 largest school districts, enabling users to compare items like teacher salaries, school year calendars, and transfer and assignment policies.[4]

Frederick Hess and Martin West (2006), writing jointly on behalf of the American Enterprise Institute and the Brookings Institution, released *A Better Bargain: Overhauling Teacher Collective Bargaining for the 21st Century*. This document is another critique of teacher contracts—castigating what the authors describe as outmoded compensation programs, inefficient and ineffective assignment procedures, and a generally rule-bound system.[5]

The Harvard-based Rennie Center on Education Policy in 2005 published a set of cases on "win-win" or collaborative bargaining and what author Linda Kaboolian (2005), a professor at Harvard's Kennedy School of Government, describes as "value added unionism." This report, unlike the ones previously described, is a "best practices" handbook that catalogues innovative labor-management practices aimed at improving teacher quality and, by extension, student achievement. Finally, a new report by Harvard professor Susan Moore Johnson describes interviews with 30 local union presidents in areas such as teacher compensation, evaluation, and transfer and assignment (Johnson, Donaldson, Munger, Papay, & Qasibash, 2007).

Why the Current Interest in Collective Bargaining?

The current interest in teacher unions stems at least in part from the continuing prominent place of education on the policy agenda, the focus on accountability and fixing responsibility for education results, and the policy cachet of developing new strategies designed generally to improve education outcomes and specifically to increase scores on standardized tests. These policies have exerted a centralizing pressure on the management of schools. Subsequently, these policy thrusts, among their other impacts, have served to shine a spotlight on teacher unions, collective bargaining, and the contracts that are the result of this process.

Collective bargaining agreements are instruments of politics and policy. These legally binding pacts, the product of negotiations between a local school board and the teachers' union elected by the teachers in a local school district, shape much about the operation of the education institu-tion, the distribution of local education resources, and, of course, the structure of teachers' work. Yet, it remains the case that teacher unions are a woefully under-researched field. A bare handful of academic and policy researchers ventures into this territory. In fact, it is relatively rare to find an article in an education-oriented academic journal that concerns the topic of teacher unions or contracts. A Web search, for example, in Google Scholar under "teacher unions," "collective bargaining in education," and "education labor-management relations," calls up only a few works published post-1990. A review of the articles published in *Educational Evaluation and Policy Analysis*, AERA's flagship policy journal, reveals no articles on teacher unions or contracts in at least a decade.

As large and complex organizations that have significant influence on much about a school district's operation, understanding the motivations and actions of teacher unions, and the results of their actions, requires a more thorough review of the data and a more subtle analysis than the topic is often granted. Hannaway and Rotherham (2006) and Loveless (2000) each took a first step toward this objective when they published a series of articles by a variety of authors on collective bargaining. Together these 19 articles begin a dialogue about an important research agenda. While Hannaway and Rotherham (2006) described the landscape of literature and analysis on collective bargaining as "sparsely populated" and frequently polarized, they noted the importance of bringing all sides of the debate to the fore in order to promote the interests of students. They argue that today's educational climate requires greater research attention be dedicated to collective bargaining.

This chapter explores some of what is known about teacher unions and collective bargaining, raises questions where data are lacking, and suggests a policy research agenda that might begin to fill in the gaps.

The Context for Teacher Collective Bargaining

In 1974, 1 in 4 workers in the public and private sectors was a member of a labor union. Two decades later, by 2004, only 1 in 12 private sector workers belonged to a union. Yet in the public sector (federal, state, and local government employees), nearly 1 in 3 workers was a union member (Farber, 2006).

The higher percentage of union membership among public sector employees is boosted, in part, by the education sector. Eighty percent of teachers belong to one of the two major national teacher unions, the National Education Association (NEA) or the American Federation of Teachers. All told, the NEA boasts a membership of 3.2 million, including teachers, classroom aides, higher education faculty, and retirees (Keller, 2007). The smaller AFT includes 1.3 million members, among them as well teachers, aides, and higher education faculty (Honawar, 2007) . Total membership numbers for the NEA and AFT include members in states and districts in which teachers do not have collective bargaining rights (Hess & Kelly, 2006).[6]

Teacher union locals (affiliates of the AFT or NEA) exist in all 50 states. Some localities—the states of New York, Montana, and Minnesota and the school districts in Los Angeles and San Francisco, for example—have merged organizations in which teachers are dual members of both national unions. Thirty-three states plus the District of Columbia require collective bargaining. Of the 17 states that do not require negotiated contracts, 11 have districts that nevertheless have such agreements. Some states (e.g., Georgia, Kentucky, Missouri, North Carolina, Texas, and Virginia) prohibit collective bargaining by state law.[7] Nevertheless, it is not unusual, particularly in urban districts in these states, to find written agreements, developed jointly by the local teachers' union and local school district (through a process of "meet and confer" or "consultation"), which look much like "contracts" in bargaining states. In the school districts that the majority of American school children attend, then, labor-management relations significantly influences the conditions under which teachers teach and students learn. How and why did collective bargaining come to education?

A Short Course in Collective Bargaining History Collective bargaining in education is a relatively new development. The National Labor Relations Act ([NLRA]; 1935), signed into law by President Franklin Roosevelt, shifted the locus of decision-making authority for determining employees' terms and conditions of employment from the exclusive province of management to shared decision making between management and workers through representatives of their own choosing. Enacted during heightened public support for organized labor in the period of the New Deal, the NLRA gave private sector employees (mostly working in the nation's factories) the right to "form, join, or assist labor organizations" (§ 157) and to bargain legally binding contracts specifying the terms and conditions of their employment.

Teachers, as public sector employees, did not come under the provisions of the NLRA or gain the right to negotiate contracts with its passage (Kahlenberg, 2006). Teachers' terms and conditions of employment typically were set by a process called "meet and confer." In some jurisdictions, such as California, this process was supported by statute, but often its conduct was simply a matter of custom. Local management representatives would meet with various groups of teachers (rather than a single organization representing all teachers) to discuss issues of salaries and working conditions. Sometimes the results of these conversations were set to writing in memoranda of understanding. These memoranda were not legally binding.

In some jurisdictions, meet and confer did not take place at all. Local school boards and administrators simply determined the salaries and other conditions under which teachers would work without consultation with employees. Under meet and confer, teachers were assumed to achieve their influence because their interests coincided with school district goals. In other words, teachers were powerful, or assumed to be so, because they wanted what school districts wanted. They were expected to express a selfless interest in what was good for the students. Open displays of self-interest, including lobbying for better salaries or working conditions, were frowned upon and sometimes even resulted in dismissal (Kahlenberg, 2006; Kerchner & Mitchell, 1988).

Meet and confer was a classically paternalistic system. Teachers were spoken for; they did not speak for themselves. Decisions of any importance, from salary to transfer and assignment to class size, were made by school boards and administrators (Kerchner, Koppich, & Weeres, 1997). Under this system, it was the duty of the institution to look after teachers' welfare. Administrators were to function as teachers' advocates, school boards as trustees of the common good. Teacher organizations were seen as legitimate only so long as they recognized the ultimate authority of the administration and governing board and did not challenge it publicly. When teachers' goals diverged from those of management and school boards, they were expected to defer and acquiesce (Kerchner & Mitchell, 1988).

By the 1950s, industrial-style collective bargaining—the process legitimized by the NLRA—began to look more appealing to teachers. Private sector unions were winning substantial wage increases. At the same time, wages of college-educated teachers were lagging substantially behind those of blue-collar factory workers. In addition, teachers were chaffing under nearly uniformly poor working conditions, including large class sizes, a plethora of assigned non-teaching duties, and multitudes of administrative directives (Kahlenberg, 2006). The bonds of meet and confer finally frayed irreparably with the social activism of the 1960s. Teachers came to see their interests as different from administrators' and began to seek an alternative means for dealing with their employer. They turned from meet and confer to industrial-style collective bargaining (Koppich, 2006).

Older forms of worker organization—guilds, artisan associations, and craft unions—had, by this time, largely disappeared. In public education, industrial unionism was labor's answer to an education system constructed on the principles of scientific management, a system in which the content and pacing of work was designed not by teachers, but by school administrators (Kerchner, 2001).

Unions and collective bargaining gained strength among teachers in the 1960s and 1970s because school district officials were perceived as being arbitrary, punitive, and politically motivated (Johnson & Donaldson, 2006). The kind of bargaining teachers adopted—called industrial bargaining because of its antecedents in the nation's factories—gave teachers voice through a legally binding contract that shaped the terms and conditions of their employment (Kerchner & Koppich, 1993). As teachers adopted industrial-style bargaining, teacher unionism came to be identified by its hallmarks. These included separation of labor and management, adversarial labor-management relations, a limited scope of bargaining, and a focus on individual interests. In other words, under the "rules" of industrial unionism, teachers and administrators had distinctly different, clearly defined responsibilities; the relationship between management and the union was consistently tense and often angry; contracts were constrained by a narrow list of acceptable topics; and, negotiated agreements centered around the self-interests of those who were covered by it.

Teachers' contracts[8] developed in response to centralized education decision making. As power and authority accrued to school district headquarters, so, too, did teacher unions consolidate their efforts in master contracts to influence the terms and conditions of those whom they represented (Kerchner et al., 1997). Early contracts, especially those negotiated in the years in which teacher collective bargaining was in its infancy, served important, but frequently limited, purposes. They applied a district-wide template to teachers' employment conditions, codifying, often for the first time, the terms and conditions that shaped teachers' work lives. They created a modicum of fairness in a bureaucracy by applying equitable, across-the-board treatment, uniform policies, and standardized procedures. And they protected teachers from arbitrary and capricious actions of the employer (Kahlenberg, 2006; Johnson & Kardos, 2000; Kerchner et al., 1997).

As bargaining evolved, so, too, did the topics contained within the pages of the contract. In bargaining's early days, labor-management negotiations focused squarely on the plain meaning of the legally described scope of negotiations, wages, hours, and terms and conditions of employment. Contracts were used to contain provisions on salaries, benefits, work day and work year, class sizes, transfer and assignment, requirements and opportunities for professional development, systems of evaluation, tenure, leaves of absence, non-teaching duties, personnel files, and academic freedom.

While contracts often contained similar provisions district-to-district (largely because the NEA, the larger of the two national unions, provided its local affiliates with boilerplate provisions that became the language of many negotiated contracts), there was also a fair amount of variation among agreements in different districts. The provisions that composed the contract developed as a result of the nature of a district's labor-management relations (more adversarial or less so), the substance of preceding contracts (often called "past practice"), broader state and local labor contexts, and the personalities and priorities of the participants in the negotiations process (Koppich, 2006; Johnson & Donaldson, 2006). Many contracts also came to embody the cumulative scar tissue of the battles between the negotiating parties (Johnson & Donaldson, 2006). Particularly in the early years of collective bargaining, as unions and management jousted for influence and authority, they often built up an enduring history of failed issues, lasting antagonisms, and nagging contract-to-contract dilemmas.

A Shift Begins Such was the nearly universal legacy of collective bargaining from the late 1960s until the mid-

1980s. Then, among some local unions, changes began to take place in the form of bargaining and in the substance of contracts. In 1983, Albert Shanker, then president of the AFT (formerly president of that organization's largest local affiliate located in New York City and one of the earliest and most vocal advocates for industrial-style teacher collective bargaining) came before the AFT's national convention in Los Angeles to proclaim the need for fundamental change in collective bargaining. *A Nation at Risk*, the report of the National Commission on Excellence in Education, had recently been released to substantial press fanfare and policy discussion. That report took the nation's public school system to task for failing its students with low expectations, lax curricula, too little time devoted to academics, and an inadequately prepared and compensated teaching force (National Commission on Excellence in Education, 1983). It was widely anticipated that Shanker would use the opportunity of the AFT gathering to excoriate the report as just another unwarranted example of teacher bashing. He did not.

Instead, Shanker (1983) publicly acknowledged problems with the education system, said the system needed to change, and asserted that teachers and their union needed to be part of the solution. The president of the AFT called for better, more comprehensive systems of teacher evaluation, advocated standards for students and teachers, supported the testing of beginning teachers, raised the prospect of differentiated pay, and called for more rigorous accountability systems. In short, he called not only for fundamental changes in public education, but for a new form of unionism based on teacher professionalism (Koppich, 2006). It would be a few years before the larger NEA started down a similar path.

The NEA, for some years, resisted reform, just as it had previously resisted collective bargaining.[9] In February 1997, the organization's then-new president, Robert Chase, gave a speech before the National Press Club in Washington, DC. Titled *It's Not Your Mother's NEA*, Chase acknowledged the NEA as a traditional, narrowly focused union, inadequate to the needs of contemporary education. He called for higher academic standards, less bureaucracy, schools better connected to parents and communities, and contract bargaining focused on school and teacher quality (Chase, 1997).

Shanker's, and later Chase's, pronouncements about the need for new kinds of labor-management relations began to trigger some localized changes in collective bargaining. A handful of districts and unions (admittedly, a quite small number) together found new ways of fostering labor-management collaboration and expanding their contract repertoire (Johnson & Kardos, 2000). The form of bargaining they adopted came to be called "reform" or "professional" bargaining. In the mid-1980s, two reports affirmed this need for new ways of bargaining. *A Nation Prepared: Teachers for the 21st Century* (Carnegie Forum, 1986) and *Tomorrow's Teachers* (Holmes Group, 1986) called for a new role for teachers as agents of change.

These reports highlighted the value of teachers as partners in reform efforts.

Over the next decade, a select number of union locals and their school districts gained notoriety both for their innovative approaches to labor-management relations and for enlarging the content of their contracts to encompass some of the issues high on education reformers' agendas. Minneapolis, Cincinnati, Toledo, Rochester, Montgomery County, Maryland, and Columbus, among others, took up the challenge to reform their labor relations and their contracts.

Describing Reform Bargaining Reform bargaining is premised on the idea that labor and management share interests and responsibilities for improving education (Johnson & Kardos, 2000). Kerchner and Koppich (1993) promoted and defined the attributes of professional unionism in *A Union of Professionals: Labor Relations and Educational Reform*. This book was composed of a series of case studies profiling local unions and district managements—among them Pittsburgh, Cincinnati, Rochester, and Chicago—engaged together in fledgling efforts to transform industrial unionism with negotiated programs around teacher evaluation, professional development, shared decision making, and budget development (Kerchner & Koppich, 1993). In the book the authors described four conditions requisite to unions and districts moving down the road toward professional unionism.

First, both parties recognize that the status quo is not an option, that if their organizations do not adapt to changing times, new systems will be thrust upon them. Second, both union and management find ways to keep day-to-day politics at bay as they give schools and teachers the flexibility to experiment and try new things, and the permission to fail without having their efforts publicly criticized or scrutinized. Third, in order for professional unionism to take root, union and management move beyond their usual antagonistic stances toward one another and deal in a professional manner. This does not mean the parties always agree; they do not. But their disagreements tend to be about substantive matters of education reform and improvement. Finally, in order for districts and their unions to move toward professional unionism, both sides accept and believe in greatly expanded professional roles for teachers. Those who maintained a belief in the centralized web of controlling rules—in either the union or the school district—simply were not candidates for professional unionism (Kerchner & Koppich, 1993).

The districts that had begun to engage in so-called reform or professional bargaining included in their negotiated agreements many of the usual contract topics, including salaries and benefits, transfers and assignments, grievance procedures and the like. But often the substance of these contract provisions changed (Kerchner & Koppich, 1993). Some union locals and districts began modestly to venture into the territory of alternative compensation, edging away from the standard single salary schedule on which teachers were paid exclusively on the basis of years of experience and college credits earned. In the area of transfer and assignment, seniority was often eliminated in these contracts as the principal criterion for voluntary transfers (Kerchner & Koppich, 1993).

Minneapolis replaced the typical pro forma tenure review system with a rigorous 3-year approach that included professional development and peer and administrator review, culminating in a portfolio presentation to a joint teacher-administrator panel to decide whether or not to award tenure. A number of districts—Toledo (beginning, actually, in 1981), Cincinnati, Columbus, and Montgomery County—began to substitute a standards-based peer assistance and review program for standard (and typically not well-regarded) longstanding systems of teacher evaluation (Bloom & Goldstein, 2000).

These reform agreements thus incorporated a number of issues in which those who were influencing education policy regarded as part and parcel of moving teaching from a job to a profession and improving educational outcomes for students. These included provisions on topics that today are individually and collectively high on the policy agenda—new forms of teacher pay, strategies to encourage high quality teachers to choose assignments in hard-to-staff schools, new forms of professional evaluation, and differentiated staffing designed to shape career pathways for teachers (Koppich, 2007).

The reform districts also engaged in a different kind of bargaining—collaborative bargaining. Collaborative, win-win, or interest-based bargaining first came to prominence as a result of the Harvard Negotiations Project (Fisher & Ury, 1983), whose original work had nothing to do with education labor-management relations, but was widely adapted for this arena. In the collaborative mode, whose functional slogan is, "Hard on the problem, not hard on each other," union and management break away from their traditional adversarial contract stances and find mutual ground for common understanding and agreement. These new labor-management relationships that are formed as a result of collaborative bargaining can lead to new kinds of contracts that are more closely in the professional unionism mold (Kerchner & Koppich, 1993; Kaboolian, 2005; Koppich, 2007).

The argument the authors made for a new system of collective bargaining was a straightforward one: Industrial unionism had given teachers' organizations the wherewithal to respond to teachers' concerns about essential matters of wages, hours, and working conditions. McDonnell and Pascal (1988) argue that this is a necessary precondition to facilitate reform bargaining. But industrial bargaining failed to recognize teachers' expertise as professionals, their need and desire to exercise professional judgment in the performance of their duties, the interests they legitimately share with management, or the obligation to involve them in significant decisions about policies affecting their professional lives (Kerchner et al., 1997).

They concluded that fundamental changes in education

required a new conception of collective bargaining, including a shift in the expectations for negotiated agreements. Policy shifts to acknowledge this new conception would require contracts that would sanction labor-management cooperation; agreements that would center on mutually determined, measurable student achievement goals; and an expansion of the scope of labor-management discussions to include a broader swath of significant education policy (Kerchner et al., 1997; Kerchner & Koppich, 2006).

The Current State of Labor Management Relations: Two Kinds of Bargaining

Collective bargaining is an evolutionary process. As some districts and their unions have moved in the direction of professional unionism, others have remained firmly wedded to traditional bargaining. Which districts are in which camp of bargaining is not a matter of organizational affiliation (AFT or NEA), geographic locale, or size. But as a result of collective bargaining's evolution, two distinct types of negotiated agreements have emerged: traditional (or industrial-style) and reform (or professional) contracts. Table 24.1 below illustrates the different traits of each.

As the table illustrates, these two forms of bargaining reflect significant differences. Traditional contracts draw clear lines of distinction between labor and management roles, specifically delineating the jobs administrators do from the jobs teachers do. Reform contracts blur these lines of distinction, emphasizing the collaborative and collective nature of education work. Traditional labor-management bonds are shaped by adversarial relationships. The tenor of discussions can often be shrill and angry as union and management vie for the upper negotiating hand. In reform bargaining relationships, both sides work through procedures to gain mutual understanding of issues and mutual solutions to problems.

Traditional contracts prescribe a set of work rules and conditions that applies to all teachers in a given district regardless of their demonstrated levels of knowledge, skills, or accomplishment. The standard single salary schedule, for example, applies the same compensation template to all teachers, granting salary increases based on years of teaching and units accrued. Voluntary transfers typically are governed by seniority, the length of time a teacher has taught in a district. Moreover, in districts with traditional

TABLE 24.1
Characteristics of Traditional and Reform Bargaining

Traditional (Industrial) Bargaining	Reform (Professional) Bargaining
Separation of labor and management	Blurred labor-management distinctions
Adversarial, positional negotiations	Collaborative, interest-based negotiations
Limited scope of negotiations	Expanded scope of negotiations
Protection of individual interests	Protection of teachers and teaching

bargaining arrangements, the scope of negotiations—the topics union and management discuss—is limited to the classic wages, hours, and employment conditions.

Reform contracts begin to acknowledge that teachers are different, that they have differing levels of skill and knowledge, as well as differing professional aspirations. Thus, these agreements may include various forms of differentiated compensation as well as differentiated roles. They also tend to pay more attention to matching teachers to assignments rather than relying exclusively on length of service. In Cincinnati, for example, by contract, a group of teachers and the principal interview potential candidates for open teaching positions and selects from among the available applicants based on "fit" with the posted job.

Industrial-style contracts little emphasize the ongoing development of teachers' professional capacity. Professional development (its frequency and content) is often limited by contract; there is little if any mention of career development, and professional evaluation is pro forma at best. Reform contracts tend to include multiple provisions for building teachers' professional skills. Sections on professional development are both more targeted and more expansive, career ladders designate differentiated roles and the means for achieving these, and rigorous, standards-based evaluation, often in the form of peer review, becomes part of standard operating procedures[10] (Koppich, 2007).

Traditional contracts center on both protecting and expanding the rights of individual teachers (Kerchner et al., 1997). In this bargaining tradition, the contract is more about how teachers as solitary practitioners interact with the system that employs them than it is a collective professional compact about how the work of teaching gets done (Koppich, 2006). Reform agreements, on the other hand, are about protecting the teaching profession. They maintain teachers' due process protections, but also focus much more fundamentally than do traditional contracts on protecting and enhancing the quality of teaching.

Finally, industrial contracts make little reference to student achievement. Traditional collective bargaining is about monetary benefits and workplace conditions. Improving student achievement is not explicitly part of the contract calculus. Reform agreements, on the other hand, make improving student achievement a stated goal of the contract. In so doing (as well as by including matters such as building teachers' professional capacity and improving teacher quality), these agreements expand the scope of labor-management discussions well beyond those items that are included in traditional negotiations and focus, at least to some extent, on education's bottom line: student learning (Koppich, 2007).

The contract differences and evolution briefly outlined above would seem to suggest wide and rich territory for research. Negotiated contracts are school district policy, with considerable local and state policy implications. These documents took the place of school board-determined work rules once collective bargaining was in play. In jurisdictions with collective bargaining, contracts govern matters from salaries and benefits to teachers' workday and work year and the school calendar, class size, the assignment of non-teaching duties, professional development and evaluation, and teacher transfer and assignment. These collected policies—the contract—shape not only teacher work rules, but also much about the way a large percentage of school district resources are allocated and procedures that govern the operation of the system. They also have tremendous spill-over effects. What is negotiated in one district's contract often shapes what becomes part of others.

What are the trends in negotiated agreements? To what extent does their content mirror the policy emphases of the times? Under what circumstances do contracts evolve from traditional to reform? Under what circumstances do labor relations and the resulting contracts remain in the industrial mode? How has the local, state, and national policy emphasis on education reform and accountability impacted collective bargaining agreements? Do teacher unions behave differently now than they did previously? Does management?

These are all questions the answers to which should inform educational policy. Yet, the pool of research about teacher unions—their roles and responsibilities, changes they have faced, embraced, and rejected, the outcomes and impact of their work, remains both shallow and spotty. Despite much rhetoric and a wealth of policy pronouncements about teacher unions, there is remarkably little comprehensive research or analytic work.

What Might the Future Hold for Collective Bargaining?

In the years since professional unionism first made its way onto the collective bargaining stage, the number of districts and unions actively engaged in it has waned. School management, feeling hemmed in by the increasing pressures for accountability in the form of higher test scores, often refuses to see unions as partners in the work of education improvement. Unions themselves are often reluctant to assume the kind of added responsibility that goes hand-in-hand with the kinds of reforms envisioned (and, in some cases, implemented) in the 1990s.

A number of reform-minded union leaders (e.g., in Cincinnati, Minneapolis, and Chicago) have been defeated in recent years at the polls in their local elections. They have been replaced by leaders who take a more traditional, industrial-style view of unions. Union critics crow that this outcome was bound to occur, that reform leaders, once they stray from the narrow boundaries of members' self-interests, sound their own political death knell (Moe, 2001). Others, less skeptical, suggest that these electoral losses were idiosyncratic and location-specific, representing less a pattern and more a series of electoral coincidences (Kahlenberg, 2006).

What caused these electoral turnovers? Did the defeated leaders' advocacy of reform unionism somehow doom them with their members? Were there other internal or external causes for their electoral losses? Did common across-the-board circumstances prevail in each of these instances, or were each particular to local circumstances? To what extent do these electoral turnovers foretell a new era of industrial unionism? Again, there are insufficient research data to provide complete answers to these questions, but some emerging research is suggesting possibilities.

Harvard education professor Susan Moore Johnson has for several years been following the aspirations and trials of a group of individuals who have recently joined the teaching profession. Her work on the "new generation of teachers" reveals that newer teachers, those hired in the last decade or so, have different expectations of their union than do their more veteran colleagues. Earlier generations of teachers, particularly Baby Boomers hired in the 1960s and 1970s, preferred the isolation of the classroom, eschewed differentiated pay and staffing, and looked to the union to protect them in all work-related circumstances. This was a good match with industrial unionism (Johnson, 2000). Teachers newer to the profession, by contrast, welcome collaboration, support differentiated compensation and roles, and want the union to be the organization that both ensures them fair treatment and helps them become more accomplished professionals (Johnson, 2000). In short, less experienced teachers are looking for a different kind of union—one that more closely follows the lines of professional unionism.

The work of Farkas, Johnson, and Duffett (2003) published by the Public Agenda Foundation confirms these findings. Veteran teachers are, indeed, more attached to the status quo, especially when it comes to the kinds of job protections unions historically have afforded them. In the Public Agenda research, 81% of all teachers report that, "without the union, teachers would be vulnerable to school politics or administrators who abuse their power," and "without collective bargaining, teachers' salaries and working conditions would probably be worse" (p. 17). But younger teachers in particular want help building their careers and improving their practice. They are hard-pressed to see the union as a source of innovation and profession building (Farkas et al., 2003).

Thus unions face a dilemma: How do they balance what is essentially a bifurcated membership, with some members clinging to the traditional unionism they have known and others—those who represent the future of the union—longing for change? How do they sustain and build an organization that simultaneously meets the needs and professional aspirations of veteran and novice teachers?

Where, then, do union leaders themselves stand? Are they more inclined toward industrial unionism, professional unionism, or something quite different from either of these? Recent research suggests that newer union leadership recognizes that strict adherence cannot be the wave of the future. Interviews with 30 local union presidents, all of whom were elected to office within the last 8 years,[11] reveal they, too, hold expanded visions for their union beyond the traditional concerns of wages, hours, and conditions of employment.

The increasing expectations of new teachers for professional support, continuing system demands for improved student achievement, and pressures from growing competition from nontraditional forms of schooling (such as charters) are causing these newer union leaders to take a second look at their organizations. Under the banner, "Teacher quality is union business" they seek to insure that their union locals participate in matters such as enhanced teacher induction programs, alternative approaches to pay, and designing new and expanded roles for teachers (Johnson et al., 2007). Follow-on research will be needed to assess the extent to which these leaders' actions follow their intentions.

Additional Big Unanswered Questions

This chapter has suggested some potential policy issues surrounding teacher collective bargaining that could be informed by more comprehensive research. There are others. For example, what has been the measurable impact of new kinds of agreements and new forms of provisions on issues such as attracting and retaining high-quality teachers or improving student achievement? Scattered studies examine specific negotiated reform programs, such as peer review (Goldstein & Noguera, 2006; Stroot et al., 1999) or new forms of teacher compensation (Odden & Kelley, 1997; Jupp, 2005; Koppich, 2005). But the literature is hardly conclusive with regard to the net impact of unions on important measures such a teacher quality or student achievement (Goldhaber, 2006).

What are the costs of collective bargaining? A new publication by Marguerite Roza (2007) of the University of Washington's Center on Reinventing Public Education examines dollars that go toward salary increases on the standard salary schedule, money used for professional development days, and dollars attached to sick leave, class size limits, and teachers' health and retirement benefits. This report, according to its author, examines "only those [contract] provisions that research suggests have a weak or inconsistent relationship to student learning" (p. 2). These contract costs are placed in the category of "frozen assets," dollars Roza says could be freed up if contracts were substantially changed—health and retirement benefits scaled back, salary plans altered, and the like.

While Roza's conclusions raise some serious questions, such as, does it make good policy sense to reduce or eliminate employees' pensions or health care benefits, this is nevertheless the first piece of contemporary research that attempts to break out some of the costs of collective bargaining. Knowing the costs of bargaining may not provide guidance about whether, or how, to use resources differently. But it certainly is a necessary piece of information requisite to designing and implementing useful education policy.

Likewise, there have been some research attempts to compare the costs of collective bargaining effects and how they benefit student achievement. For example, Eberts and Stone (1984) studied the impact of collective bargaining on education and found that unions increased the costs of education by improving rates of pay, fringe benefits, and working conditions, such as class size, for teachers. At the same time, unionized schools helped the average student achieve slightly better scores on standardized exams than non-unionized schools. Unionized schools, however, had a slightly negative effect on students performing at the high or low extremes of achievement. Eberts and Stone attributed this to standardization in the delivery of educational services.

Hoxby (1996) also found that unionized schools had greater rates of dropouts than non-unionized schools, a finding that is consistent with the Eberts and Stone study. In contrast, Loeb and Page (2000) found that raising teacher pay positively affects student achievement but only if researchers take into account alternative labor market opportunities and non-wage characteristics of districts. These examples of current research point to the complexity of understanding educational processes and the importance of a more nuanced research agenda to support policy decision making.

These studies also underscore some of the methodological challenges for this research. For example, another important question is, how does context influence content? Recent research on teacher collective bargaining uses econometric methodology to analyze contract outcomes (see, e.g., Koski & Horng, 2007). But collective bargaining is a process. Bargaining practices and outcomes are highly decentralized, and the unions that negotiate them can be quite variable. This variability is rarely acknowledged in the little research that does exist (Johnson & Donaldson, 2006). How can researchers extrapolate what is found to be true in one context and draw inferences about its effects in another? What data sources exist that support an understanding of bargaining within a particular context and across different contexts? What are the affordances of quantitative versus qualitative research in answering these types of questions? How does the political nature of policymaking affect research design?

As Deborah Stone (1988) notes, "Every idea about policy draws boundaries" (p. 25). Goals of public policy and their notions of equity and efficiency are contested values. How do the questions that are taken up by researchers straddle and articulate the competing interests inherent in public policies about education? Can research do more than define the polarity of the debate? Can it delineate and assess the middle ground where both parties to the bargaining share interests? Educational reforms have often hinged on simplistic assumptions—more pay will lead to better teacher quality, elimination of collective bargaining will free administration to improve schools, parental choice will improve urban schools. The challenge of researchers is to examine under what conditions some of these assumptions may be true and what other factors interact with these assumptions. The task is daunting but not impossible.

As Hannaway and Rotherham (2006) conclude in their recent edited volume on collective bargaining, "The lack of empirical evidence on the effects of collective bargaining on educational practice, finance, and operations is striking" (p. 260). But the gathering of diverse opinions can at least inform policy actors, educational stakeholders, and researchers as to new directions warranting further research. Additionally, the nature of the questions that currently make up the research agenda point to the saliency of reform bargaining in the future. While some critics may believe that unions are incapable of moving beyond the status quo (Moe, 2006), others recognize that the tenets of reform bargaining hold the greatest promise for experimentation and risk-taking (Johnson & Kardos, 2000; Eberts, 2007).

Considering an Agenda for Policy Research This chapter has raised just some questions that might be better informed, and provide the basis for sounder education policy, with a stronger research base. The dilemma for policy makers is clear: they must make sense of the limited body of teacher union-related research that does exist as they shape policy. Yet many of the "research" conclusions about those issues about which policy makers are likely to care deeply, such as the relationship between collectively bargained agreements and teacher quality (or student achievement) often are shaped more by rhetoric and ideology than by disinterested, thorough inquiry (Johnson & Donaldson, 2006).

Much of the recent writing and research about unions that has received public play and policy attention (including the previously mentioned think-tank reports) has tended to focus on the conservative critics who favor a continuation of industrial-style work and workers, with tight managerial authority (see, e.g., Moe, 2001, 2005; Hoxby, 1996). Moreover, the conventional view of unions, that they are mired in the traditional, resistant to change, and preoccupied with the narrow self-interests of their members, continues to be reinforced by the mainstream media, though this coverage, too, is sketchy and sporadic.

According to a recent report from Becker and Vlad (2006) for the Hechinger Institute, between 2003 and 2005, the 24 largest circulation newspapers in communities with collective bargaining published 5,835 articles that dealt with teacher unions or bargaining. A mere 10% of these articles referred at all to collective bargaining. Those articles that did tackle union-oriented issues took a decidedly traditional approach. They were written from the point of view of traditional labor negotiations and focused primarily on strikes and salary issues. Issues of teacher quality or educational outcomes, even if they were topics of labor-management discussions, did not even appear as part of the story. Thus, policy makers are in the unenviable position of designing education policy on the basis of incomplete information, and points of view reinforced by a narrow range of research and stories in the popular press.

With near universal agreement that unions play an important role in educational policy setting, it seems natural that a research agenda should emerge that addresses issues that the union and other policy actors affect. This chapter suggests that researchers who choose to understand the multidimensional relationships of bargaining and its impacts on education can shed light on how current reform agendas align (or fail to align) with reform bargaining principles. If traditional bargaining precludes risk-taking and experimentation, then it seems fruitful to study how an alternative approach to bargaining might resolve long-standing problems in education.

It has been more than 15 years since Kerchner and Koppich published case studies on unions negotiating about tough educational problems with a different type of bargaining while forging new labor-management relationships. At a minimum, researchers within the union and without, could take another look at this landscape and report on the status of reform bargaining and its effects. What are promising practices? What are fledgling, yet interesting ideas held by unions? Researchers could pair this work with the prevalent research agenda on education and note the places where interests align and further research could be promising. Assuming policy interest in empirical relevant research in the area of teacher unions and collective bargaining, what might be an agenda for such work? What are some topics that might be fruitful areas of study that could lead to productive policy?

Below are suggested six broad topics for potential study. They may simply be the topics that appeal to these authors. Certainly there are many other possibilities, and each of those suggested lends itself to multiple smaller, more intense pieces of work. But this represents a place to begin.

1. *Gauging the costs of collective bargaining.* What are the monetary costs attached to negotiating and implementing collectively bargained agreements? What would a reasonable calculus look like and how would it be devised in a way that is credible and comprehensible to both union and management? What do cost data reveal about the process of contract development? What do they reveal about the implementation of the education policy that composes the contract? Are costs different for "traditional" and "reform" agreements? If so, what is the nature of the differences and what do these differences reveal?

2. *Charting teacher unionism's course.* To what extent have contracts in collective bargaining jurisdictions changed in the last 30 years? To what extent have they remained the same? What do contract trends portend for teacher unions in a nation still struggling with education reform?

3. *Reexamining scope.* The scope of negotiated agreements has long been a debated issue. Should contract negotiations be confined to the classic wages, hours, and terms and conditions of employment, as industrial union advocates suggest, or should scope be expanded to include (and, in fact, require) that issues of professionalism, career building, and student achievement be part of the agreement, as reformers advocate? What has been the measurable impact, if any, of negotiated reform programs, such as peer assistance and review and alternative compensation on teacher quality and, by extension, on student achievement?

4. *Union organizational capacity.* Should teacher unions, as organizations, assume greater responsibility for educational improvement? If so, how would they accomplish this? Union locals tend to operate according to long ago-designed policies and procedures. What kinds of changes are necessary for these organizations to take on members' concerns such as professional development and career options? How have unions that have begun to encompass these issues changed their organizational structures?

5. *The influence of state and federal policy on local collective bargaining.* Education policy increasingly is influenced by federal and state policy. In addition to No Child Left Behind's expansion of the federal role in the education arena through accountability and testing, the original version of this statute proposed allowing districts to override collectively bargained contracts. This proposal has resurfaced as part of the reauthorization of this statute. What are the implications of allowing federal law to supersede locally negotiated contracts? No state has undertaken major changes in its collective bargaining law, but state reform efforts clearly have influenced bargaining and the resulting contracts. In what ways have state-led education reform programs impacted local collective bargaining?

6. *Examining labor law.* Collective bargaining laws have changed little since they were enacted several decades ago. The laws were constructed for a different era, and, arguably, for a different education system. In *United Mind Workers,* written a decade ago, the authors began to suggest a framework, more a skeletal outline, for a new law befitting a 21st century system of education. What might such a prototypical law look like? How might it differ from current collective bargaining statutes? Who might support and oppose such an initiative? How might it influence broader education policy (Kerchner et al., 1997)?

These are suggested topics that might begin to form a research agenda on teacher unions and collective bargaining. Data gathered from studies such as these could serve to inform more comprehensive education policy.

As the political scientist Charles Lindblom (1959) observed more than four decades ago, most policy change is incremental. Changes in collective bargaining policy and negotiated contracts, if they are desired at all, happen slowly, incrementally, and by accretion. Or, as stated more prosaically by teacher union leader Adam Urbanski (1998), "Real change is real hard and takes real time" (p. 190). Policy change can be informed by good research, research that is neither an unrelieved attack on nor unabashed support of unions. In the absence of a larger body of research, the weight of the rhetoric on either side of the "unions are good, unions are bad" debate will continue to rest on shaky empirical ground (Goldhaber, 2006). Education policy on collective bargaining will likely continue to be made largely on the basis of partial information and personal belief. The education system, its teachers, administrators, and staff, and the students it serves, deserve better.

Notes

1. Proponents of this theory include Susan Moore Johnson, Charles Kerchner, Linda Kaboolian, and Julia Koppich.
2. Proponents of this theory include Terry Moe, Dale Ballou and Michael Podgursky, Chester Finn, and Caroline Hoxby.
3. The former director of the New Teacher Project, Michelle Rhee, was named Chancellor of the Washington, DC Public Schools in June 2006.
4. http://www.nctq.org/tr3/
5. This report, however, also acknowledges that, in some circumstances, contract language is less confining than critics allege.
6. Courts have ruled that, while states may prohibit bargaining or make it permissive, prohibiting teachers from joining unions is a violation of the First Amendment right to free association.
7. These states are sometimes erroneously referred to as "right-to-work" states. Actually, so-called right-to-work states are those that make it illegal to require union membership as a condition of employment.
8. While commonly referred to as "teachers' contracts," this term actually is a misnomer. Contracts are not legally binding unless they are agreed to by both the union and the school board, making them bilateral, not unilateral, agreements.
9. The NEA, though it counted teachers among its members, was long dominated by school and college administrators and eschewed collective bargaining as "unprofessional." By the early 1970s, as collective bargaining was gaining an increasing foothold in districts in which the AFT held majority membership, the NEA began its own shift, eliminating administrators from its membership ranks and embracing industrial-style collective bargaining for teachers.
10. For a more detailed treatment of the specifics of contracts, see Koppich (2007).
11. These individuals have been local union president for 8 or fewer years. Several of them have been long-time members of their unions.

References

Becker, L. B., & Vlad, T. (2006, May). *Newspaper coverage of collective bargaining in local school systems* (Report prepared for the Hechinger Institute on Education and the Media). New York: Teachers College.

Bloom, G., & Goldstein, J. (Eds.). (2000). *The peer assistance and review reader.* Santa Cruz: University of California at Santa Cruz, The New Teacher Center.

Carnegie Forum on Education and the Economy. (1986). *A nation prepared: Teachers for the 21st century.* Washington, DC: Author.

Chase, R. (1997, February 5). *It's not your mother's NEA.* Speech before the National Press Club, Washington, DC.

Eberts, R. W. (2007). Teacher unions and student performance: Help or hindrance? *Future of Children, 17*(1), 175–200.

Eberts, R. W., & Stone, J. A. (1984, April). Teacher unions and productivity of public schools. *Industrial and Labor Relations Review, 40,* 354–363.

The Education Partnership. (2005, March). *Teacher contracts: Restoring the balance.* Providence, RI: Author.

Farber, H. (2006). Union membership in the United States. In J. Hannaway & A. Rotherham (Eds.), *Collective bargaining in education: Negotiating change in today's schools* (pp. 27–52). Cambridge, MA: Harvard Education Press.

Farkas, S., Johnson, J., & Duffett, A. (2003). *Stand by me: What teachers really think about unions, merit pay, and other professional matters.* New York: Public Agenda Foundation.

Fisher, R. & Ury, W. (1983). *Getting to yes: Negotiating agreement without giving in.* New York: Penguin Books.

Goldhaber, D. (2006). Are teachers unions good for students? In J. Hannaway & A. Rotherham (Eds.), *Collective bargaining in education: Negotiating change in today's schools* (pp. 141–158). Cambridge, MA: Harvard Education Press.

Goldstein, J., & Noguera, P. (2006). A thoughtful approach to teacher evaluation. *Educational Leadership, 63*(6), 31–37.

Hannaway, J., & Rotherham, A. (2006). Conclusion. In J. Hannaway & A. Rotherham (Eds.), *Collective bargaining in education: Negotiating change in today's schools* (pp. 257–266). Cambridge, MA: Harvard Education Press.

Hess, F., & Kelly, A. (2006). Scapegoat, albatross, or what? The status quo in teacher collective bargaining. In J. Hannaway & A. Rotherham (Eds.), *Collective bargaining in education: Negotiating change in today's schools* (pp. 53–88). Cambridge, MA: Harvard Education Press.

Hess, F., & West, M. (2006). *A better bargain: Overhauling teacher collective bargaining for the 21st century.* Cambridge, MA: Harvard University, Program on Education Policy and Governance.

Holmes Group. (1986). *Tomorrow's teachers.* East Lansing, MI: Author.

Honawar, V. (2007, January 24). AFT no longer a major player in reform arena. *Education Week, 26*(21), 1, 16–17.

Hoxby, C. (1996). How teacher unions affect education production. *Quarterly Journal of Economics, 111*, 671–718.

Johnson, S. M. (2000, June 7). Teaching's next generation: Who are they? What will keep them in the classroom? Retrieved on May 28, 2008, from http://web.ebscohost.com/ehost/detail?vid=1&hid=106&sid=cf3703ee-8dc9-4b98-8296-388dd1e7e3d3%40sessionmgr109

Johnson, S. M., & Donaldson, M. (2006). The effects of collective bargaining on teacher quality. In J. Hannaway & A. Rotherham (Eds.), *Collective bargaining in education: Negotiating change in today's schools* (pp. 111–140). Cambridge, MA: Harvard Education Press.

Johnson, S. M., Donaldson, M. L., Munger, M. S., Papay, J. P., & Qasibash, E. K. (2007, June 28). *Leading the local: Teacher union presidents speak on change, challenges.* Retrieved March 18, 2008, from http://www.educationsector.org/research/research_show.htm?doc_id=507216

Johnson, S. M., & Kardos, S. M. (2000). Reform bargaining and its promise for school improvement. In T. Loveless (Ed.), *Conflicting missions? Teachers unions and educational reform* (pp. 7–46). Washington, DC: Brookings Institution.

Jupp, B. (2005). The uniform salary schedule. *Education Next, 5*(1), 10–12.

Kaboolian, L. (2005). *Win-win labor-management collaboration in education: Breakthrough practices to benefit students, teachers, and administrators.* Cambridge, MA: Education Week Press.

Kahlenberg, R. (2006). The history of collective bargaining among teachers. In J. Hannaway & A. Rotherham (Eds.), *Collective bargaining in education: Negotiating change in today's schools* (pp. 7–26). Cambridge, MA: Harvard Education Press.

Kerchner, C. T. (2001). Deindustrialization: Why teachers must come to regard—and organize themselves—as mind workers. *Education Next, 1*(3), 46–50.

Kerchner, C. T., & Koppich, J. E. (Eds.). (1993). *A union of professionals: Labor relations and education reform.* New York: Teachers College Press.

Kerchner, C. T., & Koppich, J. E. (2006, March). *Negotiating what matters most: Student achievement.* Paper presented at the Claremont Graduate University Labor Conference.

Kerchner, C. T., Koppich, J. E., & Weeres, J. (1997). *United mind workers: Unions and teaching in the knowledge society.* San Francisco: Jossey-Bass.

Kerchner, C. T., & Mitchell, D. E. (1988). *The changing idea of a teachers' union.* New York: Falmer Press.

Keller, B. (2007, January 24). NEA wants role in school improvement agenda. *Education Week, 26*(21), 1, 16–17.

Koppich, J. E. (2005). All teachers are not the same: A multiple approach to teacher compensation. *Education Next, 5*(1), 13–15.

Koppich, J. E. (2006). The as-yet unfulfilled promise of reform bargaining. In J. Hannaway & A. Rotherham (Eds.), *Collective bargaining in education: Negotiating change in today's schools* (pp. 203–228). Cambridge, MA: Harvard Education Press.

Koppich, J. E. (2007, May). Resource allocation in traditional and reform-oriented collective bargaining agreements (Working paper No. 18). Seattle: University of Washington School Finance Redesign Project at the Center on Reinventing Public Education.

Koski, W., & Horng, E. (2007). Facilitating the teacher quality gap? Collective bargaining agreements, teacher hiring and transfer rules, and teacher assignment among schools in California. *Education Finance and Policy, 2*, 262–299.

Levin, J., Mulhern, J., & Schunk, J. (2005). Unintended consequences: The case for reforming the staffing rules in urban teachers union contracts. New York: The New Teacher Project.

Lindblom, C. E. (1959). The science of muddling through. *Public Administration Review, 19*, 79–88.

Loeb, S., & Page, M. E. (2000). Examining the link between teacher wages and student outcomes: The importance of alternative labor market opportunities and non-pecuniary variation. *The Review of Economics and Statistics, 82*, 393–408.

Loveless, T. (2000). Conflicting missions?: Teachers unions and educational reform. Washington, DC: Brookings Institution.

McDonnell, L., & Pascal, A. (1988). *Teacher unions and educational reform.* Santa Monica, CA: Center for Policy Research in Education, RAND.

Moe, T. M. (2001). Teachers unions and the public schools. In T. M. Moe (Ed.), *A primer on America's schools* (pp. 151–184), Stanford, CA: Hoover Press.

Moe, T. M. (2005). A union by any other name. *Education Next, 1*(3), 40–45.

Moe, T. M. (2006). Union power and the education of children. In J. Hannaway & A. Rotherham (Eds.), *Collective bargaining in education: Negotiating change in today's schools* (pp. 229–256). Cambridge, MA: Harvard Education Press.

National Commission on Excellence in Education. (1983, April). *A nation at risk: The imperative for educational reform.* Washington, DC: Author.

National Labor Relations Act, 29 U.S.C. §§ 151-169 (1935).

Odden, A., & Kelley, C. (1997). *Paying teachers for what they know and can do: New and smarter compensation strategies to improve schools* (1st ed.). Thousand Oaks, CA: Corwin Press.

Roza, M. (2007). *Frozen assets: Rethinking teacher contracts could free billions for school reform.* Retrieved March 18, 2008, from http://www.educationsector.org/usr_doc/FrozenAssets.pdf

Shanker, A. (1983, July). *Address to the AFT Convention.* Speech presented at the American Federation of Teachers Conference, Los Angeles.

Stone, D. (1988). *Policy paradox: The art of political decision making.* New York: W. W. Norton & Company.

Stroot, S., Fowlkes, J., Langholz, J., Paxton, S., Stedman, P., Steffes, L., et al. (1999). Impact of a collaborative peer assistance and review model on entry-year teachers in a large urban school setting. *Journal of Teacher Education, 50*, 27–41.

Urbanski, A. (1998). TURNing unions around. *Contemporary Education, 69*, 186–190.

25

The Voice of the People in Education Policy

Rebecca Jacobsen
Michigan State University

Public Education and Democracy

Since the founding of this country, a system of public education has been closely linked to a healthy democracy. Early political leaders, such as Washington and Jefferson, stressed the importance of a public education system to ensure the newly formed representative government would survive. They saw schools as a key component to creating citizens who knew their rights and responsibilities. George Washington stressed in the very first State of the Union address that educational institutions must teach citizens "to value their own rights" and to protect themselves against those who would infringe upon them (Washington, 1790/1966, p. 3). Jefferson was an advocate of public education both before and after his presidency and he too felt that a system of public education was necessary to:

> illuminate, as far as practicable, the minds of the people at large, and more especially to give them knowledge of those facts which history exhibiteth, that, possessed thereby of the experience of other ages and countries, they may be enabled to know ambition under all its shapes, and prompt to exert their natural powers to defeat its purposes. (cited in Wagoner, 2004, p. 35)

These beliefs led Jefferson to propose a full system of public education to the Virginia Legislature in 1779. In the bill, which did not pass, Jefferson argued that the main aim of free public education was to prevent tyranny and ensure the development and stability of the new democracy. Since the beginning of this country, public schools have served in the development and maintenance of democracy by educating future citizens who are capable of making wise political decisions about representatives and policy issues and are able to know and defend their rights and liberties.

There are private benefits to public education that the founding fathers most certainly recognized as well, but the emphasis on private benefits has only recently become the dominating objective of public education (Labaree, 1997). Even beyond developing citizens, however, public education offers a number of public benefits. Schools teach students critical and creative thinking skills that contribute to the economic progress of the nation. Schools contribute to "cultural and scientific progress and to the defense of the nation" (Levin, 1987, p. 630). Even Milton Friedman (1962), who advocated for a voucher program, believed that the importance of "neighborhood effects" provided a motivating factor for governments to fund public education. He stated that "schooling is financed because other people benefit from the schooling of those of greater ability and interests" and therefore, "the gains are sufficiently important to justify some government subsidy" (p. 88). For all of these reasons, public schools are critical for the development of citizens and our society.

Schools also serve a second role in our democracy. Public education is itself a democratically run institution. Public schools are open to all, are paid for by public funds, and are accountable to the public. The people make important decisions about whether and to what degree to support its public education system and for this reason, it is imperative that the voice of the people be incorporated into the running of this democratic institution. Ultimately, the public education system derives its legitimacy from the consent of the electorate. In order for public schools to function, they must be responsive to the people. Recent focus on accountability policies continue to show that providing the public with information regarding the performance of their public schools is a key component to this democratic institution.

But the public has grown increasingly dissatisfied with its public schools which has put this democratically run institution at risk. As surveys have shown over the last half century, there has been a steady downward trend in confidence or satisfaction with multiple public institutions (Newton & Norris, 1999; Nye, 1997) and specifically in education over the last 30 years, confidence has declined significantly (Loveless, 1997). For example, in 1977, over half (53%) of respondents reported that they had a "great

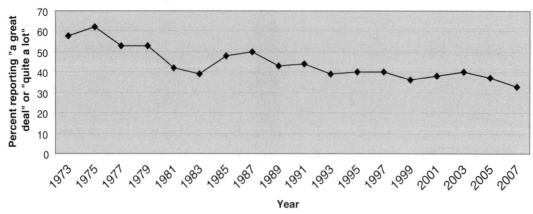

Figure 25.1 Confidence in public education.

deal" or "quite a lot" of confidence in the public schools (Gallup Organization, 1977). Today, only one-third of respondents express this same level of confidence (Gallup Organization, 2007). As is shown in the graph above, there has been steady erosion in reported confidence levels in education.

While certainly declining confidence in education may just be part of a larger trend, understanding public dissatisfaction with education is particularly important due to the unique dual role of the public education system in our democracy discussed above; it is both a place for developing citizenship but also a place where citizens can voice their opinions and have input into a democratic institution. Declining confidence and dissatisfaction with the public schools, possibly a result of the frequent discussions of "failing" public schools,[1] has led to an increased willingness on the part of the public to consider alternative governance structures that are no longer democratic (Plank & Boyd, 1994). Yet schools as developers of future citizens and schools as democratic institutions are intertwined. "Seeking to provide a democratic education though organizations deliberately placed at arm's length from democratic control must be an ultimately self-defeating exercise … Day-to-day practices serve to contradict the democratic values being imparted in the schools" (Mintrom, 2001, p. 623). Thus, loss of democratic control in education necessarily hurts the development of future citizens.

While the declining confidence trend above has been well-documented, thus far limited research has examined the nature of public beliefs and support for education. In other words, little work has considered what the people want and why they are dissatisfied with what they are getting. Certainly a degree of skepticism on the part of the public is healthy in a representative democracy as it helps to keep elected leaders in check, but extremely low confidence in public education may signal a legitimacy crisis. Therefore, understanding the public's opinions towards the educational system is important as ignoring them results in increased difficulty garnering needed public support for new policy initiatives and may even threaten the stability of education as a democratically run institution altogether (McDonnell, 2000; Yang & Holzer, 2006).

While research into public views on the goals of education ostensibly should be at the core of educational policy-making and research in education policy, instead, we find that many policy and research debates are focused on issues of accountability, school governance, curricular reform, improving teaching quality, and so forth. Because research and policymaking have focused almost exclusively on determining which reform effort will lead to success, the question of what the public believes and wants from its public schools has been ignored. No Child Left Behind (NCLB) presupposes that the ultimate goal of public education is the teaching of academic skills. The public may agree with this; however, we have limited—and often flawed—data to support this conclusion. If this assumption proves incorrect and we do not listen to what the people have to say, the risks to the institution may be quite high as people become increasingly dissatisfied, quit voicing their opinions, and simply exit the public school system because their voices are not being considered. Therefore, this chapter considers the options that the public may exercise when dissatisfied with an institution: exit and voice. It considers the limited research available on the public's voice for what it wants from its public schools. In doing so, this chapter points out ways in which public opinion questions have often been flawed and offers possible remedies for these flaws using new polling modes and question formats. Because scholarly research on public opinion on educational issues is severely lacking, the concluding section highlights potential areas for future research that can bring attention to the voice of the people on educational issues.

The Public's Options when Dissatisfied

Hirschman (1970), in his classic analysis of responses to declining performance in "any economic, social, or political system" (p. 1), identified two main courses of action: exit and voice. The exit option is when individuals stop purchasing a product or leave an organization. In the case of public education, the exit option has long existed; parents are (and have been) free to send their children to private schools and thus, exit the public school system. Alternatively, individuals may use voice as a mechanism to express their dissatisfaction. Public schools offer several routes for voice including parent-teacher organizations where parents are able to express their views collectively to school administrators and teachers and school board meetings which are open to the public and often include time for the public's comments.

These options are not intended to work in an either/ or fashion. Indeed, voice and exit work best when both are available and viable alternatives. Further, each has its benefits. Exit can be particularly powerful and exact an immediate cost on the institution. Voice, on the other hand, can be more costly to the individual as it requires more time. However, voice provides the institution in decline with greater insight as to the reasons for dissatisfaction and possible remedies that would be acceptable.

While Hirschman presents important theoretical considerations for the way in which individuals respond to dissatisfaction with an institution and how these methods must work together, researchers have documented a number of more tangible consequences for public institutions and their leaders when confidence sinks. Again, some skepticism is healthy; the real problem is when dissatisfaction becomes more extreme and in these cases, both voice and exit can become harmful, rather than helpful.

One possible voice response is that the public, when dissatisfied, often calls for rapid change in leadership or quick fixes in policy (Levi & Stoker, 2000; Orren, 1997). This can result in ill-conceived policies, more symbolic than substantive, that superficially meet the immediate demands of the public's outcry for change. Such "policy churn" has been documented in education where "an endless stream of new initiatives" are being implemented in many large, urban school districts without enough time or follow through to see substantive change (Hess, 1999, p. 52). Increasingly, more schools are being labeled as "failing" under NCLB. As of 2005-2006, 11,648 schools—or 12% of the nation's public schools—had been identified as in need of improvement (Stullich, Eisner, & McCrary, 2008, p. 59). While the majority of schools identified are large, urban districts, similar to the ones studied by Hess, 9% of suburban schools and 4% of low poverty schools have been identified for improvement as well (Stullich et al., 2008, p. 62). While Hess found that it was the urban schools districts he studied that were proposing more reforms in an effort to appear as if they were proactively improving the schools, it may be expected that as the list of schools in need of improvement continues to grow and spread to suburban and low poverty schools, as it has been doing over the past few years, his findings of policy churn are likely to occur there as well. Thus, when trust is low and the above attitude prevails, the public's demand for rapid change can make the implementation of longer term, more effective, policies more difficult.

The public may also voice its dissatisfaction through a refusal to support governmental services with taxes. Glaser and Hildreth (1999) found that approximately half of the citizens they studied were satisfied with the performance of their local government and therefore were willing to pay additional taxes to support their local governments. If the people do not trust the public school system to spend its resources wisely, they will not support increased taxes and may not even continue to comply with current tax regulations. Without such resources, the public institutions cannot possibly perform well and the downward spiral continues (Nye, 1997). In its most extreme form, low levels of trust can be used to attack government programs, reduce funding, and ultimately jeopardize the very existence of government programs (Yang & Holzer, 2006). Abernathy (2005) found in his study of New Jersey school districts that voters in districts with charter schools were actually less likely to approve the school budget. While charters remain part of the public school system and thus this finding seems somewhat perplexing, one can also consider the existence of charter schools as a sign of dissatisfaction with the traditional public school system. This dissatisfaction may also result in the decreased probability of fiscal support for the public education system as this study seems to imply.

As the public becomes increasingly disillusioned with a public institution, researchers often find that the public quits voicing, or participating, altogether. Research on voter turn out has linked low confidence levels to declining voter turnout rates (Putnam, 2000). Public education already suffers from unusually low rates of turnout in school board elections. These low rates are partly due to the timing of school board elections which are often apart from the general elections. Allen and Plank (2005) found that turnout rates for the school board elections they studied ranged from 19% to just 4%. These already low rates do not have much further to sink. But increased dissatisfaction with schools may further depress turnout as the public simply quits voicing its views regarding how the public school system should be run.

Eventually, people may become so frustrated that they turn to the exit option and leave the public education system all together. While it is not always possible to exit some public institutions, leaving the public education system has become an increasingly popular response to perceived failure in public education. The increased number of voucher programs (both publicly and privately funded), rising rates of homeschooling, and increased charter school options signal the increasing willingness of the public to simply leave public school system behind entirely.

The Rise of Exit in Education Today

While Hirschman (1970) originally theorized that the existence of both exit and voice are needed to improve institutions, he also noted that exit can too easily become the favored alternative. In this case, Hirshman warns that ease of exit can "tend to *atrophy the development of the art of voice*" (p. 43). Hirschman's use of the term "art" for voice is intentional for he stresses that unlike exit, voice must be learned and developed through practice. Without such practice, the loss of voice is not easily recaptured. Key then to maintaining the important balance between exit and voice is loyalty because it "holds exit at bay and activates voice" (p. 78). Yet the sinking satisfaction in public education discussed above erodes loyalty and the ease of exit becomes increasingly common.

The eroding loyalty to the public education institution as evidenced by declining satisfaction levels and increased exit from the public education system provides motivation to understand what the public does say when it voices its opinions on public education. Given public education's unique role in our democracy to both develop citizens and provide them with a place to participate, we cannot run the risk of eroding further support for this public institution. However, democratic control over public education has been criticized by advocates and researchers who favor privatization and market options for education. Chubb and Moe (1990), for example, charge that the fundamental causes of problems in public education "are, in fact, the very institutions that are supposed to be solving the problem: the institutions of direct democratic control" (p. 2). Those supporting this position have been making use of the exit option more widely available. Today, parents may exit the public schools through an increasing number of routes.

While exit to private schools have long existed, the majority of students have, and continue to remain, in the public education system. However, the numbers of students exercising this option has been increasing as can be seen in the table below. The percentage of students attending both private, church-related, and private, non church-related private schools has grown over the past decade.

Vouchers have become a way for students to exit the public education system and enter private schools. Vouchers, which are currently funded through public dollars in only four places (Milwaukee, WI, Ohio,[2] Washington, DC, and New Orleans, LA) provide about 40,000 students the option to exit the public school system to attend private schools (Center on Education Reform, 2008b). Additionally, there exists a wide range of private scholarship funds that also provide students with vouchers for private school tuition. These programs, as they continue to grow, will increase the number of students attending private schools, both church-related and non church-related.

Table 25.1 also shows the growth in the number of students enrolling in public school choice programs. While not a complete exit from the public education system, charter schools do represent a form of exit from the larger public education system. The Center on Education Reform, an organization which tracks and promotes choice in education, notes that there are nearly 4,000 charter schools across the country which enroll more than 1 million students and new schools continue to open each year (Center on Education Reform, 2008a).

Recent years have also seen tremendous growth in the numbers of students who are exiting the public school system for homeschooling options. As of 2003, about 1.1 million or 2.2% of all students were being homeschooled (National Center for Education Statistics, 2005, p. 32). In 1999, the number homeschooled was just 850,000. The jump demonstrates the rapid growth of this exit option over just a 4-year time period.

The increased exit option in education signals that the public is turning away from voice as its means of improving the public institution. Apparently, many of the people do not feel that their voices are being heard or responded to. Their loyalty has declined and they are not getting what they want from the public schools so they are choosing to exit.

Bringing the Public's Voice Back into Education Policy

While research on public school exit has been receiving a good deal of attention, understanding the voice of the people on educational issues and how it may balance the exit option has long been neglected by researchers. Few researchers who specialize in public opinion and policy-making have examined questions related specifically to education. When educational issues have been studied, they have been grouped into the broader category of "social welfare" (see, e.g., Monroe, 1998). But education, as discussed above, should be considered unique and worthy of study in its own right, because unlike other social welfare programs such as health care, education both serves and creates citizens.

Pollsters have asked the public many questions on a wide range of educational issues, but little scholarly attention to the public's response to such questions exists. Indeed, Hochschild and Scott (1998) open a paper on public opinion and education by saying that they "found very few scholarly analysis of public opinion about schooling" (p. 79),[3] and Loveless (1997) notes that "research on public attitudes toward education is confined to a handful of texts and articles" (p. 128). Yet understanding the public's views is critical if policy makers want to build support for reform efforts. We must bring the public's voice back into the public education debates and seek to understand how their opinions impact policy.

Public Capacity of Informing Public Policy

Although we may want people to be engaged and to offer their opinions on educational issues, are they capable

TABLE 25.1
Percentage Distribution of Students in Grades 1–12, by Type of School: 1993 and 2003

Type of school	1993	2003
Public, assigned	79.9	73.9
Public, chosen	11.0	15.4
Private, church-related	7.5	8.4
Private, not church-related	1.6	2.4

Source: U.S. Department of Education, National Center for Education Statistics, 2006, Table 36-1a

of offering meaningful opinions upon which to build educational policies? Early public opinion research seemed to confirm fears that the public was too ill-informed on particular policy issues to offer sound opinions. Some of the earliest studies of public opinion demonstrated that the public did not rely upon policy knowledge when providing answers on opinion polls and instead often made decisions based on sociological attachments such as socioeconomic status, religious affiliation, and other group memberships (Lazarsfeld, Berelson, & Gaudet, 1948) or the people relied upon attachments to political parties to determine their choices (Campbell, Converse, Miller, & Stokes, 1960).

Another criticism of public opinion is that the people's views are inconsistent and subject to seemingly random change. Hamilton argued in Federalist Paper 63 that the government should be immune to the "whims" and "violent passions" of the people and that the government should protect the people against their "own temporary errors and delusions." National Election Survey panel data which examines the same group of respondents at multiple time points has documented these "whims" and "violent passions" that Hamilton feared. Indeed, Converse (1964) found that only about 20% of the respondents he studied gave consistent responses across time. Based on this, he coined the term "nonattitudes" to describe the apparently random answers that respondents provided to public opinion surveys. Such "nonattitudes" continue to appear in polls on educational issues and are used to dismiss public opinion research. For example, as of 2006, 4 years after the No Child Left Behind Act was signed into law, 55% of the public reported that they knew very little or nothing at all about the law and yet they were willing to offer opinions on various aspects of the act (Rose & Gallup, 2006). Such findings can be used as a reason to ignore the voice of the people altogether.

However, some of the appearance of instability in attitudes is due to measurement error. Public opinion experts now know that poorly constructed survey instruments contribute greatly to the seemingly random answers given by respondents. Researchers today now consider the many ways in which measurement error can be introduced into a survey. Respondents can be influenced by the use of loaded terms in a question or by using the names of political leaders in a question stem. Issues of question order and the number of response categories offered can also influence survey outcomes. Simply including a middle choice can greatly affect the percentage of people who say they agree or disagree with a certain policy (Asher, 2001; Converse & Presser, 1986; Sudman, Bradburn, & Schwarz, 1996). These many points of potential measurement error can explain some of the early findings of "nonattitudes" as well as the continued confusion seen in today's public opinion polls that have not been crafted with rigor. By paying attention to issues of question wording and poll format, public opinion survey research on educational issues can bring the public's voice into educational policy debates.

Public Opinion on Public School Expectations: A Review of Existing Polls

So, what does the public want? A simple search of the iPoll databank at the Roper Center for Public Opinion Research resulted in over 4,600 questions containing the word education. The oldest question in the database dates back to 1936 and asked about the importance of a college education (Gallup Organization, 1936). Just 2 years later in 1938, the public was asked to consider whether Congress should create a new Cabinet Department of Public Welfare to handle public health, education, and welfare (Gallup Organization, 1938). As these questions indicate, from very early in the development of public opinion polls, educational issues have been included. Moreover, the number of questions posed to the public about educational issues has increased dramatically in the recent past with just over three-quarters of the iPoll databank questions being posed after 1987. The rapid increase in the number of questions is a result, in part, of the expansion of telephone interviewing and polling more generally but is also due to the increased attention that educational issues have received at the national level. But this rapid rise in the number of questions has not been matched by a rapid rise in research related to public opinion and educational issues.

Surely, in these thousands of existing questions, we should be able to find the needed data in order to understand the public's expectations for public education. Indeed, several surveys have specifically asked people to assess their priorities and expectations for public education. However, as will be shown below, there are some fundamental measurement issues with each of the existing surveys which makes it impossible to accurately determine how the public views educational priorities or what the public says it wants from the school system.

The first issue that arises when considering existing questions is that because the poll has been commissioned by a particular group interested in a narrow set of issues, the questions often consider only one specific educational area. For example, in a 2000 presidential election poll conducted by Time/CNN/Yankelovich Partners, the public was asked, "In your view, should gym class have more importance or less importance in the school curriculum than it does now?" The survey found that 51% of the respondents felt that gym classes should have more importance in the school day (Time, Cable News Network, & Yankelovich Partners, 2001). This response seems to indicate that a large percentage of the public expects schools to make physical fitness an important aspect of the school day.

Similarly, the National Association of Music Merchants conducted a poll through the Gallup Organization in 1994 where they asked only questions pertaining to music education. The poll asked respondents to consider the role and importance of music education. One question asked respondents to rate the following statement using a four-point scale: "Music education should be mandated by the states to ensure every child has an opportunity to study music in school." Seventy-one percent of the survey respondents agreed or mostly agreed that states should mandate music education (Gallup Organization, 1994). Taken at face value, it would appear that nearly three-quarters of the public expects that music education should be taught in the public schools.

However, the problem with the data presented above is that people were asked to evaluate one goal in isolation. Even if we were able to locate survey questions for all of the multiple goals of public education and aggregate the results, these questions may not accurately reflect the public's voice because respondents were not prompted to consider a full range of goals. We do not know, for example, if the public expects that less time be spent on some area in order to increase time spent on music or physical education. Therefore, in order for poll data to be useful in assessing the public's voice on educational goals, it must present more than one educational goal area.

Some polls have asked respondents to consider a much broader set of educational goals and state their expectations across goals, but if the set of goals presented was ill-designed, the results can still be misleading. For example, Reading is Fundamental, a national organization that donates books to children in disadvantaged communities and encourages family literacy programs, commissioned a poll with funding from the Jell-O Desserts company (Reading is Fundamental, 1988). The poll asked respondents to rate each educational area using a four-point ratings scale. Results are shown in Table 25.2.

While the survey does cover multiple educational areas, the list presented to respondents remains incomplete. There are many non-cognitive outcomes of education as well which were not considered. One of the original reasons for establishing public education was to develop citizenship skills as discussed above. This important aspect of public education is missing from the poll. Additionally, employers often state that they expect schools to help students develop social skills such as the ability to communicate and work

TABLE 25.2
Jell-O Desserts Family Reading Survey

	Very or Somewhat Important	Not that Important	Not at all Important	Don't Know
Arithmetic or math	99%	0%	0%	1%
Reading	99%	0%	0%	1%
Physical education	93%	7%	1%	
History	95%	4%	1%	
Science	97%	3%	0%	1%
Social studies or geography	96%	3%	0%	1%
Music or art	90%	9%	1%	
Writing	99%	1%	0%	
Foreign languages	79%	17%	4%	

effectively in a group and work ethic skills such as punctuality (Cappelli, 2001). These goals were not considered and therefore, while the Reading is Fundamental poll included more than one goal, we still do not have a complete picture of how the public prioritizes different goals.

Phi Delta Kappan and the Gallup Organization conduct one of the most well-known surveys on public education annually. For 40 years, they have published the results of a national public opinion poll on the public's attitudes toward the public schools. In the 2000 version of the poll (see Table 25.2), respondents were asked to consider a broader range of educational goals, including non-cognitive skills. Respondents were asked to indicate how important the goal is to the public education system by selecting a number between 1 and 10—with 10 being the highest importance and 1 being not at all important. The poll then used the average ratings for each goal to develop a rank order. The poll included seven goal areas and the following results were obtained though the poll.

Respondents stated that they expected schools to focus on developing responsible citizens as their number one goal and it received a mean rating of 9 out of 10 (Rose & Gallup, 2000). The lowest rated goal, to dispel inequalities in people's lives, received an average rating of 7.5. Thus, the average for each goal fell between 7.5 and 9. This narrow range again seems to imply that the public expects each of these goal areas to be developed by schools with only minimal differentiation among the goals.

While somewhat improved over previous polls considered thus far, this poll too presents an incomplete list of public education goals. Teaching children academic skills was not included in the poll's list of options. Thus saying that preparing citizens is the top expectation, as these results would indicate, could be misleading and yet this finding was widely reported. If teaching students academic skills had been included, would preparing students to become responsible citizens still be listed as the most important goal?

But even more problematic for the purposes of informing policy is that even if the polls above had included a complete list of educational goals for the public to consider, all of the polls rely upon ratings scales to assess expectation levels. Ratings scales are popular for telephone polls because they are relatively simple to understand and can be communicated easily via the telephone. But there are also problems with this polling technique. Researchers find that when respondents are asked to use ratings scales, they often report very high, undifferentiated levels of importance in each particular goal (Alwin & Krosnick, 1985; Krosnick & Alwin, 1988). As was seen above, the majority of goals received a very high rating, making it appear as if the public expected everything to be nearly equally emphasized and that every area is extremely important. The results of questions posed using ratings scales provide little indication as to true public views, and they provide educational leaders and policy makers with little direction because simply doing more of everything is impossible. Time and resources are limited and thus priorities must be established and public

TABLE 25.3
Phi Delta Kappan/Gallup Poll 2000, Importance of Purpose Ranking

	Mean	Rank
To prepare people to become responsible citizens	9	1
To help people become economically self-sufficient	8.6	2
To ensure a basic level of quality among schools	8.5	3
To promote cultural unity among all Americans	8	4
To improve social conditions for people	7.8	5
To enhance people's happiness and enrich their lives	7.5	6–7
To dispel inequities in education among certain schools and certain groups	7.5	6–7

opinion results provide little information regarding how the public expects choices between goals to be made. The voice of the people, when assessed in this manner, does not become included in policy debates.

Innovative Polling on Educational Issues

If we want more attention paid to what people are saying, researchers must pay close attention to how we are asking the people to contribute their opinions. New data are needed to accurately assess the public's opinions on what they want from their public education system. While phone polling is a more common method for assessing the opinions of a representative sample of the public and is considered highly reliable, new polling techniques using the Internet are becoming more widely available. This relatively new mode of polling enables the public to offer more meaningful and considered options. The online format allows respondents to move at their own pace, thus providing time for respondents to think more deeply about the content of the survey. Moreover, the visual format allows the survey to present respondents with more complete descriptors on a survey. It is important that all respondents be considering the same set of ideas when they were evaluating a topic. The online format enables more detailed descriptions of policy issues because respondents can read and reread definitions at anytime throughout a survey simply by clicking on key words which are linked to detailed descriptions.

Knowledge Networks, an online polling firm that maintains a nationally representative panel of the American public that is accessible via the Internet (www.knowledge-networks.com/knpanel/index.html), completed a survey on what the public wants from its public schools using many of the ideas discussed above. Unlike other Internet polling firms, Knowledge Networks develops their panel though a conventional random-digit telephone dialing to ensure representativeness.[4] Knowledge Networks' panel was the universe from which to draw a sample of the general public. The response rate of the panel for this survey was 64%.[5] The final sample size was 1,297 valid responses.

Eight goals for public education were randomized and presented to respondents for their consideration.[6]

1. *Basic Academic Skills in Core Subjects:* Providing students with basic skills in reading, writing and math, and knowledge of science and history.
2. *Critical Thinking and Problem Solving:* Providing students with critical thinking and problem-solving skills, such as being able to analyze and interpret information, use computers to develop knowledge, and apply ideas to new situations.
3. *Social Skills and Work Ethic:* Providing students with social skills and a good work ethic, such as good communication skills, personal responsibility, the ability to get along well with others, and work with others from different backgrounds.
4. *Citizenship and Community Responsibility:* Providing students with good citizenship skills and a sense of public ethics so that they know how government works and how to participate in civic activities like voting, volunteering, and becoming active in their communities.
5. *Physical Health:* Providing students with a foundation for lifelong physical health, including good habits of exercise and nutrition.
6. *Emotional Health:* Providing students with the tools to develop self-confidence, respect for others, and the ability to resist peer pressure to engage in irresponsible personal behavior.
7. *The Arts and Literature:* Providing students with the opportunity to participate in and appreciate the musical, visual, and performing arts and helping students develop a love of literature.
8. *Vocational Education:* Providing students with the opportunity for vocational, career, and technical education that will qualify them for skilled employment that does not require a college degree.

Efforts were made to balance the clarity and uniqueness of each goal with a recognition that respondents must be presented with a manageable number of goals.

Respondents were asked to express their expectations for schools by assigning a relative importance of each goal area using a constant sum allocation exercise.[7] This method was selected because it forces respondents to compare the relative importance of each goal as they allocate 100 points across the eight goals. Unlike the surveys discussed above that used ratings scales, this method provides a high degree of differentiation between goals and a more accurate set of expectations for public education, making the public's voice useful for policy makers.[8]

The Public Voice on their Expectations for Public Schools

The results of the survey presented below are the average number of points allocated to each area by respondents. The

TABLE 25.4
Constant Sum Allocation Results for the General Public

Goal Area	Mean	SD
Basic Academic Skills	19.9	12.2
Critical Thinking and Problem Solving	16.1	7.8
Social Skills and Work Ethic	14.0	7.9
Citizenship and Community Responsibility	10.5	6.2
Physical Health	10.8	7.2
Emotional Health	9.9	7.2
The Arts and Literature	8.2	5.1
Vocational Education	10.6	7.1

Note: n = 1,297

results suggest that the public expects a range of skills to be taught in schools but it does not see all areas as equally important. As is shown in the table above, teaching basic academic skills and critical thinking/problem solving received just over one-third of the total emphasis. This is certainly a large share, but not so much more important that the public would be satisfied if all other areas were ignored.

There were a few people who did express that they expected schools to focus the majority of their attention on academic skills. But these respondents were in the minority. Only 5% of the respondents allocated 50 or more points to the basic academic skills category and just 2 people allocated all 100 of their points to this category. Less than 1% of the respondents allocated 50 or more points to the critical thinking and problem solving category. If one combines these two areas together as a broader "academics" area, approximately 22% of the respondents allocated 50 or more points to academics. Again, this demonstrates that a large majority of respondents view academics as important, but do not expect schools to make this their overwhelming focus. The poll indicates that the general public disagrees with political leaders and educational leaders who frequently discuss the need to increase focus on improving academic outcomes without any mention of the other goal areas of public education. Instead, they expect that academics are an important part of education, but should not be the sole focus of the public education system. However, it does not seem that this public voice is part of the current policy debates focused on increased accountability for academic scores alone.

The public also expressed that they expected schools to make a significant contribution to the development of students' social skills and work ethic. It is possible that the public recognizes that skills such as one's ability to get along with others and personal responsibility are becoming increasingly important in our ever-changing economy and for this reason, they expect schools to make a significant contribution to the development of skills in this area.

The public seems most split on its expectations in the area of emotional health. Indeed, some respondents expressed that they do not expect the public schools to develop this area at all. Almost 8% of the respondents allocated no points to this goal area. More respondents allocated zero

points to this goal than any other. However, most people (approximately 65%) expressed that they expected schools to develop students' emotional health but to a more limited extent by allocating under 10 points.

Citizenship, which many early political leaders felt was the most important goal for public education, received less emphasis by the public today. Yet the public still expects that schools will contribute to the development of citizenship skills in students. Over 80% of the public allocated between 5 and 15 points to this area. The public expects that schools pay some attention to this area.

The goal for which the public expects the least amount of emphasis by schools is the development of skills in the arts and literature. Only 1% of respondents allocated more than 20 points to this goal area. This seems to imply that the public does not want this goal ignored, but does not expect that great emphasis would be placed on this area.

Lastly, much of the media and political rhetoric focuses on increasing college attendance to raise the international competitiveness of the United States. Lost in this discussion is the reality that many jobs do not require a college degree. But the public seems to recognize this fact and thus allocated just over 10% of their total points on to the vocational goal.

Conclusion

The seeming perpetual failure of schools to reach the goals of education has led some to argue that democratic governance of the public system is the problem (Chubb & Moe, 1990). The public too seems to indicate that they are losing faith in their public schools and have turned increasingly to the exit option. Plank and Boyd (1994) discuss this trend and note that there is a sentiment of "antipolitics" today where reforms seek to "move educational issues out of the realm of politics and public debate" (p. 265). There is an increasing willingness to turn over popular control of the public schools system to private interests through reforms such as vouchers and other privatizations efforts which place the locus of control in the hands of parents who then make private decisions for their individual children.

The loss of the public education system as a democratically run institution necessarily impacts the lessons we teach our next generation about what it means to participate as citizens. While exit must certainly exist, as Hirshman points out, it cannot completely replace voice if we hope to see real improvement in our schools. Understanding what the people have to say about their public schools is critical if we hope to maintain satisfaction and loyalty such that voice can become activated. Thus far, we have done a poor job of asking the public to contribute their voice in meaningful ways. However, when asked questions that have been well-crafted, the voice of the people can provide policy makers with important direction.

In part, the lack of work in this area stems from the belief that politics should be removed from education. This view of politics is rooted in the notion that politics is about "wheeling and dealing, backroom maneuvering, and ... corruption" (Stone, Henig, Jones, & Pierannunzi, 2001, p. 3). Given this, many have worked keep politics out of education policy rather than study how and where it works best. But politics need not be defined so negatively. Politics can also mean "activity by which a diverse citizenry reconcile, put aside, or in some manner accommodate their differences in order to pursue their common well-being" (Stone et al., 2001, p. 8). Rather than shun politics from education, we must find ways to understand how our diverse citizenry speaks about its public education system and how they reconcile different opinions such that policy makers can be responsive to their constituents and preserve the collective nature of public education. Ultimately, we need to understand how and when these different opinions work together to improve education policy and build support for the public education system. And when they do not, we should want to know how we can turn this tide.

Future Research on Public Opinion and Education

Because the field of public opinion and education has remained largely understudied, there is much work to be done. However, attention to following areas would certainly contribute to our understanding of how we can bring the public's voice back into educational policy debates.

The Need for Subnational Data While the majority of public opinion polling occurs at the national level, education policies are often crafted at the state level. For this reason, it is important that scholars of public opinion and education examine state-level polls. Unfortunately, as a recent review of research on state polling notes, "scholars of U.S. state politics have been in the data-scrounging business for decades" (Parry, Kisida, & Langley, 2008, p. 198). While some data do exist, often these data have been collected by campaigns, parties, or media and thus, are not always shared for scholarly research. Moreover, polls conducted for these political purposes often do not contain the kinds of questions researchers would need for analysis. Further complicating subnational data is the fact that cross-state comparisons cannot be made if question wording is altered across states or if questions are asked at different time points. Therefore, Parry et al. urge for better coordination between state level polls. Educational researchers can join in these efforts to coordinate state-level polling so that important comparative work can be done. It would be helpful to know whether there is a wide variety of opinions across states on educational issues and if so, does this make some state populations more likely to comply with federal regulations.

Variation among Sub-Populations Early public opinion researchers Lazarsfeld, Berelson, and Gaudet (1948) noted that "a person thinks, politically, as he is, socially" (p. 27). Therefore, in addition to comparisons across states, scholars of public opinion and educational issues need to pay at-

tention to variation among different subgroups. In order to do so, expanded sample sizes will be needed as a standard national poll typically does not contain enough cases for careful analysis of demographic subgroups.

One of the most enduring and thoroughly documented political cleavages in the United States is between African Americans and non-Hispanic Whites. In an era in which, paradoxically, there is an increasing presence of minorities in formerly all-White suburban neighborhoods and schools, *and* schools are growing more racially segregated due to the rapid re-segregation of central cities and inner suburbs (Frey, 2001), it is important to understand how these changes affect public attitudes towards educational policies. The racial composition of the United States and its under-18 population in particular is undergoing rapid transformation due, in part, to higher birth rates for Latinos and has major effects on the racial contexts of public schools. Limited research has found that race is a significant predictor of support for educational spending even after controlling for other demographic factors such as income and age (Brown & Saks, 1985; Tedin, Matland, & Weiher, 2001). Future studies should continue to explore these relationships and include greater attention to the changing nature of different racial and ethnic sub groups. Attention to these issues will require that scholars commission their own public opinion polls that contain the needed over samples of racial and ethnic subgroups so that rigorous analysis may be completed.

The role that age plays in support for educational funding is one of the few topics that has been debated by public opinion scholars. Some see the aging population as the "grey peril" for educational funding (Preston, 1984). Because the elderly no longer have children in the public school system, raising taxes to support education is not in their direct self-interest. Thus, a common finding has been that age is a significant and negative predictor of support for educational funding. But the relationship between age and support for public school funding has become increasingly complex as researchers delve into the self-interest hypothesis. The lack of support for additional funding faded in one study when questions moved from the more general to the more specific (Ponza, Duncan, Corcoran, & Groskind, 1988). Further, Berkman and Plutzer (2004) found that when the number of years of residence was controlled for—thus testing a loyalty hypothesis—the lack of support decreased; it was the older respondents who had recently moved to a new location that were far less supportive of educational funding initiatives. Such issues should continue to be explored and updated as the population ages.

As noted above, large, urban school districts face unique challenges. People who live in these areas may have significantly different views regarding educational policy issues than those who live in suburban or rural communities. How these different groups think about educational issues is currently unknown. But the divide may not be as great as one might assume. As mentioned above, an increasing number of suburban schools have been labeled in need of improvement. For this reason, the views of suburban residents may be changing as the number of schools which are labeled as failing becomes wider.

Not all voices are heard equally in our political system (Bartels, 2002; Verba, Schlozman, & Brady, 1995). Therefore, an understanding of how opinions on educational policy issues vary among different demographic populations is important to understand how different populations may respond to new policy initiatives.

Stability of Public Opinion on Educational Issues As national attention to education has grown, so has the range and number of new educational policies. How do these new policies shape opinions? In particular, efforts to make schools more accountable have led to increased efforts to provide the public with data regarding school achievement. For example, No Child Left Behind has mandated that the public be provided with objective measures of reading and math performance for every school. Such data are published annually in the form of school "report cards." Are policies that are aimed at providing the public with evidence regarding public school outcomes affecting how the public views their education system? Do such data lead to further erosion of confidence or do they provide the public with examples of growth and improvement such that they boost confidence in the public system?

Responsiveness of Educational Leaders Key (1961) stated that "unless mass views have some place in the shaping of policy, all the talk about democracy is nonsense" (p. 7). Ultimately, we want to study public opinion so we can understand how it does or does not shape policy. In education, policy is created and/or shaped by many policy actors. However, two main groups are formally charged with educational policy and are held accountable by the public for their decisions: state legislators and school board members. These representatives are responsible for deliberating on policies that impact public education and in doing so, they have a responsibility to represent the interests of the people. Representatives should "look after the public interest and be responsive to public opinion, except insofar as nonresponsiveness can be justified in terms of the public interest" (Pitkin, 1967, p. 224). Few studies exist of responsiveness on educational issues to test whether representatives are actually representing the views of the people (see Berkman & Plutzer, 2004, for one of the few examples). Do state legislators consider constituents views on educational issues? If so, when do they listen? To whom do they listen? While studies of responsiveness of state and national legislators have been completed for other policy issues, these important questions remain unanswered for education.

School board members are directly responsible for creating and carrying out educational policy. However, since the 1970s, studies of schools boards have faded and are "startling sparse" (Howell, 2005). In the 1970s, some scholars debated the responsiveness of school boards to their local constituents. Boyd (1976) suggested that school boards "may well be *more*, rather than *less*, responsive than most other branches of local government" because public schools "stand out as peculiarly conspicuous and accessible" (p. 574). Yet this suggestion of greater school board responsiveness has not been rigorously examined in the past few decades. Changes in school board composition over the past few decades, as well as increased state authority in public education, may yield different conclusions than those of scholars in the 1970s. Returning to questions of how school boards do or do not respond to their local constituents would certainly contribute to our understanding of the way in which the voice of the people is considered by local officials. Bringing the opinions of the people into both scholarly and policy debates is critical if we hope to garner sustained support for those new initiatives needed to improve the public educational system.

Notes

1. Whether this public education "crisis" in confidence is warranted has been debated (see, e.g., Berliner & Biddle, 1995; Rothstein, 1998).
2. Ohio currently has two voucher programs: The Cleveland Scholarship and Tutoring Program and The Ohio Educational Choice Scholarship Program (EdChoice).
3. The exception to this is the public's views on school funding and support for school bonds referendums. For a review of this literature, see Berkman and Plutzer (2004).
4. Those without Internet service are provided with WebTV hardware so that the sample is not biased in favor of those with preexisting Internet access. However, there is a slight overrepresentation of those in the middle income categories and slight underrepresentation of those in the upper income categories in the KN panel. Additionally, those over 64 are slightly underrepresented. To correct for these variations, the final sample from the Knowledge Networks panel was weighted using the Current Population Survey to correct for this variation.
5. The response rate for this study must also include the response rate for the initial panel solicitation. For the initial contact, 56% agreed to join the panel when they received the phone call for recruitment. Eighty percent of those who agreed to join the panel allowed the hardware needed to participate in the panel to be installed. This results in an overall response rate of 29%. While the final response rate may appear low when calculated in this way, the benefits gained by using the online format outweigh this drawback.
6. The order in which the goals were presented was randomized by the computer to prevent any bias due to ordering effects.
7. Exact question wording was as follows: "We would now like you to think about how important you feel the following goals are. In this question we would like you to allocate a total of 100 points across the eight goals based on the level of importance you feel each should receive."
8. To avoid the loss of invalid answers (those that did not sum to 100), the online mode supported respondents in accurately completing this task by alerting respondents if their sum did not total 100. This enabled respondents to revise their responses and resubmit. The computer system would allow a respondent to move on even if the allocation exceeded 100 points if the respondent clicked "enter" two times. Approximately 1% of all respondents who completed this exercise allocated more than 100 points even after receiving the prompt. These respondents were dropped from the analysis.

References

Abernathy, S. F. (2005). *School choice and the future of American democracy*. Ann Arbor: The University of Michigan Press.

Allen, A., & Plank, D. N. (2005). School board election structure and democratic representation. *Educational Policy, 19*, 510–527.

Alwin, D., & Krosnick, J. (1985). The measurement of values in surveys: A comparison of ratings and rankings. *Public Opinion Quarterly, 49*, 535–552.

Asher, H. (2001). *Polling and the public: What every citizen should know* (5th ed.). Washington, DC: CQ Press.

Bartels, L. (2002). *Economic inequality and political representation*. New York: Russell Sage Foundation. Retrieved January 17, 2007, from http://www.russellsage.org/publications/workingpapers/bartels2/document

Berkman, M., & Plutzer, E. (2004). *Ten thousand democracies: Politics and public opinion in America's school districts*. Washington, DC: Georgetown University Press.

Berliner, D. C., & Biddle, B. J. (1995). *The manufactured crisis: Myths, fraud, and the attack on America's public schools*. New York: Perseus Books.

Boyd, W. L. (1976). The public, the professionals and educational policy-making: Who governs? *Teachers College Record, 77*, 539–577.

Brown, B., & Saks, D. (1985). The revealed influence of class, race and ethnicity on local public school expenditures. *Sociology of Education, 58*, 181–190.

Campbell, A., Converse, P., Miller, W., & Stokes, D. (1960). *The American voter*. Chicago: University of Chicago Press.

Cappelli, P. (2001). The national employer survey: Employer data on employment practices. *Industrial Relations, 40*, 635–647.

Center on Education Reform. (2008a). *K-12 facts*. Retrieved May 12, 2008, from http://www.edreform.com/index.cfm?fuseAction=section&pSectionID=15&cSectionID=97

Center on Education Reform. (2008a). School choice programs. Retrieved October 21, 2008, from http://www.edreform.com/index.cfm?fuseAction=document&documentID=2880

Chubb, J. E., & Moe, T. M. (1990). *Politics, markets and America's schools*. Washington, DC: The Brookings Institution.

Converse, J., & Presser, S. (1986). *Survey questions: Handcrafting the standardized questionnaire*. London: Sage.

Converse, P. (1964). The nature of belief systems in mass publics. In D. Apter (Ed.), *Ideology and discontent* (pp. 206–261). New York: Free Press.

Frey, W. H. (2001, June). *Melting pot suburbs: A census 2000 study of suburban diversity*. Ann Arbor: University of Michigan, Populations Study Center.

Friedman, M. (1962). The role of government in education. In M. Friedman (Ed.), *Capitalism and freedom* (pp. 85–107). Chicago: University of Chicago Press.

Gallup Organization. (1936). *Survey results by Gallup Organization, December 2–December 7, 1936*. Washington, DC: Author.

Gallup Organization. (1938). *Survey results by Gallup Organization, December 25–December 30, 1938*. Washington, DC: Author.

Gallup Organization. (1977). *Survey results by Gallup Organization, January–January 10, 1977*. Washington, DC: Author.

Gallup Organization. (1994). *National Association of Music Merchants poll results, March 21–April 11, 1994*. Washington, DC: Author.

Gallup Organization. (2007). *Survey results by Gallup Organization, January 15–January 18, 2007*. Washington, DC: Author.

Glaser, M. A., & Hildreth, W. B. (1999). Service delivery satisfaction and willingness to pay taxes: Citizen recognition of local government performance. *Public Productivity and Management Review, 23*, 48–67.

Hess, F. M. (1999). *Spinning wheels: The politics of urban school reform*. Washington, DC: Brookings Institution Press.

Hirschman, A. O. (1970). *Exit, voice, and loyalty: Responses to decline in firms, organizations, and states*. Cambridge, MA: Harvard University Press.

Hochschild, J., & Scott, B. (1998). Trends: Governance and reform of public schools in the United States. *Public Opinion Quarterly, 62*, 79–120.

Howell, W. G. (2005). Introduction. In W. G. Howell (Ed.), *Besieged: School boards and the future of education politics* (pp. 1–23). Washington, DC: Brookings Institution.

Key, V. O., Jr. (1961). *Public opinion and American democracy*. New York: Alfred A. Knopf.

Krosnick, J., & Alwin, D. (1988). A test of the form-resistant correlation hypothesis: Ratings, rankings, and measurement of values. *Public Opinion Quarterly, 52*, 526–538.

Labaree, D. (1997). Public goods, private goods: The American struggle over educational goals. *American Educational Research Journal, 34*, 39–81.

Lazarsfeld, P., Berelson, B., & Gaudet, H. (1948). *The people's choice: How the voter makes up his mind in a presidential campaign*. New York: Columbia University Press.

Levi, M., & Stoker, L. (2000). Political trust and trustworthiness. *Annual Review of Political Science, 3*, 475–507.

Levin, H. M. (1987). Education as a public and private good. *Journal of Policy Analysis and Management, 6*, 628–641.

Loveless, T. (1997). The structure of public confidence in education. *American Journal of Education, 105*, 127–159.

McDonnell, L. M. (2000). Defining democratic purposes. In L. M. McDonnell, P. M. Timpane, & R. Benjamin (Eds.), *Rediscovering the democratic purposes of education* (pp. 1–18). Lawrence: University of Kansas Press.

Mintrom, M. (2001). Educational governance and democratic practice. *Educational Policy, 15*, 615–643.

Monroe, A. (1998). Public opinion and public policy, 1980–1993. *Public Opinion Quarterly, 62*, 6–28.

National Center for Education Statistics (NCES). (2005). *The condition of education 2005* (NCES 2005-094). Washington, DC: Author.

National Center for Education Statistics (NCES). (2006). *The condition of education 2006* (NCES 2006-071). Washington, DC: Author.

Newton, K., & Norris, P. (1999, September). *Confidence in public institutions: Faith, culture or performance?* Paper presented at the annual meeting of the American Political Science Association, Atlanta, GA.

Nye, J. S., Jr. (1997). Introduction: The decline of confidence in government. In J. S. Nye, Jr., P. D. Zelikow, & D. C. King (Eds.), *Why people don't trust government* (pp. 1–18). Cambridge, MA: Harvard University Press.

Orren, G. (1997). Fall from grace: The public's loss of faith in government. In J. S. Nye, Jr., P. D. Zelikow, & D. C. King (Eds.), *Why people don't trust government* (pp. 77–108). Cambridge, MA: Harvard University Press.

Parry, J. A., Kisida, B., & Langley, R. E. (2008). The state of state polls: Old challenges, new opportunities. *State Politics and Policy Quarterly, 8*, 198-216.

Pitkin, H. F. (1967). *The concept of representation*. Berkeley: University of California Press.

Plank, D. N., & Boyd, W. L. (1994). Antipolitics, education and institutional choice: The flight from democracy. *American Educational Research Journal, 31*, 263–281.

Ponza, M., Duncan, G., Corcoran, M., & Groskind, F. (1988). The guns of autumn? Age differences in support for income transfers to the young and old. *Public Opinion Quarterly, 52*, 441–466.

Preston, S. (1984). Children and the elderly: Divergent paths for America's dependents. *Demography, 21*, 435–457.

Putnam, R. D. (2000). *Bowling alone: The collapse and revival of American community*. New York: Simon and Schuster.

Reading is Fundamental. (1988). *Poll results, February 6–February 26, 1988*. Washington, DC: Author.

Rose, L., & Gallup, A. (2000). The 32nd annual Phi Delta Kappa/Gallup Poll of the public's attitudes toward the public schools. *Phi Delta Kappan, 82*, 41–58.

Rose, L., & Gallup, A. (2006). The 38th annual Phi Delta Kappan/Gallup Poll of the public's attitudes toward the public schools. *Phi Delta Kappan, 88*, 41–56.

Rothstein, R. (1998). *The way we were? The myths and realities of America's student achievement*. New York: Century Foundation Press.

Stone, C. N., Henig, J. R., Jones, B. D., & Pierannunzi, C. (2001). *Building civic capacity: The politics of reforming urban schools*. Lawrence: University Press of Kansas.

Stullich, S., Eisner, E., & McCrary, J. (2008). *National Assessment of Title I: Final report*. Washington, DC: Institute for Education Sciences.

Sudman, G., Bradburn, N., & Schwarz, N. (1996). *Thinking about answers: The application of cognitive processes to survey methodology*. San Francisco: Jossey-Bass.

Tedin, K., Matland, R., & Weiher, G. (2001). Age, race, self-interest and financing public schools through referenda. *Journal of Politics, 63*, 270–294.

Time, Cable News Network, & Yankelovich Partners. (2001). *Presidential election poll, January 10–January 11, 2001*. Chapel Hill, NC: Authors.

Verba, S., Schlozman, K. L., & Brady, H. E. (1995). *Voice and equality: Civic voluntarism in American politics*. Cambridge, MA: Harvard University Press.

Wagoner, J. L., Jr. (2004). *Jefferson and education*. Chapel Hill: University of North Carolina Press.

Washington, G. (1966). First annual address. In F. L. Israel (Ed.), *The State of the Union messages of the presidents: Vol. 1, 1790–1860* (pp. 2–4). New York: Chelsea House-Robert Hector Publishers. (Original address given 1790)

Yang, K., & Holzer, M. (2006). The performance-trust link: Implications for performance measurement. *Public Administration Review, 66*, 114–126.

26

Assessment Policy and Politics of Information

Jane Clark Lindle
Clemson University

U.S. assessment policy has generated increasing political activity over nearly a generation at the state level and federal level. This writing coincides with legislative time limits on U.S. federal policy known as the No Child Left Behind (NCLB) Act of 2001, a 6-year-old reauthorization of the 1965 Elementary and Secondary Education Act (ESEA). Although 2008 is the deadline for NCLB reauthorization, Congressional consideration suffers disruption by the U.S. presidential election. NCLB provides fertile ground for contention due to its omnibus nature affecting several aspects of federal education policy, including assessments. This chapter focuses on current political attention to NCLB assessment policy issues and the degree to which *political discourse* analysis illuminates the implementation and redesign of U.S. federal assessment policy.

Political discourse analysis derives from the political sciences and contrasts with policy analysis conducted by assessment experts who use the technical core of psychometrics (Beck, 2007; Cizek, 2001, 2005). Multiple sources provide a substantial foundation for understanding the technical questions associated with testing students and assessing the efficacy of public education systems (e.g., Cuban, 2004; Gipps, 1999; Hamilton, 2003; Haertel & Herman, 2005; Heck, 2006; Hursh, 2005; Linn, 2005a, 2005b; McDonnell, 1994; Wainer, 2004; Wiliam, 2000). Political actors, agencies, and professional organizations offer recommendations for addressing assessment requirements. These multiple sets of voices intersect in the policy arena as political discourse and shape policy agenda (Baumgartner & Jones, 1993; Birkland, 2001; Jones & Baumgartner, 2005; Kingdon, 2003; Sabatier & Jenkins-Smith, 1993, 1999).

Given the immediate environment for U.S. educational policy and politics, this chapter provides a snapshot of a dynamic set of political trends impacting assessment policy. This snapshot uses a narrow scope, the implementation of NCLB from 2002–2008. A brief overview of NCLB sets the context for analysis of the political discourse concern-

ing assessment. Next, a summary of literature sketching the political influence of technical experts is presented. The next section of the chapter describes a common method from the political sciences, media analysis. The section includes sources from public print media assessment policy discourses. The chapter concludes with a projection of implications for the continued political agenda-setting discourse.

Assessment and No Child Left Behind

Assessment is the centerpiece of many accountability policies (Armstrong, 2002; Carnoy & Loeb, 2002; Elmore, Abelmann, & Fuhrman, 1996; Fuhrman, 1999, 2003; Goertz & Duffy, 2003; McDermott, 2007; McDonnell, 1994). Other than the tool of assessment, educational accountability policies also include mandates for curriculum interventions as well as personnel qualifications (Goertz, 2005; Wong & Nicotera, 2004, 2007). Because assessments typically received the highest weights in accountability formulae, test results can determine penalties, resources, or even public perceptions about schools, personnel, and students. Given this weighting, testing may be considered a potent policy instrument overshadowing other features of accountability policies (Hamilton, 2003; McDonnell, 1994).

The title of current U.S. legislation known as No Child Left Behind is derived from political discourse noted across years of U.S. test results. The catch-phrase, "no child left behind," refers to federal efforts to remedy persistent gaps in student achievement results in comparisons among majority student performance and groups of minority, low-income, English language learners, and students with disabilities. The evidence of lower performance among these groups was captured across repeated administrations of the National Assessment of Educational Progress (NAEP; Education Trust, 1996; Haycock, Jerald, & Huang, 2001; Lee, 2002). Since 1969, the National Center for Education Statistics (NCES) administered NAEP as a nationally representative test of student achievement ("About NAEP," 2007; "NAEP–Frequently Asked Questions," 2007).

By the late 1990s, the political discourse about federal allocations to elementary and secondary schools focused on NAEP results and remedies to address gaps through re-authorization of ESEA, known variously as America 2000, Improving America's Schools Act (IASA, P.L. 103-382) and Goals 2000: Educate America Act (P.L. 103-227; DeBray, McDermott, & Wohlstetter, 2005; McDonnell, 2005; Riddle & Stedman, 2001). By 1994, the existing version of ESEA required that states establish curriculum standards in academic subjects and an assessment and accountability system by 2001 (Council of Chief State School Officers, CCSSO, 2002; Education Commission of the States [ECS], 2002; Riddle & Stedman, 2001). Because several states were not ready to implement standards-based assessment and accountability systems by the 2000–2001 school year, reauthorization attached more specificity to requirements for the four students groups with historically lower achievement (CCSSO, 2002; DeBray, McDermott, & Wohlstetter, 2005; ECS, 2002; McDonnell, 2005; Riddle & Stedman, 2001). Given more specific attention to these groups, the reauthorization of ESEA in 2001 became known as the No Child Left Behind (NCLB) Act (P. L.107–110).

NCLB mandates that states have an accountability system that includes annual assessments of state-set standards in math, reading, and science, grades 3 through 8, and continued testing in those subjects at the secondary level (ECS, 2004). Also, states needed to define accountability through indicators of Adequate Yearly Progress (AYP) for the four groups of students for whom achievement exhibited historical lags (CCSSO, 2002; DeBray, McDermott, & Wohlstetter, 2005; ECS, 2002, 2004; McDonnell, 2005; Riddle & Stedman, 2001). The provisions for AYP depend on connections among assessment, standards, and accountability calculations. Table 26.1 shows different attempts to simplify NCLB mandates for implementation (ECS, 2004; Palmer & Coleman, 2003; U.S. Department of Education, 2004).

Both the ECS and U.S. Department of Education offered seven categories and around 40 decision points. At least one other Department of Education document highlighted even more NCLB provisions including establishing English Language Proficiency standards and assessments (U.S. Department of Education, 2005). CCSSO provided a work plan for states that divided NCLB into eight areas. These different versions demonstrate NCLB's complexity to which states had to respond.

At the state-level, complexity heightened because more than two-thirds of the states had some form of school or student accountability by 2000 (Carnoy & Loeb, 2002; Cobb, 2002, 2004; Goertz & Duffy, 2003). Yet, only a minority met earlier federal provisions or could retrofit into the new requirements of NCLB (Jennings, 2003). Research on both assessment and accountability across the states show wide divergence in rigor of standards and quality of assessments (Goertz, 2005; Goertz & Duffy, 2003; Heck, 2006; Linn, 2005a; National Center for Education Statistics, 2007). As a consequence of NCLB, some argue that standards have dropped in those states that had adopted educational accountability systems prior to NCLB (Koretz & Barton, 2003–2004; Linn, 2005b; National Center for Education Statistics, 2007). The distinction between *curriculum standards* and *performance standards* seems obscure even to some professional educators, much less to students, their parent/guardians, or the general public.

Curriculum standards can be called content or academic standards, core content frameworks, or expectations. Despite the varying terms, such standards refer to knowledge that students should acquire across subject matter and grade levels. These curriculum standards typically develop through some deliberative process, which differs across locales (Beck, 2007; Popkewitz, 2004; Popkewitz & Lindblad, 2004; Schafer, 2005). Colorado, Michigan, and New York state education agencies' Web sites offer examples of curriculum standards:

Colorado Model Content Standards for Reading and Writing:
STANDARD 1: Students read and understand a variety of materials. (Colorado Department of Education, 1995, p. 5)
Michigan Grade Level Content Expectations for third grade Math:

TABLE 26.1
NCLB Mandates and States' Decisions

Council of Chief State School Officers (Palmer & Coleman, 2003)	Education Commission of the States (2004)	U.S. Department of Education (2004)
• Accountability with 7 key issues/tasks • Standards and Assessments with 5 key issues/tasks • Teacher Quality with 2 key issues/tasks • Data and Reporting with 3 key issues/tasks • English Language Learners with 2 key issues/tasks • Students with Disabilities with 2 key issues/tasks • School Safety with 2 key issues/tasks • General Systemic Matters with 3 key issues/tasks	• Standards and Assessments with 11 requirements • Adequate Yearly Progress with 10 requirements • School Improvement with 7 requirements • Safe Schools with 3 requirements • Supplemental Services with 4 requirements • Report Cards with one requirement • Teacher Quality with 5 requirements	• Standards and Assessments with 2 decisions • AYP with 12 decisions • AYP and State Accountability with 7 decisions • Students with Special Needs with 4 decisions • AYP for unique schools with 2 decisions • Definition of Persistently Dangerous Schools with one decision • Highly Qualified Teachers with 9 decisions.

Number and Operations: Understand and use number notation and place value … Read and write numbers to 10,000 in both numerals and words, and relate them to the quantities they represent, e.g., relate numeral or written word to a display of dots or objects. (Michigan Department of Education, 2006, p. 3)

New York Elementary Science Curriculum:

STANDARD 1—Analysis, Inquiry, and Design:

Students will use mathematical analysis, scientific inquiry, and engineering designs, as appropriate, to pose questions, seek answers, and develop solutions. (New York State Department of Education, 2000, p. 5)

These samples show how states define knowledge students need to learn. In these three samples, the Colorado and New York examples show overall standards for reading/writing and science respectively. The Michigan example shows a specific task requirement for math in Grade 3. Other states variously structure content standards from broad descriptions of knowledge in subject areas to specific tasks across subject and grade level. Curriculum standards offer guidance on learning activities, but no measures of how well students might perform those activities.

Performance standards offer that level of measurement (Cizek, 2001; Crane & Winter, 2006). Performance standards are the degrees of performance on specific assessment or curriculum tasks deemed by some negotiated criteria as acceptable or unacceptable (Cizek, 2001, 2005; Haertel & Herman, 2005; Hamilton, 2003; Popkewitz, 2004). Multiple points of contention surround these deliberations (La Marca, Redfield, Winter, Bailey, & Despriet, 2000; Linn, 2005b; Linn, Baker, & Betebenner, 2002; Rothman, Slattery, Vranek, & Resnick, 2002).

One of the challenges in setting performance standards is the use of a scale that makes sense regardless of the grade level (Buckendahl, Huynh, Siskind, & Saunders, 2005; National Research Council, 1998). Standards-based assessments reference knowledge expectations that may be more narrowly prescribed in a specific grade and perhaps not referenced at all in succeeding grade levels (Cizek, 2005; Reckase, 2004). Even so, presumably success on one grade level's test should lay the foundation for success in the next grade (Buckendahl, Huynh, Siskind, & Saunders, 2005; Lissitz & Huynh, 2003).

Prior to NCLB, many states were sampling grade levels in their assessment rather than practicing yearly assessment (Carnoy & Loeb, 2002; Goertz & Duffy, 2003). The requirements of NCLB demand yearly testing from grades 3 through 8, mandating only three levels of performance standards (basic, proficient, and advanced; CCSSO, 2002; Cizek, 2005; Roeber, 2003). The following examples from state agency websites show variation in performance standards by the states of California, Kentucky, and Vermont:

Overall scores are reported on a scale ranging from 150 to 600. The CST results for each subject area tested also are reported by performance levels: advanced, proficient, basic, below basic, or far below basic. Each performance level indicates how well a student is achieving the state content standards tested. The state target is for all students to score at the proficient or advanced level on the CSTs. (California Department of Education, 2007, p. 1)

Kentucky's Commonwealth Accountability Testing System (CATS) reports statewide test results as percentages of students scoring at any of four performance levels: novice, apprentice, proficient and distinguished. Kentucky's goal is to reduce the number of students performing at the lowest of these levels (novice and apprentice), while increasing the number performing at the higher levels (proficient and distinguished). (Kentucky Department of Education, 2007)

[Florida] Achievement levels range from 1 to 5, with Level 1 being the lowest and Level 5 being the highest. (See Figure 26.1)

These examples show differences in the amount of detail explaining performance levels. California and Florida use five levels. California, like Kentucky, uses descriptive terms to differentiate among levels. California shows a scale range from 150 to 600 without explaining how its descriptors fit on to the scale. Kentucky's and Florida's explanations omit scaling information, although all three states have such information on other portions of their Web sites. These states' distribution of information surrounding performance levels provides evidence of the complexity of negotiating among stakeholders (Beck, 2007; Schafer, 2005).

The negotiated nature of performance standards means that all such criteria are arbitrary, even though some may be more reasonable or defensible than others (Cizek, 2005; Hamilton, 2003; Schafer, 2005). Developers must be wary of bias and unintended consequences (Crane & Winter, 2006; Stiggins, Arter, Chappuis, & Chappuis, 2004; U.S. Department of Education, 2003).

Standards development issues swirl, not just around alignment between curriculum and performance levels, but

Achievement Level Definitions	
Level 5	This student has success with the most challenging content of the *Sunshine State Standards*. A student scoring in Level 5 answers most of the test questions correctly, including the most challenging questions.
Level 4	This student has success with the challenging content of the *Sunshine State Standards*. A student scoring in Level 4 answers most of the test questions correctly, but may have only some success with questions that reflect the most challenging content.
Level 3	This student has partial success with the challenging content of the *Sunshine State Standards*, but performance is inconsistent. A student scoring in Level 3 answers many of the test questions correctly but is generally less successful with questions that are the most challenging.
Level 2	This student has limited success with the challenging content of the *Sunshine State Standards*.
Level 1	This student has little success with the challenging content of the *Sunshine State Standards*.

Figure 26.1 Achievement level definitions. *Source:* Florida Department of Education, 2005.

also policy entanglement of assessment with accountability (Carnoy & Loeb, 2002; Jennings, 2003; Riddle & Stedman, 2001). NCLB intensified the overlap of standards, assessment, and accountability with its requirement for AYP.

Appearing in the 1994 iteration of ESEA, AYP mandated state definitions and assessments for measuring student achievement in schools receiving Title 1 funds (Jennings, 2003; McDonnell, 2005; Riddle & Stedman, 2001). By 2000, two-thirds of the states had adopted some performance measures for AYP based on one of three approaches: (a) a cut-score for proficiency, (b) meeting an improvement target based on past performance, or (c) improvement of scores from the lowest performing group/s of students (Goertz & Duffy, 2003, p. 7). NCLB specified performance targets each year to be recalibrated every 3 years to ensure that all students reach proficiency by 2014. States had to ensure that their accountability systems triggered consequences for schools and districts failing to close achievement gaps. States' systems that featured one-dimensional reports of aggregate student results had to add reports for the four groups (Goldschmidt et al., 2005; Joint Study Group on Adequate Yearly Progress, 2002; Riddle & Stedman, 2001).

AYP requirements added complexity to states' accountability and assessment systems. State agencies then turned to help from assessment experts. With such expertise came a variety of perspectives on the demands of NCLB with potential for politicizing that discourse.

Expert Discourse on Assessment Policy

Policy makers and implementers turn to experts for insights into complex social issues (Baumgartner & Jones, 1993; Johnson, 1999; Kingdon, 2003). Because knowledge provides power, specialized expert knowledge creates a political platform, intended or not, for assessment experts (Beck, 2007; Buckendahl et al., 2005; Johnson, 1999; McDonnell, 1994; Sabatier & Jenkins-Smith, 1993). Despite insights experts can provide, and despite policy makers' appreciation or use of such insights, historically, the general public ignores expert advice (Bohman, 1999; Darmofal, 2005; Lau & Redlawsk, 2001). Some of the public suspicion, or ignorance, of expert advice stems from complexity (Goren, 1997; Johnson, 1999; Darmofal, 2005; Lau & Redlawsk, 2001; McDonnell, 1994). In turn, complexity of decision conditions shape experts' advice politically (Larocca, 2004; McDonnell, 1994; Shulock, 1999). Experts often engage in advocacy, partially because many experts provide services to organizations with political identifications and missions (Bane, 2001; Denham & Garnett, 2006; Shulock, 1999). Those organizations use technical and research-based information to frame policy discourse and the issues shaping policy agenda (Birkland, 2001; Jones & Baumgartner, 2005; Kingdon, 2003; Nelson & Oxley, 1999; Sabatier & Jenkins-Smith, 1993).

Assessment policy, in general, provides opportunities for involving experts in political deliberations surround-

ing decisions necessary in construction of assessment systems (McDonnell, 1994). By any count, the number of decisions associated with NCLB offers a complex deliberative environment (ECS, 2004; Palmer & Coleman, 2003; U.S. Department of Education, 2004). Therefore, policy discourse analysis permits insight into the degree to which assessment expertise engages NCLB's political discourse (McDonnell, 1994; McGuinn, 2006).

Political Discourse Analysis

Political discourse is fundamental to democratic policy processes (Dewey, 1954; Knight & Johnson, 1999; Nelson & Oxley, 1999; Opfer, 2007; White, 1994; Woolley, 2000). Political systems depend on information processing to establish policy agenda (Baumgartner, Green-Pedersen, & Jones, 2006; Glenn, 2007). Political discourse ranges from public media to policy elites, including technical experts (Jones & Baumgartner, 2004; Kingdon, 2003). In U.S. public education, the tensions over degrees of professional and public participation have been documented from schoolhouses to school boards to state houses and the U.S. Congress (Berkman & Plutzer, 2005; Spring, 1993; Wirt & Kirst, 1992). The use of evidence from academics and evaluators supposedly legitimizes political agendas (Glenn, 2007; Haas, 2007; Kingdon, 2003). One result of these actors' involvement is a presumptive political role for the expert sector (Glenn, 2007; Sabatier & Jenkins-Smith, 1993; Weaver & McGann, 2000). The political discourse surrounding educational assessment policy represents interaction among publics, professionals, and assessment experts.

A variety of methods support analysis of political discourse. Perhaps the most direct form, media content analysis, focuses on public media associated with the social construction of political agenda (Althaus, Edy, & Phalen, 2001; Anderson, 2007; White, 1994; Woolley, 2000). These analyses can range from thematic narrative to structural equations (Howlett & Rayner, 2006; White, 1994). Narrative analyses offer a way of situating policy discourse contextually while exposing how policy agenda is framed (Howlett & Rayner, 2006; Nelson & Oxley, 1999; White, 1994). The archives of *Education Week* and *LexisNexis* bibliographic database (2002–2008) provide narrative sources.

Data Sources *Education Week* offers print and Web formats and is one of several publications produced by Editorial Projects in Education ("About EPE," n.d.). EPE dates its origins to 1958 generating a series of communication texts from college alumni magazines' collaborative reports to the *Chronicle of Higher Education* in 1966 to *Education Week* in 1981. *Education Week* claims a subscription rate of at least 50,000 and an editorial policy aimed at K-12 school reform ("Editorial Projects in Education History," n.d.).

LexisNexis dates its origins to publishing archives created in the late 19th century. Today it is a comprehensive electronic bibliographic source claiming billions of documents. For the purposes of this work, the sources of interest included news outlets only. *Education Week* is listed among *LexisNexis's* archived news outlets. Because results of discourse analyses vary given content, such as editorial indexing, article titles, abstracts, or body text, the current analysis required confirmatory matching of titles with body text. This permitted a means of confirming results from selected terms given the methodological limits of content analysis of media (Althaus, Edy, & Phalen, 2001). To avoid confusion, *selected terms* and *terms of interest* refer to methodological search criteria. *Discourse concepts* refer to the results from the current analysis.

In the current era, the terms *assessment* and *accountability* are often conflated (Carnoy & Loeb, 2002; Resnick, 2006). Both terms were used in the selection criteria for news sources. As a delimiter for this analysis, the term *No Child Left Behind* was used to capture this moment in the discourse. Specific delimitation on news content was also achieved by confining the dates of publication to post-January 1, 2002.

In the *Education Week* archives, the combined terms of *assessment, accountability*, and *No Child Left Behind* yielded 517 articles and editorials from January 2002 through February 2008. These same terms in *LexisNexis* produced 699 articles across 126 newspapers. One-hundred thirty-three of those articles were from *Education Week*. The next largest source of news articles was the *Washington Post* with 36 items. The *Washington Post* is known for its large circulation and influence on policy discourses in a variety of political arenas across a number of sectors and agendas (Tedesco, 2005). Given its relevance to political discourse analysis concerning assessment policy and the fact that the rest of the newspapers each published less than 30 articles, the analysis was limited to *Education Week* and the *Washington Post* for a total of 169 published items.

Analysis Procedures Each article was downloaded in full text and read for relevance to emergent political agenda for NCLB assessment policy across state and national arenas. Themes were identified as points of contention, that is, *discourse concepts*, surrounding NCLB. While more than 50% of the *Washington Post* items included editorials provided by various individuals, the selected items from *Education Week* included only one editorial commentary.

The textual analysis sought quotes and/or statements attributed to specific sources.

Presumably, sources for the discourse concepts may be important to the policy-setting process. The sources of the political discourse were divided into the following agents: *political elites, professional elites*, and *assessment experts*. Political elites included elected officials and their appointees, such as government agency heads. Professional elites included those identified as permanent employees of professional or policy organizations. Assessment experts included those identified for their technical backgrounds and research-based résumés in assessment. The boundaries on these groups are somewhat permeable, if not overlapping, due to the way that individuals move from one sector to another. For example, in the earlier selected articles one person is quoted as a deputy of the U.S. Department of Education and in later articles identified as primary spokesperson for a DC-based think tank.

Descriptive Results Table 26.2 shows the distribution of quotes and attributions among the different sources. These results are reported as counts and percents within categories of sources.

Political elites dominated the sources with 918 attributions and quotes (57%). Most of those quotes and attributions traced directly to President George W. Bush (260, 26%) and his second appointment to Secretary of Education, Margaret Spellings (195, 21%). The various states' education agency officials offered the next largest group of sources (21%). Although 10 states had none, the rest of the states averaged around 4 among these texts. States with the most quotes/attributions included Connecticut (34), Texas (23), Delaware (18), California (13), and Tennessee (9). Most of Connecticut's discourse surrounded early phases of the implementation of NCLB, where Connecticut officials protested the cost of retooling their existing assessments. Although Utah's resistance to NCLB's implementation requirements was well-vetted in the early news items, most of these stories described state-level elected officials' positions with only eight attributions to the state education agency.

The category of professional elites provided a healthy source of quotes and attributions (33%). The vast majority (77%) came from 67 national organizations based mostly in Washington DC or nearby. These averaged about six

TABLE 26.2
Sources of Discourse and Frequency of Quotes/Attributions

Political Elites		Professional Elites		Assessment Experts	
National Elected	443	National Organization	409	University	130
National Appointed	226	State Organization	6	Institutes/Centers	33
State Elected	48	Local Organization	20	Total	163
State Appointed	195	Business	46		
Local Elected	6	Principals	25		
Total	918	Teachers	14		
		Students	13		
		Total	533		

quotes or attributions. The top groups providing quotes included Education Trust (50, 12%), CCSSO (47, 11%), National Education Association (NEA; 36, 8%), Center on Education Policy (26, 6%), and American Federation of Teachers (AFT; 20, 5%).

The assessment experts category provided about 10% of the attributions and quotes. At least 33 of the attributions and quotes were ascribed to 11 institutes, centers, and consortia based at 12 to 15 universities, as described by spokesperson's affiliation. Forty universities were represented among personnel quoted as professors or experts on assessment for the total of 130 attributions. The quotes/attributions averaged slightly more than 3 per university. The universities with the most included Stanford (19, 15%), Harvard (15, 11.5%), University of California, Los Angeles (8, 6%), and University of Pennsylvania (7, 5%).

Not surprisingly, the discourse about NCLB assessment was shaped primarily by political elites and national advocacy groups among the professional elites (Baumgartner & Leech, 2001). Table 26.3 shows the content of those quotes and attributions, the discourse concepts. The selection terms connected to discourse phrases at roughly 40% of each of the news sources. Across both news sources, accountability discourse covered models for calculating student and school success, such as status or absolute ratings. News items also showed recommendations for allowing growth models. The discourse phrases associated with *assessment* included issues associated with testing formats and recommendations about national testing. A fair number of articles described annual results from states' assessments per NCLB's requirements.

Discourse Concepts among Political Elites, Professional Elites, Assessment Experts *Standards* were often described in the reporting of the yearly assessment results. The term,

standards, also appeared as a political justification for NCLB. Sample quotes demonstrate such rhetorical use by political elites as well as assessment experts. For example, two editorials from the *Washington Post* show political elites' use. These editorials came from each party. From the Democrats' side, Senator Kennedy (2007) argued reauthorization noting:

> We need a national commitment to attract and keep our best teachers in the neediest classrooms and more rigorous and relevant standards that expect more of students and schools. (p. A15)

The Republican rhetoric differed little as in this example from former Florida Governor Jeb Bush and New York Mayor Michael Bloomberg (2006):

> Make standards meaningful. Ensure that every state sets a high standard for proficiency. The existing law left room for states to define proficiency levels, and some have dumbed them down to create the illusion of progress. We need a uniform measuring stick. (p. B07)

The single *Education Week* commentary supported the editorial positions of the two *Washington Post* examples. The *Education Week* commentary was an analysis by an individual, identified as an assessment expert, who offered insights into AYP requirements' possible exploitation:

> For example, some states have lowered the test scores that the states' students must earn to be classified as "proficient." … Those early low-level demands, however, mean that the final years of these "equal increment" timelines call for huge, altogether unrealistic annual improvements by students. …Some states, therefore, are requiring outlandishly large numbers of students to establish a subgroup's statistical reliability. (Popham, 2003)

TABLE 26.3
Discourse Concept Frequencies

Education Week			Washington Post		
Discourse Concepts	Occurrences	Percent	Discourse Concepts	Occurrences	Percent
Accountability	550	23.6	Accountability	110	23.7
Assessment	495	21.3	Standards	90	19.4
High schools	257	11.0	Assessment	78	16.8
Standards	256	11.0	High schools	33	7.1
AYP	244	10.5	AYP	28	6.0
Funding	138	5.9	Failing schools	27	5.8
Consequences	104	4.5	TQ	24	5.2
Flexibility	70	3.0	Consequences	24	5.2
Failing schools	59	2.5	Funding	18	3.9
Choice	58	2.5	Choice	15	3.2
ECE	54	2.3	Flexibility	12	2.6
TQ	35	1.5	ECE	5	1.1
Safe schools	4	0.2	Total	464	
Tech lit	2	0.1			
Total	2326				

As noted, the *Washington Post* items were dominated by editorials and assessment experts appear in news items only twice as follows:

Education specialists are divided on whether the federal law has succeeded in raising achievement for all students or in narrowing the historic achievement gaps between demographic groups....But some scholars do not credit the education law. NAEP scores, for example, rose in some states and fell in others, and the general upward trend began well before No Child Left Behind. "My general view of this is that the president has been serially dishonest in claiming that No Child is accomplishing its mission," said Bruce Fuller, a professor of education and public policy at the University of California at Berkeley. (Baker, 2007)

... Help low-income students perform better in public schools deemed in need of improvement by giving them tutors. And let the federal government pick up the tab... "Nobody really knows how effective the providers are in a highly valid way with regard to helping kids," said Steven M. Ross, director of the Center for Research in Educational Policy at the University of Memphis. He is helping several states devise statewide assessment tools. (Strauss, 2005)

Both of these quotes serve as evidence for questions about NCLB's efficacy. The appearance of assessment experts in *Education Week* also was slim, and results from that periodical begin with the quotes/attributions from the dominant groups of political and professional elites.

AYP emerged as a discourse concept concerning issues with two groups of historically low-scoring students, students with disabilities (SWD) and English-language learners (ELL). AYP discussion focused on overall participation of students and N-size, that portion of SWD that states can declare as a small-enough group to exclude from AYP.

The following set of quotes from political and professional elites reported by *Education Week* came early in NCLB's implementation process pertained to the general issues of participation-rates in the annual assessments:

Georgia was among the states where a big problem was an insufficient level of participation in state tests ... Nick Smith, a spokesman for the Georgia education department ... said officials there aim to work hard over the coming year to correct the problem ... Merchuria Chase Williams, the president of the Georgia Association of Educators, criticized..."A 95 percent [participation] rate is ludicrous." (Robelen, 2003)

A year later, *Education Week* reported that due to the U.S. Department of Education's relaxation of the 95% participation rate rule, Georgia and other states had fewer schools missing AYP (Olson, 2004). Since then, reauthorization projections generated controversy over N-size:

Nancy Reder, the director of governmental relations for the National Association of State Directors of Special Education in Alexandria, Va., said... "We need to have high expectations for students with disabilities, but we also need to have an element of realism"... however, Candace Cortiella,

the director of the Marshall, Va.-based Advocacy Institute ... said she was disappointed to see the testing flexibility in the draft ... allows too many students with disabilities to take easier tests. (Samuels, 2007)

Meeting AYP for both SWD and ELL proved an ongoing challenge as in this quote justifying such pressure:

Another prominent advocate for the law acknowledges that schools are having a hard time ensuring that special education students and English-language learners reach the achievement levels set under the law ... designed to force educators to pay attention to students who otherwise might not be presented with challenging curricula, said Kati Haycock, the director of the Education Trust ..."We make them acknowledge that they have to have better services for special education kids or ELL kids." (Hoff, 2007b)

In an *Education Week* article about bilingual education, a research-validated approach to increased English language acquisition, professional elites noted the ways in which NCLB mandates depress the use of bilingual education:

California's 55,000-student Santa Ana Unified School District served 6,000 English-learners in bilingual programs in the 2002–03 school year, but now has only 800 students ... Howard M. Bryan, the director of English-language development and bilingual programs, said ... Because of the need to test students in English for both state and federal accountability systems, he doubts that most principals want to return to offering such programs. (Zehr, 2007b)

The suggestions on the table for reauthorization provisions aimed at ELL drew mixed reactions:

The idea of requiring assessments in the native language drew the strongest early reactions last week from ELL advocates. Mari B. Rasmussen, the director of programs for English-learners in North Dakota, called the proposal "ridiculous" because at least 10 percent of her state's ELLs come from Ojibwa-speaking homes and, presumably, the state would have to create a test in that Native American language. But Peter Zamora, the Washington regional counsel for the Mexican American Legal Defense and Educational Fund, favored the requirement, saying it might encourage more school districts to implement bilingual education. (Zehr, 2007a)

Political and professional elites populate NCLB's political discourse. Assessment experts served a couple of roles: (a) reactors and critics of the political and professional elites' opinions or actions and (b) translators for complexity of accountability models. Rarely did the attributions and quotes appear instigated by the work of assessment experts.

Education Week's quotes and attributions to assessment experts served as a check and balance on the claims of political elites, as in these examples:

"No Child Left Behind is working," Ms. Spellings declared in a statement ... Mr. Porter [the dean of the University of Pennsylvania graduate school of education and a member of the National Assessment Governing Board, which sets policy for NAEP] and other experts, however, are skeptical of attempts to link rising or falling NAEP scores to the nearly 6-year-old law … Those who seek to establish that connection, he said, ignore the potential positive or negative impact on test scores brought by myriad state and local education efforts, many under way before the federal law took effect…"The problem is, you'd have to say, 'The only thing in play here has been No Child Left Behind.'" (Cavanaugh & Manzo, 2007)

"Over the past four years, 'No Child' proponents have made very strong claims that this reform is raising student achievement," said lead author Bruce Fuller, a professor of education and public policy at the University of California, Berkeley, and the director of the Policy Analysis for California Education research center based at Berkeley and Stanford University. "In fact, after NCLB, earlier progress made by the states actually petered out." (Cech, 2007c)

Throughout the 2002–2008 period of NCLB's implementation, several questionable incidents encircled testing. Assessment experts were called upon to explain the likelihood of intentional misconduct versus genuine mistakes.

Although reports of cheating on standardized tests are not uncommon across the country, the extent of the allegations in Texas appear [sic] to be unprecedented…"This is an ethical failure on the part of the U.S. education system, not just on Texas," said Daniel Koretz, a testing researcher at Harvard University. "There isn't an expectation in this country that we will carefully evaluate the impact of holding people accountable for scores." (Manzo, 2005)

"[Testing companies] work hard, and they know what they're doing," said David Miller, a professor of educational psychology at the University of Florida who writes often about assessment. "With the amount of testing going on … It doesn't take much for problems to appear." (Cech, 2007a)

In the complexity of determining AYP, assessment experts encouraged alternative models for assessing improvement, not just the NCLB-required status model.

… Steven Rivkin, an economist at Amherst College in Massachusetts … [said] the way schools are now judged "is just clearly wrong, and my sense is using the value-added or growth models is going to get you closer to the right answer." Rob Meyer, who directs a center on value-added research at the University of Wisconsin-Madison, agreed: "The attainment model is so obviously flawed that we ought to work really hard to figure out whether we can get value-added to work." (Olson, 2005a)

Twenty states applied for the [pilot] program [for growth models], and proposals from eight states were forwarded to a panel of reviewers … Eric A. Hanushek, a senior fellow at the Hoover Institution at Stanford University and the head of the review panel … said that a major factor in evaluating the plans submitted by the states was that they must have proposed to get all students to proficiency by the NCLB deadline of 2014. (Samuels & Davis, 2006)

Nebraska's resistance to participating in NCLB requirements, like many states, was associated with its pre-NCLB initiatives (Borja, 2007). In Nebraska's case, the state had made an investment in teacher-developed assessments, known as School-based Teacher-led Assessment and Reporting System, or STARS. One unintended consequence of high-stakes accountability testing may have been the suppression of more immediate measures of student learning. Formative assessments typically refer to ongoing tests of student performance at the classroom, school, or district levels. Eventually, assessment experts appeared in the emergent discourse on formative assessments. Assessment experts' quotes and attributions emerged in this discourse.

"I do believe that three years from now, certainly five years from now, no one will remember a time when there weren't benchmarks," said Robert E. Slavin, the director of the Center for Data-Driven Reform in Education, at Johns Hopkins University…Lorrie A. Shepard, the dean of the school of education at the University of Colorado at Boulder … [suggested] Good benchmark assessments … should include rich representations of the content students are expected to master, be connected to specific teaching units, provide clear and specific feedback to teachers so that they know how to help students improve, and discourage narrow test-preparation strategies. (Olson, 2005b)

Call them "formative," "internal," or "enhanced,"… a new wave of federally financed assessments being piloted this fall in 10 states … are a sign … that standardized end-of-grade tests are not the end-all …"It's a conceptual shift," said Elliot Weinbaum, a researcher at the University of Pennsylvania's Consortium for Policy Research in Education. (Cech, 2007b)

In summary, the political discourse revealed by this analysis of select newsprint media focused on NCLB assessment policy revealed dominance of the discourse by political and professional elites. Nevertheless, assessment experts provided about 10% of the quotes and attributions. In the mix of political discourse, assessment experts served a couple of functions: (a) check-and-balance on political, or professional, rhetoric about policy successes or defeats and (b) interpreters of assessment/accountability policy initiatives or unintended outcomes. In very rare instances, assessment experts promoted policy direction such as expansion of accountability models and formative and summative testing.

Agenda for Policy Research

… NCLB's emphasis on testing and accountability would remain the center of federal K-12 policy under a new … president, said Ms. McDonnell, the UC-Santa Barbara political scientist. "The horse is out of the barn. Whatever happens, we're going to have a pretty heavily testing-driven accountability system," she said. "It's pretty deeply embedded now in state institutions." (Hoff, 2007a)

Psychometrics is now a politicized field due to U.S. assessment policy. Evidence from other countries suggests that this is a global phenomenon (Black & Wiliam, 2005). The results of this analysis demonstrate that today's assessment experts have a role in political discourse about policy consequences as they appear in media to react to political rhetoric and/or to explain complex policy requirements. This analysis provided a bit of evidence that assessment experts also support policy initiatives, but begs the question of to what extent they may be more than reactors or commentators on test policy into the future. As the current assessment-driven accountability environment is sustained, how will assessment experts play their expanding role?

Analyses of accountability policy often point to the general intent that accountability assures equity in public school outcomes, especially for historically underserved and low-performing students (Delandshere, 2001; Fulton, 2007; McDermott, 2007). Nevertheless, other than reports on implementation status or unintended consequences, to date, no definitive claims link assessment policy to improved student outcomes. Will assessment experts choose to address this question publicly? Or will their role continue to be tweaking the details of test-construction and accountability calculations?

Professional elites have issued official positions setting agenda for NCLB's reauthorization debate (Fulton, 2007). Their accountability issues include at least three common areas of recommendations: (a) adequate funding for NCLB, (b) expansion of accountability models, and (c) flexibility for inclusion of students with disabilities and English language learners (Fulton, 2007). The latter two policy points offer room for participation of assessment experts.

Depending on the organization, demands for increased funding are spread across a number of related issues in accountability and assessment systems. Some of the requests are general issues of local capacity for building adequate responses to NCLB requirements. The new allocations would go to assessment development along with related data systems (Fulton, 2007; Thorn & Meyer, 2006). Allocations also are needed for intervention in the lowest performing and/or highest need students, schools, and districts (Fulton, 2007; Jennings & Rentner, 2006).

The recommendations for expansions of accountability models include a particular focus on growth models and the associated challenges of adequate data systems for the required growth model calculations (Burke & Christie, 2006; "Data Collection Booms," 2006; Fulton, 2007; Thorn & Meyer, 2006). Naturally, this relates to the lobbying for increased funding. Nevertheless the architecture of the data systems can prove a technical challenge and an opportunity for participation by assessment experts. The question remains to what degree these experts may be pulled in, at what point, and how proactive a role they may play in these designs.

Finally, the knottiest questions remain with inclusion of students with disabilities and English language learners among the groups associated with AYP requirements (Cox, Demczyk, & Nieberding, 2006; Koretz & Barton,

2003–2004). To some extent, these issues are matters associated with test-construction and administration. To another extent, these issues are represented in the agenda for calibrating models of accountability. At heart is the moral question concerning the adequacy of the services provided these students, of which, supposedly, the assessments are at least one measure. With accountability and assessment now inexorably intertwined in U.S. federal education policy, assessment experts face an increasing role in the policy discourse. Will this participation continue along the sidelines or will it move into a more influential position as assessment policy is sustained in the political agenda?

References

Note: References marked with an asterisk (*) indicate studies included in the meta-analysis.

About EPE. (n.d.). Retrieved February 15, 2008, from http://www2.edweek.org/info/about/

About NAEP. (2007). Retrieved February 15, 2008, from http://nces.ed.gov/nationsreportcard/about/

Althaus, S. L., Edy, J. A., & Phalen, P. F. (2001). Using substitutes for full-text news stories in content analysis: Which text is best? *American Journal of Political Science, 45*, 707–723.

Anderson, G. L. (2007). Media's impact on educational policies and practices: Political spectacle and social control. *Peabody Journal of Education, 82*(1), 103–120.

*Anderson, N. (2005, March 24). Scrutiny increases at ailing schools; 4 in Pr. George's may get assistance. *Washington Post,* Final metro edition, p. B01.

*Anderson, N. (2005, November 11). Md. test of English reveals wide gaps; Pr. George's falters; Howard leads state. *Washington Post,* Final edition, p. B01.

*Anderson, N. (2005, November 11). New Md. test of English shows wide disparities. *Washington Post,* Final edition, p. B06.

*Anderson, N. (2006, January 24). The 'No Child' Law's flexible enforcer; As she assesses progress, the Education Secretary who helped craft the measure develops a lighter touch. *Washington Post,* Final edition, p. A10.

*Anderson, N. (2006, February 25). Districts in Md. miss special-ed testing targets. *Washington Post,* p. B01.

*Anderson, N. (2006, August 20). Proposal to boost schools' offerings; Pr. George's chief would expand AP. *Washington Post,* Final edition, p. C01.

*Anderson, N., & Aratani, L. (2005, June 21). Maryland releases schools watch list; 39 in Prince George's face stricter oversight. *Washington Post,* Final edition, p. B01.

*Archer, J. (2005, May 25). States eyeing expense of hand-scored tests in light of NCLB rules. *Education Week, 24*(38), 1, 21.

Armstrong, J. (2002, May). "Next-generation" accountability models: Principles from interviews (3 p.). Education Commission of the States Briefing Paper. Retrieved July15, 2003, from http://www.ecs.org/clearinghouse/40/29/4029.htm

*Baker, P. (2007, September 27). An extra 'S' on the report card; Hailing a singular achievement, President gets pluralistic. *Washington Post,* Met 2 Edition, p. A10.

Bane, M. J. (2001). Expertise, advocacy and deliberation: Lessons from welfare reform. *Journal of Policy Analysis and Management, 20,* 191–197.

Baumgartner, F. R., Green-Pedersen, C., & Jones, B. D. (2006). Comparative studies of policy agendas. *Journal of European Public Policy, 13,* 959–974.

Baumgartner, F. R., & Jones, B. D. (1993). *Agendas and instability in American politics.* Chicago: University of Chicago Press.

Baumgartner, F. R., & Leech, B. L. (2001). Interest niches and policy bandwagons: Patterns of interest group involvement in national politics. *The Journal of Politics, 63*, 1191–1213.

Beck, M. D. (2007). Review and other views: "Alignment" as a psychometric issue. *Applied Measurement in Education, 20*, 127–135.

Berkman, M. B., & Plutzer, E. (2005). *Ten thousand democracies: Politics and public opinion in America's school districts.* Washington, DC: Georgetown University Press.

Birkland, T. A. (2001). *An introduction to the policy process: Theories, concepts, and models of public policy making.* Armonk, NY: M. E. Sharpe.

Black, P., & Wiliam, D. (2005). Lessons from around the world: How policies, politics and cultures constrain and afford assessment practices. *The Curriculum Journal, 16*, 249–261.

Bohman, J. (1999). Democracy as inquiry, inquiry as democratic: Pragmatism, social science, and the cognitive division of labor. *American Journal of Political Science, 43*, 590–607.

Borja, R. R. (2007, February 21). Nebraska swims hard against testing's tides. *Education Week, 26*(24), 32–34.

*Bradley, A. (2005, May 25). Union campaigns to change how NCLB assesses progress. *Education Week, 24*(38), 4.

Buckendahl, C., Huynh, H., Siskind, T., & Saunders, J. (2005). A case study of vertically moderated standard setting for a state science assessment program. *Applied Measurement in Education, 18*, 83–98.

Burke, M., & Christie, K. (2006). *State data systems.* Denver, CO: Educational Commission of the States. Retrieved June 6, 2007, from http://mb2.ecs.org/reports/Report.aspx?id=913

*Bush, J., & Bloomberg, M. R. (2006, August 13). How to help our students; Building on the 'No Child' law. *Washington Post,* Final edition, p. B07.

California Department of Education. (2007, May). *Spotlight on STAR 2007: Standardized testing and reporting (STAR) program.* Retrieved February 15, 2008, from http://www.cde.ca.gov/ta/tg/sr/documents/spotlightstar.doc

Carnoy, M., & Loeb, S. (2002). Does external accountability affect student outcomes? A cross-state analysis. *Education Evaluation and Policy Analysis, 24*, 305–331.

*Cavanaugh, S. (2006, July 12). California study questions validity of gains under NCLB. *Education Week, 25*(42), 19.

*Cavanaugh, S. (2006, August 9). Perkins Bill is approved by Congress. *Education Week, 25*(44), 1, 27.

*Cavanaugh, S. (2007, May 23). Test gains reigniting old debate: Did NCLB law play a role in history, civics scores? *Education Week, 26*(38), 1, 16.

Cavanaugh, S., & Manzo, K. K. (2007, October 3). NAEP gains: Experts mull significance. *Education Week, 27*(6), 1, 16–17.

Cech, S. J. (2007a, June 13). Florida scoring glitch sparks broad debate. *Education Week, 26*(41), 19.

*Cech, S. J. (2007b, June 13). Nebraska moves to statewide reading, math exams. *Education Week, 26*(41), 18, 21.

*Cech, S. J. (2007c, August 1). 12-state study finds falloff in testing gains after NCLB. *Education Week, 26*(44), 9.

Cech, S. J. (2007d, August 15). 10-state pilot preparing teachers to develop tests. *Education Week, 26*(45), 10.

*Cech, S. J. (2008, January 30). Tests of tech literacy still not widespread despite NCLB goals. *Education Week, 27*(1), 1, 12.

*Chan, S. (2004, October 1). New D.C. learning standards weighed; Schools will adopt Mass. or Calif. Plan. *Washington Post,* Final edition, p. A19.

Cizek, G. J. (2001). *Setting performance standards: Concepts, methods, and perspectives.* Mahwah, NJ: Erlbaum.

Cizek, G. J. (2005). Adapting testing technology to serve accountability aims: The case of vertically moderated standard setting. *Applied Measurement in Education, 18*, 1–9.

Cobb, C. D. (2002, February). *Performance-based accountability systems for public education.* Retrieved February 15, 2008, from http://www.nhpolicy.org/reports/caseyreport.pdf

Cobb, C. D. (2004). Looking across the states: Perspectives on school accountability. *Educational Foundations, 18*(3/4), 59–79.

Colorado Department of Education. (1995). *Colorado model content standards: Reading and writing.* Retrieved February 15, 2008, from http://www.cde.state.co.us/cdeassess/documents/standards/reading.pdf

Council of Chief State School Officers (CCSSO). (2002). *No Child Left Behind Act: A description of state responsibilities.* Washington, DC: Division of State Services and Technical Assistance.

Cox, M. L., Demczyk, M. J., & Nieberding, J. J. (2006). Provision of testing accommodations for students with disabilities on statewide assessments: Statistical links with participation and discipline rates. *Remedial and Special Education, 27*(6), 346–354.

Crane, E., & Winter, P. C. (2006). *Setting coherent performance standards.* Retrieved February 15, 2008, from http://www.ccsso.org/publications/details.cfm?PublicationID=338

Cuban, L. (2004). Looking through the rearview mirror at school accountability. In K. A. Sirotnik (Ed.), *Holding accountability accountable: What ought to matter in public education* (pp. 18–34). New York: Teachers College Press.

Darmofal, D. (2005). Elite cues and citizen disagreement with expert opinion. *Political Research Quarterly, 58*, 381–395.

Data collection booms, but states need systems to use effectively. (2006, June 2). *Electronic Education Report, 13*(10), 4–5.

*Davis, M. R. (2005, February 9). Utah is unlikely fly in Bush's school ointment. *Education Week, 24*(22), 1, 21.

*Davis, M. R. (2006, May 3). Spellings addresses testing, NCLB issues. *Education Week, 25*(34), 27, 29.

*Davis, M. R. (2006, May 17). NCLB panel gathers views on testing and data collection. *Education Week, 25*(37), 25.

*Davis, M. R. (2006, May 24). Displaced students' test scores won't count for AYP. *Education Week, 25*(38), 27–28.

*Davis, M. R. (2006, June 21). Ed. Dept. to weigh NCLB subgroup issues. *Education Week, 25*(41), 33, 35.

*Davis, M. R. (2006, September 20). Students displaced by storms score lower on state tests. *Education Week, 26*(4), 22.

*Davis, M. R., & Archer, J. (2005, May 11). Complaint targets Utah NCLB law. *Education Week, 24*(36), 22.

*Davis, M. R., & Hoff, D. J. (2005, April 20). Questions linger over NCLB policy shifts. *Education Week, 24*(32), 21–22.

*Davis, M. R., & Richard, A. (2004, September 15). Bush test proposal for high schoolers joins wider trend. *Education Week, 24*(3), 1, 32–33.

DeBray, E. H., McDermott, K. A., & Wohlstetter, P. (2005). Introduction to the special issue on federalism reconsidered: That case of the No Child Left Behind Act. *Peabody Journal of Education, 80*(2), 1–18.

Delandshere, G. (2001). Implicit theories, unexamined assumptions and the status quo of educational assessment. *Assessment in Education: Principles, Policy & Practice, 8*(2), 113–133.

Denham, A., & Garnett, M. (2006, April). 'What works'? British think tanks and the 'end of ideology.' *Political Quarterly, 77*, 156–165.

Dewey, J. (1954.) *The public and its problems.* Athens, OH: Swallow.

*Dobbs, M. (2005, May 8). Conn. stands in defiance on enforcing 'No Child.' *Washington Post,* Final edition, p. A10.

Editorial Projects in Education History. (n.d.). Retrieved February 15, 2008, from http://www2.edweek.org/info/about/history.html

Education Commission of the States (ECS). (2002). *No state left behind: The challenges and opportunities of ESEA 2001.* ECS Special Report. Denver, CO: Author.

Education Commission of the States (ECS). (2004). *ECS report to the nation: State implementation of the No Child Left Behind Act—Respecting the diversity among states.* Denver, CO: Author.

Education Trust. (1996). *Education watch: The 1996 Education Trust state and national data book.* Washington, DC: Author.

Elmore, R. F., Abelmann, C. H., & Fuhrman, S. H. (1996). The new accountability in state education reform: From process to performance. In H. F. Ladd (Ed.), *Holding schools accountable: Performance-based reform in education* (pp. 65–99). Washington, DC: Brookings Institute.

*Fletcher, M. A. (2002, August, 29). Failing schools find hole in law; Ark. shows Bush initiative's limits. *Washington Post,* Final edition, p. A01.

*Fletcher, M. A. (2003, January 2). States worry new law sets schools up to fail; Use of test scores would label most poor performers. *Washington Post,* Final edition, p. A01.

*Florida Department of Education. (2005, December). *FCAT achievement levels.* Retrieved February 15, 2008, from http://fcat.fldoe.org/pdf/achieveleveldefine.pdf

Fuhrman, S. H. (1999). The new accountability. *CPRE Policy Briefs* (CPRE RB-27). Philadelphia: University of Pennsylvania, Consortium for Policy Research in Education.

Fuhrman, S. H. (2003). Redesigning accountability systems for education. *CPRE Policy Briefs* (CPRE RB-38). Philadelphia: University of Pennsylvania, Consortium for Policy Research in Education.

Fulton, M. (2007, September 5). Who's saying what about NCLB reauthorization? ECS reauthorization database. *ECS Briefing Report.* Retrieved February 15, 2008, from http://www.ecs.org/html/educationIssues/NCLBreauthorization/NCLBReauthBriefingRpt.pdf

*Gewertz, C. (2003, November 26). Educators endorse rules on accountability. *Education Week, 23*(13), 16.

*Gewertz, C. (2005, April 6). Urban districts report steady academic gains. *Education Week, 24*(30), 5.

*Gewertz, C. (2005, May 11). Urban districts create "subsets" of schools. *Education Week, 24*(36), 3, 15.

*Gewertz, C. (2006, August 30). 3 Houston schools fight to keep doors open. *Education Week, 26*(1), 5, 20.

Gipps, C. (1999). Socio-cultural aspects of assessment. *Review of Research in Education, 24,* 355–392.

Glenn, D. (2007). Scholars who counsel candidates wield power but face risks. *Chronicle of Higher Education, 54*(7), A1–A16.

Goertz, M. E. (2005). Implementing the No Child Left Behind Act: Challenges for the states. *Peabody Journal of Education, 80*(2), 73–89.

Goertz, M. E., & Duffy, M. (2003). Mapping the landscape of high-stakes testing and accountability programs. *Theory into Practice, 42,* 4–11.

Goldschmidt, P., Roschewski, P., Choi, K., Auty, W., Hebbler, S., Blank, R., et al. (2005). *Policymakers' guide to growth models for school accountability: How do accountability models differ?* Washington, DC: Council of Chief State School Officers (CCSSO).

Goren, P. (1997). Political expertise and issue voting in presidential elections. *Political Research Quarterly, 50,* 387–412.

Haas, E. (2007). False equivalency: Think tank references on education in the news media. *Peabody Journal of Education, 82*(1), 63–102.

Haertel, E., & Herman, J. (2005). A historical perspective on validity arguments for accountability testing. *Yearbook of the National Society for the Study of Education, 104*(2), 1–34.

Hamilton, L. (2003). Assessment as a policy tool. *Review of Research in Education, 27,* 25–68.

Haycock, K., Jerald, C., & Huang, S. (2001). Closing the gap: Done in a decade. *Thinking K-16, 5*(2), 3–21.

*Haynes, V. D. (2005, August 6). D.C. elementary scores rise as secondary results decline. *Washington Post,* Final edition, p. B01.

Heck, R. H. (2006). Assessing school achievement progress: Comparing alternative approaches. *Educational Administration Quarterly, 42,* 667–699.

*Hoff, D. J. (2002, October 19). Budget woes force states to scale back testing programs. *Education Week, 22*(6), 24.

*Hoff, D. J. (2005, March 9). Texas stands behind own testing rule. *Education Week, 24*(26), 1, 23.

*Hoff, D. J. (2005, April 13). States to get new options on NCLB law. *Education Week, 24*(31), 1, 38.

*Hoff, D. J. (2005, April 27). Chiefs' group, federal department on better terms. *Education Week, 24*(33), 22, 25.

*Hoff, D. J. (2005, September 28). States address academic concerns. *Education Week, 25*(5), 1, 17.

*Hoff, D. J. (2006, March 1). Foreseeing errors in test industry. *Education Week, 25*(25), 18.

*Hoff, D. J. (2006, October 4). NCLB panel favors retaining law's core measures. *Education Week, 26*(6), 21–22.

*Hoff, D. J. (2006, October 18). Big business going to bat for NCLB. *Education Week, 26*(8), 1, 24.

*Hoff, D. J. (2006, October 25). State chiefs offer views on NCLB renewal. *Education Week, 26*(9), 31, 33.

*Hoff, D. J. (2006, November 8). Education Dept. poised to approve more states for growth-model pilot. *Education Week, 26*(11), 21.

*Hoff, D. J. (2006, December 13). GOP era wrought unexpected changes. *Education Week, 26*(15), 10–11.

*Hoff, D. J. (2006, December 20). Miller brings ambition to helm of ed. panel. *Education Week, 26*(16), 22, 24–25.

*Hoff, D. J. (2007, February 4). State chiefs offer their prescription for renewing NCLB. *Education Week, 26*(22), 21.

*Hoff, D. J. (2007b, February 7). The view from Rockland. *Education Week, 26*(22), 22–25.

*Hoff, D. J. (2007, March 28). Growth models for NCLB accountability are weighed. *Education Week, 26*(29), 20.

*Hoff, D. J. (2007, April 18). Not all agree on meaning of NCLB proficiency. *Education Week, 26*(33), 1, 23.

*Hoff, D. J. (2007, June 6). State tests show gains since NCLB. *Education Week, 26*(39), 1, 20.

*Hoff, D. J. (2007, September 5). Draft bill heats up NCLB-renewal debate. *Education Week, 27*(2), 1, 20.

*Hoff, D. J. (2007, September 12). Spellings takes issue with NCLB draft. *Education Week, 27*(3), 21–22.

*Hoff, D. J. (2007, October 3). Bush pushes NCLB as renewal percolates. *Education Week, 27*(6), 23–24.

*Hoff, D. J. (2007, October 17). Bush, others want law to go beyond basics. *Education Week, 27*(8), 18, 21.

*Hoff, D. J. (2007a, November 7). The next education president? *Education Week, 27*(11), 24–27.

*Hoff, D. J. (2007, December 18). "Growth models" gaining in accountability debate. *Education Week, 27*(16), 22–25.

*Hoff, D. J., & Manzo, K. K. (2007, March 9). Bush claims about NCLB questioned. *Education Week, 26*(27), 1, 26–27.

*Hoff, D. J., & Richard, A. (2005, October 5). Storms force Louisiana, Mississippi to review K-12 policies. *Education Week, 25*(6), 21.

*Honawar, V. (2006, March 22). SAT glitches prompt broader testing worries. *Education Week, 25*(28), 8–9.

Howlett, M., & Rayner, J. (2006). Understanding the historical turn in the policy sciences: A critique of stochastic, narrative, path dependency and process-sequencing models of policy-making over time. *Policy Sciences, 39,* 1–18.

Hursh, D. (2005). The growth of high-stakes testing in the USA: Accountability, markets, and the decline in educational equality. *British Educational Research Journal, 31,* 605–622.

*Hurst, M. D. (2004, October 4). Nevada report reveals spike in test irregularities. *Education Week, 24*(6), 19, 22.

*Jacobson, L. (2006, November 15). Early-childhood issues raised for NCLB law. *Education Week, 26*(12), 24, 26.

Jennings, J. (2003). From the White House to the schoolhouse: Greater demands and new roles. *Yearbook of the National Society for the Study of Education, 102*(1), 291–309.

Jennings, J., & Rentner, D. S. (2006). Ten big effects of the No Child Left Behind Act on public schools. *Phi Delta Kappan, 88,* 110–113.

Johnson, B. L., Jr. (1999). Politics of research-information use in the education policy arena. In B. S. Cooper & E. V. Randall (Eds.), *Accuracy or advocacy: The politics of research in education* (pp. 17–30). Thousand Oaks, CA: Corwin.

Joint Study Group on Adequate Yearly Progress. (2002). *Making valid and reliable decisions in determining Adequate Yearly Progress.* Washington, DC: Council of Chief State School Officers (CCSSO).

Jones, B. D., & Baumgartner, F. R. (2004). Representation and agenda setting. *The Policy Studies Journal, 32,* 1–24.

Jones, B. D., & Baumgartner, F. R. (2005). *The politics of attention: How government prioritizes problems.* Chicago: The University of Chicago Press.

*Keller, B. (2006, July 26). States' standards, tests are a mismatch, study finds. *Education Week, 25*(43), 5, 20.

*Kennedy, E. M. (2007, March 26). No retreat on school reform. *Washington Post,* Regional edition, p. A15.

Kentucky Department of Education. (2007, April 5). Progress in the

Commonwealth Accountability Testing System. Retrieved February 15, 2008, from http://www.kentuckyschools.net/KDE/HomePageRepository/Proof+of+Progress/CATS+Progress.htm

Kingdon, J. W. (2003). *Agendas, alternatives, and public policies* (2nd ed.). New York: Longman, Pearson.

*Klein, A. (2006, March 29). U.S. Panel weighs accountability in higher education. *Education Week, 25*(29), 32, 34.

*Klein, A. (2006, June 7). Indian students outperform blacks on NAEP. *Education Week, 25*(39), 16–17.

*Klein, A. (2006, October 25). No Child Left Behind on the campaign trail. *Education Week, 26*(9), 34–36.

*Klein, A. (2006, December 20). Democratic Congress to step up department oversight. *Education Week, 26*(16), 22, 24–25.

*Klein, A. (2007, February 7). School board members hit D.C. to weigh in on NCLB. *Education Week, 26*(22), 19–20.

*Klein, A. (2007, February 12). Bush budget would boost NCLB efforts. *Education Week, 26*(23), 1, 25.

*Klein, A. (2007, February 23). Critics of NCLB ask Congress to overhaul it. *Education Week, 26*(25), 1, 26.

*Klein, A. (2007, March 14). Texan nominated for key K-12 post. *Education Week, 26*(27), 21.

*Klein, A. (2007, April 6). Governors enter fray over NCLB. *Education Week, 26*(32), 1, 28.

*Klein, A. (2007, April 18). Education Trust offers NCLB renewal plan. *Education Week, 26*(33), 21–22.

*Klein, A. (2007, May 9). House OKs reauthorization of Head Start. *Education Week, 26*(36), 25–26.

*Klein, A. (2007, June 20). Accountability forum backs local tests. *Education Week, 26*(42), 30.

*Klein, A. (2007, June 20). Panel: "persistently dangerous" tag for schools needs to be reworked. *Education Week, 26*(42), 30.

*Klein, A. (2007, September 5). Host of lawmakers offer bills to revise NCLB. *Education Week, 27*(2), 19.

*Klein, A. (2007, September 26). On senate panel, a different dynamic for NCLB renewal. *Education Week, 27*(5), 20–22.

*Klein, A. (2007, December 19). Impact is slight for early states using "growth." *Education Week, 27*(16), 24–25.

Knight, J., & Johnson, J. (1999). Inquiry into democracy: What might a pragmatist make of rational choice theories? *American Journal of Political Science, 43*, 566–589.

Koretz, D., & Barton, K. (2003–2004). Assessing students with disabilities: Issues and evidence. *Educational Assessment, 9*(1 & 2), 29–60.

*Labb, T. (2007, September 14). Eastern High's missing scores scrutinized. *Washington Post,* Metro Edition, p. B04.

La Marca, P. M., Redfield, D., Winter, P. C., Bailey, A., & Despriet, L. H. (2000). *State standards and state assessment systems: A guide to alignment.* Washington, DC: Council of Chief State School Officers (CCSSO).

Larocca, R. (2004). Strategic diversion in political communication. *The Journal of Politics, 66*, 469–491.

Lau, R. R., & Redlawsk, D. P. (2001). Advantages and disadvantages of using cognitive heuristics in political decision making. *American Journal of Political Science, 45*, 951–971.

Lee, J. (2002). Racial and ethnic achievement gap trends: Reversing the progress toward equity? *Educational Researcher, 31*(1), 3–12.

Linn, R. L. (2005a). Conflicting demands of No Child Left Behind and state systems: Mixed messages about school performance. *Education Policy Analysis Archives, 13*(33), 1–17.

Linn, R. L. (2005b). Issues in the design of accountability systems. *Yearbook of the National Society for the Study of Education, 104*(2), 78–98.

Linn, R. L., Baker, E .L., & Betebenner, D. W. (2002). Accountability systems: Implications of requirements of the No Child Left Behind Act of 2001. *Educational Researcher, 31*(6), 3–16.

Lissitz, R. W., & Huynh, H. (2003). Vertical equating for state assessments: Issues and solutions in determination of adequate yearly progress and school accountability. *Practical Assessment, Research & Evaluation, 8*(10). Retrieved February 15, 2008, from http://PAREonline.net/getvn.asp?v=8&n=10

Manzo, K. K. (2005, January 19). Texas takes aim at tainted testing program. *Education Week, 24*(19), 1, 14.

Manzo, K. K. (2005, September 25). Union-funded study finds fault with high-stakes testing. *Education Week, 25*(5), 9.

Manzo, K. K. (2006, June 21). Study questions NCLB law's links to achievement gains. *Education Week, 25*(41), 11.

*Manzo, K. K. (2007, October 10). Report pans how states set the bar. *Education Week, 27*(7), 1, 16.

*Manzo, K. K., & Cavanaugh, S. (2005, July 27). South posts big gains on long-term NAEP in reading and math. *Education Week, 24*(43), 1, 16.

*Matthews, J. (2004, November 4). No one need feel left behind by federal education mandate. *Washington Post,* Final edition, Fairfax Extra, p. T08.

McDermott, K. A. (2007). "Expanding the moral community" or "blaming the victim"? The politics of state education accountability policy. *American Educational Research Journal, 44*, 77–111.

McDonnell, L. M. (1994). Assessment policy as persuasion and regulation. *American Journal of Education, 102*, 394–420.

McDonnell, L. M. (2005). No Child Left Behind and the federal role in education: Evolution or revolution? *Peabody Journal of Education, 80*(2), 19–38.

McGuinn, P. (2006). Swing issues and policy regimes: Federal education policy and the politics of policy change. *The Journal of Policy History, 18*, 205–240.

*McNeil, M. (2007, April 25). State lawmakers weigh issue of national standards. *Education Week, 26*(34), 20, 22.

Michigan Department of Education. (2006). *Mathematics content grade level expectations, v. 12.05.* Lansing, MI: Author. Retrieved February 15, 2008, from http://www.michigan.gov/documents/Math-GLCE_140486_7.pdf

NAEP—Frequently Asked Questions. (2007). Retrieved February 15, 2008, from http://nces.ed.gov/nationsreportcard/faq.asp

National Center for Education Statistics. (2007). *Mapping 2005 state proficiency standards onto the NAEP scales* (NCES 2007-482). Washington, DC: U.S. Department of Education.

National Research Council. (1998). *Uncommon measures: Equivalence and linkage among educational tests.* Washington, DC: National Academy Press.

Nelson, T. E., & Oxley, Z. M. (1999). Issue framing effects on belief importance and opinion. *The Journal of Politics, 61*, 1040–1067.

New York State Department of Education. (2000, November 17). *Elementary science core curriculum K-4.* Retrieved February 15, 2008, from http://www.emsc.nysed.gov/ciai/mst/pub/elecoresci.pdf

*Olson, L. (2002, September 4). Secretary picks fellow Texan to head assessment board. *Education Week, 22*(10), 40–41.

*Olson, L. (2003, December 10). In ESEA wake, school data flowing forth. *Education Week, 23*(15), 1, 16–18.

Olson, L. (2004, September 8). Data show schools making progress on federal goals. *Education Week, 24*(2), 1, 24–25, 28.

*Olson, L. (2004, September 22). No Child Left Behind Act changes weighed. *Education Week, 24* (4), 31, 34.

*Olson, L. (2004, October 13). Wyoming signs innovative test contract with Harcourt assessment. *Education Week, 24*(7), 20.

*Olson, L. (2004, December 8). Taking root; Despite ongoing complaints. *Education Week, 24*(15), S1, S3, S7.

*Olson, L. (2005, February 2). States revive efforts to coax NCLB changes. *Education Week, 24*(21), 1, 29.

Olson, L. (2005a, May 18). States hoping to "grow" into AYP success. *Education Week, 24*(37), 15, 20.

*Olson, L. (2005, July 13). Education Department convenes working group on "growth" models. *Education Week, 24*(42), 20–21.

*Olson, L. (2005, July 13). Requests win more leeway under NCLB. *Education Week, 24*(42), 1, 20–21.

*Olson, L. (2005, September 7). Defying predictions, state trends prove mixed on schools making NCLB targets. *Education Week, 25*(2), 1, 26–27.

*Olson, L. (2005, September 14). Secretary to weigh NCLB waivers for crisis on a case-by-case basis. *Education Week, 25*(3), 21.

*Olson, L. (2005, September 21). AYP rules miss many in spec. ed. *Education Week, 25*(4), 1, 24–25.

*Olson, L. (2005, October 19). Small states find benefits in jointly developed tests. *Education Week, 25*(8), 1, 14.

Olson, L. (2005b, November 30). Benchmark assessments offer regular checkups on student achievement. *Education Week, 25*(13), 13–14.

*Olson, L. (2006, February 24). 20 States seek to join pilot on NCLB "growth models." *Education Week, 25*(25), 21.

*Olson, L. (2006, November 15). 3 states get OK to use "growth model" to gauge AYP. *Education Week, 26*(12), 24.

*Olson, L. (2007, January 31). School accountability systems seen as unlikely to face major overhaul. *Education Week, 26*(21), 11.

*Olson, L., & Jacobson, L. (2006, April 28). Analysis finds minority NCLB scores widely excluded. *Education Week, 25*(33), 5, 21.

Opfer, D. (2007). Developing a research agenda on the media and education. *Peabody Journal of Education, 82*(1), 166–177.

*Paige, R. (2004, February 27). Focus on the children. *Washington Post,* Final edition, editorial copy, p. A23.

Palmer, S. R., & Coleman, A. L. (2003). *NCLB Work Plan*. Retrieved February 15, 2008, from http://www.ccsso.org/content/pdfs/NCLBWorkplan.pdf

*Popham, W. J. (2003, September 24). Commentary, The 'No Child' noose tightens—but some states are slipping it. *Education Week, 23*(4), 48.

Popkewitz, T. (2004). Educational standards: Mapping who we are and are to become. *Journal of the Learning Sciences, 13*, 243–256.

Popkewitz, T., & Lindblad, S. (2004). Historicizing the future: Educational reform, systems of reason, and the making of children who are the future citizens. *Journal of Educational Change, 5*, 229–247.

Reckase, M. D. (2004). The real world is more complicated than we would like. *Journal of Educational and Behavioral Statistics, 29*, 117–120.

Resnick, L. (2006). Making accountability really count. *Educational Measurement: Issues & Practice, 25*(1), 33–37.

*Richard, A. (2004, September 15). NCLB law's focus turns to districts. *Education Week, 24*(3), 1, 20.

*Richard, A. (2005, May 18). Press secretary; Spellings offers her thoughts on news coverage of education. *Education Week, 24*(37), 22.

Riddle, W., & Stedman, J. (2001, December). *Elementary and secondary education: Reconsideration of the federal role by the 107th Congress* (CRS Issue Brief). Retrieved February 15, 2008, from http://www.ecs.org/clearinghouse/32/01/3201.pdf

*Robelen, E. W. (2002, March 13). Agency looks for balance policing ESEA. *Education Week, 21*(26), 1, 21.

*Robelen, E. W. (2002, September 9). An ESEA primer. *Education Week, 21*(16), 28–29.

*Robelen, E. W. (2002, September 18). Kress update. *Education Week, 22*(3), 22.

*Robelen, E. W. (2003, September 3). State reports on progress vary widely. *Education Week, 23*(1), 1, 37.

*Robelen, E. W. (2004, October 4). Paige: It's not too early to call school law a success. *Education Week, 24*(6), 23, 25.

Robelen, E. W. (2005, April 13). 40 years after ESEA. *Education Week, 24*(31), 1, 42.

*Robelen, E. W. (2005, February 9). Bush's high school agenda faces obstacles. *Education Week, 24*(22), 22, 24.

Roeber, E. D. (2003). *Assessment models for No Child Left Behind*. Retrieved June 10, 2007, from http://www.ecs.org/clearinghouse/40/09/4009.doc

Rothman, R., Slattery, J. B., Vranek, J. L., & Resnick, L. B. (2002). *Benchmarking and alignment of standards and testing* (CSE Technical Report 566). Los Angeles: University of California, Center for the Study of Evaluation, National Center for Research on Evaluation, Standards, and Student Testing.

Sabatier, P. A., & Jenkins-Smith, H. C. (Eds.). (1993). *Policy change and learning: An advocacy coalition approach*. Boulder, CO: Westview Press.

Sabatier, P. A., & Jenkins-Smith, H. C. (1999). The advocacy coalition framework: An assessment. In P. A. Sabatier (Ed.), *Theories of the policy process* (pp. 117–166). Boulder, CO: Westview Press.

*Sack, J. L. (2005, April 27). Utah passes bill to trump "No Child" law. *Education Week, 24*(33), 22, 25.

*Samuels, C. A. (2006, March 15). Study: States including special education students in tests. *Education Week, 25*(27), 11.

*Samuels, C. A. (2006, March 29). Wide variation seen in testing of students with disabilities. *Education Week, 25*(29), 11.

*Samuels, C. A. (2006, August 9). GAO: Growth models promising. *Education Week, 25*(44), 26.

*Samuels, C. A. (2006, September 13). Regulations on "2 percent" testing awaited. *Education Week, 26*(3), 31–32.

*Samuels, C. A. (2006, October 11). Alternate assessments proving to be a challenge for states. *Education Week, 26*(7), 12.

*Samuels, C. A.. (2007, April 4). Panel weighs NCLB and students with disabilities. *Education Week, 26*(31), 22.

*Samuels, C. A. (2007, September 5). Plan would codify several rules adopted to ease testing of students with disabilities. *Education Week, 27*(2), 20.

*Samuels, C. A. (2008, January 28). Report: NCLB may be aiding students with disabilities. *Education Week, 27*(22), 9.

*Samuels, C. A., & Davis, M. R. (2006, May 24). 2 states selected for "growth model" pilot. *Education Week, 25*(38), 27–28.

Schafer, W. D. (2005). Criteria for standards setting from the sponsor's perspective. *Applied Measurement in Education, 18*, 61–81.

Shulock, N. (1999). The paradox of policy analysis: If it is not used, why do we produce so much of it? *Journal of Policy Analysis and Management, 18*, 226–244.

*Spellings, M. (2005, April 2). Our high schools need help. *Washington Post,* Final edition, p. A21.

Spring, J. (1993). *Conflict of interests: The politics of American education* (2nd ed.). New York: Longman.

Stiggins, R. J., Arter, J. A., Chappuis, J., & Chappuis, S. C. (2004). *Classroom assessment for student learning: Doing it right—Using it well*. Portland, OR: Educational Testing Service.

*Strauss, V. (2005, October 24). As "No Child" answer, tutoring generates complex questions; Schools, state officials question accountability of providers. *Washington Post,* Final edition, p. A10.

Tedesco, J. C. (2005). Issue and strategy agenda setting in the 2004 presidential election: Exploring the candidate-journalist relationship. *Journalism Studies, 6*, 187–201.

Thorn, C. A., & Meyer, R. H. (2006). *Longitudinal data systems to support data-informed decision making: A tri-state partnership between Michigan, Minnesota, and Wisconsin* (WCER Working Paper No. 2006-1). Retrieved February 21, 2007, from http://www.wcer.wisc.edu/publications/workingPapers/Working_Paper_No_2006_1.swf

*Trotter, A., & Davis, M. R. (2006, January 18). At 4, NCLB gets praise and fresh call to amend it. *Education Week, 25*(19), 26, 30.

United States Department of Education. (2003, March 10). Standards and assessment: Non regulatory guidance. Retrieved June 6, 2007, from http://www.ed.gov/policy/elsec/guid/saaguidance03.pdf

United States Department of Education. (2004, January 14). Charting the course: States decide major provisions under *No Child Left Behind* [Press release]. Retrieved February 15, 2008, from http://www.ed.gov/print/news/pressreleases/2004/01/01142004.html

United States Department of Education. (2005, February). *No Child Left Behind Act of 2001: Annual report to Congress*. Retrieved February 15, 2008, from http://www.ed.gov/about/reports/annual/nclb/nclbrpt2005.pdf

*Viadero, D. (2005, February 2). Researchers connect lower achievement, high school exit tests. *Education Week, 24*(21), 10.

*Viadero, D. (2005, April 13). Researchers compare Florida testing, NCLB, but critics pan study. *Education Week, 24*(31), 12.

*Viadero, D. (2005, May 11). Second look at tougher accountability yields new results. *Education Week, 24*(36), 12.

*Viadero, D. (2005, June 15). Ed. Dept. seeks bids for new NCLB help centers. *Education Week, 24*(40), 22.

*Viadero, D. (2007, June 20). Teachers say NCLB has changed classroom practice. *Education Week , 26*(42), 6, 22.

*Viadero, D. (2007, November 14). No easy answers about NCLB's effect on "poverty gap." *Education Week, 27*(12), 12.

Wainer, H. (Ed.). (2004). Value-added assessment [Special issue]. *Journal of Educational and Behavioral Statistics, 29*(1).

*Walsh, M., & Klein, A. (2007, August 15). Miller's NCLB priorities spark fresh debate. *Education Week, 26*(45), 23–24.

Washington Post. (2004, September 23). The choice on schooling. Final edition, editorial copy, p. A28.

Washington Post. (2005, January 16). High school reform. Editorial copy, p. B06.

Washington Post. (2005, January 22). Elected and accountable. Editorial copy, p. A16.

Washington Post. (2006, December 7). Students with disabilities benefit from challenging curricula. Montgomery extra, p. T08.

Washington Post. (2007, February 15). Cheating on tests; Geography should not determine standards of learning. Final edition, p. A26.

Washington Post. (2007, June 10). Measurable progress in school; No Child Left Behind is helping. The next step will take courage. Bulldog edition, p. B06.

Washington Post. (2007, August 14). A vote for "no child"; Welcome support in the house for the law that brought accountability to public education. Regional edition, p. A12.

Washington Post. (2007, September 10). Leaving No Child Behind. Regional edition, p. A15.

Washington Post. (2007, September 10). Save school standards; Congress should resist attempts to water down the No Child Left Behind law. Regional edition, p. A14.

Washington Post. (2007, September 11). Editorial copy. Regional edition.

Washington Post. (2007, September 27). Individual student improvement should trump all else. p. LZ08.

Weaver, R. K., & McGann, J. (2000). Think tanks and civil societies in a time of change. In R. K. Weaver & J. McGann (Eds.), *Think tanks and civil societies: Catalysts for action* (pp. 1–35). New Brunswick, NJ: Transaction.

White, L. G. (1994). Policy analysis as discourse. *Journal of Policy Analysis and Management, 13*(3), 506–525.

*Whorisky, P. (2006, October 23). Political backlash builds over high-stakes testing; Public support wanes for tests seen as punitive. *Washington Post,* Final edition, p. A03.

Wiliam, D. (2000). The meanings and consequences of educational assessments. *Critical Quarterly, 42*(1), 105–127.

*Wills, G. (2003, March 2). Shame: School reform's weak weapon. *Washington Post.* Final edition, editorial copy, p. B07.

Wirt, F. M., & Kirst, M. W. (1992). *Schools in conflict: The politics of education* (3rd ed.). Berkeley, CA; McCutchan.

Woolley, J. T. (2000). Using media-based data in studies of politics. *American Journal of Political Science, 44*, 156–173.

Wong, K. K., & Nicotera, A. (2004) Educational quality and policy redesign: Reconsidering the NAR and federal Title I policy. *Peabody Journal of Education, 79*(1), 87–104.

Wong, K. K., & Nicotera, A. (2007). *Successful schools and educational accountability: Concepts and skills to meet leadership challenges.* Boston: Pearson Allyn & Bacon.

*Zehr, M. A. (2003, November 26). States developing tests for English-learners. *Education Week, 23*(13), 13, 15.

*Zehr, M. A. (2005, June 15). State testing of English-learners scrutinized. *Education Week, 24*(40), 3, 12.

*Zehr, M. A. (2005, December 7). Spellings: English-learners need more help. *Education Week, 25*(14), 30.

*Zehr, M. A. (2006, January 11). Scholars seek best ways to assess English-learners. *Education Week, 25*(18), 10.

*Zehr, M. A. (2006, September 20). Spellings issues final regulations for testing of English-learners. *Education Week, 26*(4), 29.

*Zehr, M. A. (2006, November 15). Reacting to reviews, states cut portfolio assessments for ELL students. *Education Week, 26*(12), 7.

*Zehr, M. A. (2007, January 24). States adopt new tests for English-learners. *Education Week. 26*(20), 26, 31.

*Zehr, M. A. (2007, February 7). Pilot program could help English-learners. *Education Week, 26*(22), 15–16.

*Zehr, M. A. (2007, March 28). California launches new ELL assessment. *Education Week, 26* (29), 11.

*Zehr, M. A. (2007b, May 9). NCLB seen a damper on bilingual programs. *Education Week, 26*(36), 5, 12.

*Zehr, M. A. (2007a, September 5). Language provision in NCLB draft plan criticized. *Education Week, 27*(2), 21.

27

What Works in Defining "What Works" in Educational Improvement

Lessons from Education Policy Implementation Research, Directions for Future Research

MEREDITH I. HONIG
University of Washington, Seattle

What works in educational improvement? Debates about this question have played out in education and other circles for many decades (Cremin, 1988; Kaestle, 1983; Kliebard, 1987). Arguably these debates entered a new era at the turn of this century as the United States Department of Education, private foundations, universities, and others issued various calls for evidence-based approaches to educational improvement and made unprecedented investments in identifying specific interventions that might improve student learning—often called "what works" (http://ies. ed.gov/ncee/wwc/; http://dww.ed.gov/). An intensive focus on what works marks an important evolution in education policymaking that for decades promoted educational improvement strategies for a host of reasons other than whether or not they might actually help all students learn at high levels. Some have suggested that this shift is particularly essential to addressing persistent race- and class-based achievement gaps.

As appealing as it may be, the question of "what works" is deceptively simple and arguably misleading. Debates about what works in mainstream education presses generally take for granted that researchers *should* build knowledge around that question and focus on which research methodologies would better ground their knowledge-building efforts (for an exception, see Hess & Henig, 2008). For example, in recent publications of the American Educational Research Association, such as the 2008 issue of *Educational Researcher* (vol. 37), researchers have debated how to measure the impacts of particular interventions. However, such methodological debates generally have not questioned a primary assumption underlying the matter of what works—namely, that policies, programs, or interventions can and should be categorized as either those that work or those that do not. This approach to knowledge-building, with its focus on rendering summary judgments

about program success or failure, has deep roots in fields such as policy evaluation and intervention research in a variety of disciplines. However, this approach ironically does not build on a significant body of contemporary policy implementation research that suggests alternative approaches might better reflect the on-the-ground realities of what it takes to strengthen school and youth outcomes. This research suggests that implementation researchers should recognize that any one policy that has been studied generally rests on a body of evidence that both confirms and questions its impacts. For example, some research on class size reduction links smaller class sizes with increases in student performance but other research reveals no improvement (Finn & Achilles, 1990; Gilman & Kiger, 2003; Zahorik, Halback, Earle, & Molnar, 2004).

Such typically mixed results may stem in part from the different methodologies researchers have used to derive their findings. To continue with the example of research on the implementation of class size reduction, the researchers cited here and others argue and often disagree about how to measure the effects of smaller class sizes; perhaps equivocal results across studies stem in part from the different research methods researchers have brought to bear in their empirical studies. However, such findings also reflect a well-worn lesson of implementation research: what works *depends*. My reviews of decades of implementation research suggest that whether or not a policy works is not an inherent property of the program or intervention itself. Rather, its outcomes depend on interactions between that policy, people who matter to its implementation and conditions in the places in which people operate. Given these findings, educational researchers should reframe their "what works" debates to ask: what works for whom where, when, and why? This question reflects an approach to knowledge building that is far more nuanced than many present debates about what works suggest and calls researchers' attention to the importance of uncovering various implementation contingencies.

In the subsections that follow, I elaborate this argument with a review of research on education policy implementation. I demonstrate how the field of education policy implementation research has evolved in ways that aim to unpack the contingent, situated nature of what works in educational improvement. One main finding of this research review is that implementation outcomes can be understood as a product of the interaction among policy, people, and places. Some researchers use theory to elaborate these interactions and to explain implementation dynamics and outcomes. The use of theory seems to be helping researchers accumulate knowledge about patterns in how policies, people, and places interact across sites and studies in ways that promise to serve up rich evidence-based guides for practice. Following this discussion, I briefly feature several theories that seem to provide particularly promising anchors for a next generation of implementation research.

Some might argue that focusing research on such implementation complexities perpetuates many of the problems a "what works" approach to educational improvement emerged to address: namely that too much educational research examines process, not outcomes, and reveals so many different factors that matter to implementation that it provides overly complex guides for action that are difficult to use; the parsimony of a "what works" approach at least focuses educational leaders' attention on results and some unequivocal courses of action. This chapter starts from the premise that such concerns about understanding educational outcomes and generating useful and useable knowledge are extremely well-founded and should ground debates and research across educational arenas. However, I demonstrate that various education policy implementation researchers are aiming to generate useful and useable knowledge about educational outcomes not by side-stepping the complexity of how implementation unfolds but by confronting it head-on (Honig, 2006a).

A Brief History of Education Policy Implementation Research[1]

Reviews of education policy implementation research typically aim to reveal how policy approaches and research findings have evolved since the field formally began in the 1960s (e.g., Odden, 1991a, 1991b; see also Goggin, Bowman, Lester, & O'Toole, 1990; Radin, 2000; Wildavsky, 1996). For example, in a frequently cited review, Odden (1991a) distinguished three waves of implementation research by the decades in which studies were produced and showed how findings about implementation have changed over time. I elaborate that these waves also vary by predominant patterns in how researchers aimed to build knowledge about implementation (Honig, 2006a). In this subsection I summarize that argument. I show that the field of education policy implementation research has developed from its roots

in evaluation research to include a substantial program of basic research that aims to accumulate contextually and theoretically rich knowledge about how implementation unfolds. When viewed in this historical context, the current focus on what works in education as elaborated in the introduction reflects an approach to knowledge building in education that many education policy implementation researchers have moved well beyond.

Early Decades of Implementation Research, 1970–1990

Education policy implementation research began as a formal field of inquiry shortly after the broader field of public policy analysis took root in the 1950s and 1960s (Pressman & Wildavsky, 1984; Radin, 2000). Both developments corresponded with the growth of the federal government's participation in various policy arenas. In education these developments brought with them new federal funding for both educational programs and evaluations of those programs. For example, as other scholars have chronicled, the Elementary and Secondary Education Act (ESEA) of 1965 ushered in unprecedented federal funding for education (Elmore & McLaughlin, 1988; Murphy, 1971). In tandem, the education unit of the federal Health, Education, and Welfare agency (later to become the U.S. Department of Education) issued then-significant contracts for the evaluation of various parts of ESEA. Such evaluation included those that focused on ESEA's Title I that provided new funding for the education of "disadvantaged" students and other programs related to sparking what the policy referred to as "educational innovation."

Many of these studies, in traditional evaluation fashion, probed whether or not these programs worked. Specific questions about what worked generally centered on whether the federal programs succeeded at ensuring local implementers delivered specific services to eligible students and otherwise appropriately used the new federal funds. With these questions about implementers' fidelity to policy designs as their main frame, these studies typically found that implementers rarely carried out the policies as designed by their hierarchical superiors. Some researchers traced root causes of these failures to conflicts between policy makers' and implementers' interests and to implementers' overall lack of capacity and will to carry out those instructions (Murphy, 1971; see also Derthick, 1972; Pressman & Wildavsky, 1984). Such assumptions seemed to stem in part from conventions of particular academic disciplines such as economics and political science—dominant in implementation research at that time—that viewed implementers as driven by self-interest to behave in ways not always congruous with policy designers' wishes. The knowledge generated from these studies generally focused on elaborating approaches policy makers might employ to exert greater control over implementers. For example, some researchers used these findings to argue in later publications that policy makers would improve implementation if they provided clearer instructions to implementers (Sabatier & Mazmanian, 1979, 1980), allowed more time for implementers to come into compliance

(Farrar & Milsap, 1986; Knapp, Stearns, Turnbull, David, & Peterson, 1991), or built alliances with implementers to better align implementers' interests with policy makers' interests (Elmore, 1979–1980).

Around the same time, other studies also funded by federal evaluation contracts focused on more basic research questions related to the dynamics of educational change and how such knowledge could help improve the functioning of education systems. Arguably, most prominent among these projects was the RAND Change Agent Study (Berman & McLaughlin, 1976, 1978). In contrast to the orientations of some other early evaluations that, arguably, aimed to understand what works in shoring up gaps in implementers' actions and policy designers' intentions, the RAND Change Agent Study also focused on uncovering "what's happening" when implementers participate in federal programs.

Berman and McLaughlin found that implementers such as teachers generally did aim to carry out federal policies. In the process, implementers adapted both policy demands and local conditions to improve the fit between the two—a process Berman and McLaughlin called "mutual adaptation." In this way, the RAND Change Agent Study reflected and also fueled early approaches to knowledge building about implementation research that did not aim primarily to understand implementation success or failure. Rather, studies in this line focused on the dynamics of implementation processes that might help explain success or failure of particular approaches or provide important information for policy makers in and of itself.

These early studies began to herald the importance of understanding policy, people, and places as interacting influences on implementation dynamics. For example, Peterson, Rabe, and Wong (1986, 1991) highlighted that policy designs differed not only in the details of their provisions but also in terms of their underlying mechanisms for allocating resources. The implementation of redistributive programs (those that required government to provide more services to certain generally underprivileged groups) led to more conflicts at various points in the policy process than developmental programs (those that made infrastructure investments and promised benefits for wider groups; see also Lowi, 1969). Studies began to cast implementers not as individuals who lacked the motivation to change. Rather implementers began to appear as diverse and engaged actors trying to cope with the sheer number of new policy requirements that converged on the "street level" or in implementers' local workplaces in ways that mattered substantially to implementation (Weatherley & Lipsky, 1977; see also Radin, 1977).

These and other landmark studies began to herald *that* variations among policy, people, and places mattered to implementation. However, elaborations on these dimensions and *how* they mattered were few. For example, education researchers generally did not disagree that place or local context mattered to implementation. But instructions to attend to context said little about the dimensions of context

that mattered, under what conditions they mattered, whether context could be attended to, and if it could, how policy makers should do so (Kirst & Jung, 1980).

In the 1980s, some approaches to education policy implementation research reflected knowledge-building strategies that aimed to determine policy success or failure (e.g., Anderson et al., 1987). However, other research focused on building more nuanced understandings of the significance of policy, people, and places to implementation dynamics and outcomes. For example, McDonnell and Elmore (1987) expanded on the notion that differences in policy designs matter to implementation by distinguishing policies by their "instruments" or tools. They highlighted that these instruments—mandates, incentives, capacity building, and systems change—reflected different underlying assumptions about how to motivate implementers to change. They argued that an analysis of policy designs at this level would help reveal why policies of certain types were more or less effective with particular implementers in certain circumstances (see also Schneider & Ingram, 1990).

A wider range of people emerged as the focus for implementation studies. For example, various researchers began to illuminate the importance of state educational agency leaders and staff as designers and implementers of policy (Cohen, 1982; Fuhrman, 1993; Fuhrman, Clune, & Elmore, 1988). For example, Clune (1983) and others revealed policy implementation as a negotiated process involving at least the federal government, states, and local districts through which the terms of policy compliance were constructed. While school teachers and principals had long been topics of study in the fields of teacher education and educational leadership, research explicitly located within the field of policy implementation began to explore how these school-based professionals shaped implementation processes and outcomes (Elmore & McLaughlin, 1988; McLaughlin, 1991a, 1991b; Rosenholtz, 1985). Consistent with conventions of terminology in federal legislation, studies during this period tended to refer to implementers by broad categories such as "teachers" and "state educational agencies" and not to explore how differences among individuals within these broad categories shaped implementation. Nevertheless, this research helped solidify a focus on implementers' agency as an important avenue for implementation research.

Studies in the 1980s also began to elaborate the places that mattered to implementation in several respects. For one, places included geographic locations and jurisdictions such as states that had received little attention in prior waves of reform and research. Such studies revealed that these locations and jurisdictions varied in terms of their politics, culture, and histories in ways that helped to explain their differing responses to policy directives (Fuhrman et al., 1988, p. 64). Places also included new units of analysis such as "teacher networks" and "communities." Studies of these places revealed how these non-legislated associations among implementers operated as powerful influences on implementers' work (Anderson et al., 1987; Fuhrman et al., 1988; Lieberman & McLaughlin, 1992; Little, 1984; Marsh & Crocker, 1991).

Some implementation researchers went so far as to make places rather than policies their main concern. That is, past decades' implementation studies generally asked how a given policy was implemented. By the 1980s, a growing cadre of implementation researchers focused on high performing schools and asked: "What are the policy and other conditions that explain that performance?" This approach of tracking backwards from practice to policy was a particular hallmark of the effective schools movement (Purkey & Smith, 1983; Sizer, 1986). Reinforcing this approach, McLaughlin (1991a) argued that implementation researchers should move away from mainly trying to understand which policies get implemented to elaborating the various conditions that matter to enabling effective practice (p. 155).

The Current State of the Field   Whereas past research generally revealed that policy, people, and places affected implementation, contemporary implementation research specifically aims to uncover *their various dimensions* and *how and why interactions among these dimensions* shape implementation in particular ways.

Policy Designs as Implementation Influences   Contemporary studies generally suggest that policy designs have three key dimensions—goals, targets, and tools—and aim to reveal how differences at this analytic level influence implementation. Researchers now commonly highlight that policies with *goals* relate to the core of schooling—teachers' relationships with students, their subject matter, and their workplaces—pose fundamentally different implementation challenges than policies that seek more peripheral changes such as new course schedules or classroom seating arrangements (Cuban & Tyack, 1995; Elmore, 1996; Lee & Smith, 1995; Siskin, 1994). For example, mathematics teachers in Hill's (2006) research faced distinctly different implementation challenges when it came to implementation of certain state mathematics standards. These differences depended in part on whether the standards demanded a core or fundamental change in their practice versus a more peripheral or modest change.

Goals also differ in their scope: Policies that aim to impact schools district-wide require a different degree of engagement by district central offices and other educational leaders than policies that aim for a limited number of schools. Policies that focus on changes in the short-term have different consequences in implementation than those that allow for a longer implementation horizon. For example, Hess (2002) highlights that accountability policies in general aim to deliver diffuse benefits to many people over the long term; but because costs in the short term are so high, implementation of such policies typically meets strong immediate resistance, particularly among the communities the policies aim to benefit over the long term (Hess, 2002). Failure to attend to the different challenges

and opportunities such policies present in short and long terms may significantly curb implementation.

Policy designers' choices of policy *targets*—those specifically named in policy designs as essential to achieving policy goals—appear in implementation research as influences on implementation in their own right. For example, Malen (2006) highlights that those who stand to win or lose from particular policies significantly shape the mobilization of groups either in support of or against implementation (see also Hess, 2002; Stone, 1998). How various groups are named or labeled in policy designs sends signals about targets' value in ways that significantly shape policy outcomes (Mintrop, 2003; Schneider & Ingram, 1993; Stein, 2004). For example, Pillow argues that the social construction of teen mothers as a target group within education policy designs has resulted in systematic curbs on their access to educational opportunity despite the provision of other resources (Pillow, 2004; see also Schram, 1995). Stein (2004) has revealed implementers' themselves as significant creators and reinforcers of group labels and has demonstrated how such labels may frustrate precisely the equity and other policy goals that implementers aim to advance (see also Datnow et al., 2001).

Policy *tools* also exert their own influences on implementation and have differential benefits depending on other implementation conditions. For example, Coburn and Stein (2006) demonstrate how in some settings teacher professional communities may be reinforced by central mandates whereas in other districts such mandates are unnecessary or prohibitive (see also McLaughlin & Talbert, 2001). The same accountability policies are met with different degrees of resistance within states depending on teacher motivation, capacity, incentives, and other factors (Mintrop, 2003). I have highlighted that bottom-up reform initiatives as designed generally rely on systems change and learning tools and at a minimum can spark a rethinking of relationships between school district central offices and schools; however, their strength as levers of change seems to depend on supportive contextual conditions, the starting capacity of district central offices and schools, and the assistance of intermediary organizations (Honig, 2001, 2003, 2004a, 2004b).

People as Implementation Influences   The people who ultimately implement policy significantly mediate implementation in a wide variety of ways that have begun to take center stage in contemporary studies. First, to be sure, researchers continue to examine how those targets formally named in policy designs respond to policy demands. But given the expansion of the types of formal policy targets noted above, a focus on targets now means that studies are more likely than in past decades to consider a host of individuals both inside and outside the formal education system including parents, youth workers, health and human service providers, and comprehensive school reform designers to name a few (e.g., Crowson & Boyd, 1993). A battery of new policy initiatives and related research highlight school district central office administrators as key mediators of policy outcomes (e.g., Burch & Spillane, 2004; Hightower, Knapp, Marsh, & McLaughlin, 2002; Honig, 2003; Spillane, 1996).

Second, researchers also focus on individuals who are not formally named as targets in policy designs but who nevertheless impact implementation. For example, Shipps (1997) has shown how business leaders had a profound effect on implementation of various Chicago reform efforts over the course of nearly two decades even though they were not named specifically in policy designs as targets. City mayors play increasingly prominent roles in education policy implementation not only as policy makers, but as implementers themselves (Cuban & Usdan, 2003; Katz, Fine, & Simon, 1997; Kirst & Bulkley, 2000).

Third, past decades' research tended to focus on groups of implementers based on their formal professional affiliations (e.g., "teachers," "central office administrators") and to assume that such groups on the whole held certain interests, beliefs, values, ideas, knowledge, and other orientations that shaped their participation in implementation. Contemporary studies are more likely to probe differences among sub-groups within these broad categories. Louis has demonstrated that implementers' functional roles—such as stimulator, storyteller, networker, and coper—reveal important implementation dynamics not always obvious from formal employment categories such as "teacher" (Louis, 1994). Likewise, school district central offices have begun to appear in research not as monolithic agents (Spillane, 1998) but as networks of highly differentiated staff who each face different demands, opportunities, and constraints in implementation (Burch & Spillane, 2004; Hannaway, 1989; Honig, 2003, 2006b).

Research in this vein sometimes highlights the processes whereby various individual and group orientations shape implementation. For example, Spillane, Reiser, and Gomez (2006) reveal that implementers' identities and experiences extend well beyond their formal professional positions; these authors elaborate the individual, group, and distributed sense-making processes through which implementers draw on various identities and experiences to shape their choices during implementation. In this view, opportunities for people—policy makers and implementers alike—to learn about policy problems, policy designs, and implementation progress essentially shape how implementation unfolds (Cohen & Hill, 2000; Louis, 1994; O'Day, 2002; see also Honig, 2006a).

Fourth, researchers have come to reveal that people's participation in various communities and relationships is essential to implementation. For example, researchers have shown that teachers within schools and districts are situated in different professional communities that help shape their beliefs and world views and ultimately their interpretations of policy messages (Cobb, McClain, Lamberg, & Dean, 2003; Coburn, 2001; Coburn & Stein, 2006; McLaughlin & Talbert, 2001). Hill argues that teachers and others belong to different discourse communities that significantly shape their responses to ambitious standards-based reform demands (Hill, 2006). Pollocks' school-based ethnography examines in part how such communities in schools influence how teachers talk about and act on potentially racially charged issues in their educational improvement efforts; she recounts multiple instances in which teachers aimed to use race-neutral language in an effort not to generate negative racial stereotypes of students but in the process actually reinforced the very categories they sought to avoid (Pollock, 2001). Smylie and Evans (2006) discuss how other forms of social interactions and trusting relationships both fuel and frustrate reform (see also Knapp, 1997).

Importantly, contemporary education policy implementation research also continues to move beyond traditional distinctions between policy makers and implementers and teaches that both are consequential sets of people who shape how a policy is designed and implemented. For example, Malen (2006) reveals how policy design and implementation are overlapping processes that unfold in a series of games through which those in formal designated policy-making roles and those in implementation roles shape both processes—even in cases such as school reconstitution in which traditional top-down control dynamics are a fundamental aspect of policy design. Datnow (2006) argues that education policy systems are nested systems in which local, state, and federal actors play key roles in co-constructing policy design and implementation. In my own work I have flipped these traditional policymaking and implementing roles on their heads to reveal implementers as significant drivers of policy and policy makers as key implementers (Honig, 2003, 2004a).

Place as Implementation Influence Contemporary researchers also are elaborating dimensions of places as fundamental to implementation outcomes in several respects. First, as in the past, these researchers find that governmental organizations and agencies such as state educational agencies are important settings where implementation unfolds (Hamann & Lane, 2004; Lusi, 1997). As noted above, a growing cadre of researchers explores school district central offices as particularly important implementations settings. Such organizations operate as particular types of complex systems in ways that lead to implementation processes different from those of some other organizations (O'Day, 2002). Similarly, an emerging literature on *urban* districts teaches that these districts have particular political and institutional resources for implementation that mark them as a distinct subset of districts (Kirst & Bulkley, 2000; Orr, 1998; Stone, 1998).

Second, many contemporary researchers name their districts and states in their studies in an effort to build a body of knowledge about implementation in particular locations and to call attention to how particular deep seated historical-institutional patterns shape implementation outcomes. For example, the implementation literature now includes a substantial sub-strand concerning Chicago school reform (e.g., Bryk & Sebring, 1991; Bryk, Sebring,

Kerbow, Rollow, & Easton, 1998; Katz et al., 1997; O'Day, 2002). Dumas and Anyon (2006) reveal implementation as significantly shaped by race- and class-based tensions that may seem familiar nationwide but that are deeply rooted in particular local educational, economic, and political institutions (see also Anyon, 1997).

Some contemporary research—what I call "place-based studies"—focuses on particular geographic locations as their main concern and asks which policies and other conditions account for education outcomes in that particular setting. For example, Anyon's (1997) research for *Ghetto Schooling* began as an investigation into school experiences of students in Newark, New Jersey's elementary schools and ultimately revealed important lessons about Marcy School's main policy implementation challenge at that time—school restructuring. Orr's (1998, 1999) examination of Baltimore addressed the trajectory of multiple policies in which the city was engaged over more than a decade to reveal not only how particular policy initiatives fared but also more broadly how Baltimore as a community and urban system managed change.

Some of this "place-based" research has shown that schools are inextricably linked to other places—namely the urban institutions they operate within and alongside—despite Progressive Era reforms and other efforts to separate "school" from "city" (Bartelt, 1995; Yancey & Saporito, 1995). Such interdependencies mean policy makers, researchers, and others should cast a broad net when considering which places matter to implementation and, on the flipside, aim to uncover the educational impact of policies in other sectors such as community development, health care, and social services (Anyon, 2006).

Overall, these three dimensions of implementation—policy, people, and places—come together to form a conception of implementation as a highly contingent and situated process. In this view, the benefits or limitations of one dimension cannot be adequately understood separate from the other. For example, some have noted that how teachers and central office administrators make sense of standards-based curricular reform depends on the policy tool employed within the given policy design, their own prior knowledge and experiences, and the broader institutional setting in which they operate (Hill, 2006). Maryland superintendents, such as the one featured by Malen (2006) in her research on school reconstitution, seem to face different obstacles to implementing high-stakes accountability policies than the Chief Executive Officer in Chicago (Finnigan & O'Day, 2003) or state-level leaders (Massell, 2001). These studies suggest that a given policy may work for some people in some places and researchers aim to understand how different dimensions of policies, people, and places combine to shape implementation processes and outcomes.

Distinct Approach to Knowledge Building

The discussion above reveals that contemporary education policy implementation research also may be distinguished epistemologically—by its orientation to the nature of knowledge and knowledge building about implementation. What are the main dimensions of the epistemological approach reflected in the kinds of research presented here? First, as already noted, a significant strand of contemporary implementation research tends not to seek summary judgments of a policy's success or failure. Rather, this research aims to uncover how particular policies, people, and places interact to produce particular results and to accumulate knowledge about these contingencies. This research seems to take to heart McLaughlin's (1991a) admonition that "generalizations decay"—few if any findings hold true across all contexts or across all time. For example, in the early years of education policy implementation research some researchers argued that policy makers could not mandate what matters to educational improvement—that mandates were insufficient instruments for changing teachers' underlying beliefs about and engagement in their work; however, over time researchers have shown that mandates did sometimes leverage core changes in schooling (McLaughlin, 1991a). This orientation to uncovering contingencies—what I call confronting complexity—stems not from a lack of rigor or scientific-basis for educational research. Rather, this approach reflects the basic operational realities of complex systems in education and many other arenas (Honig, 2006a). The challenge for education policy implementation researchers then becomes how to uncover the various factors that combine to produce implementation results and to accumulate enough cases over time to reveal potentially predictable patterns (Majone, 1989).

Second, contemporary research increasingly reflects the orientation that variation in implementation is not a problem to be avoided but a reality of complex systems that could be better understood and harnessed to enhance the "capacity of program participants to produce desired results" (Elmore, 1983, p. 350; see also Honig, 2003; O'Day, 2002). This view stems in part from contemporary research on student and teacher learning that suggests one size does not fit all when it comes to educational improvement, especially in diverse urban school systems; supports provided to students should vary depending on what students, teachers, and other implementers already know and can do (Darling-Hammond, 1998; Villegas & Lucas, 2002). This orientation also reflects relatively recent policy implementation findings about sensemaking, interpretation, and learning as unavoidable dimensions of implementation processes. Studies in this vein uncover how individual and group cognitive processes contribute to implementers' variable policy responses and, for certain implementers in some settings, the achievement of policy goals (Spillane, Reiser, & Reimer, 2002).

Third, many contemporary implementation researchers use theory to strengthen the rigor of their research. Theory provides criteria for site selection and guides data collection and analysis; it also helps explain why certain interactions among policy, people, and places contribute to particular implementation outcomes. Such research aims not to come up with a universal theory about implementation as an overall enterprise but to use theory to elaborate particular significant dimensions of implementation processes that contribute to implementation outcomes.

The theories upon which education policy implementation researchers now draw come in part from disciplines familiar in implementation arenas such as political science and economics but researchers have begun to apply those theories in new ways. For example, applications of economics to policy implementation have tended to assume a singular implementation actor with certain almost automatic responses to policy demands; some economists argue that many contemporary economic analyses of implementation include significantly deeper explorations of how implementers' agency and context matter to how implementation unfolds (Loeb & McEwan, 2006). At the same time, the field of education policy implementation research has expanded to embrace theoretical constructs from disciplines not traditionally applied to implementation such as those from anthropology, cognitive science, psychology, and learning theory. Critical and sociocultural theories have contributed to particularly vibrant lines of analysis within the education policy implementation field (Anyon, 1997; Lipman, 2004; Stein, 2004; Sutton & Levinson, 2001).

Perhaps in a related development, qualitative research designs and methods have become important sources of knowledge for implementation researchers. In particular, strategic qualitative cases—cases that provide special opportunities to build knowledge about little understood and often complex phenomena—have long informed implementation in other fields and seem to be becoming more standard fare within education. Such methods and research designs, especially when grounded in theory, have allowed contemporary researchers to elaborate the dimensions of and interactions among policy, people, and places that comprise implementation in contemporary educational systems. In fact, the more complex portrait of implementation processes advanced here may have become possible only recently thanks in part to the use of theoretically grounded qualitative methods for capturing such complexity.

Promising Directions for the Future

These developments in the field suggest that research going forward would do well to confront the complexity of policy implementation. Lines of analysis productively begun by the contemporary education policy implementation researchers highlighted here and others suggest that confronting complexity means aiming: (a) to understand patterns of variation as the inevitable and arguably desirable result of implementation dynamics and the various contingencies that shape such patterns; (b) to use rich theoretical frameworks and deep qualitative methods among others not to surface universal or comprehensive theories of implementation but to capture particular dimensions of policies, people, and places that shape implementation dynamics; (c) when possible, to use theoretical frameworks that capture how implementation unfolds through implementers, socially constructed understandings of policy demands and opportunities and as influenced by cultural, historical, and institutional factors.

Which conceptual frameworks seem particularly ripe to ground this new work? Among the various frameworks I could have featured, I highlight three here that are generally not represented in the review above in part because they are just gaining currency among some education policy implementation researchers: complexity theory, organizational learning theory, and critical race theory. These theories seem particularly promising for capturing the complex realities of how policies, people, and places interact over time and within and across various institutional contexts. In this subsection I outline selected major dimensions of each of these conceptual frameworks and how they have been and might be used to ground programs of research around education policy implementation.

Complexity Theory[2] Educational researchers primarily outside the United States have begun to explore how ideas from complexity theory elaborate and explain leadership and change dynamics in education. These ideas move away from framing implementation as a relatively linear process that unfolds within hierarchical or nested systems of influence. Rather, complexity theorists cast educational systems as complex systems—organizations that consist of multiple, dynamic, interacting interdependent elements (Wheatley, 1992) or "ecologies of participation" (Radford, 2006, p. 178). Within such systems, "interconnections [among the elements] at any one point may be temporary, their strength may vary and sequential orders may be multidirectional dependent on particular circumstances" (Radford, 2006, p. 178). These systems do not move in a straightforward or predictable trajectory toward improvement. Rather they evolve in and out of various states of equilibrium at which performance outcomes may not show improvement but which are still essential for systems stability and ongoing change (Salem, 2002) and possible future improvement.

For example, a complexity theorist might frame a district central office bureaucracy as a network of multiple organizations each of which is a locus of control for some aspect of the system essential to its survival and success. While people in each sub-unit continually make their own decisions about how to participate in their work, their actions affect and are invariably affected by the actions of people in other sub-units. In this view, a central office human resources department, for example, operates as a sub-unit of a larger system in which their decisions about how to recruit teachers necessarily shape and constrain decisions by other units such as the high school programs office regarding the types of high school reform approaches it may pursue; likewise, the work of the high schools programs office impacts human resources decisions. Such effects may be direct and explicit as when a human resources department takes stock of the kinds of high school programs in its schools and seeks staff that might be appropriate to those programs. However, such effects may be virtually invisible to participants. This characterization of a school district central office as a dynamic intra-dependent network is a far cry from some traditional characterizations of school district central offices as bureaucratic machines with hierarchically ordered departments each managing some distinct aspect of school district operations. But this characterization is arguably far truer to the workplace dynamics in mid-sized to large urban district central offices.

The survival and success of such systems depends on each of its elements absorbing information and other resources from its external and internal environments and using that information to adapt and change. Consistent with interpretive approaches to policy implementation (e.g., Yanow, 1996), productive use of information in such systems cannot stem from cause-and-effect reasoning because the sheer volume of information and interdependencies encountered by subunits means that direct connections between actions and results will be difficult if not impossible to draw. Accordingly, change and improvement results as systems actors continually collect, interpret, and make sense of their experience and adapt to changing internal and external environmental conditions. Such change processes necessarily are non-linear and fundamentally dependent on actors' learning (Davis & Sumara, 2001) or sense-making processes and relationships within system units and across entire systems.

Complexity theorists argue that organizations are "a world in which many players are all adapting to each other and where the emerging future is very hard to predict" (Axelrod & Cohen 1999, p. xi). The behavior of implementers in this context must be understood not as a reflection of their willingness or capacity (or unwillingness and lack of capacity) to participate in reform. Rather, implementation outcomes are the "emergent consequence of the holistic sum of all the myriad behaviors embedded within" their systems (Marion, 1999, pp. 27–28). In other words, policy does not act on individual implementers but enters a system consisting of multiple actors, layers of work, and institutional histories. Like a ray of light hitting rippling water, that policy necessarily will be refracted in a host of directions that may appear chaotic. But if studied over time through multiple iterations, like the light, regularities in how policy twists and turns under different conditions will emerge that may suggest how complexity can be harnessed to strengthen systems performance (Axelrod & Cohen, 1999).

Harnessing complexity involves strategies that build systemic capacity for self-organization—"the ability to rearrange and reform … patterns of operation in mutual adaptation to changing needs and capacities of their components as well as changing demands and opportunities from the environment" (Comfort, 1994, p. 4). In such systems, levers of top-down control are blunt instruments for change because they ignore that in such systems autonomy of local systems levels, not directives from the top, fosters the system's self-organization and ultimately its coordination and potential productivity. Complexity theorists have modeled that "allowing autonomy at the local level creates freedom that finds a natural order through self-organizing." While it

may seem paradoxical, "the result [of such autonomy and freedom] is more coherence and continuity" throughout the system (Wheatley, 1992, p. 66). Productive levers of change aim to foster ownership over reform goals and strategies and allow solutions to systems failures to emerge from systems participants.

When viewed through the lens of complexity theory, school failure stems not from the efficacy of a particular policy—or the actions of a teacher, a group of teachers, or a school. Rather, school failure is a systems failure—the product of how all the elements of the school system function together (Perrow, 1984). Change results in part not from new technocratic solutions such as better policy designs but by efforts to reshape relationships within and between system levels.

As an example of an application of ideas from complexity theory to education policy implementation, O'Day (2002) examined the implementation of a 1990s accountability policy in Chicago Public Schools (CPS). She demonstrates that such a policy functioned as a weak lever for increasing school accountability and ultimately school improvement in part because policy designers crafted the policy based on assumptions that CPS operated as a hierarchical system of top-down control in which mandates function as effective change levers. Rather, she frames CPS and other urban districts as complex systems. As such, these systems require relevant feedback and mechanisms for attending to information as part of a continuous improvement process; face challenges of interpreting cause-and-effect in using such information; and grow, change, survive, and improve in part through local ownership over problems and solutions. In such systems, accountability policies would be more productive if they aimed to "generate and focus attention on information relevant to teaching and learning and to changes in the information as it is continually fed back into and through the system," "motivate educators and others to attend to relevant information and to expend the effort necessary to augment or change strategies in response to this information," and "develop the knowledge and skills to promote valid interpretation of information and appropriate attribution of causality at both the individual and system level" (p. 9).

This line of theory has a number of implications for implementation research methodology. First, this theory suggests that researchers will not understand how implementation unfolds by focusing on individual systems elements such as a school or group of schools. Rather, understanding change demands a focus on the total system in which implementers participate. What counts as the total system is an empirical question that researchers should build into their research programs.

Second, as Radford (2006) argues, researchers should avoid "analytic reductionist" approaches because they seek to distill complex systems into discrete, independent factors and link factors to outcomes. Complexity theory suggests this approach is inappropriate because complex systems consist not of variables but of various actors in interdependent, non-linear relationships. Accordingly, researchers should focus on the nature of connections among systems actors over time and the flow of information within and between systems and its effect on systems outcomes. The primary role of policy research must shift from prescription to description and explanations that promise to inform but not direct policy-makers' decisions (Radford, 2006). Descriptive questions that might productively ground such analyses include: "Who are the social actors? How do they interact? What were the initial conditions? What were the disruptions or changes in these factors? What are the feedback loops?" (Salem, 2002, p. 447). Such questions must be addressed in real time over time and traced back historically to create a trajectory of systems dynamics that ultimately help explain present outcomes.

Third, researchers should aim to accumulate cases of how organizations adapt to changing conditions and the circumstances that seem to explain adaptation and change and look for regularities or patterns in how these dynamics play out. Social network analyses seem particularly promising for capturing these dynamics in part because they allow researchers to track different types of relationships among implementers with varying characteristics under changing circumstances over time. In the absence of data sets conducive to social network analysis, education policy implementation researchers might consider how advances in computer software may allow them to model such dynamics with considerable predictive power.

Theories of Organizational Learning[3] Educational scholars long have called for conceptualizing educational change as learning (e.g., Cohen, 1982). However, educational researchers only recently have begun to demonstrate how various theories of learning as a socially situated phenomenon can productively ground implementation research. These theories have far too many strands to capture fully here and go by such names as communities of practice (Hubbard, Stein, & Mehan, 2006) and distributed social cognition (Spillane et al., 2002). As one example, theories of organizational learning under conditions of ambiguity (also called learning from experience) help to elaborate how complex systems manage the flow of information that complexity theorists view as essential to implementation (e.g., Argyris & Schon, 1996; Fiol & Lyles, 1985; Huber, 1991; Levitt & March, 1988) and shed important light on implementation dynamics in their own right. These theories seem particularly promising because they rest on assumptions shared with complexity theory that feedback on performance is often slow in coming in complex systems and that available feedback is typically ambiguous regarding what it means and how decision-makers might use it for organizational improvement (Kanter, 1988; March, 1994). Accordingly, implementation and other organizational processes demand that policy makers and implementers engage in particular activities: the search for information; the storage or encoding of that information (or deliberate decisions not to use that information) into forms accessible

by a broader range of organizational members than those who searched for it; and the retrieval or ongoing use of that encoded information.

Briefly, search, also called exploration (Levitt & March, 1988) and knowledge acquisition (Huber, 1991), refers to a variety of processes by which information enters an organization. For example, an organization may hire staff who carry information with them into the organization or designate individuals, organizational subunits, and other so-called "boundary spanners" to gather information (Huber, 1991; Kanter, 1988).

Encoding, sometimes called exploitation, involves the integration of that new information (or deliberate decisions not to employ that information) into organizational rules or "any semi-stable specification of the way in which an organization deals with its environment, functions, and prospers" (Levinthal & March, 1981, p. 307; see also Argyris, 1976; Argyris & Schon, 1996; Cohen, 1991; Huber, 1991; Levitt & March, 1988). In education policy contexts, such forms include formal policies such as administrative procedures and resource allocations. Information also may be encoded into informal policies including individual implementers' decisions about their own work (Weatherley & Lipsky, 1977) as well as changes in implementers' frames for decision-making (Brown & Duguid, 1991; see also Barley, 1996) and where they choose to look for models of how they should behave as professionals (March, 1994).

Retrieval refers to processes by which organizational members continually draw on information from experience, encoded in various forms, to guide their subsequent choices and actions (Levitt & March, 1988). Retrieval then is a sort-of internal variation on search and encoding in that it involves organizational members mining experience—in this case already-encoded information—for guides regarding how to respond to new situations and using that information in new situations to make sense of whether and how the already-encoded information should be reinforced or changed.

For organizational learning theorists and learning theorists in other arenas, interpretation is at the heart of learning. In this view, new information rarely presents itself in a form that suggests whether or how it should be used (Yanow, 1996). Even when information is encoded those encoded forms generally are not unambiguous regarding whether and how they apply to new situations (March & Olsen, 1975; van de Ven, 1986; van de Ven & Polley, 1992). Accordingly, implementers must interpret or make sense of information from experience. That is, they grapple with whether and how to attend to information and, in the process, render information meaningful and actionable; what some scholars call "interpretation sensemaking" (Weick, 1995).

Cognitive, historical, normative, social, and political influences shape implementers' interpretations. For example, from a cognitive perspective, implementers notice information that is relatively easy to understand and can be divided into discrete action steps or phases that decision-makers believe they can undertake with relative ease and success. Individuals attend to information that confirms their competencies and fits their prior understandings (Kanter, 1988; Levitt & March, 1988; March, 1994). Through interpretation individuals reshape information so that it takes on these simpler, familiar, confidence-building forms to increase the likelihood that the information will be understood and that organizational decision-makers will view it as information on which they can take action confidently and successfully. These cognitive manipulations of information are *history dependent* in that they are shaped by past experiences. Individuals are likely to favor information that they experienced more recently than other information (March, 1994). Interpretation is also history-dependent in that it involves fitting information to individual and collective "prior knowledge"—essentially a body of information that has already been encoded/reified and that is retrieved or retrievable for use in interpretation.

Some theorists argue that interpretation also has *normative dimensions* in the sense that when individuals interpret information they fit new information to or otherwise call on particular identity conceptions—what some call "logics of appropriateness"—to guide their decisions. In this view, as part of interpretation individuals notice and attend to particular information that they believe fits identities they associate with successful or legitimate professional practice. In the process, implementation involves policy makers and implementers grappling with such normative, identity-based questions as: "Who would I like to be? What kind of information is this? How would the person I would like to be interpret this information/situation?" (adapted from March, 1994).

Interpretation also unfolds as *political struggles for power* (Steyaert, Bouwen, & Van Looy, 1996). In these struggles, individuals and collectives vie with one another to control the meanings or logics brought to bear in interpreting information (Ibarra, 1993; Kanter, 1983). As they negotiate these struggles, individuals might band together in coalitions or dedicate resources (e.g., allocate meeting agenda time) to consider some but not other interpretations. Such political struggles are not problematic or barriers to implementation that should be minimized. Rather, such political conflicts are an inherent, unavoidable, and arguably valuable dimension of interpretive processes. Through political conflicts, implementers make certain issues and priorities explicit, marshal evidence and argument to defend positions, attract resources to ground particular views, and work to convince others of their world views— all important contributors to implementation.

A handful of educational researchers have used these and related ideas to frame empirical inquiries into how implementers manage information as part of policy implementation and other processes of public bureaucracies. For example, in relatively early applications of these ideas, Kennedy and Hanaway each studied decision-making in school district central offices. They revealed in part how biases in how individual decision-makers interpret information in complex settings shaped their participation in various policy initiatives (Hannaway, 1989; Kennedy,

1982a, 1982b). More recently, I have demonstrated how search, encoding, and retrieval capture how central office administrators managed information in ways that sometimes enabled the implementation of school-community partnership initiatives and other educational policies that called for non-traditional partnership relationships between district central offices, schools, and community agencies (Honig, 2003, 2004b). Some educational leadership scholars have applied these ideas to elaborate what they variably call cycles of inquiry or continuous improvement processes within school-based teacher learning communities. In these studies, teachers' implementation of ambitious curricular reform efforts gains strength from opportunities to work with colleagues to examine and analyze their practice (Scribner, 1999; Scribner, Cockrell, Cockrell, & Valentine, 1999). Leithwood, Leonard, and Sharratt (1998) have conducted a series of mixed-method studies that link particular in-school and out-of-school conditions to principals' and teachers' engagement in such processes.

Theories of organizational learning under conditions of ambiguity have a number of implications for the design and methods of education policy implementation research. First, this line of theory moves beyond the metaphor that implementation involves learning to call researchers' attention to specific activities involved in learning such as search, encoding, and retrieval and to interpretive processes that cut across all three activities. Consistent with emerging conceptions of control as spread throughout implementing systems, these organizational learning processes include policy development activities that may be found at all points of implementing systems at individual, group, and systems levels. As I have argued elsewhere, organizational learning theory blurs traditional lines between policy designers or those who determine policy direction and implementers or those who carry out policy directives to reveal policy design and implementation as overlapping processes throughout educational systems (Honig, 2004a, 2006b).

Second, the ambiguity inherent in such activities demands that implementation researchers aim not for summary judgments of implementation success or failure but rather seek to understand how these information processes unfold over time and the conditions that shape them. In this view, process-based indicators such as whether policy actors engage in search, encoding, and retrieval, are fundamental and valued implementation outcomes.

Given the centrality of interpretation or sense-making to these processes, implementation researchers using organizational learning as conceptual frame should employ data collection methods that tap how implementers make sense of their experience over time. As noted above, semi-structured interview formats may capture implementers' reports of events but they do not always reveal how implementers interpret experience. Researchers might consider how to craft interview questions and other data collection methods specifically to explore such interpretations. For example, Ikemoto (2007) has used observations of principals' practice to surface representations of principals' experience working with teachers to improve their teaching practice; she then probed how principals made sense of these experiences through a line of questions that aimed to tap how principals did or did not link those particular activities with more abstract ideas about what instructional leaders do. Argyris and Schon (1996) have demonstrated with cases outside education how questions that tap interpretation and sense-making probe implementers' theories of action—or how they connect goals and actions in a chain of logic that reflects how they believe the world works.

Critical Race Theory Critical race theory is one promising conceptual framework for confronting complexity that centrally addresses how various forms of oppression matter to interactions among policy, people, and places. Per Delgado (1995), three notions underlie critical race theory (see also Crenshaw, Gotanda, Peller, & Thomas, 1995). First, racism is a normal feature of life that has become embedded in various forms throughout American institutions, even institutions that promise to address disadvantage. Racism has become so enmeshed in these institutions that it has become virtually invisible (Ladson-Billings, 1999). Accordingly, legal, social, and other kinds of inquiry should seek to uncover these manifestations of racism and their influences on implementation and other social processes.

Second, experiential knowledge should ground these inquiries. This focus on experiential knowledge—on implementers' reports of their lived experiences—stands in direct challenge to allegedly objective approaches to gathering evidence about implementation and other outcomes and White normative standards as the basis for gauging various outcomes (Lynn & Parker, 2006). Through the telling of their own stories, implementers and other actors tap and reveal their own experiences with oppression otherwise invisible through positivist research designs and other research methods that do not elevate and make explicit the importance of specific forms of oppression (Barnes, 1990).

Third, critical race theory rejects "liberalism" as a source of remedies for racial and other injustices. In this view, liberalism works incrementally within current legal paradigms to understand and address social injustice. Critical race theorists argue that understanding and addressing social injustice demand changes that fundamentally disrupt mainstream paradigms.

These framing ideas privilege racism as a form of oppression and in particular the experiences of African Americans in the context of the legacy of slavery. However, Carbado (2002) and others have argued that a new generation of scholarship embraces the experience of other racial and ethnic minority groups in its elaboration of these ideas. This new generation also considers other forms of oppression such as sexism and homophobia as relevant to these dynamics and how these oppressions play out in various ways for individuals even of the same status groups (Valdes, Culpe, & Harris, 2002).

Critical race theorists argue that interest convergence helps explain policy implementation and other social outcomes. Based mainly on analysis of legal cases, the concept of interest convergence highlights that policies that benefit people of color and other traditionally disadvantaged groups are enacted and implemented when they are linked to advantages for Whites (Bell, 1980, 1992; Dumas & Anyon, 2006).

As a lens on implementation processes, critical race theory is in its nascent stages. However, some educational researchers have begun to reveal how critical race theory and related ideas can begin to frame implementation analyses. For example, in a study in this tradition (though utilizing a framework the author calls "political economy" analysis), Anyon (1997) examined how school restructuring policies played out in the context of elementary schools in Newark, New Jersey. She demonstrates how such school-focused policies seem destined for failure in part because the race- and class-neutral, school-focused framing of such policies does not address how various forms of disadvantage and oppression embedded in urban political and economic institutions impede their implementation. Likewise, Taylor's (2000) analysis of Washington State's I-200 initiative to end Affirmative Action revealed how the passage of that policy could be viewed as an inevitable outcome of democratic legal systems that function to reinforce White mainstream privilege. He argues that I-200 was successful in part because these systems of privilege fueled the casting of affirmative action laws not in terms of making mainstream benefits available to people of color and women but as a vehicle for victimizing Whites.

Other researchers do not bill their work as implementation research per se but nevertheless have conducted studies of implementation dynamics from a critical race perspective. For example, Pollock's 3-year ethnography of an urban California school demonstrates how even social-justice-minded teachers' engage in talk about race in ways that actually reinforce racist power dynamics that they actively seek to avoid (Pollock, 2001).

These and other early writings in this line suggest that education policy implementation research methods should take racism and other forms of oppression as their main framing ideas. Solórzano and Yosso (2002) have called this approach a key dimension of a critical race methodology—a methodology that "foregrounds race and racism in all aspects of the research process" (p. 24).

Critical race theory also suggests that implementation research methods should aim to tap policy actors' lived experiences with various forms of oppression, such as through first-hand narrative. Researchers should structure such storytelling opportunities to help participants grapple with how aspects of their situation (e.g., their schools and classrooms) may reflect racist biases but also how they themselves carry such views and act in ways that frustrate implementation—especially the implementation of policies that aim to confer benefits on traditionally disadvantaged students and groups. This approach embraces subjectivity of perspective (Ladson-Billings, 1999) and personalizes qualitative research (Ladson-Billings, 2000) as a vehicle to reveal how mainstream institutional structures constrain individual agency.

Such methods take the individual respondents' experiences as the main analytic frame rather than other standards that view mainstream White experiences as normative (Williams, 1991; Solórzano & Yosso, 2002). For example, Lopez (2001) examined the involvement of a Spanish-speaking immigrant family in their children's education. He argues that by mainstream standards, such a family might be considered not involved in their children's education because they do not participate in activities sanctioned by schools such as Parent Teachers' Associations and bake sales. However, by privileging his respondents' cultural meaning systems, he revealed that these parents were heavily involved in their children's education for example creating opportunities for their children to learn about the demands of various kinds of workplaces and the importance of education to expanding their workplace opportunities—a form of parental involvement in education of particular value to his focal family.

Theory but not Theory Alone In sum, the field of education policy implementation research seems to be on a promising trajectory—one that focuses attention not simply on what works but on what works for whom where, when, and why? I view this trajectory as promising because it aims to confront the complex day-to-day realities in educational systems. Ideas from complexity theory, organizational learning theories, and critical race theory, among other theoretical traditions seem particularly promising for shedding light on these dynamics. Future researchers might deepen knowledge of education policy implementation by following along this trajectory.

But the power of these and other theories may lie in the extent to which researchers use them not only to ground single studies but to galvanize programs of research across settings that lead to an accumulation of cases and evidence about various implementation dynamics. When viewed in this way, future researchers might consider not only which theoretical traditions should ground their work but how to create and affiliate with communities of researchers examining common problems with similar tools.

The learning sciences may provide some guidance in this regard—as may other fields that have rich traditions of focusing on situated phenomena while also accumulating cases that contribute to a broader body of knowledge. Some learning scientists organize themselves into research laboratories—communities of scholars convened for some period of time around a particular line of inquiry. Such labs may enable sustained collaborative attention on pressing implementation challenges and the accumulation of rich situated knowledge about common cases. In lab-like settings, implementation researchers may focus on shared implementation questions over time and deliberately draw conclusions across multiple studies in ways otherwise uncommon in the traditional field of implementation research replete with individual policy entrepreneurs competing for evaluation contracts.

Notes

1. This subsection is adapted with permission from The State University of New York Press © 2006 from the following publication: Honig (2006a).
2. Thanks to Sue Feldman for her assistance with the subsections on complexity theory and critical race theory.
3. I adapted the text in this subsection from the following publications: Honig (2004) and Honig (2008).

References

Anderson, B., Odden, A., Farrar, E., Fuhrman, S., Davis, A., Huddle, E., et al. (1987). State strategies to support local school improvement. *Knowledge: Creation, Diffusion, Utilization, 9*(1), 42–87.

Anyon, J. (1997). *Ghetto schooling: A political economy of urban educational reform.* New York: Teachers College Press.

Anyon, J. (2006). *Radical possibilities: Public policy, urban education, and a new social movement.* New York: Routledge.

Argyris, C. (1976). Single-loop and double-loop models in research on decision making. *Administrative Science Quarterly, 21,* 363–375.

Argyris, C., & Schon, D. A. (1996). *Organizational learning II: Theory, method, and practice.* Reading, MA: Addison-Wesley.

Axelrod, R., & Cohen, M. D. (1999). *Harnessing complexity: Organizational implications of a scientific frontier.* New York: Free Press.

Barnes, R. (1990). Race consciousness: The thematic content of racial distinctiveness and critical race scholarship. *Harvard Law Review, 103,* 1864–1871.

Barley, S. R. (1996). Technicians in the workplace: Ethnographic evidence for bringing work into organization studies. *Administrative Science Quarterly, 41*(3), 404–441.

Bartelt, D. W. (1995). The macroecology of educational outcomes. In L. C. Rigsby, M. C. Reynolds, & M. C. Wang (Eds.), *School-community connections: exploring issues for research and practice* (pp. 159–191). San Francisco: Jossey-Bass.

Bell, D. A., Jr. (1980). Brown v. Board of Education and the interest-convergence dilemma. *Harvard Law Review, 93,* 518–533.

Bell, D. (1992). *Faces at the bottom of the well: The permanence of racism.* New York: Basic Books.

Berman, P., & McLaughlin, M. (1976). Implementation of educational innovation. *The Educational Forum, 40,* 345–370.

Berman, P., & McLaughlin, M. (1978). *Federal programs supporting educational change: Vol. 8. Implementing and sustaining innovations.* Santa Monica, CA: Rand Corporation.

Brown, J. S., & Duguid, P. (1991). Organizational learning and communities-of-practice: Toward a unified view of working, learning, and innovation. *Organization Science, 2,* 40–57.

Bryk, A., & Sebring, P. B. (1991). *Achieving school reform in Chicago: What we need to know. A research agenda.* Chicago: Consortium on Chicago School Research.

Bryk, A. S., Sebring, P. B., Kerbow, D., Rollow, S., & Easton, J. Q. (1998). *Charting Chicago school reform: Democratic localism as a lever for change.* Boulder, CO: Westview Press.

Burch, P., & Spillane, J. (2004). Leading from the middle: Mid-level district staff and instructional improvement. Chicago: Cross City Campaign for Urban School Reform.

Carbado, D. W. (2002). (E)racing education. *Equity and Excellence in Education, 35*(2), 181–194.

Clune, W. H., III. (1983). A political model of implementation and implications of the model for public policy, research, and the changing roles of law and lawyers. *Iowa Law Review, 69,* 47–125.

Cobb, P., McClain, K., Lamberg, T. D., & Dean, C. (2003). Situating teachers' instructional practices in the institutional setting of the school and district. *Educational Researcher, 32*(6), 13–24.

Coburn, C. E. (2001). Collective sensemaking about reading: How teachers mediate reading policy in their professional communities. *Educational Evaluation and Policy Analysis, 23,* 145–170.

Coburn, C. E., & Stein, M. K. (2006). Communities of practice theory and the role of teacher professional community in policy implementation. In M. I. Honig (Ed.) *New directions in education policy implementation: Confronting complexity* (pp. 25–46). Albany: The State University of New York Press.

Cohen, D. K. (1982). Policy and organization: The impact of state and federal educational policy on school governance. *Harvard Educational Review, 52*, 474–499.

Cohen, D. K., & Hill, H. C. (2000). Instructional policy and classroom performance: The mathematics reform in California. *Teachers College Record, 102*, 294–343.

Cohen, M. D. (1991). Individual learning and organizational routine: Emerging connections. *Organization Science, 2*(1), 135–139.

Comfort, L.K. (1994). Self-organization in complex systems. *Journal of Public Administration Research and Theory, 4*(3), 393–410.

Cremin, L. A. (1988). *American education: The metropolitan experience, 1876–1980.* New York: Harper and Row.

Crenshaw, K., Gotanda, N., Peller, G., & Thomas, K. (Eds.). (1995). *Critical race theory: The key writings that formed the movement.* New York: Free Press.

Crowson, R. L., & Boyd, W. L. (1993). Coordinated services for children: Designing arks for storms and seas unknown. *American Journal of Education, 101*, 140–179.

Cuban, L., & Tyack, D. (1995). *Tinkering toward utopia: A century of public school reform.* Cambridge, MA: Harvard University Press.

Cuban, L., & Usdan, M. (2003). *Powerful reforms with shallow roots: Improving America's urban schools.* New York: Teachers College Press.

Datnow, A. (2006). Connections in the policy chain: The "co-construction" of implementation in comprehensive school reform. In M. I. Honig (Ed.), *New directions in education policy implementation: Confronting complexity* (pp. 105–124). Albany: The State University of New York Press.

Datnow, A., Hubbard, L., & Conchas, G. Q. (2001). How context mediates policy: The implementation of single gender public schooling in California. *Teachers College Record, 103*(2), 184–206.

Darling-Hammond, L. (1998). Policy and change: Getting beyond bureaucracy. In A. Hargreaves, A. Lieberman, M. Fullan, & D. Hopkins (Eds.), *International handbook of educational change* (pp. 642–667). Dordrecht, The Netherlands: Kluwer.

Davis, B., & Sumara, D. (2001). Learning communities: Understanding the workplace as a complex system. *New Directions in Adult and Continuing Education, 92*, 85–95.

Delgado, R. (Ed.). (1995). *Critical race theory: The cutting edge.* Philadelphia: Temple University Press.

Derthick, M. (1972). *New towns in-town: Why a federal program failed.* Washington, DC: The Urban Institute.

Dumas, M. J., & Anyon, J. (2006). Toward a critical approach to education policy implementation: Implications for the (battle) field. In M. I. Honig (Ed.), *New directions in education policy implementation: Confronting complexity* (pp. 149–168). Albany: The State University of New York Press.

Elmore, R. F. (1979–1980). Backward mapping: implementation research and policy decisions. *Political Science Quarterly, 94*, 601–616.

Elmore, R. F. (1983). Complexity and control: What legislators and administrators can do about implementing public policy. In L. S. Shulman & G. Sykes (Eds.), *Handbook of teaching and policy* (pp. 342–369). New York: Longman.

Elmore, R. F. (1996). Getting to scale with good educational practice. *Harvard Education Review, 66*(1), 1–24.

Elmore, R. F., & McLaughlin, M. W. (1988). *Steady work: Policy, practice, and the reform of American education.* Santa Monica, CA: RAND.

Farrar, E., & Milsap, M. A. (1986). *State and local implementation of Chapter I.* Cambridge, MA: ABT Associates.

Finn, J. D., & Achilles, C. M. (1990). Answers and questions about class size: A statewide experiment. *American Educational Research Journal, 27*(3), 557–577.

Finnigan, K., & O'Day, J. (2003, July). *External support to schools on probation: Getting a leg up?* Philadelphia: Consortium for Policy Research in Education.

Fiol, C. M., & Lyles, M. A. (1985). Organizational learning. *Academy of Management Review, 10*, 803–813.

Fuhrman, S. H. (1993). The politics of coherence. In S. H. Fuhrman, (Ed.), *Designing coherent education policy: Improving the system* (pp. 1–34). San Francisco: Jossey-Bass.

Fuhrman, S. H., Clune, W., & Elmore, R. F. (1988). Research on education reform: Lessons on the implementation of policy. *Teachers College Record, 90*(2), 237–258.

Gilman, D. A, & Kiger, S. (2003). Should we try to keep class sizes small? *Educational Leadership 60*(7), 80–85.

Goggin, M. L., Bowman, A., Lester, J. P., & O'Toole, L. J., Jr. (1990). *Implementation theory and practice: Toward a third generation.* New York: Harper Collins.

Hamann, E., & Lane, B. (2004). The roles of State Departments of Education as policy intermediaries: Two cases. *Educational Policy, 18*(3), 426–455.

Hannaway, J. (1989). *Managers managing: The workings of an administrative system.* New York: Oxford University Press.

Hess, F. M. (2002). I say "refining" you say "retreating": The politics of high-stakes accountability. *Taking account of accountability: Assessing politics and policy.* Cambridge, MA: Harvard Program on Education Policy and Governance.

Hess, F. M., & Henig, J. R. (2008, February 7). "Scientific research" and policymaking: A tool not a crutch. *Education Week.* Retrieved February 15, 2008, from http://www.edweek.com

Hightower, A. M., Knapp, M. S., Marsh, J. A., & McLaughlin, M. W. (Eds.). (2002). *School districts and instructional renewal.* New York: Teachers College Press.

Hill, H. C. (2006). Language matters: How characteristics of language complicate policy implementation. In M. I. Honig (Ed.), *New directions in education policy implementation: Confronting complexity* (pp. 65–82). Albany: The State University of New York Press.

Honig, M. I. (2001). *Managing ambiguity: The implementation of complex education policy.* Unpublished doctoral dissertation, Stanford University School of Education, Stanford, CA.

Honig, M. I. (2003). Building policy from practice: District central office administrators' roles and capacity for implementing collaborative education policy. *Educational Administration Quarterly, 39*, 292–338.

Honig, M. I. (2004a). Where's the "up" in bottom-up reform. *Educational Policy, 18*, 527–561.

Honig, M. I. (2004b). The new middle management: Intermediary organizations in education policy implementation. *Educational Evaluation and Policy Analysis, 26*, 65–87.

Honig, M. I. (2006a). Complexity and policy implementation: Challenges and opportunities for the field. In M. I. Honig (Ed.) *New directions in education policy implementation: Confronting complexity* (pp. 1–24). Albany: The State University of New York Press.

Honig, M. I. (2006b). Street-level bureaucracy revisited: Frontline district central office administrators as boundary spanners in education policy implementation. *Educational Evaluation and Policy Analysis, 28*, 357–383.

Honig, M. I. (2008). District central offices as learning organizations: How socio-cultural and organizational learning theories elaborate district-central-office administrators' participation in teaching and learning improvement efforts. *American Journal of Education, 114*, 627–664.

Hubbard, L., Stein, M. K., & Mehan, H. (2006). *Reform as learning: When school reform collides with school culture and community politics.* New York: Routledge.

Huber, G. P. (1991). Organizational learning: The contributing processes and the literatures. *Organization Science, 2*, 88–115.

Ibarra, H. (1993). Network centrality, power, and innovation involvement: Determinants of technical and administrative roles. *Academy of Management Journal, 36*, 471–501.

Ikemoto, G. S. (2007). Supporting principals' sensemaking: Lessons from the Institute for Learning's Instructional Leadership Program in Baltimore, MD. Unpublished doctoral dissertation, University of Maryland, College Park.

Kaestle, C. F. (1983). *Pillars of the republic: Common schools and American society, 1780–1860.* New York: Hill and Wang

Kanter, R. M. (1983). *The change masters: Innovation and entrepreneurship in the American corporation* . New York: Simon and Schuster.

Kanter, R. M. (1988). When a thousand flowers bloom: Structural, collective, and social conditions for innovation in organization. *Research in Organizational Behavior, 10,* 169–211.

Katz, M. B., Fine, M., & Simon, E. (1997). Poking around: Outsiders view Chicago school reform. *Teachers College Record, 99,* 117–157.

Kennedy, M. M. (1982a). Evidence and decision. In M. M. Kennedy (Ed.), *Working knowledge and other essays* (pp. 59–103). Cambridge, MA: The Huron Institute.

Kennedy, M. M. (1982b). Working knowledge. In M. M. Kennedy (Ed.), *Working knowledge and other essays* (pp. 1–28). Cambridge, MA: The Huron Institute.

Kirst, M., & Bulkley, K. (2000). "New, improved" mayors take over city schools. *Phi Delta Kappan, 81,* 538–546.

Kirst, M., & Jung, R. (1980). The utility of a longitudinal approach in assessing implementation: A thirteen-year view of Title I, ESEA. *Educational Evaluation and Policy Analysis, 2*(5), 17–34.

Kliebard, H. M. (1987). *The struggle for the American curriculum, 1983–1958.* New York: Routledge.

Knapp, M. S. (1997). Between systemic reforms and the mathematics and science classroom: The dynamics of innovation, implementation, and professional learning. *Review of Educational Research, 67,* 227–266.

Knapp, M. S., Stearns, M. S., Turnbull, B. J., David, J. L., & Peterson, S. (1991). Cumulative effects of federal education policies at the local level. In A. R. Odden (Ed.), *Education policy implementation* (pp. 105–124). Albany: State University of New York Press.

Ladson-Billings, G. (1999). Preparing teachers for diverse student populations: A critical race perspective. *Review of Research in Education, 24,* 211–247.

Ladson-Billings, G. (2000). Racialized discourses and ethnic epistemologies. In N. K. Denzin & Y. S. Lincoln (Eds.), *Handbook of qualitative research* (2nd ed., pp. 257–278). Thousand Oaks, CA: Sage.

Ladson-Billings, G., & Tate, W. F. (1995). Toward a critical race theory of education. *Teachers College Record, 97,* 47–68.

Lee, V. E., & Smith, J. (1995). Effects of high school restructuring and size on gains in achievement and engagement for early secondary students. *Sociology of Education, 68,* 241–270.

Leithwood, K., Leonard, L., & Sharratt, L. (1998). Conditions fostering organizational learning in schools. *Educational Administration Quarterly, 34,* 243–276.

Levinthal, D., & March, J. G. (1981). A model of adaptive organizational search. *Journal of Economic Behavior and Organization, 2*(4), 307–333.

Levitt, B., & March, J. G. (1988). Organizational learning. *Annual Review of Sociology, 14,* 319–340.

Lieberman, A., & McLaughlin, M. W. (1992). Networks for educational change: Powerful and problematic. *Phi Delta Kappan, 73,* 673–677.

Lipman, P. (2004). *High stakes education: Inequality, globalization, and urban school reform.* New York: Routledge Falmer.

Little, J. W. (1984). Seductive images and organizational realities in professional development. *Teachers College Record, 86,* 84–102.

Loeb, S., & McEwan, P. J. (2006). An economic approach to education policy implementation. In M. I. Honig (Ed.), *New directions in education policy implementation: Confronting complexity* (pp. 169–186). Albany: The State University of New York Press.

Lopez, G. R. (2001). The value of hard work: Lessons on parent involvement from an (im)migrant household. *Harvard Educational Review, 71,* 416–437.

Louis, K. S. (1994). Beyond "managed change:" Rethinking how schools improve. *School Effectiveness and School Improvement, 5,* 2–24.

Lowi, T. (1969). *The end of liberalism.* New York: Norton.

Lusi, S. F. (1997). *The role of state departments of education in complex school reform.* New York: Teachers College Press.

Lynn, M., & Parker, L. (2006). Critical race studies in education: Examining a decade of research on U.S. schools. *The Urban Review, 38,* 257–290.

Majone, G. (1989). *Evidence, argument, and persuasion in the policy process.* New Haven, CT: Yale University Press.

Malen, B. (2006). Revisiting policy implementation as a political phenomenon: The case of reconstitution policies. In M. I. Honig (Ed.), *New directions in education policy implementation: Confronting complexity* (pp. 83–104). Albany: The State University of New York Press.

March, J. G. (1994). *A primer on decision making: How decisions happen.* New York: The Free Press.

March, J. G., & Olsen, J. P. (1975). The uncertainty of the past: Organizational learning under ambiguity. *European Journal of Political Research, 3,* 147–171.

Marion, R. (1999). *The edge of organization: Chaos and complexity theories of formal social systems.* Thousand Oaks, CA: Sage.

Marsh, D. D., & Crocker, P. S. (1991). School restructuring: Implementing middle school reform. In A. R. Odden (Ed.), *Education policy implementation* (pp. 259–278). Albany: State University of New York Press.

Massell, D. (2001). The theory and practice of using data to build capacity: State and local strategies and their effects. In S. H. Fuhrman (Ed.), *From the capitol to the classroom: Standards-based reform in the states. One hundredth yearbook of the National Society for the Study of Education* (pp. 148–169). Chicago: National Society for the Study of Education.

McDonnell, L. M., & Elmore, R. F. (1987). Getting the job done: Alternative policy instruments. *Educational Evaluation and Policy Analysis, 9,* 133–152.

McLaughlin, M. W. (1991a). Learning from experience: Lessons from policy implementation. In A. R. Odden (Ed.), *Education Policy Implementation* (pp. 185–196). Albany: State University of New York Press.

McLaughlin, M. W. (1991b). The Rand Change Agent Study: Ten years later. In A. R. Odden (Ed.), *Education policy implementation* (pp. 143–155). Albany: State University of New York Press.

McLaughlin, M. W., & Talbert, J. E. (2001). *Professional communities and the work of high school teaching.* Chicago: University of Chicago Press.

Mintrop, H. (2003). *Schools on probation: How accountability works (and doesn't work).* New York: Teachers College Press.

Murphy, J. T. (1971). Title I of ESEA: The politics of implementing federal education reform. *Harvard Educational Review, 41,* 35–63.

Oakes, J., & Rogers, J. (2006). *Learning power: Organizing for social justice.* New York: Teachers College Press.

O'Day, J. A. (2002). Complexity, accountability, and school improvement. *Harvard Educational Review, 72,* 293–329.

Odden, A. R. (1991a). The evolution of education policy implementation. In A. R. Odden (Ed.), *Education policy implementation* (pp. 1–12). Albany: State University of New York Press.

Odden, A. R. (1991b). New patterns of education policy implementation and challenges for the 1990s. In A. R. Odden (Ed.), *Education Policy Implementation* (pp. 297–327). Albany: State University of New York Press.

Orr, M. (1998). The challenge of school reform in Baltimore: Race, jobs, and politics. In C. N. Stone (Ed.), *Changing urban education* (pp. 93–117). Lawrence: University Press of Kansas.

Orr, M. (1999). *Black social capital: The politics of school reform in Baltimore, 1986–1998.* Lawrence: University Press of Kansas.

Perrow, C. (1984). *Normal accidents: Living with high-risk technologies.* New York: Basic Books.

Peterson, P., Rabe, B., & Wong, K. (1986). *When federalism works.* Washington, DC: Brookings Institution.

Peterson, P., Rabe, B., & Wong, K. (1991). The maturation of redistributive programs. In A. R. Odden (Ed.), *Education Policy Implementation* (pp. 65–80). Albany: State University of New York Press.

Pillow, W. S. (2004). *Unfit subjects: Education policy and the teen mother.* New York: Routledge Falmer.

Pollock, M. (2001). How the question we ask most about race in education is the very question we most suppress. *Educational Researcher,* *30*(9), 2–12.

Pressman, J. L., & Wildavsky, A. (1984). *Implementation: How great expectations in Washington are dashed in Oakland* (3rd ed.). Berkeley, CA: University of California Press.

Purkey, S. C., & Smith, M. S. (1983). Effective schools: A review. *Elementary School Journal, 83*, 427–452.

Radford, M. (2006). Researching classrooms: Complexity and chaos. *British Educational Research Journal, 32*, 177–190.

Radin, B. A. (1977). *Implementation, change, and the federal bureaucracy: School desegregation policy in H.E.W., 1964–1968.* New York: Teachers College Press.

Radin, B. A. (2000). *Beyond Machiavelli: Policy analysis comes of age.* Washington, DC: Georgetown University Press.

Rosenholtz, S. J. (1985). Effective schools: Interpreting the evidence. *American Journal of Education, 93*, 352–358.

Sabatier, P., & Mazmanian, D. (1979). The conditions of effective implementation: A guide to accomplishing policy objectives. *Policy Analysis, 5*, 481–504.

Sabatier, P., & Mazmanian, D. (1980). The implementation of public policy: A framework of analysis. *The Policy Studies Journal, 8*, 538–560.

Salem, P. (2002). Assessment, change, and complexity. *Management Communication Quarterly, 15*, 422–450.

Schneider, A., & Ingram, H. (1990). Behavioral assumptions of policy tools. *Journal of Politics, 52*, 510–529.

Schneider, A., & Ingram, H. (1993). Social construction of target populations: Implications for politics and policy. *American Political Science Review, 87*, 334–347.

Schram, S. F. (1995). *Words of welfare: The poverty of social science and the social science of poverty.* Minneapolis: University of Minnesota Press.

Scribner, J. P. (1999). Professional development: Untangling the influence of work context on teacher learning. *Educational Administration Quarterly, 35*, 238–266.

Scribner, J. P., Cockrell, K. S., Cockrell, D. H., Valentine, J. W. (1999). Creating professional communities in schools through organizational learning: An evaluation of a school improvement process. *Educational Administration Quarterly, 35*, 130–160.

Shipps, D. (1997). The invisible hand: Big business and Chicago school reform. *Teachers College Record, 99*, 73–116.

Siskin, L. S. (1994). *Realms of knowledge: Academic departments in secondary schools.* Washington, DC: Falmer Press.

Sizer, T. R. (1986). Rebuilding: First steps by the Coalition of Essential Schools. *Phi Delta Kappan, 68*, 38–42.

Smylie, M., & Evans, A. E. (2006). Social capital and the problem of implementation. In M. I. Honig (Ed.), *New directions in education policy implementation: Confronting complexity* (pp. 187–208). Albany: The State University of New York Press.

Solórzano, D. G., & Yosso, T. J. (2002). Critical race methodology: Counter-storytelling as an analytical framework for education research. *Qualitative Inquiry, 8*, 22–43.

Spillane, J. P. (1996). School districts matter: Local educational authorities and state instructional policy. *Educational Policy, 10*, 63–87.

Spillane, J. P. (1998). State policy and the non-monolithic nature of the local school district: Organizational and professional considerations. *American Educational Research Journal, 35*, 33–63.

Spillane, J. P., Reiser, B. J., & Gomez, L. M. (2006). Policy implementation and cognition: The role of human, social, and distributed cognition in framing policy implementation. In M. I. Honig (Ed.), *New directions in education policy implementation: Confronting complexity* (pp. 47–64). Albany: The State University of New York Press.

Spillane, J. P., Reiser, B. J., & Reimer, T. (2002). Policy implementation and cognition: Reframing and refocusing implementation research. *Review of Educational Research, 72*, 387–431.

Stein, S. J. (2004). *The culture of education policy.* New York: Teachers College Press.

Steyaert, C., Bouwen, R., & Van Looy, B. (1996). Conversational construction of new meaning configurations in organizational innovation: A generative approach. *European Journal of Work and Organizational Psychology, 5*(1), 67–89.

Stone, C. N. (1998). Introduction: Urban education in political context. In C. N. Stone (Ed.), *Changing urban education* (pp. 1–22). Lawrence: University Press of Kansas.

Sutton, M., & Levinson, B. (Eds.). (2001). *Policy as practice: Toward a comparative sociocultural analysis of educational policy.* Westport, CT: Ablex.

Taylor, E. (2000). Critical race theory and interest convergence in the backlash against affirmative action: Washington State and Initiative 200. *Teachers College Record 102*(3), 539–560.

Valdes, F., Culpe, J. C., & Harris, A. (Eds.). (2002). *Crossroads, directions, and a new Critical Race Theory.* Philadelphia: Temple University Press.

van de Ven, A. H. (1986). Central problems in the management of innovation. *Management Science, 32*, 590–607.

van de Ven, A. H., & Polley, D. (1992). Learning while innovating. *Organization Science, 3*, 92–116.

Villegas, A., & Lucas, T. (2002). *Preparing culturally responsive teachers: A coherent approach.* Albany: State University of New York Press.

Weatherley, R., & Lipsky, M. (1977). Street-level bureaucrats and institutional innovation: Implementing special-education reform. *Harvard Educational Review, 47*, 171–197.

Weick, K. E. (1995). *Sensemaking in organizations.* Thousand Oaks, CA: Sage.

Wheatley, M. J. (1992). *Leadership and the new science: Learning about organization from an orderly universe.* San Francisco: Berrett-Koehler.

Wildavsky, A. (1996). *Speaking truth to power: The art and craft of policy analysis.* New Brunswick, NJ: Transaction.

Williams, P. J. (1991). *The alchemy of race and rights: Diary of a law professor.* Cambridge, MA: Harvard University Press.

Yancey, W. L., & Saporito, S. J. (1995). Ecological embeddedness of educational processes and outcomes. In L. C. Rigsby, M. C. Reynolds, & M. C. Wang (Eds.), *School-community connections: Exploring issues for research and practice* (pp. 193–227). San Francisco: Jossey-Bass.

Yanow, D. (1996). *How does a policy mean? Interpreting policy and organizational actions.* Washington, DC: Georgetown University Press.

Zahorik, J., Halback, A., Ehrle, K., & Molnar, A. (2004). *Teaching practices for smaller classes. Educational Leadership, 61*, 75–77.

28

Conceptualizing Policy Implementation

Large-Scale Reform in an Era of Complexity

AMANDA DATNOW
University of California, San Diego

VICKI PARK
RAND Corporation

The purpose of this chapter is to examine contemporary policy aimed at instituting large-scale change, specifically focusing on reform strategies and policy instruments. We begin by explaining various perspectives or theories for examining the policy implementation process: technical-rational, mutual adaptation, and sense-making/co-construction. We argue that the sense-making and co-construction perspectives are particularly useful for examining the dynamics involved in the implementation of current educational policies in the United States. After describing prevalent policy instruments, we then use these complementary perspectives to examine research and the theories of action behind three recent reform movements or policies: No Child Left Behind (NCLB), comprehensive school reform, and data-driven decision making (DDDM) initiated at the district level. We summarize with conclusions and implications for further research.

Perspectives on the Policy Process

Before delving into a discussion of current reform efforts, we provide an overview of policy perspectives which often go hand in hand with approaches to policy implementation. Part of our rationale for doing so is the belief that whether or not policy perspectives are explicitly discussed, assumptions and theories of action underlie every policy design and implementation. We discuss three major perspectives on policy implementation: technical-rational, mutual adaptation, and sense-making/co-construction. In Table 28.1, we provide a comparative overview of the three perspectives (fidelity, mutual adaptation, and sense-making/co-construction) in order to help summarize the features of each and how we see them playing out along various dimensions.

We specifically analyze how these perspectives differ along key dimensions including beliefs about the direction of change, assumptions about the process of change, sphere of influence, role of context, and values. Just as reform strategies and policy instruments have developed and matured in order to create a greater scale of change, we find that perspectives on policy processes need to become more sophisticated and multi-faceted to capture the complexity of education reform (Honig, 2006).

Technical-Rational The technical-rational perspective traditionally has been the most extensively used approach to understanding policy implementation (Snyder, Bolin, & Zumwalt, 1992). Many educational reforms originated by the U.S. government circa 1965 until 1980 (e.g., Follow Through, Education for All Handicapped Students, Vocational Education) embody this perspective which builds on classical management theory (Sabatier & Mazmanian, 1981). By doing so, it places a premium on planning, organization, coordination, and control. A key presumption underlying these policy designs was that "...authority and responsibility should flow in a clear unbroken line from the highest executive to the lowest operative..." (Masie, as cited in Smith & Keith, 1971, p. 241). This would exemplify what Elmore (1979/1980) calls "forward mapping," noting that it is problematic because it assumes that policy makers control the organization, political, and technical processes that affect implementation. In this view, the causal arrow of change travels in one direction—from active, thoughtful designers to passive, pragmatic implementers. Accordingly, the policy process tends to be viewed as a sequential development with discrete linear stages.

Tending to be top-down oriented, the technical-rational perspective attends to the administrative and procedural aspects of policy implementation while ignoring or downplaying the influence of context. Consequently, studies utilizing this standpoint are more likely to view local variation in implementation as a dilemma rather than as inevitable or potentially desirable (Sabatier & Mazmanian, 1981; Snyder et al., 1992). Earlier studies of reform implementation that exemplify the technical-rational perspective include Hall and

TABLE 28.1
Policy Perspectives

Assumptions	Perspectives		
	Technical-rational	*Mutual Adaptation*	*Sense-making/Co-construction*
Direction of Change	Uni-directional	Bi-directional between policy and site of implementation	Multi-directional
Policy Process	Treats policy process as discrete linear stages	Treats policy formation and implementation separately; focuses on mismatch between policy intentions and implementation outcomes. Thus, some mutual adaptation perspectives are viewed as variation of fidelity viewpoint	Treats policy formation and implementation as part of one process; focuses on the role of actors in shaping policy and interrelationships between multiple institutional layers and actors
Sphere of Influence	Top-down and hierarchical	Bottom-up	Open multi-layered system
Role of Context	Generalized view of context (macro)	Importance of local context and culture (micro)	Relational sense of context; includes socio-political and intergovernmental relationships (in co-construction perspective, less so in sense-making)
Value	Fidelity; planning and control, views variation as a dilemma	Adjustment and negotiation; views variation as expected outcome of local context	Adjustment and negotiation but also contingent maneuvers resulting from policy context

Loucks (1977) and Gross, Giacquinta, and Berstein (1971). In these studies, implementation is measured according to an objectified standard: fidelity to the policy design. Furthermore, because it treats policy design and implementation as two distinct processes, it also neglects to assess the degree to which political and ideological differences embedded within the overall policy development affect policy implementation. Since the design phase is often left unproblematized, the failure of policy is placed on the implementation stage rather than the formulation of the policy itself. There is an assumption in the implementation literature that execution, not the formulation of the policy, is the root of unsuccessful outcomes; but the formulation of a policy can also be based on false/incomplete assumptions or understanding about the nature of change, curriculum, instruction, and so forth. To be sure, there is an important distinction between successful policy execution and successful outcomes. A policy can be successfully implemented in terms of fidelity to procedures but executing policy faithfully does not mean that it will produce intended outcomes.

Mutual Adaptation The mutual adaptation perspective reflects an important departure from the technical-rational view of policy, which has been criticized for not being sensitive to the culture of schools or the daily lives of educators (Berman & McLaughlin, 1978; Sarason, 1982). The groundbreaking Rand Change Agent study helped to usher in a new era of policy research that started to take seriously the importance of local level implementation and adaptation (Berman & McLaughlin, 1978; Fullan & Pomfret, 1977). The 5-year study (1973–1978) examined federal programs and found that effective projects were characterized by a process of "mutual adaptation" rather than uniform implementation (Berman & McLaughlin, 1978). They found that although policies can enable preferred outcomes, even fully

planned, highly coordinated, and well-supported policies ultimately depended on how individuals within the local context interpreted and enacted policies; in other words, local factors dominated policy outcomes (McLaughlin, 1987). Berman and McLaughlin argued that implementation should be seen as a "mutually adaptive process between the user and the institutional setting—that specific projects goals and methods be made concrete over time by the participants themselves" (McLaughlin, as cited in Snyder et al., 1992). As Berman and McLaughlin imply, not only was mutual adaptation inevitable, it was desirable. Thus, support for bottom-up policy design processes (e.g., backward mapping) entered the policy development stage (Elmore, 1979/1980).

In contrast to the technical-rational view, research examining policy implementation using the mutual adaptation perspective drew attention to previously neglected aspects of policy implementation. Because research on implementation demonstrated again and again that while pressure from the top can only provide the catalyst for change rather than guarantee effective implementation or sustainable change, scholars utilizing this viewpoint began to highlight the importance of local context in understanding policy outcomes. Rather than a top-down, hierarchical view of the change process, mutual adaptation underscored the importance of bottom-up interpretations and responses to policy intentions. Bottom-up theorists argued that policy is really made at the local level and emphasized the actions, perceptions, and interaction among implementers. Studies adopting this perspective all suggest that reform implementation involves an active and dynamic interaction between local educators, the reform policy, and the social, organizational, and political life of the school (Mehan, Hertweck, & Meihls, 1986; Popkewitz, Tabachnick, & Wehlage, 1982). Considering that conditions and needs vary by local context, negotiation, flexibility, and adjustment on the part of educators and reform designers were keys to successful reform (McLaughlin, 1990).

A limitation of the mutual adaptation perspective, however, is that it does not fully capture the differential relationships amongst multiple actors and agencies in the policy process. By focusing on the micro-level aspects of change, this branch of policy research did not examine the extent to which macro-level factors, differential access to power, and actors' positions may support, constrain, or coerce responses (Fitz, 1994; Matland, 1995). Additionally, by treating policy formation and implementation as separate processes, mutual adaptation also tends to locate local implementers as the main source of policy success or failure. Similar to the technical-rational orientation, there is an assumption that execution (e.g., lack of fidelity) rather than the design of a policy, is the root of failed implementation (Snyder et al., 1992). Nevertheless, the mutual adaptation perspective broke new ground in helping us understand why and how policies were adapted to suit local contexts and it continues to be a useful framework for these reasons.

Sense-making and Co-construction The technical-rational and mutual adaptation perspectives have been the two dominant views on policy design and implementation (Snyder et al., 1992) and reflect larger debates surrounding the macro-micro theoretical divide (i.e., top-down vs. bottom-up; Fitz, 1994; Matland, 1995). Realizing the limitations of such dichotomies, researchers acknowledge the need to examine the interconnections between policy design and implementation (Cohen, Moffitt, & Goldin, 2007; Matland, 1995; McLaughlin, 1990). As Cohen et al. (2007) point out, there is a "mutual dependence" between policy and practice; policy relies on implementers to realize goals while practice depends on policy to frame action and offer resources. More importantly, "Public policy, to put it flatly, is a continuous process, the formulation of which is inseparable from its execution. Public policy is being formed as it is being executed, and it is likewise being executed as it is being formed" (Friedrich, 1941 as cited in Cohen et al., 2007, p. 66). Furthermore, the relationship between policy and practice are not static or linear but may vary along several dimensions (e.g., clarity/ambiguity of goals, clarity/ambiguity of means, and conflict/cooperation; Matland, 1995).

The sense-making and co-construction perspectives build upon on the importance of context in the mutual adaptation view by elaborating on the interconnections between actors and explaining just exactly how context has shaped policy implementation. These two complementary perspectives share a number of similarities and are used in numerous current research studies examining educational reform and policy (e.g., Coburn, 2001, 2006; Datnow, Hubbard, & Mehan, 2002; Hubbard, Stein, & Mehan, 2006; Spillane, Reiser, & Reimer, 2002). There are far more studies using the sense-making perspective, whereas the co-construction framework is at an earlier stage of development.

Both the sense-making and co-construction perspectives assume some level of social construction at the local level. They place implementers (e.g., educators) at the forefront of reform efforts, highlighting the process by which they interpret, adapt, or transform policy (Bascia & Hargreaves, 2000; Coburn, 2001; Fullan, 2000). Both perspectives show how actors (i.e., teachers, principals) mediate reform, and how their beliefs and experiences influence the implementation of reform.

Both the sense-making and co-construction perspectives share a relational sense of context. Researchers in these traditions assume that people's actions cannot be understood apart from the setting in which the actions are situated; reciprocally, the setting cannot be understood without understanding the actions of the people within. A relational sense of context does not privilege any one context; rather it highlights the reciprocal relations among the social contexts in the policy chain (Hall & McGinty, 1997). Of course, at a given point in time, a researcher will foreground interactions among social actors in one context and locate others in the background; but in order to allow for complete analysis, the interconnections among contexts throughout the system need to be described (Sarason, 1997; McLaughlin & Talbert, 1993; Hall & McGinty, 1997). For example, Spillane et al.'s (2002) examination of standards-based reform in math shows that teachers' implementation of reform is mediated by their own experiences, the context in which they are working, and the policy environment— three separate but intersecting planes that together produce policy implementation and outcomes. However, sense-making theory, as Coburn (2006) argues, tends to focus most on these implementers (i.e., teachers), and less on other actors in the system, which co-construction attempts to do.

Sense-making theory's main contribution has been to explicate in detail how local actors interpret and enact policy (Spillane et al., 2002; Coburn, 2001, 2006). Studies utilizing sense-making theories have produced crucial insights of how organizational change occurs because it provides a lens to understand how human agency alters environments. Rooted in social psychology and organizational theory, the sense-making framework presents social actors as complex meaning-makers who do not merely *react* to external stimuli but engage in interpretation in order to act upon their environment (Weick, 1995). Weick, Sutcliffe, and Obstfeld (2005) summarize the process:

> Sensemaking involves the ongoing retrospective development of plausible images that rationalize what people are doing. Viewed as a significant process of organization, sensemaking unfolds as a sequence in which people concerned with identity in the social context of other actors engage ongoing circumstances from which they extract cues and make plausible sense retrospectively, while enacting more or less order into those circumstances. (p. 409)

In other words, people socially construct their world as they interact with others and their environment.

Sense-making theories underscore the complex interrelationship between meaning and action. By nature, sense-making is incremental, fluid, and recursive. The process always begins with "chaos" as a person or group attempt to organize the constant flood of information that surrounds them (Weick et al., 2005). The first step in organizing begins with attending to certain cues and then bracketing information from their experiences. This is then followed by a process of labeling and categorizing in an effort to construct meaning. Thus, sense-making is a process theory in which perceptions, interpretations, and actions build on each other (Weber & Glynn, 2006). Recent research has focused on how meaning actually emerges from social interaction in educational reform contexts, using frame analysis as a complement to sense-making theory to examine how reading policy is defined (Coburn, 2006) and how progressive education is framed and legitimated (Davies, 2002).

Sense-making theory highlights how policy implementation is not just a problem of will and organizational structure but also one of social learning and cognitive capacity. Because sense-making occurs in a social context and is shaped by interactions at various levels and groups, there can be different interpretations of the same message even within a single organization such as a school. Siskin's (1994) study on secondary studies indicates that teachers' responses to reform were dependent on their departmental context and their professional identities. More recently, Coburn's (2001) study of elementary schools implementing a new reading policy found that the interpretation and practical application of the policy message were mediated by both formal (e.g., grade level) and informal teacher groupings. As teachers attend to information from the environment, they construct understandings within the confines of their current cognitive frameworks (e.g., knowledge and beliefs) and enact their interpretations in a way that creates new ways of thinking, relational patterns, and practices. Thus, as researchers have suggested in order to improve organizational capacity for improvement, educational systems need to restructure learning for teachers and pay attention to how knowledge is socially constructed (Spillane et al., 2002; Coburn, 2006).

Sense-making theory tends to stress cognitive processes. It also tends to downplay other aspects of human relations, including the dynamics of power and ideology (Weick et al., 2005). Sense-making tends not to address contestation, emphasizing shared understanding, as noted by Coburn (2006). Meanwhile, differential access to decision-making positions, as well as resources, means that some social actors have more power to shape social reality. Studies of school and organizational change show those in power often have more opportunities and leverage to regulate behavior by shaping what is valued or discounted and what is privileged or suppressed (Firestone, Fitz, & Broadfoot, 1999; Scott, 2001). In schools, for instance, leaders have strong voices in the construction of messages: they can shape where and how sense-making happens, they can frame policy messages and its interpretation, and they can provide material support (Coburn, 2001; Datnow, Park, &

Wohlstetter, 2007). The ways in which policy makers and other decision makers generate confidence in the policy maintains its legitimacy. Therefore, sense-making needs to be considered within a wider institutional context that may set the conditions for the process and frames the types of sense-making that may occur.

Co-construction has many of the same assumptions as sensemaking, but it also takes into consideration political and cultural differences, acknowledging the role of power (Datnow et al., 2002; Hubbard et al., 2006). As in the sense-making perspective, the co-construction perspective recognizes that agents at all levels contribute to the policy-making process and that that process is characterized by continuous interaction among agents and actors within and between levels of the system. However, differential access and use of power are affected by an actor's position in the system (e.g., formal role, positionality; Firestone et al., 1999). Moreover, unlike policy makers whose main role is to help design policy, implementers (whether they are situated at the state, district, or school levels) are simultaneously the object of reform and the agents of change. Consequently, implementers tend to carry the bulk of the weight in adjusting or conforming to policy mandates, and although this gives them power in shaping outcomes, it does not always equate to power in setting policy. For example, Hubbard et al.'s (2006) study of reform in San Diego City schools, which builds from the co-construction framework, shows how the district's top-down vector of change challenged educators' deep-seated roles and routines, resulting in a great deal of organizational conflict within the system.

The co-construction perspective also calls attention to wider social and political dynamics existing *outside* the policy system. Co-construction draws upon the sociocultural tradition and views organizations as embedded within successively contextualized layers (McLaughlin & Talbert, 1993) or planes of interaction (Rogoff, 1995; Tharp, 1997) but it extends the context to include the broader social system and political economy. Political dimensions of race, social class, language, and culture shape—and are shaped by—educators in interaction with their local context. For example, Hubbard and Mehan's (1999) study of the Achievement Via Individual Determination (AVID) program explains how educators' beliefs about student ability and intelligence (and how they overlap with race and social class) interact with local context and with reform implementation. Fleisch's (2002) study of the state and school reform in South Africa also illustrates how power relations around race and class influence and are influenced by educational reform efforts. So too, Oakes, Quartz, Ryan, and Lipton's (2000) study of middle grades reform in several states also illustrates these dynamics. While neither Fleisch nor Oakes et al. use the term co-construction, it is clear that the same theoretical assumptions about the role of power and perspective underlie their conceptions of educational change.

As noted above, political and cultural differences do not simply constrain reform in a top-down fashion. Rather, the causal arrow of change travels in multiple directions among active participants in all domains of the system and over time. This grammar makes the reform process "flexible" and enables people who have "different intentions/interests and interpretations [to] enter into the process at different points along the [reform] course. Thus many actors negotiate with and adjust to one another within and across contexts" (Hall & McGinty, 1997, p. 4).

In fact, both the sense-making and co-construction frameworks appear to move beyond the embedded sense of context notion that has dominated many analyses up to now. The embedded sense of context can be susceptible to the conceptual traps of structural determinism and uni-directionality, implying that policy only travels in one direction, usually from the top down. If we were to take an embedded sense of context, we would assume that events at higher levels of the context occur first and are more important analytically. We might also assume that policies originating in "higher" levels of context cause or determine actions at lower levels. However, the theory of co-construction, the causal arrow of change travels in multiple directions among active participants in all domains of the system and over time. As with Elmore's (1979/1980, "backward mapping" concept, the sense-making and co-construction perspectives also do not assume that policy is the only, or even major, influence on people's behavior. Individuals at the local level do indeed make decisions that affect not only policy implementation, but sometimes also the policy itself (as we have seen with the amendments to NCLB). This emphasis upon multidimensionality marks the sense-making and co-construction perspectives of reform implementation and departs from the technically driven, uni-directional focus of the technical-rational perspective.

Formulating policy implementation as a process that involves sense-making and co-construction is helpful in making sense of the complex, and often messy, process of school reform. Even when policies are seemingly straightforward, they can look quite different across localities, schools, and classrooms (Elmore & Sykes, 1992), as peoples' actions shape both the implementation and the outcomes of a policy, and even the policy itself. We will call up the sense-making/co-construction framework in particular as we discuss numerous current reform policies later in the chapter.

Types of Policy Instruments

Before examining the current state of reform strategies and the types of leverages that are being utilized for educational improvement in light of the co-construction framework, we want to ground our discussion in common language by building on the work of McDonnell and Elmore (1987). In their definition, policy instruments are "the mechanism[s] that translate substantive policy goals into concrete actions" (p. 134). In other words, "Policy instruments are socially created tools: their aim is to encourage assent to policy and offer resources to change practice" (Cohen et al., 2007, p.

73). More specifically, policy instruments include incentives, sanctions, rules, flexibility to adapt policy, technical assistance, and so forth.

McDonnell and Elmore (1987) classify policy instruments into four distinct categories: mandates, inducements, capacity-building, and system-changing. Mandates are generally described as rules and regulations intended to produce compliance. Inducements are compensations, usually with conditions, offered in exchange for performance outcome. Capacity-building refers to monetary investments directly tied to developing material, intellectual, and human capacity. System-changing is defined as mechanisms that re-distribute formal authority and decision making for the purposes of altering delivery of goods and services.

In addition to these four instruments, we also add symbolic leverage (e.g., political rhetoric) as an important tool for policy. By including symbolic moves, we wanted to draw attention to the ways in which actors and groups attempt to influence the policy process and gain legitimacy through rhetoric and ideas. Traditionally, the federal government used its bully pulpit to influence education policy as evidence by the oft-cited *A Nation at Risk* and more recently, the rhetoric of the No Child Left Behind (2002) policy. Coalitions and other interest groups have also relied on such symbolic leverage to influence policy (Honig, 2006; Malen, 2006; McDonnell, 2007).

In general, these different types of mechanisms for policy implementation are used in various combinations to produce intended outcomes. As Cohen et al. (2007) argue, "instruments vary in strength, or their influence in practice, and in salience, or how closely they connect with what must happen in practice to achieve policy aims" (p. 74). The use of each policy instrument, or their combinations, reflect various sets of assumptions and ultimately leads to different consequences (McDonnell & Elmore, 1987). We will attempt to bring to light these different mechanisms as we discuss current policies below.

Moving Towards Large-Scale Change

The contemporary education policy period marks a shift away from the idea that change happens organically, one school at a time. Instead, there is a focus on creating a systematic infrastructure to support change and the goal was to achieve change across a large number of schools at the same time. Within this decade, we have witnessed several types of large-scale reform efforts in the United States and across other Western countries, including district-driven change initiatives, state and federal systems of standards and accountability, and comprehensive school reform. In this section, we briefly review the several major large-scale reform efforts in education policy, focusing generally on their aims, scale, and main policy instruments.

During the 1960s and 1970s, federal policies viewed equity in terms of equalizing educational opportunities and thus, policy initiatives expanded student access to educational services. Propelled by the Civil Rights Movement and the War on Poverty, this period saw an increase in educational funding and the development of intervention programs aimed at mitigating racial and class inequalities (Tyack & Cuban, 1995). The scale of the policies tended to be modest in nature, although the aims were certainly lofty and ambitious. Court mandates for desegregation and finance equalization attempted to produce equal access and opportunities. Additionally, most federal initiatives such as Title I and Education for All Handicapped Children Act in 1975 were targeted at providing additional resources to specific groups of students where funds were distributed into categorized services. Overall, the main policy instruments were court rulings, categorical funding, the development of supplementary services, and the delivery of goods and services (Honig, 2006; Moore, Goertz, & Hartle, 1983). The modus operandi for education agencies—including federal and state governments and districts—was to allocate funds and broadly regulate schools (Fuhrman, Goertz, & Weinbaum, 2007).

Reflecting the technical-rational perspective on the policy process, failure of implementation was often defined in terms of lack of motivation and capacity while policy success was often measured in terms of fidelity (i.e., compliance to mandates and regulations). To address these underlying assumptions, policy solutions focused on presenting clearer instructions and stronger incentives. As noted by Fuhrman et al. (2007), the federal governance system helped to ensure compliance to policy mandates but did little to improve the quality of these programs. The policy instruments, which focused on appropriating funds, regulating resources, and providing general oversight, did little to penetrate school and classroom practices mainly because these policy tools were insufficient to affect practice. Given the assumptions about policy and educational change, very few resources were targeted at building capacity.

Standards, Assessments, and Accountability Systems With mounting evidence suggesting that American schools were unable to close the performance gap between diverse groups of students and failed to compete on an international level, the standards-based reform period entered the policy stage during the mid-1980s and 1990s (Firestone, Fuhrman, & Kirst, 1991; Murphy & Adams, 1998; National Commission on Excellence in Education, 1983). The commissioned report, *A Nation at Risk*, was an important symbolic leverage that provided the impetus for change. It sounded the alarm to America's declining student performance especially with respect to international competition. While some criticized it for being overly alarmist and inaccurate (Berliner & Biddle, 1995), the nation began to question the value of public education in terms of its effectiveness and outcomes given the past two decades of increased investment.

Following the recommendations made by the report, policy aims turned to improving the academic and professional quality of American schools. Policies focused on establishing minimum competency standards targeted at students and teachers. More specifically, the recommendations focused on raising high school curriculum and teacher education standards. Consequently, the main policy tools along with the symbolic move reflected by the commissioned report and the subsequent America 2000 summit meeting (which called for national education goals), included increasing academic standards, adding teacher credentialing requirements, and intensifying school-related practices (e.g., increasing school hours and types of services).

However, most state systems lacked coherence in their overall approach to reform (Firestone et al., 1991). States and local education agencies also tended to respond to federal policy agendas based on their unique history and habits. For example, states that historically relied on large-scale implementation continued to do so while states that focused on incentives and mandates also followed their patterns (Firestone et al., 1991; Walker, 2004). While beginning to focus on mechanisms that would produce system changes, policy makers continued to utilize policy instruments that focused on mandates, inducements, and symbolic gestures while shortchanging tools to build capacity. As Cohen et al. (2007) succinctly summarized the period of reform leading up to the current NCLB federal policy, "weak policy instruments, modest capability in practice, and political dependence combined with flexibility to promote weak response in practice" (p. 75). Thus while the underlying hope of the policy initiatives were to improve teacher and student performance, the policy designs focused on fidelity and establishment of programs rather than the quality of programs.

As the standards-based reform era developed momentum, the policies of the 1990s explicitly focused on improving the quality and delivery of school-related services, especially instruction and curricula. With arguments and research suggesting against piecemeal approaches to reform (Smith & O'Day, 1991; Fullan, Rolheiser, Mascall, & Edge, 2001), the strategy of system alignment and coherence entered into the policy lexicon. Policy instruments were developed to produce systems-level reform by emphasizing alignment of resources, coordinating efforts amongst government agencies, and re-distributing authority. During this period, new governance structures such as site-based management and charter schools took stage. Re-distribution of authority (e.g. vouchers), comprehensive school reform models, and public-private partnerships also emerged as important features of the reform landscape.

The shift to large-scale reform was crystallized in the No Child Left Behind Act of 2001 which instituted a new accountability system based on assessments and standards. As the reauthorization of the Elementary and Secondary Education Act (ESEA), NCLB followed up on the ideas set by Presidents George H. Bush's America 2000 and Bill Clinton's Goal 2000 plans. This new policy gave the federal government unprecedented authority in several ways by "creat[ing] stern directives regarding test use and consequence; put[ting] federal bureaucrats in charge of approving state standards and accountability plans; set[ting] a single nationwide timetable for boosting achievement; and prescrib[ing] specific remedies for under-performing schools" (Finn & Hess, 2004, p. 2).

NCLB is the first federal comprehensive educational framework consisting of standards, assessments, and accountability. NCLB is particularly noteworthy because it moves past the traditional focus on schooling "inputs" and holds educators responsible for student performance results (Dembosky, Pane, Barney, & Christina, 2005; Ingram, Louis, & Schroeder, 2004; Lafee, 2002). Under this system, the mechanisms for accomplishing these goals emphasize data-driven decision making (i.e., test scores, yearly progress reports), the implementation of evidence-based practices, and increased school choice for parents. Specifically, it requires states to have standards detailing content for student learning. Testing is also mandatory for grades 3 through 8 and results must be used to drive instruction and teaching practices. In addition, student performance data must be disaggregated based on major demographic classifications such as race/ethnicity, socioeconomic status (SES), gender, disability, English language learner, and so forth. Systematic testing is also coupled with prescriptive intervention remedies for schools not meeting Adequate Yearly Progress (AYP). Schools are pushed to improve under threat of sanctions that ultimately allow parents to opt out of low-performing schools. Additionally, guidelines for enhancing teacher quality are laid out.

Previous policy reliance on instruments around resources, incentives, and compliance audits shifted to the current reform trinity of standards, assessments, and accountability. These new policy tools are held together by assumptions on the need for policy coherence, system alignment, and coordination among various education agencies. Standards, tests aligned to standards, and accountability systems are stronger policy instruments because they attempt to directly influence instruction and student outcomes. However, the instruments are still relatively weak because the how and why of teaching and learning remain unaddressed. Standards provide guidance on classroom content but do not assist teachers in translating standards into effective instructional practices. Given the flexibility that states have in determining standards and proficiency levels, student performance can also be misleading, since some states opt for less rigorous standards and minimum competency measures of learning rather than the world-class standards touted by NCLB (National Center for Education Statistics, 2007). Determining effective instructional practices and measuring learning remains an elusive goal. In sum, capacity building for the core technology of education, teaching and learning, is not apparent in NCLB. Without developing the capabilities for deeper knowledge of school improvement, superficial engagement with policy expectations will likely lead to implementers reverting back to the status quo (Spillane et al., 2002).

With the aim of improving the effectiveness of schooling practices and a focus on student outcomes, the scale of its intended impact leads to increased centralization and standardization across all levels of the system. Historically, U.S. education policy has been driven by values of equity, efficiency, and the balance between local and federal authority (Fusarelli, 2004; Tyack & Cuban, 1995). Typically, state and local communities controlled education policies while the federal government acted primarily as a funding source (Fusarelli, 2004). With NCLB, the federal government intervened on local communities, past powers to determine their own educational goals and outcomes. However, in attempting to balance federal and state powers, NCLB is a mixture of clarity and ambiguity. While the deadline for meeting AYP and sanctions are specified, the actual content of the goals are ambiguous. The policy has a built-in flexibility that allows states to define proficiency levels and the content of the standards towards AYP. Thus with NCLB, we see the co-construction of the policy design process as the federal government attempts to balance regulation of outcomes with flexibility of state and local education agencies to determine how to meet proficiency levels.

It is also interesting to examine NCLB with respect to how race is constructed within the law. Critical scholars who have done detailed analyses of the law have argued that NCLB is an example of color-blindness (Freeman, 2005; Leonardo, 2007). Leonardo (2007) argues that NCLB perpetuates a form of Whiteness as policy, deeming racial disparities as unfortunate outcomes of group competition, uneven social development, or cultural inferiority. Freeman (2005) similarly argues that the non-recognition of race in NCLB is a form of political power to tacitly allow the colorblind ideal to steer educational policy towards the maintenance of the status quo. However, we do not have a sense as to how these dynamics play out in the process of implementation and whether local educators make sense of NCLB in these ways.

We do know, though, that how the federal government has framed the policy has impacted how districts and schools have engaged with it, with some schools and districts (i.e., those serving large numbers of low-income students) much more impacted by NCLB than others. Overall, NCLB has strengthened the role of the federal and state government while increasing pressure on districts and schools. However, it is clear that states and districts are playing an active role as they co-construct NCLB implementation and outcomes at the local level, with some states pushing back on the federal government in order to better suit NCLB to their needs and others considering opting out of NCLB altogether.

Comprehensive School Reform A feature of NCLB is the emphasis on research-based educational programs. This governmental focus was also apparent in the federal Comprehensive School Reform (CSR) legislation which preceded NCLB. Comprehensive school reform is built upon the policy assumption, based upon prior research, that changing most or all elements of a school's functioning is more likely to lead to school improvement than tinkering around the edges with piecemeal efforts. As we will explain, the case of CSR illuminates how policy is co-constructed as it moves through the design and implementation. Activities at the various policy levels—federal, state, district, design, and school—influence implementation.

The former federal CSR program, also known as the Obey-Porter initiative, allocated federal funds to schools for the adoption of "research-based" school reform models. The "purpose [of CSR was] to stimulate schools to revamp their overall educational operation by implementing a comprehensive reform program" (U.S. Department of Education, 2002). One hundred forty-five million dollars were initially allocated for CSR in 1998, and by 2003 the federal allocation increased to $310 million and continued at that level for several years until its cessation in 2007. Most of the funds were designated for Title I schools or schools that met federal definitions of serving high numbers of low-income students.

In drafting the CSR legislation, policy makers originally delineated nine components (two additional components were since added) of comprehensive school reform which include: (a) effective, research-based methods and strategies; (b) comprehensive design with integrated components, including instruction, assessment, classroom management, professional development, parental involvement, and school management; (c) professional development; (d) measurable goals and benchmarks; (e) majority of faculty/staff members support model implementation; (f) parental and community involvement; (g) external technical support and assistance; (h) evaluation strategies; and (i) coordination of resources (U.S. Department of Education, 2002).

Most schools applied for CSR funds to pay for the costs associated with implementing externally developed, comprehensive school reform models, such as Success for All, Accelerated Schools, and the Comer School Development program, among others. That is, schools partnered with external organizations—often groups of individuals located in universities or non-profit organizations—to assist them in their school improvement efforts. Most CSR models first originated in one or several locations and since have been "scaled up" to schools elsewhere. In fact, the scale up of CSR models occurred rapidly, involving thousands of schools. Through the reform models differed in their approaches to change, common to many of them is an interest in whole-school change, strong commitments to improving student achievement, new conceptions about what students should be expected to learn, and an emphasis on prevention rather than remediation (Oakes, 1993).

The federal CSR program increased federal and state involvement in the implementation of comprehensive school reform and thus provides an interesting case for examining how multiple layers of educational systems interact over the course of implementation. Federal Title I funds have been available since 1994 to pay for the costs associated with whole school reform models as regular part of Title I implementation. However, CSR signaled a significantly expanded federal role in supporting comprehensive school reform. Moreover, it involved states in ways heretofore unseen in the CSR movement. While the CSR was a federal program, execution of the program took place mainly at the state level. State educational agencies typically made decisions about which schools should receive funds. While the CSR legislation listed 17 reform models as examples, schools could apply for funding for any whole school reform (including a model of their own creation), providing it had research support. States made decisions regarding whether the schools' applications meet the federal criteria.

Though some research on CSR has found that states were not very significant in supporting schools' actual implementations of reforms, apart from their resource provision role (Datnow & Kemper, 2003), other work by Hamann and Lane (2004) specifically focus on the role of states as intermediaries in CSR and find that states can forge positive relationships that support CSR implementation. That said, the level of support for CSR and the relative importance of CSR in a state's overall schools improvement agenda was due in part to the circumstances, priorities, and knowledge of the individuals placed in charge of CSR at the state level (Datnow, 2005). At the same time, that there were differences in everything from funding guidelines to criteria for selection from state to state (see Datnow, 2005) with regard to CSR, also pointing to the relatively loose connections between states and the federal government regarding CSR and among the states themselves.

More significantly, however, states' testing and accountability systems greatly affected CSR implementation throughout the movement's history. Even early studies of CSR documented that in schools where state accountability demands were high, reform strategies were abandoned in favor of test preparation (Bodilly & Berends, 1999; Datnow, Borman, & Stringfield, 2000; Desimone, 2002). The continued implementation of CSRs often depends on whether the reforms help schools meet accountability demands and whether test score gains were realized.

Studies on CSR also point to districts as important mid-level policy actors in the implementation chain. That is, we do see some patterns with regard to CSR support (or lack thereof) when we look at particular districts. District and school leadership is very important to successful CSR implementation (Murphy & Datnow, 2003). Studies specifically discuss the need for district support for reform implementation, but often find that what exists is insufficient. For example, Berends, Bodilly, and Kirby (2003) state that, "many of the NAS [New American Schools] districts failed to provide organizational, public, and instructional leadership to the schools implementing the designs. Even where initial support existed, often support for NAS designs was often limited to one individual, the superintendent, rather than to the central office staff" (p. 127). They further add: "In many districts, the failure to protect the NAS reform effort from conflicting regulations and mandates put in place by district leaders anxious to show improvement again caused the reform to be virtually abandoned" (p. 127).

Whereas there developed a growing body of knowledge on state and district influences on CSR, much of the prior research on CSR focused on school-level issues such as school-level processes of selecting a CSR model (Bodilly, 1998; Consortium for Policy Research in Education, 1998; Desimone, 2000; Education Commission of the States, 1999; U.S. Department of Education, 1999), the level of teacher support for CSR (Berends, 2000; Datnow & Castellano, 2000; Smith et al., 1998), and leadership in CSR schools (Hall & Placier, 2003; Murphy & Datnow, 2003). In general, this research tends to downplay or regard as background key dimensions of context. In doing so, prior research tended to miss some important elements of how CSR implementation unfolds.

However, there is some indication in the CSR literature that broader dynamics of race, class, and language shaped reform efforts. A study by Kirby, Berends, and Naftel (2001) revealed that CSR schools serving numbers of poor and minority students tended to have lower levels of reform implementation. Datnow and colleagues (2002) found that educators resisted or thwarted the implementation of reforms that they felt were not well suited for their student populations. For example, a teacher in one school felt that their chosen reform required adaptations for low-income, recent immigrant Hispanic students, who were "culturally" more accustomed to teacher-directed rather than student-centered instruction. The researchers also encountered schools where English language learners did not receive as many benefits of the reform because they were perceived to be unable to understand material, or when policies dictated a different form of instruction for them (Stringfield, Datnow, Ross, & Snively, 1998).

Prior studies that examined state and district contexts in CSR implementation mainly highlight context as an implementation barrier. In short, the literature on CSR was poised to move beyond lessons about states, and districts as implementation barriers to more clearly reveal how schools, districts, and states interacted in particular ways to enable implementation. The co-construction story with respect to CSR involved an additional player: reform design teams. The advent of the CSR program spurred tremendous growth in the demand for services from design teams. In several cases, the design teams further specified their reform models, or at least what was required to implement their models, in order to make them more marketable in the CSR landscape. Bodilly (2001) and her team at the RAND Corporation studied the development of the New American Schools (NAS) comprehensive school reform design teams over a period of several years. Bodilly (2001) also found that the mounting political pressure on schools to improve also led to changes in the reform models, as the design teams grew to meet increasing demands for services. During the period of the RAND study (the mid-1990s), the teams were required to evolve from small, often research-oriented organizations, into entrepreneurial enterprises. They were expected to serve more schools as well as deliver quality in sound implementation and improved student outcomes. All teams suffered growing pains, particularly from the turnover of staff, which affected their ability to work with schools.

Design teams also had to adapt to their policy environments by adapting or modifying their programs. Bodilly (2001) found that many NAS design teams changed their models to reflect growing accountability demands from state and federal governments. If they did not adapt accordingly, they found that they could not stem competition from other design teams who had adapted. Not surprisingly, these forces sometimes converged when, for example, schools implementing NAS reform models demanded assistance in meeting new accountability systems or state standards. For example, the Modern Red Schoolhouse Institute responded by developing a targeted reading program that addressed the need for improving outcomes on state tests. Additionally, both Modern Red and Success for All have "unbundled" program components from the rest of the model for specific use in schools (Datnow et al., 2002; Datnow & Park, 2006). Similarly, the Comer School Development Program (SDP) added curricular components to its model in order to assist schools in meeting state standards (Datnow et al., 2002).

Although most of the changes that occurred in the reform models took the reformers away from their original intents, in one respect, there were improvements. That is, over time, NAS design teams began to provide more implementation support, assistance, and guidance regarding the process of reform model selection. These changes were based on demands from locals practitioners working in schools and districts, but were also due to the policy and political pressures placed on schools for increased accountability (Bodilly, 2001).

In sum, events in the local, policy, or market context had a strong influence on the development of CSR models. Consequently, actions taken by the design team were inextricably connected to actions taken within schools. Design team actions were also bound up with actions occurring on the Senate floor, in state legislative chambers, in district offices, in the public domain, and in other design teams with whom they compete. The relationship between the actions in these various sites can be understood as a "thick chain or braid," not a one-directional process emanating from the "top" or the "bottom" of the reform process (Datnow et al., 2002).

In theory, the "highest" policy levels (the federal government and the state) would serve as important supports for CSR at the local level. However, Datnow (2005) suggests that high-level policies are not as enabling of true reform as one might think. To be sure, the findings of studies indicate that CSR policy provided financial support, which was much needed by schools. Yet, the goals of whole school improvement and components that guided the creation of the CSR project did not fully make the transitions from the federal legislations to the state to the district and to the school in many cases (Datnow, 2005). In part, this was due to the loose connections among the policy levels and the fact that CSR was overshadowed by state accountability systems, which shaped how educators made sense of CSR models. Perhaps this is not surprising as the CSR policies at the federal and state levels were latecomers to the entire CSR movement and were laid on top of (or had to exist alongside) state accountability systems, which had much more importance than CSR for schools. The multiple policy levels implicated in CSR help to show the need for tighter connections among the levels and more explicit implementation activities at multiple levels.

District Level Reform and Data-Driven Decision Making

As we have seen with CSR, districts, like other key policy players within the education system, have the power to enable or constrain reform efforts. Conversely, district reforms efforts may be hindered or supported by federal and state systems and local schools. Thus, districts-wide change is co-constructed by multiple actors as they interact with accountability systems and local school needs.

In the current policy environment, districts have emerged as key players in school reform. They are helping schools to focus on student achievement and quality of instructions (McIver & Farley, 2003; Tognieri & Anderson, 2003). They have done so by learning to strategically engage with state reform policies and resources, with data-driven decision making being a key ingredient. With the advent of NCLB, the push for increased accountability and improved student achievement in U.S. schools has never been greater, and much of the pressure is falling on districts. For instance, a recent national study of the impact of NCLB reveals that indeed districts are allocating resources to increase the use of student achievement data to inform instruction in schools identified as needing improvement (Center on Education Policy, 2004). Summarizing findings across several major recent studies of school districts, Anderson (2003) writes:

> Successful districts in the current era of standards, standardized testing, and demands for evidence of the quality of performance invest considerable human, financial and technical resources in developing their capacity to assess the performance of students, teachers and schools, and to utilize these assessments to inform decision making about needs and strategies for improvement, and progress towards goals at the classroom, school, and district levels. (p. 9)

Some educational researchers have long decried education as a field in which practitioners make decisions based on intuition, gut instinct, or fads (Slavin, 2002). Supporters of DDDM practices argue that effective data use enables school systems to learn more about their school, pinpoint successes and challenges, identify areas of improvement, and help evaluate the effectiveness of programs and practices (Mason, 2002). Previous research, though largely without comparison groups, suggests that DDDM has the potential to increase student performance (Alwin, 2002; Doyle, 2003; Johnson, 1999, 2000; Lafee, 2002). Student achievement data can be used for various purposes including evaluating progress toward state and district standards, monitoring student progress, evaluating where assessments converge and diverge, and judging the efficacy of local curriculum and instructional practices (Cromey, 2000). When school-level educators become knowledgeable about data use, they can more effectively review their existing capacities, identify

weaknesses, and better chart plans for improvement (Earl & Katz, 2006). Data-driven decision making is also critical to identifying and finding ways to close achievement gaps between White and minority students (Walsh, 2003; Olsen, 1997).

Studies indicate that an important aspect of the continuous improvement process throughout schools is a commitment to using data as a key feature in reform plans rather than a supplemental or sporadic activity (Datnow, Park, & Wohlstetter, 2007; Supovitz & Taylor, 2003; Tognieri & Anderson, 2003). Furthermore, the effective use of data must occur at the district, school, and classroom levels (Armstrong & Anthes, 2001; Datnow et al., 2007; Kerr, Marsh, Ikemoto, Darilek, & Barney, 2006; Supovitz & Taylor, 2003; Tognieri & Anderson, 2003; Wayman & Stringfield, 2006). As part of engaging in DDDM, districts often create a closer alignment between the curriculum and state standards. This might involve creating benchmarks and standards for each grade level. Some districts also implement regular assessments throughout the school year in order to make sure that student progress towards standards is regularly monitored and that instructional adjustments are made accordingly (Armstrong & Anthes, 2001; Petrides & Nodine, 2005). Scorecards are also utilized as a management tool to monitor and measure the progress of schools as well as assist districts and school in aligning their goals (Petrides & Nodine, 2005).

However, data need to be actively used to improve instruction in schools, and individual schools often lack the capacity to implement what research suggests (Wohlstetter, Van Kirk, Robertson, & Mohrman, 1997). The implementation of NCLB has set the stage for schools to become "data-rich" but not necessarily for teachers to be effective data users; in other words, the presence of data alone does not lead to substantive and informed decision making. NCLB prescribes the need to use data but does not prescribe exactly how data should be used beyond the collection and monitoring of student achievement and subgroup data. Educators at the local level have to operationalize data use in a meaningful way and develop a process that actually informs their decision making. The process of framing suggests factors that influence the extent to which implementers develop shared goals and actions.

Thus, districts play a key role in framing DDDM and in developing capacity and structures (and thereby influencing teachers' meaning-making) to enable effective data use. Previous studies on the implementation of DDDM confirm that structural enablers, effective leadership, and positive socialization towards data use impact its effectiveness (Armstrong & Anthes, 2001; Datnow et al., 2007; Ingram et al., 2004). In districts that support DDDM, the superintendent and school board members often know how to lead and support data use. Districts often have district staff that work as liaisons with principals and individual schools (Armstrong & Anthes, 2001). Some districts are hiring instructional guides for each school to help faculty interpret student achievement data and to develop plans for improving outcomes. Other strategies include using assessment staff to hold meetings with individual schools to explain assessment data; networking schools with similar demographics but varying achievement levels (Wohlstetter, Malloy, Chau, & Polhemus, 2003) and using data as a means to identify directions for professional development (Massell, 2000).

Studies consistently suggest that as part of their capacity-building efforts, districts often provide professional development for principals and teachers so that they can learn to use data effectively (Petrides & Nodine, 2005; Tognieri & Anderson, 2003). This is very important, as a perpetual problem that many schools face in making data-driven decisions is the lack of training regarding how to incorporate data into the school improvement process (Cromey, 2000). The onslaught of "drive-by" training sessions (Elmore, 2003) that do little to address the specific needs of schools and teachers cannot support the ongoing learning that is required for capacity-building (Darling-Hammond & McLaughlin, 1995). Instead, effective professional development provides teachers with continuous and intensive opportunities to share, discuss, and apply what they are learning with other practitioners (Garet, Porter, Desimone, Birman, & Yoon, 2001; Wilson & Berne, 1999). In order for this to occur, system-level support needs to be in place. In addition to consistent structured time for collaboration and professional learning, schools need strategies for planning, sharing, and evaluating their efforts.

Thus, developing teachers' capacity to become effective at using data to inform their instruction requires actions at multiple levels. Studies have suggested that school systems empower teachers to use data to inform their instruction and learning by: (a) investing in user-friendly data management systems that are accessible to teachers; (b) offering professional development for staff in how to use data and how to make instructional decisions on the basis of data; (c) providing time for teacher collaboration; and (d) connecting educators within and across schools to share data and improvement strategies (see Datnow et al., 2007). However, it is important to note that teachers need not only the capacity, but also the *empowerment* to make instructional decisions based on data. School and system leaders need to provide scaffolds of support, but at the same time allow teachers enough flexibility to act on the basis of an informed analysis of multiple sources of data about their students' progress.

Also, in districts where DDDM is prevalent, there is often a culture of inquiry (Earl & Katz, 2006) that supports data use at all levels. Districts are actively transforming their professional development practices to build the capacity of their staff to participate in decision-making processes and to create an organizational culture of inquiry (Petrides & Nodine, 2005). A culture of continuous improvement accompanies this culture of inquiry. Inclusiveness in the data-driven decision-making process is often prevalent. Not only are principals privy to repositories of assessment data, but teachers as well. Teachers are often encouraged

to take a close look at grade-level and classroom data and share and discuss the data with each other (Armstrong & Anthes, 2001).

Overall, school systems play an increasingly pivotal role in leading and partnering with school sites to make data-driven practices an engine of reform. However, it is at the school level where everything comes together. Schools provide time for meeting to discuss data, flexibility for re-teaching, and curriculum and material resources in order to facilitate data-driven instruction. Schools also develop their own assessments and tools for acting on data, which were often created by teachers working together. Like the systems, schools also function as places to build human and social capital in the form of building the knowledge and skills of teachers, a process that occurs through professional development, instructional leadership, and networking among teachers. Schools also play a critical role in framing the expectations for DDDM among teachers, as well as creating a climate of trust and collaboration so that teachers can work in professional learning communities to improve their practice (Datnow et al., 2007).

Thus, in DDDM, we see that reform success is a joint accomplishment of individuals and policies at multiple levels of the system. Broader federal and state accountability policies provide an important frame for the work that happens at the system and school levels. Thus, although the crux of the work around data use takes place at the school and district levels, NCLB has helped to provide the political leverage needed in order for districts to stimulate improvement at the school level. The federal government holds states, districts, and schools accountable for student performance. States set curriculum standards and also hold schools and districts accountable. However, DDDM is operationalized and develops meaning at the school level in the work of teachers and administrators. As Dowd (2005) explains, "data don't drive," and therefore local educators co-construct the outcomes of this reform in their daily work with each other and with students.

Conclusion

The three policy movements we have reviewed all reveal how—to varying degrees and in different ways—actors at multiple levels make sense of and indeed co-construct the implementation and outcomes of educational reform. By looking at the events and actions across various contextual levels in the policy chain, we find that conditions at the federal, state, district, school, and design-team levels all influence implementation efforts in complex, interactive ways. Whereas the technical-rational policy implementation would suggest that implementation is an activity restricted to a group of people in schools at the bottom of the policy chain, we see here that policy implementation is a system-wide activity, even when the desired chain is mainly at the school level. However, the various policy levels have varying degree of influence, and varying levels of connection with each other in the schools and districts. These findings point to the need for viewing events in broader contextual levels not just as "background" or "context" but as important dynamic shaping forces in the reform process.

In order to fully understand the co-construction of a multi-level reform like the ones discussed here, researchers would ideally gather detailed, longitudinal case study data on the district, state, community, and other systemic linkages that might influence school-level reform efforts. Multiple schools and school systems would be involved. The study might employ a mixed-methods design, that supplements the qualitative data with valid and reliable measures of student achievement over at least a 3-year period. Survey data gathered from teachers and principals would also be very useful in assessing the extent to which educators at the school level have been engaged in reform efforts. For example, teachers and principals could be asked about the presence of systemic structural supports (e.g., collaboration time, networks), professional development, and resources devoted to assist in the reform effort.

Examining how reforms are mediated in their local contexts and the linkages across the educational system would likely provide insights that can inform the fields of educational research, policy development, and evaluation. However, there is a dearth of empirical research that has as its primary goal identifying or describing such linkages. This gap in the reform literature reflects a systemic weakness in understanding why reform efforts have not been more successfully sustained. Clearly, educational reform involves formal structures, such as district offices, state policies, and so on. It also involves both formal and informal linkages among those structures. Yet, reform involves a dynamic relationship, not just among structures but also among cultures and people's actions in many interlocking settings. It is this intersection of culture, structure, and individual agency across contexts that helps us better understand how to build positive instances of educational reform.

Finally, there is a need for additional research using frame analysis and the sense-making framework to understand how policy makers and educators ascribe meaning to educational reforms and policies. Ideally, such research would bridge these theories with the co-construction framework to illuminate how and why broader social and political dynamics enable and constrain policy implementation and reform. Taken together, these frameworks may offer rich new insights into examinations of current educational policies.

References

Alwin, L. (2002). The will and the way of data use. *School Administrator, 59*(11), 11.

Anderson, S. (2003). *The school district role in educational change: A review of the literature* (ICEC Working Paper No. 2). Ontario, Canada: International Centre for Educational Change, Ontario Institute of Studies in Education, International Centre for Educational Change.

Armstrong, J., & Anthes, K. (2001). *Identifying the factors, conditions, and policies that support schools' use of data for decision making and school improvement: Summary of findings*. Denver, CO: Education Commission of the States.

Bascia, N., & Hargreaves, A. (2000). Teaching and leading on the sharp edge of change. In N. Bascia & A. Hargreaves (Eds.), *The sharp edge of educational change: Teaching, leading, and the realities of reform* (pp. 3–26). London: Falmer Press.

Bay Area School Reform Collaborative (2003). *After the test: Using data to close the achievement gap*. San Francisco: Author.

Berends, M. (2000). Teacher-reported effects of New American School Designs: Exploring relationships to teacher background and school context. *Educational Evaluation and Policy Analysis, 22*(1), 65–82.

Berends, M., Bodily, S., & Kirby, S. (2003). District and school leadership for whole school reform: The experience of New American Schools. In J. Murphy & A. Datnow (Eds.), *Leadership for school reform: Lessons from comprehensive school reform designs*. Thousand Oaks, CA: Corwin Press.

Berliner, D., & Biddle, B. (1995). *The manufactured crisis: Myths, fraud, and the attack on America's public schools*. White Plains, NY: Longman.

Berman, P., & McLaughlin, M. W. (1978). *Federal programs supporting educational change, Vol. VIII8: Implementing and sustaining motivation*. Santa Monica, CA: Rand.

Bodily, S. (1998). *Lessons from New American Schools' scale up phase: Prospects for bringing designs to multiple schools*. Santa Monica, CA: RAND.

Bodily, S. (2001). *New American Schools' concept of break the mold designs: How designs evolved and why*. Santa Monica, CA: RAND.

Bodily, S. J., & Berends, M. (1999). Necessary district support for comprehensive school reform. In G. Orfield & E. H. DeBray (Eds.), *Hard work for good schools: Facts not fads in Title I reform* (pp. 111–119). Boston, MA: The Civil Rights Project, Harvard University.

Center on Education Policy. (2004). *From the capital to the classroom: Year 2 of the No Child Left Behind Act*. Washington, DC: Author.

Coburn, C. E. (2001). Collective sense-making about reading: How teachers mediate reading policy in their professional communities. *Educational Evaluation and Policy Analysis, 23*(2), 145–170.

Coburn, C. E. (2006). Framing the problem of reading instruction: Using frame analysis to uncover the micro-processes of policy implementation. *American Educational Research Journal, 43*(3), 343–379.

Cohen, D. K., Moffitt, S. L., & Goldin, S. (2007). Policy and practice. In S. Furhman, D. Cohen, & F. Mosher (Eds.), *The state of education policy research* (pp. 63–85). Mahwah, NJ: Erlbaum.

Consortium for Policy Research in Education (1998). *States and districts and comprehensive school reform. CPRE Policy Brief*. Philadelphia: University of Pennsylvania Graduate School of Education.

Cromey, A. (2000). *Using student assessment data: What can we learn from schools?* Oak Brook, IL: North Central Regional Educational Laboratory.

Darling-Hammond, L., & McLaughlin, M. W. (1995). Policies that support professional development in an era of reform. *Phi Delta Kappan, 76*(8), 597–604.

Datnow, A. (2005). Happy marriage or uneasy alliance? The relationship between comprehensive school reform and state accountability systems. *Journal of Education for Students Placed At Risk, 10*(1), 115–138.

Datnow, A., Borman, G., & Stringfield, S. (2000). School reform through a highly specified curriculum: A study of the Implementation and effects of the Core Knowledge Sequence. *The Elementary School Journal, 101*(2), 167–192.

Datnow, A., & Castellano, M. (2000). Teachers' responses to Success for All: How beliefs, experiences, and adaptations shape implementation. *American Educational Research Journal, 37*(3), 775–799.

Datnow, A., Hubbard, L., & Mehan, H. (2002). *Extending educational reform: From one school to many*. London: RoutledgeFalmer Press.

Datnow, A., & Kemper, E. (2003). Connections between state, district, school and design team levels in the implemented of comprehensive school reform. Paper presentation at the annual meeting of the American Educational Research Association, Chicago.

Datnow, A., & Park, V. (2006). *Research into practice: A case study of how Success for All builds knowledge for school improvement*. In W. Hoy & C. G. Miskel (Eds.), Contemporary issues in educational policy and school outcomes, (pp. 193–213). Greenwich, CT: Information Age.

Datnow, A., Park, V., & Wohlstetter, P. (2007). *Achieving with data: How high-performing school systems use data to improve instruction for elementary students.* A report commissioned by the NewSchools Venture Fund. Los Angeles, CA: Center on Educational Governance, University of Southern California, Center on Educational Governance.

Davies, S. (2002). The paradox of progressive education: A frame analysis. *Sociology of Education, 75,* 269–286.

Dembosky, J. W., Pane, J. F., Barney, H., & Christina, R. (2005). *Data driven decisionmaking in Southwestern Pennsylvania School Districts.* (Working paper). Santa Monica, CA: RAND

Desimone, L. (2000). *Making comprehensive school reform work.* New York: ERIC Clearinghouse on Urban Education. (ERIC no. ED441915)

Desimone, L. (2002). How can Comprehensive School Reform models be successfully implemented? *Review of Educational Research, 72*(3), 433–479.

Dowd, A. C. (2005). *Data don't drive: Building a practitioner-driven culture of inquiry to assess community college performance.* Boston: University of Massachusetts, Lumina Foundation for Education.

Doyle, D. P. (2003). Data-driven decision-making: Is it the mantra of the month or does it have staying power? *Technological Horizons in Education Journal, 30*(10), 19–21.

Earl, L., & Katz, S. (2006). *Leading schools in a data rich world: Harnessing data for school improvement.* Thousand Oaks, CA: Corwin Press.

Education Commission of the States. (1999). *Comprehensive school reform: Five lessons from the field.* Denver, CO: Author.

Elmore, R. (2003, November). A plea for strong practice [Electronic version]. *Educational Leadership, 62*(3), 6–10. Retrieved May 2006, from http://www.oaesa.org/k-8/library

Elmore, R. F. (1979/1980). Backward mapping: Implementation research and policy decisions. *Political Science Quarterly, 94*(4), 601–616.

Elmore, R. E., & Sykes, G. (1992). Curriculum policy. In P. Jackson (Ed.), *Handbook of research on curriculum* (pp. 185–215). New York: Macmillan.

Finn, C. E., Jr., & Hess, F. M. (2004). On leaving No Child Left Behind. *Public Interest, 157,* 35–57.

Firestone, W. A., Fitz, J., & Broadfoot, P. (1999). Power, learning, and legitimation: Assessment implementation across levels in the United States and the United Kingdom. *American Educational Research Journal, 36*(4), 759–793.

Firestone, W. A., Fuhrman, S. H., & Kirst, M. W. (1991). State educational reform since 1983: Appraisal and the future. *Educational Policy, 5*(3), 233–250.

Fitz, J. (1994). Implementation research and education policy: Practice and prospects. *British Journal of Educational Studies, 42*(1), 53–69.

Fleisch, B. (2002). *Managing educational change: The state and school reform in South Africa.* Johannesburg, South Africa: Heinemann.

Freeman, E. (2005). No Child Left Behind and the denigration of race. *Equity and Excellence in Education, 38*(3), 190–199.

Fuhrman, S. H., Goertz, M. E., & Weinbaum, E. H. (2007). Educational governance in the United States: Where are we? How did we get here? Why should we care? In S. Furhman, D. Cohen, & F. Mosher (Eds.), *The state of education policy research* (pp. 41–61). Mahwah, NJ: Erlbaum.

Fullan, M. (2000). The return of large-scale reform. *Journal of Educational Change, 1,* 1–23.

Fullan, M., & Pomfret, A. (1977). Research on curriculum and instruction implementation. *Review of Educational Research, 47*(1), 335–397.

Fullan, M., Rolheiser, C., Mascall, B., & Edge, K. (2001). *Accomplishing large scale reform: A tri-level proposition.* Toronto: Ontario Institute for Studies in Education.

Fusarelli, L. D. (2004). The potential impact of the No Child Left Behind Act on equity and diversity in American education. *Educational Policy 18*(1), 71–94.

Garet, M., Porter, A. C., Desimone, L., Birman, B. F., & Yoon, K. S.

(2001). What makes professional development effective? Results from a national sample of teachers. *American Educational Research Journal, 38*(4), 915–945.

Gross, N., Giacquinta, J., & Bernstein, M. (1971). *Implementing organizational innovations: A sociological analysis of planned educational change.* New York: Basic Books.

Hall, G. E., & Loucks, S. F. (1977). A developmental model for determining whether the treatment is actually implemented. *American Educational Research Journal, 14*(3), 263–276.

Hall, P. M., & McGinty, P. J. W. (1997). Policy as the transformation of intentions: Producing program from statutes. *The Sociological Quarterly, 38,* 439–467.

Hall, P. M., & Placier, P. (2003). The Coalition of Essential Schools: Leadership for putting the Common Principles into practice: Leadership in CES schools and the transformation of intentions. In J. Murphy, & A. Datnow (Eds.), *Leadership for school reform: Lessons from comprehensive school reform designs* (pp. 209–238). Thousand Oaks, CA: Corwin Press.

Hamann, E. T., & Lane, B. (2004). The role of state departments in comprehensive school reform. *Benchmark: The Quarterly Newsletter of the National Center for Comprehensive School Reform, 5*(2), 1–11.

Honig, M. (2006). Complexity and policy implementation: Challenges and opportunities for the field. In M. Honig (Ed.), *New directions in education policy implementation: Confronting complexity* (pp.1–23). Albany State University of New York Press.

Hubbard, L., & Mehan, H. (1999). Race and reform: Educational "niche picking" in a hostile environment. *Journal of Negro Education, 1268*(1), 115213–130226.

Hubbard, L., Stein, M. K., & Mehan, H. (2006). *Reform as learning: School reform, organizational culture, and community.* New York: RoutledgeFalmer Press.

Ingram, D., Louis, K. S., Schroeder, R. G. (2004). Accountability policies and teacher decision-making: Barriers to the use of data to improve practice. *Teachers College Record, 106,* 1258-1287.

Johnson, J. H. (1999). Educators as researchers. *Schools in the Middle, 9*(1), 38–41.

Johnson, J. H. (2000). Data-driven school improvement. *Journal of School Improvement, 1*(1), 16–19.

Kerr, K. A., Marsh, J. A., Ikemoto, G. S., Darilek, H., & Barney, H. (2006). Strategies to promote data use for instructional improvement: Actions, outcomes, and lessons from three urban districts. *American Journal of Education, 112*(3), 496–520.

Kirby, S., Berends, M., & Naftel, S. (2001). *Implementation in a longitudinal sample of New American Schools: Four years into scale-up.* Santa Monica, CA: RAND. Retrieved February 23, 2004, from http://www.rand.org/publications/MR/MR1413/

Lafee, S. (2002). Data-driven districts. *School Administrator, 59*(11), 6–7, 9–10, 12, 14–15.

Leonardo, Z. (2007). The war on schools: NCLB, nation creation, and the educational construction of whiteness. *Race, Ethnicity, and Education, 10*(3), 261–278.

MacIver, M., & Farley, E. (2003). *Bringing the district back in: The role of the central office in improving instruction and student achievement* (Report No. 65). Baltimore: John Hopkins University, Center for Research on the Education of Students Placed at Risk.

Malen, B. (2006). Revisiting policy implementation as a political phenomenon: The case of reconstitution policies. In M. I. Honig (Ed.), *New directions in education policy implementation: Confronting complexity* (pp. 83–104). Albany: State University of New York Press.

Mason, S. (2002, April). *Turning data into knowledge: Lessons from six Milwaukee public schools.* Paper presented at the annual conference of American Educational Research Association, New Orleans.

Massell, D. (2000). *The district role in building capacity: Four strategies.* Philadelphia: Consortium for Policy Research in Education.

Massell, D., Kirst, M., & Hoppe, M. (1997). *Persistence and change: Standards-based systematic reform in nine states* (CPRE Policy Brief RB-21). Philadelphia: Consortium for Policy Research in Education (CPRE).

Matland, R. E. (1995). Synthesizing the implementation literature: The ambiguity-conflict model of policy implementation. *Journal of Public Administration Research and Theory, 5*(2), 1435–174.

McDonnell, L. M. (2007). The politics of education: Influencing policy and beyond. In S. Furhman, D. Cohen, & F. Mosher (Eds.), *The state of education policy research* (pp.19–393). Mahwah, NJ: Erlbaum.

McDonnell, L. M., & Elmore, R. F. (1987). Getting the job done: Alternative policy instruments. *Educational Evaluation and Policy Analysis, 9*(2), 133–152.

McIver, M., & Farley, L. (2003). *Bringing the district back in: The role of the central office in improving instruction and student achievement* (Report No. 65). Baltimore: Center for Research on the Education of Students Placed at Risk, John Hopkins University.

McLaughlin, M. W. (1987). Learning from experience: Lessons from policy implementation. *Educational Evaluation and Policy Analysis, 9*(2), 171–178.

McLaughlin, M. W. (1990). The Rand Change Agent Study revisited: Macro perspectives and micro realities. *Educational Researcher, 19*(9), 11–16.

McLaughlin, M., & Talbert, J. E. (1993). *Contexts that matter for teaching and learning: Strategic opportunities for meeting the nation's standards educational goals.* Stanford, CA: Stanford University Center for Research on the Context of Secondary School Teaching.

Mehan, H. A., Hertweck, A., & Meihls, J. L. (1986). *Handicapping the handicapped: Decision making in students' educational careers.* Stanford, CA: Stanford University Press.

Moore, M., Goertz, M., & Hartle, T. (1983). Interaction of federal and state programs. *Education and the Urban Society, 15*(3), 452–478.

Murphy, J., & Adams, J. E. (1998). Reforming America's schools 1980–2000. *Journal of Educational Administration, 360*(5), 426–444.

Murphy, J., & Datnow, A. (Eds.). (2003). *Leadership lessons from comprehensive school reforms.* Thousand Oaks, CA: Corwin Press.

National Center for Education Statistics. (2007). *The condition of education 2007.* Washington, DC: Institute for Education Sciences, U.S. Department of Education.

National Commission on Excellence in Education. (1983). *A nation at risk: The imperative for educational reform.* Washington, DC: U.S. Government Printing Office.

No Child Left Behind Act of 2001. Public. Law. No. 107-110, 115 Stat. 1425 (2002).

Oakes, J. (1993). *New standards and disadvantaged schools.* Background Paper prepared for research forum on Effects of New Standards and Assessments on High Risk Students and Disadvantaged Schools. Cambridge, MA: Harvard University.

Oakes, J., Quartz, K. H., Ryan, S., & Lipton, M. (2000). *Becoming good American schools: The struggle for civic virtue in educational reform.* San Francisco: Jossey-Bass.

Olsen, L. (1997). The data dialogue for moving school equity. In *California Tomorrow Perspectives, Vol. 5* (pp. 48–65). Oakland, CA: California Tomorrow.

Petrides, L., & Nodine, T. (2005). *Anatomy of school system improvement: Performance-driven practices in urban school districts.* San Francisco: NewSchools Venture Fund.

Popewitz, T., Tabachnick, B., & Wehlage, G. (1982). *The myth of educational reform: A study of school responses to a program of educational change.* Madison: University of Wisconsin Press.

Rogoff, B. (1995). Observing sociocultural activity on three planes: Participatory appropriation, guided participation, and apprenticeship. In J. V. Wertsch, P. Del Río, & A. Alvarez (Eds.), *Sociocultural studies of mind* (pp. 139–164). Cambridge, UK: Cambridge University Press.

Sabatier, P., & Mazmanian, D. (1981). The implementation of public policy: A framework of analysis. In D. Mamanian & P. Sabatier (Eds.), *Effective policy implementation* (pp. 3–36). Lexington, Massachusetts: Lexington Books.

Sarason, S. (1982). *The culture of the school and the problem of change* (2nd ed.). Boston: Allyn & and Bacon.

Sarason, S. (1997). Revisiting the creation of settings. *Mind, Culture, and Activity, 4*(3), 175–182.

Scott, R. W. (2001). *Institutions and organizations* (2nd ed.) Thousand Oaks, CA: Sage.

Siskin, L. S. (1994). *Realms of knowledge: Academic departments in secondary schools.* Washington, DC: Falmer Press.

Slavin, R.E. (2002). Evidence-based education policies: transforming educational practice and research. *Educational Researcher, 31*(7), 15–21.

Smith, L., & Keith, P. (1971). *Anatomy of an educational innovation.* New York: Wiley.

Smith, L., Ross, S., McNelis, M., Squires, M., Wasson, R., Maxwell, S., et al. (1998). The Memphis Restructuring Initiative: Analysis of activities and outcomes that affect implementation success. *Education and Urban Society, 30*(3), 276–325.

Smith, M. S., & O'Day, J. (1991). Systemic school reform. In S. Fuhrman & B. Malen (Eds.), *The politics of curriculum and testing. Politics of Education Association Yearbook 1990* (pp. 233–267). London: Taylor & Francis.

Snyder, J., Bolin, F., & Zumwalt, K. (1992). Curriculum implementation. In P. Jackson (Ed.), *Handbook of research on curriculum* (pp. 402–435). New York: Macmillan.

Spillane, J. P., Reiser, B. J., & Reimer, T. (2002). Policy implementation and cognition: Reframing and refocusing implementation research. *Review of Educational Research, 72*(3), 387–431.

Stringfield, S., Datnow, A., Ross, S. M., & Snively, F. (1998). Scaling up school restructuring in multicultural, multilingual contexts: Early observations from Sunland County. *Education and Urban Society, 30,* 326–357.

Supovitz, J., & Taylor, B. S. (2003). *The impacts of standards-based reform in Duval County, Florida,: 1999–2002.* Philadelphia: Consortium for Policy Research in Education.

Tharp, R. G. (1997). *From at risk to excellence: Research, theory, and principles for practice* (Research report No. 1). Santa Cruz: University of California, Center for Research on Education, Diversity and Excellence.

Tognieri, W., & Anderson, S. (2003). *Beyond islands of excellence: What districts can do to improve instruction and achievement in all schools.* Washington, DC: Learning First Alliance.

Tyack, D., & Cuban, L. (1995). *Tinkering towards utopia: A century of public school reform.* Cambridge, MA: Harvard University Press.

U.S. Department of Education. (1999). *CSR in the field: Fall 1999 update.* Washington, DC: Author.

U.S. Department of Education. (2002). *Guidance on the Comprehensive School Reform Demonstration Program.* Washington, DC: Author.

Walker, E. M. (2004). The impact of state policies and actions on local implementation efforts: A study of whole school reform in New Jersey. *Educational Policy, 18*(2), 338–363.

Walsh, K. (2003). *After the test: How schools are using data to close the achievement gap.* San Francisco: Bay Area School Reform Collaborative.

Wayman, J., & Stringfield, S. (2006). Technology-supported involvement of entire faculties in examination of student data for instructional improvement. *American Journal of Education, 112*(4), 549–571.

Weber, K., & Glynn, M. A. (2006). Making sense with institutions: Context, thought and action in Karl Weick's theory. *Organization Studies, 27*(11), 1639–1660.

Weick, K. E. (1995). *Sensemaking in organizations.* Thousand Oaks, CA: Sage.

Weick, K. E., Sutcliffe, K. M., Obstfeld, D. (2005). Organizing and the process of sensemaking. *Organization Science, 16*(4), 409–421.

Wilson, S., & Berne, J. (1999). Teacher learning and the acquisition of professional knowledge: An examination of research on contemporary professional development. *Review of Research in Education, 24,* 173–209.

Wohlstetter, P., Malloy, C. L., Chau, D., & Polhemus, J. (2003). Improving schools through networks: A new approach to urban school reform. *Educational Policy, 17*(4), 399–430.

Wohlstetter, P., Van Kirk, A. N., Robertson, P. J., & Mohrman, S. A. (1997). *Organizing for successful school-based management.* Alexandria, VA: Association for Supervision and Curriculum Development.

29

Public Choice and the Political Economy of American Education

Martin West
Brown University

Much research now being conducted on American education is motivated by a simple, yet vexing, puzzle: While real per pupil spending on elementary and secondary education increased steadily since the 1960s, student outcomes have remained basically flat. And despite considerable progress toward equalizing resources across school districts, gaps in basic skills along lines of ethnicity and income remain alarmingly wide. Solving this puzzle is no mere academic concern. A good explanation for the evident failure of resource investments to improve student performance and equalize educational opportunities should also indicate the most promising avenues for reform.

Some of the most influential—and surely the most provocative—recent work on the American education system's flagging productivity has come from scholars influenced by the research program known as public choice. Public choice theory applies the tools of neoclassical economics to the study of political behavior in an attempt to explain the structure and performance of public institutions. Spanning the disciplinary divide between economics and political science, public choice is distinguished from traditional approaches to the study of political behavior by three core elements:

1. *Methodological individualism.* The basic unit of analysis is the individual political actor. Collective behavior is not ignored, but it is modeled as the sum of decisions made by independent individuals.
2. *Primacy of self-interest.* Political behavior is assumed to be motivated primarily by self-interest. Although political actors may have altruistic motives, they are treated as secondary or incorporated into the definition of self-interest.
3. *Rationality postulate.* Finally, political actors are assumed to pursue their self-interest rationally. While recent work in psychology and behavioral economics casts doubt on the validity of this assumption as

an accurate description of human decision making, public choice scholars contend that it retains sufficient predictive validity to be useful in explaining aggregate behavior.[1]

It is widely accepted that insights derived from public choice theory have revolutionized the discipline of political science.[2] The extent of its influence on education research, however, is more controversial. Some critics of public choice assert that it is now the reigning paradigm in the field, shaping not only research priorities but also the design of reform efforts (Devine, 2004). Others lament its lack of impact on education research, even as they recognize its limitations (Boyd, Crowson, & van Geel, 1995). Direct citations to public choice scholarship in education research remain rare and almost exclusively limited to scholars trained in economics and political science.

In this chapter, after reviewing the approach taken by scholars working in the public choice tradition, I explore in detail a body of work motivated by the perceived inefficacy of new resource investments in public education in improving student outcomes. I argue that this puzzle has led scholars (a) to reassess the origins of publicly provided education, (b) to offer new explanations for the missing link between resources and performance in American education, and (c) to propose institutional reforms designed to enhance performance. In particular, two of the most prominent reform strategies pursued during the past decade, test-based accountability and school choice, reflect the influence of the public choice tradition. At the same time, I argue that a public choice perspective raises doubts about the potential of both of these reforms, as currently implemented, to accomplish their objectives.

This conclusion is important to bear in mind, as it is often assumed that public choice scholarship leads incontrovertibly to conservative or libertarian policy conclusions. The conflation is understandable in light of the field's historical origins. Writing in the 1950s and 1960s, early public choice scholars saw themselves as correcting what they perceived as a bias within the scholarly community in favor of sweeping government interventions in the economy. Specifically, they argued that economists had become adept at identifying ways in which markets failed to produce an optimal or equitable distribution of resources while paying scant attention to analogous problems inherent in the government's efforts to remedy those failures (Buchanan & Tullock, 1962). Public choice scholars have undoubtedly been among the most prominent academic proponents of market-oriented reforms across a range of policy domains. The perspective's only necessary implications, however, are the need for careful attention to the role of institutional design in shaping policy outcomes and for theoretically grounded, empirically based comparisons between the performance of the public and private sectors in achieving desired goals. The appropriate balance between market and government provision of education, in particular, is an empirical question that may have a different answer for each society, time period, and level of education.

A Short Introduction to Public Choice

The point of departure for the development of public choice theory was the recognition of an inconsistency in the models of human decision making traditionally employed by economists and political scientists in their respective fields. Since the time of Adam Smith (1776), economists had generally assumed that individuals in the marketplace act in their own self-interest, without regard for the collective good. Most political scientists, in contrast, assumed that the decisions of elected officials, bureaucrats, and voters were guided by their understandings of what would benefit the nation as a whole. The early proponents of public choice rejected this "bifurcated view of human behavior" (Tullock, Seldon, & Brady, 2003). Given that they were economists, it is no surprise which perspective they found most compelling.

Yet the claim that political actors are primarily motivated by self-interest is only a first step. It is also necessary to identify the particular set of interests that are most relevant for a given decision. In the economic sphere, neoclassical economists assume that individuals maximize their own utility and firms maximize profits. But what do political actors maximize? In the case of elected officials, finding a suitable analogue is relatively straightforward. Politicians earn their living by winning elections, of course, and must remain in office in order to accomplish any policy goals. Indeed, a remarkable amount of the behavior of elected officials can be explained by assuming them to be single-minded seekers of re-election without independent policy goals (Mayhew, 1974).

Things quickly become more complicated in other contexts, however. Bureaucratic officials, for example, may plausibly be assumed to internalize and rationally pursue the expansion of their agency's budget, their own professional advancement, or simply the status quo, to list just a few possibilities.[3] Each of these alternatives takes seriously the notion that government employees have their own interests that may not coincide completely with those of their political superiors or the public to which they are responsible. Each therefore suggests the usefulness of viewing bureaucratic policymaking through the lens of what economists refer to as the principal-agent problem (Pratt & Zeckhauser, 1985).

In a nutshell, a principal-agent relationship exists whenever one individual (the principal) who wants to attain a given set of goals relies on another party (the agent) to act on his or her behalf. Such relationships are ubiquitous throughout society, from patients hiring doctors to cure their ailments, to drivers hiring mechanics to fix their cars. As political scientist Terry Moe (1984) has explained, a democratic political system can also be understood as "a chain of principal-agent relationships, from the citizen to politician to bureaucratic superior to bureaucratic subordinate and on down the hierarchy of government to the lowest-level bureaucrat who actually delivers services" (p. 765–766). Clearly, these types of relationships are essential and beneficial, as principals typically lack the time or capacity to do everything on their own, while agents often have the capacity to pursue the principals' goals more effectively than principals could do on their own.

Public choice theorists, however, emphasize that principal-agent relationships also have important drawbacks. First, agents inevitably have their own interests that may not be perfectly aligned with those of the principal. Second, agents often have better information about their performance in pursuing their principals' goals than the agents themselves. As a result, principals face a basic problem of control. They must devise mechanisms that will provide incentives for agents to substitute the principals' goals for their own. The optimal choice of such mechanisms obviously depends upon the circumstances, but could include more extensive monitoring of agents' behavior or the adoption of performance-related compensation systems.

Critics of this approach to the study of bureaucratic politics argue persuasively that it is unable to explain the behavior of bureaucrats who engage in altruistic or public-spirited behavior, even in the absence of material incentives to do so. As John J. Dilulio, Jr. (1994) puts it, principal-agent models cannot account for the existence of "'principled agents'—workers who do not shirk, subvert, steal on the job even when the pecuniary and other tangible incentives to refrain from those behaviors are weak or non-existent" (p. 277). He contends that the public choice theorists are wrong to discount evidence of such behavior and to deny the capacity of agency leaders to create an organizational culture that fosters it. Similarly, Julian Le Grand (2003) uses the terms "knaves" and "knights" to contrast the motivations of public sector officials, which he suggests range from the self-interested to the purely altruistic. Le Grand (1997) worries in particular that policies based on the assumption that most bureaucrats are self-interested may erode the altruistic motivations of those who are not.

It is important to note that these critiques do not necessarily undermine the utility of an approach to bureaucratic politics rooted in public choice. Broadly defined, public choice theory makes no overarching assumptions about how individuals conceive of their self-interest. Altruistic concern for the recipients of government services, values, and ideology, to the extent that they can be clearly specified, can all be readily incorporated into the definition of self-interest. Yet it is fair to say that this would deviate from the dominant strands of research in the field, which emphasize the role that individuals' material interests are likely to play in their decision making—and the predictive value of models based on that assumption.

Perhaps the most important step in the public choice approach to modeling political behavior, then, is the specification of the objectives that a political actor will pursue. It is assumed that individual actors pursue these goals rationally, subject to the constraints imposed by available resources and their institutional setting. Predictions can then be derived about behavior and outcomes which, if confirmed, lend credibility to the underlying model. This explicit commitment to model-building distinguishes public choice scholarship from the growing body of applied policy analysis examining the effects of the incentives created by specific educational policy innovations, such as accountability programs, pay-for-performance schemes, or teacher benefit systems. As in any field of social science, the most valuable public choice models are those which are able to make a number of successful predictions using only a few assumptions.

Public schools, though they are not often recognized as such, are bureaucratic agencies. The public choice approach to the study of the politics of education assumes that the behavior of teachers and other actors within the public school system does not fundamentally differ from that of other government employees. As Jacob Michaelson (1977) put it, "we may assume that bureaucrats, including schoolmen, seek … to survive, to enlarge the scope of their activities, to gain prestige, to control the organization and content of their daily round as much as possible. All these are, as it were, profit in kind" (p. 329). Though the assumption that educators are not solely concerned with the welfare of their students was and remains novel, it should not be rejected out of hand. The ultimate test of the approach is whether it is able to explain parsimoniously otherwise puzzling features of the educational scene.

Of course, the collection of the evidence needed to make this judgment raises considerable methodological challenges. Unlike, say, competing pedagogical approaches to language instruction, hypotheses concerning the consequences of different governing institutions for educational quality are often (though not always) not amenable to the types of experimental evaluation methods that are rightly valued in the current era of education research. Perhaps for this reason, however, scholars working in the public choice tradition have paid particular attention to the challenges of making causal inferences based on observational data.

As discussed below, they have often applied many of the same econometric methods (e.g., instrumental variables, fixed effects, and the like) widely used by education researchers when randomized experiments are not feasible or inappropriate (Schneider, Carnoy, Kilpatrick, Schmidt, & Shavelson, 2007).

Public Choice Theory and the Productivity Puzzle

No educational issue has prompted more research among public choice scholars than the inconsistent track record of increased investments in elementary and secondary education in bringing about improved educational outcomes for American students. The basic facts on this point are by now well established. Per pupil spending on public education, adjusted for inflation, has more than doubled since 1970, yet the test scores of 17-year-olds have remained stagnant (see, e.g., Hanushek, 2003). Although casual observers often attribute the growth in school spending in recent decades to the expansion of services for students in need of special education, research indicates that special education spending accounts for only a fraction of the overall increase (Hanushek & Rivkin, 1997).

Recent statistics on high school completion rates are even more alarming. The percentage of American students completing high school has actually fallen since 1970—a trend masked in official statistics by the growing number of students receiving alternative credentials like the General Educational Development, or GED, certificate (Heckman & LaFontaine, 2008; Chaplin, 2002). The latest data indicate that the on-time graduation rate is below 50% for African American students and only slightly higher for Hispanics ("Diplomas count," 2007). This ongoing dropout crisis, along with the arrival of a growing immigrant population with relatively low levels of education, has bequeathed the United States a pool of low-skilled adults without parallel in the developed world (Blau & Kahn, 2001).

The problem of declining educational productivity, however, is hardly unique to the United States. As German economist Ludger Wössmann (2002) has documented, real spending on public education throughout most of the developed world has increased dramatically in recent decades, even taking into account the labor-intensive nature of the educational process. Yet these increases are largely unrelated to changes in school quality as measured by international assessments of student performance. Differences in the level of spending are also uncorrelated with student achievement across countries. And the bulk of within-country analyses indicate that, given current spending levels, increased resource investments in public education on their own do not notably improve the quality of schooling students receive.

From an historical perspective, the distinguishing characteristic of contemporary education systems worldwide is the extent of government involvement in the finance, provision, and regulation of elementary and secondary education. Over the past century, state-run mass education systems have become the norm throughout the developed world. Approximately 90% of American students attend schools that are publicly financed and operated, and similar figures apply in the majority of the industrialized world (Toma, 1996). Public choice scholars have accordingly explored the origins of state-provided education systems, attempted to identify the roots of their performance troubles, and offered proposals for reform.

Origins of Publicly Provided Education In one of the earliest applications of public choice theory to the politics of education, E. G. West (1994) offered a detailed historical account of the origins of publicly provided education in Great Britain. Of particular interest was his finding that, prior to the advent of state involvement in the provision of education in England and Wales in 1870, both school attendance and literacy rates exceeded 90%. Most working-class parents were choosing to invest in their children's education, and churches and other voluntary organizations provided free education for the most disadvantaged segments of the population. The most significant expansion of mass education in England and Wales therefore took place without compulsion in a free-market setting prior to the establishment of state-run schools. When the British government entered the education scene, West (1994) wrote, it was "as if it jumped into the saddle of a horse that was already galloping"(p. 173).

Why, then, did the British state intervene at all? West argues that W. E. Forster, the author of the 1870 legislation introducing fee-paying government schools, intended merely to fill in the gaps in an extensive and rapidly growing network of private and charity schools that was already meeting the educational needs of the bulk of the working-class population. Forster's bureaucratic officials, however, overestimated the magnitude of these gaps and, after constructing vast numbers of government schools, were embarrassed by their surplus capacity. Their next step was to lower or eliminate tuition fees in government schools, which predictably led to the collapse of most private schools serving the poor.

Furthermore, once education was made compulsory in 1880, government officials reasoned that it was wrong to compel disadvantaged families to pay fees that they could not easily afford. Rather than establish a system of means-tested grants, however, elected officials attempted to maximize their political benefits by waiving fees for rich, middle-class, and poor families alike. West similarly attributes their decision to restrict public funding to government-run schools to a desire to minimize objections from religious groups. Government officials assumed that Protestant taxpayers would object to using public funds to support Catholic education, and vice versa. In short, West portrays the development of a state financed and operated system of mass education in Great Britain as a consequence of expansionism on the part of bureaucratic officials, opportunism on the past of elected politicians, and lobbying on the part of religious interests.

While West's public choice account of the origins of publicly provided education is rooted in historical analysis, economist John Lott, Jr. (1990) starts from the observation that virtually all government activity involves the transfer of wealth between different segments of society. Elected officials seek to maximize their political support by controlling the size and distribution of these transfers, subject to the costs of creating them. Government-provided schooling, he contends, can help to reduce these costs by predisposing students to support a particular set of transfers. The government can control the content of the curriculum to which students are exposed by paying teachers a rent—that is, better compensation than they would receive in other fields—that provides an incentive for them to conform to the government's preferred views. Lott (1999) thus portrays government-provided schooling primarily as a means by which the state can indoctrinate students with the preferences of the ruling party. His empirical evidence, while merely correlational, indicates that spending on public education is in fact higher in totalitarian regimes and that spending on education and other government transfers are positively correlated across countries.

As Eugenia Toma (2004) points out, "a definitive argument, either conceptually or factually, for why the state provides schooling is still outstanding" (p. 184). Meyer, Ramirez, and Soysal (1992) demonstrate the importance of international norms about the role of the nation-state in the diffusion of such systems, a factor that has so far been ignored in public choice accounts. Yet one does not need to accept either West's or Lott's account without reservation to recognize the useful challenge they provide to the presumption that existing institutions for the provision of education evolved solely to meet the needs of the students they serve. Indeed, it is reasonable to assume that their design also reflects the interests of the politicians and public officials responsible for their establishment and expansion.

Explanations for Low Productivity In addition to reexamining the origins of state-provided education systems, public choice scholars have also worked to explain their contemporary struggles to operate efficiently and equitably. In the U.S. context, these accounts have centered primarily on the weakness of market forces in the education sector, the unionization of educational employees, and incentives for unhealthy bureaucratization.

The relative absence of market forces in public education stems from the institutional design of American schooling (Friedman, 1955). Specifically, the combination of geographically distinct school districts and the lack of government funding for private schooling effectively offers school districts local monopolies on the provision of education. Families who cannot afford to send their child to a private school and are unable to teach their child at home have no option but to send their child to the local public schools. If district officials, teachers, and other employees could be relied upon to serve their students as efficiently as possible, or if parents and other voters were able to monitor their behavior adequately, this would not be a concern. Public choice scholars, however, suggest that there are reasons to doubt each of those claims.

First, they argue that district officials and teachers are likely to be concerned primarily with their own welfare. Note that this may well include the quality of schooling received by their students. All else equal, teachers surely prefer to work in effective schools in which students are learning. Yet it also likely encompasses material interests in better compensation, more leisure time, and a reduced workload—all of which are likely to increase the costs of providing a given level of educational services. Public choice scholars also emphasize the difficulty local residents face in monitoring the efforts of teachers and other school employees, the inputs into the schooling process (which include hard-to-measure factors such as the abilities of the district's students), and student outcomes. Given these difficulties, there is reason to suspect that American schools are less productive than would be the case if they operated in a fully competitive environment.

Of course, the monopoly power exercised by American school districts is not absolute. As Charles Tiebout (1956) demonstrated, the ability of residents to "vote with their feet" by moving to a different jurisdiction if they are dissatisfied with the quality of schooling or with the local level of taxation partially constrains rent-seeking by local governments. Although in reality only a few families are in a position to move at any point in time, their observations about school quality influence housing values in all school districts. Over the long run, districts which operate inefficiently should experience budget reductions. This competitive dynamic should be strongest when there is more choice among districts, as changes in property values will depend more on the quality of schools and less on other factors.

This last insight motivated economist Caroline Hoxby's (2000) seminal analysis of the effects of competition among public school districts on student performance and spending on schools. Hoxby recognized that the extent of choice among school districts available to residents in a given metropolitan area varies widely throughout the United States. In some cases, the lack of choice among districts may actually be the result of differences in school productivity rather than its cause. An unusually productive school district, for example, may expand through consolidation or by attracting more families with school-age children, thereby reducing the extent of choice available to future residents. As a result, simple comparisons of the performance of public schools in metropolitan areas with more and less inter-district choice may not provide reliable information about the causal effects of competition. Hoxby addressed this concern by using an instrumental variables strategy to limit her analysis to variation in the number of school districts related to geographic features that determined the historical development of district boundaries—and should therefore be unrelated to contemporary school quality. Her results indicate that student achievement is higher in metropolitan areas with more school districts despite

notably lower levels of spending on public education. By demonstrating that competition among districts enhances productivity, Hoxby's analysis suggests that the relative absence of market forces may hinder the productivity of the American school system.[4]

While the extent of competition among public school districts has remained relatively constant in recent decades, other scholars examining school productivity have called attention to changes in the political economy of American education, most notably the unionization of the teaching workforce. Prior to the 1960s, unions were virtually unheard of throughout most of the public sector, including public education. The situation soon changed, however, as states began passing laws that made it considerably easier for public sector employees to organize and win collective bargaining rights. Union membership among teachers skyrocketed and, by the early 1980s, virtually all large school districts outside of the South engaged in collective bargaining with organizations designated as the exclusive representative of local employees (Kahlenberg, 2006).

One of the most important insights to emerge from early public choice scholarship involves the barriers to collective action of any kind in the absence of compulsion (Olson, 1965). Most of the benefits provided by unions or other interest groups take the form of public goods; if they are offered to anyone in the potential group, no one in that group can be excluded. This creates a situation in which rational, self-interested individuals have little incentive to join groups or to contribute to their efforts. Because the costs of participation to a potential group member almost surely outweigh the additional benefits that would result from his or her contribution to the group's efforts, the rational strategy is to free ride on the contributions of others. The widespread adoption of laws that permitted unions to collect agency fees equivalent to negotiating expenses from all teachers covered by collective bargaining agreements helped nascent teacher organizations solve this "free-rider problem" by all but eliminating the additional costs of union membership. The adoption of such laws, while in part a response to lobbying by organizations sympathetic to organized labor, contributed importantly to the dramatic increase in unionization rates (Saltzman, 1985, 1988).

Public choice also provides insight into the impact of unionization on school district performance. Once again, the work of Caroline Hoxby (1996) has been especially influential in this area. Hoxby outlines two competing models of why teachers would demand a union and the likely impact of unionization on district operations. The first assumes that teachers demanding collective bargaining rights pursue the same objectives as parents, taxpayers, and district officials, but that they do so with better information that leads them to prefer different policies and spending levels. The second model, which falls more squarely within the public choice tradition, assumes that teachers have a different set of objectives than school districts, one that places greater weight on the policies such as salaries, benefits, and workloads that directly affect their material interests. Under the first model, the presence of a teachers union should enhance the productivity of district operations. Under the second, the union will pursue policy changes that provide rents for its members without improving school quality.

Because both of these models likely capture important aspects of the behavior of teachers unions, which of them dominates in practice is an empirical question. Hoxby finds that collective bargaining increases district budgets by 12%, on average, but also lowers district productivity by enough that the overall impact on high school graduation rates is negative. Interestingly, the detrimental effects of unionization are less strong in metropolitan areas with more independent school districts, suggesting that the rent-seeking behavior of unions may be constrained in areas where districts have less monopoly power.

Hoxby's analysis is only one piece of a large literature examining differences in student performance in unionized and non-unionized school districts, some of which has reached different conclusions.[5] It is again distinguished, however, by the rigorous strategies she uses to make causal inferences based solely on observational data. Simple comparisons of the quality and productivity of education in unionized and non-unionized districts fail to account for unmeasured characteristics of school systems that make teachers more likely to unionize. Hoxby therefore restricts her analysis to variation in unionization status due to the adoption of state collective bargaining laws, which should be unrelated to conditions in local districts. For this reason, her analysis provides uniquely compelling evidence concerning the overall impact of unionization on educational production.

Additional insight into the effects of unionization on school district operations comes from a series of papers by Terry Moe. Moe (2006a) argues that the advent of collective bargaining in education fundamentally altered the structure of governance in K-12 education. Traditionally, public schools were managed from the top down by political authorities including school boards, state legislatures, the federal government, and the courts. Political power in public education rested mainly with elected officials and administrators, subject to judicial oversight. Under the current system, however, teachers unions are able to exert influence both by lobbying state and federal policy makers and by negotiating the collective bargaining contracts that shape district operations. As a result, Moe (2006a) suggests, "Much of the structure of public schooling actually comes from below, not from above, and is a reflection of the power and interests of the employees who run the schools" (p. 7). In terms of the principal-agent models discussed above, the agents have gained considerable power.

Moe contends that the primary source of the power wielded by teachers unions in contemporary education politics is their ability to shape election outcomes. Using data from a sample of California school districts, he demonstrates that teachers and other district employees are far more likely to vote in school board and bond elections than are ordinary voters. Interestingly, the gap in turnout between teachers and other citizens is especially high for those teachers who live in the same district in which they work—and therefore have the opportunity to shape the policies in the schools in which they teach. Moe (2006b) interprets this finding as evidence that it is occupational self-interest, not interest in public education or favorable background characteristics, that explains their higher voting rates.

Perhaps because of the high levels of turnout among teachers, unions appear to be successful in getting their preferred candidates elected to school boards. Indeed, across 245 California school district elections and the 1,228 candidates who competed in them during the years 1998–2001, Moe (2006b) found that the effect of a union endorsement on the probability that a new candidate will win a spot on a school board is comparable in magnitude to the effect of incumbency. Another study, based on interviews with 526 school-board candidates in 253 California districts, confirms that unions are often the most active participants in school-board elections and that their influence is not limited to large urban districts. Predictably, the candidates endorsed by the unions have considerably more favorable views toward collective bargaining than do other candidates (Moe, 2005).

In sum, the unionization of teachers has led to a fundamental shift in the political economy of American education. The most rigorous research available suggests that the rise of collective bargaining has increased the costs of public education without improving student performance. From a public choice perspective, this outcome is unsurprising. Unions primarily exist to advance the interests of their members. While the interests of teachers likely encompass the well-being of students, they also include their own interests as employees.

A final area of concern for public choice scholars studying the recent performance of the American public education system has been excessive bureaucratization. In the most fully developed statement of this critique, John Chubb and Terry Moe (1990) argue that the bureaucratic rigidities that characterize American districts and schools are fundamentally incompatible with the effective provision of education, which requires that schools and teachers have sufficient autonomy to respond to the particular needs of their students. Moreover, they argue that increasing bureaucratization is an unavoidable byproduct of the democratic institutions by which schools are controlled.

Synthesizing insights derived from public choice and the new economics of organization, Chubb and Moe (1990) outline two distinct routes by which the political control of education may bring about excessive bureaucratization. First, the hierarchical nature of educational governance leads education authorities to rely heavily on procedural rules and regulations in order to ensure that schools comply with their preferences. With no way to monitor what goes on in schools directly, they face a critical information asymmetry. Recognizing that school employees inevitably have independent values and preferences that shape their views on education—and therefore incentives to do what they think is best—they are forced to devise various *ex post* and *ex ante* mechanisms to generate information, reshape staff incentives, and constrain their behavior along preferred lines.

This natural tendency to bureaucratize is enhanced by a second fundamental feature of democratic institutions: political uncertainty. In a school system controlled by democratic means, today's authorities have no sure way of knowing if they will still be in power after the next election. If they want their policies to persist over the long haul, they need to insulate them from the influence of future political authorities who may disagree. The most common strategy for doing so is the aggressive formalization of procedures to limit the discretion of their successors.

Chubb and Moe combine their theoretical analysis with an attempt to demonstrate the empirical relationship between bureaucratization and student achievement in a nationally representative data set. To evade the selection bias inherent in making comparisons of students in public and private schools, their main analysis considers only students within the public sector. Their main results, which show students in less bureaucratized public schools performing at higher levels, are consistent with their prediction that schools granted greater autonomy are more effective. Yet the causality of this relationship is difficult to establish, as the students served by such schools may differ from students in more bureaucratic school systems in ways that their analysis is not able to take into account.

Taken at face value, however, their theoretical critique has radical implications. The two dynamics fostering bureaucratization and undermining school effectiveness are endemic to the democratic control of education. That is, they hold regardless of which particular groups exercise the most influence in school politics. The only solution, in Chubb and Moe's view, is to end the direct democratic control of schools. They propose instead a regulated voucher system in which parents are able to use government funds to send their child to the school of their choice.

Proposals for Reform As this last discussion implies, public choice analyses of the shortcomings of the American education system have also shaped the development of contemporary reform strategies. In particular, they have led to the consideration of reform proposals intended to increase self-interested incentives to improve the quality of education. Most prominent among these are test-based accountability and school choice, two strategies that were widely pursued at the state and local level in the 1990s and which shaped the federal No Child Left Behind Act of 2002 (Peterson & West, 2003).

The accountability movement emerged in the 1990s and quickly became the most widely pursued strategy for improving performance and equalizing opportunities in public education. State after state adopted formal curriculum standards, tests aligned to those standards, new requirements for promotion and graduation, procedures for ranking schools based on student test performance, and rewards and sanctions based on those rankings.[6] Under No Child Left Behind, all states are now required to establish standards in mathematics and reading, to test students annually in grades 3–8 and once in high school to ensure those standards are being met, and to intervene in schools failing to make adequate yearly progress toward the goal of universal proficiency by 2014 (Peterson & West, 2003).

The chief rationale for accountability policies is the recognition that political authorities who desire to improve the performance of public schools face a difficult control problem. Distant political authorities lack the capacity to regulate or even to monitor behavior in districts and schools. In order to improve student achievement, they need to create incentives for district officials, school administrators, teachers, and students to reduce opportunistic behavior and become more productive. The introduction of explicit rewards and sanctions based on student performance on state-wide exams is an attempt to do just that. And there is mounting evidence that accountability policies have in fact generated modest improvements in student achievement in tested subjects.[7]

Yet accountability policies themselves emerge from the same political system that governs public education, and a public choice analysis of the process by which this occurs suggests important limits on their potential to drive educational improvement over the long haul. As Frederick Hess (2003) has shown, while tough-minded accountability policies are broadly popular among voters when they are first announced, they often face strong resistance from the groups most affected by the sanctions they impose, including teachers unions and organizations representing disadvantaged and minority students. In addition, elected officials such as mayors, governors, and even presidents who have invested political capital in the passage of accountability policies have strong incentives to show progress. Over time, there is natural tendency for standards to be lowered, exemptions granted, and penalties postponed as aspirational goals go unfulfilled.[8]

A second major thrust of contemporary school reform has been the attempt to expand parental choice over the school their child attends. These efforts generally take one of two forms: policies that expand choice within the public sector and policies that reduce the costs of private school attendance through tuition tax credits or school vouchers. The former include intra- and inter-district choice programs and state laws allowing for the formation of charter schools, which are public schools of choice that are privately managed under a renewable performance contract that exempts them from many of the regulations on traditional public schools. In the 2007–08 school year, more than 1.2 million students attended one of almost 4,000 charter schools operated in 40 states and the District of Columbia.[9] The No Child Left Behind Act also requires that students attending schools that fail to make adequate yearly progress for 2 consecutive years be given the option to attend another non-failing school within the same district. Arizona, Florida, Illinois, Iowa, Minnesota, and Pennsylvania currently offer tax credits for either private school tuition or for donations to scholarship organizations, while school voucher programs operate in Cleveland, Milwaukee, Florida, and the District of Columbia.

In addition to offering new choices for families unsatisfied with their current school, school choice programs are also intended to provide healthy competition that will force traditional public schools to improve their performance. And some research using quasi-experimental methods suggests that the implementation of voucher and charter school programs has led to improved student achievement in those traditional public schools most directly affected by the new competition.[10] Critics of school choice reforms nevertheless complain that this literature ignores these program's consequences for equity or for other goals, such as the inculcation of civic values.[11] Proponents, on the other hand, respond that there is no evidence that private schools undermine civic values and that the outcomes of market-based reforms should be compared to those of the existing public education system, not a utopian ideal.

A critical factor often missing from the discussion of existing school choice programs, however, is the extent to which they shelter traditional public schools and the individuals who work in them from the consequences that typically accompany competition in private markets (Hess, 2002). Many voucher and charter school laws contain provisions that protect school districts from financial loss or even increase their budgets, if they lose students. Such provisions are often essential in order to win political support, but they obviously limit the competitive pressures for improvement that public choice scholars contend would exist under a full-fledged market system.

School voucher programs have also been limited mainly to large urban school districts, poor families, or students attending failing schools, a pattern that is consistent with public choice models of voter behavior and further limits the competitive pressures exerted on traditional public schools. Homeowners in districts with high-quality schools will typically see their property values fall if a universal voucher program is adopted, and will therefore be more likely to oppose them. In addition, the short-run tax implications of traditional voucher plans, in which vouchers are available to all children attending a private school, are ambiguous. Because voucher amounts are typically less than average per pupil spending in public schools, the overall tax burden will fall if many students use them to switch from public to private schools. If most voucher students were already attending private schools, however, taxes will increase. Programs that limit vouchers to poor families or to families in specific public schools eliminate this ambiguity and have predictably been more successful politically than more sweeping proposals (Kenny, 2005).

Conclusion

Over the past 50 years, public choice theory has radically challenged traditional approaches to political analysis across a broad range of policy domains. Nowhere was its impact more jarring than in the field of education, in which it had long been assumed that teachers and administrators were doing as well as they could and that the only way to improve America's schools was to provide them with more resources, expertise, training, and support. The notion that educators might be motivated by anything other than the needs of their students was considered anathema. However, as economic changes increased the demands placed on the nation's education system, as evidence mounted that additional investments in capacity had not worked to make American schooling more adequate or more equitable, and as economists and political scientists outside of education schools increasingly took an interest in public school performance, public choice perspectives on education policy gained in stature and influence.

The resulting scholarship has directed reformers' attention to the incentives facing the elected officials, administrators, and teachers responsible for educating American students—and to the institutions that structure those incentives. It does not deny that many educators have altruistic motives, but it suggests that mechanisms that provide them with self-interested incentives to improve student achievement are a promising strategy for improving the performance of the system as a whole. Many public choice theorists continue to see merit in the potential of test-based accountability and school choice—the policies most explicitly tied to the creation of such incentives—to lift school quality and ultimately student outcomes. It remains unclear, however, whether political realities will allow for their ideas to be given a full test.

Notes

1. For a comprehensive overview of public choice theory, see Mueller (2003).
2. For contrasting assessments of the contributions made by public choice theory to political science, see Riker (1991); Green and Shapiro (1994).
3. See, e.g., Tullock (1965); Downs & Rand Corporation (1967); Niskanen (1971). For an overview of public choice models of bureaucratic decision making, see Moe (1997).
4. A paper by Jesse Rothstein (2007) argues that Hoxby's result is not robust to plausible alternative specifications. For Hoxby's reply, see Hoxby (2007).
5. For a recent review of the literature on the impact of teachers unions on student outcomes, see Goldhaber (2006).
6. By 2002, laws in 25 states explicitly linked student promotion or graduation to performance on state or district assessments, 20 states sanctioned staff in low-performing schools, and 18 states rewarded staff for exemplary student performance (Quality Counts, 2002).
7. See, e.g., Hanushek & Raymond (2005); Carnoy & Loeb (2002); Jacob (2005); Wössmann (2003); Bishop (1997).
8. On the role of teachers unions in accountability politics, see Moe (2003).
9. Information on the number of charter schools and students comes from the Center for Education Reform http://www.edreform.com/_upload/ncsw-numbers.pdf [Accessed May 1, 2008].
10. See, e.g., Hoxby (2003); West & Peterson (2006).
11. See, among others, Brighouse (2000); Ladd (2002).

References

Bishop, J. H. (1997). The effect of national standards and curriculum-based exams on achievement. *American Economic Review, 87,* 260–264.

Blau, F., & Kahn, L. (2001). *Do cognitive test scores explain higher U.S. wage inequality?* (NBER Working Paper 8210). Cambridge, MA: National Bureau of Economic Research.

Boyd, W. L., Crowson, R. L., & van Geel, T. (1995). Rational choice theory and the politics of education: Promise and limitations. In J. D. Scriber & D. H. Layton (Eds.), *The study of educational politics, The 1994 commemorative yearbook of the Politics of Education Association, 1969–1994* (pp. 127–146). Bristol, PA: Falmer Press.

Brighouse, H. (2000). *School choice and social justice.* Oxford, UK: Oxford University Press.

Buchanan, J. M., & Tullock, G. (1962). *The calculus of consent: Logical foundations of constitutional democracy.* Ann Arbor: The University of Michigan Press.

Carnoy, M., & Loeb, S. (2002). Does external accountability affect student outcomes? A cross-state analysis. *Educational Evaluation and Policy Analysis, 24,* 305–331.

Chaplin, D. (2002). Tassels on the cheap. *Education Next, 2*(3), 24–29.

Chubb, J. E., & Moe, T. M. (1990). *Politics, markets, and America's schools.* Washington, DC: Brookings.

Devine, N. (2004). *Education and public choice: A critical account of the invisible hand in education.* Westport, CT: Praeger.

Dilulio, J. J., Jr. (1994). Principled agents: The cultural bases of behavior in a federal government bureaucracy. *Journal of Public Administration, Research and Theory, 4,* 277–318.

Diplomas count 2007: Ready for what? Preparing students for college, careers, and life after high school. (2007, June 12). *Education Week, 26*(40). Retrieved October 21, 2008, from http://www.edweek.org/ew/toc/2007/06/12/index.html

Downs, A., & Rand Corporation. (1967). *Inside bureaucracy.* Boston: Little, Brown.

Friedman, M. (1955). The role of government in education. In R. A. Solo (Ed.), *Economics and the public interest* (pp.123–144). New Brunswick, NJ: Rutgers University Press.

Goldhaber, D. (2006). Are teachers' unions good for students? In J. Hannaway & A. J. Rotherham (Eds.), *Collective bargaining in education: Negotiating change in American schools* (pp. 141–159). Cambridge, MA: Harvard Education Press.

Green, D. P., & Shapiro, I. (1994). *Pathologies of rational choice theory: A critique of applications in political science.* New Haven, CT: Yale University Press.

Hanushek, E. A. (2003, February). The failure of input-based schooling policies. *The Economic Journal, 113,* F64–F98.

Hanushek, E. A., & Raymond, M. E. (2005). Does school accountability lead to improved student performance? *Journal of Policy Analysis and Management, 24,* 297–327.

Hanushek, E. A., & Rivkin, S. G. (1997). Understanding the 20th century growth in U.S. school spending. *Journal of Human Resources, 32,* 35–68.

Heckman, J. J., & LaFontaine, P. A. (2008). *The American high school graduation rate: Trends and levels* (NBER Working paper 13670). Cambridge, MA: National Bureau of Economic Research.

Hess, F. M. (2002). *Revolution at the margins: The impact of competition on urban school systems.* Washington, DC: Brookings Institution.

Hess, F. M. (2003). Refining or retreating? High-stakes accountability in the states. In P. E. Peterson & M. R. West (Eds.), *No Child Left Behind? The politics and practice of school accountability* (pp. 55–79). Washington, DC: Brookings Institution.

Hoxby, C. M. (1996). How teachers unions affect education production. *Quarterly Journal of Economics, 111,* 671–718.

Hoxby, C. M. (2000). Does competition among public schools benefit students and taxpayers? *The American Economic Review, 90,* 1209–1238.

Hoxby, C. M. (2003). School choice and school productivity: Could school choice be a tide that lifts all boats? In C. M. Hoxby (Ed.), *The economics of school of choice* (pp. 287–341). Chicago: University of Chicago Press.

Hoxby, C. M. (2007). Does competition among public schools benefit students and taxpayers? Reply. *The American Economic Review, 97,* 2038–2055.

Jacob, B. A. (2005). Accountability, incentives, and behavior: The impact of high-stakes testing in the Chicago public schools. *Journal of Public Economics, 89,* 761–796.

Kahlenberg, R. D. (2006) The history of collective bargaining among teachers. In J. Hannaway & A. J. Rotherham (Eds.), *Collective bargaining in education: Negotiating change in American schools* (pp. 7–26). Cambridge, MA: Harvard Education Press.

Kenny, L. W. (2005). The public choice of educational choice. *Public Choice, 124,* 205–222.

Ladd, H. (2002). School vouchers: A critical view. *Journal of Economic Perspectives, 16*(4), 3–24.

Le Grand, J. (1997). Knights, knaves, or pawns? Human behaviour and social policy. *Journal of Social Policy, 26*(2), 149–169.

Le Grand, J. (2003). *Motivation, agency, and public policy: Of knights and knaves, pawns and queens.* Oxford, UK: Oxford University Press.

Lott, J. R., Jr. (1990). An explanation for public provision of schooling: The importance of indoctrination. *Journal of Law and Economics, 33*(1), 199–231.

Lott, J. R., Jr. (1999). Public schooling, indoctrination, and totalitarianism. *Journal of Political Economy, 107,* S127–S157.

Mayhew, D. R. (1974). *Congress: The electoral connection.* New Haven, CT: Yale University Press.

Meyer, J. W., Ramirez, F. O., & Soysal, Y. N. (1992). World expansion of mass education, 1870–1980. *Sociology of Education, 65,* 128–149.

Michaelson, J. B. (1977). Revision, bureaucracy, and school reform. *School Reviews, 85,* 208–241.

Moe, T. M. (1984). The new economics of organization. *American Journal of Political Science, 28,* 739–777.

Moe, T. M. (1997). The positive theory of public bureaucracy. In D. C. Mueller (Ed.), *Perspectives on public choice: A handbook* (pp. 455–480). Cambridge, UK: Cambridge University Press.

Moe, T. M. (2003). Politics, control, and the future of school accountability. In P. E. Peterson & M. R. West (Eds.), *No Child Left Behind? The politics and practice of school accountability* (pp. 80–106). Washington, DC: Brookings Institution.

Moe, T. M. (2005). Teacher unions and school board elections. In W. G. Howell (Ed.), *Besieged: School boards and the future of education politics* (254–287). Washington, DC: Brookings Institution.

Moe, T. M. (2006a). *Bottom-up structure: Collective bargaining, transfer rights, and the plight of disadvantaged schools.* Fayetteville: University of Arkansas.

Moe, T. M. (2006b). Political control and the power of the agent. *Journal of Law, Economics, and Organization, 22,* 1–29.

Mueller, D. C. (2003). *Public choice III.* Cambridge, UK: Cambridge University Press.

Niskanen, W. A. (1971). *Bureaucracy and representative government.* Chicago: Aldine-Atherton.

Olson, M. (1965). *The logic of collective action: Public goods and the theory of groups.* Cambridge, MA: Harvard University Press.

Peterson, P. E., & West, M.R. (Eds.). (2003). *No Child Left Behind? The politics and practice of school accountability.* Washington, DC: Brookings Institution.

Pratt, J. W., & Zeckhauser, R. J. (Eds.). (1985). *Principals and agents: The structure of business.* Boston: Harvard Business School Press.

Quality Counts 2002: Building blocks for success. (2002, January 10). *Education Week, 21*(17). Retrieved October 21, 2008, from http://www.edweek.org/media/ew/qc/archives/QC02full.pdf

Riker, W. A. (1991). Political science and rational choice. In J. E. Alt & K. A. Shepsle (Eds.), *Perspectives on positive political economy* (pp. 163–181). Cambridge, UK: Cambridge University Press.

Rothstein, J. (2007). Does competition among public schools benefit students and taxpayers? Comment. *The American Economic Review, 97,* 2026–2037.

Saltzman, G. M. (1985). Bargaining laws as a cause and consequence of the growth of teacher unionism. *Industrial and Labor Relations Review, 38,* 335–351.

Saltzman, G. M. (1988). Public sector bargaining laws really matter: Evidence from Ohio and Illinois. In R. B. Freeman & C. Ichniowski (Eds.), *When public sector workers unionize* (pp. 41–78). Chicago: University of Chicago Press.

Schneider, B., Carnoy, M., Kilpatrick, J., Schmidt, W. H., & Shavelson, R. J. (2007). *Estimating causal effects using experimental and observational designs.* Washington, DC: American Educational Research Association.

Smith, A. (1776). *The nature and causes of the wealth of nations.* Retrieved June 9, 2008, from http://geolib.com/smith.adam/woncont.html

Tiebout, C. M. (1956). A pure theory of local expenditures. *Journal of Political Economy, 64,* 416–424.

Toma, E. F. (1996). Public funding and private schooling across countries. *Journal of Law and Economics, 39,* 121–148.

Toma, E. F. (2004). Education and the state. In C. K. Rowley & F. Sch-neider (Eds.), *The Encyclopedia of Public Choice, Vol. 2* (pp. 183–186). Dordrecht, The Netherlands: Kluwer.

Tullock, G. (1965). *The politics of bureaucracy.* Washington, DC: Public Affairs Press.

Tullock, G., Seldon, A., & Brady, G. L. (2003). *Government failure: A primer in public choice.* Washington, DC: Cato Institute.

West, E. G. (1994). *Education and the state: A study in political economy* (3rd ed.). Indianapolis, IN: Liberty Fund.

West, M. R., & Peterson, P. E. (2006). The efficacy of choice-threats within school accountability systems: Results for legislatively induced experiments. *Economic Journal, 116*(510), C46–C62.

Wössmann, L. (2002). *Schooling and the quality of human capital.* New York: Springer.

Wössmann, L. (2003). Central exit exams and student achievement: International evidence. In P. E. Peterson & M. R. West (Eds.), *No Child Left Behind? The politics and practice of school accountability* (pp. 292–323). Washington, DC: Brookings Institution.

30

Research in the Policy Process[1]

MARSHALL S. SMITH
William and Flora Hewlett Foundation

MATTHEW L. SMITH
International Development Research Centre

Introduction

This chapter explores the relationship between education research and policy. Our approach is intended to be provocative and informative, rather than comprehensive. We use examples that demonstrate how and when research influences policy, argue that many education policies and interventions have little effect on important educational outcomes due to their very nature, suggest interventions that have had substantial effects, and indicate dimensions of these interventions that might have contributed to the substantial effects. We then explore ways of improving the quality and utility of education research to address issues of causality and external validity. Finally, we make a few observations about what we have covered in the chapter, propose four recommendations for policy makers and policy researchers, and then suggest several innovations that might result in large effects on student achievement. We favor a broad, practical conception of policy research along the lines that Lindblom and Cohen (1979) suggest by the label "social problem solving," which is the systematic study of processes that are intended to result in improving social conditions (p. 4).

How Does Research Influence Policy?

Historical Examples of How Research Has Influenced Education Policy Although researchers often bemoan the fact that their current favorite study is not being used in the policy arena, research is continually cited in policy considerations and often plays a major, if typically under-estimated role.[2] Examples abound at all levels of education governance.

For the past 45 years, the large contours of federal education policy have been shaped by the interaction of research with politics and ideology. Head Start, initiated in the summer of 1965, was prompted by the emerging civil rights movement, the tragedy of President John F.

Kennedy's death, and the ability of President Lyndon Johnson to move legislation through Congress; however, it was based on significant bodies of bench and field research concerning the importance of variations in early childhood experiences for children's intellectual and physical development and the vast differences between the environments of children of low-income families and those from middle-income homes. Jerome Bruner, Benjamin Bloom, and Edward Zigler were among the well-known psychologists who influenced the early design of Head Start. David Weikert's development work on the Ypsilanti Perry Preschool project was also helpful to a committee of scholars, including Julius Richmond, who shaped the requirements for Head Start (Vinovskis, 2005). Similarly, research on the relationship between poverty and children's learning helped shape the views of John Gardner and Francis Keppel as they put together the framework for Title I of the Elementary and Secondary Education Act, which was implemented in the summer of 1966 (Kaestle & Smith, 1982; Bailey & Mosher, 1968).

The summer of 1966 also saw the release of sociologist James Coleman's famous *Equality of Educational Opportunity* report together with the data from the massive survey of 560,000 students, teachers, and principals that provided the grist for the report (Coleman et al., 1966). The report and follow-up analyses influenced U.S. education policy throughout the 1960s and 1970s, first by challenging conventional wisdom about the effects of schooling on the variation of achievement among groups of students and later by stimulating research on inequality in the United States and on the effects of various components of schooling on achievement (Jencks et al., 1972; Mosteller & Moynihan, 1972; Bowles & Gintis, 1976).

Studies in the 1960s and early 1970s of the incidence, treatment, and best practices for educating disabled students led to a few states passing legislation and, in 1975, to the federal government's landmark legislation, the Individuals with Disabilities Education Act. For the past 33 years, the Department of Education has run a credible research program focused on the treatment of disabilities in schools; this program has influenced policy and practice on special education in government and classrooms.

Throughout the entire second half of the century, the education arm of the federal government produced program evaluations that the Office of Management and Budget and Congress regularly used in budget and policy work. These include evaluations of Title I of the Elementary and Secondary Education Act (ESEA), some of which had a direct impact on the provisions of that act (McLaughlin, 1975; Kaestle & Smith, 1982).

University-based centers and regional laboratories created by Title IV of the ESEA in 1966 have had a steady and sometimes creative role in providing research and analyses that have influenced federal and state policy. The centers focus on research while the laboratories were intended to serve as translators and disseminators of the research, though their mission expanded as they diversified their funding sources to include states and foundations. For 40 years, the UCLA Center for the Study of Evaluation, now called the National Center for Research on Evaluation, Standards, and Student Testing, has influenced federal and state policy in its areas of interest; and research and policy analysis carried out by the Consortium for Education Policy Research (CPRE) helped shape much of the states' education policy activity in the 1980s. Part of the impetus for the CPRE policy work was the federal report, A Nation at Risk, whose authors relied heavily on data and research to support their arguments (National Commission on Excellence in Education, 1983; Fuhrman, 1993).[3] CPRE's work was also instrumental in the late 1980s and early 1990s in formulating a research-based argument and a federal role in promoting state standards-based reforms (Smith & O'Day, 1991; O'Day & Smith, 1993; Vinovskis, 1996; Cross, 2004).[4]

Arguably, there is considerable variation in the use of research across the last 40 years that might be a function of the various policy positions of federal administrations and political leadership.[5] For example, some researchers argue that parts of the No Child Left Behind (NCLB) legislation were not grounded in research evidence when the act was passed by Congress. The areas included the use of student choice, after-school tutoring, and strategies to improve failing schools as components of sanctions for schools that do not meet their state's achievement level requirements (Hess & Finn, 2007). Yet, what is probably meant by the criticism is that the research is ambiguous; there are some studies that support interventions of this sort and others that find no effects or negative effects. Research has been used, but perhaps badly.

Research also regularly influences policy issues at the state and local levels. Many states have research and evaluation staffs in their Departments of Education and analysts that work for their legislatures to provide policy makers with up-to-date information about research. Findings, good and bad, make their way into local practice in a variety of ways. One avenue is through textbooks and other instruc-

tional materials, where promotional materials regularly reference research that has shaped the product. In the best instances, this research provides guidance in the construction and use of the materials. For example, following the launch of Sputnik, from the late 1950s through the 1960s, the National Science Foundation's support of new science and mathematics curricula, based in part on research, helped to alter instruction in many schools in those fields by emphasizing exploration, problem solving, and hands-on learning (Welch, 1979). Another way that research changes practice is when consultants provide "research-based," professional development to people at all levels of school systems across the nation. For example, Madeline Hunter's tireless and amazingly influential work training teachers to implement her instructional strategies during the 1980s and early 1990s was based on her interpretation of a large body of research (Wolfe, 1998).

Research has also influenced education policy made in the highest court. The Supreme Court cited research in the 1954 Brown v. Board of Education case, which struck down de jure racial segregation in the South.[6] Data and analyses of the slow progress of southern states in meeting the Court's requirements led to further court decisions in the late 1960s, which then led to widespread implementation. Later policies to desegregate northern school systems were based firstly on principle and law and secondly on studies that showed the positive effects of integrated classrooms and schools on the achievement of minority students (U.S. Commission on Civil Rights, 1967; Schwartz, Pettigrew, & Smith, 1968; Weinberg, 1977).[7] Just recently, the Supreme Court cited research in its ruling on affirmative action in college admissions (Grutter v. Bollinger et al., 2003).

Finally, some policy ideas are not directly based on research in schools and schooling but on ideas and theory drawn from other sectors.[8] Perhaps the most prominent is the idea that school choice can drive educational improvement. First put forth by economist Milton Friedman (1955), the proposal to create a market in K–12 education by using vouchers originates from theory supported by numerous examples that predict that competition and incentives within markets tend to enhance quality and efficiency.[9] Since then, numerous research efforts have examined the efficacy of different approaches to education policies that embody choice as a primary dimension.

Overall, we suspect that every important education policy at the federal level over the past 50 years has been based on a body of evidence supported by aggressive researchers and advocates. Of course, this does not mean that policy makers are unbiased in their selection of research or that politics, ideology, lobby groups, or ambitious researchers do not exert enormous influence. It does mean, however, that policy makers regularly make use of research as they conduct their business.

This understanding changes the question from: Does research influence policy? to Why isn't research better used? and leads to the question, How might education research and development better serve the making of policy?

The remainder of this chapter explores these questions. As background to this exploration, we first look at two other factors in the research/policy environment: the role of foundations and the importance of effective ways of aggregating knowledge.

The Increasing Role of Foundations in the Education Research and Policy World Recently, a variety of publications have espoused the idea that large foundations should develop programs that are guided by a well-defined theory (logic model) with an end goal of improving some aspect of the world's condition. The logic model is assumed to be based on evidence and have measurable goals in a measurable time frame (Fleishman, 2007). Very often the work defined by these models includes funding directed research and advocacy, leading to policy change. The importance and visibility of such work has increased over the past few years, in part due to the increases in the size of foundations, including the entry of the Gates Foundation into the field in 2000.

Since many foundations carry a reputation of bipartisanship, their voices are often powerful. Moreover, a foundation has the opportunity to fund policy-changing strategies over a sustained period of time, from conception through research and analysis, policy formation and advocacy, and implementation and evaluation. The capacity of foundations for such long-term commitments makes them especially formidable.

While the realization of the power of foundations may be recent, their role in deliberately supporting policy-oriented research has been influential in education for years. The Carnegie Corporation's support of research on inequality in America, funded by Frederic Mosher in the late 1960s and early 1970s, led to dozens of publications that fueled national policy debates throughout the time period (Mosteller & Moynihan, 1972; Jencks et al., 1972; Bowles & Gintis, 1976). Another early and more focused example is the Ford Foundation's work on state school finance reform in the 1970s. Many of the arguments and political impetus for equalizing funding grew out of the research and advocacy activities supported by James Kelly (1980) at the Ford Foundation, and a substantial number of states passed legislation designed to do so. Ford also invested in policy research focused on promoting and later understanding a movement for community control of schools in New York City. In fact, Ford commissioned an important, interesting report—*A Foundation Goes to School* (Ford Foundation, 1972)—which examines the effectiveness of the foundation's work in New York in the 1960s.

In the 1980s, the Carnegie Corporation, led by David Hamburg, provided resources to draw together evidence and make and disseminate policy recommendations in the fields of early childhood and middle schools. In the early 1990s, Robert Schwartz of the Pew Charitable Trust supported an extensive portfolio on standards-based reform that helped influence both the policy and the implementation of that reform across the nation.

In recent years, a large number of foundations—including the Atlantic Philanthropies, the Carnegie Corporation, and the Gates, Hewlett, MacArthur, Mott, and Packard Foundations—have funded policy-oriented research in such areas as standards-based reform, state and district reform, early childhood development, curriculum development, charter schools, after-school programs, small schools, teacher training, and secondary schools. Much of this work is guided by focused strategies that incorporate indicators to assess interim outcomes and ultimate goals. The strategy provides a structure for accumulating the knowledge and the support necessary to reach the goal.

Though policy-focused foundation work has been around for a century, its growth and recent emphasis on top-down strategic activities has potential implications, both positive and negative, for the relationship between research and policy. On the positive side, foundations: (a) can be much more nimble than government in focusing on important problems, (b) can serve as a countervailing force in society by representing views and providing grants in areas that are different from policy positions held by a government, (c) often have direct access to policy makers, (d) are capable of focusing a clear strategy on difficult issues for a sustained period of time, and (e) have the opportunity to be innovative without fear of lobby groups. On the other hand, many critics are concerned with certain aspects of foundations: (a) the lack of transparency of their activities; (b) the lack of peer review in many funding decisions; (c) the focusing of great power in the hands of a few; (d) the lack of clear accountability beyond transparency; (e) the ability to focus for long periods of time on one strategy or issue, thereby having an extraordinary influence; and, based on the preceding concerns, (f) their ability to unilaterally "distort" policy priorities.

However this tension between these two faces of philanthropy plays out, the power of foundations to influence education policy with strategies that extend from research through advocacy will continue to grow as foundations increase in number and size.

The Accumulation of Knowledge in Policy Research In most examples of the use of research in policy, no single study can be identified as the principal causal influence. Rather, the accumulation of knowledge and relevant examples lead to a gradually increasing understanding that the nation, state, or local jurisdiction is facing a problem that should be addressed by a deliberate intervention. Lindblom and Cohen (1979) argue that a succession of studies that invalidate current beliefs can help alter conventional wisdom and result in policy makers reconsidering their decision-making framework, operating philosophy, or ideology.[10] These considerations suggest that the systematic accumulation of knowledge can play a critical role in the way that research influences policy.

In this section we distinguish between *meta-analysis* (Light & Smith, 1971; Glass, 1976),[11] which effectively pools the results of many studies of the same or similar interventions and their relationship to similar outcome variables to derive an average and a distribution of effect sizes, and the *aggregation of bodies of knowledge* to inform the development of a theory, intervention, or policy. Many researchers and "best practice" centers use meta-analysis to determine whether an intervention or education program is effective. Part of the idea behind meta-analysis is to increase the reliability or power of an inference by drawing on multiple studies. Another motivation is to address the issue of external validity because the studies are generally based in different sites with different populations. Meta-analysis has been made popular by the Cochrane Collaboration for medical research, the Campbell Collaboration for educational research, and the British and U.S. governments' education best practice Web sites (see www.cochrane.org; www.campbellcollaboration.org; http://ies.ed.gov/ncee/wwc). The intent of the Campbell Collaboration and the governments' Web sites are to provide information directly to policy makers, mostly at the local school or district levels since the interventions on which they focus are mostly locally based.

The deliberate accumulation of knowledge to develop theory, design an intervention, or help create a policy starts with different goals and strategies than does meta-analysis, and makes use of different methods.[12] One distinction is whether the strategy is to create *new* knowledge or to aggregate *existing* knowledge to address an issue. Systematically planning and accumulating a *new* body of research to address a social problem starts with the assumption that the problem needs to be more completely researched to meet the needs of policy makers. This contrasts with an assumption that there may be *sufficient* research in a field but that it is not well-organized and presented. Such an assumption leads to the idea of developing a well-done, policy-oriented synthesis of prior research and theory.[13] In many instances of systematic aggregation, however, both new and prior knowledge are used to make a coherent case. Foundation programs that use a theory/logic model approach often employ both methodologies.

National research and development centers at UCLA, Johns Hopkins, the University of Wisconsin, and the University of Pittsburgh, among others, provide examples of long-term, programmatic R&D that created new knowledge and influenced policy. These centers carried out multi-study R&D agendas, some lasting longer than a decade, which often resulted in the implementation of strong, research-based products (Atkinson & Jackson, 1992).

Another approach to systematically developing and accumulating new knowledge came from National Institute of Education (NIE) research programs in the 1970s on reading, teaching, methodology, and governance, each of which led to new directions for research and development. These programs began with theoretically structured research planning and field-building conferences and resulted in research and development products funded by the government that went on to influence publishers and local and state policies. The research programs also heavily influenced the work of other researchers, helping to build the base of knowledge for future policy (Venezky, 1977).

The policy synthesis is an example of using *existing* knowledge to explicitly build a case for developing an intervention to address a problem or promote a new policy goal. The best of syntheses examine alternative approaches as well as the potential for unintended effects. To be most effective, the synthesis should tell a compelling story that engages the reader in understanding the problem(s) and possible solution(s). The NIE study of Title I carried out in the mid-1970s is one example of purposefully using a coherent collection of research to influence policy, while California's recent, well-coordinated school finance and governance studies is another (Kaestle & Smith, 1982; Loeb, Bryk, & Hanushek, 2007). Coordinated and focused syntheses of research can help change the hearts and minds of policy makers about the potential importance of changes in policy. While actively participating in the release of the reports on the condition of California education in the spring of 2007, Governor Arnold Schwarzenegger announced that for the first time in his governorship, he was optimistic about the possibilities for making serious change in California's policies and that 2008 would be the "year of education" (Loeb et al., 2007).[14] The syntheses on systemic reform supported by the Center for Education Policy Research are also examples of documents that significantly affected policy (Cross, 2004; Vinovskis, 1996).

Much of the work of the National Research Council (NRC) provides a variation on the policy synthesis. NRC syntheses are generally consensus documents that, by their nature, are nuanced (i.e., on the one hand, on the other hand). Nevertheless, they fit the general definition of careful and unbiased syntheses of existing research that are designed to provide policy-focused assistance to a government or philanthropic funder, and many have had significant effects on education policy (National Academy of Sciences, 2008a).

Without systematic and objective aggregations of knowledge in policy areas, the opportunity for the development of useful, quality theory and policy would be dramatically reduced. In the social sciences, where the behavior of humans and their institutions are the objects of research, there are few, if any, fundamental laws that are universally applicable. Interventions that are effective in changing behavior are generally complex, working in a way that may be susceptible to conditional probabilistic modeling, but are not deterministic. The systematic accumulation of knowledge and evidence supports theory and provides a potential understanding of how an intervention may operate under a variety of conditions.

When Does Research Influence Policy?

Our two central points in the prior section are that policy makers do use research and that there is some rhyme and reason that helps to determine how and in what form research influences policy. But even well-organized research, presented in what the researcher believes is a compelling manner, is by and large not enough to have an influence. This section explores some of the factors that are generally under the control of the education researcher and that lead to research being used by policy makers.[15]

Let's start with an obvious but potentially frustrating truth: Most research does not directly influence policy. Lindblom and Cohen (1979) argue that much of the most important *policy* research helps to shape the environment of thought for eventual policy action and, consequently, does not initially appear to be influential.

Even though policy makers do regularly use research, most studies never cross their desks. Whether a study is useful for policymaking depends on many things, including the nature of the knowledge produced in the study, how and in what context policy makers might use the research, and how it is packaged. "Basic" research in areas such as learning, teaching, motivation, and the nature of organizations is critical to the advancement of knowledge, but typically such research is not directly useful to policy makers, though it may eventually be part of a chain of evidence that leads to policy.

Similarly, a study that is useful at one level of government may not be useful at another. Studies designed to provide information about how to teach a specific, important concept in elementary mathematics will not be useful to policy makers in federal and state governments or even in most district offices, though they may be useful to teachers, principals, and publishers. Some research does not even indirectly influence policy because it lacks methodological or theoretical quality.[16]

Various factors associated with the content of the research influence whether a piece of research that is potentially pertinent to a possible policy actually has an influence on policy makers. One factor is whether the proposed policy is easily accepted or is threatening to vested interests and, therefore, difficult for many policy makers to support. A research study or synthesis that is appropriately used to support a policy, is not disruptive or excessively expensive, is supported by the unions and business, and sounds good to voters stands a good chance of being influential. Apparently technical policy fixes that are easy to describe and have potential results that are countable—such as increasing the amount of required testing, reducing the student/computer ratio in a school, or building new schools—are attractive and easy to understand by policy makers. However, research on the use of performance incentives to augment teachers' salaries or on the use of technology in ways that would alter the role of the teacher will attract attention but probably not serious policy proposals until the relevant lobby groups indicate their support.[17]

Another important determinant of use is how research is presented. Few policy makers or even their staff will read a study or report. Policy briefs and other short syntheses can be important vehicles for change if they succinctly present the material, are written in a style that laypeople can understand, and give arguments and data to policy makers who want to tackle the issue. Framing the problem addressed by the research in a larger social context, such as providing equality of opportunity, enhancing the economy, or supporting a democratic society, provides a useful rhetorical rationale. Clear, compelling text about the research and its implications is powerful since well-written materials help coalesce thinking by creating general agreement on the problem, framing the issues, and explaining how the research findings address the problem. Coherent anecdotes and stories are powerful, especially when they present a compelling causal argument about how the policy will address and "solve" a particular problem. At their best, the stories involve taking the findings from a number of different studies (from research syntheses) to build a causal narrative that is both easily understandable and connects to the experiences of the policy makers (Tilly, 2006; George & Bennett, 2005). In the legislature, a compelling story presented in testimony can be effective and in an administration, short, informative syntheses and compelling stories are the grist of good policy memos such as those that often precede a proposed piece of legislation.

Concrete examples of the implementation of a potential policy are quite useful. These may come from demonstration projects or naturally occur within the educational environment. They may push policy change by providing useful data or by capturing the attention of policy makers with pictures and stories that help them reach an understanding of the importance of the proposed policy. In some cases, the demonstration projects have experimental or quasi-experimental designs that provide concrete evidence of effect sizes. The Tennessee class-size study altered the entire class-size debate because it was a widely promoted randomized experiment indicating that reducing the number of students in primary school classrooms had modest positive effects on achievement, particularly that of minority students (Mosteller, 1995; Finn & Achilles, 1990).[18] The combination of an experiment with the apparent backing of a state and a finding that was enthusiastically endorsed by a powerful constituent group—the teacher unions—as well as a number of influential academics who praised the study's quality, led the federal government and several states to adopt class-size reduction policies even though a large body of literature showed mixed effects.

Marketing also matters. Publishing in an AERA research journal or even in a widely read education practitioner journal such as *Phi Delta Kappan* or *Education Leadership* is not enough. Op Ed articles in local newspapers may make local or even state policy makers take notice, but unless they appear in one of the dozen major newspapers, they stand no chance of having an effect at the federal level. Providing a briefing for a trusted assistant to an important policy maker is sometimes very useful, and convincing one of more of the major nongovernmental players (e.g., the unions, school boards, business coalitions, civil rights groups) of the worth of the research at the state and federal level is very important because many of these groups are powerful and well-funded lobbies.

Finally, in the big cities and states and at the federal level, the policy-focused think tanks are important purveyors of research findings and new reform ideas; in Washington, DC, these include Education Sector, the American Enterprise Institute, the Center on Education Policy, the Center for American Progress, the Heritage Foundation, and the Brookings Institution. These intermediary organizations, spanning the right, middle, and left, churn out large numbers of well-written policy briefs, hold meetings with many legislative and administration staffers in the audience, and personally promote policy ideas and research on the Hill. Many organizations do their own syntheses of research, sometimes gather original data, and respond to concerns addressed by Congress or the Administration in succinct, easy-to-read policy briefs. Their proximity and level of access to policy makers far exceeds that of researchers or even the Washington-based representatives of researchers. From the perspective of the researcher looking at the policy briefs from a think tank, the work may appear to lack in scholarship because it does not present the detail necessary to understand the nuances of the research. From the perspective of the researcher trying to market her wares, however, the success of the think tanks in disseminating ideas and information might suggest the need for partnerships.[19]

Most of these ideas address making research palatable on the supply side, but the demand side may be even more important. Is there need and energy on the demand side of the equation? One demand-side condition is atmospherics or general context, such as the condition of the budget or which party controls Congress; these may increase or decrease the chances that policy makers will respond to a growing body of evidence. Another factor is whether particular policy makers are ready for the research. Timing is everything. A study of NCLB that arrives just as the President is signing a 5-year reauthorization bill is too late; 1 or 2 years earlier, just as Congress starts debating the bill, is the right time for the study to appear.

The right combination of these factors—for example, the atmospherics are positive, the policy will not be disruptive and is supported by strong lobbies, the presentation is powerful and tells a story, the project is demonstrated in the legislator's district or state, and there is demand for the research—can lead to the research having a powerful influence in policy development and implementation.

In addition to the desired positive benefit of promoting a promising idea, however, all the supply-side strategies also have potentially negative effects. Compelling stories often simplify complex materials and provide a distorted and misleading linear path for the reader. Marketing may leave the interpretation partially in the hands of people who are professional communicators but who do not understand the science and therefore emphasize the parts of the idea that will "sell" rather than the complete picture, warts and all. And the interpreters in think tanks who work in the same town as the policy makers often are blinded by their environment (suffering from "Beltway myopia") and their desire to have influential people listen to them. This latter problem can lead in two unproductive directions: the environmental influence constrains thinking and promotes ideas that will not alienate powerful lobbyists and policy makers, while the desire to be listened to often stimulates ideological and/or exaggerated claims.

A final potentially negative effect of these strategies is that they may turn out to be more important than the quality and importance of the research itself. For example, the issue of the quality of research often is masked by the way the work is presented or by the authority of the presenter. Rarely will the size of an effect in a research study become a major factor in a policy maker's equation—the results must point in the right direction but the size of the effect is typically not considered. As we discuss in the next section, a policy maker's lack of interest in the size of effects is not good for the public but it is good for a legislator who wants to pad his or her resume by supporting or passing another bill.[20] This is an important problem since few enacted policies in education ultimately have been effective at substantially improving student achievement.

Why Have so Many Reforms Failed to Live Up to Expectations? Why Do so Many Reforms Have Small Effects on Education Achievement?[21]

Many so-called research- or evidence-based policies have been designed to improve educational achievement or attainment and have been touted by advocates as having important and sustaining effects (as measured by standardized assessments of achievement and by attainment of a particular grade level or graduation). Few lived up to the expectations of policy makers. Evaluations of federal and state programs and policies such as Title I, Head Start, school choice, desegregation, class-size reduction, curriculum changes, high school reform, violence and drug prevention, and many other reforms demonstrate this unfortunate reality.[22] Exacerbating the problem is the fact that it is quite difficult to eliminate a significant social program because it does not work as the designers wished.[23] By the time the first evaluation is published, the program has amassed sources of political and ideological strength that cross party lines and protect it from major change or elimination. Thus, weak and even negative results typically lead to minor corrective changes rather than to a change in policy that significantly alters or eliminates the unproductive reforms.

There are a variety of reasons why reforms have small or nonexistent effects.[24] Raw politics often compromise the potential effectiveness of policy, both in its initial crafting and its implementation. A politician from a very well-to-do suburban district may believe in the theory that funds should be targeted to concentrations of the poor but will feel obligated to ensure his or her constituents have a share, thereby reducing the potential impact of the policy. Research indicates that uncertified teacher aides in the classroom have a zero or negative effect on student learning, but many aides belong to teacher unions so, after pressure from the teacher unions, a proposed policy during the Clinton administration to phase them out of Title I classrooms was rejected.

Another example of a policy decision based primarily on politics was seen in the debates within the Clinton administration about how to provide enough resources so that tuition would be free for all students to attend community college. The debate concerned whether the Pell Grant Program or a new tuition tax credit would be the policy vehicle. If the policy was enacted via the Pell Grant, the students would receive the money before the school year, which would ease their financial burden; if the policy was enacted through the tax system, the money would come well after the school year. While some modest research suggested that the Pell Grant approach would create a stronger incentive for students to go to college, it would also require increasing the discretionary budget—the legislators would be asked to expand a government program. The tax credit, by contrast, would be seen by the legislators as a "tax cut," and this approach won the debate.[25]

Beyond politics, the dilution of effects of a policy that is widely implemented, compared to the effects from the original study or studies that prompted the policy, often occurs when policy makers, and researchers, ignore the challenges of implementation and generalization (Elmore & McLaughlin, 1988; McLaughlin, 1976; O'Day, 2002; Spillane, 2004). Implementation and generalization are two separate and critical hurdles to overcome for a policy to be effective.

First, let's consider implementation. Most national and state education interventions are inherently complex. They involve action on the part of many layers of education governance including states, districts, and schools. Imagine the path of a complex federal law: after being introduced, the original idea undergoes compromise to pass through the House and Senate; the Department of Education writes regulations and "nonregulatory" guidance that often takes on the weight of law in state and local districts; the 50 states reinterpret the federal regulations and guidance and sometimes add their own guidance, as do the big city central offices and sometimes the county offices. By the time the law reaches the school, principals, and teachers, the policy itself may have substantially changed and it has certainly become more highly specified. Policies by their very nature are typically top-down designs for change, buttressed by regulations and guidance, sometimes written by people who put their own spin on the specifications.[26] All this transformation typically occurs without prior consultation with the teachers and others who will carry out the changes, which often leads to misunderstanding, opposition, and other distortions in the policy (McLaughlin, 1990; Spillane, 2004).

Implementing an intervention well is challenging. Implementing it well and expecting comparable effects in many sites, that is, generalizing it, presents an even greater challenge. Because of dozens of differences among sites in resources, history, and culture, a policy cannot be expected to operate uniformly in local districts around the nation or even at different schools within a district. The problem is that the mechanisms and requirements embedded in the intervention will interact in unknown ways with the different characteristics of districts and schools, their staff, and students. Policies that require few changes in structure and human behavior may be absorbed seamlessly into the system, creating few waves and little effect. Policies that require more significant changes in structure and behavior are more likely to be altered or compromised during implementation in multiple sites. In some circumstances, the result is a creative adaptation of the policy at best, but other times, a policy may be distorted and end up disrupting effective practices.[27]

California's program to reduce class size in the early grades is a classic example of the problem of implementing an apparently straightforward policy on a large scale. In the spring of 1996, when California discovered it had a budget surplus, Governor Pete Wilson, supported by the legislature, rushed through a bill with money for class-size reduction to take place in the upcoming school year. The result was chaos as districts had to find extra teachers and extra space, often when schools were already overcrowded. Well-to-do districts raided poor districts for their best early-grade teachers, and classes in some schools took place in halls, teacher rooms, and auditoriums. The evaluations of the intervention indicated little or no effect on achievement (Bohrnstedt & Stecher, 1999). The Governor and legislature apparently believed that simply passing the legislation would insure effective implementation across the state.[28]

One implication of this discussion and example is that those who create and implement policy from the federal or state level ought to be required to have two theories, one to set the assumptions and intended causal mechanisms in the intervention and the second to develop a plan for implementing the change. The preceding reasons about why reforms have a small effect focus on politics, implementation, and generalization. What about the efficacy of the reforms themselves? In general, should they be expected to have the promised large and robust effects if they are well implemented and politics stays out of the way?

Many policy changes operate largely within the comfort zone of the education establishment—the teacher unions, administrators, and school boards—and fail to alter the basic structure and priorities of the school or the school system, the relationships within the school, the manner or intensity of teaching, or the opportunities for students to increase their achievement. Examples of such policies include reductions or increases in school size, most class-size reduction efforts,[29] many curriculum changes (including most battles over reading and mathematics), changes in requirements for teacher certification, increases in testing requirements, and school uniforms.[30] These policies typically have small effects at best.

From the perspective of the policy makers, the policies are often easy wins. From the perspective of students and teachers, changes made due to these policies rarely seriously interrupt the normal flow of the school or the behavior of teachers.[31] Newly required practices often find the path of least resistance. As a consequence, the effects of these efforts are swamped by variations in the skills and commitment of adults in the school—especially teachers and principals—which may have far more to do with the quality of the educational experience for students than do such policies (Schneider, Carnoy, Kilpatrick, Schmidt, & Shavelson, 2007).[32]

Even most examples of choice policy, which the education establishment views as threatening and as a significant change in the nature of public education, fit into the category of marginal change. Studies of choice interventions, including vouchers, charters, and magnet schools, indicate only small effects on achievement at best (Hill, 2007). A plausible explanation is that schools of choice typically are little different on any important educational dimension than the schools the students left. Not only are their curricula roughly the same (in most states, schools must adhere to state standards), but the pool from which the schools draw teachers, the class sizes, and the time spent in school are roughly the same. Given these circumstances, why would we expect improvement in achievement?

Changes to reading and mathematics curricula provide more examples of why reforms have little effect. Within grade levels, the differences among the curricula used in the United States in content and pedagogy generally are modest and the materials and the expectations for learning are roughly equivalent. Moreover, the time allocated to teaching reading or mathematics is roughly the same from curriculum to curriculum. Since the teachers, students, and tests are also the same, we would not expect significant effects if the curricula are contrasted to each other.[33] Given some reasonable professional development and time to perfect their teaching, competent teachers are able to accommodate, adapt, and effectively use whatever available and acceptable curriculum they must use, but less competent teachers and teachers in low-support environments will struggle with whatever curriculum they have.[34]

Even though their effects are tiny, many such education policies are vehemently debated in school districts, states, and the nation's capital. The research on choice has been regularly ambiguous about effects on achievement, but the argument over whether choice has an independent and important effect on achievement has not abated. This is partly due to the continued efforts of one small set of scholars who regularly discover positive trends and another small group who regularly find no effects or negative effects, often using the same data (Fuller, Elmore, & Orfield, 1996; Peterson & Campbell, 2001; Kruger & Zhu, 2003; Program on Education Policy and Governance, n.d.; EPE Research Center, 2004).

Indeed, one reason for vigorous debate is that the policies have small effects on average, leading to a distribution of both positive and negative findings. Thus, advocates on both sides of the argument can amass studies to support their position; if the estimates of effect for the policies were large and stable—either positive or negative—there would

be little room for empirically based argument. A second reason is that these policies often are easy to study and attract many researchers, only some of whom are competent, which generates a large corpus of studies from which policy makers can choose.

We should not be surprised that most policies and education interventions have small effects at best. Tyack and Cuban (1995) argue that stability is a necessary characteristic of our school system. Students need to be schooled near their home by responsible adults. Parents must trust the schools to take care of their children.[35] Schools, unlike small businesses, cannot come and go over the short term. Their existence and, for many, their practice must be predictable and familiar.

In this context, teachers and parents often challenge policies that require major change. There are few incentives for elected officials, who generally are not held accountable for school results, to advocate major alteration. The major stakeholders—teachers, parents, and their representatives—are suspicious of change and, in a political environment, hold great sway. This practically guarantees small effects.

Not Every Policy Has Small Effects

We Know a Lot We do not want to sound too pessimistic. Research has contributed to some powerful, promising reforms. Too often we forget the obvious fact that we hold enormous amounts of knowledge about the factors and conditions that enable and support student learning, make up powerful teaching, motivate or discourage students, and explain why some schools and districts are effective, efficient organizations and why others are not. We know (a) that time and practice improve adult and student learning; (b) that the education system is complex; (c) that implementation of significant, top-down interventions are difficult and take time in single sites and very difficult in multiple sites; (d) that coherence around goals, effort, and urgency are important in making change; (e) that teachers vary in their measured effectiveness; (f) that teacher effectiveness can be improved under the right conditions; (g) that lack of motivation of students is a major problem that can be, but rarely is, addressed in our secondary schools; (h) that it is hard to introduce serious change/innovation into our schools and districts; and (i) that politics and ideology play a substantial role in policymaking at all levels of the system. We know a great deal about effective instructional practice from researchers and practitioners in various areas, some of which becomes accurately incorporated into larger interventions and perhaps into commercial products.

Our focus in this discussion is to explore policies that have weaved together what we know to create strategies that appear to substantially improve the effectiveness of our schools. We have deliberately not included the important and generally effective civil rights rulings and legislation that have led to dramatic changes in education opportunity. Our sense is that the circumstances and moral strength of the movements for desegregation, special education, and women's rights (Title IX) make their experiences difficult to generalize to other kinds of interventions not protected under civil rights law.

At the risk of leaving out better examples, we have selected a few that represent disparate kinds of reforms and offer insight into how and why dramatic change has been or could be introduced into the system. Our examples start with the more general and national influences on student achievement and move to quite specific school and classroom interventions.

A Way of Thinking about Reforms that Influence Student Achievement In 1969, Jack Carroll, a Harvard psychologist, in the context of looking at an early international assessment, pointed out that those countries that teach foreign languages in their schools were more likely to have multilingual graduates than countries that taught only one language. Being taught content has a big effect if the comparison group has not been taught the content. This is not a trivial observation—it is a powerful example of "opportunity to learn" and might lead researchers to hypothesize about what has been or has not been taught or taught well. In an earlier article, Carroll (1963) hypothesized that the central ingredients of learning include appropriate content and instruction, student motivation, and adequate student time to learn the material, with the understanding that adequate time will not be the same for all children. As we describe a few examples of successful reform, it is useful to think about how often these three ingredients are part of the reform.

National Reform and Improvement The extraordinary increase in the national high school graduation rate over the first 60 to 70 years of the last century did not reflect the effects of a single policy or even of several actively and stra-tegically researched and coordinated policies. Rather, the effect seems to have been prompted by significant changes in the economy and urbanization, which created a national climate of investment and support for helping students to complete secondary school.

Another similar, more current example of a national emphasis on providing opportunity has been a long-term concerted social and educational press for improving mathematics achievement. This "policy" is arguably the largest generalized effect on achievement in the last few decades. Over the past 30 years, math achievement for 9-year-olds on the Long-Term Trend National Assessment of Education Progress (NAEP) assessments has increased by an average of roughly 0.8–1.0 grade level *per decade* for White, Hispanic, and African American students. For 13-year-olds, White students have seen an average increase of a little over one-half a grade level per decade while African American and Hispanic students have gained an average of roughly one full grade level per decade (see Tables 30.1 and 30.2).[36] Moreover, there has been a substantial decrease in the achievement gap between White students, on the one hand, and Hispanic and African American students, on the other hand, especially for 13-year-olds.

The NAEP scores are supported by substantial gains for all groups on the math SAT assessment and a dramatic increase in the number of students taking Advanced Placement (AP) courses in math. No particular curricular approach to math or single intervention or policy can account for these gains. Rather, since 1978 there seems to have been an overall national orientation, an "environment of thought" (Lindblom and Cohen, 1979), focused on improving math achievement. This national effort was spurred by a changing economy; the minimum competency movement; the rhetoric and reforms of the *A Nation at Risk* report; the National Council of Teachers of Mathematics standards and other

TABLE 30.1
Long-Term Trend NAEP Math Scale Scores — Age 9

GROUPS	YEARS			GAINS (RATE GAIN/YEAR)	
	1978	**1994**	**2004**	**1978–1994**	**1994–2004**
Nation	219	231	241	+12 (0.8)	+10 (1.0)
White	224	237	247	+13 (0.8)	+10 (1.0)
African American	192	212	224	+20 (1.3)	+12 (1.2)
Hispanic American	203	210	230	+7 (0.4)	+20 (2.0)

Note: A scale score gain of 10-11 points is roughly the equivalent of a grade level.
Source: National Assessment of Education Progress (http://nces.ed.gov/nationsreportcard)

TABLE 30.2
Long-Term Trend NAEP Math Scale Scores — Age 13

GROUPS	YEARS			GAINS (RATE GAIN/YEAR)	
	1978	**1994**	**2004**	**1978–1994**	**1994–2004**
Nation	264	274	281	10 (0.6)	7 (0.7)
White	272	281	288	9 (0.6)	7 (0.7)
African American	230	252	262	22 (1.4)	10 (1.0)
Hispanic American	238	256	265	18 (1.1)	9 (0.9)

Source: National Assessment of Education Progress (http://nces.ed.gov/nationsreportcard/)

education professional reform efforts; the efforts of the National Science Foundation, various states, and the standards movement; and lots of work at the local level. These factors have led many schools and teachers to take mathematics instruction in K–12 more seriously. The allocation of time and rigor of instruction probably increased as well as did the use of professional development and coaching. Consequently, children have been taught more and better math than they otherwise would have been, which increased their level of achievement.[37] Our nation may be nowhere near the level of achievement in mathematics learning that we desire or need, but the results over the past three decades have been dramatic.[38]

Both of these examples, high school graduation in the early and mid-1990s and mathematics achievement over the past 30 years, highlight the idea that significant and widespread effects on student attainment and achievement require multiple and reinforcing efforts from all levels of government. In each of these examples, there was no single or even a coordinated set of policies or interventions that spurred the changes.

Federal/State Reform State standards-based reform, initiated by federal legislation in 1994, is a more deliberate policy intervention also affecting the nation (Jennings, 1995; Cross, 2004). Using the NAEP Long-Term Trend data and comparing the rates of gain before and after 1994, the year that federal legislation supporting state standards-based reforms in all states was passed, we see that standards-based reform does not seem to influence the *rates of gain* of math scores (see Tables 30.1 and 30.2 and compare the two right-hand columns of rates of gain). The rates of gain are substantial, but appear roughly similar across the two time periods indicating that for math the reforms have not shown an independent effect.

State standards-based reforms, however, appear to have had substantial positive effects on student *reading* achievement, particularly for Hispanic and African American students.[39] On average, 9-year-old Hispanic and African American students gained at a rate of less than a quarter grade level per decade before 1994 but increased to roughly one-and-a-half grade level gains for the decade after 1994, while 13-year-old Hispanic and African American students more than doubled their rates of gain to approximately 0.7 and 1.0 grade levels during the decade after 1994 (see the right-hand columns of Table 30.3 and Table 30.4). These are substantial differences in rates of gain again favoring standards-based reforms. As in the case of the math gains, White students achieved at slower rates than Hispanic and African American students with the consequence that the test score gaps for reading also show signs of closing.

If implemented as initially conceived, standards-based reforms align resources to help students achieve at high levels established by state standards (Smith & O'Day, 1991, O'Day & Smith, 1993; Cross, 2004). States, through their governance and finance systems, support districts and schools. At the state and local levels, professional development, curriculum, assessment, and accountability are aligned with state content and performance standards. The state provides direction and support but allows districts and local schools the flexibility to decide how best to meet the needs of their students. The districts and schools focus on improving instruction and using other strategies to meet student achievement goals. Of course, there are wide differences among states, districts, and schools in implementation. The development of the logic model for state standards-based reforms was built on the experiences of a few states and many other nations, research on organizational behavior and change including studies of effective

TABLE 30.3
Long-Term Trend NAEP Reading Scale Scores — Age 9

GROUPS	YEARS			GAINS (RATE GAIN/YEAR)	
	1975	**1994**	**2004**	**1975–1994**	**1994–2004**
Nation	210	211	219	+1 (0.1)	+8 (0.8)
White	217	218	226	+1 (0.1)	+8 (0.8)
African American	181	185	200	+4 (0.2)	+15 (1.5)
Hispanic American	183	186	205	+3 (0.2)	+19 (1.9)

Source: National Assessment of Education Progress (http://nces.ed.gov/nationsreportcard/)

TABLE 30.4
Long-Term Trend NAEP Reading Scale Scores — Age 13

GROUPS	YEARS			GAINS (RATE GAIN/YEAR)	
	1975	**1994**	**2004**	**1975–1994**	**1994–2004**
Nation	256	258	259	2 (0.1)	1 (0.1)
White	262	265	266	3 (0.2)	1 (0.1)
African American	226	234	244	8 (0.4)	10 (1.0)
Hispanic American	232	235	242	3 (0.2)	7 (0.7)

Source: National Assessment of Education Progress (http://nces.ed.gov/nationsreportcard/)

schools, and on research on teaching and learning conducted from the 1970s through the early 1990s.

Just as with the example of gains in graduation rates and mathematics achievement, the reading gains from 1994–2004 reflect multiple efforts. In this case there was an organizing framework, but one that allowed very substantial state and local discretion to meet local needs.

District Reforms Aggressive and focused reform approaches in districts provide two more examples of promising reforms (see Sykes, O'Day, & Ford, this volume). For the past decade, a substantial number of school districts have attempted to improve the quality of instruction in their schools. This work is based directly or indirectly on research on improving instruction conducted over the past 40 years and on the results from District 2 in New York City, which successfully implemented a set of instructional reforms in the 1990s (Rivlin & Timpane, 1975; Cohen, 1990a, 1990b; Cohen, Raudenbush, & Ball, 2002; National Academy of Sciences, 2008b, 2008c; Snow, Burns, & Griffin, 1998; Elmore & Burney, 1997a, 1997b, 1998; Gewirtzman & Fink, 1998; Cohen, Moffitt, & Goldin, 2007). San Diego, Austin, and Los Angeles are recent examples of this genre of district reform. For the most part, the instructional reforms have been initiated by a centrally controlled team working from the district office that orchestrates a coherent and system-wide strategy for implementation in the schools. The work generally involves the intensive use of coaches and other forms of professional development to train teachers about how and when to use effective instructional strategies, and full implementation takes several years. Studies of this work are under way or just recently completed (Betts, Zau, & King, 2005).[40] Though many of these reforms have been initially effective, their long-term influence is not as clear due to the turnover of superintendents, which often leads to new policies, and the tendency of teacher unions and school boards to withhold or withdraw support if they perceive their positions are threatened.

A different approach to district reform highlights the use of evidence from careful and thorough data collection and local research to improve practice. The process goal in districts implementing this reform is to establish the practice of continuous improvement—put another way, the goal is to turn the districts and all of their schools into learning organizations. School districts such as Long Beach and Garden Grove have institutionalized the practice of data-driven decision making and improvement. Using well-functioning information systems, thoughtful interpretation of data, and a willingness to experiment and learn from the experience, the districts incorporate data-based feedback loops that result in small, often bottom-up improvements that can lead to changes in policy as well as practice throughout the entire system (Austin, Schwartz, & Suesse, 2004; Honan, Schwartz, & Suesse, 2004; Austin, Grossman, Schwartz, & Suesse, 2006). The approach to improvement is used in the district office, in the relationships between the front office and the schools, within the schools themselves, and

inside the classrooms through such strategies as formative assessment (Black & Wiliam, 1998). Creating this form of high-quality learning environment takes time, focus, and a stable environment; Long Beach has been working at it for over a decade. Successive school boards, the unions, and new superintendents all need to buy in and willingly persist in their support. This may explain why the strategy is not standard practice in large districts.

A number of districts that show clear success in improving achievement fall in between these two models. Boston and the Aldine Independent School District in Texas are good examples of districts that have simultaneously tried to implement a centrally directed instructional improvement reform while simultaneously creating elements of sophisticated, continuous improvement strategy. Both districts also have benefited from long-term, committed superintendents (Childress, Elmore, Grossman, & Johnson, 2007).

School-Based Reform At the school building level, Success for All (SFA), an extensively evaluated comprehensive school reform program for elementary grades, epitomizes another type of reform. It was developed over the past 20 years by a team from Johns Hopkins University, headed by Robert Slavin and Nancy Madden,[41] and is a school-based strategy. In dozens of studies, SFA routinely is judged to be effective with modest to strong effect sizes (Borman, Hewes, Overman, & Brown, 2003; Aladjem & Borman, 2006).[42] Its initial design was based on best practice research of the components that make up reading instruction and the organization of elementary schools, but the program exemplifies the use of continuous improvement processes. Over time, the team carried out extensive formative evaluation, and the program and professional development have evolved in design and implementation strategy. Another level of continuous improvement is represented by the use of formative assessment in classrooms as a fundamental strategy to personalize instruction (Black & Wiliam, 1998).

The Knowledge Is Power Program (KIPP) is another example of an apparently effective school-based model. Unlike SFA, KIPP Academies are generally charter middle schools that start at the fifth grade. They dramatically extend the time of the school day and year, create a strong culture with high expectations, expect their teachers to be available for large amounts of time outside of school, have aggressive human resource policies, and make every effort to personalize their instruction. There are now over 70 KIPP Academies across the country. Though there are not yet any well-controlled studies of KIPP, the data on gains in student achievement by individual schools indicate that the intervention has substantial and sustained effects (David et al., 2008; KIPP Foundation, 2008).[43]

Curriculum and Classroom Reform Finally, the federal government's What Works Clearinghouse reviews of K–5 reading interventions on student achievement indicates that well-structured, intensive, one-on-one adult tutoring (and even one-on-three tutoring); some forms of peer tutoring; and greater experience reading books at home all *may* positively affect reading achievement.[44] These are examples of classes of interventions that have been locally sponsored and that systematically alter or extend the time, intensity, and, in the case of tutoring, the personalization of learning experiences. They also provide the conditions of a motivating experience since they are different from a regular classroom and place the student in a close relationship with a respected other person.

A problem with these reviews and others like them is that the programs found effective often are based on only one or two studies; where there are more studies, the findings are decidedly mixed (for results of promising programs in middle school math, see What Works Clearinghouse, 2007). The What Works Clearinghouse receives many studies that collectively have looked at dozens of programs but does not judge the majority of programs because the studies do not meet their criteria for quality. One or two acceptable studies or even half a dozen with variable results provide little positive information about whether the programs' effects generalize over various contexts. Another problem is that the Clearinghouse provides no information about how difficult it is to implement the programs. There is also not enough information to understand the characteristics, or causal influences, that separate effective curricula from those that are not.

We recognize that we have selected a small, non-random, and easily criticized sample of "effective" reforms. Our purpose has been to choose a variety of types that appear to have substantial and widespread effects. Except for some of the curriculum programs that we refer to from the What Works Clearinghouse, we have briefly sketched the logic models/theories of how and why we think the intervention worked. Along with our observations about the interventions and policies that have small or non-existent effects, this analysis gives us some grist for creating dimensions that distinguish between effective and apparently ineffective reforms.

What Are the Characteristics of Policies with Large Effects, and How Do They Differ from Policies with Small Effects?

This is a speculative section. We propose five dimensions that appear to distinguish between policies and interventions that give evidence of large and sustainable effects and those that have small or nonexistent effects.[45] There are multiple interpretations for some of the dimensions. The dimensions should be viewed as providing tendencies rather than predictions.

Distant versus Proximate This dimension has two interpretations. The first is that the further away from the desired outcome in terms of layers of bureaucracy that the intervention is initiated, the less likely that it will be well-implemented and the effects predictable; in other words, the expectation is that an intervention from the federal or

state level will have less chance of succeeding than the same intervention initiated from the local or school level. A major reason for this increased difficulty is that as the bureaucratic layers increase, the success of a policy intervention becomes more dependent on understanding a large body of critical information. A successful intervention requires the designers of the intervention to have a good idea beforehand how the different aspects of the intervention will interact and be altered and also alter the system as it travels through the series of bureaucratic layers. Without sufficient learning from prior experience, more distant interventions become more difficult and precarious.[46] The failure of important highly specified federal legislation and the California Class Size Reduction reform to work as expected are important and powerful examples.

A second interpretation is that the further away from the desired outcome that the intervention is focused, the less likely that the intervention will be effective. Thus, an intervention that is intended to improve *achievement* by reducing school size will probably have less chance of succeeding than an intervention that focuses on changing the immediate conditions for student learning, such as the interaction between students and their teacher.

Fits into the System versus Disruptive We argued in an earlier section that many reforms slip quietly into the system without creating a serious political or organizational ripple and that these reforms generally have little effect. These politically acceptable reforms do not often add to or change the routines and responsibilities of the implementers. If other conditions are equal, however, a disruptive or innovative intervention or policy has the chance of creating a major effect on the intended outcome. Increasing the length of a school day by two hours is a major and potentially disruptive policy, as would be dramatically increasing the emphasis on oral language and vocabulary development in grades K–8 of low-income schools, or using Web-based full courses as the primary content for teaching in mathematics and science in secondary schools. When well done, such interventions could cause powerful and disruptive changes in routines, responsibilities, and content that could have a big effect. This is a complicated dimension because, as we have argued, a disruptive intervention is usually more difficult to implement well and, therefore, less likely to work effectively.

Rigidity versus Flexibility in Approach and Design Rigidly designed interventions provide little reinforcement for professional work and ownership and will interact in unexpected ways in different contexts, creating anxiety and frustration. Several examples of effective interventions indicate that a balance between structure and flexibility is critical. Flexibility built into the implementation must be *appropriate* for the type of intervention and theory of change and be sensitive to the context. An effective intervention will have a structure that grows from theory, which is translated into design and provides strategic direction, while allowing flexibility at the points where the intervention requires adaptation by local actors to their specific context. The adaptation of the intervention can be facilitated in different ways. One is by applying the principles of systematic continuous improvement. The Long Beach instructional reforms are supported by continuous improvement feedback loops throughout their system that provide information about how and when to adapt the reforms to meet local needs. The KIPP Academies have a set of operating principles, known as the Five Pillars, but give individual principals great flexibility in implementing them. The design and redesign of SFA is characterized by a continuous improvement orientation. A major focus in the instructional reforms in San Diego and Long Beach and in SFA and KIPP is the personalization of instruction (through flexibility and adaptation to individual students) using formative assessment techniques in the classroom.

Short Time versus Sustained Appropriate Effort Time is a factor in learning for children and adults as well as for the implementation of reform at all levels. People learn at different speeds depending on their context and experience. When substantially longer school days are implemented well, students experience greater learning. When teachers are given more time and practice teaching a new curriculum, they often provide better instruction. It takes time to put any reform in place and to implement it well. In general, we expect too much too soon. This perspective could be viewed as inaccurate in situations having to do with continuous improvement and formative assessment where the faster the feedback becomes available and used, the more powerful the intervention seems to be. However, it does take sustained effort and time for a system to become an effective learner and user of a continuous improvement approach or for teachers to learn how to effectively use formative assessments to inform their work in the classroom.[47]

Lack of Clarity versus Coherence All deliberate policies or interventions that we mention have a clear focus on a goal or goals and a strategy or theory about how to achieve the goal. Standards-based reform is designed to support the creation of coherence and focus within a system. A continuous improvement strategy embodies an approach to improving coherence and focus. The district instructional reforms and school-based models that we discussed each attempt to be crystal clear in their efforts. Focus and coherence do not mean rigidity—they mean that the implementers of a reform know what their goal is and have a thoughtful strategy/theory/logic model to help achieve it. We want to emphasize that coherence and adherence to a logic model of the reform should not indicate a set of concrete actions to achieve the goal—they preferably refer to a structure and process that provides flexibility and that, itself, contains self-correcting feedback loops that create a continuous improvement process.

We recognize that these dimensions are not grounded in a serious theory of interventions—the careful reader should be skeptical. Nevertheless, we have a few general comments. We think of these five dimensions as scalar rather than dichotomies, and we would expect that any intervention that would be placed on the right-hand side of a scale would have a better chance of improving student achievement than if it were on the left-hand side of the scale. (Distant, fits into the system, rigidity, short time, and lack of clarity are on the left sides of their dimensions.) Of course, an intervention or policy might fit in the middle of some dimensions and on the edges of others, which could complicate that expectation. One of many caveats in this overly simplified model is that extremism, even on the right-hand side of the scales, is probably not conducive to effective results. For example, interventions that are too disruptive and/or too flexible may not be successful. Our instinct is that balance on many dimensions is very important in education reform, as it is in much of life. We need theories of "right effort and right action."

If these five dimensions are treated as rough guidelines for the development of effective policy or interventions, they have a number of implications. One is that, other things being equal, a policy initiated at the local level to improve student achievement probably is preferable to one initiated at the federal or state level. If a policy does emanate from the federal or state level, it should build in flexibility and allow for creative adaptation at the local level. Another implication is that an intervention or policy that is implemented in different places may look and behave quite differently from one place to another. Indeed, the designer should be able to specify the causal mechanisms in the intervention that would indicate which of its aspects are less or more changeable and adaptable to context than others. Still another implication is that it may take longer and take greater effort than we normally expect for significant change to have the desired effects. For example, the most effective district reforms have been carried out under the long-term leadership of a few superintendents who have had clear goals and a flexible set of strategies. Yet, the average length of a superintendent in a large school district in the United States is 3 to 4 years, far too short for these superintendents to have a serious and lasting influence.

At the heart of a design of an effective policy or intervention is the theory that provides coherence in its development and implementation. If the policy or intervention lacks a clear underlying theory, it is impossible to know what components should be involved in the design and legislation, what its implementation should look like, how to think about improving its effectiveness, and how to generalize it. The theory behind the policy or intervention is critical to its effectiveness.

The Role of Theory in Design, Implementation, and Internal Validity

Every policy and intervention should have a purpose, behind which should be a theory (logic model) that represents a reasoned conception of how the policy would work. The theory knits together and identifies the processes by which the various components, or causal mechanisms, of a policy or intervention produce the intended outcome. Typically, developing theory requires prior knowledge from related research that may have been based on observation, quasi-experiments or case studies, or even earlier experiments. A decent theory helps guide development and implementation, fosters self-correcting feedback loops, and helps explain the failure or success of the policy.

The use of theory emerges in a variety of places in this chapter. When Slavin put together the initial evidence-based components for SFA, he had a theory for how to teach reading and one for how to manage an elementary school classroom (Slavin, Madden, & Datnow, 2007). The researchers in the Learning Research and Development Center at the University of Pittsburgh and the Wisconsin Center for Education Research at the University of Wisconsin at Madison generally have one or more theories of learning and teaching to guide their development of each of their products as well as theories to help disseminate and implement their work. The papers on standards-based reform drew on theories of organizational development, school reform, and learning (Vinovskis, 1996).

A study of the implementation of a particular intervention in a single site only makes sense if it examines the theory that drives the intervention. For example, in a study of the San Diego reform, Jennifer O'Day is examining whether achievement in the school district increased and whether the components of the logic model (theory) set out by the district administrators worked as designed.[48] If the theory behind the reform did not work in the expected fashion but the district still had improved test scores, this would weaken the argument that the intervention caused the improvement.

Causality is the critical component. Typically, causality is implied by a theory of how some new action might change an outcome. For example, the San Diego blueprint presented a theory that coaching the principals, who would then train the teachers, would improve the quality of instruction and thereby improve achievement. The logic model might be that A affects B, which affects C and D, which together affect E, the ultimate outcome. Although policy is made for a variety of reasons including raw politics, symbolism, and signaling intent or interest, causal inferences are at the heart of responsible policymaking (see also George & Bennett, 2005; Pawson & Tilley, 1997). Policy makers want to change something that will cause something else; that is, A causes B. If they do not believe and/or cannot tell a convincing story about how a causal relationship exists, they lose their strongest policy argument. As a consequence, there are many advocates for the position that studies providing the strongest evidence of causal relationships are particularly useful for policy makers. After all, the purpose of most policy is to create some sort of change, so it is particularly comforting to have evidence that the proposed policy intervention actually has been shown to "create" the intended change (Cook & Gorard, 2007; Schneider et al., 2007).

Given this somewhat self-evident view, it is a short step to make the argument that the best design for policy research is the one that gives the most evidence of causality.

For many empiricists, the criterion of causality leads to the true randomized trial as the most efficient and effective research design. Over the past decade, this view has led some advocates to believe that it is the only research methodology appropriate for providing evidence to policy makers. This perspective appears to be attractive to the current federal administration, and it is certainly possible that this design has great weight in the thinking of many policy makers. Though a randomized trial has an important place in the mix of methodologies available to education policy research, it is not the only methodology that provides knowledge useful for policy makers nor is it the only one useful for making causal inferences (for other methodological approaches for determining causality see Shadish, Cook, & Campbell, 2002; Schneider et al., 2007).

The fact is that, like other research designs, the utility of a randomized design rests on the quality and validity of the theory (logic model) that undergirds the program or policy intervention. Thus, it is not uncommon for many studies to be carried out on a particular intervention in order to improve both the theory underlying it and the quality of its implementation. When the theory and implementation strategies reach a level where the designers are comfortable, the intervention might then be ready for a randomized experiment. SFA has been the treatment in a number of randomized design studies and provides an excellent example of a type of policy or intervention where, after development and improvement, a randomized design may be effectively used. The SFA intervention is carried out at the school level where randomization is possible though sometimes difficult. Moreover, the fact that the SFA program is based on a theory allows the experimenter to determine whether the theory works as expected in the experimental setting as well as to reach an unbiased estimate of the effect of the intervention. This process of testing the operation of the model helps to close the loop on the causality argument. If the logic model of the intervention (SFA, in this example) does not work as expected, there should be considerable concern about the internal validity of the inference that the SFA intervention caused the effect—something did but it may not be the intended intervention.

Class-size reduction is another example of a treatment that appears to be a perfect subject for an experiment. However, since the intensity of the treatment (reduction amount and initial level) and its grade could vary, a truly useful class-size reduction experiment would require a very sophisticated design. Moreover, the reduction in class size by itself may have no influence. Rather, a reasonable hypothesis is that the influence may come from the opportunity that a smaller class gives teachers to alter and improve their instruction. For this reason, a plausible class-size experiment would include some systematic and theoretically based professional development for teachers to make use of the opportunity that they will have when their class size is reduced. To help ensure that the effect that may emerge from the experiment is due to the reduction in class size rather than to the less expensive professional development, a control group that maintained existing class size should also receive the professional development.

In many class-size experiments, however, the theory of how class size might enable better instruction has not been fully explicated or assessed nor have the important ingredients of intensity and change in instruction been varied or even considered in the design of the intervention or its interpretation. In our view, it is a waste of money to conduct a randomized trial without also examining whether the treatment works in the way that its theory predicts. The causality argument is incomplete for policy purposes if the experiment does not also demonstrate an understanding of why the intervention works (for a different perspective, see Cook, 2007).

Even after a randomized trial is completed and a validation study determines beyond a reasonable doubt that the treatment "caused" a good-sized effect, that is, assured the internal validity of the study, we are still left with the problem of generalization, or external validity.

The Role of Theory in External Validity

External validity addresses the question: will the intervention have similar causal effects in a variety of different contexts (e.g., with different aged children; with various instruments intended to measure the same or slightly different outcomes; with different gender, class, and cultural groups; in cities, suburbs, and rural areas)? Though few analysts view a single experiment as a case study with a sample of one, that is exactly what it is in most cases, and for the most part, in the social sciences it is practically impossible to legitimately generalize from a sample of one. Only if the subjects in the experimental and control groups are random samples from a well-defined population may the results be legitimately generalized, and then only to that population.[49] Policy makers almost always base their actions on the belief that their proposal is generalizable, though they rarely have carefully amassed evidence to support that view. This, we believe, is the most ignored and important of the criteria for credible research for policy makers. President Bill Clinton understood this problem when, while discussing education reform, he asked the frustrating question, "Why don't ideas travel?"[50]

In their volume, William Shadish and his colleagues carefully treat the methodological issues for determining external validity (Shadish et al., 2002). Though the authors strongly support the use of methodologies such as randomized trials to examine causal relationships, they also are candid about the difficulties of carrying out studies using these methodologies. In addition, they make clear that establishing external validity is an even more challenging task than establishing internal validity because of the possibilities of interactions between the intervention and the context within which it is being implemented.

It is possible that the magic of methodology may eventually solve this problem. Certainly with the computing power now available, the possibilities for fast, complex modeling make possible solutions we now can barely imagine. In the meantime, we believe that we need more than methodology to advance our understanding of external validity.

We have argued that a simple experiment that does not include validation of the theory of the intervention is not useful to social policy makers. Even simple social science interventions involve complex interactions and transactions and often multiple causal mechanisms carried out in settings where the actors have numerous and sometimes conflicting motivations and influence.

A starting point is the basic theory of the intervention. Unless that is understood and examined to see that it works as intended—"process tracing" in Alexander George and Andrew Bennett's terminology—there is little chance of effectively replicating the intervention in another setting, much less of generalizing it to a wide range of other settings, which is ordinarily the goal of a policy maker (for information on "process tracing," see George & Bennett, 2005, chapter 10).

A research focus on the *causal mechanisms* that underlie social changes has emerged for the most part from some relatively new developments in the philosophy of science.[51] This particular philosophical position has been gaining broad support among methodologists and researchers, including from those who focus on experimental or quasi-experimental design methodologies. The basic idea is that if there is a causal connection between an input and an output variable, there must be a causal mechanism that connects the two (Hedström & Swedberg, 1998; Little, 1998; Bhaskar, 1978; Bunge, 2004a, 2004b).

Understanding causal mechanisms, however, is more complex than simply identifying a process theory that links two variables, although that is part of the equation. It is also a fundamentally *contextual* notion of causality (Sayer, 2000). Different contexts may influence the causal mechanism in different ways. In contrast to the billiard ball notion of causality, that is, if A then B, the contextual causal mechanism notion of causality can be stated generically as A generates B in situation C.[52] In this conceptualization, an explanation or understanding of the causal mechanism A (in its generation of B) is incomplete without knowing what aspects of the context (C) enable or impede the operation of the causal mechanism. For example, a reduction in class size will probably not improve achievement if a school does not provide appropriate professional development to support teachers to use the smaller class size to improve instruction or if a school is unable to hire high-quality teachers to teach the extra classes created by the reduction in the other classes. As another example, because some math teachers are less knowledgeable and less effective than others, a particular program might help to compensate for these teachers and produce a positive effect. But when used with more knowledgeable teachers, the new program might show little effects or even negative ones. This discussion suggests that causality is inherently nondeterministic; that is, the ability of causal mechanism A to generate B is a tendency rather than a predictive certainty and the causal mechanism in an intervention should always be considered a partial cause (it is dependent on the characteristics of the environment; Sayer, 2000).

Adopting this way of thinking about causality has important ramifications for how we think about external validity. We need to be able to answer: How, for whom, to what extent, and in what circumstances does the intervention have a clear influence on the outcome? (Pawson & Tilley, 1997; Pawson, Greenhalgh, Harvey, & Walshe, 2005) To do so, we need to:

1. Know that the logic model (theory) works as intended, more or less. This includes identifying the degree to which the causal mechanisms exist. In some interventions, the actual mechanisms of change vary when implemented, not just because of variations in context but because the original theory was incomplete or inaccurate in terms of the nature of the inputs necessary to implement the intervention.
2. Understand the important causal aspects of the context that enable the intervention and those that disable it (and how those may be overcome with other mechanisms).
3. Translate the theory to a middle-range theory, that is, identify the necessary causal mechanisms of the theory. These mechanisms, along with an understanding of contexts that enable or disable their effectiveness, constitute a middle-range theory that enables the intervention to "travel."

Making use of this conceptualization requires that the logic model (theory of causal mechanisms) is powerful enough to support implementation and potential generalization. If the logic model is too general or abstract, it may be useless. On the other hand, if the logic model is highly detailed, the specifics may not be generalizable. An important goal, then, is to have middle-range theory, which spells out the causal mechanisms that drive the effects of the intervention; this middle-range theory must be specific enough to indicate the core causal mechanisms within the theory, yet general enough that it makes sense to think the intervention can be generalized to other sites.[53]

The great variance in contextual factors, such as settings, circumstances, population, and resources, form some of Shadish et al. (2002) and Cronbach's (1982) concerns about understanding external validity. Appropriate-level middle-range theory sets out the causal mechanisms that power the effects of an intervention and gives us a start toward understanding whether contextual variation will influence the intervention's effectiveness. Just knowing what the causal mechanisms are, however, is not enough to ensure external validity. A second theory is needed: one that helps identify what contextual factors might interact to support or impede the causal mechanisms of the intervention.

A question then might be whether a specific theory of context is necessary for each intervention or type of intervention or whether it might be possible to have a more generalized approach to the problem through some sort of meta-theory of context. Most likely, similarities between the ways interventions interact with the context will allow for the establishment of a set of general theory of context principles, in effect, generalizable theories of context. At the very least, providers of any intervention that is being touted as generalizable ought to provide a clear statement about the contextual factors that they believe would favor or disfavor the intervention's success in multiple contexts.

A third theory is probably necessary: a theory of implementation. Understanding the causal mechanisms of the logic model and their interactions with various contexts is not enough. New policy or interventions require time, expertise, other resources, and supporting institutions to be effectively implemented. If these are shortchanged, the intervention will not be as successful as desired. Some policies, for example, might have to be phased in after teachers are appropriately trained. Yet, policy makers and education leaders who have explicit and well-informed theories of implementation are few and far between. As a result of not paying any attention to implementation, Governor Wilson's administration mishandled California's class-size reduction policy in 1998.

As one final thought, earlier in this chapter we observed that many of the major and minor education policies implemented in the United States have had, at best, small effects on student achievement. We argued that small effects occur due to a variety of reasons, not least among them the interaction of the context with the intervention. Our understanding of the way that context influences causal mechanisms could help explain small effects. It might also help us to imagine causal mechanisms that would produce big effects. As Shadish et al. (2002) point out, it is statistically easier to identify big effects than small effects.[54] Presumably, the interventions that produce big effects would have strong causal mechanisms that would be robust and, thus, more easily generalizable across various contexts. This suggests that large effects can simplify the identification of both internal and external validity. Since large effects on matters that we are interested in are desired (e.g., improving the achievement of low-income students), perhaps that is the direction for future research.

Observations, Recommendations for Policy Makers and Policy Researchers, Thoughts about Innovation, and Conclusions

Observations This chapter has little to say about *most* educational research. We have not considered basic research that is driven by only theory or practical research that is not. And we have not dealt with the research on practice, which is often built into larger interventions, sometimes to its detriment. Our interests have been directly in Pasteur's Quadrant where research and development are informed by theory and driven by social and educational concerns;

research and development that might be useful through direct or indirect contributions to policy (Stokes, 1997). In that realm we made a number of observations throughout the chapter that could influence the conduct of policy research. First, we argued that policy makers, more often than not, use research in their work, that good syntheses of research that provide strong evidence and tell a good story are especially useful for policy makers, and that there are effective and ineffective ways of communicating research to and for policy makers. We also observed that foundations are playing an increasing role in education policy, a role that has some positive attributes but also some potentially problematic ones.

We then made the case that most education policy and interventions focused on student outcomes have small to modest effects at best. The reasons for this are many including politics, social norms, prevailing incentives, weakness of theory, and inattention to issues of implementation and generalization. But, there are exceptions and, based on a small sample of arguably larger-effect interventions and policies, we suggested some dimensions of interventions that distinguish between ineffective and effective policy. We followed this with sections on the role of theory in implementation and external validity. Finally, we explored how theory and an approach to thinking about causality help us postulate that interventions are populated by causal connections that are mediated by context and that by understanding the causal mechanisms and their relationship to context we can develop middle-range theory for interventions that can "travel."

Recommendations for Policy Makers and Policy Researchers

There are a variety of possible recommendations that may be taken from our discussion. We focus on four.

Policy Researchers and Policy Makers Should Think about How to Develop Interventions and Policy That Would Lead to Large Rather Than Small Effects We have proposed five dimensions that appear to distinguish between interventions that have small effects and those that have large effects. These dimensions, or others, might be useful in thinking about how to design large-effect interventions. Beyond that, at a minimum, every piece of research on policy or an intervention should be crystal clear in its theory about what causal mechanisms are expected to change the desired outcome, why they have promise of having a significant effect on the desired outcome, and what might be the contextual conditions that enable or disable their effectiveness.

Policy Researchers and Policy Makers Should Be Clear about What Kinds of Policies Are More Appropriately Initiated at the Various Levels of Government We need to sort out appropriate roles for federal, state, local, and school governance. Our discussions about the effects of policy and interventions indicate a few lessons in this area. Over the long run, the federal government has justifi-

ably worried about the least able in the society and about research and statistics including national assessment. The civil rights rulings by the courts in education stand as very significant policy and symbolically powerful statements about our nation's goals. However, most of the legislation and policy that is outside the sphere of the court's rulings has failed in its attempts to effectively address the nation's education problems.

Our observations about the political and somewhat incoherent nature of federal policy and legislation, in addition to the inherent difficulties of implementation from a great distance through layers of government, suggest why current approaches taken by the federal government are inappropriate and ineffective. A more effective approach might be to design federal strategies that support society's needy through technical and transparent mechanisms that are firmly focused on inequalities. This would include policies to redress imbalances among states in their ability to fund education as well as funding policies within states for students with disabilities and for schools with substantial percentages of low-income students. This is an appropriate role for the federal government to take if it is approached carefully with the understanding that the more the federal requirements need adaptation at the state, local, and school levels, the less likely they are to work. Research, development, innovation, experimentation, information sharing, and data collection and analysis are also straightforward federal responsibilities. At the current time these responsibilities are miserably underfunded and should be greatly expanded and managed through a network of national organizations that have strong protection from political interference.

States should set goals and standards, provide funding, assess progress, and support local education governments. Serious, innovative, and possibly disruptive policies that hold promise of major effects might emanate from the state levels so long as the local authorities have sufficient authority and flexibility to allow them to adapt the policy to their environment. Policies and interventions that are close to the school and classroom and that have had a history of small effects (e.g., choice, class size, most curriculum decisions) should be left to the local government and individual schools to be carried out in continuous improvement systems. If state and federal governments continue in these areas of small effects, they will continue to muddle the policies with political and ideological modifications. The balance between coherence and flexibility is critical and has been very hard for the various governments to get right.

Policy Researchers Should Focus More Than They have on the Theory (Logic Model) That Drives the Proposed Policy or Intervention and Extend That Theory to More Deeply Understand How it Informs Issues of Implementation and Generalization Understanding how the policy or intervention is expected to cause the intended outcome is critical in determining whether the intervention "works" and how to implement it. At the core of understanding is the determination of the causal mechanisms that are embedded in the model. This provides a guide to understanding the necessary components that must be implemented and indicates how to balance top-down direction with bottom-up initiative, flexibility, and ownership. The determination of causal mechanisms also influences ways of thinking about external validity. The variations in the basic conditions of education among schools, districts, and states pose significant problems in effectively generalizing interventions. Causal mechanisms should be seen as context-dependent, that is, they work or fail depending on what conditions exist in the site where the intervention is being implemented. This is a core idea and leads to the notion that there should be at least three theories operating for an intervention: one theory sets out the basic functioning of the intervention and identifies the causal mechanisms. A second theory, a theory of context, illuminates the conditions under which the causal mechanisms work or fail, and a third theory guides implementation.

Policy Researchers Must Be More Aggressive in Systematically Examining Ways of Improving Practice   Over the last half century, significant research efforts have engaged scholars and practitioners to identify important questions from the field and then work together to design and conduct high-quality, field-based research to figure out how to substantially improve practice (Stokes, 1997). The Learning Research and Development Center and other R&D centers in the 1970s and 1980s practiced variations of the model. The work of Bryk and others in Chicago has the same general approach and goals. A recent version of this genre is the Strategic Education Research Partnership (SERP), which holds some promise for improving the quality of the connections between research, policy, and practice at the local level (Pellegrino & Donovan, 2003; Bryk & Gomez, 2008). All of these examples employ theory in the conception and implementation of their interventions and are aware of the challenge of external validity. We think the new work in Chicago and at SERP show promise.

One recommendation to policy researchers is to consider how the theory they are using helps identify the causal mechanisms and the potential inhibitors and facilitators that exist in various contexts. To the extent that SERP researchers, including teachers, gather their ideas from local problems and fit their solutions into a local context, they might be thought of as high-powered contributors to district continuous improvement systems. However, a solution that is locally developed to meet a particular problem within a particular context may not be easily generalized and implemented in other settings, which makes it all the more important to have theory that provides an understanding of the causal mechanisms of the intervention and that can help guide implementation and use in other sites.

Another recommendation addresses the length of time that, for example, the SERP work in Boston appears to be taking. A significant challenge for any action research of this sort, of course, is to maintain a stable environment for conducting research within a school system. On the other hand, a legitimate goal for any district is to continuously improve, thereby changing the environment of the research.[55] Districts interested in continuous improvement are unlikely to wait for the years it could take researchers operating on a deliberate and often academic timetable to come up with the "right" answer to their problem. The continuous improvement implementers would be much more interested in fast, successive approximations of solutions.

Technology developers have put together a "rapid prototype" model that bears attention. This model uses fast feedback loops to continually assess the quality of the emerging product. The analogy to education R&D is clear: If the theories of the development and implementation of the proposed product (e.g., a curriculum, an approach to teaching, a measurement instrument) are explicit, it ought to be possible to carry out a continuous analysis of whether the intervention is behaving in the way the theories predict. In the product's early, unfinished stages, if it is not behaving the way it should, there are four possible explanations: the theory is wrong, the product does not track the theory, both the theory and the product are sufficient but the testing is too early or inaccurate, or the context is not appropriate to the design (i.e., the context contains mechanisms that inhibit the causal mechanisms of the intervention). All four possibilities provide powerful information for the developer and the implementers. The latter reason is particularly important since it suggests an inherent problem in using rapid prototyping in settings that are fundamentally stable. Of course, like continuous improvement, the act of rapid prototyping is itself an intervention that could have disruptive properties that could alter the context and create inhibitors for the intervention (Surry & Farquhar, 1996).[56] This problem is partly ameliorated by careful thought prior to development about the intervention's causal mechanisms and how they might interact within various contexts. But, even with this initial attention, intervention developers must be fully aware of the complexities of working in a social context in a way that has hitherto been foreign.

Finally, it is possible that a SERP-like approach could be used to design and test a serious, non-incremental, or disruptive intervention, but it would take a deliberate and gutsy decision by the local administration and researchers, because the natural instinct in those settings is to take the small view. The problem, of course, is that serious innovation can threaten traditional ways of doing business, which may threaten teachers and administrators. By and large, the business of SERP and SERP-like endeavors has been to improve rather than substantially change or innovate.

Innovation   Most of our focus to this point has been on gradual, incremental change. In the background of the discussion has been an implied, preferred model of the education system with a basic structure of state standards-based reforms, clear goals and standards, aligned resources, and appropriate accountability. This structure is supported by a data-driven continuous learning system that pervades the entire state system. Districts and schools would be expected to focus steadfastly on improving student achievement, especially for children from low-income families. In addition, there would be social and professional press for educational improvement.

In our discussion of policies that appear to work, each of the four components of this model (standards reform, continuous improvement, focus on achievement, social press) separately appears to show significant, substantial, and sustained results. To work well, this four-component model must be in place for a sustained period of time and must not be distracted by irrelevant and politically driven requirements and interference. We believe that in the best of worlds, this model would "keep giving" by facilitating smart, relevant modifications based on data and, with slight modifications, would create over time a system as robust and effective as most of the national systems that we admire for their effectiveness. Yet there are few, if any, jurisdictions in the United States that combine reasonably mature versions of all four of these components. Massachusetts probably comes closest as a state and Long Beach as a city, though it suffers from being in California.

Our point is that there is great opportunity for improvement *without* bringing disruptive change into the system. Fundamentally, this requires our system to become more professional and less political. The challenge for policy makers is to realize that their actions can hurt our children as well as help them learn; policy makers should leave most educational decisions to professionals, as they are left out in many other nations' systems, and create supportive rather than bureaucratic and regulatory environments for our districts and schools. The challenge for policy researchers is to develop systematic knowledge and strategies to improve state standards-based reform systems and to design and implement powerful, useful data systems to support continuous improvement within states, districts, and schools.

We believe, however, that even effective continuous improvement systems within states and districts and schools will not be enough to enable our education system to attain the goals that we have set for it. To reach these goals we suggest four potentially disruptive reforms that have promise of providing substantial improvement.[57] We address three in a cluster because we believe that they are critical in the nation's effort to substantially improve the levels of achievement and attainment for children from low-income families, thereby helping to substantially close the achievement gap. The fourth, which is the smart use of technology, should provide greatly increased opportunities for all children.

Improving Achievement for Students from Low-Income Families One of the three proposed policies falls outside of our traditional thinking about school. We have known for years the links between health and learning, yet large numbers of children from low-income families lack health insurance and have only erratic health care. Untreated cavities leading sometimes to fatal infections, vision and hearing issues, undiagnosed children's diseases,

and unhealthy diets are only a few of the health problems that plague high proportions of low-income children and substantially impede their learning (Hough, 2008). This concept should be simple for educators, yet in federal and state politics many of the education groups seem to view this as someone else's problem. Educators must take seriously the idea of "coming to school ready to learn." Apart from good health insurance for all children, there are a variety of other models—including mobile diagnostic labs—that work with local clinics and schools to provide necessary health services for young children. The delivery system does not have to be expensive or time consuming. This is a promising "big effect" intervention because it directly influences the readiness of the children, can be delivered in a variety of ways to meet the needs of the local community, and is not a replacement for another similar treatment.

A second large-effect policy focuses directly on the need to expand the language experiences and capacity of low-income children. The size of the working vocabulary of 4-year-old children from low-income families is approximately one-third that of children from middle-income families (Hart & Risley, 1995). The relative lack of fluency in academic language of children from low-income families and children who are English language learners has been documented in multiple studies. The research indicates that large percentages of students from all groups learn the skills of reading, such as decoding, phonemic awareness, and reading sight words (August & Shanahan, 2006). Yet, even though these skills are learned, many low-income and English language learning students fail in their comprehension of text at fourth grade and beyond, thus greatly reducing their chances of becoming competent, self-directed learners. The lack of a rich vocabulary and mastery of academic language substantially increases the odds of school failure and deserves far more attention than it currently receives.

While this is a critical problem that must be addressed while a student is young, many of the nation's K–3 language and reading classes focus on students being seen but not heard, students who are not expected to read more than scripted paragraphs. These young students start out behind; they will not catch up through enriching out-of-school experiences because they generally will not receive them and they will not catch up through traditional in-school experiences as they often are not expected to actively use oral language to enrich their language by storytelling, making logical arguments, conversing with an adult, and giving directions, even though such verbal activities will be required of them later in school. In order to have a chance to succeed to a reasonable level of proficiency, for their first 5 years of school these students should receive an aggressive, well-researched, motivating program in language development that extends their skills, knowledge, and experience using oral language and academic vocabulary building.

This policy and related interventions would require substantial changes in our reading and language curriculum; the curriculum policies of many states, districts, and schools; and the training and professional development of teachers.

The policy is disruptive but potentially powerful because it directly addresses teaching and learning, closes a serious gap in the necessary knowledge and skills of many of our students, and could be developed rapidly into a coherent set of interventions with measurable outcomes that are sustained over a long period of time.

The third area of change for children from low-income families is to dramatically extend their time in school, especially in the early years. We see this as a critical partner of the challenge to address vocabulary and academic language development. Increasing the time in school by two to three hours a day extends class time by 40% to 60%. A variety of successful charter school models, including KIPP, extend their school days and years and, in Massachusetts, first-year evaluations of sets of interventions that have used extended school time have produced promising results (KIPP Foundation., 2007; Massachusetts 2020, n.d.). We believe that the data indicate that an effective design is to fully integrate the extra time with the traditional school schedule to create a different schedule that allows for more work on language, arts, and music and for providing a substantially greater number of students with individual or small-group tutoring experiences. This formulation combines more language, time, and motivation with intensive instructional experiences, all key ingredients of large effect size interventions.

Improving Achievement and Opportunities for All Students   The time has come in education for technology. We have heard that mantra for 40 years and past and recent scholars have argued that the time may never come (Oettinger & Marks, 1969; Cuban, 2001). Analysts said the same thing about digital technology and the business world in the late 1980s, just before the business world understood that the added value of technology appears when it changes the way business is conducted rather than just provide a little greater efficiency in doing work the same way it has always been done. We are now at the time when technological change is moving faster than ever before, when it is essentially ubiquitous, powerful, connected, and a deep part of the lives of almost all students in ways that many older than 40 can barely understand.

There is no question that technology has changed the way that we can think about learning. Structured school learning experiences are now available 180 days a year for five hours a day, but, in the very near future, as the world of technology responds either with proprietary or open course materials, the student will have a rich array of opportunities available 365 days a year, 24 hours a day (Smith & Casserly, 2006; Borgman et al., 2008). A recent randomized trial at Carnegie Mellon University indicates that students who use Web-based cognitive tutors that are available anytime can learn the material of a college statistics course in half a semester as well as students who take a full semester in a conventional lecture course (Lovett, Meyer, & Thille, 2008). At the secondary school level, a technology cognitive tutor provides algebra instruction, apparently in a way

that is more effective than learning from only a teacher (Institute of Education Sciences, 2007; Carnegie Learning, Inc., 2008). The use of games and other immersive environments on the Web for student learning, sometimes with peer support through virtual communication, shows great promise (Borgman et al., 2008). Problem solving in new environments by young people is happening every day on the Web at hundreds of sites. Media-rich textbooks are now being prepared for many high school courses. The increase in voice recognition capability means that in a few years even our youngest students will be able to have controlled conversations with their computer and handheld device, a possibility that greatly extends the opportunities for all sorts of language learners. Our understanding of all of these phenomena is at a very early stage. Within 5 to 10 years, we expect that many school environments for students 10 years and older all over the world, possibly even in the United States, will have technology deeply embedded into every aspect of schooling.

In a recent book, Clay Christensen, a professor at Harvard Business School, argues that in 10 to 12 years upwards of 50% of student courses in U.S. secondary schools will be taken online (Christensen, Johnson, & Horn, 2008, pp. 98–99). The online courses he and others foresee will have built-in capacities to engage students with multimedia and interactive components and will use formative assessment methodologies to personalize instruction (see Smith & Casserly, 2006). We can imagine that the courses will be available on multiple platforms including hand-held computers. The course content would be vetted and regularly updated by content and teaching experts, often in response to user comments. The learning experience provided by these courses will almost certainly be more powerful, engaging, and effective for many students than the teaching they receive from average or even above-average teachers. Christensen sees the courses as entering into the schools in nonintrusive, nonthreatening ways, such as by offering opportunities for AP courses that did not exist in the school or language learning in languages that were not part of the curriculum, by providing opportunities for charter schools and home learning, and by helping students who are "credit deficient." Over time, the intervention would move into mainstream courses. This will have a transformative effect on teachers, who will take on a role of supporting and enabling student learning rather than functioning primarily as information providers. This reform would create new opportunities for many students to take courses that would not have been available to them and perhaps opportunities to learn more and faster than in courses that are traditionally given by teachers.

Conclusion

This chapter makes a number of recommendations for policy researchers and policy makers and suggests a few innovations that might be usefully tried. Underlying the chapter is a set of five ideas about policy research and change in education within the United States. One is that policy or intervention that requires complex adaptive change in the behavior of adults in schools is not only difficult to do because of political and institutional constraints, it seems to be difficult to imagine. As a consequence most policies tinker on the margins with little positive effect. A second idea is that when federal and state governments introduce and require such marginal policies the implementation of the policies becomes distorted as they move through levels of government and the emphasis becomes compliance rather than improvement. A third idea is that policy researchers and policy makers should think more deeply about the theory embedded in a policy or intervention and use the theory to try to understand how, when, and where the policy might be effectively used, before they propose the policy and while they implement it. A fourth idea is that the current system could be substantially improved without radical change by more thoughtful implementation of the basic structures and policies now in place. This would require a system of continuous improvement at the state, district, and local levels. Within this framework marginal improvements could be intelligently chosen and implemented and, hopefully, accumulate in effect over time. The fifth and last idea is that more radical, innovative change outside and inside schools and classrooms is necessary for the United States to reach the performance goals of equality among class and racial/ethnic groups of students while also reaching a high level of quality. We suggest some new policies or interventions that might help. However, the passage and implementation of such policies will take considerable political will by a leadership that will have to take steps that substantially disrupt the current way of doing business.

Notes

1. We thank George Bohrnstedt, Gary Sykes, Michael Feuer, Tom Toch, and Jennifer O'Day for comments on an earlier draft. We also thank Sally Tracy for her assistance and editing.

2. On a personal note, the senior author served in significant policy roles at the federal level for 11 of the 12 years of the Carter and Clinton administrations and recalls few debates over budget, legislation, or regulatory matters where research studies and data were not advanced, often to support both sides of an issue.

3. *The Nation at Risk* report was controversial as are many reports that stimulate policy (Stedman & Smith, 1983).

4. During the late 1980s and early 1990s, the senior author was the Dean at Stanford University, one of the university partners in CPRE; he later became the Under-Secretary of Education in the Clinton administration. The chair of the CPRE board was former Governor Richard Riley of South Carolina, soon to become the Secretary of Education.

5. One important reason that education research was taken seriously in the federal government during the second half of the 20th century was the quality of the people who served as analysts for the policy makers. For example, when education was housed in the Department of Health, Education and Welfare up until 1980 scholars like Alice Rivlin and Henry Aaron led the planning offices, the education research arm of the government was led by Thomas Glennan, Harold Hodgkinson, Patricia Graham, and P. Michael Timpane, all with active interests in policy, and education leaders John Jennings and Christopher Cross were key Congressional staffers. Later in the century, Chester Finn, Charles Kolb, and Terry Peterson served

in key policy positions and Isabel Sawhill ran the OMB Office that oversaw education. Finn, along with Daniel Patrick Moynihan, worked in the White House in the late 1960s and early 1970s. Also, throughout this entire period, senior civil servants such as Emerson Elliott, Bernard Martin, and Barry White in OMB and Alan Ginsburg, Thomas Skelly, Joseph Conaty, Garry McDaniels, and others in the Department of Education have been steady, honest brokers of the importance of good research in the development of policy.

6. The Supreme Court's ruling in *Brown v. Board of Education* (1954) contains a well-known footnote citing a psychological study of racial identity indicating the negative effects of racial isolation published by Kenneth Clark, an eminent African American psychologist.

7. Policy also influences research. For example, as the reforms of the 1960s were implemented, the federal government sponsored major evaluations of programs such as Head Start and Title I. As evaluation research became available during the 1970s that showed desegregation had little effect on student achievement and as distaste for bussing increased, enthusiasm for desegregation waned. By the late 1980s, desegregation had essentially disappeared as a reform strategy.

8. Another example is organizational research, which was initially focused on for-profit business and recently applied to the governmental sector.

9. An early analysis of the theory and practicality of vouchers and a trial intervention was carried out by a group of policy researchers from Harvard University on a grant from the Office of Economic Opportunity (Jencks et al., 1970; Levinson, 1976).

10. Though it is rare for a single study to itself have a determinative impact on policy, there are apparent exceptions, such as the Tennessee class-size study in the mid-1980s and the Perry Preschool study in the early 1960s. In fact, both studies were preceded by large bodies of prior research that shaped the nature of the interventions and prepared the policy environments to act on the basis of the studies. The Tennessee study tilted the balance of a large body of inconclusive evidence about the importance of differences in the number of pupils in a school classroom. The sheer size of the study and the fact that it was a randomized trial were important as the study operated as a "signal" for policy makers to act on a class-size reduction policy. The Perry Preschool study also has served as a signal. Its continuing power to influence policy results in significant part from the intervention's apparent long-lasting effect on its participants, well beyond their preschool years. It is possible to argue that many studies have played the role of triggering policy action in various areas, though few have reached the iconic status of the Tennessee and Perry Preschool studies. Our point, however, is that such apparently conclusive studies or interventions were built on the backs of large bodies of prior research and analysis.

11. Gene Glass (1976) first used the term *meta-analysis* and proposed systematic procedures to combine results from a variety of studies of the same issue. Richard Light and Paul Smith (1971) earlier had addressed the same problem.

12. In many instances, knowledge in a particular area of education seems to grow haphazardly with no apparent overall strategy guiding it. Haphazard growth develops where an individual researcher, often with his or her students, explores a topic in education research, while other researchers (sometimes known and sometimes not, but working independently) explore the same issue. If the independently created research is published or otherwise made available and the topic is popular so that large numbers of independent researchers engage in its study, the haphazard (or creative bottom-up approach, depending on your view) process sometimes results in a significant body of research that may then be systematically aggregated.

13. The process of how to create a synthesis is rarely explicitly taught, in contrast to analysis, and is often underestimated. As a process, it is at the heart of theory and policy research.

14. In the 33 days following the release, 18 editorials, 21 television stories, and at least 30 radio stories were published, and at least 192 print articles mentioned the research project. Although the Governor's commitment was clearly heartfelt the very substantial

state budget deficit he encountered early in 2008 has distracted his attention from education.

15. Carol Weiss (1999) has written extensively about this as have others. The senior author's ideas are surely influenced by all of them. The set of factors we suggest is less a distillation of their work and more a reflection of the senior author's own experiences. This is the reason that many of the examples are either from the federal government or from California.

16. Much of the research in the behavioral and social sciences and, for that matter, in the biological and physical sciences is not of sufficient caliber to be published and certainly does not deserve consideration in policy debates. Our policy makers rarely have the expertise to reach such a judgment, which leaves the responsibility in the hands of the academy.

17. At all levels of education government, education groups often resist major change because it may alter conditions for their constituents. This creates a powerful barrier to many important innovations.

18. The Tennessee study was a three-phase randomized trial study designed to determine the effect of smaller class sizes in the earliest grades on short-term and long-term pupil performance, beginning in 1985.

19. The Consortium for Education Policy Research (CPRE) is a collection of researchers drawn from the University of Pennsylvania, Columbia University, Harvard University, University of Wisconsin, and Stanford University. CPRE has been in existence for more than 20 years and has developed an effective strategy to disseminate research findings to policy makers at the state and federal levels. CPRE uses a combination of policy briefs, the Internet, meetings in Washington, DC, and partnerships with many of the national constituent groups, which often publish their materials in their own journals. But even CPRE cannot compete with the Washington-based think tanks in access to policy makers.

20. In the California legislature, each member of the Assembly may only initiate a set number (40) of different bills per 2-year session though members may "sign on" to other bills. The rule was put into place in order to control the insatiable appetite of legislators for proposing legislation. The appetite is fueled by the press, which often rates legislators and legislative bodies on the basis of the number of bills they pass rather than on the quality of the legislation. A limit of 40 bills, however, will not stem the appetite much.

21. We focus on educational achievement and attainment because policy makers use them as their primary measures for accountability purposes. We recognize that many policies have other intended outcomes. For example, creating new small schools, a reform heavily promoted and funded by the Gates Foundation, was very successful in creating schools and places that are considered relatively safe by students and staff. However, evaluations of the small schools do not indicate that school achievement clearly improved (The National Evaluation of High School Transformation, American Institutes for Research, & SRI International, 2006; Strategic Measurement and Evaluation, 2007).

22. See the U.S. Department of Education's What Works Clearinghouse Web site and, more specifically, the reviews of the effectiveness of a variety of different reading and math programs (http://ies.ed.gov/ncee/wwc/). Also, examine the various programs in the federal ESEA Act or Vocational Education Act and consider whether there is one program that has been demonstrated to have an important, lasting effect on school achievement. For the results of a study carried out in the early years of Head Start, see Westinghouse Learning Corporation and Ohio University (1969). The initial impact of Head Start on achievement generally dissipates over a few years, although some recent data indicate that effects on other outcomes such as grade repetition, special education, and high school graduation may persist (Barnett, 1998). The widely touted Perry Preschool Program and other boutique programs that have shown sustained effects have been single or a few cite early childhood programs with far more extensive and different resources than those available to children in Head Start. Kaestle and Smith (1982) consider the impact on achievement of Title I of ESEA from 1965 to 1980 and argue that the role of Title I

is mostly symbolic rather than effectively remedial. Many policies, such as Head Start and desegregation, have had multiple expected outcomes, some of which were or are being accomplished. Yet, even in these two cases, the most prominent and influential research used student achievement as the primary outcome of the reform. See Paul Hill's (2007) article for an interesting discussion of choice. While Hill favors choice, he is candid about the lack of effects on school achievement that choice interventions have had, but he sees other benefits from the policy. These few observations suggest that our focus on student achievement as currently assessed may be far too myopic a goal.

23. The Drug Abuse Resistance Education (DARE) program is a classic example. The program is run through police departments around the nation, which provide police personnel to administer the program at the schools. During the 1990s, a variety of studies showed the program was ineffective and perhaps even counterproductive. However, lobbying by police organizations and other supporters made the program impossible to limit. Only in the late 1990s was any headway made toward limiting the program. In 2003, the federal administration decided not to allow the use of federal funds for the program (Hanson, n.d.).

24. By small effects, we mean that systematic comparisons of the intervention do not show consistent and positive differences in results from comparison settings that are not implementing the intervention. This leads to a distribution of effect sizes that has values that span zero (0) and may fall on the negative or positive side. The mean of the effects may statistically be slightly greater than zero, a condition that may reflect the true average for the population represented in the studies or may represent the fact that the reports describing the studies were more likely to be published if their results were positive rather than negative. There are other interpretations as well.

25. As the senior author recalls the discussion in the White House Chief of Staff's office, he was arguing for the "evidence-based policy" when a key presidential aide entered the office and, after a few moments, exclaimed, "There goes another liberal trying to take a tax cut and turn it into a spending program."

26. The hidden history of Title I of the ESEA has myriad examples of this point. One classic story in the 1970s and 1980s has to do with some states retaining requirements for pulling out Title I children from their classes for separate classes long after the federal law was altered to remove this requirement; the federal rules had changed but some states kept their own guidance in place.

27. Maybe we need to figure out a way to encourage creative and productive adaptation of complex policy.

28. The systematic effort to starve state education departments provides another example of the effect of capacity on implementation. Over the past two decades, although state agencies have been given the responsibility for overseeing the implementation of large, complex programs, such as No Child Left Behind, policy makers at the state level have taken away their capacity and resources to implement the programs. The political motivations—including governors' desires to increase their authority and legislators' clumsy attempts to reduce bureaucratic inefficiency—have led to reductions in capacity of the state education departments. This seriously compromises the quality of implementation of all the federal and state programs (Tucker, 2004; Minnici & Hill, 2007). There is reason to change the functions and structure of state education departments by eliminating their stovepipe structures, increasing their analytic capacity, and strengthening their ability to provide support for districts. Approximately 80% of the people in the California Department of Education are paid with federal categorical funds.

29. The Tennessee class-size study focused on the early grades and reduced class size from the mid-20s to 17 pupils and, in some classes, to 13, but most policy reforms based on the study reduced class size to a lesser extent (e.g., to 20 pupils in California). Although some of the results of the Tennessee study were statistically significant and favored low-income and African American children, they varied substantially by group and grade level. Barrow and Rouse argue that there are a number of well-done class-size studies other

than Tennessee's, and they indicate that class-size reduction has a generalizable effect (Barrow & Rouse, 2007). One study the authors cite used regression discontinuity analyses on data from Israel where the class sizes ranged from 40 to 21 and found differences for fourth- and fifth-grade students but not for third-grade students. Another study carried out in Connecticut found mixed effects. A third used national survey data to find that smaller class sizes improve achievement. Taken with the Tennessee study and the large number of other non-experimental studies of class size that show little to no effect we do not find that the overall results present a compelling case for class-size reduction. Rather they indicate that class-size reduction may work somewhat well in some situations and not well at all in others. Given the uncertainty and relatively small size of even the most positive effects we classify this intervention in the small effects category.

30. We are not suggesting that there are no battles over such policies. Indeed, there are sometimes vigorous tussles over these issues. Our point is that the lives and practices of teachers, administrators, and board members are not altered or threatened in significant ways—these battles are simply part of American schooling.

31. There are always exceptions to the arguments made here. One is that a steady stream of generally disconnected changes emanating from outside may be disruptive, even if the changes are only marginal.

32. See pages 58 to 69 of Schneider, Carnoy, Kilpatrick, Schmidt, and Shavelson (2007) for an interesting discussion of the problems of estimating teacher effects and one solution, as well as a variety of references.

33. Of course, if the study compares the use of a reading or math curriculum to groups that do not receive any instruction in reading or math, we would expect the effects to be very large.

34. Cohen, Moffitt, and Goldin (2007) suggest another reason for small effects. Their position is that, as an education community, we know too little about identifying good teaching and training teachers to design programs that effectively teach our students. As a field, we lack the knowledge necessary to understand the fundamental processes of teaching and learning. These are wise observers and scientists, but we are skeptical about their argument. Surely, we do not "know" even a small fraction of everything there is to learn about the fundamental processes of teaching and learning but, more than likely, we know enough to greatly improve practice if we had the political will and resources.

35. Countless surveys and polls show that people think their neighborhood school is fine, no matter what objective data indicate, even when they think the rest of the education system is failing.

36. Data are drawn from the results from the Long-Term Trend NAEP on the Web. See http://nces.ed.gov/nationsreportcard/ltt/. We used the full sample of public and private school students. An estimated grade level is roughly 10 to 11 points. Since the composition of the sample changes over time, examining the performance of the key subgroups is the best way to look at NAEP results over time if one is interested in estimating possible school effects. In the United States, the change in the percentage of Hispanics in schools increased dramatically over the years covered by the charts. This presents a similar problem to needing a balanced design when estimating effects sizes in an analysis of variance design. Comparing the total sample mean changes over time with subgroup mean changes in a situation where there are substantial changes in composition of subgroups may lead to some very odd results, for example, all of the subgroup mean changes being larger than the total sample mean change. See Simpson Paradox at: http://en.wikipedia.org/wiki/Simpson%27s_paradox. However, the key point is that if one is interested in school effects the gains of sub-groups is the right measure while, if estimating the overall human capital potential represented in the schools is the goal, the total sample means and mean changes would seem more useful since they provide a measure of the average knowledge and skills of all of the students. The gain score data on the total national sample present a less positive picture than do the data on the subgroups.

37. Reading achievement did not increase as much during this time period even though there was arguably a similar level of social press to improve it. A probable reason for this is that math achievement appears to be far more sensitive to variations in school resources than is reading achievement. This fact has been known for years (Smith, 1972; Jencks et al., 1972). A variety of studies indicate that the effect of variations in home and community environment is much more important for reading and language than for mathematics. By the time a student reaches the point where math problems are "word problems," the impact of lack of language appears to affect math scores.

38. To help estimate how well the United States could do under its current general system of educational governance, it is useful to see how well individual states have done. According to a recent study, in eighth-grade math, Massachusetts ranks just behind five Asian countries or regions, including Singapore and Hong Kong, and well ahead of any European country (Phillips, 2007).

39. There is considerable variation in the effectiveness of states using standards-based reforms on State NAEP scores. In particular, we note that Massachusetts, Connecticut, North Carolina, and Texas have all progressed substantially since 1994.

40. In a number of these districts (including Los Angeles and Austin), some of the work was guided by a third party operating as a provider of professional development to the district's leadership.

41. SFA is administered by a not-for-profit foundation (Slavin, Madden, & Datnow, 2007).

42. Other research-based programs such as "America's Choice" also show considerable promise.

43. A final report with longitudinal data on the Bay Area KIPP Academies will be available from SRI in the late summer of 2008. In addition the planning for a randomized field trial for KIPP is underway.

44. The What Works Clearinghouse (http://ies.ed.gov/ncee/wwc/) indicates these interventions are only promising, in part because there have not been more than one or two well-done randomized trials for each of the interventions and the Clearinghouse's criteria for acceptance beyond "promising" require a greater number of randomized trials. In the elementary math area, one curriculum is seen as having substantial promise, while in middle school math, there were five curricula with promising effects.

45. The dimensions are not necessarily orthogonal.

46. This argument mirrors Karl Popper's (1962) critique of utopian engineering as impossible, for the most part due to the epistemic impossibility of being able to know enough to plan a society. As a consequence, he argues for piecemeal engineering based upon prior experience and learning from error.

47. The level of dosage (effort, resources etc.) that is applied to an intervention is an important possible other dimension.

48. The San Diego school system produced a blueprint for reform for their interventions (San Diego City Schools Institute for Learning, 2000).

49. There is some debate about how strongly this statement should be made (Shadish, Cook, & Campbell, 2002; Yin, 2003). This is really a debate between two different types of generalization—one is statistical and inductive, and the other is analytical.

50. Personal recollection of Marshall S. Smith.

51. This approach is generally associated with "realist" social science, although such a moniker encompasses a wide variety of different epistemological and ontological perspectives (Psillos, 1999). It has been introduced into a variety of social science fields, including education (Maxwell, 2004).

52. For interesting work on causality see Cartwright (2003, 2004).

53. Middle-range theory is a theory that falls between the highly concrete working hypotheses in everyday research and the non-testable, all-inclusive unifying theories. Such theory is still close enough to the empirical that it can be tested, but it is also abstract enough to be generalizable (Merton, 1967; Pawson & Tilley, 1997; Maxwell, 2004).

54. See Shadish et al. (2002, p. 230): "When treatment effects are large and coincide with the introduction of the treatment, the effects are often plausible without statistical analysis."

55. Changes in school boards, superintendents, and mayors may also influence the conduct of long-term research within a district.
56. "Planning for adoption requires an evolutionary advance in the models instructional developers use. Emerging theories that place an emphasis on the user and on the social context in which a product will be used can be incorporated into existing product-development models. Adoption analysis, user-oriented instructional development, rapid prototyping, and field testing are only a few of the tools that developers can use to determine and account for adoption factors" (Surry & Farquhar, 1996, p. 6.7).
57. There are other powerful candidates for this list. Chief among them is to develop a powerful human resource strategy for the nation, states, and districts. We are skeptical about strategies that imagine system-wide changes in the pool of teachers because of the cost and time it would take to make the strategies pay off. We believe, however, that it is possible to rigorously train principals, coaches, and superintendents and to hold them to initiate rigorous hiring standards based on their knowledge of skills demanded by these jobs. This approach could be systemically carried out relatively quickly and at far less cost than policies designed to attract a different set of teachers into the overall workforce. Yet, the challenge in carrying out such a policy is enormous and would require aggressive work by policy researchers.

References

Aladjem, D., & Borman, K. M. (2006, April). *Summary of findings from the National Longitudinal Evaluation of Comprehensive School Reform.* Paper presented at the annual meeting of the American Educational Research Association, San Francisco.

Atkinson, R. C., & Jackson, G. B. (Eds.). (1992). *Research and educational reform: Roles for the Office of Education Research and Improvement.* Washington, DC: National Academy Press.

August, D., & Shanahan, T. (Eds.). (2006). *Developing literacy in second-language learners: Report of the National Literacy Panel on language-minority children and youth.* Mahwah, NJ: Erlbaum.

Austin, J. E., Grossman, A. S., Schwartz, R. B., & Suesse, J. M. (2006). *Managing at scale in the Long Beach Unified School District* (PEL-041). Cambridge, MA: Harvard Business Publishing .

Austin, J. E., Schwartz, R. B., & Suesse, J. M. (2004). *Long Beach Unified School District (A): Change that leads to improvement, 1992–2002* (PEL-006). Cambridge, MA: Harvard Business Publishing.

Bailey, S. T., & Mosher, E. K. (1968). *The office of education administers a law.* Syracuse, NY: Syracuse University Press.

Barnett, W. S. (1998). Long-term effects on cognitive development and school success. In W. S. Barnett & S. S. Boocock (Eds.), *Early care and education for children in poverty: Promises, programs, and long-term outcomes* (pp. 11–44). Buffalo: State University of New York Press.

Barrow, L., & Rouse, C. E. (2007). Causality, causality, causality: The view of education inputs and outputs from economics. In S. H. Fuhrman, D. K. Cohen, & M. Mosher (Eds.), *The state of education policy research* (pp. 137–156). Mahwah, NJ: Erlbaum.

Betts, J. R., Zau, A. C., & King, K. (2005). *From blueprint to reality: San Diego's education reforms.* San Francisco: Public Policy Institute of California.

Bhaskar, R. (1978). *A realist theory of science* (2nd ed.). Sussex, England: Harvester Press.

Black, P., & Wiliam, D. (1998). Inside the black box: Raising standards through classroom assessment. *Phi Delta Kappan, 80,* 139–144.

Bohrnstedt, G., & Stecher, B. (Eds.). (1999). *Class size reduction in California: Early evaluation findings, 1996–1998.* Palo Alto, CA: American Institutes for Research.

Borgman, C. E., Abelson, H., Dirks, L., Johnson, R., Koedinger, K., Linn, M. C., et al. (2008). *Fostering learning in the networked world: The cyberlearning opportunity and challenge.* Washington, DC: National Science Foundation.

Borman, G., Hewes, G., Overman, L. T., & Brown, S. (2003). Comprehensive school reform and achievement: A meta-analysis. *Review of Educational Research, 73,* 125–230.

Bowles, S., & Gintis, H. (1976). *Schooling in capitalist America: Educational reform and the contradictions of economic life.* New York: Basic Books.

Brown v. Board of Education of Topeka, 347 U.S. 483 (1954).

Bryk, A., & Gomez, L. (2008). *Ruminations on reinventing an R&D capacity for educational improvement* (IREPP Working Paper No. 2008-05). Stanford, CA: Institute for Research on Education Policy and Practice.

Bunge, M. (2004a). Clarifying some misunderstandings about social systems and their mechanisms. *Philosophy of the Social Sciences, 34,* 371–381.

Bunge, M. (2004b). How does it work? The search for explanatory mechanisms. *Philosophy of the Social Sciences, 34,* 182–210.

The Campbell Collaboration. (n.d.). *The Campbell Collaboration: What helps? What hurts? Based on what evidence?* Retrieved June 18, 2008, from http://www.campbellcollaboration.org

Carnegie Learning, Inc. (2008). *Welcome to Carnegie Learning, Inc.* Retrieved June 18, 2008, from Carnegie Learning: http://www.carnegielearning.com/

Carroll, J. (1963). A model of school learning. *Teachers College Record, 64,* 723–733.

Cartwright, N. (2003). *Causation: One word, many things.* London: Centre for Philosophy of Natural and Social Science.

Cartwright, N. (2004). From causation to explanation and back. In B. Leiter (Ed.), *The future for philosophy* (pp. 230–245). Oxford, UK: Oxford University Press.

Childress, S., Elmore, R. F., Grossman, A. S., & Johnson, S. M. (Eds.). (2007). *Managing school districts for high performance.* Cambridge, MA: Harvard Education Press.

Christensen, C. M., Johnson, C. W., & Horn, M. (2008). *Disrupting class: How disruptive innovation will change the way the world learns.* New York: McGraw-Hill.

The Cochrane Collaboration. (n.d.). *The Cochrane Collaboration: The reliable source of evidence in health care.* Retrieved June 18, 2008, from http://www.cochrane.org

Cohen, D. K. (1990a). A revolution in one classroom: The case of Mrs. Oublier. *Educational Evaluation and Policy Analysis, 12,* 327–345.

Cohen, D. K. (1990b). Teaching practice: Plus ça change. In P. W. Jackson (Ed.), *Contributing to educational change: Perspectives on research and practice* (pp. 27–94). Berkeley, CA: McCutchan.

Cohen, D. K., Moffitt, L., & Goldin, S. (2007). Policy and practice. In S. H. Fuhrman, D. K. Cohen, & M. Mosher (Eds.), *The state of education policy research* (pp. 63–86). Mahwah, NJ: Erlbaum.

Cohen, D. K., Raudenbush, S. W., & Ball, D. L. (2002). Resources, instruction, and research. In F. Mosteller & R. Boruch (Eds.), *Evidence matters: Randomized trials in education research* (pp. 80–119). Washington, DC: Brookings Institution.

Coleman, J. S., Campbell, E. Q., Hobson, C. J., McPartland, J., Mood, A. M., Weinfeld, F. D., et al. (1966). *Equality of educational opportunity.* Washington, DC: U.S. Government Printing Office.

Cook, T. D. (2007). Randomized experiments in education: Assessing the objections to doing them. *Economics of Innovation and New Technology, 16*(2), 331–355.

Cook, T. D., & Gorard, S. (2007). What counts and what should count as evidence. In Centre for Educational Research and Innovation (Ed.), *Evidence in education: Linking research and policy* (pp. 33–49). Paris: Organisation for Economic Co-operation and Development.

Cronbach, L. J. (1982). *Designing evaluations of educational and social programs.* San Francisco: Jossey-Bass.

Cross, C. T. (2004). *Political education: National policy comes of age.* New York: Teachers College Press.

Cuban, L. (2001). *Oversold and underused: Computers in the classroom.* Cambridge, MA: Harvard University Press.

David, J., Woodworth, K., Grant, E., Guha, R., Lopez-Torkos, A., & Young, V. M. (2008). *San Francisco Bay Area KIPP Schools: A study of early implementation and achievement.* Menlo Park, CA: SRI International Center for Education Policy.

Elmore, R. F., & Burney, D. (1997a). *Investing in teacher learning: Staff development and instructional improvement in community school district #2, New York City*. New York: National Commission on Teaching and America's Future.

Elmore, R. F., & Burney, D. (1997b, October). *School variation and systemic instructional improvement in community school district #2, New York City*. Pittsburgh, PA: University of Pittsburgh, High Performance Learning Communities Project, Learning Research and Development Center.

Elmore, R. F., & Burney, D. (1998). District 2, NYC: Teacher learning comes first. *Strategies, 5*(2), 11–13.

Elmore, R. F., & McLaughlin, M. W. (1988). *Steady work: Policy, practice, and the reform of American education*. Santa Monica, CA: The RAND Corporation.

EPE Research Center. (2004, September 10). Choice. *Education Week*. Retrieved June 30, 2008, from http://www.edweek.org/rc/issues/choice/

Finn, J. D., & Achilles, C. M. (1990). Answers and questions about class size: A statewide experiment. *American Educational Research Journal, 27*, 557–577.

Fleishman, J. L. (2007). *The foundation: A great American secret*. New York: Public Affairs.

Ford Foundation. (1972). *A foundation goes to school*. New York: Author.

Friedman, M. (1955). The role of government in education. In R. A. Solo (Ed.), *Economics and the public interest: Essays written in honor of Eugene Ewald Agger* (pp. 123–144). New Brunswick, NJ: Rutgers University Press.

Fuhrman, S. H. (Ed.). (1993). *Designing coherent education policy: Improving the system*. San Francisco: Jossey-Bass.

Fuller, B., Elmore, R. F., & Orfield, G. (1996). Policy making in the dark: Illuminating the school choice debate. In B. Fuller & R. F. Elmore (Eds.), *Who chooses? Who loses? Culture, institutions, and the unequal effects of school choice* (pp. 1–21). New York: Teachers College Press.

George, A. L., & Bennett, A. (2005). *Case studies and theory development in the social sciences*. Cambridge, MA: MIT Press.

Gewirtzman, L., & Fink, E. (1998). *Realignment of policies and resources*. Chicago: Cross City Campaign for Urban School Reform.

Glass, G. V. (1976). Primary, secondary, and meta-analysis of research. *Educational Researcher, 5*, 3–8.

Grutter v. Bollinger et al. (02-241), 539 U.S. 306 (2003).

Hanson, D. J. (n.d.) *Drug Abuse Resistance Education: The effectiveness of DARE*. Retrieved June 30, 2008, from http://www.alcoholfacts.org/DARE.html

Hart, B., & Risley, T. (1995). *Meaningful differences in the everyday experiences of young American children*. Baltimore: Paul H. Brookes.

Hedström, P., & Swedberg, R. (Eds.). (1998). *Social mechanisms: An analytical approach to social theory*. New York: Cambridge University Press.

Hess, F., & Finn, C. (2007). *No remedy left behind: Lessons from a half-decade of NCLB*. Washington, DC: AEI Press.

Hill, P. (2007). New political economy of public education: Policy and research. In S. H. Fuhrman, D. K. Cohen, & M. Mosher (Eds.), *The state of education policy research* (pp. 87–104). Mahwah, NJ: Erlbaum.

Honan, J. P., Schwartz, R. B., & Suesse, J. M. (2004). *Long Beach Unified School District (B): Working to sustain improvement, 2002–2004* (PEL007). Cambridge, MA: Harvard Business School Case Study.

Hough, L. (2008). Can you hear me now? A look at what happens when quiet health problems go undetected in students. *Ed.Magazine, LI*(3), 22–27.

Institute of Education Sciences. (2007, May 29). *Intervention: Cognitive Tutor® Algebra I*. Retrieved June 18, 2008, from http://ies.ed.gov/ncee/wwc/reports/middle_math/ct_algebra1/info.asp

Jencks, C. (Ed.). (1970). *Education vouchers: A report on financing education by payments to parents*. Cambridge, MA: Center for the Study of Public Policy.

Jencks, C., Smith, M., Acland, H., Bane, M. J., Cohen, D., Gintis, H. et al. (1972). *Inequality: A reassessment of the effect of family and schooling in America*. New York: Basic Books.

Jennings, J. F. (Ed.). (1995). *National issues in education: Goals 2000 and school-to-work*. Bloomington, IN: Phi Delta Kappa Educational Foundation.

Kaestle, C., & Smith, M. S. (1982). The federal role in elementary and secondary education, 1940–1980. *Harvard Educational Review, 52*, 384–408.

Kelly, J. A. (1980, May). *Looking back, moving ahead: A decade of school-finance reform*. Paper presented at the Conference on the Politics of Equity, San Antonio, TX.

KIPP Foundation. (2007). *Welcome to KIPP*. Retrieved June 18, 2008, from http://www.kipp.org

KIPP Foundation. (2008). *KIPP: Report card 2007*. San Francisco: Author.

Kruger, A. B., & Zhu, P. (2003). *Another look at the New York City school voucher experiment* (NBER Working Paper 9418). Cambridge, MA: National Bureau of Economic Research.

Levinson, E. (1976, April). *The Alum Rock Voucher Demonstration: Three years of implementation*. Santa Monica, CA: RAND Corporation.

Light, R. J., & Smith, P. V. (1971). Accumulating evidence: Procedures for resolving contradictions among research studies. *Harvard Educational Review, 41*, 429–471.

Lindblom, C. E., & Cohen, D. K. (1979). *Usable knowledge: Social science and social problem solving*. New Haven, CT: Yale University Press.

Little, D. (1998). *Microfoundations, method, and causation: On the philosophy of the social sciences*. New Brunswick, NJ: Transaction Publishers.

Loeb, S., Bryk, A., & Hanushek, E. (2007). *Getting down to facts: School finance and governance in California*. Stanford, CA: Stanford University.

Lovett, M., Meyer, O., & Thille, C. (2008, May). Open Learning Initiative: Measuring the effectiveness of the OLI statistics course in accelerating student learning. *Journal of Interactive Media in Education*. Retrieved June 30, 2008, from open online journal http://jime.open.ac.uk/

Massachusetts 2020. (n.d.). *What's new*. Retrieved June 18, 2008, from http://www.mass2020.org/

Maxwell, J. A. (2004). Causal explanation, qualitative research, and scientific inquiry in education. *Educational Researcher, 33*(2), 3–11.

McLaughlin, M. (1976). Implementation of ESEA Title I: A problem of compliance. *Teachers College Record, 77*, 397–415.

McLaughlin, M. W. (1975). *Evaluation and reform: The elementary and secondary education Act of 1965, Title I*. Cambridge, MA: Ballinger.

McLaughlin, M. W. (1990). The RAND change agent study revisited: Macro perspectives and micro realities. *Educational Researcher, 19*(9), 11–16.

Merton, R. K. (1967). *On theoretical sociology: Five essays, old and new*. New York: The Free Press.

Minnici, A., & Hill, D. D. (2007). *Educational architects: Do state education agencies have the tools necessary to implement NCLB?* Washington, DC: Center on Education Policy.

Mosteller, F. (1995). The Tennessee study of class size in the early school grades. *The Future of Children, 5*, 113–127.

Mosteller, F., & Moynihan, D. P. (Eds.). (1972). *On equality of educational opportunity*. New York: Random House.

National Academy of Sciences. (2008a). *Division of Behavioral and Social Sciences and Education*. Retrieved June 18, 2008, from http://www7.nationalacademies.org/dbasse/

National Academy of Sciences. (2008b). *Mathematical Sciences Education Board, Publications*. Retrieved June 18, 2008, from http://www7.nationalacademies.org/MSEB/MSEB_Publications_List.html

National Academy of Sciences. (2008c). *Mathematical Sciences Education Board, Related Publications*. Retrieved June 18, 2008, from http://www7.nationalacademies.org/MSEB/MSEB-Related_Publications_List.html

National Commission on Excellence in Education. (1983). *A nation at risk: The imperative for educational reform*. Washington, DC: U.S. Government Printing Office.

The National Evaluation of High School Transformation, American Institutes for Research, & SRI International. (2006, August). *Evaluation of the Bill & Melinda Gates Foundation's high school grants initiative: 2001–2005 Final report.* Washington, DC: Authors.

O'Day, J. (2002). Complexity, accountability, and school improvement. *Harvard Educational Review, 72*(3), 293–329.

O'Day, J., & Smith, M. S. (1993). Systemic school reform and educational opportunity. In S. Fuhrman (Ed.), *Designing coherent education policy: Improving the system* (pp. 250–312). San Francisco: Jossey-Bass.

Oettinger, A., & Marks, S. (1969). *Run, computer, run: The mythology of educational innovation.* Cambridge, MA: Harvard University Press.

Organisation for Economic Co-operation and Development. (OECD). (2007). *Evidence in education: Linking research and policy, Part 2. Mediating the research/policy interface: The role of brokerage agencies.* Paris: Author.

Pawson, R., Greenhalgh, T., Harvey, G., & Walshe, K. (2005). Realist review—a new method of systematic review designed for complex policy interventions. *Journal of Health Services Research and Policy, 10*(Suppl. 1), 21–34.

Pawson, R., & Tilley, N. (1997). *Realistic evaluation.* London: Sage.

Pellegrino, J. W., & Donovan, M. S. (Eds.). (2003). *Learning and instruction: A SERP research agenda.* Washington, DC: National Academies Press.

Peterson, P. E., & Campbell, D. E. (Eds.). (2001). *Charters, vouchers and public education.* Washington, DC: Brookings Institution.

Phillips, G. (2007). *Chance favors the prepared mind: Mathematics and science indicators for comparing states and nations.* Washington, DC: American Institutes for Research.

Popper, K. R. (1962). *The open society and its enemies: Volume 1: The spell of Plato.* Princeton, NJ: Princeton University Press.

Program on Education Policy and Governance. (n.d.). *Program on education policy and governance at Harvard University.* Retrieved June 18, 2008, from http://www.hks.harvard.edu/pepg/

Psillos, S. (1999). *Scientific realism: How science tracks truth.* London: Routledge.

Rivlin, A., & Timpane, M. (1975). *Planned variation in education: Should we give up or try harder?* Washington, DC: Brookings Institution.

San Diego School City Schools Institute for Learning. (2000, March 14). *Blueprint for student success in a standards-based system: Supporting student achievement in an integrated learning environment.* San Diego: Author.

Sayer, A. (2000). *Realism and social science.* London: Sage.

Schneider, B., Carnoy, M., Kilpatrick, J., Schmidt, W. S., & Shavelson, R. J. (2007). *Estimating causal effects: Using experimental and observational designs.* Washington, DC: American Educational Research Association.

Schwartz, R., Pettigrew, T., & Smith, M. S. (1968). Is desegregation impractical? *The New Republic, 157,* 27–29.

Shadish, W. R., Cook, T., & Campbell, D. T. (2002). *Experimental and quasi-experimental designs for generalized causal inference.* Boston: Houghton Mifflin.

Slavin, R., Madden, N., & Datnow, A. (2007). Research in, research out: The role of research in the development and scale-up of Success for All. In S. H. Fuhrman, D. K. Cohen, & M. Mosher (Eds.), *The state of education policy research* (pp. 261–280). Mahwah, NJ: Erlbaum.

Smith, M. S. (1972). *Equality of educational opportunity: The basic findings reconsidered.* In F. Mosteller & D. P. Moynihan (Eds.), *On equality of educational opportunity* (pp. 230–342). New York: Random House.

Smith, M. S., & Casserly, C. M. (2006, September/October). The promise of open educational resources. *Change,* 8–17.

Smith, M. S., & O'Day, J. (1991). Systemic school reform. In S. H. Fuhrman & B. Malen (Eds.), *The politics of curriculum and testing, Politics of Education Association Yearbook* (pp. 233–267). London: Taylor and Francis.

Snow, C., Burns, M., & Griffin, P. (Eds.). (1998). *Preventing reading difficulties in young children.* Washington, DC: National Academies Press.

Spillane, J. P. (2004). *Standards deviation: How schools misunderstand education policy.* Cambridge, MA: Harvard University Press.

Stedman, L. C., & Smith, M. S. (Fall 1983). Recent reform proposals for American education. *Contemporary Education Review, 2*(2), 85–104.

Stokes, D. E. (1997). *Pasteur's quadrant: Basic science and technological innovation.* Washington, DC: Brookings Institution.

Strategic Measurement and Evaluation. (2007, September). *An evaluation of the Oakland New Small School Initiative.* Oakland, CA: Author

Surry, D. W., & Farquhar, J. D. (1996). *Incorporating social factors into instructional design theory.* In M. Bailey & M. Jones (Eds.), *Work, education, and technology.* (pp. 6.1–6.8) Dekalb, IL: LEPS Press. Retrieved June 18, 2008, from http://www2.gsu.edu/~wwwitr/docs/social/index.html

Tilly, C. (2006). *Why? What happens when people give reasons...and why.* Princeton, NJ: Princeton University Press.

Tucker, M. S. (2004, March). Hire ed: The secret to making Bush's school reform law work? More bureaucrats. *Washington Monthly, 36*(3)*,* 30–37.

Tyack, D., & Cuban, L. (1995). *Tinkering toward utopia: A century of public school reform.* Cambridge, MA: Harvard University Press.

U.S. Commission on Civil Rights. (1967). *Racial isolation in the public schools, Vol. 1.* Washington, DC: U.S. Government Printing Office.

Venezky, R. L. (1977). Research on reading processes: A historical perspective. *American Psychologist, 32*(5), 339–345.

Vinovskis, M. A. (1996). An analysis of the concept and uses of systemic educational reform. *American Educational Research Journal, 33,* 53–85.

Vinovskis, M. A. (2005). *The birth of Head Start: Preschool education policies in the Kennedy and Johnson administrations.* Chicago: University of Chicago Press.

Weinberg, M. (1977). *A chance to learn: A history of race and education in the United States.* New York: Cambridge University Press.

Weiss, C. (1999). The interface between evaluation and public policy. *Evaluation, 5,* 468–486.

Welch, W. W. (1979). Twenty years of science curriculum development: A look back. *Review of Research in Education, 7,* 282–306.

Westinghouse Learning Corporation and Ohio University. (1969). *The impact of Head Start: An evaluation of the effects of Head Start on children's cognitive and affective development, Vols. 1 and 2.* Athens, OH: Author.

What Works Clearinghouse. (2007). WWC Topic report: Middle school math. Retrieved June 27, 2008, from http://ies.ed.gov/ncee/wwc/pdf/MSM_APP_07_30_07.pdf

Wolfe, P. (1998). Revisiting effective teaching. *Educational Leadership, 56*(3), 61–64.

Yin, R. K. (2003). *Case study research: Design and methods, Vol. 5* (3rd ed.). Thousand Oaks, CA: Sage.

31

COMMENTARY
Politics and the Policy Process

JANE HANNAWAY
The Urban Institute and CALDER

The chapters in this section paint a stark picture of the multi-faceted complex nature of the education policy process. Indeed, after reading these chapters it is a wonder that coherent policy in education ever develops. It is also not surprising that significant shifts in policy direction are rare. Changes tend to be marginal and incremental. The situation is probably similar in most policy arenas, but the chapters here suggest that policymaking in education may be particularly likely to have marginal effects.

The reasoning in the chapters is well buttressed with empirical observations. But something seems to be missing. What about standards-based reform? And what about test-based accountability? Are these not major shifts? How do we explain them?

What I attempt to do in these comments is to review the case for marginal change made in the chapters and then suggest that we may be limiting our vision of what is possible, even what is likely. Most of the theories and research presented explain why education policies tend to produce only marginal changes; they do less well explaining marked shifts, as rare as they might be. Perhaps this is a limitation of standard social science theory and research. Or is it?

The Case for Marginal Policy Effects

At least four basic reasons suggested in the chapters argue for marginal change from education policy. The first is the role of the courts. The second is the right of participation given to different actors and the bargaining process that results. The third is the decentralized and complex nature of the U. S. education system, and the fourth is the dominance of elites and vested interest groups.

Consider the role of the courts. Mead describes how the law "bounds" education policy to practice. It "not only defines (the) limits (of education policy), but has limitations itself." As Mead put it so clearly, it both proscribes and prescribes, attempting to answer two questions for educators: "May we?" "Must we?" Is it within the bounds of the law, for example, to use publicly funded vouchers to pay for tuition at religiously affiliated schools?[1] Must school officials have an Individualized Education Plan (IEP) in place before the beginning of the school year to be in compliance with IDEA?[2] The limitation of legal analysis is that it does not answer the question of "should we?" Its purpose is not to determine whether resulting policy is likely to make education better. What it does is define the parameters of education policy and practice through legislation and litigation.

Other actors with more direct interests also participate in the policymaking and policy implementation process. Teachers unions are a prime example. While there is little empirical research on the effect of collective bargaining on education policy and practice, observers agree that teachers' unions are a major player that significantly influences resource allocation patterns within a school district, teacher hiring and firing decisions, and the scope of management prerogative. Shifts in any policy that affects human resource management in education, a labor intensive industry, invariably have heavy union involvement front and center at the table. In general, to the extent that policies affect the interests of unions, we would expect unions to moderate them.

The chapter by Koppich and Callahan contrasts two views of unions today that have different implications for the ways in which unions shape policy. The first view is a traditional adversarial industrial style collective bargaining where teachers' bread and butter interests and protection from arbitrary management treatment are the focus. The second view, called "reform unionism," assumes that teachers and management have shared interests in improving education. Reformed unionism has not fared well in recent years, but it is not dead. The extent to which it takes hold—which is far from clear—will affect the span of education issues affected by union influence and is something to watch.

Unions, of course, are not alone. Other professional associations and institutions of higher education also have interests in different aspects of education policy, such as teacher training, and get involved to shape policies that fit their preferences.

Actors that are not formally part of the education policy system, but have societal legitimacy, also insert themselves in the education policy process. Big city mayors and business leaders, for example, have become increasingly involved, and in the case of mayors even changed the participation rules by taking over schools. The broader the set of actors involved in education policymaking, each with their own interests and perspectives, the greater the number of bargains that must be struck for a policy to be established, often resulting in a diffusely defined policy. One of the rationales for mayoral takeover is to reduce diffused participation rights and more sharply locate responsibility and accountability in the mayor's office. We are still watching this play out.

A third condition contributing to marginal change—the multi-level decentralized structure of education in the United States—is related in the sense that it affects the number of players in the process. Datnow and Park focus on the dynamics of the policy implementation process. Actors at the federal, state, district, school, and classroom levels interpret, adapt, and transform policies as they pass through. Principals and teachers are the ultimate mediators of reform, adjusting it to the school and classroom context influenced by their own personal experiences. Indeed, the number of levels in the policy system and the extent of discretion at each level, perhaps, is a distinguishing feature of education. What starts at, say, the federal level is transformed in multiple ways before it gets to the classroom. Policies are remade and moderated as they are implemented; they can look different in different places and at different times. Attempts to estimate the impact of a particular policy, thus, can be misleading since there may be more than one policy operating in actual practice.

Honig also focuses on the implementation process, again stressing the complexity of the system. She uses organizational learning theory as one of the vehicles for describing how policy makes its way through the system. Learning theory posits that organizations are naturally conservative in the sense that learning is history dependent. Decision makers, in this case local implementers, make sense of policies on the basis of what has happened before and tend to shape actions to fit existing patterns. Another reason suggested by Honig for limited intended policy effects is simply local capacity. Educators may clearly understand and agree with the intent of a policy, say, increase reading achievement for middle grade students, but not be able to successfully produce desired outcomes.

There are also political explanations offered for limited policy effects. Minority and disadvantaged students are the neediest students in the U. S. education system and they have long been the least well served, as the Mickelson chapter persuasively argues. Issues associated with race

and class, for example, could effectively inhibit appropriate policy analysis and policy development. The chapters by Honig, by Torres and van Heertum, and by Stovall discuss critical race theory as a framework for confronting the limited impact of policy where it is most needed. This framework assumes that racism is embedded in American institutions to the point that is invisible. Standard forms of social inquiry simply miss it, and thereby contribute to the problem. The real conditions affecting minorities are simply not effectively brought to bear as policy is shaped.

The views of other informed actors are also often not sufficiently heard. The Lindle chapter shows that, even when technical issues call for experts, political elites and organized interests dominate. Lindle used political discourse analysis to examine the set of voices in the policy arena that together shaped the policy agenda on assessment policy. She analyzed articles from the *Washington Post* and *Education Week* from January 2002 through February 2008. Technical experts accounted for only 10% of the discourse. Political elites—federal and state elected and appointed officials—dominated the discourse, accounting for 57% of the quotes and attributions. Professional elites—national organizations mostly based in Washington and generally, advocacy organizations—followed with 33%. In short, powerful actors, with established interests, tend to define the parameters of policy discussions and hence the dimensions of policy alternatives presented to the public.

The Jacobsen chapter is related in that it stresses the importance of democratic involvement in education, both for society and for the appropriate functioning of schools. But the public appears to be increasingly disillusioned and uninvolved. As a consequence, a critical feedback loop for policy guidance is largely missing in American education and established interests prevail.

The Drivers of Policy Change: A Macro View

The above review offers explanations for why policy effects tend to be relatively weak. Many chapters in this section take a micro-analytic perspective and provide key insights into policy effects by analyzing how implementers interpret a policy, especially in terms of how closely it fits with their interests, values, experience, and existing practice. The closer the fit, the more likely it is to be implemented as intended, but the more marginal the effect. For reasons well articulated by the authors, this line of analysis generates important information about policy effects and their limitations. It shows how and why policies become modified as they move through the system to implementation. In addition, the chapters suggest that policy elites dominate the design of policy, thereby also contributing to the status quo.

But policies do change and they change education practice in significant ways. Consider the Elementary and Secondary Education Act (ESEA) of 1965 that ushered in a major expansion of the federal role in K-12 education and established its core mission as helping disadvantaged students. And consider No Child Left Behind (NCLB) that established performance-based accountability as a national policy in education. These policies may not have solved all the education problems in the United States, but they have had major effects on practice. What were the conditions that led to these breakthroughs?

A macro-analytic focus may be worthwhile to examine how and why policies change over time. This vantage point is not given much attention in the chapters. It requires research at a higher unit of analysis. What are the factors and forces shaping the institutions and players that, in turn, shape policies? The strategy is to study the mouse, not by analyzing the mouse, but by analyzing the cat. Paradoxically, the drivers of change are likely embedded in the environments of the institutions and groups described above as the guardians of the status quo, as well as in the institutions themselves.

Consider the union discussion. As noted above, the extent to which teachers' unions take on a reformed union position will widen the range of issues over which they have influence and, perhaps more importantly, their stance on many issues may change. For example, if they take on more responsibility for student outcomes, they will likely confront in a direct way tradeoffs between policies that treat all teachers as equally valuable and policies that differentiate teachers in terms of student performance. The question is the extent to which any union reforms will result in teacher interests and student interest becoming more or less aligned. Additionally, as Koppich and Callahan note, survey findings suggests that newer teachers have different views about the role of unions in their professional work life than veteran teachers. In short, unions could change from within and use their influence to sway education policy in ways that would not have been predicted a few years ago.

Similarly, the courts change. The Warren Court that decided *Brown v. Board of Education* in 1954, thereby ending racial segregation in schools, is a very different institution philosophically from the Roberts Court that decided that race could not be used in student assignment to schools in 2007. Indeed, Justice John Paul Stevens noted his "firm conviction that no Member of the Court that I joined in 1975 would have agreed with (the 2007) decision." The legal boundaries of policies could shift with new Court appointments.

New policies not only have their own effects, but also modify older policies. For example, Datnow and Park describe how the introduction of test-based accountability policies undermined comprehensive school reform policies. While the two policies were not in obvious conflict at inception, school level actors rejected comprehensive school reform policies that had been heralded in the 1990s if they did not clearly contribute to measured student achievement. Similarly, new policies may create demand for other new policies. For example, performance-based accountability policies may generate demand for complementary initiatives, such as teacher policies or curriculum policies, that link more directly to student performance.

The entry of new players can also change the dynamics and outcomes of the policy game. The involvement of mayors and business leaders was noted above. Smith and Smith point out that foundations are playing an increasingly important role in the shaping of policy. They have a number of advantages over publicly led efforts. For example, funding decisions are made privately within the foundation and, thus, less influenced by wider interests, politics, and the strictures of government. In short, they have more control over their agenda than a public body. Partly for the same reasons, they can sustain a course of action, including both research and advocacy, to shape policies and the public agenda over the long term. The emergence of the Gates Foundation, bringing its substantial resources to bear, has made foundations a particularly formidable force in shaping current education policy debates.

In addition, there are new breeds of actors, such as The New Teacher Project and Teach for America that, to a large extent, are taking on much of the teacher recruitment function for large urban districts. Charter Management Organizations are another. How these new and increasingly recognized organizations will affect policy, either by example or influence, and the balance between the status quo and change is an open question.

New information about production possibilities in education is also becoming available. Indeed, large fast-developing state administrative data systems may be the most important consequence of the accountability movement in education. Almost every state now has a system that allows individual student files to be linked over time so student academic gains can be calculated and many systems also allow students to be linked to their teachers. These data systems allow us to address questions never before possible and to do so with rigorous research methods. They are unprecedented. Emerging findings are already questioning conventional wisdom about strategic investments in the education system. For example, variation in effectiveness across teachers is huge, but it is not related to years of teaching experience (beyond the first couple of years) or advanced degrees (except in the subject taught) that form the bases for much of teacher compensation. With the ability to turn around research on policy effects relatively quickly, these data systems are likely to play a large role in shaping and refining policies in the near future and possibly change the political dynamics. These data systems introduce new transparency into the workings of education. How will they affect policymaking? Do states with highly developed data systems exhibit more evidence-based sequential policy development? Are the policy players more likely to coalesce around courses of action?

Technology is likely to play a larger role in education in the near future, as Smith and Smith discuss. While it is difficult to predict, it is probably likely that education will be less place-bound and perhaps more under the control of clients than providers. More alternatives in terms of curriculum, courses of study, and assessments will be open to students. What might the effects be in terms of who the policy players are and their interests and objectives?

Views and perceptions of the role of policy could also change. Jacobsen cites the work of Plank and Boyd (1994) who observed that public dissatisfaction with the performance of schools in the United States contributed to the public's willingness to consider alternative governance arrangements and to dispense with democratic governance. Such a climate made room for school choice, charter schools, and the use of education management firms as viable policy alternatives. Smith and Smith also discuss how the accumulation of research findings can shape world views and the thought environment that generates policy action. And in this era of globalization, international education comparisons may have a significant effect on views of appropriate education policy.

As Dylan says, "the times they are a-changin'." Education is in a time of flux; demands for better performance are coming from many corners of society. The old ways of doing business are being questioned. New demands, new players, and new information may possibly combine to usher in a new era of educational policymaking. While we should no doubt continue with the detailed analysis of the policy implementation that characterizes much of the research presented in this section, we should not lose sight of the bigger picture—the wider societal trends that are likely to have a great influence on the policy game itself and the types of policies likely to emerge.

Notes

1. *Zelman v. Simmons-Harris*, 2002.
2. *E.P. v. San Ramon Valley Unified School District*, 2007.

32

COMMENTARY
Getting "Critically Real"[1] About the State of Education Politics and Policy Process Research

V. Darleen Opfer
Cambridge University

The chapters in Section 3: "Politics and the Policy Process" demonstrate the vast range of topics, methods, and epistemological positions that exist in the field. My role, in this commentary, is not to try to create a meta-narrative that encompasses politics and policy processes as we currently understand them. Rather, my role here is as an "Under-Labourer in clearing the ground a little, and removing some of the rubbish, that lies in the way to knowledge" (Locke, 1690/1997, p. 11). My goals are therefore modest: to characterize the educational politics and policy process research as represented in the chapters in this section and to identify a "way to knowledge" in the future. In so doing, I hope to illustrate the ways that our research can address the common educational concerns of equity, efficiency, student learning, and educational outcomes, resulting in useful guidance for the design of effective educational policies.

To this end, I begin by characterizing educational politics and policy process research as being a "post-normal" policy domain that is dominated by high stakes, uncertain knowledge, and disputes over epistemological positions. Further, the dualistic separation of the field into structural versus agential research camps has rendered us unable to fully address many of the most pressing educational policy problems. I conclude my commentary by arguing for a transdisciplinary approach to educational politics and policy research in order to better address the complexity present in this post-normal domain.

Characterizing the Field as a Post-Normal Research Domain

The chapters in this section identify a series of issues over which there is much agreement in the educational policy process and politics research. The chapters in this section point out the virtual universality of education as a political enterprise:

- Politics and education intersect continually, and a neutral, objective educational practice is thus impossible (Torres & Van Heertum, p. 225).
- Arguments about vouchers have played out in political venues (Mead, p. 291).
- A dynamic set of political trends impacts assessment policy (Lindle, p. 319).

Politics in education, while acknowledged as a fundamental condition, is not considered by all the research to be negative. Jacobsen (this volume, citing Stone et al., 2001, p. 8) suggests that "Politics can also mean 'activity by which a diverse citizenry reconcile, put aside, or in some manner accommodate their differences in order to pursue their common well-being'" (p. 315). And Honig indicates, Politics are, "inherent, unavoidable, and arguably valuable dimension[s]" (p. 29).

However, many of the chapters have further shown that the political nature of education has expanded to the research itself with negative repercussions:

- [Research studies] often are shaped more by rhetoric and ideology than by disinterested, thorough inquiry (Koppich & Callahan, p. 304).
- The discourse about NCLB assessment was shaped primarily by political elites and national advocacy groups (Lindle, p. 324).
- [Policy research is] based primarily on politics (Smith & Smith, p. 378).
- [Research on collective bargaining is] "sparsely populated" and frequently polarized (Hannaway & Rotherman, 2006, cited in Koppich & Callahan, p. 297).
- Data is a political prisoner of governments, and we would add, of political ideologies as well (Torres & Van Heertum, p. 236).

In addition to the political aspects of the educational enterprise, each of the chapters identifies a raft of outstanding issues, many of them quite substantive and seemingly of foundational priority. For example, Smith and Smith summarize their chapter by discussing two enduring educational problems: improving achievement for students from low-income families and improving achievement and opportunities for all students. Similarly, West highlights how "gaps in basic skills along lines of ethnicity and income remain alarmingly wide" (p. 362). Jacobsen shows that there has been a steady erosion of public support for education and that this lower confidence is causing both exit and voice on the part of the public, thus imperiling education as a democratic institution.

We also seem to know much about what we do not know and less about how we might address some of these gaps. "The literature reflects a systemic weakness in understanding why reform efforts have not been more successfully sustained" (Datnow & Park, p. 359) and "determining effective instructional practices and measuring learning remains an elusive goal" (Datnow & Park, p. 354). Further, "little work has considered what the people want and why they are dissatisfied with what they are getting" (Jacobsen, p. 308). And, Koppich and Callahan contend, "We do not know nearly as much as we should from available research to be able to extract adequate data and craft worthwhile education policy. Nor do we know nearly as much as we should from available research and data to use the results…to improve education decision-making" (p. 296).

This combination of politics, complexity, and the immediacy of problems creates a post-normal policy domain. Funtowicz and Ravetz (1990) have characterized post-normal domains as those in which:

- decisions need to be made before conclusive evidence is available;
- the potential impacts of wrong decisions can be large;
- values are in dispute;
- the knowledge-base is characterized by large uncertainties, multi-causality, knowledge gaps, and imperfect understanding;
- research methods are dominated by models, cases, scenarios, perceptions, assumptions, and extrapolations; and
- hidden values reside in problem framing, chosen indicators and the research assumptions being made.

For example, Rosen (citing Rowan, 1984) characterizes education as an area where uncertainty, social conflict and distress are most evident. And Koppich and Callahan conclude that educational "policy makers are in the unenviable position of designing education policy on the basis of incomplete information, and points of view reinforced by a narrow range of research and stories in the popular press" (p. 304).

A combination of this post-normal situation and our current research practices results in less impact than we would wish for our research. Lindle, in an analysis of media coverage of assessment and accountability, contends that assessment researchers are portrayed in the coverage as reactors, critics or translators of assessment and accountability policies, but rarely as instigators of new ideas. She concludes from her analysis, "In very rare instances, assessment experts promoted policy direction such as expansion of accountability models and formative or summative testing" (p. 326). Smith and Smith also state that we "have very little effect on important educational outcomes" (p. 372).

While the methodologies developing in other post-normal policy contexts such as globalization, global warming, and HIV/AIDS may not be appropriate for studying education, the concept of post-normality is an apt one for the current state of our field. However, in recognizing education as a post-normal policy domain, we must acknowledge that identifying the educational truth in its entirety may be unfeasible; we must let go of our notions of speaking truth to power (Wildavsky, 1987) and expecting truth-based policy to emerge. We are unlikely to address the complex educational needs identified, or those that can be expected to emerge in the future, if we maintain entrenched epistemological positions. The chapters in this section portray a field of policy process and politics research that is dualistic, where research frameworks can be characterized as focusing *either* on the structures that impact education *or* on the agents of/in education.

Structural Versus Agential Dualism in Educational Politics and Policy Processes

The central split in the educational politics and policy process research is between those who appear committed to methodological individualism—the assumption that individuals act independently and make their own choices—and those who are committed to methodological holism—the assumption that structures such as social class, gender, ethnicity and norms limit or influence the opportunities available to individuals. Torres and Van Heertum identify that, "within education, neoliberal reforms have profoundly challenged holistic notions of education, replacing them with instrumental, corporate models" (p. 221). This split is demonstrated both across and within the chapters in this section.

Koppich and Callahan, while discussing theories of the role of unions in the collective bargaining process, illustrate the structural versus agential split. "One theory holds that unions are necessary to preserve and protect teachers' workplace rights, serve to advance the place of teachers as professionals, and further the cause of educational reform" (p. 296)—an agential notion of the role of unions. "A second and competing theory holds that unions are obstructionist organizations" (p. 296)—a structural notion of the place of unions in the educational context. Mickelson discusses "how students construct their racial identity" (p. 241), assuming an agential notion of race, yet also avows that these self-constructs depend on "social structural features in the student's environment" (p. 241). Honig and Datnow and Park illustrate the distinction between agential and structural epistemological positions in research on policy implementation by characterizing the two camps as those favoring "forward mapping" (assuming agency) and those favoring "backward mapping" (assuming structural impediments). Rosen (citing Kertzer, 1988, p. 42) reproduces this split in her own discussion by claiming "In capitalist countries this commonly entails attributing an individual's power position to his or her individual virtues—for example, intelligence or hard work—rather than conceiving of inequality as created and perpetuated by the economic system itself" (p. 272). Numerous other examples of structural or agential politics and policy process research are found in the chapters in this section. Further examples are provided in Table 32.1 below.

On their own, both epistemological positions lack the capacity to undertake the examination of complex, open systems such as education. And, Honig shows that "such typically mixed results may stem in part from the different methodologies researchers have used to derive their findings" (p. 333). With the structural research approach, there is a danger of it becoming critique qua critique and failing to achieve its emancipatory aims. Rorty (1989) claims "Socialisation [sic] … goes all the way down" (p. 185). In relying entirely on a methodology of holism, "man would be erased, like a face drawn in sand at the edge of the sea" (Foucault, 1970, p. 387). Thus, emancipation is asphyxiated by social forces (Archer, 2001).

Stovall illustrates this problem when he discusses the way a structural approach, specifically critical theory, was used in Chicago to help residents critique and ultimately stop the "revitalization" of inner-city neighborhoods and the construction of new schools built to attract middle-class families to them. While this was obviously a successful critique, the neighborhoods are still left unchanged, their residents have not been emancipated from poverty, crime,

low expectations, poor schools, and the limited futures that result from residing in these conditions. The residents stopped the city's hegemony but were not helped, within this structural approach, to develop a vision and a plan for transformational action. Likewise, in discussing prevalent theories used to account for the racial and ethnic gaps in student success, Mickelson highlights the uniformly structural orientation of these theories—from social reproduction theory to school characteristics to cultural capital to biological determinism. In so doing, Mickelson shows how each theory is unable to fully explain the persistent gap that remains.

Strict reliance on methodological individualism also has limitations. In agential research, we identify a pattern of events representing, hopefully, cause and effect. However, we do not produce a causal law that explains the complete reality of education or schooling. Rather, we produce a causal explanation of our research conditions. Agential research therefore assumes that events occur in a closed system. It thus presupposes that objects of study are intransitive. Agential researchers collapse evidence of reality with reality itself. In so doing, they make it virtually impossible to identify all the mechanisms beyond agency which may account for outcomes and effects.

Rosen identifies the problems with strict agentialism when she describes "policy analyses typically focus[ing] on the purposes and functions of policies and the extent to which they produce the outcomes stated or intended by their creators. This emphasis has led policy analysts to adopt a 'naïve rationalism'" (p. 267, citing Cohen & Rosenberg, 1977, p. 136). Jacobsen also identifies "fundamental measurement issues with each of the existing surveys which makes it impossible to accurately determine how the public views educational priorities or what the public says it wants from the school system" (p. 311). The main problem with these data "is that people were asked to evaluate one goal in isolation" (p. 312). As Torres and Van Heertum conclude,

TABLE 32.1
Structural and Agential Research in Education Politics and Policy Process

Examples of the Structural Approach to Education Politics and Policy Process Research	Examples of the Agential Approach to Education Politics and Policy Process Research
"Marshall McLuhan, in his seminal book *Understanding Media*, came to a similar conclusion, placing media and technology at the center of reality, controlling individuals who simply adapt to their imperatives and rationality." (Torres & Van Heertum, p. 223)	"Legal scholarship seeks to construct a legal theory that might be used to move jurisprudential thinking in one direction or another." (Mead, p. 288)
Stovall, in discussing gentrification by upper middle-class African-American families in low income African-American neighborhoods, claims, "it should be understood as a complex system of oppressions where members of historically oppressed racial groups can be individually rewarded to enact and enforce the policies of the dominant society." (p. 263)	Koppich and Callahan discuss the predominant econometric methodology used to analyze teacher collective bargaining contract outcomes but show that this singular method fails to account for the process and contextual variability that mediate these outcomes.
Mickelson (citing Matute-Bianchi 1986, 2008) identifies generational issues, ethnicity, social class, English-language proficiency, and immigration status (all structural conditions) as shaping Latino/a educational achievement, attainment and outcomes (agential conditions). Mickelson also shows that patterns of achievement among Whites are also influenced by the structural conditions of social class and gender.	"Public choice is distinguished from traditional approaches to the study of political behavior by…*methodological individualism*. The basic unit of analysis is the individual political actor." (West, p. 362, emphasis in original)

"attempts to adopt the methods of [agency] have led toward scientism, where intellectual work cultivated by specialists fragmented knowledge and extricated it from broader social phenomena" (p. 229).

The problems identified here go beyond the recognized split between qualitative and quantitative research (Hammersley, 1993; Salomon, 1991; Howe & Eisenhart, 1990) and between post-positivists and post-modernists (Schick, 1999; Schrag, 1992). It requires more than a call for the use of mixed methods (Johnson & Onwuegbuzie, 2004) to resolve the post-normal policy problems we face. The dualist split between structural and agential research in education politics and policy process represents epistemological disagreements about knowledge of education which have been acknowledged in the quantitative versus qualitative and post-positivist versus.. post-modernist literature. However, these arguments reproduce the "epistemic fallacy" (Bhaskar, 1997, p. 36) and suppose that the ontology of education itself can be transposed through resolving the epistemological debate. As Datnow and Park successfully argue "Clearly, educational reform involves formal structures, such as district offices, state policies, and so on. It also involves both formal and informal linkages among those structures. Yet, reform involves a dynamic relationship, not just among structures but also among cultures and people's actions in many interlocking settings. It is this intersection of culture, structure, and individual agency across contexts that helps us better understand how to build positive instances of educational reform" (p. 359).

Integrating the Structural and the Agential in Education Policy Research

At a basic level, elements in education policy research cross the structural and agential divide—it is not an either/or policy domain. The chapters in this section have clearly described the ways in which various aspects of the educational enterprise can act as *both* generative structures that support/impede educational progress *and* as agents responsible for outcomes, effects, and the reproduction of the existing structures. One of the dilemmas identified by Datnow and Park is that "policy can be successfully implemented in terms of fidelity to procedures but executing policy faithfully does not mean that it will produce intended outcomes" (p. 349). Because elements of the educational context cross this "false" divide, research and research outcomes currently appear at odds with one another, with each epistemological position making claims to knowledge supremacy. However, if we start seeing them as each providing part of the puzzle, we may begin to develop a fuller understanding of the multi-causal, multivariate nature of educational politics and policy processes. As the sociologist Margaret Archer (2001) has indicated, "Both humanity and society have their own sui generis properties and powers, which makes their interplay the central issue of social theory for all time" (p. 17).

Many of the authors of the chapters in this section rec-

ognize this need and call for such an approach for future research on educational politics and policy processes. Stovall says, we need "'engaged researchers' where theoretical assumptions are secondary to the experiential knowledge of the groups in question" (p. 260, citing Knofke, 1997, p. 61). Koppich and Callahan argue that "both theories have merit and neither alone is entirely accurate … because the two theories represent opposite poles," (p. 296) and that "the challenge of researchers is to examine under what conditions some of these assumptions may be true and what other factors interact with these assumptions. The task is daunting but not impossible" (p. 303). Rosen avers that "different models, moreover, draw attention to different kinds of phenomena and away from others. Thus, research methods should be understood as tools for mapping or modeling, not mirroring, the social and natural world" (p. 279).

The Need for Transdisciplinary Research in Education Policy and Politics

Because of the dualistic nature of the research on educational politics and policy, guidance for the design of effective educational policies has been limited. The field suffers from a severe case of epistemic fallacy—where knowledge about education has been confused with the reality of education. This epistemic fallacy results in incomplete understandings of that thing with which we are all concerned—education. While there has been a loud call for more scientific knowledge on education, a primary omission from this call is an understanding of the way scientific knowledge accumulates. Rarely in the natural sciences would you find an instance where one theory, explanation, or type of knowledge is simply overthrown by another. Rather, incorporation is the key mechanism of the scientific process—scientists develop more inclusive views of a problem by incorporating new information into previously existing theories (Bhaskar, 1998; Kuhn, 1970).

Natural scientists are also finding themselves with more post-normal scientific problems as well. For example, at the advent of genetic studies, geneticists held out the belief that genes could be identified as specific causal agents for disease. More recently, geneticists have come to understand that a specific disease is often the result of hundreds of different genes interacting with an infinite number of environmental factors. In this vein, psychologists and geneticists working together at the University of Virginia have identified poverty (an environmental factor) as having a negative impact on IQ (a factor thought to be genetic). However, they have been unable to identify specific elements of poverty that have the biggest impact on IQ—in fact, no single poverty factor accounts for much variation in IQ. Ultimately, the researchers conclude that they are not close to identifying a linear causal connection (A leads to B) and because poverty has a holistic impact, they probably never will (Turkheimer, Haley, D'Onofrio, Waldon, & Gottesman, 2003).

Recognizing the cumulative nature of knowledge

production and the growing post-normal character of scientific problems, the natural sciences have begun to identify the need for transdisciplinary research as a way to understand causality. As "trans" indicates, transdisciplinarity[2] is concerned with that which is between the disciplines, across the disciplines, and beyond each individual discipline. The goal of transdisciplinary research is the understanding of the present world and it assumes that to achieve this, an overarching unity of knowledge is imperative. Transdisciplinarity is not a super- or supra-discipline, it is constituted by disciplinary research. In turn, disciplinary research is furthered and clarified by the cumulative nature of transdisciplinary research. In this sense, disciplinary and transdisciplinary research are not antagonistic but complementary. Transdisciplinary research does not attempt to resolve or dismiss contradictory perspectives of the world, but instead it incorporates multiple viewpoints into the same problem-solving process (Gibbons, Limoges, Schwartzman, Scott, & Trow, 1994; Scott & Gibbons, 2001).

Some of the authors in this section have identified the importance of knowledge accumulation to achieving our aims of providing useful guidance to the resolution of post-normal problems in education policy. Honig argues that "the challenge for education policy implementation researchers then becomes how to uncover the various factors that combine to produce implementation results and to *accumulate* enough cases over time to reveal potentially predictable patterns" (p. 338, emphasis added). Smith and Smith show in their chapter that "in most examples of the use of research in policy, no single study can be identified as the principal causal influence. Rather, the *accumulation of knowledge* and relevant examples lead to a gradually increasing understanding" (p. 374, emphasis added). John Dewey also understood the importance of such an approach to educational policy research: "When a certain state of accumulated knowledge, of techniques and instrumentalities is obtained, the process of change is so accelerated, that, it appears externally to be the dominant trait" (Dewey, Hickman, & Alexander, 1998, p. 299).

For educational politics and policy process research to adopt a transdisciplinary approach will require considering more purposefully the ways that structure and agency interplay in educational contexts. It will also mean recognizing more fully "that agents at all levels contribute to the policymaking process and that that process is characterized by continuous interaction among agents and actors within and between levels of the system" (Datnow & Park, p. 351) and that "the causal arrow of change travels in multiple directions among active participants in all domains of the system and over time" (Datnow & Park, pp. 351–352). More importantly however, it means recognizing that different types of knowledge are necessary if we are to be more successful. As an example of what is needed, Rosen, in making a case for symbolic analysis of education policy states that it "should complement, rather than supplant, more instrumentally oriented studies" (p. 280).

As Smith and Smith conclude, "Too often we forget the obvious fact that we hold enormous amounts of knowledge

about the factors and conditions that enable and support student learning, make up powerful teaching, motivate or discourage students, and explain why some schools and districts are effective, efficient organizations and why others are not" (p. 379). It is time that the field of educational politics and policy process research remembers this and shifts from a reductionist, dualistic, research-camp mentality toward a transdisciplinary, cumulative field.

Notes

1. This commentary is heavily influenced by my participation in the Principles of Critical Realism for Education Workshop, Sessions I–V, conducted at the Institute of Education, London, July 18–20, 2008, by Roy Bhaskar.
2. Piaget is credited with coining the term *transdisciplinarity* at the Organization for Economic Cooperation and Development (OECD) workshop, *Interdisciplinarity—Problems of Teaching and Research in Universities,* held in Nice, France, September 7–12, 1970.

References

Archer, M. (2001). *Being human: The problem of agency.* Cambridge, UK: Cambridge University Press.

Bhaskar, R. (1998). The logic of scientific discovery. In M. Archer, R. Bhaskar, A. Collier, T. Lawson, & A. Norrie (Eds.), *Critical realism: Essential readings* (pp. 48–103). London: Routledge.

Bhaskar, R. (1997). *A realist theory of science.* London: Verso.

Dewey, J., Hickman, L., & Alexander, T. (1998). *The essential Dewey, Vol. 1: Pragmatism, education and democracy.* Bloomington: Indiana University Press.

Foucault, M. (1970). *The order of things.* New York: Random House.

Funtowicz, S., & Ravetz, J. (1990). *Uncertainty and quality in science for policy.* Netherlands: Kluwer.

Gibbons, M., Limoges, C., Schwartzman, S., Scott, P., & Trow, M. (1994). *The new production of knowledge: The dynamics of science and research in contemporary societies.* London: Sage.

Hammersley, M. (Ed.). (1993). *Social research: Philosophy, politics and practice.* Newbury Park, CA: Sage.

Howe, K., & Eisenhart, M. (1990). Standards for qualitative (and quantitative) research: A prolegomenon. *Educational Researcher, 19*(4), 2–9.

Johnson, R. B., & Onwuegbuzie, A. (2004). Mixed methods research: A research paradigm whose time has come. *Educational Researcher, 33*(7), 14–26.

Kuhn, T. (1970). *The structure of scientific revolutions.* Chicago: University of Chicago Press.

Locke, J. (1997). *An essay concerning human understanding.* New York: Penguin Classics. (Original work published 1690)

Rorty, R. (1989). *Contindency, irony and solidarity.* Cambridge, UK: Cambridge University Press.

Salomon, G. (1991). Transcending the qualitative-quantitative debate: The analytic and systemic approaches to educational research. *Educational Researcher, 20*(6), 10–18.

Schick, T. (1999). *Readings in the philosophy of science: From positivism to postmodernism.* New York: McGraw-Hill Humanities.

Schrag, F. (1992). In defense of positivist research paradigms. *Educational Researcher, 21*(5), 5–8.

Scott, P., & Gibbons, M. (2001). *Re-thinking science: Knowledge and the public in an age of uncertainty.* Cambridge, UK: Polity Press.

Stone, C. N., Henig, J. R., Jones, B. D., & Pierannunzi, C. (2001). *Building civic capacity: The politics of reforming urban schools.* Lawrence: The University of Kansas Press.

Turkheimer, E., Haley, A., D'Onofrio, B., Waldon, M., & Gottesman, I. (2003). Socioeconomic status modifies heritability of IQ in young children. *Psychological Science, 14,* 623–628.

Wildavsky, A. (1987). *Speaking truth to power: Art and craft of policy analysis.* Edison, NJ: Transaction Publishers.

Section IV

Policy Implications of Educational Resources, Management, and Organization

SECTION EDITOR: LINDA SKRLA

33

Notes on Reframing the Role of Organizations in Policy Implementation

Resources for *Practice,* in *Practice*[1]

JAMES P. SPILLANE, LOUIS M. GOMEZ, AND LEIGH MESLER

Northwestern University

Introduction

Scholars have long recognized that local factors dominate the policy implementation process (McLaughlin, 1987, 1990). Despite the ever-increasing presence of state and federal agencies in educational policymaking, local conditions still appear critical to policy implementation (Cohen, 1990; Coburn, 2001; Fullan, 1991; Hill, 2001; Elmore & Fuhrman, 1995; Firestone, Fitz, & Broadfoot, 1999; Spillane, 2004). This is to be expected, especially considering that state and federal policy makers have developed an unprecedented appetite for influencing the core work of schools—teaching and learning. Several decades of educational policymaking designed to bring systemic reform through the development of standards-based curricula and increasing use of student testing to hold teachers and administrators accountable all reflect efforts to more tightly couple policy to instruction. State and federal agencies that had mostly taken a "hands-off," or at least "an arms-length," approach on instruction developed policies that held locals accountable for what teachers taught, acceptable levels of mastery, and in some cases even how teachers taught. But as state and federal policy makers' appetite for instructional improvement increased, local educators were still left to figure out the particulars of improvement and procure the resources for these efforts.

Under these changed policy circumstances, it is not surprising that policy implementation still depends in important measure on local conditions. These conditions are often described in terms of the capacity and will (or motivation) of local actors and agencies (Firestone, 1989; McLaughlin, 1990). Local actors such as teachers and administrators are important to the successful implementation of education policy; after all, while the practice of these local actors may be the problem policy makers seek to ameliorate it is also the case that these very same actors are the primary agents through which policy can enable change in instruction (Cohen, 1990).

Still, teachers and administrators do not practice in a vacuum; they work in organizations and these organizations influence their practice for better or worse. More specifically, the circumstances of local practice are intimately connected to how local actors encounter and perceive the policy directives of federal and state agencies. While these organizational circumstances are similar in many respects from one local jurisdiction to another, they also differ. For example, as might be expected in a federal system where local government is still a major source of funding, some organizations are much better endowed than others in terms of conventional resources such as money and curricular materials.

While individuals on their own are important in understanding how policy is interpreted and adapted into local daily practice, the social and physical arrangements of their work is also influential. A cursory review of the literature suggests a laundry list of organizational arrangements and conditions that enable and constrain efforts to implement policy and educational reform in general. These include but are not limited to: resources such as human capital and curricular materials, workplace norms including trust and collective responsibility for student achievement, leadership support, local will or motivation, and organizational arrangements that de-privatize the core work and support collaboration among staff (see, e.g., Berman & McLaughlin, 1977; Bidwell, 1965; Bryk & Driscoll, 1985; Newmann & Wehlage, 1995; Rosenholtz, 1989; Lieberman, Falk, & Alexander, 1994; Little, 1982, 1993; Lortie, 1977; Spillane & Thompson, 1998). Scholars have identified these and other organizational "conditions" as important in understanding the success or failure of instructional reform initiatives whether they are orchestrated through government agencies, some extra-system agency, or even from within the local school system. The literature is vast and originates from different subfields in education including educational administration, policy implementation, curriculum and instruction, teacher work contexts, and the school organization.

In this chapter we revisit the local organization and its role in policy implementation. Rather than review the literature, our goal is to sketch a (re)framing of this familiar terrain in the hope of influencing future empirical work in the area of organizations and policy implementation. We use "sketch" intentionally as we broadly outline our ideas for reframing the role of local organizations in policy implementation rather than fleshing out in-depth each particular component of the framework. Our goal is to generate discussion.

Our framing is as follows: Policy typically involves planned change though it is sometimes prompted by unplanned change and often has to contend with unplanned change as it is apprehended by locals in schools, district offices, and extra-system organizations. These local organizations matter in the implementation of policy makers' planned changes. We argue for a particular way of thinking about the role of these local organizations in policy implementation. First, we conceptualize organization as *organizing* and argue for exploring dyadic and triadic subunit interactions as the basic unit for understanding the role of organizations in policy implementation (Weick, 1979). Rather than centering our frame on formal organizational structures, our approach foregrounds *practice*—an emergent property of the interactions among two or more individuals as mediated by aspects of the situation. Hence, our framing includes interactions among individuals both within organizations (e.g., school, district office, professional development provider) and interactions among individuals in different organizations; work practice as we conceptualize it can extend across formal organizational boundaries. Second, our framing centers on resources for and in practice. Specifically, we see resources as both constitutive of and constituted in practice; that is, resources such as human capital and social capital (among others) structure interactions among people while at the same time these resources are defined and potentially redefined in practice. To understand this relationship, we argue for attention to both the ostensive and performative aspects of resources (Feldman & Pentland, 2003; Latour, 1986). Whereas the ostensive aspect of a resource serves as a sort of broad script for the resource, the performative aspect refers to the resource in practice in particular places at particular times. Third, in addition to resource distribution, our framing attends to resource access and activation by putting practice center stage.

Thus, we begin by examining "change" and "organization"—two key constructs in the study of the role of local organizations in policy implementation. Our discussion points to the complexity of the term *change* and, following Karl Weick (1979), argues for thinking about organizations in terms of organizing. Next, we argue for thinking about organizing and implementation in terms of resources; that is, resources that enable and constrain practice as it unfolds in the interactions among two or more people. Resources are constellations of physical, financial, human, and social assets that individuals and organiza-

tions use to accomplish their work. We argue for thinking about resources as having both ostensive and performative aspects. We then develop our argument, based on a scan of the literature, by focusing on four key resources: (a) human capital, (b) social capital, (c) technology, and (d) organizational routines. These resources feature prominently in the literature on organizational change in general and we consider how they might be differentially distributed, accessed and activated through policy. Our list of resources is illustrative rather than exhaustive. Some of the resources we attend to have received considerable attention in work on educational policy implementation, others have figured less prominently. We conclude with a discussion of what our sketching and musing might suggest for research that focuses on understanding the nexus of policy implementation and organizations.

Change and Organization

Discussions of policy implementation would be difficult without the words "change" and "organization." Policy analysts, policy makers, and practitioners often use these terms with an ease that belies their ambiguity. Some taken as shared understanding of these core constructs is essential if we are to engage in meaningful and fruitful discussions of policy implementation and organizations. Our goal in this section is to underscore the ambiguity surrounding these constructs.

What Change for Policy Analysis?   Change is a constant in school systems. It comes in many forms. Change is sometimes intentional, but other times not. Some change is of the revolutionary sort, but change is often, perhaps even mostly, evolutionary rather than revolutionary, gradually creeping up on us and on the organizations we inhabit. Of course, gradual change that often goes unnoticed at any point in time can over time culminate in dramatic unforeseen changes in schools and school systems. Change is ubiquitous in school systems but our ease with employing the term belies its slippery nature and many forms.

Policy is an intentional effort on the part of government agencies to change existing behavior or practice. And, for policy analysts, a key concern is whether practice changes in a direction that is roughly analogous with policy makers' intentions. One analytic distinction we make is between planned change and unplanned change (Poole, 2004). Scholarship on organizations typically focuses on change in one of two ways—theories of change and theories of changing (Bennis, 1966; Poole, 2004). Unplanned change is typically not the result of some design decision by an organizational member or some external agent or agency. Planned change involves a conscious design effort by policy makers or school reformers to transform some existing way of doing things in schools. Policy makers—mostly though not always, sometimes their motives are symbolic—want to bring about change in how the agents and agencies they target behave or practice. In this respect, policy is mostly about planned change—it seeks to change practice in schools and school districts.

Policy analysis then is about the study of the planned change orchestrated by policy makers. In these accounts, schools and local school districts are often portrayed as hostile to change—bastions of constancy. As a result, implementation scholarship often reads as laments for policy failure—that is, the failure of schools and local school systems to change in response to policy makers' "good" intentions—their planned change. Constancy and change—often of the unplanned sort—is the rule rather than the exception in local school systems.

Still, policy scholars cannot ignore unplanned change. To begin with, policy makers are sometimes prompted by unplanned change—a widening achievement gap, declining student achievement, a teacher shortage, changing demographics in a neighborhood or city, an increase in fertility in a jurisdiction, and so on—to make policy. Continuous, evolutionary change that often goes unnoticed—neighborhood or city demographics that shift slowly but surely over a decade—with time can produce dramatic and unplanned changes that prompt policy makers to act. Further, policy makers' planned changes frequently butt heads with unplanned change in the organizations it targets. As planned change, policy plays out in organizations where unplanned change is a constant.

Policy makers often fail to take into account that their planned changes are meant to percolate or trickle down into organizations where change is a constant. They often appear to work on an outdated model of organizational change where freezing, changing, and refreezing is the standard operating procedure (Lewin, 1951; Kanter, 1983), rather than the model of where change is a constant. As Rosabeth Kanter (1992) puts it, planned change is better conceptualized as being about grabbing part of the constant motion in an organization and steering it so that the members of the organization will interpret it as a new way of "doing business." In this view, policy is an attempt to harness and nudge the continuous unplanned change in local schools and school systems in a particular direction. Understanding and fomenting planned change necessitates careful attention to unplanned change—you cannot understand one without the other.

In considering change, planned or unplanned, it is important to not forget about constancy; it is a critical ingredient in understanding change in organizations. *Some* things change, and *other* things remain the same. Larry Cuban captures it most aptly in the title to his book *Change and Constancy...* (Cuban, 1988). Change and constancy co-exist in organizations; close relatives rather than the distant cousins. Many of us who labor in the implementation research vineyard tend to be preoccupied with the constancy in the wake of the planned changes we investigate. As James March (1981) notes, "changes in organizations depend on a few stable processes. Theories of change emphasize either the stability of the processes or the changes they produce, but a serious understanding of organizations requires attention

to both" (p. 563). Change and constancy go together, and we need to treat them accordingly.

Planned change—even when successfully implemented—never eradicates the past in its attempts to craft the future. Policy makers' grand designs do not play out on blank slates, rather they are layered on and entangled in current ways of doing things. In this way, the past lives even when things change. In those immortal words of Faulkner (1951, p. 92), "The past is never dead. In fact, it's not even past."

Policy makers try to orchestrate planned change by manipulating resources. But what policy makers rarely do is take account of the fact that organizations are not frozen but in constant motion (Kanter, Stein, & Jick, 1992). Policy makers do not acknowledge this constant because it is much easier to imagine frozen organizations that will be subjected to policy and then unfrozen. Further, for policy makers' to acknowledge unplanned change would amount to recognizing the limits of policy in enabling planned change in a constantly changing world. But planned change is perhaps best thought about as trying to tap into, capitalize on, align with, and nudge different elements of the unplanned change in organizations. Unplanned change and planned change are about the intentional and unintentional alignment of resources.

Consider, for example, human capital—a critical resource for policy implementation. Over time policy makers have attempted to influence human capital in schools mostly by focusing on teacher quality. Most recently, the federal government, through No Child Left Behind (NCLB) and other initiatives, has put in place a series of policies intended to ensure that every American child would have a quality teacher. But the quality of America's teaching force is a product of an array of factors (many of them unplanned or the consequences of prior policies beyond the education sector) that are difficult to nudge let alone control from the halls of congress or even the statehouse. Moreover, these unplanned changes are often localized such as the supply of high quality teachers in larger urban centers (Reininger, 2006).

What Organization for Policy Implementation? In education policy implementation, the notion of organization is ambiguous. Some readers may have assumed that by local organization in the preceding discussion we mean the school. There is good reason for such thinking; much of the literature on organizations and instructional improvement has focused on the schoolhouse. Much of the literature dwells on the school organization, suggesting that the school is the key local organizational unit in instructional reform (Bidwell, 1970; Bryk & Driscoll, 1985; Lortie, 1977; Meyer & Rowan, 1977; Purkey & Smith, 1983). Strong instructional leadership, trust among teachers and among teachers and administrators, and a sense of collective responsibility for students learning can create incentives and opportunities for teachers to implement policy and revise their practice (Bryk & Schneider, 2002). In our reference to local organizational circumstances in the introduction, however, we have intentionally not confined ourselves to the schoolhouse. We also mean local school systems—the Local Education Agency (LEA), commonly referred to as the school district with its school board and district central office.

Schools are situated in LEAs that research suggests are influential in the implementation process (Berman & McLaughlin, 1977; Elmore & McLaughlin, 1988; Spillane, 1996, 1998; Supovitz, 2007). District administrators' "constant and active support" for a reform is a necessary condition for local implementation (Berman & McLaughlin, 1978, p. 33). The LEA as a government jurisdiction and its administrative wing—the district office—are important aspects of the local organization when it comes to policymaking and policy implementation. District offices' organizational arrangements can be consequential for policy implementation (Spillane, 1996, 1998). Some larger LEAs have district offices with multiple subunits for assessment, human resources, professional development, school subjects, compensatory education, and so on, a product of what John Meyer (1983) calls "fragmented centralization." Each subunit with its own responsibilities and jurisdictions often works relatively independently of one another and posing challenges for state and federal policies that attempt to align the guidance about instruction that teachers are given (Spillane, 1998).

Looking within the schoolhouse, what counts as the relevant unit of analysis for examining the role of the organization in implementation is also murky. Most scholars focus on either the attributes of teachers and administrators or on school level attributes which they typically measure by aggregating up the responses of school staff to say something about the organizational conditions in the school. While those who focus on the individual focus on things such as expertise or years of experience, those who focus on the organization examine things like social trust or collective responsibility. Both approaches have merit but together they miss or gloss over another key organizational dimension—the subgroup or subunit within schools.

At the high school level, subject matter departments can be an important context for teachers' work (Ball & Lacey, 1984; Little, 1993; McLaughlin & Talbert, 1993; Siskin, 1990, 1991, 1994). High school teachers differ in their conceptions of the subjects they teach, and these differences have consequences for curricular practices such as teachers' control of content and curriculum coordination and standardization, differences that may mediate the influence of reform on practice (Stodolsky & Grossman, 1995). In a study of high school departments in the United Kingdom, Ball (1981) showed that teachers' responses to a multi-ability classroom initiative varied by subject departments; the English department embraced the initiative while foreign language teachers argued against the reform. Even beyond the high school with its departmentalized structure around school subjects, subgroups of staff within a school are likely a critical organizational dimension in any investi-

gation of implementation (Penuel, Frank, & Krause, 2006; Hayton & Spillane, 2008).

To put one final wrinkle on what counts as the organization at the local level, various extra-system agencies and agents are also an important consideration (Burch, 2007; Cohen, 1982; Hill, 1999; Rowan, 2006). Teachers' participation in professional networks that extend beyond the schoolhouse are often critical to the implementation of reform (Huberman, 1995; Talbert & McLaughlin, 1994; Little, 1993). This is especially the case in professional organizations where linkages to professional networks that transcend organizational boundaries are common (Clark, 1983; Scott & Cohen, 1995). Various other for-profit and non-profit agencies also thrive right alongside local school systems, offering an expanding array of goods and services to the formal system. Local school systems have long relied on these extra-system agencies for services such as student assessment. But the number of these agencies and the services and goods they offer have expanded many fold over the past several decades. Local school systems can now purchase from testing companies systems that enable teachers to engage in formative assessment of their students in preparation for annual tests. Moreover, an array of firms have emerged that offer school systems more or less comprehensive models for school improvement. Any effort to understand change in schools would be remiss without serious attention to these extra-system organizations (Rowan, 2006; Hill, 2007)—some local, others national or even international—but all interacting with local school organizations, thought the intimacy of these interactions vary, sometimes tremendously. Moreover, these extra-system organizations can influence the resources critical for school improvement and policy implementation.

What counts as the relevant unit of analysis then with respect to the nexus of policy implementation and organizational behavior is not immediately obvious. Further, we contend that the interactions among these various levels of the local school system and the extra system are paramount for examining the nexus of organizations and policy implementation. Investigations that focus on one level—the high school department or grade level, the school building, or district office—while foregrounding that particular level need to be sensitive to other levels and how they interact with the level under investigation. We argue for a reframing of how we think about organizations and policy implementation by taking up the challenge posed by Karl Weick (1979) and thinking about organizing (rather than organizations)—"a consensually validated grammar for reducing equivocality by means of sensible interlocked behaviors" (p. 3). Weick argues that small units such as double interacts, dyads, and triads are "sensible as places to understand the major workings of organizations" (p. 236). Such an approach enables us to conduct analysis that cuts across organizational boundaries (e.g., school—school district or school—external consultant) and that is driven by a consideration of work practice as it unfolds in the interactions among people.

While many of the examples we use in the following sections reference the school building, we believe that taking into account the multiple levels of the system, the extra system, and their interactions is critical in understanding the nexus of organizations and policy implementation. Interactions among people both within organizations (e.g., district office and extra-system organizations) as well as interactions that cut across these units shape the distribution of, access to, and activation of resources that matter for policy implementation. Focusing on resources enables analysts to move back and forth among different levels of the local school system, and the extra system and lends itself to a consideration of organizing rather than organization. Resources are useful analytical lens because they offer a common frame that can be applied across different levels while simultaneously allowing us to examine how they become instantiated in practice in different ways depending on the level and interactions. Moreover, the focus on resources underscores the inter-dependency among levels of the system and the extra system.

An institutional perspective is helpful here in that it acknowledges that all levels of social aggregation from sub-groups within schools to the district office and extra-system agents and agencies have the potential to influence how people work (Bidwell, 2006; Rowan & Miskel, 1999). These systems of human interaction provide "cognitive, normative, and regulative structures and activities … that provide stability and meaning" to work practice (Scott, 1995, p. 33). Institutional theorists have tended to over-play aggregation and determinism (DiMaggio, 1988), curtailing the frames usefulness for investigating leadership practice. Focusing on institutional sectors, institutional theory has stressed the emergence of dominant organizational forms rather than work practice in particular organizations and smothering attention to human agency in the process (Whittington, 1991). By not attending to the micro-processes through which people in organizations make sense of, and enact their environments of which policy is an element, institutional theory runs the risk of being overly deterministic (Dimaggio & Powell, 1991; Powell & Colyvas, 2008). Further, as Powell and Colyvas (2008) state, "institutional analysis needs more attention to everyday processes than momentous events" (p. 277). In our framing, a focus on work practice enables us to engage and examine everyday processes.

Our account to this point underscores that "change" and "organization" are complex and ambiguous constructs. Any effort to understand how local organizations mediate relations between policy and classroom instruction must first grapple with settling on working definitions of these core constructs. We offered a particular take on both constructs.

Policy Implementation, Practice, and Resources

The term *organizational behavior* should not be taken too literally. Organizations after all do not implement policy. People in schools and school districts do. Still, it is important to think about the behavior or more accurately, the interactions, of people in organizations as more than the sum of their parts. Hence, we focus on practice rather than organizational or individual behavior in organizations. In our view, practice is constituted or defined in interactions among people and is not equivalent to the actions of an individual or a set of behaviors. It is in the interactions among the men and women in the district office, schoolhouse, and other organizations who make sense of policy and figure out something by way of response to their understandings of that policy.

Organizational members are not free agents; their sense-making and practice is shaped or structured by the organizations in which they work. Though frequently used in sociology and related fields the concept of structure has definitional problems. Some scholars focus on institutional structure, others relational structure, and still others on embodied structure (Lopez & Scott, 2000). Some perspectives (Althusser, 1971) overplay the determinism of organizational structure smothering human agency (for critiques, see Giddens, 1984; Weick, 1995; Rowan & Miskel, 1999). Structure is necessary for human practice (Archer, 1995). But, structure should not be construed as determining practice in organizations, at least not exclusively. Following Giddens (1979, 1984), we view structure as both the medium and the outcome of practice. Practice is constituted by organizational structure (and indeed broader societal social structure) that provides the rules and resources upon which it is based. At the same time practice is constitutive of organizational structure as it is created, reproduced, and potentially transformed in practice by human agents in interaction (Giddens, 1979). The structural properties that enable practice in organizations exist as they are "instantiated in activity" or remembered as rules of conduct or "rights to resources" (Whittington, 1992, p. 696).

We use the term *practice* to refer to patterns of behavior that emerge from people's interactions with each other, as mediated by aspects of the situation over time (Bourdieu, 1981). Hence, practice is not a synonym for best practices or strategies or individual actions, because ignoring the situation disconnects behavior from the "urgency of practice" (Bourdieu, 1980/1990). Individuals act, but they do so in relation to others—and it is in these interactions that practice takes form in organizations. Although practice unfolds in the present, it is tied to the past as people draw on a logic that is informed by their past interactions (Bourdieu, 1980/1990, p. 86). While actions are obviously important in understanding practice, interactions are paramount. Our framing of practice then departs from the rather narrow psychological framing of cognition and behavior. Rather than equating practice with the actions of individual school staff—school principal, assistant principal, literacy coach, teacher—we see school work practice as fundamentally about interactions among people, interactions that are mediated by aspects of the situation (Spillane, 2006; Spillane & Diamond, 2007). We can think of at least some of these aspects of the situation as resources.

Practice is resource-dependent. For example, the practice that we might observe at a school improvement planning meeting as participants toil to define a set of problems to work on for the coming school year will depend, in part, on the knowledge and skill of the staff present, their trust of one another, the data they have available about their school, and so on. Of course, the availability of these resources is not everything. Some people, by virtue of their position, may not have access to some resources. Further, the knowledge and skill of certain individuals may not be activated; a junior teacher with extensive expertise on a topic critical to the school improvement planning process may feel it is not in her best interest to use her knowledge and skill. Practice depends in important measure on the distribution of, access to, and activation of resources.

Below we define what we mean by resources. We then conceptualize resources through a bipartite lens that allows for both structure and agency. We consider the public or idealized characterization of the resource—its ostensive aspect and we consider what people do with the resource in particular places and at particular times—its performative aspect (Feldman & Pentland, 2003). Using this frame, we consider four organizational resources—human capital, social capital, technology, and organizational routines— examining how they enable and constrain practice and thereby policy implementation. We also consider whether and how they might be influenced through public policy.

Organizational Resources: Ostensive and Performative Aspects We conceptualize organizational structure in terms of resources that enable and constrain practice. A focus on resources has at least two advantages. First, it underscores that organizational structure is dynamic and not necessarily fixed or static. Second, it gives us traction on how that structure can simultaneously be both constitutive of and constituted in practice. Resources enable us to bridge two distinctly different perspectives on how organizations matter in practice and thereby for policy implementation.

As noted earlier, we define resources as a constellation of physical, financial, human, and social assets that people, both individually and collectively, used to accomplish organizational work. For resources to effect an organization's output they must be available *and* they have to be *recognized* and *used* by organizational members. For organizational members to use resources they have to have some awareness of them. Cohen, Raudenbush, and Ball (2003) argue that what students and teachers do with resources is as important as the resources with which they work. Resources work in the improvement of student achievement only if are recognized and used by administrators, teachers, and indeed students (Cohen et al., 2003; Hanushek, 1998). We argue that the same holds for organizational resources in work practice in schools, district offices, and other organizations.

Building on Latour's work (1986), we can think about resources as having two aspects—an ostensive aspect and a performative aspect (see also, Feldman & Pentland, 2003).

The *ostensive aspect* is the abstract, generalized idea of the resource (Feldman & Pentland, 2003). The ostensive aspect serves as a script for the resource, the resource as designed or intended. It is the resource "by the book" or ideal form of its design. The performative aspect refers to the resource in use in particular places and at particular times. It is the performative aspect of a resource that allows for agency as the resource is used, in practice, in particular situations at particular times (Feldman & Pentland, 2003).

Hence, to understand how policy implementation is enabled and constrained by the local organizations we must examine the role that resources play in daily practice in these local organizations. The issue is *how* resources are both constitutive of and constituted in practice. By and large, policy (especially from the policy makers' perspective) centers on the ostensive aspect. However, on the ground it is how people make sense of—notice and understand— the resource, distributed by policy, and use it in practice that is important for policy implementation. Thus to get analytic traction we must attend to both the ostensive and performaive aspects of resources and, most importantly the relations between the two.

Resources do not determine practice. Rather, people draw on resources through which they deploy strategies of action to address issues they face (Swidler, 1986). In this way resources from human capital to organizational routines might be conceptualized as, to borrow Swidler's term, a *tool kit* that does not determine action but instead provides resources for action from which people pick and choose to create desired strategies.[2] Focusing on practice in terms of interactions rather than actions, means that individual choices are dependent in part on those with whom they are interacting. Hence, how resources are configured in practice is critical and these configurations may differ when "objective" resources are similar or even identical.

While resource distribution is important, resource access and activation are also important (Lin, 2002). The *distribution* of particular resources within and between local organizations is a function of both planned and unplanned change. In a federal system such as the United States, the distribution of resources among local jurisdictions is uneven. A second issue concerns access to resources. An organization may be rich in a particular resource, but *access* to that resource is more or less constrained, depending on where one is situated in the organization. Some organizational members by virtue of who they are (e.g., knowledge, skill, personality), their formal position in the organization, and their professional affiliations (among other things) may have greater access to a particular resource than others in the same organization or even subunit within that organization. A third issue concerns the activation of resources.[3] By activation here we mean the use of a resource for instrumental purposes—in practice—to attain a particular goal or end. Access to a resource does not guarantee its activation. For example, novice teachers may not share their knowledge and expertise in a literacy committee meeting even though it is critical to addressing the issue at hand because they feel their veteran colleagues will resent it or they fear the literacy coordinator will feel threatened and retaliate in some way. Hence, the availability of resources in an organization, or even access to these resources, is not all that matters in understanding relations between organizations and policy implementation.

Human Capital Human resources refer to individual knowledge, skill, and expertise that are part of the stock of resources available to an organization for doing its work. Human capital involves investing in these human resources in order to improve productivity and thus generate higher returns to the organization (Smith, 1776/1937; Schultz, 1961; Becker, 1964). As Becker (1964) puts it, "expenditures in education, training, medical care, etc. are investments in [human] capital …" (p. 16). Improving teachers' or administrators' knowledge about teaching or learning enables them (at least in theory) to practice in new ways, and this new practice can, in turn, improve student achievement either directly or indirectly.

In the education policy world, human capital has received considerable attention especially in efforts to improve teacher quality (Kane, Rockoff, & Staiger, 2007). Policy makers appear intent on improving the quality of America's teachers. There is good reason for this: the available evidence suggests that a school's productivity in terms of student achievement depends at least in part on the quality of its teaching staff. Research has indicated that teacher ability, as measured by test scores or the selectivity of undergraduate institution, and experience are related to student achievement (Ehrenberg & Brewer, 1994; Hanushek, 1997; Hanushek, Kain, O'Brien, & Rivkin, 2005; Nye, Konstantopoulos, & Hedges, 2004; Boyd, Lankford, Loeb, & Wyckoff, 2008). While novice teachers become more effective at raising student achievement as they gain more experience, the value added in terms of student achievement levels off after the initial few years of teaching (Hanushek, Kain, O'Brien, Rivkin, 2005; Nye et al., 2004; Rockoff, 2004). In addition, although many studies have found the relationship between teachers' credentials, including certification status and master's degrees, and student achievement to be insignificant (see, e.g., Hanushek, 1997), recent work has indicated that teacher credentials do affect student achievement in significant ways (Darling-Hammond & Youngs, 2002; Clotfelter, Ladd, & Vigdor, 2007; Boyd, Lankford, Loeb, & Wyckoff, 2008).

While there is variation in the estimation of teacher quality, the evidence suggests that students whose teachers are near the top of the quality distribution learn significant amounts more than students whose teachers are near the bottom of the distribution (Hanushek, 1992; Rowan, Correnti, & Miller, 2002). A one standard deviation increase in teacher quality is associated with between one- and three-tenths of a standard deviation in student achievement gains (Rockoff, 2004; Rivkin, Hanushek, & Kain, 2005; Hanushek, Kain, O'Brien, Rivkin, 2005).

Perhaps most troubling from a policy perspective is that the best teachers are unevenly distributed across schools. Work in New York state, for example, shows that teachers in urban schools are less qualified (based on their experience, schooling, certification, and certification test pass rates), and that low-achieving and non-White students tend to be taught by the least qualified teachers (Lankford, Loeb, & Wyckoff, 2002). Further, teacher effects are much greater in low-socioeconomic states (SES) schools than in high-SES schools (Nye et al., 2004). Still, the evidence suggests that there is substantial within school variation in teacher quality even in schools that enroll large numbers of students living in poverty (Rivkin et al., 2005).

Even more troubling from the perspective of schools that enroll poor, minority, and underachieving students is that the racial, achievement, and income composition of the student population in the school contributes to teacher mobility and choice of school as much or more than wages do (Boyd, Lankford, Loeb, & Wyckoff, 2005; Hanushek, Kain, & Rivkin, 2001; Lankford, Loeb, & Wyckoff, 2002). Teachers are more likely to leave low-achieving schools that mostly enroll students living in poverty or minority students (Boyd, Lankford, Loeb, & Wyckoff, 2005; Stinebrickner, Scafidi, & Sjoquist, 2005). These "unplanned" changes are difficult for policy makers to manipulate through public policy. Moreover, these trends in teacher movement have major implications for policy designed to improve student achievement and narrow the achievement gap. Specifically, if schools that serve the lowest performing students are indeed the weakest in terms of the human capital of staff, then these same schools are the least likely to successfully implement policy. Moreover, if work conditions are stronger motivators than monetary rewards, the reach of public policy in transforming the imbalance among schools in human capital distribution may be limited.

From a policy perspective, improving teacher quality appears to be a safe bet. Still, scholars have rather poor measures for quality—test scores, selectivity of college attended, teacher credentials—though some recent work is promising with respect to developing more refined measures (Hill, Rowan, & Ball, 2005). Moreover, there is limited agreement about how policy might most effectively and efficiently invest in the development of human capital in local school systems. In contrast to some other countries, U.S. state and federal policy makers also exercise limited influence over teacher preparation and professional development programs.

From a policy implementation perspective, human capital—the knowledge and skill of teachers and other local staff used in practice—is critical in that it influences relations between policy and practice in at least two ways. First, what teachers and administrators understand about reforming their existing practice depends in part on their existing knowledge (Cohen, 1990; Hill, 1999; Spillane, 2004). For example, if teachers in a particular school understand mathematics as being mostly about procedural knowledge (ostensive sense) then they are unlikely to appreciate the import of a state or district policy mandating or urging mathematics instruction that balances principled and procedural knowledge. In the classroom, such teachers are likely to emphasize the facts of mathematics rather than its core constructs or principles. It is not that teachers ignore policy. Rather, they are implementing what they understand about practice from the policy and what they understand depends in part on their existing knowledge and skill. Teachers' and administrators' existing knowledge and skills not only influence their understanding, but also their ability to put the ideas mandated or encouraged by policy into practice: pressing teachers to ensure that students understand the idea of place value is unlikely to influence practice if the teachers who are charged with implementing these policies do not understand place value in the first place. Policy usually implies learning and what we learn depends in part on what we already know (Cohen & Barnes, 1993). Hence, if policy makers want to transform students' opportunities to learn in order to improve their achievement their success will depend in great part on the human capital of local educators.

As local organizations vary in human capital, the ways that local educators make sense of and implement policy will also vary (Spillane, 2004). Still, even in organizations where human capital is limited, some organizational members can forge ties through formal and informal networks to individuals in other organizations (Spillane & Zeuli, 1999). The implementation challenge is accentuated by the current patterns of human capital distribution, in which schools and school districts that enroll the most disadvantaged students are least well-endowed with human capital. Many of those schools that policy makers are intent on improving lack the human capital necessary to successfully implement the policies that are designed to improve achievement and narrow the achievement gap.

State and federal policy makers can leverage some change in the ostensive aspect of human capital by attempting to increase the supply of high quality teachers and other professionals through improved preparation and professional development programs. Teacher and administrator assessments are yet another tool that might contribute to human capital development. Of course, the extent to which policy makers can do this depends, in important measure, on knowing what knowledge and skill contributes to improvement in instruction and thereby student achievement. The reach of policy, however, is much more limited with respect to the performative aspect of human capital—how human capital is used in practice in particular places and at particular times. At the same time, it is the performative aspect that is crucial for the success of state and federal policies designed to improve classroom instruction order to improve student achievement and narrow the achievement gap. Unplanned changes, such as the tendency for highly qualified teachers to migrate to better performing schools and school districts, reduce the human capital available in the poorest performing schools and school districts and thereby undermines the planned changes pressed through public policy.

Social Capital Social capital concerns the relations among individuals in a group or organization (Adler & Kwon, 2002; Coleman, 1988; Bourdieu, 1980; Lin, 1982; Burt, 1992). Organizations or a society can invest in the development of social capital just as they do in the development of physical or human capital. Developing social capital involves investing in social relations by changing the way people relate with each other in order to achieve particular goals and enhance outcomes of practice. These new ways of relating enable people to do things that would not be possible in the absence of these relations. Social capital is a resource for action (Coleman, 1988). Just as physical capital and human capital facilitate productive activity, social capital does as well.

Work on schools conceptualizes social capital in various ways but the evidence suggests that social capital influences policy implementation and school reform in general in a number of ways. First, social capital influences the flow of information within an organization and between organizations. Coburn (2001), examining teachers' formal and informal networks in schools, shows how social capital, in the form of ties, shapes how policy messages are understood by teachers and implemented in the classroom. Specifically, teachers' collective sense-making from and about policy was shaped by their patterns of interaction—who is talking with whom—and the nature of the conversations. To whom teachers spoke was important in the collective sense-making process, as different groups of teachers often made different sense of the same policy. Information exchanges or flow is one ingredient in developing new knowledge and skill—human capital development.

In addition to information flow, social capital is also used to refer to social influence or pressure. Frank and Zhao (2004), for example, in a study of the implementation of technology show how social capital, conceptualized as the potential to access resources through social relations, influences the diffusion of innovative technology. They argue that the effects of social capital (perceived social pressure, help and talk), though moderate, were as important as the effects of teachers' perceived value of the technology and adequacy of the resources. As Frank and Zho point out, social capital is a critical consideration in implementation because it leverages human capital—expertise and knowledge.

Social capital is also used to refer to the nature of the relations among organizational members, especially norms and habits of trust and obligation among organization members. Specifically, it concerns norms and habits of trust and obligation among individuals within an organization and with organizations in their environment: "A group within which there is extensive trustworthiness and extensive trust is able to accomplish much more than a comparable group without that trustworthiness and trust" (Coleman, 1988, p. S101–S102). Bryk and Schneider (2002) conceptualize social capital as relational trust and argue that it operates as a resource for school improvement in four ways. First, organizational change involves risks for all participants, as teachers, parents, and principals must engage with changes that they are not certain will work. When relational trust in a school community is strong, the sense of uncertainty and vulnerability is moderated as participants confront the demands of school reform. Therefore, relational trust helps act as a catalyst for innovation by making change seem less daunting. Second, relational trust improves problem solving in the organization because participants trust one another and are less likely to question the motives behind changes. Third, schools with high levels of relational trust benefit from clear understandings about role responsibilities that are regularly reinforced. This makes everyone, including teachers who are isolated in their classrooms, more likely to implement reforms to the best of their ability because they understand that others will do the same. Fourth, relational trust adds a moral dimension to improvement efforts by pressing school staff to constantly work to advance the best interests of students. Bryk and Schneider found much higher levels of trust in top quartile schools than in bottom quartile schools. Further, they found evidence linking improvements in relational trust to increased gains in student performance. Schools that had stronger base levels of relational trust were more likely to improve than schools with weak base levels of trust. Research on school districts also suggests that social capital is an important resource when it comes to policy implementation (Spillane & Thompson, 1998).

The available evidence suggests that an organization's social capital is an important predictor of policy implementation. Schools and school districts that are better endowed with social capital are better equipped to implement policy. Further, if the policy involves substantial changes in existing practice, then social capital is even more critical for implementation. Again, social capital is not equally distributed among local school systems. For example, schools with stable school communities are likely to have higher levels of relational trust, as it is easier for school professionals to develop and maintain social relationships with students and parents who remain in the school community for an extended period of time (Bryk & Schneider, 2002). Here again unplanned change (e.g., teacher and student mobility) is consequential for the local implementation of policy makers' efforts to forge planned change through public policy.

This work and others suggest that implementation depends on the social capital of the local organizations that are charged with implementing policy. How local actors understand policy and put these understandings into practice are sensitive to the pattern and quality of social ties in the organization. For example, consider risk. Policies that are interpreted to demand significant change in existing practice may be more likely to be embraced in settings where relational trust is high. While in organizations where relational trust is low, organizational members may interpret policies in ways that minimize changes in existing practice.

An organization's social capital and human capital work in tandem. Social capital can be instrumental in policy implementation in local organizations, but the extent to which it is will depend in part on the organization's human capital. After all, if the knowledge and skill of organizational members is generally weak, social ties among organizational members will have limited influence in enabling policy implementation. Similarly, the extent to which an organization's human capital enables implementation will depend on access to and activation of the organization's social capital. For example, the likelihood that the human capital of a handful of expert teachers will be accessed and activated in the cause of implementing a policy school-wide is substantially reduced in a school where social ties are weak and/or these relations lack trust.

While scholars mostly dwell on the benefits of social capital for individuals and organizations, social capital can have negative consequences (Adler & Kwon, 2002; Portes, 1998). Aspects of social capital such as strong ties and trust among school staff that enable policy implementation in one school can in another school bring staff together to build a coalition in opposition to the policy that undermines its implementation. Further, strong ties among school staff can also promote conformity in organizations that can stymie innovation and undermine policy implementation. In some urban schools trusting relations among teachers contribute to reinforcing low expectations of students from particular backgrounds (Diamond, Randolph, & Spillane, 2004; Diamond & Spillane, 2004).

A key issue concerns whether district, state, and federal policy can reach into schools to influence social capital distribution, access, and activation. Coburn and Russell (2006) suggest that policy can in fact play a role in influencing some dimensions of teachers' social networks, including tie strength, access to expertise, and depth. Their analysis also suggests that some aspects of teachers' social networks are perhaps beyond policy intervention—social networks are an emergent phenomenon. A related question concerns the unintended consequences of federal and state policies for social capital in local organizations. For example, what are consequences of policies that reward individual teachers for student performance for social capital in schools? With respect to school district policymaking, an important question that remains unexamined is how teacher and administrator school placement decisions influence the social capital in schools. Finally, while building social ties among organizational members might improve access to social capital it does not guarantee that the social capital will be activated or mobilize in practice to support policy implementation.

Organizational Routines Often a taken-for-granted aspect of organizational life, routines of various sorts structure daily practice in organizations (March & Simon, 1958). Routines, from assemblies to grade-level meetings, pattern work in schools offering a rhythm to the workday, week, and month. Organizational routines involve two or more actors in "a repetitive, recognizable pattern of interdependent actions" (Feldman & Pentland, 2003, p. 96). Routines can be thought about as agreements about how to do organizational work as well as means of storing organizational experiences and thereby enable efficient coordinated action, even in the face of substantial change (Levitt & March, 1988; March, 1991; Argote, 1999). Of course, organizational routines also can contribute to inertia, mindless action, worker deskilling and demotivation, and inappropriate responses (Feldman & Pentland, 2003).

Practice in organizations is structured by organizational routines that are incorporated into daily life through planned and unplanned changes (Cyert & March, 1963; Nelson & Winter, 1982). Organizational routines are important with respect to policy implementation in that school and district staff often encounter and make sense of state and federal policy through their participation in organizational routines. Moreover, local efforts to change existing practice by way of implementing policy are typically worked out in organizational routines from school district committees to grade level meetings in a school. The particular organizational routine to which a policy is assigned by a school district, for example, influences how the policy is understood and put into practice in a school district (Sproull, 1981).

The design and deployment of organizational routines or redesign of existing routines is another means of leveraging change in local practice (Resnick & Spillane, 2006; Spillane, Mesler, Croegaert, & Sherer, 2007). Policy makers attempt to leverage change directly and indirectly using organizational routines. Many school districts, for example, mandate that schools perform particular organizational routines such as School Improvement Planning, monitoring instruction, and Walkthroughs. In this way policy makers mandate particular routines and specify more or less the various components that need to be included (i.e., the ostensive aspect of the routine). Federal, state, and school district policy makers also work indirectly to change organizational routines in schools through supporting the development of extra-system providers (e.g., Comprehensive School Reform models) and either mandating or providing inducements for schools to adopt these models. Each of these models includes a set of routines and a more or less specified process about implementing the routine with varying degrees of support in the form of coaching and monitoring. Both planned and unplanned change are important considerations with respect to organizational routines.

These efforts at planned change through organizational routines, however, face a number of challenges. Organizational routines involve multiple actors, meaning that their implementation involves distributed expertise making them difficult to observe, analyze, and transfer from one situation to the next (Cohen & Bacdayan, 1996). The knowledge of different parts of an organizational routine is in part tacit or inarticulate. Hence, policy makers and school reformers can at best provide broad scripts for organizational routines (i.e., the ostensive aspect) leaving a substantial tacit component that is difficult to codify to be worked out in local practice. Even when these scripts are more specified and accompanied with various tools and supports (e.g., coaching, modeling) to sustain their implementation much remains tacit. Further, efforts to leverage change in organizations through routines must also contend with unplanned change in organizational routines. Organizational routines often undergo continuous change through experiential learning rather than purposeful design decisions of organizational members (Cohen & Bacdayan, 1996).

The implementation of a routine in practice—the performative aspect—depends in part on an organization's human and social capital. For example, consider the LearningWalk, an organizational routine designed to engage school and district leaders in ongoing conversations about classroom instruction and its improvement (Resnick & Spillane, 2006). The social and human capital in a school district will influence that take-up of the LearningWalk and the fidelity of its implementation. In organizations that are rich in social capital the LearningWalk will be more readily taken up compared with organizations that have limited social capital. Further, the fidelity of implementation will depend in important part on the human capital of the walkers. If walks lack the knowledge and skill to be able to observe and notice important dimensions of instruction, it is unlikely that the conversations about instruction resulting from the LearningWalk will have the results intended by the designers of the routine. Organizational members can go through the motions of an organizational routine—following each of the prescribed steps to the letter, but lacking the human or social capital failing to realize the underlying intent or purpose of these steps—the spirit of the organizational routine. While policy can specify the ostensive aspects of routines and develop technologies to help with their implementation in local practice, the reach of policy is much more constrained when it comes to the performative aspect of organizational routines.

Technology and Tools The term *technology* is expansive and can encompass many tools. Organizational members do not act directly on the world nor interact directly with one another. Various tools mediate human interactions in organizations (Wertsch, 1991; Barley, 1986). Tools are neither accessories to interactions nor devices that merely allow individuals to practice more or less efficiently. Instead, tools, by virtue of their affordances and constraints, structure interactions in a manner that is constitutive of practice. Tools do more than simply enable organizational members to execute their plans of action more or less efficiently and effectively. Tools can foreground some elements in interactions and background other elements or they change the power relations among organizational members (Barley, 1986; Spillane, 2006). Although this added structure limits the ways in which practice can unfold, tools never constrain practice completely—the same tool in different hands can be used in different ways. Tools can also be studied apart from practice in order to understand their general affordances, but it is only *in* practice that the researcher is able to comprehend how tools *constitute* practice (Cole, 1996).

When we refer to technology we mean to encompass the standard suite of desktop productivity tools including word processors, presentation managers, and spreadsheets. We also include what is emerging as the standard suite of networking tools: email, web browsers, synchronous and asynchronous[4] text-based conferencing, and synchronous video and audio conferencing. In addition to these, we mean to incorporate tools that find special utility in particular domains of practice, for example simulation, modeling, and visualization tools in science, and text analysis tools in literature. Finally, we believe it is important to add to this list technological tools that aid in reflection. A key member of this category is video tools that allow learners to consider and analyze their personal practice and the practice of others. Another category tools are protocols and templates of various sorts designed to scaffold practice by engaging organizational members in observation, reflection, and decision making.

Organizational routines as designed by policy makers and school reformers are often encapsulated within protocols designed to assist in the execution of the routine. The introduction of new technology has the potential to change practice in planned and/or unplanned or unanticipated ways. The introduction of new technology into an organization can alter institutional roles and patterns of interaction among organizational members—practice—that in turn transform the organizational structure (Barley, 1986).

For the better part of two decades, technology has been a hot topic in the conversations about improving education. As the capabilities of readily available technologies have improved, discussions of their potential utility as a resource to teaching and learning have proliferated. With some notable exceptions (e.g., Blumenfeld, Fishman, Krajcik, Marx, & Soloway, 2000), the conversations about education and technology have been tightly focused on how particular technologies or suites of technologies can contribute to the solution of rather tightly construed teaching and learning problems. Some of these discussions, for example Kaput (2002) and diSessa (2000), suggest how computation can open up new ways that allow learners to represent complex problems in math and science. In a similar vein Roschelle, Kaput, and Stroup (2000) and Pea and Gomez (1992) suggest how existing and emerging telecommunications technology can transform teaching and learning. Others like Gee (2003) make compelling arguments concerning the advent of out-of-school opportunities for technology use like video games can transform the landscape of education.

A relatively large and growing literature documents examples in relatively circumscribed settings, like science and math classrooms, that suggest that technology can have a positive impact on student learning. For example, the Cognition and Technology Group (1990) demonstrated that technology-augmented curricula where students are anchored by a compelling problem can lead to reliable gains in learning. Other findings suggest that intelligent tutoring systems (Koedinger, Anderson, Hadley, & Mark, 1997) can be used to transform the practice that learners receive in domains like mathematics. From these we conclude that there are pockets of results across a very wide range of literatures

that suggest the potential power of technology to improve student learning and change teacher practice.

While noteworthy, this literature gives little insight into how technology and tools are constitutive of and constituted in work practice in organizations. What is not well understood is how technology unfolds in implementation in schools and school districts as it is understood and put to use in practice. For example, Bryk and Gomez (2007) argue that to assess the role a technology tool has in the context of schooling, we need theory that jointly accounts for the interests of local actors, specific problems of instructional practice, and the background context of formal and informal organizational norms. By and large, work focused on technology and its impact on education is not framed within larger organizational contexts and work practice. We believe framing of this sort is critically important to characterize the sustained organizational impact of technology beyond a more circumscribed effect of a classroom or school trial. This need is, perhaps, at the root of conclusions like Cuban's (1993, 2001), who argues that computers, at least in their current incarnations in schools, are ill-suited to the interpersonal rhythms of teaching and schooling. These "interpersonal rhythms" could be thought of as daily practice and as proxies for other resources like human and social capital. From a resource deployment perspective, technology, when activated in particular settings, may not fit well into practice and the various configurations of other resources such as human capital and organizational routines. A simple organizational routine like 55-minute class periods can fail to accommodate a new tool. If a tool needs long periods of uninterrupted time to work effectively, a short class period would be a poor configuration for its use. For example, Becker (2000) suggests that when computers are found in classrooms and schools where depth of instruction is valued over breadth and students have time for inquiry, computers find use and utility. In a similar vein, Wenglinsky (1998), in a summary report, suggests that when systemic factors like teacher preparation to use technology are taken into account, the use of computers can be shown to be associated improvements in student performance. Fishman, Marx, Blumenfeld, Krajcik, and Soloway (2004) suggest that to deeply appreciate the potential of technology as a resource for change we need better theories of its integration into local contexts. We argued that understanding local contexts necessitates attention to work practice in schools and school districts. When practice is richly accounted for and technologies are designed based on an understanding of practice, new technology is more likely to be taken up in local organizations.

Resources in Practice in Situ: The Case of Curricular Domains We argue that understanding the role of organizations in policy implementation necessitates attention to *practice* in local organizations, and subunits within these organizations, that is mindful that practice can involve interactions that cross formal organizational boundaries. Specifically, the interdependencies among different organizations and subunits within organizations are critical in understanding the distribution, access to, and activation of resources in practice. For example, a decision by a set of schools or subdistrict in an urban school district to build human capital by firing weak teachers and recruiting high quality teachers through various incentive arrangements can contribute to weakening the human capital in other subdistricts or schools within the school district.

Practice is situated in various ways and the situation or context is an important consideration with respect to resource distribution, access, and activation. One way to think about how practice is situated is in terms of fields of interaction; practice unfolds within fields of interaction (Bourdieu, 1977, 1980/1990, 1991; Thompson, 1990; Lareau & Horvat, 1999). Fields of interaction have rules and schemata that influence interaction within them (Thompson, 1990). Within the education sector different curricular domains (e.g., mathematics, reading/language arts, science) are important subfields (Spillane, Diamond, Walker, Halverson, & Jita, 2001). Thus, the school subject is an important consideration in examining the distribution and activation of organizational resources.

There are pervasive differences in the distribution and activation of resources by school subjects. Elementary schools, for example, are much more likely to have a full- or part-time specialist for literacy than for mathematics (Price & Ball, 1997). Elementary teachers' access to and activation of resources differs from language arts to mathematics, influencing how they implement policy (Spillane, 2000; Drake, Spillane, & Hufferd-Ackles, 2001). There is evidence to suggest that elementary school leaders and teachers are more likely to activate social capital for language arts than for mathematics or science (Spillane, 2005; Hayton & Spillane, 2008). In high schools, the cognitive and normative assumptions embedded in disciplinary cultures are reflected in departmental subcultures and influence teachers' practice and their response to reform (Ball, 1981; Little, 1993; Siskin, 1994; Rowan, 2002; Stodolsky & Grossman, 1995). Overall, the available evidence suggests that the distribution, access, and activation of resources such as human capital and social capital may differ depending on the school subject.

These school subject differences in the distribution of and access to resources in part reflect the broader policy environment. State and federal agencies regulate the different school subjects differently with mathematics and language arts receiving far more attention than other subjects (Rowan, 2006; Spillane & Burch, 2006). Differences across school subject areas are also reflected in the organization and activities of extra-system agencies, including textbook and test publishers, professional associations, and the university sector. Some subject specific professional networks, for example, are much better organized both locally and nationally than others. When it comes to the distribution of, and access to, key resources such as social capital and human capital, these professional networks can be especially relevant.

Still, we know relatively little about how resources are activated in practice and why activation differs across school subjects. Developing a better understanding of how resources are activated in schools will necessitate closer attention to practice—double interacts, dyadic and triadic interactions—the building blocks of organizing.

Research at the Nexus of Organizations and Implementation

Prospectively, we see at least three potential fruitful lines for research that explores the nexus of policy implementation and organizations. To begin with, we believe that the study of work practice in, and between, local organizations (e.g., schoolhouse, district office, extra-system agencies) is critical in any effort to understand the role of organizations in implementation. A focus on practice moves us beyond static frozen state descriptions of organizational conditions that are associated with successful or unsuccessful implementation. Specifically, focusing on practice we can investigate structure as patterned action, interaction, behavior, and cognition (Barley, 1983; Weick, 1979; Van Maanen & Schein, 1979). Conceptualizing organizational structure as resources for and in practice, we can investigate organizational structure as internal rather than external to practice.

Work practice is difficult to access and study systematically. We often gloss over these difficulties by simply extracting discrete actions from practice, and/or aggregating up from discrete actions to styles, and in the process de-contextualizing practice and masking critical interdependencies. But understanding practice in and between organizations necessitates attention to interactions as well as how aspects of the situation mediate these interactions. Moreover, it involves an acknowledgement of the emergent property of practice. While qualitative ethnographic field methods are well-suited to such work, we believe that other methodological approaches are also important in the study of practice. Logs or diaries and archival research methods all have promise in the systematic study of practice.

Studying practice involves attending to the micro- while not losing the meso- and macro-levels (Powell & Colyvas, 2008). While analyzing work practice in schools and school districts, we must still treat the broader institutional system as a relevant unit of analysis (Rowan & Miskel, 1999). We have to develop an understanding of *what* people do, *how* they do it, and *why* they do it, while simultaneously attending to the institutional structures at various levels of the system that enable and constrain practice at the street level. Scholars working in education often confine their work to one organizational level. For example, research on teaching practice often treats teachers' development of their instructional practice as occurring in an institutional vacuum, ignoring or treating lightly the broader school and school system organization. At the same time, many scholars who study the institutional context have tended to ignore, or treat as a black box, work practice in schools and districts instead focusing on understanding those institutional structures, roles, functions, and norms that enable and constrain change in student outcomes. Thinking about structure in terms of resources gives us considerable leverage in that it enables us to attend to structure across multiple levels while simultaneously attending to practice.

The issue here is that resource distribution, access, and activation operate at multiple levels within and beyond local school systems. Hence, understanding how resources matter in practice. Such frameworks, necessitates multi-level frameworks, include, but are not limited to, properties of the individual, the dyad, the subgroup or network, the particular organization, and the system of organizations with which organizational members interact. A good starting point for thinking about how an organization's resources are distributed, accessed, and activated in practice in an organization is Adam Smith's (1776/1937) multilevel framework for understanding the mobilization of social capital.

Another research challenge involves moving beyond a primary focus on studying "natural" variation in organizations to examine whether, and how, we can design interventions that actually produce change in practice in organizations, change that enables the implementation of policies designed to improve the core work of the organization (Resnick & Spillane, 2006). Stated more bluntly, can policy makers and school reformers intervene with planned change to produce significant change in work practice in organizations such as schools and school districts? Such work would involve a combination of design experiments and randomized trials to help identify the conditions under which interventions can indeed change work practice, and in turn measure the causal effects of these interventions on practice in organizations and in turn on organizational productivity.

Conclusion

Policy and its implementation is especially a matter of local organizations. Any serious consideration of organizations has to be fundamentally about work practice in organizations—that is, not simply a consideration of the behaviors or actions of the individuals who inhabit schools or school systems or of the formal organizational arrangements. Policy makers target the behavior of local agents and agencies and in so doing they target practice, but in targeting practice they are attempting to target interactions rather than the actions of individuals. Hence, school district or schoolhouse organizational practice is not simply a matter of individual or organizational behavior; rather the practice policy makers intend to transform takes shape in the interactions among the people who inhabit these organizations as mediated by key aspects of their situation. Acknowledging the emergent property of practice complicates policy makers' task of bringing about planned change in practice in local organizations where change is a constant. At the same time, thinking systematically about the distribution of, access to, and activation of those resources essential for the performance of practice is suggestive of whether and how policy might matter in changing it.

Efforts to understand how the organizations influence policy implementation need to be anchored in work practice so that they attend to not only the distribution of resources but also access to and activation of resources in practice. Public policy is perhaps best understood as a tool for distributing resources for particular instrumental ends and thereby a somewhat blunt instrument. Policy influences work practice in schools, district central offices, and other organizations indirectly through the resources it distributes for particular purposes. It is in the activation of these resources that local practice may change.

In this chapter we have committed to paper our notes on sketching a frame for thinking about organizational behavior and policy implementation. We do so to be provocative and generative rather than comprehensive and conclusive. For us, this chapter is a beginning, rather than an end, of a conversation about the role of local organizations in policy implementation. We have argued for much more careful attention to core terms or constructs we use easily but often indiscriminately in policy implementation conversations—change and organizations. We have suggested that conceptualizing organizations as *organizing* has the potential of offering new insights as it would center research on practice as it unfolds in the interactions among people as mediated by aspects of their situation rather than formal organizational structures. Viewing *practice* as emergent, we have argued for attention to how resources are distributed, accessed, and activated in interactions among people. Seeing resources such as human capital and social capital as both constitutive of and constituted in practice, we have argued for attention to both the ostensive and performative aspects of resources. Our hope is that our thoughts on reframing the role of organizations in policy implementation will be generative, prompting others to work out this broad outline of a conceptual frame and, especially important, putting it to use in empirical studies of implementation.

Notes

1. Work on this chapter was supported by the Distributed Leadership Studies funded by the National Science Foundation (RETA Grant # EHR—0412510). We appreciate the comments of an anonymous reviewer. The ideas developed in this chapter were incubated over a number of years starting when the first two authors co-taught an undergraduate seminar at Northwestern on studies in organizational change. We gratefully acknowledge the students who enrolled in this class for participating in the conversation that enabled us to develop these ideas. Any opinions, findings, and conclusions are those of the authors and do not necessarily reflect the views of the National Science Foundation.
2. Swidler's work is concerned with understanding culture. Her primary concern is to move the sociological examination of culture away from values and toward a framework that emphasizes culture as a resource for action.
3. Our thinking here has benefited tremendously from the work of Nan Lin (2002) and Sandra Susan Smith (2005) on social capital. Lin draws a distinction between accessed social capital and mobilized social capital that we find especially helpful in thinking about organizational resources.
4. Synchronous technologies involve communication at the same time, as in a telephone conversation. Asynchronous technologies involve communication at different times, as in e-mail exchanges.

References

Adler, P. S., & Kwon, S. K. (2002). Social capital: Prospects for a new concept. *Academy of Management Review, 27*, 17–40.

Althusser, L. (1971). *Lenin and philosophy and other essays.* (B. Brewster, Trans.). London: NLB.

Archer, M. S. (1995). *Realist social theory: The morphogenetic approach.* New York: Cambridge University Press.

Argote, L. (1999). *Organizational learning: Creating, retaining and transferring knowledge.* Norwell, MA: Kluwer.

Ball, S. J. (1981). *Beachside comprehensive: A case study of secondary schooling.* Cambridge, UK: Cambridge University Press.

Ball, S., & Lacey, C. (1984). Subject disciplines as the opportunity for group action: A measured critique of subject subcultures. In A. Hargreaves & P. Woods (Eds.), *Classrooms and staffrooms: The sociology of teachers and teaching* (pp.232–245). Milton Keynes, UK: Open University Press.

Barley, S. R. (1983). Semiotics and the study of occupational and organization cultures. *Administrative Science Quarterly, 28*, 393–413.

Barley, S. R. (1986). Technology as an occasion for structuring: Evidence from observations of CT scanners and the social order of radiology departments. *Administrative Science Quarterly, 31*, 78–108.

Becker, G. S. (1964). *Human capital: A theoretical and empirical analysis with special reference to education.* New York: National Bureau of Economic Research.

Becker, H. J. (2000). Findings from the Teaching, Learning, and Computing Survey: Is Larry Cuban right? *Education Policy Analysis Archives, 8*, 51. Retrieved June 18, 2008, from http://epaa.asu.edu/epaa/v8n51/

Bennis, W. G. (1966). *Changing organizations.* New York: McGraw-Hill.

Berman, P., & McLaughlin, M. W. (1977). *Federal programs supporting educational change, Vol. 7: Factors affecting implementation and continuation.* Santa Monica, CA: RAND.

Berman, P., & McLaughlin, M. W. (1978). *Federal programs supporting educational change, Vol. 8: Implementing and sustaining innovations.* Santa Monica, CA: RAND.

Bidwell, C. E. (1965). The school as a formal organization. In J. G. March. (Ed.), *The handbook of organizations* (pp. 972–1022). Chicago: Rand McNally.

Bidwell, C. E. (1970). Students and schools: Some observations on client trust in client-serving organizations. In W. R. Rosengren, M. Lefton, & C. E. Bidwell (Eds.), *Organizations and clients: Essays in the sociology of service* (pp 37–70). Columbus, OH: Merrill.

Bidwell, C. E. (2006) Varieties of institutional theory: Traditions and prospects for educational research. In H. Meyer & B. Rowan (Eds.), *The new institutionalism in education* (pp. 33–50). Albany: State University of New York Press.

Blumenfeld, P., Fishman, B. J., Krajcik, J., Marx, R. W., & Soloway, E. (2000). Creating usable innovations in systemic reform: Scaling up technology-embedded project-based science in urban schools. *Educational Psychologist, 35*, 149–164.

Bourdieu, P. (1977). *Outline of a theory of practice.* Cambridge, UK: Cambridge University Press.

Bourdieu, P. (1980). *The logic of practice.* Cambridge, UK: Cambridge University Press.

Bourdieu, P. (1981). Men and machines. In K. Knorr-Cetina & A. V. Cicourel (Eds.), *Advances in social theory and methodology* (pp. 304–317). London: Routledge.

Bourdieu, P. (1990). *The logic of practice* (R. Nice, Trans.). Stanford, CA: Stanford University Press. (Original work published in 1980)

Bourdieu, P. (1991). *Language and symbolic power.* Cambridge, MA: Harvard University Press.

Boyd, D., Lankford, H., Loeb, S., & Wyckoff, J. (2005). Explaining the short careers of high achieving teachers in schools with low-performing students. *American Economic Review, 95*, 166–171.

Boyd, D., Lankford, H., Loeb, S., Rockoff, J. E., & Wyckoff, J. H. (2008). *The narrowing gap in New York City teacher qualifications and its implications for student achievement in high-poverty schools* (NBER Working Paper No. W14021). Cambridge, MA: National Bureau of Economic Research.

Bryk, A. S., & Driscoll, M. E. (1985). *An empirical investigation of the school as community.* Chicago: University of Chicago, Department of Education.

Bryk, A. S., & Gomez, L. M. (2007, October 25). *Ruminations on reinventing an R&D capacity for educational improvement.* Paper presented at the American Enterprise Institute Conference, Washington, DC.

Bryk, A. S., & Schneider, B. L. (2002). *Trust in schools: A core resource for improvement.* New York: Russell Sage Foundation.

Burch, P. (2007). Educational policy and practice and institutional theory: Crafting a wider lens. *Educational Researcher, 36*(2), 84–95.

Burt, R. S. (1992). The social structure of competition. In N. Nohria & R. G. Eccles (Eds.), *Networks and organizations: Structure, form, and action* (pp. 57–91). Boston: Harvard Business School Press.

Clark, B. (1983). *The higher education system: Academic organization in cross-national perspective.* Berkeley: University of California Press.

Clotfelter, C. T., Ladd, H. F., & Vigdor, J. L. (2007). Teacher credentials and student achievement: Longitudinal analysis with student fixed effects. *Economics of Education Review, 26,* 673–682.

Coburn, C. E. (2001). Collective sensemaking about reading: How teachers mediate reading policy in their professional communities. *Educational Evaluation and Policy Analysis, 23*, 145–170.

Coburn, C. E., & Russell, J. (2006). *Exploring the determinants of teacher social networks.* Paper presented at the Annual Meeting of the American Sociological Association, Montreal, Canada.

Cognition and Technology Group at Vanderbilt. (1990). Anchored instruction and its relationship to situated cognition. *Educational Researcher, 19,* 2–10.

Cohen, D. K. (1982). Policy and organization: The impact of state and federal educational policy on school governance. *Harvard Educational Review, 52,* 474–499.

Cohen, D. K. (1990). A revolution in one classroom: The case of Mrs. Oublier. *Educational Evaluation and Policy Analysis, 12,* 327–345.

Cohen, D. K., & Barnes, C. A. (1993). Pedagogy and policy. In D. K. Cohen, M. W. McLaughlin, & J. E. Talbert (Eds.), *Teaching for understanding: Challenges for policy and practice* (pp. 207–239). San Francisco: Jossey-Bass.

Cohen, D. K., Raudenbush, S. W., & Ball, D. L. (2003). Resources, instruction, and research. *Educational Evaluation and Policy Analysis, 25*, 119–142.

Cohen, M. D., & Bacdayan, P. (1996). Organizational routines are stored as procedural memory: Evidence from a laboratory study. In M. Cohen & L. S. Sproull (Eds.), *Organizational learning* (pp. 403–429). Thousand Oaks, CA: Sage.

Cole, M. (1996). *Cultural psychology: A once and future discipline.* Cambridge, MA: Belknap Press of Harvard University Press.

Coleman, J. S. (1988). Social capital in the creation of human capital. *The American Journal of Sociology, 94*, S95–120.

Cuban, L. (1988). *The managerial imperative and the practice of leadership in schools.* Albany: State University of New York Press.

Cuban, L. (1993). *How teachers taught: Constancy and change in American classrooms, 1890–1990* (2nd ed.). New York: Teachers College Press.

Cuban, L. (2001). *Oversold and underused: computers in the classroom.* Cambridge, MA: Harvard University Press.

Cyert, R. M., & March, J. G. (1963). *A behavioral theory of the firm.* Englewood Cliffs, NJ: Prentice-Hall.

Darling-Hammond, L., & Youngs, P. (2002). Defining "highly qualified teachers": What does "scientifically-based research" actually tell us? *Educational Researcher, 31*(9), 13–25.

Diamond, J., Randolph, A., & Spillane, J. (2004). Teachers' expectations and sense of responsibility for student learning: The importance of race, class, and organizational habitus. *Anthropology and Education Quarterly, 35*(1), 75–98.

Diamond, J., & Spillane, J. (2004). High stakes accountability in urban elementary schools: Challenging or reproducing inequality? *Teachers College Record, 106*, 1145–1176.

DiMaggio, P. (1988). Interest and agency in institutional theory. In L. Zucker (Ed.), *Institutional patterns and organizations* (pp. 3–22). Cambridge, MA: Ballinger.

DiMaggio, P. D., & Powell, W. (1991). The iron cage revisited: Institutional isomorphism and collective rationality in organizational fields. In W. W. Powell & P. J. DiMaggio (Eds.), *The new institutionalism in organizational analysis.* Chicago: University of Chicago Press.

diSessa, A. A. (2000). *Changing minds: Computers, learning, and literacy.* Cambridge, MA: MIT Press.

Drake, C., Spillane, J., & Hufford-Ackles, K. (2001). Storied identities: Teacher learning and subject matter context. *Journal of Curriculum Studies, 33,* 1–23.

Ehrenberg, R., & Brewer, D. (1994). Do school and teacher characteristics matter? Evidence from "High School and Beyond." *Economics of Education Review, 13,* 1–17.

Elmore, R., & Fuhrman, S. (1995). Ruling out rules: The evolution of deregulation in state education policy. *Teachers College Record, 97,* 279–309.

Elmore, R., & McLaughlin, M. W. (1988). *Steady work: Policy, practice, and the reform of American education.* Santa Monica, CA: RAND.

Faulkner, W. (1951). *Requiem for a nun.* New York: Random House.

Feldman, M. S., & Pentland, B. T. (2003). Reconceptualizing organizational routines as a source of flexibility and change. *Administrative Science Quarterly, 48,* 94–121.

Firestone, W., Fitz, J., & Broadfoot, P. (1999). Power, learning, and legitimation: Assessment implementation across levels in the United States and the United Kingdom. *American Educational Research Journal, 36,* 759–793.

Firestone, W. A. (1989). Using reform: Conceptualizing district initiative. *Educational Evaluation and Policy Analysis, 11*(2), 151–64.

Fishman, B., Marx, R. W., Blumenfeld, P., Krajcik, J., & Soloway, E. (2004). Creating a framework for research on systemic technology innovations. *Journal of the Learning Sciences, 13,* 43–76.

Frank, K. A., & Zhao, Y. (2004). Subgroups as a meso-level entity in the social organization of schools. In L. Hedges & B. Schneider (Eds.), *The social organization of schooling* (pp. 279–318). New York: Sage.

Fullan, M. (1991). *The new meaning of education change.* New York: Teacher's College Press.

Gee, J. P. (2003). *What video games have to teach us about learning and literacy.* New York: Pulgrave Macmillan.

Giddens, A. (1979). *Central problems in social theory: Action, structure, and contradiction in social analysis.* Basingstoke, UK: Macmillan.

Giddens, A. (1984). *The constitution of society: Outline of the theory of structuration.* Cambridge, UK: Polity.

Hanushek, E. A. (1992). The trade-off between child quantity and quality. *Journal of Political Economy, 100,* 84–117.

Hanushek, E. A. (1997). Assessing the effects of school resources on student performance: An update. *Educational Evaluation and Policy Analysis, 19,* 141–164.

Hanushek, E. A., (1998). Conclusions and controversies about the effectiveness of school resources. *Economic Policy Review, 4*(1). Retrieved November 12, 2008, from http://ssrn.com/abstract=1023710

Hanushek, E. A., Kain, J., O'Brien, D., & Rivkin, S. (2005). *The market for teacher quality* (NBER Working Paper No. W11154). Cambridge, MA: National Bureau of Economic Research.

Hanushek, E. A., Kain, J., & Rivkin, S. (2001). Why public schools lose teachers (NBER Working Paper No. 8599). Cambridge, MA: National Bureau of Economic Research.

Hayton, P., & Spillane, J. (2008). Professional community or communities? School subject matter and elementary school teachers' work environments. In J. MacBeath & Y. C. Chen (Eds.), *Leadership for learning: International perspectives* (pp. 59–71). Rotterdam, Netherlands: SENSE Publishers.

Hill, H. C. (1999). *Implementation networks: Nonstate resources for getting policy done.* Unpublished doctoral dissertation, University of Michigan, Ann Arbor.

Hill, H. C. (2001). Policy is not enough: Language and the interpretation of state standards. *American Educational Research Journal, 38,* 289–318.

Hill, H. C., Rowan, B., & Ball, D. L. (2005). Effects of teachers' mathematical knowledge for teaching on student achievement. *American Educational Research Journal, 42,* 371–406.

Hill, P. T. (2007). New political economy of public education: Policy and research. In S. H. Fuhrman, D. K. Cohen, & F. Mosher (Eds.), *The state of education policy research* (pp. 87–104). New York: Routledge.

Huberman, M. (1995). Professional careers and professional development: Some intersections. In T. R. Guskey & M. Huberman (Eds.), *Professional development in education: New paradigms and practices* (pp. 193–224). New York: Teachers College Press.

Kane, T., Rockoff, J. E., & Staiger, D. O. (2007). What does certification tell us about teacher effectiveness? Evidence from New York City [Electronic version]. *Economics of Education Review.*

Kanter, R. M. (1983). *The change masters: Corporate entrepreneurs at work.* London: Allen and Unwin.

Kanter, R. M., Stein, B. A., & Jick, T. D. (1992). *The challenge of organizational change: How companies experience it and leaders guide it.* New York: The Free Press.

Kaput, J. (2002). Implications of the shift from isolated, expensive technology to connected, inexpensive, diverse and ubiquitous technologies. In F. Hitt (Ed.), *Representations and mathematical visualization* (pp. 79–109). Mexico: Departmento de Matematica Educativa del Cinvestav-IPN.

Koedinger, K. R, Anderson, J. R., Hadley, W. H., & Mark, M. A. (1997). Intelligent tutoring goes to school in the big city. *International Journal of Artificial Intelligence in Education, 8,* 30–43.

Lankford, H., Loeb, S., & Wyckoff, J. (2002). Teacher sorting and the plight of urban schools: A descriptive analysis. *Educational Evaluation and Policy Analysis, 24,* 37–62.

Lareau, A., & Horvat, E. M. (1999). Moments of social inclusion and exclusion: Race, class, and cultural capital in family-school relationships. *Sociology of Education, 72,* 37–53.

Latour, B. (1986). The powers of association. In J. Law (Ed.), *Power, action and belief: A new Sociology of knowledge* (pp. 264–280). New York: Routledge.

Levitt, B., & March, J. G. (1988). Organizational learning. *Annual Review of Sociology, 14,* 319–340.

Lewin, K. (1951). *Field theory in social science: Selected theoretical papers.* New York: Harper and Row.

Lieberman, A., Falk, B., & Alexander, L. (1994). A culture in the making: Leadership in learner-centered schools. In J. Oakes & K. H. Quartz (Eds.), *Creating new educational communities: Schools and classrooms where all children can be smart, The 94th NSSE Yearbook* (pp. 108–129). Chicago: National Society for the Study of Education.

Lin, N. (1982). Social resources and instrumental action. In P. V. Marsden & N. Lin (Eds.), *Social structure and network analysis* (pp. 131–145). Beverly Hills, CA: Sage.

Lin, N. (2002). *Social capital: a theory of social structure and action.* Cambridge: Cambridge University Press.

Little, J. W. (1982). Norms of collegiality and experimentation: Workplace conditions of school success. *American Educational Research Journal, 19,* 325–340.

Little, J. W. (1993). Professional community in comprehensive high schools: The two worlds of academic and vocational teachers. In J. W. Little & M. W. McLaughlin (Eds.), *Teachers' work: Individuals, colleagues, and contexts* (pp. 137–163). New York: Teachers College Press.

Lopez, J., & Scott, J. (2000). *Social structure.* Buckingham, UK: Open University Press.

Lortie, D. (1977). Two anomalies and three perspectives: some observations on school organization. In R. Corwin & R. Edelfelt (Eds), *Perspectives on organizations* (pp. 20–38). Washington, DC: American Association of Colleges for Teacher Education.

March, J. G. (1981). Footnotes to organizational change. *Administrative Science Quarterly, 26,* 563–577.

March, J. G. (1991). Exploration and exploitation in organizational learning. *Organizational Science, 2,* 71–87.

March, J. G., & Simon, H. A. (1958). *Organizations.* New York: Wiley.

McLaughlin, M.W. (1987) Learning from experience: Lessons from policy implementation. *Educational Evaluation and Policy Analysis,* *9* (2), 171–178.

McLaughlin, M. W. (1990). The Rand Change Agent Study revisited: Macro perspectives and micro realities. *Educational Researcher,* *19*(9), 11–16.

McLaughlin, M. W., & Talbert, J. E. (1993). How the world of students and teachers challenges policy coherence. In S. H. Fuhrman (Ed.), *Designing coherent education policy: Improving the system* (pp. 220–248). San Francisco: Jossey-Bass.

Meyer, J. W. (1983). Centralization of funding and control in educational governance. In J. W. Meyer, & W. R. Scott (Eds.), *Organizational environments: Ritual and rationality* (pp.199–215). Beverly Hills, CA: Sage.

Meyer, J. W., & Rowan, B. (1977). Institutionalized organizations: Formal structure as myth and ceremony. *American Journal of Sociology, 83,* 340–363.

Nelson, R. R., & Winter, S. G. (1982). *An evolutionary theory of economic change*: Cambridge, MA: Belknap Press of Harvard University Press.

Newmann, F., & Wehlage, G. G. (1995). *Successful school restructuring: A report to the public and educators.* Alexandria, VA: Association for Supervision and Curriculum Development.

Nye, B., Konstantopoulos, S., & Hedges, L. V. (2004). How large are teacher effects? *Educational Evaluation and Policy Analysis, 26,* 237–257.

Pea, R. D., & Gomez, L. M. (1992). Distributed multimedia learning environments: Why and how? *Interactive Learning Environments, 2,* 73–109.

Penuel, W., Frank, K., & Krause, A. (2006). *The distribution of resources and expertise and the implementation of schoolwide reform initiatives.* Paper presented at the 7th International Conference on Learning Sciences. Bloomington, IN.

Poole, M. S. (2004). Central issues in the study of change and innovation. In M. S. Poole & A. H. Van de Ven, (Eds.), *Handbook of organizational change and innovation* (pp. 3–31). New York: Oxford University Press.

Portes, A. (1998). Social capital: Its origins and applications in modern sociology. *Annual Review of Sociology, 24,* 1–24.

Powell, W. W., & Colyvas, J. A. (2008). Microfoundations of institutional theory. In R. Greenwood, C. Oliver, R. Suddaby, & K. Sahlin-Andersson (Eds.), *Handbook of organizational institutionalism* (pp. 276–298). London: Sage.

Powell. W. W., & Colyvas, J. (2006). Roads to institutionalization: The remaking of boundaries between public and private science. *Research in Organizational Behavior, 21,* 305–353.

Price, J., & Ball, D. L. (1997). There's always another agenda: Marshalling resources for mathematics reform. *Journal of Curriculum Studies, 29,* 637–666.

Purkey, S. C., & Smith, M. S. (1983). Effective schools: A review. *The Elementary School Journal, 83,* 426–452.

Reininger, M. (2006). *Teachers' location preferences and the implications for schools with different student populations.* Unpublished manuscript.

Resnick, L. B., & Spillane, J. P. (2006). From individual learning to organizational designs for learning. In L. Verschaffel, F. Dochy, M. Boekaerts, & S. Vosniadou (Eds.), *Instructional psychology: Past, present and future trends. Sixteen essays in honor of Erik De Corte* (pp. 259–276). Oxford, UK: Pergamon.

Rivkin, S. G., Hanushek, E. A., & Kain, J. F. (2005). Teachers, schools, and academic achievement. *Econometrica, 73,* 417–458.

Rockoff, J. E. (2004). The impact of individual teachers on student achievement: Evidence from panel data. *American Economic Review, 94,* 247–252.

Roschelle, J., Kaput, J. J., & Stroup, W. (2000). SimCalc: Accelerating students' engagement with the mathematics of change. In M. J. Jacobson & J. R. Kozma (Eds.), *Innovations in science and mathematics education: Advanced designs for technologies of learning* (pp. 47–76). Mahwah, NJ: Erlbaum.

Rosenholtz, S. (1989). *Teachers' workplace: The social organization of schools.* New York: Longman.

Rowan, B. (2002). Teachers' work and instructional management, Part 1: Alternative views of the task of teaching. In W. K. Hoy & C. G. Miskel (Eds.), *Theory and research in educational administration, Vol. 1* (pp. 129–129). Greenwich, CT: Information Age.

Rowan, B. (2006). The school improvement industry in the United States: Why educational change is both pervasive and ineffectual. In H. D. Meyer, B. Rowan, & I. NetLibrary (Eds.), *The new institutionalism in education* (pp. 67–86). Albany: State University of New York Press.

Rowan, B., Correnti, R., & Miller, R. J. (2002). What large-scale, survey research tells us about teacher effects on student achievement: Insights from the prospects study of elementary schools. *Teachers College Record, 104,* 1525–1567.

Rowan, B., & Miskel, C. G. (1999). Institutional theory and the study of educational organizations. In J. Murphy & K. S. Louis (Eds.), *Handbook of research on educational administration* (2nd ed., pp. 359–383). San Francisco: Jossey-Bass.

Schultz, T. W. (1961). Investment in human capital. *American Economic Review, 51,* 1–17.

Scott, W. R. (1995). *Institutions and organizations.* Thousand Oaks, CA: Sage.

Scott. W. R., & Cohen, R. C. (1995). Work units in organizations. In L. S. Siskin & J. W. Little (Eds.), *The subject in question: Departmental organization and the high school* (pp. 48–67). New York: Teachers College Press.

Siskin, L. S. (1990). *Different worlds: The department as context for high school teachers* (Report No. P90-126). Stanford, CA: Stanford University, Center for Research on the Context of Secondary Teaching.

Siskin, L. S. (1991). Departments as different worlds: Subject subcultures in secondary schools. *Educational Administration Quarterly, 27,* 134–160.

Siskin, L. S. (1994). *Realms of knowledge: Academic departments in secondary schools.* London: Falmer.

Smith, A. (1937). *The wealth of nations.* New York: Modern Library. (Original work published 1776)

Smith, S. S. (2005). "Don't put my name on it": Social capital activation and job-finding assistance among the black urban poor. *The American Journal of Sociology, 111,* 1–58.

Spillane, J., Mesler, L, Croegaert, A., & Sherer Zoltners, J. (2007). *Organizational routines and school-level efforts to establish tight coupling: Changing policy, changing work practice?* Unpublished manuscript.

Spillane, J., & Zeuli, J. (1999). Reform and teaching: Exploring patterns of practice in the context of national and state mathematics reforms. *Educational Evaluation and Policy Analysis, 21,* 1–28.

Spillane, J. P. (1996). School districts matter: Local educational authorities and state instructional policy. *Educational Policy, 10,* 63–87.

Spillane, J. P. (1998). State policy and the non-monolithic nature of the local school district: Organizational and professional considerations. *American Educational Research Journal, 35,* 33–63.

Spillane, J. P. (2000). Cognition and policy implementation: District policymakers and the reform of mathematics education. *Cognition and Instruction, 18,* 141–179.

Spillane, J. P. (2004). *Standards deviation: How schools misunderstand education policy.* Cambridge, MA: Harvard University Press.

Spillane, J. P. (2005). Distributed leadership. *The Educational Forum, 69,* 143–150.

Spillane, J. P. (2006). *Distributed leadership.* San Francisco: Jossey-Bass.

Spillane, J. P., & Burch, P. (2006). The institutional environment and instructional practice: Changing patterns of guidance and control in public education. In B. Rowan & H. D. Meyer (Eds.), *The new institutionalism in education* (pp. 87–102). Albany: State University of New York Press.

Spillane, J. P., & Diamond, J. (Eds). (2007). *Distributed leadership in practice.* New York: Teachers College Press.

Spillane, J. P., Diamond, J., Walker, L, Halverson, R., & Jita, L. (2001).

Urban school leadership for elementary science instruction: Identifying and activating resources in an undervalued subject area. *Journal of Research in Science Teaching, 38*, 918–940.

Spillane, J. P., & Thompson, C. L. (1998). *Looking at local districts' capacity for ambitious reform* (CPRE Policy Bulletin). Philadelphia: Consortium for Policy Research in Education.

Sproull, L. S. (1981). Beliefs in organizations. In P. C. Nystrom & W. H. Starbuck (Eds.), *Handbook of organizational design* (Vol. 2, pp. 203–224). New York: Oxford University Press.

Stinebrickner, T. R., Scafidi, B., & Sjoquist, D. L. (2005). *Race, poverty, and teacher mobility* (Andrew Young School of Policy Studies Research Paper Series No. 06-51). Atlanta: Georgia State University.

Stodolsky, S. S., & Grossman, P. L. (1995). The impact of subject matter on curricular activity: An analysis of five academic subjects. *American Educational Research Journal, 32*, 227–249.

Supovitz, J. A. (2007). *The case for district-based reform: Leading, building, and sustaining school improvement.* Cambridge, MA: Harvard Education Press.

Swidler, A. (1986). Culture in action: Symbols and strategies. *American Sociological Review, 51,* 273–286.

Talbert, J., & McLaughlin, M. (1994). Teacher professionalism in local school contexts. *American Journal of Education, 102,* 123–153.

Thompson, J. B. (1990). *Critical hermeneutics: A study in the thought of Paul Ricouer and Jurgen Habermas.* Cambridge, UK: Cambridge University Press.

Van Maanen, J. E., & Schein, E. H. (1979). Toward a theory of organizational socialization. In B. Staw (Ed.), *Annual review of research in organizational behavior* (Vol. 1, pp. 209–266) New York: JAI Press.

Weick, K. (1979). *The social psychology of organizing* (2nd ed.). New York: McGraw-Hill.

Weick, K. (1995). *Sensemaking in organizations.* Thousand Oaks, CA: Sage.

Wenglinsky, H. (1998) *Does it compute? The relationship between educational technology and student achievement in mathematics.* Princeton, NJ: Educational Testing Service.

Wertsch, J. V. (1991). A sociocultural approach to socially shared cognition. In L. B. Resnick, J. M. Levine, & S. D. Teasley (Eds.), *Perspectives on socially shared* cognition (pp. 85–100). Washington, DC: American Psychological Association.

Whittington, R. (1992). Putting Giddens into action: Social systems and managerial agency. *Journal of Management Studies, 29,* 693–712.

34

What Do We Know About Reducing Class and School Size?

JUNE AHN AND DOMINIC J. BREWER
University of Southern California

Introduction

Education reform is a continuous and often controversial process. With rising concerns about the level and distribution of student performance, the last several decades have seen a multitude of reforms. These interventions have touched almost every aspect of schooling from the classroom to the federal level. Standards-based accountability systems, comprehensive school reform designs, changes to state funding formulas, new curricula innovations, modified professional development programs, and many other programs have been attempted. These reforms are multifaceted and complex, implementation is tricky and effects on outcomes are diffuse and slow to appear. Two policies that have been popular with educators for generations are reducing class size and school size.

Smaller classes are widely believed to have beneficial effects. Scholars note that "of all the ideas for improving education, few are as simple or attractive as reducing the number of pupils per teacher" (Ehrenberg, Brewer, Gamoran, & Willms, 2001b, p. 68). Teachers expect less classroom disruption and more time for flexible teaching strategies (Finn & Achilles, 1990). Parents, teachers, and other stakeholders also hope for individualized attention for their children and higher student achievement (American Federation of Teachers, n.d.; Class Size Matters, n.d.). Similarly, supporters of smaller school size hope that smaller learning environments mean more attention to student needs and a more "personal" environment. Other benefits proposed by small schools advocates include cost-effectiveness, greater sense of community, and improved safety (Small Schools Project, n.d.). Recent philanthropic efforts have poured millions of dollars into initiatives to establish small high schools or "schools within schools" and many school districts have adopted similar efforts (Gewertz, 2006).

While smaller schools and classes make intuitive sense, there remain questions of whether such policies are the most effective ways to improve student achievement given their immense financial costs (Brewer, Krop, Gill, & Reichardt, 1999). As with many educational policies, the specifics of how smaller classes and smaller schools are actually designed and implemented are likely to be important in terms of expected effects. Important considerations include what constitutes small and whether there is an "optimal" size for a particular type of student, subject, or geographic area. For example, "small" in some countries might mean class sizes of 25 or 30 pupils, while in the United States today it might mean 15 students. A small elementary and small high school could be very different in terms of enrollment numbers. Finally, smallness in and of itself cannot be separated from other changes that accompany the reduction of enrollment or classroom size, such as the effects of physical facilities, teacher quality, and curriculum materials.

Since smaller class and school sizes evoke a great deal of emotion from supporters and opponents, there is a large advocacy literature interwoven with the research and a great deal of conventional wisdom based on anecdote and deeply held prior expectations of what works. Researchers have examined the phenomenon of smaller classes and schools in different ways, sometimes examining the underlying basic relationship between "size" and outcomes of interest. The common outcomes of study have been student achievement and the implementation and impact of policy efforts. The research literature is diffuse and spans across academic disciplines and fields. For example, economists have studied outcomes including long-term effects, psychologists have studied the effects on classroom dynamics and student self-efficacy, and sociologists have studied the relationship of size to within school stratification.

In this overview of research on class and school size, we first outline the popular justifications and expectations for these policies. The common theories of action surrounding class and school size reduction help frame the research opportunities for understanding their effects. The expected impacts of class and school size interventions define the causal-relationships that stakeholders want to uncover and education researchers have attempted to answer. Second, we briefly summarize the past research literature on class and school size effects on various student outcomes. In each level of analysis, both the class and school level, we suggest some opportunities for future research that can more fully explicate the relationships between size and student achievement. Finally, the chapter concludes with a discussion of cost effectiveness and the need for more rigorously designed research before large–scale policies are implemented.

Why Class and School Size? Theories of Action

Policy makers and practitioners give great attention to class and school size policy because of the fundamental belief that these two variables have some deterministic relationship to student outcomes such as measured student achievement. There are certainly some other rationales. For example, class and school size are very easy to grasp conceptually, and can be explained to parents, teachers, and other stakeholders who themselves have experienced being in classrooms and schools. More complex reforms that bundle changes to curriculum, pedagogy, technology, and school organization are not as easily explained and persuasive. In relating class and school size to student outcomes, a large number of possible intermediate variables may be what provides the link. For example, teacher morale, individualized attention for students, covering more curriculum, better personal relationships, reduced disruptions or violence, and other factors influence the size and student outcomes relationship. Most of the ideas that suggest class and school size matter have considerable "face validity"—they seem to accord with common sense—but there is surprisingly little rigorous or systematic evidence that have *proven* the causal linkages or suggested which are most important.

Class size reduction is supported by a wide coalition of stakeholders. The National Education Association's (NEA) position is that classes should be reduced to 15 students or less (National Education Association, n.d.). According to the NEA, small classes help teachers provide individual attention to students, enhance safety and minimize disruptive behavior, and ultimately lead students to learn more. The American Federation of Teachers (AFT) also strongly supports class size reduction. The benefits claimed by the AFT include: more opportunity for individualized instruction, flexibility to use different pedagogical approaches, less classroom disruption, and personalized relationships between teachers and students (American Federation of Teachers, n.d.). Parent and public coalitions also advocate for class size reduction. For example, Class Size Matters (CSM) is a non-profit organization of parents and citizens in New York City. CSM promotes class size reduction and asserts that smaller classes lead to higher student achievement for underserved students, increased parental involvement, less discipline issues, improved teacher morale, and lower dropout rates (Class Size Matters, n.d.).

The arguments in support of smaller classes directly impact the classroom unit. For teachers, smaller classes can lead to better and easier working conditions. In theory, there should be more time to devote to each student and less classroom disruption. Teachers can cover more curricular material, change their pedagogy to be more engaging, and use small groups or a variety of other changes that may positively affect student learning. For parents, smaller classes promise more attention for their children and personalized learning experiences. For policy makers and education reformers, small classes offer the tantalizing promise of better student achievement, especially for historically disadvantaged and underserved children. Ehrenberg et al. (2001b) note that "with its uncomplicated appeal and lack of a big, powerful group of opponents, class-size reduction has lately gone from being a subject of primarily academic interest to a policy juggernaut" (p. 68).

Class size is one of the most studied topics in education research. The findings are mixed in terms of academic achievement. However, stakeholders have learned much about what actually happens in classrooms when the number of students is reduced as well as how implementation proceeds under different policy designs. The popular arguments of class size reduction can be summarized as follows (see Biddle & Berliner, 2002; Ehrenberg et al., 2001b):

- Teachers report less stress and dissatisfaction with working conditions.
- Teachers may have more time for individual attention.
- Student motivation may increase, leading to better learning.
- Behavioral and classroom management issues are less frequent.
- Achievement scores in grades K-3 improve for students exposed to classes of 17 or less.
- Achievement gains increase with longer exposure to small classes in grades K-3.
- Achievement gains are seen for historically underserved and disadvantaged student populations in grades K-3.

Ultimately, the theory behind small class size remains a simple and intuitive way to improve student achievement. Education stakeholders have tried to apply a similar idea to influence the size of schools.

In the past, education scholars viewed larger schools as more economically efficient, and better able to provide for the diverse needs of a student body. Lindsay (1982) writes, "The dominant assumption has been that the larger the school, the more economical, specialized, comprehensive, and effective it must be" (p. 57). However in the past 30 years, education researchers have shifted their preference to smaller schools. They also ascribed a variety of benefits to smaller schools just as scholars once attached expected benefits to large schools (Howley & Howley, 2004).

Advocates for small schools often juxtapose the expected benefits against the problems of comprehensive schools, or factory-model schools. A publication from the

Bill & Melinda Gates Foundation (n.d.), which has provided substantial financial support for the creation of small schools states, "In the early 1900s, large comprehensive high schools were designed to educate all of a community's students efficiently, providing different programs, or tracks…" (p. 3). The publication asserts that in the effort to serve all students efficiently, schools in fact serve most students very poorly. The authors state, "The philosophy underlying the comprehensive high school was problematic in the early 20th century; it is catastrophic now" (p. 4). The intuitive ideas concerning the relationship of school size to student programs underlies the small school movement. Advocates hope that more focused and intimate schools will perform better than comprehensive, factory-model schools that are only focused on efficiency.

The Small Schools Project (n.d.) defines small schools along several dimensions that highlight the hopes for school restructuring. They promote schools that are:

- limiting student enrollment to usually no more than 400 students;
- autonomous and allow for the school to make its own decisions;
- distinctive and focused rather than providing a comprehensive program for students;
- personal, where students are known by many people and have personal relationships with faculty and staff;
- parent-friendly and encourage intimate parental involvement in school activities;
- schools of choice where parents and students actively choose to enroll.

The coalition also asserts that small schools can provide better opportunities for student achievement, more cost-effective schools, increased personalization and sense of community, and increased safety. Small school advocates do not merely promote a direct connection between enrollment size and student achievement. Instead, the underlying theory of small schools is that smaller enrollments have an effect on the structural and social elements of the schooling process.

In theory, smaller schools should create institutional structures that enable certain modes of work, personal relationships, and development of community. Linda Darling-Hammond (n.d.) writes concerning comprehensive schools, "The problem with these schools does not lie with the people in them, but with the institutional structures that organize their work" (p. 2). She stresses that small schools are effective when they promote certain institutional practices such as personalized programs, close relationships between individuals, high standards, adaptive pedagogy, skilled teachers, parent involvement, democratic decision making, and collaborative work environments.

The kind of underlying theories of action as to why school size might matter suggests specific research considerations. For example, a recommendation of enrollments no larger than 400 students speaks to questions of an optimal school size, or an effective threshold for size. The call for school-level autonomy suggests that local decision making has some relationship to school size and student achievement. The suggestion of personal relationships and parental involvement suggests that school size has some relationship with those processes, which in turn affect student achievement. The promotion of collaborative teacher practice, personalized pedagogy, and skilled teachers underlie some expected effect of those institutional practices on student achievement. The role of school size on these institutional practices, and furthermore on student achievement, is still unclear, however. The popular media has covered the mixed student achievement of small schools (Gewertz, 2006), which speaks to the difficulty of finding a causal school size effect. As we discuss later in this chapter, future research on school size effects may benefit from a reorganization of the question. The onus for school size research may be to find a relationship between school size, positive institutional practices, and student achievement.

Much of the argument for smaller class and school sizes is based on intuitive beliefs about the various ways in which these phenomena may affect intermediate variables that ultimately impact student achievement. However, there isn't a comprehensive well-developed theory of action underlying the belief that smaller classes and smaller schools make a difference that provides clues as to what size is optimal, when effects might be expected to be biggest and for who, or how the effects can be maximized. Despite this lack of rigorous conceptual framework, the simple appeal of small classes and small schools continues to make them a popular policy option. In the next two sections we review the empirical evidence on the effects of class and school size on student outcomes, as well as other salient research.

Research on Class Size

Education researchers have extensively studied class size policy, particularly the effects of different class sizes on student achievement. At the outset, one must note that "class size" typically refers to the number of students who are present in a classroom with a single teacher. In the empirical literature, however, this definition is often stretched due to data or policy limitations. For example, much early work relating "naturally occurring" variation in class size to student achievement did in fact use student-teacher ratios rather than actual class size. These ratios were computed by dividing total student enrollment by total teachers employed in a school (or district). Student-teacher ratio tends to include professional instructional staff members that are not actually assigned to a specific class, and hence is not an accurate measure of the class size any given student might experience. Table 34.1 shows U.S. student-teacher ratios since 1969. The current ratio suggests about 1 teacher for every 16 students, with the number declining by more than 30% over the past four decades, despite increasing or level student enrollment numbers (National Center for Education Statistics, n.d.). This trend implies that the public school

TABLE 34.1
Student-Teacher Ratio in United States 1969–2005

1969*	1974*	1979*	1984*	1989*	1993*	03–04**	04–05**
22.6	20.8	19.1	18.1	17.2	17.3	15.9	15.8

Source: * http://nces.ed.gov/pubsearch/pubsinfo.asp?pubid=95122
          ** http://nces.ed.gov/ccd/pub overview.asp, retrieved July 15, 2007.

system has hired a tremendous number of additional staff over the past four decades.

In terms of actual class sizes, data suggest a U.S. average of around 23 students at the primary level, where class sizes tend to be smaller, and around 24 at the high school level (see Table 34.2). Relative to other countries, the United States is slightly higher than the Organisation for Economic Co-operation and Development (OECD) average. However, the high student performance nations of Japan and Korea have significantly higher class size averages, and often provide a comparison point for discussion.

Class size studies that employ non-experimental and quasi-experimental data have many limitations. Many inter-related factors contribute to the relationship between class size and student achievement and all factors must be adequately accounted for in any analysis of non-experimental data (Ehrenberg, Brewer, Gamoran, & Willms, 2001a). For example, class size reduction may give teachers more flexibility, but teachers may or may not change their pedagogical practices to take advantage of the new class structure. Reducing class sizes also precipitates a need for additional teachers and facilities. The quality of those resources may confound any class size effect. There are many other possible variables that cloud our understanding of a class size effect. The key limitation of non-experimental data is the

TABLE 34.2
Average Class Size, International — Various OECD Countries (2004)

	Primary*	Secondary*
Australia	24.3	24.9
Austria	20.1	24.3
Czech Republic	20.6	23.2
Denmark	19.5	19.4
France	NA	24.1
Germany	22.1	24.7
Greece	18.3	25.2
Hungary	20.2	21.5
Iceland	17.1	18.5
Italy	18.4	20.9
Japan	28.6	33.8
Korea	33.6	35.5
Mexico	20.1	29.9
Poland	20.4	24.3
Portugal	16.4	23.5
Slovakia	19.9	22.9
Spain	20.7	24.9
Switzerland	19.2	18.7
United Kingdom	24.3	21.0
United States	23.1	24.3
OECD Avg.	21.4	24.1

Note: *Average from both public and private institutions
Source: www.oecd.org/edu/eag2006, retrieved July 15, 2007.

presence of those variables that confound how class size may or may not be effective.

In their comprehensive review of the class size literature, Ehrenberg et al. (2001a) outline the major problems researchers face when trying to account for the relevant factors that may confound class size effects. Not surprisingly, conclusions about class size effects are mixed when using non-experimental data. When summarizing the evidence, some scholars suggest that data "gives little support to the idea that smaller classes will lead to general improvements in performance" (Hanushek, 1999, p. 148). Others, using different meta-analytic methods, contend that there is some evidence for the relationship between smaller classes and improved student achievement (Hedges & Greenwald, 1996). Ehrenberg et al. (2001a) suggest that very little can be concluded from the debate because, "many if not all, of the studies that they summarize have methodological problems, which almost guarantee that the estimates of the relationship between pupil/teacher ratio and student learning that each study reports will not be unbiased" (p. 11).

Although the non-experimental analyses of class size data produce conflicting assertions, the Tennessee Project STAR studies provide compelling causal evidence of a class size effect. Subsequently, the research literature on class size is dominated by one major randomized experiment in the Tennessee Student/Teacher Achievement Ratio (STAR) study. This experimental study has its own limitations that hinder stakeholders' abilities to generalize from findings. Thus, we briefly summarize and update earlier reviews of the evidence and offer several recommendations for needed research on class size effects.

The STAR project was an ambitious randomized trial that aimed to find a causal relationship between class size and student outcomes. Students were randomly assigned to one of three classroom sizes: a classroom of 13–17 students, 22–26 students, and 22–26 students with a teacher aide. In addition, teachers were randomly assigned to the classroom treatments each year. The class size treatments continued for students from grades K-3, after which students returned to normal classrooms in Grade 4. The study included a final sample about 6,500 students in 328 classrooms, and 70 schools in the first year (Finn & Achilles, 1990). The overall student sample included nearly 12,000 students over the 4-year program. Although there are some questions about student attrition and possible contamination effects (whereby students switched into and out of small classes) the general consensus is that STAR was a well-done demonstration and that the data exhibit a high degree of integrity (Ehrenberg et al., 2001a).

Since the researchers isolated class size in their randomized, experimental design, the STAR study provides relatively compelling evidence for the basic causal relationship between class size and student achievement. Finding a causal class size effect is profoundly important; however, there remain questions about how the findings generalize to broader contexts. Following from the study's design, the STAR findings are most generalizable to students in grades K-3, in Tennessee, and in the types of schools used for the study. As we discuss later in this section, the issues of generalizing the positive STAR findings to other contexts proves challenging. However, such challenges illuminate future needs and opportunities for class size research.

The main, unambiguous finding of the STAR study was that smaller classes lead to improved student achievement in grades K-3 (Finn & Achilles, 1990). A particularly interesting finding was a significant relationship between race and class size on reading achievement. Minority students in smaller classes had significantly higher reading scores, providing a strong indication that "the performance of minority students is enhanced in the small-class setting" (Finn & Achilles, 1990, p. 574). In addition, the researchers found evidence that staying in the small class treatment in subsequent years after kindergarten led to significantly greater growth in student achievement. There were no differences between classes of 22–26 students, with or without a teaching aide.

Recent studies have continued to expand the range of results utilizing the STAR data. For example, Nye, Hedges, and Konstantopoulos (2002) analyze STAR data to explore a hypothesis that small classes benefit low-performing students more than their high-performing peers. The authors find some evidence that a small class effect was larger for low-performing students in reading. However, they found that high-performing students accrued larger benefits in mathematics. Finally, the researchers find that "all differential effects were statistically insignificant when the statistical analyses were conducted at each grade separately" (p. 215). The authors conclude that the evidence for larger class size effects for low performing students is weak. However, there is still a clear, unambiguous class size effect overall for student achievement.

Among the findings of the STAR data, there also seem to be evidence that the benefits of small classes seem to *persist* for students as they reach the upper grades. A study by Finn, Gerber, and Boyd-Zaharias (2005) examines the long-term effects of early school experiences with small classes. The authors find that students graduated at higher rates depending on the number of years they experienced small classes. Students who experienced 3 or 4 years of small classes graduated at higher rates than those who only attended 1 year. Furthermore, the benefit of 3 or 4 years of small classes was greater for free lunch students than for non-free lunch students. However, there were no significant differences in class size effects on the graduation rates of minority and non-minority students, and 1 year of small classes did not appear sufficient to realize long-term graduation rates. In another study exploring the class size effect on high school course taking, researchers found that students who were in small class treatments for 3 or more years: (a) took more foreign language classes, (b) took more advanced foreign language classes, and (c) took more higher level mathematics coursework. However, there were no differences in class size effect for low or high socioeconomic

status (SES) students (Finn, Fox, McClellan, Achilles, & Boyd-Zaharias, 2006).

Following the Tennessee STAR experiment, various states and school districts implemented class size reduction policies. The notable examples are Wisconsin and California, and case studies of both contexts highlight the limitations of assuming that experimental effects of class size on student achievement can be replicated in real world, large-scale settings. Beginning in 1996–1997, Wisconsin implemented a 5-year pilot study called SAGE, in which one of the interventions was to reduce class sizes to 15 students. The unique component of the SAGE study was that it was targeted to schools that served a significant percentage of low-income student populations. Wisconsin allows school districts to use a variety of measures to determine low-income students, and a common measure is eligibility for free or reduced lunch. The evaluation of the program involved a quasi-experimental strategy to compare SAGE schools with matched schools with similar SES, achievement, enrollment, and racial compositions. Researchers found that first grade students in SAGE improved their test scores at greater rates than their peers in comparison schools. Similarly, African American students who participated in SAGE made significantly larger gains in test scores than their peers in comparison schools (Molnar et al., 1999).

Researchers also examined different classroom configurations—15:1 teacher to student, 15:1 with shared classroom, 30:2 with 2 team teachers, and 30:2 with a roaming teacher—and the teacher responses to those variations. Researchers observed that in comparison to other SAGE teachers: (a) those in the regular 15:1 classrooms used more problem-solving activities, (b) 15:1 shared space teachers used more hands-on activities, (c) 30:2 two team teacher classrooms used more prior student knowledge in teaching, and (d) 30:2 with a roaming teacher classrooms used more instruction time. Finally, in teacher interviews the SAGE teachers voiced that they had greater knowledge of their students, spent less time in classroom management, and had more time for direct instruction and individualized instruction (Molnar et al., 1999).

In a matched, quasi-experimental design one cannot fully isolate a relationship between class size and student outcomes. While the researchers do their best to match their samples, based on variables such as SES or race, one cannot rule out any other confounding variables that might affect the results. For example, perhaps the teachers in particular schools were markedly different in their teaching philosophies. Without randomly assigning teachers to classes, one cannot be entirely sure that those using more problem-solving activities are causally attributed to being in smaller classes. Although one cannot determine an unambiguous, conclusive causal relationship between class size, institutional practices, and student outcomes from SAGE, the program is a nice example of a targeted intervention with a strong evaluative component all too rare in education.

Perhaps the most infamous implementation of a class

size reduction (CSR) policy was California's in 1996. The key difference with Wisconsin's strategy is that the Golden State attempted a statewide, across-the-board reduction to 20 students per class in grades K–3. The state spends approximately $1.5 billion annually on the program. California's CSR implementation exacerbated already existing teacher shortages and limited facilities, particularly in poorer urban districts already struggling to improve student achievement. The subsequent results included the need to hire many un-credentialed and inexperienced teachers and the use of portable or non-classroom spaces to accommodate heightened space needs. The negative effect of a blanket CSR policy on factors, such as teacher distribution, may be critical. For example, a study by Clotfelter, Ladd, and Vigdor (2005) suggests that Black students in North Carolina and students in remedial courses were more likely to have inexperienced, novice teachers. The authors posit that various systemic pressures may work to distribute teachers unequally across a district. Differential levels of parental pressure, or experienced teachers' preferences for teaching in better performing schools and classrooms, may influence unequal access to quality instruction. Widespread CSR policies, such as that in California, may exert extreme stress on education systems and exacerbate inequalities. These unintended consequences, along with the lack of a strong evaluation plan hinder the data analysis and conclusions of California's experience (Ehrenberg et al., 2001a).

Despite the less-than-ideal state of data from California's CSR implementation, scholars have attempted to find some evidence of class size effects. The major evaluation of California CSR found tiny achievement advantages for small classes in reading, writing, and mathematics. Finally, the researchers found that CSR had an influence on hiring less qualified teachers and students appeared to receive more individual attention in class, but instructional practice and curriculum remained unchanged (Bohrnstedt & Stecher, 2002). Since the effects of teacher quality and facilities cannot be untangled convincingly, it is impossible to discern how class size, and other factors, actually impacted student achievement in California.

In a later analysis, Stecher, McCaffrey, and Bugliari (2003) examine whether intensity of student exposure (number of years in K-3) in small classes influenced student achievement. The researchers find that 1 year of exposure to small classes seemed to have no effect on student achievement gains. They conclude that:

> Scores at the elementary level have been rising at the same time that increasing percentages of students have been taught in reduced size classes. However, many other educational reforms were enacted during this period that might have contributed to the achievement gains, and it is impossible for us to determine how much the various factors may have influenced trends in overall student achievement. Our analyses that used differences in group means to control for the other factors showed that a one-year difference in exposure occurring in first grade is not associated with

greater gains in achievement. (Stecher et al., 2003, Conclusions section, para. 1)

The examples of Tennessee STAR, Wisconsin SAGE, and California CSR highlight the challenges of fully understanding a class size effect on student achievement. The STAR study utilized a fully randomized trial by randomly assigning students and teachers to classes of different sizes. The study also benefited by targeting a particular subset of schools, such that the pressures of hiring teachers and requiring new facilities were lessened. For example, Finn and Achilles (1990) note that, "the final sample consisted of 76 elementary schools that were large enough to have at least three kindergarten classes" (p. 559). By taking such measures in the implementation of the study, Tennessee's STAR attempts to *isolate* class size as the intervention. Thus, one can make the most convincing argument that class size has a causal link to student achievement from the randomized trial in STAR. The Wisconsin SAGE evaluation also attempts to isolate a class size effect, working within the limitation of not conducting a randomized experiment. The main issue of the quasi-experimental design of SAGE is that one cannot rule out possible confounding variables. Taken together, the cases of Tennessee and Wisconsin offer compelling evidence that smaller class size affects student achievement in positive ways.

However, as the California policy case has revealed, there are limitations in translating this finding into real world settings that are not able to replicate the original experimental conditions. Ehrenberg et al. (2001a) note that "an experiment and its findings may be very dependent on the conditions under which it was conducted" (p. 17) and go on to note "there are a number of factors that lead us to question whether the external validity of the Tennessee experiment has been established sufficiently to warrant generalizing across different populations and settings in the United States" (p. 25). The STAR study examined a class size effect in particular conditions: for grades K-3, in the state of Tennessee, and for a limited sample of schools that already had the ability to add more classes. One cannot make the same causal claim that smaller class size would be as effective in other conditions such as: middle or high school, classes taught by less qualified teachers, or insufficient classrooms and resources. In the case of California, where a blanket class size reduction was implemented, these confounding variables cloud our understanding of a class size effect. In the ideal evolution of a research area, further experimental studies would be conducted to test additional conditions and questions that remain unanswered from the initial trial. Unfortunately, class size research has not developed past the initial Tennessee experiment while huge expenditures have been committed to support CSR policies across the country.

What is next for class size research? First, rarely are definitive conclusions made with a single experimental study (however many academic papers it may produce). A history of experiments is needed to build a stronger evidence base

TABLE 34.3
Future Questions for Research on Class Size Effects

Question	Current Understanding
Do students experiencing smaller class sizes learn more, as measured by student achievement tests, than otherwise similar students?	Strong experimental evidence from Tennessee STAR suggests that students reap advantages from attending classes of 17 or less.
Do classes at various levels (20 students, 17, 15, etc.) make a difference for outcomes?	Tennessee STAR provides strong evidence for class sizes of 17 or less. California CSR evaluations yield weak understanding for classes of 20 students. Wisconsin SAGE evaluations yield similar results to STAR, but no definitive conclusions.
Does the impact of class size vary across grade levels, subjects being taught, school and community contexts, and student characteristics?	No definitive experimental evidence past grades K-3, or the contexts explored in Tennessee STAR.
How does timing and exposure to small classes affect student outcomes?	Evidence from STAR suggests that the greatest benefits accrue for students who are exposed to 3-4 years of smaller classes. No experiments to date that directly isolate this question.
Do the effects have long-term consequences?	Analysis of STAR data suggests that students exposed to smaller classes have higher graduation rates, and advanced course taking patterns in some subjects such as foreign language.
Why do smaller classes affect (or not affect) student achievement? How does class size interact with teacher practice to influence student achievement?	No clear experimental evidence of the causal mechanisms in smaller classrooms that may or may not affect student achievement, beyond exploratory findings. Some studies suggest that teaching practice does not change substantially in smaller or larger classes. Clearer understanding is needed in this area.

Source: Ehrenberg et al., 2001a

and most importantly, to fully explicate the theory behind a causal mechanism. Second, the findings from STAR suggest a number of intriguing effects that merit further and more refined examination. Further experimental trials are needed that examine other factors in relation to class size reduction. Table 34.3 offers a solid framework for organizing some future research questions.

A final consideration, often ignored in class size research that is intent on finding effects on student achievement, is whether the benefits of class size reduction outweigh the costs associated with the resources required. Brewer et al. (1999) note that at minimum, class size reduction requires additional teachers and facilities to accommodate the smaller classes, and both of these necessities are expensive. When comparing against other reform options for schools, smaller classes are often the more expensive option. If a hypothetical implementation of CSR across the nation required an estimated $5–6 billion per year to hire enough teachers, the next logical question would be whether those funds might instead "…purchase computers, to upgrade facilities, to promote early-childhood programs, to improve counseling, to subsidize lunches, to increase the array of electives, to assist after-school programs, to hire teachers' aides, or to support widely varying local priorities" (p. 188). This critical issue of cost effectiveness requires considerably more attention as different variants of class size reduction polices are implemented and as achievement effects are established for alternative reforms.

Research on School Size

In this section, we examine the evidence on school size. As with class size, the primary question of interest is the causal one, that is, does school size affect student achievement? However, given that schools are complex places and students are nested within classrooms in schools, effects are mediated through many different potential mechanisms. Researchers have examined whether smaller schools are correlated with higher student engagement, participation in school life such as extracurricular activities, improved attendance, and lower rates of attrition. Average school sizes in the United States have generally been around 500 students. However, there is a difference by type of school with high schools much larger than elementary schools (see Table 34.4). In addition, these national averages mask very considerable variation—from just a handful of students to the many thousands found in urban high schools.

The research literature on school size effects is largely non-experimental and based on correlational methods using cross-sectional data. There are a handful of studies using richer longitudinal data (e.g., High School and Beyond [HSB], National Educational Longitudinal Study of 1988, NELS:88) employing multivariate modeling techniques but lacking sufficient rigor to establish causality. Caroline Hoxby (2006), in a presentation for a Brookings conference on school and class size, notes that there are almost *no* studies of school size effects that (a) utilize random assignments of students or schools to isolate school size effects, (b) use even quasi-random assignment of students or schools, (c) try to identify sources of arbitrary variation in school size, and (d) compares students before or after intervention, or use matching or other comparison methods to eliminate self-selection. Table 34.5 organizes the studies reviewed here, using Hoxby's taxonomy, to illustrate the lack of causal understanding of school size effects in the current literature.

TABLE 34.4
Average School Enrollment Size in the United States, by Type*

	1982–83	84–85	88–89	90–91	92–93	94–95	96–97	98–99	00–01	02–03	03–04
Elementary	399	403	433	449	464	471	478	478	477	476	476
Secondary	719	721	689	663	688	696	703	707	714	720	722
Combined	478	476	412	398	423	412	387	290	274	265	269
Overall Avg.	478	482	494	497	513	520	527	524	519	519	521

Note: *Size of public schools only

Source: http://nces.ed.gov/programs/digest/d05/tables/dt05_093.asp , retrieved July 15, 2007.

Fowler and Walberg (1991) exemplify a typical school size study, which examines the relationship of 23 different school characteristics, including school size, with the test scores of students in 293 New Jersey public schools. Using regression models, they find that school size is correlated with student achievement, possibly interacting with student socioeconomic status (SES) The authors note that, "although this study shows an inverse relationship between school size and student outcomes, it does not explain why this effect occurs" (p. 200). Similarly Friedkin and Necochea (1988) examine school census data from the California Department of Education, and find school size effects on student achievement. They hypothesize that:

> Positive effects of size on performance may emerge in high SES contexts because in such contexts increases in school system size generate many opportunities for improved system performance and few constraints on allocation of system resources. Conversely, negative effects of size on performance may emerge in low SES contexts because in such contexts increases in size generate few opportunities and many constraints. (p. 245)

Lee, using NELS:88, produced a series of studies examining school size. For example, in a 1995 paper Lee and Smith (1995) develop a theoretical relationship between various school restructuring reforms and student achievement, identifying practices such as collaborative staff decision making, parental volunteers, or interdisciplinary teaching teams as part of school restructuring reforms. Using hierarchical linear modeling (HLM) they find that schools that employ restructuring reforms "have strong, positive, and significant effects on students' cognitive gains in the first two years of high school" (p. 256). Conversely, schools that do not employ restructuring reforms show consistently negative relationships to student achievement gains. Finally, the authors assert that smaller school size is positively associated with achievement gains and other measures of effectiveness. In a follow-up analysis, the authors assert that schools employing restructuring practices show greater positive gains for high school students in the last 2 years when compared to traditional-practice schools or school employing no reforms. In addition, they again find a strong association between smaller schools

TABLE 34.5
Recent School Size Studies by Method

	Random Assignment of Students or Schools	Quasi-Random Assignment of Students or Schools	Attention to Sources of Arbitrary Variation in School Size	Compares same students before/after or Uses Matching/other methods to eliminate self selection
(Bryk, Camburn, & Louis, 1999)	No	No	No	No
(Darling-Hammond, Ancess, & Ort, 2002)	No	No	No	No
(Fetler, 1989)	No	No	No	No
(Fowler & Walberg, 1991)	No	No	No	No
(Friedkin & Necochea, 1988)	No	No	No	No
(Gamoran & Weinstein, 1998)	No	No	No	No
(Haller, 1992)	No	No	No	No
(Howley & Howley, 2004)	No	No	No	No
(Lee & Smith, 1995)	No	No	No	No
(Lee, Smith, & Croninger, 1997)	No	No	No	No
(Lee & Smith, 1997)	No	No	No	No
(Lee & Loeb, 2000)	No	No	No	No
(Lindsay, 1982)	No	No	No	No
(Monk, 1987)	No	No	No	No
(Monk & Haller, 1993)	No	No	No	No
(Pittman & Haughwout, 1987)	No	No	No	No

Source: Hoxby, 2006

and learning in mathematics and science (Lee, Smith, & Croninger, 1997).

In a more recent analysis, Lee and Smith (1997) note that "school size appears to matter more in schools that enroll less-advantaged students" (p. 214). The largest learning differences between low SES and high SES schools occurred at enrollment levels of under 300 students and over 900 students. Their analysis of high school size and student achievement using NELS:88 also highlights a major debate on an ideal or optimal school size. Lee and Smith suggest that the largest learning gains occurred in schools that enrolled 600–900 students, with lesser gains in other enrollment categories. The authors propose that schools could be too small or too large, and that there seems to be an ideal size in relation to student achievement in mathematics and reading. In response, Craig and Aimee Howley (2004) take issue with what they see as a limitation of national data sets such as the NELS, which tend to over sample larger schools. Their particular interest lies in small, rural schools and they conclude from their analysis that small school size and achievement are significantly related in all SES categories, except for high SES students. Additionally, they suggest that size effects are significant for the smallest of schools and take issue with the idea of an "ideal" school size.

A number of studies have attempted to explore relationships between school size and intermediate factors that may ultimately impact student achievement. Pittman and Haughwout (1987) explore the relationship between school size, a measure of school social climate, curricular diversity, and dropout rate. They conclude from their regression models that school size seems to affect dropout rate, but is mediated through some manifestation of school social climate. Fetler (1989), in his analysis of California data, also finds a modest correlation between enrollment size and dropout rate. Haller (1992) explores the relationship of school size with measures of student discipline and behavior and finds that "truancy and more serious forms of misconduct are likely to become worse when small rural schools are consolidated. But barely. Indeed, the increase may border on the imperceptible" (p. 154).

A promising area of research explores the relationship between school size and various institutional structures. For example, Monk (1987) analyzes the relationship between school size and academic course offerings and finds several surprising results. First, there is little evidence in Monk's analysis that larger schools offer more academic specialization or take advantage of economies of scale. Rather, small schools are likely to have similar course offerings to larger schools. Larger schools may offer more classes, but any new classes tend to be introductory courses in secondary subjects and do not offer any more depth in subject area than smaller schools. In another study utilizing data from the HSB, researchers find that school size affects academic program offerings in different ways as mediated by SES, urban versus rural locations, and the presence of a teachers union (Monk & Haller, 1993). While providing some compelling theoretical arguments for school size effects on

academic course offerings and equity, the authors note that "unfortunately, the present study is not adequate to show how urbanization and unionization" affect academic course offerings (p. 18).

Some studies show strong relationships between school size and institutional practices such as measures of teacher and staff professional community (Bryk, Camburn, & Louis, 1999). Similarly, other studies highlight educational processes that may theoretically influence student achievement. Gamoran and Weinstein (1998) explore practices such as ability grouping and high-quality instruction, and find that "evidence on restructured schools indicates that heterogeneous grouping neither ensures nor prohibits high-quality instruction for a wide range of students" (p. 398). Their qualitative study posits that aspects of leadership, strong teacher culture of collaboration, a strong academic focus, high-quality teaching, and a commitment to using tracking that does not inhibit a focus on equity are key influences on student achievement.

Lee and Loeb (2000) utilize HLM to find an association between smaller schools and positive teacher attitudes towards their students. Furthermore, their model finds a relationship between school size and student achievement as mediated by teachers' attitudes concerning their students. Finally, in a descriptive evaluation of several small schools, researchers identified several factors that may influence student achievement including: small size, structures that facilitate personalization and relationships, effective curricular design and pedagogy, and collaborative teacher practice (Darling-Hammond, Ancess, & Ort, 2002). Future research on school size effects may make the most impact by developing clearer causal understandings between school size and institutional practices that are shown to influence student outcomes. We offer some perspectives on this approach later in this section.

Scholars have examined the relationship between school size and student achievement, dropout, course offerings, and institutional practices. In addition to these theoretical studies, Lindsay (1982) finds a relationship between school size and student participation in activities. Lindsay examines the National Longitudinal Study (NLS) of the 1972 High School class for evidence of student participation in school activities. He finds that smaller schools show the highest percentages of students who report participation in school activities and sports. For example, 66% of students in schools that enroll 100 or less participate in sports compared to 52% of students in schools with populations over 400.

The trends of higher participation and satisfaction hold for smaller schools across the various measures that Lindsay (1982) explores. However, the author correctly understands that such evidence does not present a causal explanation of small school effects. Lindsay notes that, "this study does not answer the question of why school size has these effects" (p. 64) and that theoretically, one could organize a large school to provide increased opportunities and encouragement for participation. The author posits that smaller schools may require a higher percentage of students to participate in activities, due to the sheer interaction of supply and demand. A football team requires 22 starters on offense and defense, regardless of whether the total school enrollment is 100 or 400 students.

This brief overview of some of the findings on school size illustrates the relatively undeveloped nature of the research base. Table 34.6 summarizes the research evidence reviewed in this chapter around major themes. The research literature is far from providing clear findings on the critical causal relationship between school size and student outcomes. Unlike STAR in the case of class size, the evidence is overwhelmingly non-experimental with weak correlations taken to imply causation. This trend is troubling given how many programs, interventions, and policies advocating small school size have been enacted. The financial, social, and academic costs of school size interventions are large, and clearly more rigorous evidence is needed to determine if such efforts are likely to be successful.

Future research on school size is needed in two directions. First, establishing the causal relationship (if any) between school size and student achievement should be a top priority. This research stream requires either advanced quasi-experimental methods such as a regression discontinuity design, propensity score matching, or an experimental trial. Clearly such research methods pose significant logistical challenges—for example, randomly assigning students to schools of different size is unlikely to be feasible. However, it may be possible to take advantage of the current wave of school restructuring interventions, particularly in high schools such as "schools within schools" to attempt planned variation with students randomly assigned.

We note a series of promising analyses by Schneider, Wyse, and Keesler (2007) that critically examine the role of selection bias when examining data sets used in small schools research. Using the Education Longitudinal Study of 2002, the authors test several expected outcomes of small schools such as: mathematics achievement, student knowledge of post-secondary education, future aspirations, and college application. Their first set of analyses utilizes hierarchical linear models to examine the impact of school and individual variables on the outcome variables. The authors did not find clear, significant effects of school size in any of their models. Most interesting, however, was their use of propensity score matching to directly compare students who have similar characteristics and likelihood of receiving a treatment.

Schneider et al. (2007) computed propensity scores for the students in the data set, and then used the scores in regression models to compare matched groups. This technique attempts to further isolate the school size variable to develop stronger conclusions of a treatment effect. Using a matched-group strategy, the authors find no significant effect of school size on mathematics achievement. For other outcome variables, the authors find no clear relationship between school size and post-secondary knowledge or expectations. Furthermore, in some models the researchers find the opposite of the expected effect. For example, they find that "small schools have a negative effect on students' expectations to obtain an advanced degree" (p. 36) for particular matched groups. Their series of analyses shed doubt on a direct effect of school size on measures such as test scores and college aspiration.

Second, further research is needed to nail down how school size matters. Most of the past research literature

TABLE 34.6
Possible School Size Effects

Theoretical Implication	Citation
Small schools may promote more student participation in school activities.	(Lindsay, 1982)
A relationship between enrollment size and available opportunities for student involvement may explain rates of student participation in school life.	
Small schools may promote less dropout or discipline issues.	
The relationship between school size and dropout or discipline may be **mediated** by measures of school social climate such as SES.	(Pittman & Haughwout, 1987) (Fetler, 1989) (Haller, 1992)
School size may influence institutional practices such as academic course offerings, tracking, professional community, and instruction.	(Monk, 1987) (Monk & Haller, 1993)
This relationship between school size and practice may be **mediated** by variables such as SES, urbanization, or unionization.	(Gamoran & Weinstein, 1998) (Bryk et al., 1999) (Darling-Hammond et al., 2002)
School size may impact student achievement but is **mediated** by variables such as SES, or institutional practices such a teacher attitudes, team teaching, or other restructuring reforms.	(Friedkin & Necochea, 1988) (Fowler & Walberg, 1991)
There may be an ideal school size to achieve the best balance of student achievement, equity, and economy of scale.	(Lee & Smith, 1995) (Lee et al., 1997) (Lee & Smith, 1997) (Lee & Loeb, 2000)
There may not be an ideal school size, but rather an appropriate school size as mediated by contexts (variables) such as SES or urbanization versus rural.	(Monk, 1987) (Monk & Haller, 1993) (Lee & Smith, 1997) (Howley & Howley, 2004)

views school size as mediated by other variables such as SES. Future studies might examine how school composition, student demographics, teacher characteristics, community and location variables, and other factors interact with school size. In addition, there is only suggestive evidence of how school size relates to school organization, culture and community, academic programs, and teacher practice.

The key question is whether smaller schools lead to positive practices, and whether those practices influence higher student achievement. For example, popular justifications for small schools include the creation of more communal, personal environments that imply better student experiences. However, studies such as one by Meredith Phillips (1997) suggest that other factors may be more important than a sense of community for student achievement. Using hierarchical modeling, she finds that communal organization was not related to higher mathematics achievement. Rather, high expectations and challenging curriculum (what she terms academic press) were related to higher achievement. Ultimately, the onus on future school size researchers will be to provide evidence that small schools are a necessary condition for various institutional practices that are in turn linked to improved student achievement.

Conclusions

Class and school size policies are some of the most intuitive and popular education reforms. Such policies easily mobilize stakeholders and enjoy widespread support. However, such strategies are decidedly expensive, requiring physical and human resources that are costly and time consuming to procure. In some settings, particularly urban areas with little available space for new buildings and difficulties attracting qualified teachers, such policies may be especially difficult to implement and may have the unintended consequence of exacerbating inequalities between students. Whether smaller class and school sizes are *cost effective* is far from established. Clearly, the importance of a strong research base on class and school size is critical.

Existing work on class and school size effects provide varying degrees of definitive evidence to support the widespread adoption of respective policies. School size research has produced plausible arguments as to why it might be expected to affect student outcomes, but no compelling evidence on the existence of such a relationship. The extensive number of small school programs around the country resting on such a fragile research base is striking, but their popularity does at least hold out the prospect of new findings emerging over the next decade that can provide more depth to our understanding of how school size may matter.

Due to the existence of a well-done randomized trial in Project STAR, class size research has produced more believable findings that are useful for policy makers. A reasonable conclusion is that when there are no deleterious effects on teacher supply or physical facilities, classes of around 15 students for grades K-3 produce noticeable increases in student achievement particularly for poor and minority children. Nevertheless, the implementation of class size reduction in California clearly demonstrates that the experimental conditions under which these findings hold may not be easy to replicate in large-scale settings. Future research will need to further examine the effects of class size for different subgroups of students, effects on instructional practice, and cost effectiveness of the intervention relative to other reforms.

References

American Federation of Teachers. (n.d.). *Benefits of small class size*. Retrieved June 6, 2007, from http://www.aft.org/topics/classsize/index.htm

Biddle, B. J., & Berliner, D.C. (2002). Small class size and its effects. *Educational Leadership*, 59(5), 12–23.

Bill & Melinda Gates Foundation. (n.d.). *High schools for the new millennium: Imagine the possibilities*. Retrieved June 4, 2007, from http://www.gatesfoundation.org/nr/downloads/ed/edwhitepaper.pdf

Bohrnstedt, G. W., & Stecher, B. M. (2002). *What we have learned about class size reduction in California*. Retrieved July 15, 2007, from http://www.classize.org/techreport/CSR_Capstone_prepub.pdf

Brewer, D. J., Krop, C., Gill, B. P., & Reichardt, R. (1999). Estimating the cost of national class size reductions under different policy alternatives. *Educational Evaluation and Policy Analysis, 21*, 179–192.

Bryk, A., Camburn, E., & Louis, K. S. (1999). Professional community in Chicago elementary schools: Facilitating factors and organizational consequences. *Educational Administration Quarterly, 35*, 751–781.

Class Size Matters. (n.d.). *The benefits of smaller classes: What the research shows*. Retrieved June 6, 2007, from http://www.classsize-matters.org/benefits.html

Clotfelter, C. T., Ladd, H. F., & Vigdor, J. (2005). Who teaches whom? Race and the distribution of novice teachers. *Economics of Education Review, 24*, 377–392.

Darling-Hammond, L. (n.d.). *Redesigning schools: 10 features of effective design*. Stanford, CA: Stanford University, School Redesign Network.

Darling-Hammond, L., Ancess, J., & Ort, S. W. (2002). Reinventing high school: Outcomes of the coalition campus schools projects. *American Educational Research Journal, 39*, 639–673.

Ehrenberg, R. G., Brewer, D. J., Gamoran, A., & Willms, J. D. (2001a). Class size and student achievement. *Psychological Science in the Public Interest, 2*, 1–30.

Ehrenberg, R. G., Brewer, D. J., Gamoran, A., & Willms, J. D. (2001b). Does class size matter? *Scientific American, 285*(5), 78–85.

Fetler, M. (1989). School dropout rates, academic performance, size, and poverty: Correlates of educational reform. *Educational Evaluation and Policy Analysis, 11*, 109–116.

Finn, J. D., & Achilles, C. M. (1990). Answers and questions about class size: A statewide experiment. *American Educational Research Journal, 27*, 557–577.

Finn, J. D., Fox, J. D., McClellan, M., Achilles, C. M., & Boyd-Zaharias, J. (2006). Small classes in the early grades and course taking in high school [Electronic version]. *International Journal of Education Policy and Leadership, 1*(1).

Finn, J. D., Gerber, S. B., & Boyd-Zaharias, J. (2005). Small classes in the early grades, academic achievement, and graduating from high school. *Journal of Educational Psychology, 97*, 214–223.

Fowler, W. J., & Walberg, H. J. (1991). School size, characteristics, and outcomes. *Educational Evaluation and Policy Analysis, 13*, 189–202.

Friedkin, N. E., & Necochea, J. (1988). School system size and performance: A contingency perspective. *Educational Evaluation and Policy Analysis, 10*, 237–249.

Gamoran, A., & Weinstein, M. (1998). Differentiation and opportunity in restructured schools. *American Journal of Education, 106*, 385–415.

Gewertz, C. (2006). Chicago's small schools see gains, but not on tests

[Electronic version]. *Education Week*, *25*(44), 5, 14. Retrieved June 6, 2007, from http://www.edweek.org/ew/articles/2006/08/09/44chicago.h25.html?tmp=464574480

Haller, E. J. (1992). High school size and student indiscipline: Another aspect of the school consolidation issue? *Educational Evaluation and Policy Analysis*, *14*, 145–156.

Hanushek, E. A. (1999). Some findings from an independent investigation of the Tennessee STAR experiment and from other investigations of class size effects. *Educational Evaluation and Policy Analysis*, *21*, 143–163.

Hedges, L. V., & Greenwald, R. (1996). Have times changed? The relation between school resources and student performance. In G. Burtless (Ed.), *Does money matter? The effect of school resources on student achievement* (pp. 74–92). Washington, DC: Brookings Institution.

Howley, C. B., & Howley, A. A. (2004). School size and the influence of socioeconomic status on student achievement: Confronting the threat of size bias in national data sets *Education Policy Analysis Archives*, *12*(53). Retrieved June 5, 2007, from http://epaa.asu.edu/epaa/v12n52/

Hoxby, C. M. (2006, May). *Comments on high school size, structure, and content: What matters for student success?* Paper presented at the Brookings Papers on Education Policy Conference, Washington, DC.

Lee, V. E., & Loeb, S. (2000). School size in Chicago elementary schools: Effects on teachers' attitudes and students' achievement. *American Educational Research Journal*, *37*, 3–31.

Lee, V. E., & Smith, J. B. (1995). Effects of high school restructuring and size on early gains in achievement and engagement. *Sociology of Education*, *68*, 241–270.

Lee, V. E., & Smith, J. B. (1997). High school size: Which works best and for whom? *Educational Evaluation and Policy Analysis*, *19*, 205–227.

Lee, V. E., Smith, J. B., & Croninger, R. G. (1997). How high school organization influences the equitable distribution of learning in mathematics and science. *Sociology of Education*, *70*, 128–150.

Lindsay, P. (1982). The effect of high school size on student participation, satisfaction, and attendance. *Educational Evaluation and Policy Analysis*, *4*, 57–65.

Molnar, A., Smith, P., Zahorik, J., Palmer, A., Halbach, A., & Ehrle, K. (1999). Evaluating the SAGE program: A pilot program in targeted pupil-teacher reduction in Wisconsin. *Educational Evaluation and Policy Analysis*, *21*, 165–177.

Monk, D. H. (1987). Secondary school size and curriculum comprehensiveness. *Economics of Education Review*, *6*, 137–150.

Monk, D. H., & Haller, E. J. (1993). Predictors of high school academic course offerings: The role of school size. *American Educational Research Journal*, *30*, 3–21.

National Center for Education Statistics. (n.d.). *Historical summary of public elementary and secondary school statistics: Selected years 1869–70 through 2002–2003*. Retrieved July 15, 2007, from http://nces.ed.gov/programs/digest/d05/tables/dt05_032.asp?referrer=list

National Education Association. (n.d.). *Class size*. Retrieved June 6, 2007, from http://www.nea.org/classsize/index.html

Nye, B., Hedges, L. V., & Konstantopoulos, S. (2002). Do low achieving students benefit more from small classes? Evidence from the Tennessee class size experiment. *Educational Evaluation and Policy Analysis*, *24*, 201–217.

Phillips, M. (1997). What makes schools effective? A comparison of the relationships of communitarian climate and academic climate to mathematics achievement and attendance during middle school. *American Educational Research Journal*, *34*, 633–662.

Pittman, R. B., & Haughwout, P. (1987). Influence of high school size on dropout rate. *Educational Evaluation and Policy Analysis*, *9*, 337–343.

Schneider, B., Wyse, A. W., & Keesler, V. (2007). Is small really better? Testing some assumptions about high school size. In T. Loveless & F. Hess (Eds.), *Brookings papers on education policy: 2006–2007* (pp. 15–46). Washington DC: Brookings Institution.

Small Schools Project. (n.d.). *What are small schools?* Retrieved June 6, 2007, from http://www.smallschoolsproject.org/index.asp?siteloc=whysmall&section=whatss

Stecher, B. M., McCaffrey, D. F., & Bugliari, D. (2003). The relationship between exposure to class size reduction and student achievement in California. *Education Policy Analysis Archives*, *11*(40). Retrieved June 8, 2007, from http://epaa.asu.edu/epaa/v11n40/

35

Conceptions, Measurement, and Application of *Educational Adequacy* and *Equal Educational Opportunity*

BRUCE D. BAKER
Rutgers University

PRESTON C. GREEN, III
The Pennsylvania State University

Introduction

This chapter provides an overview of emerging issues in state school finance policy in the United States. We begin with an introduction to conceptions of equity and adequacy in education finance, specific to the policy context of U.S. states. In particular, we focus on the concepts of *equity* and *adequacy* in education finance, reviewing traditional conceptions and terminology that have evolved over the past several decades and providing new insights regarding both the intersections and points of divergence between *equity* and *adequacy* conceptions.

This chapter begins by providing a conceptual overview, addressing the historical roots of language used in school finance for describing conditions of equity and adequacy. The section that follows addresses the shift from input-oriented equity to outcome-oriented equity that accompanied the emergence of the accountability and outcome assessment movement, then further explains how this shift necessitates reconsidering our conventional framing of equity and adequacy conceptions. Next, the chapter moves on to summarize approaches used for estimating education costs and determining empirically the underlying costs of educational adequacy and cost variation associated with providing equal educational opportunity across children and settings. Following this summary are in-depth analyses and discussion of the use of empirical information on basic and marginal costs of education in the context of state school finance litigation in Arkansas, Wyoming, Kansas, New York, and Texas.

We conclude this chapter with a discussion of three major points of contention that have emerged through recent school finance litigation: (a) the balance between adequacy and equity, (b) the balance between judicial and legislative roles in guiding school finance reform, and (c) the balance between politics and empirical evidence in guiding state school finance reform.

Equity Conceptions in School Finance

School finance policy lies at the intersection of the fields of public finance, law, and other social sciences. As first comprehensively framed by Robert Berne and Leanna Stiefel in 1984, school finance equity may be viewed from either or both the perspectives of the *taxpayer* or the *child*. Because equity measurement evaluates the distribution of objects, there exists the critical underlying question—across which units of organization should the distribution of objects be evaluated? Ideally, equity would be measured across each individual child or taxpayer, if one could measure precisely the educational inputs available to each child or tax burden shouldered by each individual taxpayer. Most U.S. states organize public schooling into local education agencies, or school districts with school buildings within districts, Hawai'i being a notable exception where the school district intermediate level of governance is effectively non-existent.[1] In most states, the primary role for the intermediate governance unit—the school district—is financial management, including authority over local taxation for annual operations of schools and infrastructure.[2] State government interventions to resolve inequities have been designed to compensate primarily inequities in revenue raising capacity across school districts.[3] State aid is allocated primarily to districts, not schools or children. As such, most school finance distributional analyses focus on distribution across school districts, masking potentially large disparities across school buildings, and children within buildings.[4]

Berne and Stiefel (1984) offer the following four guiding questions for evaluating equity in school finance: (a) who, (b) what, (c) how, and (d) how much. Under the question of *who*, various constituents might be addressed, including children, teachers, or taxpayers. Most often, children, clustered within school districts, have been the emphasis in school finance equity analysis.

Under the question of *what*, one may focus on (a) fiscal inputs to schooling; (b) resources purchased with those fiscal inputs including teachers, equipment, materials, supplies, as well as facilities and transportation; (c) educational processes, including time spent on specific activities and student participation rates in specific courses of study; or (d) student outcomes, ranging from measures of academic achievement to measures of economic productivity. Historically, analyses have focused on the first of these—financial inputs to schooling, usually per pupil expenditure, measured at the school district (local education agency) level.[5] Further, most analysts have evaluated state-level systems of financing public education, excluding children in private and homeschooling. Cross-state analyses have been relatively rare, as have analyses that include private schooling or more recently charter schooling.[6]

In response to the question of *how*, Berne and Stiefel (1984) discuss equal opportunity and draw on public finance concepts of horizontal equity or the *equal treatment of equals*, and vertical equity or the *unequal treatment of unequals*. In their framing of the *equal opportunity* concept, Berne and Stiefel defined equal opportunity as what is now typically called fiscal neutrality. Fiscal neutrality means that variations in resources across children should not be a function of the wealth of the community in which a child happens to live.

The *how much* question requires statistical measures, which can be distinguished by their emphasis on different ranges of the resource distribution.[7] These measures address questions such as how much variation in resources across similarly situated students is acceptable? How much variation across differently situated students is necessary and on what basis?

Origins of the Berne and Stiefel Framework
Theories underlying Berne and Stiefel's (1984) framework came from two discrete sources that were adapted for evaluating the raising of public education revenue and distribution of expenditures across public schools. The first of these sources was public finance principles applied to tax policy. The second was legal theory. Given this context, the frameworks addressed herein are unique to the public education system in the United States, a nation where defining educational rights has been left largely to the states and where no broader guarantee of education as a basic human right is explicitly acknowledged.

Public Finance Origins   Though applied by Berne and Stiefel to the expenditure side of the school finance equation, the basic concepts of *horizontal* and *vertical* equity were drawn from a lengthy literature in public finance that focuses on tax policy. Within the context of the literature on tax policy, horizontal equity refers to the equal treatment of equals, and is a concept around which there is little dispute. Simons (1950) notes that "it is generally agreed that taxes should bear similarly upon all people in similar circumstances" (p. 8).

The concept of vertical equity (VE) in tax policy, like its counterpart in school finance, is more controversial. In general, VE in tax policy refers to the progressiveness of a tax, or how much more certain individuals should be asked to pay in taxes, and on what basis. As such, horizontal equity accepts that unequals should be treated unequally. Scholars of tax policy suggest two possible standards for determining the fair treatment of taxpayers that are unequal: (a) the benefit standard, and (b) the ability (to pay) standard (Monk & Brent, 1997). Under the benefit standard, individuals or groups who stand to reap the greatest benefit from a tax should pay higher taxes, as is assumed to be the case with consumption taxes on luxury goods or special assessments on property for sidewalks. Under the ability standard, individuals with greater ability to pay a tax should pay higher taxes relative to their income, as would be the case with a progressively structured income tax.[8] In the tax policy context, one is still left with the value-laden concern over just how progressive is progressive enough? We suggest at a later point that this vertical equity question is more easily answered in the context of modern public education finance.

Legal Origins   The second major element of the origin of Berne and Stiefel's (1984) framework was the emergence of early legal theories on how best to challenge and resolve significant disparities across school districts, schools, or students in the quality of public schooling. Legal theorists of the late 1960s suggested frameworks for evaluating variation in educational resources, with the particular goal of showing that wealth-based resource variation violated the Equal Protection Clause. Such frameworks sought to build on the Supreme Court's treatment of the Equal Protection Clause in the 1950s and 1960s (Enrich, 1995). Especially important was the Supreme Court's suggestion in *Brown v. Board of Education* (1954) that governments had an affirmative duty to ensure that educational services were equally available to all. Horowitz (1966) suggested that variations in resources that were geographically arbitrary should be considered by courts to violate equal protection—the principle of *geographic uniformity*. Coons, Clune, and Sugarman (1969), building on this argument, proposed the principle of *fiscal neutrality*. They argued that children in property-poor school districts were discriminated against by state policies that allowed heavy reliance on local property taxation for public schooling.

The framework of Coons et al. (1969) provided the basis for arguments in two seminal early school finance cases—*Serrano v. Priest* (1971) in California state court and *San Antonio Independent School District v. Rodriguez* (1973) in federal court. Both were equal protection challenges, and both challenged disparities in funding across school districts that resulted from differences in local taxable property wealth and local taxing decisions under state policy. The California State Supreme Court agreed that property wealth-related disparities in school district funding were unacceptable, in part on the assumption that wealth was a suspect class and that differential treatment by wealth should be reviewed under *strict scrutiny*. The U.S. Supreme Court viewed Texas' wealth-related school funding disparities differently, ruling that under the U.S. Constitution, individuals residing in property-poor school districts were not a suspect class, and that only *rational basis* scrutiny was required. In their final analysis, the U.S. Supreme Court accepted under rational basis that Texas had a legitimate interest in maintaining locally controlled taxation for public schooling. In part, testimony in *Rodriguez* revealed the complexities of evaluating the relationship between school funding and community attributes, while shutting off all future federal court challenges to property wealth-related disparities in educational funding.[9] While the arguments failed in federal court, there were some additional early successes in state courts beyond *Serrano*.[10]

The Shift from Input Equity to Outcome Equity in School Finance

Early legal challenges to state financing of public schools sought to achieve the modest and oversimplified goal of providing more equal dollar inputs to schooling, with little consideration for how the value of those dollar inputs varied across children and settings. The shift toward greater emphasis on vertical equity, as we have come to know it, is in large part associated with a shift away from a focus on the equality of educational inputs toward the equality of educational outcomes.

Interest in input-outcome relationships in public schooling grew in the aftermath of the Coleman et al. (1966) report which cast doubt on the role of schooling resources relative to family resources in influencing student outcomes. Interest in the input-outcome relationships in state school finance policy have become more central to policy discussions in recent decades with the implementation of state accountability standards and assessments across many states in the 1990s, and federal codification of accountability requirements under the No Child Left Behind Act of 2001 (NCLB). Other chapters in this volume provide thorough treatment of the accountability movement during these periods.

While shifting focus toward educational outcomes, the Coleman report (1966) raised more questions than it answered. In particular, the Coleman report raised questions that would linger through current school finance litigation about the tenuous nature of the relationship between schooling quality—as measured by student outcomes—and financial inputs to schooling. Does money matter? Will equal inputs lead to equity defined in terms of educational outcomes? Or are differential inputs needed to account for different needs and costs of achieving common outcomes? Plecki and Castañeda (this volume) explore the literature on input-outcome relationships in schooling.

Vertical Equity as Outcome Equity In the tax policy literature, no standard provides a definitive answer to the question of *how much* progressiveness is enough. Arguably, in school finance policy, the *how much* question is easier to address. At least at the conceptual level, how much, in terms of the differential input required for groups with different educational needs, can be defined in terms of the relative sufficiency of those resources toward improving equity of educational outcomes. Those outcomes may be measured either in normative terms or against specific criteria. Such criteria might include acceptable minimum performance on state assessments, graduation rates, or successful matriculation to and participation in postsecondary education. In that sense, vertical equity as a school finance conception might simply be redefined as horizontal equity of outcomes or horizontal equity of opportunity to achieve a defined outcome. Stated differently, equality of outcomes requires differentiation of financial inputs.

This statement further highlights that separate conceptions of horizontal and vertical equity are not warranted in school finance. Vertical equity, as we have come to use the term, simply refers to horizontal equity of educational outcomes or equal opportunity to attain specific educational outcomes. Focusing on outcomes in place of financial inputs, children typically classified under state school finance and regulatory policies, including children with disabilities, English language learners, and economically disadvantaged children are not "differently situated" from other children, thus requiring "different" treatment. Rather, they all are similarly situated, requiring similar treatment, where the "treatment" in question is the expectation that all children can achieve specific educational outcomes. As such, a general conception of equity (usually referred to as horizontal equity) is sufficient. To expect more or less in terms of outcomes from some children than others is to apply different treatment. The required differentiation of dollar inputs to schooling to achieve common goals is a function of the different value of a dollar input from one location to another, one year to another, and one child or group of children to another. The cost of equal treatment varies from one location to another, one year to another, and one child or group of children to another.

Shifting the focus toward outcomes raises the question of *which outcomes* are of greatest interest. The most common outcome in school finance litigation is student achievement as measured by state standardized test scores. Test scores have become the centerpiece of school finance litigation, in part because of their role in state performance based accountability systems. Further, most statistical analyses of the costs of achieving state-mandated educational outcome levels have focused on the costs either of achieving specific test score levels on state assessments or on the costs of achieving specific percentages of children scoring proficient or higher on state assessments. Less attention has been paid to longer term outcomes such as college attendance and completion, future earnings or harder-to-measure *quality of life outcomes* addressed in disability literature (Turnbull, Turnbull, Wehmeyer, & Park, 2003). In contrast to the narrow focus on test scores in cost studies, judicial decrees based on state education clauses have expressed a far broader conception of the desired outcomes of schooling, focusing most often on economic and civic participation (Rebell, 2002).

Educational Adequacy and Vertical Equity In the early 1990s, on the heels of influential state court rulings including *Rose v. Council for Better Education in Kentucky* (1989), scholars began presenting arguments for an approach to *leveling up* state education systems rather than *equalizing* them. Clune (1994), in "The Shift from Equity to Adequacy in School Finance," argued for a target of high minimum adequacy funding to be provided as a base across school districts and children within a state. This shift in emphasis from equity to a common basic floor of funding raised new questions as to how such a floor would be determined, and whether such an exercise was feasible or appropriate (Hanushek, 1994). Further, the shift toward identifying a basic floor of funding raised new questions as to how that floor might vary across children of varied needs.

Authors, including Underwood (1995), sought a connection between conceptions of vertical equity and the new educational adequacy. Underwood (1995) chose to frame vertical equity as synonymous with educational adequacy, asserting that each individual child requires a specific set of educational programs and services to achieve the desired educational outcomes for that child. As such, those inputs are necessarily differentiated. In fact, under this conception, while horizontal equity theoretically exists, it may not practically exist, since no two children's educational needs are exactly the same. Underwood's framework, while useful, applies under two very limited conditions. First, it applies only to vertical equity pertaining to individual student educational needs and it requires that a level of desired educational outcome be specified for each child or all children. Underwood's framework is primarily an adequacy framework, pegged to a specific level of outcome, with emphasis on state-mandated outcome levels.

Conditions that influence vertical equity for students (other than an individual child's needs) include concentrations of children from economically disadvantaged backgrounds, children with limited English language proficiency, minority student concentrations, or average peer group prior achievement level. While Underwood's conception addresses the student's individual needs, Underwood's approach fails to acknowledge the potential effects of peers on students' individual outcomes and different costs of improving those outcomes as peer composition varies. Underwood's conception also fails to address the fact that costs of outcomes vary due to labor market costs (cost of attaining sufficient quantity of teachers of specific quality) and economies of scale, among other things. Individual student background attributes are but one small piece of a complex integrated puzzle in which the specific educational needs of individual students interact with the composition

of students' peer groups and the context in which children are schooled, all of which affect comprehensively the costs of achieving specific educational outcomes.

To return to a previous point, we may separate conceptions of equity and adequacy, setting aside vertical equity. Educational adequacy speaks to a specific level of education outcome that is to be considered adequate or sufficient. That is, how much education is enough? What level of academic achievement outcome or other, broader social, economic or political outcome is sufficient? Some hypothetical level of financial and other inputs to schooling would be required for achieving the adequate outcome, in the aggregate, across all the children in any state.

Adequacy does not speak to equity concerns unless the adopted conception of adequacy assumes that the children of the state should have equal opportunity to achieve the adequate outcome. When equal opportunity to achieve the "adequate" level of outcome is considered, the cost in dollar inputs of achieving that outcome will vary across settings and children. This condition is analogous to Underwood's "vertical equity as adequacy." But, the conception of equity or equal educational opportunity exists and is measurable even when no "adequate" outcome goal is identified. If a state school finance system is funded such that on average, children receive only a sub-par, sub-adequate education, one can still measure the equal opportunity across children and settings with respect to existing outcomes—adequate or not.

Koski and Reich (2006) cast additional doubt on the usefulness of a minimum educational adequacy conception as proposed by Clune (1994), or vertical equity as adequacy conception as proposed by Underwood (1995). Koski and Reich argue that the quality of educational outcomes is largely relative because education is primarily a competitive *positional good.* Hirsch (1976) describes positional competition as follows:

> By positional competition is meant competition that is fundamentally for a higher place within some explicit or implicit hierarchy and that thereby yields gains for some only by dint of loss for others. Positional competition, in the language of game theory, is a zero-sum game: what winners win, losers lose. (p. 52)

If education is to be considered a competitive positional good, the extent of disparity in educational outcomes above a minimum outcome standard codified in state policies matters a great deal. Under a *vertical equity as adequacy* conception, it matters only whether individuals have sufficient resources to achieve a state mandated minimum outcome level. Yet, Koski and Reich argue that the value of achieving that minimum standard is largely contingent on the variation above it. In a system where children are guaranteed only minimally adequate K-12 education, but where many receive far superior opportunities, those with only minimally adequate education will have limited opportunities in higher education or the workplace.

Koski and Reich's point is not new. In the aftermath of

the *Rodriguez* decision in which the courts first raised the question of *minimum educational adequacy,* Arthur Wise (1976) explained that it is likely that the least fair state school finance systems in the nation might surpass the minimum adequacy standard by allowing no one school or child to fall below a meaningless minimum outcome threshold, but allowing dramatic degrees of opportunity surplus beyond that minimum threshold.

Outcome Standards, State Constitutions, and Education Costs

Since the 1990s, spawned in part by the educational adequacy movement, there has been increased attention to measuring education costs, and how those costs vary across children and settings. Notably, studies of education costs intended for use in setting policy targets date back to at least the 1930s. Mort and Reusser (1951), in reference to a study conducted in 1930–31, describe setting foundation funding according to the average "expenditures of the well-organized districts of average wealth" (p. 388). In the early 1980s, Chambers (1984) and Chambers and Parrish (1982) conducted detailed analyses of the resources required for providing a funding base for education in Illinois and in Alaska.

Studies of average spending, like those described in Mort and Reusser (1951) are studies of how much, on average, is being spent by local public school districts, toward achieving current average levels of educational outcomes, but without actually measuring outcomes. If current outcomes are "adequate," one might consider current average spending, given the average productive efficiency with which schooling resources are used, to be adequate. That is, studies of average spending assume the current technology of producing education outcomes to be reasonable, and identify a single target of average spending associated with the average outcome. Extending this logic to U.S. education systems as a whole, if we believe that on average, U.S. public schooling produces adequate educational outcomes, then the average amount spent on U.S. public schooling is adequate (setting aside the undersupply concern that the current average outcome is produced across only the 85%–90% of children attending public schools).[11] Such analysis provides no insight into equal educational opportunity—whether the low income child from Alabama has equal chance of achieving the national average outcome as the child in an affluent Connecticut suburb.

Studies conducted by Chambers and colleagues in the 1980s evaluated detailed programming inputs to schooling, based on existing and recommended practices (service delivery methods and models). These studies went a step further than average spending studies, because they included not only estimates of the costs of core, regular education programs, but also estimates of additional expenditures required on special services for identified student populations. Further, these studies considered how competitive wages of school staff might vary from one location to another. In short, these resource-cost-model, input-oriented studies

began to consider the ways in which costs of providing appropriate educational services vary from one location to the next and one child to the next. These studies did not, however, link explicitly those differentiated services to common outcomes.

These two approaches, spending-based analysis and resource input-based analysis, provided the groundwork for the more recent proliferation of *education cost studies* geared to identifying the absolute level of funding required for achieving adequate educational outcomes and identifying how the costs of achieving any given level of educational outcome vary across children and settings. The most significant difference between early and more recent studies is the attempt in more recent studies to address the connection between educational inputs and outcomes.

Two general approaches exist for estimating base and marginal costs in education: (a) resource cost, or input-oriented analysis; and (b) statistical modeling, or outcome-oriented analysis.[12]

Input-Oriented Analysis The *resource cost model* (RCM) is a method that has been used extensively for measuring the costs of educational services—existing or hypothetical, adequate or not (Chambers, 1999; Hartman, Bolton, & Monk, 2001). The RCM methodology typically involves three steps: (a) identifying and/or measuring the resources (people, space, stuff, and time) used in providing a particular set of services, (b) estimating resource prices and price variations from school to school or school district to school district, and (c) tabulating total costs of service delivery by totaling the resource quantities (resource intensity) and the prices. Resource cost methods have been used for calculating the cost of providing adequate educational services since the early 1980s, including legislatively sponsored statewide resource cost studies in Illinois and Alaska.

Recent applications of RCM have been tailored specifically to measure the costs of an "adequate" education— *professional judgment*-driven RCM and *evidence-based* RCM. The difference between them lies in the strategy for identifying the resources required to provide an adequate education. In professional judgment studies, focus groups of educators and policy makers are convened to prescribe the "basket of educational goods and services" required for providing an adequate education. In evidence-based studies, resource needs for staffing and staff development are derived from "proven effective" Comprehensive School Reform (CSR) models like Robert Slavin's *Roots and Wings/Success for All*, that focus on improving educational outcomes in high poverty schools (Odden, 2000). More recent evidence-based analyses have attempted to integrate a variety of "proven effective" input strategies such as class size reduction, specific interventions for special student populations, and comprehensive school reform models, rather than relying on a single reform model.

Outcome-Oriented Analysis Increasingly common among recent analyses of educational adequacy are statistical methods that may be used either to estimate (a) the quantities and qualities of educational resources associated with higher or improved educational outcomes or (b) the costs associated with achieving a specific set of outcomes, in different school districts, serving different student populations. The first of these methods is known as the education production function and the second of these methods is known as the education cost function.

Education production function analysis can be used to determine which quantities and qualities of educational resources are most strongly, positively associated with a measured set of student outcomes. For example, is it better for a school to have more teachers or fewer teachers with stronger academic preparation at the same total cost to maximize some desired outcome? Further, education production function analysis can be used to determine whether different resource quantities and qualities are more or less effective in districts serving different types of students (economically disadvantaged, English language learners), or in different types of districts (large urban, small remote rural).

It is difficult, however, to use education production function analysis directly in the prediction of financial resource levels needed toward achieving specific levels of student outcomes across children and settings. When one estimates a production function model, one must estimate statistically the relationship between the spending input and student outcome measure, with the spending input measure as an independent variable. Many production function analyses which attempt to link spending in the aggregate and student outcomes find a relatively weak, or fuzzy and insensitive relationship between spending and outcomes, a problem which occurs because the aggregate spending measure includes inefficiently used resources. Extrapolating total costs of desired outcomes from this weak relationship can produced strange if not absurd results (Imazeki, 2007) and it remains difficult if not infeasible to correct for inefficiency when the inefficiency is contained in the key explanatory variable in the statistical model (Duncombe & Yinger, 2007).

Production function studies may be more useful for sorting out which, among resource uses, show clearer positive relationships to student outcomes, like class size or specific teacher qualifications. However, production functions of specific resource uses provide little insights into how resources should be aggregated, or the resulting costs of aggregation at the school or district level.

In contrast, several authors have applied education cost function analysis, which involves estimating statistical models of spending across school districts (Downes & Pogue, 1994; Duncombe & Yinger, 2006, 2007; Reschovsky & Imazeki, 2004; Gronberg, Jansen, Taylor, & Booker, 2004). Cost function models use data on education spending across districts as the dependent variable, and educational outcomes as a key independent variable, along with a variety of other factors assumed to influence the costs of achieving specific outcome levels. Cost factors commonly include district characteristics such as economies of scale and geographic

location (as influences competitive wages) and student population characteristics. That is, the cost function asks, what spending level is associated with specific levels of educational outcomes, across varied settings and children?

Unlike production function studies, cost function studies do attempt to account for differences in the efficiency with which educational resources are used across districts. Education cost function models include additional variables that attempt to capture the extent that some districts, more than others, are likely to spend more than would be needed at minimum to achieve a specific level of educational outcomes. Recent cost function studies identify factors associated with the behavior of public bureaucracies that may influence relative efficiency (Duncombe & Yinger, 2008). Notably, in cost function models based on existing spending data, efficiency can only be considered in a relative sense. How much more or less productive is one district than another at producing a given level of outcomes with a given level of spending, in a specific context serving specific students? Under this framework, one can estimate needed spending associated with specific educational outcomes, if all districts were to produce outcomes at comparable levels of efficiency.[13]

Critique and Comparison of Methods　When it comes to estimation of a single cost figure for the underlying costs of providing an "adequate" education, both input- and outcome- oriented methods are significantly problematic. The central assumption in identifying the "costs of adequacy" is that one can identify the minimum financial input needed for achieving a level of outcomes defined as adequate in a specific state context. In professional judgment RCM studies, panels suggest resource configurations they assume to be reasonable toward achieving desired outcomes in the state context, drawing on their experiences in that context. But, any specific connection between inputs and outcomes is only speculative. Evidence-based RCM is even more problematic in that external consultants propose input configurations based on aggregation of reform models and strategies that may ill-fit specific schooling contexts within a state and that may not be geared toward the desired outcomes. For example, reform strategies may have been selected on the basis of positive reading outcomes in large urban districts, but proposed for implementation in remote rural locations.

Cost function models may also be of limited use in pinning down the minimum costs of producing "adequate" levels of educational outcomes statewide because cost function models cannot fully account for inefficiency. Further, where desired outcome levels are well beyond those currently achieved by some or all districts, using the statistical model to extrapolate predicted spending to meet those levels may be an unreasonable exercise. And cost function models can estimate only those costs associated with reliably measured outcomes. But the goals of schooling in any state may be much broader than outcomes measured through the state testing system.

The alternative, and perhaps more important use of both

methods, is in the measurement of how the costs of providing equal educational opportunity vary from one setting to the next and one child to the next. Under professional judgment strategies for identifying how resources vary from one child to the next and one school to the next, panels propose alternative resource configurations—primarily staffing ratios—based on their understanding of best practices and based on personal experiences, all while considering the common outcome goal. As with setting "adequate" funding, the relationship between these proposed staffing ratios and desired outcomes remains somewhat speculative. As will be discussed later, evidence based RCM studies frequently propose little or no variation in resources across settings, assuming evidence-based models of schooling to be good for all kids in all settings.

Education cost functions may be a particularly useful tool for estimating how spending varies across settings and children in a given state, toward achieving a common outcome, so long as the outcome remains within the boundaries of commonly achieved outcomes. Further, failure to measure inefficiency perfectly in this context is less problematic because the goal is to determine how costs vary from one setting to the next and one child to the next, at a common level of efficiency. Failure to fully capture inefficiencies is only problematic if those inefficiencies are systematically related to the different contexts and populations in question. In a review of cost analysis methods, Downes (2004) notes: "Given the econometric advances of the last decade, the cost function approach is the most likely to give accurate estimates of the within-state variation in the spending needed to attain the state's chosen standard, if the data are available and of a high quality" (p. 9). Where such data are unavailable, methods including professional judgment based RCM may provide the only reasonable alternative.

Cost Analysis, School Finance Litigation, and Reform

Taylor, Baker, and Vedlitz (2005) discuss over 30 cost studies performed across states as of 2004. Since that time,

numerous additional studies have been conducted. Table 35.1 provides a list of recent cost studies in states where those studies have been intertwined in at least some way with state constitutional challenges to the school finance formula. In Arkansas, in *Lake View v. Huckabee* in November 2002, the State Supreme court declared the system of school funding unconstitutional, and among other things, ordered that the legislature discern the costs of a constitutionally adequate system. The court also established a panel of special masters to evaluate legislative progress in complying with the Supreme Court order. This mandate led to the formation of the Joint Committee on Educational Adequacy, and eventually to an input-oriented education cost study by Lawrence O. Picus and Associates, applying their *evidence-based* model for estimating education costs. Within the year, the legislature made substantial adjustments to the school aid formula in order to *level up* toward a base funding of $5,400 those districts currently operating with less revenue per pupil. That said, the consultants-proposed model and resulting policy included only minimal adjustment for student needs, well out of line with nearly all other studies of marginal costs (Baker, 2006).[14] The Supreme Court of Arkansas dismissed the case, but when the legislature backed off from second year funding promises, the court chose, in a rather bold move, to re-open the case and reinstate the special masters.

Wyoming provides a similar example of reasonably expedient compliance. In 1995, the Wyoming Supreme Court first ruled the school funding system unconstitutional (*Campbell County School District v. State*), mandating that the legislature conduct a cost study and base future policy on their findings. This decision led to the first of the recent wave of professional judgment cost analyses, performed initially by Management Analysis and Planning, Inc. (MAP) and released in 1997 as the proposed Wyoming Cost Based Block Grant formula. A unique aspect of the Wyoming cost analyses and resulting policies is that the process of developing the cost-based block grant formula involves political negotiation of the empirical analysis between leg-

TABLE 35.1
Recent Cost of Adequacy Studies

State	Initiation	Sponsor	Author (year)	Method
Arkansas	Court Mandate (Nov. 2002)	Joint Committee on Educational Adequacy	Picus & Assoc. (2003)	Evidence Based
Wyoming	Court Mandate (1995, 2001)	Legislature (2006) Legislature (1998, 2001)	Picus & Assoc. (2006) MAP (1998, 2002)	Evidence Based Professional Judgment
New York	Court Mandate (2003)	Plaintiff Zarb Commission (Governor) Independent	AIR/MAP (2004) Standard & Poors (2004) Duncombe & Yinger (2008)	Professional Judgment Successful Schools Cost Function
Texas	West Orange Cove Plaintiffs	West Orange Cove Plaintiffs	MAP (2004) Reschovsky & Imazeki (2004)	Professional Judgment Cost Function
	Edgewood Intervenors Legislature	Edgewood Intervenors Legislature	AIR (2004) Taylor et al. (2004)	Simulation Cost Function
Kansas	Legislature (LEPC) & Governor's Task Force Legislature Legislature (Court Mandate)	Legislature	Augenblick & Myers (2002) Legislative Division of Post Audit Duncombe & Yinger	Professional Judgment Evidence Based Cost Function

islators and consultants. The legislature has the final word on adoption, with court oversight. The Wyoming Court intervened for a second time in 2001, requesting specific changes and/or justification for cost differences associated with small schools, variations in teacher wages across the state, and certain student characteristics. A second series of reports was released in 2002, also by MAP, and the block grant revised. Most recently, in 2005 Lawrence O. Picus and Associates substituted an evidence-based model for the previous professional judgment model, in their recalibration of the cost-based block grant.[15] Certain features of the evidence-based model were revised through political deliberation, but the block grant model, based on the Picus and Associates recommendations, was largely adopted. Again, expedient compliance in the most recent round of re-calibration may have been driven partly by the fact that consultants' proposed a "cost-based" model that included negligible adjustments for children from economically disadvantaged backgrounds and children with limited English proficiency, in significant conflict with the vast majority of empirical evidence on marginal costs.[16]

Table 35.2 expands on three cases also listed in Table 35.1 where the interactions of courts, cost analyses, plaintiffs, and legislatures become more complicated—Kansas (*Montoy v. State,* 2003), New York (*Campaign for Fiscal Equity v. State*), and Texas (*Neeley v. West Orange-Cove*

Consolidated Independent School District, 2005). We enter this discussion with the assumption that it is first the legislature's obligation to produce the operational definition of a state's constitutional mandate regarding the provision of public schooling. Where legislators fail to uphold their duty to interpret their constitutional obligation, there comes a time when courts must take the first step. We adopt a similar stand on the production and interpretation of empirical evidence. Where legislators and other elected officials have provided the operational definition of their constitutional obligation, and have sponsored and overseen the production of evidence regarding the costs of meeting their constitutional obligation, the role of the judiciary may be quite passive and deferential. However, there may come that point in time where the judicial branch must order legislators to fulfill these requirements or provide more specific judicial interpretation to guide legislative remedies. Further, the court may need to defer to cost evidence provided by plaintiffs or other parties.

Kansas   Table 35.2 indicates that in Kansas, the first attempt to operationalize the definition of the state education clause, in adequacy terms, was made by the Kansas legislature in response to a recommendation provided by a Governor's task force, which specifically recommended that the legislature develop an operational definition of the

TABLE 35.2
Cost Analysis and Court Action in Kansas, New York, and Texas

State	Preliminary Operational Definition	Detailed Operational Definition (specific standards)	Cost Analysis	Cost Study Findings	Lower Court Disposition	High Court Disposition
Kansas	Legislature	Legislature & State Board of Education	Legislative oversight of Augenblick & Myers	$853 million underfunded in 2002 (over 2.2 billion)[1] & significant vertical equity problems	Legislature failed to comply with own definition and findings (violates EP and Education Article)	Legislature failed to comply with own definition and findings (violates Education Article)
	Legislature	Legislature & State Board of Education (Court order to include SBOE)	Legislative Division of Post Audit (with Duncombe & Yinger)	$399 million underfunded in 2006-07 (over $2 billion)[2] & significant vertical equity problems		
New York	Lower Court (on Plaintiff Advisement)	Plaintiff	Plaintiffs, AIR/MAP	NYC $5.63 billion underfunded (over $13 to $14 billion)	Mandated $5.63 billion increase to NYC (appellate division modified ruling to range of two values)	Mandated $1.93 billion increase based on lower bound of Governor's reform commission recommendation.
		Zarb Commission (Governor)	Zarb Commission & S&P	NYC $4.7 billion underfunded (over $13 to $14 billion)		
Texas	Legislature	Legislature & Texas School Finance Project	Legislature & Texas School Finance Project (Taylor et al.)	$374 to $402 million under-funded in 2004 (of 31 billion)	Legislature failed to comply with own definition and plaintiff definition and findings.	System likely underfunded, but not yet unconstitutionally underfunded. Both cost estimates likely too low.
	Plaintiff	Plaintiff	Imazeki & Reschovsky	$1.7 to $6.2 billion under-funded in 2004 (of 31 billion)	Expressed preference for plaintiff findings.	

Note: [1]total of general fund budgets for 2002; [2]total of general fund budgets for 2006.

education clause (Art. 6, § 6) and conduct a study of costs of implementing the operational definition.[17] Kansas legislators responded by appropriating funding for the study and collaborating with the Kansas State Board of Education[18] on developing operational definitions of *suitable provision*, tied to current statutes and department regulations prescribing curricular programs consisting of the subjects and courses required by state statute. Members of the Legislative Coordinating Council then oversaw the study through its implementation and completion. The study was conducted by Augenblick, Myers, Silverstein, & Barkis (2002) of Denver, Colorado, and applied both successful districts analysis and professional judgment analysis, producing base cost figures of $4,547 and $5,811, respectively. The study was released in May 2002, immediately following the legislative session of that year.

Meanwhile, a legal challenge to the state school finance formula (*Montoy v. Kansas*) went to trial in the fall of 2003, at which time, the Augenblick and Myers study became a key piece of evidence presented by plaintiffs. The school finance system at the time fell at least $853 million short (nearly 40%) of the legislature's own cost estimates presented in the Augenblick et al. study. More importantly, the study showed that funding was substantially short for children in the state's highest need districts. On December 2, 2003, district court Judge Terry Bullock issued a preliminary ruling that unless the legislature substantially revised the school funding formula during the spring 2004 legislative session, he would declare the system unconstitutional. Of the Augenblick and Myers study as evidence, the district court noted:

> The Augenblick & Myers' cost study, commissioned by the State Board and the Legislature, found current funding levels dramatically short of that necessary to provide a suitable education *by the Legislature's own standards*. That is the issue at bar and on this overarching point the evidence is uncontroverted. (p. 43)

On January 5, 2005, the Kansas Supreme Court concurred with the lower court that the system failed to comply with the state constitution. Like the lower court, the state Supreme Court used as evidence, the legislature's own operational definition and cost estimate of "suitable."

During the legislative session of 2005, the legislature adopted modest changes to the school finance formula, adding approximately $143 million in new funding (HB 2247 & SB 3), well short of the recommended target of the Augenblick and Myers study, and more importantly, well short of estimated costs in higher need districts, serving higher percentages of children in poverty and with limited English speaking skills. In June 2005, the Supreme Court again invoked the Augenblick and Myers study to declare HB 2247 and SB 3 insufficient.

Among relatively small increases in total funding across districts, Kansas legislators also proposed to conduct a new cost study to replace the A&M study in future deliberations. The study would be carried out this time, by the legislature's own research arm—Legislative Division of Post Audit. Legislators initially proposed a study that would look only at inputs required for providing a basic education program. The high court agreed with the state board of education's request to require the legislature to include the board's outcome standards. The court ordered the legislature to hold an immediate special session to add $142 million in school funding for the 2005–06 school year, rationalizing that with the initial $143 million under HB 2247, the total amount of $285 million, about one-third of the total increase estimated by Augenblick and Myers. The legislature partially responded to the court mandate, adding $148 million, though not distributed across districts as would be required under the A&M study (Baker, 2005).

In January 2006, the cost studies of the Legislative Division of Post Audit were released. The Division of Post Audit had conducted an analysis of the appropriate inputs for delivering mandated curricula and had contracted William Duncombe and John Yinger of the Maxwell School at Syracuse University to estimate an education cost function of the costs of achieving the State Board of Education's mandate outcome levels. The outcome-based estimates of Duncombe and Yinger (2006) estimated, for 2006-07, the need for approximately $399 million in increased funding, with the majority to be allocated to high need urban schools. For high need urban districts, findings were strikingly similar to those of the Augenblick and Myers study. That is, the court granted the Kansas Legislature a *redo*, and the legislature got roughly the same finding in terms of districts facing the greatest shortfalls, at a somewhat lower total cost.

During the spring legislative session of 2006, the legislature offered up a new proposal which for 2006–2007 would add a total of about $195 million, with subsequent increases proposed for 2007–08 and 2008–09. First year increases were far short of the legislature's own second set of estimates, especially for high poverty districts. On July 28, 2006, the court rejected the state attempt to exclude the Duncombe and Yinger cost studies as evidence on the ground that those studies had not been subjected to fact-finding at the trial court. Nevertheless, in a turn of events that would appear to conflict significantly with their June 3, 2005, order, on July 28, 2006, the Kansas Supreme Court dismissed the case, declaring that revisions to the formula under SB 549 constituted substantial compliance with its previous orders, but leaving open "for another day" the question of whether SB 549 is actually constitutional, and whether constitutionality should be measured against the new Division of Post Audit estimates.

New York Unlike Kansas, in New York, legislators had never carried out their own exercise of developing an operational definition of their obligation for financing public schools. Nor had they attempted to estimate the costs of meeting that obligation. In January 2001, trial court judge Leland DeGrasse issued his opinion in *Campaign for Fiscal Equity v. State* that the current system of financing schools in New York, with specific emphasis on New York City, failed to provide for a *sound basic education*, or constitutionally minimally adequate education. In his remedial order, Judge DeGrasse noted, "In the course of reforming the school finance system, a threshold task that must be performed by defendants is ascertaining, to the extent possible, the actual costs of providing a sound basic education in districts around the State" (*Campaign for Fiscal Equity v. State,* 2001, p. 550). But, further action this matter would be on hold until two more rounds and three more years of court deliberation.

The appellate court, in 2002, reversed the trial court ruling, arguing that the appropriate standard for *sound basic education* is approximately an eighth-grade level of education and that on average, children in New York City were achieving just that. Eventually, in June 2003, the Court of Appeals reversed the appellate court's decision, defining a sound basic education as "a meaningful high school education, one which prepares [young people] to function productively as civic participants" (*Campaign for Fiscal Equity v. State,* 2003, p. 332). Through three rounds of deliberations, the New York courts took the initial steps of operationalizing the phrase *sound basic education,* to guide the cost analyses that would follow.

Following the high court ruling, the plaintiffs and the state released their studies of the costs of providing a meaningful high school education, largely pegged to Board of Regents Standards. Plaintiff's study was conducted via professional judgment analysis, by Management Analysis and Planning, Inc., along with the American Institutes for Research. The state's own study was conducted by Standard and Poors (S&P) School Evaluation Services, for the Zarb Commission, appointed by Governor George Pataki in September 2003. Standard and Poors applied a *Successful Districts* model for calculating costs. S&P simply took the average expenditures of districts currently meeting state Regents standards. It then lopped off the higher spending (top half) districts meeting those standards, referring to this procedure as an *efficiency filter.* Finally, S&P selected[19] weights to account for differences in need due to varied poverty concentrations (35%), limited English Proficiency (20%), and disabilities (110%). No actual cost analysis was provided for justifying these weights.

A blue-ribbon panel of referees was appointed by the trial court, under order of the high court, with responsibility of reviewing the state's remedial actions. The referees issued their review of the two competing cost studies in November 2004, recommending a 4-year phase in of an additional $5.63 billion to New York City schools. The phase-in amount was based largely on aggregate cost increases identified in the plaintiffs' professional judgment analysis (*Campaign for Fiscal Equity v. State,* 2006b). The referees criticized various aspects of the state Successful Schools analysis, including the "efficiency" filter, the arbitrarily low weight for poverty, and inappropriate regional wage adjustments (*Campaign for Fiscal Equity v. State,* 2006b).

The trial court accepted the referees' recommendations

in full. However, the appellate court reversed, declaring that allowing referees and lower court to dictate specifics of the remedy would constitute violation of separation of powers. The appellate court then suggested that any broad range of remedies based on either or both cost studies might sufficiently comply with the constitutional mandate, while respecting the legislature's authority: "The record establishes a range of between $4.7 billion and $5.63 billion, a difference of $930 million, in additional annual operating funds, that would satisfy the State's constitutional education funding obligations" (*Campaign for Fiscal Equity v. State,* 2006a, p. 2). On November 20, 2006, the High Court of Appeals, which had previously supported a higher standard of adequacy than the appellate division, retreated to a lower dollar value, mandating that the legislature immediately add $1.93 billion, rather than $4.7 to $5.63 billion in funding for New York City schools (*Campaign for Fiscal Equity v. State,* 2006b). The court, in a 4-2 decision noted that the $1.93 billion represented a minimum threshold. The $1.93 billion figure was based on a reform commission recommendation to outgoing Governor Pataki—a political, rather than empirical, recommendation.

Texas   Finally, among these three cases, the case of Texas is the one case in which the state supreme court eventually decided that current funding levels were *not yet* unconstitutionally inequitable or inadequate. *Neeley v. West Orange-Cove Consolidated Independent School District* asserted two basic claims of state constitutional violation. First, and tangential to our main point herein, plaintiffs asserted that because the majority of Texas school districts had implemented their maximum local property tax authority of $1.50 (64 cents above the minimum required rate in the state) simply in order to finance an adequate education, that the $1.50 tax had become a statewide property tax and that statewide property taxes (except for the minimum requirement of 64 cents, according to an earlier ruling) were prohibited under the Texas constitution. Second, plaintiffs and more specifically interveners (Edgewood districts) asserted that the current system (Foundation School Plan) failed to provide for a "thorough and efficient" education.

Arguably because the *West Orange-Cove* case followed earlier cases in which cost studies had been influential, leading up to the trial, there was a flurry of activity among plaintiffs and consultants to generate their own version of the legislature's constitutional obligation. Two sets of analyses predated or were planned in advance of this flurry. First, the Texas Legislature had convened a Joint Committee on Public School Finance and had allocated funding for the Texas School Finance Project, a collaborative effort among researchers at Texas A&M University and other external consultants. Among other things, the Joint Committee decided to pursue a cost function methodology for estimating education costs to guide future legislative deliberations on school finance reform, and the Joint Committee determined that a 55% pass rate on state's new assessment (Texas Assessment of Knowledge and Skills) would provide the baseline outcome standard for cost estimation. In addition, Andrew Reschovsky and Jennifer Imazeki (2004) had conducted and published an independent cost function analysis on Texas schools and presented an updated version of those analyses for plaintiffs in the case.

The cost function analysis of the Texas School Finance Project was released in March of 2004. According to Taylor (2004), "the GJTB[20] model identifies a number of districts where projected costs exceeded expenditures for 2003" (p. 2). The additional spending required to meet the cost projections in those districts, holding all other districts harmless at their actual spending per pupil, is between "$374 million and $402 million, or less than 1.3 percent of the $31 billion spent operating Texas schools in 2003" (p. 2). The legislature convened a special session in the summer of 2004 to consider how the findings of the Taylor study, among other things, might guide school finance redesign. Other studies were released at the deadline for submitting evidence in the *West Orange Cove* case, including the Reschovsky and Imazeki cost function, which indicated a range of required expenditure increases from $1.7 to $6.2 billion for achieving the same 55% passing standard, with increases targeted primarily to high poverty urban districts.

The trial court in Texas, unlike Kansas and New York courts, was flooded with contradictory "costing out" evidence, from multiple sources, applying multiple methods of cost analysis. In addition to the two statistical models, evidence included professional judgment analysis introduced on behalf of plaintiffs and a separate analysis transposing findings from New York State onto Texas districts introduced by intervener districts (see Table 35.1). In his findings of fact, lower court Judge John Dietz chose to focus on the differences between cost function estimates provided by Reschovsky and Imazeki, and by Taylor and colleagues at Texas A&M on behalf of the legislature. Dietz ruled in favor of plaintiffs on the adequacy claim ("thorough and efficient") relying most heavily on evidence from the Reschovsky and Imazeki cost function, and noting that it is likely that both the Reschovsky and Imazeki, and Taylor cost function underestimated the full costs of adequate outcomes the state's newly adopted test.

On November 22, 2005, the Supreme Court of Texas issued its ruling in the case, finding that the school finance system did violate the state constitution, but only in terms of establishing a statewide property tax. The court found in favor of the state on the question of whether the Foundation School Program failed to provide adequate resources. Like the New York appellate division, the Texas Supreme court was less willing than the lower court to make value judgments on the cost function evidence before the court. Acknowledging the lower court finding that both studies likely underestimated actual costs of succeeding on the state's new assessments, the court concluded: "the cost studies and [trial] court findings overlook the reality that almost all schools are meeting accreditation standards with current funding" (*Neeley v. West Orange-Cove Consolidated Independent School District*, 2005, p. 770). The Texas

high court's logic is strikingly similar to that applied by the *Rodriguez* court in evaluating whether the 1973 Texas school finance system resulted in deprivation of a minimally adequate education for groups of children.

Conclusions and Implications

As a result of recent school finance litigation like the cases discussed herein, the political environment surrounding school finance policy has become increasingly divisive in recent years, with pundits on all sides aggressively staking their ground. Amidst the punditry and more scholarly deliberations are three major points of contention, each revealed to some extent by the cases discussed herein: (a) the balance between adequacy and equity, (b) the balance between judicial and legislative roles in guiding school finance reform, and (c) the balance between politics and empirical evidence in guiding state school finance reform and judicial oversight.

Balancing Adequacy and Equity The adequacy ideology emergent from the early to mid-1990s, first summarized by Clune (1994), seemed to create a new politically convenient—everyone wins—solution for state school finance policy. We argue that this approach was and is oversimplified and shortsighted. Such a solution is only feasible: (a) where there is sufficient funding for everyone to win, and/ or (b) where there is sufficient political will to raise that funding, and (c) where student needs and educational costs are relatively uniformly distributed.

As discussed earlier, the pure adequacy, level-up all ships proposal significantly compromises equal educational opportunity. We argue that equal educational opportunity is a far more noble and democratic goal—one that requires redistribution and targeted distribution of resources rather than simply adding more. Solving equity concerns in many states may, in fact, be less costly than leveling up all ships, but remains less politically palatable.

Where legislators cannot muster the political will for need-based redistribution, courts must take on this responsibility. Courts should, however, avoid the temptation of playing the very same political games in which they've been asked to intervene, accepting solutions on the basis of total dollars added rather than whether inequities have been sufficiently mitigated.

Balancing Judicial and Legislative Roles Perhaps the most contentious issue raised in recent school finance litigation and reform is when, whether, and how state courts should become involved in defining educational adequacy and vertical equity and evaluating whether state legislatures have met their obligations to fund adequate and vertically equitable schooling. We see the Kansas case as clearest among the three discussed herein.[21] The state court deferred (without order), twice, to the Kansas legislature to define and cost out their constitutional obligation. Yet the legislature failed to address at all the shortcomings of school funding relative to either of their cost analyses. Where the Kansas Supreme Court erred, arguably favoring a politically palatable solution over upholding their own previous interpretation of the Constitution and available evidence, was in their acceptance of a solution based on a total sum of additional funding, rather than focusing on those districts and children most harmed under current policy.

On the one hand, the actions of the New York courts may be called into question in that the New York courts have, at each stage, deliberated over the meaning of *sound basic education* and further that the lower court in New York ordered and subsequently evaluated the estimation of costs of providing a *sound basic education,* translated as *meaningful high school education.* The New York case raises the questions of: At what point must courts take a more active role? How long should a state court wait before requiring the legislature to show that they have met their constitutional obligation? What evidence can or should legislators provide in their defense to show that they have met their constitutional obligation? And what evidence, if not externally funded cost analysis, can plaintiffs show to prove how state school finance policy has produced harm?

More recent events in New Hampshire (*Londonderry v. State SAW No. 12*, 2006) are also illustrative. In 1997, the New Hampshire high court issued four mandates: "define an adequate education, determine the cost, fund it with constitutional taxes, and ensure its delivery through accountability." To date, legislators are still stuck on task 1, and in September of 2006, the New Hampshire Supreme Court issued the following ruling:

> Respectful of the roles of the legislative and executive branches, each time this court has been requested to define the substantive content of a constitutionally adequate public education, we have properly demurred. Deference, however, has its limits. We agree with Justice Galway's concern that this court or any court not take over the legislature's role in shaping educational and fiscal policy. For almost thirteen years we have refrained from doing so and continue to refrain today. However, the judiciary has a responsibility to ensure that constitutional rights not be hollowed out and, in the absence of action by other branches, a judicial remedy is not only appropriate but essential….We urge the legislature to act. (*Londonderry School District SAW No. 12 v. State*, 2006, pp. 995–996)

We suspect that while the recent decision in New Hampshire has been pitched by many as a conclusion to a long-running court battle, that in fact, there is no clear end in sight as a result of the court's most recent *urging.*

Balancing Empirics and Politics   Finally, Hanushek (2006), among others, has become a vocal opponent of education cost analysis, specifically in the context of state school finance litigation. Hanushek argues that cost studies should be interpreted only as "political documents" and interpreted loosely, if at all, for guiding political deliberations over state school finance policy. Hanushek further notes that cost studies "are most frequently contracted for by parties interested in increasing spending for education (including teachers unions, state departments of education, and litigants), although they sometimes involve defensive reactions of parties trying to neutralize a rival costing out study that calls for large increases in spending. They are seldom used as analytical tools to aid in policy deliberations" (p. 258). Of the studies addressed in detail herein, nearly all were sponsored by, and conducted under oversight of, state officials and not special interests. In fact, initial studies in both Kansas and Texas were conducted to be used as analytical tools with the specific purpose of guiding policy deliberations, not litigation. While Hanushek suggests that such studies should never be considered as evidence in school finance litigation, we find it difficult to extend this argument to the case where no other contradictory evidence exists, and where available cost analysis, regardless of quality, represent the only available measure of the legislature's constitutional obligation.

We acknowledge that the delineations between political and empirical are not as distinct as we imply herein. Further, the separation between empirical analyses conducted on behalf of elected officials versus those conducted on behalf of non-elected special interests is not always clear. However, the alternative to introducing cost analysis evidence is to allow determination of not only total levels of education funding, but also variations in education costs across settings and children to be determined by consensus alone. Baker and Duncombe (2004) have shown, by contrasting Texas and Kansas school finance policies, that purely political control over marginal costs in particular can lead to very different patterns of advantage and disadvantage in school funding distributed by legislators across school districts and children on the argued basis of educational need. Baker and Green (2005) go further to show how legislators in some states have manipulated cost adjustment systems to create racial disparities in school funding, building facially neutral cost-adjustment policies on prior policies that may have been tied directly to racially segregated schooling and housing in the pre-*Brown* era.

Perhaps in such extreme cases, state courts can negate arbitrary marginal cost adjustments on face value alone, and under equal protection clauses in place of or in addition to education clauses. In most cases, state legislative actions that directly advantage some and disadvantage others in state school finance policy have been more subtle and less completely absurd than those of the Kansas legislature. As such, courts require at least some empirical guidance for evaluating the reasonableness of state school finance policy, especially where marginal costs are concerned. Ideally, state legislators would proactively attempt to guide school finance policies with reasonably rigorous empirical evidence, especially where marginal costs are concerned.

Education cost analysis is and will be for the foreseeable future, less precise and more art than science for identifying the absolute level—base costs—of funding that makes a school finance system statutorily or constitutionally adequate, suitable, or thorough and efficient. It is a formidable task to begin with, for judges and/or legislators to link broad constitutional language to measured levels of student outcome proficiency and further to the costs of achieving those outcomes.

Notes

1. The Hawai'i school system is often described as a single school district. Baker and Thomas (2006) describe the system as direct state control over schools, where only the state legislature has taxing and revenue raising authority for those schools.

2. Often only that level of authority granted directly by state legislative action.

3. See also Yinger (2004).

4. In New York State, for example, a cross-district distributional analysis would fail to capture disparities that may exist across more than one-third of the state's children because they all attend schools within a single district. Hawai'i has generally been exempted from distributional analysis despite significant inequities in financial resources and teacher quality across Hawai'i schools (Baker & Thomas, 2006).

5. Exceptions include Stiefel, Rubenstein, and Berne (1998).

6. See Murray, Evans, and Schwab (1998).

7. For example, measures which evaluate spending at the top and bottom of the distribution only (ranges and range ratios), the pattern of distribution across all districts (coefficients of variation, Gini coefficients, or distribution just among those districts in the lower half of the distribution—McLoone indices).

8. The two are not entirely irreconcilable. Adam Smith argued that individuals "ought to contribute to the support of the government, as nearly as possible, according to their respective abilities [ability-to-pay taxation]; that is, in proportion to the revenue which they respectively enjoy under the protection of the state [benefit taxation]" (Smith, 1904, as cited in Steuerle, 1999, p. 310). Printed in an edited collection, 114 years posthumously.

9. Arguably, *Rodriguez* was not the best case for early federal court application of Coons, Clune, and Sugarman's framework as it could be too easily shown in Texas in particular, that taxable property wealth per pupil at the school district level was not highly associated with financial well-being of families and children in those districts.

10. See *DuPree v. Alma School District* (1983); *Horton v. Meskill* (1977); *Pauley v. Kelley* (1979); *Robinson v. Cahill* (1973); *Seattle School District No. 1 v. State* (1978); *Washakie County School District No. 1 v. Herschler* (1980). *Pauley v. Kelley,* 255 S.E.2d 859 (W. Va. 1979).

11. Analysis of data from the 2006 American Community Survey (ACS) indicates that approximately 11% of 5- to 17-year-olds attended private school. (Ruggles et al., 2008).

12. This section draws heavily on a working paper by Taylor, Baker, and Vedlitz (2005) prepared in 2004 for the Texas Legislature, titled *Measuring Educational Adequacy in Public Schools,* retrieved November 19, 2008, from http://bush.tamu.edu/research/working_papers/ltaylor/measuring_edu_adequacy_in_public_schools.pdf

13. Arguably, it would be unreasonable to assert that all existing public school districts are too inefficient in their use of resources to provide any basis for estimating costs without providing some evidence of substantially more efficient, unutilized education technologies.

14. In fact, Baker (2006) shows a slope of only .17 between subsidized lunch rates and proposed adequacy cost per pupil for Arkansas, with the next lowest marginal cost slope being double in size. Further, Baker (2006) concludes "it is difficult to imagine that Little Rock, at approximately 56% subsidized lunch, 42% proficient in reading and 19% proficient in math, would require only $393 more per pupil (6280-5887) than Bentonville, with only 24% qualifying for subsidized lunch, 72% proficient in reading, and 55% proficient in math. It would appear that this substantial deflation of the need weight in Arkansas is not offset by substantial inflation of the base" (p. 199).

15. http://legisweb.state.wy.us/2006/interim/schoolfinance/schoolfinance.htm.

16. For example, consultants built marginal cost estimates for children with limited English proficiency on specialist caseloads of 1 specialist per 100 limited English proficient students, compared to typical caseload recommendations from input-based studies of 1 per 20 and leading to a marginal cost estimate well less than 1/10 the magnitude (nearer 1/20) of marginal cost estimates from statistical models (see Baker, Markham, & Green, 2004). Baker and Green (2008) show that on average, the slope between poverty and evidence-based funding proposals in Wyoming is negative and the slope between limited English proficient student populations and funding is mildly positive. No other cost study has yielded a negative relationship between costs and poverty concentration. While it is conceivable that the sparcity of Wyoming's population and relatively limited urbanization leads to this result, we find it highly suspect, especially given the underlying staffing proposals that lead to this result. The argument that higher poverty schools must simply leverage their resources differently than lower poverty schools and that these schools do not legitimately face higher marginal costs is yet unfounded in literature, with substantial sources both directly and indirectly refuting this assumption (Krueger, 2001; Levin, 2002, 2006; Baker & Green, 2007).

17. Final Report of the *Vision 21st Century Task Force,* December 2000. See Brant et al. (2000).

18. Where, in the state of Kansas, the State Board of Education is independently elected and holds independent constitutional authority for the *general supervision of schools* under Article 6.

19. This is the best term we could come up with for a process which appears, by evaluating all relevant documentation on the S&P study, to have been almost entirely arbitrary.

20. Timothy Grongerg, Dennis Jansen, Lori Taylor, and Kevin Booker.

21. Our judgment that the Kansas case is clearest is made on the basis of the way in which evidence was considered and the relative roles of legislators and the judicial branch, and not necessarily on the magnitude or types of problems that may exist in the state school finance systems of Kansas, Texas, or New York.

References

Augenblick, J., Myers, J., Silverstein, J., & Barkus, A. (2002). *Calculation of the cost of an adequate education in Kansas in 2000–2001 using two different analytic approaches.* Topeka: Legislative Coordinating Council, State of Kansas.

Baker, B. D. (2005). *Nebraska's state school finance policy fails to provide equal opportunity for Nebraska school children.* Expert testimony in the case of *Douglas County School District v. Johannes.* Lawrence: University of Kansas.

Baker, B. D. (2006). Evaluating the reliability, validity and usefulness of education cost studies. *Journal of Education Finance, 32*(2), 170–201.

Baker, B. D., & Duncombe, W. D. (2004). Balancing district needs and student needs: The role of economies of scale adjustments and pupil need weights in school finance formulas. *Journal of Education Finance, 29*(2), 97–124.

Baker, B. D., & Green, P. C. (2008). Conceptions of equity and adequacy in school finance. In H. F. Ladd & E. B. Fiske (Eds.), *Handbook of Research in Education Finance and Policy* (pp. 203–221). New York: Routledge.

Baker, B. D., & Green, P. C. (2005). Tricks of the trade: Legislative actions in school finance that disadvantage minorities in the post-Brown Era. *American Journal of Education, 111,* 372–413.

Baker, B. D., & Green, P. C. (2007, April). *Vertical equity and the distribution of state aid to schools: Can or should school racial composition be a factor?* Paper presented at the annual meeting of the American Education Research Association, Chicago.

Baker, B. D., Markham, P., & Green, P. C. (2004, February). *A comprehensive legal and empirical framework for evaluating state financial aid for the provision of services to English language learners.* Paper presented at the annual meeting of the National Association for Bilingual Education (NABE), Albuquerque, NM.

Baker, B. D., & Thomas, S. L. (2006). *Review of Hawaii's weighted student formula.* Honolulu: Hawaii Board of Education.

Berne, R., & Stiefel, L. (1984). *The measurement of equity in school finance.* Baltimore, MD: Johns Hopkins University Press.

Brant, D., Baker, B., Ballard, B., Ferguson, L., Jones, D., & Vratil, J. (2000). *Final report of the Governor's 21st Century Vision Task Force.* K-12 Education: Financing for Results.

Brown v. Board of Educ., 347 U.S. 483 (1954).

Campaign for Fiscal Equity v. State, 719 N.Y.S.2d 475 (N.Y. Sup. Ct. 2001).

Campaign for Fiscal Equity v. State, 801 N.E.2d 326 (N.Y. 2003).

Campaign for Fiscal Equity v. State, 814 N.Y.S.2d 1 (N.Y. App. Div. 2006a).

Campaign for Fiscal Equity v. State, 861 N.E.2d 50 (N.Y. 2006b).

Campbell County Sch. Dist. v. State, 907 P.2d 1238, 1278 (Wyo. 1995).

Chambers, J. G. (1984). *The development of a program cost model and cost-of-education model for the State of Alaska. Vol. 2: Technical Report.* Stanford, CA: Associates for Education Finance and Planning, Inc.

Chambers, J. G. (1999). *Measuring resources in education: From accounting to the resource cost model approach* (National Center for Education Statistics Working Paper No. 1999-16). Washington, DC: U.S. Department of Education.

Chambers, J. G., & Parrish, T. B. (1982). *The development of a resource cost model funding base for education finance in Illinois.* Springfield: Illinois State Board of Education.

Clune, W. (1994). The shift from equity to adequacy in school finance. *Educational Policy, 8,* 376–394.

Coleman, J. S., Campbell, E. Q., Hobson, C. J., McPartland, J. M., Mood, A. M., Weinfeld, F. D., et al. (1966). *Equality of educational opportunity.* Washington, DC: U.S. Government Printing Office.

Coons, J. E., Clune, W. H., III, & Sugarman, S. D. (1969). Educational opportunity: A workable constitutional test for state financial structures. *California Law Review, 57,* 305–421.

Downes, T. (2004). *What is adequate? Operationalizing the concept of adequacy for New York State.* Medford, MA: Tufts University, Department of Economics.

Downes, T., & Pogue, T. (1994). Adjusting school aid formulas for the higher cost of educating disadvantaged students. *National Tax Journal, 47,* 89–110.

Duncombe, W., Lukemeyer, A., & Yinger, J. (2004). Education finance reform in New York: Calculating the cost of a "sound, basic education" in New York City (Working Paper No. 28). Syracuse, NY: Maxwell School of Syracuse University. Retrieved March 1, 2006, from http://www-cpr.maxwell.syr.edu/pbriefs/pb28.pdfp.3

Duncombe, W., & Yinger, J. (2006). *Estimating the costs of meeting student performance outcomes mandated by the Kansas State Board of Education.* Retrieved March 1, 2006, from http://www.kslegislature.org/postaudit/audits_perform/05pa19a.pdf

Duncombe, W., & Yinger, J. (2007). *A comment on school district level production functions estimated using spending data.* Syracuse, NY: Syracuse University, Maxwell School of Public Affairs.

Duncombe, W., & Yinger, J. (2008). Measurement of cost differentials. In H. F. Ladd & E. B. Fiske (Eds.), *Handbook of research in education finance and policy* (pp. 238–256). Mahwah, NJ: Erlbaum.

DuPree v. Alma School District No. 30, 651 S.W.2d 90 (Ark. 1983).

Enrich, P. (1995). Leaving equality behind: New directions in school finance reform. *Vanderbilt Law Review, 48,* 101–194.

Equal Educational Opportunities Act, 20 U.S.C. §§ 1701-21 (2006).

Green, P. C., & Baker, B. D. (2002). Circumventing *Rodriguez*: Can plaintiffs use the Equal Protection Clause to challenge school finance disparities caused by inequitable state distribution policies? *Texas Forum on Civil Liberties and Civil Rights, 7,* 141–165.

Gronberg, T., Jansen, T., Taylor, L., & Booker, K. (2004). *School outcomes and schools costs: The cost function approach.* College Station, TX: Texas A&M University, Busch School of Government and Public Service.

Hanushek, E. A. (2006, October). *The alchemy of "costing out" an adequate education.* Palo Alto, CA: Stanford University, Hoover Institution.

Hanushek, E. A. (1994). A jaundiced view of "adequacy" in school finance reform. *Educational Policy, 8,* 460–469.

Hartman, W. T., Bolton, D., & Monk, D. H. (2001). A synthesis of two approaches to school level financial data: The accounting and resource cost model approaches. In W. Fowler, Jr. (Ed.), *Selected papers in school finance, 2000–01* (pp. 77–119). Washington, DC: National Center for Education Statistics, Office of Educational Research and Improvement.

Hirsch, F. (1976). *Social limits to growth.* Cambridge, MA: Harvard University Press.

Horowitz, H. (1966). Unseparate but unequal: The emerging Fourteenth Amendment issue in public school education. *UCLA Law Review, 13,* 1147–1172.

Horton v. Meskill, 376 A.2d 359 (Conn. 1977).

Imazeki, J. (2007). *Assessing the costs of K-12 education in California public schools.* San Diego, CA: San Diego State University, Department of Economics.

Koski, W. S., & Reich, R. (2006). When "adequate" isn't: The retreat from equity in educational law and policy and why it matters. *Emory Law Journal, 56,* 545–617.

Krueger, A. B. (2001, March). *Would smaller class sizes help close the Black-White achievement gap?* (Working Paper #451). Princeton, NJ: Princeton University. Department of Economics, Industrial Relations Section.

Lake View Sch. Dist. No. 25 of Phillips County v. Huckabee, 91 S.W.3d 472 (Ark. 2002).

Levin, H. M. (2002). *The cost effectiveness of whole school reforms* (Urban Diversity Series No. 114). New York: Teachers College, Columbia University, Institute for Urban and Minority Education.

Levin, H. M. (2006, May). *The public returns to public educational investments in African American males.* Paper presented at the Dijon Conference, Dijon, France.

Londonderry Sch. Dist. SAU No. 12 v. State, 907 A.2d 988 (N.H. 2006).

Monk, D. H., & Brent., B. O. (1997). *Raising money for education: A guide to the property tax.* Thousand Oaks, CA: Corwin Press.

Montoy v. State, 2003 WL 22902963 (Kan.Dist.Ct., Dec 2, 2003).

Mort, P. R., & Reusser, W. C. (1951). *Public school finance: Its background, structure, and operation.* New York: McGraw-Hill.

Murray, S. E., Evans, W. N., & Schwab, R. M. (1998). Education finance reform and the distribution of education resources. *American Economic Review, 88,* 789–812.

Neeley v. West Orange-Cove Consol. Indep. Sch. Dist., 176 S.W.3d 746 (Tex., 2005).

Odden, A. R. (2000) Costs of sustaining educational change via comprehensive school reform. *Phi Delta Kappan, 81,* 433–438.

Pauley v. Kelley, 255 S.E.2d 859 (W.Va. 1979).

Rebell, M. (2002) Educational adequacy, democracy and the courts.. In T. Ready, C. Edley Jr., & C. Snow (Eds.), *Achieving high educational standards for all: Conference summary* (pp. 218–270). Washington DC: National Academy Press.

Reschovsky, A., & Imazeki, J. (2004). Estimating the costs of meeting the Texas Educational Accountability Standards. Testimony provided on behalf of plaintiffs in the case of *West Orange Cove v. Neeley.*

Robinson v. Cahill, 303 A.2d 273 (N.J. 1973).

Rose v. Council for Better Education, 790 S.W.2d 186 (Ky., 1989)

Ryan, J. (1999). Schools, race, and money. *Yale Law Journal, 109,* 249–316.

San Antonio Indep. Sch. Dist. v. Rodriguez, 411 U.S. 1 (1973).

Seattle School District No. 1 v. State, 585 P.2d 71 (Wash. 1978).

Serrano v. Priest, 487 P.2d 1241 (Cal. 1971).

Simons, H. (1950). *Federal tax reform.* Chicago: University of Chicago Press.

Smith, A. (1904). *An inquiry into the nature and causes of the wealth of nations: Vol. 2* (E. Cannan, Ed.). London: Cambridge University Press.

Steuerle, C. E. (1999, December). *An equal (tax) justice for all.* Washington, DC: Tax Policy Center of the Urban Institute and Brookings Institution.

Taylor, L. L. (2004, August). *Estimating the cost of education in Texas, revised report.* College Station: Texas A&M University.

Taylor, L. L., Baker, B. D., & Vedlitz, A. (2005). *Measuring educational adequacy in public schools* (Bush School Working Paper No. 80). College Station: Texas A&M University, Bush School of Government and Public Service.

Turnbull, H. R., III, Turnbull, A., Wehmeyer, M., & Park, J. (2003). A quality of life framework for special education outcomes. *Remedial and Special Education, 24,* 67–74.

Underwood, J. K. (1995). School finance adequacy as vertical equity. *University of Michigan Journal of Law Reform, 28,* 493–519.

Washakie County School District No. 1 v. Herschler, 606 P.2d 310 (Wyo. 1980).

Wise, A. E. (1976). Minimum educational adequacy: Beyond school finance reform. *Journal of Education Finance, 1,* 468–483.

Zarb Commission. (2004). *Resource Adequacy Study for the New York State Commission on Education Reform.* New York: Standard and Poors School Evaluation Services.

Yinger, J. (2004) State aid and the pursuit of educational equity: An overview. In J. Yinger (Ed.), *Helping children left behind: State aid and the pursuit of educational equity* (pp. 3–58). Cambridge, MA: MIT Press.

36

Whether and How Money Matters in K-12 Education

MARGARET L. PLECKI AND TINO A. CASTAÑEDA
University of Washington, Seattle

Introduction: Why the Focus on Does Money Matter?

When policy makers make decisions about the amount, type, and distribution of revenues, they are faced with the issue of educational productivity. Given limited resources, multiple goals, and a wide range of possible approaches, policy makers must choose a course of action. Questions such as the following are key considerations in policy debates: How do we ensure that we getting the most for our educational dollar? How do we target resources to help students achieve at higher levels? What are the best strategies for better educating those students who are not being well-served by our schools? How do we eliminate existing inequities in the distribution of resources? What have we learned from prior efforts to allocate resources efficiently and effectively?

The answers to these questions are complex and variable. The nature and the extent of the educational challenges differ in important ways at each level of the policymaking system (state, district, school, and classroom) and the specific conditions for students and teachers within each level of the system vary considerably. Expected educational outcomes are multidimensional and sometimes even in conflict with one another. Attributing outcomes to specific interventions strategies is problematic, as much of student learning results from numerous types of interwoven interactions that are very difficult to model or measure. Nevertheless, the effective and efficient use of public funds is a prime expectation of the taxpayers who provide the majority of revenue for public schools, and for the policy makers who represent those taxpayers. Some have argued whether spending additional public money on education will improve student achievement or whether additional money would be wasted by inefficiencies that may exist in the education system. Thus, the question is often posed: Does money matter, and if so, in what ways? As Ladd and Hansen (1999) summarize, "There are, however, no easy solutions to this challenge, because values are in conflict, conditions vary widely from place to place, and knowledge about the link between resources and learning is incomplete" (p. 1). Numerous studies have focused on the extent to which specific levels and types of investments produce positive educational outcomes. Among other issues, studies have examined the relation between student achievement and: (a) overall expenditure levels, (b) the types of resources purchased (e.g., teachers, support staff, facilities, technology, etc.), and (c) the way in which resources are allocated and used (e.g., lower student-teacher ratios, additional supports for struggling students, compensation differentials, etc.).

The focus of this chapter is to describe what we have come to understand about research on the efficient and effective allocation of resources to support the improvement of student learning in K-12 public education. There are three main sections to this chapter. The first section provides an analysis of the context and the nature of the policy debate surrounding the question: Does money matter, and if so, in what ways? It includes a portrayal of the conceptual and methodological issues involved in the research concerning this question, along with a discussion of the numerous ways in which this research has been critiqued. The second section of the chapter describes some of the common policy approaches designed to make money matter that have been implemented in one manner or another over the past two decades. The chapter concludes with a discussion of the emerging topics and methods that are shaping the future of analyses about how money matters.

Overview of Trends in the Relation between Expenditures and Student Outcomes

At the heart of the debate about whether money matters is the examination of the relationship between the level of educational expenditures and student outcomes. Put most simply, the critique is that the rise in educational expenditures has outpaced any growth in student achievement (Hoxby, 2002; Walberg, 2003). An additional critique involves long-standing disparities that exist in educational attainment when students are grouped by ethnicity, race, and class, often referred to as the "achievement gap" (Hunter & Bartee, 2003; Harris & Herrington, 2006). National Assessment of Educational Progress (NAEP) and SAT scores are measures often used to indicate insufficient growth in student achievement. There is disagreement, however, about what change (or lack of change) in average scores on such tests signify as measures of educational outcomes. While this thorny problem about how to best measure educational outcomes will be discussed later in this chapter, there is general agreement that we expect the outcomes of our educational system to improve. Consequently, a brief review of the trends in educational expenditures is provided to frame both the historical context and current conditions.

Without question, spending for K-12 public education is a major enterprise of state and local governments, forming a large—if not the largest—share of the total budget for most state and local governments. In 2003–04, public school revenues totaled $475.5 billion, representing 4.5% of personal income and 3.8% of the nation's Gross Domestic Product (National Center for Education Statistics, 2005). In fiscal year 2006, per pupil expenditures averaged $9,154. Table 36.1 provides data about expenditure levels over a 50-year period. The data from this table indicate that growth in expenditures (as compared in constant dollars) as been steady and significant.

Characterizing educational expenditure patterns is complicated by the fact that wide variation exists between the highest and lowest spending states. For example, in fiscal year 2006, the average per pupil expenditure in New York State was $14,615 while Utah spent $5,464 on average (National Center for Education Statistics, 2008). Differential expenditure patterns also exist among districts in the same state, primarily due to the substantial variation in the fiscal capacity of school districts that requires some districts to impose much heavier tax burdens on residents to offer the same level of educational services that more wealthy districts can raise with ease. Addressing the interdistrict

variation in resources has been at the heart of school finance policy and research for more than 30 years. While this research has primarily examined spending differentials as an equity issue, differences in spending levels and patterns are also an integral part of the inquiry surrounding educational adequacy and productivity.[1]

Considerable differences also exist in the sources of funding for K-12 education. Numerous states have seen a dramatic shift in funding away from local sources of funds (primarily from local property taxes) towards state sources of revenue. For example, nationwide in 1919–20, state funds comprised approximately 17% of total education revenue, while in 2002–03 almost half of all education funding (49%) came from state sources. Here again, significant variation is found among states with Michigan, for example, drawing 72% of its revenue from state sources while the state share of education revenue in Illinois amounts to only 33% of all funds (National Center for Education Statistics, 2005). This shift towards state sources of funding is attributable in large part to a state's attempts to remedy longstanding disparities in the distribution of revenues. These changes in state school finance systems were often brought about through litigation, including cases such as *Serrano v. Priest* (1971) in California and *Robinson v. Cahill* (1973) in New Jersey.

These variations in total spending amounts and sources of revenue add further complexity to any overall characterization of expenditure trends over time. However, despite these considerable differences in the amounts and sources of funds, the examination of trends in the objects of expenditure reveal striking similarity across states and districts throughout the nation (Picus & Wattenbarger, 1995; Monk, Pijanowski, & Hussain, 1997). These analyses consistently indicate that the vast majority of the operating expenditures in education are allocated to pay for the cost of employing school personnel, with the largest portion of those expenditures allocated to classroom teachers. Total spending on all school personnel, including salaries and benefits, comprised 89.1% of all spending nationwide in fiscal year 2006 (National Center for Education Statistics,

TABLE 36.1
Current Expenditure per Pupil in Public Elementary and Secondary Schools

School year	Current expenditure[1] per pupil[2]		
	Unadjusted dollars	Constant 2004–05 dollars[3]	Percent increase in constant dollars from previous decade
1951–52	215	1,571	NA
1961–62	393	2,507	59.6
1971–72	908	4,228	68.6
1981–82	2,525	5,143	21.6
1991–92	5,023	6,967	26.2
2001–02	7,727	8,313	19.3

Note: [1]Current expenditures include instruction, student support services, food services, and enterprise operations but exclude capital outlay and interest on debt. Also excludes expenditures such as community services, private school programs, adult education and other programs not allocable to expenditures per student at public schools. Beginning in 1980-81, state administration expenditures are excluded from "current" expenditures. [2]Based on fall enrollment except for data for 1951-52 based on school-year enrollment. [3]Constant dollars based on the Consumer Price Index, prepared by the Bureau of Labor Statistics, U.S. Department of Labor, adjusted to a school-year basis.
Source: National Center for Education Statistics, Digest of Educational Statistics, 2005

2008). The largest share of these personnel expenditures is comprised of salaries and benefits for teachers.

Arguably, the quality of education is ultimately dependent on the classroom teacher's ability to impact student learning (Eide, Goldhaber, & Brewer, 2004; Rice, 2008). Consequently, numerous educational improvement policies have focused on the quality of the classroom teacher as a prime consideration in improving student learning. We discuss this policy approach alongside other investment strategies attempting to produce positive educational outcomes in the next section of this chapter.

Characterizing the Debate about whether Money Matters

A variety of methods have been used in the research literature to inquire into questions of educational productivity in K-12 schooling. One of the most frequently used approaches is the education production function model. This model attempts to describe the relation between a variety of inputs into the education process with specified outcomes. Often statistical and econometric techniques are used to estimate the production function, with regression methods being the most common method used during the past 30 years. While certainly not the only way to address questions of efficiency and effectiveness in education, the production function model has dominated the research literature that addresses questions of the relation between spending and educational outcomes. Production function studies also have played a role in policy debates regarding both the level of resources that should be expended in education and the way in which resources might be productively used. We now turn to a discussion of what we have learned from these types of studies, followed by an analysis of the limitations of this type of approach. We then describe some of the alternative, but less widely used approaches to addressing questions of educational productivity.

Numerous education production studies have been conducted over the past three decades, and numerous reviews of this production function literature have also been undertaken. Both the studies themselves and the meta-analyses of the research have been distinguished by mixed findings. Most analysts of the literature in this field point to the 1966 report, *Equality of Educational Opportunity* (Coleman et al., 1966) as a seminal piece which concluded that a variety of factors, most notably peer characteristics, influence student achievement. The report concluded that variables outside the purview or control of schools have a bearing on student success in school. Findings from the Coleman report prompted numerous additional studies that focused on identifying those variables which are most consistently and significantly associated with improved student achievement. Eric Hanushek (1986, 1989, 1991, 1996, 1997) published several analyses of the research on educational productivity in which he concluded that there is little evidence of a systematic relationship between the level of funding and student outcomes. Hanushek's method

for conducting his meta-analysis (called vote-counting) was challenged by Hedges, Laine, and Greenwald (1994) in their analysis of the same body of literature. Using a different method for conducting the meta-analysis (called combined significance), these authors arrive at the conclusion that money does indeed matter. They found that teacher education, ability, and experience, along with small schools and lower teacher-pupil ratios, are all positively associated with student achievement.

Others who have reviewed prior production function research (Ferguson & Ladd, 1996) claim that many of the earlier analyses did not critically sort out the methodologically weak studies from consideration, thus casting doubt on the validity of the conclusions being drawn. This classic debate regarding whether money matters continues today in both research and policy contexts. Numerous other scholars have provided additional critiques of educational productivity research and have offered suggestions in an attempt to improve the extent to which these types of studies can be used to help inform educational investment and improvement policies (Monk, 1992; King & MacPhail-Wilcox, 1994; Burtless, 1996; Card & Krueger, 1992; Ladd, 1996; Odden & Clune, 1995; Grissmer, 2001; Rice, 2001; Rolle, 2004).[2]

Conceptually, the lack of agreement about the elements of a theoretically sound "theory of production" in education plagues the research in this area. In other words, the forces and conditions that comprise the human "equation" of student learning are neither obvious nor fully understood. The lack of agreement is understandable, given that education is characterized by interactive and developmental processes and conditions stretching across many years of schooling, and individuals vary in multiple and important ways along a number of dimensions which are extraordinarily difficult to fully and reliably capture (Cullen, Jacob, & Levitt, 2005; Goldhaber & Brewer, 1997). Given this lack of an agreed-upon theory of educational production, it is little wonder that technical issues abound, such as the specification and measurement of proxies to best represent the important elements in the educational process. A further complication exists in the predominance of linear models in production function studies when most education processes are complex and non-linear in nature. Hence, the choice of inputs and their metric specifications may rest on other than strong theoretical grounds, further contributing to inconsistent research results. Thus, the selection of variables to use in these types of studies is inconsistent and less than fully reliable. Instead of using generally agreed-upon elements of production which might characterize work in other fields of study, production function researchers in education typically choose particular input or output measures because information is readily available, the variable has some policy relevance, or because the variable is intuitively plausible (Monk, 1990). The constraints surrounding the availability of data are particularly problematic and may obscure differences among students, teachers, and schools which may be important to consider (Hanushek, Rivkin, &

Taylor, 1996). For example, information about the amount of time students spend learning a particular subject, the quality of texts and curricula, and the contributions made by parents and volunteers in school settings are typically not included in these studies, primarily due to the lack of access to this type of data.

Murnane (1991) provides two critiques of studies of the relation between school resources and student outcomes that lend support to his observation that, while useful, "it is simply indefensible to use the results of quantitative studies of the relationship between school resources and student achievement as a basis for concluding that additional funds cannot help public school districts" (p. 457). His first concern is that education production function studies do not address questions of causation. This issue of implied causality is echoed by Rolle and Fuller (2007) in a similar review conducted more recently than that of Murnane. The second critique is that some productivity studies in education presume that waste or inefficiency exists when spending levels do not appear as being positively related to student outcomes. To support this claim, Murnane (1991) draws from examples of studies in private sectors that document how firms often pay for inputs that do not show a direct positive relationship to productivity but these findings are not interpreted as evidence that the firm is inefficient. Rather, the interpretation is that firms have a rationale for these expenditures, even if their reasons are not obvious.

In a later analysis of production function research, Taylor (2001) describes five types of differences that exist among the various studies of school inputs and student outcomes. Taylor finds that productivity studies vary in: (a) the identification of variables and the way in which variables are measured, (b) the level of analysis (e.g., state, district, school), (c) the geographic scope of schools under analysis, (d) the specification of the particular model under consideration, and (e) the analytic techniques employed.

One of the most contested issues of productivity studies is the manner in which outcome measures of student achievement are defined and treated. Student scores on standardized tests are measures that are used most frequently (Burtless, 1996). Critics of this approach to identifying student outcomes point to the numerous other goals of education that the public typically hold as important. Improved physical and mental health, ability to participate in a democracy, competitiveness in a global economy, crime reduction, and improved race relations are a few of the nonacademic student outcomes that are expected of elementary and secondary schools. However, even if the decision is made to focus more narrowly on the widely held expectation that schools should, at a minimum, contribute to increases in the academic performance of students, serious disagreements exist as to the extent to which the test scores that are available for use by researchers actually capture what is most important to uncover about student achievement (Ladd & Hansen, 1999; Monk, 1997). In a recent discussion of the use of student test scores in the examination of school performance, Stiefel, Schwartz, Rubenstein, and Zabel

(2005) note both psychometric and policy-related cautions about the use of student test scores. These include issues of refraining from the use of test scores for purposes other than intended, and caveats surrounding how test scores are aggregated. In particular, some forms of aggregation may mask important differences or distinctions among districts, schools, or subgroups of students. Figlio (2005) notes three ways in which states often approach the aggregation of test score data in designing accountability systems: across time, across subject areas, and across sub-groups. Each of these types of aggregation strategies addresses different approaches to characterizing student achievement levels. These dynamics and potential pitfalls in how test scores are treated can influence the policy implications of productivity studies.

A number of productivity studies have employed a more microanalytic approach using disaggregated data (Murnane, 1975; Summers & Wolfe, 1977; Thomas, Kemmerer, & Monk, 1982; Brown & Saks, 1987; Rossmiller, 1986; Monk, 1989). These studies have focused on school and classroom levels, in contrast to the analyses which have used more global measures from macro-level databases. Findings from the microanalytic studies reveal a similar pattern of mixed results. However, several production function studies in this tradition have demonstrated positive relationships between teachers' ability levels (often a measure of verbal aptitude) and student achievement (Ehrenberg & Brewer, 1995; Summers & Wolfe, 1977). Ferguson (1991) examined school districts in Texas and concluded that there are systematic relationships between educational inputs and student outcomes which he estimated to account for between one-quarter and one-third of student achievement differences. Ferguson and Ladd (1996) examined Alabama schools and concluded that there is evidence that the input variables of teacher's test scores, the percentage of teachers with master's degrees, and small class size are positively associated with student test scores. These authors and others (Rice, 2001; Schwartz & Stiefel, 2001) assert that the use of more methodologically sound analytic techniques (e.g., value-added specification)[3] combined with a more disaggregated and longitudinal analyses can address some of the perplexing problems which have been associated with production function research.

In addition to the challenges with productivity studies described above, other concerns have been raised regarding research on the relation between resources and student outcomes. A recent critique of productivity studies (Rolle & Fuller, 2007) points to the inadequacy of using family income, race, and ethnicity to "control" for differences in background characteristics of students. The authors assert that this variable cannot capture the important ways in which families and communities, especially communities of color, may contribute in a positive way to students' educational attainment.

The upshot of these lines of thinking and research to date are that we know less about the productive impact of policy makers' investments in education than we might wish. To be sure, some analyses highlight certain variables that appear to bear some relationship to student learning. Other studies establish no clear or discernible relationships. The lack of connections and the mixed nature of results across studies may be due to the weaknesses in underlying theory or specification of measures. Or, these models have yet to represent adequately important variables intervening between the allocation of resources and their enactment in practice. By a similar argument, production function models take little account of the actual allocation and expenditure dynamics within public education systems, and hence we are unable to tell whether increased levels of resource investment overall were actually targeted to inputs of immediate relevance to improved classroom performance (Stiefel et al., 2005).

In one manner of thinking, education productivity research might be best considered as a means rather than an end in itself. It can serve as an analytic tool to help uncover not only the types and levels of resources that might make a difference, but also to better understand the ways in which those resources can be effectively used in pursuit of specific education goals. Based in part on results from productivity research, educators and policy makers have been pursuing some specific strategies to improve the effectiveness of resource allocation and use. These policy approaches are discussed in the next section of this chapter.

Policy Approaches to Making Money Matter

Numerous state, district, and school level policies are aimed at improving student learning in effective ways. Some of the most common approaches in recent years fall into the following categories: (a) improving teacher quality, (b) lowering pupil-teacher ratios, (c) expanding early childhood programs, (d) improving high school, (e) decentralizing spending authority, and (f) providing incentives to improve performance. While each of these types of policy strategies have numerous goals, each strategy involves either providing additional resources or altering the way in which existing resources are used to improve student performance. A description of each policy strategy follows.

Investments in Teacher Quality As discussed earlier in this chapter, the largest share of expenditures in education is on personnel. Thus, policies that invest in human resources are a particular focus for policy makers. In addition, results from a number of productivity studies suggest that the quality of the teacher is one of the most important variables in producing improved student learning (Hanushek, Kain, O'Brien, & Rivkin, 2005; Eide et al., 2004; Rice, 2008; Sanders & Rivers, 1996). However, the specific ways in which particular teacher attributes impact student learning is still under debate (Clotfelter, Ladd, & Vigdor, 2007). Some of the lack of clarity in the research findings can be traced to the complexities involved in measuring teacher quality. At least three elements are involved in understanding how investments in teachers impact student learning: (a) the quality of the teacher workforce, typically measured

in terms of degrees, experience, verbal aptitude, etc.; (b) the quality of the interaction between the teacher and the learners; and (c) the quality of support for teachers' work, including school working conditions and teachers' collaborative efforts. However, for the most part, attention has been focused in the first category regarding individual teacher attributes (Plecki, 2000; Plecki & Loeb, 2004).

In an analysis of the literature on teacher quality, Rice (2003) emphasizes the complexities encountered when attempting to identify the specific qualifications of teachers who make the greatest contributions to student learning. For example, variations in teacher effects were found by school level (i.e., elementary school as compared to high school) and by subject matter (e.g., greater effects for mathematics as compared to reading achievement). She found evidence to support the following general observations: (a) teacher experience makes a difference, as higher performance is associated with those teachers who have more than 5 years of experience; (b) teachers with advanced degrees in mathematics and science had a positive influence on high school student achievement in those subjects, but mixed results were found for the elementary level; (c) no clear impact exists for those teachers trained through alternative routes to teacher certification as compared to traditional routes; and (d) measures of teacher verbal ability are associated with higher levels of student achievement.

An important dimension emerges in the literature about teacher quality and its relation to student learning with respect to the inequity of distribution of qualified teachers across schools and classrooms. Numerous studies have pointed to the need to examine the extent to which less experienced and less qualified teachers (e.g., teachers assigned to courses for which they lack proper certification, training, or subject matter knowledge) are located in high-poverty schools or schools serving larger proportions of students from racial and ethnic minorities and the extent to which these schools experience higher teacher turnover than schools which serve a more advantaged population of students (Lankford, Loeb, & Wyckoff, 2002; Boyd, Lankford, Loeb, & Wyckoff, 2003; Ingersoll, 2001; Clotfelter, Ladd, & Vigdor, 2005).

As already mentioned, some consensus has emerged that the effects of teacher quality on student performance in mathematics is higher than that for reading (Hanushek et al., 2005). In a recent study using 10 years of data on North Carolina teachers, Clotfelter, Ladd, and Vigdor (2007) found that teachers' experience, test scores, and licensure status were all positively related to student achievement measures, with larger effects for mathematics achievement than for reading. They go on to state that these effects are greater than those found for changes in class size or in indicators of socioeconomic factors such as parental education level.[4] While policy makers have primarily relied on identifiable teacher traits such as education level, certification status, and years of experience as measures of teacher quality, results from research studies do not consistently find these attributes as predictive of teacher effectiveness (Goldhaber, 2007).

Another important development regarding research on teacher quality involves using more precise data that matches teachers and students as well as more longitudinal approaches to assessing teacher effects. For example, recent work by Rivkin, Hanushek, and Kain (2005) noted the following: (a) teachers have significant effects on reading and mathematics achievement, (b) little of the variation in mathematics and reading achievement is explained by experience or education levels, and (c) the benefits of improving teaching quality are greater than reducing class size by 10 students.

Class Size[5] Reducing class size is a popular education policy reform of educators, parents, and policy makers. It is also one of the most costly policy strategies aimed at improving student learning. However, the impact of class size on student achievement has been debated by researchers for several decades (Glass & Smith, 1979; Odden, 1990; Grissmer, 1999; Peevely, Hedges, & Nye, 2005; Krueger, 2003). Many of these studies point to other factors which may need to accompany class size reduction, such as changes in pedagogical approaches and placing well-qualified teachers in each classroom (Imazeki, 2003). An important distinction to bear in mind when examining the evidence about class size is the difference between class size and student-teacher ratios. For example, a body of research has found that a class size of 15 in the primary grades is associated with improved student learning, particularly for students from low-income families and students from racial and ethnic minority groups (Achilles, 1996; Finn & Achilles, 1999; Grissmer, 1999, 2001; Laine & Ward, 2000). This form of class size reduction is not the same as a class of 30 with a teacher and a full-time instructional aide (Gerber, Finn, Achilles, & Boyd-Zaharias, 2001). Nor is it equivalent to classes of 18–20 students who also have access to certificated instructional coaches or specialized teachers that provide additional small group instruction for targeted students for a part of the school day. However, in policy and practice, the most common metric for class size is the number of students per certificated staff member.

The Importance of Early Intervention[6] Scholars have documented the gap that exists between children living in poverty and their more economically advantaged peers in terms of their readiness to learn when they begin kindergarten (Lee & Burkham, 2002). States, cities, and school districts are increasingly investing in pre-kindergarten programs, and evidence exists to support the wisdom of that investment. One of the most extensive longitudinal studies of the impact of a quality preschool program is the High/Scope Perry Preschool Project. The study began in the 1960s and used random assignment to a treatment and a control group to assess the effects of a preschool program for at-risk children. Evaluation of the follow-up data on these individuals through childhood and into adulthood (up to age 27) showed that gains for those participating in the preschool program outweighed the cost of the program by a factor

of seven (Barnett, 1996). Additional follow-up conducted on these same individuals who were reaching the age of 40 indicated that gains continue to be sustained over time, particularly in higher lifetime earnings and lower criminal activity, as well as reduced costs in terms of welfare and other social costs (Nores, Belfield, Barnett, & Schweinhart, 2005). Nores and colleagues (2005) estimated that the program repaid $12.90 for every $1.00 invested in the program. Other research has confirmed this finding of the long-term individual and social benefits of high-quality preschool programs, particularly for children living in poverty (Barnett, 1998; Currie & Neidell, 2007; Temple & Reynolds, 2007; Barnett & Masse, 2007). An important policy concern about the capacity to provide high quality preschool programs is the difficulty in recruiting and retaining well-qualified teachers, as wages for preschool teachers are significantly lower than elementary and secondary teachers.

Improving High School Significant policy attention nationwide has been focused on the matter of improving high school education. One of the most popular improvement strategies is to create smaller schools or learning environments that provide students with more personalized attention. The question of whether smaller schools impact student learning is a matter that has been examined by scholars for many years, often in an effort to determine if there is an optimal school size (Barker & Gump, 1964; Cohn, 1968; Riew, 1986; Fowler & Walberg, 1991; Monk, 1984; Lee & Smith, 1997). For some time, larger schools were viewed as more cost-effective and potentially more comprehensive given economies of scale that could potentially be realized. However, while improved curricular comprehensiveness is theoretically possible in larger high schools, evidence exists that this potential is not fully realized in practice (Monk, 1987; Haller, Monk, Spotted Bear, Griffith, & Moss, 1990).

It has been suggested that high school size should be within a range of 400–600 students (Lee & Smith, 1997). This range is much smaller than most comprehensive high schools across the nation. However, it is also important to note that the relationship between high school size and student outcomes is an indirect one (Lee, 2004), and simply creating smaller schools does not guarantee positive outcomes in student learning. Additional concerns have been raised about whether or not smaller high schools would be more costly. However, some microanalytic research that examines budgetary implications of high school size (Stiefel, Berne, Iatarola, & Fruchter, 2000) uses a cost per graduate approach and concludes that smaller academic high schools have about the same cost per graduate as larger high schools.

Decentralizing Spending Authority While many factors influence and contribute to student learning, leadership in all its forms is often cited as a factor that contributes to the learning process (Leithwood & Riehl, 2003). In recent years, attention has been focused on the extent to which leadership is distributed throughout the education system, including providing additional decision-making authority and responsibility at the school level, as well as distributing leadership roles within a school. The central idea is that those who are closest to the point of instruction are better positioned to make decisions tailored to the needs of individual schools, classrooms, and students. One emerging strategy for making money matter more is to provide school principals with more control and discretion over school budgets. For example, budgeting practices in the United Kingdom, Canada, and Australia allow for the majority of operational funding (85–90%) to flow directly to individual schools (Committee for Economic Development, 2004). In the United States, several urban districts are implementing this approach of providing more site-level authority for school budgets, including Chicago and New York City. However, this additional authority comes with new responsibilities for school principals and others at the school site to pay closer attention to and assume accountability for additional resource-related matters. It also implies that school leaders have the knowledge, skills, and supports that are needed to make well-informed decisions about budget and finance (Plecki, Alejano, Knapp, & Lochmiller, 2006).

Providing Incentives to Improve Performance

An issue often debated by policy makers concerns the role of incentives in educational improvement. Examples of incentive-related policies include merit pay for teachers and other forms of performance-based rewards, bonuses for teachers locating in hard-to-staff schools, and differentiated pay for teachers working in subject matter shortage areas. A number of these incentive-based approaches imply departures from the traditional approach to determining teacher salaries that relies almost exclusively on years of teaching experience and college degrees and credits earned (Odden & Kelley, 1997; Kelley, 1997). While economic theory suggests that merit pay could help attract able people into teaching and serve to motivate individuals to be more productive (Goldhaber & Player, 2005; Ballou & Podgursky, 2001), early attempts at merit pay strategies were problematic, particularly regarding the subjective nature of teachers' performance evaluations and the limited nature of the cases in which merit pay was attempted (Murnane & Cohen, 1986; Freiberg & Knight, 1991; Firestone, 1991; Cornett & Gaines, 1994). As an alternative to individual-based rewards, another incentive-based approach focuses on group-based rewards for improved performance in which all those working at a school that meet specified performance improvement targets receive additional compensation or increased funds allocated to the school (Mohrman, Mohrman, & Odden, 1996; Kelley, Heneman, & Milanowski, 2002). Such an approach may not adequately account for conditions that are not within the control of those at the individual school level (Goorian, 2000).

Yet another approach that is being attempted in a limited number of locations is some type of knowledge and skills-based pay structure (Milanowski, 2003). These pay systems

provide additional compensation for teachers who demonstrate they have particular expertise in areas that have been identified as particularly critical by the school or school district, such as the ability to teach English-language learners or advanced-placement physics. In the case of teachers who have received certification from the National Board for Professional Teaching Standards (NBPTS), several states have provided incentives for those NBPTS-certified teachers to work in hard-to-staff or low-performing schools (Humphrey, Koppich, & Hough, 2005). Other types of incentives are also being considered such as loan forgiveness programs and housing assistance as a means to attract teachers to districts and schools in need. However, non-monetary factors and conditions in the workplace also serve to shape teachers' motivation and job satisfaction (Loeb & Page, 2000; Boyd, Lankford, & Loeb, 2004). School factors such as well-behaved students, supportive principals, and strong collaborative working environments may be just as or more important to teachers than increased compensation or other forms of monetary incentives (Farkas, Johnson, Foleno, Duffett, & Foley, 2000).

Emerging Topics and Future Directions in the Field

A substantial portion of the suggestions for improvement in the field of education productivity research can be characterized as falling into three main categories: (a) inadequacies regarding the statistical techniques employed; (b) the quality, specificity, and timeliness of data to accurately address aspects of education production thought to be important; and (c) the assumptions and theoretical underpinnings of how the issue of improving productivity in education is framed. These issues are outlined in this final section of the chapter.

As previously discussed, numerous scholars have pointed to the inadequacy of statistical strategies used in much of the productivity literature and have posited that improvements in measurement and methodology would yield more accurate and useful results. For example, Alexander (1998) describes the central issue as follows:

> More poorly designed studies that use inaccurate determinations of input and productivity measures frequently result in the finding that money doesn't matter, not because no relationship exists, but rather because of improperly specified research models. Imprecise research designs usually produce results that tend toward randomness resulting in erroneous conclusions that fail to identify relationships that may well exist. (p. 239)

Some advances in recent years have attempted to address these concerns through the use of statistical techniques other than multiple regression. One of those techniques is hierarchical linear modeling (HLM). A number of scholars find HLM to be particularly well-suited for examining the nested nature of classroom, school, and district effects (Raudenbush, 1988; Raudenbush & Bryk, 2002; Odden, Borman, & Fermanich, 2004). Advocates of HLM techniques point to ways in which this approach can model the contexts and conditions in which the educational process typically occurs (i.e., within states, districts, schools, and classrooms, each with its own unique influences). Statistical and methodological techniques in addition to HLM that are emerging in this field of inquiry include data envelopment analysis (Rubenstein, 2005) and stochastic frontier analysis (Rolle & Fuller, 2007). The promise and the limitations of these emerging techniques are being debated.[7] As they develop, these methodological advances represent a means for improving the degree to which productivity analyses can contribute to our knowledge of the effectiveness of a variety of educational investments.

Addressing data insufficiencies have also been an important part of improving our understanding of the relationship between school resources and student learning. Much has been written about the need for more detailed data that captures a larger and more sophisticated picture of the factors that impact student learning (Monk, 1997). For example, a more robust portrayal of teaching quality, leadership, and district support might further our understanding of the necessary conditions that help make investments matter more (Grubb, 2006). A number of states have worked on improving the quality of their data systems to build capacity for more detailed and timely analyses, such as value-added and longitudinal approaches to examining student learning and related factors and conditions. Results from a survey of states conducted by the Data Quality Campaign and the National Center for Educational Accountability (2006) identified 10 data elements essential to developing robust longitudinal analyses, including the ability to match teachers to students and to examine student performance data over time and across key databases.

In addition to the development of more detailed and sophisticated methodological techniques and improved data capacity, policy makers have noted an increasing preference for randomized trial studies and other "scientifically based" evidence of the impact of investments on outcomes (Boruch & Mosterller, 2001; Raudenbush, 2002). However, in a critique of the role of randomized trials in education, Murnane and Nelson (2005) assert that the methodology of randomized trials is more effective in guiding very troubled schools than in helping average-performing schools in their efforts to become high-performing organizations. The authors also question the common assumption that the advances made in medical practice have come primarily from discoveries in laboratories using randomized control trials and that education should adopt this approach to advance knowledge as is done in the field of medicine.

Some scholars who have been examining the state of education productivity research have adopted a critical framework that calls into question some of the traditional conceptual and philosophical underpinnings of the constructs that guide the design and conduct of analyses about making money matter (Rodriguez & Rolle, 2007). For example, Rolle and Fuller (2007) call for the design of productivity studies that help us understand the full inequity

of efficiencies in education instead of just focusing on average efficiency which may well be masking inequities. They recommend that measures of efficiency used in productivity studies "…should focus on relative comparisons of the best observed performers to the worst" (p. 76). Rodriguez (2007) uses the case of California's school finance system to examine the theoretical and conceptual challenges involved in traditional school finance theory and points out how diverse students and communities are most likely to be represented only from a perspective that identifies their deficiencies. For example, school finance models typically provide additional resources to districts and schools that serve higher percentages of students living in poverty in an effort to provide greater equity. However, this approach also carries an assumption of cultural deficiency that is rarely explicitly surfaced as a consideration in policy design. She offers the following observation:

> In the case of school finance policy, the key issue that would benefit from the introduction of critical analysis is the persistence of disappointing or frustrating results from the educational system despite years of reform in the distribution of financial and non-financial resources to public schools. Moreover, the repetitive cycle involves the stigmatized characterizations of large (and growing) numbers of students—those who are from low-income backgrounds and/or of color—such that their potential as learners and contributors to our society is obscured and remains untapped. (p. 118)

These perspectives challenge both researchers and policy makers to consider the underlying assumptions and theoretical constructs that shape how student ability and performance is gauged and how variation across states, districts, communities, schools, classrooms, and families is considered. While the puzzles regarding the precise ways in which money matters for improving student learning are not yet solved, progress has been made in informing our understanding about the vital role that resources play. Through the use of improved data and more finely tuned methods, substantial progress has been made in the past two decades, and a greater focus is now on understanding the ways in which money makes a difference, rather than simply debating the importance of resources. Certainly, more work remains to be done in order for research to become more closely tied to informing policy and practice. Significant challenges persist in addressing the ways in which students who have not fared well in our education system can be effectively and equitably served. Research can continue to contribute to the continuous improvement of the decisions that are made in policy design and in practice regarding effective, equitable, and efficient resource allocation and use.

Notes

1. For a detailed discussion of financial equity and adequacy please refer to Baker and Green, this volume.
2. For a recent detailed discussion of a variety of methods in productivity

studies, including production functions, adjusted performance measures, cost functions, and data envelopment analysis, please see Stiefel, Schwartz, Rubenstein, and Zabel (2005).

3. A significant amount of contemporary research provides an alternative for measuring growth in student performance. This approach, often called "value-added," measures gains in student learning based on the prior performance of the individual student rather than the performance relative to a uniform aggregate standard (Sanders, 1998).

4. For additional discussion of teacher quality, please see Béteille and Loeb, this volume.

5. For a detailed discussion of the topic of class size, please see Ahn and Brewer, this volume.

6. For a detailed discussion of early childhood education, please see Schweinhart and Fulcher-Dawson, this volume.

7. See, for example, Ruggiero (2006) for a critique of data envelopment analysis.

References

Achilles, C. M. (1996). Response to Eric Hanushek—Students achieve more in smaller classes. *Educational Leadership*, *53*(5), 76–77.

Alexander, K. (1998). Money matters: Commentary and analyses. *Journal of Education Finance, 24*, 237–242.

Ballou, D., & Podgursky, M. (2001). Let the market decide. *Education Next*. Retrieved June 1, 2006, from http://www.hoover.org/publications/ednext/3390886.html

Barker, R., & Gump, P. (1964). *Big school, small school: High school size and student behavior*. Palo Alto, CA: Stanford University Press.

Barnett, W. (1996). *Lives in the balance: Age-27 benefit-cost analysis of the High/Scope Perry Preschool Project* (High/Scope Educational Research Foundation Monograph 11). Ypsilanti, MI: High/Scope Press.

Barnett, W. (1998). Long-term cognitive and academic effects of early childhood education on children in poverty. *Preventive Medicine, 27*, 204–207.

Barnett, W., & Masse, L. (2007). Comparative benefit-cost analysis of the Abecedarian program and its policy implications. *Economics of Education Review, 26*, 113–125.

Boruch, R., & Mosterller, F. (Eds.). (2001). *Education, evaluation and randomized trials*. Washington, DC: Brookings Institution.

Boyd, D., Lankford, H., & Loeb, S. (2004). Improving student outcomes: The role of teacher workforce policies. In D. Monk & J. Wyckoff (Chairs), *Proceedings from the Symposium on the Teaching Workforce* conducted at the State of New York Education Finance Research Consortium, Albany.

Boyd, D., Lankford, H., Loeb, S., & Wyckoff, J. (2003). *The draw of home: How teachers' preferences for proximity disadvantage urban schools* (NBER Working Paper No. W9953). Cambridge, MA: National Bureau of Economic Research.

Brown, B., & Saks, D. (1987). The microeconomics of the allocation of teachers' time and student learning. *Economics of Education Review, 6*, 319–332.

Burtless, G. (Ed.). (1996). *Does money matter? The effect of school resources on student achievement and adult success*. Washington, DC: Brookings Institution.

Card, D., & Krueger, A. B. (1992). Does school quality matter? Returns to education and the characteristics of public schools in the United States. *Journal of Political Economy, 100*, 1–40.

Clotfelter, C., Ladd, H., & Vigdor, J. (2005). Who teaches whom? Race and the distribution of novice teachers. *Economics of Education Review, 24*, 377–392.

Clotfelter, C., Ladd, H., & Vigdor, J. (2007). *How and why do teacher credentials matter for student achievement?* (NBER Working Paper No. 12828). Cambridge, MA: National Bureau of Economic Research.

Cohn, E. (1968). Economies of scale in Iowa high school operations. *Journal of Human Resources, 3*, 422–434.

Coleman, J. S., Campbell, E. Q., Hobson, C. J., McPartland, J., Mood, A. M., Weinfield, F. D., et al. (1966). *Equality of educational opportunity*. Washington, DC: U.S. Government Printing Office.

Committee for Economic Development. (2004). *Investing in learning: School funding policies to foster high performance*. Washington, DC: Author.

Cornett, L. M., & Gaines, G. F. (1994). *Reflecting on ten years of incentive programs: The 1993 SREB Career Ladder Clearinghouse Survey*. Atlanta, GA: Southern Regional Education Board.

Cullen, J., Jacob, B., & Levitt, S. (2005). The impact of school choice on student outcomes: An analysis of the Chicago Public Schools. *Journal of Public Economics, 89*, 729–760.

Currie, J., & Neidell, M. (2007). Getting inside the "black box" of Head Start quality: What matters and what doesn't. *Economics of Education Review, 26*, 83–99.

Data Quality Campaign and the National Center for Education Accountability. (2006). Results of the 2006 NCEA survey of state P-12 data collection issues related to longitudinal analysis. Retrieved June 16, 2008, from http://www.dataqualitycampaign.org/survey_results/

Ehrenberg, R. G., & Brewer, D. J. (1995). Did teacher's race and verbal ability matter in the 1960s? Coleman revisited. *Economics of Education Review, 14*, 291–299.

Eide, E., Goldhaber, D., & Brewer, D. (2004). The teacher labour market and teacher quality. *Oxford Review of Economic Policy, 20*, 230–244.

Farkas, S., Johnson, J., Foleno, T., Duffett, A., & Foley, P. (2000). *A sense of calling: Who teaches and why*. Washington, DC: Public Agenda.

Ferguson, R. F. (1991). Paying for public education: New evidence on how and why money matters. *Harvard Journal on Legislation, 28*, 465–497.

Ferguson, R. F., & Ladd, H. (1996). How and why money matters: An analysis of Alabama schools. In H. Ladd (Ed.), *Holding schools accountable: Performance-based reform in education* (pp. 265–298). Washington, DC: Brookings Institution.

Figlio, D. (2005). Measuring school performance: Promises and pitfalls. In L. Stiefel, A. Schwartz, R. Rubenstein, & J. Zabel (Eds.), *Measuring school performance and efficiency: Implications or practice and research* (pp. 119–135). Larchmont, NY: Eye on Education.

Finn, J. D., & Achilles, C. M. (1999). Tennessee's class size study: Findings, implications, misconceptions. *Education Evaluation and Policy Analysis, 21*, 97–110.

Firestone, W. A. (1991). Merit pay and job enlargement as reforms: Incentives, implementation, and teacher response. *Educational Evaluation and Policy Analysis, 13*, 269–288.

Fowler, W., & Walberg, H. (1991). School size, characteristics, and outcomes. *Educational Evaluation and Policy Analysis, 13*, 189–202.

Freiberg, J., & Knight, S. (1991). Career ladder programs as incentives for teachers. In S. C. Conley & B. S. Cooper (Eds.), *The school as a work environment: Implications for reform*. Boston: Allyn and Bacon.

Gerber, S. B., Finn, J. D., Achilles, C. M., & Boyd-Zaharias, J. (2001). Teacher aides and students' academic achievement. *Educational Evaluation and Policy Analysis, 23*, 123–143.

Glass, G. V., & Smith, M. L. (1979). Meta-analysis of research on class size and achievement. *Educational Evaluation and Policy Analysis, 1*, 2–16.

Goldhaber, D. (2007). Teachers matter, but effective teacher quality policies are elusive: Hints from research for creating a more productive teacher workforce. In H. Ladd & E. Fiske (Eds.), *Handbook of research on education finance and policy* (pp. 146–165). New York: Routledge.

Goldhaber, D., & Brewer, D. (1997). Why don't schools and teachers seem to matter? Assessing the impact of unobservables on educational productivity. *Journal of Human Resources, 32*, 505–523.

Goldhaber, D., & Player, D. (2005). What different benchmarks suggest about how financially attractive it is to teach in public schools. *Journal of Education Finance, 30*, 211–230.

Goorian, B. (2000). Alternative teacher compensation. *ERIC Digest No. 142*. Retrieved June 17, 2008, from http://www.ericdigests.org/2001-3/teacher.htm

Grissmer, D. (Ed.). (1999). Class size: Issues and new findings [Entire issue]. *Educational Evaluation and Policy Analysis, 21*(2).

Grissmer, D. (2001). Research directions for understanding the relationship of educational resources to educational outcomes. In S. Chaikind & W. J. Fowler (Eds.), *Education finance in the new millennium: The 2001 Yearbook of the American Education Finance Association* (pp. 139–155). Larchmont, NY: Eye on Education.

Grubb, W. (2006). When money might matter: Using NELS88 data to examine the weak effects of school funding. *Journal of Education Finance, 31*, 360–378.

Haller, E., Monk, D., Spotted Bear, A., Griffith, J., & Moss, P. (1990). School size and program comprehensiveness: Evidence from "High School and Beyond." *Educational Evaluation and Policy Analysis, 12*, 109–120.

Hanushek, E. A. (1986). The economics of schooling: Production and efficiency in public schools. *Journal of Economic Literature, 24*, 1141–1177.

Hanushek, E. A. (1989). The impact of differential expenditures on school performance. *Educational Researcher, 18*(4), 45–51.

Hanushek, E. A. (1991). When school finance "reform" may not be good policy. *Harvard Journal on Legislation, 28*, 423–456.

Hanushek, E. A. (1996). The quest for equalized mediocrity: School finance reform without consideration of school performance. In L. O. Picus & J. L. Wattenbarger (Eds.), *Where does the money go? Resource allocation in elementary and secondary schools* (pp. 20–43). Thousand Oaks, CA: Corwin Press.

Hanushek, E. A. (1997). Assessing the effects of school resources on student performance: An update. *Educational Evaluation and Policy Analysis 19*, 141–164.

Hanushek, E. A., Kain, J., O'Brien, D. M., & Rivkin, S. (2005). *The market for teacher quality* (NBER Working Paper 11154). Cambridge, MA: National Bureau of Economic Research.

Hanushek, E. A., Rivkin, S., & Taylor, L. (1996). The identification of school resource effects. *Education Economics, 4*, 105–125.

Harris, D., & Herrington, C. (2006). Accountability, standards, and the growing achievement gap: Lessons from the past half-century. *American Journal of Education, 112*, 209–238.

Hedges, L., Laine, R., & Greenwald, R. (1994). Does money matter? A meta-analysis of studies of the effects of differential school inputs on student outcomes. *Educational Researcher, 23*(3), 5–14.

Hoxby, C. (2002). *School choice and school productivity (Or, could school choice be a tide that lifts all boats?* (NBER Working Paper No. W8873). Washington, DC: National Bureau of Economic Research.

Humphrey, D., Koppich, J., & Hough, H. (2005). Sharing the wealth: National Board certified teachers and the students who need them most. *Education Policy Analysis Archives, 13*(18). Retrieved September 23, 2006, from http://epaa.asu.edu/epaa/v13n18/

Hunter, R., & Bartee, R. (2003). The achievement gap: Issues of competition, class, and race. *Education and Urban Society, 35*, 151–160.

Imazeki, J. (2003). Class-size reduction and teacher quality: Evidence from California. In M. Plecki & D. Monk (Eds.), *School finance and teacher quality: Exploring the connections. The 2003 Handbook of the American Education Finance Association* (pp. 159–178). Larchmont, NY: Eye on Education.

Ingersoll, R. (2001). Teacher turnover and teacher shortages: An organizational analysis. *American Educational Research Journal, 38*, 499–534.

Kelley, C. (1997). Teacher compensation and organization. *Educational Evaluation and Policy Analysis, 19*, 15–28.

Kelley, C., Heneman, H., III, & Milanowski, A. (2002). Teacher motivation and school-based performance awards. *Educational Administration Quarterly, 38*, 372–401.

King, R., & MacPhail-Wilcox, B. (1994). Unraveling the production equation: The continuing quest for resources that make a difference. *Journal of Education Finance, 20*, 47–65.

Krueger, A. (2003). Economic considerations and class size. *Economic Journal, 113*(485), F34–63.

Ladd, H. F. (Ed.). (1996). *Holding schools accountable: Performance-based reform in education.* Washington DC: Brookings Institution.

Ladd, H. F., & Hansen, J. S. (Eds.). (1999). *Making money matter: Financing America's schools.* Washington, DC: National Academy Press.

Laine, S., & Ward, J. (Eds.). (2000). *Using what we know: A review of the research on implementing class-size reduction initiatives for state and local policymakers.* Naperville, IL: North Central Regional Educational Laboratory.

Lankford, H., Loeb, S., & Wyckoff, J. (2002). Teacher sorting and the plight of urban schools: A descriptive analysis. *Educational Evaluation and Policy Analysis, 24*, 37–62.

Lee, V. (2004). Effects of high school size on student outcomes: Response to Howley and Howley. *Education Policy Analysis Archives, 12*(53). Retrieved June 17, 2008, from http://epaa.asu.edu/epaa/v12n53/

Lee, V., & Burkham, D. (2002). *Inequality at the starting gate: Social background differences in achievement as children begin school.* Washington, DC: Economic Policy Institute.

Lee, V., & Smith, J. (1997). High school size: Which works best, and for whom? *Educational Evaluation and Policy Analysis, 19*, 205–227.

Leithwood, K., & Riehl, C. (2003). *What we know about successful school leadership.* Philadelphia: Temple University, Laboratory for Student Success.

Loeb, S., & Page, M. (2000). Examining the link between teacher wages and student outcomes: The importance of alternative labor market opportunities and non-pecuniary variation. *Review of Economics and Statistics, 82*, 393–408.

Milanowski, A. (2003). The varieties of knowledge and skill-based pay design: A comparison of seven new pay systems for K-12 teachers. *Education Policy Analysis Archives, 11*(4). Retrieved May 6, 2006, from http://epaa.asu.edu/epaa/v11n4/

Mohrman, A. M., Jr., Mohrman, S. A., & Odden, A. R. (1996). Aligning teacher compensation with systemic school reform: Skill-based and group-based performance rewards, *Educational Evaluation and Policy Analysis, 18*, 51–71.

Monk, D. (1984). The conception of size and the internal allocation of school district resources, *Educational Administration Quarterly, 20*, 39–67.

Monk, D. (1987). Secondary school size and curriculum comprehensiveness. *Economics of Education Review, 6*, 137–150.

Monk, D. (1989). The education production function: Its evolving role in policy analysis, *Educational Evaluation and Policy Analysis, 11*, 31–45.

Monk, D. (1990). *Educational finance: An economic approach.* New York: McGraw-Hill.

Monk, D. (1992). Education productivity research: An update and assessment of its role in education finance reform. *Educational Evaluation and Policy Analysis, 14*, 307–332.

Monk, D. (1997). Challenges surrounding the collection and use of data for the study of finance and productivity. *Journal of Education Finance, 22*, 303–316.

Monk, D., Pijanowski, J., & Hussain, S. (1997). How and where the education dollar is spent. *The Future of Children, 7*(3), 51–62.

Murnane, R. J. (1975). *The impact of school resources on the learning of inner city children.* Cambridge, MA: Ballinger.

Murnane, R. J. (1991). Interpreting the evidence on "Does money matter." *Harvard Journal on Legislation, 28*, 457–464.

Murnane, R., & Cohen, D. (1986). Merit pay and the evaluation problem. *Harvard Educational Review, 56*, 1–17.

Murnane, R., & Nelson, R. (2005). *Improving the performance of the education sector: The valuable, challenging, and limited role of random assignment evaluations* (NBER Working Paper No. W11846). Cambridge, MA: National Bureau of Economic Research.

National Center for Education Statistics. (2005). *Total and current expenditure per pupil in public elementary and secondary schools: Selected years, 1919–20 through 2002–03.* Retrieved June 9, 2007, from http://nces.ed.gov/programs/digest/d05/

National Center for Education Statistics. (2008). *Education Finance Statistics Center: Public information on elementary/secondary education.* Retrieved March 8, 2008, from http://nces.ed.gov/edfin/tables.asp

Nores, M., Belfield, C., Barnett, W. S., & Schweinhart, L. (2005). Updating the economic impacts of the High/Scope Perry Preschool Program. *Educational Evaluation and Policy Analysis, 27*, 245–261.

Odden, A. (1990). Class size and student achievement: Research-based policy alternatives. *Educational Evaluation and Policy Analysis, 12*, 213–227.

Odden, A., Borman, G., & Fermanich, M. (2004). Assessing teacher, classroom, and school effects, including fiscal effects. *Peabody Journal of Education, 79*(4), 4–32.

Odden, A., & Clune, W. (1995). Improving educational productivity and school finance. *Educational Researcher, 24*(9), 6–10.

Odden, A., & Kelley, C. (1997). *Paying teachers for what they know and do: New and smarter compensation strategies to improve schools.* Thousand Oaks, CA: Corwin Press.

Peevely, G., Hedges, L., & Nye, B. (2005). The relationship of class size effects and teacher salary. *Journal of Education Finance, 31*, 101–109.

Picus, L., & Wattenbarger, J. (Eds.). (1995). *Where does the money go? Resource allocation in elementary and secondary schools. The 1995 Yearbook of the American Education Finance Association.* Thousand Oaks, CA: Corwin Press.

Plecki, M. (2000). Economic perspectives on investments in teacher quality. *Education Policy Analysis Archives, 8*(33). Retrieved June 17, 2008, from http://epaa.asu.edu/epaa/v8n33.html

Plecki, M., Alejano, C., Knapp, M., & Lochmiller, C. (2006). *Allocating resources and creating incentives to improve teaching and learning.* Seattle: University of Washington, Center for the Study of Teaching and Policy.

Plecki, M., & Loeb, H. (2004). Examining state and federal efforts to improve teaching quality: Lessons for policy design and implementation. In M. Smylie & D. Miretsky (Eds.), *Developing the teacher workforce: The 103rd Yearbook of the National Society for the Study of Education* (pp. 348–389). Chicago: University of Chicago Press.

Raudenbush, S. (1988). Educational applications for hierarchical linear models: A review. *Journal of Educational Statistics, 13*, 85–116.

Raudenbush, S. (2002, February 6). *Identifying scientifically-based research in education.* Paper presented at the Scientifically Based Research Seminar, Washington, DC.

Raudenbush, S., & Bryk, A. (2002). *Hierarchical linear models: Applications and data analysis methods* (2nd ed.). Thousand Oaks, CA: Sage.

Rice, J. K. (2001). Illuminating the black box: The evolving role of education production productivity research. In S. Chaikind & W. J. Fowler (Eds.), *Education finance in the new millennium: The 2001 Yearbook of the American Education Finance Association* (pp. 121–138). Larchmont, NY: Eye on Education.

Rice, J. K. (2003). *Teacher quality: Understanding the effectiveness of teacher attributes.* Washington, DC: Economic Policy Institute.

Rice, J. K. (2008). From highly qualified to high quality: An imperative for policy and research to recast the teacher mold. *Education Finance and Policy, 3,* 151–164.

Riew, J. (1986). Scale economies, capacity utilization, and school costs: A comparative analysis of secondary and elementary schools. *Journal of Education Finance, 11*, 433–446.

Rivkin, S., Hanushek, E., & Kain, J. (2005). Teachers, schools and academic achievement. *Econometrica, 73*, 417–458.

Robinson v. Cahill, 62 NJ, 303 A.2d 273 (1973).

Rodriguez, G. (2007). Cycling on in cultural deficit thinking: California school finance and the possibilities of critical policy analysis. In G. Rodriguez & R. A. Rolle (Eds.), *To what ends and by what means?*

The social justice implications of contemporary school finance theory and policy (pp. 107–143). New York: Routledge.

Rodriguez, G., & Rolle, R. A. (Eds.). (2007). *To what ends and by what means? The social justice implications of contemporary school finance theory and policy.* New York: Routledge.

Rolle, R. A. (2004). Out with the old—in with the new: Thoughts on the future of educational productivity research. *Peabody Journal of Education, 79*, 31–56.

Rolle, R. A., & Fuller, A. (2007). Measuring educational productivity in the face of social justice influences: A discussion of the efficacy of relative economic efficiency for determining school improvement factors. In G. Rodriguez & R. A. Rolle (Eds.), *To what ends and by what means? The social justice implications of contemporary school finance theory and policy* (pp. 59–84). New York: Routledge.

Rossmiller, R. A. (1986). *Resource utilization in schools and classrooms: Final report.* Madison: University of Wisconsin, Wisconsin Center for Education Research.

Rubenstein, R. (2005). The reliability of school efficiency measures using data envelopment analysis. In L. Stiefel, A. Schwartz, R. Rubenstein, & J. Zabel (Eds.), *Measuring school performance and efficiency: Implications for practice and research. The 2005 Yearbook of the American Education Finance Association* (pp. 93–118). Larchmont, NY: Eye on Education.

Ruggiero, J. (2006). Measurement error, education production and data envelopment analysis. *Economics of Education Review, 25*, 327–333.

Sanders, W. (1998). Value-added assessment. *School Administrator, 55*(11), 24–27.

Sanders, W., & Rivers, J. (1996). Cumulative and residual effects of teachers on student achievement. Knoxville, TN: University of Tennessee Value-Added Research and Assessment Center.

Schwartz, A., & Stiefel, L. (2001). Measuring school efficiency: Lessons from economics, implications for practice. In D. Monk, H. Walberg, & M. Wang (Eds.), *Improving educational productivity: Research in educational productivity, Vol. 1* (pp. 115–137). Greenwich, CT: Information Age.

Serrano v. Priest, 5 Cal. 3d 584, 96 Cal. Rptr. 601, 487 P.2d 1241 (1971).

Stiefel, L., Berne, R., Iatarola, P., & Fruchter, N. (2000). High school size: Effects on budgets and performance in New York City. *Educational Evaluation and Policy Analysis, 22*, 27–39.

Stiefel, L., Schwartz, A. E., Rubenstein, R., & Zabel, J. (Eds.). (2005). *Measuring school performance and efficiency: Implications for practice and research. The 2005 Yearbook of the American Education Finance Association.* Larchmont, NY: Eye on Education.

Summers, A., & Wolfe, B. (1977). Do schools make a difference? *American Economic Review, 67*, 639–652.

Taylor, C. (2001). The relationship between student performance and school expenditures: A review of the literature and new evidence using better data. In D. Monk, H. Walberg, & M. Wang (Eds.), *Improving educational productivity: Research in educational productivity, Vol. 1* (pp. 167–182). Greenwich, CT: Information Age.

Temple, J., & Reynolds, A. (2007). Benefits and costs of investments in preschool education: Evidence from the Child-Parent Centers and related programs. *Economics of Education Review, 26*, 126–144.

Thomas, J., Kemmerer, F., & Monk, D. (1982). Efficiency in school finance: The classroom perspective. In W. W. McMahon & T. Geske (Eds.), *Financing education: Overcoming inefficiency and inequity* (pp. 100–118). Urbana: University of Illinois Press.

Walberg, H. (2003). *Improving educational productivity* (Publication Series No. 1). Champaign: University of Illinois. Retrieved February 4, 2008, from http://www.temple.edu/lss/pdf/publications/pubs2003-1.pdf

37

School Reconstitution and School Improvement

Theory and Evidence

BETTY MALEN AND JENNIFER KING RICE
University of Maryland

Introduction

School reconstitution is one of many "corrective action" strategies for "turning around" low-performing schools (Mintrop & Trujillo, 2005; Brady, 2003). No Child Left Behind incorporates this strategy in its set of graduated sanctions (Malen & Porton, 2003; Fuhrman, & Elmore, 2004). States and districts also employ this strategy as a way to give low-performing schools a fresh start (Goertz, Duffy, & LeFloch, 2001; Malen, Croninger, Muncey, & Redmond-Jones, 2002). This approach to reform warrants attention because, if current trends continue, many schools may be reconstituted or, in the latest vernacular, "restructured" (Brady, 2003; U.S. Department of Education, 2001; Neuman-Sheldon & Jennings, 2007). This approach to reform also warrants attention because, like other high-stakes education reform initiatives, school reconstitution may be driven more by the urgency of the problem than the viability of the solution (Airasian, 1988). Given these prospects, a clearer understanding of this approach to school reform is required. In this chapter, we try to advance that broad purpose by defining and characterizing reconstitution as a school reform strategy, by making explicit its theoretical foundations and pivotal assumptions, by examining how a distinctive version of reconstitution plays out in practice, and by highlighting the implications of this analysis for policy and research.[1]

Definition and Description of Reconstitution Reforms

The term "reconstitution" surfaced in the early 1980s and was used, initially, to refer to a human capital reform that targets the personnel dimension of public schools and relies heavily on various combinations of incentives and sanctions to improve organizational performance (Rice & Malen, 2003; Rice & Croninger, 2005). Subsequently, the term has been expanded to include a broader set of reforms that focus on the privatization of management structures and on the development of charter schools as mechanisms to rectify chronically low-performing schools (Brady, 2003; Hettleman, 2000). In this chapter we concentrate solely on the original and more common understanding of reconstitution, namely, the blanket replacement of personnel in schools that continue to be units within the extant management structures and governance arrangements of public school systems. Throughout the chapter, reconstitution refers to this blanket replacement of school personnel.

Whether applied to individual schools, to groups of schools in a single district, or to categories of schools throughout a state, reconstitution assumes that the school's stock of human capital is the critical ingredient in school improvement and that enhancing the stock of human capital in low-performing schools is accomplished better through sweeping replacement of personnel rather than through targeted development of personnel (Rice & Croninger, 2005; Rice & Malen, 2003). Accordingly, reconstitution initiatives replace (or threaten to replace) large percentages of a school's administrators, teachers, and support staff with individuals who are presumably more capable and committed (Malen et al., 2002). Typically, employees in reconstituted schools are not terminated (Mintrop & Trujillo, 2005); teachers and support staff members are permitted to reapply for positions at the school being reconstituted or to transfer to other positions in the system. School administrators may be retained or reassigned (Malen et al., 2002). In terms of management and governance, the reconstituted schools remain units of the local district.

This en masse shift in staff has been tried in a number of locations (Hendrie, 1997, 1998; Fuhrman, 2001; Ladd, 1996; Mintrop & Trujillo, 2005). For example, early experiments occurred in San Francisco, as a result of desegregation decrees (Fraga, Erlichson, & Lee, 1998; Rojas, 1996; Khanna, et al., 1999). More recently, low-performing schools in Chicago have been placed on probation (a classification that signals the school may be reconstituted), and, in some instances, restaffed (Wong, Anagnostopoulos, Rutledge,

Lynn, & Dreeben, 1999; Wong & Anagnostopoulos, 1998; Anagnostopoulos, 2003; Spillane et al., 2002). Schools in Colorado Springs (Hansen, Kraetzer, & Mukherjee, 1998), Portland, Oregon (Christensen, 1998), and Washington, DC (Blum, 2001; Moreno, 2001, 2003) have been restaffed. Several schools in Texas (Ressel, 1999a, 1999b) and three systems in Maryland—Baltimore City, Prince George's County, and Anne Arundel County—also have experience with reconstitution reforms (Wan, 2007; Brady, 2003; Frazier, 1997; Portner, 1997; Adcock & Winkler, 1999). Some of these experiments have been the subject of systematic study (e.g., Finkelstein, Malen, Muncey, Rice, & Croninger, 2000; Mintrop, 2004b; Sunderman, 2001; Spillane et al., 2002; Ladd & Zelli, 2002); some have been the topic of commentaries (e.g., Hendrie, 1998; Ressel 1999a); and some have been described in press accounts (e.g., Ruenzel, 1996, 1997; Moreno, 2003), dissertations (e.g., Rojas, 1996; Retana, 1997), policy evaluations, and policy papers (e.g., Hansen et al., 1998; Archibald & Odden, 2000; Odden & Archibald, 2000; Designs for Change, 2005).

School reconstitution resonates with research regarding the central role that improved teaching plays in school reform (Rice, 2003) and with characterizations of low-performing schools as dysfunctional organizations that can not be rectified by the more gradual, incremental strategies (e.g., individually tailored "growth plans" and ongoing professional development programs for administrators, teachers and support staff) embodied in personnel evaluation processes (Ruenzel, 1996, 1997; Brady, 2003). As the argument goes, dysfunctional organizations have to be dismantled and reinvented by a dramatically different cadre of employees who not only bolster the stock of human capital in low-performing schools but also create a culture of success in those educational settings (Rojas, 1996; Rice & Malen, 2003; Malen et al., 2002).

Theoretical Assumptions

Reconstitution reforms pivot on sets of assumptions about how organizational incentives and organizational capacity affect organizational performance. We discuss the underlying theory behind reconstitution policies by looking at how incentives and capacity operate to engender school improvement. Although we discuss incentives and capacity separately, like others, we recognize that they are essential and interdependent components of school improvement (see, e.g., G. A. Hess, 1999; Mintrop, 2004a, 2004b; O'Day, 2002, 2007). For that reason, we consider how those two constructs might work together to improve school performance.

Incentives Incentives are an integral part of a broad range of accountability policies including reconstitution initiatives (O'Day, 2002; Fuhrman & O'Day, 1996). Typically, the incentive provisions incorporate different combinations of rewards and sanctions targeted at different categories of people in the education system, such as teachers, princi-

pals, school staff, students, parents, and business partners. Depending on the specific purpose and design of the accountability system, these rewards and sanctions may take a variety of forms, notably public recognition (of strong or weak performance), group or individual financial enhancements for improved or outstanding performance (Kelly & Protsik, 1997; Kelly, 1999; Heneman & Milanowsi, 1999), requirements to restructure or close a particular school or group of schools, loss of autonomy, and imposition of tighter regulations (O'Day, 2002; Mintrop & Trujillo, 2005). The application of rewards and sanctions may make schools eligible for additional resources including personnel, technical assistance, and professional development opportunities (U.S. Department of Education, 2001; Finnigan & O'Day, 2003; Neuman-Sheldon, 2006). In these instances, policies assume that the incentives are required to ensure that school personnel will make effective use of these new resources. Where additional resources are not provided, policies assume that incentives will motivate personnel to make more efficient use of extant resources. However the policy is designed, the incentive component is pivotal (Mintrop, 2004a, 2004b; Finnigan & Gross, 2007).

The policy literature draws on various theories of motivation and studies of educator responses to accountability systems to identify some of the conditions under which incentive systems might motivate educators to increase effort and to improve performance (Mintrop, 2000; O'Day, 1996; O'Day, 2007; Finnigan & Gross, 2007). This literature suggests that the targeted groups must view the threat of sanction (or the promise of reward) as credible, if not imminent (Firestone, Mayrowetz, & Fairman, 1998; Finnigan & O'Day, 2003); the rewards and/or sanctions as meaningful and consequential (Stronge, Gareis, & Little, 2006; O'Day, 2002; Mohrman & Lawler, 1996; Finnigan & Gross, 2007); and the performance standards as realistic and obtainable (Linn, Baker, & Betebenner, 2002; Linn, 2003; Stronge et al., 2006; Mohrman & Lawler, 1996; Finnigan & Gross, 2007). The literature is much less explicit about how accountability systems may or may not meet these criteria (Fuhrman & Elmore, 2004; Adams & Kirst, 1999; Mintrop & Trujillo, 2005).

School reconstitution relies on incentive systems to motivate individuals across levels of the education system to improve organizational performance. It relies on both the *threat* of sanction as well as the *application* of sanction. The basic assumption is that threatening to restaff schools by placing them on "alert status," on "probation," or on "reconstitution eligible" lists will motivate the people who work in them to exert greater effort (Mintrop, 2004a, 2004b). The underlying theory posits that the impact of that threat is contingent on the target populations' perception of the threat. Theoretically, the target population must believe that policy makers will carry out the sanctions, that the sanctions themselves matter, and that the performance standards can be met (Finnigan & Gross, 2007). Once a school has been reconstituted, it may operate under the same set of rewards and sanctions as other schools in the district and state, or it may operate under a unique set of rewards and sanctions that districts or states may create especially for reconstituted schools.

While many reconstitution policies are driven primarily, if not exclusively, by an emphasis on incentives (Mintrop, 2004b; Stringfield & Yakimowski-Srebnick, 2005), like others, we recognize that capacity is also an essential component of school improvement (Darling-Hammond, 2004; G. A. Hess, 1999; Shipps, Kahne, & Smylie, 1999; Elmore, 2002; O'Day, 2007). Since schools cannot improve unless they have the will *and* the capacity to do so, in the next section we consider how reconstitution policies affect school capacity.

Capacity Since school improvement is a function of capacity as well as will, reconstitution policies typically include provisions that affect school capacity (Finnigan & O'Day, 2003; U.S. Department of Education, 2001; Rojas, 1996; Mintrop & Trujillo, 2005). As we have argued elsewhere (Malen & Rice, 2004), much of the existing literature on school capacity defines capacity in terms of different but largely complementary taxonomies for (a) identifying fundamental resources that schools require to carry out their instructional functions and (b) describing the degree to which those resources are present in the organization (e.g., see Corcoran & Goertz, 1995; Spillane & Thompson, 1997; Youngs & King, 2001). Reflecting this tradition, Rice and Croninger (2005), in their analysis of reconstitution, developed a framework for analyzing school capacity that includes fiscal, human, social, and cultural capital, as well as information resources. Since this set of categories constitutes a relatively comprehensive scheme for mapping how various policies may (or may not) alter the resource base of schools, we use that typology later in this chapter to analyze how reconstitution policies affect school capacity.

Although much of the literature on capacity focuses on taking an inventory of resources, some researchers argue that the productivity of those resources must be considered as well (Corcoran & Goertz, 1995; Malen & Rice, 2004). This second dimension of capacity takes into account the ability of schools to translate resources into expected outcomes. Theoretically, many factors can affect an organization's ability to use resources productively. Two constructs are particularly helpful in understanding how policies like school reconstitution may affect the productivity of extant or additional resources.

The first construct, alignment, refers to the degree of correspondence between the resources that are provided and the resources that are required to accomplish organizational goals (Rice, 2002). This construct reminds us that additional resources, by themselves, do not translate into increased capacity, especially if the resources provided are not the resources required to accomplish the organizational tasks that are essential to the realization of central policy aims. The second construct, organizational context, relates to both the degree of fragmentation and the degree of freneticism found in organizations. This construct reminds us that poli-

cies may precipitate or exacerbate organizational dynamics that enhance or undercut productivity (Hatch, 2002; F. M. Hess, 1999; Newmann, King, & Youngs, 2000). For example, policies may affect the degree of organizational fragmentation (i.e., the number of distinct and disjointed tasks and responsibilities embedded in the work of the organization), and/or the degree of organizational freneticism (i.e., the volume, pace, and intensity of the work to be done; Malen & Rice, 2004). For these reasons, both the alignment of resources to organizational goals and features of the organizational context are of paramount concern.

School reconstitution is advanced as a mechanism to affect both the resource and the productivity dimensions of capacity through the threat as well as the application of sanction. Typically, sanctions are not applied immediately. Rather, schools are warned (or threatened), often by being placed on "probation," on "alert," or on other "reconstitution-eligible" lists that signal further sanctions may be imposed if they do not improve. As earlier noted, these designations may make schools eligible for additional resources such as support teams, coaches, professional development programs, and more personnel (Rice & Croninger, 2005; Wong & Anagnostopoulos, 1998; U.S. Department of Education, 1998; Finnigan & O'Day, 2003; Neuman-Sheldon, 2006). The application of the sanction also may alter school capacity. Policies that reconstitute schools may alter the school's resource base through enticements such as the promise of better work environments, improved work conditions (e.g., lower class sizes, additional supports, materials), and the prospects of being part of a newly created "model" school (Finkelstein et al., 2000; Mintrop, 2004b; Neuman-Sheldon, 2006; Neuman-Sheldon & Jennings, 2007; U. S. Department of Education, 1998). These policies may make adjustments to other elements of the resource base such as fiscal capital, social capital, cultural capital, and relevant information (Rice & Croninger, 2005). These policies also may affect the productivity dimension of capacity. The assumption is that changing the composition of the faculty will eliminate dysfunctional organizational cultures and replace them with work groups that exhibit more constructive and productive orientations to school improvement (Rojas, 1996; U. S. Department of Education, 1998; Malen et al., 2002).

Improving Performance by Intensifying Incentives and Enhancing Capacity The theory regarding how incentives and capacity interact to affect organizational performance in general and school performance in particular is underdeveloped. In the realm of education, scholars recognize that each of these components is necessary, but not sufficient, for school improvement (Mintrop, 2004a, 2004b; G. A. Hess, 1999). Some allude to the interdependence of incentives and capacity. For example, scholars argue that incentives are essential in order for organizations to use resources productively (Hanushek, 1994); yet capacity is required to secure the individual and organizational responses that incentives are supposed to inculcate (Mintrop, 2004a, 2004b;

G. A. Hess, 1999; Darling-Hammond, 2004; O'Day, 2007). Since existing theories on the interaction between incentives and capacity in schools are primitive, it is not clear whether or how reconstitution policies might be engineered to capitalize on the interactive, and potentially synergistic, effect of incentives and capacity on school performance. Given that situation, we review empirical studies that document the impact of reconstitution policies on the incentive and the capacity to improve school performance as a necessary step in building a stronger understanding of this approach to education reform.

Empirical Evidence

In our search for empirical evidence on how school reconstitution plays out in practice, we turned to the growing body of literature on educators' responses to high-stakes accountability policies. We discovered that the specific policy provisions being examined in these studies are, at times, difficult to identify. In other words, we could not always tell whether the threat or application of reconstitution was the subject of study. Given these ambiguities, we adopted a conservative decision rule. We chose to include only those empirical analyses that explicitly identify school reconstitution (or its conceptual equivalent) as a part of the high-stakes policy environment and an aspect of the study. In trying to walk the fine line between mining all relevant evidence and distorting the findings, we err on the side of certainty about the subject of study and the relevance of the evidence.

In assessing this more explicitly and narrowly defined body of research, we found that direct evidence on the impact of reconstitution is limited in scope and uneven in quality.[2] Moreover, the specific policies (or treatments) under study vary considerably, as do the purposes and the foci of the analyses.[3] These features of the database constrain our ability to analyze, systematically and empirically, all the reconstitution experiments that have been highlighted in popular press and website commentaries, to aggregate findings across studies, let alone, to render definitive statements about how either the threat or the application of this sanction operates to affect school performance. Thus we adopt the modest aim of providing *provisional observations* regarding how reconstitution appears to play out in practice. In the following sections we describe the empirical evidence on the threat and the application of this approach to reconstitution. In each section we identify the research base, report key findings, and then discuss what the empirical evidence says about how reconstitution may affect a school's incentive and capacity to improve its performance.

Evidence on the Threat of Reconstitution
The research base we uncovered and reviewed is comprised of a survey of elementary school principals (Ladd & Zelli, 2002), a survey of teachers (Firestone et al., 1998), a longitudinal analysis of various accountability reforms, including school reconstitution in Baltimore (Stringfield & Yakimowski-Srebnick,

2005), fairly open-ended case studies of educator responses to the threat of reconstitution in other locations (e.g., Diamond & Spillane, 2004; Mintrop, 2004b; Anagnostopoulos & Rutledge, 2007), a mixed-methods analysis of teacher motivation in ten elementary schools placed on probation (Finnigan & Gross, 2007) and more focused examinations of how educators in "reconstitution-eligible" schools respond to some of the additional resources that may accompany that designation (Finnigan & O'Day, 2003; Neuman-Sheldon, 2006; Neuman-Sheldon & Jennings, 2007). Most of the case study research is carried out in urban, metropolitan schools in Chicago and Maryland. While research carried out in Kentucky includes two cases in small towns (Mintrop, 2004b), we found only one study of a more rural site in Maryland (Malen & Porton, 2003). The majority of the studies focus on schools in a particular district, but several offer cross-state analyses (e.g., Mintrop, 2004b; Firestone et al., 1998). Although the case studies include elementary, middle, and high schools, most track educator responses to the threat of reconstitution in a small number of schools over a 1- or 2-year time period. Thus, data on the effect of the threat of reconstitution across settings and overtime are sparse. Nevertheless, taken together, these studies generate insights about how the threat of reconstitution might affect schools that are targeted for sanction. Since knowledge of the immediate policy context affects how findings may be interpreted, we organize our review of this literature by the sites of study. After we report key findings from research in various locations, we discuss what this research suggests about the impact of the threat of reconstitution on the incentive and capacity of schools to improve their performance.

Chicago-Based Research and Related Studies in Urban Districts Case studies of Chicago schools examine responses to a probation policy that makes low-performing schools subject to restaffing and eligible for additional resources. These resources are intended "to assist schools in strengthening their internal operations, raising expectations for students and improving instruction so as to foster increased student achievement" (Finnigan & O'Day, 2003, p. v). Schools on probation receive assistance from multiple sources including external partners (required by the district but selected by the schools from a menu of organizations that provide professional development and instructional support to teachers), probation managers (sent by the district to monitor school operations, to supervise and to mentor principals) as well as a regional education officer, a business manager or intern, and an assistant from the district's accountability division to provide technical assistance (Finnigan & O'Day, 2003). While the district fully funds the external partner for 1 year, individual schools share that cost with the district the second year and absorb the full price of this service thereafter, often by using Title I funds to foot the bill (Sunderman, 2001). In this setting, students are also subject to sanction (e.g., retention in grade). The district abolished "social promotion" and added a student accountability provision to its package of school reform policies (Wong et al., 1999) so students, like teachers and principals, are clear targets in the district's package of school reform policies.

On the incentive dimension, studies carried out in Chicago paint a mixed picture. Some studies indicate that the threat of reconstitution has had little if any motivational impact on site-level personnel largely because "[f]ew believed that the school would be closed down or reconstituted" (Finnigan & O'Day, 2003, p. 47). Other studies indicate that the threat of reconstitution has prompted site-based personnel to increase effort, but not necessarily to increase effectiveness. For example, several studies report that both elementary and high school principals have responded to the threat of reconstitution by becoming more directive, rigid, and controlling in their interactions with teachers even though this new style of play strained relationships, pressured teachers to conform to questionable practices, and failed to translate into stronger instructional programs and more equitable learning opportunities (e.g., Spillane et al., 2002; Anagnostopoulos, 2003; Anagnostopoulos & Rutledge, 2007). Studies also suggest that teachers were motivated to work harder but that their intensified effort focused on short-term, superficial, and arguably detrimental strategies that may hold promise for getting schools off probation, rather than on long-term, substantive changes that may help all children improve academically. To illustrate, studies found that teachers tended to focus on "low-level" test preparation activities in the domains tested (Finnigan & O'Day, 2003, p. 45) at the expense of other dimensions of the curriculum and other elements of classroom instruction (Spillane et al., 2002; Wong & Ananostopoulos, 1998; Lipman, 2006; Anagnostopoulos & Rutledge, 2007). They also tended to invest their time, energy, and instructional resources on students in benchmark grades who were most likely to pass the test rather than on the students who required extensive assistance to perform well at any grade level (Anagnostopoulos, 2003; Diamond & Spillane, 2004; White & Rosenbaum, 2008). School personnel were inclined to adopt multiple programs that they could not implement or to make superficial adjustments (e.g., altering classroom posters and work displays that might impress the monitors) that were viewed by the researchers and, at times, the study participants as unlikely to improve the quality or equity of education experiences in the school (Sunderman, 2001; Diamond & Spillane, 2004; Designs for Change, 2005; O'Day, 2002, 2007). Whether these patterns are typical is an open question. What can be said is that the threat of reconstitution in this policy context appears to trigger greater effort at least in the short run (Finnigan & Gross, 2007). However, the extra effort may be directed toward practices that run counter to broadly recognized conceptions of effective professional practice and equitable educational programs (White & Rosenbaum, 2008).

In terms of capacity, the studies document that schools on probation received additional human resources in the form of external partners, monitors, and special assistants. We were not able to discern whether these additional personnel enhanced the social and cultural capital in the schools. Studies suggest the additional personnel brought informational resources to the site, usually in the form of professional development workshops for teachers and direct consultations with principals. While it is not clear whether schools received additional fiscal resources, it is clear that they were required to absorb additional costs. As previously noted, the district paid for the external partner the first year, but the site was required to pay half that cost in the second year and the full cost the third year and thereafter (Finnigan & O'Day, 2003).

A relatively extensive analysis of the resources granted schools on probation suggests that the additional resources "are simply not strong enough to overcome the deep problems in educator and organizational capacity necessary to fundamentally improve instruction" (Finnigan & O'Day, 2003, p. 50). That assessment relates not only to the inventory of resources provided but also to their productive use. Although the policy sought to "customize the assistance to meet the individual needs of each school" (Finnigan & O'Day, 2003, p. 7) by allowing schools to select their external partners, the resources provided were not necessarily aligned with the resources required to engender major improvements in the school. For example, the professional development programs were not structured to deliver the content knowledge or the follow-up coaching that teachers may need to improve instruction (Finnigan & O'Day, 2003). At times additional personnel engaged in "capacity substitution" instead of capacity development activities (Finnigan & O'Day, 2003, p. 38). That is, they elected to do the tasks themselves rather than to equip principals and teachers to carry out those responsibilities. Moreover, the multiple sources of support contributed to fragmentation in the organization because each source of support brought a discrete and often disconnected set of activities and expectations to the school (Finnigan & O'Day, 2003). The infusion of new, often external actors as well as the pressure to improve performance and to avert sanction also created considerable stress as educators tried to address the additional demands placed upon them, as monitors and principals competed for authority and as teachers resisted, and, at times sabotaged, the work of "partners" they distrusted and resented (Wong & Anagnostopoulos, 1998; Sunderman, 2001). Some research suggests that the stigma associated with the probation designation and the strain educators in these schools experienced may have contributed to faculty, staff (and student) departures that "drain resources needed for improvement away from these schools" (Wong et al., 1999, p. 7; see also, Lipman, 2006). For these and perhaps other reasons, the resources that accompanied reconstitution reform in this setting did little to enhance capacity (O'Day, 2007). Ironically, the policy may have operated in ways that undercut capacity even when additional resources were provided to the schools on probation.

Kentucky and Maryland-Based Research   Since much of the research on the threat of reconstitution was carried out in a joint, cross-state project and reported in texts that merge findings from both states (Mintrop, 2003, 2004a, 2004b), we follow suit in our review of that research and other Maryland-specific studies. We define the policy context of each state and then summarize key findings.

Four case studies conducted in Kentucky focus on elementary and middle schools that the state determined to be "in crises" (Mintrop, 2004b). Subject to various penalties and sanctions including rapid and extensive restaffing, these schools received a "highly skilled educator….who worked with the schools to improve their curriculum and instruction and to implement the school improvement planning process by assisting in the collection and analysis of data, identification of causes of decline, and provision of feedback about goals and suggestions of possible strategies for reaching those goals" (Mintrop, 2004b, p. 10). These individuals were authorized to evaluate staff members every 6 months, and to "recommend the dismissal or transfer of any school staff member who failed to meet the growth goal [specified on individual growth plans] or was judged to be acting in a manner resistant to improvement efforts" (Mintrop, 2004b, p. 10). Although this approach to restaffing was based on an analysis of individual cases, not a blanket requirement that all staff must reapply for their positions, this process carried the threat of recurrent and large-scale staff changes that are the hallmarks of school reconstruction.

Seven case studies carried out in Maryland (Mintrop, 2004b) examine elementary and middle schools identified by the state as "reconstitution-eligible." These schools were subject to the personnel replacement and the privatized management versions of reconstitution and slated to receive technical assistance and supplemental funds from the state (Neuman-Sheldon, 2006). Technical assistance typically took the form of state monitors, audit teams, and templates for the development of school improvement plans (Mintrop, 2004b). Study sites facing the threat of reconstitution received additional financial and informational resources from the district in part because the state allocated a portion of its school improvement funds to districts and required districts to document how they were supporting the reconstitution-eligible schools[4] (Neuman-Sheldon, 2006; Mintrop, 2004b).

This body of research (Mintrop, 2004b) documents patterns strikingly similar to those found in the Chicago-based studies. For example, the response to the threat of sanction was uneven, in part because some educators simply did not believe that the state would carry out the threat. In their view, it was not realistic to think that the state could reconstitute the relatively large and growing number of schools on the "in crisis" or "reconstitution eligible" list. Others responded to the threat by intensifying effort often in the same ways that Chicago educators reacted. Principals across school levels tried to take control of the instructional program, to monitor teachers and classrooms more regularly and to inject new degrees of standardization into the teaching-learning process. Teachers tended to invest effort in a host of short-term, expedient activities that might allow them to escape the label. While the threat of reconstitution was accompanied by different packages of resources, the research suggests that the modest increases in fiscal and informational resources did not enable the schools to address, effectively, the challenges they faced. The stigma, anxiety, and embarrassment associated with the reconstitution reform, the frenetic efforts to raise test scores, the loss of autonomy, and the limited organizational capacity prompted teachers to leave the schools. Taken together, these case studies reveal how the threat of reconstitution can translate into a high effort, high exit dynamic that confounds, if not undercuts, the prospects for meaningful school improvement.

These results are generally consistent with a longitudinal case study that analyzed the impact of the "reconstitution-eligible" designation on schools in Baltimore (Stringfield & Yakimowski-Srebnick, 2005). That designation had little, if any, positive effect on the motivation of educators or the capacity of schools to alter their performance. As the authors put it, the threat of sanction seemed to "induce anxiety and stress among teachers and administrators" but these emotional responses did not translate into more robust learning opportunities for students, in part because the individual schools, the district, and the state education agency all "lacked the capacity to successfully guide improvement in historically underperforming schools" (Stringfield & Yakimowski-Srebnick, 2005, p. 55).

A more limited case study of a rural elementary school's response to the threat of reconstitution documents different, but still problematic, effects (Malen & Porton, 2003; Malen & Rice, 2004). In this case, the principal and most if not all of the teachers took the threat of sanction seriously. However, the principal did not try to seize control of the instructional program; rather, she intensified her effort to create authentic opportunities for teachers to collaborate and to participate in an array of site-based professional development programs. Teachers also intensified effort. Most if not all invested heavily in professional development, grade-level planning, school-wide committees, and new program implementation. While they invested a good deal of time teaching to the test, they did not siphon services to select students who might boost the scores of the school. Since the school received funds to support collaborative planning for teachers, the initiative appeared to enhance the stock of social capital at the site. The initiative did not alter the composition of the staff, so the quantity of human and cultural capital at the site remained constant. However, the status of the school gave it a competitive advantage in its bid for professional development grants and support. As a result, the threat of reconstitution operated to enhance substantially but indirectly, the informational resources of the school. The professional development also may have enhanced the quality of human capital of the school.

While the increased effort and the additional resources in this particular case sketch an encouraging picture of how the threat of reconstitution, accompanied by relevant foundational resources, might enhance both capacity and will, that characterization masks how the threat of sanction may intensify incentives and precipitate responses that diminish school capacity, even when they enlarge the resource base of the school. This counterintuitive outcome occurred in part because the resources provided were not sufficiently aligned with the resources the school needed to address racial issues and to provide the individualized coaching required to alter the instructional strategies of teachers. It also occurred because the threat of sanction prompted the school to adopt, rapidly, and at times, indiscriminately, a broad array of initiatives that ended up being only partially or symbolically implemented. The sheer volume of initiatives the school was trying to incorporate, the pace at which those initiatives were being introduced, and the anxiety that such an ambitious agenda can create eclipsed efforts to coordinate and integrate these initiatives in ways that might enable them to complement and reinforce rather that to compete and offset one another. In short, reform-related pressures precipitated a fragmented reaction and a frenetic response that spread resources across multiple, discrete initiatives and diluted the school's capacity for substantial, sustained improvements (Malen & Rice, 2004; Malen & Porten, 2003).

A small-scale survey of middle school math teachers in select districts in Maryland (where the state accountability system included reconstitution) and Maine (where the state accountability system had not incorporated this sanction) is generally consistent with case study findings regarding how educators interpret the threat of reconstitution (Firestone et al., 1998). Some teachers in Maryland viewed reconstitution as unlikely because "many schools would have to be reconstituted before the state would get to any of the schools" (Firestone et al., 1998, p. 108); others took the threat more seriously and "felt compelled to respond" (Firestone et al., 1998, p. 109) by adjusting the content of their courses and by investing time in test preparation activities. While Maine educators reported making some changes in response to their state's accountability systems, Maryland educators responded with a stronger "sense of urgency" and a more extensive series of changes in terms of course content and test preparation (Firestone et al., 1998, p. 109). Thus, this study suggests that the threat of reconstitution may capture educators' attention and alter their perception of the necessity, but not necessarily the desirability, of either the curricular accommodations or the test preparation priorities.

North Carolina-Based Research   Studies that can inform our understanding of how the threat of reconstitution operates in this state draw on elementary school principal surveys to gauge how educators may be responding to the state's accountability policy which includes reconstitution as a sanction but explicitly states that this sanction is to be applied only in "rare instances" (North Carolina Department of Public Instruction, as cited in Ladd & Zelli, 2002, p. 500). Under the state's ABCs program, elementary schools were identified as low-performing if fewer than 50% of their students performed at grade level or if the schools failed to

meet their specific growth standards. This program recognized a small number of highly successful schools through public ceremonies and financial stipends for the teachers and principals of those schools. Low-performing schools received "mandatory assistance from a state assistance team" and were subject to state intervention that could take the form of extensive restaffing. Principals reported redirecting resources to the areas emphasized by the ABCs program, namely basic skills in reading, math, and writing, and "focusing additional attention on low-performing students" (Ladd & Zelli, 2002, p. 522), adjustments that were consistent with the purposes of the ABCs incentive program. However, the combination of symbolic and financial rewards for principals and teachers in successful schools and the threat of state intervention and related sanctions for educators in low-performing schools may have prompted "mobile high-quality teachers and principals to leave the schools with low-performing students" and confounded efforts to recruit and retain "high-quality personnel in schools designated as low-performing" (Ladd & Zelli, 2002, p. 523). Thus the program may have diminished the capacity of low-performing schools to improve. As the researchers put it, "over time, the schools serving the most disadvantaged and low-performing students could end up with even higher proportions of the lower quality teachers than would otherwise have been the case" (Ladd & Zelli, 2002, p. 52). Moreover, the ABCs program may have prompted principals of low-performing schools to leave the profession. While it is difficult to disentangle precisely what educators may have been responding to because the state's package of policies designed to improve school performance contained a mix of rewards and sanctions, it appears that the threat of sanction as well as the promise of reward may have prompted principals to make adjustments consistent with policy goals. But that set of incentives also may have yielded deleterious effects on school capacity.

Discussion of Key Findings   Studies of educator responses to the threat of reconstitution support common themes about the potential impact of this approach to reform on organizational incentives, capacity, and performance. Some of those themes are strikingly similar to those found in studies of site-level responses to high-stakes accountability policies more broadly construed.

In terms of incentive effects, the threat of reconstitution gets mixed reviews. In some cases, educators may dismiss the threat. But, in other cases, the threat of reconstitution can be a motivating force. If educators view the threat as credible, they may adjust their behavior. Apparently the threat of reconstitution need not be seen as imminent to have impact. Even in settings where reconstitution was perceived as a fairly remote possibility, some educators still took notice and altered, albeit in different ways and to varying degrees, prior instructional practices. In low-performing schools where the threat of reconstitution was more immediate, educators tended to exert greater effort and to make more extensive changes in the nature of administrative oversight, the content of the curriculum, the allocation of instructional time and personnel, the distribution of instructional resources, and the number of initiatives to be implemented at the school.

These patterns are consistent with the broader research on educator responses to various high-stakes accountability policies (Herman, 2004; Malen & Muncey, 2000). A small but growing body of case study and survey data indicates that high-stakes accountability policies are intensifying the pressure on educators to raise student test scores (Pedulla et al., 2003) and changing (for better or worse) the content of curriculum (Dorgan, 2004; Firestone, Fitz, & Broadfoot, 1999; Herman, 2004; Sandholtz, Ogawa, & Scribner, 2004; Trujillo, 2005); the pace if not the pedagogy of instruction (Dorgan, 2004; Herman, 2004; McNeil, 2000; Swanson & Stevenson, 2002); the adoption of new initiatives; the allocation of time and personnel (Herman, 2004; Stecher & Barron, 1999; Pedulla et al., 2003); and the distribution of instructional opportunities and services. One pronounced tendency seems to be to "pull resources away from the most needy students…. [in order to concentrate] on students most likely to improve school-wide achievement test scores" (Sunderman, 2001, p. 526; see also Booher-Jennings, 2005; Elmore, 2002; Pedulla et al., 2003; White & Rosenbaum, 2008). These policies also may influence other important aspects of schooling such as the quality of principal-teacher relationships, the attractiveness of educators' work, and the prospects of recruiting and retaining the high-quality personnel required to improve school performance (Pedulla et al., 2003; Lipman, 2006).

In terms of school capacity, the threat of reconstitution can affect both the inventory of resources and their productive use in unexpected and, at times, counterproductive ways. Schools that are subject to reconstitution may receive additional human, informational and, at times, fiscal resources. The human resources rarely take the form of new, full-time positions at the school site. Typically, additional personnel provide some professional development workshops, intermittent technical assistance, and periodic oversight. While most studies do not address, directly, how the threat of reconstitution might affect the stock of social and cultural capital at the site, they document conditions (e.g., the intensification of demands, the controlling behavior of principals, the tensions between educators and external actors assigned to the school) that make the development of strong social networks and collaborative structures more difficult. When additional fiscal resources accompany the threat of reconstitution, the allocations tend to be modest, short-term deposits rather than sizeable, dependable increases in the school's operating budget (Mintrop, 2004a; Malen & Rice, 2004; O'Day, 2007). While resource allocations and configurations vary across policy contexts, generally speaking, the threat of reconstitution is accompanied by relatively small increases in select components of the schools' resource base and by growing concerns about the negative effect that this threat may have on the stock of human capital in low-performing schools. Since the threat of sanction may be a disincentive for highly capable and committed educators to work in low-performing schools, it may reduce the stock of human capital in these schools and function as an impediment to, rather than a stimulus for, school improvement.

Even if the net effect is to increase the stock of foundational resources available to target schools, these resources may not translate into increased capacity, in part because the resources provided may not align with the resources required to engender improvement in a particular school. Since schools "get stuck" for different reasons, they may require different kinds and combinations of resources to improve (Mintrop, 2004b; see also O'Day, 2007; Neuman-Sheldon, 2006; Neuman-Sheldon & Jennings, 2007). The package of supports often attached to the threat of reconstitution may not accommodate these variations. Further, the threat of reconstitution can undercut school capacity because the threat may create or exacerbate organizational dynamics that limit the ability of the school to use resources productively. The pronounced tendency of schools facing severe sanction to become even more fragmented and frenetic workplaces is well-documented in the broader literature on site-level responses to high-stakes accountability policies (O'Day, 2002; Hatch, 2002; Newmann et al., 2000) as well as a prominent pattern in the more limited literature on the threat of reconstitution as an education reform strategy.

Whether the threat of reconstitution operates to improve school performance is not directly or extensively addressed in the research we uncovered. The big picture patterns, however, are disconcerting. For example, although the threat of reconstitution has been present in Maryland for over a decade, only a few schools have come off the "reconstitution eligible" list and many more have been added. While such gross measures may be more misleading than illuminating, they are not, on face, encouraging. More site-specific assessments are also troubling. For example, the threat of reconstitution seems to engender changes that run counter to partial but prominent theories of the conditions under which schools might improve their performance (Newmann, Smith, Allensworth, & Bryk, 2001). High-quality principals and teachers, coherent instructional programs, and equitable opportunities for learning are three critical ingredients of school improvement that may be affected adversely by the threat of reconstitution.

Evidence on the Application of Reconstitution The database on the application of reconstitution contains accounts of San Francisco's early experiment with reconstitution in three elementary schools and one middle school (Rojas, 1996; Khanna, Flores, Bergum, & Desmond, 1999; Fraga et al., 1998) and a more recent analysis of professional community among teachers in one of the reconstituted middle schools in that city (Achinstein, 2002). The data base also includes an analysis of seven reconstituted high schools in Chicago (Hess, 2003), an evaluation of two reconstituted elementary schools in Colorado Springs (Hansen et al., 1998), and case studies of four reconstituted elementary schools and one reconstituted middle school in three unidentified school districts (Archibald & Odden, 2000; Odden & Archibald, 2000; Malen et al., 2002). Although these accounts include elementary, middle, and high schools, they do not support broad or confident claims about the impact of reconstitution on the incentive and the capacity of schools to improve their performance. The small number of cases and the focus on distinct and different aspects of reconstitution generate suggestive insights rather than definitive conclusions about the efficacy of this reform. As earlier noted, knowledge of the immediate policy context affects how findings may be interpreted. Therefore, we organize this portion of our literature review by the sites of study, report key findings, and then discuss of the implications of this research for our understanding of this reform.

San Francisco-Based Studies   A general description of the initial reconstitution experiment, produced by the superintendent who advocated for and oversaw the initiative (Rojas, 1996), documents that the reconstitution initiative implemented as part of a desegregation decree was accompanied by a national teacher recruitment strategy as well as major investments in faculty planning time, professional development programs, class size reductions, facility improvements, technology enhancements, and new instructional materials and services.[5] This description suggests that the principals hired to head the schools reconstituted in 1984 were more ethnically diverse than their predecessors and that the new teachers had stronger academic and linguistic qualifications than their predecessors. Unfortunately, this account does not examine how changes in the stock of human and cultural capital or changes in fiscal and informational resources affected work roles, relationships, and responsibilities in the school. Rather, it concentrates on student test scores and claims that students in the reconstituted schools outperformed their peers in other schools on district administered tests in reading and mathematics (Rojas, 1996; see also Khanna et al., 1999). However, these data do not constitute compelling evidence of the efficacy of reconstitution, given the changes in the student body that occurred when these schools were reclassified as magnet rather than neighborhood schools, the difficulty of disentangling the many factors that may affect students' test scores, and the inability to demonstrate comparable accomplishments in subsequent experiments with reconstitution in this setting (Fraga et al., 1998).

A more recent study carried out in a reconstituted middle school maps the challenges that a group of teachers who were hired because they presumably share the same general philosophy of education face when they meet to examine and assess their policies and practices (Achinstein, 2002). This study suggests that shared values may foster the development of social capital in schools, but it does not establish (nor was it intended to establish) that reconstitution is either a necessary or sufficient condition for the creation of strong collaborative networks or critical appraisals of instructional policies and practices in schools.

Chicago-Based Studies   This research mapped developments in reconstituted high schools over a 2-year period. While the number of administrators, teachers, and support staff replaced varied across the schools, restaffing the reconstituted schools proved problematic on several counts. Since teachers were not eager to transfer to these schools, and since the number of vacancies created by reconstitution outstripped the supply of qualified candidates, reconstituted schools ended up hiring one another's rejects, leaving some positions unfilled, and "plugging gaps with substitute teachers for several years" (Hess, 2003, p. 308). Although the district provided some "people development and management support" (Hess, 2003, p. 301) to assist the reconstituted schools, the researchers observed little change in school structures or in instructional practices. Efforts to get at the impact of reconstitution on student achievement indicate that students in reconstituted schools did not outperform their counterparts in the district. Moreover, the modest gains in student achievement were not due to reconstitution, but to changes in who was admitted to the schools and to other developments in the school system. As the author summarized it:

> [R]econstitution in Chicago turned out to be a one-time event which was not particularly successful, either in creating significant change in the seven subject schools or in occasioning significant improvements in student achievement. Standardized test results did improve modestly (at about half the rate experienced citywide), and passing rates in core subjects did improve. But these improvements in student achievement more reflect the better preparation of entering freshmen than improvement in learning once students enrolled in these seven high schools. (Hess, 2003, p. 326)

Colorado Springs-Based Study   This study (Hansen et al., 1998) evaluates an experiment that involved sweeping administrative and faculty changes in two elementary schools. These personnel changes were accompanied by reductions in class size, additional instructional support staff, additional technical assistance from the district office, intensive professional development programs, regular team planning time, a community advisory board, and an extensive menu of before and after school activities. Even with these workplace enticements, the restaffing initiative did not bring more experienced, better educated, or more diverse faculty and staff to the school. The evaluation suggests faculty were dedicated educators, but it is not clear that they exerted greater effort than their predecessors or their counterparts in other schools. Nor is it clear that they were more committed to working in low-performing schools. The evaluation mentions concerns about teacher turnover but it is difficult to discern whether the degree of turnover was greater under reconstitution or due to the strains of reconstitution. The evaluation alludes to the stressful work contexts in the newly reconstituted schools but does not indicate whether these conditions prompted teachers and administrators to leave the school. However, the evaluation suggests that the stressful conditions may have diminished opportunities for the new staffs to concentrate on developing and delivering more robust and responsive instructional programs.

For example, the evaluation notes that the first year of reconstitution was marred by discipline problems that staff attributed to "students coming back to school unprepared to encounter an almost entirely new array of school staff," to lack of time to develop a school-wide discipline plan, and to issues in their home environments (Hansen et al., 1998, p. v). Since these problems undermined the learning environment of the school, the newly organized faculty focused more on interventions that might reestablish "an orderly and disciplined environment" (Hansen et al., 1998, p. iv) than on innovative instructional programs. The evaluation acknowledges that scores on various student achievement tests did not show improvement in reading, language, or mathematics and adds that "given the extreme nature of the changes made at each school, general improvement in student achievement would have been surprising" (Hansen et al., 1998, p. ix).

Studies in Undisclosed Settings Case studies of two reconstituted elementary schools in an undesignated district tell us more about how districts and schools might reallocate time, money, and personnel than about the impact of reconstitution per se (Archibald & Odden, 2000; Odden & Archibald, 2000). Designed as case studies of resource reallocation models and site-based budgeting strategies rather than in-depth examinations of reconstitution, these works do not specify the scope of staff changes that occurred, compare the new recruits with their predecessors in terms of their capacity for and commitment to school improvement, or describe the processes through which new staffs worked to incorporate the whole school reform models and other district initiatives they were expected to implement. While the studies conclude that the schools are making impressive strides, the profiles of progress are not arrayed or explained. Given the sheer number of concurrent personnel, programmatic, and resource allocation changes in these schools, it is extremely difficult, if not impossible, to unravel the causal connections required to make claims about how restaffing may be influencing school incentives, capacity, and performance.

Case studies that mapped how a large metropolitan district's reconstitution initiative played out in two elementary schools and one middle school challenge the major premises of reconstitution reform (Malen et al., 2002). The restaffing initiative carried the promise of additional resources and inviting work environments (e.g., smaller class sizes, ample supplies and materials, master/mentor teachers), but those promises were largely unfulfilled. The district provided modest fiscal supplements and additional professional development and technical support during the first year of the reform, but it did not carry through on the commitment to provide smaller class sizes, cadres of master and mentor teachers, new materials and other workplace enhancements. The district provided no special forms of assistance during the second year of the reform. In this setting, reconstitu-

tion resulted in sweeping staff changes in all schools but not major staff improvements in any school. The initiative dismantled the organizational infrastructure at the target sites but it did not engender improvements in the operation or performance of these schools.

To illustrate, the reconstituted schools lost experienced principals and reputedly effective veteran teachers in part because the reconstitution initiative was so insulting that some of the most talented teachers refused to reapply for their positions. A few teachers found the promise of a fresh start and the opportunity to develop a "model" school attractive (Malen et al., 2002). But those rhetorical appeals did not generate large pools of highly qualified applicants to the vacancies created by the reconstitution reform. Given chronic teacher shortages and no organized strategy to get master teachers within or outside the system to apply for the positions, reconstituted schools were forced to fill openings with inexperienced teachers. As a result, 75% of the teachers hired to restaff the schools were new to the profession; many were not certified and hence were required to enroll in courses to complete state certification requirements. The reconstituted schools also relied on novice administrators who had no prior experience as "turn-around" principals. While the initial staff changes increased the diversity of the staffs and added cultural capital to some schools, the reconstitution reform did not create the cadres of strong principals and master teachers or the stable staffing patterns the district sought to establish in these schools. For a variety of reasons, including but not limited to the human costs of this reform (Rice & Malen, 2003), during the first 2 years of the reform, faculty departure rates increased in all the reconstituted schools and exceeded the pre-reform turnover rates in all but one school (Malen et al., 2002). Their replacements were often teachers who were new to the profession. In addition, during the first 2 years of this reform, several principals were reassigned and replaced by relatively inexperienced administrators.

Since the reconstitution initiative wiped out the organizational infrastructure of the schools and provided little time for the new, novice staffs to figure out how they would structure, regulate, and manage their work, this reform created considerable chaos in the schools. New staffs worked frantically to handle the day-to-day operations, to address the increase in discipline problems, and to meet basic classroom responsibilities. Opportunities to develop collegial networks, collaborative relationships, innovative programs, and comprehensive, coordinated approaches to school improvement were trumped by the organizational disarray the reform created, the staff turnover it fostered, and the failure of the district to deliver the full body of assistance and support it had promised to provide. While this study was not designed to get at the impact of reconstitution on student achievement, it suggests that reconstitution may weaken rather than strengthen organizational performance by depleting the stock of human capital in schools and by engendering organizational dynamics that undercut the productivity of the remaining resources.

Discussion of Key Findings   Taken together, the empirical data on school reconstitution support several more general observations about both the nature of the evidence and the efficacy of this strategy. We organize those observations around the central dimensions of interest: incentives, capacity, and performance of schools.

Evidence regarding the impact of school reconstitution on organizational incentives is indirect, but discouraging. Studies have not focused on how the en masse replacement of personnel affects the effort of the new staffs or the effort of educators in other schools that may be subject to reconstitution. Extant research provides some evidence that new staffs work long hours and exert considerable effort, but they do not indicate whether these educators are more motivated, let alone more effective, than either their predecessors or their counterparts. Studies offer some evidence that the promise of a new beginning and a better work environment may be a mild incentive for new recruits to apply for positions in low-performing schools and for a few reputedly effective veteran teachers to stay. But those studies also indicate that the punitive character of the process and the intense stress in the workplace may be a strong incentive for seasoned teachers to avoid seeking employment in reconstituted schools or to transfer out of these schools. Clearly, we need more explicit, extensive, and comparative data on the impact of en masse restaffing to unpack how the mix of positive and perverse incentives might affect the "will" component of school improvement and to gauge whether en masse restaffing policies can be crafted in ways that enhance both the effort and the effectiveness of educators in low-performing schools.

Evidence on the impact of reconstitution on organizational capacity is incomplete, but disconcerting. Unfortunately the studies we reviewed do not provide detailed accounts of the types of resource investments that may accompany reconstitution initiatives or the ultimate impact of restaffing initiatives on the level of foundational resources available to the targeted schools. The available information indicates that restaffing may alter the stock of human capital in unintended and, at times, counterproductive, ways.

For instance, several studies demonstrate that on general indicators (e.g., education, experience, turnover), newly hired staffs may be less equipped and less committed than the educators they replaced. Although several studies suggest school reconstitution may enhance the human and cultural capital available at the school, these results are not dependable or inevitable outcomes, particularly in settings marked by chronic shortages of certified teachers and experienced administrators. Most studies do not address the impact of reconstitution on social capital, but several give credence to the claim that reconstitution may diminish social capital by creating highly stressful, and, at times, chaotic conditions that make it extraordinarily difficult to develop strong social networks, collaborative structures, and robust instructional programs. In short, reconstitution may enhance the stock of human and cultural capital in schools, but the evidence we reviewed does not establish

that reconstitution is a dependable or effective mechanism for attracting and retaining large pools of highly qualified educators to low-performing schools or for enhancing social capital in those settings. Indeed, some studies reveal that reconstitution may deplete those critical resources.

While districts may provide additional fiscal and informational resources, at least in the short-term, it is hard to discern whether these resources are sufficient for or aligned with the tasks at hand. Moreover, even where reconstitution is accompanied by gains in some of the foundational resources required for school improvement, the strategy may not enhance the "capacity component" of school improvement. The financial and informational resources provided at the outset and any increases in cultural capital may be offset by the drain on the human capital and the social capital resources that are so essential for school improvement (Rice & Croninger, 2005). Moreover, the resource misalignments and the organization freneticism and fragmentation that may accompany this strategy can undermine the productivity of the remaining resources and further diminish the schools' capacity to improve. While these deleterious effects are not inevitable, they are present even when reconstitution is implemented in a small number of schools and when it is accompanied by additional, if not altogether sufficient, institutional supports.

Whether reconstitution could enhance school capacity if the sponsoring institutions (a) incorporated incentives to attract and retain experienced administrators and master teachers; (b) granted staffs the time, autonomy, and opportunity to envision alternative organizational designs; or (c) dedicated sufficient financial, informational, and human resources to the experiment remains an open, empirical question. Even impressive levels of institutional backing may not be able to counter the disruption, stigma, and strain the reform may engender and to create the resource alignments and organizational contexts that are necessary in order for resources to be put to productive use (Rice & Malen, 2003; Wong et al., 1999).

Evidence on the impact of reconstitution on school performance, or, more precisely, the student achievement proxy, is fragile and mixed. Some studies attribute actual or anticipated gains in student achievement to en masse restaffing even though the controls required to make such attributions are not part of the design; some avoid this issue or address it indirectly by discussing, as we have done here, how reconstitution may affect the organizational conditions that influence organizational performance. Since the evidence suggests that reconstitution may have a negative impact on both the incentive and the capacity dimensions of school organization, it is not a prudent strategy for improving school performance.

Implications for Policy and Research

This chapter sought to develop a clearer understanding of school reconstitution by examining the theory underlying this reform and the empirical evidence regarding how the threat and the application of reconstitution play out in practice. In this closing section, we draw on that analysis to offer tentative conclusions about the viability of this reform strategy and to identify directions for future research.

Since school reconstitution seeks to improve the stock of human capital and to create arrangements that make more productive use of that human capital, we focus on whether this approach is a sound strategy for advancing those aims. The evidence to date suggests that school reconstitution is, at best, a very risky strategy. Its espoused benefits are not well documented in the extant literature. Its actual effects may harm rather than help struggling schools. Both the threat and the application of reconstitution may create incentives that intensify effort but undercut effectiveness. That is, administrators and teachers may work harder but be prompted to engage in practices that run counter to prominent theories of school effectiveness and core principles of equitable practice. Further, evidence suggests that reconstitution can undercut commitment to the organization and weaken capacity for school improvement. Even when implemented on a very small scale and accompanied by supplemental resources, reconstitution may deplete the stock of human capital in schools and undercut productivity by imposing intense human costs and engendering organizational inefficiencies that make it less rather than more likely that the school will improve its performance. Hence, our analysis calls for restraint in the deployment of this strategy until we have a stronger theoretical and empirical understanding of and justification for this reform.

Our analysis suggests that future research should address both the threat and the application of reconstitution. The current policy context offers a natural laboratory for analyses of how the threat of reconstitution operates to affect incentives, capacity, and performance. Both longitudinal and comparative studies would enable us to document how the threat of reconstitution affects incentives and capacity in different contexts. A deeper understanding of these dimensions would allow us to design studies that have the power to address, more fully, the relationship between reconstitution initiatives and school improvement. Understanding the application of reconstitution is more difficult given the limited use of this strategy and our call for restraint in employing this strategy. However, carefully crafted studies of reconstitution experiments, even if done retrospectively, could help policy makers identify the underlying assumptions and inspect the critical conditions that must hold if this strategy is to realize its stated aims.

Notes

1. We thank Rick Mintrop, James Lytle, and two anonymous reviewers for their feedback on an earlier version of this chapter.
2. We found multiple references to school reconstitution experiments in various policy papers, website commentaries, and press accounts. Some references praised the experiments and credited them with improving student test scores (e.g., Ressel, 1999a, 1999b); others maintained that reconstitution experiments failed to meet their stated aims. Our analysis does not encompass all these examples because we could not locate systematic studies that would enable us to determine

whether any of the purported positive or negative effects that were attributed to school reconstitution occurred because of, in spite of, or apart from this intervention. Put differently, we based our analysis on empirical data, not anecdotal claims.

3. For example, we found a study that focused on how two principals tried to exercise leadership in the initial phase of reconstitution (Retana, 1997). While that focus is arguably important, it does not coincide with the focus of this chapter.
4. For an updated description of supports provided to "reconstitution eligible" schools in the Maryland context, see Neuman-Sheldon & Jennings (2007).
5. The initial experiments were carried out during a period of "teacher underemployment" in California. In 1984, the district was able to hire back good people who had been laid off during the earlier fiscal crash....precipitated by the Prop 13 tax rebellion" (Mintrop, personal communication, May 15, 2007).

References

Achinstein, B. (2002). *Community, diversity and conflict among school-teachers: The ties that blind.* New York: Teachers College Press.

Adams, J. E., Jr., & Kirst, M. (1999). New demands and concepts for educational accountability: Striving for results in an era of excellence. In J. Murphy & K. S. Louis (Eds.), *Handbook of research on educational administration* (2nd ed., pp. 463–489). San Francisco: Jossey-Bass.

Adcock, E. P., & Winkler, L. (1999, April). *Jump higher or else! Measuring school reconstitution.* Paper presented at the American Educational Research Association Conference, Montreal, Quebec, Canada.

Airasian, P. W. (1988). Symbolic validation: The case of state mandated, high stakes testing. *Educational Evaluation and Policy Analysis, 10,* 301–313.

Anagnostopoulos, D. (2003). The new accountability, student failure, and teachers' work in urban high schools. *Educational Policy, 17,* 291–316.

Anagnostopoulos, D., & Rutledge., S. A. (2007). Making sense of school sanctioning policies in urban high schools. *Teachers College Record, 109,* 1261–1302.

Archibald, S., & Odden, A. (2000). *A case study of resource reallocation to implement a whole school reform model and boost student achievement: Parnell Elementary School.* Retrieved May 16, 2000, from University of Wisconsin-Madison, Wisconsin Center for Education Research: http://www.wcer.wisc.edu/CPRE/papers/Parnell%20SF%203-00.pdf

Blum, J. (2001, June 7). Vance plans overhaul of up to 9 schools. *Washington Post,* p. B2.

Booher-Jennings, J. (2005). Below the bubble: "Educational triage" and the Texas accountability system. *American Educational Research Journal, 42,* 231–268.

Brady, R. C. (2003, January). *Can failing schools be fixed?* Washington, DC: Thomas Fordham Foundation. Retrieved June 6, 2003, from http://www.edexcellence.net/doc/failing_schools.pdf

Christensen, L. (1998). Reconstituting Jefferson. *Rethinking Schools, 13*(1), 1–4.

Corcoran, T., & Goertz, M. (1995). Instructional capacity and high performance schools. *Educational Researcher, 24*(9), 27–31.

Darling-Hammond, L. (2004). Standards, accountability, and school reform. *Teachers College Record, 106,* 1047–1085.

Designs for Change. (2005). *The big picture: School-initiated reforms, centrally initiated reforms, and elementary school achievement in Chicago (1990–2005).* Chicago: Author.

Diamond, J. B., & Spillane, J. P. (2004). High-stakes accountability in urban elementary schools: Challenging or reproducing inequality? *Teachers College Record, 106,* 1145–1176.

Dorgan, K. (2004). A year in the life of an elementary school: One school's experiences in meeting new mathematics standards. *Teachers College Record, 106,* 1203–1228.

Elmore, R. F. (2002). *Bridging the gap between standards and achievement:*

The imperative for professional development in education. Washington, DC: Albert Shanker Institute.

Finkelstein, B., Malen, B., Muncey, D., Rice, J. K., & Croninger, R. C. (2000). *Caught in contradictions: The first two years of a reconstitution initiative.* College Park: University of Maryland.

Finnigan, K. S., & Gross, B. (2007). Do accountability policy sanctions influence teacher motivation? Lessons from Chicago's low-performing schools. *American Educational Research Journal, 44,* 594–629.

Finnigan, K., & O'Day, J. (2003). *External support to schools on probation: Getting a leg up?* Philadelphia: University of Pennsylvania, Consortium for Policy Research in Education.

Firestone, W. F., Fitz, J., & Broadfoot, P. (1999). Power, learning and legitimation: Assessment implementation across levels in the United States and the United Kingdom. *American Educational Research Journal, 36,* 759–793.

Firestone, W. A., Mayrowetz, D., & Fairman, J. (1998). Performance-based assessment and instructional change: The effects of testing in Maine and Maryland. *Educational Evaluation and Policy Analysis, 20,* 95–113.

Fraga, L. R., Erlichson, B. A., & Lee, S. (1998). Consensus building and school reform: The role of the courts in San Francisco. In C. N. Stone (Ed.), *Changing urban education* (pp. 66–90). Lawrence: University Press of Kansas.

Frazier, L. (1997, May 31). Six P.G. schools face purge. *Washington Post,* p. A1, A10.

Fuhrman, S. H. (Ed.). (2001). *From the capital to the classroom: Standards-based reform in the states.* Chicago: University of Chicago Press.

Fuhrman, S. H., & Elmore, R. F. (Eds.). (2004). *Redesigning accountability systems for education.* New York: Teachers College Press.

Fuhrman, S. H., & O'Day, J. A. (Eds.). (1996). *Rewards and reform: Creating educational incentives that work.* San Francisco: Jossey-Bass.

Goertz, M. E., Duffy, M. C., & LeFloch, K. C. (2001). *Assessment and accountability systems in the 50 states: 1999–2000* (CPRE Research Report No. RR-046). Philadelphia: University of Pennsylvania, Consortium for Policy Research in Education.

Hansen, J. B., Kraetzer, A. V., & Mukherjee, P. (1998, August). *Adams-Hunt achievement initiative final evaluation report.* Colorado Springs: Colorado Springs School District.

Hanushek, E. A. (1994). *Making schools work: Improving performance and controlling costs.* Washington, DC: Brookings Institution.

Hatch, T. (2002). When improvement programs collide. *Phi Delta Kappan, 83,* 626–639.

Hendrie, C. (1997, September). Reconstitution gaining new momentum. *Education Week, 24,* 1, 12–13.

Hendrie, C. (1998, July 8). A mixed record for reconstitution flashes a yellow light for districts. *Education Week, 17*(42).

Heneman, H. G., III, & Milanowski, A. T. (1999). Teacher attitudes about teacher bonuses under school-based performance award programs. *Journal of Personnel Evaluation in Education, 12,* 327–341.

Herman, J. L. (2004). The effects of testing on instruction. In S. H. Fuhrman & R. F. Elmore (Eds.), *Redesigning accountability systems for education* (pp. 141–166). New York: Teachers College Press.

Hess, F. M. (1999). *Spinning wheels: The politics of urban school reform.* Washington, DC: Brookings Institution.

Hess, G. A., Jr. (1999). Expectations, opportunity, capacity and will: The four essential components of Chicago school reform. *Educational Policy, 13,* 494–517.

Hess, G. A., Jr. (2003). Reconstitution—three years later: Monitoring the effects of sanctions on Chicago high schools. *Education and Urban Society, 35,* 300–327.

Hettleman, K. R. (2000, September 13). A fair test of state privatization? *Education Week, 20*(2) 40, 45.

Kelly, C. (1999). The motivational impact of school-based performance awards. *Journal of Personnel Evaluation in Education, 12,* 309–326.

Kelly, C., & Protsik, J. (1997). Risk and reward: perspectives on the implementation of Kentucky's school-based performance award program. *Educational Administration Quarterly, 33,* 474–505.

Khanna, R., Flores, J. R., Bergum, B., & Desmond, D. (1999, April).

The history and practice of reconstitution in San Francisco. Paper presented at the American Educational Research Association Conference, Montreal, Quebec, Canada.

Ladd, H. (Ed.). (1996). *Holding schools accountable: Performance-based reform in education.* Washington, DC: Brookings Institution.

Ladd, H., & Zelli, A. (2002). School-based accountability in North Carolina: The responses of school principals. *Educational Administration Quarterly, 38,* 494–529.

Linn, R. E. (2003). Accountability: Responsibility and reasonable expectations. *Educational Researcher, 32*(7), 3–13.

Linn, R. L., Baker, E. L., & Betebenner, D. W. (2002). Accountability systems: Implications of requirement of the No Child Left Behind Act of 2001. *Educational Researcher, 31*(6), 3–16.

Lipman, P. (2006). "This *is* America" 2005: The political economy of education reform against the public interest. In G. Ladson-Billings & W. F. Tate (Eds.), *Education research in the public interest: Social justice, action and policy* (pp. 98–116). New York: Teachers College Press.

Malen, B., Croninger, R., Muncey, D., & Redmond-Jones, D. (2002). Reconstituting schools: Testing the theory of action. *Educational Evaluation and Policy Analysis, 24,* 113–132.

Malen, B., & Muncey, D. (2000). Creating "a new set of givens"? The impact of state activism on school autonomy. In N. D. Theobald & B. Malen (Eds.), *Balancing local control and state responsibility for k-12 education* (pp.199–244). Larchmont, NY: Eye on Education.

Malen, B., & Porton, H. (2003). *An elementary school's quest for school improvement* (Research monograph prepared for the site and district). College Park: University of Maryland.

Malen, B., & Rice, J. K. (2004). A framework for assessing the impact of education reforms on school capacity: Insights from studies of high-stakes accountability initiatives. *Educational Policy, 18,* 631–660.

McNeil, L. M. (2000). *Contradictions of school reform: Educational costs of standardized testing.* New York: Routledge.

Mintrop, H. (2000). Towards an understanding of school reconstitution as a strategy to educate children at risk. In M. Sanders (Ed.), *Schooling students placed at risk: Research, policy and practice in the education of poor and minority adolescents* (pp. 231–259). Mahwah, NJ: Erlbaum.

Mintrop, H. (2003). The limits of sanctions in low-performing schools [Electronic version]. *Education Policy Analysis Archives, 113*(3), 1–30.

Mintrop, H. (2004a). High-stakes accountability, state oversight, and educational equity. *Teachers College Record, 106,* 2128–2145.

Mintrop, H. (2004b). *Schools on probations: How accountability works (and doesn't work).* New York: Teachers College Press.

Mintrop, H., & Trujillo, T. (2005). Corrective action in low performing schools: Lessons for NCLB implementation from first-generation accountability systems [Electronic version]. *Education Policy Analysis Archives, 13*(48).

Mohrman, S. A., & Lawler, E. E., III. (1996). Motivation for school reform. In S. H. Fuhrman & J. A. O'Day (Eds.), *Rewards and reform: Creating educational incentives that work* (pp. 115–143). San Francisco: Jossey-Bass.

Moreno, S. (2001, June 23). Nine D.C. schools to be reborn; continued failures prompt makeovers. *Washington Post,* pp. B1, B4.

Moreno, S. (2003, June 26). Transformed D. C. schools show progress. *Washington Post,* pp. B1, B5.

Neuman-Sheldon, B. (2006). *Building on state reform: Maryland school restructuring.* Washington, DC: Center on Education Policy.

Neuman-Sheldon, B., & Jennings, J. (2007). *Making mid-course corrections: School restructuring in Maryland.* Washington, DC: Center on Education Policy.

Newmann, F. M., King, M. B., & Youngs, P. (2000). Professional development that addresses school capacity: Lessons from urban elementary schools. *American Journal of Education, 108,* 259–299.

Newmann, F. M., Smith, B., Allensworth, E., & Bryk, A. S. (2001). Instructional program coherence: What it is and why it should guide school policy improvement. *Educational Evaluation and Policy Analysis, 23,* 297–321.

O'Day, J. A. (1996). Incentives and school improvement. In S. Fuhrman & J. A. O'Day (Eds.) *Rewards and reform: Creating educational incentives that work* (pp. 1–16). San Francisco, CA: Jossey-Bass.

O'Day, J. A. (2002). Complexity, accountability, and school improvement. *Harvard Educational Review, 72*, 293–329.

O'Day, J. A. (2007). NCLB and the complexity of school improvement. In A. R. Sadovnik, J. A. O'Day, G. W. Bohrnstedt, & K. M. Borman (Eds.), *No Child Left Behind and the reduction of the achievement gap: Sociological perspectives on federal educational policy* (pp.25–52). New York: Routledge.

Odden, A., & Archibald, S. (2000). *A case study of resource reallocation to reduce class size, enhance teacher planning time, and strengthen literacy: Clayton Elementary School.* Retrieved May 16, 2000, from University of Wisconsin-Madison, Wisconsin Center for Education Research: http://www.wcer.wisc.edu/cpre/papers/Clayton%20SF%20 3-00.pdf

Pedulla, J. J., Abrams, L. M., Madaus, G. F., Russell, M. K., Ramos, M. A., & Miao, J. (2003). *Perceived effects of state-mandated testing programs on teaching and learning: Findings from a national survey of teachers.* Chesnut Hill, MA: National Board on Educational Testing and Public Policy.

Portner, J. (1997). Six suburban schools in Md. to be "reconstituted" [Electronic version]. *Education Week, 16*(37).

Ressel, B. (1999a). A fresh start for troubled schools. *Fiscal Notes.* Retrieved February 14, 2008, from http://www.window.state.tx.us/ comptrol/fnotes/fn9907/fna.html#fresh

Ressel, B. (1999b). Reconstituted schools' performance improves. *Fiscal Notes.* Retrieved February 14, 2008, from http:www.window.state. tx.us/control/fnotes/fn9907/fna.html

Retana, N. M. (1997). *Radical school restructuring: A case study of principal leadership in reconstituted urban high schools.* Unpublished doctoral dissertation, University of Texas-Austin.

Rice, J. K. (2002). Making economically grounded decisions about comprehensive school reform models: Considerations of costs, effects and contexts. In N. C. Wang & K. K. Wong (Eds.), *Efficiency and equity issues in Title I school-wide program implementation* (pp. 29–55). Greenwich, CT: Information Age.

Rice, J. K. (2003). *Teacher quality: Understanding the effectiveness of teacher attributes.* Washington, DC: Economic Policy Institute.

Rice, J. K., & Croninger, R. C. (2005). Resource generation, reallocation, or depletion: An analysis of the impact of reconstitution on school capacity. *Leadership and Policy in Schools, 4*, 73–104.

Rice, J. K., & Malen, B. (2003). The human costs of education reform: The case of school reconstitution. *Educational Administration Quarterly, 39*, 635–666.

Rojas, W. (1996). *Reconstitution, reculturing, and reform: Adding options for urban education.* Unpublished doctoral dissertation, Teachers College, Columbia University, New York.

Ruenzel, D. (1996). Mission impossible. *Teacher Magazine.* Retrieved May 25, 2001, from http://www.teachermagazine.org/tm/ articles/1996/04/01/07mingo.h07.html?qs=mission_impossible

Ruenzel, D. (1997). Do or die. *Teacher Magazine.* Retrieved May 25, 2001, from http://www.teachermagazine.org/tm/articles/1997/03/01/06sf2. h08.html?qs=do+or+die

Sandholtz, J. H., Ogawa, R. T., & Scribner, S. P. (2004). Standards gaps: Unintended consequences of local standards-based reform. *Teachers College Record, 106*, 1177–1202.

Shipps, D., Kahne, J., & Smylie, M. A. (1999). The politics of urban school reform: Legitimacy, city growth, and school improvement in Chicago. *Education Policy, 13*, 518–545.

Spillane, J. P., Diamond, J. B., Burch, P., Hallet, T., Jita, L., & Zolterns, J. (2002). Managing in the middle: School leaders and the enactment of accountability policy. *Educational Policy, 16*, 731–762.

Spillane, J. P., & Thompson, C. L. (1997). Reconstructing conceptions of local capacity: The local education agency's capacity for ambitious instructional reform. *Educational Evaluation and Policy Analysis, 19*, 185–203.

Stecher, B. M., & Barron, S. (1999, April). *Test-based accountability: The perverse consequences of milepost testing.* Paper presented at the Annual Conference of the American Educational Research Association, Montreal, Quebec, Canada.

Stringfield, S. C., & Yakimowski-Srebnick, M. E. (2005). Promise, progress, problems and paradoxes of three phases of accountability: A longitudinal case study of the Baltimore City Public Schools. *American Educational Research Journal, 42*, 43–75.

Stronge, J. H., Gareis, C. R., & Little, C. A. (2006). *Teacher pay and teacher quality: Attracting, developing, and retaining the best teachers.* Thousand Oaks, CA: Corwin Press.

Sunderman, G. L. (2001). Accountability mandates and the implementation of Title I schoolwide programs: A comparison of three urban districts. *Educational Administration Quarterly, 37*, 503–532.

Swanson, C. B., & Stevenson, D. L. (2002). Standards-based reform in practice: Evidence on state policy and classroom instruction from the NAEP state assessments. *Educational Evaluation and Policy Analysis, 24*, 1–27.

Trujillo, A. (2005). Politics, school philosophy, and language policy: The case of Crystal City schools. *Educational Policy, 19*, 621–654.

U. S. Department of Education. (1998, May). *Turning around low-performing schools: A guide for state and local leaders.* Retrieved May 25, 2001, from http://www.ed.gov/pubs/turning/intervene.html

U.S. Department of Education. (2001, January). *School improvement report: Executive order on actions for turning around low performing schools. First Annual Report.* Washington, DC: Author.

Wan, W. (2007, January 25). Annapolis High workers sanctioned; All jobs open. *Washington Post*, p. B1, B2.

White, K. W., & Rosenbaum, J. E. (2008). Inside the black box of accountability: How high-stakes accountability alters school culture and the classification and treatment of students and teachers. In A. R. Sadovnik, J. A. O'Day, G. W. Bohrnstedt, & K. M. Borman (Eds.), *No Child Left Behind and the reduction of the achievement gap: Sociological perspectives on federal educational policy* (pp. 97–114). New York: Routledge.

Wong, K. K., & Anagnostopoulos, D. (1998). Can integrated governance reconstruct teaching? Lessons learned from two low-performing Chicago high schools. *Educational Policy, 12*, 31–47.

Wong, K. K., Anagnostopoulos, D., Rutledge, S., Lynn, L., & Dreeben, R. (1999). *Implementation of an educational accountability agenda: Integrated governance in the Chicago public schools enters its fourth year.* Chicago: University of Chicago and Irving R. Harris Graduate School of Public Policy Studies.

Youngs, P., & King, M. B. (2001). Principal leadership for professional development to build school capacity. *Educational Administration Quarterly, 38*, 643–670.

38

Charter School Policy Issues and Research Questions

Sandra Vergari
State University of New York at Albany

The first charter school law was adopted by Minnesota in 1991 and the first charter school opened there in 1992.[1] Sixteen years and 40 additional charter school laws later, charter school issues continue to attract attention and controversy among educators, education leaders, researchers, political interest groups, and policy makers.

This chapter begins with a review of the charter school idea and current numbers. Then, I examine issues and questions that have shaped recent research on charter schools. The analysis focuses on the following concepts: equity and choice, deregulation and innovation, accountability, and student achievement. Finally, I discuss the politics of charter school policy and research and offer comments in conclusion. Throughout the chapter, I highlight questions that merit new research.

The Charter School Idea

What is a charter school? According to a 2006 survey of the American public, 53% of the respondents indicated that charter schools are not public schools, 50% said that charter schools are free to teach religion, 60% said charter schools can charge tuition, and 58% said that charter schools can select students according to ability (Rose & Gallup, 2006). In each case, the respondents were mistaken.

Charter schools are nonsectarian, publicly funded entities that operate free from many of the regulations that apply to traditional public schools. The amount of regulatory freedom varies across charter school laws and individual school charters. While charter schools embody elements of privatization, they must also abide by certain rules that pertain to public schools. For example, charter schools may not charge tuition and their admissions processes must be nondiscriminatory.[2] Moreover, as public schools, charter schools are subject to state academic standards and the federal No Child Left Behind Act of 2001 (NCLB).

In return for regulatory relief, charter schools are supposed to be held accountable by their respective public authorizers and through parental choice in the education marketplace. As publicly funded entities, charter schools are expected to be accountable not only to families who have selected the schools but also to the general public. A charter school authorizer is the public's agent for holding charter schools accountable. Authorizers have three key responsibilities. First, they review and make decisions on applications for proposed charter schools. Second, they monitor school compliance with the charter and applicable laws and rules. Third, they decide whether to renew or revoke charters.[3]

State charter school laws vary in terms of the types of eligible authorizers permitted. Most charter school laws permit school district boards to authorize charter schools. More than 30 states permit entities other than local school boards to serve as charter school authorizers. Such authorizers include special purpose charter school boards (e.g., in Arizona, the District of Columbia, and Utah); universities and colleges (in nine states); state boards of education, education commissioners, and departments of education; regional educational entities; the mayor in Indianapolis, Indiana; the city council in Milwaukee, Wisconsin; and certain nonprofit entities in Minnesota and Ohio (Hassel, Ziebarth, & Steiner, 2005).

The concept of a "charter school" in the United States was first advanced in the 1970s and 1980s by Ray Budde (1974, 1988, 1989) and Albert Shanker (1988a, 1988b).[4] Budde and Shanker envisioned a group of teachers applying to a school board for permission to operate a charter school. In contrast, the concept developed subsequently by Minnesota policy entrepreneurs Ted Kolderie (1990) and Joe Nathan (1996) emphasizes that charter schools herald the end of the "exclusive franchise" in public education long enjoyed by school districts.

When it comes to the creation of charter schools, some political interests maintain that a charter school should not be able to operate without approval from the school district in which it is located. Charter school advocates avow that charter schools should be able to operate without district permission. Given that charter schools typically compete with traditional public schools for enrollments, school districts may be reluctant to authorize charter schools. In addition, school districts may lack capacity and will to oversee charter schools they have authorized. The behavior of a given school district authorizer is shaped in part by external political pressure and the state and local political climate pertaining to school choice (Teske, Schneider, & Cassese, 2005).

A majority of charter schools are located in states with multiple authorizers (Center for Education Reform, 2007b). By 2006, 5 state-level authorizer boards, 24 public and 12 private college and university boards, 2 municipal offices, and 24 nonprofit organizations had authorized one or more charter schools. In Arizona, the State Board for Charter Schools had granted 90% of the state's charters; universities had granted 81% of the charters schools in Michigan; and, in Indiana, Ball State University and the Indianapolis mayor had authorized 93% of the charter schools (Palmer, 2006).[5]

Charter School Numbers

As of 2008, 10 states did not have charter school laws.[6] Charter school laws and numbers vary significantly across the states and the District of Columbia. Laws characterized by advocates and some analysts as "strong" or "permissive" generally promote the proliferation of charter schools while "weak" or "restrictive" laws typically inhibit charter school growth. Given different charter school laws and varying approaches to policy implementation both across and within states, it is important that analysts consider different legal and political contexts across states and localities. For example, the degree of autonomy enjoyed by charter schools varies across state laws and authorizers (Center for Education Reform, 2006a; Green & Mead, 2004; Lacireno-Paquet & Holyoke, 2007; Shober, Manna, & Witte, 2006; Vergari, 2002a; Wohlstetter, Wenning, & Briggs, 1995).

In 2007–08, there were about 4,000 charter schools in operation across the United States with a total enrollment of about 1.2 million students (Center for Education Reform, 2007c). Charter school enrollment composes only about 2% of total public school enrollment; however, this aggregate figure masks an uneven distribution of charter schools and students.[7] In April 2007, the six states with the most charter schools and the largest charter school enrollments were Arizona, California, Florida, Michigan, Ohio, and Texas. Each of these states had at least 240 charter schools.[8] There were more than 100 charter schools in each of four additional states: Colorado, Minnesota, Pennsylvania, and Wisconsin. Eleven states had fewer than 20 charter schools each (Center for Education Reform, 2007a).[9]

In some communities, charter schools enroll a substantial proportion of the local student population. In 2006–07, New Orleans had the highest percentage of public school students attending charter schools at 57%. Dayton, Ohio;

Southfield, Michigan; and Washington, D.C. ranked second, each with about 27% of public school students attending charter schools. In 15 additional jurisdictions, at least 15% of public school students were enrolled in charter schools (Ziebarth, 2007).

Global Context

The focus of this chapter is on a particular form of school choice in one country, the United States. From a broader perspective, charter school policy is part of a global trend of interest in school choice policies that challenge "one size fits all" approaches to education. Moreover, policy makers in various nations have demonstrated interest in market-based policies that make the funding and ultimate survival of a school dependent on its ability to attract and retain students (Plank & Sykes, 2003a; Salisbury & Tooley, 2005). According to international evidence, market-based theories focused on competition and consumer choice have "not translated easily into the real world of schools and classrooms" (Ladd, 2003, p. 22). Markets generate "winners and losers," and some countries are taking steps back or attempting to address unintended consequences of school choice policies (Plank & Sykes, 2003b; Ladd, 2003).

U.S. Education policy is shaped by particular historical features and values embedded in the constitutional, federal system. However, analysts of charter school issues can benefit by examining school choice policy adoption and implementation across national contexts. For example, Great Britain's experiment with grant-maintained schools offered early lessons for charter school policy makers and leaders in the United States (Wohlstetter & Anderson, 1994). Ladd (2003) advises charter school advocates to consider the inspectorate approach to school accountability in Great Britain and New Zealand. Indeed, charter school authorizers in Massachusetts and New York State based their charter school accountability processes partly on the British inspection model.[10]

Policy Issues and Research Questions

The charter school concept embodies multiple objectives. Accordingly, there are numerous charter school issues that merit attention from researchers and policy makers. Researchers have demonstrated greater interest in some key issues (e.g., student achievement) over others (e.g., school governance). Below, I discuss several ways to think about charter school policy and research questions raised by each perspective.

Equity and Choice The charter school reform may be thought of as an equity policy that expands opportunities for students to attend high-quality public schools (Rofes & Stulberg, 2004). In the traditional public education system, some families have ready access to schools that are aligned with their values and preferences while others do not. Low-income families, in particular, have not enjoyed the educational choices long available to other families. Low-income families may not be able to afford to live in areas with high-quality public schools or the tuition expense of private schools of their choice. Choice in public education refers to the opportunity to select schools based on not only academic performance but also other criteria such as values and school culture, safety, and location. As discussed below, the equity and choice elements of charter school policy provoke numerous research questions.

Parental Choice   According to Nathan (1996), a founder of the charter school concept, the charter school movement "gives real power…to parents and children to choose the kind of school that makes sense for them" (pp. xv–vi). Indeed, the charter school idea embodies formidable roles and responsibilities for parents in terms of gathering information, choosing schools, and evaluating school performance.

The parental choice functions at the heart of charter schooling raise a number of questions. For example, what are the consequences of different levels of parental capacity, and will to study various education options carefully in order to choose high-quality schools? Do school choosers have equitable access to reliable, valid information in the education marketplace? If schools compete to appeal to families, what are the consequences for children whose parents are not active choosers?

For parents to be able to make wise choices in the education marketplace, they must have ready access to valid information about schools. Van Dunk and Dickman (2003) identified significant information gaps in the Milwaukee school choice setting, and a study of school choice in China found that some parents may base their choices on misinformation about schools (Lai, 2007). Other studies in Chile, the Netherlands, and United States and the have identified differences in school choice decision-making processes across different socioeconomic groups (Bell, 2005; Elacqua, Schneider, & Buckley, 2006; Karsten, Ledoux, Roeleveld, Felix, & Elshof, 2003; Lankford & Wyckoff, 2005).

A study of parents who chose charter schools and parents who chose private schools in Denver, Milwaukee, and Washington, DC, found some differences between the two groups. For example, parents choosing charter schools were more likely to learn about educational options from written school communications while parents choosing private schools were more likely to gain information from social networks. Compared to private school parents, charter school parents were more likely to cite academic factors as key reasons for selecting a school. Compared to charter school parents, private school parents were almost twice as likely to focus on school culture when selecting a school (Teske & Reichardt, 2006).

In survey research, parents typically point to academic quality as a key factor in their choice of a school (e.g., Teske & Reichardt, 2006). However, examinations of what parents say they do and what they actually do when choosing schools reveal that parents may place more emphasis on the demographic composition of a school's student body than they acknowledge to survey researchers (Buckley & Schneider, 2007; Hamilton & Guin, 2005).

Some analysts suggest that the school choices and monitoring on the part of some parents can benefit others because the education marketplace will respond to the preferences of active choosers in ways that also benefit less active consumers (Schneider, Teske, & Marschall, 2000). Other scholars have raised concerns that the choices of parents based on private interests may not serve the broader public interest (Abernathy, 2005; Henig, 1994; Miron & Nelson, 2002; Smith, 2003; Wells, 2002).

As noted above, charter school choosers in three cities relied heavily on school-provided information (Teske & Reichardt, 2006). Thus, it is important to examine the types of information available to parents and whether some charter schools deliberately target recruitment efforts toward particular groups of parents, thereby placing some parents at a disadvantage in the education marketplace (Bell, 2005). In their examination of the distribution of charter schools in the Detroit, Michigan region, Lubienski and Gulosino (2007) report that profit-oriented charter schools avoid locating in communities with more disadvantaged students.

Charter school advocates often tout charter school waiting lists and reportedly high satisfaction rates among parents of charter school students.[11] However, studies of parental satisfaction are typically snapshots of one point in time. In their study of parental choice and charter schools in Washington, DC, Buckley and Schneider (2007) report the intriguing finding that favorable evaluations of charter schools by parents declined over time. Additional longitudinal studies of parent ratings of schools would be useful for determining whether Buckley and Schneider's finding holds elsewhere and would enable researchers to develop more nuanced assessments of parental satisfaction dynamics.

It is useful to examine the extent to which parents are satisfied with charter schools. However, measures of parental satisfaction are not direct indicators of school effectiveness and student performance. There is a need for more research on the extent to which parental assessments of the qualities of various schools are accurate. Moreover, it is important to study non-choosers in regions that have charter schools to find out why they have not chosen charter schools, and to compare their evaluation and decision-making processes with those who have selected charter schools.

Student Mobility Rates   Charter school admissions processes are supposed to be nondiscriminatory, yet there are many unanswered questions regarding the mobility rates of charter school students. The research and policy communities would benefit from data on student attrition rates across different types of charter schools. It would be helpful to examine whether there are patterns in the types of students who are exiting charter schools before graduation. For example, are low-achieving students more likely to leave charter schools than other students? The research literature lacks examination of reasons offered by students' families for their exit from particular charter schools, and how their explanations compare to those provided by leaders of the respective charter schools. There is also a lack of data on where students who leave charter schools end up. Finally, in any given community, how do the student mobility rates for charter schools compare to those of traditional public schools? There is a need for systematic research on student recruitment and retention in charter schools.

Social Stratification Depending on policy design, school choice policies such as charter schools can lead to either more or less student integration than is already the case in public education (Gill, 2005). Are charter school students similar to those in traditional public schools? Would charter school proliferation lead to greater student segregation and social stratification? According to the most recent data available, 52% of charter schools are located in central cities, compared to 25% of traditional public schools.[12] As indicated in Table 38.1, charter schools enroll a substantially larger percentage of Black students and fewer White students than do traditional public schools. Charter schools also enroll slightly more American Indian/ Alaska Native and Hispanic students, and fewer Asian/ Pacific Islanders.

An examination of the racial composition and segregation of charter schools nationally and by state noted that charter schools are often located in segregated neighborhoods; little evidence was found that the charter school reform is reducing segregation in public education (Frankenberg & Lee, 2003). Studies of comprehensive, relatively unregulated school choice policies in Chile and New Zealand have revealed patterns of disadvantage for less-educated, lower-income families (Fiske & Ladd, 2000; Carnoy & McEwan, 2003).

Scholars have also raised the possibility of potentially negative peer effects that result from school choice policies such as charter schools. As explained by Goldhaber, Guin, Henig, Hess, and Weiss (2005, p. 108), if nonchoosers tend to be lower achieving students, if lower achieving students benefit from being in class with higher achieving students, and if school choice policy results in less mixing of low- and high-achieving students, then non-choosers are likely to suffer negative consequences.

The research literature contains very little reliable,

TABLE 38.1
Percentages of Students in Traditional Public Schools and Charter Schools According to Race/Ethnicity, 2004–05

Race/Ethnicity	Traditional Public Schools	Charter Schools
American Indian/Alaska Native	1.2	1.5
Asian/Pacific Islander	4.6	3.3
Black	16.9	31.3
Hispanic	19.4	21.8
White	58.0	42.0

Source: U.S. Department of Education (2007).

national data regarding the extent to which charter schools enroll students with disabilities. Studies of charter schooling in states such as Arizona, Massachusetts, Michigan, North Carolina, New York, Texas, and Wisconsin suggest that special education students may suffer implicit and explicit barriers to equitable treatment (Fusarelli, 2002; Herdman, 2002; Hess & Maranto, 2002; Mead, 2002; McNiff & Hassel, 2002; Miron & Nelson, 2002; Vergari, 2002b). Charter school champions Finn, Manno, and Vanourek (2000) have stated that charter schools should serve special education students more adequately.

In 1998–99, students with disabilities composed about 8% of charter school students compared to 11% for all public schools in the charter school states (RPP International, 2000). More recent national studies suggest that, on average, about 12% of charter school students receive special education services (SRI International, 2002; Rhim, Lange, Ahearn, & McLaughlin, 2007). In 2005–06, about 14% of all public school students received special education services (U.S. Department of Education, 2007). Some analyses suggest that charter schools may be more likely than traditional public schools to enroll special needs students who are not formally labeled as such (Horn & Miron, 2000; Mintrom, 2002; Rhim, Ahearn, Lange, & McLaughlin, 2004).

Socialization and Civic Values According to the "common school" ideal, public schools serve as socialization agents for diverse student populations and promote good citizenship and a healthy democracy. A charter school is focused on serving the families who have chosen the school. This choice factor means that teachers, leaders, board members, and families associated with a given charter school are supposed to be "on the same page" in terms of the school culture and curriculum. Theoretically, there are fewer disputes as the school can focus on its own vision of schooling and need not please everyone (Chubb, 1997). The values of choice, deregulation, and autonomy that are characteristic of the charter school idea lead to questions about the extent to which charter schools overall will promote civil society principles and the nurturance of common core values among the nation's youth.

If charter schools expanded substantially to serve a much larger segment of the student population, and if these schools did not have some common curricular elements pertaining to the development of good citizens, one consequence might be increased social fragmentation. As publicly funded entities, it is reasonable to subject charter schools to particular mandates that serve the public interest such as curriculum requirements focused on development and nurturance of traits and values essential for good citizenship in a democracy.

Studies of civic values and school choice have focused mostly on comparisons between private schools and traditional public schools. Upon reviewing published studies on the matter, Wolf (2005) concluded that private schools rarely harm the development of civic values among students and may often enhance such development.[13] He noted that the generally favorable results found in available studies of schools of choice and civic values may also be due to unexamined factors that motivate parents to enroll their children in schools of choice. Thus, there is a need for more research that focuses specifically on charter schools and civic values.

Deregulation and Innovation   In addition to equity and choice, the charter school idea emphasizes deregulation, site-based management, and innovation. According to school choice advocates, the divisive politics that sometimes plague public school governance may be avoided in a decentralized system such as charter schooling (Chubb & Moe, 1990). A charter school is formed by like-minded founders who have the opportunity to assemble a governing board whose members support the values and objectives of the school. Charter school governing boards are typically appointed rather than elected.[14] Moreover, a charter school serves students whose families have chosen the school and employs a faculty and staff who have done the same. Thus, there is supposed to be a greater sense of school community and more cooperation among stakeholders than might be found in some traditional public school districts. Several questions raised by the deregulation and innovation elements of the charter school idea are discussed below.

Charter schools are typically free from collective bargaining agreements between school districts and unions. Unrestricted by many of the regulations that apply to traditional public schools, charter schools may serve as laboratories for innovation in public education from which school leaders and policy makers can learn. Charter school advocates maintain that deregulation also makes it possible for charter schools to use public dollars more efficiently than traditional public schools.

In an investigation of how charter school behavior might differ according to founder type, Henig, Holyoke, Brown, and Lacireno-Paquet (2005) report mixed results and suggest that the external environment and core educational tasks of charter schools may result in similar behaviors regardless of founder type. Henig et al. (2005) focused their analysis on school themes, size and grade configurations, target populations, and marketing. Their study objectives did not include assessing student outcomes according to founder type.

It would be helpful for researchers to conduct comparative studies of student performance in charter schools that are managed by different for-profit and non-profit entities. With this information, charter school founders would be able to make better decisions about the desirability of partnering with a given entity. Such data would also be useful to charter school authorizers when they are reviewing applications for new charters. Reliable, valid data on the track records of different charter school management entities could help authorizers to form conclusions about the probability of success of a proposed charter school.

Public Education for Profit   In many states, charter schools are permitted to contract with private providers to manage all or part of school operations, including curriculum and instruction. About 19% of charter schools are operated by for-profit management companies (Molnar, Garcia, Bartlett, & O'Neill, 2006). To what extent does the operation of public schools by for-profit entities conflict with or support public purposes? Some charter schools have given up a great deal of their autonomy by contracting with school management companies (Bulkley, 2004; Finnigan, 2007).

There are few studies on the effectiveness of management companies. A six-city analysis of state reading and math test scores "did not show a consistent pattern of superior student performance between schools managed by private companies and demographically similar traditional public schools" (U.S. General Accounting Office, 2003, p. 3). An analysis of research on seven management companies identified some positive student achievement results for Edison Schools, Inc. but could not draw conclusions about the other six companies due to missing data (American Institutes for Research, 2006).

New Ideas and Knowledge   What types of innovation are evident in charter schools and what have been the results of particular innovative practices? Some studies suggest that charter schools are not remarkably different from traditional public schools, and that governance and organizational innovations are more typical than new practices in curriculum and instruction (Arsen, Plank, & Sykes, 1999; Mintrom, 2000; Lubienski, 2004; Teske, Schneider, Buckley, & Clark, 2001).

A study of eight charter schools deemed to have exemplary student performance identified distinctive features of the schools such as teachers serving on charter school governing boards, parent pledges to donate time to the school, extended school day or year, multi-age classrooms, classes that work with the same teacher for more than 1 year, and an emphasis on character education. While many of these measures have already been devised and implemented in some traditional public schools, charter school proponents assert that strategic combinations of practices and careful implementation often lead to extraordinary, productive charter school structures and cultures (U.S. Department of Education, 2004).

A number of recent studies have examined charter school innovations pertaining to teacher recruitment, compensation, and evaluation. These studies indicate that many charter schools hire uncertified teachers, do not use a tenure system, do not offer salary rewards for years of experience or degrees earned, are unlikely to be unionized, use pay incentives to attract teachers in high demand-low supply subject areas such as math and science, use performance-based pay, and have higher teacher turnover than traditional public schools (Harris, 2006; Kellor, 2005; Kowal, Hassel, & Hassel, 2007; Miron & Applegate, 2007; Podgursky & Ballou, 2001).[15]

"Cyber charter schools" and "home-school charter schools" are innovations that diverge from traditional brick-and-mortar classroom settings. In both the research literature and state policy, there are conceptual ambiguities regarding these schools. For example, in some states, home-school charter schools are prohibited, yet cyber charter schools are permitted (Huerta, Gonzalez, & d'Entremont, 2006).

In a cyber charter school, (also called a virtual charter school or an online charter school), students attend school in their homes or other locations. The primary sources of instruction may involve prepackaged software programs, teacher-directed distance learning, and live or recorded instruction via the Internet from a teacher or other instructor. In a home-school charter school, the primary source of instruction is the parent and there are supplemental sources of instruction such as third-party curricula, resource centers, and paraprofessionals (Huerta et al., 2006).

In 2002–03, there were about 60 cyber charter schools across 13 states (Education Commission of the States, 2003). By 2006–07, these numbers had risen to about 170 cyber charter schools serving 92,000 students across 20 states (Robelen, 2007). Twenty-seven charter school laws explicitly prohibit home-based charter schools, the California and Alaska charter school laws explicitly permit home-based charter schools, and the remaining laws are vague on the matter.[16] By comparison, about 10 state laws explicitly permit cyber charter schools (Huerta et al., 2006).

In several states, including California, Pennsylvania, and Wisconsin, political conflicts have arisen over funding and gaps in accountability policies for cyber charter schools. There are few findings in the research literature regarding the features and consequences of these alternative delivery charter schools. The research and policy communities would benefit from careful studies of student demographics, student performance, civic values, funding, and accountability challenges pertaining to cyber and home-school charter schools.[17]

School District Responses   According to Kolderie (1995), "the real purpose" of charter schools is to provoke the traditional public education system to improve (p. 7). More than 15 years following the opening of the first charter school, there are few published, systematic examinations of school district responses (and non-responses) to charter schools. Rofes (1998) conducted the pioneering study on the matter. A majority of the 25 school districts he examined had "gone about business-as-usual and responded to charters slowly and in small ways" (p. 2). Few leaders in the traditional public school system viewed charter schools as laboratories for education innovations that could be incorporated into other schools. However, 24% of the districts examined had responded to charter schooling energetically and altered their educational programs.

A study of 49 school districts found that all had made changes in either administration or education that district leaders attributed to the existence of charter schools. The changes across the districts varied according to district enrollments, financial conditions, and whether the authorizer of the charter schools was the school district (RPP International, 2001). Other case studies have identified district responses to charter schools that include implementation of full-day kindergarten and alternative curricula such as Montessori schools, stepped-up public relations campaigns, and attempts to thwart the reform via political actions such as lobbying lawmakers (Vergari, 2002a).

Charter School Finance   Charter schools are not permitted to levy taxes and many do not receive state or local funds for facilities. Charter school funding sources include public funding from school districts, states, and the federal government; financial assistance from for-profit entities; and grants from nonprofit organizations and philanthropists (Vergari, 2004). The foremost public funding difference between charter schools and traditional public schools is lack of charter school access to comparable facilities funding (Thomas B. Fordham Institute, 2005).

Policy makers and charter school analysts are confronted with the question of whether the establishment of a parallel system of public schooling is an effective use of public funds. In terms of results and opportunity costs, are charter schools superior to other options for investing in public education? There have been few scholarly analyses focused on charter school finance issues.[18]

A preliminary study in a planned long-term analysis of California charter schools includes a pioneering analysis of academic productivity. The researchers found that while charter schools typically received less per-pupil public funding their academic productivity was roughly equivalent to that of traditional public schools in their districts. Moreover, charter schools lagged traditional public schools in absolute academic performance but had more rapid rates of improvement in academic performance than traditional public schools. The authors conclude that California charter schools are getting more "more bang for their buck" (Center on Educational Governance, 2007, p. 6). As data are gathered in subsequent years, it will be important to examine whether these trends endure.

Charter school funding rules typically amount to a zero sum game for school districts: When a student chooses to attend a charter school rather than a traditional public school, the per-pupil funding follows the student to the charter school. Charter school advocates maintain that public education funds should be treated as entitlements for students and their families rather than for school districts. They suggest that families should be able to decide whether per-pupil funds are allocated to charter schools or traditional public schools. In contrast, charter school critics often assert that charter schools are "draining" or "raiding" funds from traditional school districts (Vergari, 2004, pp. 156–157).

Traditional public school advocates claim that when students leave to attend charter schools, their exit does not necessarily translate into staff reductions or lower costs in other facets of school operations. Students leaving a traditional public school to attend a charter school may not be concentrated in the same grade levels in ways that make trimming the teaching staff practical. Moreover, overhead costs (e.g., maintenance and utilities) remain when students leave to attend a charter school (Little, Roberts, Ward, Bianchi, & Metheny, 2003).

Accountability In return for regulatory relief, charter schools are supposed to be held to a high standard of performance accountability. Charter schools are immersed in two accountability processes: market accountability and bureaucratic or public accountability (Vergari, 2000). The decision to enroll a child in a charter school is made by a parent or guardian, not by a government entity. When a traditional public school student switches to a charter school, the public funds that would otherwise be allocated to the school district follow the student to the charter school. Thus, under market accountability, charter schools are supposed to be responsive to families that have chosen the schools and may exit if dissatisfied.

Competition in public education is supposed to motivate both traditional public schools and charter schools to be accountable to families of students and the tax-paying public. Charter schools that fail to attract sufficient numbers of students are forced to close. Similarly, traditional public schools that lose student market share to charter schools may face calls from taxpayers and policy makers to downsize or close.

As noted earlier, charter schools are also held accountable by agents who act on behalf of the public. These "authorizers" are obligated to oversee the use of public dollars and serve as a check on market accountability processes.[19] In 1993, Massachusetts was among the first few states to adopt a charter school law and its first 15 charter schools opened in 1995. The Massachusetts Department of Education developed a charter school accountability system that was used as a model by policy implementers in several other jurisdictions.[20] The Massachusetts model focuses on three questions: (a) Is the academic program of the school a success? (b) Is the school a viable organization? (c) Is the school faithful to the terms of its charter? (Herdman, 2002). Charter school accountability processes and outcomes vary across states and authorizers (Bulkley, 1999; Gau, Finn, & Petrilli, 2006; Hill & Lake, 2002; Lake, 2006; SRI International, 2004; Vergari, 2000; Wohlstetter et al., 1995). Several questions pertaining to charter school accountability are reviewed below.

Private Interests and the Public Interest In order for market-based accountability to occur, parents must have access to good information about schools and the will and capacity to analyze and act upon that information. Depending on a range of factors, market-based accountability processes may not function as intended. For example, in regions where the supply of high-quality traditional public and charter schools does not meet demand, some parents may be motivated to settle for a mediocre or poorly performing charter school if they judge it to be better than or equal to other options (in terms of academics, school culture, safety, or location).

The accountability functions assigned to charter school authorizers indicate that policy makers are wary of relying solely on market processes to ensure charter school accountability. Across the states, authorizers are assigned weighty responsibilities in the charter school arena. Yet capacity and determination to meet these obligations competently vary across authorizers.[21] Authorizers must not only manage a range of technical tasks, they are also confronted with significant political pressures.[22]

While some authorizers may avow that "our state is unique and every charter school law is different," authorizers share common fundamental obligations and experience similar pressures even under different laws. Thus, it is important to assess how different authorizers are fulfilling their responsibilities and managing challenges. For example, thus far, the mayor of Indianapolis is the only mayor in the U.S. permitted to authorize charter schools.[23] Researchers and policy makers would benefit from studying this unique case. In cases where authorizers are not well-equipped or eager to fulfill their responsibilities, to what extent do policy makers hold authorizers accountable and consider permitting new types of authorizers?

Charter School Closures The ultimate accountability mechanism in the charter school arena is the possibility that a school may be required to close. About 11% of all charter schools ever opened have closed. As of 2007, 494 charter schools had closed since 1992 (Center for Education Reform, 2006b, 2007a). When a charter school closes, the public funds and human capital invested in the school have yielded a negative return. Most importantly, a charter school closure is disruptive for children enrolled in the school, many of whom may have already experienced disadvantage as low-income and minority students "at risk."

Some charter school advocates note that it is important for authorizers to address lagging charter schools by exercising their power to close such schools, even when sometimes faced with pleas from parents to keep failing charter schools open (Carroll, 2008). Another way to think about charter school closures is to focus on how they can be prevented in the first place. Indeed, it would be useful for researchers to analyze authorizer policies and practices pertaining to review and approval of charter school applications, oversight of charter schools and provision of technical assistance, and charter renewal. There have been few scholarly analyses of authorizer issues and there are some recent policy reports and advocacy pieces (Gau et al., 2006; Hill & Lake, 2002; National Association of Charter School Authorizers, 2004; Palmer, 2006; Vergari, 2000). Authorizer issues merit considerable new attention from both researchers and policy makers.

One of the largest gaps in the charter school research literature pertains to charter school closures. The research and policymaking communities would benefit from systematic analyses that identify patterns and trends among charter school closures. Some of the various questions that merit inquiry include the following: Are younger charter schools more likely to be closed than older schools? What are the charter school closure rates across different types of authorizers? What reasons do charter school leaders provide for closures of their schools? What do authorizers say about the schools that they have closed? Can particular charter school application, approval, oversight, and renewal processes be linked to higher or lower rates of charter school closures across authorizers? Research findings on these matters could be used to shape policies intended to minimize the number of charter schools that must be closed.

Student Achievement The equity, choice, deregulation, and accountability processes embodied in the charter school idea are all supposed to lead, ultimately, to improved student achievement among individual students and in the public school system overall. Analysts seeking to assess charter school effectiveness in terms of student achievement face significant technical challenges (Betts, Hill, & Charter School Achievement Consensus Panel, 2006). "Snapshot" analyses that examine aggregate student populations at a given point in time are less useful than studies that track the performance of the same students over time.

A substantial part of the political and scholarly discourse on charter school policy is focused on comparing student achievement in charter schools to that of traditional public schools (Carnoy, Jacobsen, Mishel, & Rothstein, 2005; Hassel & Terrell, 2006; Henig, 2008; Lubienski & Lubienski, 2006; Miron & Nelson, 2004; U.S. Department of Education, 2006). Given the many different types of charter schools that exist across varying state and local contexts, analyses of a given type of charter school are not generalizable to all charter schools.

Rather than focusing on comparisons between charter schools as a single form of public school and traditional public schools as a whole, it is more meaningful to compare different types of schools (Hassel & Terrell, 2006; Henig et al., 2005; Hess & Loveless, 2005; Hill, 2005; Kolderie, 2003; Plank & Sykes, 2004; Van Ryzin, 2007). In this manner, researchers can begin to isolate particular school characteristics and practices that are associated with favorable student outcomes. For example, do charter schools managed by particular companies or nonprofit organizations perform better than others? Moreover, are certain forms of charter school autonomy correlated with particular charter school outcomes? Researchers who found that Wisconsin charter schools performed somewhat better than traditional public schools suggest that authorizer type and quality of school leadership may be key factors in predicting charter school performance (Witte, Weimer, Shober, & Schlomer, 2007).

Politics of Charter School Policy and Research The charter school policy issues discussed in this chapter are not simply technical matters that might be resolved easily on

the basis of new research; they are subjects of substantial political controversy (Henig, 2005, 2008; Vergari, 2007). After all, charter school policy involves two huge political issues in public education: money and power. Indeed, some charter school leaders seek to partner with particular community organizations and companies in order to boost their own clout and reduce vulnerability in the face of often challenging political circumstances (Wohlstetter, Smith, & Malloy, 2005).

The fundamental task of charter school researchers is to address empirical questions such as those highlighted in this chapter. The research literature would be enhanced significantly by more contributions from researchers who do not have a direct stake in charter schooling and who strive to minimize the impact on the research process of their own biases regarding charter schooling.

Charter school policy makers, on the other hand, are charged with guarding the public interest and are confronted with challenging normative questions. Such questions include: How good is good enough to merit continued public investment in a charter school? What are the criteria by which charter schools should be judged? If a charter school yields about the same academic results as neighboring traditional public schools, but is safer and more appealing to families than other schools, does that justify continued public funding of the school?

The future of charter schooling depends largely on amendments to charter school laws and regulations, and there are heated political debates over the amount of regulation that is appropriate for charter schools (Fusarelli, 2003).[24] Policy makers are responsible for addressing the normative question of how much regulatory freedom is appropriate for schools that are publicly funded. Charter school researchers can assist policy makers by providing empirical data on extant and potential consequences of various types of regulation. For example, researchers can investigate whether charter schools that operate under particular forms of autonomy are more likely to flourish or close than other charter schools.

National aggregate data on the charter school sector mask significant heterogeneity within and across states. Thus, it would be useful if resources were allocated toward the maintenance of nonpartisan research centers in each state that could compile easily-accessible, timely, reliable state data on charter schools. Among other items, such data might include characteristics of charter school students, teachers, leaders, management entities, governing boards, and authorizers; number and types of charter schools per authorizer; and, charter school performance and closure information. If nonpartisan approaches can be ensured, it would be logical for state departments of education to fulfill this role.

The Center for Education Reform is presently one of the best sources of relatively up-to-date data on matters such as the contents of charter school laws, and the number of charter schools in each state. However, it is an advocacy entity. Other pro-charter organizations that release data and analysis include the National Alliance for Public Charter Schools, National Association of Charter School Authorizers, and the Thomas B. Fordham Institute. In contrast to the aforementioned entities, the Education Commission of the States (ECS) is noteworthy for its nonpartisan character. It offers some useful charter school information on its website. An enhanced ECS role in collecting and disseminating timely charter school information would be beneficial to the research and policymaking communities.

There are several scholarly research centers with a focus on charter schools. For example, the National Charter School Research Project at the University of Washington "aims to bring rigor, evidence, and balance to the national charter school debate" (National Charter School Research Project, 2008). The project is funded by about a dozen foundations and has an advisory board of academics, researchers, and practitioners. In addition to other publications, the project produces an annual report that examines facets of the charter school sector. The federally funded National Center on School Choice at Vanderbilt University conducts studies on school choice, including charter schools.[25] Moreover, the foundation-funded National Center for the Study of Privatization in Education at Teachers College, Columbia University conducts analyses and disseminates research on privatization initiatives including charter schools. Finally, a new academic journal, the *Journal of School Choice,* offers a venue for research and commentary focused on charter schools and other school choice reforms.

Conclusion

More than 15 years after the first charter school opened, charter schooling remains an intriguing, dynamic area of education policy. The charter school idea has received support from policy makers at the federal, state, and local levels of government in the United States. In many states, charter schools enjoy bipartisan political support, and charter schooling is becoming an institutionalized segment of public education.

While the charter school idea has not always been translated into policies and outcomes that advocates and school founders had preferred and anticipated, the concept has passed the "legitimacy test" in many public policy arenas. For example, under NCLB, a school that fails to make annual yearly progress for 5 consecutive years is designated as in "restructuring status" and required to establish alternative governance arrangements consistent with state law. Under the NCLB list of governance arrangements for a school required to restructure, the first option listed is to reopen the school as a charter school; this NCLB provision is one symbol of the legitimacy of the charter school idea.

As noted by Christensen and Lake (2007), analysts not long ago questioned whether charter schooling would endure as a feature of public education. In contrast, current policy debates on charter schools are focused largely on "the conditions under which they will exist, not their existence itself" (p. 6). However, there are now questions as to whether charter schools will continue to proliferate. Charter school growth rates have declined significantly over the years and some observers suggest that the growth rates may have peaked (p. 6).

There is substantial variation across the charter school sector in terms of state laws, charter school numbers, and enrollments; school founders, operators, and teachers; curricula and pedagogy; authorizers and accountability regimes; state and local political contexts; and student outcomes. Thus, it is important that researchers and policy makers avoid characterizing charter schools erroneously as composing a homogenous education reform.

As indicated throughout this chapter, there are many compelling charter school policy issues that merit substantial new research. More than 15 years into the charter school movement, there are huge gaps in the research literature on various key questions. For example, there is a need for much more research on charter school ripple effects, finance, authorizers, and closures. While charter schools have gained legitimacy as institutionalized features of public education, the performance of charter schools and their authorizers has been uneven and the charter school idea remains the subject of substantial political controversy. It is important that the research community investigate the various key questions posed in this chapter and disseminate research findings in ways that serve to inform the public and policy makers. Such a course of events would enhance opportunities for policy makers to adopt policies based on sound evidence and careful scholarly analysis as opposed to the passions and rhetoric of particular political interests on either side of ongoing debates over charter school policy.

Notes

1. Thanks to three anonymous reviewers for helpful comments on an earlier draft of this chapter.
2. In cases where demand exceeds capacity, admission is to occur by lottery. In some states, a charter school may offer admissions priority to students with a sibling already attending the charter school.
3. A charter term is often 5 years. Charter terms are designated in state law. Authorizers may choose to award or renew a charter for a shorter term but not for a term that is longer than permitted by state law.
4. Budde, a retired education professor and former school teacher and principal, introduced the term "charter school" in a 1974 conference paper and in writings in the late 1980s (Kolderie, 2005). In 1988, American Federation of Teachers President Al Shanker presented a "charter school" concept at an address to the National Press Club and in a *New York Times* column. Budde and Shanker (now both deceased) thought of charter schools as a form of teacher empowerment whereby teachers could implement new instructional ideas and strategies.
5. The Indianapolis mayor's office can authorize charter schools only within the city boundaries.
6. The 10 states were AL, KY, ME, MT, NE, ND, SD, VT, WA, WV.
7. Charter schools compose 3.5% of all public schools. Charter schools are more likely than traditional public schools to be small: 71% of charter schools enroll fewer than 300 students, compared with 31% of traditional public schools (U.S. Department of Education, 2007).
8. The numbers of charter schools per state were AZ (462), CA (637), FL (347), MI (241), OH (301), and TX (283) (Center for Education Reform, 2007a).
9. The 11 states and the number of charter schools per state were

AR (15), CT (19), DE (19), IA (8), MS (1), NH (8), OK (15), RI (11), TN (12), VA (3), and WY (3) (Center for Education Reform, 2007a).

10. A consulting firm named SchoolWorks has been hired by charter school authorizers in Massachusetts and New York State to conduct inspections of charter schools.

11. For a recent survey regarding parental satisfaction with charter schools, see Teske and Reichardt (2006).

12. Data from 2004-05 (U.S. Department of Education, 2007).

13. For additional analyses of school choice and civic values in several countries, see Wolf, Macedo, Ferrero, and Venegoni (2004).

14. A charter school authorizer may specify particular criteria for the boards of schools it authorizes.

15. These aggregate findings mask heterogeneity in the charter school sector.

16. According to Huerta et al. (2006), 52,000 students were enrolled in home-based charter schools in Alaska and California.

17. For a review of data and research issues pertaining to K-12 online learning, see Smith, Clark, and Blomeyer (2005).

18. See, for example, Nelson, Muir, and Drown (2000) and Vergari (2004).

19. Depending on state law, eligible authorizers include local and state school boards, university boards, the city of Milwaukee, the Indianapolis mayor's office, statutorily created charter school authorizer boards in Arizona and the District of Columbia, and nonprofit organizations in Minnesota and Ohio (see Palmer, 2006).

20. Such jurisdictions include Chicago, Colorado, Connecticut, New York, and Washington, DC.

21. For example, in 2007, the San Diego Unified School District superintendent indicated that the district could not fulfill its authorizer responsibilities adequately and asked the state to permit universities to authorize charter schools in the district (Gao, 2007).

22. For example, in 1998, the Texas State Board of Education rejected Texas Education Agency recommendations and responded to dozens of angry charter school applicants by approving charters for their proposed schools; several of these schools have since had serious problems (Benton & Hacker, 2007).

23. For a discussion of mayors as charter school authorizers, see Hassel (2004).

24. For a discussion of earlier political battles over school choice, including charter schools, see Morken & Formicola (1999).

25. Partner institutions include the Brookings Institution, Brown University, Harvard University, the National Bureau of Economic Research, the Northwest Evaluation Association, Stanford University, and the Center of Excellence in Leadership of Learning at the University of Indianapolis.

References

Abernathy, S. F. (2005). *School choice and the future of American democracy*. Ann Arbor: University of Michigan Press.

American Institutes for Research. (2006). *CSRQ center report on education service providers*. Washington, DC: Comprehensive School Reform Quality Center, American Institutes for Research.

Arsen, D., Plank, D., & Sykes, G. (1999). *School choice policies in Michigan: The rules matter*. East Lansing: Michigan State University.

Bell, C. (2005). *All choices created equal? How good parents select "failing" schools* (NCSPE Occasional Paper No. 106). New York: National Center for the Study of Privatization in Education.

Benton, J., & Hacker, H. K. (2007, June 4). Cheating's off the charts at charter schools: Loosely regulated schools among state's worst offenders on TAKS. *The Dallas Morning News*.

Betts, J., Hill, P. T., & Charter School Achievement Consensus Panel. (2006). *Key issues in studying charter schools and achievement: A review and suggestions for national guidelines*. Seattle: University of Washington, National Charter School Research Project.

Buckley, J., & Schneider, M. (2007). *Charter schools: Hope or hype?* Princeton, NJ: Princeton University Press.

Budde, R. (1974). *Education by charter*. Paper presented to Society for General Systems Research.

Budde, R. (1988). *Education by charter: Restructuring school districts*. San Francisco: Jossey-Bass.

Budde, R. (1989). Education by charter. *Phi Delta Kappan, 70*, 518–520.

Bulkley, K. E. (1999). Charter school authorizers: A new governance mechanism? *Educational Policy, 13*, 674–697.

Bulkley, K. E. (2004). Balancing act: Educational management organizations and charter school autonomy. In K. E. Bulkley & P. Wohlstetter (Eds.), *Taking account of charter schools: What's happened and what's next?* (pp. 121–141). New York: Teachers College Press.

Carnoy, M., & McEwan, P. J. (2003). Does privatization improve education? The case of Chile's national voucher plan. In D. N. Plank & G. Sykes (Eds.), *Choosing choice: School choice in international perspective* (pp. 24–44). New York: Teachers College Press.

Carnoy, M., Jacobsen, R., Mishel, L., & Rothstein, R. (2005). *The charter school dust-up: Examining the evidence on enrollment and achievement*. Washington, DC: Economic Policy Institute & Teachers College Press.

Carroll, T. W. (2008, February 13). *Charter schools in Albany: The Brighter Choice experience*. Presentation at Rockefeller Institute of Government, Albany, NY.

Center for Education Reform. (2006a). *Charter schools: Changing the face of American education; Part 2: Raising the bar on charter school laws, 2006 ranking and scorecard* (9th ed.). Washington, DC: Center for Education Reform.

Center for Education Reform. (2006b, February 27). Charter schools serve more poor children than district schools; accountability backed by closures data [Press release]. Washington, DC: Center for Education Reform.

Center for Education Reform. (2007a). *Charter school enrollment and closures, by state*. Washington, DC: Center for Education Reform.

Center for Education Reform. (2007b). Multiple authorizers in charter school laws. Washington, DC: Center for Education Reform.

Center for Education Reform. (2007c). *National charter school data; 2007–08 new school estimates*. Washington, DC: Center for Education Reform.

Center on Educational Governance. (2007). *Charter schools indicators*. Los Angeles: University of Southern California.

Christensen, J., & Lake, R. J. (2007). The national charter school landscape in 2007. In R. J. Lake (Ed.), *Hopes, fears, and reality: A balanced look at American charter schools in 2007* (pp. 1–15). Seattle: University of Washington, National Charter School Research Project.

Chubb, J. E. (1997). Lessons in school reform from the Edison Project. In D. Ravitch & J. P. Viteritti (Ed.), *New schools for a new century: The redesign of urban education* (pp. 86–122). New Haven, CT: Yale University Press.

Chubb, J. E., & Moe, T. M. (1990). *Politics, markets, and America's schools*. Washington, DC: Brookings Institution.

Education Commission of the States. (2003). *Cyber charter schools*. Denver, CO: Author.

Elacqua, G., Schneider, M., & Buckley, J. (2006). School choice in Chile: Is it class or the classroom? *Journal of Policy Analysis and Management, 25*, 577–601.

Finn, C. E., Jr., Manno, B. V., & Vanourek, G. (2000). *Charter schools in action: Renewing public education*. Princeton, NJ: Princeton University Press.

Finnigan, K. S. (2007). Charter school autonomy: The mismatch between theory and practice. *Educational Policy, 21*, 503–526.

Fiske, E. B., & Ladd, H. F. (2000). *When schools compete: A cautionary tale*. Washington, DC: Brookings Institution.

Frankenberg, E., & Lee, C. (2003, September 5). Charter schools and race: A lost opportunity for integrated education. *Education Policy Analysis Archives, 11*(32). Retrieved April 25, 2008, from http://epaa.asu.edu/epaa/v11n32/

Fusarelli, L. D. (2002). Texas: Charter schools and the struggle for equity. In S. Vergari (Ed.), *The charter school landscape* (pp. 175–191). Pittsburgh, PA: University of Pittsburgh Press.

Fusarelli, L. D. (2003). *The political dynamics of school choice: Negotiating contested terrain.* New York: Palgrave Macmillan.

Gao, H. (2007, March 24). Cohn wants to let others run charter schools; S.D. unified's leader sees huge demands on district. *San Diego Union-Tribune,* p. B1

Gau, R., Finn, C. E., Jr., & Petrilli, M. J. (2006). *Trends in charter school authorizing.* Washington, DC: Thomas B. Fordham Institute.

Gill, B. (2005). School choice and integration. In J. R. Betts & T. Loveless (Eds.), *Getting choice right: Ensuring equity and efficiency in education policy* (pp. 130–145). Washington, DC: Brookings Institution.

Goldhaber, D., Guin, K., Henig, J. R., Hess, F. M., & Weiss, J. A. (2005). How school choice affects students who do not choose. In J. R. Betts & T. Loveless (Eds.), *Getting choice right: Ensuring equity and efficiency in education policy* (pp. 101–129). Washington, DC: Brookings Institution.

Green, P. C., III, & Mead, J. F. (2004). *Charter schools and the law: Establishing new legal relationships.* Norwood, MA: Christopher-Gordon.

Hamilton, L. S., & Guin, K. (2005). Understanding how families choose schools. In J. R. Betts & T. Loveless (Eds.), *Getting choice right: Ensuring equity and efficiency in education policy* (pp. 40–60). Washington, DC: Brookings Institution.

Harris, D. C. (2006). Lowering the bar or moving the target: A wage decomposition of Michigan's charter and traditional public school teachers. *Educational Administration Quarterly, 42,* 424–460.

Hassel, B. C. (2004). *Fast break in Indianapolis: A new approach to charter schooling.* Washington, DC: Progressive Policy Institute.

Hassel, B. C., & Terrell, M. G. (2006). *Charter school achievement: What we know* (3rd ed.). Washington, DC: National Alliance for Public Charter Schools.

Hassel, B., Ziebarth, T., & Steiner, L. (2005). *A state policymaker's guide to alternative authorizers of charter schools.* Denver, CO: Education Commission of the States.

Henig, J. R. (1994). *Rethinking school choice: Limits of the market metaphor.* Princeton, NJ: Princeton University Press.

Henig, J. R. (2005). Understanding the political conflict over school choice. In J. R. Betts & T. Loveless (Eds.), *Getting choice right: Ensuring equity and efficiency in education policy* (pp. 176–209). Washington, DC: Brookings Institution.

Henig, J. R. (2008). *Spin cycle: How research is used in policy debates: The case of charter schools.* New York: Russell Sage Foundation and The Century Foundation.

Henig, J. R, Holyoke, T. T., Brown, H., & Lacireno-Paquet, N. (2005). The influence of founder type on charter school structures and operations. *American Journal of Education, 111,* 487–522.

Herdman, P. (2002). The Massachusetts charter school initiative: A model for public school accountability? In S. Vergari (Ed.), *The charter school landscape* (pp. 113–132). Pittsburgh, PA: University of Pittsburgh Press.

Hess, F. M., & Loveless, T. (2005). How school choice affects student achievement. In J. R. Betts & T. Loveless (Eds.), *Getting choice right: Ensuring equity and efficiency in education policy* (pp. 85-100). Washington, DC: Brookings Institution.

Hess, F. M., & Maranto, R. (2002). Letting a thousand flowers (and weeds) bloom: The charter story in Arizona. In S. Vergari (Ed.), *The charter school landscape* (pp. 54–73). Pittsburgh, PA: University of Pittsburgh Press.

Hill, P. T. (2005). Assessing achievement in charter schools. In R. J. Lake & P. T. Hill (Eds.), *Hopes, fears, & reality: A balanced look at American charter schools in 2005* (pp. 21–32). Seattle: University of Washington, National Charter School Research Project.

Hill, P. T., & Lake, R. J. (2002). *Charter schools and accountability in public education.* Washington, DC: Brookings Institution.

Horn, J., & Miron, G. (2000). *An evaluation of the Michigan charter school initiative: Performance, accountability and impact.* Kalamazoo, MI: Western Michigan University, The Evaluation Center.

Huerta, L. A., Gonzalez, M., & d'Entremont, C. (2006). Cyber and home school charter schools: Adopting policy to new forms of public schooling. *Peabody Journal of Education, 81,* 103–139.

Karsten, S., Ledoux, G., Roeleveld, J., Felix, C., & Elshof, D. (2003). School choice and ethnic segregation. *Educational Policy, 17,* 452–477.

Kellor, E. M. (2005, January 23). Catching up with the Vaughn express: Six years of standards-based teacher evaluation and performance pay. *Education Policy Analysis Archives, 13*(7). Retrieved April 25, 2008, from http://epaa.asu.edu/epaa/v13n7

Kolderie, T. (1990). *Beyond choice to new public schools: Withdrawing the exclusive franchise in public education.* Washington, DC: Progressive Policy Institute.

Kolderie, T. (1995). The charter idea: Update and prospects [Policy memo]. Saint Paul, MN: Center for Policy Studies.

Kolderie, T. (2003). "Chartering": How are we to evaluate it? Are charter laws working? *Education Week, 23*(6), 30, 40.

Kolderie, T. (2005). *Ray Budde and the origins of the "charter concept."* Washington, DC: Center for Education Reform.

Kowal, J., Hassel, E. A., & Hassel, B. C. (2007). *Teacher compensation in charter and private schools: Snapshots and lessons for district public schools.* Washington, DC: Center for American Progress.

Lacireno-Paquet, N., & Holyoke, T. T. (2007). Moving forward or sliding backward: The evolution of charter school policies in Michigan and the District of Columbia. *Educational Policy, 21,* 185–214.

Ladd, H. F. (2003). Introduction. In D. N. Plank & G. Sykes (Eds.), *Choosing choice: School choice in international perspective* (pp. 1–23). New York: Teachers College Press.

Lai, F. (2007, April). *The effect of winning a first-choice school entry lottery on student performance: Evidence from a natural experiment* (Occasional Paper No. 139). New York: National Center for the Study of Privatization in Education.

Lake, R. J. (2006). *Holding charter authorizers accountable: Why it is important and how it might be done* (NCSRP White Paper Series No. 1). Seattle: University of Washington, National Charter School Research Project.

Lankford, H., & Wyckoff, J. (2005). Why are schools racially segregated? Implications for school choice policy. In J. T. Scott (Ed.), *School choice and diversity: What the evidence says* (pp. 9–26). New York: Teachers College Press.

Little, D., Roberts, G., Ward, D., Bianchi, A., & Metheny, M. (2003). *Charter schools: Investment in innovation or funding folly?* Latham: New York State School Boards Association.

Lubienski, C. (2004). Charter school innovation in theory and practice: Autonomy, R&D, and curricular conformity. In K. E. Bulkley & P. Wohlstetter (Eds.), *Taking account of charter schools: What's happened and what's next?* (pp. 72–90). New York: Teachers College Press.

Lubienski, C., & Gulosino, C. (2007). *Choice, competition, and organizational orientation: A geo-spatial analysis of charter schools and the distribution of educational opportunities.* (NCSPE Occasional Paper No. 148). New York: National Center for the Study of Privatization in Education.

Lubienski, S. T., & Lubienski, C. (2006). School sector and academic achievement: A multi-level analysis of NAEP mathematics data. *American Educational Research Journal, 43,* 651–698.

McNiff, M. G., & Hassel, B. C. (2002). Charter schools in North Carolina: Confronting the challenges of rapid growth. In S. Vergari (Ed.), *The charter school landscape* (pp. 209–229). Pittsburgh, PA: University of Pittsburgh Press.

Mead, J. F. (2002). Wisconsin: Chartering authority as educational reform. In S. Vergari (Ed.), *The charter school landscape* (pp. 133–154). Pittsburgh, PA: University of Pittsburgh Press.

Mintrom, M. (2000). *Leveraging local innovation: The case of Michigan's charter schools.* East Lansing: Michigan State University.

Mintrom, M. (2002). Michigan's charter school movement: The politics of policy design. In S. Vergari (Ed.), *The charter school landscape* (pp. 74–92). Pittsburgh, PA: University of Pittsburgh Press.

Miron, G., & Applegate, B. (2007). Teacher attrition in charter schools. Tempe: Arizona State University, Education Policy Research Unit.

Miron, G., & Nelson, C. (2002). *What's public about charter schools? Lessons learned about choice and accountability.* Thousand Oaks, CA: Corwin Press.

Miron, G., & Nelson, C. (2004). Student achievement in charter schools: What we know and why we know so little. In K. E. Bulkley & P. Wohlstetter (Eds.), *Taking account of charter schools: What's happened and what's next?* (pp. 161–175). New York: Teachers College Press.

Molnar, A., Garcia, D. R., Bartlett, M., & O'Neill, A. (2006). *Profiles of for-profit education management organizations, eighth annual report, 2005–2006*. Tempe: Arizona State University, Commercialism in Education Research Unit.

Morken, H., & Formicola, J. R. (1999). *The politics of school choice*. Lanham, MD: Rowman & Littlefield.

Nathan, J. (1996). *Charter schools: Creating hope and opportunity for American education*. San Francisco: Jossey-Bass.

National Association of Charter School Authorizers. (2004). *Principles and standards for quality charter school authorizing*. Chicago: Author.

National Charter School Research Project. (2008). *About us*. Retrieved March 2, 2008, from http://www.ncsrp.org/cs/csr/print/csr_docs/index.htm

Nelson, F. H., Muir, E., & Drown, R. (2000). *Venturesome capital: State charter school finance systems*. Washington, DC: U.S. Department of Education.

Palmer, L. B. (2006). *"Alternative" charter school authorizers: Playing a vital role in the charter movement*. Washington, DC: Progressive Policy Institute.

Plank, D. N., & Sykes, G. (Eds.). (2003a). *Choosing choice: School choice in international perspective*. New York: Teachers College Press.

Plank, D. N., & Sykes, G. (2003b). Why school choice? In D. N. Plank & G. Sykes (Eds.), *Choosing choice: School choice in international perspective* (pp. vii–xxi). New York: Teachers College Press.

Plank, D. N., & Sykes, G. (2004). Conclusion. Lighting out for the territory: Charter schools and the school reform strategy. In K. E. Bulkley & P. Wohlstetter (Eds.), *Taking account of charter schools: What's happened and what's next?* (pp. 176–183). New York: Teachers College Press.

Podgursky, M., & Ballou, D. (2001). *Personnel policy in charter schools*. Washington, DC: Thomas B. Fordham Foundation.

Rhim, L. M., Ahearn, E. M., Lange, C. M., & McLaughlin, M. J. (2004). Balancing disparate visions: An analysis of special education in charter schools. In K. E. Bulkley & P. Wohlstetter (Eds.), *Taking account of charter schools: What's happened and what's next?* (pp. 142–157). New York: Teachers College Press.

Rhim, L. M., Lange, C. M., Ahearn, E. M., & McLaughlin, M.J. (2007). *Project intersect Research report no. 6: Survey of charter school authorizers*. College Park: University of Maryland.

Robelen, E. W. (2007). E-Learning curve: A boom in online education has school leaders and policymakers struggling to stay one click ahead. *Education Week, 26*(30), 34–36.

Rofes, E. (1998). *How are school districts responding to charter laws and charter schools?* Berkeley: University of California, Policy Analysis for California Education.

Rofes, E., & Stulberg, L. M. (Eds.). (2004). The emancipatory promise of charter schools: Toward a progressive politics of school choice. Albany: State University of New York Press.

Rose, L. C., & Gallup, A. M. (2006). The 38th annual Phi Delta Kappa/Gallup poll of the public's attitudes toward the public schools. *Phi Delta Kappan, 88*, 41–56.

RPP International. (2000). *The state of charter schools, 2000: Fourth-year report*. Washington, DC: U.S. Department of Education.

RPP International. (2001, June). *Challenge and opportunity: The impact of charter schools on school districts*. Washington, DC: United States Department of Education, Office of Educational Research and Improvement.

Salisbury, D., & Tooley, J. (Eds.). (2005). *What America can learn from school choice in other countries*. Washington, DC: Cato Institute.

Schneider, M., Teske, P., & Marschall, M. (2000). *Choosing schools: Consumer choice and the quality of American schools*. Princeton, NJ: Princeton University Press.

Shanker, A. (1988a, 31 March). Address to National Press Club. Washington, DC.

Shanker, A. (1988b, July 10). A charter for change. *New York Times,* p. E7.

Shober, A. F., Manna, P., & Witte, J. F. (2006). Flexibility meets accountability: State charter school laws and their influence on the formation of charter schools in the United States. *Policy Studies Journal, 34*, 563–587.

Smith, K. B. (2003). *The ideology of education: The commonwealth, the market, and America's schools*. Albany: State University of New York Press.

Smith, R., Clark, T., & Blomeyer, R. L. (2005). *A synthesis of new research on K–12 online learning*. Naperville, IL: Learning Point Associates, North Central Regional Educational Laboratory.

SRI International. (2002). *A decade of public charter schools*. Washington, DC: U.S. Department of Education.

SRI International. (2004). *Evaluation of the public charter schools program: Final report*. Washington, DC: U.S. Department of Education.

Teske, P., & Reichardt, R. (2006). Doing their homework: How charter school parents make their choices. In R. J. Lake & P. T. Hill (Eds.), *Hopes, fears, & reality: A balanced look at American charter schools in 2006* (pp. 1–9). Seattle: University of Washington, National Charter School Research Project.

Teske, P., Schneider, M., Buckley, J., & Clark, S. (2001). Can charter schools change traditional public schools? In P. E. Peterson & D. E. Campbell (Eds.), *Charters, vouchers and public education* (pp. 188–214). Washington, DC: Brookings Institution.

Teske, P., Schneider, M., & Cassese, E. (2005). Local school boards as authorizers of charter schools. In W. G. Howell (Ed.), *Besieged: School boards and the future of education politics* (pp. 129–149). Washington, DC: Brookings Institution.

Thomas B. Fordham Institute. (2005). *Charter school funding: Inequity's next frontier*. Dayton, OH: Author.

U.S. Department of Education. (2004). *Innovations in education: Successful charter schools*. Washington, DC: Office of Innovation and Improvement.

U.S. Department of Education. (2006). *A closer look at charter schools using hierarchical linear modeling* (NCES 2006-460). Washington, DC: National Center for Educational Statistics.

U.S. Department of Education. (2007). *The condition of education 2007* (NCES 2007-064). National Center for Education Statistics. Washington, DC: U.S. Government Printing Office.

U.S. General Accounting Office. (2003). Public schools: Comparison of achievement results for students attending privately managed and traditional schools in six cities. Washington, DC: Author.

Van Dunk, E., & Dickman, A. M. (2003). *School choice and the question of accountability: The Milwaukee experience*. New Haven, CT: Yale University Press.

Van Ryzin, M. J. (2007). *A call for an empirical taxonomy of schools* (Working paper). Minneapolis: University of Minnesota.

Vergari, S. (2000). The regulatory styles of statewide charter school authorizers: Arizona, Massachusetts, and Michigan. *Educational Administration Quarterly, 36*, 730–757.

Vergari, S. (Ed.). (2002a). *The charter school landscape*. Pittsburgh, PA: University of Pittsburgh Press.

Vergari, S. (2002b). New York: Over 100 charter applications in year one. In S. Vergari (Ed.), *The charter school landscape* (pp. 230–252). Pittsburgh, PA: University of Pittsburgh Press.

Vergari, S. (2004). Funding choices: The politics of charter school finance. In K. DeMoss & K. K. Wong (Eds.), *Money, politics and law* (pp. 151–168). Larchmont, NY: Eye on Education.

Vergari, S. (2007). The politics of charter schools. *Educational Policy, 21*, 15–39.

Wells, A. S. (Ed.). (2002). *Where charter school policy fails: The problems of accountability and equity*. New York: Teachers College Press.

Witte, J., Weimer, D., Shober, A., & Schlomer, P. (2007). The performance of charter schools in Wisconsin. *Journal of Policy Analysis and Management, 26*, 557–573.

Wohlstetter, P., & Anderson, L. (1994). What can U.S. charter schools learn from England's grant-maintained schools? *Phi Delta Kappan, 75*, 486–491.

Wohlstetter, P., Smith, J., & Malloy, C. L. (2005). Strategic alliances in action: Toward a theory of evolution. *Policy Studies Journal, 33*, 419–442.

Wohlstetter, P., Wenning, R., & Briggs, K. L. (1995). Charter schools in the United States: The question of autonomy. *Educational Policy, 9*, 331–358.

Wolf, P. J. (2005). School choice and civic values. In J. R. Betts & T. Loveless (Eds.), *Getting choice right: Ensuring equity and efficiency in education policy* (pp. 210–244). Washington, DC: Brookings Institution.

Wolf, P. J., & Macedo, S. (Eds.), Ferrero, D.J., & Venegoni, C. (2004). *Educating citizens: International perspectives on civic values and school choice*. Washington, DC: Brookings Institution.

Ziebarth, T. (2007). *Top ten charter communities by market share* (2nd annual ed.). Washington, DC: National Alliance for Public Charter Schools.

39

Vouchers

JOHN F. WITTE
University of Wisconsin–Madison

In the United States there has always been a shifting balance between private and public schools (Witte, 2000, pp. 29–31). Fully funded public schools were not commonplace until after our Civil War. Private schools developed independently, with a surge of Catholic schools as a mass private school movement between 1880 and 1920. Private schools grew to between 10% and 12% of our Kindergarten through Grade 12 school population by the 1950s. It has remained remarkably stable since, with the religious composition remaining at about 80%, although the denominational composition has varied since the 1960s.[1]

The foundation of the modern movement for vouchers is rightly focused on Milton Friedman's (1955) article in a National Bureau of Education Research (NBER) publication. It was later republished in very similar form in his classic, and widely disseminated volume *Capitalism and Freedom* (Freidman, 1962). The arguments of the article were very simple. First, because of a pure market failure that produced spillover effects for education that positively affect the community (a neighborhood effect), education qualified for public subsidy as opposed to a purely private system in which all families would purchase the desired amount of education for their children. Second, he criticized the monopoly control of education that might have been justified earlier in rural communities where only one school could be supported. But applied to most modern settings, that system was devoid of consumer input or reaction and provided no incentives for public schools to offer more efficient services. Instead he proposed:

> Governments could require a minimum level of schooling financed by giving parents vouchers redeemable for a specified maximum sum per child if spent on "approved" educational services. Parents would then be free to spend this sum and any additional sum they themselves provided on purchasing educational services from an "approved" institution of their own choice. The educational services could be rendered by private enterprises operated at a profit, or by non-profit institutions. The role of the government would be limited to insuring that schools met certain minimum standards, such as inclusion of minimum common content in their programs, much as it now inspects restaurants to insure that they maintain minimum sanitary standards. (Friedman, 1962, p. 89)

The "voucher" was to be equal to the per pupil expenditures in their current local district.

This chapter will summarize what we know, as of 2007, of the status of major educational voucher type systems in countries throughout the world. As we will see, voucher plans differ considerably and thus it is difficult to provide a common definition in practice. However, for general discussion in the first part of this chapter I will conceptually rely on the original Friedman proposal as defining a *universal voucher program*. In that proposal, every child received a voucher for approximately the full cost of funding a child in the current public school system. That voucher could be used to "purchase" education from any school provider.[2] Providers would be unconstrained in terms of accepting or rejecting applicants and would be allowed to charge in excess of the voucher amount. Finally, the system would be generally unregulated in terms of curriculum content, teachers, length of time in school, and so forth.

I modify that definition to allow for situations where, in practice, vouchers are only given to those going to new schools (private or public) under specific programmatic conditions. Examples in the United States would be vouchers in Milwaukee, Cleveland, or Florida to go to private schools or public school vouchers for students in need of improvement under No Child Left Behind. The presumption is that other students would continue to go to their assigned area (however done) public school or private schools using private resources. This admittedly arbitrary definition does not include nations or programs in which governments routinely subsidize both public and private schools. This restricts the general discussion considerably by excluding, for example, many European systems that fund all forms of schools, but also often heavily regulate them. These programs are rarely referred to as voucher systems, and often the distinction between public and private schools are blurred.

This chapter is organized in a very straightforward fashion. I first review the major points of contention in the voucher debate, providing both arguments for and against; I then briefly describe the legal issues as they pertain to the United States. Following that, I describe the types of voucher programs that have been instituted. I then review the empirical evidence on voucher research for a select set of countries, both fulfilling the definition given above and for which rigorous research has been undertaken. I conclude with brief remarks concerning the future of vouchers and voucher research.

The Voucher Debate

Arguments for Vouchers There are several arguments for vouchers. The first two invoke efficiency (Friedman's original emphasis) and equality. In addition, there is an argument for vouchers apart from efficiency and organizational improvements that stresses opportunity and freedom of choice—often for families who have little.

The main efficiency argument involves not so much moving toward a better system, than moving away from a current monopoly system that is bureaucratically controlled and operates without primary regard for the quality of education produced. It is this argument, echoing Friedman's initial position, which was central to the voucher proposal contained in the landmark book by John Chubb and Terry Moe (1990), *Politics, Markets, and America's Schools.* In this view, because professional school administrators and teachers unions dominate the system, there are no incentives to improve, and considerable incentives to retain the status quo. Going one step further, administrators and teachers may add resources for themselves (shirking) because there is little accountability in the system. Parents cannot exert themselves because they cannot afford (in general) to go outside the system and the system assigns their children to a school, usually based on residential location. Their only choice is to move their residence to find better schools. And it is the poorest, who cannot make such moves, who suffer the most in failing schools.

The second argument favoring vouchers is that they will improve overall educational quality as schools have to compete for students, and parents shop for the greatest educational opportunities for their children. Quality of educational outcomes is the equivalent metric for both price and profit. Parents will seek to maximize quality as they define it for their children; schools will maximize quality for the students in the school.[3] As this process is replicated across the system, unsuccessful schools that do not attract students will go out of business. The remaining schools will be those providing the greatest quality of results and thus the overall quality will continue to rise.

Following these arguments, the institution of a voucher system, as described above, would simultaneously produce improved quality and eliminate the public educational monopoly. I separate these two arguments because they are advanced in policy and political debates in very different ways. And, one could envision ways to greatly reduce the "monopoly problem" without resorting to vouchers.[4] Similarly one could use the monopoly-busting argument to favor vouchers, without believing the quality maximization arguments held by market enthusiasts.

A final argument is really independent of the efficiency-based arguments. That argument is a normative argument that specifies that education is a public good that should be distributed equally—at least equally in terms of opportunities for children to excel to the level of their capability. Educational opportunity should not be dependent on exogenous family wealth or income that allows some families to purchase private education or to move to wealthy neighborhoods where schools are well funded, quality teachers want to work, and peer effects insure an overall high quality of education. In this argument, those who do not have wealth are trapped in the poorest schools in the poorest neighborhoods and vouchers would provide them something of a ticket out of those schools. People who stress this argument may favor *targeted voucher* programs, making vouchers available only to low-income families in specific geographic areas.

Arguments against Vouchers The most consistent, general argument against vouchers is that they will primarily benefit the most well-off in societies at the expense of the least well-off. The economically well-off, who are often the dominant racial group, will use vouchers to subsidize their children's education and, as a consequence, drain resources from those left in traditional public schools.

The second and third arguments against vouchers, derivative from the first, are that vouchers will leave public schools with the most difficult-to-educate students, and that will mean racial and/or income segregation of "schools left behind." Schools that serve the rich will remain close to their neighborhoods, but the schools will now have even more resources than before (as private and public schools become amalgamated), and they will be able to select students they want either through overt admission requirements, covert omission procedures, or through requiring tuition add-ons to drive away the poor. The end result will be a highly balkanized education system with schools in poor neighborhoods with reduced funds and the hardest to educate children, and schools in wealthy neighborhoods with enhanced resource advantages and with open license to select the "best" students.[5] Both because of the link between socioeconomic status (SES) and race, and because of racial prejudice, the results may also lead to increased segregation by race.

A fourth argument against universal vouchers is less often used, but may have considerable impact politically in the United States. The argument is that by introducing vouchers, you may be switching some private education to public funds and in essence paying people with public money to do what they would have done on their own. This increases the total public cost of education and, because private school parents are considerably more well-off than public school parents, subsidizes upward in the income stream. This argument resonates to a degree both with egalitarians and those who favor smaller government and fewer taxes.[6]

Legal Issues Obviously legal issues with vouchers vary from country to country. And in this regard America is quite unique. The uniqueness occurs in two ways. The First Amendment to the U.S. Constitution begins with the following clause: "Congress shall make no law respecting the establishment of religion, or prohibiting the free exercise thereof…" The first phrase is termed the establishment clause, and the latter the free exercise clause. These clauses were interpreted relative to government support for private school in a series of Supreme Court rulings. The most important case until recently was *Lemon v. Kurtzman* (1971). That decision established a tripartite test for determining if government actions in support of private schools were constitutional. The tests, all of which had to be met included: "1) the action must promote a secular purpose; 2) its primary effect must neither advance nor inhibit religion; and 3) there must be no excessive entanglement between the state and religion" (Witte, 2000, p. 21). Until *Zelman v. Simmons-Harris* (2002), in which the Supreme Court ruled the Ohio voucher program constitutional on a 5–4 vote, the *Lemon* test was thought to be a barrier to voucher programs that included religious private schools.

Since *Zelman* there has not been the outpouring of new voucher programs primarily because of clauses in the various state constitutions. Many of these were added late in the 19th and early in the 20th centuries as a result of a nationwide campaign by Congressman James Blaine (R-ME). He argued the rapid growth of Catholic schools would put undue pressure on states to provide financial support for the new schools being created by parishes and dioceses throughout the country. These "Blaine Amendments" took various forms, but were geared specifically at barring the use of state money to further religious schools. Thus they were much more direct than the U.S. First Amendment, which relied on shifting interpretations to apply to schools. State constitutions also often have clauses that specify that the state shall provide "free and uniform" or "free and equal" education (Huerta & d'Entremont, 2007). As of this writing, the state of Florida is appealing a state court ruling barring its voucher program based on such a clause in the Florida Constitution. Thus even with a monumental U.S. Supreme Court ruling favoring vouchers, they still face considerable legal challenges.

Types of Voucher Programs

There are probably as many types of voucher programs as there are programs. However, five distinctions, with one mostly relevant to the United States, provide broad dif-

ferentiating categories. Relevant differences are whether the program is: (a) financed by giving parents vouchers or by public payments directly to choice schools, (b) either universal or targeted, (c) includes both public and private schools, (d) includes religious private schools, and (e) the degree of state regulation over the schools.

Financing Choice Schools The classic model of vouchers portrayed by Friedman would have provided families with vouchers to send their children to any school (public or private) of their choice. This provides the consumers with funds to purchase the educational product they desire. A much older form of financing in many countries simply pays to support all schools, or all schools accepting a specified degree of government regulation and supervision. As we shall see in the next section, this has been the case for a long time in many European countries. Whether this matters in terms of the market nature of these systems probably relies less on the exact form of the payment and more on the degree of choice and regulation in the various systems. I doubt very much that Friedman would applaud the Dutch or French systems, which require considerable centralized regulation of all schools accepting financing.

Targeted and Universal Voucher Programs The definition used in the introduction exemplifies a universal voucher program. It applies to all schools, blurring, if not eliminating, the differences between public and private schools. It also applies to all students, providing each with a public voucher to be spent on education in the school of their choice, assuming they are accepted.

Targeted vouchers are constrained by any of a number of conditions. The most common are geographic and income restrictions. In the United States and Germany, any state-created program would be targeted to the extent it would only operate in the state. However, all voucher programs in the United States have also been targeted geographically (Milwaukee, Cleveland, Washington, DC) or by student or family characteristics (income or disability status in Florida), or both.[7] The voucher program in Colombia is also income-targeted.

Inclusion of Public and Private Schools Although the original and most common meaning for voucher programs entails vouchers that may be used in private schools (some only in private schools), there is also the possibility that a voucher system could be limited to choices among only public schools. This is important currently in the United States because it is an option under the No Child Left Behind legislation for students in schools that fail to achieve Adequate Yearly Progress. This option, which rarely entails actual vouchers rather than simply a school transfer, is parallel to various types of intra- and inter-district open enrollment programs.

Inclusion of Religious Private Schools Perhaps most relevant is the inclusion of religious private schools because of the constitutional issues discussed above. Because of this the first voucher program enacted in the United States in Milwaukee was originally limited to only secular private schools. Such limitations have also been enacted or suggested in other countries. The religious issue also involves the degree of regulation of voucher schools in that some religious orders and sects may choose not to accept vouchers because they fear their schools will lose their unique religious qualities.

Regulation of Voucher Schools   American readers may be somewhat confused by this categorization because schools in the United States are regulated primarily by the states, and because most private schools are religious schools, states require only minimal regulation of them.[8] That is not the case, however, in most countries of the world. For example, in one of the countries with the oldest voucher type program—The Netherlands—from the beginning private schools, religious or not, were provided public funds, but also had to follow state guidelines on its national curriculum, take state tests, and be subject to state inspections. In essence, they were treated very much like their purely public school counterparts. As we will see in the next section, that is the case in several countries in which voucher programs have been enacted.

Voucher and School-Choice Programs in International Context

Many countries have introduced a variety of school-choice programs, some going back centuries. There are important program differences and different levels of research across these countries. Some, such as the Netherlands, have been in existence for a very long time and provide comprehensive choices across both public and private schools. Some are recent, such as the United States, and provide geographically and income-targeted vouchers. Some countries, but very few, have instigated educational choice programs, and later abandoned them.[9]

In keeping with the focus on vouchers in this paper, the countries discussed below met three criteria: (a) public subsidies must include subsidies for private schools, (b) parents must have choice beyond an assigned geographic or catchment area, and (c) there must be some quality research on either the segregation or student outcome effects of the program (hopefully both). The subsidy could occur directly to parents in the form of a voucher (as Friedman suggested), or, following application and qualification of the child, go directly to the school. The intent is not to provide detailed critical analysis of these programs or their apparent impacts, but rather to provide a snapshot, as of 2007, of vouchers and private school subsidies and what research tells us about the impacts of these programs.

My concerns with these descriptions are to first categorize the programs, then their apparent impacts on segregation of students by race or income, and finally what is known or their impact on student achievement, both in choice schools and more broadly across the educational systems.[10] A tabular outline is presented in Table 39.1.

The Netherlands   The oldest system of educational choice in modern times is in the Netherlands. It dates to the Pacification Act of 1917, which ended considerable religious turmoil and established the system of "pillarization." That system divided the country by religious denomination and included separate religious groups, social structures, economic organizations, and schools. As a result of the act, all schools were subsidized by the state, including both Protestant and Catholic schools. However, unlike private schools in the United States, religious private schools in the Netherlands are subject to regulations of teaching requirements, working conditions, general curriculum and time devoted to subjects, national examinations, and budget matters. Schools are not allowed to have additional tuition or exceed nationally set budgets. However, private schools are run by autonomous boards and schools control the precise content of what is taught and how (Dijkstra, Dronkers, & Karsten, 2001, pp. 6–7).

Because class differences have never been large in the Netherlands, and because of resource equality between schools, the level of between school segregation was never extreme. For example, a study by Dors, Karsten, Ledoux, and Steen (1991) estimated that only 23% of the primary schools experienced concentration by socioeconomic class. However, Protestant, Dutch Reform, and Catholic schools developed a reputation of higher achievement in some of the larger cities. The curious fact about the Dutch system is that the majority of students continue to attend private religious schools even as the post-World War II society has become extremely secular. Some researchers have speculated that the Reform and Catholic schools remain popular because they continue to admit high-achieving students—a fact well-known to parents (Karsten & Teelken, 1996; Dijkstra, Dronkers, & Karsten, 2001).

A recent development may be changing the equitable nature of Dutch schools to a degree. That development is the increasing immigration into the Netherlands of families from Muslim nations. They have created and there seems to be unmet demand for Muslim schools. These recent immigrants tend to be poorer than the average Dutch families and thus there is a degree of ethnic and socioeconomic segregation occurring. The numbers, however, as of the early 1990s were relatively small with only 29 Muslim or Hindu schools in the country (Dors et al., 1991).

A consistent set of research findings based on data up through the 1980s indicate that Protestant and Catholic school students, after controlling for background characteristics and selection effects, did better on cognitive tests than students in other private schools or in public schools (see Dronkers, 2001, pp. 12–13 for a summary). However, a recent study by Dijkstra, Driessen, and Veenstra (2001), using more recent data and better controls for selection, found essentially no differences in language and math scores once appropriate controls were included.

TABLE 39.1
School-Choice and Vouchers in International Context

Country	Program Type	Opportunity and Segregation Effects	Achievement Effects	Effects on Non-Voucher Schools
Netherlands	Public and private funding of schools; government regulations on testing and curriculum affect all schools	Many non-religious attending religious schools; SES segregation changing with Muslim immigrants.	Mixed: Catholic and Protestant schools more effective; but some public and other religious do not vary.	None exist. Longstanding, universal voucher system.
Scotland	Open enrollment and public funding of secondary schools and many elementary schools since 1982.	Segregation by religion (Catholic), which also leads to segregation by SES (poorer Catholic schools).	Based on 1986 study, after proper controls, poorer Catholic schools do better than public schools.	NA
England and Wales	Subsidies of all schools willing to submit to some regulations. Independent schools may opt out and religious schools pay 15% of costs.	Mixed results. A number of small studies found cream skimming and covert selection. Nationwide study findings lessening segregation over period of reforms.	Very few reliable public-private or school type difference studies.	Nationwide study using 2000 data find improvements in passing national secondary school exams from 1985–2000.
Chile	Universal vouchers for admission to public or private schools with only a small sector of private independent schools.	Data on schools prior to the 1980 reform do not exist. But strong evidence exists that the current system is highly stratified with poorer, less education and lower achieving students in public schools.	Mixed results of numerous studies. Most recent studies demonstrate public schools do at least as well or better than private schools under "uniform" conditions.	Suggestive studies that vouchers harmed public schools with no system-wide improvement.
Colombia	Income targeted vouchers for sixth graders already accepted into private schools.	Elite private schools (40%) did not accept voucher students. The remainder was very similar to public school counterparts.	Voucher winners did better on achievement tests, grade retention, college entrance, and entrance exams.	NA
United States	Targeted voucher programs in several cities and Florida.	None. If anything the targeted nature of these programs have led to more opportunities for the poor and racial minorities. Studies vary on the effects on school segregation.	Very mixed results ranging from very positive (one study of Milwaukee in 1996) to no differences between voucher and public schools (Milwaukee, Cleveland, Washington, DC).	Study results on Milwaukee are mixed. One study (Hoxby, 2003) finds positive results of vouchers for public schools. A more recent study (Carnoy et al., 2007) finds no effects. Studies in Florida find response activity in failing schools, but hard to attribute to vouchers.

Source: Compiled by author from works cited in this chapter.

Scotland Prior to the election of Margaret Thatcher in 1979, school assignment in England, Wales, and Scotland was almost exclusively based on residency in a catchment area. The local education authority (LEA) controlled schools in those areas. With the 1980 Education Act applying to England and Wales, that began to change. In addition to a number of other changes, the act for the first time allowed families to easily enroll their children in public schools outside of their assignment area. In 1981 the act was applied to Scotland and extended that right to Scottish children. In addition it made it more difficult than the 1980 act for local educational authorities to deny parental requests for transfer to schools outside of the LEA. Scottish law also provided for compulsory appeals in the case of denial.

Sociologists and education experts were immediately drawn to the radical changes in education policy in the United Kingdom. Douglas Willms and Frank Echols (1992) were among the first to report results on the segregating effects of school transfers. Utilizing data from three LEAs, they prepared samples of students who stayed in their assigned schools and of those who chose to move. They found that the "stayers" were consistently of lower socioeconomic status that the "choosers." This applied to both mothers' and fathers' education and occupation. Also, for the one sample for which they had prior test data, the stayers scored lower on verbal reasoning. This also had an impact on the receiving schools in which mean socioeconomic status and educational attainment increased (Willms & Echols, 1992). A later study, relying on four large surveys of secondary school students between 1985 and 1991 demonstrated again that choice was being exercised by more middle and upper SES students than working-class students, that students tended to select schools with higher SES student bodies, and that between school social class segregation was increasing

(Willms, 1996). These studies confirmed earlier work by Adler and his colleagues (Adler & Raab, 1988; Adler, Petch, & Tweedie, 1989).

This general conclusion as it applies to Scotland was not reversed by subsequent research. Given the difficulty of schools in denying requests for transfer, the patterns of increasing segregation are primarily the result of parent choice and not school decisions. As we will see, that is not the case in some other countries.

There has been only one study, using proper controls for selection, on the differences in outcomes by sector for public and private schools. Students in Catholic schools have remained relatively poor compared to the few students in other religious schools or students in public schools. That has resulted in lower absolute test scores and a reputation of poor Catholic schools in Scotland. However, McPherson and Willms (1986) found that once controls for background and other factors were introduced, Catholic students did significantly better than other Scottish students.

England and Wales The array of types of schools and parental choice in England and Wales has increased considerably in the last 25 years, beginning with the Education Act of 1980 and the Education Reform Act (ERA) of 1988.[11] At present there are four different sets of schools, and some shifting between categories is allowed. They are: (a) maintained schools, (b) grant-maintained schools, (c) voluntary schools, and (d) independent schools. Maintained schools are by far the most numerous and can be considered the closest to "traditional public" schools in other countries. They were traditionally run by geographically determined LEAs which established admission criteria that were usually rigidly based on their catchment area. That all changed with open enrollment created by the 1980 and 1988 acts. ERA also established grant-maintained schools of several forms. These were schools outside of the maintained school's orbit that were provided financing by the central government. Some of these schools have subsided under the Blair Labor government, but have been replaced in part by public-private partnership schools (Machin & Wilson, in press).

Voluntary schools are funded by LEAs but sponsored by other organizations, the most prevalent being the Church of England or the Roman Catholic Church. Admission to these schools may be affected by student/parent membership in the sponsoring organization. The sponsors must pay at least 15% of costs of the school.

Finally, independent schools were the traditional private (called "public") schools, often in the past providing education for the English elite. All of these schools prior to 1980 had considerable, if not exclusive, control over their admission. That is still the case for most independent schools, although some of them have crossed over into grant-maintained status. Thus, the legislation in the 1980s and 1990s dramatically loosened up the system to the point that a team of leading scholars of educational choice has called the system "a national 'voucher' scheme" (Gorard, Fitz, & Taylor, 2001).

Research on England and Wales is not as conclusive as that on Scotland. The most important research on England and Wales followed the Education Reform Act of 1988. Research conducted in the early 1990s focused often on the choice process and the factors parents considered in choosing schools. That research tended to indicate that, as in Scotland, parents would choose to align their children with children at or above their socioeconomic status. In a famous study centered at Kings College in Oxford, very different processes of school selection were described for working, middle-, and upper-class families. Thus the early research suggested that selective enrollment would occur (e.g., Gerwitz, Ball, & Bowe, 1995).

Although this research was challenged on methodological grounds, it, combined with research on a limited number of districts, suggested that selective enrollment, using overt or covert methods, was widespread (see West, Pennell, & Edge, 1997, for a summary). Recently Stephen Gorad, John Fitz, and Chris Taylor challenged that conclusion using large national data bases (Gorard & Fitz, 2000; Gorard et al., 2001). Their studies used census data on all schools at both the primary and secondary levels. The data are for every year from 1989 through 2000. The data include school aggregates for poverty, race, first language, and special needs. Regardless of the aggregate measure they use or the type of index of segregation, their results indicate a considerable decline in segregation by poverty, ethnicity, etc. from 1990 to 1996, with increases occurring again after 1997. Despite the later increases, which may have been partly induced by a 1996 act partially reintroducing catchment area assignment by LEAs, segregation appears to be lower in year 2000 than in 1990.

Thus the current results for England and Wales are mixed. Early research, based on a few districts, concluded that selective enrollment seemed to have produced greater segregation by socioeconomic status. However, more recent national data, that include the census of all school populations, point in the opposite direction. With changes introduced by the Blair government, that may be reversing somewhat.

There is also some confusion over the effects of increased choice on student outcomes. First, there has not been the focus on the public-private division that has so mesmerized American scholars. Several smaller studies early in the process argued that achievement effects followed the segregation effects. They often lacked the types of controls that make it difficult to separate education effects from selection effects. The recent study by Gorard, Fitz, and Taylor (2001) looked at the longer-term trends in countrywide outcomes. They relied on national tests called the General Certificate of Secondary Education (GCSE), which are given primarily to 15-year-olds in a many subject areas. They provided data from 1985 to 2000 for the percentages of students getting five or more "good passes" on these subject-certifying exams. The percentage of students achieving at least that goal increased linearly from 26.9% in 1985 to 46.4% in 2000 (Gorard et al., 2001, Table 2, p. 20). Although it is hard to argue that this does not represent some progress, as they note, there have been major changes in these examinations over this period involving both the testing format and scoring and the number of subject-area tests being offered.

While the research on both segregative and outcome effects is somewhat difficult to judge in England and Wales, there is no denying that the English education scene today is far removed from the education system of several decades ago. Parents have widespread choices, new and innovative schools have emerged, and there appears to be a considerable improvement across the broad population at least in terms of secondary school success.

Chile Chile's educational choice and voucher reforms began in 1980 when the military regime headed by Pinochet took power. When the reforms were concluded, the educational system contained two important characteristics: (a) each student received a considerable subsidy that would go to the school they attended; and (b) subsidies could be used at public or private schools including religious and secular schools. The subsidy was large enough so that most private schools would not cost families anything. Based on a study by McEwan and Carnoy (2000, p. 218), the reforms produced six types of schools, five of which accepted vouchers: (a) public schools run by the national Department of Education, (b) by municipal corporations (58.5% of students in 1996), (c) Catholic private schools (10.3%), (d) Protestant private schools (1.5%), (e) nonreligious private schools (21.4%), and (f) private schools that did not take vouchers (8.3%).

Unfortunately, no enrollment statistics by social class seem to exist prior to the reforms. However, all the existing post-reform data does point toward considerable selective enrollment based on social class and socioeconomic status. This includes a study by Parry of 50 basic (grades 1--8) public and private schools in Santiago and national level data cited by Parry (1996) and McEwan and Carnoy (2000). The Santiago study by Parry was based primarily on interviews with principals of the schools concerning the characteristics of their student body and their admission practices. The differences in both were striking between public and private schools. Private voucher schools reported that their students came from families with considerably higher socioeconomic status on all measures such as income, parents' education, and occupation. What may be even more revealing is what the principals had to say about admission practices. For example, private schools were four or five times more likely than public schools to use entrance exams or minimum grade criteria for admission. Public schools were also much more likely to have nutrition programs and differential classes for those with learning disabilities than private schools. These would, of course, benefit and attract the poor more than the well off (Parry, 1996, Table 1). Parry also states that because education policies in the 1960s under Allende were much more conducive to equity, the selective enrollment practices she described must have been a result of the Pinochet reforms (p. 825).

National data from 1990, reported by numerous researchers (Parry, 1996; McEwan & Carnoy, 2000; McEwan, 2001; Bellei, in press) clearly indicate considerable differences in average socioeconomic status and parental education between public, subsidized private schools, and non-voucher private schools. The differences between either public or subsidized private schools and non-voucher private schools were extremely large.[12] It is well known in Chile that these tuition-supported private schools are more or less exclusively for the very wealthy and have been for many decades.

Current research by Bellei (in press) traces the impact on achievement of both differences in school selection (admissions tests), school retention policies (e.g., expulsion for not passing a grade), and school-level variables such as mean school parent education and books in a household. Bellei also analyzed the enormous between-school variation in Chile compared to other countries.[13] The conclusion was: "this very large between-schools variation explains why school-level predictors are so successful to estimate Chilean students' test-scores: Chilean students' academic achievement is highly predictable depending on the schools they attend" (Bellei, in press, p. 28). Thus although the evidence on the effects of introduction of vouchers per se is indirect, it is quite clear that schools in Chile are currently very stratified by socioeconomic status.

Studies of the effectiveness of vouchers in Chile are extremely mixed. A number of studies have found positive effects for private schools (voucher and non-voucher) relative to the public sector. Bellei summarizes 10 studies that make 13 comparisons between public and subsidized private schools. Of those, seven studies found significant achievement score results favoring private schools, five no difference, and one favored public schools. However, the sizes of effects, sometimes using the same data, ranged considerably. When cost effectiveness is taken into account, McEwan and Carnoy (2000) found the slightly higher test scores in the private schools were offset by lower public-school costs. McEwan (2001) also finds that when controlling both for student background factors and a selection correction, the advantages of private schools become statistically insignificant. In the most recent study, when Bellei (in press) controls for student background, school-level selection policies, peer effects, and parent cultural capital, public schools outperform private schools on mathematics and language tests. As indicated above, that work emphasizes the point that school differences in selection and retention, and the social, economic, and academic composition of schools matters a great deal in Chile.

Finally, there are several studies attempting to determine if the voucher system has had a positive or negative effect on public schools and on the system as a whole. Hsieh and Urquiola (2003) conducted studies at the commune level and found the density of private schools after vouchers were introduced was related to lower public school achievement. Similarly Gallego (2002, 2004) attempted the same type of study but used instrumental variables to control for private school density (the number of priests per capita). All these studies concluded that the voucher reforms hurt public schools and offered no evidence that the system as a whole was any better off. Bellei notes that these studies have statistical problems and rely only on post-reform data. Thus without reliable pre-voucher data this issue will remain very difficult to study.

Chile remains one of the premier voucher countries in that the voucher system is truly universal, with only a small private sector refusing vouchers. The results have clearly not produced equality between schools, which are highly stratified by social class and achievement. It is unclear that private schools are doing better than public schools when efforts are made to put them on uniform footing in terms of selection and school composition. Thus Chile stands at best as an uncertain poster child for universal vouchers.

Colombia Colombia enacted a targeted voucher program (lowest one-third in income deciles) in 1991 in part to aid in relieving crowding in public schools. Private schools had excess capacity (Bellei, in press). By 1997 the program had grown to 125,000 students. As part of the program, oversubscribed schools (most of them) had to select by lottery from applicant students who had already been admitted to a private school. Thus a large natural experiment was established. Several research teams have studied the results.

Although 40% of the private schools did not accept voucher students, a study of the differences between those that did and public schools indicated that resources, test scores, class sizes, and technology were very similar between the private-voucher schools and the public schools (King, Rawlings, Gutierrez, Pardo, & Torres, 1997).[14] There is no evidence on student-level variables, but the income-targeting aspect of the program almost ensures that the program would not have a negative impact on segregation by school sector, and it may have improved the situation.

In terms of outcomes, several research groups have done quite sophisticated work. The analyses are necessarily limited to "the intent to treat" comparison between voucher winners and losers, rather than a direct treatment effect of attending a private school. That is because although they can observe winners who declined, they cannot observe losers who may have declined the voucher. This creates a selection bias problem. The limitation is somewhat mitigated by the fact that 90% of the winners actually attended private schools using the voucher.

The results between winners and losers are quite consistent and favorable for voucher winners. They were more likely to remain in private schools after 3 years, have lower grade retention, score higher on achievement tests, and more likely to take and score higher on a national college entrance examination (Angrist, Bettinger, Bloom, King, & Kremer, 2002; Angrist, Bettinger, & Kremer, 2006; Bettinger, in press). Since nearly 90% of high school graduates take that examination, it becomes a proxy for completion of high school. What is questionable in the results is a condition of the program that required students who were retained in

grades to give up their voucher in the subsequent year. This, and the fact that students had to be accepted to a private school prior to the lottery for a voucher, do not necessarily bias the results, but they do affect generalizability to programs without these two strong conditions.

United States Vouchers have occurred in the United States in two forms: privately funded vouchers, and public programs in Milwaukee, Cleveland, Washington, DC, and Florida. In this chapter, I will only include the latter. The first public voucher program began as the Milwaukee Parental Choice Program (MPCP) in 1990. Together with many colleagues, I, along with several other researchers, extensively analyzed that program in its early years.[15] The program was established as a targeted low-income program that required schools to randomly select students if they were oversubscribed. In terms of segregation, the general result was that those families applying for vouchers were somewhat more likely to be Black or Hispanic, quite poor, very likely from single-parent families, and likely to be on government assistance. In addition, if anything, students were achieving at a lower-than-average level prior to entering the program. An anomaly to this lack of creaming was that parent education, parental involvement, and parent expectations were higher than the averages in Milwaukee public schools (Witte, 2000, chapter 4; Legislative Audit Bureau, 2001).

As indicated in Table 39.1, segregation impacts in Cleveland were mixed and not as clear. In terms of SES, one study found those who accepted vouchers as poorer than those who declined (Greene, Howell, & Peterson, 1998). A second study in Cleveland also determined that voucher receivers had lower incomes and were more likely to come from single-parent households, but that the mothers had higher education than those in a control group (Metcalf, 1999). That study also found that voucher-receiving children had slightly higher achievement prior to entering the voucher program. Studies consistently found that minority children were more likely to receive vouchers than non-minority children. These results may be the result of a program condition that gave preference to low income students but did not require it.

The results from the second-year evaluation of the Washington, DC, voucher program, which again is targeted on low-income students (185% of poverty or less), did not have a comparison with all students in DC, but had data on both treatment and control students in this random assignment voucher program. However, all the statistics indicate that families were very poor, with the control group having somewhat higher income than the treatment group. The voucher was $7,500, which probably was one reason that a number of private schools chose not to participate. The composition of voucher winners and losers was also affected by a condition in the law that students from public schools in need of improvement (SINI) were to be given a priority in the lotteries (Wolf, Gutmann, Puma, & Silverberg, 2006).

The state of Florida has three separate voucher programs. The first was the opportunity scholarship program, which allowed students in schools that received failing (grade F) scores on state tests for 2 consecutive years to receive vouchers to go to other public or private schools. The second was a program that provided vouchers for low-income students using funds derived from a corporate tax credit on state taxes. The third was a program that allowed students with disabilities to attend any school of their choice with a publicly funded voucher. There has been very limited study of any of these programs.

By almost any measure, the outcome results to date of these voucher programs in terms of student achievement as measured by standardized tests have not been spectacular. Although there remains some controversy over results in Milwaukee, no researchers found any difference after 4 years (1990–1994) in reading score growth. My research found a slight, but insignificant math effect favoring voucher students; while that of Rouse (1998), using a different method of including students in the treatment and control groups, found a somewhat higher, and statistically significant math effect. Neither the Cleveland nor the DC voucher programs generated significant differences in achievement, although the DC program did have a positive effect after 1 year for students *not* in SINI schools (Wolf et al., 2007).

There have been no studies in Florida adequately testing effects of receiving vouchers versus students who chose not to exercise their rights to a voucher after their school failed state tests several times. There have been studies that have looked at failing (grade F) school responses and they have found considerable activity to attempt to raise test scores in these schools. However, the studies have been unable to attribute these reactions to vouchers rather than a simple "stigma" effect (Figlio & Rouse, 2006).

Finally, there have been several attempts, with divergent results, to test for competitive effects for vouchers. The studies have been done on Milwaukee using two types of comparisons. In the first, researchers took advantage of a "natural experiment" that pitted Milwaukee public schools against similar schools in terms of SES characteristics in other districts. The natural experiment took advantage of the rapid expansion of voucher students following 1998 due to an affirmative court ruling. Hoxby (2003) found that during this expansion of private school students using vouchers, the scores of Milwaukee public school students also went up, but that did not occur in her comparison cities. In a partial replication of that study, Carnoy et al. questioned that result as being linked to vouchers. They also employed a second methodology that looked at direct competition between traditional, voucher, charter, and magnet schools based on distance and the enrollment changes and found insignificant differences for voucher schools, but some mild effects for charter schools (Carnoy, Adamson, Chudgar, Luschei, & Witte, 2007). Thus in the United States, as of 2007, the competitive effects of private schools using vouchers remains indeterminate.

Conclusions

The importance of educational vouchers throughout the world is dependent on one's reference point. In the scope of all kindergarten through secondary school education, in the vast majority of countries, vouchers play a limited role. However, if one views vouchers and other forms of school choice in terms of changes in education policy, then they are extremely important reforms that have affected many countries in the last several decades. With the exception of the Netherlands that earlier combined public and private school funding, with considerable regulation of both sectors, most of the countries described in this review have created their educational choice systems in the last three decades. That is true for the United States, Scotland, Wales, England, Chile, and Colombia. In those countries the education landscape looks much different today than it did in 1980.

Research on vouchers and school choice in general has also increased dramatically in volume and quality in the last several decades. There remain a number of important issues, both statistical and in research design. For example, the problem of selection continues to haunt the research. The work of Bellei in Chile points the way in one important direction. Selection is not only the subject of families, but also of schools. As he shows, and many have suspected in a wide range of settings based on anecdotal evidence, private schools appear to both select in and select out in Chile. Although this is a start, further research directly targeted on the decision process of parents and schools is critically needed.

Another important and often neglected area of research has to do with the infamous "black box." This gets at the "why" question. If, for example, there is a positive effect on either student achievement or attainment of voucher systems, why does this occur? What is it that schools are doing differently? If all schools went to voucher-type systems, this may become trivial. As Milton Friedman would say, it is only the prediction that matters. But that is not and will not be the case in the foreseeable future. Thus, if traditional schools are to learn from voucher experiences, we first need to know what causes the positive effects. That research is not easy, but it is necessary.

Finally, it is very difficult to speculate on the future of vouchers and educational choice. The general trend has been to continue to expand choice options once the movements have begun.[16] However, in most places where vouchers have been introduced as conscious policy options in recent years, with the exception perhaps of Chile, they have been targeted either by income group, or geography, or both. That, of course, may well be an appropriate policy response that focuses resources where educational systems are failing (Witte, 2000, chapter 8). However, it suggests that vouchers per se will not have a major impact relative to educational systems as a whole. Indeed the strength of the voucher movement may be in the idea itself. The fundamental idea is that parents should have considerable say in where their children attend school. That say should not be limited to where one can afford to live, or more importantly *not to live*.

Notes

1. In 1965, 90% of private schools in America were Roman Catholic. That percentage has declined to less than 50 % in 2006–07. However, Christian, evangelical schools have made up the difference, thus religious private schools still make up over 80% of all private schools.
2. It is unclear if the public/private distinction would even apply in the Friedman voucher world.
3. How quality is conceptualized and measured is not clearly specified. For example, parents may seek to improve their child's knowledge as measured by subject-based standardized tests, and school would advertise the mean scores of their current students—much as colleges now advertise the SAT averages of their students. Quality could also be measured, as one private voucher school does in a large banner on its school in Milwaukee, by its graduation rate. And there will be other concepts and measures as well.
4. Some have argued that that is exactly what No Child Left Behind has done by requiring a focus on quality outcomes and providing for some parental choice (public school only) when students find themselves in a failing school. For an interesting discussion of the two-prong strategy of standards, assessment, and accountability accompanied by choice options, see the work of the Koret Task Force in Peterson (2003).
5. For detailed descriptions of overt and covert omission processes in England see West, Pennell, and Edge (1997). Bellei (in press), analyzing Chile's national voucher system, provides the best modeling to date of the effects of school selection and retention policies on school composition and student achievement.
6. This plays into the odd politics of vouchers in the United States where opposition may come from the Democratic left that resists paying for private schools for the middle- and upper-class families, and from smaller-government conservative Republicans who want to keep public budgets and taxes low.
7. There are also numerous privately funded voucher or scholarship programs in the United States. Almost all of these are targeted on low-income students.
8. To do otherwise would bring a legal challenge based on the First Amendment entanglement clause. The most common requirements are health, safety, and corporal punishment regulations, insistence on linked multi-year curricula, and often yearly time of instruction requirements. Ironically, that has not changed in voucher schools in Cleveland and Milwaukee following the *Zelman* decision because that decision was carefully argued as only an establishment clause issue.
9. For example, New Zealand instituted an extensive open enrollment program in the 1990s and has since completely eliminated it. Similarly, England created grant-maintained private schools under Margaret Thatcher, but they were limited under Tony Blair.
10. These are referred to in the literature as "competitive effects." They specifically would include the effects of vouchers on remaining public schools (usually in terms of achievement tests). Another aspect of this research, which has drawn much less attention, are the supply side effects in terms of the creation of new schools.
11. Much of this section comes from the work of Christine Teelken (1998).
12. Private schools in Chile have unlimited means to select students including student admissions tests and extensive parent and student interviews. Similarly, they can expel those they wish and many schools automatically expel students who fail a grade (Parry, 1996; Bellei, in press).
13. Reporting on OECD data, Bellei notes that countries with the smallest between-school variation are in the range of 12–18% of total student variation explained by schools. In the United States it is 30%, but in Chile it is 57%.

14. Bettinger (in press) notes that the non-participating private schools were among the most elite in Colombia. Also, with 37% of the secondary students in private schools, the private-school sector is very large.
15. Evaluations were terminated in 1995 when the program was expanded to include religious private schools. It grew from 1995 from 1,400 students to over 17,000 currently. A law enacted in 2006 requires a longitudinal evaluation that is headed up by a consortium from Georgetown, the University of Arkansas, and the University of Wisconsin. We have just completed collecting baseline data for a random sample of MPCP students and matched panel of Milwaukee Public School students.
16. The exceptions noted above were New Zealand and England's changes and restrictions in grant maintained schools.

References

Adler, M., & Raab, G. (1988). Exit, choice, and loyalty: The impact of parental choice on admissions to secondary schools. *Journal of Education Policy, 3*, 155–179.

Adler, P., Petch, A., & Tweedie, J. (1989). *Parental choice and education policy*. Edinburgh, Scotland: Edinburgh University Press.

Angrist, J., Bettinger, E., Bloom, E., King, E., & Kremer, M. (2002). Vouchers for private schooling in Colombia: Evidence from a randomized natural experiment. *American Economic Review, 92*, 1535–1558.

Angrist, J., Bettinger, E., & Kremer, M. (2006). Long-term educational consequences of secondary school vouchers: Evidence from administrative records in Colombia. *American Economic Review, 96*, 847–862.

Bellei, C. (in press). The private-public controversy in Chile. In R. Chakrabarti & P. Peterson (Eds.), *School choice international: Exploring public-private partnerships*. Cambridge, MA: MIT Press.

Bettinger, E. (in press). School vouchers in Colombia. In R. Chakrabarti & P. Peterson (Eds.), *School choice international: Exploring public-private partnerships*. Cambridge, MA: MIT Press.

Carnoy, M., Adamson, F., Chudgar, A., Luschei, T., & Witte, J. (2007). *Vouchers and public school performance: A case study of the Milwaukee Parental Choice Program*. Washington, DC: Economic Policy Institute.

Chubb, J., & Moe, T. (1990). *Politics, markets, and America's schools*. Washington, DC: Brookings Institution.

Dijkstra, A. B., Driessen, G., & Veenstra, R. (2001, April). *Academic achievement in public, religious, and private schools: Sector and outcome differences in the Netherlands*. Paper presented at the Annual Meeting of the American Educational Research Association, Seattle, WA.

Dijkstra, A. B., Dronkers, J., & Karsten, S. (2001, April). *Private schools as public provision for education: School choice and marketization in the Netherlands and elsewhere in Europe*. Paper presented at the Annual Meeting of the American Educational Research Association, Seattle, WA.

Dors, H. G., Karsten, S., Ledoux, G. & Steen, A. H. M. (1991). *Etnische segregatie in hetonderwijs: beleidsaspecten* [Ethnic segregation in education: Policy aspects]. Amsterdam: SCO-Kohnstamm Institute.

Dronkers, J. (2001). *More parental involvement in Europe? Overview of effectiveness differences between religious schools and public schools in several European societies* (Working paper). Amsterdam: Amsterdam School for Social Science Research.

Figlio, D., & Rouse, C. (2006). Do accountability and voucher threats improve low-performing schools? *Journal of Public Economics, 90*, 239–255.

Freidman, M. (1955). The role of government in education. In R. A. Solow (Ed.), *Economics and the public interest* (pp. 123–144). New Brunswick, NJ: Rutgers University Press.

Freidman, M. (1962). *Capitalism and freedom*. Chicago: University of Chicago Press.

Gallego, F. (2002). Competencia y resultados educativos. Teoria y evidencia para Chile [Educational competition and results: Theory and evidence for Chile]. *Cuadernos de Economia, 39*(318), 309–352.

Gallego, F. (2004). *School choice, incentives and academic outcomes: Evidence from Chile*. Cambridge, MA: MIT.

Gerwitz, S., Ball, S. J., & Bowe, R. (1995). *Markets, choice and equity in education.* Buckingham, England: Open University Press.

Greene, J., Howell, W., & Peterson, P. (1998). Lessons from the Cleveland Scholarship Program. In P. Peterson & B. Hassel (Eds.), *Learning from school choice* (pp. 357–394)*,* Washington DC: Brookings Institution.

Gorard, S., & Fitz, J. (2000). Markets and stratification: A view from England and Wales. *Educational Policy, 14,* 405–428.

Gorard, S., Fitz, J., & Taylor, C. (2001). School choice impacts: What do we know? *Educational Researcher, 30*(7), 18–23.

Hoxby, C. (2003). School choice and school competition: Evidence from the United States. *Swedish Economic Policy Review, 10,* 11–67.

Hsieh, C-T., & Urquiola, M. (2003). *When schools compete: How do they compete? An assessment of Chile's nationwide school voucher program* (NBER Working Paper No. W10008). Cambridge, MA: National Bureau of Economic Research.

Huerta, L. A., & d'Entremont, C. (2007). Tax credits as legal, political and policy alternative to vouchers. *Educational Policy, 21*(1), 73–109.

Karsten, S., & Teelken, C. (1996). School choice in the Netherlands. *Oxford Studies in Comparative Education, 6*(1), 17–31.

King, E., Rawlings, L., Gutierrez, M., Pardo, C., & Torres, C. (1997). *Colombia's targeted voucher program: Feature, coverage, and participation* (Impact Evaluation of Education Reforms Working Paper No. 3). Copenhagen, Denmark: The World Bank, Development Economics Research Group.

Legislative Audit Bureau. (2001). *An evaluation: Milwaukee Parental Choice Program.* (Report 00-2). Madison, WI: Author.

Lemon v. Kurtzman, 403 U.S. 388, 103 S. Ct. 3062, 77L. Ed. 2nd 745 (1971).

Machin, S., & Wilson, J. (in press). Public and private schooling initiatives in England. In R. Chakrabarti & P. Peterson (Eds.), *School choice international: Exploring public-private partnerships.* Cambridge, MA: MIT Press.

McEwan, P. (2001). The effectiveness of public, Catholic, and non-religious private schools in Chile's voucher system. *Education Economics, 9,* 103–128.

McEwan, P., & Carnoy, M. (2000). The effectiveness and efficiency of private schools in Chile's voucher system. *Educational Evaluation and Policy Analysis, 22,* 213–239.

McPherson, A., & Willms, D. (1986). Certification, class conflict, religion, and community: A socio-historical explanation of the effectiveness of contemporary school. In A. C. Kerkoff (Ed.), *Research in sociology of education and socialization, Vol. 6* (pp. 227–302). Greenwich, CT: JAI Press.

Metcalf, K. K. (1999). *Evaluation of the Cleveland scholarship and tutoring grant program, 1996–1999.* Bloomington: Indiana University, Indiana Center for Evaluation.

Parry, T. R. (1996). Will pursuit of higher quality sacrifice equal opportunity in education? An analysis of the education voucher system in Santiago. *Social Science Quarterly, 77,* 821–841.

Peterson, P. (Ed.). (2003). *Our schools and our future: Are we still at risk?* Stanford, CA: Hoover Institution Press.

Rouse, C. E. (1998). Private school vouchers and student achievement: an evaluation of the Milwaukee Parental Choice Program. *Quarterly Journal of Economics, 113,* 553–602.

Teelken, C. (1998). *Market mechanisms in education, a comparative study of school choice in the Netherlands, England and Scotland.* Unpublished Doctoral Dissertation, Rijksuniversiteit Groningen, the Netherlands.

West, A., Pennell, H., & Edge, A. (1997). Exploring the impact of reform on school-enrollment policies in England. *Educational Administration Quarterly, 33,* 170–182.

Willms, J. D. (1996). School choice and community segregation: Findings from Scotland. In A. Kerckhoff (Ed.), *Generating social stratification: Toward a new research agenda* (pp. 133–151) Denver, CO: Westview Press.

Willms, J. D., & Echols, F. (1992). Alert and inert clients: The Scottish experience of parental choice in schools. *Economics of Education Review, 11,* 339–350.

Witte, J. (2000). *The market approach to education: An analysis of America's first voucher program.* Princeton, NJ: Princeton University Press.

Wolf, P., Gutmann, B., Puma, M., Rizzo, L., Eissa, N., & Silverberg, M. (2007). *Evaluation of the DC Opportunity Scholarship Program: Summary of experimental impacts after one year.* Washington, DC: Institute of Education Sciences.

Wolf, P., Gutmann, B., Puma, M., & Silverberg, M. (2006). *Evaluation of the DC Opportunity Scholarship Program: Second year report on participation.* Washington, DC: Institute of Educational Sciences.

Zelman v. Simmons-Harris, 536, U.S. 639 (2002).

40

A Market for Knowledge?

FREDERICK M. HESS
American Enterprise Institute

For more than a decade, market-oriented education reformers have touted the ability of competition to improve American education. While arguing that competition will nevertheless promote quality, efficiency, and innovation, these advocates have avoided the blunt, self-interested language of markets. The result has been a strange politics of half-hearted debate. Proponents of deregulation have hesitated to use the instrumental language of markets. Even the champions of reform have opted for the gentler language of "choice"—while paying homage to the societal mission of schooling and its value as a public good. This has made for some astonishing, or astonishingly inept, efforts at market making. In K–12, for instance, champions of competition have chosen to ignore questions about existing incentives for schools or managers, or the manner in which collective bargaining agreements restrict the ability of schools to respond to competition.

In the context of deregulatory politics, it is vital to understand that American education is not a regulated system in any conventional sense. K–12 schooling is, quite simply, a government-operated system with a small private sector. As for "deregulation," most such policy is not concerned with reducing government restrictions on private entities but with encouraging publicly managed entities to act "as if" they were private entities. These realities of the education sector have seldom been recognized by proponents and opponents of market-based reform, whose debates rest on the unstated assumption that publicly governed schools and colleges will behave like traditional profit-seeking firms when confronted with students empowered to attend the school of their choice.

In K–12 education, there is substantially less competition and much more ambivalence about whether schools and educators should be subject to competition. Nevertheless, teachers compete to win positions in advantaged districts, superintendents and principals vie for the career-making accolades showered upon innovators, school districts compete with private firms to provide tutoring under the federal

No Child Left Behind Act (NCLB), and principals eagerly explain how they contend for students who could attend other schools. More obviously, for-profit firms have always competed to supply schools with academic products and services such as testing, textbooks, curricula, professional development, and instructional supplies.

In short, rather than suggesting that competition does not exist in education, it is more accurate for proponents of market reform to argue that education is currently subjected to inadequate or unhealthy competitive pressures, and that market-based reform will yield more constructive dynamics. This, however, places a particular burden upon reformers. If the problem is that existing competition is unproductive or toothless, then simply promoting increased choice is an insufficient solution. It becomes paramount for reformers to embrace changes that will trump existing pressures, alter the rules of the game, and rationalize behavior in the intended manner.

Education has two purposes: a "private" purpose and a "public" purpose. Education is a private good to the extent that individuals benefit from the skills and training produced by schooling and is a public good insofar as one is learning skills, dispositions, or values that make for a better citizen and neighbor. It is generally agreed that the public content of schooling is highest in the elementary grades and declines through secondary school and higher education, though there is no objective way to determine the size of the public component at any particular grade level. To the extent that education is a private matter, proponents of choice-based reform contend that public officials should regulate with a light hand and should not privilege state-run institutions. Those who see education as primarily a public good, meanwhile, argue that the state should oversee its provision and ensure product quality.

Insofar as elementary and secondary schooling is a public good, states and local school districts provide all children with a free K–12 education. The resulting arrangements buffer institutions from the choices students make and limit the ability of students and families to shop for schools. In education, state subsidies and rules defining an acceptable product shape consumer behavior. Producers operate in accord with state mandates, under stringent requirements for permissible operations, staffing, and responsibilities, and on the basis of the need to attract public funds.

In both K–12 and postsecondary education, a persistent difficulty for market proponents has been the disparity between the rhetoric and reality of competition. Confusingly, there has been a tendency to conflate two very different dynamics and call them both "competition": one is the unleashing of self-interested incentives to compel public providers to improve, and the other is a loosening of restraints that hobble nontraditional and private providers.

Quite notably, the most influential volume penned on educational competition, *Politics, Markets and America's Schools*, quietly failed to grapple with the central question of whether student choice would suffice to create effective competition (Chubb & Moe, 1990). In that volume, political scientists John Chubb and Terry Moe used a national study of school performance to argue that autonomy and freedom from bureaucratic rulemaking enabled private K–12 schools to outperform their public counterparts. However, nowhere in the volume—despite an explicit assertion that policy makers should consider school vouchers a possible "panacea" for K–12 schooling—did the authors argue that these private schools compel public institutions to better serve students.[1] In short, even those scholars cited by proponents of educational competition have often paid limited attention to how or why competition works. Claims on behalf of the peculiarly designed public school choice and supplemental service provisions of NCLB have suffered from the same lack of clarity regarding the ways and means of competition.

It is vital to distinguish between competition intended to force public school systems to change in desirable ways and competition intended to permit new providers to emerge and thrive. This distinction yields two theories of change. The most straightforward way to unleash competition is to make it relatively simple for private providers to receive public funding for their educational services. If the accompanying regulation does not erect immense barriers to entry, this kind of displacement can yield immense change whether or not existing institutions respond productively. The alternative course is to use the threat from private providers and changes in public agency funding to compel a productive public sector response, trusting that self-interest will drive public schools to improve in response to competitive pressure. In contemporary policy debates, the rhetoric of public sector response is more common than that of displacement.

The Landscape of Education Competition

After health care, education constitutes the second largest sector of the American economy. In 2005–06, American taxpayers spent a total of $909 billion on education—$536 billion on K–12 and $373 billion on postsecondary—with 90% of the funding supplied by state and local governments (U.S. Department of Education, 2005). In fiscal 2005, states devoted 21.8% of their spending to education (National Association of State Budget Officers, 2006). Medicaid is the largest category of state spending, accounting for 22.9% of total fiscal 2005 expenditures. Other than health care, there is no other sector in which improvements in quality or efficiency would have as large an impact on the public purse or on quality of life.

Although American higher education features a diverse mix of private for-profit, private nonprofit, and public providers competing across geographic markets, K–12 schooling operates in a much more hidebound market. Public school districts enrolled 48.1 million students in 2003–04, just under 90% of the nation's 54 million K–12 students. Nonprofit institutions—primarily religiously affiliated—enrolled nearly all of the 6.3 million students in private schools.

All of the approximately 15,000 school districts across the country are nonprofit public entities. With a handful of exceptions, these districts derive more than 99% of their funding from tax revenues. While funding arrangements vary from state to state, in 2004–05 the majority of education funds were provided by the states, with local districts contributing about one-third of school expenditures and the federal government contributing about 10%. The national average per pupil expenditure in this period was $8,618, with the total cost (including construction and debt service) some 15% to 20% higher. Across states, average per pupil expenditures ranged from more than $12,000 in New York to less than $6,000 in Arizona and Utah (National Education Association, 2005).

Public school principals and teachers are licensed in accordance with state credentialing rules. Although many districts employ large numbers of unlicensed educators, these individuals are typically regarded as stopgaps and are required to fulfill credentialing requirements or be replaced. Public school teachers and administrators are state employees and subject to relatively stringent state and local statutes, as well as contractual language that specifies pay scales and work conditions. In most states, teachers are tenured into their positions after 2 to 3 years, making it very difficult to remove them without an extended and often expensive process.

In private schooling, few of these conditions hold—though, for reasons of their own, private educators rarely use their advantages to maximize profitability or gain market share. Private K–12 schools operate free from state regulations. They can hire without regard to licensure provisions, pay employees as they see fit, and readily remove or reward employees. In 1999–2000, the most recent year for which data are available, the Department of Education identified 25,138 private schools. Of those, just 21% charged $5,000 or more in annual tuition, while 41% charged less than $2,500 (Snyder & Hoffman, 2002).

The private school sector illustrates some of the challenges confronting market reforms in education. As Teachers

College professor Henry Levin noted in 2000, more than two dozen New York City schools charged annual tuition in excess of $20,000 and had extensive wait lists through good times and bad, yet sought neither to maximize revenues nor attract revenue-maximizing competitors (Levin, 2001). In fact, most religious and secular schools heavily subsidize tuition with endowments, church funds, or similar sources of revenue. This makes for a peculiar marketplace, one in which key competitors to public provision are themselves unconcerned with profitability. The result is that many traditional private providers have little interest in exploiting market opportunities, maximizing revenues, or gaining market share—the objectives that market models typically assume when anticipating the nature and consequences of competition.

Perhaps surprising to those unfamiliar with schooling is that for-profit providers typically operate public schools rather than private schools, most often opening "charter" schools that have more independence than the typical public school. In 2005–06, there were 51 education management companies operating 521 schools and enrolling 237,179 students in 29 states and the District of Columbia. More than 80% of these schools were charter schools (Molnar, Garcia, Bartlett, & O'Neill, 2006).

Competitive forces are most evident in four areas of K–12 education, each a product of relatively recent changes to state or federal policy. First, somewhere between 1% and 1.5% of children are currently homeschooled. State laws rendered homeschooling illegal in nearly all states until the 1970s, when Christian groups spearheaded an effort to relax school attendance laws and ensure the right of parents to educate their children at home. Today, homeschooling is legal in all 50 states, operating under a variety of statutory restrictions. Estimates vary, but most place the homeschooling population at about 1 million (for a detailed review, see Lugg & Rorrer, this volume). This has fostered a variety of opportunities for entrepreneurial providers, as families seek curricular materials and web-based instructional support.

Second, as of fall 2006, 1,150,000 students were enrolled in 3,977 charter schools nationwide. These schools held charters from state-designated entities that permitted them to operate independently from the local school district. Charter school legislation, first enacted in Minnesota in 1991, funds schools with formulas based on enrollment, thus linking competitive performance to revenue. States fund charters to varying degrees, some at the same level as other public schools but many at a considerably reduced level. Only a few states offer charter schools substantial support when it comes to facilities and construction. As a result, entrepreneurs have encountered significant difficulty in getting charter schools started, often relying on philanthropic support and using third-rate facilities. In addition, public school districts and teachers unions have played a leading role in seeking to deny charter operators access to public capital for construction or facilities, have harassed them through legal and procedural means, and have supported caps on the number of permissible charter schools.

In short, charter schools have developed amid pinched resources, inferior facilities, and political uncertainty.

Third, publicly funded school voucher programs, first enacted in Milwaukee in 1990, now operate in some cities (e.g., Cleveland and Washington, DC) and on a limited statewide basis in Florida. Under voucher arrangements, the government provides individuals with a specified amount of money to be used toward tuition at any eligible provider (see Witte, this volume). In each case, students are able to use the vouchers to attend private schools, including religious schools. Vouchers make the financial state of a school directly dependent on whether students enroll there, though most programs set per-pupil funding at a substantially lower level than for local public schools. In 2005–06, the Milwaukee program enrolled more than 15,000 students and offered a maximum voucher of $6,351; Cleveland enrolled about 5,700 students and offered a maximum voucher of $3,450, and Florida's statewide voucher program for students in low-performing schools enrolled about 760 students with an average voucher of about $4,100.

Fourth, the landmark No Child Left Behind Act of 2001 requires low-performing districts to use federal funds to create a competitive market for after-school tutoring services. More than 2,500 state-approved supplemental service providers are now competing for federal funds that average $800–$900 per eligible student. While many of the approved providers are school districts themselves or other nonprofits, a number of small for-profits and larger national for-profits—Platform Learning and Catapult Learning, for example—are competing within this emerging sector. Harvard University business professor Clayton Christensen has argued that most disruptive innovation tends to be pioneered by low-cost "down-market" providers who find ways to undercut established, pricey producers by delivering functional substitute products at dramatic savings (Christensen, 1997; Christensen & Raynor, 2003). Historically, the absence of for-profits, coupled with K–12 funding formulas, has stifled the emergence of cost-effective education providers.

Outside of these new market niches where displacement is driving change, public school systems have proven remarkably unresponsive to competition or shrinking student enrollment. This is due in part to state financing arrangements that buffer school districts from losing the full dollar amount associated with enrollment declines. For instance, from 1996 to 2004, Detroit public schools lost 35,000 of their 175,000 students to residential flight, charter schools, and private schooling. This 20% loss in district enrollment was accompanied by a real increase in total revenues and a double-digit percentage increase in total per pupil funding. Yet the district's refusal to close schools or cut personnel as enrollment declined led it to explore issuing bonds to help cover a $250 million shortfall in 2004–05 in lieu of imminent layoffs (Gehring, 2004).

Further, existing arrangements insulate educational leaders, administrators, and teachers from the consequences of their performance. Because individual teachers are not promoted or rewarded for exemplary performance, and because they do not face termination or demotion for poor performance, it is difficult for even determined leadership to spur employee effort beyond that which they are disposed to put forth. Moreover, because neither school principals nor district superintendents are rewarded for attracting enrollment, they have little incentive to engage in controversial or unpopular measures to do so. Lacking the ability to readily assess, reward, or select subordinates, and in an environment where only the rarest school systems resort to layoffs, most principals and superintendents lack the means to answer market forces. In short, the flow of students into or out of public school systems has remarkably little impact on the administrators and teachers who staff those systems.

Competition in Practice

Across and within the worlds of K–12 and higher education, competition operates very differently, and efforts to promote it play out in unexpected ways. Both sectors have a significant public good component and are dominated by nonprofits with a structure of intrinsic and extrinsic rewards built largely on acquiring prestige and attracting higher-quality students. Beyond those broad similarities, educational competition is shaped by funding arrangements and the type of education being pursued.

On one hand, instruction in applied skills lends itself readily to commodification. Remedial tutoring services and training in vocational activities are straightforward; results are readily measured, and firms can construct focused delivery models that provide a reasonable rate of return. Because 2-year institutions like community colleges are particularly focused on vocational preparation, the less prestigious reaches of postsecondary education have proved particularly fertile ground for market forces. Meanwhile, broader and more experiential education does not fit as neatly into the classic market model. Elementary schools and liberal arts colleges are expected to cultivate social behaviors, expose students to various skills and areas of interest, and provide a supportive atmosphere for development. They are not as readily judged on straightforward criteria and may find it difficult to boost profitability without sacrificing program elements deemed important to their mission.

In K–12 schooling, the research most frequently invoked by proponents of choice-based reform is that of Harvard economist Caroline Hoxby and the University of Arkansas' Jay Greene. In studying the effects of school vouchers and charter school programs on performance, Hoxby and Greene concluded that with the introduction of the programs, student achievement improved measurably in the public schools subjected to the most direct threats (see Hoxby, 2001, 2002; Greene, 2001; Greene, Peterson, & Jiangtao, 1999). Greene found that low-performing Florida schools significantly improved their student test performance when the state threatened to issue vouchers to students in the lowest-performing schools. Greene's findings are consistent with data from other states that have introduced high-stakes tests. Schools subjected to concerted pressure of any kind tend to improve student test results as employees seek to avert sanctions—whether those sanctions are vouchers, a state takeover, or more intrusive district monitoring.

My own research, meanwhile, has suggested that a lack of meaningful incentives or consequences in existing school choice programs generally limits the scope and ambition of public agency response. In examinations of voucher programs in Milwaukee, Cleveland, and Edgewood, Texas, and of charter schooling in these locales and in Arizona, my colleagues and I have found that competition provoked little substantive change. Except for a few Arizona districts that lost a quarter or more of their enrollment in a short period, public school systems responded with little more than symbolic appeals, advertising, and organizational add-ons (see, e.g., Hess, 2002; Hess & McGuinn, 2002; Hess, Maranto, & Milliman, 2001a, 2001b).

In vital ways, these findings are actually complementary to those of Greene and Hoxby. Competition does appear to have an impact on schooling, but its initial effects are modest and incremental and depend heavily on the structure of competition and the market context. At present, the research on the competitive effects of existing choice programs is too limited to be determinative, while the resulting analyses and policy recommendations fail to entertain any theory of how competition is likely to play out in public schools or colleges.

Competitive Response of Public Schools

Markets work precisely because they are neither gentle nor forgiving. They are impersonal mechanisms that gain their power by harnessing self-interest and drawing on desire and fear. The power of the market resides in the knowledge that dominant firms may be an innovation away from being overthrown, and hungry garage inventors a breakthrough away from success. It is the handful of entrepreneurs who take chances and embrace risk that drive innovation and growth, as has been the case with entrepreneurs who have exploited new opportunities in vocational colleges or in providing curricula to homeschooling families.

Most individuals, however, are risk-averse, and fear losses much more than they value potential gains. Consequently, markets more typically work not by presenting opportunities, but by forcing resistant organizations to live in a constant state of low-level fear. There is little that is truly "voluntary" about responding to the fear of losing one's job or the desire for a promotion. The efforts of a single principal in the San Diego City Schools, a department chair at Penn State, or a manager at IBM or Disney are unlikely to have a significant impact on the bottom line or reputation of the larger organization. Accordingly, competitive models presuppose that these individuals will be primarily motivated not by a tenuous investment in aggregate outcomes, but by rewards and sanctions linked to their own work. This requires that organizations have leeway to select, terminate, reward, and sanction employees on the basis of performance—a state of affairs that does not apply to most of public K–12 schooling.

Naturally, people seek to protect or insulate themselves from this relentless pressure. Investors and executives seek the security afforded by favorable government statute or by monopoly status. Employee unions seek ways to counter the pressures of the market and protect their members by restricting layoffs, curtailing the rights of employers to terminate workers, providing wage security, and limiting the monitoring and evaluation of workers. In the case of K–12 schooling, the nation's two teachers unions—the National Education Association and the American Federation of Teachers—have won statutory and collective bargaining language that protects employees from termination, standardizes compensation, restricts staffing, and otherwise minimizes uncertainty (see, e.g., Koppich & Callahan, this volume).

In the private sector, when competition is threatening enough—such as when American electronic manufacturers were met with an onslaught of Japanese competitors in the 1980s—it can bring these protective edifices crashing down. Firms either cast off inefficient rules and procedures or are overtaken by new providers. However, the very nature of public organizations such as schools, colleges, and universities makes it possible to limit the effects of markets in two key ways. First, the market threat can be neutralized by political fiat. Public agencies are not threatened by bankruptcy in the same way that private firms are. Legislatures may require a public agency to begin competing against other entities, but they are free to buffer schools and colleges from the revenue losses that might attend a shrinking clientele. For instance, between 1990 and 2004, when Milwaukee lost nearly 15,000 students (more than 10% of its enrollment), per pupil spending in the district more than doubled. Of course, because public agencies depend on public revenue—and therefore on legislative sentiment—schools and colleges are not unconcerned with the loss of clients. However, without legislative action to base revenues strictly on student enrollment, schools and colleges are threatened less by revenue lost through consumer flight than by a loss of political support, whether due to a shrinking clientele or to steps that alienate friends and allies. This reality has crucial implications for leadership, especially when considering how public agencies will "compete."

Second, the incentives for officials in public school districts are fundamentally different from those for executives of private firms. Private firms are driven by investors anxiously watching profitability (or by owner-managers who have their own wealth riding on the future of the firm). When confronted by competitors, the overriding pressure to improve profitability propels executives to find new market opportunities, root out organizational inefficiencies, and pursue increased profitability. If executives do not take these steps, they risk being displaced by leaders who will.

Public organizations are, obviously, governed by public officials. Whereas private sector officials are judged by investors primarily on the basis of corporate profitability and growth, public officials are judged by more ambiguous criteria. Voters care little whether schools are attracting new clients (that is, boosting enrollment); thus officials are typically not rewarded for doing so.[2] Moreover, while voters naturally wish the government to operate efficiently, they rarely have clear measures to assess the efficiency of schools (though the growing prominence of test scores in the era of NCLB has begun to provide a more uniform, if imperfect, metric, in K–12 schooling). What voters do care about is perceived quality of service, responsiveness, and evidence that the leadership is effective.

Because public school leaders depend on the support of elected officials and the public, their effectiveness and future prospects turn on the breadth of their backing and on their ability to cultivate—or at least avoid provoking—influential and attentive constituencies. Key organized interests, especially teachers unions and civil rights groups, are invested in the rules that protect employees and ensure equitable service provision.

Given their environment, school leaders have good reason to focus more on accommodating influential constituencies and assuaging public opinion than on pursuing new efficiencies. The notion that provosts or superintendents will hesitate to make painful decisions may appear to contradict existing scholarship regarding the desire of agency heads to accumulate and preserve bureaucratic "slack" (for further reading, see Nohria & Gulati, 1996; Schneider & Teske, 1992). "Slack" refers to the extra resources and personnel that an official controls, and the accumulation of slack is a goal because it insulates the official from changes in the environment, is a mark of prestige, and can provide power. In fact, there is no contradiction here. The desire to accumulate slack arises largely because extra resources permit officials to avoid hard choices and strengthen their position, so they are able to more readily manage the disruptions due to competition or changes in policy. Nothing in the scholarship on bureaucratic slack has ever suggested that officials will imperil their position to collect slack—only that their default position is to seek more staff and resources. The experience of subjecting public agencies to competition suggests that officials are likely to deploy slack in an effort to dull the threat posed rather than respond aggressively in an effort to preserve slack.

Suggesting that public officials will hesitate to tackle inefficiencies is not to say they will ignore the challenges posed by competition. If market competition threatens to embarrass the organization or its community or increase local attention to services and their failings, the resulting air of crisis and scrutiny will press officials to provide a satisfactory response. Typically, political leaders are risk-averse and inclined to caution. There are times, though, when confronted with sufficient pressure, that inaction becomes costly. To do nothing in a crisis is to appear ineffectual; activity calms public concerns and positions leaders to claim credit for any perceived improvement (see Edelman, 1972; Stone, 1997).

However, public schools are not well suited to act boldly. Public employees face extensive procedural requirements. Given substantial penalties for violating a statute and few rewards for effective performance, public servants have incentives to hew to procedural requirements—even when the requirements seem inefficient. Employees who respect these prosper, while entrepreneurs who violate norms or offend constituencies encounter difficulties. Consequently, when compelled to launch a public response to the threat of market competition, leaders are considerably constricted in their course of action. One response is to enhance advertising and public outreach. These measures are cheap, inoffensive, upset no routines, build public support, and can easily be tacked onto existing practices. A second, more interesting, response is the tendency of officials to relax procedures so as to permit the development of new programs and initiatives.

Even for managers in the private sector, it can be arduous and unpleasant to undertake significant organizational changes. Most will only do so when they have to, relying upon their capacity to recruit and promote supportive managers, reward cooperative employees, monitor performance, and sanction or fire the uncooperative. Managers in public schools generally lack such tools; thus rather than forcing change upon their subordinates, they prefer reforms that allow entrepreneurial employees to step forward. The result is enhanced opportunities for principals to launch new specialty schools. This solution avoids the conflicts provoked by coercion, while producing visible evidence of organizational change.

Unorthodox opportunities to provide new services appeal to entrepreneurial personalities—the same individuals marginalized in process-oriented public sector agencies. In fields such as education, these entrepreneurs are rarely motivated by self-interest as traditionally understood in economic discourse. Having forgone the more lucrative opportunities of the private sector, they are frequently motivated by a sense of calling, intrinsic desire, or a desire for new challenges.

Competition-induced pressure can encourage influential constituencies to accept some relaxation of procedures, enabling entrepreneurs to punch small holes through regulatory barriers. Though inefficient practices are not rooted out, new initiatives—such as new schools, departments, or hiring programs—may spring up beside existing practices. Pressured to provide a visible response, officials may chip holes in the regulations and procedures that run like kudzu through public sector organizations. These holes permit entrepreneurs to bypass traditional gatekeepers, creating new pockets of reform, and possibly starting to topple the existing edifice. It is also possible, however, that these efforts will amount to nothing more than an occasional weed growing limply through an organizational crack.

Public Sector Response in K–12: The Case of DC Vouchers

An example of how educational competition may work in ways other than intended may be found in Washington, DC. There, in early 2004, Congress enacted the nation's most richly funded school voucher program, offering vouchers of up to $7,500 to more than 1,000 students in DC's public schools. Proponents such as Congressman Jeff Flake (R-Ariz.), who introduced the voucher program, rendered grand pronouncements about its likely impact: "Not only will these scholarships help students who take advantage of them, but they'll help the students who remain in the public school system by freeing up resources and creating a competitive environment where both public and private will thrive" (Flake, 2003). Mayor Anthony Williams bragged that "introducing choice and ensuring competition" would improve the schools while holding the public schools "harmless" ("Mayor Defends," 2003).

Williams's comment was telling. The voucher program did ensure that the public schools would be held harmless. In a design compromise typical of most charter school and school voucher legislation, the program provided for the DC public school system to receive $13 million a year in addition to its current budget as a condition for potentially sending 1,000 students to private schools. In other words, the voucher program ensured that the total size of the District's school budget would grow, while public school enrollment declined. Despite the logical flaws in this kind of "market" design, the rhetoric offered by Flake, Williams, and the program's other champions mirrored arguments made a decade before in promoting DC charter school legislation.

When charter school legislation passed in the District in 1995, grand claims were made on its behalf. One charter proponent, Lex Towle of the Appletree Institute, explained: "When you get a critical mass of good independent public schools, particularly in the inner city where they are most important, that will help create the competition that will raise the level of other public schools" (as cited in Hess, 2004). Critical mass ensued. By 2004, more than 20% of the District's public school students were enrolled in charter schools. Yet after 9 years of charter "competition," the U.S. Census Bureau reported that the District was spending more than $15,000 per student, yet its system was still among the worst-achieving in the nation—wracked by scandal and plagued by managerial incompetence.

How can this be, given the basic tenets of market logic? Well, imagine if a Wal-Mart store manager were told that losing customers would have no impact on his salary, evaluation, or job security, while attracting new customers would require him to hire more employees, assume greater responsibilities, and erect a trailer in the parking lot to handle the added business—all without additional compensation or recognition. In such an environment, only the clueless would be compelled to "compete." The sensible manager's preference would be for a stable customer population (although the truth is, he would probably rather lose customers than gain them).

This is exactly how schools compete under the DC voucher program and in other voucher and charter plans nationwide. Consider the principal of an average elementary school in DC that was built to house 400 students and currently enrolls 375. What happens if that principal loses 75 students to charter schools or to the voucher program? Typically, three retiring teachers are not replaced, the school is less crowded, and the tiny amount of discretionary money that flowed to the school to support those students does not come in. In short, the principal's job gets a little easier. She earns the same salary and has the same professional prospects she would have otherwise, yet has fewer teachers to lead, fewer students to monitor, and a less crowded school.

Take the same school and assume that the principal reacts effectively to the incitement to increase enrollment, prompting the school to add 75 students. What happens? The principal takes on responsibility for three new teachers, must squeeze students into the last available classroom, adds two trailers out back to hold two additional classrooms, and crowds the school's cafeteria and corridors. This principal is now responsible for two teachers who are not happy about teaching all day in a trailer and 50 families who feel the same way about their child's classroom. In return for these headaches, the "successful" principal receives what? At best, a small pool of discretionary funds, typically amounting to less than $50 per student, more responsibilities, dissatisfied constituents, and no more recognition or pay.

The bottom line is that existing statutes, regulations, and personnel create difficulty for even aggressive, gifted reformers. The visibility of district officials, however, means that school systems cannot simply ignore the emergence of competition. The result is an incentive to forgo painful steps while focusing on symbolically potent appeals. The post-NCLB increase in attention to state test results is altering this calculus and increasing the importance of bottom-line performance, though the significance of the change is yet to be seen.

Five Wrinkles for Educational Competition

The effects of educational competition depend on several marketplace considerations that are a function of the educational process and the evolution of American education. Disagreements about the nature of effective schooling, the limited capacity of competitors, incentives to enhance outcome quality by attracting desirable students, and the transaction costs implicit in switching schools all present particular challenges for educational markets.

Education as an Ambiguous Good Producers have more incentive to attend to consumer preferences when consumers can easily evaluate products. In the case of educational venues such as traditional elementary schools or compre-

hensive high schools, disagreements about the nature of a quality education and the ambiguity of educational outcomes complicate evaluation. As University of California professor Liane Brouillette (1996) has noted, "Most people agree, at least in a general way, about what constitutes good health. Agreement on what constitutes a 'good' education is harder to come by" (p. 2). While there are clear expectations for SAT preparation courses or literacy programs, there frequently is public disagreement about exactly what elementary schools, high schools, or colleges are expected to teach or look like. For instance, some urge schools to foster self-expression, while others call for more discipline and structure.

For providers seeking to fill a particular niche in a free market, such heterogeneity is more an opportunity than a concern. For public agencies charged with serving a broad public or a discrete geographic area, however, it can inhibit a coherent focus on productivity or strategy for improvement. In K–12, state accountability testing is forcing a consensus on the primacy of measured achievement in reading, language arts, and math that is far more uniform—and more similar to that in Europe or Japan—than has traditionally been the case in the United States.

Even when agreement about the goals of education is stipulated, however, there is concern that testing instruments and technology do not accurately measure school performance or instructional quality.[3] Since education is ultimately a long-term endeavor whose benefits may not be fully evident for decades, there is always room to debate the utility of any short-term proxy.

In truth, clarity of service quality is often a function of how consumers *think* about quality and their willingness to define it on the basis of a few specified dimensions. This is particularly relevant in higher education. Most sophisticated observers argue that the relative quality of colleges is difficult to judge, involves multiple factors, and depends on the student. Such nuanced cautions, while sensible, offer little practical guidance. As a result, various consumer guides rank institutions on specified criteria. While derided by experts, these rankings influence where students apply and have consequently prompted colleges to take steps to boost their rankings. Defining quality on the basis of certain criteria encourages producers to focus on those criteria—regardless of disputes about what quality "truly" entails.

Constraints on Competitive Capacity The competitive threat to traditional schools is partly a function of how many students can be educated by alternative providers or new ones that are likely to emerge. In K–12, private schools are generally much smaller than public schools and have a limited number of available seats, minimizing the number of students they can absorb. Existing private and charter schools are often hesitant to increase enrollment for fear of losing the sense of a tight-knit community. They also tend to be located in small buildings ill-suited to expansion and lack the capital that would be required to expand their size. Although charter schooling did expand rapidly during the mid- and late 1990s and a handful of charter school operators continue to explicitly seek growth, it is not clear whether the educator enthusiasm and charitable giving that helped launched new charters will operate on a scale necessary to sustain continued expansion.

Meaningful competition requires new schools to open or existing schools to expand. However, the development of future capacity is limited by various factors, primarily in K–12 schooling. First, most existing choice programs are funded less generously than district schools, and potential competitors are denied the kind of support for construction and facilities that public institutions enjoy. Second, many choice-related programs include strictures relating to admissions, staffing, or curricula that may dissuade possible operators. Third, in K–12, most educators who want to open schools are motivated to do so because they have a vision of the school community they would like to create. These entrepreneurs prefer their communities to be relatively small, and few evince interest in "franchising."

Finally, the political opposition and legal uncertainty of choice-based reform can undermine the development of competitive capacity. Launching a new school or college, or expanding an existing one, requires an immense investment of resources and psychic energy. Investors and entrepreneurs are willing to make this commitment, but they want to be materially or emotionally compensated for their efforts. The fear of adverse political or legal action can reduce the number of investors willing to launch or expand schools.

The "Cherry-Picking" Temptation

The fact that education is a service "done to," rather than "provided for," a clientele has important implications for school operators. Unlike most producers, schools can make their performance appear much more impressive by adjusting the mix of their clientele (see Epple & Romano, 1998). They are able to do so precisely because they enhance the consumer's capacities rather than provide a defined product or service. It is difficult to assess the extent of such enhancement, however, so educational providers are often judged on the basis of a final product, such as test scores or graduation rates. This is true even though observers recognize that such outcomes are heavily influenced by factors beyond the control of schools.

Schools can make themselves more attractive to consumers by accepting successful students and screening out those with difficulties. In a competitive marketplace, individual institutions have intrinsic and reputational incentives to actively pursue promising or high-performing students. The result is that elite K–12 schools engage in fierce efforts to maximize the quality of the student population. This does not mean that schools will necessarily "cherry-pick" students—institutions may refuse to do so for moral or philosophical reasons—but the market will penalize schools that do not.

This phenomenon is not unique to education; it holds whenever an individual's experience is affected by the nature or identity of his or her fellow consumers. Hip restaurants and stylish resorts, selling ambiance as part of their appeal, strive to attract the "right" clientele. Because society is unconcerned about unequal access to nightspots or beach clubs, this behavior is typically not regarded as problematic—nor is the implication that only a limited number of providers will be elite. In the case of schooling, however, policy makers care deeply about equity and access. Educational choice programs therefore include eligibility and admissions provisions designed to limit cherry-picking, simultaneously hindering the ability of producers to shape their product, target customers, or cater to client preferences.

Transaction Costs

Consumers are more likely to change goods when it is simple to procure the necessary information and arrange for service provision. They are less likely to do so if significant switching costs are involved. For example, changing schools may separate children from their friends, interfere with extracurricular activities, involve logistical or scheduling difficulties, or require students to adapt to new teachers and programs. If logistical constraints limit the number of families that can or will switch schools, the degree of competition is tempered—this is a particular limitation for efforts to promote K–12 competition in sparsely populated areas. In communities where performance information is readily available, where choices are easy to access, and where logistical support is high, families are more likely to behave like active consumers.

Price Competition

Price competition necessitates incentives for low-cost providers. Currently, choice-based reforms such as charters, vouchers, and supplemental services require the state to send a specified amount of money to the student's new provider. As a consequence, providers have no incentive to provide low-cost service options. For-profit providers do have an incentive to cut their own costs, but neither for-profits nor nonprofits have an incentive to cut prices to attract customers if the state sets the per pupil payout at a specified minimum. It is not clear if there is a way around this problem without the risk of students investing less in schooling than the government prefers or without introducing concerns of inequity. Nevertheless, this is a challenge worth significant reflection.

The Politics of Education Competition

Most proposals to reform education through enhanced competition fail to wrestle seriously with what that course of action entails. In areas where competition is driving change, providers have exploited new opportunities to offer narrowly defined services and displace existing public agencies. Efforts to compel public schools to respond through market-based measures have enjoyed less success. There is a stark difference between reforms that create new room for nonpublic operators and those that harness competition to force public providers to change. Ambivalence toward this distinction is at the heart of market-based reform. On one hand, reformers highlight the need for competition to challenge insulated institutions, unleash entrepreneurial energies, focus attention on productivity, and create incentives to find efficiencies. On the other hand, they hesitate to violate established notions of educational decorum, worry that vulnerable students may be harmed by marketplace dislocations, feel uncertain about for-profit educators, and prefer a "kinder, gentler" competitive regime.

Proponents of educational competition have proceeded with studied inattention to the central truth of market-based reform. Competition requires that producers have incentives to address consumer demands in ways that promote performance and productivity. However, this is precisely where public agencies—especially those with high levels of public support—can pursue rules and regulations that stifle potential competitors and buffer themselves from the consequences of competition. When asked to compete with private providers, public providers have strong incentives to choke-off entry, lobby for protections, and satisfy constituents with symbolic gestures, while also using the resulting slack to insulate themselves from structural changes that competition is specifically designed to engender. Incentives of this nature suppress the pressures driving the technology of change. Labor-saving or efficiency-enhancing advances such as distance learning, Web-based instruction, and automated assessment are adopted more slowly, unevenly, and with less attention to cost-savings than would otherwise be the case. Intellectual support for these efforts is provided by academics and policy makers who argue that schooling should not be analogous to the provision of other goods, and that insulating schools from incipient competition is sensible policy rather than an indulgence (Cuban, 2004).

Although the public might be expected to support efficiency-minded proposals intended to control costs, there is no evidence of a constituency for cost-effectiveness at the K–12 level. For instance, after-inflation school spending has tripled in the past 40 years, while student performance has essentially remained stagnant (Chubb & Hanushek, 1990). Nevertheless, rather than express any concerns about productivity, public opinion has consistently supported increased spending, and a plurality of the public routinely says that a lack of money is the greatest single challenge facing schools. While some observers trace undisciplined spending to the influence that teachers unions exert on school boards, the reality is that President George W. Bush increased federal spending on K–12 education more rapidly than any previous president—and was criticized primarily for not spending enough. Ultimately, the centrality of education to American notions of opportunity and meritocracy, sensitivity to questions of educational access and equity, and the public's abiding affection for educators and local institutions make it inordinately difficult to promote radical policy change in this area or to rally support on behalf of productivity or cost containment.

Not surprisingly, Americans are highly sensitive to any risk their schools face, have faith in the ideal of public schooling, express a high rate of satisfaction with their local school, and are averse to proposals for radical change (Moe, 2002). Hence, they are uncomfortable with importing into education the "creative destruction" that is the signature of market-driven improvement. Regarding public education as a shared national faith and their local schools with sentimental eyes, Americans are reluctant to embrace the kind of ongoing opening, closing, and franchising that open competition implies. There is also much ambivalence about embracing a new breed of educators who are expansionist, profit-seeking, or focused on cost-efficiencies, especially when it cannot be proven that they will be more effective than traditional educators. In fact, efforts to import new educators through "radical" new programs such as Teach For America and New Leaders for New Schools are actually *more* mission-driven than traditional training programs and seek individuals focused single-mindedly on equity and social betterment.[4] Given the hesitance of both the public and reformers toward market-based school reform, political efforts to promote specific deregulatory measures—such as relaxing the licensure of teachers and administrators, allowing money to follow students more readily from school to school, or instituting more flexible compensation—might ultimately prove to have a more dramatic effect on educational provision than proposals for choice-based reform.

Such a prediction is tenuous, however, and depends on how the politics of choice evolve. Today, the strongest popular support for educational choice is found among those who are worst served by the present system: African Americans and the urban poor. The vision of school choice embraced by these communities has nothing to do with a commitment to free markets; it is a much more prosaic concern for gaining access to improved educational options. Such concerns make for a constituency that cares little about regulatory burdens or heightened productivity. In fact, many advocates of "public school choice" and similar measures also embrace an aggressive regulatory presence. Meanwhile, it is white-collar suburbanites who are most reticent about radical education reform. The reasons for these stances are unsurprising. Suburbanites have already invested in buying homes in communities with good schools, while urban families feel trapped in cities with low-performing schools.

However, these stances are at odds with the suburban affinity for "market-based" solutions and the urban skepticism about "deregulation." An unusual political alliance has often resulted, in which Republican legislators from suburbs join grassroots Black figures from central cities to promote choice-based reforms, while Black officeholders and Democrat legislators stand opposed. It is not yet clear whether Republicans will ultimately use choice-based reform to help win the allegiance of a new generation of Black officials, whether Democrats will oppose school choice to help recapture suburban voters, or how long the present stalemate might continue.

These political calculations matter greatly for program design and for educational competition. One concern of Black officials is that the limitations imposed on existing voucher programs, such as admissions lotteries and eligibility criteria, might be weakened or eliminated if small-scale programs become national policy. This makes them highly receptive to bureaucratic rules and oversight designed to minimize potential inequities. Neither the proponents nor the opponents of choice-based reform are particularly concerned with "creative destruction" or the requirements of dynamic markets. Conservative reformers who are committed to market-based reform, through the dictates of political convenience as well as a lack of considered attention to the requirements of market making, have sought to put Black and urban faces out front while minimizing divisive talk about what it takes to make education truly competitive.

The K–12 sector is dominated by public-operated, democratically governed providers. These organizations are bound by contracts, statutes, and public officials eager to placate influential constituencies. Consequently, "deregulation" or consumer choice—absent moves to transfer control and responsibility for public entities to profit-seeking management—is likely to yield only the faintest market imperatives. This reality has been routinely, and conveniently, overlooked by progressives who regard choice as a mechanism for promoting social equity and by conservatives seeking to make school choice as palatable as possible. Even when buffeted by consumer choice, as in higher education, nonprofit and publicly governed educational institutions have good structural, organizational, and political incentives to compete on bases other than cost or productivity. The ascendance of efficiency-conscious competition in education is not merely a question of deregulating but may well require the introduction of a degree of privatization that the public appears disposed to reject. Of course, such a determination necessarily precedes the more nuanced attention to the political economy of regulation that is thoughtfully portrayed in the companion chapters of this volume.

In the end, deregulating a marketplace can mean very different things, depending on the sector, the politics, and the context. Thatcherite reform in Great Britain consisted of dismantling state monopolies and creating competitive markets. Deregulation of the airline and trucking industries was a matter of the government making it easier for firms to pursue profit-driven agendas. In education, not even the most ardent champions of markets wish to see the government dismantle its system of schools. Meanwhile, the vast majority of non-state providers are nonprofit institutions, in which concerns about culture, comfort, and prestige, for example, often take precedence over the imperatives of maximizing revenues or minimizing costs. Exactly how deregulation will proceed in such an environment is unclear. How will it impel a public that regards educational expenditure as a rough proxy for quality to endorse cost-effectiveness? And how will it spur publicly managed schools to compete as if they were private sector organizations or encourage nonprofits to behave more like profit-maximizing firms? If the success of market-based reform ultimately hinges upon the entry and expansion of

for-profits, precious little consideration has been devoted to either desirable regulatory measures or the political implications. Given that markets do not implement themselves but depend on the rules of the game and the fidelity with which their rules are monitored and maintained, this inattention leaves unclear what meaningful educational deregulation would even look like.

The abiding American faith in markets and in public institutions comes to a head in the case of schooling, where strong and passionate defenders of existing public institutions exist. But K–12 education is being gradually modified by changes in technology and society. How these changes will be accentuated or accelerated by efforts to promote educational competition may well turn on whether the nascent political alliance for school choice deepens and expands into an alliance for expansive choice-based reform. However, even this alliance is focused more on limited and controlled forms of school choice than on educational competition. Ultimately, the fate of educational markets may be dimmed by the reality that there exists a powerful constituency for equity in American education and no such similar constituency for efficiency.

Notes

1. The full context for the discussion of vouchers as a possible panacea reads, "Without being too literal about it, we think reformers would do well to entertain the notion that choice is a panacea ... choice is not like other reforms and should not be combined with them as part of a reformist strategy for improving America's public schools. Choice ... has the capacity all by itself to bring about the kind of transformation that, for years, reformers have been seeking to engineer in myriad other ways" (Chubb & Moe, 1990, p. 217).

2. Policy makers could choose to reward public agency officials for attracting clients, but such incentives are generally considered to be at odds with the larger mission of public agencies. For a brief survey of the ethical dimension of this question, see Dilulio (1994).

3. For critiques of simple, standardized outcome assessments, see Kennedy (1999); Linn (2000).

4. Examples of this can be found on the organizations' Web sites, www.teachforamerica.org and www.nlns.org.

References

Brouillette, L. (1996). *A geology of school reform: The successive restructurings of a school district. SUNY series, restructuring and school change.* Albany: State University of New York Press.

Christensen, C. M. (1997). *The innovator's dilemma.* Cambridge, MA: Harvard Business School Press.

Christensen, C. M., & Raynor, M. E. (2003). *The innovator's solution.* Cambridge, MA: Harvard Business School Press.

Chubb, J. E., & Hanushek, E. A. (1990). Reforming educational reform. In H. J. Aaron (Ed.), *Setting national priorities: Policy for the nineties* (pp. 213–248). Washington, DC: Brookings Institution.

Chubb, J. E., & Moe, T. M. (1990). *Politics, markets, and America's schools.* Washington, DC: Brookings Institution.

Cuban, L. (2004). *The blackboard and the bottom line: Why schools can't be businesses.* Cambridge, MA: Harvard University Press.

Dilulio, J. J., Jr. (1994). *Deregulating the public service: Can government be improved?* Washington, DC: Brookings Institution.

Edelman, M. J. (1972). *The symbolic uses of politics.* Urbana: University of Illinois Press.

Epple, D., & Romano, R. (1998). Competition between private and public schools, vouchers, and peer-group effects. *American Economic Review, 88*(1), 33–62.

Flake, J. (2003, May 9). *D.C. parents deserve the right to choose where their kids go to school.* Press release.

Foster, J. L. (1975). Innovation in government structures: Minnesota school district reorganization. *American Journal of Political Science, 14*, 455–474.

Gehring, J. (2004). Detroit schools facing massive cuts, layoffs. *Education Week, 24*, 5.

Greene, J. P. (2001). *An evaluation of the Florida A-plus accountability and school choice program.* New York: Manhattan Institute.

Greene, J. P., Peterson, P. E., & Jiangtao, D. (1999). Effectiveness of school choice: The Milwaukee experiment. *Education and Urban Society, 31*(2), 190–213.

Hess, F. M. (2002). *Revolution at the margins: The impact of competition on urban school systems.* Washington, DC: Brookings.

Hess, F. M. (2004). *Without competition, school choice in not enough.* Washington, DC: American Enterprise Institute. Retrieved May 23, 2008, from http://www.aei.org/publication16747

Hess, F. M., Maranto, R., & Milliman, S. (2001a). Coping with competition: The impact of charter schooling on public school outreach in Arizona. *Policy Studies Journal, 29*(3), 388–404.

Hess, F. M., Maranto, R., & Milliman, S. (2001b). Little districts in big trouble: How four Arizona school systems responded to charter competition. *Teachers College Record, 103*, 1102–1124.

Hoxby, C. M. (2001). Rising tide. *Education Next, 1*(4), 68–74.

Hoxby, C. M. (2002). *School choice and school productivity (Or, could school choice be a tide that lifts all boats?).* (NBER Working Paper No. 8873). Cambridge, MA: National Bureau of Economic Research.

Kennedy, M. M. (1999). Approximations to indicators of student outcomes. *Educational Evaluation and Policy Analysis, 21*(4), 345–363.

Levin, H. (2001). Bear market. *Education Matters, 1*(1), 6–15.

Linn, R. L. (2000). Assessments and accountability. *Educational Researcher, 29*(2), 4–16.

Mayor defends voucher stance, accountability policy. (2003, July 7). *The Washington Post,* p. T7.

Moe, T. M. (2002). *Schools, vouchers, and the American public.* Washington, DC: Brookings Institution.

Molnar, A., Garcia, D. R., Bartlett, M., & O'Neill, A. (2006). *Profiles of for-profit education management companies: Eighth annual report, 2005–2006.* Tempe: Arizona State University, Commercialism in Education Research Unit.

National Association of State Budget Officers. (2006). State expenditure report. Retrieved May 25, 2008, from http://www.nasbo.org/Publications/PDFs/2005ExpendReport.pdf

National Education Association. (2005). *Rankings & estimates: Rankings of the states 2004 and estimates of school statistics 2005.* Retrieved May 17, 2008, from http://www.nea.org/edstats/images/05rankings-update.pdf

Nohria, N., & Gulati, R. (1996). Is slack good or bad for innovation? *Academy of Management Journal, 39*, 1245–1264.

Schneider, M., & Teske, P. (1992). Toward a theory of the political entrepreneur: Evidence from local government. *American Political Science Review, 86*, 737–747.

Snyder, T. D., & Hoffman, C. M. (2002). *Digest of education statistics 2001.* Washington, DC: National Center for Education Statistics, Office of Educational Research and Improvement

Stone, D. A. (1997). *Policy paradox: The art of political decision making.* New York: W.W. Norton.

U.S. Department of Education. (2005). 10 facts about K–12 education funding. Retrieved May 12, 2005, from http://www.ed.gov/about/overview/fed/10facts/10facts.pdf

41

Market Reforms in Education

CLIVE R. BELFIELD
Queens College, City University of New York

HENRY M. LEVIN
Teachers College, Columbia University

Introduction

For at least a century and a half, universal schooling has been viewed as a primary obligation of government. In the United States, state and local governments, with federal support in recent years, have accommodated this responsibility by making substantial legal commitments and by providing funding and facilities. Although private schools existed prior to the historical establishment of public schools, today they account for only about 11% of enrollments at the elementary and secondary level (National Center for Educational Statistics [NCES], 2003b, Table 3). Thus, the provision of elementary and secondary schooling has long been accepted as a government function and responsibility.

Historically, public schools have reflected the preferences of local communities; these communities were able to mold their schools to reflect their political, educational, and religious values (Katz, 1971). Resources available to schools depended heavily on local property wealth so that schools in richer communities were better endowed than those in poorer communities (Murray, Evans, & Schwab, 1998). Parents with adequate means could move to neighborhoods that had better schools or ones that more closely matched their childrearing and educational values or could send their children to private schools. Yet, these differences have been reduced considerably in recent decades by court and legislative decisions that have: more nearly equalized school funding; reduced racial inequalities; provided more rights and opportunities for the handicapped, the poor, and females; and proscribed religious practices. These court and legislative decisions forced school policies and practices to become more alike, at least procedurally (Husted & Kenny, 2002).

However, this homogenization of schools has been countered by pressures to reassert differentiation. Starting in the 1970s cities began to create district-wide schools based upon academic or vocational themes that might attract students from among different neighborhoods. These magnet schools were designed primarily to encourage racial integration by drawing students away from segregated neighborhoods (Wells & Crain, 2005). By the 1980s and early 1990s, broader intra-district and inter-district options were expanded, the most prominent example being the establishment of charter schools. These schools are exempt from most state and local regulations in exchange for a school commitment to particular educational goals and results. As of September 2006 there were almost 4,000 charter schools in 40 states across the country (Consoletti & Allen, 2007, p. 2).

Even more profound—and politically contentious—is the emergence of proposals to shift schools from government sponsorship to the private marketplace with government funding via educational vouchers or tuition tax credits (Belfield & Levin, 2002a). Under these funding approaches, a private market of schools would substitute for public schools. Parents would be provided with a voucher (a certificate for tuition that could be redeemed with the state), or tax credits (reductions in tax burdens for all or a portion of tuition). In some cases, parents would be able to supplement these public funds with their own finances to obtain more costly schooling for their children. Again, the motivation is to provide greater freedom of choice of schools as a right and more alternatives for families as a response to increasing uniformity.

But an additional argument was made that market competition would make all schools more effective and efficient (see Hoxby, 2003). As government agencies, public schools were held to be overly bureaucratic, slow to innovate, and subject to rapidly rising costs without any improvement in academic outcomes. For example, over the period from 1973 to 1996, Hanushek (1998) charts falling NAEP Science scores and stable NAEP Math scores for students, even as real current expenditure per pupil increased by around 45% (but see Grissmer, Flanagan, & Williamson, 1998). Competition and choice would mean that only the most effective schools would prosper and that schools would face an automatic pressure (declining enrollments and funding) to improve.

These twin ideas of choice and efficiency have provided a powerful ideological and political impetus toward educational privatization (Ryan & Heise, 2002; Viteritti, 1999; Smith, 2003). Unfortunately, the ideological belief in these ideas has often overwhelmed the thrust of the accumulated evidence (Levin & Belfield, 2005).

In this chapter we evaluate the possible options for an educational marketplace. We show that all educational arrangements, including market approaches, face a conflicting set of goals, and they require tradeoffs—that is, sacrifice of some goals in order to obtain others. The movement to an educational marketplace must confront this dilemma, particularly the conflicts that may arise between the private and public purposes of education. We review the possible educational options and the tools that can be used to orient educational market approaches towards specific goals and their consequences. We provide a brief review of the available evidence on the impacts of educational markets. There is now a considerable amount of evidence on education markets, from researchers in political science, law, education, sociology, and economics (e.g., Godwin & Kemerer, 2002; Wolfe, 2003; Hoxby, 2003). Our goal is to provide an overview of the issues. Finally, we consider what this portends for the future, in terms of research and policy.

Internal Anatomy of Markets

Support for markets is predicated on simple economic theory. Markets are places (literally or figuratively) where buyers and sellers come together to purchase goods and services at an agreed upon price. The purely competitive market is considered the ideal. In such a market there are a very large number of buyers and sellers so that no one buyer or seller can influence the price. There is perfect information on the alternatives open to market participants. There is freedom of entry into the market by either buyers or sellers, meaning that there are no obstacles to either producing or purchasing the good or service. Buyers wish to maximize total satisfaction or utility subject to the limitation of their resource capacity or income. Sellers wish to maximize profits.

Critically, demanders and suppliers operate independently and in their own private best interests. The former want the best product at the cheapest cost; the latter want to sell their product at the highest price. Although suppliers may want a price that is higher than the market price, competition for clientele will push down the price to that point where firms simply cover all of their costs plus a minimal profit, enough to stay in business. Firms have a choice of which goods or services to produce, so they can decide to enter or leave the industry if they cannot succeed at the equilibrium price. Firms that are less efficient and cannot produce their output at the market price will fail and leave the marketplace. Consumers may wish to get a price below the market equilibrium, but they will be unable

to purchase goods at a below market price in the long run, because firms will not be able to sustain themselves at a price below the cost of production. The key dynamics of the market are choice and competition. Households have a choice of suppliers, so firms must compete for their business by providing goods or services at the lowest price.

In contrast to the market, government-run education systems are often heavily criticized: Public schools may have excessive rules or rules applied to all schools regardless of circumstance, and they may be run "democratically," making them fraught with conflicts and compromises to appease the demands of special interest groups, which may or may not have strong connection to students' educational needs (Chubb & Moe, 1990). Costs may be inflated, because politicians feel that spending on public services is politically popular and because of corruption, fraud, and waste (taxpayers cannot escape these as easily as shareholders can divest themselves of stock). In contrast, private owners have incentives—profits, typically—to closely monitor their companies to make sure that they are meeting their objectives. With more market freedom, private schools could be taken over by more efficient providers, or a for-profit company could franchise its schooling technology, for example. Whichever development takes place in the open educational marketplace, the profit motive or educational mission will induce owners and managers to raise educational quality and efficiency to attract an optimal number of students.

It is this model that provides claims for those who seek to shift the production of schooling from governments to the private marketplace. They believe that by providing choice and competition, the quality of schooling will rise when costs are constant or the costs will fall for a given quality. In addition, advocates may wish to provide greater choice in types of schooling, providing a range of sub-markets for families because of differences in educational preferences (values, religion, and philosophy) rather than requiring each school to provide a uniform type of education (Chubb & Moe, 1990). By replacing a local school monopoly with market competition, efficiency can be brought to the consumer in two ways. First, there will be incentives to compete by providing schooling services at the lowest possible costs. Second, households will be better matched to the types of schooling that meet their needs because of the variety of schools that will emerge and the incentives of schools to be responsive to the needs of clientele.

Market advocates would argue that the market approach leads to choice and competition overall, increasing productive behavior on the part of parents and students as well as schools. Parents and students have incentives to choose schools wisely. They also have incentives to keep schools attentive with the implicit option of switching to other schools if they are dissatisfied. Schools have incentives to be responsive to student needs to both attract and retain students and to get to the maximum size consistent with good education. At the same time, they have incentives to innovate over the long run to gain market advantages, a dynamic that can make the industry technologically and organizationally progressive as other competitors imitate those improvements to increase their own effectiveness. These incentives arise primarily from choice and competition promoted by the marketplace.

Finally, even in markets where there is considerable competition, government regulation is necessary. Governments should set basic standards to capture the public interest in schooling. The issue is how extensive this regulatory framework should be, not whether it should exist.

Market theory accommodates the reality that few markets are perfectly competitive. In many cases there are few suppliers of a particular product or service, and even these firms may choose to collude rather than compete. Further, a key resource used by firms may be controlled by a single entity such as another firm or a union. Consumers may not have good information, and the nature of the good or service may make accurate information difficult to acquire.

Certainly, all of these factors are a reality in education. Particularly in rural areas, there may be too few potential students to establish competitive schools that can operate efficiently. Teachers' unions may constrain the ability of schools to adjust employment, benefits, and salaries to market realities or to change the organization of educational services. And, parents may have difficulties obtaining and evaluating school quality with schools providing information that is designed primarily for marketing and promotional goals rather than for useful comparisons. Though each of these may reduce the efficiency of the marketplace, the issue is whether greater choice and competition *is introduced* that improves educational processes and outcomes, not whether the improvement is optimal.

Even with only limited choice and competition, it is believed that the outcomes will be better than when there are no choices at all. This does not mean that only competition can be used to obtain efficiency in the use of educational resources to gain maximal performance. In his classic book, *Exit, Voice, and Loyalty* (1970), Albert Hirschman suggests that both exit (market choice) and voice (informing the provider of how to improve) are important to efficiency and that the easy option of abandoning a supplier may undermine the incentive to guide and pressure them directly to improve services. In the case of education, such school involvement may also be a key to student and family engagement that contributes to learning. McMillan (2000) has found some evidence of this in reviewing the impact of choice on parental participation and student achievement.

Thus, market theory suggests that any opportunities to motivate agents to operate in their own private interests will improve outcomes and that reforms to the education system should be restructured to encourage these opportunities.

Education and the Public-Private Nexus

Probably the greatest challenge to the view of market efficiency in education is created by the presence of externalities. Externalities refer to effects that "spillover" to the larger society from the individual transactions of the marketplace. That is, by virtue of producing and selling goods and services, firms may have an impact that extends beyond the internal production and sale of products to consumers. At the same time, the choice of such services and their consumption by consumers may also have effects beyond the purchasers.

Schooling is considered to be a primary source of external social benefits because the results of an education benefit not only the individual, but the society of which she is a part. That is, even those who are not in school are expected to benefit from a more highly educated society. It has long been held that one of the central purposes of schools is to improve the cohesion and stability of society through the provision of a common experience that prepares the young for adult roles and responsibilities (Guttman, 1986). Schools are expected not only to educate students as individuals, but also to contribute to the overall effectiveness of society through creating competent adult citizens. Even Friedman's (1962, p. 86) proposals acknowledged this external benefit of schools by asserting that a democracy requires a minimal level of literacy and knowledge and a common set of values to function effectively. This supposition motivated Friedman's argument for public funding of education. He asserted that this externality (or "neighborhood" effect) can addressed by setting "minimum standards" for schools in a marketplace without further government intervention. Friedman did not attempt to suggest what these minimum standards might be or how they might be satisfied, providing a blank canvas on which other designers may sketch their own interpretations. That there is broad agreement that schools must meet not only the narrower requirements of individual students and their families is evident. The larger question is how to reconcile the private choices of families with the public requirements of education for democratic knowledge and values.

When families choose the type of education that they want for their children, the decision revolves primarily upon their values as well as their perception of their child's needs. That education yields private benefits to the child and her family is obvious. More and better education is closely associated with higher income and status and greater access to worldly knowledge, both technical and cultural. Since parents want their children to succeed, they will prefer schools that meet high standards. Beyond that, parents usually have political, religious, and philosophical values that they believe are important and should be transmitted to their children. Accordingly, they will seek schools that reflect these values or, at least, do not undermine them. The range of household choices for schooling will be largely predicated on the diversity of backgrounds and educational beliefs of the heterogeneous populations that are found in the United States (Hochschild & Scovronick, 2003). Increasingly, this diversity is reflected in other nations, as immigration and religious radicalism increase throughout much of the world. However, many families may make choices based on racial and class composition of the student body, leading to communities segregated along these lines.

Also, disadvantaged families are less likely to participate in voucher programs than advantaged ones. Thus, choice may allow the latter set to further distance themselves from children born into disadvantaged families.

If the market responds only to these diverse demands, schools will not be predicated on a homogeneous set of school offerings with substantially common experiences for all students. Instead they will tend to divide into market segments (or niches) that appeal to a particular group of households, segments based upon religion, child philosophy, instructional approaches, and so on. James (1987, 1993) has found that diversity in the population is an important statistical predictor of the extent of private schooling internationally. Coons and Sugarman (1978) and Chubb and Moe (1990) argue that this is the most appropriate way to serve competing needs rather than expecting a single institution to serve all needs. Under a market approach, schools will seek market niches through product differentiation. That is, they will compete by matching their appeal to particular educational preferences of parents, rather than trying to produce a standardized educational product. The problem is that serving well a wide variety of different values and preferences is likely to undermine the social goals of providing a unifying educational experience around societal institutions and values.

In general, the social purpose of schools is to prepare the young for democratic participation in the political, social, and economic institutions that unite society into nations, regions, and communities. Successful citizen participation in a free and democratic society requires common language, values, and knowledge for economic and political understanding and participation, and an acquaintance with a common set of social goals. In addition, democratic societies are also concerned with the provision of fairness in access to life's rewards so that effort and talent, rather than private privilege, are the determinants. These goals argue for a common educational experience, rather than one that is differentiated according to family political, religious, and philosophical preferences. That is, the very externalities of education that justify public support argue in favor of a common educational experience rather than one premised upon private choice.[1]

Educational Privatization Policy Alternatives

Voucher Programs The most prominent market attempt to shift education to private auspices is that of educational vouchers. The concept is found as early as the 18th century in a plan proposed by Thomas Paine (West, 1967). However, the present discussions on vouchers date back to an important essay published by Milton Friedman (1962), which asked what the government role should be in education. Friedman concluded that "a stable and democratic society is impossible without a minimum degree of literacy and knowledge on the part of most citizens and without widespread acceptance of some common set of values" (p. 86). Since education contributes substantially to these goals,

Friedman agrees that some minimal public subsidy is justified. But, he argues that public funding for schooling is not an argument for government schools. Rather, the operation of a private marketplace of schools will provide greater benefits in efficiency and technical progress by promoting choice and competition. To combine public funding with private provision, Friedman proposed that "Governments could require a minimum level of schooling financed by giving parents vouchers redeemable for a specified maximum sum per child per year if spent on 'approved' educational services" (Friedman 1962, p. 89). All educational voucher plans utilize this basic concept, although each may contain different provisions with respect to the size of the voucher, the opportunities for parents to add to the voucher, and other details.

Potentially, voucher programs are privatization reforms with very significant ramifications.[2] In their most liberal design, they can allow for all forms of schooling to be publicly supported—this would not just include variants of public schools, but also private schools with religious curricula or cyber-schools with enrollments across the United States. Families would be free to choose any type of school such that the enrollment decision would be completely privatized. Families would also be free to pay extra for additional educational services. Schools would be free to offer any form of instruction and education, subject only to the market test that they had sufficient enrollments to cover their costs. Potentially, the government might conduct very minimal oversight over these enrollment decisions—by enrolling at a particular school, families would be revealing their preferences as to which education suited them best; schools that failed to secure enough students and the concomitant funding would close. However, in practice these reforms have been highly regulated by local authorities and given to disadvantaged families. Also, the value of the voucher is typically much below the tuition at most private schools (with one notable exception in Washington, DC).

By 2006, publicly funded voucher programs had been implemented in Milwaukee, Cleveland, and Washington, DC; voucher legislation had passed in the state of Utah (later rejected by the voters in 2007 in a statewide referendum), and been frustrated by the courts in the state of Florida. But, the total number of participants has been small as a proportion of public school enrollments (there is also a network of privately funded voucher programs, providing scholarship grants to over 100,000 students; see Howell & Peterson, 2002, Table 2.1). Also, both Maine and Vermont have allowed students in rural areas to attend private schools if there is an inadequate supply of local public schooling. These state policies are largely in response to the high costs of providing education in sparsely populated areas, and not developed to expand the education market per se.

The first voucher program was established in Milwaukee in 1990. The Milwaukee Parental Choice Program was limited to low-income families and to no more than 1% of students from the Milwaukee Public Schools (raised later to 1.5%, and more recently, no cap on enrollment). The amount of the voucher rose from $2,446 in 1990 to $4,894 in 1998, and $5,882 in 2003–04, amounts predicated upon the amount of state aid to local school districts. Until 1995 the Milwaukee voucher was limited to attendance in non-religious schools. In 1998, religious schools were declared eligible by state law for the voucher, an action that was upheld subsequently by Wisconsin courts and left to the state's decision by the U.S. Supreme Court. This broadening of school eligibility promoted a large expansion in enrollments.

The second voucher plan was established by the state of Ohio for the city of Cleveland beginning in 1995. Known as the Cleveland Scholarship and Tutoring Program, it has particular prominence because it was the focus of a U.S. Supreme Court decision which resulted in the legal approval of inclusion of religious schools in a voucher plan (*Zelman vs. Simmon-Harris*, 2002). Low-income families were given preference for vouchers in Cleveland, with those below 200% of the poverty level provided with 90% of tuition or $2,250, whichever is lower. Families above 200% of the poverty level were provided with 75% of tuition or $1,875, which is lower. About one-quarter of the students came from the latter group. The vast majority of students in the program chose religious schools; this was not surprising, since such schools represent three-quarters or more of existing private enrollments more generally, and are the only ones available at the tuition levels of the Cleveland voucher.

The Florida voucher program, the Opportunity Scholarship Plan, was established in 1999 and has two components. Schools that received an F for 2 years out of 4 on the Florida educational assessment system were required to allow their students to select another public school or to receive a voucher to go to a private school. The voucher has a value of up to about $4,500. Relatively few students actually used the voucher prior to its rejection by the Florida Supreme Court in 2006. Florida also sponsors the McKay Scholarships for students with disabilities, a voucher approach. Parents who decide that their handicapped child is not progressing in public schools can use what is spent in the public school to apply towards private schools. In 2002–03, almost 9,000 out of 375,000 students with disabilities were taking advantage of this finance mechanism. The amount that could be allocated to the voucher was a maximum of more than $21,000, depending upon the services that were being provided in the public school for that child. Parents could add on to the voucher amount to pay for a more expensive placement.

Other voucher programs have been proposed, but each program has been met with some opposition. For example, in Spring 2003, the State of Colorado passed a plan to provide vouchers to students from low-income families with low-academic performance if they are in districts where 8 or more schools in 2001–02 had low or unsatisfactory performance. The plan would start with a maximum of 1% of student enrollments in eligible districts, and rise to no more than 6% by 2007 (see Lenti, 2003). But in December 2003, the Colorado plan was struck down, being judged to violate the Colorado Constitution by depriving local school boards of control over instruction in their districts. Legal challenges are likely to continue, however. The Utah legislation passed in 2006 has not been implemented while it is under legal challenge.

Tuition Tax Credits An alternative way of encouraging a private educational marketplace is a tuition tax credit (TTC; Belfield & Levin, 2002a; Huerta & d'Entremont, 2006). A TTC provides a reduction in tax burden equal to a portion of tuition paid to a private school. For example, a TTC on income tax could be enacted that reduces the tax liability of the taxpayer by some sum (e.g., up to $1,000 a year). Since 1997, 6 states have enacted tuition tax credits for education, and 13 states have tax deduction programs (for schooling expenditures). A tax credit is different from a tax deduction: Some states allow a portion of tuition to be deducted from income in computing a tax, but this only reduces the tax burden by the tax rate on the allowable deduction, rather than providing a reduction in the tax burden of that amount. Some states also permit businesses to contribute up to some maximum amount to cover the tuition of students in private schools. The TTC serves as a subsidy to households with children in private schools, reducing the effective tuition cost to them, thus increasing the demand for private enrollments. Poorer households can take less advantage of a tax credit because they have less tax liability, although it is possible to design a plan that refunds the credit if tax liability is not adequate to offset it.

Charter Schools Charter schools are public schools that are able to waive compliance with state and local regulations in exchange for adhering successfully to a specific mission, their charter. As of 2006, there were almost 4,000 charter schools serving almost 1 million students in 40 states and Washington, DC according to the Center for Educational Reform (Consoletti & Allen, 2007, p. 2). These schools simulate some of the dynamics of a private market by increasing the supply of alternatives to parents and by competing with existing public schools. In addition, many of them contract with for-profit, educational management organizations (EMOs) to operate their schools (Miron & Nelson, 2002, pp. 170–193). Typically, they also have their own boards of trustees and considerable autonomy relative to public schools in their states. Although they are not strictly private, they contain features of choice and competition which some analysts believe are good predictors of behavior in such a marketplace (see Kane & Lauricella, 2001; Sugarman, 2002).

Because the intention of charter school legislation is to encourage flexible educational provision in response to local needs, charter schools themselves are heterogeneous (on virtual/cyber charter school laws, see Huerta & Gonzalez, 2004). As well as exemption from regulations in hiring unionized teachers, charter schools can choose a non-traditional pedagogy and or curriculum; they can also select the mode of delivery (classroom-based or through distance-learning) and school facilities. Given this heterogeneity, the evidence on charter schools' performance (at least as reflected in test score comparisons) is mixed (on charter schools in California, see Zimmer, 2003). For advocates, the charter school movement represents a freedom from government intrusion—not only in how the education is provided, but also in how it should be assessed.

Educational Management Organizations In the last decade, for-profit businesses have risen to manage schools. Businesses have long sold products and services and managed some operations of schools such as transportation, cafeterias, maintenance, and construction, as well as school textbooks, supplies, and equipment, such as furnishings and computers (even to include curricular packages and assessment systems). But, the rise of educational management organizations (EMOs) has represented a marketplace in itself where such entities compete to manage entire schools under contract to school districts or to charter school boards. In general, the EMOs and their schools are in competition, because they typically are premised upon school choice of clientele and promise to out-perform comparable schools administered by the school district. In fact, school districts often contract with EMOs to operate schools that have done poorly under district administration. Thus, they provide two major dimensions of a market, choice and competition.

Evaluating Market Reforms of Education

On the one hand, the right to influence the way in which one's child is reared means that parents should have the options of choosing the school that matches most closely their childrearing preferences. On the other hand, the right of a society to maintain an effective and stable democracy and a fair society requires that children have a common educational experience. How are these conflicting goals to be reconciled in light of the range of possible market reforms in education? That conflict is at the heart of all educational systems. The existing U. S. educational system, in which 90% of students are in government-sponsored schools, has faced this historic challenge. But, even more so, a market system that bases its appeal on differentiation and choice must adopt a mechanism to ensure common experiences across schools to prepare students for their civic rights and responsibilities.

Clearly, there is no perfect system as much as a search for a "best system" in providing a balance among these and competing aims (Tyack, 1974). In this context, one can denote four major criteria for addressing an effective educational system: (a) freedom of choice; (b) productive efficiency; (c) equity; and (d) social cohesion:

1. *Freedom to Choose*: This criterion places a heavy emphasis on the private benefits of education and the liberty to ensure that schools are chosen that are consistent with the child-rearing practices of families. Voucher advocates typically place great weight on this criterion relative to detractors.

2. *Productive Efficiency*: This criterion refers to the maximization of educational results for any given resource constraint. Educational voucher advocates assume that market competition among schools for students will create strong incentives, not only to meet student needs, but to improve educational productivity. Voucher detractors believe that the assumptions that make competition effective will not be present in the educational marketplace.

3. *Equity*: This criterion refers to the quest for fairness in access to educational opportunities, resources, and outcomes by gender, social class, race, language origins, handicapping condition, and geographical location of students. Voucher advocates argue that the ability to choose schools will open up possibilities for students who are locked into inferior neighborhood schools and that the competitive marketplace will have great incentives to meet the needs of all students more fully than existing schools. Challengers argue that vouchers will create greater inequities because parents with education and income are better informed and have greater resources such as access to transportation. Also, they believe that the choices, themselves, will further segregate the poor and disenfranchised as those with power and status will select schools with students like themselves and schools will also select students by such criteria.

4. *Social Cohesion*: This criterion refers to the provision of a common educational experience that will orient all students to grow to adulthood as full participants in the social, political, and economic institutions of our society. This is usually interpreted as necessitating common elements of schooling with regard to curriculum, social values, goals, language, and political institutions. Voucher advocates believe that this will take place in schools without making special provisions or that it will only require minimal regulations.

These criteria are in conflict such that there must be tradeoffs. Some goals cannot be attained without sacrificing others. Although some design provisions would improve outcomes along more than one criterion, almost all would also reduce outcomes on other criteria. Provision of information and transportation will improve choice options for all participants, but especially for those from families with the least access to information and transportation—the poor. But, such provision would also raise the costs of the overall educational system, probably reducing productive efficiency unless gains from competition due to better information and access offset the costs of the transportation and information. The establishment of regulations with continuous monitoring and enforcement could be used to increase equity and social cohesion, but at the sacrifice of freedom of choice and productive efficiency (see the discussion in Levin & Belfield, 2005; Coons & Sugarman, 1978; Godwin & Kemerer, 2002).

This means that there is no optimal system that provides maximal results among all four criteria. Ultimately, the choice of design features will depend upon specific preferences and values as transmitted through democratic institutions. Those who place a high value on freedom of choice will probably be willing to sacrifice some equity and social cohesion provisions by eschewing regulations and support services and allowing parental add-ons to vouchers. Conversely, those who place a high value on social cohesion will be willing to sacrifice some freedom of choice through establishing a common curriculum core and other standardized features of schools. Ultimately, much of the debate over the specifics of educational voucher plans revolves around the political power and preferences of the stakeholders.

Evidence on Market Reforms

Although market reforms may offer the potential for dramatic reform of the education system, at present they apply to only a very small proportion of U.S. school populations. Even among these situations, there have been relatively few evaluations, and virtually none that address consequences for all four of the criteria that we have set out. Nevertheless, it is possible to provide the contours of findings for each criterion.

Freedom of Choice Advocates of the marketplace emphasize that parents will have greater freedom of choice than they would under a government system. In an open market, families will have the right to choose schools for their children that are premised on their values, educational philosophies, religious teachings, and political outlooks. Where there are varied preferences and/or abilities across students, this freedom of choice becomes especially important—it is too expensive and complicated for a government provider to collect and process all the information needed to allocate students to their most preferred school. For libertarians, allowing families to make their own choices—almost by definition—improves educational outcomes.

The evidence on choice favors the view that vouchers will increase choice considerably in terms of the numbers and diversity of options and that those who take advantage of choice will express higher satisfaction with their schools than comparable groups. Doubters of the expansion of choice often start out with the existing numbers of openings at private schools in a particular region, showing that the available openings are miniscule in comparison with the potential number of vouchers. Certainly, in the short run, this is likely to be true with little expansion of openings in response to voucher demands. Existing schools have capacity limitations, which can only be relieved through longer run expansion, and there is a time lag between the stimulus to establish new schools and the ability to plan, construct, and staff them. However, in response to the new private market demand, the long-run supply of school places will increase (as evidenced in Milwaukee between 1998 and 2002). But, there is another reason that the number of school choices should expand under a market system relative to government sponsorship of schools. Private schools (and charter schools too) tend to be about half of the size of public schools in the United States (NCES, 2003a). This means that for any given population there are likely to be twice as many schools under a market regime.

The U.S. evidence strongly supports the conclusion that parents value freedom of choice (Peterson & Hassel, 1998). Many families report higher satisfaction from participation in voucher programs (Howell & Peterson, 2002), and from being able to choose charter schools over regular public schools (Zimmer, 2003). There is also evidence that parents do make rational choices—that is, preferring schools with better outcomes holding other factors constant (Reback, 2005). Indeed, the very fact that parents in large numbers choose different types of schools when given options is prima facie evidence of the benefits of choice, and guaranteeing freedom of choice is an important way to raise satisfaction levels within the education system (Teske & Schneider, 2001).

But, there are several caveats to bear in mind when depending on increased choice to substantially improve the quality of education. One is that some families may not have the resources or the capacity to make choices that are in their children's best interests; there may be a role for education professionals to guide, monitor, or regulate these choices. Also, in sparsely populated areas, the limited population size may preclude the establishment of alternatives. A second is that some families may choose schools that will lead to de facto segregation of groups; individual families may feel better off, but society as a whole may be worse. A third caveat is that there may be only limited options to increase the range of choices: in the United States, many families already have as much choice as they feel they need—fully three-quarters of families appear satisfied with their choice of school (Henig & Sugarman, 1999). And, when a sample of low-income families was offered a voucher of $1,400 toward attendance at private school, only between 29% and 70% used the voucher for at least 3 years (Howell & Peterson, 2002, p. 44). Fourth, private schools might deny some students access. For example, a religious private school is likely to bar enrollment to students with atheist beliefs (or belief in an alternative faith; around 75% of all U.S. private schools currently in operation are religiously affiliated). The final caveat is that private schools may be subject to increased regulations if they accept vouchers: these regulations may discourage new supply (Muraskin & Stullich, 1998, p. 49).

Each of the above factors suggests that the gains from enhanced freedom of choice in a market—although positive overall—may not be profound and may be particularly limited for some groups. It must be borne in mind that many U.S. families already take advantage of choice through charter schools, magnet schools, within district and among district choice, and neighborhood housing choices. Henig and Sugarman (1999) estimate that more than half of all households already exercise these choices.

Efficiency   Some economists contend that an educational system with a greater reliance on the marketplace through choice and competition would be more efficient, that is, it would generate better academic outcomes for the same or less resource investment. However, very few evaluations have genuinely investigated the issue of efficiency in comparing outcomes to resources used. Instead, they have focused on whether the outcomes are better (implicitly assuming that market reforms do not require additional resources beyond what is currently being spent).

Effectiveness of Market Reforms   Evidence on the relative effectiveness of voucher programs is weakly positive. An evaluation by Rouse (1998), making considerable adjustments for data problems, showed no difference in achievement for reading and only a slight advantage for the voucher students in mathematics. But these evaluations of the impact of the Milwaukee voucher plan on academic achievement cover only the period 1990–95, which is before religious schools were eligible to participate (Witte, 1999). Similarly, an evaluation of the Cleveland Scholarship Program showed no differences in achievement in any subject between voucher and non-voucher students over the period from Kindergarten to Grade 4 (Metcalf, West, Legan, Paul, & Boone, 2003). Finally, evidence on the Florida program shows some academic benefits, but most of the gains are attributable to student characteristics, rather than the introduction of the voucher (Figlio & Rouse, 2006).

Experimental evidence also shows weak educational effects from participation in a voucher program. Using an experimental design, Howell and Peterson (2002) randomly assigned educational vouchers among a group of voucher applicants from low-income families, forming a group of voucher recipients and a similar control group. The voucher amount of about $1,400 a year was applied mainly to tuition at low-cost Catholic schools for up to 3 years in three cities (New York, Washington, DC, and Dayton, Ohio). The full results are reported in Howell and Peterson (2002) for voucher recipients who used their voucher at a private school. Overall, no achievement advantages were found for educational vouchers after 3 years. There are positive gains for one specific group—African Americans, after 3 years of voucher enrollment—but even these results pertain mainly to a single grade in one city. These findings have been challenged by a reanalysis that concludes that these gains may not be robust to more consistent racial classification and alternative sampling schemes (see Krueger & Zhu, 2004a, 2004b; and in rebuttal, see Peterson & Howell, 2004).

Competitive Pressures   As noted above, economists believe that marketplace competition forces providers of a service to be more efficient. The impact of competition can be assessed in terms of test scores and other outcomes from the education system. Belfield and Levin (2002b) review over 40 published studies from 1972 to 2002, which explicitly test for a link between competition and educational outcomes in U.S. schooling. These studies use large-scale cross-sectional datasets, employing over 400 individual tests for the impact of competition. Competition is measured either between schools within districts, between districts, or between the public and the private sectors. The impact is measured as the effect on educational outcomes when the extent of competition is increased by one standard deviation.

Their results are summarized in Table 41.1. The first row indicates that the evidence from over 200 tests in 25 separate studies shows that competition does have a beneficial effect on the academic outcomes of students in public schools. In general, test scores rise with the extent of competition. However, the effects are substantively modest: Around three-fifths of the tests show no correlation, and the mean effect of increasing competition by 1 standard deviation is to raise academic test scores in public schools by approximately 0.1 standard deviations, equivalent to

TABLE 41.1
Summary of the Effects of Increases in Competition by One Standard Deviation

Outcome Variable	Stat. Sig. Estimations (n)[a]	Competition Measure	Effect of Increasing Competition by 1 Standard Deviation
Academic outcomes	38% (*206*)	Herfindahl Index Private school enrollments or other proxies for competition	Outcome scores in public schools rise by 0.1 s.d. Outcome scores in public schools rise by <0.1 s.d.
Attainment, graduation rates, drop-out rates	42% (*52*)	Number of districts or schools Private school enrollments	Drop-out rates are not affected Graduation rates are higher by 0.08–0.18 s.d.
Spending	42% +ve 22% -ve (*33*)	Number of districts in state Private school enrollments	Spending is lower by 12% Spending effect is ambiguous (higher by 0.2–0.4 s.d. *or* lower by 7%)
Efficiency	66% (*64*)	Herfindahl Index Private school enrollments	Efficiency is higher, only in concentrated markets Efficiency is higher, by approximately 0.2 s.d.

Note: [a] Number of separate studies: academic outcomes, 25; attainment, graduation rates, dropout rates, 6; spending, 11; efficiency, 13; teaching quality, 8; private school enrollments, 6. Final column effects are calculated using all studies, where both significant and insignificant coefficients are reported.
Source: Belfield & Levin (2002b).

about 10 points on the verbal SAT, about 4 percentiles, or one-tenth of the test score gap between Anglo and African American students.

If competition presses schools to offer more effective schooling, students may respond by enrolling longer or by applying to college in greater numbers. No effect of competition on dropout rates is evident, but a 1 standard deviation increase in competition from private schools is associated with public school graduation rates of approximately 0.08 to 0.18 standard deviations. The effects of competition on spending are harder to predict. From the evidence, there is no clear link between educational expenditures and competition.

Fundamentally, competition in the marketplace should raise educational efficiency (see Hoxby, 2000). Indirectly, the evidence suggests that competition raises test scores modestly, but does not raise expenditures. There is also some direct support: The evidence given in Table 41.1 shows an increase of 1 standard deviation in private-school enrollments raises public-school efficiency (ratio of test scores to per-pupil spending) by as much as 0.2 standard deviations.

Overall, this evidence supports the argument in favor of introducing more marketplace competition into education: Increasing competition—either intradistrict, interdistrict, or from private schools—may raise effectiveness and efficiency of public schools, as well as address other educational objectives. It is important to note that the substantive effect is modest and does not support the contention that market competition will produce radical improvements in educational results. Also, the magnitude of the reform is important. Case studies of Cleveland and San Antonio show very few pressures to improve when the competitive stimuli are limited to small-scale reforms (Hess, Maranto, & Milliman, 2001). Also, less is known about which types of competition are strongest. Buddin and Zimmer (2006) found much weaker effects of competitive pressures in California from charter schools on public schools (but for Texas, see Booker, Gilpatric, Gronberg, & Jansen, 2005).

However, this evidence only establishes the benefits of competition, and does not consider any necessary reorganizational costs to foster, regulate, and monitor competition, or to promote competition broadly across the education system. For example, Levin and Driver (1997) estimate the additional costs of a statewide voucher system for record-keeping and monitoring of students, transportation, adjudication, and information services and conclude that these added costs would be substantial, perhaps as much as one-fourth of existing per-pupil expenditures. Bear in mind that the centralized administration of an extremely decentralized activity (funding and regulating household and school choice) entails a huge increase in transactions and their costs. For example, in the case of California, the state would have to shift its attention from monitoring somewhat over 1,000 school districts to concerning itself with the establishment of individual accounts for almost

7 million individual students and a doubling of existing numbers of schools to 25,000 or more.

More Efficient School Managers and Owners Another argument that the marketplace may deliver higher quality education rests on the belief that private owners and managers of schools will be more efficient than government ownership and management. The evidence here is also only moderately supportive.

The evidence on the relative effectiveness in producing academic achievement of private schools over public schools has been reviewed by McEwan (2000). The evidence for Catholic schools is summarized in Table 41.2 (the results for nonreligious schools are similar). Overall, it shows only small differences between private and public school types (when student intake differences are accounted for), indicating that there are not large differences in results across management and ownership structures (see also Figlio & Stone, 1999). For achievement, there appear to be modest effects for mathematics of poor, minority students in grades 2–5 (but not in grades 6–8 or among non-Black students) from attendance at Catholic schools. But there are no consistent effects for reading. For educational attainment (i.e., years of schooling), Catholic schools increase

TABLE 41.2
Summary of Catholic School Effects

Academic Outcome	Number of positive and significant estimates / Total number of studies	Average effect (all studies)
K-8 Math:		
Full sample	1 / 4	0.02
Minority	2 / 7	0.05
White	1 / 7	0.04
K-8 Reading:		
Full sample	1 / 3	0.03
Minority	0 / 7	0.00
White	2 / 7	0.10
Secondary Math:		
Full sample	2 / 5	-0.05
Minority	1 / 6	0.00
White	3 / 4	0.10
Secondary Reading:		
Full sample	1 / 4	-0.05
Minority	0 / 2	0.00
White	1 / 2	0.00
High school graduation:		
Full sample	4 / 5	0.07
Minority	5 / 6	0.14
White	5 / 6	0.06
College attendance:		
Full sample	3 / 4	0.06
Minority	5 / 6	0.15
White	5 / 6	0.06

Source: McEwan (2000, Table 5).

Clive R. Belfield and Henry M. Levin

the probability of high school completion and of college attendance (particularly for minorities in urban areas).[3]

Other studies have compared the school effectiveness of specific types of choice arrangements such as charter schools or magnet schools (Gamoran, 1996). Miron and Nelson (2002) compared charter schools with traditional public schools. Summarized in Table 41.3, the evidence indicates that, although results vary from state to state, charter schools appear on average to be no more (but also no less) effective than traditional public schools. Evidence on charter schools is continuing to accumulate. Recent micro-level analysis from 10 states indicates that charter school students may perform better (Wisconsin), broadly equivalent (Texas), or worse (California, North Carolina, and the Great Lakes states) than students in other school settings (see respectively, Witte, 2003; Hanushek, Kain, & Rivkin, 2003; Buddin & Zimmer, 2003; Bifulco & Ladd, 2003; Miron, Coryn, & Mackety, 2007). In Florida, charter schools start off behind regular public schools but their performance gradually converges (Sass, 2006). National evidence using NAEP data comparing charter and public school students in fourth and eighth grades also shows a mixed picture (Lubienski & Lubienski, 2007). These micro-level analyses also find considerable variation in academic achievement across types of charter school. Overall, the evidence on charter schools' relative effectiveness is mixed—some charter schools are better than public schools, but others are not (Zimmer & Buddin, 2006). In itself, this finding is not supportive of the views of advocates, because it suggests that the public schools are not performing especially badly. Nevertheless, it does motivate inquiry into which charter schools are superior. Unfortunately, this inquiry too has not yielded clear guidance—comparing charter schools is not straightforward, because they vary on so many dimensions (e.g., student body, organizational processes, goals); results tend to be sensitive to the estimation technique applied (Ballou, Teasley, & Zeidner, 2007).

Another potential school type that might be expected to take advantage of an educational marketplace is for-profit schooling. The largest for-profit provider of education in the United States is Edison Schools, which managed 76 schools in 2007, a reduction from about 130 in earlier years. However, many of the private for-profit companies have faced difficulties in achieving profitability and in competing with non-profit religious schools. In general, the for-profit companies have not been able to innovate more efficiently than public schools, and have had difficulties in establishing brand equity (Levin, 2001). Overall, private for-profit schools have not established themselves as clearly superior to public schools (Gill et al., 2005), and the evidence on improved managerial competence is ambiguous (for insights into the challenges of establishing and maintaining a profitable educational management organization, see Levin, 2002; McGuinn, 2007).

Considering all the evidence on the efficiency and effectiveness of markets in education, the following conclusion appears to be robust: markets do improve educational quality slightly over what would be provided in a fully public system, but the differences in performance are variable and do not always favor the private or market alternatives. To the degree that students are stratified into schools with more nearly homogeneous student populations, the peer effects of diversity on achievement may be reduced for some groups of students as well. The educational marketplace has advantages in matching students to the types of schools that their families prefer relative to traditional assignment by attendance area. This advantage is less evident where intra-district or inter-district or extensive charter school choice exists. The additional costs of the infrastructure required to monitor and administer a voucher system are substantial and may outweigh the modest achievement advantages.

Equity The concern that school systems—whether provided by markets or the state—be fair and equitable is an important one. Equity can be assessed in terms of inputs—do all students get an appropriate amount of funding and

TABLE 41.3
Summary of Charter School Effects

Academic outcome	Grade level	State	Results for charter schools relative to comparison group
Math	2–11	AZ	+ve (very weak)
Reading	3,4, and 7	CO	+ve (weak)
Reading			+ve (2/3rds outperformed comparison schools)
Writing	3,4, and 7	CO	+ve
Math	3,4, and 7	CO	No difference
Reading / Math	4,6,8, and10	CT	+ve
Reading / Math		DC	-ve (less likely to have improved; more 'below basic')
Reading / Math	3,5 +	GA	No difference
Reading / Math	4,5,7,8, and11	MI	-ve
Reading / Math	5,6,8,9, and11	PA	-ve (lower scores in cross-section) +ve (faster gains)
Reading / Math	3–8	TX	-ve, all schools +ve, at-risk schools

Source: Miron & Nelson (2002, Table 3).

resources, commensurate with their needs? Equity can also be assessed in terms of outcomes—do all students finish their schooling with sufficient skills and a fair opportunity to progress in life?

Those who challenge education markets argue that they will produce greater social inequities, as parents with higher incomes may benefit most. First, families already paying for private schooling may receive a government subsidy for tuition fees, which previously they were willing to pay for independently. This windfall is intrinsic to universal voucher programs, for example, and is also likely with the introduction of a tax credit or deduction. Second, wealthier families will have the most resources to purchase educational services in a private market, allowing them to purchase more education if "add-ons" are permitted, resulting in greater inequities in inputs. Also, highly educated parents may gain extra benefits when choices are expanded; as Schneider, Teske, and Marschall (2000) have shown, these parents are probably better informed about what is available to them in the market, and will be best-placed to take advantage of new school services. The likely result is that children from wealthy families will use the marketplace to greater advantage. Social stratification will increase. However, there is little direct evidence that this source of advantage is significantly greater in practice than the inequities of a public school system with local financing where families with adequate income can choose school neighborhoods, except for families with the highest incomes.

Markets can be regulated so as to avoid inequities and, in fact, help low-income families or students in failing schools. Many voucher programs—particularly the small-scale programs—have an income threshold applied to them: Only families below a certain income level are eligible for a voucher. Similarly, tuition tax credits can be allocated on a merit-based or income-based criterion. The general idea is to enable low-income and minority families to enter the market with more "purchasing power" given to them from government subsidies. Furthermore, markets may make the education system more equitable through open enrollment (Godwin & Kemerer, 2002). Advocates argue that the ability to choose schools will open up possibilities for students who are locked into inferior neighborhood schools, and that the competitive marketplace will produce greater incentives to meet the needs of all students more fully than existing government schools. Also, the existing system already has very little within-school heterogeneity; that is, many children are already sorted into schools with their immediate peers (Walsh, 2005).

Other influences on equity should also be considered. First, private schools may refuse to admit some types of students, denying them an appropriate education (it is difficult to find direct evidence that private schools do this overtly; see Lacireno-Paquet, Holyoke, Moser, & Henig, 2002), but voucher advocates such as Friedman (1962) believe that schools should have complete discretion in admissions. Second, families may seek schools that enroll students from their backgrounds with the direct or subtle exclusion of other types of students. Simply creating a curriculum and marketing appeal that is friendly to some types of ethnic and social groups can discourage others from applying. There is a reasonable amount of evidence that—where families are given school choice—they prefer enrollment at schools that are the same racial and socioeconomic group as their own (Witte, 1999; Martinez, Godwin, & Kemerer, 1996; Buckley & Schneider, 2003; Fairlie & Resch, 2002; Weiher & Tedin, 2002). Families wish to enroll their children with peers of high ability and social class backgrounds. If families sort themselves according to ability, high-achieving students will help each other, and gain further advantages over other students. Persistent and significant educational inequities may result. Recent literature has emphasized the impact that different peer groups have on the education of fellow students, and the peer consequences of choice would appear to be negative (Levin 1998; Zimmer & Toma, 2000). Given the largely neutral impact of vouchers on participants' test scores, these sorting effects may be critical in a full evaluation of the educational marketplace.

Social Cohesion Schools should promote the social good; this is the main reason they are publicly funded. What constitutes "the social good" will vary across societies, but in a democracy, the purpose of schooling is usually interpreted as necessitating common elements of schooling with regard to curriculum, values, goals, language, and political orientation. After compulsory schooling, citizens should possess the skills and knowledge necessary for civic and economic participation in society. By introducing markets and choice into the education system, therefore, there is a risk that these common elements will be undermined.

There are two routes through which an education system can generate social cohesion and order. One is by the design of the system itself: social goods are created when collective action is undertaken, that is, when all students are offered the same system of education. This is the idea of "common schooling": Social goods are created through communal activities. Reliance on the market would undermine this common schooling; where families can opt out of public schools, or when they can provide extra funds for their children's education, they will not be part of this communal activity (see Levinson & Levinson, 2003). Where richer families can buy more elitist and exclusive education for their children, social cohesion may be adversely affected. However, it is difficult to find empirical research that substantiates the importance of common schooling in promoting social order.

The second route to producing social goods is through the instruction that students receive within school. When students are taught socialization skills and the importance of civic virtues, social cohesion may be enhanced. Some schools may include courses such as Civics or Political Science or Religious Education as part of the curriculum; others may encourage charitable acts by the students or offer instruction on, for example, environmental issues. At issue is whether private schools can inculcate more of these capacities than public schools; whether families would—if schooling choices were more open—demand more of this type of education, and whether schooling does influence social cohesion.

Opponents of the marketplace argue that families will want education that only conveys private advantages and not social benefits. But precisely how to measure the student behavior that connotes these social benefits is not settled. For example, some would measure student knowledge of political and economic institutions and modes of participation in civic life. Others would measure attitudes towards civic participation. Others yet might measure orientations towards contributing to society.

Indeed, when measuring some of these dimensions, research evidence for the United States suggests that private schools offer more civic education than public schools do. National Household Education Survey (Institute for Educational Services, 1996, 1999) data has been used to examine differences in civic engagement across students from different schools (Campbell, 2001; Belfield, 2003). Although not fully consistent, the results broadly indicate that private schools produce more community service, civic skills, civic confidence, political knowledge, and political tolerance than is generated in public schools. The explanatory power of the type of school a student attends on actual levels of civic-mindedness is, however, very low. Nevertheless, there is certainly no direct evidence that, were families to choose a private school from the marketplace of providers, social cohesion would fall (unless the types of schools that would arise under a voucher plan were to differ from those currently operating, which is theoretically possible as schools differentiate themselves from their competitors). Similarly, there is some evidence that charter schools engage in more community participation and civic activities, but the effect is not substantial (Buckley & Schneider, 2004).

Future Developments

What are the prospects for market approaches to education, and where are the needs for research? In some respects, the market approach to education is proceeding apace in elementary and secondary education. Much of the momentum derives from the political tides that have swept in privatization more generally in recent decades. But, other reasons are the quest for many different forms of school choice and the search for radical alternatives to counter the failure of inner-city schools. Federal legislation under No Child Left Behind (NCLB) is also an important force for privatization as an extension of school choice; three main provisions serve to increase choice. Under Unsafe Schools Choice Options, students can transfer from a school identified as "persistently dangerous" or one where they were victims of a crime. Under Public School Choice, a school that fails to meet academic Adequate Yearly Progress targets (AYP) must offer students transfer alternatives to other schools. Finally, under Supplemental Educational Services, schools failing to meet AYP targets for three years must offer low-income students additional tutoring or remediation outside the regular school day. Each of these provisions will open up the educational market, both from the parents' perspective—many students may be affected—and from the providers' perspective—where private companies may offer tutoring or remediation services or charter schools may grow. Such provisions may also be politically attractive, in that choice is only triggered when the current set of educational options is deemed inadequate. As states are responsible for identifying unsafe schools and setting AYP targets, there is latitude in how much market provision is encouraged. However, given the difficulty of meeting NCLB standards over time, especially for highly mobile students who do not attend a particular school long enough to benefit from enriched services, it is possible that more and more schools will be declared "failures." This will provide political ammunition to push for educational market approaches and further privatization as a promising alternative to that "failure."

Yet, there are two developments which suggest that market reforms will not proliferate extensively. First, few voucher programs—often idealized as the most wide-ranging market reform—have been set up. Where they do exist, they are small-scale and confined to a subset of the populations in large urban areas. This is despite the best efforts of advocates for almost two decades to proliferate the voucher approach. Second, the evidence on charter schooling is sufficient to conclude that this type of schooling will not revolutionize U.S. public education. The numbers of students served are still only a tiny fraction of the population (about 2%), and there has been no definite case that charter schools are superior to public schools in student achievement, often the main rationale for their existence.

Generally, the evidence base for market reforms is far from complete; hard and fast conclusions are hard to come by. About the only conclusions that we can draw at this time are: (a) market approaches increase choice considerably; (b) competition and choice may be associated with small improvements in academic achievement, but nothing approximating the revolutionary changes argued by advocates; (c) there is some evidence that universal market approaches will lead to greater inequalities, but restricted ones limited to the poor may have the opposite impacts; and (d) the effects of educational markets on social cohesion are unknown and depend heavily on how social cohesion is defined and measured and what types of schools will emerge in a market expansion.

Although we have been able to set out a policy and evaluation framework for educational privatization with some confidence, the evidence needed to fill in that framework is much less comprehensive. There are a number of reasons for this. First, educational vouchers and tuition tax credits, as well as charter schools and for-profit educational management organizations, are a relatively recent phenomenon. They embrace only a tiny fraction of U.S. schools and students. This has meant that the empirical universe from which one can derive evidence is extremely limited. Hence, in the absence of more solid and persuasive evidence of superiority and the complications of tradeoffs among goals, it is difficult to initiate more extensive market demonstrations. Another important consideration is that there are so many variants of market reform and clearly the outcomes of an educational marketplace depend on the specific design of the reform. Therefore, generalization is limited from the few implementations that exist today in the United States or in other countries. In reality, evidence must be limited to a particular application of educational vouchers or other forms of the educational marketplace, and the existing variants are too limited from which to draw extensive generalizations. Finally, evaluating these reforms is expensive and time-consuming, because they typically involve system-wide changes. Yet, without more evidence to ascertain the probable impact of market reforms in education on different educational outcomes, the multiplicity of educational goals, and the thinness of the evidence suggest that a priori views and ideological stances will probably dominate in terms of educational policy on this topic.

Notes

1. Moreover, in order to make appropriate choices families need to have good information. In part, this is the motivation for more prescriptive standards and testing in schools—so that families will have information about school quality and will be able to compare schools and hold them accountable. However, there has been considerable debate over whether school quality can be easily codified and quantified (or even manipulated), leading to the possibility that parents will be making choices based on false information (for discussion, see Kane & Staiger, 2002). In addition, although the intentions of most families are aligned toward their children's well-being, some families may make poor or inappropriate choices.
2. There is not a single voucher plan. Plans differ according to three design instruments: finance, regulation, and support services (Levin, 2002). Finance refers to the overall magnitude of the educational voucher, how it is allocated and whether schools can add tuition charges to the government voucher for families willing and able to purchase a more costly education. Regulation refers to the requirements set out by government for eligibility of schools to participate in the voucher system, as well as any other rules that must be adhered to by schools and families in using educational vouchers. Support services refer to those types of publicly-provided services designed to increase the effectiveness of the market.
3. There have been a number of attempts to identify alternative outcomes for schooling besides test scores, and to compare these across school types. Comparisons between private religious and public schools show the former reduce teen involvement in sexual activity, arrests, and the use of hard drugs, but there is no difference in alcohol, tobacco, or soft drug usage (Figlio & Ludwig, 2001).

References

Ballou, D., Teasley, B., & Zeidner, T. (2007). *A comparison of charter schools and traditional public schools in Idaho* (NCSPE Occasional paper No. 135). New York: National Center for the Study of Privatization in Education.

Belfield, C. R. (2003). *Democratic education across school types: Evidence from the NHES99.* (NCSPE Occasional paper No. 73). New York: National Center for the Study of Privatization in Education.

Belfield, C. R., & Levin, H. M. (2002a, November). *The economics of tuition tax credits for U.S. schools.* Paper presented at National Tax Association 95th Annual Conference on Taxation, Orlando, FL.

Belfield, C. R., & Levin, H. M. (2002b). The effects of competition between schools on educational outcomes: A review for the United States. *Review of Educational Research, 72,* 279–341.

Bifulco, R., & Ladd, H. (2003, November). *Charter school impacts on student performance: Evidence from North Carolina.* Paper presented at the Association for Public Policy Analysis and Management, Washington, DC.

Booker, K., Gilpatric, S., Gronberg, R., & Jansen, D. (2005). *The effect of charter schools on traditional public schools* (NCSPE Occasional paper No. 104). New York: National Center for the Study of Privatization in Education.

Buckley, J., & Schneider, M. (2003). Making the grade: Comparing DC charter schools to other DC public schools. *Educational Evaluation and Policy Analysis, 25,* 203–216.

Buckley, J., & Schneider, M. (2004). *Do charter schools promote student citizenship?* (NCSPE Occasional paper No. 91). New York: National Center for the Study of Privatization in Education.

Buddin, R., & Zimmer, R. (2003, November). *Student achievement in charter schools: New evidence from California.* Paper presented at the Association for Public Policy Analysis and Management, Washington, DC.

Buddin, R., & Zimmer, R. (2006). *Is charter school competition in California improving the performance of traditional public schools?* (NCSPE Occasional paper No. 122). New York: National Center for the Study of Privatization in Education.

Campbell, D. E. (2001). Making democratic education work. In P. E. Peterson & D. E. Campbell (Eds.), *Charters, vouchers and American education* (pp. 241–267). Washington, DC: Brookings Institution.

Chubb, J., & Moe, T. (1990). *Politics, markets, and America's schools.* Washington, DC: Brookings Institution.

Consoletti, A., & Allen, J. (Ed.). (2007). *Annual survey of America's charter schools 2007.* Washington, DC: Center for Education Reform.

Coons, J. E., & Sugarman, S. D. (1978). *Education by choice: The case for family control.* Berkeley: University of California Press.

Fairlie, R. W., & Resch, A. M. (2002). Is there "white flight" into private schools? Evidence from the National Educational Longitudinal Survey. *Review of Economics and Statistics, 84,* 21–33.

Figlio, D., & Ludwig, J. (2001). *Sex, drugs and Catholic schools: Private schooling and adolescent behaviors* (NCSPE Occasional paper No. 30). New York: National Center for the Study of Privatization in Education.

Figlio, D. N., & Stone, J. A. (1999). Are private schools really better? *Research in Labor Economics, 18,* 115–140.

Figlio, D., & Rouse, C. E. (2006). Do accountability and voucher threats improve low-performing schools? *Journal of Public Economics, 90,* 239–255.

Friedman, M. (1962). The role of government in education. In M. Friedman (Ed.), *Capitalism and freedom* (pp. 85–107). Chicago: University of Chicago Press.

Gamoran, A. (1996). Student achievement in a public magnet, public comprehensive, and private city high schools. *Educational Evaluation and Policy Analysis, 18,* 1–18.

Gill, B. P., Hamilton, L. S., Lockwood, J. R., Marsh, J., Zimmer, R., Hill, D., & Pribesh, S. (2005). *Inspiration, perspiration, and time: Operations and achievement in Edison Schools.* Arlington, VA: RAND.

Godwin, R. K., & Kemerer, F. R. (2002). *School choice trade-offs.* Austin: University of Texas Press.

Grissmer, D., Flanagan, A., & Williamson, S. (1998). Does money matter for minority and disadvantaged students? Assessing the new empirical evidence. In W. J. Fowler (Ed.), *Developments in school finance* (pp. 13–30; NCES Publications No. 98-212). Washington, DC: U.S. Government Print Office.

Guttman, A. (1986). *Democratic education.* Princeton, NJ: Princeton University Press.

Hanushek, E. A. (1998). Conclusions and controversies about the effectiveness of schools. *Federal Reserve Bank of New York Economic Policy Review, 4*(1), 11–27.

Hanushek, E. A., Kain, J., & Rivkin, S. (2003, November). *New evidence on the impact of charter schools on academic achievement.* Paper presented at the Association for Public Policy Analysis and Management, Washington, DC.

Henig, J. R., & Sugarman, S. D. (1999). The nature and extent of school choice. In S. D. Sugarman & F. R. Kemerer (Eds.), *School choice and social controversy: Politics, policy and law* (pp. 13–35). Washington, DC: Brookings Institution.

Hess, F., Maranto, R., & Milliman, S. (2001). Small districts in big trouble: How four Arizona school systems responded to charter competition. *Teachers College Record, 103,* 1102–1124.

Hirschman, A. O. (1970). *Exit, voice, and loyalty: Responses to decline in firms, organizations, and states.* Cambridge, MA: Harvard University Press.

Hochschild, J. L., & Scovronick, N. (2003). *The American dream and the public schools.* New York: Oxford University Press.

Howell, W. G., & Peterson, P. E. (2002). *The education gap: Vouchers and urban public schools.* Washington, DC: Brookings Institution.

Hoxby, C. M. (2000). Does competition among public schools benefit students and taxpayers? *American Economic Review, 90,* 1209–1238.

Hoxby, C. M. (Ed.). (2003). *The economics of school choice.* Chicago: University of Chicago.

Huerta, L., & d'Entremont, C. (2006). *Education tax credits in a post-Zelman era: Legal, political, and policy alternatives to vouchers* (NCSPE Occasional paper No. 131). New York: National Center for the Study of Privatization in Education.

Huerta, L., & Gonzalez, M-F. (2004). *Cyber and home school charter schools: How states are defining new forms of public schooling.* (NCSPE Occasional paper No. 87). New York: National Center for the Study of Privatization in Education.

Husted, T. A., & Kenny, L. W. (2002). The legacy of *Serrano*: The impact of mandated equal spending on private school enrollment. *Southern Economic Journal, 68,* 566–583.

James, E. (1987). The public/private division of responsibility for education: An international comparison. In T. James & H. M. Levin (Eds.), *Comparing public and private schools* (pp. 212–227). New York: Falmer Press.

James, E. (1993). Why do different countries choose a different public–private mix of educational services? *Journal of Human Resources, 28,* 571–592.

Kane, P. R., & Lauricella, C. J. (2001). Assessing the growth and potential of charter schools. In H. M. Levin (Ed.), *Privatizing education: Can the market deliver freedom of choice, productive efficiency, equity and social cohesion?* (pp. 203–233). Boulder, CO: Westview Press.

Kane, T. J., & Staiger, D. O. (2002). The promise and pitfalls of using imprecise school accountability measures. *Journal of Economic Perspectives, 16*(4), 91–114.

Katz, M. B. (1971). *Class, bureaucracy, and schools: The illusion of educational change in America.* New York: Praeger.

Krueger, A. B., & Zhu, P. (2004a). Another look at the New York City school voucher experiment. *American Behavioral Scientist, 47,* 658–698.

Krueger, A. B., & Zhu, P. (2004b). Inefficiency, subsample selection bias, and nonrobustness: A response to Paul E. Peterson and William G. Howell. *American Behavioral Scientist, 47,* 718–728.

Lacireno-Paquet, N., Holyoke, T. T., Moser, M., & Henig, J. R. (2002). Creaming versus cropping: Charter school enrollment practices in response to market incentives. *Educational Evaluation and Policy Analysis, 24,* 145–158.

Lenti, L. (2003). *New wave of voucher programs? The Colorado Opportunity Contract Pilot Program* (NCSPE Occasional Paper No. 78). New York: National Center for the Study of Privatization in Education.

Levin, H. M. (1998). Educational vouchers: effectiveness, choice and costs. *Journal of Policy Analysis and Management, 17,* 373–392.

Levin, H. M. (2001). *Thoughts on for-profit schools* (NCSPE Occasional Paper No. 14). New York: National Center for the Study of Privatization in Education.

Levin, H. M. (2002). A comprehensive framework for evaluating educational vouchers. *Educational Evaluation and Policy Analysis, 24,* 159–174.

Levin, H. M., & Belfield, C. R. (2005). Vouchers and public policy: When ideology trumps evidence. *American Journal of Education, 111,* 548–567.

Levin, H. M., & Driver, C. (1997). Costs of an educational voucher system. *Education Economics, 5,* 303–311.

Levinson, M., & Levinson, S. (2003). "Getting religion": Religion, diversity, and community in public and private schools. In A. Wolfe (Ed.), *School choice. A moral debate* (pp. 104–125). Princeton, NJ: Princeton University Press.

Lubienski, S. T., & Lubienski, C. (2007). Charter, private, public schools and academic achievement: New evidence from NAEP mathematics data. *American Educational Research Journal, 43,* 651–698.

Martinez, V., Godwin, K., & Kemerer, F. (1996). Public school choice in San Antonio: Who chooses and with what effects? In B. Fuller & R. Elmore (Eds.), *Who chooses? Who loses? Culture, institutions, and the unequal effects of school choice* (pp. 50–69). New York: Teachers College Press.

McEwan, P. J. (2000). *Comparing the effectiveness of public and private schools: A review of evidence and interpretations* (NCSPE Occasional Paper No. 3). New York: National Center for the Study of Privatization in Education.

McGuinn, P. (2007). *The policy landscape of educational entrepreneurship* (NCSPE Occasional Paper No. 138). New York: National Center for the Study of Privatization in Education.

McMillan, R. (2000). Competition, parental involvement, and public school performance (Doctoral dissertation, Stanford University, 1999). *Dissertation Abstracts International, 61,* 280.

Metcalf, K. K., West, S. D., Legan, N. A., Paul, K. M., & Boone, W. J. (2003). *Evaluation of the Cleveland Scholarship and Tutoring Program: Summary Report 1998–2002.* Bloomington: Indiana University, School of Education.

Miron, G., & Nelson, C. (2002). *What's public about charter schools? Lessons learned about choice and accountability.* Thousand Oaks, CA: Corwin Press.

Miron, G., Coryn, C., & Mackety, D. (2007, June). *Evaluating the impact of charter schools on student achievement: A longitudinal look at the Great Lakes states.* Kalamazoo: Western Michigan University, The Evaluation Center.

Muraskin, L., & Stullich, S. (1998). *Barriers, benefits, and costs of using private schools to alleviate overcrowding in public schools* (ED 432 063). Washington, DC: U.S. Department of Education, Planning and Evaluation Service.

Murray, S. E., Evans, W. N., & Schwab, R. M. (1998). Education-finance reform and the distribution of education resources. *American Economic Review, 88,* 789–812.

National Center for Educational Statistics (NCES). (2003a). *A brief portrait of private schools.* Washington, DC: National Center for Educational Statistics.

National Center for Educational Statistics (NCES). (2003b). *Digest of educational statistics 2002.* Washington, DC: National Center for Educational Statistics.

Institute for Educational Sciences. (1996). *National Household Education Survey.* Washington, DC: Author. Retrieved November 5, 2008, from http://nces.ed.gov/nhes/dataproducts.asp#1999dp

Institute for Educational Sciences. (1999). *National Household Education Survey.* Washington, DC: Author. Retrieved November 5, 2008, from http://nces.ed.gov/nhes/dataproducts.asp#1991dp

Peterson, P. E., & Hassel, B. C. (Eds.). (1998). *Learning from school choice.* Washington, DC: Brookings Institution.

Peterson, P. E., & Howell, W. (2004). Efficiency, bias and classification schemes: A response to Alan B. Krueger and Pei Zhu. *American Behavioral Scientist, 47,* 699–717.

Reback, R. (2005). *Supply and demand in a public school choice program* (NCSPE Occasional Paper No. 99). New York: National Center for the Study of Privatization in Education.

Rouse, C. E. (1998). Private school vouchers and student achievement:

An evaluation of the Milwaukee Parental Choice Program. *Quarterly Journal of Economics, 113*, 553–603.

Ryan, J., & Heise, M. (2002). The political economy of school choice. *Yale Law Journal, 111*(8), 2043–2136.

Sass, T. (2006). Charter schools and student achievement in Florida. *Education Finance and Policy, 1*, 91–122.

Schneider, M., Teske, P., & Marschall, M. (2000). *Choosing schools: Consumer choice and the quality of American schools.* Princeton, NJ: Princeton University Press.

Smith, K. B. (2003). *The ideology of education: The commonwealth, the market, and America's schools.* Albany: State University of New York Press.

Sugarman, S. D. (2002). Charter school funding issues. *Education Policy Analysis Archives, 10*(34).

Teske, P., & Schneider, M. (2001). What research can tell policymakers about school choice. *Journal of Policy Analysis and Management, 20*, 609–632.

Tyack, D. B. (1974). *The one best system: A history of American urban education.* Cambridge, MA: Harvard University Press.

Viteritti, J. P. (1999). *Choosing equality: School choice, the Constitution and civil society.* Washington, DC: Brookings Institution.

Walsh, P. (2005). *Is there any cream to skim? Sorting, within-school heterogeneity, and the scope for cream-skimming* (NCSPE Occasional Paper No. 109). New York: National Center for the Study of Privatization in Education.

Weiher, G. R., & Tedin, K. L. (2002). Does choice lead to racially distinctive schools? Charter schools and household preferences. *Journal of Policy Analysis and Management, 21*(1), 79–92.

Wells, A. S., & Crain, R. (2005). Where school desegregation and school choice policies collide: Voluntary transfer plans and controlled choice. In J. Scott (Ed.), *The context of school choice and student diversity* (pp. 59–76). New York: Teachers College Press.

West, E. G. (1967). Tom Paine's voucher scheme for public education. *Southern Economic Journal, 33*, 378–382.

Witte, J. (2003, November). *Charter schools in Wisconsin: Assessing form and performance.* Paper presented at the Association for Public Policy Analysis and Management, Washington, DC.

Witte, J. F. (1999). *The market approach to education: An analysis of America's first voucher program.* Princeton, NJ: Princeton University Press.

Wolfe, A. (Ed.). (2003). *School choice: The moral debate.* Princeton, NJ: Princeton University Press.

Zelman v. Simmons-Harris, 536 U.S. 639 (2002).

Zimmer, R. (Ed.). (2003). *Charter school operations and performance: Evidence from California.* Santa Barbara, CA: RAND Corporation.

Zimmer, R., & Buddin, R. (2006). *Charter school performance in urban school districts: Are they closing the achievement gap?* (NCSPE Occasional paper No. 118). New York: National Center for the Study of Privatization in Education.

Zimmer, R., & Toma, E. (2000). Peer effects in private and public schools across countries. *Journal of Policy Analysis and Management, 19*, 75–92.

42

COMMENTARY
A Call to Studied Action

*Lessons from Research on Policies Designed to Improve
the Organization and Management of Schooling*

STEVE CANTRELL
Bill & Melinda Gates Foundation

Policies designed to improve the organization and management of schooling have not yet delivered game changing results at scale. As the authors in this section report, the various policy solutions to difficult educational problems have not disrupted the status quo. Many of the recent and hotly debated policies, proposals that promised to deliver significant changes in school organization and management, merely reflect the familiar historical pattern of tinkering around the edges (Tyack & Cuban, 1995). A bit of choice, fewer kids in the school or classroom, more money, and still the predominant forms of schooling persist for most American students. Moreover, the infusion of resources and innovative structures has not led to performance improvements for most American students.

Moving forward, ostensibly toward the aims advocated within much of this literature, greater equity, efficiency, effectiveness, and autonomy, it will be useful to examine the research captured within this chapter as a record of what we do and do not know, as a guide to what we need to know and how best to achieve this, and as a framework for thinking about the organization and management of schooling more generally. These three purposes roughly map to the interests of the policy maker, the applied researcher, and the organizational theorist. As explicitly stated or hinted at in several of the articles in this section, the work of members within each role group is usefully informed by considering its core problems through the lens of the others. If, for example, policy makers do not immediately see their world reflected in the work of organizational theorists, this should signal to the theorists the need to think more deeply. For when they get it right, Kurt Lewin's (1951) dictum pertains, "There is nothing so practical as a good theory" (p. 169).

What We Know (and Don't Know)

This collection of articles clearly demonstrates the limits of the knowledge base to guide the organization and management of schooling. Most of the articles cited here explore one or more solutions within a set of strategies toward more equitable, efficient, or effective schools. The policy solutions examined can be divided into two categories: organization-based solutions and market-based solutions. Organization-based solutions reflect policies designed to influence organizational inputs, processes, and/or outputs. Market-based policy solutions, at least in concept (Hess, this volume), are intended to pressure schools to make more appropriate use of resources.

What we know, and is the focus of most of the research in this chapter, is limited to the impact of policies upon outcomes. We know far less about how action, the behaviors of organizations and actors, mediates the impact of policy upon outcomes. Also missing from our knowledge base is an understanding of the policy and implementation conditions that moderate the impact of policies upon outcomes. Finally, we do not know enough about those details of a particular policy that may reflect compromises designed to undermine the policy, effectively building into the policy the seeds of its own destruction (Moe, 1989).

Organization-Based Solutions Organization-based solutions are forms of management control designed to encourage appropriate behavior (Merchant, 1998). The organization's work may be characterized as a combination of the inputs used by the organization, the transformation processes used by the organization, and the outputs of the organization (Scott, 1992). Control over work can address one or more of these stages. The goals of control always concern behavior, even though the form of control targets something other than behavior. The two forms of control included in this chapter target organizational inputs and organizational outputs.

Policies that Target Inputs   The most obvious input is money, though as evident by the wide range of dollars spent per pupil across and within states, there is sharp disagreement over what constitutes adequate funding for schooling. The fact that large increases in total educational spending have not increased performance as measured by student performance on the NAEP and SAT (Plecki & Casteñeda, this volume), suggests that money alone is insufficient to improve schools' ability to serve all students. Since a core task of the school organization is to deploy available resources most effectively, input-based policies attempt to assist schools by directing resources to their most productive use. The authors in this chapter discuss both the debate over school funding and the policy responses designed to productively assign resources.

Resources matter, but the specifics of how, why, and by what measure remain contested. The biggest policy question revolves around what it costs or what it should cost to educate students. To answer this question requires the resolution of two separate questions: First, by what standard are schools to educate the great majority of students, minimum standards or post-secondary success? Second, what resources are required to bring different students to the same standard?

Politically, the easier course leads to fiscal policy aimed at "leveling all ships" (Baker & Green, this volume), but a policy assuring a minimal threshold for the per-pupil resources provided to school districts untenably assumes equivalent costs for all pupils, irrespective of their needs. The redistribution of resources required to attain equal educational opportunity for all requires greater political courage. Recently, a few districts[1] have instituted fiscal policies using student-based (or weighted) funding formulas and others are exploring this option. These settings provide an opportunity to examine how and to what extent the particular funding formulas pursue need-based redistribution to achieve equal educational opportunity.

A few input-based policies have captured widespread attention including class size reduction, smaller schools, and early childhood learning. Class size reduction received strong empirical support from the Tennessee STAR experiment, a randomized controlled trial that demonstrated meaningful and persistent effects on student performance for K-3 students in small (13–17 students) classrooms (Finn & Achilles, 1990), with greater benefits accruing to students with multiple years in small classes and the greatest benefits accruing to the low-socioeconomic students (SES) among the multi-year students (Finn, Gerber, & Boyd-Zaharias, 2005).

Policy makers were quick to jump on the class size reduction bandwagon, most notably in California, where class size was reduced to 20 students across grades K-3 statewide. Unfortunately, while popular, this $1.5 billon annual investment did not immediately yield student performance gains. Instead, class size reduction led to teacher shortages, especially in urban areas where teachers fleeing to newly created jobs in the suburbs exacerbated the additional recruitment challenges faced by urban districts as they struggled (and often failed) to fill new and recently vacated positions with qualified candidates. While these consequences were unintended, they were also predictable, and unfortunately the costs were born by those high-need students with the most to gain from a well-implemented class size reduction policy. The lesson learned is this: Even in the face of solid evidence of positive impact, policy makers still need to attend to the implementation context and be able to anticipate the behavior of actors within the system as implementation goes to scale.

The small schools movement lacks any rigorous studies and suffers somewhat because small, by itself, is not the desired condition, but the factor that facilitates school qualities theorized to impact student performance, such as personalization and collegiality. Whether small schools are costlier depends on the metric. When cost is measured in terms of dollars per graduate, small schools cost no more, on a per graduate basis, than larger schools (Stiefel, Berne, Iatorola, & Frutcher, 2000).

Researchers in early childhood learning have estimated extraordinary returns on investment for pre-kindergarten programs developed for at-risk children. These estimates of return range from $7 to $13 in long-term individual and social benefits for each dollar invested (Barnett, 1996; Nores, Belfield, Barnett, & Schweinhart, 2005). Perhaps most striking about these results is the fact that they are presented in terms that the layperson can understand. While the studies certainly include measures of central tendency and dispersion, the message is not confused by reliance upon standard deviation units or even effect sizes. The studies have captured the total cost information for the programs, which allows comparisons to be made among programs competing for scarce educational resources.

Policies that Target Outputs   Output-based policies, by contrast, specify a valued organizational outcome and establish rewards or sanctions according to performance against the outcome. The federal government has established Adequate Yearly Progress (AYP) as the desired outcome within the No Child Left Behind Act (NCLB). Accountability provisions of NCLB include school choice, offered to parents after a school fails to meet AYP for 2 consecutive years, Supplemental Educational Services, offered to parents after a school fails to meet AYP for 3 consecutive years, and an option to reconstitute schools, offered to school districts and/or state educational agencies when a school fails to meet AYP for 4 or more consecutive years. NCLB's bark may be worse than its bite. As of 2006, few students and few districts exercised their rights under NCLB, limiting the impact of the consequences for not meeting AYP. NCLB's version of school choice is restricted to under-enrolled public schools, which may eliminate the best schools from consideration. As such, fewer than 2% of eligible students exercised this option in 2005–06 (Center for Educational Policy, 2006). More students, though still far less than the number eligible, used Supplemental Educational Services, with estimates ranging from 3% to 20% (Ascher, 2006). Similarly, reconstitution is seldom used by district administrators, who appear to favor a "lighter touch" (Olson, 2006).

It is not clear that, even if exercised, the consequences would have had their intended effect. Studies of reconstitution suggest that external threat, even when combined with additional resources, does not lead to improvement. Threat does increase effort, but not necessarily toward effective practice (Malen & Rice, this volume). Additional resources, typically in the form of assistance from external partners, were not sufficient for schools to improve. Whether this is due to frenzy created by the reality of imminent takeover or whether this is simply further evidence that the chronically underperforming school cannot mobilize resources effectively is unclear. Although it is unfortunate that teachers and administrators suffer the frenetic response to pressure, to let these schools remain chronic underperformers cannot be an acceptable alternative.

Furthermore, schools labeled chronically underperforming or targeted for reconstitution have difficulty attracting and retaining highly talented teachers and administrators (Malen & Rice, this volume). Again, it is not clear whether the label or the toxic environment repels talented staff. We need to better understand the ill effects attributable to having been labeled a school targeted for intervention. To do this requires a contrast between equally poor performing schools under different accountability rules.

Market-Based Solutions For over half a century, scholars have advocated unleashing the power of markets to transform educational institutions (Friedman, 1955). As Hess (this volume) observes, "education is currently subject to *inadequate* or *unhealthy* competitive pressures." Market proponents, argues Hess, have shied away from Schumpeter's creative destruction in favor of tamer rhetoric. Instead of touting how new and better schools will displace poorly performing schools, advocates have highlighted parental choice and promised improvement for existing schools that learn from their competitors' innovative practices. Unlike the limited use of school choice under NCLB, large numbers of students in troubled urban school systems such as New Orleans and Washington, DC, have opted to enroll in schools beyond the local school district, primarily in charter schools. For parents of students such as these, choice is valued and those who exercise choice are more satisfied with their choice (Belfield & Levin, this volume), however

there is some indication that the satisfaction can diminish over time (Vergari, this volume).

There is no strong evidence linking schools of choice to equity outcomes, however there is some evidence that the act of choosing may itself increase social capital, a finding that is especially important for low-SES families (Schneider, Marschall, Teske, & Roch, 1997). Families seek to enroll their students in schools with kids like their own (Belfield & Levin, this volume; Vergari, this volume), however, it is not clear whether this homogeneity is any greater than what occurs within residential neighborhoods, especially within elementary school attendance areas.

Schools of choice are at least as effective as comparable public schools (Booker, Zimmer, Gill, & Sass, 2008), sometimes more effective (Witte, 2002), and have been shown as more effective for subgroups, such as African Americans (Howell & Peterson, 2002). Also, since funding is not equivalent, some have argued that charters and voucher schools demonstrating equivalent performance with less funding must be more efficient (Center on Educational Governance, 2007).

Most of the research tends to lump all schools of a certain category together (vouchers, charters), though it is critical to understand that variability within category exists (Zimmer & Buddin, 2006). Charters, for example, operate under different rules across jurisdictions. Charters likely also represent a range of effectiveness, some of this may be due to the rules under which they operate, some of this is simply variation in quality among schools. How and why charter school performance differs, and what charter authorizers do to weed out poorly performing charter schools, can help us better understand the current and potential impact of charters and how this impact is enabled and constrained by current rules.

While in theory an increase in parental choice opportunity will increase the supply of schooling options and threaten the existence of underperforming schools, the experience has been otherwise. For most schools, the threat of closure has not been credible. Only under the most direct threats have public systems responded positively in terms of increased student performance (Hoxby, 2002).

Our understanding of the impact of charters and/or vouchers on public school systems faces two problems: First, supply has been limited by barriers to entry, such as limits on the number of available charters within a state or jurisdiction and limits on voucher participation. Second, the threat to poor performers has been minimized by funding formulas that limit the loss of funding due to student exit to less than the per-pupil funding allotment. Furthermore, few incentives exist for a school administrator to actively seek to retain the portion of students most likely to exit. Especially in urban environments, where most charter schools and voucher programs operate, for existing public schools fewer students equal fewer problems with overcrowding and the accompanying dissatisfaction for families and staff who suffer substandard teaching and learning environments (Hess, this volume).

What We Need—A Call to Studied Action

As practitioners, policy makers, and researchers within the field of education we should be, to quote Hebert Simon (1982), "concerned not with the necessary but with the contingent—not with how things are but with how they might be—in short, with design" (p. xi). "How things might be" suggests dissatisfaction with the results obtained by our current system. A design orientation, to reframe our collective work as improving the fit between actions and purposes, suggests a way to recalibrate our system toward less and less dissatisfaction. The implication is that what we practice, prescribe, and examine, should be motivated by and evaluated against "how things might be."

Worthwhile goals, visions, and missions notwithstanding, "how things might be" need not be restricted to sincere efforts at wishful thinking. Our thinking about "how things might be" needs to be rigorous and, most of all, pragmatic. We cannot be rigorous or pragmatic without credible information. Obtaining and applying this information cannot simply be left to chance. We need to be systematic in our production of information if it is to become knowledge useful to the system. I will argue that applied research, rightly defined as a collaborative activity, provides educators and education policy makers with relevant information that can be obtained no other way.

The research plan for our design task is twofold: describe and evaluate. The aim is to serve both immediate system goals and knowledge building. This combination keeps the research practical and the hope for greater application alive. We seek to answer two primary questions about the management and organization of schooling: What exists? and, What works? As we describe what exists, we do so not as an end in itself, but as a means toward better design. As we assess the impact of a given practice (how well does it work, for whom, under what conditions), we begin to build a contrast between current and desired practice.

Our understanding is advanced by strong contrasts. We are concerned with what the school managers who get the best results do, but even more concerned with what they do differently from their peers whose results are less impressive. Likewise, we ought to be concerned with what those managers whose results far lag their peers are doing, and how this differs from more accomplished managers. We then ought to have the courage to name specific practices as malpractice and direct leaders away from such actions.

Increasing Demand for Quality Research through Better Informed Consumers Consumer demand can help applied research become more policy-relevant and more accessible. Consumers—both policy makers and practitioners—need to understand the extent that research is applicable to their situation and whether the findings are valid. It is tempting, in the face of technical expertise, for practitioners to defer to the technocrat—the researcher with expertise and language beyond lay comprehension. Unfortunately, technical skills and language too often mask how and in what ways a given study is or is not applicable to the practitioners' situation. Researchers can help practitioners and policy makers appropriately apply lessons from research by demystifying the three most critical methodological aspects of their studies.

First, practitioners and policy makers deserve to know the extent that the findings in a given study apply to their situation. Clarity of detail about the participants in the study can help practitioners and policy makers determine the extent that results are generalizable to their situation. Also, clarity around response rate and/or study attrition can help readers understand the extent that the data is still representative of the original sample and still generalizable to the intended population.

Second, practitioners and policy makers deserve to know how the researcher measured the phenomena of interest. This addresses both the nominal fallacy and construct validity. If a study reports findings on teacher quality in charter schools, it is important to clarify how teacher quality was measured, since using credentials and experience versus an experiential log makes a difference to the meaning of the construct and should influence readers' interpretation of the results.

Third, practitioners and policy makers deserve to know what alternative explanations also fit the findings. This is especially important for causal findings. Most research is subject to some sort of threat to validity of the causal claim. In most cases, it is too costly and too difficult to eliminate every threat. When applicable, the study should report plausible, but unmeasured, effects on the outcome. Otherwise, the study has provided too much support to a strong claim—that in the absence of treatment the observed outcome differences would not have occurred.

The consequences of not recognizing the limits of the available data have been seen in the general disregard for educational research. The common assertion from practitioners is that it is easy to find research support on both sides of a given policy or intervention. Policy makers routinely pick and choose among studies to support their position. Clearer statements regarding the limits of the available data can build confidence and mitigate some of the worst abuses of research findings.

Increasing the Supply of Quality Research through More Process Data While data quality is likely improving, the range of data available to inform many educational decisions remains limited. To better understand these limits, I will suggest that helping schools and school systems turn data into information is a design challenge. The challenge, simply stated, is to collect and analyze data correspondent to the theory-of-action driving the system. The recent push toward more accurate and more complete data sets offers school systems an opportunity to go beyond compliance and to design data systems worthy of analysis and useful for informing school improvement efforts.

Ultimately, managers of school systems are interested in data because they want their employees to know what they should do. Informative data allow for analysis of action and allow one to determine the extent that the given action achieved its intended result. By "action," I mean to include not only specific behaviors of employees, but also programs and materials designed to further the system's educational goals.[2] Unless the data used to inform decisions addresses actions, it will be insufficient to guide practice. This is not to say that the current data in use are unimportant, just that they are not sufficient for system improvement purposes. Disaggregated student performance data is important, however, unless it can be linked with specific practices, it is like weighing the pig, useful for the judges, but not for farmers who want to increase the size of their pigs.

The primary danger of a data-driven system is that the system follows the data. Where the data are incomplete, a data-driven system will minimize those areas of schooling. The antidote, in the move from data to information, is to have decision making be driven not by data, but by a theory-of-action (Resnick & Glennan, 2002; Resnick, Besterfield-Sacre, Mehalik, Sherer, & Halverson, 2007). Data analysis alone will not lead to school improvement. Information-driven school improvement is possible when the data collected and analyzed allow a system to test the efficacy of its theory-of-action. A good test will require high-quality data about the full range of variables that comprise the theory-of-action. If data are unavailable for any key element of the theory-of-action and no good approximation exists, then it will be difficult to ascertain whether the theory-of-action is having its intended effect or not.

Thus, the most glaring data gap for school systems concerns action. It is hard to imagine a good test of a system's theory-of-action without information about the actions theorized to make a difference. Yet, many school systems do not systematically collect and/or use data pertaining to teacher behaviors, including the programs that they attend, the curriculum they use, and the methods they employ.

Increasing the Volume of Quality Research by Capitalizing on Constraints   This vision of how things might be is ultimately a pragmatic one. The aim is to build the knowledge base for education—to get beyond our best guesses, however well intentioned, and to make decisions based upon the rigorous examination of credible data. The problem is that the current knowledge base is thin. To illustrate the point, the IES's What Works Clearinghouse was and remains a great idea, but it preceded a sufficient supply of rigorous educational research to the extent that it spent its first several months online nearly void of content. U.S. Secretary of Education Margaret Spellings once referred to it as "the Nothing Works Clearinghouse." In recent months, the What Works Clearinghouse has become populated with dozens of studies, many emanating from IES-funded projects.

Several practical steps can lead toward expansion of the knowledge base for education. The first step, paradoxically, is to recognize the value of resource constraints. It is not uncommon for school systems to begin the implementation of a significant initiative without the resources to assure a high-quality implementation across all intended sites. Most frequently the missing resource is the money. School systems often lack the funds needed for materials or for teachers' professional development. Sometimes, the missing resource is talent. School systems may begin to implement an initiative that requires experienced and informed mentors to assist with training, implementation, and coaching, and then, to their chagrin, discover that too few qualified personnel are available to provide services system-wide. What happens all too frequently is that the pressing need to serve all students becomes the dominant goal and resources are spread too thin to assure a high-quality implementation. When the initiative fails to fully meet the intended outcomes, the field does not know whether the initiative was faulty or whether the implementation was so flawed as to negate the positive intended effects of the initiative.

There is a better way. Systems can learn a tremendous amount by using constrained resources to justify a phased implementation or pilot test of an initiative. Whenever a decision is made to provide services to a portion of the students, schools, or districts, within a jurisdiction, *and assignment to treatment is non-voluntary*, it becomes possible to design a low-cost evaluation to yield high-quality data. With this information a system can know the extent that a given initiative worked for which students and under which conditions, and thus, make an informed decision whether to continue, expand, or abandon a given program. Additionally, with proper documentation, the evaluation can contribute to the knowledge base for education. In time, fewer dollars will be spent on unpromising initiatives, and more attention and resources can flow to those initiatives that have been working for students in schools characteristically similar to theirs.

Practical Theory

Interestingly, none of the solutions in this section on organization and management address process-based solutions, policies intended to direct managerial actions toward intended results. The lack of attention to this issue leaves district and school personnel without clear guidance for action. The notable exception is Spillane et al.'s (this volume) framing of organization in terms of practice (situated interactions among organizational actors) and resources (physical, financial, human, and social assets). For the other articles, the policy solutions examined were designed to alter some of the conditions of practice (smaller classes and schools, beginning formal education earlier in a child's life) or to create incentives for excellence (either through competition for parents' selection or through threats of reconstitution for chronically underperforming schools). In both cases, it was assumed that more effective practices and tools would result, but in neither case were these practices specified.

For theory-building to yield practical results, it must focus on organizational practice. A closer inspection of organizational routines, for example, can reveal whether they work for good or for ill. At best, the organizational routine captures best practices and, in this way, transfers learning over time across individuals and groups. Drawing on management research on the technical basis for control system design (Merchant 1985, 1998), the effectiveness of the organizational routine relates directly to the knowledge content embedded within the routine itself. An organizational routine that prescribes process, but does not contain the knowledge required to successfully execute the practice, will be dependent upon the existing knowledge base of the user. To restate, if the goal is improvement, then a prescription for process is not enough, the routine must also embed the knowledge and skill components. Otherwise, the process could be carried out without achieving its intended aim. Spillane and colleagues describe an organizational routine, learning walkthroughs, where the principal and others did not possess the requisite knowledge or skill to fulfill the aims of the process—to quickly assess the overall quality of instruction at a school site. For this process to work, it will have to support what is likely to be an uncertain knowledge or skill base. Without embedded knowledge and skill, the learning walkthrough is just a walkthrough, there is no guarantee of learning.

In closing, I will echo Spillane and colleagues' call for a richer theory of school organization, one that recommends close study of action and interaction, "We have to develop an understanding of *what* people do, *how* they do it, and *why* they do it, while simultaneously attending to the institutional structures at various levels of the system that enable and constrain practice at the street level."

Notes

1. Edmonton, Canada, pioneered the use of student-based funding formulas. School districts in the U.S. that have adopted student-based funding formulas include Hawaii, Cincinnati, Houston, and San Francisco.
2. For brevity's sake, I mean to avoid consideration of school system's business services and attempts to improve these services through Enterprise Resource Planning or other mechanisms. Suffice it to say that efficiencies realized in business services will free up resources for the school system to accomplish its educational mission.

References

Ascher, C. (2006). NCLB's supplemental educational services: Is this what our students need? *Phi Delta Kappan, 88*(2), 136–141.

Barnett, W. (1996). *Lives in the balance: Age 27 benefit-cost analysis of the High/Scope Perry Preschool Project. High/Scope Educational Research Foundation Monograph 11.* Ypsilanti, MI: High Scope Press.

Booker, K., Zimmer, R., Gill, B., & Sass, T. (2008) *Achievement and attainment in Chicago charter schools.* Santa Monica, CA: RAND Corporation.

Center for Educational Policy. (2006). *From the capital to the classroom: Year 4 of the No Child Left Behind Act.* Washington, DC: Center for Educational Policy.

Center on Educational Governance. (2007). *Charter schools indicators.* Los Angeles: University of Southern California.

Finn, J., & Achilles, C. (1990). Answers and questions about class size: A statewide experiment. *American Educational Research Journal, 27,* 557–577.

Finn, J., Gerber, S., & Boyd-Zaharias, J. (2005). Small classes in the early grades and course taking in high school. *International Journal of Educational Policy and Leadership, 1*(1), 1–13.

Friedman, M. (1955). The role of government in education. In R. Solo (Ed.), *Economics and the public interest* (pp. 127–134). New Brunswick, NJ: Rutgers University Press.

Howell, W., & Peterson, P. (2002). *The education gap: Vouchers and urban public schools.* Washington, DC: Brookings Institution.

Hoxby, C. (2002, April). *School choice and school productivity (Or, could school choice be a tide that lifts all boats?).* (NBER Working Paper No. 8873). Cambridge, MA: National Bureau of Economic Research

Lewin, K. (1951). Behavior and development as a function of the total situation. In D. Cartwright (Ed.), *Field theory in social science: Selected theoretical papers* (pp. 238–303). New York: Harper & Row.

Merchant, K. (1985). *Control in business organizations.* Boston: Pitman.

Merchant, K. (1998). *Modern management control systems.* Englewood Cliffs, NJ: Prentice-Hall.

Moe, T. (1989). The politics of bureaucratic structure. In J. Chubb & P. Peterson (Eds.), *Can the government govern?* (pp. 267–329). Washington, DC: Brookings Institution.

Nores, M., Belfield, C., Barnett, S., & Schweinhart, L. (2005). Updating the economic impacts of the High/Scope Perry Preschool Project. *Educational Evaluation and Policy Analysis, 22*(1), 27–39.

Olson, L. (2006, December 6). U.S. urged to rethink NCLB "tools": Districts seen as using light touch for schools required to restructure. *Education Week, 26*(14), 1, 19.

Resnick, L., Besterfield-Sacre, M., Mehalik, M., Sherer, J., & Halverson, E. (2007). A framework for effective management of school system performance. In P. Moss (Ed.), *National Society for the Study of Education (NSSE) yearbook on evidence and decision making* (pp. 155–185). Chicago: National Society for the Study of Education.

Resnick, L., & Glennan, T. (2002). Leadership for learning: A theory of action for urban school districts. In A. Hightower, M. Knapp, J. Marsh, & M. McLaughlin (Eds.), *School districts and instructional renewal* (pp. 160–172). New York: Teachers College Press.

Schneider, M., Marschall, M., Teske, P., & Roch, C. (1997). Institutional arrangements and social capital: Public school choice. *American Political Science Review, 91,* 82–93.

Scott, W. (1992). *Organizations: Rational, natural, and open systems.* Englewood Cliffs, NJ: Prentice Hall.

Simon, H. (1982). *The sciences of the artificial.* Cambridge, MA: The MIT Press.

Stiefel, L., Berne, R., Iatorola, P., & Frutcher, N. (2000). High school size: Effects on budgets and performance in New York City. *Educational Evaluation and Policy Analysis, 27,* 245–261.

Tyack, D., & Cuban, L. (1995). *Tinkering toward utopia.* Cambridge, MA: Harvard University Press.

Witte, J. (2002). *The market approach to education: An analysis of America's first voucher program.* Princeton, NJ: Princeton University Press.

Zimmer, R., & Buddin, R. (2006). *Charter school performance in urban school districts: Are they closing the achievement gap?* (NCSPE Occasional Paper No. 118). New York: National Center for the Study of Privatization in Education.

43

COMMENTARY
Improvement or Reinvention

Two Policy Approaches to School Reform

RODNEY T. OGAWA
University of California, Santa Cruz

Much of contemporary educational policy in the United States seeks to improve the performance of K-12 education. While some of the policy discourse emphasizes the general goal of improving the academic performance of students, the majority seems to focus on the more pointed issue of closing the so-called "achievement gap." This is reflected in efforts to enact policies that will equalize educational opportunity (Baker & Green, this volume) and thus end historical disparities in educational attainment across class, race, and culture (Plecki & Castañeda, this volume). This policy intent is reflected in the nine chapters that comprise this section of the *Handbook on Educational Policy Research*. They examine how educational finance policy (Baker & Green) and the allocation of resources (Plecki & Castañeda), class-size reduction (Ahn & Brewer), school reconstitution (Malen & Rice), and market pressures (Belfield & Levin; Hess; Vergari; Witte) might generally improve the performance of the nation's K-12 education system and specifically improve educational opportunities for low-income and racially and culturally non-dominant communities.

Another theme cuts across the chapters in this section: Organizations are principal mechanisms for implementing educational policy. Spillane, Gomez, and Mesler's chapter explicitly addresses this subject. Other chapters assess policies that focus on organizational units, ranging from classrooms to schools to school districts. To improve education, we reduce the size of classes and schools (Ahn & Brewer); reconstitute schools (Malen & Rice); seek to equalize inputs and outcomes across schools (Baker & Green) and effectively allocate resources in schools (Plecki & Castañeda); expose schools and districts to market pressures (Belfield & Levin; Hess) with charter schools (Vergari) and vouchers (Witte). The reliance on educational organizations as policy mechanisms reflects dominant social and cultural norms. As Zucker (1983) reminds us, organizations are "the preeminent institutional form in modern society" (p. 1). What we do as a society, we largely accomplish though organizations.

Thus, in this commentary I will emphasize the second word in the title of this handbook section: "organization." From a perspective that is informed by the new institutionalism in organization theory, I discuss two policy approaches for improving education. One seeks to "improve" existing forms of educational organizations, principally schools. The second seeks to foster conditions to innovate and thus "reinvent" schools.

Background

A handful of concepts from institutional theory illuminate these two policy approaches.[1] Organizations develop structures that correspond to institutions, or societal rules (Meyer, Boli, & Thomas, 1987), in order to gain and maintain social legitimacy (Meyer & Rowan, 1977). The development of the K-12 public education system in the United States and the organizational form of "school" has been traced to the 19th century (Tyack, 1974). Political, business, and educational elites in the nation's urban centers developed schools to quell the social chaos that they attributed to the burgeoning population of immigrants, who were drawn to work in the nation's rapidly expanding industries. The elites looked to the models around them, such as the factory and the railroad, to develop a blueprint for schools that embodied the administrative hierarchy and organizational systems of the industrial model and was reproduced across the nation (Rury, 2002).

Organizations that are homogeneous in their structure and purpose, arising from the influence of institutions at the time of their emergence, constitute an organizational archetype or form (Greenwood & Hinings, 1993). In aggregate, organizations of a particular form comprise an organizational population (Hannan & Freeman, 1977). Schools in the United States form an organizational population.

Organizational forms tend to retain the social structures that were present at their creation (Stinchcombe, 1965), resulting in substantial inertia (Scott, 2008). As North (1990) explains, "History matters...because the present and future are connected to the past by the continuity of a society's institutions" (p. vii). The basic structures of schools have not changed since the 19th century and remain ubiquitous. We can all recite the basic elements of school organization. Students are grouped by age, the curriculum is organized by subject matter, teachers instruct classes of roughly 20–35 students, students are categorized by achievement level, and so on.

As a result of this tendency for organizational forms to retain the fundamental structures with which they were imprinted at their origin, the locus of dramatic changes in organizational structure lies at the level of population, not at the level of the organization. That is, organizations of an existing form can change marginally in adapting to their environments. However, dramatic change in the structure of organizations occurs when a new organizational form emerges to fill an environmental niche and stands beside existing organizational populations or replaces populations that can no longer survive in the environment. For more than a century, U.S. schools have adapted to changes in the social, cultural, and political environment but have not altered their core structures or operations. Some scholars and policy makers are now seeking ways to encourage the development of novel ways to organize schools.

Improving Schools

Contemporary educational policy continues to seek and employ strategies for improving the performance of schools without altering their fundamental structures. The chapters in this section of the handbook highlight three general approaches. One affects improvement through the allocation of financial resources. Baker and Green weigh the balance between educational adequacy and equity and conclude that primacy should be given to the latter. They argue that this will require redistributing and targeting financial resources to schools and programs serving populations that are documented to be underserved by the educational system. Plecki and Castañeda take this a step further by considering whether money matters in the academic performance of schools. The authors note that—despite the absence of a clear answer to this fundamental question, the lack of consensus on a theory of educational production, and disputes over how to assess academic performance—policy makers have tended to invest in a handful of approaches, a majority of which are intended to directly affect schools by improving teacher quality, lowering pupil-teacher ratios, improving high school, and providing performance incentives. This foreshadows a second and related approach to improving schools: changing particular aspects of schools.

Other chapters in this section analyze policies aimed at altering four aspects of schools: class size, school size, staff reconstitution, and teaching and learning. None alter the basic organizational structure of schools. Ahn and Brewer analyze policies that reduce the size of classes, concluding that research provides compelling evidence that smaller class size positively affects student achievement. They, however, acknowledge that broad implementation of class-size reduction is complicated by numerous real-world challenges, including schools having to hire less qualified teachers to fill additional classes and teachers not changing curriculum or instructional practices to take advantage of having fewer students. Ahn and Brewer also examine small schools and conclude that research does not provide definitive evidence on the relationship between school size and student achievement. Malen and Rice assess the impact of school reconstitution, which involves replacing the professional staffs of schools that fail to meet performance standards over time. Reconstitution relies on the threat and application of sanctions to motivate educators to exert greater efforts to improve educational performance and to enhance school capacity by providing additional resources to schools deemed "reconstitution eligible" or to schools after reconstitution. While the authors conclude that research has yet to determine definitively and directly if reconstitution works as intended or if it positively affects the academic performance of schools, they note that existing evidence suggests that reconstitution might well negatively affect both incentive and capacity in schools. Spillane, Gomez, and Mesler note that policy makers are engaging in an unprecedented campaign to influence teaching and learning. The authors do not analyze the impact of these policies on school performance; rather, they conceptualize policy implementation as being deeply affected by local, organizational contexts, emphasizing the centrality of practice that emerges from interactions among two or more actors as shaped by but also shaping resource allocated by policy makers.

A third approach to changing schools takes a very different tack. Hess explains that one possible result of market pressures is that public schools will change. Chapters in this section highlight two prominent policy strategies in the United States to introduce market-like competition in education: charter schools and vouchers. Vergari's review of research on charter schools reveals that the presence of charter schools has done little to change public schools. She concludes that the presence of charter schools has left public schools largely unaffected, with only occasional, minor changes having been documented by research. Vouchers (Witte) might be expected to have greater potential for affecting public schools because they enable parents to select from a host of schools, not simply charter schools. Belfield and Levin's review of research on market reforms indeed indicates that vouchers may affect public schools. However, they report that tests scores have been found to rise only modestly with greater competition, leading them to conclude that research does not support the contention that market competition will produce marked changes and consequent improvements in the academic performance of schools generally and public schools specifically.

The public school, as an organizational form in the United States, took root over a century ago and is supported by a broad and deep institutional web of government regulations and professional affiliations (Hess, this volume). The core structures of "school" are "taken-for-granted;" it is difficult, if not impossible, to conceive of a formal educational setting that does not organize "students" by age in "classes" taught by "teachers" and the like. Thus, it is predictable that policies aimed at improving educational outcomes focus on change within the existing structural features of schools. Changing the size of classes and schools implicitly accepts how schools are organized for instruction. Reconstituting schools that chronically fall below performance standards implicitly emphasizes that it is the people who failed not the organization of schools. Directing teachers on what and how to teach implicitly focuses on activity within the "taken-for-granted" organization of schools. The deeply institutionalized status of public schools might also account for the failure to induce change by exposing public schools to market-like competition through the introduction of charter schools and vouchers. Two possible accounts come to mind. One, our view of "school" is imprinted with the core structures present at the creation of the organizational form. Thus, schools can only change marginally and, instead, will work to maintain the legitimacy that is attached to their institutionalized status. Vergari (this volume) notes that public schools have responded to the presence of charter schools by increasing public relations and lobbying efforts. Two, the deeply institutionalized conception of "school" inhibits innovation. Thus, alternatives to public schools— charter schools and private schools—have the same core structures as public schools and thus cannot inspire change in public schools. This brings me to the second general, organizational strategy for improving education in the United States: reinventing "school."

Reinventing "School"

Scholars from widely divergent perspectives are coming to a similar conclusion: The school, which was created in 19th century urban America, was not designed to fulfill the nation's 21st century aspiration of providing equity in education for its culturally and linguistically diverse students. While not invoking institutional theory, these scholars seem to agree that the basic structures of schools have not and cannot be changed, leaving reformers to make relatively minor adjustments (Tyack & Cuban, 1995), which produce marginal improvements in educational performance. Indeed, after decades of educational reform there is abundant evidence that the so-called achievement gap between White students and students from non-dominant racial and cultural backgrounds has not significantly diminished. To substantially enhance educational performance and equity of educational opportunity, these scholars argue, the nation must reinvent school; we must innovate by designing schools with organizational structures that reflect 21st century expressions of educational excellence and equity.

A few of the chapters in this section address this second general strategy for improving education in the United States. None articulate an innovative design for school but examine a strategy for fostering innovation. Hess explains that a possible result of competition in an educational market is the emergence of "new providers." Other chapters review evidence on the impact of two particular approaches to introducing market-like competition in education: charter schools and vouchers. Vergari notes that charter schools are promoted as "laboratories for innovation" because they are freed from many of the regulations with which public schools must comply. However, research suggests that charter schools do not vary much and, apart from teacher recruitment and compensation, seem not to differ significantly from traditional public schools. In reviewing research on educational vouchers, Belfield and Levin report that for-profit schools "have not been able to innovate more efficiently than public schools…" Thus, current approaches to promoting market-like competition in education have not encouraged the development of innovative school designs. This might be attributed to the fact that the traditional conception of school, with its roots in the 19th century U.S. industrialization, is deeply enmeshed culturally and socially. Consequently, private schools, whether religiously based or for-profit, tend to resemble traditional public schools. Relatedly, Hess argues that market-oriented educational reform has been compromised by a reluctance to directly invoke the language and mechanisms of the market in part because of the "abiding American faith in markets and public institutions," which serve efficiency and equity, respectively. Thus, it seems that for the foreseeable future market-based reform is unlikely to produce schools that differ substantially from the traditional public school.

Another American institution is being revived as a possible source of educational innovation and reinvention. Community-based movements in several parts of the country are working to develop educational programs to serve the needs of low-income and non-dominant racial and cultural communities. Some locate programs in the communities; others work in conjunction with local schools and districts. Scholars argue that educational opportunities for low-income and racially and culturally non-dominant communities can be expanded by incorporating the cultural and intellectual resources of these communities in curriculum and pedagogy. Thus, the people who live in the communities can be an important source of educational innovation to enhance equity. Little if any research documents these community-based efforts to develop innovative educational approaches. Thus, it remains to be seen if such projects will produce settings for learning that depart from the organizational structures of traditional public schools.

Implications for Policy and Practice

As reflected in the chapters in this section, contemporary U.S. educational policy focuses on improving education, generally, and enhancing educational equity, specifically. The key mechanisms for implementing educational policy are educational organizations, principally schools. Schools, as an organizational form, are rooted in 19th century origins, where structures that mirror industrial models were developed and imprinted. Policy makers predictably have sought to enhance educational performance and equity by improving schools within their existing organizational configurations. Contemporary policies aim to equalize educational funding and outcomes across schools and allocate resources to effect particular aspects of schools, including class size, school size, teacher quality, curriculum and instruction, and the like.

For organizations, such as schools, to undergo fundamental structural and operational changes, entirely new forms of organization must be developed and flourish. A growing number of scholars and policy makers are expressing the view that, in order to make substantial advances in educational performance and equity, we can no longer rely on improving the old model of school. Instead, we must reinvent school. This approach to educational reform is less developed than the improvement strategy in both research and policy circles. The chapters in this section do not identify or examine alternative organizational models of school. Instead, some of the chapters explore how market-like competition through charter schools and educational vouchers can encourage innovation. But deeply embedded conceptions of school and societal commitments to the pursuit of equity through public agencies blunt the impact of competition in an educational market. Nascent, community-based educational reform movements seem promising because they draw on members of low-income and racially and culturally non-dominant communities for ideas about how best to serve their educational needs. But, little research has been reported on these efforts, leaving unanswered the question of their ability to break from traditional conceptions to reinvent school.

Policy makers must carefully distinguish between these two general approaches to educational change. In light of research indicating that market-like competition has neither placed substantial pressure on public education to change nor produced innovative models of school, it seems that working to improve schools within their existing core structures is the more feasible approach. If this is the approach that policy makers pursue, they must be clear about its limitations. They must acknowledge the core structural features of schools, identify aspects of schools that can be altered within the parameters established by the core structures, and determine which of those aspects have been documented to affect educational performance and equity. The research reviewed in this section identifies many aspects of schools that can be influenced by policy and affect educational outcomes. In addition, policy makers would be well advised to work closely with educational practitioners. If the strategy is to improve education within existing structures, or social arrangements, then policy should be informed by the experiences of the people who teach students and manage schools. In their chapter, Spillane, Gomez, and Mesler explain that policy is interpreted and implemented through practice, which involves interactions among two or more actors as shaped by but also shaping

resource allocated by policy makers. Thus, practice can and should shape policy.

The second approach to reforming education through the "reinvention" of school is, according to authors of chapters in this section, less politically viable and fraught with uncertainties. However, I would urge policy makers to consider ways in which the state can provide incentives to encourage the development of new forms of educational organization. In pursuing this strategy, policy makers might keep a couple of issues in mind. One, employ multiple, alternative mechanisms to foster innovation. Chapters in this section highlight market-based competition. I have raised another possibility: community-based educational reform efforts. Perhaps some combination of these two American institutions—markets and local democracies—can produce truly innovative ways to organize for educating a highly pluralistic society. Two, think beyond schools. Arguably, the traditional conception of school in the United States, which is deeply embedded in society and culture, inhibits imagining new conceptions of school. To escape this pull, policy makers might develop initiatives to organize for learning in non-school settings. Already, learning and teaching is organized in a wide variety of out-of-school contexts, including libraries, museums, after school programs, and the like. Policies could be adopted to support the development of non-school learning organizations, whose innovations might augment learning and teaching in schools and even reshape how learning and teaching are approached by schools.

Note

1. For in-depth treatments of institutional theory see Scott (2008) and the application of institutional theory to educational organizations see Rowan and Miskel (1999).

References

Greenwood, R., & Hinings, C. R. (1993). Understanding strategic change: The contributions of archetypes. *Academy of Management Journal, 37*, 467–498.

Hannan, M. T., & Freeman, J. (1977). The population ecology of organizations. *American Journal of Sociology, 82*, 929–964.

Meyer, J. W., Boli, J., & Thomas, G. (1987). Ontology and rationalization in Western cultural account. In G. Thomas, J. Meyer, F. Ramirez, & J. Boli (Eds.), *Institutional structure: Constituting the state, society and the individual* (pp. 12–40). Newbury Park, CA: Sage.

Meyer, J. W., & Rowan, B. (1977). Institutionalized organizations: formal structures as myth and ceremony. *The American Journal of Sociology, 83*, 340–363.

North, D. C. (1990). *Institutions, institutional change and economic performance*. Cambridge, UK: Cambridge University Press.

Rowan, B., & Miskel, C. (1999). Institutional theory and the study of educational organizations. In J. Murphy & K. Lewis (Eds.), *Handbook of research on educational administration* (Vol. 2, pp. 359–383). San Francisco: Jossey Bass.

Rury, J. L. (2002). *Education and social change: Themes in the history of American schooling*. Mahwah, NJ: Erlbaum.

Scott, W. R. (2008). *Institutions and organizations* (3rd ed.). Thousand Oaks, CA: Sage.

Stinchcombe, A. L. (1965). Social structure and organizations. In J. G. March (Ed.), *Handbook of organizations* (pp. 142–193). Chicago: Rand McNally.

Tyack, D. (1974). *The one best system: A history of American urban education.* Cambridge: Harvard University Press.

Tyack, D., & Cuban, L. (1995). *Tinkering toward utopia: A century of public school reform.* Cambridge, MA: Harvard University Press.

Zucker, L. G. (1983). Organizations and institutions. In S. B. Bacharach (Ed.), *Research in the sociology of organizations* (Vol. 2, pp. 1–47). Greenwich, CT: JAI Press.

Section V

Teaching and Learning Policy

SECTION EDITOR: GARY SYKES

44

Opportunity to Learn

WILLIAM H. SCHMIDT AND ADAM MAIER
Michigan State University

Opportunity to learn (OTL) is a rather uncomplicated concept: What students learn in school is related to what is taught in school. This notion, although seemingly tautological, undergirds much of schooling. Schools are organized around the idea of providing distinct learning opportunities in multiple academic disciplines. Yet in the United States the opportunities to learn this academic content are not equally distributed among districts, schools, classrooms, or students.

This unequal distribution stems primarily from the structure of the American educational system. Unlike many other countries, the American educational system lacks national curricular standards. Although most states have codified a set of standards, their implementation is only weakly enforceable.[1] Consequently, it may be more realistic to depict U.S. students' opportunities to learn at the district or school level. Yet even within these levels, when students are exposed to ostensibly similar content, variation often remains. So, while nearly all students study a range of school subjects and within these subjects most students take similarly titled courses (e.g., algebra I, biology, or English), students often still encounter different curricular opportunities.

In particular, Schmidt et al. (2001) identify three characteristics of curricular content—focus, rigor, and coherence—that can and often do, vary among various sets of content expectations and even among similarly titled courses. As any of these characteristics vary, so varies the resulting content exposure. In other words, algebra I in one school may not be algebra I in another; biology in one classroom may not be biology in another. Consequently, some have suggested that there is as much variation in students' opportunities as there is number of teachers.

The American educational structure, therefore, engenders, or at least allows, an environment where districts, schools, and teachers have a certain level of curricular decision-making autonomy, and thus also a significant influence on students' opportunities to learn. As a result, students are not assured the same educational opportunities during their school years. Related to this, students' performance varies appreciably across the country in ways suggesting that certain regions and certain demographics lead to higher performance than others.

These regional and demographic achievement patterns—observable in countless research studies, beginning most prominently with the Coleman report (Coleman et al., 1966)—have led many to suggest that the most important influence on educational attainment is the student's social class background. These achievement patterns are often subsumed in the larger debate in the U.S. over what matters most for achievement: schooling or family background?

Typically lost within this achievement gap debate is the opportunity to learn concept. Understanding students' underlying OTL, we argue, is vital to understanding why such gaps exist. Without taking into account students' OTL, achievement differences are most easily attributed to the obvious—usually social class and racial ethnic background. In this chapter we argue that in the No Child Left Behind (NCLB) era, the issue of opportunity to learn and its distribution across the educational system is an especially important factor in realizing NCLB's vision. The point is simple: If no child is to be left behind on important subject matter such as mathematics, reading, science, and others, then all children must be guaranteed the necessary opportunities to learn.

Others have already argued that students' OTL mediates achievement gaps. Part of this is due to OTL's ambiguity. Since its theoretical and empirical development, different researchers and commentators have defined and used the concept to encompass multifarious ideas: equal or equitable per-pupil funding, adequate school organization, a suitable amount of time in the school year, or equal access to qualified teachers, challenging curricula, and resources, to name a few (see McPartland & Schneider, 1996, pp.

541

73–75 for a discussion of OTL's multiple meanings). The definition of opportunity to learn has been cast wide, and so stretched thin.

In this chapter, we focus on opportunity to learn in the narrowest sense: students' content exposure. Though the many uses and definitions of OTL have often been valid, amalgamating all of these factors into the single opportunity to learn concept would deprive OTL of its empirical value. Moreover, we argue that all the factors of production are relevant *only if* the actual content that serves as the focal point of instruction is truly equal. For example, providing a group of students the best teachers and resources as well as additional instructional time and tutoring, while neglecting to equalize content exposure, would result in improved instruction surrounding content that differs from the content exposure of those students not requiring additional services. In many cases, this implies a less demanding set of content expectations and hence a lesser set of opportunities. So we do not quarrel with the broader view of equal educational opportunity, but instead choose to focus on the part of equality that we argue is most central.

This chapter reviews some of the work that has been done around opportunity to learn, including its origins as a concept. Additionally, we discuss specific features or dimensions of content that are important toward understanding OTL. Finally, we argue that the structure of U.S. schooling yields variation in content exposure so great that ignoring OTL in educational research will imperil the results. Educational research typically looks across classrooms and tries to understand student achievement in relationship to some other characteristic such as class size, the presence of site-based management, and so forth. However, concomitant with the variation across schools or classrooms on the dimension being studied is the large variation in the actual content exposure associated with students in different schools. We later provide data in support of this point, but the argument is simple: to study other educational characteristics which themselves are related to content exposure, while omitting a measure of content exposure could lead to erroneous conclusions and bad public policy.

The organization of this chapter centers on four broad questions: (a) what is OTL, (b) how do we measure it, (c) what have we learned, and (d) why is it important? For each, we review the relevant literature and provide explanatory examples. In order to make this discussion more explicit, the examples chosen come from mathematics and science. This not only reflects two topics deemed important by NCLB legislation, but it also reflects the availability of data. Some of those data come from the Third International Mathematics and Science Study (TIMSS). This chapter, however, will not centrally focus on international studies but rather closely examine the U.S. policy context.

What is OTL?

Carroll's Model. The opportunity to learn concept originated in the early 1960s with the work of John B. Carroll

(1962, 1963). Although many ideas and arguments centering on educational opportunity had underpinned educational research prior to this time, Carroll's work gave OTL a specific theoretical meaning and distinguished it from the more generic "educational opportunity." Carroll first developed the OTL concept in attempting to explain why aptitude varied, depending on the study, in its ability to predict achievement (Anderson, 1985; Carroll, 1984). He developed a theoretical model for school learning that used time as a metric, and introduced opportunity to learn as a measure of the time allowed for learning. He argued that anyone would succeed in learning a given task, as long he or she spends the needed amount of time. Further, the needed amount of time varied with each individual and depended solely on aptitude, the quality of instruction, and the ability to understand instruction. Using this model, Carroll posited that one's degree of learning could be represented by Formula 44.1:

$$Degree\ of\ Learning = f\ \left(\frac{time\ actually\ spent}{time\ needed} \right)$$

According to this model, the degree of learning relied heavily on the time actually spent learning. Logically, degree of learning also depended on the amount of time allocated to the individual. If we assume that a student stops working when he or she learns the task, then the time actually spent learning depends only on one's perseverance and/or the opportunity to learn. This means that a student will cease learning if the task takes longer to learn than he or she is willing to spend; or not enough time is allocated to the student. It is the latter constraint that defined OTL. Carroll's model argued that an individual cannot learn a task if he or she is not allowed enough time to do so. Carroll thus introduced OTL as a measurable concept that represented allocated learning time.

Carroll's notion of OTL remained relatively dormant for several years after its introduction (Carroll, 1984). It was eventually assimilated, however, into the work of Benjamin Bloom (1968; Block & Burns, 1976). Bloom (1968) argued that by adjusting the controllable variables in Carroll's model (i.e., OTL and quality of instruction), any child could achieve some preset level of "mastery performance" (see also Block & Burns, 1976). Bloom took Carroll's notion of OTL and framed it as a manageable variable. He further argued that "if teachers and curriculum makers can define an appropriate criterion of achievement, it then becomes the responsibility of the teachers and the schools to provide the time necessary for the students to attain the criterion" (Bloom, 1974, p. 683). With Bloom, the opportunity to learn concept began to shed its theoretical origins to become a practical way for educators to enhance achievement.

Carroll and Bloom introduced their concepts of opportunity to learn during a time in which the effects of schooling were powerfully challenged by two seminal reports. Coleman et al.'s (1966) *Equality of Educational Opportunity* found that differences in measured school inputs were not closely associated with differences in school achievement. Then Jencks et al.'s (1972) *Inequality* argued that differences between schools seemed to have little effect on any measurable attribute of students, and that "eliminating differences between schools would do almost nothing to make adults more equal" (p. 16). These reports did not argue that schooling was useless, but that differences between schools—as they measured them—could only minimally explain differences in achievement. To many, these reports questioned the effects of schooling.

The Work of Wiley, Harnischfeger, and Berliner Wiley and Harnischfeger, however, viewed this situation differently (Harnischfeger & Wiley, 1976; Wiley & Harnischfeger, 1974). They argued that school learning only takes place through pupils' pursuits. Put differently, one could not frame school inputs as directly affecting school achievement (as Coleman and Jencks had done). Rather, inputs could affect achievement only to the extent that they affected the amount of time students spent engaged in learning. The upper limit to this engaged learning time was one's opportunity to learn. Wiley and Harnischfeger contended that Coleman and Jencks did not adequately consider opportunity to learn in their analyses and thus underplayed the effects of schooling. Coleman and Jencks had inappropriately incorporated time (i.e., time in school) into their studies. These studies treated attendance—and thus the amount of schooling—as a qualitative effect (schooling or no-schooling) rather than a quantitative variable. Using Carroll and Bloom's models as theoretical lenses, Wiley and Harnischfeger (1974) contended that the amount of schooling students partake in—i.e., their opportunity to learn—is a "major determinant of school outcomes" (p. 8). By considering differences in students' exposure to schooling, Wiley and Harnischfeger found an "enormous variation" between schools—mostly due to variations in the length of the school year and the length of the school day. Ultimately, Wiley and Harnischfeger argued that students in both Jencks and Coleman's studies differed in their opportunity to learn and consequently differed in their achievement.

Some of the work that went in to developing Wiley and Harnischfeger's notion of OTL was done in collaboration with the project staff of the Beginning Teacher Evaluation Study (BTES; Berliner, 1990). The BTES staff had developed their own model of academic learning, and consequently their own, albeit quite similar, notion of OTL (Berliner, 1979, 1990; Fisher et al., 1980). In doing so, the BTES staff attached an important caveat to the opportunity to learn concept. They argued that for a student to attain a particular achievement criterion, the student needed to be provided not only enough time to do so (Carroll and Bloom's OTL), but also that that time needed to be spent engaged with a curriculum that was logically related to the criterion (Berliner, 1979).[2] Put differently, it was not enough to define OTL as allocated time, for that time could be spent engaged in infinitely many tasks. If this time is spent engaged in a task unrelated to the desired outcome, however, it could not enhance achievement on the outcome measure. Thus, the BTES staff argued it was imperative that

time be allocated to a curriculum aligned with the outcome measures (Berliner, 1990).

Implicit in both the BTES staff's and Wiley and Harnischfeger's conceptions of OTL is the teacher's role in determining students' opportunities. Both models recognized that the time allocated to a specific topic was largely dependent on the teacher. Teachers had "great flexibility in realizing curricular guidelines in the classroom" and could thus allocate time to various topics as they saw fit (Harnischfeger & Wiley, 1976, p. 7). The amount of allocated time had to be reduced by the amount of time the teacher engaged in managerial tasks (e.g., discipline, organizing groups, etc.). Furthermore, teachers varied in the amount of time they spent on these managerial tasks. Thus, Wiley and Harnischfeger argued that a student's opportunity to learn varied considerably and depended on not only the length of the school day and year (institutional structures), but also on individual teachers within the school (Hallinan, 1976).

The Institute for Research on Teaching How teachers make curricular decisions has important consequences for students' OTL and this became the focus of the Content Determinants Project in the Institute for Research on Teaching (IRT) at Michigan State University under the leadership of Porter, together with Schwille, Schmidt, Floden, and Freeman (Porter, Floden, Freeman, Schmidt, & Schwille, 1986, 1988). The IRT studies were based on the notion that teachers are presented with multiple, sometimes contradictory, statements of what mathematics content should be included in a particular grade level. These statements come from, among others, standardized tests, textbooks, and administrators. In order to study teacher decision making, IRT researchers had to examine both the content actually covered by teachers and the content implicit in the many curricular statements aimed at teachers.

Whereas the IRT studies initially focused on how various sources influence teachers' choices of what content to teach, Porter and his colleagues' later work shifted to the *match* between two potential content-providing sources. In other words, their work shifted away from content coverage and toward alignment. As a result, an instrument was developed that could not only determine classroom-level content coverage, but also the content coverage implicit in state and national standards as well as various standardized assessments. This instrument not only examined the amount and nature of content teachers provided students or was expected of them via standards or tests but—in an attempt to understand the cognitive demand associated with content coverage—also examined what teachers, tests, and standards required students to *do* with those particular topics. We say more about the nature of this measurement issue in the next section.

The IEA Studies Other ways to view opportunity to learn and other historical lines of development emerged as well. Indeed, another body of research developed OTL somewhat separately from Carroll's work. The International Study of

Achievement in Mathematics (later called FIMS) framed OTL as a content-covered variable without specific regard to allocated time.[3] Launched in 1963, FIMS' main objective was "to investigate the 'outcomes' of various school systems by relating as many as possible of the relevant input variables (to the extent that they could be assessed) to the output assessed by international test instruments" (Husen, 1967a, p. 30). In other words, FIMS set out to measure the "productivity of school systems" by examining the efficacy of various school inputs on achievement scores (Husen, 1967a). FIMS' researchers realized that, "one of the factors which may influence scores on the achievement examination was whether or not the students had an opportunity to study a particular topic or learn how to solve a particular type of problem presented by the test" (Husen, 1967b, pp. 162–163). This is an obvious problem when comparing countries that have different national curricula or countries with decentralized educational systems that have no national curriculum; variations in what content is taught are bound to occur. FIMS researchers consequently found it necessary to include an "opportunity to learn" variable in their study. Their OTL variable differed, however, from Carroll's original conception.

Instead of defining opportunity to learn as allocated time directly as Carroll and Bloom had done, FIMS researchers introduced OTL as a measure of the teachers' perception of students' opportunity to become acquainted with the material covered by the test item. FIMS researchers had teachers examine each test item and report "whether or not the topic… has been covered by the students…" by choosing one of the following:

A. All or most (at least 75%) of this group of students have had an opportunity to learn this type of problem
B. Some (25% to 75%) of this group of students have had an opportunity to learn this type of problem
C. Few or none (0% to 25%) of this group of students have had an opportunity to learn this type of problem. (Husen, 1967b, p. 167–168)

FIMS' definition of OTL does not necessarily exclude allocated time. Teachers could have easily factored in the amount of time spent teaching a given topic in their classification of what constitutes an adequate opportunity. Nevertheless, FIMS' researchers' use of OTL was not the same as Carroll's. FIMS' researchers had introduced OTL as a necessary tool to compare nations, and so were thus more interested in OTL's ability to represent content covered than in allocated time.

Including OTL in FIMS led to many interesting findings. As expected, they found a small but statistically significant positive correlation between the scores and the teachers' ratings of opportunity to learn. Further, FIMS' researchers argued that a considerable amount of the variation between countries in mathematics scores could be attributed to the differences between students' opportunities to learn the material that was tested (Husen, 1967b). In part, these find-

ings spurred the Second International Mathematics Study (SIMS), in which OTL would take a more pivotal role.

One of the main objectives of SIMS centered on the curriculum. Specifically, it was to focus, "on the content of what is being taught, the relative importance given to various aspects of mathematics, and the student achievement relative to these priorities and content…" (Wilson, as cited in Travers & Westbury, 1989, p. 5). In order to compare curricula across nations, SIMS' researchers developed a three-level model of the curriculum (Travers & Westbury, 1989), including:

1. *The Intended Curriculum*: The curriculum set by officials at the national or system (school district, educational region, etc.) level that embodies the nation or system's goals and traditions;
2. *The Implemented Curriculum*: The curriculum that the teacher actually transmits into reality; and
3. *The Attained Curriculum*: The body of knowledge a student has acquired over a given amount of time.

Because SIMS framed the curriculum in this manner, OTL became an effective measure of the implemented curriculum. SIMS' researchers also refined their measurement of OTL by supplementing the original "did you teach the mathematics needed to answer item *n*" question with a measure of why an item had not been taught (e.g., it had been taught previously, it will be taught later, it is not in the curriculum, or for some other reason). These questions taken together enabled SIMS' researchers to define OTL as the proportion of items taught prior to and including the year in which the data were collected (Schmidt, Wolfe, & Kifer, 1992).

Using their conception of OTL, SIMS' researchers found influential results that would eventually play a role in U.S. policy. Most interesting was the extent to which OTL levels varied within nations. For example, when researchers examined OTL distributions in algebra, they found that some countries demonstrated relatively homogenous OTL ratings (Japan ranged from 60% to 100% with a median of 85% and France ranged from about 50% to 100% with a median of 85%) whereas other countries displayed considerably more variation (the U.S. ranged from 0% to 100% with a median of 75%; Schmidt et al., 1992). Some posited that much of the U.S. variation was due to curricular differentiation (Kifer, 1992). SIMS' researchers found that when eighth grade algebra classes were divided into remedial, regular, and enriched sections, remedial courses had a median OTL of about 30% whereas the "highest-tracked" algebra had a median OTL upwards of 90% (Kifer, 1992). SIMS demonstrated that students in lower-tracked classes had much less opportunity to learn and were thus not exposed to all (or even a majority) of the content needed to demonstrate learning on outcome measures. Simply stated, "it is extremely difficult for a student to learn something that is not taught" (Kifer 1992, p. 307).

Although SIMS refined the OTL concept and found substantial differences in learning opportunities between and within (some) countries, the study did not find large effects of OTL on achievement. Given what was known about the varying country curricula, this finding was puzzling and suggested that the currently employed measures of OTL were inadequate. An initial R&D effort was undertaken to refine the OTL measures—the Survey of Mathematical Opportunities (SMSO); this work then informed the third major IEA study (i.e., TIMSS). Based on the tripartite model of SIMS, Schmidt and his colleagues set out to improve the measures at each curricular level: the intended curriculum, the implemented curriculum, and the achieved curriculum.

Consider first the *intended curriculum*. In all IEA studies, researchers obtained some indication of the types of learning opportunities each country intended to provide. This work, however, was often separated from the study's quantitative aspects, and, as a result, became more of a qualitative description. Consequently, SMSO proposed, and TIMSS later used, more direct curricular measures. Instead of relying on subjective interpretations of the intended curriculum, TIMSS gleaned this information from official curricular documents. Using these documents, TIMSS researchers asked influential educators from each country—typically from the ministry of education—to detail the actual content that was intended to be covered at each grade level (K-12). Particulars of this measurement scheme follow in the next section, but the key instrument necessary to carry out this work was a mathematics and science framework that, from an international point of view, detailed the topics typically covered across the primary and secondary levels.

The biggest change to the OTL measure was for the *implemented curriculum*. As noted, both FIMS and SIMS asked teachers to indicate the implemented curriculum by responding to individual assessment items. Based on the SMSO findings—TIMSS researchers discovered that teachers found this task particularly difficult for two reasons: teachers had to review (too) many items and it required teachers to abstract the content related to performance from each particular item. Consequently, the difficulty of the task produced erroneous judgments.

To remedy this situation, Schmidt and colleagues developed an entirely different approach. Based on the curricular frameworks developed from analyses of the intended curriculum, a list of topics was generated/modified to be appropriate for each grade level; and for each topic asked teachers to indicate the amount of instruction they provided students. Moreover, working with teachers in each country, topics were phrased in a way that was consistent with how teachers at each specific grade level describe the particular mathematical topic.

Additionally, SMSO included a fourth curricular area: the *potentially implemented curriculum*. Throughout the world, the most ubiquitous educational element across countries is the textbook. Studies preceding TIMSS—and corroborated by analyses of TIMSS data—suggested that textbooks powerfully impact instruction, especially in math-

ematics. It made sense for SMSO researchers to examine the opportunities provided by various countries' textbooks. As a result, TIMSS included textbooks as a source of OTL recognizing that in many classrooms the textbook becomes the de facto curriculum ranging from whole to partial to little use at all; this factor was then labeled the potentially implemented curriculum.

The last curricular area SMSO refined was the *achieved curriculum*. As stated previously, this refers to what students actually learn. SMSO researchers advanced this concept by closely tying assessment to the curricular framework. They also designed a series of subtest scores that, from an international perspective, were more specific to the nature of the curriculum. This moved the measurement of the achieved curriculum away from total test scores to scores more closely aligned with the nature of school instruction.

The Sociological Perspective Concerns with variation in students' learning opportunities have hardly been unique to the work of Carroll and the subsequent refinements or the IEA studies. A growing body of sociological research had similarly examined the effects of curricular differentiation on achievement measures. Partly influenced by Wiley and Harnischfeger and largely in response to Jencks and Coleman, some argued that the effects of schools could only be understood through the process of schooling (Barr & Dreeben, 1983; Bidwell & Kasarda, 1980; Sørensen & Hallinan, 1977, 1986). As Bidwell and Kasarda (1980) put it, the "failure [of school effects research] is the confusion of *school*, an organization, with *schooling*, a process that individual students experience….Schooling, which is comprised of acts by students and teachers, is conditioned by the social organization of classrooms, curricular tracks, and other instructional units within schools" (p. 402). Put differently, student achievement can only be affected through *schooling*, and thus schools affect achievement only through the opportunities to learn they provide students. Logically, then, students in the same school who undergo different types of schooling will exhibit different outcomes as a result of those processes.

The most salient example of within school differentiation is tracking. Much of the early tracking research demonstrated that the different curricular tracks could help explain the large variation in school outcomes (Alexander & Eckland, 1975; Alexander & McDill, 1976; Heyns, 1974). These researchers not only found an association between curricular placement or ability group and achievement, but also that stratifying students within schools affects achievement as a process in itself. Students in high-ranking groups or tracks achieve more, even when controlling for prior ability (Alexander, Cook, & McDill, 1978; Alexander & McDill, 1976; Rosenbaum, 1975; Weinstein, 1976). Much of this research was descriptive, however, and focused more on whether curricular differentiation could explain achievement variation and less on how this process did so. Later researchers have identified three different mechanisms that may produce the effects of tracking (Gamoran & Berends,

1987; Lucas, 1999): social factors, that is, tracks create stratified social contexts governed by different norms where high-tracked students have more opportunities to befriend academically motivated and high-achieving peers (Alexander & McDill, 1976; Oakes, 1985; Vanfossen, Jones, & Spade, 1987); institutional factors, that is, the symbolic meanings intrinsic to track locations that convey different images of its occupying students so that teachers, parents, peers, and society in general may expect different outcomes of students in different tracks (Meyer, 1977, 1980); and instructional factors, that is, the differential content and instruction provided to students in different tracks.[4]

Both social and institutional explanations have become more difficult to attach to tracking because schools no longer, at least overtly, assign students to school-wide tracks (Lucas, 1999). It is therefore possible for a student to simultaneously be in both high- and low-tracked courses. Consequently, students may have access to academically orientated peers in some classes but not in others. Institutional effects may be similarly dampened, as a student's multiple track locations convey a less coherent symbolic meaning. The magnitude of the social and institutional contexts of tracking therefore depend partly on how connected students' track levels are across courses (Lucas, 1999), and partly on the influential weight consigned to different academic subjects.

Whereas the social and institutional contexts of tracking may be blurred by the lack of overarching curricular programs, the instructional context remains theoretically unchanged. Instructional effects consist of both the quantity and quality of education that students receive. Track-differences in either the amount or quality of education may cause differences in student learning. Prior research has found that less experienced, energetic, qualified, and/or successful teachers teach low-tracked classes (Achinstein, Ogawa, & Speiglman, 2004; Oakes, 1985, 1990; Talbert, 1990), and that these classes tend to provide a less patient, prepared, and/or challenging atmosphere (Oakes, 1985; Vanfossen et al., 1987).

The most salient instructional aspect of tracking, though, and the one that most closely resembles OTL, is how that tracking differentiates students' coursework. This is expected, as the purpose of tracking is to separate students into substantively different classes, but studies have found that it is precisely because students take different courses that tracking is associated with increasing achievement inequality (Gamoran, 1987; Gamoran, Porter, Smithson, & White, 1997; Ma, 2000; Rock & Pollack, 1995; Schneider, Swanson, & Riegle-Crumb, 1998; Stevenson, Schiller, & Schneider, 1994). These different courses provide students with different opportunities to learn specific mathematics content. Many studies posit that the curricular opportunities available in high-tracked classes facilitate higher achievement rates.

Overall, sociologists developed opportunity to learn into a concept not unlike that found in the IEA studies or originating with Carroll. Like the SIMS study, sociologists

argued that curricular differentiation in schools restricted students' opportunities-to-learn by exposing them to different amounts and types of content. Sociologists, however, also attached other instructional effects—such as teacher quality and teaching methods—to their conception of OTL. Eventually, the confluence of both formulations of OTL became appealing to U.S. policy makers (McDonnell, 1995). After all, if differences in OTL were related to differences in achievement, then a solution presents itself nicely: ensure that all students have an adequate opportunity to learn.

How Do We Measure OTL?

As noted, OTL is a fairly straightforward notion: You cannot expect students to know what they have not been taught. Actually *measuring* OTL, however, is not so clear. To understand the learning opportunities provided to students requires information on the day-to-day activities of teachers and students. It would be nice to have trained researchers to observe thousands (or even hundreds) of teachers in their classrooms. This type of research would surely provide strong data on learning opportunities but it would also be insurmountably costly. Moreover, measuring students' classroom-level opportunities to learn specific content is relatively meaningless if we do not also have a systematic way of classifying such content. Attempting to analyze OTL raises two concomitant questions: how to classify the content that different curricular sources (i.e., standardized tests, textbooks, standards) prescribe, and how to measure what actually happens in classrooms.

Some of the earliest work around the measurement of OTL was descriptive. In an attempt to capture students' country-, classroom-, and even textbook-level opportunities, researchers provided long verbal records. This research was obviously limited in that the lack of quantitative measurements made it difficult to explore more complex relationships, such as the relationship between OTL and achievement. For example, when the focus was to compare two different specifications of opportunity to learn, researchers typically used a set of paired comparisons. Although still qualitative in nature, paired comparisons were an attempt to indicate the extent of overlap between the two different OTL sources. Yet, like the aforementioned descriptive approach, using paired comparisons was also severely limited; with several rather than just two OTL sources, the number of paired comparisons grew unmanageably large.

Various efforts ensued to measure OTL; here we focus on three recent and prominent approaches. These include the extension of work begun in TIMSS, the University of Michigan's Study of Instructional Improvement, and work begun in the IRT project. All three of these projects have employed OTL measures.

TIMSS and Beyond As indicated, much of OTL's popularity stems from the three IEA studies, most recently TIMSS. To measure OTL, TIMSS had to develop a framework for classifying both mathematics and science content and to devise a method for measuring what happens in classrooms. Adding to this already difficult challenge as an international study all participating nations had to agree to TIMSS' mathematics and science content frameworks.

Consequently, the frameworks were developed by a group of mathematicians and math educators from multiple countries. The creation of this framework took well over a year, as researchers encountered some difficulty agreeing upon the frameworks' grain size.[5] First attempts produced a framework that many thought too detailed.[6] Critics from multiple countries considered the original framework to be a long laundry list; that precluded interpretable responses.

In the end, TIMSS researchers agreed on a hierarchal framework that included ten broad areas representing major mathematics categories and then subdivisions of these larger topics. The TIMSS framework also included a second content dimension representing the cognitive demand associated with coverage of each topic. This was termed "performance expectation" and was meant to measure the nature of the expected student performance associated with coverage of each topic. Performance expectations included memorization of facts, simple algorithms, problem solving, and mathematical reasoning, among others. Combining topics with cognitive demand can be thought of as generating a complex signature or vector. Each signature represents a certain "type" of content. By subdividing the curriculum and then coding both the content and the performance expectation, this framework may be applied to content standards, tests, textbooks, and classroom instruction both in TIMSS and in subsequent work including PROM/SE—a 62-district study of school reform. The framework has remained the same although the level of detail employed in a given set of work has varied.

This played out differently across the four levels of curriculum. For the *intended curriculum*, two approaches have been taken. The first—termed "topic trace mapping"—used the framework to define an instrument, which was then filled out by a curriculum ministry official in each country in TIMSS or by their counterparts in the states or districts. Using the relevant standards, each topic and its coverage at various grade levels was mapped onto this instrument, with codes indicating when it was first covered, when that coverage was more focused, and the end point associated with that topic's coverage. This resulted in a complete "map" of content coverage or OTL over all the grades.

Then, the framework was used to code each county's national syllabus (or for those few countries where no national syllabus existed, various regional syllabi) or to code state and district standards in the United States. The document analysis procedures parsed the document into sections called blocks and each block was then assigned at least one content and one performance expectation code. Because coding of this type required very specific procedures, coders received extensive training and quality monitoring to assure the process produced reliable data (Schmidt, McKnight, Valverde, Houang, & Wiley, 1997; Schmidt, Raizen, Britton, Bianchi, & Wolfe, 1997).

For the *potentially implemented curriculum*, the same coding that was done with the content standards was done to the textbooks (Jakwerth, Bianchi, McKnight, & Schmidt, 1997; Schmidt et al., 1996; Valverde, Bianchi, Wolfe, Schmidt, & Houang, 2002). Additional procedures had to be defined as to how to subdivide the textbook, but, once accomplished, the coding exactly paralleled the process described above. Coding an entire textbook, however, was both arduous and time-consuming.

To measure the *implemented curriculum*, Schmidt and his colleagues have used teacher questionnaires based on the framework which included broader content categories as well as language more closely related to "school mathematics" rather than mathematics in general. Each teacher was asked to indicate the number of periods allocated to the coverage of a specific topic. Five categories were used for the coding.

In order to obtain curriculum sensitive measures of the *achieved curriculum*, TIMSS researchers used the framework in an aggregate sense to define the test blueprint. In allocating items across the blueprint, special care was taken to ensure that, at least at the country level, enough items would be available to gain more refined subtest-level measures. For example, the mathematics version of TIMSS included 20 subscales at the eighth grade. Consequently, test results at each subtest-level were available for each country (Schmidt, McKnight, Cogan, Jakwerth, & Houang, 1999). This resulted in performance that varied by country, with some countries performing well in certain areas but not in others. Measurements designed in this fashion can be dubbed "curriculum sensitive measurement." The same procedure was followed in PROM/SE where 20 to 25 subscales were developed at each of grades 3 through 12. The same basic procedure used for content standards documents and textbooks was used to code test content where the unit for coding was the test item.

The Work Begun in the IRT and Beyond Porter and colleagues' more recent measures of OTL had their roots in the original IRT project. The early IRT OTL group, dubbed "content determinants," had to develop a common mathematics framework as done in TIMSS to code standardized test items (Porter et al., 1988). This work suggested that the various standardized tests typically used in schools specified distinctly different content. Even tests that were essentially designed to measure the *same* mathematics at each grade level differed in the relative emphasis associated with various topics—in some cases, topics on one test were not even included on another.

Though the mismatch of standardized test content is disconcerting, the more interesting question—especially for a chapter on OTL—is how students' classroom-level learning opportunities matched these tests. Consequently, Porter's subsequent studies moved OTL measures into the classroom.

Most of these studies centered on mathematics content, and in all studies Porter and his colleagues classified content along two dimensions: topics and cognitive demand (Gamoran et al., 1997; Porter, 2002; Porter, Kirst, Osthoff, Smithson, & Schneider, 1993). The researchers first divided the mathematics curriculum into different general areas of mathematics and then divided each of these areas into specific topics. Each topic was then cross-classified with one of six levels of cognitive demand (e.g., memorize facts, understand concepts, etc.).[7] The resulting framework was very similar to that produced in TIMSS.

By applying this framework to both standardized tests and classroom instruction, content matrices were created for both assessments and instruction in order to evaluate the extent of alignment. For assessments they created content matrices by allowing the unit of analysis to be a test item (Gamoran et al., 1997; Porter, 2002; Porter & Smithson, 2001). Thus, each cell in the matrix represents the proportion of test items that focus on a specific topic and requiring a specific cognitive demand. This parallels the TIMSS work.

Creating content matrices for instruction is more difficult, as it requires data on teachers' classroom practice. Although early studies relied mostly on teachers' daily logs (Porter, 1989; Porter et al., 1993), more recent work employs end-of-year or end-of-semester teacher surveys (Porter, 2002). In these surveys, teachers are asked to indicate the amount of time spent on each topic, and, within each topic, the relative emphasis given to specific cognitive demands (see Porter, 2002, for an example of a teacher survey). Responses to these questionnaires again create the two-dimensional content matrix, where each cell represents the proportion of instructional time dedicated to a specific content area (i.e., topic and cognitive demand).

By measuring the content embedded in both instruction and assessments, Porter and colleagues were able to calculate an index of alignment between the two:

$$Alignment\ Index = 1 - \frac{\sum |X - Y|}{2}$$

where X represents the cells of the instructional content index, and Y represent the cells of the assessment content matrix; values closer to 1 represent better alignment (Porter, 2002; Porter & Smithson, 2001). In a sense, this alignment index became their OTL measure: students who have classroom instruction better aligned with the assessment can be expected to perform better. Indeed, Porter and colleagues found just this (Gamoran et al., 1997).

Later work by Porter generalized these alignment measures so that they could be used not only to compare classroom instruction and assessment, but also to compare states' assessments to their standards, and classroom instruction to state standards[8] (Porter, 2002). Actually constructing a content matrix for standards is not straightforward. Porter (2002) argues that the best strategy is to "analyze the content of each objective, paragraph, or phrase" (p. 4). Consequently, each cell of the content matrix would represent the proportion of objectives, paragraphs, or phrases that focus on a specific topic and require a specific cognitive demand.

In the end, Porter and colleague's alignment index helps highlight discrepancies between standards, instruction, and assessment.

Both approaches involve shortcomings or at least points of contention. To begin, many question the use of an end-of-year or end-of-semester survey to measure instruction. Although teacher logs or diaries might provide more accurate information, they are also more expensive (Porter, 1991). Moreover, for the Reform Up Close Study (Porter et al., 1993)—that used observational, survey, and log data results on instructional practices from end-of-year surveys-demonstrated a high degree of agreement with log-data (Smithson & Porter, 1994). Similar results were found in the SMSO work leading up to TIMSS (Schmidt et al., 1996).

The other limitation is the level of aggregation. In both approaches, the smallest unit analyzed is teachers' instructional practice, which implies that these studies cannot tell us how, or if, students' OTL varies *within* classrooms. In other words, we do not know how students in the same classroom may encounter different opportunities.

The Study of Instructional Improvement Another use of OTL is in the ongoing Study of Instructional Improvement (SII) at the University of Michigan. The OTL—or enacted curriculum, as these researchers have called it—aspect of the study has focused on mathematics and literacy instruction in the upper elementary grades (fourth–fifth; Rowan, Camburn, & Correnti, 2004; Rowan, Harrison, & Hayes, 2004). In both academic subjects researchers used teacher logs to collect curricular data in order to overcome some of the limitations inherent in end-of-year surveys.

These logs, however, differed in several ways from previous efforts to measure OTL. Instead of asking teachers what they taught to the entire class, Rowan and colleagues asked teachers to report on the instruction provided to a single student. For each class, a representative sample of eight "target students" was chosen, and at different times each of the eight target students was the focus of a teacher log. Using teacher logs in this manner allowed the researchers to account for the fact that curricular coverage may differ between students in the same classroom. In effect, the researchers collected curricular data at four nested levels: the lesson level, the student level, the classroom level, and the school level.

Although the teacher logs proved a fruitful way of measuring what actually happens in classrooms yielding high agreement with third-party observations (Camburn & Barnes, 2004; Hill, 2005), in order to measure OTL, SII researchers also had to develop a way of classifying the curriculum. This process differed slightly by subject (i.e., reading/writing or math), so we discuss each separately.

For reading, Rowan and colleagues characterized the curriculum along two dimensions. First, they divided the reading curriculum into nine reading and ten writing *strands* (e.g., print, word analysis, grammar, etc.). Teachers indicated the lesson's strand coverage in the logs by recording their emphasis on each strand which SII researchers later dichotomized as either "taught" or "not taught" (Rowan, Camburn, et al., 2004). Within three "focal strands" (comprehension, writing, and word analysis), the researchers also delineated the cognitive demand or "difficulty" level of the *skills* taught (e.g., writing practice, identifying story structure, editing capital, punctuations or spelling, etc.). This difficulty level of each skill depended on the frequency that the skill was taught; skills that were taught less often were assumed to be more difficult (Rowan, Camburn, et al., 2004). Teachers indicated the skills taught in each lesson by answering a series of yes/no questions (i.e., did the target student work on "generating ideas for writing" today).

Rowan and colleagues took a similar approach to classifying the mathematics curriculum. Again, the researchers asked teachers to indicate which of 10 mathematics strands were a focus of the lesson (i.e., the topic strand). Three of these (number concepts, operations, and patterns, functions, or algebra) were treated as "focal topics" and received further probing (Rowan, Harrison, et al., 2004). For each focal topic, the researchers also asked teachers about their practice—thus creating teaching measures. These teaching measures included three dimensions: (a) whether or not the teacher used "direct teaching," (b) the pacing of the content coverage (i.e., students performed tasks requiring ideas or methods already introduced, not introduced, or both), and (c) the nature of the students' academic work (routine practices, applications, or analytic reasoning; Rowan, Harrison, et al., 2004).

In general then, the mathematics curriculum was measured much like the reading and writing curriculum, except that the *skills* aspect for mathematics was not prescribed a scaled difficulty rating. In turn, SII researchers have thus far created two measures of OTL for each subject: for reading, the probability that a particular topic strand was taught in a lesson, and the difficulty of the skills associated with each topic; for mathematics, the type of content covered, and the type of teaching method used. Though SII researchers have also collected information on the amount of time teachers spent in both reading and mathematics lessons, they have yet to combine this data with their curricular variables. Instead, the measures of OTL they have used in published articles have thus far merged their lesson emphasis questions into a dichotomous taught or not-taught variable for each content strand on a specific day. It is possible that future SII reports will construct slightly different OTL variables. We discuss the SII's researchers substantive results later in the chapter.

Validity of Current Measurement Strategies Current efforts to measure OTL rely mostly on survey data. Surveys provide distinct advantages: They are less costly to administer to a greater number of teachers (compared to observations), are less burdensome for teachers to complete (compared to interviews or diaries), and typically provide data ready for quantitative analyses. Most of the debate, then, centers not on whether to primarily use surveys, but on choosing how often and when to administer them. Specifi-

cally, the decision is whether to survey teachers multiple times throughout an academic year (i.e., teacher logs), or to use end-of-year or end-of-semester questionnaires.[9] In the three preceding examples, both TIMSS and Porter's alignment work have relied primarily on once-administered surveys; SII has relied on teacher logs.

To be sure, most, including researchers in all three projects discussed above, agree that acquiring data throughout an academic year or semester via repeated teacher logs provides richer data than a one-time survey. (Neither would most disagree that teacher logs are considerably more costly than one-time surveys.) So, the question is not which method provides a more valid description of OTL, but how valid each method is. The validity of OTL measures, that is, how accurately surveys portray what teachers actually do in their classrooms (Mayer, 1999), has been examined in several studies.[10] These studies tend to make three general comparisons: the match between data reported on teacher logs to data from observations; the match between log data to one-time survey data, and the match between one-time survey data and observations.

Several studies have compared teacher logs to data procured from third-party observations, which are typically viewed as the most accurate measurement possible—the "gold standard." For example, for a subsample of teachers, SII researchers had two observers watch a teacher's lesson and complete an identical teacher log; observers' logs and teachers' logs of the same lesson could then be compared (Camburn & Barnes, 2004; Hill, 2005). In both language arts and mathematics, the match between observers and teachers was generally high. For language arts, teachers and observers agreed 81%, 90%, and 87% of the time on the three focal strands (word analysis, comprehension, and writing respectively) when the survey results were aggregated to the taught or not taught dichotomy (Camburn & Barnes, 2004). In math, the rates of exact matches varied, but were generally above 80% for the topics comprising the focal strands, though this rate decreased substantially when matches where both the observers and teachers indicated a topic was not taught were excluded (Hill, 2005).[11] For both subjects, the validity decreased as the detail of questions increased: observers and teachers matched much less frequently when the logs asked about instructional practices within focal strands—a common finding in studies exploring the validity of teacher surveys (Burstein et al., 1995; Mayer, 1999; Smithson & Porter, 1994). Validity was also lower for log items that occurred less frequently, and for topics that represented "reform-orientated" instruction, partly because different communities (i.e., observers, teachers, and log-makers) attached different meanings to the same log questions and terms (Hill, 2005).

Because one-time surveys are substantially less costly than teacher logs, researchers have also examined how closely data from one-time surveys matches log data. In an early study using Porter's alignment methodology, Smithson and Porter (1994) found that data from daily teacher logs indicating the proportion of instructional time dedicated to broad content areas was significantly correlated with similar questions from a once-administered survey in 6 of 9 mathematics content areas and 6 of 7 science areas. Eight of these 12 significant correlations were greater than 0.70. These high correlations are especially noteworthy, as Smithson and Porter indicate that questionnaire questions did not exactly correspond with the questions on the teacher logs—which would tend to attenuate their correlation. As expected, the correlations between one-time surveys and teacher logs were less for more detailed questions: for the cognitive demand questions that appeared both on the teacher logs and survey, the responses had correlations of 0.48 and 0.34 in math and science, respectively. Although they note that the match is not ideal, Porter and Smithson (2001) argue that "a single year-long survey instrument is adequate for many of the descriptive and analytic needs for program evaluation" (p. 13).

Although the match between one-time surveys and teacher logs can indicate the degree of trade-off when using either strategy, comparing surveys to logs does not necessarily test their validity; teachers could be inaccurately filling out both (Mayer, 1999). Surprisingly, studies have given less attention to how one-time surveys compare to third-party observations. Burstein et al. (1995) did not compare surveys to observations, but did compare survey data to data collected from classroom artifacts such as textbooks. Across all topics, the average rate of exact agreement was 42%, but much higher (72%) when the definition of agreement was relaxed to also include responses that were within one response category.[12] Mayer (1999) compared the match between surveys and logs for nine algebra teachers in a single district. The proportion of instructional time dedicated to reform-orientated instructional practices gleaned from surveys was strongly correlated with the same information obtained from teacher logs ($r = 0.85$), suggesting strong validity. As Mayer notes, however, this measure of classroom practice—either reform-orientated instruction or not—was highly aggregated and could not easily discern the quality of interaction between teachers and students. Moreover, Mayer focused exclusively on instructional practices, and did not test the validity of questions indicating content or topic coverage.

Though the match between one-time surveys and observations is lacking and surely warrants further research, the validity of these surveys is apparent in their relationship to student achievement gains (Floden, 2002; Porter, 2002). Invalid OTL measures from survey data would tend to weaken the observed relationship between achievement and OTL. The fact that this relationship has been repeatedly found, including with some of the OTL measures discussed above, demonstrates that these measures, though not ideal, are surely not invalid.

Summary Across these three current projects, there is considerable overlap in how OTL is measured. In all three studies, researchers develop an underlying framework outlining content. This framework guides the researchers' creation of

questionnaires and teacher logs; to measure the implemented or enacted curriculum, researchers ask teachers to indicate their coverage of the topics defined by the framework.

In addition to a framework specifying the content, all three studies employ an additional dimension defining the cognitive complexity associated with the coverage of that content. This notion of identifying content as having two aspects is important. By definition any topic, whether in a textbook, state standard, or on a test, also includes an aspect outlining what it is that students are to do with that particular topic. Rarely do standards simply suggest fractions, but generally suggest the ability to add and subtract fractions or to do this in a two-step problem. Here, problem solving is suggested in conjunction with fractions. These standards are not about instructional practice, per se; they are about defining content *expectations*, and hence defining the OTL desired. Porter calls this dimension "cognitive demand," Rowan "difficulty," and Schmidt "performance expectation."

It is important to note that none of the studies used course titles to measure OTL. This result is actually rather uncommon. Many sociologists and economists typically define OTL in terms of course titles. Yet Schmidt (Cogan, Schmidt, & Wiley, 2001) suggests that such a specification of opportunity to learn is inadequate. Eighth-grade mathematics courses were divided into regular mathematics, pre-algebra, and algebra based on course titles. The content of these courses was measured by the actual textbooks used. The results were striking. One-third of courses defined as algebra by the school, used pre-algebra or basic arithmetic textbooks. Additional work in PROM/SE found similar results: the proliferation of course titles produced many varieties of algebra yielding considerable variation in content even though they were all called algebra.

This raises a very important sub-question at what level of specificity do we need to measure opportunity to learn in order for it to be useful? There is no simple answer, but it is clear that course titles are only generic indicators, and probably capture more the nature of tracking in this country than the particulars of opportunity to learn. Yet, too much detail is overwhelming. Too much detail makes it difficult to communicate policy implications to those not immersed in the subject matter.

Our discussion of how to measure OTL raises another important question: Who should define the content frameworks that are integral to any OTL measure? Clearly, the answer lies with those who are deeply involved in and knowledgeable about the particular subject matter. For example, developing a mathematics framework is not something that can be done by those who only view mathematics in the way they experienced it when they were in primary or secondary school. Developing content frameworks takes a careful analysis by people familiar with the particular content and about what is typically taught at various grade levels. This implies the need for teams made up of those versed in schools, the subject matter involved, and the measurement associated with it.

What Do We Know?

Opportunity to learn appears in the research and policy literature as both an independent and a dependent variable. In the latter case, the concern is the characterization of OTL as an end in itself—an approach that considers opportunity to learn as an outcome variable of schooling. Given that schooling is concerned with transmitting the knowledge, skills, and thinking that the society deems appropriate, it seems reasonable to view opportunity as one of the system's outcomes. Also included in this category would be studies that examine the relationship of differently defined opportunities, such as the research employing Porter and colleagues' alignment index (Porter, 2002). The degree to which different opportunity sources (e.g., standards, instruction, state tests) align with each other is an important policy-relevant variable.

In the former case, OTL is considered a key independent variable in terms of its relationship to academic achievement or in some cases as a mediating variable. The goal in both cases is to understand how opportunity is related to student learning, sometimes in conjunction with other factors. The opportunity to learn variable can either be used as the direct goal of the study—that is, to understand its direct relationship to learning—or, to study the effects of another educational policy relevant variable where OTL then serves as a control variable.

The opportunity variable can also serve a more complex role, as in certain research studies where it becomes the mediating variable. This conception reflects the work of Carroll, Berliner, and Wiley and Harnischfeger (as summarized in a previous section). In these studies, researchers view other variables such as teacher quality or school finance as having an impact on student opportunity to learn. From this perspective, OTL serves as a mediating variable through which the other variables indirectly affect academic achievement.

Opportunity to Learn as an Outcome What do studies that focus on OTL as an outcome of schooling tell us? Unfortunately, what they tell us is often idiosyncratic to the particulars of a specific subject matter. Why this is unfortunate is that the policy implications can then be particular to the subject matter and not generalize over multiple disciplines. It is our contention that in some cases such focusing is necessary for good policy to result. However, understandably most policy analysts look for these results which are more general in nature. Below, we summarize some of these studies' more general findings that seem to transcend the particulars of the subject matter in which the study was originally done. This, however, can gloss over important distinctions. For this reason, this area of research demands deep subject matter knowledge, not only in terms of the subject matter itself, but also that related to schooling. Clearly, more studies of this sort are needed in the different school subject matter areas.

The first general finding suggests that within the U.S. educational system, there is tremendous variability in what

is taught (Rowan, Camburn, et al., 2004; Rowan, Harrison, et al., 2004; Schmidt et al., 1999; Schmidt, McKnight, & Raizen, 1997; Schmidt, McKnight, & Wang, 2005; Schmidt et al., 2001). Some of that variability is designed into the system through the process of tracking, but variability is also due to other sources, such as the variation in state and district standards (Schmidt, Wang, & McKnight, 2005), variation across states in the degree of alignment between standards and assessments (Porter, 1989), as well as the variation in how individual teachers interpret subject matter (Rowan, Camburn, et al., 2004; Schmidt et al., 1999). For example, in middle school mathematics, schools across the country offer many potential mathematics classes, ranging from remedial mathematics through the equivalent of high school algebra I or geometry (Cogan et al., 2001). As stated, this form of variability in OTL is designed into the system, and reflects a conscious decision to sort children and provide them different opportunities.

Yet many mathematics and science courses with very similar titles also exhibit tremendous variability in actual content (PROM/SE Research Report No. 3, 2008; Cogan et al., 2001). In fact, when one examines the actual titles of courses in a 30 high school sample, algebra appears to have many varieties. In addition, across these schools, there were over 100 distinct course offerings. In the NCLB era, such variability—whether structured by design or resulting from individual teacher decisions—has the same effect: students have different opportunities to learn. In fact, two students in the same school depending on their classroom may have very different OTLs.

A second general characteristic is the lack of coherence in U.S. curricula resulting in repetitive curricula that are often "slow-moving" (Porter, 1989; Schmidt et al., 2001). School subjects basically derive from a more formal academic discipline as represented at the university level. Schools take these abstract bodies of knowledge, decide what it is that should be taught, and then sequence these topics across grades and, within the year, across days. Those decisions are not arbitrary and the choices should reflect the internal structure of that discipline. This is what Schmidt et al. (2001) defined as coherence with specific reference to mathematics and science. The absence of coherence implies that the opportunities not sequenced in this fashion can become an arbitrary collection of isolated facts. Using an international benchmark, U.S. state standards were deemed incoherent, in comparison with other countries. This has a profound effect on the nature of educational opportunities: if standards are not coherent, then students and teachers alike struggle to understand the underlying curricular logic. Recent work has suggested that such incoherence is related to academic performance across countries (Schmidt & Houang, 2007).

Studies using OTL as an outcome also indicate that U.S. content coverage in mathematics, science, and civics is not consistent with that of much of the rest of the world in terms of the rigor of the learning opportunities (Schmidt et al., 2001; Schmidt, McKnight, Valverde, et al., 1997; Schmidt,

Raizen, et al., 1997; Steiner-Khamsi, Torney-Purta, & Schwille, 2002). This is the third general finding regarding OTL in the United States. Debates are possible as to what constitutes rigor in any subject matter but, the international studies provide an empirically derived benchmark by which rigor can be defined. In general, the academic rigor of the opportunities provided to U.S. students in mathematics and science did not match those in most other countries, especially high performing countries (Rowan, Harrison, et al., 2004; Schmidt et al., 2001; Valverde & Schmidt, 2000). In mathematics, for example, most U.S. middle school students focused on basic arithmetic including fractions, decimals, percents, and ratios. Middle grade students in most of the rest for the world, however, focused on algebra and geometry. Thus, excepting students tracked into the more advanced courses, U.S. students' opportunities fell short of the international norm. These findings have especially relevant policy implications as much of today's educational rhetoric centers on preparing children to be competitive in a global economy.

The rigor issue applies to science as well. In the middle grades, students in most countries—at least among the 50 countries participating in TIMSS—received learning opportunities focusing on physics, chemistry, and biochemistry. In contrast, U.S. students studied mostly descriptive biology and descriptive geology. The extent to which this is true in other fields is not as well known as international benchmarks are not generally available.

A final characteristic of U.S. OTL has to do with focus. The U.S. curriculum attempts to cover many content topics at each grade level in each subject matter—the now-familiar characterization of the U.S. curriculum as a mile wide and an inch deep. The coverage of so many opportunities to learn at each grade level simply makes it very difficult for students to learn anything in depth. In mathematics and science where the more extensive data are available, we see that the number of topics covered at each grade level is double, if not more, than the number of topics covered in most other countries (Schmidt, McKnight, & Raizen, 1997). As new topics are introduced at higher grade levels, previous topics still remain in the curriculum (Rowan, Harrison, et al., 2004). Although no formal data are available for other school subjects, an examination of the textbooks that are available suggests that the conclusion is not limited to mathematics and science.

Even textbooks exhibit a lack of focus. The number of mathematics topics presented in a typical U.S. eighth grade textbook spans some 700 pages while the international mean is around 250 pages. Because the textbook is very often the de facto curriculum in the United States, we can again classify the U.S. curriculum as unfocused.

OTL as an Independent or Mediating Variable Related to Achievement

As the previous section attests, OTL has grown from a concept used as a necessary control in international studies for comparing a nation's mathematics achievement to a concept worthy of its own study. In many ways OTL has surpassed its origins. It has changed from a methodological necessity to a policy tool—from a "technical" to "generative" concept (McDonnell, 1995). Part of this is due to OTL's appeal as one of a limited set of education variables that policy makers can ostensibly modify. Though not always easily, students' curricular opportunities can be changed. Another reason for the increasing attention to OTL is its ability to be measured, and, given the advances in OTL measurement discussed in the previous section, measured in a sophisticated way (McDonnell, 1995).

OTL's relationship with achievement has been repeatedly demonstrated. (Over 20 years ago, Brophy & Good, 1986, acknowledged OTL was consistently linked to achievement.) This is especially true in cross-national studies. As Floden (2002) notes, "a conclusion of comparative research is that OTL is related to achievement, a finding that should no longer be news, but somehow continues to be striking" (p. 252). In this section, we explore the research examining the OTL-achievement relationship that has helped cast OTL as an important policy-relevant variable. We specifically highlight research emanating from OTL's four (overlapping) historical themes: the IEA studies, studies of overall instructional time, studies of alignment, and studies from a sociological perspective.

The IEA Studies[13]   Given that many attribute much of OTL's conceptual origins to the first IEA study of mathematics achievement (i.e., FIMS), it seems surprising that FIMS researchers did not strongly emphasize OTL. FIMS did, nevertheless, demonstrate that OTL was significantly correlated with achievement. When students in all countries were pooled, correlations ranged from 0.16 to 0.30 depending on the student population (i.e., age or grade) analyzed (Husen, 1967b, Tables 6.6–6.9). The strength of correlation, however, differed by country.

The relationship between OTL and achievement was much larger when FIMS researchers looked among countries. Between-country correlations ranged from 0.40 to 0.80 across the four sampled populations. Thus, while the relationships between OTL and achievement within countries varied and were often tenuous (partly due to uniform OTL among some countries' classrooms), the between-country correlations were less equivocal: more OTL was associated with higher achievement.

The results from FIMS were mostly mirrored in SIMS. Even with a more detailed measure of OTL, SIMS researchers found small to nonexistent relationships between OTL and achievement within countries. Among all 20 countries, OTL was only significantly related to achievement in one country per topic area (i.e., arithmetic, algebra, geometry, measurement, and statistics) after controlling for student, parental, teacher, and school characteristics (Schmidt & Kifer, 1989). The results remain relatively underwhelming when SIMS researchers examined achievement growth instead of achievement status. Looking only at arithmetic, algebra, and geometry subtests, and controlling for a similar set of student, teacher, school, and parental variables, SIMS found OTL to be positively related to achievement gains among eighth grade students in only two (of eight) countries (Schmidt & Burstein, 1992). Nevertheless, OTL was the only teacher, classroom, or school characteristic that was, ceteris paribus, significantly related to achievement growth in more than one country. (The United States was one country where OTL was significantly associated to achievement gains; Gamoran, 1994; Schmidt & Burstein, 1992.)

Much like FIMS, SIMS researchers argued that the many country's nonsignificant OTL-achievement relationships were due to curricular homogeneity. "The positive results for geometry [and algebra] in the United States … reinforces the sense that curricular opportunities matter most in systems … where there is sufficient decentralization in curricular decision-making to allow some students to experience greater opportunities than others" (Schmidt & Burstein, 1992, p. 321). Systems in which OTL varied minimally exhibited more modest associations.

Also much like FIMS, SIMS demonstrated a substantially larger relationship between OTL and achievement between countries. The between-country correlation between OTL and achievement gain was 0.57, a statistic that falls within the range of correlations found in FIMS (Kifer & Burstein, 1992). Similarly, countries whose mathematics curriculum largely centered on one of the specific topics tested instead of stressing arithmetic or lacking a specific focus—a "potpourri" curriculum—tended to demonstrate higher achievement gains on such topics (Schmidt, 1992). To SIMS researchers, the implication was clear: "providing more content to more students produce more gain" (Kifer & Burstein, 1992, p. 337).

The findings from TIMSS support and amplify those discussed from FIMS and SIMS. Two types of analyses were done with country, and classroom or topic within country as the units of analysis. Similar to the findings of the two other studies the strongest evidence of a relationship of OTL to achievement at the eighth grade was found across countries. This is consistent with the findings that demonstrate the large variation in OTL across countries (Schmidt, McKnight, Valverde, et al., 1997). TIMSS as cited earlier in this chapter collected extensive curricular data from country standards, textbooks, and teachers. In all cases there were large differences in the intended and implemented curricula across countries (Schmidt et al., 1999).

These differences were found to be statistically significantly related to achievement gain using different analytical approaches including causal modeling and standard regression techniques (Schmidt et al., 2001). Gain was defined at the country level using the seventh and eighth grade results as cohort longitudinal data. TIMSS defined 20 subscales for which separate analyses were done relating gain in each of the 20 areas to those aspects of curricular content that theory would suggest to be relevant. This was done for the several manifestations of curriculum for which there were quantitative measures—emphasis in country standards, na-

tional average instructional time for a topic, proportion of a country's teachers covering a topic, proportion of textbook space devoted to a topic, and proportion of textbook space devoted to a topic but with greater complexity of student performance expected.

Across the 20 subtest areas 12 were found to be statistically significantly related to at least one of the manifestations of OTL. Teacher coverage was the factor most strongly related to most of the subtest areas—6 of the 12. Other relational analyses were also done, such as a causal model looking at the interrelationship of the various measures of OTL and their structural relationship to achievement gain. This led the authors to suggest (Schmidt et al., 2001):

> Putting these results together with those described earlier in this chapter seems to lead to a powerful, straightforward conclusion. Curriculum was related to learning in mathematics across countries in seventeen of the twenty tested topic areas as measured by the TIMSS Population 2 test. Further, the relationships with gain involved different aspects of the curriculum for different topics, but across the topics, all aspects of curriculum other than the content standards measure were represented. (p. 324)

The other types of analyses examined the relationship of OTL to achievement gain within countries. Unlike FIMS and SIMS these relationships were more frequently found. The main difference perhaps resulted from the more extensive curricular data, which was available in TIMSS. Using the same five measures of OTL, in only 5 of the 29 countries on which these analyses were done were there no statistically significant relationships to achievement gain. The estimated R^2 values ranged from 0 to .67.

Consistent with SIMS, the one country where statistically significant results were clearly found was the United States. This, of course, is due in part to the large within-country across-classroom variation in content coverage. Controlling for SESS and prior achievement multilevel analyses were performed on each of the 20 subscales. On 18 of the scales measures of instructional time in key content areas were found to be statistically significant to achievement gain. The R^2 values ranged from .38 to .63.

Given the IEA model of intended and implemented curricula, TIMSS also fitted causal models to the topic-level data within countries. These models related content coverage defined by country standards, textbooks, and teachers' instructional time to each other and then to achievement gain. Different models of influence emerged across the countries. In Japan, for example, the estimated causal structure suggested a seamless system in which the country's content standards influenced both textbook coverage and instructional time. Textbook coverage also had a direct effect on instructional time—instructional time being the mediating variable directly related to achievement gain. This is as one would expect in a system where the national standards drive the system.

In the United States, on the other hand, achievement gain

in mathematics at the eighth grade was driven mostly by content coverage as defined by the textbook. It was the only measure of OTL to be related to achievement gain. Across the 29 countries in all but ten of them statistically significant relationships were found. The estimated R^2 values for countries in which the significant relationships were found ranged from .23 to .70, where the largest value was found for the model fitted to the Japanese data.

Other early IEA studies have found similar associations between OTL and achievement. In his review of multiple international studies, Suter (2000) found that, in the First IEA Science Study (Comber & Keeves, 1973), the "measure of opportunity to learn (i.e., whether students were instructed in the topics of the test) was directly related to science score levels in middle school and high school when the separate science topics were delineated" (p. 536). Unlike FIMS and SIMS, the association between OTL and achievement within countries remained substantial: teachers' OTL ratings were correlated with students' scores for each country investigated (Comber & Keeves, 1973; Suter, 2000).

Studies of Overall Instructional Time   Early studies examining the relationship between time and achievement typically defined allocated or usable instructional time— their measure of OTL—crudely.[14] For example, Wiley and Harnischfeger (1974) calculated the average number of hours of instruction for 40 central-city Detroit schools— a subset of Coleman's EEO data—by multiplying the school's average daily attendance by the number of hours in a school day and multiplying this product by the number of school days in an academic year. The associations they found between time and achievement were significant and substantial; students in schools that provided about a quarter more usable time received, on average, reading comprehension, mathematics, and verbal scores that were two-thirds, one-third, and one-third higher, respectively.

Ambiguity has been common in studies of allocated time, though research has generally demonstrated small to moderate positive associations between time and achievement (Berliner, 1990; Karweit, 1985; Walberg & Frederick, 1983). Studies of allocated time have focused mostly on total instructional time for a subject matter or across all subject matters—not on specific topic areas such as time allocated to the study of linear equations. For example, Baker, Fabrega, Galindo, and Mishook (2004) reviewed evidence from three international studies, the Programme for International Student Assessment (PISA), TIMSS, and the IEA Study of Civics Education, and found that no study demonstrated significant associations between overall mean instructional time and country-level mean achievement.

Baker et al.'s analyses demonstrated stronger and more positive correlations when allocated time was limited to time spent teaching math, science, or civics content specifically. In fact, when Baker and colleagues examined the within-nation relationships between science instructional time and science achievement, 29 nations had significantly positive

correlations, explaining, on average, 5% of the variance in achievement (Baker et al., 2004, Table 13). Similarly, Hill, Rowan, and Ball (2005) found that third grade students in classrooms with longer average daily mathematics lessons exhibited larger mathematics achievement gains. Lesson length was the only teacher or classroom characteristic besides measures of teachers' knowledge that demonstrated a significant association.[15]

The results from both Baker et al. and Hill et al. highlight our central tenet that overall time, even if limited to an area such as mathematics, is often an inadequate measure of OTL if it does not specify time spent teaching specific content. If allocated time is expected to represent one's opportunity to learn a set of topics, then the closer this time measures time allocated to the teaching of those particular topics, the stronger we can expect the OTL-achievement relationship. Simply measuring total instructional time or even total instructional time in a subject matter such as mathematics is usually not enough.

An example of the difficulty in finding significant associations between achievement and total allocated time, independent to the extent to which this time is spent covering tested content, is well-demonstrated in Rowan, Correnti, and Miller's (2002) oft-cited analysis of the *Prospects* study. In attempting to explain the large proportion of variance in achievement that lies between classrooms, Rowan et al. included a variable representing the "average minutes per week spent in their classroom on instruction in mathematics and reading" (p. 1545). In neither subject was this variable significantly related to achievement growth. Yet, when Rowan et al. included content coverage variables from survey questions that asked teachers the amount of emphasis they gave to broad mathematics and reading curricular areas in their model,[16] they found significant associations between content coverage and reading achievement growth for both lower and upper elementary school students, and a significant positive association between mathematics growth and upper elementary school students.

Studies of Alignment   Other researchers have examined the relationship between Porter and colleagues' alignment index, which uses up to 700 possible unique topic/cognitive demand combinations to define OTL, and student achievement. In order to examine the extent to which alignment between instruction and a NAEP-based test accounted for differences in achievement between differently tracked mathematics courses, Gamoran et al. (1997) analyzed the achievement growth profiles of 882 students in predominantly low-income, low-achieving schools. Using a version of Porter's alignment index,[17] which they labeled "content coverage" Gamoran et al. found a substantial positive association between coverage and mathematics achievement growth. In fact, once content coverage was included in the model, the negative coefficient associated with taking a low-tracked course (i.e., general math or pre-algebra) diminished substantially and lost statistical significance, suggesting that a good portion of the lower rates of achievement growth in low-tracked courses was due to more limited curricular opportunities.

Smithson and Collares (2007) also explored how alignment mediates student achievement, though they investigated how instruction was aligned to state benchmarks instead of the test. Again focusing on low-achieving, low-income schools—few schools in their sample had met AYP the previous year—Smithson and Collares examined how alignment predicted achievement on Ohio's statewide English, Language Arts, and Reading assessment for over 5,000 elementary students. Employing a multi-level framework that permitted analysis at both the student and classroom level, Smithson and Collares found that alignment was significantly and positively associated with achievement gains. Though their sample was marred by substantial missing data, rendering their results tentative, they nevertheless found that, after accounting for a missing data effect, alignment accounted for about 34% of the gain in the number of correct responses and 71% of the gain in scaled scores.

Taken together, Gamoran et al. (1997) and Smithson and Collares (2007) provide evidence that OTL, as measured by Porter and colleagues' alignment index, is strongly related to achievement gains. Students with teachers whose instruction provides more opportunities to learn the content embedded in tests and/or curricular standards tend to exhibit increased achievement growth. However, these findings have been largely limited to low-income and low-achieving schools. It remains to be seen how similar these results will be when applied to more representative samples.

Studies from a Sociological Perspective   Sociological research examining the relationship between opportunity to learn and achievement typically involves studies examining how differences in students' coursework or course sequences relate to achievement. They typically represent studies of tracking defining opportunity to learn at the course-level—usually assuming that more advanced, courses represent more OTL. For example, after controlling for prior achievement, Gamoran (1987) found that taking additional math and science courses raised math and science achievement respectively. Taking *advanced* math and science courses, however, had an even stronger effect on achievement than taking additional courses (although this trend was not as salient with reading, writing, vocabulary, and civics courses).

That taking more upper-level academic coursework is associated with greater achievement has been an often replicated research finding. Using NELS:88-94, Schneider et al. (1998) found that students taking math and science course sequences that included more rigorous coursework such as calculus for math and physics and chemistry for science demonstrated, on average, significantly greater achievement gains between 10th and 12th grade.[18] Other studies using NELS have similarly found that math and science achievement gains from the beginning to end of high school are strongly related to the number of math and science courses students completed (Hoffer, Rasinski, &

Moore, 1995; Rock & Pollack, 1995; Rowan, as cited in Rowan et al., 2002).

Sociologists have also found that schools that "constrain" their curriculum so that most, if not all, students take the same academically focused courses have higher overall achievement levels, and more equitable achievement distributions among students (Gamoran, 1992; Lee & Bryk, 1988, 1989; Lee, Croninger, & Smith, 1997; Lee, Smith, & Croninger, 1997). Much of this work has focused on, or at least highlighted, differences between public and Catholic schools (Bryk, Lee, & Holland, 1993; Coleman, Hoffer, & Kilgore, 1982; Lee & Bryk, 1988, 1989). Together, these studies have argued that, on average, students in schools that present more students more opportunities to learn—as represented by making students take more academically rigorous courses—learn more.

In all, multiple studies have demonstrated a strong relationship between students' courses and their achievement. Although convincing, representing OTL with course titles is potentially problematic for two reasons. First, the extent to which similarly titled courses in two different schools represent the same curricular opportunities is questionable (Cogan et al., 2001). Second, though it seems reasonable to attribute the relationship between coursework and achievement to learning opportunities, these studies provide little information about what actually happens to students once they are in particular courses (Gamoran, 1989).

Consequently, many studies of tracking or curricular differentiation have employed more refined measures of OTL in order to examine how different tracks provide different curricular opportunities and how, or if, these differences affect achievement. These studies have typically represented OTL as a measure of content coverage. For example, studying elementary students, Rowan and Miracle (1983) found that pacing, as measured by counting the number of reading levels the students covered in an academic year, was significantly associated with achievement: students who were paced faster tended to achieve more. Students in different tracks were paced differently, however, with students in lower ability classrooms paced more slowly than students in higher ability classrooms. Gamoran (1986) found similar results looking at elementary students' vocabulary achievement; he found that the strongest predictor of the number of words a student learned was the number of words and phonics the student was taught.

Why is OTL Important?

We argue that opportunity to learn, defined in the original curricular sense of Carroll and IEA as the coverage of particular content for a given amount of time, is perhaps the single most important factor related to school learning. Moreover, OTL is an entirely malleable variable—it can be changed through policy. As we stated at the beginning of this chapter, schools are organized to provide its future citizens the knowledge, skills, and analytical procedures needed to function in an ever-increasingly complex society and to compete economically. Because schooling is essentially about providing these distinct skills and content knowledge, it becomes fairly clear that OTL and the various manifestations of it (including their measures discussed in this chapter) hold a place at the core of schooling.

Furthermore, those multiple measures of OTL—teacher responses, instructional time, coursework, content coverage, intended coverage as found in standards, textbook coverage, and alignment—have overwhelmingly demonstrated positive relationships with achievement. As with most concepts in educational research, the strength of this relationship varies by study, sample, and most importantly, by how OTL is operationalized. The weakest measures of OTL such as overall allocated instructional time tend to show the most ambiguous results. On the other hand, we find it promising that the most sophisticated measures of OTL such as those used in TIMSS and the alignment indices have also been those showing the most consistent positive associations.[19] But one thing is clear, consistently studies show that OTL is related to student learning.

Yet even though research has generally found consistent results, it is important to point out that no study reviewed provided evidence that OTL was the *only* factor significantly contributing to learning. Even if different classrooms provided relatively similar OTLs, other aspects of instruction and teaching can still produce different outcomes by impacting the effectiveness of the OTL. Specific mathematics content is the defining element of an educational opportunity in mathematics. As a result core subject matter content is separated from other "qualifying" aspects associated with the delivery of those opportunities—aspects that enhance or limit opportunities. The concept employed here is that if the instructional delivery is not fully effective due to such qualifying factors then the impact of the coverage on achievement will be reduced.

Content coverage is not the whole story but it is the core of schooling and given the overwhelming empirical evidence indicating its positive association with achievement, OTL is too important to be ignored either as an outcome itself allowing the examination of such issues as equity or as a control or mediating variable toward understanding the impact of various other policy variables on student learning. In the latter case, ignoring a measure of OTL in the analysis model runs the risk of yielding a biased estimate of the coefficient relating the policy variable under study to student learning. This results in part from the cross classroom variability in OTL which is likely correlated with the policy variable under study.

Perhaps the best example of this is teacher quality—currently a major U.S. policy issue. The allocation of teachers in this country is not random (Bacolod, 2007; Lankford, Loeb, & Wyckoff, 2002). Better teachers, as defined by such proxies as ACT/SAT scores, or selectivity of university, tend to teach in districts with the highest achieving children (Lankford et al., 2002; Loeb & Reininger, 2004). It is also true, however, that more students in those districts tend to take a more advanced curriculum, especially in the middle grades. It is likely that there is a positive correlation between teacher quality and the coherence and rigor of the curriculum. Doing statistical analyses that relate teacher quality to achievement without accounting for the variation in OTL across those same classrooms or districts would result in biased estimates of teacher quality.

In addition, we argue that with the progress made, and hopefully still to be made, in our ability to measure OTL quantitatively, we can move education forward to a more mature science. The history of various sciences follows such a pattern. Astronomy enabled us to better understand the origins of the universe once we were better able to measure such things as the universe's background microwave radiation and red shift. Recent advances in biology, such as deciphering and measuring the genome, have moved biology from a descriptive science to a much more deeply analytical one. So it might be with education as we progress in the development of measures of content coverage—the core aspect of schooling.

What Does All This Mean?

Schooling is about teaching children the essential content and skills that a society deems appropriate. The specified knowledge, skills, and analytical procedures define the heart of schooling and what we have termed OTL. Other factors can impact its effectiveness, but it is the content exposure itself which is most important in terms of learning that content. And so, educational opportunity will remain an essential aspect of educational research and public policy. In fact, we have argued that it must remain a *central* feature in understanding other policy-relevant issues reported on in this volume. Providing students learning opportunities is what schooling is about. Content coverage and its variability in the U.S. educational system, therefore, become fundamental concepts in any type of policy discussion.

Notes

1. One might argue that curricular standards are enforceable via state sponsored standardized tests. Yet the degree to which a state's test is actually aligned to its standards is often tenuous (Porter, 2002)
2. BTES researchers also included students' success rate in their model of learning. They found that students achieve more when they engage in tasks on which they have high success (Fisher et al., 1980). Though both students' engagement and success rates are surely factors in school learning, we restrict our discussion to the upper limit of students' opportunities. That is, the time allocated to learn specific content.
3. See both McDonnell (1995) and Floden (2002) for further discussions of how OTL grew out of the IEA studies.
4. See Jones and Schneider (this volume) for further discussion of education and stratification.
5. Grain size refers to the level of detail in the specification of the mathematics content.
6. For the remainder of this section, we refer to the mathematics, as opposed to the science framework.
7. The number of general areas, specific topics, and cognitive demand levels depended on the study. Usually, there were 9–10 general areas, 7–10 specific topics (thus, approximately 100 distinct topics), and 5–8 cognitive demand levels.

8. Thus, the X and Y in the alignment index can represent the cells of an assessment, instructional, or standards content matrix.

9. Compared to the debate over how often to administer surveys, there is substantially less discussion about *who* to survey. Researchers have almost unanimously surveyed teachers, though some have experimented with asking students the extent of content they were taught—usually in order to test the validity of teachers' surveys (Blank, Porter, & Smithson, 2001). Though surveying students is intriguing, especially since most research on OTL is primarily interested in investigating the curricular opportunities experienced by students, it runs into substantial logistical problems (e.g., training students to code content, providing time for students to fill out surveys, etc.).

10. The literature on measuring teachers' instructional practices is much larger than what we convey in the following few paragraphs. For the sake of brevity, we focus particularly on the validity of the recent OTL measures discussed above.

11. Hill's study of the validity of the mathematics log used an earlier version of the log. In subsequent logs, items with low validity were dropped or combined to create broader topic strands, increasing the log's overall validity (Rowan, Harrison, et al., 2004).

12. Mayer (1999) has pointed out that the "within one" methodology is somewhat undermined given that there were only four categories. Using this method, an item would match 62.5% of the time by chance alone.

13. For other discussions of the relationship between OTL and achievement stemming from IEA studies, see Floden (2002) and Suter (2000).

14. The word "early" is somewhat of a misnomer. Scholars have been interested in the relationship between time and learning since the late 19th century; see Berliner (1990) for a review.

15. The average length of mathematics lessons was not similarly associated with mathematics gains among first grade students, however.

16. Specifically, content coverage for reading was measured by combining teacher emphasis variables in a way that intended to represent a "balance reading curriculum" (p. 1548). Three content coverage variables were created for reading, including two items measuring the extent to which teachers self-reportedly (on a simple 3-point scale) emphasized word analysis and writing process, and eight items highlighting reading comprehension combined into a single Rasch scale score. Rowan et al. obtained the mathematics content coverage variable from a single, multi-item scale indexing "the difficulty of the mathematics content covered in a classroom" (p. 1548). For more details, see Rowan et al. (2002, pp. 1548–1549).

17. Gamoran et al.'s (1997) alignment or OTL variable was very similar to Porter's alignment index discussed in the previous section. But instead of creating instructional matrices with cells representing the proportion of instructional time spent on each topic compared to time spent *on all topics*, as Porter's later efforts have done (Porter, 2002; Porter & Smithson, 2001), Gamoran et al. analyzed the "degree to which the relative emphasis of tested content *that was also taught* matched the relative emphasis of tested content as a whole" (Porter, 2002, p. 6, emphasis added) and separately computed the proportion of instructional time spent teaching tested content. These two measures were multiplied to create Gamoran et al.'s "content covered" or OTL variable. Though the two alignment indices differ slightly, they were nevertheless highly correlated (Porter, 2002). Porter and Smithson (2001) argue that the index employed by Gamoran et al. better predicts student achievement gains.

18. More specifically, Schneider et al. divided students' math and science coursework into ten and six separate sequence, respectively. These sequences were ranked according to the academic difficulty of the courses comprising each sequence. Higher ranked sequences represented more academically rigorous coursework, and were associated with greater achievement gains.

19. At the time of writing, results linking Rowan and colleagues' OTL measures to achievement, besides the measure of average lesson length in Hill et al. (2005) have yet to be published or made available on their Web site.

References

Achinstein, B., Ogawa, R. T., & Speiglman, A. (2004). Are we creating separate and unequal tracks of teachers? The effects of state policy, local conditions, and teacher characteristics on new teacher socialization. *American Educational Research Journal, 41*, 557–603.

Alexander, K. L., Cook, M., & McDill, E. L. (1978). Curriculum tracking and educational stratification: Some further evidence. *American Sociological Review, 43*, 47–66.

Alexander, K. L., & Eckland, B. K. (1975). School experience and status attainment. In S. D. Dragastin & G. H. Elder, Jr. (Eds.), *Adolescence in the life cycle: Psychological change and social context* (pp. 171–210). Washington, DC: Hemisphere.

Alexander, K. L., & McDill, E. L. (1976). Selection and allocation within schools: Some causes and consequences of curriculum placement. *American Sociological Review, 41*, 963–980.

Anderson, L. W. (1985). Introduction to Part I, School learning. In L. W. Anderson (Ed.), *Perspectives on school learning: Selected writings of John B. Carroll* (pp. 3–9). Hillsdale, NJ: Erlbaum.

Bacolod, M. (2007). Who teaches and where they choose to teach: College graduates of the 1990s. *Educational Evaluation and Policy Analysis, 29*, 155–168.

Baker, D. P., Fabrega, R., Galindo, C., & Mishook, J. (2004). Instructional time and national achievement: Cross-national evidence. *Prospects, 34*, 311–334.

Barr, R., & Dreeben, R. (1983). *How schools work*. Chicago: University of Chicago Press.

Berliner, D. C. (1979). Tempus Educare. In P. L. Peterson & H. J. Walberg (Eds.), *Research on teaching: Concepts, findings, and implications* (pp. 120–135). Berkeley, CA: McCutchan.

Berliner, D. C. (1990). What's all the fuss about instructional time? In M. Ben-Peretz & R. Bromme (Eds.), *The nature of time in schools: Theoretical concepts, practitioner perceptions* (pp. 3–35). New York: Teachers College Press.

Bidwell, C. E., & Kasarda, J. D. (1980). Conceptualizing and measuring the effects of school and schooling. *American Journal of Education, 88*, 401–430.

Blank, R. K., Porter, A. C., & Smithson, J. (2001). *New tools for analyzing teaching, curriculum and standards in mathematics and science: Results from Survey of Enacted Curriculum Project, final report*. Washington, DC: Council of Chief State School Officers.

Block, J. H., & Burns, R. B. (1976). Mastery learning. *Review of Research in Education, 4*, 3–49.

Bloom, B. S. (1968). Learning for mastery (UCLA-CSEIP). *Evaluation Comment, 1*(2), 1–12.

Bloom, B. S. (1974). Time and learning. *American Psychologist, 29*, 682–688.

Brophy, J., & Good, T. (1986). Teacher behavior and student achievement. In M. C. Wittrock (Ed.), *Handbook of research on teaching* (3rd ed., pp. 328–375). New York: Macmillan.

Bryk, A. S., Lee, V. E., & Holland, P. B. (1993). *Catholic schools and the common good*. Cambridge, MA: Harvard University Press.

Burstein, L., McDonnell, L. M., Van Winkle, J., Ormseth, T., Mirocha, J., & Guiton, G. (1995). *Validating national curriculum indicators*. Santa Monica, CA: RAND.

Camburn, E., & Barnes, C. A. (2004). Assessing the validity of a language arts instruction log through triangulation. *Elementary School Journal, 105*, 49–73.

Carroll, J. B. (1962). The prediction of success in intensive foreign language learning. In R. Glaser (Ed.), *Training research and education* (pp. 87–136). Pittsburgh, PA: University of Pittsburgh Press.

Carroll, J. B. (1963). A model of school learning. *Teachers College Record, 64*, 722–733.

Carroll, J. B. (1984). The model of school learning: Progress of an idea.

In C. Fisher & D. C. Berliner (Eds.), *Perspective on instructional time* (pp. 29–58). New York: Longman.

Cogan, L. S., Schmidt, W. H., & Wiley, D. E. (2001). Who takes what math and in which track? Using TIMSS to characterize U.S. students' eighth-grade mathematics learning opportunities. *Educational Evaluation and Policy Analysis, 23,* 323–341.

Coleman, J. S., Campbell, E. Q., Hobson, C. J., McPartland, J., Mood, A. M., Weinfeld, F., et al. (1966). *Equality of educational opportunity.* Washington DC: U.S. Government Printing Office.

Coleman, J. S., Hoffer, T., & Kilgore, S. B. (1982). *High school achievement: Public, Catholic, and private schools compared.* New York: Basic Books.

Comber, L. C., & Keeves, J. P. (1973). *Science education in nineteen countries: An empirical study.* New York: Wiley.

Fisher, C. W., Berliner, D. C., Filby, N. N., Marliave, R., Cahen, L. S., & Dishaw, M. M. (1980). Teaching behaviors, academic learning time, and student achievement: An overview. In C. Denham & A. Lieberman (Eds.), *Time to learn* (pp. 7–32). Washington, DC: National Institute of Education.

Floden, R. E. (2002). The measurement of opportunity to learn. In A. C. Porter & A. Gamoran (Eds.), *Methodological advances in cross-national surveys of educational achievement* (pp. 231–266). Washington, DC: National Academy Press.

Gamoran, A. (1986). Instructional and institutional effects of ability grouping. *Sociology of Education, 59,* 185–198.

Gamoran, A. (1987). The stratification of high school learning opportunities. *Sociology of Education, 60,* 135–155.

Gamoran, A. (1989). Measuring curriculum differentiation. *American Journal of Education, 97,* 129–143.

Gamoran, A. (1992). The variable effects of high school tracking. *American Sociological Review, 57,* 812–828.

Gamoran, A. (1994). Schooling and achievement: Additive versus interactive models. In I. Westbury, C. A. Ethington, L. A. Sosniak, & D. P. Baker (Eds.), *In search of more effective mathematics education* (pp. 273–292). Norwood, NJ: Ablex.

Gamoran, A., & Berends, M. (1987). The effects of stratification in secondary schools: Synthesis of survey and ethnographic research. *Review of Educational Research, 57,* 415–435.

Gamoran, A., Porter, A. C., Smithson, J., & White, P. A. (1997). Upgrading high school mathematics instruction: Improving learning opportunities for low-achieving, low-income youth. *Educational Evaluation and Policy Analysis, 19,* 325–338.

Hallinan, M. T. (1976). Salient features of the Harnischfeger-Wiley model. *Curriculum Inquiry, 6*(1), 45–59.

Harnischfeger, A., & Wiley, D. E. (1976). The teaching-learning process in elementary schools: A synoptic view. *Curriculum Inquiry, 6,* 5–43.

Heyns, B. (1974). Social selection and stratification within schools. *The American Journal of Sociology, 79,* 1434–1451.

Hill, H. C. (2005). Content across communities: Validating measures of elementary mathematics instruction. *Educational Policy, 19,* 447–475.

Hill, H. C., Rowan, B., & Ball, D. L. (2005). Effects of teachers' mathematical knowledge for teaching on student achievement. *American Educational Research Journal, 42,* 371–406.

Hoffer, T. B., Rasinski, K. A., & Moore, W. (1995). *Statistics in brief: Social background differences in high school mathematics and science coursetaking and achievement* (NCES Report 95-206). Washington, DC: National Center for Education Statistics.

Husen, T. (1967a). *International study of achievement in mathematics: A comparison of twelve countries, Vol. 1.* New York: Wiley.

Husen, T. (1967b). *International study of achievement in mathematics: A comparison of twelve countries, Vol. 2.* New York: Wiley.

Jakwerth, P., Bianchi, L., McKnight, C. C., & Schmidt, W. H. (1997). Focus in school science: An international comparison. *Geotimes, 42*(7), 19–22.

Jencks, C., Smith, M., Acland, H., Bane, M. J., Cohen, D., Gintis, H., et al. (1972). *Inequality: A reassessment of the effect of family and schooling in America.* New York: Basic Books.

Karweit, N. (1985). Should we lengthen the school term? *Educational Researcher, 14*(6), 9–15.

Kifer, E. (1992). Opportunities, talents, and participation. In L. Burstein (Ed.), *The IEA Study of Mathematics III: Student growth and classroom processes* (pp. 279–308). Tarrytown, NY: Pergamon Press.

Kifer, E., & Burstein, L. (1992). Concluding thoughts: What we know, what it means. In L. Burstein (Ed.), *The IEA study of mathematics III: Student growth and classroom procesesses* (pp. 329–341). Tarrytown, NY: Pergamon Press.

Lankford, H., Loeb, S., & Wyckoff, J. (2002). Teacher sorting and the plight of urban schools: A descriptive analysis. *Educational Evaluation and Policy Analysis, 24,* 37–62.

Lee, V. E., & Bryk, A. S. (1988). Curriculum tracking as mediating the social distribution of high school achievement. *Sociology of Education, 61,* 78–94.

Lee, V. E., & Bryk, A. S. (1989). A multilevel model of the social distribution of high school achievement. *Sociology of Education, 62,* 172–192.

Lee, V. E., Croninger, R. G., & Smith, J. B. (1997). Course-taking, equity, and mathematics learning: Testing the Constrained Curriculum hypothesis in U.S. secondary schools. *Educational Evaluation and Policy Analysis, 19,* 99–121.

Lee, V. E., Smith, J. B., & Croninger, R. G. (1997). How high school organization influences the equitable distribution of learning in mathematics and science. *Sociology of Education, 70,* 128–150.

Loeb, S., & Reininger, M. (2004). *Public policy and teacher labor markets: What we know and why it matters.* East Lansing: Michigan State University, The Education Policy Center.

Lucas, S. R. (1999). *Tracking inequality: Stratification and mobility in American high schools.* New York: Teachers College Press.

Ma, X. (2000). A longitudinal assessment of antecedent course work in mathematics and subsequent mathematical attainment. *Journal of Educational Research, 94,* 16–28.

Mayer, D. P. (1999). Measuring instructional practice; can policymakers trust survey data? *Educational Evaluation and Policy Analysis, 21,* 29–45.

McDonnell, L. M. (1995). Opportunity to learn as a research concept and a policy instrument. *Educational Evaluation and Policy Analysis, 17,* 305–322.

McPartland, J. M., & Schneider, B. (1996). Opportunities to learn and student diversity: Prospects and pitfalls of a common core curriculum. *Sociology of Education, 69*(Special Issue), 66–81.

Meyer, J. W. (1977). The effects of education as an institution. *American Journal of Sociology, 83,* 55–77.

Meyer, J. W. (1980). Levels of the educational system and schooling effects. In C. E. Bidwell & D. M. Windham (Eds.), *The analysis of educational productivity, Vol. 2: Issues in macroanalysis* (pp. 15–63). Cambridge, MA: Ballinger.

Oakes, J. (1985). *Keeping track: How schools structure inequality.* New Haven, CT: Yale University Press.

Oakes, J. (1990). *Multiplying inequalities: The effects of race, social class and tracking on opportunities to learn math and science.* Santa Monica, CA: RAND Corporation.

Porter, A. C. (1989). A curriculum out of balance: The case of elementary school mathematics. *Educational Researcher, 18*(5), 9–15.

Porter, A. C. (1991). Creating a system of school process indicators. *Educational Evaluation and Policy Analysis, 13,* 13–29.

Porter, A. C. (2002). Measuring the content of instruction: Uses in research and practice. *Educational Researcher, 31,* 3–14.

Porter, A. C., Floden, R. E., Freeman, D. J., Schmidt, W. H., & Schwille, J. R. (1986). *Content determinants.* East Lansing: Michigan State University, Institute for Research on Teaching.

Porter, A. C., Floden, R. E., Freeman, D. J., Schmidt, W. H., & Schwille, J. R. (1988). Content determinants in elementary school mathematics. In D. A. Grouws & T. J. Cooney (Eds.), *Perspectives on research on effective mathematics teaching* (pp. 96–113). Hillsdale, NJ: Erlbaum.

Porter, A. C., Kirst, M. W., Osthoff, E. J., Smithson, J. L., & Schneider, S. A. (1993). *Reform up close: An analysis of high school mathematics and science classrooms. Final report.* Madison: Wisconsin Center for Education Research.

Porter, A. C., & Smithson, J. L. (2001). *Defining, developing, and using curriculum indicators* (CPRE Research Report Series RR-048). Philadelphia: Consortium for Policy Research in Education.

Promoting Rigorous Outcomes in Mathematics and Science Education (PROM/SE). (2008). *Dividing opportunities: Tracking in high school mathematics, Research report, Vol. 3.* East Lansing: Michigan State University.

Rock, D. A., & Pollack, J. M. (1995). *Mathematics course-taking and gains in mathematics achievement* (NCES Report 95-714). Washington, DC: National Center for Education Statistics.

Rosenbaum, J. S. (1975). The stratification of socialization processes. *American Sociological Review, 40,* 48–54.

Rowan, B., Camburn, E., & Correnti, R. (2004). Using teacher logs to measure the enacted curriculum: A study of literacy teaching in third-grade classrooms. *Elementary School Journal, 105,* 75–101.

Rowan, B., Correnti, R., & Miller, R. (2002). What large-scale survey research tells us about teacher effects on student achievement: Insights from the Prospects study of elementary schools. *Teachers College Record, 104,* 1525–1567.

Rowan, B., Harrison, D. M., & Hayes, A. (2004). Using instructional logs to study mathematics curriculum and teaching in the early grades. *Elementary School Journal, 105,* 103–127.

Rowan, B., & Miracle, A., Jr. (1983). Systems of ability grouping and the stratification of achievement in elementary school. *Sociology of Education, 56,* 133–144.

Schmidt, W. H. (1992). The distribution of instructional time to mathematical content: One aspect of opportunity to learn. In L. Burstein (Ed.), *The IEA Study of Mathematics III: Student growth and classroom processes* (pp. 129–145). Tarrytown, NY: Pergamon Press.

Schmidt, W. H., & Burstein, L. (1992). Concomitants of growth in mathematics achievement during the population A school year. In L. Burstein (Ed.), *The IEA study of mathematics III: Student growth and classroom processes* (pp. 309–327). Tarrytown, NY: Pergamon Press.

Schmidt, W. H., & Houang, R. T. (2007). Lack of focus in the mathematics curriculum: Symptom or cause? In T. Loveless (Ed.), *Lessons learned: What international assessments tell us about math achievement* (pp. 65–84). Washington, DC: Brookings Institution.

Schmidt, W. H., Jorde, D., Cogan, L. S., Barrier, E., Gonzalo, I., Moser, U., et al. (1996). *Characterizing pedagogical flow: An investigation of mathematics and science teaching in six countries.* Dordrecht, The Netherlands: Kluwer.

Schmidt, W. H., & Kifer, E. (1989). Exploring relationships across Population A systems: A search for patterns. In F. D. Robitaille & R. A. Garden (Eds.), *The IEA study of Mathematics II: Contexts and outcomes of school mathematics* (pp. 209–231). Tarrytown, NY: Pergamon Press.

Schmidt, W. H., McKnight, C. C., Cogan, L. S., Jakwerth, P. M., & Houang, R. T. (1999). *Facing the consequences: Using TIMSS for a closer look at U.S. mathematics and science education.* Dordrecht, The Netherlands: Kluwer.

Schmidt, W. H., McKnight, C. C., Houang, R. T., Wang, H., Wiley, D., Cogan, L. S., et al. (2001). *Why schools matter: A cross-national comparison of curriculum and learning.* San Francisco: Jossey-Bass.

Schmidt, W. H., McKnight, C. C., & Raizen, S. A. (1997). *A splintered vision: An investigation of U.S. science and mathematics education.* Dordrecht, The Netherlands: Kluwer.

Schmidt, W. H., McKnight, C. C., Valverde, G. A., Houang, R. T., & Wiley, D. E. (Eds.). (1997). *Many visions, many aims (TIMSS Volume 1): A cross-national investigation of curricular intentions in school mathematics.* Dordrecht, The Netherlands: Kluwer.

Schmidt, W. H., Raizen, S., Britton, E. D., Bianchi, L. J., & Wolfe, R. G. (Eds.). (1997). *Many visions, many aims (TIMSS Volume 2): A cross-national investigation of curricular intentions in school science* Dordrecht, The Netherlands: Kluwer.

Schmidt, W. H., Wang, H. A., & McKnight, C. C. (2005). Curriculum coherence: an examination of us mathematics and science content standards from an international perspective. *Journal of Curriculum Studies, 37,* 525–529.

Schmidt, W. H., Wolfe, R. G., & Kifer, E. (1992). The identification and description of student growth in mathematics achievement. In L. Burstein (Ed.), *The IEA Study of Mathematics III: Student growth and classroom processes* (pp. 59–100). Tarrytown, NY: Pergamon Press.

Schneider, B., Swanson, C. B., & Riegle-Crumb, C. (1998). Opportunities for learning: Course sequences and positional advantages. *Social Psychology of Education, 2,* 25–53.

Smithson, J. L., & Collares, A. C. (2007, April). *Alignment as a predictor of student achievement gains.* Paper presented at the annual meeting of the American Educational Research Association, Chicago.

Smithson, J. L., & Porter, A. C. (1994). *Measuring classroom practice: Lessons learned from efforts to describe the enacted curriculum—the Reform Up Close Study.* New Brunswick, NJ: Consortium for Policy Research in Education.

Sørensen, A. B., & Hallinan, M. T. (1977). A reconceptualization of school effects. *Sociology of Education, 50,* 273–289.

Sørensen, A. B., & Hallinan, M. T. (1986). Effects of ability grouping on growth in academic achievement. *American Educational Research Journal, 23,* 519–542.

Steiner-Khamsi, G., Torney-Purta, J., & Schwille, J. (Eds.). (2002). *New paradigms and recurring paradoxes in education for citizenship: An international comparison.* Amsterdam: Elsevier Science.

Stevenson, D. L., Schiller, K. S., & Schneider, B. (1994). Sequences of opportunities for learning. *Sociology of Education, 67,* 184–198.

Suter, L. E. (2000). Is student achievement immutable? Evidence from international studies on schooling and student achievement. *Review of Educational Research, 70,* 529–545.

Talbert, J. E. (1990, April). *Teacher tracking: Exacerbating inequalities in the high school.* Paper presented at the annual meeting of the American Educational Research Association, Boston.

Travers, K. J., & Westbury, I. (1989). *The IEA Study of Mathematics I: Analysis of mathematics curricula.* Elmsford, NY: Pergamon Press.

Valverde, G. A., Bianchi, L. J., Wolfe, R. G., Schmidt, W. H., & Houang, R. T. (2002). *According to the book: Using TIMSS to investigate the translation of policy into practice through the world of textbooks.* Dordrecht, The Netherlands: Kluwer.

Valverde, G. A., & Schmidt, W. H. (2000). Greater expectations: Learning from other nations in the quest for "world-class standards" in U.S. school mathematics and science. *Journal of Curriculum Studies, 32,* 651–687.

Vanfossen, B. E., Jones, J. D., & Spade, J. Z. (1987). Curriculum tracking and status maintenance. *Sociology of Education, 60,* 104–122.

Walberg, H., & Frederick, W. C. (1983). Instructional time and learning. In H. E. Mitzel, J. H. Best, & W. Rabinowitz (Eds.), *Encyclopedia of educational research, Vol. 2* (5th ed., pp. 917–924) New York: The Free Press.

Weinstein, R. S. (1976). Reading group membership in first grade: Teacher behaviors and pupil experience over time. *Journal of Educational Psychology, 68,* 103–116.

Wiley, D. E., & Harnischfeger, A. (1974). Explosion of a myth: Quantity of schooling and exposure to instruction, major educational vehicles. *Educational Researcher, 3*(4), 7–12.

45

The Reading and Math Wars

Alan H. Schoenfeld and P. David Pearson
University of California, Berkeley

Introduction

The reading and math wars rocked California's education system in the mid-1990s. Discussions of curricular frameworks and efforts to develop guidelines for state textbook adoptions in both areas were contentious and ideological. Soon afterward, both curricular conflicts went nationwide. They grew in severity to the point where U.S. Secretary of Education Richard Riley made a plea at the January 1998 annual mathematics meetings for a ceasefire, for civility and restraint in discussions of curricula. His calls for peace went unheeded. Curricular issues in both reading and mathematics have remained highly contentious through the early years of the 21st century, although the battles took on different forms with the ascendance of a politically and educationally conservative federal administration and the enactment of the No Child Left Behind Act (NCLB).

This chapter examines similarities and differences in the causes and evolution of the reading and math wars. We begin with a historical backdrop, characterizing longstanding tensions regarding the goals of education in America. We then describe the two curricular conflicts in sequence—first reading, then mathematics, following a common narrative structure. With those stories told, we identify unifying themes. A case can be made that both wars are cut from the same political cloth, reflecting the same historical tensions regarding the role of education in American society. Perhaps all that differs between the two is the garment to be made from the common cloth.

Historical Tensions: The Goals of Education

To establish a context for what follows, we point to a long-standing historical tension regarding the roles and purposes of education. In the main narrative, it will be seen that the reading and math wars reflect this historical tension. In addition, the narrative will reveal an epistemological (and thus instructional) tension regarding the nature of understanding,

which occurs both in reading and mathematics. Parallels between the historical and epistemological tensions will be addressed in the final discussion.

The goals of education have been contested from the very beginnings of this nation. Rosen (2000) claims that there have been three "master narratives" regarding the role of education in the United States:

> *Education for democratic equality* (the story that schools should serve the needs of democracy by promoting equality and providing training for citizenship); *education for social efficiency* (the story that schools should serve the needs of the social and economic order by training students to occupy different positions in society and the economy); and *education for social mobility* (the story that schools should serve the needs of individuals by providing the means of gaining advantage in competitions for social mobility). (p. 4)

Stanic (1987) offers a slightly different decomposition. Like Rosen, Stanic identifies *social efficiency educators* and *social meliorists* (similar to those who believed in education for social mobility); he adds *humanists* (those who value the discipline for its contributions to humankind) and *developmentalists*, who would organize schooling according to their perception of psychological development.

There are nuances of difference in historical analyses, but the points of overlap in these two categorizations provide a rough dichotomy of purposes. Broadly speaking, those in the social mobilist or social meliorist camp see education as a powerful, egalitarian, democratizing force—as a mechanism for facilitating the American Dream, the "belief in the freedom that allows all citizens and residents of the United States of America to achieve their goals in life through hard work" (Wikipedia, 2008). According to this view, universally accessible education provides the meritocratic mechanism by which class and race can be transcended. The idea is that everyone should have access to high-quality education, and that those who do well can advance in society. Indeed, this is the official position of the U.S. Department of State (2008):

> Education is a universal human right. It also is a means of achieving other human rights and it is an empowering social and economic tool. Through the Universal Declaration of Human Rights, the world's nations have agreed that everyone has the right to education. (¶ 1)

This is one view. In stark contrast, critical theorists take as their starting point that the text quoted above is rhetoric and no more—that the real, rather than rhetorical, purpose of education is the maintenance and reproduction of the status quo, and that the educational system in the United States is largely designed to "keep people in their place."

Social realities are complex, and these diametrically opposite perspectives can and do coexist in both theory and practice. In historical terms, one can take the biographies of George Washington Carver and Booker T. Washington as archetypical examples of liberation through education and hard work; but one can also find ample evidence for the social efficiency perspective, for example, the fact that in the mid-19th century the explicit intention was for slaves to be illiterate and the penalty for teaching a slave to read was death. Similarly, the current rhetoric in mathematics education points to the potential for quantitative literacy to serve a democratizing function.

> Today…the most urgent social issue affecting poor people and people of color is economic access. In today's world, economic access and full citizenship depend crucially on math and science literacy. I believe that the absence of math literacy in urban and rural communities throughout this country is an issue as urgent as the lack of Black voters in Mississippi was in 1961. (Moses & Cobb, 2001, p. 5)

However, the very fact that Moses and Cobb feel the need to plead this case points to the fact that social realities have historically dictated otherwise. To provide an example from more than a century prior to Moses and Cobb's argument, L. Resnick (personal communication, July 9, 2000) discusses a memorandum from a late 19th century school principal instructing mathematics teachers at his school to provide instruction in the four basic arithmetic operations and no more, because the students are going to be mercantile clerks and that is all the mathematics that they will need.

In sum, there are longstanding tensions regarding the purposes of education (e.g., is education to serve as the path of opportunity for all citizens, especially the poor and powerless, to aspire to upward social mobility and political enfranchisement? Or, is the primary purpose of education to train workers just skilled enough to fill the jobs needed but not skilled enough to question the inequities of power and wealth in the society, perpetuating the status quo by reproducing the social and economic order in each generation?). These tensions provide a useful backdrop for our narratives about the reading and math wars, for they play out in the very conceptions of what it means to be literate and to do mathematics.

The Reading Wars

Demographic Trends and their Import For as long as there have been free public schools in the United States, learning to read and spell in the early grades of grammar school has been a common cultural expectation, almost reaching the status of a developmental task (Havighurst, 1972), of a kind with learning to walk at about 1 year of age and talk at about 1½ years. The expectation was that any student who attended a free public school would learn to read by the end of the primary grades. The only exceptions would be a few very resistant students, most likely those born with what was called then called congenital word blindness (now dyslexia). Of course, learning to read—at least until the 1920s—did not mean what it means today. Understanding was not the goal; instead accurate, efficient, and perhaps even eloquent oral reading was the prevailing standard prior to the 1920s. That may have seemed reasonable to educators of that era.

Once the standard for reading competence shifted to efficient comprehension following silent reading, as it did in the 1920s, assessment experts developed a new tool, the multiple-choice reading test, which was capable of monitoring growth and trends more efficiently; unlike oral reading measures, these silent multiple-choice measures could be administered to large groups of students, even entire schools, at once. Whether cause or consequence of the demographic changes that took place in the first quarter of the 20th century, these new indicators certainly "fit" the changing demographics. Most notable among these pressures were the extension of free compulsory education through the middle teens and the dramatic increase in student populations as a function of immigration. Also the need to know the level of literacy of citizens (particularly citizen soldiers) propelled by the new "science" of education (see Thorndike, 1910) provided additional pressure for a new, more efficient indicator of reading competence. These forces conspired to create a readiness for the new standard for reading—the ability to read short passages silently and answer multiple-choice test questions about the ideas in the passages.

Interestingly, there is little evidence of strong demographic influences on the literacy curriculum between the 1920s and the 1960s. This was a quiet time in reading policy and practice, with each decade bringing some refinements to the emerging "giant," the look-say basal reader with early grade stories that "serialized" the life of Dick, Jane, Sally, Mother and Father, and the pets (or one of the sets of competing "cousins" such as Tom and Susan or Alice and Jerry).

The next big wave of demographic influences would await another watershed in literacy assessment—the development of the National Assessment in Educational Progress (NAEP) in the late 1960s. The big news from the early administrations of NAEP, beginning in 1971, was clear evidence that there was an unconscionably large achievement gap between the educational haves and have-nots at every age level (9, 13, and 17) at which NAEP was administered, as defined by ethnicity or economic status. These ethnic and economic disparity trends have been mapped over the last 35 years, with the general finding that gaps gradually but steadily closed from 1971 through 1990, opened from 1990 through about 2000, and have once again decreased over the decade of the 2000s. The gradual closing of the gap through 1990 was generally viewed by policy makers and educators as evidence of the positive impact of 25 years of compensatory education through Title I funding (although no such causal inferences are warranted or, for that matter, claimed by anyone close to NAEP or Title I implementation). Conversely, claims have recently been made, most notably by Secretary of Education Spellings (see, e.g., Tough, 2006), that the gap-closing realized between 1999 and 2004 is attributable to the No Child Left Behind Act. Like the earlier overoptimistic conclusions about Title I in the 1970s and 1980s, even a cursory analysis of the timing of NCLB, particularly its Reading First program, in relationship to the performance improvements for ethnic minorities and poor students does not support any causal attributions.

Perhaps the most significant consequence of an ever-increasing federal role in compensatory education, through the various instantiations of Title I, has been to promote a consistent focus on the achievement gap. NAEP contributed to this awareness and sensitivity by reporting performance, for the nation, by ethnicity, language, and income—and Title I, at least until it became a school-based funding formula in the early 1990s, added to the awareness by requiring that dollars follow students who were "disadvantaged" by virtue of either income or achievement. This sensitivity reached its peak—and took a new turn—in 2002 with the NCLB requirement of disaggregated reporting by categories based on ethnicity, economic group, disability labeling, or linguistic background. What disaggregated reporting at the school level means for reading policy and practice is that the achievement gap phenomenon, which used to be characterized as an aggregate phenomenon—a problem that plagues the nation, or a state, or a district—has now become a school phenomenon—it is the Latino, African American, or poor students in *our* school who exhibit the achievement gap.

The most important consequence of this newfound sensitivity to demographic characteristics and achievement was the elevation of testing in American schools. It is a perverse but important—and wholly plausible—chain of events in the history of reading policy, one worth remembering in each generation. Once the federal government, through Title I, began giving money to states and schools, it was only a matter of time until some "accounting" of the impact of the resources was demanded. This came during the first reauthorization of Title I in 1967. States had to report on the progress being made with those dollars. And NAEP played an important backup role by allowing the nation to examine the overall impact of Title I at the national level, especially the question of whether the achievement gap was widening or closing. But states soon developed state testing programs—beginning with Michigan, Minnesota, and New Jersey in the very early 1970s—as indexes of progress that they could use to report back to the federal government on the wise use of federal resources, among other uses. The next important link in the chain was the standards movement in the late 1980s and early 1990s, which elevated curriculum standards (what kids should know and be able to do), performance standards (how much is enough to indicate whether they know) and assessments (how to measure that performance) to an even more important role. Next came the requirement, this time as part of Clinton's administration in the form of the Improving America's Schools Act (1994), that all states had to send to the federal government the standards (deadline of 1998) and assessments (deadline of 2000) that they were going to use to demonstrate progress on the national goal of school improvement. The final link in the chain came in January 2002, in the form of the Bush administration's version of Title I, NCLB. Its big contribution was the requirement of disaggregated reporting of progress down to the level of the school. By late in the decade of the 2000s, it was fair to conclude that tests had become the tacit blueprint for American reading curriculum and that teaching to the test had become a virtue not a vice, no matter how narrow the curricular focus of those tests had become (see Pearson, 2004). And all this carried out in the name of closing the achievement gap.

Curricular Context   Until the early years of the 20th century, notwithstanding a few vocal critics (e.g., Horace Mann in the mid 19th century and Francis Parker at the turn of the 20th century), the age-old synthetic, or alphabetic, approach to teaching reading prevailed. The principles and stages are straightforward:

- First teach the letter names and sounds.
- Then teach two- and three-letter syllables.
- Then teach monosyllabic real words.
- Then teach multi-syllabic words.

In this synthetic approach, once these component skills are acquired, students are deemed ready to read (and understand) connected text. The underlying view of reading comprehension is what we have since come to call the simple view of reading. In the simple view, reading comprehension is thought of as the product of decoding and listening comprehension:

$$(RC = Dec \times LC) \qquad (1)$$

An instructional implication of the simple view is that the major task of instruction is to ensure that students master the code (the cipher that governs the translation of letters into sounds) so they can translate print into sound representations and then comprehend more or less by listening to what they decode. Within the simple view, if decoding is taught well to all students, it follows that their ability to comprehend is determined mainly by their oral language comprehension. Oral language competence, in turn, is shaped by the knowledge students acquire with experience (in the world outside of school) and education (in the world of disciplinary experiences inside the school).

Once wide-scale standardized assessment took hold, as it did in the 1920s, the standard for reading competence was set. It has, as a matter of policy, remained fundamentally unchanged and only occasionally challenged since that time, although, as we pointed out earlier (and will emphasize again later), we pay a high price in terms of consequences for using multiple-choice test scores as our standard of progress. Also correlated with this change in the standard was a change in pedagogy. The highly synthetic (letters to words) alphabetic approach, which had prevailed since colonial times, was challenged by two decidedly analytic alternatives. The first, dubbed the words-to-letters approach, introduced words in the very earliest stages and, for each word introduced, immediately asked children to decompose it into component letters. Words-to-letters is the obverse of the alphabetic, or letters-to-words, logic of the alphabetic approach. However, with the alphabetic approach, it shares the goal of ensuring that children learn the sound correspondences for each letter and the same set of underlying assumptions about the nature of teaching, learning, and reading. Today we would call it analytic (whole-to-part) phonics.

The second reform, dubbed words-to-reading, later came to be known as the look-say or whole word method of teaching reading. Here, no attempt was made to analyze words into letter-sounds *until* a sizeable corpus of words were learned as sight words. Contrary to popular opinion, which would have us believe that phonics was never taught in the look-say approach, some form of analytic phonics (a modified version of words-to-letters) usually kicked in after a corpus of a hundred or so sight words had been learned. It was different from a strict word-to-letters approach, though, because the strict requirement for decomposing each word into its component letters was dropped in favor of what might be called focused analysis. For example, a teacher might group several words that start with the letter f (e.g., *farm, fun, family, fine*, and *first*) and ask students to note the similarity between the initial sounds and letters in each word. As it turned out, this approach (a combination of look-say with analytic phonics) persevered to become the "conventional wisdom" from 1930–1970. It was the basic premise in the infamous Dick and Jane series developed first by William Elson (Elson & Keck, 1911) and then Elson and William S. Gray (1936) for Scott Foresman's *Curriculum Foundation Series* in the 1930s.

The remainder of reading curricular history in the 20th century can be aptly characterized by any one of the popular metaphors describing tensions among different camps in a profession—a *struggle* between competing goals, a *war* between opposing ideological forces, or a *pendulum* that swings back and forth between opposing curricular viewpoints. Even though the war metaphor is rhetorically appealing, we think the most appropriate metaphor is perpetual motion pendulum. The pendulum swing in reading entails several dimensions, but only one is clearly dominant, the

focus of the curriculum in the early grades—Kindergarten through Grade 2. And the perennial question is, should our early reading curriculum emphasize *cracking the code* (the successors of the alphabetic approach), the cipher detailing how print maps onto sound, or *constructing meaning* in response to a text (the successors to the look-say approach)?[1] Confounded in this fundamental distinction is a dimension focused on how reading develops: Does reading develop as students acquire an increasingly larger set of *component skills* that lead eventually to understanding *or* does reading involve the successive application of an *ever-increasing store of knowledge and metacognitive strategies* to the task of making meaning in response to text? In general, code-emphasis approaches also emphasize acquiring an increasingly complex set of subskills (the assembly line metaphor fits), while meaning-emphasis approaches emphasize the continual quest for meaning at every age and stage and the reciprocal relationship between knowledge and comprehension—knowledge begets comprehension begets knowledge (the metaphor of a machine that is fully operational from the start but is able to perform those operations on increasingly sophisticated content fits). In the first metaphor, students get better by adding more components to their repertoires; in the second, by adding more potent fuel, in the form of more sophisticated world knowledge and experience in managing the metacognitive monitoring functions of reading, to the mix.

From the 1920s through the 1960s, the pendulum swung farther and farther to the meaning end of the pendulum's arc (see Chall, 1967 for a meticulous—and delightful—account of this trend), only to be challenged, initially in the popular press by pundits such as Rudolph Flesch (1955), who was confident about the source of the problem (we had forsaken simple but enduring phonics rules in favor of this gibberish about meaning and whole words), and at the end of the 1960s by the revitalization of a host of code-emphasis curriculum programs (Chall, 1967; Bond & Dykstra, 1967). This brief return to phonics first, however, would be short-lived because it was almost immediately challenged by the paradigm shift that lay just around the corner in the 1970s. Then, after a two-decade period of dormancy during the late 1970s and 1980s, the back to phonics/basics was once again re-energized in the mid-1990s by a complex set of political forces.

A Paradigm Shift in Reading Theory and Practice Somewhere in the 1970s—the exact point of departure is hard to fix—the field of reading curriculum experienced a paradigm shift that lasted until some point in the mid-1990s (depending on how one assesses the end of a paradigm). The underlying theoretical tenets of behaviorism upon which reading pedagogy and reading assessment had been built throughout the initial 70+ years of the century were challenged, overturned, and replaced by a succession of pretenders to the theoretical throne of reading. Along the way the reading field confronted fundamental shifts in the prevailing views of reading and writing that led to the creation of a variety of serious curricular alternatives to the conventional wisdom of the 1970s. Reading became an ecumenical scholarly enterprise; it was embraced by scholars from many different fields of inquiry (see Pearson & Stephens, 1993, for a complete account of this phenomenon). First came the linguists, who claimed that reading (and writing) was a language process closely allied to its sibling oral language processes of speaking, and listening. They were soon joined by psycholinguists who studied the psychological implications, if not the psychological reality, of these linguistic principles. Taken together, the linguistic and psycholinguistic perspectives (Brown, 1970) prompted several leading reading theorists (e.g., Smith, 1971, or Goodman, 1967) to propose a "reading is natural—just like oral language" theory of reading processes and reading development. Just as the young child needs both a motive (participation in a social world) and data (the oral language of surrounding adults and older children) to infer the language system used in her environment, so the reader needs both a motive (crypto-analytic intent—the motive to learn how print maps onto sound) and data (the thousands of stories, words, and letters in that world of print) to infer the regularities of the "cipher"—the code that maps letters onto sound).

Then came the cognitive psychologists, who pushed beyond a brain with a language-specific natural learning device toward a more general cognitive "module" that sought pattern and predictability in all data it encountered—language, perception, attention, and even executive monitoring. The capacity to learn, not just the capacity to learn language, was the domain and object of this alternative biological device. And the quest of the young learner was for cognitive structure, clarity, and predictability. The enterprise of constructing meaning became the primary focus of the curriculum.

Soon afterward came the sociolinguists (Heath, 1983), literary critics (Rosenblatt, 1978), and critical theorists (Gee, 1988); each new discipline brought a critique of its immediate predecessor, and each offered a new perspective to reshape the operative theory of reading development. Each also bore implications for instructional practice and assessment. If the psycholinguists pushed beyond the word to the contextual influences of surrounding sentences and the cognitivists (joined, albeit unintentionally, by the literary critics) pushed beyond the text to the knowledge base the reader brings to the task, the sociolinguists pushed us to a different kind of context, the context of the community, be it in the classroom, the home, or the neighborhood, in which reading develops. And the critical theorists established an even broader context—the context of discursive, political, and economic forces—in which reading is shaped. In fact, the metaphor of an ever-broadening notion of context nicely characterizes the intellectual forces that shaped our dynamic notions of reading development over the last 30 years of the 20th century.

This highly interpretive, decidedly constructivist perspective reached the zenith of its influence on pedagogy and assessment in the mid-1990s. At a pedagogical level, this was the era of whole language, literature-based reading, and process writing—all radically constructivist pedagogical approaches that placed the interpretive powers of the individual reader at the center of the teaching-learning context. At a policy level, the movement played itself out in the advent of the highly influential California Reading Framework (California Department of Education, 1987). In curriculum, the movement was witnessed by a spurt of short-lived literature-based basal reading series that emerged between the mid-80s and mid-90s; all the major publishers of that era were implicated, but none was more influential than the Houghton-Mifflin series adopted in California in the early 1990s. In assessment, the state assessments in many states, such as California, Maryland, Vermont, and Washington, as well as the coalition of states and districts involved in the New Standards examinations (see Myers & Pearson, 1996) paralleled the movement in constructivist curriculum and called for performance tasks that not only mirrored the pedagogy but were themselves enactments of the pedagogical principles inherent in these curricula. In short, assessment became repurposing good curriculum and pedagogy for assessment purposes, rendering the potential divide between assessment and instruction irrelevant. The motto of this era was, "well, if people are going to teach to the test, let's have tests worth teaching to!" But there was one important proviso—that the "tests worth teaching to" emerged from the curriculum, rather than the other way around.

A Second Paradigm Shift   Toward century's end, just when it appeared as if this suite of constructivist approaches (whole language, process writing, literature-based reading, and performance assessment) was about to assume the position of conventional wisdom for the field, the movement was challenged seriously, and the pendulum of the pedagogical debate began to swing back toward the skills/code end of the continuum. Several factors converged to make the challenge credible, among them (a) unintended curricular casualties of whole language, (b) questionable applications of whole language, (c) the growth of balanced literacy as a mediating force in the debate, (d) a paradigm shift in reading research, and (e) loss of the moral high ground. All of these forces, but especially the shift in reading research, came together in one place—the Reading First component of NCLB. In the Bush administration, Reading First assumed the role of conventional wisdom in reading instruction, albeit by mandate rather than groundswell, and only a few traces of whole language, which seemed so dominant only a decade earlier, could be found in our schools and curricula.

Unintended Curricular Consequences   In its ascendancy, whole language changed the face of reading instruction, and in the process, left behind some curricular casualties, few of which were intended by those who supported whole language. Those, including many curricular moderates, who supported practices that were discarded in the rise of whole language, had difficulty supporting the whole language movement even though they might have been philosophically and curricularly sympathetic to many of its principles and practices (see Pearson, 1996). This lack of enthusiasm from curricular moderates meant that whole language failed to build a base of support that was broad enough to survive even modest curricular opposition, let alone the political onslaught that it would experience at century's turn.

There were four casualties of the short-lived constructivist ascendancy: skills instruction, strategy instruction, text structure, and content area instruction. When the field accepted whole language, it tacitly accepted the premise that skills, strategies, and structural elements are better caught in the act of reading and writing genuine texts for authentic purposes than taught directly and explicitly by teachers. These entities may be worthy of learning, but they are unworthy of teaching. This position presents a serious conundrum for a profession. Admit, for the sake of argument, that the skills instruction of the 1970s and earlier, with decontextualized lessons and practice on "textoids" in workbook pages, deserved the criticism accorded to it by whole language advocates (and scholars from other traditions). But a retreat from most skills instruction into a world of "authentic opportunity" did not provide a satisfactory answer for teachers and scholars who understood the positive impact that instruction can have. Many young readers do not "catch" the alphabetic principle by sheer immersion in print or by listening to others read aloud. It was the same story with strategies and an appreciation of the role of text structure. There was a fear among many professionals that an approach that championed learning over teaching would privilege those who acquired the knowledge naturally, without explicit instruction on the part of teachers—and that this privilege would discriminate along lines of race, language, ethnicity, and class (see Delpit, 1988; Reyes, 1992).

Content area reading also suffered during the ascendancy of literature-based reading. Content area texts—expository texts in general, but especially textbook-like entries—were not privileged in a world ruled by literature. To add to the problem, the prevailing practices in middle and high school subject matter classrooms did not help to promote competence with expository text either. Faced with classrooms of students who either could not or would not read the texts, teachers resorted, quite understandably, either to reading the text to the students or more commonly, to telling them what they would have encountered had they or could they have read the text. While understandable, this approach is ultimately counterproductive for it creates an unhealthy dependence on the teacher as the source of knowledge. This dependence worked through secondary school, but it would not wash in college or enter the world of work—both sites where others expected them to read and understand informational texts on their own and in printed form rather than through oral or video transformation.[2]

The constructivist movement could not easily accommodate structural- and content-focused curricular practices. As a consequence, those who championed one or another of these practices were uneasy allies of constructivism, even though they had much in common.

Questionable Applications of Whole Language   One of the dilemmas faced by any curricular initiative is sustaining the integrity of the movement without imposing the very sorts of controls it is trying to eliminate. Whole language did not find a way to manage this dilemma, and it suffered as a consequence. Many schools, teachers, and institutions appropriated the whole language label without honoring its fundamental principles of authenticity, integration, and empowerment. Basal reader publishers made the most obvious and widespread appropriation, some even positioning their basal series as "whole language" programs. The most egregious misapplication was the conflation of whole language with whole-class instruction. Nowhere was this conflation more extreme than in the implementation of the California literature framework. The logic that prevailed in many classrooms was that it was better to keep the entire class together, all experiencing the same texts; even if it meant that the teacher had to read the text to those children who lacked the skills to read it on their own. Implicit in this practice are two interesting assumptions: (a) that getting the content of the stories is the most important goal for reading instruction, and (b) that the skills and processes needed to read independently will emerge somehow from this environment in which many students are pulled through texts that far exceed their grasp, given the sophistication of their current skills repertoire. Needless to say, whole language had enough on its hands dealing with its own assumptions and practices; these philosophical and curricular misapplications exposed the movement to a whole set of criticisms that derived from practices not of its own making (Pearson, 2004).

A plausible explanation for the misapplication of whole language was its lack of an explicit plan for professional development. Given its grassroots political assumptions, it is not surprising that whole language gave teachers a wide berth for making curricular and instructional decisions. It assumed that teachers who are empowered, sincere, and serious about their work would be able to tailor programs and activities to the needs and interests of individual children. Such an approach makes sense only when teacher knowledge is widely and richly distributed in our profession. To offer these prerogatives in the face of narrow and shallow knowledge is to guarantee that misguided practices, even perversions of the very intent of the movement, will be widespread. The puzzle, of course, is where to begin the reform—by ensuring that the knowledge precedes the prerogative, or by ceding the prerogative to teachers as a way of leveraging their motivation for greater knowledge. Similar arguments have been made for the reform movements in mathematics, that is, that the reforms got out ahead of the professional knowledge base; interestingly the reform movement in mathematics has experienced a fate similar to that of the whole language movement (see Good & Braden, 2000; Schoenfeld, 2004).

Balanced Literacy   While it has reached its peak in the last 5 years, concern about extreme positions, be they extremely child-centered (such as the more radical of whole language approaches) or extremely curriculum-centered (such as highly structured, unswerving phonics programs) is not new. Voices from the middle, extolling balanced approaches or rationalizing the eclectic practices of teachers, began to be heard even in the earliest days of whole language's ascendancy.[3] Scholars and teachers raised a number of concerns about the assumptions and practices of the whole language movement. Most importantly, they expressed concern about the consequences of whole language outlined earlier in this essay. They questioned the assumption that skills are best "caught" during the pursuit of authentic reading activity rather than "taught" directly and explicitly. They also questioned the insistence on authentic texts and the corollary mistrust of "instructional" texts written to permit the application of skills within the curriculum. They questioned the zeal and commitment of the movement qua movement, with its strong sense of insularity and exclusivity. Finally, they worried that the press toward the use of authentic literature and literature-based reading would eradicate, albeit unintentionally, what little progress had been made toward the use of informational texts and teaching reading in the content areas (Pearson, 1996).

Ironically, from the mid-1990s to the mid-2000s, these voices from the middle found themselves responding more to those who hold steadfastly to the phonics first position because there is so little political pressure from those who maintain a radical whole language position. Even so, the fact that those with centrist positions were not inclined to defend whole language when the political campaign against it began in the mid-1990s undoubtedly hastened the demise of whole language as the pretender to the title of conventional wisdom.

Changing Research Paradigms   Prior to the 1980s, qualitative research in any form had little visibility within the reading research community. Among the array of qualitative efforts, only miscue analysis[4] and some early forays into sociolinguistic and anthropological accounts of literacy had achieved much in the way of archival status.[5] However, the situation changed dramatically in the mid- to late 1980s and early 1990s. Qualitative research more generally, along with more specific lines of inquiry taking a critical perspective on literacy as a social and pedagogical phenomenon, became more widely accepted as part of the mainstream archival literature.[6] Treatises pointing out the shortcomings of traditional forms of quantitative inquiry, especially experimental research, appeared frequently in educational research journals.[7] Much of the research that undergirds the suite of constructivist pedagogies comes from this more qualitative, interpretive, critical tradition. Thus, the credibility of this type of research increased in concert with the influence of whole language, literature-based reading, and the like.

Sometime in the mid- to late 1990s, a new force and a new paradigm began to take shape. It was first visible in a new discourse stimulated by research supported by the National Institute for Child Health and Human Development. We began to see and hear a "new" brand of experimental work that had been quietly but steadily gathering momentum for over a decade (Lyon, 1995; Lyon & Chhabra, 1996). This was experimentalism reborn from the 1950s and 60s, with great emphasis placed upon "reliable, replicable research," large samples, random assignment of treatments to teachers and/or schools, and tried and true outcome measures. Its aegis was in the experimental rhetoric of science and medicine and in the laboratory research that was so prominent in those earlier periods. Although this effort was not broadly accepted by the reading education community, it found a very sympathetic ear in the public policy arena.[8]

This new research paradigm became officially codified by the appearance, in rapid succession, of two research syntheses—the publication of the report of the National Academy of Science's Committee on Preventing Reading Difficulties (PRD; Snow, Burns, & Griffin, 1998) and the report of the National Reading Panel (NRP, National Institute of Child Health and Human Development [NICHD], 2000). The PRD report was conducted in the tradition of "best evidence" syntheses: Well-established scholars meet, decide on the issues, the domain of relevant research, and some subdivision of labor, do the work, write up the results, and turn the manuscript over to a set of editors to bring some synthetic clarity to the entire effort. As such, it considered a range of studies conducted within very different research traditions using very different research methods. The result was a strong plea for a balanced view of reading instruction, but with a special nod to phonemic awareness and phonics first and fast.

Authorized by congressional mandate, the NRP report used what they considered to be the most "scientific" review approaches (i.e., meta-analysis, at least wherever they could) available to them to distill from existing research what is known about the efficacy of teaching phonemic awareness, phonics, fluency (instantiated as either guided reading instruction or independent reading), comprehension, and vocabulary; additionally, they investigated the status of the research base on teacher education and professional development and attempted to review research on technology and literacy.

These two reports were different in style, tone, and effect. PRD was a best evidence synthesis, while NRP was largely a meta-analysis. PRD was at least partially grounded in a broad set of research traditions, including a great deal of conventional reading research, along with much of the research from the emerging "scientific" paradigm. PRD was received by the field with great fanfare, but it lived a very short life of influence due, in large part, to the pre-emptive effect of the NRP report. The NRP has exerted a great deal of influence for nearly a decade since its release. It is interesting to note that Catherine Snow (2001), one of the lead authors of the PRD report, acknowledges that officials like G. Reid Lyon and Duane Alexander from NICHD, one of the sponsoring agencies of the NRP, were concerned about the PRD report because it was vague and did not discriminate between trustworthy and untrustworthy research.

The NRP was, indeed *is*, noteworthy on several grounds. First, the actual conclusions in the main report are consistent with earlier attempts to summarize the knowledge base on these key issues, such as *Becoming a nation of readers* (Anderson, Hiebert, Scott, & Wilkinson, 1984) and *Preventing reading difficulties* (Snow, Burns, & Griffin, 1998), and point to a balanced approach to teaching reading. Second, while the vote of confidence in teaching phonics and phonemic awareness was strong and direct, it was moderated by important caveats that limit the applicability of these important instructional tools. For example, phonics was found to be a useful instructional approach but only in a particular time frame (grades K-1); it was not effective for older students. Moreover, while the analysis privileged systematic phonics, nothing in the analysis implicated a particular approach (e.g., synthetic or letter-by-letter phonics versus analytic phonics), nor was there any explicit support for decodable text. Also, the authors of the report were careful, in their conclusions, to suggest that phonics by itself was not the total reading program:

> Finally, it is important to emphasize that systematic phonics instruction should be integrated with other reading instruction to create a balanced reading program. Phonics instruction is never a total reading program. (NICHD, 2000, p. 2-135)

Third, the authors of the report were very clear about which topics and studies would be included. It would review only those topics for which there existed a sufficiently large pool of "potentially viable" experimental studies. Hence issues of grouping, the relationship of reading to writing, the role of texts in reading acquisition—just to name a few of the more obvious issues that schools and teachers must address in crafting local reading programs—are not addressed at all (Pearson, 2004). Regarding specific studies, they would include only those that met minimal criteria: employ an experimental or quasi-experimental design with an identifiable comparison group, measure reading as an outcome, describe participants, interventions, study methods, and outcome measures in sufficient detail to contribute to the validity of any conclusions drawn. Natural experiments of the sort found in large-scale evaluation efforts or epidemiological investigations of relationships between methods and outcomes were excluded.[9]

As important as the NRP was in shaping the professional conversation about reading research as soon as it came out in 2000, it was not until the passage of NCLB in January of 2002 that it achieved its real impact. It is no small accident that the Reading First section of NCLB employs the phrase "Scientifically based reading research" no less than 110 times. And in the implementation of Reading First, the science of reading is instantiated very directly as what have come to be known as the "big five": phonics, phonemic awareness, fluency, comprehension, and vocabulary. In

state after state, Reading First plans for selecting programs, creating or selecting assessments, and developing professional development initiatives were to demonstrate their adherence to this new science of reading.

One of the great ironies of NRP's enactment within NCLB is the domination of the Big Five. It is clear, both from the methodological approach of the NRP as well as commentary and conversations with the authors of NRP (e.g., Samuels, 2006), that no one meant for reading curriculum to be limited to the Big Five. But those other curricular issues already mentioned (grouping, writing, and texts) just did not make it into the report, either because the areas failed to meet the minimal numbers criteria (not enough experimental studies for a meta-analysis) or the interest standard (no one on the panel was willing to champion them). Thus, the NRP, by adopting a narrow focus, actually denied consideration of a large number of scientific studies. Had the panel adopted a different approach or standard for entry into the policy conversation (e.g., more like that used for entry into the handbooks of reading research), we might have had a different policy menu in No Child Left Behind and Reading First.[10]

What this meant is that research played a new role in influencing policy, curriculum, and practice. In particular eras of the past, research has been regarded just as one among many information sources consulted in policy formation—including expert testimony from practitioners, information about school organization and finance, and evaluations of compelling cases. But those expectations were dramatically elevated the late 1990s, even before the passage of NCLB. In the past decade, research, at least selective bits of research, has never been taken more seriously. Several laws in California make direct references to research. For example, in 1997 Assembly Bill 1086 (California Assembly, 1998) prohibited the use of Goals 2000 money for professional developers who advocated the use of context clues over phonics or supported the use of "inventive" spellings in children's writing. The federally sponsored Reading Excellence Act of 1999, which allocated $240 million for staff development in reading, required that both state and local applications for funding base their programs on research that meets scientifically rigorous standards. The "scientifically rigorous" phrase was a late entry; in all but the penultimate version of the bill, the phrase was "reliable, replicable research," which had been interpreted as a code word for experimental research. As of early 1999, "phonics bills" (bills mandating either the use of phonics materials or some sort of teacher training to acquaint teachers with knowledge of the English sound symbol system and its use in teaching) had been passed or were pending in 36 states, most often pointing to NICHD research documenting the efficacy of phonics. These and other reading policy matters were well documented in a series of pieces in *Education Week* by Manzo (1997, 1998a, 1998b).

This new set of relationships between research, policy, and practice represented a watershed. These new elements became the stuff of policymaking in the era of accountability. Scientific research was the driver of the system and the basis on which we established standards for the primary policy levers—curriculum, assessment, and professional development. Then monitoring tools (observations and checklists) were added to ensure fidelity to the standards, and sanctions (rewards and penalties) were implemented to motivate schools and teachers to higher achievement and stricter adherence to reforms. This was not the benign "sowing the seeds of knowledge" logic of marketplace of ideas. It was reform by mandate and monitoring.

Above all, the enactment of reading policy in NCLB meant that research had become fully politicized, both in the neutral sense of the term (i.e., became a part of the process by which laws are made, policies are established, and reform is enacted in our schools) and in its pejorative sense (i.e., manipulated to achieve particular political ends). The changes in the dominant paradigm that have occurred in the past 15 years all but invalidated the research base on which many of the constructivist reforms of the previous decade; all of those close ethnographies of individual class-rooms and teacher action stories were no longer privileged in official conversations about "research-" based practice. Numbers, not compelling stories, were the order of a new day; and it was not clear whether there was a place for con-structivist pedagogy in these new conversations—unless, of course, it could play by the new rules.

Loss of the Moral High Ground One other factor, while difficult to document, seems to be operating in the rhetoric of the field in the first decade of the 21st century. Constructivist approaches have traditionally privileged the role of the teacher as the primary curriculum deci-sion maker. Teachers, the argument goes, are in the best position to serve this important role because of their vast knowledge of language and literacy development, their skills as diagnosticians (they are expert "kid watchers"), and the materials and teaching strategies they have at their disposal. And in the arguments against more structured approaches, this is exactly the approach advocates of the more radical approaches took (indeed still take): "Don't make these decisions at the state, district, or even the school level. Arm teachers with the professional prerogative—and corollary levels of professional knowledge—they need in order to craft unique decisions for individual children." While this may seem a reasonable, even admirable position, it has recently been turned into an apology for self-serving teacher ideology.[11] The counterargument suggests that the broad base of privilege accorded to teachers may come at the expense of students and their parents. Thus, those who advocate a strong phonics-first position often take the moral high ground: "We are doing this for America's children (and for YOUR child!)—so that they have the right to read for themselves." Even if one opposes this rhetorical move, it is hard not to appreciate the clever repositioning on the part of those who want to return to more phonics and skills.

The Current Situation As we near the end of the first decade of the 21st century, it is clear that the balance of curricular power for teaching reading has once again shifted back to the basics. We are in an era of first things first, pho-nics first and fast, and interventions designed to guarantee that all students get ample opportunity to learn to decode well enough to "get the message" that resides in school texts. The simple view of reading (that comprehension is the product of decoding and listening comprehension) is alive and well. Complex assessments for nuanced understandings of text have been replaced by frequent monitoring of reading fluency (how many words correct per minute can you read?), and high fidelity to core reading programs and interventions for those who struggle most is the order of the day. But as we set this manuscript aside, there are signs of a crack in the armor of Reading First and NCLB. The pendulum appears posed to begin a swing back to the center, and the march to Lake Wobegon, where all children are (quite literally) above average (all children at state standards for proficiency), may be halted. Bad management, the politics of privilege (some would say cronyism), and unfavorable scientific evidence (ironically the very basis for the ascendancy of this conservative turn in the late 1990s) have all played a role. The scandals of Reading First that were unearthed in 2006 by the Department of Education's own Inspector General and in 2007 by congressional committees (Chair-man's Staff of the U.S. Senate Health, Education, Labor, and Pensions Committee, 2007) discredited the program and the department substantially. And the release of the findings of a carefully designed evaluation study from the Institute of Education Sciences, demonstrating that Read-ing First produced virtually no gains over business as usual programs, in April of 2008 dealt a hard blow to a program and a group of supporters that had placed all of its bets on science as its champion.

The Math Wars

There are surface differences and deep similarities between the stories of reading and mathematics. Our description of the math wars follows the same narrative structure as our description of the reading wars, beginning with a discussion of demographic trends (corresponding to the democratiza-tion of schooling, with the need for more mathematics for more people) and curricular trends (spurred by periodic crises, during which attention to mathematics waxed and then waned). In the details, mathematics differs from read-ing. But, these surface differences matter little. Over the past half century cognitive research in both reading and mathematics revealed the power of teaching and learning for deep understanding, rather than for "mastery." This motivated attempts at curricular change, which in turn catalyzed major warfare. As will be seen, there are far more similarities than differences in the character and outcomes of the warfare in both disciplines.

Demographic Trends and their Import In the late 1800s, "universal education" stopped at elementary school; second-ary education was for the select few. Only 6.7% of the 14-

year-olds in the United States attended high school in 1890, and only 3.5% of the 17-year-olds graduated. Elementary school mathematics consisted of arithmetic (i.e., preparation for the workplace), while secondary school mathematics included algebra and geometry, and prepared students for more advanced study. Hence there was a sharp break between "mathematics for the masses" and "mathematics for the elite" (Stanic, 1987). A hundred years later, "the percentage of young adults receiving either a high school diploma or an alternative credential has remained [stable at] about 85 percent" (National Education Goals Panel, 2001, p. 1) and more than half of the nation's students go on to college at some point.

The democratization of schooling has led to curricular difficulties in mathematics at various times. In the mid-20th century, when the mathematics once reserved for the elite (e.g., algebra and geometry) became available to large numbers of students, high failure rates resulted. In response to these pressures, such courses became elective, and vocational courses became available as an alternative (Jones & Coxford, 1970). Functionally, there were two mathematics tracks in the latter part of the 20th century. All students studied arithmetic in elementary school. The elite track in secondary school—9th-grade algebra, 10th-grade algebra, 11th-grade advanced algebra/trigonometry, 12th-grade analysis or pre-calculus (or possibly calculus, if the track was accelerated)—was for "college-intending" students. Most states required 1 or 2 years of high school mathematics, which might include algebra but might, for the non-college-intending, be vocational mathematics or something else. According to the National Research Council (NRC), enrollments in mathematics dropped roughly 50% per year from ninth grade on; the dropout rate for minorities was higher (Madison & Hart, 1990). This drop-off rate was a serious concern for those who believe that schooling in general, and mathematics learning in particular, are mechanisms for entry into the American social and economic mainstream. Perhaps the most eloquent spokesman for this perspective is civil rights leader Robert Moses (2001), who wrote: "the most urgent social issue affecting poor people and people of color is economic access … I believe that the absence of math literacy in urban and rural communities throughout this country is an issue as urgent as the lack of registered Black voters in Mississippi was in 1961" (p. 5).

The issue of racial performance gaps, and the role of mathematics as a barrier to minority access to economic enfranchisement, remains a persistent problem (see, e.g., Lee, 2002). Indeed, the problem may become worse, given a confluence of two related forces that have an extremely powerful impact on the schools: the "standards" movement as currently conceived and the "high-stakes" accountability movement catalyzed by the NCLB legislation.

California, for example, now mandates a High School Exit Examination (CAHSEE) for all potential high school graduates. CAHSEE has two parts—one part in English Language Arts, the other in mathematics. Students who fail either examination are not granted diplomas, receiving instead "certificates of attendance" commemorating their years of high school work.[12] In the first year that results were legally binding, 2006, roughly 10% of the potential 2006 graduating class in California was denied diplomas. Minority students were very disproportionately represented in this group. The CAHSEE has been challenged in the courts, but thus far without success. Legal arguments surrounding the use of CAHSEE are concerned with opportunity to learn: There are some claims that high-minority, low-SES schools had a disproportional percentage of uncredentialed teachers, and that students are being held responsible for learning material that they have not been taught (Holme & Rogers, 2005). Moreover, studies are now beginning to appear indicating that states that have exit exams have higher dropout rates than states that do not, and that the dropout problem is especially severe for African American males (Glenn, 2006).

Curricular Context

Periodic Crises In contrast to the persistent worry about reading (one rarely hears of "literacy crises" and concomitant bursts of attention to literacy instruction, because it always seems to be in the limelight), attention to mathematics curricula has waxed and waned over the course of American history—waxing in times of perceived crisis, waning in the in-between times. For example: "In the 1940s it became something of a public scandal that army recruits knew so little math that the army itself had to provide training in the arithmetic needed for basic bookkeeping and gunnery. Admiral Nimitz complained of mathematical deficiencies of would-be officer candidates and navy volunteers. The basic skills of these military personnel should have been learned in the public schools but were not." (Klein, 2003, paragraph 23). Such concerns led to temporary overhauls of mathematics curricula, but not to lasting change. A more significant change occurred during the cold war. In the wake of the Soviet launch of the satellite Sputnik, American mathematicians contributed to the development of mathematics curricula known collectively as the "new math," which flowered in the 1960s. These curricula, which were controversial, held sway for a few years until, in the 1970s, they were swept away by another "back to basics" movement, representing a reemergence of skills as the focus of the curriculum. Later, in the late 1970s and early 1980s, the crisis was economic. In an oft-quoted report, *A Nation at Risk,* the U.S. National Commission on Education made the case in the bluntest terms:

> Our Nation is at risk. Our once unchallenged preeminence in commerce, industry, science, and technological innovation is being overtaken by competitors throughout the world…The educational foundations of our society are presently being eroded by a rising tide of mediocrity that threatens our very future as a Nation and a people … if an unfriendly foreign power had attempted to impose on America the mediocre educational performance that exists today, we might well have viewed it as an act of war. As

it stands, we have allowed this to happen to ourselves. We have even squandered the gains in student achievement made in the wake of the Sputnik challenge. Moreover, we have dismantled essential support systems which helped make those gains possible. We have, in effect, been committing an act of unthinking, unilateral educational disarmament. (National Commission on Excellence in Education, 1983, p. 1)

This climate of crisis ushered in by *A Nation at Risk* opened the door for something new. And as it happened, there was a new research base on mathematical cognition waiting in the wings. Accompanied by a pendulum swing toward the democratizing (rather than reproductive) goals of education, these two forces combined to produce the "reform mathematics" that grew steadily (though never holding even close to a dominant market share) through the mid- to late 1990s.

A New Research Base   In the 1970s and 1980s research on thinking and learning broke new paradigmatic ground. Researchers in the social sciences generally, and in education in particular, emerged from the statistical straightjacket that had held them in tow for decades. In the 1960s and early 1970s, almost all research in mathematics education was quantitative in nature, consisting of "treatment A versus treatment B" experimental studies, factor analyses of complex arrays of mathematical subtests, and the like. Much of this work was grounded in simplistic epistemological assumptions, often rooted in behaviorism or trait theory. The "constructivist movement" brought with it its own set of excesses, but it also brought a reexamination of what it means to perceive and understand. The "cognitive revolution" brought a new framework for thinking about what it means to be proficient in a domain. In mathematics and other fields, it became clear that in examining proficiency, one needs to look at:

- the knowledge base,
- problem-solving strategies,
- metacognition (including monitoring and self-regulation),
- beliefs and dispositions, and
- practices typifying productive disciplinary engagement. (Schoenfeld, 1985)

There were both positive and negative aspects to this story. On the positive side, research revealed dimensions of mathematical competency that are important to attend to in instruction. On the negative side, the research pointed out that some of the negative things affiliated with mathematics—unproductive beliefs and dispositions, and a general absence of problem-solving strategies and productive metacognitive behaviors—could be seen as consequences of the traditionalist program of mathematics instruction focused primarily on mastery of facts and procedures that had dominated curriculum in the 1970s and into the early 1980s.

A Novel (Proposed) Synthesis   A combination of circumstances led the National Council of Teachers of Mathematics (NCTM), a professional organization of mathematics teachers, to play a catalytic role in stimulating "reform" in mathematics instruction. First, there was the perceived crisis in mathematics education, as trumpeted by *A Nation at Risk*. Second, for political reasons, the National Science Foundation (NSF) was unable to spearhead curricular change, as it had in the post-Sputnik days; the initiative had to come from elsewhere. Third, NCTM's leadership was well aware of this new breed of cognitive and meta-cognitive research. Fourth, the two dozen writers that NCTM assembled took a broad view of the goals of mathematics instruction. The result was NCTM's (1989) *Curriculum and Evaluation Standards for School Mathematics,* which to everybody's surprise (including the mathematics part of this article's authorship team) wound up changing the landscape of American public education.

The *Standards,* as they are known, were undoubtedly progressive in their intention. They explicitly turned away from the idea of school mathematics serving primarily as a training ground for professionals in mathematics and the sciences, taking a much broader perspective on the roles of education:

> New social goals for education include (1) mathematically literate workers, (2) lifelong learning, (3) opportunity for all, and (4) an informed electorate.(p. 3).

More generally, mindful of the negative consequences of traditional instruction and the research base described above, the *Standards* specified

> "five general goals for all students: (1) that they learn to value mathematics, (2) that they become confident in their ability to do mathematics, (3) that they become mathematical problem solvers, (4) that they learn to communicate mathematically, and (5) that they learn to reason mathematically. (p. 5)

The substance of the *Standards* consisted of a delineation of curricular desiderata at three grade bands: K–4, 5–8, and 9–12. For the first time, and in direct response to the problem-solving research of the preceding decade, instructional goals were process-oriented as well as content-focused. At each of the three grade bands, the first four curriculum standards were:

1. Mathematics as problem solving
2. Mathematics as communication
3. Mathematics as reasoning
4. Mathematical connections

These were followed by the more familiar content-based standards, which were concerned with number sense, patterns, algebra, geometry, statistics, probability, and measurement.

Beyond its reform (i.e., process-oriented and democratic) orientation, the *Standards* had another major characteristic that turned out to be consequential. In many ways, the content of the *Standards* was underspecified. Specification of content was given at the level of grade bands rather than grades. Hence there was no specified scope-and-sequence outline. This gave the designers of standards-based curricula tremendous latitude in designing curricula that fit with (their perceptions of) the ethos of the *Standards*. Generally speaking, guidance was broadly framed: in addition to delineating and exemplifying mathematical content at the grade band level, the *Standards* provided lists of topics that (in comparison to extant, "traditional" curricula) should receive "increased attention" or "decreased attention." How these phrases should be interpreted was left to curriculum designers.

The Research Base   The literature in mathematics education differs substantially from the literature in reading, both at the micro and macro levels.

At the micro level, the literature contains numerous studies of student understandings and difficulties with particular topics (e.g., understanding fractions, or graphing). Unlike the literature in reading, however, such descriptions tend not to be developmental; they do not map out a sequence of understandings that build upon one another. The presumption in mathematics has been that the hierarchy of mathematical complexity, not the stage of development of the learner, should shape the development of the curriculum: for example, fractions are more complex mathematically than whole numbers, so students should become familiar with whole number operations (addition, subtraction multiplication, division) before encountering fractions and the same operations with fractions. Different arenas of mathematics (the study of number; of patterns, functions and algebra; of geometry; of measurement; and of probability and statistics) each have their hierarchies. But, tradition and common sense aside, there is no agreed-upon sense of developmental pathways through mathematics; and there is certainly no analogue to the diagnosis and remediation found in the reading community. Thus, while statements such as "this student reads at the fourth-grade level" are a commonplace in the reading community, there is no analogous phrase for mathematics.

At the macro level, there was by 1989 a substantial amount of evidence characterizing the downside of the traditional curriculum. Large dropout rates from mathematics, the development of counterproductive belief systems, and an absence of problem-solving skills were well documented. However, the *Standards* proposed a new approach—hence there was little or no evidence that curricula whose development was premised on the *Standards* would achieve the new set of goals described above. In a special issue of the *Journal of Mathematical Behavior* entitled "What Should Students Learn?" Schoenfeld (1994) summarized the state of the art as follows:

> In the United States we have no real existence proofs—that is, there do not exist substantial numbers of students who have gone through the reform curricula and emerged demonstrably competent to do further work either in collegiate mathematics or in the workplace…Why abandon the old content specifications, some would say, until you can replace them with something that is demonstrably better?…The fact is that, in the absence of either large-scale empirical proof of success or the existence of compelling and documentable standards, there *is* reason to be cautious. The traditionalists are nervous for good reason. It should be noted, however, that the resistance to change is not based on the purported success of current curricula (one is hard-pressed to find people who say that we are doing things well!), but on the fear that the replacement will be even worse. Here it is worth returning to the notion of a zero-based curriculum planning process. Suppose we declared that any proposed curriculum must, in order to be implemented, make a plausible case that it would do well. The reform curricula would fail because they cannot yet produce real proof, or real standards. But current mainstream curricula would fail even more strongly because there exists a massive body of evidence indicating that they do not work. Conclusion: we can not and must not inhibit the extensive field testing of well-designed reform curricula, but we must at the same time be vigilant. (pp. 73–74)

To presage what comes later in this section: It was clear that there was significant promise to standards-based approaches, and some preliminary evidence of their effectiveness (see, e.g., Cognition and Technology Group at Vanderbilt, 1993; Schoenfeld, 1985; Silver, 1996; for the broader case, see NRC, 2000). However, given the timing (NSF began supporting standards-based curriculum development in the early 1990s, and it took a decade for those curricula to be refined and for data on them to be gathered), the first real data on the effectiveness of the new, standards-based curricula emerged in the early years of the 21st century. The math wars heated up on the mid-1990s, reaching their acrimonious peak in the late 1990s. That is, *the most vehement anti-reform battles were fought in the absence of any solid data one way or the other regarding the effectiveness of the NSF-supported curricula.*

As it happens, the data that came in subsequently weighed in overwhelmingly on the side of reform. Senk and Thompson (2003) provide evaluations of all of the NSF-supported standards-based curricula. Broadly speaking, all of the evaluations converge on the following findings. When tested on skills, students in standards-based courses perform more or less the same as students who studied traditional curricula. When tested on conceptual understanding and problem solving, students in standards-based courses do far better than students who studied traditional curricula. A large-scale comparative study (ARC Center, 2003) examined performance data on matched samples of students spread widely across Illinois, Massachusetts, and Washington state.

> The principal finding of the study is that the students in the NSF-funded reform curricula consistently outperformed the comparison students: All significant differences favored the reform students; no significant difference favored the comparison students. This result held across all tests, all

grade levels, and all strands, regardless of SES and racial/ethnic identity. The data from this study show that these curricula improve student performance in all areas of elementary mathematics, including both basic skills and higher-level processes. Use of these curricula results in higher test scores. (p. 5)

Status at the Start of the Wars: How much of the Curriculum was "Traditional," How much was "Reform"?   Here too there is a significant difference between the reading and mathematics literatures. Before the reading wars erupted, whole language had nearly attained the status of conventional wisdom in the reading community. The same never happened in mathematics. In the early 1980s, there had been a "problem-solving" movement that was quickly co-opted by the publishing industry. In 1980 the NCTM issued a slim pamphlet entitled *An Agenda for Action: Recommendations for School Mathematics of the 1980s*, declaring that problem solving was to be the theme of the 1980s. In short order, publishers responded by producing "problem-solving editions" of their standard texts. Typically, the main text was unchanged, but there was, at the end of each chapter, a set of new problems intended to exemplify the "problem-solving" approach.

When the *Standards* was produced in 1989, it was clear that it called for wholesale change. The reaction of the publishers was simple: It could not be done.[13] It soon became clear that the standard commercial mechanisms for producing texts would not result in change. Hence the NSF issued a request for proposals for curriculum development in mathematics in 1991. Roughly speaking, curriculum development on most standards-based curricula took place in the early to mid-1990s;[14] implementation of early versions of those curricula took place in the mid-to-late 1990s; the first cohorts of students to emerge from them "graduated" from them at the turn of the 21st century.

Thanks to the tireless efforts of NCTM, "teaching for reform" or "teaching in ways consistent with the *Standards*" gained some currency in the mathematics teaching community. This was especially the case at the secondary level, where NCTM has the bulk of its membership. (Elementary school teachers are generalists, and therefore less likely to align with specific disciplines. NCTM's total membership, roughly 100,000, pales against the number of elementary school teachers in the United States, which is roughly 2,000,000 (U.S. Census Bureau, 2004). (Thus, the degree to which a standards-based philosophical approach permeated the elementary schools is open to question.) Textbook adoption figures would be a good guide to overall impact, but publishers are less than fully forthcoming about their text circulation. However, it seems safe to say that at the peak of "reform," at most 25% of the texts being sold were standards-based. Thus, standards-based mathematics never came close to reaching the status of conventional wisdom in the mathematics community.

The Demise   Although there are some significant differences between the conflicts over reading and mathematics,

the stories are parallel in many ways. The math wars came hard upon the heels of the reading wars, first in California and then in the nation. Indeed, one might suspect that the anti-reform warriors in mathematics learned many techniques from their anti-whole-language compatriots in the reading wars. In some cases, they were aided by the naïve actions of reformers, which set reform up for ridicule.

Unintended Curricular Consequences and Questionable Applications   The *Standards* were less a scope-and-sequence description than a vision statement, allowing wide latitude in interpretation. (Less kindly, Michael Apple, 1992, referred to the *Standards* as a "slogan system.") This allowed people to project their understandings onto it, in some cases creating "standards-based" instruction that might well have come as a surprise to the authors of the *Standards*. In particular, the "decreased emphasis/increased emphasis" lists in the *Standards* were an invitation to excess, or at least caricatures of excess. For example, "two column proofs" had been a mainstay of geometry classes for decades; according to some, a call for decreased emphasis meant eliminating proof from the curriculum. Similarly, there were pitched battles over whether students should be exposed to the traditional procedures for basic operations on whole numbers, or whether students should discover the procedures for themselves—the argument being that introducing the traditional procedures would stifle students' creativity. There were some extremes in practice, which led to claims that that reformers were urging a return to the already discredited "discovery math" of the 1960s.

Pedagogical reformers urged group work, on the basis that collaboration was a good thing, and that learning to communicate mathematics is important. However, those who took it seriously learned rapidly that it is one thing to sit a group of students down at a table and ask them to talk about mathematics; it is quite something else to select the tasks and orchestrate the conversations in ways that result in *productive* interactions.

Finally (in the sense of coup de grâce), the emphasis on process and communication in reform mathematics provided significant opportunity for caricature. The California state assessment program, the California Learning Assessment System (CLAS), had already made a fundamental political mistake in assigning comprehension passages from a novel by Alice Walker, and CLAS was under attack. Then, a CLAS mathematics item asked students to make a decision and write a memo justifying it. The publicly released scoring rubric gave a lower score to a student who arrived at the correct answer but did not defend it well than to a student whose answer was wrong but who wrote a good memo. That was the straw that broke the CLAS's back: conservative columnists could now write that the right answer no longer counted in mathematics—that the ability to write a perfunctory response was more important than the ability to get the right answer (see Saunders, 1995).

Politics   In a word: brutal. Simply put, it is hard for someone who believes in intellectual integrity to apprehend the ways in which the process became political—and vicious. For a balanced description of the evolution of the wars, see Jackson (1997a, 1997b). For a broad overview, see Schoenfeld (2004). For a detailed description of historical context and of California state politics, see Rosen (2000). For a view of the combat from the liberal side, see Becker & Jacob (2000), Jacob (1999, 2001), and Jacob and Akers (2003). For a view of the combat from the traditional side, see the website of the most well-known anti-reform organization, Mathematically Correct (http://www.mathematicallycorrect.com/).

Simply put, the anti-reform forces in reading and mathematics grew strong at a time of the resurgence of the right wing in California politics. San Diego politician Pete Wilson had ridden "wedge politics" (appeals to the fears of the White middle-class voting majority regarding the rising populations and rights of minorities) to become mayor of San Diego. Wilson was a strong supporter of Proposition 187, a 1994 ballot initiative designed to deny illegal immigrants social services, health care, and public education. (The proposition won at the ballot box, with non-Latino Whites being the largest voting block in favor; it was later declared unconstitutional.) In 1996, California voters passed Proposition 209, which abolished affirmative action programs in public institutions (Office of Legislative Analysis, State of California, 1996). In 1998, voters passed Proposition 227, which "requires all public school instruction be conducted in English" (California Voter's Guide, 1998) and severely curtailed bilingual education.

The *Standards* represented a clear tilt toward the "democratic access" view of education. Advocates of reform believed in "mathematics for all"—in particular that it was possible to achieve excellence *and* equity, without sacrificing one for the other. There are many who believe that the goals of equity and excellence are in tension, and that making mathematics accessible to many more students necessarily entails "dumbing down" the mathematics. If one believes this, then two consequences of the democratization of mathematics as proposed by reform are (a) a weakening of the mathematical preparation of our best students, and a concomitant weakening of the nation's base of mathematically and scientifically prepared elite; and (b) a different demographic mix of those who are considered to be prepared for entry into elite institutions and professions. It is interesting to note that the first two major "anti-reform" organizations in California developed in Palo Alto (the organization was Honest Open Logical Debate [HOLD] on math reform, whose Web site is http://www.dehnbase.org/hold/), where the feared dumbing-down of curricula would threaten a record of success in placing students in elite institutions, and in the San Diego area (see http://mathematicallycorrect.com), where governor-to-be Wilson's wedge politics was developed.

This is not the place for a blow-by-blow description of the battles engaged and tactics used in the math wars; see the papers referenced in the first paragraph of this section for detail. Here we highlight some major events.

The routine revision of the California mathematics *Framework* began in late 1988 and was completed in 1991; the *Mathematics Framework for California Public Schools, Kindergarten through Grade 12* was published in 1992. The *Framework,* very much in the spirit of the *Standards,* catalyzed a backlash fomented by groups like those in Palo Alto and San Diego. The anti-reform movement gained steam with the help of newspaper columnists like the *San Francisco Chronicle's* Debra Saunders, whose columns bore titles like "New-New Math: Boot Licking 101" (March 13, 1995) and "Creatures from the New-New Math Lagoon" (September 20, 1995). Wilson-appointed California State Secretary of Child Development and Education Maureen DiMarco referred publicly to reform curricula as "fuzzy crap" (Ginsburg, 1997, p. 228). The California Assembly Education Committee held public hearings on the *Frameworks* in 1995 and 1996, forcing an early revision of the mathematics *Frameworks.* The state legislature enacted AB 170, which "requires the State Board of Education to ensure that the basic instructional materials it adopts for reading and mathematics in grades 1 to 8, inclusive, are based on the fundamental skills required by these subjects, including, but not limited to, systematic, explicit phonics, spelling, and basic computational skills" (see http://www.cde.ca.gov/board/readingfirst/exhibit-i.pdf).

As a result of pressure from the right, the state began the process of revising the mathematics *Framework* early. In violation of established practice, the State Board of Education overrode the recommendations of its curriculum commission and objections from the California Mathematics Council, altering the membership of the Curriculum Framework and Criteria Committee, whose task it was to revise the *Framework.*

The California Education Code (§ 60200c-3) requires that that state-adopted instructional materials "incorporate principles of instruction reflective of current and confirmed research." (California Education Code, 2008). The State Board of Education has an obligation, then, to make sure that the work it commissions is grounded in research. But which research?

> The Framework Committee Chair announced that E. D. Hirsch would speak to the board and urged committee members to attend since he would supply the research for the *Framework.* However, during the 8 months of meetings, the chair refused to allow discussion of research articles as agenda items, so at best, research was mentioned in incidental remarks during committee work. At the July meeting, when the Framework Committee was assembling its final draft, board member Janet Nichols announced that Professor Douglas Carnine from the University of Oregon would write the research basis for the document. (Jacob & Akers, 2003, p. 12)

Thus, from the universe of scholars who might inform the Board and the Committee about current research in mathematics education, the board solicited information from two: E. D. Hirsch, Jr. and Douglas Carnine. Hirsch, well known for his emphasis on "core knowledge," is not exactly central to mathematics education research. Becker and Jacob (2000) describe his appearance before the board:

> The state board invited E. D. Hirsch, Jr., to speak on this issue in April 1997. In the written version of his comments, Hirsch ridiculed "mainstream educational research," as found in "journals such as the *Educational Researcher*," explicitly stating, "This is a situation that is reminiscent of what happened to biology in the Soviet Union under the domination of Lysenkoism, which is a theory that bears similarities to constructivism ..."
>
> Citing math education experts John Anderson, David Geary, and Robert Siegler on the matter of what research shows that math students need, he goes on, "They would tell you that only through intelligently directed and repeated practice, leading to fast, automatic recall of math facts, and facility in computation and algebraic manipulation can one do well at real-world problem solving." (p. 535)

Hirsch, then, was openly contemptuous of mainstream educational research. Douglas Carnine's role was more problematic. The Board commissioned Carnine to write a review of the research in mathematics education, which would ultimately frame the criteria for textbook adoptions used by the state. (In California, school districts receive reimbursements for the purchase of textbooks that meet the criteria for adoption established by the Curriculum Framework and Criteria Committee.) Given that his research review would shape textbook adoption policy, it would seem obvious that Carnine, lead author of major programs of direct instruction in mathematics, had a conflict of interest. Nevertheless, he was the sole expert on research allowed to present evidence to the Curriculum Framework and Criteria Committee. Carnine's approach in framing his review was to accept only experimental research, thus enabling him to ignore almost all of the classroom and other research conducted over the past 20 years. Not surprisingly, the "Carnine report," as it is known (Dixon, Carnine, Lee, Walling, & Chard, 1998). focused on an out-of-date body of research that had little to say about current instructional practices, indicated that the kind of direct instruction Carnine favored was the only effective way to teach mathematics.

It should be noted that the experimental studies Carnine reviewed focused almost exclusively on skills-related outcomes, ignoring the kinds of problem solving and other process goals that were central to the newer curricula. Moreover, contemporary research, which includes experimental methods, shows that the skills level of students who emerge from standards-based curricula is on a par with the skills level of students who study from "traditional" curricula—and the students who emerge from standards-based curricula do far better on tests of problem solving and conceptual understanding than students who study from "traditional" curricula (see, e.g., ARC Center, 2003; Senk & Thompson, 2003).

The Standards Commission's draft was completed in 1997. By this time, however, conservatives held a majority of positions on the state board, and they used their power without restraint:

> At the request of two state board members, these [draft] standards were substantially revised by four Stanford University mathematics professors prior to their December approval. Although California's public meeting act requires that any committee of more than two appointed by a state board member must give public notice of its work sessions, the revisions were drafted in secret and were approved without input from K-12 educators or the public. (Becker & Jacob, 2000, p. 2)

There were attempts to address the board regarding the wisdom and propriety of its actions. Among many others, William Schmidt, who had conducted the mathematics component of the Third International Mathematics and Science Study (TIMSS), and Hyman Bass, chair of the National Research Council's Mathematical Sciences Education Board, wrote the state board to claim that both the process of revising the draft and the outcome of the revisions were travesties. The board ignored the criticisms (Schoenfeld, 2004).

The revised standards were a major nail in the coffin of reform. The next, equally large nail, was the process by which textbooks were reviewed for statewide adoption, using the criteria elaborated in the frameworks. There were significant irregularities in process: Jacob (1999) indicates that much more lax evaluation standards were applied to traditionalist texts than to reform texts. The bottom line is the list of state-adopted textbooks contained none of the reform text series. Thus, school districts across the state were reimbursed for their purchase of traditional texts, but they had to use their own funds to purchase "standards-based" materials. Finally, the state revised its high-stakes examination system, aligning it with the new mathematics standards. Given the extreme pressures to teach to the test—at one point the state offered large cash bonuses to teachers whose students did well on state tests, and now, under NCLB, schools ultimately face closure if students do not score well enough—it is extremely difficult for teachers, even if they are so inclined, to teach in ways consistent with reform.

The Issue of Balance   The situation in mathematics differs from the situation in reading. From 1995 on, traditionalists have had the upper hand within California, and they have seen no need to compromise. Some of Governor Wilson's most influential education advisors (e.g., Williamson Evers and David Klein) went on to become advisors to President Bush and are now influencing federal policy.

Changing Research Paradigms.   In mathematics as well as in reading, the zeitgeist has changed: With the creation of the Institute of Educational Sciences in the U.S. Department of Education, the current administration's emphasis has been on "scientifically based" educational research, which has been narrowly interpreted to mean experimental studies—preferably randomized controlled trials. IES established the What Works Clearinghouse to review the literature, and to summarize "what works"—but there are serious questions as to whether the Clearinghouse's work is indeed scientific (Schoenfeld, 2006a, 2006b; Herman, Boruch, Powell, Fleischman, & Maynard, 2006), and whether the administration has sanctioned ideologically driven policies under the cover of "science."

Measurable Results versus Political Positioning (and the Loss of the High Moral Ground)   At the time of the reading wars, there existed some reasonably robust data concerning the appropriate timing and use of phonics instruction. There was nothing analogous regarding reform mathematics. As noted above, data on failure rates, dropout rates, and overall lack of mathematical success provided motivation for the creation of standards-based materials. However, performance data played no role in the math wars. The wars reached their height in the mid- to late 1990s. At that time not a single cohort of students had emerged from a complete, "beta-version" standards-based curriculum; hence no rigorous data were available to assess the curricula's effectiveness. The wars themselves were fought on the basis of anecdote, with examples (e.g., letters from upset parents, complaints from mathematicians about errors in the texts, etc.) used to tar the whole standards-based approach. The traditionalists gained the high moral ground with regard to content (Do you want a return to the new math? Do you want kids who cannot add and subtract? Do you want kids to get credit for mechanical responses rather than for getting the right answer?) and with regard to the stringent, no-exceptions application of testing standards (So you think all kids should not be held to high standards? Which kids do you want to sacrifice?).[15]

Ironically, when the data did begin to come in, the reform approach was favored. The inescapable conclusion is that politics trumps research. That, alas, is a point of commonality between reading and mathematics.

Synthesis

There are similarities and differences in the stories of the reading and math wars. The differences pertain to the intellectual and instructional histories of the disciplines, and the availability of relevant data—that is, at the height of the reading wars there were data regarding the impact of various literacy practices, but those data were mostly sidelined by the political process, whereas there was little by way of relevant data during the height of the mathematics wars. However, there are far more similarities than differences.

The first set of similarities is political and ideological. In California and the nation, the same conservative forces have played a strong hand in enforcing what is, in essence, a "back to basics" agenda. Across the boards, the rhetoric has been lofty and the implementation brutal, with the results serving to reinforce the status quo.

The strong-handed tactics are clearly more visible in reading, thanks to the U.S. Office of the Inspector General's (2006) *Final Inspection Report* of the Reading First Program's grant application process. This blistering report describes the ways in which the program's actions, which channeled millions of federal dollars into states for the purchase of reading materials, was ideologically driven. Here are the conclusions of the report concerning the actions of the Department of Education:

Specifically, the report concluded that the department:

- Developed an application package that obscured the requirements of the statute;
- Took action with respect to the expert review panel process that was contrary to the balanced panel composition envisioned by Congress;
- Intervened to release an assessment review document without the permission of the entity that contracted for its development;
- Intervened to influence a State's selection of reading programs; and
- Intervened to influence reading programs being used by local educational agencies (LEAs) after the application process was completed.

These actions demonstrate that the program officials failed to maintain a control environment that exemplifies management integrity and accountability. (p. 2)

Where it was unable to control panels that produced results that, contrary to ideology, the Department of Education worked to either delay their publication or put a different spin on them after they were released—the history of the report of the National Reading Panel and the subsequent public dissemination of panel "results" are instructive in this regard.

Though not as dramatic in scope, the Department of Education has acted similarly in mathematics. Schoenfeld (2006a, 2006b) describes the ways in which the What Works Clearinghouse, at the behest of the Department of Education, attempted to suppress evidence contrary to the department's ideology. Of course, reading and mathematics are not isolated cases in this regard—the best documented long-running case of the administration's suppression of evidence in the service of ideology is denial of the reality of global warming and its attempts to suppress evidence that the phenomenon is real. What we have seen, first in California and then in Washington, DC, is a series of ideological moves that attempt to define both methods and outcomes in very narrow ways, claiming the rhetorical "high ground" (e.g., demanding "scientifically based research") while in fact acting in ways that violate the very principles of scientific research.

To establish the base for our final comments, we turn briefly to a discussion of the epistemological stances underlying current approaches to reading and mathematics instruction. We note that there is a fundamental epistemological similarity between "traditionalists" and "reformers" in both reading and mathematics, and a curious linkage between those intellectual values and some of the fault lines in both the reading and math wars.

One consequence of the cognitive revolution has been a reconceptualization of the very nature and purpose of learning as an act of sense-making. The traditional metaphor for learning is one of acquisition: One learns facts and procedures, masters vocabulary and skills, and so forth. Knowledge and skills are to be used in fixed ways. A prime exemplar of this perspective is E. D. Hirsch's "cultural literacy." According to Hirsch, one is culturally literate when one knows a particular body of information. His intellectual program, thus, is to provide a body of facts that people can master (see, e.g., Hirsch, Kett, & Trefil, 2002), and thus become culturally literate. Note the passive character of the learner in this enterprise: when the learner has ingested a certain body of knowledge (determined by others), the learner is declared to be literate.

This perspective contrasts dramatically with the current view of skills, be they literacy- or mathematics-related, as tools for sense-making. In the current conception of literacy, a major purpose of reading is being able to understand written information and argument, in order to take in that information, judge it using what one knows, reflect on it, and come to one's own conclusions about the topic at hand, with the text and the cultural models of our society as important ballasts in avoiding complete solipsism. The same is the case in mathematics: The ideas behind *modeling* and *problem solving* are that mathematics provides a wide array of tools with which one can interpret and understand real-world as well as purely symbolic phenomena. In both cases, knowledge is seen as empowering and the individual is seen as agentive.

It interesting to note that there are direct parallels between the active and passive epistemological stances described in this and the previous paragraph and the social positions described in the historical introduction to this chapter. The social efficiency stance toward education—the stance that that schools should serve the needs of the social and economic order by training students to occupy socially predetermined positions in society and the economy, and that the reproduction of the status quo is a desired outcome of the educational system—is entirely compatible with the epistemological stance that treats learners as passive and learning as the ingesting of a fixed body of knowledge. In contrast, education for democratic equality and social mobility are entirely compatible with an epistemological stance that treats individuals as agentive and knowledge as empowering.

That said, we can now see how the system works at present, to reinforce traditionalism and a form of social efficiency. The rhetoric of the No Child Left Behind Act, "high standards for all," is noble, but its implementation is something else altogether. In an era of high-stakes testing, a major curricular outcome is WYTIWYG—What You Test is What You Get. When students' academic careers, teachers' and administrators' jobs, and a school district's status all depend on test scores, then teaching to the test increasingly becomes the norm—in an interestingly differentiated way. In California, as in many states around the nation, standards and tests are relatively skills-oriented. As was discussed above, there is ample evidence that a balanced diet of skills, concepts, and problem solving in instruction produces respectable scores on skills, as well as positive outcomes with regard to concepts and problem solving. Thus, high-performing districts can continue with the kinds of rich instructional practices that have gotten them there, without worrying overmuch about skills. Low-performing districts face another picture altogether. Their very survival depends on improving skills, and skills become the almost exclusive focus of instruction. This phenomenon of differential curriculum has been documented in the 1980s and 1990s by Herman and her colleagues (Dorr-Bremme & Herman, 1983; Herman & Golan, 1991): Students in schools with lots of compensatory education programs are much more likely to have their daily curricular diet fed by test scores rather than the collective pedagogical imagination of the teaching staff, while just the opposite is true in schools with few compensatory education resources. For poor schools, in essence, the curriculum becomes test prep. And when it does, students are denied the kinds of critical thinking skills that are needed for social mobility. Examined from a somewhat different perspective, it is a conspiracy of good intentions that might be labeled the "basic skills conspiracy": First you have to get the words right and the facts (including number facts) straight before you can do the "what ifs" and "I wonder whats" of the school curriculum. And the conspiracy is that for many poor and initially low-achieving students, they spend their entire school careers getting the words right and the facts straight—and never get to the what ifs and I wonder whats. And we wonder why students leave our schools so ill-prepared to solve problems and critique the texts of politicians and advertisements of global business.

We should also note that test results can be deceptive. The question is, just what do improvements on a high-stakes test mean? The answer can be "not much." Haney (2000), for example, shows that significant increases on high-stakes accountability tests do not necessarily correlate with independent measures such as the National Assessment of Educational Progress. Thus, students who have been drilled to pass a particular test may learn the skills necessary to pass that test—but whether they have truly become better readers or gotten better at mathematics may be open to question.

Concluding Comments At present the right wing is in its ascendancy, and ideology seems to drive the policy agenda, under the cover of the rhetoric of "science." This agenda prizes a narrow band of experimental work, which if not properly executed, can itself be unscientific; it fails to recognize the complexities of both qualitative and quantitative research, and the contributions that each, properly employed, can make to the advancement of the educational enterprise (see Schoenfeld, 2007, for an extensive discussion of methodological issues). It is useful to note that educational research is not alone here. Other areas of research, most notably environmental research, have suffered similar treatment (Union of Concerned Scientists, 2008). Is there hope for those who believe in the potential of truly scientific base for educational policy, and for teaching and testing that focus on having students learn to think?

One cannot be overly optimistic, but a long-term view helps. Both of us have been involved in our respective research and curricular communities for several decades, and we recall various pendulum swings in the national policy zeitgeist. We highlight a few compelling examples. There was significant federal funding for educational R&D in mathematics and science following Sputnik in the 1960s, funding that vanished after the MACOS scandal and the "back to basics" movement. In the late 1970s, education flourished at NSF, with James Rutherford being asked by President Carter to build a 10-year plan for an investment in the nation's science and mathematics education. Rutherford worked on it from 1978 to 1980, only to have newly elected President Ronald Reagan line-item education out of the NSF budget soon after he took office. There were similar swings in reading policy: periods of optimism as chronicled by the Right to Read movement in the early 1970s, the reading research centers of the 1970s, 1980s, and 1990s, and increasing infusions of Title I resources into poor schools, alternating with pessimism and frustration at continued attempts by the field to resist a return to the basics of code-emphasis approaches. There was much sadness, and pessimism, among those who valued educational research—could things possibly get worse? In the 1990s, however, Congress began to fund education once again, and the research enterprise flowered. It did for some time, until the current repoliticization of the educational research and policy agenda. Today the policy environment is clearly hostile to the kinds of research that would best serve America's youth. But a long view suggests that this too shall pass.

Notes

1. Many would argue that the look-say approach, at least as enacted in the early part of the 20th century, was no more meaning-based than the alphabetic approach. However, as it evolved and became ensconced in the work of William S. Gray and the Curriculum Foundation Series, it was clearly meaning-based (see Chall, 1967).

2. For a compelling account of this "no text" phenomenon, see Schoenbach et al. (1999). In this account the staff developers and teachers of a middle school academic literacy course document the role of (or lack of a role for) text in middle school as well as attempts to turn the tide to help students tackle the texts that so often serve as their nemesis.

3. In 1989, a special interest group with the apocryphal label of Balanced Reading Instruction was organized at the International Reading Association. The group was started to counteract what they considered the unchecked acceptance of whole language as *the* approach to use with any and all students and to send the alternate message that there is no necessary conflict between authentic activity (usually considered the province of whole language) and explicit instruction of skills and strategies (usually considered the province of curriculum-centered approaches). For elaborate accounts of balanced literacy instruction, see Gambrell et al. (1999, 2003, 2007) and Pearson (1996).

4. As early as 1965, Kenneth Goodman had popularized the use of miscues to gain insights into cognitive processes. The elaborate version of miscue analysis first appeared in Y. Goodman and Burke (1972).

5. See Guthrie and Hall (1984) and Bloome and Greene (1984) for in-progress indices of the rising momentum of qualitative research in the early 1980s.

6. As a way of documenting this change, examine the *Handbook of Reading Research*, Volumes I and II (Pearson, Barr, Kamil, & Mosenthal, 1984; Barr, Kamil, Mosenthal, & Pearson, 1991). Volume I contains only two chapters that could be construed as relying on some sort of interpretive inquiry. Volume II has at least eight such chapters. For an account of these historical patterns in non-quantitative inquiry, see Siegel & Fernandez (2000).

7. Starting in the mid-1980s and continuing until today, the pages of *Educational Researcher* began to publish accounts of the qualitative-quantitative divide. It is the best source to consult in understanding the terms of the debate.

8. Allington and Woodside-Jiron (1998) document the manner in which an unpublished manuscript *30 Years of Research: What We Now Know About How Children Learn to Read* by Bonnie Grossen (1997), which is an alleged summary of the research sponsored by NICHD, was used in several states as the basis for reading policy initiatives.

9. At a meeting of the International Reading Association in 2006, S. Jay Samuels, one of the members of the NRP, announced that another criterion was at work in determining topics—the research interests of the panel members. This revelation suggests the strong possibility that some things did not get studied because no one on the panel found them compelling.

10. There have been three handbooks since 1984: Pearson, Barr, Kamil, and Mosenthal (1984); Barr, Kamil, Mosenthal, and Pearson (1991); and Kamil, Mosenthal, Pearson, and Barr (2000).

11. An interesting aside in all of the political rhetoric has been the question of who is de-skilling teachers. As early as the 1970s, whole language advocates were arguing that canned programs and basal reader manuals were de-skilling teachers by providing them with preprogrammed routines for teaching. In the ascendancy of phonics in the mid-1990s, whole language was accused of the de-skilling, by denying teachers access to technical knowledge needed to teach reading effectively (see McPike, 1995).

12. Starting in their sophomore year, students have multiple opportunities to take (and pass) the CAHSEE. However, despite strong statements from the American Educational Research Association (http://www.aera.net/policyandprograms/?id=378), the American Psychological Association (http://www.apa.org/releases/testing.html), the International Reading Association (http://www.reading.org/resources/issues/positions_high_stakes.html), the National Council of Teachers of English (http://www.ncte.org/about/over/positions/category/assess/107357.htm), and the National Council of Teachers of Mathematics (http://www.nctm.org/about/position_statements/highstakes.htm), that a single test should never be used by itself for "high-stakes" decisions, the California Department of Education has taken an uncompromising stance, going to the courts to bar alternative forms of certification of competence for possible graduates who had met all other graduation requirements besides the CAHSEE.

13. Schoenfeld served on the committee who wrote California's 1992 mathematics Standards. The most assiduous attendees of the committee's (open) meetings were publishers' representatives, who spoke with one voice: creating texts along the lines suggested by the *Standards* was not compatible with their development procedures, and was too great a risk fiscally to warrant undertaking.

14. A small number of curricula, including the *University of Chicago School Mathematics Project* and the *Interactive Mathematics Project*, predated the NSF curriculum RFPs. The vast majority of reform curricula were generated with the help of NSF funding.

15. As noted above, California has taken a "no exceptions" stance with regard to its dependence on one test for high school graduation. Lofty rhetoric is used to defend a policy that has serious consequences—often for children denied the resources to learn the skills they are being tested on.

References

Allington, R., & Woodside-Jiron, H. (1998). Decodable texts in beginning reading: Are mandates based on research? *ERS Spectrum, 16*(2), 3–11.

Anderson, R. C., Hiebert, E. H., Scott, J., & Wilkinson, I. (1984). *Becoming a nation of readers.* Champaign, IL: Center for the Study of Reading.

Apple, M. (1992). Do the standards go far enough? Power, policy, and practice in mathematics education. *Journal for Research in Mathematics Education, 23*, 412–431.

ARC Center. (2003). *The ARC Tri-State Student Achievement Study.* Lexington, MA: Author.

Barr, R., Kamil, M. L., Mosenthal, P., & Pearson, P. D. (Eds.). (1991). *Handbook of reading research, Vol. 2.* New York: Longman.

Becker, J., & Jacob, B. (2000). The politics of California school mathematics: The anti-reform of 1997–99. *Phi Delta Kappan, 81*, 527–539.

Bloome D., & Greene, J. (1984). Directions in the sociolinguistic study of reading. In P. D. Pearson, R. Barr, M. Kamil, & P. Mosenthal (Eds.), *Handbook of reading research* (pp. 394–421). New York: Longman.

Bond, G. L., & Dykstra, R. (1967). The cooperative research program in first-grade reading instruction. *Reading Research Quarterly, 2*(4), 5–142.

Bowler, M. (1998, August 9). Experts' bias complicates lesson debate. *Baltimore Sun,* p. 2B.

Brown, R. (1970). *Psycholinguistics: Selected papers by Roger Brown.* New York: Macmillan.

California Assembly. (1998). *Assembly Bill 1086: Reading Instruction.* Retrieved July 4, 2006, from http://www.leginfo.ca.gov/pub97-98/bill/asm/ab_1051-1100/ab_1086_bill_199708_chaptered.html

California Department of Education. (1987). *English-language arts framework for California public schools: Kindergarten through grade twelve.* Sacramento, CA: Author.

California Education Code. (2008). Retrieved June 18, 2008, from http://www.leginfo.ca.gov/cgi-bin/displaycode?section=edc&group=60001-61000&file=60200-60206

California Department of Education. (1992). *Mathematics framework for California public schools: Kindergarten through grade twelve.* Sacramento, CA: Author.

California Voter's Guide. (1998). *Official title and summary prepared by the attorney general: English language in public schools, Initiative statute.* Retrieved July 4, 2006, from http://primary98.sos.ca.gov/VoterGuide/Propositions/227.htm

Chairman's Staff of the U.S. Senate Health, Education, Labor, and Pensions Committee (2007, May 9). *The chairman's report on the conflicts of interest found in the implementation of Reading First at three regional technical assistance centers.* Retrieved May 12, 2008, from http://kennedy.senate.gov/imo/media/doc/CORRECTED%20reading%20first.pdf

Chall, J. (1967). *Learning to read: The great debate.* New York: McGraw-Hill.

Cognition and Technology Group at Vanderbilt. (1993). The Jasper series: Theoretical foundations and data on problem solving and transfer. In L. A. Penner, G. M. Batsche, H. M. Knoff, & D. L. Nelson (Eds.), *The challenge in mathematics and science education: Psychology's response* (pp. 113–152). Washington, DC: American Psychological Association.

Delpit, L. D. (1988) The silenced dialogue: Power and pedagogy in educating other people's children. *Harvard Educational Review, 58,* 280–297.

Dixon, R., Carnine, D. W., Lee, D.-S., Walling, J., & Chard, D. (1998). *Report to the California State Board of Education and addendum to principal report of high quality experimental mathematics research.* Eugene, OR: National Center to Improve the Tools of Educators.

Dorr-Bremme, D., & Herman, J. (1983). *Assessing student achievement: A profile of classroom practices.* Los Angeles: UCLA, Center for the Study of Evaluation.

Elson, W. H., & Gray, W. S. (1936). *Elson-Gray basic readers: Curriculum foundation series.* Chicago: Scott, Foresman.

Elson, W. H., & Keck, C. M. (1911). *The Elson readers, Book Five.* Chicago: Scott, Foresman.

Flesch, R. (1955). *Why Johnny can't read—and what you can do about it.* New York: Harper and Row.

Foorman, B. R., Francis, D. J., Fletcher, J. M., Schatschneider, C., & Mehta, P. (1998). The role of instruction in learning to read: Preventing reading failure in at-risk children. *Journal of Educational Psychology, 90,* 37–55.

Gambrell, L. B., Morrow, L. M., Newman, S. B., & Pressley, M. (Eds.). (1999). *Best practices in literacy instruction.* New York: Guilford.

Gambrell, L. B., Morrow, L. M., Newman, S. B., & Pressley, M. (Eds.). (2003). *Best practices in literacy instruction* (2nd ed.). New York: Guilford.

Gee, J. P. (1988). The legacies of literacy: From Plato to Freire through Harvey Graff. *Harvard Educational Review, 58,* 195–212.

Ginsburg, H. P. (1997). *Entering the child's mind.* Cambridge, UK: Cambridge University Press.

Glenn, D. (2006). High-school exit exams are associated with higher dropout rates, researchers find. *The Chronicle of Higher Education, 52*(45), A. 14.

Good, T., & Braden, (2000). Reform in American education: A focus on vouchers and charters. Mahweh, NJ: Erlbaum .

Goodman, K. S. (1967). Reading: A psycholinguistic guessing game. *Journal of the Reading Specialist, 6,* 126–135.

Goodman, Y. M., & Burke, C. L. (1972). *Reading miscue inventory manual procedure for diagnosis and evaluation.* New York: Macmillan.

Grossen, B. (1997). *30 years of research: What we now know about how children learn to read.* Santa Cruz, CA: The Center for the Future of Teaching and Learning.

Guthrie, L. F., & Hall, W. S. (1984). Ethnographic approaches to reading research. In P. D. Pearson (Ed.), *Handbook of reading research* (pp. 91–110). New York: Longman.

Haney, W. (2000, August 19). The myth of the Texas miracle in education. *Education Policy Analysis Archives, 8*(41). Retrieved June 11, 2008, from http://epaa.asu.edu/epaa/v8n41/part1.htm

Havighurst, R. (1972). *Developmental tasks and education* (3rd ed.). New York: McKay.

Heath, S. B. (1983). *Ways with words: Language, life, and work in communities and classrooms.* New York: Cambridge University Press.

Herman, J., & Golan, S. (1991). *Effects of standardized testing on teachers and learning—another look* (CSE Technical Report no. 334). Los Angeles: Center for the Study of Evaluation.

Herman, R., Boruch, R., Powell, R., Fleischman, S., & Maynard, R. (2006). Overcoming the challenges: A response to Alan H. Schoenfeld's "What doesn't work." *Educational Researcher, 35*(2), 22–23.

Hirsch, E., Jr., Kett, J., & Trefil, J. (2002). *The new dictionary of cultural literacy: What every American needs to know* (3rd ed.). New York: Houghton-Mifflin.

Holme, J. H., & Rogers, J. (2005, May). *UCLA/IDEA research brief: Are California high schools ready for the exit exam?* Retrieved July 1, 2006, from http://www.idea.gseis.ucla.edu/publications/exitexam3/pdf/HumRROResponse.pdf

Improving America's Schools Act of 1994, Pub. L. No. 103-382, 108 Stat. 3518.

Jackson, A. (1997a). The math wars: California battles it out over mathematics education, Part 1. *Notices of the American Mathematical Society, 44,* 695–702.

Jackson, A. (1997b). The math wars: California battles it out over mathematics education, Part 2. *Notices of the American Mathematical Society, 44,* 817–823.

Jacob, B. (1999). Instructional materials for K-8 mathematics classrooms: The California adoption, 1997. In E. Gavosto, S. Krantz, & W. McCallum (Eds.), *Contemporary issues in mathematics education* (Mathematical Sciences Research Institute Publications 36, pp. 109–122). Cambridge, UK: Cambridge University Press.

Jacob, B. (2001). Implementing standards: The California mathematics textbook debacle. *Phi Delta Kappan, 83,* 264–272.

Jacob, B., & Akers, J. (2003). *Research-based mathematics education policy: The case of California 1995–1998.* Retrieved on June 27, 2003, from Exeter University, Centre for Innovation in Mathematics Teaching Web site http://www.cimt.plymouth.ac.uk/journal/bjcalpol.pdf

Jones, P. S., & Coxford, A. F., Jr. (1970). Mathematics in the evolving schools. In P. S. Jones (Ed.), *A history of mathematics education in the United States and Canada* (pp. 11–92). Washington, DC: National Council of Teachers of Mathematics.

Kamil, M., Mosenthal, P., Pearson, P. D., & Barr, R. (Eds.). (2000). *Handbook of reading research, Vol. 3*. Mahwah, NJ: Erlbaum.

Klein, D. (2003). *A brief history of American K-12 mathematics education in the 20th century*. Retrieved July 1, 2003, from http://www.csun.edu/~vcmth00m/AHistory.html

Lee, J. (2002). Racial and ethnic achievement gap trends: Reversing the progress towards equity? *Educational Researcher, 31*(1), 3–12.

Lyon, G. R. (1995). Research initiatives in learning disabilities: Contributions from scientists supported by the National Institute of Child Health and Human Development. *Journal of Child Neurology, 10*, 120–126.

Lyon, G. R., & Chhabra, V. (1996). The current state of science and the future of specific reading disability. *Mental Retardation and Developmental Disabilities Research Reviews, 2*, 2–9.

Madison, B., & Hart, T. (1990). *A challenge of numbers: People in the mathematical sciences*. Washington, DC: National Academy Press.

Manzo, K. K. (1997). Study stresses role of early phonics instruction. *Education Week, 16*(24), 1, 24–25.

Manzo, K. K. (1998a). New national reading panel faulted before it's formed. *Education Week, 17*(23), 7.

Manzo, K. K. (1998b). NRC panel urges end to reading wars. *Education Week, 17*(28), 1, 18.

McPike, E. (1995). Learning to read: Schooling's first mission. *American Educator, 19*, 3–6.

Moses, R. P., & Cobb, C. E., Jr. (2001). *Radical equations: Math literacy and civil rights*. Boston: Beacon Press.

Myers, M., & Pearson, P. D. (1996). Performance assessment and the literacy unit of the New Standards Project. *Assessing Writing, 3*, 5–29.

National Commission on Excellence in Education. (1983). *A nation at risk: The imperative for educational reform*. Washington, DC: U. S. Government Printing Office.

National Council of Teachers of Mathematics (NCTM). (1980). *An agenda for action: Recommendations for school mathematics of the 1980s*. Reston, VA: Author.

National Council of Teachers of Mathematics (NCTM). (1989). *Curriculum and evaluation standards for school mathematics*. Reston, VA: Author.

National Education Goals Panel. (2001, June). *High school completion rates stay level despite rising academic standards*. Retrieved June 28, 2006, from http://govinfo.library.unt.edu/negp/issues/publication/othpress/rel0601.pdf

National Institute of Child Health and Human Development (NICHD). (2000). *Report of the National Reading Panel, Teaching children to read: An evidence-based assessment of the scientific research literature on reading and its implications for reading instruction—Reports of the subgroups*. Washington, DC: Author.

National Research Council. (2000). *How people learn: Brain, mind, experience, and school* (Expanded edition). Washington, DC: National Academy Press.

No Child Left Behind Act of 2001, Pub. L. No. 107-110, 115 Stat. 1425. (2002).

Office of Legislative Analysis, State of California. (1996). *Analysis of Proposition 209 by the Legislative Analyst*. Downloaded June 18, 2008, from http://vote96.sos.ca.gov/BP/209analysis.htm

Pearson, P. D. (1996). Reclaiming the center. In M. Graves, P. van den Broek, & B. M. Taylor (Eds.), *The first R: Every child's right to read* (pp. 259–274). New York: Teachers College Press.

Pearson, P. D. (2004). The reading wars: The politics of reading research and policy, 1988 through 2003. *Educational Policy, 18*, 216–252.

Pearson, P. D., Barr, R., Kamil, M. L., & Mosenthal, P. (Eds.). (1984). *Handbook of reading research*. New York: Longman.

Pearson, P. D., & Stephens, D. (1993). Learning about literacy: A 30-year journey. In C. J. Gordon, G. D. Labercane, & W. R. McEachern

(Eds.), *Elementary reading: Process and practice* (pp. 4–18). Boston: Ginn Press.

Reading Excellence Act of 1999, Pub. L. No. 105-277 (1999).

Reyes, M. d. l. L. (1992). Challenging venerable assumptions: Literacy instruction for linguistically different students. *Harvard Educational Review, 62*, 427–446.

Rosen, L. (2000). *Calculating concerns: The politics or representation in California's "math wars."* Unpublished doctoral dissertation, University of California, San Diego.

Rosenblatt, L. (1978). *Literature as exploration* (3rd ed.). New York: Appleton Century Croft.

Samuels, S. J. (2006, May). *No Child Left Behind: A panel discussion*. Panel comments presented at the annual conference of the Internatonal Reading Association, Chicago.

Saunders, D. (1995, February 1). There is no one answer. *San Francisco Chronicle*, p. A-21.

Schoenbach, R., Greenleaf, C., Cziko, C., & Hurwitz, L. (1999). *Reading for understanding: A guide to improving reading in middle and high school classrooms*. San Francisco: Jossey-Bass.

Schoenfeld, A. H. (1985). *Mathematical problem solving*. Orlando, FL: Academic Press.

Schoenfeld, A. H. (1994). What do we know about mathematics curricula? *Journal of Mathematical Behavior, 13*(1), 55–80.

Schoenfeld, A. H. (2004). The math wars. *Educational Policy, 18*, 253–286.

Schoenfeld, A. H. (2006a). Reply to comments from the What Works Clearinghouse on "What doesn't work." *Educational Researcher, 35*(2), 23.

Schoenfeld, A. H. (2006b). What doesn't work: The challenge and failure of the What Works Clearinghouse to conduct meaningful reviews of studies of mathematics curricula. *Educational Researcher, 35*(2), 13–21.

Schoenfeld, A. H. (2007). Method. In F. Lester (Ed.), *Handbook of research on mathematics teaching and learning* (2nd ed., pp. 69–107). Charlotte, NC: Information Age.

Senk, S., & Thompson, D. (Eds.). (2003). *Standards-oriented school mathematics curricula: What does the research say about student outcomes?* Mahwah, NJ: Erlbaum.

Siegel, M., & Fernandez, S. L. (2000). Critical approaches. In M. Kamil, P. Mosenthal, P. D. Pearson, & R. Barr (Eds.), *Handbook of reading research, Vol. 3* (pp. 141–152). Mahwah, NJ: Erlbaum.

Silver, E. A. (1996). Moving beyond learning alone and in silence: Observations from the QUASAR project concerning communication in mathematics classrooms. In L. Schauble & R. Glaser (Eds.), *Innovations in learning: New environments in education* (pp. 127–160). Mahwah, NJ: Erlbaum.

Smith, F. (1971). *Understanding reading: A psycholinguistic analysis of reading and learning to read*. New York: Holt, Rinehart, and Winston.

Snow, C. E. (2001). Preventing reading difficulties in young children: Precursors and fallout. In T. Loveless (Ed.), *The great curriculum debate* (pp. 484–504). Washington, DC: Brookings Institution.

Snow, C., Burns, S., & Griffin, P. (Eds.). (1998). *Preventing reading difficulties in young children*. Washington, DC: National Academy Press.

Stanic, G. M. A. (1987). Mathematics education in the United States at the beginning of the twentieth century. In T. S. Popkewitz (Ed.), *The formation of school subjects: The struggle for creating an American institution* (pp. 145–175). New York: Falmer Press.

Thorndike. E. L. (1910). The contribution of psychology to education. *Journal of Educational Psychology, 1*, 5–12.

Tough, P. (November 26, 2006). What it takes to make a student. *New York Times Magazine*. Retrieved June 18, 2008, from http://www.nytimes.com/2006/11/26/magazine/26tough.html?_r=1&oref=slogin

Union of Concerned Scientists. (2008). *Scientific integrity: Examples of political interference in science*. Retrieved May 19, 2008, from http://www.ucsusa.org/scientific_integrity/interference/a-to-z-alphabetical.html

U.S. Census Bureau. (April 22, 2004). *Facts for Features*. Retrived June

18, 2008, from http://www.census.gov/Press-Release/www/releases/ archives/facts_for_features_special_editions/001737.html

U.S. Department of Education, Office of the Inspector General. (2006, September). *The Reading First Program's grant application process final inspection report* ED-OIG/I13-F0017. Washington, DC: Author.

U.S. Department of State. (2008). *Principles of democracy: Education and democracy*. Retrieved April 23, 2008, from http://usinfo.state. gov/products/pubs/principles/education.htm

Wikipedia. (2008). *American dream*. Retrieved April 23, 2008, from http:// en.wikipedia.org/wiki/American_Dream

46

Language Policy in Education

PATRICIA GÁNDARA
University of California, Los Angeles

M. CECILIA GÓMEZ
University of California, Davis

Language, in its varied forms—spoken, written, understood, articulated verbally, through signs, or in body language—in many ways defines who we are and allows us to, in turn, define the world. It certainly shapes our personal identity and has implications for how others see us (Ryan & Carranza, 1977; Schmidt, 2000). Thus, it should be no surprise that it is a hotly contested area both in education and in politics. And sometimes the two overlap greatly. Whose language is to be taught? Whose linguistic variety constitutes the "standard" for a given idiom? Shall a particular language be the *medium of instruction* or shall it be solely an object of instruction? This latter question has been at the center of bitter debates and considerable legislation in the United States, most prominently represented in the "bilingual wars" that have been waged in a number of states and within the U.S. Department of Education over how English Learners should best be educated. However, as Tollefson and Tsui (2004) point out, the debate is about much more than effective pedagogical strategies; it is in fact about social, political, and economic hegemony. The issue of which language will be used to test and assess students also gives rise to considerable controversy, as it often dictates the language of instruction as well as signaling which language(s) will be valued in society. The stakes are high for such policies as decisions about which language(s) may be taught or used for public purposes carry important social and economic consequences for both groups and individuals. The rapid growth of language minority populations in the United States (and in the rest of the developed world) has lent particular urgency to this policy area.[1]

A clear definition of *language policy*, however, remains elusive. Because the field of language policy and planning (LPP) is relatively new, a consensus on its definition has not yet been attained. Crawford (2000) defines language policy as:

(1) what government does officially—through legislation, court decisions, executive action, or other means—to (a)

determine how languages are used in public contexts, (b) cultivate language skills needed to meet national priorities, or (c) establish the rights of individuals or groups to learn, use, and maintain language, and (2) government regulation of its own language use, including steps to facilitate clear communication, train and recruit personnel, guarantee due process, foster political participation, and provide access to public services, proceedings, and documents. (¶ 1)

Crawford thus understands language policy as largely political activity. For Ricento (as cited in Herriman & Burnaby, 1996), language policy is also an instrument of social control. Tollefson (2002), in turn, views language policy as "the roles of government and other powerful institutions in shaping language use and language acquisition" (p. 3). The United States, a nation without a formal language policy, has nevertheless promulgated a number of specific language policies in education.

Ruiz (1984) suggested three ways or orientations by which policy makers conceptualize language planning. Ruiz defines orientations as "a complex of dispositions toward language and its role, and toward languages and their role in society" (p. 16), and he argues that these orientations are, in fact, what drive the formulation of language policy in education. Regarding the first of these orientations, *language-as-problem,* Ruiz asserts that the bulk of writing on language policy in multilingual settings has been concerned with the notion of identification and resolution of language problems caused by the presence of more than one language in the society. Policies that result from this orientation are generally remedial with the goal of moving students from their native language into the dominant language.

The second orientation is *language-as-right,* in which the right to use one's language in activities of communal life and the right not to be discriminated against because of language are asserted. He further argues that, while this orientation is important in securing civil rights for linguistic minorities, it does little to promote thoughtful language planning in education. The third orientation, that of *language-as-resource*, is, according to Ruiz, acknowledged in U.S. society, and periodic concerns are voiced about the need for fluent multilinguals to promote business, commerce, and international cooperation, but there is little acknowledgement that language planning and policy in the U.S. is fundamentally at war with those aims. Very little support has been voiced in federal or state policies for maintaining the non-English languages that exist in the United States. In fact, with the exception of a brief period in the 1970s, and later in the mid-1990s, when there was official support for *maintenance* bilingual education as the preferred method, the emphasis has been on *transitional* bilingual education, that is, use of the primary language only until it can be replaced by English, and that should occur as quickly as possible.

U.S. Language Policy—A Brief History

During British rule, English was established as the dominant language through what Wiley and Wright (2004) term "language status achievement." They argue that English was used as a tool of social control and as a means of maintaining the social and economic advantage of the English settlers over, for instance, the native populations; since then, it has always operated as if it were the official language. Nevertheless, a laissez-faire government policy towards language education allowed non-English speaking immigrant groups to use and teach their languages, for the most part without government intrusion (Crawford, 1999, 2000, 2004). For example, German communities were able to print German-language newspapers and teach their children in German at private or parochial schools. However, the beginning of the 20th century saw the first federal language law requiring English proficiency to gain naturalization and citizenship (1906). Subsequent to this, and until the end of World War I, legislation was passed in several states to establish English as the official language of instruction. Amid an increasing climate of xenophobia, brought on by economic tensions and World War I, tight immigration quotas soon followed in the 1920s, which generally set a preference for Northwestern European immigrants who were viewed as more easily assimilated than other groups. Overall, the period from the late 1890s to the mid-1920s was notably one of anti-immigration sentiment (Del Valle, 2003).

A small reversal in this trend was found in the Supreme Court decision, *Meyer v. Nebraska* (1923), in which Robert Meyer, a Nebraska parochial high-school teacher had been dismissed from his job for teaching German in an English-only state. The justices affirmed the right of teachers to have control over their own curriculum and the right of parents to make decisions about what their children would be taught, and removed the most extreme limitations on foreign language instruction, citing a violation of Due Process in the 14th Amendment. Scholars have questioned, however, whether the courts would provide similar protections for teachers in publicly supported schools (Del Valle, 2003). It was not until 1974 that another case reached the Supreme

Court that would spell out students' rights to access education regardless of their primary language. *Lau v. Nichols* (1974) recognized the right of linguistic minority students to have access to the same education as English-speaking students, and that it was incumbent upon the schools to facilitate that access through whatever effective means they chose, including bilingual education.

With respect to federal intervention on behalf of racial and linguistic minorities, Title VI of the Civil Rights Act (1964) was, and continues to be, the most important legislation ever passed. Title VI is particularly important as it prohibits discrimination in government programs or programs receiving federal funds. This was followed closely by the passage of the Elementary and Secondary Education Act (ESEA) in 1965, of which Title VII (added in 1968), also known as the Bilingual Education Act (BEA), represented the first official federal bilingual education policy in the United States. Although titled "bilingual," it did not initially stipulate that schools had to offer instruction in a language other than English in order to receive federal funds. Still, it opened the doors to bilingual education. With all its importance in matters of bilingual education, the BEA's focus was mostly on eliminating poverty among poor, "deprived," limited-English children. Its philosophy was not connected to the development of additive bilingualism, rather, it was a good example of the instrumental approach to language education that ascribes learning deficits to use of the mother tongue and supports the assimilation of minority groups to the majority culture (Churchill, as cited in May, 2001). In fact, for political reasons, the prime sponsor of the BEA, Senator Ralph Yarborough of Texas, left the aim of the legislation purposely vague, telling his fellow lawmakers:

> It is not the purpose of the bill to create pockets of different languages throughout the country … not to stamp out the mother tongue, and not to make their mother tongue the dominant language, but just to try to make those children fully literate in English. (Crawford, 2004, p. 107)

Bilingual education, inextricably associated with the "war on poverty" legislation, was, from the beginning, largely a compensatory program to remediate the language deficits of limited English speakers.

The Lau Remedies (1975) and the Lau Compliance Reviews, promulgated by the U.S. Department of Education, followed soon after the Lau decision, and provided the regulatory framework for its implementation. The Lau Remedies established how school districts should assess and instruct English Learners (ELs) and required schools to offer bilingual education to students who were not proficient in English when it could be demonstrated that their civil rights had been violated. Even though the Remedies, which were widely viewed as supporting primary language maintenance, were guidelines and lacked the legal status of federal regulations, in the political environment of the mid-1970s and following on Lau, they were rigorously enforced by the Office for Civil Rights (OCR).

The end of the 1970s and the 1980s saw an increase

in opposition to bilingual education. In 1978, Title VII was reauthorized and the amendments excluded the native language maintenance component of the bilingual programs. Federal funding would support only transitional bilingual programs and there was an increase in seats for English speakers, ostensibly to serve as language models for English Learners. By the early 1980s, the growth of the foreign-born population, especially of Spanish speakers, and the challenges faced by non-English speaking minorities met with the rise of conservative forces in the U.S. government and in groups such as the English-only movement. The movement redefined bilingual education as a barrier to cultural assimilation and citizen participation and successfully lobbied for the closure of bilingual education programs in several states. It put forth a series of arguments for English-only education: (a) that language diversity can lead a nation into ethnic and political conflict and separation (erroneously likened to that of Canada with Quebec), (b) that the English language is the "social glue" that unites all Americans, and (c) that the new immigrants refused to learn English and were not assimilating as fast as those before them (Crawford, 2004). The English-only movement had anti-immigration and nativist political goals that were similar to those of the Americanization movement of the early 20th century (Wiley & Wright, 2004).

Starting in 1981, the English-only movement, led by a former senator from California, S. I. Hayakawa, and a Michigan physician, John Tanton, who had founded an anti-immigration lobby, tried to introduce several constitutional amendments to make English the official language of the country. Even though they were unsuccessful at the federal level, up to 23 states passed similar measures (Wiley & Wright, 2004). Their political agenda was incorporated into the policy of the Reagan administration and, in 1984, the BEA was reauthorized with modest funding for developmental bilingual and a guarantee that, at least 25% of funds would be allocated to "special alternative" (all-English) programs (Crawford, 2004).

The anti-bilingual and anti-multicultural tenor of the times continued to build through the 1980s and 1990s, with increasing immigration, rising numbers of English Learners, and a "close the borders" mentality gripping the nation. Arthur Schlesinger, Jr., a well-known historian and self-admitted political liberal, sounded an alarm in 1991 with the publication of *The Disuniting of America: Reflections on a Multicultural Society*. In that volume he lamented that, with the new immigration of the 20th century, "a cult of ethnicity had erupted" whose only result can be "the fragmentation, resegregation, and tribalization of American life" (p. 21), and that "institutionalized bilingualism remains another source of the fragmentation of America" (p. 109). Multiculturalism, anathema to the political Right, was linked with bilingual education by an avowed spokesman of the political Left. With the Democrats moving away from support of the bilingual education legislation, the future of federal policy was bound to shift.

In 1994, Title VII of ESEA, newly named Improving America's School Act (IASA), was reauthorized, and this time the cap on English-only programs was effectively removed. Any district that claimed it could not mount a bilingual program was authorized to proceed with English only. Nevertheless, the 1994 legislation signaled a new, more positive attitude toward primary language instruction and a preference for programs that served to conserve native languages and expand bilingualism was once again established, however briefly. With the reauthorization of the legislation under the new title of No Child Left Behind in 2001, all references to any bilingual instruction were removed. The former Office of Bilingual Education was renamed the Office of English Language Acquisition, Language Enhancement, and Academic Achievement for Limited English Proficient Students. The eradication of any mandate to support the development of native language, or support academic instruction through the native language, was complete (Gándara, Moran, & García, 2004).

In the meantime, during the 1990s a new state-level movement was underway, financed by a wealthy would-be politician from California's Silicon Valley. Ron Unz spearheaded the movement against primary language as medium of instruction that began with the passage of Proposition 227 (English for the Children) in California in 1998, and then moved to Arizona and Massachusetts. Proposition 227 made English-only instruction in "structured immersion" classes "not normally to last more than one year" the default instruction for all English Learners. Anything else required an elaborate waiver process that proved difficult to mount for many families and communities, and ultimately reduced the percentage of students receiving bilingual education in California from about 30% of all EL students to less than 6% by 2007 (California Department of Education, 2008). In 2000, Arizona voters chose to replace bilingual education with intensive, English-only instruction in public schools with the adoption of Proposition 203, and by 2007 bilingual instruction had been virtually eradicated from the state.[2] Massachusetts, the first state to enact bilingual education more than 30 years ago, rejected it with the approval of Question 2 in 2002. It has been pointed out that state referenda may not be the best way to shape language policy and other complex issues that the public cannot possibly be sufficiently informed about (Herriman & Burnaby, 1996). The trend was not the same throughout the states, though. Supporters of bilingual education organized English-Plus responses and some states (i.e., New Mexico, Oregon, and Washington) declared themselves to be multilingual during that same period.

Romero-Little and McCarty (2006) point out that:

> Of 210 Native languages still spoken in the U.S. and Canada, only 34 (16 percent) are still being acquired as a first language by children. Unlike "world" languages, such as Spanish, Indigenous languages have no external pool of speakers to replace dwindling speech communities; the loss of an Indigenous language is terminal. (p. 3)

There have been several efforts to reverse the loss of native, immigrant, and refugee languages (a.k.a., heritage languages). In the 1980s, many Native American Nations adopted policies to encourage the use of their languages in reservation schools and in other community activities, and the approval of the Native American Language Act in 1990 by the U. S. Congress was an important, although largely symbolic, step in the protection of these linguistic resources (Crawford, 1999; Wiley, 2005). The NCLB of 2001, however, has posed new challenges to Native American communities as high-stakes testing in English has placed heavy counter pressures on heritage language programs attempting to rescue their languages (Wright, 2007).

In the late 1990s, a heritage language movement emerged, and the first national conferences on heritage languages were held in the United States (in 1999 and 2002), thereby leading the way to a series of publications, formal policy statements, and an online journal on heritage language teaching. The movement has been key in the development of specific programs in schools, such as the Spanish-for-heritage-speakers educational programs, as well as in differentiating and addressing the particular needs of heritage and foreign-language learners. In the post-9/11 world, calls from language educators and native communities for increased attention to the language rights of heritage speakers have coincided with the national defense interest in a number of strategically important languages (e.g., Arabic, Farsi), as well as diplomatic and business interest in more and better linguistic resources among the U.S. population. However, no "macro" language policy and no funding provisions have supported the development of heritage languages. Furthermore, Cummins (2005) considers that no large-scale policy changes for heritage languages are in view in the near future, especially considering that NCLB only assesses yearly progress in English. In fact, the accountability and high-stakes testing provisions of NCLB have, at a minimum, discouraged the implementation of several quality heritage language programs and, at worst, seriously weakened or eliminated many of them, although there is no evidence that the dismantling of heritage language programs helps English learners acquire English faster (Wright, 2007).

In sum, the development of language policy in U.S. education has been characterized by contestation, accommodation, and controversy (San Miguel, 2004). The U.S. approach to language policy in education during the 20th and the early 21st centuries has encompassed an orientation to English-only, a drive for cultural uniformity, and the accommodation to the language rights of some minority groups, but with a notable lack of fiscal and policy support for maintaining heritage languages. The United States has no formal overarching language policy, only language policies in education, and these have been ad hoc rather than systematically designed and implemented (Crawford, 2004). Because language is the primary vehicle for instruction in school, educational policies often directly and indirectly invoke the issue of language use, and language policy, as it affects youth, will almost inevitably intersect with education policies. The two, while they may be developed independently, are closely related. For example, policies about academic standards (education policy) need to clarify in which languages a student may be considered to have met the standards; policies about instruction of a second or other languages (language policy) should specify what is to be taught through these languages. Here we focus on the development and diffusion of language policies in educational contexts, primarily school.

How do Language Policies Vary among Nations?

While the United States has been undergoing dramatic demographic transformations, resulting in very large increases in speakers of languages other than English, so too have many other parts of the world. Almost all nations are multi-ethnic and most other nations are more multilingual than the United States (Schmidt, 2000). Almost all incorporate multiple languages within their borders, and while most have a *de facto* official language, most European nations have language policies that tolerate and encourage the acquisition and use of multiple languages, as do many other nation-states (Dicker, 2003).

Inasmuch as language policy can be applied to many facets of life—workplace, voting, education, governmental functions and services—policies may evolve in some areas and not in others. For example, some nations regulate the teaching of multiple languages, but do not regulate their use in the workplace (Dicker, 2003). Language policy in other nations reaches into the spoken and written forms of the national or regional language, as in France and Spain, where an official body is charged with judging and policing language correctness. There is no such body equivalent to the Real Academia Española or the Académie Française in the United States that regulates the use of the English language. Nevertheless, there are frequent complaints by linguistic nationalists that "standard English" be taught without consideration of regional or ethnic dialects/varieties. A case in point is the brouhaha created by the Oakland Unified School District when in 1996 it sought to teach Ebonics in an effort to bridge the gap, and acknowledge the existence, of two forms of English spoken by African Americans in that community. The issue created a national firestorm, and attempts were made to oust the school board members who voted for the policy; yet there is some research evidence that such an approach can, indeed, foster stronger standard English skills (Rickford & Rickford, 1995). An interesting twist on this attempt to incorporate Ebonics into the English curriculum, however, was the school board's reference to the federal Bilingual Education Act and the appropriateness of extending these resources to Black children who they characterized as bilingual. Some saw this as an attempt to move resources targeted to the Latino and Asian communities to other purposes. Thus the policy, which was quickly abandoned, was politically explosive on a number of fronts—pitting the African American community against other minorities as well as the standard English-speaking White majority.

Migration, political changes, and internationalization and globalization dynamics, among other forces, play an important role in the development of language policies. As Suárez-Orozco and Suárez-Orozco (1995) have pointed out, migration is historically the norm—people move to better their circumstances and improve their chances of survival. There have also been important political realignments over the last several decades that have resulted in greater multilingualism in various parts of the world. English has grown in world importance and there are now more speakers of English as a second language than native speakers of English (Wiley, 2007). This fact can give rise to a certain smugness on the part of English speakers that there is no need to speak other languages if the rest of the world learns English. However, there is a danger in this position, since most of the rest of the world will speak English *plus* one or more other languages, while Americans remain limited to a monolingual world. Much can be learned from the experiences of other nations in crafting language policy that serves their social and economic needs and respects the language rights of their minority language groups.

Spolsky (2004, p. 60) presents a model (see Table 46.1) that correlates states with their perceptions and ideologies about how to manage language. His model encompasses monolingual, bi/trilingual, and multilingual polities. Although several modern states have constitutionally declared themselves to be monolingual, different language groups are present in their territory. In fact, scholars note that true monolingual polities are by far the exception in sociolinguistic terms. Bilingual and trilingual polities (e.g., Canada, Singapore, Switzerland, South Africa, Paraguay, Belgium) partition their linguistic space based on historical, political, and social/ethnic considerations. Multilingual and supranational polities include mosaic polities (e.g., India, South Africa) and entities such as the European Union (EU).

At the multilingual end we find nations that tend to accommodate to various types of cultural and linguistic diversity, multiculturalism, and multilingualism. For that purpose, they have developed more pluralist and inclusive language policies (e.g., India) than the more assimilationist and restrictive ones found at the monolingual end. Polities with monolingual ideologies, although oftentimes multilingual in practice, have generally adopted state monolingualism in their language-related practices and sometimes in their Constitution. Historically, these nations' ethnocentric views can be found in their restrictive and/or assimilationist language policies towards groups that speak other languages. Japan offers an example of such a state. In Japan, the notions of nation, state, and language meant the same thing for a long time. Although Japan has ethnic minorities, it has operated under the ideology of ethnolinguistic and social homogeneity typical of monolingual states. There is agreement in the literature that language policies created under the nation-state ideology (one nation = one language) have become increasingly problematic. As Spolsky (2004) points out, not only are monolingual polities in ideology and practice quite rare, but they also generally face more pressure from both their multilingual reality and that introduced by international migration and globalization.

Bilingual or trilingual polities (e.g., Canada, Singapore, Switzerland, Paraguay) partition their linguistic space in two or more languages based on historical, political, and social/ethnic considerations. Since their realities and ideologies are different and complex, these polities vary in how they grant language rights to regional and minority speech communities at the national level. They generally use one of two principles: the "territorial language principle" (e.g., Quebec, Switzerland, Belgium, and Catalonia in Spain) and the "personality language principle" (Canada—outside Quebec, South Africa, and India). The territorial language principle has been most used by bi/trilingual polities for their autochthonous (indigenous) groups. It grants "legally exclusive rights to a specific language within a precisely defined territory" (Wise, 2006, p. 2) and aims to protect a single linguistic community. Minorities that move to regions that operate under this principle generally need to learn and use the language of the territory in the public space. On the other hand, the personality language principle "grants language rights to individuals irrespective of their geographical location within a state territory" (Wise, 2006, p. 3). Theoretically, these rights follow individuals as they move from one linguistic region to another. For instance, outside of Quebec, French-speaking Canadians can claim French-language services from the federal government notwithstanding their location. In practice, however, such

TABLE 46.1

Models of Language Planning

Type	Attitude	Ideology	Usual Activity	Examples
I	One language is associated with the national identity; others are marginalized	Monolingual	Corpus planning (normativism), foreign-language acquisition, diffusion	*France, Portugal, Syria, Turkey, Japan, several Latin American countries, U.S.*
II	Two or three languages associated with the national identity; others are marginalized	Bi- or trilingual	Status planning	*Canada, Israel, Singapore, Paraguay, Switzerland*
III	No one language is seen as motivated by the national identity	Multilingual, with varying official status for several favored languages	Corpus and acquisition planning	*India, South Africa, EU.*

Note: The examples provided (in italics) are not part of Spolsky's (2004) model.

rights are provided only when there are sizable speakers of a particular language in an area. These principles are designed to offer a higher degree of linguistic equality and linguistic choice (with some limitation to the latter) to language minorities. It must be noted, however, that they do not refer to immigrant groups, but only to the incorporation of national minority groups.

The EU has embraced multilingualism at the institutional and educational levels in its declarations. It has a policy of institutional multilingualism with 23 official languages as per the last official declaration (EU, 2007) and the promotion of a linguistically and a culturally diverse Europe supported by language learning and intercultural dialogue. Such a language policy aims, first of all, for communication with citizens and heads of government in their mother tongues. Although the EU does not have an official lingua franca, scholars find that it has been using a more restricted set of working languages (i.e., English, French, and German) when operating internally for pragmatic reasons. In educational terms, the language policy supports the "mother tongue plus two foreign languages" principle for every EU citizen, including the study of English, which is seen as a necessity to participate in the international community, and the study of local and community languages. The EU emphasizes multilingualism (for nation-states), plurilingualism (for EU citizens), and cultural diversity for pragmatic, economic, political, and ideological reasons.

Implementing such a policy in a setting where member states have control over their language policies and educational systems is not without obstacles. Scholars point out that there are currently two levels of language policy within the EU: (a) a top-down, plurilingual language policy based on the personality principle adopted at the supranational level, and (b) bottom-up activities of member states, which are still based on the territoriality principle. The forward-looking policies of the EU are sometimes in dissonance with those implemented at the state level. In terms of linguistic minorities, the EU has provided protection to autochthonous and culturally and linguistically diverse minorities through documents such as The European Charter for Regional or Minority Languages (ECRML) of 1992. These minorities, however, are composed of EU citizens exclusively. Immigrants face a different situation. Even though several Western European countries have become the destination of heterogeneous groups of immigrants, there are still no specific EU documents on their language rights.

In sum, monolingual polities face many challenges. Their language policy ideology has become increasingly problematic. They lack flexibility to deal both with internal and external multilingual realities and global changes. In contrast, bi/trilingual polities have generally adopted the territorial language principle to address the needs of their autochthonous groups. Still, there is disagreement in the literature about whether this is the most flexible system. In a context characterized by fluid national identities and flex-

ible boundaries between local, national, and global levels, several nations and communities have given more attention to multilingualism and to the rights of linguistic minorities. However, polities tend to focus more on the language and cultural needs of autochthonous/national minority language groups than those of immigrants. In some cases, this may be due to the fact that some immigrant-receiving nations have not yet acknowledged their new status.

The United States has no explicit policy regarding the use of particular languages in the public sphere, though implicitly, it is clear that it is an English-speaking nation. There have been attempts over the last few decades to forge policy about the use of non-English languages in the education of language minority students, and this certainly has enormous consequences for the use and viability of non-English languages. These policies have, however, been inconsistent. For example, the U.S. Constitution is written only in English and does not mention any other languages. Nor is a right to an education mentioned in the Constitution and is therefore left to the individual states to determine. Likewise, as the Constitution is silent on the issue of official language, regulation of language (as long as it does not violate the Bill of Rights) is left to the discretion of the states. Although all states use English for governmental purposes, some (e.g., New Mexico) have required in their state constitutions that students be educated bilingually, and others (e.g., Hawaii and Louisiana) either require or permit the use of non-English languages for various governmental activities (Dicker, 2003). Although Spolsky (2004) does not include the United States in his model, he wonders whether the country has a language policy/policies or simply civil rights.

On the other hand, nearly every attempt to fashion immigration legislation in the United States has carried with it declarations of English as the official language and requirements that immigrants learn it. The last major immigration legislation, the Immigration Reform and Control Act (Public Law 99-603) of 1986, required that unauthorized persons in the United States learn English to gain legal status, and the most recent attempt at a bi-partisan compromise on immigration legislation in 2007 likewise included a section on "strengthening assimilation of new immigrants" by enacting "accelerated English requirements" (see Department of Homeland Security, 2007). The requirement that immigrants learn English is "boiler plate" for any immigration bill in the U.S. Congress.

Language policies may be overt or covert, principally; however, they regulate the use of languages in public contexts when more than one language competes for status in the society. In such cases, language becomes a critical marker of social and political status and language policy is promulgated to arbitrate issues of regional and national identity. Schmidt (2000), in fact, argues that "the dispute [over language policies] is essentially a disagreement over the meanings and uses of group identity in the public life of the nation-state, and not language as such" (p. 47).

Why is Language Policy such a Hot Button Issue?

Nation-states have frequently used language as an instrumental and a symbolic tool for the process of building one "national culture" and integrating different ethnic groups into it. Language is generally a key element of ethnic and national identity. In fact, Fishman (as cited in May, 2001) points out that ethnocultural identity and language are inextricably connected, and language choice and language use always have sociopolitical and socioeconomic consequences. Schmidt (2000) describes the policy quandary as a conflict between assimilationist and pluralist perspectives:

> Assimilationists are unrealistic because their ideology posits a monocultural and monolingual country that does not exist in the real world … the consequence … is the continued unjust subordination of language minority groups … Pluralists too are unrealistic in that they assume that an egalitarian society of multiple cultural communities can be achieved through a combination of individualistic rights-based free choice measures and moral exhortations.… (p. 209)

In either case, Schmidt argues that minority language groups face "continued racialized and marginalized subordination" (p. 209). Of course, such cultural subordination always carries economic consequences. In sum, language policy—whether overt or covert—is very high stakes as it speaks to the core identity of groups of people as well as their social, educational, and economic opportunities.

Three Primary Questions

In this section we address three major questions relevant to language policy in education:

1. *What are the policy issues and research questions that have oriented current language policy?* Under this question we review issues of migration, notions of language proficiency, debates over the "best" way to educate and assess language minority students, and, ultimately, whether the United States should have an overt language policy, and if so, what should it be?
2. *What research methods or strategies have proven to be most fruitful in the field of language policy in education?* Here we examine the strands of research, both programmatic and theoretical, that have formed the body of investigation in language policy, and provide an overview of the most fruitful methods.
3. *What is and should be the research agenda for language policy in education? Which issues demand attention? And, which methods are most likely to yield important gains in knowledge?* While both quantitative and qualitative methods are critical in the next stages of research, only a few of the most important questions will be answered through experimental methods. Because of the different goals being pursued by different

regions and language communities and the enormous diversity of the language minority population groups in the United States, it is difficult, if not impossible, to statistically control for the myriad variables that describe and affect speakers of non-English languages, their choices of language use, and their acquisition of English.

What are the Policy Issues and Research Questions that have Oriented Current Language Policy? Five primary, and recurring, issues have framed the debates over language policy in education for the last few decades in the United States. The first is migration. The entire history of humanity is one of movement from one geographic space to another in search of better living conditions. If people had not continuously migrated, the species would have very likely died out. Migration is a normal, adaptive, and inevitable response of humans to changing conditions in society, economy, climate, and forces of nature, like earthquakes, fires, and floods. When groups move, they take their cultural practices, beliefs, and languages with them. Every sending and receiving society must grapple with how to incorporate the newcomers. Often the newcomers enhance and build on the existing culture and language. Certainly the entire history of the United States is one of increasing wealth and power brought about, in good part, by the waves of ambitious, productive immigrants that peopled and built the nation. In fact, it has long been noted that migrants tend to be the most ambitious of their group (Suárez-Orozco & Suárez-Orozco, 1995). Myers (2007), for example, argues that immigration to the United States at the beginning of the 21st century is the only thing standing between this generation and serious economic decline because native-born U.S. citizens no longer reproduce at replacement levels. According to Myers, without significant immigration, the country will lack the necessary workforce to sustain the economy into the next generation.

In spite of the net cultural and economic gains represented by immigration, U.S. history has been punctuated by great debates over the rights of immigrants to retain any vestige of their culture and language. During periods when the economy has been strong and the country has not been at war with any significant group represented in the immigrant pool, considerable concession has been made to the teaching of immigrant languages in the schools. For example, German was widely taught in many midwestern schools prior to World War I, but was prohibited in its wake (Schlossman, 1983; Kloss, 1998). On the heels of the great migration from Europe at the turn of the century, when there was concern about how the country could incorporate so many newcomers, Teddy Roosevelt, in 1919, was famously quoted as weighing in on the issue with the following sentiments:

> We have room for but one language here and that is the English language, for we intend to see that the crucible turns our people out as Americans, and American nationality, and

not as dwellers in a polyglot boarding house. (as cited in Hart & Ferleger, 1989, p. 243)

More recently, steep increases in immigration have incited new movements to prohibit the use of non-English languages through the Official English or U.S.-English organization. Half of American states have had an official English clause added to their constitutions, most since the 1980s when immigration hit a new peak (Schmid, 2001). However, the 1990s saw new efforts to prohibit the teaching of students in their native (non-English) languages. California, Arizona, and Massachusetts all passed voter initiatives either banning or severely curtailing bilingual education on the grounds that it retarded students' English acquisition and was, in fact, responsible for Spanish-speaking students' failure in the U.S. education system (Unz, as cited in Marca, 2001). While English-only crusaders couched the language of prohibition of bilingual education in terms of "English for the Children" (Proposition 227, California, 1998) or helping children succeed in school—the movement was deeply rooted in identity politics (Schmid, 2001; Schmidt, 2000) with undertones of xenophobia about immigrants usurping the English language (Krashen, 1996). It is notable that the U.S. Census estimates that about 75% of English Learner students are in fact native-born U.S. citizens, and not immigrants themselves (Capps et al., 2005).

Two more related issues are: How long does it take to learn English? What constitutes English proficiency? These questions have been at the heart of much of the debate around what kinds of services schools need to provide for English Learners, by whom, and at what cost. Although there is a consistent finding that it takes from 5 to 7 years, at least, for the typical English Learner to learn the language well enough to be considered fluent (Collier, 1987; Hakuta, Butler, & Witt, 2000; Parrish et al., 2006), there is great skepticism in public policy circles on this issue. It appears to be counterintuitive to many general observers. Most immigrants learn to communicate in English relatively quickly; however, many limited English speakers will remain in the category of English Learner for seven and more years. A recent study in California found that the typical English Learner in California schools had only a 40% chance of reclassifying to a fluent English speaker by high school graduation (Parrish et al., 2006). Of course, a great deal depends on when students begin school and what kind of exposure they have to English. The primary problem, however, is that while many EL students appear to be orally fluent in English, they lack facility with *academic* English and the English Language Arts curriculum—skills in reading comprehension, vocabulary, text analysis, and writing. In fact, the problem for many so-called English Learners is not an inability to communicate orally in English, but an inability to pass grade level tests in the use of the language in academic contexts (Parrish et al., 2006). Recent research (see Harklau, Losey, & Seigal, 1999; Meltzer & Hamann, 2005) has focused on identifying the unique characteristics of academic English and in determining how best to teach

it, but the term "English Learner" or "Limited English Proficient" conjures up visions of a student who cannot speak English, obscuring the real problem of inadequate literacy instruction.

Research over time has shown that immigrants are exceptionally anxious to learn English, and immigrant parents are especially supportive of this goal for their children (Pew Hispanic Center and The Henry J. Kaiser Family Foundation, 2004). Spanish speakers, however, are increasingly isolated in neighborhoods where they are unlikely to hear English spoken (Asian immigrants are much less isolated; Orfield & Lee, 2006; Rumberger, Gándara, & Merino, 2006). Moreover, a recent national study of adult ESL programs found that more than half have long waiting lists and many of the classes exceed 40 students (Tucker, 2006). Limited English students are also often tracked into low-level courses where they receive few opportunities to actually use the language they are learning (Callahan, 2003). Notwithstanding these impediments, Spanish-speaking immigrants—and their children—are actually acquiring English at a more rapid rate than previous generations, and simultaneously losing their ability to speak Spanish more quickly as well (Tienda & Mitchell, 2006). A recent survey by the Pew Hispanic Center (2004) found that by the second generation, only 7% of Hispanics counted themselves as Spanish dominant, down from 72% in the first generation.

Fourth, of all the issues in language policy, nothing is more contentious than the question of how best to educate immigrants and students who do not speak English fluently. This is the sole question to which most federal research funds have been devoted. Put simply, is bilingual education or English immersion more effective in teaching English Learners? Of course, it is critical to specify *effective at what*? The general assumption is that schooling goals for all students include achieving grade-level proficiency in the academic curriculum, or meeting state grade-level standards. In keeping with this, large scale federal studies have incorporated measures of reading and mathematics skills as well as English proficiency as outcome measures (Ramírez, Yuen, Ramey, Pasta, & Billings, 1991; Danoff, Coles, McLaughlin, & Reynolds, 1977a, 1977b); however, most of the rhetoric and overt concern has been around having English Learners become proficient in English, largely to the exclusion of any other goal. For example, the rhetoric that drove the various state initiatives to prohibit bilingual education during the late 1990s and early 2000s featured prominently the idea that students in bilingual programs were not learning English and that if they could just learn English their academic problems would be solved (see, e.g., Marca, 2001). The prescribed amount of time to learn English, and therefore to be eligible to enter mainstream instruction and presumably catch up academically with English-speaking peers, was "not normally to exceed one year" (Proposition 227, 1998). In fact, few English Learners have been able to learn the language this rapidly and gaps in academic achievement between English Learners and English speakers have barely narrowed at all in spite of recent increased attention to these students (Grissom, 2004; Parrish et al., 2006; Rumberger & Gándara, 2004). A recent study commissioned by the U.S. Department of Education and the National Institute of Child Health and Human Development concluded that, "Where differences were observed [in studies comparing English-only and bilingual instruction] on average they favored the students in the bilingual program. The meta-analytic results clearly suggest a positive effect for bilingual instruction that is moderate in size" (August & Shanahan, 2006, p. 397). What must be concluded from these studies is that factors in addition to the language of instruction are important contributors to the academic achievement of English Learners since neither English immersion nor bilingual education *alone* has been able to close the achievement gaps for these students. Unfortunately, the obsession with the question of English-only versus bilingual education has obscured the more critical social and pedagogical issues that need to be studied.

Fifth, related to the issue of language of instruction is that of language of assessment. NCLB, with its focus on accountability and testing of all students, has resulted in much-needed attention to the academic plight of English Learners, but it has also placed inordinate pressure on schools and teachers to raise test scores at almost any cost (Sunderman & Orfield, 2006). Although NCLB encourages states to test EL students "in a valid and reliable manner … including, to the extent practicable assessments in the language and form most likely to yield accurate data" (No Child Left Behind, 2001, § 6311.b.3.C.ix.ix.III), states that were not prepared to test students who had been instructed in their primary language have largely ignored this provision of the law. Moreover, bilingual educators, knowing that their students would have to perform on English-only tests, in many cases curtailed instruction in the primary language in favor of test preparation in English only (Parrish et al., 2006), a case of the test driving instructional decisions. Some states, such as New York and Texas, have attempted to maintain primary language assessment for purposes of accountability under NCLB, but not without challenges by the U.S. Department of Education. Overwhelmingly, however, states are simply including their English Learners in the regular testing regimen with minimal and often unrelated accommodations that cannot be expected to ameliorate the problem of being tested in a language that is not understood by the examinee (Abedi, Lord, Hofstetter, & Baker, 2000; Rivera, Stansfield, Scialdone, & Sharkey, 2000).

In sum, education policies such as NCLB have driven language policy in education in covert ways, while the politics of language and identity have driven educational policy in more overt ways. However, without an overarching language policy, these decisions tend to be *ad hoc* and respond more to political climate than to thoughtful assessment of what would best serve the nation's interests and its peoples. Americans' infamous lack of familiarity with languages other than English is particularly ironic given that so many come from homes in which a language other than English is spoken. If more attention were given to broader social and economic goals, biliteracy—which is achievable for most English speakers and English Learners at little additional cost (Gándara & Rumberger, 2007)—would likely be a national priority (Cziko, 1992). Instead, it is viewed as a threat to national unity.

What are the Research Strategies or Methods that have Proven Most Fruitful in the Study of Language Policy in Education? U.S. educators and policy makers pay relatively little attention to the experiences of other nations, and the general public has only passing acquaintance with the practices in other countries, such as the rather widespread, and completely erroneous, belief that the political turmoil that erupts periodically in Quebec is due to Canada's liberal bilingual education policy (Schmid, 2001). So, neither historical nor contemporary analysis of other nations' education policy has played any significant role in formulating U.S. policies. The primary research strategies supported by the federal government have been program evaluation and research syntheses. Very little support has gone to the development of theory or studies that improve on our understanding of second language acquisition.

The federal government has supported several attempts to evaluate the effectiveness of English immersion versus bilingual programs. All of these efforts have been based on the notion that if one can hold enough variables constant, it is possible to determine that one approach or the other is clearly superior with respect to academic outcomes for English Learners (Cziko, 1992). However, Cziko (1992) and others (see, e.g., Crawford, 2004) have argued that it is impossible to draw such a conclusion because of the enormous diversity of students, languages, program implementations, and goals. Two expensive, multi-year experimental studies have been devoted to answering this question nevertheless. The American Institutes for Research (AIR) study published in 1978 found that there had been no consistent significant impact of Title VII bilingual education on English Learners (Danoff, Coles, McLaughlin, & Reynolds, 1978). In 1991 a second federally sponsored longitudinal study was released with similarly ambiguous results. Although the principal investigator David Ramírez argued that the trajectories of student achievement strongly favored the students in the late exit bilingual programs, he conceded that the 4-year duration of the study was insufficient to draw definitive conclusions. Importantly, the study also noted that in several cases programs had shifted their language emphasis and no longer looked distinctly different from other categories of programs (Ramírez et al., 1991). Criticism of both the AIR and Ramírez studies has focused on insurmountable methodological challenges in trying to compare students and programs that are not in reality comparable (Crawford, 2004). Without the ability to completely control programs, assign demographically and linguistically identical students to different treatments, and mandate that students stay in the same programs over many years, this kind of research has yielded limited insights.

The second type of research that the federal government has sponsored has been research syntheses. The first of these was the now infamous Baker-de Kanter (1981) study, which was requested by the Office of Planning and Budget in 1980. The authors were charged with reviewing the research literature to determine the effectiveness of bilingual education. Baker and de Kanter included 28 studies of bilingual education that they considered sufficiently methodologically sound to conduct a simple meta-analysis, and concluded that there was not enough evidence in its favor to mandate transitional bilingual education (TBE) as the preferred approach for educating English Learners. The study was cited widely for many years afterward as bilingual education came under increasing attack during the Reagan administration.

The Baker-de Kanter study itself, however, was widely criticized for being biased in its choice of studies and in its simple "up or down vote" methods and gave rise to a series of re-analyses, most of which concluded that, when strict methodological criteria were applied to study selection and analyses, bilingual programs tended to fare better than English only (Willig, 1985; Greene, 1997; Rolstad, Mahoney, & Glass, 2005). In the mid-1990s the National Research Council commissioned a major study of the extant knowledge base and research needs for educating language minority students. The book that resulted, authored by Diane August and Kenji Hakuta (1998), concluded that research needs were indeed lengthy, but that some conclusions could be drawn. Among these were that "When socioeconomic status is controlled, bilingualism shows no negative effects on the overall linguistic, cognitive, or social development of children, and may even provide general advantages in these areas of mental functioning" and that "use of the child's native language does not impede the acquisition of English" (p. 28).

A subsequent study commissioned by the National Research Council in 1998 on preventing reading difficulties in young children also concluded that "If language minority children arrive at school with no proficiency in English but speaking a language for which there are instructional guides, learning materials, and locally available proficient teachers, they should be taught how to read in their native language …" (Snow, Burns, & Griffin, 1998, p. 325). More recently, the previously cited study by August and Shanahan (2006), commissioned by the U. S. Department of Education, likewise found that use of the primary language was preferable for teaching students to read where it could be provided. Thus, while the debates over primary language—or bilingual—instruction have continued unabated, the major research syntheses that have been commissioned by the federal government have increasingly concluded that use of the primary language in instruction probably holds certain benefits, and does not impede EL students' learning, lending evidence to the argument that English-only efforts are likely based, at least in part, on something other than a simple concern for English Learners' academic welfare.

The more fruitful, but less attended to, research that relates to language policy is that on second language acquisition (SLA) theory, cognitive science, sociolinguistics and sociocultural studies. Large bodies of research developed in these areas can provide considerable guidance to policy makers on best practices for educating English Learners, and therefore for formulating language policy in education. Each area uses methods specific to the discipline to frame and guide inquiry, and some, such as the study of SLA, are still largely at a stage of theory building. Whole volumes have been written merely synthesizing the major studies, but below we briefly review the key insights from this research.

Linguistics and Second Language Acquisition (SLA) Theory Understanding *how* students learn a second language in the context of schooling is critical for determining how to approach their instruction, and therefore what kinds of instructional policies should be fashioned. Do students transfer what they learn in one language to another, or must they relearn what they have been taught in the first language? Does learning proceed in all languages in a more or less similar pattern? Is all language learned in the same way, or are there certain languages that require different instructional approaches? These are some of the questions that have shaped the area of SLA. Cummins has been exceptionally influential in developing theory of second language acquisition in the context of education policy. Two of his primary contributions have been in elaborating a theory that multiple languages occupy a *common underlying proficiency,* or CUP, in the brain (1981, 1984a) suggesting that knowledge acquired in any language is shared with other languages that an individual knows. Second, his theorizing that language can be organized into two types—*basic interpersonal communicative skills* (BICS) and *cognitive/academic language proficiency* (CALP; 1984b) presaged what would become an increasingly important area of research one and two decades later, as educators began to note that students who appeared to have good oral English skills were not necessarily capable of using the language in cognitively demanding ways in the classroom. The distinction in skills has come increasingly into focus with the pressures of accountability testing: many students who pass English language proficiency tests at high levels nevertheless fail grade level tests of English Language Arts (Gándara & Rumberger, 2007), both because the constructs of language proficiency and language arts are different and because they call on different linguistic skills. It should be noted nevertheless that Cummins' theories have not been uniformly accepted by linguists and some have argued that the notion of BICS and CALP, in fact, lead to social constructions of English Learners as students who have basic cognitive deficiencies, rather than simply being developmentally at different stages of language acquisition (see, e.g., MacSwan, 2000).

A number of researchers have pursued the question of whether knowledge in one language transfers to another (related to the common underlying proficiency hypothesis), and there is emerging evidence for the transfer of some skills, such as phonemic awareness and decoding, providing evidence for cross-linguistic transfer (August & Shanahan, 2006). It has also been widely observed that students who have mastered literacy in their first language are much quicker to attain literacy in the second language than those who do not have this advantage (August & Hakuta, 1998; August & Shanahan, 2006). Yet, much research remains to be done to better understand how literacy in a first language can contribute to literacy in a second. Most SLA research has been conducted on small samples of students, observing and describing language use and development, and using measures developed by the researchers themselves for specific purposes. Most of these studies do not incorporate true experimental methods or monolingual control groups (August & Shanahan, 2006).

Cognitive Studies Two primary questions of particular policy importance come out of the area of cognitive sciences: whether additional time on task results in more rapid or better acquisition of a second language, and whether bilingualism or biliteracy confers special cognitive advantages. If a student spends more minutes or hours in the day studying *in* English to learn English and this results in superior and more rapid acquisition of English, then this would argue for English immersion, and if bilingualism or biliteracy confers cognitive advantages, then this would argue for (additive) bilingual or dual language education. The first question has been pursued for years, but without sufficient controls to answer definitively. Both of the major federal studies testing bilingual versus English immersion (Danoff et al., 1978; Ramírez et al., 1991) could find no significant difference in the ultimate rate or quality of acquisition of English by program type, and studies of rate of acquisition of English proficiency similarly find little difference with respect to type of educational program to which students are assigned (Hakuta et al., 2000). In fact, socioeconomic status and prior exposure to English are generally better predictors of rate of acquisition (August & Hakuta, 1998).

Given the importance of the topic, relatively few studies have been conducted of the cognitive advantages of bilingualism and biliteracy. There is some evidence in the literature, however, that some specific cognitive advantages accrue to individuals who have command of more than one language—creativity, problem solving, and perceptual disembedding (Reynolds, 1990; Bialystok, Craik, Klein, & Viswanathan, 2004), as well as cognitive flexibility (August & Hakuta, 1998). To what extent these advantages enhance learning or provide academic achievement advantages is not known. Most of the research in cognitive science is conducted by psychologists and psycholinguists. They are inclined to use experimental methods, often testing small samples of experimental (e.g., bilingual) and control (e.g., monolingual) groups for differences in cognitive function on specific tasks. Some questions are only answerable with large data sets, such as examining trends in language or academic learning over time for specified population groups.

Sociocultural Studies A very large body of literature has accrued under the topic of sociocultural studies. This research attempts to capture the social context of language learning and has large implications for language policy in education. Under what social conditions do English Learners learn most effectively? What kinds of peer groups and interactions are likely to foster optimal learning for these students? Do students from different language groups learn at different rates? Why? To briefly summarize this literature, studies find that attitudes toward language learning do, indeed, affect acquisition and that teachers, as well as others, are influenced by the primary language (or dialect) that students speak, holding higher expectations for some language groups than others (Snow, 1992; August & Hakuta, 1998) and that accented speech can also cause students to be judged (and judge themselves) in negative ways (Lippi-Green, 1997). Researchers have also found that immigrant language minority students, on average, hold more positive attitudes toward learning than subsequent generations and, as a result, often outperform native-born members of their own ethnic group scholastically, even when the latter have greater proficiency in English (Suárez-Orozco & Suárez-Orozco, 1995; Rumbaut, 1995). Reasons given for this generally focus on the negative effects of socialization into low-income and low-status communities, and the loss of hopefulness that comes when second and third generations fail to realize the American dream and are left behind in an unforgiving economy. Researchers have also concluded that intergroup relations can be positively affected by educating students in contexts in which the first and second languages share equal status, such as in dual language classrooms (Genesee & Gándara, 1999). Sociolinguistic studies, generally conducted by anthropologists, social psychologists, and sociolinguists, range from small samples to very large, typically incorporating observation, survey, interview, and focus group methodologies to try to understand the attitudes and experiences of individuals in learning language in a specific social context.

What Is and Should Be the Research Agenda for Language Policy in Education?

In 1997 the National Research Council published a comprehensive volume entitled *Improving Schooling for Language-Minority Children*, which included specific recommendations for the research agenda needed to improve these students' academic outcomes (August & Hakuta, 1998). It included such things as improving knowledge about how best to educate these students in content areas, not just in learning English; how and when to introduce literacy instruction in English; what conditions promote positive inter-group relations and how to address the problem of lowered expectations for EL students on the part of teachers; how best to incorporate the resources of linguistic minority families and communities to support students' schooling; how to organize preschool and secondary instruction for English Learners and to identify the particular characteristics and needs of a variety of language groups and students with disabilities, to name a few.

It would be hard to improve on that list, given that not much of that agenda has been accomplished in the interim because, as the authors of the volume point out, the resources have not been available to conduct that research. There are, however, three topics in the area of educating students who are learning English and other languages that over the last decade have come into sharper focus: (a) How can we most effectively prepare, support, and retain qualified teachers for English Learners?; (b) What are the appropriate ways to assess the learning of students who are not proficient in the language of instruction?; and (c) How can we begin to close the enormous achievement gaps between English Learners and English-speaking students?

The extreme emphasis on accountability that has come about as a result of NCLB has focused educators' and researchers' attention on the huge divide between the academic performance of different groups of students, with English Learners typically being the lowest performers in the school, other than special education students (Parrish et al., 2006). A consensus has been developing over time that the most critical resource for all students is the quality of their teachers—this is no less true for English Learners (Sanders & Rivers, 1996; Goldhaber & Anthony, 2003; Wayne & Youngs, 2003). However, they are more likely than all other students to have teachers who are not qualified to teach them, who have little experience in the classroom, and who admit to being unprepared for the task (Gándara, Maxwell-Jolly, & Driscoll, 2005; Zehler, Fleischman, Hopstock, Pendzick, & Stephenson, 2003; Esch, Chang-Ross, Guha, Tiffany-Morales, Shields, 2004). A recent report issued by the Commission on No Child Left Behind (2007) recommended, among its most urgent priorities, strengthening the teaching force as a means of raising the academic performance of the nation's students. While it is clear that teachers are frustrated and feel unprepared to teach EL students, there is no consensus in the research literature on what the critical competencies of teachers of English Learners should be, and NCLB has provided no standard for highly qualified teachers of English Learners. While some excellent work has been done on identifying important characteristics of these teachers (Milk, Mercado, & Sapiens, 1992; García, 1996; Wong-Fillmore & Snow, 2002), there is no consensus on what every teacher of English Learners should know before entering the classroom, and on what professional development should focus to strengthen their skills. Teacher preparation programs cannot teach everything that would be optimal, but they must teach what is critical. Research is needed to identify what those critical competencies are.

Under NCLB the stakes are very high for assessment outcomes, and yet the testing regime for English Learners is not designed to collect either valid or reliable information on what they have learned and can do. Tests designed for native English speakers, normed on native English speakers, and presented in English only to EL students (who by definition do not understand English well) provide inaccurate information about both the students' English language development and academic proficiency. Much research needs to be done to determine how best to assess the educational progress of students who have different levels of English proficiency, who speak different primary languages, and who have been educated partially or wholly outside of the United States. Over 90% of English Learners in the U.S. speak one of four languages and more than three-fourths speak just one other language—Spanish (Zehler et al., 2003). Thus the challenge in creating valid and reliable instruments is for most English Learners is substantial, but not insurmountable.

With the reporting of sub-group scores, and with sanctions being applied to schools that do not demonstrate progress for all subgroups, the spotlight has shone on the problem of enormous disparities in performance between English speakers and English Learners. National data show that these gaps, where they are narrowing, are narrowing very slowly and in many places they are actually growing larger over time (Losen, 2008). The most hopeful outcomes that have been produced for English Learners occur in dual language, or dual immersion programs where both English speakers and English Learners study together and where the two languages share equal status (Genesee, Lindholm-Leary, Saunders, & Christian, 2006). Such programs, when well implemented, draw on much of the research on SLA and sociocultural studies. It cannot be overlooked, though, that an element of their success is the additional social capital provided by middle class parents who often seek out these programs. It has been well established that schools respond to parents with resources and influence (Lareau, 2000), and that all children can benefit from this. If dual language education provides the advantage of a second language for all students as well as narrowing of the achievement gap among groups, it would seem to be an area ripe for serious research attention.

Conclusion

Politics is the negotiation of interests represented by various constituencies. Language use and status have tremendous consequences for language minority groups as well as for the majority population and so it is not surprising that its regulation would be a highly politicized arena. While many educators decry the fact that the education of English Learners has been turned into what appears to be a purely political activity, without particular concern for the actual learning of these students, it could hardly be less political. Group identities and economic welfare and opportunity are the stakes. While a language policy that was thoughtful, respectful of the language rights of minorities, and promotes the general social and economic welfare of the state would be an important advance, it is not likely to happen soon in the United States. Ideology still holds sway over public policy and issues of identity and its relationship to language are unresolved. In the meantime, language policy in education can promote better educational outcomes for all students if it shifts from the narrow research focus on which program best addresses the "language problem" to a richer research agenda on the possibilities for enhanced achievement for all students by examining language policy through the lens of language as a personal and societal resource.

Notes

1. Over the last 25 years, the linguistic minority population in the United States has grown by 130%, while the English-only population has actually declined by 1.3%. In 2005, 10.5 million children ages 5–17 spoke a language other than English, representing 20% of the school age population. In California, the state with the largest number of linguistic minority students, 44% of school age children come from homes in which a language other than English is spoken (University of California Linguistic Minority Research Institute, 2006).

2. The Arizona Department of Education does not publish the numbers of students who continue to be served in bilingual programs, so exact figures are not available. However, the waiver process is stricter than in California, making it more difficult for parents to seek such a program.

References

Abedi, J., Lord, C., Hofstetter, C., & Baker, E. (2000). Impact of accommodation strategies on English Language Learners' test performance. *Educational Measurement: Issues and Practice, 19*(3), 16–26.

August, D., & Hakuta, K. (1998). *Educating language minority children.* Washington, DC: National Research Council.

August, D., & Shanahan, T. (Eds.). (2006). *Developing literacy in second-language learners: Report of the National Literacy Panel on Language Minority Children and Youth.* Mahwah, NJ: Erlbaum.

Baker, K. A., & de Kanter, A. A. (1981). *Effectiveness of bilingual education: A review of the literature.* Washington, DC: U.S. Department of Education, Office of Planning, Budget and Evaluation.

Bialystok, E., Craik, F. I. M., Klein, R., & Viswanathan, M. (2004). Bilingualism, aging, and cognitive control: Evidence from the Simon Task. *Psychology and Aging, 19*, 290–303.

California Department of Education. (2008). *Statewide English Learners enrolled in and receiving instructional services.* Retrieved April 1, 2008, from http://dq.cde.ca.gov/dataquest/ElP2_State.asp?RptYear=2006-07&RptType=ELPart2_1a

Callahan, R. (2003). *Opportunity to learn English in a California high school: Tracking and secondary English Learners.* Unpublished doctoral dissertation, University of California, Davis.

Capps, R., Fix, M., Murray, J., Ost, J., Passel, J., & Herwantoro, S. (2005). *The new demography of America's schools: Immigration and the No Child Left Behind Act.* Washington DC: Urban Institute.

Collier, V. (1987). Age and rate of acquisition of second language for academic purposes. *TESOL Quarterly, 21*, 617–643.

Commission on No Child Left Behind. (2007). *Beyond NCLB: Fulfilling our promise to our nation's children.* Aspen, CO: The Aspen Institute.

Crawford, J. (1999). *Bilingual education: History, politics, theory, and practice* (4th ed.). Los Angeles: Bilingual Educational Services.

Crawford, J. (2000). *Language policy.* Retrieved September 8, 2006, from http://ourworld.compuserve.com/homepages/JWCRAWFORD/langpol.htm

Crawford, J. (2004). *Educating English Learners: Language diversity in the classroom* (5th ed.). Los Angeles: Bilingual Educational Services.

Cummins, J. (1981). The role of primary language development in promoting educational success for language minority students. In Office of Bilingual, Bicultural Education (Ed.), *Schooling and language minority students: A theoretical framework* (pp. 3–49). Sacramento: California State Department of Education.

Cummins, J. (1984a). *Bilingualism and special education: Issues in assessment and pedagogy.* Clevedon, UK: Multilingual Matters.

Cummins, J. (1984b). Wanted: A theoretical framework for relating language proficiency to academic achievement among bilingual students. In C. Rivera (Ed.), *Language proficiency and academic achievement* (pp. 2–19). Clevedon, UK: Multilingual Matters.

Cummins, J. (2005). A proposal for action: Strategies for recognizing heritage language competence as a learning resource within the mainstream classroom. *The Modern Language Journal, 89*, 585–592.

Cziko, G. (1992). The evaluation of bilingual education. From necessity and probability to possibility. *Educational Researcher, 21*(2), 10–15.

Danoff, M. N., Coles, G. J., McLaughlin, D. H., & Reynolds, D. J. (1977a). *Evaluation of the impact of ESEA Title VII Spanish/English bilingual education programs: Vol. 1. Study design and interim findings.* Palo Alto, CA: American Institutes for Research.

Danoff, M. N., Coles, G. J., McLaughlin, D. H., & Reynolds, D. J. (1977b). *Evaluation of the impact of ESEA Title VII Spanish/English bilingual education programs: Vol. 2. Project descriptions.* Palo Alto, CA: American Institutes for Research.

Danoff, M. N., Coles, G. J., McLaughlin, D. H., & Reynolds, D. J. (1978). *Evaluation of the impact of ESEA Title VII Spanish/English Bilingual Education Programs: Vol. 3. Year two impact data, educational process, and in-depth analyses.* Palo Alto, CA: American Institutes for Research.

Del Valle, S. (2003). *Language rights and the law in the United States: Finding our voices.* Clevedon, UK: Multilingual Matters.

Department of Homeland Security. (2007, May 17). Administration and bipartisan group of senators reach bipartisan agreement on comprehensive immigration reform. Retrieved May 5, 2008, from http://www.dhs.gov/xnews/releases/pr_1179511978687.shtm

Dicker, S. J. (2003). *Languages in America: A pluralist view* (2nd ed.). Clevedon, UK: Multilingual Matters.

Esch, C. E., Chang-Ross, C. M., Guha, R., Tiffany-Morales, J., & Shields, P. M. (2004). *California's teaching force 2004: Key issues and trends.* Santa Cruz, CA: The Center for the Future of Teaching and Learning.

European Union (EU). (2003). *Promoting language learning and linguistic diversity: An action plan 2004–2006.* Brussels: European Commission.

European Union (EU). (2005). *A new framework strategy for multilingualism.* Brussels: European Commission.

European Union (EU). (2006). *Eurobarometer survey: Europeans and languages.* Retrieved August 20, 2006, from http://ec.europa.eu/education/policies/lang/languages/eurobarometer06_en.html

European Union (EU). (2007). *FAQ. Frequently asked questions about the European Union's policy on languages.* Retrieved January 17, 2007, from http://europa.eu/languages/en/document/59

Gándara, P., Maxwell-Jolly, J., & Driscoll, A. (2005). *Listening to teachers of English Language Learners.* Santa Cruz, CA: Center for the Future of Teaching and Learning.

Gándara, P., Moran, R., & García, E. (2004). Legacy of Brown: Lau and language policy in the United States. *Review of Research in Education, 28*, 27–46.

Gándara, P., & Rumberger, R. W. (2007). *Resource needs for California's English Learners.* Retrieved May 4, 2008, from Stanford University School of Education, Institute for Research on Educational Policy and Practice Web site: http://irepp.stanford.edu/documents/GDF/SUMMARIES/Gandara.pdf

García, E. (1996). Preparing instructional professionals for linguistically and culturally diverse students. In J. Sikula (Ed.), *Handbook of research on teacher education* (pp. 802–813). New York: Simon & Schuster.

Genesee, F., & Gándara, P. (1999). Bilingual education programs: A cross-national perspective. *Journal of Social Issues, 55*, 665–686.

Genesee, F., Lindholm-Leary, K. J., Saunders, W., & Christian, D. (2006). *Educating English Language Learners: A synthesis of empirical evidence.* New York: Cambridge University Press.

Goldhaber, D., & Anthony, E. (2003). *Teacher quality and student achieve-*

ment (Urban Diversity Series No. UDS 115). New York: Teachers College, Institute for Urban and Minority Education.

Greene, J. (1997). A meta-analysis of the Rossell and Baker review of bilingual education research [Electronic version]. *Bilingual Research Journal, 21.*

Grissom, J. B. (2004). Reclassification of English Learners [Electronic version]. *Education Policy Analysis Archives, 12.*

Hakuta, K., Butler, Y., & Witt, D. (2000). *How long does it take English Learners to attain proficiency?* Santa Barbara: University of California Linguistic Minority Research Institute.

Harklau, L., Losey, K., & Seigal, M. (1999). *Generation 1.5 meets college composition: Issues in the teaching of writing to U.S.-educated learners of ESL.* Mahwah, NJ: Erlbaum.

Hart, A. B., & Ferleger, H. R. (Eds.). (1989). *Theodore Roosevelt cyclopedia* (rev. 2nd ed.). Westport, CT: Meckler Corporation and Theodore Roosevelt Association.

Herriman, M. L., & Burnaby, B. (Eds.). (1996). *Language policies in English-dominant countries: Six case studies.* Clevedon, UK: Multilingual Matters.

Kloss, H. (1998). *The American bilingual tradition* (2nd ed.). Washington, DC: Center for Applied Linguistics and Delta Systems.

Krashen, S. (1996). *Under attack: The case against bilingual education.* Culver City, CA: Language Education Associates.

Lareau, A. (2000). *Home advantage: Social class and parental intervention in elementary education* (2nd ed.). New York: Rowman & Littlefield.

Lau v. Nichols, 414 U.S. 563 (1974).

Lippi-Green, R. (1997). *English with an accent: Language, ideology and discrimination in the United States.* New York: Routledge.

Losen, D. (2008, May). *Challenging limitations: How improved opportunities for English Language Learners might result from new data, law and policy.* Paper presented at the University of California Linguistic Minority Research Institute Conference, Sacramento, CA.

MacSwan, J. (2000). The threshold hypothesis, semilingualism, and other contributions to a deficit view of linguistic minorities. *Hispanic Journal of Behavioral Sciences, 22,* 3–45.

Marca, P. (Director). (2001). Bye-bye, bilingual [Television series episode]. In W. Free (Executive producer), *Uncommon Knowledge.* San Jose, CA: KTEH.

May, S. (2001). *Language and minority rights: Ethnicity, nationalism, and the politics of language.* Essex, UK: Longman.

Meltzer, J., & Hamann, E. T. (2005). *Meeting the literacy development needs of adolescent English Language Learners through content area learning. Part one: Focus on engagement and motivation.* Providence, RI: Northeast and Islands Regional Educational Laboratory at Brown University.

Meyer v. Nebraska, 262 U.S. 390 (1923).

Milk, R., Mercado, C., & Sapiens, A. (1992). Rethinking the education of teachers of language minority children: Developing reflective teachers for changing schools [Electronic version]. *Focus: Occasional papers in bilingual education, 6.* Washington, DC: National Clearinghouse for Bilingual Education.

Myers, D. (2007). *Immigrants and boomers: Forging a new social contract for the future of America.* New York: Russell Sage Foundation.

No Child Left Behind Act of 2001, 20 U.S.C. § 6311 (2002).

Orfield, G., & Lee, C. (2006). *Racial transformation and the changing nature of segregation.* Cambridge, MA: The Civil Rights Project at Harvard University.

Parrish, T. B., Perez, M., Merickel, A., Linquanti, R., Socia, M., Spain, A. et al. (2006). *Effects of the implementation of Proposition 227 on the education of English Learners, K–12: Findings from a five-year evaluation.* Palo Alto, CA: American Institutes for Research and WestEd.

Pew Hispanic Center and The Henry J. Kaiser Family Foundation. (2004). *Assimilation and language* (Publication No. 7052). Retrieved March 13, 2007, from http://pewhispanic.org/files/factsheets/11.pdf

Ramírez, J. D., Yuen, S. D., Ramey, D. R., Pasta, D. J., & Billings, D. (1991). *Final report: Longitudinal study of immersion strategy, early-exit and late-exit transitional bilingual education programs for language-minority children.* San Mateo, CA: Aguirre International. (ERIC Document Reproduction Service No. ED330216)

Reynolds, A. (1990). The cognitive consequences of bilingualism. In A. G. Reynolds (Ed.), *Bilingualism, multiculturalism, and second language learning: The McGill conference in honour of Wallace E. Lambert* (pp. 145–182). Hillsdale, NJ: Erlbaum.

Rickford, J. R., & Rickford, A. E. (1995). Dialect readers revisited. *Linguistics and Education, 7,* 107–128.

Rivera, C., Stansfield, C., Scialdone, L., & Sharkey, M. (2000). *An analysis of state policies for the inclusion and accommodation of ELLs in state assessment programs during 1998–1999: Final Report.* Arlington, VA: George Washington University, Center for Equity and Excellence in Education.

Rolstad, K., Mahoney, K., & Glass, G. (2005). Effectiveness of programs for English Language Learners. *Educational Policy, 19,* 572–594.

Romero-Little, M. E., & McCarty, T. (2006). *Language planning challenges and prospects in Native American communities and schools.* Tempe: Language Policy Research Unit (LPRU), Education Policy Studies Laboratory, Arizona State University.

Ruiz, R. (1984). Orientations in language planning. *NABE Journal, 8*(2), 15–24.

Rumbaut, R. (1995). The new Californians: Comparative research findings on the educational progress of immigrant children. In R. Rumbaut & W. Cornelius (Eds.), *California's immigrant children: Theory, research, and implications for educational policy* (pp. 17–70). San Diego: University of California, Center for US-Mexican Studies.

Rumberger, R. W., & Gándara, P. (2004). Seeking equity in the education of California's English Learners. *Teachers College Record, 106,* 2032–2056.

Rumberger, R. W., Gándara, P., & Merino, B. (2006). Where California's English Learners attend school and why it matters. *UC LMRI Newsletter, 15*(2), 1–2.

Ryan, E. B., & Carranza, M. A. (1977). Ingroup and outgroup reactions to Mexican American language varieties. In H. Giles (Ed.), *Language, ethnicity, and intergroup relations* (pp. 59–82). New York: Academic Press.

San Miguel, G. (2004). *Contested policy: The rise and fall of federal bilingual education in the United States, 1960–2001.* Denton: University of North Texas Press.

Sanders, W., & Rivers, J. (1996). *Cumulative and residual effects of teachers on future student academic achievement.* Nashville: University of Tennessee Value-Added Research and Assessment Center.

Schlesinger, A., Jr. (1991). *The disuniting of America: Reflections on a multicultural society.* New York: W.W. Norton.

Schlossman, S. (1983). Is there an American tradition of bilingual education? German in the public elementary schools, 1840–1919. *American Journal of Education, 91,* 139–186.

Schmid, C. L. (2001). *The politics of language: Conflict, identity and cultural pluralism in comparative perspective.* Oxford, UK: Oxford University Press.

Schmidt, R. (2000). *Language policy and identity politics in the United States.* Philadelphia: Temple University Press.

Snow, C. (1992). Perspectives on second-language development: Implications for bilingual education. *Educational Researcher, 21*(2), 16–19.

Snow, C., Burns, S., & Griffin, P. (Eds.). (1998). *Preventing reading difficulties in young children.* Washington, DC: National Academy Press.

Spolsky, B. (2004). *Language policy.* Cambridge, UK: Cambridge University Press.

Suárez-Orozco, M., & Suárez-Orozco, C. (1995). *Trans-formations: Migration, family life, and achievement motivation among Latino adolescents.* Palo Alto, CA: Stanford University Press.

Sunderman, G. L., & Orfield, G. (2006). *Domesticating a revolution: No Child Left Behind and state administrative response.* Cambridge, MA: The Civil Rights Project at Harvard University.

Tienda, M., & Mitchell, F. (Eds.). (2006). *Multiple origins, uncertain destinies: Hispanics and the American future.* Washington DC: National Academies Press.

Tollefson, J. W. (Ed.). (2002). *Language policies in education: Critical issues*. Mahwah, NJ: Erlbaum.

Tollefson, J. W., & Tsui, A. (Eds.). (2004). *Medium of instruction policies: Which agenda? Whose agenda?* Mahwah, NJ: Erlbaum.

Tucker, J. T. (2006). *The ESL Logjam: Waiting times for adult ESL classes and the impact on English Learners.* Los Angeles: NALEO Educational Fund.

University of California Linguistic Minority Research Institute (UC LMRI). (2006). The growth of the linguistic minority population in the U.S. and California, 1980–2005 [Electronic version]. *EL Facts, 8.*

Wayne, A. J., & Youngs, P. (2003). Teacher characteristics and student achievement gains: A review. *Review of Educational Research, 73,* 89–122.

Wiley, T. G. (2005). The reemergence of heritage and community language policy in the U.S. national spotlight. *The Modern Language Journal, 89,* 594–601.

Wiley, T. G. (2007, March). *Language policy in international perspective.* Paper presented at the Second Binational Symposium, Monterrey, Mexico.

Wiley, T. G., & Wright, W. E. (2004). Against the undertow: Language-minority education policy and politics in the "age of accountability." *Educational Policy, 18,* 142–168.

Willig, A. C. (1985). A meta-analysis of selected studies on the effectiveness of bilingual education. *Review of Educational Research, 55,* 269–317.

Wise, M. (2006). Defending national linguistic territories in the European Single Market: towards more transnational geolinguistic analysis. *Area, 38,* 204–212.

Wong-Fillmore, L., & Snow, C. E. (2002). What teachers need to know about language. In C. T. Adger, C. E. Snow, & D. Christian (Eds.), *What teachers need to know about language* (pp. 7-54). Washington, DC: Center for Applied Linguistics.

Wright, W. E. (2007). Heritage language programs in the era of English-only and No Child Left Behind. *Heritage Language Journal, 5,* 1–26.

Zehler, A., Fleischman, H., Hopstock, P., Pendzick, M., & Stephenson, T. (2003). *Descriptive study of services to LEP students and LEP students with disabilities.* Washington, DC: U.S. Department of Education Office of English Language Acquisition, Language Enhancement, and Academic Achievement of Limited English Proficient Students (OELA).

47

Teacher Quality and Teacher Labor Markets

Tara Béteille and Susanna Loeb
Stanford University

Introduction

Students experience schools through their classrooms and their teachers. The ability of a teacher to motivate students and facilitate learning affects each student's educational attainment, perhaps more than any other single characteristic of schooling. A large body of research generated over the last 50–60 years has improved our understanding of who teachers are, how they make decisions on whether to teach and where to teach, and how these factors ultimately impact students. This chapter reviews the evidence on teacher labor markets. It asks what factors influence the career decisions of teachers and potential teachers, and how these career decisions then affect the overall teacher workforce, the distribution of teachers across schools, and students' educational opportunities.

The chapter is organized as follows: We begin by looking at the size and composition of the teaching labor force in the United States and changes therein over time. We discuss teacher attributes found to be associated with student learning, as well as attributes for which there is ambiguity, drawing upon recent literature and data from the latest Schools and Staffing Survey (SASS) and Teacher Follow-up Survey (TFS).[1] The section that follows describes the distribution of teachers across schools and discusses our understanding of why the teacher workforce appears the way it does, drawing on insights from extant research on both supply and demand-driven factors. We then study the transfer and quit behavior of teachers using existing literature and data from the latest TFS (2004–05); next, we consider teacher-focused policy measures and their impact on student achievement, and briefly review the research on charter schools and private schools in the United States and how the country fares vis-à-vis teacher labor markets in other developed countries. The chapter then concludes with suggestions for areas for future research.

Teacher Characteristics

Size of the Teaching Force The number of elementary and secondary school teachers in public schools in the United States has grown steadily over the last 50 years. In 1955, there were 1.14 million public elementary and secondary school teachers. The 2003–04 SASS puts this number at 3.25 million for the country's 15,500 school districts, serving approximately 47.3 million students (Strizek, Pittsonberger, Riordan, Lyter, & Orlofsky, 2006). The increase in teaching staff has been driven primarily by rising student enrollment, falling student-teacher ratios, and increased demand for teachers in specific areas such as special education.

Student enrollment increased in the 1950s and 1960s due to the post-war baby boom. It declined by approximately 5 million between 1970 and 1990, but has been increasing since then (NCES, 2008). Immigration into the United States explains some part of the increase in enrollment rates, especially in California. Another important factor driving the increase in demand for school teachers is the change in student-teacher ratios. These ratios decreased from 26.9 in 1955 to 14.5 in 2003–04 (Strizek et al., 2006). Part of this decline comes from class size reduction policies targeted at all students, while another part comes from laws making the provision of education to all handicapped children mandatory.[2] The special education sector has become more staff-intensive; from 194,802 special education teachers in 1978, the number of teachers in this sector rose to 307,575 in 1990 and 412,750 in 2003–04 (Hanushek & Rivkin, 2002).[3]

Age and Experience The average age of teachers has increased over the last 30 years. The median age of teachers was 41 years in 1961, falling to 33 years in 1976, but increasing thereafter. The average age of public school teachers was 42.5 years in 2003–04 (Strizek et al., 2006). At least two forces have been driving the increase in the average age of teachers. First, teachers hired to educate the children of the baby boom era have aged and are now reaching retirement. Approximately 31% of public school teachers were aged 50 years or more in 2004–05 (Marvel, Lyter, Peltola, Strizek, & Morton, 2007). These teachers are likely to retire over the next 10–15 years, creating a demand for new teachers. Second, those entering teaching today are older than in the past. For example, over 80% of new teachers in New York were under 25 years of age in 1970. By the mid-1980s this had decreased to roughly 40%. It has continued to decline slowly ever since (Loeb & Reininger, 2004).

In keeping with the changing age distribution of teachers, experience levels have changed over time. Whereas the 1987–88 SASS found that only 9.9% of all public school teachers had taught for 3 or fewer years, the 2003–04 SASS found that 17.8% of all full-time public school teachers had teaching experience of 3 or fewer years. Roughly the same percentage of teachers have been teaching for 20 or more years in 2003–04 as in 1987–88. In terms of numbers, however, there were more than 160,000 teachers in 2003–04 with teaching experience of 20 or more years than there were in 1987–88. The latest SASS also tells us that approximately 57% have been teaching at their current school for more than 4 years (Strizek et al., 2006).

Multiple studies have estimated the effects of teaching experience on students' learning, though few have looked at the effects of teachers' age. Using data on New York City schools for grades 4–8, Boyd, Lankford, Loeb, Rockoff, and Wyckoff (2007) found that, on average, first and second year teachers did not add as much to student learning in English Language Arts (ELA) or math as more experienced teachers did. Gains accrued thereafter, but stopped being substantial after the fifth year. Using a 10-year panel from North Carolina, and focusing on students from grades 3, 4, and 5, Clotfelter, Ladd, and Vigdor (2007a) found that the more experienced a teacher was, the more student test scores in reading and math increased over the course of a year. Compared to a teacher with no experience, the benefits of experience rose continuously, peaking at 21–27 years of experience. They too found that more than half of the gain occurred during the first couple of years of teaching. This is consistent with other studies in Texas and New Jersey (for Texas, see Hanushek, Kain, & Rivkin, 2004; for New Jersey, see Rockoff, 2003). The evidence from New Jersey, however, suggests that the effect of experience may vary by subject matter. Using a panel from New Jersey, Rockoff (2003) found that the impact of teacher experience on student vocabulary achievement increased until the sixth year of teaching after which it flattened. The impact on reading comprehension, however, increased monotonically past the tenth year. The effect of teacher experience on math computation skills, on the other hand, increased until year 3, after which it began to decrease. All of these studies

suggest that experience matters for student learning, but that on average, the gains to experience are greatest in the first years of teaching.

The better performance of more experienced teachers could reflect either improvement with experience or the differential attrition of ineffective teachers. If those who are less effective, on average, are also the ones to leave initially, then what looks like gains to experience might simply be gains to more effective teachers regardless of experience. In other words, we might see more experienced teachers, on average, registering higher student test scores, even if they as individuals did not get any better with experience. Using a Florida Panel for grades 3–10, Harris and Sass (2006) find that while experience generated positive effects for student learning in both math and reading, those effects became very small when teacher fixed effects were included. This suggests it may be differential attrition, not improvement in teaching skills, which drive the better performance of more experienced teachers. Clotfelter et al. (2007a), however, find little support for the differential attrition hypothesis from their analysis of North Carolina schools. They argue that positive returns to experience in their models come primarily from experience and not from a sample biased by the attrition of ineffective teachers. Thus, while it is clear that on average more experienced teachers are more effective than first-year teachers, the extent to which this is driven by learning or attrition is less clear. There are likely to be differences in learning opportunities available to teachers from place to place, which could influence the effect of teacher experience on student learning, as well.

Gender Approximately 75% of public school teachers are female, with 83.8% in elementary schools and 57.3% in secondary schools (Strizek et al., 2006). These proportions are similar across the urban and rural spectrum, though schools in the South and Midwest employ relatively more women than other schools (Bacolod, 2005). The proportion of female teachers has *not* changed dramatically over the last 50 years. Two things, however, have changed. First, the number of women completing college has risen dramatically. As a result, the test score of the average college graduate is now lower relative to the full distribution of high school students in a given cohort, than was previously the case, when a smaller proportion of high school students went onto college.[4] Second, as Corcoran, Schwab, and Evans (2004) note, the labor market for women has changed considerably since the mid-1960s with traditionally male-dominated professions such as law and medicine becoming increasingly open to women. Using data from five longitudinal surveys of high school graduates spanning the classes of 1957 to 1992, they found that while the math and verbal test scores of the average new teacher had fallen only slightly, the likelihood that a female from the top of her class would enter teaching had fallen dramatically. Bacolod (2005) reached similar conclusions. Using indices of teacher quality such as test scores and selectivity of undergraduate institution, she establishes an empirical link between an increase in professional opportunities for women and a decline in the quality of teachers as measured by these indices. [5]

The research literature assessing the effect of teachers' gender on student outcomes is relatively small. Ehrenberg, Goldhaber, and Brewer (1995) did not find a systematic relationship between teacher gender and student outcomes; while Nixon and Robinson (1999) found no relationship between gender and outcomes for boys, but found that girls attending high schools with a higher proportion of female teachers had higher educational attainment. In a recent study of the relationship between teacher gender and student outcomes, Dee (2007) finds that same gender matches between teachers and students improves student learning. In particular, boys appear to learn less with female teachers.

Teacher and Student Race The racial and ethnic makeup of teachers does not reflect that of their students in most school districts. The share of non-White students is much larger than the share of non-White teachers. For instance, the proportion of African American and Hispanic students (16.8 and 17.7%, respectively) is nearly three times the percentage of African American and Hispanic teachers (7.9 and 6.2%).

The underrepresentation of racial and ethnic minority teachers stems largely from their underrepresentation in the college-educated population. Among college graduates in 1976–77, for example, 90% were White, 7% were African American, and 2% were Hispanic. By 1999–2000, the gap had decreased slightly to 78%, 9%, and 6%, respectively. Nevertheless, non-Hispanic White teachers were considerably overrepresented in the group of college graduates.

How important is having a teacher of the same race for student achievement? A recent study using data from the Tennessee STAR experiment in which students and teachers were randomly assigned to each other found that an additional year with an own-race teacher increased student performance by two to four percentile points (Dee, 2004). As Dee (2004) notes, a comparison with other estimated effects suggests these gains are considerable. Specifically, they are comparable to those associated with a small-class assignment. The results are in tune with those from a large school district in Texas, where Black students' scores improved by 0.1 standard deviations when they had a Black teacher compared to when they had a White teacher (Hanushek, Kain, O'Brien, & Rivkin, 2005). These results should be interpreted with caution to the extent that teacher quality varies systematically with school-level student racial composition, making it difficult to separate teacher quality from teacher race. If, for instance, the best White teachers self-select themselves into more affluent schools, leaving the least competent White teachers in schools with a high share of low-income, low-achievement Black students, then such studies might end up comparing the "average" Black teacher with a set of "below-average" White teachers, leading one to overstate the benefit of having a same-race teacher (Jacob, 2007).

Educational Attainment Almost all public school teachers have bachelor's degrees and nearly 41% have master's degrees as their highest degree earned (Strizek et al., 2006). In 1961, 15% of teachers did not have a bachelor's degree, but by the early 1980, nearly all teachers had completed an undergraduate degree. As an example, in 2003–04, only 1.1% of all public school teachers did not have a bachelor's degree. The percentage of teachers with master's degrees as their highest degree has risen considerably, from approximately 23% in 1961 to 41% in 2003–04 (Strizek et al., 2006). Degree attainment varies by the grade the teacher teaches, with high school teachers more likely to hold a master's degree than middle school teachers, who in turn are more likely to hold a master's degree than primary school teachers. However, there is little difference across community types (rural, suburban, and urban) in the percentage of teachers with masters' degrees.

The increase in master's degree attainment, at least in part, is related to changes in state requirements and the additional pay linked to educational attainment in district or state salary schedules. The incentives that encourage teachers to get a master's, unfortunately, are not likely to have benefited students. Master's degrees have *not* been found to predict higher student achievement, except for content specific masters' degrees in high school mathematics. For example, using North Carolina data, Clotfelter et al. (2007a) found no impact of master's degrees on student achievement in elementary school; in some cases, the impact was negative; thought they find more positive effects in high schools. A study using Florida panel data also found that advanced degrees were not effective, on average, in increasing teacher productivity. There was some evidence that teachers with subject-specific master's degrees had students who learned more over the course of a year, but, as just mentioned, this was only found to hold for high school math, and has yet to be confirmed using current empirical techniques (Harris & Sass, 2006). Even here, it is unclear whether it is the master's degree per se, or greater interest in math (which presumably led them to the master's) which leads to better student performance. If it is the latter, then these teachers might have helped improve student performance even without the master's (Boyd, Goldhaber, Lankford, & Wyckoff, 2007).

Subject-Matter Knowledge Basic reasoning would lead one to expect teacher effectiveness to be linked to adequate subject-matter knowledge. There are several ways of measuring a teacher's subject-matter knowledge; for instance, scores in field-specific examinations, such as the Praxis series, teaching certificates, or undergraduate or graduate course-taking. While none of these captures subject-matter knowledge completely, they nevertheless give us some sense on average of a teacher's content knowledge.

Most teachers have a graduate or undergraduate major or minor in their primary teaching field, and this has been increasing over the years (Ingersoll, 2003). As of 1997–98, 86% of 7th- to 12th-grade English teachers, 89% of social science teachers, 82% of math teachers, and 88% of science teachers reported having an undergraduate or graduate major or minor in their main teaching assignment field. The types of majors teachers have vary substantially by school level. High school teachers are far more likely to have degrees in traditional academic fields such as math or history (66%) than are middle school teachers (44%) or elementary school teachers (22%; Loeb & Reininger, 2004). Many teachers, however, also teach classes outside their primary teaching assignment—and they are much less likely to hold a major or minor in these areas. In 1999–2000, Ingersoll (2003) found that 38% of all 7th- to 12th-grade teachers who taught one or more math classes did not have either a major or a minor in math, math education, or related disciplines like engineering, statistics, or physics. A third of all 7th- to 12th-grade teachers who taught one or more English classes had neither a major or minor in English or related subjects such as literature, communications, speech, journalism, English education, or reading education. In science and social studies, the numbers were slightly lower. Approximately 28% of all 7th- to 12th-grade teachers who taught one or more science classes did not even have a minor in one of the sciences or in science education. Finally, roughly 25% of those who taught one or more social studies classes were without a minor in any of the social sciences, in public affairs, in social studies education, or in history (Ingersoll, 2003).

The No Child Left Behind (NCLB) Act of 2001 mandated that every student be taught by a "highly qualified" teacher by 2006. NCLB defines a highly qualified teacher as a fully state-certified teacher, who holds a bachelor's degree and demonstrates competency in the core academic subject or subjects he or she teaches.[6] In order to be fully state-certified, as per these standards, a teacher must obtain a certificate appropriate to his or her level of experience and must not be in a position where certification or licensure requirements are waived on an emergency, temporary, or provisional basis. The law provides states considerable flexibility in determining the exact criteria for certification within the broad framework laid out. States, for instance, are allowed to determine their own requirements for indicators of subject-matter competence. Twenty-five states require high school teachers to have a major in their primary subject area and to have passed a subject-matter exam. Six states require high school teachers to only have an undergraduate major in the area, while 18 other states require teachers to only pass a subject-matter test in their primary teaching field (Boyd, Goldhaber, et al., 2007). Note, however, that there is considerable variation in the level of knowledge that constitutes a major or that which is necessary for certification exams.

While there is much rhetoric around the importance of subject-matter competence on teacher effectiveness, to date most research does not show a strong relationship between teachers' subject matter knowledge and student test-score gains. For example, in their study of New York City schools, Boyd et al. (2006) do not find a relationship

between teacher's undergraduate degree and student performance. Similarly, using data from the San Diego Unified School District, Betts, Zau, and Rice (2003) find no clear link between a student's rate of learning at the elementary level and the number of college courses completed by his/her teacher in a particular subject. This should not be taken as evidence that content knowledge is not important, but simply that it may not be the factor that most differentiates teachers' effectiveness in the classroom, especially in the early grades.

There is some recent evidence that suggests it is not content knowledge per se, but pedagogical knowledge that is important for student learning. Hill, Rowan, and Ball (2005) find that pedagogical knowledge for teaching math is significantly associated with student achievement for first- and third-graders, after controlling for key student and teacher-level covariates. In high school, however, recent literature finds that even the more general measures of teacher content knowledge might be associated with learning. For instance, Clotfelter, Ladd, and Vigdor (2007b) find some evidence that teachers who obtained a masters' degree while teaching add more value to student learning in high school than do teachers without masters' degrees.

Teacher Ability: Test Scores and Selectivity of Undergraduate Institution While there is little evidence on the importance of content knowledge for student learning, there is some evidence that teachers with greater general knowledge and academic ability are more effective in the classroom. This relationship, however, appears weak.

Teachers, on average, score below the typical college graduate on standardized aptitude tests (see Corcoran et al., 2004; Hanushek & Pace, 1995; Bacolod, 2005). Focusing on the average alone, however, masks the fact that many teachers score well on standardized aptitude tests. In a study of more than 300,000 prospective teachers who took a Praxis test between 1994 and 1997, Gitomer, Latham, and Ziomek (1999) found that prospective teachers in academic subject areas had SAT/ACT scores that were comparable, if not better, than the larger college graduate population. At the same time, those seeking licenses in non-academic fields such as elementary education had much lower scores (Gitomer et al., 1999). The academic ability of teachers has also changed over time. More than 20% of young female teachers in the 1960s scored in the top 10% of their high-school graduating cohort. By 2000, this number had dropped to 11% (Corcoran et al., 2004). For men in the top two decile groups, the drop in the probability of entering teaching was comparatively lower. While 6.3% of men in the ninth and tenth deciles of their high school graduating cohort entered teaching in 1964, this figure had dropped to 3.8% in 2000.[7] Bacolod's (2005) findings complement this; she shows that among those with higher test scores, the predicted probability of entering alternative professions has increased dramatically.[8]

Students of teachers with higher test scores tend to learn slightly more as measured by test score performance than other students. The relationship appears stronger in math than in reading. Using North Carolina data, Clotfelter et al. (2007a) find that teachers who had scored two or more standard deviations above the average boosted students test scores by 0.068 standard deviations while those who scored two or more below the average reduced achievement gains by 0.62 standard deviations.[9] They conclude that having a teacher at either extreme of the test score distribution has a far bigger effect on student math achievement than having an average teacher. Using data on New York City school teachers, Boyd et al. (2006) find that teachers who passed the Liberal Arts and Sciences Test (LAST) state teacher-certification exam on their first attempt produced higher student math achievement than those who did not (Boyd, Lankford, et al., 2007). They find no effects for student ELA performance. Importantly, however, they find that higher scoring teachers on average have a greater effect on students with higher prior test scores. When teaching students with lower prior test scores, they tended to do no better and in some cases worse than lower scoring teachers.

Caveats It is important to emphasize that the findings from many of the studies cannot be treated as definitive, but only suggestive. Some of them fail to establish causality because they are unable to estimate the counterfactual, that is, what would happen in the absence of the particular intervention being studied. This happens for several reasons. First, it is not always clear what the counterfactual means. For instance, does it mean being taught by the average teacher in the district or by the least effective teacher? Second, even if one can establish the effect of a particular teacher on a group of students, it is not always possible to extrapolate those findings to an entirely different group of students (Murnane & Steele, 2007). It is also hard to disentangle contextual effects (such as school and classroom effects) from teacher effects in many studies. Since teachers choose where they wish to teach, it is likely that teacher assignment is related to student, classroom, and school characteristics. This makes it difficult to distinguish statistically between effects that are due to teachers per se, and those that are due to characteristics of the students' classroom, school, and district environment. Large longitudinal data sets that follow students over time and match them to their schools and teachers have substantially increased our ability to sort among possible causes for the relationships that we see.

An important reason why it has been difficult to know the impact of many policy interventions is that large micro-education data sets gather very little information on the policy variables we are interested in. For instance, Figlio and Kenny (2006) explain that there has been little quantitative work linking teacher incentives to student performance because most data sets do not provide us the detail we need on school's personnel practices. Moreover, most data sets provide cross-sectional information. Cross-sectional studies, being specific to one time-period, are unable to capture *gains* in student achievement for a given cohort of students. As a result, they are not very helpful in

telling us how student achievement gains relate to specific characteristics of teachers. Comparing across cohorts is not a very effective method of understanding these gains since cohorts are likely to vary in measurable and unmeasurable characteristics. Value-added studies, in contrast, track the performance of individual students over time, thereby attempting to isolate the learning that a specific teacher adds to his or her students. They attempt to control for factors that are unrelated to a particular teacher's potential influence, such as student background characteristics (including past test scores), and classroom and school characteristics that likely impact a student's performance. How well this is done will determine whether we can glean any causal information from the study. As Murnane and Steele (2007) point out, the use of multi-year data on student achievement requires specifying statistical models that account for correlations between an individual student's test scores from any given year to the next. Such models make statistical assumptions about the constancy of teacher effects over time. Using different assumptions, one can generate different estimates of teacher effectiveness.

A final challenge stems from the lack of precise measures of teaching quality. As a result, we are left to look at measured attributes of teachers such as their years of teaching experience and their own test performance. To understand the effect of these measured attributes on student learning, quantitative work, including all the quantitative literature discussed in this paper, has primarily studied the average achievement gains of students on standardized tests in their classrooms. Relying entirely on student test scores to gauge the impact of a teacher on student learning is problematic. First, the test itself may not be the most precise instrument to capture all that a student has learned. Second, because we are interested in measuring students' achievement gains from one period to the next, it is important that the tests measure comparable content and scores be measured on comparable scales. Third, it is important that the tests measure content that a particular teacher has covered. This becomes difficult to ascertain in higher grades given the greater curricular differentiation among classrooms (Murnane & Steele, 2007).

Variation in Teacher Characteristics across Schools

The description of the teacher workforce above masks the substantial variation in teacher characteristics across schools and school districts. Nationwide, schools with the highest minority enrollment, largest low-income enrollments, and the most academically struggling students are also the ones most likely to have teachers with the weakest qualifications.

Certain features of the distribution of teachers stand out. First, there is greater variation in teacher credentials *within* individual cities than *across* cities. For instance, there are larger variations in teacher credentials, such as selectivity of undergraduate institution and average experience, among the schools in the Phoenix metropolitan area, than there are between the metropolitan areas of Phoenix and Detroit (Loeb & Page, 2001).

This variation across schools within metropolitan areas is systematic. Schools with high minority enrollments also have higher proportions of teachers in their first 3 years of teaching, higher proportions of teachers with less than 10 years experience, and the lowest proportion of teachers with more than 20 years experience. They also have the lowest share of teachers with certification in their primary or secondary teaching assignment. In the New York City school district, for example, there are large differences in teacher characteristics across racial and income groups (Loeb & Reininger, 2004). As of 2000, 21% of non-White students had teachers who were not certified in any subject taught, compared to only 15% of White students. Twenty-six percent of non-White students had teachers who failed the general knowledge certification exam, compared to 16% of White students. Similarly, 22% of low-income students had teachers who were not certified in any subject they taught, compared to 17% of higher income students. Thirty percent of low-income students had teachers who failed the certification exam, compared to 21% of higher income students.

There is also some variation across community type. Approximately 50% of all school teachers work in suburban settings, with the other half evenly distributed between rural and urban areas. Teachers in these settings are similar in terms of gender, experience, and certification, yet fairly different when it comes to race, age, and educational attainment (Loeb & Reininger, 2004). Not surprisingly, non-White teachers more frequently teach in central cities than in urban fringe/large towns or rural/small towns. Fewer rural teachers hold masters degrees compared to teachers in urban and suburban settings (Strizek et al., 2006).

The choices individual teachers make with regard to job postings are influenced by multiple measured and unmeasured factors. The research literature has identified and assessed a number of these including wages and benefits, working conditions, entry requirements, and school location. These are believed to affect the *supply* decisions of teachers. They tell us whether college graduates will choose teaching as a profession, and if they make this choice, where they are likely to teach. The eventual outcome is, however, also influenced by factors originating from the school system, that is, from those who *demand* teachers. Important among these factors are district hiring practices, contracts, and bureaucratic features. We look at each in turn.

Wages A large literature suggests that teachers are more likely to choose teaching when starting wages are high relative to wages in other occupations (see Corcoran et al., 2004; Bacolod, 2005; Hanushek & Rivkin, 2006). Drawing upon multiple data sources, Bacolod (2005) finds that highly qualified teachers are especially sensitive to changes in relative wages. The lower teachers are paid relative to professionals, the less likely high-quality educated women are to choose teaching (see Corcoran et al., 2004). Ap-

proximately 16.5% of public school teachers who decided to move to another school between 2003–04 and 2004–05 reported having done so for better salary or benefits. For those who left teaching in 2004–05, nearly 15% cited salary related reasons (Marvel et al., 2007).

Teacher wages have increased dramatically over the last 40 years. Nevertheless, since the 1970s, they have fallen behind salaries in non-teaching jobs for individuals with similar qualifications. Lawyers, doctors, scientists, and engineers earn substantially more, as do managers and sales and financial service workers (Corcoran et al., 2004). The opportunity cost of becoming a teacher, in terms of salary forgone in alternative professions, is high. However, teachers may work fewer hours and fewer days, at least partially compensating for this forgone income.

In 2003–04, the average base salary of regular full-time teachers was $44,400 per annum. Public school teachers on average earned considerably more than their private school counterparts, the former making $44,500 on average and the latter $31,700.[10] Regular full-time teachers in rural/small towns had, on average, lower base salaries than their counterparts in urban fringe/large towns and central cities (Strizek et al., 2006).

Teachers' salaries increase with years of experience and additional education (Hanushek & Rivkin, 2006). The average salary of beginning teachers in 2004–05 was $31,753 per annum. There is considerable variation across states, with new teachers making up to $39,259 per annum in Connecticut and approximately $24,872 per annum in North Dakota. If we look at all teachers, and not just new teachers, we find considerable statewide variation. Average teacher salaries are the highest in Connecticut at $57,760 per annum and the lowest in South Dakota at $34,039 (American Federation of Teachers, 2007). Much of this variation in salary mirrors variation in the wages of non-teaching college graduates and thus the differences in dollars overstate the differences in the relative wages (and thus appeal of teaching) across regions.

Within a state, there are differences across counties, and within counties, between districts. The within-county differences, compared with differences across states, more closely reflect differences in relative wages and thus in the appeal of teaching relative to other occupational choices. Thus, salaries can affect not only whether an individual chooses to become a teacher, but also where they choose to teach. In Florida, for instance, teachers with a bachelor's degree as their highest degree earned anywhere between $32,283 and $45,613 in 2005–06 depending on where they taught in the state (Florida Department of Education, 2006). In Santa Clara County in California, teachers with similar educational qualifications were paid $66,652 per annum in Alum Rock Union Elementary school district during 2005–06, but $80,041 per annum the same year in a neighboring district (California Department of Education).[11]

A number of factors explain the variation in teacher salaries seen above. For example, districts with greater resources have more money to spend on teacher salaries.

Alternatively, a district could have greater demand for teachers because of policy preferences for smaller class sizes or more skilled teachers; they may be willing to spend the money they have available on more teachers instead of potentially increasing the quality of their teachers by spending more on wages per teacher. Salaries could also be higher in one district than another because the region does not produce many teachers, or because the job opportunities for college graduates are very good in other fields and thus the district has to pay more to attract equally skilled individuals into teaching.

Non-Wage Job Characteristics Salaries are only one criterion influencing individuals' decisions about whether and where to teach. Non-wage job characteristics, including attributes of students, class size, school culture, facilities, teaching assignments, leadership, and safety, also affect teachers' choices and these characteristics often vary more dramatically across schools than do salaries.

Studies in Georgia, New York, and Texas all find that teacher mobility is heavily influenced by characteristics of the student body, especially race and achievement (Scafidi, Stinebrickner, & Sjoquist, 2003; Boyd, Lankford, Loeb, & Wyckoff, 2005; Hanushek et al., 2004). Georgia elementary teachers move from schools with higher proportions of minority students and from low-performing schools, but the latter appears to be explained by teacher preferences for fewer minority students. Texas and New York data, on the other hand, find that teachers prefer higher-achieving students even after controlling for student racial composition. Teachers, especially highly qualified teachers, are more likely to transfer or quit when teaching lower-achieving students. As further evidence of the weight some teachers put on student-body characteristics, when class size reduction in California increased the demand for teachers across the state, many teachers in schools with low-achieving

students switched to schools with higher-achieving students (Shields et al., 2001).

While student characteristics are important by themselves, teachers also choose schools with more high-achieving and wealthy students because these schools often offer other characteristics that teachers prefer, such as better facilities or more preparation time. A recent survey of teachers in California, Wisconsin, and New York found that schools serving large numbers of low-income students had a much higher incidence of inadequate facilities relative to other schools, evidence of vermin (cockroaches, mice, and rats) in school buildings; dirty, closed or inoperative student bathrooms; inadequate textbooks and science equipment; and higher personal expenditures by teachers to compensate for insufficient classroom materials and supplies (Carroll, Fulton, Abercrombie, & Yoon, 2004).

The 2004–05 TFS asked teachers who moved across schools and why they moved. Table 47.1 shows that approximately 38% of teachers reportedly moved to another school due to a better teaching assignment. Interview studies also reveal that new teachers resent teaching subjects they do not know, subjects requiring extensive class preparation, being split between two subjects, or teaching very large classes. While there is little evidence that these factors by themselves explain high turnover rates, it is likely that they cause stress and dissatisfaction, thereby precipitating teachers' transfers and resignations (Johnson, Berg, & Donaldson, 2005).

School leadership is another important factor in teachers' decision making. In the 2004–05 TFS, more than 37% of teachers indicated that this was an important factor in their decision to switch schools. Similarly, for teachers who left teaching altogether, Ingersoll and Smith (2003) found that of the 29% of leaving teachers who cited dissatisfaction as their reason for leaving, more than three-fourths linked their quitting to low salaries. However, the next two most important factors were student discipline problems and lack of support from the school administration.

Teacher peers also affect teachers' decisions. In a study of California schools, Shields et al. (2001) found that credentialed teachers complained of the lack of professionalism of those who were not credentialed and the resulting instructional burden they had to carry to compensate for the teaching inadequacies of their colleagues.

Differences across schools in non-wage attributes of the job will be particularly important when there is little variation in wage to compensate, as is the case in large urban districts in which all schools operate under the same salary schedule. Policies that attract effective administrators, increase preparation time, decrease class size, or provide funds to renovate facilities can improve working conditions and thus help to equalize the distribution of teachers across schools.

Location In addition to wages and working conditions, school location has a strong influence on the distribution of teachers. Research shows that most teachers prefer to

TABLE 47.1

Percentage of Public School Teacher Movers Who Rated Various Reasons as Very Important or Extremely Important in Their Decision to Move to Another School: 2004-05

Reason for Moving to Another School	Percentage of Teachers
Opportunity for a better teaching assignment (subject area/ grade)	38.1
Dissatisfaction with support from administrators at previous school	37.2
Dissatisfaction with workplace conditions at previous school	32.7
Higher job security	19.1
Dissatisfaction with changes in job description or responsibilities	18.3
Dissatisfaction with opportunities for professional development in previous school	12.8
Did not have enough autonomy over classroom at previous school	10.4

Source: Marvel et al. (2007).

teach close to where they grew up and in districts that are similar to the districts they attended as high school students. Of all public school teachers who chose to move from one school to another between 2003–04 and 2004–05, 26.2% cited closeness to home as a very or extremely important factor in their decision to move. Of those who left teaching, 11.2% cited changing residence as very or extremely important.

Sixty-one percent of teachers who entered public school teaching in New York state between 1999 and 2002 started teaching in a school district located within 15 miles of the district where they went to high school. Eighty-five percent entered teaching within 40 miles of their high school. Even when teachers go far away to college, they tend to come home to teach (Loeb & Reininger, 2004). A recent study using the NELS 1988–2000 dataset and Common Core of Data finds that these results are consistent nationwide: teachers are indeed local. Further, in comparison to college graduates in nearly 40 other occupations, teachers were significantly more likely to live locally 8 years after high school graduation (Reininger, 2006). Cannata (2007a) argues that teachers tend to sort themselves into schools that are socially proximal to them, in terms of race and class, and resemble the schools they attended as children. She finds that teacher candidates tend to have a clear notion of where they want to teach and where they do not, despite knowing little about these schools. Thus, she concludes, even though teacher candidates espouse preferences for specific school characteristics, such as beginning teacher support, the eventual decision on where to teach is based more on feelings of familiarity, comfort, and fit (Cannata, 2007b).

Teachers' preferences to teach close to home or in similar settings pose serious concerns for urban districts since these tend to be net importers of teachers. Urban areas do not produce as high a proportion of college graduates as suburban areas. Using schools with large minority enrolments and large percentages of students receiving free and reduced-price lunch as proxies for difficult-to-staff schools, Reininger (2006) finds these schools produce significantly lower percentages of students earning bachelor's degrees—a prerequisite for teaching (Reininger, 2006). As a result, schools in these regions need to attract teachers from other regions, for which they have to pay a premium to get equally qualified candidates. If they are unable to find qualified candidates, then they will be forced to hire from a less-qualified pool of applicants.

Entrance Requirements In addition to factors affecting the appeal of a particular job, such as wages, working conditions, and location, requirements for entry into teaching can also affect who goes into teaching and the distribution of teachers across schools. While teacher preparation and certification requirements could improve student outcomes by increasing skills and knowledge, they also impose costs on current teachers and would-be teachers for tuition and the opportunity cost of time. On the one hand, the willingness to incur such costs might signal those who are likely to be more motivated to teach; on the other hand, the costs per se could be prohibitively high for some, decreasing the potential pool of talented applicants. Licensure exams play a role similar to certification. While they have the merit of establishing a floor on the measured knowledge teachers must have, if the tests are unable to effectively distinguish between better and worse candidates, or assess applicants on material unrelated to student learning, they may exclude teachers who might have been very effective in the classroom (see Boyd, Goldhaber, et al., 2007).

Until recently many schools, particularly those serving high concentrations of students in poverty, staffed their classrooms with uncertified teachers, despite the fact that in theory certification was required of all teachers. As an example, in New York City in 2000, 35% of teachers in the highest-poverty quartile of schools had failed the general knowledge certification exam the first time they took it and approximately half of all new teachers held a temporary license (were not certified to teach). As described above, NCLB changed the landscape, requiring that *all* students be taught by a "highly qualified" teacher by the end of the 2006–07 school year. At least partially as a result, between 2000 and 2005 there was a remarkable narrowing in the gap in teacher qualifications between high-poverty schools and low-poverty schools in New York City. By 2005, only some 10% of new teachers in the highest-poverty quartile had failed their certification exam on the first attempt (see Boyd, Lankford, Loeb, Rockoff, & Wyckoff, 2007).

Teacher Hiring Practices Factors that affect teachers' decisions are only one side of the story. Factors affecting demand for teachers are important as well. Teacher hiring practices, for example, explain part of why some schools and districts end up with better teachers than others. A recent study by the New Teacher Project in three large urban districts in the southwestern, midwestern, and eastern regions and one mid-sized urban district in the Midwest found that some schools that appeared difficult-to-staff did not have a problem *attracting* teachers, but they did have a problem when it came to actually *hiring* them. While there were between 5 to 20 times as many applicants as available positions in these districts, with up to 37% of the applicants in difficult-to-staff subjects such as math, science, special education, and English Language Learners, each of the districts failed to make offers until mid-to-late summer. By that time, many of the applicants (31–60%) had withdrawn their applications. Of those who had withdrawn, 50–70% cited late timelines as a major reason for taking another job. Furthermore, the study indicates that applicants who withdrew from the process were significantly better qualified than new hires in terms of the likelihood of having a higher undergraduate GPA, a degree in their teaching field, and completed educational coursework (Levin & Quinn, 2003). This suggests that districts with effective hiring practices such as aggressive recruitment strategies and spring job offers are likely to end up with higher quality teaching staff even if initially faced with the same pool of applicants. These districts are able to recruit their top choices while other districts are left with teachers who could not find jobs elsewhere.

Principals also do not always have the information needed to accurately assess teacher quality and judge future performance. In a recent paper, Jacob and Lefgren (2005) argue that while principals are able to identify the best and the worst teachers in their schools, they are not able to identify where the rest fall in the ability distribution. Principals, according to this study, also discriminated systematically against male and untenured faculty (Jacob & Lefgren, 2005).

Liu and Johnson (2006) stress the importance of information-rich and timely hiring processes in improving the match between teachers, schools, and teaching assignments. In a survey of new teachers in California, Florida, Massachusetts, and Michigan, they found that the hiring process relied heavily on reviews of paper credentials and interviews. Importantly, schools and districts rarely observed a candidate's teaching. In much the same way, applicants rarely got much experience of the school to which they had applied. While most new teachers met with the school principal during the hiring process, very few interviewed with current teachers or met with students to get a feel of the school culture and requirements. As a result, new teachers in these states formed only a moderately accurate picture of what their job likely entailed, increasing the chances for job-related disappointments and turnover.

The timing of the hiring process might be the most severe impediment to information-rich hiring processes. Many new teachers are hired in summer, when school is not in session; teachers are unlikely to be available for interviews and classes cannot be observed in action. Further, Liu and Johnson (2006) found that approximately a third of new teachers in California and Florida were hired only after the school year had started, when principals were in a rush to fill a position, teachers were busy with their classes and there was little time for an informative hiring process. The combination of these factors underscores the difficulty—and necessity—of achieving effective hiring practices.

Bureaucratic Hurdles The problem of suboptimal staffing is driven, at least in part, by bureaucratic and contractual requirements. Three district-level policies may be particularly important: vacancy notification requirements, teachers' union transfer requirements, and late budget timetables and poor forecasting (Levin, Mulhern, & Schunck, 2005). Vacancy notification requirements allow resigning or retiring teachers to provide very late notice of when they intend to leave. In the study of hiring practices in four districts conducted by the New Teacher Project, three had a summer notification deadline or none at all, while one had a mid-May deadline. Late notification deadlines make it very difficult to know which posts will be available in September when the school year typically starts. Local laws and union contracts make it possible for experienced teachers to ask

for last-minute transfers. Further, many principals delay advertising vacancies for fear of being required to hire a transferring teacher they do not want. Finally, late state budget deadlines lead to chronic budgetary uncertainties as a result of which administrators do not know which positions will be funded in their schools.[12]

Collective Bargaining Agreements Collective bargaining agreements also influence hiring and retention practices and may affect the distribution of teachers across schools. Rules in these contracts, for instance, often make it very difficult to fire tenured teachers even when they are performing poorly. To the extent that parents can exert power to have such teachers removed from their children's schools, they may be more likely to end up in schools serving students with the fewest available resources and the greatest needs. Similarly, the least effective teachers may end up in poorly performing schools if the administrators are less effective as well. The collective bargaining process may also distort the allocation of resources toward easily measured factors such as salary, with other important aspects of schooling such as working conditions, bearing the brunt. Since non-wage factors such as working conditions are important in determining whether high-quality teachers will come to teach in low-achieving and poor schools, this over-emphasis on pecuniary measures may be detrimental. Finally, policies tend to standardize across schools—salaries are just one example. If the needs of some schools are much greater than that of others, such standardization might put high-needs schools at a relative disadvantage.

In summary, the differences in teachers across schools are systematic and often striking. A variety of factors combine to create these differences. On the supply side, wages, working conditions, location, and entry requirements all contribute to the variation. On the demand side, hiring practices, bureaucratic hurdles, and collective bargaining practices are all important factors.

Teacher Mobility and Turnover

Once the decision to teach is made, the next question is where to teach. Differences in the characteristics of teachers across schools get determined, to a large extent, by teachers' initial choice of posting. From an aggregate nationwide perspective, the magnitude of teacher turnover is not very large. Between 2003–04 and 2004–05, for instance, 83.5% of teachers stayed in the same school, while only 8.1% transferred between schools and 8.4% left teaching (Marvel et al., 2007).[13] From the perspective of the individual school that loses teachers, however, knowing that the magnitude of attrition nationally is very small in relative terms is of little consolation. For the school in question, not only is there the risk of losing a good teacher, the school's learning environment likely suffers as instructional continuity gets disrupted.

From Table 47.2 we see that while the percentage of those who move to another school (henceforth called mov-

TABLE 47.2
Percentage Distribution of Teacher Stayers, Movers, and Leavers in Public Schools[a]

Year	Stayers (%)	Movers (%)	Leavers (%)
1991–92	87.6	7.3	5.1
1994–95	86.3	7.2	6.6
2000–01	84.9	7.7	7.4
2004–05	83.5	8.1	8.4

Note. [a]Stayers are teachers who were teaching in the same school in the current school year as in the year before (base year). Movers are teachers who were still teaching in the current school year but had moved to a different school after the base year. Leavers are teachers who left the teaching profession after the base year. Note, this does not rule out the possibility of their re-entering teaching at a later date.
Source: Compiled from Marvel et al. (2007)

ers) has been fairly stable over the years, the percentage of those who stay on in a school (henceforth called stayers) has been decreasing gradually. Those who leave the teaching profession altogether (henceforth called leavers) has been rising steadily.

Characteristics of Movers and Leavers Younger teachers tend to leave a given school or teaching more frequently than older ones. Between 2003–04 and 2004–05, for instance, 14.7% of teachers under the age of 30 years had moved to another school, while 9% had left teaching altogether. For teachers between the ages of 40–49 years, on the other hand, only 7.1% had moved to another school and 5.3% had left teaching altogether.

According to TFS data, between 2003–04 and 2004–05, the category of teachers with *no* full-time teaching experience was the most likely to move out of a school as well as leave teaching altogether. For teachers with full-time teaching experience, those with 1–3 years of experience were both the most likely to move to another school as well as leave teaching altogether. The corresponding figures for teachers with more experience are lower; for instance, for teachers with 10–19 years of experience, 6.3% moved to another school, while 5.5% left teaching.

The difference by sex is not striking, although a larger percentage of female teachers left teaching altogether between 2003–04 and 2004–05. White teachers relative to Black and Hispanic teachers had the lowest percentage of movers and leavers for the same period. The data suggests that Hispanic teachers had the highest percentage of movers, while Black teachers had the highest percentage of leavers.

Not surprisingly, teachers whose base salary was $30,000 per year or less were the most likely to move to another school or leave teaching compared to teachers who earned more. With regard to main teaching assignment, special education teachers were the most likely to switch schools as well as leave teaching between 2003–04 and 2004–05. This stands in contrast to the period between 1999–2000 and 2000–01 when special education teachers were among those least likely to leave teaching (though not among those less likely to move to another school).

Teachers who have a regular or standard certification type are the least likely to move to another school or leave teaching altogether. Between 2003–04 and 2004–05, 7.2% of teachers who had a regular or standard certification type had switched schools, while 8.2% of them had left. Those with a provisional or temporary certification type were the most likely to move, while those who had none of the common types of certification were the most likely to leave.[14]

Better qualified teachers (but not necessarily more effective teachers) are also more likely to leave teaching, at least in some geographical regions. In New York City, for example, there are considerable differences between teachers who stay on in a particular school and those who transfer or quit (Loeb & Reininger, 2004). Those who stay on in a particular school have failed the certification exams twice as often as those transferring to another district (Boyd et al., 2005). Moreover, the latter are twice as likely to have attended a highly competitive college, and half as likely to have attended a less competitive college. New York City teachers who quit teaching in New York State are also substantially more qualified than those who remain in terms of their test scores. For example, 20% of new teachers in the top quartile on the general-knowledge certification exam left high-achieving schools after 1 year, while 34% of those in low-achieving schools left after 1 year. By contrast, 14% of bottom-quartile teachers left high achieving schools after 1 year, and 17% left low-achieving schools.

More qualified teachers are also substantially more likely to leave schools having the lowest-achieving students. For example, of the new teachers hired in New York City's lowest-achieving schools in 1996–1998, 28% scored in the lowest quartile on the general-knowledge certification exam. Of those remaining in the same schools 5 years later, 44% had scores in the lowest quartile. In contrast, 22% of the new teachers in the higher-achieving schools were in the lowest quartile, which increased to only 24% for those remaining after 5 years.

Teacher mobility also varies by geographical region and community type. Turnover rates in the Northeast region of the country are lower than in other regions, and larger schools face fewer turnovers than do smaller schools. Urban areas tend to have a slightly higher turnover rate than suburban areas in general, but there are certain urban areas where the situation is particularly bad. For example, in New York City approximately 62% of teachers switch schools within 5 years compared to 54% in the suburbs. Thirty-five percent of New York City teachers leave teaching altogether within 5 years, compared with 25% of teachers in the suburbs (Boyd et al., 2005).

Turnover rates in schools with higher proportions of African American and Hispanic students are higher than in schools that are predominantly White. Scafidi et al. (2003) found that Georgia elementary teachers moved from schools with higher proportions of minority students and from low-performing schools, and that the latter is explained by teacher preferences for fewer minority students. Hanushek et al. (2004), using a similar model and Texas data, find that teachers prefer higher-achieving students even after controlling for student racial composition.

Implications of Turnover Teacher turnover may affect student learning in several ways. First, in high-turnover schools, students may be more likely to have inexperienced teachers who we know are less effective, on average (Rockoff, 2003; Rivkin, Hanushek, & Kain, 2004; Kane, Rockoff, & Staiger, 2006). Second, high turnover creates instability in schools, making it more difficult to have coherent instruction. This instability may be particularly problematic when schools are trying to implement reforms, as the new teachers coming in each year are likely to repeat mistakes rather than improve upon implementation of reform. Third, high turnover can be costly in that it takes time and effort to continuously recruit teachers.

Transfer and quit behavior would be especially worrying if more effective teachers had higher attrition rates. This does not appear to be the case. Using data on a large urban school district in Texas, Hanushek and Rivkin (2006) find no conclusive evidence suggesting that more effective teachers, in terms of student test score gains, have higher exit rates. They find that those who exit are in fact less effective, on average, than non-movers, both in that district and in general. Further, those who move between schools within the same school district are, on average, less effective than those who do not. They go beyond average performances, and compare the quality distributions of teachers who either change schools or exit public schools to get a more nuanced picture of what is happening with teachers at the top and bottom end of this distribution.[15] They find that the distribution of these teachers falls distinctly below the distribution of those who stay, indicating that at every level, it is the less effective teachers who are more likely to change schools or exit public schools.

Their finding is echoed in a recent study of new teachers in New York City schools (Boyd, Grossman, Lankford, Loeb, & Wyckoff, 2007). This study also found no reason to believe that those who exited were better than those who stayed. Specifically, they found that first-year teachers identified as being less effective in improving student test scores had higher attrition rates than those identified as more effective. They found that it was relatively ineffective teachers, on average, who transferred within New York City; again, however, averages mask important variation. For teachers transferring from a given low-performing school, the more effective ones tended to transfer to schools with fewer low-scoring and non-White students, exacerbating the inequities in teacher quality across schools.[16]

Policy Approaches

In the 2003–04 school year, 74% of all public schools had teaching vacancies. Of the schools with vacancies, 16.4% reported having to hire a less than fully-qualified teacher (see Strizek et al., 2006). Vacancies were highest in special education (67.4%), followed by English Language Arts (57.1%) and then math (55.6%). In each, the shortages were most pronounced at the secondary level and in urban schools (versus suburban and rural schools). While only 8.1% of schools with vacancies in ELA found it very difficult or were not able to staff their schools, the numbers for special education and mathematics were much higher at 29.2% and 28.8%, respectively. This section looks at the impact of different supply-side and demand-side strategies that aim to improve teacher labor market outcomes.

Incentives As discussed previously, teachers' salaries are important in the decision to teach and the decision to stay in a particular school. Nearly 17% of teachers who moved from their base school between 2003–04 and 2004–05 reported better salary and benefits as being very or extremely important in their decision to change schools. Approximately 14% of those who left teaching in the same period cited salaries and benefits as being at least very important (Marvel et al., 2007).

Teachers' salaries can be increased in two ways: (a) across-the-board increases in salaries, and (b) targeted increases, for example, by focusing on difficult-to-staff schools and difficult-to-staff fields. The economic argument for increasing the pay of teachers already content to work in a given school is weak. Since it is unlikely that such schools will face staffing difficulties, it makes sense to target resources at teachers in difficult-to-staff schools and difficult-to-staff subject areas.

Many states and a large number of school districts are pursuing pay-related methods to recruit and retain highly qualified teachers. While retention bonuses are the most widely used of these methods, a few states offer housing incentives and a few offer signing bonuses to new teachers. Most of these policies are, however, not targeted at increasing the quality of the teaching force in shortage fields or in high-poverty or low-performing schools. Of the 35 states providing retention bonuses for teachers in 2003, only 5 targeted teachers in high-need schools.

The evidence on the effectiveness of pay-related incentives on retaining teachers and improving student performance is small and mixed. The Massachusetts Signing Bonus Program for New Teachers, which started in 1998, combined a national recruitment campaign, $20,000 in signing bonuses, and a 7-week "fast-track" certification program, but met with limited success in its stated goals. Twenty percent of the first cohort of bonus recipients left teaching after 1 year, and more than 50% of its second cohort ended up *not* teaching where policy makers said they should—in 13 state-designated, high-need school districts (Fowler, 2001). In 2001, North Carolina began giving $1,800 in annual bonuses to teachers in specific fields (math, science, and special education) for middle or high schools serving low-income or low-performing students. This program mildly increased the retention of teachers, but it also suffered from complicated eligibility requirements and implementation problems (Jacob, 2007).

Incentives can also directly target success, rewarding

teachers or schools that seem most effective. In a study of Dallas' school-based accountability program, where *every* member of the staff of the most effective schools was rewarded, Clotfelter and Ladd (1996) found that the pass rates of students in the city increased relative to five other large Texas cities. Figlio and Kenny (2006), using data from the National Education Longitudinal Survey and their own survey conducted in 2000, however, found that test scores were higher in schools that offered individual-level financial incentives but *not* in schools that offered indiscriminate merit pay. While they were able to demonstrate that students learned more in schools in which individual teachers received financial incentives as reward for superior performance, data limitations prevented them from making causal linkages from their findings.

Incentives can also take the form of reduced costs of entry into teaching. Teachers have traditionally entered teaching after taking courses in four broad areas—foundational courses, pedagogical courses, subject-matter knowledge courses, and field experiences—during either their undergraduate education or their master's program. Many states, in an attempt to reduce the cost of entry for college graduates interested in teaching, now allow them to take alternative route programs with fewer course requirements prior to beginning teaching. Forty-seven states and the District of Columbia have some form of alternative-route program to recruit, train, and certify teachers (Boyd, Lankford, et al., 2007). Many states rely heavily on alternative routes for teachers. New Jersey, Texas, and California, for instance, obtain more than a third of their new teachers from alternative routes (Boyd, Lankford, et al., 2007).

Alternative route programs typically allow teachers to enter the classroom by delaying or bypassing many of the requirements for entry that are part of traditional teacher preparation programs. These programs require teachers to be college graduates and approximately 80% of them require demonstration of subject matter knowledge by completing coursework, passing an exam, or some combination of the two. This apart, they vary greatly in requirements. ITeachTexas, a statewide alternative certification program in Texas, for instance, is a Web-based alternative certification program which does not require any onsite pre-service meetings. The New York City Teaching Fellows Program (NYCTF), on the other hand, requires an intensive onsite 7-week pre-service training session.

The most commonly studied alternative route program, Teach for America (TFA), is able to recruit teachers with stronger qualifications than those recruited through the traditional route. For instance, in 2003 TFA had 16,000 applicants, most from highly selective undergraduates, for 1,800 available slots, as a result of which it could be highly selective in terms of teacher qualifications—this is not true of all alternative route programs. Studies of the effectiveness of TFA teachers have found that these teachers are equally effective, or more effective, than other teachers in math, though the results for reading are not quite as positive. For instance, in a randomized evaluation of the program in 17 schools covering Chicago, Los Angeles, Houston, New Orleans, and the Mississippi Delta, researchers from Mathematica found that while the average TFA student increased his/her rank in math by 3 percentile points over the course of a year, the average non-TFA student did not register any change. In contrast, there was no difference between the average TFA and non-TFA student in reading gains, with both having registered an increase of a percentile. Note, TFA teachers in the sample differed from non-TFA teachers considerably in terms of selectivity of college, education-specific training, certification and experience (Decker, Mayer, & Glazerman, 2004). Similar, though not quite as positive, results hold for the New York City Teaching Fellows (NYCTF). Early estimates suggest that Teaching Fellows are less effective in their first year of teaching but that the differences in student achievement between NYCTF teachers and traditional route teachers diminish with experience (Boyd, Grossman, Lankford, Loeb, & Wyckoff, 2006). Both TFA and NYCTF include substantial recruiting efforts as well as efforts to continuously improve, making it difficult to generalize the findings to alternative route programs, many of which may be less selective and put less effort into quality. In a recent study of alternative certification programs, Humphrey and Wechsler (2005) find a great deal of variation both between and within alternative certification programs, leading them to question the worth of comparing different alternative certification programs. Further, the individuals who take up these programs have considerably different backgrounds, school placements, and learning outcomes, making comparisons across programs problematic.

Districts have also been trying out various strategies to recruit people into teaching, especially minorities and people who belong to difficult-to-staff neighborhoods. Typically, these involve partnerships between K-12 school districts and local colleges to encourage students to enter teaching or scholarship and loan forgiveness programs for candidates who commit to teaching for a certain period (Jacob, 2007). Broward County Public Schools in Florida, one of the five largest school districts in the United States, initiated the Urban Teacher Academy Project (UTAP) to address a major challenge that faced the district: the need for 13,000 new teachers over the next 10 years. The program recruits students when they are as young as 14 years old, grooms them in teaching techniques, classroom theory, and pairs them with teacher mentors. After high school, they move on to community colleges and universities for a 4-year, tuition-free teaching degree with a guaranteed job at the end. The program not only generates a larger number of teachers, but by drawing students from difficult-to-staff schools and minority areas, it also creates a teaching force that is unlikely to face culture shocks when it goes back to those schools to teach.[17] Evidence on the success of these programs, in terms of student achievement and teacher quality and retention, remains sparse—a recent review of research by analysts at RAND and the Education Commission of the States (ECS) found very little research on the impact of recruitment strategies employed in most states and districts (Jacob, 2007).

Regulating Entry Incentives are not the only way to influence the teaching workforce. One of the most common tools policy makers use to regulate the teaching profession is certification requirements. Most teachers in the United States are certified. For instance, in 1999–2000, 94.4% of public elementary and secondary teachers were certified in their main teaching assignment. In theory, certification keeps individuals who are likely to be poor teachers out of the classroom. The evidence on the effect of certification is, however, mixed. Recent studies in New York City and North Carolina found that students of certified teachers learned more, on average, than did students of uncertified teachers, though a similar study in Florida found no difference (Boyd et al., 2006; Goldhaber, 2007; Harris & Sass, 2006). Similarly, studies in New York and North Carolina found that teachers who passed their certification exam (the Liberal Art and Science Test in New York and the Praxis II in North Carolina) showed higher student achievement in math. For example, teachers who passed the Praxis II produce on-average student achievement gains that were in the range of 3 to 6% of a standard deviation higher (in math) than those who failed. Comparing the effect of this gain to that produced by experience, the study found that the average teacher who failed the test, were he/she allowed to teach regardless, would likely produce the same level of math achievement in his/her second or third year of teaching as a novice teacher who passed the test. The study also shows how test cut-off criteria can generate a number of false negatives (individuals who fail to pass the test but might have been high-quality teachers) and false positives (individuals who make the cut-off might turn out to be poor teachers), calling into question the signal value of certification tests (Goldhaber, 2007). Raising cut-off scores might also be detrimental if it reduces the supply and racial/ethnic diversity of the prospective teacher pool (Gitomer et al., 1999; Angrist & Guryan, 2004).

Supporting Teachers In addition to regulating teachers, policy makers and educational leaders can affect the teacher workforce through policies that support teachers' development. Surveys have found that the lack of support services ranks high in teachers' decisions to quit teaching (Jacob, 2007). Of teachers who changed schools between 1999–2000 and 2000–01, 33.4% of new teachers (1–3 years of experience) reported dissatisfaction with support from administrators as being very important in their decision to move. Almost 21% of those who left teaching over the same period reported dissatisfaction with job description or responsibilities as a very important factor in their decision to quit. Nearly 15% said that a very important reason for quitting was related to not feeling prepared to implement or not agreeing with new reform measures. Many districts have, as a consequence, adopted programs aimed at providing support, guidance, and orientation services to elementary and secondary teachers as they begin their teaching career. The goal of these programs is to reduce teacher attrition by making teaching more manageable (Smith & Ingersoll, 2004).

Participation in induction programs increased during the nineties. In 1990–91, approximately 40% of new teachers had participated in a teacher induction program; by 1999–2000, 80% had participated in an induction program (Smith & Ingersoll, 2004). Induction programs typically involve meetings, informal classes for new teachers, and the formation of new-teacher peer support groups. Mentoring programs typically pair new teachers with experienced ones, although the details vary across programs. In a review of 10 studies on induction and mentoring programs, Ingersoll and Kralik (2004) find empirical support for the claim that induction programs for new teachers and, in particular, mentoring programs, have a positive impact on teachers' decision to stay in the same school and continue in the teaching profession. Using 1999–2000 SASS data, Smith and Ingersoll (2004) find that certain types of activities, such as having a mentor from the same field and having common planning time with other teachers on instruction, were more effective in reducing turnover than other types of activities such as the provision of seminars or classes for beginning teachers (Smith & Ingersoll, 2004). A study of 141 teachers in New Mexico who participated in a teacher mentoring program found that the attrition rate was only 4% annually compared with the statewide average rate of 9%. In an analysis of the Beginning Teacher Support and Assessment Program (BTSA), a mentorship program in California, Strong and Vilar (2005) found that in addition to reducing teacher attrition rates, the program resulted in aggregate reading scores for students of new teachers being comparable to those of mid-career teachers.

Professional development programs provide teachers with continuing education opportunities once they have joined the profession. These programs encompass traditional workshops, in-services, graduate coursework, school-based teacher study groups, mentoring relationships, and advanced credentials such as that provided by the National Board for Professional Teaching Standards (NBPTS). Of teachers who moved from one school to another between 2003–04 and 2004–05, nearly 13% reported dissatisfaction with opportunities for professional development in their previous school as a very important reason for their decision.

Unfortunately, the research literature does not provide a clear understanding of the extent to which professional development programs improve student achievement. While specific professional development programs have shown positive effects on student learning in randomized trials, there is considerable variation in the quality of professional development programs, and, on average, professional development programs do not appear to benefit students (Hill, 2007). Teacher self-reports of the quality of their own professional development experiences are not encouraging. In a recent study, only 20% of science teachers and 25% of math teachers said that their professional development program had changed their teaching practices (Horizon, 2002).

Selective Retention According to an informal survey of the human resources departments in several large urban districts, less than 1% of the teaching workforce is dismissed each year (Jacob, 2007). Yet, selective dismissal or, similarly selective promotion, could affect the teacher workforce. In a recent study using data from New York City schools, Gordon, Kane, and Staiger (2006) argue that it is possible to predict the performance of a teacher in later years from student achievement scores in the first 2 years of teaching. On average, a teacher whose students make above average gains is likely to produce such gains in later years; similarly, a teacher who performs badly in the first 2 years is unlikely to improve dramatically. Making somewhat conservative assumptions about the costs of replacing ineffective teachers, they conclude that denying tenure to the bottom quarter of new teachers would substantially improve student achievement. This study, however, does not account for the potential change in teaching such a policy might facilitate, including a need to compensate teachers for the additional risk and the potential for undesirable narrowing or targeting of instruction (Gordon et al., 2006).

Looking Outside Traditional Public Schools Charter schools and private schools may offer insights into teachers' preferences and how to develop policies to attract and retain effective teachers. In a case study of 40 charter schools in Arizona which had completed their fifth year of operation in 1999–2000, Gifford, Phillips, and Ogle (2000) found that in general charter schools aimed to hire staff that had a philosophical connection with the school. They also sought less experienced teachers with the expectation that it would be easier to train and assimilate new teachers into the school environments. The literature more generally identifies three reasons teachers are attracted to charter schools. First, teachers perceive charter schools as offering increased freedom, flexibility, and empowerment (Finn, Manno, & Vanourek, 2000; Koppich, Holmes, & Plecki, 1998; Wohlstetter & Griffin, 1998); second, teachers want to work in schools that share similar educational philosophies (Finn et al., 2000; Hill et al., 2001; Koppich et al., 1998; Wohlstetter & Griffin, 1998); and third, teachers believe charter schools offer smaller classes (Finn et al., 2000). Nevertheless, Ballou and Podgursky (1998) found teacher turnover to be significantly higher in charter schools relative to public schools. A study conducted by NEA concluded that charter school teachers were dissatisfied with their salaries and the lack of job security (Koppich et al., 1998).

Private schools share characteristics with charters. Researchers have found that religious beliefs and moral training at Catholic schools contributes to a sense of community and common purpose that improves teacher efficacy and morale (Bryk, Lee, & Holland, 1993). This said, the percentage of private-school teachers leaving teaching since 1988–89 has remained consistently higher than the percentage of public-school teachers leaving teaching. This higher attrition may be driven either by teachers' decisions to leave (e.g., because of relatively low wages) or by greater administrative flexibility to dismiss teachers. Ballou (1996) suggests that private schools are more successful in retaining the best of their new teachers because of greater flexibility in structuring pay, more supervision and mentoring of new teachers, and freedom to dismiss teachers for poor performance. This may well be true, but there is no research to date that verifies or contradicts this proposal.

Schools outside of the United States can also provide useful insights because of the great variation in approaches seen throughout the world. In a review of the research on teacher labor markets in developed countries, Ladd (2007), for instance, finds that in most developed countries teachers' relative pay is higher than in the United States. That being said, she finds no clear relationship across countries between teacher salaries and student achievement.

Conclusion

Teacher labor markets are huge and they are complex. Approximately 3.5 million adults teach in elementary and secondary schools in the United States. Teachers are a diverse group by any measure: gender, race, age, experience, academic achievement, preparation, or effectiveness at improving student test performance. They are also systematically distributed across schools, with the least experienced and least prepared often teaching in schools with the highest proportion of low-income, non-White, and academically struggling students.

The supply and demand model provides a simple framework for analyzing these markets. Wages and non-pecuniary job attributes combine to determine the supply of individuals interested in teaching in a given school, district, or state. A large body of research suggests that potential and current teachers respond to wage changes, although research on the degree of this response is inconclusive. Non-pecuniary aspects of teaching influencing teacher supply include working conditions, school location, and ease of entry into the occupation and the school. Feelings of success in the classroom also appear to be important for the retention of teachers already in the workforce.

The demand for teachers and the institutional constraints within which these demands are expressed also affect the teacher workforce. The number and characteristics of teachers demanded is a function of many factors including local preferences, ability and willingness to pay for teachers, the student population, teacher retirements, and attrition. Institutional constraints such as the skill and efficiency of hiring authorities, available information on the quality of individual teachers, budget timing, certification and licensure policies, tenure policies, and teacher contract provisions can all affect the ability of districts to recruit and retain effective teachers.

A wide variety of policies now aim to improve the teaching workforce and alleviate disparities in teachers' knowledge and skills across schools. Direct incentives are one such policy approach. Higher wages targeted at difficult-to-staff schools, difficult-to-staff fields, or particularly effective teachers are all potential avenues for affecting teachers and teaching. Similarly, regulations governing who can enter teaching by establishing criteria for course-taking or test performance can change the teacher workforce. Further, policies targeted at teacher supports, through mentoring or professional development, can potentially increase retention and improve teaching if implemented well.

To date, the research on the effectiveness of different policy approaches is, however, sparse. Our inability to make convincing causal assessments is partly a consequence of the fact that policies and practices are rarely implemented in a manner that allows for rigorous impact evaluation. As a result, we have not learned very much from our experiences. Nevertheless, there are signs of change. Recent investments in policy innovations and evaluations combined with enhanced information collection may well increase our understanding of teacher labor markets, and our ability to improve teaching across all schools. We may soon know more about which teachers are effective; how preparation and continued professional development can increase teacher effectiveness; how instructional materials, curriculum, and instructional leadership and collaboration at the school site affect teaching; and how to design teachers' work life to increase the retention of the most effective teachers. With such knowledge, policies and practices could be improved, good policies expanded, and ineffective or detrimental ones abolished.

Notes

1. The Schools and Staffing Survey (SASS) is conducted by the United States Census Bureau and sponsored by the National Center for Education Statistics (NCES). It collects extensive data on U.S. public and private elementary and secondary schools, providing data on important aspects of teacher supply and demand, the qualifications of teachers and principals, and the working conditions in schools. SASS has been conducted five times: 1987–88, 1990–91, 1993–94, 1999–2000, and 2003–04. The most recent SASS, conducted in 2003–04, went out to approximately 5,400 public school districts, 13,300 schools, 13,300 principals, and 62,000 teachers. The Teacher Follow-up Survey (TFS) is a follow-up of a sample of the school teachers who participated in the previous year's SASS. The TFS sample includes teachers who continued to teach a year after the SASS data collection, teachers who had moved schools and teachers who had left teaching in the year the TFS was conducted. The 2004–05 TFS was completed by 7,429 current and former teachers. Of these, 2,864 were still teaching at the same school in 2004–05 as in the previous year; 1,912 were still teaching, but in a different school; and 2,653 had left the teaching profession.
2. The Federal Law enacted through the Education for All Handicapped Children Act in 1975 makes the provision of educational services to all mentally and physically handicapped children compulsory.
3. http://nces.ed.gov/surveys/sass/das.asp
4. The test score here is a centile ranking or standardized score based on the combined math and verbal portions of a standardized test administered to five cohorts of high school students. The content of these tests are similar to the ACT and SAT. See Corcoran et al. (2004) for more.
5. Bacolod points out that the results from her analysis on selectivity of undergraduate institution need to be interpreted in the light of

two facts: (a) During the period under study, many universities curtailed undergraduate education programs, and (b) there is no empirically verified one-to-one link between majoring in education and becoming a teacher. Furthermore, while changes in female labor markets appear to be the major source of the decline in highly qualified women entering teaching, Bacolod points out the potential for additional explanations. For instance, women's admission to professional programs, their increased access to credit markets for loans to pursue skill acquisition and even access to the pill, as well as unionization in teaching and deunionization in non-teaching, and the general rise in skill returns might also explain the above pattern. See Bacolod (2005) for more.
6. The law defines core academic subjects as the following: English, reading or language arts, mathematics, science, foreign language, civics and government, economics, arts, history, and geography (P.L. 107-110 §9101.11). "Arts" as a subject was not further defined in the law.
7. Corcoran et al. (2004) point out that these results should be interpreted with caution since the sample for men was much smaller than that for women. Also, male teachers are much more likely to be secondary school teachers.
8. As mentioned previously, Bacolod notes certain problems in using data on the selectivity of undergraduate institutions. First, during the period under study, many institutions curtailed undergraduate education programs. Second, there is no one to one link between education majors actually becoming teachers.
9. From the early 1960s through the mid-1990s, all elementary school teachers in North Carolina were required to take either the Elementary Education or Early Childhood Education test. The former included material on curriculum, instruction, and assessment. Starting in the mid-1990s, teachers were required to take both that basic elementary test and one focusing on content. See Clotfelter et al. (2007a) for more.
10. The figure for public schools excludes charter schools.
11. California Department of Education: http://www.ed-data.k12.ca.us/. The educational qualification referred to above is a bachelor's degree and 60 Continuing Education units.
12. In 46 states, the fiscal deadline is not until June 30, and even then, states can get extensions. See Levin and Quinn (2003) and Jacob (2007).
13. New teachers are more likely to leave than more experienced ones. While this might be because teaching turns out to be somewhat more difficult than expected, it is important to note that data on recent college graduates show that young workers tend to switch jobs more, regardless of occupation.
14. A probationary certificate is issued after an individual completes all the regular certification requirements except the completion of the probationary period. A provisional certificate is issued to individuals who are still participating in what states call "alternative certification programs." Temporary certification requires some additional college coursework, student teaching, and/or passage of a test before regular certification can be awarded (Strizek et al., 2006).
15. They measure teacher quality by looking at value-added in terms of standardized average student test score gains.
16. A final point on transfer and quit behavior. Exit decisions could just as well be driven by an especially unruly class in a particular year or a personal emergency. In fact, approximately 21% of teachers who quit teaching between 2003–04 and 2004–05 cited family or personal reasons as being very important in their decision to quit (Marvel et al., 2007).
17. http://www.browardschools.com/press/release.asp?press_id=243

References

American Federation of Teachers. (2007). *Survey and analysis of teacher salary trends 2005*. Washington, DC: AFT.
Angrist, J., & Guryan, J. (2004). Teacher testing, teacher education and teacher characteristics. *American Economic Review, 94*(2), 241–246.

Bacolod, M. (2005). Do alternative opportunities matter? The role of female labor markets in the decline of teacher quality. *The Review of Economics and Statistics, 89*, 737–751.

Ballou, D. (1996). Do public schools hire the best applicants? *Quarterly Journal of Economics, 111*, 97–133.

Ballou, D., & Podgursky, M. (1998). Teacher recruitment and retention in public and private schools. *Journal of Policy Analysis and Management, 17*, 393–417.

Betts, J., Zau, A., & Rice, L. (2003). *Determinants of student achievement: New evidence from San Diego.* San Francisco: Public Policy Institute of California.

Boyd, D., Goldhaber, D., Lankford, H., & Wyckoff, J. (2007). The effect of certification and preparation on teacher quality. *The Future of Children, 17*(1), 45–68.

Boyd, D., Grossman, P., Lankford, H., Loeb, S., & Wyckoff, J. (2006). How changes in entry requirements alter the teacher workforce and affect student achievement. *Education Finance and Policy, 1*, 176–216.

Boyd, D., Grossman, P., Lankford, H., Loeb S., & Wyckoff, J. (2007). *Who leaves? Implications of teacher attrition for student achievement.* Unpublished manuscript.

Boyd, D., Lankford, H., Loeb, S., Rockoff, J., & Wyckoff, J. (2007). *The narrowing gap in New York City teacher qualifications and its implications for student achievement in high poverty schools.* Unpublished manuscript.

Boyd, D., Lankford, H., Loeb, S., & Wyckoff, J. (2005). Explaining the short careers of high-achieving teachers in schools with low-performing students. *American Economic Review, 95*(2), 166–171.

Bryk, A., Lee, V., & Holland, P. (1993). *Catholic schools and the common good.* Cambridge, MA: Harvard University Press.

Cannata, M. (2007a, April). *Understanding the teacher job search process: Espoused preferences and preferences in use.* Paper presented at the annual meeting of the American Educational Research Association, Chicago.

Cannata, M. (2007b). *Where to teach? Developing a more comprehensive framework to understand teachers' career decisions.* Unpublished doctoral dissertation, Michigan State University, East Lansing.

Carroll, T. G., Fulton, K., Abercrombie, K., & Yoon, I. (2004). *Fifty years after Brown v. Board of Education: A Two-tiered education system.* Washington, DC: National Commission on Teaching and America's Future.

Clotfelter, C., Ladd, H., & Vigdor, J. (2007a). *How and why do teacher credentials matter for student learning?* (NBER Working Paper No. 12828). Cambridge, MA: National Bureau of Economic Research.

Clotfelter, C., Ladd H., & Vigdor, J. (2007b). *Teacher credentials and student achievement in high school: A cross-subject analysis with student fixed effects* (NBER Working Paper No. 13617). Cambridge, MA: National Bureau of Economic Research.

Clotfelter, C., & Ladd, H. (1996). Recognizing and rewarding success in public schools. In H. Ladd (Ed.), *Holding schools accountable: Performance-based reform in education* (pp. 23–64). Washington, DC: Brookings Institution.

Corcoran, S., Schwab, R., & Evans, W. (2004). Women, the labor market and the declining relative quality of teachers. *Journal of Policy Analysis and Management, 23*, 449–470.

Decker, P. T., Mayer, D. P., & Glazerman, S. (2004). *Quality in the classroom: How does Teach for America measure up?* (Issue Brief No. 1). Princeton, NJ: Mathematica Policy Research, Inc.

Dee, T. (2004). Teachers, race, and student achievement in a randomized experiment. *Review of Economics and Statistics, 86*, 195–210.

Dee, T. (2007). Teachers and the gender gaps in student achievement. *Journal of Human Resources, 42*, 528–554.

Ehrenberg, R., Goldhaber, D., & Brewer, D. (1995). Do teachers' race, gender and ethnicity matter? Evidence from the National Educational Longitudinal Study of 1988. *Industrial and Labor Relations Review, 48*, 547–561.

Figlio, D., & Kenny, L. (2006). *Individual teacher incentives and student performance* (NBER Working Paper No. 12627). Cambridge, MA: National Bureau of Economic Research.

Finn, C. E., Jr., Manno, B. V., & Vanourek, G. (2000). *Charter schools in action: Renewing public education.* Princeton, NJ: Princeton University Press.

Florida Department of Education. (2006). Teacher salary, experience and degree level. *Statistical Brief Series 2006–23B.* Tallahassee, FL: Bureau of Education Information and Accountability Services.

Fowler, R. C. (2001). *An analysis of the recruitment, preparation, attrition, and placement of the Massachusetts Signing Bonus teachers.* Unpublished manuscript.

Gifford, M., Phillips, K., & Ogle, M. (2000). *Five year charter school study.* Phoenix, AZ: Goldwater Institute Center for Market-Based Education.

Gitomer, D. H., Latham, A. S., & Ziomek, R. (1999). *The academic quality of prospective teachers: The impact of admissions and licensure testing.* Princeton, NJ: Educational Testing Service.

Goldhaber, D. (2007). Everybody's doing it, but what does teacher testing tell us about teacher effectiveness? *Journal of Human Resources, 52*, 765–794.

Gordon, R., Kane, T. J., & Staiger, D. O. (2006, April). *Identifying effective teachers using performance on the job* (The Hamilton Project Discussion Paper No. 2006-01). Washington, DC: Brookings Institution.

Hanushek, E., Kain, J. F., O'Brien, D., & Rivkins, S. (2005). The market for teacher quality (NBER Working Paper No. W11154). Cambridge, MA: National Bureau of Economic Research.

Hanushek, E., Kain, J. F., & Rivkin, S. (2004). Why public schools lose teachers. *Journal of Human Resources, 39*, 326–354.

Hanushek, E., & Pace, R. (1995). Who chooses to teach (and why)? *Economics of Education Review, 14*, 101–117.

Hanushek, E., & Rivkin, S. (2002). Understanding the twentieth century growth in U.S. school spending. *Journal of Human Resources, 32*, 65–68.

Hanushek, E., & Rivkin, S. (2006). Pay, working conditions, and teacher quality. *The Future of Children, 79*(1), 69–86.

Harris, D. & Sass, T. (2006). *Teacher training and teacher productivity.* Unpublished manuscript.

Hill, H. (2007). Learning in the teaching workforce. *The Future of Children, 17*(1), 111–127.

Hill, H. C., Rowan, B., & Ball, D. L. (2005). Effects of teachers' mathematical knowledge for teaching on student achievement. *American Educational Research Journal, 42*, 371–406.

Hill, P., Lake, R., Celio, M. B., Campbell, C., Herdman, P., & Bulkley, K. (2001). *A study of charter school accountability.* Washington, DC: U.S. Department of Education, University of Washington and Office of Educational Research and Improvement, Center on Reinventing Education.

Humphrey, D., & Wechsler, M. (2005). Insights into alternative certification: Initial findings from a national study. *Teachers College Record, 109*, 483–530.

Ingersoll, R. (2003). *Out-of-field teaching and the limits of teacher policy.* Center for the Study of Teaching and Policy, and The Consortium for Policy Research in Education.

Ingersoll, R., & Kralik, J. M. (2004). *The impact of mentoring on teacher retention: What the research says.* Denver, CO: Education Commission of the States.

Ingersoll, R., & Smith, T. (2003). The wrong solution to the teacher shortage. *Educational Leadership, 60*(8), 30–33.

Jacob, B. (2007). The challenges of staffing urban schools with effective teachers. *The Future of Children, 17*(1), 1–26.

Jacob, B., & Lefgren, L. (2005). *Principals as agents: Subjective performance measurement in education* (NBER Working Paper No. 11463). Cambridge, MA: National Bureau of Economic Research.

Johnson, S., Berg, J., & Donaldson, M. (2005). *Who stays in teaching and why: A review of the literature on teacher retention.* Cambridge, MA: Harvard Graduate School of Education, The Project on the Next Generation of Teachers.

Koppich, J., Holmes, P., & Plecki, M. L. (1998). *New rules, new roles? The professional work lives of charter school teachers.* Washington, DC: National Education Association.

Ladd, H. (2007). Teacher labor markets in developed countries. *The Future of Children, 17*(1), 201–217.

Levin, J., Mulhern, J., & Schunck, J. (2005). *Unintended consequences: The case for reforming the staffing rules in urban teachers' union contracts.* New York: New Teacher Project.

Levin, J., & Quinn, M. (2003). *Missed opportunities: How we keep high-quality teachers out of urban classrooms.* New York: New Teacher Project.

Liu, E., & Johnson, S. M. (2006). New teachers' experiences of hiring: Late, rushed, and information poor. *Educational Administration Quarterly, 42,* 324–360.

Loeb, S., & Page, M. (2001). *The role of compensating differentials, alternative labor market opportunities and endogenous selection in teacher labor markets. Final report.* Chicago: Spencer Foundation.

Loeb, S., & Reininger, M. (2004). *Public policy and teacher labor markets: What we know and why it matters.* East Lansing: Michigan State University, The Education Policy Center.

Marvel, J., Lyter, D. M., Peltola, P., Strizek, G. A., & Morton, B. A. (2007). *Teacher attrition and mobility: Results from the 2004–05 Teacher Follow-up Survey.* Washington, DC: National Center for Education Statistics.

Murnane, R., & Steele, J. (2007). What is the problem? The challenge of providing effective teachers for all children. *The Future of Children, 17*(1), 15–43.

National Center for Education Statistics (NCES). (2008). *Fast facts.* Retrieved May 5, 2008, from http://nces.ed.gov/fastfacts/display.asp?id=65

Nixon, L. A., & Robinson, M. D. (1999). The educational attainment of young women: Role model effects of female high school faculty. *Demography, 36,* 185–194.

Reininger, M. (2006). *Teachers' location preferences and the implications for schools with different student populations.* Unpublished manuscript.

Rockoff, J. (2003). The impact of individual teachers on student achievement: Evidence from panel data. *The American Economic Review, 94,* 247–252.

Scafidi, B, Stinebrickner, T., & Sjoquist, D. L. (2003). *The relationship between school characteristics and teacher mobility* (Working paper). Atlanta: Georgia State University, Andrew Young School of Policy Studies.

Shields, P. M., Humphrey, D. C., Wechsler, M. E., Riel, L. M., Tiffany-Morales, J., Woodworth, K., et al. (2001). *The status of the teaching profession 2001.* Santa Cruz, CA: The Center for the Future of Teaching and Learning.

Smith, T., & Ingersoll, R. (2004). Do teacher induction and mentoring matter? *NASSP Bulletin, 88*(638), 28–40.

Strizek, G. A., Pittsonberger, J. L., Riordan, K. E., Lyter, D. M., & Orlofsky, G. F. (2006). *Characteristics of schools, districts, teachers, principals, and school libraries in the United States: 2003–04 Schools and Staffing Survey* (NCES 2006313). Washington, DC: National Center for Education Statistics.

Strong, M., & Vilar, A. (2005). *Is mentoring worth the money? A benefit-cost analysis and five-year rate of return of a comprehensive mentoring program for beginning teachers.* Santa Cruz: University of California, New Teacher Center.

Wohlstetter, P., & Griffin, N. (1998). *Creating and sustaining learning communities: Early lessons from charter schools.* Philadelphia: University of Pennsylvania Consortium for Policy Research in Education.

48

Teacher Preparation and Teacher Learning

A Changing Policy Landscape

LINDA DARLING-HAMMOND, RUTH CHUNG WEI,
WITH CHRISTY MARIE JOHNSON
Stanford University

The last two decades have witnessed a remarkable amount of policy directed at teacher education—and an intense debate about whether and how various approaches to preparing and supporting teachers make a difference. Beginning in the mid-1980s with the report of the Carnegie Task Force on Teaching as a Profession, the Holmes Group (1986), and the founding of the National Board for Professional Teaching Standards (NBPTS) in 1987, a collection of analysts, policy makers, and practitioners of teaching and teacher education argued for the centrality of expertise to effective practice and the need to build a more knowledgeable and skillful professional teaching force. A set of policy initiatives was launched to design professional standards, strengthen teacher education and certification requirements, increase investments in induction mentoring and professional development, and transform roles for teachers (see, e.g., National Commission on Teaching and America's Future [NCTAF], 1996).

Meanwhile, a competing agenda was introduced to replace the traditional elements of professions—formal preparation, licensure, certification, and accreditation—with market mechanisms that would allow more open entry to teaching and greater ease of termination through elimination of tenure and greater power in the hands of districts to hire and fire teachers with fewer constraints (see, e.g., Thomas B. Fordham Foundation, 1999). Some have argued that teaching does not require highly-specialized knowledge and skill, and that such skills as there are can be learned largely on the job (e.g., Walsh, 2001). Others see in these "systematic market attacks" a neo-liberal project that aims to privatize education, reduce the power of the teaching profession over its own work, and allow greater inequality in the offering of services to students (Barber, 2004; Weiner, 2007).

Particularly contentious has been the debate about whether teacher preparation and certification are related to teacher effectiveness. For example, in his Annual Report on Teacher Quality (USDOE, 2002), Secretary of Education

Rod Paige argued for the redefinition of teacher qualifications to include little specific preparation for teaching. Stating that current teacher certification systems are "broken," and that they impose "burdensome requirements" for education coursework comprising "the bulk of current teacher certification regimes" (p. 8), the report suggested that certification should be redefined to emphasize verbal ability and content knowledge and to de-emphasize requirements for education coursework, making student teaching and attendance at schools of education optional and eliminating "other bureaucratic hurdles" (p. 19). Associated policy initiatives, encouraged by the federal government under No Child Left Behind, have stimulated alternative certification programs and, in a few states, pathways to certification with no professional preparation at all.

Some commentators have also argued that certification of teachers should be abandoned by states in order to remove "regulatory barriers" to teaching. Their arguments are linked to concerns that state requirements for teacher preparation are burdensome and unlinked to teacher performance (see, e.g., Walsh, 2001, pp. 1–2), and that "professionalization" of teaching is an unnecessary barrier to school choice (Ballou & Podgursky, 1997, p. 44). Debates about the value of teachers' preparation have generally focused on technical analyses of studies on the topic (see, e.g., Ballou & Podgursky, 1997; Darling-Hammond, 1997, 2000a, 2002; Darling-Hammond & Youngs, 2002; Walsh, 2001; Walsh & Podgursky, 2001), but there are substantial social, political, and economic implications of how teacher education is treated by policy. These include implications for school funding and allocations of teaching resources to students of different socioeconomic backgrounds, as well as for the nature of the teaching career.

This chapter will examine research about the outcomes of different kinds of preparation and professional learning opportunities that emerge from these different policy perspectives. We treat not only governmental policy but also "professional policy" made by professional bodies (e.g., standards boards, accrediting agencies, professional associations) as they develop and implement standards for preparation and practice. In the process, we examine the emergence of a standards movement in teaching and what has been learned about the challenges and effects of implementing such standards.

Framing the Issues of Teacher Preparation and Teaching Quality

The importance of these questions is increasingly clear. Recent studies of teacher effects have found that teachers strongly determine differences in student learning, far outweighing the effects of differences in class size and composition (Rivkin, Hanushek, & Kain, 2005; Rockoff, 2004; Sanders & Rivers, 1996), and sometimes matching the sizable effects of student background variables like family income and education (Clotfelter, Ladd, & Vigdor, 2007; Ferguson, 1991). Teacher effects appear to be sustained and cumulative; that is, the effects of a very good or poor teacher spill over into later years, influencing student learning for a substantial period of time, and the effects of multiple teachers in a row who are similarly effective or ineffective produce large changes in students' achievement trajectories.

Furthermore, in the United States, teachers are the most inequitably distributed resource. On any measure of qualifications—extent of preparation, level of experience, certification, content background in the field taught, advanced degrees, selectivity of educational institution, or test scores on college admissions and teacher licensure tests—studies show that students of color, low-income and low-performing students, particularly in urban and poor rural areas, are disproportionately taught by less-qualified teachers (Darling-Hammond, 1997, 2004; Hanushek, Kain, & Rivkin, 2001; Ingersoll, 2002; Jerald, 2002; Lankford, Loeb, & Wyckoff, 2002). In some high-minority schools, a majority of teachers are inexperienced and uncertified, and in those with more than 90% students of color, the odds of having a math or science teacher with a certification and a degree in the field taught are less than 50% (Oakes, 1990).

It is worth noting that, among industrialized nations, this circumstance is virtually unique to the United States. Most high-achieving countries fund their schools centrally and equally, and pay teachers on a common scale that is competitive with other professions, sometimes with additional stipends for working in remote or high-need schools. Furthermore, these countries support a well-prepared teaching force—funding high-quality teacher education (usually 3 to 4 years, completely at state expense, plus a living stipend), beginning teacher mentoring, and ongoing professional development for all teachers. These teachers work in schools where they have continuous access to their colleagues for planning and fine-tuning curriculum and to professional learning opportunities inside and outside the school. Most of the highest-achieving nations attribute much of their educational success to these investments in teacher education (Darling-Hammond, 2005, 2008).

Because of public attention to the importance of teacher quality for student learning and the unequal access U.S. students have to well-qualified teachers (see, e.g., NCTAF, 1996), the federal Congress included a provision in No Child Left Behind Act of 2001 that states should create plans to ensure that all students have access to "highly qualified teachers," defined as teachers with full certification and demonstrated competence in the subject matter field(s) they teach (defined as completing a college major or passing a test in the field). This provision was historic, especially since the students targeted by federal legislation—students who are low-income, low-achieving, new English language learners, or identified with special education needs—have been in many communities those least likely to be served by experienced and well-prepared teachers (NCTAF, 1996).

At the same time, reflecting the differences in views among policy makers, the law encouraged states to expand alternative certification programs, now operating in at least 47 states, and regulations later developed by the U.S. Department of Education allowed candidates who had just begun—but not yet completed—such a program to be counted as "highly qualified." Policies across the states since then have both increased expectations for teacher education and certification—for example, adding subject matter requirements and testing—and, in some states, reduced the expectations for pre-service preparation for those undertaking alternative routes. In a few states, candidates can gain a license without pedagogical preparation if they pass a content test. In some others, meanwhile, requirements for pedagogical preparation and assessment of skill have increased. Although research is not yet dispositive on the wisdom of these distinctive policy choices, it sheds some light on the implications of these choices.

Influences of Teacher Attributes and Knowledge on Teacher Quality

Over the years, researchers have analyzed how differences in teacher characteristics, including educational background and teacher training, are related to student learning. Various lines of research looking at teacher effectiveness since the 1960s have suggested that many kinds of teacher knowledge and experiences may contribute to teacher effects, including teachers' general academic and verbal ability; subject matter knowledge; knowledge about teaching and learning; teaching experience; and the set of qualifications measured by teacher certification, which typically includes the preceding factors and others (for reviews, see Darling-Hammond, 2000b; Wilson, Floden, & Ferrini-Mundy, 2002; Rice, 2003). Other studies have also found that traits like adaptability and flexibility are also important to teacher effectiveness (for a review, see Schalock, 1979).

In particular, a review commissioned by USDOE's Office of Educational Research and Improvement, which analyzed 57 studies that met specific research criteria and were published after 1980 in peer-reviewed journals, concluded that the available evidence from technically sound studies demonstrates a relationship between teacher education and teacher effectiveness (Wilson, Floden, & Ferrini-Mundy, 2001). The review showed that empirical relationships between teacher qualifications and student achievement have been found across studies using different units of analysis and different measures of preparation and in studies that employ controls for students' socioeconomic status and prior academic performance.

While there is some research supporting the importance of each of these traits or areas of knowledge, there are debates about the relative importance of various elements and about how strong the research is supporting different correlates of teacher effectiveness. One reason for these debates is that few studies have examined multiple elements of teacher knowledge, skills, and abilities at the same time. For example, some analysts argue on the basis of studies in the 1960s through 1980s that general academic or verbal ability matters most for teacher effectiveness, as there were a number of studies finding small but significant effects of teachers' test scores on both general ability and tests of teaching knowledge during this time. However, none of these studies included measures of teacher education or certification which became available in large data sets during the 1990s. Later studies that include measures of teacher preparation find effects of teachers' knowledge about subject matter and pedagogy, above and beyond general intellectual ability (for a review, see Darling-Hammond & Youngs, 2002).

During the period of time that teacher characteristics have been examined, requirements for teaching have also evolved. Since the mid-1980s, states have taken steps to strengthen their licensure requirements, which are now substantially stronger than they were 20 or more years ago. In most states, candidates for teaching must now earn a minimum grade point average and/or achieve a minimum test score on tests of basic skills, general academic ability, or general knowledge in order to be admitted to teacher education or gain a credential. In addition, they must generally secure a major or minor in the subject to be taught and/or pass a content test, take specified courses in education and, sometimes, pass a test of teaching knowledge and skill. In the course of teacher education and student teaching, candidates are typically judged on their teaching skill, professional conduct, and the appropriateness of their interactions with children.

A few well-controlled studies have been able to compare the relative influences on student achievement of some of these aspects of teacher qualifications. In a large-scale study of mathematics and science achievement, for example, Monk (1994) found that teachers' content preparation, as measured by coursework in the subject field, was positively related to student achievement in mathematics and science but that the relationship was curvilinear, with diminishing returns to student achievement of teachers' subject matter courses above a threshold level (e.g., five courses in math-

ematics). He also found that the number of content-specific pedagogical courses had a positive effect on student learning and was in some cases more influential than additional subject matter preparation.

Goldhaber and Brewer (2000) also found influences of both content and pedagogical preparation on teachers' effectiveness in math and science. They found that the effects of teachers' certification exceeded those of a content major in the field, suggesting that what licensed teachers learn in the pedagogical portion of their training adds to what they gain from a strong subject matter background:

> [We] find that the type (standard, emergency, etc.) of certification a teacher holds is an important determinant of student outcomes. In mathematics, we find the students of teachers who are either not certified in their subject ... or hold a private school certification do less well than students whose teachers hold a standard, probationary, or emergency certification in math. *Roughly speaking, having a teacher with a standard certification in mathematics rather than a private school certification or a certification out of subject results in at least a 1.3 point increase in the mathematics test. This is equivalent to about 10% of the standard deviation on the 12th grade test, a little more than the impact of having a teacher with a BA and MA in mathematics.* Though the effects are not as strong in magnitude or statistical significance, the pattern of results in science mimics that in mathematics. (p. 139, emphasis added)

This study also found that beginning teachers on probationary certificates (those who were fully prepared and completing their initial 2- to 3-year probationary period) from states with more rigorous certification exam requirements had positive effects on student achievement, suggesting the potential value of recent reforms to strengthen certification.

The individual and cumulative effects of various kinds of teacher qualifications were recently estimated in a large-scale study using North Carolina data to examine learning gains of high school students. This study found that teachers were more effective if they held a standard license (as compared to those who entered without having completed training), had a license in the specific field taught, had higher scores on the teacher licensing test (especially in mathematics), had taught for more than 2 years, had graduated from a more competitive college, and went through the process of National Board certification to demonstrate their teaching skills (Clotfelter, Ladd, & Vigdor, 2007).

While each of these variables was statistically significant in its own right, the combined influence on student achievement of a teacher with low overall qualifications (no experience, low licensure test scores, no prior teacher preparation, certification in a field other than the one taught, no board certification, no graduate degree, and from an uncompetitive college) as compared to one having most of them was 0.30 standard deviations lower. Using a more conservative measure representing a comparison between teachers whose mix of qualifications were in the top 10% versus those in the bottom 10%, the effect on student achievement of 0.18

standard deviations was larger than that of race and parent education (e.g., the average difference in achievement between a White student with college-educated parents and a Black student with high-school educated parents).

These very large effects suggest the importance of focusing on what teachers have had the opportunity to learn through their general education, subject matter training, and preparation for teaching, as well as their experience and professional learning opportunities such as National Board certification (discussed further below). A similar study of teachers in New York City (Boyd, Lankford, Loeb, Rockoff, & Wyckoff, 2007) also found that teachers' certification status, pathway into teaching, teaching experience, graduation from a competitive college, and math SAT scores were significant predictors of teacher effectiveness in elementary and middle grades mathematics. Certified teachers who graduated from university pre-service programs and who had attended a competitive college were the most effective as beginners. Additional experience also had strong positive effects. In combination, improvements in these qualifications reduced the gap in achievement between the schools in deciles serving the poorest and most affluent student bodies by 25%. Changes in the mix of teacher qualifications available to students appear to influence student achievement, thus suggesting that policies which tackle the twin problems of inadequate and unequally distributed teacher quality may help improve school outcomes.

These studies and other evidence suggest that it is a mistake to believe that only one or two characteristics of teachers can explain their effects on student achievement. The message from the research is that multiple factors are involved and teachers with a combination of attributes—strong general ability, solid grasp of subject matter, and knowledge of effective methods for teaching that subject matter, including the knowledge acquired in teacher education about how to instruct, motivate, manage and assess diverse students—appear to hold the greatest promise for producing student learning.

Pathways into Teaching This conclusion, which undergirds the approach of contemporary teacher certification systems, is disputed by some (though not all) proponents of fast-track alternative certification programs, who have argued that individuals with higher academic ability are likely to produce stronger student achievement gains than other teachers, even without the benefit of teacher preparation (e.g., Ballou & Podgursky, 1997; Raymond, Fletcher, & Luque, 2001; Schaefer, 1999).

Evidence on Routes into Teaching That Reduce Pre-Service Training This hope has not yet been borne out by controlled studies on the topic. In the North Carolina study cited above, the largest negative effect on student achievement was found for teachers who had entered teaching on the state's "lateral entry" program, an alternate route that allows entry for mid-career recruits who have subject matter background but no initial training for teaching. In

addition, three recent, large well-controlled studies, using longitudinal individual-level student data from New York City and Houston, Texas, found that teachers who enter teaching without full preparation—as emergency hires or alternative route candidates—were less effective than fully-prepared beginning teachers working with similar students, especially in teaching reading (Boyd, Grossman, Lankford, Loeb, & Wyckoff, 2006; Darling-Hammond, Holtzman, Gatlin, & Heilig, 2005; Kane, Rockoff, & Staiger, 2006). This was equally true of alternate routes like the New York City Teaching Fellows and the highly selected Teach for America (TFA) recruits as it was of other entrants who entered without pre-service preparation.

All three studies also found that by the third year, after the alternate route teachers had completed their required teacher education coursework for certification, there were few significant differences in their effectiveness and that of the traditionally prepared teachers. Indeed, in two of the studies, students of experienced Teach for America recruits had larger gains on average in mathematics. However, 80% of the TFA entrants and one-half of other alternatively prepared teachers had left the profession, leaving questions about whether the measured effectiveness of later year recruits was a result of selection (since less effective teachers were found to leave earlier) or of gains in performance.

Findings from analyses of teacher effectiveness depend substantially on the nature of the comparison groups examined. For example, two studies of TFA recruits have found them to be as effective as other teachers in their school or district who were even less likely to be trained and certified than the TFA candidates (Decker, Mayer, & Glazerman, 2004; Raymond, Fletcher, & Luque, 2001). TFA recruits' 5 weeks of pre-service training—including a few weeks of student teaching—plus the additional coursework for a credential they took while on the job gave them more preparation than many recruits entering on emergency permits.

In these studies and others, the schools staffed by such under-prepared teachers invariably serve concentrations of low-income students of color in disadvantaged communities where non-competitive salaries, poor working conditions, and personnel policies have allowed shortages to fester (NCTAF, 1996, 2004). However, some states and districts have changed this outcome for low-income schools by putting in place strong incentives and supports for recruiting and retaining teachers (for examples, see Darling-Hammond & Sykes, 2003). From a policy perspective, then, the questions of how to recruit and prepare teachers depend on the expectations policy makers and the public are willing to hold for the education of different groups of students and the strategies they are willing to put in place to achieve these expectations.

Even given evidence that teacher education may support teacher effectiveness, important questions arise about what pathways into teaching can recruit academically able individuals, prepare them adequately for the challenges they face, and keep them in the profession so that students can benefit from both the knowledge they have when they enter and the skills they gain with experience. Furthermore, it is clear from recent studies of program models that there is so much variability in the features of so-called "traditional" teacher education programs and within the newer set of "alternative" programs—and considerable overlap among the groups of programs described under these different labels—that these descriptors do not really help much in guiding policy or practice (see e.g., Zeichner & Schulte, 2001; Humphrey, Wechsler, & Hough, 2008).

Evidence on Routes into Teaching That Reconfigure Pre-Service Preparation The term "traditional teacher education" is often used to compare and contrast the features of university-based teacher preparation and teacher preparation routes that are organized and run by non-university entities such as state and district internship programs and other recruiting programs that fast-track the placement of individuals into classrooms. However, most "alternative" certification programs are actually operated by universities (Feistritzer, 2005), and they range widely in design—from post-baccalaureate master's degree programs that provide a year or more of pre-service preparation, including a year-long internship or residency in the classroom of a veteran teacher (such as the MAT models launched in the 1960s), to designs that offer a few weeks of summer training before becoming a teacher of record. Many alternative certification policies were initially created to provide post-baccalaureate options to the traditional undergraduate pathways, rather than to reduce preparation; thus, the range of strategies is quite large (Zeichner & Hutchinson, in press). Furthermore, there are widely varying practices among "traditional" teacher preparation programs—including the kinds and organization of coursework and the extent, quality, and structure for clinical work.

The format and content of teacher education programs are shaped both by state laws professional associations, such as general and professional accrediting bodies. What teachers encounter when they try to become prepared for their future profession depends on the state, college, and program in which they enroll, and the professors with whom they study. Prospective teachers take courses in the arts and sciences and in schools of education, and they spend time in schools. What they study and who teaches it vary widely. Unlike other professions, where the professional curriculum is reasonably common across institutions and has some substantive coherence, the curriculum of teacher education is often idiosyncratic to the professors who teach whatever courses are required, which are different from place to place. These courses are distributed widely, often with little coordination (Darling-Hammond & Ball, 1997).

What is considered "traditional" teacher preparation has evolved over the last nearly 200 years that teachers have received professional preparation for their work. Feiman-Nemser (1990) describes three historic traditions that have influenced approaches to teacher education: the normal school tradition, the liberal arts tradition, and professionalization through graduate preparation and research. The

liberal arts tradition has dominated since the 1950s, with teachers earning their credentials through 4-year college programs. From the time when normal schools were the primary pathway for entry into teaching, reformers have continually sought to improve the status and quality of teaching by lengthening programs and adding requirements. In the past, reformers have sought to create alternatives to undergraduate teacher education, which has been criticized as lacking rigor (Conant, 1963; Koerner, 1963) and practical relevance (Lanier & Little, 1986; Lortie, 1975). These alternatives have included extending undergraduate programs to 5 years (e.g., blended undergraduate and graduate programs, fifth-year programs), moving professional studies to the graduate level (e.g., MAT programs and M.Ed. programs), and on-the-job training programs (e.g., alternate route and internship programs; Feiman-Nemser, 1990).

Five-year extended programs were seen as having an advantage over 4-year programs because of greater flexibility in the organization of fieldwork and education coursework, allowing for a gradual induction into the teaching profession and a better integration of theory and practice. This flexibility also allowed for early field experiences throughout the undergraduate portion of the program and for extending the amount of student teaching time. Graduate-level MAT programs, promoted in the 1930s by James Conant, president of Harvard University, were seen as more academically rigorous than undergraduate programs and as a means to attract a stronger pool of applicants (those who had already completed a liberal arts education with a specific content major). MAT programs were a particularly favorable strategy for recruitment in times of teacher shortages, as they open up new pools of potential recruits and can be completed in 1 or 2 years, combining educational coursework with clinical internships.

The Educational Masters (Ed.M.) was promoted by Henry Holmes, dean of the Harvard Graduate School of Education in the 1920s and namesake of the Holmes Group of education deans and chief academic officers from 120 research universities. In their 1986 report *Tomorrow's Teachers*, this group argued for the elimination of undergraduate degrees in education in favor of graduate-level programs and called for improved articulation between coursework and field experiences through the creation of school-university partnerships called professional development schools (Holmes Group, 1986). In these sites, new teachers are expected to learn to teach alongside more experienced teachers who plan and work together, and university and school-based faculty work collaboratively to design, implement, and conduct research about learning experiences for new and experienced teachers, as well as for students (Holmes Group, 1990). Ideally, the university program and the school develop a shared conception of good teaching that informs their joint work. Thus PDSs aim to develop *school practice* as well as the *individual practice* of new teacher candidates.

In large part because of reform efforts of groups like the Holmes Group, the 1990s saw important structural changes in some teacher education programs. A growing number of teachers are now prepared in 5- or 6 -year programs of study that include a disciplinary degree at the undergraduate level, graduate-level education coursework, and intensive year-long internships, often in professional development schools that seek to model state-of-the-art practice. Levine's (2006) study *Educating School Teachers* reported that in 2002–03, the nearly 1,200 schools and departments of education in the United States produced 106,000 teachers in undergraduate programs, 63,000 teachers in masters programs, and about 4,000 teachers in certificate programs. Thus, it appears that although colleges and universities continue to prepare the most teachers at the undergraduate level (about 61%), there has also been an increase in the number of teachers prepared at the graduate level (36% in master's programs and 3% in post-baccalaureate credential programs). In addition, as of 1998, the American Association of Colleges for Teacher Education estimated that there were more than 1,000 professional schools in 47 states in operation across the country (Abdal-Haqq, 1998).

Some studies have found that, on average, teachers prepared in extended teacher education programs, such as the Holmes Group's recommended 5-year models, feel better prepared, are more committed to the profession, and enter and remain in teaching at higher rates than teachers in traditional 4-year programs and at even higher rates than those prepared in short-term alternative certification programs (Andrew & Schwab, 1995; Applegate & Shaklee, 1988; Baker, 1993; Denton & Peters, 1988; Shin, 1994).

Recent research on professional development schools associated with both 4- and 5-year teacher education programs has also shown some promise in improving teacher retention (Kenreich, Hartzler-Miller, Neopolitan, & Wiltz, 2004; Hunter-Quartz, 2003; Fleener, 1998; Latham & Vogt, 2007). Although most of these studies had small sample sizes and followed graduates only a few years after program completion, Latham and Vogt's (2007) longitudinal study of about 1,000 graduates compared the retention rates of teachers prepared in PDS programs versus traditional elementary education programs over 8 years, between 1996 and 2004. They found that controlling for teacher background and academic qualifications, teachers prepared in PDS programs had higher rates of entry into teaching and retention in the teaching profession. Given the range of PDS models included in this and other studies, such findings are suggestive only, and more research is needed to evaluate what kinds of models and features influence teacher commitment and practice for various kinds of prospective teachers.

Nevertheless, it is reasonable to conjecture that the full year of clinical training such programs often provide may be associated with some of these outcomes, as several studies have found a relationship between the experience of student teaching and feelings of preparedness (California State University, 2002a, 2002b), as well as retention in teaching (Henke, Geis, Giambattista, & Knepper, 1996; Henke, Chen, & Geis, 2000; NCTAF, 2004).

Indeed, given the large differences in attrition rates associated with teachers' preparation and entry pathways, the National Commission on Teaching and America's Future (1997) estimated that by the third year of a teacher's career, based on the costs of preparation and the costs of teacher attrition, it actually costs substantially less to have underwritten the costs of an extended program than it does to prepare candidates in shorter programs who leave much sooner.

However, other changes in teacher education may be improving the capacity of undergraduate programs to attract and prepare candidates who are more committed to the profession than was once the case when many undergraduates, especially young women, were advised to take an education major as "insurance" in case they did not get married or find another job. Most states have substantially raised requirements for admission into teacher education programs by requiring either a basic skills test or minimum grade point average, and nearly all have revised the teacher education curriculum, requiring more content courses as well as education courses including more clinical training. Many now require that prospective teachers major in an academic content area, rather than solely in education (Council of Chief State School Officers [CCSSO], 1998; Darling-Hammond & Youngs, 2002). A recent study of graduates of bachelor's degree programs in teacher education using the longitudinal Baccalaureate and Beyond data set found that nearly 80% of those who finished university-based pre-service programs remained in teaching 5 years after graduation (Henke, Chen, & Geis, 2000).

Furthermore, a study of seven teacher education programs that graduate extraordinarily well-prepared candidates—as judged by observations of their practice, administrators who hire them, and their own sense of preparedness and self-efficacy as teachers—found exemplars among 4-year, 5-year, and graduate-level programs, which suggests that program structure is not the determinative factor in predicting program success (Darling-Hammond, 2006).

The programs did, however, have a number of features in common, including a strong, shared vision of good teaching and well-defined standards of practice guiding coursework, clinical placements, and performance assessments; a common core curriculum grounded in substantial knowledge of development and learning in cultural contexts, as well as subject matter pedagogy, taught in the context of practice, using case methods and other pedagogies that connect theory and practice; extended clinical experiences (at least 30 weeks), interwoven with coursework and carefully mentored; and strong partnerships between universities and schools. Similar program features and pedagogical tools are noted in other studies of strong programs (e.g., Cabello, Eckmier, & Baghieri, 1995; Graber, 1996) that have documented program influences on candidates' preparedness and performance.

Teacher Education Program Effects   Although the kinds of case studies described above are suggestive of teacher education program features that may make a difference, there are relatively few well-controlled studies that look at the effects of specific aspects of teacher education on teacher effectiveness as measured by student achievement. Recent reviews by the Center for the Study of the Teaching Profession (Wilson, Floden, & Ferrini-Mundy, 2001), the American Educational Research Association (Cochran-Smith & Zeichner, 2005), and the National Academy of Education (Darling-Hammond & Bransford, 2005) capture both the limitations of that literature and the relatively small number of studies that signal potentially fruitful directions.

While research on the effects of specific teacher education program elements on teacher effectiveness is slim, there is considerably more evidence from research on teaching about kinds of preparation or professional development that have been found to enable teachers to engage in practices that influence student learning. For example, teachers trained to use formative assessment to provide feedback to students and opportunities for them to revise their work have been found in many dozens of studies to have large effect sizes on student learning gains (Black & Wiliam, 1998), as have teachers prepared to use cooperative learning strategies effectively (for reviews, see Cohen & Lotan, 1995; Johnson & Johnson, 1989). Teachers who have learned to teach students specific meta-cognitive strategies for reading, writing, and mathematical problem solving have been found to produce increased student learning of complex skills (for a review, see Darling-Hammond & Bransford, 2005). Mathematics and science teachers who have learned to engage in hands-on learning, such as the use of manipulatives in math or laboratory experiments in science, and who emphasize higher-order thinking skills appear to produce stronger student achievement (Perkes, 1967–1968; Wenglinsky, 2002). Similarly, preparation in how to work with diverse student populations appears to have an effect on teacher effectiveness, in particular, training in multicultural education, teaching limited English proficient students, and teaching students with special needs (Wenglinsky, 2002).

There is also evidence that teachers learn different things from different programs and pathways and feel differentially well-prepared for specific aspects of teaching depending on the program or pathway completed (Darling-Hammond, Chung, & Frelow, 2002; Cohen & Hill, 2000; Denton & Lacina, 1984; Desimone, Porter, Garet, Yoon, & Birman, 2002). While research does not offer precise guidance about many of the program features that may be associated with differential effectiveness, a growing body of evidence points toward some considerations that appear to be important.

For example, *the content, sequencing, and connections among coursework* and other learning experiences may matter as much as their number or duration (Kennedy, 1998, 1999). For example, a number of large-scale studies suggest that the extent of content-specific study of teaching methods may influence teacher effectiveness (Begle, 1979; Druva & Anderson, 1983; Ferguson & Womack, 1993; Goldhaber & Brewer, 2000; Harris & Sass, 2006; Monk, 1994; Monk & King, 1994; Sykes et al., 2006). Further-

more, in a number of experimental studies, teachers who participated in targeted learning opportunities on effective teaching practices in specific content areas, with immediate opportunities to apply these practices, have produced student achievement gains that were significantly greater than those of comparison group teachers (Angrist & Lavy, 2001; Crawford & Stallings, 1978; Ebmeier & Good, 1979; Good & Grouws, 1979; Lawrenz & McCreath, 1988; Mason & Good, 1993). In the pre-service context, courses that occur while or after candidates have been in the field may be more salient than front-loaded courses where theory is learned in the absence of practice (Denton, 1982; Denton, Morris, & Tooke, 1982; Henry, 1983; Ross, Hughes, & Hill, 1981; Sunal, 1980).

The *quality, duration, and timing of clinical experiences* may also matter. Research suggests that candidates learn more from their fieldwork and coursework when they have opportunities to connect their coursework in real time to practice opportunities in the classroom. Carefully constructed field experiences can enable new teachers to reinforce, apply, and synthesize concepts learned in coursework (Denton, 1982; Denton, Morris, & Tooke, 1982; Henry, 1983; Ross et al., 1981; Koerner, Rust, & Baumgartner, 2002; Sunal, 1980). For example, Denton (1982) found that teacher candidates with early field experiences performed significantly better in their methods courses than those without early field experiences. Other work suggests that the care with which placements are chosen, the quality of practice that is modeled, and the quality and frequency of mentoring candidates receive may influence candidates' learning (Feiman-Nemser & Buchmann, 1985; Goodman, 1985; Knowles & Hoefler, 1989; Laboskey & Richert, 2002; Rodriguez & Sjostrom, 1995).

In addition, the quality and intensity of supervision, and the evaluation tools used to guide supervision, are factors that may be potentially important elements of teacher learning. The match between placements in which candidates learn to teach and their eventual teaching assignments—in terms of the type of students, grade level, and subject matter—appear to be associated with stronger teaching in the early years (Koerner et al., 2002; Goodman, 1985). Some research also suggests that the duration of student teaching experiences may influence teachers' later teaching practice and self-confidence (Koerner et al., 2002; Chin & Russell, 1995; Denton & Lacina, 1984; Denton, Morris, & Tooke, 1982; Denton & Smith, 1983; Denton & Tooke, 1981-1982; Laboskey & Richert, 2002; Orland-Barak, 2002; Sumara & Luce-Kapler, 1996).

Perhaps because of the presence of several of these elements, studies of highly developed professional development schools—those that have managed to create a shared practice between the school and the university curriculum—have suggested that teachers who graduate from such programs often feel more knowledgeable and prepared to teach (Gettys, Ray, Rutledge, Puckett, & Stepanske, 1999; Sandholtz & Dadlez, 2000; Stallings, Bossung, & Martin, 1990; Yerian & Grossman, 1997). Although research has also demonstrated how difficult these partnerships are to enact, studies polling employers and supervisors showed graduates of highly developed PDSs were viewed as much better prepared than other new teachers (Hayes & Wetherill, 1996; Mantle-Bromley, 2002). Veteran teachers working in highly-developed PDSs have reported changes in their own practice and improvements at the classroom and school levels as a result of the professional development, action research, and mentoring that are part of the PDS (Tracht-man, 1996; Crow, Stokes, Kauchak, Hobbs, & Bullough, 1996; Houston Consortium of Professional Development, 1996; Jett-Simpson, Pugach, & Whipp, 1992).

Comparison group studies have found that PDS-prepared teachers have been rated stronger in various areas of teaching, ranging from classroom management and uses of technology to content area skills (Gill & Hove, 1999; Neubert & Binko, 1998; Shroyer, Wright, & Ramey-Gassert, 1996). A small set of studies has documented gains in student performance and achievement tied directly to curriculum and teaching interventions resulting from the professional development and curriculum work professional development schools have undertaken with their university partners (e.g., Frey, 2002; Gill & Hove, 1999; Glaeser, Karge, Smith, & Weatherill, 2002; Fischetti & Larson, 2002; Houston et al., 1995; Judge, Carrideo, & Johnson, 1995; Wiseman & Cooner, 1996).

Finally, *program standards* may matter in several ways: Recent work on the use of standards to guide teacher development and assessment suggests that the clarity and salience of standards and performance tasks against which candidates are judged—and the extent to which they represent research-based elements of teaching—may organize teacher learning in important ways (Darling-Hammond, 2006; Hammerness & Darling-Hammond, 2002). Also the rigor of the expectations the program holds for students—as seen in course expectations, grading policies, and whether weak candidates are counseled out of the program—may signal both aspects of selection and program quality. Finally, the extent to which the program holds itself accountable by engaging in self-study and continual improvement may be an indirect measure of program quality.

As we describe below, the emergence of new professional standards for teaching has been an important element of the policy context for teacher education and teacher learning over the last 20 years and may offer new possibilities for means to improve professional practice in the years ahead.

The Emergence of Standards for Teaching

The last two decades have marked the emergence of professional standards for teaching, stimulated in large part by the view that heightened expectations for student learning can be accomplished only by greater expectations for teaching quality. As part of the standards-based reform movement initiative launched in the late 1980s, new standards for teacher education accreditation and for teacher licensing,

certification, and ongoing evaluation have become a prominent lever for promoting system-wide change in teaching. For example, the National Commission on Teaching and America's Future (NCTAF, 1996) argued that:

> Standards for teaching are the linchpin for transforming current systems of preparation, licensing, certification, and ongoing development so that they better support student learning. [Such standards] can bring clarity and focus to a set of activities that are currently poorly connected and often badly organized ... clearly, if students are to achieve high standards, we can expect no less from their teachers and from other educators. Of greatest priority is reaching agreement on what teachers should know and be able to do to teach to high standards. (p. 67)

Professions generally set and enforce standards in three ways: (a) through professional accreditation of preparation programs; (b) through state licensing, which grants permission to practice; and (c) through advanced certification, which is a professional recognition of high levels of competence.[1] In virtually all professions other than teaching, candidates must graduate from an accredited professional school in order to sit for state licensing examinations that test their knowledge and skill. The accreditation process is meant to ensure that all preparation programs provide a reasonably common body of knowledge and structured training experiences that are comprehensive and up-to-date. Licensing examinations are meant to ensure that candidates have acquired the knowledge they need to practice responsibly. The tests generally include both surveys of specialized information and performance components that examine aspects of applied practice in the field: Lawyers must analyze cases and, in some states, develop briefs or memoranda of law to address specific issues; doctors must diagnose patients via case histories and describe the treatments they would prescribe; engineers must demonstrate that they can apply certain principles to particular design situations. These examinations are developed by members of the profession through state professional standards boards.

In addition, many professions offer additional examinations that provide recognition for advanced levels of skill, such as certification for public accountants, board certification for doctors, and registration for architects. This recognition generally takes extra years of study and practice, often in a supervised internship and/or residency, and is based on performance tests that measure greater levels of specialized knowledge and skill. Those who have met these standards are then allowed to do certain kinds of work that other practitioners cannot. The certification standards inform the other sets of standards governing accreditation, licensing, and re-licensing: They are used to ensure that professional schools incorporate new knowledge into their courses and to guide professional development and evaluation throughout the career. Thus, these advanced standards may be viewed as an engine that pulls along the knowledge base of the profession. Together, standards for accreditation, licensing, and certification comprise a "three-legged stool" (NCTAF, 1996) that supports quality assurance in the mature professions.

This three-legged stool, however, has historically been quite wobbly in teaching, where each of the quality assurance functions has been much less developed than in other professions. Until recently, there was no national body to establish a system of professional certification. Meanwhile, states have managed licensing and the approval of teacher education programs using widely varying standards and generally weak enforcement tools. Furthermore, the utility of each of these functions has been hotly contended within and outside the profession on a variety of ideological and political grounds. In recent years, these debates have led to an array of empirical studies seeking to establish whether and how licensing, accreditation, and certification make a difference for teacher quality, as well as teacher learning and the distribution of teachers. We note that this phenomenon is largely unique to education, as the mature professions have adopted such quality controls without questioning their outcomes. In this section, we review much of this research and consider its implications for policy.

The National Board for Professional Teaching Standards A set of efforts to set standards for teaching has been led by the National Board for Professional Teaching Standards (the National Board), an independent organization established in 1987 as the first professional body—-comprised of a majority of classroom teachers—to set standards for the advanced certification of highly accomplished teachers. The board's mission is to "establish high and rigorous standards for what accomplished teachers should know and be able to do, to develop and operate a voluntary national system to assess and certify teachers who meet those standards, and to advance related education reforms—all with the purpose of improving student learning" (Baratz-Snowden, 1990, p. 19). These standards stimulated the development of beginning teacher licensing standards developed by the Interstate New Teacher Assessment and Support Consortium (INTASC; 1992), a consortium of states working together on "National Board-compatible" licensing standards and assessments. Both of these have been reinforced by the National Council for Accreditation of Teacher Education (NCATE), which recently incorporated the performance standards developed by both.

The standards developed by the National Board, INTASC, and NCATE incorporate knowledge about teaching and learning that supports a view of teaching as complex, contingent on students' needs and instructional goals, and reciprocal—that is, continually shaped and reshaped by students' responses to learning events. The new standards and assessments take into explicit account the teaching challenges posed by a student body that is multicultural and multilingual and that includes diverse approaches to learning. By reflecting new subject matter standards for students which were articulated by the national professional associations in the 1990s, the demands of learner diversity, and the expectation that teachers must collaborate with col-

leagues and parents in order to succeed, the standards define teaching as a collegial, professional activity that responds to considerations of subjects and students. By examining teaching in the light of learning, they put considerations of effectiveness at the center of practice. This view contrasts with that of the previous "technicist" era of teacher training and evaluation, in which teaching was seen as the implementation of set routines and formulas for behavior, unresponsive to the distinctive attributes of either clients or curriculum goals.

Another important attribute of the new standards is that they are *performance-based*: that is, they describe what teachers should know, be like, and be able to do rather than listing courses that teachers should take in order to be awarded a license. This shift toward performance-based standard-setting is in line with the approach to licensing taken in other professions and with the changes already occurring in a number of states. This approach aims to clarify what the criteria are for determining competence, placing more emphasis on the abilities teachers develop than the hours they spend taking classes.

To achieve National Board certification (NBC) candidates must complete a rigorous two-part assessment. The assessment includes a portfolio completed by the teacher at the school site, which incorporates student work samples, videotapes of classroom practice, and extensive written analyses and reflections based upon these artifacts. The portfolio is meant to allow teachers to present a picture of their practice as it is shaped by the particular needs of the students with whom the teachers work and the particular context of the teacher's school. The assessment also includes a set of exercises completed at a local assessment center during which candidates demonstrate both content knowledge and pedagogical content knowledge through tasks such as analyzing teaching situations, responding to content matter prompts, evaluating curriculum materials, or constructing lesson plans.

Influences of the Board By 2007, the National Board for Professional Teaching Standards had offered advanced certification to 63,821 accomplished teachers, about 2% of the U.S. teaching force. This represents about 40% of those who apply for certification. However, the board has had much greater impact than the initial numbers of certified teachers suggested. As the first professional effort to define accomplished teaching, it has also had an enormous influence on standard-setting for beginning teacher licensing, teacher education programs, teacher assessment, on-the-job evaluation, and professional development for teachers throughout the United States.

The standard-setting work completed by the National Board for Professional Teaching Standards influenced the setting of national standards for the licensing of beginning teachers through the work of the Interstate New Teacher Assessment. These standards have been adopted or adapted by most states as part of their licensing standards and incorporated into the standards of NCATE. NCATE then began working with universities to help them design advanced master's degree programs focused on the development of teaching practice and organized around the standards of the National Board.

As a result of these combined initiatives, systems of licensing and accreditation that seek to assess what teachers know and can do are gradually replacing the traditional methods of tallying specific courses as the basis for granting program approval or a license. Furthermore, because these three sets of standards are substantively connected and form a continuum of development along the career path of the teacher, they conceptualize the main dimensions along which teachers can work to improve their practice. By providing vivid descriptions of high-quality teaching in specific teaching areas, some analysts argue, "[the standards] clarify what the profession expects its members to get better at … profession-defined standards provide the basis on which the profession can lay down its agenda and expectations for professional development and accountability" (Ingvarson, 1997, p. 1).

These standards and the board's assessment process have stimulated initiatives in teacher education to focus coursework on standards of practice and to use portfolios to evaluate teaching. Documenting the spread of portfolio assessments throughout teacher education, and into teacher evaluation and teacher development enterprises as well, Nona Lyons (1998a) directly attributes to the National Board the widespread move to performance assessments focused on documentation of practice. In addition, Lyons argues that portfolios hold the seed of a "new professionalism" that supports teaching quality in a number of ways:

> Portfolio assessment systems hold out standards of rigor and excellence; require evidence of effective learning; foster one's own readiness to teach, to author one's own learning; make collaboration a new norm for teaching, creating collaborative, interpretive communities of teacher learners who can interrogate critically their practice; and uncover and make public what counts as effective teaching in today's complex world of schools and learners. (p. 21)

This is an ambitious set of aspirations, and not easily met. As Lee Shulman (1998)—who launched the design work for the board's portfolios—noted, these great possibilities are accompanied by potential dangers as well. These include the possibilities that showmanship might trump substance, that portfolios—like other assessments—might eventually begin to trivialize teaching by measuring what is easy rather than what is important, that they might misrepresent teachers' actual practice, and that the amount of work they require might be viewed as not worth the benefits (pp. 34–35).

As the National Board certification process has spread, policy makers and researchers have begun to look for evidence about its effects on teacher learning as well as its validity as a measure of teacher effectiveness. As of 2005, 31 states encouraged teachers to pursue National Board certification by offering support for the hefty application fee, and 32 states provided incentives in the form of salary supplements to teachers who earn such certification. A number of states also provided full or partial license reciprocity on the basis of National Board status, and 28 used certification status as a proxy for full or partial license renewal. More than 500 school districts provided incentives in the form of fee support and/or salary increases, often in addition to state incentives (Humphrey, Koppich, & Hough, 2005). In addition, a number of districts have incorporated National Board certification into teacher evaluation processes, compensation systems, and career ladders that identify teachers for new roles and responsibilities, such as master or mentor teacher positions.

The Effectiveness of Board Certified Teachers　　As initiatives to recognize board certified teachers for compensation and advanced responsibilities have grown, the question of whether the certification process indeed recognizes individuals who are more effective than other teachers has given rise to a number of studies, most of which have answered the question in the affirmative. For example, Cavaluzzo (2004) examined mathematics achievement gains for nearly 108,000 high school students over 4 years in the Miami-Dade County Public Schools, controlling for a wide range of student and teacher characteristics (including experience, certification, and assignment in field, as well as board certification). Each of the teacher quality indicators made a statistically significant contribution to student outcomes. Students who had a typical NBC teacher made the greatest gains, exceeding gains of those with similar teachers who had failed NBC or had never been involved in the process. The effect size for National Board certification ranged from 0.07 to 0.12, estimated with and without school fixed effects. Students with new teachers who lacked a regular state certification, and those who had teachers whose primary job assignment was not mathematics instruction made the smallest gains.

Goldhaber and Anthony (2005), using 3 years of linked teacher and student data from North Carolina representing more than 770,000 student records, found the value-added student achievement gains of National Board certified teachers (NBCTs) were significantly greater than those of unsuccessful NBCT candidates and non-applicant teachers. Students of NBCTs achieved growth exceeding that of students of unsuccessful applicants by about 5% of a standard deviation in reading and 9% of a standard deviation in math.

In two other large-scale North Carolina-based studies using administrative data at the elementary and high school levels, Clotfelter, Ladd, and Vigdor (2006, 2007) found positive effects of National Board certification on student learning gains, along with positive effects of other teacher qualifications, such as a license in the field taught. Comparing NBC teachers to all others (rather than to those who had attempted and failed the assessment, where the differences are greatest in most studies), they found effect sizes of .02 to .05 across different content areas and grade levels, with fairly consistent estimations using student and school fixed effects.

Using randomized assignment of classrooms to teachers in Los Angeles Unified School District, Cantrell, Fullerton, Kane, and Staiger (2007) found that students of NBC teachers outperformed those of teachers who had unsuccessfully attempted the certification process by 0.2 standard deviations, about twice the differential that they found between NBC teachers and unsuccessful applicants from a broader LAUSD sample not part of the randomized experiment, but analyzed with statistical controls.

Significant positive influences of NBC teachers on achievement were also found in much smaller studies by Vandevoort, Amrein-Beardsley, and Berliner (2004) and Smith, Gordon, Colby, and Wang (2005). Smith and colleagues also examined how the practices of their 35 NBCTs compared to those of 29 who had attempted but failed certification, finding significant differences reflecting the ways in which NBCTs fostered deeper understanding in their instructional design and classroom assignments.

Not all findings have been as clearly positive. Using an administrative data set in Florida, Harris and Sass (2007) found that NBC teachers appeared more effective than other teachers in some but not all grades and subjects—and on one of the two different sets of tests evaluated (the Florida Comprehensive Assessment Test and the SAT-9). This study did not compare NBCs to those who had attempted certification unsuccessfully, which is the strongest comparison for answering the question of whether the board's process differentiates between more and less effective teachers. Finally, using a methodology different than that used in most other studies, Sanders, Ashton, and Wright (2005) found effect sizes for NBCTs similar to those of other studies (about .05 to .07 in math), but most of the estimates were not statistically significant because of the increased size of the standard errors when allowing for teacher random effects in a small sample.

The weight of the evidence does suggest that the board's certification process differentiates in a meaningful way between teachers who are more and less effective, which provides some support for policy decisions to use the certificate as a basis for differentiating compensation and responsibilities. It also suggests that use of the board's standards and assessments to guide preparation, licensing, and professional development may be warranted. Indeed, many have justified the time and expense associated with the certification process in part by the gains in teacher learning and practice that are thought to occur as teachers go through the process of certification and, in some cases, assume leadership roles.

Effects of Board Certification on Teacher Learning Early studies examining teachers' reactions to the assessment process, along with testimonials from individual teachers, have consistently reported that teachers become more conscious of their teaching decisions and change their self-reported practices as a result (see, e.g., Chittenden & Jones, 1997; Sato, 2000; Tracz, Sienty, & Mata, 1994; Tracz et al., 1995). National Board participants often say that they have learned more about teaching from their participation in the assessments than they have learned from any other previous professional development experience (Areglado, 1999; Bradley, 1994; Buday & Kelly, 1996). David Haynes' (1995) statement is typical of many:

> Completing the portfolio for the Early Adolescence/Generalist Certification was, quite simply, the single most powerful professional development experience of my career. Never before have I thought so deeply about what I do with children, and why I do it. I looked critically at my practice, judging it against a set of high and rigorous standards. Often in daily work, I found myself rethinking my goals, correcting my course, moving in new directions. I am not the same teacher as I was before the assessment, and my experience seems to be typical. (p. 60)

In an early pilot of portfolios in the Stanford Teacher Assessment Project (1987–1990), which led to the National Board's work, 89% of teachers who participated felt that the portfolio process had had some effect on their teaching. Teachers reported that they improved their practice as they pushed themselves to meet specific standards that had previously had little place in their teaching (Athanases, 1994). A 2001 survey of more than 5,600 National Board candidates found that 92% believe the National Board certification process has made them a better teacher, reporting that it helped them create stronger curricula, improved their abilities to evaluate student learning, and enhanced their interaction with students, parents, and other teachers (80%; NBPTS, 2001a).

Another survey which reported similar results regarding self-reported improvements in practice also found that most (80%) teachers who had gone through the certification process felt it was more productive than other professional development experiences they had had. Nearly 80% of teachers involved as assessors similarly felt that serving as an assessor was more useful than professional development activities. Large majorities of both the board certified teachers and assessors felt their experiences had a strong effect on their teaching (NBPTS, 2001b).

Another study of teachers' perceptions of their teaching abilities before and after completing portfolios for the National Board found that teachers reported statistically significant increases in their performance in each area assessed (planning, designing, and delivering instruction, managing the classroom, diagnosing and evaluating student learning, using subject matter knowledge, and participating in a learning community; Tracz et al., 1994; Tracz et al., 1995). Teachers commented that videotaping their teaching and analyzing student work made them more aware of how to organize teaching and learning tasks, how to analyze student learning, and how to intervene and change course when necessary.

In a longitudinal, quasi-experimental study that investigated learning outcomes for high school science teachers who pursued National Board certification, Lustick and Sykes (2006) found that the certification process had a significant impact upon candidates' understanding of knowledge associated with science teaching, with a substantial overall effect size of 0.47. Teachers' knowledge was assessed before and after candidates went through the certification process through an assessment of their ability to analyze and evaluate practice.

In an ingenious design, each candidate was sent an identical interview packet containing a sealed 6-minute video clip of a whole class discussion in science, student artifacts, and classroom situations to be discussed during the interview. The specific questions they would be asked about these materials were not included in the packet. During an extended telephone interview (ranging from 40 to 90 minutes), teachers examined and analyzed the artifacts, responded to the interview questions, and watched the videotape for the first time. After the audiotaped interview was transcribed, a "processed" version of the transcription was then scored by at least two assessors using rubrics associated with the 13 standards of the National Board certification process. The 13 assessed scores for each candidate were then aggregated to the group level so that means representing different observations could be compared for significant differences at the overall, set, and individual standard level of analysis. The greatest gains—as measured by data from interviews and examination of portfolio entries—were associated with standards dealing with *scientific inquiry* and *assessment*.

More recent research that followed comparison groups of teachers over time found that teachers who undertook National Board certification did indeed change their assessment practices significantly more over the course of their certification year than did teachers who did not participate in the certification process (Sato, Chung, & Darling-Hammond, 2008). This study tracked National Board candidates' assessment practices over 3 years—a year prior to pursuing certification, a year of candidacy, and the post-candidacy year—along with those of a comparison group of teachers who were interested in pursuing certification but who postponed their candidacy until the study was completed. Evidence of teachers' practices on 6 dimensions of formative assessment included classroom data (lesson plans, videotaped lessons, and student work samples), student surveys, and teacher interviews. Although the National Board group began the study with lower mean scores than the comparison group on all 6 dimensions of formative assessment, by the second year of the study, the group had higher mean scores on all dimensions, with statistically significant gains on 4 of them, and they continued to demonstrate substantially higher scores in the year after they completed in the certification process. The most pronounced changes were in the ways teachers used a range of assessment information to support student learning.

Other studies have looked at how National Board teachers may influence the learning of other teachers through mentoring, assistance, and other leadership activities. A 2001 national survey of nearly 2,200 board certified teachers indicated substantial involvement in such activities, with 99.6% reporting they were involved in at least one leadership activity and most involved in as many as ten (Yankelovich Partners, 2001). Among these, 90% reported mentoring or coaching candidates for board certification, 83% reported mentoring or coaching new or struggling teachers, 80% reported developing or selecting programs or materials to support or increase student learning, and 68% reported district or school leadership roles. A large majority (81%) agreed that the certification opened up new leadership activities for them.

Another study surveyed nearly 1,600 teachers from 47 elementary schools in two states, evaluating the helping behavior of NBTs compared to others who were comparable in experience and other background characteristics. Based on other teachers' reports of which teachers had helped them, the study found that National Board certified teachers helped, on average, 40% more teachers than other similar colleagues (Frank & Sykes, 2006). This research suggests that National Board certified teachers may contribute in important ways to school improvement beyond the contributions they make in their own classrooms.

Policy Implications From a policy perspective, then, encouraging teachers to pursue National Board certification may both improve their own teaching effectiveness and support the learning of other teachers through mentoring, coaching, and other leadership activities. It also appears to provide a useful marker for teacher performance for purposes of recognition and reward. Yet, NBCTs frequently find that their schools and districts have not begun to envision new roles that will allow them to share their expertise. Often these potential teacher leaders feel they are "all dressed up with nowhere to go," even in states like North Carolina that have provided substantial base salary increments for board-certified teachers and have grown a sizable cadre of NBCTs (see, e.g., Southeast Center for Teaching Quality, 2002; Williams & Bearer, 2001; Loeb, Elfers, Plecki, Ford, & Knapp, 2006). From this perspective, much policy development work is yet to be done to develop differentiated teacher roles and collegial workplace settings that provide the time and opportunity for expertise to be shared—and, in particular, to create means for such investments in organizational learning to occur in the schools that most need them.

For example, Humphrey, Koppich, and Hough (2005) found that, of the more than 30 states offering various incentives for board certification, only two had made any effort to equalize the distribution of such teachers through their policies. Among six states they examined more closely, only California—which offers a $20,000 bonus (paid out over 4 years) to NBCTs who teach in underperforming schools—showed a reasonably equitable distribution of board certified teachers to schools serving poor, minority, and lower performing students. Other incentives may also contribute to this finding, since a large proportion of NBCTs working in low performing, minority, and poor schools were in Los Angeles, which not only has a large number of the states' underperforming schools, it is also one of a very few California districts providing a 12% base salary increase to NBCTs.

A modest beginning on this agenda has occurred in local career ladder plans in a few districts such as Rochester, New York; Cincinnati, Ohio; and Denver, Colorado, and state incentives for career ladder plans in Arizona, Iowa, and Minnesota, among others. Some federal legislative proposals have aimed to increase leverage for local experimentation with these ideas. For example, the TEACH Act, introduced by George Miller in the House and Edward Kennedy in the Senate, encouraged career ladders and authorized incentive pay to attract "effective" teachers to high-need schools and to pay them stipends to serve as mentors or master teachers.

These new proposals represent the growing political interest in moving beyond traditional measures of teacher qualifications—such as experience, degrees, and licensing status—to evaluate teachers' actual performance and effectiveness as the basis for making decisions about hiring, tenure, licensing, compensation, and selection for leadership roles. In addition to measures like National Board certification, measures of effectiveness have included other performance-based evaluations.

Often based on those of the National Board, standards-based teacher evaluations used by some districts have been found to be significantly related to student achievement gains for teachers and to help teachers improve their practice and effectiveness. Like the board's performance assessments, these systems for observing teachers' classroom practice are based on professional teaching standards grounded in research on teaching and learning. They use systematic observation protocols to examine teaching along a number of dimensions. All of the career ladder plans mentioned earlier use such evaluations as part of their systems and many use the same or similar rubrics for observing teaching. The Denver compensation system, which uses such an evaluation system as one of its components, describes the features of its system as including: well-developed rubrics articulating different levels of teacher performance, inter-rater reliability, a fall-to-spring evaluation cycle, and a peer and self-evaluation component.

In a study of three districts using standards-based evaluation systems, researchers found significant relationships between teachers' ratings and their students' gain scores on standardized tests (Milanowski, Kimball, & White, 2004). In the schools and districts studied, assessments of teachers are based on well-articulated standards of practice evaluated through evidence including observations of teaching along with teacher interviews and, sometimes, artifacts such as lesson plans, assignments, and samples of student work.

The set of studies on standards-based teacher evaluation suggest that the more teachers' classroom activities and behaviors are enabled to reflect professional standards of practice, the more effective they are in supporting student learning—a finding that would appear to suggest the desirability of focusing on such professional standards in the preparation, professional development, and evaluation of teachers. Yet the policy community is still divided about whether preparation for teachers should be universally guided by and held to common professional standards.

Standards for Licensing Beginning Teachers While the emergence of the INTASC standards for licensing beginning teachers have created a substantially common set of standards for teaching across the states, there are still important differences in the ways that states manage licensing and the approval of teacher education programs. States issue many types of licenses, endorsements, and certifications, and in some states, there is a wide variety of loopholes and exceptions for any requirement. Furthermore, standards for teaching candidates vary with the wide range of licensing examinations enacted across the 48 states, plus the District of Columbia, that require them (Goldhaber, 2006). These exams, too, set different standards of knowledge and skill for both content and levels of performance.

Whereas a few states require examinations of subject matter knowledge, teaching knowledge, and teaching skill and use relatively high standards for evaluating those assessments, others require only basic skills or general knowledge tests that do not seek to measure teaching knowledge or performance. In 2004, 34 states required basic skills tests for admission to teacher education or for an initial license, 38 required tests of subject matter knowledge, 25 required tests of pedagogical knowledge, and 13 states required successful completion of a state performance assessment to obtain the advanced license (NASDTEC, 2004). In most states, prospective teachers are required to pass at least two tests and sometimes as many as four.

The nature, content, and quality of tests constructed and selected across the states vary greatly, as do their cutoff scores (NCTAF, 1996; Strauss, 1998). A report by the Committee on Assessment and Teacher Quality of the National Research Council (Mitchell, Robinson, Plake, & Knowles, 2001) noted that while the initial licensure tests used by states are designed to identify candidates qualified for minimally competent beginning practice, the several hundred different tests currently in use, despite their quantity, do not provide information about some of the most important competencies relevant to beginning practice. Haertel (1991) summarized the many concerns as follows:

> The teacher tests now in common use have been strenuously and justifiably criticized for their content, their format, and their impacts, as well as the virtual absence of criterion-related validity evidence supporting their use...these tests have been criticized for treating pedagogy as generic rather than subject-matter specific, for showing poor criterion-related validity or failing to address criterion-related validity altogether, for failing to measure many critical teaching skills, and for their adverse impact on minority representation in the teaching profession. (pp. 3–4)

While teacher tests have evolved some over the last decade, many of these concerns remain. Over the years, a number of studies have examined the relationship between teachers' scores on traditional licensing tests and teacher ratings or their contributions to student achievement. The findings of these studies have been mixed. Although many studies have found little or no relationship between teachers' scores on licensing tests and teacher effectiveness (Ayers, 1988; Ayers & Qualls, 1979; Boyd et al., 2007; Dybdahl, Shaw, & Edwards, 1997; Haney, Madaus, & Kreitzer, 1987; Hanushek, 1971), some studies have found that teachers' scores on tests that include aspects of professional knowledge are related to their effectiveness in raising student achievement (Clotfelter, Ladd, & Vigdor, 2006; Ferguson, 1991; Goldhaber, 2005, 2006; Sheehan & Marcus, 1978; Strauss & Sawyer, 1986).

Some of these tests do appear to measure aspects of the knowledge base specific to teaching. For example, Gitomer, Latham, and Ziomek (1999) found that teachers who were never enrolled in a teacher education program had the lowest pass rates on the PRAXIS II curriculum tests, even though they had comparable SAT scores to those who had completed teacher education programs.

Given the uncertain relationship between teachers' performance on the multiple licensure tests they are required to take and the effectiveness of their teaching practice, some have voiced concerns about the effects on teacher supply of the requirements. For example, while Goldhaber (2006) found a small positive relationship between the PRAXIS Curriculum test and student achievement, he also pointed out that the high rate of Type I and Type II errors results in significant tradeoffs: Cut scores allow some teachers with little contribution to student achievement to become licensed based on their performance on these tests, while others who would be effective teachers are ineligible to receive licensure.

Furthermore, there is evidence that many licensing tests have served to limit the diversity of the teaching force. Several studies have found a differential impact of teacher exams (the now-ended National Teacher Examinations, the currently used PRAXIS series, and a number of state-developed exams) on teacher candidates of different races, with African Americans and Hispanics having lower pass rates than Whites (Angrist & Guryan, 2003; Garibaldi, 1991; Gitomer et al., 1999; Murnane & Schwinden, 1989; Texas Education Agency, 1994). Finally, some teacher educators have argued that state licensing tests may undermine accountability for teaching and learning if they are not aligned with the programs' goals for their teacher candidates (Graham, Lyman, & Trow, 1995).

All of these concerns—and a desire to create stronger measures for both developing and assessing readiness to teach—have led to recent experimentation with performance assessments for beginning teacher licensure.

Beginning Teacher Performance Assessments The need for licensing examinations that can better predict teachers' effectiveness in the classroom and for a way to support the professional development of beginning teachers has led some states and school districts to adopt performance-based assessments that measure teachers' application of their pedagogical and content-area knowledge as the basis for licensure and professional development. Over the last decade, teaching performance assessments have also begun to find wide appeal in the context of teacher education programs and teacher licensing for their innovative ways of assessing teacher knowledge and skill but also for their potential to promote teacher learning and reflective teaching. Such assessments come in a variety of formats, including tasks that ask teachers to analyze student work, evaluate textbooks, analyze a teaching video, or solve a teaching problem; lesson planning exercises; videotapes and direct observations of teaching in the classroom.

Within individual programs, locally-developed assessments represent distinctive conceptualizations of teaching tasks, a wide range of quality, and differential attention to concerns for reliability and validity. These assessments, no doubt, also vary in how much they affect candidate competence, program planning, and improvement. However, with pressures on programs to demonstrate their effects—and with public policy concerns for gauging teachers' practice and effectiveness—more systematic, cross-cutting approaches to performance assessment have been undertaken in a number of states.

In some states, teacher performance assessments for new teachers, modeled after the National Board assessments, are being used either in teacher education, as a basis for the initial licensing recommendation (California, Oregon), or in the teacher induction period, as a basis for moving from a probationary to a professional license (Connecticut). These assessments require teachers to document their plans and teaching for a unit of instruction, videotape and critique lessons, and collect and evaluate evidence of student learning. Like the National Board assessments, beginning teachers' ratings on the Connecticut BEST assessment have been found to significantly predict their students' value-added achievement on the state reading test (Wilson & Hallam, 2006). As more states begin to implement performance-based assessments for teacher licensure on a wide scale, we can anticipate that there will be additional opportunities to examine the predictive validity of these assessments.

The Impact of Performance Assessments on Beginning Teacher Learning Because teacher education programs have been experimenting with the use of portfolios and other forms of performance-based assessment (such as teaching cases and exhibitions) since the 1980s, they have provided opportunities to study the effects of these alternative assessments on the learning of pre-service teachers. Across the country, a number of studies have examined the impact of performance assessments on pre-service teachers' learning and have suggested that, in some programs with highly-developed internal systems, such assessments have provided candidates with opportunities to put into practice the knowledge, principles, and skills they learned in their coursework, and to reflect on and learn from their teaching experiences (e.g., Anderson & DeMeulle, 1998; Davis & Honan, 1998; Lyons, 1996, 1998a, 1998b, 1999; Richert, 1987; Shulman, 1992; Stone, 1998; Zeichner, 2000).

Like those of the National Board, there is also some evidence that performance assessments may help beginning teachers improve their practice. Connecticut's process of implementing INTASC-based portfolios for beginning teacher licensing involves virtually all educators in the state in the assessment process, either as beginning teachers taking the assessment or as school-based mentors who work with beginners, as assessors who are trained to score the portfolios, or as expert teachers who convene regional support seminars to help candidates learn about the standards. Educators throughout the system develop similar knowledge about teaching and learn how principles of good instruction are applied in classrooms. These processes can have far-reaching effects. By the year 2010, an estimated 80% of elementary teachers, and nearly as many secondary teachers, will have participated in the new assessment system as candidates, support providers, or assessors (Pecheone & Stansbury, 1996).

A new teacher who participated in the assessment described the power of the process, which requires planning and teaching a unit, and reflecting daily on the day's lesson to consider how it met the needs of each student and what should be changed in the next day's plans. He noted: "Although I was the reflective type anyway, it made me go a step further. I would have to say, okay, this is how I'm going to do it differently. It made an impact on my teaching and was more beneficial to me than just one lesson in which you state what you're going to do ... the process makes you reflect on your teaching. And I think that's necessary to become an effective teacher."

Similar learning effects are recorded in research on the PACT assessment used in California teacher education programs. California recently enacted a new state law that will require all pre-service teachers in the state to pass a Teaching Performance Assessment (TPA) to qualify for a preliminary teaching credential beginning in 2008. Since 2003, teacher credential programs across the state have been piloting either the CA Teaching Performance Assessment (created in partnership with ETS) or the Performance Assessment for California Teachers, an alternative assessment designed by a consortium of 31 public and private universities (see Pecheone & Chung, 2006).

The assessment requires student teachers or interns to plan and teach a week-long unit of instruction mapped to the state standards; to reflect daily on the lesson they have just taught and revise plans for the next day; to analyze and provide commentaries of videotapes of themselves teaching; to collect and analyze evidence of student learning; to reflect on what worked, what did not and why; and to project what they would do differently in a future set of lessons. Candidates must show how they take into account students' prior knowledge and experiences in their planning. Adaptations for English language learners and for special needs students must be incorporated into plans and instruction. Analyses of student outcomes are part of the evaluation of teaching.

The Impact of Performance Assessment on Teaching and Teacher Education   Faculty and supervisors score these portfolios using standardized rubrics in moderated sessions following training, with an audit procedure to calibrate standards. Faculties use the PACT results to revise their curriculum. Like the National Board and Connecticut assessments, these promise to have learning effects that may affect the system more broadly, through the learning that occurs for assessors as well as for candidates (Darling-Hammond, 2006). For example:

> For me the most valuable thing was the sequencing of the lessons, teaching the lesson, and evaluating what the kids were getting, what the kids weren't getting, and having that be reflected in my next lesson ... the "teach-assess-teach-assess-teach-assess" process. And so you're constantly changing—you may have a plan or a framework that you have together, but knowing that that's flexible and that it has to be flexible, based on what the children learn that day. (Prospective teacher)

> This [scoring] experience ... has forced me to revisit the question of what really *matters* in the assessment of teachers, which—in turn—means revisiting the question of what really *matters* in the *preparation* of teachers. (Teacher education faculty member)

> [The scoring process] forces you to be clear about "good teaching;" what it looks like, sounds like. It enables you to look at your own practice critically, with new eyes. (Cooperating teacher)

> As an induction program coordinator, I have a much clearer picture of what credential holders will bring to us and of what they'll be required to do. We can build on this. (Induction program coordinator)

Significantly, early validation studies of the PACT have found no disparate impact of the assessment by race and ethnicity, in contrast to many other teach teacher tests (Pecheone & Chung, 2006.) Whether teachers' effectiveness actually improves as a result of completing performance-based assessments has not been established. However, there is some evidence that beginning teachers are capable of enacting what they report learning from a performance assessment in their actual classroom practice. Research on student teachers who had completed the Performance Assessment for California Teachers (see Chung, 2007, 2008) found that pre-service teachers did change their teaching practices as a consequence of their experiences with the performance assessment. Another study (Sloan, Cavazos, & Lippincott, 2007) found that first-year secondary science teachers who had completed the Performance Assessment for California Teachers during their pre-service year reported continued influences of the assessment on their teaching. Follow-up studies currently underway will reveal more about the relationship between PACT assessment ratings and beginning teacher practice and effectiveness, including evidence of students' value-added learning.

Standards for Accrediting Teacher Education A final element of the professional standards picture is the increasing use of such standards and performance assessments for evaluating schools of education. Until recently, the program approval process for schools of education, generally coordinated by the state's department of education, has typically assessed "the types of learning situations to which an individual is exposed and ... the time spent in these situations, rather than ... what the individual actually learned" (Goertz, Ekstrom, & Coley, 1984, p. 4). The 20th century practice of admitting individuals into practice based on their graduation from a state-approved program was a wholesale approach to licensing. It assumed that program quality could be well-defined and monitored by states; that programs would be equally effective with all of their students; and that completion of the courses or experiences mandated by the state would be sufficient to produce competent practitioners. The state approval system also assumed that markets for teachers were local: that virtually all teachers for the schools in a given state would be produced by colleges within that state, a presumption that has become increasingly untrue over time.

Most states, meanwhile, have routinely approved virtually all of their teacher education programs, despite the fact that these programs offer dramatically different kinds and qualities of preparation (Goodlad, Soder, & Sirotnik, 1990; NCTAF, 1996; Tom, 1997). Many state education agencies have inadequate budgetary resources and person-power to conduct the intensive program reviews that would support enforcement of high standards (David, 1994; Lusi, 1997). And even when state agencies find weak programs, political forces make it difficult to close them down. Teacher education programs bring substantial revenue to universities and local communities, and the availability of large numbers of teaching candidates, no matter how poorly prepared, keeps salaries relatively low. As Dennison (1992) notes, "the generally minimal state-prescribed criteria remain subject to local and state political influences, economic conditions within the state, and historical conditions which make change difficult" (p. A40).

Since the 1990s, however, states have been moving toward a common set of accreditation and teacher preparation standards linked to the National Board's professional standards for accomplished teachers and INTASC's standards for beginning teachers. This movement has been facilitated by a growing interest in national accreditation. In 1989, NCATE launched a new state partnership program in which its professional review of colleges of education is integrated with states' own reviews. The number of partnerships increased from 19 in 1990 to 48 in 2000. The partnerships eliminate duplication in an institution's preparation for state program approval and professional accreditation. One important result of these state partnerships is the alignment of state and professional standards. As of 2007, 39 states have adopted or adapted NCATE unit standards as their own unit standards, and NCATE's professional program standards have influenced teacher preparation across the 48 partnership states plus the District of Columbia and Puerto Rico.

In addition, beginning in the early 1990s, NCATE moved away from a curriculum-based review of programs to performance-based accreditation, in which institutions must provide evidence of competent teacher candidate performance rather than showing that candidates have been exposed to curriculum. In the 1995 version of its standards, NCATE required institutions to use multiple measures of performance to demonstrate candidate ability, and in the late 1990s, began developing performance-based accreditation standards. At the same time, NCATE also incorporated the INTASC model state licensing principles and the National Board standards into its accreditation standards. Additionally, NCATE aligned its teacher preparation standards with national standards for P–12 students. NCATE expects national standards for teacher preparation in the various subject matter areas to be congruent with P–12 student standards.

A somewhat different approach has been pursued by the newly-created Teacher Education Accrediting Council (TEAC), which was launched in 1997 by a group of education school deans and college presidents as an alternative to NCATE accreditation, and which has accredited 41 institutions over the last decade. TEAC audits education programs based on their performance in relation to internally derived objectives and standards, rather than against a common set of national or professional standards. To be accredited, a program must present evidence that its faculty have accomplished its own objectives. While critics of TEAC's approach assert that allowing a program to determine its own set of objectives and standards could lower or ignore key standards, TEAC counters that its accreditation process relies on "a common standard all TEAC programs must meet, viz. (1) credible evidence of their common claim that their graduates are competent, etc., (2) evidence that the means by which they establish the evidence is valid, (3) evidence that program decisions are based on evidence, and (4) evidence that the institution is committed to the program" (Murray, 2004, p. 8).

TEAC also anchors its review in part in state licensing standards to which programs are expected to be responsive, which, in turn, generally reflect the INTASC standards incorporated into NCATE's review. TEAC claims a high degree of alignment between its own principles and most of the NCATE standards (TEAC, n.d.). Thus, while their approaches to professional standards differ, both national accreditation systems currently emphasize the importance of credible evidence of candidate outcomes as the basis for accreditation and a set of standards against which programs are evaluated. While, in the past, evidence of inputs (i.e., the curriculum of teacher education) was sufficient for state and national accreditation, there has been a clear shift at the national level to a focus on evidence of outcomes of teacher education.

There have been few studies that have systematically examined the impact of accreditation on teacher education programs. Some studies indicate that negative NCATE reviews have led to substantial changes in weak education programs (e.g., Altenbaugh & Underwood, 1990; Williams, 2000), highlighting the fact that professional accreditation can spur program reform efforts. A study by Gitomer, Latham, and Ziomek (1999) of the Educational Testing Service (ETS) also found that graduates of NCATE accredited colleges of education pass ETS subject matter and pedagogy examinations at a higher rate than do graduates of unaccredited colleges of education and those who did not prepare. At the state policy level, Darling-Hammond (2000b) found an indirect relationship between accreditation, teacher quality, and student achievement, showing that states with a higher percentage of NCATE-accredited institutions had a significantly higher percentage of teachers with full certification, which in turn was strongly and positively associated with average student achievement on the National Assessment of Educational Progress. This, however, likely reflects a general policy climate with respect to teacher education investments in states—and perhaps overall education support—rather than a direct effect of the accreditation process.

There is also some evidence from NCATE that accreditation can act as a policy lever and that programs engaged in the accreditation process may also engage in program improvement efforts. For example, the initial failure rate for programs seeking NCATE accreditation in the 3 years after NCATE strengthened its standards in 1987 was 27%. During the first 3 years of implementation, almost half of the schools reviewed could not pass the new "knowledge base" standard, which specified that schools must be able to describe the knowledge base on which their programs rest. However, most of these schools made major changes in their programs, garnering new resources, making personnel changes, and revamping curriculum, and were successful in their second attempt at accreditation. NCATE upgraded its standards again in 1995 to incorporate the INTASC and National Board standards, and in 2005 introduced performance-based accreditation, requiring evidence of candidate outcomes. This means that many programs that want to secure or maintain professional accreditation will need to upgrade their efforts further.

In addition, recent reforms in teacher education seem to have resulted in improved perceptions of the quality of teacher preparation. Since 1990, surveys of beginning teachers who experienced teacher education (Gray et al., 1993; Howey & Zimpher, 1993; Kentucky Institute for Education Research, 1997; California State University, 2002a, 2002b) have found that more than 80% felt that they were well prepared for nearly all of the challenges of their work, while a somewhat smaller majority (60 to 70%) felt prepared to deal with the needs of special education students and those

with limited English proficiency. Veteran teachers and principals who work with current teacher preparation programs, particularly 5-year programs and those that feature professional development schools, have also reported their perception that their newly-trained colleagues are much better prepared than they were some years earlier (Andrew & Schwab, 1995; Baker, 1993; Darling-Hammond, 1994; National Center for Education Statistics [NCES], 1996, tables 73 and 75).

Nevertheless, issues of teacher education quality and the efficacy of contemporary accreditation remain contentious. While identifying a few teacher education programs he deemed excellent, Levine's (2006) report on U.S. teacher education echoed the historically common complaints of low quality for the field as a whole. In addition, the study used Northwest Evaluation Association student test score data to examine the relationship between students' achievement and the accreditation status of the college where their teachers were prepared. Controlling for teachers' years of experience, students taught by teachers prepared by NCATE institutions had slightly higher, but non-significant, gains in reading and math test scores than non-NCATE teachers. Having found that deans and faculty members most commonly cited accreditors as one of the most powerful forces in determining the organization and content of their curricula, Levine concluded that neither state regulations nor current accreditation processes are able to assure a minimum quality of teacher education. His critique centered on the need for greater attention to outcomes, implicitly discounting the value of such things as licensing examinations or even on-the-job ratings as evidence of teacher quality:

> Process trumps outcomes; teachers overshadow students; and teaching eclipses learning. Today quality control focuses principally on teaching; for instance, it emphasizes the components that make up a teacher education program and focuses on attempts to measure teaching ability (passage rates on certification exams, principals' assessments of new teachers) rather than learning outcomes. (p. 61)

Although Levine does not acknowledge the moves toward outcome-based accreditation that are already occurring, his expressed concern represents the drumbeat of the times.

Evaluating Teacher Education Based on Learning Outcomes

Interest in basing decisions about teachers—and their preparation institutions—on evidence of student learning has been growing. After all, if student learning is the primary goal of teaching, it appears straightforward that it ought to be taken into account in determining a teachers' competence. A prominent proposal is to use value-added student achievement test scores from state or district standardized tests as a key measure of teachers' effectiveness. The value-added concept is important, as it reflects a desire to acknowledge teachers' contributions to students' progress, taking into account where students begin. Furthermore, as our review illustrates, value-added methods are increasingly used for research on the effectiveness of specific populations teachers (e.g., those who are National Board certified or those who have had particular preparation or professional development experiences) and on the outcomes of various curriculum and teaching interventions.

Some analysts and policy makers are now urging that states develop data sets that link student test score data to their teachers' identifications so that it can be routinely used to evaluate individual teachers as well as the teacher education programs that prepared them. However, there are serious technical and educational challenges associated with using this approach to make strong inferences. In addition to the fact that curriculum-specific tests that would allow gain score analyses are not typically available in most teaching areas and grade levels, these include concerns that readily available tests do not measure many important kinds of learning, are inaccurate measures of learning for specific populations of students (e.g., new English language learners and some special education students), and that what appear to be the "effects" of a given teacher may reflect other teachers and learning experiences, home differentials, or aspects of the school environment that influence teaching (e.g., curriculum choices, resources and supports, class sizes, whether a teacher is assigned out-of-field, etc.).

Furthermore, value-added analyses have found that teachers look very different in their measured effectiveness depending on what statistical methods are used, including whether and how student characteristics are controlled, whether school effects are controlled, and how missing data are treated. In addition, effectiveness ratings appear highly unstable: a given teacher is likely to be rated differently in his or her effectiveness from class to class and from year to year. (For a summary of concerns, see Braun, 2005.)

Thus, while value-added models may prove useful for looking at groups of teachers for research purposes, and they may provide one measure of teacher effectiveness among several, they are problematic as the primary or sole measure for making evaluation decisions about individual teachers or even teacher education programs. More sophisticated judgments will be needed that take into account analyses of the teachers' students and teaching context, the nature of teachers' practices, and the availability of other learning opportunities if judgments are to reflect all the factors that influence student learning and teacher effects. Furthermore, evaluations of student learning will need to include both more comprehensive and more curriculum-connected measures of what students know and can do than are provided by most state-required standardized tests, which evaluate only a small, superficial set of learning objectives that are often a remote proxy for what is actually taught.

Conducting the kind of research that is necessary will be costly and difficult, though not impossible. Over the last few years, universities that are part of the "Teachers for a New Era" initiative funded by the Carnegie Corporation have been seeking to develop evidence of the learning out-

comes of teacher education, and, despite difficulties with small sample sizes, inaccessible student learning data, and a host of other feasibility issues, some promising studies that carefully evaluate the teaching process, context, and outcomes are underway.

One example of such research, conducted at the University of Virginia over the course of 2 years was designed explicitly "to examine the value added to pupil learning by contrasting teachers with and without formal pedagogical training, and to do so within the context of a theoretical model that more fully accounts for the complexity of teachers' and pupils' educational lives than do other value-added schemes" (Konold et al., 2008, p. 2). The study used an experimental design to assign 680 middle school pupils to instructional groups taught by two groups of university arts and sciences students, roughly half of whom had formal teacher training (N = 43) and half without (N = 47). University students within each of these two groups were matched on educational backgrounds and assigned in pairs to the randomly formed instructional groups of middle school pupils. Each student taught four lessons to his or her instructional group, and administered pre- and post-test measures on the content delivered in the four lessons and a reflection scale on lesson difficulty at the end of each lesson. Teachers' behaviors were recorded and scored independently by two trained observers. Data were analyzed using structural equations modeling and statistical procedures that accounted for the multi-level nesting of teachers within programs. The researchers found that teacher education candidates used teaching behaviors that had a statistically significant influence on pupils' acquisition of content knowledge, application, and interpretation of basic data analysis concepts, accounting for about 20% of the variation in gain scores. Students who were not enrolled in a teacher education program failed to demonstrate teaching behaviors that influenced student outcomes.

A teacher who scored high on the five sets of teaching behaviors might simply be described as one who provided support for learning. As noted by Konold and colleagues (2008): "These teachers gave clues and reminders, encouraged serious thought, broke problems into steps, provided examples, asked questions, gave feedback, and the like. Generally speaking, Teaching Behavior that worked appeared to be responsive to pupil understanding of the material and aimed at producing independent learners" (p. 23). Not included in the report of the study, but plausible to conduct, would be the companion research that reveals how these candidates learned to develop the kinds of teaching sensibilities and strategies that allowed them to be more effective.

A program of such careful research, conducted across subject matter domains, teaching contexts, and learning goals, and included teacher education graduates as well as current candidates, could begin to develop traction on many of the knotty questions of preparation strategies, as well as overall teacher education effects. The Carnegie-supported institutions engaged in this kind of research have been supported with grants of $5 million each over 5 years to develop and study the implementation of a set of teacher education principles. It is unlikely that individual institutions, studying themselves, will be able to build the needed corpus of research in the years ahead. Furthermore, many important research questions will need to be examined with larger samples across institutions and contexts.

This endeavor will require research funding on a scale that is not currently available. Sharp decreases in the funding available for teacher education research that occurred in the 1980s have not yet been reversed. Furthermore, the now-discontinued National Center for Research on Teacher Education, formerly located at Michigan State University, has not been replaced. A major federal investment in research on teacher education and learning—on the scale of that last undertaken in the 1970s—will be needed to build the knowledge base for increasingly sound policy and practice.

Conclusion

Debates about teacher education policy have arisen from both technical and political disagreements about what qualifications and preparation predict effectiveness and what principles should guide teacher selection and learning opportunities. At the root of some of these debates is the question of whether all students are equally entitled to teachers of comparable quality, as well questions of what kinds of qualifications and training matter most.

Current research suggests that there are many teacher characteristics and abilities which, in combination, predict teaching effectiveness. The fact that teachers' effectiveness is greatly enhanced when they have had many opportunities to learn—including high-quality general education, deepening of both content and pedagogical knowledge, teaching experience, and opportunities to develop specific practices through professional development and assessment—suggests a multi-faceted approach to policy development on behalf of stronger teaching. Evidence suggests that if policies were to support the recruitment of well-educated candidates into high-quality preparation programs that ensure substantial opportunities to learn subject matter and pedagogy, and support their ongoing learning focused on effective practices, the overall quality of teaching could be expected to be significantly higher.

Such policies would need to include effective incentives for recruiting, retaining, and distributing teachers to the places where they are needed (for examples, see Darling-Hammond & Sykes, 2003) as well as professional policies governing accreditation, licensure, and advanced certification that encourage schools of education to adopt the kinds of connected coursework and clinical experiences that enhance teachers' capacities and effectiveness.

Promising among these policy possibilities are supports for teacher assessment strategies—such as standards-based teacher evaluations and assessments like those of the National Board for Professional Teaching Standards and the Performance Assessment for California Teachers—that have been found not only to measure features of teaching associated with effectiveness, but actually to help develop effectiveness at the same time. Particularly useful are those approaches that both develop greater teaching skill and understanding for the participants and for those involved in mentoring and assessing these performances. These approaches may be particularly valuable targets for policy investments, as they may provide an engine for developing teaching quality across the profession—through their contributions to program improvement and to measures of how teachers contribute to student learning.

Finally, continued efforts to conduct careful, contextualized research on the outcomes of teacher education—in terms of teachers' retention in teaching, classroom practices, and associated learning results—will likely be essential to the development of policies that can both leverage program improvement and ensure that prospective teachers have access to the preparation that will allow them to teach effectively.

Notes

1. In education, the term "certification" has often been used to describe states' decisions regarding admission to practice, commonly termed licensing in other professions. Until recently, teaching had no vehicle for advanced professional certification. Now, advanced certification for accomplished veteran teachers is granted by a National Board for Professional Teaching Standards. To avoid confusion between the actions of this professional board and those of states, we use the terms licensing and certification here as they are commonly used by professions: "licensing" is the term used to describe state decisions about admission to practice and "certification" is the term used to describe the actions of the National Board in certifying accomplished practice.

References

Abdal-Haqq, I. (1998). *Professional development schools: Weighing the evidence.* Thousand Oaks, CA: Corwin Press.

Altenbaugh, R. J., & Underwood, K. (1990). The evolution of normal schools. In J. I. Goodlad, R. Soder, & K. Sirotnik (Eds.), *Places where teachers are taught* (pp. 136–186). San Francisco: Jossey-Bass.

Anderson, R. S., & DeMeulle, L. (1998). Portfolio use in twenty-four teacher education programs. *Teacher Education Quarterly, 25*(1), 23–32.

Andrew, M., & Schwab, R. L. (1995). Has reform in teacher education influenced teacher performance? An outcome assessment of graduates of eleven teacher education programs. *Action in Teacher Education, 17*(3), 43–53.

Angrist, J. D., & Guryan, J. (2003). *Does teacher testing raise teacher quality? Evidence from state certification requirements.* (NBER Working Paper No. 9545). Cambridge, MA: National Bureau of Economic Research, Inc. Retrieved June 11, 2008, from http://www.nber.org/papers/w9545

Angrist, J. D., & Lavy, V. (2001). Does teacher training affect pupil learning? Evidence from matched comparisons in Jerusalem public schools. *Journal of Labor Economics, 19*, 343–369.

Applegate, J. H., & Shaklee, B. (1988). Some observations about recruiting bright students for teacher preparation. *Peabody Journal of Education, 65*(2), 52–65.

Areglado, N. (1999). I became convinced: How a certification program revitalized an educator. *Journal of Staff Development, 20*, 35–37.

Athanases, S. Z. (1994). Teachers' reports of the effects of preparing portfolios of literacy instruction. *Elementary School Journal, 94,* 421–439.

Ayers, J. B. (1988). Another look at the concurrent and predictive validity of the National Teacher Examinations. *Journal of Educational Research, 81,* 133–137.

Ayers, J. B., & Qualls, G. S. (1979). Concurrent and predictive validity of the National Teacher Examinations. *Journal of Educational Research, 73*(2), 86–92.

Baker, T. (1993). A survey of four-year and five-year program graduates and their principals. *Southeastern Regional Association of Teacher Educators Journal, 2*(2), 28–33.

Ballou, D., & Podgursky, M. (1997). *Teacher pay and teacher quality.* Kalamazoo, MI: W. E. Upjohn Institute for Employment Research.

Baratz-Snowden, J. (1990). The NBPTS begins its research and development program, *Educational Researcher, 19*(6), 19–24.

Barber, B. R. (2004). Taking the public out of education: The perverse notion that American democracy can survive without its public schools. *School Administrator, 61*(5), 10–13.

Begle, E. G. (1979). *Critical variables in mathematics education: Findings from a survey of the empirical literature.* Washington, DC: Mathematical Association of America; Reston, VA: National Council of Teachers of Mathematics.

Black, P. J., & Wiliam, D. (1998). Assessment and classroom learning. *Assessment in Education, 5*(1), 7–74.

Boyd, D., Grossman, P., Lankford, H., Loeb, S., & Wyckoff, J. (2006). How changes in entry requirements alter the teacher workforce and affect student achievement. *Education Finance and Policy, 1,* 178–216.

Boyd, D., Lankford, H., Loeb, S., Rockoff, J., & Wyckoff, J. (2007, August). *The narrowing gap in New York City teacher qualifications and its implications for student achievement in high-poverty schools.* Unpublished manuscript.

Bradley, A. (1994, April 20). Pioneers in professionalism. *Education Week, 13,* 18–21

Braun, H. I. (2005). *Using student progress to evaluate teachers: A primer on value-added models.* Princeton, NJ: Educational Testing Service.

Buday, M., & Kelly, J. (1996). National Board certification and the teaching professions commitment to quality assurance. *Phi Delta Kappan, 78,* 215–219.

Cabello, B., Eckmier, J., & Baghieri, H. (1995). The comprehensive teacher institute: Successes and pitfalls of an innovative teacher preparation program. *Teacher Educator, 31*(1), 43–55.

California State University. (2002a). *First system wide evaluation of teacher education programs in the California State University: Summary Report.* Long Beach, CA: Author.

California State University. (2002b). *Preparing teachers for reading instruction (K-12): An evaluation brief by the California State University.* Long Beach, CA: Author.

Cantrell, S., Fullerton, J., Kane, T. J., & Staiger, D. O. (2007). *National Board Certification and teacher effectiveness: Evidence from a random assignment experiment.* Unpublished manuscript. Retrieved March 18, 2008, from http://harrisschool.uchicago.edu/Programs/beyond/workshops/ppepapers/fall07-kane.pdf

Cavaluzzo, L. (2004). *Is National Board Certification an effective signal of teacher quality?* (National Science Foundation No. REC-0107014). Alexandria, VA: The CNA Corporation.

Chin, P., & Russell, T. (1995, June). *Structure and coherence in a teacher education program: Addressing the tension between systematics and the educative agenda.* Paper presented at the annual meeting of the Canadian Society for the Study of Education, Montreal, Quebec, Canada.

Chittenden, E., & Jones, J. (1997, April). *An observational study of National Board candidates as they progress through the certification process.* Paper presented at the annual meeting of the American Educational Research Association, Chicago.

Chung, R. R. (2007, April). *Beyond the ZPD: When do beginning teachers learn from a high-stakes portfolio assessment?* Paper presented at the annual meeting of the American Educational Research Association, Chicago.

Chung, R. R. (2008). Beyond assessment: Performance assessments in teacher education. *Teacher Education Quarterly, 35*(1), 7–28.

Clotfelter, C., Ladd, H., & Vigdor, J. (2006). *Teacher-student matching and the assessment of teacher effectiveness* (NBER Working paper 11936). Cambridge, MA: National Bureau of Economic Research.

Clotfelter, C., Ladd, H., & Vigdor, J. (2007). *How and why do teacher credentials matter for student achievement?* (NBER Working Paper 12828). Cambridge, MA: National Bureau of Economic Research.

Cochran-Smith, M., & Zeichner, K. M. (Eds.). (2005). *Studying teacher education: The report of the AERA Panel on Research and Teacher Education.* Mahwah, NJ: Erlbaum.

Cohen, D. K., & Hill, H. C. (2000). Instructional policy and classroom performance: The mathematics reform in California. *Teachers College Record, 102,* 294–343.

Cohen, E. G., & Lotan, R. A. (1995). Producing equal-status interaction in the heterogeneous classroom. *American Educational Research Journal, 32*(1), 99–120.

Conant, J. B. (1963). *The education of American teachers.* New York: McGraw-Hill.

Council of Chief State School Officers (CCSSO). (1998, December). *Key state education policies on K-12 education standards: Standards, graduation, assessment, teacher licensure, time and attendance, 1998.* Washington, DC: Author.

Crawford, J., & Stallings, J. (1978). *Experimental effects of in-service teacher training derived from process-product correlations in the primary grades.* Stanford, CA: Center for Educational Research at Stanford, Program on Teaching Effectiveness.

Crow, N., Stokes, D., Kauchak, D., Hobbs, S., & Bullough, R.V., Jr. (1996, April). *Masters cooperative program: An alternative model of teacher development in PDS sites.* Paper presented at the annual meeting of the American Educational Research Association, New York.

Darling-Hammond, L. (Ed.). (1994). *Professional development schools: Schools for developing a profession.* New York: Teachers College Press.

Darling-Hammond, L. (1997). *Doing what matters most: Investing in quality teaching.* New York: National Commission on Teaching and America's Future.

Darling-Hammond, L. (2000a). *Solving the dilemmas of teacher supply, demand, and standards: How we can ensure a caring, competent, and qualified teacher for every child.* New York: National Commission on Teaching and America's Future.

Darling-Hammond, L. (2000b). Teacher quality and student achievement: A review of state policy evidence. *Educational Policy Analysis Archives, 8*(1). Retrieved June 10, 2008, from http://epaa.asu.edu/epaa/v8n1

Darling-Hammond, L. (2002). *Access to quality teaching: An analysis of inequality in California's public schools.* Los Angeles: University of California, Institute for Democracy, Education, and Access.

Darling-Hammond, L. (2004). Inequality and the right to learn: Access to qualified teachers in California's public schools. *Teachers College Record, 106,* 1936–1966.

Darling-Hammond, L. (2005). Teaching as a profession: Lessons in teacher preparation and professional development. *Phi Delta Kappan, 87*(3), 237–240.

Darling-Hammond, L. (2006). *Powerful teacher education: Lessons from exemplary programs.* San Francisco: Jossey-Bass.

Darling-Hammond, L. (2008). Educating teachers: How they do it abroad. *Time, 171*(8), 34.

Darling-Hammond, L., & Ball, D. L. (1997). *Teaching for high standards: What policymakers need to know and be able to do.* Paper prepared for the National Education Goals Panel, Washington, DC.

Darling-Hammond, L., & Bransford, J. (Eds.). (2005). *Preparing teachers for a changing world: What teachers should learn and be able to do.* San Francisco: Jossey-Bass.

Darling-Hammond, L., Chung, R., & Frelow, F. (2002). Variation in teacher preparation: How well do different pathways prepare teachers to teach? *Journal of Teacher Education, 53*(4), 286–302.

Darling-Hammond, L., Holtzman, D. J., Gatlin, S. J., & Heilig, J. V. (2005). Does teacher preparation matter? Evidence about teacher certification, Teach for America, and teacher effectiveness. *Education Policy Analysis Archives, 13*(42). Retrieved June 10, 2008, from http://epaa. asu.edu/epaa/v13n42/

Darling-Hammond, L. & Sykes, G. (2003). Wanted: A national teacher supply policy for education: The right way to meet the "highly qualified teacher" challenge. *Educational Policy Analysis Archives, 11*(33). Retrieved June 10, 2008, from http://epaa.asu.edu/epaa/v11n33/

Darling-Hammond, L., & Youngs, P. (2002). Defining "highly qualified teachers:" What does "scientifically-based research" actually tell us? *Educational Researcher, 31*(9), 13–25.

David, J. L. (1994). *Transforming state education agencies to support education reform.* Washington, DC: National Governors' Association.

Davis, C. L., & Honan, E. (1998). Reflections on the use of teams to support the portfolio process. In N. Lyons (Ed.), *With portfolio in hand: Validating the new teacher professionalism* (pp. 90–102). New York: Teachers College Press.

Decker, P. T., Mayer, D., & Glazerman, S. (2004). *The effects of Teach For America on students: Findings from a national evaluation* (Discussion paper no. 1285–04). Madison: University of Wisconsin-Madison, Institute for Research on Poverty.

Dennison, G. M. (1992). National standards in teacher preparation: A commitment to quality. *The Chronicle of Higher Education, 39*(15), A40.

Denton, J. J. (1982). Early field experiences influence on performance in subsequent coursework. *Journal of Teacher Education, 33*(2), 19–23.

Denton, J. J., & Lacina, L. J. (1984). Quantity of professional education coursework linked with process measures of student teaching. *Teacher Education and Practice, 1,* 39–64.

Denton, J. J., Morris, J. E., & Tooke, D. J. (1982). The influence of academic characteristics of student teachers on the cognitive attainment of learners. *Educational and Psychological Research, 2*(1), 15–29.

Denton, J. J., & Peters, W. H. (1988). *Program assessment report curriculum evaluation of a non-traditional program for certifying teachers.* College Station: Texas A&M University.

Denton, J. J., & Smith, N. L. (1983). *Alternative teacher preparation programs: A cost-effectiveness comparison.* Portland, OR: Northwest Regional Educational Lab, Research on Evaluation Program.

Denton, J. J., & Tooke, J. (1981–82). Examining learner cognitive attainment as a basis for assessing student teachers. *Action in Teacher Education, 3,* 39–45.

Desimone, L. M., Porter, A. C., Garet, M. S., Yoon, K. S., & Birman, B. F. (2002). Effects of professional development on teachers' instruction: Results from a three year longitudinal study. *Educational Evaluation and Policy Analysis, 24,* 81–112.

Druva, C. A., & Anderson, R. D. (1983). Science teacher characteristics by teacher behavior and by student outcome: A meta-analysis of research. *Journal of Research in Science Teaching, 20,* 467–479.

Dybdahl, C. S., Shaw, D. G., & Edwards, D. (1997). Teacher testing: Reason or rhetoric. *Journal of Research and Development in Education, 30*(4), 248–254.

Ebmeier, H., & Good., T. L. (1979). The effects of instructing teachers about good teaching on the mathematics achievement of fourth grade students. *American Educational Research Journal, 16,* 1–16.

Feiman-Nemser, S. (1990). Teacher preparation: Structural and conceptual alternatives. In W. R. Houston (Ed.), *Handbook for research on teacher education* (pp. 212–233). New York: Macmillan.

Feiman-Nemser, S., & Buchmann, M. (1985). Pitfalls of experience in teacher preparation. *Teachers College Record, 87,* 53–65.

Feistritzer, C. E. (2005). *Profile of alternate route teachers.* Washington, DC: National Center for Alternative Certification.

Ferguson, P., & Womack, S. T. (1993). The impact of subject matter and education coursework on teaching performance. *Journal of Teacher Education, 44*(1), 55–63.

Ferguson, R. F. (1991). Paying for public education: New evidence on how and why money matters. *Harvard Journal on Legislation, 28,* 465–498.

Fischetti, J., & Larson, A. (2002). How an integrated unit increased student achievement in a high school PDS. In I. N. Guadarrama, J. Ramsey, & J. L. Nath (Eds.), *Forging alliances in community and thought: Research in professional development schools* (pp. 227–258). Greenwich, CT: Information Age.

Fleener, C. E. (1998). *A comparison of attrition rates of elementary teachers prepared through traditional undergraduate campus-based programs and elementary teachers prepared through centers for professional development and technology field-based programs by gender, ethnicity, and academic performance.* Unpublished doctoral dissertation, Texas A&M University, Commerce.

Frank, K. A., & Sykes, G. (2006, April 10). *Extended influence: National Board Certified Teachers as help providers.* Paper presented at the annual meeting of the American Educational Research Association, San Francisco.

Frey, N. (2002). Literacy achievement in an urban middle-level professional development school: A learning community at work. *Reading Improvement, 39*(1), 3–13.

Garibaldi, A. M. (1991). Abating the shortage of Black teachers. In C. V. Willie, A. M. Garibaldi, & W. L. Reed (Eds.), *The education of African-Americans* (pp. 148–158). New York: Auburn House.

Gettys, C. M., Ray, B. M., Rutledge, V. C., Puckett, K., & Stepanske, J. (1999, November). *The professional development school experience evaluation.* Paper presented at Mid-South Educational Research Association Conference, Gatlinburg, TN.

Gill, B., & Hove, A. (1999). *The Benedum collaborative model of teacher education: A preliminary evaluation.* Santa Monica, CA: RAND.

Gitomer, D. H., Latham, A. S., & Ziomek, R. (1999). *The academic quality of prospective teachers: The impact of admissions and licensure testing.* Princeton, NJ: Educational Testing Service.

Glaeser, B. C., Karge, B. D., Smith, J., & Weatherill, C. (2002). Paradigm pioneers: A professional development school collaborative for special education teacher education candidates. In I. N. Guadarrama, J. Ramsey, & J. L. Nath (Eds.), *Forging alliances in community and thought: Research in professional development schools* (pp.125–152). Greenwich, CT: Information Age.

Goertz, M. E., Ekstrom, R. B., & Coley, R. J. (1984). *The impact of state policy on entrance into the teaching profession.* Princeton, NJ: Educational Testing Service.

Goldhaber, D. (2005). *Teacher licensure tests and student achievement: Is teacher testing an effective policy?* Seattle: University of Washington and the Urban Institute.

Goldhaber, D. (2006). *Everybody's doing it, but what does teacher testing tell us about teacher effectiveness?* Seattle: University of Washington and the Urban Institute.

Goldhaber, D., & Anthony, E. (2005). *Can teacher quality be effectively assessed?* Seattle: University of Washington and the Urban Institute.

Goldhaber, D. D., & Brewer, D. J. (2000). Does teacher certification matter? High school certification status and student achievement. *Educational Evaluation and Policy Analysis, 22,* 129–145.

Good, T. L., & Grouws, D. A. (1979). The Missouri mathematics effectiveness project: An experimental study in fourth-grade classrooms. *Journal of Educational Psychology, 71,* 355–362.

Goodlad, J. I, Soder, R., & Sirotnik, K. A. (Eds.). (1990). *Places where teachers are taught.* San Francisco: Jossey-Bass.

Goodman, J. (1985). What students learn from early field experiences: A case study and critical analysis. *Journal of Teacher Education, 36*(6), 42–48.

Graber, K. C. (1996). Influencing student beliefs: The design of a "High Impact" teacher education program. *Teaching and Teacher Education, 12,* 451–466.

Graham, P. A., Lyman, R. W., & Trow, M. (1995). *Accountability of colleges and universities.* New York: Columbia University Press.

Gray, L., Cahalan, M., Hein, S., Litman, C., Severynse, J., Warren, S., et al. (1993). *New teachers in the job market, 1991 update.* Washington, DC: U.S. Department of Education.

Haertel, E. H. (1991). New forms of teacher assessment. In G. Grant (Ed.), *Review of research in education, 17,* 3–29. Washington, DC: American Educational Research Association.

Hammerness, K., & Darling-Hammond, L. (2002). Meeting old challenges and new demands: The redesign of the Stanford Teacher Education Program. *Issues in Teacher Education, 11*(1), 17–30.

Haney, W., Madaus, G., & Kreitzer, A. (1987). Charms talismanic: Testing teachers for the improvement of American education. In E. Z. Rothkopf (Ed.), *Review of research in education: Vol 14* (pp. 169–238). Washington, DC: American Educational Research Association.

Hanushek, E. (1971). Teacher characteristics and gains in student achievement: Estimation using micro data. *American Economic Review, 61,* 280–288.

Hanushek, E. A., Kain, J. F. & Rivkin, S. G. (2001). *Teachers, schools, and academic achievement* (NBER Working paper No. W6691). Cambridge, MA: National Bureau of Economic Research.

Harris, D., & Sass, T. R. (2006). *Value-added models and the measurement of teacher quality.* Unpublished manuscript. Retrieved June 10, 2008, from http://itp.wceruw.org/vam/IES_Harris_Sass_EPF_Value-added_14_Stanford.pdf

Harris, D., & Sass, T.R. (2007). The effects of NBPTS-certified teachers on student achievement. Unpublished manuscript. Retrieved June 11, 2008, from http://www.nbpts.org/userfiles/file/harris_sass_final_2007.pdf

Hayes, H. S., & Wetherill, K. S. (1996, April). *A new vision for schools, supervision, and teacher education: The professional development system and Model Clinical Teaching Project.* Paper presented at the annual meeting of the American Educational Research Association, New York.

Haynes, D. D. (1995). One teacher's experience with National Board assessment. *Educational Leadership, 52*(8), 58–60.

Henke, R. R., Chen, X., & Geis, S. (2000). *Progress through the teacher pipeline: 1992–1993 College graduates and elementary/secondary school teaching as of 1997.* Washington, DC: U.S. Department of Education, National Center for Education Statistics.

Henke, R. R., Geis, S., Giambattista, J., & Knepper, P. (1996). *Out of the lecture hall and into the classroom: 1992–1993 College graduates and elementary/secondary school teaching.* Washington, DC: U.S. Department of Education, National Center for Education Statistics.

Henry, M. (1983). The effect of increased exploratory field experiences upon the perceptions and performance of student teachers. *Action in Teacher Education, 5*(1-2), 66–70.

Holmes Group. (1986). *Tomorrow's teachers: A report of the Holmes Group.* East Lansing, MI: Author.

Holmes Group. (1990). *Tomorrow's schools: Principles for the design of professional development schools: A report of the Holmes Group.* East Lansing, MI: Author.

Houston Consortium of Professional Development. (1996, April). *ATE Newsletter,* p. 7.

Houston, W. R., Clay, D., Hollis, L. Y., Ligons, C., Roff, L., & Lopez, N. (1995). *Strength through diversity: Houston Consortium for Professional Development and Technology Centers.* Houston, TX: University of Houston, College of Education.

Howey, K. R., & Zimpher, N. L. (1993). *Patterns in prospective teachers: Guides for designing preservice programs.* Columbus: Ohio State University.

Humphrey, D., Koppich, J., & Hough, H. (2005). Sharing the wealth: National Board Certified Teachers and the students who need them most. *Education Policy Analysis Archives, 13*(18). Retrieved June 10, 2008, from http://epaa.asu.edu/epaa/v13n18/v13n18.pdf

Humphrey, D., Wechsler, M., & Hough, H. (2008). Characteristics of effective alternative certification programs. *Teachers College Record, 110,* 1–63.

Hunter-Quartz, K. (2003). "Too angry to leave": Supporting new teachers' commitment to transform urban schools. *Journal of Teacher Education, 54,* 99–111.

Ingersoll, R. M. (2002). *Out-of-field teaching, educational inequality, and the organization of schools: An exploratory analysis.* Seattle: University of Washington, Center for the Study of Teaching and Policy.

Ingvarson, L. (1997). *Teaching standards: Foundations for professional development reform.* Melbourne, Australia: Monash University.

Interstate New Teacher Assessment and Support Consortium (INTASC). (1992). *Model standards for beginning teacher licensing, assessment, and development: A resource for state dialogue.* Washington, DC: Council for Chief State School Officers.

Jerald, C. D. (2002). *All talk, no action: Putting an end to out-of-field teaching.* Washington, DC: Education Trust.

Jett-Simpson, M., Pugach, M. C., & Whipp, J. (1992, April). *Portrait of an urban professional development school.* Paper presented at the annual meeting of the American Educational Research Association, San Francisco.

Johnson, D. W., & Johnson, R. T. (1989). *Cooperating and competition: Theory and research.* Edina, MN: Interaction Book Co.

Judge, H., Carrideo, R., & Johnson, S. M. (1995). *Professional development schools and MSU: The report of the 1995 review.* East Lansing: Michigan State University.

Kane, T. J., Rockoff, J. E., & Staiger, D. O. (2006). *What does teacher certification tell us about teacher effectiveness? Evidence from New York City* (NBER Working paper no. 12155). Cambridge, MA: National Bureau of Economic Research.

Kennedy, M. (1998). *Form and substance in inservice teacher education. Research Monograph* (No. No-13). Wisconsin: National Institute for Science Education, University of Wisconsin-Madison.

Kennedy, M. M. (1999) The role of preservice teacher education. In L. Darling-Hammond & G. Sykes (Eds.) *Teaching as the learning profession: Handbook of teaching and policy* (pp. 54–86). San Francisco: Jossey Bass.

Kenreich, T., Hartzler-Miller, C., Neopolitan, J. E., & Wiltz, N. W. (2004, April). *Impact of teacher preparation on teacher retention and quality.* Paper presented at the meeting of the American Educational Research Association, San Diego, CA.

Kentucky Institute for Education Research. (1997). *The preparation of teachers for Kentucky Schools: A survey of new teachers.* Frankfort, KY: Author.

Knowles, J. G., & Hoefler, V. B. (1989). The student-teacher who wouldn't go away: Learning from failure. *Journal of Experiential Education, 12*(2), 14–21.

Koerner, J. (1963). *The miseducation of American teachers.* Baltimore: Penguin Books.

Koerner, M., & Rust, F., & Baumgartner, F. (2002). Exploring roles in student teaching placements. *Teacher Education Quarterly, 29*(2), 35–58.

Konold, T., Jablonski, B., Nottingham, A., Kessler, L., Byrd, S., Imig, S., et al. (2008). *Adding value to public schools: Investigating teacher education, teaching, and pupil learning.* Charlottesville: University of Virginia.

Laboskey, V. K., & Richert, A. E. (2002). Identifying good student teaching placements: A programmatic perspective. *Teacher Education Quarterly, 29*(2), 7–34.

Lanier, J., & Little, J. (1986). Research on teacher education. In M. C. Wittrock (Ed.), *Handbook of research on teaching* (3rd ed., pp. 527–569). New York: Macmillan.

Lankford, H., Loeb, S., & Wyckoff, J. (2002). Teacher sorting and the plight of urban schools: A descriptive analysis. *Educational Evaluation and Policy Analysis, 24*(1), 37–62.

Latham, N. I., & Vogt, W. P. (2007). Do professional development schools reduce teacher attrition? Evidence from a longitudinal study of 1000 graduates. *Journal of Teacher Education, 58*(2), 153–167.

Lawrenz, F., & McCreath, H. (1988). Integrating quantitative and qualitative evaluation methods to compare two teacher inservice training programs. *Journal of Research in Science Teaching, 25*(5), 397–407.

Levine, A. (2006). *Educating school teachers.* Washington, DC: The Education Schools Project.

Loeb, H., Elfers, A. M., Plecki, M. L., Ford, B., & Knapp, M. S. (2006). *National Board Certified teachers in Washington state: Impact on professional practice and leadership opportunities.* Seattle: University of Washington, College of Education, Center for Strengthening the Teaching Profession.

Lortie, D. (1975). *Schoolteacher: A sociological study.* Chicago: University of Chicago Press.

Lusi, S. F. (1997). *The role of state departments of education in complex school reform.* New York: Teachers College Press.

Lustick, D., & Sykes, G. (2006). National Board Certification as professional development: What are teachers learning? *Education Policy Analysis Archives, 14*(5). Retrieved June 10, 2008, from http://epaa.asu.edu/epaa/v14n5/

Lyons, N. P. (1996). A grassroots experiment in performance assessment. *Educational Leadership, 53*(6), 64–67.

Lyons, N. P. (1998a). Portfolio possibilities: Validating a new teacher professionalism. In N. P. Lyons (Ed.), *With portfolio in hand: Validating the new teacher professionalism* (pp. 247–264). New York: Teachers College Press.

Lyons, N. P. (1998b). Reflection in teaching: Can it be developmental? A portfolio perspective. *Teacher Education Quarterly, 25*(1), 115–127.

Lyons, N. P. (1999). How portfolios can shape emerging practice. *Educational Leadership, 56*(8), 63–65.

Mantle-Bromley, C. (2002). The status of early theories of professional development school potential. In I. Guadarrama, J. Ramsey, & J. Nath (Eds.), *Forging alliances in community and thought: Research in professional development schools* (pp. 3–30). Greenwich, CT: Information Age.

Mason, D. A., & Good, T. L. (1993). Effects of two-group and whole-class teaching on regrouped elementary students' mathematics achievement. *American Educational Research Journal, 30*, 328–360.

Milanowski, A. T., Kimball, S. M., & White, B. (2004). *The relationship between standards-based teacher evaluation scores and student achievement.* Madison: University of Wisconsin, Consortium for Policy Research in Education.

Mitchell, K. J., Robinson, D. Z., Plake, B. S., & Knowles, K. T. (2001). *Testing teacher candidates: The role of licensure tests in improving teacher quality.* Washington, DC: National Academy Press.

Monk, D. H. (1994). Subject area preparation of secondary mathematics and science teachers and student achievement. *Economics of Education Review, 13*(2), 125–145.

Monk, D. H., & King, J. A. (1994). Multilevel teacher resource effects on pupil performance in secondary mathematics and science: The case of teacher subject-matter preparation. In R. G. Ehrenberg (Ed.), *Choices and consequences: Contemporary policy issues in education* (pp. 29–58). Ithaca, NY: ILR Press.

Murnane, R. J. & Schwinden, M. (1989). Race, gender, and opportunity: Supply and demand for new teachers in North Carolina, 1975–1985. *Educational Evaluation and Policy Analysis, 11*, 93–108.

Murray, F. (2004). *On some differences between TEAC and NCATE.* Washington, DC: Teacher Education Accreditation Council.

National Association of State Directors of Teacher Education and Certification (NASDTEC). (2004). *NASDTEC Knowledge Base.* Retrieved June 10, 2008, from http://www.nasdtec.info/

National Board for Professional Teaching Standards (NBPTS). (1989). *Toward high and rigorous standards for the teaching profession.* Detroit, MI: Author.

National Board for Professional Teaching Standards (NBPTS). (2002). *What teachers should know and be able to do.* Detroit, MI: Author.

National Board for Professional Teaching Standards (NBPTS). (2001a). *"I am a better teacher:" What candidates for National Board certification say about the assessment process.* Arlington, VA: Author.

National Board for Professional Teaching Standards (NBPTS). (2001b). *The impact of National Board Certification on teachers: A survey of National Board certified teachers and assessors.* Arlington, VA: Author.

National Center for Education Statistics (NCES). (1996). *NAEP 1992, 1994 National Reading Assessments, Data Almanac, Grade 4.* Washington, DC: Author.

National Commission on Teaching and America's Future (NCTAF). (1996). *What matters most: Teaching for America's future.* Washington, DC: Author.

National Commission on Teaching and America's Future (NCTAF). (1997). *Doing what matters most: Investing in quality teaching.* Washington, DC: Author.

National Commission on Teaching and America's Future (NCTAF).

(2004). *Special report: Fifty years after Brown v. Board of Education: A two-tiered education system.* Washington, DC: Author.

Neubert, G. A., & Binko, J. B. (1998). Professional development schools: The proof is in the performance. *Educational Leadership, 55*(5), 44–46.

Oakes, J. (1990). *Multiplying inequities: The effects of race, social class, and tracking on opportunities to learn mathematics and science.* Santa Monica, CA: RAND.

Orland-Barak, L. (2002). The impact of the assessment of practice teaching on beginning teaching: Learning to ask different questions. *Teacher Education Quarterly, 29*, 99–122.

Pecheone, R., & Stansbury, K. (1996). Connecting teacher assessment and school reform. *Elementary School Journal, 97*, 163–177.

Pecheone, R., & Chung, R. R. (2006). Evidence in teacher education: The performance assessment for California teachers. *Journal of Teacher Education, 57*, 22–36.

Perkes, V. A. (1967–1968). Junior high school science teacher preparation, teaching behavior, and student achievement. *Journal of Research in Science Teaching, 5*(2), 121–126.

Raymond, M., Fletcher, S., & Luque, J. (2001). *Teach For America: An evaluation of teacher differences and student outcomes in Houston, Texas.* Stanford, CA: Hoover Institution, Center for Research on Education Outcomes.

Rice, J. (2003). *Teacher quality: Understanding the effectiveness of teacher attributes.* Washington, DC: Economic Policy Institute.

Richert, A. E. (1987). *Reflex to reflection: Facilitating reflection in novice teachers.* Unpublished doctoral dissertation. Stanford University School of Education, Stanford, CA.

Rivkin, S.G., Hanushek, E.A., & Kain, J.F. (2005). Teachers, schools, and academic achievement. *Econometrica 73*(2), 417–458.

Rockoff, J. E. (2004). The impact of individual teachers on student achievement: Evidence from panel data. *American Economic Review, 94*(2), 247–252.

Rodriguez, Y., & Sjostrom, B. (1995). Culturally responsive teacher preparation evident in classroom approaches to cultural diversity: A novice and an experienced teacher. *Journal of Teacher Education, 46*, 304–311.

Ross, S. M., Hughes, T. M., & Hill, R. E. (1981). Field experiences as meaningful contexts for learning about learning. *Journal of Educational Research, 75*, 103–107.

Sanders, W., Ashton, J. J., & Wright, P. S. (2005). *Comparison of the effects of NBPTS certified teachers with other teachers on the rate of student academic progress.* Retrieved June 10, 2008, from http://www.nbpts.org/UserFiles/File/SAS_final_report_Sanders.pdf

Sanders, W. L., & Rivers, J. C. (1996). *Cumulative and residual effects of teachers on future academic achievement.* Knoxville, TN: University of Tennessee Value-Added Research and Assessment Center.

Sandholtz, J. H., & Dadlez, S. H. (2000). Professional development school trade-offs in teacher preparation and renewal. *Teacher Education Quarterly, 27*(1), 7–27.

Sato, M. (2000, April). *The National Board for Professional Teaching Standards: Teacher learning through the assessment process.* Paper presented at the annual meeting of American Educational Research Association, New Orleans, LA.

Sato, M., Chung, R., & Darling-Hammond, L. (2008). Improving teachers' assessment practices through professional development: The case of National Board Certification. *American Educational Research Journal, 45*, 669–700.

Schaefer, N. (1999). Traditional and alternative certification: A view from the trenches. In M. Kanstoroom & C. E. Finn, Jr. (Eds.), *Better teachers, better schools* (pp. 137–162). Washington, DC: Thomas B. Fordham Foundation.

Schalock, D. (1979). Research on teacher selection. In D. C. Berliner (Ed.), *Review of research in education: Vol. 7* (pp. 364–417). Washington, DC: American Educational Research Association.

Sheehan, D. S., & Marcus, M. (1978). Teacher performance on the National Teacher Examination and student mathematics and vocabulary achievement. *Journal of Educational Research, 71*, 134–136.

Shin, H. S. (1994, April). *Estimating future teacher supply: An application of survival analysis.* Paper presented at the annual meeting of the American Educational Research Association, New Orleans, LA.

Shroyer, G., Wright, E., & Ramey-Gassert, L. (1996). An innovative model for collaborative reform in elementary school science teaching. *Journal of Science Teacher Education, 7,* 151–168.

Shulman, L. (1992). Toward a pedagogy of cases. In J. Shulman (Ed.), *Case methods in teacher education* (pp.1–30). New York: Teachers College Press.

Shulman, L. (1998). Teacher portfolios: A theoretical activity. In N. P. Lyons (Ed.), *With portfolio in hand: Validating the new teacher professionalism* (pp. 23–37). New York: Teachers College Press.

Sloan, T., Cavazos, L., & Lippincott, A. (2007, April). *A holistic approach to assessing teacher competency: Can one assessment do it all?* Paper presented at the Annual Meeting of the American Educational Research Association, Chicago.

Smith, T., Gordon, B., Colby, S., & Wang, J. (2005). *An examination of the relationship between the depth of student learning and National Board certification status.* Boone, NC: Appalachian State University, Office for Research on Teaching.

Southeast Center for Teaching Quality. (2002, April). Teacher leadership: An untapped resource for improving student achievement. *Teaching quality in the Southeast: Best practices and policies, 1*(11). Retrieved June 10, 2008, from http://www.teachingquality.org/BestTQ/issues/v01/issue11.pdf

Stanford Teacher Assessment Project. (1987–1990). *Technical reports of the Teacher Assessment Project.* Stanford, CA: Stanford University School of Education.

Stallings, J., Bossung, J., & Martin, A. (1990). Houston Teaching Academy: Partnership in developing teachers. *Teaching and Teacher Education, 6,* 355–365.

Stone, B. A. (1998). Problems, pitfalls, and benefits of portfolios. *Teacher Education Quarterly, 25*(1), 105–114.

Strauss, R. P. (1998). *Teacher preparation and selection in Pennsylvania: Ensuring high performance classroom teachers for the 21st century.* Pittsburgh, PA: Carnegie-Mellon University, The H. John Heinz III School of Public Policy and Management.

Strauss, R. P., & Sawyer, E. A. (1986). Some new evidence on teacher and student competencies. *Economics of Education Review, 5,* 41–48.

Sumara, D. J., & Luce-Kapler, R. (1996). (Un)Becoming a teacher: Negotiating identities while learning to teach. *Canadian Journal of Education, 21,* 65–83.

Sunal, D. W. (1980). Effect of field experience during elementary methods courses on preservice teacher behavior. *Journal of Research in Science Teaching, 17,* 17–23.

Sykes, G., Anagnostopoulos, D., Cannata, M., Chard, L., Frank, K., McCrory, R., et al. (2006). *National Board Certified Teachers as an organizational resource: Final report to the National Board for Professional Teaching Standards.* Retrieved June 10, 2008, from http://www.nbpts.org/UserFiles/File/NBPTS_final_report_D_-_Sykes_-_Michigan_State.pdf

Teacher Education Accreditation Council (TEAC). (n.d.). *The alignment of NCATE's unit standards and TEAC's program quality principles and standards.* Retrieved June 10, 2008, from http://www.teac.org/literature/teacandncateframeworkscompared.pdf

Texas Education Agency. (1994). *Texas teacher diversity and recruitment: Teacher supply, demand, and quality policy research project* (Report no. 4). Austin: Author.

Thomas B. Fordham Foundation. (1999). *The teachers we need and how to get more of them.* Washington, DC: Author.

Tom, A. R. (1997). *Redesigning teacher education.* Albany: State University of New York Press.

Trachtman, R. (1996). *The NCATE professional development school study: A survey of 28 PDS sites.* Unpublished manuscript.

Tracz, S. M., Sienty, S., & Mata, S. (1994, February). *The self-reflection of teachers compiling portfolios for National Certification: Work in progress.* Paper presented at the annual meeting of the American Association of Colleges for Teacher Education, Chicago.

Tracz, S., Sienty, S., Todorov, K., Snyder, J., Takashima, B., Pensabene, R., et al. (1995, April). *Improvement in teaching skills: Perspectives from National Board for Professional Teaching Standards field test network candidates.* Paper presented at the annual meeting of the American Educational Research Association, San Francisco.

United States Department of Education (2002). *Meeting the Highly Qualified Teachers Challenge: The secretary's annual report on teacher quality.* Washington, DC: Author. Retrieved June 10, 2008, from http://www.ed.gov/news/speeches/2002/06/061102.html

Vandevoort, L. G., Amrein-Beardsley, A., & Berliner, D. C. (2004). National Board certified teachers and their students' achievement. *Education Policy Analysis Archives, 12*(46), 117.

Walsh, K. (2001, October). *Teacher certification reconsidered: Stumbling for quality.* Baltimore, MD: The Abell Foundation.

Walsh, K., & Podgursky, M. (2001, November). *Teacher certification reconsidered: Stumbling for quality, A rejoinder.* Baltimore, MD: The Abell Foundation.

Weiner, L. (2007). A lethal threat to U.S. teacher education. *Journal of Teacher Education, 58,* 274–286.

Wenglinsky, H. (2002). How schools matter: The link between teacher classroom practices and student academic performance. *Education Policy Analysis Archives, 10*(12). Retrieved June 10, 2008, http://epaa.asu.edu/epaa/v10n12/

Williams, B. C. (Ed.). (2000). *Reforming teacher education through accreditation: Telling our story.* Washington, DC: National Council for the Accreditation of Teacher Education and American Association of Colleges for Teacher Education.

Williams, B., & Bearer, K. (2001). *NBPTS-parallel certification and its impact on the public schools: A qualitative approach.* Akron, OH: University of Akron.

Wilson, S. E., Floden, R. E., & Ferrini-Mundy, J. (2002). Teacher preparation research: An insider's view from the outside. *Journal of Teacher Education, 53*(3), 190–204.

Wilson, M., & Hallam, P. J. (2006). *Using Student Achievement Test scores as evidence of external validity for indicators of teacher quality: Connecticut's Beginning Educator Support and Training program.* Unpublished manuscript.

Wiseman, D. L., & Cooner, D. (1996). Discovering the power of collaboration: The impact of a school-university partnership on teaching. *Teacher Education and Practice, 12,* 18–28.

Yankelovich Partners. (2001). *Accomplished teachers taking on new leadership roles in schools; Survey reveals growing participation in efforts to improve teaching and learning.* Chapel Hill, NC: Author.

Yerian, S., & Grossman, P. L. (1997). Preservice teachers' perceptions of their middle level teacher education experience: A comparison of a traditional and a PDS model. *Teacher Education Quarterly, 24*(4), 85–101.

Zeichner, K. M. (2000). Ability-based teacher education: Elementary teacher education at Alverno College. In L. Darling-Hammond (Ed.), *Studies of excellence in teacher education: Preparation in the undergraduate years* (pp.1–66). Washington, DC: American Association of Colleges for Teacher Education.

Zeichner, K. M. & Hutchinson, E. (in press). The development of alternative certification policies and programs in the U.S. In P. Grossman & S. Loeb, *Taking stock: An examination of alternative certification.* Cambridge, MA: Harvard Education Press.

Zeichner, K. M., & Schulte, A. K. (2001). What we know and don't know from peer-reviewed research about alternative teacher certification programs. *Journal of Teacher Education, 52,* 266–282.

49

School Improvement by Design

Lessons from a Study of Comprehensive School Reform Programs[1]

BRIAN P. ROWAN
University of Michigan

RICHARD J. CORRENTI
University of Pittsburgh

ROBERT J. MILLER
University of Michigan

ERIC M. CAMBURN
University of Wisconsin

Introduction

After four decades of education reform aimed at improving the academic achievement of poor and minority students in the United States, No Child Left Behind has once again drawn attention to the problem of America's "failing schools." Forty years ago, when federal policy makers first addressed this problem, a solution seemed easy. All that was needed, it seemed, was to give failing schools more money and (without much additional guidance) the natural capacity of education professionals to improve instruction and schooling would yield gains in student achievement. Within a decade, however, policy makers came to doubt the efficacy of this approach, and as a result, during the 1980s and 1990s, Congress and the states developed additional reform strategies. During this time, agencies at various levels of the education system worked to raise academic standards for students, hold schools accountable for students' test scores, and devise new ways to increase parental choice in schooling. Over this same time period, the tested achievement of American students improved—especially the achievement of poor and minority students. But after more than a decade of higher academic standards, more test-based accountability, and expanded school choice, nearly one-fourth of U.S. schools are still "failing" by the standards of No Child Left Behind (Basken, 2006), and a disproportionate number of these schools serve America's poor and minority students.

Researchers who study school improvement are not surprised by this. Many believe that education policies built around high academic standards, tough accountability, and more school choice are necessary, but *not* sufficient, conditions for improving instruction and student achievement in schools. Higher standards, increased accountability, and expanded school choice, this argument goes, can motivate educators to work harder at improving schools, but motivation alone cannot produce the magnitude of gains in student learning needed to turn troubled schools around. Instead, many analysts argue that what low-performing schools in the United States need is a fundamental overhaul of instructional practice. Some reformers would encourage this overhaul through macro-level changes in education policy—for example, by making it easier and more attractive for smarter people to enter (and stay in) the teaching force, or by developing strategies that bring more highly qualified teachers into America's most academically troubled schools. Others call for locally driven approaches to instructional improvement, where teachers and school leaders build strong professional communities—one school at a time—in order to discover and implement more productive approaches to instruction. The evidence on both these approaches, however, is discouraging. For example, teachers with higher academic test scores and better professional training do, in fact, promote increased learning gains in their classrooms, but research shows that these gains are discouragingly small on average (Wayne & Youngs, 2003); and, while locally driven change efforts have produced some dramatic cases of instructional improvement in troubled schools, research shows that locally driven approaches to instructional improvement most often work on a hit-or-miss basis, with only a few (of many) schools trying this approach actually showing real signs of instructional improvement (Berends & King, 1994).

The Concept of School Improvement by Design

By the late 1990s, the uneven progress of education reform was leading many in the education community to become interested in what we call "school improvement by design." As defined here, this approach to school improvement occurs when local schools work with outside agencies to implement new designs for educational practice. As we see it, two elements of this definition warrant attention. First, the concept of "design" suggests a school improvement process guided by a preexisting blueprint or specification of educational practices that can be replicated in *many* school settings. Such a design can include core instructional or curricular components, such as new curricular materials and/or sets of teaching routines, but equally important, these designs also frequently include blueprints for organizational practices that allow the core instructional parts of the design to be implemented faithfully and used effectively in schools. Second, our definition of school improvement by design focuses on situations where local schools work with *outside* organizations to stimulate instructional change. This is important because many researchers and reformers want to study approaches to school improvement that can be replicated reliably and faithfully in many settings (not just a single school), and because the outside organizations that support design-based school improvement make such replication possible. In principle, the organizations referred to in our definition can be governmental agencies, but in American education, they are more often for-profit and/or not-for-profit vendors of instructional materials (e.g., textbooks or software), professional development and/or technical assistance services, or increasingly a blend of the two. In fact, situations where local schools enter into contractual relationships with outside organizations to implement new designs for educational practice are ubiquitous in American education (Rowan, 2001).

This chapter discusses a particular type of design-based assistance to local schools—assistance that is offered by organizations known as Comprehensive School Reform providers. In discussing such providers, however, it is important to remember that they are just a single example of a larger movement toward design-based, technical assistance that has been present in the U.S. education system for at least 50 years. Indeed, the movement toward design-based school improvement has its origins in the federal government's attempts since the 1950s to build a research and development (R&D) infrastructure in the field of education. This movement originated with the Cooperative Research Act of 1954 (1954), which authorized the U.S. Office of Education to conduct research with universities and state departments of education, and then expanded in the 1960s, as first the National Science Foundation, and then the U.S. Office of Education (and its successors), sponsored curriculum development projects, contracted with universities and other non-governmental organizations to build a network of education laboratories and R&D centers, and funded a set of special-purpose organizations to promote the dissemination

and utilization of innovative designs for practice. In building this infrastructure, federal policy makers and education researchers hoped to create a "research-based" process of school improvement that would begin with research on practical problems, and then move to the development of new educational programs and practices, which would be disseminated widely to schools, where they would be utilized in practice. This was the well-known "RDDU" (or *r*esearch, *d*evelopment, *d*issemination, *u*tilization) paradigm of school improvement that captured the attention of policy makers and researchers during the expansive period of educational R&D in the 1960s and 1970s.

Although our definition of school improvement by design is not restricted to research-based designs, "research-based" designs for school improvement are especially important today. In 2002, for example, Congress declared that a primary goal of No Child Left Behind was to "ensure the access of children to effective, scientifically based instructional strategies ...," and it peppered the bill with over 100 references to "scientifically based research." Around the same time, Grover Whitehurst, the first Director of the U.S. Department of Education's newly created Institute for Education Sciences, also testified before Congress, arguing that "there is every reason to believe that if we invest in the education sciences and develop mechanisms to encourage evidence-based practices, we will see progress and transformation [in education] ... of the same order and magnitude as we have seen in medicine and agriculture" (Whitehurst, 2002). For these reasons, information about the conditions under which "research-based" designs for school improvement can be successfully implemented in local schools, and the conditions under which such implementation can be expected to improve student learning, is especially important.

The Emergence of Comprehensive School Reform

This chapter addresses these questions by examining a particular approach to design-based school improvement that came to be known in the 1990s as comprehensive school reform (CSR). During this time, the movement toward comprehensive school reform arguably became the "poster child" for scientifically based reform in American education, having been supported initially by business leaders and philanthropists, and then by the Comprehensive School Reform Demonstration Act, and finally by Part F of No Child Left Behind, which gave states funding to award competitive grants to local schools to facilitate adoption of CSR programs locally. Representative David Obey (D-WI), who co-sponsored the first federal bill supporting comprehensive school reform, called this movement "the most important education reform effort since Title I because CSR programs give local schools the tools ... they [need to] raise student performance to ... high standards" (Congressional Record, 1997).

Interestingly, the CSR movement was not the creation of the federal government. Rather, it was first initiated in 1991 by a private, not-for profit organization known as the New

American Schools Development Corporation (NASDC). Founded as part of President George H.W. Bush's America 2000 initiative, NASDC (later re-named New American Schools [NAS]) provided the kinds of venture philanthropy and political capital that were needed to catapult comprehensive school reform to national prominence. Under the leadership of David Kearns, Chairman emeritus of the Xerox Corporation and a former Deputy Secretary of Education, NAS raised more than $130 million in contributions from the nation's top businesses and foundations with the explicit goal of fostering what it called "a new generation of American schools." Researchers at the RAND Corporation who studied NAS during this key period reported that the organization's "core premise was that all high quality schools possess, de facto, a unifying design that ... integrates research-based practices into a coherent and mutually-reinforcing set of effective approaches to teaching and learning" (Berends, Bodilly, & Kirby, 2002, p. xv).

To make this core idea a reality, NAS funded the development of several new, "break-the-mold" designs for school improvement that it called "whole-school reforms." After selecting 11 organizations from a competitive request for proposals responded to by over 600 applicants, NAS began its work in 1992 with a 1-year development phase, during which time the selected organizations (known as "design teams") created new designs for schooling. This was followed by a 2-year demonstration phase, during which these organizations worked in a small number of demonstration sites to get their new designs implemented, and then by a 5-year scale-up phase in which the organizations worked in a larger set of school districts chosen by NAS to get the new designs implemented even more broadly.

Although the NAS scale-up effort met with uneven success (only 7 of the original 11 design teams made it out of the scale-up phase), NAS nevertheless gave a tremendous boost to the idea of school improvement by design. In 1997, for example, when the NAS scale-up phase ended, the surviving NAS design teams were working with over 685 schools around the country. Then, with federal funding from the Comprehensive School Reform Demonstration Act, and later from Part F of NCLB, nearly 7,000 schools across the country adopted CSR designs provided by well over 600 different organizations. By any count, this was a remarkable rate of uptake for an educational innovation. In a few short years, roughly 10% of all public schools in the United States had adopted a CSR design, more than twice the number of schools that were operating as charter schools during the same time period.

The Focus of this Chapter

This chapter takes a closer look at design-based school improvement by reporting on the results of a multi-year study of three of America's most widely disseminated comprehensive school reform (CSR) programs. The study described here (known as A Study of Instructional Improvement [SII]) was conducted between 1999 and 2004 and was a large-scale, quasi-experiment involving three well-known CSR programs: the Accelerated Schools Project (ASP), America's Choice (AC), and Success for All (SFA). At the time of this study, these three CSR programs were operating in more than 2,500 elementary schools across the United States. Our approach to studying these programs was to form a sample of 115 elementary schools (31 AC schools, 30 SFA schools, 28 ASP schools, and 26 Comparison schools) located in 17 different states in all geographic regions of the country and to balance the schools in this sample, as much as possible, in terms of geographic location and school demographic characteristics. By design, however, the final sample in the study over-represented schools in the highest quartiles of socioeconomically disadvantaged schools in the United States, since a major goal of the research was to study instructional improvement in high-poverty settings.

In describing the results of this study, we discuss three important issues. First, we look at the strategies each of these CSR programs used to promote instructional change inside of schools. Our aim in this section of the chapter is to develop some conceptual models to describe the "designs" external agencies use as they go about organizing schools for instructional change. Next, we examine whether or not these designs do, in fact, promote changes in school organization and instructional practice, and if so, in what direction. As we shall see, making changes to school organization and instruction were major goals of each of the CSR programs under study, but each program had a different vision of what this should look like. Finally, we provide some preliminary data on whether or not each of these CSR programs succeeded in improving student achievement in the schools where they worked.

In addressing each of these questions, we hope to address various puzzles that researchers studying school improvement have confronted over several decades. Among these puzzles are theoretical questions about: (a) how instructional improvement programs can be designed; (b) the relationships between design characteristics and program implementation; and (c) why some externally designed programs work to increase student achievement while others do not. These questions have animated research on school improvement for decades, and they are controversial. For this reason, we turn to a discussion of how these questions have been addressed in previous research on design-based school improvement.

Background

In many ways, research on the design, implementation, and instructional effectiveness of CSR programs echoes familiar themes in research on education reform in the United States. Like many previous reform efforts, the CSR movement began when an influential and dedicated group of reformers (in this case business and government leaders) succeeded in promoting (and, through legislation, institutionalizing) a new template for school improvement. This new template then diffused widely and quickly through the education system, as several thousand schools adopted one or another CSR program. But, while adoption of CSR programs was seemingly quick and easy, implementation at local sites turned out to be difficult (Bodilly, 1996; Berends et al., 2002; Desimone, 2002; Mirel, 1994), and program evaluations gradually uncovered a pattern of weak effects on the reform's intended goal—to improve the academic achievement of students (Borman, Hewes, Overman, & Brown, 2003). As a result, enthusiasm for the new reform strategy waned, and American education policy veered away from what was once considered a promising approach to school reform in order to find a new magic bullet for school improvement.

There is a problem with this story, however. First of all, while a meta-analysis of CSR program evaluations conducted by Borman et al. (2003) showed that CSR program effects on student achievement were quite small on average (Cohen's dsd = .12 in comparison group studies), the analysis demonstrated that there was a great deal of program-to-program variability in effect sizes (with Cohen's dsd varying from −.13 to +.92 in comparison group studies). Thus, some CSR programs apparently worked much better than others in improving student achievement, a common finding in evaluations of externally-designed school improvement programs dating to the earliest evaluations of Follow Through designs (see, e.g., House, Glass, McLean, & Walker, 1978; Gersten, 1984).

The central objective of this chapter is to develop an explanation for the variable effects on student achievement that occur when schools embrace design-based, instructional improvement programs. Previous research on this issue has tended to focus on three determinants of program success: the nature of the problem being addressed by a social policy or program (e.g., the problem's inherent complexity or uncertainty); the nature of the program itself (e.g., features of the program's design); and the social context in which the intervention or policy change is attempted (e.g., the degree of conflict present over policy or program goals, the coherence of the policy environment in which change is attempted, the motivation and skill of personnel implementing the program or intervention, and the organizational culture, climate, and authority structure under which implementing personnel work). By holding constant the problem being addressed by the CSR programs we studied (i.e., instructional improvement), and by limiting the social context in which these CSR programs operate (to matched samples of elementary schools), our work focuses on an examination of program designs as the key factor explaining program outcomes.

Table 49.1 shows our assumptions about how a design-based explanation might be used to explain CSR program outcomes. Simply put, this explanation assumes that effective designs resolve two problems of intervention simultaneously. First, organizations providing design-based assistance to schools cannot succeed in raising student achievement unless their designs for instructional practice are different from (and more effective than) existing instructional practices. This statement is akin to the old adage

that if you keep on doing the same old things, you cannot expect to get different outcomes. But second, Table 49.1 also shows that building a CSR program around an effective instructional design does not guarantee improved student learning unless there also exists an effective strategy for getting that instructional design implemented in schools. From this perspective, school improvement by design works under limited circumstance and can go wrong in several ways. An externally-developed program works when it is built around an effective instructional design and a sound implementation strategy. Programs can fail, however, if they are built around an instructional design that is more effective (in principle) than existing practice when it has a poor design for implementation. Alternatively, a program can fail if it has a very strong design for program implementation but is built around a weak and ineffective instructional design. Finally, in the worst case scenario, an external program might be built around poor ideas about both instruction and implementation. From this perspective, building an effective design is difficult and requires attention to both instructional design and implementation support.

It is worth noting that while this basic idea seems obvious, much prior research on design-based instructional improvement has failed to gather data on these twin issues of instructional design and implementation simultaneously. As a case in point, consider the large body of research on curriculum development projects supported by the National Science Foundation (NSF) in the 1960s—arguably America's first attempt at large-scale school improvement by design. Research on this educational reform effort often took for granted that these NSF-supported curricular designs were more effective than existing materials (especially since the innovative curricula were developed by universities and prestigious not-for-profit organizations). One result of this assumption was that a great deal of research on this reform effort focused on problems of implementation. Indeed, a major finding from this body of this research was that few NSF curricula were implemented with any fidelity at all (for reviews of this literature, see Welch, 1969; Darling-Hammond & Snyder, 1992; Elmore, 1996). Obviously, this is an important finding, but it does *not* tell us whether the new curricula—if implemented—would have improved student outcomes, and so we, in fact, gained only partial

TABLE 49.1
Relation of Design to Instructional Improvement

	Effective Instructional Design?	
Effective Implementation Strategy?	Yes	No
Yes	Changes in instruction and learning	Change in instruction without effects on learning
No	No change in learning or instruction	No change in instruction or learning

information about the process of school improvement by design from this research.

A somewhat different problem plagued the next generation of research on innovative programs. Consider, for example, the so-called "planned variation" experiment designed to evaluate alternative Follow Through designs. Here, researchers focused on measuring student outcomes, but as a result of funding problems, failed to collect measures of program implementation (House et al., 1978). A major finding in this research was that there was great variability in effects on student outcomes across different Follow Through designs. But explanations for this finding were the subject of a huge debate, largely because researchers could never tell if the variability in program effects was due to differences in the effectiveness of the instructional designs across programs themselves, differences in the ability of program designers to get their instructional designs faithfully implemented in the multiple school settings where they operated, or both (for a review of this literature, see the essays in Rivlin & Timpane, 1975).

Approach

Fortunately, much has been learned in succeeding decades about how to study design-based intervention programs. The general idea has been to build a "logic model" that describes the "theory of action" underlying a particular reform effort, and to use that model to lay out both the intermediate and final outcomes that reformers hope to achieve as a result of their reform efforts. Our effort to formulate such a model for the process of school improvement by design is shown in Figure 49.1. That figure begins on the left-hand side with the assumption that *any* provider of design-based assistance has a program design, which we earlier defined as a blueprint for change laid out along two dimensions: (a) an instructional design, and (b) a design for school organizational practices that encourage faithful implementation and productive use of that instructional design. Moving to the right in the figure, we have included a set of arrows describing our assumption that these designs influence the ways schools are organized to manage and support instruction and to encourage the use of particular instructional practices in schools. Finally, the arrows in Figure 49.1 suggest that organizational and instructional practices in schools are reciprocally related and affect student outcomes.

In the field of education policy research, much effort has gone into building highly general conceptual frameworks to describe each step of this process. For example, Berman (1978) developed an influential conceptual framework that described intervention designs as either "programmed" or "adaptive" in order to capture the fact that programs can be more (or less) explicit and directive about the kinds of organizational and instructional practices they want to implement in schools. Others have developed conceptual frameworks to describe organizational practices for managing instruction, for example, the contrast between "mechanistic" or "organic" forms of management that Miller and

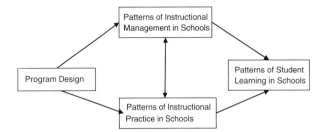

Figure 49.1 Logic model of design-based instructional improvement.

Rowan (2006) used to signal the extent to which patterns of instructional supervision, monitoring, and decision making in schools are either centralized, standardized, and routinized, or decentralized and flexible. Finally, attempts have been made to characterize instructional practices in schools as oriented either to "basic" or to "higher order" instructional goals (e.g., Cohen, McLaughlin, & Talbert, 1993), or to "reform" versus "traditional" practices (Stecher et al., 2006).

In what follows, we depart from these familiar categories to describe how the CSR programs we studied actually worked. That is not because we have a quarrel with these more generalized conceptual frameworks. In fact, we find them useful. However, in our own work, we have found that such general categories do not provide the kinds of nuanced descriptions of CSR program designs, intended organizational practices, or intended instructional practices that are needed to explain program-specific outcomes in a logically compelling fashion, either at the intermediate stage of our model (where we are looking at organizational and instructional change resulting from CSR participation) or at the final step of our model (where we are looking at student achievement outcomes that result from working with a specific CSR program).

The remainder of this chapter is divided into four sections that mirror Figure 49.1 and sketch out our logic model for studying the process of school improvement by design. The section immediately following this one provides an overview of this logic model by briefly reviewing the main findings from A Study of Instructional Improvement. In this section of the chapter, we provide brief "portraits" of the three CSR designs we studied, and discuss what was found about how they were implemented in schools, and to what effects on student learning. The following three sections then report in more detail on these portraits. Here, we follow Figure 49.1 by discussing in turn: (a) how the different CSR models organized to promote instructional change in classrooms; (b) whether the CSR programs succeeded in moving schools toward their preferred instructional designs; and (c) whether, once implemented, the CSR programs succeeded in improving student achievement at the schools under study. Considering these topics as a whole, we seek to shed light on the specific mechanisms through which the CSR designs under study influenced student achievement, particularly reading achievement, a major emphasis of improvement in all of the schools we studied.

Brief Portraits of the CSR Programs under Study

Over a 4-year period, SII researchers used program documents, field research, and survey data to examine the design,[2] implementation, and instructional effectiveness of the three CSR programs examined in A Study of Instructional Improvement. Not surprisingly, these analyses showed that each of the CSR programs studied had different "designs"—that is, ideas about the kinds of instructional practices they wanted to implement in schools and the ways they wanted to organize schools to support the process of instructional change. More importantly, we have found that these designs had important consequences for the schools working with these programs. For example, we have found that schools working with the different programs varied in: (a) how they were organized to manage instruction, (b) the kinds of literacy instruction they provided to students, and (c) the patterns of student achievement growth that occurred at different grade levels. This section lays out our findings in these areas and provides a preview of results that will be discussed in more detail at later points in the chapter.

The Accelerated Schools Project In previous studies (Rowan, Camburn, & Barnes, 2004; Correnti & Rowan, 2007; Rowan & Miller, 2007), we have argued that at the time of our study, ASP was using a pattern of "cultural controls" to bring about instructional change in schools. We use that description because ASP's approach to working with schools revolved around promoting a normative commitment among school leaders and faculty to the program's abstract vision or ideal of "powerful learning" for all students. Indeed, from the onset of working with schools, ASP facilitators used the staff development process to emphasize the program's commitment to this abstract construct, and to define powerful learning as constructivist in nature, with an emphasis on authentic, learner-centered, and interactive forms of instruction. However, ASP was not prescriptive in nature. For example, it did not target particular school subjects for improvement, nor did it provide teachers with a great deal of explicit guidance about curriculum objectives or teaching strategies. Instead, ASP facilitators helped schools use a systematic process of organizational development to design a unique path toward powerful learning and to adopt locally appropriate forms of instructional practice consistent with this approach. In this sense, ASP had a design best labeled as "adaptive" in form.

This description, it is worth noting, suggests that ASP's approach to producing instructional change is at least partially at odds with many of the design features that previous research on educational innovation has identified as promoting implementation success. For example, at the time we studied ASP, the program's goals for change were generic in form—aiming at broad changes across the board rather than targeting specific areas of the curriculum for change. By contrast, prior research on design-based assistance suggests that successful programs often focus on changing specific,

curriculum-embedded elements of instructional practice as opposed to more diffuse elements that cut across curricular areas or represent generic forms of teaching (Cohen & Hill, 2001; Desimone, Porter, Garet, Yoon, & Birman, 2002; Fennema et al., 1996). Moreover, the kinds of changes teachers were expected to make as a result of participating in ASP were not formally specified, and instead, each school (and each teacher within a school) was asked to "discover" the most appropriate means to producing powerful learning within his or her own particular context. Again, this differs from the stance taken by more successful programs, which tend to have clearly defined goals for change in particular curricular areas, that is, a clear specification of what features of curriculum and instruction will be changed, and of the steps to be taken to achieve these changes (McLaughlin & Marsh, 1978; Elmore & Burney, 1997; Nunnery, 1998). For these reasons, schools and teachers had a great deal of autonomy in the ASP system, with the result that there was little real focus on implementation fidelity, either from external program facilitators, or from internal leaders. In fact, in previous research, we have found that ASP schools had the lowest reported levels of instructional leadership of all the schools in our study sample (Camburn, Rowan, & Taylor, 2003). This too contrasts with previous research, which suggests that successful programs are those in which program designers, local program facilitators, and local administrative leaders demand fidelity to planned changes in instructional practice (Loucks, Cox, Miles, & Huberman, 1982; Huberman & Miles, 1984; Stringfield & Datnow, 1998).

In light of these patterns, it is not surprising that a particular pattern of instructional improvement emerged in ASP schools. First, as we report below, staff in ASP schools reported that school improvement plans were weakly (not highly) specified, that is, they saw plans as centered more on shared values and group investigation than on specific curricular goals and objectives. In this environment, teachers in ASP schools were trusted to make innovations in their classrooms as they saw fit, so long as these innovations were consistent with the normative ideal of powerful learning. The autonomy afforded by this system of instructional control promoted high levels of motivation for improvement among faculty. But, as we demonstrate below, the approach did *not* promote implementation of distinctive forms of literacy instruction in schools; instead, we will show that literacy instruction in ASP schools looked very much like literacy instruction in our sample of comparison schools. Moreover, because instructional practices were so similar, patterns of student achievement were also quite similar across ASP and comparison schools.

America's Choice The America's Choice (AC) program took a contrasting approach to instructional change at the time of our study, stimulating instructional improvement using what we have called a pattern of "professional controls" (Rowan, Camburn, & Barnes, 2004; Correnti & Rowan, 2007; Rowan & Correnti, 2006; Rowan & Miller,

2007). The AC program had its origins in the standards-based reform movement, and, as a result, the program was built around some definite ideas about the curricular content and methods of teaching it wanted to occur inside classrooms, especially in the area of language arts. At the time of our study, for example, AC typically began its work in local schools by focusing on the school's *writing* program (moving only later to changes in reading and mathematics programs). Moreover, AC typically provided teachers with a great deal of instructional guidance. For example, teachers in AC schools received a curriculum guide, were taught a set of recommended instructional routines for teaching writing (called "writers' workshop"), and worked with locally appointed AC coaches and facilitators to develop "core writing assignments" and clear scoring "rubrics" for judging students' written work. Thus, in the area of writing instruction at least, AC was trying to implement a well-specified, standards-based curriculum grounded in professional consensus about what constitutes a desirable instructional program. AC also expected schools that adopted the program to create two new leadership positions—a design coach and a literacy coordinator. Design coaches were expected to help principals implement the program, while AC literacy coordinators were expected to work with classroom teachers. Previous research showed that levels of instructional leadership were highest in the AC schools in our study sample (Camburn, Rowan, & Taylor, 2003).

Our findings (discussed below) show that the "professional" control strategy used by AC had strong effects in the schools where they worked. First, AC schools tended to organize for instructional improvement in ways that were quite different from schools in the control group or in ASP schools. For example, given all the instructional guidance that AC teachers and leaders received, it is not surprising to find that staff in AC schools viewed their school improvement plans as clear and well-specified. Moreover, as a result of extensive coaching, AC schools tended to be characterized by strong instructional leadership. But this pattern of strong leadership and clear instructional guidance came at a price—with teachers in AC schools reporting lower levels of autonomy of practice than did teachers in comparison group schools. Still, as we shall see, the presence of strong instructional leadership—coupled with a well-specified instructional design—produced distinctive instructional practices in AC schools. As our findings demonstrate, AC teachers were much more likely than other teachers to emphasize writing instruction as part of their literacy program, and to place more emphasis on students' production of extended written text. This approach to literacy instruction, in turn, seemed to produce accelerated growth in students' literacy achievement at the upper elementary grades.

Success for All Success for All (SFA) illustrates yet a third model for promoting instructional change in schools: what we elsewhere have called "procedural controls" (Rowan et al., 2004; Correnti & Rowan, 2007; Rowan & Miller, 2007). Of the three programs under study, SFA gave schools the clearest and most highly-specified plan for instructional improvement by producing a set of highly-specified instructional routines for the teaching of reading. In particular, the SFA program was built around two core principles: (a) offering students cooperative learning opportunities during class instruction, and (b) a clear and well-defined reading curriculum that provided teachers with a weekly lesson sequence, where each lesson in this sequence was designed around a "script" intended to guide teaching activities through a 90-minute reading period. In grades K-1, moreover, these scripts were accompanied by program-provided curricular materials for use throughout the school. For grades 2–6 these scripts were designed to be used in conjunction with existing reading curricula in the school.

SFA schools also were more centrally managed than other schools in our study. For example, the SFA design sought to intervene on the students (e.g., through tutoring and family support) in order to increase their attendance in school and to better prepare them to benefit from classroom instruction. Additionally, schools implementing SFA were expected to appoint a full-time literacy coordinator, and this staff member was given substantial responsibility for school-wide coordination of the reading program, including the task of constituting reading groups and making teaching assignments to these groups on a school-wide basis every eight weeks. In addition, instructional leaders in SFA schools and SFA linking agents were asked to supervise implementation of SFA instructional routines. In prior research, levels of instructional leadership in SFA schools were not statistically different from AC schools, but were higher than levels of instructional leadership found in ASP schools (Camburn et al., 2003).

Given SFA's approach to promoting instructional change, it is not surprising that the SFA schools in our study were characterized not only by distinctive patterns of organizing for school improvement, but also by distinctive patterns of literacy instruction and student achievement. For example, as we demonstrate below, staff in SFA schools saw school improvement plans as highly specified and as focused squarely on a particular instructional target (reading). In addition, school leaders worked mainly to monitor instruction, reducing teacher autonomy and standardizing instruction. This emphasis on faithful implementation of instructional routines, we found, produced a distinctive pattern of teaching practices that was generally faithful to the program's instructional design. In particular, more than any group of teachers in our sample, SFA teachers enacted what we have called a "skills-based" reading program focused on direct/explicit teaching of reading comprehension strategies and an emphasis on having students demonstrate their reading comprehension through simple, direct responses to oral questions and/or short written work. As we shall see, this instructional approach appeared to accelerate students' reading achievement in the early elementary grades.

Findings on Instructional Improvement Processes in CSR Schools

Having presented initial portraits of the CSR schools under study, we turn now to several detailed discussions of the data analyses from which these portraits were constructed. The first analysis to be discussed in this chapter examines the organizational processes for school improvement found in the four groups of schools under study. A detailed discussion of these findings has been presented in Rowan and Miller (2007). That paper used measures of organizational processes constructed from surveys administered annually over the 4-year course of the study to approximately 5,500 teachers and about 800 school leaders. Specifically, measures of organizational processes for school improvement were developed from teacher and school leader survey responses in four analytic domains: (a) the degree of *instructional guidance and standardization* in schools; (b) the degree of intensive *instructional leadership* present in schools; (c) schools' emphasis on faculty *innovation, discretion, and autonomy*; and (d) the strength of faculty *professional communities* in schools.

Overall, a total of 12 separate measures of these organizational processes were constructed in three steps. First, person-level scale scores were created by applying the Rasch model (a one parameter item response theory model) to the survey responses of teachers and school leaders (see Bond & Fox, 2001, for an accessible discussion of the Rasch model). Second, these scores were modeled as outcome measures in three-level hierarchical linear models (HLM) which nested individuals' annual scores on a particular scale within individuals, who were then nested within schools. In a third step, school-level scores on the outcome measures were derived from these HLM models. Specifically, the variables reported in this section are school-level empirical Bayes residuals from the models and indicate a school's average score on a measure, aggregated across all teachers (or leaders) and all 4 years; after controlling for staff characteristics, student characteristics, and school size. In all instances, these empirical Bayes (EB) residuals are standardized scores with mean = 0 and standard deviation = 1. The results reported below are based on comparisons of the overall means of the four quasi-experimental groups on the 12 outcome measures, where group means were "bracketed" by their standard errors. By comparing the ranges defined by the standard errors of the means, we were able to get a sound understanding of both the magnitude and degree of uncertainty of group mean differences in these organizational measures.

Findings As expected, the four quasi-experimental groups differed in important ways with respect to the amount of instructional guidance and standardization that was reported to exist in schools. Here, three separate measures of instructional guidance were examined: (a) school leaders' reports of the extent to which there was a press for a standardization of practice in the school, (b) teachers' reports of how closely

their improvement efforts were monitored, and (c) teachers' reports of instructional guidance they received.

Rowan and Miller (2007) showed that schools participating in the AC and SFA programs exhibited much higher levels of instructional guidance and standardization than schools participating in the ASP program and comparison schools. For example, we have found that among the four quasi-experimental groups in SII, the press for standardization was reported to be much greater in schools implementing AC and SFA than in comparison or ASP schools. In addition, teachers in AC and SFA schools felt that their improvement efforts were monitored more closely than did teachers in ASP and comparison schools. Teachers in schools implementing AC and SFA also reported receiving greater levels of instructional guidance than teachers in ASP and comparison schools, however, mean differences on the instructional guidance variable were not statistically significant.

The second domain of organizational processes examined was instructional leadership. Here, school leaders reported on three dimensions of instructional leadership—their involvement in staff development, their advising of teachers on matters of instruction, and their efforts at setting a vision for teaching and learning in the school. The data indicate that schools implementing the AC design were higher than schools in the other three groups on all three dimensions of instructional leadership. The differences between AC schools and schools in the other three groups are statistically significant in nearly every case. These findings on leadership processes illustrate a key difference in implementation strategy between SFA and AC. Both programs provided teachers with strong instructional guidance. However, SFA's strategy of procedural controls relied heavily on scripted lesson routines to secure faithful implementation, complemented by school leaders working closely with teachers to monitor and reinforce the use of scripted lesson routines. By contrast, AC relied more on having school leaders work closely with teachers to help them develop the knowledge and capabilities to use the design effectively.

The third organizational process we examined was schools' emphasis on teacher autonomy and innovation. Here, we examined a measure of leaders' reports of teacher autonomy, leaders' reports of the prevalence of values-based decision making in the school, and teachers' reports of support for innovation in the school. Given ASP's strategy of cultural control, we anticipated that ASP schools would have higher average scores than AC and SFA schools on these three measures. The results confirmed this prediction. The means for schools implementing the Accelerated Schools Project design were higher than the means of the three other quasi-experimental groups on all three measures of teacher autonomy and innovation, and with only a few exceptions, these mean differences were statistically significant.

The fourth and final organizational process examined was the strength of professional community in the schools under study, which was assessed through three measures: teachers' reports of trust and respect among the faculty, the prevalence of collaboration on instruction, and the prevalence of critical discourse among school staff. Recall that the ASP strategy of cultural control relied strongly on teachers to generate locally proposed instructional improvements. For this approach to be successful, however, schools would seem to need strong professional communities in which high levels of trust, critical discourse, and collaboration were evident. We found evidence that this was indeed the case in ASP schools. As with the indicators of teacher autonomy and innovation, ASP schools were higher than the other three quasi-experimental groups on all three measures of professional community, though the differences on these indicators were not as large as differences found in the areas of autonomy and innovation. In particular, ASP teachers reported substantially greater levels of trust among faculty members than did teachers in AC schools; and further, ASP teachers also reported a greater prevalence of critical discourse among colleagues than did teachers in AC schools.

Summary Our analyses of data on organizational processes in schools illustrate how externally designed and operated instructional improvement programs can pursue very different strategies to produce instructional change in schools. In particular, the survey data just discussed show that ASP's strategy of cultural control led to the development of school environments that were quite strong in professional community (i.e., trust among faculty, critical discourse, and teacher collaboration) and led to a great deal of teacher autonomy in pursuit of classroom instructional innovations. In contrast, AC and SFA used very different approaches to instructional reform. SFA, for example, pursued a strategy of "procedural controls" to promote instructional change, and as our data show, this approach led to relatively high levels of instructional guidance and to an associated press for instructional standardization. But, as we saw, SFA relied heavily on procedures and routines, with school leaders monitoring and reinforcing the enactment of routines. However, this approach failed to stimulate a sense of strong professional community. Finally, America's Choice also emphasized a significant amount of guidance and press for instructional standardization as part of its instructional improvement strategy, but it did so not by emphasizing scripted instructional routines, but rather by encouraging development of strong instructional leadership in schools. As with SFA, this emphasis on standardization and leadership worked against the formation of strong professional communities and also decreased the press for innovation and autonomy in AC schools.

Patterns of Literacy Instruction in CSR Schools

An interesting question is whether these different approaches to promoting instructional change were consequential, especially in promoting distinctive instructional practices in the schools under study. Results from *SII* provide evidence on this issue. As we are about to see, both AC and SFA managed to get their preferred instructional practices implemented faithfully in schools, whereas instruction in ASP schools was indistinguishable from that observed in comparison schools.

To examine instructional practices in the schools under study, SII researchers analyzed data from 75,689 instructional logs that were collected from 1,945 classroom teachers in grades 1 through 5 over the course of the study. In general, log data have been analyzed by SII researchers using three-level hierarchical linear models that nest multiple log reports within teachers within schools (see, e.g., Rowan, Camburn, & Correnti, 2004). The point of the analyses reported here was to test for mean differences in instructional practices across schools in the different quasi-experimental groups after adjusting, through propensity score stratification for many different school-level, pre-treatment covariates, as well as important lesson and teacher level characteristics that might differ across quasi-experimental groups.

Results The results of these analyses have been discussed in considerable detail in Correnti and Rowan (2007). In particular, these researchers reported very distinctive patterns of instruction for schools in the AC and SFA quasi-experimental groups, but little distinctiveness of instruction for the ASP schools in the sample. In the analyses presented here, we discuss the findings from this paper in three main areas of literacy instruction: word analysis, reading comprehension, and writing.

We begin by noting that we observed *no* significant differences in literacy teaching practices between ASP schools in the study and the comparison schools. That means that, on average, students in ASP schools would have experienced instructional opportunities that were virtually the same as students in comparison schools. This result is not surprising, especially in light of the school improvement strategy pursued by the ASP program. ASP's strategy of "cultural controls" did not prescribe specific instructional practices in the area of literacy but rather left it up to individual schools and their teachers to determine which instructional practices to implement. When left largely to their own devices, teachers in ASP schools apparently implemented the same patterns of instruction that were common in comparison schools. This indicates that ASP's approach to reform, similar to at least some other unsuccessful reform efforts, is not well-suited for creating large-scale instructional changes.

By contrast, Correnti and Rowan (2007) found substantial differences in literacy instruction between teachers in AC and comparison schools. Moreover, these differences occurred precisely where the AC instructional design was *most* prescriptive—in the area of writing and in the production of written text by students. In fact, the magnitude of these differences was quite large by social science standards. Controlling for lesson, teacher, and school characteristics, for example, Correnti and Rowan (2007) showed that AC teachers focused on writing in 54% of all lessons, whereas comparison teachers focused on writing in just 38% of all lessons. AC teachers also differed in the instructional practices and curricular content they covered when they taught writing. For example, on days when writing was taught, AC teachers were more likely than comparison teachers to have engaged in 6 of the 10 writing-related instructional practices measured by SII researchers. In particular, when they taught writing, AC teachers were more likely than comparison teachers to also have the lesson focus on reading comprehension and to directly integrate work in reading comprehension with their work in writing. They also were more likely to explicitly teach the writing process, more likely than comparison teachers to provide instruction on literary techniques or different writing genres, and more likely to have students share their writing and do substantive revisions to their writing. Additionally, AC teachers were more likely than comparison teachers to have their students write multiple connected paragraphs as they taught writing. Sensitivity analyses revealed that these findings were not likely due to omitted variable bias (Correnti & Rowan, 2007). Finally, we have recently examined measures of variability of these measures of writing instruction. This evidence is compelling because a measure of variability—the confidence interval for the coefficient of dispersion (Bonett & Seier, 2006)—reveals that variability in writing instruction among AC teachers was less than it was for comparison teachers, or indeed, for teachers in each of the other CSR designs. Thus, not only did AC teachers have higher means, on average, they also were less variable in their use of these instructional strategies. This is further evidence of the design's effect on literacy instruction. Moreover, this reduction in variation was largely due to a reduction in variance among teachers within schools and less to a reduction in variation across schools.

Correnti and Rowan (2007) also found large differences in instruction between SFA and comparison schools. In SFA schools, teachers were more likely to teach reading comprehension on a daily basis and they also taught comprehension differently from comparison teachers when it was taught. Here, for example, the average SFA teacher taught reading comprehension in 65% of all lessons, while the average comparison school teacher taught comprehension in 50% of all lessons. Moreover, when reading comprehension was taught, SFA teachers were more likely than comparison group teachers to use teacher-directed instruction, to focus on literal comprehension strategies, to check students' comprehension by eliciting brief answers from students, and (due to extensive use of cooperative grouping arrangements) to have students discuss text with one another. It is noteworthy also that teachers in SFA schools did *not* compromise any other aspect of comprehension instruction in order to obtain these significant differences. That is, in lessons where comprehension was taught, teachers in SFA schools were no less likely than comparison school teachers to focus on more advanced reading strategies or write extended text

about what they read. They did, however, more frequently provide direct instruction on reading strategies with more frequent checks for student understanding requiring brief oral or written answers from students. And, as was the case with AC schools, teachers in SFA showed less variability in their reading comprehension instruction than did teachers in the comparison schools or teachers in schools participating in the other CSR designs.

Summary The analysis of literacy instruction practices in CSR schools is important for two reasons. First, it suggests that the ways in which CSR programs organized schools for instructional improvement was consequential, not only for the kinds of organizational processes that emerged to support instructional change within schools, but also for the kinds of instructional practices that ended up being implemented. The evidence presented thus far suggests that although ASP's use of cultural controls promoted a strong professional community of teachers working hard on instructional innovation, the lack of a clear instructional design or strong instructional guidance for teachers, coupled with weak instructional leadership, tended to produce quite ordinary instruction that was not different from what was observed in comparison schools. By contrast, AC and SFA were far more prescriptive in their instructional designs. Both used different, but apparently quite effective strategies of "professional" and "procedural" controls to stimulate instructional change, and in both cases, SII researchers observed very distinctive forms of instructional practice in program schools.

A second point is that although both AC and SFA were "prescriptive" in instructional design and developed organizational processes in schools that emphasized faithful implementation of their preferred instructional designs, the instructional designs implemented in AC and SFA schools were quite different. Literacy instruction in AC schools was "literacy-based" in emphasis. As a result, students were far more likely to be exposed to direct instruction in writing and to work on extended writing assignments than were students in other schools. By contrast, SFA's instructional design placed more of an emphasis on what might be called "skills-based" reading instruction, that is, explicit instruction in reading comprehension tasks, coupled with a tendency to have students work on providing brief written and oral answers to check for basic comprehension. As we demonstrate in the next section, these differences in instructional practices provide at least one explanation for the patterns of reading achievement found in SII schools.

The findings presented here are based on cross-sectional comparisons of *teachers'* instruction in treatment and comparison schools. But it is important to consider these results from the students' perspective, since the instructional differences observed in a single year add up over time for students who remain in the treated schools. For example, across grades 3–5 in our study, students in SFA schools experienced about 28% more reading comprehension instruction (341 days vs. 265) than did students in comparison schools.

Similarly, students in AC schools experienced about 36% more writing instruction (264 days vs. 194) than students in the comparison schools. These differences are quite substantial for that portion of students who did not move out of the treated schools. Unfortunately, however, rates of student mobility in high poverty schools can be very high. In the SII sample, for example, only 46% of the students originally sampled in third grade remained in their same school by the end of fifth grade.[3] Given our logic model (that differences in achievement growth are likely to be caused by differences in instruction), the accumulated instructional histories of students provide two working hypotheses. One hypothesis is that students in SFA and AC schools are more likely to show differences in achievement growth due to the large differences in accumulated instruction in target areas. A second hypothesis is that such gains will be especially true for non-mobile students who remain in treated schools for multiple years and thus benefit from a greater increase in instructional opportunities than do mobile students in those schools.

Patterns of Literacy Achievement in CSR Schools

The final step in our work has been to study patterns of literacy achievement in the schools under study. To do so, SII researchers followed two cohorts of students as they passed through the schools under study, examining differences in achievement growth among students in the four quasi-experimental groups. One cohort of students in the study was followed as it passed from kindergarten to second grade over the course of the study, with SII researchers assessing these students' achievement in spring of kindergarten, the fall and spring of first grade, and the fall and spring of second grade. A second cohort of students was followed as it passed from third to fifth grade over the course of the study, and this group was assessed during the fall and spring of third, fourth, and fifth grades. The kindergarten cohort included approximately 3,600 students, while the third-grade cohort included approximately 4,000 students. Students in the sample analyzed here were enrolled in a total of 114 schools: 28 ASP schools, 31 AC schools, 29 SFA schools, and 26 comparison schools.

SII researchers used the *TerraNova* assessment published by CTB McGraw-Hill to measure students' growth in literacy achievement. This assessment produced two literacy scale scores for students at each administration—a *Reading Comprehension* score and a *Language* score. The Reading Comprehension scale charted students' academic growth as they moved beyond basic oral and reading comprehension to a level at which they are able to analyze and evaluate more extended text by employing various reading comprehension strategies. The Language scale charted the degree to which students moved from a basic understanding of sound/symbol relationships to a more complex understanding of the structure of the English Language. In both the lower and upper grades, the findings from the language scale score closely mirror findings from the reading comprehension scale score. As a result, in this chapter, we discuss only the findings from the reading comprehension scale score.

The sample of students assessed during the course of the study was more disadvantaged than a representative sample of U.S. students, reflecting the fact that schools in the SII sample were disproportionately drawn from high and medium poverty neighborhoods in order to study the effects of specific instructional interventions on student achievement in high poverty settings. For example, over half of the students in the SII sample were African American, while another 19% were Hispanic. Moreover, over half the parents of SII students had only a high school education or less, and over 40% of the students' mothers were single parents. Finally, substantial percentages of students in the SII sample were at risk of school failure. For example, 20% of SII students received services for learning difficulties, 18% received special education services, and 13% repeated a grade early in their elementary school career. Although schools in the SII sample varied in their degree of disadvantage, on average the schools served a highly disadvantaged student population.

Achievement Growth Models To examine general patterns in reading achievement in the schools under study, we have been fitting a series of three-level hierarchical linear models (HLM) in which multiple test scores per student are nested within students, who are nested within schools. In these analyses, we have been especially interested in examining differences in rates of literacy achievement growth between each set of CSR schools and the set of comparison schools. In the evaluation literature, such analyses are commonly referred to as "intent-to-treat" models since they examine achievement patterns for any schools nominally involved with a CSR program regardless of its level of implementation. Since schools were not randomly assigned to treatments, we also have been using propensity score stratification to statistically equate schools on 34 observed pre-treatment characteristics and then match the schools (using optimal matching) based on their propensity to have received treatment. Under the assumption of strongly ignorable treatment assignment, the average treatment effect in our statistical models is determined by pooling within-stratum treatment effects—the difference in mean rates of achievement growth between treated and untreated schools with similar pre-treatment characteristics. We caution the reader that the results about to be presented are *preliminary* and have yet to be peer-reviewed.

We also have been examining differences between each set of CSR schools and all other schools in our sample (e.g., SFA schools vs. comparison, ASP and AC schools). Once again, we are using propensity score stratification to statistically equate schools on 34 pre-treatment covariates and to match them using an optimal matching program. In many ways this comparison is superior to the one between each set of CSR schools and the set of comparison schools, not only because the larger sample of schools provides for better matches between treated and untreated schools, but also because some of the schools in our so-called "comparison" group participated in a variety of whole-school reform programs (e.g., Expeditionary Learning/Outward Bound, Direct Instruction, etc.).

To date, the findings of all of these analyses seem to follow logically from our discussion to this point. For example, thus far, we have found that the school improvement strategy followed in ASP schools failed to produce instructional practices that were different from instructional practices in comparison schools. As a result, it is not surprising that patterns of achievement in ASP schools were also indistinguishable from patterns of achievement in comparison schools. For both cohorts of students (K–2 and 3–5), our preliminary analyses failed to find any significant differences in students' rates of achievement *growth* over time across ASP and comparison schools—or across ASP and all other schools. Again, given the lack of differences in instructional practices across ASP and control schools, this finding is not surprising.

In contrast, we *have* found differences in patterns of achievement between SFA and comparison schools (under certain model conditions) and between SFA and all other schools. In our preliminary analyses, these differences are most apparent for the lower grades cohort, but the magnitude of these differences varies depending on the statistical adjustments used in the models. In a model with no controls other than the propensity score, for example, SFA students gain about 6 points more than comparison students over the 2-year interval from the spring of kindergarten to the spring of second grade. After adjusting for patterns of student mobility in the schools under study, however, the SFA advantage over comparison schools during the same interval increases to more than 10 points. A similar 10-point advantage holds when SFA students are compared with all other students in AC, ASP, and comparison schools. This SFA advantage is especially impressive considering that students in the SII study gained in percentile rank over this interval relative to the norming population. An average student beginning our study at the 30th percentile in a comparison school, for example, finished the end of second grade at about the 40th percentile. The SFA effect moved a comparable student in the average SFA school from the 30th percentile to the 50th percentile.

In a similar vein, our preliminary analyses have found statistically significant differences in patterns of achievement growth for students in AC schools in the upper grades. Students in AC schools grew at a significantly faster rate than students in comparison schools and faster than students in all other schools. From the beginning of third grade to the end of fifth grade, for example, our analyses suggest that students in AC schools, on average, scored an additional 9 to 12 points on the reading comprehension outcome, depending on the model adjustments. The size and interpretation of the AC effect on reading comprehension is similar to the one found for SFA schools in early grades reading, except that in the upper grades cohort, students in the SII were losing ground relative to the norming population. For example,

our statistical models suggest that the average student in a comparison school who began third grade at about the 40th percentile nationally ended the study at about the 30th percentile; by contrast, our models suggest that the equivalent student in the average AC school who began third grade at the 40th percentile would achieve at or above the 40th percentile nationally at the end of fifth grade.

We should note that the effects on reading comprehension for SFA schools in the lower grades and for AC schools in the upper grades represent the average "intent-to-treat" effects of those interventions. We have also have been examining whether exposure to the treatment has influenced student growth in our schools. In preliminary work we have been able to demonstrate effects of exposure to the treatment in a number of ways. For example, we examined the degree of implementation at each school by examining the organizational, instructional, and staff development profiles of schools and the degree to which they reflected the aims of the SFA and AC designs, respectively. Using this strategy, we have found that, in both interventions, schools with better implementation scores show higher rates of achievement growth. Additionally, we also observed an implementation effect for SFA schools in the upper grades. Within our sample, a number of SFA schools indicated that they participated in Roots and Wings, while others indicated they did not. Thus, while all of the schools considered themselves SFA schools, Roots and Wings schools were more resource intensive, especially in the upper grades, where the *Wings* curriculum (grades 2 through 6) is enacted immediately upon completion of reading *Roots* (Grade 1). Indeed, in the upper grade models, SFA schools that participated in *Roots* and *Wings* had students with greater achievement growth than students in other SFA schools that was also significantly better than the growth rates for students in comparison schools.

Additionally, it has become apparent in our work that student mobility plays a large role in moderating effects of the CSR programs on student achievement. For example, we have shown that the overall effects of both SFA in the lower grades and AC in the upper grades increase when the statistical models adjust for student mobility, thus demonstrating that students who stay in treated schools for a longer period of time make greater gains in achievement. These same effects can also be demonstrated when a variable indicating students' entry into the study at the initial starting point is entered into the model. Students remaining longer in an SFA school (in the lower grades) or an AC school (in the upper grades) show significantly higher achievement growth. Third, we have run statistical models adjusting for student demographic characteristics and for school-level propensity strata (but without the CSR program variables entered into the analysis). We then examined student-level residuals, calculating the model predicted gains for each student. When we examined bar plots with 95% confidence intervals for SFA versus other students in the lower grades and for AC versus other students in the upper grades, we found that students making the greatest gains were less mobile and located in schools with less student mobility. More importantly, the *magnitude of the CSR program effect* was greatest for those same students, presumably because they received greater exposure to the treatment.

These results are important for two reasons. First, the fact that the CSR program effect varies with exposure to the treatment strengthens our causal arguments about the effects of program designs on achievement gains. Since students varied in their treatment dosages and since higher dosages tended to predict higher achievement gains, we can infer that the treatment is more likely than not the causal agent producing the achievement gains. Second, the results also show that the potential for achievement growth after the adoption of one of these interventions is greater than the average "intent-to-treat" effect *if schools have a faithful implementation of the design.* In addition, our results show that the "intent-to-treat" effect on students is a lower bound *if students are present to receive the treatment in successive years.* Consider, for example, that the SFA effect in the lower grades is averaged over all SFA students in the model. But, of these students, only 29.6% received SFA-like instruction in both first and second grade. Another 15.4% were present both years and had 1 year of SFA-like instruction, while only 4.1% were present both years and received instruction very similar to students in comparison schools in both years of the study. About half of the SFA students were only present for 1 year of the study. Thus, 37.2% of the SFA students in our achievement models received SFA-like instruction in the 1 year they were present, while the remaining 13.2% received instruction that was very similar to the instruction received by students in the comparison schools in the 1 year they were present.[4] Thus, even for an intervention with high rates of implementation fidelity, the transfer of the treatment to individual students over successive years reaches less than one-third of all SFA students in our achievement models. When we examine "intent-to-treat" effects, we must keep in mind that not only is implementation fidelity incomplete (a condition that is potentially manipulable by CSR design), but also that student mobility severely limits the treatment dosage received by students (a condition that is less easily manipulated by CSR programs or, indeed, by social policies).

Conclusions and Recommendations for Future Research

What do the specific findings from A Study of Instructional Improvement tell us about the process of school improvement by design and how to study this process in the future? First, our findings suggest that design-based instructional improvement can come in many and varied forms. Intervention providers, for example, can vary in terms of how they organize schools to manage the process of instructional improvement *and* in the kinds of instructional practices they seek to put in place in schools. As we argued at the beginning of this chapter, and as we demonstrated through a discussion of SII findings, both of these design elements must be explicitly studied if we are to understand the conditions under which design-based instructional improvement efforts actually succeed in improving student learning. Indeed, SII illustrates this lesson in a telling way. As we have seen in this chapter, one program studied by SII researchers (ASP) managed to produce a very distinctive pattern of instructional management in schools, but that pattern did *not* produce any real changes in instruction, and as a consequence, the program had very little effect on students' reading achievement in the schools where it worked. By contrast, two other programs that were studied by SII researchers appear to have changed schools in ways that *did* promote instructional change. Here, however, the patterns of instruction produced were differentially effective. The AC program, for example, produced what we called a "literacy-based" pattern of reading instruction in schools, but that type of instruction appeared to promote reading gains only at the later grades—not in earlier grades. By contrast, the SFA program produced a pattern of "skills-based" reading instruction in schools that—in some analyses at least—was only effective at the early grades. The obvious implication for future studies is the need to closely examine not only how schools organize to make instructional change, but also to examine explicitly the kinds of instructional changes being made in these schools. Only then can researchers understand if null effects on student achievement that emerge in many studies are due to implementation failures or to implementation of ineffective instructional practices.

Our findings also show the benefits of moving beyond highly generalized conceptual frameworks for describing program designs, patterns of instructional management, and specific instructional practices in schools. For example, we argued earlier in this chapter that program designs are often discussed as being either "programmed" or "adaptive" in form (Berman, 1978). Yet SII demonstrates why this dichotomy is simplistic. In this chapter, we advanced an alternative (and more nuanced) conceptual framework. To be sure, the design features emphasized by ASP appear to be consistent with Berman's discussion of "adaptive" designs, and to a large degree, SFA appears to have been built around a design that can easily be labeled as "programmed" in nature. But the AC program, which we also studied, is not easily classified within this dichotomy, incorporating as it does at least some features of programmed designs and some features of adaptive designs. A similar point can be made about the patterns of instructional management that emerged in AC schools. While organization theorists in education often contrast mechanistic with organic forms of instructional management (e.g., Miller & Rowan, 2006), AC's organizational design once again incorporates features of both. The implication for future research is to continue to look in more fine-grained ways at programs designs, for it is not at all clear that the patterns that we labeled as cultural control, procedural control, and professional control exhaust the "types" of designs that might be encountered as the design-based school reform movement progresses.

Third, we would argue that A Study of Instructional Improvement shows the benefits of looking closely at instruction when studying the process of instructional improvement. While that point seems obvious, it is nevertheless amazing how much research on school reform avoids directly measuring instructional practice when trying to explain student achievement outcomes. Indeed, in SII, the pattern of achievement results that were found makes sense only if we appeal to our findings about instructional practices in schools. Why, for example, would two well-implemented instructional programs produce very different patterns of reading growth in the schools where they worked? After looking at instruction in the schools under study, the answer is obvious—because instruction differed across schools implementing these programs.

Finally, we would argue that the results of SII confirm the larger "logic model" of school improvement by design that we described earlier in this chapter. That logic model points to the importance of two dimensions of design—the way designs organize schools to produce instructional change, and the kinds of instructional changes the design envisions. Obviously, the results of SII show just how fragile school improvement by design is: A design can fail because of a poor approach to implementation, it can fail because of an ineffective approach to instruction, or it can fail on both counts. That is an important lesson, and one that should guide all future research and development in the area.

Notes

1. Work on this chapter was supported by grants from the U.S. Department of Education to the Consortium for Policy Research in Education (CPRE) at the University of Pennsylvania (Grant # OERI-R308A60003), the National Science Foundation's Interagency Educational Research Initiative to the University of Michigan (Grant #s REC-9979863 & REC-0129421), the William and Flora Hewlett Foundation, and the Atlantic Philanthropies. Opinions expressed in this chapter are those of the authors, and do not reflect the views of the U.S. Department of Education, the National Science Foundation, the William and Flora Hewlett Foundation, or the Atlantic Philanthropies. We thank Deborah L. Ball and David K. Cohen (co-PIs of the study), Carol Barnes, and Stephen W. Raudenbush for critical contributions at various points in our work.

2. It is important for the reader to keep in mind that our analysis of the design of the CSR programs reflects the designs as they existed at the time of our data collection (from 2000 to 2004). The designs evolved during the course of the study, and continue to evolve in response to research, current demands of the reform environment, and their own intuitions about the school improvement process.

3. Rates of attrition did not vary substantially by treatment or comparison group.

4. Daily log data submitted by teachers was used in a discriminant analysis to identify teachers as being AC-like, SFA-like, ASP-like, or comparison-like in their instruction (see Rowan & Correnti, 2006). Once teachers' instruction was identified as being in one of these groups, the instructional-type was written back to individual students. We then constructed instructional profiles for students across the years of the study. The discriminant analysis correctly identified 76% of SFA teachers as being such, 62% of AC teachers as such, only 44% of ASP teachers as such, and only 36% of comparison school teachers as such. These data show that even when intervention

programs produce strong effects on instruction (as did SFA and AC), many teachers do not implement the intended instructional regimes faithfully. The analysis also shows that teachers in both comparison and ASP schools implemented patterns of instruction that were close to the preferred regimes of SFA and AC.

References

143 Cong. Rec. S97-100, H6849-H6890. (September 4, 1997) (statement of David Obey). Retrieved July 29, 2008, from http://frwebgate3.access.gpo.gov/cgi-bin/waisgate.cgi?WAISdocID=3583079271+2+0+0&WAISaction=retrieve

Basken, P. (2006, March 29). States have more schools falling behind. *Washington Post.* Retrieved July 28, 2008, from http://www.washingtonpost.com/wp-dyn/content/article/2006/03/28/AR2006032801794.html

Berends, M., Bodilly, S., & Kirby, S. (2002). *Facing the challenges of whole school reform: New American schools after a decade.* Santa Monica, CA: RAND.

Berends, M., & King, B. (1994). A description of restructuring in nationally nominated schools: Legacy of the iron cage? *Educational Policy, 8,* 28–50.

Berman, P. (1978). *Designing implementation to match policy situation: A contingency analysis of programmed and adaptive implementation.* Santa Monica, CA: RAND.

Bodilly, S. (1996). *Lessons from New American Schools Development Corporation's demonstration phase.* Santa Monica: RAND.

Bond, T. G., & Fox, C. M. (2001). *Applying the Rasch model: Fundamental measurement in the human sciences.* Mahwah, NJ: Erlbaum.

Bonett, D., & Seier, E. (2006). Confidence interval for a coefficient of dispersion in nonnormal distributions. *Biometrical Journal, 48,* 144–148.

Borman, G. D., Hewes, G. M., Overman, L. T., & Brown, S. (2003). Comprehensive school reform and achievement: A meta-analysis. *Review of Educational Research, 73,* 125–230.

Camburn, E., Rowan, B., & Taylor, J. (2003). Distributed leadership in schools: The case of elementary schools adopting comprehensive school reform models. *Educational Evaluation and Policy Analysis, 25,* 347–373.

Cohen, D. K., & Hill, H. C. (2001). *Learning policy: When state educational reform works.* New Haven, CT: Yale University Press.

Cohen, D., McLaughlin, M. W., & Talbert, J. (Eds.). (1993). *Teaching for understanding: Challenges for policy and practice.* San Francisco: Jossey-Bass.

Cooperative Research Act of 1954, Pub. L. No. 83-531, 83rd Cong., 2d Sess. (1954).

Correnti, R., & Rowan, B. (2007). Opening up the black box: Literacy instruction in schools participating in three comprehensive school reform programs. *American Educational Research Journal, 44,* 298–338.

Darling-Hammond, L., & Snyder, J. (1992). Curriculum studies and traditions of inquiry: The scientific tradition. In P. W. Jackson (Ed.), *Handbook of research on curriculum* (pp. 41–77). New York: MacMillan.

Desimone, L. (2002). How can comprehensive school reform models be implemented? *Review of Educational Research, 72,* 433–480.

Desimone, L., Porter, A., Garet, M., Yoon, K., & Birman, B. (2002). Effects of professional development on teachers' instruction: Results from a three-year longitudinal study. *Educational Evaluation and Policy Analysis, 24,* 81–112.

Elmore, R. (1996). Getting to scale with good educational practice. *Harvard Educational Review, 66*(1), 1–26.

Elmore, R., & Burney, D. (1997). *Investing in teacher learning: Staff development and instructional improvement in school district #2, New York City.* Philadelphia: Consortium for Policy Research in Education and the National Commission on Teaching and America's Future.

Fennema, E., Carpenter, T., Franke, M., Levi, L., Jacobs, V., & Empson, S. (1996). A longitudinal study of learning to use children's thinking in mathematics instruction. *Journal for Research in Mathematics Education, 27,* 403–434.

Gersten, R. (1984). Follow Through revisited: Reflections on the site variability issue. *Educational Evaluation and Policy Analysis, 6,* 411–423.

House, E., Glass, G., McLean, L., & Walker, D. (1978). No simple answer: Critique of the follow-through evaluation. *Harvard Educational Review, 48,* 128–160.

Huberman, A., & Miles, M. (1984). *Innovation up close: How school improvement works.* New York: Plenum.

Loucks, S., Cox, P., Miles, M., & Huberman, M. (1982). *People, policies and practices: Examining the chain of school improvement, Vol. 2: Portraits of the changes, the players and the contexts. A study of the dissemination efforts supporting school improvement.* Andover, MA: Network of Innovative Schools.

McLaughlin, M., & Marsh, D. (1978). Staff development and school change. *Teachers College Record, 80,* 69–94.

Miller, R. J., & Rowan, B. (2006). Effects of organic management on student achievement. *American Educational Research Journal, 43,* 219–253.

Mirel, J. (1994). *The evolution of the New American Schools: From revolution to mainstream.* New York: Fordham Foundation.

Nunnery, J. (1998). Reform ideology and the locus of development problem in educational restructuring. *Education and Urban Society, 30,* 277–295.

Rivlin, A. M., & Timpane, P. M. (Eds.). (1975). *Planned variation in education: Should we give up or try harder?* Washington, DC: Brookings Institution.

Rowan, B. (2001). The ecology of school improvement. *Journal of Educational Change, 3,* 283–314.

Rowan, B., Camburn, E., & Barnes, C. (2004). Benefiting from comprehensive school reform: A review of research on CSR implementation. In C. Cross (Ed.), *Putting the pieces together: Lessons from comprehensive school reform research* (pp. 1–52). Washington, DC: National Clearinghouse for Comprehensive School Reform.

Rowan, B., Camburn, E., & Correnti, R. (2004). Using teacher logs to measure the enacted curriculum in large-scale surveys: Insights from the Study of Instructional Improvement. *Elementary School Journal, 105,* 75–102.

Rowan, B., & Correnti, R. (2006, April). *Interventions to improve instruction: How implementation strategies affect instructional change.* Paper presented at the annual meeting of the American Educational Research Association, San Francisco.

Rowan, B., & Miller, R. J. (2007). Organizing strategies for promoting instructional change: Implementation dynamics in schools working with comprehensive school reform providers. *American Educational Research Journal, 44,* 252–297.

Stecher, B., Le, V-N., Hamilton, L., Ryan, G., Robyn, A., & Lockwood, J. R. (2006). Using structured classroom vignettes to measure instructional practices in mathematics. *Educational Evaluation and Policy Analysis, 28,* 101–130.

Stringfield, S., & Datnow, A. (1998). Scaling up school restructuring designs in urban schools. *Education and Urban Society, 30,* 269–276.

Wayne, A. J., & Youngs, P. (2003). Teacher characteristics and student achievement gains: A review. *Review of Educational Research, 73,* 89–122.

Welch, W. W. (1969). Curriculum evaluation. *Review of Educational Research, 39*(4), 429–443.

Whitehurst, G. (2002, June 25). *Statement before the Senate Committee on Health, Education, Labor and Pensions.* Retrieved July 28, 2008, from http://ies.ed.gov/director/speeches2002/06_25/2002_06_25.asp

50

Measurement and Improvement of Teacher-Child Interactions

Implications for Policy and Accountability Frameworks of Standardized Observation

ROBERT C. PIANTA AND BRIDGET K. HAMRE
University of Virginia

Many children spend more of their waking hours in classrooms than they do at home; within these settings they are exposed to experiences that for better or worse, intended and unintended, shape their development—they may learn to read, write, and think critically; they make friends and face the inevitable challenges of peer relationships; and they are increasingly oriented to become productive, independent members of a larger society. Interest is keen in the extent of these effects of classrooms, the methods of producing and reproducing them at various levels of scale, and understanding the mechanisms responsible for them. In fact it could be argued that interest in classroom effects is among the core foci of educational policy at the present time, with teacher effects at the epicenter. The scale is staggering, with millions of classroom teachers working each day in public education settings; more than 200,000 of which are new entrants to the profession each year, 87% of which leave the profession before a decade of experience (Béteille & Loeb, this volume; Anderson, 2008).

The focus of this chapter is the consequences for policy-making of research on teachers' interactions with students within classrooms, particularly the implications of research on standardized observations and their use in large-scale policy-relevant contexts. Implications are outlined not only for education policy that aims to improve student achievement but also policy that influences the nature and focus of education research. The overall goal is to invigorate and inform policymaking that takes classrooms seriously as settings for learning (Tseng & Seidman, 2007; Shinn & Yoshikawa, 2008). The chapter takes a course that is somewhat unconventional for research handbooks. Rather than collect, synthesize, and present an encyclopedic review of the evidence on teacher or classroom effects and related policies published over the past several years, the chapter advances a "proof of concept" argument for a set of policies relevant to improving teacher effectiveness based on a set of contemporary studies on observations of classrooms, drawn primarily from the last decade of literature on classroom and teacher effects, and how to improve them, in early childhood education.

Because the field of early childhood education is less tightly regulated with regard to teacher qualifications and credentials and observations of the features and qualities of early education classroom settings are both accepted in practice and used as policy levers, there is ample evidence to develop an argument that could apply to K–12 classroom settings and policies pertaining to teacher effectiveness in those settings. In fact, nearly half the states with publicly funded pre-kindergarten programs are considering some form of observation of teachers' practices with children as part of state policy aimed to not only monitor and improve quality but to also make such information available publicly as a means to subject classrooms to market forces (see discussions of "Quality Rating Improvement Systems," Mitchell, in press). As just one example, the federal preschool program, Head Start, has used direct observations of classroom settings as a means of program development and monitoring for more than a decade; the Early Childhood Environmental Rating Scales (Harms, Clifford, & Cryer, 1998) has arguably been the cornerstone of program development in Head Start and other early childhood programs, with evidence clearly pointing to its value in identifying clear and observable targets for improvement, with subsequent effects on children's learning gains. States have scaled-up capacity to conduct observations and have paired these protocols with incentives and resources, suggesting, again from the early education sector perspective, that such efforts are feasible (see Mitchell, in press).

To preview, advances in theory, in measurement, and in intervention, particularly in early education settings, have led to policies in that sector of public education, that reach into classrooms through the use of standardized observations of teacher behavior and the classroom environment, taking shape in metrics for "quality" that rely neither on the proxies of degrees or experience that bear only indirectly or not at all (Gordon, Kane, & Staiger, 2006) on student outcomes nor on the tautology that effective teachers are those who produce achievement gains (Rivkin, Hanushek, & Kain, 2005; Rockoff, 2004). If, as is argued herein, the lessons from early childhood education translate, it may now be feasible to experiment in K–12 with policy that utilizes regular, direct assessments of teachers' performance in the classroom as one of several bases for merit pay, tenure decisions, allocation of professional development resources, and planning of support programs for teachers. Finally, placing observational assessment of teachers' classroom instruction and interactions more squarely into the realm of policy and accountability frameworks would in turn spur research and development efforts in teacher training likely to lead to more regular and efficient production of effective teaching by higher-education based training programs and through professional development supports that are linked with outcomes. In short, the lesson from early childhood is that policies that pertain to teachers and teaching, if centered on *performance-based observations of classroom teaching behaviors*, could function in a coordinated fashion to more systematically and directly produce better teaching in classrooms.

Policy and Classroom Effects

The politics of school reform are a powerful force directing attention to classrooms and teachers' behavior. As the results of widespread accountability and state standards-testing used to identify schools that do not meet established proficiency levels and rates of performance, attention is quickly turning to classrooms as the locus of effects and solutions. Re-authorization of NCLB is launching a range of discussions that shift the dynamic of accountability to focus on how inputs such as teacher behavior produce achievement through the expected debate about "effective" or "qualified" teachers (e.g., Appalachian Regional Advisory Committee [ARAC], 2005; Foundation for Child Development [FCD], 2005; Gordon et al., 2006; Hamre, Pianta, Mashburn, & Downer, 2007; Ladd, 2008). Clearly, classrooms are the hotspot as states and districts scramble to find the right mix of curriculum, professional development, and instructional supports that will raise students' achievement levels (e.g., Educational Testing Service [ETS], 2004; Lasley, Siedentop, & Yinger, 2006).

A second impetus for orienting policy toward teachers' behavior in classrooms is illustrated in the widespread and persistent arguments being made for state-supported pre-kindergarten as a means of addressing a range of social and economic concerns (Bogard & Takanishi, 2005). This evidentiary stream pertains to the present focus on teacher interactions because it draws from empirical work on class-rooms as interventions for high-risk young children. Over the past two decades, a host of studies describing results of randomized controlled trials and highly controlled quasi-experimental work have shown quite clearly that significant gains in achievement accrue as a function of enrollment in pre-K classrooms, and that children's interactions with teachers are in large part the source of these effects (see Mashburn et al., 2008). Thus the argument for pre-K is predicated on the convergence of three streams of evidence: (a) for an achievement gap starting before children enter school (e.g., Bogard & Takanishi, 2005), (b) the role that early education plays in closing this gap, and (c) recent evidence that once programs are implemented in any form, it is the nature and quality of children's experiences in classrooms that are the source of program effects (Bogard & Takanishi, 2005; Burchinal et al., 2008; Hamre & Pianta, 2005; Howes et al., 2008; Mashburn et al., 2008). The focus on pre-K is not intended here as an end in itself, but illustratively; to the extent there is a body of well-controlled studies of educational effects of teachers' actions in classrooms, it exists for pre-kindergarten educational programs.

The third body of evidence in support of teacher behavior as a focus of policy draws directly from studies that indicate quite clearly that teachers (and presumably their behaviors) matter. In studies of large-scale statewide testing programs in which multi-level analysis has been used to isolate sources of variance to which achievement growth can be attributed (e.g., Nye, Kostantopoulous, & Hedges, 2004), classrooms are more often than not the level at which the greatest source of variation in what students learn and gain as a function of attending school can be attributed (at least in achievement-related domains; it is not as clear with regard to social outcomes). Value-added modeling of achievement data that takes into consideration student performance over many years clearly isolates a definable "teacher effect" to the extent that such effects are a major focus of policy discussions and debate (Gordon et al., 2006; Ladd, 2008). Recent work, largely motivated by NCLB's focus on highly qualified teachers and an assortment of concerns related to teacher licensing systems, has focused on teacher characteristics such as degrees, experience, qualifications, and test performance, and shows significant but modest and somewhat inconsistent returns to achievement as a function of each of these features, and policy-relevant effect sizes when considering their cumulative benefits (see Ladd, 2008; Béteille & Loeb, this volume). However plausible it may be to infer that the student achievement literature demonstrates the importance of teacher behaviors as the source of the teacher effect, it should be noted that these studies do not directly assess teacher behavior. It should also be pointed out that teacher behaviors are implicated as significant moderators of treatment effects in highly controlled experimental studies (Battistich, Watson, Solomon, Lewis, & Schaps, 1999). And within classrooms, differences in teachers' implementation of treatments (e.g., curricula) appear to be the single biggest factor determining effects on child outcomes (Domitrovich & Greenberg, 2004), even when they are instructed to deliver the intervention in a standardized manner and provided with regular and intensive supports to maintain fidelity. Thus in both value-added research and experimental studies not only is a good part of the value of attending school conveyed at the level of classrooms, but it also appears that teachers play a major role in determining the value of the classroom environment for student learning and development.

As the focus of research seeking to locate and maximize the benefits of education recognizes and considers the processes within classrooms that could account for such benefits, whether in value-added or experimental frameworks, the evidence shows that experiences with teachers can matter. The remainder of this chapter focuses on one source of teacher effects on achievement—teacher-student interactions—and the consequences for policy when an evidence base is accrued regarding the measurement, production, and improvement of interactions that are effective in producing achievement gains. Teachers can be a point of great leverage for policymaking; the production of teachers (and presumably teaching quality) is under considerable regulatory control at the state and Federal levels, and has extraordinarily high stakes attached to its success or failure—as just one example, see Pianta, Belsky, et al. (2008) for observational descriptions of thousands of U.S. classrooms taught by certified teachers that indicates only 25% provide a level of instructional or emotional support consistent with the production of learning gains. As another, refer to the report by Clotfelter, Ladd, and Vigdor (2007) that certain profiles of teacher characteristics actually have negative effects on achievement for certain student groups. Policies that place direct assessment of actual teaching as a central feature of accountability frameworks and provisions for equity of educational opportunity are likely to accomplish several interlocking aims that in a coordinated fashion could result in substantial shifts in the nature and quality of instruction, socialization, mentoring, and tutelage that takes place in classrooms. If the lessons learned from widespread use of classroom observations in early childhood education programs translate to K–12, such policies will result in better teaching in classrooms; will lead to improved student outcomes; and will drive a research and development enterprise that will advance measurement efficiency and validity.

Teacher-Student Interactions and Classroom Effects

A major question occupying the attention of education science and policy has been to determine the degree to which placement in a particular classroom accounts for variability in children's academic performance. As suggested above, numerous studies have indicated that: (a) a significant portion of variance in student learning is explained at the classroom level (see Nye, Konstantopoulos, & Hedges, 2004), and (b) deflections in the trajectory of student learning across years can be attributed to their experiences in specific classrooms (see Ladd, 2008; Rivkin et al., 2005).

Although these studies have been important in laying a foundation for inquiry into classroom effects, they fail to articulate the mechanisms through which experiences in classrooms, specifically teacher behaviors, lead to student learning and positive social adjustment. If there is no focus on identifying these mechanisms responsible for achievement, then policy is left to rely on Hanushek's (2002) definition of teacher quality, "Good teachers are ones who get large gains in student achievement for their classes; bad teachers are just the opposite" (p. 3). Even much of the research using the value-added paradigm for identifying effective teachers (see Gordon et al., 2006, for an overview) provides virtually no guidance to evidenced-based strategies to produce effective teaching (Cochran-Smith & Zeichner, 2005). A critical component of the effort to produce effective teaching is the identification of mechanisms responsible for teacher effects. Perhaps with value-added models as one source, one course of action would be to identify a set of conceptually sensible and empirically valid teaching practices and assign students randomly to teachers exhibiting those practices; or to build programs (interventions) for training teachers to exhibit those behaviors and test their efficacy on teacher and student outcomes. The research programs likely to have the greatest impact, for *both* policy and for designing approaches that produce effective teaching, are likely to go beyond asking to what degree classrooms or teachers matter and instead focus on why they matter— the processes through which they influence learning and development. Taking this approach requires a conceptual framework and valid measurements that can be applied at scale if they are to have any relevance for policy.

Domains and Measurement of Teacher-Child Interaction Perhaps the key ingredient of any classroom or school environment, with regard to learning and development, is the nature and quality of interaction between adults and students (Bronfenbrenner & Morris, 1998). This premise has been reflected in the voluminous and influential literature describing and conceptualizing what teachers do in classrooms that produces learning (e.g., Brophy, 1999; Brophy & Good, 1986; Eccles & Roeser, 1999; Gage, 1978; Pressley et al., 2003; Soar & Soar, 1979). For example, Brophy (1999) describes 12 principles of effective teaching, including supportive classroom climates, opportunities to learn, curricular alignment, thoughtful discourse, scaffolding engagement, and achievement expectations, each of which are based on research findings and theories of teaching and learning. Others organize teachers' practices into larger domains of teaching and classroom environments. Pressley and colleagues (2003) draw from their studies of effective teachers (e.g., Bogner, Raphael, & Pressley, 2002; Pressley, Allington, Wharton-McDonald, Block, & Morrow, 2001; Wharton-McDonald, Pressley, & Hampston, 1998) to suggest that effective teaching strategies can be organized into categories regarding motivational atmosphere, classroom management, and curriculum and instruction. Similarly, Eccles and Roeser (1999) suggest that schooling is characterized by organizational, social, and instructional processes that help regulate children's and adolescents' development across cognitive, social-emotional, and behavioral domains.

These conceptual frameworks have made significant contributions to advancing an understanding of classroom and teacher effects, but there have been far fewer attempts, in K–12, to operationalize these concepts in measurement systems that can be scaled, and so their impact on policy has been modest. The following discussion outlines conceptual frameworks and measurement systems developed for early education settings that have been in widespread use, one for more than a decade (Harms et al., 1998), which has been foundational to policy and program development in early education. Again, these are presented to illustrate the possibility that conceptualization, measurement, and widespread implementation of standardized observations of classroom settings and teacher behavior can play a fundamental role in education policy.

The Early Childhood Environment Rating Scale-Revised (ECERS-R; Harms et al., 1998) has been in use for more than a decade as the gold standard for observation in early education settings. The ECERS-R is perhaps the most widely-used observational assessment of classroom settings in the world, implemented in literally tens of thousands of classrooms globally. The ECERS-R conceptualizes classroom settings in terms of characteristics of the physical environment, structural features of how the setting is organized, and aspects of teacher behavior with children. Included are features of the setting that support young children's development such as: Space and Furnishings, Language-Reasoning resources, Interaction, and Program Structure (e.g., schedule, group time, provisions for children with disabilities). From a measurement standpoint, these features are operationalized both in terms of the physical environment (e.g., Language-Reasoning includes games available) and interactions (e.g., Language-Reasoning also includes teachers' stimulation of thinking). These "dimensions" of the classroom setting's resources are then scored on a 1–7 scale. In addition to an overall score, factor analysis of the ECERS-R yields two factors that reflect molar aspects of the setting: Teaching and Interactions is a composite of several indicators including staff-child interactions, discipline, supervision, encouraging children to communicate, and using language to develop reasoning skills and Provisions for Learning is a composite of indicators such as furnishings, room arrangement, gross motor equipment, art, blocks, dramatic play, and nature/science.

For the purposes of the present discussion, the use of the ECERS-R as an indicator of setting quality in large-scale studies of program effects repeatedly has produced evidence demonstrating that features of the setting, particularly interactions, account for gains in children's performance on assessment of school readiness skills (e.g., Burchinal, Peisner-Feinberg, Bryant, & Clifford, 2000; Burchinal, Peisner-Feinberg, Pianta, & Howes, 2002; Peisner-Feinberg & Burchinal, 1997; Peisner-Feinberg et al., 2001). Furthermore, this evidence has been used as the basis for policies

at state or program levels that identify adequate "quality" using a specific cutoff score on the ECERS-R and subsequent program development and investments that are tied directly to the metrics and items in efforts to raise a specific score to the desired level. States such as Georgia have used this form of program monitoring and development in their statewide pre-K system, with observation of settings at the core. This dynamic of policy and program development centers on observed features of the classroom, assessed through a standardized system validated to child outcomes, that in turn triggers investment and action tied directly to those classroom features (see Mitchell, in press).

Building on the dynamic just described and the need for further measurement refinement focused solely on teacher-child interactions, Hamre and Pianta (2007) presented a multi-level framework for conceptualizing and measuring teacher-student interactions and applied it extensively in early education settings as the Classroom Assessment Scoring System (CLASS; Pianta, La Paro, & Hamre, 2008). At the most molar level, the conceptual framework posits three major domains—Emotional Supports, Classroom Organization, and Instructional Supports—each of which is reflected by a set of specific dimensions of teacher behavior. These dimensions are then defined in terms of key indicators of behavioral interaction. A similar approach has been taken by McCaslin and colleagues (2006) in their measuring of elementary classroom setting effects on student motivation. The result is a multi-level conceptual and measurement model that can be subjected to empirical tests and evaluation. This latent structure for organizing teaching behaviors poses explicit, testable hypotheses regarding the organization of teachers' interactive behaviors. For example, the domain of Emotional Supports includes three dimensions: Positive Classroom Climate, Teacher Sensitivity, and Regard for Student Perspectives, while the Instructional Support domain includes Concept Development and Quality of Feedback dimensions. Within each of these dimensions are posited a set of behavioral indicators reflective of that dimension, For example, Positive Classroom Climate includes observable behavioral indictors such as the frequency and quality of teacher affective communications with students (smiles, positive verbal feedback) as well as the degree to which students appear to enjoy spending time with one another.

Empirical support for this organization of classroom processes derives from large-scale studies of several thousand classrooms (Hamre et al., 2007). Drawing from a sample of over just under 4,000 preschool to fifth grade classrooms that were a part of several large national and regional studies, Hamre and colleagues (2007) first examined observational instruments and sorted observed dimensions into the domains described by this three-domain, multi-level framework. Confirmatory factor analysis was used to examine the extent to which this organization of classroom interactions was consistent with actual observations in these settings and to test alternative organizational structures. Results suggested adequate fit of the three-factor model and that the fit of this model was superior to a one- or two-factor model. These findings provide evidence that the three-domain structure suggested by the CLASS Framework (Hamre & Pianta, 2007) fits reasonably well to the natural variation of teacher-child interaction in early education and elementary classrooms.

Finally, evidence has accumulated that measurement of teacher-child interactions using CLASS has shown to be useful in accounting for gains in children's performance on standardized achievement tests assessed at the beginning and end of the year during which their classroom was observed. In pre-kindergarten, teachers' instructional support predicts to gains in vocabulary and literacy that remain stable into kindergarten (Howes et al., 2008; Mashburn et al., 2008). These effects appear stronger for children from low income backgrounds (Burchinal et al, 2008). In the elementary grades, both emotional support and instructional support in first grade account for significant gains in children's performance on literacy assessments, with effects such that children from disadvantaged backgrounds or children demonstrating adjustment problems show the same gains as high achieving students when placed in classrooms rated as high on these dimensions (Hamre & Pianta, 2005). Gazelle (2006) has reported a similar risk-moderating effect of the classroom environment for children with a prior history of anxiety and inhibition. And across the elementary years, emotionally supportive classrooms predict greater gains in children's performance on math achievement tests (Pianta, Belsky, et al., 2008). Thus, a similar pattern of results as was shown for the ECERS has emerged with use of the CLASS as a tool for assessing teacher-child interactions in large-scale studies, which observed features of interaction, both emotional and instructional, regularly account for gains in student performance on achievement tests. Across all these studies, the effect sizes for observational metrics are consistent with the effect sizes for the "teacher effect" in value-added modeling of student achievement data, in the range of d =.15 to .25.

Ecometrics Despite the promise of observational tools to provide a different, policy-relevant lens on teacher quality and effectiveness, there are a number of questions pertaining to standardized classroom observational protocols (Danielson, 1996; Jacob & Lefgren, 2006) that give pause, or at least constrain their widespread and unmonitored use. These issues revolve around reliability and validity. With regard to reliability, questions pertain to decomposing variance attributable to factors such as raters, time of day, time of year, length of observational window, and unit of analysis, all issues that are addressed in ecometric approaches to modeling features of settings (Raudenbush & Sadoff, 2008). In the ecometric modeling framework, each of these parameters is treated as error in models attempting to isolate effects of teachers, and so to the extent they can be modeled in analysis of teacher effects, the precision of prediction improves as does the effect sizes of teacher-related variables (Raudenbush & Sadoff, 2008).

As just one example of the application of the ecometric approach, CLASS ratings from multiple studies across multiple grades were examined in relation to these basic generalizability theory-informed questions. The evidence suggested that indeed rater-related variance, even after raters pass stringent tests for interrater agreement and reliability, are substantial in these global dimensions of classroom interaction, but that such effects are attenuated with increased numbers of raters within a given data collection system, and pale in comparison to time of day and window effects for frequency-related codes (Chomat-Mooney et al., 2008). Indeed the evidence suggests that observational instruments assessing teacher-child interactions do capture aspects of the teacher's behavior that are stable across a specific day, across days, across students, and across content area of instruction.

Clearly, much more research of this type is needed if observational tools are to become a prominent feature in the policy and program development landscape (Jacob & Lefgren, 2006). However, the key point from this discussion, for the purposes of the illustration being presented in this chapter, is that large-scale observational assessments of teacher-child interactions in classrooms are feasible, can be conducted reliably, account for significant proportions of variance in student achievement gains, and can be subjected to rigorous measurement-focused analysis that in turn can be used to improve precision of measurement and estimates of validity. Although these conclusions rest primarily on observations conducted in early childhood and elementary classrooms, they stand as an example of what might also be the case in the K–12 grades.

Epidemiology and Change of Classroom Environments

The health sciences rely heavily on epidemiological studies to provide population estimates of certain conditions and precursors that can be used to both drive health policy as well as research. It is stunning, given the importance of classroom settings, that little-to-no population-level data exist pertaining to exposures to classroom practices either known to relate to academic success or failure, or desired on the basis of certain policies or values. Although there is evidence emerging for early education and elementary classrooms, in secondary classrooms there is no current work that provides national-level, observational data on these environments. Two large national studies conducted over the past 10 years do provide some of the first "epidemiological" data on preschool to fifth grade U.S. classrooms (Early et al., 2005; National Institute of CHild Health and Human Development [NICHD ECCRN], 2002, 2005; Pianta et al., 2005; Pianta, La Paro, & Hamre, 2008).

Overall, these studies suggest that the average child is exposed to moderate levels of emotional support and classroom organization, and fairly low levels of instructional support throughout preschool to elementary school (Early et al., 2005; NICHD ECCRN, 2002, 2005; Pianta et al., 2005, 2008). In general, teachers are fairly positive in their interactions with students and examples of teacher or student negativity are relatively rare (NICHD ECCRN, 2002, 2005). However, these interactions between teachers and students appear to be fairly impersonal, with very few instances in which individual students have positive, one-to-one interactions with their teachers. For example, in fifth-grade classrooms, positive, individual interactions with a teacher occurred in only 1% of observed intervals across a school day (Pianta et al., 2008). The typical student also has few interactions with teachers around behavior management issues in schools, either positive or negative (NICHD ECCRN, 2005). However, one clear indication of problems in classroom organization comes from consistent findings that students spend a great deal of their time in classrooms without being exposed to any learning activity at all, ranging from 42% of the time in preschool classrooms to 30% of time in fifth-grade classrooms. Evidence on the quality of instructional supports is particularly concerning—with consistent evidence that children across grades are unlikely to be exposed to high-quality supports such as concept development and feedback. For example, children in fifth-grade classrooms are exposed to instructional activities (across any content area) that are basic-skill focused in contrast to a focus on analysis, inference, or synthesis of information by a ratio of nearly 5:1 (Pianta, Belsky, Houts, Morrison, & NICHD ECCRN, 2007).

Most notable in these and other studies, however, is the high degree of variability across classrooms. A typical school day for some students includes spending the majority of time engaged in productive instructional activities with caring and responsive adults who consistently provide feedback and challenge students to think critically. For others a typical day consists of spending most of the time sitting around, watching the teacher deal with behavioral problems, and engaged in boring and rote instructional activities such as completing worksheets and spelling tests (Early et al., 2005; NICHD ECCRN, 2002, 2005; Pianta et al., 2005, 2007). These problems of inconsistent exposure to high-quality classrooms are compounded by clear evidence of inequity. Students coming from disadvantaged backgrounds are more likely than their peers to be exposed to poor quality (Hamre & Pianta, 2005; Pianta et al., 2005). Further troubling is evidence that even the student lucky enough to experience a high-quality classroom one year is very unlikely to be systematically exposed to high quality over a period of years, even if they remain in the same school (NICHD ECCRN, 2005; Pianta et al., 2007), suggesting that school-level resources such as professional development supports and school climate are insufficient to ensure high-quality classroom environments. Taken together these studies suggest that very few of the students who are in greatest need of high-quality classroom experiences receive them and the few that do are unlikely to receive them consistently, making it unlikely that the positive effects will be sustained.

In sum, despite the importance of teacher-student interactions in classrooms as an influence on student achievement and other outcomes, the fact that such processes can be reliably assessed and have been shown to predict to achievement, only one major national study has been conducted that provides information on the nature and quality of these key educational assets for large numbers of students. Moreover, this study, although large in nature, is not representative of national or state demographics and actually underrepresents students of color or from families of varying language or economic backgrounds. Although there are no representative studies of classroom environments that could drive education policy, there are literally dozens of large-scale epidemiological studies of health-related inputs that drive policy on health services.

Intervention and Policy A final set of issues to be addressed in this discussion of teacher-student interactions and their consequences for educational policy concerns the extent to which such interactions can be improved and the mechanisms by which such improvement can be engendered. By and large, these issues concern the nature and effectiveness of professional development and certification. At present, there is virtually consensus agreement that the vast machinery of teacher licensing, certification, entry-level and advanced degrees, and in-service professional development plays far to0 little a role in producing achievement gains for students (or effective teacher-student interactions as evinced in the Pianta et al. study described above). The one exception to this pattern is the set of findings showing that teachers with degrees and courses in math tend to produce higher math scores for their students (see Goldhaber, 2008). Rather, the general conclusion to be drawn from this work is that the metrics and processes used in the preparation and certification of teachers are very hard to link, either directly or indirectly, to student achievement gains or to observed effectiveness of teachers' interactions in classrooms. One argument that has been advanced as an explanation for this is that the metrics used to regulate, certify, license, and produce teacher quality are not tied to direct observation (measurement) of what teachers do. And like pre-service teacher preparation in K–12, there is virtually no evidence linking in-service training experiences to children's learning or to observed practices (NICHD ECCRN, 2002, 2005; Walsh & Tracy, 2005; Pianta, La Paro, Payne, Cox, & Bradley, 2002).

Again drawing from the literature in early childhood education, there is evidence that observed teacher-child interactions can change as a function of incentives and policy investments (see Mitchell, in press) and specific interventions focused on coaching and feedback to teachers regarding their behaviors (e.g., Pianta, Mashburn, Downer, Hamre, & Justice, in press; Raver, Jones, Li-Grining, Metzger, Smallwood, & Sardin, 2008; Rimm-Kaufman & Chiu, 2007). For example, the ECERS-R forms the basis of a number of higher education-based initiatives in teacher preparation, including coursework. Several of these have been evaluated and shown to be promising avenues for producing higher-rated classroom settings (www.fpg.unc.

edu/ECERS). Recently there has been exponential growth in the use of observational tools such as the ECERS as program monitoring and improvement tools in the context of government regulation. States such as Colorado, North Carolina, Tennessee, and Louisiana use systematic, periodic observationally based data collection in their program quality monitoring systems, with findings from these observations (using the ECERS) triggering program development and professional development, as well as entering the public record in market-based systems for informing consumers about quality. In short, in the realm of early childhood education, standardized observational monitoring of teacher behavior, periodically conducted, is mandated by state policy and tied to resource allocation decisions, precisely some of the issues that are the focus of K–12 school reform effects (Jacob & Lefgren, 2006). Perhaps it is time for K–12 to consider these possibilities.

Policy Implications

Drawing from the lessons from the early education sector, there is a reasonable body of evidence (see Gordon et al., 2006; Jones, Brown, & Aber, 2008; McCaslin et al., 2006; Pianta et al., 2007) that teachers' performance in classrooms, in terms of their actual behavioral interactions with students, can be assessed observationally using standardized protocols, analyzed systematically with regard to various sources of error and in turn shown to be valid for predicting student learning gains, changed (improved) as a function of specific and aligned supports provided to teachers, and that exposure to such supports is predictive of greater student learning gains. Although modest, these effects are robust and consistent across investigator groups, samples of teachers, and samples of students that vary by grade and socioeconomic and geographic background. They are particularly strong with regard to early education teachers and classrooms, where these ideas and tools have been scaled into policy frameworks. Below we briefly summarize the implications of this work for policy.

Research Policy A major and unique advantage of observational assessments of teachers for leveraging improvements in educational outcomes is that they can be directly related to the investigation and experimentation of specific interventions aimed at improving teaching. For this reason, these methods have considerable promise. Yet measurement challenges, some of which are noted above pertaining to psychometric issues, are not inconsequential. In addition to those challenges described earlier, observational assessments require technical supports that enhance efficiency and lower costs when used at scale. The questions related to psychometrics, efficiency, and costs compel attention and rigorous study, yet the investment in research related to assessments of such "inputs" pale in comparison to research investments in outcomes, specifically standardized tests. Nevertheless, recent Institute of Education Sciences' requests for applications do include research centers on

teacher effectiveness and specific topical areas on teacher quality; however, the assessment and measurement goals in the IES framework do not include research on assessment of teachers' performance in classrooms.

It seems important that investment in measurement studies, cost efficiency studies, investigations of the determinants and regulators of the quality of teacher-child interactions, and the value of teacher preparation programs for improving such interactions, could be key areas for research and development support. Studies could identify early predictors of teacher competence, effective supports that improve teaching, virtual reality environments that accelerate teacher development, and networks of teacher preparation programs studying the natural history and course of teachers' competence in these performance domains. Again drawing from the early childhood world, although this work could indeed be informed by value-added metrics of teacher quality and effectiveness, the route to eventual useful interventions and tools will be quicker and perhaps more efficient if focused on teacher-child interactions (see Mashburn et al., 2008).

Education Policy Here is it is important to recognize the limitations of the work described above—measurement issues, small effect sizes, and logistic challenges that impede efficiency and scalability. Yet despite these challenges, the consistency and nature of the results suggests several implications for education policy, and again the lessons are clear from use in the early childhood sector (Mitchell, in press) that standardized observations of settings can indeed be a tool used by policy that results in improvement of classroom settings' value for learning and as well as gains in child outcomes.

In the realm of accountability, teacher quality and teacher effectiveness are critical "inputs" that counterbalance the focus on student achievement outcomes and potentially address value-laden issues such as equality of opportunity. Given the rather meager results related to teacher characteristics such as education, training, and experience as they relate to outcomes, the results presented herein with regard to observational metrics merit attention as a complementary feature of a comprehensive system.

With regard to production of effective teaching, using teacher preparation programs, and credentialing and licensing systems, observational metrics have potential to provide anchors in actual performance that could be used to drive these systems toward higher levels of impact on student performance (providing the observation system is validated). Furthermore, if these systems used observations of performance as an outcome or competence metric, it is highly likely that collateral professional development supports would be developed that were oriented to producing performance at levels specified in licensing and credentialing systems. Finally, performance-based metrics anchored in observations in classrooms may also be compatible with market-based approaches to incentivizing performance such as merit pay structures.

Thus, on the one hand, standardized observational approaches to measuring teacher performance represent a credible complement to the current focus on teacher credentials and degrees, and value-added metrics of student performance, on the other. Furthermore, observational approaches may link more easily to systems of producing teaching that in the long run, despite costs and logistic challenges, they represent an alternative that has greater long-range benefits for building capacity and quality.

References

Anderson, S. (2008). *Teacher career choices: Timing of teacher careers among 1992–93 bachelor's degree recipients* (NCES 2008-153). Washington, DC: National Center for Education Statistics.

Appalachian Regional Advisory Committee (ARAC). (2005, March 31). *Education challenges and technical assistance needs of the Appalachian region.* Washington, DC: Author.

Battistich, V., Watson, M., Solomon, D., Lewis, C., & Schaps, E. (1999). Beyond the three R's: A broader agenda for school reform. *The Elementary School Journal, 99,* 415–429.

Bogard, K., & Takanishi, R. (2005). PK-3: An aligned and coordinated approach to education for children 3 to 8 years old. *SRCD Social Policy Report, 19*(3), 1–23.

Bogner, K., Raphael, L., & Pressley, M. (2002). How grade 1 teachers motivate literate activity by their students. *Scientific Studies of Reading, 6,* 135–165.

Bronfenbrenner, U., & Morris, P. A. (1998). The ecology of developmental processes. In W. Damon & R. M. Lerner (Eds.), *Handbook of child psychology: Vol. 1. Theoretical models of human development* (5th ed., pp. 993–1029). New York: Wiley.

Brophy, J. E. (1999). *Teaching* (Educational Practices Series-1). Geneva, Switzerland: International Academy of Education and International Bureau of Education, UNESCO.

Brophy, J. E., & Good, T. (1986). Teacher behavior and student achievement. In M. Wittrock (Ed.), *Handbook of research on teaching* (3rd ed., pp. 328–375). New York: Macmillan.

Burchinal, M., Howes, C., Pianta, R., Bryant, D., Early, D., Clifford, R. et al. (2008). Predicting child outcomes at the end of kindergarten from the quality of pre-kindergarten teacher-child interactions and instruction. *Applied Developmental Science, 12,* 140–153.

Burchinal, M. R., Peisner-Feinberg, E., Bryant, D. M., & Clifford, R. (2000). Children's social and cognitive development and child care quality: Testing for different associations related to poverty, gender, or ethnicity. *Journal of Applied Developmental Sciences, 4,* 149–165.

Burchinal, M. R., Peisner-Feinberg, E., Pianta, R., & Howes, C. (2002). Development of academic skills from preschool through second grade: Family and classroom predictors of developmental trajectories. *Journal of School Psychology, 40,* 415–436.

Chomat-Mooney, L. I., Pianta, R. C., Hamre, B. K., Mashburn, A. J., Luckner, A. E., Grimm, K. J., et al. (2008). *A practical guide for conducting classroom observations: A summary of issues and evidence for researchers.* Charlottesville: University of Virginia.

Clotfelter, C., Ladd, H., & Vigdor, J. (2007). *Teacher credentials and student achievement in high school: A cross-subject analysis with student fixed effects* (NBER Working Paper No. 13617). Cambridge, MA: National Bureau of Economic Research.

Cochran-Smith, M., & Zeichner, K. (Eds.). (2005). *Studying teaching education: The report of the AERA panel on research and teacher education.* Mahwah, NJ: Erlbaum.

Danielson, C. (1996). *Enhancing professional practice: A framework for teaching.* Alexandria, VA: Association for Supervision and Curriculum Development.

Domitrovich, C. E., & Greenberg, M. T. (2004). Preventive interventions with young children: Building on the foundation of early intervention programs. *Early Education and Development, 15,* 365–370.

Early, D., Barbarin, O., Bryant, B., Burchinal, M., Chang, F., Clifford, R. et al. (2005). *Pre-kindergarten in eleven states: NCEDL's multi-state study of pre-kindergarten and state-wide early educational programs (SWEEP) study.* Retrieved September 30, 2005, from http://www.fcd-us.org/usr_doc/Prekindergartenin11States.pdf

Eccles, J. S., & Roeser, R. W. (1999). School and community influences on human development. In M. H. Bornstein & M. E. Lamb (Eds.), *Developmental psychology: An advanced textbook* (4th ed., pp. 503–554). Mahwah, NJ: Erlbaum.

Educational Testing Service (ETS). (2004). *Where we stand on teacher quality: An issue paper from ETS.* Retrieved February 15, 2006, from http://www.ets.org/Media/News_and_Media/position_paper.pdf

Foundation for Child Development (FCD). (2005). *Getting there: PK-3 as public education's base camp.* New York: Author.

Gage, N. L. (1978). *The scientific basis of the art of teaching.* New York: Teachers College Press.

Gazelle, H. (2006). Class climate moderates peer relations and emotional adjustment in children with an early childhood history of anxious solitude: A child-by-environment model. *Developmental Psychology, 42,* 1179–1192.

Goldhaber, D. (2008). Teachers matter, but effective teacher quality policies are elusive. In H. F. Ladd & E. B. Fiske (Eds.), *Handbook of research in education finance and policy* (pp. 146–165). New York: Routledge.

Gordon, R., Kane, T. J., & Staiger, D. O. (2006). *Identifying effective teachers using performance on the job* (Discussion Paper No. 2006-01). Washington, DC: The Hamilton Project, Brookings Institution.

Hamre, B. K., & Pianta, R. C. (2005). Can instructional and emotional support in the first grade classroom make a difference for children at risk of school failure? *Child Development, 76,* 949–967.

Hamre, B. K., & Pianta, R. C. (2007). Learning opportunities in preschool and early elementary classrooms. In R. Pianta, M. Cox, & K. Snow (Eds.), *School readiness and the transition to kindergarten in the era of accountability* (pp. 49–84). Baltimore: Brookes.

Hamre, B. K., Pianta, R. C., Mashburn, A. J., & Downer, J. T. (2007). *Building a science of classrooms: Application of the CLASS framework in over 4,000 U.S. early childhood and elementary classrooms.* New York: Foundation for Child Development.

Hanushek, E. A. (2002). *The long run importance of school quality* (NBER Working Paper No. W9071). Cambridge, MA: National Bureau of Economic Research.

Harms, T., Clifford, R. M., & Cryer, D. (1998). *Early Childhood Environment Rating Scale* (Rev. ed.). New York: Teachers College Press.

Howes, C., Burchinal, M., Pianta, R., Bryant, D., Early, D., Clifford, R., et al. (2008). Ready to learn? Children's pre-academic achievement in pre-kindergarten programs. *Early Childhood Research Quarterly, 23,* 27–50.

Jacob, B., & Lefgren, L. (2006). When principals rate teachers: The best—and the worst—stand out. *Education Next, 6*(2), 58–64.

Jones, S. M., Brown, J. L., & Aber, J. L. (2008). Classroom settings as targets of intervention and research. In M. Shinn & H. Yoshikawa (Eds.), *The power of social settings: Transforming schools and community organizations to enhance youth development* (pp. 58–79). New York: Oxford University.

Ladd, H. F. (2008, May). *Teacher effects: What do we know?* Paper presented at the Teacher Quality Conference, Evanston, IL.

Lasley, T. J., II, Siedentop, D., & Yinger, R. (2006). A systemic approach to enhancing teacher quality: The Ohio Model. *Journal of Teacher Education, 57,* 13–21.

Mashburn, A. J., Pianta, R. C., Hamre, B. K., Downer, J. T., Barbarin, O., Bryant, D., et al. (2008). Measures of classroom quality in prekindergarten and children's development of academic, language, and social skills. *Child Development, 79,* 732–749.

McCaslin, M., Good, T. L., Nichols, S., Zhang, J., Hummel, C., Bozack, A. R., et al. (2006). Comprehensive school reform: An observational study of teaching in grades 3 through 5. *Elementary School Journal, 106,* 313–331.

Mitchell, A. (in press). Quality rating and improvement systems. In C.

Howes & R. Pianta (Eds.), *Pre-kindergarten in the United States.* Baltimore: Brookes.

National Institute of Child Health and Human Development, Early Child Care Research Network (NICHD ECCRN). (2002). The relation of global first-grade classroom environment to structural classroom features and teacher and student behaviors. *The Elementary School Journal, 102,* 367–387.

National Institute of Child Health and Human Development, Early Child Care Research Network (NICHD ECCRN). (2005). A day in third grade: A large-scale study of classroom quality and teacher and student behavior. *The Elementary School Journal, 105,* 305–323.

Nye, B., Konstantopoulos, S., & Hedges, L. (2004). How large are teacher effects? *Educational Evaluation and Policy Analysis, 26,* 237–257.

Peisner-Feinberg, E. S., & Burchinal, M. R. (1997). Relations between preschool children's child-care experiences and concurrent development: The cost, quality, and outcomes study. *Merrill-Palmer Quarterly, 43,* 451–477.

Peisner-Feinberg, E. S., Burchinal, M. R., Clifford, R. M., Culkin, M. L., Howes, C., & Kagan, S. L. (2001). The relation of preschool child care quality to children's cognitive and social developmental trajectories through second grade. *Child Development, 72,* 1534–1553.

Pianta, R., Belsky, J., Houts, R., Morrison, F., & NICHD ECCRN. (2007). Opportunities to learn in America's elementary classrooms. *Science, 315,* 1795–1796.

Pianta, R. C., Belsky, J., Vandergrift, N., Houts, R., Morrision, F., & NICHD ECCRN. (2008). Classroom effects on children's achievement trajectories in elementary school. *American Educational Research Journal, 45,* 365–397.

Pianta, R. C., Howes, C., Burchinal, M., Bryant, D., Clifford, R., Early, D., et al. (2005). Features of pre-kindergarten programs, classrooms, and teachers: Do they predict observed classroom quality and child-teacher interactions? *Applied Developmental Science, 9,* 144–159.

Pianta, R. C., La Paro, K., & Hamre, B. K. (2008). *Classroom Assessment Scoring System (CLASS).* Baltimore: Brookes.

Pianta, R. C., La Paro, K., Payne, C., Cox, M., & Bradley, R. (2002). The relation of kindergarten classroom environment to teacher, family, and school characteristics and child outcomes. *Elementary School Journal, 102,* 225–238.

Pianta, R., Mashburn, A., Downer, J., Hamre, B., & Justice, L. (in press). Effects of web-mediated professional development resources on teacher-child interactions in pre-kindergarten classrooms. *Early Childhood Research Quarterly.*

Pressley, M., Allington, R., Wharton-McDonald, R., Block, C. C., & Morrow, L. M. (2001). *Learning to read: Lessons from exemplary first grades.* New York: Guilford.

Pressley, M., Roehrig, A. D., Raphael, L. M., Dolezal, S. E., Bohn, C., Mohan, L. et al. (2003). Teaching processes in elementary and secondary education. In W. M. Reynolds & G. E. Miller (Eds.), *Handbook of psychology, Vol. 7: Educational psychology* (pp. 153–175). New York: Wiley.

Raudenbush, S., & Sadoff, S. (2008). Statistical inference when classroom quality is measured with error. *Journal of Research on Educational Effectiveness, 1,* 138–154.

Raver, C. C., Jones, S. M., Li-Grining, C., Metzger, M., Smallwood, K., & Sardin, L. (2008). Improving preschool classroom processes: Preliminary findings from a randomized trial implemented in Head Start settings. *Early Childhood Research Quarterly, 63,* 253–255.

Rimm-Kaufman, S. E., & Chiu, Y. I. (2007). Promoting social and academic competence in the classroom: An intervention study examining the contribution of the Responsive Classroom approach. *Psychology in the Schools, 44,* 397–413.

Rivkin, S. G., Hanushek, E. A., & Kain, J. F. (2005). Teachers, schools, and academic achievement. *Econometrica, 73,* 417–458.

Rockoff, J. (2004). The impact of individual teachers on student achievement: Evidence from panel data. *American Economic Review, 94,* 247–252.

Shinn, M., & Yoshikawa, H. (Eds.). (2008). *The power of social settings: Promoting youth development by changing schools and community programs.* New York: Oxford University Press.

Soar, R. S., & Soar, R. M. (1979). Emotional climate and management. In P. Peterson & H. Walberg (Eds.), *Research on teaching: Concepts, findings and implications* (pp. 97–119). Berkeley, CA: McCutchan.

Tseng, V., & Seidman, E. (2007). A systems framework for understanding social settings. *American Journal of Community Psychology, 39,* 217–228.

Walsh, K., & Tracy, C. O. (2005). *Increasing the odds: How good policies can yield better teachers.* Washington, DC: National Council on Teacher Quality.

Wharton-McDonald, R., Pressley, M., & Hampston, J. M. (1998). Outstanding literacy instruction in first grade: Teacher practices and student achievement. *Elementary School Journal, 99,* 101–128.

51

Closing Achievement Gaps

GEORGE FARKAS
University of California, Irvine

Introduction

Social class-based educational and/or cognitive achievement gaps have long been with us. In all societies, and during all time periods (at least since the Industrial Revolution), adults with greater social status, income, wealth, power, and better living and working conditions have been, on average, better educated and higher performing in the cognitive skills associated with such education, than those with lower social status. They have also generally succeeded in passing these educational advantages on to their children. Thus, if cognitive achievement tests were given to the children of the haves and the have-nots across multiple nations and time periods, studies of achievement gaps and efforts to close them might be a universal phenomenon.

However, such data collection and public policy discussion exercises have rarely, if ever, been undertaken. Indeed, the U.S. focus on national, state, and school-level test results at the beginning of the 21st century, the ubiquitous public discussion of "achievement gaps" between ethnic minority and White students, or between low-income and middle-class students, and the enormous pressure on the schools to narrow these gaps, is unique in world history. In this chapter we examine the reasons for this focus, the causes and characteristics of the gaps uncovered, the efforts and progress that have been made to close these gaps, and implications for educational policy in the years ahead.

Post-World War II interest in group differences in cognitive achievement was stimulated by Michael Young's (1958) focus on intelligence as a determinant of social achievement in his book, *The Rise of the Meritocracy*. This was followed by Arthur Jensen's (1969) *Harvard Education Review* article, "How much can we boost IQ and scholastic achievement?" Jensen argued that the answer was "not much," since intelligence is strongly determined by genetics. This occasioned responses from Jencks et al. (1972, 1979) and Bowles and Gintis (1976). Jencks et al. presented evidence that while test scores *do* affect socioeconomic attainment,

so too do "non-cognitive traits" such as work habits, leadership, and other personality traits. Bowles and Gintis argued that such non-cognitive traits and behaviors are far more important than test scores, and that both working-class parents and schools in working-class neighborhoods seek to inculcate into working-class students the traits of rule-following and docility that they will need for success within the capitalist factory system. Meanwhile, in 1966, President Johnson's War on Poverty funded programs such as Head Start and Title I (of the Elementary and Secondary Education Act), with the intention of raising the school achievement of low-income students.

Data on achievement and achievement gaps have been collected by the National Center for Education Statistics and other agencies at least since the 1970s, but the subject faded somewhat from public and scholarly discussion until it gained renewed attention from publication of Herrnstein and Murray's (1994) volume, *The Bell Curve*. These authors argued, with extensive data analyses, that test scores are key determinants of socioeconomic success. They also argued that test scores are genetically determined, so that they are passed from parent to child by biological inheritance, and cannot be significantly changed by social interventions. Herrnstein and Murray emphasized the large magnitude of Black-White differences in test scores, which had remained substantial over a long time period.

At least partly in reaction, Jencks and Phillips (1998) published a wide-ranging set of scholarly papers focusing on the determinants and consequences of the Black-White test score gap. This greatly increased detailed empirical knowledge of the magnitude and determinants of the gap, as measured at any particular point in time, and as it evolved over time. In addition, Arrow, Bowles, and Durlauf (2000) and Bowles, Gintis, and Groves (2005) published collections of papers further examining the role of cognitive skills and noncognitive traits and behaviors as determinants of socioeconomic inequality.

Also during the 1990s, President Bill Clinton built on

scholarly and policy-oriented discussion and research that had been ongoing since *A Nation at Risk* was published in 1983, proclaiming that cognitive skills are crucial to the nation's competitiveness and productivity, as well as to upward mobility for America's workers. He emphasized efforts to improve educational outcomes, and announced a Reading Initiative focused on improving basic reading skills among elementary school students, particularly those from low-income households.

This emphasis was continued by President George W. Bush. When, shortly after his election, the Elementary and Secondary Education Act (ESEA) came up for its scheduled reauthorization, the Bush administration worked with Senator Ted Kennedy and a bipartisan group of senators to pass a revision titled No Child Left Behind (NCLB). This declared many ambitious goals, including all children proficient in reading and mathematics by the close of the 2013–2014 academic year. Concretely, it required the states to set specific achievement-level goals on reading and mathematics assessments, and for all schools and districts and all subgroups of students within these schools and districts to make "adequate yearly progress" (AYP) toward the goal of 100% proficiency. Subgroups that must each make AYP include low-income students, those belonging to racial or ethnic minorities, students with disabilities or limited English proficiency, and others. Schools receiving Title I funds that fail to make AYP for several years face a variety of interventions, including the provision of Supplemental Educational Services (SES) for their students (typically after-school tutoring), parental options to move their students to other schools (taking their tuition with them), as well as possible restructuring, state takeover, or management by private firms. One consequence has been that the NCLB requirement to close achievement gaps, both nationally and within every district and school, has created a more intense public focus on these gaps than was the case previously.

Achievement Gaps over the Educational Life Course

The Preschool Period An important feature of achievement gaps for low-income and ethnic minority children is that they first develop in the preschool period. The cognitive skills that teachers want students to have at the beginning of kindergarten include, on the pre-reading side, oral vocabulary knowledge, letter-sound knowledge, and phonological awareness (particularly the ability to identify the beginning sounds in spoken words). On the pre-mathematics side they include knowledge of shapes, numbers, and simple counting. The National Longitudinal Survey of Youth, 1979 Cohort (NLSY79) and the Infant Health and Development (IHDP) surveys administered vocabulary tests to preschool children in the 1980s and 1990s. The ECLS-K administered tests of these skills to a national sample of children entering kindergarten in 1998. The results showed that, on average, the highest scores were earned by Asians, followed in order by Whites, African Americans, and Hispanics. The magnitudes of the racial gaps are shown in Table 51.1.

TABLE 51.1

Reading, Mathematics, and Behavior Gaps when School Begins, Selected Estimates (standard deviation units)

	White-Black	White-Hispanic
PPVT-R, NLSY79	1.15	
PPVT-R, IHDP	1.63	
Reading Test, ECLS-K	0.40	0.43
Math Test, ECLS-K^2	0.64	0.72
Approaches to Learning, ECLS-K	0.36	0.21

Source: Collected by Rock & Stenner (2005) ^{2}Fryer & Levitt (2004)

The gaps are measured in standard deviation units, with Whites as the reference category. The largest gaps are found for oral language vocabulary, with the Black-White gap being more than one standard deviation. For supporting analyses of the NLSY79 data, showing that Black-White oral vocabulary gaps are already large as early as 36 months of age, see Jencks and Phillips (1998) and Farkas and Beron (2004). These results are important, because the finding that large achievement gaps begin so early suggests that preschool programs will be an important feature of public policies designed to close the gaps.

Perhaps the most recent large sample evidence concerning this issue comes from the Early Childhood Longitudinal Study-Kindergarten Cohort (ECLS-K), which tested a large nationally representative sample of kindergartners in the fall of 1998. The ECLS-K reading test shows African Americans averaging 0.40 standard deviation, and Hispanics averaging 0.43 standard deviation, below Whites. The mathematics gaps are 0.64 and 0.72 standard deviation, respectively. However, these are simple mean differences between the groups. When they are adjusted for social class, family structure, parenting behaviors, birth weight, and other determinants of child outcomes, these gaps decline to only approximately one-sixth this size. This suggests that preschool interventions aimed to supplement the parental instruction received by low-income children may be able to significantly narrow these gaps.

This study also asked teachers to report on the behaviors of their students. This is important because success at formal schooling requires that the student have appropriate learning-related behaviors. In the ECLS-K, this was estimated by a scale called Approaches to Learning, comprising measures of attentiveness, ability to focus, flexibility, organization, eagerness to learn, and independence. As we see in Table 51.1, Whites score 0.36 standard deviation higher than African Americans, and 0.21 standard deviation higher than Hispanics, on this scale. Table 51.2 examines race/ethnicity gaps in these behaviors in greater detail, using three items from the Approaches scale—persists at tasks, seems eager to learn, and pays attention.

We see that 75% of White kindergartners are rated by their teachers as persisting at tasks. Comparable figures are 67% for Hispanics and 61% for Blacks. Similar race gaps are observed for "seems eager to learn" and "pays

TABLE 51.2
Percentage of Students Demonstrating Specific Learning-Related Behaviors when Schooling Begins

	White	Black	Hispanic
Persists at Tasks	75	61	67
Seems Eager to Learn	79	66	72
Pays Attention	70	56	62

Source: West, Denton, and Reaney (2001: Table 7)

attention." These emotional and behavioral maturity measures—key features of school engagement—are, alongside academic readiness, key determinants of elementary school achievement (Duncan, Dowsett et al., 2007). Also, as with academic readiness, race/ethnic gaps in these behaviors narrow substantially after social class, parenting behaviors, birth weight and related variables are controlled (Duncan & Magnuson, 2005; Reichman, 2005; Brooks-Gunn & Markman, 2005). Thus, well-designed preschool programs can be expected to improve these behaviors by the beginning of kindergarten (Magnuson & Waldfogel, 2005). Phillips, Crouse, & Ralph (1998) found that half the twelfth grade Black-White achievement gap came into existence during the preschool period, so that narrowing or eliminating this preschool gap will likely be an important feature of future policy efforts.

Achievement Gaps in Elementary School Table 51.3 shows the National Assessment of Educational Progress (NAEP) performance levels and the magnitude of the reading and mathematics achievement gaps for African American and Hispanic students aged 9 in 2004, when most were in fourth grade. These scores, and other NAEP results presented here, are from the Long Term Trend Data, which are comparable across time.

White students averaged a score of 226 in reading. Black and Hispanic students scored, respectively, 26 and 21 points lower. White students averaged 247 in mathematics, with Black and Hispanic students 23 and 17 points below them. These achievement gaps are substantial and are generally somewhat larger for African American than for Hispanic students.

How important, in practical terms, are these gaps? One way to gain some perspective on this is to look at achievement on the specific skill measures underlying the composite scales used in the ECLS-K data collection. One such measure is mastery of multiplication and division,

TABLE 51.3
Reading and Mathematics NAEP Scores and Gaps for White, Black, and Hispanic Students Aged 9 in 2004

	White	Black (Gap)	Hispanic (Gap)
Reading	226	200 **(26)**	205 **(21)**
Mathematics	247	224 **(23)**	230 **(17)**

Source: Retrieved from Long-Term Trends Data at http://nces.gov/nationsreportcard/nde on 2/23/2008.

from the mathematics assessment. When measured in spring 2002 for the ECLS-K study sample of students 3 years after kindergarten, 84% of Whites and 75% of Hispanics had achieved mastery of multiplication and division. However, only 58% of African Americans had achieved such mastery (Rathbun & West, 2004). These are the sorts of important gaps in practical skills, occurring for higher level skills at higher grade levels, which underlie the important White-Black and White-Hispanic achievement gaps.

Fitting growth curve models to the ECLS-K data for the same children as they age from the fall of kindergarten through spring of first grade, Downey, von Hippel, and Broh (2004) have shown that attending school *does* matter for cognitive achievement. All students learn significantly more when school is in session than during the summer. And individual achievement inequalities tend to increase less when school is in session than during the summer; that is, they are decreased by schooling. As for trends in race/ethnic group achievement gaps as children age, these calculations show that, when school is in session between approximately September and June, these gaps tend to increase for African Americans and stay relatively unchanged for Hispanics.

The finding that the Black-White cognitive skills gap is not only significant when schooling begins, but also widens substantially as children move up through the grade levels, was first reported by Phillips et al. (1998), utilizing a variety of data sets. The ECLS-K calculations presented by Downey et al. (2004) further corroborate this result. Both sets of authors also report that the reasons for this finding are somewhat mysterious—most variables show little ability to explain the increasing gap. And yet, some variables are obvious candidates for this task. To learn successfully, students need adequate basic skills, a good quantity and quality of instruction, an appropriate level of attentiveness and effort, and parental support. Yet, as compared to Whites, African American students begin school with lower basic skills, lower attentiveness and effort, typically come from a single-parent family with very much lower SES, and typically attend lower quality schools. These factors likely play a role in the lower gains of African American students during grades K–12.

Achievement Gaps in Middle and High School Table 51.4 shows NAEP results for students aged 13 and 17 in 2004. We see that as students move up through the grade levels, from age 9 to 13, and from age 13 to 17, their scale scores in reading and mathematics rise substantially. This occurs in a roughly parallel manner for the three race/ethnic groups, so that achievement gaps generally remain in the 17–30 point range observed among 9-year-olds. There is, however, a tendency for these gaps to be largest among 17-year-olds, particularly in reading, where for both African Americans and Hispanics, they approach 30 points. Neal (2006) compared the detailed test score distributions of White and Black teenagers, using both NAEP data and data from the Armed Forces Qualification Test available

TABLE 51.4
Reading and Mathematics NAEP Scores and Gaps for White, Black, and Hispanic Students Aged 13 and 17 in 2004

	White	Black (Gap)	Hispanic (Gap)
Reading			
Age 13	266	244 (**22**)	242 (**24**)
Age 17	293	264 (**29**)	264 (**29**)
Mathematics			
Age 13	288	262 (**26**)	265 (**23**)
Age 17	313	286 (**27**)	289 (**24**)

Source: Retrieved from Long-Term Trends Data at http://nces.gov/nationsreportcard/nde on 2/23/2008.

on the NLSY79 and NLSY97 databases. He found that, in general, the median Black score fell at about the 20th percentile of the White distribution. Only a very small percentage of African Americans achieved a score falling within the top 25% of White scores. These results highlight the large magnitude of the continuing achievement gaps between the groups.

Since White 17-year-olds have higher academic achievement than African American and Hispanic 17-year-olds, it is not surprising that Whites also have higher enrollment in, and graduation rates from, 4-year colleges. Whites also have higher grade point averages in college. Further, the wage premium for a 4-year college degree versus a high school degree has been increasing over time, and, in our technologically demanding economy, continues to increase. Thus, increased economic advancement for African Americans and Hispanics, and a closing of the economic gaps between these groups and Whites, will require increased college success for African Americans and Hispanics, and a narrowing of the gaps between the college graduation rates of Whites and each of these groups.

A great many factors underlie the academic achievement differentials examined above. African American, Hispanic, and White students generally live in different neighborhoods, attend different schools, belong to different peer groups, and are being raised by families with different economic, social, and cultural experiences and resources. To date, and despite much effort, researchers have not achieved definitive estimates of the separate contributions of teachers, instructional curricula, school policies, peers, parents, and other factors to these achievement patterns and gaps. For reviews of these research efforts, see Jencks and Phillips (1998), Chubb and Loveless (2002), and Neal (2006). For the argument that a central issue in closing achievement gaps is the need to improve the parenting skills and behaviors of African American parents, see Ferguson (2005).

Trends in Achievement Gaps

The achievement gaps shown in Table 51.3 and Table 51.4 are large in magnitude. When the full distribution of student scores is examined for each race/ethnic group, we find

that the great majority of African American and Hispanic students perform well below the average level of White students, and below national grade-level standards for instruction (Farkas, 1996; Neal, 2006). As a consequence, African American and Hispanic students have higher school dropout, retention in grade, and special education placement rates than Whites. They also have lower high school grade point averages, lower college enrollment, lower college grade point averages, and lower college graduation rates than Whites. As a consequence, they have lower occupational attainment and earnings trajectories than Whites.

For all of these reasons, there is a great desire to narrow and ultimately eliminate these achievement gaps. With the enactment of NCLB, it was made national policy to do so. And certainly, efforts to narrow these gaps have been ongoing for a great many years. In this section we look at how these gaps have changed over time, as well as some of the demographic trends that affect these changes.

Table 51.5 shows over-time trends in reading and mathematics NAEP scores (from the Long-Term Trend NAEP data) for 13-year-olds. Focusing on this age group allows us to examine achievement for students who have had about 8 years of formal schooling, while avoiding distortions due to missing data for students who drop out in high school.

In reading, White students gained little between 1980 and 2004. By contrast, African Americans showed significant reading gains during this period, with greater gains during the 1980s than subsequently. The result was a significant narrowing of the Black-White reading gap during this time period. Hispanics also gained in reading, but not by as much as African Americans. By 2004, the Black and Hispanic reading gaps were similar—approximately 23 points.

Mathematics is a different story, with Whites showing significant gains, from an average score of 272 in 1978 to 288 in 2004, with most of these gains occurring after 1990. Fortunately for gap closing, both African Americans and Hispanics increased their mathematics performance even more rapidly than Whites during this period. Both groups made strong gains from 1978 to 1990, and from 1990 to 2004. As

TABLE 51.5
Reading and Mathematics NAEP Scores and Gaps for White, Black, and Hispanic Students, Age 13, Trends Over Time

	White	Black (Gap)	Hispanic (Gap)
Reading			
1980	264	233 (**31**)	237 (**27**)
1990	262	241 (**21**)	238 (**24**)
2004	266	244 (**22**)	242 (**24**)
Mathematics			
1978	272	230 (**42**)	238 (**34**)
1990	276	249 (**27**)	255 (**21**)
2004	288	262 (**26**)	265 (**23**)

Source: Retrieved from Long-Term Trends Data at http://nces.gov/nationsreportcard/nde on 2/23/2008.

a consequence, mathematics gaps in 2004 were at a similar level to those for reading—in the 23–26 point range.

These patterns of over-time growth remind us that closing achievement gaps requires catching a moving target—to narrow their achievement gaps with Whites, Blacks and Hispanics must actually improve their performance *more rapidly* than Whites. Their ability to do so at least partly depends on the parental resources that these groups have available for their children. We now examine how these have varied over time.

As has been demonstrated by many studies, parental education is a particularly powerful determinant of children's academic achievement. Further, we know that (a) at any one point in time, African American and Hispanic adults have lower average educational levels than Whites, and (b) adults born in this country at later time periods have trended upward in their levels of completed education. Table 51.6 uses census data to show how the details of these patterns evolved between 1980 and 2000.

Between 1980 and 2000, the share of White adults at least 25 years of age with at least a high school education rose from 69% to 84%, so that by 2000, only 16% did not have at least this level of schooling. For African Americans, the percentage rose even more dramatically, from 51% to 72%. By contrast, Hispanic adults with a high school education rose from 44% to 52%. This slower rate of Hispanic educational growth was likely due to the recently high rate of immigration by less-well-educated Latin Americans.

During this period, the share of Whites with at least a college education rose from 17% to 26%. For African Americans this rate rose from 8% to 14%, and for Hispanics, from 8% to 10%. Thus, the average educational attainment of adults in all groups moved upward, with Whites maintaining, and in some cases increasing, their educational lead over African Americans and Hispanics. As a consequence, White parents have, on average, greater educational resources to draw on in assisting their children with school achievement. This at least partly explains the rising educational performance of all children, and the fact that efforts to close the achievement gaps between Whites and the other groups must cope with the fact that White performance is a moving target, which is likely to

TABLE 51.6

Trends in the Educational Attainment of Adults 25 and Over, by Race/Ethnicity

	White %	Black %	Hispanic %
HS or Higher			
1980	68.8	51.2	44.0
1990	77.9	63.1	49.8
2000	83.6	72.3	52.4
BA or Higher			
1980	17.1	8.4	7.6
1990	21.5	11.4	9.2
2000	26.1	14.3	10.4

Source: U.S. Census.

TABLE 51.7

Trends in the Percent of Children under 18 Living with Two Parents, by Race/Ethnicity

	White %	Black %	Hispanic %
1980	82.7	42.2	75.4
1990	79.0	37.7	66.8
2000	75.3	37.6	65.1

Source: U.S. Census.

continue to increase, if only because of the continuously rising educational level of White parents.

Of course, parental resources include more than parental educational levels. They also include the time and money available to parents to keep their household in order, with everyone's needs being met. Central to this is the number of parents in the household—single-parent households with children are typically under enormous physical and financial strain, particularly when compared with two-parent households. And it has been shown that single-parent households produce less positive child outcomes than do two-parent households (McLanahan & Sandefur, 1994). Table 51.7 shows trends in the percentage of children living in two-parent households for each of the race/ethnic groups.

For all groups, the share of children in two-parent households declined between 1980 and 2000. For Whites in 2000, 75% of children were being raised in two-parent households. By contrast, 65% of Hispanic children and 38% of African American were being raised in such households. The latter figure is particularly striking. Almost two-thirds of African American children are being raised under the stressful conditions typically experienced by single-parent households. This will continue to present a serious obstacle to efforts to close achievement gaps for these children.

Thus we see that the demographic composition of African American, Hispanic, and White households has been changing over time, and these changes affect the achievement levels of these groups. One way to get a clearer picture of these changing achievement levels is to control at least a portion of the compositional effects by examining over-time

TABLE 51.8

Reading and Mathematics NAEP Scores and Gaps for White, Black, and Hispanic 13-Year Olds Whose Parents Had a High School Education, Trends Over Time

	White	Black (Gap)	Hispanic (Gap)
Reading			
1980	258	232 (**26**)	240 (**18**)
1990	256	236 (**20**)	238 (**18**)
2004	258	239 (**19**)	243 (**15**)
Mathematics			
1978	268	232 (**36**)	244 (**24**)
1990	267	247 (**20**)	253 (**14**)
2004	279	253 (**26**)	264 (**15**)

Source: Retrieved from Long-Term Trends Data at http://nces.gov/nationsreportcard/nde on 2/23/2008.

achievement patterns for students whose parents have a given educational level. Table 51.8 shows these trends for 13-year-olds whose parents had (exactly) a high school education; Table 51.9 repeats the calculation for the children of parents with (exactly) a 4-year college degree.

Table 51.8 shows that, between 1980 and 2004, White students with high school-graduate-parents showed essentially no change in their level of reading performance. By contrast, African American students whose parents had this educational level showed improvement, narrowing their gap with Whites from 26 to 19 points. The reading performance of Hispanic students with high school-educated parents also moved upward slightly, narrowing their gap with Whites to 15 points.

A somewhat different story emerges for mathematics performance. Here, White students with high school-educated parents showed significant gains, entirely between 1990 and 2004, so that by 2004 their average score had increased by 11 points over its 1978 level, to 279. However, Blacks and Hispanics with this parental educational level did even better. Black students whose parents had a high school education improved their mathematics performance from 232 in 1978 to 253 in 2004, thereby decreasing their achievement gap with Whites from 36 to 26 points. Similarly, Hispanics improved from 244 in 1978 to 264 in 2004, reducing *their* achievement gap from 24 to 15 points.

Thus, among students whose parents had a high school education, both African Americans and Hispanics made substantial progress in narrowing reading and mathematics achievement gaps with Whites during the 25 or so years prior to 2004. This is a real accomplishment, particularly since, at least in mathematics, scores for Whites were themselves moving upward.

Table 51.9 presents a similar analysis for 13-year-old students whose parents had a college education. As in the previous table for students of high school-educated parents, White children of college-educated parents showed no gains in reading over the 1980–2004 period. And once again, Black students did show such gains (although they

occurred almost entirely during the 1980s). The result is that, for these students of college-educated parents, the Black-White achievement gap in reading declined from 34 to 22 points.

Similar reading gains did not occur for Hispanics. Instead, their reading scores actually declined between 1980 and 2004, so that their gap with Whites increased from 18 to 22 points over this period. This decline occurred during the 1980s, and there is no obvious explanation for it.

Mathematics trends for children of college-educated parents resemble those already observed for the children of high school-educated parents. Whites showed modest average gains, from 288 to 297. Blacks and Hispanics showed larger gains, thereby reducing their achievement gaps. Black gains were from 246 to 268, reducing their achievement gap to 29 points in 2004. Hispanics gained from 264 to 279, reducing their achievement gap to 18 points in 2004.

To summarize, using the long-term trend data for 2004 as an ending point, and restricting attention to the children of parents with either a high school or a college education, we found that African Americans in both groups made substantial gains in closing achievement gaps in both reading and mathematics. Some of this progress occurred after 1990, a revision of the conclusion reached by scholars prior to the availability of the 2004 data (Hedges & Nowell, 1998; Grissmer, Flanagan, & Williamson, 1998; Neal, 2006). Hispanics also made substantial gains in closing achievement gaps, with the exception of reading performance among college-educated Hispanics, where the gap widened slightly.

This progress, over this 25-year period, is encouraging. On the other hand, the remaining gaps with Whites are of a magnitude (20 points, plus or minus) that is approximately twice as large as the progress made over these 25 years. Thus, an additional 50 years of similar progress may be necessary before we will be able to close these gaps that exist after controlling parental education. There will then still be the additional compositional effects due to the higher average educational levels, and rates of two-parent households, of White, compared to African American and Hispanic parents.

Programs and Policies to Close the Gaps

Since 1965, when the Head Start and Title I programs were inaugurated, many programs and policies, some widely disseminated, others smaller and experimental, have been introduced in efforts to improve the school readiness and achievement of children from low-income households. Because higher poverty rates among African American and Hispanic families are responsible for portions of the race/ethnic achievement gaps, programs aimed to increase the performance of low-income children should serve to narrow these gaps. Further, NCLB contains provisions and policies focused on narrowing achievement gaps for groups defined by race/ethnicity. Thus, there is a relatively long history of efforts to create programs and policies

TABLE 51.9

Reading and Mathematics NAEP Scores and Gaps for White, Black, and Hispanic 13-Year Olds Whose Parents Had a College Education, Trends Over Time

	White	Black (Gap)	Hispanic (Gap)
Reading			
1980	276	242 (**34**)	258 (**18**)
1990	271	251 (**20**)	251 (**20**)
2004	274	252 (**22**)	252 (**22**)
Mathematics			
1978	288	246 (**42**)	264 (**24**)
1990	287	251 (**36**)	262 (**25**)
2004	297	268 (**29**)	279 (**18**)

Source: Retrieved from Long-Term Trends Data at http://nces.gov/nationsreportcard/nde on 2/23/2008.

designed to narrow the achievement gaps. In this section I summarize some of the lessons learned from these program and policy efforts.

Preschool Programs Policies aimed to improve instruction for children in grades K–12 can have no effect on the gaps that already exist when students begin kindergarten. Instead, we must look to preschool programs to narrow these gaps. The only such program implemented on a large scale is Head Start. However, a number of smaller, experimental programs have also been implemented, and many of these have been evaluated.

High-quality programs (where quality is measured by higher levels of teacher education and training, lower student/teacher ratios, the quality and intensity of instructional curricula, and related variables) have been found to have positive effects on both student cognitive and behavioral outcomes (Magnuson & Waldfogel, 2005). Program implementation quality, however, varies widely across locations, even within the same program (e.g., Head Start), with a tendency for the most disadvantaged children to be enrolled in the lowest quality programs. Estimated program effects thus typically represent averages of results from more- and less-well implemented program sites. With program implementation varying relatively widely, it is not surprising that program effect estimates have also varied. Reviewing the results of non-experimental studies of Head Start, Magnuson and Waldfogel (2005) found evidence of positive effects on both cognitive performance and behavior, but they also concluded that the magnitudes of these effects, their persistence as children age, and their differences across race/ethnic groups "remain unclear" (pp. 174–175).

Some critics of Head Start have argued that the program has had an insufficiently strong emphasis on instruction, and that, as a consequence, it has achieved at best modest-sized cognitive gains for participants (Whitehurst & Massetti, 2004). Support for this position is provided by the recent Head Start Impact Study, a designed experiment in which some low-income students were randomly assigned to Head Start, while others were not. The impacts on 4-year-olds are shown in Table 51.10. We see that of six standardized tests, Head Start had no significant effect on three. For the other three tests, it did have a significant positive effect, but with an effect size of about 0.2. That is, the program raised students' performance by .2 of a standard deviation on each of these tests. Since, for example, preschool White-Black cognitive skills gaps may approximate one standard deviation, effects of this magnitude narrow these gaps by only about 20% for three of the tests, and not at all for the other three. Head Start effects will have to increase substantially in size and scope if the program is to substantially narrow White-Black and White-Hispanic preschool academic readiness.

As for the effects of Head Start on the problem behaviors, social skills and competencies, and approaches to learning of 4-year-olds, no significant effects were found. Here too, the program will have to improve its performance if it is to

TABLE 51.10

Significant Effects and Effect Sizes for 4-Year-Olds, Head Start Impact Study (June, 2005: Exhibit 1 of the Executive Summary)

Test Scores	
Woodcock-Johnson Letter-Word ID	.22
Letter Naming	.24
McCarthy Draw-A-Design	NS
Woodcock-Johnson Spelling	.16
PPVT Vocabulary	NS
PPVT Color Naming	NS
Problem Behaviors	
Total Behavior Problems	NS
Hyperactive Behavior	NS
Aggressive Behavior	NS
Withdrawn Behavior	NS
Social Skills and Approaches to Learning	NS
Social Competencies	NS

NS = Not significant.
Source: Retrieved on 2/23/08 from http://www.acf.hhs.gov/programs/opre/hs/impact_study/

play a significant role in reducing poverty and race/ethnic disparities.

A relatively large number of small, experimental preschool intervention prototypes have been tried over the past 40 years. Some, including the Perry Preschool Program, the Abecederian Program, and the Chicago Child-Parent Centers appear to produce larger effects than Head Start, including effects that persist through to adulthood (Magnuson & Waldfogel, 2005). However, these programs tend to have relatively high costs per child, and have not been implemented on a large scale. It is disappointing that 40 years of research in this area have not produced greater success in narrowing the school readiness gaps of children from low-income families. (For the view that we may be asking these programs to accomplish more than is possible, see Brooks-Gunn, 2003.) On the other hand, it is promising that a consensus appears to be emerging that it *must* become national policy to provide preschool programming that succeeds in closing the school readiness gap experienced by low-income children (Heckman & Krueger, 2003; Duncan, Ludwig, & Magnuson, 2007).

Programs and Policies for Grades K–12 In addition to Head Start, the War on Poverty created a second program targeted at the school achievement of low-income children (typically those enrolled in the elementary school grades), the Title I program, which has been continuously reauthorized by Congress since 1966 as part of the Elementary and Secondary Education Act. Funding for Title I in 2005 was approximately $12 billion, approximately twice the amount for Head Start. Yet evaluations of this program mandated by Congress have found it to have little positive effect on the achievement of students enrolled in it (Farkas & Hall, 2000).

Why has Title I been ineffective in raising the elementary school performance of disadvantaged students? As discussed by Farkas and Hall (2000), this program has always been more of a funding stream than a structured program. In low-income schools, the lowest performing students were pulled out in groups of three to eight or more students, to work with specially designated teachers. Unfortunately, these teachers had little effective curriculum or training, the students were at different performance levels and had different learning problems, their school engagement was often poor, and the resulting program was stigmatizing and demoralizing. Meanwhile, students in the regular class were moving ahead, creating a moving target of grade-level performance that was difficult for the Title I children to catch up with. Little wonder that the program was largely ineffective.

Beginning around 1990, a number of smaller scale programs began trying to develop more successful intervention models for at-risk elementary school students. Many of these focused on structured curricula, and one-to-one or small group tutoring in reading and language arts. Such programs, for example, one-to-one tutoring programs, and large-scale interventions that include tutoring, such as Success for All, have been able to show effect sizes in the .25–.50 standard deviation range (Invernizzi, 2002; Borman et al., 2005). Now that NCLB has greatly increased funding for supplemental educational services, including tutoring, it seems possible that these services will be deployed on a much larger scale than previously. However, the expansion of tutoring services under NCLB is only now occurring, with results that are not fully encouraging (Farkas & Durham, 2007).

As for intervention programs to assist middle and high school students with their schoolwork, systematic work on such programs, accompanied by program evaluations with adequate research designs, is just beginning. This is a likely growth area in the years ahead.

Conclusion

Where Have We Been? Educational policy has been a contentious and dramatic arena from the War on Poverty in 1966 to No Child Left Behind in 2001. Landmark events have occurred in each decade, including the following. First, the invention of the Head Start and Title I programs, their continuation for more than 40 years, and their at-best modest positive effects. Second, the Coleman report (Coleman et al., 1966), its surprising finding that family characteristics exert a more powerful effect on student achievement than do school characteristics, subsequent controversy over this finding, and its confirmation over 40 years of further investigation (Rumberger & Palardy, 2004). Third, the attempt to implement school busing nationwide, struggles over this, "White flight," and the ultimate national retreat from busing. Also, the failure to find, controlling other factors, positive effects of school integration on minority test scores (Angrist & Lang, 2004; Card & Rothstein, 2007). Fourth,

publication of *A Nation at Risk* in 1983, and the subsequent and continuing efforts to increase school accountability. Fifth, the emergence of Hispanics as the nation's largest minority group, with associated struggles over the high dropout rates for this group, their achievement gaps, and efforts, such as bilingual education, to improve the performance of this group. Sixth, President Clinton's Reading Initiative"and focus on the importance of cognitive skills for individual and the nation's economic competitiveness. Seventh, the curricular debates known as the "reading wars" (phonics versus whole language) and a similar conflict over mathematics instruction (for a review, see Loveless, 2001). Eighth, struggles over "school choice," including vouchers and charter schools. Ninth, Herrnstein and Murray's (1994) *The Bell Curve*, the ensuing Jencks/Phillips (1998) volume on *The Black-White Test Score Gap*, and the emergence of achievement gaps as a constant discussion issue among policy makers, scholars, and the public at large. Tenth, No Child Left Behind, and the embodiment in legislation of the demand that schools succeed in closing achievement gaps for Blacks, Hispanics, low-income students, and other subgroups, or face harsh penalties.

In education policy, the new century began with struggles over the details of implementing NCLB. Near the end of the first decade of this century, and despite progress over the past 25 years, achievement gaps remain large. The question then becomes—how *can* we make progress in narrowing these achievement gaps?

How Can We Do Better? On the one hand, the answer must lie in the details of instructional and learning-related time-on-task by low-income students and their teachers. These efforts must begin early, and continue through every grade level. On the other hand, statistical studies of student achievement reveal that the most powerful factors determining educational inequality lie outside school walls. More comprehensive efforts addressing various aspects of the well-being of American children and their families will surely be required if these gaps are to be completely closed.

First, we must strive to eliminate the pre-reading and pre-mathematics gaps that exist when children enter kindergarten. Table 51.1 showed the relatively large size of these gaps, and Table 51.10 showed that Head Start provides only a modest effect in closing them. Preschool program must provide more effective and intensive instruction in basic knowledge of letters, sounds, numbers, and shapes. There must also be more attention to behavioral training, so that low-income and ethnic minority children begin kindergarten with the same ability to pay attention and do their schoolwork that is currently shown by middle-class and White children.

In this context an example of a successful early intervention is relevant. The Abecedarian project, although a relatively small-scale program, showed significant positive effects on the educational achievement and attainment of the students who participated in its intensive intervention program. Low-income, mostly minority children, were exposed to a full-time intervention from infancy to age 5, and then supported during the early elementary years (Campbell & Ramey, 1994; Campbell, Pungello, Miller-Johnson, Burchinal, & Ramey, 2001). Certainly such an intense, long-term program is expensive. However its costs should be examined within the context of the potential costs of school failure for these children—low lifetime wages, unemployment, and other negative life consequences such as depression, substance abuse, and delinquent and criminal behavior.

Second, kindergarten must be more successfully used as a learning opportunity for at-risk students. The fact that low-income and ethnic minority youngsters are more likely than middle-class White students to attend full-day kindergarten has been shown to modestly improve their learning (Bodovski & Farkas, 2007). But more needs to be done. By beginning with those kindergartners who are the most developmentally ready, it is possible to take at least some of them closer to pre-reading, and even reading, as well as numeracy skills during the kindergarten year. Not only will this ensure that more students are ready for first grade, but it will also provide early identification, and thus a better opportunity for remediation, of those in need of help.

Third, first grade is a "make or break" year. In most schools, first-grade teachers aim to have the children reading independently by the winter break. When they fall too far behind this schedule, students are unprepared for the more demanding curriculum of second grade. Thus, student progress during first grade should be closely monitored, and tutoring and other forms of supplementary assistance should be offered to students who are falling behind schedule.

Fourth, student progress during second and third grade should also be closely monitored. Basic skills in reading and mathematics are typically only taught in grades K–3. After this, the curriculum (as well as teacher training) calls for teachers to use these student basic skills as a foundation for instruction on more advanced material. (This is the source of the saying "K–3 involves learning to read, 4–6 involves reading to learn.") Thus, it is crucial that students reach the end of third grade with the full set of foundational skills in reading, mathematics, and other subjects that will be required for progress in subsequent grades. This would best be achieved if data were collected monthly on student progress on specific skills, with extra resources (such as tutoring) immediately brought to bear when remediation is needed.

Fifth, and finally, the same sort of close monitoring of academic progress by at-risk students should be provided in grades 4–12. This might be difficult to implement, and also quite expensive. However, such monitoring is routinely provided to their children by middle-class parents. Surely low-income students will be unable to perform at the same level as middle-class children if their academic work does not receive the same level of monitoring and assistance.

Can these suggestions be implemented for all low-income children? Doing so would surely not be easy. However, significant progress might be made toward achieving at least the first several of these suggestions. Perhaps more important, all five suggestions provide a template, sharply focused on teaching and learning, against which to judge our efforts toward that most difficult of goals—closing the achievement gaps.

The framing of these goals must also be addressed. Currently, each state is charged to achieve "proficiency for all groups" by 2014. Each state is required to set the standard for proficiency, and then achieve it. However, the NCES has already set a standard for proficient performance on tests such as the NAEP. They have marked off different scores as constituting "proficient," "basic," and "below basic." This use of "proficient" defines a standard which is achieved by only the highest-performing group of students. Given the importance of family background in student achievement, it is unlikely that the schools will ever be able to completely equalize the performance of low- and middle-income students, with all students performing at this high level. A more realistic goal is to minimize the share of low-income students scoring "below basic." For example, it is clearly both shameful and avoidable that more than 40% of all fourth graders in the Washington, DC, school district score below basic in reading and mathematics. That is, their skills and knowledge are below minimally acceptable levels in these subjects. Setting a goal of moving most low-income students out of the below basic category in all grades in reading and mathematics, and focusing instruction intensively to achieve this, including the five steps listed above, would be an appropriate, and realistic, goal for which to aim.

Although more targeted efforts are necessary within schools and classrooms, such efforts alone will not be sufficient. Studies show the importance of close cooperation between teachers, students, and parents for the achievement of school success (Lareau, 2003). School outreach activities must be expanded, and focused on providing parents with educational resources, including improving parents' own academic skills, as well as building their confidence and increasing their ability to work collaboratively with their child's teacher. A successful example of this type of intervention is reported in the Chicago Longitudinal Study (Miedel & Reynolds, 1999; Reynolds & Temple, 1998).

Students cannot be fully engaged with academic tasks when their minds are preoccupied with external problems, particularly when these are caused by family poverty, mental and physical health issues within families, and neighborhood disintegration and violence. American schools will not achieve the goals stated by NCLB without comprehensive efforts to reduce the ill effects of family and neighborhood poverty on children, and to make American schools and neighborhoods safe for students and their families. As shown in Table 51.8 and Table 51.9, the past 25 years have seen progress in narrowing the achievement gaps. Further progress is possible. Achieving it is an urgent national priority.

References

Angrist, J. D., & Lang, K. (2004). Does school integration generate peer effects? Evidence from Boston's Metco Program. *American Economic Review, 94*, 1613–1634.

Arrow, K., Bowles, S., & Durlauf, S. (Eds.). (2000). *Meritocracy and economic inequality.* Princeton, NJ: Princeton University Press.

Bodovski, K., & Farkas, G. (2007). Do instructional practices contribute to inequality in achievement? The case of mathematics instruction in kindergarten. *The Journal of Early Childhood Research, 5*, 301–322.

Borman, G., Slavin, R. E., Cheung, A., Chamberlain, A., Madden, N., & Chambers, B. (2005). The national randomized field trial of success for all: Second-year outcomes. *American Educational Research Journal, 42*, 673–696.

Bowles, S., & Gintis, H. (1976). *Schooling in capitalist America.* New York: Basic Books.

Bowles, S., Gintis, H., & Groves, M. O. (Eds.). (2005). *Unequal chances: Family background and economic success.* New York: Russell Sage Foundation.

Brooks-Gunn, J. (2003). Do you believe in magic? What we can expect from early childhood intervention programs. *Society for Research on Child Development Social Policy Report, 17*(1). Retrieved November 19, 2008, from http://nccf.tc.columbia.edu/pdf/Do%20You%20Believe%20In%20Magic.pdf

Brooks-Gunn, J., & Markman, L. (2005). The contribution of parenting to ethnic and racial gaps in school readiness. *The Future of Children, 15*(1), 139–168.

Campbell, F. A., & Ramey, C. T. (1994). Effects of early intervention on intellectual and academic achievement: A follow-up study of children from low-income families. *Child Development, 65*, 684–698.

Campbell, F. A., Pungello, E. P., Miller-Johnson, S., Burchinal, M., & Ramey, C. T. (2001). The development of cognitive and academic abilities: Growth curves from an early childhood educational experiment. *Developmental Psychology, 37*, 231–242.

Card, D., & Rothstein, J. (2007). Racial segregation and the Black-White test score gap. *Journal of Public Economics, 91*, 2158–2184.

Chubb, J. E., & Loveless, T. (Eds.). (2002). *Bridging the achievement gap.* Washington, DC: Brookings Institute.

Coleman, J. S., Campbell, E. Q., Hobson, C. J., McPartland, J., Mood, A. M., Weinfeld, F. D., et al. (1966). *Equality of educational opportunity.* Washington, DC: U.S. Department of Health, Education, and Welfare.

Downey, D. B., von Hippel, P., & Broh, B. A. (2004). Are schools the great equalizer? Cognitive inequality during the summer months and the school year. *American Sociological Review, 69*, 613–635.

Duncan, G., Dowsett, C. J., Claessens, A., Magnuson, K., Huston, A. C., Klebanov, P., et al. (2007). School readiness and later achievement. *Developmental Psychology, 43*, 1428–1446.

Duncan, G., Ludwig, J., & Magnuson, K. (2007). Reducing poverty through pre-school interventions. *The Future of Children, 17*(2), 143–160.

Duncan, G., & Magnuson, K. (2005). Can family socioeconomic resources account for racial and ethnic test score gaps? *The Future of Children, 15*(1), 35–54.

Farkas, G. (1996). *Human capital or cultural capital? Ethnicity and poverty groups in an urban school district.* New York: Aldine de Gruyter.

Farkas, G., & Beron, K. (2004). The detailed age trajectory of oral vocabulary knowledge: Differences by class and race. *Social Science Research, 33*, 464–497.

Farkas, G., & Durham, R. (2007). The role of tutoring in standards-based reform. In A. Gamoran (Ed.), *Standards-based reform and the poverty gap* (pp. 201–228). Washington, DC: Brookings Institute.

Farkas, G., & Hall, L. S. (2000). Can Title I attain its goal? In D. Ravitch (Ed.), *Brookings Papers on Education Policy 2000* (pp. 59–103). Washington, DC: Brookings Institute.

Ferguson, R. F. (2005). Why America's Black-White school achievement gap persists. In G. C. Loury, T. Modood, & S. Teles (Eds.), *Social mobility and public policy* (pp. 309–341). Cambridge, UK: Cambridge University Press.

Fryer, R. G., & Levitt, S. D. (2004). Understanding the Black-White test score gap in the first two years of school. *Review of Economics and Statistics, 86*, 447–464.

Grissmer, D., Flanagan, A., & Williamson, S. (1998). Why did the Black-White score gap narrow in the 1970s and 1980s? In C. Jencks & M. Phillips (Eds.), *The Black-White test score gap* (pp. 182–228). Washington, DC: Brookings Institute.

Heckman, J. J., & Krueger, A. B. (Eds.). (2003). *Inequality in America: What role for human capital policies?* Cambridge, MA: MIT Press.

Hedges, L., & Nowell, A. (1998). Black-White test score convergence since 1965. In C. Jencks & M. Phillips (Eds.), *The Black-White test score gap* (pp. 149–181). Washington, DC: Brookings Institute.

Herrnstein, R., & Murray, C. (1994). *The bell curve: Intelligence and class structure in American life.* New York: The Free Press.

Hobb, F., & Stoops, N. (2002). *Demographic trends in the 20th century* (Census 2000 Special Reports, Series CENSR-4). Washington, DC: U.S. Government Printing Office.

Invernizzi, M. (2002). The complex world of one-on-one tutoring. In S. Neuman & D. Dickinson (Eds.), *Handbook of early literacy research* (pp. 459–470). New York: Guilford.

Jencks, C., Bartlett, S., Corcoran, J., Crouse, D., Eaglesfield, G., Jackson, R., et al. (1979). *Who gets ahead? The determinants of economic success in America.* New York: Basic Books.

Jencks, C., & Phillips, M. (Eds.). (1998). *The Black-White test score gap.* Washington, DC: Brookings Institute.

Jencks, C., Smith, M., Acland, H., Bane, M. J., Cohen, D., Gintis, H. et al. (1972). *Inequality: A reassessment of the effect of family and schooling in America.* New York: Basic Books.

Jensen, A. (1969). How much can we boost IQ and scholastic achievement? *Harvard Education Review, 39*, 1–123.

Lareau, A. (2003). *Unequal childhoods: Class, race, and family life.* Berkeley: University of California Press.

Loveless, T. (Ed.). (2001). *The great curriculum debate: How should we teach reading and math?* Washington, DC: Brookings Institute.

Magnuson, K., & Waldfogel, J. (2005). Early childhood care and education: Effects on ethnic and racial gaps in school readiness. *The Future of Children, 15*(1), 169–196.

McLanahan, S., & Sandefur, G. (1994). *Growing up with a single parent: What hurts, what helps.* Cambridge, MA: Harvard University Press.

Miedel, W. T., & Reynolds, A. J. (1999). Parent involvement in early intervention for disadvantaged children: Does it matter? *Journal of School Psychology, 37*, 379–402.

Neal, D. (2006). Why has Black-White skill convergence stopped? In E. Hanushek & F. Welch (Eds.), *Handbook on the economics of education* (pp. 511–576). Amsterdam: Elsevier.

Phillips, M., Crouse, J., & Ralph, J. (1998). Does the Black-White test score gap widen after children enter school? In C. Jencks & M. Phillips (Eds.), *The Black-White test score gap* (pp. 229–272). Washington, DC: Brookings Institute.

Rathbun, A., & West, J. (2004). *From kindergarten through third grade: Children's beginning school experiences* (NCES 2004-007). Washington, DC: U.S. Department of Education.

Reichman, N. (2005). Low birth weight and school readiness. *The Future of Children, 15*(1), 91–116.

Reynolds, A. J., & Temple, J. A. (1998). Extended early childhood intervention and school achievement: Age thirteen findings from the Chicago Longitudinal Study. *Child Development, 69*, 231–246.

Rock, D., & Stenner, A. J. (2005). Assessment issues in the testing of children at school entry. *The Future of Children, 15*(1), 15–34.

Rumberger, R. W., & Palardy, G. J. (2004). Multilevel models for school effectiveness research. In D. Kaplan (Ed.), *The Sage handbook of quantitative methodology for the social sciences* (pp. 235–258). Thousand Oaks, CA: Sage.

West, J., Denton, K., & Reaney, L. (2001). *The kindergarten year: Findings from the Early Childhood Longitudinal Study, Kindergarten Class of 1998–99* (NCES 2001-023). U.S. Department of Education.

Whitehurst, G., & Massetti, G. (2004). How well does Head Start prepare children to learn to read? In E. Zigler & S. Styfco (Eds.), *The Head Start debates* (pp. 251–262). Baltimore: Paul Brookes.

Young, M. (1958). *The rise of the meritocracy, 1870–2033.* London: Thames and Hudson.

52
New Technology

Yong Zhao
Michigan State University

Jing Lei
Syracuse University

This chapter examines the role of policymaking in the development of school technology and the policy challenges brought by the rapid development of new technologies. We start this chapter with two questions: First, why do policy makers continue to invest in technology in schools despite the lack of confirming evidence? Second, why has technology improved productivity and saved costs in sectors outside education, but failed to achieve the same effect in schools? To answer these questions, we first examine the disconnection between policymaking and policy implementation in school technology, followed by a review of technology in the world beyond education in the hope of borrowing effective strategies from successful stories; we then analyze factors that help answer the two questions, examine the new changes and challenges brought by new technologies, and discuss new policies needed to move school technology to a new phase. We conclude the chapter with recommendations for research, practice, and policymaking.

Unfulfilled Promises of and Continued Enthusiasm in Educational Technology

A typical morning at a middle school connected to the information superhighway might begin as one group of students arrives early to update the school's home page on the World Wide Web. This home page signals to other schools that also have electronic access to the Web that they have a sister school here whose students and teachers are interested in exchanging ideas about world events and other educational topics. At the same time, another group of early arrivals works with the vice principal to prepare the morning broadcast. Each school day formally starts with a live television presentation about the day's events; these presentations are written, directed, and produced by rotating teams of students and broadcast internally to all the classrooms. In the quiet minutes before this broadcast airs and classes start, a young language teacher is using his desktop computer to access an electronic bulletin board to see how language teachers from schools across the state

have responded to his question about the best ways for explaining prepositions. Meantime, the principal is reviewing the electronic mail that parents sent her the evening before, prior to sending voice mail to all her teachers suggesting a schedule for the upcoming parent-teacher "open house."

Later in the morning, in a first-period modern history class, the same video technology that carried the local morning broadcast now enables this class to tour the Smithsonian's aerospace museum. In the classroom next door, the subject is anthropology. Students are grouped in teams of 3 and 4 around the classroom's computers, engrossed in a computer simulation that allows them to play the role of archaeologists on-site in Egypt, exploring ancient Egyptian culture as revealed in its artifacts. In a classroom down the hall, each individual student is working math problems pitched at exactly the pace and level of difficulty appropriate for him or her, and getting immediate feedback on the answers, thanks to interactive software. At the same time, students in a writing class are drafting an essay assignment on their computers and employing electronic mail to get rapid feedback on their work from their peers.... (McKinsey & Company, 1996, p. 8)

This scenario is included in a 1996 report commissioned by the National Information Infrastructure Advisor Council (NIIAC)[1] to drum up support for investment in computers and Internet technology in schools. Entitled *Connecting K-12 Schools to the Information Superhighway*, the report projects expenditures of equipping U.S. schools based on the level of uses. The most expensive and ideal model—to equip all classrooms so that every five students have access to one Internet-connected computer—would require an initial investment of over $47 billion U.S. dollars and subsequently an annual operation expense of $14 billion (McKinsey & Company, 1996, p. 33).

Policy makers responded to scenarios like this with great enthusiasm. Governments at all levels acted quickly to put computers in schools and connect them to the Internet. Today, about a decade later, American schools have more than what was recommended in terms of hardware and connectivity: Every 3.8 students have access to an instructional computer and every 3.9 students have access to an instructional computer connected to the Internet; almost 100% of schools are connected to the Internet (Fox, 2005). The goal of a ratio of 5 to 1 was achieved in 2002. Compared with schools in most countries, American schools have better access to technology. According to a 2005 OECD Programme for International Student Assessment (PISA) report, the United States ranked first in OECD countries in the number of computers per student (OECD, 2005, p. 27)

The Reality of Technology in Schools While schools have more technology than what was believed to be necessary to realize the scenario used to justify the billions of dollars in education technology, the scenario has not become commonplace in American schools. In fact, technology in schools has long been criticized as "oversold but underused" (Cuban, 2001). As of 2004, although almost all classrooms were connected to the Internet, more than half of the teachers in 23% of schools nationwide did not use the Internet for instruction (Fox, 2005). Today, schools are falling behind their students in using technology (*Education Week*, 2007; Levin & Arafeh, 2002). Teachers' use of technology is still sporadic (*Education Week*, 2007). It would be quite difficult to find many meaningful differences in how and what students study in school today and how and what they studied in school in 1996. The third National Educational Technology Plan released by the U.S. Department of Education in 2004 quotes Education Secretary Rod Paige (2002):

> Indeed, education is the only business still debating the usefulness of technology. Schools remain unchanged for the most part despite numerous reforms and increased investments in computers and networks. The way we organize schools and provide instruction is essentially the same as it was when our Founding Fathers went to school. Put another way, we still educate our students based on an agricultural timetable, in an industrial setting, but tell students they live in a digital age. (U. S. Department of Education, 2004)

Moreover, what schools do now in regard to technology is hampering teaching new technology knowledge and skills. Under the pressure of meeting standards set out by the No Child Left Behind Act (NCLB), schools are targeting curriculum toward high-stakes assessments, narrowing teaching and learning, pushing instruction toward lower order cognitive skills (e.g., Darling-Hammond, 2004; Meier & Wood, 2004), and inevitably, cutting back the time and opportunities students can learn about and with technology. Research suggests that standards-based reforms are at odds with efforts to increase technology integration in K–12 schools because standardized testing discourages the constructivist learning supported by technology (Keller & Bichelmeyer, 2004).

Even when technology is provided, schools often merely focus on how to use specific technology hardware and software, but not the deep understanding of the nature of technology (Campbell, 1998; Yannie, 2000). The report titled *Technically Speaking: Why all Americans Need to Know More about Technology* (Committee on Technological Literacy, National Academy of Engineering, National Research Council, Pearson, & Young, 2002) points out that although the use of technology is ubiquitous, people have a poor understanding of the nature of technology and how technology interacts with people and society:

> Thus the paradox: Even as technology has become increasingly important in our lives, it has receded from view. Americans are poorly equipped to recognize, let alone ponder or address, the challenges technology poses or the problems it could solve. And the mismatch is growing. Although our use of technology is increasing at a breathtaking pace, there is no sign of a corresponding improvement in our ability to deal with issues relating to technology. (pp. 1–2)

Contradictory Evidence on Effectiveness The continuous investment in school technology has been fueled by the hope that technology can bring significant improvement to education. However, the hope has not been consistently supported by empirical evidence. Uncertainty about the effectiveness of technology still exists despite years of heavy investment and widespread euphoric claims about the power of technology for transforming education (Dynarski et al., 2007). Various studies examining the effect of technology on learning have yielded contradictory findings. Some studies found positive impact of technology use on student outcomes in the areas of literacy development (Blasewitz & Taylor, 1999; Tracey & Young, 2007), reading comprehension and vocabulary (Scrase, 1998; Stone, 1996; Woehler, 1994), writing (Nix, 1998), mathematics (Elliott & Hall, 1997; MacIver, Balfanz, & Plank, 1999), and science (Harmer & Cates, 2007; Lazarowitz & Huppert, 1993; Liu, Hsieh, Cho, & Schallert, 2006; Reid-Griffin, 2003). Positive impact was also found in developmental areas including attitude toward learning and self-esteem (Sivin-Kachala & Bialo, 2000), motivation, attendance, and discipline (e.g., Mathew, 1997).

But other studies came to very different conclusions. They suggest that technology use may not have any positive impact on student outcomes and may even harm children and their learning (e.g., Healy, 1998; Stoll, 1999). For example, Waight and Abd-El-Khalick (2007) found that the use of computer technology restricted rather than promoted "inquiry" in a sixth-grade science classroom. Mixed findings have also emerged from large-scale international studies. The PISA 2003 study found that students using computers most frequently at school do not necessarily perform better than students using technology less frequently (OECD, 2005). A TIMSS 1999 study reported that technology use was negatively related to science achievement amongst eighth graders in Turkey (Aypay, Erdogan, & Sozer, 2007). A TIMSS 2003 study found that while medium-level use of computer technology was related to higher science scores, extensive use was related to lower science scores (Antonijevic, 2007). Similarly, based on data collected from 175,000 15-year-old students in 31 countries, researchers at the University of Munich announced that performance in math and reading had suffered significantly among students who had more than one computer at home (MacDonald, 2004). Schacter (1999) also found negative impact on student achievement after a review of five large-scale studies that employed diverse research methods to examine the impact of educational technology.

The lack of impact is further confirmed by a widely cited report entitled *Effectiveness of Reading and Mathematics Software Products: Findings from the First Student Cohort*, released by the U.S. Department of Education in April 2007. This study, intended to assess the effects of 16 computer software products designed to teach first- and fourth-grade reading and sixth-grade math, found that "test scores in treatment classrooms that were randomly assigned to use products did not differ from test scores in control classrooms by statistically significant margins" (Dynarski et al., 2007).

Cost of Having Technology in School Not only has investment in technology not resulted in consistently positive educational outcomes, technology seems to have increased costs of running school and brought unintended consequences to schools. Schools, teachers, students, and parents are now faced with a series of new challenges, including the constant demand in keeping up with new technology development and concerns over misuse and abuse of technology.

Cost of Owning Technology In addition to the initial investment of putting computers in schools and wiring them to the Internet, schools must not only upgrade software, but also buy new hardware almost every 3 to 5 years just in order to keep the same level of access, much like what the Red Queen tells Alice in Lewis Caroll's *Through the Looking Glass*: "It takes all the running *you* can do to keep in the same place." With the rapid development of information and communication technology, schools are constantly running to catch a moving train (Becker, 1998). Upgrading software and hardware is only one part of the total ownership of technology. Other factors must also be considered to make technology accessible and useable, such as changes and upgrade in administration, planning, technical support, resource allocation, and teacher professional development (Freeman, 2002; McIntire, 2006). The costs in terms of money, teacher time and energy, as well as the lost opportunity for teachers to engage in other potentially more beneficial activities can be significant.

Cost of Unintended and Unanticipated Consequences Schools have to exert effort to deal with the undesirable uses by students and staff, and must address the potentially harmful or distractive effects of technology, particularly the Internet. The Internet and computers enhance the ways we access, process, and store information and communicate with others, but they themselves do not differentiate the quality of information and communication, making it possible for students to be exposed to all sorts of potentially harmful information and communications. Stories about children being addicted to surfing the Internet, playing computer games, and chatting with strangers online pose problems and reveal the potential harms of technology (Finkelhor, 2007; Lavy, 2007). In schools, common concerns include students being distracted by the Internet, e-mail, games, and music, and students' attention spans being shortened by multimedia (Paulson, 2007). Another concern is related to how to teach students to be more critical and not to take everything online for granted. Teachers are concerned that students might just copy and paste from the Internet, that they do not think critically, and took everything online as facts without careful scrutiny (Lei, Conway, & Zhao, 2008).

More serious concerns come from the complexity of technology, especially the Internet. The online world is full of wonders as well as complications and dangers, such as hacking, viruses, privacy and security issues, inappropriate content, cyber-bullying, and crime. Research shows an increasing number of students are exposed to online pornography, harassment, and bullying (eSchool News, 2007a; Wolak, Mitchell, & Finkelhor, 2006). Online victimization experiences often leave youth upset, afraid, distressed, or embarrassed, but rarely are the incidents reported or talked to adults (Wolak et al., 2006).

Schools are legally responsible for protecting children against the potential harms brought about by technology. Besides compliance with the federal Children's Internet Protection Act (CIPA), schools have to work with state and local regulations. Schools have been drawn into legal, ethical, and ideological battles over the uses of the Internet and other technologies (e.g., eSchool News, 2007b; Irmas, 2008). For example, in 2003, a school district in Illinois was sued over not addressing parents' concerns in its WLAN planning (Fleishman, 2003). In 2006, parents in the New York City School District sued the city's Department of Education for a cell phone ban (Hartocollis, 2006).

The concern over misuses of the Internet and potential harms it may bring to students is so grave that most schools use a number of strategies to protect students, such as the use of filters, adult supervision, monitoring student online activities, and signed acceptable-use policies. A recent study on cyber security reports that 95% of school districts surveyed block or limit Web sites and 38% maintain a closed district network (CDW-G, 2007). Many schools completely block certain forms of online activities, especially synchronous communication (e.g., chat) and publishing on the Web (e.g., blogging and access to social Web sites such as MySpace and Facebook).

Such practices are the educational cost of filters. Filters often block Web sites inappropriately, blocking children-friendly information (Electronic Privacy Information Center, 1997) but leaving access to many inappropriate sites. Students frequently experience "overblocking" and "underblocking" (Sutton, 2005). Schools with the most restrictive filtering criteria can block up to 70% of the search results based on state-mandated curriculum topics (Electronic Frontier Foundation & Online Policy Group, 2003). Limited access to necessary information and resources seriously limit the depth of the research of some topics, and cause frustration to teachers and students (NetDay, 2006). According to the National Report on NetDay's 2005 Speak Out Event, on average, 40% of students in grades 6–12 think filters are obstacles that prevent them from finding the information they need for their schoolwork, with a steady increase in the percentage of students thinking so as the grade advances, growing from one-fifth of the students in sixth grade to more than 50% in grade 12 (NetDay, 2006, p. 16). This grade/age difference in their response to filters reflects a problem pointed out by Levinson (1998) that the category "children" pertains "a range of human beings from under 1 to 18 years of age, at the opposite ends of Piaget's cognitive stages of development" (p. 155). In addition, filters in schools also block and limit teachers' access to the Internet, further complicating and restricting student educational experience (Electronic Frontier Foundation & Online Policy Group, 2003).

Moreover, filters are relatively easy to break, and give parents and teachers a false sense of security (Johnson, 2004). Filters do not block access for students who are determined to find what they want to find online. Children have become very adept at getting around the restrictions and often "outsmart" filters to break the locks on materials and visit Web sites blocked by their school districts (Olsen, 2006; Sutton, 2005). As Stager (2006) points out, limiting Internet access, as well as unimaginative use of the Internet, results in "over-promising and under-delivering reliable Internet functionality and subsequent benefits" (¶ 25).

A History of Unfulfilled Promise and Continued Enthusiasm

This is not the first time that the claimed educational benefits of technological innovation have failed to be realized. In fact, none of the major modern information and communication technological innovations touted to significantly improve education over the past century have succeeded. In 1922, Thomas Edison proclaimed: "I believe that the motion picture is destined to revolutionize our educational system and that in a few years it will supplant largely, if not entirely, the use of textbook" (Weir, 1922, p. 54). Today, textbooks remain the primary learning tool in American classrooms while motion pictures have no place in them. In 1932, Benjamin Darrow, who founded Ohio School of the Air in 1929, suggested that radio would "bring the world to the classroom, to make universally available the services of the finest teachers, the inspiration of the greatest leaders ... and unfolding events which through the radio may come as a vibrant and challenging textbook of the air" (p. 79). Radio

is nowhere to be seen in today's classrooms. The television then became the next technology that could improve education. Despite early enthusiasm and investment, the TV once again failed to deliver what was promised by its proponents. Then came the computer. In 1984, Seymour Papert, the MIT professor and inventor of the Logo language, claimed that "There won't be schools in the future ... I think the computer will blow up the school" (Papert, quoted in Clark & Wentworth, 1997, p. 9). After two decades, schools are still here and will likely continue to be here.

However, neither the repeated unfulfilled promises of technology nor the unintended consequences of technology seemed to have curbed the enthusiasm of policy makers. Today, schools continue to invest in technology. Over the past few years, the student-computer ratio continued to drop (Fox, 2005), suggesting that schools have been buying more computers. More significantly, there is a growing trend for schools to equip every student with a computing device with wireless connection. Currently at least 33 states in the United States have one-to-one laptop programs, ranging from individual schools to school districts to statewide projects (Lei et al., 2008). In the last decade, the United States has spent more than $66 billion in school technology (Quality Education Data, 2004). More money is being invested. According to the 2005–2006 National Technology Assessment conducted by Quality Education Data (2006), 47% of the school districts surveyed expect to mount a major technology initiative or upgrade effort focused on desktops, laptops, and handhelds during the next 24 months. Most telling of this continued faith in technology is the recent U.S. National Educational Technology Plan entitled *Toward a New Golden Age in American Education: How the Internet, the Law, and Today's Students are Revolutionizing Expectations*, which promises:

> As these encouraging trends develop and expand over the next decade, facilitated and supported by our ongoing investment in educational technology, and led by the drive, imagination and dedication of a reenergized educational community at every level, we may be well on our way to a new golden age in American education. (U.S. Department of Education, 2004, pp. 8–9)

In summary, in the last two decades, policy makers have always embraced new information and communication technologies with enthusiasm, despite past failures, and policy makers have always been able to garner sufficient support for the technology agenda and been able to fund the technology initiatives. However, short of isolated cases of success, the considerable investment in school technology has not paid off. This observation raises a significant question: Why do policy makers continue to invest in technology despite a long history of unfulfilled technology promises?

Technology in the World Beyond Education

Although technologies have not transformed education as promised, they have led to irreversible changes in how we work, live, and entertain (CNN, 2005). They have had significant impact on economy, politics, and practically every aspect of human society (Horrigan, 2008; Kohut, 2008). They have led to the development of new industries, new laws, and new areas of research. Technology has also proven to improve productivity and save costs in sectors outside education. For example, a study conducted in 2002 found that the Internet "has already yielded a current, cumulative cost savings of $155.2 billion to U.S. organizations that have adopted Internet business solutions. In addition, these organizations indicate that their Internet business solutions have also helped to increase revenues cumulatively to approximately $444 billion" (Varian, Litan, Elder, & Shutter, 2002, p. 5). The same study projected that these organizations will realize more than $.5 trillion in cost savings once all Internet businesses solutions have been fully implemented by 2010 and "the Net Impact of these cumulative cost savings is expected to account for .43 percentage points of the future increase in the annual U.S. productivity growth rate" (Varian et al., 2002, p. 6). A more recent study of the impact of the Internet focused on the public sector. This 2004 study found that public sector organizations using the identified best practices in using the Internet could experience 45% improvement in efficiency, 40% in service volume, 25% in financials, and 55% in citizen satisfaction (Brown, Elder, & Koenig, 2004).

These data show that technology has already generated significant cost savings and improved productivity in other sectors outside education. The technologies that failed to transform education have already resulted in life-altering changes in our society in general, attesting to their transformative power and impact (e.g., Lynskey, 2006).

The stark contrast between the effect of technology in other industries and that in education begs the question: Why does the same technology that has proven very effective in improving productivity and saving costs in sectors outside education fail to achieve the same effect in schools? In the following sections, we explore answers to this question along with the question raised in the first section.

Why Do Policy Makers Continue to Invest Despite Unfulfilled Promises?

Why technology has not been used enough and why there has been continued investment despite the lack of empirical evidence? To answer these questions, we need to examine the disconnected nature of technology policymaking and policy implementation. Policy is often disconnected from the reality and evidence (Hunter, 2003). Similarly, educational technology policymaking has been largely separated from the reality of implementation. This disconnectedness between policy setting and policy implementation resulted in a puzzling phenomenon: In spite of repeated failures, policy makers' enthusiasm over technology remains unwavering. This disconnectedness also partially explains the massive "resistance" (passive and active) among teachers, hence the under-utilization of technology in schools.

Technology Policymaking

After the Symbolic Value   Technology, similar to other artifacts, has use value and socio-symbolic value (Biggs, 1993). The use value, or the practical value, comes from the utilitarian role technology plays, such as how it can be used and what problems it can solve. For example, a distance learning system helps students in remote areas to receive education they need without spending time and money on transportation. The symbolic value of technology is what representational benefit a technology can bring to the decision makers, the adopter, or the institution. Just like wearing brand name clothing can make people feel trendy, having cutting-edge technology can serve as an advertisement and set a high profile for the school. Many schools purposefully create such images to increase their reputations or reputation of the school district (Stager, 2006).

Although it seems that the utility of technology is the most important element as practical functions are to help improve teaching and learning, the symbolic function of technology plays an even more important role in the decision-making process. Schools have been using purchasing or upgrading technology as a common strategy to improve their image (e.g., Weiss, 2001). The education system has always been shaped by the political need to be competitive and ahead of others (Besser, 1993). Technology in education has been promoted as a key element to make and maintain progress, an unquestioned concept that has been enthusiastically and adamantly pursued by American society since the Industrial Revolution (Besser, 1993; Douglas, 2007). Thus, we started equipping schools with technology not because there was any conclusive evidence that showed that technology improved teaching and learning—the practical value, but because it was a politically correct and the right thing to do.

The symbolic value of technology is signified in comparisons, based on which strong arguments for technology investment are frequently made: we must have technology in our classrooms because other schools, states, or countries have technology in their classrooms (e.g., U.S. Department of Education, 1996). At the national level, technology is believed to be able to improve the country's competency in an increasingly globalized economy, and thus improving education with technology is ubiquitously considered critical to the nation's global competitiveness (CEO Forum on Education and Technology, 2001). The notion is that without technology, we, our children, and our nation, will be worse off (Besser, 1993). Hence, national technology plans cite examples from other countries to illustrate the grand technology vision they depict and to defend the technology goals they set for the nation (Zhao, Lei, & Conway, 2006). Similarly, at the school or district level, technology plans use numbers from other schools or districts to justify their technology decisions (Palozzi & Spradlin, 2006). The argument is simple and strong: Other people are doing it, and we cannot be left behind.

It is then not surprising to find that national educational technology plans and other policy documents universally associate technology with such phrases as "key-driven element," "essential," and "crucial" (Zhao, Lei, & Conway, 2006, p. 686). Investing in technology in schools is viewed as a "longstanding national priority" and a "national urgency" of "preeminent national importance" (e.g., CEO Forum on Education and Technology, 2001, p. 4), and must remain "at the center of school reform and improvement efforts" (U.S. Department of Education, 2000, p. 11).

Policy discourse like this has created a "national infatuation with computers" (Cordes & Miller, 2000, p. 1) by emphasizing the unlimited opportunities and great potentials for students. For example, technology is often portrayed as a magic wand that has the potential to provide "any time, any place, any pace" learning to "all children" (Bogden, 2001, p. 4), and to "enhance the achievement of all students, increase families' involvement in their children's schooling, improve teachers' skills and knowledge, and improve school administration and management" (U.S. Department of Education, 1996, p. 6). How could anyone who cares about the future of our children and our nation resist such magical tools?

By emphasizing the symbolic value of technology, policymaking tends to include mostly references to the future and point to long-term trends. Unlike other educational policies, policy about technology does not even have to be bound by references to the past because each technology is new and what was impossible before can surely be possible in the future. When comparing the technology policymaking process with "normal" policymaking processes, researchers at the Institute on Governance identified a number of differences at all seven stages of policymaking: advent, initial analysis, expert consultation, publication of policy intention, public consultation, implementation of policy decision, and feedback (Woodley, 2002). These differences show that the technology policymaking process is more chaotic, less rational, more risky, and with less measurable goals than regular policymaking. Therefore, although there are many repeated failures in infusing technology in education, each time the new technology seems to be better and more powerful. Perhaps the added power is the tipping point for the next revolution. Thus policy is often glib and not necessarily supported by a genuine understanding of how technology can be used effectively to achieve desired outcomes (Brown, 1994), nor does it soberly weigh new technology against existing technologies (Seidensticker, 2006). Instead, policies always chase after the newest technological innovations with great enthusiasm and try to replace the relative older ones that were advocated with passion only a while ago, creating waves of technological fads and fashion (Zhao, Lei, & Conway, 2006).

Hope and Fear   The promise of technology is so great, and the risk of not adopting technology is so grave: Without technology we will not be able to compete with other countries, and the future of our children and the nation will be "threatened" (CEO Forum on Education and Technology, 2001). The importance of innovation in technology to

maintaining the economic and political dominance of the United States is emphasized and specified in policy documents (Culp, Honey, & Mandinach, 2003). For instance, the first educational technology plan asks this question: "Can schools afford the investment? The real question is, can they afford not to make the investment?" (U.S. Department of Education, 1996, p. 13).

With such a strong sense of urgency, education policy makers find they "do not have the luxury of time" to carefully consider important issues such as how to effectively use technology in order to assume the leadership role (Bogden, 2001). Because the decisions to invest in technology are made in a hasty fashion and driven by political vision and speculations, the investment is often in what is visible (e.g., hardware) and standard (e.g., student to computer ratio, connectivity rate). More importantly, political decisions often go after the immediate image and cash in the symbolic value and thus short-term outcomes are sought after without considering the long-term implications (Davis, 2008; Freyta & Renaud, 2004; Whitfield & Jones, 2007).

The shortsightedness of educational technology decisions affects how technology is used and evaluated. In the pursuit of immediate symbolic value, some critical details on technology integration are often neglected: Technology integration is a slow process (Byrom & Bingham, 2001). It is largely guided by pragmatic constraints in the local context, social interactions in a school, and experiences of the user. Without a host of peripherals and sufficient support, technology breaks down and becomes the problem. The effects of technology depend on how it is used, by whom, and for what purposes. In addition, changes are gradual. It takes time for technology to have any impact and it takes even longer to observe the impact (Honey, Culp, & Spielvogel, 2005). By focusing on the immediate effect and symbolic value of technology, technology project evaluation has been largely "summative," focusing on short-term changes associated with independent technologies, but omitting more important overall long-term effects, and thus it fails to provide practical information for future technology decisions and implementation.

Blaming the Implementers   Technology policy makers also tend to blame the users rather than the product for unrealized claims. It is often pointed out that most problems with the implementation of information technology relate to human rather than technical factors (e.g. Bowns, Rotherham, & Paisley, 1999). Schools have long been criticized for not being able to meet expectations set by policy makers (Berliner & Biddle, 1995). In fact, the history of education reform can be interpreted into a history of complaints about schools (Schlechty, 2001, p. 4), and "bashing schools and teachers is common fare in the rhetoric of reform" (Cuban, 2001, p. 1). Schools are criticized as being "retrospective, even conservative," resistant to changes despite many education reform efforts (Brown, 1994), and inclined to fall into "regression to the mean(ingless)" (Jerald, 2005, p. 4). School leaders are blamed for not having the full understanding of the core challenges raised by technology and the urgency to adopt it (e.g., Bogden, 2001).

At the center of the criticism are teachers, whose image in relation to technology has been not very positive—in fact, quite negative. In the early days, teachers were compared to Luddites in the Industrial Revolution who destroyed machines (Bryson & Castell, 1998; Conway & Zhao, 2003). Later, a more common description of teachers was as gatekeepers because teachers actually decided what technologies may enter the classroom and whether and how they could be used (Cuban, 1986; Noble, 1996). In general, teachers are characterized as reluctant and unwilling to use new technologies (MacMillan, Liu, & Timmons, 1997). Even when they do, most teachers hold an incrementalist viewpoint and they only use technology to support what they have been doing, not to make fundamental changes expected by policy makers (Cuban, 1986, 2001; Schofield, 1995, p. 104). This portrayal of teachers, on the one hand, recognizes the important role that teachers play in the process of technology implementation; on the other hand, however, it exaggerates how teachers often foil the best-laid technology plans (Conway & Zhao, 2003).

Because teachers have been identified as the key factor (and the major obstacle) in using technology in schools, teacher technology professional development has consistently been emphasized in technology policies and reports in the last two decades as "the single most important step" toward integrating technology into education (Culp et al., 2003; CEO Forum on Education and Technology, 1999). For example, the national information and communication technology (ICT) plan specifies its first goal as "All teachers in the nation will have the training and support they need to help students learn using computers and the information superhighway" (U.S. Department of Education, 1996, p. 5), and the second national educational technology plan continue to stress that "we must provide teachers with the skills necessary to integrate technology effectively into the curriculum" (U.S. Department of Education, 2000, p. 13). Specific projects and grants have been dedicated to improving teacher technology preparation. For example, the U.S. Department of Education's Preparing Tomorrow's Teachers to Use Technology (PT3) program has spent $337.5 million and awarded 441 grants since 1999 (U.S. Department of Education, 2006). Similarly, teacher technology professional development remains the most common top priority for educational technology spending in most states besides hardware (Fox, 2005).

To summarize, the continued enthusiasm about and investment in technology despite the lack of consistent evidence of positive impact has been sustained at the policy level by three factors. First, the symbolic value of technology is often sufficient to justify the investment because by simply bringing the newest technology to schools or sometimes even calling for such actions gives the policy makers what they are looking: to appear progressive and on the cutting edge. Additionally with any new technology, it is always possible to identify a few exemplary cases of educational benefits. Second, the future-oriented yet uncertain nature of new technologies can always bring hope and engender fear, making it almost impossible to resist act against the new possibilities. Third, when all fails, one can always point to the teachers, the existing practices, and traditions as the causes without serious questioning the policy itself, making it an issue of poor implementation rather than bad policy.

Policy Implementation Unlike policymaking, implementation of polices or actual making use of technology in schools is much more difficult than imagined by policy makers. The symbol-driven policymaking process makes technology infusing in education appear straightforward and smooth: You buy the stuff, train the teachers, and voila, you have better students and better education. However, putting ideas into practice is a process far more complex than expected (Fullan, 2001, p. 5).

Innovation as Invasion Technological innovations are often talked about with enthusiasm and passion. They are invariably viewed as something good and should be adopted without question by policy makers (Zhao, Lei, & Frank, 2006). But innovation is, in essence, a disturbance to an existing organization: "innovation implies change" (Lubrano, 1997, p. 3). Almost all technology policies and decisions are about changes that require specific changes in schools, such as reengineering the system and revising learning standards (Bogden, 2001). In all policies advocating for investment in technology, technology is universally viewed as a change agent that can catalyze various changes in learning, teaching, and the learning environment (Culp et al., 2003). These changes have significant impact on the organization.

All organizations, like ecosystems, have the tendency or ability to maintain internal equilibrium (Odum, 1975). The introduction of new innovations, intentional or unintentional, affects this equilibrium to varying degrees. A new technology project often requires the installation of new facilities, modification of existing policies or establishment of new policies and regulations, reallocation of resources, changes in the informal and formal activities, and may also affect the social relationships of different groups of people (Nardi & O'Day, 1999, p. 17). In this way, technology innovations introduced to schools are essentially invaders from the outside (Zhao & Frank, 2003). Whether they can be successfully adopted and become permanently established depends on their compatibility with the teaching and learning environment and the co-adaptation between the technology and the system (Lei, 2005; Zhao & Frank, 2003).

Policy's faithful pursuit of the most cutting-edge technology creates constant disturbance to schools. In the last two decades we have seen dramatic development of technology hardware, software, and connectivity. Computers have developed from mainframe to desktop to laptop and handhelds, software has been updated every few months, and Internet connection has changed from dial-up to cable and then to wireless. The fast development roughly followed Moore's law which predicts that technology advances double in every 18 to 24 months. There is always something new emerging, so there are always more innovations being introduced to schools, and they are not necessarily connected with or complementary to each other, further complicating the situation. As Michael Fullan (2001) points out, the main problem in schools is that there are "too may disconnected, episodic, fragmented, superficially adorned projects" (p. 21), which creates constant disturbance to schools.

The Process of Implementation   Policy implementation in schools is a continuous social process that takes place in a dynamic, ever-evolving society (Brown, 1994; Bruce, 1993; Noble, 1977). Its complicated and dynamic nature resembles that of a new species introduced to an ecosystem. A school system can be viewed as an example of an ecosystem that is a combination of diverse components and various relationships (Bronfenbrenner, 1979; Zhao & Frank, 2003). In this complex social environment, various groups are closely connected with each other and form a network of changes (Honey et al., 2005). An innovation is not independent and isolated, but is situated in this network and connected with the context. What happens to an innovation is, to a great extent, determined by the existing goals and practices of the organization and the individuals (Bruce, 1993). A newly introduced innovation often requires simultaneous innovations in pedagogy, curriculum, assessment, and school organization (Dede, 1998). It also affects the relationships in the network, and the ongoing interaction catalyzes changes in social relationships (Bruce, 1993). Changes in the organization and individuals, in return, affect whether or not and how the innovation is adopted. So changes in schools are bidirectional or even circular (Keiny, 2002), which is akin to the ecological process, in which gene, organisms and the environment continuously interact with each other, co-evolve, and co-adapt to each other, and these interactions shape not only the organism but also the environment (Lewontin, 2000). Similarly, changes caused by the interactions between an innovation and the school system not only determine how the innovation is adopted, but also affect the organization and operation of the school system. The dynamic co-adaptation and co-evolution of users, the innovation, resources, and the system determines whether the utility of the innovation can be realized in schools (Bruce, 1993; Zhao & Frank, 2003).

Conditions for Successful Technology Integration
Therefore, a healthy co-adaptation of technology and the school system is influenced and constrained by many conditions. These conditions can be factors related to the school technology resources, characteristics of the school culture, readiness and experiences of teachers and students on using technology, and the dynamics of social interactions in the school system. The successful implementation of a technology project depends on not only a working technological infrastructure to ensure that the technology can be used, but more importantly, an effective human infrastructure that supports and facilitates the meaningful use of technology (Byrom & Bingham, 2001; Lei, 2005; Zhao, Pugh, Sheldon, & Byers, 2002).

These conditions are not independent of one another, and their impact on technology implementation is not a simple and linear one. On the contrary, they are entangled with each other. Their influence varies from case to case. Their interactions and relationships change as the school environment evolves with the technology implementation, and the changes are situated in local contexts (Bruce, 1993; Buckenmeyer, 2001; Fullan, 2001, p. 92; Honey et al., 2005). The school context gradually evolves, changing the characteristics of teachers, students, and their technology uses, which further change the challenges the school faces at different stages. Since technology uses in schools constantly change and so do all of the other members of the ecosystem—the users, the school system, and the relationships between these subsystems—there is no "once and for all" solution to technology implementation in schools. A technology implementation plan that works at one time may not work at another time, so a dynamic plan that reflects changes works better than a static plan (Hoffman, 2002). Even if a technology project has been successful, to continue its successful implementation, old policies need to be updated, new policies need to be made, more money needs to be spent on upgrading software and updating hardware, resources and support need to be provided to both teachers and students, and more investment needs to be put in sustaining and improving sufficient technical support. All these changes depend on consistently strong leadership. Thus it is important to provide ongoing technology planning and evaluation, to continuously refine current practices, and to provide timely support (November, Staudt, Costello, & Huske, 1998).

Lack of Specific Goals or Criteria to Judge Success
However, even if all the necessary conditions are in place, it is still difficult to judge the success of technology implementation because there lacks specific goals. Policymaking about technology at high levels can be vague and generic as long as it can project sensational images: every student connected to the Internet, students learning with real scientists, learning with a tireless teacher, bringing the world into the classroom, learning anywhere and anytime from anyone, to name just a few examples. Although researchers have repeatedly suggested that successful policy implementation requires clearly defined goals directly connected to student learning (e.g., Buckenmeyer, 2001; Fullan, 2001, p. 76; Hawkes, 1995), no specific educational goals are defined in educational technology policy documents except for tangible intermediary goals such as figures for hardware, student to computer ratio, and connection speed. In a paper that reviews educational technology policy in the last 20 years, Culp, Honey, and Mandinach (2003) identify six major recommendations that have remained highly consis-

tent over time, but none of which is about the educational outcomes of technology investment. Most of these policy documents are not clear what goals they intend to help policy makers achieve.

Although specific quantitative data (such as numbers, percentile, or test scores) are commonly used in policy documents to demonstrate the current "crisis" in education and to justify the need for technology, they are not often set as the specific goal for technology to achieve. Even in the few cases where student outcomes are mentioned, it is done using vague and unmeasured terms (Besser, 1993). For example, the most recent national educational technology plan concludes that students must have "the knowledge and competence to compete in an increasingly technology-driven world economy" (U.S. Department of Education, 2004, p. 45), however, it is not clear what exactly the "knowledge and competence" is and how technology can help attain it. Similarly, the No Child Left Behind Act requires that every student must be "technologically literate by the time the student finishes the eighth grade" (No Child Left Behind Act, 2001, p. 248), but the requirement does not define the knowledge and skills students need to be qualified as "technologically literate," nor does it suggest the mechanism for accountability (Honey et al., 2005). Other fashionable terms such as "technological literacy" (U.S. Department of Education, 1996; Committee on Assessing Technological Literacy, National Academy of Engineering, National Research Council, Gamire, & Pearson, 2002), "technology and information literacy skills" (U.S. Department of Education, 2000), "21st century skills" (CEO Forum on Education and Technology, 2001) and "quality education" (Bogden, 2001) are often used in the rhetoric of educational technology policy, but neither the nature of these outcomes (i.e., what they are and mean), nor the ways to achieve them or the expected growth is clearly identified. Nevertheless, dramatic improvement in education by "any measure" and "the greatest leap forward in achievement in the history of education" (U.S. Department of Education, 2004, p. 11) is expected.

A convenient criterion is student academic achievement. However, it is very difficult to establish causal relationships between technology use and student academic achievement, because student achievement is influenced by many factors. The impact of technology use on student outcomes is not determined merely by the particular technology uses, but rather mediated by environmental factors, the users, and the constantly changing interactions and mutual influences. In addition, the use of technology in schools is part of a complex network, and changes in classroom technologies correlate to changes in other educational factors (Honey et al., 2005). Thus, it is unrealistic to draw simple cause-effect relations or to expect dramatic changes in student performance through one or two specific technology projects.

Consequently, schools can only guess what is expected from their technology investment (Moore, 2001). Most school leaders do not have a clear sense of how to evaluate effective use of technology (Russell, Bebell, O'Dwyer, &

O'Connor, 2003), and teachers do not know much about their school/districts' vision for the use of technology in their classrooms (Higgins & Russell, 2003).

As a result of lacking a sound understanding of the specific goals of technology integration, the use of technology per se has become the goal. Schools, as well as educational technology research, often turn to how much time students use technology and what technology is available as indicators of successful technology integration, but do not measure whether or not, or how, technology is being used in meaningful ways in teaching and learning (Lei & Zhao, 2007; Moore, 2001).

In summary, the lack of consistent evidence of positive effects on education can be attributed to four factors. First, the complexity of the implementation process makes it difficult to realize the potentials of technology claimed by policy makers, at least not consistently across the board. Some of the claims may be overstated anyway in order to attract support for investment. Second, technology changes rapidly but schools do not. Policy makers, in their pursuit of the symbolic value, tend to jump on the latest technology. As a result, new technologies are introduced while schools are still working to digest the old ones. Third, many schools do not have the required conditions to realize the potential of technology or not sufficient resources and time are provided to enable such realization. Many technology policies tend to be generous with investment in hardware and infrastructure, but not on software and human resources, which are equally important for successful implementation. Fourth, the lack of specific goals makes it difficult to come up with universally accepted measures of success of technology, resulting in conflicting conclusions.

Why Is Technology Effective Outside Schools but Not In Schools?

The significant impact of technology on human society and the improvement of productivity in certain industries have always been used by education policy makers to justify their proposals to put technology in schools. They argue that technology has changed the world in which future citizens, today's students, will work. Thus, schools must infuse technology into classrooms to make sure that their graduates will be able to cope with the changed society (e.g., U.S. Department of Education, 1996, 2000, 2004). Furthermore, in the hope of replicating the effects of technology in other industries to improve the efficiency of education, policy makers argue that schools should also modernize themselves through technology (Mehlinger, 1996; Murray, 2006). These arguments sound reasonable. Indeed, if the business sector can improve their productivity through technology, why not the education sector?

How is Efficiency Achieved in Other Industries? As discussed earlier in this chapter, technology has greatly improved productivity and has saved costs in sectors outside education. In other industries, efficiency is pursued by following a fundamental principle of reducing the cost and/or increasing the output, and this is achieved through a number of strategies: effective use of technology, re-organization, relocating jobs, training, and specific and measurable goals.

First, efficiency in other industries is achieved by the effective use of technology to replace human workers. Although the society has long been uncomfortable with machines doing human work, not only because of job loss, but also because of a sense of dignity loss (Seidensticker, 2006, p. 12), industries have been relentless in replacing human workers with technology. In the pursuit of efficiency, businesses are pioneers in inventing and adopting new technologies. From machines in the industrial revolution to the Internet, PDAs, and RFID tags in the IT revolution, technology is employed widely in businesses to increase productivity and lower labor costs (Panel of the National Academy of Public Administration, 2006, p. 8), increase and maintain the quality and consistency of products (Magaziner, n.d.), cut human errors, and enable the talent of employees to be spent on more critical and productive jobs. The role of technology has been vital to creating business value (Hall & Suh, 2004). For example, the use of bar codes saves the food industry $17 billion per year, or 50 times the savings initially forecast (Stone, 2003).

Second, efficiency is also often achieved by following cost-benefit analysis to move production to wherever the cost is lower. Relocating activities to developing countries greatly lowered the cost and improved the efficiency, and technology has made this process easier and more convenient. Nowadays companies are breaking their functions into discrete fragments and performing each function in "whatever location allows them to minimize costs" (Bernanke, 2006, p. 7).Offshore outsourcing offers feasible combinations of cost and service that helps U.S. companies to remain competitive in the world market (Pollack, 2004). For example, the expected savings by outsourcing services to India are at least 40% and can be as high as 80% (Dossani & Kenney, 2003). Globalized production makes IT hardware some 10% to 30% less expensive than it otherwise would have been (Institute for International Economics, 2003). By sending jobs to developing countries, some companies not only save 75% on wages, but also gain a 100% increase in productivity (Friedman, 2005, p. 260). To lower cost, an estimated 3.5 to 6 million U.S. jobs will be offshored by 2015 (Dossani & Kenney, 2006, p. 194).

In addition, reorganization and restructuring is a strategy commonly used to reduce cost. Companies sometimes sell non-profitable portions to improve their balance, sell underutilized assets, and reorganize functions such as sales, marketing, and distribution.

To ensure efficiency, changes and reforms in other industries are frequent, dramatic, and sometimes relentless. The Trade Unions Anticipating Change in Europe (TRACE), a large-scale project that serves the European trade unions to respond to economic and industrial changes, summarizes it well: "Not a day goes by without announcements of further cases of restructuring—closures, relocations, privatisations, mergers and acquisitions, decentralisation, outsourcing and offshoring" (Holman, 2006, p. 1).

Can Schools Achieve the Same Effects and Why Has Technology not Transformed Schools?

But schools have not been able to take the same strategies and perhaps never will for a number of reasons. First, education is considered a human business. Schools are still structured around human teachers, with one teacher instructing a group of students. Technology is primarily considered an aid for the teacher. To have better-qualified teachers and more teachers (thus smaller classes) is what policy makers and the public want. One of the most significant elements of NCLB, for example, is highly qualified teachers. It is thus unlikely that schools can propose to begin to replace or reduce human teachers because of technology. In addition, reshuffling of jobs and personnel is not easy in schools because school principles, unlike business managers, do not have sufficient control over personnel, which makes it difficult to change school personnel or hire teachers who are a good fit with the reform (Jerald, 2005; Levin & Quinn, 2003)

Second, it is unlikely that the possibility of outsourcing parts of the education process enabled by technology will be fully realized soon because of long-held traditions—education is local and physical. It has been suggested that deeply held cultural beliefs about the nature of teaching and learning steer towards certain forms of instruction and ways of organizing instruction (e.g., Cuban, 1986, 1993a, 1993b; Warschauer, 2003). Schools, as Papert (1993) points out, remain largely committed to the late nineteenth century's educational philosophy that attempts to "impose a single way of knowing on everyone" (p. 3). The traditional belief that children "should be educated in a specific place, for a certain number of hours, and a certain number of days during the week and year" (Ravitch, 1993, p. 45) is directly at odds with the "Anytime, anywhere, any pace" learning supported by ICT. As individual productivity tools, computers demand personalization and they offer students the flexibility of learning. By nature, they are a "children's machine" that gives students control over what to learn, how to learn, and at what pace (Papert, 1993; Zhao, Tan, & Mishra, 2000). Learning supported by technology is increasingly constructivist, nonlinear, and sometimes chaotic, and it happens far beyond the borders of the conventional classroom. However, both the physical and conceptual structure of school, such as the view of teaching as transmission of knowledge from teachers to students instead of students' exploration, the limited classroom space and the bulky size of computers, and the 45-minute period, is quite incompatible with effective use of technology (Collins, 1996, p. 61). The constraining effect of school traditions on technology leads to trivialization of technology reforms rather than the transformation of learning in schools (Feldman, Konold, & Coulter, 2000). As a result technology integration in schools has been very slow and using technology to improve efficiency in schools has been mostly unsuccessful.

Third, there lack specific measures to spread effective practices. It would be unfair to categorically characterize technology investments as a complete waste or to suggest that technology has no educational benefits. In fact, there are plenty of "success stories" and empirical studies to show that when used properly, technology does lead to a wide range of educational benefits (e.g., see U.S. Department of Education, 2004; President's Committee of Advisors on Science and Technology [Panel on Educational Technology], 1997). These investments can serve as important steps towards better informed technology decision making and improved technology investment efforts. However, because educational technology policies and decisions do not specify measurable educational outcomes, it is difficult to identify effective practices for integrating technology in teaching and learning, let alone to replicate and spread effective practices. The problem is that the effects seem to be confined to a very small number of schools. Somehow, unlike hardware, connectivity, and software, the practices that lead to positive educational outcomes have had a difficult time to spread across classrooms and schools to lead the promised transformation.

Additionally, there is no sufficient social pressure on spreading effective practices. In line with the pursuit of symbolic value of technology in policymaking, schools often pursue the symbolic value of technology instead of the practical value, because it is often the technology initiatives and bold technology decisions that make the news, not what happens after. By emphasizing the symbolic value, many schools adopt reforms that they do not have the capacity to implement (Fullan, 2001, p. 6). Schools may even deliberately disregard the lessons of their predecessors to appear cutting-edge and ahead of others (Stager, 2006). Failing to take full advantage of lessons from previous efforts, schools are making very slow, if any, progress in integrating technology in education.

However, changes that are happening outside of education have significant impact on education. Information technology that is transforming our society is also posing significant challenges to schools. Schools will face increasing pressure and challenges as technology further alters our society.

What Comes Next: New Context for Technology Policymaking

Thus far, we have examined two significant questions in educational technology policy, namely why, despite consistent evidence of significant returns of investment in school technology, policy makers continue their enthusiasm about and investment in putting more technology into schools and why, despite the continued investment, technology has not produced changes of similar magnitude to those in sectors outside education. While technology has not produced the intended and planned changes inside schools, it has, ironi-

cally, resulted in significant changes that are very likely to affect schools in fundamental ways. These changes pose new challenges for education policy makers and practitioners and demand new ways of thinking about technology and education.

The Changes

The Online World   One of the significant changes brought about by technology is the emergence of the online world. Modern information and communication technology is not only, as traditionally conceived, a new tool that we use to enhance our lives in the physical world. It has also created a whole new world. In this new world we use different technologies to seek and provide resources and information, express ourselves, communicate with others, create, consume, and entertain, often assuming new identities. The scope of the online world is comparable to that of the physical world. From online gaming, online dating, and virtual marriage, to e-learning, e-business, and e-governance, activities that are happening online include everything imaginable. The size of this online world is phenomenal and the growth dramatic, in terms of both the mere population of users and the amount of time people spend involving online activities. There were about 800 million Internet users around the world in 2004 (Zooknic, n.d.). This number increased to about 1.41 billion as of March 2008 (Internet World Stats, 2008a). Among them more than 210.6 million are Americans (Internet World Stats, 2008b), who account for 73% of the U.S. population (Madden, 2006), spent an average of three hours a day online (Stone, 2005), and approximately $170 billion in 2006 (comScore Networks, 2006).

Many people are spending their physical world time living a second or third life in the online world. Second Life, a popular 3-D virtual world, has over 1.67 million residents. A recent study on massively multiplayer online games (MMOPG) finds that the current global player populations of three popular game titles (Lineage I, Lineage II, and The World of Warcraft) total over 9.5 million, which is greater than any U.S. metropolis (Steinkuhler, 2006). An increasing number of individuals are merging their physical world life with their virtual one through mobile technology and dynamic Web sites such as blogs, discussion forums, personal Web sites, and social networking Web sites such as MySpace. In the United States, two out of every three people online visit social networking sites (Lamb, 2006).

Moreover, the online world penetrates the physical world, as more and more activities are consigned to and performed by means of digital resources. We learn, work, entertain, and stay connected with family and friends in a world that is mediated by ICT that has become an essential part of our daily lives. People are seeking real world information from the digital world, as they move away from traditional media such as TV and daily newspaper to stay informed online, using niche news channels, blogs, podcasts, and Web sites (Estabrook, Witt, & Rainie, 2007; Haller, 2005; Horrigan, 2008). For Americans with high-speed connections at home, the Internet is the most popular source for science news and information (Pew Internet and American Life Project & The Exploratorium, 2006). Today, an average American home has 26 different electronic devices for communication and media, thereby making the home media ecology much more complicated than 30 years ago (Rainie, 2006b).There is no doubt that in the future more of our worldly activities will be conducted online. This is even more so, both now and in the future, for our children, who, by their nature, are the digital generation.

The Digital Generation   The second significant change that will affect education is the coming of age of the digital generation. Also called the N(et) generation (Tapscott, 1998), Generation M(-edia/-ultitasker; Rideout, Foehr, & Roberts, 2005), or the Digital Natives (Prensky, 2001), the digital generation is the first generation of people growing up with digital technology, first computers, then the Internet, and other ubiquitous information and communication devices such as game consoles, cell phones, PDAs, and iPods. When referred to as the "digital natives," it is in contrast to the "digital immigrants," that is, their parents and teachers, who have not had technology as a natural part of their lives. Digital natives are considered to be more comfortable with the digital technology and to be innovative users of available technology as well as eager adopters of new technology, often setting trends of technology use both in school and at home (Rideout et al., 2005). They are using more kinds of technology, using increasingly more sophisticated technology, at an increasingly earlier age, and they are using technology more regularly (NetDay, 2006). The average time this generation spends on all types of media every week is equivalent to a full time job (Rideout et al., 2005). Today a typical 21-year-old has, on average, exchanged 250,000 e-mails, instant messages, and phone text messages, spent 5,000 hours on game playing, 10,000 hours of cell phone use, and 3,500 hours online (Rainie, 2006a).

Their digital experiences have changed not only the ways today's young people communicate, socialize, and entertain, but also fundamentally altered how they approach learning (Prensky, 2006). They are technology-savvy, confident in the positive value of technology, and reliant upon technology as an "essential and preferred component of every aspect of their lives" (U.S. Department of Education, 2004, p. 19). They are multi-taskers, often working on two or more tasks using two or more technology devices simultaneously (Rideout et al., 2005; Shifrin, 2006, p. 450). To them there is no clear distinction between play and learning. They have been learning from playing and have been playing while learning. They are not passive consumers of information, but energetic participants of and active contributors to the digital world. *Growing Up Digital* (Tapscott, 1998), they are natural participants in the online world, and they are shaping and creating it.

Globalization and Outsourcing Education   Another significant change cannot be completely attributed to technology, but it is a major and essential contributing factor. This change is globalization or the "flattening of the world." According to Thomas Friedman (2005), the world has been "flattened" by a number of global forces: the convergence of advanced technologies, new ways of doing business, the removal of economic and political obstructions, and the rapid introduction of millions of young professionals from all over the world. Advances in transportation, information, and communication technologies have shrunk the physical distances between places on the globe, making it possible for easier, cheaper, and faster movements of people, goods, money, and data. As a result, businesses can now locate different parts of their business process globally in order to achieve efficiency and stay competitive (Bernanke, 2006).

The opportunities and pressures afforded by globalization to other industries apply similarly to education. When global outsourcing (or offshoring) has become a common, albeit controversial, practice for all businesses, it is also becoming increasingly common in education. Outsourcing in the field of education has a long history, but it has been mainly contracting services and some organizational functions such as dining and bookstore operations to instructions to an external provider (Adams, Guarino, Robichaux, & Edwards, 2004), mostly within the country and within the same region (Pollack, 2004). But now teaching is being conducted in other locations, physical or virtual. For example, online tutoring now accounts for 6% of the entire tuition market in the United States, and the service provider can be from anywhere on the globe. Singapore and India are offering online math tutoring to American students, and Pakistan is predicted to be a rising star in the global educational services outsourcing market ("Why Pak will have more online tutors," 2006).

Education globalization also brings opportunities for global collaboration. Students can work on projects with peers from other schools or states, or other countries. Organizations such as the World-links and the ORACLE education foundation are connecting students from the world. Learning is becoming increasing diversified and globalized (e.g., Hay, 2008; Smith & Ayers, 2006).

Online Courses and Virtual Schools   Online education is yet another significant change brought about by technology that will have a long-lasting impact on education. Started and successful in higher education, online education has spread to K–12 education and is experiencing explosive growth (U.S. Department of Education, 2004). For K–12 students, using online learning systems, taking online courses, and attending online schools are becoming common practices. The 2005 NetDay Speaking Out Event finds that 17% of 6th graders, 28% of 9th graders, and 46% of 12th graders say that they or someone they know have taken an online class (NetDay, 2006). Students take virtual field trips, attend e-conferences, and learn with peers from other schools, states, and even students from other countries (e.g., Blachowicz & Obrochta, 2005; Stainfield, Fisher,

Ford, & Solem, 2000). Currently 57% of American school districts host online instructional applications via a Web-hosting model (Quality Education Data, 2005). Schools employ a variety of technologies such as streaming audio and video, computer animations, e-mail, newsgroups, chat rooms, bulletin boards, and digital portfolios to provide enriched learning experiences and more options to students. Many organizations offer online learning opportunities for K–12 students. For example, NASA held e-conferencing on science programs including aviation history, planetary exploring, and weather tracking (McDermon, 2005).

The growth of virtual schools is even more impressive. The Virtual High School, one of the first pre-collegiate level online schools, started offering Internet-based courses for the first time in September 1997, to about 500 students in 27 schools in 10 states (U.S. Department of Education, 2000). At the time of this writing, the Virtual High School offers 296 courses to 10,111 students in 520 U.S. schools, located in 30 states and 39 international schools (Virtual High School, 2008). As of January 2007, 24 states in the U.S. operate state-level virtual schools (Mehta, 2007), such as Michigan Virtual High School, Illinois Virtual High School and Colorado Online Learning (Shambles, n.d.). Indiana University offers more than 100 high school courses through its Independent Study Program.[2] In Hawaii, about 200 to 400 students coming from 30 to 48 secondary schools in the Hawaii Department of Education school system take online courses from the Hawaii E-School every semester (Hawaii Department of Education, n.d.). In April 2006, the State of Michigan passed a law making online learning experience part of its high school graduate requirement (Michigan Virtual University, 2006).

After nearly two decades of development, virtual schools have developed into a broad range of varieties. The courses offered vary from general K–12 curriculum to specific subjects such as science, mathematics, or foreign languages; the targeted audience varies from all students to targeted groups of students such as gifted students, students with special needs, and homeschoolers; the level of curriculum varies from general courses and remedial courses to advanced courses and college preparation courses; and the pace varies from accelerated, standard, or extended learning pace (Müller & Ahearn, 2004). With expanded options and flexible scheduling, virtual schools are providing students with unprecedented learning opportunities.

The rapid growth of virtual schools are posing unprecedented pressure on traditional schools to compete for students, teachers, and funding. Virtual schools offer an appealing option to homeschoolers as well as traditional school students because of the flexibility and choices that can serve more students (Long, 2004). Virtual schools are also attractive to teachers because they are not limited by the geographic boundaries, physical settings, or regular daily schedules. For example, teachers who cannot teach in regular school settings due to health problems can teach for online schools (Anderson, 2003), and they do not have to reside in the same state where the virtual school is located.

In addition, virtual schools are gaining the same status as traditional schools in receiving public funding. Take the Florida Virtual School as an example. Founded in 1997 as the first statewide virtual high school, the Florida Virtual School has become one of the public school districts in Florida. It now receives state aid through a set per-pupil amount in the same ways as any other regular school district does (Fox, 2005) and has a $43-million annual budget (Mehta, 2007). In the 2006-2007 academic year, this virtual school had over 576 teachers from Florida and beyond, offered more than 90 courses for grades 6 to 12, and served more than 52,000 students in all Florida school districts and around the nation, up from 31,000 students from the previous academic year.[3] It is reasonable to expect more virtual schools similar to the Florida Virtual School are on the way (Mehta, 2007).

Homeschooling and Privatization of Education   Homeschooling and the privatization of education are certainly not the result of technology but technology has been fully employed by both to advance their causes. Home-schooling has experienced a rapid growth in the last decade. The population of homeschoolers is larger than that of either vouchers program or charter schools (Bauman, 2002). As of 2003, about 1.1 million students were being home-schooled in the United States. The percentage of home-schoolers in all school-age population increased to 2.2% in 2003 from 1.7% in 1999 (National Center for Education Statistics [NCES], 2004). It is estimated that about 2.2 million students are homeschoolers (Apple, Inc., n.d.).

As a radical departure from traditional education, homeschooling has profound impact on traditional schools, and has the potential to force traditional schools to make significant adjustment to current practices (Bauman, 2002). Bauman (2002) predicts that with the growth of homeschooling, the demand for educational services from public schools and other organizations will also grow. At least two models can meet this demand, and technology has been used to support both. The first model is that teachers or schools form online schools and offer their educational services to homeschoolers. Parents can buy these online courses with their vouchers. This, in fact, has been happening. Public schools have begun to provide various services to homeschoolers including allowing them to take regular courses or participating in extracurricular activities (Bauman, 2002). Several states have developed courses that can be taken online for credits by homeschoolers and others (e.g., Carothers, 2000; Trotter, 2001). The other model is that groups of parents organize "schools" and buy online courses from all over the world. With the help of ICT, homeschooling families can connect with and rely on one another much more easily than before. This makes it possible for them to form new educational institutions (Hill, 2000).

Many private organizations and enterprises entered the K–12 education field to target homeschooling families (Hill, 2000). But now privatizing a range of educational services is widespread even for public schools. Schools are outsourcing more services than ever to reduce cost. A national study shows that half of the 2,318 superintendents surveyed in a study in 2003 are open to the possibility of privatization of instructional services (Belfield & Wooten, 2003). According to the annual privatization report conducted by Reason Public Policy Institute, private companies make up the majority of providers of after-school tutoring services required by NCLB for students who fail to make adequate yearly progress, and an estimated 15,000 for-profit education businesses across the United States offered their services for K–12 education in areas such as tutoring, student assessment, and online content and made a revenue of $50.1 billion (Segal, 2004).

Education has become diversified, with charter schools, magnet schools, voucher programs, homeschooling, and virtual schools co-existing with traditional public schools. Although these institutions have been in existence for some time, their magnitude and impact are farther-reaching than ever before due to the fact that ICT has become "an appliance." If traditional public schools are not able to keep up with the changes, an increasing proportion of the population will seek alternatives, and the continuing existence of public schools will be threatened (Good, 2001; Schlechty, 2001, p. 32).

The Challenges These changes pose serious challenges to policy makers and education leaders. In different ways, these changes challenge policy makers and leaders to adopt a new way of thinking about technology. Instead of viewing technology as simply a tool that holds tremendous potential for improving student learning of the traditional curriculum, they must consider technology as a new context for education. This context is not a choice but an inescapable new reality. This new reality is full of controversy and questions await policy decisions and empirical research.

To Block or Not to Block: Internet Safety verus. Freedom to Access The online world is a classic example of a double-edged sword. While policy makers and education leaders have been enthusiastic about its vast educational benefits, they are equally, perhaps more, concerned about the potential harms it can bring to students. In order to protect students from harmful content and prevent students from misconduct, virtually all schools in the United States censor what students can do on the school computer and network through what is commonly called Acceptable Use Policy (AUP). As early as 1995, when the Internet was still in its infancy, U.S. lawmakers introduced bills to control what can be transmitted online to minors (under age 18). A version of these bills became the Communications Decency Act of 1996 (CDA), which criminalized the transmission of materials that were "obscene or indecent" to persons known to be under 18 and impose criminal sanctions on anyone who:

> knowingly (A) uses an interactive computer service to send to a specific person or persons under 18 years of age, or (B) uses any interactive computer service to display in a

> manner available to a person under 18 years of age, any comment, request, suggestion, proposal, image, or other communication that, in context, depicts or describes, in terms patently offensive as measured by contemporary community standards, sexual or excretory activities or organs. (p. 80)

Although part of the CDA was blocked by a panel of federal judges in 1996 and the Supreme Court upheld their ruling in 1997, the lawmakers did not give up their efforts. Since the Supreme Court overturned the CDA, Congress has made two narrower attempts to regulate children's exposure to Internet indecency: the Child Online Protection Act (COPA) in 1998 and the Children's Internet Protection Act (CIPA) in 2000. COPA was eventually overturned but CIPA was found constitutional by the Supreme Court in 2004 and has since become the rule of the land. CIPA requires that all public schools and public libraries block or filter out obscene materials, child pornography, and materials harmful to minors. Recently, social-networking Web sites have become the center of contention. While the use of social-networking sites has become a regular component of many young people's daily lives, schools are ambiguous with the use of such sites (eSchool News, 2006). Meanwhile, policy makers see more danger than benefit of such sites and have proposed a number of policies to ban them in schools. The controversial Deleting Online Predators Act of 2006 was proposed in the U.S. Congress out of concern for children's online safety. This bill proposed to impose age-limits on users who visit social-networking sites such as MySpace.com to 18 years and older (Brumfield, 2006). This bill was reintroduced in 2007 as the Deleting Online Predators Act of 2007 and was referred to the House Committee on Energy and Commerce. Another bill, Protecting Children in the 21st Century Act, introduced in the U.S. Senate in February 2007, seeks to ban Wikipedia and social-networking sites in schools and libraries (Racoma, 2007).

Blocking access seems to have been the dominating mindset for policy makers and schools must comply in order to receive federal funds. However, while the effectiveness of blocking is largely questionable, as discussed earlier in this chapter, the negative impact seems clear. Schools not only over-block Web sites that are of educational value, but also block access to forms of using the Internet for more engaging ways of learning, such as using synchronous communication tools (e.g., Skype or other video/audio conferencing systems, chatting, and instant messaging) to interact with experts, instructors, and peers outside school. In essence, school computers with Internet access have become a little more than a static library, a place to access pre-selected materials rather than a dynamic, multi-modal, multi-functional online world.

Depriving students of access to the full capacity of the Internet can also bring harmful consequences. Researchers argue that blocking represents a simplistic view of a one-way child-Internet relationship, treating children as passive recipients of information rather than teaching them about the complexity of the online world, in which they regularly participate outside of school (Yan, 2008). Furthermore, because many low-income students only have access to the Internet at school while their more affluent peers have access at home, blocking access to the full functions of the Internet deprive these children of educational opportunities such as online courses, tutoring, creating and posting media products, and interacting with experts and peers outside school. Hence, it further widens the digital divide (Yan, 2008).

Policy makers and education leaders need to reexamine this issue based on more empirical research about the psychological and cognitive impact of participation in the online world, the probability and extent of potential harms and benefits, and the effectiveness of various blocking practices and their impact on educational practices in schools.

What is Worth Teaching and Learning? Technology redefines talents. That is, technology can increase the value of certain knowledge and skills while decreasing the value of others. For example, the widespread use of printing technology has made the ability to read and write much more worthwhile than before. The invention of stairways enabled us to build houses higher than one story, but defined people who cannot climb the stairways as handicapped (Office of the Deputy President of South Africa, 1997). The wide spread of mass media has made a whole cluster of talents such as playing sports, singing, dancing, and performing much more valuable than before because these talents can now reach many people as entertainment products and services (Fang, 1997; Schoenherr, 2005). Technology also creates new talents in various ways. New technology requires new uses, so people need to learn new skills in order to adopt it. New technology also needs creative users who can take existing technology and re-invent it. Innovators drive technology development from one stage to another, and the development of technology in return inspires creativity (Basalla, 1988). Steam-engines in the 18th century initially allowed the transportation and control of power, which inspired the creative use of steam-engine in other technologies such as power loom, trains, boats, and other machines, and it further facilitated urbanization and modernization, and hence fundamentally changed our world and our lives (Derry & Williams, 1993).

In a similar fashion but at a much more rapid rate, information and communication technology is fundamentally changing what talents are valuable. Many new professions have emerged around ICT, especially since the advent of the World Wide Web. IT-producing and IT-using industries employ more than 10 million Americans (Information Technology Association of America [ITTA], 2003) and contributed half of the acceleration in U.S. economic growth (Jorgenson, Ho, & Stiroh, 2005; Jorgenson, 2005). Computer programming, database management, Web-design, network security, digital animation, and technology support are just some of the more commonly known professions that emerged along with the growth of the IT industry. These professions require new skills, new knowledge, and new talents.

The online world has also increased the value of other talents. For example, YouTube and podcasting make it possible for any individual to operate what essentially would be considered a TV or radio station. Blogging and Web publishing make it possible for anyone with the ability to operate a "newspaper." Thus individuals with media talents do not need a media network to reach a worldwide audience, neither do those who have other special talents and knowledge to share or sell. Consequently, the ability to design, produce, and distribute multi-media products becomes a very valuable commodity.

The new technologies have changed the role of consumers as well. They do not simply purchase and consume. But rather they take on multiple roles, becoming "producers, collaborators, researchers and publishers" (Stead, 2006, p. 6). For example, 64% of teenagers online have created content for the Internet through various activities including maintaining blogs, creating personal Web sites, creating and maintaining sites for others or business, sharing original artwork, videos, or stories (Lenhart, Madden, Macgill, & Smith, 2007). The contribution of online gamers from around the globe makes the economy of some popular MMOPG game worlds rival the economies of many real world countries (Castronova, 2001).

With the ever-decreasing cost in computers and Internet connection, the threshold of starting an online business is lower than ever before. A wave of Internet entrepreneurs is rising and the new "dot-economy" is booming (Sipress, 2006). Physical products or services can be exchanged and sold online as well as virtual products and services: textures, programs, pictures, models, movies, videos, animations, games, or Web sites (e.g., Dibbell, 2006). Playing online games, which did not exist a few decades ago and was mainly an entertainment or even viewed as a waste of time, is a new talent that can help players to earn not only respect from other players, but also, at times, earn real money. Thousands of "gold farmers" around the real world are making real money in a game world by selling virtual items valued in online games (Jin, 2006). For a real life investment of $9.95, Anshe Chung, an online personality in the 3-D virtual world of Second Life, has become the first online millionaire (in U.S. dollars) in 2 years. Her empire now hires more than 80 real world employees and is seeking to double the size.[4] It was estimated that the market for virtual-asset trading to come in at $2.7 billion in 2006 (Knowledge@Wharton, 2005).

In a recent study conducted by Pew Internet & American Life Project, a majority of people surveyed agreed that "by the year 2020, virtual reality on the internet will come to allow more productivity from most people in technologically-savvy communities than working in the 'real world'" (Anderson & Rainie, 2006, p. iii). It is safe to predict that many current jobs in the real world will be replaced by new jobs, and new talents will be created and nurtured in the digital world.

The online world creates unprecedented opportunities and demand for new talents (McIntosh, 2007; Zhao, 2007).

But schools in general are not deliberately cultivating these talents or teaching their students the knowledge and skills that have become valuable in this new world. Policy makers and education leaders need to reconsider what schools should teach to prepare students for this online world, which is both similar and different from the physical world. It is similar in that it is an extension of the real, face-to-face, physical world and thus many general principles that operate in the physical world apply in the digital world. But it is significantly different in many fundamental ways, including the tools we use to participate, the rules that govern online activities, the consequences of participation, as well as the characteristics of the participants (Balkin & Noveck, 2006; Benkler, 2007; Castronova, 2005; Lessig, 2006; Thompson, 2003; Turkle, 1984, 1995; Zigurs, 2001).

We propose the concept of digital citizenship. Digital citizenship is the ability to live in the digital world productively and be a contributing member to the society. It includes the following fundamental concepts: (a) knowledge of the nature of the digital world, including a sound understanding of the differences and connections between the physical and virtual worlds, the nature of technology and how different media work together, the nature of online/virtual activities, and the nature of the digital world as a constantly expanding and evolving global network of individual and collective participants, and the ability to tell fantasy from reality; (b) positive attitude toward the digital world, including an appreciation of the complexity and uncertainty of the digital world, positive attitude toward technical problems, effective strategies to approach technical problems (knowing where and how to obtain assistance), and effective strategies to learn new ways of communication and information sharing; (c) ability to use different tools to participate and lead in the digital world, such as online communities, to entertain, learn, and work, and to obtain and share information; and (d) ability to use different tools to create digital products and lead in the digital world (i.e., to create and manage online communities).

Are Virtual Schools Schools? The Legitimacy of Online Education Although online education seems to have grown significantly, and research suggests that online education is as effective or as ineffective as face-to-face education (Zhao, Lei, Yan, Tan, & Lai, 2005), it is not without controversy. For example, while the Florida Virtual High school has been receiving state aid as one of Florida's public school districts, the Wisconsin Virtual Academy was cut off from state funding by a recent court ruling (Foley, 2008). Not all schools are willing to cover the cost of online courses for their students. The ruling of the Wisconsin case put the role of online education at the center of national policy debate: What is the role of virtual schools? Should institutions offering e-learning be treated the same way as institutions offering traditional face to face learning? Can public funds be spent on supporting individual's online learning? Should public schools pay for online courses their students take from other institutions? Should online courses be accepted as a legitimate component of schooling?

Can Education be Offshored? Education as a Global Business Online education is a form of outsourcing. But what if the provider is a foreign company and the instructors reside in a foreign country? To cut cost or meet some special instructional need, it is technically possible for students to take courses offered by a foreign institution online or for a school to contract a teacher from overseas. But is it politically acceptable? Policy makers and education leaders will have to confront this issue and work with teachers' unions, parents, and the local community to develop better policies about contracting services. Additionally, this may force state education authorities to rethink teacher certification, performance assessment, and funding strategies.

What to Do With iPhones: Student-Owned Technology Tools Everett Rogers (1995) describes the process of innovation reaching different groups of people, from a small number of "innovators," to "early adopters," to "early majority," and then finally to "late majority." In general, technologies that reached the "early majority" and "late majority" have gone through a transformation from innovations to appliances (Zhao, Lei, & Frank, 2006). An innovation is something new or the act of "introducing something new."[5] Innovations are normally rare, expensive, unstable, unreliable, and with functions that are often uncertain and evolving. Compared to innovations, appliances are more affordable, widespread, more reliable, with fixed functions, and often disappear into the context where they are used (Lei et al., 2007). Information and communication technology has gone through this evolutionary transformation from innovation to appliance. Only a few decades ago, computers were very expensive to operate and maintain, belonging to companies or universities, and only accessible to a few experts. Now they are becoming increasingly portable, powerful, efficient, reliable, and ubiquitous, and becoming so enmeshed in many people's daily experiences that they "disappear" (Bruce & Hogan, 1998). Many students have at least one piece of powerful digital equipment, be it cell phones, iPods, or video game consoles. But what should schools do with these ubiquitous tools?

Schools in general have been discouraging their uses in school. The wisdom of this general practice is questionable because these technologies can have as much power as a computer, something the school works hard to provide each student, when they already have one. Why do schools not take advantage of what is already available?

Conclusions and Recommendations

We tend to overestimate the short-term effect of technology, but underestimate the long-term effect, as Amara's law states. Although we have not observed dramatic changes in schools as expected, technology is changing today's learners and the ways they learn, and this change in turn affects how technology is used. In fact, technology and learning have always shaped and been shaped by each other. On the one hand, how educational organizations function affects what technology survives in schools, what technology is selected out, and how technology evolves (Bruce, 1993; Lei, 2005; Tan, Lei, Shi, & Zhao, 2003; Zhao & Frank, 2003). Television has taken root in most classrooms, but instructional film has never found a secure niche; whiteboards are replacing blackboards; computer projectors are replacing overhead projectors. Many stories illustrate how the survival and prosperity of a technology in schools is determined by its interactions with other components in the school system.

Meanwhile, technology is playing an active role in changing schools and education. For example, the book can be seen as one of the first mobile and personal learning tools. Even before that, tablet and chalk provided (and still do in many developing countries) a mobile and personal learning tool for students. When everyone was able to afford a pencil, it changed how people learned (Papert, 1980). Similarly, when everyone regularly uses one or more personal computing device, changes in learning can be expected (Chan et al., 2006).

We have noticed the changes that are happening. For example, technology certainly has changed some physical aspects of traditional schools. Libraries are changed into computer labs and then media centers. Classrooms are wired, rewired (and un-wired). Furniture is rearranged to allow for the mobility within the classroom. Instructors' computers sit next to the TV. More outlets are installed. After two decades of heavy investment in technology hardware, the outlook of schools has certainly changed.

But more importantly, technology is changing how schools function and how teaching and learning is conducted. Learning is extended outside formal class sessions and outside of school, and becomes more inter-curriculum (i.e., Twining et al., 2006). Students are the driving force in changing the learning and teaching environment within schools (U.S. Department of Education, 2004). Students take their digital devices on field trips, or take virtual field trips using their digital technologies. They are sharing their work and collaborating on projects with peers in the same class, outside of the school, or even from other countries. Characterized by increasing access to new mobile and personal digital technologies out of school, today's students expect to use mobile, connected, personal computing devices within school (Chan et al., 2006). Technology has shaped the way they entertain and learn, and they are pushing traditional learning to learning with technology, to e-learning, and to m-learning.

In reviewing the development and current situation of policy, research, and practices on educational technology, we make the following recommendations.

Policy Recommendations Successful technology use in schools depends, to a great extent, on a supportive policy environment. Policymaking can support effective technol-ogy integration into schools through providing holistic support, providing ongoing technology planning, setting realistic and specific educational goals for technology use, and supporting rigorous research on technology use.

First, we need to recognize both the symbolic value and the practical value of technology innovations. As social organizations, schools have been investing and will continue to invest in technology for its symbolic value. However, the pursuit of only the symbolic value of technology will put schools in a position of constantly trying to catch the newest technology fad, and the lack of emphasis on the practical value of technology innovations will put the users' benefit at risk. Without seeing strong evidence on the utility of technology innovations, the public can become less enthusiastic than before to support adopting new technologies.

Second, we need data-driven policymaking that is based on evidence provided by scientific research, to learn from history and from success and failures made by previous efforts. Whether or not human societies can make progress depends on our ability to learn from the past, so as to replicate, expand, and adapt successful experiences and to avoid repeating the same mistakes. In the last two decades, we have been experimenting with investing technology in schools. These investments can serve as important steps towards better informed technology decision making and improved technology investment efforts. We need serious scientific evaluation to examine the comprehensive effects of our technology investments and to support data-driven decision making. Based on what we learn from previous investment efforts, we can make better technology investment decisions on what to invest, when to invest, how much and how to invest, but also on how to best implement technology projects so that we can receive educational returns from our continuous investment in educational technology. Meanwhile, formal mechanisms need to be established for advising policymaking. Technology policymaking and decision making should be based upon evidence found in scientific research. Formal advising mechanism should be established as a bridge between scientific research and policymaking to help translate scientific findings into practical suggestions and to advise policymaking.

Third, policymaking must expand its focus from traditional physical learning to including online learning. As we discussed in this chapter, the digital world has become an increasingly important component of our lives. Competent citizens of the digital economy need a sound understanding of the nature of the digital world, a positive attitude about its complexities, and the ability to create digital products and services in order to participate in and lead its activities. Yet schools are not preparing the next generation of citizens to live and work competently in a digital economy. Research reveals that the "digital natives," in fact, have a poor understanding of the complexity of the digital world and their digital literacy is limited in nature and scope (Livingstone, 2008, pp. 103–106; Tannenbaum & Kartz, 2008; Yan, 2006). Policymaking should provide both the directions and the regulations on how schools should and can prepare students to be contributing members and creative leaders in the digital era. Given the fact that the digital world is still a new phenomenon and research in this area is scarce, policymaking should also encourage and support innovative research efforts to understand the nature of the digital world, the essence of digital citizenship, and the effective strategies to prepare students with digital citizenship.

Any policymaking with regard to education cannot deny the fact that technology has transformed the society and will likely transform education institutions but we also have to be mindful that educational institutions cannot be easily transformed. The impact of technology on education, as discussed in this chapter, has been limited because of the disconnectedness between policymaking and policy implementation, as well as the unwillingness of educational institutions to engage in transformative actions. Future policies need to be more closely aligned with the reality of technology implementation, to involve stakeholders in the decision-making process, and to bridge the gap between the promises and the reality of technology use in schools.

Research Recommendations The public, policy makers, and educators are in desperate need of rigorous research to guide their technology decisions and technology project implementations. First, research needs to provide evidence to address broad policy issues. In order to do so, we need to develop large-scale comprehensive research studies. Technology provides great opportunities for education but at the same time also poses new challenges. Too often it is the beneficial aspects of technology that are talked about but the pitfalls ignored. Therefore, research should use a variety of strategies to detect changes in students, teachers, administrators, parents, and the public, and also use a variety of indicators to measure the breadth and depth of the impact of technology on individuals and institutions, capturing both the anticipated and unanticipated, desirable and undesirable, short-term and long-term changes technology may bring about.

Second, today's children are spending more and more time in the digital world, which differs from the physical world in fundamental ways, yet little is known about the nature of the digital world and the impact of children's engagement in that world on their development. Future research needs to explore the psychological and cognitive impacts of technology use on children, to understand how time spent on the Internet affect children developmentally, and more importantly, to examine what challenges educators face and how to deal with these challenges.

Third, as virtual schools and virtual learning become an increasingly common practice, extensive research is needed to investigate the institutional impact of virtual learning. For example, how does online teaching affect traditional teaching jobs? How are teacher unions dealing with losing students, and as a consequence, losing teaching jobs to virtual schools? How can virtual schools be funded? How can e-learning programs be evaluated and accredited?

Fourth, the digital society requires a complete suite of

cognitive and psychological abilities and perspectives that enable the individual to intelligently consume and creatively develop digital products, ethically participate, and courageously lead in a world that has become increasingly mediated by technology. We need a sound understanding of what strategies, activities, and experiences are most effective in equipping students with these necessary abilities and perspectives. Research along this line will greatly help today's education to prepare students to live, work, and lead competently in a digital economy.

Fifth, there is a need to develop research methods and instruments that can rigorously study and evaluate student learning with technology. Student technology use and learning is experience-related and, at times, hidden and subtle; consequently, it cannot be assessed through traditional outcome evaluation. Some alternative assessment methods such as performance assessment, essays, and portfolios might be more effective in assessing student learning with and about technology.

Notes

1. The NIIAC was a high-level advisory group established by President Bill Clinton in 1993 under executive order EO 12864 to advise on national information infrastructure issues (available at http://nodis3.gsfc.nasa.gov/displayEO.cfm?id=EO_12864_).
2. Indiana University High School Web site: http://www.indiana.edu/~scs/hs/highschoolcourses.html
3. Florida Virtual School Web site: http://www.flvs.net/educators/fact_sheet.php
4. Anshe Chung Studio web site: http://acs.anshechung.com/
5. Merriam-Webster Online (2006).

References

Adams, O. L., Guarino, A. J., Robichaux, R. R., & Edwards, T. L. (2004). A comparison of outsourcing in higher education, 1998–99 and 2003–04 [Online submission]. *Journal of Educational Research and Policy Studies, 4*(2), 90–110.

Anderson, A. B. (2003, May). *Charter schools: Cyber charter schools.* Retrieved March 15, 2004, from http://www.ecs.org/clearinghouse/44/13/4413.htm

Anderson, J. Q., & Rainie, L. (2006). *The future of the internet II.* Retrieved November 15, 2006, from http://www.pewinternet.org/pdfs/PIP_Future_of_Internet_2006.pdf

Antonijevic, R. (2007, March/April). *Usage of computers and calculators and students' achievement: Results from TIMSS 2003.* Paper presented at the International Conference on Informatics, Educational Technology and New Media in Education, Sombor, Serbia.

Apple, Inc. (n.d.). *Apple's home for homeschools.* Retrieved November 17, 2006, from http://www.apple.com/education/shop/homeschool/

Aypay, A., Erdogan, M., & Sozer, M. A. (2007). Variation among schools on classroom practices in science-based on TIMSS-1999 in Turkey. *Journal of Research in Science Teaching, 44*, 1417–1435.

Balkin, J. M., & Noveck, B. S. (2006). *The state of play: Law, games, and virtual worlds.* New York: New York University Press.

Basalla, G. (1988). *The evolution of technology.* Cambridge, UK: Cambridge University Press.

Bauman, K. J. (2002). Home schooling in the United States: Trends and characteristics. *Education Policy Analysis Archives, 10*(26). Retrieved December 23, 2006, from http://epaa.asu.edu/epaa/v10n26.html

Becker, H. J. (1998). Running to catch a moving train: Schools and information technologies. *Theory into Practice, 37*, 20–30.

Belfield, C. R., & Wooten, A. L. (2003). *Education privatization: The attitudes and experiences of superintendents* (Occasional Paper No. 70). New York: Columbia University, Teachers College.

Benkler, Y. (2007). *The wealth of networks: How social production transforms markets and freedom.* New Haven, CT: Yale University Press.

Berliner, D. C., & Biddle, B. J. (1995). *The manufactured crisis: Myths, fraud, and the attack on America's public schools.* New York: Basic Books.

Bernanke, B. S. (2006, Auguest 25). *Global Economic Integration: What's New and What's Not?* Remarks at the Federal Reserve Bank of Kansas City's Thirtieth Annual Economic Symposium, Jackson Hole, Wyoming. Retrieved February 10, 2007, from http://druckversion.studien-von-zeitfragen.net/FRB%20Speech,%20Bernanke%20Jackson%20Hole.pdf

Besser, H. (1993). Education as marketplace. In R. Muffoletto & N. Knupfer (Eds.), *Computers in education: Social, historical, and political perspectives* (pp. 37–69). Cresskill, NJ: Hampton Press.

Biggs, S. (1993). *The Sentient Sign: Some speculations on the Totemic value of the artificial Author.* Retrieved January 9, 2007, from: http://hosted.simonbiggs.easynet.co.uk/texts/sentientsign.htm

Blachowicz, C. L. Z., & Obrochta, C. (2005). Vocabulary visits: Virtual field trips for content vocabulary development. *Reading Teacher, 59*(3), 262–268.

Blasewitz, M. R., & Taylor, R. T. (1999). Attacking literacy with technology in an urban setting. *Middle School Journal, 30*(3), 33–39.

Bogden, J. (2001). *Any time, any place, any path, any pace: Taking the lead on e-Learning policy.* Washington, DC: National Association of State Boards of Education (NASBE).

Bowns, I. R., Rotherham, G., & Paisley, S. (1999). Factors associated with success in the implementation of information management and technology in the NHS. *Health Informatics Journal, 5,* 136–145.

Bronfenbrenner, U. (1979). *The ecology of human development: Experiments by nature and design.* Cambridge, MA: Harvard University Press.

Brown, G., Jr. (1994, February 25). *External factors forcing change on education: How can they work for us?* Retrieved June 3, 2008, from http://www.towson.edu/csme/mctp/Essays/ExternalForces.txt

Brown, S., Elder, A., & Koenig, A. (2004). *Net impact: From connectivity to creativity.* Austin, TX: Momentum Research Group.

Bruce, B. C. (1993). Innovation and social change. In B. C. Bruce, J. K. Peyton, & T. Batson (Eds.), *Network-based classrooms: Promises and realities* (pp. 9–32). New York: Cambridge University Press.

Bruce, B. C., & Hogan, M. P. (1998). The disappearance of technology: Toward an ecological model of literacy. In D. Reinking, M. C. McKenna, L. D. Labbo, & R. D. Kieffer (Eds.), *Handbook of literacy and technology: Transformations in a post-typographic world* (pp. 269–281). Hillsdale, NJ: Erlbaum.

Brumfield, R. (2006, May 16). Bill calls for MySpace age limit: Deleting Online Predators Act aims to restrict use of social networking sites by minors. *eSchool News.* Retrieved June 3, 2008, from http://www.eschoolnews.com/news/top-news/index.cfm?i=36991&CFID=4218450&CFTOKEN=82756348

Bryson, M., & Castell, S. (1998). New technologies and the cultural ecology of primary schooling: Imagining teachers as Luddites In/Deed [Electronic version]. *Educational Policy, 12,* 542–567.

Buckenmeyer, J. (2001, November). *Lessons learned from a university partnership established to promote the adoption of educational technology: One size does not fit all.* Annual proceedings of selected research and development and practice papers presented at the national convention of the Association for Educational Communications and Technology, Atlanta, GA.

Byrom, E., & Bingham, M. (2001). *Factors influencing the effective use of technology for teaching and learning: Lessons learned from the SEIR-TEC Intensive Site Schools.* Retrieved June 3, 2008, from http://www.serve.org/seir-tec/publications/lessons.pdf

Campbell, R. J. (1998). Hyperminds for hypertimes: The demise of rational, logical thoughts? *Educational Technology, 38*(1), 24–31.

Carothers, M. L. (2000). *Florida home education programs, 1999–2000.* Tallahassee: Florida Department of Education.

Castronova, E. (2001). *Virtual worlds: A first-hand account of market and society on the cyberian frontier* (CESifo Working Paper Series No. 618). Bloomington: Indiana University.

Castronova, E. (2005). *Synthetic worlds: The business and culture of online games.* Chicago: University of Chicago Press.

CDW-G. (2007). *CDW-G K-12 School Safety Index 2007.* Vernon Hills, IL: Author.

CEO Forum on Education and Technology. (1999). *Professional development: A link to better learning. The CEO Forum school technology and readiness report–Year two.* Washington, DC: Author.

CEO Forum on Education and Technology. (2001). *Education technology must be included in comprehensive education legislation: A policy paper.* Washington, DC: Author.

Chan, T., Roschelle, J., Hsi, S., Sharples, M., Brown, T., Patton, C., et al. (2006). One-to-one technology-enhanced learning: An opportunity for global research collaboration [Electronic version]. *Research and Practice in Technology Enhanced Learning, 1*(1), 3–29.

Clark, M., & Wentworth, C. (1997). *Constructivism and the development of multimedia applications.* Proceedings of the 30th Annual Small College Computing Symposium, April 17–19, University of Wisconsin-Parkside.

CNN. (2005, December 30). How technology is changing our lives. CNN.com. Retrieved March 11, 2008, from http://www.cnn.com/2005/TECH/10/27/humantech.emails/

Collins, A. (1996). Whither technology and schools? Collected thoughts on the last and next quarter centuries. In C. Fisher, D. C. Dwyer, & K. Yocam (Eds.), *Education and technology: Reflections on computing in classrooms* (pp. 51–66). San Francisco: Jossey-Bass.

Committee on Assessing Technological Literacy, National Academy of Engineering, National Research Council, Elsa Gamire, E., & Pearson. G. (2002). *Tech tally: Approaches to assessing technological literacy.* National Academies Press.

Committee on Technological Literacy, National Academy of Engineering, National Research Council, Pearson, G., & Young, A. T. (Eds.). (2002). *Technically speaking: Why all Americans need to know more about technology.* Washington, DC: National Academy Press.

comScore Networks. (2006, October 26). *U.S. non-travel e-commerce spending by consumers increased 23 percent in Q3 2006 versus year ago, according to comScore Networks* [Press release]. Retrieved November 20, 2006, from http://www.comscore.com/press/release.asp?press=1050

Conway, P., & Zhao, Y. (2003). From Luddites to designers: Portraits of teachers and technology in political documents. In Y. Zhao (Ed.), *What should teachers know about technology? Perspectives and practices* (pp. 15–30). Greenwich, CT: Information Age.

Cordes, C., & Miller, E. (Eds.). (2000). *Fool's gold: a critical look at computers in childhood.* College Park, MD: Alliance for Childhood.

Cuban, L. (1986). *Teachers and machines: The class room use of technology since 1920.* New York: Teachers College Press.

Cuban, L. (1993a). Computer meets classroom: Classroom wins. *Teachers College Record, 95,* 185–210.

Cuban, L. (1993b). *How teachers taught: Constancy and change in American classrooms 1890–1980* (2nd ed.). New York: Longman.

Cuban, L. (2001). *Oversold and underused: Computers in the classroom.* Cambridge, MA: Harvard University Press.

Culp, K. M., Honey, M., & Mandinach, E. (2003). *A retrospective on twenty years of education technology policy.* Washington, DC: U.S. Department of Education, Office of Educational Technology.

Darling-Hammond, L. (2004). Standards, accountability, and school reform. *Teachers College Record, 106,* 1047–1085.

Darrow, B. (1932). *Radio, the assistant teacher.* Columbus, OH: R.G. Adams.

Davis, M. (2008, February 4). *2020 vision: Rudd summit to map future.* Retrieved March 11, 2008, from http://www.smh.com.au/news/national/2020-vision-pm-looks-ahead/2008/02/03/1201973740462.html?page=fullpage

Dede, C. (1998). The scaling-up process for technology-based educational innovations. In C. Dede (Ed.), *Learning with technology. 1998 ASCD yearbook* (pp. 199–215). Alexandria, VA: Association for Supervision and Curriculum Development.

Derry, T. K., & Williams, T. I. (1993). *A short history of technology: From the earliest times to A.D. 1900*. New York: Dover Publications.

Dibbell, J. (2006). *Play money: Or how I quit my day job and made millions trading virtual loot*. Basic Books: New York.

Dossani, R., & Kenney, M. (2003). *Went for cost, Stayed for quality? Moving the back office to India*. Retrieved June 6, 2008, from http://iis-db. stanford.edu/pubs/20337/dossani_kenney_09_2003.pdf

Dossani, R., & Kenney, M. (2006). The relocation of service provision to developing nations: The case of India. In J. Zysman & A. Newman (Eds.), *How revolutionary was the digital revolution? National responses, market transitions, and global technology* (pp. 193–216). Palo Alto, CA: Stanford University Press.

Douglas, A. J. (2007, September). *Politics and policymaking in science and technology: An assessment of the U.S. high tech advantage, state based initiatives, and the process of globalization*. Paper presented at the OECD International Conference, Valencia, Spain.

Dynarski, M., Agodini, R., Heaviside, S. N. T., Carey, N., Campuzano, L., Means, B., et al. (2007). *Effectiveness of reading and mathematics software products: Findings from the First Student Cohort. Report to Congress*. Washington, DC: Institute of Education Sciences.

Education Week. (2007). *Technology counts 2007*. Retrieved March 11, 2008, from http://www.edweek.org/media/ew/tc/2007/tc07_press_release.pdf

Electronic Frontier Foundation & Online Policy Group. (2003). *Internet blocking in public schools: A study on internet access in educational institutions*. Retrieved June 5, 2008, from http://www.eff.org/Censorship/Censorware/net_block_report/net_block_report.pdf

Electronic Privacy Information Center. (1997). *Faulty filters: How content filters block access to kid friendly information on the internet*. Retrieved June 4, 2008, from http://www2.epic.org/reports/filter_report.html

Elliott, A., & Hall, N. (1997). The impact of self-regulatory teaching strategies on "at-risk" preschoolers' mathematical learning in a computer-mediated environment. *Journal of Computing in Childhood Education, 8*, 187–198.

eSchool News. (2006, November 20). *Social-networking sites confound schools*. Retrieved March 12, 2008, from http://hb1.eschoolnews.com/resources/minimizing-classroom-disruptions/articlesmcs/index.cfm?rc=1&i=42038;_hbguid=5e029fb4-d29c-4dcf-9788-a27b99cc7eb2&d=resources

eSchool News. (2007a). *Despite filters, more kids exposed to online porn*. Retrieved March 11, 2008, from http://www.eschoolnews.com/resources/minimizing-classroom-disruptions/articlesmcs/index.cfm?i=45728&page=1

eSchool News. (2007b). *Teacher gets new trial in web-porn case*. Retrieved June 4, 2008, from http://www.eschoolnews.com/news/top-news/index.cfm?i=46362&CFID=4218450&CFTOKEN=82756348

Estabrook, L., Witt, E., & Rainie, L. (2007, December 30). *Information searches that solve problems: How people use the Internet, libraries, and government agencies when they need help*. Retrieved March 12, 2008, from http://www.pewinternet.org/pdfs/Pew_UI_LibrariesReport.pdf

Fang, I. (1997). *A history of mass communication: Six information revolutions*. Boston: Focal Press.

Feldman, A., Konold, C., & Coulter, B. (2000). *Network science, a decade later: The Internet and classroom learning*. Mahwah, NJ: Erlbaum.

Finkelhor, D. (2007, July 24). Online sex crimes against juveniles: Myth and reality (Testimony before the U.S. Senate, Committee on Commerce, Science, and Transportation). Retrieved June 4, 2008, from http://unh.edu/news/pdf/Senate072407_Finkelhor.pdf

Fleishman, G. (2003, October 6). School district sued over WLAN planning. *WNN Wi-Fi Net News*. Retrieved March 12, 2008, from http://wifinetnews.com/archives/002303.html

Foley, R. (2008, January 16). Court ruling threatens schools. *FoxNews. Com*. Retrieved June 4, 2008, from http://www.foxnews.com/wires/2008Jan16/0,4670,VirtualSchools,00.html

Fox, E. (2005). Tracking U.S. trends. *Education Week*. Retrieved June 4, 2008, from http://www.edweek.org/ew/articles/2005/05/05/35tracking.h24.html

Freeman, J. (2002). The total cost of technology. *School Business Affairs, 68*(9), 23–26.

Freyta, A., & Renaud, S. (2004). From short-term to long-term orientation—Political economy of the policy reform process. Retrieved March 12, 2008, from http://www.wiwi.uni-jena.de/Papers/wp-sw1204.pdf

Friedman, T. L. (2005) *The world is flat: A brief history of the twenty-first century*. New York: Farrar, Straus, and Giroux.

Fullan, M. (2001). *The new meaning of educational change* (3rd ed.). New York: Teachers College Press.

Good, D. G. (2001). *Investing in K-12 technology equipment: Strategies for state policymakers, ECS Issue Paper*. Education Commission of the States.

Hall, J., & Suh, B. (2004). Breaking away: Creating business value through information technology. *Outlook Special Edition*. Retrieved June 4, 2008, from http://www.accenture.com/Global/Research_and_Insights/Outlook/By_Alphabet/BreakingTechnology.htm

Haller, S. (2005, September 12). iPod era of personal media choices may be turning us into an iSolation nation. *The Arizona Republic*. Retrieved November 28, 2006, from http://www.azcentral.com/arizonarepublic/arizonaliving/articles/0912customize0912.html

Harmer, A., & Cates, W. (2007). Designing for learner engagement in middle school science: Technology, inquiry, and the hierarchies of engagement. *Computers in the Schools, 24*(1–2), 105–124.

Hartocollis, A. (2006, July 13). Parents to sue over schools' cellphone ban. *New York Times*. Retrieved February 20, 2008, from http://www.nytimes.com/2006/07/13/nyregion/13phones.html?_r=1&oref=slogin

Hawaii Department of Education. (n.d.). *Some questions you may have on e-school*. Retrieved June 6, 2008, from http://www.eschool.k12.hi.us/Pages/some_answers.html

Hawkes, M. (1995, October 6). *Educational technology dissemination: Its impact on learning, instruction, and educational policy*. Paper presented at the National Rural Education Association (NREA), Salt Lake City, UT.

Hay, I. (2008). Postcolonial practices for a global virtual group: The case of the International Network for Learning and Teaching geography in higher education (INLT). *Journal of Geography in Higher Education, 32*(1), 15–32.

Healy, J. M. (1998). *Failure to connect: How computers affect our children's minds—and what we can do about it*. New York: Touchstone.

Higgins, J., & Russell, M. (2003). *Teachers' beliefs about vision and leadership*. Boston, MA: Boston College, Technology and Assessment Study Collaborative.

Hill, P. T. (2000). Home schooling and the future of public education. *Peabody Journal of Education, 75*(1&2), 20–31.

Hoffman, E. S. (2002, April). *Can research improve technology planning policy?* Paper presented at the annual meeting of the American Educational Research Association, New Orleans, LA.

Holman, K. (2006). Trade unions anticipating change in Europe: Project Report. Retrieved June 4, 2008, from http://www.traceproject.org/files/884_TraceReport_EN_rep01-revNov.pdf

Honey, M., Culp, K., & Spielvogel, R. (2005). *Critical issue: Using technology to improve student achievement*. Retrieved June 4, 2008, from http://www.ncrel.org/sdrs/areas/issues/methods/technlgy/te800.htm#goal

Horrigan, J. B. (2008). *Online shopping: Internet users like the convenience but worry about the security of their financial information*. Retrieved March 11, 2008, from http://www.pewinternet.org/pdfs/PIP_Online%20Shopping.pdf

Hunter, D. (2003). Evidence-based policy and practice: Riding for a fall? *Journal of the Royal Society of Medicine, 96*, 194–196.

Information Technology Association of America (ITAA), (2003). *2003 Workforce Survey*. Presented at the National IT Workforce Convocation, May 5, 2003. Arlington, VA Retrieved on November 20, 2006, from http://www.itaa.org/workforce/studies/03execsumm.pdf

Institute for International Economics. (2003). *Globalization of IT services and white collar jobs: The next wave of productivity growth* (International Economics Policy Briefs No. PB03-11). Retrieved June 4, 2008, from http://www.iie.com/publications/pb/pb03-11.pdf

Internet World Stats. (2008a). *Internet usage statistics—The Internet big picture: World internet users and population stats.* Retrieved June 6, 2008, from http://www.internetworldstats.com/stats.htm

Internet World Stats. (2008b). *Top 43 countries with the highest Internet penetration rate.* Retrieved June 6, 2008, from http://www.internetworldstats.com/top25.htm

Irmas, J. (2008, February 7). Parents ask for school cell phone ban to be lifted. *The New York Sun.* Retrieved March 11, 2008, from http://www.nysun.com/article/70906

Jerald, C. (2005, August). *The implementation trap: Helping schools overcome barriers to change.* Washington, DC: Center for Comprehensive School Reform and Improvement Policy Brief.

Jin, G. (2006). Chinese gold farmers in the game world. *Consumers, Commodities and Consumption, 7*(2). Retrieved June 4, 2008, from https://netfiles.uiuc.edu/dtcook/www/CCCnewsletter/7-2/jin.htm

Johnson, D. (2004). *Intellectual freedom and Internet filters: Can we have both?* Retrieved June 4, 2008, from http://www.doug-johnson.com/handouts/filter1p.pdf

Jorgenson, D. (2005). Accounting for growth in the information age. In P. Aghion & S. Durlauf (Eds.), *Handbook of economic growth, Vol 1* (pp. 743–815). Retrieved November 5, 2008, from http://www.economics.harvard.edu/faculty/jorgenson/files/acounting_for_growth_050121.pdf

Jorgenson, D., Ho, M. S., & Stiroh, K. J. (2005). *Information technology and the American growth resurgence.* Cambridge, MA: MIT Press.

Keiny S. (2002). *Ecological thinking: A new approach to educational change.* Lanham, MD: University Press of America.

Keller, J. B., & Bichelmeyer, B. (2004). What happens when accountability meets technology integration. *TechTrends: Linking Research & Practice to Improve Learning, 48*(3), 17–24.

Knowledge@Wharton. (2005, November 2). *The new new economy: Earning real money in the virtual world.* Retrieved June 4, 2008, from http://knowledge.wharton.upenn.edu/article.cfm?articleid=1302

Kohut, A. (2008). *The Internet gains in politics.* Retrieved March 11, 2008, from http://www.pewinternet.org/PPF/r/234/report_display.asp

Lamb, P. (2006). Have YourSpace call MySpace (Commentary). *The Christian Science Monitor.* Retrieved December 5, 2006, from http://www.csmonitor.com/2006/1108/p09s02-coop.html

Lavy, I. (2007). A case study of dynamic visualization and problem solving. *International Journal of Mathematical Education in Science and Technology, 38,* 1075–1092.

Lazarowitz, R., & Huppert, J. (1993). Science process skills of 10th-grade Biology students in a computer-assisted learning setting. *Journal of Research on Computing in Education, 25,* 366–382.

Lei, J. (2005). *The dynamics of technology use in schools.* Unpublished doctoral dissertation, Michigan State University, East Lansing.

Lei, J., Conway, P., & Zhao, Y. (2008). *The digital pencil: One-to-one computing for children.* New York: Erlbaum.

Lei, J., & Zhao, Y. (2007). Technology uses and student achievement: A longitudinal study. *Computers and Education, 49,* 284–296.

Lenhart, A., Madden, M., Macgill, A. R., & Smith, A. (2007). *Teens and social media: The use of social media gains a greater foothold in teen life as they embrace the conversational nature of interactive online media.* Retrieved March 12, 2008, from http://www.pewinternet.org/pdfs/PIP_Teens_Social_Media_Final.pdf

Lessig, L. (2006). *Code: Version 2.0.* New York: Basic Books.

Levin, D., & Arafeh, S. (2002). *The digital disconnect: The widening gap between Internet-savvy students and their schools.* Retrieved March 21, 2007, from http://www.pewinternet.org/pdfs/PIP_Schools_Internet_Report.pdf

Levin, J., & Quinn, M. (2003). *Missed opportunities: How we keep high-quality teachers out of urban classrooms.* New York: The New Teacher Project.

Levinson, P. (1998) *The soft edge: A natural history and future of the information revolution.* New York: Routledge.

Lewontin, R. (2000). *The triple helix: Gene, organism, and environment.* Cambridge, MA: Harvard University Press.

Liu, M., Hsieh, P., Cho, Y., & Schallert, D. (2006). Middle school students' self-efficacy, attitudes, and achievement in a computer-enhanced problem-based learning environment. *Journal of Interactive Learning Research, 17,* 225–242.

Livingstone, S. (2008). Internet literacy: Young people's negotiation of new online opportunities. In T. McPherson (Ed.), *Digital youth, innovation, and the unexpected* (pp. 101–122). Cambridge, MA: MIT Press.

Long, A. (2004, April). Cyber schools. *Education Commission of the States StateNotes.* Retrieved June 4, 2008, from http://www.ecs.org/clearinghouse/51/01/5101.pdf

Lubrano, A. (1997). *The telegraph: How technology innovation caused social change.* New York: Garland.

Lynskey, M. J. (2006). Transformative technology and institutional transformation: Coevolution of biotechnology venture firms and the institutional framework in Japan. *Research Policy, 35,* 1389–1422.

MacDonald, G. (2004, December 6). Contrarian finding: Computers are a drag on learning. *Learning.* http://www.csmonitor.com/2004/1206/p11s01-legn.html

MacIver, D. J., Balfanz, R., & Plank, S. B. (1999). An "elective replacement" approach to providing extra help in math: The Talent Development Middle Schools' Computer- and Team-Assisted Mathematics Acceleration (CATAMA) Program. *Research in Middle Level Education Quarterly, 22*(2), 1–23.

MacMillan, R. B., Liu, X., & Timmons, V. (1997). Teachers, computers, and the Internet: The first stage of a community-initiated project for the integration of technology into the curriculum. *Alberta Journal of Educational Research, 43*(4), 222–234.

Madden, M. (2006). *PEW Internet Penetration Report.* Retrieved November 20, 2006, from http://www.pewinternet.org/pdfs/PIP_Internet_Impact.pdf

Magaziner, N. (n.d.). *Packaging automation increases efficiency, reduces costs.* Retrieved June 4, 2008, from http://www.mrotoday.com/mro/archives/exclusives/PackagingAutomation.htm

Mathew, K. (1997). A comparison of the influence of interactive CD-ROM storybooks and traditional print storybooks on reading comprehension. *Journal of Research on Computing in Education, 29,* 263–274.

McDermon, L. (2005). Distance learning: It's elementary! *Learning and Leading with Technology, 33*(4), 28–30.

McKinsey & Company. (1996). *Connecting K-12 Schools to the information superhighway.* Retrieved June 4, 2008, from http://www.tcet.unt.edu/research/cnctk12.htm

McIntire, T. (2006). Enough to go 'round? Thinking smart about total cost of ownership (educational technology). *Technology and Learning, 26*(12), 20–22.

McIntosh, E. (2007, July 20). *Technology refines talents.* Retrieved March 12, 2008, from http://edu.blogs.com/edublogs/2007/07/technology-re-1.html

Mehlinger, H. (1996). Achieving school reform through technology. *TECHNS Quarterly, 5*(1).

Mehta, S. (2007, February 4). New K-12 elective: Class online; One educator predicts the shift 'is going to reinvent high school in the U.S.' Loss of social interaction is a worry. *Los Angeles Times,* p. A1.

Meier, D., & Wood, G. (Eds.). (2004). *Many children left behind: How the No Child Left Behind Act is damaging our children and our schools.* Boston: Beacon Press.

Michigan Virtual University. (2006, April 21). *Michigan first state to require online learning.* Retrieved June 6, 2008, from http://www.mivhs.com/upload_2/MIOnlineRequirment42106.pdf

Moore, B. (2001). Taking stock of teacher technology use. *Multimedia Schools, 8*(1), 26–31.

Müller, E., & Ahearn, E. (2004). Virtual schools and students with disabilities. Retrieved June 4, 2008, from http://www.projectforum.org/docs/virtual_schools.pdf

Murray, C. (2006, December 8). Ruling: Schools must archive eMail; New rules make eMail, instant messages subject to legal review. *eSchool News.* http://www.eschoolnews.com/news/top-news/index.cfm?i=42051&CFID=2844512&CFTOKEN=46694510

Nardi, B. A., & O'Day, V. L. (1999). *Information ecologies: Using technology with heart.* New York: MIT Press.

National Center for Education Statistics (NCES). (2004, July) *1.1 Million homeschooled students in the United States in 2003* (NCES 2004-115). Retrieved June 4, 2008, from http://nces.ed.gov/pubs2004/2004115.pdf

NetDay. (2006). *Our voice, our future: Student and teacher views on science, technology and education*. Irvine, CA: Author.

Nix, C. A. G. (1998). The impact of e-mail use on fourth graders' writing skills (Doctoral dissertation, The University of Texas at Arlington, 1999). *Dissertation Abstracts International, 60/03-A*, 726.

No Child Left Behind Act. (2001). Retrieved June 7, 2008, from http://www.ed.gov/policy/elsec/leg/esea02/107-110.pdf

Noble, D. D. (1977). *America by design: Science, technology, and the rise of corporate capitalism*. New York: Alfred A. Knopf.

Noble, D. D. (1996). Mad rushes into the future: The overselling of educational technology. *Educational Leadership, 54*(3), 18–23.

November, A., Staudt, C., Costello, M. A., & Huske, L. (1998). *Critical issues: Developing a school or district technology plan*. Retrieved June 5, 2008, from http://www.ncrel.org/sdrs/areas/issues/methods/technlgy/te300.htm

Odum, E. P. (1975). *Ecology: The link between the natural and the social sciences* (2nd ed.). New York: Holt, Rinehart and Winston.

Office of the Deputy President of South Africa. (1997). *South African Integrated National Disability Strategy* (White Paper). Retrieved January 30, 2007, from http://www.independentliving.org/docs3/sa1997wp.pdf

Olsen, S. (2006). Kids outsmart Web filters. *CNET News.com*. Retrieved February 24, 2007, from http://news.com.com/2009-1041_3-6062548.html

Organisation for Economic Co-operation and Development (OECD). (2005). *Are students ready for a technology-rich world? What PISA studies tell us*. Paris: Author.

Paige, R. (2002). Forward. In Office of Technology Policy and Technology Administration (Eds.), *2020 Visions: Transforming education and training through advanced technologies* (pp. 4–5). Washington, DC: U.S. Department of Commerce.

Palozzi, V., & Spradlin, J. (2006). Educational technology in Indiana: Is it worth the investment? *Center for Evaluation and Education Policy Education Policy Brief, 4*(4), 1–12.

Panel of the National Academy of Public Administration. (2006). *Off-shoring: An elusive phenomenon*. Retrieved November 27, 2006, from http://www.napawash.org/Pubs/Off-ShoringJan06.pdf

Papert, S. (1980). *Mindstorms: Children, computers, and powerful ideas*. New York: Basic Books.

Papert, S. (1980). Trying to predict the ruture. *Popular Computing, 3*(13), 30–44.

Papert, S. (1993). *The children's machine: Rethinking school in the age of the computer*. New York: Basic Books.

Paulson, N. (2007, April 5). Technology ruining attention spans, lecturer says. *Iowa State Daily*. Retrieved March 11, 2008, from http://media.www.iowastatedaily.com/media/storage/paper818/news/2007/04/05/News/Technology.Ruining.Attention.Spans.Lecturer.Says-2824571.shtml

Pew Internet and American Life Project & The Exploratorium. (2006, November 20). Seeking science in cyberspace: *A Pew Internet/Exploratorium project finds wide use of the Internet by science seekers*. Retrieved April 18, 2007, from http://pewresearch.org/pubs/274/seeking-science-in-cyberspace

Pollack, T. A. (2004, June). The potential impact of offshore outsourcing on information systems education programs. In *Proceedings of the 2004 Association of Small Computer Users in Education Conference* (pp. 205–210). Myrtle Beach, SC: Association of Small Computer Users in Education.

Prensky, M. (2001). Digital natives, digital immigrants. *On the Horizon, 9*(5), 1–2.

Prensky, M. (2006). *"Don't bother me mom—I'm learning!" How computer and video games are preparing your kids for twenty-first century success—and how you can help*. St. Paul, MN: Paragon House.

President's Committee of Advisors on Science and Technology (Panel on Educational Technology). (1997). *Report to the President on the use of technology to strengthen K-12 Education in the United States*. Washington, DC: Author.

Quality Education Data (QED). (2004). *2003–2004 Technology Ppurchasing forecast*. http://www.qeddata.com/marketkno/researchreports/techpurchaseforecast.aspx

Quality Education Data (QED). (2005). *2004–2005 Technology purchasing forecast* (10th ed.). Denver, CO: Author.

Quality Education Data (QED). (2006). *2005–2006 National Technology Assessment*. http://www.qeddata.com/MarketKno/ResearchReports/nta.aspx

Racoma, J. A. (2007). *Senator wants Wikipedia, blogs, social networking sites banned from U.S. schools and libraries*. Retrieved March 11, 2008, from http://www.blogherald.com/2007/02/22/senator-wants-wikipedia-blogs-social-networking-sites-banned-from-us-schools-and-libraries/

Rainie, L. (2006a). *Digital "natives" invade the workplace: Young people may be newcomers to the world of work, but it's their bosses who are immigrants into the digital world*. Retrieved April 14, 2007, from http://pewresearch.org/pubs/70/digital-natives-invade-the-workplace

Rainie, L. (2006b). *How the Internet is changing consumer behavior and expectations* [Speech to ThinkTank06]. http://www.pewinternet.org/ppt/2006%20-%206.7.06%20ThinkTank%20Seton%20Hall.pdf

Ravitch, D. (1993). When school comes to you. *The Economist, 328*, 45–46.

Reid-Griffin, A. (2003). Technology: A tool for science learning. *Meridian: A Middle School Computer Technologies Journal, 6*(2). Retrieved on February 15, 2008, from http://www.ncsu.edu/meridian/sum2003/science/index.html

Rideout, V. J., Foehr, U. G., & Roberts, D. F. (2005). *Generation M: Media in the lives of 8–18 year-olds*. Washington, DC: Kaiser Family Foundation.

Rogers, E. M. (1995). *Diffusion of innovation* (4th ed.). New York: The Free Press.

Russell, M., Bebell, D., O'Dwyer, L., & O'Connor, K. (2003). Examining teacher technology use: Implications for preservice and inservice teacher preparation. *Journal of Teacher Education, 54*(4), 297–310.

Schacter, J. (1999). *The impact of education technology on student achievement: What the most current research has to say*. Santa Monica, CA: Milken Family Foundation.

Schlechty, P. (2001). *Shaking up the schoolhouse: How to support and sustain educational innovation*. San Francisco: Jossey-Bass.

Schofield, J. W. (1995). *Computers and classroom culture*. New York: Cambridge University Press.

Schoenherr, S. (2005). *Recording technology history*. Retrieved March 12, 2008, from http://history.sandiego.edu/gen/recording/notes.html

Scrase, R. (1998). An evaluation of multi-sensory speaking-computer bases system (Starcross-IDL) designed to teach the literacy skills of reading and spelling. *British Journal of Educational Technology, 29*(3), 221–224.

Segal, F. F. (Ed.) (2004). *Annual privatization report 2004—Education*. Los Angeles: Reason Foundation.

Seidensticker, B. (2006) *Futurehype: The myths of technology change*. San Francisco: Berrett-Koehler.

Shambles. (n.d.). *Virtual schools*. Retrieved June 6, 2008, from http://www.shambles.net/pages/school/vschools/

Shifrin, D. (2006). Effect of media on children and adolescents: It's about time. *Archives of Pediatric and Adolescent Medicine, 160*, 448–450.

Sipress, A. (2006, December 5). The new dot-economy: Plummeting costs give rise to a wave of internet entrepreneurs. *Washington Post*, p. D01.

Sivin-Kachala, J., & Bialo, E. (2000). *2000 Research report on the effectiveness of technology in schools* (7th ed.). Washington, DC: Software and Information Industry Association.

Smith, D. R., & Ayers, D. F. (2006). Culturally responsive pedagogy and online learning: Implications for the globalized community college. *Community College Journal of Research and Practice, 30*, 401–415.

Stager, G. (2006, October 2). *Has educational computing jumped the shark?* Paper presented at the Australian Computers in Education Conference 2006, Cairns, Australia.

Stainfield, J., Fisher, P., Ford, B., & Solem, M. (2000). International virtual field trips: A new direction? *Journal of Geography in Higher Education, 24*(2), 255–262.

Stead, G. (2006). Mobile technologies: transforming the future of learning. Retrieved April 12, 2007, from http://www.m-learning.net/links/papers/Mobile%20technologies%20-%20Geoff%20Stead%20for%20Becta.pdf

Steinkuhler, C. (2006). Virtual worlds, learning, and the new pop cosmopolitanism [Online article]. *Teachers College Record, 12843.*

Stoll, C. (1999). *High-tech heretic: Why computers don't belong in the classroom and other reflections by a computer contrarian.* New York: Random House.

Stone, B. (2003, September 29). Is that a radio in your cereal? *Newsweek,* p. E34.

Stone, B. (2005, April 11). Hi-tech's new day. *Newsweek,* p. 2, 62.

Stone, T. T., III. (1996). The academic impact of classroom computer usage upon middle-class primary grade level elementary school children (Doctoral dissertation, Widener University, 1996). *Dissertation Abstracts International, 57/06-A,* 2450.

Sutton, L. (2005). Blocked: Experiences of high school students conducting term paper research using filtered internet access [Online article]. *Teachers College Record,* 12248.

Tan, S., Lei, J., Shi, S., & Zhao, Y. (2003, April). *The adult-children tension: Activity design and selection in after-school programs.* Paper presented at American Educational Research Association Annual Meeting, Chicago.

Tannenbaum, R. J., & Kartz, I. R. (2008, February). *Setting standards on the core and advanced iSkills™ assessments* [Research memorandum]. Princeton, NJ: Educational Testing Services.

Tapscott, D. (1998). *Growing up digital: The rise of the net generation.* New York: McGraw Hill.

Thompson, R. (2003). *MAYA: The world as virtual reality.* Alachua, FL: Govardhan Hill.

Tracey, D. H., & Young, J. (2007). Technology and early literacy: the impact of an integrated learning system on high risk kindergartners' achievement. *Reading Psychology, 28,* 443–467.

Trotter, A. (2001, January 24). Cyber learning at online high. *Education Week, 24*(19).

Turkle, S. (1984). *The second self: Computers and the human spirit.* New York: Simon and Schuster.

Turkle, S. (1995). *Life on the screen: Identity in the age of the Iinternet.* New York: Simon and Schuster.

Twining, P., Evans, D., Cook, D., Ralston, J., Selwood, I; Jones, A., et al. (2006). *Tablet PCs in schools: Case study report.* Coventry, UK: BECTA ICT Research.

U.S. Department of Education. (1996). *Getting America's students ready for the 21st century—Meeting the technology literacy challenge: A report to the nation on technology and education.* Washington DC: Author.

U.S. Department of Education. (2000). *e-Learning: Putting a world-class education at the fingertips of all children.* Washington, DC: Author.

U.S. Department of Education. (2004). *Toward a new golden age in American education: How the Internet, the law and today's students are revolutionizing expectations: The National Educational Technology Plan.* Washington DC: Author.

U.S. Department of Education. (2006). *Preparing Tomorrow's Teachers to Use Technology: Performance fast facts.* Retrieved June 6, 2008, from http://www.ed.gov/programs/teachtech/performance.html

Varian, H., Litan, R. E., Elder, A., & Shutter, J. (2002). *The Net Impact Study: The projected economic benefits of the Internet in the United States,* United Kingdom, France and Germany V2.0. Retrieved June 6, 2008, from http://www.netimpactstudy.com/nis_2002.html

Virtual High School. (2008). *VHS member profile.* Retrieved June 6, 2008, from http://www.govhs.org/Pages/AboutUs-MemberProfile

Waight, N., & Abd-El-Khalick, F. (2007). The impact of technology on the enactment of "inquiry" in a technology enthusiast's sixth grade science classroom. *Journal of Research in Science Teaching, 44*(1), 154–182.

Warschauer, M. (2003). The allures and illusions of modernity: Technology and educational reform in Egypt. *Education Policy Analysis Archives, 11*(38). Retrieved June 6, 2008, from http://epaa.asu.edu/epaa/v11n38/

Weir, H. (1922). The story of the motion picture. *McClure's,* p. 54.

Weiss, S. (2001, May 2). St. John's works to shake its commuter school image. *New York Times.* Retrieved March 12, 2008, from http://query.nytimes.com/gst/fullpage.html?res=9902EEDA1738F931A35756C0A9679C8B63

Whitfield, L., & Jones, J. (2007). *Ghana: Economic policymaking and the politics of aid dependence* (GEG Working Paper 2007/32). Oxford, UK: University College, Global Economic Governance Programme.

Why Pak will have more online tutors than India. (2006, November 17). *The Times of India.* Retrieved June 6, 2008, from http://timesofindia.indiatimes.com/NEWS/India/Why_Pak_will_have_more_online_tutors_than_India/articleshow/462236.cms

Woehler, C. (1994). The evaluation of a computer-assisted reading program for at-risk students. (Doctoral dissertation, Texas A&M University, 1994). *Dissertation Abstracts International, 55/07-A,* 1816.

Wolak, J., Mitchell, K., & Finkelhor, D. (2006). *Online victimization of youth: Five years later.* Alexandria, VA: National Center for Missing and Exploited Children.

Woodley, B. (2002). *The impact of transformative technologies on governance: Some lessons from history.* Ottowa, Ontario, Canada: Institute on Governance.

Yan, Z. (2006). What influences children's and adolescents' understanding of the complexity of the Internet? *Developmental Psychology, 42,* 418-428.

Yan, Z. (2008, May). *Internet and child development: The past decade of efforts and the next decade of tasks.* Plenary speech at the 12th Global Chinese Conference on Computers in Education, East Lansing, MI.

Yannie, M. (2000). Technology is us: Do we have time to learn? A librarian's perspective. *TechTrends, 44*(4), 42–43.

Zhao, Y. (2007, July). *Digital citizenship in a global economy: The internet revolution and its implications for education.* Keynote address at Building Learning Communities Conference, Boston.

Zhao, Y., & Frank, K. (2003). Factors affecting technology uses in schools: An ecological perspective. *American Educational Research Journal, 40,* 807–840.

Zhao, Y., Lei, J., & Conway, P. (2006). A global perspective on political definitions of e-learning: Commonalities and differences in National Educational Technology strategy discourses. In J. Weiss, J. Nolan, J. Hunsinger, & P. Trifonas (Eds.), *The international handbook of virtual learning environments* (pp.673–697). Dordrecht, The Netherlands: Kluwer/Springer Verlag.

Zhao, Y., Lei, J., & Frank, K. (2006). The social life of technology: An ecological analysis of technology diffusion in schools. *Pedagogies: An International Journal, 1*(2), 135–149.

Zhao, Y., Lei, J., Yan, B., Tan, S. & Lai, C. (2005). What makes the difference? A practical analysis of research on the effectiveness of distance education. *Teachers College Record, 107,* 1836–1884.

Zhao, Y., Pugh, K., Sheldon, S., & Byers, J. L. (2002). Conditions for classroom technology innovations. *Teachers College Record, 104,* 482–515.

Zhao, Y., Tan, S. H., & Mishra, P. (2000). *Going beyond the teacher's machine: Reading online.* Retrieved June 6, 2008, from http://www.readingonline.org/electronic/elec_index.asp?HREF=/electronic/jaal/12-00_Column/index.html

Zigurs, I. (2001). *Our virtual world: the transformation of work, play and life via technology.* Hershey, PA: IDEA Group.

Zooknic. (n.d.). *Geography of Internet users.* Retrieved June 6, 2008, from http://www.zooknic.com/Users/index.html

53

Education and the Shrinking State

DAVID N. PLANK
Policy Analysis for California Education (PACE)

VENESSA KEESLER
Michigan State University

When he first ran for Prime Minister of the United Kingdom in 1997, Tony Blair was asked to list his policy priorities. "Education, education, education," he replied. Informed of Blair's response, his Tory opponent asserted that his policy priorities were the same, "but in a different order."
—Wolf, 2002, p. 13

Britain's political consensus that more and better education is the critical policy lever for addressing a host of economic and social issues is echoed daily in the United States and in countries around the world. Providing young people with an ever-increasing quantity of schooling of constantly rising quality is adduced as the key to economic competitiveness (e.g., Reich, 1992; Marshall & Tucker, 1993), equality of opportunity (Hochschild & Scovronick, 2003), and civic engagement (Gutmann, 1999). In addition, governments have come to rely on schools to accomplish a variety of other goals, ranging from improving childhood nutrition (Sedlak, 1995) to limiting drug use and combating AIDS. As schools have taken on ever more diverse and ambitious goals they have emerged as the critical and in some respects, unique, site for children's maturation and preparation for legitimate adult roles, providing an array of services that were once the province of the family, the workplace, or the church (Meyer, 2000).

Even as the importance ascribed to education has grown, however, the capacity of the State to deliver the quantity and quality of educational services that would be required to accomplish these goals successfully is subject to growing challenges, on both practical and ideological grounds. On the one hand, governments from Afghanistan to Zimbabwe are vexed by the challenge of meeting ever-higher expectations for educational access and quality without overwhelming the fiscal and administrative resources of the State.

On the other hand, generations of critics have questioned whether State provision of schools is the most efficient or effective strategy for expanding educational access and improving educational quality, often proposing greater reliance on private markets as an alternative (e.g., Friedman, 1955; Chubb & Moe, 1990).

Much of the policy ferment that has agitated the education sector over the past quarter-century originates in the growing distance between constantly rising public and private expectations for education and the capacity of the State to satisfy these expectations. Even as public expenditure on education steadily increases, and national education systems enroll more and more young people for more and more years, the central role traditionally played by the State in the education system has begun to shrink. As other chapters in this volume make clear, a diverse and growing array of non-State actors now play a critical role in providing educational services, and a growing share of the cost of education has come to be borne by private rather than public agencies.

This is partly a function of the State's success in institutionalizing education as the key to social and individual advancement. The normative importance nearly universally ascribed to more and better schooling generates demands that exceed the capacities of the State, leading parents and others to seek educational advantage outside or beyond the State system, often relying on private resources to do so. The shrinking of the State's role is simultaneously a function of the persistent failure of governments around the world to mobilize resources on a scale sufficient to extend educational access and opportunity to all young people, including especially those facing the largest initial disadvantages. The stakes attached to education are increasingly high, and the quantity of resources that would be needed to ensure even basic educational opportunities for all significantly exceeds already high levels of State expenditure. In the absence of State action, however, it is unlikely that many young people will be able to escape political and economic marginalization.

694

Constructing Education Systems

The centrality of education in modern societies is mainly a consequence of State action. Before the 19th century, the primary responsibility for the education of young people was left to households, with training for specialized occupations provided by guilds or by the Church (Aries, 1962). For more than a century, however, modern States have devoted vast quantities of resources to building and expanding comprehensive education systems, financed largely at public expense (Archer, 1982). They have encouraged and sometimes compelled young people to attend school, and they have fostered rewards systems that make adult success increasingly contingent on academic persistence and performance (Collins, 1979; Scott, 1999).

National education systems grew inexorably in the 19th and 20th centuries, in two distinct ways. On the one hand, the State worked systematically to extend educational opportunities both socially and spatially, to incorporate previously excluded groups including rural children, girls, linguistic and ethnic minorities, and the disabled. On the other hand, the State sponsored and supported policies that require young people to spend an ever-increasing share of their time within the education system. In many countries these have evolved from the introduction and enforcement of child labor and compulsory education laws (which at first typically required 4 years of schooling, and now often require 12 or more) to current initiatives aimed at ensuring universal access to pre-school and post-secondary education.

Modern States constructed national education systems in the service of political, economic, and military goals. The traditional rationale for the public provision of schools was political: Schools were expected to foster civic unity and national integration by providing young people with canonical knowledge including familiarity with national languages and civic traditions, and incorporating them into the State as citizens. In France, for example, the State extended the public school system to all corners of the nation in a generally successful effort to limit the use of local dialects and reduce the sway of local loyalties, and to construct a sense of shared national identity in their place (Weber, 1976). In the United States, State action supported the expansion, integration, and standardization of previously local educational systems (Tyack, 1974; see also Cohen-Vogel & McLendon, this volume).

The drive to fully incorporate citizens has expanded over time to include successively wider classes of persons, including girls, rural residents, racial and linguistic minorities, and the handicapped (Ramirez, 1989). The U.S. Congress enacted a series of federal laws aiming to address the special educational needs of diverse populations. The Elementary and Secondary Education Act was passed in 1965, and was quickly followed by legislation providing support for the education of English language learners in 1967 and handicapped children in 1975 (Fuhrman, Goertz, & Weinbaum, 2007). The United Nations and the World Bank have encouraged and financed the construction and expansion of national education systems in countries around the world, with a particular focus on the education of girls, in an effort to guarantee the "right" to education and to achieve the goal of Education for All by 2015 (UNICEF, 2000).

More recently, an economic rationale has been put forward to warrant the public provision of schooling. Like other goods including housing and haircuts, the consumption of schooling confers private benefits on those who participate in it. The knowledge and skills that young people acquire in school prepare them for productive employment, and for effective civic participation. People with more education enjoy higher wages, along with a variety of non-pecuniary benefits including better health and longer lives. As national economies have become more sophisticated and the average level of education has risen, the quantity of schooling that young people must complete in order to gain access to these benefits has steadily increased.

Beyond these private benefits, however, the education that individuals receive also produces benefits for the broader society and for the State. In addition to educated individuals' increased tax payments and reduced demand for social welfare expenditures (Belfield & Levin, 2007), a literate society functions more smoothly, with reduced communications costs, stronger democratic institutions, and a higher degree of social cohesion (Belfield, 2000; Stiglitz, 2000). Education also has a strong positive impact on health and fertility, both within and across generations. Educated mothers have fewer, healthier children, and the children of educated mothers are more likely to enroll and remain in school (Becker, 1991; Barrera, 1990; Colclough & Levin, 1993; Schultz, T. P., 1988; Schultz, T. W., 1981). As Eric Hanushek argues elsewhere in this volume, increases in educational quality and attainment produce large public benefits in the form of enhanced competitiveness in global markets and accelerated economic growth, which benefit the State and all of its citizens.

Over the course of the past century, State action to expand and improve national education systems in countries around the world has also been justified by reference to the imperatives of economic and military competitiveness. Following the "opening" of Japan in 1853, for example, the Japanese State created a new education system, modeled on those in Prussia and the United States, in an effort to keep up economically and militarily with its Western rivals (Passin, 1965). In the United States, successive waves of State-sponsored educational reform have gained their impetus from public anxieties about keeping up with the Germans, the Russians, the Japanese, the Chinese, and now the Finns (National Center on Education and the Economy, 2006).

The century-long push to keep young people in school longer has more recently been joined by State initiatives aimed at getting them into school earlier. Efforts to expand and institutionalize publicly funded childcare and early education for children prior to the age of compulsory attendance are accelerating in countries around the world, but wide variation nevertheless persists in access to pre-school and kindergarten, both across and within nations (see Table

TABLE 53.1
Pre-Primary Gross Enrollment Ratio

	1991	2000	2005
Australia	70.75	103.54[a]	104.02
Brazil	48.00	60.36	68.60
China*	22.47	38.40	39.29[b]
France	83.27	113.63	116.97
India	3.33	23.50	38.82
Japan	48.13	83.84	85.11
Mexico	63.10	74.47	96.03
Netherlands	99.18	96.64	89.75
Republic of Korea	55.42	78.05	90.61
Sweden	64.71	73.49	93.05
United States	62.86	58.96	61.42

Note: Gross enrollment ratio is calculated as the number of pupils enrolled in a given level of education, regardless of age, expressed as a percentage of the population in the theoretical age group for the same level of education.
[a]Data from 2001, due to missing 2000 data
[b]Data from 2006, due to missing 2005 data
Data Source: UNESCO

53.1). The State's efforts to bring children into the education system at younger ages are justified on both equity and efficiency grounds. Economists argue that the returns to high-quality pre-school education are very large, especially for poor children (e.g., Heckman & Masterov, 2007; Barnett, 1985). Others argue that achieving the goals of equal educational opportunity and full citizenship requires early interventions to overcome the initial disadvantage of children growing up in poverty (e.g., Rothstein, 2004).

The consequence of all of these efforts has been that more and more young people spend more and more years in school (see Table 53.2). Expectations about who should attend school have steadily expanded, along with expectations about how much schooling is sufficient to prepare young people for productive adult citizenship. Virtually every nation in the world has committed itself to the goal of ensuring that all young people complete 6 years of basic education by 2015. In countries where this target has long been achieved, governments now seek to ensure that all students complete secondary school, and many pursue efforts to expand enrollments in post-secondary education. In the United States, for example, the share of young people completing secondary education has risen steadily toward universality over the course of the 20th century; the share of adults with at least some college now exceeds 50%. The rate of change has been even faster in several European and Asian countries, where rates of post-secondary enrollment and completion now exceed those in the United States (see Table 53.3).

As formal education has come to occupy an ever-increasing share of young people's time, governments have sought to take advantage of children's compulsory presence in school to provide them with additional services, from nutrition to health care via sex education and recreational services. There have been frequent efforts in the United States to incorporate comprehensive services into schools as

a way both of addressing the full array of children's needs and also of ensuring that children enter the classroom ready to learn (e.g., Lindle & McClure, 1997; Rothstein, 2004). Programs including *Progresa* in Mexico and *Bolsa Escola* in Brazil have approached the question of children's services from the opposite side, providing income supplements and additional social services to households that promise to keep their children in school (e.g., International Food Policy Research Institute, 2002).

After more than a century of steady growth, however, there are signs that the State's role in national education systems has begun to shrink. The central importance of more and better education for the accomplishment of multiple public purposes remains unchallenged, but questions arise as to the appropriate nature and scale of the State's role in providing educational services. Efforts to expand access to post-secondary education have run into difficulties rooted partly in questions about whether the State should pay for the further education of young adults who stand to reap large private benefits from their college education (Hansen & Weisbrod, 1969; Fairweather, 2007) and partly in the cost of expanding opportunities at this level. Efforts to expand the State's role in early childhood and pre-school education have run into significant opposition, based in part on resistance to increased taxes and public spending, and in part on aversion to the idea that very young children should be placed under the care of the State rather than their families and communities (Fuller, 2007). The constantly rising cost of education at all levels produces political dissatisfaction and resistance. In Europe and elsewhere, groups defined by communal, religious, and linguistic affinities have begun to demand increased control over the education of their own children, including the right to establish their own schools (Plank, 2006). For now, though, it remains an open question whether this marks a genuine turning point in the history of education or a brief pause in the steady expansion of the State's role in the education system.

Why the State's Role Is Shrinking

The central role of the State in the development of modern economies and societies is under increasing challenge, and not just in education. The increasing mobility of capital makes it increasingly difficult for national governments to regulate or manage the national economy, or to raise the revenues necessary to provide social services including education (Ohmae, 1996; Reich, 2007). The growing influence of transnational agencies, including the World Bank, challenges the authority of national governments in education as in other areas of public policy (Plank, 1993; see also Mundy & Ghali, this volume). The proliferation of transnational and subnational institutions and loyalties challenge the State's role as the arbiter of citizenship and the guarantor of national interest (Guéhenno & Elliott, 2000).

With specific reference to the education system, there are both practical and ideological reasons why the State's

TABLE 53.2
Gross Enrollment Rates for Primary and Secondary Levels

Primary Gross Enrollment Rate

	1970	1975	1980	1985	1990	1991	1992	1993	1994	1995	1996	1997	1998	1999	2000	2001	2002	2003	2004	2005	2006
Australia	115	107	112	107	108	108	108	107	106	101	101	101	100	100	101	101	103	103	104	104	105
Brazil	119	87	98	100	105	104	109	110	112	118	120	125	...	154	150	147	145	141	140	137	...
China	91	122	113	123	125	126	119	117	117	118	120	123	...	...	...	117	116	115	...	...	111
France	117	109	111	109	108	108	106	106	106	106	105	105	...	107	107	106	106	105	104	110	110
India	78	81	83	96	99	94	100	101	101	100	100	97	114	93	94	93	94	102	110	115	112
Japan	100	99	101	102	100	100	101	102	103	103	102	102	102	101	101	101	101	100	100	100	100
Korea, Rep.	103	107	110	97	105	105	103	101	98	95	94	94	94	95	98	100	102	104	105	105	105
Mexico	106	111	120	118	114	112	114	114	115	115	114	114	...	111	110	110	111	112	112	112	113
Netherlands	102	99	100	99	102	102	97	108	107	107	108	108	...	108	108	107	107	107	107	107	107
Sweden	94	101	97	98	100	100	104	105	105	106	107	111	...	110	109	110	110	110	100	98	96
United States	88	89	99	99	103	103	101	101	102	102	101	102	101	101	100	101	99	99	98	98	98

Secondary Gross Enrollment Rate

	1970	1975	1980	1985	1990	1991	1992	1993	1994	1995	1996	1997	1998	1999	2000	2001	2002	2003	2004	2005	2006
Australia	82	72	71	80	82	83	84	132	131	142	148	153	156	157	162	154	153	155	149	149	150
Brazil	26	26	33	35	38	40	43	43	45	50	56	...	...	99	104	107	109	102	106	105	...
China	24	46	46	40	49	49	55	57	61	66	69	59	...	62	63	65	67	70	...	...	76
France	73	82	85	90	98	98	102	110	111	111	111	111	...	111	110	109	109	109	109	114	114
India	24	26	30	38	44	42	49	49	49	49	49	47	34	44	46	46	48	50	52	54	...
Japan	87	92	93	95	97	97	96	99	100	103	107	102	102	102	102	102	103	102	102	102	101
Korea, Rep.	42	56	78	92	90	90	91	95	98	101	102	102	102	100	98	94	91	90	91	93	96
Mexico	23	35	49	57	53	53	54	56	58	61	64	68	...	70	72	74	77	81	83	85	87
etherlands	75	89	93	117	120	120	123	140	139	137	132	129	...	124	123	123	121	121	118	118	118
Sweden	86	78	88	91	90	90	121	127	132	137	140	157	...	157	152	148	144	137	103	103	103
United States	84	84	91	97	92	92	97	99	97	97	97	98	96	95	94	94	93	94	94	94	94

Source: The World Bank Group, 2007

TABLE 53.3
Enrollment in Tertiary Education (Gross Enrollment Ratio)

	1991	2000	2005
Australia	38.95	65.57	72.57
Brazil	11.25	16.06	25.48
China	2.96	7.68	21.58
France	39.64	52.88	56.08
India	6.10	9.60	11.03
Japan	29.61	47.40	55.31
Mexico	14.70	19.51	25.25
Netherlands	39.83	52.15	58.98
Republic of Korea	38.58	72.58	89.94
Sweden	32.00	67.17	81.62
United States	73.31	69.03	82.24

*Data from 2006; 2005 data not available

Note: Gross enrollment ratio is calculated as the number of pupils enrolled in a given level of education, regardless of age, expressed as a percentage of the population in the theoretical age group for the same level of education.

role is shrinking. In practical terms, the growing weight of expectations that schools bear is a challenge that the education system is almost certain to fail. Under circumstances where more and better education is proposed as the solution to a wide array of social and economic problems, no amount of education can ever suffice; even being "best in the world" falls short, as rivals strive to catch up. Moreover, the persistence of the problems that the education system is expected to solve breeds cynicism and distrust about the capacity of schools and teachers to accomplish public goals, and a corresponding reluctance to increase the quantity of resources in the system without solid evidence of success.

Practical skepticism originating in the observed failure of the education system to achieve large public purposes finds its justification in theoretical and political arguments that assert that the State cannot and will not succeed in

the pursuit of large public objectives. Proponents of these theories argue on behalf of institutional arrangements that rely less on the State, including administrative decentralization, community control, and an increased role for private markets.

How the State Fails

The Growing Financial Burden   The construction of comprehensive education systems is a monumental undertaking, and the cost of meeting the ever more ambitious goals assigned to the education system is constantly increasing. The provision of sufficient schools and teachers to keep all young people in school for 6, 10, 12, or more years ensures that education is almost invariably among the largest items of public expenditure in national budgets (see Table 53.4). The level of schooling that students must complete to "keep up" with their local and international rivals and compete successfully in the global economy rises steadily, as does the level of qualifications that teachers must have to keep ahead of their students.

In the quest to improve the performance of schools and students the demand for additional resources is insatiable, but there is argument about whether increased expenditure in fact leads to better outcomes (Hanushek, 1986; Hedges, Laine, & Greenwald, 1994). The levels of taxation that would be required to accomplish ambitious public expectations are strongly resisted, but even sustaining current levels of performance implies continuously rising costs. The history of mass education has consequently been characterized at every turn by concerns about cost, and demands for increased efficiency in the use of scarce public resources (Callahan, 1962; World Bank, 2001).

Current strategies for controlling costs in the education system include increased reliance on new technologies, reduction in administrative and non-classroom personnel, and privatization of ancillary services but—as with previous

TABLE 53.4
Public Expenditure by Percent of GDP and Total Government Expenditure

	Percent of GDP			Percent of Total Government Expenditure		
	1991	2000	2005	1991	2000	2005
Australia	4.73	4.68	4.53	14.76	13.32	...
China	2.23	1.91a	...	12.71	12.97a	...
Japan	...	3.69	3.54	...	10.49	9.17
Republic of Korea	3.78	3.76a	4.63c	25.60	13.12a	16.48c
Brazil	...	4.01	4.01c	...	12.01	...
Mexico	3.83	4.86	5.54	15.33	23.62	25.61c
France	5.55	5.67	5.70	...	11.39	10.57
Netherlands	5.38	4.58a	5.26	14.28	10.44a	11.49
Sweden	7.07	7.32	7.13	13.77	13.40	12.95c
United States	5.09	5.08a	5.33	12.34	17.15b	13.72
India	3.65	4.41	3.25	12.24	12.71	...

aData from 1999, not available in 2000
bData from 2001, not available in 2000
cData from 2004, 2005 not available
Source: UNESCO

efforts—there is little evidence that any of these strategies has had much effect on the upward trend in educational spending. Vast expenditures on educational technology have had little discernible impact on student learning (Zhao & Lei, this volume) and there is little evidence that private management of schools is less costly or more efficient than public (Belfield & Levin, this volume). Popular dissatisfaction with the financial demands of the education system consequently continues to grow.

Arbitrary and Unattainable Aspirations   In the quest to provide more and better education for their citizens, governments often define arbitrary and unattainable goals, which may or may not reflect genuine gains in the knowledge and skills of students or enhanced competitiveness in local or global labor markets. Americans are especially susceptible to adopting high-minded but practically meaningless goals. At President George H. W. Bush's Charlottesville education summit, for example, the assembled governors proclaimed that U.S. students should be "best in the world" in science and math, within a decade (Vinovskis, 1999). President George W. Bush was the strongest advocate for the No Child Left Behind Act (NCLB), which requires "proficiency" for all U.S. students by 2014 (Darling-Hammond, 2007). The first goal was not achieved, and it is now clear that the second will not be achieved either. Elsewhere, as 2015 approaches, the goal of Education for All—which has already been postponed twice—appears increasingly distant.

Even as the goals assigned to national education systems become more ambitious, however, the challenge of providing even minimally adequate and equitable educational opportunities for disadvantaged schools and students remains daunting. Achievement gaps in the United States and in other countries leave behind students facing initial disadvantage, including poor students, linguistic and racial minorities, and students with special needs. These disadvantages are compounded in schools where similarly poor students are concentrated, whether in the inner cities of the U.S. or the *banlieues* of France. Programs aimed at improving the performance of these schools and students include NCLB in the United States, the establishment of *zones d'education prioritaires* (ZEPs) in France, and the P-900 program in Chile, among many others. None has shown systematic success, which calls governments' even more ambitious goals into serious question (Plank & Smith, 2007).

The challenges to the State's role in the education system are exemplified in the international commitment to provide 6 years of quality education to all of the world's children by 2015 (UNICEF, 2000). Careful analyses by the World Bank and others (Bruns, Mingat, & Rakotomalala, 2005; Colclough & Lewin, 1993) have shown that the goal is attainable, with sufficient funding and "political will." Quite apart from the question whether sufficient funding and political will can in fact be mobilized, however, skepticism as to whether the goal of Education for All will be achieved persists for two main reasons. The first is the practical question whether national governments in places where the goal remains to be achieved have the administrative capacity and political legitimacy to build, staff, and manage schools for all of their nations' children. The second is whether reliance on the State is the most promising strategy for expanding educational opportunities, or whether the goal can be achieved in some other way.

Positional Goods and the Receding Horizon   Education is in significant part what economists call a "positional good"; much of the value of a given educational credential derives from the fact that the available supply is strictly limited and only a few people have one. Students may gain positional advantage by attending schools in pricy suburbs, earning straight As, or obtaining degrees from prestigious universities, but the value of these accomplishments is diminished as they become more widely available and therefore less distinctive. Pervasive grade inflation, for example, reduces the positional value of a student's grade point average; the opportunity to earn a PhD from a mail-order university reduces the positional advantage conferred upon those with doctoral degrees. Tyack and Cuban (1995) attribute much of the resistance to educational reform in the United States to concerns about the potential redistribution of opportunities and rewards through the education system.

The contest for positional advantage is observed not only among students, but among States as well. Having the best-educated workforce confers a notional advantage in the global economy that is only available to a few countries, which must strive to maintain their advantage while others strive to catch up. To the extent that educational "success" is defined in positional terms, however, the consequence is an educational arms race; no amount of education can be sufficient to ensure a permanent advantage over one's rivals.

The increasing availability of internationally comparable assessment results has raised the stakes in the contest for positional advantage, as States are able to measure the performance of their schools and students against those in other countries. Relatively poor results on international assessments have exacerbated dissatisfaction with schools in the United States, Germany, and other countries, and have strengthened arguments for institutional reforms aimed at making local students "the best in the world" (Herman & Baker, this volume). The proposed standard begs the question, however, of how much education—and of what kind—would be enough to satisfy the demands of the local or even the global labor market, in light of constant increases in the general standard.

Why the State Fails   Practical concerns with the rising cost and unsatisfactory outcomes of national education systems find their political justification in the resurgence of theories and ideologies that identify the costs of excessive State intervention in society and the economy, and that call for alternative institutional arrangements better suited to accomplish the large public purposes to which the education system is dedicated. The most influential of these proposes greater reliance on the free operation of competitive markets to accomplish a variety of public purposes including more and better education for young people. A competing argument laments the damage that State action does to local communities and popular initiative, and proposes greater reliance on local actors and social capital to provide social services including education (e.g., Fuller 2007; Coleman & Hoffer, 1987; Bryk, Lee, & Holland, 1995).

In the decades following the Great Depression and World War II, the prevailing "liberal consensus" put the State at the center of national policy debates, as the essential unit of international relations, as the provider of key social services, and as the engine of economic and social progress (Polanyi, 2001; Bell, 1960; Galbraith, 1968). In Europe and North America, the State provided an expanding variety of services, from social security to interstate highway systems. These efforts included a steady and dramatic expansion in access to educational opportunities, including universal secondary education and "free" higher education (Hansen & Weisbrod, 1969). In less developed countries, national and international agencies worked to build the capacity of new and weak States to lead the process of national development, including the provision of educational and other services for their citizens (e.g., Nyerere, 1968).

The claim that the State had a large and essentially benign role to play in sponsoring development and social progress was subject to challenge from the beginning, on a number of different grounds, including the loss of freedom entailed by the growth of powerful State institutions (Hayek, 2007; Friedman, 1955); the economic costs imposed by the self-serving behavior of politicians and officials (Buchanan, 2000); the inefficiency of State efforts to manage national economies (Bauer, 1972; Stiglitz, 1996); and the obstacles to flexibility and innovation created by the increased power of occupational and other interest groups over State action (Olson, 1971).

In the view of James Buchanan and other public choice economists, the State's apparent failure to provide the quantity and quality of services that citizens expect is not a problem of insufficient resources or "political will," but is instead intrinsic to the State itself (Buchanan, 2000; Tullock, Seldon, & Brady, 2002). The State's role as the primary if not exclusive provider of educational services fosters self-interested behavior among teachers and other educators, and the absence of competition weakens incentives for diligence and innovation in schools (e.g., Chubb & Moe, 1990). The State's inability to acquire sufficient information about educational practice and performance undermines local initiative and fosters inefficiency in the use of public resources (Stiglitz, 1996). The rise of scholarship rooted in public choice theories and the simultaneous rise of political parties committed to shrinking the State have provided a compelling public explanation for the persistent failure of the education system to meet public expectations. These theories have offered arguments against relying on the State as the main or monopoly provider of educational and

other public services, and a justification for experimenting with alternative institutional arrangements.

Informed by these critiques, a very different view of the State and its role has taken hold in recent years (Blyth, 2002). The critics' ideas have found political expression in the ascendancy of parties and politicians committed to reducing the State's role in the economy and society, in countries including France and Sweden as well as the U.S. and the U.K. (Feigenbaum, Henig, & Hamnett, 1998; Daun, 2003; Meuret, 2007). Their calls for cutting taxes, limiting social activism, and scaling back welfare and other redistributive policies were grounded both in skepticism about the State's capacity and competence to address complex social problems, and also in popular resistance to the equalizing and inclusionary project that governed State policies.

This view of the State has had a large impact in the education system, as in other sectors. The consequence has been an extended period of policy ferment, accompanied by both active and passive shrinking of the State's role. The ensuing policy debate turns on whether alternative institutions—notably markets—can accomplish the large public purposes assigned to the education system more effectively or efficiently than the State can do, or whether a smarter and more competent State is the essential guarantor of public goals.

Shrinking the State

If the State is shrinking, the burden of expectations that the education system now bears requires that goals once pursued mainly or exclusively through the State must be accomplished under alternative institutional arrangements. Policy debates in recent decades have therefore focused on strategies for streamlining the State's role and making State provision more efficient, or else on identifying alternatives to State provision. These debates have been conducted in a policy environment in which the relative importance of State provision has steadily shrunk, notably as the demand for higher education has exceeded the State's capacity to expand educational provision. The question that arises is whether the State's role should be sustained or even expanded, or whether shrinking the State further and relying on other institutions offers greater promise.

Funding versus Provision One central question with regard to the State's role in national education systems is whether the State should be directly involved in providing schools, or whether the State should simply provide the funds that make it possible for other actors to provide educational services. At the limit, the State might provide vouchers to parents, and allow them to purchase educational services for their children on the open market (e.g., Friedman, 1955); alternatively, the State might subsidize the provision of educational services by a variety of private agencies, including community-based and religious organizations (Gintis, 1995). Even conceding that the State has a fundamental interest in ensuring adequate education for all citizens, and a unique responsibility to ensure that all young people have access to educational services that advance this goal, the question remains whether maintaining public school systems that deliver educational services under direct State control is the most efficient or effective way to accomplish public objectives.

U.S. higher education policy has separated public funding from State provision for several decades, although state and local governments continue to maintain extensive networks of public colleges and universities. Federal programs including the G.I. Bill and Pell Grants provide funds to students for use in public or private institutions; state scholarship programs are typically available for use in all in-state institutions, whether public or private. The tax breaks available to non-profit organizations represent a further subsidy to private colleges and universities (Fairweather, 2007). As demand for post-secondary education has grown, the number and variety of private agencies providing higher educational services has expanded significantly, and this trend is likely to continue (Levine, 2001).

A more recent development in the United States has been the emergence of private-sector education management organizations providing administrative and support services for charter schools and traditional public school systems as well. These include companies like Edison Schools or National Heritage Academies that manage far-flung networks of schools under contract, along with local companies managing one or two charter schools (Levin, 2001; Bulkley, 2003). Reliance on non-State actors for the direct provision of educational services funded by the State has been further institutionalized in the Supplementary Educational Services provisions of NCLB, which have led to the proliferation of for-profit and non-profit organizations offering tutoring and other services to disadvantaged students at public expense (Hess & Finn, 2008). The constitutional boundary between Church and State continues to block most forms of public financial support for religious schools in the United States, but recent court challenges have opened the door more widely (Feinberg, 2000).

The question whether the State should subsidize private institutions in basic and post-secondary education is less controversial in many other countries. In Australia, Chile, and Sweden the provision of State subsidies to non-State providers of educational services extends to religious as well as secular schools (Plank & Sykes, 2003; McDonough & Feinberg, 2003). As governments in Africa and elsewhere seek to achieve the goals of Education for All, they find themselves obliged to rely on a wide variety of partners to provide schools, including non-governmental organizations, local communities, and religious organizations, many of which rely on public funds to support their educational efforts (World Bank, 2001).

Cost-shifting and Privatization The financial challenge of providing a growing number of young people with an increasing number and variety of educational services has led to significant cost-shifting in the education system, as a rising share of the cost of schooling now falls on the shoulders of students and their families (OECD, 2007, Table B3.2a). This is especially the case with regard to higher education, where State subsidies for both students and institutions have fallen steadily over time and the private cost of obtaining advanced education has commensurately increased (Fairweather, 2007). The same dynamic is observed in other countries, as reduced public support for universities and their students has been matched by dramatic increases in the number and variety of private and for-profit higher education institutions (e.g., Altbach & Levy, 2005).

Similar debates have emerged in the pre-school sector, producing disagreements along two distinct dimensions. On the one hand, there is disagreement about whether the State should fund universal pre-school, underwriting the cost for all children, or whether State subsidies should be targeted to the neediest households. On the other hand, there is controversy over whether the State should provide pre-school services itself, or instead whether State funds should underwrite the provision of pre-schooling by other agencies (Fuller, 2007).

Even in the basic education system, State funding for a variety of ancillary services including libraries, school nurses, and others has been reduced or eliminated. Private resources including mandatory fees (e.g., "pay to play"), financial contributions to local foundations (Addonizio, 1998; Brunner & Imazeki, 2005), and volunteer labor have replaced State resources in some schools, but in schools serving less prosperous students many services have simply disappeared. In addition, the provision of privately provided and privately financed "shadow" education services aimed at ensuring positional advantage in the education system are a large and growing industry in countries around the world (Lee, Park, & Lee, this volume).

Administrative Decentralization One critical front in the contest over the State's role in the education system has been the continuing debate over administrative decentralization, which originates partly in concerns about the relative efficiency and efficacy of central versus local administrative control, but more profoundly in concerns about the central State's capacity to exercise effective leadership across a dispersed system of schools (e.g., McGinn & Welsh, 1999). The key policy question revolves around which responsibilities should be decentralized, and which should remain under the control of the State. A frequent response to this question promotes what Ladd and Fiske have characterized as "tight-loose-tight" administrative arrangements, under which the State defines clear performance objectives and conducts rigorous assessments to determine whether these have been achieved, leaving local actors free to adopt whatever policies and practices are best suited to local circumstances (Ladd & Fiske, 2000). This administrative approach to the problem of central versus local control in the education system is emerging as the modal pattern in countries around the world (Plank & Smith, 2007).

As with other efforts to shift costs off the State's budget, initiatives that aim to decentralize administrative control are often motivated in part by the hope that shifting authority and responsibility to the local level will make it possible for schools to tap additional sources of financial and other support through partnerships with local organizations including businesses, religious organizations, and local governments (Bray, 1996).

The debate over administrative decentralization has been especially sharp in developing countries, where States are struggling—often with limited success—to build national education systems capable of meeting the goals of Education for All. It has become apparent that this remains a distant goal in many parts of the world, well beyond the capacity of States and local authorities alike. The World Bank and other international agencies have consequently invested a great deal of attention in the problem of how to expand educational opportunity and improve educational quality without relying on the traditional institutions of State provision and control (World Bank, 2001).

Other Challenges to the State Other challenges to the State's role in the education system arise from questions about the legitimacy of centralized educational provision, and fundamentally about the virtues of universal citizenship in a modern, secular State. These challenges arise from a variety of sources: resurgent nationalisms, religious loyalties, and doubts about the appropriate balance between the State and parents in the education of young people. All of them call into question the State's role as the main or monopoly provider of educational services (Plank, 2006).

One set of challenges originates in the resurgent power of subnational (or, in some instances, transnational) ethnic and linguistic loyalties. In Belgium, for example, three Ministries of Education administer separate systems of schools for Dutch-, French-, and German-speaking children, respectively. Regional authorities in Spain provide education in local languages including Basque and Catalan, and exercise growing authority over the regional curriculum as well. The ebb and flow of Quebecois separatism in Canada is similarly reflected in the provincial education system (Bourhis, 1984). These regional movements are a direct refutation of the nation-building efforts that supported the construction and expansion of national education systems in the 19th and 20th centuries.

A parallel but quite different set of challenges has emerged with the rise of transnational institutions including the OECD, the European Union, and the World Bank, which constrain the policy discretion of national governments by encouraging convergence around transnationally legitimated educational policy arrangements (e.g., "tight-loose-tight" accountability systems). States face powerful incentives to adopt policies endorsed by these agencies in order to demonstrate their commitment to economic competitiveness and in many countries to ensure the continued flow of public and private financial resources (Mundy & Ghali, this volume).

In the United States and some other countries, a third challenge has arisen among parents who question whether the State should play any role at all in the education of their children, and who consequently choose to educate their children at home. The grounds for questioning the State's "right" to educate children are sometimes located in religious belief, and at other times in doubts about the quality or utility of standardized State provision (Lugg & Rorrer, this volume).

A New Role for the State? In light of the heavy and growing burden of expectations placed on the education system, the fundamental question for scholars and policy makers is whether the ambitious goals for schools will best be accomplished by reinvigorating the State and providing educational services through direct public action, or whether these goals can be accomplished more efficiently or effectively by relying on other actors, including households, community and religious organizations, and for-profit firms. This question has come to the fore in policy debates over issues ranging from early childhood education through school choice to university finance, raising fundamental disagreements over the responsibilities and capacities of the State.

Even as the shrinking of the State has accelerated in recent years, a new recognition of the State's importance has begun to emerge (World Bank, 1997; Fukuyama, 2004). This originates partly in apprehension about the growing number of weak and failed States in critical regions of the world, but also in acknowledgment that key social objectives including Education for All cannot be accomplished in the absence of an effective State. The urgent question for policy makers and scholars is what set of institutional arrangements will be able to bear the weight of expectations and responsibilities that now rests on the education system. It is a question that will remain with us for some time to come.

References

Addonizio, M. F. (1998). *Private funding of public schools: Local education foundations in Michigan.* Washington, DC: Aspen Institute.

Altbach, P. G., & Levy, D. C. (2005). *Private higher education: A global revolution.* Rotterdam: Sense Publishers.

Archer, M. (Ed.). (1982). *The sociology of educational expansion.* Beverly Hills, CA: Sage.

Aries, P. (1962). *Centuries of childhood: A social history of family life.* New York: Vintage.

Barnett, W. S. (1985). Benefit-cost analysis of the Perry Preschool Program and its policy implications. *Educational Evaluation and Policy Analysis, 7*(4), 333–342.

Barrera, A. (1990). The role of maternal schooling and its interaction with public health programs in child health production. *Journal of Development Economics, 32,* 69–91.

Bauer, P. T. (1972). *Dissent on development: Studies and debates in development economics.* Cambridge, MA: Harvard University Press.

Becker, G. (1991). *A treatise on the family.* Cambridge, MA: Harvard University Press.

Belfield, C. R. (2000). *Economic principles for education: Theory and evidence.* Cheltenham, UK: Edward Elgar.

Belfield, C. R., & Levin, H. M. (2007). *The price we pay: Economic and social consequences of inadequate education*. Washington D.: Brookings Institution.

Bell, D. (1960). *The end of ideology: On the exhaustion of political ideas in the fifties*. Glencoe, IL: Free Press.

Blyth, M. (2002). *Great transformations: Economic ideas and institutional change in the twentieth century*. New York: Cambridge University Press.

Bourhis, R.Y. (1984). *Conflict and language planning in Quebec*. Bristol, UK: Multilingual Matters.

Bray, M. (1996). *Counting the full cost: Parental and community financing of education in East Asia*. Washington, DC: The World Bank.

Brunner, E., & Imazeki, J. (2005). Fiscal stress and voluntary contributions to public schools. In Fowler, W. J. (Ed.), *Developments in School Finance: 2004* (pp. 39–54).Washington, DC: NCES.

Bruns, B., Mingat, A., & Rakotomalala, R. (2005). *Achieving universal primary education by 2015: A chance for every child*. Washington, DC: World Bank.

Bryk, A., Lee, V., & Holland, P. (1995). *Catholic schools and the common good*. Cambridge: Harvard University Press.

Buchanan, J. M. (2000). *Politics as public choice*. Indianapolis: Liberty Fund.

Bulkley, K. E. (2003). Balancing act: Educational management organizations and charter school autonomy. In K. E. Bulkley & P. Wohlstetter (Eds.), *Taking account of charter schools: What's happened and what's next?* (pp. 121–141). New York: Teachers College Press.

Callahan, R. (1962). *Education and the cult of efficiency*. Chicago: University of Chicago.

Chubb, J., & Moe, T. (1990). *Politics, markets, and America's schools*. Washington, DC: Brookings Institution.

Colclough. C., & Levin, K. M. (1993). *Educating all the children: strategies for primary education in the south*. Oxford, UK: Clarendon

Collins, R. (1979). *The credential society: An historical sociology of education and stratification*. New York: Wiley.

Coleman, J. S., & Hoffer, T. (1987). *Public and private high schools: The impact of communities*. New York: Basic Books.

Darling-Hammond, L. (2007). The flat earth and education: How America's commitment to equity will determine our future. *Educational Researcher, 36*(6), 318–334.

Daun, H. (2003). Market forces and decentralization in Sweden: Impetus for school development or threat to comprehensiveness and equity? In D. N. Plank & G. Sykes (Eds.), *Choosing choice: School choice policies in international perspective* (pp. 92–111). New York: Teachers College Press.

Fairweather, J. (2007). *Higher education and the new economy*. East Lansing: The Education Policy Center at Michigan State University.

Feigenbaum, H., Henig, J., & Hamnett, C. (1998). *Shrinking the state: The political underpinnings of privatization*. New York: Cambridge University Press.

Feinberg, W. (2000). On public support for religious schools. *Teachers College Record, 102*(4), 841–856.

Friedman, M. (1955). The role of government in education. In R. A., Solo (Ed.), *Economics and the public interest* (pp. 123–144). New Brunswick: Rutgers University Press.

Fuhrman, S. H., Goertz, M. E., & Weinbaum, E. H. (2007). Educational governance in the United States: Where are we? How did we get here? Why should we care? In S. Fuhrman, D. Cohen. & F. Mosher (Eds.) *The state of education policy research* (pp. 41–62). Mahwah, NJ: Erlbaum.

Fuller, B. (2007). *Standardized childhood: The political and cultural struggle over early education*. Stanford, CA: Stanford University Press.

Fukuyama, F. (2004). *State-building: Governance and world order in the 21st century*. Ithaca, NY: Cornell University Press.

Galbraith, J. K. (1968). *The affluent society*. New York: Penguin.

Gintis, H. (1995). The political economy of school choice. *Teachers College Record, 96*, 492–5110.

Guéhenno, J., & Elliott, V. (2000). *The end of the Nation State*. Minneapolis: University of Minnesota Press.

Gutmann, A. (1999). *Democratic education*. Princeton, NJ: Princeton University Press.

Hansen, W. L., & Weisbrod, B. A. (1969). *Benefits, costs and finance of public higher education*. Chicago: Markham.

Hanushek, E. (1986). The economics of schooling: Production and efficiency in public schools. *Journal of Economic Literature, 24*, 1141–1178.

Hayek, F. A. (2007). *The road to serfdom*. Chicago: University of Chicago Press.

Heckman, J. J., & Masterov, D. V. (2007) The productivity argument for investing in young children. *Review of Agricultural Economics, 29*, 446–493.

Hedges, L. V., Laine, R. D., & Greenwald, R. (1994). Does money matter? A meta-analysis of studies of the effects of differential school inputs on student outcomes. *Educational Researcher, 23*(3), 5–14.

Hess, F., & Finn, C. (2006). *No remedy left behind: Lessons from a half-decade of NCLB*. Washington, DC: AEI Press.

Hochschild, J. L., & Scovronick, N. (2003). *The American Dream and the public schools*. New York: Oxford University Press.

International Food Policy Research Institute (2002). *Progresa: Breaking the cycle of poverty*. Washington, DC: IFPRI.

Ladd, H. F., & Fiske, E. B. (2000). *When schools compete: A cautionary tale*. Washington, DC: Brookings Institution.

Levin, H. M. (2001). *Privatizing education: Can the marketplace deliver choice, efficiency, equity, and social cohesion?* Denver, CO: Westview Press.

Levine, A. (2001). Privatization in higher education. In H. M. Levin, (Ed.), *Privatizing education: Can the marketplace deliver choice, efficiency, equity, and social cohesion?* (pp. 133–148). Denver, CO: Westview Press.

Lindle, J. C., & McClure, M.W. (1997). *Expertise versus responsiveness in children's worlds: Politics in school, home and community relationships*. New York: Routledge.

McDonough, K., & Feinberg, W. (2003). *Citizenship and education in liberal-democratic societies*. New York: Oxford University Press.

McGinn, N., & Welsh, T. (1999). *Decentralization of education: Why, when what, and how?* Paris: UNESCO.

Marshall, R., & Tucker, M. (1993). *Thinking for a living: Education and the wealth of nations*. New York: Basic Books.

Meuret, D. (2007). *Gouverner l'ecole: Une comparaison france/etats-unis*. Paris: Broché.

Meyer, J. (2000). Reflections on education as transcendence. In L. Cuban & D. Shipps (Eds.), *Reconstructing the common good in education* (pp. 206–222). Stanford, CA: Stanford University Press.

National Center on Education and the Economy. (2006). *Tough choices or tough times*. Washington, DC: NCEE.

Nyerere, J. (1968). *Freedom and socialism. Uhuru na ujamaa; a selection from writings and speeches, 1965–1967*. Dar Es Salaam, Tanzania: Oxford University Press.

Ohmae, K. (1996). *The end of the Nation State: The rise of regional economies*. New York: Free Press.

Olson, M. (1971). *The logic of collective action: Public goods and the theory of groups*. Cambridge: Harvard University Press.

Organisation for Economic Cooperation and Development. (2007). *Education at a glance, 2007*. Paris: OECD.

Passin, H. (1965). *Society and education in Japan*. New York: Teachers College Press.

Plank, D. N. (1993). Aid, debt, and the end of sovereignty: Mozambique and its donors. *Journal of Modern African Studies, 31*, 407–430.

Plank, D. N. (2006). Unsettling the State: How 'demand' challenges the U.S. education system. *European Journal of Education, 41*(1), 13–27.

Plank, D. N., & Smith, B.A. (2007). Autonomous schools: Theory, evidence and reality. In H. F. Ladd & E. B. Fiske (Eds.), *Handbook of research in education finance and policy* (pp. 402–444). London: Routledge.

Plank, D. N, & Sykes, G. (2003) *Choosing choice: School choice policies in international perspective*. New York: Teachers College Press.

Polanyi, K. (2001). *The great transformation*. Boston: Beacon Press.

Ramirez, F. O. (1989). Reconstituting children: Extension of personhood and citizenship. In D. Kertzne & K. W. Schaie (Eds.), *Age structuring in comparative perspective* (pp. 143–165). Mahwah, NJ: Erlbaum.

Reich, R. (1992). *The work of nations*. New York: Vintage.

Reich, R. (2007). *Supercapitalism: The transformation of business, democracy, and everyday life*. New York: Knopf.

Rothstein, R. (2004). *Class and schools: Using social, economic, and educational reform to close the Black-White achievement gap*. New York: Teachers College Press.

Schultz, T. P. (1988). Education, investments and returns. In H. Chenery & T. N. Srinivasan, (Eds.), *Handbook of development economics Vol. 1* (pp. 544–630). Amsterdam: Elsevier.

Schultz, T. W. (1981). *Investing in people*. Berkeley: University of California Press.

Scott, J. C. (1999). *Seeing like a state: How certain schemes to improve the human condition have failed*. New Haven, CT: Yale University Press.

Sedlak, M. (1995). Attitudes, choices, and behavior: School delivery of health and social services. In D. Ravitch. & M. Vinovskis (Eds.) *Learning from the past: What history teaches us about school reform* (pp. 57–94). Baltimore: Johns Hopkins University Press.

Stiglitz, J. E. (1996). *Whither socialism?* Cambridge: MIT Press.

Stiglitz, J. E. (2000). *Economics of the public sector*. Palo Alto: Stanford University Press.

Tullock, G., Seldon, A., & Brady, G. L. (2002). *Government failure: A primer in public choice*. Washington, DC: Cato Institute.

Tyack, D. B. (1974). *The one best system: A history of American urban education*. Cambridge. MA: Harvard.

Tyack, D., & Cuban, L. (1995). *Tinkering toward utopia: A century of public school reform*. Cambridge, MA: Harvard University Press.

UNESCO. (1991). *UNESCO Institute for Statistics Data Centre, Custom Tables*. Retrieved July 25, 2008, from http://stats.uis.unesco.org/unesco/TableViewer/document.aspx?ReportId=136&IF_Language=eng&BR_Topic=0

UNESCO. (2000). *UNESCO Institute for Statistics Data Centre, Custom Tables*. Retrieved July 25, 2008, from http://stats.uis.unesco.org/unesco/TableViewer/document.aspx?ReportId=136&IF_Language=eng&BR_Topic=0

UNESCO. (2005). *UNESCO Institute for Statistics Data Centre, Custom Tables*. Retrieved July 25, 2008, from http://stats.uis.unesco.org/unesco/TableViewer/document.aspx?ReportId=136&IF_Language=eng&BR_Topic=0

UNICEF. (2000). *Basic education programme, plan of action*. New York: UNICEF.

Vinovskis, M. (1999). *The road to Charlottesville: The 1989 education summit*. Washington, DC: National Education Goals Panel.

Weber, E. (1976). *Peasants into Frenchmen*. Palo Alto, CA: Stanford University Press.

Wolf, A. (2002). *Does education matter?: Myths about education and economic growth*. London: Penguin.

World Bank. (1997). *World development report 1997: The state in a changing world*. Washington, DC: The World Bank.

World Bank. (2001). *A chance to learn: Knowledge and finance for education in Sub-Saharan Africa*. Washington, DC: World Bank.

World Bank. (2007). *World Bank Data and Research*. Retrieved July 25, 2008, from http://web.worldbank.org/WBSITE/EXTERNAL/DATASTATISTICS/0,,contentMDK:20535285~menuPK:1192694~pagePK:64133150~piPK:64133175~theSitePK:239419,00.html

54

COMMENTARY
Research on Teaching and Learning

BARBARA R. FOORMAN
Florida State University

Over the past 50 years, U.S. education policy has not diminished its dual emphases on equal access to education for minorities and the right to education for individuals with disabilities. A third emphasis on educational excellence was added in 1983 with the report *A Nation at Risk* (National Commission on Excellence in Education, 1983). Commitments to these fundamental rights to quality education were couched within the social reform spurred by Lyndon Johnson's 1965 War on Poverty (Foorman, Kalinowski, & Sexton, 2007). Although the role of the nation in Johnson's War on Poverty shrank in the Reagan years, the greatest retreat came at the turn of the millennium with 8 years of the George W. Bush administration that squandered a surplus on a misguided war and tax benefits to the wealthy and mismanaged the most ambitious retooling of national educational policy for disadvantaged children, the No Child Left Behind act of 2001 (NCLB; Pub. L. No. 107-110). At the end of the first decade of the second millennium, we are in danger of "throwing the baby out with the bathwater" as we seek to correct the mistakes of NCLB and its primary-grade component, Reading First. Against this backdrop of U.S. education policy, I present my commentary on the Teaching and Learning section of this handbook on educational research policy in three parts: (a) solid findings and points of consensus that have emerged from recent policy research, (b) critical questions policy researchers should address, and (c) research strategies that show particular promise for addressing these questions.

Points of Consensus

The major point of agreement in these chapters on teaching and learning is that the *quality* of teaching matters to students' learning and achievement. Teaching quality is not adequately captured by the degrees and certification required by NCLB, except in the case of high school mathematics (Béteille & Loeb, this volume). Instead, as Pianta and Hamre (this volume) point out, teaching quality can be

observed reliably in the classroom and is part of the effective implementation of curriculum. Teaching quality is not randomly distributed, as Schmidt and Maier (this volume) remind us in their chapter on opportunity to learn. Better teachers teach better students with more coherent, rigorous curricula. Less experienced teachers are disproportionately in the inner cities and are not providing minority students with opportunities to learn academic content.

A common first step in addressing teaching quality is to promote the *quantity* of instructional time. Indeed, increasing reading instruction to 90 uninterrupted minutes was one of the first requirements of Reading First. To ensure that the increased time was spent delivering worthwhile curriculum, another requirement was to implement curriculum based on scientifically based reading research. The term "scientifically based reading research" was named in the Reading First legislation 110 times and quickly was reduced to the acronym SBRR. The research wing of the U.S. Department of Education—the Institute of Education Sciences—developed a What Works Clearinghouse to vet educational interventions, but few effective reading interventions were found to guide the selection of Reading First curricula. Thus, the application of SBRR to curricula did *not* mean empirically validated effective curricula because educational publishers had no tradition of investing in research and development. Rather, curricula labeled SBRR were those that claimed to be based on the National Reading Panel Report (NRP; National Institute of Child Health and Human Development [NICHD], 2000). The NRP reported meta-analyses of the research on phonemic awareness and phonics and summaries of quality research in fluency, vocabulary, and comprehension. These five areas of reading came to be addressed as separable curricular components with isolated outcomes, with the emphasis on increasing instructional time so as to increase achievement gains. When the interim report of the Reading First Impact Study (Gamse, Jacob, Horst, Boulay, & Unlu, 2008) reported that increased time in these five components was *not* associated with gains in reading comprehension, many were quick to brand Reading First a failure. But the real failure was ignoring the systemic context within which teaching quality exists and expecting increased time allocation alone to produce gains in reading comprehension.

Teachers and their students exist within organizational structures that have direct and indirect affects on teaching and learning. For example, tracking affects the content covered and the nature of instructional interactions. Schmidt and Maier (this volume) explain that alignment of state standards and tests with curriculum coverage interacts with teacher's pedagogical content knowledge to influence students' achievement gains. In international comparisons of middle school mathematics, Japan had the closest alignment. In the United States, achievement gains were highly correlated with content coverage in the textbooks. Students' achievement was hampered by the lack of opportunity to learn the mathematics covered on the test. Schmidt and Maier point out that this important construct—opportunity to learn—is often lost in discussions of closing the achievement gap. Pianta and Hamre (this volume) make a related point when they remark that there is only one national study of classroom quality (i.e., the National Institute of Child Health and Human Development, Early Child Care Research Network [ECCRN], 2002) while there are dozens of large-scale epidemiological studies of health-related inputs. The ECCRN study documented the huge proportion of time in classrooms where no learning took place—42% in pre-kindergarten to 30% in fifth grade—and where the focus was more on basic skills than on analysis, inference, or synthesis. Pianta et al. (2005) found that teachers who used strategies to focus students on higher order thinking, who gave consistent, timely, and process-oriented feedback, and who worked to extend students' oral language skills, had students with greater gains in literacy achievement. Two related sets of findings are worth noting. The first set is Taylor, Pearson, and Rodriquez's (2003) study that revealed an association between teachers' inferential reading comprehension questions and students' achievement gains. The second set of findings is from Foorman and colleagues and concerns the relationship between the quantity and quality of writing instruction to gains in students' literacy (Mehta, Foorman, & Branum-Martin, 2005; Moats, Foorman, & Taylor, 2006).

Critical Questions Policy Researchers Should Address

The elephant in the policy room is how to improve teaching quality and how to measure the impacts of quality teaching on gains in student achievement. The measurement issues will be addressed in the next section. Before considering how to improve teaching quality, two conceptual issues will be raised. First, discussions of teaching and learning are grounded in theoretical discussions of the nature of human behavior. Second, the content of teaching and learning is subject to national debate.

Theoretical Views on Teaching and Learning No one disputes that human learning is a product of gene-environment interactions. However, where one stands on this balance beam affects one's views of teaching. Is teaching a matter of releasing pure reason through leading questions, much as Socrates did with Meno? The constructivist tradition alive and well in American education is imbued with such optimism. Or, in the tradition of Locke and Skinner, is the teacher the social engineer who can maximize opportunities to learn? Most would agree that the engineering is constrained by the raw materials available and that it occurs within a set of social conventions. In fact, the social conventions interact with the subject matter to complicate the discussion of teaching and learning even further. For example, Aristotle said in the Nicomachean Ethics (Bk. I, Ch. 3; see McKeon, 1947, pp. 309–310) that you can only expect as much precision as the subject matter allows and that it would be foolish to expect the precision of geometry when the subject matter is ethics or politics. And yet we learn from Schoenfeld and Pearson (this volume) that the math and reading wars have many similarities when it comes to the interference of politicians in determining what, when, and how mathematics and literacy are taught.

National Debate on the Content of Teaching and Learning It is noteworthy that the National Council of Teachers of Mathematics (NCTM) passed a set of standards in 1989 that has become the de facto national mathematics standards. In contrast, the Primary Literacy Standards for Kindergarten through Third Grade (National Center on Education and the Economy, 1999) were never adopted by any state in spite of a stellar panel of reading experts guiding their development. It is also noteworthy that the mathematics curricula developed with funding from the National Science Foundation were not widely adopted (Schmidt & Maier, this volume) and that their evaluations revealed the highly variable implementation evident in the evaluation of Reading First's SBRR curricula (Gamse et al., 2008). One conclusion that can be drawn is that in spite of the rhetoric of standards-based reform, the commercial textbook publishers in fact dictate what is taught. As mentioned above, there is no incentive for the publishers to invest in the research and development that would test contrasting theories of learning in their materials. For example, my colleagues and I developed a relational database to examine lexical, semantic, and syntactic features of six first-grade reading programs (Foorman, Francis, Davidson, Harm, & Griffin, 2004). We found that 70% of the words in the lessons in a 6-week grading period were singletons. That is, a word appeared only once in a 6-week interval. A similar high percentage was documented in Hiebert's examination of first-grade reading materials (Hiebert, 2002). No theory of learning would suggest that a single appearance is sufficient for beginning readers. Additionally, the programs varied extensively in the extent to which a word's sound-spelling patterns had been taught prior to encountering the word in the student edition. Moreover, the programs varied greatly in the oral and printed word frequency of the words in the student anthology and in the percentage of sentences in the reading selections with embedded clauses or prepositional phrases. Thus, no theory of vocabulary learning or syntactical complexity was evident in constructing passages.

Indeed such relational databases, coupled with models of different reader ability levels, could be field tested to develop differentiated curricula for teachers to use. However, it will take a national effort to convince the commercial textbook publishers that it is in their interest to invest in such research. Reviews of primary-grade reading programs are conspicuously absent in the What Works Clearinghouse.

What is Quality Teaching? Assuming a modicum of conciliation regarding a theory of teaching and learning and agreement about national standards, could we agree on how to develop quality teaching? Authors of the chapters in this section agree that we must look beyond degrees and certification to pedagogical content knowledge (Darling-Hammond & Wei, this volume). Teacher knowledge about reading instruction can be increased by professional development and induction programs, but effects on student achievement gains are small (Foorman & Moats, 2004; Pianta & Hamre, this volume). Effects of mentoring or coaching on gains in student achievement are mixed. This appears to be due to a number of factors having to do with the coach (e.g., her role, expertise, and acceptance by the teacher) and with the student composition of the classroom. For example, Pianta and Hamre (this volume) report a positive effect of a consultancy model of coaching compared to a web-based model on pre-kindergarten teacher sensitivity, instructional learning formats, and language modeling ($d = .21$). These improvements in observed teacher-student interactions were associated with gains in students' language and literacy skills.

In contrast, Foorman and colleagues found a small, significant effect ($d = .124$) on a standardized reading test administered at the end of kindergarten when teachers screened 3,635 English-speaking students for risk in the fall and received Web rather than on-site mentoring coaches (Santi, York, Foorman, & Francis, 2008). Moreover, *no* significant effect of mentoring with coaches or via the Web was apparent on second-grade fluency outcomes when 3,058 Spanish-speaking students in 67 schools read Spanish texts (Foorman, York, Francis, & Santi, 2008). In fact, students of teachers who received no mentoring from coaches or from the Internet had significantly higher fluency outcomes as school-level variability increased in first grade. Also, as between-class variability increased, effects on fluency outcomes of web mentoring decreased, effects of handheld devices to score fluency increased, and effects of post-hoc data entry into a website decreased. The use of the handheld device to score fluency outcomes was popular with teachers (Foorman, Santi, & Berger, 2007) and yielded more accurate fluency scores than teachers' computation of words correct per minute. Also, as soon as the handheld device was synched, teachers had immediate access to assessment results on the Web. An important finding was the negative effect of coaching and Web mentoring on Spanish fluency outcomes when heterogeneity increased from first to second grade. As Gándara and Gómez point out (this volume), we know little about the conditions under which English-language learners learn literacy skills. Mentoring of teachers working with diverse classrooms of English learners needs to include professional development about the interaction of language proficiency with literacy learning (Francis & Rivera, 2007).

Promising Research Strategies

The pressing policy question raised in the previous section was how to promote quality teaching. Strides have been made in answering this question in the past two decades with the use of multilevel statistical modeling to capture contextual effects. Such models allow us to move conceptually beyond explaining gains in student achievement through interactions of method by teacher or aptitude by treatment. Instead, we can model a host of teacher-level variables as moderators of relations between students' initial status and outcome. We can also model school-level and district-level variables. Additionally, we can create latent variables to account for the inter-correlations among predictors or outcomes. Finally, we can measure growth in student learning and achievement, taking into account changing classroom contexts.

Policy decisions demand that we model reliably the multiple contexts within which teaching quality and student achievement are linked. Once we better understand the significant contextual variables, we can manipulate teaching quality in an intervention study to promote gains in student achievement. This is precisely what Pianta and Hamre (this volume) did. They identified conceptually and empirically valid teaching practices and then randomly assigned teachers to two different professional development approaches to learning these practices—a consultancy approach and a web-based approach. As described earlier, the consultancy model was more effective in changing teacher behavior (more sensitive, more instructional learning formats, more language modeling) and in enhancing student language and literacy skills. Pianta and Hamre (this volume) also acknowledge the very real concerns raised about reliability of classroom observation systems due to rater-related variance, time of day, and window effects for frequency-related codes (Raudenbush & Sadoff, 2008). Reliability is improved by increasing the number of raters within a data collection period. Pianta and Hamre (this volume) and others (e.g., Foorman et al., 2006; Mehta et al., 2005) have found stability in observations of teacher-student interactions within and across days, students, and instructional content.

Assessing teaching quality within bilingual settings can be particularly challenging. In one study with 1,387 children followed from kindergarten through second grade in 36 schools in urban Texas, urban California, and border

Texas, ratings of teachers' language proficiency and whether reading/language arts was taught separately by language or in an integrated fashion predicted literacy gains in students' achievement in Spanish and in English (Cirino, Pollard-Durodola, Foorman, Carlson, & Francis, 2007; Saunders, Foorman, & Carlson, 2006). The variability in language usage in these classrooms was so great that the ratio of Spanish to English predicted language and literacy gains above and beyond the label given to the bilingual program (Foorman, Carlson, & Santi, 2007).

Effects of instruction, program, and locale were evident in a multivariate, multilevel analysis focused on reading comprehension in first-grade primary-language and English immersion classrooms in 34 schools in border Texas and urban California and Texas (Foorman, Branum-Martin, Francis, & Mehta, 2008). Mean differences in English reading comprehension showed a split by locale favoring urban schools. The Texas border immersion programs did not perform as highly as urban immersion programs in Texas and in California. Mean differences in Spanish reading comprehension were split by program rather than locale. Urban immersion may have grown more slowly due to a lack of environmental Spanish. In cross-language correlations, controlling for instructional language, border Texas again stood out: (a) prior status in Spanish explained the strong L1-L2 transfer in immersion classrooms; (b) zero correlations between L1 and L2 in the spring in primary-language classrooms suggested that factors other than instruction contributed strongly to relative standing of classrooms; and (c) negative correlations between L2 in the fall and L1 in the spring suggested some sort of interference, such as schools or parents transitioning or switching their students to English instruction.

Conclusion

As we near the end of the first decade of the second millennium, we consider the policy implications of the major conceptual and empirical advances in research on teaching and learning. Neuroscience research has improved our understanding of gene-environment interactions and how learning affects brain development. Statistical modeling techniques now allow us to capture the nested contexts within which teaching and learning take place. The next step is for education policy to be based on the advances made. At the turn of the millennium, this next step seemed within our grasp with the bipartisan passage of NCLB in 2001, the passage of the Institute for Education Sciences Reform Act in 2002 (IES; Pub. L. No. 107-279), and the reauthorization in 2004 of the Individuals with Disabilities Education Improvement Act (IDEA; Pub. L. No. 108-446)). Yet 8 years later these bold new initiatives to foster educational equity and scientific rigor have fallen prey to bipartisanship and lack of national leadership. In spite of improved management and conflict of interest procedures, Reading First continues to suffer from inside-the-beltway politics and from an under-powered effectiveness evaluation

(Gamse et al., 2008) that ignored the central question of the conditions under which quality teaching and learning occur (Francis, 2008). The fact that some districts have scaled-up Reading First district wide, have increased the percentage of students on grade level each year, and have reduced referrals to special education by implementing prevention and early intervention practices was lost in the regression discontinuity design employed (Foorman & Robinson, 2008). Instead, we learned that from 2004 to 2005 Reading First had null results when average student outcomes from schools on one side of the funding cutpoint within a district were compared with average student outcomes from schools on the other side of the funding cutpoint. None of the moderating effects of Reading First treatment (e.g., the role of the reading coach, availability of layered interventions) or student-level moderators such as length of time in Reading First was considered.

Education science will continue to yield null effects as long as students' initial status accounts for the majority of variability in achievement outcomes. This reality requires a policy focus on early education to reduce achievement gaps in preschool (as suggested by Farkas, this volume; Fielding, Kerr, & Rosier, 2007) and an education science that captures the contexts that facilitate quality teaching and improvements in student learning.

References

Cirino, P., Pollard-Durodola, S. D., Foorman, B. R., Carlson, C. D., & Francis, D. J. (2007). Teacher characteristics, classroom instruction, and student literacy and language outcomes in bilingual kindergarteners. *Elementary School Journal, 107*, 341–364.

Fielding, L., Kerr, N., & Rosier, P. (2007). *Annual growth for all students, catch-up growth for those who are behind.* Kennewick, WA: The New Foundation Press.

Foorman, B. R., Branum-Martin, L., Francis, D. J., & Mehta, P. (2008, May). *Contextual effects of bilingual programs on beginning reading.* Paper presented at the annual meeting of the International Reading Association, Atlanta, GA.

Foorman, B. R., Carlson, C. D., & Santi, K. L. (2007). Classroom reading instruction and teacher knowledge in the primary grades. In D. Haager, J. Klingner, & S. Vaughn (Eds.), *Evidence-based reading practices for response to intervention* (pp. 45–72). Baltimore, MD: Brookes.

Foorman, B. R., Francis, D. J., Davidson, K., Harm, M., & Griffin, J. (2004). Variability in text features in six grade 1 basal reading programs. *Scientific Studies in Reading, 8*, 167–197.

Foorman, B. R., Kalinowski, S. J., & Sexton, W. L. (2007). Standards-based educational reform is one important step toward reducing the achievement gap. In A. Gamoran (Ed.), *Standards-based reform and the poverty gap: Lessons from "No Child Left Behind"* (pp. 17–24). Washington, DC: Brookings Institution.

Foorman, B. R., & Moats, L. C. (2004). Conditions for sustaining research-based practices in early reading instruction. *Remedial and Special Education, 25*(1), 51–60.

Foorman, B. R., & Robinson, S. (2008, May). *Reading First in Florida.* Presentation at the annual meeting of the International Reading Association in Atlanta, GA.

Foorman, B. R., Schatschneider, C., Eakin, M. N., Fletcher, J. M., Moats, L. C., & Francis, D. J. (2006). The impact of instructional practices in grades 1 and 2 on reading and spelling achievement in high poverty schools. *Contemporary Educational Psychology, 31*, 1–29.

Foorman, B. R., Santi, K., & Berger, L. (2007). Scaling assessment-driven instruction using the Internet and handheld computers. In B.

Schneider (Ed.), *Scale up in practice* (pp. 69–89). Lanham, MD: Rowan & Littlefield.

Foorman, B. R., York, M., Francis, D. J., & Santi, K. L. (2008, July). *Contextual effects in early reading assessment in Spanish.* Paper presented at the annual meeting of the Society for the Scientific Study of Reading, Asheville, NC.

Francis, D. J. (2008, June). *Reading First Impact study: What have we learned and where do we go from here?* Paper presented at the Institute of Education Sciences Research Conference, Washington, DC.

Francis, D. J., & Rivera, M. (2007). Principles underlying English language proficiency tests and academic accountability for ELLs. In J. Abedi (Ed.), *English language proficiency assessment in the nation: Current status and future practice* (pp. 13–32). Davis: University of California Press.

Gamse, B. C. Jacob, R. T., Horst, M., Boulay, B., & Unllu, F. (2008). *Reading First Impact Study: Final Report* (NCEE 2009-4038). Washington, DC: National Center for Education Evaluation and Regional Assistance, Institute of Education Sciences, U.S. Department of Education.

Hiebert, E. H. (2002). Standards, assessments, and text difficulty. In A. E. Farstrup & S. J. Samuels (Eds.), *What research has to say about reading instruction* (pp. 337–391). Newark, DE: International Reading Association.

Individuals with Disabilities Education Improvement Act of 2004 (IDEA), Pub. L. No. 108-446, 118 Stat 2647-2808, (2004).

Institute of Education Sciences Reform Act of 2002, Pub. L. No. 107-279, 116 Stat 1425, (2002).

McKeon, R. (Ed.) (1947). *Introduction to Aristotle.* New York: Random House.

Mehta, P., Foorman, B. R., Branum-Martin, L., & Taylor, W. P. (2005). Literacy as a unidimensional multilevel construct: Validation, sources of influence, and implications in a longitudinal study in grades 1–4. *Scientific Studies of Reading, 9,* 85–116.

Moats, L. C., Foorman, B. R., & Taylor, W. P. (2006). How quality of writing instruction impacts high-risk fourth graders' writing. *Reading and Writing: An Interdisciplinary Journal, 19,* 363–391.

National Center for Education and the Economy. (1999). *Primary literacy standards for kindergarten through third grade.* Washington, DC: Author.

National Commission on Excellence in Education. (1983). *A nation at risk: The imperative for educational reform.* Retrieved November 8, 2008, from http://www.ed.gov/pubs/NatAtRisk.html

National Institute of Child Health and Human Development, Early Child Care Research Network. (2002). The relation of global first-grade classroom environment to structural classroom features and teacher and student behaviors. *The Elementary School Journal, 102*(5), 367–387.

National Institute of Child Health and Human Development. (2000). *National Reading Panel–Teaching children to read: Reports of the subgroups* (NIH Pub. No. 00-4754). Washington, DC: U.S. Department of Health and Human Services.

No Child Left Behind Act of 2001, Pub. L. No. 107-110, 115 Stat.1425 (2001).

Pianta, R. C., Howes, C., Burchinal, M., Bryant, D., Clifford, R., Early, D., et al. (2005). Features of pre-kindergarten programs, classrooms, and teachers: Do they predict observed classroom quality and child-teacher interactions? *Applied Developmental Science, 9,* 144–159.

Raudenbush, S. W., & Sadoff, S. (2008). Statistical inference when classroom quality is measured with error. *Journal of Research on Educational Effectiveness, 1*(2), 138–154.

Santi, K. L., York, M., Foorman, B. R., & Francis, D. J. (2008). *The timing of early reading assessment in kindergarten.* Manuscript submitted for publication.

Saunders, W. M., Foorman, B. R., & Carlson, C. D. (2006). Do we need a separate block of time for oral English language development in programs for English learners? *Elementary School Journal, 107*(2), 181–198.

Taylor, B. M., Pearson, P. D., & Rodriquez, M. C. (2003). Reading growth in high-poverty classrooms: The influences of teacher practices that encourage cognitive engagement in literacy learning. *Elementary School Journal, 104,* 3–28.

55

COMMENTARY
Informing Teaching and Learning Policy

Robert E. Floden
Michigan State University

Chapters in this section of the handbook can inform policy by summarizing information about the current condition of education, by describing the range of existing policies, by reviewing current understandings of policy-related instrumental connections, by highlighting normative dimensions of education, by reporting on the processes of policy change, and by recommending priories for further policy-useful research. The chapters here make contributions to policy in all these ways. Comments below are organized according to these types of contribution. For each area, a selection of key points from across the chapters is accompanied by thoughts about the trustworthiness of these points and the ways they can contribute to policy.

The Condition of Education

Many contemporary education policies are aimed at affecting student achievement or improving the quality of teaching. Arguments for one policy or another typically start with a review of information about students, pointing to some combination of overall low performance and gaps among demographic groups. Litanies of the U.S. education system's poor performance have been a perennial feature of policy discussions, with occasional events or reports that heighten awareness—Sputnik, *A Nation At Risk*, the TIMSS reports. Teaching and teachers enter these discussions through statements about their centrality as influences on student achievement.

Handbook chapters can inform policy by indicating where the standard statements of these problems do and do not match the best available evidence. Farkas (this volume), for example, describes changes in the achievement gaps among Whites, African Americans, and Hispanics over the past 30 years. He shows that the gaps among these groups are substantial and persistent, with variation over time and some overall narrowing of the gaps. Cross-comparisons with family characteristics like parental education explain some, but not all, of the gaps. Farkas gives a basis for understanding persistent significance of the gaps by pointing out that achievement levels are a moving target for every group: Bringing any group up to a given level is an accomplishment, but if other groups also improve, a gap remains. Given the broad policy interest in increasing access to pre-school, these detailed descriptions of the magnitude and persistence of the gap are important considerations. A comparison of the size of the gaps to the likely effects of additional schooling show that good instruction would help, but instruction alone appears unlikely to eliminate gaps completely.

Policies cannot directly affect student achievement; they must work through influencing children's learning experiences, primarily by altering who teaches, what they teach, and how they teach. Discussions about such policies are based on assumptions about the current situation, assumptions that can be informed by chapters in this volume. Béteille and Loeb (this volume), for example, describe characteristics of the current teaching force, some probably familiar, some surprising. The sheer magnitude of the teaching force, now 3.25 million K–12 teachers, implies that widespread change would require comparably massive policies. Historical changes in basic demographics—median age swings from 41 to 33 and back to 42 over four decades—may signal needs for changes in policies as the typical life stage of teachers shifts. The fact that most teachers are employed close to where they went to school suggests that labor markets are local, a condition that will shape the impact of policies. For policies motivated by the achievement gap, one key result, echoed by Darling-Hammond and Wei (this volume), is that typical teacher characteristics vary substantially across schools. For a wide range of teacher variables, some likely linked to teaching quality, teachers are unevenly distributed, more so within cities than across. If policies depend on teachers, their effects will likely vary due these differences in teachers.

The chapters also describe variability in instructional content and pedagogy. Rowan, Correnti, Miller, and Camburn (this volume) describe how instruction varies according to broad models some schools adopt. Schmidt and Maier (this volume) point how widely classrooms vary in their mathematics and science content, variation associated with student demographics in the US, but much less so in other nations. Pianta and Hamre (this volume) look at large-scale, though not nationally representative, data on student-teacher interactions, and see overall levels that disturb them.

For the most part, descriptive summaries of the condition of education are trustworthy documents. Especially when based on government surveys, such as those conducted by the National Center for Education Statistics (NCES), they can draw on nationally representative samples, conducted by agencies that strive to remain non-partisan. Nevertheless, descriptive reports may suggest varying conclusions, depending on which particular statistics are presented. Conclusions about trends over time in the achievement gap, for example, may vary, depending on the start and end dates selected, or on whether the trend presented is for a single demographic group or for a comparison among groups. Those presented in the descriptive report may also suggest an interpretation that incorporates a value position. Pianta and Hamre, for example, see the data from their national sample of classroom observations as disturbing, but others might have a different opinion.

Policies in Place

Policy makers are eager to know what policies other jurisdictions have in place. They look for possible avenues *they* might take, or wish to keep up with the latest trends. In any case, descriptions of *current* policies can inform *new* policies. A clearer idea of what policies are already in place might help to avoid policy layering that leads to conflicts and unintended restrictions of flexibility.

Plank and Keesler's chapter (this volume) gives an overarching picture of a policy trend, a movement toward a reduced role for government. That global context suggests a new option for policy makers to consider—eliminating policies rather than creating new ones.

For language policy, Gándara and Gómez (this volume) argue that the current situation represents confusion or unclarity about the central principles that would guide the establishment of specific policies. Perhaps the close connections between language policy and other key domains—immigration, multiculturalism—obstruct progress toward clarity about language education. Understanding the inconsistencies among language education policies could inform further developments, which must either find a way to agree on core principles or continue to work piecemeal.

Other chapters offer descriptions about the range of current policies about teacher assignment, teacher compensation, teacher certification, curriculum standards, education technology, and curriculum policies. As with the reports on the condition of education, researcher descriptions of current policies are generally trustworthy, though varying conclusions can be drawn, depending on how policies are

defined and what features are specified. Reports about "alternative routes" in teacher education, for example, come to different conclusions about policy prevalence, depending on how "alternative" is defined.

Instrumental Connections

When policies are established, deliberations often build on assumptions about a policy's likely effects. Policy makers ask researchers what is known about the likely consequences of a policy change. Several chapters in this volume report on the best current understanding about these instrumental connections. The chapter authors sometimes report confidently about likely causal links; at other times they report the current limits of research evidence. They report on the probable impact of policies in four areas: *instructional content, pedagogy, resources, and human capacity*.

For policies about *instructional content*, one well-established connection is that between opportunity to learn and learning. As Schmidt and Maier (this volume) report, the connection between what is taught and what is learned has been studied in national and international research, with significant positive associations when variance in opportunities is large. Moreover, the variability in content taught to different demographic groups of students is high in the United States, compared with other developed countries. Policies that reduce content variability thus seem likely to reduce variability in achievement.

The evidence about the differential effects of competing *pedagogical approaches* is less consistent. As Schoenfeld and Pearson (this volume) report, the dominant view about the superiority of a particular teaching approach has swung from one extreme to another, driven in part by which research approaches are seen as most credible. The two national reports about reading differ from one another in their conclusions; the mathematics report says that little research (done using the methods preferred by the report authors) exists to support particular methods of instruction. As a result, research consistently supports policies that favor one particular pedagogical approach.

For research on pedagogical approaches to teaching English Language Learners, Gándara and Gómez (this volume) report that most of the federal research investment has gone into program evaluations, which yielded unclear, inconsistent, or contested conclusions. Research syntheses have given support to teaching in students' primary language, but the results have not been sufficiently persuasive to affect policy. Recent work from cognitive science is promising, but remains suggestive, rather than definitive.

Other chapters make general claims about links between pedagogical practices and student outcomes, but the claims are either too general to guide policy or remain restricted in grade and subject matter. Darling-Hammond and Wei (this volume) refer to research on teaching as a general source of guidance. Pianta and Hamre (this volume) report on studies of patterns of teacher-student interaction that are promising, but evidence to date remains restricted to early grades.

The chapter that seems best able to guide policies about *pedagogical practice* is Rowan, Correnti, Miller, and Camburn's report (this volume) on three models of comprehensive school reform. Working from the Study of Instructional Improvement, they carefully elaborate the evidence that supports two specific models of school reform—America's Choice and Success for All—and indicates general principles that support models of these types.

Prior debates about the general impact of increases in *resources* (e.g., Hanushek, 1994; Hedges, Laine, & Greenwald, 1994a,b) have concluded that sheer increases in dollars invested are unlikely to affect student outcomes; connections between level of resources and student achievement depends on how dollars are invested. Zhao and Lei's chapter (this volume) examines the impact of investments in educational technology. That chapter concludes that investments in technology have so far had little effect in education, a contrast to results from technology investments in business. That negative result can inform policy by suggesting that current patterns of investment in educational technology are unlikely to boost achievement.

Descriptions of the connections between student learning and *human capital* investments—more or higher quality teachers and school administrators—are intriguing. Virtually all policy analysts agree that teacher quality is one of the most important determinants of student learning. Analysts agree less on what teacher characteristics are most important and on how policies can reliably affect those characteristics. For some content areas and grades, research has shown a link between teacher content knowledge and student learning; likewise for teacher pedagogical knowledge. Teachers' general academic ability has a positive, weak effect. Teachers in their first few years of teaching tend to be less effective, though this also varies by subject and grade. Overall, research generally, but weakly, supports connections consistent with common sense: teachers with relevant knowledge and experience tend to be more effective. Hence, policies to support teacher quality—content knowledge, pedagogical skill, and experience—have some basis in research.

All conclusions about instrumental connections are based on causal inferences, which are more subject to threats to validity than the conclusions from descriptive research. Much of research supporting claims about the impact of content, instruction, resources, and educator quality comes from a mixture of studies, most of which provide weak or modest support for causal conclusions. Arguments from these studies to the likely effects of a policy have other weak links, because so much depends on the way in which a policy attempts to change teaching and learning. The link between teacher content knowledge and student learning, for example, suggests that increasing teachers' knowledge would affect learning, but different policies might change teacher knowledge (e.g., mandated professional development, changes in hiring practices, financial incentives for taking courses), possibly with different effects on student learning.

Darling-Hammond and Wei (this volume) make the positive case for connections to teacher education, professional development, and standards for teacher licensure. Their account is a helpful walk through the policy issues around teacher education and certification. They note that the research linking teacher policies to student learning remains inconclusive, suggesting that better measures of teacher knowledge and performance are needed to make strong conclusions about the likely impact of particular policies.

Normative Considerations

Although some policy discussions presume consensus about the goals of education, people are divided about what policies should try to accomplish. In the current climate, great emphasis in placed on academic achievement, as measured by the state tests used for determining Adequate Yearly Progress. Chapters in this section inform policy by documenting the consider differences in goals people see as most important.

At a macro level, Plank and Keesler (this volume) describe reduction in the overall expectation that government policies should influence education. Based on skepticism that national investments in education can be effective in meeting their stated goals, they argue that citizens are inclined to allow private initiatives and market forces to guide the direction of education. This understanding of the changing macro context can inform the development of education policies, which may either work against that trend or identify the areas where government policies remain important.

In the chapters on curriculum "wars," language policy, and classroom processes, the variation in educational goals is particularly salient. The debates about language policy have been driven more by differences in desired outcome than by arguments about what effects are most likely to result from one policy or another. As Gándara and Gómez's analysis (this volume) makes clear, education language policy choices are based on differences in the value assigned to integration of immigrant populations or maintenance of group identity, as well as to the value of gaining language proficiency and academic skill. The chapter can inform policy by making clear that some debates are about *how much* effect a policy will have on a particular outcome, but policies have thus far been based more on *which* effects are desired.

Schoenfeld and Pearson (this volume) provide a parallel look at debates about educational policies in reading and mathematics. In both content areas, the dominant policy directions have swung from one position to another, driven in part by emerging understandings about teaching and learning, but also driven by different views about what children should learn. The question of whether it is more important to master computational procedures or approaches to problem solving is answered in part by empirical studies of consequences for later learning, but the answer also depends on value judgments about what knowledge is of most worth. Their chapter can inform policy by revealing how past shifts in policy have been affected by the mix of empirical research and value positions.

In their discussion of classroom observation measures, Pianta and Hamre (this volume) argue both for greater knowledge about teacher-student interactions and for added attention to student outcomes beyond academic achievement. Drawing on research on child development, they argue that teaching should be improving students' lives across a range of dimensions, rather than only improving performance on tests of core academic subjects.

These handbook chapters illuminate normative issues both by describing differences the authors observe and by arguing for positions the authors themselves take. In reading these chapters, policy makers can see illustrations of the range of educational goals that are embraced, but none of these attempts a systematic account of which goals are currently embraced by which groups of citizens, with what degree of enthusiasm.

Policy Formulation and Implementation

Most chapters in this section address, explicitly or implicitly, issues about how policies are developed and implemented. Researchers sometimes think, perhaps naively, about policy development as a process in which policy makers have a goal in mind, consider several possible policies aimed at reaching that goal, and select the one for which evidence of likely success is strongest. Policy makers are probably well aware that other considerations play a large part in determining what policy is ultimately approved and how the formal policy is modified during implementation.

Several chapters describe how other political considerations affect policy. Zhao and Lei (this volume), for example, document the continued investments in educational technology, despite consistent evidence that the investments have not led to positive increases in student outcomes. The symbolic value of new technology, plus the eternal hope that newer technologies will produce better results, have outweighed any doubts about the real effects of these continued investments.

For mathematics, reading, and language policy, Schoenfeld and Pearson (this volume) and Gándara and Gómez (this volume) argue that political considerations are more important than research results in shaping policies. Research results show that primary language is more effective for teaching reading, but policies prescribe instruction only in English. Both the reading and mathematics "wars" had people taking sides based on associations with political views, rather than on the weight of evidence about the effects of instruction on student learning.

In other chapters, the extra-scientific considerations can also be seen influencing policy choices. Policies about teacher education are connected to general commitments to market models, rather than regulation. Policies about the assignment of teachers to schools are tied to political ne-

gotiations between unions and school boards. Approaches to reducing achievement gaps connect to policies about broad social service provision, including health, nutrition, and employment. The policies highlighted in this handbook section put teaching and learning at the forefront, but each policy is linked to broader policies and political alignments.

The web of political connections is especially dense in education; questions about education are questions about the shape of future society. Education policies affect the relative positions of social groups, as well as the life courses of individual students and educators. Many educational goals are difficult to measure, elevating the role of symbolism. The chapters in this section shed light on the condition of education and the connections between elements in the system, but some of them include clear reminders that the nature and effects of policies will be shaped by political and normative considerations. Experienced policy makers may have a clearer implicit sense of how policy is actually made than any of the scholars writing these chapters, but the chapters may inform policy by making such implicit understandings explicit.

Research Investments

Each chapter reports on current knowledge and recommends directions for future research. The overall level of investment in education research and the distribution of resources across possible studies can both be seen as policy choices for potential funds, federal, state, or private. Choices will be affected by judgments about the relative importance of research areas or topics, the likelihood that research will make a substantial contribution, and the capacity of the field to conduct needed studies. As with other policies, political symbolism and connections to other policy issues will also affect what research is and is not supported.

In a caricature of a research article, the final conclusion is always, "more research is needed." The chapters here avoid the caricature by making specific recommendations for priority research efforts, with supporting arguments for the recommendations. The amount of funds needed to support all the recommendations undoubtedly exceeds available resources, so choices will be required. Policy makers can draw on these chapters to inform decisions about research funding. Each author is likely to view his or her area as of highest importance, so details of the *arguments* for needed research should be carefully considered.

Conclusion

Research on teaching and learning has much to offer policy deliberations. Descriptions about the current state of U.S. education have grown more detailed. Representative samples undergird descriptions of trends in student achievement and in many characteristics of teachers, classrooms, and schools. Knowledge about the causal linkages among student learning, content, pedagogy, teachers, and other resources is growing and significant, but remains thin in many areas. The chapters here document and illustrate the interactions among empirical studies of education, normative dimensions, and education policy.

The information and insights in these chapters can inform policy development and implementation. The contributions of researchers, however, will inevitably be only a part of what policy makers consider as they craft and revise policies, and as they attempt to see that their intentions are carried out. Education policy is, and ought to be, deeply connected to other social policies. The education system, broadly construed, is a key influence on the shape of society. Policy can be informed by research, but will also be guided by policy makers' understandings of where society should be headed.

References

Hanushek, E. A. (1994). Money might matter somewhere: A response to Hedges, Laine, and Greenwald. *Educational Researcher, 23*(4), 5–8.

Hedges, L. V., Laine, R. D., & Greenwald, R. (1994a). A meta-analysis of the effects of differential school inputs on student outcomes. *Educational Researcher, 23*(3), 5–14.

Hedges, L. V., Laine, R. D., & Greenwald, R. (1994b). Money does matter somewhere: A reply to Hanushek. *Educational Researcher, 23*(4), 9–10.

Section VI

Actors and Institutions in the Policy Process

SECTION EDITOR: CAROLYN HERRINGTON

56

International and Transnational Policy Actors in Education

A Review of the Research

KAREN MUNDY WITH MONA GHALI
Ontario Institute for Studies in Education, University of Toronto

Introduction

Why do we have international institutions with educational mandates, and how do these institutions matter for educational policy? Has the nature or degree of influence these international actors have on educational policy processes changed over time—particularly in the context of globalization? In this chapter we will seek to answer these questions by reviewing a growing body of research on the education policy activities of international (intergovernmental) organizations and other transnational (non-state) policy actors, as well as the related literatures and theoretical debates on globalization and global governance.

Most educational policy research frames education policy as an arena of domestic rather than international politics. Recent research, however, suggests that the impact of international and transnational actors and policy processes in education is growing, and deserves heightened attention from education policy scholarship. While research on the policy impact of international organizations and transnational policy processes from within the field of education still lacks some of the theoretical precision and empirical rigor employed by sociologists and political scientists who study international processes in other domains, there is an exciting new body of research that looks at the increasingly "pluri-scalar" nature of contemporary educational policy processes, which increasingly involve multiple levels of government (from local to international), new kinds actors (including professional networks, nongovernmental organizations, and private sector actors with a transnational reach); and new processes (including heightened reference to international standards and norms).

The chapter is organized as follows: We begin by presenting a historical overview of the origins, mandates, and expansion of formal intergovernmental organizations and other transnational (i.e., non-state) actors in education between 1945 and 1980. A subsequent section considers the evolution of inter- and transnational policy actors in

education in the period between the mid-1980s and the present, alongside debates about globalization. A final section highlights the importance of further research based on our identification of significant puzzles and gaps in present research, and explores research on global governance in the field of political science as a possible impetus for new research directions.

International and Transnational Actors in Education: Historical Background

For at least the last century, the idea that educational issues require intervention at the international level has been commonplace. Well before World War I, a burgeoning number of transatlantic educational associations committed to the universalization of progressive educational ideals emerged, each working, in the words of one organization, to "represent comprehensively the forces working for universal free public education" (World Federation of Education Associations, 1923, p. 1). At world fairs, through the development of international teachers' organizations, the expansion of colonial policies on education, and the increase in international educational borrowing by China and Japan from the West, an international educational policy arena had emerged by 1920. Initiated both by "transnational" (i.e., non-state) and governmental actors, these global level interactions helped to produce world-level models for educational development that increasingly set the standard for national educational development (Boli, Ramirez, & Meyer, 1985; Anderson, 1983; Meyer, Boli, Thomas, & Ramirez, 1997; McNeely & Cha, 1994).

However, efforts to create formal, intergovernmental organizations with an educational mandate met with great resistance from nation-states before World War II. In 1919, for example, the founders of the League of Nations dismissed a petition by suffragette organizations, the British Workers Educational Association, international peace networks, and international federations of teachers to include an education organization under the League (Fuchs, 2007, p. 398). This was because, in the view of leading member states: "national education lies outside and will always lie outside the competence of any official committee of the League" (Davies, 1943, p. 12). The League's mandate was later extended just far enough to allow it to sponsor a mechanism for international intellectual cooperation.[1] In the absence of a League body, nongovernmental actors formed the International Bureau of Education (IBE), which gradually recruited states to a program of intergovernmental information sharing in the period between 1929 and 1945, through its annual International Conference on Public Education (UNESCO 1997, p. 58). The International Labour Organization (ILO) also became marginally involved in education in this period, especially as related to issues of child labor, worker education, and the protection of teachers' rights as workers. But the general message of the period was clear: education was an unsuitable arena for intergovernmental policy action.

The end of World War II marked the beginning of an era of rising multilateralism (defined by Ruggie, 1993, as "coordinated behavior among three or more states on the basis of generalized principles of conduct," p. 8), most notably, through the creation of the United Nations and the Bretton Woods Organizations (the International Monetary Fund and the World Bank). Although concerns continued about national sovereignty in education, state representatives at the founding conference of the United Nations agreed to include educational cooperation in Article 55 of the UN charter:

With a view to the creation of conditions of stability and well-being which are necessary for peaceful and friendly relations among nations based on respect for the principle of equal rights and self-determination of peoples, the United Nations shall promote: a. higher standards of living, full employment, and conditions of economic and social progress and development; b. solutions of international economic, social, health, and related problems; and international cultural and educational cooperation.... (Charter of the United Nations, 1945, Chap. 9, Art. 55)

Shortly thereafter, the United Nations Educational, Scientific and Cultural Organization (UNESCO) was established (Jones, 1988). One of the most important features of UNESCO's constitution highlighted state parties support for "full and equal opportunities for education for all," guiding the organization to "give fresh impulse to popular education…by instituting collaboration among the nations to advance the ideal of equality of educational opportunities without regard to race, sex or any distinctions, economic or social" (Constitution of the United Nations Educational, Scientific, And Cultural Organization, 1945, Art. 1).[2] The idea of "education for all" was later reinforced by the Universal Declaration of Human Rights (1948), and the development of a number of additional UN conventions which support equal educational opportunity as a fundamental right.[3]

Competing state views about how to define education as an arena for international action shaped intergovernmental education policy activities in the post-World War II era. This is especially well illustrated in UNESCO's history.

TABLE 56.1
UN Conventions and Other International Legal Instruments in Education

1945	**Constitution of UNESCO.** Signed London November 16, 1945.
1948	**Universal Declaration of Human Rights.** Adopted and proclaimed by General Assembly resolution 217 A (III) of 10 December 1948 Paris France.
1960	**Convention against Discrimination in Education.** Adopted by the UNESCO General Conference at its 11th session, Paris 14 December 1960.
1964	**Declaration on the Eradication of Illiteracy in the United Nations Development Decade.** General Conference of UNESCO at its Thirteenth Session, 19 November 1964.
1966	**International Covenant on Economics, Social and Cultural Rights.** UN General Assembly resolution 2200A (XXI), 21 U.N.GAOR Supp (No. 16) at 49, U.N. Doc. A/6316 (1966), entered into force Jan. 3, 1976.
1975	**Literacy, Declaration of Persepolis.** International Symposium for Literacy, Persepolis, 3-8 September 1975.
1976	**Recommendation on the Development of Adult Education.** UNESCO General Conference 19th session, Nairobi, 26 October to 30 November 1976, at its nineteenth session.
1979	**International Convention on the Elimination of All Forms of Discrimination against Women.** General Assembly resolution 34/180.
1987	**Resolution on International Literacy Year.** Adopted by the UNESCO General Assembly at the 93rd plenary meeting, 7 Dec. 1987.
1989	**Convention on the Rights of the Child.** Adopted, United Nations General Assembly, 1989.
1990	**World Declaration on Education for All.** World Conferece on Education for All, Jomtien, Thailand, 5-9 March 1990.
1994	**Resolution on United Nations Decade for Human Rights Education.** Adopted by the UNESCO General Assembly at the 94th plenary meeting, 23 Dec. 1994.
1995	**Declaration and Programme of Action of the World Summit for Social Development.** Adopted during Copenhagen World Summit Organized by the United Nations.
1997	**Hamburg Declaration on Adult Learning.** Adopted by the Fifth International Conference on Adult Education held in Hamburg, 14-18 July 1997.
2000	**Dakar Framework for Action on Education for All.** Adopted by the World Education Forum, Dakar Senegal.
2000	**United Nations Millennium Declaration.** Adopted by the UN General Assembly, Sept. 18, 2000.

At UNESCO's formation, the United States advocated for an international agency focused on post-war reconstruction and the expansion of Anglo-American scientific supremacy, while the French argued for a more elite organization focused on high-level intellectual cooperation (Jones, 1988). Meanwhile, several Latin American states hoped for an organization devoted to the expansion of mass literacy and schooling for all. Non-state actors (including groups of progressive educators and teachers associations) strongly supported a UNESCO mandate to use education to build peace and international understanding. Not surprisingly, education emerged as a loosely defined arena for policy action within the new UNESCO: its mandate includes the promotion of peace through education, education for economic and social development, and the setting of educational norms and standards at all levels of educational systems (as through the creation of its standard classification of educational systems, an annual international yearbook of education, and various legal conventions and declarations). With a budget never larger than that of small university, a one-nation-one-vote governance structure and increasingly politicized membership, it is little wonder that UNESCO is widely perceived having failed as an effective policy actor. Nevertheless, it clearly played a role in establishing common standards for educational development (see Table 56.1 and Figure 56.1.[4]

In the vacuum created by UNESCO's increasing Cold War politicization, a growing number of intergovernmental organizations began to adopt education as a focus for their activities in the 1960s and 1970s (see Table 56.2). Established in 1961, the Organization for Economic Cooperation and Development (OECD), whose mandate lay primarily in the promotion of policies for economic growth and development among its Western member states, gradually emerged to play a leading role in facilitating information-sharing and cross-national policy learning about education among Western governments (Papadopoulos, 1994). The OECD's education sector activities were initially funded by the United States in response to its perception of Soviet scientific superiority.[5] By the late 1960s, the OECD began to respond to the rapid expansion of its member states' educational systems by initiating peer reviews of member countries' educational performance. Increasingly, the OECD also became the locus for member state debates about educational equality and the potentially redistributive impacts of educational systems—with competing arguments from Anglo-American governments and more social democratic member states (Papadopoulos, 1994; Rinne, Kallo, & Hokka, 2004). Throughout the 1970s the OECD diffused a wide range of policy research on innovations in such areas as special and disability education, multiculturalism, participatory pedagogy, and recurrent education. These became themes and benchmarks in assessments of member states' educational systems.

Far and away the most active international policy actors in education to appear after World War II were those focused on international development: UNICEF, the World Bank (since 1963 through both its International Bank for Reconstruction and Development facility and its more highly concessional loan arm for least developed countries, the International Development Association), and a large number of bilateral development agencies (coordinated and monitored to some degree by the OECD's Development Assistance Committee). Along with UNESCO and a few major foundations (e.g., Rockefeller & Ford-Arnove, 1980b; Berman, 1979, 1983), these multilateral organizations played a significant role in structuring the educational development policies of the post-colonial world, both by

Level	Age Range	Stage	Examples
4	22–25	6	Postgraduate Study
3	21–22	5	Professional Schools Higher stage of University study Teacher training
	18–19	4	Advanced technical schools Lower stage of University study Teacher training
2	14–15	3	Full- and part-time vocational schools Upper section of high schools Grammar schools Gymnasiums Teacher training
	10–11	2	Upper section of elementary schools Lower section of high schools Grammar schools Gymnasiums
1	5–7	1	Primary schools
Compulsory School Begins		Pre-School Education	Nursery and Kindergarten

Figure 56.1 International Standard Classification of Education (ISCED97). *Note:* The stages are illustrated by typical examples; ages stated are also illustrative. *Source:* Adapted from Holmes and Robinsohn (1963); and UNESCO (1997), p. 57.

working with developing country governments, and by exerting normative influence over bilateral aid donors such as the Canadian, Swedish, and United States Agencies for International Development. While bilateral aid organizations continued to provide the largest share of international finance for education, and often channeled their aid to meet the particular geo-political objectives of their home governments, multilateral intergovernmental organizations played an increasing role in shaping the policy agenda for bilateral spending (King, 1991; Weiler, 1983; McNeely, 1995; Ginsburg, Cooper, Raghu, & Zegarra, 1990).

Important differences emerged in the policy roles played by these "development-focused" intergovernmental organizations. Both UNESCO and UNICEF attempted to use legal standards (such as conventions and declarations) and norm-setting (through world conferences) to protect a more rights-centric and social development-oriented vision of educational change (Jones, 1988, 2005; Mundy, 1998;

Phillips, 1987; Black, 1996; Chabbott, 2003). However, over time it was the World Bank, with its more instrumental view of education as an investment in human capital, which came to dominate education policy making in the developing world (Jones, 2007; Mundy, 1998; Heyneman, 2003; Resnik, 2006). Furthermore, each organization has been shaped by its specific resource base and governance structure: UNESCO, which is governed on the basis of one nation one vote, has tended to suffer from a high level of politicization, particularly during the Cold War period, when Western governments became increasingly wary of supporting the initiatives of organizations with large socialist bloc votes (Sewell, 1975; Imber, 1989; Preston, Herman, & Schiller, 1989; Sack, 1986). In contrast, UNICEF is governed by a nominated board, and has been able to preserve a higher degree of organizational autonomy by focusing on children's issues at the country level, and using this focus as the foundation for fundraising drawn both from voluntary

TABLE 56.2
Major Transnational and International Policy Actors in Education

	Pre-1945	1945–1985	1985–Present
Transnational	**International Teachers Associations** (eg, World Education Association)	**International Teachers Associations**	**Education International** (and other Regional Associations of Teacher Organizations and Unions)
	Child Protection Organizations (International Save the Children Union, f. 1920 – Declaration of Geneva, on children's rights, 1923)	**International Nongovernmental Development Organizations**	**Corporate-like Nongovernmental organizations** (Save the Children, CARE, Catholic Relief OXFAM, PLAN International, World Vision)
		Philanthropic Foundations (Rockefeller, Ford, Carnegie)	**New Philanthropic Foundations** (Soros Foundation, Hewlett and Gates Partnership for Education
			Transnational Advocacy Networks Children's Rights Network; Global Campaign for Education; International Network on Education in Emergencies (INEE) – etc.
			Private Sector Actors World Economic Forum: Information Technology Corporations such as Microsoft, CISCO, Intel etc.
Inter-governmental	**International Bureau of Education** (IBE, formed 1929)	**UNESCO** (formed 1945) (incorporates IBE)	**World Bank** (IBRC, IDA and IFC)
	International Institute for Intellectual Cooperation (formed 1921 under the League of Nations)	**UNICEF (f. 1946; education after 1960)**	**OECD**
	International Labour Organization (formed 1919, Treaty of Versailles)	**World Bank (f. 1946, education after 1963).** Loans from International Bank for Reconstruction and Development & the International Development Association facilities	**World Trade Organization** (f. 1995; General Agreement on Trade In Services (GATS)
		OECD (f. 1961: education after 1968) Centre for Educational Research and Innovation (f. 1968); Education Committee of Ministers from 1970.	**OECD** Education Directorate Centre for Educational Research and InnovationEducation Committee (Ministerial)
			UN Organizations UNESCO, UNICEF, UNDP, ILO
			Regional Organizations with new activities in education: European Union, ASEAN, APEC, SADC, G8, Mercusor, etc.

contributions of UN member governments and the donations of individuals. Of the three organizations, the World Bank has the greatest fiscal autonomy (it uses the promises of capital from member states as the basis for raising funds on the international bond market, which it later offers to developing countries as repayable loans). However, the Bank's identity as a financial lending institution, along with the fact that its governors are member country Finance Ministers, with voting privileges weighted by contribution level, has led it to adopt an approach to education that is driven by economists and Anglo-American states.

In conclusion, several things are worth remarking about this first cycle in the development of international and transnational educational policy actors. First, although nongovernmental "transnational" actors, including NGOs, teachers' organizations, women's organizations, and networks of progressive educators initially played a key role in getting education included in the mandates of international institutions, they were increasingly marginalized from decision making within the expanding intergovernmental educational policy arena (Mundy & Murphy, 2001). Second, while nation-states remained committed to preserving domestic sovereignty on educational matters, sometime between 1924 and 1945, Western states in particular came to view expanding systems of public education as essential not only for statehood, but also for the functioning and stability of an international system. This shift allowed for the establishment of the first formal intergovernmental bodies with educational mandates, who in turn began to play a significant role in influencing domestic policies, especially in the developing world. To a lesser extent, these international organizations also emerged as arenas within which major powers debated key policy directions and benchmarks for education.

Finally, it is important to point out that although many governments became members of international organizations and signatories to international conventions on education as a human right, the general trend was towards a more limited, economic, and instrumental view of international cooperation in education. One part of the work of intergovernmental organizations continued to be shaped by a deepening set of redistributive or compensatory, universal (liberal) educational norms, captured in the idea that the international community and its bodies should act as a guarantor of educational rights and educational equality (Mundy, 2007; Spring, 2000; Tomasevski, 2005; Chabbott, 2003). But in practice, nation-states came to view the purposes of educational multilateralism in much more instrumental terms, either as an opportunity to advance national economic and geopolitical interests (as in bilateral aid programs or through the OECD's benchmarking initiatives), or as a collective investment in human capital expected to produce the levels of economic growth and modernization in the developing world that Western governments have long argued is essential to the political stability of the larger world system.

Globalization and the Changing Influence of International Educational Policy Actors

In the 1970s and 1980s, major shifts in the world economy and the interstate system began to emerge. Often captured in the term "globalization," such shifts are typically described as increasing the influence of international and transnational policy actors and processes on domestic decision-making in education. Interest in globalization, the changing role of the nation-state, and the rise of nongovernmental organizations has fed the rapid growth of new research on intergovernmental and transnational policy actors on education.

Almost any definition of globalization begins with the idea that the integration of human societies across pre-existing territorial units has sped up, assisted in part by the development of new technologies that compress time and space (Harvey, 1989; Mundy, 2005). For most authors, the main motor of integration is economic—the expansion of truly global chains of commercialized production and consumption.[6] Central to all theories of globalization is also the notion that interregional and "deterritorialized" flows of all kinds of social interaction have reached new magnitudes since the early 1980s. Deterritorialized flows are thought to impact the capacity of nation-states to steer domestic policies, not least in the form of an increasing number of non-state based policy actors (Ruggie, 1994; see also Table 56.2). Deterritorialized flows of ideas, people, goods, and money have been supported by new information and communications technologies.

For intergovernmental and transnational policy actors in education, the globalization story begins in the mid- to late 1970s, when the Keynesian economic policies of Western states came under increasing pressure and many developing countries began to suffer from declining raw materials prices and mounting international debt. In both contexts the ability of governments to generate the tax resources needed to sustain their social welfare and redistributive policies began to be questioned. Governments began to adopt neoliberal approaches to public policy, focusing on shrinking the state's expenditures and increasing economic competitiveness (Carnoy, 1995; Rodrik, 1997). Such policies were often promoted by those intergovernmental organizations with predominantly economic mandates—most notably by the OECD, the IMF, and the World Bank. A new approach to sound public policy was deeply influenced by what John Williamson described as the "Washington consensus," with its focus on fiscal constraint, trade liberalization, and state privatization (Helleiner, 1994; Williamson, 1993; Maxwell, 2005; Colclough, 1993). The Washington consensus had significant implications for education, pointing to reduced or more targeted state spending on educational goods, a focus on forms of education that could be directly linked to the creation of a competitive workforce, and the introduction of market-like mechanisms (vouchers, private schools) to increase system efficiencies (Carnoy, 1999; Ball, 1998; Dale, 1997; Davies & Guppy, 1997; World Bank, 1995).

Driven in part by the rise of the Washington consensus, as well as more directly by member state concerns about economic globalization, both the scope and the content of the activities of intergovernmental policy actors in education shifted in the 1980s and 1990s. For international organizations working primarily on educational development, the most important initial change was the gradual ebb of northern government support for international development. This can be seen most starkly in the decline of development assistance funding from the U.S. and the U.K. (the earliest neo-liberal reformers); both governments also withdrew from UNESCO in the 1980s, and became highly critical of the United Nations (Augelli & Murphy, 1988; Lee, 1995). It can also be observed in the overall stagnation of development assistance flows in real terms from many OECD countries, and the first prolonged decline of bilateral aid for education. Instead of a peace dividend, the collapse of the Soviet Union actually created less incentive for bilateral flows of development aid (Griffin, 1991). Western governments only began to renew their interest in global equity and development after 2000, a point we consider in more detail below.

In the context of globalization, intergovernmental organizations with economic development as their primary mandate have steadily risen to supremacy, often eclipsing UN bodies. The World Bank, for example, emerged from a decade of involvement in structural adjustment programs (which typically called for cost constraints in education) to become the most influential multilateral policy actor in education in the 1990s (Carnoy, 1995; Reimers, 1994; Samoff, 1993, 1996). Not only did the World Bank come to house the largest cadre of education policy staff (mainly

TABLE 56.3
Washington Consensus—Key Recommendations

1. Fiscal policy discipline;

2. Redirection of public spending from subsidies ("especially indiscriminate subsidies") toward broad-based provision of key pro-growth, pro-poor services like primary education, primary health care and infrastructure investment;

3. Tax reform – broadening the tax base and adopting moderate marginal tax rates;

4. Interest rates that are market determined and positive (but moderate) in real terms;

5. Competitive exchange rates;

6. Trade liberalization – liberalization of imports, with particular emphasis on elimination of quantitative restrictions (licensing, etc.); any trade protection to be provided by low and relatively uniform tariffs;

7. Liberalization of inward foreign direct investment;

8. Privatization of state enterprises;

9. Deregulation – abolition of regulations that impede market entry or restrict competition, except for those justified on safety, environmental and consumer protection grounds, and prudent oversight of financial institutions; and,

10. Legal security for property rights.

Note: Based on Williamson (1993).

trained in the economics of education), it also emerged as the largest single external source of finance for education and the leading source of policy research on education (Samoff & Stromquist, 2001). Led by its education sector staff, the bank increased its lending to basic education from the late 1980s and throughout the 1990s (World Bank, 1995; Heyneman, 2003). Such a shift in bank lending proved a highly effective response to the mounting criticisms of its structural adjustment policies by UN actors, middle power countries, and nongovernmental organizations (Jolly, 1991; Mundy, 2002, 2007). But the bank's emergent framework for financing improvements in education diverged quite significantly from earlier "education for all" activities. In virtually all of its education sector lending, the World Bank introduces a standard menu of reform policies, including decentralization, the restructuring of the public service (especially teachers terms of employment), standardized educational testing programs, the inclusion private service providers, and in some cases cost recovery (Psacharopoulos, Tan, & Jimenez, 1986; World Bank, 1988, 2005a; Jones, 1992, 2007; Alexander, 2001; Bonal, 2002).

Since 2000, the World Bank has been delegated the lead role in the recent resurgence of rich country efforts to support "education for all" (Sperling, 2001; Birdsall & Vaishnav, 2005; Bruns, Mingat, & Rakotomalala, 2003). It is widely viewed as the most effective international organization in the international development arena, and as such is at the center of the development of a new global development compact among western governments that marries neo-liberal and more social welfare-oriented approaches to development. It is in this context that the bank (not UNESCO) has been delegated the task of managing a newly created "Fast Track" facility, which both acts as a global fund for achieving universal access to education, and sets benchmarks for educational quality and expenditure (Rose, 2003). The bank increasingly receives trust funds from European Union (EU) governments, who push the bank towards greater emphasis on poverty and equity issues. It is often caught in a web of new expectations that arise as a result of changes in international relations—for example the World Bank was expected to use education to enhance democracy and social cohesion in post-Soviet countries, and it is currently at the center of donor efforts to support post-conflict reconciliation through education (World Bank, 2005b; Novelli & Lopes Cardozo, 2008). Some scholars now believe that despite the bank's centrality and power as a global governor, it suffers increasingly from mission creep and competing mandates in ways that undermine its efficacy.

The centrality of the OECD as a policy actor in education also grew substantially in the 1990s. Beginning with its first interministerial conference on education in 1978, the OECD emerged as the pre-eminent forum for discussions about economic adjustment to globalization among Western governments, as well as the main multilateral provider of cross-national educational statistics and research in the north. In the 1980s and 1990s, its work was profoundly re-shaped by U.S. funding for research and policy development focused on issues of privatization, choice, standards, and (most elaborately) cross-national testing of the kind found its Program for International Student Assessment (PISA; OECD 2006a, 2006b, 2007c; Bottani & Walberg, 1992). Both the PISA program and the annual *Education at a Glance* report (launched by the OECD in 1992), mark an important shift in the type of policy role being played by intergovernmental organizations. From a somewhat benign forum for information exchange and cross-national learning in education, the OECD has emerged at the center of much more muscular efforts to compare educational performance across nations. In the 1990s it began to use statistical indicators to rank member countries' educational systems in league tables, and actively advocated the use of such comparisons to leverage domestic educational policy change. Throughout the 1990s, the OECD's education sector work clearly shifted away from an earlier focus on educational equity, towards a central focus on educational reform in the context of economic globalization (Papadopoulos, 1994; Henry, Lingard, Rizvi, & Taylor, 2001; Rinne et al., 2004). This trend is now offset by an increasing interest in social cohesion (Green, Preston, & Germen Janmaat, 2006). Many researchers have argued that OECD programs have come to play an increasingly influential role in the reordering of domestic education policies in Western welfare states, by teaching member governments to think about the relationships between education, society and the economy in new ways, and by introducing new technologies for comparing their systems with others (Henry et al., 2001; Martens, 2007, Steiner-Khamsi, 2003, 2006; Smith & Baker, 2001). Its emphasis on using statistical indicators to measure and compare educational performance has now also reached non-Western and non-OECD member countries, either through accession to the OECD (e.g., Korea, Mexico, many Soviet bloc countries); non-member participation in PISA (often with support from the World Bank), or through the creation of regional assessment programs (such as the Southern and Eastern African Consortium for Monitoring Educational Quality [SACMEQ] and the Latin American Laboratory for Evaluating the Quality of Education [OREALC]).[7]

Two other intergovernmental organizations emerged as significant policy actors in the context of globalization: the European Union and the World Trade Organization (WTO). Formed in 1995, the World Trade Organization has as its central mandate the progressive liberalization of world markets. The rapid expansion of demand for certain kinds of educational services (particularly technology training and higher education) has created increasing opportunities for cross-border provision by transnational corporations and higher education institutions, who, in turn, press for liberalized access to educational markets (Heyneman, 2001; Knight, 2003, 2005, 2006; Martens & Starke, 2008; Ziguras, McBurnie, & Reinke, 2003). Many countries expanded the use of their diplomatic and international trade machineries to promote export of educational services in the 1980s, but the formation of the WTO and the initiation

of the General Agreement on Trade in Services (GATS), for the first time, created a mechanism for such services to become the focus of international negotiations for trade liberalization (Larsen, Martin, & Morris, 2002; Adlung & Roy, 2005; Adlung, 2006). GATS negotiations prompt countries to commit to liberalization by level and form of educational service. If commitments to liberalization are not fulfilled, the WTO provides machinery for intergovernmental litigation and penalty. In the context of globalization, many researchers view the GATS framework as playing a pivotal role in legitimating the expansion of forms of private transnational corporate authority in a space previously imagined as national and public (Robertson, Bonal, & Dale, 2002; Robertson & Dale, 2006; Schugurensky & Davidson-Harden, 2003; Sidhu, 2007; Verger, 2008). In addition, the GATS negotiations have issued a swell of criticism from civil society organizations on the grounds that the liberalization of trade in education services will exacerbate inequalities and degrade the advances associated with public education (Association of Universities and Colleges of Canada [AUCC], 2003; Education International, 2005; Verger & Bonal, 2006). Others, however, argue that the GATS poses much less threat to public education than critics assume (Sauvé, 2002; OECD, 2007a; Vlk, Westerheijden, & van der Wende, 2008). In either case, the debate about the GATS and rising levels of international trade in educational services underscores how little we know about the policy influence wielded by "private" forms of transnational authority in education, such as Microsoft, Cisco, the Apollo Corporation, or the World Economic Forum, who are also increasingly engaged in public-private partnerships (Bull & McNeill, 2007; Bhanji, 2008).

A second new intergovernmental organization to emerge as a significant policy actor in the context of globalization is the EU. After many decades of existence, the EU emerged in the 1990s as the locus of efforts to create an integrated European economy capable of withstanding global economic competition. While the EU is formally limited to "supporting and supplementing" national systems of education, it has steadily expanded its efforts to harmonize the structure and content of the educational systems of its member states (Field, 1997; Keeling, 2006; Corbett, 2005; Neave, 1984, 2003; Lawn, 2001; Novoa & Lawn, 2002). The EU sponsors large-scale programs to enhance student mobility across its member states. Working through interministerial meetings and working groups of senior public administrators in a process sometimes described as "comitology" (governance by intergovernmental committee), the EU has also come to influence general education policy trends across EU members (Slaughter 2005a, 2005b; Dale & Robertson, 2002).

Many researchers believe that the EU is responsible for the introduction of market-like mechanisms into European educational systems: it is widely blamed for the trend toward the commoditization of education, particularly at the tertiary level (Lawn & Lingard, 2002; Dale & Robertson, 2002; Robertson & Dale, 2006; Ceri Jones, 2005; Davies,

2003). However, other researchers focus on the role the EU educational activities play in producing a new, novel form of post-national citizenship (Soysal, 2002; Habermas, 2001). More empirical research is needed on whether the EU's main impact is in harmonizing educational provision for economic competitiveness, or attaching its member citizens to a new form of social democratic citizenship that transcends the nation-state. Such research could also extend to the rising number of other regional or thematic intergovernmental membership organizations with activities in education: recent literature suggests that bodies as diverse as the Group of 8 industrialized nations, Mercusor, the Association of South East Asian Nations (ASEAN), the organization for Asia-Pacific Economic Cooperation (APEC), and the Southern African Development Community, (SADC), are becoming increasingly active in education (Dale & Robertson, 2002; Dale, 2004; de Prado Yepes, 2006, 2007; Kirton & Sunderland, 2006; Hahn, 2005; Jaramillo & Knight, 2005; Lamarra, 2003; Louisy, 2004; Robertson, 2007a; Teferra, 2005). While we know little about the global effects of this regionalization of intergovernmental educational activity, it would seem to be at odds with the more universal goals established for education under the UN and UNESCO, which emphasized the construction of a single world educational community.

Globalization has also led to the expansion of transnational (nongovernmental) policy actors in education, and the emergence of new types of transnational actors. The 1990s saw an explosion of educational policy activities among such transnational actors as international nongovernmental organizations (e.g., CARE, Save the Children, Oxfam), new foundations (e.g., Soros, Hewlett, Gates, the World Economic Forum); and transnational advocacy networks (in areas such as children's rights, education for all, etc.). Much recent research has focused on the rise of global social movement activism in response to the emergence of increasingly globalized forms of political and economic power (Scholte, 2005; Tarrow, 2005; Keck & Sikkink, 1998; Smith, Chatfield, & Pagnucco, 1997). In education, there has clearly been a substantial recent growth of transnational social movement activism (Mundy & Murphy, 2001). For example, teachers unions and other collective actors have successfully blocked GATS negotiations on educational services in several countries (Schugurensky & Davidson-Harden, 2003; Klein, 2001; Fredriksson, 2004; Chan, 2007). Transnational advocacy networks have also been effective in promoting reform of the international regime for educational development—prompting, for example, the World Bank to rethink its policies for promoting user fees (Mundy, 2007). Some researchers have argued that these organizations are helping to construct forms of "global social citizenship" through their emphasis on universal rights (Habermas, 2001; Cornwall & Nyamu-Musembi, 2005; Kabeer, 2005; Finnemore & Sikkink, 1998; Nelson & Dorsey, 2003, 2007; Held, 2005; Ruggie, 2004). But there is much further research to be done on the policy influence of specific groups of nongovernmental actors.

For example, we know that international nongovernmental organizations play surprisingly contradictory roles: They are often heavily dependent on bilateral aid funding and are increasingly corporate-like in the scale and organization of their operations and fundraising.[8] Such international non-government organizations (INGOs) often bypass national policy control in the educator sector by directly providing services (Archer, 1994; Edwards & Hulme, 1996), but the implications of this in particular country contexts has rarely been followed (e.g., see Silova & Steiner-Khamsi, 2008; Murphy, 2005). Furthermore, many of the new transnational advocacy networks—such as the Global Campaign for Education, or the Inter-Agency Network on Education in Emergencies, are threatened by dependency on the major international organizations for funding and research. Much more research is needed on these issues, as well as on other neglected transnational actors in education, such as professional networks (including international teacher unions), private philanthropies (Arnove, 1980b; Berman, 1979; Arnove & Pinede, 2007; Bhanji, 2008), and non-state education actors from non-western backgrounds (e.g., transnational Islamist organizations).

In summary, the period since 1985 can be characterized as introducing several key changes in the scope and content of the educational policy activities of international and transnational policy actors. First, as we have seen, the period saw the rise of a much tighter relationship between education and the economy in the work of intergovernmental organizations, partly in response to the competitive pressures arising from global economic integration. In a related movement, intergovernmental organizations have become much more muscular and evaluative in their use of cross-national statistics on educational performance. Second, the period has seen an increasing number of international actors in new fields of competence—like the World Trade Organization and the European Union becoming engaged in educational policy processes—again often for reasons tightly tied to economic globalization. Finally, a considerable number of transnational (nongovernmental) educational policy actors have emerged, who often oppose the official policy directions promoted by leading intergovernmental organizations. However, while there is some indication that transnational nongovernmental actors have shifted the focus of both international and domestic educational policies back to topics of equity and equality, many operate in a contradictory fashion.

Debates and Gaps in Current Research

Educational policy researchers are sharply divided in the ways they interpret and analyze the effects that this recent proliferation of intergovernmental and transnational policy actors has on education, and there appear to be significant gaps in our understanding of the multiple policy roles being played by intergovernmental and transnational actors in education. Despite an increasing volume of research on intergovernmental and transnational actors in education, efforts to assess their activities and influence are still in their infancy. Below, we first review the central theoretical debates that have shaped recent research on international organizations, noting the need for alternative approaches. A second section looks at recent research and debates about international policy actors from political science, in order to suggest potential new avenues and direction for educational scholarship on this topic.

Theoretical Debates and Research Directions among Education Researchers Educational researchers have commonly interpreted the expansion of the educational policy roles of international organizations by referring to macro-sociological theories of world order, world society, or world system. Two central theoretical schools of thought have emerged.

The first school views international policy actors in education through critical theories of a world capitalist system. Most well-known studies draw from a variety of critical sociological traditions: Wallerstein's world systems theory (Arnove 1980a, 1980b; Ginsburg et al., 1990; Weiler, 1983; Clayton, 1998), dependency theories (Carnoy, 1972; Altbach, 1977; Mazrui, 1975; Berman, 1979, 1983; Samoff, 1993, 1999), and postcolonial theory (Rizvi, Lingard, & Lavia, 2006); the work of Gramsci (Mundy, 1998; Scherrer, 2005), Foucault (Popkewitz, 2000; Olssen, 2004; Sidhu, 2007), and Jessop (Dale, 1999a; Dale & Robertson, 2002; Robertson & Dale, 2006). In each of these instances, studies by educational researchers have focused on showing the way in which international organizations extend inequitable and exploitative relations and structures within a capitalist world system, extending the economic and geopolitical hegemony of specific states and capitalist forces. Much of the conceptual and empirical research on the World Bank and education relies on this framework, as does more recent work on newer international organizations like the World Trade Organization, the European Union, and the OECD. In this view international organizations involved in poverty or equity-driven policy work in education are understood as providing a legitimating function that allows for a "cooling off" of popular demands for equality and redistributive justice at national and international scales (Carnoy, 1972; Cox, 1979; Carnoy & Levin, 1985; Ilon, 1994; Dale, 2007; Offe, 1984).

A second, and increasingly influential macro-sociological framework used for studying international actors in education draws on John Meyer's sociological institutionalism (Meyer et al., 1997; Ramirez & Boli, 1987; McNeely & Cha, 1994; McNeely, 1995; Chabbott, 2003; Ramirez, 2006). Using cross-national data sets, Meyer and his colleagues have documented the expansion of schooling as a taken-for-granted and relatively homogenous institutional form around the world. To explain this pattern of isomorphism, Meyer and his students argue that schooling has developed an institutional logic and momentum at the level of a world society—it has become part of a world cultural script that reinforces norms of bureaucratic rationalism, scientific

progress, and a notion of equality among human individuals (Meyer et al., 1997). In contrast to the critical sociological approach described above, in this research, international organizations are not viewed as agents of specific geopolitical and economic interests. Instead, intergovernmental and transnational organizations are conceptualized as "carriers" of a world cultural script, responsible for deepening institutional isomorphism at the global level. Subsequent research by Meyer's students, using both large scale data sets and case study methodologies, has indeed shown that states that are more closely linked into the international system through memberships in international organizations are more likely to mirror international norms in their policies and bureaucratic structures (Chabbott, 2003; McNeely & Cha, 1994; Finnemore, 1993, 1996a).

Many critics have pointed out the limitations of both these macro-sociological approaches. Critical sociological accounts tend to ignore progressive forms of agency among international actors, favoring research on activities that are more easily linked to a critique of capitalism (McLean, 1983; Psacharopoulos, 1990). In world institutionalist accounts, conflict or contradiction in the policies of international organizations, and the surprising variation of impact they achieve at the country level, are often underplayed or neglected (Dale, 2000; Finnemore, 1996b; Anderson-Levitt, 2003). While these two macro-sociological accounts have generated an impressive research literature, they rarely use empirical evidence to weigh the validity of competing conceptions of world politics and world order. They also tend to focus on broad questions of international political economy or macro-institutional change, at the expense of more detailed accounts of the variable and changing effects of international actors on specific domestic educational policy processes.

Recent research has tried to complicate these theoretical debates, by focusing on policy borrowing and transfer, rather than the policies and characteristics of individual international actors or macro-sociological accounts of world order. Rich empirical case studies of policy borrowing have begun to document how international policies are "indigenized" by receiving countries (Halpin & Troyna, 1995; Phillips & Ochs, 2003; Steiner-Khamsi, 2004, 2006; Levin, 1998), and often suggest that globalization-driven educational reform movements are sharply modified by national contexts (Ozga & Jones, 2006; Brown & Lauder, 1996; Green, 2006; Rhoten, 2000; Welmond, 2002; Benveniste, 2002; Astiz, Wiseman, & Baker, 2002). Some scholars have made tentative efforts to develop typologies of policy borrowing and policy diffusion mechanisms (Dale, 1999b; Schriewer, 2000). Researchers are also beginning to pay greater attention to the role of strategic decision-making in processes of educational policy borrowing, and increasingly look at non-traditional actors in such processes. There is mounting recognition that international actors work together in formations that operate more like networks than traditional bureaucratic hierarchies. Many researchers focus on the development of specific policy issues or issue arenas across networks of international organizations, for example, the issue of life-long learning (Schuetze & Casey, 2006; Schuetze, 2006; Field, 2006, Edwards, 2002; Torres, 2002); and the right to education (Tomasevski, 2003, 2005; Spring, 2000; Robeyns, 2006; Fuchs, 2007); human rights education (Suárez, 2007); and curricular homogenization (Ramirez & Meyer, 2002).

International organizations themselves contribute mightily to such research efforts, both by commissioning research on specific issues and by conducting evaluations of their practices, as well as through corporate efforts to redefine their policy roles vis-à-vis nation-states and the international community (see, e.g., UNESCO, 2005, 2006; OECD, 2007c; Nielsen, 2006; World Bank, 1995, 2005a; United Nations Millennium Development Project, 2005; European Council, 2000).

However, despite the richness of this recent research, efforts to explain why specific policies are more often adopted than others, and why they are adopted in some places (and not others) are relatively rare. The development of "testable" hypothesis about patterns of international policy borrowing and the policy influence of international actors (as is quite common in the field of political science), is uncommon.[9] Yet the existence of more extensive data sets, including those generated by the OECD Program for International Student Assessment (PISA), Freedom House, Afro and Euro-Barometer, and so forth, should allow for more, and better, cross-national research on how international policies impact the functioning of national educational systems and education-society relationships. The overall goal of such research would be to develop and explore competing theoretical and causal arguments that address detailed questions about the operation of power within the world system. Such research could also address the question of whether and how the expansion of international policy actors in education shifts approaches to domestic forms of inequality and democratic participation in education, as for example, in terms of race, class, gender, and ethnicity.

We also note that there is virtually no formative modeling of alternative institutional arrangements for global governance in education of the kind quite common in political science (e.g., Held, 1995; Galtung, 1980). This may stem from the fact that neither the critical nor the institutionalist theoretical approaches most commonly used in education policy research provides much justification for thinking that transformative political agency can emerge at the level of the world polity. Yet some authors have argued that the tension between the rights/redistribution and the human capital investment mandates of international educational actors may be creating new impetus for the collective provision of global public goods in education, precisely because they engender new forms of political contest at the global scale (Mundy, 2006, 2007; see also Robertson, 2007b). At a time when global governance in education seems to be increasing in scope and gaining greater public attention, it is certainly surprising to find so few aspirational attempts to model "good" global governance in education.

Drawing from the Political Science-Global Governance Literature

International relations scholarship—the field within political science that most closely tracks changes in international politics and the relationship between international and national politics—offers some guidance on how to meet the research challenges posed by debates about globalization and the rising influence of international actors on domestic educational policies. While political scientists have paid relatively limited attention to the educational mandates and roles of international organizations per se,[10] they have engaged in extensive theoretical and empirical research on international policy actors and their effects on both domestic policies and the world system. Recently, the field has seen a resurgence of interest in international social policy making and its effects, as well as a mounting debate about the nature and prospects for "global governance."

After 1990, the field of International Relations (IR) began an important movement away from its traditional, tripartite interparadigm debate about the nature of the world system. For many years, thinking about international policy actors in the field had been divided between realist, liberal, and (highly marginalized) neo-Marxist conceptual frames.[11] However, in the early 1990s the field reorganized itself around a newly reconstructed debate about "global governance." IR scholars recognized that the emergence of new actors and changes in their influence had not been adequately captured in realist, liberal, or neo-Marxist paradigms (Biersteker & Hall, 2002; Price & Reus-Smit, 1998). Furthermore, the argument that states have less control over domestic policy arenas in the face of economic and technological globalization has particularly important implications for conceptualizations of the world polity: it implies that territorial nation-states are no longer the sole or most significant building blocks of the global order (Harvey, 1989; Ruggie, 1994).

There has thus been growing effort among IR scholars to study "global governance," a term typically used to capture the fact that the global polity is an evolving set of processes and interactions (rather than a fixed rule system and administrative hierarchy) that by definition involves heterogeneous private and public actors at multiple levels or scales of action: local, national, international, and transnational (Castells, 2000; Higgott, 2000; Barnett & Duvall, 2005; Jessop, 2005). The concept of global governance draws from an expanding literature about "governance" from the policy sciences, where the notion of governance is used both normatively—to draw attention to the value of public/private partnerships and less state-driven action—and analytically, to describe the increasingly disaggregated nature of public action in the context of globalization and neo-liberal approaches to public policy (Reinicke, 1998; Smouts, 1998; Dale, 2004). Governance signals a new interest in networked (as opposed to bureaucratically hierarchical) forms of interdependence (Slaughter, 2004; Rhodes, 1997; Castells et al., 1999).

Initially, research on global governance fell into three distinct camps. In the first camp, where research is informed by a liberal idealist tradition, are scholars whose major interest lies in the development of alternative models or institutional arrangements to augment global governance (Held, 1995; Commission on Global Governance, 1995; Kaul, Conceição, Le Goulven, & Mendoza, 2003; Galtung, 1980). A second group of researchers utilizes a liberal-rationalistic conceptualization of the world political system, and is more empirically driven. In this camp, international organizations are seen as the outgrowth of rational and strategic decisions by nation-states to pool their sovereignty in order to meet collective action problems; international organizations are efficient for states because they reduce information and transaction costs, lower uncertainty, and are perceived by domestic constituencies as more legitimate (Krasner, 1983; Keohane, 1984; Koremenos, Lipson, & Snidal, 2004). Research in this vein emphasizes the conditions under which binding intergovernmental regimes are established, using game theory and principal agent theory as analytical tools to model decision-making processes and answer questions about why states coordinate their activities or allow international norms to have bearing on domestic decision making (Moravcsik, 2000; Drezner, 2003). This group of researchers has convincingly shown that the movement towards cooperation and the construction of binding international rules has strong, rational roots within state polities—indicative of a robust expansion of forms of interstate coordination. However, scholars working in the liberal-rationalist paradigm have remained cautious, arguing that the impact of the immediate strategic interests of states, and the overall anarchy of the interstate system, is likely to limit the growth of a more complete system of interstate coordination, and could even produce oppressive or exploitative international institutions (Keohane, 2001). Their research is primarily focused on modeling the limits and prospects for new forms of interstate cooperation.

A third school of political science research has developed in a very different direction. In what later came to be described as a "constructivist turn," these scholars argue that normative or ideational structures have always mattered at least as much as material factors in the world polity, primarily because systems of meaning define how actors interpret and work on their material environment (Ruggie, 1982; Finnemore, 1996a, 1996b; Price & Reus-Smit, 1998, p. 266). A steady stream of careful empirical case studies shows, for example, that state behavior in armed conflicts changed significantly over the course of the 20th century (e.g., through the Geneva Conventions, the banning of chemical weapons and more recent ban on landmines; Finnemore, 1996b; Price & Reus-Smit, 1998). Such changes could not be attributed solely to a change in the material/strategic interests of states; instead they depended on the ability of international non-state actors and intergovernmental organizations to make normative claims that states later adopted in order to preserve domestic and international legitimacy (Keck & Sikkink, 1998; Finnemore & Sikkink, 1998; Barnett & Finnemore, 2004).

By emphasizing examples of norm-driven change in the international system, empirical research by constructivists opened the way to a new discussion about global governance that would have seemed purely idealistic a decade earlier. Constructivist scholarship directly challenged both realist and liberal-rationalist paradigms, first by claiming that states are historically constructed actors, with interests that are not primordial but which are continuously modified through normative and social processes. Second, constructivist scholars argue that actors other than states could also wield substantial transnational power, often using norms and ideas as tools of power (Biersteker & Weber, 1996; Ruggie, 1998a, 1998b; Finnemore, 1996b). Some constructivists highlight technical knowledge and bureaucratic organization as the source of the influence wielded by major international organizations (Finnemore, 1996b; Barnett & Finnemore, 2004; Boli & Thomas, 1999; Smouts, 1998). Other constructivist scholars highlight more popular processes, such as the moral authority wielded by transnational advocacy and issue networks (Keck & Sikkink, 1998; Finnemore & Sikkink, 1998; Lipschutz, 1992, 2005; O'Brien, Goetz, & Scholte, 2000; Risse, Ropp, S. C., & Sikkink, 1999; Smith et al., 1997; Scholte, 2005; Biersteker & Hall, 2002).

More recently there have been efforts to synthesize constructivist and liberal-rationalist frames in analysis of international actors—the argument here being that both long-term ideational processes and shorter-term strategic issues fuel political interactions in the international arena (Nielson, Tierney, & Weaver, 2006). There has also been a substantial contribution to the debate about global governance from those who emphasize the role of policy networks as a new mode of governance (Resnik, 2006; Benner, Reinicke, & Witte, 2004; Rhodes, 1997; Börzel, 1999; Marsh & Smith, 2000; Coleman & Perl, 1999; Castells, 1997). Network approaches cut across theoretical frameworks, and may incorporate rational choice, or institutional or constructivist approaches in order to understand different aspects of the policy process. Network approaches have focused attention on such issues as the importance of "policy entrepreneurs," processes of cognition and learning, and communicative mechanisms such as persuasion and argumentation (Keck & Sikkink, 1998; Sabatier, 2007; Maxwell & Stone, 2005).

In sum, understanding the relative and varied power wielded by different kinds of international actors and normative processes has emerged at the epicenter of contemporary international relations scholarship. Even in the context of post-9/11 and the Iraq crisis, the realist idea that hegemonic nation-states can go it alone seems unsustainable to political scientists (Grande & Pauly, 2005; Held, 2005; Keohane, 2003). Today the field of international relations is densely populated with efforts to use empirical data to analyze the relative power of various transnational forms of political authority. Liberal-rationalistic IR theorists continue to employ sophisticated game-theoretic methodologies to study the extent and changing influence of transnational forms of authority on states. Constructivists use case study methods to present arguments about the normative processes that shape state actions, and to highlight the roles played by supranational non-state actors. Other contributors focus on specific mechanisms of diffusion or model ideal alternatives. Research across all camps is aggregated in an overarching debate about the limits and possibilities for more just global governance.

Attention to current debates about global governance in political science may offer new ways forward for educational policy research. Not only does such research alert us to the need for more attention to new kinds of international actors and new forms of organization and coordination. It also directs our attention to the need for better empirical research into the causes of variation in the influence of international actors, guiding us towards deeper consideration of both the normative processes and the strategic interests that shape the way nation-states, intergovernmetal organizations, and non-state actors identify their international policy interests in the education. We need a much richer understanding of how both intergovernmental and transnational policy processes are working in education, addressing questions such as the following: Are forms of transnational private authority influencing the educational decision-making power of states? Is supranational elite or expert authority in education thickening, and if so, then how does this affect the global educational policy field? What are the democratic openings in the intergovernmental and transnational policy arena? Can we model better or more effective international actors and actor behavior?

Conclusion

Educational researchers have increasingly argued that after two decades of rapid economic globalization, heightened human mobility, and the end of the Cold War, the nature of governments' strategic interests in education and their ability to contain educational demand within nationally controlled educational systems has changed (Mundy, 1998; Carnoy, 1999; Dale, 1999b). As Dale (1997, 2007) notes, the idea that the relationship between the state and education is complete is no longer taken for granted: governments are no longer expected to be the funders, providers, regulators, and owners of educational systems, and they work in an environment increasingly dense with intergovernmental and non-state policy actors. International policy actors are now a permanent and expanding feature of an increasingly multilevel (or what Dale and Robertson term "pluriscalar") and fragmented arena for educational governance. Such changes have important implications, both for the trajectories of national systems of education, and for the development of broader systems of global level governance.

Despite the recent expansion of research on the international and transnational actors in education, three key gaps in research call out for more systematic attention. First, more effort should be focused on using case studies of in-

dividual international policy actors and issue networks, and other empirical evidence, to adjudicate among competing theories of globalization and global governance. Research on inter- and transnational policy actors in education has been characterized by a sharp ideological divide, creating "silos" within which empirical evidence is rarely used to weigh competing hypotheses about global governance. Second, we need to learn to use empirical evidence to build more robust theories of explanation for the varied patterns of policy borrowing and diffusion occurring as result of international level policy intervention, focusing more attention on answering the questions, why do some internationally generated policies get adopted (and not others) in some places and contexts (and not others). Finally, we need to pay more attention to formative modeling of alternative institutional arrangements for global governance in education. Renewed attention needs to be paid to the question of how new forms of transnational political authority can contribute to the creation of more democratic "operating rules" for the world polity. In all three regards, global governance research from the field of political science offers important guidance and direction from which education policy researchers can draw and to which they can fruitfully contribute.

Notes

1. The International Institute for Intellectual Cooperation (formed in 1921) focused primarily on scientific and cultural exchange, but also did significant work in the area of textbook revision to promote peace.
2. Adopted November 16, 1945, London. Available at: http://www.icomos.org/unesco/unesco_constitution.html
3. Article 26 states: "Everyone has the right to education. Education shall be free, at least in the elementary and fundamental stages. Elementary education shall be compulsory" (Universal Declaration of Human Rights, 1948, Art. 26.1). For the full declaration see http://www.un.org/Overview/rights.html
4. The International Organization for Standardization (ISO) defines a standard as a "document established by consensus that provides, for common and repeated use, rules, guidelines or characteristics for activities or their results, aimed at the achievement of the optimum degree of order in a given context" (as cited in Borraz, 2007, p. 57).
5. In 1958, following the success of the USSR's Sputnik mission, the United States provided funding for the creation of an office for Scientific and Technical Personal within the OECD, under whose auspices emerged an OECD program to support new science curricula, and better trained scientists and science teachers across member states.
6. Others focus on the cultural and political dimensions of globalization as driving forces (Appadurai, 1996).
7. Information about the SACMEQ and the OREALC programs can be found online at: http://www.sacmeq.org/ and http://www.unesco.cl/ing/
8. The "big five" in education—Care, Save the Children, World Vision, Plan International, Oxfam—have annual budgets that dwarf those of smaller developing countries.
9. In the field of political science, variation in the receptivity of different nation-states to transnational policies has generated detailed causal arguments (e.g., those based on differences in type of nation-state, such as social democracies vs. Anglo-American democracies, or on the idea of regional cluster in the diffusion neo-liberalism), as well as elaborate empirical efforts to test competing hypothesis, this is rare in research on transnational policy actors in education (Hega & Hokenmaier, 2002; Simmons & Elkins, 2004).

10. The only examples of IR scholarship on education are Cox's 1968 article and a variety of studies of UNESCO.

11. Realist accounts argued that international politics revolve around the maximizing interests of territorial sovereign nation-states, leading to a research on international organizations that emphasized their manipulation by states seeking greater power within a world system (Holsti, 1985; McKinlay & Little, 1986; Mearsheimer, 1994; Morgenthau, 1967). Liberal accounts, in contrast, argued that state actors increasingly saw an advantage in ceding some part of their sovereignty to international organizations, in order to achieve specific goals, such as security and economic coordination. In doing so, they fundamentally changed the nature of state power itself, creating a world system characterized by increasingly sustained habits of interdependence (Claude, 1966; Keohane & Nye, 1977). Critical and neo-Marxist scholars felt that both the realist and liberal views underestimated the role played by the evolution of a capitalist world economy within which all politics were deeply embedded (Cox, 1981; Murphy, 1994).

References

Adlung, R. (2006). Services negotiations in the Doha Round: Lost in flexibility? *Journal of International Economic Law, 9*, 865–893.

Adlung, R., & Roy, M. (2005). *Turning hills into mountains? Current commitments under the GATS and prospects for change* (WTO Staff Working Paper No. ERSD-2005-01). Geneva, Switzerland: World Trade Organization, Economic Research and Statistics Division.

Alexander, N. C. (2001). Paying for education: How the World Bank and the International Monetary Fund influence education in developing countries. *Peabody Journal of Education, 76*(3 & 4), 285–338.

Altbach, P. G. (1977). Servitude of the mind? Education, dependency, and neo-colonialism. *Teachers College Record, 79*, 187–204.

Anderson, B. R. (1983). *Imagined communities: Reflections on the origin and spread of nationalism.* New York: Verso.

Anderson-Levitt, K. (Ed.). (2003). *Local meanings, global schooling: Anthropology and world culture theory.* New York: Palgrave Macmillan.

Appadurai, A. (1996). *Modernity at large: Cultural dimensions of globalization.* Minneapolis: University of Minnesota Press.

Archer, D. (1994). The changing roles of non-governmental organizations in the field of education (in the context of changing relationships with the state). *International Journal of Educational Development, 14*, 223–232.

Arnove, R. F. (1980a). Comparative education and world-systems analysis. *Comparative Education Review, 24*, 48–62.

Arnove, R. F. (Ed.). (1980b). *Philanthropy and cultural imperialism: The foundations at home and abroad.* Boston: G. K. Hall.

Arnove, R. F., & Pinede, N. (2007). Revisiting the "big three" foundations. *Critical Sociology, 33*, 389–425.

Association of Universities and Colleges of Canada (AUCC). (2003). *The GATS and higher education in Canada: An update on Canada's position and the implications for Canadian universities.* Retrieved June 10, 2006, from http://www.aucc.ca/_pdf/english/reports/2003/gats_update_e.pdf

Astiz, M. F., Wiseman, A. W., & Baker, D. P. (2002). Slouching towards decentralization: Consequences of globalization for curricular control in national education systems. *Comparative Education Review, 46*, 66–88.

Augelli, E., & Murphy, C. (1988). *America's quest for supremacy and the third world: A Gramscian analysis.* London: Pinter.

Ball, S. J. (1998). Big policies/small world: An introduction to international perspectives in education policy. *Comparative Education, 34*, 119–130.

Barnett, M., & Duvall, R. (Eds.). (2005). *Power in global governance.* Cambridge, UK: Cambridge University Press.

Barnett, M., & Finnemore, M. (2004). *Rules for the world: International organizations in global politics.* Ithaca, NY: Cornell University Press.

Benner, T., Reinicke, W. H., & Witte, J. M. (2004). Multisectoral networks in global governance: Towards a pluralistic system of accountability. *Government and Opposition, 39*(2), 191–210.

Benveniste, L. (2002). The political structuration of assessment: Negotiating state power and legitimacy. *Comparative Education Review, 46*(1), 89–118.

Berman, E. H. (1979). Foundations, United States foreign policy, and African education, 1945–1975. *Harvard Educational Review, 49*(7), 145–179.

Berman, E. H. (1983). *The ideology of philanthropy: The influence of the Carnegie, Ford, and Rockefeller Foundations on American Foreign Policy.* Albany: State University of New York Press.

Bhanji, Z. (2008). Transnational corporations in education: Filling the governance gap through new social norms and market multilateralism. *Globalisation, Societies and Education, 6*(1), 55–73.

Biersteker, T. J., & Hall, R. B. (2002). Private authority as global governance. In R. B. Hall & T. J. Biersteker (Eds.), *The emergence of private authority in global governance* (pp. 3–22). Cambridge, UK: Cambridge University Press.

Biersteker, T. J., & Weber, C. (Eds.). (1996). *State sovereignty as social construct.* Cambridge, UK: Cambridge University Press.

Birdsall, N., & Vaishnav, M. (2005). Education and the MDGS: Realizing the Millennium Compact. *Journal of International Affairs, 58*(2), 257–264.

Black, M. (1996). *Children first: The story of UNICEF, past and present.* New York: Oxford University Press.

Boli, J., Ramirez, F., & Meyer, J. (1985). Explaining the origins and expansion of mass education. *Comparative Education Review, 29*, 145–170.

Boli, J., & Thomas, G. (Eds.). (1999). *Constructing world culture: International Nongovernmental Organizations Since 1875.* Stanford, CA: Stanford University Press.

Bonal, X. (2002). Plus ça change... the World Bank global education policy and the post-Washington consensus. *International Studies in Sociology of Education, 12*, 3–22.

Borraz, O. (2007). Governing standards: The rise of standardization processes in France and in the EU. *Governance, 20*(1), 57–84.

Börzel, T. (1999). Organizing Babylon: On the different conceptions of policy networks. *Public Administration, 76*, 253–273.

Bottani, N., & Walberg, H. J. (1992). What are international education indicators for? In OECD/CERI, *The OECD international education indicators: A framework for analysis* (pp. 7–22). Paris: OECD.

Brown, P., & Lauder, H. (1996). Education, globalization and economic development. *Journal of Education Policy, 11*(1), 1–25.

Bruns, B., Mingat, A., & Rakotomalala, R. (2003). *Achieving universal primary education by 2015: A chance for every child.* Washington, DC: The World Bank.

Bull, B., & McNeill, D. (2007). UNESCO and the software companies. In *Development issues in global governance: Public-private partnerships and market multilateralism* (pp. 115–134). London: Routledge.

Carnoy, M. (Ed.). (1972). *Schooling in a corporate society: The political economy of education in America.* New York: McKay.

Carnoy, M. (1995). Structural adjustment and the changing face of education. *International Labour Review, 134*, 653–673.

Carnoy, M. (1999). *Globalization and education reform: What planners need to know.* Paris: UNESCO, International Institute for Educational Planning (IIEP).

Carnoy, M., & Levin, H. (1985). *Schooling and work in the democratic state.* Stanford, CA: Stanford University Press.

Castells, M. (1997). *The power of identity—The Information Age: Economy, society and culture: Vol. 2.* Oxford: Blackwell.

Castells, M. (2000). *The rise of the network society* (2nd ed.). Oxford: Blackwell.

Castells, M., Flecha, R., Freire, P., Giroux, H. A., Macedo, D., & Willis, P. (1999). *Critical education in the new Information Age.* Lanham, MD: Rowman & Littlefield.

Ceri Jones, H. (2005). Lifelong learning in the European Union: Wither the Lisbon strategy? *European Journal of Education, 40*, 247–260.

Chabbott, C. (2003). *Constructing education for development: International Organizations and Education for All*. New York: Routledge/Falmer.

Chan, J. (2007). Between efficiency, capability and recognition: Competing epistemes in global governance reforms. *Comparative Education, 43*, 359–376.

Clayton, T. (1998). Beyond mystification: Reconnecting world-system theory for comparative education. *Comparative Education Review, 42*, 479–496.

Claude, I. L., Jr. (1966). Collective legitimization as a political function of the United Nations. *International Organization, 20*, 367–379.

Colclough, C. (1993). Who should learn to pay? An assessment of neo-liberal approaches to education policy. In C. Colclough & J. Manor (Eds.), *States or markets? Neo-liberalism and the development policy debate* (pp. 197–213). New York: Oxford University Press.

Coleman, W. D., & Perl, A. (1999). Internationalized policy environments and policy network analysis. *Political Studies, 47*, 691–709.

Commission on Global Governance. (1995). *Our global neighborhood: Report of the Commission on Global Governance*. Oxford, UK: Oxford University Press.

Corbett, A. (2005). *Universities and the Europe of Knowledge: Ideas, institutions and policy entrepreneurship in European Union higher education policy, 1955–2005*. Basingstoke, UK: Palgrave.

Cornwall, A., & Nyamu-Musembi, C. (2005). Why rights, why now? Reflections on the rise of rights in international development discourse. *IDS Bulletin, 36*(1), 9–18.

Cox, R. W. (1968). Education for development. In R. Gardner & M. F. Millikan (Eds.), *The global partnership: International agencies and economic development* (pp. 310–331). New York: Praeger.

Cox, R. W. (1979). Ideologies and the new international economic order: reflections on some recent literature. *International Organization, 33*(2), 257–302.

Cox, R. W. (1981). Social forces, states and world orders: Beyond international relations theory. *Millennium: Journal of International Studies, 10*(2), 126–155.

Dale, R. (1997). The state and the governance of education: An analysis of the restructuring of the state-education relationship. In A. H. Halsey, H. Lauder, P. Brown, & A. S. Wells (Eds.), *Education, culture, economy, society* (pp. 273–282). Oxford, UK: Oxford University Press.

Dale, R. (1999a). Globalization: A new world through comparative education? In J. Schriewer (Ed.), *Discourse formation in comparative education* (pp. 87–109). Berlin, Germany: Peter Lang.

Dale, R. (1999b). Specifying globalization effects on national policy: A focus on the mechanisms. *Journal of Education Policy, 14*, 1–17.

Dale, R. (2000). Globalization and education: Demonstrating a "common world educational culture" or locating a "globally structured educational agenda"? *Educational Theory, 50*, 427–448.

Dale, R. (2004). Forms of governance, governmentality and the EU's open method of coordination. In W. Larner & W. Walters (Eds.), *Global governmentality: Governing international spaces* (pp. 174–194). London: Routledge.

Dale, R. (2007). Globalization and the rescaling of educational governance: A case of sociological ectopia. In C. A. Torres & A. Teodoro (Eds.), *Critique and utopia* (pp. 25–44). Lanham, MD: Rowman & Littlefield.

Dale, R., & Robertson, S. L. (2002). The varying effects of regional organisations as subjects of globalisation of education. *Comparative Education Review, 46*, 10–36.

Davies, G. (1943). *Intellectual cooperation between the two wars*. London: Council for Education and World Citizenship.

Davies, P. (2003). Widening participation and the European Union: Direct action—indirect policy? *European Journal of Education, 38*(1), 99–116.

Davies, S., & Guppy, N. (1997). Globalization and educational reforms in Anglo-American democracies. *Comparative Education Review, 41*, 435–459.

de Prado Yepes, C. (2006). World regionalization of higher education: Policy proposals for international organizations. *Higher Education Policy, 19*, 111–128.

de Prado Yepes, C. (2007). Regionalisation of higher education services in Europe and East Asia and potential for global change. *Asia Europe Journal, 5*, 83–92.

Drezner, D. W. (2003). The hidden hand of economic coercion. *International Organization, 57*, 643–659.

Education International. (2005, December). *Statement of the delegations to the 6th WTO Ministerial concerning GATS and education*. Paper presented at the Higher Education International Conference, Melbourne, Australia.

Edwards, M., & Hulme, D. (1996). Too close for comfort? The impact of official aid on nongovernmental organizations. *World Development, 24*, 961–973.

Edwards, R. (2002). Mobilizing lifelong learning: Governmentality in educational practices. *Journal of Education Policy, 17*, 353–365.

European Council. (2000). *Presidency conclusions: Lisbon European Council*. Retrieved June 6, 2007, from http://consilium.europa.eu/ueDocs/cms_Data/docs/pressData/en/ec/00100-r1.en0.htm

Field, J. (1997). The learning society and the European Union: A critical assessment of supranational education policy formation. *Journal of Studies in International Education, 1*(2), 73–92.

Field, J. (2006). *Lifelong learning and the new international order*. Sterling, VA: Trentham Books.

Finnemore, M. (1993). International organizations as teachers of norms: The United Nations Education, Scientific, and Cultural Organization and science policy. *International Organization, 47*, 565–597.

Finnemore, M. (1996a). *National interests in international society*. Ithaca, NY: Cornell University Press.

Finnemore, M. (1996b). Norms, culture, and world politics: Insights from sociology's institutionalism. *International Organization, 50*, 325–347.

Finnemore, M., & Sikkink, K. (1998). International norm dynamics and political change. *International Organization, 52*, 887–917.

Fredriksson, U. (2004). Studying the supra-national in education: GATS, education and teacher union policies. *European Educational Research Journal, 3*, 415–441.

Fuchs, E. (2007). Children's rights and global civil society. *Comparative Education, 43*, 393–412.

Galtung, J. (1980). *The true worlds: A transnational perspective*. New York: The Free Press.

Ginsburg, M., Cooper, S., Raghu, R., & Zegarra, H. (1990). National and world system explanations of educational reform. *Comparative Education Review, 34*, 474–499.

Grande, E., & Pauly, L. W. (Eds.). (2005). *Complex sovereignty: Reconstituting political authority in the twenty-first century*. Toronto: University of Toronto Press.

Green, A. (2006). Models of lifelong learning and the "knowledge society." *Compare, 36*, 307–325.

Green, A., Preston, J., & Germen Janmaat, J. (2006). *Education, equality and social cohesion: A comparative analysis*. New York: Palgrave Macmillan.

Griffin, K. (1991). Foreign aid after the Cold War. *Development and Change, 22*, 645–685.

Habermas, J. (2001). *The postnational constellation: Political essays* (M. Pensky, Trans.). Cambridge, MA: MIT Press.

Hahn, K. (2005). Towards a SADC area of higher education (NEPRU Research Report No. 30). Retrieved June 10, 2007, from http://www.uni-kl.de/wcms/fileadmin/isgs/pdf/Publikationen_Hahn/SADC_NEPRU_Research_Report.pdf

Halpin, D., & Troyna, B. (1995). The politics of education policy borrowing. *Comparative Education, 31*, 303–310.

Harvey, D. (1989). *The condition of postmodernity: An enquiry into the origins of cultural change*. Cambridge, MA: Blackwell.

Hega, G. M., & Hokenmaier, K. G. (2002). The welfare state and education: Comparison of social and educational policy in advanced industrial societies. *German Policy Studies, 2*, 1–29.

Helleiner, E. (1994). *States and the reemergence of global finance: From Bretton Woods to the 1990s*. Ithaca, NY: Cornell University Press.

Held, D. (1995). *Democracy and the global order: From the modern state to cosmopolitan governance*. Stanford, CA: Stanford University Press.

Held, D. (2005). At the global crossroads: The end of the Washington Consensus and the rise of global social democracy? *Globalizations, 2*, 95–113.

Henry, M., Lingard, B., Rizvi, F., & Taylor, S. (2001). *The OECD, globalisation and education policy.* Oxford, UK: Pergamon.

Heyneman, S. P. (2001). The growing international commercial market for educational goods and services. *International Journal of Educational Development, 21*, 345–359.

Heyneman, S. P. (2003). The history and problems in the making of education policy at the World Bank 1960–2000. *International Journal of Educational Development, 23*, 315–337.

Higgott, R. (2000). Contested globalization: The changing context and normative challenges. *Review of International Studies, 26*(5), 113–153.

Holmes, B., & Robinsohn, S. (1963). *Relevant data in comparative education.* Hamburg, Germany: UNESCO Institute for Education.

Holsti, K. J. (1985). *The dividing discipline: Hegemony and diversity in international theory.* Boston: Allen & Unwin.

Ilon, L. (1994). Structural adjustment and education: Adapting to a growing global market. *International Journal of Educational Development, 14*(2), 95–108.

Imber, M. (1989). *The USA, ILO, UNESCO, and IAEA: Politicization and withdrawal in the specialized agencies.* New York: St. Martin's Press.

Jaramillo, I. C., & Knight, J. (2005). Key actors and programs: Increasing connectivity in the region. In H. de Wit, I. C. Jaramillo, J. Gacel-Ávila, & J. Knight (Eds.), *Higher education in Latin America: The international dimension* (pp. 301–339). Washington, DC: The World Bank.

Jessop, B. (2005). Multi-level governance and multi-level metagovernance: Changes in the European Union as integral movements in the transformation and reorientation of contemporary statehood. In F. Kratochwil & E. D. Mansfield (Eds.), *International organization and global governance: A reader* (2nd ed., pp. 355–367). New York: Pearson Longman.

Jolly, R. (1991). Adjustment with a human face: A UNICEF record and perspective on the 1980s. *World Development, 19*, 1807–1821.

Jones, P. W. (1988). *International policies for third world education: UNESCO, literacy and development.* New York: Routledge.

Jones, P. W. (1992). *World Bank financing of education: Lending, learning and development.* New York: Routledge.

Jones, P. W. (2005). *The United Nations and education: Multilateralism, development and globalisation.* New York: Routledge Falmer.

Jones, P. W. (2007). *World Bank financing of education: Lending, learning and development* (2nd ed.). New York: Routledge.

Kabeer, N. (Ed.). (2005). *Inclusive citizenship: Meanings and expressions.* London: Zed Books.

Kaul, I., Conceição, P., Le Goulven, K., & Mendoza, R. U. (Eds.). (2003). *Providing global public goods: Managing globalization.* New York: Oxford University Press.

Keck, M. E., & Sikkink, K. (1998). *Activists beyond borders: Advocacy networks in international politics.* Ithaca, NY: Cornell University Press.

Keeling, R. (2006). The Bologna Process and the Lisbon research agenda: The European Commission's expanding role in higher education discourse. *European Journal of Education, 42*, 203–223.

Keohane, R. O. (1984). *After hegemony: Cooperation and discord in the world political economy.* Princeton, NJ: Princeton University Press.

Keohane, R. O. (2001). Governance in a partially globalized world. *American Political Science Review, 95*, 1–13.

Keohane, R. O. (2003). Global governance and democratic accountability. In D. Held & M. Koenig-Archibugi (Eds.), *Taming globalization: Frontiers of governance* (pp. 160–186). Cambridge, UK: Polity Press.

Keohane, R., & Nye, J. S. (1977). *Power and interdependence: World politics in transition.* Boston: Little and Brown.

King, K. (1991). *Aid and education in the developing world: The role of the donor agencies in educational analysis.* Harlow, UK: Longman.

Kirton, J., & Sunderland, L. (2006). *The G8 and global education governance.* Retrieved July 10, 2006, from http://www.g7.utoronto.ca/scholar/kirton2006/kirton_education_060530.pdf

Klein, N. (2001). Reclaiming the commons. *New Left Review, 9*, 81–89.

Knight, J. (2003). Higher education and trade agreements: What are the policy implications? In G. Breton & M. Lambert (Eds.), *Universities and globalization, private linkages, public trust.* Paris: UNESCO, Laval/Economica.

Knight, J. (2005). Higher education in the trade context of GATS. In B. Kehm & J. W. de Wit (Eds.), *Internationalisation in higher education: European responses to the global perspective.* Amsterdam: European Association for International Education and the European Association for International Research.

Knight, J. (2006). *Higher education crossing borders: A guide to the implications of General Agreement on Trade of Services (GATS) for cross-border education.* Paris: Commonwealth of Learning and UNESCO.

Koremenos, B., Lipson, C., & Snidal, D. (Eds.). (2004). *The rational design of international institutions.* Cambridge, UK: Cambridge University Press.

Krasner, S. D. (Ed.). (1983). *International regimes.* Ithaca, NY: Cornell University Press.

Lamarra, N. F. (2003). Higher education, quality evaluation and accreditation in Latin America and Mercosur. *European Journal of Education, 28*(3), 253–269.

Larsen, K., Martin, J. P., & Morris, R. (2002). Trade in educational services: Trends and emerging issues. *The World Economy, 25*, 849–868.

Lawn, M. (2001). Borderless education: Imagining a European education space in a time of brands and networks. *Discourse, 22*, 173–184.

Lawn, M., & Lingard, B. (2002). Constructing a European policy space in educational governance: The role of transnational policy actors. *European Educational Research Journal, 1*, 290–307.

Lee, K. (1995). A neo-Gramscian approach to international organization: An expanded analysis of current reforms to UN development activities. In J. MacMillan & A. Linklater (Eds.), *Boundaries in question: New directions in international relations* (pp. 144–162). New York: St. Martin's Press.

Levin, B. (1998). An epidemic of education policy: (What) can we learn from each other? *Comparative Education, 34*(2), 131–141.

Lipschutz, R. (1992). Reconstructing world politics: The emergence of global civil society. *Millennium: Journal of International Studies, 21*, 389–429.

Lipschutz, R. D. (2005). Global civil society and global governmentality: Or, the search for politics and the state amidst the capillaries of social power. In M. Barnett & R. Duvall (Eds.), *Power in global governance* (pp. 229–248). Cambridge, UK: Cambridge University Press.

Louisy, P. (2004). Whose context for what quality? Informing education strategies for the Caribbean. *Compare, 34*, 285–292.

Marsh, D., & Smith, M. (2000). Understanding policy networks: Toward a dialectal approach. *Political Studies, 48*, 4–21.

Martens, K. (2007) How to become an influential actor--the "comparative turn" in OECD education policy. In K. Martens, A. Rusconi, & K. Leuze (Eds.), *New arenas of education governance: The impact of international organisations and markets on education policy making* (pp. 40–56). Basingstoke, UK: Palgrave Macmillan.

Martens, K., & Starke, P. (2008). Small country, big business? New Zealand as education exporter. *Comparative Education, 44*, 3–19.

Maxwell, S. (2005). *The Washington Consensus is dead: Long live the meta-narrative!* (Working Paper No. 243). Retrieved August 12, 2007, from http://www.odi.org.uk/publications/working_papers/wp243.pdf

Maxwell, S., & Stone, D. L. (2005). Global knowledge networks and international development: Bridges and boundaries. In D. Stone & S. Maxwell (Eds.), *Global knowledge networks and international development: Bridges across boundaries* (pp. 1–17). Abingdon, UK: Routledge.

Mazrui, A. (1975). The African university as a multinational corporation: Problems of penetration and dependency. *Harvard Educational Review, 45*, 191–210.

McKinlay, R. D., & Little, R. (1986). *Global problems and world order.* London: Pinter.

McLean, M. (1983). Educational dependency: A critique. *Compare, 13*, 25–42.

McNeely, C. L. (1995). Prescribing national education policies: The role of international organizations. *Comparative Education Review, 39*, 483–507.

McNeely, C. L., & Cha, Y.-K. (1994). Worldwide educational convergence through international organizations: Avenues for research [Electronic Version]. *Education Policy Analysis Archives, 2*(14).

Mearsheimer, J. (1994). The false promise of international institutions. *International Security, 19*(3), 5–49.

Meyer, J., Boli, B., Thomas, G., & Ramirez, F. (1997). World society and the nation-state. *American Journal of Sociology, 103*, 144–181.

Morgenthau, H. J. (1967). *Politics among nations: The struggle for power and peace* (4th ed.). New York: Knopf.

Moravcsik, A. (2000). The origins of human rights regimes: Democratic delegation in Postwar Europe. *International Organization, 54*, 217–252.

Mundy, K. (1998). Educational multilateralism and world (dis)order. *Comparative Education Review, 42*, 448–478.

Mundy, K. (2002). Discussion. Retrospect and prospect: Education in a reforming World Bank. *International Journal of Educational Development, 22*(5), 483–508.

Mundy, K. (2005). Globalization and education change: New policy worlds. In N. Bascia, A. Cumming, A. Datnow, K. Leithwood, & D. Livingstone (Eds.), *International Handbook of Educational Policy* (pp. 3–18). Dordrecht, The Netherlands: Springer.

Mundy, K. (2006). Education for All and the new development compact. *International Review of Education, 52*, 23–48.

Mundy, K. (2007). Education for All: Paradoxes and prospects of a global promise. In D. Baker & A. W. Wiseman (Eds.), *The impact of comparative education research on institutional theory* (pp. 1–30). Amsterdam: Elsevier/JAI Press.

Mundy, K., & Murphy, L. (2001). Transnational advocacy, global civil society? Emerging evidence from the field of education. *Comparative Education Review, 45*, 85–126.

Murphy, C. (1994). *International organization and industrial change: Global governance since 1850*. Cambridge, UK: Polity Press.

Murphy, J. (2005). The World Bank, INGOs and Civil Society: Converging agendas? The Case of universal basic education in Uganda. *Volunatas: International Journal of Voluntary and Non-Profit Organizations, 16*, 353–374.

Neave, G. (1984). *Education and the EEC*. Stoke-on-Trent, UK: Trentham Books.

Neave, G. (2003). The Bologna Declaration: Some of the historic dilemmas posed by the reconstruction of the community in Europe's systems of higher education. *Educational Policy, 17*(1), 141–164.

Nelson, P., & Dorsey, E. (2003). At the nexus of human rights and development: New methods and strategies of global NGOs. *World Development, 31*, 2013–2026.

Nelson, P., & Dorsey, E. (2007). New rights advocacy in a global public domain. *European Journal of International Relations, 13*, 187–216.

Nielsen, H. D. (2006). *From schooling access to learning outcomes, an unfinished agenda: An evaluation of World Bank support to primary education*. Washington, DC: World Bank.

Nielson, D. L., Tierney, M. J., & Weaver, C. E. (2006). Bridging the rationalist-constructivist divide: Re-engineering the culture of the World Bank. *Journal of International Relations and Development, 9*(2), 107–139.

Novelli, M., & Lopes Cardozo, T. A. (2008). Conflict, education and the global south: New critical directions. *International Journal of Educational Development, 28*, 473–488.

Novoa, A., & Lawn, M. (Eds.). (2002). *Fabricating Europe: The formation of an education space*. Boston: Kluwer.

O'Brien, R., Goetz, A. M., & Scholte, J. A. (2000). *Contesting global governance: Multilateral economic institutions and global social movements*. Cambridge, UK: Cambridge University Press.

Offe, C. (1984). *Contradictions of the welfare state*. Cambridge, MA: MIT Press.

Organization for Economic Cooperation and Development (OECD). (2006a). *Education at a glance* [Electronic version]. Paris: Author.

Organization for Economic Cooperation and Development (OECD).

(2006b). *First results from PISA: Executive summary. Programme for International Student Assessment* [Electronic version]. Paris: Author.

Organization for Economic Cooperation and Development (OECD). (2007a). *Cross-border tertiary education: A way towards capacity development*. Paris: OECD, CERI and the World Bank.

Organization for Economic Cooperation and Development (OECD). (2007b). *Education at a Glance 2007*. Paris: OECD.

Organization for Economic Cooperation and Development (OECD). (2007c, February) *The OECD Programme for International Student Assessment (PISA) brochure*. Retrieved March 3, 2008, from http://www.pisa.oecd.org/dataoecd/51/27/37474503.pdf

Olssen, M. (2004). Neoliberalism, globalisation, democracy: Challenges for education. *Globalisation, Societies and Education, 2*, 231–275.

Ozga, J., & Jones, R. (2006). Traveling and embedded policy: The case of knowledge transfer. *Journal of Education Policy, 21*, 1–17.

Papadopoulos, G. S. (1994). *Education 1960–1990: The OECD Perspective*. Paris: OECD.

Phillips, D., & Ochs, K. (2003). Processes of policy borrowing in education: Some analytical and explanatory devices. *Comparative Education, 39*, 451–461.

Phillips, H. M. (1987). *Unicef and education: A historical perspective*. New York: Unicef.

Popkewitz, T. (2000). National imaginaries, the indigenous foreigner and power: Comparative educational research. In J. Schriewer (Ed.), *Discourse formation in comparative education* (pp. 261–294). Berlin, Germany: Peter Lang.

Preston, W., Herman, E., & Schiller, H. (1989). Hope and folly: The United States and UNESCO, 1945–1985. Minneapolis: University of Minnesota Press.

Price, R., & Reus-Smit, C. (1998). Dangerous liaisons? Critical international theory and constructivism. *European Journal of International Relations, 4*, 259–294.

Psacharopoulos, G. (1990). Comparative education: From theory to practice, or are you A:\neo.* or B:*.ist? *Comparative Education Review, 34*, 369–380.

Psacharopoulos, G., Tan, J-P., & Jimenez, E. (1986). *Financing education in developing countries: An exploration of policy options*. Washington, DC: The World Bank.

Ramirez, F. O. (2006). *From citizen to person? Rethinking education as incorporation* (Working Paper No. 53). Center on Democracy, Development, and the Rule of Law (CDDRL). Retrieved June 10, 2007, from http://iis-db.stanford.edu/pubs/21085/Ramirez_No_53.pdf

Ramirez, F. O., & Boli, J. (1987). Global patterns of educational institutionalization. In G. M. Thomas, J. W. Meyer, F. O. Ramirez, & J. Boli (Eds.), *Institutional structure: Constituting the state, society and the individual* (pp. 150–172). Beverly Hills, CA: Sage.

Ramirez, F. O., & Meyer, J. W. (2002). National curricula: World models and national historical legacies. In M. Caruso & H.-E. Tenorth (Eds.), *Internationalization: Comparing educational systems and semantics* (pp. 91–107). Frankfurt, Germany: Peter Lang.

Reimers, F. (1994). Education and structural adjustment in Latin America and Sub-Saharan Africa. *International Journal of Educational Development, 14*, 119–129.

Reinicke, W. H. (1998). *Global public policy: Governing without government?* Washington, DC: Brookings Institution.

Resnik, J. (2006). International organizations, the "education-economic growth" black box, and the development of world education culture. *Comparative Education Review, 50*, 173–195.

Rhodes, R. A. W. (1997). *Understanding governance: Policy networks, governance, reflexivity, and accountability*. Buckingham, UK: Open University Press.

Rhoten, D. (2000). Education decentralization in Argentina: A "global-local conditions of possibility" approach to state, market and society change. *Journal of Education Policy, 15*, 593–619.

Rinne, R., Kallo, J., & Hokka, S. (2004). Too eager to comply? OECD education policies and the Finish response. *European Educational Research Journal, 3*, 454–485.

Risse, T., Ropp, S. C., & Sikkink, K. (Eds.). (1999). *The power of human *rights: International norms and domestic change*. Cambridge, UK: Cambridge University Press.

Rizvi, F., Lingard, B., & Lavia, J. (2006). Postcolonialism and education: Negotiating a contested terrain. *Pedagogy, Culture and Society 14*, 249–262.

Robertson, S. L. (2007a). *Regionalism, "Europe/Asia" and higher education*. Retrieved June 12, 2007, from http://www.bris.ac.uk/education/people/academicStaff/edslr/publications/16slr/

Robertson, S. L. (2007b). Globalisation, rescaling, national education systems and citizenship regimes. In K. Roth & N. Burbules (Eds.), *Citizenship education in national, trans-national and global contexts* (pp. 136–150). Rotterdam, The Netherlands: Sense.

Robertson, S. L., Bonal, X., & Dale, R. (2002). GATS and the education service industry, the politics of scale and global reterritorialisation. *Comparative Education Review, 46*, 472–496.

Robertson, S. L., & Dale, R. (2006). *Changing geographies of power in education: The politics of rescaling and its contradictions*. Retrieved May 5, 2008, from http://www.bris.ac.uk/education/people/academicStaff/edslr/publications/03slr/

Robeyns, I. (2006). Three models of education: Rights, capabilities and human capital. *Theory and Research in Education, 4*, 69–84.

Rodrik, D. (1997). *Has globalization gone too far?* Washington, DC: Institute for International Economics.

Rose, P. (2003). *The education fast track initiative: A global campaign for education review*. London: Action Aid and the Global Campaign for Education.

Ruggie, J. G. (1982). International regimes, transactions, and change: Embedded liberalism in the postwar economic order. *International Organization, 36*(2), 379–415.

Ruggie, J. G. (1993). *Multilateralism matters: The theory and practice of an institutional form*. New York: Columbia University Press.

Ruggie, J. G. (1994). At home abroad, abroad at home: International liberalisation and domestic stability in the new world economy. *Millennium: Journal of International Studies, 24*, 507–526.

Ruggie, J. G. (1998a). *Constructing the world polity: Essays on international institutionalization*. New York: Routledge.

Ruggie, J. G. (1998b). What makes the world hang together? Neoutilitarianism and the social constructivist challenge. *International Organization, 52*(4), 855–885.

Ruggie, J. G. (2004). Reconstituting the global public domain – issues, actors, and practices. *European Journal of International Relations, 10*(4), 499–531.

Sabatier, P. A. (Ed.). (2007). *Theories of policy process* (2nd ed.). Boulder, CO: Westview Press.

Sack, R. (1986). UNESCO: From inherent contradictions to open crisis. *Comparative Education Review, 30*, 112–119.

Samoff, J. (1993). The reconstruction of schooling in Africa. *Comparative Education Review, 37*, 181–222.

Samoff, J. (1996). Which priorities and strategies for education? *International Journal of Educational Development, 16*, 249–271.

Samoff, J. (1999). Institutionalizing international influence. In R. F. Arnove & C. A. Torres (Eds.), *Comparative education: The dialectic of the global and the local* (pp. 51–89). Lanham, MD: Rowan & Littlefield.

Samoff, J., & Stromquist, N. P. (2001). Managing knowledge and storing wisdom? New forms of foreign aid? *Development and Change, 32*, 631–656.

Sauvé, P. (2002). Trade, education and the GATS: What's in, what's out, what's all the fuss about? *Higher Education Management and Policy, 14*(3), 47–76.

Scherrer, C. (2005). GATS: Long-term strategy for the commodification of education. *Review of International Political Economy, 12*, 484–510.

Scholte, J. A. (2005). Civil society and democratically accountable global governance. In D. Held & M. Koenig-Archibugi (Eds.), *Global governance and public accountability* (pp. 87–109). Malden, MA: Blackwell.

Schriewer, J. (2000). Comparative education methodology in transition: Towards a science of complexity? In J. Schriewer (Ed.), *Discourse formation in comparative education* (pp. 3–52). Berlin, Germany: Peter Lang.

Schuetze, H. G. (2006). International concepts and agendas of lifelong learning. *Compare, 36*, 289–306.

Schuetze, H. G., & Casey, C. (2006). Models and meanings of lifelong learning: Progress and barriers on the road to a learning society. *Compare, 36*, 279–287.

Schugurensky, D., & Davidson-Harden, A. (2003). From Cordoba to Washington: WTO/GATS and Latin American education. *Globalisation, Societies and Education, 1*, 321–357.

Sewell, J. P. (1975). *UNESCO and world politics: Engaging in international relations*. Princeton, NJ: Princeton University Press.

Silova, I., & Steiner-Khamsi, G. (Eds.). (2008). *How NGOs react: Globalization and education reform in the Caucasus, Central Asia and Mongolia*. Bloomfield, CT: Kumarian Press.

Sidhu, R. (2007). GATS and the new developmentalism: Governing transnational education. *Comparative Education Review, 51*, 203–228.

Simmons, B., & Elkins, Z. (2004). The globalization of liberalization: Policy diffusion in the international political economy. *American Political Science Review, 98*, 171–189.

Slaughter, A.-M. (2004). *A new world order*. Princeton, NJ: Princeton University Press.

Slaughter, A.-M. (2005a). Disaggregated sovereignty: Towards the public accountability of global government networks. In D. Held & M. Koenig-Archibugi (Eds.), *Global governance and public accountability* (pp. 35–66). Malden, MA: Blackwell.

Slaughter, A.-M. (2005b). Governing the global economy through government networks. In F. Kratochwil & E. D. Mansfield (Eds.), *International organization and global governance: A reader* (2nd ed., pp. 124–140). New York: Pearson Longman.

Smith, J., Chatfield, C., & Pagnucco, R. (Eds.). (1997). Transnational social movements and global politics: Solidarity beyond the state. Syracuse, NY: Syracuse University Press.

Smith, T. M., & Baker, D. P. (2001). Worldwide growth and institutionalization of statistical indicators for education policy making. *Peabody Journal of Education, 76*(3&4), 141–152.

Smouts, M. C. (1998). The proper use of governance in international relations. *International Social Science Journal, 50*(155), 81–89.

Soysal, Y. N. (2002). Locating Europe. *European Societies, 4*(3), 265–284.

Sperling, G. B. (2001). Toward universal education: Making a promise and keeping it. *Foreign Affairs, 80*(5), 7–13.

Spring, J. H. (2000). *The universal right to education: Justification, definition and guidelines*. Mahwah, NJ: Erlbaum.

Steiner-Khamsi, G. (Ed.). (2004). *The global politics of educational borrowing and lending*. New York: Teacher's College Press.

Steiner-Khamsi, G. (2003). The politics of league tables. *Journal of Social Science Education*. Retrieved March 5, 2008, from http://www.jsse.org/2003-1/tables_khamsi.htm

Steiner-Khamsi, G. (2006). The economics of policy borrowing and lending: A study of late adopters. *Oxford Review of Education, 32*, 665–678.

Suárez, D. (2007). Education professionals and the construction of human rights education. *Comparative Education Review, 51*, 48–70.

Tarrow, S. G. (2005). *The new transnational activism*. Cambridge, UK: Cambridge University Press.

Teferra, D. (2005). The Bologna Process: The experience—and challenges—for Africa. Paper presented at the Third Conference on Knowledge and Politics. Retrieved June 10, 2007, from http://ugle.svf.uib.no/svfweb1/filer/1359.pdf

Tomasevski, K. (2003). *Education denied: Costs and remedies*. London: Zed Books.

Tomasevski, K. (2005). Has the right to education a future within the United Nations? A behind-the-scenes account by the Special Rapporteur on the Right to Education 1998–2004. *Human Rights Law Review, 5*, 205–237.

Torres, R. M. (2002). Lifelong learning in the North, Education for All in the South. In C. Mendel-Añonuevo (Ed.), *Integrating lifelong learning perspectives* (pp. 3–12). Hamburg, Germany: UNESCO Institute for Education.

UNESCO. (1945). *Constitution of the United Nations Educational,*

Scientific, and Cultural Organization. Retrieved March 1, 2008, from http://portal.unesco.org/ci/en/ev.php-URL_ID=5288&URL_DO=DO_TOPIC&URL_SECTION=201.html

UNESCO. (1997). *International Standard Classification of Education ISCE97* [Electronic version]. Paris: Author.

UNESCO. (2005). *Global Monitoring Report 2006.* Paris: Author.

UNESCO. (2006). *Global Action Plan: Improving support to countries in achieving EFA Goals* (Edition of 10 July 2006). Paris: Author.

United Nations. (1945). *Charter of the United Nations.* Retrieved March 1, 2008, from http://www.un.org/aboutun/charter/

United Nations. (1948). *Universal Declaration of Human Rights.* Retrieved March 1, 2008, from http://www.un.org/Overview/rights.html

United Nations Millennium Project. (2005). *Toward universal primary education: Investments, incentives and institutions. Report from the Task Force on Education and Gender Equality* [Electronic version]. London: Earthscan and the UN Millennium Project.

Verger, A. (2008). Measuring educational liberalization. A global analysis of GATS *Globalisation, Societies and Education, 6*(1), 13–31.

Verger, A., & Bonal, X. (2006). Against GATS: The sense of a global struggle. *Journal of Critical Education Policy Studies, 4.* Retrieved January 16, 2007, from http://www.jceps.com/index.php?pageID=article&articleID=55

Vlk, A., Westerheijden, D., & van der Wende, M. (2008). GATS and the steering capacity of a nation state in higher education: Case studies of the Czech Republic and the Netherlands: *Globalisation, Societies and Education, 6*(1), 33–54.

Weiler, H. (1983). *Aid for Education: The political economy of international cooperation in educational development* (International Development Research Centre Manuscript Report No. MR84e). Ottawa, Canada: International Development Research Center (IDRC).

Welmond, M. (2002). Globalization viewed from the periphery: The dynamics of teacher identity in the Republic of Benin. *Comparative Education Review, 46,* 37–65.

Williamson, J. (1993). Democracy and the Washington Consensus. *World Development, 21,* 1329–1336.

World Bank. (1988). *Education in sub-Saharan Africa: Policies for adjustment, revitalisation, and expansion.* Washington, DC: Author.

World Bank. (1995). *Priorities and strategies for education: A World Bank review.* Washington, DC: Author.

World Bank. (2005a). *Education sector strategy update: Achieving Education for All, broadening our perspective, maximizing our effectiveness.* Washington DC: IBRD.

World Bank. (2005b). *Reshaping the future: Education and post-conflict reconstruction.* Washington, DC: Author.

World Federation of Education Associations. (1923, July). *World conference on education.* Proceedings held under the auspices of the National Education Association of the United States, San Francisco, CA.

Ziguras, C., McBurnie, G., & Reinke, L. (2003). Hardly neutral players: Australia's role in liberalising trade in education services. *Globalisation, Societies and Education, 1,* 359–374.

57

New Approaches to Understanding Federal Involvement in Education

Lora Cohen-Vogel
Florida State University

Michael K. McLendon
Vanderbilt University

The influence of the federal government in education has never been greater. In the K-12 system, federal law now requires states to develop and administer proficiency tests to all students in grades three through eight, mandates that all students be taught by a qualified teacher, and raises the stakes—for states, districts, and schools—for failure to demonstrate steady progress towards 100% student proficiency. In higher education, new pressures at the national level for increased "accountability" have fueled recent national debates over so-called student-unit records, new accreditation approaches, college affordability and calls from the federal level for rigorous assessments of college student learning. In its final report in late 2006, U.S. Secretary of Education Margaret Spellings' Commission on the Future of Higher Education characterized American universities as "increasingly risk-averse, at times self-satisfied, and unduly expensive" (Commission on the Future of Higher Education, 2006). The creation of the high-profile commission itself symbolized for many a growing willingness by national authorities to intervene in areas long considered the exclusive domain of states and of campuses.

Preoccupied with (important) questions about the effects and outcomes of federal policy, educational researchers have largely failed to consider equally-important questions about the escalating influence of the federal government in education. As a result, our understanding of the factors that spur and dampen educational policy reform by federal officials is incomplete. What conditions lead the federal government to undertake major policy reforms in education? Do policy reforms come about gradually or through "sudden bursts" and "open windows"? Do recent federal educational initiatives in the K-12 and higher education arenas represent revolutionary change or incremental "tinkering"? More generally, what explains policy stasis and change in education? Educational researchers, focused on policy analysis, and political scientists, with their emphasis on health and social welfare policies, have paid too little systematic attention to

these questions and to building, testing, and refining theories that explain federal education policy reform (Hochschild, 2004; McGuinn, 2006; McGuire, 2004).

As far back as 1994, Sroufe problematized what he saw as "the virtual abandonment of politics in favor of policy studies" (p. 87) in educational research and studies of federal education programs in particular. The singular policy focus, he argued, "makes little contribution to the problem of explanation or prediction, which is generally considered a desirable aspect of scientific endeavors" (p. 79). He urged scholars to work toward recombining policy and politics into a new synthesis, and cited Sundquist's 1968 analysis of the federal Elementary and Secondary Education Act as a model. Tracing the development of ESEA over a decade, Sundquist explored the problems the legislation addressed, the policy effects it achieved, and the political outcomes it produced (e.g., ideological shifts; congressional reforms). With Sundquist as a guide, Sroufe encouraged education policy scholars to build in-depth, longitudinal case studies illuminated by rich conceptual approaches to explain policy outcomes in the context of political phenomena: "While it is clearly a moral responsibility to pay attention to policy concerns (e.g., equity issues) at any point in time, it is equally imperative for scholars to seek to explain why such policies exist and under what circumstances they might be changed" (p. 79). But, in the ensuing fourteen years, relatively little has changed.

By contrast, over this same period, political scientists have continued—even rejuvenated—their long debate over the nature of the American political system and the amenability of the federal government to major policy reform (McGuinn, 2006). This attention among political scientists has been motivated by numerous factors, including a growing awareness of the limitations inherent in existing theories of policy making, a revival in the study of political institutions and of the dynamics leading to institutional change, and a resurgent interest in the study of public policy, generally (March & Olsen, 1989; McLendon & Cohen-Vogel, 2008; Olsen, 2001; Sabatier, 1999a,b; Stimson, MacKuen, & Erikson, 1995). Scholarly attention among political scientists has led to the development and elaboration of conceptual approaches, approaches that hold promise for shoring up studies of federal involvement in education and the education policy literature more generally.

The approaches can be organized into three schools of thought.[1] The first school—the *stasis school*—stresses the intractability of the American political system. Numerous inertial forces—a political culture that emphasizes local control, powerful and vested interests, and institutional configurations, among them—make the policy-making process and its outputs (i.e., policies) highly stable and path dependent (Berry, 1989; Cuban, 1990; Downs, 1967; Hayes, 2001; Pierson, 2000; Sabatier & Jenkins-Smith, 1999; Tyack & Cuban, 1995). Second, the *dynamic school*, underscores the openness and adaptability of our system of government. Electoral competition and exogenous forces (e.g., hurricanes, school shootings) ensure that extant policies will be frequently challenged and that politicians will forward their own ideas for reform (Berry & Baybeck, 2005; Bailey & Rom, 2004; Cohen-Vogel & Ingle, in press; Cohen-Vogel, Ingle, Albee, & Spence, 2008; Dye, 1990; Mayhew, 1974; Schattschneider, 1975; Stimson et al., 1995; Walker, 1969). Most recently, what we will call the *synthetic school* draws upon and integrates approaches from both the stasis and dynamic schools to argue that the national policy-making process is responsive to reform pressures at certain moments on certain issues and unresponsive at others; it is, in other words, time- and context-sensitive (Beck, Katz, & Tucker, 1998; Pierson, 2000, 2004). Table 57.1 displays the conceptual approaches, unifying premises, and major constructs that characterize these three distinct schools of thought.

In the remainder of the chapter, we will describe three synthetic approaches from the political science literature—namely, the Multiple Streams approach (MS; Kingdon, 1984, 1995), the Punctuated Equilibrium approach (PE; Baumgartner & Jones, 1991, 1993; True, Jones, & Baum-

gartner, 1999), and the Policy Regimes approach (PR; Skowronek, 1993)—and analyze the ways these approaches can help answer some persistent questions about the role of the federal government in education. For each framework, we identify its origins, delineate its defining elements, and discuss the major works that have utilized or refined the approach. At the end of each section, we discuss opportunities for the frameworks' application and elaboration in future research on federal education policy. We pose key research questions that connect the study of federal education reforms to larger bands of work in the political science literature on policy development in the United States. Additionally, we identify the data and methodologies through which the questions might be addressed. Before doing so, however, we briefly discuss the limited body of recent work on federal education politics and the policies they reveal.

Recent Titles on Federal Involvement in Education Despite ongoing exhortations by politics of education scholars for theoretically rich examinations of policy phenomena (M. Kirst, personal communication, 1993; Kirst, 2006; Crowson et al., 2003), the recent literature on federal education policy focuses primarily on description and/or outcome analysis, nearly all of it exclusively on the No Child Left Behind Act of 2001, President Bush's signature K-12 education law. Scott Abernathy's book, *No Child Left Behind and the Public Schools* (2007), for example, argues that the overarching intent of the law to increase student performance and close the achievement gap will not be fulfilled until the strategies for doing so are rethought. Urging policy makers and researchers alike to recognize the resource inequities with which children come to school, Abernathy writes that "Under NCLB, all of the factors that affect measured achievement but lie beyond a school's control will largely determine that school's success or failure." Rather than "trying to extract this information [about educational quality] from student test scores" (p. 23), he suggests that assessment and accountability systems incorporate "process indicators." Specifically, he calls for detailed surveys of teachers, parents, and students at the individual school level

TABLE 57.1
Understanding the Evolution of Federal Education Policy in the U.S.: Three Schools of Thought

	Schools of Thought		
	Stasis	**Dynamic**	**Synthetic**
Conceptual Approaches	Fragmentation; Incrementalism; Institutionalism; Path Dependency	Electoral Competition; Public Opinion; Policy Innovation Diffusion; Crisis–Response	Multiple Streams; Punctuated Equilibrium; Policy Regimes
Unifying Premise	The American political system possesses inertial forces that uphold the status quo, make policies highly stable, and constrain major policy change	Crises and competition for votes and among governmental units make the American political system very responsive to changing public demands	Because space and time matter for policy development, the American political system is capable of both stasis and major reform
Major Constructs	Multiple veto points; closed system; iron triangles; bureaucratic inertia; institutional "stickiness"; limited policy options; organized beneficiaries	Mobilization of public pressure; open system; expanding "scope of conflict"; bellwether status; policy emulation; exogenous shocks	Open windows; policy venues; policy images; (dis)equilibrium; non-incremental bursts; shifting coalitions; fluctuating power centers

to measure leadership quality; the safety and orderliness of the school environment; the commitment to high standards; and parent involvement. A crowd of other evaluations and critiques of the federal law have also been published (see, e.g., Center on Education Policy's series, 2006).

Drawing primarily from his lived experiences as an official in the United States Department of Education and congressional advisor, in a second example, Christopher Cross (2004), takes an historical evolutionary approach to study the federal government's role in education since the mid-20th century. In nine chapters that align with the administrations of Harry S. Truman through George W. Bush, Cross chronicles federal policy around schools and schooling from the 1940s and 50s when attempts to make education a federal issue were met with loud resistance to the first decade of the 21st century and a U.S. president who called education reform his number one domestic achievement. Cross focuses on the contributions of key political figures and events (e.g., *Brown v. Board* decision; Sputnik; the publication of *A Nation at Risk*) in accounting for the shift. Similarly, a shorter manuscript by the Center on Education Policy (1999) in Washington, DC, provides a historical look at federal involvement over time, recording the key federal programs and policies beginning with the Northwest Ordinance of 1787 encouraging new western territories to establish schools. In it, Jack Jennings and associates argue that an analysis of these policies illustrates four major reasons that the federal government has become involved in education: to promote democracy, to ensure equality of educational opportunity, to enhance national productivity, and to strengthen national defense.

In examining the details of congressional legislation over time, a few recent studies have focused on American educational governance before and after NCLB. Contrasting the Bush administration's claim that NCLB redefined federal involvement in education, Cohen-Vogel (2005), Kaestle (2006), and McDonnell (2005) argue that the sixth reauthorization of the Elementary and Secondary Education Act does not as much signal a shift in the federal role as much as a step in a march that commenced a decade earlier.

Among recent studies of federal education politics, three stand out for their linkages to the broader literatures in political science and policy studies. First, drawing on interviews with congressional aides and interest group members during the reauthorization process that would result in NCLB, DeBray-Pelot (2007) applies Kingdon's Multiple Streams model of agenda setting and alternative specification to explain the consideration but ultimate failure of two private school voucher proposals during the 106th and 107th Congresses. In summarizing Kingdon, she writes that when the "political stream," composed of election results, ideological shifts, swings in public opinion, and related factors, converge with the "policy stream," a policy "window" for adoption is said to open. In applying the framework to the legislative activities of the two successive Congresses, DeBray-Pelot finds that "the window for approving a limited privatization measure in Title 1

finally opened in 2001, nearly 20 years after the Reagan administration had proposed such measures" (p. 932). She further demonstrates that the "problem" to which the policy solution—privatization—was tied was the failure of billions of dollars in compensatory federal aid to improve the achievement of economically disadvantaged students. According to DeBray-Pelot, however, "the Kingdon model... does not explain why these two Republican-dominated Congresses voted down private school vouchers as part of sanctions in Title 1, and did so by a larger margin in the 107th than the 106th" (p. 933). Instead, she proposes an electoral explanation wherein congressional Republicans perceived that a vote for vouchers was to take a risk with their mostly suburban constituents who were largely content with their neighborhood public schools. In a more detailed book on the topic, DeBray-Pelot (DeBray, 2006) demonstrates how shifting interest group politics and the demographic and ideological realignment of the Democratic and Republican parties over the past 20 years intersected to shape the substance of recent education policy proposals in Congress.

Second, Paul Manna's *School's In: Federalism and the National Education Agenda* (2006) uses a new view of federalism to frame his study of federal education policy and the emergence of NCLB, in particular. Whereas traditional models of federalism proposed that the preferences of those with more power tend to marginalize the preferences of those with less, Manna's "borrowing strength" model considers how government actors can share power for greater influence at crucial policy moments. Through the analysis of public opinion surveys, secondary databases, interviews with the DC policy elite, presidential speeches, and other documents, Manna shows that the passage of NCLB was possible only because policy entrepreneurs at the national level were able to borrow capacity—in the form of standards and assessments—from state governments. Careful to note that the process can work in reverse, wherein states can borrow strength from federal officials, Manna argues that policy change cannot be explained in simple top-down or bottom-up models and thus has been praised for its potential for theory-expansion (McDonnell, 2006; Robinson, 2007; Simon, 2007).

Finally, in *No Child Left Behind: The Transformation of Federal Education Policy, 1965–2005*, McGuinn (2006) argues that the emergence of the No Child Left Behind Act of 2001, which he contends signifies a major change in the federal government's involvement in education, is a story of policy regime destruction and reconstruction. Employing content analysis of federal legislation, media coverage, polling data, and the like, McGuinn measures changes in public opinion and in the rules of electoral competition to track the gradual shift from an "equity regime" to an "accountability regime" over four decades. According to McGuinn, the policy paradigm, policy-making arrangement, and power alignment at the center of the Elementary and Secondary Education Act of 1965 shaped the foundation for an equity policy regime that would persist for two decades—well into the 1980s. During that time, power over federal education policy making was vested in a few groups, with little public input—conditions that thwarted efforts to substantially expand or reform the federal role. During the late 1980s and 1990s, however, public pressures began to mount for a larger federal role in response to evidence that the K-12 public school system was in trouble and calculations by politicians of both parties to use the issue for electoral gain. Eventually, as both citizens and politicians pressed for federal solutions to what was perceived as a broken system, powerful interest groups on the left (i.e., unions) and right (i.e., religious groups) that opposed an expanded federal role were gradually pushed aside. McGuinn uses his findings to maintain that policy change cannot be understood in punctuated equilibrium terms wherein longstanding policy monopolies are "rapidly punctured and replaced in a single decision stroke" (p. 209). Instead, he argues, that "federal education policy demonstrates how the *gradual* shifting of ideas, interests, and institutions in a policy area and their interaction with changes in the broader political context over time ultimately brings about major reform" (p. 209).

Together, the DeBray, Manna, and McGuinn studies offer models of promising research for those who study educational politics and policy, remind readers of the value of understanding the political dimensions behind the development and implementation of federal reform programs, and showcase the potential for politics of education scholars to contribute to theory-building and elaboration in policy arenas beyond education. At the same time that these three studies represent promising models of research, they also evoke new questions about what some characterize as an "evolving," "sweeping," even "revolutionary" expansion of the federal government's involvement in education: When, if ever, is Kingdon's streams model of policy making sufficient for the adoption of major education reforms by Congress? When do government actors invest in borrowing strength, rather than their own capacity-building? "What distinguishes successful attempts at borrowing strength from unsuccessful attempts?" (Robinson, 2007, p. 167). How preciously does regime change happen? Are there instances when regime change does not lead to policy change? Finally, how do policy streams, strength borrowing, and policy regimes help explain policy contraction (as opposed to policy change)? That is to say, when, if ever, will the federal government's involvement in education begin to contract, and why?

Synthetic Perspectives on Federal Transitions in Federal Education Policy

Answers to these and other questions require an increased focus among education policy researchers on federal involvement in pre-K, K-12, and higher education. It is our contention that education policy scholars should build new databases of legislative and executive policy activity (e.g., bills, laws, regulations) in education, develop deep and, where possible, longitudinal case studies of federal initia-

tives (e.g., choice, national tests), and that both quantitative and qualitative research be illuminated by theory-rich approaches that have been emblematic of much of the recent political science literature. Moreover, we believe that the most promising frameworks to explain policy in the context of political phenomena are those we have earlier called "synthetic."

The synthetic school of political thought conceives of the American political system as neither an inherently closed nor open system. Instead, it posits that reform ideas interact with the broader political environment to either condition change or reinforce stasis. Stated differently, the school seeks to explain how the political system can promote both long-term policy inertia (e.g., categorical school funding schemes) and abrupt shifts in course (e.g., performance benchmarks for all students). Scholars subscribing to the perspective suggest that the key to understanding federal policy is in the transitions between stasis and change, an orientation that requires study across space and time. Three conceptual approaches from the political science literature meet the requirements and describe the transitions as a function of converging streams, punctuated equilibrium, and gradual regime change, respectively. There are other frameworks that could arguably be described as synthetic (e.g., Moe's (1990) politics of structural choice frame). Yet, we focus on these three policy frameworks because of the prominence they have achieved in the larger political science and public policy literatures. All three have been the subject of application and elaboration over the past two decades, and are included in recent surveys of contemporary theories of the public policy process (e.g., Dodd & Jillson, 1994; John, 1998; Sabatier, 2007). In a sense, these frameworks have become "standards" in the literature on American public policy making (McLendon, 2003b). Too infrequently, however, have the frameworks been deployed by policy scholars in K-12 education and higher education.

Multiple Streams Framework Our first model of the transitions from stasis to reform in federal education policy—Kingdon's (1984, 1994, 1995) so-called Multiple Streams approach—remains one of the most cited theories of policy formation, if also one of its least systematically applied. At the heart of the MS^2 perspective lies an interest in explaining *agenda change*—how and why some issues move onto and up the decision agenda of government, while others do not. In Kingdon's words: "How do subjects come to officials' attention? How are the alternatives from which they choose generated? How is the governmental agenda set? Why does an idea's time come when it does" (1995, p. xi)? Through case studies of federal policy making in the areas of transportation and health and an impressive panel-design consisting of 247 interviews with policy makers over a 4-year period, Kingdon developed an explanation of policy change that accommodated some elements of rationalism and incrementalism, while rejecting as inadequate the traditional problem-solving and incremental models of policy formation.

The federal government, according to MS thinking, can be viewed as an arena through which three "streams" of separate, simultaneous activity surge. The *problem stream* consists of those conditions which policy makers have chosen to interpret as problems. The *policy stream* consists of the various "solutions" developed by specialists in the countless policy communities that surround and engulf the nation's capitol. The *politics stream* consists of developments involving macro political conditions: the public mood, interest group politics, and turnover in the administrative and legislative branches. These streams—of problems, policies, and politics—flow, Kingdon asserts, through the federal governmental system largely independent of one another and each according to its own set of internal dynamics. As a result, change within one stream may occur independently of change in other streams, a principal assumption of the MS model.

Turning first to the problem stream, Kingdon maintains that conditions become defined as *problems* principally due to the ways in which officials learn about conditions and the ways in which conditions become defined. Officials tend to convert conditions into problems in three ways: conditions that violate important values can become perceived as problems, conditions can become problems via comparison with relevant units (e.g., what a neighboring unit may have done), and, conditions can become problems through their reclassification into one or another class of condition (e.g., is a waterway-usage proposal a question of transportation, of water resource management, or something else).

The process of solution generation (the policy stream), according to Kingdon (1995), is not unlike that of biological natural selection. Specialists in policy communities may experiment with many ideas over time. These ideas float in and around government in a sort of "policy primeval soup," combining, recombining, and mutating. Here one finds incrementalism at work, in the manner in which specialists within particular policy communities develop solutions over time. In Kingdon's conception, one also finds a degree of rationalism at work inasmuch as policy makers use certain decision criteria, such as technical feasibility, value congruence, and the anticipation of future constraints, in winnowing ("selecting out") some ideas for survival and others for extinction.

In discussing the third stream (the politics stream), Kingdon describes the forces that "soften-up" the political system and make it possible for an issue to move onto the agenda. These developments may be both predictable (as in the cyclical turn-over among officeholders that results from regularized elections) and unforeseen (as in the case of political scandal, sudden shifts in public opinion, or economic downturn). Regardless, interest groups play a crucial role in mobilizing over time support for, and opposition to, certain policy ideas.

In the MS formulation, an issue gains traction on the policy agenda only when the three separate streams of activity *couple* with a choice opportunity. This coupling of streams constitutes the single-most important feature of the

model. Stream-convergence may occur when a "window of opportunity" opens, allowing policy entrepreneurs brief moments in time to push attention towards their pet problems or to push their pet solutions. According to Kingdon (1995), entrepreneurs "lie in wait in and around government with their solutions [already] in hand, waiting for problems to float by to which they can attach their solutions, waiting for a development in the political stream they can use to their advantage" (p. 165). Although the forces that guide activity within the streams possess a discernable pattern, one finds in the process of stream convergence a certain arbitrary quality. Kingdon paraphrases Cohen, March, and Olsen (1972) in portraying, counter-intuitively, the agenda setting process as one whereby choices look for issues, problems look for decision situations in which they can be aired, solutions look for problems to which they might be the answer, and politicians look for pet problems or policies by which they might advance their careers.

Kingdon's framework diverges markedly with older conceptions of policy formation rooted in equilibrium and stasis. For example, whereas the "muddling" of policy *incrementalism* (Lindblom, 1965) emphasizes marginal adjustments, Kingdon's model conceives an environment in which policy trajectories can change rapidly and in unpredictable-seeming ways. When streams converge, an issue may suddenly be seen to "take off," becoming the hot topic of the day (Kingdon, 1994, p. 84).[3]

Many of the ideas Kingdon introduced (e.g., policy entrepreneurs, windows of opportunity) have both influenced the development of other contemporary theories of policy making and been the subject of serious and sustained analytic examination. Studies have applied the model to examine policy decisions in the domains of healthcare, the environment, and national defense (e.g., Baird, 1998; Blaukenau, 2001; Durant & Diehl, 1989; Kamieniecki, 2000; Kawar, 1989; Oliver, 1991). Others have recently begun to use it to study K-12 and higher education policy (e.g., DeBray-Pelot, 2007; Larson, 2004; Leslie & Berdahl, 2006; McDermott, 2005; McLendon, 2003a; Mills, 2007; Ness, 2005; Portz, 1996; Protopsaltis, 2004; Stout & Stevens, 2000; Van Der Slik, 1999). The bulk of this work has examined the suitability of MS in the states, rather than at the federal level. The research designs of these studies typically consist of single-case studies within a particular state or, less frequently, multiple-case studies across states. In the main, these works have tended to find strong support for the MS framework.

Among the few studies that have reflected thoughtfully on the applicability of the MS perspective to higher-education policy phenomena at the federal level are two essays by Hearn (1993, 2001). Hearn portrayed as "paradoxical" the remarkable growth in federal student aid programs during the 1980s and 1990s in the face of a welter of problematic program characteristics. He wondered what might account for increased growth in federal support of these programs despite the fact these policies lacked many of the attributes assumed, under rationalist models of policy development, to be prerequisites for such growth: philosophical coherence, programmatic clarity and distinctiveness, access to managerially needed information, a strong and supportive interest-group coalition, a beneficent resource environment, and a robust client base (2001, p. 317). Having explored several competing explanations for the federal-aid paradox at the heart of his chapter, Hearn observed that the failure of reform and cutback efforts may be traced to the "nonlinear, anarchic qualities of federal policy making in education" (Hearn, 1993, p. 136)—the author settles, in other words, on the possibility of an organized-anarchy explanation for the phenomenon that closely resembles Kingdon's MS model. To our knowledge, no subsequent efforts have yet undertaken systematic analysis of federal higher-education policy along the lines Hearn's essay proposed.

Federal Education Reform Through a Multiple-Streams Lens The MS framework provides scholars of federal education reform a counter-intuitive theoretical perspective on policy making that challenges traditional views of federal involvement as inherently stable and preconditioned for incremental rather than sweeping change. The MS framework suggests that reform ideas emerge on the federal policy agenda, neither as a function of the problem-solving efforts of technically-rational policy actors, nor as the result of the steady and seemingly irresistible momentum of issue evolution. Instead, it suggests that major federal reforms can be characterized by an "irrational" sequence of problem-identification and solution-generation: ambivalences toward education and the goals of federal education policy may abound, policy solutions may long precede the problems to which they become publicly attached, and, federal education reform may suddenly emerge when policy entrepreneurs recognize politically propitious moments at which to couple their pet solutions with previously unrelated public problems.

Numerous questions for both the study of federal education reforms and the literature on policy making generally could frame future research using a MS approach. To what extent do proposals to alter federal involvement in education develop independently—indeed, in advance—of the "problems" for which proponents later claim these solutions may be the "answer?" What are the criteria that condition specialists' development of ideas within particular policy communities over time? What is the nature of the "policy windows" whose brief openings may make possible the coupling of problems, solutions, and politics in ways that make federal school accountability initiatives ripe for passage? What and who open these windows, under what sets of conditions, and for what reasons? What is the nature of the policy entrepreneurism that Kingdon's framework maintains must precede and attend the opening and maintenance of these windows? How does the specific content of federal education proposals (e.g., policies bearing regulatory, distributive, or redistributive elements) influence their amenability to coupling with certain kinds of problems? Do reforms that increase sanctions for school performance, for

instance, tend to be coupled with specific kinds of federal problems (e.g., global competitiveness)?

Most studies utilizing the MS framework have typically relied on case-study methods building on large numbers of interviews and historical documents. Interviewing hundreds or, even dozens, of policy makers poses notable challenges both in terms of access to participants and of concerns about the validity of data and the conclusions drawn from them. What is more, because elements of loose-coupling may be at work, the boundaries among policy domains, episodes, issues, and actors over time may appear indistinct, thus frustrating the efforts of the case-method researcher in answering a foundational design question: what are the precise parameters of the case? These conditions may compel the analyst to collect vast amounts of interview and archival data as s/he attempts to triangulate competing or incomplete understandings in search of a clear explanatory narrative. A sample of the research questions the frameworks invite as well as the data sources for answering these questions may be found in Table 57.2.

Future research applying the MS lens to federal education policy reform would profit from various improvements in methodology. First, more sophisticated sampling approaches are warranted. Scholars who deploy case methods at the federal level often focus primarily on a single case. This approach enjoys many advantages and can yield valuable perspective. Important insights, however, can also be gained by examining multiple cases at once. Such an approach affords the advantage of "controlling" for certain differences in governmental design, while permitting the analyst to assess how changing contextual conditions may influence reform trajectories. For example, pursuing this design would allow one to examine the dynamics of policy windows under consistently *similar* structural conditions (legal-structural arrangements), but meaningfully *dissimilar* contextual ones (e.g., across different periods in political control of institutions, different environmental influences, and different issue episodes). The finding that MS holds up well as an explanatory lens across these varied conditions could lend stronger support than the results obtained from only a single case.

Second, future applications of the MS model might be improved with the use of more comprehensive data-collection efforts, including surveys, interviews with policy elites, and archival analysis. Integrating the case study approach with survey data drawn from elected officials, staffers, issue specialists, non-governmental education-issue advocates, and others would permit analysts to better gauge the extent to which the core elements in Kingdon's conceptualizing (e.g., independent policy streams, windows, and entrepreneurs) hold in the distinctive context of federal policy making in the K-12 and higher education arenas.

A major archival resource for MS scholars conducting research at the national level is the *Policy Agendas Project*, a publicly-available archive housed at the University of Washington. The Web site (http://www.policyagendas. org/) provides archived historical data on the U.S. budget,

House, Senate, and joint-committee hearings of the U.S. Congress, Executive Orders, Gallup Poll information, State of the Union addresses, Supreme Court cases, and data on public laws passed between 1948–1998. Additionally, the Library of Congress continues to support its Thomas project (http://thomas.loc.gov/), a comprehensive online source of bills introduced in the House and/or Senate beginning with the 101st Congress. The site also allows visitors to search the *Congressional Record*, the official account of all floor proceedings and debates of the U.S. Congress, reports from Senate, House and Joint/Conference Committees since the 104th Congress, and the United States Code. At the Web site of the Government Printing Office (http://www.gpoaccess.gov/index.html), visitors can view dockets of cases heard by the U.S. Supreme Court, read the oral arguments, and locate judicial opinions, read State of the Union addresses, and search proposed, pending, and final regulations and executive orders since 1994 in the *Federal Register*.

Punctuated Equilibrium Framework Punctuated equilibrium has become a widely recognized phrase since paleontologists Niles Eldredge and Stephen Jay Gould (1972) coined it as an alternative to the Darwinian model of phyletic gradualism that dominated evolutionary theory throughout much of the 20th century. In its original usage, the phrase characterized evolutionary change as one taking place over long periods of "stasis," in which species remain virtually unchanged, "punctuated" by relatively brief periods of intense change when new species are introduced, old ones become extinct, and existing ones experience sudden permutations. Whereas traditional views of evolution suggested a gradual and linear process of speciation in which ancestors and descendants are linked by a "long sequence of continuous, insensibly graded intermediate forms"

(Eldredge & Gould, 1972, p. 89), the fossil record reveals a pattern of interruptions in the process. Addressing this discrepancy, Eldredge and Gould's punctuated equilibrium notion thus characterized natural history as one of long periods of stability and gradualism, punctuated by rapid and transformative episodes of intense change.

By the 1980s, similar ideas had gained traction in political science, where analysts had begun elaborating on them in an effort to better explain the dynamics of change in American governmental systems.[4] In this context, the term *punctuated equilibrium* came to refer to a "sudden, transformative change in an otherwise stable system" (Kelly, 1994, p. 165). Baumgartner and Jones' (1991, 1993) PE theory emerged as the most comprehensive, well-developed and prominent application of this principle (Sabatier, 1999b). Drawing heavily on the case of civilian nuclear policy since World War II, Baumgartner and Jones (1991, 1993) argue that, when viewed over the long run, American public policy exhibits periods of "relative gridlock [equilibrium] interspersed by episodes of dramatic change [disequilibrium]," rather than the steady, predictable incremental-like tendencies conventionally attributed to it (1993, p. 10).[5]

Periods of *equilibrium* are those in which issues are captured by a subsystem of policy actors and issue experts and "policy monopolies" are established. Periods of *disequilibrium* occur when policy monopolies are challenged or overthrown and issues are forced into the macropolitical arena. What explains this process, the creation and destruction of policy monopolies? According to Baumgartner and Jones (1993), the answer lies in interactions between shifting policy *venues* and shifting policy *images*.

Baumgartner and Jones (1993) describe policy monopolies as associated strongly with a (a) "definable institutional structure" (a particular venue) in which advocacy

TABLE 57.2
Research Questions and Data Requirements Generated from the MS, PE, and PR Frameworks

	Synthetic Frameworks		
	Multiple-Streams	**Punctuated-Equilibrium**	**Policy Regimes**
Research Questions	To what extent do proposals to alter federal involvement in education develop in advance of the "problems" for which proponents later claim these solutions may be the "answer?"	What are the alternative policy venues through which education reformers seek to bypass existing policy monopolies?	What key actors and issue specialists are routinely part of the education policy regime at the federal level?
	Do the processes that attend solution generation in the education policy domain resemble those described by Kingdon in other domains?	Within the context of education policy change at the federal level, does Baumgartner and Jones' interpretation of the "mobilization of interest" hold up?	What are the alternative policy paradigms through which education reformers try to unseat existing policy regimes?
	What is the nature of "policy windows" whose brief openings may make possible the coupling of problems, solutions, and politics in ways that make federal school initiatives ripe for passage?	To what extent is equilibrium an accurate characterization of the policy history of K-12 education reform at the national level, where "reform" as of late has been the rule not the exception?	To what extent and in what ways do politicians and leaders from outside of government work to shape public opinion around federal fixes for education?
Selected Data	Interviews with policy elites; Observations; Survey responses; Federal legislation, bills, agency reports, and judicial papers	News articles; Press releases; Transcripts of Congressional committee hearings; Executive orders; Case summaries	Interviews with policy elites; Congressional voting records, media coverage, polling data, interest group memos, and Presidential papers

and conflict over the policy occurs and (b) a powerful supporting image (p. 7). Venues may include federal agencies, state and local authorities, interest groups and professional associations, the open market, and various other institutions. When such venues involve governments, they are referred to as policy subsystems. Subsystems dampen participation by "outsiders" because they tend to be dominated by small groups of issue specialists in the interest-groups community, in the government bureaucracy, and in congressional committees who operate out of the public eye. Second, policy monopolies tend to be associated with dominant supporting images—images so powerful that they produce only support among those involved or indifference by those not involved. While the establishment and maintenance of policy monopolies enable policy equilibria, destruction of these monopolies facilitates policy punctuations.

According to Baumgartner and Jones (1991), when issues move from the subsystem arena into the macropolitical arena large-scale policy change can occur. As noted, shifting policy venues and images help account for an issue's movement from the policy subsystem to the macropolitical arena. The "venue shopping" efforts of strategically minded political actors play a vital role in this process. By crafting new ways of understanding old problems, disempowered issue advocates "shop" for new venues in which different political actors and governmental institutions can claim jurisdiction over issues previously of little interest to them. In reformulating these images, advocates make the policies more amenable to previously-disinterested actors. As policy images become redefined over time, new participants become attracted to the emerging debate and newer venues surface as legitimate arenas for deliberation of the issue (True et al., 1999). This process is iterative and cyclical: "as venues change, images may change as well; as the image of a policy changes, venue changes [also] become more likely" (Baumgartner & Jones, 1991, p. 1046–1047). The net effect of these shifts in policy image and venue is the crumbling of existing monopolies of policy ownership, substantial bursts of new policy activity, and the subsequent return to a steady-state as those interests that previously were marginalized become institutionalized.

Over the past decade, PE has found application to a variety of political phenomena and substantive policy domains. The literature on PE's application to educational policy making is less robust than that to electoral politics (Kelly, 1994), budget setting (Breunig & Koske, 2005; Jordan, 2003; True, 2000), and environmental policy (Baumgartner & Jones, 1991, 1993; Repetto, 2006), but a growing body of work has emerged. Robinson (2004), for example, examined how PE theory might help explain the twin phenomena of "bureaucratization" and school budgetary change by comparing changes in instructional spending per pupil among schools facing different levels of bureaucracy. The PE model has rarely been applied to policy change in higher education, though Orr-Bement's (2002) application of the Baumgartner and Jones framework to study legislative decision making for higher education in the state of Washington serves as

one particularly rigorous undertaking. In a series of recent applications of the theory to K-12 education policy at the national level, Miskel and colleagues (Sims & Miskel, 2001, 2003) find strong support for a PE interpretation of child and adult literacy policies. These authors interpret their findings as lending support for one key tenet of PE: As policy images change over time, advocates will find new policy venues more suitable and, thus, the locus of policy activity within a given policy domain shifts accordingly. As with the MS framework, the number of such PE studies of similar rigor at the national level is few.

Federal Education Reform Through a Punctuated Equilibrium Lens   The PE perspective focuses the attention of scholars of federal education reform on the dynamics by which issues move from monopolistically controlled policy subsystems to the macropolitical arena, creating possibilities for dramatic education policy change. According to the framework, analyses of federal education policy trajectories over time should reveal long periods of stable, incremental change interrupted by bursts of lurching, large-scale change, followed again by stability and gradualism. The policy record should reveal a shift, prior to the policy punctuations, in both the prevailing imagery surrounding the particular education policy and the institutional assignment for the policy. These shifts in policy images and policy venues facilitate the punctuation. Thus, application of the PE framework to federal education reform requires researchers to focus on at least four interdependent concepts: the functioning of policy subsystems of issue specialists which routinely make education policy at the federal level, the ways that policy images contribute to the monopolistic control over education policy within a particular subsystem, policy entrepreneurs' strategic use of issue-redefinition to mobilize previously disinterested parties, leading to issue expansion, and, the "punctuation" that is alleged to occur when shifting images and venues permit macropolitical institutions to intervene into the education arena (McLendon, 2003b).

These four concepts give rise to a host of questions that future researchers may wish to pursue in applying the PE perspective to education reform at the national level. For instance, the existence of multiple policy venues is a foundational assumption of the PE framework, as those excluded from a monopoly must have other venues to which they may appeal. What are the alternative policy venues through which education reformers seek to bypass existing policy monopolies? Additionally, to what extent are the dynamics of issue redefinition and venue change truly interactive and simultaneous in nature; by contrast, does one set of processes tend to precede another, temporally? Within the context of education policy change at the federal level, does Baumgartner and Jones' (1991, 1993) interpretation of the "mobilization of interest" hold up? Does the mobilization of interests surrounding NCLB or the increasing federal push to make higher education more accountable stem from a mobilization of the previously disinterested, or did mobilization require "conversion" of those parties previously opposed to change? To what extent can *equilibrium*—a foundational concept for the PE perspective—be considered an accurate characterization of the policy history of K-12 education reform at the national level, where "reform" over the past 15 years seems to have been the rule, rather than the exception? What are the most effective strategies of issue redefinition that policy entrepreneurs employ to export education reform to new venues? How does venue shopping differ across the K-12 and the higher education arenas—arenas whose legal, financial, governance, and political contexts differ markedly?

The PE framework focuses heavily on shifting policy images over time. Fortunately, collecting, organizing, and coding trend data on media coverage of education reform (i.e., the conventional approach to appraising changes in policy image) has been eased over the past decade with the enhancement of electronic databases of newspapers with national circulation (e.g., the *New York Times, Los Angeles Times*, and *Washington Post*). The ProQuest Historical Newspapers™ digital archive, for example, offers full-text and full-image articles in the nation's leading newspapers dating back to the 18th century. The archive includes the complete collection of the *New York Times*, beginning with its first issue in 1851. New additions to the archive include the Black Newspapers Collection, providing access to the *New York Amsterdam News, Pittsburgh Courier, Los Angeles Sentinel*, and *Atlanta Daily World*. Many libraries also allow you to search the Readers' Guide Retrospective: 1890–1982 on WilsonWeb. The Retrospective indexes articles from over 375 leading magazines, many dating back to their inaugural issues. Moreover, a webpage created by the United States Department of Education, http://www.ed.gov/news/landing.jhtml, allows visitors to search official DOE press releases and speeches given by the Secretary of Education and other key DOE officials since 2001. There is also a link to an archive of speeches from previous administrations back through 1994.

Assessing change in policy venues might be captured in interviews with aides, advocates and the political elite, in conjunction with databases available on-line. The Advocacy and Public Policymaking Project is a data source that has been compiled by Frank Baumgartner and others at Pennsylvania State University. On this Web site (http://lobby.la.psu.edu), researchers will find case summaries and political resources across multiple domains, including education. The case summaries provide overviews that include background information, key proponents/opponents, arguments used, lobbying activities, venues of government decision making, among other information. For each case, the site also includes links to advocacy group statements, bills introduced in Congress, transcripts of House and Senate committee hearings, statements and press releases by members of Congress, and media coverage (print and television).

These data provide the necessary information for testing key tenets of the PE framework and for elaborating new conceptions distinctively tailored to studying federal education policy reform.

Policy Regime Framework The Policy Regime approach is the newest of the synthetic models, and grew out of the international relations literature (Dougherty & Pfaltzgraff, 1997; Kratochwil & Ruggie, 1997). Though the bulk of work has concentrated on international regimes, other political scientists have applied the regime model to urban (Stone, C., 1989), presidential (Skowronek, 1993), and regulatory (Harris & Milkis, 1996) policy making in the United States. Policy regimes are organized around specific issue areas, like environmental protection, civil rights, or education, and consist of three dimensions: a power arrangement, a policy paradigm, and an organizational arrangement (Wilson, 2000).

In terms of its power arrangements, a policy regime may involve governmental and nongovernmental actors, single or multiple interests, traditionally friendly or competitive groups, and policy beneficiaries. Next, policy paradigms shape both the way that problems are defined (e.g., their cause and severity) and how they should be solved (e.g., responsible party). Finally, organizational arrangements refer to the institutional and procedural contexts in which policy decisions get made and are implemented. A policy, therefore, will reflect the regime's conception of the means and ends of governmental action, the institutional arrangements that structure policy making and implementation in the arena, and the goals of regime members (McGuinn, 2006).

According to Wilson (2000), each dimension of PR contributes to long-term policy stability. Power arrangements themselves tend to be stable. The paradigms of those in power are reinforced through media coverage and bully pulpits, and promote public perceptions that existing arrangements are rational. Finally, organizations, with their institutional rules, regulations and routines, tend to resist change and innovation (Wilson, 1989). Stability can be disrupted according to the PR model, however, when conditions become favorable for regime change.

Policy regime changes themselves do not happen spontaneously. They occur gradually "when regimes become stressed, alternative policy paradigms arise, legitimacy crises occur, and shifts in power become evident" (Wilson, 2000, p. 266). *Stressors* consist of natural or man-made disasters, cumulative processes like demographic shifts, new discoveries, or scandals. Cobb and Elder (1983) refer to "trigger events," Sabatier (1999b) to "external perturbations," and Jones, Baumgartner, and True (1995) to "exogenous shocks." They can generate stress on organizational arrangements, undermine dominant policy paradigms, and raise the visibility of new problems. Paradigm shifts occur when events or stressors arise that are inconsistent with the dominant policy narrative. If this occurs, new paradigms or discourses may emerge or existing (but dormant) alternatives may gain traction. Stressors and paradigm shifts sometimes interact, producing crises of legitimacy. By questioning the stories, images, and authority upon which established regimes are based, politicians and nongovernmental leaders may gradually propel a loss of public confidence in them (Stone, D., 1988, 1989). Power shifts are sometimes enabled by stressors, paradigm shifts, and legitimacy crises, but can also occur "naturally." They can occur with changes in the composition of Congress or the White House, through the defection of a bloc of policy elite, or because of the mobilization of advocacy coalitions (Wilson, 2000).

PR's application to the literature on educational policy making has been limited, though the framework has enjoyed increased attention among school researchers in the last 9 years. That work has been influenced by a study by Clarence Stone (1989) who explained the success of Atlanta's downtown development in terms of the gradual establishment of new "urban regimes" brokered between public- and private-sector actors, and (mostly White) civic leaders and members of the Black community. Henig, Hula, Orr, and Pedescleaux (1999) were the first to apply regime theory to the education policy arena. As part of a larger study of school politics, each of the four led a research team and interviewed people from schools, local governments, and civic organizations in one of four Black-led cities (i.e., Washington, DC, Detroit, Baltimore, and Atlanta). They collaborated on a book comparing school reform efforts in the four cities, and Orr (1999) wrote another detailing Baltimore's experience. Both books conclude that neither good ideas nor inspired leaders are sufficient for successful education reform. Instead, what is needed is the construction of new regimes that link civic elites across institutional sectors and social boundaries (Neckerman, 2000).

Also in 1999, Gittell and McKenna reported on a 3-year, 9-state comparative study of state education policy-making regimes and the roles of various stakeholders within each regime. They used the PR framework to document the construction of new state education regimes during the mid-1990s that included governors, segments of the business community, and religious groups. During this period, governors in all sampled states "gained new formal powers over education, formed coalitions with powerful interest groups, and overcame resistance of other interest groups" to effectively replace a policy orientation focused around equity with another on standards, choice, and efficiency (p. 289).

Finally, as discussed earlier in the chapter, McGuinn (2006) finds support for the PR framework in explaining accountability policies at the national level. According to the author, the emergence of NCLB, which he contends signifies a major change in the federal government's involvement in education, is a story of policy regime destruction and reconstruction.

Rarely has the PR model been applied to policy change in higher education. In 2006, Shattock employed the framework in an historical piece about the higher education system in the United Kingdom. Arguing that higher education policy—while once driven from the inside—has since the 1970s largely been driven from outside the university system, he sought to unpack the shift in the balance of power. Drawing largely on personal experiences, Shattock

concludes that higher education policy enjoyed an extended period of stability, when policy guidance came from a hands-off University Grants Committee (UGC) which was in essence a "benign" policy regime "operating at the university/state interface" (p. 134). The British system of higher education was subject to major reforms (e.g., a new funding mechanism [the "RAE"], star rating system, formal quality audit system) when a new paradigm took hold, fostered by the OECD and the European Union, arguing that investment in postsecondary education and research is linked with economic competitiveness. The UGC's power was replaced by a legislatively created Quality Assurance Agency responsible to the new state Higher Education Funding Councils.

Federal Education Reform Through a Policy Regimes Lens Like the other synthetic approaches, PR offers an explanation for prolonged policy stability and dramatic, short term change. The PR framework suggests that policy solutions at the federal level arise neither as the result of the steady, path-dependent evolution of ideas nor dynamically as a function of an open, adaptable political system. Instead, PR focuses on the transition from policy stasis to reform, and illuminates the shift in terms of factors that condition the gradual replacement of one policy regime with another: stressors and natural cycles (e.g., elections) may undermine existing power arrangements, new or dormant policy narratives may emerge that challenge dominant paradigms, and people may lose confidence in the old regime. In short, federal education reform emerges when political leaders and leaders outside of government who favor policy change exploit stressors, establish popular doubt in the stories, images, and authority upon which the old regime is based, and, ultimately join with others to construct new regimes. The model demands that scholars consider at least three domains in any systematic application of the PR framework to the study of federal education reform. They are the policy narratives that help build and maintain regime control over education policy at the federal level, politicians' monitoring and exploitation of public opinion to shape or redefine issues and solutions in ways that give them electoral advantage, and, the reform ideas that arise when gradually shifting power arrangements, paradigms, and institutional structures interact with the broader political environment to permit the intervention of the federal government in education.

These domains lead to a host of questions that researchers might ask in applying the PR lens in future studies of federal education reform and trends. What key actors and issue specialists are routinely part of the education policy regime at the federal level? What are the alternative policy paradigms through which education reformers try to unseat existing policy regimes? To what extent and in what ways do politicians, as well as leaders from outside of government, work to shape public opinion around federal fixes for education? When does politicians' responsiveness to public opinion outweigh their allegiances to narrow interest and constituent groups? How does the behavior of stakeholders in the K-12 and higher education arenas differ in response to the construction of new policy regimes at the federal level? To what extent can *shifting power and institutional arrangements*—key components of the PR model—be considered an accurate characterization of the history of federal higher education reform?

Using the PR framework to answer these questions—questions that are fundamentally about "shifts in governing authority"—requires a particular kind of methodology: "the study of shifts, by definition, resists containment within predefined institutional boundaries and because relationships among variables are altered as these boundaries change over time" (Orren & Skowronek, 2004, p. 184). Regimes, shifting over space and time, do not easily conform to conventional methods in political science that look for causal relationships between an independent and dependent variable. Instead, policy development research that highlights authority shifts "presumes configurative and crosscutting effects, in which feedback and interdependency are omnipresent" (p. 184).

In studies that use the PR framework, data might be collected from retrospective interviews with current and former policy elites. The challenges that the MS model poses in terms of access to policy officials to interview are also likely to confront the PR scholar. Moreover, the boundaries among policy regimes, much like the boundaries between policy episodes, issues, and actors are often blurry, impeding efforts to isolate true regime shifts (Wilson, 2000) and requiring the analyst to collect archival data from a host of documentary sources as she attempts to confirm observed patterns in the interview data.

Data to be gathered and analyzed may also include current and past lists of advocacy organizations, signatories on petitions, editorials, lawsuits, and reports, and witnesses called to testify before relevant congressional committees. Documents to be collected may include voting records, media coverage, congressional speeches, polling data, interest group memos, and presidential papers. In addition to The University of Washington and Pennsylvania State University archives previously mentioned, The Lexis-Nexis Congressional service will be a valuable resource for those who aim to apply and extend the PR framework to the study of federal education reform. This comprehensive collection of historic and current congressional information provides access to full text congressional publications and public laws. It includes, for example, selected transcripts and full-text statements from congressional hearings since 1988, committee reports since 1990, GAO reports since 2004, public law texts, U.S. Code, Code of Federal Regulations, campaign finance data, member profiles, and political news from *The Hill* and *Roll Call*. Additionally, the American Presidency Project is a searchable online resource housing state of the union addresses, proclamations, press conferences, inaugural addresses, radio addresses, addresses to Congress, FDR's fireside chats, veto messages, executive orders, addresses to foreign legislatures, party conventions,

and college commencements, the messages and papers of the presidents from Washington to Taft (1789–1913), the public papers of the presidents from Hoover to G. H. W. Bush (1929–1993), and the weekly compilation of presidential documents from Clinton to G. W. Bush (1993–2008).

Conclusion

Our premise here is twofold. First, we have argued that recent federal initiatives to reform K-12 and higher education compels researchers to pay closer attention not only to the effects—intended and otherwise—of such policies but also to the political dynamics that shape their development and implementation. If federal actors continue to benefit politically by attending to schools (primary, secondary, and postsecondary) and, consequently, their influence continues to grow, understanding these dynamics takes on added importance. Today, at the K-12 level, policy makers in Washington are debating whether to standardize federal testing and performance requirements across states as part of the next reauthorization of the Elementary and Secondary Education Act. At the postsecondary level, the Secretary of Education's Commission on the Future of Higher Education has recommended that colleges and universities be required to measure student achievement on a "value-added" basis and to report that information so that policy makers and consumers have a way of comparing their relative effectiveness.

Second, we maintain that understanding the changing federal role would be well served by employing synthetic approaches in studies of education policy at the national level. Previous research has in general looked narrowly at the federal government's role in education, focusing on individual events, players, or policies (McGuinn, 2006). But, synthetic approaches place reform developments in their broader historical context and emphasize that policy inertia can sometimes be overcome when features of the political and policy-making environment shift. Through the use of these frameworks, we can learn whether patterns exist in how reform is supported at the federal level, by whom it is opposed, and how issues are defined and redefined in ways that reinforce existing policy trajectories or condition changes in course. If the research agenda that this chapter enables is pursued, the information gleaned might be used to better explain, predict, and alter the direction of national education reform efforts.

Notes

1. This discussion is indebted to Patrick McGuinn's recent book No Child Left Behind and the Transformation of Federal Education Policy, 1965–2005.
2. For reasons noted below, Kingdon originally referred to his framework as the "revised garbage can" model in homage to Cohen-March's foundational work on garbage-can decision making in organizations. Analysts subsequently coined the term Multiple Streams in recognition of the stream-like features that the model suggests flow though government. We follow this more recent convention.

3. Kingdon acknowledges that incrementalism often seems capable of capturing the stream-level dynamics that determine the evolution of potential policy solutions; rather, it is at the macro-level of stream convergence where the explanatory power of incrementalism seems to falter.

4. Kelly (1994) observes how similar notions had already become incorporated into the literature; for example, Burnham (1970) on "electoral realignments," Mayhew (1991) and Schlesinger (1986) on "mood cycles," and Sundquist (1983) on "party systems."

5. In the remainder of this section, describing the core punctuated-equilibrium model, we draw on McLendon (2003b).

References

Abernathy, S. (2007). *No Child Left Behind and the public schools*. Ann Arbor: The University of Michigan Press.

Bailey, M. A., & Rom, M. C. (2004). A wider race? Interstate competition across health and welfare programs. *Journal of Politics, 66*, 326–347.

Baird, K. L. (1998, April). *The NIH and FDA new medical research policies*. Paper presented at the annual meeting of the Midwest Political Science Association, Chicago.

Baumgartner, F. R., & Jones, B. D. (1991). Agenda dynamics and policy subsystems. *Journal of Politics, 53,* 1044–1074.

Baumgartner, F. R., & Jones, B. D. (1993). *Agendas and instability in American politics*. Chicago: University of Chicago Press.

Beck, N., Katz, J. N., & Tucker, R. (1998). Taking time seriously: Time-series—cross-section analysis with a binary dependent variable. *American Journal of Political Science, 42,* 1260–1288.

Berry, F. S., & Baybeck, B. (2005). Using geographic information systems to study interstate competition. *American Political Science Review, 99*, 505–519.

Berry, J. (1989). *The interest group society* (2nd ed.). New Haven, CT: Yale University Press.

Blaukenau, J. (2001). The fate of national health insurance in Canada and the United States: A multiple streams explanation. *Policy Studies Journal, 29*, 38–55.

Breunig, C., & Koske, C. (2005). *Punctuated equilibria and budgets in the American states*. Seattle, WA: Center for American Politics and Public Policy.

Burnham, W. D. (1970). Revitalization and decay: Looking toward the third century of American electoral politics. *Journal of Politics, 38*(3), 146–172.

Center on Education Policy. (1999). *A brief history of the federal role in education: Why it began and why it's still needed*. Washington, DC: Author.

Center on Education Policy. (2006, March). From the capital to the classroom: Year four of the No Child Left Behind Act. Washington, DC: Author. Retrieved November 20, 2008, from http://commongood.org/assets/attachments/CEP-NCLB-Report-4.pdf

Cobb, R. W., & Elder, C. D. (1983). *Participation in American politics: The dynamics of agenda building* (2nd ed.). Baltimore: Johns Hopkins University Press.

Cohen, M., March, J., & Olsen, J. (1972). A garbage can model of organizational choice. *Administrative Science Quarterly, 17,* 1–25.

Cohen-Vogel, L. (2005). Federal role in teacher quality: "Redefinition" or policy alignment? *Educational Policy, 19*, 18–43.

Cohen-Vogel, L., & Ingle, K. (2007). When neighbours matter most: Innovation, diffusion and state policy adoption in tertiary education. *Journal of Education Policy, 22*(3), 241–262.

Cohen-Vogel, L., Ingle, K., Albee, A., & Spence, M. (2008). The "spread" of merit-based college aid: Politics, policy consortia and interstate competition. *Educational Policy, 22,* 339–362.

Commission on the Future of Higher Education. (2006). A test of leadership: Charting the future of U.S. higher education. A report of the commission appointed by Secretary of Education Margaret Spellings. Retrieved February 28, 2008, from http://www.ed.gov/about/bdscomm/list/hiedfuture/reports/final-report.pdf

Cross, C. T. (2004). *Political education: National policy comes of age*. New York: Teachers College Press.

Crowson, R. L., Firestone, W., Johnson, B., Levin, B., Mitchell, D., Scribner, J., et al. (2003). The future of the Politics of Education Association: A committee report. Retrieved February 28, 2008, from http://www.fsu.edu/~pea/committee.html

Cuban, L. (1990). Reforming again, again, and again. *Educational Researcher, 19*(1), 3–13.

DeBray, E. (2006). *Politics, ideology, and education: Federal policy during the Clinton and Bush Administrations*. New York: Teachers College Press.

DeBray-Pelot, E. (2007). School choice and educational privatization initiatives in the 106th and 107th Congresses: An analysis of policy formation and political ideologies. *Teachers College Record, 109*, 927–972.

Dodd, L., & Jillson, C. (Eds.). (1994). *New perspectives on American politics*. Washington, DC: Congressional Quarterly Press.

Dougherty, J., & Pfaltzgraff, R. (1997). *Contending theories of international relations: A comprehensive survey* (4th ed.). New York: Longman.

Downs, A. (1967). *Inside bureaucracy*. Boston: Little, Brown.

Durant, R. F., & Diehl, P. F. (1989). Agendas, alternatives, and public policy: Lessons from the U.S. foreign policy arena. *Journal of Public Policy, 9*, 179–205.

Dye, T. R. (1990). *American federalism: Competition among governments*. Lexington, MA: Lexington Books.

Eldredge, N., & Gould, S. J. (1972). Punctuated equilibria: An alternative to phyletic gradualism. In T. Schopf (Ed.), *Models in Paleobiology* (pp. 82–115). San Francisco: Freeman.

Gittel, M., & McKenna, L. (1999). Redefining education regimes and reform: The political role of governors. *Urban Education, 34*, 268–291.

Harris, R. A., & Milkis, S. M. (1996). *The politics of regulatory change: A tale of two agencies* (2nd ed.). New York: Oxford University Press.

Hayes, M. (2001). *The limits of policy change*. Washington, DC: Georgetown University Press.

Hearn, J. C. (1993). The paradox of growth in federal aid for college students: 1965–1990. In J.C. Smart (Ed.), *Higher education: Handbook of theory and research: Vol 9* (pp. 94–153). New York: Agathon.

Hearn, J. C. (2001). Epilogue to 'The paradox of growth in federal aid for college students: 1965–1990.' In M. B. Paulsen & J. C. Smart (Eds.), *The finance of higher education: Theory, research, policy, and practice* (pp. 316–320). New York: Agathon.

Henig, R., Hula, R. C., Orr, M., & Pedescleaux, D. S. (1999). *The color of school reform: Race, politics, and the challenge of urban education*. Princeton, NJ: Princeton University Press.

Hochschild, J. (2004). Three puzzles in search of an answer from political scientists (with apologies to Pirandello). *Political Science and Politics, 37*, 225–229.

John, P. (1998). *Analyzing public policy*. London: Pinter.

Jones, B. D., Baumgartner, F. R., & True, J. L. (1995). The shape of change: Punctuations and stability in U.S. budgeting, 1946–95. *Journal of Politics, 66*, 1–33.

Jordan, M. M. (2003). Punctuations and agendas: A new look at local government budget expenditures. *Journal of Policy Analysis and Management, 22*, 345–360.

Kaestle, C. (2006). Foreword. In E. H. DeBray (Ed.), *Politics, ideology, and education: Federal policy during the Clinton and Bush administrations* (pp. xi–xiv). New York: Teachers College Press.

Kamieniecki, S. (2000). Testing alternative theories of agenda setting: Forest policy change in British Columbia, Canada. *Policy Studies Journal, 28*, 176–189.

Kawar, A. (1989). Issue definition, democratic participation, and genetic engineering. *Policy Studies Journal, 17*, 719–744.

Kelly, S. Q. (1994). Punctuated change and the era of divided government. In L. Dodd & C. Jillson (Eds.), *New perspectives on American politics* (pp. 162–190). Washington, DC: Congressional Quarterly Press.

Kingdon, J. W. (1984). *Agendas, alternatives, and public policies*. Boston: Little, Brown.

Kingdon, J. W. (1994). Agendas, ideas, and policy change. In L. Dodd & C. Jillson (Eds.), *New perspectives on American politics* (pp. 215–299). Washington, DC: Congressional Quarterly Press.

Kingdon, J. W. (1995). *Agendas, alternatives, and public policies* (2nd ed.). New York: Harper Collins.

Kirst, M. (2006). A forty-year perspective on the politics of education and its association, *PEA* [Electronic version]. *Politics of Education Bulletin, 31*(1), 1, 4.

Kratochwil, F., & Ruggie, J. G. (1997). International organizations: The state of the art. In P. F. Diehl (Ed.), *The politics of global governance: International organizations in an interdependent world* (pp. 29–40). Boulder, CO: Lynne Rienner.

Larson, T. E. (2004, November 3). *Decentralization in U.S. public higher education: A comparative study of New Jersey, Illinois, and Arkansas.* Paper presented at the annual meeting of the Association for the Study of Higher Education, Kansas City, MO.

Leslie, D. W., & Berdahl, R. A. (2006, September 3). *More freedoms, more controls simultaneously in U.S. state accountability patterns: The Virginia experience.* Paper presented at the annual meeting of the European Association for Institutional Research, Rome, Italy.

Lindblom, C. E. (1965). *The intelligence of democracy: Decision-making through mutual adjustment.* New York: Free Press.

Manna, P. (2006). *School's in: Federalism and the national education agenda.* Washington, DC: Georgetown University Press.

March, J., & Olsen, J. P. (1989). *Rediscovering institutions: The organizational basis of politics.* New York: Free Press.

Mayhew, D. (1974). *Congress: The electoral connection.* New Haven, CT: Yale University Press.

Mayhew, D. (1991). *Divided we govern: Party control, lawmaking, and investigations, 1946–1990.* New Haven, CT: Yale University Press.

McDermott, K. (2005). In MINT Condition? The politics of alternative certification and pay incentives for teachers in Massachusetts. *Educational Policy, 19*, 44–62.

McDonnell, L. (2005). No Child Left Behind and the federal role in education: Evolution or revolution? *Peabody Journal of Education, 80*(2), 19–38.

McDonnell, L. (2006). School's in: Federalism and the national education agenda [Review of the book *School's in: Federalism and the national education agenda*]. *Teachers College Record.* Retrieved March 22, 2007, from http://www.tcrecord.org

McGuinn, P. J. (2006). *No Child Left Behind and the transformation of federal education policy, 1965–2005.* Lawrence: University Press of Kansas.

McGuire, M. (2004, April). *Are political scientists ignoring education policy at their own risk?* Paper presented at the Midwest Political Science Association Meeting, Chicago.

McLendon, M. K. (2003a). Setting the governmental agenda for state decentralization of higher education. *Journal of Higher Education, 74*, 479–516.

McLendon, M. K. (2003b). State governance reform of higher education: Patterns, trends, and theories of the public policy process. In J. Smart (Ed.), *Higher education: Handbook of theory and research: Vol. 18* (pp. 57–143). London: Kluwer.

McLendon, M., & Cohen-Vogel, L. (2008). Understanding educational policy-making in the American states: Lessons from political science. In B. S. Cooper, L. Fusarelli, & J. Cibulka (Eds.), *Handbook of educational politics and policy* (pp. 30–51). Mahwah, NJ: Erlbaum.

Mills, M. (2007). Stories of politics and policy: Florida's higher education governance reorganization. *Journal of Higher Education, 78*, 162–187.

Moe, T. (1990). The politics of structural choice: Toward a theory of public bureaucracy. In O. Williamson (Ed.), *Organizational theory from Chester Bernard to the present* (pp. 116–153). Oxford, UK: Oxford University Press.

Neckerman, K. M. (2000). Good politics [Review of the book *The color of school reform: Race, politics, and the challenge of urban education*]. *American Journal of Education, 108*, 135–145.

Ness, E. C. (2005, November 15). *Deciding who earns HOPE, PROMISE, and SUCCESS: Toward a comprehensive model of the merit aid eligibility policy process.* Paper presented at the Association for the Study of Higher Education, Philadelphia.

Oliver, T. R. (1991). Health care market reform in Congress: The uncertain path from proposal to policy. *Political Science Quarterly, 106*, 453–477.

Olsen, J. P. (2001). Garbage cans, new institutionalism, and the study of politics. *American Political Science Review, 95*, 191–198.

Orr, M. (1999). *Black social capital: The politics of school reform in Baltimore, 1986–1998.* Lawrence: University Press of Kansas.

Orr-Bement, D. M. (2002, November 21). *A theoretical perspective of the state policy process for higher education policy decisions.* Paper presented at the annual meeting of the Association for the Study of Higher Education, Sacramento, CA.

Orren, K., & Skowronek, S. (2004). *The search for American political development.* New York: Cambridge University Press.

Pierson, P. (2000). Increasing returns, path dependence, and the study of politics. *American Political Science Review, 94*, 251–267.

Pierson, P. (2004). *Politics in time: History, institutions and social analysis.* Princeton, NJ: Princeton University Press.

Portz, J. (1996). Problem definitions and policy agendas: shaping the educational agenda in Boston. *Policy Studies Journal, 24*, 371–386.

Protopsaltis, S. (2004, November 3). *Political and policy dynamics of higher education governance and finance reform: The Shaping of the first college voucher system.* Paper presented at the Association for the Study of Higher Education, Kansas City, MO.

Repetto, R. (Ed.).(2006). *By fits and starts: Punctuated equilibrium and the dynamics of US environmental policy.* New Haven, CT: Yale University Press.

Robinson, S. E. (2004). Punctuated equilibrium, bureaucratization, and budgetary changes in schools. *Policy Studies Journal, 32*, 25–39.

Robinson, S. E. (2007). Schools in: Federalism and the national education agenda [Review of the book *School's in: Federalism and the national education agenda*]. *Perspectives of Politics, 5*(1), 166 – 167.

Sabatier, P. A. (1999a). The need for better theories. In P. A. Sabatier (Ed.), *Theories of the policy process* (1st ed., pp. 3–18). Boulder, CO: Westview Press.

Sabatier, P. A. (Ed.). (1999b). *Theories of the policy process* (1st ed.). Boulder, CO: Westview Press.

Sabatier, P. A. (Ed.). (2007). *Theories of the policy process* (2nd ed.). Boulder, CO: Westview Press.

Sabatier, P. A., & Jenkins-Smith, H. C. (1999). The advocacy coalition framework: An assessment. In P. A. Sabatier (Ed.), *Theories of the policy process* (pp. 97–116). Boulder, CO: Westview Press.

Schattschneider, E. E. (1975). *The semi-sovereign people.* New York: Wadsworth.

Schlesinger, A. M. (1986). *The cycles of American history.* Boston: Houghton Mifflin.

Shattock, M. (2006). Policy drivers in UK higher education in historical perspective: 'Inside out', 'outside in' and the contribution of research. *Higher Education Quarterly, 60*, 130–140.

Simon, C. A. (2007). Schools in: Federalism and the national education agenda [Review of the book *School's in: Federalism and the national education agenda*]. *Political Science Quarterly, 122*(1), 177–178.

Sims, C. H., & Miskel, C. G. (2001, March). *The punctuated equilibrium of national reading policy: Literacy's changing images and venues.* Paper presented at the annual meeting of the American Educational Research Association, Seattle, WA.

Sims, C. H., & Miskel, C. G. (2003). The punctuated equilibrium of national reading policy: Literacy's changing images and venues. In W. Hoy & C. Miskel (Eds.), *Studies in leading and organizing schools* (pp. 1–26). Greenwich, CT: Information Age.

Skowronek, S. (1993). *The politics presidents make: Leadership from John Adams to George Bush.* Cambridge, MA: Harvard University Press.

Sroufe, G. E. (1994). Politics of education at the federal level. In J. D. Scribner & D. H. Layton (Eds.), *The study of educational politics* (pp. 75–88). Washington, DC: Falmer Press.

Stimson, J., MacKuen, M., & Erikson, R. (1995). Dynamic representation. *American Political Science Review, 89*, 543–565.

Stone, C. (1989). *Regime politics: Governing Atlanta, 1946–1988*. Lawrence: University Press of Kansas.

Stone, D. (1988). *Policy paradox and political reason*. Glenview, IL: Scott, Foresman/Little, Brown.

Stone, D. (1989). Causal stories and the formation of policy agendas. *Political Science Quarterly, 104*, 281–300.

Stout, K., & Stevens, B. (2000). The case of the failed diversity rule: A multiple streams analysis. *Educational Evaluation and Policy Analysis, 22*, 341–355.

Sundquist, J. L. (1968). *Politics and policy: The Eisenhower, Kennedy, and Johnson years*. Washington, DC: Brookings Institution.

Sundquist, J. L. (1983). Whither the American party system? *Political Science Quarterly, 98*(4), 573–593.

True, J. L. (2000). Avalanches and incrementalism. *American Review of Public Administration, 30*, 3–18.

True, J. L., Jones, B. D., & Baumgartner, F. R. (1999). Punctuated-equilibrium theory. In P. A. Sabatier (Ed.), *Theories of the policy process* (pp. 97–115). Boulder, CO: Westview Press.

Tyack, D., & Cuban, L. (1995). *Tinkering toward Utopia: A century of public school reform*. Cambridge, MA: Harvard University Press.

Van Der Slik, J. (1999, April). *Beyond incrementalism: Changing higher education governance in Illinois*. Paper presented at the annual meeting of the Midwest Political Science Association, Chicago.

Walker, J. L. (1969). The diffusion of innovations among the American states. *American Political Science Review, 67*, 1174–1185.

Wilson, J. Q. (1989). *Bureaucracy: What government agencies do and why they do it*. New York: Basic Books.

Wilson, C. (2000). Policy regimes and policy change. *Journal of Public Policy, 20*, 247–274.

58

The Expansion of State Policy Research[1]

KATHRYN A. MCDERMOTT

University of Massachusetts, Amherst

Over the past 50 years, the state role in education policy has expanded to an extent that would once have seemed unbelievable. Indeed, it is now more accurate to speak of state *roles* in education policy rather than of "*the* state role." State legislatures and state boards of education enact policies that set the general framework within which local school districts operate. The states are the key guarantors of equal educational opportunity in the U.S. federal system. Since the Elementary and Secondary Education Act of 1965, the states have stood in the center of the complex intergovernmental network that governs public education. As state education policy has expanded, so has state education policy research.

This chapter identifies major trends and themes in state policy research, but does not claim to identify all studies of all policy areas or states. In order to keep its scope manageable, this chapter focuses on policy research related to elementary and secondary education, and emphasizes studies that include all 50 states, compare a subset of states, or generalize about patterns in state education policy, rather than single-state case studies. I begin with a brief discussion of the key methodological and data issues that scholars of state education policy must confront. I then examine the areas in which scholarship on state education policy has made contributions to knowledge about education policy in general, emphasizing several state roles. The final section of the chapter discusses potential future directions in which state policy research might move.

Methodological and Data Issues

The research surveyed for this chapter includes scholarly publications as well as many reports produced for more general audiences of policy makers and educators. This sort of report might not warrant inclusion in a survey of research on a different policy area, but the enormous volume and political salience of reports on state policy, many written by university-based scholars with federal funding, makes this genre worthy of inclusion. Relevant studies were identified by searching ERIC, visiting the Web sites of several national organizations, and browsing key journals.[2]

Issues of scope, research methods, and data arise in all studies of state education policy. Researchers must decide whether to emphasize depth or breadth of coverage, and thus whether they wish to study all 50 states, or to select only a few for case studies. National organizations interested in particular areas of state education policy often produce tables, or brief descriptions, of state policies. Examples (by no means a comprehensive list) include state requirements related to social studies (Council of State Social Studies Specialists, 1986); school choice (Fossey, 1992; Greene, 2000); charter schools (American Federation of Teachers, 2001; Center for Education Reform, 2008); special education (National Association of State Directors of Special Education, 1998a, 1998b; Thompson, Erickson, Thurlow, Ysseldyke, & Callender, 1999; Linehan, 2000; Linehan & Markowitz, 2002; Ahearn, 1995; Beard, Bull, & Montgomery, 1991; Place, Gallagher, & Harbin, 1989; Koyanagi & Gaines, 1993; Harbin, Gallagher, & Lillie,1989; Harbin, Terry, & DaGuio, 1989; Harbin, Gallagher, Lillie, & Eckland, 1990; Harbin, Gallagher, & Terry, 1991; Meisels, Harbin, Modigliani, & Olson, 1988); alternate routes to teacher certification (Feistritzer, 2007); assessments and content standards (Council of Chief State School Officers, 2007a, 2007b); and implementation of the No Child Left Behind Act (NCLB; Education Commission of the States, 2004). For years, the Education Commission of the States also has produced thorough and well-done summaries and citations of state laws and regulations in a vast range of policy areas, which can be found on their Web site (www. ecs.org) under headings such as the StateNotes series, a compilation of education proposals from governors' State of the State addresses, and a project entitled *The Progress of Education Reform*.

Challenges for Quantitative Research In order to move from description to analysis or explanation, a researcher who wishes to include all 50 states will need to use quantitative methods, since it is usually impractical to produce case studies of all the states.[3] One approach to quantitative analysis of state policies is cross-sectional modeling, in which the unit of analysis is the state (thus, $N = 50$), and the goal is to explain how the states vary at a given point in time. Examples of cross-sectional analysis include Amrein and Berliner (2002), Carnoy and Loeb (2002), and McDermott (2003).

The major statistical challenge of cross-sectional analyses is that a universe of 50 cases is too small to permit inclusion of more than a few independent variables. Some researchers enlarge their sample sizes, and also include variation over time, by shifting from cross-sectional to time-series or event-history analysis (Box-Steffensmeier & Jones, 2004). Grissmer and Flanagan (2001) used time-series techniques to analyze the effects of state reform policies. Event-history analysis (EHA) shows how change in the value of an independent variable affects the probability that a certain event (usually a policy enactment, in policy research) will happen to a particular member of the population (a state) in a given year (examples include Wong & Shen, 2002; Mintrom, 2000). EHA treats each state-year, such as Alabama in 1970 or Virginia in 1987, as a separate case, which greatly expands the universe of cases. For example, instead of an N of 50, a national study of change in a particular state policy over the period 1970–1990 would have an N of 1,050 (50 states multiplied by 21 years) and could thus include far more independent variables. However, a plausible argument can be made that "Alabama in 1970" and "Alabama in 1985" are not, in fact, different cases, but rather the same case at different points in time (Abbott, 1992).

Quantitative studies of the effects of state policy face an additional methodological challenge in untangling the effects of variables that affect both the likelihood that a state will enact a policy and the educational outcomes of its students. Amrein and Berliner (2002) examined trends in SAT, ACT, Advanced Placement, and the National Assessment of Educational Progress (NAEP) tests in 18 states with "high-stakes" tests (defined as tests whose results had effects on students or schools) for evidence that increasing scores on the states' own tests indicated actual learning rather than the results of narrowly-focused test preparation. This study received a great deal of press attention, including articles in the *Boston Globe* (Kurtz, 2003) and the *New York Times* (Winter, 2002). Amrein and Berliner concluded that states with high-stakes tests had worse student achievement than states without such policies. They did find some improvements, but argued that these were the result of decreasing participation rates rather than better student performance. Amrein and Berliner noted that the states with high-stakes tests tend to be in the South or Southwest, and to have lower levels of per-pupil spending than states without such tests. However, their analysis of test-score trends does not attempt to control for the demographic characteristics of these region's populations, in particular their greater poverty and larger populations of African American and Latino students than other states, each of which would have tended to produce lower levels of achievement regardless of state policy.[4]

It is also possible that states with high-stakes tests had lower test scores because states with bigger educational problems, or populations that include large numbers of educationally disadvantaged students, are likelier *both* to have enacted high-stakes tests and to have lower test scores. One approach to this problem is a recursive model like the one used by Carnoy and Loeb (2002). First, they use a regression analysis to identify the characteristics of states with the most extensive accountability policies. Then, they use the variables that predicted the extent of a state's accountability policies as controls in a second equation that measures the association between these policies and student outcomes. Carnoy and Loeb concluded that states with "stronger" accountability policies (more consequences attached to test scores) had larger increases in their scores on the mathematics NAEP examination, and that there was no strong relationship between accountability policies and either grade-retention or high-school-completion rates.

However, Marchant, Paulson, and Shunk (2006) criticize Carnoy and Loeb for failing to control for variables that are important predictors of student performance that are not also predictors of policy enactment, such as family income, parental education levels, ethnicity, and exclusion of students with disabilities and students with limited English proficiency. Controlling for all these factors, Marchant, Paulson, and Shunk find that there is little evidence of a positive relationship between high-stakes testing and achievement.

Another possible way of handling the complicated causal connections among state conditions, policies, and educational outcomes is to employ hierarchical linear modeling (HLM). HLM is a method for analyzing data that is "nested," such as test scores earned by students in different schools in different states (Willms, 1999). For example, Braun, Wang, Jenkins, and Weinbaum (2006) used HLM to analyze the contribution of state policies to change in the test-score gap between White and Black students. The debate on the educational effects of testing and accountability policies continues, and will be discussed in more detail later in this chapter.

Case Selection for Qualitative Research Policy makers and educators often want information about policy characteristics or effects that are not easily quantified. Thus, there is a great deal of case-study research on policy implementation and effects. Although random selection of cases seems like an obvious strategy to use, and has actually been used (Kohl, McLaughlin, & Nagle, 2006), it has serious shortcomings. King, Keohane, and Verba (1994), in a book on scientific inference in qualitative research, point out that random selection for qualitative research risks not including important cases, and also offer a formal proof that random selection "will often cause very serious biases" in qualitative research (p. 126).

Rather than selecting randomly, researchers tend to choose cases based on the characteristics of their policies. One common method is to select states whose policies embody of range of alternatives in a particular policy area (e.g., see Clarke et al., 2003). Less commonly, some researchers select states based on a characteristic of their education governance institutions, such as their degree of centralization (see, e.g., Cibulka & Derlin, 1998a, 1998b). Often, researchers use several selection criteria. For example, in a 1989 study of education reform in six states, the Consortium for Policy Research in Education chose cases according to whether their reform approach was comprehensive or incremental, the kinds of policy instruments on which the reforms relied, and location in different regions of the country (Firestone, Fuhrman, & Kirst, 1989). For their influential study of state education governance, Campbell and Mazzoni (1976) categorized states according to whether the chief state school officer and state board of education members were elected or appointed, and then chose a group of states from each category that had large populations and were located in various regions.

In order to permit valid causal inferences, a research design needs to include at least as many cases as possible combinations of independent variables. Researchers' selection of cases for studies of state education policy often does not attempt to do this. Frequently, if one were to lay out the dimensions of variation among a set of cases in a matrix, there would be one or more empty cells. For example, to include all possible combinations of incremental versus comprehensive reform, policy instruments, and regions, Firestone et al. (1989) would have needed more than the six states they studied. In addition, one extreme end of the policy continuum is generally unrepresented: qualitative studies of state education policies generally have little or nothing to say about what is going on in states that have not enacted a particular policy (for a critique of case selection on this and other grounds, see Burlingame & Geske, 1979).

These case selection patterns do *not* indicate collective methodological sloppiness, but rather give a clue about what the authors intend to accomplish with their case selection. Most multiple-case qualitative studies are not designed to make causal inference possible, or even to generalize about how the state-level differences used as case selection criteria affect the policy of interest, but rather to draw conclusions about how a particular kind of policy is working in an approximately representative group of states, or a group of states that are important because of their large populations. For example, the Firestone et al. (1989) study cited above was intended to draw general conclusions about the goals and content of state reforms, not to explain differences among state policies or to develop theories about the effects of particular kinds of state policy.

Data Challenges Both qualitative and quantitative researchers on state education policy face challenges in obtaining data. The dependent variable poses a challenge for quantitative researchers interested in student performance on standardized tests. The SAT and ACT are taken by high-school students across the United States, but only by those who aspire to attend college, and states have very different college-application rates. In the Northeast, very few students take the ACT. In the Midwest and West, the only students who take the SAT are those who are applying to highly selective Eastern colleges. The result is that attempts to compare these test scores across states are complicated by differences in the populations tested.

NAEP has the advantage of being administered to a representative group of students at various grade levels in each of the states participating, but there are no state-level scores available from years prior to 1990, and until very recently, there were not state-level NAEP scores for all states. Consequently, scholars whose goal is to draw conclusions about all states are limited to analyzing only the smaller set of states for which NAEP data are available. For example, Carnoy and Loeb's (2002) models of the relationship between accountability policies and NAEP scores include between 25 and 37 states (Carnoy & Loeb, 2002, Table 2, p. 314). This makes the already small population of 50 states even smaller, and limits the number of independent variables that can meaningfully be included in analysis.

For qualitative researchers who want to use press coverage or legislative records, the main data challenge is that the quality and availability of these sources varies greatly among states. Although the state role in education policy is at least as important as the federal role, the federal role is far better documented. State "newspapers of record" often do not cover state politics as closely as the *New York Times* or *Washington Post* cover federal policy making. Increasingly, small-market news sources are included in NEXIS, but not necessarily for any given time period. Adding to this difficulty, state governments devote widely different levels of resources to maintaining and indexing their archives. A researcher interested in four states' enactment of a particular policy may find that one of the states has full transcripts of legislative hearings and debates indexed and available online, one has un-indexed transcripts of hearings but not of debates, one has transcripts of debates but not of hearings, and that the fourth has 30 hours of cassette tapes, which can be listened to at the state library but not borrowed or duplicated. The New York State Archives has taken a step towards rectifying this situation by beginning to collect documents relevant to any state education policies (not just New York's) that have influenced federal education policy (see http://www.archives.nysed.gov/edpolicy/index.shtml).

Major Contributions of State Policy Research

Since the 1960s, scholars have produced an immense body of work on state education policy, which contributes to four major areas of education policy research. First, scholars of state education policy have built a base of knowledge on how state government works. Second, because states are the key constitutional guarantors of equal educational opportunity, a great deal of research has analyzed how state policy affects educational equity, particularly with regards to equity of educational funding. Third, the states took a leading role in several education reform movements of the 1970s, 1980s, and 1990s, which are well-documented and analyzed in research, including studies of how reform ideas spread among the states and of the reforms' implementation and effects. Finally, because states occupy the middle ground between federal and local government, studies of state education policy have contributed to knowledge about intergovernmental relations, including state implementation of federal policies, state-local relations during the waves of state reform, and, most recently, how federal NCLB changed state policy and federal-state relations.

The range of research on state education policy has grown apace with the state role. As researchers expand the range of what they investigate, the research community also continues research on existing topics. Thus, rather than "waves" of policy research, there are layers of policy research that accrete over time, increasing the overall volume of research on state education policy and the range of topics under consideration.

How State Government Works The characteristics and operations of state education governance systems were among the earliest topics of research in state education policy. Some research spanned all 50 states. One early—and large—such effort was funded by the U.S. Office of Education, carried out by the Council of Chief State School Officers, and published by the National Education Association. The first volume (Pearson & Fuller, 1969) is a collection of histories of all 50 states' departments of education since 1900, and the second (Fuller & Pearson, 1969), consists of essays on "areas of concern to all state departments of education" (p. iii). The Lawyers' Committee for Civil Rights under Law (1974) summarized the states' laws and regulations on education in an effort to determine what their constitutional commitments to equal educational opportunity entailed in practice. Wirt (1977, 1978) used the 1974 Lawyers' Committee survey to classify the states on the basis of their degree of centralization or local control. Other research examined smaller groups of states. In the 1960s, the Carnegie Corporation funded studies of state education policy, emphasizing the relationships between educators and general state government (Bailey, Frost, Marsh, & Wood, 1962; Masters, Salisbury, & Eliot, 1964; Usdan, 1963), on which Iannaccone (1967) based a fourfold typology of "linkage structures" in state education policy. Other classifications of state education policy systems include Campbell and Mazzoni's (1976) federally-funded identification and evaluation of "alternative models of state education governance" (p. 4), based on research in 12 states.

Although, as the Lawyers' Committee for Civil Rights Under Law (1974) first noted, it is difficult to generalize about what educational areas states do and do not regulate, states have on the whole increased their influence over what

schools teach and how students' progress will be assessed. Ironically, despite a deep-seated distrust of government and preference for local control of public education, Americans have strengthened state agencies and expanded the state role in education policy (Tyack & James, 1986). Apart from a few experiments with deregulation for certain kinds of schools and districts, the states have not moved *out* of any major fields of educational regulation. The trend towards alternative certification for teachers at first seems to be an area of reduced state influence, but no state has actually stopped certifying or licensing educators.

Many researchers have examined what goes on inside state government institutions. After the increase in state legislative activity related to education, scholars focused on the legislatures themselves, including legislative leadership and influence (Fuhrman & Rosenthal, 1981; Rosenthal & Fuhrman, 1981a), legislative staffing (Rosenthal & Fuhrman, 1981b), state policy-making culture (Marshall, Mitchell, & Wirt, 1989; Placier, 1993; Sacken & Medina, 1990; Wirt & Kirst, 1997), and the different possible arenas of state education policy making (Mazzoni, 1991; Fowler, 1994). Other scholars have investigated changes in state education agencies (SEAs). These agencies have grown from sparsely staffed, minimally influential entities to those that take on a central role in implementing both the expanded state policies and the even more dramatically increased range of federal education policies (Timar, 1997). The federal government actually subsidized major growth in state agencies during the 1960s and 1970s through the Elementary and Secondary Education Act of 1965 (ESEA), especially Title V, which included funds to strengthen state education agencies. The federal government also sponsored research on how the new funds were affecting state education agencies (McDonnell & McLaughlin, 1982; Murphy, 1971, 1973, 1974; Milstein, 1976). Increased state activism in the 1980s and 1990s also inspired some researchers to examine how state education agencies were implementing their expanded roles (Lusi, 1997; Madsen, 1994). The Center on Education Policy (2007a) has, more recently, investigated the challenges posed for state departments of education by the requirements of the federal NCLB.

State Education Policy and Equal Educational Opportunity Constitutionally, the states have the responsibility to provide public education, and the state constitutions have generally been interpreted as guaranteeing equal educational opportunity (McCarthy & Deignan, 1992). A large group of scholars has analyzed education finance, the policy area most closely linked to state education guarantees. Over the years, the emphasis of finance policy has shifted from equity in spending to adequacy of educational outcomes, which may entail spending more on students with greater educational needs (see Baker & Green, this volume).

Equity of Education Funding In the 1970s, the Ford Foundation stood at the center of a "national reform network" that sought to change states' policies for financing public education (Fuhrman, Berke, Kirst, & Usdan, 1979, p. 81), and to "bring intellectual strength to a field that for years had not attracted broad scholarly interest." Ford's grants totaled $27 million between 1970 and 1981 (Ford Foundation, 1981, p. iii) for work done at the Rand Corporation, the Education Commission of the States, the Center for Education Policy Research at the Educational Testing Service, the Syracuse University Research Corporation, the Childhood and Government Project at the University of California-Berkeley, the National Urban Coalition, and the Lawyers' Committee for Civil Rights under Law. The Ford Foundation supported research on alternative models of education finance, and also on the politics of finance reform (Cohen, Levin, & Beaver, 1973). Ford funded state-level citizens' groups and state agencies researching finance reform issues, a study by the National Urban Coalition of the effects of reforms in 10 states, and citizen education on finance reform by the League of Women Voters (see Ford Foundation, 1976). Joel Berke, who served as director of the ETS Center for Education Policy Research, and later as U.S. Deputy Assistant Secretary for Education Policy Development, participated in much of this research (Berke, 1974a, 1974b; Berke, Bailey, Campbell, & Sacks, 1971a, 1971b; Berke, Shalala, & Williams, 1975).

The Ford Foundation's interest in education-finance reform went beyond research sponsorship to supporting the lawyers and activists who actually brought the suits, including the path-breaking *Serrano v. Priest* case in California. Kirst (1979) stated that pressure for school finance reform had come not from the grass roots but rather from "an alliance of educational finance scholars, lawyers, foundation officers, the USOE, and the NIE" (p. 428). In a later paper, Kirst (1981) credited Ford with having provided "publicity, grants, travel, and recognition as resources to motivate and bond together" the members of this alliance (p. 16).

The U.S. Office of Education and the National Institute of Education (NIE) also sponsored research on education finance during this period, sometimes in conjunction with Ford (Berke et al., 1975; Kirst, 1979). An NIE-supported report on education finance reform undertaken by the National Conference of State Legislatures notes that the U.S. Congress had directed NIE to fund "goal oriented, school finance research" (Callahan & Wilken, 1976, p. v). In addition to work specifically analyzing education finance, the NIE funded the Lawyers' Committee 1974 study. Other research sponsored by the NIE examined "the implications of slowing or declining state-local support" for the federal government's own education spending (Berke, 1979, p. 19), the changing relationship between education and state government (Fuhrman et al., 1979), and the state financial difficulties caused by recession, tax revolts, and the changed federal tax structure (Adams, 1982).

One important area of research was the interaction between policies that increased the extent to which states' education finance systems redistributed funds from wealthier to less wealthy communities and policies that addressed other areas of education and tax policy. Shortly after activists began to advocate for more equality in state school finance laws, citizen groups in some states "revolted" against rising tax burdens and supported enactment of tax-limitation measures such as Proposition 13 in California and Proposition 2½ in Massachusetts. Kirst (1979) portrayed the funding-equity and tax-limitation advocates as two movements on a collision course with each other; voters' increasing sense that government could not spend money effectively was fueling the tax-reduction movement and also posing political challenges for advocates of increased education spending. Palaich, Kloss, and Williams (1980) analyzed the politics of tax and expenditure limitations in four states, and Palaich, Wendling, and Flakus-Mosqueda (1983) concluded that "each state has its own breed of school finance politics" (p. 351).

During the 1980s, as states began enacting policies intended to improve the quality of education, scholars also considered how the newer policies affected equity of school finance. Kirst (1984a) identified a key tension between the "excellence" policies, which often gave school districts flat grants to support initiatives like mentor teachers, curriculum improvement, and longer school days, regardless of district wealth, and the policies that redistributed funds from wealthier to poorer districts. Conceivably, one state policy could be attempting to narrow a spending gap while another inadvertently worsened it. Augenblick (1986) drew a similar conclusion to Kirst's, also noting that the separate funding for excellence policies made them more vulnerable to future cuts.

Adequacy of State Education Funding During the 1990s, scholars noted that school-finance plaintiffs were increasingly basing their claims on states' constitutional guarantees of public education, rather than arguing that equal protection of the laws required equal educational spending (Clune, 1994; Verstegen & Whitney, 1997). Verstegen and Whitney (1997) pointed out that whether plaintiffs succeeded with this strategy depended on whether state courts interpreted "adequacy" to mean a bare minimum of schooling, or a quality education for all children. If the former, the plaintiffs tended to lose; if the latter, they tended to win. Education-finance plaintiffs found there to be a synergy between the "adequacy" emphasis and the state policies of the 1980s and 1990s that enacted standards for what children should learn at various points in their schooling. The standards-based policies made it harder for courts to interpret constitutional guarantees as requiring only a bare minimum (Odden, 1998, 1999).

After several decades of experience with school finance litigation, scholarship on state education policy attempted to take stock of the movement's effects. DeBartolome (1997) found that the inflation-adjusted value of state aid for education had doubled between 1970 and 1990, although economic trends rather than judicial decisions appeared to account for the change. Evans, Murray, and Schwab (1997) concluded that judicial decisions in favor of plaintiffs led to increased state spending on education, and also to more redistributive state finance policy. DeMoss (2003) and Reed (2001) both found that court decisions favoring plaintiffs tend to reduce funding disparities between school districts. Wong (1999) found that states' education finance policies had not converged on a common model, despite the nationwide reform movement, and that specifically targeted spending policies tend to produce a more distinct service-delivery structure than do more diffuse policies. Scholars have also analyzed the meaning of "adequacy" in education finance policy, including the increased use by courts of studies that attempt to determine what an adequate education costs (Augenblick, Sharp, Silverstein, & Palaich, 2004). Recently, some scholars have criticized these studies, and the overall effects of the adequacy movement, as leading to inefficient use of resources and circumventing legislatures' appropriate role in setting spending priorities (e.g., see West & Peterson, 2007).

Movements for State Education Reform Legislatures often changed state education finance systems at the same time as they enacted other education reform laws. Many such laws expanded the state role in curriculum, testing, and evaluation of school and district performance. This chapter emphasizes the assessment and accountability components of standards-based reform, although it should be kept in mind that many states also enacted changes to teacher certification and evaluation during this period (see, e.g., Darling-Hammond, 2000; Furtwengler, 1995). Unlike earlier state policies, the new policies enacted during the 1970s and 1980s were intended to change the schooling experience of all students, not just special populations such as students with disabilities and limited-English-proficient students (Kirst, 1984b). Many analysts describe this heightened state activity as occurring in two waves. For example, Smith and O'Day (1990) identify a first wave of reforms that emphasized increasing educational inputs and improving students' basic skills, and a second wave in which reformers rethought structure and process. Minimum-competency tests for high school graduation were a major part of this first wave (Ramsbotham, 1980; Pipho, 1980a, 1980b; Marshall, Serow, & McCarthy, 1987). Airasian (1987) pointed out that these policies departed from past uses of educational tests, in that they had implications beyond placement of students, including effects on resource allocation.

The state-level origins of the standards-based reform idea have been obscured by the tremendous political impact of the federal *A Nation at Risk* report released in 1983. In fact, the states began moving in this direction—and issuing their own commission reports calling for change—several years before *A Nation at Risk* (Kirst, 1984a; Toch, 1991). It is important to note that although the states were following the same general reform model, they did not all enact the same sort of policies; each state's version of the policies responds to local conditions and political values (Fuhrman, 1989b; Firestone, Fuhrman, & Kirst, 1991; McDermott, 2007). The spread of standards-based reform definitely shifted the emphasis of state policy making. However, like the other changes identified in this chapter, the shift entailed some states adding a new area of policy making while others continued the older ones, with the net effect of expanding state activity. For example, Firestone, Fuhrman, and Kirst (1990) point out that even after the standards-based reform movement began, states kept enacting minimum-competency tests.

Many studies identified central trends in the rapidly-changing state reforms. Mitchell and Encarnation (1984) identified 7 policy mechanisms common to the reforms, and McDonnell and Elmore (1987) drew on political science research to produce a classic piece on four alternative policy instruments: mandates, inducements, capacity building, and system changing. McDonnell (2004) later wrote a book on state testing as "hortatory policy" in action. Other typologies of state education assessment and accountability policies were developed by Clarke et al. (2003), Pedulla et al. (2003), and Desimone, Smith, Hayes, and Frisvold (2005).

The expansion of state education policy making that began in the 1970s produced a corresponding expansion in state education policy research. The U.S. Office of Educational Research and Improvement funded a great deal of research, often by contracting with the Consortium for Policy Research in Education (CPRE). Much of the CPRE research of the 1980s and 1990s applied common analytical frameworks to sets of state case studies, beginning with a six-state study in the 1980s (Firestone et al., 1989). By 1994 the Consortium had investigated so many states that it could release a policy brief drawing on research from 19 states (Fuhrman, 1994). State regulation of school districts was an enduring concern of the CPRE studies, with deregulation and state takeover seen as the ends of a continuum of state intervention or non-intervention (Fuhrman, 1989a; Fuhrman & Elmore, 1992, 1995). CPRE produced many policy briefs in addition to full reports and academic journal publications. In 2001, CPRE released findings from a survey of all 50 states' assessment and accountability systems, which shows the diversity of states' approaches to these issues prior to increased federal pressure for uniformity.

Since the 1980s, there has been a great deal of research, both by university-based scholars and by stakeholder organizations, on the characteristics and quality of states' standards. The American Federation of Teachers rates standards (American Federation of Teachers, 2001). Achieve, Inc., a non-profit organization funded by business organizations, contracts with states to evaluate the quality of their standards (see http://www.achieve.org/publications/state_report_view). The Council on Basic Education has also weighed in on the subject (Joftus & Berman, 1998), as has the Fordham Institute (Finn, Petrilli, & Vanourek, 1998).

In addition to identifying what was new about the reforms of the 1970s, 1980s, and 1990s, researchers have investigated why these ideas appealed to so many policy makers. One factor was a broadening of the players in the education policy process (Cohen, 1987), in particular the involvement of business groups who saw a connection between improving schools and improving economic conditions amid losses of industrial jobs in the Rust Belt and competition for factories among states in the Sun Belt (McDonnell & Fuhrman, 1986; Toch, 1991; Vold & DeVitis, 1991). One policy that created interest in more policy making was education finance reform. According to McDonnell and Fuhrman (1986), the increased state role in funding education, at a time of rising costs, made state policy makers likely to intervene, and the public had indicated a willingness to pay more for education if the quality of schooling improved (p. 54–55). Airasian (1988) adds that the policies made sense symbolically to the public, even though they had not previously been shown to work.

Diffusion of policy ideas was a significant topic of research. State policy makers often look to other states, or national organizations, or both, for ideas about policies that might work. Examining patterns of state policy enactment thus provides an excellent opportunity to learn about how ideas spread or diffuse among policy makers. One such idea was education finance reform, which began to spread among the states in the 1970s largely through the Ford Foundation's efforts to fund research on alternatives and also to bankroll legal challenges to existing state finance systems. Around the same time, the idea of minimum-competency testing gained popularity. The minimum-competency testing movement provides an interesting contrast to both the earlier finance reforms and the later spread of standards-based reform because it did not depend on national organizations. As Pipho (1980b) notes, minimum-competency testing spread through 38 states "without any centralized support and no single agency or group of people playing an advocate role" (1980b, p. 2).

The enactment of standards-based reform and the accountability policies associated with it have been examined by several scholars (Carnoy & Loeb, 2002; McDermott, 2003). State accountability policies also spread upward in the intergovernmental system, influencing the design of the 1994 reauthorization of the Elementary and Secondary Education Act (also known as the Improving America's Schools Act) and the 2001 reauthorization as the No Child Left Behind Act (McDonnell, 2005; Manna, 2006; McDermott & DeBray-Pelot, in press). Enactment of policies on school choice and charter school authorization has also been analyzed (Lacireno-Paquet & Holyoke, 2007; Mintrom, 2000; Mintrom & Vergari, 1998; Renzulli & Roscigno, 2005; Wohlstetter, Wenning, & Briggs, 1995; Wong & Shen, 2004). National organizations and individual "policy entrepreneurs" were active in promoting both standards-based reform and school choice policies. The role of these networks is generally acknowledged, but less often specifically included in studies of state policy enactment. An exception is the work of Mintrom (2000) and Mintrom and Vergari (1998), which included the role of policy entrepreneurs in school choice policy diffusion. Song and Miskel (2007) apply a new method of analysis to the network of people who are active in state reading policy.

Implementation of State Reforms   Early on, there was

skepticism that the states' standards-based reform policies could be successfully implemented (see Turnbull, 1984). The same increase in the diversity of interest groups involved in the education policy process that produced the standards-based reforms complicated efforts to keep a focus on implementation (Massell, Kirst, & Hoppe, 1997). Legislatures' natural tendency is to move on to other issues once they have passed legislation, unless an individual legislator makes it her or his business to act as a "fixer" when challenges arise (McDonnell & Fuhrman, 1986; Wohlstetter, 1989, 1991). One challenge to successful implementation is that policy makers do not always pay sufficient attention to the need to increase capacity to act, both at the state and local levels (Massell, 1998, 2000).

In part because they posed such large challenges, the state reforms have been the subject of important research on policy implementation, which focuses on schools and classrooms, emphasizing how district and school staffs interpret state policies, and how their interpretations shape the policies' effects on teaching. Even if teachers embrace a reform, and feel responsible for carrying it out, the message of a policy or program may be distorted in transmission. In an introductory essay to a special issue of *Educational Evaluation and Policy Analysis*, which was devoted to research on classroom-level implementation of California's state mathematics-education reform program, Cohen and Ball (1990) note that teachers' role in state reform is paradoxical: teachers are both the target of the reforms and the essential means for carrying out the reforms. In order to implement state policies that attempt to change classroom practices, teachers must "teach a mathematics that they never learned, in ways they never experienced" (p. 233).

They tend to respond to this challenge by incorporating the reforms into their familiar practices, as new topics to cover, or as new ways of engaging student interest, rather than as fundamentally new ways of understanding and teaching mathematics. Spillane and Zeuli (1999), writing of mathematics reform in Michigan, note that it easier to change "behavioral" patterns than "epistemological" ones. Part of the challenge is the multiple signals state policies send to teachers. In California, as Sykes (1990) points out, the state was also requiring that students take tests, whose format and content were more consistent with the "old" style of teaching the teachers were supposed to be discarding than with reform pedagogy. Spillane's book *Standards Deviation* (2005) extends analysis of how teachers make sense of policies, and how their sense-making affects their responses. The process of sense-making is not specific to teachers, and the research on how teachers' understandings shape policy implementation is relevant to any policy that depends on relatively autonomous frontline workers for its implementation, adding to older ideas about teachers and other kinds of public employees as "street-level bureaucrats" (Lipsky, 1980).

Effects of State Assessment and Accountability Policies   The area of state policy in which the largest number of researchers have examined the same sets of quantitative data and directly engaged with each other's findings concerns the effects of state testing and accountability policy on students' academic attainment. Most of these studies specifically concern the impact of state-mandated high school graduation tests (Catterall, 1989; Coates & Wilson-Sadberry, 1994; Muller & Schiller, 2000; Jacob, 2001; Warren & Edwards, 2005; Warren, Jenkins, & Kulick, 2006). All of these studies are quantitative, although they draw upon different sources of data. Generally, they find that graduation tests do not lead to lower rates of high-school completion (Muller & Schiller, 2000; Schiller & Muller, 2003; Warren & Edwards, 2005). Warren, Jenkins, and Kulick (2006) concluded that graduation tests are associated with lower rates of high-school completion and higher rates of GED test-taking, but cautioned, "these findings should only be considered in conjunction with other findings about the potential positive consequences of state [graduation tests]" (p. 132).

The Center on Education Policy, a relatively new but influential research organization, has tracked controversy over, and effects of, graduation tests since its founding in 2002. Most recently, the Center on Education Policy (2007b) reports have emphasized how the tests affect students of color, who are likelier than average to live in states with graduation tests. The center has also found that controversy over the tests tends to drop a few years after they are first implemented, but state funding for remediation programs for students who fail tends to drop at the same time (Center on Education Policy, 2006).

Other studies concern the effects of a broader set of assessment and accountability policies, not just graduation tests (Amrein & Berliner, 2002; Carnoy & Loeb, 2002; Rosenshine, 2003; Amrein-Beardsley & Berliner, 2003; Schiller & Muller, 2003; Hanushek & Raymond, 2005). Grissmer and Flanagan (2001) analyzed NAEP data and information about states' education spending and reforms, concluding that Texas and North Carolina had made the greatest "nonresource-related gains" (p. 204), and attributing these gains to the states' accountability policies. Carnoy and Loeb (2002) found a positive correlation between the extent of state accountability policies and NAEP score gains after controlling for characteristics that affect both accountability policies and student outcomes. Swanson and Stevenson (2002) generated a linear measurement scale of states' policy activism and policies' levels of difficulty and examined how those policy attributes related to classroom practices, based on data from the eighth-grade NAEP examination in mathematics and found that state policy has a significant effect on the classroom practices that teachers report using. Desimone et al. (2005) identified consistency, specificity, authority, and power as four key attributes of state policy and found that some attributes had a positive relationship with gains in specific areas of mathematical performance. Hanushek and Raymond (2005) also found that state accountability sanctions led to increased test scores without also causing more students to be identified for special education. Braun et al. (2006)

ranked the coherence and consistency of the policies of 10 states that collectively enrolled over 40% of the nation's Black students. They found that the achievement gaps are "pervasive, profound, and persistent," and that their measure of the coherence and consistency of state policies correlated "moderately" with gains in Black student achievement, but were less useful in predicting their record with respect to closing the achievement gaps" (p. 2).

Intriguingly, although state assessment and accountability policies are known to have influenced the federal No Child Left Behind Act, at the time when Congress passed the law relatively little was known about the state policies' effects. The studies cited above appeared during NCLB debate, or after the law was implemented, as did studies by Malen, Croninger, Muncey, and Redmond-Jones (2002), Mintrop (2003), and Mintrop and Trujillo (2005) on the effects of state sanctions against low-performing schools, a key component of NCLB.

Intergovernmental Relations in Education Policy NCLB continues a general increase in the complexity of intergovernmental relations in education policy. According to Elmore (1984), "Education invites intergovernmental politics because it is such a versatile good; it can be used as the medium for delivering both public and private benefits and for accomplishing allocative, developmental, and redistributive objectives" (p. 134). States stand in the middle of this intergovernmental network, both geographically and functionally. Federal policies, beginning with the National Defense Education Act (NDEA) of 1957, and most dramatically including the Elementary and Secondary Education Act of 1965 and the Education for All Handicapped Children Act of 1975, have added the intergovernmental role of federal policy implementer to the states' home-grown policy roles as equal-opportunity guarantors and school regulators. This section of the chapter surveys research on how states implemented the first major federal education policies, how state reforms affected state-local relations, and how federal-state relations changed as a result of standards-based reform and NCLB. The focus is on Title I (known as Chapter 1 from 1981–1994); other important areas of study include special education, and surveys of states' policies pursuant to various other federal policies.[5]

Title I and Chapter 1 in the States The relationship between state and federal education policy since the 1960s has been complex, sometimes mutually reinforcing, and sometimes contradictory. The Elementary and Secondary Education Act of 1965 is remarkable not only because it authorized the first general federal aid to elementary and secondary education, but also because of its effect on state education agencies (SEAs). The SEAs were responsible for distributing ESEA Title I compensatory education funds. ESEA also provided funds for SEAs to use for "innovative programs" and, through Title V, to use specifically to increase their staffing and administrative capacity. Not surprisingly, then, federally funded research has addressed the extent to which the states use the federal funds as intended and implement federal policies faithfully (Berke et al., 1971a; McDonnell & McLaughlin, 1980, 1982; Hamann & Lane, 2004).

Following early revelations that some school districts were treating Title I funds as general aid, rather than spending it on disadvantaged children as the law required, SEAs had to take a more aggressive stand towards local districts' regulatory compliance than many had previously (Murphy, 1971). A 1977 report by the Syracuse University Research Corporation concluded that although some states lacked sufficient administrative resources for Title I implementation, the federal role was maintaining or enhancing the efficiency of eight SEAs (Syracuse University Research Corporation, 1977).

One influential idea in studies of states as federal policy implementers was that states' modifications of federal policies were often entirely appropriate. McDonnell and McLaughlin (1980, 1982) drew the conclusion that analysis of the state-federal relationship had to go beyond simple regulatory compliance. Some states implement federal programs "basically as [they come] to them from the federal government," while others shape federal programs to fit better with state policies and priorities, and others fall between these extremes (1980, p. 80). Even the states that reshape federal programs generally are acting consistently with the federal government's policy, understood as "a statement of broad aims and purposes" (McDonnell & McLaughlin, 1980, p. 82). In a similar vein, Elmore (1982) argued that uneven federal influence across the states did not mean that some states were good and others bad, but rather that "federal policy objectives are picked up and amplified by the economic and political structure of some states, while in other states they are deflected and damped" (p. 46). Because federal policies interact differently with different state policies, Elmore argued that federal policy should be flexible enough to treat states differently, where differential treatment would meet federal goals more effectively than would uniform treatment, and that state implementation of federal policy should be evaluated not according to its uniformity, but rather by "the degree to which federal actions resulted in the formation of state-level policies, and state-level coalitions supporting them" (p. 48). Another important concept was the federal government as the defender of vulnerable populations in state-level politics. McDonnell and McLaughlin's (1980, 1982) analyses, and that of Elmore (1982), concluded that federal programs were crucial in serving populations with special needs that often lacked political strength at the state level. Similarly, Moore, Goertz, and Hartle (1983) found that federal programs provided important political and financial support for services to special populations.

Many, but not all, analyses of the states in their role as implementers of federal policy were carried out under the aegis of the National Assessments of Title I (or Chapter 1) which have been federally mandated since the Education Amendments of 1974 (Birman et al., 1987). In addition to evaluating the effects of federal programs on students, the National Assessments have considered issues such as the effects on the states of the shift to more block grants and fewer categorical federal programs early in the Reagan administration (Birman et al., 1987; Farrar et al., 1986) and the fit between federal and state programs (United States Department of Education [USED], 1996).

Some states already had compensatory, special, or bilingual education policies in place when they began implementing federal policies, which raised the question of how the programs would interact. An early study found that the programs tended not to overlap, and when they did overlap, federal programs strengthened state programs (Moore et al., 1983). When federal policy first began requiring states to assess the quality of their federally-funded programs, rather than simply ensuring that funds were being spent on the right students (see Plunkett, 1991), the assessment activities shifted emphasis. Milne and Moskowitz (1983) found that the states monitored federal programs more closely than state-funded programs. Milstein (1976) had found states moving only slowly in the direction of setting statewide goals for education programs, but also noted that "… the increasing policy initiatives and resource inputs of both the states and the federal government are forcing SEAs to move into such activities" (p. 57).

State-Local Relations and State Reforms   Just as federal and state programs have the potential to interact, the state reforms of the 1980s and 1990s raised the possibility of conflict between state and *local* policies, or state encroachment on local prerogatives. Scholars have considered the ways in which increased state policy activism has affected the long-standing tradition of local control of education. Most studies converge on an intriguing finding: that shifts in intergovernmental relations are not a zero-sum game in which one level's influence expands at the expense of another's. Instead, increased state activism leaves room for local discretion (Tyree, 1991, 1993) and seems to produce an increase in local policy activity (Murphy, 1982; Kirst, 1988; Fuhrman, Clune, & Elmore, 1988; Fuhrman & Elmore, 1990). Some district-level policy makers used state policies as a way of promoting their own priorities (Firestone et al., 1990, p. 80). One dissenting voice comes from Malen (2003), who argues that the remaining extent of local freedom of action has been overestimated, and that this view may "underestimate the importance of agenda control" (p. 201), "equate ingenuity with autonomy" (p. 201), and "cast the exception as the rule" (p. 202).

Interactions Between the Post-1994 Title I and State Policies   Many states responded to federal requirements to assess the quality of Title I/Chapter 1 policies by administering norm-referenced tests of basic skills to students in the program. By the early 1990s, the states' own standards-based reform policies were also requiring mainstream students to meet higher performance standards, and state policy makers were beginning to want Chapter 1 assessments to be better aligned with their tests based on state standards. One of the National Assessments of Chapter 1 made the point that the isolation of Chapter 1 from related state programs meant that the federal program "could not adequately support children in achieving the National Education Goals" (cited in USED, 1996, p. 6).

The 1994 reauthorization of the Elementary and Secondary Education Act, greatly influenced by President Bill Clinton and U.S. Education Secretary Richard Riley's prior experiences as "education governors," cited the National Education Goals and for the first time required states to have rigorous academic standards and assessments in order to receive Title I funds. As part of this shift, the new law also required that students in Title I programs take the same assessments as their non-Title I peers. The U.S. Office for Educational Research and Improvement (OERI) funded research (carried out by CPRE) of the extent to which the 1994 ESEA had led states to unify their assessments of Title I and non-Title I students. A study of two states and three school districts concluded that "despite attempts to make the systems coherent, Title I schools often appear to be subject to dual systems of accountability" (O'Day & Gross, 1999, p. viii). A later study of all 50 states' assessment and accountability systems, carried out near the end of the implementation period for the 1994 requirements, found a great deal of variation among the states' systems, and determined that despite the 1994 law, only 22 states would have a "single or unitary accountability system" by the deadline (Goertz & Duffy, 2001). The National Assessments of Title I drew similar conclusions (USED, 1996, 1999, 2001). USED granted many waivers and extensions to the states. One important area of flexibility was that USED allowed states to design tests before setting standards, rather than the other way around, as IASA required. State education officials had found the required sequence did not fit well with how test design works (Cohen, 2002, p. 44).

In contrast, NCLB tightened the requirements for state accountability policies (McDonnell, 2005). Early on, the USED took a very hard line on implementation, declaring that there would be little if any flexibility on requirements and deadlines (DeBray, 2006, p. 136–138). Later, the USED's approach to implementation became more flexible. Manna (2006) developed the concept of "borrowing strength" to explain how federalism influences the education policy agenda. According to Manna, state and federal policy makers may draw on each other's "license" to act and capacity to act; in the case of NCLB, the states' difficulties implementing the law, and their resentment of what they saw as federal overreaching, "sapped Bush's license to expand the law's reach" (p. 157). The U.S. Department of Education funded creation by ECS of a database on states' policy responses to NCLB (Education Commission of the States, 2004), rating each state as "on track," "partially on track," or "not on track" towards meeting various NCLB requirements. This database has been used as a source of data for publications both by ECS-affiliated researchers

(Wanker & Christie, 2005) and researchers outside ECS (Ritter & Lucas, 2003).

Interaction between NCLB and states' previously developed accountability systems has been a key issue. National organizations of state-level officials, such as the National Council of State Legislatures and the Council of Chief State School Officers, have turned an often critical eye on how the federal law has affected state policy (see, e.g., Erpenbach, Forte-Fast, & Potts, 2003). Linn (2005), reporting on research funded by the federal Institute of Education Sciences, took note of the "mixed messages" that NCLB and the states' own accountability systems send to schools. Linn concluded, "… it is clear that the likelihood that a school will be identified as failing to meet AYP targets in a given year, or be placed in the needs improvement category, or be subject to more serious sanctions, depends to a substantial degree on the state in which the school is located and not exclusively on the effectiveness of the school" (p. 14). Clarke (2007) classified states according to the initial congruence of their policies with NCLB requirements, and concluded that the NCLB model does not appear to represent an improvement over states' earlier policies in terms of improving performance and narrowing achievement gaps.

One especially important question, given that NCLB bases a great deal on students' reaching "proficiency" as states define it, is the whether states' proficiency standards are sufficiently rigorous, and the extent to which "proficiency" means the same thing in different states. Peterson and Hess (2005, 2006) have analyzed these questions in an index published in the Hoover Institution's journal *Education Next*, concluding most recently that some states have gamed the system by lowering their proficiency definitions, and that states with low standards have not increased them. Others have improved, or have maintained high standards. A Center on Education Policy (2007b) study compared states' passing standards for graduation with the cut scores on the same high-school tests that the states used for assessing "proficiency" under NCLB, and concluded that about half the states have a graduation standard below the NCLB-influenced proficiency standard.

One strand of studies of state responses to IASA and NCLB has come from the civil rights community. The Citizens' Commission on Civil Rights has followed the states' efforts to include students with disabilities and students with limited proficiency in English in their assessments (Citizens' Commission on Civil Rights, 1998; Yu & Taylor, 1999; Piché, 2001). The Citizens' Commission's complaint that states were using the federal government's flexibility to enable perpetuation of lower expectations for Title I students was one of the reasons why a bipartisan majority in Congress supported making the NCLB's assessment and accountability provisions more stringent than the IASA had been (DeBray, 2006). The Civil Rights Project at Harvard University also analyzed the effects of NCLB on students of color (Kim, 2003; Sunderman, 2006).

Future Directions for State Policy Research

Since the 1960s, research on state education policy has followed state policy into a wide range of areas. Research on the structure and functions of state education governance institutions began with describing the systems and moved on to examine how legislatures and state education agencies participated in the education reforms of the 1970s, 1980s, and 1990s. Through this entire period, state education finance policy was a key issue because of its close relationship to the states' guarantees of equal educational opportunity. Education reforms focused on standards, tests, and accountability spread through the state during this same period, with controversial results. All of this policy activity, along with changes in federal law, made intergovernmental relations increasingly complex. All the issues that comprise the broadened state policy role will continue to be important in education policy research. There is a need for more research on state policy making, including how research interacts with policy advocacy. Some evidence suggests that education finance policy is entering a new phase. Scholars can continue to examine states' accountability policies, and to synthesize what has been learned. Finally, intergovernmental relations promise to remain interesting and controversial.

How State Governments Work It is unlikely that states will become less involved in education policy, although the precise nature of their involvement will continue to change. There has not been much recent research on how state legislators view education policy. Questions that future researchers might consider include how legislators think about education as a policy area, what they believe the goals of a state's public education system should be, and what they perceive their constituents want them to do. One current issue, the ongoing fiscal crisis of state government, echoes concerns from the 1980s, and is worthy of new study, particularly the challenges created by interactions between states' education policies and their policies in other areas. Rising costs of healthcare programs have squeezed out some education spending, and states' tax policies affect the amount of revenue they have available for spending in all areas. Do any states show signs of having come up with better solutions to these problems? Research on the states' education reform policies of the 1980s and 1990s emphasized the role of business interests and concerns about the economy. In the late 20th century, the large corporations that participate in the Business Roundtable believed it was worth their while to support education reform, but the global political economy of the early 21st century is different from that of the late 20th. To what extent does the shift of manufacturing formerly done in the United States to other countries with lower labor costs affect business's participation in, and goals for, state education policy making?

The concept of state political culture is now ripe for updating. It seems intuitively obvious that states have different political cultures, and that these political cultures probably matter in policy making. However, it has been nearly 20 years since the publication of Marshall et al.'s (1989) work on the cultures of state education policy makers. When scholars want to use some measure or index of state political culture, they generally still have to fall back on the late Daniel Elazar's (1984) typology of "moralistic," "traditionalistic," and "individualistic" political cultures, which is based on research that is now several decades old. Since then, new immigrants have entered the country, populations have moved within the country, and new generations have moved into civic and political leadership. A full updating of Elazar might be more than scholars of educational politics and policy want to undertake, but it would still be interesting to look for patterns in political culture that specifically affect education, or to inquire into the educational implications of conflicts between political cultures within states (on intrastate cultural conflict, see Gimpel & Schuknecht, 2003).

Research as Advocacy The political use of state education policy research is another important area of inquiry. Despite educators' frequent assertions that their work should be kept separate from politics, research on states' education policy has generally been closely linked with efforts to influence states' education policy. If we understand the term "politics" broadly, as the process by which a society decides what goals it values and how to allocate resources toward those goals, rather than narrowly, as a synonym for "partisanship," this means that research on education policy has been part of the politics of education. One early example of this relationship was the Ford Foundation's education finance program.

One common strategy that combines research and advocacy is to produce a survey or "report card" that rates or grades states' policies against a rubric related to an organization's priorities. For example, the Center for Education Reform (2008) notes on its Web site that it advocates "strong charter school laws," and it grades the states on the extent to which their policies facilitate the growth of charter schools. Knowing the organization's mission makes a difference to how one interprets its "A" grade for Arizona and "F" for Mississippi. Scott and Barber (2002) critiqued the ratings given to states' charter-school laws by both the Center for Education Reform and the American Federation of Teachers, which is critical of the charter-school concept, and concluded that both are flawed. Another organization, the Center for Educational Opportunity, which opposes much about current bilingual education policies, rated state bilingual education policies according to their flexibility and the ease with which a parent can have a child exempted from participating in them. No state rated higher than a C+, largely because the grading criteria represented characteristics that existing policies did not have, but which the Center wanted to advocate (Amselle, 1997).

The goal of such ratings is to have them picked up by

the media and reported without much information about the context in which the ratings were given. During 1997, the Massachusetts state legislature was considering changes to the state's bilingual education laws. An editorial in the Worcester, Massachusetts, *Telegram and Gazette* called for a more radical overhaul than the legislature seemed willing to make, citing the Center for Educational Opportunity report as evidence of the need for change: "In a recent nationwide report card on bilingual education issued by the Center for Educational Opportunity, a Washington-based think tank, Massachusetts scored D-minus, ranking dead last with New York" ("Reform bilingual ed," 1997). This grade appears to be particularly damning if a reader does not know that the "think tank" is an advocacy organization, and also does not know that C+ was the highest grade given. The criteria for the grades given by *Education Week*'s annual *Quality Counts* report have less of an advocacy edge, but have still been criticized for embodying a particular set of assumptions about school finance (Finn, 2001).

Political scientists have recently noted the increasing importance of "think tanks" that generate research in support of particular policy and political agendas (Rich, 2004; Graetz & Shapiro, 2005). There is some evidence that this trend is crowding out more neutral research. The Education Commission of the States (ECS) has long been the major source of neutral compilations of what the states are doing in various policy areas. However, ECS has recently struggled financially, in part because of its member states' budget difficulties, and in part because of shifting foundation priorities. In 2006, former ECS president Ted Sanders told *Education Week* that "Many of the foundations are getting far more strategic about their agendas and are investing in particular advocacy for something" (Hoff, 2006). The article went on to note that the emphasis on advocacy was making it difficult for organizations like ECS that are "neutral analysts of state policy" to raise funds. There is room for a great deal more inquiry that would unite what is known about how policy makers use education research (see Hess, 2008; Henig, 2008) and research on how foundations seek to influence state-level policy debates (Bushouse, 2009).

The States and Equal Educational Opportunity

In the area of education finance, scholars have recently begun to question whether "adequacy studies" are the best way to inform policy decisions about education finance (West & Peterson, 2007). It is also possible that the peak of successful plaintiff arguments on the basis of adequacy is past. If the 2005 Massachusetts Supreme Judicial Court decision in *Hancock v. Driscoll*, which declined to order more state education spending in the name of adequacy, does mark the beginning of a retreat from adequacy-based rulings for plaintiffs, then it will be important to study the resulting state education finance politics, and how defeat of adequacy-based arguments in court affects education spending and outcomes. Scholarship on state education finance policies should track these issues, in particular whether state fiscal crises are contributing to a backlash against adequacy arguments.

Equity issues related to student achievement also persist. Research on states' implementation of No Child Left Behind has made it clear that states' definitions of "proficient" student performance vary greatly. Some activists are now calling for policies that would try to reduce differences among states, such as national standards or a federal-level guarantee of educational opportunity. This movement raises the empirical question of what differences currently exist among students' experiences in different states, as well as the normative question of what differences ought, or ought not, to exist.

State Education Reform and Accountability

As described earlier in this chapter, the widespread state education reform activity of the last quarter of the 20th century generated a great deal of research. Much of this reform was based on the idea of accountability, which also was important in other policy areas (Radin, 2002, 2006). Research on state education reform has the potential to inform scholarship on accountability more broadly, since educational accountability and its effects have been so widely studied.

State Education Policy and Intergovernmental Relations

Now that the state response to increased federal accountability pressure is well underway, the time is ripe for replications and extensions of the influential studies of state-federal interaction. The case-study based research on how federal education policy affects state education agencies, and how federal and state policies interact, is at this point mostly several decades old, even though the federal-state relationship has obviously changed greatly since the 1994. Federal policy on assessment and accountability is far more prescriptive than it used to be, and it also makes new demands on state education agencies that are at least as large as the new demands made by the original ESEA.

The long-standing assumption that federal policies are a key to protecting vulnerable populations, like low-income students, students with limited English proficiency, and students with disabilities, that otherwise cannot compete successfully for state and local resources, should be reexamined. One of the most influential books in American politics (Schattschneider, 1960) claimed that disadvantaged groups *always* gain when the scale of politics increases from local or state to national. The civil rights movement of the 1960s is the textbook case of this phenomenon. However, politics has changed at all levels, in part because of the civil-rights successes of the 1960s, but also because of the way the media affects national political debate. Some evidence suggests that, as a result of these changes, vulnerable groups now can be more successful in local than in national politics (Miller, 2007). Because education policy is so intergovernmental, it would be an excellent area in which to investigate this possibility.

One challenge to future research on intergovernmental relations is that much of the earlier research was federally funded, but the federal government's funding priorities for education research have changed dramatically. A companion law to NCLB reorganized federal education research and replaced the Office of Educational Research and Improvement and the National Institute of Education[6] with the Institute for Education Science (IES), whose mission is to "provide national leadership in expanding fundamental knowledge and understanding of education from early childhood through postsecondary study," through "scientifically valid" research (Education Sciences Reform Act of 2002, §§ 102 & 111). The National Center for Education Evaluation, a subunit of IES, took over responsibility for the National Assessment of Title I. According to the most recent National Assessment, the assessment's emphasis has shifted from policy implementation to scientific studies of curriculum and program effectiveness (USED, 2007). Unless the priorities change again, the likely implication of this shift is that future Title I National Assessments will focus less on the details of state implementation and more on student outcomes. Unless other funders step in, there will be less opportunity for research on state policy questions that cut across issue areas and do not fit within the "what works" conception of research.

* * *

Former U.S. Speaker of the House Tip O'Neill is often quoted as having said that "all politics is local." In education, it would be accurate to paraphrase O'Neill and say that all policy is state policy. This is even true of local or national-level educational change efforts. Local-level education reformers work within the constraints and opportunities produced by state laws and regulations. As Wirt (1977) said, "Local policy services are manifestations of state structures for allocating resources and values; trying to move the former without affecting the latter is like throwing an elephant by grabbing first the end of his trunk" (p. 186). Barring major federal legislative or constitutional change, education reformers with national aspirations will also find that their path lead through 50 state capitals. State policy researchers are certain to be following closely behind them.

Notes

1. This research received support from the Center for Public Policy and Administration at the University of Massachusetts Amherst, where Lisa Hilt provided research assistance. Thanks also to the interlibrary loan and microfoms staff of the W. E. B. DuBois Library at the University of Massachusetts, Peg Goertz, Paul Manna, and two anonymous reviewers whose comments greatly improved the chapter.
2. The Web sites were those of the Education Commission of the States, the National Conference of State Legislatures, and the Council of Chief State School Officers. The journals browsed were *Educational Policy, Educational Evaluation and Policy Analysis, Education Policy Analysis Archives, Policy Studies Journal*, and the *Journal of Policy Analysis and Management*.
3. Usually, but not always. The 1968 Council of Chief State School Officers study *Education in the States* included histories of all 50 state education agencies (Fuller & Pearson, 1969; Pearson & Fuller, 1969). In 2001, the Consortium for Policy Research in Education produced detailed, narrative descriptions of all 50 states' assessment and accountability systems (Goertz, 2001; Goertz & Duffy, 2001).

4. Another methodological flaw of the 2002 Amrein and Berliner study was that it included only states with high-stakes tests, rather than comparing them with states that did not have high-stakes tests. Rosenshine (2003) replicated Amrein and Berliner's analysis with a control group and found that the NAEP gains by states with high-stakes tests actually exceeded those of the states with low-stakes tests. Amrein-Beardsley and Berliner (2003) acknowledged Rosenshine's criticism, but repeated the claim that NAEP gains could still be attributable to exclusion of certain students from the tests, and stood by their original claims about trends in SAT, ACT, and AP test scores.
5. See, for example, Meisels et al. (1988); Harbin, Gallagher, et al. (1989); Harbin, Terry, et al. (1989); Harbin et al. (1990); Harbin et al. (1991); Rivera, Stansfield, Scialdone, & Sharkey (2000); Abedi (2001).
6. The National Institute of Education had been created through federal legislation in 1971, and was later incorporated into the Office of Educational Research and Improvement; see Shavelson & Towne (2002).

References

Abbott, A. (1992). What do cases do? Some notes on activity in sociological analysis. In C. C. Ragin & H. S. Becker (Eds.), *What is a case? Exploring the foundations of social inquiry* (pp. 53–82). New York: Cambridge University Press.

Abedi, J. (2001). *Assessment and accommodations for English language learners: Issues and recommendations* (CRESST Policy Brief 4). Los Angeles: Center for Research on Evaluation, Standards, and Student Testing.

Adams, E. K. (1982). *A changing federalism: The condition of the states*. Denver, CO: Education Commission of the States. (ERIC Document Reproduction Service No. ED220915)

Ahearn, E. M. (1995). *State compliance monitoring practices: An update*. Alexandria, VA: National Association of State Directors of Special Education. (ERIC Document Reproduction Service No. ED304034)

Airasian, P. W. (1987). State mandated testing and educational reform: Context and consequences. *American Journal of Education, 95*, 393–412.

Airasian, P. W. (1988). Symbolic validation: The case of state-mandated, high-stakes testing. *Educational Evaluation and Policy Analysis, 10*, 301–313.

American Federation of Teachers. (2001). *Making standards matter: A fifty-state report on efforts to implement a standards-based system*. Retrieved March 17, 2008, from http://www.aft.org/pubs-reports/downloads/teachers/msm2001.pdf

Amrein, A. L., & Berliner, D. C. (2002). High-stakes testing, uncertainty, and student learning. *Education Policy Analysis Archives, 10*(18). Retrieved February 1, 2003, from http://epaa.asu.edu/epaa/v10n18/

Amrein-Beardsley, A., & Berliner, D. C. (2003, August 4). Re-analysis of NAEP math and reading scores in states with and without high-stakes tests: Response to Rosenshine. *Education Policy Analysis Archives, 11*(25). Retrieved Feburary 9, 2007, from http://epaa.asu.edu/epaa/v11n25/

Amselle, J. (1997). *Bilingual education: A ten state report card*. Washington, DC: Center for Equal Opportunity. (ERIC Document Reproduction Service No. ED421876)

Augenblick, J. (1986). The current status of school financing reform in the states. In V. D. Mueller & M. P. McKeown (Eds.), *The fiscal, legal, and political aspects of state reform of elementary and secondary education: Sixth annual yearbook of the American Education Finance Association* (pp. 3–20). Cambridge, MA: Ballinger.

Augenblick, J. G., Sharp, J. A., Silverstein, J. R., & Palaich, R. M. (2004). Politics and the meaning of adequacy: States work to integrate the concept into K to 12 school finance. In K. DeMoss & K. K. Wong (Eds.), *Money, politics, and law: intersections and conflicts in the provision of educational opportunity. American Education Finance Association 2004 Yearbook* (pp. 17–35). Larchmont, NY: Eye on Education.

Bailey, S. K., Frost, R. T., Marsh, P. E., & Wood, R. C. (1962). *School-men and politics: A study of state aid to education in the Northeast.* Syracuse, NY: Syracuse University Press.

Beard, J., Bull, K. S., & Montgomery, D. (1991). *State directors of special education transition programs: State definitions, and real and ideal teacher competencies.* (ERIC Document Reproduction Service No. ED 342543)

Berke, J. S. (1974a). Recent adventures in school finance: A saga of rocket ships and glider planes. *School Review 82,* 183–206.

Berke, J. S. (1974b). *Answers to inequity: An analysis of the new school finance.* Berkeley, CA: McCutchan.

Berke, J. S. (1979). Federal education policy on school finance after Proposition 13: Short- and long-run implications. *Educational Evaluation and Policy Analysis 1*(5), 19–27.

Berke, J. S., Bailey, S. K., Campbell, A. K., & Sacks, S. (1971a, April). *The pattern of allocation of federal aid to education.* Paper presented at Annual Meeting of the American Educational Research Association. (ERIC Document Reproduction Service No. ED056370)

Berke, J. S., Bailey, S. K., Campbell, A. K., & Sacks, S. (1971b). *Federal aid to education: Who benefits?* Syracuse, NY: Syracuse University Research Corporation. (ERIC Document Reproduction Service No. ED 051441)

Berke, J. S., Shalala, D. E., & Williams, M. F. (1975). *The politics of school finance reform: State referenda, state legislation, and federal incentives.* Paper presented at 18th National Education Finance Conference. (ERIC Document Reproduction Service No. ED173901)

Birman, B. F., Orland, M. E., Jung, R. K., Anson, R. J., Garcia, G. N., Moore, M.T. et al. (1987) *The current operation of the Chapter 1 program: Final report from the National Assessment of Chapter 1.* Washington, DC: United States Department of Education. (ERIC Document Reproduction Service No. ED 289935)

Box-Steffensmeier, J. M., & Jones, B. S. (2004). *Event history modeling: A guide for social scientists.* New York: Cambridge University Press.

Braun, H. I., Wang, A., Jenkins, F., & Weinbaum, E. (2006). The black-white achievement gap: Do state policies matter? *Education Policy Analysis Archives, 14*(8). Retrieved March 12, 2008, from http://epaa.asu.edu/epaa/v14n8/

Burlingame, M. & Geske, T. G. (1979). State politics and education: An examination of selected multiple-state case studies. *Educational Administration Quarterly, 15*(2), 50–75.

Bushouse, B. K. (2009). *Universal preschool in the United States: Policy change, stability, and the Pew Charitable Trusts.* Albany: State University of New York Press.

Callahan, J. J., & Wilken, W. H. (Eds.). (1976). *School finance reform: A legislator's handbook.* Washington, DC: National Conference of State Legislators. (ERIC Document Reproduction Service No. ED122403)

Campbell, R. F., & Mazzoni, T. L., Jr. (1976). *State policymaking for the public schools: A comparative analysis of policy making for the public schools in twelve states and a treatment of state governance models.* Berkeley, CA: McCutchan.

Carnoy, M., & Loeb, S. (2002). Does external accountability affect student outcomes? A cross-state analysis. *Educational Evaluation and Policy Analysis, 24,* 305–331.

Catterall, J. S. (1989). Standards and school dropouts: A national study of tests required for high-school graduation. *American Journal of Education, 98,* 1–34.

Center for Education Reform (2008). *2008 Charter school laws at-a-glance: Current rankings from first to worst.* Retrieved May 7, 2008 from http://www.edreform.com/_upload/ranking_chart.pdf.

Center on Education Policy. (2006). *State high school exit exams: A challenging year.* Retrieved March 17, 2008, from http://www.cep-dc.org/_data/n_0001/resources/live/HSEE2006FINAL.pdf

Center on Education Policy. (2007a). *Educational architects: Do state education agencies have the tools necessary to implement NCLB?* Washington, DC: Author. Retrieved March 17, 2008 from http://www.ecs.org/clearinghouse/74/03/7403.pdf.

Center on Education Policy. (2007b). *State high school exit exams: Work-ing to raise test scores.* Retrieved March 17, 2008, from http://www.cep-dc.org/document/docWindow.cfm?fuseaction=document.viewDocument&documentid=224&documentFormatId=3704

Cibulka, J. G., & Derlin, R. L. (1998a). Accountability policy adoption to policy sustainability: Reforms and systemic initiatives in Colorado and Maryland. *Education and Urban Society, 30,* 502–515.

Cibulka, J. G., & Derlin, R. L. (1998b). Authentic education accountability policies: Implementation of state initiatives in Colorado and Maryland. *Educational Policy, 12,* 84–97.

Citizens Commission on Civil Rights. (1998). *Title I in midstream: State examples.* Washington, DC: Author.

Clarke, M. (2007). State responses to the No Child Left Behind Act: The uncertain link between implementation and "proficiency for all." In C. F. Kaestle & A. E. Lodewick (Eds.), *To educate a nation: Federal and national strategies of school reform* (pp. 144–174). Lawrence: University Press of Kansas.

Clarke, M., Shore, A., Rhoades, K., Abrams, L., Miao, J., & Li, J. (2003). *Perceived effects of state-mandated testing programs on teaching and learning: Findings from interviews with educators in low-, medium-, and high-stakes states.* Chestnut Hill, MA: National Board on Educational Testing and Public Policy. Retrieved May 7, 2008 from http://escholarship.bc.edu/lynch_facp/20/.

Clune, W. H. (1994). The shift from equity to adequacy in school finance. *Educational Policy, 8,* 376–394.

Coates, R. D., & Wilson-Sadberry, K. R. (1994). Minimum-competency testing: Assessing the effects of assessment. *Sociological Focus, 27,* 173–185.

Cohen, D. K., & Ball, D. L. (1990). Policy and practice: An overview. *Educational Evaluation and Policy Analysis, 12,* 233–239.

Cohen, M. (1987). State boards in an era of reform. *Phi Delta Kappan, 69,* 60–64.

Cohen, M. (2002). Unruly crew: Accountability lessons from the Clinton administration. *Education Next, 2*(3), 42–47.

Cohen, M. A., Levin, B., & Beaver, R. (1973). *The political limits to school finance reform.* Washington, DC: The Urban Institute. (ERIC Document Reproduction Service No. ED078521)

Council of Chief State School Officers. (2007a). *State content standards.* Retrieved March 14, 2007, from http://www.ccsso.org/content/pdfs/2006-07%20Content%20Standards%20FINAL.pdf

Council of Chief State School Officers. (2007b). *Statewide student assessment: By subject, 2006–07.* Retrieved March 14, 2007, from http://www.ccsso.org/content/pdfs/2006-07%20Assessment%20053007.pdf

Council of State Social Studies Specialists. (1986). *Social studies education, kindergarten-grade 12: National survey.* Richmond: Virginia Department of Education. (ERIC Document Reproduction Service No. ED289800)

Darling-Hammond, L. (2000). Teacher quality and student achievement: A review of state policy evidence. *Education Policy Analysis Archives 8*(1). Retrieved March 14, 2008, from http://epaa.asu.edu/epaa/v8n1/

DeBartolome, C. A. M. de (1997). What determines state aid to school districts? A positive model of foundation aid as redistribution. *Journal of Policy Analysis and Management, 16,* 32–47.

DeBray, E. H. (2006). *Politics, ideology, and education: Federal policy during the Clinton and Bush administrations.* New York: Teachers College Press.

DeMoss, K. (2003). Who's accountable to the constitution? Thirty years of judicial politics in state education finance litigation. *Peabody Journal of Education, 78*(4), 44–65.

Desimone, L. M., Smith, T. M., Hayes, S. A., & Frisvold, D. (2005). Beyond accountability and average mathematics scores: Relating state education policy attributes to cognitive achievement domains. *Educational Measurement: Issues and Practice, 24*(4), 5–18.

Education Commission of the States. (2004). *ECS report to the nation: State implementation of the No Child Left Behind Act.* Retrieved March 14, 2008, from http://www.ecs.org/html/Special/NCLB/ReportToTheNation/docs/Report_to_the_Nation.pdf

Education Sciences Reform Act of 2002, P.L. 107-279 (2002).

Elazar, D. J. (1984). *American federalism: A view from the states* (3rd ed.). New York: Harper and Row.

Elmore, R. F. (1982). Differential treatment of states in federal education policy. *Peabody Journal of Education, 60*(1), 34–52.

Elmore, R. F. (1984). The political economy of state influence. *Education and Urban Society, 16*(2), 125–144.

Erpenbach, W. J., Forte-Fast, E., Potts, A. (2003). *Statewide educational accountability under NCLB: Central issues arising from an examination of state accountability workbooks and US Department of Education reviews under the No Child Left Behind Act of 2001.* Washington, DC: Council of Chief State School Officers. (ERIC Document Reproduction Service No. ED481838)

Evans, W. N., Murray, S. E., & Schwab, R. M. (1997). Schoolhouses, courthouses, and statehouses after *Serrano. Journal of Policy Analysis and Management 16*, 10–31.

Farrar, E., Millsap, M. A., Nutt-Powell, B., Wilber, N. R., Greene, J. C., Turnbull, B. J., et al. (1986). *State and local administration of the Chapter 1 program, Vol. 1* (Report No. NIE-400-85-1017). Cambridge, MA: ABT Associates, Inc. (ERIC Document Reproduction Service No. ED285965)

Feistritzer, C. E. (2007). *Alternative teacher certification: A state-by-state analysis 2007.* Washington, DC: National Center for Education Information.

Finn, C. E., Jr. (2001). Selective reporting: Quality counts only sometimes in *Education Week's* signature report. *Education Next, 1*(3),69–73.

Finn, C. E., Jr., Petrilli, M. J., & Vanourek, G. (1998). The state of state standards, *Fordham Report, 2*(5).

Firestone, W. A., Fuhrman, S. H., & Kirst, M. W. (1989). *The progress of reform: An appraisal of state education initiatives.* New Brunswick, NJ: Center for Policy Research in Education. (ERIC Document Reproduction Service No. ED315901)

Firestone, W. A., Fuhrman, S. H., & Kirst, M. W. (1990). Implementation, effects of state education reform in the '80s. *NASSP Bulletin, 74*(523), 75–84.

Firestone, W. A., Fuhrman, S. H., & Kirst, M. W. (1991). State educational reform since 1983: Appraisal and the future. *Educational Policy 5*, 233–250.

Ford Foundation. (1976). *Paying for schools and colleges: A Ford Foundation report.* New York: Author. (ERIC Document Reproduction Service No. ED130436)

Ford Foundation. (1981). *The political economy of education: A bibliography of Ford Foundation-supported publications, 1968–1980.* New York: Author.

Fossey, R. (1992). School choice legislation: A survey of the states. New Brunswick, NJ: Consortium for Policy Research in Education.

Fowler, F. C. (1994). Education reform comes to Ohio: An application of Mazzoni's arena model. *Educational Evaluation and Policy Analysis, 16*, 335–350.

Fuhrman, S. H. (1989a). *Diversity amidst standardization: State differential treatment of districts.* New Brunswick, NJ: Center for Policy Research in Education. ED315903)

Fuhrman, S. H. (1989b). State politics and education reform. In J. Hannaway & R. Crowson (Eds.), *The politics of reforming school administration: The 1988 yearbook of the Politics of Education Association* (pp. 61–75). New York: Falmer.

Fuhrman, S. H. (1994). *Challenges in systemic education reform.* New Brunswick, NJ: Consortium for Policy Research in Education. (ERIC Document Reproduction Service No. ED377562)

Fuhrman, S. H., Berke, J., Kirst, M., & Usdan, M. (1979). *State education politics: The case of school finance reform.* Denver, CO: Education Commission of the States. (ERIC Document Reproduction Service No. ED185663)

Fuhrman, S. H., Clune, W. H., & Elmore, R. F. (1988). Research on education reform: Lessons on the implementation of policy. *Teachers College Record, 90*, 237–257.

Fuhrman, S. H., & Elmore, R. F. (1990). Understanding local control in the wake of state education reform. *Educational Evaluation and Policy Analysis 12*, 82–96.

Fuhrman, S. H., & Elmore, R. F. (1992). *Takeover and deregulation: Working models of new state and local regulatory relationships.* New Brunswick, NJ: Consortium for Policy Research in Education. (ERIC Document Reproduction Service No. ED345368)

Fuhrman, S. H., & Elmore, R. F. (1995). Ruling out rules: The evolution of deregulation in state education policy. *Teachers College Record 97*, 279–309.

Fuhrman, S. H., & Rosenthal, A. (Eds.). (1981). *Shaping education policy in the states.* Washington, DC: Institute for Educational Leadership. (ERIC Document Reproduction Service No. ED208550)

Fuller, E. & Pearson, J. B. (Eds.) (1969). *Education in the states, Vol. 2: Nationwide development since 1900.* Washington, DC: National Education Association.

Furtwengler, C. B. (1995). State actions for personnel evaluation: Analysis of reform policies, 1983–1992. *Education Policy Analysis Archives, 3*(4). Retrieved March 14, 2008, from http://epaa.asu.edu/epaa/v3n4.html

Gimpel, J. G., & Schuknecht, J. E. (2003). *Patchwork nation: Sectionalism and political change in American politics.* Ann Arbor: University of Michigan Press.

Goertz, M. E. (2001, April). *The long march: School performance goals and progress measures in state accountability systems.* Paper presented at the American Educational Research Association, Seattle, WA.

Goertz, M. E., & Duffy, M. C. (2001). *Assessment and accountability across the 50 states.* Philadelphia: Consortium for Policy Research in Education. (ERIC Document Reproduction Service No. ED480401)

Graetz, M. J., & Shapiro, I. (2005). *Death by a thousand cuts: The fight over taxing inherited wealth.* Princeton, NJ: Princeton University Press.

Greene, J. P. (2000). *The education freedom index.* New York: The Manhattan Institute. (ERIC Document Reproduction Service No. ED 448246)

Grissmer, D., & Flanagan, A. (2001). Searching for indirect evidence for the effects of statewide reforms. In D. Ravitch (Ed.), *Brookings Papers on Education Policy 2001* (pp. 181–229). Washington, DC: Brookings.

Hamann, E. T. & Lane, B. (2004). The roles of state departments of education as policy intermediaries: Two cases. *Educational Policy 18*(3), 426–455.

Hanushek, E. A., & Raymond, M. E. (2005). Does school accountability lead to improved student performance? *Journal of Policy Analysis and Management, 24*, 297–327.

Harbin, G. L., Gallagher, J. J., & Lillie, T. (1989). *States' progress related to fourteen components of PL 99-457, Part H.* Chapel Hill, NC: Carolina Policy Studies Program. (ERIC Document Reproduction Service No. ED319169)

Harbin, G. L., Gallagher, J. J., Lillie, T., & Eckland, J. (1990). *Status of States' progress in implementing Part H of P.L. 99-457: Report #2 and Executive Summary.* Chapel Hill, NC: Carolina Policy Studies Program. (ERIC Document Reproduction Service No. ED328030)

Harbin, G. L., Gallagher, J. J., & Terry, D. (1991). Defining the eligible population: Policy issues and challenges. *Journal of Early Intervention, 15*, 13–20.

Harbin, G. L., Terry, D., & DaGuio, C. (1989). *Status of the States' progress toward developing a definition for developmentally delayed as required by P.L. 99-457, Part H.* Chapel Hill, NC: Carolina Policy Studies Program. (ERIC Document Reproduction Service No. ED312865)

Henig, J. R. (2008). *Spin cycle: How research is used in policy debates: the case of charter schools.* New York: Russell Sage Foundation.

Hess, F. M. (Ed.). (2008). *When research matters: How scholarship influences education policy.* Washington, DC: American Enterprise Institute.

Hoff, D. J. (2006, May 10). ECS resignations raise questions of fiscal health: Leader of state policy group says problems can be fixed. *Education Week, 25*(36), 1, 24.

Iannaccone, L. (1967). *Politics in education.* New York: Center for Applied Research in Education.

Jacob, B. A. (2001). Getting tough? The impact of high school graduation exams. *Education Evaluation and Policy Analysis, 23,* 99–121.

Joftus, S., & Berman, I. (1998). *Great expectation?: Defining and assessing rigor in state standards for mathematics and English language arts.* Washington, DC: Council for Basic Education.

King, G., Keohane, R. O., & Verba, S. (1994). *Designing social inquiry: Scientific inference in qualitative research.* Princeton, NJ: Princeton University Press.

Kim, J. (2003, April). *The initial response to the accountability requirements in the No Child Left Behind Act: A case study of Virginia and Georgia.* Paper presented at the annual meeting of the American Educational Research Association, Chicago.

Kirst, M. W. (1979). The new politics of state education finance. *Phi Delta Kappan, 60,* 427–432.

Kirst, M. W. (1981). *The state role in education policy innovation.* Stanford, CA: California Institute for Research on Educational Finance and Governance. (ERIC Document Reproduction Service No. ED207160)

Kirst, M. W. (1984a). State policy in an era of transition. *Education and Urban Society 16,* 225–237.

Kirst, M. W. (1984b). The changing balance in state and local power to control education. *Phi Delta Kappan, 66,* 189–191.

Kirst, M. W. (1988). Recent state education reform in the United States: Looking backward and forward. *Educational Administration Quarterly, 24,* 319–328.

Kohl, F. L., McLaughlin, M. J., & Nagle, K. (2006). Alternate achievement standards and assessments: A descriptive investigation of 16 states. *Exceptional Children, 73,* 107–123.

Koyanagi, C., & Gaines, S. (1993). *All systems failure: An examination of the results of neglecting the needs of children with severe emotional disturbance. A guide for advocates.* Alexandria, VA: National Mental Health Association. (ERIC Document Reproduction Service No. ED366146)

Kurtz, M. (2003, January 9). Study questions benefit of high-stakes testing. *Boston Globe,* p. A14.

Lacireno-Paquet, N., & Holyoke, T. T. (2007). Moving forward or sliding backward: The evolution of charter schools in Michigan and the District of Columbia. *Educational Policy, 21,* 185–214.

Lawyers' Committee for Civil Rights Under Law. (1974). *A study of state legal standards for the provision of public education.* Washington, DC: Author.

Linehan, P. (2000). *Statewide behavior initiatives.* Alexandria, VA: National Association of State Directors of Special Education. (ERIC Document Reproduction Service No. ED440505)

Linehan, P., & Markowitz, J. (2002). *Special education data reporting to the public. Revised. Quick turn around (QTA).* Alexandria, VA: National Association of State Directors of Special Education. (ERIC Document Reproduction Service No. ED471796)

Linn, R. L. (2005). Conflicting demands of No Child Left Behind and state systems: Mixed messages about school performance. *Education Policy Analysis Archives, 13*(33). Retrieved March 12, 2008, from http://epaa.asu.edu/epaa/v13n33/

Lipsky, M. (1980). *Street-level bureaucracy: Dilemmas of the individual in public services.* New York: Russell Sage Foundation.

Lusi, S. F. (1997). *The role of state departments of education in complex school reform.* New York: Teachers College Press.

Madsen, J. (1994). *Education reform at the state level: The politics and problems of implementation.* Washington, DC: Falmer Press.

Malen, B. (2003). Tightening the grip? The impact of state activism on local school systems. *Educational Policy, 17,* 195–216.

Malen, B., Croninger, R., Muncey, D., & Redmond-Jones, D. (2002). Reconstituting schools: "Testing" the "theory of action." *Educational Evaluation and Policy Analysis, 24,* 113–132.

Manna, P. (2006). *School's in: Federalism and the national education agenda.* Washington, DC: Georgetown University Press.

Marchant, G. J., Paulson, S. E., & Shunk, A. (2006). Relationships between high-stake testing policies and student achievement after controlling for demographic factors in aggregated data. *Education Policy Analysis Archives, 14*(30). Retrieved March 12, 2008, from http://epaa.asu.edu/epaa/v14n30/

Marshall, C., Mitchell, D., & Wirt, F. (1989). *Culture and education policy in the American states.* Bristol, PA: Falmer Press.

Marshall, J. C., Serow, R. C., & McCarthy, M. M. (1987). *State initiatives in minimum competency testing for students.* Bloomington, IN: Consortium on Educational Policy Studies. (ERIC Document Reproduction Service No. ED292205)

Massell, D. (1998). *State strategies for building local capacity: Addressing the needs of standards-based reform.* Philadelphia: Consortium for Policy Research in Education. (ERIC Document Reproduction Service No. ED424697)

Massell, D. (2000). *Special education in an era of school reform: Building the capacity for standards-based reform.* Washington, DC: Federal Resource Center for Special Education. (ERIC Document Reproduction Service No. ED448571)

Massell, D., Kirst, M., & Hoppe, M. (1997). *Persistence and change: Standards-based reform in nine states.* Philadelphia: Consortium for Policy Research in Education. (ERIC Document Reproduction Service No. ED407718)

Masters, N. A., Salisbury, R. H., & Eliot, T. H. (1964). *State politics and the public schools: An exploratory analysis.* New York: Alfred A. Knopf.

Mazzoni, T. L. (1991). Analyzing state school policymaking: An arena model. *Educational Evaluation and Policy Analysis 13*(2), 115–138.

McCarthy, M. M. & Deignan, P. T. (1992). *What legally constitutes an adequate public education?* Bloomington, IN: Phi Delta Kappa Educational Foundation.

McDermott, K. A. (2003). What causes variation in states' accountability policies? *Peabody Journal of Education, 78*(4), 153–176.

McDermott, K. A. (2007). 'Expanding the moral community' or 'blaming the victim?': The politics of state accountability policy. *American Educational Research Journal, 44,* 77–111.

McDermott, K. A., & DeBray-Pelot, E. H. (in press). Accidental revolution: State policy influences on the No Child Left Behind Act. In L. D. Fusarelli, B. C. Fusarelli, & B. S. Cooper (Eds.), *The rising state: How state power is transforming our nation's schools.* Albany: State University of New York Press.

McDonnell, L. M. (2004). *Politics, persuasion, and educational testing.* Cambridge, MA: Harvard University Press.

McDonnell, L. M. (2005). No Child Left Behind and the federal role in education: Evolution or revolution? Peabody Journal of Education, 80(2), 19–38.

McDonnell, L. M., & Elmore, R. F. (1987). Getting the job done: Alternative policy instruments. *Educational Evaluation and Policy Analysis, 9*(2), 133–152.

McDonnell, L. M., & Fuhrman, S. H. (1986). The political context of reform. In V. D. Mueller & M. P. McKeown (Eds.), *The fiscal, legal, and political aspects of state reform of elementary and secondary education: Sixth annual yearbook of the American Education Finance Association* (pp. 43–64). Cambridge, MA: Ballinger.

McDonnell, L. M., & McLaughlin, M. W. (1980). *Program consolidation and the state role in ESEA Title IV.* Santa Monica, CA: Rand. (ERIC Document Reproduction Service No. ED192464)

McDonnell, L. M., & McLaughlin, M. W. (1982). *Education policy and the role of the states.* Santa Monica, CA: Rand.

Meisels, S. J., Harbin, G., Modigliani, K., & Olson, K. (1988). Formulating optimal state early childhood intervention policies. *Exceptional Children, 55,* 159–165.

Milne, A. M., & Moskowitz, J. (1983). Implications of state programs: The case of special needs pupils. *Education and Urban Society, 15,* 500–524.

Miller, L. L. (2007). The representational biases of federalism: Scope and bias in the political process, revisited. *Perspectives on Politics, 5,* 305–321.

Milstein, M. (1976). *Impact and response: Federal aid and state education agencies.* New York: Teachers' College Press.

Mintrom, M. (2000). *Policy entrepreneurs and school choice.* Washington, DC: Georgetown University Press.

Mintrom, M., & Vergari, S. (1998). Policy networks and innovation diffusion: The case of state education reforms. *Journal of Politics, 60,* 126–148.

Mintrop, H. (2003, January 15). The limits of sanctions in low-performing schools: A study of Maryland and Kentucky schools on probation. *Education Policy Analysis Archives, 11*(3). Retrieved March 12, 2008, from http://epaa.asu.edu/epaa/v11n3.html

Mintrop. H., & Trujillo, T. M. (2005). Corrective action in low-performing schools: Lessons for NCLB implementation from first-generation accountability systems. *Education Policy Analysis Archives, 13*(48). Retrieved March 12, 2008, from http://epaa.asu.edu/epaa/v13n48/

Mitchell, D. E., & Encarnation, D. J. (1984). Alternative state policy mechanisms for influencing school performance. *Educational Researcher, 13*(5), 4–11.

Moore, M. T., Goertz, M. E., & Hartle, T. W. (1983). Interaction of federal and state programs. *Education and Urban Society, 15,* 452–478.

Muller, C., & Schiller, K. S. (2000). Leveling the playing field? Students' educational attainment and states' performance testing. *Sociology of Education, 73,* 196–218.

Murphy, J. T. (1971). Title I of ESEA: The politics of implementing federal education reform. *Harvard Educational Review, 41,* 35–63.

Murphy, J. T. (1973). Title V of ESEA: The impact of discretionary funds on state education bureaucracies. *Harvard Educational Review, 43,* 362–385.

Murphy, J. T. (1974). *State education agencies and discretionary funds: Grease the squeaky wheel.* Lexington, MA: Lexington Books.

Murphy, J. T. (1982). Progress and problems: The paradox of state reform. In A. Lieberman & M. W. McLaughlin (Eds.), *Policy making in education: Eighty-first yearbook of the National Society for the Study of Education* (pp. 195–214). Chicago: University of Chicago Press.

National Association of State Directors of Special Education. (1998a). *Involvement of general education teachers in the IEP process.* Alexandria, VA: Author. (ERIC Document Reproduction Service No. ED426542)

National Association of State Directors of Special Education (1998b). *Performance goals and indicators. Quick turn around (QTA) Forum.* Alexandria, VA: Author. (ERIC Document Reproduction Service No. ED428491)

O'Day, J., & Gross, B. (1999). *One system or two? Title I accountability in the context of high stakes for schools in local districts and states.* Paper presented at American Educational Research Association annual meeting, Seattle, WA. (ERIC Document Reproduction Service No. ED434388)

Odden, A. (1998). *Creating school finance policies that facilitate new goals.* Philadelphia: Consortium for Policy Research in Education. (ERIC Document Reproduction Service No. ED424696)

Odden, A. (1999). *Improving state school finance systems: New realities create need to re-engineer school finance structures.* Philadelphia: Consortium for Policy Research in Education. (ERIC Document Reproduction Service No. ED428462)

Palaich, R., Kloss, J., & Williams, M. F. (1980). *The politics of tax and expenditure limitations: An analysis of public opinion, voting behavior, and the campaigns in four states.* Denver, CO: Education Commission of the States. (ERIC Document Reproduction Service No. ED189694)

Palaich, R., Wendling, W., & Flakus-Mosqueda, P. (1983). *State legislative voting and leadership: The political economy of school finance.* Denver, CO: Education Commission of the States. (ERIC Document Reproduction Service No. ED238094)

Pearson, J. B., & Fuller, E. (Eds.). (1969). *Education in the states: historical development and outlook.* Washington, DC: National Education Association.

Pedulla, J. J., Abrams, L. M., Madaus, G. F., Russell, M. K., Ramos, M. A., & Miao, J. (2003). *Perceived effects of state-mandated testing programs on teaching and learning: Findings from a national survey of teachers.* Chestnut Hill, MA: National Board on Educational Testing

and Public Policy. Retrieved May 7, 2008, from http://escholarship.bc.edu/lynch_facp/51/.

Peterson, P. E., & Hess, F. M. (2005). Johnny can read…in some states: Assessing the rigor of state assessment systems. *Education Next, 5*(3), 52–53.

Peterson, P. E., & Hess, F. M. (2006). Keeping an eye on state standards: A race to the bottom? *Education Next, 6*(3), 28–29.

Piché, D. M. (2001). *Closing the deal: A preliminary report on state compliance with final assessment and accountability requirements under the Improving America's Schools Act of 1994.* Washington, DC: Citizens' Commission on Civil Rights. (ERIC Document Reproduction Service No. ED460200)

Pipho, C. (1980a). *State minimum competency testing programs: Resource guide. Legislation and state policy authorizing state minimum competency testing* (NIE-G-79-0033). Denver, CO: Education Commission of the States. (ERIC Document Reproduction Service No. ED190656)

Pipho, C. (1980b). *Analysis of state minimum competency testing programs* (NIE-G-79-0033). (ERIC Document Reproduction Service No. ED190675)

Place, P., Gallagher, J. J., & Harbin, G. (1989). *State Progress in Policy Development for the Individualized Family Service Plan (P.L. 99-457, Part H).* Chapel Hill, NC: Carolina Policy Studies Program. (ERIC Document Reproduction Service No. ED 312864)

Placier, M. L. (1993). The semantics of state policy making: The case of 'at risk.' *Educational Evaluation and Policy Analysis, 15,* 380–395.

Plunkett, V. R. L. (1991). The states' role in improving compensatory education: Analysis of current trends and suggestions for the future. *Educational Evaluation and Policy Analysis, 13,* 339–344.

Radin, B. A. (2002). *The accountable juggler: The art of leadership in a federal agency.* Washington, DC: Congressional Quarterly Press.

Radin, B. A. (2006). *Challenging the performance movement: Accountability, complexity, and democratic values.* Washington, DC: Georgetown University Press.

Ramsbotham, A. (1980). *The status of minimum competency programs in twelve southern states.* Jackson, MS: Southeastern Public Education Program.

Reed, D. S. (2001). *On equal terms: The constitutional politics of equal opportunity.* Princeton, NJ: Princeton University Press.

Reform bilingual ed; Non-English speakers penalized by status quo. (1997, June 5). *Telegram & Gazette,* p. A14.

Renzulli, L. A., & Roscigno, V. J. (2005). Charter school policy, implementation, and diffusion across the United States. *Sociology of Education, 78,* 344–366.

Rich, A. (2004). *Think tanks, public policy, and the politics of expertise.* New York: Cambridge University Press.

Ritter, G. W., & Lucas, C. J. (2003). Puzzled states. *Education Next, 3*(4), 55–61.

Rivera, C., Stansfield, C. W., Scialdone, L., & Sharkey, M. (2000). *An analysis of state policies for the inclusion and accommodation of English language learners in state assessment programs during 1998–1999. Final Report.* Arlington, VA: George Washington University Center for Equity and Excellence in Education.

Rosenshine, B. (2003). High-stakes testing: Another analysis. *Education Policy Analysis Archives, 11*(24). Retrieved February 9, 2007, from http://epaa.asu.edu/epaa/v11n24/

Rosenthal, A., & Fuhrman, S. (1981a). *Legislative education leadership in the states.* Washington, DC: Institute for Educational Leadership. (ERIC Document Reproduction Service No. ED208549)

Rosenthal, A. & Fuhrman, S. (1981b). Legislative education staffing in the states. *Educational Evaluation and Policy Analysis, 3*(4), 5–16.

Sacken, D. M., & Medina, M., Jr. (1990). Investigating the context of state-level policy formation: A case study of Arizona's bilingual education legislation. *Educational Evaluation and Policy Analysis, 12,* 389–402.

Schattschneider, E. E. (1960). *The semisovereign people: A realist's view of democracy in America.* New York: Holt, Rinehart, and Winston.

Schiller, K. S., & Muller, C. (2003). Raising the bar and equity? Effects of state high school graduation requirements and accountability policies on students' mathematics course taking. *Educational Evaluation and Policy Analysis, 25,* 299–318.

Scott, J. T., & Barber, M. E. (2002). *Charter schools in California, Michigan, and Arizona: An alternative framework for policy analysis* (National Center for the Study of Privatization in Education Occasional Paper #40). Retrieved March 12, 2008, from http://www.ncspe.org/publications_files/468_OP40_v7.pdf

Shavelson, R. J., & Towne, L. (Eds.). (2002). *Scientific research in education.* Washington, DC: National Academies Press.

Smith, M., & O'Day, J. (1990). Systemic school reform. In S. Fuhrman & B. Malen (Eds.), *The politics of curriculum and testing* (pp. 233–267). Philadelphia: The Falmer Press.

Song, M., & Miskel, C. G. (2007). Exploring the structural properties of the state reading policy domain using network visualization technique. *Educational Policy, 21,* 589–614.

Spillane, J. P. (2005). *Standards deviation: How schools misunderstand education policy.* Cambridge, MA: Harvard University Press.

Spillane, J. P., & Zeuli, J. S. (1999). Reform and teaching: Exploring patterns of practice in the context of national and state mathematics reforms. *Educational Evaluation and Policy Analysis, 21,* 1–27.

Sunderman, G. (2006). The unraveling of No Child Left Behind: How negotiated changes transform the law. Cambridge, MA: The Civil Rights Project at Harvard University.

Swanson, C. B., & Stevenson, D. L. (2002). Standards-based reform in practice: Evidence on state policy and classroom instruction from the NAEP state assessments. *Educational Evaluation and Policy Analysis, 24,* 1–27.

Sykes, G. (1990). Organizing policy into practice: Reactions to the cases. *Educational Evaluation and Policy Analysis, 12,* 349–353.

Syracuse University Research Corporation. (1977). *A study of the administration of the Elementary and Secondary Education Act (ESEA) Title I in eight states and thirty-two school districts (Executive Summary).* Syracuse, NY: Author. (ERIC Document Reproduction Service No. ED147984)

Thompson, S., Erickson, R., Thurlow, M., Ysseldyke, J., & Callender, S. (1999). *Status of the states in the development of alternate assessments.* Minneapolis, MN: National Center on Educational Outcomes.

Timar, T. B. (1997). The institutional role of state education departments: A historical perspective. *American Journal of Education, 105,* 231–260.

Toch, T. (1991). *In the name of excellence: The struggle to reform the nation's schools, why it's failing, and what should be done.* New York: Oxford University Press.

Turnbull, B. J. (1984). States propose, schools dispose: Prospects for state initiatives in quality improvements. *Education and Urban Society, 16,* 207–224.

Tyack, D., & James, T. (1986). State government and American public education: Exploring the 'primeval forest.' *History of Education Quarterly, 26,* 39–69.

Tyree, A. K., Jr. (1991, April). *Examining the evidence: Have states eliminated local control of the curriculum?* Paper presented at the annual meeting of the American Educational Research Association, Chicago. (ERIC Document Reproduction Service No. ED335753)

Tyree, A. K., Jr. (1993). Examining the evidence: Have states reduced local control of curriculum? *Educational Evaluation and Policy Analysis, 15,* 34–50.

United States Department of Education. (1996). *Mapping out the national assessment of Title I: The interim report.* Washington, DC: Author. (ERIC Document Reproduction Service No. ED401284)

United States Department of Education. (1999). *Promising results, continuing challenges: The final report of the National Assessment of Title I.* Washington, DC: Author. (ERIC Document Reproduction Service No. ED434418)

United States Department of Education. (2001). *High standards for all students: A report from the National Assessment of Title I on progress and challenges since the 1994 reauthorization.* Washington, DC: author. (ERIC Document Reproduction Service No. ED457280)

United States Department of Education. (2007). *National Assessment of Title I Final Report: Key Findings.* Washington, DC: Author. (ERIC Document Reproduction Service No. ED499016)

Usdan, M. D. (1963). *The political power of education in New York State.* New York: Teachers College, Columbia University, Institute of Administrative Research.

Verstegen, D. A., & Whitney, T. (1997). From courthouses to schoolhouses: Emerging judicial theories of adequacy and equity. *Educational Policy, 11,* 330–352.

Vold, D. J., & DeVitis, J. L. (1991). Introduction. In D. J. Vold & J. L. DeVitis (Eds.), *School reform in the Deep South: A critical appraisal* (pp.1–15). Tuscaloosa: University of Alabama Press.

Wanker, W. P., & Christie, K. (2005). State implementation of the No Child Left Behind Act. *Peabody Journal of Education, 80*(2), 57–72.

Warren, J. R., Jenkins, K. N., & Kulick, R. B. (2006). High school exit examinations and state-level completion and GED rates, 1975 through 2002. *Educational Evaluation and Policy Analysis, 28,* 131–152.

Warren, J. R., & Edwards, M. R. (2005). High school exit examinations and high school completion: Evidence from the early 1990s. *Educational Evaluation and Policy Analysis, 27,* 53–74.

West, M. R., & Peterson, P. E. (2007). The adequacy lawsuit: A critical appraisal. In M. R. West & P. E. Peterson (Eds.), *School money trials: The legal pursuit of educational adequacy* (pp. 1–22). Washington, DC: Brookings.

Willms, J. D. (1999). Basic concepts in hierarchical linear modeling with applications for policy analysis. In G. Cizek (Ed.), *Handbook of educational policy* (pp. 473–493). New York: Academic Press.

Winter, G. (2002, December 28). Make-or-break exams grow, but big study doubts value. *New York Times,* p. A3.

Wirt, F. M. (1977). School policy culture and state decentralization. In J. Scribner (Ed.), *The politics of education: The seventy-sixth yearbook of the National Society for the Study of Education* (pp. 164–187). Chicago: University of Chicago Press.

Wirt, F. M. (1978). What state laws say about local control. *Phi Delta Kappan 59,* 517–520.

Wirt, F. M., & Kirst, M. W. (1997). *The political dynamics of American education.* Berkeley, CA: McCutchan.

Wohlstetter, P. (1989). *Oversight of state education reforms: The motivations and methods of program 'fixers.'* New Brunswick, NJ: Center for Policy Research in Education. (ERIC Document Reproduction Service No. ED336861)

Wohlstetter, P. (1991). Accountability mechanisms for state education reform: Some organizational alternatives. *Educational Evaluation and Policy Analysis 13,* 31–48.

Wohlstetter, P., Wenning, R., & Briggs, K. L. (1995). Charter schools in the United States: The question of autonomy. *Educational Policy 9,* 331–358.

Wong, K. K. (1999). *Funding public schools: politics and policies.* Lawrence: University Press of Kansas.

Wong, K. K., & Shen, F. X. (2002). Politics of state-led reform in education: Market competition and electoral dynamics. *Educational Policy, 16,* 161–192.

Wong, K. K., & Shen, F. X. (2004). Political economy of charter school funding formulas: Exploring state-to-state variations. In K. DeMoss & K. K. Wong (Eds.), *Money, politics, and law: intersections and conflicts in the provision of educational opportunity: 2004 Yearbook of the American Education Finance Association* (pp. 169–196). Larchmont, NY: Eye on Education.

Yu, C. M., & Taylor, W. L. (Eds.). (1999). *Title I in midstream: The fight to improve schools for poor kids.* Washington, DC: Citizens' Commission on Civil Rights. (ERIC Document Reproduction Service No. ED438372)

59

The District Role in Instructional Improvement[1]

GARY SYKES
Michigan State University

JENNIFER O'DAY
American Institutes for Research

TIMOTHY G. FORD
Michigan State University

Introduction

From its inception, the American school district has been regarded as a primary agent of local control meant to keep schools close to those it served. Celebrated as one of the unique inventions of American democracy—perhaps even a cornerstone—the local district has stood as a great exception to the world-wide pattern of centralized governance via national ministries of education. Over much of the past half-century, however, school districts—both in reality and in their conceptualization—have fallen into disfavor, regarded by some as an anachronism and a stubborn impediment to school-level educational improvement (Chubb, 2001; Finn, 1991). Such skepticism coincides with recent policy developments that emphasize instructional improvement as a primary responsibility of educational organization and management. At question is whether districts can learn to exercise this function, with their ability to do so likely to define their effectiveness in the coming years.

While districts have assumed a variety of roles throughout American educational history (as agents of local democratic control, financiers of school construction and operation via local levies, and mediators of state and federal policies), to an increasing degree they now are called on to manage and lead the systematic improvement of instruction and its outcomes for students. A small but growing body of research suggests how districts might fulfill this role, but much remains to be learned.

Our purpose in this chapter is to set an agenda for policy research focused on the role of districts in instructional improvement, with particular attention to large minority and high poverty districts where improving student learning is perhaps most challenging. Our orientation to this purpose is systemic, meaning that we are interested in improvement across whole systems of schools rather than just isolated units or parts. Indeed, it is important to note that when we refer to the "district," we are often referring not simply to the central office or local governing body (although these may be the most obvious policy initiators), but to the whole complex system of interacting actors (teachers, administrators, students, support staff, even parents and communities), units (schools, departments, formal and informal networks), roles, and purposes.

Equally important, we treat districts both as policy systems in their own right and as actors nested within the larger policy systems operating at the state and federal levels. We are thus interested in districts both as policy *initiators* that attempt to coordinate and direct the work of schools within their jurisdiction and as policy *interpreters* and *enactors*, implementing decisions and requirements that originate outside local boundaries and context. We see the coordination of these policy roles—initiator, interpreter, and enactor—as a task of great complexity and consequence and thus an important subject of research. Finally, in this chapter we are particularly interested in the *learning* that is required at all levels of the system to effectively turn attention to the improvement of instruction and student performance, and the relationship of such systemic learning to policy design.

Given this orientation, the chapter advances both a policy argument and a research argument. The policy argument proposes that the interacting systems of federal, state, and local policies—which are today oriented primarily toward holding subunits accountable for a mixture of input and outcome specifications—require emphasis on learning as a policy focus, where learning involves all the actors up and down the system as well as the system itself. This argument necessarily implies that policy instruments and institutions should attend to system-wide learning as a goal and purpose co-equal and in conjunction with the recent emphasis on accountability. This focus, in turn, requires greater understanding of and attention to the relationship between accountability and system-wide learning.

To a large extent, this argument is a contemporary formulation of an older policy wisdom that change requires a combination of pressure and support; one or the other alone is unlikely to prevail against deeply ingrained structures and practices (Huberman & Miles, 1984; McLaughlin, 1987). It also reflects earlier work of Schon (1971), Cohen and Barnes (1993), and others who have argued that policy itself could play an instructive role in school systems. Indeed, joint emphasis on accountability and system-wide learning requires that external policies be reconciled with district organization and management of instruction. We argue that how districts develop as learning organizations in the midst of the contemporary accountability thrust is one of the great challenges facing these organizations. The implication of this theme is two-fold: that districts learn new behaviors, and that external policies better support such learning. We explore these ideas later in this chapter.

On the research side, this chapter proposes that inquiry on districts be expanded to include more and better use of multiple genres, investigators, and methods. Because school districts are complex organizations set within complex environments, we argue that building a base of usable knowledge involves reliance on the full range of inquiry approaches within the arsenal of the social sciences. To date, single and multi-site case studies have comprised the bulk of research on districts. This work has produced provocative and useful knowledge, as well as exemplars for practice—but the expansion of such knowledge calls for ecumenism in methods, approaches, investigators, and purposes of inquiry. One particularly important aspect of this ecumenism is the incorporation of more practice-based inquiry and data analysis into our understanding of what constitutes "research" on districts. Such forms of knowledge development (e.g., documentation research and formative evaluation, systematic internal data collection and analysis, etc) are crucial to continuous improvement of these organizations and systems, and have much to offer the broader field as well.

We return to both these policy and research arguments later in this chapter, but first it is important to address two fundamental questions about districts and instructional improvement. The first is why study districts at all? What evidence is there that districts are a meaningful locus for research if the goal is instructional improvement in classrooms and schools? We address this question in the next section. Second, what is the historical legacy of districts on which a new systemic focus on instruction is to be built, and what does this legacy imply for research in this arena? This is our focus in the following section. We follow these discussions with a brief synopsis of current research on districts and an expansion of the policy and research arguments above. These arguments, then, serve as a frame for the final sections of the chapter, which address the specific topics and approaches for a future research agenda on districts and instructional improvement.

Prospects for the District Role in Instructional Improvement

The argument for the importance of school districts to instructional reform contends with considerable skepticism about their current operation. The research and policy literature is rife with writings critical of the American school district as a policy actor. Such skepticism has both theoretical and empirical standing. For example, Chubb and Moe (1990) advanced an influential critique that laid the failures of school reform squarely at the feet of the American school district. They argue that democratic governance has spawned a top-heavy bureaucracy that interferes with the school-level autonomy necessary for improvement. The process occurs through a distinctive politics: Each political administration (at federal, state, and local levels) seeks to insulate its reforms both from implementation resistance in subordinate bodies and from successive and potentially opposing administrations by relying on detailed rules and regulations. Over time, this body of regulation grows increasingly thick, progressively robbing schools of the freedom they need to respond genuinely to their clientele. Ironically, political processes rising out of the democratic control of schooling beget bureaucracy that foils school improvement (see also West and Mintrom, this volume).

Hess (1999) adds to this account by documenting how urban districts engage in ad hoc program "adoption" in order to make it appear they are "reforming." In attempting to respond to multiple, competing constituencies, district leaders adopt many reforms, but the sum of all this "policy churn" is fragmentation and overload, not steady improvement. Institutional incentives, Hess argues, favor adoption but not steady, coherent implementation of improvement programs or strategies. Ogawa and colleagues (2003) add yet another critique with their description of a district that adopted standards-based reforms in purely symbolic manner absent much substantive change. One of the earliest district studies noted that labor peace, steady school board support, and community acceptance were requirements for an improvement agenda to succeed (Murphy & Hallinger, 1988), yet these "pre-conditions" are infrequently present—particularly in today's urban settings—and their absence fatally weakens the steady progress of an instructional agenda.

Karl Weick's (1976) seminal work on educational organizations as loosely coupled systems provides a theoretical explanation for the district's weak instructional role from a systems perspective. Contrary to Chubb and Moe (1990), Weick argues that loose coupling in both the technical core and authority of office allows for a substantial degree of local innovation and adaptation (i.e., at the school site) on the one hand while limiting the spread of such local innovations on the other. Weick's perspective goes a long way toward explaining the seeming intransigence of American education as an institution despite the constant churn of reforms and reformers. As Cohen (1998) and others have noted about education: *Plus que ça change, plus c'est la meme chose* (The more things change, the more they stay the same).

At the same time, Weick's analysis presents a potential way out of this dilemma. For if we could change what is tightly and loosely coupled in educational systems, might we not actually enable effective practice on a large scale? Indeed, much of the current attention to school districts, as well as basic tenets of standards based reform, rests on the assumption that it is possible to tighten the linkages around the instructional core—while loosening other deleterious controls—such that outcomes for students might be markedly improved.

Evidence of District Effects and Potential Effectiveness

What evidence, then, is there that demonstrates that districts do—or at least could—exert positive, sustained effects on instruction within most, if not all, of the schools under their jurisdiction? First, an accumulating body of evidence from studies of vanguard districts suggests that the district itself can have important effects on matters of teaching, curriculum, and assessment (Elmore & Burney, 1998a, 1998b, 1999; Snipes, Doolittle, & O'Herlihy, 2002; Supovitz, 2006; May & Supovitz, 2006; Togneri & Anderson, 2003). These accounts relate the crucial role that districts play in establishing vision and strategy, working on the technical core (e.g., aligning curriculum district-wide to state standards and assessments and using data for systematic instructional improvement), managing human and fiscal resources, and intervening in low-performing schools to improve their results. Attention to these and other matters marks a shift in focus from improvements that schools alone might accomplish to processes through which *systems of schools* may be improved.

While cross-district studies have not uncovered a large, stable effect size uniquely attributable to the district, there is increasing evidence that distinguishes some districts over time on common outcome measures. To illustrate, Figure 59.1 arrays 7 of California's largest districts over a period of 4 years. While overall reading scores in grades 2–5 improved modestly during this period, stable and sustained differences among these districts, net of their demographic composition, suggest a district effect on student performance. In addition, qualitative and quantitative investigations into what was happening in these systems during these years suggest some hypotheses about what might be contributing to the districts' different trajectories (e.g., see Bitter et al., 2005). Accounts of Long Beach and San Diego, for example, describe the systematic efforts taken to improve instruction and its outcomes across many schools (see Childress, Elmore, Grossman, & Johnson, 2007; O'Day, 2007; Woody, Bae, Park, & Russell, 2006).

Coincidently, while early efforts at standards-based, accountability-oriented reform tended to bypass districts in favor of a policy model that favored a direct line from statehouse to schoolhouse, empirical research suggests that districts may, in fact, play a critical role in how instructional reforms—including standards-based reforms—are implemented at the school level (Berman & McLaughlin, 1977; Elmore & McLaughlin, 1988; Firestone, 1989; Spillane, 1996; Spillane & Thompson, 1997). Indeed, most of the district success stories unfolded in the early years of standards-based reform, suggesting that these ideas had impact at the level of district leadership, particularly in large urban districts that were the first to respond. As a result, analysts now are exploring and documenting how district actions have both positive and adverse consequences for how instructional policies are interpreted and implemented (Bulkley, Fairman, & Martinez, 2004; Spillane, 1996, 2004).

These developments are beginning to revise the dominant neo-institutional theory which posits that management, structure, and process in educational organizations have been decoupled from the technical core of schooling—teaching, curriculum, and assessment (Meyer & Rowan, 1977). To an increasing degree, policy-initiated developments are "tightening" organizational couplings around the

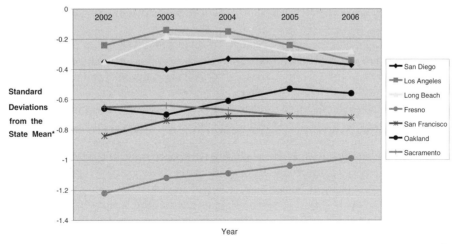

Figure 59.1 District differences in estimated English Language Arts Scores, California Standards Test, Elementary (Grades 2–5), All schools, controlling for differences in school demographics. *Note:* Scale scores are standardized against the state mean in each year; Estimated scores control for differences among schools in school-level demographics (% poverty, % ELL, % African-American, % Hispanic/Latino, % Asian). *Data Source:* CDE (star.cde.ca.gov), official school-level data; Analyses by AIR, 2008

core technology, and the district is playing a significant role in this process (Rowan & Miskel, 1999). While state and federal policy has had a lot to do with this trend, districts are beginning to respond to the new imperatives in the policy system by creating greater alignment and linkage among organizational management, structure, process, and results; district actions now seem more consequential.

In addition to emerging evidence and theory suggestive of a role for districts, there is also a policy argument in favor of districts as instructional actors. Institutional choice theory emphasizes the trade-offs inherent in placing decision-making and implementation authority at one versus another level of the institutional framework (Clune, 1987). Two factors—agreement on substantive goals and capacity to achieve them—are posited to underlie policy choice of institutions. Comparative institutional advantage begins with distrust of existing institutions that are perceived as failing. In a world filled with imperfect institutions, institutional choice typically centers on the "least worst alternative."

The application of institutional choice theory to our discussion of districts is straightforward, if evolving. For example, the original conceptualization of standards-based reform and accountability placed schools at the center of the reform effort with the state as the principal policy actor (Smith & O'Day, 1991). The logic behind this rationale was that the state has both the constitutional authority for education but also controls important policy levers relevant to instructional improvement (teacher preparation and credentialing, textbook adoption, testing), and that coherence among these policy levers would go a long way to producing the conditions necessary for widespread improvement in instruction and student learning in schools. While many believe this logic still holds, after more than a decade of standards-based reform implementation, policy-makers have increasingly come to recognize that districts may hold a comparative advantage over states for certain aspects of standards implementation—particularly with regard to mobilizing support and capacity in schools. Districts seem better suited to allocating resources to spur improvements, especially in low-performing schools; to creating and maintaining political support; and to carrying out other functions that neither the state nor the individual school alone can accomplish. Distrust of school districts undoubtedly was an important factor in choosing states as the key policy actor in standards-based reform, but subsequent developments have come to emphasize a more central role for districts. In other words, districts can play a more consequential role in the accountability—and capacity building—chain between the statehouse and the schoolhouse. Thus, policy makers today have increasingly turned to districts as middle-ground agencies that, in principle, might scale up effective practice.

The District in Historical Perspective

All change is to some extent history dependent. To understand adequately what districts might *become* and how they might realize their potential for instructional improvement, it is important to note several aspects of their historical evolution, and how the "hand of history" exerts influence on current improvement efforts, creating constraints and possibilities for the future.

First, current structures and roles in school districts were developed to serve functions other than the guidance and improvement of instruction. Districts originally were established as political and administrative bodies assigned to manage the growth and establishment of the school system itself (Spring, 1990). From the mid-19th to the mid-20th centuries, attention was focused on dramatically increasing enrollments of an increasingly diverse student population; extending schooling for all through secondary education; building the needed schools; and raising funds in local communities to support such growth (Tyack, 1974). Managing growth, not performance, was the main preoccupation of communities and their schools over the founding and successive decades; significantly less prominent in the daily preoccupations of district superintendents was attention to instruction (Elmore, 1993; Rowan, 1982).

The new organizations also served from their inception as agents of local democracy, as represented in school boards and committees and the administrators who served at their will (Kirst, 1995). Local control of schooling meant that districts confronted a precarious politics tied to often unstable preferences as represented by elected citizens, plural constituencies, and community power brokers (Cremin, 1961; Kaestle, 1983). Cosmopolitan, progressive, or professional claims often collided with desires rooted in particular locales and special interest groups. Schoolmen and women were vulnerable to what some might call whims and vagaries, others the will of the people (Callahan, 1967; Iannacconne & Lutz, 1995). The implication here is that democratic politics with its attendant instabilities in governance regimes will continue to thwart the mobilization of consistent approaches to instructional improvement.

Both institutionalist and organizational perspectives also reckon how history has created impediments to district-wide instructional improvement. Institutionalists, for example, emphasize how cultural scripts arise and come to define what is right, proper, and accepted, and research has identified the cultural script for instruction that is embedded in most schools and districts (see Stigler & Hiebert, 1999). The organizational form that arose in the early years of system growth was bureaucracy, and, as Chubb and Moe (1990) have described, it became in part the creature of democratic politics at all levels of the federal system. Typical features included the early use of testing for decision making, the batch processing of children, a command and control administrative structure, and others. The great promise of efficiency and effectiveness that bureaucracy once promised has left a legacy, especially in large urban districts, of high administrative costs, a thicket of rules and regulations, and a body of personnel policies and practices that serves neither efficiency, effectiveness, nor equity. Bureaucratic structures and processes, then, serve as context and constraint for systematic improvements in instruction.

Districts and their contexts also have evolved in ways that make generalizations suspect due to the variability among them. The long-term trend has been toward consolidation and concentration. Once numbering over 100,000, the current number stands at just under 15,000 (National Center for Education Statistics, 2006). While some states (e.g., California) have over 1,000 districts, others such as Maryland or Delaware have only a handful. As the numbers of districts declined, their size increased. Districts with over 10,000 serve over half the student population; 731 cities alone harbor nearly 30% of all U.S. students (Hoffman, 2007). At the same time, nearly one fifth of all students still attend relatively small rural districts, and one quarter of rural students are members of minority groups; nearly one half of all English Language Learners attend rural schools (Snyder, Dillow, & Hoffman, 2007). Another dimension of variation is grade configuration; while the majority of districts are K–12, some are pre-K to Grade 9, some are high school only, and others are pre-K to Grade 6. Scale, size, and grade configurations are likely factors in district approaches to instruction.

Governance structures also vary among districts. Some (e.g., Boston and Chicago) have school boards appointed by the mayor while in other districts the boards are elected, often by smaller geographical areas within a city. Similarly, some school budgets (e.g. Syracuse and New York City) are part of the larger city budget while others are independent of city finances. Some states have both county districts and city districts within counties, further complicating the interpretation of "district" within these states. Differing governance structures have implications for policy and politics and thus for the context of instructional improvement and policy stability.

If some accounts of instruction tend to portray uniformity in practices, other accounts emphasize variability, particularly around "opportunity to learn" as defined by exposure to curriculum content (see Schmidt & Maier, this volume). Measures for example on such variables as time allocations to topics, coherence across grade levels, and degree of curricular complexity turn up considerable variation within and between schools. Not unexpectedly, much of this variability tends to disadvantage poor and minority students located in urban and rurally isolated communities; large inequalities in instructional resources of various kinds have plagued the system of education to the detriment of many students. In many cases through both inattention and explicit policies, districts have contributed to these inequalities. Whether they can now transcend these historical patterns to foster more equitable student outcomes is the challenge.

Districts also have come to define the social geography of schooling. Particularly over the years since World War II, students of color and poverty, children of immigrants, and those with special needs have come to be concentrated in large urban districts. The effort to desegregate schools following *Brown vs. The Board of Education* appears to have been ineffective; districts are more segregated along race and class lines than ever.[2] While some analysts (e.g.,

Kahlenberg, 2001; Frankenburg, Lee, & Orfield, 2003) have argued that desegregation is a needed and powerful means for improving educational equity, this solution looks to be off the table (especially following the 2007 Supreme Court decision in the cases of Seattle, Washington, and Louisville, Kentucky that prohibited race as a factor in balancing school populations).[3] It seems, then, that one of the great challenges facing districts concerns how to assemble and focus the full array of resources needed to educate the most challenging populations of students. Peer effects are implicated in this task (see Zimmer & Toma, 2000) but also basic resources such as a stable stock of qualified and effective teachers. The social geography contributes to existing inequalities, calling not just for educational but also for social policies to assist in the effort.

A final historically significant development has been increased policy activism at federal and state levels. External policy pressures and the demand for results-based accountability are likely to continue with new policies penetrating more powerfully to the core of schooling—standards for learning, highly specified curriculum content, pacing guides, testing and disaggregated data analysis, new stakes and incentives around learning results, targeted professional development for teachers. Policy development proceeds additively via the accretion of centralized directives. California, for example, has upwards of 100 categorical programs. An older wisdom about policy argued that in a federal system, policy was not a zero-sum game, meaning that increased authority at one level might well stimulate increased authority at other levels (Fuhrman & Elmore, 1990). We may, however, be reaching the limits of this perspective in light of the dramatic increase in the number, reach, and power of the new state and federal policies. Forging instructional coherence out of a fragmented and overloaded policy environment has emerged as a critical task for districts.

At the same time, however, are pressures of new sorts on districts that take the form of market-based solutions, including charter schools, interdistrict enrollment policies, the rise of educational management organizations, and others. If certain pressures conduce to more centralized and standardized instructional policy, other perspectives argue for greater school autonomy, decentralized management, and a "portfolio of schools" approach that would alter the district role dramatically. The future will probably include both strategies as exhibited in one or more of the Nation's large urban districts.

We underscore several points from this brief historical tour. First, managing instructional improvement is a relatively recent development in the history of U.S. school districts, and the R & D track record is modest. In certain respects, policy developments have set the stage for district actions by providing aligned bundles of instruments as resources for use. In other respects, however, the institutional and organizational history of districts has created impediments to improvement in the form of large, unwieldy and unresponsive bureaucracies and governance structures together with significant inequalities in access to resources for improvement at all levels within the system of schooling. Studies of vanguard districts (as we sketch below) point to promising developments, but the tension between centralized management of school improvement and decentralizing policies in support of more autonomous schools will continue to play out. As well, the large variability among districts means that solutions crafted for one district may not transfer easily to others with different characteristics. Theories of action, reform programs, and implementation strategies may not be readily diffused from one district to another, thus research and policy must contend with context and diversity of district types and circumstances. Various theoretical frames and theories of action might be employed to study future developments, and we turn next to an examination of ideas that place learning in the theoretical and practical cross-hairs.

A Framework for Research: Districts and Learning

The preceding commentary on districts suggests that they must make some substantial changes if they are to play a more powerful role in supporting and guiding instructional improvement. Neo-institutional theory includes a framework for understanding the factors that might impel such change. Dimaggio and Powell (1991), for example, have posited three factors that impel change in fields of institutions. *Coercive mechanisms* involve, "…formal and informal pressures exerted on organizations by other organizations upon which they are dependent and by cultural expectations in the society within which the organizations function" (p. 67). In recent years, combinations of pressure from state and federal policies are supplying structuration in districts around instruction. *Mimetic mechanisms* come into play in response to uncertainty. Organizations borrow and adopt from other organizations in response to new imperatives; districts copy one another, especially from those that appear to be managing the new uncertainties successfully. A third mechanism, *normative pressure*, is associated with the professionalization of workers, particularly as it involves development of a cognitive knowledge base and the growth of professional networks that span organizations and across which new models diffuse.

We see each of these factors operating today in school districts, but whether the resulting structuration comes to exert widespread and substantial influence on instruction is still an open question, particularly as theorists have specified organizational responses to institutional processes that range from acceptance to avoidance to defiance (Oliver, 1991). Teacher organizations are implicated in such responses, but also teachers individually and in their workgroups who play a key sense-making role relative to policy pressures so that factors such as congruence with prior practice, intensity and pervasiveness of policy messages, and normative pressures can combine over time to exert influence on teachers' reactions and on their instruction (Coburn, 2004). Absent favorable conditions, such influence is less likely.

From a policy perspective such developments look like the combination of pressure and support that prior research has shown to be effective (e.g., McLaughlin, 1987). Both are necessary because educational institutions often lack the capacity to change in the desired ways—coercion (pressure) without capacity building (support) is insufficient. In today's climate, accountability mechanisms are providing more than ample pressure and are generally accompanied by some attempt at capacity building as well (support). Indeed, one important line of research has sought to tease apart the dimensions of organizational—in this case district—capacity. Spillane and colleagues (this volume), for example, posit three dimensions of capacity at the district level—human, material, and social—that must be cultivated together (to which we would add administrative capacity; see below).

Inherent in Dimaggio and Powell's (1991) institutional change factors and in much of the current policy discussions regarding the need for support and capacity building are notions of individual and organizational learning. Indeed, if as a nation we are to significantly improve instruction and student outcomes, then adults in the system must not only be *motivated* to change what they do (e.g., through policy pressure), but they must actually *learn to do their work in different and more productive ways*. It is in recognition of this need for adult learning that much current policy incorporates attention and resources for professional development, particularly of teachers but to a lesser extent of school and system leaders as well. Yet evidence of large scale impacts of such professional development efforts remains mixed. One important reason for this is that the ability of adults to improve their practice significantly and at scale through learning is constrained by the organizations (schools, departments, central offices) in which they work. Organizational structures, routines, and culture produce shared cognitive maps and practices, influence the degree to which individuals come into contact with new and potentially more productive practices, and help to shape individuals' interpretation of results. Some such routines and structures may help to support individual learning to improve practice while others impede it.

At the same time, organizational theorists have argued that those structures and routines are themselves manifestations of learning—in this case learning at the organizational level. They have developed as the organizations have accumulated experience, interpreted results, and responded to their environments. Indeed, the picture of districts presented in the previous section, for better or worse, can be viewed as the result of over 200 years of such organizational learning. Consequently, if school districts are to become effective actors in the work of instructional improvement, they must themselves learn how to better support the learning/ improvement of individuals and units within them. The question, then, becomes two-fold: How can district systems support the learning of individuals and subunits, and how can district systems themselves learn (change) to work in more productive ways?

A construct that has emerged in the literature—nested or embedded learning systems—is one example of this general perspective on individual and organizational learning (Resnick & Glennan, 2002). The idea of nested learning systems provides a particular descriptive and normative orientation to the internal operation of school districts and to their role in the larger policy systems in which they reside. Viewed from the inside, districts develop policies aimed at instructional improvements; they constitute systems of learning, and, as part of their operation, also help to constitute schools as learning communities. Viewed from the outside, districts are actors within policy systems developed by federal, state, and other authorities. In what has been characterized as a fragmented, decentralized system beaming many, often conflicting, signals into districts and schools (Cohen & Spillane, 1992), a main challenge for districts is to forge coherence out of the policy cacophony (Honig & Hatch, 2004) such that schools and the educators within them can better learn how to continuously modify their practice to improve outcomes for students.

These external and internal views serve to describe districts, but several explicitly normative orientations also propose ways of theorizing district activity. In the High Performance Learning Communities research, Resnick and Glennan (2002) began developing a set of design principles for "nested learning communities" that they defined as, "… organizations in which all individuals and units are expected to upgrade their capacities continuously in accord with a shared set of instructional principles and strategies. In this design, instructional leadership, coupled with reciprocal accountability between 'layers' of the organization, provides professional learning opportunities specifically geared to the district's version of instruction" (p. 165). This conception of districts as part of a nested system takes on normative dimensions, in which the primary responsibility of administrative leadership becomes the professional learning of organizational members, cohered around a common instructional vision. Learning thus becomes an explicit strategy for change and a primary orientation for district leadership. This view opens up a range of topics for the next generation of district studies. It also has implications for the policy systems within which districts are embedded.

The other broad orientation to districts conceives them as actors within the system made up primarily of state and federal policies, as well as of initiatives that stem from such private sector actors as philanthropies, regional agencies, professional associations, and others. As noted earlier, the dominant thrust of current federal and state policy is accountability, although some analysts argue strongly for a learning orientation to accompany if not replace the accountability orientation (see, e.g., Elmore, 2004; O'Day, 2007).

Schon (1971) was an early proponent of this view, and his ideas bear revisiting. He argued that social policy should be conceived as a learning system in which central government acts as the hub. From this perspective, innovation is likely to occur in far flung organizations where practices

are located, rather than in the centralized institutions of governance. Government, in this conception of policy as a learning system, would play a supporting role in the spread of good ideas that originated in the contexts of practice. He wrote:

> Government cannot play the role of 'experimenter for the nation', seeking first to identify the correct solution, then to train society at large in its adaptation. The opportunity for learning is primarily in discovered systems at the periphery, not in the nexus of official policies at the center. Central's role is to detect significant shifts at the periphery, to pay explicit attention to ideas in good currency, and to derive themes of policy by induction. The movement of learning is as much from periphery to periphery, or periphery to center, as from center to periphery. Central comes to function as facilitator of society's learning rather than as society's trainer. (p. 177–178)

Districts may lack the focus, the pressures, and the incentives to improve that external accountability policy may provide (see Rouse, Hannaway, Goldhaber, & Figlio, 2008), but they also may lack the know-how. We argue that a main question for the future is how to develop what some analysts have called "learning policy" (Cohen & Hill, 2006) as a necessary accompaniment to accountability policy. This perspective requires certain kinds of capacity distributed across institutions that range from government agencies to districts to communities and their schools. Districts in this conceptualization play a critical intermediary role between the central agencies of government and the schools that serve as the primary setting for education (see Hubbard, Mehan, & Stein, 2006).

A Synopsis of District Studies We find this notion of nested learning systems to be a particularly useful lens for exploring and planning research on the district role in instructional improvement. Within it, a mounting body of research has described how district actions can enable and/or constrain the work of schools. This includes both the ways in which district policies and actions can support schools as communities of learning and the ways in which lessons and promising practices that emerge from those communities can be spread to other parts of the district system. Across this body of research, a number of threads have emerged that can help inform directions for future research. We turn now to a very brief overview of some of these threads with respect to the district as an instructional system.

First, as Cuban (1988) originally noted, three spheres of action are implicated in discussion of district leadership— the political, the administrative, and the professional. District leaders must manage the politics of their community in order to build and sustain a coalition around instructional reforms. Such a coalition is critical in providing the stability necessary for individual and organizational learning to occur. When districts and the schools within them are buffeted by constantly changing external pressures and by multiple and conflicting messages about what is important to do, they cannot identify, attend to, and use emerging information on strategies and results to alter behavior in a way to improve outcomes. Put another way, they cannot learn. Studies thus reveal that political work is a necessary precursor to systematic instructional improvement

Districts must also manage a set of administrative tasks with skill and competence in order to carry out routine functions while also attending to the instructional agenda. Building "administrative capital" in districts where leadership throughout the organization works in concert on core functions is critical. From a learning perspective, administrative capital helps creates the spaces within which those engaged in instruction can focus on and interpret information about both the strategies they employ and the results those strategies produce so as to yield productive changes in practice. Finally, the district also must organize the activities of teachers around exchanges and interchanges that support the basic tenets of professionalism. As Dimaggio and Powell (1991) point out, professionalism can be a strong factor in institutional change. Important aspects of professionalism include commitment to the client (adult responsibility for student learning), a focus on the specialized knowledge and skills needed for effective practice, and engagement in norms of professional interchange (professional community). Hearts and minds are involved in this work; cultural attributes of districts loom large, and factors such as relational trust, collective efficacy and responsibility are implicated in this process.

Table 59.1 uses these spheres of activity to array factors that have emerged from multiple studies of district effectiveness. Several key ideas serve to unify these elements. One is the concept of district-wide instructional coherence (see, e.g., Childress et al., 2007; Thompson, Sykes, & Skrla, 2008). Broadly speaking, coherence has both sociocultural and technical dimensions. On the social side, it refers to processes through which agreement is forged up and down the district around mission and strategy. Also implicated is a district culture that fosters trust and legitimacy around the instructional mission, together with creation of collective efficacy and responsibility oriented to strong academic press. Studies are accumulating that show a relationship between teachers' collective belief that "we can be successful with these students," and a belief that "we are responsible for these students." (Goddard, Hoy, & Woolfolk, 2000; Hoy, Sweetland, & Smith, 2002; Tschannen-Moran, Woolfolk, Hoy, & Hoy, 1998; Lee & Smith, 1996). Further, when such beliefs are oriented around a rigorous academic curriculum featuring a combination of high demand with high support for learning, positive results for students are obtained (Shouse, 1996; Phillips, 1997). Theory proposes that in districts where these cultural features are common across many if not most schools, academic achievement will be both high and equitable.

On the technical side, district-wide coherence refers to how primary elements of instruction are aligned and coordinated. These include: learning standards, curriculum

TABLE 59.1

Elements of District-Wide Instructional Effectiveness

Political Sphere

—Forming and sustaining a community-based political coalition around vision and strategy

—Building staff consensus around an explicit, focused instructional vision and strategy

—Managing the external environment of the district to achieve focus and coherence around vision and strategy

—Acquiring and allocating fiscal resources to support the instructional mission

Administrative Sphere

—Creating alignment district-wide among standards of learning, curriculum materials, assessments, and instruction

—Creating instructional guidance tools, routines, and resources shared among teachers and administrators

—Using data to support cycles of continuous improvement around program implementation and results

—Instituting a variety of "second chance" learning opportunities for students

—Creating mechanisms of accountability and support for low performing schools in the district

—Managing human resources to support the instructional vision, including staff recruitment, placement, retention, and ongoing professional development; also, attention to new roles (i.e., instructional coaches) that support systematic improvement of instruction

—Managing support operations such that they contribute to rather than distract from the instructional mission

Professional Sphere

—Creating high levels of relational trust among teachers around district mission and strategy

—Formation of communities of practice among teachers within and across schools

—Building in hallmarks of professional community including deprivatized practice, shared values, reflective dialogue, focus on student learning, and collaboration

—Enhancing collective efficacy and responsibility

materials, and assessments; "second-chance" learning opportunities; instructional guidance and cycles of feedback and adjustment around program implementation and outcomes; ongoing organizational and professional learning for staff; and mobilization of human and fiscal resources. Technical elements of coherence have both conceptual and administrative dimensions. The very concept of alignment is multi-dimensional and requires further exploration (Webb, 2005), as do the administrative mechanisms for producing and sustaining such alignment.

Instructional coherence has been shown to be an important property of schools (Newmann, Smith, Allensworth, & Bryk, 2001) so that from one perspective, district-wide coherence might be regarded just as the sum of coherence school by school. But for several reasons the concept of systemic coherence at the district level may add value to its school-level counterpart. First, certain functions conducive to instructional coherence reside naturally at the district level. These include, for example, managing the external environment to "pull in" elements supporting mission and strategy while "buffering" elements that distract and fragment effort and attention (Honig & Hatch, 2004). Relatedly, fiscal resource acquisition and allocation is another key function coordinated primarily by the district. In effective districts, funds to support program development, technology infrastructure, professional development, and other key priorities are mobilized and allocated in support of the district mission. Also critical to coherence is the district's human resource function, including how teachers and administrators are selected, placed, and supported in line with the instructional mission. As stated earlier, coherence in these areas may be beneficial to learning at both the individual and school levels. But we must also ask, at what point does coherence become counter-productive to learning and improvement? Can there be too much coherence? Can the technical core be so tightly aligned that innovation and variation necessary for learning are driven out of the system? Some analysts have suggested that the current singular focus on test scores, coupled with a constrained and prescriptive approach to acceptable practice, are driving the system in this direction (see, e.g., Nichols & Berliner, 2007; Meier, 2000; O'Day & Quick, in press).

Finally, an emerging hypothesis about coherence concerns the creation of professional learning communities (PLCs), which are implicated in both individual and organizational learning. The How People Learn framework (Bransford, Brown, & Cocking, 1999) emphasizes the social dimension of individual learning. On the organizational side, professional communities potentially support the identification of effective practices and the spread of such practices across classrooms, schools, and locales. PLCs among teachers are related to district actions that include creating instructional commonalities around which collaboration can occur; allocating time and other resources to teacher exchanges; complementing professional with organizational accountability; orchestrating professional development in relation to shared mission and strategy; and mobilizing teacher leadership, including new positions and roles, in support of district-wide instruction (O'Day, 2002; Thompson, Sykes, & Skrla, 2008). A second key idea then—robust professional community among teachers—is thereby implicated not simply as a property of individual schools, but of district-wide developments. As one analysis argues, "The district is the system context of greatest significance for teachers' school-based learning communities … [T]hough it is possible for a strong school-based learning community to develop despite the district, it is unlikely that it can be sustained or extended to other schools if the district is not actively supportive" (McLaughlin & Talbert, 2006, p. 116–117).

Some Caveats Before turning to an agenda for future studies, we note that any observations about "effective districts" must be tempered in several ways. One concerns normative orientation. The idea of systemic action extends district control over the functions of teaching and learning in the name of increased rationality, improved efficiency, and productivity. Not all observers or analysts believe that these rationalizing tendencies comport well with all conceptions of "good" teaching and learning. Consequently, studies that document the pace and progress of centralized controls represent "progress" or "reform" only from particular normative perspectives (see, e.g., Fuller, this volume). An interest in "coherence" begs the question, "coherence for or around what?" While some district cases build upward from a particular normative orientation to teaching and learning (see, e.g., Stein & D'Amico, 2002), in other instances standardized tests serve as the criterion for teaching—a practice that has provoked criticisms (see, e.g., Firestone, Schorr, & Monfils, 2004).

And, as indicated above, a related issue concerns the unforeseen consequences of district actions that might compromise valued outcomes. Critics, for example, invoke "Campbell's Law" in challenging the merits of accountability policies oriented around high-stakes testing (Nichols & Berliner, 2007). Named for its author, the methodologist Donald Campbell, the law states that, "The more any quantitative social indicator is used for social decision making, the more subject it will be to corruption pressures, and the more apt it will be to distort and corrupt the social processes it was intended to monitor" (Nichols & Berliner, 2007, pp. 26–27). A debate has emerged in U.S. society around the No Child Left Behind legislation and related state accountability policies that implicates district responses to the accountability pressures represented in this law. While reforms of the legislation itself are likely to unfold in future, questions arise as to the institutional changes that this law and parallel state laws may engender in districts. To some observers, accountability demands may be creating the framework for tighter coupling among elements of structure, process, and resource allocation around instruction. To other observers, such tightening may improve organizational rationality but degrade the quality of teaching and learning. Studies, then, are needed not simply to judge whether implementation is occurring, but also to determine its effects, as these are nested in various conceptions of educational quality and equity.

And finally there is the issue of context. Findings from existing district studies must be tempered with an understanding that context matters and that generalizations framed at high levels of abstraction conceal important differences, nuances, and challenges. In addition, little knowledge is available concerning processes that move districts from being less effective to being more so. Static accounts of district characteristics, together with context-bound case histories, compose the bulk of the literature. Thus, the emerging literature on districts has substantial holes, though we acknowledge that it contains more complexity and nuance than this thin portrayal allows. Nevertheless, the threads outlined above suffice as a basis for turning next to an emerging agenda for future research.

An Agenda for District Policy Research

Based on our argument that a focus on system-wide learning is a necessary accompaniment to a focus on accountability, and drawing on our outline of the historical and institutional foundations of districts and findings from existing district literature, our purpose in this section is to set forth recommendations for the future study of districts. We first consider the processes within districts directed to the organization and management of teaching and learning and then move to questions concerning how districts respond to policies and other influences in their environments. In this section we recommend seven topics for study based on our review of the district literature, and our central argument concerning systemic learning.

District-Wide Instructional Coherence   A logical place to begin is with the issue of district-wide instructional coherence. Coherence has emerged as a defining issue due both to its promise for improvement and to the many challenges externally and internally to its creation. As already indicated, a fragmented policy environment will likely contribute to a fragmented district. One aspect of the challenge for districts, therefore, is the manner in which they forge coherence in response to the many competing and conflicting stimuli from the environment.

A second aspect is how districts forge coherence as a characteristic of internal district-wide instructional functioning. The assumption here is that districts bring together many aspects of their operations to support the instructional mission. Knapp and colleagues (2003), for example, identify 23 separate strategies and argue these must be selected and combined in various ways depending on features of the local context. Hill and Celio (1998) recommend using "multiple approaches" after noticing that most theories of action are incomplete to some degree. Particular elements and their sequencing are likely to vary from district to district but might include staffing patterns, professional development, curriculum alignment, common assessments, data-based decision making around outcomes, and others. Because districts are in charge of and also have the capacity to coordinate functions and processes, they are in position to construct coherence using a broad range of tools. While evidence from prior research suggests that systemic coherence is important, we still have relatively little information about how districts not only align their instructional and operational programs but also how they create and sustain the needed coherence over time and across other changes in internal and external conditions.

A third aspect of the challenges of coherence concerns district actions in forging school-level instructional coherence. Studies have revealed how districts can monitor individual schools, then intervene as needed to build capacity (e.g., Elmore & Burney, 1998b). Given the likelihood of variability across schools in a district, a key role for districts is to assist those schools that may be under-performing. Because one key dimension of performance is school-wide instructional coherence (Newmann et al., 2001), district actions can be critical in moving schools toward this ideal. Understanding how school-level coherence is related to district coherence and how both can be purposefully gen-

erated in a variety of contexts is an important issue for further study.

The Politics of Instructional Improvement   Set within the political sphere, a host of questions arise concerning how districts establish and sustain the political pre-conditions necessary for sustained systemic learning and steady work on instructional improvement. How do districts manage the external policy environment and the contending interest groups within local communities? District accounts to date tend to start with a description of effective practices without analyzing how the district was able to create the political and social conditions that gave rise to the practices. The concept of civic capacity (Stone, Henig, Jones, & Pierannunzi, 2001) is particularly promising in this regard. Civic capacity entails the mobilization of a broad coalition of disparate interests to cooperate in addressing a commonly defined problem on a sustained basis. As Smith (2004) points out, civic capacity emphasizes "power to" rather than "power over"—the power to accomplish individual or group goals by accomplishing broader civic goals.

Like social capital, civic capacity involves relationships with high degrees of trust and reciprocity—attributes of social relationships which facilitate cooperative action (Coleman, 1990). While social capital is often construed as largely private, interpersonal, and informal, civic capacity is public, involves major groups and institutions across sectors (e.g., community-based and advocacy organizations, business associations and chambers of commerce, unions, general city or county government, and school districts themselves), and is typically formalized in collaborative organizations or compacts with reliable funding and significant staffing. Political skill and deliberate effort are required to overcome the intergroup tensions associated with group identity and advocacy and to organize cooperative action across sectors. Particularly when trusting interpersonal relationships transcend group boundaries, social capital may be a resource for skilled political leaders to use in building civic capacity—this is tempered with the understanding that social capital in the strictly interpersonal sense does not necessarily engender civic capacity.

Similarly, the problems around which civic capacity are mobilized may grow out of troubling situations, but political leaders must give problems clear and shared definition if they are to serve as a basis for cooperative action. In the sphere of urban redevelopment, the short-term material and political benefits derived by cooperating groups (e.g., contracts for minority businesses in return for political support for rezoning) play a substantial role in sustaining coalitions. But in education, political leaders' ability to persuade actors to view their long term individual and group interests in the frame of a broader civic vision may be more important. Defining problems in community-wide terms can help affect this shift in perspective, as can public forums that call on participants to see themselves as civic leaders rather than solely as representatives of private or group interests. Studies, then, are needed to explore and explain how districts manage the political and policy process as a precondition for work on instruction.

Learning the Practice of Instructional Improvement A third arena for research that cuts across the administrative and professional spheres concerns how districts learn the practice of instructional improvement and how they can learn to be better learners. As indicated, instructional guidance as a core responsibility is new for districts, and they must pursue it not instead of but alongside their traditional responsibilities. One aspect of the needed learning thus involves how to mobilize other district functions such as professional development, school staffing decisions, and resource allocations, for example, in service of the instructional mission. Another aspect concerns how districts as organizations learn the practice of instructional improvement.

Three theoretical views on this subject have emerged. One views organizational learning as the sum of individual learning within the organization. A second involves how groups acquire shared knowledge through social interactions to induce shared learning across individuals; "… when a *group* acquires the know-how associated with its ability to carry out its collective activities" (Supovitz, in press, p. 1). This usage often invokes social or cultural attributes. And the third involves embedding learning in the tools, rules, and routines of the organization. These are, respectively, the cognitive, social, and institutional bases of organizational learning (Supovitz, 2006). In his case study of Duval County, Florida, for example, Supovitz describes how the district-wide practice of using "dashboard lights"—snapshot data on program implementation—helped educators to learn about the America's Choice reform that the district was using. He argues that this third conception of organizational learning is particularly important and deserves greater study. Clearly, however, the idea of organizational learning as applied to instruction has emerged as critical to district studies and is receiving increased theoretical and empirical attention. This makes sense because a key issue is how a shared practice of teaching may be created on a district-wide basis not strictly as a function of external mandates, but of capacity building conceived in terms of organizational learning. Here, then, the central concern is for districts as learning organizations in relation to support for instructional improvement.

Learning the practice of organizational improvement is a multi-dimensional concept that calls for better measures at the individual, group, and organizational levels. As in the Duval case with its creation of implementation measures, participants may develop such measures as part of larger strategies through which districts use data for monitoring and decision making. Likewise, though, researchers also need such measures to study organizational learning as it unfolds and spreads. "Learning policy" conceived as a district phenomenon requires better measurement strategies embedded in longitudinal designs.

Scaling Up Programs and Practices A fourth broad topic for research concerns how districts scale up localized programs and practices shown to have merit, and how they can institute broad-based instructional improvement efforts at scale across the entire system. Here too are questions that span internal and external responses. In light of evidence on wide variability in both curriculum and instruction at classroom and school levels, a critical issue concerns how districts work to improve opportunity to learn for all students by reducing variability in ways that create more exposure to key content together with related instructional practices. Coburn (2003) has distinguished four dimensions of scale, identified as depth (related to deep change in instructional practices); breadth (the spread of change across many classrooms); ownership (the transfer of commitment from those initiating the change to those who must implement it); and sustainability (the changes persist over time, even in the face of turnover in key personnel).

These are useful criteria, but they require much more exploration, and many questions surround the nature of variability in district practices along these dimensions. On one hand, many studies have revealed stable patterns of inequity in the distribution of effective teachers and teaching to the disadvantage of poor and minority children. This fact argues in favor of increasing the uniformity of curriculum and instruction in the interests of equity. But critiques point out that well-meaning interventions of this kind can undercut effective teaching by creating lockstep procedures and practices, so balance is clearly needed. What, though, is the proper balance between centralized authority and direction on one hand and local initiative and professional judgment on the other? How do successful districts manage this balance? How do they learn from and spread good practices, provide teachers opportunity to develop deep understanding of new practices, and create genuine ownership? The criteria proffered by Coburn can, in fact, easily come into conflict with one another. These criteria supply fertile leads for the measurement of implementation over time, tracking how instructional improvements spread, deepen, and sustain themselves—especially in the face of staff turnover and student mobility, which have proven disruptive to learning (see Rowan and colleagues, this volume).

Furthermore, studies have shown that standards-based reforms may standardize less than meets the eye because teachers inevitably interpret and make sense of any new initiatives based on such factors as prior knowledge and experience, agreement with reform practices, and other factors (Coburn, 2004; Spillane, 2004). Professional development is likely to make a large difference in such circumstances, but developing a shared base of practice also may rely on professionalizing reforms that bring teachers more centrally into the account as actors not just enactors. Practices in other nations such as lesson study in Japan appear to cultivate teachers' professional judgment, knowledge, and experience in ways that have not emerged on a widespread basis in the United States (Stigler & Hiebert, 1999). In any event, scaling up good practice as a district-wide commitment involves evident complexities that call for greater study.

Managing Human Resources   A fifth concern rising out of existing research is how districts manage the human resource function to support better teaching and learning. Two observations frame this issue. First, studies are beginning to document the importance of teacher quality (as measured in various ways) to student achievement (Aaronson & Barrow, 2007; Rockoff, 2004; Rivkin, Hanushek, & Kain, 2005).

Second, other studies have described the difficulties that many districts have in recruiting and retaining qualified teachers. Attrition is a systemic problem in many urban and rural districts that places strains on recruitment in the face of high turnover (Ingersoll, 2001).

The hypothesis here is that inefficiencies in district recruiting, hiring, and placement practices undercut school improvement and so point to the improvement in these functions when they are attended to by top leadership. As well, the ways that districts manage professional development for all personnel—teachers and administrators alike—have emerged as a central issue. Celebrated cases such as New York City's Community District #2 place professional learning at the very center of district-wide instructional improvement (see Elmore & Burney, 1998a, 1998b, 1999).

Taken together, the pattern of studies suggests that many districts are not attending centrally to human resource management, and that such attention is one key to improved learning outcomes. Studies, then, are needed that document what districts are doing and how vanguard districts are reforming their practices in order to overcome historic and deeply entrenched dysfunctions in the management of human resources. Some work is beginning to indicate that combinations of state and district policies are capable of improving the stock of teachers in urban schools (see, e.g., Boyd, Lankford, Loeb, Rockoff, & Wyckoff, 2008), but more cases of effective district actions are needed both to highlight the importance of this district function and to demonstrate how districts can better manage it in conjunction with supportive state policy.

Managing the Organization   Sixth, and more prosaically, districts cannot lose grasp on how to maintain many routine administrative functions *upon* which the overall effectiveness of the district depends. As March (1978) famously quipped, educational administration is "…a bus schedule with footnotes by Kierkegaard" (p. 244). He notes that elementary competence in making a bureaucracy work is under-valued when compared to heroic notions of leadership. District administrators cannot fail to carry out routine administrative functions efficiently even as they attend to instruction and the requisite learning across the system.

As districts increase in size and complexity, overall organization and management are vital and consume a lion's share of administrative time and attention. Leadership too is increasingly conceived as widely distributed (Spillane, 2006), but how particular functions are distributed so that routine management is effected competently alongside instructional leadership remains an issue of central importance about which relatively little is known. Districts

must develop effective information management systems; budgeting procedures that target funds to needed areas; personnel procedures that recruit, cultivate, and match personnel to positions and other functions. In new markets of schooling ushered in by school choice regimes, they also must respond to client demands, compete for students, maintain enrollments, raise funds, and diversify offerings. At the same time, they also must respond to the increased weight of federal and state policies. By concentrating just on the importance of instructional improvement, studies have tended to overlook how the sum total of demands on leadership are being carried out.

Forging Professional Community among Teachers   While the above issues are embedded primarily in the administrative sphere of districts, a seventh issue focuses on how district administrative actions help to forge community among teachers around instruction. Teaching increasingly is conceived as a distributed practice involving interactions among teachers within and across schools (Cobb et al., 2003). As noted earlier, these communities provide rich opportunities for individual and collective learning. How district actions afford the development of "communities of practice" among teachers has thus emerged as a central topic for study. Following Wenger (1998) these analysts characterize communities of practice as involving (1) joint enterprise; (2) mutual relationships; and (3) a well-honed repertoire of ways of reasoning with tools and artifacts. O'Day (2002) adds a further element in noting that, "Standards of practice, constructed generally across the profession and more particularly within the professional community of the school, provide cognitive maps for this process of meaning creation" (p. 317). Two questions here seem critical. First, what are the means and the specifics concerning how these elements are concerted around instruction in a district? Second, in the absence of a history and tradition of strong professionalism in teaching—especially in support of an equity agenda for learning—how might districts participate in developing the requisite beliefs, attitudes, and actions?

While the school clearly is a context of high salience for professional reforms, the district also appears to be crucial for several reasons. First, mutual relations among teachers can benefit from networks that "drape" across schools as this helps extend access to valuable information (Coburn & Russell, 2008). Second, districts organize staffing patterns and allocate resources in support of professional interchanges among teachers. For example, the addition of positions such as "instructional coach" that help mediate communication and information flow among teachers typically requires district staffing decisions and resource reallocations. In this manner, districts are well-placed to provide structural supports and affordances for professional exchanges around instruction. Third, districts are responsible for instituting common "instructional regimes" that provide the basis in practice for teacher exchanges and interchanges. Raudenbush (2008) defines this idea as "…a more or less explicit set of rules for repeatedly assessing student skill and then tailoring instructional activities in response in order to achieve more or less explicit aims for student learning" (p. 210).

Such regimes may incorporate varying levels of professional judgment among teachers (compare, for example, Success for All with America's Choice as described by Rowan et al., this volume), but the emphasis is on shared approaches among teachers. Absent common practices, professional exchanges are unlikely to overcome the prevailing pattern of isolation and normative anomie that has characterized teaching (Lortie, 1975). And finally, as O'Day (2002) has noted, accountability likely depends on a combination of bureaucratic and professional forms that link district administrative actions with norms and standards of professional practice. She argues that a balance between these two forms of accountability is needed to offset the weaknesses of either one alone. Much remains to be understood about how district actions build, make use of, and sustain communities of practice among teachers for purposes of instructional improvement; nevertheless, a body of research is emerging on this issue with the district playing a pivotal role.

On all these issues it will be critical to *trace the processes* through which districts achieve and sustain coherence; build civic capacity; pursue organizational learning; scale up good practice; manage human resources; provide basic administrative competence; and create community among teachers. Moreover, we will need studies that explicate how these critical matters are accomplished *across a range of contexts*.

The District within the Broader Policy System   We turn next to districts as actors within the policy system. Recall that we have argued for a particular normative orientation to policy—that it serve as a stimulus for learning. This role overlaps with traditional calls for capacity-building policies (see, e.g., McDonnell & Elmore, 1987), but places particular emphasis on learning as interactive, reciprocal, and distributed across institutions and agencies. The assumption behind this orientation frames instructional improvement as a complex matter that requires learning on the part of all the engaged parties, and that such learning originates in many locales. If, in relation to instructional improvement, policy systems are conceived as learning systems within which districts are a nested actor, then a number of fruitful questions for future work emerge.

Learning from Outside Sources   One set of questions concerns how districts learn from one another and from other sources engaged in district-oriented improvement strategies. How, this line of inquiry asks, might districts with other actors break out of the pattern of faddish reforms that have a short shelf-life, spreading to some number of districts before fading away? Related questions here concern how to validate ideas "in good currency" (to use Schon's term), disseminate them efficiently and effectively, and determine

how they may be adapted from one context to another. While activity of this kind has always occurred among districts, relatively little is known about the process by which it occurs and how to improve it. Here the emphasis is on how districts can learn effectively from one another.

The Role of External Actors in District Learning   A related question concerns how external actors can support district-to-district learning. This calls for a novel role for state agencies (and other system actors such as universities), to study district best practices, then to create methods for disseminating information and guidance from district to district. Technology is an obvious affordance here, but traditional means such as site visits and more extended consultations also would be valuable. When districts or schools seek to disseminate good practices from teacher to teacher within or across schools, the methods typically include cycles of discussion and study, observation, guided practice, and follow up consultations. Such models at the level of teaching practice might be scaled up to accommodate learning the leadership of instruction from high performing to other districts in states or regions. Studies that explore how external actors can assist district to district learning seem another useful focus, particularly when orchestrated around "alike" districts that are facing common problems (e.g., concentrations of second language learners).

Importing vs. Exporting District Functions   An emerging element in the external environment of districts is the presence of a wide range of service providers who assist with whole-school models, supply supplemental services, intervene in low-performing schools, manage schools of choice, and others. To a greater extent than in times past, districts are facing a "service rich" environment that provokes questions about the pros and cons of external assistance, quality assurance, the functions that are best imported vs. exported, the optimal use of contracting for services, and related matters. To an increasing degree the education sector is now a mixed economy of governmental and market-based provision, raising a host of questions about effective administration under these new circumstances. A new market of service providers is growing up around districts, but how and whether such providers are genuinely adding value to district operations is a rich topic for future studies.

Policy Support for District Learning   Then, another question concerns how external policies can best support the instructional mission of school districts. Policy studies of this kind would examine how the sum of state and federal policies influence district learning as it relates to key administrative functions, professional development, and school-level learning about instruction. Contending ideas currently favor accountability as stimulus for learning together with systemic reforms that align factors of production. These are reasonable approaches, but they may prove too narrow in the long run, possibly even misdirected. We argue for policy innovations and inventions to stimulate system-wide learning, which may serve as sites for policy research. Some examples already are appearing. States such as Connecticut and North Carolina have invested in a coordinated array of policies aimed at recruiting and placing personnel in high-need districts; developing alternative assessments for learning keyed to state standards; and creating widely used courses of study to direct teaching and learning, to name a few. The important point here, though, is to understand how innovative policies support district efforts to improve teaching and learning—and to understand how districts are "using reform" to effect systematic instructional improvement (Firestone, 1989).

A parallel point concerns how actions in response to external policies may be used to inform subsequent policy making. Along these lines, Elmore (1983) characterized what he called regulatory vs. programmatic approaches to policy development. In the first, the aim was to increasingly fine-tune regulations to induce behavioral compliance at lower levels of the policy system. But in fields such as education, he argued, the issue was not only (or not simply) compliance, but also development. Policy actors needed to develop ways of responding to policy goals that were attuned to their contexts; policy makers, then, also needed to be learners in order to develop better policies. To be sure, traditional mechanisms have been in place to promote policy learning. These include hearings, commissioned studies, informal fact-finding, site visits, and surveys. An apparatus is in place that, in principle, serves to inform policy with practice, just as practice is informed by policy. At the moment, the regulatory view predominates, so there is ample need to resurrect the developmental view through which policy is informed through studies of practice, through the process described as "backward mapping."

A Medley of Methods for the Study of School Districts

Turning finally to questions of method, we argue for a broad approach that makes use of multiple methods, geared to the variety of issues that we have identified. Case studies have comprised most of the research on districts so far. A common approach has been to identify exemplar districts through an analysis of standardized test performance and then to conduct qualitative inquiry in those high-achieving districts to determine the surface factors that may be associated with high, equitable, and sustained achievement. Such studies suffer the usual defects with respect to causal inference including lack of counterfactual examples, absence of a precipitating event or intervention to study, complex causal texture within which the relationships among multiple variables are obscured, and limited generalizability. Further, this approach tends to focus on achievement in a delimited set of subjects (e.g., math, literacy) at the elementary level, leaving open questions about other important outcomes of schooling and about district effects at other levels of schooling—particularly the high school.

To pursue the kinds of issues described above, we advocate an agenda that includes multiple genres and investiga-tors, based on the multiple purposes and knowledge needs to which the research responds. Indeed, "research" might be thought of quite broadly to include knowledge development activities that range from context-bound self-study to multivariate, hierarchical analyses of large datasets. Knowledge that is particular to specific districts, the actors within them, and their external stakeholders, for example, might take continuous improvement of the system and its outcomes as the central purpose. Such research would include evaluation of policies, programs, and practices in the system to discern what is working, for whom, and under what conditions; to inform resource allocation; and to build common direction and action. Research on these and other processes may also be relevant to other juris-dictions, providing what Huber (1991) called "vicarious learning" across districts. Such research may include case studies examining improvement processes, implementation challenges, unintended consequences and self correction strategies from which other jurisdictions might learn. Equally relevant, though, is research for the broader field, in which the nature of the district role, processes, and structures may be a focus in its own right or may simply be the context for considering other research questions of interest. These differing purposes and audiences suggest R & D activities vary with respect to at least three distinct dimensions: the chief investigator, the focus or content of study, and the research genre.

Choice of Principal Investigator First, with respect to a chief investigator, choices would include: (1) research conducted in-house by district personnel, (2) research partnerships between internal and external investigators, and (3) external studies in which districts serve as sites rather than as participants. Studies conducted by external investigators that aim to establish both internal and external validity face limitations due to the cost and complexity inherent in tracking variables across multiple cases over time. Consequently, with the wide availability of data, in-house research conducted by central office personnel also has a role to play, particularly as such inquiry can be tied to improvement processes. A more expansive view of district R & D might seek to build capacity for such in-house research in service to continuous improvement. While such work may not serve to assemble a base of formally tested and accumulated knowledge about districts, we suspect that generating "local knowledge" of direct and immediate use to districts in managing cycles of implementation and improvement is an important and underutilized form. In this case, building district capacity for instructional improvement involves assistance in rigorous self-study of important organizational processes.

External actors such as private foundations or univer-sities might support capacity building for such in-house research as well as for dissemination across districts. As well, partnerships that combine external researchers with internal investigators also look promising for the assem-blage of relevant knowledge and skills. Examples such as the Bay Area School Reform Collaborative (BASRC), the Consortium on Chicago School Research, and, more recently, the Strategic Educational Research Partnership (SERP) point to the value of such inside-outside cooperation around inquiry.

The Focus of District Studies A second dimension of inquiry is the focus of research including districts as the unit of analysis or as contexts in one of two ways: as mediators of policies emanating from state and federal levels or as settings of influence over focal interests at school and classroom levels. Many questions of interest, including those listed above, concern district operations and take the district as the unit of interest and analysis. For example, districts are exploring ways of providing differential attention to schools based on their performances. To take one case, the Superintendent in Montgomery County, Maryland, divided the district into two zones and developed different strategies for the high- and low-achieving schools in the district (Olson, 2008). Studying a range of cases around a question of this kind looks to be quite fruitful in understanding the success of a range of administrative actions.

There are many important administrative processes to study including, among others, the balance of centralized direction with school-level autonomy; the creation of professional community through administrative action; management of the human resources function; and budgeting to support instructional improvement. Then, other studies seek to understand the role that districts play as strategic actors in policy or program implementation across levels of a federal system or in relation to their local community. Studies that examine questions at the school or classroom level increasingly are interested in the district context as an important element. Teacher learning is a good example here, because it is subject to influences at the individual, primary group, school, and district levels of analysis.

Research Genres and the District A final dimension of inquiry is the research genre. Studies might be variable or case-oriented, including several different kinds of cases. Many studies, especially but not exclusively employing quantitative analysis of large datasets, aim to understand co-variation of conditions across many cases or sites and use statistical controls for confounding variables. Questions about district-level factors that may be modeled in relation to other factors for influence on outcomes take a variable-oriented approach. To ensure gains from such work, strong theory is important such that measures of key constructs and variables are established in relation to a theoretical frame.

Another variable-based form of research involves secondary analysis of large-scale databases that nest achievement and other outcomes within several levels of analysis that include districts. Hierarchical linear models seem especially useful insofar as districts naturally function as one level of analysis within a nested set.

While case studies have formed the most common kind of inquiry on districts, we have in mind an expansion of this form based on several different approaches found in the literature. One is the theory-generating or testing study. Some examples of work which has concentrated on single cases include: Community District #2, New York (Elmore & Burney, 1998a, 1998b, 1999; Stein & D'Amico, 2002); Duval County, Florida (Supovitz, 2006); Chicago (Bryk, et al., 1998); and San Diego (Hubbard, Mehan, & Stein, 2006; O'Day, 2008). Others have selected multiple cases for comparison (e.g., Cuban & Usdan, 2003; Firestone et al., 2004; Snipes, Doolitle, & O'Herlihy, 2002; Togneri & Anderson, 2003). Such studies explore the syndrome of conditions within cases, together with constancies and case contrasts in relation to phenomena of interest (for greater explication, see McLaughlin & Talbert, 2001, Appendix A; and Ragin, & Becker, 1992). Work in this vein has proven provocative in generating ideas about how districts manage the instructional agenda. Such work has been the staple so far, but several other kinds of case studies can serve as useful complements.

One kind takes advantage of the narrative turn in qualitative research. In this rendering of the case, a practitioner (singly or with an external colleague) sets forth experiences associated with district work on instruction. Such "insider" stories enjoy favor in the business literature, where leaders describe what they take to be key elements in their leadership. Such narrative accounts are infrequent in the education literature, although these accounts could well be provided by superintendents, principals, or by practicing administrators working with an external colleague (combination of participant observer and amanuensis). While sparse in the literature, we submit that this line of inquiry could well add to the store of knowledge about instructionally-related district leadership. Cultivating practitioners with the time and support to reflect on lessons learned, mistakes made (and overcome), and the wisdom of practice might have high pay-off particularly as such accounts enrich the knowledge of current and future leaders.

And a third form of case also is worth considering. This is the "teaching case" as that form has been polished in professional education in other fields. Here too inside/outside investigators might be involved where the aim is to prepare cases for use in leadership education. As developed in fields such as law and business, teaching cases are the product of careful and purposeful research into actual instances (e.g., appellate court decisions, practices of the firm) selected to teach about particular concepts, practices, or dilemmas. They are, in fact, "cases of" the particular topic or phenomenon of interest. The material is thus rendered into case descriptions, not research reports, that pose problems and dilemmas, reveal ambiguities, and suggest understandings in the form of maxims, principles, and case-bound specifics. As in practitioner-based narratives, the stance is participant in the action rather than observer on the scene. Recent work from Harvard's Public Education Leadership Project (PELP) illustrates this form of case (see Childress et al., 2007), which also includes explicit comparison among cases in multiple sectors.

Conclusion

Our approach to districts in this chapter might be chided on several accounts. For some analysts, the district is the problem, not the solution, such that new organizational designs and structures are needed to take its place. The turn to privatization and choice suggests a new role for education management organizations (EMOs) working with collections of semi-autonomous charter schools. Voucher programs effectively replace the democracy of the local school board with the democracy of family choice. Still other analysts anticipate the role of technology in dramatically expanding the possibilities of online education and the creation of virtual environments for learning that will revolutionize education in ways beyond imagination. We do not mean to discourage such alternatives with the focus we have undertaken in this chapter. But for the near term at least, and in most locales, the traditional school district is likely to persist within the social geography prescribed by law and by the political economy of local communities. Particularly in large urban and rurally isolated environments, the educational fate of poor and minority children will continue to depend in no small measure on the prospects that district leaders are able to exert systematic influence over the quality of instruction. It is with this task in mind that we have framed this chapter.

Notes

1. We wish to thank Marshall Smith and Jon Supovitz for thoughtful reviews of an earlier draft of this chapter. All remaining errors are the authors' alone.
2. Exceptions appear to be large county-wide districts in states like North Carolina and Florida; however, within-district, between-school segregation is still marked.
3. Even this generalization is not absolute. Wake County, North Carolina, has implemented a plan to integrate students using socioeconomic criteria to balance school populations.

References

Aaronson, D., & Barrow, L. (2007). Teachers and student achievement in the Chicago Public High Schools. *Journal of Labor Economics, 25*(1), 95–135.

Berman, P., & McLaughlin, M. W. (1977). *Federal programs supporting educational change. Volume 7, Factors affecting implementation and continuation.* Santa Monica, CA: RAND.

Bitter, C., Pérez, M., Parrish, T., González, R., Socias, M., Salzfass, L., Chaney, K., Gubbins, P., Dawson, K., Yu, V., Delancey, D., & Esra, P. (2005). *Evaluation study of the Immediate Intervention/Underperforming Schools Program of the Public Schools Accountability Act of 1999.* Palo Alto, CA: American Institutes for Research.

Boyd, D., Lankford, H., Loeb, S., Rockoff, J., & Wyckoff, J. (2008). The narrowing gap in New York City teacher qualifications and its implications for student achievement in high poverty schools. *Journal of Policy and Management, 27,* 793–818.

Bransford, J. D., Brown, A. L., & Cocking, R. R. (Eds.). (1999). *How people learn: Brain, mind, experiences, and school.* Washington DC: National Academy Press.

Bryk, A., Sebring, P., Kerbow, D., Rollow, S., & Easton, J. (1998). *Charting Chicago school reform.* Boulder, CO: Westview Press.

Bulkley, K., Fairman, J., & Martinez, M. C. (2004). The district and test preparation. In W. A. Firestone, R. Y. Schorr, & L. F. Monfils (Eds.),

The ambiguity of teaching to the test: Standards, assessment, and educational reform (pp. 113–141). Mahwah, NJ: Erlbaum.

Callahan, R. E. (1967). *The superintendent of schools: A historical analysis, final report, S-212.* Washington DC: U.S. Office of Education.

Childress, S., Elmore, R., Grossman, A., & Johnson, S. (Eds.). (2007). *Managing school districts for high performance.* Cambridge, MA: Harvard Education Press.

Chubb, J. (2001). The system. In T. M. Moe (Ed.), *A primer on America's schools* (pp. 15–42). Stanford, CA: Hoover Institution Press.

Chubb, J., & Moe, T. (1990). *Politics, markets, and schools.* Washington, DC: Brookings.

Clune, W. (1987). Institutional choice as a theoretical framework for research on educational policy. *Educational Evaluation and Policy Analysis, 9,* 117–132.

Cobb, P., McLain, K., Lamberg de Silva, T., & Dean, C. (2003). Situating teachers' instructional practices in the institutional setting of the school and district. *Educational Researcher, 32*(6), 13–24.

Coburn, C. (2003). Rethinking scale: Moving beyond numbers to deep and lasting change. *Educational Researcher, 32*(6), 3–12.

Coburn, C. (2004). Beyond decoupling: Rethinking the relationship between the institutional environment and the classroom. *Sociology of Education, 77,* 211–244.

Coburn, C., & Russell, J. (2008). District policy and teachers' social networks. *Educational Evaluation and Policy Analysis, 30,* 203–235.

Cohen, D. (1998). Teaching practice: Plus que ça change. In P. Jackson (Ed.), *Contributions to educational change* (pp. 27–84). Berkeley, CA: McCutchan.

Cohen, D., & Barnes, C. (1993). Pedagogy and policy. In D. K. Cohen, M. McLaughlin, & J. Talbert (Eds.), *Teaching for understanding* (pp. 207–239). San Francisco: Jossey Bass.

Cohen, D., & Hill, H. (2006). *Learning policy.* New Haven, CT: Yale University Press.

Cohen, D., & Spillane, J. (1992). Policy and practice: The relations between governance and instruction. In G. Grant (Ed.), *Review of Research in Education, 18* (pp. 3–35). Washington, DC: American Educational Research Association.

Coleman, J. (1990). *Foundations of social theory.* Cambridge, MA: Harvard University Press.

Cremin, L. (1961). *The transformation of the school: Progressivism in American education (1876–1957).* New York: Knopf.

Cuban, L. (1988). *The managerial imperative and the practice of leadership in schools.* Albany: State University of New York Press.

Cuban, L., & Usdan, M. (2003). *Powerful reforms with shallow roots: Improving America's urban schools.* New York: Teachers College Press.

Dimaggio, P., & Powell, W. (1991). The iron cage revisited: Institutional isomorphism and collective rationality in organizational fields. In W. Powell & P. Dimaggio (Eds.), *The new institutionalism in organizational analysis* (pp. 63–82). Chicago: University of Chicago Press.

Elmore, R. (1983). Complexity and control: What legislators and administrators can do about implementing public policy. In L. Shulman & G. Sykes (Eds.), *Handbook of Teaching and Policy* (pp. 342–369). New York: Longman.

Elmore, R. (1993). The role of local school districts in instructional improvement. In S. Fuhrman (Ed.), *Designing coherent education policy: Improving the system* (pp. 96–124). San Francisco: Jossey Bass.

Elmore, R. (2004). *School reform from the inside out.* Cambridge, MA: Harvard Education Press.

Elmore, R., & Burney, D. (1998a). *Continuous improvement in Community District #2, New York City.* Pittsburgh, PA: University of Pittsburgh, Learning Research and Development Center, High Performance Learning Communities Project.

Elmore, R., & Burney, D. (1998b). *School variation and systemic instructional improvement in Community District #2, New York City.* Philadelphia: Consortium for Policy Research in Education, University of Pennsylvania.

Elmore, R., & Burney, D. (1999). Investing in teacher learning: Staff development and instructional improvement. In L. Darling-Hammond & G. Sykes (Eds.), *Teaching as the learning profession* (pp. 263–291). San Francisco: Jossey Bass.

Elmore, R., & McLaughlin, M. W. (1988). *Steady work: Policy, practice, and the reform of American education.* Santa Monica, CA: RAND.

Finn, C. (1991). *We must take charge: Our schools and our future.* New York: Free Press.

Firestone, W. A. (1989). Using reform: Conceptualizing district initiative. *Educational Evaluation and Policy Analysis, 11*(2), 151–164.

Firestone, W. A., Schorr, R., & Monfils, L. (Eds). (2004). *The ambiguity of teaching to the test: Standards, assessment, and educational reform.* Mahwah, NJ: Erlbaum.

Frankenburg, E., Lee, C., & Orfield, G. (2003). A multi-racial society with segregated schools: Are we losing the dream? Cambridge, MA: The Civil Rights Project, Harvard University. Retrieved, March 22, 2008, from http://www.civilrightsproject.harvarduniversity.edu/research/reseg03/AreWeLosingtheDream.

Furhman, S. H., & Elmore, R. F. (1990). Understanding local control in the wake of state educational reform. *Educational Evaluation and Policy Analysis, 12,* 82–96.

Goddard, R., Hoy, W., & Woolfolk, A. (2000). Collective teacher efficacy: Its meaning, measure, and effect on student achievement. *American Educational Research Journal, 37*(2), 479–507.

Hess, F. (1999). *Spinning wheels: The politics of urban school reform.* Washington, DC: Brookings Institution.

Hill, P. T., & Celio, M. B. (1998). *Fixing urban schools.* Washington DC: Brookings Institution.

Hoffman, L. (2007). *Numbers and types of public elementary and secondary education agencies from the Common Core of Data: School year 2005–06* (NCES 2007-353). U.S. Department of Education. Washington, DC: National Center for Education Statistics. Retrieved April 20, 2008, from http://nces.ed.gov/pubsearch/pubsinfo.asp?pubid=2007353.

Honig, M., & Hatch, T. (2004). Crafting coherence: How schools strategically manage multiple, external demands. *Educational Researcher, 33*(8), 16–30.

Hoy, W., Sweetland, S. R., & Smith, P. A. (2002). Toward an organizational model of achievement in high schools: The significance of collective efficacy. *Educational Administration Quarterly, 38*(1), 77–94.

Hubbard, L., Mehan, H., & Stein, M. K. (2006). *Reform as learning.* New York: Routledge.

Huber, G. P. (1991). Organizational learning: The contributing processes and the literatures. *Organizational Science, 2*(1), 88–115.

Huberman, M. & Miles, M. (1984). *Innovation up close: How school improvement works.* New York: Plenum Press.

Iannaccone, L., & Lutz, F. W. (1995). The crucible of democracy: The local arena. In J. D. Scribner & D. H. Leyton (Eds.), *The study of educational politics, the 1994 commemorative yearbook of the Politics of Education Association (1969–1994)* (pp. 39–52). Philadelphia: Falmer Press.

Ingersoll, R. (2001). Teacher turnover and teacher shortages: An organizational analysis. *American Journal of Educational Research, 38*(3), 499–534.

Kaestle, C. F. (1983). *Pillars of the republic: Common schools and American society, 1780–1860.* New York: Hill and Wang.

Kahlenberg, R. D. (2001). *All together now: Creating middle class schools through public school choice.* Washington DC: Brookings Institution.

Kirst, M. (1995). Who's in charge? Federal, state, and local control. In D. Ravitch & M. A. Vinovskis (Eds.), *Learning from the past: What history teaches us about school reform* (pp. 25–56). Baltimore, MD: Johns Hopkins University Press.

Knapp, M., Copland, M., Ford, B., Markholt, A., McLaughlin, M., Milliken, M., & Talbert, J. (2003, February). *Leading for learning sourcebook: Concepts and examples.* Seattle: Center for the Study of Teaching and Policy, University of Washington.

Lee, V., & Smith, J. B. (1996). Collective responsibility for learning and its effects on gains in achievement for early secondary school students. *American Journal of Education, 104*(2), 103–147.

Lortie, D. (1975). *Schoolteacher: A sociological study.* Chicago: University of Chicago Press.

March, J. (1978). American public school administration: A short analysis. *The School Review, 86*(2), 217–250.

May, H., & Supovitz, J. A. (2006). Capturing the cumulative effects of school reform: An 11-year study of the impacts of America's Choice on student achievement. *Educational Evaluation and Policy Analysis, 28,* 231–257.

McDonnell, L., & Elmore, R. (1987). Getting the job done: Alternative policy instruments. *Educational Evaluation and Policy Analysis, 9*(2), 133–152.

McLaughlin, M. (1987). Learning from experience: Lessons from policy implementation. *Educational Evaluation and Policy Analysis, 9*(2), 171–178.

McLaughlin, M., & Talbert, J. (2001). *Professional communities and the work of high school teaching.* University of Chicago Press.

McLaughlin, M. & Talbert, J. (2006). *Building school-based teacher learning communities: Professional strategies to improve student achievement.* New York: Teachers College Press.

Meier, D. (2000). *Will standards save public education?* Boston: Beacon Press.

Meyer, J. W., & Rowan, B. (1977). Institutionalized organizations: Formal structure as myth and ceremony. *American Journal of Sociology, 83,* 340–363.

Murphy, J., & Hallinger, P. (1988). Characteristics of instructionally effective school districts. *Journal of Educational Research 81*(3), 175–181.

National Center for Educational Statistics. (2006). *Table 8, Number of public school districts and public and private elementary and secondary schools: Selected years 1869–70 through 2005–06.* Retrieved July 10, 2008, from http://nces.ed.gov/pubs2002/overview/tableA-5.asp.

Newmann, F., Smith, B., Allensworth, E., & Bryk, A. (2001). Instructional program coherence: What it is and why it should guide school improvement policy. *Educational Evaluation and Policy Analysis, 23*(4), 297–321.

Nichols, S., & Berliner, D. (2007). *Collateral damage: How high-stakes testing corrupts America's schools.* Cambridge: Harvard Education Press.

O'Day, J. A. (2002). Complexity, accountability, and school improvement. *Harvard Educational Review, 72*(3), 293–329.

O'Day, J. A. (2007, April). *Using theory-based evaluation to understand district reform: The case of San Diego City Schools.* Paper presented and the Annual Meeting of the American Educational Research Association, Chicago, IL.

O'Day, J. A. (2008). NCLB and the complexity of school improvement. In A. R. Sadovnik, J. A. O'Day, G. W. Bohrnstedt, & K. M. Borman (Eds.), *No Child Left Behind and the Reduction of the Achievement Gap* (pp. 25–52). New York: Routledge.

O'Day, J. A., & Quick, H. E. (in press). Assessing instructional reform in San Diego: A theory-based approach. *Journal of Education for Students Placed At Risk, 14*(1).

Ogawa, R., Sandholtz, J. H., Martinez-Flores, M., & Scribner, S. P. (2003). The substantive and symbolic consequences of a district's standards-based curriculum. *American Educational Research Journal, 40*(1), 147–187.

Oliver, C. (1991). Strategic responses to institutional processes. *Academy of Management Review, 16*(1), 145–179.

Olson, L. (2008, February 20). When "unequal" is fair treatment. *Education Week, 27*(24), 24–27.

Phillips, M. (1997). What makes schools effective?: A comparision of the relationships of communitarian climate and academic climate to mathematics achievement and attendance during middle school. *American Educational Research Journal, 34*(4), 633–662.

Ragin, C., & Becker, H. (1992). *What is a case?: Exploring the foundations of social inquiry.* Chicago: University of Chicago Press.

Raudenbush, S. (2008). Advancing educational policy by advancing research on instruction. *American Educational Research Journal, 45*(1), 206–230.

Resnick, L., & Glennan, T. (2002). Leadership for learning: A theory of action for urban school districts. In A. Hightower, M. Knapp, J. Marsh, & M. McLaughlin (Eds.), *School districts and instructional renewal* (pp. 160–172). New York: Teachers College Press.

Rivkin, S. G., Hanushek, E., & Kain, J. (2005). Teachers, schools, and academic achievement. *Econometrica, 73*(2), 417–458.

Rockoff, J. E. (2004). The impact of individual teachers on student achievement: Evidence from panel data. *American Economic Review, 94*(2), 247–252.

Rouse, C., Hannaway, J., Goldhaber, D., & Figlio, D. (2008). *Feeling the Florida heat: How low-performing schools respond to voucher and accountability pressure.* Cambridge, MA: National Bureau of Economic Research.

Rowan, B. (1982). Instructional management in historical perspective: Evidence on differentiation in school districts. *Educational Administration Quarterly, 18,* 43–59.

Rowan, B., & Miskel, C. (1999). Institutional theory and the study of educational organizations. In J. Murphy & K. S. Louis, *Handbook of Research on Educational Administration* (2nd ed.; pp. 359–384). San Francisco: Jossey Bass.

Schon, D. (1971). *Beyond the stable state.* New York: W. W. Norton.

Shouse, R. (1996). Academic press and sense of community: Conflict, congruence, and implications for student achievement. *Social Psychology of Education, 1,* 47–68.

Smith, M. S., & O'Day, J. (1991). Systemic school reform. In S. H. Fuhrman & B. Malen (Eds.), *The politics of curriculum and testing, Politics of Education Association Yearbook* (pp. 233–267). London: Taylor and Francis.

Smith, S. (2004). *Boom for whom?: Education, desegregation, and development in Charlotte.* Albany: State University of New York Press.

Snipes, J., Doolittle, F., & O'Herlihy, C. (2002). *Foundations for success: Case studies of how urban school systems improve student achievement.* Washington, DC: MRDC, Council of Great City Schools.

Snyder, T. D., Dillow, S. A., & Hoffman, C. M. (2007). *Digest of Education Statistics 2006* (NCES 2007-017). National Center for Education Statistics, Institute of Education Sciences, U.S. Department of Education. Washington, DC: U.S. Government Printing Office.

Spillane, J. (1996). School districts matter: Local educational authorities and state instructional policy. *Education Policy, 10,* 63–87.

Spillane, J. (2004). *Standards deviation: How schools misunderstand education policy.* Cambridge, MA: Harvard University Press.

Spillane, J. (2006). *Distributed leadership.* San Francisco: Jossey-Bass.

Spillane, J., & Thompson, C. (1997). Reconstructing conceptions of local capacity: The local education agency's capacity for ambitious instructional reform. *Educational Evaluation and Policy Analysis, 19*(2), 185–203.

Spring, J. (1990). *The American school (1640–1990)* (2nd ed.). New York: Longman.

Stein, M. K., & D'Amico, L. (2002). Inquiry at the crossroads of policy and learning: A study of a district-wide literacy initiative. *Teachers College Record, 104*(7), 1313–1344.

Stigler, J. W., & Hiebert, J. (1999). *The teaching gap: Best ideas from the world's teachers for improving education in the classroom.* New York: Free Press.

Stone, C., Henig, J., Jones, B., & Pierannunzi, C. (2001). *Building civic capacity: The politics of reforming urban schools.* Lawrence: University Press of Kansas.

Supovitz, J. (2006). *The case for district-based reform.* Cambridge, MA: Harvard Education Press.

Supovitz, J. (in press). Knowledge-based organizational learning for instructional improvement. In M. Fullan (Ed.), *International handbook on educational change.*

Thompson, C., Sykes, G., & Skrla, L. (2008). *Coherent, instructionally-focused district leadership: Toward a theoretical account.* E. Lansing: Education Policy Center, Michigan State University.

Togneri, W., & Anderson, S. E. (2003). *Beyond islands of excellence: What districts can do to improve instruction and achievement in all schools.* Washington, DC: Learning First Alliance.

Tschannen-Moran, M., Woolfolk, A., Hoy, A., & Hoy, W. (1998). Teacher efficacy: Its meaning and measure. *Review of Educational Research, 68,* 202–248.

Tyack, D. B. (1974). *The one best system.* Cambridge, MA: Harvard University Press.

Webb, N. L. (2005, November). *Alignment, depth of knowledge, and change.* Paper presented at 50th Annual Meeting of the Florida Educational Research Association.

Weick, K. E. (1976). Educational organizations as loosely coupled systems. *Administrative Science Quarterly, 21,* 1–19.

Wenger, E. (1998). *Communities of practice.* New York: Cambridge University Press.

Woody, E. L., Bae, S., Park, S., & Russell, J. (2006). *Snapshots of reform: District efforts to raise student achievement across diverse communities in California.* Berkeley, CA: Policy Analysis for California Education.

Zimmer, R., & Toma, E. (2000). Peer effects in private and public schools across countries. *Journal of Policy Analysis and Management, 19*(1), 75–92.

60

Pushing on the Paradigm

Research on Teachers' Organizations as Policy Actors

NINA BASCIA
OISE, University of Toronto

What roles do teachers' organizations have with respect to educational policy? The answers depend on what one's understanding of educational policy is. If what is meant by "policy" is decisions made by governments or their designated decision makers and codified in legislation or contractual language, then in many countries teachers and their representative organizations have no formal policy role, or a carefully delimited role with respect to negotiating "industrial" or "labor" factors such as teacher compensation, benefits, and working conditions. When they think about them at all, most educational policy analysts and policy makers understand teachers' organizations only in relation to formal, system-level decision-making arenas and specifically with respect to issues of current interest at any given time. And when they think about them at all, policy researchers are often critical: A review of the research conducted over a decade ago concluded that, "Regardless of where they stand, one thing unites the few researchers who actually study unions and the many commentators who have an opinion on them: Everyone wants them to change" (Bradley, 1996). The same holds today.

In hierarchical educational systems, where policy formation is demarcated from implementation and teachers' involvement in decision making is legally controlled, teachers and their organizations participate in "policy" only at the pleasure of formally designated decision makers. If, however, "policy" is understood to include the development of policy ideas, to encompass less formal and decentralized as well as centralized forms of decision making, and if the distinction between policy making and practice is understood as somewhat permeable, the contributions of teachers' unions and their other "professional" organizations to "policy" are more numerous and more valuable. Teachers' organizations themselves can be sites for educational experimentation and innovation, teacher leadership, teacher learning, and career development, can serve as sources of system feedback about educational conditions, and can

increase the capacity of educational systems more broadly (Bascia, 1994, 1997, 1998a, 2000, 2004, 2005).

This chapter reviews the research on teachers' organizations' contributions to policy within and beyond policy-making arenas. In addition to mainstream educational policy research, it reviews less well-known historical, sociological and organizational studies on teachers' organizations, in the United Kingdom, Australia, New Zealand, and Canada, as well as the United States. It describes their emergence and presence in relation to formal policy making and the organizational and political dynamics within them that shape their viability as *teachers'* organizations in relation to formal policy making. By describing ways that teachers' organizations contribute to educational improvement in classroom, school, district, and jurisdictional settings, the chapter provides a broader conception of policy activity than that which is common to policy research.

The organizations discussed in this chapter are teacher unions and subject associations, which have as their primary (but not always exclusive) mandate to serve teachers' occupational needs (not always a straightforward prospect). Designed to be fundamentally concerned with teacher-identified issues, these organizations are grassroots and yet tend to be highly politicized (Hilferty, 2004). The tensions inherent in that dual nature are enduring and lead to a variety of different forms across time and in different jurisdictions. Teachers' organizations may have formal legal authority to speak on teachers' behalf directly with system decision makers, or to provide a conduit for closer interactions between government and teacher members. Barring this legally delineated role, they may attempt to exert their influence informally. They may focus on one or a small number of well-defined occupational needs or be open to broadening what they consider their purview as teachers' articulated needs evolve (Gaskell & Rowell, 1993). Similarly, they may claim to represent all of the teachers in a jurisdiction or only a subset in that jurisdiction;

membership may be compulsory, either legally or by social fiat; they may be large and well-funded and well-staffed, or small and dependent on members' voluntary contributions of labor and other resources. They may include a wider array of educational workers, such as university faculty, school counselors, or non-certified classroom support staff. They may act independently or in collaboration with other organized groups.

Teacher unions and teachers' subject associations are often believed to be quite different kinds of organizations with respect to notions of professionalism and exclusivity, but in practice the kinds of issues with which they concern themselves overlap. Teacher unions typically are understood as focusing their attention on the domains over which they have some legal authority as designated by labor legislation—on salary, benefits, and teachers' working conditions—but in actuality their purview often extends to professional development, program innovation, professionalizing strategies, and a broad advocacy role for public education (Bascia, 2000, 2005, 2008a). Subject teaching associations have been less well-covered in the research than teacher unions (but see, e.g., Cornbleth & Waugh, 1995; Lichtenstein, McLaughlin, & Knudsen, 1992; Lieberman & Grolnick, 1998; Little, 1993). Hilferty (2004) identifies three major functions subject organizations perform—curriculum development and subject knowledge, professional development, and professionalizing strategies—where "professional" subject associations overlap with those of teacher unions. Teachers' subject associations are sometimes subsets of teacher unions, and teachers' subject associations sometimes concern themselves with issues that extend beyond subject-specific concerns. Still other organizations, such as the U.S.-based National Association of Educational Activists, might be characterized as focused on supporting the actualizing of particular educational ideologies (e.g., Peterson & Charney, 1999). They are concerned with teaching-related issues, on the one hand, and political strategizing ideas, on the other, but this type of organization has yet to be subjected to academic scrutiny. There is much more research on unions than on any other type of teachers' organization, particularly in the policy research domain.

In much of the policy research, organizational actors such as teacher unions and subject associations are viewed positively when their actions are in alignment with system priorities, and negatively when they question the status quo or champion other issues. Further, they often are judged in ways that parallel conventional role expectations for teachers. That is, teacher organizations' interests in issues seen as within the purview of the classroom—such as curriculum development and pedagogical improvement—are viewed positively; however, teachers' organizations that concern themselves with organizational, decision making, and resource allocation issues are viewed as overstepping their bounds. For these reasons, subject associations have been viewed more favorably than "industrial" or "labor" organizations. For example, in the United States, teacher

unions' willingness to "trade" increases in teachers' salary and benefits for professional development funding has been viewed for some time as an indicator of a lack of "professionalism" more generally (e.g., Little, 1993; McDonnell & Pascal, 1988). In actuality, the line between the two kinds of teachers' organizations is blurred: unions are strong supporters of teachers' professional learning and subject associations are often concerned with issues in the policy realm.

The next section reviews some of the historical research on teaching to lay out the ways that notions of teacher professionalism underlie the very existence of teachers' organizations, the ways they are assessed by most mainstream policy research, and the logic that provides the basis for their own strategic directions. The chapter then focuses on the actions of teachers' organizations in relation to the traditional policy paradigm described earlier, centering on dynamics inherent to their involvement in legislative and collective bargaining arenas. Research on teacher leadership—both collective and individual—provides an illustration of what the traditional policy paradigm makes visible and the limits of its scope. The chapter then reviews research that places teachers' organizations, or teachers themselves, at the center of analysis. Such research reveals how teachers' organizations may help engender new policy ideas and increase educational system capacity. The chapter concludes by arguing for the utility of a broadened conception of educational policy activity.

The Paradox of Professionalism

Issues surrounding professionalism and professionalization provide increasingly common ways for educational historians and sociologists to make sense of the status of teaching as an occupation (Gitlin, 1996; Larson, 1977; Sykes, 1987). In particular, researchers have developed a number of conceptual schemes in which professionalism plays a major role by which to understand and explain the actions of teachers' organizations (Mitchell & Kerchner, 1983; Poole, 2000; Rodrigue, 2003). Contested claims—over who has the right to control occupations, and whole public sectors—have been a fundamental preoccupation of many occupational groups, as the consequences of formal decision making become evident. Fundamental to the notion of professionalism is that it assumes that status is zero-sum: Although some claim professionalization is a strategy to enhance the quality of educational delivery, it also has had the effect of reinforcing a status hierarchy that tends to inhibit rather than enhance teachers' influence on educational decisions that affect their work.

Some historians maintain that educational administrators asserted their authority over teachers by claiming special "scientific" expertise that teachers did not have (Abbott, 1981; Gitlin, 1996; Larson, 1977; Tyack, 1974). Maintaining or improving teachers' status, in contexts where states and educational systems control many aspects of educational practice, has been an ongoing struggle (Hilferty,

2004; Seddon, 1999). Teachers' subject associations have attempted to claim the sole right to determine the criteria for admission, training, performance, and evaluation (Larson, 1977) and to define subject knowledge and establish curriculum guidelines (Cornbleth & Waugh, 1995; Goodson, 1983; Layton, 1988; Phillips, 1998) or, at least, to be at the table with others when such decisions are made.

The professionalism paradigm also has resulted in a status demarcation between so-called "professional" issues (such as subject expertise) and concerns about working conditions, in the eyes of both policy researchers and teachers themselves. For example, in their analysis of U.S. teacher union priorities in the later part of the 1980s, McDonnell and Pascal (1988) made a distinction between salary and working conditions, on the one hand, and professional development on the other (see also Johnson, 1988; Little, 1993). The independent operation of subject associations and teacher unions in many (but not all) countries is the manifestation of some teachers' concerns about the relative status of these ostensibly different issues (Hilferty, 2004).

Some teachers' organization leaders are able to successfully negotiate the challenges of working in subordinate positions, either by impressing decision makers that teachers "deserve" to play in the big leagues because they care about the issues that matter most, or by reframing the prevailing discourse about the value of what teachers do (Bascia, 2008a). Others, facing attacks by politicians or administrators or attempting to counterattack their members, respond in kind, adopting the language and terminology being used against them. For example, in Ontario in the mid-1990s, after several decades of cooperative relations between the province and teachers' federations, a new government administration reduced the scope of federations' authority over teaching-related issues and began calling them "unions." Teacher organizations responded by "playing hardball" and adopted the "union" moniker. In doing so, they also reinforced conventional assumptions about what unions do and do not stand for. When unions respond to attacks that explicitly or implicitly cast teachers as selfish and teaching as technical work, with arguments that fail to contest these characterizations, teachers are thereby handicapped in challenging negative press (Bascia, 2008b).

The Standard Policy Paradigm

Educational history can shed some light on the fundamental dynamics that have shaped the functions of teachers' organizations and colored the nature of their interactions with policy makers. Canadian, American, Australian, and British historians have characterized the emergence of teachers' organizations as responses by teachers, who had been independently employed, to the systems of employment that emerged with the rise of mass education systems around the beginning of the last century (Carlson, 1993; Gitlin, 1996; Larson, 1977; Murphy, 1990; Ozga, 2000; Ozga & Lawn, 1981; Tyack, 1974). Teachers organized when and where they were confronted by entrance qualification requirements, career ladders, pay schedules, disciplinary procedures, and inspection schemes that controlled their work in ways they found unfair or unworkable. Where administrators and others had already established organizations meant to include teachers, teachers struggled to establish a meaningful presence within them, such as in the National Education Association in the United States (Murphy, 1990; Rousmaniere, 2005), or established organizations of their own (Smaller, 1991; Urban, 1982). The legacies of the rifts between teachers and educational administrators and university faculty—as well as among teachers, such as between men and women and between elementary and secondary educators—endure in the form of multiple organizations in the same jurisdictions. In the UK, currently there are seven organizations, including three for "heads" (principals) and two for women educators. In Ontario, male and female public elementary teachers merged their separate unions a decade ago, but there are still distinct organizations for secondary, Catholic, and French-speaking teachers. In the United States, where collective bargaining is legislated in 34 of the 50 states, teachers elect the union they prefer to have represent them: affiliates of the American Federation of Teachers, the National Education Association, or some other grass-roots originated organization.

To the extent that "policy action" concerns influence on and participation in formal decision making, teachers' organized involvement is rather constrained. Because education is the purview of the state, teachers' formal policy involvement tends to be provisional and episodic. They may attempt to persuade; they may be invited to participate from time to time in relation to specific spheres of educational practice (such as working conditions, curriculum development, or standards of practice); but teachers' involvement in educational decision making is subject to the willingness of the state to allow their participation.

The first rush of policy research interest in teacher unions as institutional actors of any magnitude was in response to the legalization of collective bargaining, state by state, and then actualized, school district by school district, through the 1960s and 70s in the U.S (Bascia, 1994). While Canadian teachers had had "federations" recognized in provincial Education Acts since the 1930s and 1940s, there, too, collective bargaining was not common until much later in the 20th century. Prior to that, in both countries, whether teacher organizations could claim that they represented all teachers (in Canada) or only those teachers who elected membership (in some U.S. states), they could only appeal to local administrators', trustees', and legislators' sense of fairness. In both countries, the practice of informal "meeting and conferring" was known among teacher unionists as "begging and deferring" because of the relative ineffectiveness of agreements that had no legal weight. With collective bargaining, for the first time, school and school system administrators were confronted with the legal requirement that they attend to teachers' concerns.

Teacher unions' traditional concerns about compensation and working conditions are perceived by many union researchers and the media as "self-interested," "mundane," and "non-professional" issues and yet these factors are clearly fundamental to attracting and retaining individuals to teaching careers. They are persistent points of contention in local labor relations and, where salary and working conditions are set at the state level, in legislative agendas. Resources, relationships, roles, an appropriate degree of professional autonomy, and opportunities to develop teaching skills both directly influence teaching quality and contribute to educators' sense of achievement and job satisfaction, serving to attract and retain teachers to the occupation in general as well as to particular schools and districts (Johnson, 1990; McLaughlin, 1993; McLaughlin & Talbert, 2001). They are the "necessary conditions" (Alberta Teachers' Association, 1997) for teacher quality for which teacher unions often are the only advocates. Attention to organizational arrangements and professional roles and relationships have been missing from standards-based and accountability-driven educational policy for several years (Bascia, 2005). There currently are a small number of counter examples: for example, the North Carolina Teachers' Association recently has been successful in establishing a survey of teachers' working conditions monitors and supplies feedback to state legislators. In many other jurisdictions, however, teachers' organizations' concerns about the poor quality of working conditions are not taken seriously. From policy makers' point of view, their influence on the quality of teaching and learning is not as immediate, direct, or straightforward as other factors.

The parameters of such organizations' legal purview were framed by labor law: within accepted—indeed, constitutionally defined—terms, formal authority over educational decision making originates in state/provincial (or federal) legislative bodies and their administrative deputies. As employees, teachers might, through their agents, negotiate issues of salary, other benefits, and working conditions but in no way could they formally weigh in on issues of curriculum, educational funding, or other "managerial" issues. This demarcation between teachers' and administrators' domains has been viewed as a "compromise" between teachers' desire for representative participation and the maintenance of formal legislative and administrative authority (Carlson, 1993).

Living with the compromise has proven seriously challenging for teachers. But the existence of such legal parameters seems to have done little to allay the concerns of administrators, trustees and other local decision makers about possible inroads on their authority, and the policy research on teacher unions in the U.S. during the era of collective bargaining legislation reflected that unease. Did union presence impede district- and school-level decision making? Did it increase conflict and bureaucratic response (Englert, 1979; Johnson, 1983, 1984; Russo, 1979; Williams, 1979)? What were its consequences for educational spending (Lawton, Bedard, MacLellan, & Li, 1999)? Did it stifle educational improvement? Close-up studies of interactions between administrators and union leaders undertaken

during this time period suggested that productive relationships, enhanced communications, and more informed decisions were common. While teacher unions have been blamed for favoring procedural responses at the expense of educational quality, some researchers have suggested that it tends to be administrators, not union officials, who responded bureaucratically (e.g., Johnson, 1983, 1984).

There is evidence that teachers' organizations have been influential in identifying issues and shaping legislation in policy-making arenas at state and national levels. Instigating and conducting research, drafting legislation, and other means of influencing legislators' decisions constitute an important domain of teachers' organizational activity (see Ballou & Podgursky, 2000; Boyd, Plank, & Sykes, 2000; Cibulka, 2000; Lieberman, 1997). Teachers' organizations are directly concerned not only about issues that seem to fall neatly within their purview, such as working conditions and teacher evaluation policies, but also express concern about seemingly broader concerns such as educational spending, school choice, and, in the United States recently, the reauthorization of No Child Left Behind.

In some jurisdictions, teacher unions recently have lost what limited legal ground they previously had, as decision making becomes centralized (curtailing local negotiations over working conditions or salary) or decentralized (so that teachers in certain schools are waived from collective bargaining, as in the case of many charter schools in the U.S. and with "enterprise bargaining" in some Australian states). Researchers have reported a decline in the influence teachers' organizations have on decision making because of the centralization and formalization of decisions over resource allocation and working conditions that had previously been made more locally and, in some cases, because of deliberate attempts by lawmakers to restrict the authority of teachers (see Bascia, 2005, 2008a; Boyd et al., 2000).

Teacher Leadership Given the interest in the leadership literature on the attributes of successful leaders (their skills, strategies, vision) it should be no surprise that studies of union leaders comprise one aspect of the teachers' organization literature. Albert Shanker, a controversial character credited with launching the legalization of collective bargaining through his leadership in the New York City schools starting in the early 1960s, has fascinated researchers (see Braun, 1972; Kahlenberg, 2007). What kind of person was he? Why did he have such a great influence? Biographical studies of union leaders such as Margaret Hailey (Rousmaniere, 2005; Tyack & Hansot, 1982) pull away from an exclusive focus on leaders to consider the dynamics between individuals and their organizations and the times in which they lived. But the pervasive image of organizations is as personifications of their leaders, just as faceless, striking workers and public statements by union leaders are what the media tells us teacher unions are.

In the 1980s, U.S. researchers Charles Kerchner and his colleagues, Douglas Mitchell and then Julia Koppich, began documenting and then actually supporting the development of alternatives to collective bargaining (Bascia, 1994; Kerchner & Koppich, 1993; Kerchner & Mitchell, 1988). They were concerned with how the discourse inherent to labor relations constrained relationships and encouraged adversarial dynamics between the parties to labor-management negotiations (Mitchell & Kerchner, 1983), and they proposed that there was enough goodwill to establish more positive and productive interactions. The device they invented, which they called a "trust agreement," promoted deliberate discussions about fundamental educational issues, starting with the dyadic relationships of system and union leaders, and intended to expand to include more and more varied kinds of educators. Trust agreements commonly focused on supporting educational reforms selected by local educators. Kerchner and his colleagues were optimistic that these developments heralded a new era in the development of local educational leadership capacity (see also Rosow & Zager, 1989).

Studies of the trust agreement and similar initiatives revealed how improving the relationship between system and teachers' organizational leaders was necessary but not sufficient to solve recurring educational problems (Bascia, 1994, 2005; Bascia, Stiegelbauer, Jacka, Watson, & Fullan, 1997). The development of goodwill and trust appeared to lead to greater engagement and enthusiasm between management and teacher union leadership, but external pressures could not always easily be ignored. In the volatile policy environment of the 1990s, teachers expressed concerns about standards and accountability-based policies, and serious reductions in educational budgets in many locales made it difficult for union leaders to balance their commitment to advocate for teacher members with their relationships with formal decision makers. Frequent changes in formal leadership during that time period meant that union leaders were faced with having to re-establish their credibility with educational system leaders and persuade them of the legitimacy of teachers' concerns, over and over again. Innovations attractive to leaders at the system level might look irrelevant or inadequate to teachers in the face of more fundamental issues such as resource scarcity at the school level.

There is much to be gained by studying the actions of and relationships between individual leaders. But a single-minded focus on people in formal leadership draws attention away from the milieu in which they act. However, a series of studies at both the macro and organizational level have provided some useful ways to understand the nature and complexity of the tasks faced by teachers' organizations. Close-up, comparative case studies of teachers' organizations across school districts, states, provinces, and nationalities (Bascia, 1994, 2005; Bascia et al., 1997; Humphries, 2003; Poole, 1999) challenge assumptions that union effectiveness is purely a matter of the shrewdness and character of union leadership by revealing how the history of relationships between teachers' organizations and system policy makers, and local understandings about the rightful role of teachers in relation to decision making,

also contribute to the nature of teachers' organizations' roles with respect to educational policy setting.

Pushing on the Policy Paradigm

The strength of the traditional policy paradigm is its emphasis on formal decision-making processes and the official chain of command within educational organizations, domains to which decision makers have most immediate access and direct influence. But there are limitations to the traditional policy paradigm: Without moving out of their zones of familiarity, neither policy makers nor policy researchers can fully understand the dynamics at play at other levels of the educational system or for other players, such as teachers. It is no wonder that teachers' organizations continue to puzzle and frustrate formal decision makers and researchers, given the exclusive emphasis on domains where their actions are limited and constrained.

The last section described teacher organizations' involvement in formal policy-making venues and explained the constraints under which they must operate, but there is more to what occurs within and as a result of teacher organizations' work. Clune (1990) suggested nearly two decades ago that the perspective of school context taken by policy researchers changes the way we understand how policy works: while traditional policy research either takes school organizations for granted or views them as potential confounders of policy's initial intent, respectfully recognizing the agency and discretion educators exercise can help us understand *why* policy has the effects that it does (and why its effects may not be what was intended). Clune suggested that schools mediate policy; that understanding the realities of school processes can help us assess the effectiveness of policy; and that it is useful to recognize that formal policy does not constitute the only set of priorities and agendas (see also McLaughlin, 1987). Extrapolating from Clune's suggestions about how to think about schools as policy arenas, we can look beyond legislative and bargaining arenas to put teachers and teacher organizations themselves at the center of analysis. Research guided by this paradigm can help us recognize the processes by which teachers' organization leaders decide what positions to promote in formal policy-making arenas; how teachers can be sources of policy ideas and their organizations the conduits by which such ideas are manifested and, sometimes, disseminated; how teachers and make use of their organizations to be more effective under policy realities.

Looking within Teachers' Organizations Just as schools are more than the manifestations of principals' leadership in their organizational structure and the realities of the people who work within them, teachers' organizations exert tremendous influence over the issues organizational leaders bring to formal policy-making settings. The extent to which teachers' organizations "work" in terms of identifying and articulating teachers' issues depends on a variety of factors. Micro-political dynamics among teachers are consequential.

A series of case studies of teacher subject associations reveals important differences of opinion among teachers with respect to their organizations' political strategy vis–à–vis other institutional actors. Murphy's (1990) account of the histories of both U.S. national teacher unions similarly records the overt conflict between men and women teachers over what issues might legitimately be taken up (for more on gender dynamics, see Bascia, 1998b; Smaller, 1991). Hilferty's (2004) study of two Australian subject associations describe how disciplinary differences shaped understandings of the optimal strategies for promoting curriculum reform (see also Goodson, 1983; Phillips, 1998).

Differences among teachers have many implications for what their organizations do. The diversity of teachers' experiences and values makes it difficult to arrive at unitary agendas that satisfy all members. Instead, many teacher organizations have the reputation among teachers of favoring, or "belonging to," one type of teachers over another—elementary or secondary, science or special education, one generational cohort or another, men or women—because of the patterns they see in who is elected into leadership, who participates in union activities, and what kinds of issues become organizational priorities (Bascia 1998a, 2000). Such situations tend to perpetuate and intensify, not only because teachers' perceptions of favoritism encourage or discourage them from active engagement, but also because teachers who do have access to organizational decision making lack the awareness and information that might influence them to increase opportunities to union access and union priorities. Such situations can lead to uneven commitment from teachers, leadership vacuums, antagonism, and much energy expended in internal power struggles. More rarely, teachers' organizations work to provide organizational structures to ensure participation and representation from a wide array of teachers, across subject areas, career stages, and working with different student populations (Bascia, 2008b). Looking within teachers' organizations, then, to understand which teachers' issues are taken up and how, is important in understanding the wider range of issues for which teachers seek some kind of redress.

Looking at why Teachers are Active in their Organizations A range of studies have begun documenting the reasons why teachers decide to invest time and energy in organizational activities and, as a result, reveal the value of organizational involvement to teachers. Beyond the clichés—that committed teachers focus their energy solely on their students—are a number of reasons why teachers choose to put time and energy into organizationally related activities, sometimes over long periods of their careers (Bascia, 2000; Bascia & Young, 2001; Bascia & Chassels, 2004). The actions of individual teachers working through their organizations have the potential to increase the capacity of educational systems, usually in small, incremental ways and sometimes in ways that add up to innovations and policy ideas that have a broader impact on educational practice.

Teachers' organizations have received brief mentions in some the literature on teacher leadership (Smylie, Conley, & Marks, 2002) although the major source of data tends to be on system-designated roles such as mentor teachers, and a recent meta-review of the literature (York-Barr & Duke, 2004) makes no mention of them at all. Still, both deliberately and in actual fact, teachers' organizations provide a wide range of opportunities for teachers to develop and display leadership—that is, working with educators and others to get things done that they believe will improve the quality of educational delivery.

While, as the last section suggested, teachers' organizations are not necessarily uncontested spaces, they can provide opportunities for teachers to learn and participate in the development of a variety of educational program areas that would not be possible through formal educational system channels—at least, not initially. Research on union-active teachers reveals, for example, that teachers have used these organizations to develop curriculum in new areas, particularly in the domains of equity and social justice.

Professional development is one area where both kinds of teachers' organizations—unions and subject associations—have been recognized for their innovative approaches, particularly in the United States and Australia. A close look at these organizations reveals that the professional development of members has been a major domain of activity from their inception. In some cases the intention is to help teachers respond effectively to government-mandated regulations—from early Ontario organizations providing support for teachers to study for new occupational entrance examinations (Smaller, 1991) to much more recent efforts, by British subject teaching associations, to "reskill" teachers under the implementation of the National Curriculum (Knight, 1996). American researchers have noted the role of subject associations in providing "collaborative and responsive" learning environments for teachers, much superior to the conventional training model in place in most school districts (Lieberman & Grolnick, 1998; Little, 1993; Talbert & McLaughlin, 1996). A wide variety of new types of teacher learning strategies were developed or attempted locally through teacher unions, in response to teachers' sense of a lack of appropriate professional support available to them in their schools and school systems: induction programs for new teachers, including peer review; action research; school-based professional development; teacher-facilitators that are based in school to support teachers, parents, and others develop teaching strategies appropriate to their student clientele; workshops and institutes of longer duration that allow teachers to test out teaching ideas in their classrooms and then come together with other educators to discuss what happened (see Bascia, 1998a, 2000, 2004, 2005, 2008a, 2008b). School-based student peer mediation and conflict resolution programs were initiated by teachers under the auspices of teachers' organizations. Skills development opportunities for school administrators, parents, and other community members are also increasingly provided by teachers' organizations.

Teachers elect to do this kind of work through their organizations because the formal systems in which they teach lack the capacity to make such program development possible, and are unlikely to welcome innovation—particularly when it comes to teachers. Teachers' organizations make it possible for *teachers* to test out ideas locally. If they are valued by other educators, these innovations may get picked up for inclusion in contractual or trust agreement provisions, and eventually they may become popular enough to become part of the life of school, district, or state or provincial educational practice.

Rethinking the Policy Paradigm

In educational systems characterized by clear demarcations between policy making and implementation, teachers' organizations are by definition anomalous: they exist to provide teachers with collective and individual access to decision-making arenas where teachers are not intended to be. Because teachers' organizations work in legislative arenas, on cross-jurisdictional commissions and committees, as well as in districts, schools, and classrooms, their presence and actions across levels and settings suggest a policy influence is that not neatly contained by conventional notions of policy making. Further, their relationships with other actors across formal roles reveals the unpredictability of policy influence.

The research on educational reform, teacher quality, teacher leadership, professional development, and the politics of educational research have tended to miss what teacher unions and professional associations have contributed in these areas because of the focus on formally sanctioned, system-driven activities. Teachers' organizations' contributions in these areas tend to become visible only when they are the deliberate focus of research. The extent of their contributions becomes even clearer when, rather than evaluating the impact of a single innovation or policy during a discrete time period, research focuses on educators' longer-term activities through such organizations to discover the attempts, missteps and ultimate influence teachers can have. Such alternative research strategies allow researchers to capture the more idiosyncratic, episodic, and possibly less formally sanctioned opportunities these organizations can provide.

This review of the literature on teachers' organizations suggests how policy research can broaden our understandings of the dynamics that underlie policy making at the macro-level by considering the origins of policy ideas and the organizational and network strategies that enable their dissemination and institutionalization over time. At the same time, the evidence suggests that policy making at meso- and micro-levels of educational organizations may also be appropriate and adequate responses to problems of practice. The range of influences teachers' organizations can have on educational processes suggests that a fundamental reframing of policy processes is required in order to fully understand the nature of policy influence.

References

Abbott, A. (1981). Status and status strain in the professions. *American Journal of Sociology, 86,* 819–835.

Alberta Teachers' Association (1997). *Trying to teach: Necessary conditions.* Edmonton: Alberta Teachers' Association.

Ballou, D., & Podgursky, M. (2000). Gaining control of professional licensing and advancement. In T. Loveless (Ed.), *Conflicting missions: Teachers unions and educational reform* (pp. 69–109). Washington, DC: Brookings.

Bascia, N. (1994). *Unions in teachers' professional lives: Social, practical, and intellectual concerns.* New York: Teachers College Press.

Bascia, N. (1997). Invisible leadership: Teachers' union activity in schools. *Alberta Journal of Educational Research, 43*(2–3), 69–85.

Bascia, N. (1998a). Teacher unions and educational reform. In A. Hargreaves, A. Lieberman, M. Fullan, & D. Hopkins (Eds.), *International handbook of educational change* (pp. 895–915). The Netherlands: Kluwer.

Bascia, N. (1998b). Women teachers, union affiliation, and the future of North American teacher unionism. *Teaching and Teacher Education, 14,* 551–563.

Bascia, N. (2000). The other side of the equation: Teachers' professional development and the organizational capacity of teacher unions. *Educational Policy 14,* 385–404.

Bascia, N. (2004). Teacher unions and the teaching workforce: Mismatch or vital contribution? In M. Smylie & D. Miretzky (Eds.), *Addressing teacher workforce issues effectively: Institutional, political and philosophical barriers. Yearbook of the National Society for Study of Education, Vol. 1* (pp. 326–347). Chicago: University of Chicago Press.

Bascia, N. (2005). Triage or tapestry: Teacher unions' work in an era of systemic reform. In N. Bascia, A. Datnow, & K. Leithwood (Eds.), *International handbook of educational policy, Vol. 13* (pp. 593–612). Dordrecht, The Netherlands: Kluwer.

Bascia, N. (2008a). Learning through struggle: How the Alberta Teachers' Association maintains an even keel. In K. Church, N. Bascia, & E. Shragge (Eds.), *Learning through community: Exploring participatory practices* (pp. 169–186). Dordrecht, The Netherlands: Springer.

Bascia, N. (2008b). Unions' role in the assault on teaching, teachers, and teacher unions. In L. Weiner & M. Compton (Ed.), *Reversing the global assault on teaching, teachers, and their unions* (pp. 95–108). New York: Palgrave Macmillan.

Bascia, N., & Chassels, C. (2004, December 1). *Reforming education: How teacher unions work for change.* Paper presented at Australian Association for Research in Education (AARE), Victoria, Australia.

Bascia, N., Stiegelbauer, S., Jacka, N., Watson, N., & Fullan, M. (1997, November). *Teacher associations and school reform: Building stronger connections.* Toronto: University of Toronto, Ontario Institute for Studies in Education.

Bascia, N., & Young, B. (2001). Women's careers beyond the classroom: Changing roles in a changing world. *Curriculum Inquiry, 31,* 271–302.

Boyd, W., Plank, D., & Sykes, G. (2000). Teachers unions in hard times. In T. Loveless (Ed.), *Conflicting missions: Teachers unions and educational reform* (pp. 174–210). Washington, DC: Brookings.

Bradley, A. (1996, December 4). Education's "dark continent." *Education Week, 16,* 25–27.

Braun, R. J. (1972). *Teachers and power: The story of the American Federation of Teachers.* New York: Simon and Schuster.

Carlson, D. (1993). *Teachers and crisis. Urban school reform and teachers' work culture.* New York: Routledge.

Cibulka, J. (2000). The NEA and school choice. In T. Loveless (Ed.), *Conflicting missions: Teachers unions and educational reform* (pp. 150–173). Washington, DC: Brookings.

Clune, W. (1990). Three views of curriculum policy in the school context: The school as policy mediator, policy critic, and policy constructor. In M. McLaughlin, J. Talbert, & N. Bascia (Eds.), *The contexts of teaching in secondary schools: Teachers' realities* (pp. 256–270). New York: Teachers College Press.

Cornbleth, C., & Waugh, D. (1995). *The great speckled bird: Multicultural politics and education policymaking.* New York: St. Martin's Press.

Englert, R. (1979). Collective bargaining in public education: Conflict and its context. *Education and Urban Society, 11,* 255–269.

Gaskell, P. J., & Rowell, P. (1993). Teachers and curriculum policy: Contrasting perspectives of a subject specialist and a generalist teachers' organization. *Historical Studies in Education, 5,* 67–86.

Gitlin, A. (1996). Gender and professionalization: An institutional analysis of teacher education and unionism at the turn of the twentieth century. *Teachers College Record, 97,* 588–624.

Goodson, I. (1983). *School subjects and curriculum change: Case studies in curriculum history.* London: Croom Helm.

Hilferty, F. (2004). *Teacher professionalism defined and enacted: A comparative case study of two subject teaching associations.* Unpublished doctoral dissertation, University of Sydney, Sydney, Australia.

Humphries, S. (2003). *Types of relations between states and organized teachers as exemplified in education reform.* Unpublished doctoral dissertation, Universite de Montreal, Montreal, Canada.

Johnson, S. M. (1983). Teacher unions in schools: Authority and accommodation. *Harvard Educational Review, 53,* 309–326.

Johnson, S. M. (1984). *Teacher unions in schools.* Philadelphia: Temple University Press.

Johnson, S. M. (1988). Pursuing professional reform in Cincinnatti. *Phi Delta Kappan, 69,* 746–751.

Johnson, S. M. (1990). *Teachers at work: Achieving success in our schools.* New York: Basic Books.

Kahlenberg, R. D. (2007). *Tough liberal: Albert Shanker and the battles over schools, unions, race, and democracy.* New York: Columbia University Press.

Kerchner, C. T., & Koppich, J. E. (Eds.). (1993). *A union of professionals: Labor relations and educational reform.* New York: Teachers College Press.

Kerchner, C. T., & Mitchell, D. E. (1988). *The changing idea of a teachers' union.* Philadelphia: Falmer Press.

Knight, P. (1996). Subject associations: The cases of secondary phase geography and home economics, 1976–94. *History of Education, 25,* 269–284.

Larson, M. (1977). *The rise of professionalism: A sociological analysis.* Berkeley: University of California Press.

Lawton, S., Bedard, G., MacLellan, D., & Li, X. (1999). *Teachers' unions in Canada.* Calgary, Alberta: Detselig.

Layton, D. (1988). Subject teaching associations and curriculum control in nineteenth century England: The case of science. *History of Education Review, 17*(2), 15–29.

Lichtenstein, G., McLaughlin, M. W., & Knudsen, J. (1992). Teacher empowerment and professional knowledge. In A. Lieberman (Ed.), *The changing contexts of teaching. The 91st Yearbook of the National Society for theStudy of Education* (pp. 37–58). Chicago: University of Chicago Press.

Lieberman, A., & Grolnick, M. (1998). Educational reform networks: Changes in the forms of reform. In A. Hargreaves, A. Lieberman, M. Fullan, & D. Hopkins (Eds.), *International handbook of educational change: Part 2* (pp.710–729). Dordrecht, the Netherlands: Kluwer.

Lieberman, M. (1997). *The teacher unions: How the NEA and AFT sabotage reform and hold students, parents, teachers, and taxpayers hostage to bureaucracy.* New York: The Free Press.

Little, J. W. (1993). Teachers' professional development in a climate of educational reform. *Educational Evaluation and Policy Analysis, 15,* 129–151.

McDonnell, L. M., & Pascal, A. (1988). *Teacher unions and educational reform.* Washington, DC: RAND Corporation.

McLaughlin, M. (1987). Learning from experience: Lessons from policy implementation. *Educational Evaluation and Policy Analysis, 9,* 171–178.

McLaughlin, M. (1993). What matters most in teachers' workplace context? In J. W. Little & M. W. McLaughlin (Eds.), *Teachers' work: Individuals, colleagues, and contexts* (pp. 79–103). New York: Teachers College Press.

McLaughlin, M. W., & Talbert, J. E. (2001). *Professional communities and the work of high school teaching.* Chicago: University of Chicago Press.

Mitchell, D. E., & Kerchner, C. T. (1983). Labor relations and teacher policy. In L. S. Shulman & G. Sykes (Eds.), *Handbook of teaching and policy* (pp. 214–238). New York: Longman.

Murphy, M. (1990). *Blackboard unions: The AFT and the NEA 1900–1980.* Ithaca, NY: Cornell University Press.

Ozga, J. (2000). *Policy research in educational settings: Contested terrain.* Buckingham, UK: Open University Press.

Ozga, J., & Lawn, M. (1981). *Teachers, professionalism and class: A study of organized teachers.* London: Falmer Press.

Peterson, B., & Charney, M. (Eds.). (1999). *Transforming teacher unions: Fighting for better schools and social justice.* Milwaukee, WI: Rethinking Schools, Ltd.

Phillips, R. (1998). *History teaching, nationhood and the State: A study in educational policies.* London: Cassell.

Poole, W. L. (1999). Teachers union involvement in educational policy making: Issues raised by an in-depth case. *Educational Policy, 13,* 698–725.

Poole, W. L. (2000). The construction of teachers' paradoxical interests by teacher union leaders. *American Educational Research Journal, 37,* 93–119.

Rodrigue, A. F. (2003). *The conceptualization, production and use of the rhizome of professionalism by Canadian teacher unions: Snapshots of the present, roadmaps for the future.* Unpublished doctoral dissertation, University of South Australia, Adelaide, Australia.

Rosow, J., & Zager, R. (1989). *Allies in educational reform: How teachers, unions, and administrators can join forces for better schools.* San Francisco: Jossey-Bass.

Rousmaniere, K. (2005). *Citizen teacher: The life and leadership of Margaret Haley.* Albany: State University of New York Press.

Russo, J. (1979). Changes in bargaining structures: The implications of the Serrano decision. *Education and Urban Society, 11,* 208–218.

Seddon, T. (1999). A self-managing teaching profession for the learning society. *Unicorn, 25*(1), 15–29.

Smaller, H. (1991). "A room of one's own": The early years of the Toronto Women Teachers' Association. In R. Heap & A. Prentice (Eds.), *Gender and education in Ontario: An historical reader* (pp. 103–124). Toronto: Canadian Scholars' Press.

Smylie, M., Conley, S., & Marks, H. (2002). Building leadership into the roles of teachers. In J. Murphy (Ed.), *The educational leadership challenge: Redefining leadership for the 21st century* (pp.162–188). Chicago: University of Chicago Press.

Sykes, G. (1987). Reckoning with the spectre. *Educational Researcher, 16*(6), 19–21.

Talbert, J., & McLaughlin, M. (1996). Teacher professionalism in local school contexts. In I. Goodson & A. Hargeraves (Eds.), *Teachers' professional lives* (pp. 127–153). London: Falmer Press.

Tyack, D. (1974). *The one best system: A history of American urban education.* Cambridge, MA: Harvard University Press.

Tyack, D., & Hansot, E. (1982). *Managers of virtue: Public school leadership in America, 1820–1980.* New York: Basic Books.

Urban, W. J. (1982). *Why teachers organized.* Detroit, MI: Wayne State University Press.

Williams, R. (1979). The impact of collective bargaining on the principal: What do we know? *Education and Urban Society, 11,* 168–180.

York-Barr, J., & Duke, K. (2004). What do we know about teacher leadership? Findings from two decades of scholarship. *Review of Educational Research, 74,* 255–316.

61

Local Democracy in Education

MICHAEL MINTROM
University of Auckland

The relationship between local democracy and education has long provoked discussion and debate among scholars, policy makers, and educators. Recently, the relationship has been approached from two distinct perspectives. The first perspective assumes democratic practice to be inherently good. The second has questioned the merits of democratic school governance. This chapter focuses on issues surrounding local democracy in education in the contemporary United States. However, the issues raised here are relevant to discussions of educational reform in other advanced democracies. Attention is paid to the apparent trade-offs between the pursuit of deepened democratic practice and the pursuit of improved student outcomes. I consider how contemporary educational reform efforts primarily motivated by other goals might nonetheless serve to support the advancement of local democracy. Contrary to more common claims, my central claim is that reform efforts that introduce greater top-down accountability requirements and others that use vouchers to allow private provision of public education can contribute significantly to revitalization of local democracy.

The chapter begins with a theoretical framework setting out the linkages between education and democratic citizenship. This is followed by a review of the institutions of local democracy in education. Here, the emphasis is placed on the complexity of the democratic structures that influence educational decision making in a federal system. Next, four contemporary institutional dilemmas are presented and discussed. The focus here is placed on issues that arise when the strengthening of local democratic processes and the pursuit of improved student outcomes are both recognized as vital goals for educational policy makers. Consideration is then given to contemporary strategies for improving system outcomes. These strategies are divided into those designed to incrementally improve current institutions, those designed to reform current institutions, and those that introduce new institutions. Discussion of these strategies focuses on their implications for local democracy

in education. The chapter concludes with an assessment of the future prospects for strengthening local democracy, and how this might be achieved, even when some reforms appear driven by disillusionment with local democratic control of schools.

Education and Democratic Citizenship

The substance and the quality of the education young people receive both shape their character and affect their abilities to become socially and economically engaged adults. Since our own destinies and life chances are heavily influenced by the character and actions of those around us—not just immediate family or neighbors, but our fellow citizens—all citizens have vested interests in ensuring that young people receive good and appropriate schooling. Following from Alexis de Tocqueville (1848/1988) and John Dewey (1916), a good deal of scholarship has been devoted to exploring the linkages between education and democratic citizenship. In recent times, Amy Gutmann's *Democratic Education* (1987) has served as a landmark theoretical discussion, one that offers compelling insights into what we should expect from schooling and how, in a large, complex society, schooling should be funded, delivered, and controlled. Here, I draw on Gutmann's analysis to construct a framework through which to interpret contemporary institutional dilemmas surrounding the relationship between education and democracy. The framework also serves to inform my subsequent discussion of how those dilemmas might play out in the future.

Many possible definitions of democracy exist (Held, 1996; Manzer, 2003). Throughout this chapter, I work with a definition that emphasizes citizen participation. As an ideal, I contend that societies can derive great value from allowing freedom of expression, choice among meaningful alternatives, and citizen engagement in decision making. This view is consistent with that of many contemporary political theorists who have written on democracy and, in particular, deliberative democracy. Relevant discussions of deliberative democracy and how it might be pursued are offered by James Bohman (1996), John Forester (1999), and John Gastil and Peter Levine (2005). This view of democracy is also consistent with views expressed by influential economists, such as Milton Friedman (1962) and Joseph A. Schumpeter (1976), who have emphasized the mutually-supportive relations found between political systems based on effective democratic processes and well-functioning market-based economies.

While democracy as an ideal is a highly appealing form of government, in practice, democratic systems of government often deliver disappointing outcomes. For example, in the realm of public education, the history of school segregation and efforts to achieve desegregation in the United States highlights how significant tensions can arise between majoritarian participation in local decision making and the pursuit of social justice. Asymmetries in the power of citizens can have material bearing on their abilities to engage in politics. These power asymmetries can derive from differences in economic status, differences in access to information, differences in education levels, and the legacy of historical norms of exclusion, among other things. Difficulties of this kind are not readily resolved in democratic systems of government (Dahl, 1989). Having said that, because democracies offer spaces for expression and debate, critics seeking more inclusive and fair decision-making procedures and better system outcomes have many opportunities to put forward arguments for change. Sometimes the decisions of enlightened government elites can better serve the longer term outcomes of a society than decisions left in the hands of citizens (Hochschild, 1984). In federal systems, we frequently observe actors at different levels of government seeking to exercise influence in ways that might appear to undermine local democratic processes. However, often these efforts are prompted by different understandings of the public good. Localism, and local control of schools, has its limits.

At a theoretical level, states can be characterized as taking a range of distinctive forms. In her discussion of education and democracy, Gutmann examines the merits of several idealized state forms. According to Gutmann, the core value of a democratic state is to promote "conscious social reproduction in its most inclusive form" (1987, p. 42). Education is a crucial component of this conscious social reproduction. Alternative state types cannot effectively achieve this. If the state were to accept full responsibility for the education of the young, then other influences would be banished, and the state would get on with imparting a particular, unchallenged notion of the good life and the role of the citizen. Such a state would be deeply undemocratic and deeply repressive because it would not allow expression of alternative conceptions of the good life. The state of families, where family preferences are assumed paramount, holds more appeal because it at least permits a range of conceptions of the good life. However, by granting full responsibility for education to the family, this state would allow families the option of inculcating discriminatory and exclusionary predispositions and practices in their children. It would also create conditions whereby, in dysfunctional family settings, the transmission of socially-appropriate knowledge and skills would not occur. As such, the state of families is inadequate to the task of conscious social reproduction in its most inclusive form. Further, the state of families does not guarantee conditions under which children can gain exposure to conceptions of the good life that differ from those of their family.

We seek a state that is non-repressive and nondiscriminatory. The state of individuals would seem appropriate. It would allow adults and children to develop their own conceptions of the good life. But in this state type—the extreme opposite of the fully-controlling state—there would be no possibility of people developing collective, agreed notions of the good life and effectively transmitting them to younger generations.[1]

Gutmann (1987) concludes that, in a democratic state, responsibility for education must be shared between parents, the state acting on the behalf of all citizens, and professional educators, acting as agents for the state. "States, parents, and professional educators all have important roles to play in cultivating moral character. A democratic state of education recognizes that educational authority must be shared among parents, citizens, and professional educators even though such sharing does not guarantee that power will be wedded to knowledge, that parents can successfully pass their prejudices on to their children, or that education will be neutral among competing conceptions of the good life" (p. 42).

Education for democratic citizenship must give young people the knowledge and skills to participate to their fullest as adults in social, economic, and political activities. A democratic state must recognize legitimate differences in educational philosophies and allow opportunities for local communities to pursue locally-agreed approaches to schooling. The approaches taken by any given community might at times be idiosyncratic. That is fine, so long as what occurs in the local schools is consistent with the development of democratic values and the cultivation of a common culture (see Gutmann, 1987, p. 74). In the best cases, democratic control of local schools allows citizens to participate in local school politics, identify with a community, and help to shape community development. But localism can create problems. Local control can create conditions under which discrimination occurs. Further, excessive reliance on local funding of schools can promote gross inequality in the educational opportunities open to the young.[2]

Often, politicians, educators, and social commentators fall into nostalgic and romantic talk about the linkages between education, localism, and democratic practice.[3] Of course, there is a place for idealism in discussions of education and democracy. But pragmatism is also important, especially when we are discussing issues of institutional design and practical ways to achieve improved social outcomes. Given this, education policy makers within a democratic state must recognize—and create spaces for—parents to act on their beliefs about what is best for their children. In some cases, this will lead local districts where resources are plentiful to fund their schools generously. In other cases, this will lead some parents to send their children to private schools, seeking particular educational opportunities for them or seeking a curriculum that incorporates religious instruction. In such cases, policy makers must be vigilant to ensure two basic conditions are met. First, plentiful funding of schools in some localities should not compromise the adequacy of funding in all other localities (see Gutmann, 1987, p. 134). Second, all schools—be they public or private—should impart democratic values to their students (see Gutmann, 1987, p. 117).

The two provisions noted here bring to the surface other tensions that must be managed to ensure democratic education and social reproduction in its most inclusive form. For example, imbalances in educational opportunities can create problems in a democracy. They can serve to perpetuate and exacerbate economic and political disparities that can undermine the potential for fair, inclusive political practice. Further, when well-off and politically savvy parents exit the public schools, they deprive those schools of resources that could otherwise help in the pursuit of effective education for all and advocacy for improvements. Removal of oneself, and one's children, from the public domain does send signals about one's faith in democratic institutions. At the extreme, choice options could move us from a democratic state to a state of families (see Gutmann, 1987, p. 116). Abernathy (2005) offers several empirical investigations of the consequences for public schooling and democratic participation of choice options and their potential to siphon off parents who could otherwise be strong advocates for improved public schools. The question that then arises is whether problems in public schools can be adequately addressed in the absence of market competition. If not, then loss of strong advocates must be a cost—but certainly not the greatest or most immediate cost—of poorly performing public schools.[4] In a climate where parental choice is treated as a significant policy option, exploring the implications of choice for democratic practice is essential.

Institutions of Local Democracy in Education

Public control of organizations can be exercised in many ways under democratic systems of government. In the United States, schools have traditionally been controlled through local institutional structures. Initially, these structures were quite basic, and it was common for schools to exist within their individual districts, subject to control by an elected school board whose oversight responsibilities began and ended with that one school. During the reform era of the early 20th century, the control of schools was consolidated through the creation of school districts typically containing multiple schools. Consistent with developments elsewhere in the public sector at that time, efforts were

made during the reform era to separate the administration and day-to-day practices of schooling from direct political control (Knott & Miller, 1987; Tyack, 1974). Contemporary forms of school organization and the institutions of local democracy still bear the imprint of the reform era. It is ironic that public schools in the United States remain strongly controlled by local institutions yet, especially in large, urban school districts, those institutions present few opportunities for citizens (and parents) to engage closely in decision making around school practices. This state of affairs has led Moe (2000) to observe that "...hardly anyone participates in school politics, and those who do are likely to be quite unrepresentative of the public at large and instead a reflection of the power of interest groups" (p. 133). McDermott (1999) has suggested that "[d]emocratic local control of public education is a potent ideal; it should also be regarded as a myth" (p. 7).[5]

Problems of democratic control in large, urban school districts are a function of size and interest group politics, among other things. As organizations grow larger, any sense of individual effectiveness tends to decline. In turn, this leads to weaker incentives to participate and hence, less participation (Dahl & Tufte, 1973). At the same time, large organizations—like urban school administrations—tend to develop complex systems of control that are unresponsive to calls for change. As Bish and Ostrom observed long ago, "[l]arge school systems are inflexible, lack innovation and do not adapt to changing conditions and changing student needs. Change in the performance of big school systems usually is the result of shocks generated outside the system" (1973, p. 37).

Over recent decades, scholars have offered a range of interpretations concerning local democracy in education in the United States. During the 1960s and 1970s, Laurence Iannaccone and Frank W. Lutz developed an empirically-based "dissatisfaction theory" of local educational politics. These authors argued that the majority of school elections are characterized by lack of competition and low voter turnout. This results in school district board members viewing themselves as separate from the community. They therefore tend to act as trustees rather than representatives, and they can become unresponsive to citizen voices. However, when dissatisfaction reaches a certain threshold, this can result in greater attendance at school board meetings, more competitive school board elections, increased voter turnout, defeat of incumbent board members, turnover of superintendents, and policy change (Iannaccone & Lutz, 1994; Lutz & Iannaccone, 1978). Consistent with the dissatisfaction theory, many efforts to achieve greater "community control" of schools have occurred since the 1970s. Actions taken in Chicago since 1989 to devolve school decision making have been prominent among such efforts. The results in Chicago were often positive, but not universally (Bryk, Bebring, Kerbow, Rollow, & Easton, 1998). Mixed results have also been found elsewhere (Hess, 2005; Shirley, 1997). Moves towards greater community control have served to highlight differences across communities in what Clarence

Stone (1989) has termed "civic capacity." Communities with high levels of efficacious parents, supported by powerful stakeholders, are more likely to achieve effective and sustained changes in the running of their schools than are those with fewer community resources (Stone, Henig, Jones, & Pierannunzi, 2001).

Across the United States, school districts are typically governed by elected local school boards consisting of around seven members. The school districts tend to be independent of other forms of local government, such as towns, cities, or counties. This means they have the power to raise their own revenues, and historically school districts have relied upon property taxes as their primary revenue source. The situation is different in big cities, where schools are managed as part of the city government, and some or all board members are appointed by the mayor (Berkman & Plutzer, 2005). Local school boards delegate managerial responsibilities to a district superintendent who is responsible for developing and managing district policies. In this role, superintendents are supported by a local bureaucracy that, among other things, attends to curriculum issues, school budgets, property management, personnel matters, and relations with other levels of government. Many local school districts are required to receive the approval of local citizens for increases in property taxes or new bond issues. In some instances, citizen approval is required for annual budgets. Through elections, local citizens exercise democratic control over the membership of their district school boards and the most significant financial decisions made by those boards.[6]

The Constitution of the United States does not mention education or how it is to be provided. The Founding Fathers left responsibility for educational concerns to state governments. State constitutions typically made provision for the education of state residents. Historically, states simply delegated most responsibilities concerning the provision of public education to local school districts. However, from the 1960s onwards, citizen groups established a trend of using the state courts to seek greater equality of funding of local schools (Reed, 2001). These efforts resulted in states taking on greater responsibility for the financing of school operations. With this greater responsibility, states began to seek more control over local schools and school policies. Today, it is common for state governments to play an active role in the control of schools and the monitoring of school performance. Further, beginning with federal government efforts to eliminate the practice of racial segregation within public schools since the 1950s, the role played by the government in the control of public schools has increased. Currently, the federal government funds a number of redistribution and special education initiatives. These funds are typically funneled to schools through state departments of education. In recent times, the federal government has sought to achieve greater school accountability. The passage of the No Child Left Behind Act of 2002, requiring, among other things, that all schools undertake annual testing of student performance, represented a major change in the role that the government plays in the control of public schools (Rudalevige, 2003).

In sum, local school districts, their boards, and their superintendents continue to exercise significant influence over schools within the United States. However, due to the nature of the federal system, a complex situation of intergovernmental power sharing has evolved. The system of democratic government and control ensures that various branches of government and a multitude of constituencies at the local, state, and national levels all have the potential to influence what happens in local schools (Wirt & Kirst, 1997). In this system, the voices of parents and other interested local actors can readily be drowned out. As a result, the extent to which schools might serve as spaces for the nurture and exercise of democratic citizenship is often compromised.

Contemporary Institutional Dilemmas

Earlier we noted that democratic education is necessary if we are to secure social reproduction in its most inclusive form. When thinking about education and democracy, it is important to recognize that the substance and the delivery of education cannot be meaningfully separated. Just as democratically-decided policies emerge out of the to-and-fro of debate among individuals and groups who hold different interests and visions of the good life, so too, democratic education is predicated on young people being subject to multiple influences. Education for democracy—that is, education within a democratic state—must be shared among parents, citizens, and professional educators. This suggests that questions concerning who should be making particular educational choices on behalf of children will present ongoing political challenges. At the local community level alone, this need to strike compromises and achieve balance between parents, citizens, and professional educators can be demanding (Leithwood, Jantzi, & Steinbach, 1999; Mountford, 2004; Robinson & Ward, 2005). However, as we have also noted, the federal system of democratic government and control in the United States allows actors at multiple levels of government to weigh in on educational decision making. This adds significant complexity to policy development around what schools should do and how schools should be organized and controlled.

All this complexity presents challenges for those seeking to interpret educational politics and policy. As analysts and researchers, we need to find straightforward approaches that yield insights into contemporary developments. We need to stay alert to complexity, but not allow it to undermine our efforts to achieve clarity concerning those issues of most significance. Here, the discussion is built around four contemporary institutional dilemmas. Each arises from the desire to pursue goals that, while not necessarily incommensurate, must be balanced against one another.

Dilemma 1: *How might we strengthen local democratic processes and promote continuous improvement in student outcomes?* Democratic oversight whereby well-informed and engaged citizens exercise effective control over elected and appointed administrators is most readily achieved in local settings, where the chains of accountability are shortest. However, part of the legacy of the progressive era reforms has been the greater professionalization of teaching and the buffering of school administration and practices from close public scrutiny (Brunner, 1998; Feuerstein, 2002). Add to this the strength of interest groups, especially teachers unions, and the power of states and the federal government to impose standards and systems of accountability, and the notion that public education is subject to democratic local control does begin to look farcical.[7] That said, for broader processes of democracy to be sustained, it is essential that schools serve as sites where democratic practice is nurtured and exercised. But is that possible? Terry M. Moe (2000) has suggested that "the schools have difficulty contributing to the quality of democratic government precisely because they are democratically controlled" (p. 142). Moe's prescription involves largely removing schools from top-down democratic oversight and replacing this with a system of parental choice. In this view, democratic control should be sacrificed in service of improved student outcomes. Alternative views tend to incorporate more positive interpretations of democratic processes and their potential. Among these are views that suggest greater efforts to secure democratic practice within schools, and greater efforts on the part of schools to engage with their communities, can lead to improved student outcomes (McGee Banks & Banks, 1997; Sanders & Harvey, 2002). Although limited, comparative evidence on the linkages between democratic versus market-like accountability systems and student outcomes suggests that market-like systems in themselves might not be sufficient to boost student outcomes (Harris & Herrington, 2006; Witte, 2000). Given this, we should not abandon the prospect that improved local democratic processes could support efforts to improve student outcomes.

Dilemma 2: *How might we balance local community aspirations for schools with broader societal or national aspirations?* It is well recognized that different communities, and different groups of parents, will often hold distinctive views about what matters for the education of their children. In the United States, there is a long tradition of leaving decisions around educational choices to local communities. However, without some determined efforts being made to achieve uniformity, there is a risk that broader state or national concerns might get lost within a sea of disconnected local schools or school districts. There is also the concern that some local communities will become pockets of poverty, bigotry, and educational backwardness while others engage in well-funded, inclusive practices that generate effective educational innovations that do not necessarily diffuse. Yet, when curriculums, guides for effective practice, and testing regimes are set exclusively at the national or state level, the concern arises that local preferences and practices may get ignored. In turn, this could lead to local apathy around the pursuit of educational effectiveness (Brunner, 1998). Additionally, localities could atrophy as significant

venues for the nurturing of democratic citizenship (Barber, 1984; Valelly, 1993).

Dilemma 3: *How might we pursue public educational goals when the technical core of schooling often involves private, unobserved practice?* This dilemma highlights the relationship between governance and instruction, which is not as straightforward as many people might think (Cohen & Spillane, 1992). It has often been noted that school systems are highly susceptible to problems that arise when the people who are engaging in tasks on the behalf of others have more information about the quality and effectiveness of their performance than do the people for whom they are working.[8] In the case of schooling, all adults engaged in educational decision making and the practice of teaching serve as agents for the children involved. As such, they should be striving to act in the best interests of those children. However, as a post-experience good, the quality and the benefits of education often become clear to individuals on whom it was bestowed only well after the fact.[9] At a more immediate level, the loose coupling between the efforts of school administrators to achieve control and the technical core of schooling, performed by teachers in their classrooms, raises concerns as to how effectively the wishes of parents, citizens, politicians, policy makers, and administrators are translated into educational practice.[10] To address this concern, Richard F. Elmore (2004) has proposed quite radical reform of school-level practices, all designed to achieve greater professionalism and collective learning among teachers within schools. If implemented, such reforms would potentially reduce disparities between the specification of public educational goals and the extent to which, in practice, those goals are sought.

Dilemma 4: *How might we ensure that information generated to support greater school accountability can be effectively utilized to support improved school practices?* Recent accountability efforts in the United States, undertaken both by states and by the federal government, to use annual tests to monitor student and school performance are generating significant amounts of new information on student learning. They are also promoting new efforts to carefully analyze that information (Clotfelter & Ladd, 1996; Hanushek & Raymond, 2003; Hess, 2003). Yet, questions have long been raised about the quality and usefulness of educational indicators and how they are used (Bryk & Hermanson, 1993). Evidence has also emerged concerning the barriers that inhibit teachers from using data to improve their practice (Ingram, Louis, & Schroeder, 2004). Despite this, evidence is emerging about how school leaders can structure conversations and activities among teachers to use test data in support of improved student outcomes. Significantly, the extent to which the actions of school leaders are consistent with good democratic practice can positively effect the likelihood that learning conversations will occur among teachers and, in turn, influence student learning (Leithwood, Steinbach, & Jantzi, 2002; Spillane, Halverson, & Diamond, 2004). But there are no guarantees that practices of this kind will emerge in schools simply because of the appearance of new information or even in the light of new incentives being developed to promote its use.[11]

Each of these dilemmas speaks to contemporary issues surrounding local democracy in education. The first raises the possibility that democratic oversight, as currently practiced, might inhibit what happens in schools and classrooms, to the point where good student outcomes are jeopardized. The second dilemma raises the possibility that local and broader social and national interests may sometimes be incompatible. The third raises the possibility that, due to information problems, incongruities might arise between democratically-agreed educational goals and actual educational practices. The final dilemma raises the possibility that teachers' various notions of what constitutes good professional practice might inhibit the taking of action based on relevant information concerning student and school performance. These dilemmas do not exhaust the set of dilemmas faced by contemporary educational policy-makers and administrators. But they are major dilemmas—ones that can be expected to arise in any education system intended to promote democratic purposes. Having laid out these contemporary institutional dilemmas, we can now turn to examining key strategies that have been adopted in recent times to improve system outcomes.

Strategies for Improving System Outcomes

Beginning in the 1980s, an array of reform efforts have been launched in the United States with the goal of improving the performance of public schools. Typically, performance is measured in terms of student results on standardized tests, although other measures of performance matter too, such as efficient and equitable provision of services. These reform efforts have originated mostly at the state level. The most salient reforms have included the introduction of new accountability systems, new funding systems, and provision of options for school choice, the creation of charter schools and, in some cases, the use of vouchers. But the federal government has also been active. Further, a range of less salient efforts have been made at the school district level to introduce reforms. In the sections to follow, I discuss these reform efforts and the implications they hold for local democracy in education. The reforms are presented here in three broad categories. First, I consider reform efforts that have been designed to preserve current institutional arrangements and make them more effective. I then consider reforms that have changed the current institutional arrangements. Finally, I consider reforms that have involved creating alternative institutions.

Working within Current Institutional Arrangements

While they do not gain the attention received by institutional reforms or efforts to create alternative institutions, efforts to improve the operations of current institutional arrangements often have positive consequences for student outcomes and for local democratic practice. Here, I present several examples of incremental changes to standard operating procedures that appear to generate positive results. The first concerns local school board elections. Concern is often expressed at the lack of citizen participation in such elections (McDermott, 1999). As well as this, in general, citizens often appear ignorant of important electoral issues (Kuklinski, Quirk, Jerit, Schwieder, & Rich, 2000). However, creating opportunities for citizens to acquire appropriate information can make a significant difference to voter knowledge and behavior. Allen and Plank (2005) present a careful analysis of school board elections in Michigan; they show that citizens are more likely to vote and to be well-informed on the issues when those elections coincide with general municipal elections, as opposed to the situation when special school elections are held. Berry and Howell (2005) offer another example of how changes in the information environment can lead to more rational voting in school board elections. This evidence suggests that reasonably modest changes in standard operating procedures can enhance citizen engagement in school board politics and, hence, the effective democratic control of schools.

Within schools themselves, changes in leadership style that result in more inclusive, democratic decision making among the teaching staff can have positive effects for student learning. Much has been written about the importance of leadership in schools.[12] Recent explorations based on the notion of "distributed leadership" take the focus away from the practices of a given individual—such as the school principal—and instead consider how leadership might be found "stretched over" the social and situational contexts of the school (Spillane, Halverson, & Diamond, 2004, p. 5). In this perspective, the tools and activities used to undertake given tasks, such as the development of forms, curricular documents, and methods for representing test-score data become central to the study of leadership practice. As Maxcy and Nguyễn (2006) note, the politics behind the distribution of leadership in schools should never be ignored. However, this perspective emphasizes the importance of taking context into account when devising new teaching strategies, and of listening to the voices of people with situated knowledge, not just those with formal power. Such actions can promote organization learning about how to effectively interpret and respond to student test-score data (Timperley, 2005). As such, they hold the promise of overcoming factors that would otherwise inhibit organizational use of relevant information (Ingram, Louis, & Schroeder, 2004).

Reaching out to students from diverse backgrounds and making effective connections with parents are other strategies that schools can undertake to promote student engagement with school. Culturally-relevant pedagogy might be thought of as just good teaching (Ladson-Billings, 1995), but it is often resisted and requires careful effort to undertake. School principals can do much to promote inclusive learning conditions in their schools, but this does require an awareness of need, and conscious effort to promote improvements (Cambron-McCabe & McCarthy, 2005; Marri,

2005; Norte, 1999; Riehl, 2000). Effective leadership is also required if school-community collaborations are to be established. As Hess and Leal (2001) have noted, a variety of factors, including institutional structures, can affect how much parents and other citizens will engage with their local school. Efforts to address barriers to engagement can require a great deal of energy.

Separately and in combination, activities of the type noted here can have positive effects, both in terms of promoting democratic practice in and around schools, and in promoting better educational outcomes for students. Importantly, improved outcomes for students—especially those at risk of marginalization in the school system—can have positive consequences for their future participation in society.

Reforming Current Institutional Arrangements

Three types of reform to the control and organization of public schooling have been highly salient over the past two decades. First, various states and school districts have created open-enrollment programs. These inter- and intra-district choice programs have given parents options concerning the public schools their children attend. At the margin, the introduction of such options can have positive effects for local democratic practice, although they do not set up the kind of competitive dynamics associated with other choice programs. The linkages between choice programs and local democratic practice are explored further in the next section, where the implications of charter schools and voucher programs are discussed. Second, educational management organizations—that is, private management companies—that contract to operate public schools have become much more prevalent in the past decade. Initially, such companies were established to create their own chains of schools or to manage charter schools. However, several large urban school districts have turned to such companies to improve the organization of their schools. The implications of this development for democratic practice deserve consideration. Finally, state and federal efforts to make schools more accountable for student performance represent a significant reform to current institutional arrangements.

As part of their standard operating procedures, public schools and school districts have always found it necessary to determine what services they should produce themselves and what ones they should purchase from private providers. Educational management organizations offer the prospect of school districts becoming primarily contract managers, leaving the day-to-day decisions about the operations of their schools to a private company. Since these organizations seek to build and maintain good reputations, they face strong incentives to improve outcomes for students. They also have the potential to readily transmit from site to site valuable information about effective strategies for teaching and learning and other aspects of schooling and school management. In practice, contract details could inhibit the potential for these organizations to introduce practices that

would generate significant performance improvements. This would be especially true if opponents of contracting out were able to have a hand in specifying the contract.[13]

The use of educational management organizations to run public schools could have positive or negative implications for local democratic practice, depending on the nature of the company and the contract or contracts under which it operates. On the positive side, because management organizations operate under contract, they face strong incentives to deliver good educational outcomes. Because good public relations are important to a management organization's ongoing viability, such companies also face strong incentives to see that personnel in their schools develop and maintain effective, cooperative relations with parents and other key stakeholders associated with the schools they manage. These incentives would suggest that use of management organizations could support local democratic purposes. Further, the existence of an explicit service contract increases the possibility that school board members and other interested parties can engage in well-informed, focused discussions about how effectively a company is meeting its obligations within a given school district. This can be beneficial to local democratic processes, especially the oversight element. The most significant potential negative aspect of the use of educational management organizations is that some could require the schools they manage to confirm to a fairly rigid blueprint with respect to a range of matters, including curriculum content and classroom practices. However, such rigidity could face limits. Insensitivity to local preferences would ultimately result in non-renewal of a contract.[14]

The structures of democratic control of public schools have always ensured that teaching staff and administrators are accountable to their local superintendents, local boards, and—at least in principle—to state authorities for what happens in their schools. The drive over the past two decades to achieve greater accountability has forced schools to systematically generate information on student performance. Increasingly, such information is being carefully analyzed, appropriately aggregated, and publicly disseminated (Hanushek & Raymond, 2003). As a result, administrators, teachers, parents, and other interested citizens are able to compare student performance across local schools. They can then raise pointed questions and suggest strategies for change in cases where performance appears to be lagging. There is potential here for new accountability systems to simultaneously strengthen local democratic processes and promote continuous improvement in student outcomes. At the same time, these new accountability systems have been designed to give state and federal officials more leverage over local schools, so that they can take action when schools appear to be failing. Inevitably, the details of accountability systems and how effectively they are implemented will determine the quality of the student outcome information that they generate (Hess, 2003; West & Peterson, 2003). But there is clear potential here for state and federal officials to force change at the local level when local districts or particular schools appear to be systematically underperforming. Evidence is also beginning to emerge suggesting that citizens will use publicly-available information on school performance to punish board members at election time if schools in their districts have been perceived as under-performing (Berry & Howell, 2005).

While new state and federal efforts to promote greater school accountability hold some positive consequences for local democratic practice, there is a danger that the methods used to set standards and to develop standardized tests could reduce the discretion of local boards and schools over curriculum choice and teaching methods. Strike (1998) has considered this issue in detail, focusing on how accountability systems might encourage transmission of knowledge, values, and skills that promote national goals, while recognizing the merits of multiculturalism, pluralism, and local decision making. Strike has proposed that the means of accountability should set "a high, but narrow bar" (p. 211). For example, they should require high standards to be met in reading and numeracy, but should not venture into other subject areas, such as history, science, and literature. He has also suggested that states should "coerce to adequacy but inspire to excellence" (p. 212). Strike offers clear criteria to guide standard setting: "[S]tandards should emphasize curricular areas that are central to the public interest and the welfare of all students. Arguments for such standards should show that when students fail to meet them, they are denied significant access to our society's political and economic institutions; also, when such standards are not met by significant numbers of students, the welfare of society is broadly harmed" (p. 212). When such criteria are followed, local community aspirations for schools can be effectively balanced against broader societal or national aspirations.

Creating Alternative Institutions

The school choice movement in the United States has flourished during the past two decades, giving rise to the creation of many new charter schools across the country, and opening the way for parents in some locations to use vouchers to send their children to private schools. Tax-credits for parents sending their children to private schools have also become more prevalent, as have opportunities for homeschooling. Here, I focus on the introduction of charter schools and the creation of voucher programs, because these represent significant efforts to establish institutional alternatives to the traditional public school system. Charter schools and voucher programs create new opportunities for many parents to choose the schools their children can attend. They also create opportunities for energetic teachers and administrators to establish new schools and experiment with new models of educational organization and pedagogy. There is much scope within these developments for education professionals to harness them for the advancement of democratic practices within schools, if they choose to do so. Test-score evidence is yet to demonstrate unambiguously that students exposed to these different schooling options

necessarily do better in them.[15] A major confounding factor is that many charter schools have been established to cater to students with special educational needs or who have not been performing well in traditional public schools. In addition, voucher programs have been established in urban school districts where the family backgrounds of students and their prior educational experiences have placed them at major disadvantages to begin with.

The implications of charter schools and voucher programs for local democracy in education deserve careful consideration. Several interpretations have been offered. By expanding the educational choices open to parents, the introduction of charter schools and voucher programs could be viewed as contributing positively to democratic practice. School choice can also create dynamics whereby traditional public schools, subject to market-like pressures, begin to show greater concern for the needs and concerns of students and their parents. Here, the virtues of individual liberty are played up, while the possibility is played down that creating choice options could have negative implications for democratic equality.[16] As noted earlier, Abernathy (2005) has argued that choice options pose a danger of taking some of the most able parents out of school settings where their voice and energy would otherwise be put to good use in pushing for improved conditions for their own and other children. Abernathy concludes that public school choice initiatives, including the creation of charter schools, are less of a threat than voucher programs. He views voucher programs negatively because they take parents out of the public sector and give them incentives to become advocates of full privatization of the school system.[17]

A range of issues come into play when new institutional arrangements are established that directly challenge traditional ways of doing things. If the introduction of charter schools and voucher programs is to contribute to good educational outcomes that are consistent with broader societal goals, doing more than meeting the aspirations of the parents associated with them, then some system of broader accountability must be in place. School accreditation schemes and student testing programs would appear to address this. If good quality information about schools and student outcomes is made available to parents, then the chances are raised that parents will base their choices among schools on educationally-sound criteria, as opposed to proxies, such as the income bracket and race of families attending different schools (it is important to note that the tradition of local funding of public schools in the United States, combined with limited information regarding school and student performance, has produced sorting of families to schools on exactly such proxies).

Scholars should be vigilant as to how creating alternative institutions for the delivery of schooling could prove detrimental to local democratic practice. In particular, we need to consider whether the creation of charter schools and the use of vouchers could serve to inhibit involvement of the broader citizenry in school decision making. Claims have been made that efforts to enhance parental choice have resulted in less oversight of the ways that public funds are spent in schools that are either private or quasi-private in nature. There is no reason why this should be the case, but the potential for erosion of non-parental citizen involvement is real (Lubienski, 2003). This matter deserves further scrutiny. Having said this, there is merit also in assessing the potential opportunities that such institutions present for enhancing democratic practice.[18] Drawing on work of Schneider, Teske, Marschall, Mintrom, and Roch (1997) that analyzed parental behavior under choice plans in New York and New Jersey, and upon his own analysis of parental behavior under the Milwaukee voucher program, Abernathy (2005) has noted a consistent finding that parents who face choice options and exercise them end up engaging in more activities associated with their new schools than what they did with their old schools or what non-choosing parents do. Consistent with these findings, Mintrom (2003) found that charter schools were more likely than traditional public schools to create structured opportunities for parents to contribute to school deliberations and decision making. That said, in their comparison of the practices of public and private schools, Benveniste, Carnoy, and Rothstein (2003) noted that some charter schools and private schools seek to limit the extent to which parents influence school decision making. No school can function effectively when the voices of parents dominate over those of teachers and administrators. In cases where parents dominate, we are taken back to the state of families which, as noted earlier, is inadequate to the task of conscious social reproduction in its most inclusive form. Schools need to listen closely to parents, and it is possible that the threat of parental exit makes charter schools and private schools more open to engaging in close dialogue with parents (Hirschman, 1970). But close dialogue is different from responding to every whim of every parent. It can also mean taking the time to explain clearly to parents why certain practices are followed in the school over others.

Taken together, these findings suggest that creating alternative institutions for the delivery of schooling can be a way to lay the groundwork for strengthening democratic politics more broadly.[19] If we value ways to enhance local democratic processes and admit that traditional arrangements for the local control of public schools have not delivered on their promise, then exploring the potential contributions of alternative institutions, including private schools and privately-managed public schools makes sense. With appropriate institutional design, market incentives can create dynamics that promote greater democratic participation.

Conclusion: Future Prospects for Local Democracy in Education

When discussion turns to the relationship between education and democracy, people sometimes glorify traditional systems of local control of public schools.[20] When proposals are made to reform the delivery of public schooling or to tighten up accountability systems, some opponents portray them as thinly-veiled attacks on the institutions of local democracy in education.[21] There is, of course, a vital linkage between education and democratic citizenship. The quality of the education young people receive holds implications for the future wellbeing of those young people and the future wellbeing of society in general. In addition, local democratic control of public schooling, when effectively exercised, can serve to promote the involvement of citizens in the political life of their communities. This, in turn, can raise the chances that those citizens will take an interest in the political life of the broader jurisdictions in which they reside. However, none of this should be taken to imply that local democracy in education, as currently practiced in the United States, is as good as things get. Indeed, low levels of participation in school board elections, in meetings of school boards, and in various local school events suggest that local democracy in education is not quite the wellspring of civic participation that Tocqueville found it to be in the 1840s.

Here, I noted the complexities surrounding control of education and how these can serve to inhibit local democratic engagement. I also discussed several contemporary institutional dilemmas and how these have played out across a range of recent reform efforts. From this, I conclude that local democracy in education could be enhanced both directly and indirectly through a variety of reform efforts currently in play. Importantly, local public schools should not be viewed as the exclusive preserve of effective democratic control in education. Indeed, democratic processes around local schools often work better when they are supported by the efforts of higher-level governments to promote school accountability or when local schools are subjected to competition from charter schools or private schools. The local dynamics created by institutional changes and by efforts to help parents exercise more informed voice and choice can open up new opportunities for democratic engagement. Reform efforts should always be scrutinized to assess their compatibility with good democratic practices and the advancement of democratic education. So, too, should established institutional arrangements.

When analyzing local education politics, policy researchers face a range of choices concerning the analytical strategies they employ. In the past, theorization of the linkages between structural choices concerning the delivery of schooling and the advancement of democratic practice has been somewhat limited. More theoretical work focused upon contemporary policy choices is needed. In terms of empirical work, previous studies of local education politics have been dominated by the use of historical and contemporary case studies. These have given us a large amount of rich description and have served as the basis for a fair degree of hypothesis development. Formal hypothesis testing through quantitative research has been less common in this field. Looking ahead, much room exists for the development of theory-driven, rigorous empirical analyses of relationships between aspects of institutional design and the actions of educational administrators, teachers, parents, citizens, and other interested stakeholders. The variety of reforms now underway provides excellent conditions for conducting comparative analyses of local democracy in education. Perfect systems of democratic governance will never be achieved. But evidence-based debate over what institutions for schooling work best will support improved outcomes for all students. Such debate will also keep the prospects bright for the improvement of local democracy in education.

Notes

1. These points are made by Gutmann (1987) in chapter 1, "States and Education."
2. McDermott (1999) offers a sustained analysis of tensions between localism and educational equity.
3. Meier (1995) states, "Schools embody the dreams we have for our children. All of them. These dreams must remain public property" (p. 36). McDonnell (2000) observes: "Highlighting the democratic purposes of education at the beginning of the twenty-first century may seem hopelessly romantic or quaintly outdated" (p. 1).
4. A further point not explored by Gutmann or Abernathy concerns the moral dilemma faced by individual parents with the resources to use private options. Should you act in what you see as the best educational interests of your children and use private schools, or should you put commitment to improving public schools above these more immediate, individualized interests? A few presidents and other high-profile politicians have at times struggled publicly with this issue.
5. Gutmann (1987) makes a similar point: "[O]ur public schools, especially in many of our largest cities, are so centralized and bureaucratized that parents along with other citizens actually exercise very little democratic control over local schools" (p. 70). In Gutmann's view, this state of affairs helps explain why many people see appeal in vouchers.
6. Berkman and Plutzer (2005) provide up-to-date summaries of key institutional differences across contemporary school districts in the United States. See, especially, the tables in chapters 4 and 5.
7. For comprehensive analyses of the strength of teachers union in the control of school district policies, see Berkman and Plutzer (2005, chapter 6) and Moe (2005).
8. Moe (2003, pp. 81–83) provides a useful overview of the agency problem in education. For a thorough exposition and investigation of agency problems, see Pratt and Zeckhauser (1985).
9. Weimer and Vining (2005, pp. 110–111) provide a useful discussion of post-experience goods and the unique agency problems they present.
10. Weick (1976) introduced the terms "loose coupling" and "technical core" into discussions of educational organizations.
11. Tyack and Cuban (1995) note the tendency for schools to resist administrative change and other innovations. Bennett and Desforges (1991) provide an insightful analysis of sources of resistance to change, based on a review of primary education in England.
12. For a comprehensive review, see Leithwood, Louis, Anderson, and Wahlstrom (2004).
13. Moe (2000, 2003) notes the role that compromise plays in the political control of schools. Moe's concerns about the power of teachers unions and their influence on board decision making are also relevant to this point (see Moe, 2005).
14. Bulkley (2003) and Hentschke, Oschman, and Snell (2002) offer useful analyses and discussions of the emergence, operations, and consequences of educational management organizations.
15. For reviews of available evidence, see, for example, Howell and Peterson (2002) and Witte (2000).
16. Wells, Slayton, and Scott (2002) examine the ways that advocates of school choice have emphasized democratic liberty over democratic equality.

17. Gutmann (1987, p. 116) shares this concern.
18. See Mintrom (2001) for a more detailed "democracy audit" of recent school reform efforts.
19. Valelly (1993) has observed: "Policy design can construct citizens as competent to address public problems. It can do so by providing for representation in local problem-solving processes. Such representation provides for small-scale governance that, in turn, can foster reconnected citizenship in other areas: other groups and more frequent voting" (p. 262).
20. See, e.g., Meier (1995) and Wells, Slayton, and Scott (2002).
21. Henig (1994, chapter 3) documents early arguments against school choice and vouchers. Cohen (1996) documents examples of local resistance to state accountability systems.

References

Abernathy, S. F. (2005). *School choice and the future of American democracy*. Ann Arbor: University of Michigan Press.

Allen, A., & Plank, D. N. (2005). School board election structure and democratic representation. *Educational Policy, 19*, 510–527.

Barber, B. R. (1984). *Strong democracy: Participatory politics for a new age*. Berkeley: University of California Press.

Bennett, N., & Desforges, C. (1991). Primary education in England: A system in transition. *The Elementary School Journal, 92*, 61–78.

Benveniste, L., Carnoy, M., & Rothstein, R. (2003). *All else equal: Are public and private schools different?* New York: RoutledgeFalmer.

Berkman, M. B., & Plutzer, E. (2005). *Ten thousand democracies: Politics and public opinion in America's school districts*. Washington, DC: Georgetown University Press.

Berry, C. R., & Howell, W. G. (2005). Democratic accountability in public education. In W. G. Howell (Ed.), *Besieged: School Boards and the Future of Education Politics* (pp. 150–172). Washington, DC: Brookings Institution.

Bish, R. L., & Ostrom, V. (1973). *Understanding urban government: Metropolitan reform reconsidered*. Washington, DC: American Enterprise Institute for Public Policy Research.

Bohman, J. (1996). *Public deliberation: Pluralism, complexity, and democracy*. Cambridge, MA: MIT Press.

Brunner, C. C. (1998). The legacy of disconnection between the public schools and their communities: Suggestions for policy. *Educational Policy, 12*, 244–266.

Bryk, A. S., Bebring, P. B., Kerbow, D., Rollow, S. & Easton, J. Q. (1998). *Charting Chicago school reform: Democratic localism as a lever for change*. Boulder, CO: Westview Press.

Bryk, A. S., & Hermanson, K. L. (1993). Educational indicator systems: Observations on their structure, interpretation, and use. *Review of Research in Education, 19*, 451–484.

Bulkley, K. E. (2003). *Recentralizing decentralization? Educational management organizations and charter schools' educational programs* (NCSPE Occasional Paper No. 60). New York: National Center for the Study of Privatization in Education.

Cambron-McCabe, N., & McCarthy, M. M. (2005). Educating school leaders for social justice. *Educational Policy, 19,* 201–222.

Clotfelter, C. T., & Ladd, H. F. (1996). Recognizing and rewarding success in public schools. In H. F. Ladd (Ed.), *Holding schools accountable*: *Performance-based reform in education* (pp. 23–63). Washington DC: Brookings Institution.

Cohen, D. K. (1996). Standards-based school reform: Policy, practice, and performance. In H. F. Ladd (Ed.), *Holding schools accountable*: *Performance-based reform in education* (pp. 99–127). Washington DC: Brookings Institution.

Cohen, D. K., & Spillane, J. P. (1992). Policy and practice: The relations between governance and instruction. *Review of Research in Education, 18,* 3–49.

Dahl, R. A. (1989). *Democracy and its critics*. New Haven, CT: Yale University Press.

Dahl, R. A., & Tufte, E. R. (1973). *Size and democracy*. Stanford, CA: Stanford University Press.

Dewey, J. (1916). *Democracy and education: An introduction to the philosophy of education.* New York: The Free Press.

Elmore, R. F. (2004). *School reform from the inside out: Policy, practice, and performance.* Cambridge, MA: Harvard Education Press.

Feuerstein, A. (2002). Elections, voting, and democracy in local school district governance. *Educational Policy, 16,* 15–36.

Forester, J. (1999). *The deliberative practitioner: Encouraging participatory planning processes.* Cambridge, MA: MIT Press.

Friedman, M. (1962). *Capitalism and freedom.* Chicago: University of Chicago Press.

Gastil, J., & Levine, P. (Eds.). (2005). *The deliberative democracy handbook: Strategies for effective civic engagement in the twenty-first century.* San Francisco: Jossey-Bass.

Gutmann, A. (1987). *Democratic education.* Princeton, NJ: Princeton University Press.

Hanushek, E. A., & Raymond, M. E. (2003). Lessons about the design of state accountability systems. In P. E. Peterson & M. R. West (Eds.), *No Child Left Behind? The politics and practice of school accountability* (pp. 127–151). Washington, DC: Brookings.

Harris, D. N., & Herrington, C. D. (2006). Accountability, standards, and the growing achievement gap: Lessons from the past half-century. *American Journal of Education, 112,* 209–238.

Held, D. (1996). *Models of democracy* (2nd ed.). Stanford, CA: Stanford University Press.

Henig, J. R. (1994). *Rethinking school choice: Limits of the market metaphor.* Princeton, NJ: Princeton University Press.

Hentschke, G. C., Oschman, S., & Snell, L. (2002, May). *Education management organizations: Growing a for-profit education industry with choice, competition, and innovation* (Reason Foundation Policy Brief No. 21). Los Angeles: Reason Foundation.

Hess, F. M. (2003). Refining or retreating? High-stakes accountability in the States. In P. E. Peterson & M. R. West (Eds.), *No Child Left Behind? The politics and practice of school accountability* (pp. 55–79). Washington DC: Brookings Institution.

Hess, F. M. (Ed.). (2005). *Urban school reform: Lessons from San Diego.* Cambridge, MA: Harvard Education Press.

Hess, F. M., & Leal, D. L. (2001). The opportunity to engage: How race, class, and institutions structure access to educational deliberation. *Educational Policy, 15,* 474–490.

Hirschman, A. O. (1970). *Exit, voice, and loyalty: Responses to decline in firms, organizations, and states.* Cambridge, MA: Harvard University Press.

Hochschild, J. L. (1984). *The new American dilemma: Liberal democracy and school desegregation.* New Haven, CT: Yale University Press.

Howell, W. G., & Peterson, P. E. (2002). *The education gap: Vouchers and urban schools.* Washington, DC: Brookings Institution.

Iannaccone, L., & Lutz, F. W. (1994). The crucible of democracy: The local arena. *Politics of Education Association Yearbook, 9,* 39–52.

Ingram, D., Louis, K. S., & Schroeder, R. G. (2004). Accountability policies and teacher decision making: Barriers to the use of data to improve practice. *Teachers College Record, 106,* 1258–1287.

Knott, J. H., & Miller, G. J. (1987). *Reforming bureaucracy: The politics of institutional choice.* Englewood Cliffs, NJ: Prentice-Hall.

Kuklinski, J. H., Quirk, P. J., Jerit, J., Schwieder, D., & Rich, R. F. (2000). Misinformation and the currency of citizenship. *Journal of Politics, 62,* 791–816.

Ladson-Billings, G. (1995). But that's just good teaching! The case for culturally relevant pedagogy. *Theory into Practice, 34,* 159–165.

Leithwood, K., Jantzi, D., & Steinbach, R. (1999). Do school councils matter? *Educational Policy, 13,* 467–493.

Leithwood, K., Louis, K. S., Anderson, S., & Wahlstrom, K. (2004). *How leadership influences student learning.* New York: Wallace Foundation.

Leithwood, K., Steinbach, R., & Jantzi, D. (2002). School leadership and teachers' motivation to implement accountability policies. *Educational Administration Quarterly, 38,* 94–119.

Lubienski, C. (2003). Instrumentalist perspectives on the 'public' in public education: Incentives and purposes. *Educational Policy, 17,* 478–502.

Lutz, F. W., & Iannaccone, L. (Eds.). (1978). *Public participation in local school districts: The dissatisfaction theory of American democracy.* Lexington, MA: D.C. Heath.

Manzer, R. (2003). *Educational regimes and Anglo-American democracy.* Toronto: University of Toronto Press.

Marri, A. R. (2005). Building a framework for classroom-based multicultural democratic education: Learning from three skilled teachers. *Teachers College Record, 107,* 1036–1059.

Maxcy, B. D., & Nguyễn, T. S. T. (2006). The politics of distributing leadership: Reconsidering leadership distribution in two Texas elementary schools. *Educational Policy, 20,* 163–196.

McDermott, K. A. (1999). *Controlling public education: Localism versus equity.* Lawrence: University Press of Kansas.

McDonnell, L. M. (2000). Defining democratic purposes. In L. M. McDonnell, P. M. Timpane, & R. Benjamin (Eds.), *Rediscovering the democratic purposes of education* (pp. 1–18). Lawrence: University Press of Kansas.

McGee Banks, C. A., & Banks, J. A. (1997). Reforming schools in a democratic pluralistic society. *Educational Policy, 11,* 183–193.

Meier, D. (1995, April 19). Democracy is not always convenient. *Education Week, 14,* 35–36.

Mintrom, M. (2001). Educational governance and democratic practice. *Educational Policy, 15,* 615–642.

Mintrom, M. (2003). Market organizations and deliberative democracy: Choice and voice in public service delivery. *Administration and Society, 35,* 52–81.

Moe, T. M. (2000). The two democratic purposes of public education. In L. M. McDonnell, P. M. Timpane, & R. Benjamin (Eds.), *Rediscovering the democratic purposes of education* (pp. 127–147). Lawrence: University Press of Kansas.

Moe, T. M. (2003). Politics, control, and the future of school accountability. In P. E. Peterson & M. R. West (Eds.), *No Child Left Behind? The politics and practice of school accountability* (pp. 80–106). Washington, DC: Brookings.

Moe, T. M. (2005). Teachers unions and school board elections. In W. G. Howell (Ed.), *Besieged: School boards and the future of education politics* (pp. 254–287). Washington, DC: Brookings Institution.

Mountford, M. (2004). Motives and power of school board members: Implications for school board-superintendent relationships. *Educational Administration Quarterly, 40,* 704–741.

Norte, E. (1999). 'Structures beneath the skin': How school leaders use their power and authority to create institutional opportunities for developing positive interethnic communities. *The Journal of Negro Education, 68,* 466–485.

Pratt, J. W., & Zeckhauser, R. J. (Eds.). (1985). *Principals and agents: The structure of business.* Boston: Harvard Business School Press.

Reed, D. S. (2001). *On equal terms: The constitutional politics of educational opportunity.* Princeton, NJ: Princeton University Press.

Riehl, C. J. (2000). The principal's role in creating inclusive schools for diverse students: A review of normative, empirical, and critical literature on the practice of educational administration. *Review of Educational Research, 70,* 55–81.

Robinson, V., & Ward, L. (2005). Lay governance of New Zealand's schools: An educational, democratic or managerialist activity? *Journal of Educational Administration, 43,* 170–186.

Rudalevige, A. (2003). No Child Left Behind: Forging a congressional compromise. In P. E. Peterson & M. R. West (Eds.), *No Child Left Behind? The politics and practice of school accountability* (pp. 23–54). Washington DC: Brookings Institution.

Sanders, M. G., & Harvey, A. (2002). Beyond the school walls: A case study of principal leadership for school-community collaboration. *Teachers College Record, 104,* 1345–1368.

Schneider, M., Teske, P., Marschall, M., Mintrom, M., & Roch, C. (1997). Institutional arrangements and the creation of social capital: The effects of public school choice. *American Political Science Review, 91,* 82–93.

Schumpeter, J. A. (1976). *Capitalism, socialism, and democracy* (5th ed.). London: Allen and Unwin.

Shirley, D. (1997). *Community organizing for urban school reform.* Austin: University of Texas Press.

Spillane, J. P., Halverson, R., Diamond, J. B. (2004). Towards a theory of leadership practice: A distributed perspective. *Journal of Curriculum Studies, 36,* 3–34.

Stone, C. N. (1989). *Regime politics: Governing Atlanta, 1946–1988.* Lawrence: University Press of Kansas.

Stone, C. N., Henig, J. R., Jones, B. D., & Pierannunzi, C. (2001). *Building civic capacity: The politics of reforming urban schools.* Lawrence: University Press of Kansas.

Strike, K. A. (1998). Centralized goal formation, citizenship, and educational pluralism: Accountability in liberal democratic societies. *Educational Policy, 12,* 203–215.

Timperley, H. S. (2005). Distributed leadership: Developing theory from practice. *Journal of Curriculum Studies, 37,* 395–420.

Tocqueville, A. de. (1988). *Democracy in America* (G. Lawrence, Trans. & J. P. Mayer, Ed.). New York: Harper and Row. (Original work published 1848)

Tyack, D. B. (1974). *The one best system: A history of American urban education.* Cambridge, MA: Harvard University Press.

Tyack, D. B., & Cuban, L. (1995). *Tinkering toward utopia: A century of public school reform.* Cambridge, MA: Harvard University Press.

Valelly, R. M. (1993). Public policy for reconnected citizenship. In H. Ingram & S. R. Smith (Eds.), *Public policy for democracy* (pp. 241–266). Washington, DC: Brookings Institution.

Weick, K. E. (1976). Educational organizations as loosely coupled systems. *Administrative Science Quarterly, 21,* 1–19.

Weimer, D. L., Vining, A. R. (2005). *Policy analysis: Concepts and practice* (4th ed.). Upper Saddle River, NJ: Pearson Prentice-Hall.

Wells, A. S., Slayton, J., & Scott, J. (2002). Defining democracy in the neoliberal age: Charter school reform and educational consumption. *Teachers College Record, 39,* 337–361.

West, M. R., & Peterson, P. E. (2003). The politics and practice of accountability. In P. E. Peterson & M. R. West (Eds.), *No Child Left Behind? The politics and practice of school accountability* (pp. 1–22). Washington DC: Brookings Institution.

Wirt, F. M., & Kirst, M. W. (1997). *The political dynamics of American education.* Berkeley, CA: McCutchon.

Witte, J. F. (2000). *The market approach to education: An analysis of America's first voucher program.* Princeton, NJ: Princeton University Press.

62

The Politics of (Im)Prudent
State-Level Homeschooling Policies

CATHERINE A. LUGG
Rutgers, The State University of New Jersey

ANDREA K. RORRER
University of Utah

I want to have control over what goes in my son's head, not what's put in there by people who might be on the far left who have their own ideas about indoctrinating kids.

—Glenn, a homeschooling parent,
as cited in Mehta & Landsberg, 2008, ¶ 27

This particular homeschooling parent provides a glimpse into possibly why the number of home educated students appears to be on the rise. The National Center for Educational Statistics roughly estimates 1,096,000 children were homeschooled in 2003 nationally, which was up 29% from 1990s estimate of 890,000 (see Princiotta, Bielick, & Chapman, 2006). As a percentage of the total school population, an estimated 2.2% of all students are currently homeschooled, which is an increase from 1.7% in 1999 (Princiotta et al., 2006). While the overall number of children who are educated at home has seemingly grown over the last 20 years, determining the actual numbers remains impossible, since not all adults who homeschool comply with reporting requirements, nor do all states require notification by adults who homeschool their children (Dibble, 2005). Obviously, the percentage of students who are homeschooled does not necessarily pose an immediate threat to public schools. However, we also do not know the extent of homeschooling's impact on students, the state, or how states' interests are served when parents/guardians and students engage in homeschooling.

In fact, homeschooling might be one of the most under-researched and least understood educational policy areas in the United States. This situation is due to a number of factors. First, much of the early research on homeschooling has been indelibly marked by theological and political agendas (see Apple, 2000; Detwiler, 1999; Lugg, 2000). For example, one study examining homeschooling and academic achievement used data provided by Bob Jones University (Rudner, 1999). Given the institution's history of religiously-based racial bias (see Welner & Welner, 1999), the utility of the study's findings was greatly minimized.

Additionally, homeschoolers' suspicions of government and academic researchers means they are disinclined to participate in research studies (see Collom, 2005; Detwiler, 1999). Finally, there is wide divergence in state regulations concerning those adults who homeschool their children as well as how children are homeschooled (e.g., what is taught, how often, how performance is measured). For instance, some states (e.g., New Jersey) have relatively permissive guidelines while others are far more stringent (e.g., Pennsylvania); some states have multiple options for homeschooling (e.g., California) while others currently maintain a general homeschooling option (e.g., Iowa). This variance in regulatory policy further complicates the research terrain since the appropriateness, utility, and viability of these policies remains difficult to ascertain.

Given the lack of reliable data and the diverse regulatory environment in which homeschooling takes place, this chapter seeks to better define the contemporary terrain of homeschooling in the United States. To do so, first we discuss the political and legal contexts of contemporary homeschooling. Next, we explore the varied and sometimes conflicting state regulations, as well as compare and contrast representative examples of state homeschooling policies.[1] Finally, because the extant research does not capture the scope of this policy's current existence nor its potential impact, we propose an agenda for future research based on the review of the political and policy contexts established in the prior sections, and conclude by making some tentative recommendations for educational policy makers.

This chapter departs from most of the extant educational research on homeschooling which at present is primarily rooted in traditional policy analysis and anchors its claims in objective social science. By contrast, we concur with historian Peter Novick (1988), who described the quest for objectivity as the *never-ending quest to nail jelly to the wall*. After all, this quest has been an embarrassingly elusive project, and avowedly objective social scientists have repeatedly lost their cloak of objectivity as their findings aged badly (Harding, 1993; Levine & Kaplan, 1997; Mc-Closeky, 1993; Novick, 1988). Consequently, we employ *critical policy analysis.* In doing so, we foreground our assumptions. First, we explore both intended and unintended policy outcomes as to "who gets what, where and how" (see Lasswell, 1990). In a country that has historically privileged Protestant Christianity (Ahlstrom, 1972), religious ideology matters in the politics of policy making, as does a country's racial, gender, and class assumptions. It is particularly important to interrogate homeschooling policies given recent findings that parents who homeschool do so largely out of personal beliefs (see Green & Hoover-Dempsey, 2007).[2] As a result, our second assumption entails how power and privilege is distributed and redistributed along historic lines of religion, race, gender, class, and so forth (Bobrow & Dryzek, 1987). Next, we question the rationale for and related outcomes to establishing and maintaining policies steeped in these beliefs. Finally, our analysis is consistent with Charles Lindblom and Edward Woodhouse's (1993) recommendation, who encourage researchers to pursue more politicized forms of analyses. In doing so, we extend the current discussion beyond describing homeschooling as "a powerful social and political movement" (Cooper & Sureau, 2007, p. 115).

Political and Legal Contexts of Contemporary Homeschooling in the United States

While educating children in the home in the United States dates to the colonial era, contemporary homeschooling emerged in the 1970s (Cooper & Sureau, 2007; Stevens, 2001, 2003). During this era, both the political left and right strongly critiqued public schools for their weak pedagogical delivery, stultifying content, as well as suffocating conformity (Bowles & Gintis, 1976; Buzzard, 1982; Holt, 1981). Dissatisfaction with the public schools coupled with a disdain for private schools prompted some parents to begin homeschooling. Moreover, a growing Protestant Right (see Apple, 2001; Lugg, 2000) fueled most of the growth in homeschooling during the 1980s and 1990s. Today, homeschooling appeals to a cross-section of parents and guardians in America (Cooper & Sureau, 2007; Stevens, 2001, 2003). As such, participants in homeschooling have been a varied lot, ranging from anti-establishmentarians to religiously motivated pedagogues (Cooper & Sureau, 2007; Cordes, 2000; McDowell, Sanchez, & Jones, 2000; Princiotta et al., 2006; Stevens, 2001, 2003).[3]

Nevertheless, during the last two and a half decades, Protestant Right political activists have provided much of the political and legal work in "mainstreaming" homeschooling within the larger U.S. political culture. Most prominent of these activists has been Michael Farris, who founded the Homeschool Legal Defense Association (HSLDA) in 1983 (Cooper & Sureau, 2007; Cordes, 2000; Stevens, 2001, 2003). Farris, who has been a lawyer for Concerned Women of America (CWA) and been involved with the Coalition on Revival (COR), has a long track record in Protestant Right

activism and is well-known in Christian Reconstructionist circles (Clarkson, 1997; Cordes, 2000).

A central tenant of Christian Reconstruction theology is that the U.S. public school system presents the strongest impediment to the establishment of an old-Testament style theocracy in the United States. Consequently, not only are Reconstructionists utterly hostile towards public education, many embrace homeschooling as the most legitimate form of educating children (Apple, 2001; Guzman, 2003; Lugg, 2000). Although Reconstructionists are highly controversial in Protestant Right circles, Reconstructionist thinkers and activists have provided much of the theological support for the historically apolitical fundamentalist Christians to embrace political activism (Diamond, 1995, 1998; Lugg, 2000; Phillips, 2006).[4] From the mid-1970s until the present day, Reconstructionsts have played vital behind-the-scenes roles in moving the Protestant Right, as well as the Republican Party, towards embracing more overtly religiously-oriented public policies, including homeschooling (Diamond, 1995, 1998; Goldberg, 2007; Phillips, 2006, Slevin & Bacon, 2007).[5]

This nexus between Christian Reconstructionism (e.g., Farris' role) and the U.S. Protestant Right is worth examining when considering the rise of homeschooling. After all, prior to 1983, homeschooling was rare-to-non-existent in many states (Cooper & Sureau, 2007; Cordes, 2000; Dibble, 2005; Dorman, 1990; Stevens, 2003). Through an energetic combination of litigation and lobbying, Farris and the HSLDA successfully challenged various state statutes that either tightly limited or forbade parents from educating their children at home (Dorman, 1990; Stevens, 2001, 2003). Again, this growth was aided by the larger movement of Protestant Right activists and their participation with Republican Party politics (Cordes, 2000; Phillips, 2006). Farris' involvement with various Protestant Right organizations and their causes, as well as his failed run for lieutenant governor of Virginia during the early 1990s (see Clarkson, 1997) resulted in increasing access to GOP politicians and party officials, and influence in the policy-making process relative to homeschooling (Stevens, 2001, 2003) for both Farris and the HSLDA. As Cooper and Sureau note (2007), the movement's "close relationship with the Christian right and conservative politicians remains a strong source of political access and power" (p. 129), with Farris retaining the position as the movement's long-standing leader.

Many of the philosophical justifications for homeschooling are found in literalist understandings of the Protestant Bible (Mason, 2006), which can be oft tied to Christian Reconstructionism (see Lugg, 2000). For example, homeschoolers in a 2005 HSLDA case in Pennsylvania argued that "God had given them full and exclusive authority for the children's education" (HSLDA, 2005, ¶ 1), meaning that the Commonwealth of Pennsylvania had *no* legitimate interest or authority in intervening into an area they consider to be their sole province. Such an argument is consistent with Christian Reconstructionism, which holds that the public school, by definition, is an illegitimate institution because it is *secular*, hence ungodly (Detwiler, 1999; Lugg, 2000). However, this justification for homeschooling has repeatedly proved insufficient, in and of itself, to withstand legal challenge (see HSLDA, 2005).

As a result, while Supreme Court decisions such as *Meyer, Pierce,* and *Yoder* do not directly involve homeschooling, Farris and his colleagues have cited these key decisions as providing constitutional justification for homeschooling. In particular, these cases established the parameters of what is permissible for parents in shaping their own children's education. First, in *Meyer v. State of Nebraska* (1923), the Court ruled that public schools could not be compelled by the state to instruct their charges solely in English. During WWI, in a surge of anti-German hysteria, the state of Nebraska had tried to ban German language instruction. In the *Meyer* decision, the Court agreed that the state had the power to establish compulsory education, but it also observed that parents had liberty rights regarding their children's education that were protected under the due process clause of the 14th Amendment. This included the right to provide for German language instruction in their public school (Dibble, 2005).

Second, in *Pierce v. Society of Sisters* (1925), the Court ruled that while the state of Oregon could compel school attendance for children, it could not require parents to send their children *only* to public schools. In the early 1920s, in a wave of anti-Catholic bigotry, Oregon had passed a law requiring parents and guardians to send their children to public schools—or be considered truant. Drawing on the tenets established in the recent *Meyer* decision (and under the 14th Amendment), the Court again ruled that parents had certain rights in their children's education, including the option of sending their children to private religious schools. Again, while the state could require school attendance, it could not limit this attendance solely to public schools (Dibble, 2005).

Finally, in *Yoder v. Wisconsin* (1972), the Supreme Court ruled that compulsory education until age 16, as required by the state of Wisconsin, threatened both the religious liberty of the Amish and equal protection under the law (Dibble, 2005). The Amish had objected to the Wisconsin law, because, following their religious tenets, they ceased formal education for their youngsters after eighth grade fearing greater formal education would make a child too worldly (Biedrzycki, 2006). In this decision, the court acknowledged that the state has a proper role in demanding that children be educated. However, like *Meyer* and *Pierce*, the court balanced the rights of the parents against the needs of the state. In the case of the Amish, the state role was even more curtailed, since the Amish, as a religious community, believed further education imperiled the continued existence of their way of life (Dibble, 2005). Furthermore, the health and well-being of Amish children was not an issue before the Court, consequently, the role of the state could be more circumscribed (Biedrzycki, 2006; LeFever, 2006).[6]

While Farris and HSDLA have repeatedly invoked the Supreme Court decisions from *Meyer, Pierce,* and *Yoder*

to argue parents have a right to homeschool their children largely free of state regulation (or to use their words, "interference"), a closer reading of the case law and subsequent legal theorizing indicates this right is and should be, in fact, balanced against the needs and interests of the state. In each instance, (*Meyer, Pierce,* and *Yoder*), the U.S. Supreme Court has been quite clear in stipulating that the state could require children be educated, as well as place reasonable regulations upon the educative enterprise, be it public or private (Biedrzycki, 2006; Mason, 2006).

Despite the perceived Court support of homeschooling, several other Supreme Court decisions clearly establish limits on parental and religious rights (*Prince v. Massachusetts,* 1944; *Employment Division v. Smith,* 1990) and directly bear on the development and implementation of homeschooling policies, cases which Farris and the HSDLA fail to mention. First, in *Prince v. Massachusetts* (1944), the U.S. Supreme Court ruled that religious liberty did not trump the Commonwealth's ban on child labor. The case involved a parent who, as a Jehovah's Witness, was convicted of violating Massachusetts child labor laws by permitting her 9-year old child to sell magazines on a street corner. The parent argued that her child's labor was out of religious obligation and consequently was immune from state regulation. While the Court agreed that parents do have a right to instill their religious values within their children, it disagreed with the argument that religion alone freed families from state regulation. As the Court observed:

> But the family itself is not beyond regulation in the public interest, as against a claim of religious liberty ... and neither rights of religion nor rights of parenthood are beyond limitation. Acting to guard the general interest in youth's well being, the state as parens patriae may restrict the parent's control by requiring school attendance ... regulating or prohibiting the child's labor ... and in many other ways. *Its authority is not nullified merely because the parent grounds his claim to control the child's course of conduct on religion or conscience.* Thus, he cannot claim freedom from compulsory vaccination for the child more than for himself on religious grounds. (at 167; internal citations omitted; italics added)

Importantly, the Court concluded that:

> Parents may be free to become martyrs themselves. But it does not follow they are free, in identical circumstances, to make martyrs of their children before they have reached the age of full and legal discretion when they can make that choice for themselves. (at 170)

As with the previous *Meyer* and *Pierce* decisions, the Court relied upon balancing the issues of religious liberty against the needs of the state. However, in contrast to *Meyer* and *Pierce*, the state's concern for child welfare and safety (involving child labor) outweighed religious liberty claims.

In *Employment Division, Department of Human Resources of Oregon, et al. v. Smith, et al.* (1990), the Supreme Court further delineated individual rights regarding religious liberty. The case involved two Native American employees of a drug rehabilitation clinic who were fired and then subsequently denied state unemployment insurance benefits, since they were dismissed for using the drug peyote. The employees claimed that the peyote was consumed as part of Native American religious practices, and as such, was a protected religious act. The Supreme Court ruled that the state had a reasonable interest in preventing drug abuse and the consumption of illegal drugs. Consequently, the religious rights of the employees were outweighed by the state's interests in preventing drug abuse. The U.S. Congress tried to legislate around this decision by passing the Religious Freedom Restoration Act in 1993. But in 1997, the Religious Freedom Restoration Act was invalidated by the Supreme Court in *City of Boerne v. Flores* (1997). Some legal scholars have argued that while *Smith* did not overturn *Yoder*, *Yoder* has been substantially weakened (see Biedrzycki, 2006). Despite this ruling, 12 states currently have some locally derived variation of the Religious Freedom Restoration Act (Tabone, 2006). In the post-*Flores* era, the Constitutionality of these statutes appears to be an open question.

Reading these five cases together, *Meyer*, *Pierce*, *Yoder*, *Prince*, and *Smith*, one can see that while parents have strong federal Constitutional protections in overseeing the education of their children, especially in the area of religion, these rights are not absolute (Mason, 2006). In particular, religious rights may be superseded when they undermine a "compelling state interest" like ensuring an educated citizenry. For instance, if the religious practice threatens a child's well-being and safety (and "well-being" was expansively defined in *Prince*), the state has a right to intervene. Also, practices which the state has ruled to be illegal, like the consumption of peyote, are not immune from sanction even if a religious claim is involved (Biedrzycki, 2006; Mason, 2006).

In a very recent case that touches on all of the above points, on February 28, 2008, a California Court of Appeals ruled that parents do not have a state constitutional right to homeschool their children, overturning a lower court decision that granted parents this right. The case involved reported instances of physical and emotional abuse by the children's father, and the father's claim of religious liberty to educate his eight children in a manner consistent with his religious beliefs. The court, however, ruled that under California's constitution children residing in California must be taught by a credentialed teacher. In this particular case, the children were being taught by their mother who held neither a teaching credential nor a high school diploma (Mehta & Landsberg, 2008). A lower court had stated that these parents had a constitutional right to homeschool, although the quality of their home education was described as "lousy," "meager," and "bad." By contrast, citing a previous California educational decision, the Appellant Court observed, "the educational program of the State of California was designed to promote the general welfare of all the people and was not designed to accommodate the personal ideas of

any individual in the field of education" (*Jonathan L. and Mary Grace L. v. Superior Court*, 2008, p. 11). Explicitly rejecting the parents' invocation of *Yoder*, the court reasoned the state had a compelling interest in ensuring that children received an education provided by a credentialed teacher. Since the mother was not a credentialed teacher, the parents had violated state law, and their espoused religious beliefs did not insulate them from possible criminal charges. Furthermore, given the allegations of physical abuse by the parents involving three of the eight children, merely providing an in-home credentialed tutor was also deemed not an appropriate remedy to the current situation. In this instance, the parents could only comply with the law if they would enroll their children in a public or private school. Since then, the political uproar over the decision has been fierce and the same appeals court has scheduled a rehearing of the case in June of 2008, which vacates the February 28th decision (Egelko, 2008). Nevertheless, given the evidence relating to child abuse involved in this case, it is unlikely that California homeschoolers will be successful in their attempt to be exempt from all state regulations.[7]

Under the umbrella of a "compelling state interest" position, states may establish parameters for homeschooling policies. Thus, while states cannot ban homeschooling outright, they can establish reasonable standards regarding what forms of homeschooling are permissible and not permissible, particularly in areas deemed relevant to the current and *future* well-being of children (Mason, 2006)—particularly those identified as U.S. citizens, citizens of their respective states—and the state's interests generally. Because the tension between parental rights and state's rights remains, proponents of homeschooling have and continue to lobby state legislatures and state departments of education to take more expansive views of religious liberty, and more narrow views of the state's role. In the end, the array of political cultures across the country combined with the relative strength or weakness of Protestant Right organizations in a given state, and the political clout of parents and parental groups have produced quite a bit of variance in homeschooling regulations when one makes state-by-state comparisons. This chapter now moves towards an exploration of these regulations categorically. We pay particular attention to the complexity and contradictions embedded in the regulations.

An Overview of State Regulations

By and large, U.S. homeschools are relatively free from state and local authority and/or governance when compared to traditional (even private or charter) schooling options. In many instances, local boards, superintendents, and state agencies have minimal-to-no authority regarding home education. For example, in South Carolina, local boards "shall approve" parents to provide home education when instructor and instructional conditions are met. These conditions in South Carolina include: those who homeschool must hold either a high school diploma, GED, or a baccalaureate degree; the minimum instructional time is 4.5 hours a day, 180 days a year; students are instructed in at least the basic instructional areas; records are maintained for instructional plans, and a portfolio of student work and progress is reported to the district semiannually; the student has access to a library; the student participates in the state's annual assessment program as well as in the Basic Skills Assessment Program; and that parents or guardians "release the district from liability regarding their child's education" (S.C. Code § 59-65-40). In reality, the discretion of the local board to approve or disapprove is nonexistent. Local boards are rendered largely impotent when their role is limited to approving homeschool requests upon submission of the identified conditions rather than *evaluating the quality of the individual homeschooling effort*. Similarly, the language of New Jersey's alternative statutes further demonstrates these constraints on local authority. New Jersey does not require homeschoolers to submit a notification of intent to homeschool, and the local school board has no role in authorizing, reviewing, or approving the homeschool curriculum or program. The local board, however, may request documentation of a child's attendance in home education if "credible evidence" exists that the child is not attending school or receiving instruction at home, but homeschooling adults maintain the right to ignore this request without consequence (N.J. Stat. Ann. § 18A:38-25).

The following discussion illustrates the complexity of analyzing U.S. homeschool policies by considering six dimensions of current homeschool statutes and provisions.[8] These dimensions include: types of homeschool permitted, requirements for filing and documentation regarding intent to homeschool, qualified teachers, instructional time/days, subjects, performance evaluation, or standardized testing requirements. Table 62.1 provides a state-by-state overview. While individual state's provisions regarding these seven elements vary, these dimensions reflect a common set of expectations for homeschooling, as well as the general considerations addressed in state-level homeschooling policies and regulatory guidance stemming largely from provisions in their compulsory attendance laws. Moreover, these categories reflect the areas of greatest commonality across existing state policies; thus, provides a base upon which to compare the status of homeschooling policies nationally. This type of categorical information can also be found on state department of education and other organization Web sites, including local affiliate homeschooling sites and HSLDA.

State-Level Homeschool Requirements Across the United States

Despite relatively restricted authority and/or role in homeschooling, most states have stipulated some operational parameters for homeschools. These parameters, however, range from permissive with minimal reporting requirements to more stringent requirements and monitoring of areas such as the language for instructional delivery and reporting (i.e., English), and, in some instances, accountability for student performance. For instance, five states (California, Illinois, Indiana, Pennsylvania, and Rhode Island) mandate that instruction in homeschools occur in English.[9] For those states that have existing homeschool statutes or alternative statutes that permit homeschools, most minimally outline compliance requirements.

Homeschool Configurations As mentioned previously, a few of the state statutes outline specific homeschool options, while others have a general statement permitting the existence of homeschooling. For instance, Alabama provides both church school and private tutor homeschooling options. Alaska offers a general homeschool statute as well as options for private tutors, correspondence study, and religious and private school options. In addition to homeschools that can be designated as private schools and private tutors, California adds independent study at home and private school satellite programs to their menu of homeschooling alternatives. Hawaii offers two homeschool alternatives, including a declaration to the superintendent and a superintendent-approved alternative education program. In Maryland, children may participate in homeschooling through three options, including a portfolio option, a state-approved school, and a church umbrella option. Under the portfolio option, the district superintendent retains authority to monitor a students' progress. Similarly, Pennsylvania provides general homeschooling guidance as well as options for private tutors and day school/church schools. The state also permits "a bona fide church or other religious body" to serve as a day school option, which permits these institutions to be a home education alternative (Pennsylvania Department of Education, 2005).

Several states (e.g., North Carolina, Vermont, Wisconsin, and Wyoming) restrict homeschooling to single-family arrangements and prohibit multi-family arrangements while other states permit multi-family homeschooling arrangements. For example, Delaware's alternative statute provides three options for parents to homeschool, including a single-family homeschool, multi-family homeschool, and single family homeschool coordinated with the local school district. As part of their third homeschool option, South Carolina permits parents/guardians to become members of an association for homeschools as long as the association has no fewer than 50 members (S.C. Code §59-65-47) and other state regulations are met. By contrast, South Dakota permits up to 22 children to be homeschooled together. Moreover, church school options for home education, such as those offered in Alabama, Kentucky, and Pennsylvania, permit students to be educated either in affiliation with one local church, a group, or association of churches.

Instructional Time/Day Requirements While the constitutionality of California's requirement that all who teach be certified (including parents who homeschool), is currently being challenged, most home education provisions nationally are anchored in or intertwined with state com-

TABLE 62.1
Overview of State Home School Regulations

State	Intent to Home School Filing Required and/or Documentation Required	Qualified Teachers Required		Time/Day for Instruction Required	Requires Certain Subjects Taught	Performance Evaluation or Standardized Testing Required
		Certification	Other Requirements and/ or Options			
Alabama	Y	Y		Y (PT)	N	N
Alaska	Y	Y (PT)		Y (RPS)	Y	N; Y (RPS)
Arizona	Y	N		Y	Y	N
Arkansas	Y	N		N	N	Y
California	Y	Y (PT)		Y	Y	N
Colorado	Y	Y (PT)		Y	Y	Y
Connecticut	Y	N		Y	Y	N
Delaware	Y	N		Y	Y	N
District of Columbia	N	N		Y	Y	N
Florida	Y	Y (PT)		Y	N	Y
Georgia	Y	N	DHG (PT)	Y	Y	Y
Hawaii	Y	N	BS	N	Y	optional
Idaho	N	N		Y	Y	N
Illinois	N	N		Y	Y	N
Indiana	N	N		Y	N	N
Iowa	Y	Y	SUP	Y	N	Y (when there is no certified teacher)
Kansas	Y	N	COMP	Y	N	N
Kentucky	Y	N		Y	Y	N
Louisiana	Y	N		Y	Y	Y
Maine	Y	Y (NAPS)	COMP	Y	Y	Y (HS)
Maryland	Y	N		Y	Y	N
Massachusetts	Y	N		N	Y	Y
Michigan	N (can be requested)	Y (option 2, unless religious objections)		N	Y	N
Minnesota	Y	N	SUP,TEST,COMP,BS	N	Y	Y
Mississippi	Y	N		Y	N	N
Missouri	Optional	N		Y	Y	N
Montana	Y	N		Y	Y	N
Nebraska	Y	N		Y	Y	N
Nevada	Y	N		Y	Y	N
New Hampshire	Y	N		N	Y	Y
New Jersey	N	N		N	Y	N
New Mexico	Y	N	DHG	Y	Y	N
New York	Y	N	COMP	Y	Y	Y
North Carolina	Y	N	DHG	Y	N	Y
North Dakota	Y	Y	SUP, DHG, BS, TEST	Y	Y	Y
Ohio	Y	N	DHG	Y	Y	N
Oklahoma	N	N		Y	Y	N
Oregon	Y	N		N	N	Y
Pennsylvania	Y	Y(PT)		Y	Y	Y
Rhode Island	Y	N		Y	Y	N
South Carolina	Y	N	BS, DHG	Y	Y	Y

State	Intent to Home School Filing Required and/or Documentation Required	Qualified Teachers Required		Time/Day for Instruction Required	Requires Certain Subjects Taught	Performance Evaluation or Standardized Testing Required
		Certification	Other Requirements and/or Options			
South Dakota	Y	N		Y	Y	Y
Tennessee	Y	N	BS, DHG	Y	Y	Y; N (Satellite Campus of Church)
Texas	N	N		N	Y	N
Utah	Y	N		Y	Y	N
Vermont	Y	N	DHG	N	Y	Y
Virginia	Y	Y (PT option)	SUP, DHG	Y	N	Y (HS)
Washington	Y	N	CRED, COMP	Y	Y	Y
West Virginia	Y	N	DHG, COMP	Y	N	Y
Wisconsin	Y	N		Y	Y	N
Wyoming	Y	N		N	Y	N

Cells received a "Y" if one or more of the state's statute required this provision. Information that appears in parenthesis indicates when the particular requirement applies.
DHG – Diploma, High School Equivalent or GED
CRED – College Credit
COMP – Designated as competent
BS -- Bachelors
TEST – Passed a test demonstrating competency
SUP – Supervised by a certified teacher or administrator
PT – Private tutor
HS – High School
RPS – Religious and/or Private Schools

pulsory attendance laws—not certification. For instance, Oklahoma's compulsory school attendance laws, which are embedded in Title 70 of Oklahoma's statutes, stipulate that:

> The Legislature shall provide for the compulsory attendance at some public or other school, unless other means of education are provided, of all the children in the State who are sound in mind and body, between the ages of eight and sixteen years, for at least three months in each year. (State of Oklahoma, 2005, Art. 8, § 4)

All 50 states and the District of Columbia have compulsory attendance laws, although these too vary. Across the nation, compulsory attendance laws require between 9 and 13 years of school attendance—four states require 13 years of compulsory attendance, while seven states require 12 years, eight states require 11 years, 18 states require 10 years of compulsory attendance, and 14 states require 9 years. The combination of age ranges for general compulsory attendance include: ages 5–16, 5–17, 5–18, 6–16, 6–17, 6–18, 7–16, 7–17, 7–18, and 8–17. Currently, the District of Columbia, New Mexico, Oklahoma, and Virginia require the most years of mandatory schooling—13 years of compulsory attendance. Beyond compulsory attendance laws by age, most homeschoolers are bound by time/day requirements. Indeed, 40 states currently have instructional time/day requirements for all or at least one part of their home education provisions. For instance, Missouri requires 1,000 hours of instruction and includes stipulations for the number of hours of instruction at the "regular home school location" annually and how much instructional time must

be dedicated to required subjects (i.e., reading, math, social studies, language arts, and science; Mo. Ann. Stat. § 167.031.2.2.b). Although some homeschool statutes require equivalent days/time of instruction to the public schools for that particular state, others situate the homeschool policy within its more micro-environment, such as the district. New Mexico, for example, requires homeschools to observe the same compulsory attendance regulations and instructional calendar of the district in which the student resides (N.M. Stat. Ann. § 22-12-2.B). Yet, a glance at California's home education alternative statutes illustrates the complexity and paradoxes inherent in these states where multiple homeschool provisions exist. In California, most homeschools are released from the general instructional regulations governing public schools. However, students who are instructed by a private tutor within their homeschool provisions are subject to time/day instructional restrictions.

Intent to Homeschool Filing and Documentation Required Only seven states (Idaho, Illinois, Indiana, Michigan, New Jersey, Oklahoma, and Texas) and the District of Columbia reportedly do not require parents or guardians to file an *intent to homeschool* document. In states such as Missouri, statute makes it optional for parents to declare their intent to homeschool. Despite the prevalence of filing requirements, the types of documentation necessary for parents/guardians to homeschool range from non-binding, report-only to information provided only at the explicit request of local authorities to annual information for review, from broad to specific, and from brief to extensive and protracted. For example, only five states (Arizona,

Louisiana, North Dakota, Nebraska, and Nevada) require the submission of at least a copy of the child's birth certificate. South Dakota merely requires that a copy be available for review. Indiana, which has minimized its requirements, does not require declaration of intent to homeschool, but requires parents to maintain attendance records that may be requested by the state superintendent to verify enrollment and attendance (Ind. Code Ann. § 20-33-2-20). By contrast, Minnesota (Minnesota Department of Education, 2007), which has arguably stronger controls than Indiana on homeschools, requires annual reports be submitted to the superintendent (Mn. Stat §120A.24). These annual reports must contain information on: the child's name, birth date, address, name of each instructor and evidence of teacher qualification requirements, annual instructional calendar, and when a student is instructed by the parent, a quarterly report card on achievement that indicates each of the required subjects. Virginia requires parents to notify the local superintendent annually by August 15 (or within 30 days of determining that they will homeschool) regarding their plans to homeschool.

In South Carolina parents/guardians who choose to homeschool must provide to the local district specific documentation related to instruction. This documentation must include: a plan book or record of subjects taught and activities, a portfolio of their child's work, and record of academic evaluation as well as a semiannual progress report (S.C. Code § 59-65-40). New Jersey, by contrast, does not require notification or documentation of the homeschool's instructional program, although, again, they must enforce their compulsory attendance laws (N.J.S.A. 18A:38-25) which requires "equivalent instruction elsewhere than at school." According to the New Jersey Department of Education, the district may *request* a letter of intent but may not require it. Similarly, Texas, as a result of the *Texas Education Agency v. Leeper* (1994) decision, cannot require documentation—although the decision does specify a very modest curriculum.

Teacher Qualifications Aligned with the intent of homeschool proponents to maintain some distance from government "intrusion," states generally place very few limits as to who can teach or provide home education, including requiring criminal background checks or certification requirements. For example, until 1995, Florida required parents/guardians who chose to homeschool to sign an affidavit that they had neither been named a perpetrator nor convicted of child abuse or neglect. In response to Florida's 1995 repeal of that requirement, HSLDA (1995) said, "The silver lining for this year's legislative season was that the child abuse requirements in the home school law have finally been removed" (¶ 1). Today, only Pennsylvania stipulates that a notarized affidavit must be filed verifying a person's criminal record. The affidavit must include: "a certification that the supervisor, all adults living within the home, and persons having legal custody of the children have not been convicted of certain criminal offenses within the

TABLE 62.2

Crimes Identified as "Certain Criminal Offenses" under Pennsylvania Homeschooling Law

1.	criminal homicide	13.	incest
2.	aggravated assault	14.	concealing death of child
3.	harassment and stalking	15.	endangering welfare of children
4.	kidnapping		
5.	unlawful restraint	16.	dealing in infant children
6.	rape	17.	prostitution and related offenses
7.	statutory sexual assault		
8.	involuntary deviate sexual intercourse	18.	obscene and other sexual materials and performances
9.	sexual assault	19.	corruption of minors
10.	aggravated indecent assault	20.	sexual abuse of children
11.	indecent assault	21.	and those crimes related to The Controlled Substance, Drug, Device and Cosmetic Act
12.	indecent exposure		

past five years" (Pa. Stat. Ann. tit. 24, § 13-1327.1). The statute continues that "The affidavit 'shall be satisfactory evidence' of compliance with the law." There are 21 offenses referred to as "certain criminal offenses" (Pa. Stat. Ann. tit. 24, § 1-111), displayed in Table 62.2.

Technically, Arkansas (§ 6-15-508.a) also prohibits homeschooling if an adult in the home has been registered under the Sex and Child Offender Registration Act of 1997 (§ 12-12-901 et seq.). However, its state code (§ 6-15-508.b) allows parents/guardians to petition the sentencing court to waive the restriction against homeschooling in these instances. In addition, this provision does not apply if the person who is registered under the Sex and Child Offender Registry is the child who is to be homeschooled (§ 6-15-508.c).

Generally, adults who homeschool children do not have to be qualified teachers. However in contrast, homeschool provisions that permit or require tutors or homeschools qualify as private schools frequently require certified teachers. In California, for instance, the statute (CA. EDC § 48222) indicates that persons who provide instruction under homeschools that are identified as private schools must "be capable of teaching," although the term "capable" is not qualified and is currently being litigated. When the option to provide private tutors is exercised by the parent, the tutor must hold a valid state credential for the grade taught. Similar to California's "capable of teaching" standard, Hawaii stipulates that "a parent teaching the parent's child at home shall be deemed a qualified instructor" (HI Rev. Stat. § 302A-1132.a.5, Rule § 8-12-19). Iowa's statute requires instruction to be provided by "or under the supervision of a licensed practitioner in the manner provided under section 299A.2, or other person under section 299A.3" (Iowa Code Ann. § 299A). Iowa, as will be discussed further, couples their instructor requirements with a stipulation for adequate student performance. According to Minnesota's code (M.S. § 120A.22), Minnesota expects instructors to have met at least one of the following six requirements: hold a teaching license, be directly supervised by a licensed teacher, successfully completed a teacher competency exam, provide instruction in a school that is accredited or recognized by a state recognized accrediting agency, hold a baccalaureate degree, or be the parent of a child who is assessed annually using a norm-referenced standardized examination. Currently, instructors who only meet the last provision—the child is assessed annually—must provide quarterly reports on achievement in academic areas taught. Multiple states, such as Georgia, North Carolina, North Dakota, New Mexico, Ohio, South Carolina, Tennessee, Virginia, and West Virginia stipulate that parents/guardians who homeschool must have at least a high school diploma, GED, and/or a baccalaureate. Tennessee also requires a baccalaureate for those instructing students in grades 9–12, for instance. On the other hand, Ohio's statute requires that those providing instruction to homeschoolers must submit an assurance to the local superintendent that they meet at least one of the following five criteria:

1. A high school diploma; or
2. The certificate of high school equivalence; or
3. Standardized test scores that demonstrate high school equivalence; or
4. Other equivalent credential found appropriate by the superintendent; or
5. Lacking the above, the home teacher must work under the direction of a person holding a baccalaureate degree from a recognized college until the child's or children's test results demonstrate reasonable proficiency or until the home teacher obtains a high school diploma or the certificate of high school equivalence. (Ohio Administrative Code, 3301-34-03 Notification)

Subjects to be Taught   Eleven states (Alabama, Arkansas, Florida, Indiana, Iowa, Kansas, Mississippi, North Carolina, North Dakota, Oregon, Virginia, and West Virginia) do not require a particular or minimum set of subjects to be taught within their homeschool statutes. Some states, such as Hawaii, provide direction on the types of subjects to be taught. In Hawaii's case, parents are required to file what subjects will be part of the child's at home curriculum. Hawaii's statute's guidance suggests that the elementary curriculum "may include the areas of language arts, mathematics, social studies, science, art, music, health and physical education to be offered at the appropriate development stage of the child" while the secondary curriculum "may include the subject areas of social studies, English, mathematics, science, health, physical education and guidance" (Hawaii Admin. Rules, § 8-12-15). Idaho's statute is reminiscent of Hawaii's policy language in that parents/guardians must provide "comparable instruction" in "subjects commonly and usually taught in public schools" (Idaho Code § 33-202). Similarly, in Indiana, a homeschooled child must receive instruction that is equivalent to that of the public schools (Ind. Code Ann. § 20-33-2-20). However, the state removed language that prescribes which subjects shall be taught (Ind. Code Ann § 20-33-2-12). On

the other hand, New Mexico like Missouri has stipulated the minimum subjects (reading, language arts, mathematics, social studies, and science) to be taught. However, the state also includes language "but not limited to," which provides additional freedom and flexibility for parents/guardians who homeschool (N.M. Stat. Ann. § 22-1-2.V). In contrast, North Dakota's curriculum requirements are much more specific as well as inclusive:

> English language arts, including reading, composition, creative writing, English grammar, and spelling; mathematics; social studies, including the United States Constitution, and United States history, geography, and government; science, including agriculture; physical education; health, including physiology, hygiene, disease control, and the nature and effects of alcohol, tobacco, and narcotics. (N.D. Cent. Code §§ 15.1-23-04, 15.1-21-01)

Further illustrating the variance in even those states that require certain subjects to be taught, Texas (Texas Education Agency, 2007), where homeschooling is permissible within the private school category, requires instruction in good citizenship, math, reading, spelling and grammar (Texas Education Code §25.085). Finally, some states such as North Carolina do not specify the subjects to be taught, but again, they do require that students be assessed annually.

Performance Evaluations or Standardized Testing Required   Nineteen states require or have provisions for performance evaluations and/or standardized testing. However, the type of evaluations (e.g., norm references, criterion-based), who administers the test (e.g., parent, certified teacher), rate of occurrence (e.g., annually, at certain grade levels), and the implications of these evaluations vary among these states. For instance, North Dakota monitors parents who homeschool if they have only a high school diploma or GED and if the child's performance falls below the fiftieth percentile, and it requires additional assessment and evaluation of a child whose performance falls below what is considered an acceptable level—thirtieth percentile (NDCC 15.1-23). Colorado provides two assessment options and requires the public school to be notified when students composite scores dip below the thirteenth percentile on the national standardized achievement tests for grades, 3, 5, 7, 9, and 11 (CO. § 22-33-104.5.3.f). As a result, the student must take an alternative nationally standardized assessment, including a potentially different version of the same test. In the case of students who are homeschooled Colorado, students must have a composite score above the thirteenth percentile to be exempt from the public school attendance requirements (CO. § 22-33-104.5.a.I). In Colorado, scores must be reported to either the local district or an independent or parochial school (CO. § 22-33-104.5.3.f). Similarly, Oregon requires a child whose composite score is below the fifteenth percentile to be reevaluated. If the percentile fails to improve, parents are then subjected to increasingly restrictive policies such as homeschool monitoring by a certified teacher, additional assessments, or even requiring the student to return to the public school (ORS § 339.030.1.d,- 339.035).

In Arkansas, norm-referenced achievement test selected by the state must be administered to homeschooled students in grades 3–9 and those who are 2 years beyond their appropriate grade level (AR Code § 6-15-504). The norm-referenced assessment may be used by districts to determine the appropriate placement of homeschooled students who (re)enroll in the public schools. In South Carolina, students who are homeschooled by their parents/guardians must be tested annually using in the statewide testing program as well as the Basic Skills Assessment Program. If a student is determined to not be performing at a level comparable to the public school's standard for promotion, then the school district may require that the child be reenrolled in public schools and/or provided special education services or additional instructional support services—all at the parent's expense (S.C. Code § 59-65-40). Similar regulations apply in West Virginia.

Some states have even more stringent regulations regarding assessments for homeschoolers. For example, Colorado's second assessment option relies on parents to select a "qualified person"—a certified teacher, a private school teacher, a licensed psychologist, or a person who holds a graduate degree—to administer the assessment, and the state requires the student to demonstrate "sufficient academic progress" (Colorado Department of Education, 2007). Similarly, in Arkansas, tests are administered by either the directors of the education service cooperatives or someone designated by the Arkansas Department of Education (2007; § 6-13-1001). North Carolina allows parents to administer assessments. However, the state's (§ 115C-564) requirement for making records available for an "annual inspection" has been reduced over time to simply making the scores available. Washington's statute has comparable requirements (RCW § 28A.200.010), including the administration of assessments by a "qualified person" such as certified professional (Washington Department of Education, 2007). Comparable to North Carolina, rather than reporting the results parents must merely maintain these results in the child's records. North Dakota requires a certified teacher to administer the assessment, but the parents can choose either to have the test administered at home or at the public school (N.D. Cent. Code §§ 15.1-23-09, 15.1-23-11). When homeschooled students chose to be evaluated as part of the state's assessment program, the public schools cover the costs of assessment. If, however, parents choose one of the other three options available for evaluating the academic progress of homeschooled students, then parents are responsible for the costs. Pennsylvania requires students who are homeschooled to be tested using a nationally-normed test in grades 3, 5, and 8. Results must be submitted as part of the child's annual portfolio (PA §13-1327.1.e.1).

Additional Provisions Only five states (Arkansas, Iowa, North Dakota, Oregon, and Pennsylvania) explicitly address students who are eligible for special education services in their homeschool provisions. For instance, within Pennsylvania's compulsory school attendance statute, parents who wish to homeschool students identified with disabilities must have an approved (including a notarized affidavit) home education program by a state-certified special education teacher, a licensed clinical or school psychologist (PA §13-1327; see also Tabone, 2006). North Dakota's statute requires identification of the disability by a licensed psychologist, a qualified parent to supervise, filing with the superintendent, a service plan developed and followed by both the district and the parents or substitute plan to be selected and compensated by the child's parents, and monitoring of child's progress (ND § 15.1-23-14).

While concerns regarding access to higher education have gained recent political attention, only a few states (New Mexico, North Carolina, and Texas) explicitly address access to higher education for homeschoolers. In fact, each of these states prohibits higher education institutions from discriminating against homeschoolers. For instance, the statute (§ 21-1-1.B) in New Mexico that requires certain subjects to be taught to homeschoolers stipulates that higher education institutions cannot require proof of a GED for students who have been homeschooled and who have submitted test scores consistent with the institution's admission policy.

As this overview demonstrates, the policies regarding homeschooling in the United States range from relatively permissive (e.g., New Jersey) to somewhat restrictive (e.g., Pennsylvania). Consequently, the range of policies across categories creates a high degree of policy incoherence within the country. While this incoherence does not warrant national-level policies for homeschooling, some of these policy inconsistencies may unintentionally place children as at-risk for poor educational outcomes, as well as endanger their well-being, in some instances. It is here that we now turn our attention.

Conclusion

At present, a combination of prominent state-level court and political battles and sparse regulations, coupled with increasingly strong political action among homeschool advocates afford U.S. homeschoolers a high degree of autonomy and flexibility regarding educational choices and decisions. Clearly, this autonomy and flexibility is consistent with the ideology of most homeschoolers (Apple, 2000, 2001; Knowles, Marlow, & Muchmore, 1992; Mason, 2006) who consider limiting the "intrusion" of government in their children's education to be prudent. However, when we take into account the well-being and interests of both children and the state generally, the question of (im)prudence seems central to this and future analyses of homeschooling policies and practices. In particular, as some parents/guardians retreat from public schools to homeschooling as an alternative, questions remain as to the educational efficacy, safety of homeschooling, and impact on state interests (Mason, 2006).

Unfortunately, much of what can be said about home education remains steeped in conjecture, particularly since few empirical studies have been conducted. Although some scholars have attempted to conduct research with homeschoolers, homeschoolers tend to avoid participating in these studies. Consequently, rather than using rigorous empirical research to inform policy, policy makers, practitioners, homeschool organizations, and families who homeschool are constrained by the proliferation of extant reports, advocacy research, testimonials, or analysis of current statutes such as provided here. The reality is that more questions than answers currently exist. Furthermore, as our review of existing policies demonstrates, homeschool related statutes vary widely and wildly, and there is little evidence regarding the fidelity implementation of these regulations or their impact (Collom, 2005). Lacking solid empirical evidence, we too are left to speculate what the actual impact is for students, families, communities, and public schools.[10] With this in mind, we now draw attention to specific aspects of homeschooling policy and implementation that need further examination.

First, some of the unregulated aspects of homeschooling, such as permitting sex offenders to homeschool by default, are among our greatest concern.[11] Currently, only Pennsylvania and Arkansas forbid homeschooling when registered sex offenders are present, and even the Arkansas prohibition can be appealed by the individual requesting to homeschool. Pennsylvania has the most rigorous regulations (Tabone, 2006), generally barring most violent felons from engaging in homeschooling, but even this requirement is time-limited to within 5 years after conviction. Similarly, there is a dearth of policy regarding special needs students who are homeschooled, which is also particularly troubling given the expansive statutory rights these children have in the areas of education and health. In general, most states have yet to require even the bare minimum regarding health, safety, and educational adequacy of homeschool programs, even though states have strong legal bases for doing so under the *Prince* decision, as well as the "compelling state interest" rubric (see Biedrzycki, 2006; Dibble, 2005; LeFever, 2006; Mason, 2006; Tabone, 2006).

We surmise that this hesitancy by states to require more stringent regulations has more to do with the political influence of homeschooling advocates and associations whose arguments dwell on parental sovereignty (see Cooper & Sureau, 2007) rather than an apparent lack of care for all children by these states' political leaders. We also recognize that homeschools do not receive local, state, or federal funding. Some states such as Alabama, Alaska, Arkansas, Idaho, and Louisiana explicitly address the ineligibility criteria for local, state, or federal funding in their homeschool statutes. In Alabama, for instance, one of two homeschool options includes being designated as a "church school," which ensures no local, state, or federal funding.

Nevertheless, states have a duty to ensure that all children

be educated in environments that are safe from abuse and neglect, and are actually educative (Mason, 2006). The recent legal wrangling in California underscores this very point. As such, those adults who wish to homeschool their children should pass a criminal background check at minimum. Moreover, as our review of state policies indicates, additional consideration is needed in determining what constitutes a "qualified person" to homeschool. Currently, the de facto qualification is a letter of intent to homeschool in some states and even less in others.

In addition, the current era of educational accountability raises the issue of reasonable academic standards (i.e., content, performance) for homeschoolers. Based on our review of the state regulations, we propose the following guidelines: Adults who homeschool should file with both the local district and the state department of education "an annual intent to homeschool" at the beginning of the school year, as well as file an annual progress report demonstrating a child's academic achievement comparable to at least 1 year's growth at the conclusion of the year. This would provide districts with information on homeschooled students who reside within their boundaries. Furthermore, students who have learning, behavioral, or psychological needs who are homeschooled should have their education programs evaluated and approved by the local education agency (the district) to ensure federal "adequacy and appropriate" standards are met. While local districts may establish supplemental regulations, each state, to date, retains authority to establish regulations and ensure compliance commensurate with agreed upon academic standards, knowledge, and skills. Ultimately, each state is responsible for the education of its citizenry.

We recognize the inherent contradiction in calling for additional regulatory provisions for homeschoolers, particularly given the rationale by parents/guardians to homeschool and the fact that states and districts do not fund homeschools. Despite this, without a growing body of empirical evidence to demonstrate the educational efficacy of homeschools, as well as any potential social and political benefits and/or costs for individuals, states and communities, homeschooling policies in the United States must be approached deliberately and cautiously.

Finally, we return to the consideration of whether state homeschooling policies are (im)prudent. In particular, do these policies withstand the scrutiny of meeting the minimum threshold for assuring that "compelling state interests" are met and establishing when and under what conditions individual interests supersede "compelling state interest." Lubienski's (2000) critique of homeschooling illustrates this point. He suggests that a paramount concern regarding the continuance of homeschooling is the potential for individual interests to supplant common good, and concludes:

> As an extreme form of privatizing the purpose of education, home schooling denies democratic accountability and disenfranchises the community from its legitimate interest in education. This denial of the public interest does not only affect the education of home schoolers, but it also

erodes the ability of the community to express its interest in the education of those remaining in the public schools as well. (p. 229)

As we consider the body of homeschooling policies nationally, Lubienski's observation remains remarkably pungent. That is, most states have failed to take the bare minimum to ensuring children who are homeschooled are healthy and safe, much less that homeschooled children receive an adequate education. Moreover, there is a long-standing public interest in ensuring that all children, as future voting citizens and participants in the economy, are reasonably literate and numerate. While states must recognize the liberty of adults who homeschool, these rights must be negotiated with the very real, and sometimes competing, needs of states (Mason, 2006). For instance, would the majority of homeschooling advocates continue to push for and relish in the de- and unregulation of homeschooling for gay and lesbian parents/guardians?[12] Homeschooling parents who embraced Wahhabist Islam? Probably not. Thus far, the only consistent limitation on homeschooling is that five states have issued statutes to ensure that homeschooling only occurs in English, which intentionally or not demarcates the state's perceived "compelling interests."

Both adults who homeschool their children and the local communities and states in which homeschooling occurs must live with the tensions this balancing of competing needs requires. It may be uncomfortable and complex for all involved, but children deserve an education that is accountable to parents, the local community, and the state. From a policy perspective, there is simply too much that is unknown, as well as potentially unknowable, at present given the lack of regulations and any systemic or reliable data to determine the success and impact of homeschooling. With the exception of a few scholarly studies and law review articles, homeschooling is an area of education that is literally wide-open for investigation. Specifically, as discussed here, future empirical research may consider the quality of education, the learning opportunities afforded children who are homeschooled, community benefits, and, importantly, the politics of crafting and implementing homeschooling policies, including the negotiation between exercising individual liberty and establishing compelling state interests. We recognize that to pursue these lines of inquiry, researchers and policy makers alike will need to explore these topics in ways that inform policy and practice rather than simply seek worst-case-scenarios. That said, we also acknowledge that a great deal can be learned for what has *not* served the best interests of children to date.

Notes

1. We would like to recognize graduate assistants, Cai Lun Jai, Laurie Lacy, and Mohomodou Boncana, for contributing to the compilation and verification of homeschooling policies.
2. Unfortunately, this study did not disentangle which personal belief was the strongest parental factor in homeschooling, only that personal beliefs were important.
3. While there are children of color who are homeschooled, the vast majority of homeschooled children are white and Protestant (see

Princiotta et al., 2006).
4. Prior to the influence of Christian Reconstructionism, most fundamentalist Christians were apolitical, with many refraining from even voting (see Lugg, 2000).
5. The Texas GOP 2004 party platform is emblematic of Recontructionist thinking. See Michelle Goldberg's (2007) *Kingdom Coming: The Rise of Christian Nationalism*. Additionally, homeschooling activists played a key role in the 2008 presidential campaign of Mike Huckabee, a former GOP governor of Arkansas and ordained Baptist minister (Slevin & Bacon, 2007). Huckabee has advocated amending the U.S. Constitution to comport with "God's law," a long-standing Reconstructionist goal.
6. There is some question as to *Yoder*'s viability since the facts of the case have radically changed. The Amish are increasingly "worldly," employing cell phone technology, and are moving from farming to manufacturing. This presents many dilemmas for states since Amish children work in these industries, largely in violation of standard child labor laws (including those which cover family-owned businesses), as well as health and safety laws (see Biedrzycki, 2006).
7. This case is sure to cause homeschooling advocates all matter of heartburn. While the parents are making explicit religious justifications for homeschooling their children, the allegations of child abuse and subsequent involvement by the California Dependency Court, who represented two of the children against their parents, could push some homeschool legal activists to step away from this case. Quite simply, it is not a good case to litigate and any final decision may compel even stricter regulation of homeschooling in California.
8. Information to complete and verify this description of state policies related to homeschooling was obtained from state education and state legislative Web sites. Additional provisions for particular states may exist.
9. Requiring that instruction occur only in English runs afoul of the Constitutional standard established in *Meyer v. State of Nebraska* (1923), which upheld the right of parents/guardians to educate their children in the language that they preferred (German at that time). If challenged by parents and/or guardians who homeschool, these language restrictions should fail federal Constitutional scrutiny. However, requiring that English language instruction be provided should pass scrutiny. The difference is "English-only" versus "home language plus English."
10. For instance, Medlin (2000) reviewed the research to date on socialization of homeschoolers, including the (perhaps misplaced) speculation that students suffer as a result.
11. There is a bitter irony that 49 states permit actual sex offenders to educate children, while at least 14 states can still dismiss lesbian, gay, bisexual, and transgendered public school teachers for being "statutory" sex offenders. The bigotry is simply astounding and very dangerous for queer educators and those children who are homeschooled. The present authors are planning a follow-up research project on this point.
12. If the proponent in question is a Christian Reconstructionist, the answer to this rhetorical question is "absolutely not." In fact, Reconstructionists have argued that gays and lesbians should be executed (see Diamond, 1995, 1998; Goldberg, 2007; Phillips, 2006).

References

Admission and Enrollment, Texas Education Code. § 25-085 (2007).

Ahlstrom, S. E. (1972). *A religious history of the American people*. New Haven, CT: Yale University Press.

Apple, M. (2001). *Education the "right" way: Markets, standards, God and inequality*. New York: Routledge.

Apple, M. W. (2000). The cultural politics of home schooling. *Peabody Journal of Education, 75*(1&2), 256–271.

Arkansas Department of Education. (2007). *Home schools*. Retrieved May 27, 2008, from http://arkansased.org/schools/schools_home.html

Attendance at Schools, 33 Idaho. Code. § 2-202. (2008).

Attendance Compulsory; exceptions, HI. Rev. Stat. § 302A-1132.a.5. (2007).

Attendance; exceptions, 18 N.J. Stat. Ann. §18A-38-25 (2008).

Biedrzycki , L. (2006). "Conformed to this world": A challenge to the continued justification of the *Wisconsin v. Yoder* education exception in a changed Old Order Amish society. *Temple Law Review, 79*, 249–278.

Bobrow, D. B., & Dryzek, J. S. (1987). *Policy analysis by design*. Pittsburgh, PA: University of Pittsburgh Press.

Bowles, S., & Gintis, H. (1976). *Schooling and capitalist America: Educational reform and the contradictions of economic life*. New York: Basic Books.

Buzzard, L. R. (1982). *Schools: They haven't got a prayer*. Elgin, IL: David C. Cook.

City of Boerne v. Flores, 521 U.S. 507 (1997).

Clarkson, F. (1997). *Eternal hostility: The struggle between theocracy and democracy*. Monroe, ME: Common Courage Press.

Collom, E. (2005). The ins and outs of homeschooling: The determinants of parental motivations and student achievement. *Education and Urban Society, 37*, 307–335.

Colorado Department of Education. (2007). *Home Schooling in Colorado*. Retrieved June 12, 2007, from http://www.cde.state.co.us/cdeedserv/homeschool.htm

Compulsory Attendance Exceptions, Hawaii Admin. Rules. § 8-12-15 (2006).

Compulsory Attendance, 59 S.C. Stat. Code. § 65-47 (2007).

Compulsory School Attendance, 20 Ind. Code. Ann. § 33-2-12 (2005).

Compulsory School Attendance, 20 Ind. Code. Ann. § 33-2-20 (2005).

Compulsory School Attendance, N.M. Stat. Ann. § 22-12 (1978).

Cooper, B. S., & Sureau, J. (2007). The politics of homeschooling: New developments, new challenges. *Educational Policy, 21*, 110–131.

Cordes, H. (2000, October 2). Battling for the heart and soul of homeschoolers. *Salon*. Retrieved November 19, 2000, from http://www.salon.com/mwt/feature/2000/10/02/homeschooling_battle/

Detwiler, F. (1999). *Standing on the premises of God: The Christian Right's fight to redefine America's public schools*. New York: New York University Press.

Diamond, S. (1995). *Roads to Dominion. Right-wing movements and political power in the United States*. New York: Guilford.

Diamond, S. (1998). *Not by politics alone: The enduring influence of the Christian right*. New York: Guilford.

Dibble, D. B. (2005). Parental rights movement on Utah's Capitol Hill should note make gains at the expense of the state's children. *Brigham Young University Education and Law Journal, 2005*, 1–31.

Dorman, D. D. (1990). Michigan's teacher certification requirement as applied to religious motivated home schools. *University of Michigan Journal of Law Reform, 23*, 733–768.

Education Code, CA. EDC. § 48222 (2006).

Education Code, Compulsory Attendance, M.S. Stat. § 120A-22 (2007).

Education Code, Compulsory Attendance, Mn. Stat. §120A-24 (2003).

Egelko, B. (2008, March 27). California homeschooling case to be reheard. San Francisco Chronicle. Retrieved April 21, 2008, from http://www.sfgate.com/cgi-bin/article.cgi?f=/c/a/2008/03/27/BA7CVR0TG.DTL

Employment Division, Department of Human Resources of Oregon, et al. v. Smith, et al., 494 U.S. 872 (1990).

Goldberg, M. (2007). *Kingdom coming: The rise of Christian nationalism*. New York: W.W Norton.

Green, C. L., & Hoover-Dempsey, K. V. (2007). Why do parents homeschool? A systematic examination of parental involvement. *Education and Urban Society, 39*, 264–285.

Guzman, I. M. (2003). Contesting the borders of the imagined nation: The frame of religious marginalization in grassroots socially conservative discourses about sexuality in public education. *Journal of Communication Inquiry, 27*, 29–48.

Harding, S. (1993). Rethinking standpoint epistemology: What is "strong objectivity?" In L. Alcoff & E. Potter (Eds.), *Feminist epistemologies* (pp. 49–82). New York: Routledge.

Holt, J. (1981). *Teach your own. A hopeful path for education*. New York: Delta/Seymour Lawrence.

Home Education, 15 NDCC. § 15.1-23 (2007).

Home Education, N.D. Cent. Code. § 15.1-23 (2008).

Home Education, N.D. Cent. Code. §§ 15.1-21-23 (2008).

Home Education, Pa. Stat. Ann. §13-1327 (2006).

Home School Law, 6 AR. Code. § 15-504 (2007).

Home School Law, 6 AR. Code. Ann. §15-508 (2001).

Home School Legal Defense Association (HSLDA). (1995). Florida. *The Home School Court Report, 11*(4). Retrieved January 21, 2008, from http://www.hslda.org/courtreport/V11N4/V11N4FL.asp

Home School Legal Defense Association (HSLDA). (2005, December) *Pennsylvania: Combs, et al, v. Homer-Center School District, et al.: Six families claim religious exemption from home education law*. Retrieved September 4, 2006, from http://www.hslda.org/Legal/state/pa/CombsetalvHomerCenterSchoolDistrict/default.asp

Home School Statute, Compulsory Attendance, Pa. Stat. Ann. tit. 24, § 13-1327.1 (2006).

Home School Statute, Pa. Stat. Ann. tit. 24, § 1-111 (2006).

Home Schooling Programs, 59 S.C. Stat. Code. § 65-40 (2007).

Home-Based Instruction, 28A RCW. §200-010 (1999).

Jonathan L. and Mary Grace L. v. Superior Court of California for the County of Los Angeles, No. JD00773 (Los Angeles Co. Super. Ct. Feb. 28, 2008).

Knowles, J. G., Marlow, S., & Muchmore, J. (1992). From pedagogy to ideology: Origins and phases of home education in the United States, 1970–1990. *American Journal of Education, 100*, 195–235.

Lasswell, H. D. (1990). *Politics: Who gets what, where and how*. New York: Peter Smith.

LeFever, L. E. (2006). Religious exemptions from school immunization: A sincere belief or a legal loophole? *Penn State Law Review, 110*, 1047–1067.

Levine, G., & Kaplan, E. A. (1997). Introduction. In E. A. Kaplan & G. Levine (Eds.), *The politics of research* (pp. 1–18). New Brunswick, NJ: Rutgers University Press.

Lindblom, C. E., & Woodhouse, E. J. (1993). *The policy-making process* (3rd ed.). Englewood Cliffs, NJ: Prentice Hall.

Lubienski, C. (2000). Whither the common good? A critique of home schooling. *Peabody Journal of Education, 75*(1&2), 207–232.

Lugg, C. A. (2000). Reading, writing and Reconstructionism: The Christian Right and the politics of public education. *Educational Policy, 14*, 622–637.

Mason, C. E. (2006). Faith, harm, and neutrality: Some complexities of Free Exercise law. *Duquesne Law Review, 44*, 225–273.

McCloseky, D. N. (1993). Some consequences of a conjective economics. In M. A. Ferber & J. A. Nelson (Eds.), *Beyond economic man: Feminist theory and economics* (pp. 69–93). Chicago: University of Chicago Press.

McDowell, S. A., Sanchez, A. R., & Jones, S. S. (2000). Participation and perception: Looking at home schooling through a multicultural lens. *Peabody Journal of Education, 75*(1&2), 124–146.

Medlin, R. (2000). Home schooling and the question of socialization. *Peabody Journal of Education, 75*(1&2), 107–123.

Mehta, S., & Landsberg, S. (2008, March 6). Ruling seen as a threat to many home-schooling families: State appellate court says those who teach children in private must have a credential. *Los Angeles Times*. Retrieved March 8, 2008, from http://www.latimes.com/news/local/la-me-homeschool6mar06,0,7343621.story?track=ntothtml

Meyer v. State of Nebraska, 262 U.S. 390 (1923).

Minnesota Department of Education. (2007). *Home school packet*. Retrieved April 20, 2008, from http://education.state.mn.us/mdeprod/groups/Choice/documents/Manual/031646.pdf

New Jersey Department of Education. (2005). *Homeschooling frequently asked questions*. Retrieved July 2, 2005, from http://www.state.nj.us/njded/genfo/overview/faq_homeschool.htm

North Dakota Department of Public Instruction. (2007). *North Dakota Century Code Laws*. Retrieved June 12, 2007, from http://www.dpi.state.nd.us/approve/home/

Novick, P. (1988). *That noble dream: The "objectivity" question in the American Historical profession*. New York: Cambridge University Press.

Pennsylvania Department of Education. (2005). Home education and private tutoring. Retrieved July 2, 2005, from http://www.pde.state.pa.us/home_education/site/default.asp

Phillips, K. (2006). *American theocracy: The peril and politics of radical religion, oil, and borrowed money in the 21st century*. New York: Viking Press.

Pierce v. Society of Sisters, 268 U.S. 510 (1925).

Prince v. Massachusetts, 321 U.S. 158 (1944).

Princiotta, D., Bielick, S., & Chapman, C. (2006, February). *Homeschooling in the United States: 2003*. Washington, DC: The National Center for Educational Statistics.

Private Instruction, Iowa. Code. Ann. § 299A (2001).

Public School Code, N.M. Stat. Ann. § 22-1-2.V (1987).

Pupils and Special Services, Mo. Ann. Stat. § 167-031 (2007).

Rudner, L. M. (1999). Scholastic achievement and demographic characteristics of home school students in 1998. *Education Policy Analysis Archives, 7*(8). Retrieved September 5, 2006, from http://epaa.asu.edu/epaa/v7n8/

School Attendance Law of 1963, 22 CO. Rev. Stat. § 33-104 (1968).

School Attendance; Admission; Discipline; Safety, 9 ORS. Stat. § 339.030-035 (2007).

Sex and Child Offender Registration Act of 1997, Ark. Code Ann. § 12-12-901 *et seq.*

Slevin, P., & Bacon, P, Jr. (2007, December 17). Home-school ties aided Huckabee's early rise: Early backers rallied conservative network. *The Washington Post*, A01. Retrieved December 17, 2007, from http://www.washingtonpost.com/wp-dyn/content/article/2007/12/16/AR2007121602078.html

State of Ohio Homeschooling Regulations, Ohio Administrative Code. § 3301-34-03 (1999).

State of Oklahoma. (2005). *Constitution of the State of Oklahoma*. Retrieved February 22, 2008, from http://oklegal.onenet.net/okcon/

Stevens, M. L. (2001). *Kingdom of children: Culture and controversy in the homeschooling movement*. Princeton, NJ: Princeton University Press.

Stevens, M. L. (2003). The normalization of homeschooling in the USA. *Evaluation and Research in Education, 17*(2&3), 90–100.

Tabone, S. M. (2006). Home-Schooling in Pennsylvania: A prayer for parental autonomy in education. *St. John's Journal of Legal Commentary, 21*, 371–410.

Texas Education Agency v. Leeper, 893 S.W.2d 432 (Tex. 1994).

Texas Education Agency. (2007). *Texas Education Code*. Retrieved June 12, 2007, from http://www.tea.state.tx.us/educationlaw.html

Washington Department of Education. (2007). Washington state's laws regulating home-based Instruction. Retrieved June 12, 2007 from http://www.k12.wa.us/PrivateEd/HomeBasedEd/regulations.aspx

Welner, K. M., & Welner, K. G. (1999). Contextualizing homeschooling data: A response to Rudner. *Educational Policy Analysis Archives, 7*(13). Retrieved September 5, 2006, from http://epaa.asu.edu/epaa/v7n13.html

Yoder v. Wisconsin, 406 U.S. 205 (1972).

63

Student Voice and Student Roles in Education Policy and Policy Reform

DANA L. MITRA
The Pennsylvania State University

As the pressure to equate student outcomes with test scores increases, the broader democratic mission of schools (Dewey, 1916/1966) is fading into the background. Public schools on the whole are successfully linking students to community service activities (Flanagan & Faison, 2001; Honig, Kahne, & McLaughlin, 2001). Most, however, fall short when it comes to providing students with opportunities to learn how to become citizens prepared to actively engage in their communities and participate in democracy (Kirshner, 2004; Larson, 2000).

Rather than students being viewed as actors in the school system, typically they are constructed as part of the problem that needs to be fixed. The characterization of youth in American society tends to represent teenagers as uniformly resistant, rebellious, and determined to isolate themselves from adult-dominated structures, including Coleman's famous study of teenage values and lifestyles in the Midwest that characterized the youth in some schools collectively as shirking discipline and wanting to distance themselves from traditional institutions (Coleman, 1961). The media, politicians, and researchers perpetuate perceptions of youth as disengaged and alienated from adult institutions (Males, 1996; Roberts, 1993; Takanishi, 1993). Christine Griffin described the research literature's frequent depiction of youth as "pathologized, criminalized, muted, or silenced altogether" (as cited in Pope, 1999, p. 5).

Perhaps, then, it is no surprise that high school students frequently describe their school experiences as anonymous and powerless (Earls, 2003; Heath & McLaughlin, 1993; Pope, 2001; Smyth, 2007). To make matters worse, alienation results in two-thirds of students being disengaged from high schools (Cothran & Ennis, 2000). Disengaged students attend school less, have lower self-concepts, achieve less academically, and are more likely to drop out of school (Fullan, 2001; Noguera, 2002; Rudduck, Day, & Wallace, 1997). These students often perceive their teachers as unfair and insist that they need teachers they can trust (Noddings, 1992; Poplin & Weeres, 1992). Students of color and low socioeconomic status struggle most in schools with impersonal school environments in which students do not feel that they have strong connections with teachers or peers (McLaughlin & Talbert, 2001).

Defining Student Voice

While youth tend to have few opportunities for civic engagement, a growing body of research has examined the potential role of increasing student voice in schools. Called a variety of names including student participation, active citizenship, youth leadership, and youth empowerment (McQuillan, 2005), the concept of *student voice* describes the many ways in which youth have opportunities to share in the school decisions that will shape their lives and the lives of their peers (Fielding, 2001; Goodwillie, 1993; Levin, 2000). Student voice can range from the most basic level of youth sharing their opinions of problems and potential solutions; to allowing young people to collaborate with adults to address the problems in their schools; to youth taking the lead on seeking change (Mitra, 2005b). All types of student voice, from limited input to substantial leadership, are considerably different from the types of roles that students typically perform in schools (such as planning school dances and holding pep rallies).

While the conception of "student voice" tends to be under-theorized in educational research, it fits well with the concept "youth-adult partnership" (Camino, 2000) discussed in the field of human development. Youth-adult partnerships are defined as relationships in which both youth and adults have the potential to contribute to visioning and decision-making processes, to learn from one another, and to promote change (Jones & Perkins, 2004). With appropriate guidance and coaching by adults (Camino, 2000), collaboration consists of creating a learning environment in which individuals come together in groups, with the willingness to share authority, accept responsibility, and highlight individual members' abilities and contributions (Panitz, 1996).

Fostering Opportunities for Positive Youth Development

Youth-adult partnerships, including student voice initiatives, have been shown to lead to gains in *positive youth development* indicators for the young people involved. While many typologies exist of the types of skills and assets that youth need to become productive adults,[1] one of the most parsimonious and useful descriptions consist of the "ABCs" of youth development (Carver, 1997; Mitra, 2003)—namely, agency, belonging, and competence. Research in developmental psychology supports the finding that agency, belonging, and competence are necessary factors for adolescents to remain motivated in school and to achieve academic success (Eccles et al., 1993; Goodenow, 1993; Roeser, Midgley, & Urdan, 1996; Stinson, 1993).

Agency in a youth development context indicates the ability to exert influence and power in a given situation. It connotes a sense of confidence, a sense of self-worth, and the belief that one can do something, whether contributing to society writ large, or to a specific situation (Heath & McLaughlin, 1993). Research conducted with middle school students in the United States also found that students valued their schooling the most when their teachers heard their voices and "honored" them (Mitra, 2003; Oldfather, 1995). Such initiatives can lead to an increase in youth leadership and empowerment (Larson, Walker, & Pearce, 2005), which can be a source of social capital for youth that can yield opportunities for further education, employment and other enrichment opportunities (O'Connor & Camino, 2005). Providing legitimate opportunities for youth to take on meaningful roles (Camino, 2000), including opportunities to be change-makers in their schools and communities so that they can experience making a difference—and especially by helping others in need (Mitra, 2003).

The concept of *belonging* in a youth development frame consists of developing relationships consisting of supportive, positive interaction with adults and peers and of opportunities to learn from one another (Costello, Toles, Spielberger, & Wynn, 2000; Heath & McLaughlin, 1993; Pittman & Wright, 1991; Goodenow, 1993; Roeser et al., 1996; Ryan & Powelson, 1991). Student voice activities have been found to increase students' attachment to their peers, their teachers, their school, and their broader community (Mitra, 2003; Sanders, Movit, Mitra, & Perkins, 2007). Since youth tend to spend most of their time with peers and relatively little time in formal or informal socialization or interactions with adults, opportunities to develop meaningful relationships with adults has become an increasingly important need for adolescents (Csikszentmihalyi & Larson, 1984). When students believe that they are valued for their perspectives and respected, they begin to develop a sense of ownership and attachment to the organization in which they are involved (Atweh & Burton, 1995). Scholars have found that an adolescent's belonging to their schools is positively related to academic success and motivation. By providing new opportunities to increase collaborative interactions between students and adults and to engage students in actively shaping their own learning environments, increasing student voice can help to re-engage alienated students by creating a sense of ownership in the school and building a source of intrinsic motivation (deCharms, 1976).

Competence in a youth development context consists of the need for youth to develop new skills and abilities, to actively solve problems, and to be appreciated for one's talents (Goodwillie, 1993; Takanishi, 1993; Villarruel & Lerner, 1994). Student voice initiatives also often provide a rare opportunity to value a diverse range of talents and leadership styles (Camino & Zeldin, 2002; Denner, Meyer, & Bean, 2005; Mitra, Sanders, Movit, & Perkins, 2007), including being a critical thinker, teacher, anchor, peacemaker, and supporter. Student voice initiatives also offer opportunities to learn a broad range of competencies, including physical, intellectual, psychological, emotional, and social skills; opportunities to develop social and cultural capital (Camino 2000; Larson et al., 2005; Perkins & Borden, 2003; Zeldin, Camino, Calvert, & Ivey, 2002).

Research points to the damaging effects of disingenuous student voice efforts. Often, however, attempts to involve students in school reform efforts are clumsy and poorly defined (Bragg, 2007; Muncey & McQuillan, 1991; Silva, 2003). Michael Fielding (2004) argues that many student voice efforts are problematic because schools co-opt student voices through a process of "managerialism" rather than learning from them. Roger Holdsworth and Pat Thomson (2002) have found similarly in their research in Australia that student voice can support democratic activity, but more often than not, it is a thin, conservative democracy in which advantaged students assume all of the rights to voice. In such cases, student voice is a façade of participation and consultation. Thus attention must be paid not only to having student voices heard, but also to which voices are being heard when given the opportunity. Other researchers have raised similar concerns about government-sanctioned student voice efforts in the United Kingdom that claim to improve pupil performance by building local partnerships, but in practice fail to include students in the process despite the rhetoric (Whitehead & Clough, 2004).

One issue that groups must watch vigilantly is whether student voice efforts increase the voices of the disadvantaged, or if they only raise the voices of privileged youth. In Elena Silva's (2003) research, for example, students of color began to drop out of a student panel developing recommendations for their school's accreditation process. In the end, the group was comprised primarily of wealthier white females. The students of color that were still present in the group tended to defer to these vocal privileged women in the group.

The Evolution of Student Voice Internationally

Current student voice efforts rarely fit with the student power efforts of the 1960s and 70s. During that time, young people demanded the right to expression, due process, peaceful assembly, educational opportunity, and representation on school boards (Johnson, 1991, p. 7). Current emphasis on student voice fits within present-day contexts of school reform and student assessment by suggesting that educational change will be more successful if students participate.

A focus on student voice has been officially sanctioned by government bodies in many European countries and in Australia. Encouraged by the *United Nations Convention on the Rights of the Child* and an interest in raising the voting rate among young voters, many European governments have championed student voice. These efforts include: Demark and parts of Germany requiring student representation on school boards, The Netherlands requiring all secondary schools to have student participation in Participation Councils, the United Kingdom encouraging governmental and nongovernmental agencies to ensure that students are included in decisions that affect them, and Sweden requiring students to participate in the same numbers as teachers in meetings about pedagogy and curriculum (Davies, as cited in McIntyre & Ruddock, 2007).

Australia also offers a strong set of examples of student-initiated reform efforts. Roger Holdsworth and Pat Thomson (2002) offer an in-depth review of the many ways in which student participation is fostered by Australian schools and the government at large, including student action teams focused on community safety issues such as health, drug use, safety and environment; peer tutoring; peer mediation; community research on youth needs; youth media production; review and evaluation of school policies; youth forums and community development issues. National reform initiatives containing a student voice component also exist in professional development associations, such as the United Kingdom's National College for School Leadership (NCSL).

Some critics consider the use of voice by European and Australian governments as false pretenses of equality in a time of increasing social inequality (Arnot, Reay, & Wang, 2001); others describe such efforts as neo-liberal forms of cooptation (Bragg, 2007; Whitehead & Clough, 2004). Rather than arguing for the abandonment of student voice efforts, most critiques focus on the need for authentic perspectives and for new obligations for schools to include all voices, even the disparate ones. Critique also emphasize the need to examine how social class and ethnicity can help to either empowered or silence youth voice.

In the United States and Canada, student voice instead only occurs in small pockets. In fact, Michael Fullan (2001) stated that, when writing his third edition of *The New Meaning of Educational Change*, he had considerably more new research about reform to include in his updated chapters on the roles of teachers, administrators, districts, and parents because of the ways the reform picture has evolved over the past 20 years. Yet, he had hardly any changes to make in his chapter on the role of students in educational change, because, quite simply, not much has happened. Similarly, Ernest Boyer of the Carnegie Foundation said in the early 1990s, "Throughout the entire scheme of the [educational] reform movement, students are rarely mentioned" (cited in Johnson, 1991, 7).

Student voice initiatives that do exist tend to distinguish themselves from traditional student governments, which have rarely concerned themselves with meaningful issues in schools (Johnson, 1991; Schmuck & Schmuck, 1990). Most student governments exercise little power, focus primarily on social activities, and do not represent a cross-section of the school. In fact, a nationwide study of communities found no instances where student governments engaged in formal problem solving related to either the "school's academic program or social-emotional climate. In most places, administrators told us that student council was ineffective, if not inoperative" (Schmuck & Schmuck, 1990, p. 19). Instead, student voice efforts focus on gathering perspectives of broad spectrums of students. Rather than working mainly with the best and brightest youth, who tend to form the leadership of student government and such organizations, student voice initiatives instead often seek out students from all backgrounds, cliques, and academic abilities (Mitra, 2008). With a focus on improving educational outcomes, the insight of the students who are not succeeding under current conditions are often the most important voices that need to be heard in reform efforts.

Student Voice Contributions to Educational Change

This section reviews research that has examined student voice efforts. As is typical for a field in which research is at a beginning stage, most of the reviewed literature on student voice examines small-scale research with few studies finding common theoretical groups or building upon prior research. Rather than an exhaustive review of the field,[2] this section takes a broad brush look at the literature to align the types of student voice research that has been conducted with broader patterns of educational change efforts—including students as *data sources*, as collaborators in *learning communities*, and as *co-leaders of change efforts*.[3]

Students as Data Sources In a climate of standards-based reform, researchers, practitioners, and policy makers have increasingly emphasized the importance of data-driven analyses to identify achievement gaps and other weaknesses in teaching and learning, to implement changes, and to measure the results (Massell, 2001; McLaughlin & Mitra, 2004). With growing high-stakes accountability pressures, including the advent of No Child Left Behind, standardized testing data is often prioritized over other forms of information, including grades, narrative assessments, graduation rates, and the reflections of students and teachers themselves (Wood, 2007). Such a narrow focus can ignore the important and insightful information that students themselves can provide about their learning experiences and how to improve them. Exploring differences in youth experiences, including a special focus on how students are not succeeding in current school climates, can yield new definitions of the sources of problems, as well as possible new solutions for reforming schools.

Caution also is required so as to avoid categorizing youth as having a monolithic point of view, but instead to understand youth in relationship to their respective contexts (Strobel & McDonald, 2001). Despite the potential benefits of engagement in educational change efforts, the term "student voice" and efforts to enact this concept can be viewed as problematic—particularly when students are viewed as speaking with one voice. According to Karen Strobel and Morva McDonald (2001), "The objective, outsider view seeks to make all youth fit into one mold, and follow one predetermined pathway to positive development. In order to help youth develop along a positive developmental trajectory, it is necessary to recognize the different challenges that youth face in their different communities" (p. 3). Thus, student voice research must rise to the challenge of representing the diversity of youth experiences while trying to capture the essence of student experiences.

Research examining student responses to reform efforts has included student experiences in: "schools within a school" (Sidler, 1993); whole school structuring efforts (Wasley, Hampel, & Clark, 1997), district-wide reform (MacPherson, Cohen, Portnoy, & Buchanan, 1996; Wilson & Corbett, 1999), statewide and national reform (Coe, Leopold, Simon, Sowers, & Williams, 1994; Fielding, 1999, 2006). Such studies examined the extent to which students observed changes happening in their classrooms, and, if they felt that the culture of the school was changing, such as shifts in teacher-student relationships. For example, researchers conducted student focus groups at six schools in Ontario to examine the impact of the broad-based Secondary School Reform in Ontario, Canada (Earl & Sutherland, 2003). They reported that the new curriculum increased student stress levels, reduced course selection choices, and increased teacher anxiety. An initiative at Stanford University called Stressed-Out Students (SOS) also sought to increase conversations about the stresses faced by high school students (Galloway, Pope, & Osberg, 2007; Osberg, Pope, & Galloway, 2006). As a result of a recent conference, student presenters from high schools in the San Francisco Bay area offered suggestions for reducing the culture of competition in their schools, including changing homework and testing policies, encouraging teachers to engage more with students, and increasing awareness of the high stress levels of young people.

Research seeking student perspective on educational change efforts indicates giving students a voice in such reform conversations reminds teachers and administrators that students possess unique knowledge and perspectives about their schools that adults cannot fully replicate without

this partnership (Kushman, 1997; Levin, 2000; Rudduck et al., 1997; Thorkildsen, 1994), including broaching subjects that adults are reluctant to discuss, such as systemic inequities (Fine, 1991; Mitra, 2003; Smyth, 2007). Young people have also served as researchers and witnesses documenting school policies that exacerbate achievement gaps and identifying ways in which detrimental school conditions can adversely affect students' psychological, social, and academic well-being (Fine, Torre, Burns, & Payne, 2007). Furthermore, school personnel are learning that youth have access to information and relationships that teachers and administrators do not, such as providing a bridge between the school and families reluctant to interact with school personnel, including first generation immigrant families (Mitra, 2006c).

While the above studies focused on whether whole-school restructuring efforts influence student experience, other studies gathered student data to improve classroom practice (Cushman, 2000; Daniels, Deborah, & McCombs, 2001; Nicholls, 1993; Pope, 2001; Powell, Farrar, & Cohen; 1985; Thorkildsen, 1994; Turley, 1994). When asking student opinions, a common theme across several studies was the students' desires for positive, strong relationships with their teachers, as opposed to the isolation and lack of respect and appreciation that students reported they often feel (Lynch & Lodge, 2002; Phelan, Davidson, & Cao, 1992; Poplin & Weeres, 1992; Yonezawa & Jones, 2007).

Other research aimed at why some students feel alienated and detached from school settings focused on interviewing students who were not successful in school. In Sonia Nieto's research (1994), for example, youth pointed to racism, tracking, and discrimination as major problems, and urged that schools must affirm students' languages, cultures, and experiences and must align curricula with student experiences, backgrounds, and hopes if they intend to prevent high drop-out rates. Similarly, Dana Mitra (2004) described the effort of teachers at one reforming school that invited students, who in the previous year had received at least three Ds or Fs, to participate in a focus group during a summer staff-training. When asked to explain why some students do not succeed in school, the students in their own words talked about differences in learning styles, needing additional counseling and tutoring, and having a sense of mutual respect between teachers and students. Their responses provided teachers with specific reform issues to target in the upcoming year. Other studies have focused specifically on seeking out perspectives of failing students. Such struggling students tend to cite structural and classroom procedures that hamper learning, the lack of opportunities to build caring relationships with adults, and blatant discrimination as being the actual problems (Cusick, 1973; Mitra, 2008; Nieto, 1994; Soohoo, 1993).

In addition to teachers collaborating with students, collaboration can also exist between researchers and young people. In contrast to gathering data from students, these studies involve collaborations with youth on data collection and analysis. This body of studies includes broad-scale examinations of youth experiences in schools (Phelan & Davidson, 1994), of literacy efforts in urban high schools (Clark & Moss, 1996), student experiences with whole-school change (Shaughnessy & Kushman, 1997), and of reasons for academic failure and success (Atweh & Burton, 1995; Farrell, 1990, 1994), including the psychological, social, and academic effects of unqualified teachers, poor quality structures, and insufficient materials (Fine, Burns, Payne, & Torre, 2004). These kinds of studies demonstrate that partnering with students allows for an understanding of the causes of student failure in secondary schools to emerge from the students themselves. For example, students working with Patrick Lee (1999) identified school-related causes for their academic difficulties, including teacher-centered classrooms, racism and other forms of discrimination, and lack of personalized teacher-student relationships. Based on their data analysis, the student researchers recommended that the school modify instructional practice to make it less teacher-centered and more "real."

Students as Collaborators in Learning Communities A large body of research documents the value of improving classroom practice (including Cushman, 2000; Daniels et al., 2001; Kincheloe, 2007; Nicholls, 1993; Thorkildsen, 1994; Turley, 1994). Often, this form of student voice is termed "consultation," which is defined as teachers partnering with students to discuss teaching and learning, including inviting students to provide feedback on instructional styles, curriculum content, assessment opportunities, and other issues in the classroom (Flutter & Rudduck, 2004; Rudduck, 2007). This body of research expands the notion of school-based teacher learning communities to include students in the collaboration process. Focused primarily on increasing teacher voice in decision-making and collaborative processes at the grade/departmental and school-wide levels, professional collaboration has been shown to lead to improved teaching and learning as teachers work together to critique practice, to support professional growth, and to learn together how to improve practice (Grossman, Wineburg, & Woolworth, 2001; Leonard & Leonard, 2001; Louis & Kruse, 1995; Newmann, King, & Youngs, 2000; McLaughlin & Talbert, 2001). Student voice research of this type focuses on how the involvement of students in reflections on teaching and learning affects the exchange of ideas, the development of critique, and the sharing of expertise in schools.

The largest body of research on teacher-student collaboration has taken place in the United Kingdom. As a part of the Consulting with Pupils on Teaching and Learning project in the United Kingdom, researchers worked with teachers to identify what consultation looks like in classrooms, what students say about their classroom experiences, how teachers react to student reflections about their classes, and the impact of consultation on student learning and teacher practice (McIntyre & Rudduck, 2007; Rudduck, 2007). The findings from the research project include that increasing "pupil consultation" in decisions about teaching

and learning has increased teacher confidence (MacBeath, Demetriou, & Myers, 2001) and increased student agency, self-worth, respect, and a sense of membership in the school (Rudduck & Demetriou, 2003). Research from this project also explores the criteria that teachers tend to use to define the limits of collaboration, including: the validity of the pupil accounts of classroom activities, the feasibility and commonality of student perspectives, and the extent to which the pupil perspectives affirmed a teacher's own sense of their strengths and weaknesses as a practitioner (McIntyre & Rudduck, 2007).

In the United States, Whitman High School students developed strategies for building communication between students and teachers (Mitra, 2003, 2008). Students joined in the school's reform work, including participating in staff trainings on inquiry-based research and research groups on reading strategies. During these activities, Student Forum members served as "experts" on their classroom experience by providing teachers with feedback on how students might receive new pedagogical strategies. Working with Student Forum members during professional development sessions, research groups encouraged teachers to continue to involve students as they returned to their classrooms to implement what they had learned.

Individual teachers in the United States also have engaged in consultation with students. For example, fifth- and sixth-grade students working with their teacher, Penny Oldfather (1995), researched their own processes of learning and motivation for literacy. The research partnership continued with these students throughout middle school and into high school, where the students researched how teachers make decisions about motivation in their classrooms. Student collaboration increased overtime in this project. Initially, Oldfather used students as a check to see if she "got it right." Over time, however, she and her adult colleagues stepped back as the students assumed a higher level of agency in developing and implementing the research agenda. Students and researchers struggled with power relationships between adults and students and how to best delegate responsibilities to students. The research team also wrestled with how to provide opportunities for all members to participate. A further struggle occurred in deciding whose ideas should be presented when there was a disagreement between students and adults. The students ultimately shared their findings with teacher education classes, their local school board, and scholarly meetings across the country, including the American Educational Research Association.

Students as Reformers In addition to classroom-focused collaborations, students have also participated in designing and implementing school-wide change efforts. This small slice of student voice initiatives contributes to the growing body of literature emphasizing the value of extending the notion of distributed leadership (Elmore, 2000; Lashway, 2003). While student participation in school-reform decision making is unusual, and thus research is scant and primarily case studies, student voice in decision-making processes have led to some incredible accomplishments. These include improvements in: instruction, curriculum, and teacher-student relationships (Rudduck, 2007; Soohoo, 1993), teacher preparation (Cook-Sather, 2001, 2006), assessment systems (Colatos & Morrell, 2003; Fielding, 2001), and visioning and strategic planning (Kirshner, O'Donoghue, & McLaughlin, 2003; Eccles & Gootman, 2002; Zeldin, 2004; Zeldin, Camino, & Mook, 2005), among others.

In the United Kingdom, the student researchers participating in the Students as Researcher program gathered and analyzed data on three issues—student voice, student experiences with teachers in training (student teachers), and the school's assessment system (Fielding, 2001). Taking up the student recommendations, the school changed its assessment system, examined how to partner with universities to reform teacher training, reformed the life-skills curriculum, and redesigned the advisory period. Additionally, the schools developed standings committees that included students and teachers to assist with future school reform efforts, including staff development activities and curriculum planning.

In Canada, the Ontario Secondary School Students' Association (OSSSA), in collaboration with the Institute on Governance, has published several reports detailing youth involvement in public policy at local, provincial, and federal levels throughout the country (Haid, Marques, & Brown, 1999; Marques, 1999). The OSSSA has been in existence since 1969 and holds leadership conferences across Ontario as well as working on many reform initiatives with teachers unions and working to represent secondary school students on panels and commissions. The organization has also begun a large-scale restructuring of the organization with the plan on electing an OSSSA representative at each school in Ontario (Ontario Secondary School Students' Association, 2007).

Work also occurred in the Manitoba School Improvement Program Inc. Students in three schools developed surveys to learn about student backgrounds, high school experiences, post secondary experiences, work activity and attitudes (Seven Oaks School, 2003). After receiving assistance on how to analyze the data from academics at the Universities of Winnipeg and Manitoba, the student researchers conducted professional development sessions for staff, hosted parent evenings, held school-wide workshops on teaching and learning, and participated as members of school improvement planning teams (Lee & Zimmerman, 2001). The students' findings emphasized the importance of self-directed learning opportunities for students, the need to explore connecting students' part time jobs with their coursework, and the desire to engage in less specialized coursework in their final years of high school so that they have a wider range of post secondary options. The schools devised less automated and more individualized scheduling as a result of these data. They also developed a schools-within-schools approach so that teachers have greater contact with a smaller group of students. Doing so

helped the teachers to develop interdisciplinary approaches and to provide more opportunities for students to participate in shaping the curriculum. The project also noticed the growth in students as a result of participating in the research. Student researchers who had been sullen and unreachable became some of the most passionate participants in the school reform process once they became actively involved (Earl & Lee, 1999; Lee & Zimmerman, 2001). Students participating in the research also developed a better meta-cognitive understanding of their own learning, including the differences between learning styles, multiple intelligences, and emotional intelligence (Lee & Zimmerman, 2001).

In the United States, Anthony Colatos and Ernest Morrell (2003) examined a school involved in the James Madison Futures Project. The school placed students of color in roles as critical researchers in order to "facilitate greater equity and access" at the high school (p. 119), accomplishing this through the creation of a collaborative effort that developed shared beliefs and practices of social justice. Students involved in the project successfully challenged the unfair testing policies for administering the Golden State Examinations, as well as opened up a much-needed dialogue with more privileged classmates on issues of tracking at the school, despite an atmosphere very hostile to any de-tracking reforms. The student researchers were also quite academically successful, with nearly all going on to a four-year university, as well as emerging "with a strong sense of themselves as agents of school reform and social justice" (p. 127). Colatos and Morrell, despite acknowledging that long-term systemic reform had not taken place, were encouraged by the fact that students cannot only "be catalysts during such efforts, but they also have valuable expertise to contribute" (p. 129) within this collaborative model.

The work of Suzanne Soohoo (1993) demonstrates how administrators also can collaborate with students to spark whole school reform. Middle school students identified three main barriers to learning as they interviewed their peers: learning takes place based on teacher rhythms rather than student rhythms, the need for more care and connection between teachers and students, and the valuing of students as a whole and each student individually. Students also were frustrated that teachers and administrators exclusively controlled curriculum, pedagogy, assessment, and governing rules. According to one student, "They think just because we're kids we don't know anything" (p. 391). The student researchers in this study also became change agents when they presented their results to teachers and the principal. The faculty agreed to form committees comprised of teachers, student co-researchers, and administrators to re-examine school policies.

What Conditions Enable the Creation of Student Voice Initiatives?

One of the biggest struggles in student voice efforts is *how* to engage students as active partners in school change. The power and status distinctions in school settings especially provide a dramatic form of asymmetry due to institutional norms of deference to adult authority and the separation of adult and youth roles in schools. Youth-adult partnerships must develop new ways to communicate effectively and to learn how to work together in more equitable ways. The greater the youth role in student voice efforts, the greater the need to empower young people to become strong collaborators for educational change. Creating a new set of working conditions requires developing new norms, relationships, and organizational structures (Della Porta & Diani, 1999; Oakes & Lipton, 2002). To do so, adults must relinquish some of their power and work to build a tone of trust among adults and students (Cervone, 2002). Without an intentional focus on building relationships, student voice can easily become tokenism.

To combat these challenges, some research has taken on the task of examining how adults go about empowering youth and relinquishing their power. True engagement requires a "rupture of the ordinary" (Fielding, 2004), which demands as much of teachers as it does of students. Benjamin Kirshner (2003) also has documented that students and adults struggle regarding power in youth-adult partnerships, including how to best delegate responsibilities to students, how to provide opportunities for all members to participate, and how to resolve disagreements of opinion—especially when adults and young people have opposing views.

Roger Holdsworth and Pat Thomson (2002) suggest that teachers and others concerned about student voice need to think critically about the spaces in which democratic projects and programs can occur. Some strategies for increasing student participation are better suited to occurring within the formal structures of schools and others are better suited to occur outside of the formal system through community-based organizations and other such formats. For example, the youth participation newsletter in Australia, *Connect*, survives only by subscription and unpaid labor. Holdsworth and Thomson believe that *Connect* would not be possible if it was formally supported by a school or the government because it is often critical of public policy.

An in-depth examination of conditions that enable student voice initiatives has been conducted by Dana Mitra (2006b). Overall, Mitra identified the guiding principles that are correlated with strong student voice initiative—a baseline of trust, creating meaningful but not equal roles among youth and adults, and ongoing professional development for all involved.

Baseline of Trust Often in student voice initiatives, groups are so anxious to work on improving schools and classrooms that little time is devoted to building the capacity of the group members and the overall identity of the group (Mitra, 2006b). In such cases, adults and youth may successfully complete a specific project, but without a broader vision and collective purpose, the group disbands and often even the accomplished activities disappear as well. Instead, research has found that youth-adult partnerships fail if they do not provide sufficient focus and attention to the development of trust and building of community among group members (Camino, 2005; Cook-Sather, 2002; Schön & McDonald, 1998; Zeldin et al., 2005). The creation of a safe space and open lines of communication must be given priority in the work of student voice initiatives.

Creating Meaningful, but not Equal Roles Adults and youth needed opportunities to share what they have learned based on their experiences and their beliefs. A sense of shared ownership grows when student voice initiatives encourage group members to experiment with a variety of roles, including being a critical thinker, a teacher, a learner, a peacemaker, a supporter, a facilitator, and a documenter (Denner et al., 2005; Zeldin et al., 2002). Successful student voice initiatives therefore require a clear understanding of what roles each individual plays within the group (Mitra, 2005a). They do not create an expectation of equal roles, but instead foster equal responsibility and respect through mutual understanding.

Youth-adult partnerships are much different than the common misconception that an increase in youth leadership means that adults must simply "get out of the way" (Camino, 2005). This assumption suggests that power is a zero-sum game. Instead, research has found that the more empowered adults are, the more they can enable power in others, including youth (Camino, 2000; Ginwright, 2005). Nevertheless, in instances such as the formation of youth-adult partnerships, where the imbalance of power among group members is extreme, adults often had to make explicit gestures that signaled their stepping back in order to create a space in which youth could have a shared responsibility for group decision making. Such a process does not entail handing over control to youth per se, but instead consists of creating a space in which all group members—youth and adults—could develop a common vision for their collective, could carve out an important and meaningful role for themselves in the activities, and could share responsibility for decisions and accountability for group outcomes (Mitra, 2005a).

Ongoing Professional Development Often adults are reluctant to share power until they have assurance that youth possess the skills and confidence to assume leadership (Muncey & McQuillan, 1991; Zeldin, 2004; Zeldin et al., 2005). While partnerships should capitalize on the assets and talents that youth and adults bring to a group (Camino, 2000; Perkins & Borden, 2003), research has indicated that adults and youth both need specific skill development to serve as contributing members in their youth-adult partnerships (Mitra, 2006b). Adults must to learn how to enable leadership in youth, and often the best way to do so is first to develop a theoretical understanding of youth developmental needs and cultural contexts so that they are able to act with intention as they foster youth leadership (Camino & Zeldin, 2002; Zeldin et al., 2002). Youth need to develop the capacity to assume this leadership by developing an understanding of effective communication in adult contexts and specific skills such as time management, planning, and learning to resolve differences among group members (Mitra, 2004). Building understanding of the perspectives of the other in the partnership can help the group to forge a more equitable form of interaction.

Intermediary Organizations Student voice initiatives benefit from ongoing partnerships that can help to push schools toward new forms of decision making, planning, and ultimately, teaching and learning (Mitra, in press). Working outside of a school system allows opportunities for much different types of pressure on the system, as compared to building alliances and working from the inside of an institution. Seeking increased student voice from a vantage point outside of school walls, such as through a community-based organization, trades internal legitimacy for the ability to challenge openly the practices of an organization and to provide funding and dedicated staff to make the change effort the primary goal of an organization (Mitra, 2006a). While, indeed, not a central focus of this review, some of the strongest examples of youth taking the lead in change efforts occur outside the domain of formal schooling. Community-based organizations provide the home for much of the youth organizing activities that occur in inner-cities under the banner of youth activism (Camino & Zeldin, 2002; Ginwright & James, 2002). Strong youth-led initiatives also can be found in rural communities through organizations such as 4-H (Zeldin et al., 2005).

Next Steps in Student Voice Research

The role of student voice in educational change is underutilized, and therefore, understudied. As research on student voice matures, it will benefit from stronger ties to ongoing theory and research. The growing body of literature on youth-adult partnerships and positive youth development in the field of human development offers a natural home for examining the nature of student voice initiatives.

In addition to a stronger theoretical grounding, the field is also ready for larger, more comprehensive mixed methods studies that can examine the development and outcomes of student voice initiatives in educational reform. The current body of research in this emerging field has focused primarily on qualitative case study research that examines a limited number of student voice initiatives. The current literature base has primed the field for larger studies; hopefully these will be developed in the upcoming years. It is important nevertheless to understand the challenges of studying student voice initiatives, which might help to explain why many larger scale studies have not been conducted. These questions include how students can be included in the development of a research design as well as be the subject that is being studied. The value of students as valuable sources of data and as important contributors also must keep being reemphasized because of the counter-normative nature of this conception (Cook-Sather, 2002, 2007).

The early findings from the research reviewed in this chapter demonstrates the ways in which including student voice in a reform process can strengthen the validity of reform efforts such as inquiry-based reform, improve the deliberations of professional learning communities, and facilitate the implementation of reforms. Future research could also examine how student voice can fit within policy initiatives, including comprehensive school reform and high-stakes accountability systems. The inclusion of students in the reform process therefore provides many potential benefits with little additional costs. Scaling-up of student voice efforts requires caution, however. Surface level implementation (i.e., the offering insincere gestures rather than authentic partnership) could create greater alienation among young people. As with any educational change, the quality of implementation will prove to be as important as the merit of the idea itself.

Notes

1. The youth development field does not possess a consistent set of assets that youth need to acquire to be prepared for the future and to navigate their current situations. The most common set, perhaps, is of "confidence and compassion; connection and caring; competence and character" (Eccles & Gootman, 2002; Roth & Brooks-Gunn, 2003). Other lists include "autonomy, belonging, and competence" (Schapps, Watson, & Lewis, 1997), "self-worth, belonging and competence" (Kernaleguen, 1980), "knowledge, belonging and competence" (Villarruel & Lerner, 1994), and "navigation, connection and productivity" (Connell, Gambone, & Smith, 1998).
2. The most comprehensive bibliography of student voice work occurring primarily in the United States can be found at http://www.soundout.org/bibliography.html. This annotated bibliography is updated yearly. Additionally, the *International Handbook of Student Experience* (Thiessen & Cook-Sather, 2007) provides the most comprehensive international compilation of writings on student voice in recent times.
3. This framework was developed by Dana Mitra (2007).

References

Arnot, M., Reay, D., & Wang, B. (2001, April). *Pupil consultation and the social conditions of learning: Race, class and gender*. Paper presented at the Annual meeting of the American Educational Research Association, Seattle, WA.

Atweh, B., & Burton, L. (1995). Students as researchers: Rationale and critique. *British Educational Research Journal, 21*, 561–575.

Bragg, S. (2007). "It's not about systems, it's about relationships": Building a listening culture in a primary school. In D. Thiessen & A. Cook-Sather (Eds.), *International handbook of student experience in elementary and secondary school* (pp. 659–680). Dordrecht, The Netherlands: Springer.

Camino, L. A. (2000). Youth-adult partnerships: Entering new territory in community work and research. *Applied Developmental Science, 4*(Suppl. 1), 11–20.

Camino, L. (2005). Pitfalls and promising practices of youth-adult partnerships: An evaluator's reflections. *Journal of Community Psychology, 33*, 75–85.

Camino, L., & Zeldin, S. (2002). From periphery to center: Pathways for youth civic engagement in day-to-day life of communities. *Applied Developmental Science, 6*, 213–220.

Carver, R. L. (1997). Theoretical underpinnings of service learning. *Theory into Practice, 36*, 143–149.

Cervone, B. (2002, May). *Taking democracy in hand: Youth action for educational change in the San Francisco Bay area.* Providence, RI: What Kids Can Do and The Forum for Youth Investment.

Clark, C. T., & Moss, P. A. (1996). Researching with: Ethical and epistemological implications of doing collaborative, change-oriented research with teachers and students. *Teachers College Record, 97,* 518–548.

Coe, P., Leopold, G., Simon, K., Sowers, P., & Williams, J. (1994). *Perceptions of school change: Interviews with Kentucky students.* Charleston, WV: Appalachia Educational Laboratory.

Colatos, A. M., & Morrell, E. (2003). Apprenticing urban youth as critical researchers: Implications for increasing equity and access in diverse urban schools. In B. Rubin & E. Silva (Eds.), *Critical voices in school reform: Students living through change* (pp. 113–131). London: RoutledgeFalmer.

Coleman, J. (1961). *The adolescent society: The social life of the teenager and its impact on education.* New York: Free Press of Glencoe.

Connell, J. P., Gambone, M. A., & Smith, T. J. (1998). *Youth development in community settings: Challenges to our field and our approach.* Rochester, NY: Institute for Research and Reform in Education.

Cook-Sather, A. (2001). Between student and teacher: learning to teach as translation. *Teaching Education, 12,* 177–190.

Cook-Sather, A. (2002). Authorizing students' perspectives: Toward trust, dialogue, and change in education. *Educational Researcher, 31*(4), 3–14.

Cook-Sather, A. (2006). Change based on what students say: Preparing teachers for a paradoxical model of leadership. *International Journal of Leadership Education, 9,* 345–358.

Cook-Sather, A. (2007). Translating researchers: Re-imagining the work of investigating students' experiences in school. In D. Thiessen & A. Cook-Sather (Eds.), *International handbook of student experience in elementary and secondary school* (pp. 829–872). Dordrecht, The Netherlands: Springer.

Costello, J., Toles, M., Spielberger, J., & Wynn, J. (2000). History, ideology and structure shape the organizations that shape youth. In *Youth development: Issues, challenges, and directions* (pp. 185–231). Philadelphia: Public/Private Ventures.

Cothran, D., & Ennis, C. (2000). Building bridges to student engagement: Communicating respect and care for students in urban high schools. *Journal of Research and Development in Education, 33*(2), 106–117.

Csikszentmihalyi, M., & Larson, R. (1984). *Being adolescent: Growth and conflict in the teenage years.* New York: Basic Books.

Cushman, K. (2000). Students solving community problems: Serious learning takes on a new look. *Challenge Journal: The Journal of the Annenberg Challenge, 4*(1).

Cusick, P. A. (1973). *Inside high school: The student's world.* New York: Holt, Rinehart, and Winston.

Daniels, D. H., Deborah, L., & McCombs, B. L. (2001). Young children's perspectives on learning and teacher practices in different classroom contexts: Implications for motivation. *Early Education and Development, 12,* 253–273.

deCharms, R. (1976). *Enhancing motivation: Change in the classroom.* New York: Irvington.

Della Porta, D., & Diani, M. (1999). *Social movements: An introduction.* Malden, MA: Blackwell.

Denner, J., Meyer, B., & Bean, S. (2005). Young Women's Leadership Alliance: Youth–adult partnerships in an all-female after-school program. *Journal of Community Psychology, 33,* 87–100.

Dewey, J. (1966). *Democracy and education: An introduction to the philosophy of education.* New York: The Free Press. (Original work published 1916)

Earl, L., & Lee, L. (1999, April). *Learning, for a change.* Paper presented at the American Educational Research Association, Montreal, Canada.

Earl, L., & Sutherland, S. (2003). Student engagement in times of turbulent change. *McGill Journal of Education, 38,* 329–343.

Earls, F. (2003). *Age segregation and the rights of children.* Ann Arbor, MI: Society for Research in Child Development.

Eccles, J. & Gootman, J. A. (Eds.). (2002). *Community programs to pro-mote youth development.* Committee on Community-Level Programs for Youth. Board on Children, Youth, and Families, Commission on Behavioral and Social Sciences Education, National Research Council and Institute of Medicine. Washington, DC: National Academies of Science.

Eccles, J. S., Midgley, C., Wigfield, A., Buchanan, C. M., Reuman, D., Flanagan, C., et al. (1993). Development during adolescence: The impact of stage-environment fit on young adolescents' experiences in schools and in families. *American Psychologist, 48,* 90–101.

Elmore, R. (2000). *Building a new structure for school leadership.* Washington, DC: The Albert Shanker Institute.

Farrell, E. (1990). *Hanging in and dropping out: Voices of at-risk high school students.* New York: Teachers College Press.

Farrell, E. (1994). *Self and school success: Voices and lore of inner-city students.* Albany: Statue University of New York Press.

Fielding, M. (1999). Target setting, policy pathology and student perspectives: Learning to labour in new times. *Cambridge Journal of Education, 29,* 277–287.

Fielding, M. (2001). Students as radical agents of change. *Journal of Educational Change, 2,* 123–141.

Fielding, M. (2004). Transformative approaches to student voice: Theoretical underpinnings, recalcitrant realities. *British Educational Research Journal, 30,* 295–311.

Fielding, M. (2006). Leadership, radical student engagement and the necessity of person-centered education. *International Journal of Leadership Education, 9,* 299–314.

Fine, M. (1991). *Framing dropouts: Notes on the politics of an urban high school.* Albany: State University of New York Press.

Fine, M., Burns, A., Payne, Y., & Torre, M. E. (2004). Civics lessons: The color and class of betrayal. *Teachers College Record, 106,* 2193–2223.

Fine, M., Torre, M. E., Burns, A., & Payne, Y. A. (2007). Youth research/participatory methods for reform. In D. Thiessen & A. Cook-Sather (Eds.), *International handbook of student experience in elementary and secondary school* (pp. 805–828). Dordrecht, The Netherlands: Springer.

Flanagan, C., & Faison, N. (2001). *Youth civic development: Implications of research for social policy and programs.* Ann Arbor, MI: Society for Research in Child Development.

Flutter, J., & Rudduck, J. (2004). *Consulting pupils: What's in it for schools?* London: Routledge.

Fullan, M. G. (2001). *The new meaning of educational change* (3rd ed.). New York: Teachers College Press.

Galloway, M., Pope, D., & Osberg, J. (2007). Stressed-out students-SOS: Youth perspectives on changing school climates. In D. Thiessen & A. Cook-Sather (Eds.), *International handbook of student experience in elementary and secondary school* (pp. 611–634). Dordrecht, The Netherlands: Springer.

Ginwright, S. A. (2005). On urban ground: Understanding African-American intergenerational partnerships in urban communities. *Journal of Community Psychology, 33,* 101–100.

Ginwright, S., & James, T. (2002, Winter). From assets to agents of change: Social justice, organizing, and youth development. *New directions for youth development, 96,* 27–46.

Goodenow, C. (1993). Classroom belonging among early adolescent students: Relationships to motivation and achievement. *Journal of Early Adolescence, 13,* 21–43.

Goodwillie, S. (Ed.). (1993). *Voices from the future: Our children tell us but violence in America.* New York: Crown.

Grossman, P., Wineburg, S., & Woolworth, S. (2001). Toward a theory of teacher community. *Teachers College Record, 103,* 942–1012.

Haid, P., Marques, E. C., & Brown, J. (1999, June). *Re-focusing the lens: Assessing the challenge of youth involvement in public policy.* Ottawa, Canada: The Ontario Secondary School Students' Association (OSSSA) and The Institute On Governance (IOG).

Heath, S. B., & McLaughlin, M. W. (Eds.). (1993). *Identity and inner-city youth.* New York: Teachers College Press.

Holdsworth, R., & Thomson, P. (2002, April). *Options within the regulation and containment of "student voice" and/or Students researching and acting for change: Australian experiences.* Paper presented at the Annual Meeting of the American Educational Research Association, New Orleans, LA.

Honig, M., Kahne, J., McLaughlin, M. W. (2001). *School-community connections: Strengthening opportunity to learn and opportunity to teach.* In V. Richardson, (Ed.), *Handbook of research on teaching* (4th ed., pp. 998–1028). Washington, DC: American Educational Research Association.

Johnson, J. H. (1991). *Student voice motivating students through empowerment.* Eugene: Oregon School Study Council. (ERIC Document Reproduction Service No. ED337875)

Jones, K., & Perkins, D. (2004). Youth-adult partnerships. In C. B. Fisher & R. M. Lerner (Eds.), *Applied developmental science: An encyclopedia of research, policies, and programs* (pp. 1159–1163). Thousand Oaks, CA: Sage.

Kernaleguen, A. (1980). Clothing: An important symbol for adolescents. *School Guidance Worker, 35*(3), 37–41.

Kincheloe, J. (2007). Clarifying the purpose of engaging students as researchers. In D. Thiessen & A. Cook-Sather (Eds.), *International handbook of student experience in elementary and secondary school* (pp. 745–774). Dordrecht, the Netherlands: Springer.

Kirshner, B. (2003, November). *The social formation of youth voice.* Paper presented at the International Conference on Civic Education, New Orleans, LA.

Kirshner, B. (2004). *Democracy now: Activism and learning in urban youth organizations.* Unpublished doctoral dissertation, Stanford University, Stanford, CA.

Kirshner, B., O'Donoghue, J. L., & McLaughlin, M. W. (Eds.). (2003). *New directions for youth development: Youth participation improving institutions and communities.* San Francisco, CA: Jossey-Bass.

Kushman, J. W. (Ed.). (1997). *Look who's talking now: Student views of learning in restructuring schools.* Portland, OR: Northwest Regional Educational Labratory. (ERIC Document Reproduction Service No. ED028257)

Larson, R. W. (2000). Toward a psychology of positive youth development. *American Psychologist, 55,* 170–183.

Larson, R., Walker, K., & Pearce, N. (2005). A comparison of youth-driven and adult-driven youth programs: Balancing inputs from youth and adults. *Journal of Community Psychology, 33,* 57–74.

Lashway, L. (2003). Distributed leadership. *Research Roundup, 19*(4).

Lee, L. E., & Zimmerman, M. (2001). *Passion, action, and a new vision for student voice: Learnings from the Manitoba School Improvement Program Inc.* Winnepeg, Canada: Manitoba School Improvement Program.

Lee, P. W. (1999). In their own voices: An ethnographic study of low-achieving students within the context of school reform. *Urban Education, 34,* 214–244.

Leonard, P. E., & Leonard, L. J. (2001). The collaborative prescription: Remedy or reverie? *International Journal of Leadership Education, 4,* 383–399.

Levin, B. (2000). Putting students at the centre in education reform. *Journal of Educational Change, 1,* 155–172.

Louis, K. S., & Kruse, S. D. (1995). *Professionalism and community: Perspectives on reforming urban schools.* Thousand Oaks, CA: Corwin.

Lynch, K., & Lodge, A. (2002). *Equality and power in schools: Redistribution, recognition and representation.* London: RoutledgeFalmer.

MacBeath, J., Demetriou, H., & Myers, K. (2001, April). *Supporting teachers in consulting pupils about aspects of teaching and learning, and evaluating impact.* Paper presented at the Annual meeting of the American Educational Research Association, Seattle, WA.

MacPherson, P., Cohen, J., Portnoy, D., & Buchanan, J. (1996). *Homegrown research: A guide for school communities: Vol. I. Strategies for listening to and analyzing student voices.* Philadelphia: Philadelphia Education Fund and Research for Action.

Males, M. A. (1996). *The scapegoat generation: America's war on adolescence.* Monroe, ME: Common Courage Press.

Marques, E. (1999). *Youth involvement in policy-making: Lessons from Ontario school boards* (Policy brief no. 5). Ottawa: Institute on Governance.

Massell, D. (2001). The theory and practice of using data to build capacity: State and local strategies and their effects. In S. Fuhrman (Ed.), *From the Capitol to the classroom: Standards-based reform in the states* (pp. 148–169). Chicago: University of Chicago Press.

McIntyre, D., & Rudduck, J. (2007). *Improving learning through consulting pupils.* London: Routledge.

McLaughlin, M., & Mitra, D. (2004). *The cycle of inquiry as the engine of school reform: Lessons from the Bay Area School Reform Collaborative.* Stanford, CA: Stanford University, Center for Research on the Context of Teaching.

McLaughlin, M. W., & Talbert, J. E. (2001). *High school teaching in context.* Chicago: University of Chicago.

McQuillan, P. J. (2005). Possibilities and pitfalls: A comparative analysis of student empowerment. *American Educational Research Journal, 42,* 639–670.

Mitra, D. L. (2003). Student voice in school reform: Reframing student-teacher relationships. *McGill Journal of Education, 38,* 289–304.

Mitra, D. L. (2004). The significance of students: Can increasing "student voice" in schools lead to gains in youth development? *Teachers College Record, 106,* 651–688.

Mitra, D. L. (2005a). Adults advising youth: Leading while getting out of the way. *Educational Administration Quarterly, 41,* 520–553.

Mitra, D. L. (2005b). Increasing student voice and moving toward youth leadership. *Prevention Researcher, 13,* 7–10.

Mitra, D. L. (2006a). Educational change on the inside and outside: The positioning of challengers. *International Journal of Leadership in Education, 9,* 315–328.

Mitra, D. L. (2006b, April). *Student voice in school reform: From listening to leadership.* Paper presented at the Annual Meeting of the American Educational Research Association, San Francisco.

Mitra, D. L. (2006c). Youth as a bridge between home and school: Comparing student voice and parent involvements as strategies for change. *Education and Urban Society, 38,* 455–480.

Mitra, D. (2007). Student voice in school reform: From listening to leadership. In D. Thiessen & A. Cook-Sather (Eds.), *International Handbook of Student Experience in Elementary and Secondary School* (pp. 727–744). Dordrecht, the Netherlands: Springer.

Mitra, D. L. (2008). *Student voice in school reform.* Albany: State University of New York Press.

Mitra, D. L. (in press). What really matters when sustaining educational change? An examination of the persistence among strong student voice initiatives. *Teachers College Record.*

Mitra, D., Sanders, F., Movit, M., & Perkins, D. F. (2007, April). *Examining ways in which youth conferences can spell out gains in positive youth development.* Paper presented at the annual meeting of the American Educational Research Association, Chicago.

Muncey, D., & McQuillan, P. (1991). *Empowering nonentities: Students in educational reform* (School Ethnography Project working paper No. 5). Providence, RI: Brown University, Coalition of Essential Schools.

Newmann, F. M., King, M. B., & Youngs, P. (2000). Professional development that addresses school capacity: Lessons from urban elementary schools. *American Journal of Education, 108,* 259–299.

Nicholls, J. G. (1993, March). *What knowledge is of most worth? Student perspectives.* Paper presented at the biennial meeting of the Society for Research in Child Development, New Orleans, LA.

Nieto, S. (1994). Lessons from students on creating a chance to dream. *Harvard Educational Review, 64,* 392–426.

Noddings, N. (1992). *The challenge to care in schools: An alternative approach to education.* New York: Teachers College Press.

Noguera, P. (2002, December). Joaquin's dilemma: Understanding the link between racial identity and school-related behaviors. *In Motion Magazine.* Retrieved April 29, 2004, from http://www.inmotionmagazine.com/er/pnjoaq2.html

Oakes, J., & Lipton, M. (2002). Struggling for educational equity in diverse communities: School reform as a social movement. *Journal of Educational Change, 3*, 383–406.

O'Connor, C., & Camino, L. (2005). *Youth and Adult Leaders for Program Excellence: Youth participation in research and evaluation: Outcomes for youth*. Retrieved May 22, 2008, from http://www.actforyouth.net/documents/YAE%20Issue%20Brief2.pdf

Oldfather, P. (1995). Songs "come back most to them": Students' experiences as researchers. *Theory Into Practice, 34*, 131.

Ontario Secondary School Student Association. (2007). *History*. Retrieved January 22, 2008, from http://www.osssa-aeeso.org/history.html

Osberg, J., Pope, D., & Galloway, M. (2006). Students matter in school reform: Leaving fingerprints and becoming leaders. *International Journal of Leadership Education, 9*, 329–343.

Panitz, T. (1996). *A definition of collaborative vs. cooperative learning*. Retrieved February 11, 2008, from http://www.lgu.ac.uk/deliberations/collab.learning/panitz2.html

Perkins, D., & Borden, L. (2003). Positive behaviors, problem behaviors, and resiliency in adolescence. In R. M. Lerner, M. A. Easterbrooks, J. Mistry, & Weiner, I. B. (Eds.), *Handbook of Psychology: Vol. 6. Developmental Psychology*. (pp. 273–419) Hoboken, NJ: Wiley.

Phelan, P., & Davidson, A. L. (1994). Looking across borders: Students' investigations of family, peer, and school worlds as cultural therapy. In G. Spindler & L. Spindler (Eds.), *Pathways to cultural awareness: Cultural therapy with teachers and students* (pp. 35–59). Thousand Oaks, CA: Corwin.

Phelan, P., Davidson, A. L., & Cao, H. T. (1992). Speaking up: Students' perspectives on school. *Phi Delta Kappan, 73*, 695–704.

Pittman, K., & Wright, M. (1991). *Bridging the gap: A Rationale for enhancing the role of community organizations in promoting youth development*. Washington, DC: Carnegie Council on Adolescent Development.

Pope, D. C. (1999). *Doing school: "Successful" students' experiences of the high school curriculum*. Unpublished Doctoral dissertation, Stanford University, Stanford, CA.

Pope, D. C. (2001). *"Doing school": How we are creating a generation of stressed out, materialistic, and miseducated students*. New Haven, CT: Yale University Press.

Poplin, M., & Weeres, J. (1992). *Voices from inside the classroom*. Claremont, CA: Claremont Graduate School, Institute for Education in Transformation.

Powell, A. G., Farrar, E., & Cohen, D. K. (1985). *The shopping mall high school*. Boston: Houghton Mifflin.

Roberts, D. F. (1993). Adolescents and the mass media: From "Leave It to Beaver" to "Beverley Hills 90210." In R. Takanishi (Ed.), *Adolescence in the 1990s: Risk and opportunity* (pp. 171–186). New York: Teachers College Press.

Roeser, R. W., Midgley, C., & Urdan, T. C. (1996). Perceptions of the school psychological environment and early adolescents' psychological and behavioral functioning in school: The mediating role of goals and belonging. *Journal of Educational Psychology, 88*, 408–422.

Roth, J. L., & Brooks-Gunn, J. (2003). What exactly is a youth development program? Answers from research and practice. *Applied Developmental Science, 7*(2), 94–111.

Rudduck, J. (2007). Student voice, student engagement, and school reform. In D. Thiessen & A. Cook-Sather (Eds.), *International handbook of student experience in elementary and secondary school* (pp. 587–610). Dordrecht, The Netherlands: Springer.

Rudduck, J., Day, J., & Wallace, G. (1997). Students' perspectives on school improvement. In A. Hargreaves (Ed.), *Rethinking educational change with heart and mind: 1997 ASCD Year Book*. Alexandria, VA: Association for Supervision and Curriculum Development.

Rudduck, J., & Demetriou, H. (2003). Student perspectives and teacher practices: The transformative potential. *McGill Journal of Education, 38*, 274–288.

Ryan, R. M., & Powelson., C. L. (1991). Autonomy and relatedness as fundamental to motivation and education. *Journal of Experimental Education, 60*, 49–66.

Sanders, F., Movit, M., Mitra, D., & Perkins, D. F. (2007). Examining

ways in which youth conferences can spell out gains in positive youth development. *LEARNing Landscapes, 1*(1), 49–78.

Schapps, E., Watson, M., & Lewis, C. (1997). A key condition for character development: Building a sense of community in school. *Social Studies Review, 37*(1), 85–90.

Schmuck, P., & Schmuck, R. (1990). Democratic participation in small-town schools. *Educational Researcher, 19*(8), 14–19.

Schön, D., & McDonald, J. (1998). *Doing what you mean to do in school reform: Theory of Action in the Annenberg Challenge*. Providence, RI: Brown University, Annenberg Institute for School Reform.

Seven Oaks School. (2003, April). *Student research as a force for school improvement*. Paper presented at the annual meeting of the American Educational Research Association, Chicago.

Sidler, J. (1993). *School restructuring: Building connections, adjusting to new roles and spreading the vision*. Philadelphia: Research for Better Schools.

Silva, E. (2003). Struggling for inclusion: A case study of students as reform partners. In B. Rubin & E. Silva (Eds.), *Critical voices in school reform: Students living through change* (pp. 11–30). London: RoutledgeFalmer.

Smyth, J. (2007). Toward the pedagogically engaged school: Listening to student voice as a positive response to disengagement and 'dropping out'. In D. Thiessen & A. Cook-Sather (Eds.), *International handbook of student experience in elementary and secondary school* (pp. 635–658). Dordrecht, The Netherlands: Springer.

Soohoo, S. (1993). Students as partners in research and restructuring schools. *The Educational Forum, 57*, 386–393.

Stinson, S. W. (1993). Meaning and value: Reflections on what students say about school. *Journal of Curriculum and Supervision, 8*, 216–238.

Strobel, K., & McDonald, M. A. (2001, April). *What counts from the inside: Youth's perspective on youth development*. Paper presented at the Annual Conference of the American Educational Research Association, Seattle, WA.

Takanishi, R. (1993). Changing views of adolescence in contemporary society. In R. Takanishi (Ed.), *Adolescence in the 1990s: Risk and opportunity* (pp. 1–7). New York: Teachers College Press.

Thiessen, D., & Cook-Sather, A. (Eds.). (2007). *International handbook of student experience in elementary and secondary school*. Dordrecht, the Netherlands: Springer.

Thorkildsen, T. A. (1994). Toward a fair community of scholars: Moral education as the negotiation of classroom practices. *Journal of Moral Education, 23*, 371–385.

Turley, S. (1994, April). *"The way teachers teach is, like, totally whacked": The student voice on classroom practice*. Paper presented at the Annual Meeting of the American Educational Research Association, New Orleans, LA.

Villarruel, F. A., & Lerner, R. M. (Eds.). (1994). *Promoting community-based programs for socialization and learning*. San Francisco: Jossey-Bass.

Wasley, P., Hampel, R. L., & Clark, R. W. (1997). *Kids and school reform*. San Francisco: Jossey-Bass.

Whitehead, J., & Clough, N. (2004). Pupils, the forgotten partners in education action zones. *Journal of Education Policy, 19*, 215–227.

Wilson, B. L., & Corbett, H. D. (1999). *"No excuses": The eighth grade year in six Philadelphia middle schools*. Philadelphia: Philadelphia Education Fund.

Wood, A. (2007, April). *Evidence-based practice: Prospects and problems*. Paper presented at the Annual Meeting of the American Education Research Association, Chicago.

Yonezawa, S., & Jones, M. (2007). Using students' voices to inform and evaluate secondary school reform. In D. Thiessen & A. Cook-Sather (Eds.), *International handbook of student experience in elementary and secondary school* (pp. 681–710). Dordrecht, The Netherlands: Springer.

Zeldin, S. (2004). Youth as agents of adult and community development: Mapping the processes and outcomes of youth engaged in organizational governance. *Applied Developmental Science, 8*, 75–90.

Zeldin, S., Camino, L., Calvert, M., & Ivey, D. (2002). *Youth-adult partnerships and positive youth development: Some lessons learned from research and practice in Wisconsin.* Madison: University of Wisconsin.

Zeldin, S., Camino, L., & Mook, C. (2005). The adoption of innovation in youth organizations: Creating the conditions for youth-adult partnerships. *Journal of Community Psychology, 33,* 121–135.

64

Looking Forward

Toward a New Role in Promoting Educational Equity
for Students with Disabilities from Low-Income Backgrounds

THOMAS HEHIR
Harvard University

Many education reformers decry the relative lack of change in the American education system (see, e.g., Elmore, 2004). Since the issuance of *A Nation at Risk* (National Commission on Excellence in Education, 1983), local districts, states, and the federal government have tried a number of reform initiatives, from radical decentralization reflected in the school management movement of the late 1980s and 1990s, to the current federalized model represented by NCLB. Yet, there is relatively little data showing that these attempts have resulted in widespread improvement.

An exception to this pessimistic assessment of the potential for government-initiated reform can be found in the case of the Individuals with Disabilities Education Act (IDEA). Though not all students with disabilities are being successfully educated, significant progress has been made. The implementation of this act over its 30-year history supports the thesis that a significant federal reform initiative can influence widespread improvement in the education system. Consider the following: the practice of institutionalization of students with mental retardation and severe physical disabilities has been largely eliminated, record numbers of students with disabilities are enrolling in postsecondary institutions, employment rates of people with disabilities leaving high school approach that of their non-disabled peers, and more students with significant disabilities are being educated in increasingly inclusive settings (U.S. Department of Education, 2004; Wagner, Newman, Cameto, & Levine, 2005).

One could argue that these successes are simply due to nation-wide efforts to extend educational opportunity to a previously excluded group. However, more recent data indicates that students with disabilities are continuing to experience improved outcomes at an accelerating rate long after the initial implementation of IDEA. Evidence from the first and second National Longitudinal Transition Study have shown the effectiveness of IDEA in changing educational practice, as well as the limits of IDEA for students from low-income schools and districts. Using research-based standards for best practices, the paper will argue for changes in litigation and advocacy to promote equity for all students with disabilities.

IDEA and Educational Practice for Students with Disabilities

In the mid-1980s, the federal government initiated a major longitudinal study to determine the status of students with disabilities in high school and to ascertain their attainment levels after school. Known as the National Longitudinal Transition Study (NLTS), this study of a nationally representative sample of students with disabilities gave us an accurate glimpse of what was happening for disabled students in high schools in 1987, as well as how they fared 3 and 5 years after that, also including students who graduated from high school. This study at best presented a mixed picture.

NLTS documented that disabled students were dropping out at high rates approximately double that of their non-disabled peers, and dropping out was associated with other negative outcomes such as unemployment, trouble with the law, and early pregnancies to unwed youth (Wagner, 1991; Wagner, Blackorby, Cameto, & Newman, 1993). Of particular concern were outcomes for students with emotional disturbances, of whom 59% dropped out of high school (Wagner, D'Amico, Marder, Newman, & Blackorby, 1992). Of that number, 37% had been arrested within 2 years of dropping out; 5 years after dropping out, 56% had been arrested at some point (Wagner et al., 1992). The NLTS study also documented that large numbers of students with disabilities were not enrolled in challenging classes at the high school level and that failure rates were very high among these students. In addition, a substantial number of regular education teachers had not been trained to meet the needs of disabled students in their classes (Wagner, 1991; Wagner et al., 1992).

Though the study documented results that were less than satisfying, it did identify a subpopulation who appeared to be doing well, as well as practices that were associated with improved outcomes, including greater levels of integration, avoiding course failure, more access to challenging curricula, greater access to vocational education, and greater level of parental involvement (Wagner et al., 1993). One cannot assume direct causal relationships between these variables and improved outcomes, but these practices were supported by strong evidence in this large-scale longitudinal study.

Further, the study heavily influenced the 1997 reauthorization proposal submitted by the Clinton Administration that ultimately became IDEA 97. Especially notable changes in the reauthorization included requirements that students gain access to the curriculum, that states take action to reduce drop-outs, and that special education support greater integration of disabled students into general education classrooms.

The NLTS study was reproduced again in 2000, with outcome data published in 2003. In their report on NLTS-2 findings, students with disabilities had demonstrated large improvements in educational attainment levels (Wagner et al., 2005). These improvements included:

- The school completion rate of youth with disabilities increased 17 percentage points, with 70% of the 2003 second cohort youth with disabilities completing high school.
- The dropout rate decreased by 17 percentage points between 1987 and 2003, down to 30%. Youth with emotional disturbance demonstrated a substantial improvement (16 percentage points) in their school completion rate.
- The rate of postsecondary education participation by youth with disabilities more than doubled over time, with 32% of the cohort 2 youth enrolling in a 2- or 4-year college or postsecondary school within 2 years of graduation.
- In 2003, 70% of youth with disabilities who had been out of school up to 2 years had worked for pay at some time since leaving high school; 55% had done so in 1987.

In addition to these improvements, NLTS-2 documented that many of the practices associated with improved outcomes, such as integration and taking challenging academic subjects, were more widespread in the second study (Wagner, Newman, Cameto, Levine, & Marder, 2003):

- Students' schools had a range of resources to meet students' needs.
- Students accessed a diversity of courses.
- Students typically were instructed in multiple settings.
- Within the classroom, instruction for students with disabilities typically mirrored instruction for the class as a whole, though curricular content might differ for students with disabilities.

- The vast majority (60%) of general education teachers received some support and resources for students with disabilities in their classes.
- Most accommodations in the classroom did not require modification to instructional practices.
- Most factors used in student evaluation were the same for all students in class.

Again, it is important to note that one cannot infer causation from this type of study and that individual children might not benefit from practices that had a group effect. For instance, compared with other students with disabilities, a child with mental retardation might not benefit from advanced curricula such as foreign language instruction. Further, it should be noted that diagnostic and assessment criteria resulted in some significant changes between the studies—for example, in NLTS-2 more children were being classified as having attention deficits and autism (Wagner, Cameto, & Newman, 2003). However, even with these caveats in mind, it should be noted that students from most disability groups showed major attainment gains (Wagner et al., 2005). This evidence would thus support the argument that reform is possible and that the federal law may have plausibly played a role.

Standards to Improve the Equity and Effectiveness of IDEA

However, a deeper look at the data, comparing NLTS-1 with NLTS-2, might give some reason for pause. Most of the gains experienced by students with disabilities are due to improvements in outcomes of children from middle- and upper-income homes. The outcomes of students with disabilities from low-income homes are largely flat. For example, researchers from NLTS-2 (Wagner et al., 2005) also found that:

- Youth from households in the lowest income group did not have a significant improvement in postsecondary education participation, continuing the gap between income groups that existed in NLTS-1's cohort.
- Youth from the lowest-income households did not share with their highest-income peers an increase in having been employed at some time since leaving high school, so that they lagged significantly behind that group on that measure, as well as on their rate of current employment.
- Only White youth with disabilities experienced a significant increase in postsecondary education enrollment overall, and in the pursuit of both employment and postsecondary education since high school.

Two logical questions arise from this data. First, what caused the rather large improvements in attainment levels for students with disabilities from middle-income and upper-income homes? Second, why did students from low-income families not enjoy the same improvements?

Neither of these questions is fully answerable with current data, as the attribution of causal connections is undoubtedly complex and diverse. There is likely a sea of variables that influence these results. For instance, blind students showed significant gains in employment; this is likely due to mix of improved educational opportunity, employment market changes brought about through the digital revolution that make employment of blind people more accessible, and the passage of the Americans with Disabilities Act (ADA), which may have decreased employment discrimination and other unidentified variables.

However, it also is likely that improved educational opportunity is at least partially responsible for improved life outcomes. Regarding the question of whether educational practice for students with disabilities has changed between the periods of both studies, NLTS-2 provides extensive data in this area. For many children with disabilities the answer is yes—educational practice in classrooms and schools has changed considerably (Wagner et al., 2005). These changes in practice include more children being educated in more integrated environments and enrolled in challenging academic subjects. More students benefited from earlier intervention (another factor associated with improved outcomes). Finally, more children had general education teachers who had training and resources to meet the needs of disabled students.

All of these factors appear to be happening to a lesser degree with low-income students. For instance, integration into general education classrooms is associated with greater attainment levels in both NLTS studies. Yet in big urban districts where large numbers of low-income students are clustered, a great number of these students are still being served in segregated settings. Examples include Los Angeles, New York City, San Diego, and Washington, DC (Hehir et al., 2005; Hehir & Mosqueda, 2007).

For example, within its district, Los Angeles continues to operate a large number of separate schools for students with disabilities (Hehir et al., 2005). New York City has a separate subdistrict that operates separate schools, as well as totally self-contained programs within general education schools (Hehir et al., 2005). Even in San Diego, where the district has done a good job in educating higher numbers of students within regular school buildings, only 90 students with mental retardation out of 796 are served predominantly in a general education setting, many of whom are from middle-class backgrounds, integrated only after parents have used the due process system (Hehir & Mosqueda, 2007).

It is important to note here that although integration is generally associated with improved outcomes, the effect varies by disability group (Wagner, Blackorby, Cameto, & Newman, 1993). Students with disabilities are a highly diverse group with widely varying needs. Further, poorly implemented inclusion in which students fail might be associated with higher levels of dropping out of school (Wagner, 1991). In addition, some of the practices associated with inclusive programs are not validated by research (Fuchs, Fuchs, & Bahr, 1990). The main point here is that

a factor associated with better outcomes for most students with disabilities is less apt to happen for poor children in some districts and that federal policy and implementation matter.

Another factor associated with better outcomes is earlier intervention for students experiencing significant problems with reading or behavior in the primary grades (Lyon et al., 2001). Again, districts with large numbers of low-income students appear to come up short (Lyon et al., 2001). There is also strong research evidence supporting children having access to challenging curriculum and teachers who are trained to meet their needs (Wagner et al., 1993).

Concerning the question of low-income students and their relative lack of progress, a further logical inquiry would be why schools and educational practices are not changing for low-income students as they are for more affluent students. Again, this is a question that is not fully answerable with existing data. However, the phenomenon of relatively significant change in educational practice experienced by middle-income and upper-income students is an anomaly in the public education system and therefore worthy of study. One factor may be financial resources.

This author (Thomas Hehir) was involved in an evaluative study done in conjunction with a school finance case in Massachusetts (*Hancock v. Driscoll*), which examined the degree to which districts with poor tax revenues, both urban and rural, implemented strategies associated with better outcomes for students with disabilities (Hehir, Gruner, Karger, & Katzman, 2003). Evaluators were asked to determine if students with disabilities were given access to appropriate educational options and, if not, whether inadequate financial resources were partly responsible for the breakdown. This study provided interesting findings concerning the disparities in educational opportunities available to students in poorer districts in the era of standards-based education. Further, the methodology used in the study is potentially useful to advocates and interveners who may be interested in promoting reform in districts with large numbers of low-income students.

This research asked whether students were receiving access to the curricula standards and making sufficient progress toward the attainment of such standards. The central research question was what would be expected to happen within these schools if children with disabilities were receiving effective education based on the best available research. The following three factors were used to determine whether a discrepancy existed:

1. Children who demonstrated potential problems with reading and/or behavior were identified and supported at an early age, prior to referral for special education services.
2. The process for special education referral was appropriate, culturally-sensitive, timely, and efficient.
3. Students with disabilities were educated in the least restrictive environment and have access to the general curriculum.

These three standards parallel the three stages of the special education process and therefore have a basis in law—namely, the three stages of pre-referral, referral, and the provision of services—and the consequence of these three stages—student outcomes. These three standards of effective education are intimately linked, and the report argues that an effective framework for evaluation should not only look at evidence of effectiveness for each standard, but should also look for how each standard connects with and builds upon the others.

Pre-Referral The first standard used in this study was to determine if children who demonstrated potential problems with reading and/or behavior were provided support in the primary grades, prior to referral for special education services. Pre-referral, the first stage of the special education process, has generally been viewed as a method of helping to prevent the misidentification of students with disabilities and reduce the number of inappropriate referrals (Chalfant & Pysh, 1989; Fuchs, Fuchs, & Bahr, 1990; Garcia & Ortiz, 1988; Graden, Casey, & Bonstrom, 1985). In contrast, the study's authors used the above standard of best practice, which embodied a functional definition of pre-referral focusing specifically on reading and behavior—two areas identified in the literature as important for helping all children to succeed in school (see, e.g., Eber, Sugai, Smith, & Scott, 2002; Lyon et al., 2001).

The emphasis on reading was based on important findings in the literature. First, more than half of all students who are identified for special education services are classified as having a learning disability (LD) (Vaughn & Fuchs, 2003). Of these students, approximately 80% of children with LD have problems with reading (Lyon et al., 2001). Moreover, students who do not acquire basic reading skills by the third grade do not catch up to their peers in later grades, encountering difficulty when they must read to learn, instead of simply learning to read (Lyon et al., 2001). Consequently, in order to meet the above standard of best practice, it is important for school districts to provide support in reading at an early age for all children who demonstrate potential problems in reading (Lyon et al., 2001; National Institute of Child Health and Human Development, 2000; Torgesen, 2002; Vaughn & Fuchs, 2003). School districts should also target resources toward interventions at the pre-Kindergarten level (National Institute of Child Health and Human Development, 2000; Yaden et al., 2000). This standard has been reinforced in the 2004 reauthorization of IDEA which has sought to encourage the use of Response to Intervention (RTI) practices in general education classes, prior to referral of students to special education (for details on RTI, see Haager, Snow, Vaughn, & Klingner, 2007).

Research also shows that children are often not identified as having a serious emotional disorder (SED) until the middle to late elementary years (Duncan, Forness, & Hartsough, 1995). Moreover, delays in identification and interventions can result in exacerbation of emotional and/ or behavioral problems whereas effective, early behavioral interventions can be instrumental in mitigating subsequent problems and is associated with lower attainment levels (Forness, Serna, Nielson, Lambros, Hale, & Kavale, 2000). School districts thus need well-qualified personnel who are able to develop children's social and emotional skills and address behavioral problems that develop prior to referral. In particular, the literature documents the effectiveness of comprehensive, school-wide behavior supports (Horner, Sugai, & Horner, 2000; Lewis, Sugai, & Colvin, 1998; Scott, 2001; Sprague, Walker, Golly, White, Myers, & Shannon, 2001).

Referral The second standard used in this evaluation is that once a child is referred to special education, it must be appropriate, culturally-sensitive, timely, and efficient. The effectiveness of a school district's referral process is intimately connected to the pre-referral process. If pre-referral is successful, then most students with disabilities will be identified by the third or fourth grade and will be appropriately referred to special education. In order to meet the above standard of best practice, the evaluators must also examine whether school district possesses a sufficient number of well-qualified personnel to conduct diagnostic evaluations. These included school psychologists, special education teachers, and speech/language therapists. Additionally, in order for school districts to carry out evaluations that are culturally sensitive, districts need competent bilingual evaluators (Figueroa, 2002).

The Provision of Services The next standard used in this evaluation concerns whether students with disabilities are educated in the least restrictive environments and whether they have access to the general curriculum. This third standard of best practice corresponds to the provision of services and follows directly from the referral process. While current federal and state evaluations of compliance with IDEA examine a variety of areas pertaining to services for students with disabilities, this standard focuses on two specific aspects of the provision of services that have been identified in the literature as important components for ensuring that students with disabilities achieve high outcomes: (1) education in the least restrictive environment; and (2) access to the general education curriculum.

In order for students with disabilities to attain proficiency on statewide assessments, it is important for them to receive meaningful access to the curriculum on which the exam is based. Research has shown that, in the past, the IEP goals of students with disabilities were often not connected to the general curriculum or assessments (Brauen, O'Reilly, & Moore, 1994; Giangreco, Dennis, Edelman, & Cloninger, 1994). In order to meet the above standard of best practice, one specific question was whether districts provided professional development opportunities to regular education teachers to develop the skills to provide appropriate accommodations in the classroom that do not water down the curriculum (Sands, Kozleski, & French, 2000).

In the study for *Hancock v. Driscoll* by Hehir et al. (2003), findings showed that in four low-income districts, practices were not consistent with the standards for best practice upon which the evaluation was based. Though there was some variability, data showed that in general, the low-income districts were not providing adequate support for children who demonstrated problems with reading or behavior in the early grades.

Concerning the issue of least restrictive education (LRE) and access, data showed that students in low-income districts were far more likely to be placed in more restrictive educational settings than their counterparts in more affluent districts. For instance, one low-income district educated only 24% of its students with disabilities in regular classes, 54% of its students with disabilities in resource rooms, and 11% of its students with disabilities in separate classrooms. Compared to a national average of 48% of students being educated in regular classrooms for most of the day (U.S. Department of Education, 2004), this data paints a picture of a system that is segregating its students with disabilities to a considerable degree.

The study for *Hancock* was informative because it helped explain why some of the disparity existed between high-income and low-income districts. Interviews revealed that although leadership personnel knew they should be intervening with children who demonstrated problems with reading or behavior, they did not have sufficient resources to do so. For example, the special education director in one district explained that the district did not provide robust literacy instruction in general education; rather, special education provided most of the literacy remediation. She hypothesized that fewer students would be referred for special education services if the district provided these services. The one low-income district that did provide rather systematic early intervention for students experiencing reading difficulties did so primarily through various grant resources. The entrepreneurial leaders of this district expressed concerns that these efforts could not continue if they were not able to bring in these funds.

With regard to LRE, we found that leaders and staff in districts wanted very much to practice inclusion to the greatest degree possible, but felt they did not have the resources to do it in a way that would be effective. For example, inclusion requires a collaborative relationship between special education and general education teachers that allows students with disabilities to receive both access to the general education curriculum and individualized support. In one district, schools were greatly understaffed. As a result, the most efficient way to serve students with disabilities was to educate them for most of the day in a resource room. When students went into the regular classroom, they rarely had support from a special education teacher. In addition, there was no money to provide professional development for regular education teachers on how to provide appropriate accommodations/modifications and access to the general education curriculum.

For those schools that were able to educate students with disabilities for most of the day in a regular classroom, they were forced to "cluster" all the students with disabilities in one class, because of their limited staff. As one principal explained,

> Ideally ... you want to divide them evenly in classes, but we have to cluster them together in order to use our limited special education staff efficiently. But then is that really [inclusion]? It's not really following the letter of their IEP. But we do the best we can. We compromise. (Anonymous special education director, cited in Hehir et al., 2003)

For most of the schools in this particular district, clustering wasn't even an option. Without adequate support from special education teachers, students with disabilities could not effectively access the general education curriculum in a regular education class.

Furthermore, nearly all of the students with emotional disabilities in this district were placed in self-contained classrooms. The needs of these students require staff with specialized expertise, of which there was an extreme shortage. In the four low-income districts, there was an average of 1 psychologist to 230 students, compared to a 1 to 95 psychologist/student ratio in the high-income districts. The ability to provide high-quality services to this population of students was therefore heavily compromised in the low-income districts, in turn leading to even greater difficulty in providing services in the least restrictive environment. Not surprisingly, the low-income districts spent considerably less per child in special education (see Table 64.1).

The picture that emerged from this study in Massachusetts is that the education of children with disabilities in low-income districts departed significantly from practices that would increase the students' likelihood of passing high-stakes state standard's test (Massachusetts Comprehensive Assessment System). In Massachusetts and many

TABLE 64.1

Per Pupil Expenditures for Regular Education and Special Education, by District: 2001

	Regular education	Special education
Hancock districts (low income)		
Brockton	$6,699	$12,989
Lowell	$6,503	$13,324
Springfield	$5,541	$13,662
Winchendon	$4,265	$9,638
Hancock average	$5,752	$12,403
Comparison districts (high income)		
Brookline	$7,873	$15,254
Concord-Carlisle*	$7,621	$19,246
Wellesley	$7,357	$13,456
Comparison average	$7,617	$15,985

Note: Because the high schools for Concord and Carlisle are combined, all data for Concord-Carlisle represent an aggregation of data from Concord K-8, Carlisle K-8, and Concord-Carlisle Regional High School.

Source: Massachusetts Department of Education

other states, this means that large numbers of students with disabilities will be denied diplomas. The good news is that in the high-income communities where fidelity to best practices was rather high, virtually all non-cognitively disabled students with disabilities pass these tests.

The judge in the *Hancock* case, Margot Bosford, found in favor of the plaintiffs, but her decision was later overturned by the state Supreme Court. Although the plaintiffs were unsuccessful in this case, the importance of the study is that it reinforces and supports those who contend that low-income districts' lack of financial resources may ultimately have a negative influence on student test results, and that using evaluation techniques similar to those used in this study can yield actionable findings either by advocacy attorneys or government regulators.

The Influence of Due Process

Though lack of financial resources might partially explain some of the lack of progress experienced by low-income students, in Massachusetts many low-income students do not attend districts with low financial resources. One plausible factor that may partially explain the beneficial change in practice experienced by these Massachusetts students may be the activation of the due process protections under IDEA. Research on the implementation of due process has shown that school administrators are quite attentive to parents who file, or even threaten to file for due process hearings. Directors often change programs in order to avoid these contentious, and often expensive, adversarial proceedings. Changes sought by a relatively few parents can thus impact programs serving many more (Hehir, 1990).

Some due process hearings ultimately move through the courts and provide significant legal precedence that can have a far-reaching impact. Consider the case of inclusive education. In the mid-1980s, some parents of significantly disabled children began to use the due process proceedings to promote more integration of their daughters and sons. Some school districts worked with parents and began integrating students with significant disabilities, while others opposed these efforts. As these cases began to make their way through the federal court system, the courts began to create precedence upon which later cases were built. *Daniel RR v San Antonio* was the first to provide workable tests. Though Daniel RR's parents' desire for full integration was not supported, the court developed a two-prong test that laid the foundation for future inclusion cases: (1) Can education in the regular classroom be provided with the use of supplementary supports and services? (2) If removal is necessary, is the child participating in non-academic and extra-curricular activities with nondisabled students (Hehir & Gamm, 1999)?

A few years later, parents obtained a significant victory with the *Oberti* decision, in which the court supported the integration of a student named Rafael with mental retardation and behavioral issues into a regular class. The court required the school district provide supplementary support

services in general to lessen the disruption that Rafael might cause. The court also required that curriculum be modified to meet Rafael's needs. Further, the court was persuaded by the parent's expert evidence that given the right services and training, other school districts had successfully integrated similar students like Rafael (see Hehir & Gamm, 1999, for further discussion).

Finally, the Supreme Court failed to grant cert in the *Holland v Sacramento* case, allowing the lower court ruling to stand that required integration of a child with moderate cognitive disability (Hehir & Gamm, 1999). In a relatively short time, the inclusion of students with more significant cognitive disabilities was affirmed by the courts. This undoubtedly had a significant impact throughout the country. Given this precedent, it is likely that special education directors were more apt to acquiesce to parents seeking these types of placements. What some may have considered radical in the mid-1980s became much more widespread by the late 1990s.

The expansion of inclusive education for students with significant cognitive disabilities supports my belief that change can occur through legalized mechanisms. I would also argue that some of the change that occurred for more affluent students, as documented in the NLTS studies, was probably supported by school districts being more attentive to parents as means of avoiding due process. It should be noted that many of the improved educational opportunities enjoyed by more affluent students were those that were supported in the original NLTS study, including earlier intervention, more integration, and access to more challenging curricula. It should also be noted that these changes took place at a time when state and federal laws were changing, requiring students to be included in accountability measures.

Improving Equity for Low-Income Families

So, why is the legal mechanism of due process not working as well for low-income students? First, the vast majority of parents who use this mechanism are middle and upper class (Hehir, 1990). This is probably due to both the potential expense entailed as well as the social capital necessary to challenge the authority of district administrators. Further, there is evidence that in some large cities where due process use is high (e.g., New York City and Washington, DC), the types of disputes going to hearings disproportionately involve parents seeking out-of-district placements for their children (Hehir, Blackman Jones Report, prepared for the plaintiff in *Blackman Jones* case). In Los Angeles, it appears that administrative policy changes implemented by the administration may have resulted in a rapid increase in due process hearings (Independent Monitor's Report, *Chanda Smith*). One could argue that in these districts the impact of due processes is not leading to systemic reforms as they have done in the inclusion cases, but may instead be diverting attention and resources away from fundamental reforms associated with improved results.

Another avenue employed by advocates to promote reform, class action litigation, has had mixed results. Though it appears that these litigations have brought some districts into higher levels of procedural compliance, reforming educational practice through this mechanism in large systems seems mixed at best. (It should be noted here that I have extensive experience in over a half a dozen of these cases as a defendant, consultant, and mediator.) For instance, *Blackman Jones* in Washington, DC, has failed to yield demonstrable reform in practice within the district, and New York City continued to run a segregated subdistrict many years after *Jose P.*

Strategies for Advocates

For advocates from low-income districts, the question that now arises is whether the due process mechanisms in IDEA and class action litigation can be used to promote the reform of educational practice. I believe they can and recommend the following five strategies for advocates.

Know the Research First, advocates need to know the practices most associated with better educational results and promote their use. The good news is that we know far more about what those practices are than we did when many of the class action litigations were filed. Special education research knowledge and practice has advanced enormously over the last 20 years. It is important that advocates know what these are and promote their use wherever possible. Though there might be pressure to "get kids out of the system" and into private schools, advocates should be aware that such action is unlikely to improve integration for the masses of students served within the system. Attorneys should thus work with knowledgeable practitioners and seek smart strategies designed to have a systemic impact.

Provide Free Representation to Low-Income Parents The due process mechanisms are powerful and, as the inclusion cases have demonstrated, they can have an enormous influence over educational practice. Some might argue that funding to enable poor parents to effectively use due process might, in some places, simply result in more children being placed in private schools. However, the use of due process by more advantaged parents is much more complex than that. Many parents use the threat of hearings to secure greater integration for their children with disabilities, and many of those cases never proceed to hearing because districts settle given the LRE imperative in IDEA law (Hehir, 1990). It is undoubtedly that threat that accounts for some of the movement of middle and upper income students to more inclusive settings between the two NLTS studies.

Though this proposal might sound utopian in the current political climate, there is a practical way it could be accomplished even in part: fund Protection & Advocacy Centers to selectively provide representation to parents within the centers' current legislative mandate. These centers, currently funded under the Developmental Disability Act, serve individuals with significant disabilities and their families, and their legislative mandate is to prevent institutionalization and to promote integration. Funding these centers to provide representation would thus increase pressure on districts to provide more effective integration for students with significant disabilities.

The California Protection and Advocacy Center has implemented a model of how this might be implemented. Currently, the center funds a skilled educator who works mostly with low-income parents seeking more inclusion for their children within the Los Angeles Unified School District. This educator has worked with scores of parents over the years and has helped promote more inclusive practice within the district.

Promote More Strategic Litigation Focused Systemically on Changing Practice Though it is my opinion that class action litigation has on the whole had a positive impact for students with disabilities, the primary impact has been in assuring implementation of IDEA's procedural elements. Though this is important in that children with disabilities need to be identified and receive services, the overall impact of these litigations on district instructional practice can be questioned (Hehir et al., 2005). For instance, a number of districts that have been under consent decrees for years, including Boston, New York, and Washington, DC, continue to segregate large numbers of students with disabilities at rates that are far above national averages (Hehir et al., 2003; Hehir et al., 2005; Hehir & Mosqueda, 2007).

Litigation's focus on procedural compliance is understandable, in that IDEA is a law of individual entitlement with prescribed procedural elements. These procedural elements lend themselves to oversight and enforcement (e.g., whether the child had their evaluation conducted on time or not, whether the child received a service or not). However, it is far more difficult to evaluate whether a child has received a free appropriate public education (FAPE) in the least restrictive environment (LRE). Though these are legal requirements, both contain an element of regulatory vagueness that is difficult to assess. Further, a district would likely claim that simply because they have large numbers of students in separate environments it does not mean that they are violating LRE for individual students.

Though both FAPE and LRE are relatively vague, they are central to IDEA and should be viewed as the main entitlements of the law, designed to confer benefits on children. As the research has shown, integration is associated with better outcomes for students with disabilities, and FAPE, ultimately, should ensure that the impact of a students' disability is minimized through the provision of special education services and access to general education with individualized disability accommodations.

It should be noted, however, that though these are vague concepts, class action litigations have been successful in finding districts and states in non-compliance with these elements either through court action (e.g., *Corey H et al. v Chicago Public Schools*) or through negotiated settlements (e.g., *Chanda Smith v Los Angeles Unified School District*). Of the two requirements, it may be easier to establish non-compliance with LRE, given the tests developed in the inclusion cases. A litigant could apply these tests to groups of students in districts and establish that these thresholds were not met, therefore establishing a class as was done in *Corey H.*

Regarding the issue of FAPE, past litigations such as *Jose P.* have focused on the provision of special education services. However, the issue of access to curriculum, an essential element of FAPE since IDEA 1997, has not been a main focus of these class actions. The focus on special education service delivery in these districts may well have inadvertently removed many students from accessing general education. For instance, in 2005 when I was conducting an assessment of the reorganization of special education in New York City for the plaintiffs and the district in the *Jose P.* case, I observed meetings between the parties in which the primary concern was how rapidly students were being placed in special education programs. Most of these special education programs were segregated. At the same time the plaintiffs were pushing for faster placements, the district was promulgating a policy concerning the new "small high school" initiative that largely excluded students with disabilities from enrollment. In my view, the plaintiffs were missing a major opportunity to promote integration and equity.

To increase the likelihood of districts implementing practices that will improve outcomes, class action litigation must focus more closely on educational practices and move away from their current emphasis on procedural compliance through "top down" bureaucratic intervention. They need to promote changes in educational practice at the school level where children are educated. This is admittedly difficult to do because each school is an organization that is semi-autonomous. However, the fact that schools are individual organizations may explain some of the failure of traditional bureaucratic interventions.

Moving class action litigation is possible and has been happening in several sectors, such as mental health facilities, prisons, and housing, as well as education with some initial promising results (Sabel & Simon, 2004). Two promising cases, *Chanda Smith v Los Angeles Unified School District* and *Corey H et al. v Chicago Public Schools*, have explicitly sought to change the traditional approach. There are several principles that have arisen out of both these cases that should be helpful to those seeking to promote substantive changes of educational practices for low-income students with disabilities.

Promote Data-Based Agreements   Though not all aspects of education are easily quantifiable, many are. The degree of integration a child receives, the relative participation of parents at IEP meetings, whether a child is educated in their neighborhood "home" school, the number of days children are suspended, the over-placement of students of color in special education, graduation rates, and the performance of children on statewide accountability measures are all important measurable outcomes related to IDEA compliance and educational reforms likely to benefit children and families.

These types of measures can be used in class action suits or governmental oversight to promote systemic reform. However, many traditional class action litigations have not sufficiently focused on measurable outcomes associated with educational reform. *Jose P.* is an example of a long-standing class action suit for which it is difficult to identify measurable outcomes. Concerning the work I conducted assessing the impact of the New York Chancellor's reorganization on special education in 2004, it was very hard to find measurable data that could document progress in implementing the IDEA within New York City. The agreement is not structured that way, nor were there data systems capable of answering basic questions concerning IDEA implementation. One observed meeting between the parties took on a vitriolic air, as the parties argued whether children were getting the services on their IEPs. This resulted in a costly audit, which verified that neither party was totally correct in their assessment. This class action suit is over 25 years old.

In my view, a more effective intervention would involve carefully selected measures, upon which data systems could be build that would generate valid information to the parties. If this were the case, the district could intervene when and where problems arise, and the plaintiffs would have transparent measures upon which to hold the district accountable. More importantly, such an approach would be likely to lead to substantive improvement for children and families.

Such an approach has been employed in the *Chanda Smith* case in Los Angeles. This suit originally evolved as a traditional top-down bureaucratic case that required hundreds of actions costing the district millions of dollars. The district sought to have this consent agreement modified by the federal court, due to their view that the agreement was too burdensome with little demonstrable benefit. The judge in the case refused to modify the agreement because of the unilateral action of the district without the involvement of the plaintiffs, but he did express his view that the agreement as written would never be resolved. Judge Lew stated, "The way I see it structured now, what I fear most is that there may be a never-ending conclusion to the case, and that is not right…. But there is certainly an inherent problem with how this case is structured before this court" (Proceedings, U.S. Central District Court of California, Sept 24, 2001, for *Chandra Smith* case). When the district appealed to the circuit court, they upheld the lower court but also encouraged mediation. The plaintiffs agreed to mediate a new agreement, and this author was appointed as a mediator.

The ultimate agreement reached in 2003 was based on 18 verifiable outcomes, the accomplishment of which would result in the termination of the lawsuit. The outcomes represented some traditional compliance such as timely completion of IEP meeting to student outcome measures such as graduation rate and performance on statewide assessments. The agreement established a small independent monitor's office whose primary responsibility is to verify accuracy of data and to approve a plan designed by the district to bring about compliance.

Though this district has not fully come into compliance with the agreement, measurable progress has been made. For instance, the number of students suspended more than six days has dropped from 828 in 2003–2004 to 489 in 2006–2007. The number of students with low incidence disabilities (disabilities other than speech and language or learning disabilities) placed 40% or more of their day in general education has gone from 5,687 to 9,778 during the same period. Other areas where major improvements have occurred include: timely completion of evaluations, parental participation, response to parental complaints, and translation of IEPs (Weintraub, Alleman, & Hernandez, 2007). Though data is not available at this time concerning test results and graduation rates, some progress, though slow, is happening there as well.

The early but important lesson from the *Chanda Smith* case is that progress can be made under this model. The establishment of a monitor's office charged with assuring the accuracy of data can free the parties to focus on remedies as opposed to endless disputes over data accuracy. It should be noted that recently the office uncovered major inaccuracies with the district's reporting of architectural accessibility renovations of schools. This transparency allowed the district to focus on holding contractors accountable and was reassuring to the plaintiffs that accessibility renovations would occur.

However, improving student outcomes is likely to require significantly more effort and attention. It is the hope of this author that, as the district comes into compliance with many of the more procedural aspects of IDEA, it will be free to focus its energies on improving educational practice and that the litigation will serve to assure that it will take place.

Focus Intervention As the *Chanda Smith* case is demonstrating, improving real educational opportunity and outcomes for disabled students from low-income backgrounds will require major change in practice and will not occur rapidly. Though it may be tempting for advocates to structure agreements that are comprehensive and seek many changes simultaneously, large school systems do not change that fast. Further, the organizational change literature generally acknowledges that reforms that actually impact how people in organizations do their work (in this case, teachers and administrators) require strong focus and capacity building (Elmore, 2004; Hess, 1998). Thus, in the Los Angeles case, the independent monitor is now requiring the district to develop interventions that focus on low performing schools, while also including major staff development activities (Weintraub, Alleman, Ramanathan, & Hernandez, 2006).

Another case that is relevant here is *Corey H et al. v*

Chicago Public Schools. In this case, the primary issue at hand was the failure of both Chicago and the State of Illinois to provide students' education in the least restrictive environment. The remedy in this case has involved capacity building at the school level largely funded by the State of Illinois, with over $19 million in financial support. Individual schools in Chicago have since shown impressive gains (Soltman & Moore, 2002).

Involve States The *Corey H.* suit is also notable in that the State of Illinois is joined as a defendant. As the *Hancock* case demonstrates, many districts that have large numbers of low-income students with disabilities also have significant fiscal restraints. In *Corey H.*, the state was required to provide significant funds to support reform. (It is important to emphasize here that IDEA is a state grant program and that major responsibility for its implementation resides at the state level.) From the perspective of this author, it is unfortunate that the State of California was never joined in *Chanda Smith* and that the cost of litigation rests solely on the city of Los Angeles. States should be joined in these cases. It important for all parties involved in these suits to remember that the primary statutory responsibility for the implementation of IDEA rests with the states. The strong state monitoring role envisioned in NCLB adds further importance to the state role. States therefore should always be parties. This takes on even greater importance given the states' role in funding education generally. That funding may be an issue that undergirds the lack of educational opportunity experienced by many low-income students with disabilities.

Though there is much promise in well-structured class action suits to promote change, most districts will never have such action brought against them. It is therefore important for advocates to first and foremost seek ways for states to play a greater role in enforcement and reform. States can structure interventions with school districts that incorporate many of the elements discussed above. Further, states can bring significant and diverse resources to the table, from state universities to discretionary grants. Fortunately the IDEA amendments of 2004 support a more assertive role on the part of states in enforcing IDEA.

Conclusion

Compelling data suggests that IDEA has influenced widespread research-based improvement in educational practice for students with disabilities. Despite positive effects for students and teachers, it is clear that youth from low-income backgrounds are not showing the same academic, postsecondary education, and employment gains as students from middle-income and upper-income households. One likely reason for this may be the failure of school districts that serve these students to implement practices associated with better outcomes for students with disabilities. One factor that is likely affecting this failure is lack of funding. Another factor may be the relative lack of access to due process hearings of low-income parents which is a means of change in schools.

Those interested in improving educational opportunity for low-income students with disabilities have brought lawsuits against a number of large school systems in the United States. Though I believe these have promoted some reforms, their influence, at times, may have promoted greater segregation of disabled students and may not have been as effective as they may otherwise have been. Lessons from some more recent actions show the promise that these interventions may hold for future reform if interveners concentrate more closely on focused, data-based, reforms in educational practices associated with improving results. Further, a greater involvement of states is needed to increase the likelihood that the promise of IDEA will be achieved for all students.

References

Brauen, M., O'Reilly, F., & Moore, M. (1994). *Issues and options in outcomes-based accountability for students with disabilities.* College Park, MD: Center for Policy Options in Special Education, University of Maryland.

Chalfant, J., & Pysh, M. (1989). Teacher assistance teams: Five descriptive studies on 96 teams. *Remedial & Special Education, 10,* 49–58.

Chanda Smith et al. v. Los Angeles Unified School District et al., USDC Central District of California, CV 93-7044 LEW (GHKx 1996).

Corey H et al. v. Board of Education of the City of Chicago, et al., 995 F. Supp. 900 (N.D. Ill. 1998).

Duncan, B., Forness, S. R., & Hartsough, C. (1995). Students identified as seriously emotionally disturbed in day treatment: Cognitive, psychiatric, and special education characteristics. *Behavioral Disorders, 20,* 238–252.

Eber, L., Sugai, G., Smith, C. R., & Scott, T. M. (2002). Wraparound and positive behavioral interventions and supports in the schools. *Journal of Emotional and Behavioral Disorders, 10*(3), 171–181.

Elmore, R. F. (2004). School *reform from the inside out: Policy, practice, and performance.* Cambridge, MA: Harvard Education Press.

Figueroa, R. (2002). Toward a new model of assessment. In A. Artiles & A. Ortiz (Eds.) *English language learners with special needs: Identification, assessment and instruction* (pp. 51–63). McHenry, IL: Delta Systems.

Forness, S. R., Serna, L. A., Nielson, E., Lambros, K., Hale, M. J., & Kavale, K. A. (2000). A model for early detection and primary prevention of emotional or behavioral disorders. *Education and Treatment of Children, 23*(3), 325–346.

Fuchs, D., Fuchs, L. S., & Bahr, M. W. (1990). Mainstream assistance teams: A scientific basis for the art of consultation. *Exceptional Children, 57,* 128–139.

Garcia, S. B., & Ortiz, A. A. (1988, June). Preventing inappropriate referral of language minority students to special education. *New Focus: National Clearinghouse for Bilingual Education, 5,* 1–12.

Giangreco, M., Dennis, R., Edelman, S., & Cloninger, C. (1994). Dressing your IEPs for the general education climate: Analysis of IEP goals and objectives for students with multiple disabilities. *Remedial and Special Education, 15*(3), 288–296.

Graden, J. L., Casey, A., & Bonstrom, O. (1985). Implementing a pre-referral intervention system: Part II. The data. *Exceptional Children, 51,* 487–496.

Haager, D., Snow, C., Vaughn, S., & Klingner, J. (Eds.). (2007). *Evidence-based reading practices for response to intervention.* Baltimore, MD: Paul H. Brookes.

Hancock v. Driscoll, 443 Mass. 428 (2005).

Hehir, T. (1990). Conclusions. In *The impact of due process on the programmatic decisions of special education directors* (chapter 9).

Unpublished doctoral dissertation, Harvard Graduate School of Education, Cambridge, MA.

Hehir, T., Figueroa, R., Gamm, S., Katzman, L. I., Gruner, A., Karger, J., & Hernandez, J. (2005). *Comprehensive management review and evaluation of special education* (Report submitted to the New York City Department of Education). Retrieved July 21, 2007, from http://schools.nyc.gov/Administration/mediarelations/PressReleases/2005-2006/09232005.htm

Hehir, T., & Gamm, S. (1999). Special education: From legalism to collaboration. In J. Heubert (Ed.), *Law and school reform* (pp. 205–227). New Haven, CT: Yale University Press.

Hehir, T., Gruner, A., Karger, J., & Katzman, L. (2003, June). *Hancock v. Driscoll: Special Education assessment.* Unpublished report.

Hehir, T., & Mosqueda, E. (2007). San *Diego Unified School District Special Education document.* Boston, MA: Thomas Hehir & Associates.

Hess, F. M. (1998). Spinning *wheels: The politics of urban school reform.* Washington, DC: Brookings.

Horner, R. H., Sugai, G., & Horner, H. F. (2000, February). A school wide approach to student discipline. *School Administrator,* 20–24.

Jose P. et al. v. Richard P. Mills, et al., 669 F.2d 865 (1982).

Lewis, T., Sugai, G., & Colvin, G. (1998). Reducing problem behavior through a school-wide system of effective behavioral support: Investigation of a school-wide social skills training program and contextual intervention. *School Psychology Review, 27,* 446–460.

Lyon, G. R., Fletcher, J. M., Shaywitz, S. E., Shaywitz, B. E., Torgesen, J. K., Wood, F. B., Shulte, A., & Olson, R. (2001). Rethinking learning disabilities. In C. E. Finn, A. J. Rotherham, & C. R. Hokanson (Eds.), *Rethinking special education for a new century* (pp. 259–288). Washington, DC: Thomas B. Fordham Foundation and the Progressive Policy Institute.

Mikeisha Blackman et al. v. District of Columbia, et al., 454 F. Supp. 2d 1 (D.D.C. 2006).

National Commission on Excellence in Education. (1983). A *nation at risk: The imperative for educational reform.* Washington, DC: U.S. Government Printing Office.

National Institute of Child Health and Human Development. (2000). Report *of the National Reading Panel. Teaching children to read: An evidence-based assessment of the scientific research literature on reading and its implications for reading instruction* (NIH Publication No. 00-4769). Washington, DC: U.S. Government Printing Office.

Oberti v. Board of Education, 995 F.2d 1204 (3d Cir. 1993).

Sabel, C. F., & Simon, W. H. (2004). Destabilization rights: How public law litigation succeeds. *Harvard Law Review, 117,* 1016–1101.

Sacramento City School Dist. v. Rachel H., 14 F.3d 1398 (9th Cir. 1994).

Soltman, S. W., & Moore, D. R. (2002). Ending segregation of Chicago's students with disabilities: Implications of the *Corey H.* lawsuit. In D. J. Losen & G. Orfield (Eds.), *Racial inequity in special education* (pp. 239–271). Cambridge, MA: Harvard Education Press.

Sands, D. J., Kozleski, E. G., & French, N. (2000). *Inclusive education for the 21st century: A new introduction to special education.* Belmont, CA: Wadsworth.

Scott, T. M. (2001). A school-wide example of positive behavioral support. *Journal of Positive Behavior Interventions, 3,* 88–94.

Sprague, J., Walker, H., Golly, A., White, K., Myers, D. R., & Shannon, T. (2001). Translating research into effective practice: The effects of a universal staff and student intervention on indicators of discipline and school safety. *Education and Treatment of Children, 24,* 495–511.

Torgesen, J. K. (2002). The prevention of reading difficulties. *Journal of School Psychology, 40*(1), 7–27.

U.S. Department of Education. (2004). *Twenty-sixth annual report to Congress on the implementation of the Individuals with Disabilities Education Act, 2004: Volume 1.* Washington, DC: U.S. Government Printing Office.

Vaughn, S., & Fuchs, L. (2003) Redefining learning disabilities as inadequate response to instruction: The promise and potential problems. *Learning Disabilities Research and Practice, 18*(3), 137–146.

Wagner, M. (1991). Dropouts *with disabilities: What do we know? What can we do? A report from the National Longitudinal Transition Study of Special Education Students.* Menlo Park, CA: SRI International.

Wagner, M., Blackorby, J., Cameto, R., & Newman, L. (1993). *What makes a difference? Influences on postschool outcomes of youth with disabilities: the third comprehensive report from the National Longitudinal Transition Study.* Menlo Park, CA: SRI International. (ERIC Document Reproduction Service No. ED 365 O85)

Wagner, M., Cameto, R., & Newman, L. (2003). *Youth with disabilities: A changing population. A report of findings from the National Longitudinal Transition Study (NLTS) and the National Longitudinal Transition Study-2 (NLTS-2).* Menlo Park, CA: SRI International.

Wagner, M., D'Amico, R., Marder, C., Newman, L., & Blackorby, J. (1992). *What happens next? Trends in postschool outcomes of youth with disabilities: the second comprehensive report from the National Longitudinal Transition Study of Special Education Students.* Menlo Park, CA: SRI International (ERIC Document Reproduction Service No. 356 603)

Wagner, M., Newman, L., Cameto, R., & Levine, P. (2005). *Changes over time in the early postschool outcomes of youth with disabilities. A report of findings from the National Longitudinal Transition Study (NLTS) and the National Longitudinal Transition Study-2 (NLTS-2).* Menlo Park, CA: SRI International.

Wagner, M., Newman, L., Cameto, R., Levine, P., & Marder, C. (2003). *Going to School: Instructional Contexts, Programs, and Participation of Secondary School Students with Disabilities. A Report from the National Longitudinal Transition Study-2 (NLTS-2).* Menlo Park, CA: SRI International. Retrieved August 2006 from http://www.NLTS-2.org/reports/2003_12/NLTS-2_report_2003_12_complete.pdf

Weintraub, F. J., Alleman, J. R., Ramanathan, A., & Hernandez, J. E. (2006, July 7). *Report on the progress and effectiveness of the Los Angeles Unified School district's implementation of the modified consent decree during the 2005–2006 school years—part I.* Los Angeles, CA: Office of the Independent Monitor, Modified Consent Decree. Retrieved October 20, 2007, from http://dse-web.lausd.k12.ca.us/sepg2s/mcd/im_report0706_part1.pdf

Weintraub, F. J., Alleman, J. R., & Hernandez, J. E. (2007, September 28). *Report on the progress and effectiveness of the Los Angeles Unified School district's implementation of the modified consent decree during the 2006–2007 school year—part I.* Los Angeles: Office of the Independent Monitor, Modified Consent Decree. Retrieved November 20, 2008, from http://oimla.com/pdf/annrep4_docs/200607ConsentDecree_Report1_Final.pdf

Yaden, D. B., Tam, A., Madrigal, P., Brassell, D., Massa, J., Altamirano, L. S., & Armendanz, J. (2000). Center for the Improvement of Early Reading Achievement. Early literacy for inner-city children: The effects of reading and writing interventions in English and Spanish during the preschool years. *Reading Teacher, 54*(2), 186–190.

65

COMMENTARY
Research on Actors and Institutions Involved in Education Policy

Themes, Tensions, and Topics to Explore

MARTHA MCCARTHY
Indiana University

The eight chapters addressing research on actors and institutions involved in education policy are substantive, enlightening, and diverse in their approaches as well as in the content covered. The authors contributing to this section of the handbook illuminate the range of policy actors and institutions, from students to federal policy makers to international organizations, who play important roles in determining educational practices. The chapter authors also explore various strategies to study the actors and institutions involved in education policy development and implementation.

Some of the chapters (e.g., McDermott's on the expansion of state education policy research) emphasize the types of research conducted and the theoretical and methodological underpinnings of the research. Others give greater attention to the findings from studies or to the current status of regulatory activity (e.g., Lugg & Rorrer's on homeschooling policies). Still others place more emphasis on exploring the evolution of the involvement of specific actors (e.g., Cohen-Vogel & McLendon's on the federal role in education policy). But despite their differences in approach and substance, the chapters in this section contain some commonalities, which are the primary focus here.

My intent is not to critique these excellent chapters or even to provide a summary of their major points. Any attempt to summarize the comprehensive chapters would be woefully inadequate and certainly would take more than the limited space I have been allocated. Instead, I will discuss some themes and tensions that emerge in this section, weaving points from the eight chapters into the discussion, rather than commenting on each chapter independently. The concluding section of my commentary highlights three topics that deserve additional attention in connection with research on education policy actors and institutions.

Selected Themes

Some topics are addressed in more than one chapter in this section, and several themes appear across most of the eight chapters. Given the rich content of these chapters, additional themes surely could be identified beyond the seven highlighted below.

Political Dimension of Education Policies and Policy Research It goes without saying that education policies are established in a political context, and the authors in this section emphasize how essential it is to understand the political dynamics involved in policy development and implementation. For example, it cannot be doubted that *A Nation at Risk*, distributed by the U.S. Department of Education in 1983, had a huge impact on state education agendas. Recent partisan debates over the future of the federal No Child Left Behind (NCLB) Act also vividly illustrate the impact of politics on education policies.

In exploring theoretical models of federal involvement in education, Cohen-Vogel and McLendon address the significance of political considerations in education reform efforts. They cite various perspectives including McGuinn's (2006) argument that major education reforms result from the interaction of shifts in "ideas, interests, and institutions in a policy area … with changes in the broader political context over time" (p. 209). Other chapters in this section explore from different vantage points the political aspects of school improvement initiatives.

Authors of several chapters also contend that additional thought should be given to the political use of education policy research in decisions related to politics in the broad sense, which McDermott defines as "the process by which a society decides what goals it values and how to allocate resources toward those goals" (p. 759). Cohen-Vogel and McLendon conclude that insufficient progress has been made in responding to Sroufe's (1995) concern about the "abandonment of politics in favor of policy studies" (p. 87) and his plea for researchers to recombine policy and politics to assist in explaining and predicting why certain policies exist and what stimulates policy changes. Chapters in this section reinforce that education policies cannot be adequately studied separate from their political dimensions.

Importance of Partnerships Among Policy Actors Several authors in this section mention that partnerships are significant in ensuring the implementation of effective educational policies. About half of these chapters note that partnerships among different levels of government, research and development laboratories and centers, institutions of higher education, private foundations, and/or other organizations interested in education are key in bringing about meaningful education reform—far more effective than efforts by single actors or institutions. And the importance of partnerships is not limited to formal arrangements among designated policy actors. For example, in the chapter on student voice and student roles in education policy, Mitra recognizes the importance of youth-adult partnerships where both parties learn from each other and contribute to making decisions and promoting change.

The focus on partnerships across these chapters extends beyond policy development and implementation. In their chapter on the local school district's role in instructional improvement, Sykes, O'Day, and Ford urge the formation of partnerships between internal and external researchers in conducting education policy research. As discussed below, other authors in this section also champion broader collaboration in policy research activities. These chapters underline that promising strategies for various actors and organizations to work effectively together to develop, implement, and study education policies are worthy of additional exploration.

Centrality of Standards-based Reforms and Student Test Data A theme evident in the discussion of various education policy actors is the shift in education policy emphasis beyond addressing the needs of special populations to adopting universal accountability mandates. As Mintrom notes in the chapter on local democracy in education, standards-based reforms and accountability systems tied to student test scores dominate education policies currently. Cohen-Vogel and McLendon review research on NCLB, which exemplifies this policy shift to standards-based accountability, and they mention that there is even discussion about adopting a national standardized testing program and performance requirements. Although Sykes, O'Day, and Ford argue that accountability and systemwide learning should be equally emphasized, they recognize that accountability is the central policy concern today. Several authors in this section advocate for more studies on the implementation of NCLB, its impact on policy coherence within school districts, and

whether recent accountability mandates improve the quality of teaching and learning.

Globalization of Education Policy The chapter by Mundy and Ghali specifically focuses on international and transnational education policy actors and institutions, but several other chapters in this section acknowledge that the education policy environment is now a global one, which substantially changes policy interactions and outcomes and even alters who the policy actors are. The ease of Internet communication has revolutionized international collaboration and the potential to learn from others around the globe. Also, several authors discuss the worldwide impact of international initiatives, such as the United Nations Convention on the Rights of the Child, adopted by the United Nations in 1989 and subsequently ratified by all nations except for Somalia and the United States. Regardless of one's position on the merits of globalization, the international impact of education policies cannot be denied.

Increase in Advocacy Research and Influence Across several of the chapters in this section, the authors recognize the increase in research conducted by advocacy groups seeking to promote particular positions. Think tanks and other advocacy groups often devote substantial energy to press relations, and their research reports receive considerable media attention, which may disproportionately influence the direction of education policies. Lugg and Rorrer recognize the impact of homeschooling advocacy groups even though much that the groups report continues to be based on conjecture instead of empirical studies. The mounting volume of research conducted by those advocating positions makes it imperative to have stringent mechanisms in place to assess the merits of education policy research. If the mission and orientation of a given advocacy group are downplayed in media accounts of a specific research report, this can lead to misplaced reliance on the group's findings.

Also, there is some sentiment that the prevalence of advocacy research makes it more difficult to produce neutral research and to raise funds for objective investigations. With charitable foundations becoming increasingly strategic in their agendas, data on foundations' influence on the nature of education policy research would be instructive. In the chapter on the expansion of state policy, McDermott urges analysts to conduct "more research on state policymaking, including how research interacts with policy advocacy" (p. 759). As noted previously, several other chapters in this section also acknowledge that additional attention should be given to the political use of education policy research.

Desirability of Using Multiple Approaches to Study Education Policy Actors and Institutions Chapters in this section also encourage researchers to broaden their approaches in investigating policy issues, and most contend that research on policy actors and institutions should have stronger theoretical grounding. The authors across the eight chapters note that much of the research currently available entails case studies, which are limited in nature, and they urge an expansion of the types of studies and who conducts them. Also, they assert that the research should employ more comprehensive mixed methods approaches.

Sykes, O'Day, and Ford contend that research needs to be broadly conceptualized to include development activities, and they advocate more practice-based inquiry. Cohen-Vogel and McLendon encourage researchers to design deep longitudinal case studies of federal initiatives using synthetic frameworks that explain education policies in the context of political phenomena. Mitra notes that although it is difficult to include students as researchers, instead of viewing them only as subjects of research, it is not impossible to do. A similar statement can be made regarding teachers being involved in conducting action research.

Importance of Using Credible Data

The authors across several chapters in this section note the need for greater use of reliable data in education decision making. In connection with services for children with disabilities, Hehir advocates building data systems that would generate valid information on measurable outcomes to document progress in implementing the Individuals with Disabilities Education Act. The federal government has provided incentives for school personnel to use data and to base decisions on research, but quality assessments of the data are not assured. While a few of the authors highlight the need to evaluate the merits of the data used, this important topic deserves even greater attention. If educational policy makers and practitioners are basing decisions on faulty data, it may facilitate them moving more quickly in the wrong direction.

Several chapters discuss the difficulties researchers face in gaining access to appropriate data to use in policy research. McDermott notes that a major challenge is presented by the variations in the quality of data collected across states that hamper cross-state comparisons. To solve some of the data problems, Cohen-Vogel and McLendon advocate the creation of new databases of legislative and executive education policy activity (e.g., bills, laws, regulations) that can be used in studying the impact of policy decisions.

Selected Tensions

In addition to themes evident in this section, tensions can be identified that relate to these themes and affect the actors and institutions involved in education policy. A few of the more prominent tensions are highlighted below.

Immediate Results versus Long-Term Goals

Across education policy actors, a long-standing tension exists between achieving immediate results and creating a vision for the future, and this tension certainly is portrayed in the chapters in this section. In several of the chapters, the authors specifically mention the tension between accountability policies demanding improvements in student performance *now* and education policies addressing long-term aspirations by putting structures and processes in place to affect outcomes in the future. Policy makers often want results to be produced in a short time frame—one that typically coincides with their election cycles. But education professionals counter that with realistic education goals, it may take far longer for the envisioned results to be realized. Some authors in this section call for additional research on current federal and state education policy initiatives, including the merits of their timelines and proficiency standards.

Equity Goals versus Standards-Based Reforms

Several authors of chapters in this section acknowledge the tension between advancing equity for previously disadvantaged student groups and imposing standards-based accountability for all students. As mentioned, the shift in federal policy from promoting equity for certain students to fixing what is wrong with the entire educational system through standards and high-stakes assessments has created tensions that often are played out among policy actors at the state and local levels.

Particularly controversial is the implementation of student testing policies. High-stakes testing programs have polarized policy makers and often pitted education professionals against policy makers in debates over the long-term effects on equity goals of the current emphasis on student test results (see Amrein & Berliner, 2002). McDermott's review of research on this topic reveals meager evidence of a positive correlation between the use of high-stakes tests and improvements in student achievement. Mitra further notes that under NCLB and related state accountability mandates, test results overshadow other forms of student outcome data that should be considered. Regardless of one's position on the merits of high-stakes testing, the tension this topic has created across policy actors is likely to remain for some time.

Government versus Nongovernment Actors in Education

Several chapters explore the involvement of nongovernment actors in influencing education policy and the tensions this phenomenon creates. These private actors range from parents to businesses to international organizations. Cohen-Vogel and McLendon acknowledge the current federal emphasis on increasing private participation in education decisions and the increasing influence of business coalitions. Also, Mundy and Ghali, in their chapter on international and transnational policy actors in education, recognize the increase in nongovernment policy actors and organizations that are influencing global education policy. Not only may interests of private parties and the government differ, but also the private entities may not agree among themselves.

Mintrom describes the tension between government interests and parental interests in connection with school choice policies. Lugg and Rorrer also recognize that parents and the state may have very different views regarding the best way to educate specific children and whether individual enhancement or the common good should guide education policy deliberations. Decisions made by parents in exercising choice in educational matters for their children may or may not coincide with governmental priorities in ensuring an enlightened electorate in a democratic society. Policies that facilitate parental discretion in determining their children's education allow parents to select educational settings with philosophies that reinforce their own beliefs. But such policies that enhance homogeneity within schools may exacerbate segregation based on class and race and increase fiscal inequities across schools.

Related to private actors' increased involvement in developing education policies is the movement toward privatization of education in the United States through companies managing public schools or contracting to provide remediation and enrichment services. For example, Mintrom addresses charter schools, a number of which are run by private companies. Edison Schools (2008) served 285,000 students in charter and other public schools during the 2006–07 school year. Tension is apparent between those who contend that opening education to competition of the marketplace will improve all schools, public and private (see Chubb & Moe, 1990), and those who are concerned that when private companies are involved the interests of children become secondary to meeting contractual agreements and earning profits (see Giroux, 2003).

Local Control versus the Advancement of National Education Goals
Similar to the tension between private and government interests, the tension between local control and the advancement of national goals in education permeates a number of important policy deliberations and is mentioned in connection with several policy actors in this section. Sykes, O'Day, and Ford point out that historically the school district has been considered the primary vehicle to maintain local control of public schools. Such local control traditionally has been highly valued in the United States.

As Mintrom describes, a widely publicized conflict between a national priority and sentiments in some locales pertains to school desegregation. While there is a national goal to end racial segregation and achieve social justice in our public schools, the majoritarian sentiment in some local communities favors policies that would maintain segregation and inequities across schools serving primarily different races. This tension has not been resolved even though segregation by law was struck down in our nation more than 50 years ago (*Brown v. Board of Education,* 1954).

Also, volatile conflicts have ensued over the national commitment to keep religion separate from the government and the desire in some communities to infuse sectarian beliefs in the public school program. Efforts to incorporate the dominant faith in public schools range from graduation prayers to instruction in the biblical account of creation, and church/state controversies show no signs of dissipating (Thomas, Cambron-McCabe, & McCarthy, 2009).

Another example of this tension over local control versus national goals involves the disparities across school districts in funding public education. In some property-wealthy school districts, citizens want education taxes raised lo-cally to be used to support local schools despite the large fiscal inequities across school districts that are created by reliance on property taxes to fund education. The national commitment to ensure that all students have access to an adequate public education is difficult to reconcile with local control of school funding.

Tensions across Levels and Branches of Government
Distinctive features of the U.S. system of government are the separation of powers among the legislative, judicial, and executive branches of government, and the parallel governments at the local, state, and federal levels. A tension alluded to in some chapters entails the interactions and conflicts across the levels and branches of government. With the volume of recent education policy activity at all levels, several authors acknowledge that intergovernmental relationships are extremely complex. McDermott points out that the increase in state influence in education policy over time has been particularly significant, with the most pronounced expansion in state activism occurring in the 1980s and 1990s. Mintrom cautions that with the increase in state as well as federal governmental involvement in setting education policies and determining what happens in schools, the voices of parents and other interested citizens may be lost.

Regarding tensions across *levels* of government, state and federal interests at times differ. States have been known to adopt policies that conflict with those of the federal government, such as policies governing religious influences in public schools, instruction pertaining to sex education, programs for English language learners, and many other issues. In addition, McDermott notes that some recent tension has involved the interaction between NCLB and states' previously developed accountability systems. Sykes, O'Day, and Ford remind us that there are also tensions between local schools and their school districts regarding where the focus of current reform efforts should be, especially the school district's role in getting individual schools to implement standards-based reforms. They also contend that a major challenge is for school districts to develop instructional coherence, given the conflicting policy signals districts are receiving from state and federal government.

Legislative bodies and administrative agencies generate much of the tension across levels of government, but tension is also apparent between state and federal courts. The Supreme Court may find no U.S. constitutional violation in a given practice, but state courts may conclude that a particular practice abridges state constitutional provisions. Illustrative are legal developments in the school finance arena, a topic treated extensively by McDermott in addressing the expansion of state policy research. After the U.S. Supreme Court ruled that education is not a fundamental right under the federal Constitution and rejected a challenge to the inequities in the Texas school funding scheme (*San Antonio Independent School District v. Rodriguez,* 1973), school finance litigation shifted to state courts. Since the *Rodriguez* decision was rendered, there have been challenges to school funding systems in 45 states with somewhat mixed results (see Sergiovanni, Kelleher, McCarthy, & Fowler, 2009).

The Supreme Court has emphasized that simply because a practice satisfies the U.S. Constitution does not mean that it will survive judicial scrutiny under the respective state constitution. For example, the Supreme Court has upheld states' authority to impose more stringent antiestablishment provisions in connection with religious influences in public schools and state aid to sectarian schools than required by the First Amendment to the U.S. Constitution (see *Locke v. Davey*, 2004).

Tensions are evident not only across the local, state, and federal levels of government but also among the three *branches* of government within each level. The executive branch may adopt implementation regulations that at times conflict with the intent of legislation; in short, some regulations promulgated do not reflect what the legislative bodies were attempting to achieve. Also, the courts may interpret legislative acts in ways not intended by the drafters of the provisions. Of course, legislatures can correct such judicial or administrative misunderstandings by amending the specific laws, unless the Supreme Court rules that a law abridges the U.S. Constitution.

Topics to Explore

In addition to the themes and tensions identified across these chapters, a few topics deserve greater consideration in addressing research on education policy actors and institutions. Three of these topics are addressed briefly below.

Impact of the Digital Age on Policy Actors and Institutions One topic that was not given much attention across these chapters is research on the ongoing technological advances that have revolutionized communication among policy actors, influenced who the actors are, and even changed our concept of "school" through virtual learning environments. And new technologies have dramatically increased the ability to process and customize information. As noted in the discussion of globalization, the potential for policy actors to collaborate and learn from others internationally has been greatly enhanced by technological advances. The discussions in the education policy blogosphere, for example, may significantly expand citizen interactions with policy analysts and broaden participation in education policy deliberations.

Not only is more research needed on how technology is influencing who is making education policy decisions and what those decisions are, but also analysts need to explore the remarkable recent changes in how individuals receive and share information. Indeed, the technological environment in which current students are being socialized is totally different from the environment only a few decades ago. Students and others are simply a click away from information on almost any topic, but assessing the validity and reliability of Internet material remains a major problem. Education policy has not yet caught up with the significant

implications of the digital age in terms of how, what, and where education takes place. Research pertaining to the impact of technological advances on education policy actors and institutions is in its infancy but nevertheless deserves more extensive treatment and should be prominent on the proposed agenda for future research.

Courts as Policy Actors n the 1970s the judiciary became more prominent in influencing education policies and practices. Courts became less likely to defer to policy makers, especially if constitutional rights were at stake. While the federal judiciary seems more conservative now than was true in the 1970s in terms of recognizing individual rights, it will not return to the judicial deference to the other branches of government that was prevalent in education cases prior to the mid-20th century.

Courts, of course, do not make laws as legislative bodies do. Yet, they greatly influence the nature of education policies through their interpretive powers. Courts may find certain laws unconstitutional, such as statutes calling for daily Bible reading in public schools (*School District v. Schempp*, 1963). Kagan (2004) has asserted that the most fundamental judicial policymaking in our nation comes from the courts' "authority to hold legislative statutes and executive branch decisions and actions unconstitutional" (p. 21).

The judiciary also can have a noteworthy impact in interpreting what laws mean, and at times its interpretations may go beyond legislative intent. To illustrate, the Supreme Court interpreted Title VII of the Civil Rights Act of 1964 as allowing employers to exclude pregnancy-related disabilities from disability benefits packages (*General Electric v. Gilbert*, 1976). This ruling motivated Congress to enact the Pregnancy Discrimination Act, clarifying that Title VII was intended to curtail discrimination based on an employee's pregnancy status.

A permissive judicial ruling generally stimulates legislative action. For example, after the Supreme Court found no violation of the U.S. Constitution in the use of corporal punishment in public schools (*Ingraham v. Wright*, 1977), legislation was adopted in more than half of the states barring this disciplinary technique. If the Court instead had invalidated the use of corporal punishment under the Constitution, the ruling would have reduced legislative discretion and created a national standard.

Two of the chapters in this section review some major court cases and their influence in specific areas (special education and home education policy), although they do not address the courts as policy actors more generally. Hehir discusses several court cases establishing criteria to judge whether the least restrictive environment is being provided for children with disabilities. He concludes that the expansion of inclusive education for students with cognitive disabilities supports the premise that legalized strategies can bring about change. Indeed, Hehir notes that school districts are responsive to parents who file or threaten to file lawsuits, so even the threat of litigation can influence educational policies and practices. Lugg and Rorrer also acknowledge the importance of Supreme Court decisions in providing the framework for parents to assert a right for their children to attend private schools or to be educated at home. They discuss the impact of Supreme Court decisions not only in recognizing parental rights to educate their children but also in clarifying the state's authority to compel children to be educated and to regulate education. But neither of these chapters go beyond their specific topics in exploring the significant interpretive function of the courts. Given the importance of judicial rulings, additional attention to the role of the courts in influencing education policies and practices seems appropriate.

Teachers as Policy Actors   This section should be applauded for including a chapter on students as policy actors, because as Mitra points out, students often are viewed as the problem to be addressed, rather than as policy actors in the education reform movement. However, it is somewhat surprising that the role of teachers was not given more attention across the eight chapters or perhaps covered in a separate chapter, similar to the treatment of students. A few authors, such as McDermott, note that classroom teachers ultimately determine how education policies are implemented, but this concept is not sufficiently explored in this section. Indeed, the technical core of education takes place in the classroom, and without teachers' active support, many education policies are simply words. For effective changes to occur, teachers must be key actors; teachers can derail policy decisions or give them meaning. Furthermore, teachers can be involved in conducting action policy research, and this resource has not been adequately tapped to date. The crucial role played by teachers in implementing policies and investigating their impact deserves additional study.

Conclusion

As noted in the introduction, these eight enlightening chapters reflect a range of methodological and substantive approaches. They enhance our understanding of the actors and institutions involved in developing and implementing education policy. Also, these chapters are instructive regarding the nature of research being conducted on education policy actors and institutions and the limits, as well as the promise, of such research. Moreover, the authors collectively present impressive suggestions for future investigations in this arena and provide a clarion call to broaden the research approaches and the individuals involved. The field will be enhanced by following up on these authors' excellent ideas for future research pertaining to education policy actors and institutions.

References

Amrein, A., & Berliner, D. (2002, March 28). High-stakes testing, uncertainty, and student learning. *Education Policy Analysis Archives, 10*(18). Retrieved October 10, 2006, from http://epaa.asu.edu/epaa/v10n18/

Brown v. Board of Education, 347 U.S. 483 (1954).

Chubb, J. E., & Moe, T. M. (1990). *Politics, markets and America's schools.* Washington, DC: Brookings Institution.

General Electric Co. v. Gilbert, 429 U.S. 125 (1976).

Giroux, H. A. (2003). *The abandoned generation: Democracy beyond the culture of fear.* New York: Palgrave Macmillan.

Ingraham v. Wright, 430 U.S. 651 (1977).

Kagan, R.A. (2004). American courts and the policy dialogue. In M. Miller and J. Barnes (Eds.), *Making policy, making law* (pp. 13-34). Washington, DC: Georgetown University Press.

Locke v. Davey, 540 U.S. 712 (2004).

McGuinn, P. J. (2006). *No Child Left Behind and the transformation of federal education policy, 1965–2005.* Lawrence: University Press of Kansas.

San Antonio Independent School District v. Rodriguez, 411 U.S. 1 (1973).

School District v. Schempp, 374 U.S. 203 (1963).

Sergiovanni, T., Kelleher, P., McCarthy, M., & Fowler, F. (2009). *Educational governance and administration* (6th ed.). Boston: Allyn and Bacon.

Sroufe, G. E. (1995). Politics of education at the federal level. In J. D. Scribner & D. H. Layton (Eds.), *The study of educational politics* (pp. 75–88). Washington, DC: Falmer.

Thomas, S., Cambron-McCabe, N., & McCarthy, M. (2009). *Public school law: Teachers' and students' rights* (6th ed.). Boston: Allyn and Bacon.

66

COMMENTARY
Nested Actors and Institutions

The Need for Better Theory, Data, and Methods to Inform Education Policy

MARK BERENDS
University of Notre Dame

The chapters in this section on actors and institutions are highly varied, as one might expect when thinking of the myriad actors that influence educational policy and politics. For instance, the chapters cover theories and frameworks to examine K–16 educational policies (Cohen-Vogel & McLendon), discussions of federal and state policy analysis (McDermott; Cohen-Vogel, & McLendon), links between education and local democracy (Mintrom), district policies and instructional improvement (Sykes, Ford, & O'Day), international and transnational actors in educational development and policy (Mundy & Ghali), students' voices in educational policy and reform (Mitra), homeschooling policies (Lugg & Rorrer), and the development of educational policies affecting students with disabilities (Hehir). Surely a varied lot of chapters, all merit a careful read to understand perspectives of educational policy and politics, the development of research and policy in these different areas, and suggested avenues for further research.

When considering actors and institutions in the arena of research on educational policy and politics, there are some important themes that emerge from the chapters. These themes include the importance of placing educational policy research within an historical context, the expanding role of federal and state governments in policy, the need for better theory, and the need for more theory-driven empirical studies.

Historical Context Regardless of the actor or topic addressed, each chapter carefully describes the history of the policy and its development. The authors effectively frame each of their topics within an historical context, by drawing upon a number of studies, and in many instances highlighting the key legal cases that shaped current policy. As Cohen-Vogel & McLendon argue, there is a need for approaches that place educational policy reform and politics within a

broader historical perspective, because prior "research in general looked narrowly at the federal government's role in education, focusing on individual events, players, or policies" (p. 745).

McDermott's chapter on "The Expansion of State Policy Research" focuses on the expansion of state policy research, emphasizing that states have stood at the center of the complex network of government agencies implementing federal laws, especially since the passage of the Elementary and Secondary Education Act of 1965. She is careful to outline much (although admittedly not all) of the research on state education policy that has evolved over time. This research base has investigated many topics including: how state governments work, educational equity and finance, diffusion of educational reforms, and inter-governmental relationships with states as mediators between federal and local governments.

Similarly, Mundy and Ghali in their chapter on "International and Transnational Policy Actors in Education" cover a rich history of the themes and agencies involved in educational development and reform from World War II to the present. During the first part of this time span, the authors note that although non-governmental transnational actors initially played a role, they were subsequently marginalized from policy decisions as governments expanded their role. In addition, Western governments came to view the expansion of education as critical for statehood and the stability of the international system, thus promoting the development of intergovernmental educational agencies. Finally, following World War II, the development of international and transnational organizations resulted in a more narrow view of education "toward a more limited, economic, and instrumental view of international cooperation" around education issues, even though many international education agencies held strongly the broader view of education as a human right (p. 721). Most recently, Mundy and Ghali point out that international and transnational policy actors have encouraged tighter linkages between education and the economy. In addition, the increasing number of international and transnational policy actors makes this area ripe for further research.

Although the other chapter authors also emphasize historical context as it relates to the specific policy actors and educational policies addressed within each chapter, the general point here is that the historical context of policy is fluid. A thorough understanding of the historical context within which policy actors intersect with policy development and implementation is critical to richer empirical analysis and the identification of policy actors worthy of focus in the complex educational policy arena.

Expanding Role of Policy Actors at the Federal and State Levels Another theme that emerges is the growing influence of actors at the federal and state levels. For example, in their chapter on "New Approaches to Understanding Federal Involvement in Education," Cohen-Vogel and McClendon begin by stating that the "influence of the federal government in education has never been greater" (p. 735). Most would agree with this claim as both K–12 policies and higher education policies have aimed to increase the accountability and productivity of students and teachers in K–16 institutions. No Child Left Behind has emphasized student performance on standardized tests, attendance and graduation rates, and the importance of having qualified teachers in classrooms as some of the indicators used to hold schools accountable. Similar policies of accountability for performance are being promoted for post-secondary institutions as well. Due to the expansion of federal influence in K–16 educational policies, Cohen-Vogel & McLendon argue that it is timely to pay closer attention to not only the effects of these policies, but to also be cognizant of the "political dynamics that shape their development and implementation" (p. 745).

Toward that end, their chapter discusses perspectives from political science—Kingdon's multiple streams approach, the punctuated equilibrium approach, and the policy regimes approach. All three of these perspectives are from the "synthetic school" of political science that aims to understand how the political system can either promote change or reinforce the status quo of educational policies. The authors argue that researchers need to build longitudinal databases of legislative and executive policy, develop rich longitudinal case studies of federal initiatives, and conduct both quantitative and qualitative studies that rely on the theoretical perspectives they highlight.

This chapter's section on actors and institutions effectively describes synthetic approaches that position federal reform efforts within a broad historical context to distinguish between reforms supported by the federal level, and those that are opposed by various actors. Another strength of this chapter is its explanation of how policy issues are defined to promote change or reinforce existing policy (inertia).

In addition to the expanding federal role in educational policy and the need to understand not only policy effects but the politics that inform the development, change, and status quo of policy, the role of states in educational policy continues to need further attention and research. In her chapter, McDermott covers the research related to how state governments work, educational equity and finance, diffusion of reform, and intergovernmental relations. Due to the expanding role of states, she identifies several areas in which further research is needed. For instance, she states that due to the fact that the increasing role of states will alter the historical context, the research she covers from an historical perspective may need modification.

Future Research on Actors and Institutions

The authors point to two areas in need of additional research. First, there is a need for better theory. Second, they point to the lack of data and analysis driven by theory in the area of research pertaining to educational policy actors.

Need for Better Theory As this collection of chapters reveals, it is an understatement to describe the arena of actors and institutions within education policy as complex. By focusing on international, transnational, federal, state, and local actors, the perspectives and analyses on different educational policy issues can get murky quite quickly.

Certainly, as the authors of these chapters point out, whether thinking about international agencies, federal and state governments, districts, schools, or the actors within schools (e.g., teachers, families, and students), more theoretical development is needed. When thinking about these layers of the educational system and the actors that play a key part within each, it may be helpful to revisit theoretical development through careful reflection on the interrelatedness of the system's components. For example, over 25 years ago, Barr and Dreeben (1983) emphasized looking at educational systems as "a set of nested hierarchical layers, each having a conditional and contributory relation to events and outcomes occurring at adjacent ones" (p. 7).

From this perspective, students and families are nested within schools, nested within districts, states, nation-states, and a global system of education. Within a nested-layers perspective, actors are situated hierarchically—each carrying out distinct activities, drawing upon specific resources, and engaging in politics, policy making, and policy implementation, all of which come into play in various ways depending on where actors are nested within the system. Theoretical development in this area of actors and institutions might benefit from the nested-layers perspective, which sheds light on the ways in which policies at different levels are coupled and uncoupled, how these couplings vary over time across different educational policies, and how politics in its many forms affects each of the levels nested within the system (e.g., states, districts, and schools).

Drawing on organizational theory, the Sykes et al. chapter on "The District Role in Instructional Improvement" provides a good example of how the nested-layers perspective may inform analysis of educational policy and politics and pave the way for further theoretical developments. For example, Sykes et al. describe learning communities as nested or embedded within the context of districts; that is, districts are actors who shape instructional improvement in schools and classrooms while they respond to federal and state authorities. Within this nested framework, Sykes and colleagues point out a key challenge—"to forge coherence out of the policy cacophony...such that schools and the educators within them can better learn how to continuously modify their practice to improve outcomes for students" (p. 773).

Such a perspective is helpful in thinking about the actors within and across levels of the educational system. It points to the possibilities created by an integration of viewpoints concerning the development of policy, by drawing on theories described by Cohen-Vogel and McClendon, such as multiple-streams (addressing existing policy solutions waiting for problems to arise), punctuated equilibrium (addressing the policy venues through which educational reformers circumvent exiting policy monopolies), and policy regimes (addressing the actors who are most relevant in the policy regime).

Moreover, a nested-layers perspective clarifies and adds definition to policy development, implementation, and effects at any one level. McDermott emphasizes that when looking at the various roles of states as actors, there is a need to better understand the variation in these effects (or to make sense of the policy cacophony, as Sykes and colleagues put it). McDermott notes that there is research addressing how districts shape instruction in classrooms and emphasizing how schools and teachers make sense of district level policies aimed at changing educational practice. Highlighting several examples, McDermott stresses the importance of "sense-making" when examining the relationships of actors within one nested level of the education system to actors in other levels. In addition, the chapter by Sykes et al. emphasizes the importance of "sense-making" as different actors respond to policies and pressures at many levels, suggesting that additional research and theory is needed to illuminate the functions of the many actors that comprise the layers of the education system. They state that whether actors such as districts "exert widespread and substantial influence on instruction is still an open question, particularly as theorists have specified organizational responses to institutional processes that range from acceptance to avoidance to defiance" (p. 772; see also Coburn, 2004; Spillane, 2005).

In addition, Mintrom's chapter on "Education and Local Democracy" suggests the importance of examining interrelationships among layers of the educational system. He specifically notes the complexity of democratic structures that influence educational policy decision making, the tensions that result when pursuing democratic processes at lower and higher levels of the education system; and four dilemmas that drive policy makers towards finding a balance. These dilemmas deal with (1) local democratic processes and improvement in student outcomes; (2) aspirations of the local community and the nation; (3) improvements in instructional goals in ways that are congruous with feasible instructional practices; and (4) external accountability requirements and internal accountability of schools as related to sound educational practice. Mintrom is optimistic about open enrollment programs, educational management organizations, charter schools and vouchers as means to help balance these tensions and thereby strengthen democratic politics. Although optimistic about choice and accountability, Mintrom is careful to point out that further research is necessary to examine effects of these institutional arrangements to improve educational policy aimed at providing the necessary balance of tensions so as to further democratic practices within educational systems. Attention to the balancing of these tensions would be advanced by attention to the actors within and across levels of the educational system.

Although not directly taking a nested-layers organizational perspective, some of the other chapters suggest the need to understand how educational policy affects different levels of the education system. For example, Hehir in his chapter on "Looking Forward: Toward a New Role in Promoting Educational Equity for Students with Disabilities from Low-Income Backgrounds" has a sanguine view of how policy shapes practice, highlighting the changes that have occurred in schools under the Individuals with Disabilities Education Act (IDEA). He summarizes his view by stating, "The implementation of this act over its thirty-year history supports the thesis that a significant federal reform initiative can influence widespread improvement in the education system" (p. 831). In his chapter, he highlights the historical development and effects of educational policy aimed at students with disabilities, focusing not only on the policies themselves, but the effects they have had on schools and classrooms. His chapter provides a good example of policy effects that can be observed across nested layers of the system. A promising avenue of future research would be to further articulate the key actors and interrelationships across levels, with particular attention to his finding that low-income students are not as positively affected by changes in educational policies aimed at students with disabilities when compared with students from middle- and upper-income families.

In addition, in their chapter on "The Politics of (Im) Prudent State-Level Homeschooling Policies," Lugg and Rorrer point out the limited research available on homeschoolers. Although a growing area of school choice, little is known about whether homeschooling has a positive impact on student outcomes, either academic or social. Lugg and Rorrer cover the history of homeschooling educational policies, the variation among state policies, and an agenda for future research. Although the authors do not take a nested-layers perspective, it might advance our understanding of homeschooling policies and their effects on students. For example, although Lugg and Rorrer document the variation in state homeschooling policies, we know little about how these affect students. As the authors also point out, there is wider variation in the homeschooling experiences of students, although the empirical base for such claims is thin. Within a nested-layers perspective, future research might advance this area by conducting research among homeschoolers in different states that link student learning and social experiences to variation in state laws. In addition, many homeschoolers are part of homeschooling networks, so further research could examine how homeschoolers are nested within homeschooling networks nested within different state regulatory contexts. Access to data is difficult, as Lugg and Rorrer point out, but this type of research agenda would yield important findings for research and policy.

Mitra in her chapter on "Student Voice and Student Roles in Educational Policy and Policy Reform" also points out that students, as key actors within the nested-layers perspective of the educational system, merit more attention. As she aptly observes, "Rather than students being viewed as actors with the school system, they are typically treated as part of the problem that needs to be fixed" (p. 819). She argues that researchers need to pay attention to students' voices and roles to understand how "youth have opportunities to share in the school decisions that will shape their lives and the lives of their peers" (p. 819). In particular, she points out that it is important to understand which voices are heard and which are not. Expanding research to include student perspectives on how they may shape policy and how educational policies shape their experiences in schools is critical to fully flesh out our understanding of the different actors within educational systems.

Need for Better Theory-Driven Data and Analysis Authors of these chapters articulate that a key challenge for both quantitative and qualitative researchers has been access to high quality data. They point to the growing number of data sources for improving qualitative data on educational policies and politics (e.g., Lexis-Nexis Congressional service, Policy Agendas Project, Library of Congress Thomas project, ProQuest Historical Newspapers digital archive, Advocacy and Public Policymaking Project, state data such as New York State Archives). Quantitative data from national databases (e.g., National Center of Education Statistics) and state data also provide rich data sources to examine the policy issues touched upon in these chapters. The integration of quantitative and qualitative databases holds great promise for future research.

Although there is an increase in the available data and technological advances to access and analyze data, the area of actors and institutions in educational policy is in need of theory-driven analyses that rely on state-of-the-art methods. For example, many of the authors in this section highlight the need for more specific hypothesis testing. Mintrom (p. 801) points out, "Formal hypothesis testing through quantitative research has been less common in this field," and Mundy and Ghali state, "The development of 'testable' hypotheses about patterns of international policy borrowing and the policy influence of international actors (as is quite

common in the field of political science), is uncommon" (p. 726). Even authors such as Lugg and Rorrer, who take a critical perspective emphasizing "who gets what, when, and how" (p. 806) and arguing that objective social science is "an embarrassingly elusive project" (p. 805), argue that there is a need for more rigorous empirical research to inform educational policy. And Cohen-Vogel and McLendon point out a critical challenge for researchers pursuing a research agenda that empirically tests theories is access to higher quality data, for the purpose of being able to apply more sophisticated quantitative and qualitative research methods. Although several have attempted to inform extant theory, it is often difficult to operationalize key concepts with existing data. Thus, future research should heed advice of these authors for building better databases; conducting deeper longitudinal case studies; and relying on state-of-the-art methods to operationalize, test, and inform theory in the area of educational actors and institutions.

Careful operationalization of key constructs within different nested levels and clear articulation of hypotheses relating these constructs would advance the field. For instance, several of the chapters address variation in educational policy across states and districts. Addressing key constructs that vary across state actors and examine the interrelationships of actors within the educational system (e.g., districts, schools, teachers, and students) would inform different theories, such as those described by Cohen-Vogel and McClendon or institutional theory, market theory, and social capital theory mentioned in several of the other chapters. Perhaps these theories are lacking in their explanatory power, but until we draw on existing data and create new databases by merging extant data and gathering new data, our constructs will lack operationalization, and our tests of theories will be disappointing.

What is needed is a better understanding, conceptualization, and definition of the actors within different nested layers, the consequences of their actions, and the direct and indirect effects on other actors within the system (e.g., how federal actors affect states, districts, schools, and students). Without more careful thought about the organizational actors (be they individuals or organizational units), we may be left in the short-term with a smattering of informative and useful studies (and many uninformative studies) and a lack of development of sound theory and research in the long term.

In summary, what is needed are theories that address the variation in policies at the federal, state, and local levels with clear direction about how to operationalize key concepts within empirical data. Only then can we begin to test hypotheses, either with quantitative or qualitative data, to better form our theories, refine our hypotheses, and clarify our understanding about how politics and policies interact to shape the experiences of different actors within the K–16 education system. As these chapters point out, there is clearly more work to do. The authors provide some helpful direction toward future research with their discussions of different actors within the education system, the extant research on those actors, and the need to better understand policy effects and the politics involved in shaping policy and its implementation. Yet, until better data and more rigorous methods are used to inform different theoretical perspectives on educational policy and politics, focusing on the different nested layers of educational system, researchers will have little chance of truly informing policy makers' decision making and improving educational policy. If that is the case, we will be hard pressed to overcome the Cohen (1998) observation that the more things change, the more they stay the same.

References

Barr, R., & Dreeben, R. (1983). *How schools work.* Chicago: University of Chicago Press.

Coburn, C. (2004). Beyond decoupling: Rethinking the relationship between the institutional environment and the classroom. *Sociology of Education, 77,* 211–244.

Cohen, D. (1998). Teaching practice: Plus que ça change. In P. Jackson (Ed.), *Contributions to educational change* (pp. 27–84). Berkeley, CA: McCutchan.

Spillane, J. P. (2005). *Standards deviation: How schools misunderstand education policy.* Cambridge, MA: Harvard University Press.

Section VII

Educational Access and Differentiation

Section Editor: Barbara Schneider

67

Policy and Place—Learning from Decentralized Reforms

BRUCE FULLER
University of California, Berkeley

Standardization, formulae, generalizations, principles, universals have their place, but the place is that of being instrumental to better approximation to what is unique and unrepeatable.
—John Dewey, 1938/1981, p. 97

This chapter asks, what are we learning about the social organization and effects of decentralized reforms? These initiatives, proliferating over the past quarter century, include vouchers and faith in private schools, charter schools, magnet and cross-town transfer efforts, neighborhood governance, and the spread of early education via mixed markets. In turn, the expanding field of policy research—focusing on how parental "choice" unfolds and the human-scale institutions that respond—remains quite young. Theoretical accounts abound, each alleging how decentralized action is *supposed* to energize parents, kids, and educators. The empirical haze is just beginning to lift when it comes to observing the social and economic mechanisms that actually kick in, under what local conditions, and benefiting which children and families.

After all, place is not supposed to matter under basic tenets of the modern regulatory state. The centralists instead sketch the school's problems in rather broad strokes. This invites policy remedies that are universally slathered on all schools.[1] Engineered learning outcomes and standardized ways of gauging knowledge are to raise the prospects of all children. Educators aren't working hard enough; so let's push the same curriculum package into every classroom. Test scores are flat; so why not monitor achievement trends and sanction schools from Washington, DC?

Policy researchers—at times resembling their political benefactors—often embrace universal fixes. We assume that a strong central state will serve, and redistribute resources to, children living on the outer edges of society. Being well trained in scientific mechanics and confident about hierarchical rules, we aim to rationalize and align the education

system. We like to identify "best practices" and sprinkle them like immutable apple seeds across the land.

This isn't a new role for policy thinkers. Emile Durkheim, that early R&D activist, helped to create and mold France's network of government schools in the 19th century. Run efficiently from Paris, this national system would cast a national consciousness and wipe out the messy *patois* spoken by backward villagers (Durkheim, 1956). Horace Mann returned from Prussia with a similar policy theory about how the Commonwealth must spawn "common schools." Cut from the same cloth and plopped down in any village, Mann's institution would deliver standardized knowledge and routinized pedagogy, hoping to construct a modern state of mind. The tribal boundaries of class, ethnicity, and religion would be erased—integrating the fledgling nation-state—through common schooling.

Still, few predicted how a feisty democracy like the United States—once so committed to de-centered republicanism—would come to mimic Europe's faith in nationalized schools. At first Washington focused surgically on equity, pushing local districts to desegregate their schools and beaming resources to poor students. Governors and state school chiefs by the mid-1970s were tugging at the reins as well, moving to meliorate sharp finance inequalities (sometimes shrinking the power of local boards to raise taxes). State governments were charged by Washington to implement myriad categorical aid programs, each accompanied by rules and compliance officers. The pursuit of civil rights and even liberal learning ironically came to be regulated from the political center.

Yet, the uneven payoff to escalating school spending came under scrutiny out in the states by the 1980s, not to mention inside the Reagan White House. Governors and legislatures had tired of trying to engineer optimal mixes of school inputs; now they became more intrigued with the (politically attractive) effort to regulate outputs. The school accountability script that emerged—animated by symbols of tough love and the focus on performance—was so compelling that a Texas Republican would join Democratic centralists to craft the No Child Left Behind (NCLB) Act in 2001.

The centralizing frame that now defines the school's problems—insufficient performance, not family poverty or resource disparities among schools—has proven seductive for policy researchers, not only for their political benefactors. Thus, the institutionally constrained truth now being spoken to power centers on things such as, how NCLB's moving parts are being implemented, or how well a wealthy foundation's silver-bullet is working, from small high schools to universal preschool. If politics is the art of the possible, policy research has become the art of the fundable.

Bringing the Community Back In

A widening count of researchers has moved against this grain, digging carefully and critically into how *decentralized* school organizations or localized forms of collective action may engage and motivate key actors—from parents seeking out better schools to dissident teachers crafting charter schools. Initial decentralization experiments—from magnet schools and community control, to vouchers and charters—are typically accompanied by rich polemics and impoverished research. But as the decentralization movement has matured, so have the methods and integrity of those who study these innovations. This chapter delves into what we are learning about the colorful spectrum of decentralizing reforms and the analytic tools used to illuminate the mechanisms unleashed (or not) when public authority and the architecture of schooling is reshaped locally.

Some decentralization advocates emphasize how government-run schooling—around the world—has come to resemble a total institution, similar to asylums or military academies. These bounded institutions, now tied directly to the central state, come to be insulated from the surrounding preferences and cultural forms desired by parents. It's a bedeviling paradox that the modern state has chosen to intensify the standardizing dreams of Durkheim and Mann at the very moment that Western societies are becoming ever more pluralistic (Fuller, 1999; Lloyd & Thomas, 1998; Marty, 1997). In contrast, the market does not deny the diverse tastes of local groups, or sand down their rough edges. Instead, the private sector responds to, even exploits, our diversity.

This review will address the related question of whether stronger *continuity* between schools and family preferences regarding language or social norms yield stronger benefits for children or for the wider society. Instead, should the school institution advance *discontinuity*, to widen the horizons of students and reinforce modern rules and economic values? Evidence alone will not answer this pivotal philosophical question. But educators and policy researchers are thinking anew about how place matters—what mechanisms and social architecture make or break well-meaning reforms. Beneath this question of contextual-ized versus decontextualized knowledge lay a rich array of empirical questions.

Organization   I begin with the normative debate—partially informed, yet not settled with evidence—around the ideals attached to central "public" action versus civic activism down under. This contention swivels on questions of *who gets to decide* the priority goals of schools and human learning, and *what forms of collective action* are most motivating for which social groups. That is, the debate is over both the goals for education and the social means or economic incentives that energize collective action to improve the upbringing of children. This chapter is *not* a critique of government's illiberal drift toward centralization or the frequent insularity of local schools. Instead, I focus on claims that can be informed with empirical evidence.[2]

We then delve into four types of decentralized reforms, including emergent evidence on whether these interventions work and via what social or economic mechanisms:

- Granting parents the authority to shop around and choose their preferred school, assuming that a colorful mix of schools is available (rational choice).
- Enriching organizational populations and granting neighborhood control of schools (institutional pluralism).
- Creating new forms of schooling to strengthen human relationships and engagement inside educational institutions (communitarian localism).
- Organizing schools and engaging families in ways that scaffold up from a community's cultural assets and social architecture (situated learning).

We will examine the *kinds of benefits* pursued by the decentralists, be they motivated by private or collective local interests, as well as the *dilemmas* inherent in de-centering the control of schools in a society marked by stark inequalities across locales. Some market advocates prefer to weaken the central state; others envision a diverse mixed-market of schools with equity measures that guard against segregation and inequity. We will arrive at the key point that the wealth of ideals and arguments (ideologies) about how decentralized reforms are *supposed* to work outpace the paucity of *evidence* on how they discernibly touch the everyday motivation and capacities of students and educators.

Table 67.1 captures the four kinds of decentralized social action examined. The columns specify reform examples and the theorized mechanisms that are to drive parental engagement, motivating relationships inside schools, or beneficial continuity between learning in homes and schools. Let's turn first to the ideological debates that surround decentralizing reforms, both around their educational aims and the ethics of their means. Then, we walk through extant evidence on each type of decentralization.

Should Place Matter?   Let's be clear on the kinds of issues that evidence can arbitrate. One may believe, for example, that parents should have a "right" to select their child's

TABLE 67.1
Types of and Theories Underlying Decentralized Public Action

	Program types and level of social organization	Social and economic mechanisms
Rational choice	*Liberalizing parental choice*: vouchers, magnet schools, transfer policies, tutoring options.	Family incentives to boost purchasing power; market mechanisms will raise quality; varying preferences drive diversity of school forms.
Organizational populations, new school forms	*Localized forms of schooling*: charter schools, preschools, community-based governance, new urbanism.	Public funding of locally crafted, deregulated schools, which will adapt to family preferences and localized cultural forms.
Social engagement inside and within schools	*Strengthening social ties, motivation*: small "learning communities," teacher-student relationships, parent involvement.	Stronger ties, relationships boost teacher and student motivation; small-scale organizations nurture deeper interaction inside schools.
Family and community scaffolds	*Building from family, neighborhood*: Home visits, parenting practices, adult-like roles and career academies, linguistic and cultural continuity.	Improve home support for learning; reduce insularity between family and school;, integrate adolescents into adult-like roles; scaffold up from "indigenous" social architecture.

school—even when it increases racial segregation or selection of a lousier school. Or, you may oppose paying teachers more when their students' learning curves grow steeper, arguing that extrinsic rewards displace intrinsic motivation. Empirical evidence won't settle such debates, but it can inform elements of such arguments. What's important is that we pinpoint the idealized (ideological) claims made by decentralization advocates, and then identify claims that can be informed by empirical research.

The ideological foundations of *rational choice*, the first decentralizing pathway, accents the influence of the family's purchasing power, along with parents' capacity to make informed choices, operating within a mixed market of schools. Rational choice stems from the liberal tenets of the democratic nation-state: the assumption that the individual will act from exogenous preferences to maximize his or her utility, be it shopping for hamburgers or selecting better schools (Friedman & Friedman, 1980; Howell & Peterson, 2006). Policy researchers have learned much over the past generation about supply responses to liberalized parental choice. That is, whether parents choose from among public schools, or from a rising count of charter schools, depends upon local institutional conditions, not only upon the mechanism of individual choice.

In this vein, the next two lines of work focus on the *populations of organizations* that mediate (and often constrain and/or stratify) opportunities for groups, rather than asserting that incentives or rules directly spur individual action. From preschools to Ivy League colleges, government and private agents act to spread or restrict the growth of education organizations, then often ration access to this array of schools. *Opportunity structures* are reproduced over time, with incremental adjustments to which social groups benefit from what kinds of schools. Politics matters—centrally and locally—in terms of which parents have the economic means, the knowledge, the language, and the cultural understanding to send their children to varying schools (Lareau, 2003). These institutions can be seen as differing vertically in their quality and status awarded to graduates, or horizontally in their philosophies of learning, pedagogy, or roots in local cultural norms.

At times government pushes to build new subsectors, or surround and systematize mixed-markets of local educational organizations. Historically, this goes back to the European state's incorporation of parish and small private schools—the advance of government schooling within a unified system run from Paris or Berlin (Garnier, Hage, & Fuller, 1989). The contemporary spread of charter schools in the United States, or state governments' attempt to suck community-based preschools into the public education apparatus, offer contemporary examples (Fuller, 2007). Whether this attempt at central regulation yields intended effects as seen by government actors, or actually emboldens local activists and erodes central authority, remains a provocative empirical question.

Formal organizations represent the main tool for localizing the organization of human learning under the third line of decentralizing action, one that aims to create *stronger relationships and social engagement* inside the school. This includes efforts to strengthen social bonds between teachers and students, consequential engagement with parents, and integrating adolescents into adult-like service roles in the community. Departing from the modernist tenets of Durkheim or Mann, where the state defines the official knowledge that all children should learn, transmitted via didactic teaching, localized forms of participation build from the Vygotskian notion that meaningful and animated learning is locally situated, embedded in supportive relationships between teacher and student, adult and child.

The fourth line of decentralizing action centers on how education, more broadly conceived, might *scaffold up from the cultural assets* and *social architecture* of families and neighborhoods. If effective learning is situated in local contexts, then education organizations are best nested within children's immediate environs. Instead, modern schooling is supposed to whisk children out of local settings, socializing them to national ideals, dominant cultural forms, and the competitive job market. It's the decontextualized nature of rationalized schooling that serves to erode the authority of local agents—from the stigmatized yokels who speak low-status languages to high schools that rarely connect with youths' everyday worries. From the scaffolding perspective, however, it is the social architecture of families and community that offers a firmer starting point for enhancing children's learning.

At times this fourth perspective sounds idealistic. Yet, these foundations undergird rising decentralization movements, including charters and community-based preschools, a pair of subsectors that continue to grow. And more broadly, the rational-choice and civil rights perspectives assume that a firm social architecture is in place. That is, the individual gains the liberty to choose from enabling institutions (Glendon, 1991), while the third and fourth models make no such assumption. Indeed, it's the paucity of supportive bonds—to lift poor children or the spirits of all—that is the underlying problem.

Central Institutions, Local Motivations   The rising popularity of decentralizing reforms—even within the state—suggests that some educators and parents have tired of the hyper-rationalization of contemporary schooling, the assumption that tighter *systems* best advance teaching and learning. This, of course, is not a new debate in the West. It is only during the past century that schooling has come to be controlled by central agents of the state. The initial spread of literacy was spurred by Protestant commitments and the rising count of tutors, not by secular government, going back to the 16th century (Meyer, Tyack, Nagel, & Gordon, 1979). Two-fifths of all Englishmen and about one-third of women were literate by the mid-1700s (Mitch, 1992).

Yet, western Europe and the United States would catch-up institutionally, punctuated by Margaret Thatcher's centralizing reforms in the mid-1980s, then with America's No Child Left Behind law enacted in 2002. Even conservative heads of state who otherwise sought to shrink the state, like Thatcher and George W. Bush, realized the political benefits of trying to boost the effectiveness of schools, relying on the regulatory, standardizing habits of the central state (Cross, 2003). The political Right—and elements of the Left—had come to see the ideals of Jeffersonian (local) control as being been hijacked by self-interested education interest groups, from the teacher unions to downtown school bureaucrats to parents of special education students. The lobbies for particular groups of students had secured funding and segmented regulations which hogtied principals and teachers on the ground according to this critique (Chubb & Moe, 1990).

Neighborhood schools are unlikely to be responsive to their constituent families as long as myriad funding streams, instructional materials, and pedagogical preferences are controlled by the state, a governing apparatus that's penned in by powerful interests. And the rise of accountability hawks—in part from within the New-Democrat movement led governors like Bill Clinton and Richard Reilly—was supported by a similar diagnosis. The problem underlying stagnating performance was not family poverty, nor the maldistribution of resources among schools, but rested at the feet of local educators who lacked the will or incentives to do better. Whereas the Right argued for radical decentralization, replete with faith in market competition, the new moderates argued for greater centralization, where the state would trump the local political-economy of schooling that had been captured by special interests.

These developments are spurred by a distrust of place—under the modern rules of public governance. The liberal state aims to protect market relations and centrally provide a unifying infrastructure, necessary for advancing economic growth and the well-being of particular groups. This requires universal policy remedies, from public schools to public highways to public housing. Contemporary decentralists are largely pressing against what Robert Wuthnow (2004) calls "the modernization story line." That is, if the school is to serve the modern state's interests, then children are to be readied for work in mass institutions and a competitive labor market. Students' destinations are set by this functional logic. So, variability in parents' preferences, local cultural norms, or even nearby economic relations is not supposed to matter. "You will go far," is the common adage signaling success in American schools. To stay near is a quaint, backward practice more characteristic of low-status or rural communities.

Yet, the drift toward central regulation of schools runs into a daunting motivational problem: Why would individuals or groups innovate or pursue more complex forms of teaching and learning when the technology of schooling is being engineered from above? This nettlesome question has long plagued democratic societies, drawn to the potential of a strong state, while recognizing that civil society is energized by human-scale organizations from below (Marty, 1997). And, of course, Jefferson won the constitutional debate over whether state governments or the central state should be running public schools (Rossiter, 2003).

Do Governance Reforms Matter?   Decentralizing the control of schools—even beneath the authority of district school boards—rekindles contention over which groups should be chartered to control public dollars and craft the nature of teaching and learning. As Plank and Boyd (1994, p. 4588) emphasize, "the institutions of educational governance, rather than the ends to be pursued in the educational system" often dominate reform discussion. Real changes in the social organization of teaching and learning "are too fraught politically to be carried through in pluralistic and interest-driven political systems." It's easier—not to mention politically rewarding—to debate what level of government or collectivity should control schools than to re-engineer the social relations found inside schools or classrooms. But this often distracts from the core issue of how decentralized control does, or does not, touch the nature of social relations inside classrooms.

Neoinstitutional theorists have long argued that institutions are adept at complying symbolically with novel technical demands that arise in their environment—without altering their core technologies (Meyer & Rowan, 1977). Decentralizing policies, for example, may grant authority and public dollars to seemingly inventive organizers of a fresh charter school. But as Huerta's (2000) work details, once-innovative charters often drift back toward conventional forms of organization, including traditional forms of didactic pedagogy. Simply note the count of charter schools that have come to include "academy" or "preparatory" in their names. Competitive markets ironically can push firms and institutions to become more uniform to reduce uncertainty in attracting consumers and to boost legitimacy in a field where various actors hold tacit conceptions of how work should be arranged within a school. So, whether decentralizing forces and market pressures truly yield differing forms of schooling—which recast daily social relationships or classroom technology—remains a ripe empirical question (Rowan, 2006).

Overall, policy researchers are bringing the community back in, recognizing that place matters. We no longer assume that the state's centralizing tendency or tools are necessarily more effective or motivating inside schools. This growing band of analysts is delving both into the effects and mediating mechanisms of various decentralizing reforms. We are learning to separate normative from empirically inform-able questions. And critical researchers are asking tough questions about whether the everyday social organization of teaching and learning is somehow better or different in locally crafted forms of schooling.

Let's turn next to how the four contemporary lines of decentralization have prompted fresh policy research over the past generation.

Rational Choice without Institutions

The push to liberalize parental choice—to select from a presumed panoply of schools—has received much attention since the 1950s. This movement, going back to the 18th-century roots of neoclassical economics, at first set aside state-run institutions, aiming to award parents greater authority and purchasing power. It is the individual, according to these theorists, who acts from clear exogenous preferences, seeking out reliable information about higher quality or more responsive organizations (Friedman & Friedman, 1980).

We turn first to vouchers—the lightening rod of the choice movement and a policy that is supposed to operate through neoclassical mechanisms. Yet, its effectiveness rests largely on the quality of sectarian schools, that is, *organization-level* dynamics seen in local areas, not only upon the less fettered action of the individual parent. We then review findings on related forms of parental choice, including open enrollment schemes, alternative and magnet schools. Third, we look at new lines of research that delve into legislated forms of choice under NCLB, or creating smaller school districts to advance competitive pressure on schools to improve.

Vouchers—The Lone Individual Expressing Demand?

Linking portable vouchers to the financing of private schools is a rather old idea. What is new are large-scale studies of how they work within institutional contexts and which families benefit. In 1792 Thomas Paine in *The Rights of Man* proposed vouchers with public accountability, so that "the ministers of every … denomination would certify that the duty is performed" (Kirkpatrick, 1990, p. 34). The idea would eventually catch on with how the Congress structures student aid via Pell Grants in 1972 and federal financing of child care and preschools in 1990. But moving vouchers into the K–12 institution has proven more controversial. The rise of publicly funded "choice schools" in the 1950s, as southern Whites sought to avoid desegregation, fused choice to the racist far Right (Wells, 1996). But vouchers would be embraced a decade later by the Johnson administration, as civil rights activists tried to empower low-income parents who often faced unresponsive school districts. The longest running voucher experiment, stemming from the Great Society yielded disappointing effects in the northern California district of Alum Rock (Fuller & Elmore, 1996).

The Reagan administration aimed to advance parental choice—and public financing of private schools—by unsuccessfully pushing tuition tax credits during the 1980s. Defeated at the federal level, this form of portable financing was legislated in a few states, including Arizona and Minnesota. But voucher advocates persevered, shifting tactics and pushing to demonstrate how publicly funded chits could benefit children from low-income families. The earliest publicly funded voucher initiative, established in Milwaukee in 1989, was heavily backed by African American activists and conservative allies in the Wisconsin legislature. It led to the first contemporary studies of how market dynamics unfold within the institutional field of public education.

The first evaluation by Witte (2000) and colleagues found no significant short-term achievement effects for the small number of voucher participants, compared with regular students attending Milwaukee public schools. Greene, Peterson, and Du (1997) then tracked just 67 voucher students—almost all from poor Black or Latino families—who spent 4 years in (at first non-sectarian) independent schools, compared with students who had originally applied to the program but decided against using a voucher. This was an attempt to control on selection bias. Greene's team reported a 10.7 percentile point advantage in math achievement for this small cohort of students, but no significant difference in reading scores. Rouse (1998), utilizing a larger sample of voucher students, essentially replicated Greene's finding, although the estimated advantage in math scores was smaller in magnitude.

From the beginning the Milwaukee voucher program was constrained institutionally by the state legislature. It continues to operate only within Milwaukee, exclusively targeted on low-income families. The dollar value of the voucher has increased over the years, but it still does not cover the full tuition charged by many private schools. So, many parents must "top up" the voucher's dollar value to cover tuition costs, while leaving some private schools unaffordable. In turn, a significant number of parents leave the voucher program. I have termed this *exit selection bias,* which remains present in recent studies, at times altering the composition of treatment and control groups (Fuller, Burr, Huerta, Puryear, & Wexler, 1999). The legislature also lifted the restriction on parochial school participation and raised the cap on the count of voucher recipients.

These initial studies played a key role in the logic of major judicial action on the voucher question. The U.S. Supreme Court, in 1998, allowed inclusion of parochial schools in certain federal school aid programs, but let stand a lower court ruling against public financing of vouchers going to Catholic schools. In 2002 the Supreme Court, in a 5–4 decision, ruled that a similar voucher program in Cleveland begun in 1996 was constitutional.[3] The majority argued that vouchers offered fresh school options for poor children and parents—allegedly yielding positive achievement benefits—outweighing any risk of violating church-state separation (Forman, 2007). By 2006 fully 127 private schools in Milwaukee enrolled 17,951 students; four of every five voucher students attendedsectarian schools (Dickman & Schmidt, 2007).

To more clearly establish the benefits of vouchers (and parochial school enrollment) advocates and researchers teamed up to run a series of random trials. Scholar-activists like Harvard's Paul Peterson understood that selection bias rendered as inconclusive any findings that did not employ an experimental design, since unobserved attributes of economically poor parents could be driving selection and achievement. A set of foundations and wealthy individuals capitalized scholarship funds in Dayton, Ohio, New York City, and Washington, DC. They were designed and then evaluated by Peterson and his students.

The initial privately funded effort began in DC, offering vouchers of $2,000 to parents of elementary-age children through a lottery process in 1993. This allowed researchers to randomly assign about half the applicants to the treatment: winning a voucher that varied in dollar value. Similar experiments were created in Dayton (1998; $1,785 voucher for elementary-age students) and New York City (1997; $1,400 voucher). Across the three cities about 3 in 5 voucher winners enrolled in a Catholic school.

Exit from the program ran high in some locations, presenting unanticipated methodological challenges. In Year 1 of the DC program, 29% of children left the voucher program and returned to their neighborhood schools, rising to 46% by Year 3. In New York, 70% of the original treatment group remained in a private school by Year 3, but this share fell to just 29% in DC (Howell & Peterson, 2002). Peterson and colleagues persevered to estimate 3-year effects of these allied experiments, yielding a wealth of data. Yet, the overall punch line was not encouraging. After 3 years, only Black students participating in the New York voucher program displayed stronger test scores than the control group (Howell & Peterson, 2002, table 6-1).[4]

This trio of random-assignment experiments did yield important design lessons when examining how individual and organization action unfolds within decentralizing reforms. The necessity of substantial private funding for real experiments is notable. In contrast, publicly funded randomized trials are common in other fields, especially in medicine and recent work on preschool programs and career academies (Fuller, 2007). The Howell and Peterson (2002) line also opened-up a panorama of rarely explored student and parental outcomes. They examined, for instance, the capacity of private schools to engage and hold onto students, compared with control-group kids who remained in the public schools. They found significantly lower pupil suspension rates in New York City private schools attended by voucher recipients, but higher rates among DC private schools, compared with children attending public schools. Fully one-fifth of middle-school voucher students were suspended during the first year. A more recent review of 19 studies of "choice schools" found that they, at times, impart stronger civic values and engagements, compared with public school effects (Wolf, 2005). Benefits were greatest among Latino students attending Catholic schools, including stronger tolerance of civil liberties, knowledge of political institutions, more frequent involvement in public meetings and volunteer activities. The conditioning of these benefits on particular groups of students and type of school offers a notable lesson for future designs.

The DC voucher program has survived and is now funded with congressionally allocated public funds. But first-year findings are not encouraging. In 2005 a total of 797 families accepted vouchers, out of 1,088 awardees (Wolf, Gutmann, Puma, Rizzo, & Eissa, 2007). Eligible families must earn less than 185% of the poverty line, and the voucher amount has climbed to $7,500. After 1 year of participation—most students attend parochial or private schools—no consistent gains in reading or math could be detected. Parents receiving vouchers reported that their children's schools were safer, compared with reports from public school parents, although participating children reported no significant differences in school climate.

Market Choice with Hazy Information   Markets work best, according to neoclassical logic, when consumers act from rich information about their options, including the quality of alternative goods or institutions. As school choice expands in lower-income communities, it appears that many parents do seek out information sources and channels that lead to alternative schools. Schneider, Teske, and Marschall (2000) found that most parents hold little knowledge of test scores when scanning schools in their area, although variation can be wide among social-class groups. One Massachusetts study found that only 29% of parents attending "low-performing schools" actually realized that students were achieving at dismal levels (Howell, 2006). Another survey, involving just over 800 low-income parents in Denver, Milwaukee, and Washington, DC, found that most parents visited schools, talked with teachers, and consulted printed information as they were considering school options (Teske, Fitzpatrick, & Kaplan, 2007). Yet, indicators of "quality" often come down to the racial or class composition of students and the neighborhood in which charter or other schools are located (Hamilton & Guin, 2005).

Still, competitive pressures may nudge school leaders to raise the quality of teaching. Florida's statewide voucher program—quite small in the count of families who have been granted portable chits—appears to have contributed modestly to instructional improvement in certain communities. School financing is converted into liberal vouchers only when particular schools repeatedly display low student achievement. Under this threat, schools serving large portions of African American children have lengthened instructional time, created summer classes, reduced class size, hired classroom aides, and boosted the amount of time that teachers collaborate on instructional improvements (Rouse, Hannaway, Goldhaber, & Figlio, 2007). These organizational changes, in turn, appear to have boosted achievement. By detailing institutional changes, this study illuminates the mechanisms through which competitive pressures may benefit teachers and students alike.

Open Enrollment and Magnet Schools Other forms of parental choice have matured while receiving less attention from policy researchers. Cross-town transfer and magnet schools—originally sparked by desegregation ideals in the 1970s—represent one example. The notion that children would no longer be required to attend the school in their catchment area first surfaced when the courts accepted in 1975 the idea that special-purpose magnet schools could be used as a desegregation device, hoping to stem White flight from urban centers. By 1990, over 3,100 magnet schools or programs situated in regular high schools were operating (Steel & Levine, 1994). The Los Angeles school district operates about 13,000 slots in magnet programs—for which 28,217 families remained on waiting lists in 2007 (Blume & Rivera, 2007).

Work on magnet programs sheds great light on the institutional context in which policy research unfolds. One study, for instance, focused on the question of whether magnets were more racially integrated than regular public schools in Cincinnati, St. Louis, and Nashville, that is, were they able to attract more White families than regular inner-city schools? The empirical answer was yes: enrollments in magnet schools were less Black in their composition, more integrated along racial lines, reducing social isolation (Yu & Taylor, 1997). The study also found that magnets tend to attract greater numbers of students from middle-class Black families, compared with neighboring schools. This good news, however, blurs what can be inferred from nonexperimental assessments of magnet effects, since unobserved family selection factors likely bias estimated treatment effects.

A related analytic problem is that variable features of schools or programs are insufficiently measured. Again, program funders and investigators are consumed by the summative question: Does this reform work; yes or no? Left unanswered is how, through what mechanisms, do parental choice and alternative school selection yield discernible effects? Gamoran (1996) did test to see whether school climate, social bonds among students, and course-taking patterns contributed to higher achievement levels among magnet-school students, compared with statistically similar public school students, employing a variety of regression controls. He found that magnet students outperformed their peers in reading, social studies, and science, but these organizational features failed to show significant associations with achievement. Results for New York City magnets were less encouraging, where researchers could detect few significant benefits, compared with regular public schools (Heebner et al., 1992).

Open enrollment programs, another pro-choice device, arose first in Minnesota in 1987. This abolition of catchment areas was legislated prior to the state's pioneering authorization of charter schools. Massachusetts soon followed by passing an open enrollment program. But it resulted in additional White flight from urban schools. It operated as Robin Hood in reverse, as state dollars were pulled from low-wealth school communities to follow students into wealthier areas (Armor & Peiser, 1998). Studies in California and Minnesota show that Black and Latino parents exercise their new-found transfer rights at somewhat higher rates than do White parents, as mirrored in the growth of charter schools situated in poor communities, where families are more desperate for school options (Funkhouser & Colopy, 1994). But in the aggregate does open enrollment raise the quality or effectiveness of schools within a region or school district, as market theory claims? We do not know.

Emerging work on the school exit provisions of NCLB indicates that many families do seek out schools with higher mean achievement. The expression of parental demand, however, can be institutionally conditioned. When the Charlotte-Mecklenburg district in North Carolina introduced discrete information about achievement levels in 2004, school by school, parents more readily moved their children to schools showing higher performance levels (Hastings & Weinstein, 2007). Across the sample of 1,092 participating students exiting from their original school, the average student transferred to a school that displayed a mean achievement level that was about one standard deviation higher. The propensity of students to leave a "program improvement" school was related to the proximity of a school displaying stronger achievement. But where performance differences were hazy or absent many parents operated from scarce information or relied on proxies, like student composition (Lankford & Wyckoff, 1992; Schneider & Coleman, 1993).

Does Market Competition Lift School Quality? Two promising areas of work have recently emerged from within the rational-choice tradition. The first tackles the question of whether individual demand and competition for students truly places competitive pressure on regular public schools.

Early work by Rofes (1998), based on interviews with charter educators and district officials, found that they interacted rarely over substantive issues or pedagogical innovations. But recent work—examining achievement growth trends in regions with a competitive mix of vouchers and/or charter schools—yields more optimistic findings. Hoxby (2003) tracked the performance of students attending regular schools in Milwaukee, where thousands of peers by the mid-1990s were exiting assigned schools with vouchers in-hand and heading for private schools. She ran a similar analysis in Arizona and Michigan where the count of charter schools had grown dramatically by the mid-1990s, creating competition for students among these locales.

Hoxby's innovative methodology gauged the magnitude of the voucher treatment in Milwaukee by sorting regular public schools between those with large versus small concentrations of students who were eligible to exit (with a voucher). Controlling on prior fixed-effects for schools, she found that achievement gains were steepest in public schools that faced the stiffest competitive pressure. Growth curves were also stronger in communities where the threat of exit was greater, compared with growth observed in earlier years, prior to the rise of vouchers and/or charters (when competitive pressure was less). Hoxby examined achievement trends in regular public schools before and after their respective district experienced at least 6% attrition, students bound for charter schools. Significant gains in achievement were detected after this threshold level of competition was reached. The next question on the theoretical frontier pertains to the institutional mechanisms employed by district or school-level actors in their efforts to hold onto families and raise performance.

Finally, voucher experiments in neighboring fields are yielding fresh perspectives on the advantages and limits of the rational-choice perspective. Two-thirds of all Americans receiving housing assistance accept their aid in the form of a portable voucher; just one-third still live in large housing projects. The potential utility of vouchers was pushed further in 1994 when the federal housing department created the Moving to Opportunity for Fair Housing experiment, involving 1,320 families living in 1 of 5 cities that were randomly selected and urged to move to a better-off community. An initial study found that children's achievement climbed significantly as they moved to schools in less-poor communities (Ludwig, Ladd, & Duncan, 2001). But adolescent boys were worse off in the long run, compared with peers who remained behind in public housing; family health, quality of life, and girls' well-being improved markedly. Many families simply left the experiment or indicated that they missed old friends and families in their old neighborhoods. This latter result resembles Wells (1996) finding that Black teens frequently exited the St. Louis desegregation choice program, even though they reported that their new, predominantly White school was of higher quality than their old inner-city school. The recurring lesson is that choice does not occur in a vacuum; it's conditioned by prior relationships and local settings of social integration.

Organizational Populations, Diversifying Forms of Schooling

The modernization storyline has long assumed that rational-choice and market dynamics are fine for powering economic growth—but a publicly structured set of institutions is essential to integrate markets and socialize diverse individuals. Durkheim spoke of *social facts* or norms that serve to bind large groups. Adam Smith argued that commonly held *sentiments* among individuals were necessary to support market exchange and contracts (Collins, 1984). Just as the individual aims to maximize her utility, stemming from personal preferences, the modern organization pursues crisp objectives, surviving and thriving if goals are met efficiently. Rational firms are to follow these same spare, utilitarian motives that drive the rational individual (Scott, 2001).

Organizational Diversification This idealized theoretical frame, of course, has been buffeted by ideological and empirical challenges over the past four decades. In education, one presenting issue is what some call the *supply response* problem. Parents want to exit a lousy school, but they can find few affordable alternatives close by. Or, charter schools emerge, but how do parents (and public funders) know which charters are more or less effective? Institution building is certainly required to ensure a robust supply response; but now government is pressed to invest in *decentralized organizations* that it chooses not to regulate. So, how is the *public good* defined as a variably regulated mixed market of institutions responds to liberalized family demand?

The authority of mass institutions is precious for policy makers and the interest groups that have a stake in them, from the post office to public schools. Yet, decentralists argue that government need not run schools from afar, but instead strengthen the capacity of civil society to nurture local institutions. This was the organizing principle of one-room schoolhouses during a simpler era. The school was an extension of the family, the church, the town square. On this same tack, scholars are now learning about the vitality and distribution of educational organizations that operate in mixed markets, from preschools to charter schools. Here the starting question pertains not to state-led bureaucratic controls but how government intervenes into markets (or institutional fields) to advance quality or equity goals. In some cases, the central state deregulates while setting in place new rules and resource flows to local groups. This form is illustrated below by Chicago's intriguing experiment to allow neighborhoods to elect school principals, what Anthony Bryk has called *democratic localism* (Bryk, Sebring, Kerbow, Rollow, & Easton, 1999).

Schools that Thicken Civil Society When Michael Bennett, a Yale-trained lawyer, took over the Denver public schools in 2005, he pushed quickly to toughen high school graduation requirements, hoping to prepare a larger share of teenagers to enter college. But soon the data came back that high school truancy rates remained just as high, graduation rates just as low. So, he took a new approach, walking through impoverished northeast communities, knocking on doors, trying to convince sporadic attendees that it was important to finish high school. "We've been trying to erect reforms over this weak political, economic, and cultural scaffolding," Bennett said after a long day of sitting in the homes of poor Latino families. "It's not impossible, but, God, it's really, really hard" (as cited in Boo, 2007, p. 56).

It is a discovery that is repeated over and over again—what parents demand of schools and what children bring into classrooms are conditioned by their immediate context. In the absence of economic incentives (like jobs) and sustainable social institutions (churches, civic groups), awarding parents "choice" may help at the margins but do little to alter underlying cultural and economic conditions. So, from Thomas Jefferson to Vaclav Havel, political theorists have urged a stronger public commitment to civil society and the grassroots organizing which supports families. As even Durkheim (1964) put it:

> The State is too remote from individuals; its relations with them too external and intermittent to penetrate deeply into individual consciences. A nation can be maintained only if, between the State and the individual, there is intercalated a whole series of secondary groups near enough to the individuals to drag them…into the general torrent of social life." (p. 28)

The pursuit of individual rights, from this communitarian perspective, is not sufficient. The state must enrich the mix of local organizations that engage families and their children—thickening civil society (Glendon, 1991).

This line of analysis powered the localized approaches of Dorothy Day's settlement houses, offering child care and family supports, as well as the community action movement of the 1960s, spurred by the Kennedy-Johnson White House. This gave birth to many of the same organizations that now run preschools and charter schools in communities of color (Fuller, 2000; Halpern, 1995). But little is known empirically about the effectiveness of community-based organizations (CBOs), compared to bureaucratically organized firms, like the public schools. As Weisbrod (1988, p. 70) argues with respect to nonprofit health care organizations, "In spite of the paucity of theory and evidence, judgments and assertions about the comparative behavior of private firms and nonprofit organizations abound, and these beliefs give rise to conflicting…public policy prescriptions." The ideals and "cultural inheritances" (DiMaggio & Anheier, 1990, p. 137) may differ for many nonprofit firms, even as they compete in mixed markets with publicly funded, highly regulated organizations. A variety of upbeat claims are made about how the social architecture of grassroots organizations yields motivating and engaging effects, whether the analyst leans on concepts like *gesellschaft*, social capital, or collective efficacy (Alinsky, 1969; Coleman, 1990; Tönnies, 1887/1957).

The Distribution and Quality of Community Schools Recent papers have examined how the state and market, together, shape the supply and quality of early education programs. This is a colorful and uneven mix of preschools, of which over 131,000 are run by community-based organizations nationwide. Just over two-thirds of all 4-year-olds and about one-half of all 3-year-olds spend significant time with one of these organizations or caregivers. The early education sector is now powered by $47 billion in economic activity each year; about two-fifths of these dollars come from government, the remaining three-fifths from parental fees (Fuller, 2007). Focusing just on 3- and 4-year-olds attending preschool centers, about 70% are enrolled in private programs (modest CBOs), while the remaining 30% attend preschools nested in public schools.

A robust supply response has followed rising family demand for preschool, going back to the 1950s. Market forces still drive much of the (unequal) distribution of supply. One study found that variance in preschool availability is largely explained by maternal employment, household income, and ethnic composition among 9,179 zip codes nationwide (Fuller, Loeb, Strath, & Carrol, 2004). Communities hosting more churches and nonprofit organizations displayed stronger availability of preschools. And states that spent more and regulated quality more intensively showed richer preschool supply. The magnitudes of disparity in supply (per capita) can be large. For example, affluent zip codes have over twice as many adults working in preschools or as caregivers, compared with low-income zip codes (Fuller & Strath, 2001). It is also clear that blue-collar and lower middle-class families face comparatively low availability of preschools, and their segment of this mixed market is less formalized in terms of teacher credentials, even compared with preschools in poor communities.

Government efforts to improve availability and quality in poor communities have paid off. We found that quality does covary with states' wealth and levels of maternal employment: preschool supply is higher on average in rich states where more young mothers remain in the work force (Fuller, Raudenbush, Wei, & Holloway, 1993). Quality is stronger in more heavily subsidized preschools, including state programs and those based inside public schools—evidence that public intervention into provider markets can yield equity benefits. Multilevel modeling aids this line of work, since investigators ask whether the distribution of supply or quality is moderated by state-level factors. The higher order effects are not fixed among states, they vary in terms of demographic and policy differences, moderating the supply effects of family-level demand factors.

Individual Selection within Organization Sets The expanding mixed market of preschools has sparked considerable work on parental selection. This line of work moves beyond nascent research on family selection in the K–12 arena, limiting our ability to properly estimate treatment effects of moving to another school. This applies to estimating the value-added effects of moving to a charter school or small high school, since children are not randomly assigned to decentralized organizations, especially when operating in a competitive mixed market. Early work in early education found expected patterns: The likelihood of entering preschool (compared with other forms of care) was associated with family wealth and maternal education, and with parents who report frequent reading and other pro-developmental practices (Fuller, Holloway, & Liang, 1996).

But a few surprises have emerged. Children from African American families turn out to display the highest preschool enrollment rate, compared with White and Latino children. This appears to be related to historically high maternal employment rates in the Black community, single-parenthood, and the growth of Head Start and other preschool efforts. Latino 3- and 4-year-olds enroll in preschool at low rates overall, but this is centered in Spanish-speaking communities where mothers and grandmothers still hold a cultural commitment to childrearing and preschools remain comparatively scarce (Hirshberg, Huang, & Fuller, 2005; Liang, Fuller, & Singer, 2000).

These empirical patterns help to inform understanding of how parents may operate in mixed K–12 markets, say in the charter school field. Progressive financing by government can help to equalize access to, and the quality of, educational organizations when situated in mixed markets. But in the absence of such resource equalization, mixed provider markets may reproduce familiar inequalities. Charter schools that largely serve African American students, for example, attract less experienced teachers, more frequently uncredentialed, and pay their principals less (Fuller, Gawlik, Kuboyama-Gonzalez, & Park, 2004; Bodine et al., 2008). Focusing on charters in Michigan, Ross (2005) shows how this sector disproportionately serves Black communities: 47% of Michigan charter students are African American, compared with just 17% across regular public schools. Decentralists optimistically hope that resource disparities among rich and poor communities can be overcome with local organizing and raw chutzpa. But this work on mixed markets suggests that the organizational capacity of local places is firmly constrained by the wider political-economy.

Family demand for alternative schools is often stronger in poorer communities. The supply of private schools run by churches or community-based groups is somewhat higher in lower-income neighborhoods, compared with affluent areas where parents demand quality public schools (Betts, Goldhaber, & Rosenstock, 2005). But institutional fields (supply-side conditions) also manifest factors that spur more robust growth of alternative organizations. Renzulli (2005) found that local groups submitted more applications to become a charter school, across 29 states, when the concentration of nonreligious private schools was richer and the presence of existing charters was weaker. Charter applications were higher in states that spend more per pupil on instruction. Market forces may be weaker in shaping the supply response in highly subsidized sectors, such as charter regimes. But variation in institutional conditions and competition among charter organizations appear to interact, heating-up or cooling-out supply responses.

Charter Schools—A Thousand Flowers Bloom The steady growth of charter schools reflects a huge public project, aiming to diversify the array of available schools. What's intriguing is that policy makers—mainly situated in the states—remain agnostic about the learning aims and pedagogical practices of charter schools. Somehow, a richer variety of organizations is simply good, a colorful departure from the top-down regulatory practices of the modern state. Public support of dissident teachers, determined parents, and private entrepreneurs will allegedly yield a more varied and responsive population of school organizations. Yet, as reported above, the resources and quality of many charter schools remains fused to the wealth or poverty of surrounding neighborhoods.

Within this institutionally constrained market, families have responded to charter schools in robust fashion. Overall the count of charter schools continues to grow, albeit at a slower rate than that observed in the 1990s. By fall 2006 over 4,100 charter schools were serving about 1.4 million students, according to one advocacy group (Center for Education Reform, 2008). The growth rate of new charters opening their doors remains at about 8% annually. Some states continue to limit the number of charters granted to independent educators or parents, hoping to maintain high quality standards, limit public cost, or accommodate political pressure from interest groups opposed to unregulated expansion. Dramatic failures of charters continue to be reported in the press, including virtual schools in which taxpayers support courses offered over the Web with no human contact between teacher and student.

Evidence remains quite inconsistent over whether charter schools boost achievement, on average, compared with regular public schools serving comparable students. Unlike the randomized trials in which parental vouchers have been tested, charter school evaluations have yet to benefit from experimental design. Nor have selection processes been studied systematically, beyond simple statistical controls for students' demographic background; omitted variables bias is likely in the charter school evaluations appearing in this young field.

One careful analysis examined growth trends in charter and regular public schools in California (Zimmer et al., 2003). These researchers drew three kinds of contrasts. First, they compared mean student performance in charters versus regular publics over a 3-year period on the state-defined Academic Performance Index (API), which is pegged to standardized test scores. Charter students did not outperform regular students in any of the 3 years; nor did student growth curves differ between the two groups. Achievement change did not differ between charters that had previously operated as regular schools (conversion charters) versus entirely new (start-up) charters.

The RAND analysts then examined individual-level test scores for charter and regular school students, allowing for careful controls on student demographics. But contrasts could be drawn only for individual school years, since California lacks capacity to track the same kids over time. Students in regular public schools outperformed charter students by about 2 percentile points in secondary reading and math, and elementary math but not reading, after taking into account observed student background characteristics. Students in start-up charters and "non-classroom" (virtual) charters performed at very low levels. When these programs were removed, children attending conversion charters performed at essentially the same levels as kids in regular public schools. This illustrates how the charter subsector displays enormous heterogeneity across organizations. Third, charter students showed equals levels of achievement growth in several California districts that could provide longitudinal data on the same students over time.

A stronger punchline stemmed from the RAND cost-benefit analysis, revealing that charter students were performing at comparable levels to regular school kids—at significantly lower costs. In California, charter schools receive fewer public dollars per pupil than regular publics. Charters tend to rely on younger, non-unionized, and less expensive teachers. So, within the scope conditions defined by California, the cost-effectiveness was found to be significantly higher for charters (at least among conversion charters), compared with regular public schools.

Evidence on the nationwide effectiveness of charters remains hazy. That National Assessment of Educational Progress (NAEP) administered standardized tests to about 3,400 students attending one of 150 charter schools in 2003. This yielded rich data for comparing the performance of regular students along a uniform gauge. After the NAEP governing board delayed in releasing their analysis, researchers at the American Federation of Teachers (AFT) published multivariate results, attempting to control on simple student characteristics (Nelson, Rosenberg, & Van Meter, 2004). When put up against fourth-graders attending regular public schools, charter students performed about one-half year lower in reading and math. At the eighth grade, the results were similar for math; performance levels were quite close in reading. These gaps were of similar magnitude for students eligible for lunch subsidies and for middle-class students.

When the NAEP researchers released their own analysis (Braun, Jenkins, & Grigg, 2006), they concurred with the AFT with regard to children from low-income families: These students performed at lower levels when attending charters, compared with their counterparts attending regular public schools. But when estimating test scores for the entire sample, few differences were detected, after taking into account known demographic characteristics. The NAEP governing board tried to cast these results in a positive light, emphasizing that " there was no measureable difference in performance between charter school students in the fourth grade and their public school counterparts as a whole … even though charter schools have higher proportions of students from groups that typically perform lower on NAEP" (2006, p. 1). Yet, these analysts had statistically taken into account demographic variability among students.[5]

Democratic Localism—Motivating Engagement in Organizations One way to strengthen direct forms of accountability involve putting market dynamics into play, allowing parents to vote with their feet. A second way is to alter the authority and resources that neighborhood activists can exercise in their school's daily work. Rather than regulating learning standards or "input mixes" from afar, government has occasionally devolved power to the grassroots, well beneath the school board or downtown bureaucracy. One notable example is Illinois's attempt to shift accountability of Chicago's schools down to popularly elected site councils forums that won the authority to hire and fire school principals. This form of decentralization is what Anthony Bryk (1999) has called *democratic localism,* pushing for direct accountability of school leaders via political realignment.

This local control movement also arose from Chicago's long tradition, similar to Milwaukee and Harlem in the 1960s, of community organizing and struggles between municipal elites and neighborhood leaders who sought control over small-scale institutions (Alinsky, 1969). Localized control is sometimes combined with liberalized parental choice or the creation of alternative schools, exemplified by New York's famed District 4 in East Harlem (Fliegel & MacGuire, 1993). Yet, as richer organizational populations are nurtured and subjected to direct accountability within local politics, questions arise as to *which* local interests benefit most and whether the *capacity of schools* actually grows (DiMaggio & Anheier, 1990).

The Illinois legislature in 1988:

> deliberately sought to weaken centralized bureaucratic control of school and replace it with locally rooted politics. The vertical 'problem-solution path,' where local school officials looked up into the system for guidance, was rebalanced toward a greater engagement of school professionals with their local communities. (Bryk, Sebring, Kerbow, Rollow, & Easton, 1999, p. 21)

This greater engagement was driven by direct election of local councils, each awarded the power to hire and fire their school principal. Teachers held 2 seats on each council, compared with 6 elected parents and 2 additional community members. State legislation also capped the budget of the downtown schools office and shifted some fungible resources down to the schools. Bryk and the Consortium for Chicago Public Schools spent the subsequent two decades tracking the effects of this attempt at radical decentralization.[6]

Bryk's team initially aimed to measure the extent to which the newly awarded autonomy and democratic pressures led to positive organizational changes. They cast a keen eye on the mechanisms through which democratic localism might drive school improvement. This included measuring the influence of principal leadership, via time spent on instructional change and teacher development, the ability to resolve conflicts within the school, and teacher involvement in decision-making. Drawing on themes from his earlier work inside Catholic schools, Bryk observed the extent to which teachers freely expressed their opinions and engaged school-wide efforts, rather than remaining in their classrooms. Indicators of the local council's vitality were measured as well, including the number of meetings held, cooperation between the council and principal, and the level of neighborhood voting activity (Bryk et al., 1999). These theorized links are essential. A governance reform is put in place across a large population of schools. But does localized democracy lead to stronger school leadership or greater cohesion around organization-wide improvements? And are these changes sufficiently effective to raise student learning?

Overall, the Bryk team found that most schools either displayed principals who consolidated their authority and influence over the school council (associated with less teacher participation), or schools manifest strong demo-cratic social relations, with meaningful engagement of key actors. A few schools became bogged down in adversarial politics. Only about one-third of the schools went about "actively restructuring," that is, engaging in steady teacher development and pedagogical innovations, including coop-erative learning, literature-based reading, and what came to be called hands-on math and science. These schools showed significant gains in achievement. But the degrees of organizational change were uneven or disappointing in the other two-thirds of schools where student performance remained flat.

Another lesson from Chicago was that central nodes of authority push back quickly when decentralized account-ability show flagging results. Throughout the 1990s the central schools office (and mayor) would incrementally regain control over, then reconstitute the staffing of, several schools. In 1997 the district board approved a major effort to "restructure" high schools, "increasing academic press and enhancing personalization" (Hess & Cytrynbaum, 2002, p. 19). High school test scores did inch upward in the late 1990s after declining earlier. Lee (2002) argues that this stemmed partly from creating schools within schools (SWS), which improved teacher-student relationships. Her team found that the discipline-based organization of knowledge and teaching staff worked against the stronger identity and supportive relationships formed in SWS pro-grams. Intensifying "accountability and standardization in state and federal policy" during this period had "profound and usually negative effects on the SWS organization," according to Lee (2002, p. 14). In this way, the resurgent influence of the city school's office, backed by the state legislature, worked to erode neighborhood control. Flag-ging performance in a significant share of schools invited the reassertion of central authority.

In sum, this organization-level view of decentralization illuminates the importance of local conditions and insti-tutional history—especially the strength and legitimacy of community organizations and their position in mixed markets or vis-à-vis the public schools. Local political-economies also constrain the willingness and extent to which central agents can expand the supply of diverse school organizations, equalize quality, or devolve power to neighborhood actors. Such activists in Chicago benefited from a brief window in which central agents were so impa-tient with the city schools office that they were willing to radically decentralize control. Similarly, governors and state legislatures may be under pressure to expand charter schools or preschool options, run by public schools or CBOs. But which route is taken depends on the institutional history of the state's (or city's) particular mixed market. Govern-ment can choose to expand more colorful populations of schools, or induce quality changes through local control. But government's success in pressing these decentralizing strategies depends upon the organizational tools deployed and the institutional set already in place.

Small is Beautiful—Motivating Relationships in Schools

The third form of decentralization emphasizes that it is the web of children's immediate settings at home, with peers, and in the neighborhood that most forcefully socializes chil-dren. Schools may contribute to the upbringing of children and youths when relationships inside are motivating and richly educational. In the absence of meaningful activities or uncaring adults, schools simply breed alienation and resistance, according to this viewpoint. The centralization of authority or official knowledge, along with the external control of teachers' daily work, may further undercut atten-tion to relationships and the kinds of activities that students find to be motivating. Richer relationships are likely to arise in smaller collectivities that hold shared aims and norms, not within impersonal, hierarchical institutions long bred by the modern state.

This section reviews evidence on three decentralizing reforms that have attempted to improve relationships inside schools: small schools, career academies, and bilingual instruction. This small-places approach at times renders rationalized policy irrelevant, other than efforts to decouple schools from government's regulatory tendencies.

Control versus Commitment The small-places framework stems from a recurring skepticism with the modernization storyline, particularly the central state's habitual reliance on hierarchical, industrial ways of organizing work inside public organizations.[7] It is the steady rationalization of schools, according to this perspective, which reproduces unfulfilling relationships, didactically spooned-out knowl-edge, and narrow notions of how children develop. Just like life inside commercial firms students are rewarded based on their individual, competitive performance, and merit is assessed along efficiently tested slices of facts (Dreeben, 1968). This mass processing of students through regimented classroom routines leads to stiff resistance by many, as well as demoralizing effects on teachers.[8]

Developments in learning theory also emphasize that supportive relationships in schools are founded on points of continuity with the surrounding cultural or linguistic community. Lev Vygotsky's early work stressed that children learn mostly by observing others and "apprenticing" with adults in their immediate environment, prompting the metaphor of scaffolding up from local norms and knowledge (Wertsch, 1985). Bourdieu (1993) would add the notion of *habitus*, the enveloping setting in which the child matures and feels comfortable, lent order by shared language, markers of status, and expected forms of everyday participation. Learning is more likely to stick if the knowledge or meanings move within Vygotsky's zone of proximal development, like building scaffolds higher and higher. Attempts at introducing knowledge or beliefs that are too distant from the child's everyday community will not be viewed as legitimate. Implementing what some have come to call *situated models* of learning requires loosening the ties to centralized agents who have little understanding of local context. Advocates of small places, then, argue that "learning communities" must be human scale and respectful of the mores and understandings with which students or teachers arrive.

Some American pragmatists, however, argue that education that is fully continuous with one's surrounding community may exert conserving effects, rather than opening up new opportunities, wider horizons. John Dewey (1981) is perhaps the best known pragmatist—one who emphasized that democratic social relations and the practice of civic engagement requires a *decontextualized* perspective. Small and intimate communities matter; but children and youths must also understand how their small place is positioned on a wider institutional and economic map. From this progressive theory of learning stem decentered reforms like career academies, service learning, and magnet programs. Each places adolescents in adult-like roles outside school, replete with accompanying responsibilities. In contrast, the contemporary drift toward seeing schools as total institutions means that adolescents remain confined within the school's walls, delaying entry into public roles that advance social integration and meaning *beyond* their immediate context.

Smaller Schools, Richer Engagement? This intellectual tradition informs the attraction of smaller schools, perhaps the most decentralizing social arrangement that promises to enrich daily relationships. Listen to the theory of action behind Gates Foundation-funded small high schools: "The school is designed to support sustained relationships where every student has an adult advocate. The environment is authoritative, safe, ethical, and studious. Schools publish their progress to parents and engage the community in dialog about continuous improvement" (Smerdon & Means, 2006, p. 3). Indeed, the evaluation of the Gates-funded small schools, running over a 4-year period, found that they were marked by "close interpersonal relationships, common focus, and mutual respect and responsibility" (cited by Viadero, 2006, p. 25).

Still, early findings remain mixed and evaluation designs have been uneven in quality. These studies have typically employed comparison groups of neighboring schools, failing to seriously address the likelihood of selection bias. Careful experiments, similar to work on vouchers, have yet to be undertaken. This may become increasingly difficult, especially as the small-schools movement has gained legitimacy in many urban districts, resembling the weak political support for evaluating charter schools in a tough-headed manner. On the other hand, as the Gates Foundation and other benefactors rethink their approach to high school reform, empirical evidence may become more influential.

The initial Gates-sponsored evaluation showed that some of the intended mechanisms inside small schools were unfolding, operating with greater intensity than social dynamics observed in neighboring high schools. Innovative small schools were "characterized by greater personalization, higher expectations for students, and a more cohesive teacher community than were found in large, comprehensive high schools" (Smerdon & Means, 2006, p. 4). Other mechanisms appeared to contribute to stronger outcomes, including a more rigorous curriculum and higher-quality student work in English-learner classrooms, again compared with nearby high schools serving presumably similar students. Students' confidence and belief in their own capabilities were higher, as well. Implementation of the small-schools principles unfolded more completely in start-up schools, compared with older high schools that had been cut up into smaller learning communities.

"Growing pains" were reported in the second year of operation, including "some erosion in the strength of their school climate and signs of teacher burnout" (Smerdon & Means, 2006, p. 4). Nor did students attending small schools show consistently higher test scores, compared with district averages or neighboring schools. Higher attendance rates were reported for about seven or eight additional days in the school year. But the magnitude of estimated differences may have been smaller if selection processes into small schools had first been identified. Comparisons were often made to district-wide averages, a rather imprecise point of reference. For example, small schools tended to enroll higher shares of students of color than district averages. But this relates to family selections across large urban districts, not the value-added effects on achievement or other outcomes. When lower achievement levels are found, compared with district averages, so what? This may simply be the result of enrolling larger shares of children from low-income families. And the heterogeneity within districts limits the utility of making comparisons to district averages.

In fact, this young line of work tells us little about how small-school enrollees differ from, or remain similar to, students from similar communities. Many small schools report enrolling fewer students that qualify for special education. Little data are reported on how parents and homes may differ for those children who find there way into small high schools (Miner, 2005).[9] Initial evidence suggests that small schools enroll fewer students with behavioral problems (Stiefel, Schwartz, Iatarola, & Chellman, 2008). Many findings are regression-adjusted to take into account student gender, ethnicity, and economic status of the family. But as with other research on decentralized school options, we learn little about unobserved home or parental factors that may drive selection. Researchers too often assume that all low-income families are alike, then fail to measure variability within social class or ethnic groups.

Recent findings from Chicago's small high schools are similar, in line with the notion that small places matter. Teachers in small schools were "much more likely to report working in contexts characterized by teacher influence, collective responsibility, and teacher-teacher trust," compared with teachers in other Chicago high schools (Kahne, Sporte, de la Torre, & Easton, 2006, p. 2). But only juniors reported more demanding expectations from teachers, and test score growth showed no advantage for youths attending small schools, compared with those attending regular high schools (with regression controls). First-year students attended school nine days more during the year than the comparison group, and dropout rates improved slightly. One coauthor of the evaluation denied the importance of achievement growth: "If the lower dropout rate translates into a better graduation rate, the life chances (of students) will be much more strongly impacted than a change in two or three points on the PSAE [state tests]" (Sporte, as cited in Gewertz, 2006, p. 18). Schools chief Arne Duncan reverted back to the ideals of creating small places for students: "You have to get the culture right before you start to get the academics right. Those are leading indicators. The academic gains will follow" (as cited in Gewertz, 2006, p. 18).

Another Gates-funded evaluation found that 79% of seniors graduated from 14 small schools, and about 65% had been accepted into a 2- or 4-year college (Huebner, Corbett, & Phillippo, 2006). In what reads like a celebration of the initiative's ideals, replete with glossy photos, the authors admit that New York City cannot reliably estimate graduation rates in other schools. All but two of the small schools used a lottery to accept entrants, but no data are presented that compare applicants to students city wide or in comparable neighborhoods. We never learn whether the representation of special education students or those with behavior problems differs between small schools and regular high schools. Since these schools include "heavy representation" of Black and Latino students, the reader is apparently supposed to assume that selection into these theme-focused, bright new schools is random (p. 1). Sustainability also remains a pressing issue. Small schools appear to have unit costs that range between 3% and 18% higher than comprehensive high schools (Miner, 2005).

Career Academies   Academies offer another decentralized innovation, one that also sprouted from the small-places theory of action. Over 2,500 career academies—either dedicated schools or programs nested in regular high schools—were operating in the United States at last count (Kemple & Scott-Clayton, 2004). They strive, true to Deweyian pragmatism, to integrate demanding academic study with real work in adult-like roles, whether focused on health sciences, new technology, or the arts in units of under 200 students. Rather than warehousing youths in high school classrooms, academy proponents argue that students will find greater meaning and easier transitions if serving alongside adults. Career academies "are organized as small learning communities to create a more supportive, personalized learning environment" (Kemple & Scott-Clayton, 2004, p. 1). Career academies have spread over the past generation with much less capital and political clout than has accompanied charter or small schools (Stern, Raby, & Dayton, 1992). One random-assignment evaluation is tracking the long-term effects of career academies.

After following academy graduates and a control group for a decade, Kemple and Scott-Clayton (2004) found that enrollees "reported higher levels of interpersonal support from their teachers and peers than did students in the non-academy group" (pp. 2–3). Even though students entering predominately urban career academies were at high risk of dropping out, these programs "increased the likelihood of their staying in school through the end of twelfth grade, improved attendance, and increased the number of credits earned toward graduation." However, teaching practices were no different between the academies and regular high schools, and students tended to substitute more career-oriented courses for academic courses, which may help to explain mixed labor market benefits.

Young men, 4 years after leaving high school, earned $212 more per month if they had attended a career academy, compared with the control group, or about 18% more. The jobs obtained offered more steady employment and more hours per week for the treatment group. No labor market advantages for young women were observed. The academies had a negligible effect on the pursuit of postsecondary education. The highest risk group at entry showed the strongest wage returns, although this appeared to slightly suppress the likelihood that they entered and persisted through a postsecondary school.

Researchers have moved beyond the summative question to examine why some career academies produce significant benefits while others do not (Stern, Wu, Dayton, & Maul, 2005). This parallels the work above on vouchers and charter schools where investigators are bridging over to earlier school-effects research to understand whether the mechanisms found in decentralized schools or programs may differ from the organizational behavior and pedagogical practices found in schools that remain tightly coupled to the state's agenda. Stern and his colleagues found that academy students completed more courses when compared with matched comparison groups, perhaps due to stronger engagement. He also examined implementation fidelity to the idealized academy model, including taking courses together as a tight cohort, a greater share of coursework taken in the academy, and the mix of academy and non-academy students. Thus far, findings are inconsistent. But this line of work offers important methodological directions, especially the importance of measuring fidelity of implementation and the association between key program elements and student outcomes.

Classrooms that Build from Cultural Assets Proponents of the small-places framework argue that continuity between school, home, and community will advance children's engagement and capacity to build from what they already know. Continuity is often defined in terms of language. The National Literacy Panel (August & Shanahan, 2006) reviewed this growing area of research. In terms of language continuity, they found that quality bilingual classrooms advance children's performance in English and measures of academic engagement, compared with English-immersion classrooms (Francis, Lesaux, & August, 2006). But fewer than 20 studies have run randomized trials over the past four decades; effect sizes are modest; and most work is limited to elementary classrooms. Otherwise, most research on the extent to which culturally bounded norms or skills are continuous with home practices has employed qualitative methods. Classroom methods for advancing continuity and some benefits have been observed, but the social mechanisms and effects have not been measured and tested with large samples of children and teachers (Rueda, August, & Goldenberg, 2006).

At the preschool level, classroom-level research is demonstrating how teachers can build up from the (variable) norms that Latino youngsters acquire at home, as one example. Ann Eisenberg (2002) ran an ingenious experiment, asking blue-collar and middle-class Mexican American mothers to work with their 4-year-olds on a block-building task. They then engaged in a simple baking task. Eisenberg found that mothers asked their preschoolers many more questions when engaged in the familiar baking activity, compared with a more novel collaborative task. Working inside classrooms with preschool teachers, Riojas-Cortéz (2001) created storytelling exercises where children recounted episodes and events stemming from their extended family, offering grist for discussions, which yielded more complex language and moral considerations than abstracted curriculum tasks. The challenge is to link these suggestive findings to policy strategies for advancing continuity, then carefully evaluating which forms of continuity lead to what specific learning outcomes.

Scaffolding up from Family and Community

The family represents the fourth site of decentralized action, often conceptually bridging over to how children engage the school institution. I briefly review theoretical and empirical progress in two arenas: parental involvement and home-based interventions. Rekindled policy and research interest stems from the nagging realization that schools make little difference in determining children's life chances, compared with the strong effects of parenting practices and home environments. This fourth approach to decentralization shares intellectual roots with the third. But now researchers are tracking a colorful array of family and neighborhood reforms, each attempting to touch school-related outcomes, including more inviting forms of parent participation in schools, home visiting, and early childhood efforts. These initiatives have focused on the child, the home, or the mother's own practices and economic well-being since the 1960s (for a review, see St. Pierre & Layzer, 1998).

The notion of cultural consonance even arises in the work of economists who test whether the effectiveness of teachers is conditioned by particular contexts. Dee (2005), for instance, finds that an ethnic match between teacher and student appears to contribute to higher achievement. Yet, the social or motivational mechanisms that spark this effect remain poorly understood. More broadly, the theoretical accent on the embedded nature of social life—for parents and children alike—holds implications for how far families range as they consider school alternatives. Drawing on Bourdieu's (1993) classic conception of habitus, Wells (1996) found that many high school students participating in St. Louis's metropolitan desegregation program returned to inner-city schools from predominately White schools that ringed the city. They simply did not feel comfortable going out to the suburbs each morning.

Engaging Parents Historian William Cutler (2000) reminds us that educators have long been attentive to parents and home practices. "The child is a faithful representative of his home sentiments" (p. 16) wrote one contributor to the magazine, *The Massachusetts Teacher*, in 1851, "Nothing can be right, nothing can be safe, unless all is right and safe at home" (p. 16). To this day, the rhetoric around parent partnerships remains robust: The parent should be involved in school activities, be in close touch with teachers, and watch after homework, encouraging children to achieve in school. At the same time, non-stop statistics surface reminding us that parent participation varies with social class and ethnic membership. The recent national literacy survey found that only two-fifths of the most literate parents had connected with their child's school, volunteering, attending a school meeting, speaking with an individual teacher about their child's progress (Tonn, 2007). This proportion fell to about one-quarter among illiterate parents. Spanish-speaking parents in low-income homes report the lowest degree of contact with their child's teachers (Institute for Education Sciences, 2006).

A variety of empirical work examines why parental involvement is so low, focusing on the interaction between family characteristics and features of the school organization's limited capacity to engage parents. Second, researchers continue to estimate the benefits of differing kinds of participation, from simply attending school meetings to direct work with children at home. Analytic methods continue to rely on correlational analyses and multivariate modeling with limited attention to endogeneity and establishing causal pathways.

The influence of cultural or linguistic mismatch also arises in the literature on factors that facilitate or restrict parent participation. Several scholars have shown, for example, how Latino parents feel social distance from teachers who are not seen as approachable, or simply can't speak Spanish or remain uninterested in the home practices and social norms in which children are raised (Delgado-Gaitán, 1992). We have observed how Latina mothers within preschool classrooms often feel that too much play is evident, individualistic behavior is expected, or teachers and aides simply lack fluency in Spanish (Holloway, Fuller, Rambaud, & Eggers-Piérola, 1997).

Hoover-Dempsey et al. (2005) has pushed to delineate the motivational mechanisms that may explain variation in parents' level of engagement, helping to establish a theoretically informed empirical agenda. This includes whether the parent sees her or his role as legitimately linked to teachers' own work to advancing the child's growth. The parent's feeling of efficacy when engaging educators appears to play a role, and this interacts with how inviting school staff appear to be. Social class remains an overwhelming determinant of involvement, conceptualized by Lareau (2003) as disparate levels of cultural capital and knowledge about how to resolve disputes or collaborate with educators. Middle-class parents may share with teachers particular interpersonal norms, language, and social authority in ways that equalize the relationship, whereas parents from low-income settings are often viewed as being of lower status, or less able to contribute to their children's development (Hoover-Dempsey & Sandler, 1997; Horvat, Weininger, & Lareau, 2003).

We know that public mechanisms can be mobilized to encourage greater parental engagement, especially within the early education sector. Chicago's Child-Parent Centers represent a well-known effort that heavily involves mothers whose young children attended preschool, primarily located in the poor southside area. Home visits were once conducted to encourage educational activities and discuss alternative forms of discipline; literacy centers still operate to advance mothers' own reading skills and to teach them how to engage their children through language and reading activities. Variation in mothers' involvement has been associated with their child's developmental trajectories, after taking into account home background (all children came from low-income, predominately Black families) and length of preschool exposure. Effect sizes were moderate and persisted into the elementary grades (Clements, Reynolds, & Hickey, 2004).

Researchers have distinguished between parental effects inside the home versus indirect effects from involvement at school. This typically involves regression analysis of survey data. Helping with homework, structuring a time and place for it in the home, and restricted television viewing have been associated with higher student achievement, drawing on cross-sectional data or longitudinal panel data (e.g., Epstein, 1991, Ho Sui-Chu & Willms, 1996, Muller, 1993). The count and quality of parent contacts with teachers appear to hold indirect effects, operating through the teacher's perceptions of the child's capacities and the kinds of courses and curricular tracks that students enter (Schneider & Coleman, 1993). This line of work continues to be limited by reliance on cross-sectional survey data, insufficient attention to endogeneity, and sometimes modest effect sizes.

Recent work is advancing our understanding of how parent engagement with schools and children's development is nested in wider social networks and expectations that are reproduced over time. One correlational study found that parents who are more frequent church-goers consistently show high levels of engagement with (elementary school) teachers, stronger oversight of homework, and steadier educational activities. Religious commitments varied independently of social-class background (Sikkink & Hernández, 2003). Small's (2004) recent work details how mothers' engagement with preschools can strengthen social networks, leading to new information about parenting and family-support agencies. These wider networks may yield decontextualized knowledge not available in one's immediate community. Recent studies suggest that poor children's learning curves are flatter when their parents report tight bonds ("closure" in social capital parlance) with other poor adults (Morgan & Sørensen, 1999). Parents who break out of their immediate circle, perhaps facilitated or ignored by their child's teachers, appear to acquire more novel information.

Start inside the Home Mothers in poor communities since the 1960s have been implicated across a variety of policy initiatives, from Head Start preschools to Title I parent councils. Home visiting programs—aimed at enriching educational activities and socialization practices—have involved schools and a variety of educators inside neighborhoods. As these programs grew in the 1980s, their effects on parenting practices and child outcomes were found to be uneven and often weak (Gomby, Culross, & Behrman, 1999). These disappointing benefits were linked to the infrequent or uninspiring contact between mothers and home visitors.

More recent work on the home-visiting elements of preschools and early childhood interventions has yielded encouraging results. The random-assignment evaluation of the national Early Head Start program, for instance, found significant effects on 2- and 3-year-old children in terms of steeper cognitive growth (Love et al., 2002). Over half of the families enrolled received home visitation and parent training; the other portion benefited from center-based care for their infant or toddler. Children's growth trajectories were related to treatment-group gains in mothers' use of language, reading with their children, and reduced use of harsh or negative discipline practices. The fertility rate of mothers in the treatment group also declined modestly. Effect sizes were moderate, ranging over 0.35 of a standard deviation for several outcomes. Investigators measured the extent to which key ingredients of Early Head Start were implemented by host community agencies, and this implementation scale was related to effect sizes for maternal and child outcomes.

Additional home mechanisms have been identified that affect children's early cognitive and social development. A portion overlaps with the mother's efficacy in attending to the child's growth, including her interaction with local educators. The level of intentionality with which mothers see child development as an engineered project varies across groups and individual parents. This holds implications for the kinds of activities and constraints that parents structure at home (e.g., television viewing, passive or active child roles), as well as the intensity of interaction with teachers (Bridges, Fuller, Livas, Mireles, & Scott, 2007). The recent generation of research on welfare reform confirms the powerful effects of maternal mental health, the extent to which mothers design educational activities with their children, and the mother's level of social support (Ripke & Crosby, 2002).

The study of home interventions and educational practices has long been linked to economic and family policy, and commonly employs experimental designs. This offers a useful methodological lesson. Preoccupied with the big policy questions of does Head Start or welfare reform work, randomization occurs on a global variable: enrollment in the program in question. However, after determining whether the overall intervention yields benefits, this design often fails to illuminate mediating mechanisms. The Early Head Start evaluation is a notable exception, where investigators observed program elements that were variably implemented. This yielded considerable information on how to improve the quality of the intervention, moving beyond the summative evaluation question.

Conclusions—Lessons for Decentralists

These initial findings on decentralizing reforms—both the benefits and the mediating mechanisms—are encouraging in certain ways. Most notable perhaps is the state's ability to enter mixed markets of organizations and spur greater supply, as seen with the rapid expansion of charter schools. At times, government displays a sustained capacity to equalize access and raise quality in mixed markets, as discovered in the preschool field. The decentering of public authority and dollars to neighborhoods, as we learned from the Chicago experiment, spurred civic engagement at the grassroots, while falling short in raising organizational effectiveness. And the RAND analysis in California showed that some kinds of charter schools—ironically, those charters that secede from their district boards—can operate more cost-effectively than regular public schools.

What's bedeviling along these lines of work is how local conditions can be so telling when gauging the efficacy of decentralized social organizations. The migration of children of color into parochial schools, aided by portable vouchers, has yielded quite spotty effects, depending on the city and the ethnicity and grade level of students. Start-up charter schools often display disappointing effects, but conversion charter can spark stronger achievement. Preschools appear to boost the early learning of children from poor families, but not those from middle-class homes. Crafting generalizable theory and pinpointing human-scale mechanisms that work (triggered by decentralized arrangements) will continue to be difficult when local conditions are so telling. More serious thinking should focus on prior conditions,

before casting our eye to the decentralized intervention that alights onto these local settings.

Resurgent interest in decentralizing reforms has shifted how the organizational problems of schooling and accompanying remedies are framed. Politicians and the policy researchers they embrace continue to ask how government can regulate behavior far below, inside schools and classrooms. Simpler learning objectives, routinized classroom technologies, sanctions and extrinsic rewards laid on teachers are the tools wielded by the system builders. Some decentralists accent the importance of "getting the incentives right"; others put forward intrinsically motivating mechanisms, from jump-starting civic engagement by chartering local groups to run schools, to enlisting parents to become respected partners in the upbringing of their children. Shaking off the Weberian tenets of the modern regulatory state has proven liberating for a growing count of policy researchers, not to mention their political patrons.

The field of decentralization—especially how we conceptualize progressive intervention into mixed markets—has prompted methodological advances. We reviewed work on how state government action has significantly moderated the regressive effects of local poverty or wealth when it comes to expanding family access to quality preschools. But government has yet to show such determination when it comes to equalizing the resources made available to charter schools, situated across a colorful variety of neighborhoods. Students of mixed markets also worry about family selection processes, advancing our understanding of how household and organizational factors converge to drive which families gain access to high quality educational organizations.

Research on decentralization reminds us that whether an intervention works, or not, remains a pressing question. But even with elegant randomized trials, for instance when vouchers have failed to work, investigators often come up short in explaining why. We are learning more about variability in the resources that flow to charter schools. But we remain largely in the empirical dark as to why some charters are more cost-effective than others, or when compared with regular public schools. Again, keeping both eyes on the prize—does it work?—distracts from uncovering mediating mechanisms inside schools or classrooms, and perhaps the spirit of teachers.

Decentralization advocates and allied researchers might become more candid about how human-scale organizations are situated—and regressively constrained—by their surrounding political-economies. Some advocates continue to invoke rhetoric about freedom from government control, and we researchers are illuminating how this results in organizational advantages and wider options for some parents. At the same time, charter school associations, gated communities, and major foundations—to name a few interest groups—are lobbying to secure greater funding or advantageous treatment for their favorite decentralized form of schooling. This is all part of the vibrant democratic contention energizing school improvement. But these advocates and allied researchers should recognize that they aim to influence the institutional arrangements that benefit their favored reform. These proponents, hoping to manipulate centralized policy levers, well understand that "decentralized" schooling is often engineered from above (Handler, 1996). Decentralists could find common cause in addressing the deep structural constraints that affect all schools: uneven teacher supply, unequal school financing, and levels of family poverty that undercut their own reforms.

Enthusiastic funders of decentralizing reforms should endeavor to understand how mediating mechanisms work before dumping millions of dollars into a single model based solely on their well-meaning ideals. It seems unnecessary to repeat this warning after four decades of grand experiments mounted by governments and large foundations. But rising faith in small high schools, capitalized by philanthropies and now urban school districts, has yet to yield hard evidence of consistant results. Encouraging signs have emerged, including stronger personal relationships in some small schools, along with more robust student engagement and perhaps climbing graduation rates. But this literature thus far is based on research designs that lack longitudinal data and at times simply ignore selection biases. A similar case is how urban districts, including Los Angeles and New York, are granting autonomy to some schools—eagerly mimicking the loosely-coupled governance of charter schools—with little articulation of the organizational mechanisms required to tie decentralized social arrangements to stronger teacher and student motivation.

Finally, this review demonstrates how policy researchers sometimes do work for public or private agents who honestly want to know whether their decentralizing reform works, and why. But our field also hosts analysts in reputable firms and universities who are content with employing weak designs which yield indefensible findings, the stuff of glossy reports that sing praise for their particular silver bullet. Even before getting to their technical work policy researchers might start with a normative question, then consider an ethical quandary. Is this study already bounded by the ideals held by the centralizing state or decentralization enthusiast who is footing the bill? And if so, could my research still influence how the problem is framed or how the policy remedy is weighed over time? Just like the field of decentralization, policy researchers are surrounded by normative assumptions and pivotal questions that cannot be resolved with evidence alone.

Notes

1. This chapter stems from work on state action in decentralized organizational fields supported over the years by the Hewlett, Packard, and Spencer foundations, and the federal departments of education and health and human services. Special thanks to Susan Dauber, Kristi Kimball, Mike Smith, and Marie Young. Colleagues and students have contributed enormously to my thinking about the social organization of children's development, including Ed Bodine, Margaret Bridges, Luis Huerta, Susan Holloway, Lynn Kagan, Susanna Loeb, Seeta Pai, Robert LeVine, Sandy Dornbusch, Annelie Strath, and John Vasconcellos. Timothy Ford and Sitome Mabrahtu helped enormously with editing.

2. Space does not allow for a parallel review of the forces that have contributed to the resurging popularity of the ideals and claimed benefits of decentralized social organizations. Elsewhere I offer one analysis (Fuller, 2007, chapters 1 and 2).

3. Evaluation results for the publicly funded Cleveland voucher program continue to appear (previously reviewed in Fuller, Burr, Huerta, Puryear, & Wexler, 1999; Howell & Peterson, 2002).

4. This finding was challenged by Krueger and Zhu (2004), based on their reanalysis and a dispute over how mixed-race students were classified. They pointed out that the magnitude (effect size) of the Black advantage found by Peterson was so small that shifts in coding decisions could erase statistical significance.

5. Henig (2008) details how the *New York Times* imprecisely reported the AFT's estimation of mean differences between charter and regular public school student performance with no statistical controls for demographic background, sparking a sustained debate by scholars and charter school advocates. A sound methodology—given the wide heterogeneity among charter schools—would measure organizational features and a detailed set of family characteristics, along with tracking student growth. The dueling AFT and NAEP studies could not disaggregate types of charter schools, so central to the RAND design, nor were complete student demographic measures available.

6. Research on charter schools is beginning to examine this interplay between the rising legitimacy and localized clout of community activists and their constrained capacity to sustain effective schools over time (especially, Schorr, 2002). State actors and local activists have negotiated how to share authority and diversify the organization of publicly funded schools via the charter mechanism. But this does not necessarily mean that the population of charters, say within a district, will necessarily affect the mean quality or effectiveness of regular public schools. The de-centering of authority and resource controls may be insufficient.

7. This section header borrows from Rowan's (1990, 2006) ongoing thinking on how accountability-controls or market pressures may advance or erode the intrinsic motivation expressed by teachers and students.

8. This skepticism over government's attempt to regulate social relations inside institutions stems from an old debate in the West. In the late 19th century, Tönnies (1887/1957) advanced the distinction between non-instrumental kinship bonds versus formal organizations, instruments that pursue shared goals "and (individuals) are willing to join hands for this purpose, even though indifference or even antipathy may exist at other levels" (p. 5). Writing at a time dominated by Darwinian thought and naturalistic metaphor, Tönnies argued that family-like collectives are motivated by the "natural will" of individual members, seeking without reflection the affective and expressive benefits of informal association. Whereas "rational will," exercised mainly within the capitalist class, motivated individuals to form corporations that produced or traded goods through organized means that were distinct from the end goal: profit and material well-being.

9. One of the Gates Foundation's explicit goals was to broaden family options among differing high schools. The national evaluation highlights that fully one-third of parents in host districts reported attending a "school of choice," up from 6%, between 2001 and 2005 (Smerdon & Means, 2006, p. 61). But to date no serious work has examined student migration patterns and non-random selection into particular kinds of schools.

References

Alinsky, S. (1969). *Reveille for radicals* (Rev. ed.). New York: Random House.
Armor, D., & Peiser, B. (1998). Interdistrict choice in Massachusetts. In

P. Peterson & B. Hasssel (Eds.), *Learning from school choice* (pp. 157–186). Washington DC: Brookings Institution.

August, D., & Shanahan, T. (2006). *Developing literacy in second-language learners.* New York: Routledge.

Betts, J., Goldhaber, D., & Rosenstock, L. (2005). The supply side of school choice. In J. Betts & T. Loveless (Eds.), *Getting choice right: Ensuring equity and efficiency in education policy* (pp. 61–84). Washington DC: Brookings Institution.

Blume, H., & Rivera, C. (2007, July 29). Parents still seek the elusive 'right' school: Parents scramble to claim seats for their children in magnet, charter and private programs. *Los Angeles Times.* Retrieved May 9, 2008, from http://www.satbank.net/satinfobbs/content.asp?tb=satnews&id=178&page=1&block=0

Bodine, E., Fuller, B., González, M., Huerta, L., Naughton, S., Park, S., et al. (2008). Disparities in charter school resources—The influence of state policy and community. *Journal of Education Policy, 23,* 1–33.

Boo, K. (2007, January 15). Expectations: Can the students who became a symbol of failed reform be rescued? *The New Yorker, 82*(45), 44–57.

Bourdieu, P. (1993). *The field of cultural production: Essays on art and literature.* New York: Columbia University Press.

Braun, H., Jenkins, F., & Grigg, W. (2006). *A closer look at charter schools using hierarchical linear modeling.* Washington, DC: U.S. Department of Education, National Assessment of Educational Progress.

Bridges, M., Fuller, B., Livas, A., Mireles, L., & Scott, L. (2007, March). *The daily activities of Mexican-American children.* Paper presented at the Society for Research in Child Development, Boston.

Bryk, A., Sebring, P., Kerbow, D., Rollow, S., & Easton, J. (1999). *Chartering Chicago school reform: Democratic localism as a lever for change.* Boulder, CO: Westview Press.

Chubb, J., & Moe, T. (1990). *Politics, markets, and America's schools.* Washington DC: Brookings Institution.

Center for Education Reform. (2008). *Charter school facts.* Retrieved April 8, 2008, from http://www.edreform.com/index.cfm?fuseAction=stateStats&pSectionID=15&cSectionID=44

Clements, M., Reynolds, A., & Hickey, E. (2004). Site-level predictors of children's school and social competence in the Chicago Child-Parent Centers. *Early Childhood Research Quarterly, 19,* 273–296.

Coleman, J. (1990). *Foundations of social theory.* Cambridge, MA: Harvard University Press.

Collins, R. (1984). *Three sociological traditions.* New York: Oxford University Press.

Cross, C. (2003). *Political education: National policy comes of age.* New York: Teachers College Press.

Cutler, W. (2000). *Parents and schools: The 150-year struggle for control in American education.* Chicago: University of Chicago Press.

Dee, T. (2005). A teacher like me: Does race, ethnicity, or gender matter? *American Economic Review, 95,* 158–165.

Delgado-Gaitán, C. (1992). School matters in the Mexican-American home: Socializing children to education. *American Educational Research Journal, 29,* 495–513.

Dewey, J. (1981). Experience and nature. In J. Boydston (Ed.), *The later works of John Dewey: Vol. 1.* Carbondale: Southern Illinois University Press. (Original work published 1938)

Dickman, A., & Schmidt, J. (2007). Are voucher schools putting the squeeze on the MPS? *Public Policy Forum Research Brief, 95*(1), 1–8

DiMaggio, P., & Anheier, H. (1990). The sociology of nonprofit organizations and sectors. *Annual Review of Sociology, 16,* 137–159.

Dreeben, R. (1968). *On what is learned in school.* Reading, MA: Addison Wesley.

Durkheim, E. (1956). *Education and Sociology.* Glencoe, IL: Free Press.

Durkheim, E. (1964). *Essays on sociology and philosophy.* New York: Harper and Row.

Eisenberg, A. (2002). Maternal teaching talk within families of Mexican descent: Influence of task and socioeconomic status. *Hispanic Journal of Behavioral Sciences, 24,* 204–224.

Epstein, J. (1991). Effects on student achievement and teachers' practices of parent involvement. In B. A. Hutson, T. G. Sticht, S. B. Silvern, F. R. Chang, & S. Wood (Eds.), *Advances in Reading/Language Research, Vol. 5: Literacy through family, community and school interaction* (pp. 261–276). Greenwich: JAI Press.

Fliegel, S., & MacGuire, J. (1993). *Miracle in East Harlem: The fight for choice in public education.* New York: Times Books.

Forman, J., Jr. (2007). The rise and fall of school vouchers: A story of race, religion, and politics. *UCLA Law Review, 54,* 547–604.

Francis, D., Lesaux, N., & August, D. (2006). Language of instruction. In D. August & T. Shanahan (Eds.), *Developing literacy in second-language learners* (pp. 365–413). Mahwah, NJ: Erlbaum.

Friedman, M., & Friedman, R. (1980). *Free to choose: A personal statement.* New York: Harcourt Brace Jovanovich.

Fuller, B. (Ed.). (1999). *Government confronts culture: The struggle for local democracy in southern Africa.* New York: Taylor and Francis.

Fuller, B. (Ed.). (2000). *Inside charter schools: The paradox of radical decentralization.* Cambridge, MA: Harvard University Press.

Fuller, B. (2007). *Standardized childhood: The political and cultural struggle over early education.* Palo Alto, CA: Stanford University Press.

Fuller, B., Burr, E., Huerta, L., Puryear, S., & Wexler, E. (1999). *School choice: Abundant hopes, scarce evidence of results* [Monograph]. Berkeley: Policy Analysis for California Education.

Fuller, B., & Elmore, R. (Eds.). (1996). *Who chooses? Who loses? Culture, institutions, and the unequal effects of school choice.* New York: Teachers College Press.

Fuller, B., Gawlik, M., Kuboyama-Gonzalez, E., & Park, S. (2004). Localized ideas of fairness: Inequality among charter schools. In K. Bulkley & P. Wohlstetter (Eds.), *Taking account of charter schools: What's happened and what's next?* (pp. 93–120). New York: Teachers College Press.

Fuller, B., Holloway, S., & Liang, X. (1996). Family selection of child-care centers. The influence of household support, ethnicity, and parental practices. *Child Development, 67,* 3320–3337.

Fuller, B., Loeb, S., Strath, A., & Carrol, B. (2004). State formation of the child care sector: Family demand and policy action. *Sociology of Education, 77,* 337–358.

Fuller, B., Raudenbush, S., Wei, L., & Holloway, S. (1993). Can government raise child care quality? The influence of family demand, poverty, and policy. *Educational Evaluation and Policy Analysis, 15,* 255–278.

Fuller, B., & Strath, A. (2001). The child care and preschool workforce: Demographics, earnings, and unequal distribution. *Education Evaluation and Policy Analysis, 23,* 37–55.

Funkhouser, J., & Colopy, K. (1994). *Minnesota's open enrollment option: Impacts on school districts.* Washington, DC: Policy Studies Associates.

Gamoran, A. (1996). Student achievement in public magnet, public comprehensive, and private city high schools. *Educational Evaluation and Policy Analysis, 18,* 1–18.

Garnier, M., Hage, J., & Fuller, B. (1989). The strong state, social class, and controlled school expansion in France, 1881–1975. *American Journal of Sociology, 95,* 279–306.

Gewertz, C. (2006, August 9). Chicago small schools see gains, but not on tests. *Education Week,* Retrieved November 30, 2007, from http://ccsr.uchicago.edu/news_citations/080906_edweek.html

Glendon, M. (1991). *Rights talk: The impoverishment of political discourse.* New York: Maxwell Macmillan.

Gomby, D., Culross, P., & Behrman, R. (1999). Home visiting: Recent program evaluations, analysis, and recommendations. *Future of Children, 9*(1), 4–26.

Greene, J., Peterson, P., & Du, J. (1997). *Effectiveness of school choice: The Milwaukee Experiment.* Cambridge, MA: Harvard University, Center for American Political Studies.

Halpern, R. (1995). *Rebuilding the inner city: A history of neighborhood initiatives to address poverty in the United States.* New York: Columbia University Press.

Hamilton, L., & Guin, K. (2005). Understanding how families choose schools. In J. Betts & T. Loveless (Eds.), *Getting choice right: Ensuring equity and efficiency in education policy* (pp. 40–60). Washington, DC: Brookings Institution.

Handler, J. (1996). *Down from bureaucracy: The ambiguity of privatization and empowerment*. Princeton, NJ: Princeton University Press.

Hastings, J., & Weinstein, J. (2007). *No Child Left Behind: Estimating the impact of choices and student outcomes* (NBER Working Paper No. W13009). Cambridge, MA: National Bureau of Economic Research.

Heebner, A., Crain, R., Kiefer, D., Si, Y., Jordan, W., & Tokarska, B. (1992). *Career magnets: Interviews with students and staff*. Macomb, IL: National Center for Research in Vocational Education.

Henig, J. (2008). *Spin cycle: How research is used in policy debates—The case of charter schools*. New York: Russell Sage Foundation.

Hess, G. A., Jr., & Cytrynbaum, S. (2002). The effort to redesign Chicago high schools: Effects on schools and achievement. In V. Lee (Ed.), *Reforming Chicago's high schools: Research perspectives on school and system level change* (pp. 19–50). Chicago: Consortium on Chicago School Research.

Hirshberg, D., Huang, D., & Fuller, B. (2005). Which low-income parents select child care? Family demand and neighborhood organizations. *Children and Youth Services Review, 27*, 1119–1148.

Holloway, S., Fuller, B., Rambaud, M., & Eggers-Piérola, C. (1997). *Through my own eyes: Single mothers and the cultures of poverty*. Cambridge, MA: Harvard University Press.

Ho Sui-Chu, E., & Willms, D. (1996). Effects of parental involvement on eighth-grade achievement. *Sociology of Education, 69*, 126–141.

Hoover-Dempsey, K., & Sandler, H. (1997) Why do parents become involved in their children's education? *Review of Educational Research, 67*, 3–42.

Hoover-Dempsey, K., Walker, J. M. T., Sandler, H. M., Whetsel, D., Green, C. L., Wilkins, A. S., et al. (2005). Why do parents become involved? Research findings and implications. *The Elementary School Journal, 106*, 105–130.

Horvat, E., Weininger, E., & Lareau, A. (2003). From social ties to social capital: Class differences in the relations between schools and parent networks. *American Educational Research Journal, 40*, 319–351.

Howell, W. (2006). Switching schools? A closer look at parents' initial interest in and knowledge about the choice provisions of No Child Left Behind. *Peabody Journal of Education, 81*, 140–179.

Howell, W., & Peterson, P. (2006). *The education gap: Vouchers and urban schools*. Washington, DC: Brookings Institution.

Hoxby, C. (2003). School choice and school competition: Evidence from the United States. *Swedish Economic Policy Review, 10*, 11–67.

Huebner, T., Corbett, G., & Phillippo, K. (2006). *Rethinking high school: Inaugural graduations at New York City's new high schools*. San Francisco: WestEd and the Gates Foundation.

Huerta, L. (2000). Losing public accountability: A home schooling charter. In B. Fuller (Ed.), *Inside charter schools: The paradox of radical decentralization* (177–202). Cambridge, MA: Harvard University Press.

Institute for Education Sciences (IES). (2006). *Trends in the use of school choice, 1993 to 2003* (NCES 2007-045). Washington, DC: National Center for Education Statistics.

Kahne, J., Sporte, S., de la Torre, M., & Easton, J. (2006). *Small schools on a larger scale: The first three years of the Chicago high school redesign initiative*. Chicago: University of Chicago, Consortium on Chicago School Research.

Kirkpatrick, D. (1990). *Choice in schooling: A case for tuition vouchers*. Chicago: Loyola University Press.

Kemple, J., & Scott-Clayton, J. (2004). *Career academies: Impact on labor market outcomes and educational attainment* [Monograph]. New York: Manpower Research Demonstration Corp.

Krueger, A., & Zhu, P. (2004). Another look at the New York City school voucher experiment. *American Behavioral Scientist, 47*, 658–698.

Lankford, H., & Wyckoff, J. (1992). Primary and secondary school choice among public and religious alternatives. *Economics of Education Review, 11*, 317–337.

Lareau, A. (2003). *Unequal childhoods: Class, race, and family life*. Berkeley: University of California Press.

Lee, V. (Ed.). (2002). *Reforming Chicago's high schools: Research perspectives on school and system level change*. Chicago: Consortium on Chicago School Research.

Liang, X., Fuller, B., & Singer, J. (2000). Ethnic differences in child care selection: The influence of family structure, prenatal practices, and home language. *Early Childhood Research Quarterly, 15*, 357–384.

Lloyd, D., & Thomas, P. (1998). *Culture and the state*. New York: Routledge.

Love, J. M., Kisker, E. E., Ross, C. M., Schochet, P. Z., Brooks-Gunn, J., Paulsell, D. et al. (2002). *Making a difference in the lives of infants and toddlers and their families: Impacts of Early Head Start*. Washington DC: United States Department of Health and Human Services.

Ludwig, J., Ladd, H., & Duncan, G. (2001). The effects of urban poverty on educational outcomes: Evidence from a randomized experiment. In W. Gale & J. R. Pack (Eds.), *Brookings-Wharton papers on urban affairs: 2001* (pp. 147–202). Washington DC: Brookings Institution.

Marty, M. (1997). *The one and the many: America's struggle for the common good*. Cambridge, MA: Harvard University Press.

Meyer, J., & Rowan, B. (1977). Institutionalized organizations: Formal structure as myth and ceremony. *American Journal of Sociology, 83*, 340–363.

Meyer, J., Tyack, D., Nagel, J., & Gordon, A. (1979). Public education as nation-building in America: Enrollments and bureaucratization in the American states, 1870–1930. *American Journal of Sociology, 85*, 591–613.

Miner, B. (2005). The Gates Foundation and small schools. *Rethinking Schools, 19*(4). Retrieved May 9, 2008, from: http://www.rethinkingschools.org/archive/19_04/gate194.shtml

Mitch, D. (1992). The rise of popular literacy in Europe. In B. Fuller & R. Rubinson (Eds.), *The political construction of education: The state, school expansion, and economic change* (pp. 31–46). New York: Praeger.

Morgan, S., & Sørensen, A. (1999). Parental networks, social closure, and mathematics learning. *American Sociological Review, 64*, 661–681.

Muller, C. (1993). Parent involvement and academic achievement: An analysis of family resources available to the child. In B. Schneider & J. S. Coleman (Eds.), *Parents, their children and schools* (pp. 77–113). Boulder, CO: Westview Press.

Nelson, H., Rosenberg, B., & Van Meter, N. (2004). *Charter school achievement on the 2003 National Assessment of Educational Progress*. Washington, DC: American Federation of Teachers.

Plank, D., & Boyd, W. (1994). Politics and governance of education. In T. Husén, & T. Postlethwaite (Eds.), *The International Encyclopedia of Education: Vol. 8* (2nd ed., pp. 4587–4595). Oxford, UK: Pergamon Press.

Renzulli, L. (2005). Organizational environments and the emergence of charter schools in the United States. *Sociology of Education, 78*, 1–26.

Riojas-Cortéz, M. (2001). Preschoolers' funds of knowledge displayed through sociodramatic play episodes in a bilingual classroom. *Early Childhood Education Journal, 29*, 35–40.

Ripke, M., & Crosby, D. (2002). The effects of welfare reform on the educational outcomes of parents and their children. *Review of Research in Education, 26*, 181–261.

Rofes, E. (1998). *Districts react slowly to charter schools*. Berkeley: Policy Analysis for California Education.

Ross, K. (2005). Charter schools and integration: The experience in Michigan. In J. Betts & T. Loveless (Eds.), *Getting choice right: Ensuring equity and efficiency in education policy* (pp.146–175). Washington, DC: Brookings Institution.

Rossiter, C. (Ed.). (2003). *The federalist papers: Alexander Hamilton, James Madison, John Jay*. New York: Signet Classic.

Rouse, C. (1998). Private school vouchers and student achievement: An evaluation of the Milwaukee parental choice program. *Quarterly Journal of Economics, 113*, 553–602.

Rouse, C., Hannaway, J., Goldhaber, D., & Figlio, D. (2007). *Feeling the*

Florida heat: How low-performing schools respond to voucher and accountability pressure. Washington, DC: Urban Institute.

Rowan, B. (1990). Commitment and control: Alternative strategies for the organizational design of schools. *Review of Research in Education, 16*, 353–389.

Rowan, B. (2006). The new institutionalism and the study of educational organizations: Changing ideas for changing times. In H. Meyer & B. Rowan (Eds.), *The new institutionalism in education* (pp. 15–32). Albany: State University of New York Press.

Rueda, R., August, D., & Goldenberg, C. (2006). The sociocultural context in which children acquire literacy. In D. August & T. Shanahan (Eds.), *Developing literacy in second-language learners: Report of the National Literacy Panel on Language-Minority Children and Youth* (pp. 319–340). Mahwah, NJ: Erlbaum.

Schneider, B., & Coleman, J. (Eds.). (1993). *Parents, their children, and schools.* Boulder, CO: Westview Press.

Schneider, M., Teske, P., & Marschall, M. (2000). *Choosing schools: Consumer choice and the quality of American schools.* Princeton, NJ: Princeton University Press.

Schorr, J. (2002). *Hard lessons: The promise of an inner city charter school.* New York: Ballantine.

Scott, W. R. (2001). *Institutions and organizations* (2nd ed.). Thousand Oaks, CA: Sage.

Sikkink, D., & Hernández, E. (2003). *Religion matters: Predicting schooling success among Latino youth.* Notre Dame, IN: University of Notre Dame, Institute for Latino Studies.

Small, M. (2004). *Villa Victoria: The transformation of social capital in a Boston barrio.* Chicago: University of Chicago Press.

Smerdon, B., & Means, B. (2006). *Creating cultures for learning: Supportive relationships in new and redesigned high schools.* Menlo Park, CA: American Institutes for Research and the Gates Foundation.

St. Pierre, R., & Layzer, J. (1998). Improving the life chances of children in poverty: Assumptions and what we have learned. *Social Policy Report, 12,* 1–25.

Steel, L., & Levine, R. (1994). *Educational innovation in multicultural contexts: The growth of magnet schools in American education* [Monograph]. Palo Alto, CA: American Institutes for Research.

Stern, D., Raby, M., & Dayton, C. (1992). *Career academies: Partnerships for reconstructing American high schools.* San Francisco: Jossey-Bass.

Stern, D., Wu, C., Dayton, C., & Maul, A. (2005). Learning by doing career academies. In D. Neumark (Ed.), *Improving school to work transitions* (pp.134–168). New York: Russell Sage.

Stiefel, L., Schwartz, A., Iatarola, P., & Chellman, C. (2008). *Mission matters: The cost of small high schools* (Working paper 08-03). New York: New York University.

Teske, P., Fitzpatrick, J., & Kaplan, G. (2007). *Opening doors: How low-income parents search for the right school.* Seattle: University of Washington.

Tonn, J. (2007, April 11). Adult literacy linked to parent involvement. *Education Week,* p. 14.

Tönnies, F. (1957). *Community and society* (C. Loomis, Trans.). East Lansing: Michigan State University Press. (Original work published 1887)

Viadero, D. (2006). Foundation shifts tack on studies: Scholars say Gates risks losing valuable findings. *Education Week, 26*(9), 1, 25.

Weisbrod, B. (1988). *The nonprofit economy*: Cambridge, MA: Harvard University Press.

Wells, A. (1996). *Time to choose: America at the crossroads of school choice policy.* New York: Hill and Wang.

Wertsch, J. (1985). *Vygotsky and the social formation of mind.* Cambridge, MA: Harvard University Press.

Witte, J. (2000). *The market approach to education: An analysis of America's first voucher program.* Princeton, NJ: Princeton University Press.

Wolf, P. (2005). School choice and civic values. In J. Betts & T. Loveless (Eds.), *Getting choice right: Ensuring equity and efficiency in education policy* (pp. 210–244). Washington, DC: Brookings Institution.

Wolf, P., Gutman, B., Puma, M., Rizzo, L. & Eissa, N. (2007). *Evaluation of the D.C. Opportunity Scholarship Program: Impacts after one year.* Washington, DC: U.S. Department of Education.

Wuthnow, R. (2004). *Saving America? Faith-based services and the future of civil society.* Princeton, NJ: Princeton University Press.

Yu, C., & Taylor, W. (Eds.). (1997). *Difficult choices: Do magnet schools serve children in need?* Washington, DC: Citizens' Commission on Civil Rights.

Zimmer, R., Buddin, R., Chau, D., Gill, B., Guarino, C., Hamilton, L., et al. (2003). *Charter school operations and performance: Evidence from California.* Santa Monica, CA: RAND.

68

Early Childhood Education

Lawrence J. Schweinhart
High/Scope Educational Research Foundation

Rachel Fulcher-Dawson
Michigan State University

This chapter presents what we know about the importance and impact of early childhood education, from research on the development of young children's brains and from long-term research on the effects of early childhood programs. Abuse, poor care, and harsh settings inhibit the development of young children's brains. Model early childhood programs for children from such environments contribute to their success in school and life, providing high return on investment. The United States has many early childhood programs and policies, including Head Start, the Child Care and Development Fund, preschool special education, state preschool programs, and child care programs in centers and in homes. Various studies show that typical and even special publicly funded early childhood programs have modest effects on children's literacy and social skills and parents' behavior. Certain model early childhood programs and model parent education programs contribute much to participants' lives, but many of our publicly funded programs are not of this quality and effectiveness. We need to know what ingredients are necessary to cross the threshold of quality and effectiveness so that many programs can achieve the great contributions to children's development of which they are capable.

What We Know About Early Childhood Education

Our knowledge of the importance and potential impact of early childhood education comes from the implications of brain science and the findings of evaluative studies of early childhood programs.

Early Childhood Learning and Brain Growth One source of evidence of the importance of early childhood learning is the burgeoning field of neuroscience. Essentially, neuroscientific research examines the relationship of various kinds of early childhood experience to brain status, as measured by certain imaging techniques, such as positron emission tomography and functional magnetic resonance imaging. Another type of research looks at children with localized brain damage (National Research Council and Institute of Medicine, 2000). Such research has identified the conditions that are dangerous to the developing brain from which young children should be protected, but has yet to identify the conditions that enhance their brain development. Simply put, abuse, neglectful care, and harsh environments interfere with the full development of young children's brains. Early childhood experience has a large role in shaping the developing brain, but few specific types of critical experiences have been identified. The early childhood experience that is needed is commonplace in young children's environments, except for children with sensory problems, such as blindness or deafness. A blind child, for example, has no visual experience.

The brain is a complex collection of interconnected cells that transmit information from one cell to another. It produces all our learning, abilities, and behavior. It accounts for our school achievement, social adaptation and responsibility, and workforce success. Genetics and experience are in constant interaction with each other. Genetics determines the timetable for brain development, while experience determines the actual construction of circuits between brain cells, known as brain architecture. A newborn baby has the capacity to learn any language in the world, but immediately begins to learn to discriminate the sounds of his or her home language rather than other languages. The brain begins by building basic circuits between cells, which become the basis for more complex circuits, and so on. Thus, the child first learns to discriminate language sounds and then learns to combine these sounds into words, then two-word utterances, and so forth.

Environments produce various levels of stress. Young children with supportive relationships readily handle the positive stress that arises from their everyday experience—being told no, having to share adult attention with someone else, having to get a shot from a doctor. Young children with supportive relationships also handle the extreme but tolerable stresses that arise from time to time—the death of someone close to them, serious illness or injury, and other types of calamities. But young children cannot handle the prolonged extreme stress that arises from persistent poverty in which they experience physical or emotional abuse or neglect and the absence of supportive relationships (Evans, 2004; McLoyd, 1998; Shonkoff, 2006). Most of the longitudinal studies of the effects of early childhood programs have included young children living in highly stressful environments (Galinsky, 2006; Guralnick, 1998; National Forum on Early Childhood Program Evaluation and National Scientific Council on the Developing Child, 2007; Ryan, Fauth, & Brooks-Gunn, 2006). These programs provided children with some respite from this stress as well as educational experiences that helped grow the circuitry of their brains.

Long-Term Early Childhood Program Studies Early childhood care and education are important because a great deal of learning takes place in this time before traditional schooling begins. Schooling traditionally begins at 5 or 6 years of age because most children begin to learn to read at this age, and reading is a fundamental ability that serves as a door to much other learning. But reexamination of learning by psychologists, first inspired by Jean Piaget, indicates that young children learn skills that are even more fundamental. The abilities to listen and speak precede the abilities to read and write. Working vocabulary in speech and comprehension determines how good a reader one becomes. Thinking abilities, such as categorizing, ranking, spatial thinking, and temporal and causal thinking are the components of everyday problem solving. The abilities to regulate one's own actions and resolve conflicts with other people are essential to social living. Such abilities, which can and ought to develop in early childhood, are important not only in themselves, but as doors to all the rest of learning.

Early childhood experience has large economic consequences. Economic analyses of the program cost and long-term benefits of the model early childhood programs reviewed in this chapter have found that the benefits far outweigh the costs, returning $4 to $16 for every dollar spent. In this way, they are rare among publicly funded programs.

Several long-term early childhood program follow-up studies stand out for their duration and methodological quality—the High/Scope Perry Preschool study, the Carolina Abecedarian Project study, and the Chicago Child-Parent Centers study. These three studies offer the best recent evidence of the long-term effects of good preschool programs. Studies by David Olds and his colleagues in Elmira, New York, and Memphis, Tennessee, are similar to these studies in employing random assignment of study participants, long-term follow-up, and cost-benefit analysis, but examine a different type of program—prenatal and infancy home visitation by nurses.

Table 68.1 compares the principal characteristics and outcomes of the three long-term preschool studies. On most characteristics, one of the studies can be contrasted with the other two, but not always the same two versus the other one. The Abecedarian, Chicago, and High/Scope studies differed in time, place, and program. At least two of these three studies found positive effects on children's

TABLE 68.1
Common Findings of Three Long-Term Early Childhood Program Studies

Characteristic	Carolina Abecedarian	Chicago Child-Parent Centers	High/Scope Perry
Intellectual performance tests	Ages 3–21	—	Ages 4–7
School achievement tests	Age 15	Ages 14–15	Ages 7–27
Placed in special education	25% vs. 48%	14% vs. 25%	65% vs. 60%
Retained in grade	31% vs. 55%	23% vs. 38%	35% vs. 40%
High school graduates	67% vs. 51%	50% vs. 39%	65% vs. 45%
—Males		43% vs. 29%	50% vs. 54%
—Females		57% vs. 48%	84% vs. 32%
Arrested by 21	45% vs. 41%	17% vs. 25%	15% vs. 25%
Age at birth of first child	19.1 vs. 17.7	—	20.0 vs. 21.0
Cost-benefit analysis[a]			
Program cost	$34,476	$6,956	$15,166
Program cost per year	$13,362	$4,637	$8,540
Public return, total	—	$26,637	$195,621
Public return, per dollar invested	—	$3.83	$12.90
Societal return, total	$130,300	$49,364	$244,812
Societal return, per dollar invested	$3.78	$7.10	$16.14

Note: [a] All dollar entries are per participant in constant 2000 dollars discounted at 3% annually.

intellectual performance in childhood, school achievement in adolescence, reduced placements in special education, reduced retentions in grade, improved high school graduation rate, reduced arrest rates, and older female age at first birth. All three studies found economic returns that were at least several times as great as the initial program investment. For every dollar spent on them, the Perry program returned $16, the Chicago program returned $7, and the Abecedarian program returned almost $4. Leading economists have found this evidence to be stronger than the evidence for most other public investments (Heckman, 2006; Rolnick & Grunewald, 2003).

The High/Scope Perry Preschool Study is a scientific experiment that has identified the short- and long-term effects of a high-quality preschool education program for young children living in poverty (Schweinhart et al., 2005). From 1962 through 1967, David Weikart and his colleagues in the Ypsilanti, Michigan, school district operated the preschool program for young children to help them avoid school failure and related problems. They identified a sample of 123 low-income African American children who were living in poverty and assessed to be at high risk of school failure and randomly assigned them to either a group that received a high-quality preschool program at ages 3 and 4 or a group that received no preschool program. Because of the random assignment strategy, children's preschool experience is the best explanation for subsequent group differences in their performance over the years. Project staff collected data annually on both groups from ages 3 through 11 and again at 14, 15, 19, 27, and 40, with a missing data rate of only 6% across all measures (Schweinhart et al., 2005).

The program group outperformed the no-program group on various intellectual and language tests from their preschool years up to age 7; school achievement tests at 9, 10, and 14; and literacy tests at 19 and 27. During their schooling, fewer program than no-program females were treated for mental impairment or were retained in grade. More of the program group than the no-program group graduated from high school, specifically, more program females than no-program females. At 15 and 19, the program group had better attitudes toward school than the no-program group, and program-group parents had better attitudes toward their 15-year-old children's schooling than did no-program-group parents. More members of the program group than the no-program group were employed at 27 and 40. The program group had higher median annual earnings than the no-program group at 27 and 40. More of the program group than the no-program group owned their own homes at 27 and 40. By 40, fewer members of the program group than the no-program group were arrested five or more times; fewer were arrested for violent crimes, property crimes, or drug crimes, and fewer were sentenced to prison or jail. More program than no-program males raised their own children.

Cost-benefit analysis indicates that, in constant 2000 dollars discounted at 3%, the economic return to society for the program was $244,812 per participant on an investment of $15,166 per participant—$16.14 per dollar invested. Of

that return, 80% went to the general public and 20% went to each participant in the form of increased lifetime earnings. Of the public return, 88% came from crime savings, and 1% to 7% came from each of three sources—education savings, increased taxes due to higher lifetime earnings, and welfare savings. Remarkably, 93% of the public return through age 40 was due to males because of the program's large reduction of male crime, and only 7% was due to females.

Ramey and his colleagues at the University of North Carolina at Chapel Hill began the Carolina Abecedarian Study in 1972 (Campbell, Ramey, Pungello, Sparling, & Miller-Johnson, 2002). They randomly assigned 111 infants from poor families either to a special program group or a typical child care group that used the child care arrangements in homes and centers that were prevalent in that place in the 1970s. The special program was a full-day, full-year daycare program for children that lasted the 5 years from birth to elementary school. Some of the study participants also received follow-up support from kindergarten to grade 3. The special program's goal was to enhance children's cognitive and personal characteristics so they would achieve greater school success. It offered infants and toddlers good physical care, optimal adult-child interaction, and a variety of playthings and opportunities to explore them. It offered preschoolers a developmentally appropriate preschool learning environment. The curriculum was a series of 16–18 game-like activities for each 6-month period of development, designed to enhance the overall development of infants and toddlers and the language, problem-solving skills, and emergent literacy of preschoolers. Adults learned the significance of each activity for children's development. They were taught how to conduct each activity in a playful, back-and-forth exchange with the child, praising and encouraging the child to engage in the expected behavior.

This was the first study to find preschool program benefits on participants' intellectual performance and academic achievement *throughout* their schooling. The mean IQ of the program group, which was the same as that of the no-program group at study entry, was higher at ages 3, 4½, 15, and 21, as were reading and mathematics achievement test scores at age 15. When children were 4½, more teen mothers of program-group children than teen mothers of no-program-group children were self-supporting. By age 15, fewer of the program group than the no-program group had been retained in grade or placed in special education. At age 21, more of the program group than the no-program group had graduated from high school, received a GED certificate, or attended a 4-year college. Fewer of the program group than the no-program group became teen parents. However, the program and no-program groups did not differ in number of arrests by age 19 (Clarke & Campbell, 1998).

Cost-benefit analysis of the Abecedarian program indicates that, in 2000 dollars discounted at 3% annually (converted from the 2002 dollars reported), the program cost $34,476 per child ($13,362 per child per year) and yielded benefits to society of $130,300—$3.78 return per dollar invested (Barnett & Masse, 2007). Most of the benefits came from mothers' earnings (54%), participants' earnings (28%), and health improvement due to less smoking (13%).

Beginning in 1985, the Chicago Longitudinal Study, conducted by Arthur Reynolds and his colleagues examined the effects of the Chicago Child-Parent Centers (CPC) program offered by the nation's third largest public school district (Reynolds, Temple, Robertson, & Mann, 2001). This program was citywide—much larger in scale than the research programs of the Perry Preschool and Abecedarian studies. Hence, the study sample was larger, with 1,539 low-income children (93% African American, 7% Hispanic) enrolled in 25 schools, 989 who had been in the CPC program and 550 who had not. Families in this study went to their neighborhood schools, and children were not randomly assigned to groups. Preschool-program group members attended a part-day preschool program when they were 3 and 4 years old, while the no-preschool-program group did not. At age 5, some members of both groups attended part-day kindergarten programs, while others attended full-day kindergarten programs. The CPC program involved the agency's traditional family-support services and preschool education. Parent outreach was provided by a family-support coordinator and a parent-resource teacher. The classroom program emphasized attainment of academic skills through relatively structured learning experiences presented by the teacher.

The preschool-program group did better than the no-preschool-program group in educational performance and social behavior, with lower rates of grade retention, special education placement, and high school dropout, along with almost half a year more of education and a lower rate of juvenile arrests, for both violent and nonviolent infractions. High school completion rates were higher for both males and females who had attended the program.

Analysis of the costs and benefits of the Chicago Child-Parent Centers program indicates that, in 2000 dollars discounted at 3% annually (converted from the 1998 dollars reported) the program cost $6,956 per child participating 1.5 years on average and yielded benefits of $49,564 per participant, $7.10 return per dollar invested (Reynolds, Temple, Robertson, & Mann, 2002). Benefits to the general public were $26,637 per participant, $3.83 per dollar invested, with the largest benefits coming from more taxes paid on higher earnings (28%), reduced crime victim costs (18%), and reduced costs of school remedial services (18%).

Studies by David Olds and his colleagues in Elmira, New York, and Memphis, Tennessee, are similar to these studies in employing random assignment of study participants, long-term follow-up, and cost-benefit analysis, but examine a different type of early childhood program—prenatal and infancy home visitation by nurses (Olds, Henderson, Phelps, Kitzman, & Hanks, 1993). The program involved weekly to monthly home visits from the onset of pregnancy up to the child's second birthday. It focused on the topics of maternal health, parental role, parental life course, family and friends, and linkage with services. The semi-rural Elmira (New York) efficacy study involved 400 children, 89% of them Caucasian. It found fewer verified reports of child abuse or neglect, fewer subsequent births, a longer interval to the birth of the next child, fewer months receiving welfare, fewer behavior problems due to alcohol and drug abuse, and fewer arrests of the mothers (Olds et al., 1997; Olds et al., 1998).

Cost-benefit analysis of those families in the Elmira study who were at higher risk than the other families in the study found that the program cost $7,208 (in 2000 dollars) per family and led to benefits of $29,262 per family, 4 times as much (Karoly et al., 1998). The urban Memphis (Tennessee) effectiveness study involved 1,139 pregnancies and 743 children; 92% were African American and 98% of the mothers were unmarried. It found that the nurse-visited mothers provided better care for their children and had fewer subsequent pregnancies, and their children were hospitalized for fewer days with injuries indicative of child abuse and neglect (Olds et al., 2004).

Olds and colleagues' nurse home visit program studies stand out among studies of home visit and other family support programs in their identification of long-term effects by experimental designs involving random assignment of families to receive or not receive the program. With the exception that some programs have a moderate effect on preventing child abuse, studies have found that such programs have no or small effects across a variety of child and parent outcomes, of unclear practical value (Board on Children, Youth, and Families, 1999; Layzer, Goodson, Bernstein, & Price, 2001). The most effective programs, such as Olds' program, used professional staff and targeted specific types of families.

Moore, Armsden, and Gogerty (1998) reported a 12-year follow-up of 35 children who were representative of children randomly assigned either to standard community services or a therapeutic child care program for maltreated or at-risk infants and toddlers. The therapeutic child care group displayed fewer behavior problems, violent delinquent behavior, and arrests, but the groups did not differ on school-related measures.

Some of these long-term studies have included program replication at multiple sites. The Chicago Child-Parent Centers Study was conducted at multiple sites. Olds replicated his Elmira New York study in Memphis. The Abecedarian project was replicated to some extent in the Infant Health and Development Program study, which found program effects at age 8 for the heavier low-birth-weight babies (McCormick et al., 2006). The High/Scope Perry Preschool Study was replicated in the High/Scope Preschool Curriculum Comparison Study, in which study participants were randomly assigned to three preschool curriculum models (Schweinhart & Weikart, 1997). This study found that the High/Scope model surpassed a scripted direct instruction model in preventing emotional problems and crime. Several other studies have also revealed evidence of the curriculum model's effectiveness (Epstein, 1993; Frede & Barnett, 1992; Smith, 1975).

A Picture of Early Childhood Care and Education

The focus in this chapter is on children from birth to 5 years old and so early childhood care and education are defined as serving children of these ages. Child care refers to any nonparental care arrangement for any child, but this chapter does not address out-of-school care for school-aged children. Infants are children from birth to 1 year old; toddlers are children 2 or 3 years old; and preschoolers are children 3 and 4 years old. Preschool refers specifically to a center-based arrangement for children 3 to 5 years old. Many government preschool programs limit enrollment to preschoolers who live in poverty or are otherwise at risk of school failure, but several states, including Georgia, Oklahoma, and Florida, have begun to offer preschool programs to all the state's 4-year-olds whose families choose to enroll them.

The 2001 National Household Education Survey of the National Center for Educational Statistics presents a national picture of early childhood care and education (Mulligan, Brimhall, West, & Chapman, 2005). This recurrent survey was conducted again in 2005, with results similar to those of 2001, for example, the same percentage of young children having some type of nonparental care arrangement at least weekly (60%; Iruka & Carver, 2006). However, results have not yet been reported by year of age, as they were in 2001. The U.S. Census Bureau conducted a similar survey as part of the 2002 Survey of Income and Program Participation (Overturf Johnson, 2005).[1]

According to the report by Mulligan et al. (2005), the United States in 2001 had 20.2 million children under 6 years old who had not yet entered kindergarten:

- Sixty percent of these children had *some type of nonparental care and education arrangement* at least weekly, while 40% did not; the participation rate increased from 40% for infants under 1 year old to 79% for 4-year-olds, due to the increase in the center participation rate.
- Thirty-three percent received *care and education in a center*, a proportion that grew steadily from 8% of infants, to 16% of 1-year-olds, 25% of 2-year-olds, 43% of 3-year-olds, and 65% of 4-year-olds.
- Sixteen percent received *care and education from a nonrelative in a home*, ranging from 13%–14% for infants and 4-year-olds to 18%–20% for 1- and 2-year-olds.
- Twenty-two percent received *care and education from a relative in a home,* a proportion that varied by only 1% either way from infancy to age 4.[2]

Another federal study has looked at the types and quality of care experienced by age 2. The National Center for Education Statistics and other agencies are conducting the Early Childhood Longitudinal Study—Birth Cohort. This study involves a nationally representative sample of over 10,500 children born in 2001 that is being followed from birth through first grade. To date, findings from interviews, parent and caregiver questionnaires, and developmental as-

sessments of children have been reported for ages 9 months and 2 years (Flanagan & West, 2004; Mulligan & Flanagan, 2006). At age 2, 49% of the children received nonparental care: 19% from relatives, 15% from nonrelatives in homes, 16% in centers, and 1% in two or more settings (Mulligan & Flanagan, 2006). Of those in center-based care, 24% experienced high quality, 66% experienced medium, adequate quality, and 9% experienced low quality, as measured by the Infant/Toddler Environment Rating Scale (Harms, Cryer, & Clifford, 1990). Of those in home-based arrangements, 7% experienced high quality, 57% experienced adequate, medium quality, and the remaining 36% experienced low-quality care, as measured by the Family Day Care Rating Scale (Harms & Clifford, 1989).

Early Childhood Public Policies and Evidence of their Effectiveness

Early childhood education policy spans at least three major categories of domestic social policy—education, welfare, and family policy. Thus, early childhood policy researchers should be mindful of the vast bodies of research in these three fields and the differences between them. The Child Care and Development Fund, for example, can be seen as addressing early childhood education, but was developed and is funded and measured by the government as a welfare program, with its measured outcomes being jobs of recipients and numbers of children served rather than specific children's learning. Because policies in each of these three categories have different targets, funding streams, advocates, and so forth, early childhood education policies embody differing principles. The idea of programs serving all 4-year-olds, for example, derives from the egalitarian principles of education; targeted funding on children in greatest need comes from welfare, and parent education programs embody the individualist and holistic principles of family policy.

The federal government has initiated and funded early childhood programs consistently since 1965, as well as previous to that with nursery schools funded by the Works Progress Administration in the 1930s and the Lanham Act in the 1940s. Total federal funding for early childhood programs in Fiscal Year 2005 was $16.4 billion. The U.S. Department of Health and Human Services funds early childhood programs through Head Start, Early Head Start, the Child Care and Development Fund, Temporary Assistance to Needy Families, and the Social Services Block Grant (White House, 2004). The U.S. Department of Education funds early childhood programs through Title I preschools, Early Reading First, Even Start, Special Education Preschool Grants, Grants for Special Education for Infants and Toddlers, and the Early Childhood Educator Professional Development Program.

Head Start and Similar Federal Programs Since 1965, the federal government has funded and supervised Head Start programs that provide various services for young children and their families. Head Start is the largest of the current federally funded early childhood programs, funded at $6.8 billion in FY 2005. It gives local agencies grants to fund and run comprehensive child development programs that serve children from 3 to 5 years old, with limited Early Head Start programs available for younger children. Head Start services include early childhood education, parent involvement, meals, and medical, dental, and mental health referrals. Grantees include local public agencies, private non-profit and for-profit organizations, Indian tribes, and school districts (Head Start Bureau, 2005). Program eligibility depends on family income, so that 90% of all recipients must be below the federal poverty level. In addition, 10% of the slots in a program must be reserved for children with disabilities. Most Head Start programs are center-based and are generally required to operate at least 3.5 hours a day, 4 days a week, 32 weeks of the year.

The Head Start Family and Child Experiences Survey (FACES) is a study of a representative national sample of Head Start programs in the United States (Zill et al., 2003). The first cohort of 3,200 children entered Head Start in Fall 1997; the second cohort of 2,800 children entered Head Start in Fall 2000. In Head Start, children improved on important aspects of school readiness, narrowing the gap between them and the general population, but still lagging behind. Relative to national norms, children made significant gains during their Head Start year, particularly in vocabulary and early writing skills. Children in Head Start grew in social skills and reduced hyperactive behavior, especially if they started out more shy, aggressive, or hyperactive. The study found that Head Start classrooms were rated to have good quality. Most programs used a specific integrated curriculum, particularly Creative Curriculum and High/Scope. Use of these curricula and higher teacher salaries were predictive of positive child outcomes. Teachers' educational credentials were linked to greater gains in early writing skills. In addition, provision of preschool services for a longer period each day was tied to greater cognitive gains by children. Based on follow-up of the 1997 cohort, Head Start graduates showed further progress toward national averages during kindergarten, with substantial gains in vocabulary, early mathematics, and early writing skills. The majority of Head Start graduates could identify most or all of the letters of the alphabet by the end of kindergarten, and more than half could recognize beginning sounds of words.

The Head Start Impact Study, now under way, involves a nationally representative sample of Head Start programs and random assignment of about 5,000 children to Head Start or no Head Start. This study has so far provided results for entering 3-year-olds and entering 4-year-olds after 1 year in Head Start and will follow them through the end of kindergarten and first grade (Administration for Children and Families, 2005). It has found evidence of small to moderate Head Start effects on children's literacy skills (pre-reading, pre-writing, parent-reported literacy skills, 3-year-olds' vocabulary), reduced problem behaviors of 3-year-olds, children's access to health care, parents' reading to their children, and reduced use of physical discipline of 3-year-olds.

The Head Start Comprehensive Child Development Program Evaluation randomly assigned 4,410 children and families living in poverty at 21 sites either to this program or no program and followed them for 5 years (Goodson, Layzer, St. Pierre, Bernstein, & Lopez, 2000). Although the program's comprehensive services centered on the assignment to each family of a case manager to help them meet their needs, only 58% of the program group actually met with a case manager, as did 18% of the control group due to other programs. The study found no statistically significant, positive group differences on either child or parent outcomes, suggesting that families do not really profit from case management associated with early childhood programs. However, lack of compliance with group assignment could have led to underestimation of program effects.

Two evaluations of the Even Start Family Literacy program randomly assigned children and families to Even Start or not (Planning and Evaluation Service, 1998). Somewhat greater percentages of the Even Start group than the control group received various services, 95% versus 60% participating in early childhood education, for example. Consequently, both groups experienced gains, with the Even Start group experiencing some greater gains—the pattern for adult literacy, adult GED attainment, cognitive stimulation and emotional support by the family, and children's vocabulary. Even Start children improved their basic school readiness skills (e.g., recognition of colors, shapes, and sizes), but their non-Even Start peers caught up with them a year later. Again, the lack of compliance with group assignment may have led to underestimation of program effects.

The Early Head Start program evaluation of some 3,000 infants and toddlers and their low-income families found program effects through age 2 for this federal program that began in 1995 (Love et al., 2005). When compared to a randomly assigned control group, Early Head Start children did modestly but statistically significantly better on measures of cognitive, language, and social-emotional development, and their parents scored significantly better than control-group parents on measures of parenting behavior, emotional support of their children, and knowledge of infant-toddler development.

Early Childhood in the Individuals with Disabilities Education Act The Individuals with Disabilities Education Act (IDEA) is the federal special education law. It provides regulatory guidance for states and school districts to provide special education and other services to eligible children. States are responsible for implementation and enforcement of this federal mandate. A child is evaluated by a team of experts and given an Individualized Education Program if he or she is found to have a disability and to need special education or other services in order to make progress in the general education curriculum. In 2001, IDEA served 31,378 infants and toddlers, 2.1% of all children from birth to 2 years old, under part C and 620,195 preschoolers, 5.3% of all preschoolers age 3 to 5, under part B (Office of Special Education and Rehabilitative Services, 2003).

Early Childhood in the No Child Left Behind Act Early in his presidency, President George W. Bush successfully advocated for the No Child Left Behind (NCLB) Act (2002) as a radical revision of the Elementary and Secondary Education Act through which the majority of federal K–12 funding and directives flow. Among the many problems NCLB proposes to address are the school achievement gap between disadvantaged students and their peers and the low school-achievement ranking of U.S. children against their international peers. The act sets strict standards of learning and holds schools accountable for them, based on the belief that these measures will reduce the school achievement gap and increase overall school performance. The major accountability measure of NCLB is annual testing of all public school students in reading and mathematics in grades 3–8 and high school. From these results, schools and states prepare annual report cards on school performance for the public.

President Bush has also advocated an early childhood education agenda called Good Start, Grow Smart. The main aims of this agenda are to align preschool programs with K–12 schools, increase and standardize the evaluation of early childhood programs, and increase the information on school readiness for parents and early childhood teachers and caregivers (White House, 2004). The initiative also included new accountability measures for Head Start and the other federally funded preschool initiatives. The major impact of this initiative has not been to change the basic funding streams for early childhood care and education, but rather to introduce several new programs such as Early Reading First and to require more stringent evaluation and testing of existing federally funded programs, such as the short-lived Head Start National Reporting System.

The Child Care and Development Fund The Child Care and Development Fund (CCDF; formerly called the Child Care and Development Block Grant Program) gives states funding for child care subsidies for low-income families (85% or less of the state's median family income) who are working or looking for work. While these funds can go to any children under age 13, about two-thirds go to children under 5 (Barnett & Masse, 2002). Of CCDF funds, 70% must be given for child care assistance to families receiving Temporary Assistance for Needy Families benefits. While the rules and regulations under this law changed with the new welfare laws, funding has generally increased over time.

Several studies of typical child care programs in the United States bear out the idea that high-quality programs contribute to children's development while low-quality programs do not. The Cost, Quality and Child Outcomes in Child Care Centers Study was a longitudinal study of how children's experience in center-based care and school related to their socioemotional and cognitive outcomes in early childhood and at age 7 (Cost, Quality & Child Outcomes Study Team, 1995). The study focused on a random sample of 100 nonprofit and for-profit centers in four states in the mid-1990s. Observers found that 65% of centers posted a medium score on the Early Childhood Environment Rating Scale (Harms & Clifford, 1980), 24% scored high, and 11% scored low. A follow-up examined 733 children from these settings from ages 4 to 8 as a function of their child care center experience, after adjusting for their background characteristics. The findings indicate that center quality had a modest long-term effect on children's cognitive and socioemotional development.

The NICHD Early Child Care Study is a longitudinal study initiated by the National Institute of Child Health and Human Development in 1989 to look at the relationship between child care experience and children's developmental outcomes (NICHD Early Child Care Research Network, 2005; Belsky, Vandell, Burchinal, Clarke-Stewart, McCartney, Owen, & The NICHD Early Child Care Network, 2007). The sample began with 1,364 infants in 1991 and is continuing to follow up on 1,000 of them through age 15. Higher quality child care was found to be associated with higher test scores on mathematics and reading achievement and memory through third grade and vocabulary at sixth grade. Time spent in center child care was found to be associated with better memory and more conflictual relationships with adults at third grade. More hours of child care were found to be associated with poorer work habits and poorer social skills through sixth grade.

State-Funded Preschool Programs The states are currently enacting and implementing a variety of early childhood policies. While some states target preschool-age children, others such as North Carolina have a more comprehensive approach to support early childhood care and education. A few general trends and policies are emerging in this area. Most states have added state-funded preschool programming in the last two decades. As states have implemented these programs and evidence grows on the importance of program quality to preschool outcomes, states have heightened their attention to program quality in policies on curriculum models, high teacher qualifications, and increased size and scope of the program and the children served.

Currently, 38 states fund and run preschool programs (Barnett, Hustedt, Robin, & Schulman, 2006a). Twenty states appropriate supplemental Head Start funds, either to serve more children or to support a range of things that the federal money does not sufficiently cover, such as administration and coordination of training. For four states this is the *only* state investment in early childhood. Combined, states spent more than $3.27 billion on preschool programs in FY 2006, with 12 states spending nothing. Many states decreased spending from 2001 to 2005, indicating that funding for early childhood programs is not yet stable in many state budgets.

The National Institute for Early Education Research (NIEER) now publishes an annual preschool yearbook with evaluations of preschool commitments of all 50 states and recently released its fourth such report (Barnett, Hustedt, Hawkinson, & Robin, 2006b). As of 2005–2006, NIEER reported that state-funded preschool programs serve more than 942,766 children in the United States. This includes 20% of all 4-year-olds and 3% of all 3-year-olds nationwide. Oklahoma and Georgia provide the greatest access to preschool programs, enrolling 70% and 52% of children in their state-funded programs, respectively. It is interesting to note how similar these percentages are to the national rate of 65% of 4-year-olds enrolled in both public and private center programs. Florida has passed a ballot initiative requiring preschool programs for all the state's 4-year-olds.

NIEER ranks states in three ways: access to preschool, quality standards, and resources. The *quality standards rating* depends on the presence of 10 factors that include comprehensive early learning standards, teachers' bachelors' degrees and specialized pre-kindergarten training, assistant teacher Child Development Associate credential or the equivalent, at least 15 hours a year of teacher in-service training, maximum class size of 20 or fewer children, staff-child ratio of 1 to 10 or better, required screening, referral and support services (vision, hearing, health, and at least one support service), at least one meal a day, and required monitoring by site visits. These benchmarks are not a scaled or balanced score—serving a meal counts the same as staff-child ratio, but do provide a rough measure of the extent to which states are tackling the demands of quality in their preschool programs. Only Alabama and North Carolina met all ten benchmarks, with six other states meeting nine of the ten. Of the 38 states with 45 programs (some states have as many as three), 13 have programs that meet five or fewer of the quality standards benchmarks.

The governance of state preschool and early childhood education programs also varies across the states. At the state level, oversight and regulation is done by the state department of education in 28 states, a separate state department such as family services in 8 states, and a joint agency or quasi-agency in 6 states. Likewise, the program operators vary across and within states. While 5 states allow only public schools to run state-funded preschool, others allow any agency (private non-profit, private for-profit, community agency, or public school) to run state preschools as long as they meet the program standards, such as teacher training and class size.

Barnett, Lamy, and Jung (2005) led a study of the effects of five state-funded preschool programs on the academic skills of entering kindergartners. It involved 5,071 children from Michigan, New Jersey, Oklahoma, South Carolina, and West Virginia. Children who did and did not make the age cutoff for program entry were compared using a regression discontinuity research design to avoid selection bias. The programs were found to have statistically significant, meaningful effects on children's vocabulary, print awareness skills, and early mathematics skills.

An evaluation of Oklahoma's universal pre-kindergarten program in Tulsa compared 1,461 children who just completed pre-K to 1,567 children just beginning pre-K, using a regression discontinuity design to avoid selection bias (Gormley, Gayer, Phillips, & Dawson, 2005). They found strong effects on achievement test scores for letter and word identification (.79 of the standard deviation of the control group), spelling (.64 of the standard deviation), and applied mathematics problems (.38 of the standard deviation). Findings held for Hispanic, Black, White, and Native American children, and for middle-income as well as low-income children.

Gilliam and Zigler (2001) reported that as of 1998, 13 of the 33 state preschool programs had received evaluations. They summarized these evaluations as finding modest support for positive program effects on children's developmental performance, school performance and attendance, and reduced percentages of children held back a grade.

Table 68.2 summarizes the design and findings of the short-term studies reviewed here. The programs studied were either typical or enhanced Head Start or state preschool programs and typical child care centers. While one study (the Comprehensive Child Development Program evaluation) found no effects and another (the Oklahoma evaluation) found strong effects, most found modest effects on children's literacy and social skills and parents' behavior. The consensus finding of these studies is that typical and

TABLE 68.2

Findings of Recent Short-Term Early Childhood Program Studies in the U.S.

Study	Findings
Head Start Impact Study	Modest effects on children's literacy skills, reduced problem behavior, parent reading to children
Head Start Family and Child Experiences Survey	Modest gains in children's literacy and social skills in Head Start and kindergarten years
Comprehensive Child Development Program	No effects on child or parent outcomes
Early Head Start Evaluation	Modest effects on children's development to age 2; effects on parents' behavior and knowledge
Even Start Evaluations	One-year improvement in children's readiness skills, gains in adult literacy, GED certification
Five-State Preschool Study	Improvements in children's literacy and mathematics skills
Oklahoma Preschool Study	Strong effects on literacy skills.
State Preschool Evaluations	Modest effects on children's development, school performance.
Cost, Quality and Child Outcomes Study	Quality had a modest effect on children's cognitive and socioemotional development at age 7.
NICHD Early Child Care Study	Higher quality child care was associated with higher math, reading, and memory test scores through grade 3.

even special publicly funded early childhood programs have modest effects on children's literacy and social skills and parents' behavior.

Early Childhood Around the World The IEA Preprimary Project examined various types of early childhood settings and their relationship to child outcomes, not only in the United States, but also in other countries around the world. It was sponsored by the International Association for the Evaluation of Educational Achievement (IEA) and coordinated by the High/Scope Educational Research Foundation (Montie, Xiang, & Schweinhart, 2006; Olmsted & Montie, 2001; Weikart, Olmsted, & Montie, 2003). The purpose of the study was to identify how process and structural characteristics of community preprimary settings affect children's language and cognitive development at age 7. The target population consisted of children in selected community settings who were 4½ years old when they entered the study. The original sample included over 5,000 children in more than 1,800 settings in 15 countries. Ten of the 15 countries followed the children to age 7 to collect language and cognitive outcome measures: Finland, Greece, Hong Kong, Indonesia, Ireland, Italy, Poland, Spain, Thailand, and the United States. The number of children included in the longitudinal analyses varied from 1,300 to 1,897, with an overall retention rate of 86% of the original samples in the participating countries.

Four findings emerged that are consistent across all of the countries included in the data analysis.

- Children's language performance at age 7 improves the most when the predominant types of children's activities that early childhood teachers proposed were freely chosen by children rather than personal care, group social activities, or discipline. Physical and expressive activities were second in influence and preacademic activities were third.
- Children whose early childhood teachers had more years of full-time schooling have better language performance at age 7.
- Children who spent less time in whole-group activities, in which the teachers proposed the same activity for all the children in the class, have better cognitive performance at age 7.
- Children whose preschool settings had a greater number and variety of equipment and materials have better cognitive performance at age 7.

This study is unprecedented in the number of countries participating, so these findings transcend the sample limitations of the other studies reviewed here. The fact that these findings were found internationally suggests that these process and outcome variables have common meanings across all 10 countries. Also, unlike others studies reviewed here, these findings were found across all types of early childhood settings, not just those established by a particular early childhood funding source, again testifying to their unusual robustness and durability.

Studies of early childhood care and education in countries other than the United States include studies in the United Kingdom, New Zealand, Turkey, Nepal, and Mauritius (an island in the Indian Ocean):

- The 141-center Effective Provision of Preschool Education Project in the United Kingdom (Sammons et al., 2004) found that children who went to preschool had developmental advantages over those who did not, that program quality and earlier program entry were related to better child outcomes, that disadvantaged children did better in socioeconomically mixed settings, and that home learning opportunities had effects through age 7.
- The Turkish Early Enrichment Project in Turkey (Kağiçibaşi, Sunar, & Bekman, 2001) found that a training intervention for the mothers of young children had immediate effects on the mothers and effects on their children 6 years later; in their teen years, these children had better attitudes toward school and were more likely to stay in school.
- The longitudinal Competent Children Project in New Zealand (Wylie et al., 2004) found that children beginning preschool at 1 and 2 had better attitudinal competencies than those beginning after 3; and that children in higher-quality preschools (teachers asking open-ended questions, joining in children's play, and letting children make choices) developed better than those in lower-quality ones.
- A study of Save the Children's 38 early childhood development programs in Nepal (Save the Children, 2003) found that program participants were more likely than non-participants to enter school on time, have better attendance, pass their exams, and not repeat a grade or drop out in first and second grade.
- A study of the effects of an environmental enrichment program at ages 3 to 5 in Mauritius found that participants reduced schizotypal personality traits (difficulties with relationships, cognitive distortions, and eccentric behavior) and antisocial behavior 14–20 years after the program (Raine, Melligen, Liu, Venables, & Mednick, 2003).

What We Still Need to Know

We are at a crossroads in early childhood education research. On the one hand, brain research findings suggest that early childhood education is very important, and several long-term studies have established the fact that model preschool programs and model parent education programs can have lifelong benefits and a strong economic return in investment. On the other hand, evaluations of typical and even enhanced publicly funded early childhood programs reveal only modest short-term effects on children's development. Clearly, if the goal is to provide long-term effects and financial return on investment, the general intention to run an early childhood program is not enough. Emulation of effective programming is also essential. For example, in the Head Start Impact Study, the difference between the Head Start and no Head Start groups for the Peabody Picture Vocabulary Test (version III) scores of entering 3-year-olds after 1 year of Head Start was 1.5 points. Children gained 4 points on this measure during their program year in the Head Start FACES study and in the 5-state preschool study. In contrast, children in the High/Scope Perry Preschool program gained 8 points in their first year on the PPVT (original version), and a total of 14 points in 2 years.

We are in a season of expansion of public attention to early childhood programs. All but 10 states are investing state dollars in preschool programs. Illinois, South Carolina, and a growing number of states are following North Carolina's lead with the Smart Start project to create a comprehensive, statewide early childhood system. We have not only an opportunity to gather needed research on early childhood education, but a critical opportunity to shape emerging public policy with such information.

Given this state of affairs, we need research that identifies the limits of the long-term findings we have. Some early childhood programs and parent education programs have large initial effects, long-term effects, and economic return on investment, but some do not. What are the characteristics of the ones that do and the ones that do not? These characteristics may be internal, program characteristics—such as teacher qualifications, curriculum model, style of teacher-child interaction, or parent involvement component. They may be external characteristics, such as population served or historical or geographic context. They may be combinations of internal and external characteristics.

Based on the long-term findings, we would recommend that early childhood programs meet all of several broad standards.

- Every center-based preschool classroom, whether part-day or full-day, should have qualified, fairly paid teachers who are prepared to, and actually do, contribute to children's development. A recent meta-analysis (Early et al., 2007) questioned whether teachers with bachelors' degrees are truly contributing to certain aspects of children's development. That is a secondary question; current bachelors' degrees should be, but currently may not be, a means to the end of qualified teachers. Likewise, every home visit program should be run by a qualified teacher or nurse.
- Every teacher or nurse should know how to use, and use, a validated child development curriculum that has evidence that it contributes to all aspects of children's development.
- Every program should fully engage parents as genuine partners in their children's education, through frequent home visits and other meetings.
- Every program director should focus single-mindedly on the program's contribution to children's development and should continuously assess program implementation and child outcomes to confirm that the intended teacher practices and child outcomes are taking place as planned.

Long-term research has provided evidence of the value of this constellation of standards, but their formulations require interpretation of this research, so it would be wise to conduct further research on these formulations. Are one professional teacher and an aide enough for long-term effects, or are two professional teachers needed? How much program attention must be paid to parents? Are long-term effects limited to children in poverty or do they also apply to other children as well? Do these findings apply only in economically developed countries or also in economically developing countries, as the findings from studies around the world suggest?

The bridge between the long-term studies of model early childhood programs and the short-term studies of current publicly funded early childhood programs is a long one. Efforts to cross this bridge have been made in the studies of enhanced Head Start programs. But these efforts have not yet found the hoped-for breakthrough successes. Would Head Start, state preschool programs, or other early childhood programs that embodied the proposed standards identified above provide this breakthrough success?

- About one-third of today's center-based teachers (including Head Start) and 17% of family child care providers have a bachelor's degree (Burton et al., 2002). Lack of credentials follows from low pay: The average hourly wage for U.S. preschool teachers in 2004 was only $9.34 (Bureau of Labor Statistics, 2006).
- Few early childhood programs now use validated educational models. A national survey of 400 early childhood educators conducted by Quality Education Data (2005) found that 10% of them used High/Scope as their primary curriculum, the same percentage found a decade ago (Epstein, Schweinhart, & McAdoo, 1996).
- Few early childhood programs fully engage parents as genuine partners in their children's education, through frequent home visits and other meetings. Head Start requires only two home visits a year, whereas the Perry program had weekly home visits.

These studies apply most clearly to children who are living in poverty or are otherwise at risk of school failure. What about the rest of young children, including the majority who are not enrolled in early childhood programs at a given point in time? While the research directions just described may be called confirmatory, research on the effects of early childhood programs on these children needs to be exploratory. What programs work best for them, fitting into families' lifestyles while contributing to young children's development? While 65% of all 4-year-olds enroll in center-based early childhood programs, 35% do not. How many more would enroll if high-quality programs were widely available? While nurse home visit programs are effective with some children, what of the majority of all young children whom parents and other relatives now take care of? Perhaps the lessons of highly effective programs apply to these situations in modified form: that everyone who takes care of young children can and should profit from the scientifically established lessons of early childhood education.

One final consideration involves the delicate links between research, policy and practice. This is not a concern unique to early childhood education. Given what is known about the importance of early childhood and the effects of past and current early childhood education policies, how do we move forward in a way that improves practice? The current status of early childhood education in the public realm is limited, though growing. As public policy involvement grows, it is crucial that public policy and practice are founded on solid research. Policy that will positively contribute to young children's development must do so through competent early childhood teachers. Policy and research need to focus on (a) the expertise and needs of existing teachers and caregivers, (b) developing consistent criteria for the training of competent teachers and caregivers, and (c) adequate compensation to attract and retain competent teachers and caregivers. As in K–12 education, early childhood education policy, research, and practice must center on teachers' practices and children's development.

Notes

1. The Education survey (Mulligan et al., 2005) presents parents' care and education arrangements for their young children under 6 but not in kindergarten, while the Census survey (Overturf Johnson, 2005) presents mothers' care arrangements for their young children under 5, with relative care including both mothers (while working or in school) and fathers.

2. The Census survey found that 70% of nonparental relative care came from grandparents, 8% came from siblings, and 22% came from other relatives (Overturf Johnson, 2005).

References

Administration for Children and Families, U.S. Department of Health and Human Services. (2005, June). *Head Start Impact Study: first year findings*. Retrieved December 3, 2007, from www.acf.hhs.gov/programs/opre/hs/impact_study/reports/first_yr_finds/first_yr_finds.pdf

Barnett, W. S., Hustedt, J. T., Robin, K. B., & Schulman, K. L. (2006a). *The state of preschool: 2005 state preschool yearbook (amended)*. New Brunswick, NJ: National Institute for Early Education Research).

Barnett, W. S., Hustedt, J., Hawkinson, L., & Robin, K. (2006b). *The state of preschool 2006*. New Brunswick, NJ: National Institute for Early Education Research.

Barnett, W. S., Lamy, C., & Jung, K. (2005). *The effects of state prekindergarten programs on young children's school readiness in five states*. New Brunswick, NJ: National Institute for Early Education Research, Rutgers University. Retrieved December 3, 2007, from http://www.nieer.org/docs/index.php?DocID=129

Barnett, W. S., & Masse, L. N. (2002). Funding issues for early childhood care and education programs. In D. Cryer & R. Clifford (Eds.), *Early childhood education and care in the USA* (pp.137–165). Baltimore: Paul H. Brookes.

Barnett, W. S., & Masse, L. N. (2007). Early childhood design and economic returns: A comparative benefit-cost analysis of the Abecedarian program and its policy implications. *Economics of Education Review, 26*, 113–125.

Belsky, J., Vandell, D. L., Burchinal, M., Clarke-Stewart, K. A., McCartney, K., Owen, M. T., & the NICHD Early Child Care Network. (2007). Are there long-term effects of early child care? *Child Development, 78*, 681–701.

Bureau of Labor Statistics, U.S. Department of Labor. (2006). *Career guide to industries, 2006–07 edition, Child day care services*. Retrieved December 3, 2007, from http://www.bls.gov/oco/cg/cgs032.htm

Burton, A., Whitebrook, M., Young, M., Bellm, D., Wayne, C., Brandon, R. N., et al. (2002). *Estimating the size and components of the U.S. child care workforce and caregiving population*. Washington, DC: Center for the Child Care Workforce and Human Services Policy Center. Retrieved December 3, 2007, from http://www.ccw.org/pubs/workforceestimatereport.pdf

Board on Children, Youth, and Families, Commission on Behavioral and Social Sciences and Education, National Research Council and Institute of Medicine. (1999). *Revisiting Home Visiting: Summary of a Workshop*. N. G. Margie & D. A. Phillips, Eds. Washington, DC: National Academy Press. Retrieved December 3, 2007, from http://books.nap.edu/openbook.php?record_id=9712&page=R1

Campbell, F. A., Ramey, C. T., Pungello, E. P., Sparling, J., & Miller-Johnson, S. (2002). Early childhood education: Young adult outcomes from the Abecedarian project. *Applied Developmental Science, 6*, 42–57.

Clarke, S. H. & Campbell, F. A. (1998). Can intervention early prevent crime later? The Abecedarian Project compared with other programs. *Early Childhood Research Quarterly, 13*, 319–343.

Cost, Quality & Child Outcomes Study Team (1995). *Cost, quality, and child outcomes in child care centers*, Public report, second edition. University of Colorado at Denver, Economics Department.

Early, D. M., Maxwell, K. L., Burchinal, M., Alva, S., Bender, R. H., Bryant, D., et al. (2007). Teachers' education, classroom quality, and young children's academic skills: Results from seven studies of preschool programs. *Child Development, 78*, 558–580.

Epstein, A. S. (1993). *Training for quality: Improving early childhood programs through systematic inservice training*. Ypsilanti, MI: High/Scope Press.

Epstein, A. S., Schweinhart, L. J., & McAdoo, L. (1996). *Models of early childhood education*. Ypsilanti, MI: High/Scope Press.

Evans, G. W. (2004). The environment of childhood poverty. *American Psychologist, 59*, 77–92.

Flanagan, K., & West, J. (2004). *Children born in 2001: First results from the base year of the Early Childhood Longitudinal Study, Birth Cohort (ECLS-B)* (NCES 2005-036). Washington, DC: National Center for Education Statistics, U.S. Department of Education.

Frede, E., & Barnett, W. S. (1992). Developmentally appropriate public school preschool: A study of implementation of the High/Scope Curriculum and its effects on disadvantaged children's skills at first grade. *Early Childhood Research Quarterly, 7*, 483–499.

Galinsky, E. (2006, February). *The economic benefits of high-quality early childhood programs: What makes the difference?* Washington, DC: Committee for Economic Development. Retrieved December 2, 2007, from http://www.ced.org/docs/report/report_prek_galinsky.pdf

Gilliam, W. S., & Zigler, E. F. (2001). A critical meta-analysis of all evaluations of state-funded preschool from 1977 to 1998: Implications for policy, service delivery, and program implementation. *Early Childhood Research Quarterly, 15*, 441–473.

Goodson, B. D., Layzer, J. I., St. Pierre, R. G., Bernstein, L. S., & Lopez, M. (2000). Effectiveness of a comprehensive, five-year family support program for low-income families: Findings from the Comprehensive Child Development Program. *Early Childhood Research Quarterly, 15*, 5–39.

Gormley, W. T., Jr., Gayer, T., Phillips, D., & Dawson, B. (2005). The effects of universal pre-k on cognitive development [Electronic version]. *Developmental Psychology, 41*, 872–884.

Guralnick, M. J. (1998). Effectiveness of early intervention for vulnerable children: A developmental perspective. *American Journal on Mental Retardation, 102*, 319–345.

Harms, T., & Clifford, R. M. (1980). *The Early Childhood Environment Rating Scale*. New York: Teachers College Press.

Harms, T., & Clifford, R. M. (1989). *The Family Day Care Rating Scale*. New York: Teachers College Press.

Harms, T., Cryer, D., & Clifford, R. M. (1990). *Infant/Toddler Environment Rating Scale*. New Yor: Teachers College Press.

Head Start Bureau (2005). *Head Start program fact sheet for fiscal year 2004.* Retrieved December 3, 2007, from http://www.acf.hhs.gov/programs/hsb/about/fy2004.html

Heckman, J. J. (2006, January 10). Catch 'em young [Electronic version]. *Wall Street Journal,* p. A14.

Iruka, I. U., & Carver, P. R. (2006). *Initial results from the 2005 NHES early childhood program participation survey* (NCES 2006-075). U. S. Department of Education. Washington, DC: National Center for Education Statistics.

Kağıtçıbaşı, C., Sunar, D., & Bekman, S. (2001). Long-term effects of early intervention: Turkish low-income mothers and children. *Applied Developmental Psychology, 22,* 333–361.

Karoly, L. A., Greenwood, P. W., Everingham, S. S., Houbé, J., Kilburn, M. R., Rydell, C. P., Sanders, M., et al. (1998). *Investing in our children: What we know and don't know about the costs and benefits of early childhood interventions.* Santa Monica, CA: The Rand Corporation.

Layzer, J. I., Goodson, B. D., Bernstein, L., & Price, C. (2001). *National evaluation of family support programs. Final Report Volume A: The meta-analysis.* Cambridge, MA: Abt Associates. Retrieved December 3, 2007, from http://www.abtassociates.com/reports/NEFSP-VolA.pdf

Love, J. M., Kisker, E. E., Ross, C.M., Raikes, H., Constantine, J., Boller, K., et al. (2005). The effectiveness of Early Head Start for 3-year-old children and their parents: Lessons for policy and programs. *Developmental Psychology, 41,* 885–901.

McLoyd, V. C. (1998). Socioeconomic disadvantage and child development. *American Psychologist, 53,* 185–204.

McCormick, M. C., Brooks-Gunn, J., Buka, S. L., Goldman, J., Yu, J., Salganik, M., et al. (2006). Early intervention in low birth weight premature infants: Results at 18 years of age for the Infant Health and Development Program. *Pediatrics, 117,* 771–780

Montie, J. E., Xiang, Z., & Schweinhart, L. J. (2006). Preschool experience in 10 countries: Cognitive and language performance at age 7. *Early Childhood Research Quarterly, 21,* 313–331.

Moore, E., Armsden, G., & Gogerty, P. L. (1998). A twelve-year follow-up study of maltreated and at-risk children who received early therapeutic child care. *Child Maltreatment, 3,* 3–16.

Mulligan, G., Brimhall, D., West, J., & Chapman, C. (2005). *Child care and early education arrangements of infants, toddlers, and preschoolers: 2001* (NCES 2006-039). Washington, DC: National Center for Education Statistics, U.S. Department of Education. Retrieved December 3, 2007, from http://nces.ed.gov/pubs2006/2006039.pdf

Mulligan, B., & Flanagan, K. D. (2006). *Age 2: Findings from the 2-year-old follow-up of the Early Childhood Longitudinal Study, Birth Cohort (ECLS-B)* (NCES 2006-043). Washington, DC: National Center for Education Statistics, U.S. Department of Education.

National Forum on Early Childhood Program Evaluation and National Scientific Council on the Developing Child. (2007). A science-based framework for early childhood policy. Retrieved December 2, 2007, from Harvard University, Center on the Developing Child Web site: http://www.developingchild.harvard.edu/content/downloads/Policy_Framework.pdf

National Research Council and Institute of Medicine. (2000). *From neurons to neighborhoods: The science of early childhood development.* Committee on Integrating the Science of Early Childhood Development. J. P. Shonkoff & D. A. Phillips (Eds.). Commission on Behavioral and Social Sciences and Education. Washington, DC: National Academy Press.

NICHD Early Child Care Research Network. (2005). Early child care and children's development in the primary grades: Follow-up results from the NICHD Study of Early Child Care, *American Educational Research Journal, 42,* 537–570. Related material retrieved December 3, 2007, from http://secc.rti.org

The No Child Left Behind Act of 2001. Pub. L. No. 107-110, 115 Stat. 1425 (2002).

Office of Special Education and Rehabilitative Services, U. S. Department of Education. (2003). *25th annual report to Congress on the Individuals with Disabilities Education Act: Vol. 1.* Retrieved December 3, 2007, from http://www.ed.gov/about/reports/annual/osep/2003/25th-vol-1.pdf

Olds, D. L., Eckenrode, J., Henderson, C. R., Jr., Kitzman, H., Powers, J., Cole, R., et al. (1997). Long term effects of home visitation on maternal life course and child abuse and neglect: 15-year follow-up of a randomized trial. *The Journal of the American Medical Association, 278,* 637–643.

Olds, D. L., Henderson, C. R., Jr., Cole, R., Eckenrode, J., Kitzman, H., Luckey, D., et al. (1998). Long-term effects of nurse home visitation on children's criminal and antisocial behavior: 15-year follow-up of a randomized trial. *The Journal of the American Medical Association, 280,* 1238–1244.

Olds, D. L., Henderson, C. R., Jr., Phelps, C. Kitzman, H., & Hanks, C. (1993). Effects of prenatal and infancy nurse home visitation on government spending. *Medical Care, 31,* 155–174.

Olds, D. L., Kitzman, H., Cole, R., Robinson, J., Sidora, K., Luckey, D. W., et al. (2004). Effects of nurse home-visiting on maternal life course and child development: Age 6 follow-up results of a randomized trial. *Pediatrics, 114,* 1550–1559.

Olmsted, P., & Montie, J. (Eds.). (2001). *What do early childhood settings look like?: Structural characteristics of early childhood settings in 15 countries.* Ypsilanti, MI: High/Scope Press.

Overturf Johnson, J. (2005). *Who's minding the kids? Child care arrangements: Winter 2002.* Current Population Reports, P70-101. Washington, DC: U.S. Census Bureau. Retrieved December 3, 2007, from http://www.census.gov/prod/2005pubs/p70-101.pdf

Planning and Evaluation Service. (1998). *Even Start: Evidence from the past and a look to the future.* Washington, DC: U.S. Department of Education. Retrieved December 3, 2007, from http://www.ed.gov/pubs/EvenStart/evenstart.pdf

Quality Education Data. (2005). *High/Scope early childhood curriculum final report.* Denver, CO: Author.

Raine, A., Melligen, K., Liu, J., Venables, P., & Mednick. S. (2003). Effects of environmental enrichment at ages 3–5 years on schizotypal personality and antisocial behavior at ages 17 and 23 years. *American Journal of Psychiatry, 160,* 1627–1635.

Reynolds, A. J., Temple, J. A., Robertson, D. L., & Mann, E. A. (2001). Long-term effects of an early childhood intervention on educational achievement and juvenile arrest: A 15-year follow-up of low-income children in public schools. *Journal of the American Medical Association, 285,* 2339–2346.

Reynolds, A. J., Temple, J. A., Robertson, D. L., & Mann, E. A. (2002). Age 21 cost-benefit analysis of the Title I Chicago child-parent centers. *Educational Evaluation and Policy Analysis, 24*(4), 267–303. Retrieved December 3, 2007, from http://www.irp.wisc.edu/publications/dps/pdfs/dp124502.pdf

Rolnick, A., & Grunewald, R. (2003, September). *Early childhood development: Economic development with a high public return.* Fedgazette. (Federal Reserve Bank of Minneapolis). Retrieved December 3, 2007, from http://www.minneapolisfed.org/research/studies/earlychild/abc-part2.pdf

Ryan, R. M., Fauth, R. C., & Brooks-Gunn, J. (2006). Childhood poverty: Implications for school readiness and early childhood education. In B. Spodek & O. N. Saracho (Eds.), *Handbook of research on the education of young children* (2nd ed., pp. 323–346). Mahwah, NJ: Erlbaum.

Sammons, P., Elliot, K., Sylva, K., Melhuish, M., Siraj-Blatchford, & Taggart, B. (2004). The impact of pre-school on young children's cognitive attainments at entry to reception. *British Education Research Journal, 30,* 691–712.

Save the Children. (2003). *What's the difference? The impact of early child development programs.* Katmandu, Nepal: Author.

Schweinhart, L. J., Montie, J., Xiang, Z., Barnett, W. S., Belfield, C. R., & Nores, M. (2005). *Lifetime effects: The High/Scope Perry Preschool Study through age 40.* Ypsilanti, MI: High/Scope Press.

Schweinhart, L. J., & Weikart, D. P. (1997). The High/Scope Preschool Curriculum Comparison Study through age 23. *Early Childhood Research Quarterly, 12,* 117–143.

Shonkoff, J. (2006). *The Science of Early Childhood Development: Closing the Gap Between What We Know and What We Do.* Waltham, MA: National Scientific Council on the Developing Child.

Smith, M. S. (1975). Evaluation findings in Head Start Planned Variation models. In A. M. Rivlin & P. M. Timpane (Eds.), *Planned variation in education* (pp. 101–111). Washington, DC: Brookings.

Weikart, D. P., Olmsted, P. P., & Montie, J. (Eds.). (2003). *A world of preschool experience: Observations in 15 countries.* Ypsilanti, MI: High/Scope Press.

The White House. (2004). *Good Start, Grow Smart: The Bush administration's early childhood initiative,* Executive Summary. Retrieved December 3, 2007, from http://www.whitehouse.gov/infocus/early-childhood/earlychildhood.html

Wylie, C., Thompson, J., Hodgen, E., Ferral, H., Lythe, C. & Fijn, T. (2004). *Competent children at 12.* Wellington, New Zealand: Ministry of Education/New Zealand Council for Educational Research.

Zill, N., Resnick, G., Kim, K., O'Donnell, K., Sorongon, A., McKey, R. H., et al. (2003, May). *Head Start FACES 2000: A whole child perspective on program performance—Fourth progress report.* Retrieved December 3, 2007, from http://www.acf.hhs.gov/programs/opre/hs/faces/reports/faces00_4thprogress/faces00_4thprogress.pdf

69

Social Stratification and Educational Opportunity

NATHAN D. JONES AND BARBARA SCHNEIDER
Michigan State University

An overwhelming number of research studies indicate that children in families with limited economic and social resources and from racial and ethnic minorities are less likely to achieve their educational goals and occupational aspirations than their more advantaged peers.[1] A principal contribution of educational sociological research has been to document the ways in which institutions (through specific policies, practices, and values) undermine the ability of certain students to achieve their aspirations. Families, schools, peer groups, and neighborhood communities have all been shown to influence the educational and occupational trajectories of children; however, these influences vary among groups of students—particularly those in minority groups with limited economic and social resources. Social scientists have frequently focused their research on the roles that schools can play in encouraging student ambitions and ameliorating the negative influences of other institutions.

Social stratification typically refers to the process by which societal institutions hierarchically sort individuals into particular groups based on one or more criteria. These placements have unique characteristics and subsequently affect individuals' lifestyles and educational and occupational status. One of the earliest scholars to conceptualize the process of social stratification in schools was the sociologist, Sorokin (1927/1963). Sorokin referred to schools as "channels of vertical circulation," which use testing and other measures of performance to sort and distribute students along various strata. His analogy of schools as an elevator within a social building is particularly relevant: Where there is universal or public access to education, students are presumably allowed to move up from the very bottom of the social building to the very top. In his conceptualization, the role of education is to sort students according to academic ability, with the highest performing students moving on to additional schooling, regardless of their family background characteristics, such as the occupation, income and immigrant status of their parents. Although schools hold the potential to move individuals between floors in the social building, Sorokin realized that students in families with considerable economic and social resources have easier access to the top floors than their less advantaged peers.

Schools have a serious challenge in operating as a social evaluator, for by the time children enter formal schooling, their preschool learning, skills, and knowledge have already been shaped by the first and perhaps most significant institution, their families (Heckman, Stixrud, & Urzua, 2006). For some researchers, such as Coleman et al. (1966) and Sewell and Hauser (1972), families represent the strongest predictor of educational attainment, exceeding the impact of schools. Other scholars, such as Oakes (1990, 2005) and Gamoran (Gamoran & Mare, 1989; Lucas & Gamoran, 2002), recognize the importance of families but argue that research should focus on characteristics of schools, such as courses and instruction, that can potentially lessen the impact of limited family resources. Similar arguments have been made for examining the stratifying effects of peer groups, and scholars in this area have investigated the influence of factors such as the expectations, behaviors, and performance of other students and close friends in the school; the characteristics of the student body, including the proportion of students who repeat grades and the proportion who drop out of school; and the quality of the neighborhoods where students live—including the numbers of adults unemployed, unmarried with children, and engaged in illicit activities.

This chapter traces research that examines the role of education in social stratification and reviews several major studies that have examined how schools and other institutions stratify educational opportunities for students. At the same time, we acknowledge that some forms of stratification may be hidden or difficult to detect—we certainly have not covered every experience that stratifies people or every study that has discussed stratification mechanisms in schools. Rather, we have attempted to highlight a particular set of studies in which the scope and rigor of the work appears to be linked to major educational policies over the last 50 years. Finally, the chapter discusses what issues have received less attention and what that has meant for the study of student performance and attainment and the policies designed to improve it.

Theoretical Foundations of Social Stratification and Educational Attainment

Blau and Duncan (1967) and Sewell and Hauser (1972) were among the first researchers to empirically demonstrate how family background characteristics interact with educational experiences impact students' educational attainment. Collectively, their work shows that the "vicious cycle of poverty" argument—or the direct link between a parent's occupation and their child's—is insufficient for explaining the mechanisms underlying social stratification. Instead, they argue how family effects on attainment operate through schools. To test the association between fathers' educational attainment and occupation status on their sons' educational attainment, first job, and subsequent occupation, Blau and Duncan (1967) conducted an analysis of survey data for 20,700 respondents.[2] An advance of their study over previous work was their use of a "social mobility distance ratio," which serves as an index of the influence of occupational origins on destinations (Carlsson, 1958; Glass, 1954; Rogoff, 1953).[3] From these scores, Blau and Duncan were able to examine in detail patterns of movement across generations and to locate specific spaces within the stratification system where more or less movement is likely to be found.

Their findings showed that fathers' education and occupation have an independent effect on their sons' careers, but these two factors interact as well; males in families whose fathers' held higher levels of education and occupation were more likely to attain more prestigious jobs than males in less advantaged circumstances. Subsequently, Sewell and Hauser (1972, 1980) expanded on Blau and Duncan's work by incorporating social psychological variables to explain how educational experiences mediate the relationship between socioeconomic background and educational and occupational outcomes. In their "Wisconsin Model," the authors measured educational aspirations by asking how much further beyond high school a student planned to go; a student was determined to have "high" aspirations if they planned to attend 4 years of college or higher. They found that family background characteristics are largely predictive of academic success; however, by incorporating social psychological variables a more comprehensive explanation of educational attainment can be achieved. By including social psychological variables, these researchers established a new tradition of looking beyond conventional family background characteristics into other contexts that influence student learning and motivation. Using, at the time, very sophisticated path models, Sewell and Hauser and their students showed how children are socialized through their interactions with their significant others (i.e., their family members, peers, and teachers); and through these relationships they develop aspirations that shape their educational outcomes. It is these aspirations that are integral for predicting educational and occupational outcomes (Sewell, Haller, & Portes, 1969; Sewell & Shah, 1968).

Socioeconomic status (SES) appears to impact the aspirations parents have for their children. The aspirations of peer groups also affect individuals' aspirations, although their effects are not as strong as those of one's parents. Academic ability is a stronger predictor than socioeconomic status for determining the educational expectations teachers hold for their students, although peers and parents have twice as strong an influence on students' aspirations as their teachers (Sewell & Hauser, 1972). These findings also suggests that individuals outside of the family can impact educational attainment, which holds promise for the potential impact that schools and policy makers can have on individuals. The model was less strong at predicting earnings (only 7%), given that the students had only been in the work force for a short time when the survey was completed, but subsequent studies have been able to capture a greater effect of these variables on earnings.

The Wisconsin Model has played a foundational role in the way that sociological researchers have examined the relationship between family background characteristics and educational attainment. Subsequent data collection allowed Sewell and Hauser to refine their models and extend them to include experiences of the original survey participants, tracing their occupational success through various stages of adulthood. Surveys conducted from 1992–1994, for example, provided updated data on occupations, health, wealth, marital status, childrearing, and other measures of attainment in adulthood (Hauser et al., 1992; Hauser et al., 1994). They have also expanded their model to include data on the siblings of the original participants.[4] Even with longitudinal data that follows participants and their siblings throughout their occupational careers, the role of aspirations remains prominent in explaining how plans made during childhood and adolescence have effects on educational attainment in adulthood.

The Equality of Educational Opportunity In nearly the same time period that Blau and Duncan were examining the relationship between parent occupational status and student educational attainment, Coleman was asked by the Assistant Commissioner of Education and Director of the National Center for Education Statistics (NCES) to direct a study (as mandated in the Civil Rights Act of 1964) that examined the relationship between school resources (such as per pupil expenditures, teachers' postsecondary degrees, and school facilities) and student performance. The underlying intent of the study was to document the differences in school resources that were hampering the success of African American students. What Coleman et al. (1966) found and reported in the now widely cited report, *Equality of Educational Opportunity*, was a relative lack of relationship between school resources and student achievement; he found that children from similar backgrounds did similarly well, regardless of school resources. Equal schooling did not translate into equal outcomes; even if the resources available to Whites and minority students were the same, the effects of socioeconomic status were overwhelming with respect to academic achievement. An additional finding was that the majority of America's schools were largely segregated (over 90% of White students attended schools that were primarily White and over 65% of Black students attended schools that were primarily Black). These levels of segregation had adverse effects on African American students, who were shown to benefit from being in schools with larger percentages of White students. The same positive influence was shown for Black students who attended schools with a higher percentage of students who come from backgrounds that are "strongly and effectively supportive of education." School composition did not appear to be as influential for White students; their achievement was not adversely affected by being in schools with higher percentages of minority students or students from weak educational backgrounds. Seen in the context of social mobility, although children's backgrounds are a strong predictor of their educational attainment, their own educational expectations are likely to improve if their peers have similarly high expectations.

From a policy standpoint, Coleman's evidence suggested that school reforms should target school composition, rather than school resources. Given the high rates of segregation at the time of his report, Coleman came to believe that one avenue for social mobility would be to more fully integrate schools. The report's findings were highly contested and often misinterpreted. However, it did suggest that per pupil expenditures were not the answer to erasing lack of educational opportunities, and as a result many scholars set about looking more closely in the schools for those "alterable" variables that could change student schooling trajectories. The research pursued by these investigators highlights the importance of children's experiences in schools, and points at the variety of school factors that shape their subjective feelings about education and the actions they take in schools (Alexander, Entwistle, & Kabbani, 2001). The path children take in their schooling careers is based on decisions made in conjunction with adults and peers at multiple points around a diverse group of factors (e.g., how far in school one expects to go, what courses to take in high school, whether to work hard, participate in sports, or engage in undesirable behaviors).

Mechanisms of Stratification in Schools and Neighborhoods

School Effects Beyond family effects that have enduring impact on their children's education, schools themselves have been shown to also influence educational attainment. An important distinction is how the experiences of students differ *between* schools as well as *within* schools. Research on between-school effects looks closely at how the differences in quality between schools impacts student

attainment. Within-school studies have tended to examine whether individual schools can make up for disadvantages children bring with them to school. Another subset of research on school effects looks at how teachers allocate resources and how they interact with students in their classes that can lead to unequal educational outcomes. This work deals primarily with the ways in which schools, teachers, and peers influence the educational aspirations of students, and how these plans in turn shape educational and career decisions.

Between-School Effects Even though school-level factors may not have the same level of influence on educational attainment that family effects do, it is worthwhile, from a policy perspective, to explore whether differences in the resources, racial and ethnic composition, and academic climate of schools produce diverse educational opportunities (Hallinan, 2001). Taking, for example, the issue of teacher quality, low-income and minority students are likely to attend schools with higher rates of teacher turnover and higher numbers of beginning teachers (Hanushek, Kain, & Rivkin, 2004; Lankford, Loeb, & Wyckoff, 2002). Research by Rivkin, Hanushek, and Kain (2005) suggests that these differences in teacher quality have a significant impact on student achievement (see Hanushek, this volume).

Additionally, young people are influenced by the student composition of their schools; researchers have found that high levels of achievement among the student body has a positive effect on achievement growth (Hanushek, Kain, Markman, & Rivkin, 2003; Zimmer & Toma, 2000). This effect appears to be strongest for the most low-achieving students (Zimmer & Toma, 2000). The racial composition of a school appears to matter as well; Black students who attend schools that are primarily White benefit academically (Harris, 2006; Kaufman & Rosenbaum, 1992) and are less likely to drop out of school (Rumberger & Thomas, 2000). In contrast, there is some evidence to suggest that students feel more attached to their schools when they are surrounded by a greater number of same-race students (Johnson, Crosnoe, & Elder, 2001). The lack of consensus on the effects of school classmates, despite the large body of research discussing them, exists in part because it is difficult to sort out the influence of students from other confounding variables, such as the socioeconomic status of parents. One potential source of error in these studies is that the attitudes of students in the school may represent proxies for omitted variables that impact individual attainment. In addition to issues of omitted variables, there is a problem of reciprocal effects for it is difficult to unravel the direct link between peers and individual attitudes as individual attitudes may simultaneously influence their peers' (Hanushek et al., 2003).

Another source of inequality between schools is related to school climate or community. With a lack of adequate school resources, instability in the teaching force, and large numbers of students from high-poverty neighborhoods, the culture of some urban schools is one that does not typically support high educational aspirations, nor the norms that would provide children with a model for academic success. This is evidenced in research on students in Catholic versus public schools, which highlights the academic advantages afforded to students by being in Catholic schools (Bryk, Lee, & Holland, 1993; Coleman & Hoffer, 1987). These researchers attribute increased academic performance and school completion to the positive environment fostered in Catholic schools. The academic success of students in these schools is encouraged through the communal organization within the school building, the inspirational ideology of the teachers, and the connection between their school curriculum and social norms (Bryk et al., 1993). In schools where effective social relationships exist between teachers, administrators, and parents (also conceptualized as having high degrees of relational trust), the environment is likely to be more conducive to academic improvement (Bryk & Schneider, 2002). As this and other research indicates, the presence of a strong academic school culture, which is supported by positive peer group norms, can lessen the impact of family background on attainment (Phillips, 1997).

Within-School Effects   Even for students within the same school, it has been shown that educational expectations vary considerably and this variation has been attributed to structural factors as well as teacher-student interactions. Through a variety of mechanisms, schools make decisions about children's learning environments that can create unequal educational opportunities. One frequently cited mechanism that differentiates students is ability grouping (for a comprehensive review of ability grouping and tracking, see Oakes, Gamoran, & Page, 1992).

Ability grouping has a long history in education, beginning with reading groups that differentiated young children according to their literacy skills. The rationale for ability grouping in elementary schools is that it facilitates the instructional process by allowing teachers to focus on students of different levels of reading proficiency in the same classroom. This explanation has proved somewhat inconsistent and research has shown that students in the lower groups are typically exposed to fewer opportunities to learn, leading to increased inequality of achievement (Sørensen & Hallinan, 1986). These practices of ability grouping continue through middle school, where students are often placed in academic courses that are designated as honors, general, or remedial.

In high schools, similar types of placements have occurred, primarily around the type of programs students are sorted into, although ability grouping also occurs. For most of the latter half of the 20th century, high school students were commonly grouped into academic, general, or vocational tracks, with each track consisting of a series of courses that would prepare students for different occupational outcomes. Studies indicate that when schools organize students into tracks, students in the academic track are more likely to make achievement gains over the course of high school, have higher educational aspirations, and ma-

triculate into postsecondary schools than students in other tracks (Lucas, 2001, Natriello, Pallas, & Alexander, 1989; Oakes, 2005). These academic effects are more pronounced for students who take more advanced-level courses, especially math and science in high school; these students are not only more likely to attend postsecondary school but attend more competitive prestigious universities (Adelman, 2006; Schneider, Swanson, & Riegle-Crumb, 1999).

High school tracking practices are generally viewed as limiting with respect to educational opportunity. When schools organize students into tracks, researchers have found that grouping patterns appear to be based not only on ability. A large number of students from racial and ethnic minority groups as well as from families with limited resources tend to be grouped in the lowest track (Gamoran & Mare, 1989; Lucas & Gamoran, 2002). These results have encouraged many high schools to adopt non-tracking policies which place all students in the academic program. Most high school teachers and academic counselors now report that they expect all students will attend postsecondary education (Rosenbaum, 2001). These postsecondary expectations can be found in all types of high school courses, even vocational ones, where teachers encourage students to attend 2-year colleges after high school (Schneider & Stevenson, 1999). However, as recent graduation rates indicate, the normative postsecondary expectations often articulated by school personnel do not necessarily translate into college attendance for all students (Swanson, 2004; Warren & Halpern-Manners, 2007).

Although the formalized concept of high school programmatic tracking is becoming less prevalent, new mechanisms have emerged that group students into *de facto* tracking circumstances (Lucas & Berends, 2002). De facto tracking arises when students' levels of study are associated across multiple subject areas, thus blurring the set programmatic designations that were more obvious with prior formalized tracking. Both formal and de facto tracking impede students' ability to meet their academic goals, and the negative consequences of being placed in low-level courses are disproportionately experienced by African American and low-income students (Catsambis, 1994; Hallinan, 1994; Lucas & Berends, 2002; Oakes, 1990).

These course assignments emerge out of a series of complex decisions made at "key decision points" by students and school personnel, in which choices are routinely made and re-made. Some researchers have argued that teachers are making these course decisions and that they do so from a set of expectations regarding certain students, so that minority students are more likely to be placed in lower-level courses (Ferguson, 1998). While it has not as yet been determined who is primarily responsible for course decisions, what has been more generally agreed upon is that early decisions about high school courses appear to affect later ones, placing students on trajectories that influence their educational attainment (McFarland, 2006). The most frequent one is taking algebra in the eighth grade, which has been shown to set the mathematics sequence for most students in high school. If a student fails to take algebra in eighth grade, the chances of completing a 4-year sequence of advanced level mathematics in high school is less likely.

Family, Teacher, and Peer Effects on Student Educational Expectations

Bourdieu (1984) points to the consumption patterns followed by individuals (including food, culture, and personal appearance), paying specific attention to the role of families and friends in shaping these preferences. Individuals develop certain dispositions based on their experiences that then shape their actions, beliefs, and consumption—collectively described as their *cultural capital*. Related to schooling, families play a primary role in conveying to their children appropriate ways of speaking, acting, and approaching education. The outward effect of these patterns of consumption is to signal to teachers and peers the class to which a student belongs, which may, in turn, affect how these individuals react to the child. Lareau (1987, 1989) observes that schools are primarily middle-class institutions that support middle-class values. Students are best able to succeed if they hold values and beliefs that align with those of their teachers and schools. For students from lower-class families, it is less likely that they possess the requisite attitudes and skills necessary for academic success.

As teachers develop expectations for students, they may rely on factors other than performance. At the beginning of the school year (when they have had few interactions with students), teachers may rely on more general characteristics such as race, ethnicity, social class, and gender when forming ideas about students' long-term educational success.[5] There is evidence that teachers underestimate the academic potential of African American and low-income students (Brophy, 1983; Farkas, 1996, 2003; Ferguson, 1998). Brophy (1983), for example, claims that although teachers are often accurate in their perceptions of student ability, their expectations toward Black students are more likely to be rigid than those for White students; if teachers begin with low expectations for Black students, they are less likely to change these beliefs based on student performance. Additionally, researchers have found that the expectations teachers have for their students may affect their academic performance, motivation, effort, and achievement (Brophy & Good, 1974; Jussim & Harber, 2005). Scholars argue that biased teacher expectations can lead to "self-fulfilling prophecies," in which students respond to lower expectations by exerting less effort and performing at lower levels. Although effect sizes associated with self-fulfilling prophecies are typically small, they tend to be strongest for African Americans and students from low-income backgrounds, suggesting that teacher expectations at times serve as a stratifying force in schools (Brophy, 1983; Jussim, Eccles, & Madon, 1996; Jussim & Harber, 2005).

In addition to the influence of teachers on academic attainment, peers and classmates also play an important role (Crosnoe, Riegle-Crumb, Field, Frank, & Muller, 2008). Given that friendships are most likely to form when students are close in physical space, shared classes become a primary source for building social relationships. Friendships with classmates can shape academic achievement in multiple ways, as can membership in peer groups; and location within a friendship group and the overall cohesion of the network can influence the kind of effects peers have on student aspirations, achievement and other behaviors (Crosnoe & Needham, 2004; Haynie, 2001). Friendships appear to play a protective role as well; children who have friends that do better in school or who enjoy school more have fewer academic problems and lower rates of acting out and drug use (Cook, Deng, & Morgano, 2007; Crosnoe, Cavanaugh, & Elder, 2003).

Several studies have focused on the effects of friendships on female performance. For females, academic performance of same-sex friends predicts enrollment in advanced coursework, particularly in subjects (math and science) that are commonly viewed as male-dominated domains (Riegle-Crumb, Farkas, & Muller, 2006). In addition to gender studies, researchers are examining the effects of peer groups for different racial and minority groups. Recent studies by Ream and others have examined the positive and negative effects peer groups can have on Hispanic student aspirations, suggesting that gender, grades, and teacher expectations all play a particularly strong role in shaping expectations (Ream, 2005; Valenzuela, 1999). For Black students, recent research recognizes the heterogeneous nature of Black adolescent peer groups, suggesting that friendships can coexist that both support college aspirations and provide negative influences as well (Horvat & Lewis, 2003). African American students who are able to straddle the boundary between their peer group, especially if it is not academically oriented, and their school environment appear to have greater success in school than those students who choose to follow their peers or isolate themselves from the school academic culture (Carter, 2006).

Neighborhood Effects

Neighborhood effects complicate the within/between school distinction; they manifest themselves between *and* within schools. Living in a high-poverty neighborhood is likely to shape the educational aspirations children bring with them to school, while the concentration of poverty within a community can also have consequences for the resources available to schools. Wilson (1987), Massey and Denton (1993) and others studying the effects of neighborhoods have shown how the impact of poverty and social isolation affect educational aspirations. The social norms modeled by adults and adolescents in a neighborhood can have profound socialization effects on children in low-income communities that undermine their educational aspirations and attainment.

Wilson (1987) argues that changes in the economic structures of cities have resulted in the flight of the Black middle class out of urban neighborhoods and into higher-income neighborhoods. This trend, coupled with the decrease in sustainable jobs available to urban residents has increased the concentration of poverty among many urban neighborhoods.[6] The lack of available jobs undermines the ability of individuals to use schooling to get ahead; with few legitimate avenues for gaining status, residents, in some cases, develop oppositional behaviors and values toward schooling and mainstream society more generally (Massey & Denton, 1993). Additionally, the high rates of joblessness limit the positive role models young people have access to. Rather than learn behaviors and attitudes that would lead to success in school and the labor market, children in impoverished communities are likely to be socialized in a manner that reproduces the inequalities already in place.

Empirical studies testing the influence of neighborhood-level factors on education must be careful to separate out family from neighborhood effects. Jencks and Mayer (1990) warn that many times what we attribute to neighborhoods are really qualities of family background that have not been identified in the study. Another concern, according to Duncan and Raudenbush (1999) is that in many surveys, "neighborhood-level characteristics are nothing more than the aggregation of family- and individual-level characteristics" (p. 31). This is especially the case when using census data (which several studies of neighborhood effects have relied on), which derives many "neighborhood" factors from aggregates of individual characteristics.

The complicated nature of neighborhood effects has prompted researchers to make use of several different analytic techniques. Solon, Page, and Duncan (2000) have used correlations between neighboring children and their later socioeconomic status as a means of determining the extent of neighborhood effects. Another promising advance in this area of research is the study of neighborhood effects within a causal framework. Research by Harding (2003) uses propensity score matching to approximate random assignment into treatment and control groups. Using this method, one matches students according to their propensity to be subjected to the treatment—in this case, living in a high poverty neighborhood—while taking into account numerous covariates (such as family background). Harding finds that of a variety of outcomes, dropping out of high school and becoming pregnant as a teenager are likely consequences of living in a high-poverty neighborhood, lending support to similar findings that have been reported using cross-sectional data (Brooks-Gunn, Duncan, Klebanov, & Sealand, 1993; Crane, 1991). With the movement of students in and out of neighborhoods to attend schools out of their attendance areas, these neighborhood effects may or may not prove to be important in shaping educational aspirations.

Educational Stratification from High School to College and the Labor Market

As researchers have struggled to understand the process of educational stratification, the landscape of education itself has changed. The kinds of post-high school opportunities available to students have become more diversified. While the majority of adolescents through the 1970s and 1980s sought employment after high school, by the 1990s nearly 70% of high school seniors matriculated to some sort of postsecondary institution upon graduation. Far fewer students than 30 years ago stop their education once they graduate from high school, and those that do are likely to experience negative consequences on their occupational attainment. From the perspective of educational stratification, it is important to know what role schools play in the paths students take after high school.

Dropping Out: A Consequence of Stratification

It is generally acknowledged that dropping out of high school is the culmination of a long-term multiplicative process that begins in early childhood (Alexander et al., 2001; Garnier, Stein, & Jacobs, 1997). Research indicates that the experiences students have at home and school predict high school completion, including grade retention, absenteeism, low motivation, and poor academic performance (Eckstein & Wolpin, 1999; Kaufman & Bradby, 1992; Rumberger, 1995; Stearns, Moller, Potochnick, & Blau, 2007). Young people who drop out of high school are more likely to be unemployed, to be in prison, and are more likely to be in poorer physical health than those who did not drop out (Coley, 1995; Laird, Kienzl, DeBell, & Chapman, 2007; McCaul, Donaldson, Coladarci, & Davis, 1992). The financial consequences of not completing high school are considerable; in 2005, individuals who completed their education with a high school credential made $29,700 on average while dropouts made $20,100 (Laird et al., 2007). Evidence suggests that graduation rates vary by race and ethnicity, with students from traditionally disadvantaged racial and ethnic minority groups having "little more than a fifty-fifty chance of finishing high school with a diploma," in comparison to White and Asian students who have a likely graduation rate of 75% and 77%, respectively (Swanson, 2004). Graduation rates for schools in high poverty, racially segregated, and urban districts are between 15% and 18% lower than other schools (Swanson, 2004).

This body of research has prompted questions about how best to lessen dropout rates for minority or low-income youths. One source of concern has been the role of student employment during high school (Entwistle, Alexander, & Olson, 2000; McNeal, 1997; Warren, 2002; Warren, LePore, & Mare, 2000), leading researchers to investigate whether holding a job while in school actually takes time away from academics (e.g., completing homework, participating in extracurricular activities). Students who work extensively during high school have lower grades than those who work less, are more likely to drop out, and are less likely to go on to postsecondary schooling. However, economists suggest that if we were to introduce policies that prohibited work in high school, they would likely have only limited impact on high school graduation rates because students who are likely to work during high school are likely to be students who face other risks for dropping out, such as a lack of motivation to do well in school, lower expectations of the rewards associated with high school graduation, and a history of low academic performance (Eckstein & Wolpin, 1999).

Vocational programs, the series of courses that provide students with practical skills, also have been used as a way of attracting students who would otherwise drop out of high school. These "at-risk" students—who might not see postsecondary education as an option—might be motivated to stay in school if they learn skills that would be directly relevant in the labor market. Although federal programs have scaled back on the resources available for vocational programs, research suggests that investing in such programs increases the likelihood that students graduate from high school (Arum, 1998) and that participation in such programs leads to more desirable occupations 4 years after high school (Arum & Shavit, 1995).

Stratification and Higher Education   As at previous levels of schooling, the effects of family background and previous school experiences influence decisions related to whether to go to college (Cabrera & La Nasa, 2001; Perna, 2000). High schools play a part in this process and several newer studies suggest how schools can ease the transition for students whose families lack the information and resources to assist their children in the college process (Hill, 2008). It is not clear if these policies—as well as other factors such as the financial consequences of not going to college—have influenced minority student transitions, but what has occurred is that the fastest growing segment of the population entering college are children from families whose parents did not go to college and are from low-income backgrounds (National Center for Educational Statistics, 2001).

Once enrolled in college, minority students and students from families with limited resources often face additional financial and academic problems that may lead to increased rates of dropout or transfer to other institutions. Tinto (1993) argues that colleges can increase the likelihood that students persist by holding high expectations and by providing students with continual feedback about their performance, especially in the first year. Also, when students feel supported—both academically and personally—and integrated into the college culture, they are more likely to stay. However, too often the college experiences of African American students are not marked by these characteristics, and they instead report a lack of support and lowered expectations. As a result, African American students are much less likely to complete college than their White peers; if they do complete school, they are likely to have much lower grade point averages and achieve lower class rankings than other students (Bowen & Bok, 1998; Light & Strayer, 2000; Tinto, 1993). Even if minority or low-income students persist in their postsecondary education, they are more likely than other students to transfer between institutions or experience interruptions in their schooling (Adelman, 1999; Goldrick-Rab, 2006). Both of these conditions have been shown to lessen the likelihood of timely college completion, which appears to have negative consequences for later earnings (Elman & O'Rand, 2004).

The increase in the college-going population has also led to greater variability in the quality of schools students attend. In order to compete for students, institutions are seeking to distinguish themselves vertically—by seeking out a certain level of quality in their applicants, as well as horizontally—by developing more specialized learning opportunities (Hoxby, 1997). Although the distribution of students into these various schools is based on ability, low-income and traditionally disadvantaged minority students make up only a small percentage of the student body of elite colleges and universities. To address the disparities in the number of traditionally disadvantaged minorities in more prestigious schools, Bowen and Bok (1998) investigated the consequences of considering race in the admissions process of selective universities, asking whether Black students or the universities themselves profited or were hurt by affirmative action. The authors suggest that the students admitted into select colleges did benefit from the placement; there is an advantage in graduation rates, career income and status, and life satisfaction. Also, the universities themselves benefit from the increased diversity, with a large number of White and Black students suggesting that "their undergraduate experience made a significant contribution to their ability to work with and get along with members of other races" (p. 267). Arcidiacono (2005) refines this finding by suggesting that, in fact, race-based advantages have little effect on earnings, but that removing advantages in admissions would lead to a significant loss of Black students at elite schools.

In addition to more commonly studied background characteristics such as race/ethnicity and socioeconomic status, gender also plays a critical role in how students become stratified through postsecondary education. Women attend college at a higher rate than males, are more likely to complete college and are more likely to go on to advanced degrees (Bae, Choy, Geddes, Sable, & Snyder, 2000). The finding is most pronounced for those at the lower half of the SES distribution. That women have caught up to men can be partially explained by the rise of women's participation in the labor force, the increase in the age of first marriage, and a more level playing field for women (Goldin, Katz, & Kuziemko, 2006). Diprete and Buchmann (2006) find evidence that the gap in college completion between White men and White women can be explained by the significantly greater returns to college completion for women than for men, a trend that is even more pronounced when including "returns" variables other than earnings alone (e.g. insurance against living in poverty). These differences in attainment in college will likely be manifested in differences in labor market outcomes.

Economic Benefits of High Educational Attainment
How does one quantify the economic payoff of obtaining a bachelor or associate degree? The sociological literature has explored the sources of variation in attainment, but the importance of educational attainment has also prompted economics researchers to develop more accurate predictions

of the economic and social benefits of additional schooling, and to trace trends in these benefits over time. These studies are typically conducted by comparing the added benefit of graduating from college over graduating from high school, otherwise known as the "wage premium" (Freeman, 1976; Mincer, 1962; Murphy & Welch, 1989). The premium associated with going to college has fluctuated over time, but remains substantial for shaping future status attainment. Using annual information from the Current Population Survey, Murphy and Welch (1989) determined that wage differences for males increased from 47% to 61% from 1963–1971, decreased from 61% to 48% from 1971–1979 (a decline that is attributed to the cohort of baby boomers entering college), and then rebounded from 48% to 67% from 1979–1986 (p. 25). This figure then dropped slightly to 58% in 1989 (Murphy & Welch, 1992). In addition to 4-year schools, researchers have attempted to estimate the labor market value of vocational schooling, finding that attending a 2-year college increases the rate of wage earnings beyond a high school diploma by 10% (Kane & Rouse, 1995).

Beyond the extent of education one receives, there is an added wage benefit of attending elite universities, further disadvantaging minority and low-income students who are often excluded from these schools. Existing literature shows that there are significant economic returns to attending a top-tier school (Black & Smith, 2004; Brewer, Eide, & Ehrenberg, 1999; Dale & Krueger, 2002; Grubb, 1993). These studies are noteworthy for the ways they have handled measurement issues related to selection biases in who goes to elite schools. Dale and Krueger, for example, used longitudinal data to match students who applied to and were accepted by similar colleges to determine if specific effects could be attributed to the more elite school. Although they found that, in general, students who attended top-tier universities were likely to earn similar wages as students of similar ability levels who attended less prestigious schools, students from low-income populations did benefit financially from attending more selective schools. As these and other studies suggest, research on educational stratification must be mindful of these differential effects of attending top colleges.

Strategies of Promoting Social Mobility

A major focus of school reform over the last 50 years has been to address unequal educational outcomes. Many of these policies have addressed the role that families, schools, or neighborhoods play in limiting children's educational attainment. In situations where structural factors constrain the educational decisions a student chooses, policy may be able to influence what students *want* to do with their lives (Gambetta, 1987). From this perspective, we shift our attention to strategies that policy makers have taken to raise the educational expectations of young people from disadvantaged backgrounds, as well as directions for future reforms.

One strategy for increasing the expectations of these students has been to provide them with the opportunity to attend schools that are outside of their neighborhoods (since many students from disadvantaged backgrounds do not typically have the financial means to attend private schools and are likely to be trapped in the poorest and lowest-performing schools). By providing students with opportunities to attend schools with strong academic rigor, such policies may raise these students' educational expectations. Additionally, if students use choice programs to attend schools with high percentages of academically-successful peers, it increases the likelihood that minority students forge friendships that could lead to increased academic engagement and performance. These friendships may also expose these students to new sources of cultural capital, providing access to the kinds of habits and values that have been shown to have a positive influence on educational outcomes (Lareau, 1987, 1989).

Targeting schools where low-income and minority students are already likely to attend, Comprehensive School Reform (CSR) programs emerged in the late 1990s as a strategy for raising student achievement by improving virtually all aspects of teaching and learning in a school, including a more rigorous curriculum, professional development for teachers and administrators, the use of measurable goals for students, and a greater commitment to school community (Stevenson, 2000). Through a unified approach to improving student performance, CSR programs have the potential to raise the expectations of all students, while at the same time decreasing the influence of low-performing peers and the consequences of placement in classes with unchallenging coursework. As of 2002, CSR programs have been implemented in over 3,000 U.S. schools and the Department of Education has committed $310 million to these programs. With its emphasis on testing and accountability, No Child Left Behind (NCLB) can be seen from a similar perspective. By requiring annual testing and by using sanctions to motivate low-performing schools, NCLB intends to address the racial gap in student performance. NCLB also does this by requiring that student scores be disaggregated and that results be presented for racial "subgroups." These strategies seek to bring attention to racial differences in achievement, and in so doing, attach negative consequences to lowered expectations for what students from low-income and minority backgrounds can achieve.

Sociological research has shown us the critical role that teachers can play in the formation of students' educational expectations. Policy efforts to improve teacher quality in low-performing schools may raise the quality of education that these students receive beginning at a young age, which may in turn decrease the likelihood that these students will have lowered expectations. NCLB requires that all teachers of core academic subjects be "highly qualified," meaning that all teachers be fully certified, hold a bachelor's degree from a 4-year institution, and demonstrate competency in their subject area. In addition, requiring full certification will allow us to better control entry into the profession and ensure that universities are preparing future teachers to work with students from diverse backgrounds; an increasing number of teacher training institutions have recognized this need, training their teaching candidates in "culturally-relevant pedagogy" (Ladson-Billings, 1995, 2000).

Finally, there are examples of policies that have had success in directly confronting low expectations among minority and low-income adolescents (as well as targeting students who have high expectations but lack the information and resources necessary to reach their ambitions). Several federally and privately funded programs have been initiated in high schools to help minority students make a successful transition into college. These programs often include more rigorous coursework, tutorial assistance, preparation for college entrance exams, and mentoring.[7] Examples of such programs include GEAR-UP (Gaining Early Awareness and Readiness for Undergraduate Programs), Upward Bound, AVID (Achievement via Individual Determination), and Achieve. Some of these initiatives begin even earlier than high school, to provide students with support while they are in middle school, to allow them to make educational decisions in high school that will prepare them for a more successful transition into postsecondary education. GEAR-UP, for example, is a federal grant program that supports state and partnerships to work with cohorts of students in low-income schools beginning in the seventh grade; currently, U.S. Department of Education devotes over $300 million to GEAR-UP programs, impacting over 700,000 students from low-income backgrounds.

How successful have we been? The majority of adolescents have high expectations,[8] and the prevailing culture in high schools is one where all students are expected to pursue some form of postsecondary education. However, these advances present new challenges; with more students from disadvantaged backgrounds attending college, we need to address the inequality of experiences for students once they are in college, as well as the under-representation of minority and low-income students in prestigious universities. As this chapter has demonstrated, the forces that stratify students are multiple and persistent, which suggests that it will not be a single, large-scale initiative that will improve the educational opportunities for low-income and minority youth. We are better off making small changes, recognizing that, over time, these can accumulate into larger changes. Moving forward, the next wave of reforms will require a variety of polices across all levels of schools (from early education to postsecondary schools) and all levels of policy making (from classroom and school-based reforms to state and federal initiatives). The short-term effects of these policies will likely be small, yet over time, the cumulative effects will likely have real consequences for the educational opportunities available to low-income and minority students.

Notes

1. The recent work on the achievement gap in U.S. schools has focused on understanding why certain minority racial and ethnic groups continue to academically fall behind other students (Harris & Herrington, 2006; Hedges & Nowell, 1999; Jencks & Phillips, 1998; Rothstein, 2004; Sirin, 2005).

2. The 1962 Occupational Changes in a Generation survey that Blau and Duncan employed was conducted by the U.S. Census Bureau, and was initiated to study the effects of men's background on their occupations. The study collected information from 20,700 males aged 20 to 64 on their age, ethnicity, schooling, industry, socioeconomic status, and first occupation, as well as information about their fathers (i.e., their educational attainment and occupation). To allow for comparable analysis, this survey was replicated and extended for a sample of 33,600 males in 1973, including new information on military service and mother's education.

3. The score is calculated by taking observed frequencies of occupations among respondents based on what would be expected if there were independence between father and son.

4. Research extending the Wisconsin Model has concluded that birth order does not have a significant impact on intelligence or on educational attainment (Hauser & Sewell, 1985; Retherford & Sewell, 1991). In families with fewer children, the children are likely to obtain more schooling (Hauser & Sewell, 1985; Sewell, Hauser, & Wolf, 1980), however there is greater variation in educational attainment within large sibships than within small sibships. Socioeconomic background variables affect the educational attainment of children from large families and small families similarly, meaning that large sibships feel the impact of low socioeconomic status more strongly (Kuo & Hauser, 1995). Finally, within families, gender is the largest factor in predicting educational attainment.

5. Diamond, Randolph, and Spillane (2004) find that teachers' expectations also depend on school context. In schools where the majority of students are low-income African Americans, teacher beliefs about student abilities are likely to be more deficit-oriented.

6. Additionally, as recent evidence suggests, the racial inequality of the economic status of neighborhoods persists across generations (Sharkey, 2008).

7. There are also examples of states that have initiated programs requiring students to take more rigorous coursework. The Michigan Merit Curriculum requires students to take 4 years of math and language arts as well as three years of science and social studies.

8. Over 90% of students now plan on attending college (Schneider & Stevenson, 1999).

References

Adelman, C. (1999). *Answers in the toolbox: Academic intensity, attendance patterns, and bachelor's degree attainment.* Washington, DC: U.S. Department of Education, Office of Educational Research and Improvement.

Adelman, C. (2006). *The toolbox revisited: Paths to degree completion from high school through college.* Washington, DC: U.S. Department of Education.

Alexander, K., Entwistle, D., & Kabbani, N. (2001). The dropout process in life course perspective: Early risk factors at home and school. *Teachers College Record, 103,* 760–822.

Arcidiacono, P. (2005). Affirmative action in higher education: How do admission and financial aid rules affect future earnings? *Econometrica, 73,* 1477–1524.

Arum, R. (1998). Invested dollars or diverted dreams: The effect of resources on vocational students' educational outcomes. *Sociology of Education, 71,* 130–151.

Arum, R., & Shavit, Y. (1995). Secondary vocational education and the transition to higher education. *Sociology of Education, 68,* 187–204.

Bae, Y., Choy, S., Geddes, C., Sable, J. & Snyder, T. (2000). *Trends in educational equity of girls and women* (NCES 2000-030). Washington, DC: National Center for Education Statistics.

Black, D., & Smith, J. (2004). How robust is the evidence on the effects of college quality? Evidence from matching. *Journal of Econometrics, 121,* 99–124.

Blau, P., & Duncan, O. (1967). *The American occupational structure.* New York: Wiley.

Bourdieu, P. (1984). *Distinction: A social critique of the judgment of taste* (R. Nice, Trans.). Cambridge, MA: Harvard University Press.

Bowen, W., & Bok, D. C. (1998). *The shape of the river: Long-term consequences of considering race in college and university admissions.* Princeton, NJ: Princeton University Press.

Brewer, D., Eide, E., & Ehrenberg, R. (1999). Does it pay to attend an elite private college? Cross-cohort evidence on the effects of college type on earnings. *The Journal of Human Resources, 34,* 104–123.

Brooks-Gunn, J., Duncan, G. J., Klebanov, P. K., & Sealand, N. (1993) Do neighborhoods influence child and adolescent development? *American Journal of Sociology, 99,* 353–395.

Brophy, J. (1983). Research on the self-fulfilling prophecy and teacher expectations. *Journal of Educational Psychology, 75,* 631–661.

Brophy, J., & Good, T. (1974). *Teacher-student relationships. Causes and consequences.* New York: Holt, Rinehart, and Winston.

Bryk, A. S., Lee, V. E., & Holland, P. B. (1993). *Catholic schools and the common good.* Cambridge, MA: Harvard University Press.

Bryk, A. S., & Schneider, B. (2002). *Trust in schools: A core resource for improvement.* New York: Russell Sage Foundation.

Cabrera, A. F., & La Nasa, S. M. (2001). On the path to college: Three critical tasks facing America's disadvantaged. *Research in Higher Education, 42,* 119–150.

Carlsson, G. (1958). *Social mobility and class structure.* Lund, Sweden: Glerup.

Carter, P. (2006). Straddling boundaries: Identity, culture, and school. *Sociology of Education 79,* 304–328.

Catsambis, S. (1994). The path to math: Gender and racial-ethnic differences in mathematics participation from middle school to high school. *Sociology of Education, 67*(3), 199–215.

Coleman, J. S., Campbell, E. Q., Hobson, C. J., McPartland, J., Mood, A. M., Weinfeld, F. D., et al. (1966). *Equality of educational opportunity.* Washington, DC: Government Printing Office.

Coleman, J. S., & Hoffer, T. (1987). *Public and private high schools: The impact of communities.* New York: Basic Books.

Coley, R. (1995). *Dreams deferred: High school dropouts in the United States.* Princeton, NJ: Educational Testing Service, Policy Information Center.

Cook, T., Deng, Y., & Morgano, E. (2007). Friendship influences during early adolescence: The special role of friends' grade point average. *Journal of Research on Adolescence, 17,* 325–356.

Crane, J. (1991). The epidemic theory of ghettos and neighborhood effects on dropping out and teenage childbearing. *The American Journal of Sociology, 96,* 1226–1259.

Crosnoe, R., Cavanaugh, S., & Elder, G. H. (2003). Adolescent friendships as academic resources: The intersection of friendship, race, and school disadvantage. *Sociological Perspectives, 46,* 331–352.

Crosnoe, R., & Needham, B. L. (2004). Holism, contextual variability, and the study of friendships in adolescent development. *Child Development, 75,* 264–279.

Crosnoe, R., & Riegle-Crumb, C., Field, S., Frank, K., & Muller, C. (2008). Peer group contexts of boys' and girls' academic experiences. *Child Development, 79,* 139–155.

Dale, S. B., & Krueger, A. (2002). Estimating the payoff to attending a more selective college: An application of selection on observables and unobservables. *Quarterly Journal of Economics, 117,* 1491–1528.

Diamond, J. B., Randolph, A., & Spillane, J. P. (2004). Teachers' expectations and sense of responsibility for student learning: The importance of race, class, and organizational habitus. *Anthropology & Education Quarterly, 35,* 75–98.

Diprete, T., & Buchmann, C. (2006). Gender-specific trends in the value of education and the emerging gender gap in college completion. *Demography, 40,* 1–24.

Duncan, G., & Raudenbush, S. (1999). Assessing the effects of context in studies of child and youth development. *Educational Psychologist, 34,* 29–41.

Eckstein, Z., & Wolpin, K. I. (1999). Why youths drop out of high school: The impact of preferences, opportunities, and abilities. *Econometrica, 67,* 1295–1339.

Elman, C., & O'Rand, A. M. (2004). The race is to the swift: Socioeconomic origins, adult education, and wage attainment. *American Journal of Sociology, 110,* 123–160.

Entwistle, D., Alexander, K., & Olson, L. S. (2000). Early work histories of urban youth. *American Sociological Review, 65,* 279–297.

Farkas, G. (1996). *Human capital or cultural capital? Ethnicity and poverty groups in an urban school district.* New York: Aldine de Gruyter.

Farkas, G. (2003). Racial disparities and discrimination in education: What do we know, how do we know it, and what do we need to know? *Teachers College Record, 105,* 1119–1146.

Ferguson, R. (1998). Teachers' perceptions and expectations and the black-white test score gap. In C. Jencks & M. Philips (Eds.), *The black-white test score gap* (pp. 273–317). Washington, DC: Brookings Institution Press.

Freeman, R. (1976). *The overeducated American.* New York: Academic Press.

Gambetta, D. (1987). *Were they pushed or did they jump?: Individual decision mechanisms in education.* Cambridge, UK: Cambridge University Press.

Gamoran, A., & Mare, R. D. (1989). Secondary school tracking and educational inequality: Compensation, reinforcement, or neutrality? *The American Journal of Sociology, 94,* 1146–1183.

Garnier, H., Stein, J., & Jacobs, J. (1997). The process of dropping out of high school: A 19-year perspective. *American Educational Research Journal, 34,* 395–419.

Glass, D. V. (Ed.). (1954). *Social mobility in Britain.* London: Routledge & Kegan Paul.

Goldin, C., Katz, L., & Kuziemko, I. (2006). The homecoming of American college women: The reversal of the college gender gap. *Journal of Economic Perspectives, 20*(4), 133–156.

Goldrick-Rab, S. (2006). Following their every move: An investigation of social-class differences in college pathways. *Sociology of Education, 79,* 61–79.

Grubb, W. N. (1993). The varied economic returns to postsecondary education: New evidence from the class of 1972. *The Journal of Human Resources, 28,* 365–382.

Hallinan, M. (1994). Tracking from theory to practice. *Sociology of Education, 67,* 79–91.

Hallinan, M. (2001). Sociological perspectives on black-white inequalities in American schooling. *Sociology of Education, 74*(Extra Issue), 50–70.

Hanushek, E. A., Kain, J. F., Markman, J., & Rivkin, S. G. (2003). Does peer ability affect student achievement? *Journal of Applied Econometrics, 18,* 527–544.

Hanushek, E. A., Kain, J. F., Rivkin, S. G. (2004). Why public schools lose teachers. *The Journal of Human Resources, 39,* 326–354.

Harding, D. J. (2003). Counterfactual models of neighborhood effects: The effect of neighborhood poverty on dropping out and teenage pregnancy. *American Journal of Sociology, 109,* 676–719.

Harris, D. N. (2006, November 29). *Lost learning, forgotten promises: A national analysis of school segregation, student achievement, and "controlled choice" plans.* Washington, DC: Center for American Progress..

Harris, D. N., & Herrington, C. D. (2006). Accountability, standards, and the growing achievement gap: Lessons from the past half-century. *American Journal of Education, 112,* 209–238.

Hauser, R. M., Carr, D., Hauser, T. S., Hayes, J., Krecker, M., Kuo, H. D. et al. (1994). *The Class of 1957 after 35 Years: Overview and preliminary findings* (CDE Working Paper No. 93-17). Madison: University of Wisconsin: Center for Demography and Ecology.

Hauser, R. M., & Sewell, W. H. (1985). Birth order and educational attainment in full sibships. *American Educational Research Journal, 22,* 1–23.

Hauser, R. M., Sewell, W. H., Logan, J. A., Hauser, T. S., Ryff, C., Caspi, A., et al. (1992). The Wisconsin Longitudinal Study: Adults as parents and children at age 50. *IASSIST Quarterly, 16*(1/2), 23–38.

Haynie, D. L. (2001). Delinquent peers revisited: Does network structure matter? *American Journal of Sociology, 106*, 1013–1057.

Heckman, J. J., Stixrud, J., & Urzua, S. (2006). The effects of cognitive and noncognitive abilities on labor market outcomes and social behavior. *Journal of Labor Economics, 24*, 411–482.

Hedges, L., & Nowell, A. (1999). Changes in the black-white gap in achievement test scores. *Sociology of Education, 72*, 111–135.

Hill, L. D. (2008). School strategies and the "college-linking" process: Reconsidering the effects of high schools on college enrollment. *Sociology of Education, 81*, 53–76.

Horvat, E. M., & Lewis, K. S. (2003). Reassessing the "burden of 'acting white'": The importance of peer groups in managing academic success. *Sociology of Education, 76*, 265–280.

Hoxby, C. M. (1997). *How the changing market structure of U.S. higher education explains college tuition* (NBER Working Paper No. W6323). Cambridge, MA: National Bureau of Economic Research.

Jencks, C., & Mayer, S. (1990). The social consequences of growing up in a poor neighborhood. In L. Lynn & M. McGeary (Eds.), *Inner-city poverty in the United States* (pp. 111–186). Washington, DC: National Academy Press.

Jencks, C., & Phillips, M. (Eds.). (1998). *The black-white test score gap.* Washington, DC: Brookings.

Johnson, M. K., Crosnoe, R., & Elder, G. H., Jr. (2001). Students' attachment and academic engagement: The role of race and ethnicity. *Sociology of Education, 74*, 318–340.

Jussim, L., Eccles, J., & Madon, S. (1996). Social perception, social stereotypes, and teacher perceptions: Accuracy and the search for the powerful self-fulfilling prophecy. In M. P. Zanna (Ed.), *Advances in experimental social psychology* (pp. 281–388). New York: Academic Press.

Jussim, L., & Harber, K.D. (2005). Teacher expectations and self-fulfilling prophecies: Knowns and unknowns, resolved and unresolved controversies. *Personality and Social Psychology Review, 9*, 131–155.

Kane, T., & Rouse, C. E. (1995). Labor-market returns to two-and four-year college. *American Economic Review, 85*, 600–614.

Kaufman, P., & Bradby, D. (1992). *Characteristics of at-risk students in the NELS:88.* Washington, DC: U.S. Government Printing Office.

Kaufman, J., & Rosenbaum, J. (1992). The education and employment of low-income black youth in white suburbs. *Educational Evaluation and Policy Analysis, 14*, 229–240.

Kuo, H. D., & Hauser, R. (1995). Trends in family effects on the education of black and white brothers. *Sociology of Education, 68*, 136–160.

Ladson-Billings, G. (1995). Toward a theory of culturally relevant pedagogy. *American Educational Research Journal, 32*, 465–491.

Ladson-Billings, G. (2000). Fighting for our lives: Preparing teachers to teach African-American students. *Journal of Teacher Education, 51*, 206–213.

Laird, J., Kienzl, G., DeBell, M., & Chapman, C. (2007). *Dropout rates in the United States: 2005* (NCES 2007–059). Washington, DC: National Center for Education Statistics.

Lankford, H., Loeb, S., & Wyckoff, J. (2002). Teacher sorting and the plight of urban schools: A descriptive analysis. *Educational Evaluation and Policy Analysis, 24*, 37–62.

Lareau, A. (1987). Social class differences in family-school relationships: The importance of cultural capital. *Sociology of Education, 60*, 73–85.

Lareau, A. (1989). *Home advantage: Social class and parental intervention in elementary education.* New York: The Falmer Press.

Light, A., & Strayer, W. (2000). Determinants of college completion: School quality or student ability? *Journal of Human Resources, 35*, 299–332.

Lucas, S. (2001). Effectively maintained inequality, educational transitions, track mobility, and social background effects. *The American Journal of Sociology, 106*, 1642–1690.

Lucas, S., & Berends, M. (2002). Sociodemographic diversity, correlated achievement, and de facto tracking. *Sociology of Education, 75*, 328–348.

Lucas, S., & Gamoran, A. (2002). Tracking and the achievement gap. In J. E. Chubb & T. Loveless (Eds.), *Bridging the achievement gap* (pp. 171–198). Washington DC: Brookings Institution.

Massey, D. S., & Denton, N. A. (1993) *American apartheid: Segregation and the making of the underclass.* Cambridge, MA: Harvard University Press.

McCaul, E. J., Donaldson, G. A., Coladarci, T., & Davis, W. E. (1992). Consequences of dropping out of school: Findings from high school and beyond. *Journal of Educational Research, 85*, 198–207.

McFarland, D. A. (2006). Curricular flows: Trajectories, turning points, and assignment criteria in high school math careers. *Sociology of Education, 79*, 177–205.

McNeal, R. B. (1997). Are students being pulled out of high school? The effect of adolescent employment on dropping out. *Sociology of Education, 70*, 206–220.

Mincer, J. (1962). On-the-job training: Costs, returns, and some implications. *The Journal of Political Economy, 70*(5), 50–79.

Murphy, K., & Welch, F. (1989). Wage premiums for college graduates: Recent growth and possible explanations. *Education Researcher, 18*(4), 17–26.

Murphy, K., & Welch, F. (1992). The structure of wages. *The Quarterly Journal of Economics, 107*, 285–326.

National Center for Educational Statistics. (2001). *The condition of education, 2001.* Washington, DC: Author.

Natriello, G., Pallas, A. M., & Alexander, K. (1989). On the right track? Curriculum and academic achievement. *Sociology of Education, 62*, 109–118.

Oakes, J. (1990). Opportunities, achievement, and choice: Women and minority students in science and mathematics. *Review of Research in Education, 16*, 153–222.

Oakes, J. (2005). *Keeping track: How schools structure inequality* (2nd ed.). New Haven, CT: Yale University Press.

Oakes, J. Gamoran, A., & Page, R. (1992). Curriculum differentiation: Opportunities, outcomes, and meanings. In P. Jackson (Ed.), *Handbook of research on curriculum* (pp. 570–608). New York: Macmillan.

Perna, L. W. (2000). Differences in the decision to attend college among African Americans, Hispanics, and Whites. *Journal of Higher Education, 71*, 117–141.

Phillips, M. (1997). What makes schools effective? A comparison of the relationships of communitarian climate and academic climate to mathematics achievement and attendance during middle school. *American Educational Research Journal, 34*, 633–662.

Ream, R. K. (2005). Toward understanding how social capital mediates the impact of student mobility on Mexican American achievement. *Social Forces, 84*, 201–224.

Retherford, R., & Sewell, W. (1991). Birth order and intelligence: Further tests of the confluence model. *American Sociological Review, 56*, 141–158.

Riegle-Crumb, K., Farkas, G., & Muller, C. (2006). The role of gender and friendship in advanced course-taking. *Sociology of Education, 79*, 206–228.

Rivkin, S. G., Hanushek, E. A., & Kain, J. F. (2005). Teachers, schools, and academic achievement. *Econometrica, 73*, 417–458.

Rogoff, N. (1953). *Recent trends in occupational mobility.* Glencoe, IL: Free Press.

Rosenbaum, J. (2001). *Beyond College for All: Career paths for the forgotten half.* New York: Russell Sage Foundation.

Rothstein, R. (2004). *Class and schools: Using social, economic, and educational reform to close the black–white achievement gap.* Washington, DC: Economic Policy Institute.

Rumberger, R. (1995). Dropping out of middle school: A multilevel analysis of students and schools. *American Educational Research Journal, 32*(3), 583–625.

Rumberger, R., & Thomas, S. (2000). The distribution of dropout and turnover rates among urban and suburban high schools. *Sociology of Education, 73*, 39–67.

Schneider, B., Swanson, C., & Riegle-Crumb, C. (1999). "Opportunities for learning: Course sequences and positional advantages." *Social Psychology of Education, 2*, 25–53

Schneider, B., & Stevenson, D. (1999). *The ambitious generation: American teenagers, motivated but directionless.* New Haven, CT: Yale University Press.

Sewell, W. H., Haller, A. O., & Portes, A. (1969). The educational and early occupational attainment process. *American Sociological Review, 34*, 82–92.

Sewell, W. H., & Hauser, R. M. (1972). Causes and consequences of higher education: Models of the status attainment process. *American Journal of Agricultural Economics, 54*, 851–861.

Sewell, W. H., Hauser, R. M., & Wolf, W. C. (1980). Sex, schooling, and occupational status. *The American Journal of Sociology, 86*, 551–583.

Sewell, W. H., & Shah, V. P. (1968). Social class, parental encouragement, and educational aspirations. *The American Journal of Sociology, 73*, 559–572.

Sharkey, P. (2008). The intergenerational transmission of context. *The American Journal of Sociology, 113*, 931–969.

Sirin, S. (2005). Socioeconomic status and academic achievement: A meta-analytic review of the research. *Review of Educational Research, 75*, 417–453.

Solon, G., Page, M., & Duncan, G. (2000). Correlations between neighboring children and their subsequent educational attainment. *Review of Economics and Statistics, 82*, 383–392.

Sørensen, A., & Hallinan, M. (1986). Effects of ability grouping on growth in academic achievement. *American Educational Research Journal, 23*, 519–542.

Sorokin, P. (1963). *Social and cultural mobility*. Glencoe, IL: Free Press. (Original work published 1927)

Stearns, E., Moller, S., Potochnick, S., & Blau, J. (2007). Staying back and dropping out: The relationship between grade retention and school dropout. *Sociology of Education, 80*, 210–240.

Stevenson D. (2000). The fit and misfit of sociological research and educational policy. In M. T. Hallinan (Ed.), *Handbook of the Sociology of Education* (pp. 547–564). New York: Kluwer.

Swanson, C. (2004). *Who graduates? Who doesn't? A statistical portrait of public high school graduation, class of 2001* [Executive summary]. Washington, DC: The Urban Institute Education Policy Center.

Tinto, V. (1993). *Leaving college: Rethinking the causes and cures of student attrition* (2nd ed.). Chicago: University of Chicago Press.

Valenzuela, A. (1999). *Subtractive schooling: U.S.-Mexican youth and the politics of caring*. Albany: State University of New York Press.

Warren, J. R. (2002). Reconsidering the relationship between student employment and academic outcomes: A new theory and better data. *Youth and Society, 33*, 366–393.

Warren. J. R., & Halpern-Manners, A. (2007). Is the glass emptying or filling up? Reconciling divergent trends in high school completion and dropout." *Educational Researcher, 36*, 335–343.

Warren, J. R., LePore, P. C., & Mare, R. D. (2000). Employment during high school: Consequences for students' grades in academic courses. *American Educational Research Journal, 37*, 943–969.

Wilson, W. J. (1987). *The truly disadvantaged: The inner city, the underclass, and public policy*. Chicago: University of Chicago Press.

Zimmer, R. W., & Toma, E. F. (2000). Peer effects in private and public schools across countries. *Journal of Policy Analysis and Management, 19*, 75–92.

70

Shadow Education Systems

Chong-Jae Lee and Hyun-Jeong Park
Seoul National University

Heesook Lee
Florida State University

Introduction

Private supplementary tutoring, or shadow education, has long been a major phenomenon in parts of East Asia, including Japan, Hong Kong, South Korea, and Taiwan. In recent times, shadow education has been rapidly increasing in other Asian countries as well, as it has in Europe and North America. Traditionally, private supplementary tutoring has been a neglected topic in research, though there has been much more research in recent years. A growing body of literature focuses on the shadow education system of private supplementary tutoring, which occurs in academic subjects beyond the hours of mainstream formal schooling (Bray, 1999, 2003; Kwok, 2004; Silova & Bray, 2006; Yoo, 2002).

The term "shadow education" was first coined by David L. Stevenson and David P. Baker (1992); however, Mark Bray (1999) is responsible for bringing the term to the public's attention as a worldwide education phenomenon with his comprehensive overview of the shadow education system. Stevenson and Baker use the term, "shadow" to denote the strong connection between the allocation rules in formal schooling and non-formal schooling; however, they do not imply that these activities are hidden. Bray, on the other hand, uses the term to emphasize the fact that shadow education exists in connection with the mainstream system.

Private tutoring affects a student's academic performance as well as psychological growth. Its effects on academic performance can in turn affect equal educational opportunities and the future social achievements of education, which ultimately affects the way public education is managed. The tremendous amount of money spent on private tutoring not only affects the household economy, but the overall effectiveness of investing in education. Governmental response to private tutoring has ranged from laissez-faire to restrictive control and even prohibition (Bray, 1999, pp. 74–77).

Empirical studies on the demand for private tutoring are needed. The results of such studies will help the government establish policies in response to the problem. Countries that are aware of the negative aspects of private tutoring have been implementing such countermeasures without empirical evidence. This is the main reason for the "failure of private tutoring policies" where governments have made continuous efforts to curb private tutoring to no avail. Research on the effectiveness of private tutoring will help students and their parents make the right educational decisions. Individuals' subjective expectations on the effect of private tutoring may cause excessive investment in it.

This chapter will introduce the main studies that have looked at the causes of the demand for private tutoring and its effectiveness. Despite this research, a comprehensive overview of the subject is still needed. So far, the studies on the effectiveness of private tutoring have had a limited scope; thus, they have yielded contrasting results.

The Scale of Shadow Education: Comparative Perspectives

The Concept of Shadow Education Private tutoring began with one-to-one education between a tutor and a student, and the relationship evolved into a tutor and a group of students (e.g., *juku*—tutoring school—in Japan), ranging from private one-to-one lessons to private institute classes. As it began to enter into competition with mainstream schooling, the term "supplementary private tutoring" was born. A UNESCO (1976) report showed that the existence of a "parallel system of education" alongside mainstream schooling led to supplementary private tutoring (p. 3).

The term "shadow education" was first suggested by Marimuthu et al. (1991) and coined by David L. Stevenson and David P. Baker (1992) when they used the term in the title of their research. Baker, Akiba, LeTendre, and Wiseman (2001) note that shadow education parallels mainstream schooling with school-like organized learning opportunities. Since Bray's (1999) UNESCO report, The Shadow Education System: Private Tutoring and its Implication for Planners, the term has been used to describe a worldwide private tutoring phenomenon.

Scale of Supplementary Private Tutoring Private tutoring is a familiar topic and is a very important issue in East-Asian Confucian countries such as Japan, Korea, Hong Kong, and Taiwan. There has been a plethora of research on private tutoring in these countries (Rohlen, 1983). However, international research on this topic was conducted only after Stevenson and Baker focused on the issue (1992). This led to Bray's (1999) overall review of private tutoring in Asia, the Middle East, Europe, and Africa. Baker and his colleagues analyzed data from Third International Mathematics and Science Study (TIMSS) to show the worldwide trend in private tutoring (Baker et al., 2001; Baker & LeTendre, 2005).

In Bray's (1999) report, shadow education is also common in Singapore, Sri Lanka, Burma, Brazil, Zimbabwe, Tanzania, Egypt, and Morocco. It is also prevalent in low-income countries, such as Cambodia and Bangladesh. Due to the breakdown of socialism and the introduction of market economics, private tutoring is also on the rise as an important industry in Eastern European countries that used to be part of the Soviet Union (Silova & Bray, 2006).

Although the proportion of students receiving private tutoring is low and despite different dynamics and underlying forces, participation in private tutoring is becoming increasingly evident in Western Europe and North America. Private tutoring is currently a global educational phenomenon that demands the attention of all policy makers (Baker & LeTendre, 2005).

Table 70.1 shows the global educational phenomenon, according to many regional studies. Several cross-national data confirm that private tutoring is a macro phenomenon of modern schooling through its prevalence. Based on TIMSS, Baker et al.'s research (2001) showed that 16 countries had more than 40% participation in private tutoring among the 41 countries that participated in the study of Grade 8 students (in 1995). Almost 10 years later, we came out with similar results based on the 2006 Programme for International Student Assessment (PISA) which is another cross-national data of 15-year-olds. As can be seen in Figure 70.1, 37 countries had more than 40% participation in science private tutoring, and 42 countries had more than 40% participation in math private tutoring among the 57 participating countries and regions. The OECD average of participation rate in private tutoring was 34.4% for science and 46.4% for mathematics.

The Form of Participation in Private Tutoring: Cases of Korea, Japan, Hong Kong, and the United States

Korea The history of Korea's private tutoring includes various patterns. It shows a systematic growth of private tutoring through its demand and the government's counter-measure policy to suppress that demand. Private tutoring in Korea began in the 1950s as elementary and middle school students prepared for entrance exams to progress to the next education level. At this time, most private tutoring took the form of personal one-to-one lessons. The Korean government established a policy that aimed to decrease the demand for private tutoring in order to relieve exam-oriented rote learning in schools and to prevent social problems, such as rising family expenditures on private tutoring that could have led to inequality of educational opportunities.

Middle and high school entrance exams were abolished in 1968 and 1973, respectively, to eliminate the demand for private tutoring. Instead, students were allocated to schools randomly. After that, the demand for private tutoring in elementary and middle schools temporarily decreased, while private tutoring became tied to preparing for the college entrance exam. Competition for university entrance was fierce in the 1970s. Parents believed that entrance to a university was not possible without private tutoring, giving rise to the social problem of "overheated private tutoring." In 1980, the military government issued "The July 30 Education Reform" prohibiting students and teachers from taking and giving private lessons. As a part of this reform, the government increased enrollment quotas and replaced the university entrance exams administered by each university with the government-administered National Academic Examination.

Since the 1990s, private tutoring at the elementary school level has been on the rise again. The increase of households with both parents working, which creates the necessity for childcare, and the introduction of an English education curriculum at the elementary school level have given rise to an increase in private tutoring because such demands could not be satisfied at school. Parents of elementary school students seem to focus more on the development of aptitude and long-term academic competence rather than improving school grades. Private tutoring at the middle school level is not only for improving school grades, but for the long-term development of academic competence for admission into prestigious universities (Kim, Kang, Park, Lee, & Hwang, 2006). However, specialized high schools of foreign language and science and self-running private high schools have recently developed excellent academic reputations and their graduates enjoy high admission rates to prestigious universities. The demand for private tutoring to help with the entrance exams into those high schools has also been on the rise.

Since the government did little to restrict private tutoring in the 1990s, it has greatly increased. The government began providing examination preparation and tutoring courses through broadcasts on the Educational Broadcasting Station (EBS) in the mid-1990s. In 2000, the constitutional court ruled that the government's prohibition of private tutoring was unconstitutional. To decrease the demand for private tutoring, the courts supported a new, less expensive government-based educational tutoring model. Through the government's support of after-school activities and

TABLE 70.1
Scale of Shadow Education

	Country	Year	Sample	Scale of participation	Sources
Asia	Korea	2007	34,000 parents	77% of students (88.8% of elementary, 74.6% of middle, & 55.0% of high school students) Participation hours amounted to 7.8 hours per week.	Korean National Statistical Office (2008)
	Japan	2000		37.7% of primary school, 75.7% of middle school students attended	Ministry of Education, Culture, Sports, Science & Technology-Japan (2003)
	Taiwan	1998	359 students	81.2% of secondary school students received shadow education	Tseng (1998)
	Hong Kong	1996, 1998/99	507 students, 6 secondary schools	A 1996 survey: 44% of primary, 25.6% of lower-secondary, 34.4% of middle secondary and 40.5% of upper-secondary students received shadow education. A 1998/99 follow-up survey: 35.1% of secondary grades 1–3, 46.6% of grades 4–5, & 70.3% of grades 6–7 attended.	Bray & Kwok (2003)
	Singapore	1992	1,052 households & 1,261 students	49% of primary & 30% of secondary students received shadow education.	Wong & Wong (1998)
	Turkey	2001		35% of senior high school students attended private tutoring centers. The number of private tutoring centers in 2002 was 2,100, which is close to the number of 2,500 high schools in the whole country in the same year.	Tansel & Bircan (2006)
	Vietnam	1997/98	Vietnam Living Standard Surveys, 6,000 households	31.1% of primary school, 55.9% of lower-secondary school, & 76.7% of upper-secondary school students attended shadow education.	Dang (2007)
North America	Canada	2000		14.1% of 13-year-old & 15.3% of 16-year-old students received tutoring for 1 hour a week, especially in Ontario State, where 20% of 16-year-old students received tutoring.	Davies (2002)
	U.S.	1990, 1992	NELS:88	11% of high school students enrolled in a commercial preparation program for SAT and 7% of high school students made use of a private tutor.	Buchmann, Roscigno, & Condron (2006)
Europe	Germany	1998	26,450	21% of primary & secondary school students received.	Kramer & Werner (1998)
	Greece	1999	First-year university students	During secondary school, 80% of students attended a tutoring institute, 50% received one-to-one tutoring, & 30% received both.	Psacharopoulos & Papakonstantinou (2005)
	U.K.	1998	107 middle- class households	33% of primary school students attended.	Ireson (2004)
	East Europe	2004/05	First-year university students 8,713	Of secondary school students, 92% in Azerbaijan, 31% in Bosnia and Herzegovina, 28% in Croatia, 76% in Georgia, 58% in Lithuania, 66.9% in Mongolia, 50% in Poland, 35% in Slovakia, & 68% in Ukraine received.	Silova & Bray (2006)
Africa	Egypt	2000	Egypt Demographic and Health Survey	71% of 6–15 year-old students have shadow education	Suliman & El-Kogali (2002)
	Kenya	1997	3,233 Standard 6 students	68.6% students attended, ranging from 39% in North Eastern Province to 74.4% in Nyanza Province.	Nzomo, Kariuki, & Guantai (2001)

Figure 70.1 Proportion of 15-year-olds who participated in private tutoring, using PISA 2006 data. *Note:* Countries are listed in the descending order of proportion of 15-year-olds who participated in math tutoring.

educational broadcasting, it introduced a national private tutoring model (Han, 2004). As a result, private tutoring has taken several forms, such as after-school activities, tutoring courses through educational broadcasting, and the Internet.

The Korean National Statistical Office (2008) reported that the participation rate in private tutoring was 88.2% for the elementary school level, 74.6% at the middle school level, and 55.0% at the high school level, as of 2007. The study also reveals that there are 47.2% of elementary and secondary school students participating in private tutoring institutions, 25.2% using study-at-home sheets provided by private tutoring industries, 11.8% taking small group private lessons, 9.6% taking one-to-one private lessons, and 3.2% using paid Internet or broadcasting services.

Japan   In Japan, there are two types of private tutoring industries, *juku* (private institutions offering extra-school programs) and *yobiko* (literally "prep" schools). While the *juku* are for students in grades 1 through 9, the *yobiko* serves to prepare grade 10 and above students for the college entrance examination (including upper-secondary school graduates who failed to pass the college entrance examination).

The Ministry of Education in Japan conducted nationwide surveys on the juku three times (1976, 1985, and 1993). As of 1993, 59.5% of middle school students and 24% of elementary school students (approximately 30% for the upper-graders) in Japan attended the juku on a regular basis (Ministry of Education, Culture, Sports, Science, and Technology-Japan [MEXT], 1994). Compared to 1976, when the first governmental survey was conducted, the attendance rate in private tutoring doubled for the elementary school students (increased from 12% in 1976 to 24% in 1993) and increased sharply for the middle school students (from 38% to 59.5%). Even though the governmental survey on the juku has not been conducted since 1993, the nationwide survey on educational expenditure revealed that 37.7% of primary school students and 75.7% of middle school students attended private tutoring in 2000 (MEXT, 2003).

The narrow charters of Japanese universities seem to produce intense competition for admission to the most prestigious universities (Stevenson & Baker, 1992, p. 1642). Rohlen (1980) argued that the rising of the juku in the 1960s and 1970s must be explained in terms of the interaction of many factors: high competition ratio to enter good universities, equalitarian atmosphere in public school practices, very small number of private schools, rising incomes, rising aspirations, and so on. Besides these macro-level determinants of private tutoring, Stevenson and Baker (1992) argue that students from higher socioeconomic backgrounds are more likely to participate in private tutoring based on the longitudinal data analysis of 1980 (senior students of high schools, some of whom were re-interviewed in 1982; p. 1649). Tsukada (1988) also shows that ronin students (upper-secondary school graduates, who failed to pass the college entrance examination and enrolled in the yobiko)

tend to come from higher economic status families. Additionally, Hirao (2002) found that dual-earner families are spending more on children's extra-school education, both in real terms and in proportion to the total household expenditures, based on the Japanese Government's 2002 Family Income and Expenditure Survey.

Hong Kong   In Hong Kong, the main function of private tutoring is to help students perform better on examinations and improve their academic achievement. There are two high-stakes examinations in Hong Kong: the Certificate Education Examination (HKCE) and the Advanced Level Examination (HKAL). The HKCE is administered to secondary Grade 5 students to screen qualified students to study in matriculation (secondary grades 6 and 7). After students have finished secondary Grade 7, the HKAL determines whether students are able to get admitted to the local universities.

Bray and Kwok (2003) analyzed the data from a sample of 630 students in six Hong Kong secondary schools during the 1998/1999 academic year. From this analysis, they reported that 48.8% of Hong Kong secondary school students received some amount of private tutoring, and the proportion of students receiving private tutoring increased at higher grades (35.1% for secondary grade 1–3, 46.6% for secondary grades 4–5, and 70.3% for secondary grades 6–7 students). They found that the greatest motivation for private tutoring is the "preparation for examination" at higher grades (secondary grades 4–5 and 6–7), even though "seeking guidance with homework" was the greatest motivation in secondary grades 1–3.

Based on the same data from Bray and Kwok, Kwok (2004) depicted the following sociocultural and socioeconomic factors for tutoring demand: emergence of nuclear families, affordability of tutoring fees (especially in low-income or middle-income families), insufficiency of free academic guidance from elder family members (especially for parents with higher educational qualifications), relationship between tutoring types and nature of curricula (more individual tutoring and multi-functional tutoring for lower than the secondary level due to the curricula focusing more on individual learning differences), examination-oriented school culture, selective functions or screening effects of the secondary educational system (between upper-elementary and lower-secondary levels and between upper-secondary and matriculation levels), social significance of some popular tutoring subjects, such as mathematics and English, and societal credentialism and meritocracy.

United States   In the United States, common types of shadow education include test preparation courses for the SATs and ACTs, supplementary programs for low- or under-achieving students, and private tutors. In this section, we will focus on the test preparation courses for the SATs and ACTs.

Based on a survey of a nationally representative sample of 1995/96 SAT-takers, Powers and Rock (1999) reported that 427 SAT-takers, among 3,160 respondents (13.5%), engaged in "coaching" on SAT I. In their study examining the longitudinal effects of college preparation programs on college retention, Ishitani and Snider (2006) reported that 21.1% of the National Education Longitudinal Study: 1988–2000 sample (which contained 4,445 first-time freshmen students who enrolled in 4-year institutions between 1992 and 1994) received special ACT/SAT prep courses during high school. Using the same data set of NELS:88, Briggs (2001) reported that 11% of high school students enrolled in a commercial preparation program for the SAT and/or ACT, and 7% of high school students made use of a private tutor. Using the same data set of NELS:88, Buchmann, Roscigno, and Condron (2006) reported that 11% of high school students enrolled in a commercial preparation programs for the SAT/ACT and 7% of high school students made use of a private tutor. They also argued that the high SES significantly increased the likelihood of participating in these types of private tutoring for test preparation.

From their analysis of a sample of 1995/96 SAT-takers, Powers and Rock (1999) reported that students engaged in coaching are most likely to be Asian American, English speakers of another language, have parents with more formal education, have parents with higher income, have higher grades in high school, have higher educational aspirations, have taken more foreign languages, math, and science courses in high school, have higher previous test scores, have first-choice colleges with higher mean SAT I scores, and have taken the PSAT/NMSQT.

The Demand for Shadow Education

Who wants to participate in private tutoring and why? Why is the demand for private tutoring increasing? Why is private tutoring spreading to many countries and not limited to a few countries? These are the most important questions. Theoretical models and empirical analyses on the causes of the demand for private tutoring are necessary for understanding the dynamics and problems of private tutoring and to establish countermeasure policies.

Rohlen (1980) pointed out that in Japan, the spread of private tutoring is caused by factors such as the administrative power of the government, restrictive examinations, school systems that encourage competition rather than support, and a strong connection between achievement at the elementary and middle school level and the opportunity of future education, employment, and higher social status. Blumenthal (1992) has also pointed out that several factors within the management of the educational system influenced the demand for private tutoring in Japan. Those factors include: the baby boom generation entering college; the administration of uniform public university examinations in 1979; entrusting the function of public schools to private tutoring by schoolteachers; peer-pressure from other students and parents who were participating in private tutoring; and the uniformity of the educational system in Japan which is characterized by few subject choices, the egalitarianism and uniformity of school education, and teacher-centered education.

Foondun (2002) explained the reason for the widespread private tutoring phenomenon in Africa and Southeast Asia in relation to the supply and demand side of private tutoring. On the demand side, the competition to enter prestigious universities resulted in crowded public classrooms (ineffective teaching) and large class sizes that wouldn't allow teachers time to spend with individual students. On the supply side, teachers' low salaries and low morale lead them to participate into private tutoring.

According to Bray (1999, 2003), the causes of flourishing private tutoring can be divided into cultural, societal, economical, and educational factors: (a) private tutoring is popular in Asian countries due to the emphasis placed on effort by Confucianism;, (b) the private tutoring industry rapidly increased in the 1990s in English-speaking countries with the emphasis on the competitive ability of schools based on neo liberalism. Especially in England and Australia, from the mid-1990s, the academic burden on the students increased, and the demand for private tutoring also increased after the academic achievement of schools were opened to the public due to educational reform; (c) university entrance competition is fierce in countries that expect economic profit from highly educated people. This leads to an increase in private tutoring fostering further competition. In the case of Singapore and Hong Kong, the salary of a university graduate is six times higher than that of a high school graduate. This gap in salary, based on academic background, is a major reason for increasing private tutoring; (d) since classes in public schools are mainly conducted in a teacher-centered manner, private tutoring flourishes in educational systems that do not pay enough attention to low academic achievers.

When student selection is determined by test results (in school and on the entrance examination), the demand for test-preparation private tutoring increases. Also, as the schools are vertically ranked according to a single criterion, the competition to enter the higher ranked schools strengthens. Thus, when students are enrolled based on test results, the demand for private tutoring will increase. In consideration of this, the factors behind school education inducing private tutoring can be classified into three categories: (a) the degree of vertical ranking of schools, (b) the degree to which students are selected based on school and entrance examination test scores, and (c) the level of the development of school education. If the development patterns of school education are classified by two factors (enrollment level and the level of the financial support), then there can be four kinds of patterns defined by the enrollment level and financial support to education, which is measured by the education budget compared to GDP.

When considering these factors, the causes of the demand for private tutoring are: (a) an emphasis on academic background (credentialism), (b) the high-stakes test as a gatekeeper managing the competition of academic background, (c) the educational system and the characteristics of school education, (d) the personal conditions of the pupils of private tutoring, and (e) the systematization of private tutoring. This conceptualization of the demanding factors of private tutoring suggests a hierarchical model of factors causing it at three levels. At the macro-level, credentialism operates as a belief system and action strategy for pursuing academic credentials. At the meso-level, relating the credentialism and individual's decision to participate in private tutoring, there is high-stakes testing and characteristics of the public school systems. At the micro-level, we consider individual characteristics.

Baker et al. (2001) propose the Institutional Perspective of shadow education as their theoretical model. Their research was the first attempt to analyze and compare the participation rate of private tutoring and the determining factors for the demand for private tutoring through TIMSS data analysis. This research analyzed the relationship of the pervasiveness of shadow education, strategic use of shadow education to high-stakes testing, and the national characteristics of educational systems by analyzing the Grade 8 math achievement of the 41 countries participating in the TIMSS research. The Institutional Perspective of shadow education provides a theoretical model for analyzing the macro-level factor of credentialism and the education system's external factors.

Institutional Perspective of Shadow Education: The Credentialism and Tight Linkage at Macro-Level Factors Outside of the Educational System

In the process of pursuing a meritocracy, school education was justified as an important device for social selection and public education was developed as a screening device for distributing social roles. In the process of the institutionalization of schooling, the importance of student academic achievement at schools increased. The importance of credentials as an indicator of academic achievement and its attributes has increased. The tight linkage between credentials, such as diplomas and certificates, and the social values, such as income and job opportunities, creates the demand for credentials. In the process of competing for these credentials, entrance examinations to higher-level schools or selective, prestigious universities play a critical role in the selection process. When examinations are used as the selection device, private tutoring for preparing for the examinations increases even further. These examinations become high-stakes tests. From the students' point of view, the competition for achieving high social class derives from the competition of high-stakes tests. This competition mechanism determines the institutional demands of private tutoring.

Society's pursuit of meritocracy causes the family to lose its ability to achieve a higher social status. As public education becomes more uniform and access to education is substantially guaranteed, parents turn to private tutoring as an additional method to improve social status. This forms the basis to the background to private tutoring. This is not a phenomenon occurring in just a few countries, but a worldwide one (Baker & LeTendre, 2005).

From the institutional point of view, there are three factors behind the demand for private tutoring: (a) credentialism, which values credentials as an index to the achievement of meritocracy; (b) the recognition of the tight linkage between educational background and the achievement of social value; and (c) high-stakes tests acting as social gatekeepers in the selection process for higher education. In this sense, private tutoring has become the additional effort necessary to prepare for high-stakes tests in order to maximize the expected benefit of social compensation.

Credentialism is a perspective, or value system, that regards educational credentials as an important social value and an absolute standard in judging one's ability (T. Kim, 2003). Korean society has a tendency to impose excessive value and importance on entering prestigious universities by equating entrance with success in life (Choi et al., 2003; Hyun, Lee, & Lee, 2003). This tendency translates into a strong desire to attend a prestigious university, and most students compete over this (H. Kim, 2004). The strong desire to enter the best universities influences the demand for private tutoring. There is an implication here that the desire for a good educational background is the most influential factor behind the demand for private tutoring (S-J. Lee, 2006).

The salary gap produced by educational background fortifies belief in the existence of a tight linkage between educational background and the distribution of social values. The subjective beliefs on the connection between credentialism and social achievement result in the competition to enter an excellent university. Parents, who provide the demand for private tutoring, even though they are aware of the burden on family finances, believe that the family will ultimately profit from gaining entrance into prestigious universities. Therefore, the main reason that students receive private tutoring is to prepare them for entrance examinations to high schools that raise their chance of getting into prestigious universities.

Woo et al. (2004) introduced the life-time expected welfare model from the human capital perspective. This model looks at private tutoring as an investment into the welfare of a person's lifetime expectancy. This model mainly examines the contribution of private tutoring to achievement, college entrance, academic performance at college, career placement, and performance in the career. This model examines the effects of private tutoring on advancement, placement, and performance achievements. This research indicates that although private tutoring affects college entrance, it does not affect academic performance at college, and thus sees human resource development as problematic. Also, when the universities are ranked according to SAT scores, there is an increase in income as the university rank increases. The high returns on the college investment and the high income of graduates of prestigious universities increase college entrance competition and the demand for private tutoring.

High-Stakes Testing at the Meso-Level Factor

Some scholars believed that the main reason for the high rate of participation in private tutoring in Korea, Greece, Turkey, and elsewhere is the fierce competition of going to college and the existence of the college entrance examinations as high-stakes tests. In the process of moving from middle school to high school, students have no choice but to pay for private tutoring that prepares them for entrance examinations (Bray & Kwok, 2003; Bray, 1999; Psacharopoulos & Papakonstantinou, 2005; Tansel & Bircan, 2006).

In order to verify this idea, Baker et al. (2001) proposed the following hypothesis. From the perspective that the demand for shadow education is brought on by intense competition for future educational opportunities accompanied by a "tight linkage" between academic performance and later-life opportunities in the labor market and selection by "high-stakes testing" as a public gatekeeper to education and labor market opportunities, the high-stakes testing of national educational organizations induces an enrichment strategy from private tutoring. However, their research did not show a statistically significant result of the effect of high-

stakes testing on the TIMSS Grade 8 students' decision to participate in private tutoring. The difference in participation rates in private tutoring among countries was considerable. The students participating in private tutoring more than 1 hour per week in 41 countries was 39.6%. This shows that private tutoring was not restricted to a few countries, but was widespread throughout the world. When focusing on Grade 8 students, some important results were discovered:

1. High-stakes tests are not related at all to cross national variation in the use of shadow education.
2. The main reason for participating in private tutoring was as a remedial strategy to complement academic achievement. This occurred in 30 out of 40 countries, while students in Korea, Romania, and Taiwan participated in private tutoring for competition-oriented enhancement motivation. The enrichment strategy suggested in prior research was not well supported. Figure 70.2 shows modal strategy of private tutoring in each country.

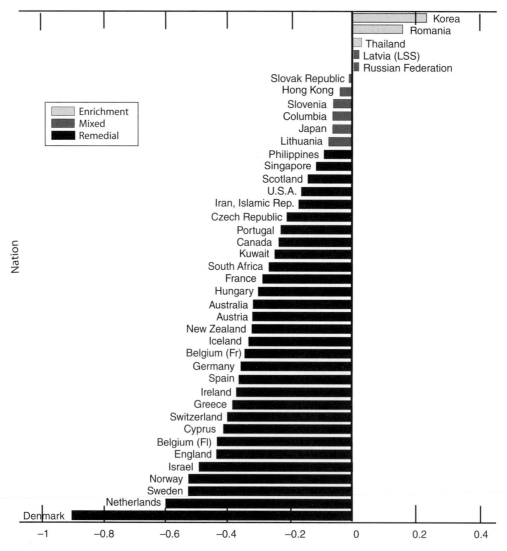

Figure 70.2 Classification of national modal strategy motivating shadow education. *Note*: The classification of national modal strategy motivating shadow education into enrichment, mixed, and remedial was based on the significance and direction of logit coefficient of effects of math score on shadow education participation, controlling for SES, home language, sex, community, remedial teaching, and the interaction term between SES and math score. Enrichment equals significant (p<.01) positive coefficient; Mixed equals non-significant coefficient; Remedial equals significant (p<.01) negative coefficient. *Source:* Reprinted with permission from Baker et al., 2001, p. 9.

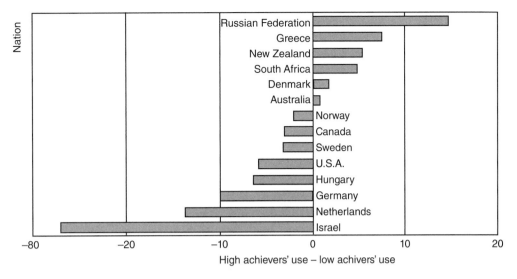

Figure 70.3 Difference in participating rate of private tutoring between high- and low-achievers: 12th graders in TIMSS 1995. *Note:* High- and low-achievers are defined as upper 1/3 and lower 1/3 of scoring group for each country. *Source:* Lee & Lee, 2007.

This research goes against credentialism which claims to tighten the linkage between educational credentials and career opportunities controlled by high-stakes tests leading to the demand for private tutoring. The result of the analysis may be due to the suitability of the measurement from the Grade 8 students, since high-stakes tests and college admittance were not an immediate concern to them.

The modal strategy as a participation strategy of private tutoring only answers the question, who mainly participates in private tutoring. In countries that used a competition strategy, the students with better grades participated in private tutoring more than the students with poor grades. Figure 70.3 shows a simple comparison of the participation rate between the high achiever and lower achiever groups using TIMSS Grade 12 students. Using a simple comparison of the participation rate between the high achiever and lower achiever groups, Lee & Lee (2007) found that some countries categorized as the remedial mode for Grade 8 students were identified enrichment mode for Grade 12 students. Looking at 12th-graders from 1995, it was discovered that students in the upper one-third ranking in math participated more in private tutoring in the countries of remedial strategy. These countries are the Russian Federation, Greece, South Africa, Denmark, and Australia. This suggests a possible trend towards using an enrichment strategy when it is time to enter college (Lee & Lee, 2007).

Since students with high grades have a high rate of participation in private tutoring in some Asian countries with internationally high levels of academic achievement, it is suggested that "tight-linkage" and "high-stakes testing" had a strong effect on the demand for participation in private tutoring (Yang, 2003; Lee & Lee, 2007; Bray, 1999).

Also, similar results came out from the cross-national data of 15-year-olds almost 10 years later. Figure 70.4 and Figure 70.5 demonstrate the relationship between the number and characteristics of 15-year-olds receiving private tutoring. The horizontal axis represents the mean difference scores in science and math domain between those who receive private tutoring and those who do not (positive numbers indicate higher-scoring students receiving private tutoring), and the vertical axis represents the proportion of 15-year-olds who received private tutoring in science and math, respectively. Therefore, countries in the upper-right corner, such as Korea, Turkey, Hong Kong (for science), Taiwan (for mathematics), Greece, and Tunisia can be described as countries with high intensity of private tutoring and enrichment motivation. Meanwhile, countries in the lower-left corner, such as Austria, Germany, Luxembourg, Belgium, and Finland can be described as countries with low intensity of private tutoring and with remedial motivation.

Characteristics of Public School Management at the Meso-Level There is a possibility that the demand for private tutoring can be dependent on the characteristics of the school's education. There is a discussion that indicates that the deficiency of school education is the main factor stimulating the demand for private tutoring. Teacher-induced private tutoring (Bray, 2003) and deficient teaching in poor school education leads to private tutoring as a way to supplement low-quality instruction. In this regard, the demand for private tutoring is brought on by the market reaction to the lack of high-quality and diversity of school education (Lee & Hong, 2001; Kim & Lee, 2002).

More pronounced qualities of mass education do not generate a higher prevalence of shadow education use. Low achievers use shadow education with a remedial strategy, while high achievers use less shadow education. This results in the pattern of private tutoring in developed countries. Shadow education is negatively associated with the level of educational expenditure and enrollment rates. Shadow education has become a private supplement to a less than fully developed education system. This suggests that, depending on development patterns of the educational system, the form and degree of participation in private tutoring could vary.

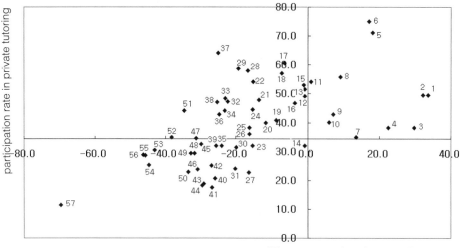

Figure 70.4 Intensity of science private tutoring and achievement gap in PISA 2006. *Note*: 1=Korea, 2=Turkey, 3=Slovak, 4=Hong Kong, 5=Greece, 6=Tunisia, 7=Taipei, 8=Indonesia, 9=Brazil, 10=Thailand, 11=Romania, 12=Colombia, 13=Denmark, 14=Czech, 15=Azerbaijan, 16=Macao, 17=Jordan, 18=Russia, 19=Serbia, 20=Poland, 21=Chile, 22=Hungary, 23=UK, 24=Israel, 25=Latvia, 26=France, 27=Australia, 28=Kyrgyzstan, 29=Norway, 30=Uruguay, 31=Croatia, 32=Bulgaria, 33=Montenegro, 34=Slovenia, 35=Portugal, 36=USA, 37=Qatar, 38=Mexico, 39=Canada, 40=Ireland, 41=Japan, 42=New Zealand, 43=Belgium, 44=Iceland, 45=Netherlands, 46=Switzerland, 47=Lithuania, 48=Spain, 49=Italy, 50=Finland, 51=Estonia, 52=Sweden, 53=Liechtenstein, 54=Argentina, 55=Germany, 56=Luxembourg, 57=Austria.

The analysis of Baker et al. (2001) indicates that depending on the developmental level of the educational system, demands for private tutoring and modal strategy could be different. In countries where enrollment was high and educational financial support was sufficient, demand of private tutoring using a small-scale remedial strategy was prevalent. In the second hypothesis of Baker et al., shadow education will be more prevalent as a remedial strategy in nations with more pronounced qualities of mass schooling, such as those with high expenditures on public education or large enrollment rates at both the elementary and secondary level. This second hypothesis was supported.

The lower the satisfaction with public education and the level of trust given to it, the higher the participation rate in private tutoring (Kim, 2004). Davies's (2002) study revealed that Canadian parents' decision to participate in private tutoring was influenced by the degree of satisfaction with public schools and the degree of preference for private tutoring rather than demographic conditions. As the dissatisfaction with public schools goes up, the rate of

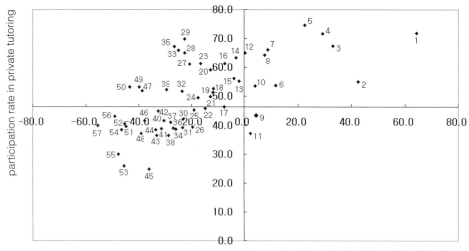

Figure 70.5 Intensity of mathematics private tutoring and achievement gap in PISA 2006. *Note*: 1=Korea, 2=Taipei, 3=Turkey, 4=Greece, 5=Tunisia, 6=Slovak, 7= Indonesia , 8=Russia, 9=Thailand, 10=Azerbaijan, 11=Japan, 12=Romania, 13=Brazil, 14=Jordan, 15=Colombia, 16=Hong Kong, 17=Serbia, 18=Chile, 19=Macao, 20=Kyrgyzstan, 21=Bulgaria, 22=Lithuania, 23=Latvia, 24=Poland, 25=Portugal, 26=Uruguay, 27=Norway, 28=Hungary, 29=Israel, 30=Czech, 31=Montenegro, 32=Mexico, 33=Qatar, 34=Australia, 35=Denmark, 36=UK, 37=Italy, 38=Argentina, 39=Estonia, 40=Spain, 41=Croatia, 42=Canada, 43=Liechtenstein, 44=Ireland, 45=Finland, 46=Netherlands, 47=France, 48=New Zealand, 49=USA, 50=Slovenia, 51=Sweden, 52=Switzerland, 53=Austria, 54=Iceland, 55=Belgium, 56=Luxembourg, 57=Germany.

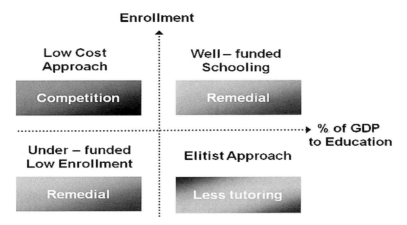

Figure 70.6 Patterns of educational development and modal strategy of shadow education.

participation in private tutoring also goes up. Davies (2002) points out that the growth of the private tutoring industry in Canada was caused by the local government's intensified comparison of students' achievement scores and the reduction of the public school budget. Particularly in Ontario, increased private tutoring was caused by education reforms, such as fortifying the competition for the college entrance examination, intensifying the math curriculum, standardized testing, writing, report cards of students' grades, and the abolishment of the 13th grade. All of these factors led to increased college entrance competition. Figure 70.6 demonstrates national strategy of shadow education according to patterns of educational development.

Under the low cost approach, where the demand for educational services is not supported by the school, private tutoring can increase with competition strategy. There is a likelihood of a high demand for private tutoring when the educational system follows the low cost approach, achievement is assessed only by test grades, and college applicants are selected by a college entrance examination. Even in well-funded school systems, private tutoring increases with high-stakes testing. In countries that have high financial support and follow an elitist approach, it can be estimated that the demand for private tutoring will be low. In the case of under-funded low enrollment, teacher tutoring may arise where teachers seek additional income from tutoring. This is a case of corruption within the school system. If the quality of public schools is low and the self-directed learning of students is also low, these conditions might result in an increased demand for private tutoring. From this idea, a countermeasure policy for private tutoring needs to include the strengthening of public school education.

The Individual Factors at the Micro-Level In order to analyze the psychological factors stimulating participation in private tutoring, the process of determination needs to be investigated theoretically. Theoretical models, such as the expectancy model and game theory, can be used to explain the determination to participate in private tutoring. Vroom's (1960) model, goal expectancy theory, explains the factors that lead to the motivation to participate in private tutoring.

Porter and Lawler's (1968) model expands on this theory by including the factors that affect this motivation.

When the goal expectancy theory is expanded to apply to the individual person's decision-making process to participate in private tutoring, the social, economic, and psychological factors stimulating participation can be defined. It shows that the motivation behind participation in private tutoring can be determined by the subjective recognition on the instrumentality that realizes: (a) the first order outcomes, (b) the second order outcomes and the value of rewards on them, (c) the probability of goal expectancy which will achieve the first order outcomes, and (d) subjective expectancy of achieving the second order outcomes. It can be explained that the subjective recognition of a result of participation in private tutoring (such as improvement in academic ability), the subjective value on entering college, and the possibility of entering college can influence the determination of participation in private tutoring. Figure 70.7 shows the mechanism of determination in private tutoring participation by expectancy theory.

Factors involved in the process of determining whether or not to participate in private tutoring on the individual level include the level of student ability, the effectiveness of private tutoring, the recognition of the possibility of realizing the final value as the effect of private tutoring, and the expenditure of private tutoring. The level of the parents' educational background, family socioeconomic status, the number of children, order of children, and subjective assessment about the expectancy of attaining the purpose are factors influencing participation in private tutoring. Factors that increase the expectation of attaining the purpose stimulate participation in private tutoring. In the case where conditions of expecting effective private tutoring exist, the motivation of participation is fortified.

The results of the surveys of those participating in private tutoring show that the group that has the highest chance of meeting their expectations through private tutoring is more likely to participate in it. This tendency shows that participation in private tutoring comes from a rational calculation and is an "investment in studying." The expectations of the positive effects of private tutoring (efficacy), the ability to

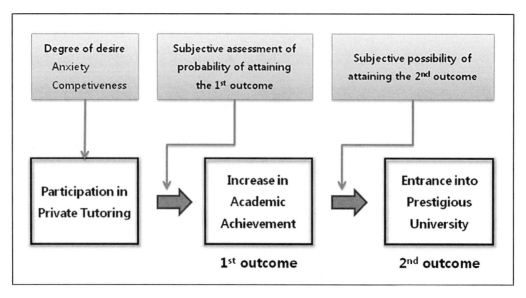

Figure 70.7 Expectancy theory model for the determination of participation in private tutoring.

afford private tutoring expenses (affordability), and the accessibility of private tutoring services (availability) affect participation in private tutoring. The participation of private tutoring is generally high in big cities, since the supply of high-quality tutoring services is plentiful. The higher the parents' academic achievement level and income, the higher the participation in private tutoring (Kim et al., 2006). The empirical analysis on the relationship between student grades and private tutoring expenditure shows inconsistent results, but on the whole, students who have higher grades spend more money on private tutoring than students who get lower grades (Lee et al., 2002).

Studies of student characteristics relate gender and birth order to the level of expenditure on private tutoring. First, it was found that the expenditure on private tutoring for girls was lower than the expenditure on private tutoring for boys. This showed that depending on the gender of the child, the expectation of parents was different and parental support was supplied discriminately (M. Lee, 1998; J. Lee, 2002). Also, in the case of firstborns, the expenditure on private tutoring is inclined to increase. It can be understood that the parents' care and resources focus on the first child (S-S Lee, 2002; J. Lee, 2002). Second, most research explains the cause and effect between student grades and the rate of participation in private tutoring. According to Bray and Kwok (2003), in the cases of Hong Kong and Taiwan, private tutoring was high in the excellent schools. Stevenson and Baker (1992) also show that if student achievement was high, participation in private tutoring was also high.

Third, Bray (2003) and Foondun (2002) also emphasized that the correlation between socio-economic status and participation in private tutoring was consistent in some countries. The level of the mother's educational background was particularly closely related to participation. In a study of private tutoring in Turkey, which was done by Tansel and Bircan (2006), the data from the 1994 Household Expenditure Survey show that household expenditure and

the education level of parents were regarded as the most important reasons behind participation in private tutoring. In the case of Japan, according to Blumenthal (1992), the upper 20% income households spent 10 times more on private tutoring than the lower 20%. Also, the demand for private tutoring was high amongst parents who worked as professionals. Stevenson and Baker (1992) analyzed the data of third-year students in Japanese high schools and showed that as the family income and the parents' educational background increased, so did participation in private tutoring. The family environmental variable accounted for a 12%–15% participation rate difference in private tutoring in Japan.

Another theoretical model of explanation is the "prisoner's dilemma" game theory model. It can be explained that, from the individual point of view, a person who does not want to participate inevitably does so because other people participate (J. Kim, 2005). This model provides a framework for understanding mutual and dependent choices when a consumptive and competitive game between rational decision makers exists. In other words, this is a strategy that is chosen in a competitive situation when each of the competitors pursues their own purpose through mutual reaction, but cannot control the outcomes themselves. The expected benefits of participation in private tutoring are defined by following equation:

$$EB = P * B + (1 - P) * 0 - C \text{ where} \tag{1}$$

EB: Expected Benefits
P: Probability of getting reward such as better grades and passing exams
B: Reward in better grades and passing exams
0: No reward in grades or passing exams
C: Cost of private tutoring

The compensation matrix of the two players is deducted from the equation of expected benefits. Figure 70.8 shows the compensation matrix of the two players which is de-

Player A \ Player B	Particiaption in Private Tutoring	No Participation
Particiaption in Private Tutoring	(B/2 – C, B/2 – C)	(B – C, 0)
No Participation	(0, B – C)	(B/2, B/2)

Figure 70.8 Compensation matrix of two players

ducted from the equation of expected benefits. In the case of B/2–C > 0, everyone decides to participate in private tutoring, and in the case of B/2–C = 0, the participation and non-participation in private tutoring is indiscriminate. In the case of B/2–C < 0, everyone decides not to participate in private tutoring. When "credentialism" and tight linkage in the institutional environment exist, both the parents and the students recognize that B/2 is much bigger than C, and everyone makes the rational decision of participating in private tutoring. Depending on the students' characteristics, the subjective value given to entering the university of choice, the level of income, and the price of private tutoring, various situations provide subjective evaluation of the probabilities and values in estimating expected benefits associated with private tutoring.

The psychological anxiety that people feel due to others taking private lessons stimulates more demand for private tutoring. The psychological anxiety is brought on in the form of "peer pressure," where a need to participate in private tutoring arises from not wanting to solely depend on school education while others are participating in it. In a study done by the Sung (1999), in answer to a question about the biggest motivation for parents to make children participate in private tutoring, 33.9% of the respondents claimed anxiety through peer pressure was the motivator. This shows the existence of a psychological group anxiety in Korea.

The Effects of Shadow Education

What will be the long-term effects of large-scale argumentation of shadow education to formal schooling? Precise information and the analysis about the effect of private tutoring will provide vital information for parents and students to participate in private tutoring. Empirical analysis on the effect of private tutoring affects rational choices. If private tutoring affects improvement of achievement, the educational inequalities can increase. Private tutoring, while systemizing it, might bring about difficulties to public education. In the case of Korea and Japan, students neglected public school education because of the advanced study provided by private tutoring (Kim et al., 2003; Stevenson & Baker, 1992).

There have been many studies about the effect of private tutoring on academic achievement, psychological dependence, and unequal education opportunity. It is, however, hard to generalize the effect of private tutoring due to its various forms and studies with contrasting results.

The Effect of Private Tutoring on Academic Achievement Based on the type of achievement data, studies on the effect of private tutoring can be classified in two groups. First, there are studies investigating the effect of private tutoring based on the subjective answers of perceived improvement. Second, there are studies based on the objective academic performance data.

Many studies claim that private tutoring affects academic achievement based on the subjective perceptions of students and parents. Parents' perception of private tutoring was not substantially different from that of the students, though sometimes parents exhibited greater trust in the effect of private tutoring than students (Paik, 1999; Yun, 1997). Kramer and Werner (1998) studied the subjective perception of students and parents on private tutoring. According to their survey conducted with 26,450 German parents, 54% of the respondents answered that private tutoring had a positive effect on academic achievement. Also, 34.1% and 27.3% of Japanese parents with their children in *juku* acknowledged these extra-school education services as necessary and useful in helping children better understand school curriculum and making children more interested in study, respectively (MEXT, 1994).

Studies that have investigated the effect of private tutoring based on the empirical data showed a mixed result with both statistically significant and non-statistically significant results. The studies with significant effect of private tutoring will be examined first.

Park, Park, and Kim (2001) and Yang and Kim (2003) analyzed the Korean data from TIMSS 1999. They showed through Hierarchical Linear Modeling (HLM) that private tutoring contributed to the improvement of the math and science scores at statistically significant levels. Lee (2001) analyzed the effect of private tutoring on middle and high school students by setting the mean score of practice examinations for high school and college entrance as a dependent variable for 3 years. A multivariate regression analysis revealed that the effect of private tutoring was small but it was the next most influential factor on after intelligence, effort, and social environment.

Sawada and Kobayashi (1986) analyzed the effect of *juku* attendance on mathematics performances using 375 elementary and lower-secondary students in 8 Japanese schools. They found that students with *juku* attendance showed higher scores on tests of arithmetic calculation and algebra, but did not have higher scores in arithmetic application and geometry. They argued that this happened because the students with *juku* attendance had greater opportunities to learn, possibly because the *juku* curriculum emphasized arithmetic calculation and algebra. Elbaum, Vaughn, Hughes, and Moody (2000) analyzed the effects of private lessons through an experimental design and showed that students who took one-to-one private lessons received two-third standard deviations higher grades than students who did not take private lessons. Mischo and Haag (2002) investigated the effects of private tutoring on 244 middle school students and showed that students who participated in it received higher grades than students who did not participate. Concerning the effects of private tutoring, Tansel and Bircan (2005) investigated high school students in Turkey. They showed that students who participated in private tutoring received better grades and had a higher probability of entering college than students who did not.

In contrast to the above research, which showed that the effect of private tutoring on academic achievement was statistically significant, there were studies that claimed it did not display a pure effect on academic achievement. Yasmeen's (1999) study reported a contrasting result with Tansel and Bircan (2005), namely that students receiving private tutoring depended on their tutor for homework, examination-related clues and all other information, so their grades did not improve. Sung (2003) analyzed the academic achievement data of the first and second year students in a high school in Seoul. The results showed no effects on academic achievement.

Han, Sung, and Gil (2001) analyzed the effect of private tutoring on the practice examination for college entrance, administered in April and August of 1999, by performing a regression analysis on the mathematics and science scores of 918 second-year high school students. In order to see the "pure" effect, preceding variables that have an effect on private tutoring, such as family background (parents' educational background, family income, cultural expenses), individual characteristics (intelligence, plans for future education), social background (sex, equalization), and previous academic achievement (scores from the April mathematics section) were controlled. The results revealed that private tutoring could not explain the additional variance of the mathematics scores.

Lee et al. (2002) analyzed the relationship between private tutoring and the academic achievement of elementary and middle school students. When they compared academic achievement between students participating in private tutoring and those not participating in private tutoring using change scores between the years 2000 and 2001, it was found that there was no statistically significant difference between them in the subjects of Korean, English, or Mathematics. Also, in order to explore the mid- to long-term effect of private tutoring, this study investigated whether second-year high school students had participated in private tutoring during the previous 5 years and compared the grade change of the two groups, where one group participated in private tutoring continuously (students who participated for at least 4 years out of the past 5 years) and the other group did not participate in private tutoring at all. The results showed that the difference between the two groups decreased or the grade was reversed.

Ban, Jung, and Yang (2005) also stated that private tutoring was not related to the improvement of grades at school and, particularly in the case of high school which is designed to prepare its students to enter a college, private tutoring even showed negative effects on school grades. It was argued that private tutoring did not provide much assistance in improving grades because it focused on instruction ahead of the school schedule and on test preparation, rather than complementing study at the individual or school levels.

When synthesizing these studies, it was recognized that they analyzed the effects of private tutoring by comparing group means or conducting multiple regression analyses; however, simply comparing the mean academic achievement between two groups or mean change in grade is not a valid way to measure the effects of private tutoring, unless the equality between the two groups is guaranteed. Otherwise, even if there is a significant difference between groups, it cannot be determined if it is due to private tutoring or some unknown difference between the groups. Also, even though a multiple regression analysis shows the degree of impact private tutoring has when variables, such as family backgrounds and previous achievements, are controlled, the relationship between private tutoring and student background variables are generally high. Additionally, different explanations could be made according to the characteristics and order of the variables.

In order to confirm the pure effect of private tutoring, the endogenous variable between the student's ability level and participation level needs to be considered, which is explained as follows: Suppose students with superior academic abilities have a tendency to participate in private tutoring in order to maintain good grades. In this case, the simple comparison between students who participate in private tutoring and students who do not is in danger of overestimating the effect of private tutoring, rather than estimating the pure effect of private tutoring. On the other hand, in the case of students with inferior academic abilities participating in private tutoring in a supplementary form in order to keep up with the school curriculum, the effect of private tutoring may be underestimated.

In this context, Kang (2005) and Choi (2007) tried to settle the problem of the endogenous variables by regarding the order of birth as the exogenous instrumental variable of the expenditure of private tutoring. In other words, even though many theoretical and empirical truths show that the parents' interests and investment can vary depending on the order of birth, it cannot be concluded that the order of birth has a systematic relationship with the ability of academic achievement. Therefore, the birth order can be a useful instrumental variable. These studies concluded that the effect of private tutoring was not statistically significant after controlling for the instrumental variables on academic achievement and college entrance.

Analysis of the Effects of Reliance on Private Tutoring on Learner Psychological Development Generally, participation in private tutoring occurs as a result of parental rather than student decision. In private tutoring, the tutors inform learners of their achievement goals and plans, causing negative emotional effects on their self-regulation and motivation. Even though Korean and Japanese students showed high achievement in PISA 2003, they were reported to have low self-regulation, interest in learning, confidence, and engagement in learning (OECD, 2004).

Using PISA 2006 data, Table 70.2 shows the average psychological characteristics related to learning for those who participate in private tutoring in science and those who do not. The scores of general interest in learning science, enjoyment of science, and science self-efficacy were scaled to have an OECD mean of 0 and a standard deviation of 1. The results from Table 70.2 indicate that in most countries students who received private tutoring showed less interest in learning, less enjoyment, and low self-efficacy of study in compared to their counterparts who did not receive private tutoring.

There have been limited studies regarding the influence of private tutoring on students' psychological characteristics, but these studies are expected to be an important field of future research. One study by Kim and Kim (2002) reported that 45.6% of the total respondents felt uncomfortable about self-learning, and 8% in Korea even found it impossible to learn by themselves. In Japan, Tsukada (1988) argued that the specialized *yobiko* had influenced its students' self-concept and educational aspiration through its tracking system and self evaluation based on the continuous practice examination process.

Analysis of the Effects of Participation in Private Tutoring on Education Inequality

There are differences in the amount of private tutoring and the expenditure on private tutoring among social classes. The difference in achievement caused by private tutoring is a universal phenomenon (Baker & LeTendre, 2005). It is also universal that there are differences in the probability of college entrance among social classes. It is reported that private tutoring affects academic achievement and that its availability is different according to social class (K. Kim, 2005). As a result, it is probable that private tutoring causes education inequality among social classes in terms of college entrance.

However, it has been pointed out that since the effect of private tutoring on academic achievement is not clear, it cannot be concluded that it actually leads to education inequality. In Korea, for example, family background is more likely to determine achievement level, causing subsequent generations to attain similar levels of achievement (Kim & Kim, 1999). It has also been reported that entrance to the most prestigious universities is limited to the higher classes (Kim et al., 2004).

There are few studies, if any, that explore the relationship between private tutoring and college entrance, despite a recent attempt to examine their relationship using longitudinal data in Korea. Yang (2007) examined the effects of 5 years of private tutoring (from 2000 [second-year middle school students] to 2004 [high school seniors]) on college entrance using longitudinal data from the Korean Labor Panel Survey. As the final participants, he analyzed 184 students, who were third-year students in high school in 2004. The results showed that students who gained entrance to 4-year colleges had been involved in private tutoring for at least 3 years. Specifically, a multinomial logistic regression analysis found that private tutoring was more effective for those who gained entrance to 4-year colleges than 2-year colleges. Therefore, it can be argued that private tutoring has an effect on college entrance. However, Choi (2007) attempted to analyze the same data in a different way. When he controlled for the birth order, which he identified as an exogenous instrumental variable of the expenditure of private tutoring, it was found that the relationship between it and college entrance was not statistically significant, even though those who participated in private tutoring were more likely to go to college than those who did not.

Until now, many studies have shown conflicting results about the effects of private tutoring on college entrance. In Japan, its role was acknowledged by social status (Stevenson & Baker, 1992). Kataoka (1998) illustrated, however, that the effect of attending private tutoring schools was not so significant in regard to admission to prestigious colleges for the younger cohort (aged 20–34) while attending a private tutoring schools had increased the chances of admission to prestigious colleges for the older cohort (aged 35–49). In Turkey, Tansel and Bircan (2005) illustrated that high school students who participated in private tutoring had a higher probability of entering college than students who did not. In the United States, Ishitani and Snider (2006) argued that participating in ACT/SAT preparation programs enhanced not only academic knowledge and test-taking skills, but also commitment and motivation to attain a college education, based on the evidence that ACT/SAT preparation programs showed positive effects on college retention after controlling for the parental involvement using NELS data.

Besides these studies on the relationship between private tutoring and college entrance, future studies examining the effects of private tutoring on the types of colleges entered, the college entrance examination scores, and social status after college graduation are needed.

Policy Responses

Bray (1999, 2003) classified policy responses into four types: (a) ignore the phenomenon, (b) prohibit private tutoring, (c) recognize and regulate, and (d) actively encourage. Two opposing views exist toward the government's response to private tutoring in terms of differences in recognition given to private tutoring and the different thoughts about the role of government.

First of all, an "ignore the phenomenon" or laissez-faire approach implies that the government lacks its own capacity, that the market controls educational systems, and that the market influences the quality and price of private tutoring. The former can be found in Nigeria and Kenya and the latter in Canada, England, and Japan. In the case of Japan, the Japanese government does not regulate any private institutes.

The second approach, such as that taken by the Korean government in the 1980s, is to prohibit students and teachers from taking and giving private lessons.

Most countries follow a third approach, "recognize and regulate." In these countries, if private tutoring becomes

TABLE 70.2

Difference in Psychological Characteristics Between 15-Year-Olds With Private Tutoring and Those Without, Using PISA 2006 Data

OECD Countries	General interest in learning science			Enjoyment of science			Science self-efficacy		
	W/O Private Tutoring	With Private Tutoring	Difference	W/O Private Tutoring	With Private Tutoring	Difference	W/O Private Tutoring	With Private Tutoring	Difference
Australia	−0.02	−0.26	−0.24	0.08	−0.11	−0.19	0.28	0.09	−0.19
Austria	0.08	0.04	−0.04	−0.15	−0.24	−0.09	−0.10	−0.11	−0.01
Belgium	0.18	−0.01	−0.19	0.08	−0.05	−0.13	−0.05	−0.11	−0.06
Canada	0.21	0.08	−0.13	0.22	0.16	−0.06	0.27	0.20	−0.07
Czech	0.08	−0.06	−0.14	0.06	−0.08	−0.14	0.25	0.13	−0.12
Denmark	0.03	−0.18	−0.21	0.04	−0.07	−0.11	−0.01	−0.08	−0.07
Finland	−0.08	−0.25	−0.17	0.16	0.11	−0.05	0.14	0.02	−0.12
France	0.28	0.17	−0.11	0.17	0.11	−0.06	0.00	−0.09	−0.09
Germany	0.17	0.19	0.02	−0.11	−0.09	0.02	0.07	0.06	−0.01
Greece	0.27	0.13	−0.14	0.14	0.03	−0.11	−0.09	−0.16	−0.07
Hungary	0.02	−0.12	−0.14	0.31	0.14	−0.17	0.05	−0.11	−0.16
Iceland	−0.24	−0.13	0.11	−0.15	−0.01	0.14	0.09	0.15	0.06
Ireland	0.01	−0.20	−0.21	−0.09	−0.22	−0.13	0.15	−0.05	−0.20
Italy	0.20	0.16	−0.04	0.12	0.12	0.00	−0.17	−0.22	−0.05
Japan	−0.01	−0.14	−0.13	−0.15	−0.27	−0.12	−0.32	−0.55	−0.23
Korea	−0.15	−0.28	−0.13	−0.15	−0.18	−0.03	−0.12	−0.25	−0.13
Luxembourg	0.14	0.13	−0.01	−0.07	−0.03	0.04	−0.15	−0.14	0.01
Netherlands	−0.27	−0.36	−0.09	−0.26	−0.34	−0.08	0.08	0.02	−0.06
New Zealand	0.03	−0.12	−0.15	0.12	−0.04	−0.16	0.09	−0.04	−0.13
Norway	0.18	−0.05	−0.23	0.09	−0.02	−0.11	0.29	0.12	−0.17
Poland	0.12	0.04	−0.08	−0.21	−0.26	−0.05	0.45	0.22	−0.23
Portugal	0.24	0.11	−0.13	0.32	0.29	−0.03	0.31	0.13	−0.18
Spain	−0.14	−0.20	−0.06	−0.12	−0.15	−0.03	−0.06	−0.07	−0.01
Sweden	0.01	−0.14	−0.15	−0.04	−0.11	−0.07	−0.06	−0.06	0.00
Switzerland	0.03	−0.01	−0.04	−0.02	−0.08	−0.06	−0.19	−0.20	−0.01
Turkey	0.44	0.19	−0.25	0.61	0.38	−0.23	0.28	−0.03	−0.31
UK	0.11	−0.04	−0.15	0.03	−0.11	−0.14	0.28	0.17	−0.11
USA	0.21	−0.01	−0.22	0.07	−0.05	−0.12	0.32	0.20	−0.12
Non OECD Countries									
Argentina	0.21	0.23	0.02	0.01	0.02	0.01	−0.02	−0.05	−0.03
Azerbaijan	0.70	0.56	−0.14	0.76	0.75	−0.01	−0.27	−0.52	−0.25
Brazil	0.54	0.49	−0.05	0.36	0.38	0.02	0.07	−0.08	−0.15
Bulgaria	0.31	0.14	−0.17	0.48	0.36	−0.12	0.11	−0.09	−0.20
Chile	0.43	0.34	−0.09	0.32	0.24	−0.08	0.19	0.05	−0.14
Colombia	1.26	1.10	−0.16	0.91	0.77	−0.14	0.14	0.07	−0.07
Croatia	0.20	0.16	−0.04	0.09	0.10	0.01	0.18	0.13	−0.05
Estonia	0.33	0.16	−0.17	0.12	−0.01	−0.13	0.07	0.02	−0.05
Hong Kong	0.23	0.18	−0.05	0.39	0.37	−0.02	0.15	0.03	−0.12
Indonesia	0.65	0.53	−0.12	0.86	0.75	−0.11	−0.53	−0.74	−0.21
Israel	−0.18	−0.24	−0.06	−0.10	−0.01	0.09	0.08	−0.03	−0.11
Jordan	0.70	0.66	−0.04	0.79	0.81	0.02	0.26	0.19	−0.07
Kyrgyzstan	0.97	0.87	−0.10	0.97	0.94	−0.03	−0.09	−0.17	−0.08
Latvia	0.24	0.13	−0.11	0.03	−0.02	−0.05	0.04	−0.05	−0.09
Liechtenstein	0.09	−0.08	−0.17	−0.27	−0.21	0.06	−0.05	−0.12	−0.07
Lithuania	0.40	0.33	−0.07	0.25	0.19	−0.06	0.12	−0.01	−0.13
Macao	0.10	0.10	0.00	0.37	0.43	0.06	−0.08	−0.12	−0.04
Mexico	0.76	0.76	0.00	0.65	0.64	−0.01	0.20	0.06	−0.14
Montenegro	0.43	0.42	−0.01	0.24	0.28	0.04	0.08	−0.06	−0.14
Qatar	0.26	0.29	0.03	0.26	0.44	0.18	−0.08	−0.10	−0.02
Romania	0.45	0.35	−0.10	0.45	0.45	0.00	−0.29	−0.37	−0.08
Russia	0.36	0.26	−0.10	0.20	0.11	−0.09	0.12	−0.05	−0.17
Serbia	0.27	0.24	−0.03	0.03	0.11	0.08	0.09	0.03	−0.06
Slovak	−0.02	−0.12	−0.10	0.01	−0.01	−0.02	0.17	0.08	−0.09
Slovenia	0.05	0.03	−0.02	−0.14	−0.13	0.01	−0.09	−0.11	−0.02
Taipei	0.15	0.07	−0.08	0.21	0.15	−0.06	0.22	0.17	−0.05
Thailand	0.85	0.77	−0.08	0.83	0.70	−0.13	0.26	0.01	−0.25
Tunisia	0.82	0.75	−0.07	0.98	1.03	0.05	−0.05	−0.13	−0.08
Uruguay	0.28	0.23	−0.05	0.14	0.06	−0.08	0.19	0.10	−0.09

a social issue, then more regulatory steps are taken to establish systems that can control the market. If the government admits the positive aspects of private tutoring, then more lenient steps are taken to lessen the restrictions and to establish supportive systems and policies that allow people to take advantage of opportunities for private tutoring. Hong Kong can be considered more regulatory, but Taiwan and Singapore have been more supportive of private tutoring.

Besides this, there are several approaches to indirectly control private tutoring. First of all, some countries have tried to control it by adopting a school equalization policy, rather than by regulating private tutoring itself. Mauritius has been implementing a middle and high school equalization policy that makes it possible for students to attend middle and high schools according to where they live, not according to their academic achievement. Also, the Japanese government tried to adopt a public high school equalization policy in Tokyo in 1976. Against expectations, however, students with high grades crowded the prestigious private schools, causing the rate of college entrance from private schools to heighten and the rate of entrance from public schools to lessen. This turned out to be an undesirable result; therefore, the Japanese government is now abolishing this equalization policy in Tokyo. Korea has also attempted to improve the public schooling system to reduce private tutoring. A number of steps have been taken, such as implementing the No Entrance Exam to Middle School Policy of 1969 and the Public High School Equalization Policy of 1973. Meanwhile, however, the variety in the curriculum in public school education has decreased and doubts have been raised about the quality of the public school system.

Another approach to indirectly control private tutoring can be found in Korea. After the constitutional court ruled that the government's prohibition of private tutoring was unconstitutional in 2000, the courts supported a new, less expensive government-supported educational tutoring model in an effort to decrease the demand for private tutoring. Since 2000, the Korean government has explored ways for public schooling to offer private tutoring services in order to regulate the practice. The government also provided financial support for the lower classes. Through the government's support of after-school activities and educational broadcasting, the government introduced a national private tutoring model (Han, 2004). As a result, private tutoring has taken several forms, such as after-school activities, tutoring courses through educational broadcasting, and the Internet. However, the effects of these national private tutoring practices have not been clear until now, and more empirical studies are called for.

Concluding Remarks

The phenomenon of private tutoring is not restricted to Korea, Japan, Hong Kong, and Taiwan; it is also prospering in North America, Asia, Africa, and countries of the former Soviet Union that are currently setting up market-based economic systems. Now is the time to conceptualize private tutoring as shadow education, which is parallel to the sphere of public education. Shadow education is exercising its own power. There is an increasing need to look into the causes and dynamics of shadow education and to formulate a countermeasure policy on it.

There are a number of theoretical models that can explain the causes of this growing demand for private tutoring. The Institutional Perspective of shadow education provides analytical frameworks for analyzing the causes of shadow education. The Institutional Perspective views this boom as an appropriate reaction to academic competition in this achievement-oriented society that is filled with meritocracy, mass schooling, credentialism, academic achievement, and high-stakes testing. However, one empirical analysis, did not support this theoretical hypothesis. An investigation into the Institutional Perspective is called for based on the collection of internationally comparable data.

Researches of the causes for and effects of private tutoring are also needed. With the increasing number of studies on the demands for private tutoring and the different forms of participation, it is still difficult to develop generalized statements about the causes and effects of private tutoring. In order to set up countermeasure policies to private tutoring, an analysis of the demand for unnecessary private tutoring and the negative effects of it is necessary. There is a great need for analytic research in the area of private tutoring for evidence-based policy making.

References

Baker, D. P., Akiba, M., LeTendre, G. K., & Wiseman, A. W. (2001). Worldwide shadow education: Outside-school learning, institutional quality of schooling, and cross-national mathematics achievement. *Educational Evaluation and Policy Analysis, 23*, 1–17.

Baker, D. P., & LeTendre, G. K. (2005). *National differences, global similarities: World culture and the future of schooling.* Stanford, CA: Stanford University Press.

Ban, S., Jung, S., & Yang, S. (2005, October). *Analyzing the effect of private tutoring on academic achievement.* Paper presented at the first Korean Education and Employment Panel conference, Seoul, Korea.

Blumenthal, T. (1992). Japan's Juken industry. *Asian Survey, 32*, 448–460.

Bray, M. (1999). *The shadow education system: Private tutoring and its implications for planners.* Paris: United Nations Educational, Scientific and Cultural Organization.

Bray, M. (2003). *Adverse effects of private supplementary tutoring: Dimensions, implications and government responses.* Paris: International Institute for Educational Planning.

Bray, M., & Kwok, P. (2003). Demand for private supplementary tutoring: Conceptual considerations and socio-economic patterns in Hong Kong. *Economics of Education Review, 22*, 611–620.

Briggs, D. C. (2001). The effect of admissions test preparation: Evidence from NELS: 88. [Electronic version]. *Chance, 14*, 10–21.

Buchmann, C., Roscigno, V., & Condron, D. (2006, August). *The myth of meritocracy? SAT preparation, college enrollment, class and race in the United States.* Paper presented in annual meeting of the American Sociological Association.

Choi, H. (2007). *Does private tutoring help advancement to higher education?* (Working paper 2007-1). Seoul: Korea Labor Institute.

Choi, S., Kim, M., Kim, O., Kim, J., Lee, M., Lee, S., et al. (2003). *Managing the private tutoring problem.* Seoul: Korean Educational Development Institute.

Dang, H-A. (2007). The determinants and impact of private tutoring classes in Vietnam. *Economics of Education Review, 26*(6), 683–698.

Davies, S. (2002). School choice by default? Understanding the growing demand for private tutoring in Canada (NALL Working Paper No.65). Toronto: University of Toronto, Ontario Institute for Studies in Education.

Elbaum, B., Vaughn, S., Hughes, M. T., & Moody, S. W. (2000). How effective are one-to-one tutoring programs in reading for elementary students at risk for reading failure? A meta-analysis of the intervention research. *Journal of Educational Psychology, 92*, 605–619.

Foondun, A. R. (2002). The issue of private tuition: An analysis of the practice in Mauritius and selected south-east Asian countries. *International Review of Education, 48*, 485–515.

Han, J. (2004). *National private tutoring.* Seoul, Korea: Hakjisa.

Han, D., Sung, B., & Gil, I. (2001). A study on the comparison between the effects of private tutoring versus in-school education on academic achievement of high school students. *The Korean Journal of Sociology of Education, 11*(1), 33–54.

Hirao, K. (2002, August). *Privatized education markets and maternal employment in Japan.* Paper presented to the annual meeting of the American Sociological Association, Chicago.

Hyun, J., Lee, J., & Lee, H. (2003). *Study on the educational fever of Korean parents.* Seoul: Korean Educational Development Institute.

Ireson, J. (2004). Private tutoring: How prevalent and effective is it? *London Review of Education, 2*(2), 109–122.

Ishitani, T. T., & Snider, K. G. (2006). Longitudinal effects of college preparation programs on college retention. *IR Applications, 9*, 1–9.

Kang, C. (2005, October). *The more, the better? The effect of private educational expenditures on academic performance: Evidence from exogenous variation in birth order.* Paper presented at the first Korean Education and Employment Panel conference, Seoul.

Kataoka, E. (1998). Kyoiku tassei ni okeru meritokuraci no kozo to kazoku no kyoiku senryaku [Meritocracy and cultural reproduction in Japan: Cultural capital investment in extra-school education and school success]. In K. Seiyama & S. Imada (Eds.), *Kyoiku to sedaikan ido* [Education and Social Mobility]. *1995 SSM Research Series: Vol. 12* (pp. 1–16). Tokyo: 1995 Social Stratification and Mobility Survey Research Group.

Kim, H. (2004). Analyzing the structure of variables affecting on private tutoring expense. *The Korean Journal of Educational Administration, 22*(1), 27–45.

Kim, J. (2005). *Study on economic decision making of the private tutoring for college entrance exam.* Unpublished doctoral dissertation, Yonsei University: Seoul, Korea.

Kim, K. (2005). Educational gap in Korea and determinant factors. *Korean Journal of Sociology of Education, 15*(3), 1–27.

Kim K., Kim, D., Seo, I., & Lee, C. (2004). *Change in university entrance system: Who enters Seoul National University?.* The Center for Social Sciences at the Seoul National University.

Kim, M., Kang, Y., Park, S., Lee, H., & Hwang, Y. (2006). *Scales of the entrance examination industry and its development: A study of the entrance examination industry and college admission policy.* Seoul: Korean Educational Development Institute.

Kim, S., & Lee, J. (2002). *Demand for education and developmental state: Private tutoring in South Korea.* Seoul: Korea Development Institute.

Kim, T. (2003). The psychological mechanism to reduce educational credentialism in Korean adults: From perspective contraction to perspective expansion. *The Korean Journal of Educational Psychology, 17*(3), 131–148.

Kim, Y., Kang, S., Ryu, H., & Namgung, J. (2003). *An analytical study on the qualitative level and actual condition of school education.* Seoul: Korean Educational Development Institute.

Kim, Y., & Kim, B. (1999). Education and social class shift in the Korean industrialization process. *The Korean Journal of Educational Research, 37*(1), 155–172.

Kim, Y., & Kim, M. (2002). *Analysis of the education of private tutoring institute.* Seoul: Korean Educational Development Institute.

Korean National Statistical Office. (2008). *Survey of private education expenditure in 2007.* Daejeon, Korea: Author.

Kramer, W., & Werner, P. (1998). *Parental and paid tutoring.* Köln, Germany: Deutscher-Institus Verlag.

Kwok, L. P. (2004). Emergence of demand for private supplementary tutoring in Hong Kong: Argument, indicators and implications. *Hong Kong Teachers' Centre Journal, 3*, 1–14.

Lee, C., & Lee, H. (2007). *Worldwide growth of shadow education: Global pervasiveness and national differences.* Unpublished manuscript.

Lee, H. (2001, September). *Educational effect of private tutoring.* Paper presented at the Korea Education Forum-3rd Educational Problem Seminar. Seoul: Korean Educational Development Institute.

Lee, J. (2002). Family environment, private tutoring and school grades. *Korean Sociology, 36*(6), 195–213.

Lee, J., & Hong, S. (2001). Schooling versus private tutoring: Choices and equity in Korean education. *The Korean Economic Review, 49*(1), 37–56.

Lee, J., Kim, Y., Lee, I., Yoon, C., Sung, K., Kim, M. et al. (2002). *Study on the effect of preceding learning.* Seoul: Korean Educational Development Institute.

Lee, M. (1998). Gender differential educational investment within family. *Korean Sociology, 32*(1), 63–97.

Lee, S-J. (2006). *Prestige-oriented view of college entrance and shadow education in South Korea: Factors influencing parent expenditures on private tutoring.* Unpublished Doctoral Dissertation, Pennsylvania State University.

Lee, S-S. (2002). Private education expenditure for children and the economic well-being of households. *Journal of the Korean Home Economics Association, 40*(7), 211–227.

Marimuthu, T., Singh, J. S., Ahmad, K., Lim, H. K., Mukherjee, H., Oman, S. et al. (1991). *Extra-school instruction, social equity and educational quality.* Report prepared for the International Development Research Centre, Singapore.

Ministry of Education, Culture, Sports, Science and Technology-Japan (MEXT). (1994). *Gakushu juku to ni kansuru jittsichosa hokokusho* [Survey on extra-school education]. Tokyo: Author.

Ministry of Education, Culture, Sports, Science and Technology-Japan (MEXT). (2003). *The survey of expenditure on education.* Tokyo: Author.

Mischo, C., & Haag, L. (2002). Spreading and effectiveness of private tutoring. *European Journal of Psychology of Education, 17*, 263–273.

Organisation for Economic Co-operation and Development (OECD). (2004). *Education at a glance 2004: OECD indicators.* Paris: Author.

Paik, I. (1999). Study on the determinants of demand for private tutoring. *The Korean Journal of Educational Administration, 17*(4), 117–136.

Park, D., Park, C., & Kim, S. (2001). The effects of school and student level background variables on math and science achievements in middle schools. The Korean *Journal of Educational Evaluation, 14*(1), 127–149.

Porter, L. W., & Lawler, E. E. (1968). *Managerial attitudes and performance.* Homewood, IL: Irwin.

Powers, D. E., & Rock, D. A. (1999). Effects of coaching on SAT I: Reasoning test scores. *Journal of Educational Measurement, 36*, 93–118.

Psacharopoulos, G., & Papakonstantinou, G. (2005). The real university cost in a "free" higher education country. *Economics of Education Review, 24*, 103–108.

Rohlen, T. P. (1980). The juku phenomenon: An exploratory essay. *Journal of Japanese Studies, 6*, 207–242.

Rohlen, T. P. (1983). *Japan's high schools.* Berkeley: University of California Press.

Sawada, T., & Kobayashi, S. (1986). *An analysis of the effect of arithmetic and mathematics education at Juku.* Tokyo: National Institute for Educational Research.

Silova, I., & Bray, M (2006). The hidden market place: Private tutoring in former socialist countries. In I. Silova, V. Būdienė, M. Bray, & A. Zabulionis (Eds.), *Education in a hidden marketplace: Monitoring of private tutoring* (pp. 71–98). Budapest, Hungary: Education Support Program of the Open Society Institute.

Stevenson, D. L., & Baker, D. P. (1992). Shadow education and allocation in formal schooling: Transition to university in Japan. *American Journal of Sociology, 97,* 1639–1657.

Suliman, E. D. A., & El-Kogali, S. (2002, October) *Why are the children out of school? Factors affecting children's education in Egypt.* Paper presented at the Economic Research Forum 9th Annual Conference, Al-Sharjah, United Arab Emirates.

Sung, G. (1999). KEDI POLL 1999. Seoul: Korean Educational Development Institute.

Sung, G. (2003, July). *Analyzing the determinants of high school students' achievement: Focused on the effect of self-directed learning attitude.* Paper presented at the 2003 International Conference on Educational Fever.

Tansel, A., & Bircan, F. (2005). *Effect of private tutoring on university entrance examination performance in Turkey* (IZA Discussion Paper No. 1609). Retrieved on April 8, 2008, from http://ssrn.com/abstract=721925

Tansel, A., & Bircan, F. (2006). Demand for education in Turkey: A tobit analysis of private tutoring expenditures. *Economics of Education Review, 25,* 303–313.

Tseng, J. L. C. (1998). *Private supplementary tutoring at the senior secondary level in Taiwan and Hong Kong.* Unpublished M.Ed. dissertation, The University of Hong Kong.

Tsukada, M. (1988). Institutionalised supplementary education in Japan: The Yobiko and Ronin student adaptations. *Comparative Education, 24,* 285–303.

Vroom, V. H. (1960). *Some personality determinants of the effects of participation.* Englewood Cliffs, NJ: Prentice-Hall.

United Nations Educational, Scientific and Cultural Organization (UNESCO). (1976). *Recommendation on the development of adult education.* Paris: Author.

Wong, T. C., & Wong, J. Y. (1998). The time management issue of tertiary students: An investigation of tuition conductors in Singapore. *New Horizons in Education, 39*(11), 1–7.

Woo, C., Cho, B., Kim, T., Kim, K., Kim, Y., Kim, J., et al. (Eds.). (2004). *Study on the effect, demand and affecting factors of private tutoring.* Seoul: Korea Development Institute.

Yang, J. (2003). Mathematics private tutoring of middle school students: An HGLM analysis of TIMSS-R. *The Korean Journal of Education, 30*(2), 261–283.

Yang, J. (2007). The effect of private tutoring on advancement to higher education. *The 8th Conference on Korean Labor and Income Panel Study,* 41–59.

Yang, J., & Kim, K. (2003). Effects of middle school organization on academic achievement in Korea: An HLM analysis of TIMSS-R. *The Korean Journal of Sociology of Education, 13*(2), 165–184.

Yasmeen, S. (1999, May). The spreading private tuitions epidemic. *Journal of Educational Excellence* [India], 21–25.

Yoo, Y. (2002). *Economics of private tutoring: In search for its causes and effective cures.* Seoul: Korea Development Institute.

Yun, C. (1997). A study on actual condition of private tutoring [Special issue]. *The Korean Journal of Economics and Finance of Education,* 231–254.

71

K-16 Transitions and Higher Education Access

Frankie Keels Williams
Clemson University

Projections from the Census 2000 indicate that by 2015, more than 19.9 million students will enroll in 2-and 4-year colleges and universities in the United States (National Center for Education Statistics [NCES], 2005; U.S. Bureau of Census, 2005). This figure includes approximately 2.2 million of the most recent public and private high school graduates and GED completers. In addition, the trajectory shows that the population is not only growing, but is becoming increasingly diverse. Moreover, the college enrollment of recent high school graduates will include an increasing number of first-generation college students, women, and young immigrants. Given these projections and myriad factors that have been reported in a large number of studies about this diverse population, both the K-12 and higher education sectors of education must prepare for the record numbers of enrollments. Accordingly, with diverse students expected over the next few decades, the transitions to college and access to higher education are more significant today than ever before.

While there is general recognition of the importance of successful K-12 transitions to college and subsequent college completion, persisting social and economic inequalities exist and are attributable to economic, racial, and gender disparities (Trent, Orr, Ranis, & Holdaway, 2007). These disparities in turn limit access and success for various groups as well as provide differential experiences for their transitions into college. Thus, considerable gaps exist in educational access, achievement, and completions for minority and ethnic groups. During the next decade, these gaps in educational achievement by minorities and ethnic groups may continue to persist (Callan, Finey, Kirst, Usdan, & Venezia, 2006). The greatest disparities are between Hispanic and Black populations and White and Asian populations. For example, 48% of Hispanics age 25 and older do not hold a high school credential compared to 20% for the total population (Organization for Economic Cooperation and Development [OECD], 2007).

Challenges for K-12 and Higher Education Transitions

The report *Closing the College Participation Gap,* published by the Education Commission of the States (Ruppert, 2003) includes three warning signs calling for attention to risks that may lie ahead for the K-12 and higher education systems in terms of improving educational transitions, access, and attainment for all groups in the future. The author suggests that the United States is falling behind other industrialized countries in college participation and other critical measures of postsecondary access and attainment. Further, current gaps in college participation and attainment based on age, race, ethnicity, and income indicate a strong risk for some individuals of losing access to a college education.

The relationship between postsecondary education and economic and social benefits is very strong. The literature consistently shows that disadvantaged and minority students are more likely to be unprepared for employment. These students are also more likely to come from families who tend to earn less and are many times minorities and first generation college students. Parents and students with lower incomes are less likely to receive adequate information about college access, participate in financial aid opportunities, or enroll in college (Flint, 1997). The challenge for the nation is to close the achievement gap and provide access and successful transitions to college for all.

While once the world leader in providing access to college for its young population, the competitive edge of the United States workforce is currently behind other developed countries in the percentage of the young working-age population enrolling in college and attaining a degree. The educational attainment of the U.S. workforce (ages 24 to 34) ranks fifth among industrialized nations (OECD, 2004). Scholars (Flint, 1997; McCabe, 2000) point out the need for postsecondary education in order for individuals to enter employment and eradicate the potential growth of what seems to be a permanent underclass. More than 70% of the fastest growing jobs in the future will require some level of postsecondary education as will almost all sectors of employment (American Diploma Project [ADP], 2006). Economists and researchers emphasize that unless the educational achievement of the young population, the competitiveness of the U.S. workforce will decline over the next decades (Carnevale & Desrochers, 2003).

In order to remain competitive in the global economy, the United States must promote economic efficiency and social equity for all citizens by developing a highly skilled workforce that begins with the K-12 educational system and continues through the higher education system. The future of the country depends on more students graduating from high school with skills to enter college and be successful in college. School districts, colleges and universities, government, businesses, foundations, and policy organizations must focus on improving higher education access and K-16 transitions. Integrated reform efforts must take place at both the K-12 and higher education systems and throughout all levels of these systems.

To examine these issues further, this chapter provides descriptions of the current landscape and predictions about the future of college access and K-16 transitions in education. Background and historical contexts provide information on college readiness, college access, transitions to college, and college completion. Implications for research and policy are included for each section.

College Readiness

Historical data show dismal statistics on the number of high school graduates who entered college and were not prepared for college. These students subsequently required remedial work or did not complete a 2- or 4-year degree. For example, a study conducted by the American Association of Community Colleges (Shults, 2000) reports that an average of 36% of entering students in community colleges enrolled in at least one remedial course in fall 1998. Further, findings from another national study show that American high school students are no better prepared for college than they were 10 years ago (Arenson, 2004). Overall, approximately 50% of students currently entering all postsecondary education institutions in the United States are required to take remedial courses (NCES, 2003). These data consistently confirm that students leaving high school are not ready for successful transitions to college.

From a historical review of the literature, Deil-Amen and Turley (2007) found that many individual, family, institutional, and system-wide factors affect a person's ability to prepare and subsequently graduate from college. Other researchers assert that many first-year students find that their college courses are fundamentally different from their high school courses (Conley, Aspengren, Stout, & Veach, 2006). These differences can make the transition to college very difficult for most students, especially students from minority groups.

Research on College Readiness Goldrick-Rab, Carter, and Wagner (2007) found that the body of research on college readiness and entry is concerned with examining inequities in academic and social participation (Cabrera & LaNasa, 2000a, 2000b; Hurtado, Inkelas, Briggs, & Rhee, 1997; Jun & Tierney, 1999; Nora & Rendon, 1990). Several researchers found that Mean difference between Blacks and Whites in college completion is most often attributable to differences in high school preparation (Cabrera, Burkum, & La Nasa, 2003; Terenzini, Cabrera, & Bernal, 2001). Other scholars found evidences within this line of research focusing on how high school preparation shapes student aspirations (Carter, 1999; McDonough, 1997; Perna & Swail, 2001; Rosenbaum & Person, 2003; Schneider & Stevenson, 1999). Differences in aspirations, dropout rates, grade-point averages, and test scores are usually attributed to socioeconomic status (Schmid, 2001). Research questions mostly focus on the relative importance of ascriptive characteristics, high school preparation, and financial aid in predicting enrollment. Deil-Amen and Turley (2007) found that the vast majority of sociological studies focus on college readiness with disadvantaged students at the center of this work. Several studies include individual attributes hypothesized to have an effect on achievement. These include gender, race, ethnicity, immigrant status, and bilingualism.

Kirst and Venezia (2004) provide a scholarly analysis of issues relating to misunderstandings that contribute to poor preparation for college. The scholars developed a theoretical framework for identifying state-specific policy signals and used case study research to explore components of K-12 and higher education systems. Kirst and Venezia's findings highlight such issues as inequalities throughout the educational systems in college counseling, high school course offerings, connections with local postsecondary institutions, information about college placement policies, and tuition costs. They conclude that there is an undeniable need for additional research on college readiness.

Policy Implications for College Readiness The literature identifies state policy dimensions for improving college-readiness opportunities for all high school students (Conley, 2003; Davies, 2006). These dimensions include the alignment of coursework and assessments, financial incentives and support to stimulate K-12 and postsecondary education to collaborate, the development of the capacity to track students across educational institutions statewide, and the ability to publicly report on student progress and success from high school through postsecondary education. Schools, colleges, and universities are deemed accountable for improving student performance from high school to college completion. Specific strategies were identified that can help high schools increase the numbers of college ready students in the future by bringing their curriculum courses and programs into alignment (Conley, 2007).

High school curriculum and instruction should align with college expectations. High school leaders should work in partnerships with local colleges to analyze the content of the school's curriculum. The content of each high school course should link to college readiness standards and state content standards. Research findings indicate that syllabi for high school courses are different from those found in college courses. Teachers should develop high-quality syllabi in all courses that link to college courses. This process of syllabi alignment is a major component of high school to college articulation and enhances the link of high school courses with college expectations. High schools should implement senior seminars that can create a college-like experience in high school. The National Commission on the High School Senior Year (ADP, 2004) notes the significance of keeping students fully engaged academically throughout the senior year. Considerable content necessary for college has been found missing from high school instruction. Missing content should be added to high school courses to ensure significant knowledge and skills are included in the curricula.

Kirst and Venezia (2004) offer actions for promising reform in the area of policy. They suggest providing all students, their parents, and educators with accurate, high quality information about, and access to, courses that will help prepare students for college-level standards. Kirst and Venezia advocate focusing on the institutions that serve the majority of students by shifting media, policy, and research attention to include broad access colleges and universities attended by the vast majority of students (approximately 80%). The focus of local, state, and federal programs must include access to college and success in college as well as access to the resources and information students need to prepare well for college and to make informed decisions.

Improving Access to Higher Education

Traditional approaches to increasing and improving college access focus mostly on the issue of college enrollment. Access to higher education in the United States has improved dramatically for all groups during the last several decades. This growth has occurred at both the 2-year and 4-year colleges and universities among all racial/ethnic and income groups. Tremendous increases have occurred in 2-year colleges, with almost 50% of all students enrolled in higher education enrolled at 2-year colleges. As mentioned earlier, the college enrollment of recent high school graduates will include an increasing number of first-generation college students, women, and young immigrants. Predictably, the number of women enrolling in both 2-year and 4-year colleges will continue to increase. Nevertheless, despite these increases in access to higher education, dramatic under representation continues. African American, Hispanic, and Native American students continue to fall behind White and Asian students throughout the K–16 pipeline (NCES, 2005). African Americans were only 12% of all college students in 2000, while they comprised over 20% of the college age population. Further, African American

and Hispanic students are disproportionately likely to earn an associate's degree when compared to White students earning a bachelor's degree (Adelman, Daniel, Berkovitz, & Owings, 2003).

Research on Access to Higher Education The demographic disparities in enrollment at colleges and universities have been a priority on the research agenda. Many studies focus on the relationship between race and access to higher education (Cabrera & La Nasa, 2000a, 2000b; Cross & Slater, 2002: Perna, 2000) and issues of socioeconomic stratification in college choice (Alon, 2001; Karen, 1991; Paulsen, 1990). In general, students from the lowest socio-economic quartile who complete high school are less likely as students from the high socio-economic quartile to enroll in college (Terenzini et al., 2001). The majority of the literature examines type of college (2- or 4-year attendance) and college admission selectivity. Other studies focus on gender differences and Latino students (Perna, 2000). Women are currently enrolling and graduating at higher rates than men (NCES, 2003).

Researchers have delved into college access and affordability. Several researchers contend that college affordability is a major reason why a disproportionate number of low-income and minority students do not enroll in college or complete degree requirements (Heller, 2001, 2002; Perna, 2002; St. John & Starkey, 1994). Long and Riley (2007) document how low-income students and students of color are likely to face substantial unmet financial needs for college. The authors suggest a greater emphasis on need-based financial aid in the future, especially grants to reduce the cost of college as a barrier to college access. Flint (1994) found that there are many inequities among contributions for college from income groups because of differences in the time spent on planning and savings for college. Long (2007) reports on studies that focus on indirect subsidies to students in higher education (Heller, 2002; Rizzo & Ehrenberg, 2004), direct financial aid to students (Johnstone, 2003; McPherson & Schapiro, 1998), and studies of changes in price for higher education (Kane, 1999; Wetzel, O'Toole, & Peterson, 1998). Concerns about studies on financial aid include the levels of aggregation that result in masking the vast heterogeneity in college price, quality, and subsidies. Other research synthesized by Long (2007) include the effects of price and grants on particular groups (Bosworth & Choitz, 2002; Seftor & Turner, 2002; St. John & Noell, 1989). The enrollment effects of loans (Baum, 2003; King, 1999), tax credits and savings initiatives (Cronin, 1997; Dynarski, 2002; Long, 2004), and aid on college choice (Dynarski, 2000; Cornwell, Mustard, & Sridhar, 2002; Long, 2004) are also reviewed by Long (2007).

The definition of "college access" has been difficult for the policy and research arenas. Conceptual and methodological issues for researchers result from new forms of postsecondary attendance definitions. Goldrick-Rab et al. (2007) illustrate this issue when considering definitions of "dual enrollment," distance education learners," "likely" postsecondary participants, and "known" postsecondary participants for research purposes.

Policy Implications for Higher Education Access Efforts to promote access to colleges intertwine with policies and programs linked to open admissions and affirmative action. While policies and practices related to affirmative action have been notably controversial, there is still strong disagreement among policymakers. Discussions will continue during the next decade regarding affirmative action and college access.

Various types of support may be presented to complement public policy-making intended to extend access for all students to the full range of opportunities and benefits of college attendance and program completion. These support services will likely continue to include early interventions designed to raise the awareness of low-income middle school children and their parents of the possibilities of college attendance and to help them secure the necessary academic qualifications for admission and success once there. Financial aid in amounts and packages will continue to be essential for allowing recipients to participate fully in the academic and nonacademic systems of their institutions.

Transitions to College

Several states are now examining how they can become more effective in facilitating and assuring a smooth transition for students graduating from high school and entering college. In response to the need to prepare students for higher education, particularly among low-income and minority students, there are several outreach and intervention programs offered both at the K-12 and higher education levels. These programs include the federal TRIO programs established to provide supplementary academic support to low-income and historically underrepresented students. Other programs include Gaining Early Awareness and Readiness for Undergraduate Programs (GEARUP), dual enrollment programs, Advanced Placement, and Early College High School. In addition to these types of programs, once students enroll, most institutions offer freshman experience programs, orientations, and seminars.

Swail (2000) evaluates the potential of these outreach programs and stresses conditions that effective programs must meet in the future to make a difference in K-16 transitions and college access. These include ensuring that each young person is offered the opportunity to be involved in an intervention or college preparation program in middle and high school. These programs must be of high instructional quality and delivery must take place in school environments. Other major components of these programs must include expanding opportunities for networking among the various programs. All of these programs should link directly to schools and long-term systemic plans must be developed. These K-12 and higher education intervention strategies require focused research and interaction between both entities to more effectively meet their goals. Further, arrangements and instructional approaches must be provided that will increase involvement and student learning, change, and development in educational outcomes (Pascarella & Terenzini, 2005).

Research on Transitions to College Researchers have examined several aspects of the K-16 transitions, mostly focusing on improving retention to degree completion. Tinto's (1993) model has been the dominant theory emphasizing the significance of academic and social integration in student persistence. Orfield (1998) hypothesizes that racial differences in college completion result from the higher dropout rates in high school and lack of college preparation. Pascarella and Terenzini (2005) contribute notable work on the college experiences of students in two volumes of *How College Affects Students*. In the second volume, Pascarella and Terenzini provide a synthesis and analysis of the research covering college outcomes, theories, and models of student change in college, cognitive skills and intellectual growth, psychosocial change, attitudes and values, moral development, educational attainment and persistence, career and economic impacts of college, and quality of life after change. The researchers conclude the need to extend college access for students, redefine educational "quality," and rethink accountability.

The extant research literature presents a need to integrate research, policy, and practice on K-12 and transitions to college (Gándara, 2002; Louie, 2007). Louie (2007) suggests that researchers adopt a K-16 perspective, rather than keeping within the boundaries of K-12 or higher education. Other scholars (Trent et al., 2007) suggest a disciplinary lens to synthesize research and inform policies and practices that guide and support college access and transitions from high school to college. These scholars present field reviews in a special issue of the *Teachers College Record* journal on the research from anthropology (Koyama, 2007) demography (Maralani, 2007), economics (Long, 2007), higher education (Goldrick-Rab et al., 2007), history (Gelber, 2007), and sociology (Deil-Amen & Turley, 2007). The scholars call for persistent inquiry through integrated research methodologies among these disciplines.

Goldrick-Rab et al. (2007) conclude in their literature field review that further work is necessary to better clarify and conceptualize the multitude of transitions occurring both into college and within college. The researchers place emphasis on differences in transitions made by different racial and ethnic groups, older and younger, and independent and dependent students. The researchers identify gaps in the research base and points to methodologies and strategies that are promising for future research. They stress that while prior research has been more critical in raising questions about race, gender, and class inequalities, this has not become normative. Other relevant disciplines mentioned (e.g., economics, political science, anthropology) might contribute both new ways to thinking about the transition to college, as well as rigorous methodologies for examining it.

Recent efforts to integrate quantitative and qualitative methods in order to address issues of both causality and process are lauded by Goldrick-Rab et al. There is relatively little research on transitions to college in the areas of demography. According to Maralani (2007), existing studies examine the relationship between educational attainment and migration, educational attainment and fertility, and educational attainment and family structures.

Policy Implications for Transitions to College There is an emerging pattern of educational continuation for older populations. This suggests an increase of research and policy implications in addressing barriers adults face in their college transitions. Researchers must go beyond studies that focus on the academic achievement and the engagement of students and realize that the experiences of students and their families vary greatly, depending on their social, cultural, political, and historical contexts (Koyama, 2007). There should be an explicit agenda to continue to study the experiences of minorities in higher education.

College Completion

During past years, college completion dominated the research when studying college readiness and access. Research findings show demographic disparities in completion rates. African American and Hispanic students are more likely to depart college prior to earning a degree at both 2- and 4-year colleges than are White and Asian students (Allen, 1992; Cabrera, Burkum, et al., 2003; Ganderton & Santos, 1995; Hatch & Mommsen, 1984; Nora, Kraemer & Itzen, 1997). Data show that only 35% of the students who entered 4-year colleges in 1998 earned a degree 4 years later in 2002, and only 56% earned degrees 6 years later in 2004 (Knapp, Kelly-Reid, & Whitmore, 2006).

Research on College Completion Goldrick-Rab et al. (2007) examine the pathways through college, beginning with initial entry and followed with a series of transitions to college completion. Many studies on the first-year experience for students enrolled at 4-year colleges are characterized by social integration (Gardner, 2001). The first-year experience for many students enrolled in community colleges may include participation in remedial courses (NCES, 2005). Further, students at all types of institutions may experience transfer to multiple institutions before college completion (Adelman, 1999). Most studies on transfer include characteristics of students who transfer from community colleges to 4-year colleges. Several studies focus on racial differences in college completion, women's educational attainment, and theories of student persistence. Pascarella and Terenzini (2005) point out that research has been limited on the effects of college for minority students and students who attend 2-year colleges. Other researchers (Choy, 2002; Knapp et al., 2006) report a need for research on institutional factors advancing retention. Goldrick-Rab et al. (2007) also call attention to how institutions shape

completion and the relationship between college completion and lifetime earnings.

Policy Implications for College Completion Goldrick-Rab et al. (2007) conclude that higher education has used multiple definitions and measures of college completion. These include measures of various groups, institutional, system-wide, state-level, and national completions. For example, the completion rates may vary depending on how the researcher defines the group of students eligible for completion. Hearn (1991) emphasizes that racial differences in college completion rates receive more attention than socioeconomic differences in completion.

The ability to improve the college-going and completion rates is dependent upon the ability of our society to address inequities that affect education and opportunity. Community Colleges and Historically Black Colleges and Universities (HBCUs) can have a significant impact on completion rates for minority populations. These types of institutions provide opportunities for access by many minority and ethnic groups that might not otherwise have such opportunities.

Linking K-12 and Higher Education

Substantial literature exists regarding the organizational structures for K-16 transitions. For the most part, current practices and policies for the K-12 system and higher education system historically have existed in two separate worlds in the United States. Correspondingly, the disconnect between the two systems of education has created barriers to college access and successful transitions for students. The literature includes documented cases of disconnect or misalignment between the public educational systems of K-12 and higher education. Many contend that the K-12 and higher education systems have operated separately and independently as well as developed different and distinct policies (Consortium for Policy Research in Education [CPRE], 2000; Kirst & Venezia, 2001; Venezia, Kirst, & Antonio, 2003). Consequently, national and state-level policies intensify the separation of the K-12 and higher education systems, sometimes requiring the two systems to compete for the same resources. Each system has promulgated policies to address what it perceives as priority issues. In attempting to address the implications for college access and transitions for students, most reform efforts are documented in the literature within the separate systems of K-12 and higher education. As a result, many of these efforts have been successful in targeting student readiness for college access at the K-12 level and transitions for college at the higher education level.

Collaborative Partnership Efforts Significant efforts of aligning K-12 and postsecondary education are being addressed by several partnerships that include organizations, state agencies, and associations. For example, Pathways to College Network (2004) is a national initiative dedicated to ensuring a smooth transition for students from high school to college. State and federal policy makers, K-12 leaders, higher education leaders, and those funding education are involved in its activities. Pathways to College Network provides research-based knowledge about effective policies and practice on improving college access and successes for underserved populations.

Numerous publications were derived from the work of organizations that includes a 50-state survey report called *Statewide College Admissions, Student Preparation, and Remediation Policies and Programs* (State Higher Education Executive Officers [SHEEO], 1998) along with a series of commissioned strategy briefs focusing on remedial education policies and partnerships to improve student performance. *Mixed Messages: What State High School Tests Communicate About Student Readiness for College* by David Conley (2003) presents an analysis of 66 state high school assessments from 20 states to determine the degree of concurrence between test items, and knowledge and skills for university success standards developed and endorsed by members of the Association of American Universities. The primary goal of the project includes identifying what students need to know and be able to do in order to succeed in entry-level university courses. A second goal of the project is to produce a database of information on state high school assessments to improve the connection between the content of high school tests and the standards for university success; faculty members and administrators at member institutions of the Association of American Universities developed the standards. These standards include content knowledge, behaviors, and attitudes expected of entering students by the professors who will teach them. Future plans of the consortium include distributing a booklet containing the results of the project to all high schools in the nation, and consulting with national testing organizations and state education departments to explore possible integration of Knowledge and Skills for University Success with state academic content standards and assessment instruments. These efforts will improve the alignment between the curriculum and assessments needed for university success.

Another project that has been at work for the past 2 years and geared toward strengthening the connections between K-12 and higher education is a collaborative of The Education Trust, Achieve, Inc., and the Thomas B. Fordham Foundation called the American Diploma Project (ADP, 2003). The goal of ADP is to determine the English and mathematics skills that high school graduates need in order to be successful in college and the workplace. The publication, *Ready or Not: Creating a High School Diploma That Counts* provides the college and workplace readiness benchmarks and samples, along with specific recommendations for states, postsecondary institutions, the president, and Congress.

Future Directions for K-16 Partnerships The new public policy agenda for linking K-12 and higher education will vary by state; however, there will be common themes across states. For example, the findings from the literature emphasize policy levers that are promising for states interested in creating sustained K-16 reform. These levers include assessments and curricula, finance, data systems, and accountability. Many states, as well as national organizations, have already begun developing and implementing policies and strategies. For example, The No Child Left Behind Act aims to close the achievement gaps of minorities and ethnic groups beginning at the K-12 level. One approach for future policy and practice implications for higher education policy involves strong, committed, visionary leadership. The approach includes appointing a leadership group, grounding the agenda and its priorities into needs of state residents, completing a higher education policy audit, meeting with key people throughout the state, and reporting to the leadership group, finalize the public agenda, and assign responsibilities (Davies, 2006).

Some policy makers and researchers advocate for a large-scale education accountability system to include all public education sectors reflecting student needs as they transition from the K-12 system to the higher education system. Some models of accountability can help in improving access and K-16 transitions. New research and policy for K-16 partnerships can view education from kindergarten through college as one system. Significant assumptions and components from a new paradigm of K-16 transitions may include new structures to help students prepare for college, resources for helping students prepare for college, curricula alignment, and strong leadership. In order to accomplish goals for all students through collaboration, concerted efforts must take place by policymakers, research scholars, educators, and parents. These new organizational structures for K-16 entities will help facilitate reforms.

Conclusions

Educational leaders and policy makers must re-conceptualize a collaborative partnership between the K-12 and higher education systems focusing on both college access and K-12 transitions to college under the umbrella of the new paradigm, called K-16 transitions. Policy approaches for improving college access and K-12 transitions to college include alignment of curriculum, instruction, and assessment; data systems, accountability, and finance through collaborative partnerships. In all likelihood, additional partnerships will form during the next few years.

Additional research is necessary to help further conceptualize the dimensions of K-16 transitions occurring both into college and within college. The types of data collected are critical along with qualitative and quantitative methodologies. The meaning of "access" is that all prospective students will be prepared for college, be able to afford the costs of attendance and be successful in achieving their learning goals. State policy makers will need to take the lead because of their primary roles in setting policy and funding public postsecondary education in each state.

The transitions from high school to college will require a

more rigorous research focus. Close attention should focus on the effectiveness of reforms that have taken place at both the K-12 educational system and the higher education system. Further work is necessary to better conceptualize the individual experiences of those gaining access and transitioning to higher education. Linking work across disciplines will enhance the rigor of future research. In addition, scholars must create data sets that link practice, policy, and research.

References

Adelman, C. (1999). *Answers in the tool box: Academic intensity, attendance patterns, and bachelor's degree attainment.* Washington, DC: U.S. Department of Education.

Adelman, C., Daniel, B., Berkovitz, I., & Owings, J. (2003). *Postsecondary attainment, attendance, curriculum, and performance.* Washington, DC: National Center for Education Statistics.

Allen, W. R. (1992). The color of success: African-American college students outcomes at predominantly White and historically Black public colleges and university. *Harvard Educational Review, 62,* 26–43.

Alon, S. (2001). *Racial, ethnic, and socioeconomic disparities in college destinations, 1982 and 1992* (Working Paper No. 2001-02). NJ: Princeton University, Office of Population Research.

American Diploma Project (ADP). (2004). Ready or not: Creating a high school diploma that counts. Washington, DC: Achieve, Inc.

American Diploma Project (ADP). (2006). Closing the expectations gap 2006: An annual 50-state progress report on the alignment of high school policies with the demands of college and work. Washington, DC: Achieve, Inc.

Arenson, K. W. (2004, October 14). Study of college readiness finds no progress in decade. New York Times, p. A26.

Baum, S. (2003). *The role of student loans in college access.* New York: National Dialogue on Student Financial Aid, College Board.

Bosworth, B., & Choitz, V. (2002). *Held back: How student aid programs fail working adults.* Belmont, MA: FutureWorks.

Cabrera, A. F., Burkum, K., & LaNasa, S. M. (2003, November). *Pathways to a four-year degree: Determinants of degree completion among socioeconomically disadvantaged students.* Paper presented at the Association for the Study of Higher Education, Portland, OR.

Cabrera, A. F., & LaNasa, S. M. (2000a). Three critical tasks America's disadvantaged face on their path to college. *New Directions for Institutional Research, 27*(3), 23–29.

Cabrera, A. F., & LaNasa, S. M. (2000b). Understanding the college choice of disadvantaged students. *New directions for institutional research. No. 107.* San Francisco: Jossey-Bass.

Callan, P. M., Finey, J. E., Kirst, M. W., Usdan, M. D., & Venezia, A. (2006). *Claiming common ground: State policymaking for improving college readiness and success.* San Jose, CA: The National Center for Public Policy and Higher Education.

Carnevale, A., & Desrochers, D. (2003). *Standards for what? The economic roots of K-16 reform,* Princeton, NJ: Education Testing Service.

Carter, D. F. (1999). The impact of institutional choice and environments on African-American and White students' degree expectations. *Research in Higher Education, 40,* 17–41.

Choy, S. P. (2002). *Access and persistence: Findings from ten years of longitudinal research on students.* Washington, DC: Center for Policy Analysis, American Council on Education.

Conley, D. T. (2003). *Mixed messages: What state high school tests communicate about student readiness for college?* Eugene: Center for Educational Policy Research, University of Oregon.

Conley, D. T. (2007). The challenge of college readiness. *Educational Leadership, 64*(7), 23–26.

Conley, D. T., Aspengren, K., Stout, O., & Veach, D. (2006). *College Board advanced placement best practices course study report.* Eugene, OR: Educational Policy Improvement Center.

Consortium for Policy Research in Education (CPRE). (2000, June). *Bridging the k-12/postsecondary divide with a coherent k-16 system* (Policy brief No. 31 RB). Philadelphia: University of Pennsylvania, Graduate School of Education.

Cornwell, C., Mustard, D., & Sridhar, D. (2002). *The enrollment effects of merit-based financial aid: evidence from Georgia's Hope scholarship.* Unpublished manuscript, University of Georgia.

Cronin, J. (1997). The economic effects and beneficiaries of the administration's proposed higher education tax subsidies. *National Tax Journal, 50,* 519–540.

Cross, T., & Slater, R. B. (2002). How bans on race-sensitive admissions severely cut Black enrollments at flagship state universities. *Journal of Blacks in Higher Education, 38,* 93–99.

Davies, G. K. (2006, December). *Setting a public agenda for higher education in the states: Lessons learned from the National Collaborative for Higher Education Policy.* Denver, CO: The National Collaborative for Higher Education Policy.

Deil-Amen, R., & Turley, R. L. (2007). A review of the transition to college literature in sociology. *Teachers College Record, 109,* 2324–2366.

Dynarski, S. (2000). Hope for whom? Financial aid for the middle class and its impact on college attendance. *National Tax Journal, 53,* 629–661.

Dynarski, S. (2002). The behavioral and distributional implications of aid for college. *American Economic Review, 92,* 279–285.

Flint, T. (1994). Ideal vs. real dependent student family contributions. *Journal of Student Financial Aid, 24*(3), 13–32.

Flint, T. (1997). Intergenerational effects on paying for college. *Research in Higher Education, 38,* 313–344.

Gándara, P. (2002). Meeting common goals: Linking k-12 and college interventions. In W. G. Tierney & L. S. Hagedon (Eds.), *Increasing access to college: Extending possibilities for all students* (pp. 81–103). Albany: State University of New York Press.

Ganderton, P. T., & Santos, R. (1995). Hispanic college attendance and completion: Evidence from the "High School and Beyond" Surveys. *Economics of Education Review, 14,* 35–46.

Gardner, J. (2001). Focusing on the first-year student. *AGB Priorities, 1–17.*

Gelber, S. (2007). Pathways in the past: Historical perspectives on access to higher education. *Teachers College Record, 109,* 2252–2286.

Goldrick-Rab, S., Carter, D. F., & Wagner, R. W. (2007). What higher education has to say about the transition to college. *Teachers College Record. 109,* 2444–2481.

Hatch, L. R., & Mommsen, K. (1984). The widening racial gap in American higher education. *Journal of Black Studies, 14,* 457–476.

Hearn, J. C. (1991). Academic and nonacademic influences on the college destinations of 1980 high school graduates. *Sociology of Education, 64,* 158–171.

Heller, D. E. (Ed.). (2001). *The states and public higher education policy: Affordability, access, and accountability.* Baltimore, MD: Johns Hopkins University Press.

Heller, D. E. (Ed.). (2002). *Condition of access: higher education for lower income students.* Westport, CT: American Council on Education/Praeger.

Hurtado, S., Inkelas, K. K., Briggs, C. L., & Rhee, B. S. (1997). Differences in college access and choice among racial/ethnic groups: Identifying continuing barriers. *Research in Higher Education, 38,* 43–75.

Johnstone, D. B. (2003). *Fundamental assumptions and aims underlying the principles of federal financial aid to students,* National Dialogue on Student Financial Aid. New York: College Board.

Jun, A., & Tierney, W. G. (1999). At-risk urban students and college success: A framework for effective preparation. *Metropolitan Universities, 9*(4), 49–60.

Kane, T. J. (1999). *The price of admission: Rethinking how Americans pay for college.* Washington, DC: Brookings.

Karen, D. (1991). The politics of class, race, and gender: Access to higher education in the United States, 1960–1986. *American Journal of Education, 99*, 208–237.

King, J. E. (Ed.) (1999). *Financing a college education: How it works, how it's changing.* Phoenix, AZ: American Council on Education, Oryx Press.

Kirst, M. W., & Venezia, A. (2001) Bridging the great divide between secondary schools and postsecondary education. *Phi Delta Kappan, 83*, 92–97.

Kirst, M. W., & Venezia, A. (Eds.). (2004). *From high school to college: Improving opportunities for success in postsecondary education.* San Francisco: Jossey-Bass.

Knapp, L. G., Kelly-Reid, J. E., & Whitmore, R. W. (2006). Table 6. In *Enrollment in postsecondary institutions, fall 2004; graduation rates, 1998 and 2001 cohorts; and financial statistics, fiscal year 2004 (NCES 2006-115).* Washington, DC: U.S. Department of Education. National Center for Education Statistics.

Koyama, J. P. (2007). Approaching and attending college: Anthropological and ethnographic accounts. *Teachers College Record, 109*, 2301–2323.

Long, B. T. (2004). Does the format of an aid program matter? The effects of in-kind tuition subsidies. *Review of Economics and Statistics, 86*, 767–782.

Long, B. T. (2007). The contributions of economics to the study of college access and success. *Teachers College Record, 109*, 2367–2443.

Long, B. T., & Riley, E. (2007). Financial aid: A broken bridge to college access? *Harvard Educational Review. 77*, 39–63.

Louie, V. (2007). Who makes the transition to college? Why we should care, what we know, and what we need to do. *College Teachers Record, 109*, 2222–2251.

Maralani, V. (2007). The transition to college from a demographic perspective: Past findings and future possibilities. *Teachers College Record, 109*, 2287–2300.

McCabe, R. H. (2000). *No one to waste: A report to public decision makers and community college leaders.* Denver, CO: Community College Press.

McDonough, P. M. (1997). *Choosing colleges: how social class and schools structure opportunity.* Albany: State University of New York Press.

McPherson, M. S., & Schapiro, M. O. (1998). *The student aid game: Meeting need and rewarding talent in American higher education.* Princeton, NJ: Princeton University Press.

National Center for Education Statistics (NCES). (2003). *The condition of education.* Washington, DC: US Department of Education.

National Center for Education Statistics (NCES). (2005). *Projections of Education Statistics to 2015.* Washington, DC: U.S. Department of Education.

Nora, A., & Rendon, L. (1990). Differences in mathematics and science preparation and participation among community college minority and non-minority students. *Community College Review, 18*(2), 29–40.

Nora, A., Kraemer, B., & Itzen, R. (1997, November). *Persistence among non-traditional Hispanic college students: A causal model.* Paper presented at the annual meeting of the Association for the Study of Higher Education.

Orfield, G. (1998). Campus resegregation and its alternatives. In G. Orfield & E. Miller (Eds.), *Chilling admissions: The affirmative action crisis and the search for alternatives* (pp. 1–16). Cambridge, MA: Harvard Educational Press.

Organisation for Economic Cooperation and Development (OECD). (2004). *Education at a Glance.* Paris: OECD Publishing.

Organization for Economic Cooperation and Development (OECD). (2007, May). *Economic survey of the United States, 2007* (Policy brief). Retrieved December 27, 2007, from http://www.oecd.org/dataoecd/56/40/38665203.pdf

Pascarella, E. T., & Terenzini, P. T. (2005). *How college affects students: A third decade of research.* San Francisco: Jossey-Bass.

Pathways to College Network. (2004). *A shared agenda: A leadership challenge to improve college access and success.* Boston: The Education Resources Institute.

Paulsen, M. B. (1990). *College choice: Understanding student enrollment behavior* (ASHE–ERIC Higher Education Report No. 6). Washington, DC: George Washington University Graduate School of Education and Human Development.

Perna, L. W. (2000). Differences in the decision to attend college among African Americans, Hispanics, and Whites. *Journal of Higher Education, 71*, 117–141.

Perna, L. W. (2002). Financing higher education at selective private institutions: Implications for college access and choice. *The Review of Higher Education, 25*, 225–235.

Perna, L. W., & Swail, W. S. (2001). Pre-college outreach and early intervention. *Thought and Action, 17*(1), 99–110.

Rizzo, M., & Ehrenberg, R. (2004). Resident and nonresident tuition and enrollment at flagship state universities. In C. Hoxby (Ed.), *College choices: The economics of which college, when college, and how to pay for it* (pp. 303–353). Chicago: University of Chicago Press.

Rosenbaum, J. E., & Person, A. E. (2003). Beyond college for all: Policies and practices to improve transitions into college and jobs. *Professional School Counseling, 6*, 252–260.

Ruppert, S. S. (2003). *Closing the college participation gap: A national summary.* Denver, CO: Education Commission of the States.

St. John, E. P., & Noell, J. (1989). The effects of student financial aid on access to higher education: An analysis of progress with special consideration of minority enrollment. *Research in Higher Education, 30*, 563–581.

St. John, E. P., & Starkey, J. B. (1994). The influence of costs on persistence by traditional college-age students in community colleges. *Community College Journal of Research and Practice, 18*, 201–213.

Schmid, C. L. (2001). Educational achievement, language-minority students, and the new second generation. *Sociology of Education, 74*, 71–87.

Schneider, B., & Stevenson, D. (1999). *The ambitious generation: America's teenagers, motivated but directionless.* New Haven, CT: Yale University Press.

Seftor, N., & Turner, S. (2002). Back to school: Federal student aid policy and adult college enrollment. *Journal of Human Resources, 37*, 336–352.

Shults, C. (2000). *Institutional policies and practices in remedial education: A national study of community college.* Washington, DC: American Association of Community Colleges.

State Higher Education Executive Officers. (1998). *Statewide college admissions, student preparation, and remediation policies and programs.* Denver, CO: Author.

Swail, W. S. (2000). Preparing America's disadvantaged for college: Programs that increase college opportunity. *New Directions for Institutional Research, 107*, 85–101.

Terenzini, P., Cabrera, A. F., & Bernal, E. (2001). *Swimming against the tide: The poor in American higher education.* New York: College Board.

Tinto, V. (1993). *Leaving college: rethinking the causes and cures of student attribution* (2nd ed.). Chicago: University of Chicago Press.

Trent, W. T., Orr, M. T., Ranis, S. H., & Holdaway, J. (2007). Transitions to college: Lessons from the disciplines. *Teachers College Record, 109*, 2207–2221.

U.S. Bureau of Census (2005). *Census Bureau projects tripling of Hispanic and Asian populations in 50 years; non-Hispanic Whites may drop to half of total population.* Retrieved June 5, 2007, from http://www.census.gov/Press-Release/www/releases/archives/population/001720.html

Venezia, A., Kirst, M., & Antonio, A. L. (2003). *Betraying the college dream: How disconnected k-12 and postsecondary education systems undermine student aspirations.* Stanford, CA: The Bridge Project.

Wetzel, J., O'Toole, D., & Peterson, S. (1998). An analysis of student enrollment demand. *Economics of Education Review, 17*, 47–54.

72

Permeability and Transparency in the High School-College Transition[1]

Jennifer L. Stephan and James E. Rosenbaum
Northwestern University

Introduction

Dramatic changes have taken place in the who, where, and how of higher education. No longer dominated by traditional undergraduates attending traditional colleges, there is great variety in the types of students who attend college, the institutions they attend, and their attendance patterns. While students' pathways through higher education have become increasingly varied, not all pathways lead to degree attainment with equal probability, even for similar students, and some research suggests that students may be unaware of the implications of the pathways they choose. This chapter proposes a conceptual framework for thinking about how higher education policies shape students' pathways through higher education. We present evidence about the operation of American higher education in terms of this framework and then use the framework to consider three policy areas: high school counseling policies, community college policies including open-admissions, and financial aid policies. We argue that while the current policies have increased accessibility and choice in higher education, they also obscure the pathway to completion.

In analyzing the school-to-work transition, Hamilton (1994) characterizes the relationship between the education system and labor-market along two dimensions: permeability, which refers to how easy it is to move between the education system and labor market, and transparency, which refers to how clearly individuals can see the implications of their early educational decisions on later occupational outcomes. Generalizing these concepts, we develop a framework to characterize higher education systems and ask: To what extent is the current U.S. higher education system permeable? To what extent is it transparent? How does the U.S. system's current location on this typology compare to its historical location? And, how can we better understand the effects of higher education policies using a permeability-transparency framework? Reviewing recent studies, we find that the U.S. higher education system

has become increasingly permeable but is characterized by low transparency. We then examine how high school counseling, community college, and financial aid policies simultaneously contribute to an increase in permeability and a decrease in transparency.

Relatively new college options which offer open admissions, low cost, proximal locations, and flexible schedules increase the permeability of the higher education system. This is an important accomplishment as it paves the way for increased opportunity for all students. However, low levels of transparency impair students' ability to navigate the increasingly complex higher education system and may disproportionately affect students with the fewest social and economic resources. This calls into question whether the opportunities provided by a more permeable system are real.

In the following section, we review Hamilton's concepts of permeability and transparency, and building on those concepts, we introduce a framework to characterize higher education systems. Next, using descriptive statistics and previous research, we review evidence about the operation of the U.S. system with respect to permeability and transparency and discuss historical changes. Finally, we consider the effects of three policies on opportunity using the developed framework.

Theoretical Background

Permeability and Transparency To characterize the link between the education system and labor market, Hamilton (1994) introduces the ideas of permeability and transparency. He defines permeability as "the ease of movement from one point in the education-labor market system to another" (Hamilton, 1994, p. 268), and transparency as "how well youth can see through the educational system and labor market and plot a course from where they are in the present to a distant future goal" (Hamilton, 1994, p. 268). Formal credentials impact permeability and transparency in opposite directions: while they make it easier to see how to obtain a particular job, they place hurdles in the way of actually obtaining one. Hamilton compares education-labor market systems in different nations to illustrate his model. Because the middle tier of the U.S. occupational hierarchy has few licensing requirements, Hamilton finds that this system is highly permeable but not transparent. The lack of occupational licensing requirements means that workers can easily switch employers and types of jobs, but at the same time, the lack of requirements obscures the pathway to a particular job. In contrast, in Germany, occupational and trade associations, collaborating with employers, stipulate highly specific skill requirements for licensing, which require apprenticeship training. The specificity of job requirements in Germany makes the system transparent, but the organization of students into different highly specialized and stratified apprenticeship tracks impairs permeability (Hamilton, 1994). Hamilton's model provides a way to conceptualize characteristics of the education-labor market link and the relationship between these characteristics.

Proposed Framework The constructs of permeability and transparency can be extended to describe the higher education system more generally (Arnett, 2004). Doing so provides insight into how educational policies shape the pathways of students into and through higher education. Similarly to Hamilton, we define *permeability* as how easy it is to move into and within the higher education system, and *transparency* as how easy it is to see a path towards educational attainment. Conceptually, researchers have considered two levels of educational attainment, enrollment and completion; we separate transparency into how it relates to these two attainments. We define *enrollment transparency* as how easy it is to see a path into college, and *completion transparency* as how easy it is to see a path from enrollment to completion. Most students enter higher education seeking a degree, and this analysis is primarily concerned with them. Over 80% of high school seniors in 1992 planned to get an associate's degree or higher (authors' calculation using NELS), and, in a national sample of all beginning postsecondary students (of all ages), 75% enter expecting to complete an associate's degree or higher (authors' calculation using BPS 96/01). We argue that policies, institutional structures, and socio-cultural expectations combine to locate a higher education system on a plane defined by permeability and transparency. For simplicity, higher education systems may be modeled as low or high on each dimension, as depicted in Figure 72.1.

Highly permeable higher education systems not only open college doors to a more diverse set of students (greater inter-individual opportunity), but they also allow greater opportunity for individuals to attend college in diverse ways (greater intra-individual opportunity), such as simultaneously taking college courses while working, or piecing together a degree from multiple postsecondary institutions. Increased inter- and intra-individual opportunity could help

	Permeability	
	High	Low
High (Transparency)	Informed Choice	Known Limits
Low (Transparency)	Uninformed Choice	Unknown Limits

Figure 72.1 Permeability-transparency framework.

equalize the social distribution of educational attainment and promote individual well-being.

However, transparency also affects the distribution of educational attainment and individuals' well-being. Highly permeable systems that are also highly transparent assure that students understand the pathways leading into college and then towards a degree. A highly permeable system provides students a variety of types and selectivity of postsecondary institutions, but high enrollment transparency is needed to provide guidance to students and their families for selecting an option that fits with their aspirations, preparation, and preferences. A system high on permeability and completion transparency would allow students to pursue multiple pathways to completion but at the same time make clear the specific steps necessary and the implications of pursuing alternative attendance patterns for completion. Based on their individual circumstances, students can then decide which path is best for them. Systems with high permeability and high transparency provide students the opportunity for educational attainment as well as adequate information on how to enroll and attain a degree. Thus, we label the high permeability/high transparency quadrant in Figure 72.1 *Informed Choice.*

On the other hand, a system with high permeability and low enrollment transparency is characterized by a variety of colleges and ways to enroll, but a poor student understanding of which institutions fit their needs or the steps required to enroll. A system with high permeability and low completion transparency allows students to take several paths through college without providing clear information about which paths are more likely to lead to degree completion. For example, a system high on permeability but low on completion transparency would give students the option of delayed college entry, but would not make it clear that delay can lead to lower degree attainment rates or persistence (Bozick & DeLuca, 2005; Horn, Cataldi, & Sikora, 2005; Kempner & Kinnick, 1990). While delayed entry is the only way some students can attend, it is optional for others (particularly if they take advantage of underutilized federal and state financial aid entitlements). We label the high permeability and low transparency quadrant in Figure

72.1 as *Uninformed Choice*. The opportunity provided by permeability may be diminished if students do not realize the negative impact of delayed entry, and students who lack social, cultural, or economic capital may be the least likely to have such knowledge. Permeability is related to, but not equivalent to, opportunity. Transparency also matters.

Higher education systems with low permeability limit access to college and the ways students attend college. Systems with high transparency and low permeability provide a clear pathway into college and then to degree completion, but only for particular students who attend college in a particular way. For example, a higher education system that caters only to recent high school graduates from middle-class families who seek to attend full-time at a 4-year college lacks permeability, but may have high enrollment and completion transparency. The limited variety of institutions and ways of attendance may make the steps to both enrollment and completion easier for students to see. In such a system, students can judge for themselves whether they can or want to fit this mold. We label the low permeability and high transparency quadrant in Figure 72.1 as *Known Limits*. Finally, a higher education system with low transparency and low permeability provides few opportunities and little direction about how to access them, and we label this quadrant in Figure 72.1 as *Unknown Limits*.

Location of the U.S. System in the Framework

Permeability—Ease of Movement Into and Within Higher Education Shifts in economic, social, and policy factors have resulted in increased diversity in the types of students attending college, their attendance patterns, and the institutions they attend, all of which attest to the increasing permeability of the higher education system. Traditional

undergraduates, defined as financially dependent students who enter college directly after attaining a high school diploma, who attend full-time, and work less than full-time, comprised just 27% of all undergraduates in 1999–2000 (Choy, 2002). Table 72.1 shows significant changes in the characteristics of college students and their attendance patterns between the 1970s[2] and 2000.

The proportion of minorities[3] increased from 15% to 28% of total fall college enrollments between 1976 and 2000 (National Center for Education Statistics [NCES], 2005, table 205). Among recent high school graduates, enrollments increased 90% for low-income students between 1972 and 2000, compared to an increase of 21% for high-income students (NCES, 2006, table 29-1). In addition, a substantial proportion of undergraduates are older. Students 25 or older made up 28% of total fall enrollments in 1970 compared to 39% in 2000, and students 35 or older increased from 10% to 18% of enrollments in the same period (NCES, 2005, table 172). Greater access to college as well as greater economic and social pressure for higher education has resulted in a shift towards a more diverse student body. This increased diversity, however, may increase the importance of transparency, since upwardly mobile students cannot rely on parents to provide college information that they need.

Permeability has also increased in terms of *how* students attend college. Part-time enrollment, discontinuous attendance, delayed entry, and college mobility have become major ways of accessing college. The incidences of part-time enrollment and employment during college have both increased significantly. Between 1970 and 2000, part-time enrollments increased from 32% to 41% of total fall enrollments. While some of the increase is due to greater enrollment among older students, part-time enrollments

TABLE 72.1
Postsecondary Student Characteristics and Attendance Patterns, 1970–2000

Fall enrollments by student characteristics	1970	2000	%Δ
	(1)	(2)	(3)
% Black, Hispanic, Asian/Pacific Islander, American Indian/Alaskan Native	14.5[a]	28.2	94.5
% Low-income[e]	26.1[b]	49.7	90.4
% High-income[e]	63.8	76.9	20.5
% Age 25 or older	27.8	39.0	40.3
% Age 56 or older	9.6	18.0	87.5
Fall enrollments by student attendance patterns			
% Part-time	32.2	41.1	27.6
% Part-time for students age 18–24	16.9	24.0	42.0
% Working while attending college full-time[e]	27.8	40.8	46.8
% Working while attending college part-time[e]	67.1	77.6	15.6
% Attending more than one institution (among those beginning at a 4-yr college)	38.8[c]	50.1[d]	29.1

Sources: Digest of Education Statistics 1971 (Table 150), 2002 (Table 383), and 2005 (Tables 172 and 205); Condition of Education Statistics 2006 (Table 29-1); and Adelman, 1999 (Table 19).

[a] Percentage in column (1) based on 1976 data.

[b] Percentage in column (1) based on 1972 data.

[c] Percentage in colum (1) based on data from the National Longitudinal Study of the High School Class of 1972.

[d] Percentage in colum (2) based on data from the Beginning Postsecondary Study of the 1989/1990 cohort limited to students age 17–23.

[e] Among recent high school completers.

have increased even for students of traditional age, from 17% to 24% (NCES, 2005, table 172). Among recent high school graduates, the percent of full-time students who were employed increased from 28% to 41% between 1970 and 2000; the percent of part-time students who work increased less, from 67% to 78% (NCES, 1971, table 150; NCES, 2002, table 383). In addition, a significant portion of students attend discontinuously. Goldrick-Rab (2006) estimates that 25% to 30% of undergraduates temporarily dropout.

Delayed entry has also become common. Inspiring stories are told of students getting great benefits from delaying college entry (Harder, 2006). In their advertising, many colleges, both 2- and 4-year, encourage students to enroll at any time, implying no costs to delayed-entry. Students have gotten the message. Among students first-entering postsecondary education in 1995–96, about one-third of students had delayed their enrollment (Horn et al., 2005). College mobility has also become more common. For students who began at a 4-year college, 39% of the 1972 high school graduation cohort attended more than one institution. This rate increased to 50% for students of traditional age entering college during 1989–1990 (Adelman, 1999, table 19).

While a significant portion of students engage in nontraditional patterns of enrollment, students from lower socioeconomic status (SES) backgrounds or those with lower academic achievement tend to do so at higher rates. This is true for part-time (Hearn, 1992; Stratton, O'Toole, & Wetzel, 2004), discontinuous, (Goldrick-Rab, 2006), and delayed enrollment (Bozick & DeLuca, 2005; Hearn, 1992). Students with lower SES work more hours (Walpole, 2003), and those with lower academic achievement are more likely to engage in multiple institution attendance (Goldrick-Rab, 2006; McCormick, 2003; Peter & Cataldi, 2005). Instead of following a direct path from high school to full-time, continuous enrollment at a single institution, today a significant portion of college students delay college, enroll in multiple institutions, attend discontinuously or part-time, and combine work with college attendance.

Variation in the types of colleges attended has also increased. Enrollments at 2-year and for-profit colleges have increased in particular. Between 1970 and 2000, total fall enrollment increased 50% for 4-year colleges compared to 156% for 2-year colleges. Across the nearly 40-year period, 1965 to 2004, the growth rates are even more divergent: 126% for 4-year colleges compared to 458% at 2-year colleges (NCES, 2005, table 171). At for-profit degree-granting institutions, enrollment increased 189% between 1996 and 2004 (NCES, 2005, table 171). Today, 42% of undergraduates are enrolled in public 2-year colleges (commonly called community colleges), 31% in public 4-year colleges, 14% in private not-for-profit 4-year colleges, and 5% in for-profit institutions (Horn, Peter, & Rooney, 2002).

Although community colleges are not a new type of college, they account for a significantly greater share of enrollments than 30 years ago, and they have changed in their mission and focus. Community colleges evolved as middle-class institutions serving as feeder schools into traditional 4-year colleges, but in recent decades, they have begun to emphasize occupational programs (Brint & Karabel, 1989; Dougherty, 1994; Grubb, 1996), which are not necessarily meant to lead to transfer. Community colleges today serve many purposes, including adult education, job training, remedial education, and vocational education. With over 1,000 institutions, community colleges offer students convenient locations as well as low tuition; the median community college student pays just $1,803 in tuition and required fees (NCES, 2005, table 314 and table 243). In addition, community colleges provide students flexible schedules, serve significantly more part-time students than other colleges (Bailey, Badway, & Gumport, 2001), and offer a variety of courses that allow students to explore potential career interests. The open admissions policies of community colleges attract students from academically and socio-economically disadvantaged backgrounds, who may not otherwise have attended college. Representing the largest share of 2-year enrollments, community colleges are characterized by diversity and access.

New institutional forms, however, have been attracting both attention and enrollments. For-profit institutions account for a small but rapidly growing share of enrollments. Two-thirds of students enrolled in a degree granting for-profit college attend a 4-year college, while the remaining one-third attend a 2-year college (NCES, 2005, table 174). The vast majority of students enrolled at (degree granting) private 2-year colleges are enrolled in for-profit institutions—in 2003, 85% of private 2-year college enrollments were at for-profit colleges (NCES, 2005, table 174). The mission and structure of for-profit colleges differs from that of more traditional institutions. Compared to community colleges, for-profits have a narrower mission, one focused on a limited number of primarily vocational program offerings (Bailey et al., 2001), and students primarily attend full-time (Bailey et al., 2001), generally as a result of the program structure (Deil-Amen & Rosenbaum, 2003). In a case study of one for-profit institution and three community colleges, Bailey et al. (2001) find that the for-profit institution has more centralized curriculum development, more applied and structured programs, and more developed student services compared to the community colleges. In a study of seven community colleges and seven high-quality private 2-year occupational colleges, Deil-Amen and Rosenbaum (2003) find that the private occupational colleges provided more structured programs, more college-initiated academic guidance, significantly greater access to counselors, and better access to financial aid. The sticker price at for-profits is relatively high, but so is financial aid; net tuition is about $4,100 higher at 2-year for-profits compared to community colleges, and about $5,400 higher at 4-year for-profits compared to public 4-year colleges (Bailey et al., 2001). For-profit colleges provide an interesting alternative model of how colleges, especially 2-year colleges, might operate.

The classic three-box model divides the life-course into schooling, work, and retirement. Increasingly, this model provides a poor description of individuals' lives (Settersten,

2005) as the patterns in who, where, and how students attend college testify. Compared to today's higher education system, the system 30 years ago was characterized by low permeability as evidenced by the high proportion of traditional college students attending traditional colleges in traditional ways. Since then, the educational system has become increasingly permeable, blurring the lines between schooling and work and redefining what counts as a college education. This suggests increased opportunity for individuals of all ages and backgrounds. Yet the extent to which this increased permeability represents real opportunity depends importantly on the transparency of the system.

Enrollment Transparency: How Easy It Is to See a Path Into College The admissions and sorting mechanisms of higher education have varied in their level of transparency over the 20th century. Between the 1920s and 1940s, the ideal college candidate was a man of "character," largely defined according to social background (Karabel, 2005; Lemann, 1999). College admissions were closely linked to where a student attended secondary school, with students from college-prep schools finding relatively easy access into college (Lemann, 1999; Powell, 1996). Unsurprisingly, this process resulted in a student body largely homogeneous with respect to race, religion, and socioeconomic status. The SAT, first administered in 1926 and widely adopted by the late 1950s, was conceived as a way to identify students, regardless of background, who had the academic aptitude for college success (Lemann, 1999). At the time, the SAT was one of just a few criteria for determining admissions (Lemann, 1999). A system of admissions based on social standing and one based on the SAT differed in their definition of merit, but both restricted admissions to an elite group of students (low permeability) and at the same time made admissions criteria clear (high transparency).

Over the past four decades, the admissions process has been characterized by increasing variance. During the 1960s, admissions departments, at least at Princeton, Harvard, and Yale, began adding new criteria and weighing them more heavily in the selection process (Karabel, 2005). Today, selective colleges, particularly highly selective ones that devote significant resources to processing applications, use multiple criteria, ones not well-specified, for selecting students. While the SAT continues to play an important role, scoring highly is not sufficient for admission to highly selective schools. Meanwhile, at 2-year colleges, open-admissions policies make the SAT unnecessary. In addition to the expansion of admissions criteria at selective colleges, the level at which students must achieve those criteria may have been increasing (Kirst & Venezia, 2004) as the competition for available places increases. Admissions criteria range from none at some 2-year colleges to expansive, unspecified, and dynamic criteria at highly selective colleges. Such changes have contributed to a decline in enrollment transparency. In recent years, there has been much public criticism of the complexity and arbitrariness of the college admissions process (Washor & Mojkowski, 2007).

The most direct consequence of the system's poor enrollment transparency is confusion or misunderstanding among students and their families. Research of students' and families' perceptions and reactions to the college process is limited. However, Kirst and Venezia (2004), in studies of six states, find that students and their parents are confused by admissions requirements regarding high school coursework, details of college placement exams, and paying for college. In case studies, McDonough (1994) finds that students from upper-middle-class families have difficulty negotiating the college selection and application process. Specifically, families at upper-middle-class schools sought supplemental help from private counselors, likely expending significant time and large financial payments to do so. Parents explained that their actions were necessary because they were confused about available choices; they needed help to organize necessary steps; and, they felt they had inadequate information to help their children navigate the process. It is noteworthy that many of these upper-middle-class parents were likely to be college educated. So, if the enrollment process is difficult for middle-class parents to navigate, what must this mean for first-generation students?

In addition to the above case studies, the vast number of programs and products to assist students in the enrollment process provides some indirect evidence for the widespread perception of problems with enrollment transparency. In 2007, for example, the Lumina Foundation for Education launched a public service campaign, KnowHow2GO, which targets low-income and first generation college students. The campaign assumes that students know why they should go to college but lack information on the steps necessary for enrollment. The plethora of guide books, software, Web sites, test-prep companies, private college counselors, and college-prep camps addressing the college admissions process may further testify to low transparency and a perception that students and their families are struggling to understand the process. Although limited, some evidence suggests that students who seek admission to any college as well as those seeking admission to the "right" college have difficulty seeing the path to enrollment. Whether these multiple resources actually increase transparency or simply add to the confusion is not clear.

Completion Transparency—How Easy It Is to See a Path from Enrollment to Completion The structure and processes of the higher education system affect how well students see both the path to enrollment as well as the path to degree completion. Poor completion transparency is most clearly indicated by students who do not understand that their choices about the where, when. and how of college affect their time to degree completion or chances of completing a degree. As noted, a significant portion of college enrollments, and much of the growth in enrollments, has occurred at community colleges. However, research reviewed below shows significant problems with transparency in these types of institutions. We know of very little research that considers these issues at 4-year colleges, but some students, particularly those at less selective 4-year colleges, may have similar experiences. As discussed below, research also indicates that non-traditional patterns of attendance can reduce completion rates. There is no indication, however, that students receive information about the association between non-traditional attendance patterns and reduced completion chances and some indication that students sometimes choose such attendance patterns without realizing their implications. The fact that students pursuing non-traditional attendance patterns are largely concentrated in community colleges potentially compounds the completion transparency problems associated with these two factors. Although permeability has increased significantly, the implications of new options for degree completion may be hard to see.

Poor Completion Transparency at 2-Year Colleges Certain aspects of 2-year colleges make it difficult for students to see what courses they need to fulfill their degree plans. Community colleges typically offer multiple levels of associate's degrees with different requirements. An associate's of applied sciences (AAS) degree requires lower-level courses than an associate's of sciences (AS) degree, and an associate's of general studies (AGS) has even lower requirements. Since employers often do not understand the distinctions among these degrees, students with achievement deficiencies could get employment benefits in less time by choosing an AAS or AGS, but it is hard to discern these options and hard to figure out which courses are required for each (Rosenbaum, Deil-Amen, & Person, 2006). Two-year colleges are often unclear about which courses count for transfer to 4-year colleges (Dougherty, 1994), although some colleges have developed explicit articulation agreements with specific 4-year colleges (Rosenbaum et al., 2006). Department heads report that school-wide counselors are often unfamiliar with specific department requirements (Deil-Amen & Rosenbaum, 2003), and students report ambiguity in course catalogs as well as poor advice from counselors regarding course requirements (Rosenbaum et al., 2006). Two-year colleges appear to be characterized by a low-level of transparency, at least with respect to course selection, a key step towards degree completion.

Low levels of transparency help explain students' reports of information problems regarding degree requirements. In a local sample of 2-year college students, Person, Rosenbaum, and Deil-Amen (2006) report that students have difficulty figuring out which courses count for their majors or for transfer credit to 4-year colleges: 35% of community college students report that they are not certain which courses they need for their degree plans, and 46% report that they have taken courses that do not apply towards their degree. In interviews, complaints about wasted time and tuition were common among disadvantaged students for whom these resources were scarce. Students' confusion about degree requirements may help explain why, in the NELS national survey, while 8% of 1992 high school seniors attained an associate's degree by 2000, another 10%

had enough credits for an associate's degree (60 or more credits) but did not have any degree (Adelman, 2004, table 3.1; Rosenbaum et al., 2006). At least at 2-year colleges, students appear to have significant information problems about the steps required to complete a degree, and they are making course choices which they later realize do not lead to their degree goal.

Remedial courses are another area where poor transparency explains some of students' problems in seeing the steps to degree completion. Remedial courses are a major component of colleges, particularly community colleges. For the high school senior cohort of 1992, 61% of students first entering community colleges and 25% of those first entering 4-year colleges took at least one remedial class (Adelman, 2004, table 7.1). However, remedial placements are difficult to anticipate and to understand. The placement test is one of the first tasks when students arrive at college (particularly for unselective colleges), yet colleges and high school guidance counselors rarely mention placement tests; some students are unaware of placement exams, and many do not know specifics about the tests (e.g., tested subjects or test formats; Kirst & Venezia, 2004; Rosenbaum, 2001). Moreover, even if students knew details about the exams, they would have no basis for predicting their performance on such exams since very few high schools give exams aligned with college placement tests (Kirst & Venezia 2004).

Seeking to avoid stigmatizing or discouraging students, community colleges sometimes are not clear about the implications of remedial courses and the fact that they do not confer college credits (Deil-Amen & Rosenbaum, 2002). As a result, remedial courses are poorly understood even by students taking them (Person et al., 2006). In a local sample of 2-year college students, analyses comparing college catalogs with students' perceptions find that only 27% of students in remedial courses realized that these courses do not count towards their degree (Rosenbaum et al., 2006). Analyses of the BPS national survey indicate that 95% of first-year students who are taking three or more remedial courses planned to complete a college degree, but less than a third had attained a degree or remained in college 6 years after entry (Deil-Amen & Rosenbaum, 2002).

Colleges are also unclear about timetables for attaining degrees. In a local sample of community colleges, a so-called "2-year associate's degree" takes an average of over 3 years (Rosenbaum et al., 2006). In a national survey (NELS), almost half of students take more than 3 years to complete this degree (Goble et al., 2007). The obstacles to quicker completion include those noted above (i.e., noncredit remedial courses, students' mistaken choices of courses that do not count towards their degree, and students' ignorance of alternative associate's degrees with lower-level requirements). In addition, some required courses are not offered in the order and at the times that students need them. This lack of completion transparency about timetables has implications for student perceptions. Students enter these colleges expecting to complete a "2-year associate's degree" in 2 years, but, even in the second-year, some students do not realize that it will take longer than 2 years to complete the degree (Rosenbaum et al. 2006).

Person et al. (2006) find that among a local sample of 2-year college students, those who are racial minorities, younger, have lower high school grades, and whose parents have low education or income were relatively more likely to report information problems. These results suggest that some students cannot see the steps necessary for degree attainment and that the students who struggle with information problems the most may be those that lack other social and economic capital.

Poor completion transparency about attendance patterns may also be a problem. As noted, increased permeability allows students to attend college in new ways (delaying entry, stopping-out, part-time enrollment, and attending multiple institutions), and these patterns have become extremely common, especially for students from disadvantaged backgrounds. However, in offering these options, society may not be clear about their implications. Media reports give the impression that non-traditional attendance patterns have no particular consequences. News magazines provide fascinating stories of affluent high school seniors delaying entry to highly selective colleges to engage in exotic activities and travels (known as taking a "gap year"). The prevalent catchphrase "lifelong learning" conjures images of more mature adults seeking out personal enrichment, but the phrase also suggests that delayed or discontinuous enrollment has no implications for degree completion. In addition, colleges make efforts not to discourage students who have pursued these pathways, which may also give the impression that these patterns have no negative implications. The enormous increase in students pursuing these pathways suggests that students may not see any disadvantages to these pathways.

Although media accounts give the impression that alternative attendance pathways are costless alternatives, research indicates that these alternative pathways are associated with reduced likelihood of degree completion. Delayed enrollment appears to lower the odds of degree attainment (Bozick & DeLuca, 2005; Horn et al., 2005; Kempner & Kinnick, 1990). Bozick and DeLuca (2005) estimate that postponing postsecondary enrollment by 1 year decreases the odds of bachelor's degree attainment by 64%; furthermore, delay is more harmful for students with the lowest SES and those with less academic preparation. Length of delay, however, may have non-linear effects. Horn et al. (2005) find that short delays (< 1 year) correspond to lower persistence, but longer delays do not. Although analyses have not ruled out influences from unmeasured variables, the evidence suggests that delayed entry may reduce the chances of degree completion. While delayed entry offers options to those who have no alternatives, the odds of graduating appear to improve if students avoid delayed entry.

College mobility seems to have a similar negative impact. For 4-year college students in general, multiple-institution enrollment is associated with lower persistence and bachelor's degree attainment rates and increased time to degree completion (Adelman, 2006; Peter & Cataldi, 2005), while discontinuous enrollment decreases the probability of bachelor's degree attainment (Adelman, 2006). Adelman (2006) finds that multiple-institution attendance decreases the probability of bachelor's degree attainment by 15% for 1992 seniors followed for 8 years after graduation, while continuous enrollment increases the probability of attainment by 43%. For students who began at community colleges, attending more than two institutions is associated with decreased bachelor's degree attainment rates and increased time to bachelor's degree completion (Peter & Cataldi, 2005). However, the details of the patterns also matter. For students beginning at 4-year institutions, transferring institutions or enrolling in a community college are associated with lower 6-year persistence rates while co-enrollment increases persistence (Peter & Cataldi, 2005).

Overall, research suggests that work or part-time enrollment negatively affect persistence, degree completion, and time to degree (Ehrenberg & Sherman, 1987; Gleason, 1993; Jacobs & King, 2002; O'Toole, Stratton, & Wetzel, 2003; Pascarella & Terenzini, 2005). However, research distinguishes between on- and off-campus work finding that off-campus work negatively affects persistence or attainment (Anderson, 1981; Ehrenberg & Sherman, 1987), while on-campus work does not appear to harm and may benefit students (Anderson, 1981; DesJardins, Ahlburg, & McCall, 2002; Ehrenberg & Sherman, 1987). Adelman (2006) finds that ever being enrolled part-time decreases the probability of bachelor's degree completion by 25% for 4-year college students in a nationally representative sample.

Students follow alternative pathways through college for a variety of reasons. Some students cannot attend college any other way. However, other students have the option of choosing traditional or alternative pathways, and the lack of completion transparency makes it difficult for them to make informed choices. Interestingly, some college counselors report that they can discourage part-time studies by strong warnings about negative impacts (Rosenbaum et al. 2006). Unfortunately, only a few counselors give such warnings, possibly because counselors may be unaware of the implications of part-time studies. Counselors generally cannot tell whether students who do not complete degrees at their college might do so at other colleges since colleges rarely collect follow-up information on their students. The only information on this question comes from studies like those we have cited, which rely on longitudinal surveys that follow students overtime (like NELS and BPS), and they indicate poor completion rates. Unfortunately, colleges rarely collect comparable follow-up information on their students. The above findings indicate the need for transparency so that students can make informed choices.

The problem of poorly informed choices leading to reduced opportunity is most clearly seen in the case of high school students. Because of poor transparency regarding remedial courses and their implications for degree completion, many high school students with college plans believe that high school is irrelevant for their future and that there is no penalty for low effort in high school. While open admissions policies make it possible to attend college despite low academic achievement, students may plan college degrees which they have little chance of attaining. Of the 1982 high school graduation cohort, 52% of seniors with low grades planned to get a college degree, but less than 20% of these students actually attained any degree over the next 10 years (Rosenbaum, 2001). Indeed, poor completion transparency seems to prevent some students from taking the increased efforts that would advance their degree goals. Two separate studies found that roughly 40% of college-bound students report that they can obtain their educational plans even if they do poorly in high school (Steinberg, 1996; Rosenbaum, 2001), and, not surprisingly, this attitude is associated with low efforts in school. Probably unaware of placement tests, noncredit remedial courses, or the connection between high school achievement and later educational attainment, these students fail to take advantage of their high school experience in a way that would promote their college degree goals.

More research is needed to better establish the level of transparency in American higher education, especially with respect to the range of 4-year colleges. Research is also needed to identify how often students choose low probability options without realizing their implications, in effect sacrificing a better opportunity because of poor transparency. The available research suggests a low level of enrollment and completion transparency. Institutions offer many different options, but they do not specify the implications of the various options. Students do not appear to have clarity about how to effectively navigate the higher education system to degree attainment or about the implications of their earlier actions for later outcomes. The lack of transparency in the system gives advantages to students with more social, economic, and cultural capital, who can call on additional resources for assistance. But, if that is the case, then high levels of permeability are not sufficient to provide opportunity for those without such resources. Instead, it is the intersection of permeability and transparency that matters; real opportunity requires high levels of both.

Assessing Educational Policies within a Permeability-Transparency Framework

The permeability-transparency framework helps us understand how policy reforms may affect the higher education system. It allows us to decompose educational policies into their effects on opening new pathways and their effects on increasing transparency regarding the pathways to enrollment and completion. Such a decomposition helps us to understand the processes encouraging or blocking opportunity, how existing policies and practices influence those processes, and perhaps how policies and practices can be reformed. The following sections use the permeability-transparency framework to consider the effects of three specific policies on higher education: community college policies, high school guidance counseling policies, and financial aid policies.

High School Counseling Policies In the 1960s and 1970s, high school counselors functioned as gatekeepers whose advice affected, and sometimes limited, students' postsecondary pathways (Cicourel & Kitsuse, 1963; Rosenbaum, 1976). However, by the 1990s, nearly all high school seniors were planning to attend college (Schneider & Stevenson, 1999), and, as noted, open admissions and low costs at community colleges erased most barriers to access. Without much public discussion, high schools adopted a college-for-all norm, which may have changed guidance counselors' behaviors. In a qualitative study of 27 counselors in 8 large high schools, Rosenbaum (2001) finds that counselors, citing open-admissions policies at community colleges, have abandoned the gatekeeper role, and they avoid discouraging students' plans, no matter how unrealistic. Other research supports this observation. Comparing national surveys of students in two successive decades, research finds that while 32% of seniors said their counselors urged them to go to college in 1982, in 1992 more than twice as many seniors reported such counselor encouragement (66%). Even among students in the bottom half academically, 57% said their counselors recommended college in 1992 (Gray, 1996). Rather than limiting students' choices and redirecting their pathways, counselors encourage all students to attend college. The changing role of counselors has increased permeability. Counselors no longer place roadblocks on the path to college.

But, do counselors provide enough guidance to students who need help with the process of college enrollment? Prior research finds that with enough involvement, counselors can play an important role in students' college choice and application process (Freeman, 1997; King, 1996; McDonough, 1997; Plank & Jordan, 2001). At the same time, however, high school counseling policies sometimes contribute to low levels of transparency with respect to enrollment. For instance, some current policies limit access to college counseling. First, there are few counselors to meet the needs of high school students. In 2002, the average ratio of students to counselors was 284:1 for public high schools nationally and more than 300:1 for large or urban schools, or those schools serving more than 20% minorities (Parsad, Farris, & Hudson, & Alexander, 2003). Further, there are significant differences in the student-to-counselor ratio by state, with some exceeding 700:1 (McDonough, 2005). Second, even when counselors are present, they are expected to take on many other tasks including administrative, discipline, and testing responsibilities (Kirst & Venezia 2004; McDonough, 2005). A majority (57%) of public high schools report that their guidance staff spends less than 20% of their time on postsecondary admissions and selections (Parsad et al, 2003). McDonough (2005) estimates that counselors, on average, spend 38 minutes per year on each student for college counseling.

Moreover, there appears to be inequity in access to counselors across schools (Lee & Ekstrom, 1987; McDonough, 1997). In a case-study of four California high schools, McDonough (1997) finds that at an affluent private school, students received 10 to 15 hours of individualized attention, compared to just 45 minutes in a public school in the same upper-middle-class neighborhood and no individualized attention at a school in a working-class neighborhood. In a highly transparent system, all students would see the steps in the application process clearly and have the necessary information and guidance to make an appropriate choice given their personal needs and aspirations. Policies regarding high school counseling can limit transparency of enrollment by not providing resources that could assist students in these tasks. Reforms that provide more counseling resources or more efficient ways of reaching high school students may increase the transparency of the system.

Policies regarding counselor training also need to be reconsidered. Although guidance counselors are the staff responsible for providing information about college, they receive little formal training about the college choice process. While some states require guidance counselors to have certain courses, courses in college counseling are not always required (Rosenbaum, 2006). Further, the formal training that counselors do receive is based on psychology, not sociology or economics. An examination of counseling textbooks suggests that while counselors are trained to help students understand their own interests and aptitudes, they do not receive training on the array of college options, their requirements, or their payoffs. While some counselors may seek out information from counselor associations or special courses on college counseling, many must rely on their own limited experiences, which may not include highly selective colleges or community colleges. Policies that rely on commonsense or counselors' own experience, however, preserve the status quo; they reproduce traditional biases and exclude new options.

Community College Policies Community college policies increase the permeability of the higher education system by increasing the diversity of students who attend college and the ways in which they attend. The low cost and open admissions policies enable socioeconomically and academically disadvantaged students who may otherwise not have enrolled in college to do so. Community colleges also try to accommodate a variety of student aspirations. In their missions, community colleges support vocational training, transfer to 4-year colleges, and non-degree enrollment (Cohen & Brawer, 2003; Cross & Fideler, 1989). Further, community colleges allow students to engage in a variety of non-traditional enrollment patterns. For example, community colleges schedule classes during evenings and weekends and operate satellite campuses for convenience, all of which allow students to combine school with other commitments (Person et al., 2006). Both with respect to diversity in students and also flexibility in attendance patterns, the policies of community colleges contribute significantly to the high permeability of American higher education. In addition to high permeability, community colleges have high enrollment transparency. Nearly everyone qualifies for admission, and the application process (though not

necessarily the financial aid process, as discussed later) is straightforward.

At the same time, however, even as they emphasize permeability and have high enrollment transparency, community college policies provide low levels of completion transparency. Community colleges try to address students' information needs by providing more information (Person et al., 2006). Information dissemination regarding financial aid and requirements is largely decentralized, however, placing the burden for gathering information on the student. In addition, the information about the range of choices and their implications is not always easy to interpret, and students are often left to tackle this on their own as well (Deil-Amen & Rosenbaum, 2003). Complicating this situation, counseling at community colleges is peripheral: there are relatively few counselors and the counseling that does occur must be initiated by students (Deil-Amen & Rosenbaum, 2003; Person et al., 2006). In the process of offering diversity and flexibility, and perhaps because of the ways they do so, community colleges appear to contribute significantly to the low levels of transparency in the higher education system.

"Cooling out" could be considered one institutional response to a system characterized by high permeability and low completion transparency. In a study of a single community college, Burton Clark (1960) described how counselors get students to lower their plans to fit their low achievement. Although he did not describe it this way, such cooling out is, in effect, required because high permeability gives students access to community colleges, but low transparency does not warn them that they may have trouble succeeding. Low transparency gives counselors more leverage to change students' plans and contributes to individuals' susceptibility to having their plans adjusted. While some have rightly criticized cooling out for being biased against minorities and low SES students (Karabel, 1972), some community college counselors have tried to avoid cooling out entirely, which allows students to continue pursuing goals without realizing their costs, timetables, and low chances of attainment (Rosenbaum et al., 2006). A more helpful strategy would be to provide advice that would increase the transparency of completion.

Alternative policies might increase the level of transparency of completion. Research by Rosenbaum et al. (2006), using a local sample of public and private 2-year colleges, finds that the private 2-year colleges provide a good model of high transparency. These private colleges (which the authors call "occupational colleges" because they focus on training in occupational fields) provide many counselors per student and require students to meet with counselors at least once per term. Information regarding financial aid and requirements is much more centralized and streamlined at the private 2-year colleges. Moreover, the private 2-year colleges decrease the need for information and guidance by structuring programs, advising, and peer support (Person et al., 2006), and student information systems monitor student progress and quickly catch student mistakes (Deil-Amen & Rosenbaum, 2003; Person et al., 2006). Like occupational colleges, community colleges could shift the burden of information from students to advisors, who would take responsibility for assuring student progress as part of their job description. Some of the advising (e.g., concerning courses, time management) does not need to be done one-on-one, and colleges could save money with group advising, particularly if students are in similar programs or have similar goals.[4]

The processes of private 2-year colleges seem to make a difference. Person et al. (2006) find, in their local college sample, that public 2-year (community) college students are significantly less likely to know what courses they need for their degree plans, less likely to know which courses give credit for their planned degree, and less likely to agree that they have enough information about requirements. This is the case even though the private and public 2-year colleges in their sample enroll similar students (and to the extent that they do not, the occupational colleges actually enroll less advantaged students; Person et al., 2006). In a national sample of degree seekers (based on NELS), students who first enter private 2-year colleges attain degrees at a rate 16 percentage points higher than similar students who first enter community colleges (52% vs. 36% rates of degree completion, respectively). With respect to permeability, community colleges offer several advantages over private 2-year colleges. These recommendations do not necessarily inhibit high levels of permeability, but they may improve completion transparency.

Significant amounts of debate revolves around whether community colleges provide opportunity or reinforce existing social stratification (see Dougherty, 1994, for a review); so suggesting that community colleges may not provide real opportunity is not a new idea. However, analyzing community college policies within the permeability-transparency framework suggests the ways in which community colleges may hinder real opportunity as well as shows ways in which such policies could be revised to lead to a system of informed choice.

Financial Aid Policies Financial aid provides an opportunity for students to attend college regardless of income, and therefore increases the permeability of the higher education system. Beyond enrollment, more financial aid is associated with a lower likelihood of stopping out and increased persistence (Bettinger, 2004; DesJardins et al., 2002), particularly for low-income students (Pascarella & Terenzini, 2005). For students in Ohio's public 2- and 4-year colleges, a $1,000 increase in Pell grants corresponded to an 8.6 percentage point decrease in the likelihood of dropping out (Bettinger, 2004). Financial aid also affects a student's choice of institution (Avery & Hoxby, 2004; DesJardins et al., 2002; Dynarski, 2004; Perna & Titus, 2004). Dynarski (2004), for example, finds that state merit-aid programs have shifted attendance towards 4-year colleges. Not only can financial aid increase opportunity for accessing the system, it can shift attendance patterns to those that research suggests are most efficient for educational attainment.

At the same time, however, the financial aid system contributes to low levels of enrollment and completion transparency. Research suggests that students and families have difficulty understanding or accessing aid. In 1999–2000, less than one-third of eligible college students claimed higher education tax credits (Long, 2004); 26% of low-income students do not apply for federal aid (Burdman, 2005); and, students and parents routinely overestimate college costs and lack information on the availability of aid (Avery & Kane, 2004; Perna, 2004). These statistics are startling examples of the importance of transparency. While policy makers may reasonably assume that students will respond to free (or low cost) money, in fact, transparency can be an important obstacle. Even with financial aid policies associated with high permeability, students and parents may not be taking advantage of available funds because financial aid systems lack transparency. In a study of high-achieving high school students, Avery and Hoxby (2004) find that "'bewildering' and 'confusing' are the modal words" (p. 290) in parents' comments about the financial aid process. Reviewing several studies, Perna (2006) concludes that awareness and understanding of college costs and financial aid is particularly low for Latino and Black students and their families as well as for parents without college experience. Free and low cost financial aid is available, but poor transparency may prevent some students and parents from taking advantage of it.

Poor transparency results, in part, from poor financial aid counseling. In colleges, the only time a student is certain to receive financial aid counseling is in a mandatory interview conducted by colleges after a student takes out loans, but even these are increasingly administered on line and in perfunctory ways (Burdman, 2005). In a study of 14 two-year colleges, Deil-Amen and Rosenbaum (2003) find that students at community colleges were confused about financial aid, and some students report that when they tried to get help, their encounters with financial aid staff were "unpleasant and even hostile" (p. 125; see also Orfield & Paul, 1994). In interviews, high school counselors suggest that they focus more on aspirations and academic preparation rather than finances, although it is not clear whether counselors do so because they are uninformed or uncomfortable with financial matters (Burdman, 2005). McDonough and Calderone (2006) found, in interviews and focus groups with counselors at 14 high schools, that most counselors did little besides discuss college costs with their students and some steered students away from more selective colleges for financial reasons.

Financial aid policies themselves also lead to confusion. The formula for the expected family contribution is not explained on the FAFSA (Kane, 1999). Some community colleges have policies that require students to request loans before staff can provide information about them, and students are not told about loans if they do not explicitly ask (Burdman, 2005). Institutional pricing and scholarship policies may also make it difficult for students to know the real cost of an education. Private college scholarships are not usually awarded based on explicitly stated criteria, and in some cases, they can be negotiated. As a result, applicants are unable to anticipate the cost of college at the time of application. In a study of 28 elite private 4-year colleges, Hill, Winston, and Boyd (2005) find that students in the lowest-income quartile paid a net price ranging from $800 to $11,390 across institutions. Students in similar economic circumstances pay significantly different amounts of tuition and would be unable to predict this before receiving aid award letters. In addition, the relationship between sticker price and net price (sticker price—grants) is increasingly decoupled. Among 10 elite private 4-year colleges, average sticker prices increased 9% over a 5-year period, but net prices went down for all institutions except one (where the rise was just 0.8%; Hill et al., 2005). One role of financial-aid policy is to mitigate lack of access to information, but the patchwork and nature of policies appears to create significant information problems. It is not clear how lack of information affects enrollment, persistence, or the choice of particular attendance patterns since students more committed to getting information may be those more committed to college anyway.

Beyond the difficulty of understanding the financial aid process, the meaning of financial aid may differ between policymakers and recipients. Affordability has a sociocultural dimension; it depends on an individual's reference points, and the meaning of money may vary by social class (McDonough & Calderone, 2006). As policymakers change the composition of financial aid (from grants to loans and from need- to merit-based grants), it is important to consider that different types of aid have a value not necessarily represented by dollar value. Loans comprised 41% of financial aid in 1980 compared to 58% in 2000 (Witkowsky, 2002). Some research suggests that low income and minority students are less willing to accept loans because of the uncertainty of being able to repay them or the size of the debt relative to family income (Baker & Velez, 1996; McDonough & Calderone, 2006). Avery and Hoxby (2004) find that the offer of a loan positively affects a students' selection of a particular college except for low income students, for whom it has no effect. With respect to the effects of loans on stop-out or persistence, the evidence is mixed. DesJardins et al. (2002) find that loans have less of an impact on stop-out compared to scholarships, work-study, and campus employment at one particular 4-year college. They estimate that converting loans to scholarships would increase the median time to stop-out from 8.9 to 11 academic terms. Other research, however, finds positive effects of loans on persistence (Pascarella & Terenzini, 2005). Loans may affect students' pathways differently than monetarily equivalent aid of a different type because of students' reluctance to take out a loan or the complexity of applying and evaluating the value of loans.

Policy makers are also increasingly awarding merit-based rather than need-based aid. The amount of aid not based on need tripled at public and private 4-year colleges between 1983 and 1991 (Kane, 1999). In this case too, the value of the type of aid goes beyond monetary value. Avery and Hoxby (2004) find that for a sample of high-achieving high school students, calling a grant a "scholarship" matters: a scholarship increases the probability of matriculation at a particular institution by 86% compared to a grant of equal monetary value. Among students who attended the University of Minnesota, DesJardins et al. (2002) find that scholarships have the greatest impact (negative) on stop-out, while grants have no significant impact. They suggest that students may interpret merit-based aid as a commitment by the institution to their success and therefore feel more committed in return. Neither of these studies, however, provides insight into the effects of this compositional change on students attending 2-year colleges, for whom financial aid may matter more or differently. The point is not that merit-based aid is better than need-based aid, but that part of the complexity of the financial aid system is the different meanings that students attach to different types of aid.

While the financial aid system increases the permeability of higher education, it also reduces transparency. While students who are able to take advantage of the system are more likely to pursue pathways with a high probability of leading to degree completion, other students are confused by the system, and still others have a sociocultural construction of aid that may be inconsistent with the structure of the system, especially given recent trends in aid composition. The structure of the system makes some students unable or uncomfortable accessing it, which could leave them unsure of their pathways into college or towards completion.

Conclusion

Expanding on Hamilton's constructs, this chapter suggests that higher education systems can be characterized along two dimensions: permeability and transparency. While *Known Limits*—a situation corresponding to low permeability but high transparency—once characterized the American system, a combination of economic, social, and policy factors have increased the permeability of the system, which paves the way for increased equality and greater flexibility for individuals to combine multiple roles with education. At the same time, however, transparency is low, which makes it difficult for students to see pathways to college and to degree completion. Students with limited access to economic and social capital may have the most difficult time negotiating the web of possible pathways to arrive at one that will efficiently lead to degree completion. We characterize the current situation of American higher education as *Uninformed Choice*, a location characterized by high permeability but low transparency.

Why has the American system developed in the way that it has, rather than retaining its high level of transparency and adding high permeability? Critics might argue that high permeability and low transparency is a deliberate strategy to give the appearance of increased opportunity while maintaining traditional patterns of social stratification (Karabel, 1972, 1986; Pincus, 1980). Brint and Karabel (1989) considered the possibility that employers somehow had a hand in influencing community college practices (testing a hypothesis suggested by Bowles & Gintis, 1976), but they discovered that the business community was remarkably indifferent and uninvolved in the development of community colleges. Moreover, detailed interviews with college staff find no indications of such motives. Indeed, community college faculty seem remarkably motivated by the idea that they are providing second chances for upward mobility to disadvantaged students, and many report working 60 hours per week to try to assist such students (Rosenbaum et al., 2006). If there is a hidden conspiracy, the conspirators have not been identified.

Another possibility is that in their focus on increasing access to college, policymakers have not paid attention to transparency. As a result, while colleges, governments, and media have encouraged dramatically greater permeability, corresponding actions have not been taken to increase transparency. While existing practices may have provided a sufficient level of transparency when just a few students were passing through higher education and these students were receiving advice from college-educated parents, it may no longer suffice given the diversity of students, institutions, and attendance patterns.

Throughout this chapter, we have often seen that policy dilemmas can result because the same procedure can have contradictory influences on permeability and transparency. American society has lowered the barriers to college access, offered remedial courses to reduce barriers of low achievement, provided many new ways to attend college (delayed, part-time, discontinuous, and multiple-institution attendance), and offered financial aid to support increased access, yet each example of increased permeability was rarely accompanied by new information and guidance about the long-term implications of the new option.

Permeability reforms, which add new low-probability paths through higher education, increase opportunity for those already on those paths and those who have no alternative. However, without transparency, some students who can choose among several paths will choose low-probability paths without realizing the implications. Research is needed to examine how often this happens, for which individuals and which circumstances. At the same time, policy makers must be aware that increasing permeability in a way that adds new low-probability pathways carries risks unless special steps are taken to improve transparency and inform students' choices.

Some may think we place too much emphasis on information, assuming an overly simple rational choice model. While information is probably not sufficient to assure appropriate choices, it is surely necessary. We cannot be certain that a student would choose a particular type of institution or attendance pattern if she were aware of the likely impact on her chances of success, but a student who lacks information on the likely consequences of her choices cannot possibly be expected to make choices that increase her likelihood of success. Future work on the risks of alternative pathways

should also attempt to better control for selection bias to separate the consequences of choosing a particular pathway from the factors that lead to the choice in the first place. Where possible, methods such as regression discontinuity may help to provide insight into this issue.

Identifying the problem as transparency, not permeability, suggests practical policy actions. The best way to reduce remedial needs in college is to improve high school preparation, provide clear warning to high school students about their likelihood of being placed in (noncredit) remedial courses (using exams aligned with college remedial tests), and give clear advice about actions students can take to improve their chances of avoiding remedial placement.

A broader conception of counseling is also needed. As noted, counselors' reliance on commonsense knowledge preserves old biases, ignores the needs of new students, and prevents students from seeing new options. Instead of merely being trained in counseling psychology, high school guidance counselors must also be trained in "counseling sociology." They must understand the new institutional and program options, various ways of attending and funding college, and how these choices affect degree completion. Permeability presents new opportunities, but improved counseling is needed to improve transparency about these opportunities.

In addition, this analysis suggests the need for system-wide reforms. The college admissions system and financial aid system have become overwhelmingly complex. At the same time that permeability reforms have sought to increase access to disadvantaged students, these systems have created such complexity that students who lack social and economic capital remain at a disadvantage. The same motivations that drove prior increases in permeability should now be redirected to increase transparency.

Notes

1. We are grateful to two anonymous reviewers and the editors of this handbook for thoughtful comments on earlier drafts of this chapter. Support for this work was provided by the Spencer Foundation, the Institute for Policy Research at Northwestern University, and the Multidisciplinary Program in Education Sciences at Northwestern University supported by the Institute for Education Sciences.

2. When available, data from 1970 and 2000 were compared. The few exceptions are noted both in the table and in the text.

3. Minority students are defined here as Black, Hispanic, Asian/Pacific Islander, and American Indian/Alaska native.

4. Some critics will object that these procedures are too expensive for community colleges. Many community colleges have faced repeated and severe budget cuts, and, from our observations, policymakers often respond to budget cuts by striving to preserve course offerings while cutting other services, including counseling. Funding agents should realize the harm that budget cuts impose. Moreover, community colleges should realize that counseling and other information sources may be necessary for improving degree completion rates, which may justify retaining counseling even if this requires cuts in course offerings. Unfortunately, funding formulas that pay community colleges for enrollment, but not for completion, create perverse incentives that do not encourage steps to improve graduation rates.

References

Adelman, C. (1999). *Answers in the tool box: Academic intensity, attendance patterns, and bachelor's degree attainment*. Washington ,DC: U.S. Department of Education, Office of Educational Research and Development.

Adelman, C. (2004). *Principal indicators of student academic histories in postsecondary education, 1972–2000*. Washington, DC: U.S. Department of Education, Institute of Education Sciences.

Adelman, C. (2006). *The toolbox revisited: Paths to degree completion from high school through college*. Washington, DC: U.S. Department of Education.

Anderson, K. L. (1981). Post-high school experiences and college attrition. *Sociology of Education, 54*, 1–15.

Arnett, J. J. (2004). *Emerging adulthood*. New York: Oxford University Press.

Avery, C., & Hoxby, C. M. (2004). Do and should financial aid packages affect students' college choices? In C. M. Hoxby (Ed.), *College choices: The economics of where to go, when to go, and how to pay for it* (pp. 239–299). Chicago: University of Chicago Press.

Avery, C., & Kane, T. J. (2004). Students perceptions of college opportunities: The Boston COACH program. In C. M. Hoxby (Ed.), *College choices: The economics of where to go, when to go, and how to pay for it* (pp. 355–394). Chicago: University of Chicago Press.

Bailey, T., Badway, N., & Gumport, P. J. (2001). *For-profit higher education and community colleges*. Stanford, CA: National Center for Postsecondary Improvement.

Baker, T. L., & Velez, W. (1996). Access to and opportunity in postsecondary education in the United States: A review. *Sociology of Education, 69*(SI), 82–101.

Bettinger, E. (2004). How financial aid affects persistence. In C. M. Hoxby (Ed.), *College choices: The economics of where to go, when to go, and how to pay for it* (pp. 207–232). Chicago: University of Chicago Press.

Bowles, S. & Gintis, H. (1976). *Schooling in capitalist America: Educational reform and the contradictions of economic life*. New York: Basic Books.

Bozick, R., & DeLuca, S. (2005). Better late than never? Delayed enrollment in the high school to college transition. *Social Forces, 84*, 527–550.

Brint, S., & Karabel, J. (1989). *The diverted dream: Community college and the promise of educational opportunity in America, 1900–1985*. New York: Oxford University Press.

Burdman, P. (2005). *The student debt dilemma: Debt aversion as a barrier to college access* (No. CSHE.13.05). Berkeley, CA: Center for Studies in Higher Education.

Choy, S. (2002). *Nontraditional undergraduates* (No. NCES 2002-012). Washington, DC: U.S. Department of Education, National Center for Education Statistics.

Cicourel, A. V., & Kitsuse, J. I. (1963). *The educational decision makers*. Indianapolis, IN: Bobbs-Merrill.

Clark, B. R. (1960). *The open door college*. New York: McGraw-Hill.

Cohen, A. M., & Brawer, F. (2003). *The American community college* (4th ed.). San Francisco: Jossey-Bass.

Cross, K. P., & Fideler, E. F. (1989). Community college missions: Priorities in the mid-1980's. *Journal of Higher Education, 60*, 209–216.

Deil-Amen, R., & Rosenbaum, J. E. (2002). The unintended consequences of stigma-free remediation. *Sociology of Education, 75*, 249–268.

Deil-Amen, R., & Rosenbaum, J. E. (2003). The social prerequisites of success: Can college structure reduce the need for social know-how? *The Annals of the American Academy of Political and Social Science, 586*, 120–143.

DesJardins, S. L., Ahlburg, D. A., & McCall, B. P. (2002). Simulating the longitudinal effects of changes in financial aid on student departure from college. *Journal of Human Resources, 37*, 653–679.

Dougherty, K. J. (1994). *The contradictory college: The conflicting origins, impacts, and futures of the community college*. Albany: State University of New York Press.

Dynarski, S. (2004). The new merit aid. In C. M. Hoxby (Ed.), *College choices: The economics of where to go, when to go, and how to pay for it* (pp. 63–96). Chicago: University of Chicago Press.

Ehrenberg, R. G., & Sherman, D. R. (1987). Employment while in college, academic achievement, and postcollege outcomes: A summary of results. *Journal of Human Resources, 22*, 1–23.

Freeman, K. (1997). Increasing African Americans' participation in higher education: African American high-school students' perspectives. *Journal of Higher Education, 68*, 523–550.

Gleason, P. M. (1993). College student employment, academic progress, and postcollege labor market success. *Journal of Student Financial Aid, 23*(2), 5–14.

Goble, L., Rosenbaum, J. E., & Person, A. E. (2007). *Individual vs. institutional explanations of college degree completion using two national longitudinal surveys*. Unpublished manuscript, Northwestern University, Evanston, IL.

Goldrick-Rab, S. (2006). Following their every move: An investigation of social-class differences in college pathways. *Sociology of Education, 79*, 61–79.

Gray, K. (1996). The baccalaureate game: Is it right for all teens? *Phi Delta Kappan, 77*, 528–534.

Grubb, W. N. (1996). *Working in the middle: Strengthening education and training for the mid-skilled labor force*. San Francisco: Jossey-Bass.

Hamilton, S. F. (1994). Employment prospects as motivation for school achievement: Links and gaps between school and work in seven countries. In R. K. Silbereisen & E. Todt (Eds.), *Adolescence in context: The interplay of family, school, peers, and work in adjustment* (pp. 267–283). New York: Springer-Verlag.

Harder, B. (2006, August 28). The credibility in your gap year. *U.S. News and World Report*, 97.

Hearn, J. C. (1992). Emerging variations in postsecondary attendance patterns: An investigation of part-time, delayed, and nondegree enrollment. *Research in Higher Education, 33*, 657–687.

Hill, C. B., Winston, G. C., & Boyd, S. A. (2005). Affordability: Family incomes and net prices at highly selective private colleges and universities. *Journal of Human Resources, 40*, 769–790.

Horn, L., Cataldi, E. F., & Sikora, A. (2005). *Waiting to attend college: Undergraduates who delay their postsecondary enrollment* (No. NCES 2005-152). Washington, DC: U.S. Department of Education, National Center for Education Statistics.

Horn, L., Peter, K., & Rooney, K. (2002). *Profile of undergraduates in U.S. Postsecondary institutions: 1999–2000* (NCES 2002-168). Washington, DC: U.S. Department of Education, National Center for Education Statistics.

Jacobs, J. A., & King, R. B. (2002). Age and college completion: A life-history analysis of women aged 15–44. *Sociology of Education, 75*, 211–230.

Kane, T. J. (1999). *The price of admission: Rethinking how Americans pay for college*. Washington, DC: Brookings Institution.

Karabel, J. (1972). Community colleges and social stratification. *Harvard Educational Review, 42*, 521–562.

Karabel, J. (1986). Community colleges and social stratification in the 1980's. In L. S. Zwerling (Ed.), *The community college and its critics* (pp. 13–30). San Francisco: Jossey-Bass.

Karabel, J. (2005). *The chosen: The hidden history of admission and exclusion at Harvard, Yale, and Princeton*. Boston: Houghton Mifflin.

Kempner, K., & Kinnick, M. (1990). Catching the window of opportunity: Being on time for higher education. *Journal of Higher Education, 61*, 535–547.

King, J. E. (1996). *The decision to go to college: Attitudes and experiences associated with college attendance among low-income students*. Washington, DC: The College Board.

Kirst, M. W., & Venezia, A. (Eds.). (2004). *From high school to college: Improving opportunities for success in postsecondary education*. San Francisco: Jossey-Bass.

Lee, V. E., & Ekstrom, R. B. (1987). Student access to guidance counseling in high school. *American Educational Research Journal, 24*, 287–310.

Lemann, N. (1999). *The big test: The secret history of the American meritocracy*. New York: Farrar, Straus and Giroux.

Long, B. T. (2004). The impact of federal tax credits for higher education expenses. In C. M. Hoxby (Ed.), *College choices: The economics of where to go, when to go, and how to pay for it* (pp. 101–165). Chicago: University of Chicago Press.

McCormick, A. C. (2003). Swirling and double-dipping: New patterns of student attendance and their implications for higher education. *New Directions for Higher Education, 121,* 13–24.

McDonough, P. M. (1994). Buying and selling higher education: The social construction of the college applicant. *Journal of Higher Education, 65,* 427–446.

McDonough, P. M. (1997). *Choosing colleges: How social class and schools structure opportunity.* Albany: State University of New York Press.

McDonough, P. M. (2005). *Counseling and college counseling in America's high schools.* Alexandria, VA: National Association for College Admission Counseling.

McDonough, P. M., & Calderone, S. (2006). The meaning of money: Perceptual differences between college counselors and low-income families about college costs and financial aid. *American Behavioral Scientist, 49,* 1703–1718.

National Center for Education Statistics. (1971). *Digest of education statistics, 1971.* Washington, DC: U.S. Department of Education.

National Center for Education Statistics. (2002). *Digest of education statistics, 2002.* Washington, DC: U.S. Department of Education.

National Center for Education Statistics. (2005). *Digest of education statistics, 2005.* Washington, DC: U.S. Department of Education.

National Center for Education Statistics. (2006). *The condition of education.* Washington, DC: U.S. Department of Education.

O'Toole, D. M., Stratton, L. S., & Wetzel, J. N. (2003). A longitudinal analysis of the frequency of part-time enrollment and the persistence of students who enroll part time. *Research in Higher Education, 44,* 519–537.

Orfield, G., & Paul, F. G. (1994). *High hopes, long odds: A major report on Hoosier teens and the American dream.* Indianapolis: Indiana Youth Institute.

Parsad, B., Alexander, D., Farris, E., & Hudson, L. (2003). *High school guidance counseling* (NCES 2003–015). Washington, DC: U.S. Department of Education, National Center for Education Statistics.

Pascarella, E. T., & Terenzini, P. T. (2005). *How college affects students: A third decade of research.* San Francisco: Jossey-Bass.

Perna, L. W. (2004). *Impact of student aid program design, operations, and marketing on the formation of family college-going plans and resulting college-going behaviors of potential students.* Boston: The Education Resources Institute.

Perna, L. W. (2006). Understanding the relationship between information about college prices and financial aid and students' college-related behaviors. *American Behavioral Scientist, 49,* 1620–1635.

Perna, L. W., & Titus, M. A. (2004). Understanding differences in the choice of college attended: The role of state public policies. *Review of Higher Education, 27,* 501–525.

Person, A. E., Rosenbaum, J. E., & Deil-Amen, R. (2006). Student planning and information problems in different college structures. *Teachers College Record, 108,* 374–396.

Peter, K., & Cataldi, E. F. (2005). *The road less traveled? Students who enroll in multiple institutions* (NCES 2005-157). Washington, DC: U.S. Department of Education, National Center for Education Statistics.

Pincus, F. L. (1980). The false promises of community colleges: Class conflict and vocational education. *Harvard Educational Review, 50,* 332–361.

Plank, S. B., & Jordan, W. J. (2001). Effects of information, guidance, and actions on postsecondary destinations: A study of talent loss. *American Educational Research Journal, 38,* 947–979.

Powell, A. G. (1996). *Lessons from privilege: The American prep school tradition.* Cambridge, MA: Harvard University Press.

Rosenbaum, J. E. (1976). *Making inequality: The hidden curriculum of high school tracking.* New York: Wiley.

Rosenbaum, J. E. (2001). *Beyond college for all: Career paths for the forgotten half.* New York: Russell Sage Foundation.

Rosenbaum, J. E. (2006). *Research approaches for understanding new patterns of college experience.* Unpublished manuscript, Northwestern University, Evanston, IL.

Rosenbaum, J. E., Deil-Amen, R., & Person, A. E. (2006). *After admission: From college access to college success.* New York: Russell Sage Foundation.

Schneider, B., & Stevenson, D. (1999). *The ambitious generation: America's teenagers, motivated but directionless.* New Haven, CT: Yale University Press.

Settersten, R. A., Jr. (2005). Social policy and the transition to adulthood: Toward stronger institutions and individual capacities. In R. A. Settersten, Jr., F. F. Furstenberg, Jr., & R. G. Rumbaut (Eds.), *On the frontier of adulthood: Theory, research, and public policy* (pp. 534–560). Chicago: University of Chicago Press.

Steinberg, L. (1996). *Beyond the classroom: Why school reform has failed and what parents need to do.* New York: Simon and Shuster.

Stratton, L. S., O'Toole, D. M., & Wetzel, J. N. (2004). Factors affecting initial enrollment intensity: Part-time versus full-time enrollment. *Economics of Education Review, 23,* 167–175.

Walpole, M. (2003). Socioeconomic status and college: How SES affects college experiences and outcomes. *Review of Higher Education, 27,* 45–73.

Washor, E., & Mojkowski, C. (2007, January 17). The college juggernaut: Just who is it that needs to get ready? *Education Week,* 31–33.

Witkowsky, K. (2002). Debating student debt: Are college students living beyond their means? *National CrossTalk, 10*(4), 1, 8–9.

73

Governmental Policy and the Organization of Postsecondary Education

JAMES C. HEARN AND T. AUSTIN LACY
University of Georgia

Little of the existing research on colleges and universities as organizations in the United States can be characterized as *policy research*. More precisely, when defining policies as courses of action adopted by governments, one finds very little analysis focused on relationships between such policies and colleges' and universities' structures, processes, and normative contexts. There is a very substantial research tradition focused on non-organizationally directed governmental policies (such as the massive state and federal efforts to finance student attendance). There have been numerous, hortatory, anecdotal, and descriptive essays written on state and federal governments' relations with institutions. But there is relatively little empirical, social-science-based research on government/institution connections.[1]

Those topics are important, however, and merit research attention. State governments shape postsecondary systems, leadership, staffing, and curricula not only through funding but also through statutory and political channels. Since the 1950s, state legislatures have periodically involved themselves in academic-freedom controversies at public institutions, most recently involving the events of 9/11 and terrorism more generally. Over the past decade, allegations of "sunshine law" violations have derailed or tarnished presidential searches at several flagship universities. Key court decisions on affirmative-action in Texas, Michigan, and California have reshaped admissions policies in those states and beyond. Clearly, even within the United States' decentralized, loosely coupled, market-driven approach to higher education, governments do influence core organizational features of colleges and universities. Very often, these influences are tied to issues of fairness and equity, and thus touch upon higher education's central role in societal stratification. Thus, government/institution relations are not trivial, and what research exists on these topics is significant. That research constitutes the focus of this chapter.

An Overview of the Research Arena

There are at least four reasons for the dearth of policy-oriented research on postsecondary organization, one historical, one technological, one methodological, and one cultural. First, for a variety of historical reasons dating back to the seventeenth-century origins of higher education in this country (Thelin, 2004), governmental authority over the organization, governance, and management of colleges and universities tends not to be nearly as expansive and direct as in K-12 education or in higher education systems in other nations. Here, governing agencies and boards tend to leave "micro" issues to institutions. Curricular coverage of various subject areas, for example, is largely left to the discretion of faculty and individual programs. Even in public colleges and universities, organization and management are driven more by institutionalized and professionalized norms and values than by externally imposed bureaucratic requirements (Clark, 1983). As Meyer, Ramirez, Frank, and Schofer (2007) have argued in comparing the European and U.S. contexts for higher education, "U.S. universities often develop as private formal organizations, with a good deal of embeddedness in both the 'civil society' and market structure, while continental universities operate more directly under the authority of the bureaucratic state" (p. 195). Thus, historically, policy makers' concerns in higher education have been less wide-ranging. Not surprisingly, this limited scope of authority has been accompanied by limited research attention.

Second, higher education organization is a difficult subject to address empirically because of the inherent complexity of its technology of production (in the broad, social-scientific sense of "technology"). The problem is especially acute in governmentally funded institutions, in which a blend of public and private purposes is imbued and infused from the beginning. Rather than a straightforward organizational technology driven by a singular goal, public institutions almost all serve multiple purposes. Of course, all organizations arguably pursue multiple goals, but the conflicts can often be minimized by timing sequences and structural separation. In contrast, in colleges and universities, purposes must often be pursued simultaneously and jointly, creating a challenge for analysis.

The classic formulation of institutional purposes focuses on research, service, and teaching, but this typology greatly oversimplifies relations among individual, unit, and campus-wide goals and definitions of success, as well as the calculus of decision making. Michael Cohen and James March (1986) explored the many ambiguities inherent in institutions' unclear internal agreement regarding goals, core technologies, and appropriate participants in decision making. In a similar vein, Karl Weick (1976) identified "loose coupling" among different organizational elements and processes as an explanation for much that happens, and does not happen, on campus, and John Meyer and colleagues (Meyer & Rowan, 1977; Meyer et al., 2007) have emphasized the institutionalized nature of U.S. higher education, the logic and transcending faith in scientific rationality that allows much of the work of higher education to proceed rather autonomously, inefficiently, and idiosyncratically. Each of these authors suggests these features pose constraints for central policy makers' efforts to drive organizational directions and reform.

Tensions around authority relations extend to governmental decision-making. Public colleges and universities are asked by legislators, private donors, research funders, and the general public to be equitably and widely accessible, to provide effective instruction, research, and service, and to provide all their services at low costs.[2] These three goals can comprise a binding "iron triangle" (Bowen, 1980; Finifter, Baldwin, & Thelin, 1991; Hearn & Anderson, 1995): although serving any two of the goals aggressively is conceivable, the pursuit of all three can invoke difficult tradeoffs. For example, pursuing affordable access can compromise effectiveness (quality), because it may require larger class sizes, use of less qualified teachers, and the like. That is, limited state dollars mean there are limits to how much can be spent per-student for delivering educational services. In effect, given budget constraints, expanding quantity of people served can mean decreasing the quality of any one person's experiences. Similarly, states pursuing effectiveness at low costs may be forced to restrict access, because there are budgetary limits on how many people can be provided the highest-cost educational services. The situation poses a dilemma of constrained institutional choice. Efforts to achieve improvements in one goal domain inevitably imply opportunity costs for serving other goal domains. In both theoretical and empirical terms, scholarship on multi-product organizations can be exponentially more difficult than work on simpler organizations, and universities are no exception.[3]

A third factor limiting policy research relating to higher education organization is methodological. Such research confronts a design constraint unlike such work in K-12 in that there are fewer decision-making bodies to investigate comparatively. Very few institutions have local, community-based governing bodies, analogous to K-12 education's school boards (California community colleges being an exception). Instead, states and statewide systems are the norm. With most states having at most only a handful of public postsecondary governing boards, the raw data for comparative organizational policy analysis are sparse. Adding a time dimension addresses some of the inherent data-analysis issues, but the idiosyncrasy of state settings, the unavailability of integrated, comprehensive datasets, and the strong variations in governance within and across states, make systematic policy research difficult (Heller, 2007; Goldrick-Rab & Shaw, 2007; Ewell & Boeke, 2007; Delaney & Doyle, 2007).

Finally, research on higher education arguably tends not to emphasize policy/organizational issues for reasons relating to the distinctive cultural origins of the field. Higher education scholarship has its roots not so much in governmental policy considerations as in more purely educational concerns. Academic researchers in higher education have historically focused less on the intersections of governmental policies with institutional structures and processes than on the interactions of students with their teachers and peers in their local institutional settings (Terenzini, 1996). This may stem from higher education researchers' typical academic training and aspirations, which tend to be oriented toward improving individual students' educational outcomes. Thus, the research field has tended to emphasize teaching/learning issues rather than the broader social, economic, and political contexts in which teaching and learning take place.[4] For example, while federal and state governments often seek to implement policies to foster student success on campus (e.g., see Spellings, 2006), researchers on student success have usually focused on its social-psychological aspects, rather than on the broader policy and societal factors affecting undergraduates from different backgrounds (Hearn, 2006).[5]

For similar reasons, the relatively small numbers of policy-oriented researchers in higher education have often delimited their work to "policy analysis" rather than "policy research." That is, the focus of much of the work in the field has been, understandably, on what educational improvements might be achieved by particular policy instruments at what costs. Thus, the costs and effects of prospective student-aid policies on student enrollment and persistence to degree constitute a frequent topic of research, but researchers have shown less interest in such related questions as how those policies shape the decision-making of administrators on admissions or diversity issues or, more broadly, what factors drive the emergence and shaping of those policies politically across the states and in Congress. Such concerns as the genesis of policy, policy maker decisions not to choose a particular policy approach, and policy makers "deciding not to decide" on policy issues have largely been ignored, but may pose research questions as important as those associated with the particular impacts an enacted policy might have. As McLendon (2003a) has noted, "The challenge confronting politics of higher education researchers is one of stimulating a systematic and sustained scholarship that is topically, conceptually, and methodologically multidimensional" (p. 166). Tending to limit policy research to the study of policy effects alone may well be typical of a professional field with shared underlying norms favoring achieving a certain desired social goal, but that tendency arguably limits not only broader understanding but also the achievement of those very social goals.

There is, nevertheless, significant research on the intersections of governmental policy and postsecondary organization, governance, and management. The goal of this chapter is to address critically the state of that research. To help ensure manageable scope and adequate clarity, institutional policies and governmental student aid and cost subsidization policies are considered only to the extent that those policies have noteworthy *organizational* implications. The chapter begins with consideration of central policy issues currently facing higher education. It moves next to research on the various contexts in which governmental policy intersects with higher education. The chapter concludes with consideration of the contexts, constraints, and directions for new and continuing research in this arena.

Key Developments in the State and Federal Policy Arenas

A number of developments in the past 30 years, taken together, arguably constitute a notable turn in the postsecondary policy arena in this country. In the late 1970s, tuitions in state institutions were still quite low by current standards, and the total amount of federal student grants was rising to rival total federal loan aid (Wilkinson, 2005). The baby boom was still buttressing enrollments, and federal research funding was growing. Energy costs were receding from earlier spikes and capital and maintenance spending were robust. Since that time, much has changed.

First, the financing system began to evolve rapidly and dramatically. Dating back to the 19th century, states had provided institutional subsidies sufficient to maintain low tuition and fee levels for students, the rationale being that offering college education to citizens at low costs served public purposes. In recent decades, however, state political leaders have been forced to address growing constraints on state tax revenues accompanied by growing demands for state spending on K-12 education, transportation, healthcare, and corrections. Seeking budgetary flexibility to respond to these conditions and expressing growing doubts over whether higher education provides public benefits commensurate with its costs, legislatures have begun to challenge longstanding state subsidization levels for public higher education (Ehrenberg, 2000; Callan, 2007). In good part as a consequence of these developments, states' institutional subsidization levels have moderated and become more unstable (Hovey, 1999), and tuition and fee levels in

public institutions have risen rapidly in dollar and percentage terms (College Board, 2007).

Second, while growth has slowed in the raw numbers of 18 to 22-year-olds in the larger population, postsecondary enrollment rates in that age group have grown, and remarkable proportions of students from all socioeconomic backgrounds now express aspirations for postsecondary attendance (Hearn, 2001). At the same time, institutions have expanded their offerings and openness to students enrolling in novel ways, that is, those enrolling well after the traditional college-going ages, those attending part-time, those pursuing distance and online education, those not having college-preparatory courses in high school, and so forth. Indeed, what was "nontraditional" in the mid 1970s is more the norm in current enrollments. For example, over a third of all college students in fall, 2006 were over 24 years old (Chronicle Almanac, 2008, p. 14).

Third, and relatedly, students' gender and racial-ethnic diversity has increased remarkably since the 1970s. Women first equaled the numbers of men among first-year students in the 1970s, but since that time have come to dominate enrollments across sectors and levels, with only certain doctoral and professional degree areas still majority male in enrollments (U.S. Department of Education, 2007). The numbers of students of color and students from immigrant backgrounds have grown dramatically as well, especially in high-growth states in the Sun Belt (notably Florida, Georgia, California, Arizona, Nevada, and Texas). As more and more sons and daughters of first-generation Americans enroll, the cultures, curricula, and organizational characteristics are influenced in new ways.

Fourth, on a more ideological level, the dominant logic of educational policy makers has arguably begun to tilt away from equity and access-oriented reasoning toward marketplace-oriented reasoning emphasizing academic quality (St. John, 2003). While these two logics are not necessarily opposed to each other, there is little question that the ideological shift has shaped not only policy goals but also the means used to pursue those goals (Wilkinson, 2005).

Finally, at both the federal and the state levels, authorities have begun demanding more performance reporting and accountability from institutions. In some cases, these demands have been explicitly linked to dollars: the federal government has increasingly tied academic progress to eligibility for student-aid programs (Wilkinson, 2005), while states have begun experiments in performance budgeting and funding, which tie institutional subsidies to schools' progress on selected key indicators, such as graduation rates, test scores, placement rates, external research funding (Burke, 2002). But funding has not always been the carrot. As states' enthusiasm for performance funding and budgeting waned somewhat in the early 2000s, stepped-up performance reporting was increasingly mandated as a routine requirement for state-supported institutions, absent any funding implications (Burke, 2005). Thus, tensions between institutional autonomy and public accountability have heightened since the 1970s, making the relationships between state governments and higher education institutions increasingly complex (Newman, 1987; Volkwein, 1987; Berdahl, 1990; Hines, 2000; McLendon, 2002; McLendon, Hearn, & Deaton, 2006).

Research on Policy and Postsecondary Organization

The emerging context noted above has created an ample supply of provocative questions for empirical research at the intersections of governmental policy and college and university organization. That research can be reasonably organized under three themes: the federal and state roles in research and graduate education, state governance and politics, and legal issues.

Federal and State Roles in Research and Graduate Education The federal government is easily the largest source of financing for campus-based research. This spending is concentrated in only a small set of the nation's over 4,000 colleges and universities, however: about four-fifths of total federal research spending of $28 billion consistently goes to 100 doctorate-granting institutions (Gladieux, King, & Corrigan, 2005; National Science Foundation, 2006). Direct governmental influences on the educational activities of colleges and universities may be small, but governments not only shape the broad context of faculty scholarship but also go to the micro-level organizational nature and conditions of research work.

Thus, academic departments are shaped by their successes in securing research funding, new research units are formed by developing governmental research agendas, and successful grants-seeking faculty receive rewards in salary, benefits, and working conditions. At the same time, institutions, departments, and faculty also confront new layers of bureaucracy in their work. Gumport's (1991) essay on the federal role in research and graduate education found that very little empirical research had been done on these organizational influences, and there is little to suggest that the pattern has changed. That is unfortunate, because the institutional effects of governmentally funded research are undoubtedly substantial and significant.

Historically, it is important to note that, while the rise of federally sponsored university research in the 20th century was incremental rather than overtly policy-driven, it carried with it expectations of contributions to the nation's defense and economic needs (Geiger, 1986). In the boom funding years after World War II, universities came to see research as a distinctive, central organizational function supported mainly by the federal government (Ben-David, 1977). Two features of this emerging federal role had critical organizational implications. First, by the 1950s, it became clear to university leaders that the national government was going to provide a robust and consistent funding stream (Gumport, 1991). Second, it was similarly clear that peer review was becoming established as the dominant basis of federal research award decisions. These two features con-

vinced institutional leaders that it was in their best interests to arrange their management structures, faculty and staff hiring, and student recruitment and employment practices in ways that effectively positioned institutions to compete for federal funds. Departments in fields favored by federal funding unquestionably benefited from these organizational moves, but the implications went further.

One important organizational effect of the federal role was in the support federal grants provided for costs not directly connected to the project activities themselves. This indirect-cost support formed a basis for improving campus research infrastructures and laboratory, computing, and information resources. The federal government, institutional administrations, and researchers each have somewhat distinct interests in the setting of rates for indirect-cost recovery, but one implication of these rates is that they shape the likelihood that researchers will remain on campus and thus train new researchers serving science and economic development. That is, if the government sets indirect-cost rates low, premier researchers may experience weaker research infrastructures relative to industry and private labs, and abandon university positions (Gumport, 1991). Thus, there are clear second-order organizational effects from governmental policies.

The emergence of ongoing federal funding has also raised a challenge rooted in the multi-purpose nature of university organization. Specifically, the rise of the grants economy on campus has reshaped the traditional nature of graduate students' organizational and disciplinary socialization. As Hackett (1990) has observed, "The roles of faculty member (mentor) and principal investigator (employer) are becoming inconsistent, straining the incumbents. Principles and practices that the *mentor* would prefer are inconsistent with the needs of the scientist as *employer*" (p. 267).

Thus, the graduate school experiences of students across fields began to diverge in accord with the extent to which the discipline was embedded in the pursuit and management of sponsored projects. Students in such fields as English, philosophy, and foreign languages, relative to fields such as engineering and chemistry, would likely spend more of their work time as teaching assistants and less as research assistants. A variety of research has highlighted the organizational differences (and distances) among units in different disciplinary areas, and the resulting differences in organizational approaches to graduate education in those areas,[6] and the rise of the grants economy in certain fields no doubt contributed further to that atomization.

Relatedly, the acquisition of an ongoing base of federal funding (in those institutions able to consistently compete well for the dollars) prompted institutions to use their own funding for industry collaborations, teaching and research assistantships for graduate students, and the like (Gumport, 1991). No doubt, the resources provided by federal effort, and the desirability of leveraging that support to obtain more support, fueled these initiatives. Also encouraging these efforts was the passage in 1980 of the Bayh-Dole Act,[7] which gave universities intellectual property rights over discoveries emanating from their research, and provided strong incentives for institutions to pursue commercialization of their academic discoveries (Mowery, Nelson, Sampat, & Ziedonis, 2001). The Bayh-Dole Act was arguably a watershed, creating an expectation that universities could actively engage in commercial activity and contribute to economic development (Bercovitz & Feldman, 2008). The act came to be a major impetus organizationally for the formation of campus technology-transfer offices, which seek to generate revenues from licenses, patents, and equity holdings emerging from the federally funded work of faculty.[8]

One must be cautious in attributing to the Bayh-Dole Act alone increases or improvements in patenting activity (Mowery et al., 2001; Mowery & Ziedonis, 2002), but there is evidence that "Universities have responded to the incentives of the government to pay attention to potential private returns to their research by redirecting their patenting efforts toward technologies that are effectively transferred through market mechanisms" (Shane, 2004, p. 148). That is, the federal policy context has influenced the nature of institutional choices regarding costs and returns of different strategic research initiatives and different organizational configurations.

Notably, as Geiger (2004) has observed, massive federal research funding, in concert with changing conditions in the markets for patient care, has contributed to the incorporation of medical schools into research universities in a special, hybrid form: offering professional education and conducting research but doing so under forms of organizational structures and oversight quite distinct from those of other university research and teaching units.

The growing federal role also has helped lead to the development of organized research units (ORUs) not conforming to the boundaries of existing academic departments (Kerr, 1963; Geiger, 2004). These units often arise around emerging areas crossing disciplinary fields, such as biotechnology and nanotechnology. In such fields, nonfaculty researchers join those with faculty appointments and graduate students in pursuing projects, and often those projects emphasize applied and commercial returns. As Gumport (1991) has noted, these units can raise organizational questions:

> The administration of research and training in ORU's evokes a new set of challenges as it is increasingly incompatible with departmental organization. Full-time nonfaculty research personnel may supervise graduate student research assistants but do not have faculty status ... Not only do faculty loyalties become divided between organizational units, but budgets for research are overseen by different managers than departmental instructional budgets. Thus, a significant component of research training ends up being staffed and financed by complex administrative arrangements in which faculty allocations and budget allocations may no longer be congruent with the actual practice of department-based graduate education. In short, the actual research training activity of graduate education has become organizationally less visible, as it falls between the lines of departmental organization. (p. 117)

Some organized research units also carry with them implications for university goals in the largest sense: Congress and the National Science Foundation have, for several decades, funded a variety of initiatives designed to foster cooperation and shared funding for applied research between corporations and institutions. The expectation of these efforts is that industries will fund work on campuses that directly aids economic development (Feller, 1990, 2004). Naturally, faculty in some academic fields may tend to question universities organizing themselves toward such ends.

While some researchers view the hyper-competitive federal funding environment as providing effective incentives for beneficial research efforts and well-targeted graduate education, a variety of contemporary scholars have employed the tools of conflict theory to examine the implications, most notably sociologist Sheila Slaughter and her colleagues' work on what they term "academic capitalism" (e.g., see Slaughter & Leslie, 1997). For Slaughter and Rhoades (2004), the new logic of higher education funding and governance has led to research funding being seen as a critical element in the survival and financial health of academic units, and thus of the nature and extent of academic offerings in institutions. Referring to academic departments, they write that "academic capitalism ... has become part of the core educational activity of that academic heartland in the form of various types of educational entrepreneurism" (p. 203).

An important development in recent years is at the state rather than the federal level. States have begun more aggressively investing in university research, most often with economic development goals in mind. Historically, states have supported their research institutions through the enrollment subsidies noted earlier, and that remains the dominant focus of state funding, but in recent years attention has increased on states' leveraging of their institutions' research capacity.

Interestingly, some of the most familiar examples of such efforts are not the most instructive. The associations of Silicon Valley with Stanford and Route 128 with MIT were more spontaneous than attributable to direct state policy intervention.[9] Nevertheless, in the 1980s and 1990s, those examples strengthened policy maker perceptions of the importance of the universities in economic development (Saxenian, 1994; Leslie & Kargon, 1996). Reviewing the history of state efforts in science and technology policy, Plosila (2004) noted that states began to reconsider their approaches to economic development after the heated interstate battles over a variety of major projects in the 1980s, including the federally funded supercollider project (pp. 115–116). Gradually, states came to see the centrality of universities in potential economic development, and universities became willing participants in state policy initiatives, partly reflecting the attractiveness of the provisions of the Bayh-Dole Act (Feller, 1990; Mowery et al., 2001). The idea quickly gaining currency was that states could adopt science and innovation policy initiatives building on their academic resources, creating incentives for commercialization and thus aiding the pursuit of new industries and development.

Illinois, Connecticut, and Georgia exemplified the trend in the 1980s and early 1990s. Of course, unsurprisingly, some states and institutions have had more difficulties in this arena than others, and some approaches have succeeded more than others (Feldman & Desrochers, 2003). Over time, states have experimented with general and targeted initiatives, different organizational forms, a variety of alternative funding mechanisms, and different inducements and incentives. Most recently, California's well-publicized $3 billion embryonic stem-cell initiative raised the fiscal magnitudes of these efforts higher than ever. Whatever the outcome of these latest policy developments, there is increasing evidence that cooperative efforts by states and institutions can stimulate innovation and broader economic development—numerous examples exist for the biotech industry alone (Feller, 2004).

There are at least three potentially significant organizational implications of these state policies and programs. First, when state research initiatives parallel federal and corporate research initiatives, they reinforce those latter initiatives. Second, states similarly reinforce those other sectors' goals when their policies incentivize faculty and institutions' engaging directly in federal and corporate research initiatives, through salary support, creation of "centers of excellence," creation of eminent-scholar programs, funding of venture-capital efforts, and the like. Thus, by incentivizing certain kinds of research activity by faculty, notably activity that may help stimulate economic development, states contribute to academic capitalism's growth and its embedding in institutional norms and values. Third, these state research-policy efforts can contribute to stratification within and across institutions, privileging some fields, academic departments, and institutional emphases over others. This phenomenon has been stimulated at the same time by federal research policies and by the ongoing commercialization of higher education more generally, raising the specter of liberal arts faculty, units, and institutions threatened by an increasingly marketized ethos on campus.

Federal and state efforts in research and graduate education raise a variety of provocative conceptual and policy questions which should stimulate further research. Important issues for attention include the proverbial question of *cui bono*. Geiger (2004) vividly addresses this question of who benefits in his look at the research university context:

> Units that conduct research, whether departments or institutes, compete with one another within a single university for resources to augment their research role. And they compete with other units elsewhere in the research system for direct support of research projects. At this level, the process is truly Darwinian. Units that succeed will increase in size or status (or both); those that fail to keep abreast of the intellectual frontiers will wither or languish, at least as far as research is concerned. (p. 133)

Whose interests are being served by the massive governmental investments in the enterprise, and the rising ascendance of research as a priority on campuses? What ends are being served by this spending, and what are the organizational, philosophical, and societal benefits and costs?

State governance and politics provide a rich context for policy research in higher education. State governments are central to the funding of public postsecondary education.[10] At the same time, however, public higher education in the United States does not operate under substantial local, state, or national bureaucratic authority. The bulk of public campuses' interactions with government take place through mediating organizational entities. These entities include institutional associations, lobbyists, and, most prominently, the state legal structures for higher education. Such structures include consolidated governing boards, coordinating boards, and planning agencies. Regarding these structures, Chambers (1961, 1965), Berdahl (1971), and McGuinness (1985) produced early, pioneering taxonomies of state governance and coordination of higher education. This largely descriptive work suggested some likely implications of the various structures for the organizational functioning of institutions. These interorganizational influences can undoubtedly be significant, flowing from governments to campuses and vice versa, but are most often rather indirect (Richardson, Bracco, Callan, & Finney, 1999; McGuinness, 1999; Zumeta, 2001).

This lack of more direct organizational influences flows from the traditions of autonomy discussed earlier. Altbach, Berdahl, and Gumport (2005) have suggested that public colleges and universities claim three types of autonomy from direct governmental oversight: academic, substantive, and procedural. Academic autonomy reflects the values of academic freedom, the right of academic professionals to pursue knowledge as they see fit. This form of autonomy is centered on individual faculty on campuses, and is guarded by professional associations and legally (although governments have sometimes sought to reduce this autonomy in the past). In contrast, substantive autonomy (the content of institutional goals and decision making) and procedural autonomy (how decision-making efforts proceed) are more inconsistently upheld, varying across time, across states, and, within states, from system to system and institution to institution.

Recent state policy developments, notably mission differentiation and accountability measures, have arguably eroded substantive autonomy at some institutions. Similarly, recent state and federal policy developments, notably emerging open meetings and open records laws and expanding human subjects requirements in research, have eroded procedural autonomy. But state and federal governments continue to balance tendencies toward more distal, "encourager" approaches (which focus on setting broad goals, creating task forces, and establishing incentives and inducements) with more aggressive "intervener" roles (which centralize authority, mandate, and regulate).[11] While the federal government has always been a relatively minor player in governing U.S. higher education, states have been major funders and have maintained more legal authority. Still, in their relations with both public and private higher education, states in recent years have maintained some distance from campuses. Most often, Zumeta (1996) argues, they have settled into a middle path, which might be termed "market competitive" for its blend of freedom and directiveness.

States can affect organizational arrangements, processes, and outcomes in a variety of ways along the intervening/encouraging continuum, including mission differentiation, funding for human resources and infrastructures on campus, creation of faculty workload policies (incorporating incentives of various kinds), constructing of tax codes to favor certain organizational activities, funding of lotteries that support students, targeting teaching and research initiatives, and creation of accountability mechanisms such as performance reporting. Within this context, a variety of studies have examined how governance, politics, and university operations are interconnected.

State postsecondary governance influences have been the focus of many studies in this arena. Lowry (2001) investigated the ways state governance arrangements affect operations on campus, including pricing and spending patterns. Notably, Lowry found that universities in states with more centralized governance and universities with elected boards or boards appointed by elected officials exhibit lower pricing and spending, and suggested that these outcomes reflect the power of institutions' political contexts. Thus, centralized and election-sensitive systems may be less directly tied to academic interests and more attentive to public sentiments favoring lower tuition and leaner institutional operations.

Addressing a similar research question in a longitudinal quantitative study, Nicholson-Crotty and Meier (2003) found that system-level organizational factors, notably the level of centralization of the system authority, help direct and shape the influences of political factors on organizational and other outcomes on campuses. While some influences may be muted by a centralized, professionalized agency, Crotty and Meier argue that transaction costs for policy makers are lowered by needing to deal with only one geographic site.

That states' organizational decisions shape such outcomes raises the importance of recent studies of governance reform. Much of that work suggests the importance of politics, as opposed to demographic, economic, or structural conditions, in the movement of states toward reforming postsecondary governance. In their review and empirical analysis of studies of state governance, Leslie and Novak (2003) concluded that political factors drive governance reform in the states more than institutional-improvement logic.

Although Leslie and Novak concluded that case studies are especially useful for understanding governance reform, several quantitative studies have addressed this issue as well, and come to similar conclusions. For example, in an event-history analysis of extensive state-level data, McLendon, Deaton, and Hearn (2007) found that governance reform in the states has been importantly stimulated and shaped for over two decades by transitions in political power, such as those when control of a state legislature shifts from one party to another, or when a new governor takes office.[12]

A variety of studies of state accountability and assessment measures has profitably detailed the many ways that institutions seek to conform to external pressures, including both reorganizations and new policies, while simultaneously maintaining goals, values, and norms that preserve institutions' strengths as organizations. Nettles and Cole (2001), for example, detail how assessment initiatives create tensions on campuses between legitimate expectations of state coordination and control and longstanding strategic commitments and practices (e.g., upholding faculty autonomy over academic domains). Similarly, Frost, Hearn, and Marine (1997) examine how the imposition of a cost-oriented measure to limit out-of-state enrollments affected varied institutions within the University of North Carolina system, including historically Black colleges and universities and the flagship campus in Chapel Hill. In the end, those campuses acted to interpret and translate the new measure in ways that minimized organizational threats and disruptions.

An important aspect of politics is establishing positions clearly attractive to constituents and stakeholders. Higher education, as a societally valued institution, is of interest to, and affected by, multiple sectors and interest groups. Decision processes in this context are rooted in institutional histories, cultures, values, and norms, and case-study analyses have often highlighted the importance of individual "policy entrepreneurs" in moving in the states' toward new postsecondary policies and organizational configurations (Berdahl, 1971; Richardson et al., 1999; Bastedo, 2007). These activists, working both in external sectors such as legislatures and interest groups and in higher education itself, maneuver among the various parties to form coalitions, stake out positions, reduce conflicts, and guide their organizations and their allies to desirable, although rarely perfect, outcomes.

Along these lines, a small number of researchers have emphasized the symbolic aspects of higher education policy making and policy compliance as it relates to organizational issues. As Bastedo (2007) and others have stressed, political actors usually seek to portray their actions in ways that soothe and satisfy various interests, an approach that aids survival and maintains established resources and values. Edelman, Petterson, Chambliss, and Erlanger (1991), for example, found that establishing affirmative action offices on campus does little to affect actual workforce diversity, but allows institutions to maintain symbolic compliance with social and legal demands and thus helps ensure continuing legitimacy and resources.

Policy makers also employ symbolic, simplifying language and imagery in their consideration of higher education issues. Notably, many political leaders in recent years have maintained publicly that higher education is wastefully inefficient and an expensive drain on state and federal budgets.[13] A number of researchers have investigated the effects of the ongoing pressures from state governments to improve productivity, suggesting that these demands have had significant impacts on faculty work lives and attitudes (e.g., see Slaughter, 1993; Gumport, 1997).

In the same vein, another important governmental influence on organizational operations is via seeking mission differentiation in public institutions, that is, aiming to reduce duplication and competition among institutions by assuring each has a distinct and visible role in the state system of higher education. Seeking a pluralistic state system pushes differing institutions to focus on differing goals, ranging among research quality and graduate education, improved access, targeted remediation, expanded service, vocational preparation, and beyond. Ideally, by narrowing each institution's focus, mission differentiation expands a system's educational scope at a decreased cost. While initially this may appear effective, mission differentiation has the potential to reduce institutional autonomy (Morphew, 2002), institutionalize advantages and disadvantages among institutions, and threaten minority students' access to the state's most resource-rich institutions (Gumport & Bastedo, 2001; Bastedo & Gumport, 2003).

Although direct empirical evidence is difficult to obtain, it is clear that the politics of state budgeting can have similarly important effects on institutional infrastructure, quality, and stability. In a pioneering study, Covaleski and Dirsmith (1988) examined the many ways a set of powerful state actors influenced critical funding decisions regarding the University of Wisconsin when the university was undergoing financial stress and the state actors' self-interests were threatened. Specifically, external interests were able to shape institutionalized expectations regarding budgeting procedures and outcomes in specific, enforceable ways.

A widely cited analysis by Hovey (1999) provided further evidence of political interests' effects on institutions. Hovey's work suggested that, because state higher education budgets are less formulaically driven than budgets for highways, elementary/secondary education, and other forms of state spending, and because higher education attracts appreciably less federal matching dollars, spending for public colleges and universities is one of the most discretionary parts of state budgets. As a result, that spending is usually finalized in the later stages of the legislative appropriations process in most states. If other claimants have succeeded politically earlier in the process, and especially if recent economic conditions in a state have been weak, there is unlikely to be much left on the table for colleges and universities. Hovey's research evidence strongly indicates that in the 1990s, state legislators across the nation chose to obtain flexibility for serving other public agendas at the expense of higher education. Although funding inevitably rebounded some in more recent years, prospects are very unsure for a return to earlier levels of state largesse, especially with the demands imposed by rising maintenance and healthcare costs. Thus, Hovey's conclusions may still hold.[14]

Strikingly, despite the perceptions of some lawmakers that higher education is resource rich and capable of significant cuts without losses in quality (Zumeta, 2001; Callan, 2002), there is evidence that cutting funding does not necessarily improve institutions' ability to become more efficient and effective guardians of public funds. In an empirical analysis of state funding in lean recent years, Robst (2001) found that larger declines in state appropriations reduced the capacity of institutions to improve their efficiency, relative to institutions suffering smaller declines, and noted that "Based on these results, states need to be cautious about simply reducing appropriations and altering universities' revenue structure as a reaction to perceived inefficiency" (p. 745).

More recently, Kane and Orszag's (2003) multivariate analysis has shown that declines in state spending per student adversely affected quality in public research universities, leading to increases in student-faculty ratios and faculty workloads, declines in faculty salaries relative to private institutions, declines in faculty faith in the quality of undergraduate education relative to faculty in private institutions, and declines in student SAT scores relative to those of students in private institutions. Noting that three-fourths of the nation's college students are enrolled in public institutions, Kane and Orszag (2003) term this "a startling and troubling deterioration in the relative quality of public universities" (p. 19).

A recent policy development with important organizational implications is the granting of increased governing autonomy to institutions in exchange for greater accountability for funds, reduced funding assurances from the state, or some combination of these two approaches. States have begun to experiment in governance by focusing on choice rather than standardization, efficiency rather than equity, performance rather than process, and outcome rather than input measures (McLendon et al., 2007). Thus, some state governments have moved toward deregulation, decentralization, and devolution of decision authority empowering local systems and campuses relative to central state agencies. These moves, in keeping with broader national trends in the new public management (Osborne & Gaebler, 1992), began in the 1980s with efforts to deregulate state procedural controls (Hyatt & Santiago, 1984; Marcus, Pratt, & Stevens, 1997). Later, states began to move toward disaggregating central governance systems and weakening statewide coordinating boards (Leslie & Novak, 2003).

Arguably most dramatically, some states have moved toward establishing "charter" or "enterprise" colleges and universities. While other elements of states' public responsibilities have been covered under this approach for decades, including some K-12 educational efforts, the approach is new to public higher education and provides a new operating framework for the relationship between public institutions and state government (Berdahl, 1998).[15] In exchange for increased flexibility in areas such as tuition setting, purchasing, internal resource allocation, and personnel, charter institutions agree to receive more constrained state funding growth. In accepting such arrangements, institutions are betting that new operational efficiencies, new capabilities to establish market-driven tuition rates, and savings from reduced state reporting requirements will lead to increased net revenues. Charter colleges and universities maintain accountability to the state through university-specific performance contracts (sometimes termed memoranda of understanding), which operationalize the new framework by defining mutual expectations between the states and their institutions (Association of Governing Boards, 2005).

It is important to note that trends in governmental approaches to higher education are not universally in the direction of decentralizing. Many state reforms in recent years have simultaneously featured elements of tightening and loosening (McLendon et al., 2007), thus continuing historic tensions over these issues. Indeed, state politicians' responses to certain academic freedom controversies on campus have often been directed toward controlling more rather than less of academic life. Along those lines, it appears that no researchers have yet undertaken empirical analyses of the legislative actions and organizational implications stemming from University of Colorado faculty member Ward Churchill's controversial statements regarding the 9/11 terror attacks (York, 2005), but such an analysis could enrich discussions of the contemporary status of institutional autonomy.[16]

Policies sometime attend more to operational systems than to overarching governance concerns. States' management policies and practices can affect institutions, for example. State postsecondary systems often are able to leverage their size through pooled purchasing of resources such as supplies, food services, health insurance, financial management services, and equipment. These efforts can reduce overall costs and thus provide resources for other organizational initiatives, but they also can reduce decision-making authority in individual institutions, and thus threaten sensitivity to local needs (Folger & Jones, 1993).

Perhaps unsurprisingly, it appears that organizational configurations for public postsecondary education can importantly shape state systems' outcomes. Rouse (1998), for example, studied how the organizational structure of state higher education systems may affect various indicators of educational quality, finding that the greater a states' investment in and reliance on community colleges in its overall enrollments, the higher the number of students attending overall but the lower the eventual educational attainments of students. Thus, policy decisions regarding organizational configurations and capacity shape important stratification outcomes.[17]

It is important to examine empirically the ways state policies can influence organization and governance in *private* colleges and universities. As conceptual background, Zumeta (1992) perceptively outlined several potential foci for states in their policy stances toward independent institutions: (a) choice: states can provide aid funding for students to consider more expensive private alternatives to public institutions in the state, (b) appropriations: states can direct state subsidies to institutions deemed to be serving state interests, (c) taxation: states can craft tax policies to help or hinder private institutions and their donors and debt purchasers, (d) tuition: states can coordinate public tuition levels with those in private institutions, (e) programming: states can consider private institution offerings in their decisions regarding existing and proposed academic offerings in public institutions, (f) governance: states can consider the interests and resources of private institutions in the way they structure authority over postsecondary education, and (g) planning: states can involve private institutions in planning relating to higher education. Empirical evidence on states' efforts in these arenas is sparse, but Zumeta's review emphasized that there is tremendous variability in the postures states take toward private higher education, with some states heavily depending on and integrating the private institutions in their policy development and others only minimally considering the sector.

Under Zumeta's (1992) framework, the dominant ways states directly affect independent institutions' organization, governance, and management are system-wide planning, academic programming, and research and technology support. Zumeta found that only six states actively provided direct general (non-targeted) operating support to private institutions: Illinois, Maryland, New Jersey, New York, Pennsylvania, and, to a much lesser degree, Michigan.[18] The great majority of states at that time involved private institutions in planning, Zumeta reported, but surveys suggested that fewer than 10 states "extensively involved" private institutions in planning. Regarding the teaching and research core of institutions, the areas of most direct state influence were academic programming in health sciences and health professions (22 states), programming in other academic fields (12 states), and research and technology support (10 states). Thus, as with public institutions, many of states' influences on private institutions are indirect.

There are numerous other examples of state policies affecting both public and private postsecondary organization indirectly. Notably, as non-profit organizations, public and private higher education institutions are the beneficiaries of state taxation policies. Through not having to pay property tax or taxes on purchased goods, institutions are able to allocate finances to other endeavors that can potentially benefit student learning, research, and service activities. Relatedly, because gifts to institutions as non-profit organizations are tax deductible under state and federal law, individuals are incentivized to give, thus providing resources for institutional development.

Much policy making affecting higher education organization takes place latently, without fanfare, without clear written expression, and sometimes, even without action. Decades ago, social scientists studying community decision making identified the importance of "non-decisionmaking" (Bachrach & Baratz, 1970), a governing authority's determination not to act on an issue, or not to consider the issue at all. More broadly, some organizational trends proceed unnoticed and unchecked, or benignly tolerated, never reaching the point of receiving active, critical attention. Among researchers who have considered what is left undecided, or considered only indirectly, in higher education, perhaps the most prominent is Sheila Slaughter, whose most recent work suggests the emergence, largely unheralded, of a neoliberal state countenancing or quietly encouraging organizational reforms unimaginable in earlier eras (see Slaughter, in press). In 1988, Slaughter argued that for a variety of reasons, public higher education in the 1960s through the 1980s became a vehicle for policy makers to address issues and grievances the private sector was unwilling to consider. In the emerging economic, social, and political conditions, however, Slaughter (in press) suggests that all of higher education, public and private, is becoming a facilitating organizational element and extension of often unwritten state policy goals and agendas:

> In many ways, higher education is … now characterized by: steep user fees (including tuition); dramatically reduced labor costs achieved by outsourcing many classified personnel as well as radically expanded use of contingent professional labor (adjunct and clinical professors); expansion of revenue generating areas (grant and contract activity, university-industry partnerships, exploitation of an array of intellectual property rights, distance education, food services, book stores); participation in making more porous the boundaries between public and private sector (economic development and innovation, start-up companies, technology transfer); heavy investment in academic fields close to the market (business schools and the biosciences).

Thus, Slaughter argues, organizational forms and norms are rapidly aligning to the needs of business, and academic freedom, in particular, is being threatened.

Legal issues shape the organization of postsecondary education in numerous ways, although research on these issues is limited. Most visibly, the organization and operations of admissions offices are significantly shaped by a variety of equal opportunity and affirmative action laws. Recent challenges to those laws have brought social scientists' work on organizational diversity to the nation's highest courts (see Gurin et al., 2004). Much of that work has suggested that a diverse student body brings measurable individual, organizational, and societal benefits (Allen & Solórzano, 2001; Gurin, Dey, Hurtado, & Gurin, 2002; Hurtado, Dey, Gurin, & Gurin, 2003; Saenz, Ngai, & Hurtado, 2006). The argument has achieved both victories and losses in court. The unfavorable decisions have fundamentally altered the extent to which institutions can favor students of color in admissions decisions, and a number of researchers have begun to analyze the implications of these decisions. Notably, analysts such as Tienda and Niu, (2006a, 2006b) have examined the effects of the state laws emerging in the decisions' aftermath. Only a few have focused directly on organizational implications, but those studies are well worth attention for their dissection of how shifting legal contexts directly affect what campus leaders do (see Duffy & Goldberg, 1998; Olivas, 2000).

Another arena in which legal statutes and regulations shape postsecondary organization, both formally and informally, is in the realm of open meetings and records laws, often labeled jointly as "sunshine laws." In a recent study, McLendon and Hearn (2006) found that such laws, which require citizen access to meetings and records of public higher education institutions, influence virtually every area of campus functioning. McLendon and Hearn's multistate study of stakeholder perspectives on mandated openness in higher education governance suggests that, although there is nearly universal support for the principle of openness, most officials see problems in the application of the laws and favor legal refinements. Specifically, while sunshine laws are increasingly accepted and institutionalized in the affairs of public colleges and universities, stakeholders are often unsure of the applications of the laws to particular circumstances, and worry about the capability of parties outside institutions to "weaponize" the laws (i.e., use them to make self-interested, sweeping demands for information) and thus add significantly to the staffing and costs of legal offices on campuses. Also, the laws can raise problems for presidential searches and for governing boards' internal communications and decision making. In an intriguing organizational effect of the laws, the analysis found increasing number of state systems in recent years have initiated new "university foundations" for research, fundraising, athletics, and other purposes—these new organizations are often not covered under sunshine statutes, and thus can conduct their business with less public scrutiny.

Legal issues surrounding privacy are also at the heart of another important organizing trend: many states have moved in recent years to establish state unit-record (SUR) systems to link students' records across institutions and time periods in a state, and across states via linkage agreements. In an event-history analysis examining the factors driving these state policy initiatives to improve organizational database efficiency and, ultimately, student success, Hearn, McLendon, and Mokher (2008) found that the adoption of these systems over the past two decades appears to have been rooted in demand and ideological factors. Larger states, states with high proportions of students of traditional college-going age, and states subject to federal civil rights monitoring, were more likely to adopt SUR systems, suggesting influences of demands posed by size and legal constraints. In addition, states with more liberal citizen ideology were more likely to adopt the systems. Interestingly, the strength of private colleges and universities in a state worked against the adoption of SUR systems, suggesting that privacy and autonomy concerns were important deterrents to adoption.

No discussion of legal influences on higher education organization can ignore academic freedom, which shapes the nature of teaching/learning environments and employment relations in fundamental ways. There appears to be very little being done empirically on the specific ramifications of emerging views of academic freedom. Concerns over terrorist threats have spurred recent developments relating to academic freedom, and student and faculty rights more generally. In several places, faculty have been dismissed or sanctioned for writing and teaching relating to terrorism (see O'Neil, 2006).

Security issues have also driven other legal cases affecting campus life. Notably, in Texas, a controversy arose over whether faculty, staff, and students have a legal right to know the precise placement and scanning schedules of security cameras on a public university campus. In that case, the court ruled that, because the University of Texas is not a police agency, it cannot keep security camera information private, even though doing so might allow criminals and terrorists to avoid detection (Young, 2003). Thus, maintaining an open organizational climate was viewed as legally more important than covert deterrence.

Two legal domains in which less work has been done, but which, no doubt, have important organizational ramifications, are laws to ensure workplace safety and laws and policies regarding the use of human subjects for research. It appears increasing attention is being paid to these arenas in the popular and professional press, but systematic organizational research is lacking.

Conclusion: Expanding the Research Arena

Policy-centered research on postsecondary organization, governance, and management merits expansion. Policy makers are reconsidering traditional levels of both centralization (e.g., state control over budgeting and tuition issues) and decentralization (e.g., institutional autonomy in quality control), university foundations are multiplying, admissions policies are being shaped by legal decisions and by taxpayer votes, governments' economic development initiatives are increasingly incorporating institutions, and federal and state science policies are taking new forms and having new influences on institutions' hiring patterns and structural configurations. This changing policy context should spur more sustained research attention targeted on emerging developments and gaps in our analytic approaches.

First, the *research traditions* of the field may be too narrow methodologically. As Bastedo (2007) has noted, research in this arena has been dominated by descriptive case studies of state policy making. While there are certainly good reasons for focusing on states, given their centrality in postsecondary policy issues in recent years, there is a need for more work at the federal and international levels, where issues of science, technology, globalization, and economic development are of increasing importance. Similarly, while descriptive work can certainly deal effectively with the complexities and uniqueness of each policy episode and setting (Leslie & Novak, 2003), it is regrettable that there is so little use of the robust theoretical ideas of political scientists, policy researchers, and organizational theorists use to understand the complexities of policy development, policy implementation, and policy effects in organizational settings. Broader conceptualizations can enrich understanding and, ultimately, policy and practice. Those conceptu-

alizations can be addressed quantitatively as well as in the qualitative traditions of the field.

Most specifically, the field would benefit from more theory-driven, quantitative analysis of (a) the political, social, structural, and economic factors driving policy formation in higher education systems, and (b) the organizational changes brought on by policy reform. Pursuing these goals would add to understanding of what conditions favor the adoption of certain policy approaches, and how those approaches may, in turn, shape and reform universities and colleges and their students, staff, and faculty. Addressing such questions requires multi-year, multi-case methods developed in a variety of disciplines. Event-history analysis, originally developed as survival analysis in biological sciences and epidemiology, provides a technique useful in discerning the roots of changes in policy contexts in states and other entities (Box-Steffensmeier & Jones, 2004). Also, systematic across-site comparative case studies and nested case studies can facilitate the field moving beyond single-site analyses often too idiosyncratic to foster generalizations (Yin, 1989).

Data limitations have imposed important barriers to research along these lines. For many researchers, leaders, and policy makers at all levels of government, the movement toward building integrated unit-record databases promises significant breakthroughs in tracking the movement of students and funds through institutions (Bailey, 2006; Ewell & Boeke, 2007). But the improvement of student-level data is only one part of the data challenge. Students are nested within multiple organizations and social contexts, which, in turn, are nested in more inclusive organizations and social contexts, and so on. Faculty, staff, leaders, and policy makers are similarly embedded in multiple contexts, each shaping their actions in proximal and distal ways. The construction of longitudinal databases with information on the welter of organizational, economic, demographic, and political factors relating to higher education constitutes a daunting, but critical goal for the field.[19]

Second, the field could more productively employ *institutional theory* in exploring policy/organization connections. Meyer and Rowan's 1977 article remains a pioneering work from this perspective—they argued that U.S. institutions have historically been allowed to decouple their internal processes from inspection to preserve symbols of effectiveness, efficiency, and order. Institutions have used listed course requirements, degree structures, organization charts, grades, and major programs to exhibit standardization and control of the organizational *form* without imposing formal standardization and control of content or pedagogical approach. Thus, college curricula vary greatly in pedagogy, content, and quality across institutions, but appear similar on the surface. Norms and values relating to academic freedom and professional autonomy lessen prospects for external intervention by states or other entities, leaving the core of the enterprise (notably, classroom instruction and learning outcomes) buffered and protected. Thus, students' learning experiences in higher education tend to be far more directly influenced by faculty's values and goals than by those of policy makers, funders, the press, or the public at large.

This provocative early formulation has been expanded in recent years.[20] Increasingly, analysts are calling for explorations of the ways colleges and universities as institutionalized settings interact with other institutionalized settings surrounding them, including legislatures, the press, the federal government, K-12 education, and the courts, each also powerfully shaped and guided by multiple constituencies and stakeholders. For example, what are the values and expectations driving the "P-16" movement (Kirst & Venezia, 2004), and in what ways are universities relating to that effort to better integrate all levels of education in this country?

Relatedly, how are emerging research and development norms, expectations, and agendas in federal and state governments affecting what research is being done and how that research is being pursued organizationally on campuses? Governments shape incentives for pursuing various research topics and for taking various methodological and theoretical approaches to research. One can investigate such issues productively from perspectives based in economic theory, conflict theory, or political theory.[21] But the issues are open for institutional analysis as well, in the style of past work on funding and incentives in other non-profit arenas (e.g., see DiMaggio, 1987).

Importantly, adopting an institutional-theory perspective does not mean simply viewing environments as deterministic and organizational leaders as powerless. As Bastedo (2007) has astutely noted, institutional theory can bring analysts to consider "the myriad cultural, cognitive, regulative, and normative pressures in the environment and to investigate why behavior that is ostensibly nonoptimal persists" (p. 303), but it can also be used to examine strategic change: whether it occurs and, when it occurs, how leaders act to bring reform into compliance with institutionalized norms and expectations, via the enriching of organizational sagas, the development of new organizational resources, and the importation of effective new organizational models.

At the same time, and conversely, it seems important to consider and investigate arenas where policy makers do not act: that is, which higher education issues do policy makers consider but decide to avoid, and which issues never reach the agenda at all? For example, if an early 21st century policy researcher were to be dropped into a faculty discussion about a prospective student at Yale in 1670 (when Yale was effectively a public institution), or at the University of Alabama in 1920, she would note much that was assumed but not being said about what kinds of people should be allowed entry, and much that might be offensive to contemporary eyes and ears. Admissions standards at those schools at those times were institutionalized to the point that certain questions would never be even raised, much less discussed. What then, might be the contemporary analogy? What issues are not even being brought to mind now? Is it possible to hope that contemporary researchers could begin to step "outside" to identify and examine those issues?

Like institutional theory, *political theory* seems underused in the field. As noted earlier, research on the connections between higher education policy and organization has until recently largely ignored state and federal politics. While Schuster (1982), Gladieux and Wolanin (1976), Wilkinson (2005), and numerous others have perceptively analyzed political issues at the state and federal level, the bulk of higher education policy studies have been either focused on policy effects or focused on student aid and tuition, rather than on issues relating to the organization of higher education. Good work is now being done on those latter issues, but clearly more can be done.

Consider the issue of policy development at the state and federal levels. Some studies have been undertaken recently (e.g., see Doyle, 2006) to explore policy-diffusion models from political science such as those of Walker (1969) and Berry and Berry (1990). Such studies investigate the extent to which a state policy development in higher education, such as the emergence of a "performance-funding" system, reflects an impulse in the states to craft policies similar to those of their neighbors, for competitive or emulative reasons. Taking this kind of political analysis to the level of campuses, however, has been more infrequent. How might adopted performance-funding policies be shaped by influence efforts by campus and system leaders, for example? Because substantial management research suggests that much of the power and politics around decisions occurs after adoption and during implementation (Pfeffer, 1992), a related and equally significant question would be how state policies come to be interpreted and further operationalized at the campus level.

In policy studies focused outside of higher education, one of the most frequently used theories is Kingdon's (2003) conceptualization of agendas, arenas, and policy making streams. Little work is being done in higher education from this perspective but, strikingly, it is directly derived from ideas Cohen and March (1986) proposed to characterize decision-making in higher education settings. Some analysts have applied Kingdon's ideas to legislative deliberations regarding higher education, but little of this work has been tied to state policies' effects on campus and system-level organizational forms and processes (McLendon, Heller, & Young, 2005; McLendon, 2003b). For example, if as McLendon et al. (2007) suggest, political transitions in states are key predictors of organizing change in postsecondary systems, how have policy entrepreneurs on campus and off maneuvered to shape these organizational decisions in the window of opportunity available to them? Questions such as this provide an intriguing invitation to apply Kingdon's work to campuses and, ironically, to circle back to that work's intellectual roots in Cohen and March's pioneering speculations on campus organization and governance.[22]

There are innumerable promising ways to study further the connections between policy and campus organization, and no chapter can encompass all that has been done, or that might be done. In closing, therefore, it may be helpful to bring the discussion to ground: In the end, the most important organizational features of colleges and universities are those relating to students. Research that can illuminate understanding of policies and policy making is valuable in its own right, but the primary societal role of colleges and universities should not be lost. Thus, for public purposes and for the purposes of this chapter, the central question is how effectively and efficiently do state and federal policies help postsecondary organizations work to improve all students' enrollment rates, educational experiences, and post-degree outcomes? Not all policies will directly deal with that question, of course, and not all research will examine it. Still, it seems reasonable to hope that work in this arena will increasingly connect productively with the multiple facets of student success.

Notes

1. That argument holds even if governmental policy is viewed as encompassing not only written and legally formalized policies but also what is taken for granted or assumed by those in authority and ultimately expressed through the nature and implications of governmental actions and inaction. Thus, broader social and political theories of the state are rarely referenced or employed in this arena (for an exception, see Slaughter & Rhoades, 2004).
2. Private institutions arguably face the same incompatibilities and parallel, if not equal, consequences of failure in meeting the three goals.
3. Some analysts have attempted to theorize and address empirically the special circumstances of public colleges as multi-purpose, multi-product firms (e.g., see James, 1978; Cohn, Rhine, & Santos, 1989; Winston, 1996; Doyle, 2007).
4. This point has been raised by others regarding educational research in general (e.g., see Clifford & Guthrie, 1988).
5. This may be an example of the gulf between how academics and policy makers think about policy issues (Birnbaum, 2000).
6. See Becher and Trowler (2001), Braxton and Hargens (1996), and Smart, Feldman, and Ethington (2000).
7. Formally, the Bayh-Dole Act is the 1980 enactment of P.L. 96-517, The Patent and Trademark Law Amendments Act.
8. See Dill (1995) for an exploration of the organizational origins and impacts of these offices.
9. A counter-example is Research Triangle Park in North Carolina, an intentional effort integrated with Duke University, North Carolina State University, and the University of North Carolina, Chapel Hill.
10. Especially in the 2-year vocational/technical and community college sectors and in non-research intensive public 4-year institutions. In the major public research universities (the "flagships"), the bulk of institutional budgets comes from the federal government, private donors, foundations, students and their families, and other non-state sources.
11. See McDonnell and Elmore (1987) and Colbeck (2002).
12. Also see McLendon and Ness (2003).
13. See extensive testimony and publications relating to the recent "Spellings Commission" (Secretary of Education's Commission, 2006).
14. For some recent supportive evidence, see Delaney and Doyle (2007).
15. Among the states experimenting with versions of this approach have been Maryland, Virginia, and Colorado.
16. For an insightful essay suggesting some directions for empirically oriented organizational research in this arena, see O'Neil (2006).
17. Also see Hearn and Griswold (1994) for an examination of policy choices empirically related to the level of centralization in postsecondary governance systems.
18. The number of states supporting private institutions has shrunk to four since that time (Hebel, 2003).
19. These issues are considered at more length in Shaw and Heller (2007).
20. For example, see the new contribution by Meyer et al. (2007).
21. Such work is indeed important and being done (e.g., see Saxenian, 1994; Slaughter & Rhoades, 2004).
22. While the McLendon et al. study (2007) was longitudinal and quantitative, examination of the relevance of Kingdon's ideas to organizational reform would most likely require deeper qualitative study of particular campus and state cases. For some examples, see Mills (2007) and Leslie and Berdahl (2008).

References

Allen, W. R., & Solórzano, D. G. (2001). Affirmative action, educational equity, and campus racial climate: A case study of the University of Michigan Law School. *Berkeley La Raza Law Journal, 12*, 237–363.

Altbach, P. G., Berdahl, R. O., & Gumport, P. J. (2005). Introduction. In P. G. Altbach, R. O. Berdahl, & P. J. Gumport (Eds.), *American higher education in the twenty-first century: Social, political, and economic challenges* (pp. 1–11). Baltimore: Johns Hopkins University Press.

Association of Governing Boards of Universities and Colleges. (2005, December). The new interest in charter universities and state performance contracts (State Policy Brief No. 3). Washington, DC: Author.

Bachrach, P., & Baratz, M. S. (1970). *Power and poverty: Theory and practice.* New York: Oxford University Press.

Bailey, T. R. (2006). *Research on institution-level practice for postsecondary student success.* Washington, DC: U.S. Department of Education, National Postsecondary Education Collaborative.

Bastedo, M. N. (2007). Sociological frameworks for higher education policy research. In P. Gumport (Ed.), *Sociology of higher education: Contributions and their contexts* (pp. 295–316). Baltimore: Johns Hopkins University Press.

Bastedo, M. N., & Gumport, P. J. (2003). Access to what? Mission differentiation and academic stratification in US public higher education. *Higher Education, 46*(3), 341–359.

Becher, T., & Trowler, P. (2001). *Academic tribes and territories: Intellectual enquiry and the cultures of disciplines* (2nd ed.). Buckingham, UK: SRHE/Open University Press.

Ben-David, J. (1977). *Centers of learning: Britain, France, Germany, United States.* New York: McGraw Hill.

Bercovitz, J., & Feldman, M. P. (2008). Academic entrepreneurs: Organizational change at the individual level. *Organization Science, 19*, 69–89.

Berdahl, R. O. (1971). *Statewide coordination of higher education.* Washington, DC: American Council on Education.

Berdahl, R. O. (1990). Public universities and state governments: Is the tension benign? *Educational Record, 71*(1), 38–42.

Berdahl, R. O. (1998). Balancing self interest and accountability: St. Mary's College of Maryland. In T. J. MacTaggart (Ed.), *Seeking excellence through independence: Liberating colleges and universities from excessive regulation* (pp. 59–83). San Francisco: Jossey-Bass.

Berry, F. S., & Berry, W. D. (1990). State lottery adoptions as policy innovations: An event history analysis. *American Political Science Review, 84*, 395–416.

Birnbaum, R. (2000). Policy scholars are from Venus, policymakers are from Mars. *Review of Higher Education, 23*, 119–132.

Box-Steffensmeier, J. M., & Jones, B. S. (2004). *Event history modeling: A guide for social scientists.* Cambridge, UK: Cambridge University Press.

Bowen, H. (1980). *The costs of higher education: How much do colleges and universities spend per student and how much should they spend?* San Francisco: Jossey-Bass.

Braxton, J. B., & Hargens, L. L. (1996). Variation among academic disciplines: Analytical frameworks and research. In J. C. Smart (Ed.), *Higher education: handbook of theory and research: Vol. 11* (pp. 1–46). New York: Agathon Press.

Burke, J. C. (2002). *Funding public colleges and universities for performance: Popularity, problems, and prospects.* Albany, NY: Nelson Rockefeller Institute Press.

Burke, J. C. (2005). The many faces of accountability. In J.C. Burke (Ed.), *Achieving accountability in higher education* (pp. 1–24). San Francisco: Jossey-Bass.

Callan, P. M. (2002, February). *Coping with recession: Public policy, economic downturns, and higher education.* San Jose, CA: National Center for Public Policy and Higher Education.

Callan, P. M. (2007, November 2). Looking under the hood of public higher ed. Retrieved November 6, 2007, from http://www.insidehighered.com/layout/set/print/views/2007/11/02/callan

Chambers, M. M. (1961). *Voluntary statewide coordination in public higher education.* Ann Arbor: University of Michigan.

Chambers, M. M. (1965). *Freedom and repression in higher education.* Bloomington, IN: Bloomcraft Press.

Chronicle Almanac, 2007–8. (2008). College enrollment by age of students, Fall 2006. *The Chronicle of Higher Education, 55*(1), 14.

Clark, B. R. (1983). *The higher education system.* Berkeley: University of California Press.

Clifford, G. J. & Guthrie, J. W. (1988). *Ed school: A brief for professional education.* Chicago: University of Chicago Press.

Cohen, M., & March, J. G. (1986). *Leadership and ambiguity: The American college president.* Boston: Harvard Business School Press.

Cohn, E., Rhine, S. L. W., & Santos, M. C. (1989). Institutions of higher education as multi-product firms: Economies of scale and scope. *The Review of Economics and Statistics, 71*, 284–290.

Colbeck, C. L. (2002). State policies to improve undergraduate teaching. *The Journal of Higher Education, 73*, 4–25.

The College Board. (2007). *Trends in college pricing, 2007.* Washington, DC: Author.

Covaleski, M., & Dirsmith, M. (1988). An institutional perspective on the rise, social transformation, and fall of a university budget category. *Administrative Science Quarterly, 33*, 562–587.

Delaney, J. A., & Doyle, W. R. (2007). The role of higher education in state budgets. In K. M. Shaw & D. E. Heller (Eds.), *State postsecondary education research: New methods to inform policy and practice* (pp. 55–76). Sterling, VA: Stylus.

Dill, D. D. (1995). University-industry entrepreneurship: The organization and management of American university technology transfer units. *Higher Education, 29*, 369–384.

DiMaggio, P. (1987). Nonprofit organizations in the production and distribution of culture. In W. Powell (Ed.), *The nonprofit sector: A research handbook* (pp. 195–220). New Haven, CT: Yale University Press.

Doyle, W. R. (2006). Adoption of merit-based student grant programs: An event history analysis. *Educational Evaluation and Policy Analysis, 28*, 259–285.

Doyle, W. R. (2007). Challenges to designing cross-state measures of state resources for higher education. In K. M. Shaw & D. E. Heller (Eds.), *State postsecondary education research: New methods to inform policy and practice* (pp. 97–120). Sterling, VA: Stylus.

Duffy, E.A., & Goldberg, I. (1998). *Crafting a class: College admissions and financial aid, 1955–1994.* Princeton, NJ: Princeton University Press.

Edelman, L., Petterson, S., Chambliss, E., & Erlanger, H. S. (1991). Legal ambiguity and the politics of compliance: Affirmative action officers' dilemma. *Law and Policy, 13*, 73–97.

Ehrenberg, R. G. (2000). *Tuition rising: Why college costs so much.* Cambridge, MA: Harvard University Press.

Ewell, P., & Boeke, M. (2007). *Critical connections: Linking states' unit record systems to track student progress.* Indianapolis, In.: Lumina Foundation for Education.

Feldman, M. P., & Desrochers, P. (2003). The evolving role of research universities in technology transfer: Lessons from the history of Johns Hopkins University. *Industry and Innovation, 10*, 5–24.

Feller, I. (1990). Universities as engines of R&D-based economic growth: They think they can. *Research Policy, 19*, 335–348.

Feller, I. (2004). Virtuous and vicious cycle in the contributions of public research universities to state economic development objectives. *Economic Development Quarterly, 18*, 138–150.

Finifter, D. F., Baldwin, R. G., & Thelin, J. R. (1991). *The uneasy public policy triangle in higher education: Quality, diversity, and budgetary efficiency.* New York: ACE-Macmillan.

Folger, J., & Jones, D. P. (1993). *Using fiscal policy to achieve state education goals: State Policy and College Learning.* Denver, CO: Education Commission of the States.

Frost, S. H., Hearn, J. C., & Marine, G. M. (1997). State policy and the public research university: A case study of manifest and latent tensions. *Journal of Higher Education, 68*, 363–397.

Geiger, R. (1986). *To advance knowledge: The growth of American research universities in the twentieth century: 1900–1940.* New York: Oxford University Press.

Geiger, R. (2004). *Knowledge and money: Research universities and the paradox of the marketplace.* Stanford, CA: Stanford University Press.

Gladieux, L. E., King, J. E., & Corrigan, M. E. (2005). The federal government and higher education. In P. G. Altbach, R. O. Berdahl, & P. J. Gumport (Eds.), *American higher education in the twenty-first century: Social, political, and economic challenges* (2nd ed., pp. 163–197). Baltimore: Johns Hopkins University Press.

Gladieux, L. E., & Wolanin, T. R. (1976). *Congress and the colleges: The national politics of higher education.* Lexington, MA: Lexington (Heath).

Goldrick-Rab, S., & Shaw, K. M. (2007). Tracking how ideas become higher education policy and practice. In K. M. Shaw & D. E. Heller (Eds.), *State postsecondary education research: New methods to inform policy and practice* (pp. 77–96). Sterling, VA: Stylus.

Gumport, P. J. (1991). The federal role in American graduate education. In J. C. Smart (Ed.), *Higher education: Handbook of theory and research: Vol. 7* (pp. 102–134). New York: Agathon.

Gumport, P. J. (1997). Public universities as academic workplaces. *Daedalus, 126*(4), 113–136.

Gumport, P. J., & Bastedo, M. N. (2001). Academic stratification and endemic conflict: Remedial education policy at CUNY. *Review of Higher Education, 24*, 333–349.

Gurin, P., Dey, E. L., Hurtado, S., & Gurin, G. (2002). Diversity and higher education: Theory and impact on educational outcomes. *Harvard Educational Review, 72*, 330–366.

Gurin, P., Lehman, J. S., Lewis, E., Dey, E. L., Gurin, G., & Hurtado, S. (2004). *Defending diversity: Affirmative action at the University of Michigan.* Ann Arbor: University of Michigan Press.

Hackett, E. (1990). Science as a vocation in the 1990s: The changing organizational culture of academic science. *Journal of Higher Education, 61*, 241–279.

Hearn, J. C. (2001). Access to postsecondary education: Financing equity in an evolving context. In M. B. Paulsen & J. C. Smart (Eds.), *The finance of higher education: Theory, research, policy, and practice* (pp. 439–460). New York: Agathon Press.

Hearn, J. C. (2006, November). *Student success: What research suggests for policy and practice.* Washington, DC: U.S. Department of Education, National Postsecondary Education Collaborative.

Hearn, J. C., & Anderson, M. S. (1995). The Minnesota financing experiment. In E. St. John (Ed.), *New directions for higher education: Rethinking tuition and financial aid strategies, No. 89* (pp. 5–25). San Francisco: Jossey-Bass.

Hearn, J. C., & Griswold, C. P. (1994). State-level centralization and policy innovation in U.S. postsecondary education. *Educational Evaluation and Policy Analysis, 16*, 161–190.

Hearn, J. C., McLendon, M. K., & Mokher, C. (2008). Accounting for student success: An empirical analysis of the origins and spread of state student unit-record systems. *Research in Higher Education, 49*, 665–683.

Hebel, S. (2003). Private colleges face cuts in public dollars. *Chronicle of Higher Education, 49*(47), A19–A20.

Heller, D. E. (2007). The challenges of comparative state-level higher education policy research. In K. M. Shaw & D. E. Heller (Eds.), *State postsecondary education research: New methods to inform policy and practice* (pp. 1–10). Sterling, VA: Stylus.

Hines, E. R. (2000). The governance of higher education. In J. C. Smart (Ed.), *Higher education handbook of theory and research: Vol. 15* (pp. 105–155). New York: Agathon Press.

Hovey, H. A. (1999). *State spending for higher education in the next decade: The battle to sustain current support.* San Jose, CA: National Center for Public Policy and Higher Education.

Hurtado, S., Dey, E. L., Gurin, P., & Gurin, G. (2003). The college environment, diversity, and student learning. In J. C. Smart (Ed.), *Higher education: Handbook of theory and research: Vol. 18* (pp. 145–189). Amsterdam: Kluwer.

Hyatt, J. A., & Santiago, A. A. (1984). *Incentives and disincentives for effective management.* Washington, DC: National Association of Colleges and University Business Officers.

James, E. (1978). Product mix and cost disaggregation: A reinterpretation of the economics of higher education. *Journal of Human Resources, 13,* 157–186.

Kane, T. J., & Orszag, P. R. (2003, September). *Funding restrictions at public universities: Effects and policy implications* (Brookings Institution Working Paper). Washington, DC: Brookings Institution.

Kerr, C. (1963). *The uses of the university.* New York: Harper and Row.

Kingdon, J. W. (2003). *Agendas, alternatives, and public policies* (2nd ed.). New York: Longman.

Kirst, M., & Venezia, A. (Eds.). (2004). *From high school to college: Improving opportunities for success in postsecondary education.* San Francisco: Jossey-Bass.

Leslie, D. W., & Berdahl, R. O. (2008). The politics of restructuring higher education in Virginia: A case study. *Review of Higher Education, 31,* 309–328.

Leslie, D. W., & Novak, R. J. (2003). Substance versus politics: Through the dark mirror of governance reform. *Educational Policy, 17,* 98–120.

Leslie, S. W., & Kargon, R. H. (1996). Selling Silicon Valley: Frederick Terman's model for regional advantage. *Business History Review, 70,* 435–472.

Lowry, R. C. (2001). Governmental structure, trustee selection and public university prices and spending: Multiple means to similar ends. *American Journal of Political Science, 45,* 845–861.

Marcus, L. R., Pratt, B., & Stevens, J. L. (1997). Deregulating colleges: The autonomy experiment. *Educational Policy, 11,* 92–110.

McDonnell, L., & Elmore, R. (1987). Getting the job done: Alternative policy instruments. *Educational Evaluation and Policy Analysis, 9,* 133–152.

McGuinness, A. C. (1985). *State postsecondary education structures handbook.* Denver, CO: Education Commission of the States.

McGuinness, A. C. (1999). The states and higher education. In P. G. Altbach, R. O. Berdahl, & P. J. Gumport (Eds.), *American higher education in the twenty-first century: Social, political, and economic challenges* (pp. 198–225). Baltimore: Johns Hopkins University Press.

McLendon, M. K. (2002). State governance reform of higher education: Patterns, trends, and theories of the public policy process. In J. C. Smart (Ed.), *Higher education: Handbook of theory and research: Vol. 18* (pp. 57–143). New York: Agathon Press.

McLendon, M. K. (2003a). The politics of higher education: Toward an expanded research agenda. *Educational Policy, 17,* 165–191.

McLendon, M. K. (2003b). Setting the governmental agenda for state decentralization of higher education. *Journal of Higher Education, 74,* 479–516.

McLendon, M. K., Deaton, R., & Hearn, J. C. (2007). The enactment of reforms in state governance of higher education: Testing the political-instability hypothesis. *Journal of Higher Education, 78,* 645–675.

McLendon, M. K., & Hearn, J. C. (2006). Mandated openness in public higher education: A field study of state sunshine laws and institutional governance. *Journal of Higher Education, 77,* 645–683.

McLendon, M. K., Hearn, J. C., & Deaton, R. (2006). Called to account: Analyzing the origins and spread of state performance-accountability policies for higher education. *Educational Evaluation and Policy Analysis, 28,* 1–24.

McLendon, M. K., Heller, D. E., & Young, S. P. (2005). State postsecondary policy innovation: Politics, competition, and the interstate migration of policy ideas. *Journal of Higher Education, 76,* 363–400.

McLendon, M. K., & Ness, E. C. (2003). The politics of state higher education governance reform. *Peabody Journal of Education, 78*(4), 66–88.

Meyer, J. W., & Rowan, B. (1977). Institutionalized organizations: Formal structure as myth and ceremony. *American Journal of Sociology, 83,* 340–363.

Meyer, J. W., Ramirez, F. O., Frank, D. J., & Schofer, E. (2007). Higher education as an institution. In P. Gumport (Ed.), *Sociology of higher education: Contributions and their contexts* (pp. 187–221). Baltimore: Johns Hopkins University Press.

Mills, M. R. (2007). Stories of politics and policy: Florida's higher education governance reorganization. *Journal of Higher Education, 78,* 162–187.

Morphew, C. C. (2002, June). *Steering colleges and universities toward distinctive missions.* Paper presented at the Research Seminar on Governance, Santa Fe, New Mexico. Retrieved October 28, 2007, from http://www.usc.edu/dept/chepa/gov/rf2002/morphew.pdf

Mowery, D. C., Nelson, R. R., Sampat, B. N., & Ziedonis, A. A. (2001). The growth of patenting and licensing by U.S. universities: An assessment of the effects of the Bayh-Dole Act of 1980. *Research Policy, 30,* 99–119.

Mowery, D. C., & Ziedonis, A. A. (2002). Academic patent quality and quantity before and after the Bayh-Dole Act in the United States. *Research Policy, 31,* 399–418.

National Science Foundation, Division of Science Resources Statistics. (2006). *Federal science and engineering support to universities, colleges, and non-profit institutions: Fiscal year 2005* (NSF No. 07-333). Retrieved October 26, 2007, from http://www.nsf.gov/statistics/nsf07333/content.cfm?pub_id=3795&id=3

Nettles, M., & Cole, J. (2001). A study in tension: State assessment and public colleges and universities. In D. E. Heller (Ed.), *The states and public higher education policy: Affordability, access, and accountability* (pp. 198–218). Baltimore: Johns Hopkins University Press.

Newman, F. (1987). *Choosing quality: Reducing conflict between the state and the university.* Denver, CO: Education Commission of the States.

Nicholson-Crotty, J., & Meier, K. J. (2003). Politics, structure, and public policy: The case of higher education. *Educational Policy, 17,* 80–97.

Olivas, M. A. (2000). The shape of the class [Review of the books *The shape of the river: Long-term consequences of considering race in college and university admissions* and *Crafting a class: College admissions and financial aid, 1955–1994*]. *Review of Higher Education, 24,* 193–201.

O'Neil, R. M. (2006). Limits of freedom: The Ward Churchill case. *Change, 38*(5), 34–41.

Osborne, D., & Gaebler, T. (1992) *Reinventing government: How the entrepreneurial spirit is transforming the public sector.* Reading, MA: Addison-Wesley.

Pfeffer, J. (1992). *Managing with power: Politics and influence in organizations.* Boston: Harvard Business School Press.

Plosila, W. H. (2004). State science- and technology-based economic development policy: History, trends, developments, and future directions. *Economic Development Quarterly, 18,* 113–126.

Richardson, R. C., Bracco, K. C., Callan, P. M., & Finney, J. E. (1999). *Designing state higher education systems for a new century.* Phoenix, AZ: Oryx Press.

Robst, J. (2001). Cost efficiency in public higher education institutions. *The Journal of Higher Education, 72,* 730–750.

Rouse, C. E. (1998). Do two-year colleges increase overall educational attainment? Evidence from the states. *Journal of Policy Analysis and Management, 17,* 595–620.

Saenz, V. B., Ngai, H., & Hurtado, S. (2006). Factors influencing positive interactions across race for African American, Asian American, Latino, and White college students. *Research in Higher Education, 48,* 1–38.

Saxenian, A. (1994). *Regional advantage: Culture and competition in*

Silicon Valley and Route 128. Cambridge, MA: Harvard University Press.

Schuster, J. H. (1982). Out of the frying pan: The politics of education in a new era. *Phi Delta Kappan, 63,* 583–591.

The Secretary of Education's Commission on the Future of Higher Education. (2006). *A test of leadership: Charting the future of U.S. higher education.* Washington, DC: U.S. Department of Education.

Shane, S. (2004). Encouraging university entrepreneurship? The effect of the Bayh-Dole Act on university patenting in the United States. *Journal of Business Venturing, 19,* 127–151.

Shaw, K. M., & Heller, D. E. (Eds.). (2007). *State postsecondary education research: New methods to inform policy and practice.* Sterling, VA: Stylus.

Slaughter, S. (1988). Academic freedom and the state: Reflections on the uses of knowledge. *Journal of Higher Education, 59,* 241–262.

Slaughter, S. (1993). Retrenchment in the 1980s: The politics of prestige and gender. *Journal of Higher Education, 64,* 250–282.

Slaughter, S. (in press). Academic freedom and the neoliberal state. In J. C. Hermanowicz (Ed.), *The American academic profession: Changing forms and functions.* Baltimore: Johns Hopkins University Press.

Slaughter, S., & Leslie, L. L. (1997). *Academic capitalism: Politics, policies, and the entrepreneurial university.* Baltimore: Johns Hopkins University Press.

Slaughter, S., & Rhoades, G. (2004). *Academic capitalism and the new economy: Markets, state, and higher education.* Baltimore: Johns Hopkins University Press.

Smart, J. C., Feldman, K. A., & Ethington, C. A. (2000). *Academic disciplines: Holland's theory and the study of college students and faculty.* Nashville, TN: Vanderbilt University Press.

Spellings, M. (2006, September 6). *An action plan for higher education* [Speech delivered to the National Press Club]. Washington, DC. Retrieved March 29, 2007, from http://www.ed.gov/news/speeches/2006/09/09262006.html

St. John, E. P. (2003). *Refinancing the college dream: Access, equal opportunity, and justice for taxpayers.* Baltimore: Johns Hopkins University Press.

Terenzini, P. (1996). Rediscovering roots: Public policy and higher education research. *Review of Higher Education, 20,* 5–13.

Thelin, J. (2004). *A history of American higher education.* Baltimore: Johns Hopkins University Press.

Tienda, M., & Niu, S. X. (2006a). Capitalizing on segregation, pretending neutrality: College admissions and the Texas top 10% law. *American Law and Economics Review, 8,* 312–346.

Tienda, M., & Niu, S. X. (2006b). Flagships, feeders, and the Texas top 10% law: A test of the "Brain Drain" hypothesis. *Journal of Higher Education, 77,* 712–739.

U.S. Department of Education. (2007). *Digest of education statistics, 2006* (National Center for Education Statistics Report 2007-017). Washington, DC: Author.

Volkwein, J. F. (1987). State regulation and campus autonomy. In J. C. Smart (Ed.), *Higher Education: Handbook of theory and research*: *Vol. 3* (pp. 120–154). New York: Agathon Press.

Walker, J. L. (1969). The diffusion of innovations among the American states. *American Political Science Review, 63,* 880–899.

Weick, K. (1976). Educational organization as loosely coupled system. *Administrative Science Quarterly, 21,* 1–19.

Wilkinson, R. (2005). *Aiding students, buying students: Financial aid in America.* Nashville, TN: Vanderbilt University Press.

Winston, G. (1996). *The economic structure of higher education: Subsidies, customer inputs, and hierarchy* (Williams Project on the Economics of Higher Education No. 40). Williamstown, MA: Williams College.

Yin, R. K. (1989). *Case study research: Design and methods* (Rev. ed.) Newbury Park, CA: Sage.

York, M. (2005). Unrest on campus over speaker who sees U.S. role in 9/11. *New York Times,* January 31, 2005. Retrieved June 2, 2008, from http://www.nytimes.com/2005/01/31/nyregion/31hamilton.html?scp=16&sq=%22ward+churchill%22&st=nyt

Young, J. R. (2003). Smile! You're on campus camera: Colleges debate increased use of surveillance devices. *Chronicle of Higher Education, 49*(40), A36–38.

Zumeta, W. (1992). State policies and private higher education: Policies, correlates, and linkages. *Journal of Higher Education, 63,* 363–417.

Zumeta, W. (1996). Meeting the demand for higher education without breaking the bank: A framework for the design of state higher education policies for an era of increasing demand. *Journal of Higher Education, 67,* 367–425.

Zumeta, W. (2001). Public policy and accountability in higher education: Lessons from the past and present for the new millennium. In D. E. Heller (Ed.), *The states and public higher education policy: Affordability, access, and accountability* (pp. 155–197). Baltimore: Johns Hopkins University Press.

74

The Invisible Hand of World Education Culture

Thoughts for Policy Makers[1]

DAVID P. BAKER
Pennsylvania State University

Education is a global institution—an observation that is as obvious as it is ignored in education policy making in modern societies worldwide. Nothing seems as fundamental to the future of a nation as its own public school system, from kindergarten to the upper reaches of higher education. Consequently, most education policy making starts from the premise that schooling is explicitly national, or as in the case of the United States, local but within an overall national context. Yet, while issues that education policy addresses seemingly come only from local concerns and situations, in actuality almost always these issues are rooted in a global institution supported by a common culture of formal education reaching across just about every nation in the world. What appears to be a burning local or national education policy issue often is the product of larger trends throughout education worldwide. Over the relatively short history of mass education, common, deeply-held values, ideas, and norms behind the practice of schooling have emerged everywhere. Policy makers react to their proximate environment and tend to be unaware of the global forces behind modern education systems; the costs of such unawareness can be missed relevant information and unworkable solutions to local problems. "All politics are local" is the sage adage given to the would-be effective educational policy maker, but the corollary that "all policy issues are global" is equally important to keep in mind.

Education as a global institution is not just a truism, it is the product of distinct historical development. In a short time, human society went from providing only very limited schooling for the masses and advanced education for the few to the now widely held idea and expected practice of schooling all children and youth. It is abundantly apparent that schooling has steadily pushed its way into lives all over the globe. Just 50 years ago one half of American adults either had no schooling or had attended only primary school, but since then we have progressed to the point where almost everyone graduates from high school and over one half of us go to colleges and universities. During the same period,

whole populations in poorer nations went from no access to any schooling to widespread primary and secondary education. Right now, as a product of widespread formal education, 80% of all humans aged 15 or over are able to both read and write a short statement about their life (UNESCO, 2003).[2] This fact would have been hard to imagine just 50 years ago, and most likely it would have been unthinkable 100 years ago. This is the result of nothing short of what can be called a worldwide education revolution (Fiala & Gordon Lanford, 1987; Meyer, Ramirez, Rubinson, & Boli-Bennett, 1977).

This chapter orients education policy makers and analysts to the facts and consequences of the educational revolution that has been occurring in modern society over the past 150 years and its ensuing institutional power worldwide. It also introduces to this audience a theoretical perspective known as neo-institutionalism that now guides considerable research on why, how, and with what impact national education systems in every respect are largely shaped by cultural forces existing beyond the political and historical particulars of individual nations (e.g., Meyer, 1977; Wiseman & Baker, 2005).

This is not to imply that a global culture of education has produced (or will produce) a fully isomorphic system of education everywhere in the world; substantial differences in education persist across nations for a number of reasons. But at the same time, from kindergarten to graduate education, basic ideas, expectations, and social rules underlying schooling have become similar as a result of an influential global culture about the role of education in society (Baker & LeTendre, 2005). Educators, students, parents, and other shareholders in most places in the world approach the workings of schooling with a remarkably consistent and persistent internalized model of what formal education should be and what it should contribute to individuals and society.

The implications of an institutional perspective on the influence of a global culture of education are significant for the forming and enacting of policy. Policy makers focus on the immediate contingencies of an educational problem and by necessity the specific policy environment (local and/or national) dominate their working model of schooling that in turn guide strategies and actions. Consequently, what is often missed in policy makers' calculations are the common and deeper cultural forces at work behind the idiosyncrasies of a specific problem at a particular time and place. There are a number of classic cases where ignorance of these deeper forces led to surprisingly unsuccessful policy and implementation; examples of a few of these are described here. The causes of these policy failures become clear when analyzed from an institutional perspective of the global culture of education. Lastly, it should be made clear to national and local policy makers that the most fundamental stuff of policy making—information—has itself also become internationalized, and will become increasingly so in the future.

The Nature of Education Policy within the Education Revolution

At the turn of the 21st century, the dimensions of education are immense in terms of its recent growth, its claim to people's time and effort, and the strength of its of impact on their lives. Most salient about this education revolution is both its relative newness to how humans live and the speed by which it grows. The rate of growth for the worldwide number of students enrolled in primary, secondary, and tertiary (i.e., higher education) schooling over the past 200 years rapidly became significant and sustained. Demographically, attending school for a considerable number of years is a new and massive change in the lives of children and youth, and supporting this endeavor is a new role and challenge for their families and communities.

There was very little formal education as we now know it before levels of industrialization, urbanization, and political consolidation into nations intensified in the 19th century. Worldwide, relatively small numbers of children attended primary schooling in the 19th century, but over the first few decades of the 20th century growth took off and by 1940 burst into a logarithmic climb in many parts of the world. And as primary schooling reached large numbers of children 20 years later, enrollment in secondary schooling rose sharply. And by the early 1970s enrollment in higher education began to grow. New advanced sectors of education are spurred on by the growth of the preceding sector. This is not just a function of population growth; for example, what education demographers call gross enrollment rates— or the percent of school-aged children and youth attending schooling—have grown steadily, with only the most extreme social and political events retarding growth at certain times in some nations (e.g., Baker, Köhler, & Stock, 2007). This stepwise revolution in school enrollments, increasingly justified as preparing all children for the adult world, was first undertaken in wealthier nations, but since the middle of the 20th century has spread globally (Benavot & Riddle, 1988; Fuller & Rubinson, 1992).

Similarly, the average length of individuals' school attainment continues to rise worldwide. In what is often referred to as the "developed world,"—rich or at least upper middle-income nations—average educational attainment across the entire population is now slightly over 12 years of schooling. Importantly, a large group of lower middle- and low-income nations now have expected attainment of over 9 years (UNESCO, 2007). The multilateral campaign to bring basic schooling to all children worldwide continues on with some definite challenges to full implementation, but with wide political support nevertheless. As shown in the world map of average length of school careers in Figure 74.1, the world is rapidly becoming a schooled society.[3]

As more people undertake formal education and longer school careers, education continues to assert its authority over their lives. Probably most illustrative of this increased integration of schooling into modern life is the consistent finding from social stratification research that adult social status (i.e., social mobility) is now overwhelmingly dictated by educational performance, attainment, and a general culture of schooling (e.g., Shavit & Blossfeld, 1993). The education revolution has reconstructed heavily traveled pathways to adult status in pre-modern society; inheritances, sinecures, prebends, and apprenticeships have all but vanished worldwide (e.g., Collins, 1979; Hout, 1988).

The overarching idea propelling this sea-change in people's attitude and behavior towards formal education is that schooling is useful, appropriate, and valuable enough to require all children to attend. Ideas about education create the belief that it is good that one's own children are schooled, as well as the belief that it is also good if everyone else's children are schooled too. So the stage is set for mass schooling, all operating under a similar model of education and hence influencing what do and do not become educational problems and solutions. Moreover, appreciation of a worldview of education helps national and local policy makers understand why education systems are constantly under pressure to reform—because they are at the core of what we consider social progress.

Identifying the forces that have shaped the education revolution historically help inform us about the current global forces are at work in shaping the basic components of education policy in the world today. There is a sizable sociological and historical research literature on why the education revolution began and what sustains it across the globe. And although it is a literature with some complicated twists and turns, it is summarized by two major findings. First, and surprisingly, the things commonly thought of as causes of educational expansion turn out, upon close examination, not to be causes. And second, the penetration of a specific set of cultural ideas, stemming mostly from the historical rise of Western society, generates a logic by which both individuals and nations actively believe in and support large amounts of formal education.

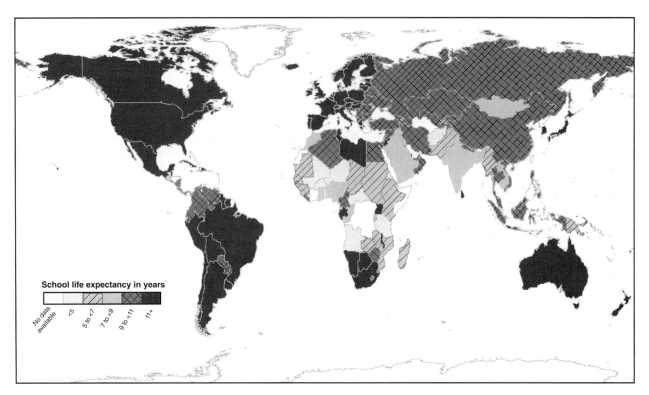

Figure 74.1 Average school life-expectancy in years for primary and secondary education by country, 2001. *Note:* Data refer to 2001 for 133 countries, 2000 for 38 countries, and 1999 for 7 countries. *Source:* Reprinted with permission, UNESCO Institute for Statistics, Figure 3, Global Education Digest, 2004, p. 11.

These two findings are well illustrated by recent research on the origins of worldwide growth of enrollments in higher education—the most current of thriving educational expansion. Evan Schofer and John Meyer (2005), two sociologists who have extensively studied why formal education grows, report on the amazing expansion of people undertaking higher education: about half a million students, or just 1% of youth were enrolled worldwide in 1900, yet 100 years later, approximately 100 million were enrolled, representing 20% of all youth (p. 898). In a number of nations, the gross enrollment rates are now rapidly climbing past 50 and even 80% (UNESCO, 2007).

When Schofer and Meyer analyze which nations have had the highest growth rate over the 20th century, an interesting three-part story emerges. First, contrary to what is often believed, the wealth of nations (as measured by indicators like the Gross Domestic Product) is only somewhat related to growth in higher education (see also Windolf, 1997). Obviously, it takes national resources and a certain standard of living to undertake large amounts of higher education, but the effect is not overwhelming nor is it the whole story, and this is consistent with other similar analyses of educational expansion (e.g., Benavot, 1992; Meyer, Ramirez, & Soysal, 1992). Second, these researchers show that over the middle third of the last century, enrollments grew the fastest in nations most connected to what they call the "world society," by which they mean a combination of factors that make up modern Western culture including scientization, rational national planning for progress, democratization, and the globalized world polity of mul-

tilateral agencies such as the United Nations and INGOs (international non-government agencies) (Drori, Meyer, & Hwang, 2006; Suárez, 2007). Nations that embraced these ideas early on and made them part of their national institutions grew higher education the fastest. Finally, by 1960 enrollment growth rates (not absolute levels) begin to converge in almost all nations as, for better or worse, the western version of a world society dominated most nations. The crux of the story is that the worldwide education revolution is not so much a product of more complex jobs, bigger labor markets, or even consumer patterns in education spending; instead, it is fundamentally a cultural product—a product that operates on a global level.

This is an important story for policy makers and analysts. The supply and demand for education are not just some reflection of economic need, or some "naturally growing" social complexity; instead, formal education expands because it is a deeply held belief for both personal achievement and collective progress. This means that policy recommendations banking on an overly rationalized notion of education supply and demand will likely fail because they miss the larger point of the promise of progress (individual as in human development and collective as in societal) that the culture of mass education has generated (Fuller & Rubinson, 1992).

At every stage of the education revolution, research on the causes of education expansion, like that of Schofer and Meyer, has shown similar results: Education grows not so much because of accelerated economies or social complexities, but because of a growing belief in the powers of education for social progress of society through academic development of individuals (Baker & Holsinger, 1996; Boli, Ramirez, & Meyer, 1985; Fiala & Gordon Lanford, 1987; Fuller & Rubinson, 1992). These findings have transformed our understanding of education's relationship to society: New beliefs about human development originating and spreading through mass academic schooling shapes society as much as, if not more, than societal development shapes schooling (Meyer, 1977).

Formal Education as a Social Institution

Perhaps the best way to come to appreciate the global nature of education is by thinking about education as a social institution. The bundle of theoretical ideas that have made this new perspective on the transforming power of global formal education possible is called "neo-institutionalism." The key to understanding this theoretical perspective is to understand the essence of a social institution. Sociologists have long considered social institutions as the building blocks of human society at any time and place. Here, institution does not mean a specific place with bricks and mortar like in the vernacular "a particular mental hospital is an institution." Instead, it is conceived as the source of sets of rules for behavior and social roles to be played in a particular sector of life. An early sociological idea about institutions argued they provided relatively tight prescription about social roles and behavior, but this hypothesis was discarded after it failed to explain results from a wave of methodologically sophisticated research on a number of aspects of human life.

The older version gave way to a new theoretical version of the social institution, hence the term neo-institutionalism (hereafter referred to as just institutionalism). In this new perspective the social institution is thought of as more of a process. At the heart of this conceptualization is the idea that society is not made up of naturally occurring entities, such as individuals or organizations that enter into institutional arrangements as autonomous agents. Rather, society at its most basic level is made up of institutionalized culture that creates, maintains, and disseminates conceptual models of the individual and the social organization. Ideas about the individual and society are socially constructed. Over the course of the production of collective reality, institutions operate more by providing conceptual models of how to act and feel than by issuing abstract roles, and hence their influence on us can be thought of as generating widely shared everyday theories of reality as opposed to tight commands; in short, they provide the "logic of action" within the social order—normative for sure, but much less scripted than what was theorized earlier (Friedland & Alford, 1991; Swidler, 1986).

The social world is a world constructed out of social institutions providing meanings about how to think and act in the everyday world. Individuals and collectives, such as formal organizations, informal groups, and the individual human, obtain realities through social institutions. There-

fore, from an institutional perspective the very essence of social change and stability are institutional change and stability (e.g., Berger, Berger, & Kellner, 1974).[4]

From this perspective, education is an institution; and like modern healthcare or the family, it may take on some different organizational forms from nation to nation and even from region to region within nations. But at a deeper level, it is strongly affixed to similar everyday ideas about what education is and how it should operate. Every individual school is still influenced by its local, regional, and national context, but the basic ideas behind schooling—what it is and what it should do—are commonly defined in the same way globally (Baker & LeTendre, 2005). Consequently, the organization of national school systems (Japanese, German, Mexican, American, etc.) are now influenced by transnational forces that are out of the control of national policy makers, politicians, and educators themselves, yet these transnational forces are part of their everyday world. This is not to say that some world government, or even overly robust multi-national agencies, overtly forces nations to do and think similarly about schooling, rather, the globalization process is much more all-encompassing. Through institutions like mass education, the globalizing of an image of Western society has led to a set of "legitimating ideas [that] are often much more than values and norms resting in sentiments: they are accounts of how the reified parts of the social world fit together and function and have a cognitive status" (Meyer 1981, p. 897). Indeed, this is exactly the point of institutionalism as a way to think about formal education and society: It describes how widely shared ideas can define what we do in schools as students, teachers, administrators, and even policy makers, regardless of one's own national education system. Widespread understandings, repeatedly communicated within and across nations, result in common acceptance of ideas that lead to standardization and similar core ideas about education, all happening in a soft, almost imperceptible, taken-for-granted way.

Turning a blind eye towards this world institutional quality of schooling that has sustained a successful and massively transforming revolution, the policy maker and education analyst can easily go astray in interpreting trends in schools and universities from a purely local or national perspective. There are a handful of major cultural ideas behind education as a global institution.

Dimensions of the Global Education Culture

A shorthand way to refer to all of the theories of everyday life that institutions produce is to say "culture" (DiMaggio, 1997). Hence, to refer to education as a global institution means assuming that schooling shares a common culture throughout the world. The global education culture provides the logic for action towards schooling at both the individual and collective levels in society. In describing these, it is important to note that they are the core ideas that drive our everyday theories of schooling and do not necessarily reflect the actual practice of formal education at every turn, in fact the opposite can, and does, happen. But the centrality of these ideas is evident in the fact that when they are grossly violated in practice, it is noticed, and over time any such violations increasingly become invitations for educational reform. As core ideas, they are deeply integrated throughout the institution, forming the foundation of the global education culture that has spread so fully over the course of the education revolution. And while there is still some debate over exactly how many dimensions make up the global culture of education, there are at least four that capture most of the scholarly discussions so far. These are briefly described here along with their organizational manifestation in schooling, and how each compares to ideas behind traditional education as practiced several centuries ago before the inception of the educational revolution:

1. *Equality of opportunity and social justice.* From the rise of "student" as a modern status that all are not only entitled to but required to adopt comes the idea that all kinds of people are educable (Meyer, 1977). Moreover, educational universalism, inculcated through mass education up through higher education, sets the stage for the idea of equality of educational opportunity that leads to a foundation for social justice. In its attempts to educate all, the organization of mass schooling, at least formally, ignores social statuses of individuals from traditional society such as gender, ethnicity, religion, family wealth, clans, and so forth. These former highly legitimate personal identities lose authority within the institution of schooling, particularly as they might be used to limit access to opportunity or the future development of the person. As mass formal education becomes a central institution of modern society, its lack of exclusionary logic about access to schooling takes on a wider theme of the universal human beyond the school, which leads rapidly to expanded notions of social justice. This is certainly one of the core ideas that sustains the demand for ever more formal education.

2. *Development of modern individuals for the collective good.* This core educational idea closely aligns human and societal development into one symbiotic process. It stems from and reinforces the modern notion of the individual as the basic social unit of society (Meyer & Jepperson, 2000). Not only is everyone educable, but an educated population, as an aggregation of schooled individuals, adds to the collective economic and social good of society. Versions of this core idea range from extreme economic ones originating out of human capital theory where education is rationalized personal investment to extreme social-political ones where education is citizenship production (Wiseman, Astiz, Fabrega, & Baker, 2007). Hence, mass schooling has increasingly moved towards comprehensive curricula and instruction (at least in its objectives) for all, dominating over specialized schooling for subgroups, regardless of special talents or deficits. This core idea completely rejects the traditional notion of explicitly different educational

experiences for different social strata. Similarly, older ideas of the alignment between "manpower planning and educational efficiency" are replaced by development of individuals in a common academic fashion (Baker & Lenhardt, 2008). In modern society, social stratification, including elite selection, are certainly a central mission of schooling, but the larger logic behind schooling itself is to educate all for a wide host of assumed benefits to all. This idea is the main one that sustains the supply of ever more formal education by nation-states and multilateral agencies.

3. *Dominance of academic intelligence.* The education revolution not only transforms our core ideas about equality, individuals, and the collective good, it also transforms the nature of knowledge itself (Young, 2008). Mass formal education makes academic intelligence primary, privileging it among all human cognition as the master capability to develop. Included in academic intelligence are problem solving, higher-order thinking, informed interpretative skills, generation of new ideas, and an active participation in academic subjects. The development of this type of cognitive ability through participation in schooling takes prominence over traditional craftsmanship, memorization and reproduction of form, emulation of high culture, erudite knowledge, and even vocational training. Official curricula all over the world have converged towards a similar academic model over the past century (Benavot, Cha, Kamens, Meyer, & Wong, 1991), and the rise of what might be called "academic intelligence" as the model of the "smart and accomplished" person has occurred simultaneously (e.g., Schaub, n.d.). This core idea mitigates against frequent revisionist calls for a return to old traditional elite and vocational educational curricula.

4. *Meritocratic achievement and education credentialism.* Formal education has previously been used as a kind of social sorter, but the education revolution takes the sorting function to an unprecedented level. Through earned degrees, chartering of educational institutions, and credentialism, the alignment of educational outcomes and social status attainment is fixed and singularly powerful in its impact on social stratification in modern society (Meyer, 1977; Shavit & Blossfeld, 1993; Werum & Baker, 2004). Moreover as access to jobs is increasingly controlled through educational credentials, personal success and failure is also defined academically to a degree unimaginable in traditional society. The supremacy of academic achievement as a core idea behind formal education is widely legitimated through the assumption that meritocratic principles should work through the schooling processes: educational achievement earns social standing. The focus on achievement and its formal links to educational credentials plays a central role in the day-to-day operation of schools and higher education institutions. Important credentials also increase the logic for expanded schooling, as well as substantiate claims of legitimate authority by formal

education through the production of educated experts, specialized academic expertise, and academically credentialed access to elite positions (Meyer, 1977).

These core ideas about education converge with broader dimensions of the world society that now drive so much of our globalized world Taken as a whole, this model translates into the specific type of education system that is now widely adopted throughout the world. And these core ideas make formal education a leading institution in modern society, and produce an overall widespread "cultural faith" in education to act in social progress well beyond narrowly defined training for jobs (Baker & LeTendre, 2005).

As shown in Figure 74.2, deeply held institutional values about education produce specific cultural products that dominate the aims, goals, and even the organization of schooling from kindergarten through advanced graduate training. For example, the core ideas of *equality of opportunity and social justice* and *development of modern individuals for the collective good* combine to generate almost unstoppable education expansion, as educational investment become a societal logic for creating social progress. Just when one stage of educational expansion becomes saturated and many think it is all that is possible, another cycle of expansion begins. Note the growth in higher education at the undergraduate level and the rise in graduate degrees; or, the growth of distance learning and the idea of "life-long learning" that is sweeping through the American culture.

Another example of institutional values producing major attributes of the culture of education is that the intersection of the core ideas of the *dominance of academic knowledge and meritocratic achievement* shape what becomes important in the day-to-day learning in classrooms. For better or

worse, vocationalism in school has died and along with it the notion of teaching specific skills for the world of work, and so has the passive appreciation of the classics (Benavot, 1983, Bloom, 1987). What has taken its place is a robust notion of academic intelligence that finds young primary school students doing sophisticated thinking exercises for ever greater amounts of time, and more of the curricula at all levels of schooling demanding active learning and the student-as-scholar behavior. As a result, the teaching of cognitive skills, particularly related to what psychologists refer to as "executive functioning," have been on the rise historically (e.g., Baker et al., n.d; Blair, Gamson, Thorne, & Baker, 2005).

A final example is how the intersection between the core ideas of *meritocratic achievement and development of* individuals as a collective good generates along with widespread use of credentials and social status defined educationally, unprecedented amounts of private investment in education, a rising culture of academic achievement at any cost, and the intensification of consumers' attention to school and university quality.

In addition to these few examples, various combinations of these core ideas go a long way in explaining many of the recent trends in schooling and higher education worldwide (e.g., Baker & LeTendre, 2005). And hence policy issues, even of the most idiosyncratic nature, have roots in these common cultural ideas, so much so that often policy success and failure can be judged on how much a particular policy aligns with these ideas. These core ideas swirl around policy in education and integrate themselves into the politics of education in an amazing fashion. They define acceptable problems for the policy apparatus to address, and even define the repertoire of acceptable solutions (March & Olsen, 1979). Of course, as with all social institutions, core

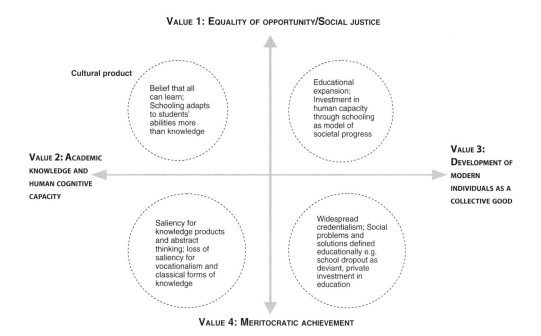

Figure 74.2 Examples of cultural products from fundamental institutional values about education.

ideas taken to extremes in practice can easily produce some internal conflict with other ideas. The list above does not in every instance yield a fully integrated and copasetic practice of schooling. Policy issues which cause such deep conflict between two or more core values are frequently thought of as the most "politically messy," and if robust enough can lead to a certain amount of institutional stretching and change (e.g., Tyack & Cuban, 1995).

Failed Education Policy and an Institutional Analysis of What Went Wrong

Two cases, one about policy analyses and recommendations about the trend of worldwide expansion of higher education, and the other about improving American mathematics and science secondary education, serve as two examples of what can happen when the deeper cultural qualities of formal education are ignored or misunderstood.

Case I: The Great Diploma Disease that Wasn't As the education revolution heated up from the 1960s to the 1980s, educators, economists, sociologists, and experts of national development predicted dire consequences from a worldwide oversupply of educated youth working in jobs "beneath" them. In wealthy nations the poster boy for seemingly run-away over-education was the embittered PhD driving a taxi for a living, while in less wealthy nations it was the angry young man with an upper-secondary diploma who could not find a prestigious job in the nation's civil service. As the first waves of the masses swelled into educational opportunities formerly reserved mostly for elites, it threatened the upper levels of the older educational order, one that had been tightly connected to a small number of elite jobs. The assumption was that the expanding enrollment would mean that as more students received higher levels of educational degrees than in the past, the upper reaches of the labor market would become full, and with their expectations for an elite future dashed the over-educated might turn disaffected and unruly, and the whole modern society would be beset by anomie and social dysfunction. Over-education was considered a looming social problem, even a disease on the verge of epidemic proportions (Dore, 1976).

Books heralding the dangers of over-education flooded into bookstores with telling titles like *The Diploma Disease* (Dore, 1976), *The Great Training Robbery* (Berg, 1970), and *The Overeducated American* (Freeman, 1976). In one version after another, over-education during the initial rise of both secondary enrollments in less wealthy nations and higher education enrollments in wealthy nations was defined as a growing social problem of wide and disastrous proportions, with each new account's pessimism outdoing the last. Some even went so far as to blame the threat of a whole societal upheaval on over-education; one report stressed that frustrations of the over-educated and under-employed is nothing less than the "central dynamic for social discontent emerging in America" (Blumberg & Murtha, as cited in Burris, 1983, p. 455) while another influential book claimed

that the "incongruence between the aspirations of college students … and the labor requirements of the economy is the chief cause of student radicalism" (Bowles & Gintis, as quoted in Burris 1983, p. 455). Even the much trumpeted international Trilateral Commission and the U.S. Government got into the act, with an influential report from the latter proclaiming "the potential for frustration, alienation and disruption resulting from the disparity between educational attainment and the appropriate job content cannot be overemphasized" (Trilateral Commission, as cited in Burris, 1983, p. 456).

At the time, experts from education, demography, and public policy all recommended controlling education expansion. And there were even some policy attempts to do so, particularly in East Bloc nations behind the iron curtain whose leaders felt the same looming over-education problem, albeit with a different take on the political problems it would cause (Baker, Kölher, & Stock, 2007). By and large, this episode was more one of failed policy analysis than actual failure of policy implementation, but it is illustrative none the less.

First, the analysts at the time underestimated or misunderstood entirely the forces driving this wave of education expansion. They took an overly technical-functional interpretation that drew a tight connection between education and fixed slots in the labor market. As described above, a growing worldwide belief in *development of modern individuals for the collective good* forges formal education as both an individual and societal good into a strong logic behind people attaining and society providing more schooling—as mass education becomes a highly valued cultural activity, expansion becomes an assumed good for all individuals and collectives.

Consider, for example, the persistent rise in secondary and higher education enrollments among females. For some reason, most of the over-education literature focuses only on males, but if more attention had been paid to the telling combination of factors behind the similarly skyrocketing enrollments of females in many nations, these experts might have realized that there is far more behind the education revolution than just a competition for jobs (e.g., Baker & LeTendre, 2005). Of course, just like the males, these newly educated females were interested in the kinds of jobs that education would bring them. The expectations for more education were not just determined by narrow economic calculations; expectations were also determined by the fact that the amount of education it took to be considered a normally developed individual in modern society kept rising, as it continues to do today. (The core idea of the universality of being a student in mass education made it increasingly difficult to exclude females from all educational opportunities. In fact, education has been so successful at the incorporation of both genders that on average, American females rapidly reached parity with males in educational attainment and now even surpass them—which in and of itself is a new threat to the core idea of universality in mass education; Bradley, 2000.)

Second, education and labor market analysts, often writing from within universities, also misunderstood how dynamic the relationship between education and the world of work had become as the rising demand and supply of education became a norm in many nations. They operated on an incorrect image of a fixed structure of jobs for which education merely produces trained individuals. So, it was no wonder that as they watched the education revolution take off into secondary and higher institutions, they predicted a volatile clash in the labor market. But no such widespread clash happened—in short, the much feared diploma disease never occurred. A decade or so later when sociologists looked for a great wave of over-education and mismatched workers, they did not find very many. Moreover, they did not detect a rise in job dissatisfaction, political radicalism, political alienation, unionism, or cynicism with an achievement ideology among American workers—all attitudes that one would expect from large numbers of people whose education and expectations for particular types of work were not met (e.g., Burris, 1983, but see Vaisey, 2006, for some evidence of job dissatisfaction).

In this massive demographic change, the over-education image failed to account for the fact that large numbers of more educated people flowing into jobs also led to changes in the world of work. Education expansion has changed jobs and the workplace: more technology entered, and instead of significant de-skilling of jobs, there was an off-setting trend of more jobs requiring skills more in line with academic intelligence type activities. And not only were more educated workers more trainable, they come with new ideas about their worth and the world around them as described above in terms of universalism and social justice. So, it is not surprising that over this period many working conditions changed as well—note, for instance, the wide scale change in rules about sexual and gender harassment in the workplace. This is not to imply that everything good or bad about the current labor markets of developed nations is a sole function of education expansion, but it certainly played and continues to play a major role, and there is evidence that similar trends are occurring in developing nations as well.[5]

Case II: If It Ain't Broke Don't Fix It Perennially, U.S. mathematics and science educators worry that the curriculum across schools in the nation is not very demanding, and that more demanding and better-implemented curricular materials would improve national achievement in comparison to the much advertised high math and science scoring nations such as Japan, Singapore, and South Korea. Since the 1960s "new math" era and even earlier during the Sputnik crises, there has been a long-standing desire by U.S. mathematics and science curricular specialists to get a real chance at setting policy that would improve, strengthen, and standardize curricula throughout the nation. In the mid-1990s, this long-standing interest in reform of American mathematics and science curricula was the solution waiting for a problem to attach itself to.

The media buzz about a fourth to eighth grade "slump" in international tests of mathematics performance of American students in comparison to students in other nations became that problem—and a politically perfect one at that, if only it had really been a problem (Baker & LeTendre, 2005, especially chapter 10).

Policy analysts and makers at the time quickly seized on the idea that U.S. math and science curricula were "broken" and that this was the chief cause of the nation's slump in achievement compared internationally. Major national and local mathematics and science forces, such as the nation's National Science Foundation, the U.S. Department of Education, non-governmental organizations of curricular expert professional associations, state Departments of Education, and some local school districts were all ready to spring into action upon hearing about this problem and, of course, they had the solution already in mind—curricular reform (Baker & LeTendre, 2005).

What is relevant about this case here is that on one hand, the whole concern was driven by the core idea of *development of modern individuals for the collective good*, but on the other hand, it went overboard on reform. This was partly because the mathematics and science constituencies pushing the agenda failed to appreciate the wide global impact of this very idea and the subsequent growing similarity in mathematics and science education everywhere. Also given the widespread cultural faith about education and its impact (realistic or not), cycles of crisis and reform easily beset education and even give the institution a certain dynamic power (Baker & LeTendre, 2005).

The mobilization of the American education establishment over mathematics and science curricula reform was primed by two longstanding ideas about the educational performance of the nation and its economic wellbeing that had been widely disseminated in the media and in scholarly works since the publication of *A Nation at Risk* in 1983. One idea was that a nation's achievement in technical fields such as mathematics and science are directly linked to its economic productivity. For example, two decades of concern over declining U.S. economic competitiveness led to the "economic threat" from East Asian national educational achievements. The other idea was that American public mass schooling was failing the nation as a producer of technically capable future workers. Both of these ideas were powerful in terms of policy, even though research on them suggests that national economic productivity is far more complicated than a one-to-one link with the performance of the school system (Ramirez, Luo, Schofer, & Meyer, 2006).

By the time a new round of international results was released in the mid-1990s, these ideas were already driving the highly ambitious federal government's *Goals 2000* reforms. The *Goals* legislation contained few concrete plans for improving education, but laid out a clear set of lofty, if unrealistic, ambitions. The United States was to become "First in the world" in math and science by the year 2000—a goal actually borrowed from the preceding George Bush administration. *Goals 2000* implicitly made the nation's performance on international tests a referendum on the quality of the entire educational system and promulgated the belief that a higher ranking was indicative of greater national economic competitiveness.

The politics behind this case of U.S. educational reform turned on two main assumptions that quickly became foregone conclusions through extensive official and media coverage. First, that the American mathematics and science curricula were indeed broken and in need of reform as compared to other nations. Second, that if the nation managed to fix its broken curricula, it would improve the nation's educational and economic competitiveness internationally. These assumptions led many U.S. education policy makers at all levels to develop ways to improve the mathematics and science curricula. And even though there were a number of other important policy messages for American education from these international studies, such as the truly extreme level of inequality in education resources in the country, the "broken curriculum" message drowned out all others.

Ironically, subsequent in-depth comparisons of the American mathematics and science curricula and other nations showed very little differences in the intent and implementation of curricula across nations. If the American curricula in these subjects were broken, they were no more or less so than in other nations. Then the analysis found that even the small variation in curricula across nations was not related to national achievement in mathematics and science:

> In all of these analyses, on a range of characteristics of national intended and implemented curricula in both mathematics and science, virtually *no* national qualities of curricula are related to any of a range of indicators of national achievement in 8th grade. High performing nations are not more likely to have curricula with a particular set of characteristics in terms of both intended content as well as implementation in classrooms. Whether it is for the full mathematics and science tests or focused sub-scores, or for indicators of the intended or implemented curricula, there is no pattern of association between the qualities of national curricula and national achievement. (Baker & LeTendre, 2005, p. 162)

What the American mathematics and science policy world failed to understand was that there has been a significant convergence of mathematics and science curricular content and implementation of eighth-grade mathematics and science from one nation to the next. In fact, research on historical curricular trends shows precisely this—national intended curricula continue to converge on similar content over time and across nations (e.g., Benavot et al., 1991). There has come to be much greater homogeneity in terms of recognized core knowledge—content for curricula—at least through the end of primary schooling across nations. Although nations vary with regard to the emphasis they place on various subtopics in the intended curriculum, virtually all nations teach mathematics and science with an increasingly standard notion of the essence and components of these subjects. In the elementary years, most students worldwide will have exposure to core concepts, so it is un-

derstandable that there is no association between intended curricula and achievement across nations.

What happened in this "not so broken curricula" case has happened in a number of well-known cases where it was assumed that if something in the education process could be "fixed," then educational outcomes would greatly improve. Rarely are there single, quick fixes in education. And this case was further complicated by the failure to understand how isomorphic mass schooling has become across nations, in large part because the deeper institutional ideas that drive it are so widely shared. Further, since the motivation for cycles of crisis and reform are deeply embedded within the institution, policy makers need to assess accurately the "real causes" behind each round of the cycle.

If the United States wishes to further enhance its mathematics and science training, these global trends suggest that the nation is not handicapped by "low achieving curricula," and that other qualities of the system, such as instruction and inequalities in resources and so forth, should receive serious empirical investigation before charging off half-cocked towards curricular reform.

Internationalized Education Information and Policy Making

One final observation about the influence of the world education culture on policy making is that the very stuff of policy—sophisticated information on education quality—has become increasingly international (Wiseman & Baker, 2005). Globalization of core ideas has led to the establishment of common definitions of educational inputs and metrics of achievement outcomes which, in turn, generate widespread cross-national comparisons with accompanying impact on national and even local policy debates and issues.

Indications of the dimensions to which educational policy making in many nations has become internationalized are everywhere. Over the past century, nations have observed and actively studied schooling in other nations for their own benefit. In the last several decades, however, the pace of production and breadth of scope of the most basic of policy resources—namely comparable international information on education from a large number of nations—has hit unprecedented levels. Similarly, over the past 30 years, observations of schooling across nations have shifted markedly from only comparing basic structures of schooling and enrollments to a laser-like focus on educational outcomes, primarily student achievement on assessments of academic subjects like language skills, mathematics, science, and social studies. This testing information, frequently packaged as a barometer of school quality, is often accompanied by in-depth information on processes and resources related to teaching and learning of academic subjects. Cross-national studies of achievement, curriculum, instruction, and school resources draw in more nations into internationalizing their education policy, which, in turn, validates a greater interest among all kinds of nations in international comparison. Very public indicators of national educational success or failure routinely now ripple through education policy making.

What was once chiefly an erratic, exotic enterprise undertaken by small groups of pioneering academics from different nations has transformed itself into multi-lateral governmental undertakings of heavily-funded, professionalized international studies of achievement. These studies produce huge amounts of information to judge one nation's performance against the other and are now routine, regularly anticipated, and widely published.

For example, groups such as the International Association for the Evaluation of Educational Achievement (IEA, which produces among others the TIMSS studies and data sources) and the Organization for Economic Co-operation and Development (OECD, which produces among others the PISA studies and data sources) have provided policy makers with publicly-available and readily-digestible information on educational achievement and attainment since the 1960s. Some multinational organizations such as the World Bank, International Monetary Fund (IMF), and the United Nations Educational, Scientific, and Cultural Organization (UNESCO) collect and disseminate their own internationally comparative data—sometimes publicly, sometimes not. In each case, the data reports made available to policy makers are largely descriptive and quantitative (LeTendre, Baker, Akiba, Goesling, & Wiseman, 2001; Marginson & Mollis, 2001).

A cascade of high quality international information about education, which would have been unimaginable just a few decades ago, continues to expand into more academic topics, grade levels, and aspects of running schools and organizing instruction. For policy analysts and makers, this means that less and less of a nation's education system can be sacredly protected from the harsh light of cross-national comparisons. Curricular streaming, social class reproduction through private schooling, gender differences, and other misapplications of well-institutionalized meritocratic principles in education have been exposed for national discussion because of cross-national studies whose results are openly reported, and in some cases, like TIMSS in the United States in the mid-1990s and PISA in Germany in the early 2000s, incessantly commented on in the national media (e.g., Robitaille, Beaton, & Plomp, 2000).

International comparative studies of education have been both praised and criticized, but either way they continue to be consistently used by policy makers. As momentum for international comparisons has increased worldwide, the frequency of international studies being used by national and multinational policy organizations has increased as well. As more policy makers become aware of these studies and are inundated with more recent and updated data from these studies, the relevance of frequent participation becomes a more pressing question (Wiseman & Baker, 2002). The surge in nations' technical capabilities to compare their educational outputs has helped make internationalization of education policy common practice. Further, and perhaps most important, is that the very institutional character of

schooling tempts many policy makers to compare systems in their work on domestic issues (Meyer, 1980; Meyer & Baker, 1996).

World Culture of Education and Policy Making

If most politics around educational policy issues are national, or even sub-national as in the United States and Canada, what do the observations that policy issues are increasingly common across nations and are made transparently so because of growing international information on education mean for the policy-maker? Obviously the trends and their institutional origins described here have been around for some time. What is new though is the degree to which local policy is now debated and formed, and even implemented, in the larger context of education worldwide. The most salient of these contexts is, of course, the image of national competition. And a competitive model easily filters down to subnational units, as witnessed by some American school districts that monitor and benchmark their educational outcomes with both national and international information.

Beyond the competition image and growing in saliency is the use of information about education across the globe as a way to understand the larger forces operating on national and sub-national politics of education. The policy maker, operating nationally or locally, has much to gain from keeping a larger institutional and international perspective.

Notes

1. The author thanks Maryellen Schaub, Saamira Halabi, Laura Salganik, Josh Pontrelli, and three reviewers for their helpful comments on earlier drafts of the chapter.
2. Most people who are still illiterate are living in very poor nations and 7 out of 10 are women (UNESCO 2003).
3. It should be pointed out that widespread enrollment does not imply equal quality of schooling, and there is still considerable variation among the school experiences of students from different nations and social groups within nations.
4. The neo-institutional perspective has spread well beyond sociology to economics, the study of political regimes, and strategic studies and international relations (e.g., Burlamaqui, Castro, & Chang, 2000; Finnemore, 1996).
5. There is a hypothesis that one reason for the lack of social unrest with over-education is that many people are duped into believing that their education is of less quality, and or value, than in past generations. But there has not been much evidence that this is the case.

References

Baker, D., & Holsinger, D. (1996). Human capital formation and school expansion in Asia: Does a unique regional model exist? *International Journal of Comparative Sociology, 37,* 159–173.

Baker, D., Knipe, H., Cummings, E., Collins, J., Gamson, D., Blair, C., et al. (n.d.). T*he fall and rise of American primary school mathematics: A content analysis and cognitive assessment of textbooks from 1900 to 2000.* Manuscript submitted for publication.

Baker, D., Köhler, H., & Stock, M. (2007). Socialist ideology and the contraction of higher education: Institutional consequences of state manpower and education planning in the former East Germany 1949 to 1989. *Comparative Education Review, 51,* 353–377.

Baker, D. & Lenhardt, G. (2008). The institutional crisis of the German research university. *Higher Education Policy, 21,* 49–64.

Baker, D., & LeTendre, G. (2005). *National differences, global similarities: World culture and the future of schooling.* Stanford, CA: Stanford University Press.

Benavot, A. (1983). The rise and decline of vocational education. *Sociology of Education, 56*, 63–76.

Benavot, A. (1992). Curricular content, educational expansion, and economic growth. *Comparative Education Review, 36*, 150–174.

Benavot, A., Cha, Y., Kamens, D., Meyer, J., & Wong, S. (1991). Knowledge for the masses: World models and national curricula, 1920–1986. *American Sociological Review, 56*, 85–100.

Benavot, A., & Riddle, P. (1988). The expansion of primary education, 1870–1940: Trends and issues. *Sociology of Education, 61*, 191–210.

Berg, I. (1970). *Education and jobs: The great training robbery.* New York: Praeger.

Berger, P., Berger, B., & Kellner, H. (1974). *The homeless mind: Modernization and consciousness.* New York: Random House.

Blair, C., Gamson, D., Thorne, S., & Baker, D. (2005). Rising mean IQ: Cognitive demand of mathematics education for young children, population exposure to formal schooling, and the neurobiology of the prefrontal cortex. *Intelligence, 33*, 93–106.

Bloom, A. (1987). *The closing of the American mind: How higher education has failed democracy and impoverished the souls of today's students.* New York: Simon and Schuster.

Boli, J., Ramirez, F., & Meyer, J. (1985). Explaining the origins and expansion of mass education. *Comparative Education Review, 29*, 145–170.

Bradley, K. (2000). The incorporation of women into higher education: Paradoxical outcomes? *Sociology of Education, 73*, 1–18.

Burlamaqui, L., Castro, A., & Chang, H-J. (Eds.). (2000). *Institutions and the role of the state.* Northampton, UK: Edward Elgar.

Burris, V. (1983). The social and political consequences of overeducation. *American Sociological Review, 48*, 454–467.

Collins, R. (1979). *The credential society: An historical sociology of education and stratification.* New York: Academic Press.

DiMaggio, P. (1997). Culture and cognition. *Annual Review of Sociology, 23*, 263–287.

Dore, R. (1976). *The diploma disease: Education, qualification and development.* London: Allen and Unwin.

Drori, G., Meyer, J., & Hwang, H. (Eds.). (2006). *Globalization and organization: World society and organizational change.* Oxford, UK: Oxford University Press.

Fiala, R., & Gordon Lanford, A. (1987). Educational ideology and the world educational revolution, 1950–1970. *Comparative Education Review, 31*, 315–332.

Finnemore, M. (1996). Norms, culture, and world politics: Insights from sociology's institutionalism. *International Organization, 50*(2), 325–347.

Freeman, R. (1976). *The overeducated American.* New York: Academic Press.

Friedland, R., & Alford, R. (1991). Bringing society back in: Symbols, practices, and institutional contradictions. In W. Powell & P. DiMaggio (Eds.), *The new institutionalism in organizational analysis* (pp. 232–263). Chicago: University of Chicago Press.

Fuller, B., & Rubinson, R. (Eds.). (1992). *The political construction of education: The state, school expansion, and economic change.* New York: Praeger.

Hout, M. (1988). More universalism, less structural mobility: The American occupational structure in the 1980s. *The American Journal of Sociology, 93*, 1358–1400.

LeTendre, G., Baker, D., Akiba, M., Goesling, B., & Wiseman, A. (2001). Teacher's work: Institutional isomorphism and cultural variation in the U.S., Germany, and Japan. *Educational Researcher, 30*(6), 3–16.

March, J., & Olsen, J. (1979). *Ambiguity and choice in organizations* (2nd ed.). Bergen, Norway: Universitetsforlaget.

Marginson, S., & Mollis, M. (2001). The door opens and the tiger leaps: Theories and reflexivities of comparative education for a global millennium. *Comparative Education Review, 45*, 581–615.

Meyer, J. (1977). The effects of education as an institution. *American Journal of Sociology, 83*, 55–77.

Meyer, J. (1980). Levels of the educational system and schooling effects. In C. E. Bidwell & D. M. Windham (Eds.), *The analysis of educational productivity: Vol. 2. Issues in macroanalysis* (pp.15–63). Cambridge, MA: Ballinger.

Meyer, J. (1981). Review essay: Kings or people [Review of the book *Kings or people: Power and the mandate to rule*]. *American Journal of Sociology, 86*, 895–899.

Meyer, J., & Baker, D. P. (1996). Forming American educational policy with international data: Lessons from the Sociology of Education [Special issue]. *Sociology of Education, 69*, 123–130.

Meyer, J. W., & Jepperson, R. L. (2000). The "actors" of modern society: The cultural construction of social agency. *Sociological Theory, 18*, 100–120.

Meyer, J., Ramirez, F., Rubinson, R., & Boli-Bennett, J. (1977). The world educational revolution, 1950–1970. *Sociology of Education, 50*, 242–258.

Meyer, J., Ramirez, F., & Soysal, Y. (1992). World expansion of mass education, 1870–1980. *Sociology of Education, 65*, 128–149.

Ramirez, F., Luo, X., Schofer, E., & Meyer, J. (2006). Student achievement and national economic growth. *American Journal of Education, 113*, 1–29.

Robitaille, D., Beaton, A., & Plomp, J. (Eds.). (2000). *The impact of TIMSS on the teaching and learning of mathematics and science.* Vancouver, BC, Canada: Pacific Educational Press.

Schaub, M. (n.d.). *Parenting for cognitive development from 1950 to 2000: The institutionalization of mass education and the social construction of parenting in the United States.* Manuscript submitted for publication.

Schofer, E., & Meyer, J. (2005). The worldwide expansion of higher education in the twentieth century. *American Sociological Review, 70*, 898–920.

Shavit, Y., & Blossfeld, H. (Eds.). (1993). *Persistent inequality: Changing educational attainment in thirteen countries.* Boulder, CO: Westview Press.

Suárez, D. (2007). Education professionals and the construction of human rights education. *Comparative Education Review, 51*, 48–70.

Swidler, A. (1986). Culture in action: Symbols and strategies. *American Sociological Review, 51*, 273–286.

Tyack, D., & Cuban, L. (1995). *Tinkering toward utopia: A century of public school reform.* Cambridge, MA: Harvard University Press.

UNESCO. (2003). *Gender and education for all: The leap to equality. EFA Global Monitoring Report 2003/4.* Paris: Author.

UNESCO. (2007). *Education for All by 2015, Will we make it? EFA Global Monitoring Report 2007/8.* Paris: Author

Vaisey, S. (2006). Education and its discontents: Overqualification in America, 1972–2002. *Social Forces, 85*, 835–864.

Werum, R., & Baker, D. (2004). Inequality and schooling as an institution: Future directions in the comparative study of educational stratification. *Research in Sociology of Education, 14*, 275–284.

Windolf, P. (1997). *Expansion and structural change: Higher education in Germany, the United States, and Japan, 1870–1990.* Boulder, CO: Westview Press.

Wiseman, A. W., Astiz, M. F., Fabrega, R., & Baker, D. P. (2007). *Making citizens for a world polity: The political socialization of youth in modern mass school systems.* Manuscript submitted for publication.

Wiseman, A. W., & Baker, D. P. (2002, April). *A preliminary study of the impact of TIMSS-related activities on U.S. education, 1996–2001.* Paper presented to the Board on International Comparative Studies in Education of the National Academy of Science/National Research Council, Washington, DC.

Wiseman, A. W., & Baker, D. P. (2005). The worldwide explosion of internationalized education policy. In D. P. Baker & A. W. Wiseman (Eds.), *Global trends in educational policy: Vol. 6* (pp. 1–22). London: Elsevier Science.

Young, M. (2008). From constructivism to realism in the sociology of the curriculum. *Review of Research in Education, 32*, 1–28.

75

COMMENTARY
Access and Differentiation

C. Kent McGuire
Temple University

As the preceding chapters in this handbook demonstrate, research on education policy as well as the development and application of research methods to educational policy issues have evolved considerably over the last quarter century. This is certainly true of research on issues related to educational access and differentiation. The chapters in this section provide a broad view of both the issues with which both research and policy makers have been concerned. They also reveal well how our knowledge about these issues has advanced over time. I will comment on the story I think this set of chapters tells about access and opportunity and what confidence we can have in the research findings presented. I will speak very briefly on the potential for new research and analytic approaches. Finally, I explore ideas and lines of inquiry not present in these chapters, but from which we might benefit if additional work could be stimulated.

Current Knowledge on Access and Differentiation

As a set, these chapters confirm the attention given in this country over the past 30 years to improving educational opportunity. The early postwar period brought several Supreme Court rulings focused on educational opportunity. Included among them was the celebrated *Brown v. Board of Education* decision putting an end to de jure school segregation in the South. The policy response to this included busing programs and related efforts to address resource disparities based on residence. In 1965, the Congress passed the Elementary and Secondary Education Act (ESEA) in pursuit of both expanded opportunity and increased experimentation and innovation. Federal education funding increased markedly over this timeframe, not only for elementary and secondary education but for student aid and support for research and development. State education and social welfare agencies developed their capacities in the 1960s and 1970s to enact categorical programs focused on the disadvantaged and to monitor the progress of special stu-

dent populations as they moved from preschool through the early grades to high school. The national ambition toward improved access and opportunity has been well examined over this time frame, and these chapters contribute to the evolving story in several important ways.

One of the questions informed by them, for instance, is whether the national investment in creating opportunities for young children will pay dividends if seriously pursued. Schweinhart and Fulcher-Dawson's review of the landscape in early childhood education is encouraging, at least on the question of whether the benefits of such programs have been demonstrated. As their review suggests, numerous studies show that federal and state investments in early childhood education are generating effects, especially in relation to costs. Fuller's chapter on decentralized reforms further confirms the effects of public investment in early childhood education and child care. The Head Start Impact Study is particularly important in this regard, since there are relatively few large-scale random assignment studies on which to depend since the High Scope Perry Preschool Study. Still a question that deserves more attention relates to quality. Schweinhart and Fulcher-Dawson note that a majority of children in the United States have access to early care/learning opportunities, especially by age 4. The variation in program features and qualifications of staff become significant as the country approaches universal access. A new series of demonstrations that explicitly test different program features or which prevailing model delivery standards would contribute mightily to policy formation.

Another is the extent to which experiments with alternative forms of school organization, management and governance are fostering the changes in school climate, professional norms, and instructional practice that have been promised. My read of Bruce Fuller's review of this literature is encouraging in terms of the aspiration of these reform initiatives, but discouraging in terms of their effects. There is little question as to the popularity of some of these "decentralizing reforms" as Fuller refers to them. I commend to readers his historical treatment of the idea as well as his critique of contemporary lines of decentralization. In the end, I think Fuller confirms long-held suspicions about the limits of these strategies for expanding access and inhibiting stratification in American society. On the other hand, it may be too soon to say, particularly as regards these new educational organizations operating in mixed markets. These organizations—charter schools and education management organizations—are ripe for greater investigation. Much of the limited inquiry into their functioning has been focused on issues of accountability and student performance. While important, we have missed opportunities to learn whether their relief from labor contract provisions or district policy enables important practices and outcomes that have been difficult to realize within state-led bureaucracies.

A third aspect of the story concerns efforts to promote college access and whether such policies and programs have increased participation and career advancement in line with stated public policy objectives. Frankie Keels provides a useful survey of the policy landscape while Jennifer Stephan and James Rosenbaum look inside this question to explore more closely the pathways through higher education. Keels notes that participation has increased markedly over the past 20 years. Yet, for underrepresented groups, completion remains disappointing. Stephan and Rosenbaum provide a very useful framework for understanding this outcome, especially as relates to enrollment and completion transparency. In fact, they make a compelling argument that more research is needed with respect to the level of transparency in American higher education. The permeability-transparency framework is useful for assessing prevailing institutional policies and future work around this framework would be of significant benefit to guidance counselors in high schools and academic advisors in colleges and universities.

So, the story across these chapters is one of national attention to access and opportunity. This is the right impulse to be sure. But we are humbled by the realization that the outcomes we have pursued—success in the K-12 system, high school graduation, persistence in college and participation in the civic, economic and political mainstream—are elusive. These chapters reveal considerably more insight into the circumstances, events, and processes within systems and institutions that mediate access and opportunity. Our ability these days to model between and within school effects, and to analyze community and neighborhood contexts sets up a much deeper understanding of the factors that influence a child's actual experience in school and explain the differential outcomes revealed in the data on participation and attainment. This capacity also holds the promise of providing stronger evidence for policy design should our political leaders develop greater interest in using government policy to reduce income inequality and promote full participation in American society.

A word or two on the question of evidence is in order. A wide range of questions have been taken up across these chapters. Different research traditions are at work here with differing standards of evidence. While these chapters provide a rich treatment of the landscape and what we have learned over time, there was relatively little attention within them to the strength of findings per se. I would encourage readers to pay close attention to comments sprinkled throughout about exploring new theoretical concepts, new disciplinary tools, and methodological possibilities associated with these efforts. Yet, a chapter that takes up specifically the question of evidence would be a terrific addition to the section.

In the end, the absence of this analysis does not trouble me greatly as it is important to note that our intellectual curiosity about access and opportunity is not a recent event. Our insights around these issues benefit from years of exploration and investigation. As a result, so much of what is presented in this section is supported through multiple investigations using a variety of research traditions. Further, the findings converge around a few overarching themes that we can probably trust. We know that the core patterns of social stratification are quite durable in spite of our consistent attempts to break the relationship between circumstance and status. Early attempts to overcome poverty must continue, recognizing that neighborhood effects, peer effects, institutional bias and discrimination will be difficult to overcome. Yet, contemporary policy research, given the improvements in measures and methods, provide specific ideas for policy adjustments. These adjustments, (preschool to K-12; K-12 and higher education, etc.), are within our reach and the differing research traditions which generate these insights should give us greater confidence as we pursue the national ambition of closing the gap between policy intent and reality.

New Questions and Analytic Approaches

Longitudinal studies are perhaps most prevalent in policy research addressing questions of educational opportunity. Data sets that follow individuals or groups of individuals over time not only permit the direct examination of educational or occupational attainment but the refinement of survey instruments over time to capture additional information revealing important patterns and relationships. The introduction of social psychological variables represents an important advancement in our efforts to predict educational or occupational attainment. And as Jones and Schneider indicate, a number of methodological developments along with progress in tackling difficult measurement issues means that researchers are now engaged in increasingly sophisticated analyses of how schooling effects educational attainment. I am optimistic that as methods continue to improve, as we extend existing data sets out in time and do more to link national data sets with state and local data, that our predictive capacity will increase. The more we understand about context and process and can model more effectively, for instance, how family structure and parenting practices influence attainment, the more we might inform institutional policies for improving student performance in schools or at least shed brighter light on the non-academic supports that matter in improving academic outcomes.

In this regard, the chapter on supplemental tutoring (Lee et al.), brings attention to a little studied phenomenon, especially here in the United States. Generating explanations for the increasing demand for tutoring in the United States is itself a useful line of inquiry. Lee et al.'s review of such traditions in Asian countries as well as in Europe begs greater examination of supplemental tutoring in the North America and the comparative analyses that might follow. With the advent of private enterprises such as Huntington and Sylvan Learning Centers and the proliferation of private tutoring especially in middle- and upper-middle-class neighborhoods, it will be important to incorporate information about supplemental learning opportunities into our predictive models of attainment.

Several chapters in this section offer new and interesting conceptual frameworks worthy of additional analysis. Fuller's four-pronged schema of decentralized action is a case in point. For instance, Philadelphia's 5-year experiment with Educational Management Organizations and the corresponding proliferation of public charters offer a unique opportunity to analyze new cases using Fuller's conceptual framework to examine the evidence on performance, community engagement, and accountability. How are parental interests reflected in these new forms of school organization and management? Do we observe more complex forms of teaching and learning in these schools? What are the central benefits to these new reform strategies?

Stephan and Rosenbaum's permeability and transparency is another. A new round of studies of college admissions processes that exploit this construct might document the complexities associated with existing admissions and financial aid policies, to include policy recommendations for simplifying and streamlining them. State policy efforts to align K-12 and postsecondary education would benefit from analyses incorporating this framework. Aligning high school curriculum standards, for instance, with the general education requirements of postsecondary institutions might serve to increase enrollment transparency. In policy contexts where such alignment already exists, using this framework to assess policy impacts on participation and retention would be instructive.

I am inclined to agree with Hearn and Lacy that research on postsecondary organization, governance, and management merits expansion, especially given the changing interests, priorities, and organizational forms in the higher education marketplace. A number of ideas about how best to extend research and expand the theoretical and methodological traditions involved were presented in this chapter, which I support but will not repeat here.

However, the ideas advanced about research on postsecondary organization and management were not so clearly linked to the question of differential outcomes. But these connections could be established. Take, for instance, the matter of research incentives to foster more attention to institutional policies that promote or inhibit retention and persistence. Greater interest in and attention to the systematic analysis of institution data will likely reveal patterns and relationships of great value to administrators interested in increasing enrollment and completion transparency.

What's Missing?

Given the broad sweep with which the authors have approached their topics, this chapter on access and differentiation has much to offer policy makers and opinion leaders. In the context of early learning and care, the body of research is well documented and nicely situated into specific policy contexts (NCLB, IDEA, State Funded Preschool Programs, etc.). To my knowledge, there is little dispute as to the current state of knowledge regarding the returns to investments in early learning. If anything is missing, it might be deeper treatment of the issues related to program quality. Current policy leaves to chance what children actually experience, and outside a handful state of states with strong early learning policy structures, I suspect the variation in quality is disturbingly high. In any event, this is work for both emerging and established scholars. New demonstrations that benefit from greater program specification and larger samples hold real promise for informing the next phase of policy debate, which is already turning toward issues of teacher quality and curricular effectiveness (Barnett, Lamy, & Jung, 2005).

Jumping to postsecondary education, pathways to completion of college should be of considerable interest to higher education administrators, who will likely feel added pressure in the coming years to demonstrate their institutions are adding value. Hopefully, examining the complex set of institutional policies and practices that appear to influence student persistence and graduation will contribute to more sophisticated research on institutional behavior generally. It is striking after all, how little of the academy's considerable intellectual capacities are turned to the analysis of factors driving policy with higher education.

A topic which is largely missed in these chapters, and of arguably of great significance to long-term success, concerns the experiences of poor and minority children at the secondary level (middle and high schools). The section on teaching and learning no doubt shed light on the matter, which may today be among the most pressing educational issues in the country. Suffice it to say that institutional practices known to foster differential outcomes (ability grouping, tracking, etc.) are most pernicious in American high schools. Several chapters in this section surface issues, for instance, in the context of early learning and postsecondary education, that could just as easily be developed in the context of secondary school reform. Given the paucity of hard evidence on what is working to improve high school persistence and reduce drop-out rates, commissioning work that carefully reviews the knowledge in this arena and that suggests opportunities for additional research may be warranted.

On balance however, these chapters have much to commend, especially as regards the well organized survey of current knowledge and research activity. Readers will find much food for thought as they ponder what we now understand about access and outcomes. And more than one author provides fresh conceptual apparatus for interpreting findings and raising new questions. This section is, it seems to me, a fitting close to a very thorough and far reaching treatment of policy research in education.

References

Barnett, W. S., Lamy, C., & Jung, K. (2005). *The effects of state pre-kindergarten programs on young children's school readiness in five state*s. New Brunswick, NJ: National Institute for Early Education Research, Rutgers University.

76

COMMENTARY
Access and Differentiation

Structuring Equality and Inequality in Education Policy

JEANNIE OAKES
Ford Foundation

Access: means of approaching, entering, exiting, communicating with, or making use of; the ability or right to approach, enter, exit, communicate with, or make use of.

Differentiation: constitute the distinction between; perceive or show the difference in or between; discriminate; make different by alteration or modification.[1]

Few education policies escape the implications of access and differentiation. How many students are granted "entry"? Which students? How is this entry negotiated? How are educational structures and practices altered for various groups of students? How do the various structures and practices differ in their character or the outcomes they foster? A primary concern has been the ways that access and differentiation relate systematically to students' race, social class, neighborhood, or other background variables, and, as a consequence, limit or increase education equity.

Access and differentiation are most often investigated in relationship to the educational opportunities, resources, and outcomes afforded to students who are disadvantaged by poverty or racism. Access and differentiation's impact on education policies is also manifest in the efficiency and effectiveness of educational systems, by shaping what and how well students learn. As the chapters in this section make clear, consequential policy-generated patterns of access and differentiation can be found throughout the educational enterprise.

Some policies are designed to shape access and differentiation directly, often by expanding the provision of education, setting admissions criteria for schools and postsecondary institutions, and establishing specialized programs and/or curriculum tracks within institutions. Other policies shape access and differentiation without such stated intent or transparency; for example, decentralization policies, school assignment and choice policies, or resource allocation mechanisms, for example. Patterns of access and differentiation are also the consequence of policies (or the absence thereof) related to educational domains outside the public sphere—preschool or "shadow systems" (private tutoring and supplemental classes, test preparation, and college counseling), for example. As the chapters in this section reveal, patterns of access and differentiation across these many domains parallel students' background characteristics. Students from more privileged backgrounds have greater educational access, generally, and, when structures and opportunities are differentiated, access to better quality or higher status education.

Jones and Schneider examine policy-driven mechanisms through which schools and other institutions differentiate educational opportunities for K–12 students, even as they provide universal access to schooling. The patterns they identify are clear: Despite decades of reforms aimed at promoting social mobility, these core schooling practices most often result in young people replicating the economic and social positions of their parents. Schools have been notably weak instruments for disrupting the intergenerational transmission of advantage and disadvantage.

Bruce Fuller poses the fundamental question of whether differentiation through decentralization schools can advance an equitable agenda rather than reinforce existing social and economic inequalities. He looks at the extent to which decentralized schooling through the mechanisms of parental choice and competition, local community control of schools, small learning communities, and stronger ties between schools and families realizes the benefits claimed by advocates for these approaches. A central theme of this chapter is that context matters in decentralization, and that significant structural and political constraints—unequal schooling resources, local poverty or wealth—differentiate school quality across neighborhoods. These constraints undercut the promise of equal access through decentralized reform.

Lee, Park, and Lee look internationally at "shadow education" systems—privately provided out-of-school learning opportunities—tutoring, supplemental classes, and preparation for high-stakes tests. The authors link the demand for shadow education to the increased importance of education credentials, to social mobility, and to the importance of tests in the attainment of high status credentials. They also show that higher income and better educated families are more likely to invest in private opportunities that promise to lead to high status credentials.

The chapters by Williams, Stephan and Rosenbaum, and Hearn and Lacy focus access and differentiation in the context of postsecondary schooling. Williams points to the increased demand for access to postsecondary credentials across diverse populations and, at the same time, to persistent social, racial, and economic inequalities that limit that access. She traces these gaps in access to the differentiation in college counseling, college preparation, and information about college going and financial aid. Stephan and Rosenbaum show how higher education access and differentiation have changed in their forms as postsecondary opportunities increased, although the stratifying effects remain. In particular, students with less economic and social capital face barriers because they are not fully apprised of different routes to degree completion and the different status and exchange value of credentials. Hearn and Lacy's review of research on policies related to the impact of government policies on higher education organization and governance finds that too little research has considered the impact of "mission differentiation" and other higher education policies on improving students enrollment rates, educational experiences and post-degree outcomes.

David Baker views access and differentiation broadly, through the lens of neo-institutionalism. He writes, "What appears to be a burning local or national policy issue often is the product of larger trends throughout education worldwide." Access to schooling has increased worldwide, and schooling across the globe has become more similar in its basic ideas, expectations, and social rules. Notable is the nearly universal belief in the value of schooling for all children in order to ensure individual opportunity and an educated populace. Also notable, however, is ubiquitous social stratification through differentiated credentials that signify educational achievement and merit—i.e., one's status in society as an adult is "overwhelmingly dictated" by school performance and attainment. Collectively, these chapters add to our store of knowledge about access and differentiation, but how does that store become the knowledge, tools, and dispositions that policy makers can use to address policy shortcomings? That, after all is said and researched, should be at least one guide to our future work. Can the research reported here and elsewhere inform policies that break tight connections between access, differentiation, and equity? Are we generally asking the correct questions? Why are even the most incontrovertible findings so often and so easily ignored?

The relationship between access and differentiation might be seen as symbiotic—access that is diminished by differential opportunity, and differentiation that distributes access inequitably. Moreover, access and differentiation are sustained by, and in return sustain, the larger social context.

In the United States, both concepts—existing side-by-side in education policy—are as old as public schooling itself. In what is often cited as the first call for universal access to public education, Thomas Jefferson proposed that the state of Virginia provide primary education to all young children. In Jefferson's view, universally provided public schools would serve the most basic purposes of the new republic:

> … to understand his duties to his neighbors and country, and to discharge with competence the functions confided to him by either; to know his rights; to exercise with order and justice those he retains, to choose with discretion the fiduciary of those he delegates; and to notice their conduct with diligence, with candor and judgment; and in general, to observe with intelligence and faithfulness all the social relations under which he shall be placed. (Jefferson, 1818)

At the same time, Jefferson also advanced policies for educational differentiation, providing increasingly advanced levels of schooling for decreasing numbers of students:

> The public education…we divide into three grades: 1. Primary schools, in which are taught reading, writing, and common arithmetic, to every infant of the State, male and female. 2. Intermediate schools, in which an education is given proper for artificers and the middle vocations of life; in grammar, for example, general history, logarithms, arithmetic, plane trigonometry, mensuration, the use of the globes, navigation, the mechanical principles, the elements of natural philosophy, and, as a preparation for the University, the Greek and Latin languages. 3. An University, in which these and all other useful sciences shall be taught in their highest degree; the expenses of these institutions are defrayed partly by the public, and partly by the individuals profiting of them. (Jefferson, 1823)

For Jefferson, this differentiation was not tied to students' backgrounds—not designed perpetuate economic privilege. He argued that a system of universal public primary schools would provide equal opportunity for talented students from all classes and would diminish the link between wealth and political power: "Worth and genius would thus have been sought out from every condition of life, and completely prepared by education for defeating the competition of wealth and birth for public trusts" (Jefferson, 1813). History has shown otherwise.

In the mid-19th century Horace Mann augmented Jefferson's vision with his own view of common public schools as mechanisms of democracy and social equity. As Fuller notes in chapter 67, Mann was confident that providing children from all social classes, ethnicities, and religions with a common body of knowledge and values would ensure a citizenry capable of grappling with the complexities of life in a modern republic. Mann also believed the common school to be a remedy for the social and economic inequality that he viewed as threatening the republic: If a common "intellectual" and "political" education were provided universally and "administered in the spirit of justice and conciliation, all the rising generation may be brought within the circle of [the common school's] reformatory and elevating influences." A system of common schools would be the "great equalizer of the conditions of men—the balance-wheel of the social machinery" and "do more than all things else to obliterate factitious distinctions in society." Such schools would "peaceably abolish all the miseries that spring from the coexistence, side by side, of enormous wealth and squalid want" (Mann, 1848). Mann's common schools would not displace the existing system of secondary academies, mostly private, attended by a small portion of young people, mostly from the upper classes. That such differentiated schooling existed seemed not to dim Mann's confidence in the salutary affect of the common schools.

Of course, neither Jefferson nor Mann could have predicted how central schools would become to the development of a smooth-running industrial economy, the critical role that access and educational differentiation would play in preparing workers for the division of labor that such an economy requires, and that, by the early 20th century, industrial elites would become drivers of education policy. Prior to the late 19th century, nobody thought schools had much relevance to the nation's workforce or economy. Except for a few "learned professions" (law, the ministry, etc.) who required advanced academic training, education was not seen as preparation for work. Most jobs were learned through apprenticeships that were completely unrelated to children's five years of common schooling. Few could imagine that the eventual link between schooling and work would grow increasingly tight—that the nation's economic health would be tied to the quality of its public schools (Grubb & Lazerson, 2006).

Early in the 20th century, the need for an "appropriate" education for immigrants converged with industry's need for trained workers. These young people seemed so different—less capable, in fact—from those who had enrolled in the traditional academic curriculum of years past. The response was both access and differentiation—access for all to comprehensive high schools, within in all would be socialized commonly for democratic participation and social cohesion, but also sorted into curriculum tracks that provided academic work and access to higher education for some, general education for others, and industrial preparation for still others.

Notably, powerful ideologies of equal opportunity, merit, and White superiority rationalized and justified this juxtaposition of access and differentiation—of equality and inequality. Justifying such differentiation as fundamentally democratic, the superintendent of Boston's public school system noted in 1908 that, "Until very recently the schools have offered equal opportunity for all to receive one kind of education, but what will make them democratic is to provide opportunity for all to receive education as will fit them equally well for their particular life work" (Boston Schools, 1908, p. 53). Not long after, a new "science" of intelligence offered theories and data to show that children of color and those from Southern and Eastern European immigrant families had mental deficits that would limit their school achievement. Intelligence-test pioneer Lewis Terman famously wrote, "Their dullness seems to be racial … Children of this group should be segregated in special classe … They cannot master abstractions, but they can often be made efficient workers" (1916, pp. 91–92). Although these views did not go uncontested, schools enacted the prevailing belief that inherent group differences caused enormous variation in students' potential for school learning. The result was that as access to secondary education increased, differentiation ensured that not all secondary education would have equal value in the capitalist economy.

Such structures and ideologies continue. New and old forms of tracking proliferate, even as reforms emphasize high standards and college preparation for all (Lucas, 1999; Oakes, 2005). In 1994, Richard Herrnstein and Charles Murray's *The Bell Curve: Intelligence and Class Structure in American Life* claimed to offer scientific proof that African Americans inherit lower IQs than White Americans and that these IQ differences are virtually impossible to change. Put bluntly, Herrnstein and Murray argued that the average African American is less well educated and less wealthy than the average White because he or she is not born with the capacity to be as smart. Therefore, educational programs that attempt to close opportunity gaps—programs such as Head Start, compensatory education, and affirmative action—are costly and useless. Just two months after its publication, 400,000 copies of *The Bell Curve* were in print.

Today, Jefferson's and Mann's goal of "universal and complete" access to public schools has been realized, but not the vision of schools as generators of social equity. By the 1970s, between 98% and 99% of young Americans ages 7–13 attended school, and about 90% were enrolled in public schools—percentages that continue today (NCES 2008). At the same time, large and pernicious social and economic divisions persist, and by the most recent accounts are growing worse (Thompson, 2007). Between 1979 and 2005, the top 5% of American families saw their real incomes grow by 81%, compared to families in the bottom 20%, whose incomes shrunk by 1%. In 2005, families in that top group, on average, earn 20.9 times more than do those in the bottom group. In 2004, the top 10% of the wealthiest Americans owned almost three-quarters of the nation's wealth, and the top 1% owned more than the bottom 90% (Bernstein, McNichol, & Nicolas, 2008).

For the past half-century, philosophers, sociologists, curriculum theorists, and economists have theorized and debated how and why various features of schooling map onto broader social and economic inequality, and why these patterns are so difficult to change. Most notably, in the 1970s, neo-Marxist analysts argued that schools are captive to the needs of hierarchical, capitalist economies. In this view, schools primary role is to prepare and socialize students for the occupations and social positions they will assume within the existing class structure. This role is enacted through the close *correspondence* of the structures and practices of schools and workplaces, including providing different curriculum and socialization to various groups of students. Specifically, through patterns of selective access and differentiation schools turn upper class children into professionals and lower-class children into subordinate workers (Apple, 1978; Bourdieu & Passeron, 1977; Bowles & Gintis, 1976).

The social reproduction just described weaves around a complex American ideology that is vaguely democratic and agentive. By holding out the promise that wealth and power are available to anyone who marshals sufficient determination and hard work, differences that otherwise appear as unfair or undemocratic are rendered sensible, even deserved. Merit, not education, is the "great equalizer." Lest too harsh a judgment be passed on young Americans who are not White or middle class, we have powerful cultural assumptions to call upon: These students come to school with deficits that make it inevitable that they will perform less well (by any objective test or criteria) than students who are less burdened by their culture. The privileges that come with being White allow the most powerful Americans to believe that their ways of knowing and being in the world represent intelligence and merit, and, therefore, they deserve the disproportionate school and life advantages they enjoy (Fine, Weis, Pruitt, & Burns, 1996).

My own studies of schools seeking to adopt and implement equity reforms (detracking, specifically), demonstrated the difficulty of disengaging the conduct (structures, or technology) of schools from the norms. Equity reforms require more than finding appropriate systems, pedagogies, class schedules, funding, and so forth. Thwarting most equity reforms are deeply entrenched beliefs about low-income students and students of color and the competition among parents to obtain for their children scarce opportunities for the "best" education and the life chances that follow. When reformers try to disrupt the uneven distribution of high status knowledge and learning opportunities, they are by definition redistributing. These efforts mobilize families who, perhaps, never saw themselves as benefiting from stratified schools and society, but who certainly know when their relative advantages are threatened (Oakes, Quartz, Ryan, & Lipton, 2000; Oakes 2005).

A recent analysis by Samuel Lucas argues that when equity reforms disrupt the access/differentiation dynamic, advantaged members of society will "effectively maintain inequality" (Lucas, in press). Lucas notes that academic advantages are not just tangible and measurable, they are also "relational"; that is, parents may be as concerned that their children's opportunities are qualitatively *superior* to other children's as they are concerned about the actual opportunities themselves. As such, universalizing *access* may not reduce educational inequality, if *differentiation* (often in the name of "special" or "appropriate" or "individualized") effectively maintain inequality.

These are undeniably gloomy analyses. However, some theorists and researchers find opportunities to increase equity and mitigate the polarizing effects of differentia-

tion; they do not deny the capitalist/democratic critique, but they suggest that society's need for democratic agents can be a contentious counterforce to blunt the libertarian individualism that coheres around elite interests, particularly in schools.

In their 1985 book, *Schooling and Work in the Democratic State*, Martin Carnoy and Henry Levin complicate the social reproduction analysis. Carnoy and Levin focus on the multiple purposes of education, generally, and in capitalist democracies specifically.[2] For democratic societies to sustain themselves, they must ensure that members of each new generation acquire the knowledge and the values they need to function effectively as democratic citizens; primary among these are the principles and practices of political equality, social equality, and equality of opportunity that form the bedrock of democracy. At the same time, however, democracies with capitalist economies must also prepare young people to assume positions in a highly differentiated workforce that the economic structure requires. Accordingly, they must also make legitimate the fundamental inequalities inherent capitalist economies. Because much of this work is shouldered by schools, schools are captive to the contradictory demands of readying students for both equality and inequality:

> Indeed, public schools in America are institutions of the State, and like other State institutions subject to the pull of two conflicting forces over their control, purpose, and operation. On the one hand, schools reproduce the unequal, hierarchical relations of the capitalist workplace; on the other, schooling represents the primary force in the United States for expanding economic opportunity for subordinate groups and the extension of democratic rights. (Carnoy & Levin, 1985, p. 144)

While not denying that school practices and outcomes reproduce socioeconomic inequality, they find the neo-Marxist focus on *correspondence* too limiting. Rather, they find in schools' credible and whole-hearted efforts to prepare young people for democratic social participation a *contradiction* to deterministic reproduction.

Access and differentiation can be understood best in this context of educational contradiction. Policies and practices that increase educational access seek to foster democratic socialization and equal opportunity—perhaps contradicting the status quo distribution of power and advantage. And, at the same time, policies and practices that increase educational differentiation legitimate economic inequality—likely corresponding to inequalities in the social and economic status quo.

Alongside the remarkable expansion of schooling over the past 200 years, policies governing access and differentiation have been key means by which schools support capitalist democracies' contradicting commitment to equality and inequality as they perform the work of socializing young people into their society. As Baker in this volume observes, belief has grown in the power of an academically educated populace for social progress. However, increased access to more schooling was paralleled by sorting students and providing differentiated of opportunities that reproduction theorists describe.

Carnoy and Levin (1985) argue that democratic coalitions—often propelled by social movements—not only have resisted the reproductive practice of schools, they have pressed their case for equity into the courts, public opinion, and the media. They end their analysis with the hopeful conclusion that "Democratic struggles for just and meaningful schooling are effective counters to the economic forces that are attempting to gain primacy over American schools and the formation of our youth" (p. 267). Often, schools are more democratic and equal places than other social institutions; they have become so by contesting many of the more blatant expressions of differentiated schooling—for example, school segregation and the denial of college preparatory coursework for traditionally underrepresented students.

My colleague, John Rogers and I have spent the past few years exploring the proposition that the active and knowledgeable engagement of communities most negatively affected by schooling inequalities can counter the obstacles that inhibit equitable reform. To investigate this proposition empirically, we've used Dewey's ideas about participatory social inquiry and action as a guide for developing collaborations with grassroots and advocacy groups pursuing higher quality schooling for California young people in low-income, communities of color. These "social design experiments" have allowed us to examine whether and how social inquiry (using both academic research and community-based action research) together with social movement organizing, may prove efficacious for equitable education reform.

Not surprisingly, issues of access and differentiation lie at the center of student- and community-based struggles for school improvement. Such groups often advance an educational justice agenda through campaigns for increased access and/or for differentiated programs that do not relegate low-income students and students of color to limited post-high school choices and chances. For example, in California, activist groups have sought policies and resources that provide the state's college preparatory curriculum to all high school students (access to the highest status programs), with a variety of approaches and programs that would support diverse groups of students success in that curriculum (a version of differentiation that is not strongly linked to status or wealth) (Oakes & Rogers, 2006).

Although much remains unknown about the efficacy of this approach for fundamental and/or lasting change, the work to date provides evidence for the following proposition on which to base further inquiry: More equitable schooling requires a technology of schooling (structures and practices), high quality teachers that enable diverse groups of students to learn well, and policy mandates (court decrees, laws, or administrative orders that require a fair distribution of resources and opportunities. Public engagement, in the form of participatory social inquiry by those impacted by inequality helps generate the knowledge and the power needed to disrupt the dominant norms and politics of privilege that sustain unequal structures of access and differentiation. In my view, this proposition, investigated through multiple theoretical frames and with a mix of social science methods, could produce important, new knowledge to guide policies aimed at disrupting gaps in educational opportunities and outcomes.

Notes

1. *The American Heritage® Dictionary of the English Language, Fourth Edition*. Retrieved July 14, 2008, from Answers.com Web site: http://www.answers.com

2. Bowles and Gintis (2002) made a similar argument that "schools and the public sector generally are loci of conflicts stemming from the contradictory rules of the marketplace, the democratic polity, and the patriarchal family" (p. 2).

References

Apple, M. W. (1978). Ideology, reproduction, and educational reform. *Comparative Education Review, 22*(3), 367–387.

Bernstein, J., McNichol, E., & Nicolas, A. (2008, April). *Pulling apart: A state by state analysis of income trends*. Washington, DC: Center on Budget and Policy Priorities and the Economic Policy Institute.

Bowles, S., & Gintis, H. (1976). *Schooling in capitalist America: Educational reform and the contradictions of economic life*. London: Routledge.

Bowles, S., & Gintis, H. (2002). Schooling in capitalist America revisited. *Sociology of Education, 75*, 1–18.

Bourdieu, P., & Passeron J. (1977). *Reproduction in education, society and culture*. London: Sage.

Boston Schools. (1908). *Documents of the School Committee*, No. 7.

Carnoy, M., & Levin, H. (1985). *Schooling and work in the democratic state*. Stanford, CA: Stanford University Press.

Fine, M., Weis, L., Pruitt, L., & Burns, A. (1996). *Off White: Readings on power, privilege, and resistance*. New York: Routledge.

Grubb, W. N., & Lazerson, M. (2006). *The education gospel: The economic power of schooling*. Cambridge, MA: Harvard University Press.

Jefferson, T. (1813). Thomas Jefferson to John Adams, 1813. ME 13:399. Retrieved July 20, 2008, from http://etext.virginia.edu/jefferson/quotations/jeff1370.htm

Jefferson, T. (1818). *Report for University of Virginia*, 1818. Retrieved July 20, 2008, from http://etext.virginia.edu/jefferson/quotations/jeff1370.htm

Jefferson, T. (1823). Thomas Jefferson to A. Coray, 1823. ME 15:487. Retrieved July 20, 2008, from http://etext.virginia.edu/jefferson/quotations/jeff1370.htm

Lucas, S. (1999). *Tracking inequality: Stratification and mobility in American high schools*. New York: Teachers College Press.

Lucas, S. (in press). Constructing equal pathways under conditions of effectively maintained inequality. In J. Oakes and M. Saunders (Eds.), *Beyond tracking: Multiple pathways to college, career, and civic participation*. Cambridge, MA: Harvard Education Press.

Mann, H. (1848). *Report No. 12 of the Massachusetts School Board*. Retrieved November 11, 2008, from http://usinfo.state.gov/infousa/government/overview/16.html

National Center for Education Statistics. (2008). *The condition of education 2008*. Retrieved July 20, 2008, from http//www.nces.ed.gov/pubs2008/2008031.pdf

Oakes, J. (2005). *Keeping track: How schools structure inequality* (2nd ed.). New Haven, CT: Yale University Press.

Oakes, J., Quartz, K. H., Ryan, S., & Lipton, M. (2000). *Becoming good American schools: The struggle for civic virtue in education reform*. San Francisco: Jossey-Bass.

Oakes, J., & Rogers, J. (2006). *Learning power: Organizing for education and justice*. New York: Teachers College Press.

Thompson, M. J. (2007). *The politics of inequality: A political history of the idea of economic inequality in America*. New York: Columbia University Press.

Author Index

Subject Index

Page numbers in italic refer to Figures or Tables.

Randomized trials (*continued*)
  logic of experiments, 130–131
  obstacles, 132–133
  Rubin's causal model, 131
  selection bias, 131–132
  withholding services, ethical and political
      dilemmas, 133–135
Rate of return, higher education, 40–41
  economic benefits to society, 41
  non-financial benefits, 41
Ratings scales, polling, 312–313, *313*
Rational choice models, 57
Rationality, public choice, 362
Rationality project, 267
Reading, achievement gap, *662,* 662–666,
      663, 664, 665, 666
Reading wars
  assessment, 563
  balanced literacy, 566
  California, 560–577
  changing research paradigms, 566–568
  current situation, 568
  curriculum
      curricular context, 562–563
      unintended curricular consequences,
          564–565
  demographic trend effects, 561–562
  history, 560
  National Assessment of Education
      Progress, 561–562
  No Child Left Behind, 567–568
  paradigm shift in reading theory and
      practice, 563–564
  paradigm shift toward skill/code, 564–568
  synthesis, 575–576
  whole language, questionable applications,
      565
Reflexive action, Critical Race Praxis,
      260–261
Regression discontinuity, selection bias, 35
Regulation, markets, 515
Religious education, 290–291
  homeschooling, 806
  vouchers, 493–494
Renaissance 2010
  Critical Race Feminism, 261–265
  Critical Race Theory, 261–265
Representation, 58
  politics of, 277
  science, 279–280
Repressive desublimation, 224
Reproduction theory
  ethnicity, 248–249
  race, 248–249
Research, *see also* Specific type
  community engagement, critical policy
      questions, 265
  post-positivist conception, 279
Research and development centers, 375
Research policy, teacher-student interaction,
      658
Research synthesis, 154–161
  background, 154–155
  causality, 156
  data analysis, 158–159
  data collection, 157–158
  data evaluation, 158
  defined, 154
  education policy, 154–155, 210

beyond external validity of single
      studies, 155–156
  contributions, 155–156
  mapping and organizing studies, 155
  relationship, 155–161
expanding questions addressed, 159–160
methods, 154
problem formulation, 157
public presentation, 159, 160
quality standards, 156–159
ruling out irrelevancies, 156
strengthening, 159–160
surface similarity, 155–156
timeliness of reviews, 160
Resistance theory
  ethnicity, 249
  race, 249
Resource cost model, 442
Resources
  constrained, quality research, 532
  ostensive aspect, 414
  performative aspect, 414
Retrieval, 341
Ritual, policy as, 272–273
Rubin-Holland model, causality, 143–145

S
SAGE study, 430, 431
*San Antonio Independent School District v.
      Rodriguez,* equity, 439–440
SAT
  ethnicity, 247, *247*
  race, 247, *247*
School attainment
  defined, 39
  international comparisons
      expected completion by country, 40–41,
          41
      upper secondary education or more, by
          country and age, 40, *40*
School board, 795
  elections
      representation, 58
      rules governing, 58
School choice, 67–68, 368–369, 373, 379,
      518, 519, 530, 800–801
  charter schools, 479–484, 486
      parental choice, 480
  Chile, *495,* 498
  Colombia, *495,* 498
  England, *495,* 496–497
  international context, 494–499, *495*
  mothers, 870–871
  Netherlands, *495, 495*
  parents, 859–862
      market choice with hazy information,
          860–861
  policy entrepreneurs, 66
  Scotland, *495,* 495–496
  United States, *495,* 498–499
  Wales, *495,* 496–497
School effects research, 74
School finance
  cost analysis, 444–448
  education law, 292–293
  equity, 438–442
      Berne and Stiefel framework origins,
          438–440
      legal origins, 439–440

public finance origins, 439
  shift from input equity to outcome
      equity, 440–442
growing financial burden, *698,* 698–699
Individuals with Disabilities Education Act
  pre-referral, 834
  provision of services, 834–836, *835*
  referral, 834
K-12 education, 453–460
  characterizing debate about whether
      money matters, 455–456
  class size, 458
  decentralizing spending authority,
      458–459
  early intervention, 458
  education production function model,
      455–456
  future directions, 459–460
  importance, 453
  improving high school, 458
  policy approaches to making money
      matter, 457–459
  productivity, 456–457
  providing incentives to improve
      performance, 459
  relation between school resources and
      student outcomes, 456
  student outcomes, 453–455, *454*
  teacher quality, 457–458
litigation, 59, 444–448
  Arkansas, 444
  Kansas, *445,* 445–446
  New York, *445,* 446–447
  Texas, *445,* 447–448
  Wyoming, 444–445
reform, 62–63, 444–448
vouchers, 493
School life-expectancy
  enrollment, 960, *960*
  global education culture, 960, *960*
  international comparison, 960, *960*
School personnel, school reconstitution,
      464–475
School production functions, education
      policy, 30–33
  effects of school variables on student
      performance, 30–31
  estimates, 30–31
School quality, 39
  competition, 861–862
  improving, 49–50
  teacher quality, 32–33
School reconstitution, 464–475
  administration, 464–475
  Chicago, 472
  Colorado Springs, 472–473
  definition, 464–465
  description, 464–465
  incentives, 465–467
  North Carolina, 470
  San Francisco, 472
  school personnel, 464–475
  school reform, 464–475
  teachers, 464–475
  theoretical assumptions, 465–467
  use, 464
School reconstruction
  Chicago, 467–468
  empirical evidence, 467–474

List of Figures

List of Tables

The Editors

Gary Sykes is a Professor of Teacher Education and Education Policy at Michigan State University. He specializes in educational policy relating to teaching and teacher education. His research interests center on policy issues associated with the improvement of teaching and teacher education, on the development of leadership preparation programs, and on educational choice as an emerging policy issue.

Barbara Schneider is a John A. Hannah University Distinguished Professor in the College of Education and Department of Sociology at Michigan State University. She holds research appointments at the University of Chicago and NORC, where she is Principal Investigator of the Data Research and Development Center (DRDC). She has published 12 books and over 100 articles and reports on family, social context of schooling, and sociology of knowledge. Professor Schneider is currently conducting a collaborative study with the Michigan Department of Education on using administrative data to make state education policy decisions. She was selected by the American Sociological Association as the editor of *Sociology of Education*.

David N. Plank is Executive Director of Policy Analysis for California Education (PACE), an independent policy research center based at the University of California-Berkeley, Stanford University, and the University of Southern California. He was previously a professor at Michigan State University, where he founded and directed the Education Policy Center. He received his Ph.D. from the University of Chicago in 1983. In addition to his work on education policy in the U.S., he has served as a consultant in the areas of educational policy and finance to international organizations including the World Bank, the UNDP, the OECD, USAID, and the Ford Foundation, and also to governments in Africa and Latin America.

The Contributors

June Ahn is a graduate student and Dean's Fellow in Urban Education in the Rossier School of Education at the University of Southern California. He studies the structural, social, and socio-psychological dynamics of education organizations and technology.

Bruce D. Baker is an Associate Professor in the Department of Educational Theory, Policy, and Administration in the Graduate School of Education at Rutgers University in New Brunswick, NJ. His recent research focuses on state aid allocation policies and practices, with particular attention to the equity and adequacy of aid for special student populations.

David P. Baker is a Professor of Education and Sociology in the College of Education at Pennsylvania State University.

Eva L. Baker is a Distinguished Professor of Education at UCLA, Graduate School of Education & Information Studies. She directs the Center for Research on Evaluation, Standards, and Student Testing (CRESST). Dr. Baker was recently the president of the American Educational Research Association and is currently a member of the National Academy of Education.

Nina Bascia is a Professor and Chair of the Department of Theory & Policy Studies at the Ontario Institute for Studies in Education of the University of Toronto (OISE/UT).

Clive R. Belfield is an Assistant Professor in the Department of Economics at Queens College, City University of New York. Dr. Belfield writes on the economics of education, with an emphasis on the economics of pre-schooling.

Mark Berends is a Professor of Sociology and Director of the Center for Research on Educational Opportunity at the University of Notre Dame.

Tara Béteille is a doctoral candidate in the Economics of Education program at Stanford University and a Stanford Graduate Fellow.

Geoffrey D. Borman is a Professor of Education at the University of Wisconsin-Madison, a Senior Researcher with the Consortium for Policy Research in Education, and the lead analyst for the Center for Data-Driven Reform in Education at Johns Hopkins University.

Kathryn M. Borman is a Professor of Anthropology and lead researcher at the Alliance for Applied Research in Anthropology and Education, Department of Anthropology, the University of South Florida.

Dominic J. Brewer is the Clifford H. and Betty C. Allen Professor in Urban Leadership and a Professor of Education in Economics and Policy at the University of Southern California. He is a labor economist specializing in the economics of education and education policy.

Mary Alice Callahan is currently a doctoral student at the University of California, Berkeley, studying educational policy. She was a teacher for 24 years and continues her work with the California Federation of Teachers both as a state vice president and as a member of the American Federation of Teachers program and policy council.

Eric M. Camburn is an Assistant Professor at the University of Wisconsin and a Senior Researcher at the Consortium of Policy Research in Education. His research focuses on urban public schools and their improvement, including programmatic efforts to improve instruction and learning and the organizational factors that promote such improvement.

Steve Cantrell is a Senior Program Officer for the Bill & Melinda Gates Foundation. Previously he directed the Regional Educational Laboratory–Midwest and was Chief Research Scientist for Los Angeles Unified School District.

Martin Carnoy is the Vida Jacks Professor of Education at Stanford University. His research focuses on the economic value of education, on the underlying political economy of educational policy, and on the financing and resource allocation aspects of educational production.

Tino A. Castañeda is a doctoral student in Educational Leadership and Policy Studies at the University of Washington, Seattle. He is currently working as a researcher on a national study of educational leadership.

Lora Cohen-Vogel earned her Ph.D. from Vanderbilt University and is currently an Assistant Professor at Florida State University. Her teaching and research focus on educational policy and politics, with particular attention to issues in teacher preparation, recruitment, and retention.

Richard Correnti is an Assistant Professor and a Research Scientist at the Learning Research Development Center at the University of Pittsburgh. His research interests focus on instruction received by students, including how to measure instructional delivery on a large scale, variability in students' accumulated instruction, and how instruction influences student learning.

Bridget A. Cotner is a graduate student in the Measurement, Research, and Evaluation Program in the College of Education, the University of South Florida.

Linda Darling-Hammond is the Charles E. Ducommun Professor of Education at Stanford University where her research, teaching, and policy work focus on issues of teaching quality, school reform, and educational equity. She is former president of the American Educational Research Association and a member of the National Academy of Education.

Amanda Datnow is Professor and Director of Education Studies at the University of California, San Diego. She was formerly a faculty member at the University of Southern California and at the Ontario Institute for Studies in Education. Her research focuses on the politics and policies of school reform, particularly with regard to the professional lives of educators, and issues of equity.

Laura M. Desimone is an Associate Professor at the University of Pennsylvania Graduate School of Education. She studies education policy effects on teaching and learning in the core academic subjects, with a focus on comprehensive school reform, standards-based reform, and teachers' professional development.

Maressa L. Dixon is a graduate student in Applied Anthropology at the University of South Florida.

George Farkas is a Professor in the Department of Education at the University of California, Irvine. His research interests include labor markets, schooling and human resources, demography, statistical research methods, evaluation research, and economic sociology.

Michael J. Feuer is the executive director of the Division of Behavioral and Social Sciences and Education in the National Research Council (NRC) of the National Academies, where he is responsible for a broad portfolio of studies and other activities aimed at improved economic, social, and educational policymaking.

Robert E. Floden is a University Distinguished Professor of Teacher Education, Measurement and Quantitative Methods, Educational Psychology, and Educational Policy at Michigan State University. He is Associate Dean for Research, director of the Institute for Research on Teaching and Learning and co-director of Teachers for a New Era (TNE).

Barbara Foorman is the Francis Eppes Professor of Education and Director of the Florida Center for Reading Research at Florida State University.

Timothy G. Ford is a doctoral candidate and Erickson Research Fellow in the Curriculum, Teaching, and Educational Policy program at Michigan State University. His primary research interests center on the sociology of education, in particular the relationship between policy and the social organization of schooling and parenting and adolescent development.

Rachel Fulcher-Dawson is a graduate student in educational policy at Michigan State University.

Bruce Fuller is Professor of Education and Public Policy at the University of California, Berkeley. He served as a legislative aide and education advisor to one California governor, then as research sociologist at the World Bank. Fuller previously taught comparative policy and cultural studies at Harvard University.

Adam Gamoran is a Professor of Sociology and Educational Policy Studies and the director of Wisconsin Center for Education Research at University of Wisconsin, Madison. His research interests include school organization, stratification and inequality in education, and resource allocation in school systems.

Patricia Gándara is Professor of Education in the Graduate School of Education and Information Studies at UCLA, and co-director of The Civil Rights Project/Proyecto Derechos Civiles at UCLA. Her research focuses on educational equity and access for low income and ethnic minority students, language policy, and the education of Mexican origin youth.

Mona Ghali is a graduate student at the Ontario Institute for Studies in Education, the University of Toronto.

Louis M. Gomez is the Aon Professor of Learning Sciences and co-director of the National Science Foundation-sponsored Center for Learning Technologies in Urban Schools (LeTUS) at Northwestern University.